OXFORD EU LAW LIBRARY

General Editors: David Anderson, QC
Barrister at Brick Court Chambers and
Visiting Professor of Law at King's College London.
Piet Eeckhout, Professor of Law at University College London.

EU PROCEDURAL LAW

OXFORD EU LAW LIBRARY

The aim of this series is to publish important and original studies of the various branches of EU law. Each work provides a clear, concise, and critical exposition of the law in its social, economic, and political context, at a level which will interest the advanced student, the practitioner, the academic, and government officials.

EU Securities and Financial Markets Regulation
Third Edition
Niamh Moloney

The General Principles of EU Law
Third Edition
Takis Tridimas

The EU Common Security and Defence Policy
Panos Koutrakos

EU Anti-Discrimination Law
Second Edition
Evelyn Ellis and Philippa Watson

EU Employment Law
Fourth Edition
Catherine Barnard

EU External Relations Law
Second Edition
Piet Eeckhout

EU Justice and Home Affairs Law
Third Edition
Steve Peers

The EC Common Fisheries Policy
Robin Churchill and Daniel Owen

EC Competition Law
Fifth Edition
Joanna Goyder and Albertina Albors-Llorens

EC Customs Law
Second Edition
Timothy Lyons

The European Union and its Court of Justice
Second Edition
Anthony Arnull

EU PROCEDURAL LAW

Koen Lenaerts
Ignace Maselis
Kathleen Gutman

Edited by
Janek Tomasz Nowak

OXFORD
UNIVERSITY PRESS

OXFORD
UNIVERSITY PRESS

Great Clarendon Street, Oxford, OX2 6DP,
United Kingdom

Oxford University Press is a department of the University of Oxford.
It furthers the University's objective of excellence in research, scholarship,
and education by publishing worldwide. Oxford is a registered trade mark of
Oxford University Press in the UK and in certain other countries

First published 2014
First published in paperback 2015

Published in the United States of America by Oxford University Press
198 Madison Avenue, New York, NY 10016, United States of America

British Library Cataloguing in Publication Data
Data available

Library of Congress Cataloging in Publication Data
Data available

ISBN 978–0–19–870733–2 (Hbk.)
ISBN 978–0–19–870734–9 (Pbk.)

GENERAL EDITORS' FOREWORD

What distinguishes the European Union from previous attempts to bind Europe together is the rule of law: a comprehensive system of judicial protection that allows individuals, entities, Member States, and European institutions to enforce their rights under the Treaties and to hold others to account for breach of the rules by which all are bound.

Ultimate authority over the interpretation and validity of Union law rests with the Court of Justice of the European Union. Its three component courts (the Court of Justice since 1952, the General Court since 1989, and the Civil Service Tribunal since 2005) have handed down many thousands of judgments and orders from their seat in Luxembourg.

Respect for the Court's authority depends on the impartiality and integrity of its members, and the quality of their reasoning as expressed in opinions and judgments. But just as important, from the perspective of the litigant, is the fairness of the Court's procedures. A degree of formalism that to some may seem excessive will readily be forgiven if the rules of the game—whether reference from a national court, direct action, or appeal—are clear, accessible, and just.

Much information is available on the Court's website, and the Registry staff are notably patient and helpful. But for the answers to the myriad procedural questions that come up in practice, a comprehensive guide is needed. To be optimally useful, that guide must reference legal instruments, academic literature, and—most elusively—the precedents afforded by past judicial determinations, some of them in little-known cases.

Lawyers and scholars are fortunate that such a distinguished team has been willing to provide precisely that guide. Koen Lenaerts, who animated the predecessor volume *Procedural Law of the European Union*, has for 25 years combined his professorial duties with judicial service first on the General Court and then on the Court of Justice of which he is now Vice-President. His combination of academic and practical expertise is echoed and amplified by the other team members. Together, they have produced a book which is clear, authoritative, and formidably well-referenced.

All those practising before the European Courts, however experienced, need to have this work close at hand. They will, if they are wise, find reason to consult it and to learn from it at every stage of every case in which they appear.

David Anderson Q.C.
February 2014

PREFACE

This book explains how to enforce Union law in court. It sets out the remedies available to enforce Union law rights as well as the mechanisms affording judicial protection against unlawful action on the part of Union institutions, bodies, offices, and agencies. It is directly oriented towards legal practice. Accordingly, competition law, State aid, and anti-dumping law are dealt with in separate sections wherever it was felt appropriate to provide guidance as to how the available remedies work concretely in these fields.

Considerable attention has been given to the central role played by the national courts in the European Union legal order, both in deciding cases alone and in dialogue with the Court of Justice under the preliminary ruling procedure. In addition, the various direct actions which can be brought before the Court of Justice, the General Court, and the Civil Service Tribunal are described and explained.

This book reflects the state of the law on 1 December 2013. Two remarks should be made in that respect.

First, the General Court is currently in the process of revising its Rules of Procedure. That revision is essentially aimed at bringing the General Court's rules into line with the recent revision of the Court of Justice's Rules of Procedure as well as at adapting them to current practice. Since the book analyses in depth the Court of Justice's Rules of Procedure as well as the General Court's practice under its current Rules of Procedure, we have decided to proceed with the publication of this book without waiting for the formal adoption of the General Court's new Rules of Procedure.

Second, as from 1 January 2012, the judgments and orders rendered by the Court of Justice, the General Court, and the Civil Service Tribunal have—in contrast to judgments and orders rendered prior to that date—only been available electronically. Indeed, it has been decided to abandon the paper version of the European Court Reports, which has led the Court to reflect also on a new citation method for its case-law. Since the citation method used in this book—copying in this respect the current citation method of the Court of Justice—refers to the actual page number on which the judgments and orders are published in the European Court Reports and given that the electronic version of the European Court Reports does not use a system of continuous page numbering, all judgments and orders rendered after 1 January 2012, are cited in this book as 'not reported'. It goes without saying that they are all published on the website of the Court: <http://www.curia.europa.eu>.

Finally, all views expressed in this book are our own.

Koen Lenaerts
Ignace Maselis
Kathleen Gutman
Janek Tomasz Nowak (editor)

SUMMARY CONTENTS

Contents   xi
Table of Cases   xxv
Table of Legislation, Treaties, and Conventions   cxxxv

1. General Introduction   1

I THE JUDICIAL ORGANIZATION OF THE EUROPEAN UNION

2. The European Courts   13
3. Cooperation Between National Courts and the Court of Justice:
   The Reference for a Preliminary Ruling   48
4. National Procedural Autonomy, Equivalence, and Effectiveness   107

II ENFORCEMENT OF UNION LAW

5. The Action for Infringement of Union Law by a Member State   159
6. Preliminary Rulings on the Interpretation of Union Law   215

III PROTECTION AGAINST ACTS OF THE INSTITUTIONS

7. The Action for Annulment   253
8. The Action for Failure to Act   419
9. The Objection of Illegality   441
10. Preliminary Rulings on the Validity of Union Law   456
11. The Action for Damages   480
12. Application for an Opinion on the Compatibility with the Treaties
    of an International Agreement to be Concluded by the Union   550

IV SPECIAL FORMS OF PROCEDURE

13. Proceedings for Interim Measures Before the Union Courts   563
14. Proceedings for Authorization to Serve a Garnishee Order on the Union 619
15. Unlimited Jurisdiction of the Union Courts in Respect of Actions
    Relating to Sanctions   622
16. Appeals   632
17. The Review Procedure   658
18. Proceedings Brought by Officials and Other Servants
    of the Union (Staff Cases)   665

19. Jurisdiction of the Union Courts to Give Judgment Pursuant to an
    Arbitration Clause or a Special Agreement   686
20. Jurisdiction of the Union Courts over Disputes Relating to Intellectual
    Property Rights   700
21. Jurisdiction of the Court of Justice under Conventions Concluded by
    the Member States   715
22. Jurisdiction of the Court of Justice of the European Union with Regard
    to the Area of Freedom, Security, and Justice   726

V PROCEDURE BEFORE THE UNION COURTS

23. Common Procedural Rules Applicable to Cases Before the Union Courts   739
24. Procedure in the Case of References for a Preliminary Ruling   783
25. Procedure in the Case of Direct Actions   798
26. Procedure in the Case of Appeals Against Decisions of the General Court   862

Index   871

CONTENTS

Table of Cases   XXV
Table of Legislation, Treaties, and Conventions   CXXXV

1. **General Introduction**
    A. Overview   1.01
    B. The complete and the coherent system of judicial protection in
       the European Union   1.02
    C. Union based on the rule of law   1.03
    D. Role of the national courts   1.04
    E. Challenges underlying the system of judicial protection of the
       European Union   1.05
    F. Former Treaty framework and the pillar structure   1.06
    G. Changes brought by the Treaty of Lisbon   1.07
    H. The two-fold task of the Union judicature   1.08
    I. Structure of the book   1.09
    J. Procedural texts applicable to the procedure before
       the Union courts   1.10

I THE JUDICIAL ORGANIZATION OF THE EUROPEAN UNION

2. **The European Courts**
    I. The National Courts   2.01
    II. The Court of Justice of the European Union   2.03
    III. The Court of Justice   2.04
        A. Composition   2.04
        B. Internal organization   2.10
        C. Basic functions   2.21
    IV. The General Court   2.23
        A. Composition   2.23
        B. Internal organization   2.29
        C. Basic function   2.35
    V. The European Union Civil Service Tribunal   2.37
    VI. Allocation of Jurisdiction Among the Union Courts   2.45
        A. The position before the Treaty of Nice   2.45
        B. The Treaty of Nice: a fundamental reallocation of jurisdiction
           in embryo   2.47
        C. The present allocation of jurisdiction   2.49
3. **Cooperation Between National Courts and the Court of Justice:**
   The Reference for a Preliminary Ruling
    I. Introduction   3.01
        A. General   3.01

B. Changes brought by the Treaty of Lisbon	3.02
C. The EAEC Treaty	3.03
D. The former ECSC Treaty	3.04
E. Objectives of the preliminary ruling procedure	3.05
F. Sole power of the Court of Justice to declare a Union act invalid	3.06
G. Topics to be discussed	3.07
II. The Initiative for Requesting a Preliminary Ruling	3.08
A. What is a 'court or tribunal of a Member State'?	3.08
B. Types of proceedings in which a preliminary ruling may be requested	3.16
C. Timing and content of a request for a preliminary ruling	3.19
D. Annulment of a request for a preliminary ruling	3.29
III. Determination of the Relevance of the Request for a Preliminary Ruling	3.31
A. Task of the national court	3.31
B. The limits set by Union law	3.34
IV. The Duty to Request a Preliminary Ruling	3.43
A. General	3.43
B. What national courts and tribunals are involved?	3.44
C. Decisions against which there is no judicial remedy under national law	3.48
D. Limits placed on the duty to request a preliminary ruling	3.50
E. Enforcement of the obligation to request a preliminary ruling	3.56
F. Obligation to request a preliminary ruling *praeter legem*	3.59
4. National Procedural Autonomy, Equivalence, and Effectiveness	
I. Introduction	4.01
A. Overview	4.01
B. National procedural autonomy	4.02
C. Judicial supervision	4.03
D. Constraints	4.04
E. Expressions of the principle of effectiveness	4.05
II. The Principle of Effective Judicial Protection	4.06
A. General	4.06
B. Access to a court	4.07
C. Equal treatment	4.08
D. Statement of reasons	4.09
E. Deficiencies in the system of judicial protection in the European Union pre-Lisbon	4.10
F. Possible solutions identified in the case-law	4.11
G. The Treaty of Lisbon	4.12
III. Constraints: The Principles of Equivalence and Effectiveness	4.13
A. General	4.13
B. *Locus standi* and interest in bringing proceedings	4.17
C. Limitation periods and rules of evidence	4.19
D. Assessment of the legality of national provisions in the light of Union law	4.36

E. Raising pleas derived from Union law of the court's own motion   4.39
F. Effects of infringements of Union law   4.42
IV. Legal Protection in Proceedings for Interim Relief   4.60
    A. Two situations   4.60
    B. Allegedly illegal national measure   4.61
    C. Allegedly illegal Union measure   4.62
    D. Appeal against a national decision   4.63
    E. Counterpart of interim relief granted by the Union judicature   4.64

II ENFORCEMENT OF UNION LAW

5. **The Action for Infringement of Union Law by a Member State**
    I. Subject-Matter   5.01
       A. General   5.01
       B. Failure of a Member State to fulfil an obligation under the Treaties   5.05
       C. Relationship with special legal procedures to obtain a declaration that a Member State has failed to fulfil its obligations under Union law   5.21
    II. Identity of the Parties   5.31
       A. The applicant   5.31
       B. The defendant   5.36
    III. Special Characteristics   5.40
       A. The pre-litigation stage of the procedure   5.40
       B. The stage of the procedure held before the Court of Justice   5.51
    IV. Consequences   5.69
       A. Result of the action   5.69
       B. Legal force of the judgment declaring that a Member State has failed to fulfill its obligations   5.70
       C. Sanctions for failure to comply with the judgment   5.75
6. **Preliminary Rulings on the Interpretation of Union Law**
    I. Introduction   6.01
       A. General   6.01
       B. Topics to be discussed   6.02
    II. Subject-Matter of a Preliminary Ruling on Interpretation   6.03
       A. Overview   6.03
       B. The Treaties   6.04
       C. Acts of Union institutions, bodies, offices, or agencies   6.08
       D. International agreements concluded by the Union and acts of bodies established by such agreements   6.13
       E. Provisions of Union law to which national law refers   6.16
    III. Content of a Preliminary Ruling on Interpretation and Limits Placed on the Jurisdiction of the Court of Justice   6.18
       A. Interpretation versus application   6.18
       B. Judicial cooperation   6.19

C. Limits placed on the jurisdiction of the Court of Justice	6.20
D. The Court of Justice does not rule on facts and points of national law	6.21
E. Reformulation of questions	6.22
F. No jurisdiction to rule on the compatibility of national rules with Union law	6.23
G. The issues raised must fall within the scope of Union law	6.24
H. Reference back to the national court	6.25
I. Jurisdiction of the national court	6.26
IV. Consequences of a Preliminary Ruling on Interpretation	6.27
A. As regards the national court deciding the case at issue in the main proceedings	6.27
B. As regards national courts generally	6.30
C. Temporal effects	6.33

III PROTECTION AGAINST ACTS OF THE INSTITUTIONS

7. **The Action for Annulment**	
I. Introduction	7.01
A. General	7.01
B. Role in the complete and coherent system of judicial protection in the European Union	7.02
C. Overview of the changes brought by the Treaty of Lisbon	7.03
D. The former second and third pillars of the Union	7.04
E. Temporal effect of the Treaty of Lisbon	7.05
F. EAEC and former ECSC Treaties	7.06
G. Overview of the chapter	7.07
II. Subject-Matter	7.08
A. The concept of a reviewable act	7.08
B. The concept of a reviewable act: some fields of application	7.30
III. Identity of the Parties	7.69
A. Defendants	7.69
B. Applicants	7.76
IV. Special characteristics	7.145
A. Grounds for annulment	7.145
B. Conduct during the administrative procedure and admissibility of pleas in judicial proceedings	7.185
C. Standard of review in competition cases	7.190
D. Time limits	7.207
E. Examination *ex officio* of the conditions governing the admissibility of an action for annulment	7.217
V. Consequences	7.219
A. Result of an application for annulment	7.219
B. Authority of the judgment	7.222

8. **The Action for Failure to Act**
    I. Subject-Matter   8.01
        A. General   8.01
        B. Subject-matter of an action for failure to act   8.04
        C. Relationship between the action for annulment and the action for failure to act   8.09
    II. Identity of the Parties   8.11
        A. Defendants   8.11
        B. Applicants   8.12
    III. Special Characteristics   8.15
        A. Pre-litigation procedure   8.15
        B. Procedure before the Court   8.21
    IV. Consequences   8.23

9. **The Objection of Illegality**
    I. Subject-Matter   9.01
        A. General   9.01
        B. Acts against which an objection of illegality may be raised   9.05
    II. Identity of the Parties   9.09
        A. Natural or legal persons   9.10
        B. Member States and Union institutions   9.11
        C. Union bodies, offices, and agencies   9.12
        D. Objection raised by the parties and exceptionally by the Union courts   9.13
    III. Special Characteristics   9.14
        A. Requirements for admissibility   9.14
        B. Actions in which an objection of illegality may be raised   9.16
        C. Pleas in law   9.18
    IV. Consequences   9.19

10. **Preliminary Rulings on the Validity of Union Law**
    I. Introduction   10.01
        A. General   10.01
        B. Topics to be discussed   10.02
    II. Subject-Matter of Preliminary Ruling Proceedings Relating to the Validity of a Union Act   10.03
        A. Acts excluded from review   10.03
        B. Union acts in the former second and third pillars of the Union   10.04
        C. Review of the validity of international agreements concluded by the Union   10.05
        D. Acts of Union institutions, bodies, offices, or agencies   10.06
        E. Acts of bodies established by international agreements concluded by the Union   10.07
        F. Review of the validity of Union acts in the light of international agreements   10.08
        G. Binding and non-binding Union acts   10.09
        H. Acts of general application   10.10
        I. Individual acts and the *Deggendorf* line of case-law   10.11
        J. Failure to act   10.12

III. Substance of the Review of the Validity of a Union Act in Preliminary
    Ruling Proceedings   10.13
    A. Review of legality of Union acts reserved to the Court of Justice
       under *Foto-Frost*   10.13
    B. Differences compared with an action for annulment   10.14
    C. Grounds on which validity may be contested   10.15
    D. Assessment of validity normally based on the situation existing
       when Union measure adopted   10.16
    E. Finding of facts necessary to assess the legality of a given
       Union act   10.17
IV. Consequences of the Review of the Validity of a Union Act in
    Preliminary Ruling Proceedings   10.18
    A. Ruling of the Court of Justice   10.18
    B. Definitive effect of a declaration of invalidity   10.19
    C. Consequences of the declaration of invalidity in the national
       legal order   10.20
    D. Declaration of invalidity comparable to declaration of nullity   10.21
    E. Temporal effects   10.22
    F. Exceptional limitation of temporal effects   10.23

11. The Action for Damages
  I. Subject-Matter   11.01
    A. General   11.01
    B. Union 'non-contractual' liability   11.06
    C. The relationship between the action for damages and other
       actions in the Treaties   11.09
  II. Identity of the Parties   11.13
    A. Applicants   11.13
    B. Defendants   11.18
  III. Special Characteristics   11.33
    A. General   11.33
    B. Substantive requirements for liability   11.36
    C. Limitation period   11.86
  IV. Consequences   11.95
    A. Judgment holding the Union liable   11.95
    B. Judgment dismissing the action for damages   11.97

12. Application for an Opinion on the Compatibility with the Treaties of
an International Agreement to be Concluded by the Union
  I. Subject-Matter   12.01
    A. General   12.01
    B. The expression 'agreement envisaged'   12.07
  II. Identity of the Parties   12.09
    A. Applicants   12.09
    B. No obligation   12.10
  III. Special Characteristics   12.11
    A. Extent of the jurisdiction to give opinions   12.11
    B. Time limit   12.14
    C. Procedure before the Court   12.18

IV. Consequences   12.20
   A. Adverse opinion   12.20
   B. Favourable opinion   12.21

IV SPECIAL FORMS OF PROCEDURE

13. Proceedings for Interim Measures Before the Union Courts
   I. Subject-Matter   13.01
    A. Introduction   13.01
    B. Types of measure   13.04
    C. The ancillary nature of proceedings for interim measures   13.07
    D. The provisional nature of interim measures   13.15
   II. Identity of the Parties   13.17
    A. The applicant   13.17
    B. The defendant   13.20
   III. Special Characteristics   13.23
    A. Competent Judge   13.23
    B. Procedure before the Union courts   13.24
    C. Other requirements for admissibility   13.25
    D. Substantive requirements   13.31
   IV. Consequences   13.44
    A. Provisional nature   13.44
    B. Costs   13.45
    C. Appeal   13.46

14. Proceedings for Authorization to Serve a Garnishee Order on the Union
   I. Subject-Matter   14.01
    A. Principle and purpose   14.01
    B. Competent court   14.02
   II. Identity of the Parties   14.03
    A. Applicants   14.03
    B. Defendants   14.04
   III. Special Characteristics   14.05
    A. Automatic immunity   14.05
    B. Limited jurisdiction   14.06
    C. Applications   14.07

15. Unlimited Jurisdiction of the Union Courts in Respect of Actions Relating to Sanctions
   I. General   15.01
    A. Legal basis   15.01
    B. Changes brought by the Treaty of Lisbon   15.02
    C. EAEC Treaty and former ECSC Treaty   15.03
    D. Objective   15.04
    E. Notion of unlimited jurisdiction   15.05
   II. Scope of Review   15.06
    A. Review of the sanction   15.06
    B. Reasonableness of the sanction   15.07
    C. Criteria   15.08
   III. Force of Unlimited Jurisdiction   15.09

16. Appeals
  I. Subject-Matter   16.01
    A. General   16.01
    B. Appeals are confined to points of law   16.02
    C. Against what decisions of the General Court will an appeal lie?   16.12
  II. Identity of the Parties   16.14
    A. Appellant   16.14
    B. Interveners   16.15
    C. Union institutions and Member States   16.16
    D. Other parties to the proceedings   16.17
  III. Special Characteristics   16.18
    A. Pleas   16.18
    B. Appeal must clearly indicate errors of law   16.19
    C. No change in the subject-matter of the proceedings   16.20
    D. Inoperative or ineffective pleas   16.21
    E. Pleas of public interest (*moyens d'ordre public*)   16.22
    F. Injury suffered as a result of the bringing of the appeal   16.23
    G. Measures of inquiry   16.24
    H. Time limits   16.25
  IV. Consequences   16.26
    A. No suspensory effect   16.26
    B. Dismissal of the appeal   16.27
    C. Successful appeal   16.28
    D. Consequences of a successful appeal   16.29
    E. Court of Justice gives final judgment   16.30
    F. Referral back to the General Court   16.31
    G. Effects of a successful appeal brought by a Member State or a Union institution   16.32

17. The Review Procedure
  I. Subject-Matter   17.01
  II. Special Characteristics   17.02
    A. Determination whether there is a serious risk of the unity or consistency of Union law being affected   17.02
    B. Procedure   17.04
  III. Consequences   17.09

18. Proceedings Brought By Officials and Other Servants of the Union (Staff Cases)
  I. Subject-Matter   18.01
    A. General   18.01
    B. Against what measures will an action lie?   18.03
  II. Identity of the Parties   18.08
    A. Applicants   18.08
    B. Defendants   18.11

III. Special Characteristics		18.13
A. The requirement for a pre-litigation procedure		18.13
B. Priority of an action brought under Art. 270 TFEU		18.27
IV. Consequences		18.28
A. Decision of the Civil Service Tribunal		18.28
B. Costs		18.29
C. Appeal		18.30
D. Review		18.31

19. Jurisdiction of the Union Courts to Give Judgment Pursuant to an Arbitration Clause or a Special Agreement

I. Art. 272 TFEU	19.01
A. Subject-matter	19.01
B. Identity of the parties	19.13
C. Special characteristics	19.15
D. Consequences	19.21
II. Art. 273 TFEU	19.22
A. Disputes between Member States	19.22
B. EAEC and now-expired ECSC Treaties	19.23
C. Special agreement	19.24
D. Dispute related to the subject-matter of the Treaties	19.25
E. Only between Member States	19.26
F. Art. 273 TEU *juncto* Art. 344 TFEU	19.27

20. Jurisdiction of the Union Courts over Disputes Relating to Intellectual Property Rights

I. Subject-Matter	20.01
II. System of Legal Protection	20.02
A. Boards of Appeal	20.02
B. The General Court	20.03
III. Identity of the Parties	20.09
A. The defendant	20.09
B. The applicant	20.11
IV. Special Characteristics	20.12
A. Pleas in law	20.12
B. Time limits	20.18
C. Content of the application	20.19
V. Consequences	20.20

21. Jurisdiction of the Court of Justice under Conventions Concluded by the Member States

I. Subject-Matter	21.01
A. General	21.01
B. What conventions are involved?	21.02
II. Survey of the Court's Powers	21.06
A. Jurisdiction to give preliminary rulings	21.06
B. Direct actions	21.09

III. Procedure Before the Court of Justice   21.12
   A. Preliminary references   21.12
   B. Direct actions   21.13
IV. Consequences   21.14
   A. Preliminary references   21.14
   B. Direct actions   21.15

22. **Jurisdiction of the Court of Justice of the European Union with Regard to the Area of Freedom, Security, and Justice**
   I. Removal of Restrictions Placed on Jurisdiction of the Court of Justice of the European Union in the AFSJ   22.02
     A. Former Treaty framework   22.02
     B. Changes brought by the Treaty of Lisbon   22.05
   II. Urgent Preliminary Ruling Procedure in the AFSJ   22.06
     A. General   22.06
     B. Scope   22.07
     C. Procedure   22.13
     D. Relationship to expedited procedure   22.19

V PROCEDURE BEFORE THE UNION COURTS

23. **Common Procedural Rules Applicable to Cases Before the Union Courts**
   I. Language Arrangements   23.02
     A. Language of a case   23.02
     B. Internal language arrangements at the Court of Justice of the European Union   23.11
   II. Parties' Representation   23.14
     A. General   23.14
     B. Rights and obligations   23.20
   III. Service   23.24
     A. Methods of service   23.24
     B. Service by e-Curia   23.25
   IV. The Calculation of Time Limits   23.26
     A. Distinction between procedural time limits and limitation periods   23.26
     B. Preliminary objection   23.27
     C. Main steps in the calculation of procedural time limits   23.28
     D. *Dies a quo*   23.29
     E. Starting point in case of publication   23.30
     F. Duration of the period   23.31
     G. Extension of ten days on account of distance   23.32
     H. *Dies ad quem*   23.33
     I. Applications   23.34
     J. The Court is never closed   23.35
     K. Lodgment at the Registry   23.36
     L. Lodgment by telefax, e-Curia, or any other means of communication   23.37
     M. Excusable error, unforeseeable circumstances, or *force majeure*   23.38

V. Procedures for Dealing with Cases	23.39
A. General	23.39
B. Joinder of cases	23.43
C. Stay of proceedings	23.46
D. Deferment of the determination of a case	23.48
VI. Written Part of the Procedure	23.49
A. Lodging of procedural documents	23.49
B. e-Curia	23.50
C. Original procedural documents must be signed	23.51
D. Copies and translations	23.52
E. Annexes and schedule	23.53
F. All procedural documents must be dated	23.54
G. Length of procedural documents	23.55
VII. The Preliminary Report and Assignment of Cases	23.56
VIII. Measures of Organization of Procedure and Measures of Inquiry	23.57
A. Burden of proof on the parties and role played by the Union courts in fact-finding	23.57
B. Measures of organization of procedure	23.62
C. Measures of inquiry	23.64
IX. Oral Part of the Procedure	23.73
A. Opening of the oral part of the procedure	23.73
B. Course of the oral procedure	23.76
C. Reopening of the oral procedure	23.82
X. Judgments and Orders	23.85
A. The judgment or order	23.85
B. Content and formal requirements	23.88
C. Legal force	23.93
24. Procedure in the Case of References for a Preliminary Ruling	
I. The Order for Reference	24.02
A. Formal and substantive requirements	24.02
B. Notification	24.06
II. The Written Part of the Procedure	24.09
A. Written observations	24.09
B. Calculation of the two-month period for submission of written observations	24.10
C. No second exchange of written observations	24.11
D. No intervention	24.12
III. The Oral Part of the Procedure	24.13
A. Oral observations	24.13
B. Reopening of the oral part of the procedure	24.14
C. Cases in which no hearing is held	24.15
IV. Expedited and Urgent Preliminary Ruling Procedures	24.16
A. General	24.16
B. Expedited preliminary ruling procedure	24.17
C. Urgent preliminary ruling procedure	24.20
V. Special Characteristics	24.22
A. General	24.22

B. Measures of organization of procedure and measures of inquiry   24.23
C. Representation   24.24
D. Withdrawal of the reference for a preliminary ruling   24.25
E. Costs   24.26
F. Legal aid   24.27
G. Language of the case   24.28
H. No appeal   24.29
I. No interpretation   24.30
J. Revision   24.31
K. Rectification   24.32
L. EEA Agreement   24.33

25. **Procedure in the Case of Direct Actions**
  I. The Written Procedure   25.02
    A. The application   25.02
    B. The defence   25.28
    C. The reply and the rejoinder   25.46
    D. Directions for preparing procedural documents   25.52
  II. Intervention   25.58
    A. Aim and manner in intervention   25.58
    B. Substantive requirements   25.61
    C. Formal requirements   25.70
  III. The Expedited Procedure   25.79
    A. General   25.79
    B. Separate document   25.80
    C. Importance of the oral part of the procedure   25.81
  IV. Discontinuance, Cases that do not Proceed to Judgment,
    and Preliminary Issues   25.82
    A. Discontinuance   25.82
    B. No need to proceed to judgment   25.84
    C. Preliminary issues   25.86
  V. The Closure of Proceedings   25.88
    A. The judgment or order   25.88
    B. Costs   25.89
    C. Legal aid   25.101
    D. Requests and applications relating to judgments and orders   25.106

26. **Procedure in the Case of Appeals Against Decisions of the General Court**
  I. The Written Part of the Procedure   26.02
    A. Appeal   26.02
    B. Response   26.03
    C. Cross-appeal   26.04
    D. Reply and rejoinder   26.05
  II. The Oral Part of the Procedure   26.06
    A. Submission of reasoned request   26.06
    B. Cases in which no hearing is held   26.07
  III. Application of General Rules and Special Characteristics   26.08
    A. Provisions applicable to appeals   26.08

Contents

B. No measures of inquiry   26.09
C. Legal aid   26.10
D. Effect on cross-appeal of dismissal of the appeal   26.11
E. Procedure when a case is referred back to the General Court   26.12

Index   871

TABLE OF CASES

COURT OF JUSTICE

1/54 *France v High Authority* [1954 to 1956] E.C.R. 1. . . . . .7.146, 7.158, 7.159, 7.182
2/54 *Italy v High Authority* [1954 to 1956] E.C.R. 37 . . . . .7.158, 7.159, 25.14
3/54 *ASSIDER v High Authority* [1954 to 1956] E.C.R. 63 . . . . 7.222
6/54 *Netherlands v High Authority* [1954 to 1956] E.C.R. 103 . . . . 7.146, 7.158
7 and 9/54 *Groupement des Industries Sidérurgiques Luxembourgeoises v High Authority*
 [1954 to 1956] E.C.R. 175. . . . . 23.43, 23.45

5/55 *ASSIDER v High Authority* [1954 to 1956] E.C.R. 135 . . . . 25.126, 25.128
8/55 *Fédération Charbonnière de Belgique v High Authority* [1954 to 1956] E.C.R. 292. . . . . . 7.181, 7.182
9/55 *Société des Charbonnages de Beeringen and Others v High Authority* [1954 to 1956]
 E.C.R. 311 . . . . 25.12
10/55 *Mirossevich v High Authority* [1954 to 1956] E.C.R. 333 . . . . 11.76, 23.58

1/56 *Bourgaux v Common Assembly* [1954 to 1956] E.C.R. 361 . . . . 19.10
2/56 *Geitling v High Authority* [1957] E.C.R. 3 . . . . 7.170
7/56 and 3-7/57 *Algera and Others v Common Assembly* [1957 and 1958] E.C.R. 39 . . .7.12, 11.66, 25.12
8/56 *ALMA v High Authority* [1957 and 1958] E.C.R. 95 . . . . 15.09, 25.16
9/56 *Meroni v High Authority* [1957 and 1958] E.C.R. 133 . . . . .7.152, 7.155, 9.03, 10.06
10/56 *Meroni v High Authority* [1957 and 1958] E.C.R. 156 . . . . 9.03

1/57 and 14/57 *Société des Usines à Tubes de la Sarre v High Authority* [1957 and 1958]
 E.C.R. 105 . . . . 7.12, 7.13
2/57 *Compagnie des Hauts Fourneaux de Chasse v High Authority* [1957 and 1958]
 E.C.R. 199 . . . . 7.181, 7.182
13/57 *Wirtschaftsvereinigung Eisen- und Stahlindustrie and Others v High Authority*
 [1957 and 1958] E.C.R. 265 . . . . 7.181, 25.04
15/57 *Compagnie des Hauts Fourneaux de Chasse v High Authority* [1957 and 1958]
 E.C.R. 211 . . . . 7.181, 9.03
17/57 *De Gezamenlijke Steenkolenmijnen in Limburg v High Authority* [1959] E.C.R. 1 . . . . 8.15
18/57 *Nold v High Authority* [1959] E.C.R. 41 . . . . 7.83, 7.146, 7.158, 7.170, 7.174

3/58 R to 18/58 R and 25/58 R to 26/58 R *Barbara Erzbergbau and Others v High Authority*
 [1960] E.C.R. 220, (order of the President of 11 April 1960) 13.26
20/58 *Phoenix-Rheinrohr v High Authority* [1959] E.C.R. 75. . . . . 7.25
21/58 *Felten und Guilleaume Carlswerk Eisen- und Stahl and Walzwerke v High Authority* [1959]
 E.C.R. 99 . . . . 25.04
24/58 and 34/58 *Chambre Syndicale de la Sidérurgie de l'Est de la France and Others v High
 Authority* [1960] E.C.R. 281. . . . . 8.21, 25.86
32/58 and 33/58 *SNUPAT v High Authority* [1959] E.C.R. 127. . . . . .7.214, 9.08, 9.16
36/58 to 38/58 and 40/58 to 41/58 *SIMET and Others v High Authority* [1959]
 E.C.R. 157 . . . . .7.85, 7.99, 7.108

14/59 *Société des Fonderies de Pont-à-Mousson v High Authority* [1959]
 E.C.R. 215 . . . . .7.146, 9.13, 9.19, 23.72
15/59 and 29/59 *Société Métallurgique de Knutange v High Authority* [1960] E.C.R. 1 . . . . 7.16
23/59 *FERAM v High Authority* [1959] E.C.R. 245. . . . . 11.58
30/59 *De Gezamenlijke Steenkolenmijnen in Limburg v High Authority* [1961] E.C.R. 1 . . . . 25.60
31/59 R *Acciaieria e Tubificio di Brescia v High Authority* [1960] E.C.R. 98, (order of the
 President of 26 June 1959). 13.35, 13.40
33/59 *Compagnie des Hauts Forneaux de Chasse v High Authority* [1962] E.C.R. 381 . . . . 11.58
33/59, 46/59, and 47/59 *Compagnie des Hauts Fourneaux de Chasse and Others v High Authority*,
 not reported, (order of 2 June 1960) 25.86

36/59 to 38/59, and 40/59 *Präsident Ruhrkohlen-Verkaufsgesellschaft and Others v High Authority*
[1960] E.C.R. 423 . . . . 23.45
41/59 and 50/59 *Hamborner Bergbau and Others v High Authority* [1960] E.C.R. 493 . . . . 8.21
42/59 and 49/59 *SNUPAT v High Authority* [1961] E.C.R. 53 . . . . 7.23, 7.74, 23.61, 23.72, 25.60
42/59 and 49/59 TO *Breedband v Société des Aciéries du Temple and Others* [1962]
E.C.R. 145 . . . . 25.108
43/59, 44/59, and 45/59 R *Von Lachmüller and Others v Commission* [1960] E.C.R. 489,
(order of the President of 20 October 1959) 13.34
46/59 and 47/59 *Meroni and Others v High Authority* [1962] E.C.R. 411 . . . . 11.58, 11.87, 25.16

1/60 *FERAM v High Authority* [1960] E.C.R. 165 . . . . 25.118
9/60 and 12/60 *Vloeberghs v High Authority* [1961] E.C.R. 197 . . . . .9.19, 11.48, 11.58, 25.14
9/60 and 12/60 TO *Belgium v Vloeberghs and High Authority* [1962] E.C.R. 171 . . . . 25.108, 25.110
14/60, 16/60 to 17/60, 20/60, 24/60, 26/60 to 27/60, and 1/61 *Meroni and Others v
High Authority* [1961] E.C.R. 161 . . . . .9.19, 11.43, 11.76, 11.85
18/60 *Worms v High Authority* [1962] E.C.R. 195 . . . . 11.78, 25.14
19/60 and 21/60, 2/61 and 3/61 *Société Fives Lille Cail and Others v High Authority* [1961]
E.C.R. 281 . . . . .7.146, 11.43, 11.58, 25.12

7/61 *Commission v Italy* [1961] E.C.R. 317 . . . . 5.47
13/61 *Bosch and Others* [1962] E.C.R. 45 . . . . 3.29, 3.30, 6.17, 6.23

16/62 and 17/62 *Confédération Nationale des Producteurs de Fruits et Légumes and Others
v Council* [1962] E.C.R. 487, (order of 24 October 1962) 25.69
18/62 *Barge v High Authority* [1963] E.C.R. 259 . . . . 7.179, 9.08
24/62 *Germany v Commission* [1963] E.C.R. 63 . . . . 7.170
25/62 *Plaumann v Commission* [1963] E.C.R. 95 . . . . .4.11, 7.85, 7.90, 7.97, 7.106,
7.110, 7.117, 7.118, 7.122, 7.124, 11.09, 11.44
26/62 *Van Gend & Loos* [1963] E.C.R. 1 . . . . 2.02, 3.44, 5.03, 24.13
28/62 to 30/62 *Da Costa en Schaake and Others* [1963] E.C.R. 31 . . . . 3.44, 3.52
31/62 and 33/62 *Wöhrmann and Others v Commission* [1962] E.C.R. 501 . . . . .3.19, 7.216, 9.01
35/62 and 16/63 *Leroy v High Authority* [1963] E.C.R. 197 . . . . 25.96
35/62 and 16/63 R *Leroy v High Authority* [1963] E.C.R. 213, (order of the President
of 16 July 1963) 13.07
36/62 *Société des Aciéries du Temple v High Authority* [1963] E.C.R. 289 . . . . 11.85

2/63 to 10/63 *Società Industriale Acciaerie San Michele and Others v High Authority* [1963]
E.C.R. 327 . . . . 25.12
15/63 *Lassalle v European Parliament* [1964] E.C.R. 31 . . . . 11.76, 25.61
18/63 *Wollast (née Schmitz) v EEC* [1964] E.C.R. 85 . . . . 18.10, 25.08
19/63 and 65/63 *Prakash v Commission* [1965] E.C.R. 533 . . . . 25.12
23/63, 24/63, and 52/63 *Usines Emile Henricot and Others v High Authority* [1963]
E.C.R. 217 . . . . .7.16, 7.27, 25.94, 25.96
26/63 *Pistoj v Commission* [1964] E.C.R. 341 . . . . 18.04
27/63 *Raponi v Commission* [1964] E.C.R. 129 . . . . 25.08
29/63, 31/63, 36/63, 39/63 to 47/63, 50/63, and 51/63 *SA des Laminoirs, Hauts
Fourneaux, Forges, Fonderies et Usines de la Providence and Others v High Authority*
[1965] E.C.R. 911 . . . . 11.43, 11.68
53/63 and 54/63 *Lemmerz-Werke and Others v High Authority* [1963] E.C.R. 239 . . . . 7.16
65/63 R *Prakash v Commission* [1965] E.C.R. 576, (order of the President of
25 June 1963) 13.16, 13.34
66/63 *Netherlands v High Authority* [1964] E.C.R. 533 . . . . 7.146
68/63 *Luhleich v Commission* [1965] E.C.R. 581 . . . . 11.76
70/63 A *High Authority v Cllotti and Court of Justice* [1965] E.C.R. 275 . . . . 25.125
73-74/63 *Handelsvereniging Rotterdam v Minister van Landbouw* [1964] E.C.R. 1 . . . . 7.158, 10.15
78/63 *Huber v Commission* [1964] E.C.R. 367 . . . . 18.05
79/63 and 82/63 *Reynier and Erba v Commission* [1964] E.C.R. 259 . . . . 25.08
80/63 *Degreef v Commission* [1964] E.C.R. 391 . . . . 25.16
83/63 *Stefan Krawczynski v Commission* [1965] E.C.R. 623 . . . . 25.16
90/63 and 91/63 *Commission v Luxembourg and Belgium* [1964] E.C.R. 625 . . . . 7.24
101/63 *Wagner* [1964] E.C.R. 195 . . . . 3.23

106/63 and 107/63 *Toepfer and Getreide-Import v Commission* [1965] E.C.R. 405 . . . . 7.95, 7.98
108/63 *Merlini v High Authority* [1965] E.C.R. 1 . . . . 13.28, 23.51
110/63 *Willame v Commission* [1965] E.C.R. 649 . . . . 11.66, 25.125
111/63 *Lemmerz-Werke v High Authority* [1965] E.C.R. 677 . . . . 25.12, 25.65

1/64 *Glucoseries Réunies v Commission* [1964] E.C.R. 413. . . . . 7.99
6/64 *Costa v ENEL* [1964] E.C.R. 585 . . . . 3.45, 6.23
6/64 *Costa v ENEL* [1964] E.C.R. 614, (order of 3 June 1964) 6.18
9/64 and 25/64 *FERAM and Others v High Authority* [1965] E.C.R. 311 . . . . 11.67
12/64 and 29/64 *Ley v Commission* [1965] E.C.R. 107. . . . . 7.29, 25.49
20/64 *Albatros* [1965] E.C.R. 29 . . . . 3.42, 6.18
21/64 *Macchiorlati Dalmas v Commission* [1965] E.C.R. 175 . . . . 7.158, 9.08
23/64 *Vandevyvere v European Parliament* [1965] E.C.R. 157. . . . . 18.08
28/64 REV *Müller v Council* [1967] E.C.R. 141 . . . . 25.120
32/64 *Italy v Commission* [1965] E.C.R. 365. . . . . 13.28
38/64 *Getreide-Import v Commission* [1965] E.C.R. 203 . . . . 7.99
45/64 *Commission v Italy* [1965] E.C.R. 857. . . . . 5.53, 23.58
55/64 *Lens v Court of Justice* [1965] E.C.R. 837. . . . . 25.16
56/64 and 58/64 *Consten and Grundig v Commission* [1964] E.C.R. 299. . . . . 7.161

8/65 *Acciaierie e Ferriere Pugliesi v High Authority* [1966] E.C.R. 1 . . . . 7.171
16/65 *Schwarze* [1965] E.C.R. 877. . . . . 3.05, 3.23, 6.18, 7.170, 10.15
18/65 R *Gutmann v Commission* [1966] E.C.R. 135, (order of the President of
    8 April 1965). 13.07, 13.15
18 and 35/65 *Gutmann v Commission* [1966] E.C.R. 103. . . . . 7.183, 7.184
25/65 and 26/65 *SIMET and FERAM v High Authority* [1967] E.C.R. 33. . . . . 7.09
28/65 *Fonzi v Commission* [1966] E.C.R. 506, (order of 10 March 1966) 25.86
32/65 *Italy v Council and Commission* [1966] E.C.R. 389. . . . . 9.08, 9.11
44/65 *Singer* [1965] E.C.R. 965. . . . . 9.17, 10.14
48/65 *Lütticke v Commission* [1966] E.C.R. 19 . . . . 5.33, 5.34, 8.10
59/65 *Schreckenberg v Commission* [1966] E.C.R. 543 . . . . 11.10
61/65 *Vaassen (née Göbbels)* [1966] E.C.R. 261 . . . . 3.08, 3.12
62/65 *Serio v Commission* [1966] E.C.R. 561. . . . . 25.12

5/66, 7/66, and 13/66 to 24/66 *Kampffmeyer and Others v Commission* [1967]
    E.C.R. 245 . . . . 11.32, 11.44, 11.48, 11.58, 11.65, 11.81, 11.94
8/66 to 11/66 *Cimenteries CBR Cementbedrijven and Others v Commission* [1967]
    E.C.R. 75 . . . . 7.16, 7.20, 7.35
24/66 bis *Gesellschaft für Getreidehandel v Commission* [1973] E.C.R. 1599 . . . . 25.126
29/66 R *Gutmann v Commission* [1967] E.C.R. 241, (order of the President of
    28 November 1966). 13.35
30/66 *Becher v Commission* [1967] E.C.R. 285 . . . . 11.44

4/67 *Muller (née Collignon) v Commission* [1967] E.C.R. 365 . . . . 7.217, 11.10, 11.85
5/67 *Beus v Hauptzollamt München* [1968] E.C.R. 83 . . . . 7.170, 10.15, 10.17
13/67 *Becher* [1968] E.C.R. 196, (order of 16 May 1968) 6.28, 24.29
16/67 *Labeyrie v Commission* [1968] E.C.R. 293 . . . . 11.44
35/67 *Van Eick v Commission* [1968] E.C.R. 329 . . . . 7.157

5/68 *Sayag and Others* [1968] E.C.R. 395. . . . . 11.23
6/68 *Zuckerfabrik Watenstedt v Council* [1968] E.C.R. 409. . . . . 7.99
7/68 *Commission v Italy* [1968] E.C.R. 423. . . . . 5.01, 5.31, 5.62, 5.65
10/68 and 18/68 'Eridania' *Zuccherifici Nazionali and Others v Commission* [1969]
    E.C.R. 459 . . . . 7.95, 7.210, 8.06, 8.10
13/68 *Salgoil* [1968] E.C.R. 453. . . . . 3.31, 6.18
25/68 *Schertzer v European Parliament* [1977] E.C.R. 1729 . . . . 7.170
29/68 *Milch-, Fett-, und Eierkontor* [1969] E.C.R. 165. . . . . 6.27, 6.28
30/68 *Lacroix v Commission* [1970] E.C.R. 301. . . . . 7.09, 25.10
31/68 *Chanel* [1970] E.C.R. 404, (order of 16 June 1970). 3.30
32/68 *Graselli v Commission* [1969] E.C.R. 505. . . . . 18.04

4/69 *Lütticke v Commission* [1971] E.C.R. 325 .... 11.01, 11.09, 25.12
6/69 and 11/69 *Commission v France* [1969] E.C.R. 523 .... 5.66
7/69 *Commission v Italy* [1970] E.C.R. 111 .... 5.56
9/69 *Sayag and Others* [1969] E.C.R. 329 .... 11.21
13/69 *Van Eick v Commission* [1970] E.C.R. 3 .... 25.117
19/69 to 20/69, 25/69, and 30/69 *Richez-Parise and Others v Commission* [1970]
    E.C.R. 325 .... 11.44, 11.59
28/69 *Commission v Italy* [1970] E.C.R. 187 .... 5.17
29/69 *Stauder* [1969] E.C.R. 419 .... 3.17
31/69 *Commission v Italy* [1970] E.C.R. 25 .... 5.14, 5.32, 5.43, 7.161
33/69 *Commission v Italy* [1970] E.C.R. 93 .... 5.68
41/69 *ACF Chemiefarma v Commission* [1970] E.C.R. 661 .... 7.34, 7.160
48/69 *ICI v Commission* [1972] E.C.R. 619 .... 7.157, 7.175, 7.215
50/69 R *Germany v Commission* [1969] E.C.R. 449, (order of the President of
    5 October 1969) 13.04, 13.05
55/69 *Cassella v Commission* [1972] E.C.R. 887 .... 7.161, 7.170
56/69 *Hoechst v Commission* [1972] E.C.R. 927 .... 7.170
63/69 *Compagnie Française Commerciale and Financière v Commission* [1970] E.C.R. 221 .... 7.99
69/69 *Alcan v Commission* [1970] E.C.R. 385 .... 7.95
75/69 *Hake v Commission* [1970] E.C.R. 535 .... 8.21, 25.91, 25.93
77/69 *Commission v Belgium* [1970] E.C.R. 237 .... 5.37

6/70 *Borromeo v Commission* [1970] E.C.R. 815 .... 8.13
8/70 *Commission v Italy* [1970] E.C.R. 961 .... 5.10, 5.38
15/70 *Chevalley v Commission* [1970] E.C.R. 975 .... 8.08, 8.09, 8.11, 8.13
18/70 *Duraffour v Council* [1971] E.C.R. 515 .... 18.08
22/70 *Commission v Council* (the AETR case) [1971] E.C.R. 263 .... 7.17, 7.20, 7.21, 7.158, 7.221, 10.05
25/70 *Köster* [1970] E.C.R. 1161 .... 7.152
40/70 *Sirena* [1979] E.C.R. 3169, (order of 18 October 1979) 6.28, 24.29
41/70 to 44/70 *International Fruit and Others v Commission* [1971] E.C.R. 411 .... 7.93
45/70 and 49/70 *Bode v Commission* [1971] E.C.R. 465 .... 7.217
48/70 *Bernardi v European Parliament* [1971] E.C.R. 175 .... 7.157
56/70 REV *Mandelli v Commission* [1971] E.C.R. 1 .... 25.118
59/70 *Netherlands v Commission* [1971] E.C.R. 639 .... 8.17
62/70 *Bock v Commission* [1971] E.C.R. 897 .... 7.95, 7.98
77/70 *Prelle v Commission* [1971] E.C.R. 561 .... 23.83

1/71 SA *X v Commission* [1971] E.C.R. 363, (order of 11 May 1971) 14.01, 14.05
5/71 *Zuckerfabrik Schöppenstedt v Council* [1971] E.C.R. 975 .... 11.09, 11.44, 11.45, 11.48, 11.76
7/71 *Commission v France* [1971] E.C.R. 1003 .... 5.02, 5.31, 5.62
8/71 *Komponistenverband v Commission* [1971] E.C.R. 705 .... 8.05, 8.10, 8.19
9/71 and 11/71 *Compagnie d'Approvisionnement, de Transport et Crédit and Others v
    Commission* [1972] E.C.R. 391 .... 7.88, 7.147, 11.07, 11.09, 11.30
10/71 *Muller* [1971] E.C.R. 723 .... 6.22
15/71 *Mackprang v Commission* [1971] E.C.R. 797 .... 8.13
24/71 *Meinhardt (née Forderung) v Commission* [1972] E.C.R. 269 .... 18.08
37/71 *Jamet v Commission* [1972] E.C.R. 483 .... 7.220, 25.120
40/71 *Richez-Parise v Commission* [1972] E.C.R. 73 .... 25.120
42/71 *Nordgetreide v Commission* [1972] E.C.R. 105 .... 7.18, 7.101, 8.10, 8.19
43/71 *Politi* [1971] E.C.R. 1039 .... 3.24
44/71 *Marcato v Commission* [1972] E.C.R. 427 .... 18.15
48/71 *Commission v Italy* [1972] E.C.R. 527 .... 5.70
96/71 *Haegeman v Commission* [1972] E.C.R. 1005 .... 11.29

6/72 *Europemballage and Continental Can v Commission* [1973] E.C.R. 215 .... 7.213, 7.214
6/72 DEP *Europemballage and Continental Can v Commission* [1975] E.C.R. 495,
    (order of 18 April 1975) 25.92
8/72 *Vereeniging van Cementhandelaren v Commission* [1972] E.C.R. 977 .... 7.157
10 and 47/72 *Di Pillo v Commission* [1973] E.C.R. 763 .... 11.59, 11.66
11/72 *Giordano v Commission* [1973] E.C.R. 417 .... 11.94
13/72 *Netherlands v Commission* [1973] E.C.R. 27 .... 7.170

21/72 to 24/72 *International Fruit Company v Produktschap voor Groenten en Fruit*
 [1972] E.C.R. 1219 . . . . 7.178, 10.14
39/72 *Commission v Italy* [1973] E.C.R. 101 . . . . 5.02, 5.19, 5.59, 5.73
40/72 *Schroeder* [1973] E.C.R. 125 . . . . 7.147
41/72 *Getreide-Import* [1973] E.C.R. 1 . . . . 10.15
43/72 *Merkur Aussenhandels v Commission* [1973] E.C.R. 1055 . . . . 7.88, 11.30
48/72 *Brasserie de Haecht v Wilkin-Janssen* [1973] E.C.R. 77 . . . . 7.34
56/72 *Goeth v Commission* [1973] E.C.R. 181 . . . . 7.23
57/72 *Westzucker v Einfuhr-und Vorratsstelle Zucker* [1973] E.C.R. 321 . . . . 7.170
62/72 *Bollmann* [1973] E.C.R. 269 . . . . 24.26
63/72 to 69/72 *Werhahn Hansamühle and Others v Council* [1973] E.C.R. 1229 . . . . 11.19, 11.50
70/72 *Commission v Germany* [1973] E.C.R. 813 . . . . .5.23, 5.49, 5.69
75/72 *Perinciolo v Council* [1973] E.C.R. 511 . . . . 7.217
81/72 *Commission v Council* [1973] E.C.R. 575 . . . . 7.221

4/73 *Nold v Commission* [1974] E.C.R. 491 . . . . 7.178
6/73 and 7/73 *Instituto Chemioterapico Italiano and Commercial Solvents v Commission*
 [1974] E.C.R. 223 . . . . 15.07
9/73 *Schlüter* [1973] E.C.R. 1135 . . . . 6.08, 7.24
15/73 to 33/73, 52/73 to 53/73, 57/73 to 109/73, 116/73 to 117/73, 123/73, 132/73 and 135/73
 to 137/73 *Schots (née Kortner) and Others v Council and Others* [1974] E.C.R. 177 . . . . 7.12, 9.19
34/73 *Fratelli Variola* [1973] E.C.R. 981 . . . . 5.19
36/73 *Nederlandse Spoorwegen* [1973] E.C.R. 1299 . . . . 3.10
40/73 to 48/73, 50/73, 54/73 to 56/73, 111/73, 113/73, and 114/73 *Suiker Unie and*
 Others v Commission [1975] E.C.R. 1663 . . . . 25.94
41/73, 43/73 to 48/73, 50/73, 111/73, 113/73 and 114/73 *Générale Sucrière and Others*
 v Commission [1973] E.C.R. 1465, (order of 11 December 1973) 25.61, 25.69, 25.131
41/73, 43/73, and 44/73 INT *Générale Sucrière and Others v Commission* [1977] E.C.R. 445 . . . . . 25.132
112/73, 144/73 and 145/73 *Campogrande and Others v Commission* [1974] E.C.R. 957 . . . . 23.43
120/73 *Lorenz* [1973] E.C.R. 1471 . . . . 5.24
127/73 *BRT* [1974] E.C.R. 51 . . . . 3.29
130/73 *Vandeweghe and Others* [1973] E.C.R. 1329 . . . . 6.13
134/73 *Holtz & Willemsen v Council* [1974] E.C.R. 1 . . . . 8.13
146/73 *Rheinmühlen-Düsseldorf ('Rheinmühlen II')* [1974] E.C.R. 139 . . . . 3.30
153/73 *Holtz & Willemsen v Council and Commission* [1974] E.C.R. 675 . . . . 11.10, 11.30, 11.36
166/73 *Rheinmühlen-Düsseldorf ('Rheinmühlen I')* [1974] E.C.R. 33 . . . . 3.01, 3.07, 3.19, 4.40
167/73 *Commission v France* [1974] E.C.R. 359 . . . . 5.17, 5.31
169/73 *Compagnie Continentale v Council* [1975] E.C.R. 117 . . . . 11.18, 11.58, 11.85
173/73 *Italy v Commission* [1974] E.C.R. 709 . . . . 5.24
175/73 *Union Syndicale and Others v Council* [1974] E.C.R. 917 . . . . 7.83, 18.10
181/73 *Haegeman* [1974] E.C.R. 449 . . . . 6.13, 7.178
185/73 *Hauptzollamt Bielefeld v König* [1974] E.C.R. 607 . . . . 7.175, 7.210
188/73 *Grassi v Council* [1974] E.C.R. 1099 . . . . 25.16

17/74 *Transocean Marine Paint v Commission* [1974] E.C.R. 1063 . . . . 7.161, 7.220
18/74 *Syndicat Général du Personnel des Organismes Européens v Commission* [1974]
 E.C.R. 933 . . . . 7.83, 18.10
19/74 and 20/74 *Kali & Salz and Kali-Chemie v Commission* [1975] E.C.R. 499 . . . . 23.43
20/74 R II *Kali-Chemie v Commission* [1974] E.C.R. 787, (order of the President of
 8 July 1974) 13.15
26/74 *Roquette Frères v Commission* [1976] E.C.R. 677 . . . . .11.29, 11.31, 11.75, 11.76
32/74 *Haaga* [1974] E.C.R. 1201 . . . . 3.17
56/74 to 60/74 *Kampffmeyer and Others v Commission and Council* [1976] E.C.R. 711 . . . . . . 11.67, 11.89
68/74 *Alaimo* [1975] E.C.R. 109 . . . . 6.30
71/74 R and RR *Fruiten Groentenimporthandel and Frubo v Commission* [1974]
 E.C.R. 1031, (order of the President of 15 October 1974) 13.06
72/74 *Union Syndicale and Others v Council* [1975] E.C.R. 401 . . . . 11.15
73/74 *Papiers peints v Commission* [1975] E.C.R. 1491 . . . . 7.170
74/74 *CNTA v Commission* [1975] E.C.R. 533 . . . . .11.50, 11.65, 11.77, 25.14
79/74 *Küster v European Parliament* [1975] E.C.R. 725 . . . . 18.05
90/74 *Deboeck v Commission* [1975] E.C.R. 1123 . . . . 18.07

95/74 to 98/74, 15/75, and 100/75 *Coopératives Agricoles de Céréales and Others v
Commission and Council* [1975] E.C.R. 1615 . . . . 11.68
99/74 *Société des Grands Moulins des Antilles v Commission* [1975] E.C.R. 1531 . . . . 11.30
100/74 *CAM v Commission* [1975] E.C.R. 1393 . . . . 7.100

Opinion 1/75 *Draft understanding on a Local Cost Standard drawn up under the auspices
of the OECD* [1975] E.C.R. 1355 . . . . 10.05, 12.01, 12.07, 12.08, 12.11
3/75 R *Johnson & Firth Brown v Commission* [1975] E.C.R. 1, (order of the President of
16 January 1975) 13.34, 13.42
9/75 *Meyer-Burckhardt v Commission* [1975] E.C.R. 1171 . . . . 18.27
23/75 *Rey Soda* [1975] E.C.R. 1279 . . . . 3.17, 7.153, 10.20
40/75 *Produits Bertrand v Commission* [1976] E.C.R. 1 . . . . 5.34
43/75 *Defrenne* [1976] E.C.R. 455 . . . . 6.34
44/75 R *Könecke v Commission* [1975] E.C.R. 637, (order of the President of 28 May 1975) 13.16
52/75 *Commission v Italy* [1976] E.C.R. 277 . . . . 5.65
56/75 *Elz v Commission* [1977] E.C.R. 1617 . . . . 25.119
58/75 *Sergy v Commission* [1976] E.C.R. 1139 . . . . 11.85, 18.22
59/75 *Manghera and Others* [1976] E.C.R. 91 . . . . 10.09
87/75 *Bresciani* [1976] E.C.R. 129 . . . . 6.13
105/75 *Giuffrida v Council* [1976] E.C.R. 1395 . . . . 7.184
109/75 R *National Carbonising v Commission* [1975] E.C.R. 1193, (order of the President of
22 October 1975). 13.05
110/75 *Mills v EIB* [1976] E.C.R. 955 . . . . 18.09
113/75 *Frecassetti* [1976] E.C.R. 983 . . . . 6.08

Opinion 1/76 *Draft Agreement establishing a European laying-up fund for inland
waterway vessels* [1977] E.C.R. 741 . . . . 7.152, 7.154, 10.07, 12.01, 12.08, 12.11
1/76 *Wack v Commission* [1976] E.C.R. 1017 . . . . 7.23
5/76 *Jänsch v Commission* [1976] E.C.R. 1027 . . . . 7.213
15/76 and 16/76 *France v Commission* [1979] E.C.R. 321 . . . . 5.01, 7.59, 7.147, 7.187
23/76 *Pellegrini and Others v Commission* [1976] E.C.R. 1807 . . . . 7.183, 19.15
26/76 *Metro v Commission* [1977] E.C.R. 1875 . . . . 7.23, 7.43, 7.86
27/76 *United Brands and United Brands Continentaal v Commission* [1978] E.C.R. 207 . . . . . 7.192, 7.220
31/76 *Hebrant (née Macevicius) v European Parliament* [1977] E.C.R. 883. . . . . 7.213
33/76 *Rewe* [1976] E.C.R. 1989 . . . . 4.01, 4.02, 4.13, 4.23, 4.40
44/76 *Milch-, Fett- und Eier-Kontor v Council and Commission* [1977] E.C.R. 393 . . . . 25.06
45/76 *Comet* [1976] E.C.R. 2043 . . . . 4.02, 4.13, 4.19, 4.23
50/76 *Amsterdam Bulb* [1977] E.C.R. 137. . . . . 5.19
52/76 *Benedetti* [1977] E.C.R. 163 . . . . 3.26, 6.27
61/76 *Geist v Commission* [1977] E.C.R. 1419. . . . . 7.170
62/76 *Strehl* [1977] E.C.R. 211 . . . . 10.15
64/76 and 113/76, 167/78 and 239/78, 27/79 to 28/79 and 45/79 *Dumortier
Frères v Council* [1979] E.C.R. 3091 . . . . 11.50, 11.70, 11.72, 11.73, 11.78
66/76 *CFDT v Council* [1977] E.C.R. 305 . . . . 7.142
78/76 *Steinike & Weinlig* [1977] E.C.R. 595 . . . . 5.65
83 and 94/76, 4, 15, and 40/77 *HNL and Others v Council and Commission* [1978]
E.C.R. 1209. . . . . 11.45, 11.48, 11.50, 11.56, 11.57
85/76 *Hoffmann-La Roche v Commission* [1979] E.C.R. 461 . . . . 7.161
88/76 *Société pour l'Exportation des Sucres v Commission* [1977] E.C.R. 709 . . . . 7.140
88/76 R *Société pour l'Exportation des Sucres* [1976] E.C.R. 1585, (order of the President of
19 October 1976). 13.07
91/76 R *De Lacroix v Court of Justice* [1976] E.C.R. 1561, (order of the President of
15 October 1976). 13.04, 13.16
97/76 *Merkur v Commission* [1977] E.C.R. 1063. . . . . 11.60
101/76 *Koninklijke Scholten Honig v Council and Commission* [1977] E.C.R. 797. . . . . 7.16, 7.85
107/76 *Hoffmann-La Roche* [1977] E.C.R. 957 . . . . 3.17, 3.44, 3.46
112/76 *Manzoni* [1977] E.C.R. 1647 . . . . 3.61, 6.32
114/76 *Bela-Mühle v Grows-Farm* [1977] E.C.R. 1211. . . . . 7.178
121/76 *Milo v Commission* [1977] E.C.R. 1971 . . . . 7.161

5/77 *Tedeschi* [1977] E.C.R. 1555 . . . . 3.31, 7.152
25/77 *De Roubaix v Commission* [1978] E.C.R. 1081. . . . . 18.05
29/77 *Roquette Frères v France* [1977] E.C.R. 1835 . . . . 7.180
31/77 R and 53/77 R *Commission v United Kingdom* [1977] E.C.R. 921,
    (order of 21 May 1977) 13.12
34/77 *Oslizlok v Commission* [1978] E.C.R. 1099 . . . . 7.09
54/77 *Herpels v Commission* [1978] E.C.R. 585 . . . . 18.21
56/77 *Agence Européenne d'Intérims v Commission* [1978] E.C.R. 2215 . . . . 23.82
61/77 R *Commission v Ireland* [1977] E.C.R. 937, (order of 22 May 1977). 13.12
61/77 R II *Commission v Ireland* [1977] E.C.R. 1411, (order of 13 July 1977) 13.12, 13.41
65/77 *Razanatsimba* [1977] E.C.R. 2229 . . . . 3.10, 3.29, 6.13
68/77 *IFG v Commission* [1978] E.C.R. 353 . . . . 11.09
70/77 *Simmenthal* [1978] E.C.R. 1453. . . . . 3.17
75/77 *Mollet v Commission* [1978] E.C.R. 897. . . . . 7.161, 11.66
77/77 *BP v Commission* [1978] E.C.R. 1513 . . . . 7.143
86/77 *Ditterich v Commission* [1978] E.C.R. 1855. . . . . 7.170
87/77 and 130/77, 22/83, 9/84 and 10/84 *Salerno and Others v Commission* [1985]
    E.C.R. 2523. . . . . 7.93, 9.01
90/77 *Stimming v Commission* [1977] E.C.R. 2113, (order of 10 November 1977) 25.06
103/77 and 145/77 *Royal Scholten Honig* [1978] E.C.R. 2037 . . . . 10.15
104/77 *Oehlschläger* [1978] E.C.R. 791. . . . . 6.21, 24.23
106/77 *Simmenthal* [1978] E.C.R. 629. . . . . 2.01, 3.20, 3.29, 4.36
113/77 *NTN Toyo Bearing v Council* [1979] E.C.R. 1185 . . . . 7.85, 7.93, 7.133, 25.98
116/77 and 124/77 *Amylum and Others v Council and Commission* [1979] E.C.R. 3479. . . . . 11.31, 11.60
116/77, 124/77, and 143/77 *Amylum and Others v Council and Commission* [1978]
    E.C.R. 893, (order of 12 April 1978). 25.65
118/77 *ISO v Council* [1979] E.C.R. 1277 . . . . 7.85, 7.93, 7.133, 25.98
119/77 *Nippon Seiko v Council and Commission* [1979] E.C.R. 1303. . . . . 7.85, 7.93, 25.98
120/77 *Koyo Seiko v Council and Commission* [1979] E.C.R. 1337 . . . . 7.93, 25.98
121/77 *Nachi Fujikoshi v Council* [1979] E.C.R. 1363 . . . . 7.85, 7.93, 25.98
123/77 *UNICME v Council* [1978] E.C.R. 845. . . . . 7.93, 7.95, 7.99
132/77 *Société pour l'Exportation des Sucres v Commission* [1978] E.C.R. 1061 . . . . 11.81
135/77 *Bosch* [1978] E.C.R. 855 . . . . 6.11, 6.27
148/77 *Hansen* [1978] E.C.R. 1787 . . . . 6.21
156/77 *Commission v Belgium* [1978] E.C.R. 1881 . . . . 5.66, 9.07

Opinion 1/78 *International Agreement on Natural Rubber* [1979]
    E.C.R. 2871. . . . . 12.01, 12.06, 12.11, 12.15
Ruling 1/78 *Draft Convention of the International Energy Agency on the Physical Protection*
    of Nuclear Materials, Facilities and Transports [1978] E.C.R. 2151 . . . . 12.06
4/78 R *Salerno v Commission* [1978] E.C.R. 1, (order of the President of 13 January 1978) 13.35
8/78 *Milac* [1978] E.C.R. 1721 . . . . 6.11, 10.18
17/78 *Deshormes v Commission* [1979] E.C.R. 189. . . . . 18.07
30/78 *Distillers v Commission* [1980] E.C.R. 2229 . . . . 7.36, 7.162, 25.76
83/78 *Pigs Marketing Board v Redmond* [1978] E.C.R. 2347. . . . . 3.31
90/78 R *Granaria v Council and Commission* [1979] E.C.R. 1081 . . . . 8.13, 11.68, 11.77
92/78 R *Simmenthal v Commission* [1978] E.C.R. 1129, (order of the President of
    22 May 1978) 13.42
92/78 *Simmenthal v Commission* [1979] E.C.R. 777. . . . . . . 7.141, 7.176, 7.181, 7.184, 7.221, 7.222, 9.03
93/78 *Mattheus* [1978] E.C.R. 2203. . . . . 3.19
98/78 *Racke* [1979] E.C.R. 69 . . . . 7.201, 7.210
101/78 *Granaria* [1979] E.C.R. 623. . . . . 11.27, 11.31
116/78 REV *Bellintani v Commission* [1980] E.C.R. 23 . . . . 25.119, 25.123
125/78 *GEMA v Commission* [1979] E.C.R. 3173 . . . . 8.19, 8.20, 25.16
141/78 *France v United Kingdom* [1979] E.C.R. 2923 . . . . 5.35, 5.69
155/78 *M v Commission* [1980] E.C.R. 1797 . . . . 23.66
159/78 *Commission v Italy* [1979] E.C.R. 3247. . . . . 5.17
166/78 R *Italy v Council* [1978] E.C.R. 1745, (order of the President of 28 August 1978) 13.40, 13.41
166/78 *Italy v Council* [1979] E.C.R. 2575 . . . . 7.76
168/78 *Commission v France* [1980] E.C.R. 347 . . . . 25.11
170/78 *Commission v United Kingdom* [1980] E.C.R. 417 . . . . 5.69

177/78 *McCarren* [1979] E.C.R. 2161 . . . . 5.25
209/78 to 215/78 and 218/78 *Van Landewyck v Commission* [1980]
    E.C.R. 3125. . . . . .7.158, 7.161, 7.167, 7.170
220/78 and 221/78 *ALA and ALFER v Commission* [1979] E.C.R. 1693 . . . . 7.214, 23.51
222/78 *ICAP* [1979] E.C.R. 1163 . . . . 3.26
232/78 *Commission v France* [1979] E.C.R. 2729 . . . . .5.65, 25.11, 25.16
238/78 *Ireks-Arkady v Council and Commission* [1979] E.C.R. 2955 . . . . .11.16, 11.30,
                                     11.48, 11.50, 11.64, 11.68, 11.70, 11.71, 11.72
241/78 to 242/78, 245/78 to 250/78 *DGV v Council and Commission* [1979]
    E.C.R. 3017. . . . . 11.30, 11.48, 11.50
243/78 *Simmenthal v Commission* [1980] E.C.R. 593. . . . . 7.142
244/78 *Union Laitière Normande* [1979] E.C.R. 2663 . . . . 3.25, 6.19
250/78 *DEKA v EEC* [1983] E.C.R. 421 . . . . 11.16, 25.37
257/78 *Devred v Commission* [1979] E.C.R. 3767 . . . . 11.44
261/78 and 262/78 *Interquell Stärke-Chemie and Diamalt v Council and Commission*
    [1979] E.C.R. 3045 . . . . .11.30, 11.48, 11.50, 23.45
278/78 *Ireks-Arkady v Council and Commission* [1979] E.C.R. 2955 . . . . 11.57

4/79 *Providence Agricole de la Champagne* [1980] E.C.R. 2823 . . . . 10.23
12/79 *Hans-Otto Wagner v Commission* [1979] E.C.R. 3657. . . . . 11.30
26/79 and 86/79 *Forges de Thy-Marcinelle and Monceau v Commission* [1980] E.C.R. 1083 . . . .23.45, 25.12
40/79 *P v Commission* [1979] E.C.R. 3299, (order of 4 October 1979). 25.65
49/79 *Pool v Council* [1980] E.C.R. 569 . . . . 11.76
51/79 R II *Buttner v Commission* [1979] E.C.R. 2387, (order of the President of 10 July 1979) 13.44
51/79 *Buttner v Commission* [1980] E.C.R. 1201, (order of 26 March 1980). 7.74
60/79 *Fédération Nationale des Producteurs de Vins de Table et Vins de Pays v Commission*
    [1979] E.C.R. 2429, (order of 11 July 1979) 8.13
61/79 *Denkavit Italiana* [1980] E.C.R. 1205. . . . . 4.19, 4.21, 4.23, 4.27, 4.56, 6.33, 6.34
65/79 *Chatain* [1980] E.C.R. 1345. . . . . 3.17
66/79, 127/79 and 128/79 *Salumi* [1980] E.C.R. 1237 . . . . 6.33
68/79 *Just* [1980] E.C.R. 501. . . . . 4.21, 4.27
72/79 *Commission v Italy* [1980] E.C.R. 1411 . . . . 5.23, 5.25
73/79 *Commission v Italy* [1980] E.C.R. 1533 . . . . 5.23
76/79 *Könecke v Commission* [1980] E.C.R. 665 . . . . 7.143
87/79, 112/79 and 113/79 *Bagusat and Others* [1980] E.C.R. 1159 . . . . 6.11
89/79 *Bonu v Council* [1980] E.C.R. 553 . . . . 7.170
102/79 *Commission v Belgium* [1980] E.C.R. 1473 . . . . 5.65
104/79 *Foglia v Novello* ('Foglia v Novello I') [1980] E.C.R. 745 . . . . 3.42
107/79 REV *Schuerer v Commission* [1983] E.C.R. 3805 . . . . 25.120
108/79 *Belfiore v Commission* [1980] E.C.R. 1769 . . . . 7.217
109/79 *Maïseries de Beauce* [1980] E.C.R. 2883. . . . . 10.23
114/79 to 117/79 *Fournier v Commission* [1980] E.C.R. 1529, (order of 7 May 1980). 8.07, 18.27
130/79 *Express Dairy Foods* [1980] E.C.R. 1887 . . . . .4.04, 4.27, 10.22
133/79 *Sucrimex v Commission* [1980] E.C.R. 1299. . . . . 7.13, 11.25
136/79 *National Panasonic v Commission* [1980] E.C.R. 2033 . . . . 7.32
137/79 *Kohl v Commission* [1980] E.C.R. 2601 . . . . 11.44
138/79 *Roquette Frères v Council* [1980] E.C.R. 3333 . . .7.100, 7.144, 7.158, 7.159, 7.160, 7.180, 25.62
139/79 *Maizena v Council* [1980] E.C.R. 3393 . . . . 7.100, 7.144, 7.158, 7.159, 7.160, 25.62
145/79 *Roquette Frères* [1980] E.C.R. 2917. . . . . 10.23
148/79 *Korter v Council* [1981] E.C.R. 615. . . . . 25.96
155/79 *AM & S Europe v Commission* [1982] E.C.R. 1575. . . . . 7.37
158/79 *Roumengous Carpentier v Commission* [1985] E.C.R. 39 . . . . 11.72
532/79, 534/79, 567/79, 600/79, 618/79, 660/79, and 543/79 *Amesz and Others v*
    Commission [1985] E.C.R. 55 . . . . 11.72
730/79 *Philip Morris v Commission* [1980] E.C.R. 2671. . . . . 7.123
737/79 *Battaglia v Commission* [1985] E.C.R. 71. . . . . 11.72
792/79 R *Camera Care v Commission* [1980] E.C.R. 119 . . . . .7.39, 13.05, 13.16
806/79 *Gerin v Commission* [1980] E.C.R. 3515 . . . . 18.15
811/79 *Ariete* [1980] E.C.R. 2545 . . . . 4.13
817/79 *Buyl v Commission* [1982] E.C.R. 245 . . . . 7.160, 7.181
819/79 *Germany v Commission* [1981] E.C.R. 21. . . . . 7.170

826/79 *MIRECO* [1980] E.C.R. 2559 .... 4.13
828/79 *Adam v Commission* [1982] E.C.R. 269 .... 7.160
1253/79 *Battaglia v Commission* [1982] E.C.R. 297 .... 7.159

1/80 *Salmon* [1980] E.C.R. 1937 .... 6.26
24/80 and 97/80 R *Commission v France* [1980] E.C.R. 1319, (order of 28 March 1980)..... 5.70, 13.16
33/80 *Albini v Council and Commission* [1981] E.C.R. 2141............................ 9.01
35/80 *Denkavit v Produktschap voor Zuivel* [1981] E.C.R. 45 .... 7.170
36/80 and 71/80 *Irish Creamery Milk Suppliers Association* [1981] E.C.R. 735 .... 3.25, 3.28
46/80 *Vinal* [1981] E.C.R. 77 .... 3.42
59/80 and 129/80 *Turner v Commission* [1981] E.C.R. 1883 .... 7.184, 11.66
66/80 *International Chemical* [1981] E.C.R. 1191 .... 3.06, 4.27, 10.18, 10.19
125/80 *Arning v Commission* [1981] E.C.R. 2539 .... 7.170
126/80 *Salonia* [1981] E.C.R. 1563 .... 3.19, 3.36
138/80 *Borker* [1980] E.C.R. 1975, (order of 18 June 1980) 3.10
142/80 and 143/80 *Essevi and Salengo* [1981] E.C.R. 1413 .... 5.31, 5.33
158/80 *Rewe* [1981] E.C.R. 1805... 4.14
179/80 *Roquette Frères v Commission* [1982] E.C.R. 3623............................ 7.142
182/80 *Gauff v Commission* [1982] E.C.R. 799 .... 7.13
184/80 *Van Zaanen v Court of Auditors* [1981] E.C.R. 1951............................ 18.26
185/80 *Garganese v Commission* [1981] E.C.R. 1785 .... 11.72
186/80 R *Suss v Commission* [1980] E.C.R. 3501, (order of the President of 3 November 1980).... 13.07
188/80 to 190/80 *France and Others v Commission* [1982] E.C.R. 2545 .... 25.94
195/80 *Michel v European Parliament* [1981] E.C.R. 2861...................... 7.147, 7.173
197/80 to 200/80, 243/80, 245/80 and 247/80 *Ludwigshafener Walzmühle and Others v
Council and Commission* [1981] E.C.R. 3211 .... 11.10, 11.78, 23.60
203/80 *Casati* [1981] E.C.R. 259.. 4.42, 4.44
244/80 *Foglia v Novello* ('Foglia v Novello II') [1981] E.C.R. 3045 .... 3.32, 3.33, 3.37, 3.41, 3.42
246/80 *Broekmeulen* [1981] E.C.R. 2311 .... 3.09
256/80 to 257/80, 265/80, 267/80, and 51/81, and 282/82 *Birra Wührer and Others v
Council and Commission* [1984] E.C.R. 3693 .... 11.16, 11.71, 11.72, 11.90
258/80 R *Rumi v Commission* [1980] E.C.R. 3867, (order of the President of
16 December 1980) 13.07
262/80 *Andersen v European Parliament* [1984] E.C.R. 195 .... 9.03
267/80 TO *Dreher v Riseria Modenese, Council and Commission* [1986] E.C.R. 390 .... 25.110
267/80 REV *Riseria Modenese v Council and Others* [1985] E.C.R. 3499.................... 25.120
275/80 and 24/81 *Krupp v Commission* [1981] E.C.R. 2489.......................... 7.158, 9.08

9/81 *Williams v Court of Auditors* [1982] E.C.R. 3301 .... 7.23
9/81 INT *Court of Auditors v Williams* [1983] E.C.R. 2859, (order of 29 September 1983) 25.125
10/81 *Farrall v Commission* [1981] E.C.R. 717, (order of the President of 26 February 1981)...... 13.25
11/81 *Dürbeck v Commission* [1982] E.C.R. 1251 .... 25.13
14/81 *Alpha Steel v Commission* [1982] E.C.R. 749 ....7.11, 25.13, 25.17
17/81 *Pabst & Richarz* [1982] E.C.R. 1331... 24.23
20/81 R *Arbed v Commission* [1981] E.C.R. 721, (order of the President of
26 February 1981) 13.16, 13.36
26/81 *Oleifici Mediterranei v EEC* [1982] E.C.R. 3057 .... 11.85
28/81 *Commission v Italy* [1981] E.C.R. 2577 .... 5.50
29/81 *Commission v Italy* [1981] E.C.R. 2585 .... 5.50
36/81, 37/81 and 218/81 *Seton v Commission* [1983] E.C.R. 1789.................... 7.170
44/81 *Germany v Commission* [1982] E.C.R. 1855..................................... 8.10
51/81 *De Franceschi v Council and Commission* [1982] E.C.R. 117 .... 11.90
54/81 *Fromme* [1982] E.C.R. 1449.. 4.04
60/81 *IBM v Commission* [1981] E.C.R. 2639....................7.17, 7.20, 7.27, 7.28, 7.34, 7.57
60/81 and 190/81 R *IBM v Commission* [1981] E.C.R. 1857, (order of the President of
7 July 1981)... 13.16
65/81 *Reina* [1982] E.C.R. 33 .... 3.29
94/81 *Commission v Italy* [1982] E.C.R. 739 .... 5.10, 5.38
96/81 *Commission v Netherlands* [1982] E.C.R. 1791..................... 5.63, 5.64, 5.65, 23.58
97/81 *Commission v Netherlands* [1982] E.C.R. 1819...................... 5.65, 23.58
102/81 *Nordsee* [1982] E.C.R. 1095 .... 3.12

104/81 *Kupferberg* [1982] E.C.R. 3641 . . . . 5.05, 6.14
106/81 *Kind v EEC* [1982] E.C.R. 2885 . . . . .11.19, 11.48, 11.50, 11.60
108/81 *Amylum v Council* [1982] E.C.R. 3107 . . . . 25.13
109/81 *Porta v Commission* [1982] E.C.R. 2469 . . . . 19.10
110/81 *Roquette Frères v Council* [1982] E.C.R. 3159 . . . . 25.49
114/81 *Tunnel Refineries v Council* [1982] E.C.R. 3189 . . . . 7.160
124/81 *Commission v United Kingdom* [1983] E.C.R. 203 . . . . 5.43, 25.16
132/81 *Vlaeminck* [1982] E.C.R. 2953 . . . . 3.36
135/81 *Groupement des Agences de Voyage v Commission* [1982] E.C.R. 3799 . . . . 7.83, 7.136
141/81 to 143/81 *Holdijk* [1982] E.C.R. 1299 . . . . 3.25, 6.31
206/81 R *Alvarez v European Parliament* [1981] E.C.R. 2187, (order of the President of
    20 July 1981) 13.16
206/81 INT *Alvarez v European Parliament* [1983] E.C.R. 2865, (order of
    29 September 1983) 25.16, 25.128
207/81 *Ditterich v Commission* [1983] E.C.R. 1359 . . . . 7.158, 11.66
210/81 *Demo-Schmidt v Commission* [1983] E.C.R. 3045 . . . . 7.43, 7.86
211/81 *Commission v Denmark* [1982] E.C.R. 4547 . . . . 5.41
213/81 to 215/81 *Norddeutsches Vieh- und Fleischkontor and Others* [1982] E.C.R. 3583 . . . . 7.152
217/81 *Interagra v Commission* [1982] E.C.R. 2233 . . . . 11.25
230/81 *Luxembourg v European Parliament* [1983] E.C.R. 255 . . . . 7.76, 7.150
232/81 R *Agricola Commerciale Olio and Others v Commission* [1981] E.C.R. 2193,
    (order of the President of 21 August 1981) 13.34
232/81 *Agricola Commerciale Olio and Others v Commission* [1984] E.C.R. 3881 . . . . 7.136
242/81 *Roquette Frères v Council* [1982] E.C.R. 3213 . . . . 7.99
244/81 *Klöckner-Werke v Commission* [1983] E.C.R. 1451 . . . . 7.170
246/81 *Lord Bethell v Commission* [1982] E.C.R. 2277 . . . . 8.13
249/81 *Commission v Ireland* [1982] E.C.R. 4005 . . . . 5.18, 5.39
256/81 *Pauls Agriculture v Council and Commission* [1983] E.C.R. 1707 . . . . 11.71, 11.72
261/81 *Rau* [1982] E.C.R. 3961 . . . . 3.42, 24.13
263/81 *List v Commission* [1983] E.C.R. 103 . . . . 25.96
267/81 to 269/81 *SPI and SAMI* [1983] E.C.R. 801 . . . . 6.13
282/81 *Ragusa v Commission* [1983] E.C.R. 1245 . . . . 7.158, 7.168
283/81 *CILFIT* [1982] E.C.R. 3415 . . . . 3.19, 3.50, 3.51, 3.52, 3.53, 3.54, 3.55, 3.56
285/81 REV I and II *Geist v Commission* [1984] E.C.R. 1789 . . . . 25.120
294/81 *Control Data v Commission* [1983] E.C.R. 911 . . . . 7.170
301/81 *Commission v Belgium* [1983] E.C.R. 467 . . . . 5.65
306/81 *Verros v European Parliament* [1983] E.C.R. 1755 . . . . 25.14
307/81 *Alusuisse v Council and Commission* [1982] E.C.R. 3463 . . . . 7.133
310/81 *EISS v Commission* [1984] E.C.R. 1341 . . . . 11.78
314/81 to 316/81 and 83/82 *Waterkeyn* [1982] E.C.R. 4337 . . . . 3.53, 3.56, 5.70, 5.72, 6.11
318/81 *Commission v CO.DE.MI.* [1985] E.C.R. 3693 . . . . 19.16

1/82 *D* [1982] E.C.R. 3709 . . . . 5.32
2/82 to 4/82 *Delhaize Frères and Others* [1983] E.C.R. 2973 . . . . 3.30
11/82 *Piraiki-Patraiki v Commission* [1985] E.C.R. 207 . . . . .7.95, 7.98, 7.100
12/82 *Trinon* [1982] E.C.R. 4089 . . . . 3.23
33/82 *Murri Frères v Commission* [1985] E.C.R. 2759 . . . . 11.24
35/82 and 36/82 *Morson and Jhanjan* [1982] E.C.R. 3723 . . . . 3.44, 3.46
41/82 *Commission v Italy* [1982] E.C.R. 4213 . . . . 5.10, 5.38
42/82 R *Commission v France* [1982] E.C.R. 841, (order of 4 March 1982) 13.34
42/82 *Commission v France* [1983] E.C.R. 1013 . . . . 5.55
43/82 and 63/82 *VBVB and VBBB v Commission* [1984] E.C.R. 19 . . . . 7.157, 7.170
43/82 R and 63/82 R *VBVB and VBBB v Commission* [1982] E.C.R. 1241, (order of the
    President of 31 March 1982) 13.05
50/82 to 58/82 *Dorca Marina and Others* [1982] E.C.R. 3949 . . . . 10.15
62/82 *Italy v Commission* [1983] E.C.R. 687 . . . . 7.227
64/82 *Tradax v Commission* [1984] E.C.R. 1359 . . . . 7.170, 8.06
74/82 *Commission v Ireland* [1984] E.C.R. 317 . . . . 5.40, 5.47, 5.50
75/82 and 117/82 *Razzouk and Beydoun v Commission* [1984] E.C.R. 1509 . . . . .9.16, 9.19, 11.72, 18.26
84/82 *Germany v Commission* [1984] E.C.R. 1451 . . . . 8.18
85/82 *Schloh v Council* [1983] E.C.R. 2105 . . . . 7.144, 18.07

86/82 R *Hasselblad v Commission* [1982] E.C.R. 1555, (order of the President of 7 May 1982) 13.06
91/82 and 200/82 *Chris International Foods v Commission* [1983] E.C.R. 417,
    (order of 23 February 1983) 7.82
92/82 *Gutmann v Commission* [1983] E.C.R. 3127 .... 25.04
107/82 *AEG v Commission* [1983] E.C.R. 3151.. 7.36
140/82, 146/82, 221/82 and 226/82 *Walzstahl-Vereinigung and Thyssen v Commission* [1984]
    E.C.R. 951 .... 7.181, 9.08
149/82 *Robards* [1983] E.C.R. 171.. 3.32
169/82 *Commission v Italy* [1984] E.C.R. 1603 .... 5.37
191/82 *Fediol v Commission* [1983] E.C.R. 2913 .... 7.104, 7.132
199/82 *San Giorgio* [1983] E.C.R. 3595 ....4.15, 4.27, 4.28
205/82 to 215/82 *Deutsche Milchkontor* [1983] E.C.R. 2633 .... 3.26, 4.31
224/82 *Meiko-Konservenfabrik v Germany* [1983] E.C.R. 2539 .... 7.178
225/82 *Verzyck v Commission* [1983] E.C.R. 1991....................................... 18.28
228/82 and 229/82 *Ford v Commission* [1984] E.C.R. 1129............................. 7.39
231/82 *Spijker v Commission* [1983] E.C.R. 2559 .... 7.99
235/82 REV *Ferriere San Carlo v Commission* [1986] E.C.R. 1799 .... 25.120
239/82 and 275/82 *Allied Corporation v Commission* [1984] E.C.R. 1005 ......7.85, 7.100, 7.131, 7.133
240/82 to 242/82, 261/82, 262/82, 268/82 and 269/82 *Stichting Sigarettenindustrie v*
    Commission [1985] E.C.R. 3831 .... 7.170
264/82 *Timex v Council and Commission* [1985] E.C.R. 849 .... 7.132, 7.221, 10.20
266/82 *Turner v Commission* [1984] E.C.R. 1 .... 7.225
267/82 *Développement and Clemessy v Commission* [1986] E.C.R. 1907 .... 11.07, 11.24
281/82 *Unifrex v Commission and Council* [1984] E.C.R. 1969............11.28, 11.30, 11.50, 25.10
284/82 *Busseni v Commission* [1984] E.C.R. 557 .... 7.208
286/82 and 26/83 *Luisi and Carbone* [1984] E.C.R. 377 .... 4.44
294/82 *Einberger* [1984] E.C.R. 1177.. 3.23
296/82 and 318/82 *Netherlands and Leeuwarder Papierwarenfabriek v Commission*
    [1985] E.C.R. 809 .... 7.123
316/82 and 40/83 *Kohler v Court of Auditors* [1984] E.C.R. 641........................ 7.16
318/82 *Leeuwarder Papierwarenfabriek v Commission* [1985] E.C.R. 3727,
    (order of 26 November 1985)... 25.93
323/82 *Intermills v Commission* [1984] E.C.R. 3809 .... 7.118, 7.123
324/82 *Commission v Belgium* [1984] E.C.R. 1861 .... 5.31, 5.62
325/82 *Commission v Germany* [1984] E.C.R. 777............................... 5.45, 5.65

13/83 *European Parliament v Council* [1985] E.C.R. 1513 .... 8.07, 8.08, 8.12, 8.18, 8.19
14/83 *Von Colson and Kamann* [1984] E.C.R. 1891.. 4.44, 6.08
28/83 *Forcheri v Commission* [1984] E.C.R. 1425 .... 5.03
29/83 and 30/83 *CRAM and Rheinzink v Commission* [1984] E.C.R. 1679 .... 7.191
41/83 *Italy v Commission* [1985] E.C.R. 873... 7.76, 7.170
51/83 *Commission v Italy* [1984] E.C.R. 2793 .... 5.42, 5.48
52/83 *Commission v France* [1983] E.C.R. 3707 .... 5.66
53/83 *Allied Corporation v Council* [1985] E.C.R. 1621 .... 7.85
59/83 *Biovilac v EEC* [1984] E.C.R. 4057...............................11.07, 11.50, 25.13
62/83 *Eximo v Commission* [1984] E.C.R. 2295.............................. 11.19, 11.30
69/83 *Lux v Court of Auditors* [1984] E.C.R. 2447....................................... 7.183
78/83 R *Usinor v Commission* [1983] E.C.R. 2183, (order of the President of 5 July 1983) 13.15
79/83 *Harz* [1984] E.C.R. 1921.. 4.44
80/83 *Habourdin International and Others* [1983] E.C.R. 3639, (order of 9 November 1983)...... 21.07
108/83 *Luxembourg v European Parliament* [1984] E.C.R. 1945 .... 7.24, 7.150
111/83 *Picciolo v European Parliament* [1984] E.C.R. 2323 .... 7.173
112/83 *Société des Produits de Maïs* [1985] E.C.R. 719.......................10.05, 10.22, 10.23
114/83 *Société d'Initiatives et de Coopération Agricoles v Commission* [1984] E.C.R. 2589.......... 11.15
118/83 *CMC v Commission* [1985] E.C.R. 2325 ....7.73, 7.95, 11.13, 11.24
120/83 R *Raznoimport v Commission* [1983] E.C.R. 2573, (order of the President of
    19 July 1983)... 13.36
126/83 *STS v Commission* [1984] E.C.R. 2769 .... 7.73, 7.96
130/83 *Commission v Italy* [1984] E.C.R. 2849 .... 5.23
145/83 *Adams v Commission* [1985] E.C.R. 3539 ....7.167, 11.59, 11.85, 11.92
147/83 *Binderer v Commission* [1985] E.C.R. 257 ....7.85, 7.99, 7.108

152/83 *Demouche and Others* [1987] E.C.R. 3833 . . . . .3.02, 6.09, 6.10
169/83 and 136/84 *Leussink-Brummelhuis v Commission* [1986] E.C.R. 2801 . . . . 11.66, 11.84
172/83 and 226/83 *Hoogovens Groep v Commission* [1985] E.C.R. 2831 . . . . . .7.143, 7.216, 7.217, 25.44
178/83 *Firma P.* [1984] E.C.R. 3033 . . . . 21.07
209/83 *Valsabbia v Commission* [1984] E.C.R. 3089 . . . . 7.208
216/83 *Les Verts v Commission and Council* [1984] E.C.R. 3325, (order of 26 September 1994) 25.42
222/83 *Municipality of Differdange and Others v Commission* [1984] E.C.R. 2889 . . . . 7.77
224/83 *Ferriera Vittoria v Commission* [1984] E.C.R. 2349. . . . . 7.208, 7.214
227/83 *Moussis v Commission* [1984] E.C.R. 3133 . . . . 7.217
251/83 *Haug-Adrion* [1984] E.C.R. 4277 . . . . 6.22
270/83 *Commission v France* [1986] E.C.R. 273 . . . . 25.11
274/83 *Commission v Italy* [1985] E.C.R. 1077 . . . . 5.41, 5.43, 5.48, 5.64
289/83 *GAARM v Commission* [1984] E.C.R. 4295 . . . . 11.15, 25.27
290/83 *Commission v France* [1985] E.C.R. 439 . . . . 5.23
293/83 *Gravier* [1985] E.C.R. 593 . . . . 24.13
294/83 *Parti écologiste 'Les Verts' v European Parliament* [1986] E.C.R. 1339
  (order of 13 July 1990) 1.03, 3.07, 3.57, 4.10, 4.11, 6.04, 7.69, 7.70,
    7.83, 7.90, 7.102, 7.106, 7.141, 7.149, 9.04, 10.05, 10.10, 25.04
296/83 *Les Verts v European Parliament* [1984] E.C.R. 3335 . . . . 25.42
297/83 *Les Verts v Council* [1984] E.C.R. 3339 . . . . 25.42
298/83 *CICCE v Commission* [1985] E.C.R. 1105 . . . . .7.43, 25.94

1/84 R *Ilford v Commission* [1984] E.C.R. 423, (order of the President of 1 February 1984) 13.25
21/84 *Commission v France* [1985] E.C.R. 1355 . . . . 5.10
29/84 *Commission v Germany* [1985] E.C.R. 1661 . . . . 5.15
35/84 *Commission v Italy* [1986] E.C.R. 545 . . . . 5.10
41/84 *Pinna* [1986] E.C.R. 1 . . . . 10.20, 10.23
42/84 *Remia v Commission* [1985] E.C.R. 2545. . . . . .7.170, 7.190, 7.193
44/84 *Hurd* [1986] E.C.R. 26 . . . . 6.13
50/84 R *Bensider v Commission* [1984] E.C.R. 2247, (order of the President of 23 May 1984) 13.25
50/84 *Bensider v Commission* [1984] E.C.R. 3991 . . . . .7.83, 7.218, 25.44
52/84 *Commission v Belgium* [1986] E.C.R. 89 . . . . 5.22, 5.66
56/84 *Von Gallera* [1984] E.C.R. 1769, (order of 18 March 1984). 21.07
59/84 *Tezi Textiel v Commission* [1986] E.C.R. 887. . . . . 7.216
71/84 and 72/84 *Surcouf and Vidou v EEC* [1985] E.C.R. 2925. . . . . 11.50
75/84 *Metro v Commission* [1986] E.C.R. 3021 . . . . 7.112
82/84 *Metalgoi v Commission* [1984] E.C.R. 2585, (order of 4 July 1984) 7.213
83/84 and 84/84 *NM v Commission and Council* [1984] E.C.R. 3571,
  (order of 17 October 1984). 8.13
103/84 *Commission v Italy* [1986] E.C.R. 1759 . . . . 5.59
121/84 *Commission v Italy* [1986] E.C.R. 107 . . . . 5.63
142/84 and 156/84 *BAT and Reynolds v Commission* [1987] E.C.R. 4487 . . . . . .7.43, 7.145, 7.190, 7.193
150/84 *Bernardi v European Parliament* [1986] E.C.R. 1375 . . . . 7.158
159/84 and 267/84, 12/85 and 264/85 *Ainsworth v Commission* [1987] E.C.R. 1579,
  (order of 1 April 1987) 7.227
160/84 R *Oryzomyli Kavallas v Commission* [1984] E.C.R. 3217, (order of the President of
  16 July 1984). 13.15
166/84 *Thomasdünger* [1985] E.C.R. 3001 . . . . 6.16
169/84 *Cofaz and Others v Commission* [1986] E.C.R. 391 . . . . 7.121, 7.124
175/84 *Krohn v Commission* [1986] E.C.R. 735 . . . . 11.09, 11.10, 11.24, 11.25, 11.28, 11.30
179/84 *Bozzetti v Invernizzi* [1985] E.C.R. 2301 . . . . 3.18
188/84 *Commission v France* [1986] E.C.R. 419 . . . . 5.63
190/84 *Les Verts v European Parliament* [1988] E.C.R. 1017 . . . . 7.25
222/84 *Johnston* [1986] E.C.R. 1651 . . . . .4.07, 4.11, 7.106
232/84 *Commission v Tordeur* [1985] E.C.R. 3027 . . . . 23.60
234/84 *Belgium v Commission* [1986] E.C.R. 2263 . . . . 7.165, 7.204
240/84 *NTN Toyo Bearing v Council* [1987] E.C.R. 1809 . . . . .7.85, 7.131, 7.205
258/84 *Nippon Seiko v Council* [1987] E.C.R. 1923. . . . . 7.131
260/84 *Minebea v Council*, not reported, (order of 20 March 1985) 25.86
279/84 to 280/84, 285/84, and 286/84 *Rau v Commission* [1987] E.C.R. 1069 . . . . 11.50, 25.13
281/84 *Zuckerfabrik Bedburg v Council and Commission* [1987] E.C.R. 49. . . . . 11.50, 11.60

292/84 TO *Bolognese and Others v Scharf and Commission* [1987] E.C.R. 3563, (order of
    22 September 1987) 25.110
297/84 *Sahinler v Commission* [1986] E.C.R. 443, (order of 29 January 1986). 25.05
309/84 *Commission v Italy* [1986] E.C.R. 599 . . . . 5.10, 5.38, 5.53, 5.59, 5.73

5/85 *AKZO Chemie v Commission* [1986] E.C.R. 2585 . . . . 7.156, 25.13
15/85 *Consorzio Cooperative d'Abruzzo v Commission* [1987] E.C.R. 1005 . . . . 7.12
20/85 *Roviello* [1988] E.C.R. 2805 . . . . 10.13, 24.07
25/85 *Nuovo Campsider v Commission* [1986] E.C.R. 1531. . . . . 8.18
27/85 *Vandemoortele v Commission* [1987] E.C.R. 1129 . . . . 11.50
42/85 *Cockerill-Sambre v Commission* [1985] E.C.R. 3749 . . . . 7.215
44/85, 77/85, 294/85, and 295/85 *Hochbaum and Rawes v Commission* [1987] E.C.R. 3259 . . . . . . 11.66
53/85 *AKZO Chemie v Commission* [1986] E.C.R. 1965 . . . . 7.10, 7.20, 7.37, 7.141, 7.167, 7.223
56/85 *Brother v Commission* [1988] E.C.R. 5655 . . . . 7.66
67/85, 68/85 and 70/85 *Van der Kooy and Others v Commission* [1988]
    E.C.R. 219 . . . . 7.104, 7.120, 7.122, 7.128
69/85 *Wünsche* [1986] E.C.R. 947, (order of 5 March 1986) 6.11, 6.27, 6.28, 6.31, 10.03, 24.29
85/85 *Commission v Belgium* [1986] E.C.R. 1149 . . . . 5.32
C-89/85, C-104/85, C-114/85, C-116/85, C-117/85, and 125–129/85 *Ahlström and Others*
    v Commission [1988] E.C.R. 5193 . . . . 7.151
C-89/85, C-104/85, C-114/85, C-116/85, C-117/85, and C-125/85, C-129/85 *Ahlström*
    and Others v Commission [1993] E.C.R. I-1307 . . . . 7.34, 7.36, 7.178, 7.191, 23.68, 25.137
97/85 *Deutsche Lebensmittelwerke v Commission* [1987] E.C.R. 2265. . . . . 7.98
98/85, 162/85 and 258/85 *Bertini* [1986] E.C.R. 1885 . . . . 3.33
103/85 *Stahlwerke Peine-Salzgitter v Commission* [1988] E.C.R. 4131 . . . . 25.17
133/85 to 136/85 *Rau and Others* [1987] E.C.R. 2289 . . . . 10.10
146/85 and 431/85 *Diezler and Others v ESC* [1987] E.C.R. 4283 . . . . 25.44
146 and 431/85 INT *Maindiaux and Others v ESC* [1988] E.C.R. 2003,
    (order of 20 April 1988) 25.125, 25.126
150/85 *Drake* [1986] E.C.R. 1995 . . . . 3.09
152/85 *Misset v Council* [1987] E.C.R. 223. . . . . 7.207, 23.33
154/85 R *Commission v Italy* [1985] E.C.R. 1753, (order of 7 June 1985). 13.41
154/85 *Commission v Italy* [1987] E.C.R. 2717 . . . . 5.14, 5.59
168/85 *Commission v Italy* [1986] E.C.R. 2945 . . . . 5.17
181/85 *France v Commission* [1987] E.C.R. 689 . . . . 9.11
185/85 *Usinor v Commission* [1986] E.C.R. 2079 . . . . 7.158, 7.174, 9.15
187/85 *Fediol v Commission* [1988] E.C.R. 4155. . . . . 7.205
201/85 and 202/85 *Klensch* [1986] E.C.R. 3477 . . . . 4.44
204/85 *Stroghili v Court of Auditors* [1987] E.C.R. 389 . . . . 7.140, 7.141
220/85 *Fadex v Commission* [1986] E.C.R. 3387 . . . . 19.16
227/85 to 230/85 *Commission v Belgium* [1988] E.C.R. 1 . . . . 5.37, 5.65
239/85 *Commission v Belgium* [1986] E.C.R. 3645 . . . . 5.37
265/85 *Van den Bergh and Jurgens v Commission* [1987] E.C.R. 1155 . . . . 11.50
281/85, 283/85 to 285/85, and 287/85 *Germany and Others v Commission* [1987]
    E.C.R. 3203. . . . . 7.150, 23.33
282/85 *DEFI v Commission* [1986] E.C.R. 2469 . . . . 7.127, 7.140
293/85 *Commission v Belgium* [1988] E.C.R. 305 . . . . 5.44, 5.50, 13.25
293/85 R *Commission v Belgium* [1985] E.C.R. 3521, (order of the President of
    25 October 1985). 4.62, 13.12, 13.25, 13.41
307/85 *Gavanas v ESC and Council* [1987] E.C.R. 2435 . . . . 7.168
309/85 *Barra* [1988] E.C.R. 355 . . . . 4.24, 6.34
310/85 R *Deufil v Commission* [1985] E.C.R. 537, (order of the President) 13.40
310/85 *Deufil v Commission* [1987] E.C.R. 901. . . . . 7.202
311/85 *VVR* [1987] E.C.R. 3801 . . . . 6.19
314/85 *Foto-Frost* [1987] E.C.R. 4199 . . . . . . 3.06, 3.59, 3.60, 10.01, 10.05, 10.13, 10.17, 10.19, 11.29
318/85 *Greis Unterweger* [1986] E.C.R. 955, (order of 5 March 1986) 3.10
331/85, 376/85, and 378/85 *Bianco and Girard* [1988] E.C.R. 1099 . . . . 4.28
338/85 *Pardini* [1988] E.C.R. 2041 . . . . 3.16
347/85 *United Kingdom v Commission* [1988] E.C.R. 1749 . . . . 25.17
351/85 and 360/85 *Fabrique de Fer de Charleroi v Commission* [1987] E.C.R. 3639 . . . . 7.181, 25.17
358/85 and 51/86 *France v European Parliament* [1988] E.C.R. 4821 . . . . 7.19, 7.150, 7.217, 25.44
383/85 *Commission v Belgium* [1989] E.C.R. 3069 . . . . 23.82

391/85 *Commission v Belgium* [1988] E.C.R. 579 .... 5.56
C-403/85 REV *Ferrandi v Commission* [1991] E.C.R. I-1215 .... 25.119
415/85 *Commission v Ireland* [1988] E.C.R. 3097 .... 5.01, 5.65
416/85 *Commission v United Kingdom* [1988] E.C.R. 3127 .... 5.01, 5.65
426/85 *Commission v Zoubek* [1986] E.C.R. 4057 .... 19.10

1/86 *Commission v Belgium* [1987] E.C.R. 2797 .... 5.37
12/86 *Demirel* [1987] E.C.R. 3719 .... 6.14
14/86 *Pretore di Salò v X* [1987] E.C.R. 2545 .... 3.08, 3.17, 3.24, 3.26, 6.11, 6.28
23/86 R *United Kingdom v European Parliament* [1986] E.C.R. 1085, (order of the
    President of 17 March 1986). 13.15, 13.16, 13.21
24/86 *Blaizot* [1988] E.C.R. 379 .... 6.34
25/86 *Suss v Commission* [1986] E.C.R. 3929, (order of 11 December 1986). 25.125
26/86 *Deutz and Geldermann v Council* [1987] E.C.R. 941 .... 7.99
31/86 and 35/86 *LAISA and Others v Council* [1988] E.C.R. 2285 .... 7.75, 11.18, 23.60
33/86, 44/86, 110/86, 226/86, and 285/86 *Stahlwerke Peine-Salzgitter and Others v
    Commission* [1988] E.C.R. 4309 .... 7.181, 7.184, 7.220
34/86 *Council v European Parliament* [1986] E.C.R. 2155 .... 7.69, 7.74, 7.220, 7.221
45/86 *Commission v Council* [1987] E.C.R. 1493. .... 7.76, 7.172, 7.221
50/86 *Grands Moulins de Paris v Council and Commission* [1987] E.C.R. 4833. . . 11.46, 11.56, 11.57, 11.60
52/86 *Banner v European Parliament* [1987] E.C.R. 979 .... 7.183
55/86 *ARPOSOL v Council* [1988] E.C.R. 13 .... 7.93
62/86 R *AKZO Chemie v Commission* [1986] E.C.R. 1503, (order of the President of
    30 April 1986). 13.16
64/86, 71/86 to 73/86 and 78/86 *Sergio v Commission* [1988] E.C.R. 1399. .... 7.173
68/86 *United Kingdom v Council* [1988] E.C.R. 855 .... 7.168
69/86 *Commission v Italy* [1987] E.C.R. 773 .... 5.74
70/86 *Commission v Greece* [1987] E.C.R. 3545. .... 5.68
74/86 *Commission v Germany* [1988] E.C.R. 2139. .... 5.17
81/86 *De Boer Buizen v Council and Commission* [1987] E.C.R. 3677 .... 11.28, 11.30
85/86 *Commission v EIB* [1986] E.C.R. 2215, (order of 3 July 1986) 25.06
89/86 and 91/86 *L'Étoile Commerciale and CNTA v Commission* [1987] E.C.R. 3005 ...... 11.24, 11.25
97/86, 99/86, 193/86, and 215/86 *Asteris v Commission* [1988]
    E.C.R. 2181. .... 7.99, 7.101, 7.221, 7.223, 16.29
104/86 *Commission v Italy* [1988] E.C.R. 1799 .... 5.17
108/86 *D.M. v Council* [1987] E.C.R. 3933 .... 7.138
113/86 *Commission v Italy* [1988] E.C.R. 607 .... 5.55
114/86 *United Kingdom v Commission* [1988] E.C.R. 5289 .... 7.25
119/86 *Spain v Council and Commission* [1987] E.C.R. 4121 .... 7.171
121/86 *Epicheiriseon Metalleftikon Viomichanikon kai Naftiliakon and Others v Council*
    [1989] E.C.R. 3919 .... 7.64
128/86 *Spain v Commission* [1987] E.C.R. 4171 .... 7.160
147/86 TO 1 *POIFXG and Others v Greece and Commission* [1989] E.C.R. 4103,
    (order of the President of 6 December 1989) 25.109
166 and 220/86 *Irish Cement v Commission* [1988] E.C.R. 6473. .... 7.23, 8.19
199/86 *Raiffeisen* [1988] E.C.R. 1169. .... 10.20
203/86 *Spain v Council* [1988] E.C.R. 4563 .... 7.172
204/86 *Greece v Council* [1988] E.C.R. 5323. .... 9.11
207/86 *APESCO v Commission* [1988] E.C.R. 2151 .... 7.10, 7.93, 7.141
214/86 R *Greece v Commission* [1986] E.C.R. 2631, (order of the President of
    24 September 1986) 13.36
221/86 R *Group of the European Right and National Front Party v European Parliament*
    [1986] E.C.R. 2969, (order of the President of 16 October 1986) 13.25
222/86 *Heylens and Others* [1987] E.C.R. 4097. .... 4.09, 7.173
229/86 *Brother Industries v Commission* [1987] E.C.R. 3757, (order of 30 September 1987) 7.19
231/86 R *Breda-Geomineraria v Commission* [1986] E.C.R. 2639, (order of the President of
    26 September 1986) 13.04
236/86 *Dillinger Hüttenwerke v Commission* [1988] E.C.R. 3761 .... 7.216
240/86 *Commission v Greece* [1988] E.C.R. 1835. .... 5.58, 5.59, 5.73
247/86 *Alsatel* [1988] E.C.R. 5987 .... 3.22

267/86 *Van Eycke* [1988] E.C.R. 4769 . . . . 3.41, 3.42

272/86 *Commission v Greece* [1988] E.C.R. 4875. . . . . 5.63

279/86 *Sermes v Commission* [1987] E.C.R. 3109, (order of 8 July 1987) 7.133

283/86 *Commission v Belgium* [1988] E.C.R. 3271 . . . . 5.59

294/86 R *Technointorg v Commission* [1986] E.C.R. 3979, (order of the President of
    17 December 1986) 13.36

294/86 and 77/87 *Technointorg v Commission and Council* [1988] E.C.R. 6077. . . . . 7.10, 7.66

295/86 *Garelly v Commission* [1987] E.C.R. 3117, (order of 8 July 1987) 7.133

298/86 *Commission v Belgium* [1988] E.C.R. 4343 . . . . 5.63

300/86 *Van Landschoot* [1988] E.C.R. 3443 . . . . 10.20

301/86 *Frimodt Pedersen v Commission* [1987] E.C.R. 3123, (order of 8 July 1987). 7.133

C-305/86 and C-160/87 *Neotype Techmashexport v Commission and Council* [1990]
    E.C.R. I-2945 . . . . 7.10, 7.85, 7.133, 23.43, 25.60

1/87 SA *Universe Tankship v Commission* [1987] E.C.R. 2807, (order of
    17 June 1987) 14.01, 14.05, 14.06

32/87, 52/87 and 57/87 *ISA v Commission* [1988] E.C.R. 3305 . . . . 7.181

38/87 *Commission v Greece* [1988] E.C.R. 4415. . . . . 5.17

45/87 R *Commission v Ireland* [1987] E.C.R. 1369, (order of the President of 13 March 1987) 13.43

45/87 *Commission v Ireland* [1988] E.C.R. 4929 . . . . 5.37

46/87 R *Hoechst v Commission* [1987] E.C.R. 1549, (order of the President of 26 March 1987) 13.16

46/87 and 227/88 *Hoechst v Commission* [1989] E.C.R. 2859. . . . . 7.32

51/87 *Commission v Council* [1988] E.C.R. 5459. . . . . 7.221

62/87 and 72/87 *Exécutif Régional Wallon and Glaverbel v Commission* [1988] E.C.R. 1573 . . . . 7.77

65/87 R *Pfizer v Commission* [1987] E.C.R. 1691, (order of the President of 8 April 1987) 13.25

76/87, 86/87 to 89/87 and 149/87 *Seguela and Others* [1988] E.C.R. 2397. . . . . 6.32

85/87 *Dow Benelux v Commission* [1989] E.C.R. 3137. . . . . 7.32

85/87 R *Dow Chemical Nederland v Commission* [1987] E.C.R. 4367, (order of the
    President of 26 March 1987). 7.32

94/87 *Commission v Germany* [1989] E.C.R. 175. . . . . 4.31

97/87 to 99/87 *Dow Chemical Ibérica and Others v Commission* [1989] E.C.R. 3165 . . . . 7.156

106/87 to 120/87 *Asteris and Others v Greece and EEC* [1988] E.C.R. 5515 . . . . 11.31

125/87 *Brown v Court of Justice* [1988] E.C.R. 1619 . . . . 18.05

126/87 *Del Plato v Commission* [1989] E.C.R. 643 . . . . 18.07, 18.26

133/87 R *Nashua v Commission* [1987] E.C.R. 2883, (order of the President of 25 June 1987). 13.20

C-133/87 and C-150/87 *Nashua Corporation and Others v Commission and Council* [1990]
    E.C.R. I-719 . . . . 7.65, 7.85, 7.133, 7.134

141/87 *Commission v Italy* [1989] E.C.R. 943 . . . . 5.63

142/87 R *Belgium v Commission* [1987] E.C.R. 2589, (order of the President of
    15 June 1987) 13.40, 13.41

C-142/87 *Belgium v Commission* [1990] E.C.R. I-959 . . . . 5.24

C-156/87 *Gestetner Holdings v Council and Commission* [1990]
    E.C.R. I-781 . . . . 7.65, 7.131, 7.133, 7.134, 7.205

165/87 *Commission v Council* [1988] E.C.R. 5545. . . . . 7.159

169/87 *Commission v France* [1988] E.C.R. 4093 . . . . 5.74

C-174/87 *Ricoh v Council* [1992] E.C.R. I-1335 . . . . 7.131, 7.205

186/87 *Cowan* [1989] E.C.R. 195 . . . . 4.42

193/87 and 194/87 *Maurissen and European Public Service Union v Court of Auditors*
    [1989] E.C.R. 1045 . . . . 7.23, 7.69, 18.10

205/87 *Nuova Ceam v Commission* [1987] E.C.R. 4427 . . . . 7.133

223/87 R *ASSIDER v Commission* [1987] E.C.R. 3473, (order of the President of
    10 August 1987) 13.36

223/87 *Commission v Greece* [1988] E.C.R. 3611. . . . . 9.07

224/87 *Koutchoumoff v Commission* [1989] E.C.R. 99 . . . . 18.26

226/87 *Commission v Greece* [1988] E.C.R. 3611. . . . . 5.27, 5.66, 7.12

229/87 *Commission v Greece* [1988] E.C.R. 6347. . . . . 5.41

247/87 *Star Fruit v Commission* [1989] E.C.R. 291 . . . . 5.34, 7.09, 8.06, 8.13

275/87 *Commission v Council* [1989] E.C.R. 259. . . . . 7.221

C-287/87 *Commission v Greece* [1990] E.C.R. I-125 . . . . 5.73

290/87 *Commission v Netherlands* [1989] E.C.R. 3083. . . . . 5.63

C-301/87 *France v Commission* [1990] E.C.R. I-307 . . . . 5.24, 7.58

302/87 *European Parliament v Council* [1988] E.C.R. 5615 . . . . .8.09, 8.19, 11.19
C-308/87 *Grifoni v EAEC* [1994] E.C.R. I-341. . . . . 11.64, 11.85
C-343/87 *Culin v Commission* [1990] E.C.R. I-225 . . . . .7.147, 7.173, 11.66
346/87 *Bossi v Commission* [1989] E.C.R. 303. . . . . .7.28, 11.10, 18.04
352/87 *Farzoo and Kortmann v Commission* [1988] E.C.R. 2281, (order of 27 April 1988). 7.214
359/87 *Pinna* [1989] E.C.R. 585 . . . . 10.20
361/87 and 362/87 *Caturla-Poch and De la Fuente Pascual v European Parliament* [1989]
    E.C.R. 2471. . . . . 7.183
374/87 *Orkem v Commission* [1989] E.C.R. 3283 . . . . 7.31
376/87 R *Distrivet v Council* [1988] E.C.R. 209, (order of the President of 27 January 1988). 13.25
377/87 *European Parliament v Council* [1988] E.C.R. 4017 . . . . 8.01, 8.05, 8.08, 8.21, 25.84
378/87 *Top Hit Holzvertrieb v Commission* [1989] E.C.R. 1359 . . . . 7.216
383/87 *Commission v Council* [1988] E.C.R. 4051. . . . . 8.01, 8.05

1/88 SA *Générale de Banque v Commission* [1989] E.C.R. 857, (order of 11 April 1989). 14.01, 14.07
C-2/88 *Imm. J.J. Zwartveld and Others* [1990] E.C.R. 3365 (order of 13 July 1990) 1.03
5/88 *Wachauf* [1989] E.C.R. 2609 . . . . 4.44
14/88 *Italy v Commission* [1989] E.C.R. 3677. . . . . 7.170
16/88 *Commission v Council* [1989] E.C.R. 3457. . . . . 7.153
20/88 *Roquette Frères v Commission* [1989] E.C.R. 1553 . . . . 11.29, 11.56, 11.93
22/88 *Vreugdenhil and Others* [1989] E.C.R. 2049. . . . . 7.153
30/88 *Greece v Commission* [1989] E.C.R. 3711. . . . . 6.15, 7.178
C-35/88 *Commission v Greece* [1990] E.C.R. I-3125 . . . . 5.23
C-49/88 *Al-Jubail Fertilizer v Council* [1991] E.C.R. I-3187. . . . . 7.166
C-54/88, C-91/88 and C-14/89 *Nino and Others* [1990] E.C.R. I-3537 . . . . 6.24
C-62/88 *Greece v Council* [1990] E.C.R. I-1527 . . . . 7.177
68/88 *Commission v Greece* [1989] E.C.R. 2965. . . . . 4.43, 4.45
C-70/88 *European Parliament v Council* [1990] E.C.R. I-2041 . . . . .7.79, 23.85, 25.88
C-70/88 *European Parliament v Council* [1991] E.C.R. I-4529 . . . . 7.79
76/88 R *La Terza v Court of Justice* [1988] E.C.R. 1741, (order of the President of
    23 March 1988). 13.04
109/88 *Danfoss* [1989] E.C.R. 3199 . . . . 3.12
111/88 R *Greece v Commission* [1988] E.C.R. 2591, (order of the President of
    6 May 1988) 13.36, 13.41
112/88 R *Crete Citron Producers Association v Commission* [1988] E.C.R. 2597,
    (order of the President of 6 May 1988) 13.41
C-119/88 *AERPO and Others v Commission* [1990] E.C.R. I-2189 . . . . 11.30, 11.48, 11.50
133/88 *Del Amo Martinez v European Parliament* [1989] E.C.R. 689 . . . . 18.22, 18.26
138/88 *Flourez v Council* [1988] E.C.R. 6393, (order of 7 December 1988) 7.94
C-143/88 and C-92/89 *Zuckerfabrik Süderdithmarschen and Zuckerfabrik Soest* [1991]
    E.C.R. I-415 . . . . .4.62, 4.64, 13.13
150/88 *Eau de Cologne & Parfumerie-Fabrik 4711* [1989] E.C.R. 3891. . . . . 3.37
152/88 R *Sofrimport v Commission* [1988] E.C.R. 2931, (order of the President of 10 June 1988). 13.36
C-152/88 *Sofrimport v Commission* [1990] E.C.R. I-2477. . . . . .7.98, 7.100,
    11.50, 11.52, 11.68, 11.72, 23.85, 25.88
160/88 *Fédération Européenne de la Santé Animale and Others v Council* [1988]
    E.C.R. 6399, (order of 7 December 1988). 7.94
160/88 R *Fédération Européenne de la Santé Animale and Others v Council* [1988] E.C.R. 4121,
    (order of the President of 13 July 1988). 7.99, 13.25
176/88 R *Hanning v European Parliament* [1988] E.C.R. 3915, (order of the President of
    11 July 1988). 13.42
C-177/88 *Dekker* [1990] E.C.R. I-3941 . . . . 4.44
C-180/88 *Wirtschaftsvereinigung Eisen- und Stahlindustrie v Commission* [1990]
    E.C.R. I-4413 . . . . 7.216
194/88 R *Commission v Italy* [1988] E.C.R. 5647, (order of the President of 27 September 1988) 13.43
C-200/88 *Commission v Greece* [1990] E.C.R. I-4299 . . . . 5.31
C-202/88 *France v Commission* [1991] E.C.R. I-1223 . . . . 5.26
C-209/88 *Commission v Italy* [1990] E.C.R. I-4313. . . . . 5.31
C-213/88 and C-39/89 *Luxembourg v European Parliament* [1991] E.C.R. I-5643 . . . . 7.24
C-221/88 *Busseni* [1990] E.C.R. I-495 . . . . 3.04, 3.05
C-229/88 *Cargill and Others v Commission* [1990] E.C.R. I-1303 . . . . 7.99

244/88 *Usines Coopératives de Déshydratation du Vexin and Others v Commission* [1989]
   E.C.R. 3811. . . . . .7.85, 7.99, 7.108
C-249/88 *Commission v Belgium* [1991] E.C.R. I-1275 . . . . .5.59, 5.63, 5.73
C-262/88 *Barber* [1990] E.C.R. I-1889. . . . . 6.34
C-262/88 INT *Peinado Guitart*, not reported, (order of 17 December 2010). 24.30
C-286/88 *Falciola* [1990] E.C.R. I-191, (order of 26 January 1990) 3.36
C-297/88 and C-197/89 *Dzodzi* [1990] E.C.R. I-3763 . . . . 3.42, 6.16, 6.17, 6.22, 6.24
C-229/88 *Cargill and Others v Commission* [1990] E.C.R. I-1303 . . . . .7.85, 7.108
322/88 *Grimaldi* [1989] E.C.R. 4407. . . . . 6.08, 10.09
C-323/88 *Sermes* [1990] E.C.R. I-3027. . . . . 7.183
C-326/88 *Hansen* [1990] E.C.R. I-2911 . . . . .4.43, 4.44, 4.45
C-330/88 *Grifoni v EAEC* [1991] E.C.R. I-1045. . . . . 19.10
C-331/88 *Fedesa and Others* [1990] E.C.R. I-4023 . . . . 7.183
C-347/88 *Commission v Greece* [1990] E.C.R. I-4747 . . . . 25.12
C-350/88 *Delacre and Others v Commission* [1990] E.C.R. I-395 . . . . 7.170
353/88 *Briantex and Di Domenico v Commission* [1989] E.C.R. 3623 . . . . 11.19
C-361/88 *Commission v Germany* [1991] E.C.R. I-2567. . . . . 5.59
C-363 and C-364/88 *Finsider and Others v Commission* [1992] E.C.R. I-359. . . . . 11.43
C-366/88 *France v Commission* [1990] E.C.R. I-3571 . . . . .7.19, 7.25

C-10/89 *CNL-SUCAL* [1990] E.C.R. I-3711 . . . . 6.32
C-38/89 *Blanguernon* [1990] E.C.R. I-83 . . . . 5.65
C-42/89 *Commission v Belgium* [1990] E.C.R. I-2821 . . . . 5.53
56/89 R *Publishers Association v Commission* [1989] E.C.R. 1693, (order of the President of
   13 June 1989) 13.34, 13.42
C-58/89 *Commission v Germany* [1991] E.C.R. I-4983. . . . . 5.37
C-59/89 *Commission v Germany* [1991] E.C.R. I-2607. . . . . 5.59
C-63/89 *Assurances du Crédit v Council and Commission* [1991] E.C.R. I-1799 . . . . 11.50, 11.52
C-69/89 *Nakajima v Council* [1991] E.C.R. I-2069. . . . . 7.169
C-73/89 *Fournier* [1992] E.C.R. I-5621 . . . . 6.16, 6.17
C-87/89 *SONITO and Others v Commission* [1990] E.C.R. I-1981 . . . . .5.31, 5.33, 7.101, 11.10
C-96/89 *Commission v Netherlands* [1991] E.C.R. I-2461. . . . . 5.62
C-100/89 and C-101/89 *Kaefer and Procacci* [1990] E.C.R. I-4647. 3.13
C-104/89 DEP *Mulder and Others v Council and Commission* [2004] E.C.R. I-1,
   (order of 6 January 2004) 25.91, 25.92, 25.93
C-104/89 and C-37/90 *Mulder and Others v Council and Commission* [1992]
   E.C.R. I-3061 . . . . 11.25, 11.50, 11.57, 11.68, 11.72, 11.85
C-152/89 *Commission v Luxembourg* [1991] E.C.R. I-3141 . . . . 5.45
C-170/89 *BEUC v Commission* [1991] E.C.R. I-5709 . . . . 7.66
C-192/89 *Sevince* [1990] E.C.R. I-3461 . . . . 6.15, 10.07
C-200/89 *FUNOC v Commission* [1990] E.C.R. I-3669. . . . . 7.157
C-201/89 *Le Pen and Front National* [1990] E.C.R. I-1183 . . . . 7.73
C-209/89 *Commission v Italy* [1991] E.C.R. I-1575. . . . . 5.09
C-213/89 *Factortame and Others ('Factortame I')* [1990] E.C.R. I-2433 . . . . 4.04, 4.10, 4.61, 13.13
C-220/89 *FUNOC v Commission* [1990] E.C.R. I-3669. . . . . 7.157
C-231/89 *Gmurzynska-Bscher* [1990] E.C.R. I-4003 . . . . .3.31, 3.40, 6.16
C-241/89 *SARPP* [1990] E.C.R. I-4695 . . . . 3.23
C-243/89 *Commission v Denmark* [1993] E.C.R. I-3353 . . . . 5.31, 5.43, 5.52, 5.60
246/89 R *Commission v United Kingdom* [1989] E.C.R. 3125, (order of the President of
   10 October 1989). 13.34
C-247/89 *Commission v Portugal* [1991] E.C.R. I-3659 . . . . 5.49
C-260/89 *ERT* [1991] E.C.R. I-2925. . . . . 5.06
C-280/89 *Commission v Ireland* [1992] E.C.R. I-6185. . . . . 5.59
C-291/89 *Interhotel v Commission* [1991] E.C.R. I-2257 . . . . 7.146, 10.15
C-298/89 *Gibraltar v Council* [1993] E.C.R. I-3605 . . . . .7.77, 7.94, 7.99
C-304/89 *Oliveira v Commission* [1991] E.C.R. I-2283 . . . . 7.146, 10.15
C-304/89 and C-37/90 *Mulder and Others v Council and Commission* [2000] E.C.R. I-203 . . . .11.68, 11.72
C-309/89 *Codorníu v Council* [1994] E.C.R. I-1853 . . . . .7.85, 7.100
C-313/89 *Commission v Spain* [1991] E.C.R. I-5231 . . . . 7.75
C-340/89 *Vlassopoulou* [1991] E.C.R. I-2357 . . . . 4.09
C-348/89 *Mecanarte—Metalúrgica da Lagoa Lda* [1991] E.C.R. I-3277. . . . . 3.20

C-354/89 *Schiocchet v Commission* [1991] E.C.R. I-1775 .... 7.180
C-355/89 *Barr and Montrose Holdings* [1991] E.C.R. I-3479 .... 3.13
C-358/89 *Extramet Industrie v Council* [1991] E.C.R. I-2501 .... 7.85, 7.133
C-368/89 *Crispoltoni* [1991] E.C.R. I-3695.. 3.36
C-370/89 *SGEEM and Etroy v EIB* [1992] E.C.R. I-6211 .... 11.20, 11.24
C-371/89 *Emrich v Commission* [1990] E.C.R. I-1555, (order of 30 March 1990) 8.13
C-377/89 *Cotter and Others* [1991] E.C.R. I-1155............................... 6.11
C-384/89 *Tomatis and Fulchiron* [1991] E.C.R. I-127 .... 6.16

C-2/90 *Commission v Belgium* [1992] E.C.R. I-4431 .... 23.82
C-6/90 and C-9/90 *Francovich and Others* [1991]
    E.C.R. I-5357 .... 3.58, 4.02, 4.46, 4.51, 5.02, 5.73, 11.27, 11.48
C-7/90 *Vandevenne* [1991] E.C.R. I-4371.. 4.43
C-12/90 *Infortec v Commission* [1990] E.C.R. I-4265, (order of 21 November 1990)........... 7.23
C-16/90 *Nölle* [1991] E.C.R. I-5163 .... 7.201, 10.17
C-18/90 *Kziber* [1991] E.C.R. I-199.. 6.13
C-29/90 *Commission v Greece* [1992] E.C.R. I-1971 .... 5.59
C-33/90 *Commission v Italy* [1991] E.C.R. I-5987 .... 5.37, 5.64, 5.65
C-48/90 and C-66/90 *Netherlands and Others v Commission* [1992] E.C.R. I-565 .... 5.26, 5.27
C-50/90 *Sunzest v Commission* [1991] E.C.R. I-2917, (order of 13 June 1991) 11.09
C-51/90 R and C-59/90 R *Comos-Tank and Others v Commission* [1990] E.C.R. I-2167,
    (order of the President of 23 May 1990) 13.11, 13.36
C-52/90 *Commission v Denmark* [1992] E.C.R. I-2187 .... 5.52, 25.10, 25.12
C-56/90 *Commission v United Kingdom* [1993] E.C.R. I-4109 .... 5.50, 5.62
C-61/90 *Commission v Greece* [1992] E.C.R. I-2407 .... 5.25
C-65/90 *European Parliament v Council* [1992] E.C.R. I-4593 .... 7.160, 7.221
C-66/90 *PTT v Commission* [1991] E.C.R. I-2723, ECJ (order of 4 June 1991) 2.54
C-68/90 R *Blot and Front National v European Parliament* [1990] E.C.R. I-2177,
    (order of the President of 23 May 1990) 13.25
C-72/90 *Asia Motor France v Commission* [1990] E.C.R. I-2181,
    (order of 23 May 1990) 2.54, 5.34, 11.27, 11.47, 11.81
C-87/90 to C-89/90 *Verholen and Others* [1991] E.C.R. I-3757 .... 4.17, 4.39
C-106/90, C-317/90, and C-129/91 *Emerald Meats v Commission* [1993] E.C.R. I-209........... 5.32
C-115/90 P *Turner v Commission* [1991] E.C.R. I-1423, (order of 20 March 1991)............. 26.07
C-126/90 P *Bocos Viciano v Commission* [1991] E.C.R. I-781, (order of 27 February 1991) 26.07
C-132/90 P *Schwedler v European Parliament* [1991] E.C.R. I-5745 .... 16.02, 16.07
C-145/90 P *Costacurta v Commission* [1991] E.C.R. I-5449 .... 16.07
C-159/90 *Society for the Protection of Unborn Children Ireland* [1991] E.C.R. I-4685 .... 3.16, 5.06
C-163/90 *Legros and Others* [1992] E.C.R. I-4625.......................... 6.34
C-185/90 P-REV *Gill v Commission* [1992] E.C.R. I-993, (order of 25 February 1992)......... 25.117
C-186/90 *Durighello* [1991] E.C.R. I-5773.......................... 3.36
C-195/90 R *Commission v Germany* [1990] E.C.R. I-2715, (order of the President of
    28 June 1990) 13.24, 13.34
C-195/90 R *Commission v Germany* [1990] E.C.R. I-3351 .... 4.62, 13.06, 13.24
C-205/90 *Les Assurances du Crédit Namur*, not reported, (order of the President of
    20 February 1997) 3.30
C-208/90 *Emmott* [1991] E.C.R. I-4269.. 4.33, 4.35
C-209/90 *Commission v Feilhauer* [1992] E.C.R. I-2613 .... 19.13, 19.15, 19.16
C-237/90 *Commission v Germany* [1992] E.C.R. I-5973........................... 5.52
C-240/90 *Germany v Commission* [1992] E.C.R. I-5383........................... 4.42, 7.153
C-242/90 P-R *Commission v Albani and Others* [1990] E.C.R. I-4329, (order of the President
    of 27 November 1990).. 16.26
C-242/90 P *Commission v Albani and Others* [1993] E.C.R. I-3839 .... 9.19, 18.28
C-255/90 P *Burban v European Parliament* [1992] E.C.R. I-2253.................. 16.07, 16.19
C-257/90 *Italsolar v Commission* [1993] E.C.R. I-9 .... 7.73
C-258/90 and C-259/90 *Pesquerias De Bermeo and Naviera Laida v Commission* [1992]
    E.C.R. I-2901 .... 7.201
C-260/90 *Leplat* [1992] E.C.R. I-643.. 3.13
C-269/90 *Technische Universität München* [1991] E.C.R. I-5469 .... 7.170, 7.198, 7.201, 7.206
C-283/90 P *Vidrányi v Commission* [1991] E.C.R. I-4339 .... 16.19
C-286/90 *Poulsen and Diva Navigation and Others* [1992] E.C.R. I-6019 .... 7.151

C-294/90 *British Aerospace and Rover v Commission* [1992] E.C.R. I-493 . . . . 5.22, 5.24
C-294/90 DEP *British Aerospace v Commission* [1994] E.C.R. I-5423, (order of
    30 November 1994) 25.91
C-295/90 *European Parliament v Council* [1992] E.C.R. I-4193 . . . . 7.221
C-295/90 REV *Council v European Parliament and Others* [1992] E.C.R. I-5299 . . . . 25.117
C-303/90 *France v Commission* [1991] E.C.R. I-5315 . . . . 7.19
C-312/90 *Spain v Commission* [1992] E.C.R. I-4117 . . . . 7.20, 7.57
C-313/90 R *CIRFS and Others v Commission* [1991] E.C.R. I-2557, (order of the President
    of 17 May 1991) 13.07
C-313/90 *CIRFS and Others v Commission* [1993] E.C.R. I-1125 . . . .7.61, 7.62, 7.104, 7.128, 7.137, 25.60
C-315/90 *Gimelec and Others v Commission* [1991] E.C.R. I-5589 . . . . 7.66
C-320/90 to C-322/90 *Telemarsicabruzzo and Others* [1993] E.C.R. I-393 . . . . 3.26, 3.28, 3.29
C-343/90 *Lourenço Dias* [1992] E.C.R. I-4673 . . . . 3.36, 6.21
C-345/90 P-R *European Parliament v Hanning* [1991] E.C.R. I-231, (order of the President
    of 31 January 1991) 13.34, 16.26
C-348/90 P *European Parliament v Virgili-Schettini* [1991] E.C.R. I-5211 . . . . 16.20
C-354/90 *Fédération Nationale du Commerce Extérieur des Produits Alimentaires and
    Others* [1991] E.C.R. I-5505 . . . . 5.24
C-356/90 R *Belgium v Commission* [1991] E.C.R. I-2423, (order of the President of
    8 May 1991) 13.41
C-362/90 *Commission v Italy* [1992] E.C.R. I-2353 . . . . 5.58
C-375/90 *Commission v Greece* [1993] E.C.R. I-2055 . . . . 5.63
C-378/90 P *Pitrone v Commission* [1992] E.C.R. I-2375 . . . . 16.03

Opinion 1/91 *Draft Agreement between the Community and the countries of the European Free
    Trade Association relating to the creation of the European Economic Area* [1991]
    E.C.R. I-6079 . . . . 1.03, 2.02, 12.01, 12.13, 12.20
Opinion 2/91 *Convention No 170 of the International Labour Organisation concerning safety
    in the use of chemicals at work* [1993] E.C.R. I-01061 . . . . 12.01, 12.06, 12.11, 12.12, 12.13
C-15/91 and C-108/91 *Buckl and Others v Commission* [1992]
    E.C.R. I-6061 . . . . 7.99, 7.101, 8.05, 8.19, 25.84
C-18/91 P *V v European Parliament* [1992] E.C.R. I-3997 . . . . 16.28
C-25/91 *Pesqueras Echebastar v Commission* [1993] E.C.R. I-1719 . . . . 8.05
C-45/91 *Commission v Greece* [1992] E.C.R. I-2509 . . . . 5.65
C-47/91 *Italy v Commission* [1992] E.C.R. I-4145 . . . . 7.57
C-59/91 *France v Commission* [1992] E.C.R. I-525, (order of 5 February 1992) 7.214
C-65/91 *Commission v Greece* [1992] E.C.R. I-5245 . . . . 5.64
C-67/91 *Asociación Española de Banca Privada and Others* [1992] E.C.R. I-4785 . . . . 3.11, 3.36
C-74/91 *Commission v Germany* [1992] E.C.R. I-5437 . . . . 5.66, 9.11
C-83/91 *Meilicke* [1992] E.C.R. I-4871 . . . . 3.28
C-88/91 *Federconsorzi* [1992] E.C.R. I-4035 . . . . 3.42, 6.16
C-94/91 *Wagner* [1992] E.C.R. I-2765 . . . . 10.09
C-97/91 *Oleificio Borrelli v Commission* [1992] E.C.R. I-6313 . . . . 4.07, 7.73
C-101/91 *Commission v Italy* [1993] E.C.R. I-191 . . . . 5.70
C-104/91 *Aguirre Borrell and Others* [1992] E.C.R. I-3003 . . . . 4.09
C-105/91 *Commission v Greece* [1992] E.C.R. I-5871 . . . . 5.53
C-109/91 *Ten Oever* [1993] E.C.R. I-4879 . . . . 6.34
C-110/91 *Moroni* [1993] E.C.R. I-6591 . . . . 6.34
C-117/91 R *Bosman v Commission* [1991] E.C.R. I-3353, (order of the President of
    27 June 1991) 13.25
C-117/91 *Bosman v Commission* [1991] E.C.R. I-4837, (order of 4 October 1991) 11.09
C-130/91 REV *ISAE/VP and Interdata v Commission* [1995] E.C.R. I-407 . . . . 25.117, 25.119
C-155/91 *Commission v Council* [1993] E.C.R. I-939 . . . . 25.59
C-157/91 *Commission v Netherlands* [1992] E.C.R. I-5899 . . . . 5.52, 5.63
C-181/91 and C-248/91 *European Parliament v Council and Commission* [1993]
    E.C.R. I-3685 . . . . 7.17, 7.73
C-182/91 *Forafrique Burkinabe v Commission* [1993] E.C.R. I-2161 . . . . 14.05
C-183/91 *Commission v Greece* [1993] E.C.R. I-3131 . . . . 5.66
C-187/91 *Société Coopérative Belovo* [1992] E.C.R. I-4937 . . . . 3.23
C-188/91 *Deutsche Shell* [1993] E.C.R. I-363 . . . . 6.15
C-199/91 *Foyer Culturel du Sart-Tilman v Commission* [1993] E.C.R. I-2667 . . . . 7.223

C-195/91 P *Bayer v Commission* [1994] E.C.R. I-5619. . . . . 7.208
C-198/91 *Cook v Commission* [1993] E.C.R. I-2487 . . . . 7.118
C-199/91 *Foyer Culturel du Sart-Tilman v Commission* [1993] E.C.R. I-2667 . . . . 7.23
C-210/91 *Commission v Greece* [1992] E.C.R. I-6735 . . . . 4.44, 5.63
C-213/91 *Abertal v Commission* [1993] E.C.R. I-3177. . . . . 7.99
C-220/91 P *Commission v Stahlwerke Peine-Salzgitter* [1993] E.C.R. I-2393. . . . . 11.03, 11.43
C-225/91 *Matra v Commission* [1993] E.C.R. I-3203. . . . . .7.118, 7.202, 25.60
C-237/91 *Kus* [1992] E.C.R. I-6781. . . . . 6.15
C-241/91 P and C-242/91 P *RTE and ITP v Commission* [1995] E.C.R. I-743 . . . . 26.08
C-267/91 and C-268/91 *Keck and Mithouard* [1993] E.C.R. I-6097. . . . . 6.32
C-271/91 *Marshall* [1993] E.C.R. I-4367 . . . . 4.44, 4.52
C-272/91 R *Commission v Italy* [1992] E.C.R. I-457, (order of the President of 31 January 1992). 13.34
C-280/91 *Viessmann* [1993] E.C.R. I-971. . . . . 3.23
C-294/91 P *Sebastiani v European Parliament* [1992] E.C.R. I-4997, (order of 30 September 1992) . . .16.04
C-306/91 *Commission v Italy* [1993] E.C.R. I-2133. . . . . 5.42, 5.52
C-314/91 *Weber v European Parliament* [1993] E.C.R. I-1093 . . . . 1.03
C-316/91 *European Parliament v Council* [1994] E.C.R. I-625 . . . . 7.21, 7.79
C-325/91 *France v Commission* [1993] E.C.R. I-3283 . . . . .7.19, 7.172, 7.178
C-326/91 P *De Compte v European Parliament* [1994] E.C.R. I-2091 . . . . 16.03, 16.18
C-327/91 *France v Commission* [1994] E.C.R. I-3641 . . . . .7.17, 7.20, 10.05, 12.03
C-328/91 *Thomas and Others* [1993] E.C.R. I-1247 . . . . 6.26
C-338/91 *Steenhorst-Neerings* [1993] E.C.R. I-5475. . . . . 4.13, 4.33

Opinion 1/92 *Draft Agreement between the Community, on the one hand, and the countries of the
    European Free Trade Association, on the other, relating to the creation of the European Economic
    Area* [1992] E.C.R. I-2821 . . . . .12.01, 12.13, 12.20
Opinion 2/92 *Competence of the Community or one of its institutions to participate in the
    Third Revised Decision of the OECD on national treatment* [1995]
    E.C.R. I-521. . . . . .12.01, 12.09, 12.11, 12.18
C-6/92 *Federmineraria and Others v Commission* [1993] E.C.R. I-6357 . . . . 7.122, 7.127
C-13/92 to 16/92 *Driessen and Others* [1993] E.C.R. I-4751 . . . . 7.160
C-24/92 *Corbiau* [1993] E.C.R. I-1277 . . . . 3.09
C-32/92 P *Moat v Commission* [1992] E.C.R. I-6379, (order of 3 December 1992) 16.27
C-35/92 P-R *European Parliament v Frederiksen* [1992] E.C.R. I-2399, (order of the President of
    3 April 1992). 13.37, 16.26
C-35/92 P *European Parliament v Frederiksen* [1993] E.C.R. I-991 . . . . 16.23
C-36/92 P *SEP v Commission* [1994] E.C.R. I-1911 . . . . 7.167
C-41/92 *Liberal Democrats v European Parliament* [1993] E.C.R. I-3153, (order of
    10 June 1993) 8.05, 25.84
C-49/92 P *Commission v Anic Partecipazioni* [1999] E.C.R. I-4125. . . . . 7.190, 16.02
C-51/92 P *Hercules Chemicals v Commission* [1999] E.C.R. I-4235 . . . . 7.36, 7.162
C-53/92 P *Hilti v Commission* [1994] E.C.R. I-667 . . . . 16.04, 16.07
C-75/92 *Gao Yao v Council* [1994] E.C.R. I-3141. . . . . 7.131
C-80/92 *Commission v Belgium* [1994] E.C.R. I-1019 . . . . 5.14
C-91/92 *Faccini Dori* [1994] E.C.R. I-3325 . . . . 4.47, 5.73
C-102/92 *Ferriere Acciaierie Sarde v Commission* [1993] E.C.R. I-801 . . . . 7.216
C-115/92 P *European Parliament v Volger* [1993] E.C.R. I-6549. . . . . 7.173, 18.25
C-128/92 *Banks* [1994] E.C.R. I-1209 . . . . 4.53
C-130/92 *OTO* [1994] E.C.R. I-3281 . . . . 6.23
C-131/92 *Arnaud and Others v Council* [1993] E.C.R. I-2573, (order of 24 May 1993). 7.98, 7.99
C-135/92 *Fiskano v Commission* [1994] E.C.R. I-2885. . . . . 7.16
C-136/92 P *Commission v Brazzelli and Others* [1994] E.C.R. I-1981 . . . . 16.02, 16.25, 25.37
C-137/92 P *Commission v BASF and Others* [1994] E.C.R. I-2555 . . . . .7.12, 7.158, 7.169, 23.32
C-188/92 *TWD Textilwerke Deggendorf* [1994] E.C.R. I-833 . . . . 7.122, 10.11
C-199/92 P *Hüls v Commission* [1999] E.C.R. I-4287 . . . . 7.12, 7.192, 16.11, 23.83, 25.75, 26.09
C-200/92 P *ICI v Commission* [1999] E.C.R. I-4399 . . . . 7.12, 16.15, 23.64, 23.83, 25.65, 25.75
C-228/92 *Roquette Frères* [1994] E.C.R. I-1445. . . . . 10.22, 10.23
C-234/92 P *Shell v Commission* [1999] E.C.R. I-4501 . . . . 16.24
C-235/92 P *Montecatini v Commission* [1999] E.C.R. I-4539 . . . . 7.12, 7.146, 7.192, 23.83, 25.75, 26.09
C-244/92 P *Kupka-Floridi v ESC* [1993] E.C.R. I-2041, (order of 26 April 1993). 16.19
C-245/92 P *Chemie Linz v Commission* [1999] E.C.R. I-4643 . . . . 7.12

C-269/92 *Bosman*, not reported, (order of the President of 8 December 1993)................. 3.30
C-278/92 to C-280/92 *Spain v Commission* [1994] E.C.R. I-4103 .... 7.204
C-295/92 R *Landbouwschap v Commission* [1992] E.C.R. I-5069, (order of the President of
    12 October 1992)... 13.25
C-296/92 *Commission v Italy* [1994] E.C.R. I-1.. 5.52
C-315/92 *Clinique Laboratoires and Estée Lauder Cosmetics* [1994] E.C.R. I-317 .... 3.23
C-317/92 *Commission v Germany* [1994] E.C.R. I-2039........................... 5.59, 5.62
C-320/92 P *Finsider v Commission* [1994] E.C.R. I-5697................................ 15.07
C-332/92 to C-333/92, and C-335/92 *Eurico Italia and Others* [1994] E.C.R. I-711 .... 3.29, 3.36
C-345/92 *Commission v Germany* [1993] E.C.R. I-1115................................. 5.74
C-354/92 P *Eppe v Commission* [1993] E.C.R. I-7027 .... 16.19, 16.20
C-360/92 *Publishers Association v Commission* [1995] E.C.R. I-23...................... 7.171
C-382/92 *Commission v United Kingdom* [1994] E.C.R. I-2435 .... 4.43, 5.63
C-383/92 *Commission v United Kingdom* [1994] E.C.R. I-2479 .... 4.43
C-388/92 *European Parliament v Council* [1994] E.C.R. I-2067 .... 7.160
C-393/92 *Almelo* [1994] E.C.R. I-1477 .... 3.12
C-398/92 *Mund & Fester* [1994] E.C.R. I-467 .... 5.08, 21.02
C-399/92, C-409/92, C-425/92, C-34/93, C-50/93, and C-78/93 *Helmig and Others* [1994]
    E.C.R. I-5727 .... 3.31
C-410/92 *Johnson* [1994] E.C.R. I-5483............................... 4.13, 4.33
C-422/92 *Commission v Germany* [1995] E.C.R. I-1097.............................. 5.31
C-424/92 *Ladbroke Racing v Commission* [1993] E.C.R. I-2213, (order of 3 May 1993)........... 2.54
C-432/92 *Anastasiou and Others* [1994] E.C.R. I-3087............................ 6.13

C-5/93 P *DSM v Commission* [1999] E.C.R. I-4695 .... 15.05, 16.07, 25.125
C-18/93 *Corsica Ferries* [1994] E.C.R. I-1783 ....3.08, 3.17, 3.36
C-19/93 P *Rendo and Others v Commission* [1995] E.C.R. I-3319............7.16, 7.43, 16.14, 16.28
C-30/93 *AC-ATEL Electronics* [1994] E.C.R. I-2305 .... 3.28
C-39/93 P *SFEI and Others v Commission* [1994] E.C.R. I-2681.................7.43, 8.20, 16.04
C-41/93 *France v Commission* [1994] E.C.R. I-1829 .... 7.170
C-44/93 *Namur–Les Assurances du Crédit* [1994] E.C.R. I-3829 ....5.22, 7.53, 7.54
C-46/93 and C-48/93 *Brasserie du Pêcheur and Factortame* [1996] E.C.R. I-1029........ 3.58, 4.15, 4.46,
                             4.47, 4.48, 4.51, 4.52, 5.73, 6.26, 11.60
C-62/93 *BP Supergaz* [1995] E.C.R. I-1883 .... 3.36
C-64/93 *Danotab and Others v Commission* [1993] E.C.R. I-3595, (order of 28 June 1993) 7.27
C-64/93 R *Donatab and Others v Commission* [1993] E.C.R. I-3955, (order of the
    President of 9 July 1993) 13.25
C-107/93 R *AEFMA v Commission* [1993] E.C.R. I-4177, (order of the President of
    16 July 1993).. 13.25
C-156/93 *European Parliament v Commission* [1995] E.C.R. I-2019 .... 7.79, 25.60
C-187/93 *European Parliament v Council* [1994] E.C.R. I-2857 .... 7.79
C-257/93 *Van Parijs and Others v Council and Commission* [1993] E.C.R. I-3335,
    (order of 21 June 1993) 7.99, 11.09
C-257/93 R *Van Parijs and Others v Council and Commission* [1993] E.C.R. I-3917,
    (order of the President of 6 July 1993)................................. 13.25
C-274/93 *Commission v Luxembourg* [1996] E.C.R. I-2019 .... 5.52, 25.31
C-275/93 P *Boessen v ESC* [1994] E.C.R. I-159, (order of 24 January 1994)................. 26.07
C-276/93 *Chiquita Banana and Others v Council* [1993] E.C.R. I-3345, (order of 21 June 1993).... 7.99
C-278/93 *Freers and Speckmann* [1996] E.C.R. I-1165.............................. 6.26
C-280/93 R *Germany v Council* [1993] E.C.R. I-3667, (order of 29 June 1993) 13.30, 13.34, 13.41
C-280/93 *Germany v Council* [1994] E.C.R. I-4973............................ 7.160, 7.169
C-293/93 *Houtwipper* [1994] E.C.R. I-4249................................... 23.14
C-296/93 R *France v Commission* [1993] E.C.R. I-4181, (order of the President of
    16 July 1993)...................................... 13.40, 13.41
C-298/93 P *Klinke v Court of Justice* [1994] E.C.R. I-3009....................... 16.27
C-299/93 *Bauer v Commission* [1995] E.C.R. I-839.............................. 19.15
C-307/93 R *Ireland v Commission* [1993] E.C.R. I-4191, (order of the President of
    16 July 1993).. 13.41
C-310/93 P *BPB Industries and British Gypsum v Commission* [1995] E.C.R. I-865 .... 15.09, 16.11
C-312/93 *Peterbroeck* [1995] E.C.R. I-4599 ....3.07, 4.40
C-316/93 *Vaneetveld* [1994] E.C.R. I-763................................... 3.26

C-322/93 P *Peugeot v Commission* [1994] E.C.R. I-2727 .... 16.07
C-329/93, C-62/95 and C-63/95 *Germany and Others v Commission* [1996] E.C.R. I-5151 .... 7.171
C-338/93 P *De Hoe v Commission* [1994] E.C.R. I-819, (order of 7 March 1994) 25.10
C-346/93 *Kleinwort Benson* [1995] E.C.R. I-615 .... 6.17
C-348/93 *Commission v Italy* [1995] E.C.R. I-673 .... 5.22
C-349/93 *Commission v Italy* [1995] E.C.R. I-343 .... 5.22
C-359/93 *Commission v Netherlands* [1995] E.C.R. I-157 .... 5.30
C-360/93 *European Parliament v Council* [1996] E.C.R. I-1195 .... 7.79, 7.221
C-363/93 and C-407/93 to C-411/93 *Lancry and Others* [1994] E.C.R. I-3957 .... 6.11, 6.34, 10.22
C-365/93 *Commission v Greece* [1995] E.C.R. I-499 .... 5.15
C-378/93 *La Pyramide* [1994] E.C.R. I-3999 .... 3.17
C-388/93 *PIA HiFi v Commission* [1994] E.C.R. I-387 .... 25.16
C-392/93 *British Telecommunications* [1996] E.C.R. I-1631 .... 4.49, 6.26
C-396/93 P *Henrichs v Commission* [1995] E.C.R. I-2611 .... 16.03, 16.13
C-412/93 *Leclerc-Siplec* [1995] E.C.R. I-179 .... 3.42
C-415/93 *Bosman* [1995] E.C.R. I-4921 .... 3.27, 3.34, 23.83
C-417/93 *European Parliament v Council* [1995] E.C.R. I-1185 .... 7.159
C-422/93 to C-424/93 *Zabala Erasun and Others* [1995] E.C.R. I-1567 .... 3.29
C-428/93 *Monin Automobiles* [1994] E.C.R. I-1707, (order of 16 May 1994) 3.36
C-430/93 and C-431/93 *Van Schijndel and Van Veen* [1995] E.C.R. I-4705 .... 4.40
C-433/93 *Commission v Germany* [1995] E.C.R. I-2303 .... 5.65
C-445/93 *European Parliament v Commission*, not reported, (order of 11 July 1996) 8.08
C-446/93 *SEIM* [1996] E.C.R. I-73 .... 3.18, 4.07
C-465/93 *Atlanta Fruchthandelsgesellschaft and Others* [1995] E.C.R. I-3761 .... 4.62, 13.13
C-472/93 *Spano and Others* [1995] E.C.R. I-4321 .... 3.29
C-473/93 *Commission v Luxembourg* [1996] E.C.R. I-3207 .... 5.44, 5.69, 5.74
C-480/93 P *Zunis Holding and Others v Commission* [1996] E.C.R. I-1 .... 7.23, 16.27
C-485/93 and C-486/93 *Simitzi* [1995] E.C.R. I-2655 .... 6.34

Opinion 1/94 *Agreement establishing the World Trade Organisation* [1994]
     E.C.R. I-5267 .... 12.01, 12.11, 12.16
Opinion 2/94 *Accession by the Communities to the Convention for the Protection of
     Human Rights and Fundamental Freedoms* [1996] E.C.R. I-1759 .. 12.01, 12.02, 12.09, 12.11, 12.15
Opinion 3/94 *GATT-WTO-Framework Agreement on Bananas* [1995]
     E.C.R. I-4577 .... 12.01, 12.03, 12.09, 12.16
C-1/94 *SA Dupret v Commission* [1995] E.C.R. I-1, (order of 10 January 1995) 14.05
C-2/94 *Denkavit International* [1996] E.C.R. I-2829 .... 4.15
C-5/94 *Hedley Lomas* [1996] E.C.R. I-2553 .... 4.48, 11.48
C-7/94 *Gaal* [1995] E.C.R. I-1031 .... 2.10
C-21/94 *European Parliament v Council* [1995] E.C.R. I-1827 .... 7.79, 7.159
C-25/94 *Commission v Council* [1996] E.C.R. I-1469 .... 7.17, 7.72
C-29/94 to C-35/94 *Aubertin and Others* [1995] E.C.R. I-301 .... 6.24
C-36/94 *Siesse* [1995] E.C.R. I-3573 .... 4.45
C-39/94 *SFEI and Others* [1996] E.C.R. I-3547 .... 3.29, 7.58
C-54/94 and C-74/94 *Cacchiarelli and Stanghellini* [1995] E.C.R. I-391 .... 3.09
C-57/94 *Commission v Italy* [1995] E.C.R. I-1249 .... 5.57
C-61/94 *Commission v Germany* [1996] E.C.R. I-3989 .... 5.05, 5.63
C-62/94 P *Turner v Commission* [1995] E.C.R. I-3177, (order of 17 October 1995) 16.19
C-68/94 and C-30/95 *France and Others v Commission* [1998]
     E.C.R. I-1375 .... 7.51, 7.93, 7.113, 7.143, 7.197, 7.220
C-79/94 *Commission v Greece* [1995] E.C.R. I-1071 .... 5.30
C-84/94 *United Kingdom v Council* [1996] E.C.R. I-5755 .... 7.145
C-87/94 R *Commission v Belgium* [1994] E.C.R. I-1395, (order of the President of
     22 April 1994) 13.26, 13.43
C-90/94 *Haahr Petroleum* [1997] E.C.R. I-4085 .... 4.19, 4.23, 4.33
C-97/94 P-R *Schulz v Commission* [1994] E.C.R. I-170, (order of the President of
     5 May 1994) 13.25
C-111/94 *Job Centre* [1995] E.C.R. I-3361 .... 3.17
C-114/94 *IDE v Commission* [1997] E.C.R. I-803 .... 19.10
C-118/94 *Associazione Italiana per il WWF and Others* [1996] E.C.R. I-1223 .... 3.40, 3.41

C-119/94 P REV *Coussios v Commission*, not reported 25.120
C-120/94 *Commission v Greece* [1996] E.C.R. I-1513, (order of the President of
    19 March 1996). 5.28, 25.83
C-126/94 *Société Cadi Surgelés and Others* [1996] E.C.R. I-5647 . . . . 6.34
C-127/94 *H. & R. Ecroyd and Rupert Ecroyd* [1996] E.C.R. I-2731. 10.20
C-129/94 *Bernáldez* [1996] E.C.R. I-1829 . . . . 3.36, 3.41
C-132/94 *Commission v Ireland* [1995] E.C.R. I-4789 . . . . 5.52
C-134/94 *Esso Española* [1995] E.C.R. I-4223. . . . . 3.31
C-137/94 *Richardson* [1995] E.C.R. I-3407. . . . . 6.33
C-143/94 *Furlanis* [1995] E.C.R. I-3633 . . . . 3.36
C-158/94 *Commission v Italy* [1997] E.C.R. I-5789. . . . . 5.40
C-159/94 *Commission v France* [1997] E.C.R. I-5815 . . . . 5.40
C-163/94, C-165/94 and C-250/94 *Sanz de Lera and Others* [1995] E.C.R. I-4821. . . . . 3.31
C-167/94 *Grau Gomis and Others* [1995] E.C.R. I-1023 (order of 7 April 1995). 1.06
C-178/94, C-179/94, C-188/94, C-189/94, and C-190/94 *Dillenkofer and Others* [1996]
    E.C.R. I-4845 . . . . 4.46, 4.48, 5.73
C-182/94 *Commission v Italy* [1995] E.C.R. I-1465. . . . . 5.31
C-192/94 *El Corte Inglés* [1996] E.C.R. I-1281 . . . . 4.47
C-193/94 *Skanavi and Chryssanthakopoulos* [1996] E.C.R. I-929. 3.31, 4.44
C-197/94 and C-252/94 *Société Bautiaa and Société Française Maritime* [1996] E.C.R. I-505 . . . . 6.34
C-199/94 P and C-200/94 P *Pevasa and Inpesca v Commission* [1995] E.C.R. I-3709. . . . . . 11.10, 25.117
C-206/94 *Brennet* [1996] E.C.R. I-2357. . . . . 6.11
C-209/94 P *Buralux and Others v Council* [1996] E.C.R. I-615 . . . . 7.100, 11.76, 16.10
C-212/94 *FMC and Others* [1996] E.C.R. I-389 . . . . 4.29, 4.33
C-241/94 *France v Commission* [1996] E.C.R. I-4551 . . . . 7.204
C-253/94 P *Roujansky* [1995] E.C.R. I-7, (order of 13 January 1995). 16.13
C-264/94 P *Bonnamy* [1995] E.C.R. I-15, (order of 13 January 1995) 16.13
C-266/94 *Commission v Spain* [1995] E.C.R. I-1975, (order of 11 July 1995). 5.40, 5.48, 5.51
C-271/94 *European Parliament v Council* [1996] E.C.R. I-1689 . . . . 7.221
C-277/94 *Taflan-Met and Others* [1996] E.C.R. I-4085. . . . . 6.15
C-279/94 *Commission v Italy* [1997] E.C.R. I-4743. . . . . 5.41, 5.47, 5.52
C-280/94 *Posthuma-van Damme and Oztürk* [1996] E.C.R. I-179 . . . . 6.11
C-283/94, C-291/94, and C-292/94 *Denkavit and Others* [1996] E.C.R. I-5063. . . . . 4.49, 6.26
C-289/94 *Commission v Italy* [1996] E.C.R. I-4405. . . . . 5.41, 5.59
C-310/94 *Garage Ardon*, not reported, (order of the President of 16 January 1996) 3.30
C-320/94, C-328/94, C-329/94, C-337/94, C-338/94, and C-339/94 *RTI and Others* [1996]
    E.C.R. I-6471 . . . . 3.31, 3.36
C-325/94 P *An Taisce and WWF UK v Commission* [1996] E.C.R. I-3727, (order of
    11 July 1996). 16.07
C-331/94 *Commission v Greece* [1996] E.C.R. I-2675 . . . . 25.83
C-334/94 *Commission v France* [1996] E.C.R. I-1307 . . . . 5.74

C-7/95 P *Deere v Commission* [1998] E.C.R. I-3111 . . . . 16.04
C-10/95 P *Asocarne v Council* [1995] E.C.R. I-4149, (order of 23 November 1995) 7.94, 7.100
C-11/95 *Commission v Belgium* [1996] E.C.R. I-4115 . . . . 5.53, 5.65
C-12/95 P *Transacciones Maritimas and Others v Commission* [1995] E.C.R. I-467,
    (order of the President of 7 March 1995). 13.36
C-19/95 P *San Marco v Commission* [1997] E.C.R. I-4435, (order of 17 September 1996). . . 16.04, 16.07
C-24/95 *Alcan-Deutschland* [1997] E.C.R. I-1591 . . . . 4.31
C-28/95 *Leur-Bloem* [1997] E.C.R. I-4161 . . . . 3.40, 6.16, 6.17
C-32/95 P *Commission v Lisrestal and Others* [1996] E.C.R. I-5373. . . . . 7.161, 16.04
C-43/95 *Data Delecta Aktiebolag and Forsberg* [1996] E.C.R. I-4661. . . . . 4.08
C-51/95 P *Unifruit Hellas v Commission* [1997] E.C.R. I-727, (order of 5 February 1997). 16.19
C-57/95 *France v Commission* [1997] E.C.R. I-1627 . . . . 7.16, 7.150
C-58/95, C-75/95, C-112/95, C-119/95, C-123/95, C-135/95, C-140/95, C-141/95,
    C-154/95, and C-157/95 *Gallotti and Others* [1996] E.C.R. I-4345 . . . . 4.42, 4.44
C-66/95 *Sutton* [1997] E.C.R. I-2163. . . . . 4.51
C-68/95 *T. Port v Commission* [1996] E.C.R. I-6065. . . . . 4.64, 8.09, 8.11, 8.13, 8.14, 10.12
C-72/95 *Kraaijeveld and Others* [1996] E.C.R. I-5403 . . . . 4.40
C-74/95 and C-129/95 *X* [1996] E.C.R. I-6609 . . . . 3.09
C-85/95 *Reisdorf* [1996] E.C.R. I-6257. . . . . 3.40

C-89/95 P *D v Commission* [1996] E.C.R. I-53, (order of 11 January 1996) 16.04
C-91/95 P *Tremblay and Others v Commission* [1996] E.C.R. I-5547 .... 26.02
C-94/95 and C-95/95 *Bonifaci and Others and Berto and Others* [1997] E.C.R. I-3969. .... 4.52
C-104/95 *Kontogeorgas* [1996] E.C.R. I-6643 .... 3.36
C-107/95 P *Bundesverband der Bilanzbuchhalter v Commission* [1997] E.C.R. I-947 .... 5.33, 7.44
C-114/95 and C-115/95 *Texaco and Olieselskabet Danmark* [1997] E.C.R. I-4263. .... 4.33
C-122/95 *Germany v Council* [1998] E.C.R. I-973 .... 7.210, 7.216, 12.03, 12.16, 12.17
C-127/95 *Norbrook Laboratories* [1998] E.C.R. I-1531. .... 4.48
C-129/95 P(R) *Commission v Atlantic Container Line and Others* [1995] E.C.R. I-2165,
   (order of the President of 19 July 1995). 13.40
C-130/95 *Giloy* [1997] E.C.R. I-4291 .... 6.16, 6.17
C-134/95 *USSL No 47 di Biella* [1997] E.C.R. I-195. .... 6.24
C-137/95 P *SPO and Others v Commission* [1996] E.C.R. I-1611, (order of 25 March 1996) 16.21
C-138/95 P *Campo Ebro Industrial and Others v Council* [1997] E.C.R. I-2027 .... 16.19
C-143/95 P *Commission v Socurte and Others* [1997] E.C.R. I-1 .... 7.214, 16.04
C-147/95 *Evrenopoulos* [1997] E.C.R. I-2057 .... 6.04
C-149/95 P(R) *Commission v Atlantic Container Line and Others* [1995] E.C.R. I-2165,
   (order of the President of 19 July 1995). 13.16, 13.32, 13.34, 16.02, 26.02
C-166/95 P-R *Commission v Daffix* [1995] E.C.R. I-1955, (order of the President of
   6 July 1995). 16.26
C-166/95 P *Commission v Daffix* [1997] E.C.R. I-983 .... 7.146, 7.158, 7.174, 16.09
C-171/95 *Tetik* [1997] E.C.R. I-329 .... 6.15
C-178/95 *Wiljo* [1997] E.C.R. I-585 .... 3.23, 3.25, 10.11
C-180/95 *Draehmpaehl* [1997] E.C.R. I-2195. .... 4.13
C-181/95 *Biogen* [1996] E.C.R. I-717, (order of the President of 26 February 1996) 24.12, 25.61
C-184/95 *Lores Guillín*, not reported, (order of 24 June 1997) 3.29
C-185/95 P *Baustahlgewebe v Commission* [1998] E.C.R. I-8417. .... 7.190, 11.20,
   16.04, 16.11, 16.18, 23.59, 23.87, 25.48
C-188/95 *Fantask and Others* [1997] E.C.R. I-6783 .... 4.33
C-191/95 *Commission v Germany* [1998] E.C.R. I-5449. .... 5.31, 5.45, 5.47
C-192/95 to C-218/95 *Comateb and Others* [1997] E.C.R. I-165 .... 4.23, 4.27
C-219/95 P *Ferriere Nord v Commission* [1997] E.C.R. I-4411 .... 16.11
C-235/95 *AGS Assedic Pas-de-Calais* [1998] E.C.R. I-4531. .... 3.28
C-241/95 *The Queen v Intervention Board for Agricultural Produce, ex parte Accrington Beef*
   [1996] E.C.R. I-6699. .... 7.122, 10.11
C-242/95 *GT-Link* [1997] E.C.R. I-4449. .... 4.28
C-245/95 P *Commission v NTN Corporation and Koyo Seiko* [1998] E.C.R. I-401 .... 23.32, 25.59, 25.67
C-245/95 P-INT *NSK and Others v Commission* [1999] E.C.R. I-1. .... 25.126, 25.131, 25.132
C-246/95 *Coen* [1997] E.C.R. I-403. .... 7.207, 18.27
C-253/95 *Commission v Germany* [1996] E.C.R. I-2423. .... 5.65
C-254/95 P-R *European Parliament v Innamorati* [1995] E.C.R. I-2707, (order of the President
   of 15 September 1995). 16.26
C-259/95 *European Parliament v Council* [1997] E.C.R. I-5303 .... 7.79
C-261/95 *Palmisani* [1997] E.C.R. I-4025 .... 3.19, 3.22, 3.36, 4.23, 4.52
C-263/95 *Germany v Commission* [1998] E.C.R. I-441. .... 7.168
C-264/95 P *Commission v UIC* [1997] E.C.R. I-1287 .... 16.21
C-265/95 *Commission v France* [1997] E.C.R. I-6959 .... 5.14
C-277/95 P *Lenz v Commission* [1996] E.C.R. I-6109, (order of 28 November 1996) 7.227
C-278/95 P *Siemens v Commission* [1997] E.C.R. I-2507 .... 16.07
C-279/95 P *Langnese-Iglo v Commission* [1998] E.C.R. I-5609 .... 7.142, 16.20
C-282/95 P *Guérin automobiles v Commission* [1997] E.C.R. I-1503 .... 7.43, 7.178, 8.20
C-285/95 *Kol* [1997] E.C.R. I-3069. .... 6.15
C-286/95 P *Commission v ICI* [2000] E.C.R. I-2341 .... 7.146
C-286/95 P-DEP *ICI v Commission* [2004] E.C.R. I-6469, (order of 8 July 2004). 25.93
C-294/95 P *Ojha v Commission* [1996] E.C.R. I-5863 .... 16.28, 16.29
C-299/95 *Kremzow* [1997] E.C.R. I-2629. .... 6.24
C-300/95 *Commission v United Kingdom* [1997] E.C.R. I-2649 .... 5.10, 5.63
C-307/95 *Max Mara* [1995] E.C.R. I-5083, (order of 21 December 1995). 3.23
C-309/95 *Commission v Council* [1998] E.C.R. I-655. .... 7.210, 7.216
C-321/95 P *Greenpeace Council and Others v Commission* [1998] E.C.R. I-1651 .... 7.97, 7.117
C-323/95 *Hayes* [1997] E.C.R. I-1711 .... 4.08, 7.105

C-326/95 *Banco de Fomento e Exterior* [1996] E.C.R. I-1385, (order of 13 March 1996) 3.26
C-334/95 *Krüger* [1997] E.C.R. I-4517. . . . . .3.23, 4.62, 4.63
C-337/95 *Parfums Christian Dior* [1997] E.C.R. I-6013. . . . . .3.14, 3.47, 3.52
C-338/95 *Wiener* [1997] E.C.R. I-6495 . . . . 3.50
C-351/95 *Kadiman* [1997] E.C.R. I-2133. . . . . 6.15
C-352/95 *Phytheron International* [1997] E.C.R. I-1729. . . . . 3.28
C-355/95 P *TWD Textilwerke Deggendorf v Commission* [1997] E.C.R. I-2549 . . . . 7.22
C-360/95 *Commission v Spain* [1997] E.C.R. I-7337 . . . . 5.15
C-361/95 *Commission v Spain* [1997] E.C.R. I-7351 . . . . 5.15
C-362/95 P *Blackspur DIY and Others v Council and Commission* [1997] E.C.R. I-4775. . . . . 16.10
C-367/95 P *Commission v Sytraval and Brink's France* [1998] E.C.R. I-1719 . . . . . 7.55, 7.61, 7.62, 7.117,
                        7.118, 7.146, 7.165, 7.170, 7.171, 7.174, 7.201, 16.22
C-373/95 *Maso and Others* [1997] E.C.R. I-4051 . . . . .3.36, 4.52, 6.08
C-375/95 *Commission v Greece* [1997] E.C.R. I-5981 . . . . 5.53
C-386/95 *Eker* [1997] E.C.R. I-2697 . . . . 6.15
C-388/95 *Belgium v Spain* [2000] E.C.R. I-3123. . . . . 5.35
C-390/95 P *Antillean Rice Mills v Council* [1999] E.C.R. I-769 . . . . 7.100, 11.52
C-392/95 *European Parliament v Council* [1997] E.C.R. I-3213 . . . . 7.79
C-395/95 P *Geotronics v Commission* [1997] E.C.R. I-2271 . . . . .7.73, 7.96, 16.21
C-399/95 R *Germany v Commission* [1996] E.C.R. I-2441, (order of the President of
      3 May 1996) 13.01
C-408/95 *Eurotunnel and Others* [1997] E.C.R. I-6315 . . . . .3.42, 10.11, 24.07

C-2/96 *Sunino and Data* [1996] E.C.R. I-1543, (order of 20 March 1996) 3.25
C-22/96 *European Parliament v Council* [1998] E.C.R. I-3231 . . . . 7.221
C-30/96 P *Abello and Others v Commission* [1998] E.C.R. I-377, (order of 5 February 1998) 16.19
C-36/96 *Günaydin* [1997] E.C.R. I-5143 . . . . 6.15
C-42/96 *Società Immobiliare SIF* [1997] E.C.R. I-7089 . . . . 3.23
C-46/96 *Germany v Commission* [1997] E.C.R. I-1189, (order of 4 March 1997) 7.141
C-48/96 P *Windpark Groothusen v Commission* [1998] E.C.R. I-2873 . . . . 26.02
C-49/96 P *Progoulis v Commission* [1996] E.C.R. I-6803, (order of 12 December 1996) 16.19, 16.20
C-50/96 *Deutsche Telekom* [2000] E.C.R. I-743. . . . . 4.56
C-53/96 *Hermès International* [1998] E.C.R. I-3603 . . . . 6.14
C-54/96 *Dorsch Consult* [1997] E.C.R. I-496. . . . . 3.08
C-55/96 *Job Centre* [1997] E.C.R. I-7119. . . . . 3.17
C-61/96, C-45/98, C-27/99, C-81/00, and C-22/01 *Spain v Council* [2002] E.C.R. I-3439. . . . . . . 7.218
C-67/96 *Albany International* [1999] E.C.R. I-5751. . . . . .3.26, 3.27
C-69/96 to C-79/96 *Garofalo and Others* [1997] E.C.R. I-5603 . . . . 3.10
C-95/96 *Clinique de la Pointe Rouge*, not reported, (order of 12 June 1996). 3.31
C-96/96 *Clinique Florens*, not reported, (order of 12 June 1996). 3.31
C-98/96 *Ertanir* [1997] E.C.R. I-5179 . . . . 6.15
C-101/96 *Italia Testa* [1996] E.C.R. I-3081, (order of 25 June 1996). 3.25
C-106/96 *United Kingdom v Commission* [1998] E.C.R. I-2729 . . . . 7.221
C-116/96 REV *Reisebüro Binder* [1998] E.C.R. I-1889, (order of 28 April 1998). 24.29, 24.31
C-122/96 *Saldanha and MTS Securities* [1997] E.C.R. I-5325 . . . . 4.08
C-137/96 *Commission v Germany* [1997] E.C.R. I-6749. . . . . 5.15
C-140/96 P *Dimitriadis v Court of Auditors* [1997] E.C.R. I-5635, (order of 16 October 1997) 16.04
C-147/96 *Netherlands v Commission* [2000] E.C.R. I-4723. . . . . 7.28
C-148/96 P(R) *Goldstein v Commission* [1996] E.C.R. I-3883, (order of the President of
      11 July 1996). 16.02
C-149/96 *Portugal v Council* [1999] E.C.R. I-8395 . . . . 7.178
C-153/96 P *De Rijk v Commission* [1997] E.C.R. I-2901 . . . . 16.20
C-156/96 P *Williams v Court of Auditors* [1997] E.C.R. I-239, (order of 21 January 1997). 16.07
C-159/96 *Portugal v Commission* [1998] E.C.R. I-7379 . . . . 7.16
C-162/96 *Racke* [1998] E.C.R. I-3655 . . . . 10.14
C-170/96 *Commission v Council* [1998] E.C.R. I-2763. . . . . 1.06
C-171/96 *Pereira Roque* [1998] E.C.R. I-4607. . . . . 3.13
C-174/96 P *Lopes v Court of Justice* [1996] E.C.R. I-6401 . . . . 23.17
C-175/96 P *Lopes v Court of Justice* [1996] E.C.R. I-6409, (order of 5 December 1996). 23.17
C-176/96 *Lehtonen and Castors Braine* [2000] E.C.R. I-2681 . . . . .3.17, 3.24, 3.26
C-188/96 P *Commission v V.* [1997] E.C.R. I-6561 . . . . 16.09

C-191/96 *Modesti* [1996] E.C.R. I-3937, (order of 19 July 1996) 3.25
C-196/96 *Lahlou* [1996] E.C.R. I-3945, (order of 19 July 1996) 3.25
C-197/96 *Commission v France* [1997] E.C.R. I-1489 . . . . 5.17
C-228/96 *Aprile* [1998] E.C.R. I-7141 . . . . 4.23
C-231/96 *Edis* [1998] E.C.R. I-4951 . . . . 4.13, 4.19, 4.21, 4.24, 4.25, 4.33
C-239 and C-240/96 R *United Kingdom v Commission* [1996] E.C.R. I-4475,
    (order of the President of 24 September 1996) 13.41
C-246/96 *Magorrian and Cunningham* [1997] E.C.R. I-7153 . . . . 4.34
C-252/96 P *European Parliament v Gutiérrez de Quijano y Lloréns* [1998] E.C.R. I-7421 . . . . 25.14
C-259/96 P *Council v De Nil and Impens* [1998] E.C.R. I-2915 . . . . 16.09, 23.63
C-260/96 *Spac* [1998] E.C.R. I-4997 . . . . 4.13, 4.24, 4.25, 4.33
C-262/96 *Sürül* [1999] E.C.R. I-2685 . . . . 6.34
C-268/96 P(R) *SCK and FNK v Commission* [1996] E.C.R. I-4971 . . . . 13.36
C-279/96, C-280/96, and C-281/96 *Ansaldo Energia and Others* [1998]
    E.C.R. I-5025 . . . . 4.13, 4.25, 4.30, 4.33
C-285/96 *Commission v Italy* [1998] E.C.R. I-5935 . . . . 25.31
C-288/96 *Germany v Commission* [2000] E.C.R. I-8237 . . . . 7.59
C-298/96 *Oelmühle Hamburg and Schmidt Söhne* [1998] E.C.R. I-4767 . . . . 4.31
C-303/96 P *Bernardi v European Parliament* [1997] E.C.R. I-1239, (order of
    6 March 1997) 16.13, 16.19
C-314/96 *Djabali* [1998] E.C.R. I-1149 . . . . 3.29
C-319/96 *Brinkmann* [1998] E.C.R. I-5255 . . . . 4.48, 6.26
C-326/96 *Levez* [1998] E.C.R. I-7835 . . . . 4.35
C-328/96 *Commission v Austria* [1999] E.C.R. I-7479 . . . . 5.30, 5.49, 5.50
C-337/96 *Commission v IRACO* [1998] E.C.R. I-7943 . . . . 19.10
C-340/96 *Commission v United Kingdom* [1999] E.C.R. I-2023 . . . . 5.52
C-343/96 *Dilexport* [1999] E.C.R. I-597 . . . . 3.29, 4.23, 4.24, 4.25, 4.27, 4.28
C-353/96 *Commission v Ireland* [1998] E.C.R. I-8565 . . . . 5.30, 5.31, 5.39
C-386/96 P *Dreyfus v Commission* [1998] E.C.R. I-2309 . . . . 7.91, 7.93, 7.96
C-391/96 P *Compagnie Continentale v Commission* [1998] E.C.R. I-2377 . . . . 7.96
C-393/96 P(R) *Antonissen v Council and Commission* [1997] E.C.R. I-441, (order of the
    President of 29 January 1997) 13.11, 13.16, 16.29
C-401/96 P *Somaco v Commission* [1998] E.C.R. I-2587 . . . . 16.04, 16.09
C-403/96 P *Glencore Grain v Commission* [1998] E.C.R. I-2405 . . . . 7.96
C-404/96 P *Glencore Grain v Commission* [1998] E.C.R. I-2435 . . . . 7.96
C-409/96 P *Sveriges Betodlares Centralförening and Henrikson v Commission* [1997]
    E.C.R. I-7531, (order of 18 December 1997) 7.99
C-415/96 *Spain v Commission* [1998] E.C.R. I-6993 . . . . 7.223
C-416/96 *Eddline El-Yassini* [1999] E.C.R. I-1209 . . . . 3.08

C-1/97 *Birden* [1998] E.C.R. I-7747 . . . . 6.15
C-2/97 *IP* [1998] E.C.R. I-8597 . . . . 6.17
C-5/97 *Ballast Nedam Groep* [1997] E.C.R. I-7549 . . . . 6.11
C-9/97 and C-118/97 *Jokela and Pitkäranta* [1998] E.C.R. I-6267 . . . . 3.08
C-10/97 to C-22/97 *IN.CO.GE. '90 and Others* [1998] E.C.R. I-6307 . . . . 3.18, 4.24
C-26/97 *Giolfo and Others*, not reported, (order of the President of 30 April 1999) 3.29
C-35/97 *Commission v France* [1998] E.C.R. I-5325 . . . . 5.71
C-55/97 P *AIUFFASS and AKT v Commission* [1997] E.C.R. I-5383, (order of
    6 October 1997) 16.04
C-61/97 *FDV* [1998] E.C.R. I-5171 . . . . 3.26
C-69/97 *Commission v SNUA* [1999] E.C.R. I-2363 . . . . 19.10
C-70/97 P *Kruidvat v Commission* [1998] E.C.R. I-7183 . . . . 7.112, 10.10
C-73/97 P *France v Comafrica and Others* [1999] E.C.R. I-185 . . . . 16.12, 16.16
C-75/97 *Belgium v Commission* [1999] E.C.R. I-3671 . . . . 7.170
C-78/97 P(R) *Goldstein v Commission*, not reported, (order of the President of 10 March 1997) 13.44
C-87/97 *Consorzio per la Tutela del Formaggio Gorgonzola* [1999] E.C.R. I-1301 . . . . 3.23
C-89/97 P(R) *Moccia Irme v Commission* [1997] E.C.R. I-2327, (order of the President of
    30 April 1997) 13.04
C-95/97 *Régione Wallonne v Commission* [1997] E.C.R. I-1787, (order of
    21 March 1997) 2.54, 5.37, 7.77, 7.125
C-103/97 *Köllensperger and Atzwanger* [1999] E.C.R. I-551 . . . . 3.09

C-104/97 P *Atlanta v EC* [1999] E.C.R. I-6983 .... 16.20, 25.13
C-111/97 *EvoBus Austria* [1998] E.C.R. I-5411. .... 4.09
C-113/97 *Babahenini* [1998] E.C.R. I-183 .... 6.13
C-119/97 P *Ufex and Others v Commission* [1999] E.C.R. I-1341 .... 16.24, 23.59
C-124/97 *Läuarä and Others* [1999] E.C.R. I-6067 .... 3.23
C-126/97 *Eco Swiss China Time* [1999] E.C.R. I-3055 .... 3.12, 4.39, 4.41
C-131/97 *Carbonari and Others* [1999] E.C.R. I-1103. .... 3.23, 4.52
C-134/97 *Victoria Film* [1998] E.C.R. I-7023 .... 3.10, 3.11
C-140/97 *Rechberger and Others* [1999] E.C.R. I-3499. .... 4.46, 4.49, 6.26
C-150/97 *Commission v Portugal* [1999] E.C.R. I-259 .... 5.09
C-151/97 P(I) and C-157/97 P(I) *National Power and PowerGen v British Coal and Commission*
  [1997] E.C.R. I-3491, (order of the President of 17 June 1997)................... 25.65
C-161/97 P *Kernkraftwerke Lippe-Ems v Commission* [1999] E.C.R. I-2057.................. 26.02
C-164/97 and C-165/97 *European Parliament v Council* [1999] E.C.R. I-1139 .... 7.221
C-166/97 *Commission v France* [1999] E.C.R. I-1719 .... 5.58, 5.63, 5.65
C-172/97 *Commission v SIVU and Hydro-Réalisations* [1999] E.C.R. I-3363 .... 25.31, 25.32
C-172/97 OP *SIVU du plan d'eau de la Vallée du Lot v Commission* [2001] E.C.R. I-6699 ...... 25.32, 25.33
C-180/97 *Regione Toscana v Commission* [1997] E.C.R. I-5245,
  (order of 1 October 1997). 2.54, 7.77, 7.125
C-181/97 *Van der Kooy* [1999] E.C.R. I-483. .... 3.26
C-189/97 *European Parliament v Council* [1999] E.C.R. I-4741 .... 7.79
C-198/97 *Commission v Germany* [1999] E.C.R. I-3257. .... 5.31
C-200/97 *Ecotrade* [1998] E.C.R. I-7907 .... 3.23, 3.31
C-207/97 *Commission v Belgium* [1999] E.C.R. I-275 .... 5.56
C-210/97 *Akman* [1998] E.C.R. I-7519 .... 6.15
C-221/97 P *Schröder and Others v Commission* [1998] E.C.R. I-8255 .... 16.04, 26.02
C-224/97 *Ciola* [1999] E.C.R. I-2517 .... 2.01
C-226/97 *Lemmens* [1998] E.C.R. I-3711 .... 4.42
C-233/97 *KappAhl Oy* [1998] E.C.R. I-8068 .... 6.04
C-239/97 *Ireland v Commission* [1998] E.C.R. I-2655, (order of 7 May 1998) 23.38
C-248/97 P(R) *Chaves Fonseca Ferrão v OHIM* [1997] E.C.R. I-4729, (order of the President
  of 10 September 1997). 13.32
C-252/97 *N v Commission* [1998] E.C.R. I-4871, (order of 16 July 1998). 26.02
C-265/97 P *VBA v Florimex and Others* [2000] E.C.R. I-2061 .... 7.146
C-272/97 *Commission v Germany* [1999] E.C.R. I-2175. .... 5.31
C-274/97 *Commission v Coal Products* [2000] E.C.R. I-3175 .... 19.10
C-295/97 *Piaggio* [1999] E.C.R. I-3735 .... 3.23, 7.54
C-301/97 *Netherlands v Council* [2001] E.C.R. I-8853. .... 7.180
C-302/97 *Konle* [1999] E.C.R. I-3099 .... 4.51, 6.26
C-310/97 P *Commission v AssiDomän Kraft Products and Others* [1999] E.C.R. I-5363...... 7.223, 7.226
C-312/97 P *Fichtner v Commission* [1998] E.C.R. I-4135, (order 25 June 1998) 18.25
C-319/97 *Kortas* [1999] E.C.R. I-3143. .... 13.10
C-321/97 *Andersson and Wåkerås-Andersson* [1999] E.C.R. I-3551 .... 6.14
C-329/97 *Ergat* [2000] E.C.R. I-1487 .... 6.15
C-334/97 R-EX *Comune di Montorio al Vomano v Commission* [2001] E.C.R. I-4229,
  (order of the President of 30 May 2001) 5.02, 23.94
C-336/97 *Commission v Italy* [1999] E.C.R. I-3771 .... 5.15
C-341/97 *Commission v Netherlands* [2000] E.C.R. I-6611, (order of 13 September 2000)......... 5.41
C-348/97 *Commission v Germany* [2000] E.C.R. I-4429. .... 5.09
C-359/97 *Commission v United Kingdom* [2000] E.C.R. I-6355 .... 5.71
C-365/97 *Commission v Italy* [1999] E.C.R. I-7773 .... 5.54
C-371/97 *Gozza and Others* [2000] E.C.R. I-7881. .... 3.29
C-372/97 *Italy v Commission* [2004] E.C.R. I-3679. .... 7.202, 7.222
C-387/97 *Commission v Greece* [2000] E.C.R. I-5047 .... 5.74, 5.76, 5.78
C-404/97 *Commission v Portugal* [2000] E.C.R. I-4897 .... 5.66
C-408/97 *Commission v Netherlands* [2000] E.C.R. I-6417. .... 5.64
C-412/97 *ED* [1999] E.C.R. I-3845. .... 4.02
C-414/97 *Commission v Spain* [1999] E.C.R. I-5585 .... 5.68
C-421/97 *Tarantik* [1999] E.C.R. I-3633 .... 3.36
C-422/97 P *Sateba v Commission* [1998] E.C.R. I-4913, (order of 17 July 1998)........... 5.39, 7.18
C-424/97 *Haim* [2000] E.C.R. I-5123 .... 4.47, 4.51, 11.61

C-429/97 *Commission v France* [2001] E.C.R. I-637 . . . . 5.52
C-433/97 P *IPK v Commission* [1999] E.C.R. I-6795. . . . . 16.05
C-437/97 *EKW and Wein & Co.* [2000] E.C.R. I-1157 . . . . 6.34
C-443/97 *Spain v Commission* [2000] E.C.R. I-2415 . . . . 7.21, 7.25

C-1/98 P *British Steel v Commission* [2000] E.C.R. I-10349 . . . . 16.03, 16.18, 16.20
C-2/98 P *De Compte v European Parliament* [1999] E.C.R. I-1787 . . . . 16.07, 25.119
C-9/98 *Agostini* [1998] E.C.R. I-4261, (order of 8 July 1998) 3.26
C-15/98 and C-105/99 *Italy and Sardegna Lines v Commission* [2000]
   E.C.R. I-8855 . . . . 7.117, 7.120, 7.122
C-17/98 *Emesa Sugar* [2000] E.C.R. I-665 . . . . 2.15, 4.62, 23.81, 24.14
C-28/98 and C-29/98 *Charreire and Hirtsmann* [1999] E.C.R. I-1963, (order of
   21 April 1999) 3.26
C-35/98 *Verkooijen*, not reported, (order of 17 September 1999) 23.82, 24.14
C-38/98 *Renault* [2000] E.C.R. I-2973. . . . . 21.07
C-57/98 P *ATM v Commission*, not reported, (order of 5 May 1999) 7.138
C-61/98 *De Haan Beheer* [1999] E.C.R. I-5003. . . . . 3.23
C-64/98 P-REV *Odette Nicos Petrides v Commission* [2010] E.C.R. I-65*, Summ. pub.,
   (order of 20 May 2010) 23.03, 25.122
C-76/98 P and C-77/98 P *Ajinomoto and NutraSweet v Council and Commission* [2001]
   E.C.R. I-3223 . . . . 7.66
C-78/98 *Preston and Others* [2000] E.C.R. I-3201 . . . . 4.14, 4.25, 4.32
C-83/98 P *France v Ladbroke Racing and Commission* [2000] E.C.R. I-3271 . . . . 7.201
C-95/98 P *Edouard Dubois and Fils v Council and Commission* [1999] E.C.R. I-4835,
   (order of 8 July 1999). 11.18
C-97/98 *Jägerskiöld* [1999] E.C.R. I-7319. . . . . 6.24
C-104/98 *Buchner and Others* [2000] E.C.R. I-3625 . . . . 6.34
C-106/98 P *Comité d'entreprise de la Société française de production and Others v Commission*
   [2000] E.C.R. I-3659 . . . . 7.123, 7.124, 7.128, 7.129
C-107/98 *Teckal* [1999] E.C.R. I-8121. . . . . 3.23
C-108/98 *RI.SAN.* [1999] E.C.R. I-5219 . . . . 6.24
C-110/98 to C-147/98 *Gabalfrisa and Others* [2000] E.C.R. I-1577 . . . . 3.08, 3.09, 3.10
C-151/98 P *Pharos v Commission* [1998] E.C.R. I-5441, (order of the President of
   28 September 1998). 25.69
C-152/98 *Commission v Netherlands* [2001] E.C.R. I-3463. . . . . 5.31
C-154/98 P *Guérin Automobiles v Commission* [1999] E.C.R. I-1451, (order of 5 March 1999). 7.13
C-155/98 P *Alexopoulou v Commission* [1998] E.C.R. I-4935, (order of the President of
   23 July 1998). 25.67
C-162/98 *Hartmann* [1998] E.C.R. I-7083, (order of 12 November 1998) 6.13
C-164/98 P *DIR International Film and Others v Commission* [2000] E.C.R. I-447 . . . 7.145, 7.219, 16.05
C-165/98 *Mazzoleni and ISA* [2001] E.C.R. I-2189. . . . . 3.32
C-168/98 *Luxembourg v European Parliament and Council* [2000] E.C.R. I-9131. . . . . 7.170
C-175/98 and C-177/98 *Lirussi and Bizzaro* [1999] E.C.R. I-6881. . . . . 3.28
C-180/98 to C-184/98 *Pavlov and Others* [2000] E.C.R. I-645. . . . . 3.26
C-186/98 *Nunes and De Matos* [1999] E.C.R. I-4883 . . . . 4.44
C-193/98 *Pfennigmann* [1999] E.C.R. I-7747 . . . . 6.09
C-195/98 *Österreichischer Gewerkschaftsbund* [2000] E.C.R. I-10497. . . . . 3.08, 3.11
C-200/98 *X and Y* [1999] E.C.R. I-8261 . . . . 3.10
C-205/98 *Commission v Austria* [2000] E.C.R. I-7367 . . . . 5.05
C-210/98 P *Salzgitter v Commission and Germany* [2000] E.C.R. I-5843 . . . . 7.146, 10.15
C-214/98 *Commission v Greece* [2000] E.C.R. I-9601 . . . . 5.63
C-219/98 *Anastasiou and Others* [2000] E.C.R. I-5241. . . . . 6.11
C-225/98 *Commission v France* [2000] E.C.R. I-7445 . . . . 5.41
C-228/98 *Dounias* [2000] E.C.R. I-577 . . . . 4.09, 4.20
C-237/98 P *Dorsch Consult v Council and Commission* [2000] E.C.R. I-4549. . . . . 11.07, 16.04
C-240/98 to C-244/98 *Océano Grupo Editorial and Salvat Editores* [2000]
   E.C.R. I-4941 . . . . 4.40, 4.41, 6.26
C-256/98 *Commission v France* [2000] E.C.R. I-2487 . . . . 5.52
C-258/98 *Carra and Others* [2000] E.C.R. I-4217 . . . . 3.26
C-283/98 P *Mooch Domsjö v Commission* [2000] E.C.R. I-9855 . . . . 16.11
C-291/98 P *Sarrió v Commission* [2000] E.C.R. I-1213, (order of 9 March 2000) 26.06

C-291/98 P *Sarrió v Commission* [2000] E.C.R. I-9991 . . . . 16.11
C-295/98 *Italy v Commission* [2000] E.C.R. I-111, (order of 11 January 2000) 7.207
C-297/98 P *SCA Holding v Commission* [2000] E.C.R. I-10101 . . . . 7.185
C-300/98 and C-392/98 *Parfums Christian Dior and Others* [2000] E.C.R. I-11307 . . . . 6.14
C-310/98 and C-406/98 *Met-Trans and Sagpol* [2000] E.C.R. I-1797. . . . . 4.20
C-325/98 *Anssens* [1999] E.C.R. I-2969 . . . . 3.26, 3.33
C-337/98 *Commission v France* [2000] E.C.R. I-8377 . . . . 5.63
C-340/98 *Italy v Council* [2002] E.C.R. I-2663 . . . . 7.170
C-343/98 *Collino and Chiappero* [2000] E.C.R. I-6659 . . . . 3.32
C-344/98 *Masterfoods and HB Ice Cream* [2000] E.C.R. I-11369 . . . . 3.60
C-347/98 *Commission v Belgium* [2001] E.C.R. I-3327 . . . . 5.63
C-352/98 P *Bergaderm and Goupil v Commission* [2000] E.C.R. I-5291. . . . . .4.46,
                                          11.44, 11.45, 11.48, 11.52, 11.56
C-358/98 *Commission v Italy* [2000] E.C.R. I-1255. . . . . 5.17
C-364/98 P(R) *Emesa Sugar v Commission* [1998] E.C.R. I-8815, (order of the President
   of 17 December 1998) 13.32
C-372/98 *Cooke* [2000] E.C.R. I-8683 . . . . 6.34
C-376/98 *Germany v European Parliament and Council* [2000] E.C.R. I-8419 . . . . . . .7.151, 7.220, 25.50
C-377/98 R *Netherlands v European Parliament and Council* [2000] E.C.R. I-6229,
   (order of the President of 25 July 2000). 13.35
C-377/98 *Netherlands v European Parliament and Council* [2001] E.C.R. I-7079 . . . . 25.59
C-378/98 *Commission v Belgium* [2001] E.C.R. I-5107 . . . . 5.58
C-383/98 *Polo/Lauren* [2000] E.C.R. I-2519. . . . . 3.23
C-390/98 *Banks* [2001] E.C.R. I-6117 . . . . 10.11
C-393/98 *Gomes Valente* [2001] E.C.R. I-1327 . . . . 3.53
C-397/98 and C-410/98 *Metallgesellschaft and Others* [2001] E.C.R. I-1727 . . . . .4.23, 4.30, 4.52
C-399/98 *Ordine degli Architetti and Others* [2001] E.C.R. I-5409 . . . . 3.26
C-402/98 *ATB and Others* [2000] E.C.R. I-5501. . . . . 3.22
C-405/98 *Gourmet International Products* [2001] E.C.R. I-1795. . . . . 3.30
C-407/98 *Abrahamsson and Anderson* [2000] E.C.R. I-5539. . . . . 3.08
C-422/98 *Colonia Versicherung and Others* [1999] E.C.R. I-1279, (order of 2 March 1999) 3.26
C-425/98 *Marca Mode* [2000] E.C.R. I-4861 . . . . 3.23
C-426/98 *Commission v Greece* [2002] E.C.R. I-2793 . . . . 5.71
C-432/98 P and C-433/98 P *Council v Chvatal and Others* [2000] E.C.R. I-8535 . . . . 9.08
C-434/98 P *Council v Busacca and Others* [2000] E.C.R. I-8577. . . . . 9.19, 16.16
C-440/98 *RAI* [1999] E.C.R. I-8597, (order of 26 November 1999) 3.10
C-441/98 and C-442/98 *Michailidis* [2000] E.C.R. I-7145 . . . . 3.32, 4.28
C-446/98 *Fazenda Pública* [2000] E.C.R. I-11435. . . . . 6.27
C-448/98 *Guimont* [2000] E.C.R. I-10663 . . . . 3.33, 3.38, 6.24
C-449/98 P *IECC v Commission* [2001] E.C.R. I-3875 . . . . 7.147
C-450/98 P *IECC v Commission* [2001] E.C.R. I-3947 . . . . 16.20
C-451/98 *Antillean Rice Mills v Council* [2001] E.C.R. I-8949 . . . . 7.100
C-452/98 *Nederlandse Antillen v Council* [2001] E.C.R. I-8973 . . . . 7.85, 7.100
C-458/98 P *Industrie des Poudres Sphériques v Council* [2000] E.C.R. I-8147. . . . . 7.223, 16.19
C-462/98 P *Mediocurso v Commission* [2000] E.C.R. I-7183. . . . . 7.161
C-471/98 *Commission v Belgium* [2002] E.C.R. I-9681 . . . . 5.31, 25.37, 25.49
C-472/98 *Commission v Luxembourg* [2002] E.C.R. I-9741 . . . . 5.31
C-475/98 *Commission v Austria* [2002] E.C.R. I-9797 . . . . 5.62
C-476/98 *Commission v Germany* [2002] E.C.R. I-9855. . . . . 5.31

C-1/99 *Kofisa Italia* [2001] E.C.R. I-207. . . . . 6.17
C-6/99 *Greenpeace France and Others* [2000] E.C.R. I-1651. . . . . 3.59
C-7/99 P *Campoli v Commission* [1999] E.C.R. I-2679, (order of 30 April 1999). 16.25
C-8/99 P *Gòmez de Enterría y Sanchez v European Parliament* [2000] E.C.R. I-6031,
   (order of 13 July 2000). 7.223
C-17/99 *France v Commission* [2001] E.C.R. I-2481 . . . . 5.66
C-29/99 *Commission v Council* [2002] E.C.R. I-11221. . . . . 7.220, 12.06
C-36/99 *Idéal Tourisme* [2000] E.C.R. I-6049. . . . . 3.27, 3.41
C-52/99 and C-53/99 *Camarotto and Vignone* [2001] E.C.R. I-1395 . . . . 4.13
C-56/99 *Gascogne Limousin Viandes* [2000] E.C.R. I-3079. . . . . 3.26
C-59/99 *Commission v Pereira Roldão & Filhos and Others* [2001] E.C.R. I-8499 . . . . 25.28, 25.31

C-68/99 *Commission v Germany* [2001] E.C.R. I-1865................................ 5.63
C-70/99 *Commission v Portugal* [2001] E.C.R. I-4845 .... 5.26
C-77/99 DEP *Commission v Oder-Plan Architektur and Others* [2004] E.C.R. I-1267,
    (order of 4 February 2004) 25.92
C-80/99 to C-82/99 *Flemmer and Others* [2001] E.C.R. I-7211 .... 11.06, 19.16, 19.17
C-83/99 *Commission v Spain* [2001] E.C.R. I-445................................. 5.65
C-88/99 *Roquette Frères* [2000] E.C.R. I-10465............... 3.22, 3.23, 4.25, 4.33, 6.33
C-89/99 *Schieving-Nijstad and Others* [2001] E.C.R. I-5851........................ 6.14
C-100/99 *Italy v Council and Commission* [2001] E.C.R. I-5217..................... 7.170
C-107/99 *Italy v Commission* [2002] E.C.R. I-1091 .... 7.168, 25.60
C-109/99 *ABBOI* [2000] E.C.R. I-7247 .... 3.26
C-110/99 *Emsland-Stärke* [2000] E.C.R. I-11569 .... 4.28
C-120/99 *Italy v Council* [2001] E.C.R. I-7997.................................. 7.170
C-127/99 *Commission v Italy* [2001] E.C.R. I-8305 .... 5.76
C-145/99 *Commission v Italy* [2002] E.C.R. I-2235 .... 5.17
C-150/99 *Stockholm Lindöpark AB* [2001] E.C.R. I-493........................ 4.48, 4.49
C-153/99 P *Commission v Giannini* [2000] E.C.R. I-2891 .... 7.223
C-154/99 P *Politi v European Training Foundation* [2000] E.C.R. I-5019 .... 16.07, 18.22
C-159/99 *Commission v Italy* [2001] E.C.R. I-4007............................... 5.48
C-163/99 *Portugal v Commission* [2001] E.C.R. I-2613 ....5.26, 5.65, 7.44
C-176/99 P *ARBED v Commission* [2003] E.C.R. I-10687......................... 7.161
C-178/99 *Salzmann* [2001] E.C.R. I-4421 .... 3.10
C-177/99 and C-181/99 *Ampafrance and Sanofi Synthelabo* [2000] E.C.R. I-7013 .... 10.22
C-184/99 *Grzelczyk* [2001] E.C.R. I-6193....................................... 6.34
C-194/99 P *Thyssen Stahl v Commission* [2003] E.C.R. I-10821 .... 7.162
C-196/99 P *Aristrain v Commission* [2003] E.C.R. I-11005 .... 15.04
C-197/99 P *Belgium v Commission* [2003] E.C.R. I-8461..................... 16.05, 16.09
C-198/99 P *Ensidesa v Commission* [2003] E.C.R. I-1111.......................... 26.09
C-199/99 P *Corus UK v Commission* [2003] E.C.R. I-11177 .... 16.18, 23.61
C-202/99 *Commission v Italy* [2001] E.C.R. I-9319............................... 5.63
C-208/99 *Portugal v Commission* [2001] E.C.R. I-9183, (order of 27 November 2001) 7.21
C-212/99 *Commission v Italy* [2001] E.C.R. I-4923.............................. 5.17
C-213/99 *De Andrade* [2000] E.C.R. I-11083.................................... 4.45
C-216/99 and C-222/99 *RiccardoPrisco and CASER* [2002] E.C.R. I-6761 .... 4.25, 4.30
C-223/99 and C-260/99 *Agorà and Excelsior* [2001] E.C.R. I-3605................. 3.23
C-226/99 *Siples* [2001] E.C.R. I-227 .... 4.07, 4.61
C-228/99 *Silos e Mangimi Martini* [2001] E.C.R. I-8401......................... 10.22
C-236/99 *Commission v Belgium* [2000] E.C.R. I-5657....................... 5.65, 5.68
C-238/99 P, C-244/99 P, C-245/99 P, C-247/99 P, C-250/99 P, C-252/99 P,
    and C-254/99 P *Limburgse Vinyl Maatschappij and Others v Commission* [2002]
    E.C.R. I-8375 .... 7.178, 15.05, 16.09, 16.19, 23.87, 25.13
C-239/99 *Nachi Europe* [2001] E.C.R. I-1197.............. 3.23, 7.131, 7.133, 7.223, 9.07, 10.11
C-242/99 *Vogler* [2000] E.C.R. I-9083, (order of 20 October 2000)...................... 24.15
C-248/99 P *France v Monsanto and Commission* [2002] E.C.R. I-1 .... 16.09, 16.19, 25.60
C-249/99 P *Pescados Congelados Jogamar v Commission* [1999]
    E.C.R. I-8333, (order of 18 November 1999) 8.15, 8.18
C-261/99 *Commission v France* [2001] E.C.R. I-2537 .... 5.66
C-263/99 *Commission v Italy* [2001] E.C.R. I-4195 .... 5.63
C-267/99 *Adam* [2001] E.C.R. I-7467 .... 6.16
C-271/99 *Commission v Belgium*, not reported, (order of 11 July 2000)................. 25.99
C-274/99 P *Connolly v Commission* [2001] E.C.R. I-1611 .... 16.09
C-278/99 *Netherlands v Commission* [2001] E.C.R. I-1501....................... 7.170
C-280/99 P, C-281/99 P, and C-282/99 P *Moccia Irme and Others v Commission* [2001]
    E.C.R. I-4717 .... 16.19
C-294/99 *Athinaïki Zythoppoïïa* [2001] E.C.R. I-6797........................... 6.34
C-302/99 P and C-308/99 P *Commission and France v TF1* [2001] E.C.R. I-5603 .... 16.21, 25.84
C-306/99 *BIAO* [2003] E.C.R. I-1.. 6.17
C-307/99 *OGT Fruchthandelsgesellschaft* [2001] E.C.R. I-3159, (order of 2 May 2001) 24.15
C-309/99 *Wouters and Others* [2002] E.C.R. I-1577 .... 23.82, 24.14
C-310/99 *Italy v Commission* [2002] E.C.R. I-2289 .... 7.170
C-315/99 P *Ismeri v Court of Auditors* [2001] E.C.R. I-5281 .... 16.24

C-321/99 P *ARAP and Others v Commission* [2002] E.C.R. I-4287 . . . . 7.61, 7.62
C-329/99 P(R) *Pfizer Animal Health v Council* [1999] E.C.R. I-8343,
 (order of the President of 18 November 1999) 25.60
C-333/99 *Commission v France* [2001] E.C.R. I-1025 . . . . 5.31, 5.62
C-335/99 P(R) *HFB and Others v Commission* [1999] E.C.R. I-8705,
 (order of the President of 14 December 1999) 13.36
C-340/99 *TNT Traco* [2001] E.C.R. I-4109 . . . . 3.54
C-349/99 P *Commission v ADT Projekt* [1999] E.C.R. I-6467, (order of 4 October 1999) 16.12
C-351/99 P *Eridania and Others v Council* [2001] E.C.R. I-5007, (order of 28 June 2001) 16.19
C-353/99 P *Council v Hautala* [2001] E.C.R. I-9565. . . . . 1.06
C-354/99 *Commission v Ireland* [2001] E.C.R. I-7657 . . . . 4.44
C-356/99 *Commission v Hitesys* [2000] E.C.R. I-9517 . . . . 19.07, 25.31
C-363/99 *Koninklijke KPN Nederland* [2004] E.C.R. I-1619 . . . . 3.47
C-364/99 P(R) *DSR-Senator Lines v Commission* [1999] E.C.R. I-8733, (order of the President
 of 14 December 1999) 13.36
C-365/99 *Portugal v Commission* [2001] E.C.R. I-5645 . . . . 25.31
C-366/99 *Griesmar* [2001] E.C.R. I-9383 . . . . 6.34
C-381/99 *Brunnhofer* [2001] E.C.R. I-4961 . . . . 6.26
C-382/99 *Netherlands v Commission* [2002] E.C.R. I-5163. . . . . 7.204
C-383/99 P *Procter & Gamble v OHIM* [2001] E.C.R. I-6251 . . . . 16.14
C-384/99 *Commission v Belgium* [2000] E.C.R. I-10633 . . . . 5.58
C-387/99 *Commission v Germany* [2004] E.C.R. I-3751. . . . . 5.10
C-390/99 *Canal Satélite Digital* [2002] E.C.R. I-607 . . . . 3.32
C-393/99 and C-394/99 *Hervein and Others* [2002] E.C.R. I-2829 . . . . 10.03
C-400/99 *Italy v Commission* [2001] E.C.R. I-7303. . . . . 7.53, 7.57, 7.58
C-400/99 *Italy v Commission* [2005] E.C.R. I-3657 . . . . 7.54, 7.57, 7.142, 7.165, 7.181, 7.183
C-404/99 *Commission v France* [2001] E.C.R. I-2667 . . . . 5.65
C-424/99 *Commission v Austria* [2001] E.C.R. I-9285 . . . . 4.11
C-430/99 and C-431/99 *Sealand Service and Nedlloyd Lijnen* [2002] E.C.R. I-5235. . . . . 3.36
C-439/99 *Commission v Italy* [2002] E.C.R. I-305 . . . . 5.58
C-449/99 *EIB v Hautem* [2001] E.C.R. I-6733 . . . . 26.07
C-451/99 *Cura Anlagen* [2002] E.C.R. I-3193 . . . . 3.42
C-453/99 *Courage and Crehan* [2001] E.C.R. I-6297. 4.53, 4.54, 7.189
C-470/99 *Universale-Bau and Others* [2002] E.C.R. I-11617 . . . . 4.25
C-473/99 *Commission v Austria* [2001] E.C.R. I-4527 . . . . 5.65
C-474/99 *Commission v Spain* [2002] E.C.R. I-5293 . . . . 5.31
C-478/99 *Commission v Sweden* [2002] E.C.R. I-4147 . . . . 5.15
C-480/99 P *Plant and Others v Commission and South Wales Small Mines Association*
 [2002] E.C.R. I-265 . . . . 16.06, 23.45, 23.61
C-481/99 *Heininger* [2001] E.C.R. I-9945 . . . . 6.34
C-496/99 P *Commission v CAS Succhi di Frutta* [2004] E.C.R. I-3801 . . . . 7.136, 7.141
C-514/99 *France v Commission* [2000] E.C.R. I-4705 . . . . 7.23
C-515/99, C-519/99 to C-524/99, and C-526/99 to C-540/99 *Reisch and Others* [2002]
 E.C.R. I-2157 . . . . 3.38, 6.24
C-516/99 *Schmid* [2002] E.C.R. I-4573 . . . . 3.09
C-518/99 *Gaillard* [2001] E.C.R. I-2771, (order of 5 April 2001) 24.15

Opinion 1/00 *Proposed Agreement between the European Community and non-Member States on the
 establishment of a European Common Aviation Area* [2002] E.C.R. I-3493. . . . . 12.01, 12.13
Opinion 2/00 *Cartagena Protocol* [2001] E.C.R. I-9713 . . . . 12.01, 12.03, 12.11, 12.12, 12.16
C-1/00 *Commission v France* [2001] E.C.R. I-9989 . . . . 5.44, 5.50, 5.51, 5.66, 5.68
C-1/00 SA *Cotecna Inspection v Commission* [2001] E.C.R. I-4219,
 (order of 29 May 2001) 14.01, 14.06, 14.07
C-11/00 *Commission v ECB* [2003] E.C.R. I-7174. . . . . 5.66, 9.07, 9.10, 9.11, 10.11
C-13/00 *Commission v Ireland* [2002] E.C.R. I-2943 . . . . 5.07, 25.60
C-15/00 *Commission v EIB* [2003] E.C.R. I-7281 . . . . 1.03, 7.70
C-17/00 *De Coster* [2001] E.C.R. I-9445 . . . . 3.09
C-23/00 P *Council v Boehringer* [2002] E.C.R. I-1873 . . . . 7.66, 7.89, 16.12, 25.43
C-27/00 and C-122/00 *Omega Air and Others* [2002] E.C.R. I-2569 . . . . 4.11, 7.170
C-40/00 *Commission v France* [2001] E.C.R. I-4539 . . . . 5.62
C-43/00 *Andersen og Jensen* [2002] E.C.R. I-379 . . . . 6.16

C-44/00 P *Sodima v Commission* [2000] E.C.R. I-11231, (order of 13 December 2000). 8.05, 8.19
C-50/00 P *Unión de Pequeños Agricultores v Council* [2002] E.C.R. I-6677. . . . . 2.16, 4.10, 4.11, 7.106, 9.04
C-52/00 *Commission v France* [2002] E.C.R. I-3827 . . . . 5.52, 5.65, 5.66
C-62/00 *Marks & Spencer* [2002] E.C.R. I-6325 . . . . 3.23, 4.26
C-92/00 *HI* [2002] E.C.R. I-5553 . . . . 3.08, 4.38
C-94/00 *Roquette Frères* [2002] E.C.R. I-9011. . . . . 7.32
C-97/00 *Commission v France* [2001] E.C.R. I-2053 . . . . 5.15
C-99/00 *Lyckeskog* [2002] E.C.R. I-4839. . . . . 3.48
C-116/00 *Laguillaumie* [2000] E.C.R. I-4979, (order of 28 June 2000). 3.33
C-118/00 *Larsy* [2001] E.C.R. I-5063. . . . . 4.48
C-119/00 *Commission v Luxembourg* [2001] E.C.R. I-4795 . . . . 5.58, 5.59
C-123/00 *Bellamy and English Shop Wholesale* [2001] E.C.R. I-2795. . . . . 3.26
C-129/00 *Commission v Italy* [2003] E.C.R. I-14637 . . . . . . 3.56, 3.57, 4.23, 4.28, 5.10, 5.12, 5.37, 5.38
C-137/00 *Milk Marque and National Farmers' Union* [2003] E.C.R. I-7975 . . . . 3.27
C-139/00 *Commission v Spain* [2002] E.C.R. I-6407 . . . . 5.52
C-140/00 *Commission v United Kingdom* [2002] E.C.R. I-10372 . . . . 5.01, 5.65
C-142/00 P *Commission v Nederlandse Antillen* [2003] E.C.R. I-3483. . . . . 7.100
C-147/00 *Commission v France* [2001] E.C.R. I-2387 . . . . 5.58, 5.63
C-150/00 *Commission v Austria* [2004] E.C.R. I-3887 . . . . 5.10
C-153/00 *der Weduwe* [2002] E.C.R. I-11319. . . . . 3.08, 3.28, 3.36, 3.37
C-159/00 *Sapod Audic* [2002] E.C.R. I-5031 . . . . 4.36
C-171/00 P *Libéros v Commission* [2002] E.C.R. 451. . . . . 2.29
C-182/00 *Lutz and Others* [2002] E.C.R. I-547. . . . . 3.08, 3.10
C-185/00 *Commission v Finland* [2003] E.C.R. I-14189 . . . . 5.48, 5.52, 25.60
C-190/00 *Balguerie and Others* [2001] E.C.R. I-3437. . . . . 3.23
C-204/00 P, C-205/00 P, C-211/00 P, C-213/00 P, C-217/00 P, and C-219/00
    P *Aalborg Portland and Others v Commission* [2004] E.C.R. I-123 . . . . 7.36, 7.43,
                                    7.145, 7.190, 7.193, 16.04, 16.05, 16.09, 16.18, 16.19, 26.07
C-211/00 P *Ciments Français v Commission*, not reported, (order of 5 June 2002) 26.07
C-217/00 P *Buzzi Unicem v Commission*, not reported, (order of 5 June 2002) 16.09, 23.87
C-242/00 *Germany v Commission* [2002] E.C.R. I-5603. . . . . 7.21
C-252/00 *Vandeweerd*, not reported, (order of 6 December 2000) 3.26
C-255/00 *Grundig Italiana* [2002] E.C.R. I-8003 . . . . 4.26
C-260/00 to C-263/00 *Lohmann and Medi Bayreuth* [2002] E.C.R. I-10045. . . . . 6.18
C-265/00 *Campina Melkunie BV* [2004] E.C.R. I-1699 . . . . 3.47
C-273/00 *Sieckmann* [2002] E.C.R. I-11737. . . . . 23.82
C-274/00 P *Simon v Commission* [2002] E.C.R. I-5999 . . . . 23.54
C-275/00 *First and Franex* [2002] E.C.R. I-10943. . . . . 11.04
C-277/00 *Germany v Commission* [2004] E.C.R. I-3925. . . . . 7.147
C-280/00 *Altmark Trans and Regierungspräsidium Magdeburg*, not reported, (order of
    18 June 2002) 23.82, 24.14
C-281/00 P *Una Film 'City Revue' v European Parliament and Council*, (order of
    23 October 2001). 11.12
C-287/00 *Commission v Germany* [2002] E.C.R. I-5811. . . . . 5.40, 5.51
C-290/00 *Duchon* [2002] E.C.R. I-3567. . . . . 2.01
C-298/00 P *Italy v Commission* [2004] E.C.R. I-4087 . . . . 7.120, 7.122, 7.217
C-301/00 P-REV *Meyer v Commission*, not reported, (judgment of 7 November 2002) 25.117
C-304/00 *Strawson and Gagg & Sons* [2002] E.C.R. I-10737 . . . . 3.23
C-312/00 P *Commission v Camar and Tico* [2002] E.C.R. I-11355 . . . . 7.99, 7.106, 11.45, 11.67
C-313/00 P *Zino Davidoff and Davidoff & Cie v European Parliament and Council*
    (order of 23 October 2001). 11.12
C-318/00 *Bacardi-Martini and Cellier des Dauphins* [2003] E.C.R. I-905 . . . . 3.28, 3.37
C-323/00 P *DSG Dradenauer Stahlgesellschaft v Commission* [2002] E.C.R. I-3919. . . . . 7.201
C-325/00 *Commission v Germany* [2002] E.C.R. I-9977. . . . . 5.39
C-330/00 P *AICS v European Parliament* [2001] E.C.R. I-4805 . . . . 16.04
C-347/00 *Barreira Pérez* [2002] E.C.R. I-8191 . . . . 6.34
C-366/00 *Commission v Luxembourg* [2002] E.C.R. I-1749 . . . . 5.60
C-378/00 *Commission v European Parliament and Council* [2003] E.C.R. I-937 . . . . 7.220
C-383/00 *Commission v Germany* [2002] E.C.R. I-4219. . . . . 5.31
C-404/00 *Commission v Spain* [2003] E.C.R. I-6695 . . . . 5.24
C-409/00 *Spain v Commission* [2003] E.C.R. I-1487 . . . . 7.202

C-411/00 *Felix Swoboda* [2002] E.C.R. I-10567 . . . . 3.08
C-418/00 and C-419/00 *Commission v France* [2002] E.C.R. I-3969 . . . . 5.14, 5.31
C-430/00 P *Dürbeck v Commission* [2001] E.C.R. I-8457. . . . . 25.14
C-445/00 R *Austria v Council* [2001] E.C.R. I-1461, (order of the President of
     23 February 2001) 13.32, 13.36
C-445/00 *Austria v Council* [2002] E.C.R. I-9151, (order of 23 October 2002). 23.60
C-445/00 *Austria v Council* [2003] E.C.R. I-8549 . . . . 7.29
C-446/00 P *Cubero Vermurie v Commission* [2001] E.C.R. I-10315 . . . . 16.09
C-447/00 *Holto* [2002] E.C.R. I-735 . . . . 3.17
C-453/00 *Kühne & Heitz* [2004] E.C.R. I-837 . . . . 4.56, 4.57
C-454/00 *Vis Farmaceutici Istituto Scientifico delle Venezie*, not reported, (order of 26 April 2002). . . . 6.16
C-456/00, C-138/01, and C-139/01 *Österreichischer Rundfunk and Others* [2003] E.C.R. I-4989 . . . . 3.17
C-466/00 *Kaba* [2003] E.C.R. I-2219. . . . . 6.11
C-471/00 P(R) *Commission v Cambridge Healthcare Supplies* [2001] E.C.R. I-2865,
     (order of the President of 11 April 2001) 13.42
C-472/00 P *Commission v Fresh Marine* [2003] E.C.R. I-7541 . . . . 11.37, 11.45, 11.52, 11.54, 11.85
C-473/00 *Cofidis* [2002] E.C.R. I-10875 . . . . 4.25
C-480/00 to C-482/00, C-484/00, C-489/00 to C-491/00, C-497/00–C-499/00 *Azienda
     Agricola Ettore Ribaldi and Others* [2004] E.C.R. I-2943 . . . . 3.27, 3.31

C-2/01 P and C-3/01 P *BAI and Commission v Bayer* [2004] E.C.R. I-23 . . . . 16.05, 16.07, 16.24
C-6/01 *Anomar and Others* [2003] E.C.R. I-8621 . . . . 6.24
C-20/01 and C-28/01 *Commission v Germany* [2003] E.C.R. I-3609. . . . . 5.09
C-24/01 P and C-25/01 P *Glencore and Compagnie Continentale v Commission* [2002]
     E.C.R. I-10119 . . . . 16.04, 16.20, 16.24
C-29/01 *Commission v Spain* [2002] E.C.R. I-2503. . . . . 5.58
C-42/01 *Commission v Portugal* [2004] E.C.R. I-6079 . . . . 7.46
C-62/01 P *Campogrande v Commission* [2002] E.C.R. I-3793. . . . . 16.10
C-63/01 *Evans* [2003] E.C.R. I-14447 . . . . 4.46, 4.47
C-76/01 P *Eurocoton and Others v Council* [2003] E.C.R. I-10091 . . . . 7.14, 7.64, 7.66, 11.48, 11.51
C-80/01 *Michel* [2001] E.C.R. I-9141, (order of 22 November 2001) 24.15
C-82/01 P *Aéroports de Paris v Commission* [2002] E.C.R. I-9297 . . . . 16.04, 16.07, 26.02
C-87/01 P *Commission v CCRE* [2003] E.C.R. I-7617. . . . . 7.15, 25.37
C-121/01 P *O'Hannrachain v European Parliament* [2003] E.C.R. I-5539. . . . . 16.22
C-125/01 *Pflücke* [2003] E.C.R. I-9375 . . . . 4.25, 4.32
C 129/01 *Condominio Facchinei Orsini*, not reported, (order of 2 May 2002) 3.36
C-136/01 P *Autosalone Ispra dei Fratelli Rossi v Commission* [2002] E.C.R. I-6565 (order of
     18 July 2002). 2.24, 11.92, 11.94
C-145/01 *Commission v Italy* [2003] E.C.R. I-5581 . . . . 5.42, 5.47
C-147/01 *Weber's Wine World and Others* [2003] E.C.R. I-11365. . . . . 4.23, 4.24, 4.27, 4.28
C-165/01 *Betriebsrat der Vertretung der Europäischen Kommission in Österreich* [2003]
     E.C.R. I-7683 . . . . 18.08
C-167/01 *Inspire Art* [2003] E.C.R. I-10155. . . . . .3.31, 3.32, 4.44
C-172/01 P, C-175/01 P, C-176/01 P, and C-180/01 P *International Power and Others
     and Commission v NALOO* [2003] I-11421 .7.171, 16.05, 16.15, 25.65
C-184/01 P *Hirschfeldt v European Environment Agency* [2002] E.C.R. I-10173. . . . . 23.82
C-189/01 *Jippes and Others* [2001] E.C.R. I-5689 . . . . 24.19, 25.81
C-193/01 P *Pitsiorlas v Council and ECB* [2003] E.C.R. I-4837 . . . . 7.214, 9.15
C-194/01 *Commission v Austria* [2004] E.C.R. I-4579 . . . . 5.66
C-207/01 *Altair Chimica* [2003] E.C.R. I-8875 . . . . 3.25, 6.08
C-209/01 *Schilling and Fleck-Schilling* [2003] E.C.R. I-13389, (judgment of
     13 November 2003). 24.14
C-211/01 *Commission v Council* [2003] E.C.R. I-8913. . . . . 7.221
C-222/01 *British American Tobacco Manufacturing* [2004] E.C.R. I-4683 . . . . 6.16
C-224/01 *Köbler* [2003] E.C.R. I-10239. . . . . .3.56, 3.58, 4.07, 4.47,
     4.50, 4.51, 4.58, 5.73, 6.11, 11.60
C-226/01 *Commission v Denmark* [2003] E.C.R. I-1219 . . . . 5.65
C-227/01 *Commission v Spain* [2004] E.C.R. I-8253 . . . . 5.09
C-228/01 and C-289/01 *Bourrasse and Perchicot* [2002] E.C.R. I-10213 . . . . 3.23
C-230/01 *Penycoed Farming Partnership* [2004] E.C.R. I-937 . . . . 4.43, 4.44
C-239/01 *Germany v Commission* [2003] E.C.R. I-10333. . . . . 7.220

C-241/01 *National Farmers' Union* [2002] E.C.R. I-9079 . . . . .3.23, 9.11, 10.11
C-257/01 *Commission v Council* [2005] E.C.R. I-345. . . . . 7.153
C-261/01 and C-262/01 *Van Calster and Cleeren* [2003] E.C.R. I-12249 . . . . 5.24
C-271/01 *COPPI* [2004] E.C.R. I-1029 . . . . 3.23
C-278/01 *Commission v Spain* [2003] E.C.R. I-14141 . . . . 5.78
C-296/01 *Commission v France* [2003] E.C.R. I-13909 . . . . 5.15
C-299/01 *Commission v Luxembourg* [2002] E.C.R. I-5899 . . . . 5.59
C-300/01 *Salzmann* [2003] E.C.R. I-4899 . . . . 6.24
C-314/01 *Siemens and ARGE Telekom & Partner* [2004] E.C.R. I-2549 . . . . 3.32, 3.35
C-315/01 *GAT* [2003] E.C.R. I-6351. . . . . 3.32
C-341/01 *Plato Plastik Robert Frank* [2004] E.C.R. I-4883. . . . . 3.26, 3.42
C-353/01 P *Mattila v Council and Commission* [2004] I-1073. . . . . 7.173
C-358/01 *Commission v Spain* [2003] E.C.R. I-13145 . . . . 5.48
C-362/01 *Commission v Ireland* [2003] E.C.R. I-11433 . . . . .5.40, 5.48, 5.51
C-380/01 *Schneider* [2004] E.C.R. I-1389. . . . . 3.24, 3.35, 23.80
C-387/01 *Weigel* [2004] E.C.R. I-4981. . . . . 3.23, 3.32
C-397/01 to C-403/01 *Pfeiffer and Others* [2004] E.C.R. I-8835 . . . . 2.01, 4.37
C-404/01 P(R) *Commission v Euroalliages and Others* [2001] E.C.R. I-10367,
     (order of 14 December 2001) 13.36
C-428/01 *Fratelli Costanzo and Others*, not reported, (order of 27 January 2004). 24.15
C-429/01 *Commission v France* [2003] E.C.R. I-14355 . . . . 5.15
C-430/01 *Herbstrith*, not reported, (order of 21 March 2002). 3.26
C-439/01 *Cipra and Kvasnicka* [2003] E.C.R. I-745 . . . . 6.14
C-440/01 P(R) *Commission v Artegodan* [2002] E.C.R. I-1489, (order of 14 February 2002) 13.44
C-447/01 *DLD Trading Company Import-Export*, not reported, (order of 21 March 2002) 3.26
C-463/01 *Commission v Germany* [2004] E.C.R. I-11705. . . . . 5.48
C-465/01 *Commission v Austria* [2004] E.C.R. I-8291 . . . . 5.07
C-467/01 *Eribrand* [2003] E.C.R. I-6471 . . . . 4.09
C-475/01 *Commission v Greece* [2004] E.C.R. I-8923 . . . . .5.20, 5.67, 7.12, 9.11, 9.13, 10.21
C-478/01 *Commission v Spain* [2003] E.C.R. I-4141 . . . . 5.74
C-482/01 and C-493/01 *Orfanopoulous and Others* [2004] E.C.R. I-5257 . . . . 6.21, 6.25
C-486/01 P *Front National v European Parliament* [2004] E.C.R. I-6289 . . . .7.69, 7.91, 7.92, 16.14, 26.11
C-488/01 P *Martinez v European Parliament* [2003] E.C.R. I-13355. . . . . 7.69, 7.92, 16.04, 16.05, 26.02
C-491/01 *British American Tobacco and Imperial Tobacco* [2002]
     E.C.R. I-11453 . . . . .4.11, 7.105, 10.09, 10.18
C-494/01 *Commission v Ireland* [2005] E.C.R. I-3331 . . . . .5.10, 5.11, 5.14, 5.31, 5.37, 5.64

C-1/02 SA *Antippas v Commission* [2003] E.C.R. I-2893, (order of 27 March 2003) 14.01, 14.06, 14.07
C-4/02 and C-5/02 *Schönheit and Becker* [2003] E.C.R. I-12575 . . . . 6.26
C-9/02 *De Lasteyrie du Saillant* [2004] E.C.R. I-2409 . . . . 3.28
C-24/02 *Marseille Fret* [2002] E.C.R. I-3383. . . . . 21.07
C-30/02 *Recheio* [2004] E.C.R. I-6053 . . . . .3.23, 4.04, 4.21, 4.23, 4.26, 6.23
C-32/02 *Commission v Italy* [2003] E.C.R. I-12063 . . . . 25.31
C-34/02 *Pasquini* [2003] E.C.R. I-6515 . . . . 4.14
C-41/02 *Commission v Netherlands* [2004] E.C.R. I-11375. . . . . 5.10
C-57/02 P *Acerinox v Commission* [2005] E.C.R. I-6689 . . . . 16.09
C-60/02 *X* [2004] E.C.R. I-651 . . . . .3.17, 3.24, 4.44
C-66/02 *Italy v Commission* [2005] E.C.R. I-10901 . . . . 25.14
C-69/02 *Reichling* [2002] E.C.R. I-3393 . . . . 21.07
C-71/02 *Herbert Karner Industrie-Auktionen* [2004] E.C.R. I-3025 . . . . 3.33, 3.36
C-87/02 *Commission v Italy* [2004] E.C.R. I-5975. . . . . 5.32, 5.37
C-93/02 P *Biret International v Council* [2003] E.C.R. I-10497 . . . . 11.51
C-94/02 P *Biret & Cie v Council*. 11.25, 11.45, 11.51, 11.88
C-99/02 *Commission v Italy* [2004] E.C.R. I-3353 . . . . .4.31, 5.22, 5.24, 5.58, 5.65
C-103/02 *Commission v Italy* [2004] E.C.R. I-9127 . . . . 5.65
C-104/02 *Commission v Germany* [2005] E.C.R. I-2689. . . . . 5.69
C-105/02 *Commission v Germany* [2006] E.C.R. I-9659. . . . . 5.68
C-110/02 *Commission v Council* [2004] E.C.R. I-6333. . . . . 5.22, 7.55, 7.150
C-111/02 P *European Parliament v Reynolds* [2004] E.C.R. I-5475 . . . . 7.161, 18.03
C-116/02 *Gasser* [2003] E.C.R. I-14693 . . . . 3.26, 3.32
C-117/02 *Commission v Portugal* [2004] E.C.R. I-5517 . . . . 5.52

C-141/02 P *Commission v T-Mobile Austria* [2005] E.C.R. I-1283 . . . . .5.33, 7.44, 8.06
C-153/02 *Neri* [2003] E.C.R. I-13555 . . . . .3.22, 3.36, 6.21
C-164/02 *Netherlands v Commission* [2004] E.C.R. I-1177, (order of 28 January 2004) 7.21, 7.22
C-166/02 *Messejana Viegas*, not reported, (order of 24 July 2003) 24.15
C-167/02 P *Rothley and Others v European Parliament* [2004]
    E.C.R. I-3149 . . . . 4.10, 4.11, 7.69, 7.100, 7.105, 7.106
C-170/02 P *Schlüsselverlag J.S. Moser and Others v Commission* [2003] E.C.R. I-9889. . . .8.06, 8.17, 16.27
C-174/02 *Streekgewest Westelijk Noord-Brabant* [2005] E.C.R. I-85. . . . . 4.17
C-184/02 and C-223/02 *Spain and Finland v European Parliament and Council* [2004]
    E.C.R. I-7789 . . . . 25.06
C-186/02 P *Ramondín and Others v Commission* [2003] E.C.R. I-2415, (order of the President
    of 6 March 2003). 25.65, 25.67
C-189/02 P, C-202/02 P, C-205/02 P to C-208/02 P, and C-213/02 P *Dansk Røyrindustri
    and Others v Commission* [2005] E.C.R. I-5425 . . . . 9.08, 15.07
C-190/02 *Viacom* [2002] E.C.R. I-8287, (order of 8 October 2002). 3.26
C-195/02 *Commission v Spain* [2004] E.C.R. I-7857 . . . . 25.60
C-209/02 *Commission v Austria* [2004] E.C.R. I-1211 . . . . 5.59
C-225/02 *Garciá Blanco* [2005] E.C.R. I-523 . . . . 3.29
C-232/02 P(R) *Commission v Technische Glaswerke Ilmenau* [2002] E.C.R. I-8977, (order of
    the President of 18 October 2002). 13.36, 13.44
C-233/02 *France v Commission* [2004] E.C.R. I-2759 . . . . .7.19, 7.25, 25.43
C-234/02 P *European Ombudsman v Lamberts* [2004] E.C.R. I-2803 . . . . .5.31, 5.34,
                                                  11.09, 11.20, 11.55, 16.14, 26.11
C-235/02 *Saetti* [2004] E.C.R. I-1005 (order of 15 January 2004) 3.17, 3.32
C-236/02 *Slob* [2004] E.C.R. I-1861 . . . . 3.22
C-238/02 *Douwe Egberts* [2004] E.C.R. I-7007. . . . . 6.24
C-245/02 *Anheuser-Busch* [2004] E.C.R. I-10989 . . . . 6.14
C-248/02 *Commission v Italy*, not reported, (judgment of 16 September 2004) 5.63, 5.65
C-249/02 *Portugal v Commission* [2004] E.C.R. I-10717 . . . . 7.16, 7.157
C-250/02 to C-253/02 and C-256/02 *Telecom Italia Mobile*, not reported,
    (order of 8 June 2004) 24.15
C-258/02 P *Bactria Industriehygiene-Service v Commission* [2003] E.C.R. I-15105,
    (order of 12 December 2003) 7.97, 7.106, 26.02
C-259/02 *La Mer Technology and Others* [2004] E.C.R. I-1159, (order of 27 January 2004) 24.15
C-263/02 P *Commission v Jégo-Quéré* [2004] E.C.R. I-3425 . . . . 4.11, 7.99, 7.100, 7.106, 9.04
C-275/02 *Ayaz* [2004] E.C.R. I-8765 . . . . 6.15
C-276/02 *Spain v Commission* [2004] E.C.R. I-8091 . . . . 7.204
C-279/02 P *Antas de Campos v European Parliament*, not reported, (judgment of
    14 October 2004). 16.24
C-286/02 *Bellio Fratelli* [2004] E.C.R. I-3465. . . . . 3.27, 3.36
C-289/02 *AMOK Verlags* [2003] E.C.R. I-15059. . . . . 5.13
C-294/02 *Commission v AMI Semiconductor Belgium and Others* [2005] E.C.R. I-2175. . . . . . 19.14, 19.15
C-299/02 *Commission v Netherlands*, not reported, (order of 28 October 2004) 25.133
C-301/02 P *Tralli v ECB* [2005] E.C.R. I-4071 . . . . 16.13
C-304/02 *Commission v France* [2005] E.C.R. I-6263 . . . . 5.77, 5.78, 5.79, 23.82
C-309/02 *Radlberger Getränkegesellschaft and S. Spitz* [2004] E.C.R. I-11763. . . . . 3.29
C-315/02 *Lenz* [2004] E.C.R. I-7063 . . . . .3.16, 3.32, 3.36
C-340/02 *Commission v France* [2004] E.C.R. I-9845 . . . . 5.47
C-350/02 *Commission v Netherlands* [2004] E.C.R. I-6213. . . . . 5.47, 5.48, 5.51, 5.52
C-360/02 P *Ripa di Meana v European Parliament* [2004] E.C.R. I-10339,
    (order of 29 October 2004). 25.42, 26.02
C-383/02 *Commission v Italy*, not reported, (judgment of 9 September 2004) 5.65
C-387/02, C-391/02, and C-403/02 Berlusconi and Others [2005] E.C.R. I-3565 . . . . 4.44
C-394/02 *Commission v Greece* [2005] E.C.R. I-4713 . . . . .5.30, 5.49, 5.58
C-417/02 *Commission v Greece* [2004] E.C.R. I-7973 . . . . 5.52
C-434/02 *Arnold André* [2004] E.C.R. I-11825. . . . . 10.18
C-441/02 *Commission v Germany* [2006] E.C.R. I-3449. . . . . .5.06, 5.10, 5.52
C-445/02 P *Glaverbel v OHIM* [2004] E.C.R. I-6267, (order of the President of
    28 June 2004) 16.14, 25.76
C-455/02 P *Sgaravatti Mediterranea v Commission*, not reported,
    (order of 22 March 2004) 7.178, 25.70

C-456/02 *Trojani* [2004] E.C.R. I-7573 . . . . 3.23
C-464/02 *Commission v Denmark*, not reported, (order of 20 October 2005). 25.133
C-469/02 *Commission v Belgium*, not reported, (judgment of 7 September 2004). 5.52
C-470/02 P *UER v Commission and Others*, not reported, (order of 27 September 2004) 16.06, 23.58

Opinion 1/03 *Competence of the Community to conclude the new Lugano Convention
    on jurisdiction and the recognition and enforcement of judgments in civil and commercial
    matters* [2006] E.C.R. I-1145 . . . . 2.10, 12.01, 12.09, 12.11, 12.15, 21.02
C-12/03 P *Commission v Tetra Laval* [2005] E.C.R. I-987 . . . . 7.145, 7.193, 7.196, 7.197, 7.201
C-12/03 P-DEP and C-13/03 P-DEP *Tetra Laval v Commission* [2010] I-67*, Summ. pub. 25.93
C-29/03 *Commission v ITEC* [2003] E.C.R. I-12205 . . . . 25.31
C-37/03 P *BioID v OHIM* [2005] E.C.R. I-7975 . . . . 25.14
C-38/03 *Commission v Belgium*, not reported, (judgment of 13 January 2005). 25.59
C-39/03 P *Commission v Artegodan and Others* [2003] E.C.R. I-7885 . . . . 25.81, 26.08
C-39/03 P-R *Commission v Artegodan and Others* [2003] E.C.R. I-4485, (order of the
    President of 8 May 2003) 13.14
C-40/03 P *Rica Foods v Commission* [2005] E.C.R. I-6811 . . . . 7.810, 16.14
C-42/03 *Commission v Spain*, not reported, (judgment of 2 December 2004). 5.62
C-44/03 *Horn*, not reported, (order of 24 July 2003) 3.36
C-45/03 *Oxana Dem'Yanenko*, not reported, (order of 18 March 2004) 3.10, 3.23, 22.02
C-46/03 *United Kingdom v Commission* [2005] E.C.R. I-10167 . . . . 7.23, 7.42
C-51/03 *Georgescu* [2004] E.C.R. I-3203, (order of 31 March 2004) 22.02
C-53/03 *Syfait and Others* [2005] E.C.R. I-4609 . . . . 3.11
C-54/03 *Austroplant Arzneimittel*, not reported, (order of 12 March 2004) 3.26, 6.21, 6.25, 24.23
C-55/03 *Commission v Spain*, not reported, (judgment of 14 October 2004) 25.10
C-61/03 *Commission v United Kingdom* [2005] E.C.R. I-2477 . . . . 5.03
C-72/03 *Carbonati Apuani* [2004] E.C.R. I-8027 . . . . 3.26, 6.34
C-78/03 P *Commission v Aktionsgemeinschaft Recht und Eigentum* [2005] E.C.R. I-10737 . . . . 7.118, 16.30
C-80/03 *Commission v Netherlands*, not reported, (order of 21 October 2003) 25.99
C-82/03 *Commission v Italy* [2004] E.C.R. I-6635 . . . . 5.14, 5.64
C-86/03 *Greece v Commission* [2005] E.C.R. I-10979 . . . . 9.11, 9.15
C-87/03 and C-100/03 *Spain v Council* [2006] E.C.R. I-2915 . . . . 7.177
C-91/03 *Spain v Council* [2005] E.C.R. I-2267 . . . . 7.177
C-98/03 *Commission v Germany* [2006] E.C.R. I-53 . . . . 5.53
C-105/03 *Pupino* [2005] E.C.R. I-5285 . . . . 3.09, 22.03
C-106/03 P *Vedial v OHIM* [2004] E.C.R. I-9573 . . . . 20.10
C-114/03 P *Piscioneri v European Parliament*, not reported, (order of 11 November 2004) 25.10
C-118/03 *Commission v Germany*, not reported, (judgment of 15 July 2004) 5.65, 5.66, 9.11
C-123/03 P *Commission v Greencore* [2004] E.C.R. I-11647 . . . . 7.14, 7.226, 8.09, 16.02
C-125/03 *Commission v Germany*, not reported, (judgment of 9 September 2004) 5.58
C-129/03 *Commission v Italy* [2003] E.C.R. I-14637 . . . . 5.10
C-131/03 P *R.J. Reynolds Tobacco Holdings and Others v Commission* [2006]
    E.C.R. I-7795 . . . . 5.31, 7.18, 7.20, 7.21, 7.42, 11.12, 23.45
C-134/03 *Viacom Outdoor* [2005] E.C.R. I-1167. . . . . 3.26, 3.27
C-136/03 *Dörr* [2005] E.C.R. I-4759 . . . . 4.09
C-138/03, C-324/03, and C-431/03 *Italy v Commission* [2005] E.C.R. I-10043 . . . . . . 7.21, 7.23, 7.217
C-139/03 *Commission v Germany*, not reported, (judgment of 15 July 2004) 9.11
C-145/03 *Keller* [2005] E.C.R. I-2529 . . . . 3.22, 3.25, 3.31
C-147/03 *Commission v Austria* [2005] E.C.R. I-5969 . . . . 5.13
C-150/03 *Hectors v European Parliament* [2004] E.C.R. I-8691 . . . . 7.173
C-151/03 P *Meyer v Commission*, not reported, (order of 22 June 2004) 11.39
C-152/03 *Ritter-Coulais* [2006] E.C.R. I-1711. . . . . 3.34
C-157/03 *Commission v Spain* [2005] E.C.R. I-2911 . . . . 5.09
C-159/03 *Pflugradt v ECB*, not reported, (order of 9 March 2004) 18.04
C-160/03 *Spain v Eurojust* [2005] E.C.R. I-2077. . . . . 7.04, 18.09, 22.04
C-161/03 *CAFOM and Samsung Electronics France*, not reported, (order of 11 July 2003) 3.09, 24.15
C-168/03 *Commission v Spain* [2004] E.C.R. I-8227 . . . . 5.59
C-170/03 *Feron* [2005] E.C.R. I-2299 . . . . 6.16
C-173/03 *Traghetti del Mediterraneo* [2006] E.C.R. I-5177 . . . . 3.58, 4.47, 4.50, 4.51
C-176/03 *Commission v Council* [2005] E.C.R. I-7879. . . . . 1.06, 4.42, 7.04, 22.03, 25.62, 25.64
C-177/03 *Commission v France* [2004] E.C.R. I-11671 . . . . 5.53, 5.62

C-178/03 *Commission v European Parliament* [2006] E.C.R. I-107 . . . . 7.221
C-182/03 and C-217/03 *Belgium and Forum 187 v Commission* [2006] E.C.R. I-5479. . . . . . 7.122, 7.126
C-182/03 R and C-217/03 R *Belgium and Forum 187 v Commission* [2003] E.C.R. I-6887,
    (order of the President of 26 June 2003) 7.57, 7.63, 7.178
C-182/03 and C-217/03 *Belgium and Forum 187 v Commission* [2006] E.C.R. I-5479. . . . . 7.98
C-197/03 *Commission v Italy* [2006] E.C.R. I-60*, Summ. pub. 4.24
C-198/03 P *Commission v CEVA Santé Animale and Pfizer Enterprises* [2005]
    E.C.R. I-6357 . . . . 11.46, 11.61
C-203/03 *Commission v Austria* [2005] E.C.R. I-935 . . . . 5.52, 5.53
C-208/03 P-R *Le Pen v European Parliament* [2003] E.C.R. I-7939, (order of the President
    of 31 July 2003) 13.32, 13.42
C-208/03 P *Le Pen v European Parliament* [2005] E.C.R. I-6051 . . . . 7.16
C-209/03 *Bidar* [2005] E.C.R. I-2119 . . . . 6.33, 6.34
C-210/03 *Swedish Match* [2004] E.C.R. I-11893. . . . . 10.18
C-213/03 *Syndicat professionnel coordination des pêcheurs de l'étang de Berre et de la région*
    [2004] E.C.R. I-7357 . . . . 6.14
C-220/03 *ECB v Germany* [2005] E.C.R. I-10595. . . . . 19.05, 19.14
C-222/03 P *APOL and AIPO v Commission*, not reported, (order of 16 December 2004) 16.19
C-224/03 *Italy v Commission* [2003] E.C.R. I-14751, (order of 9 December 2003) 7.219, 25.42
C-229/03 *Herbstrith*, not reported, (order of 1 April 2004). 3.26
C-230/03 *Sedef* [2006] E.C.R. I-157 . . . . 6.15
C-235/03 *QDQ Media* [2005] E.C.R. I-1937 . . . . 6.21
C-236/03 P *Commission v CMA CGM and Others*, not reported, (order of 28 October 2004) 16.21
C-239/03 *Commission v France* [2004] E.C.R. I-9325 . . . . 6.14
C-240/03 P *Comunita Montana della Valnerina v Commission* [2006] E.C.R. I-731 . . . . 16.19
C-244/03 *France v European Parliament and Council* [2005] E.C.R. I-4021. . . . . 7.220
C-250/03 *Mauri* [2005] E.C.R. I-1267, (order of 17 February 2005) 3.38, 6.24
C-253/03 *CLT-UFA* [2006] E.C.R. I-1831. . . . . 6.21
C-265/03 *Simutenkov* [2005] E.C.R. I-2579 . . . . 6.13
C-266/03 *Commission v Luxembourg* [2005] E.C.R. I-4805 . . . . 5.13
C-267/03 *Lindberg* [2005] E.C.R. I-3247 . . . . .3.22, 3.28, 6.21
C-239/03 *Commission v France* [2004] E.C.R. I-9325 . . . . 5.07
C-278/03 *Commission v Italy* [2005] E.C.R. I-3747 . . . . 5.17
C-279/03 *Commission v Implants*, not reported, (judgment of 24 February 2005). 25.28, 25.31, 25.32
C-280/03 *Commission v Lior and Others*, not reported, (order of 21 November 2003) 19.07
C-287/03 *Commission v Belgium* [2005] E.C.R. I-3761 . . . . 5.10, 5.63
C-301/03 *Italy v Commission* [2005] E.C.R. I-10217 . . . . 7.20, 7.21, 7.22
C-320/03 R *Commission v Austria* [2003] E.C.R. I-7929, (order of the President of
    30 July 2003). 13.24
C-320/03 *Commission v Austria* [2005] E.C.R. I-9871 . . . . 5.44, 5.50
C-320/03 R *Commission v Austria* [2003] E.C.R. I-7929, (order of the President of
    30 July 2003). 4.62, 13.12
C-320/03 R *Commission v Austria* [2003] E.C.R. I-11665, (order of the President of
    2 October 2003) 13.12, 13.15, 13.24
C-320/03 R *Commission v Austria* [2004] E.C.R. I-3593, (order of the President of
    27 April 2004). 13.12, 13.15, 13.24
C-321/03 *Dyson* [2007] E.C.R. I-687 . . . . 6.22
C-325/03 P *Zuazaga Meabe v OHIM* [2005] E.C.R. I-403, (order of 18 January 2005) 16.14, 23.38
C-346/03 and C-529/03 *Atzeni and Others* [2006] E.C.R. I-1875 . . . . 7.122, 10.11
C-348/03 P(R) *Asian Institute of Technology v Commission*, not reported, (order of
    30 September 2003). 13.24
C-358/03 *Commission v Austria* [2004] E.C.R. I-12055 . . . . 5.65
C-366/03, C-368/03, C-390/03, C-391/03, and C-394/03 P *Associazione Bancaria Italiana
    and Others v Commission*, not reported, (order of 26 November 2003) 2.55, 16.12
C-374/03 *AJ Gürol*, not reported, (order of 16 November 2004) 25.101
C-377/03 *Commission v Belgium* [2006] E.C.R. I-9733 . . . . 5.09, 5.68
C-379/03 P *Pérez Escolar v Commission*, not reported, (order of 1 October 2004). 8.13
C-380/03 *Germany v European Parliament and Council* [2006] E.C.R. I-11573 . . . . 7.151
C-396/03 P *Killinger v Germany, Council and Commission* [2005] E.C.R. I-4967,
    (order of 3 June 2005) 4.51, 5.13, 5.38, 16.02, 16.27, 25.136

C-397/03 P *Archer Daniels Midland and Archer Daniels Midland Ingredients v
  Commission* [2006] E.C.R. I-4429 . . . . .7.194, 15.07, 16.09
C-402/03 *Skov and Bilka* [2006] E.C.R. I-199 . . . . 6.22, 6.33
C-410/03 *Commission v Italy* [2005] E.C.R. I-3507 . . . . 5.15
C-414/03 *Commission v Germany*, not reported, (judgment of 3 March 2005) 5.60
C-415/03 *Commission v Greece* [2005] E.C.R. I-3875 . . . . 5.22
C-419/03 *Commission v France*, not reported, (judgment of 15 July 2004). 5.63
C-432/03 *Commission v Portugal* [2005] E.C.R. I-9665 . . . . 5.14
C-433/03 *Commission v Germany* [2005] E.C.R. I-6985. . . . . 5.13
C-438/03, C-439/03, C-509/03, and C-2/04 *Cannito and Others* [2004] E.C.R. I-1605 . . . . . 3.27, 24.15
C-442/03 P and C-471/03 P *P&O European Ferries (Vizcaya) and Others v Commission*
  [2006] E.C.R. I-4845 . . . . 16.22, 26.02
C-451/03 *Servizi Ausiliari Dottori Commercialisti* [2006] E.C.R. I-2941 . . . . 6.19, 6.24
C-452/03 *RAL and Others* [2005] E.C.R. I-3947. . . . . 3.23
C-453/03 *ABNA and Others*, not reported, (order of the President of 30 March 2004). 24.12
C-453/03, C-11/04, C-12/04 and C-194/04 *ABNA and Others* [2005]
  E.C.R. I-10423 . . . . 3.34, 4.62, 10.18, 10.20, 25.61
C-456/03 *Commission v Italy* [2005] E.C.R. I-5335 . . . . 5.16, 5.64, 25.12, 25.14, 25.16, 25.96
C-458/03 *Parking Brixen and Others*, not reported, (order of the President of
  25 May 2004) 24.12, 25.61
C-459/03 *Commission v Ireland* [2006] E.C.R. I-4635 . . . . 5.03, 5.05, 5.13, 5.14, 13.12, 19.27
C-461/03 *Gaston Schul Douane-expediteur* [2005] E.C.R. I-10513 . . . . 3.55
C-470/03 *AGM.-COS.MET Srl* [2007] E.C.R. I-2749. . . . . 4.46, 4.47, 4.48, 4.52
C-475/03 *Banco popolare di Cremona* [2006] E.C.R. I-9273 . . . . 6.34, 24.14
C-475/03 *Banca popolare di Cremona*, not reported, (order of 21 October 2005) 23.82
C-485/03 to C-490/03 *Commission v Spain* [2006] E.C.R. I-11887 . . . . 5.22
C-495/03 *Intermodal Transports* [2005] E.C.R. I-8151. . . . . 3.55, 3.58
C-499/03 P *Biegi Nahrungsmittel and Commonfood v Commission* [2005] E.C.R. I-1751. . . . . 16.19, 26.02
C-502/03 *Commission v Greece*, not reported, (judgment of 6 October 2005). 5.11
C-508/03 *Commission v United Kingdom* [2006] E.C.R. I-3969 . . . . 5.62, 25.11
C-511/03 *Ten Kate Holding Musselkanaal and Others* [2005] E.C.R. I-8979 . . . . . 4.64, 7.76, 8.14, 10.12
C-513/03 *van Hilten-van der Heijden* [2006] E.C.R. I-957. . . . . 6.22
C-515/03 *Eichsfelder Schlachtbetrieb* [2005] E.C.R. I-7355 . . . . 4.28
C-517/03 *IAMA Consulting v Commission*, not reported, (order of 27 May 2004) 19.10
C-519/03 *Commission v Luxembourg* [2005] E.C.R. I-3067 . . . . 5.68
C-521/03 *Internationaler Hilfsfonds v Commission*, not reported, (order of
  7 December 2004) 7.23, 16.24
C-525/03 *Commission v Italy* [2005] E.C.R. I-9405 . . . . 5.58
C-540/03 *European Parliament v Council* [2006] E.C.R. I-5769 . . . . .7.73, 7.76, 7.220, 25.81
C-552/03 P *Unilever Bestfoods (Ireland) v Commission* [2006]
  E.C.R. I-9091, (order of 28 September 2006) 16.21
C-555/03 *Warbecq* [2004] E.C.R. I-6041, (order of 10 June 2004). 22.02
C-580/03 *Commission v United Kingdom* [2006] E.C.R. I-3969 . . . . 5.52, 5.63

Opinion 1/04 *Proposed Agreement between the European Community and the United States
  of America on the processing and transfer of Passanger Name Record data*, not reported,
  (order of the President of 29 April 2004) 12.18
C-1/04 SA *Tertir-Terminais de Portugal v Commission* [2004] E.C.R. I-11931, (order of
  14 December 2004) 14.01, 14.07
C-3/04 *Poseidon Chartering* [2006] E.C.R. I-2505 . . . . 6.17
C-7/04 P(R) *Commission v Akzo Nobel and Others* [2004] E.C.R. I-8739, (order of the
  President of 29 September 2004). 13.36, 13.40
C-15/04 *Koppensteiner* [2005] E.C.R. I-4855. . . . . 4.07, 4.10
C-18/04 P(R) *Krikorian v European Parliament and Others*, not reported, (order of the
  President of 13 September 2004). 13.26
C-18/04 P *Krikorian and Others v European Parliament and Others* 11.20
C-23/04 to C-25/04 *Sfakianakis* [2006] E.C.R. I-1265 . . . . 6.13
C-27/04 *Commission v Council* [2004] E.C.R. I-6649. . . . . 7.08, 7.14, 7.17, 7.66, 25.81
C-33/04 *Commission v Luxembourg* [2005] E.C.R. I-10629 . . . . 5.31, 5.62
C-36/04 *Spain v Council* [2006] E.C.R. I-2981 . . . . 7.220, 25.86
C-36/04 *Spain v Council*, not reported, (order of 30 September 2004) 23.60

C-40/04 *Yonemoto* [2005] E.C.R. I-7755 .... 4.42
C-53/04 *Marrosu and Sardino* [2006] E.C.R. I-7213 .... 4.45
C-70/04 *Swiss Confederation v Commission*, not reported, (order of 14 July 2005) 2.53, 2.54, 7.82
C-73/04 AJ *Klein*, not reported, (order of 21 October 2004) 24.27
C-82/04 P *Audi v OHIM*, not reported, (order of 19 January 2006) 16.14
C-94/04 and C-202/04 *Cipolla and Others* [2006] E.C.R. I-11421 .... 3.22, 3.34, 3.38, 6.24
C-95/04 P *British Airways v Commission* [2007] E.C.R. I-2331.......................... 16.07
C-96/04 *Standesamt Stadt Niebüll* [2006] E.C.R. I-3561 .... 3.10
C-105/04 P *Nederlandse Federatieve Vereniging voor de Groothandel op Elektrotechnisch
    Gebied v Commission* [2006] E.C.R. I-8725 .... 16.30
C-110/04 P *Strintzis Lines Shipping v Commission* [2006] E.C.R. I-44*, Summ. pub....... 15.09
C-111/04 P *Adriatica di Navigazione v Commission* [2006] E.C.R. I-22*, Summ. pub........ 15.09
C-113/04 P *Technische Unie v Commission* [2006] E.C.R. I-8831 .... 15.07, 16.05, 16.30
C-119/04 *Commission v Italy* [2006] E.C.R. I-6885 .... 5.76, 5.78
C-121/04 P *Minoan Lines v Commission*, not reported, (order of 17 November 2005) 15.09
C-125/04 *Denuit and Cordenier* [2005] E.C.R. I-923.................................. 3.12
C-144/04 *Mangold* [2005] E.C.R. I-9981 ....3.36, 3.42
C-145/04 *Spain v United Kingdom* [2006] E.C.R. I-7917............................... 5.35
C-154/04 and C-155/04 *Alliance for Natural Health and Others*, not reported, (order of the
    President of 7 May 2004) 24.18
C-156/04 *Commission v Greece* [2007] E.C.R. I-4179 .... 5.10
C-167/04 P *JCB Service v Commission* [2006] E.C.R. I-8935 .... 16.21, 16.27, 16.30
C-177/04 *Commission v France* [2006] E.C.R. I-2461 .... 5.09, 5.76
C-180/04 *Vassallo* [2006] E.C.R. I-7251... 4.45
C-184/04 *Uudenkaupungin kaupunki* [2006] E.C.R. I-3039............................. 6.34
C-195/04 *Commission v Finland* [2007] E.C.R. I-3351 .... 5.52
C-196/04 *Cadbury Schweppes and Cadbury Schweppes Overseas* [2006] E.C.R. I-7995............. 6.22
C-199/04 *Commission v United Kingdom* [2007] E.C.R. I-1221 .... 5.52
C-210/04 *FCE Bank* [2006] E.C.R. I-2803... 6.22
C-212/04 *Adeneler and Others* [2006] E.C.R. I-6057 .... 3.36, 4.37, 4.42, 4.45
C-213/04 *Burtscher* [2005] E.C.R. I-10309.. 3.29
C-214/04 *Commission v Italy*, not reported, (judgment of 7 July 2005) 5.17
C-221/04 *Commission v Spain* [2006] E.C.R. I-4515 .... 5.55, 5.58
C-222/04 *Cassa di Risparmo di Firenze and Others* [2006] E.C.R. I-289............... 6.21, 10.11
C-227/04 P *Lindorfer v Council* [2007] E.C.R. I-6767 .... 16.30
C-234/04 *Kapferer* [2006] E.C.R. I-2585 .... 4.56, 4.58
C-237/04 *Enirisorse* [2006] E.C.R. I-2843... 6.23
C-243/04 P *Gaki-Kakouri v Court of Justice*, not reported, (judgment of 14 April 2005) 16.24, 23.63
C-255/04 *Commission v France* [2006] E.C.R. I-5251 .... 5.52
C-259/04 *Emanuel* [2006] E.C.R. I-3089 .... 3.08, 3.09
C-273/04 *Poland v Council*, not reported, (order of 15 November 2006)............... 23.58, 23.66
C-292/04 *Meilicke and Others* [2007] E.C.R. I-1835 .... 6.33, 6.34
C-295/04 to C-298/04 *Manfredi and Others* [2006] E.C.R. I-6619..................... 3.31, 4.54
C-300/04 *Eman and Sevinger*, not reported, (order of the President of 18 March 2005) 24.18
C-301/04 P *Commission v SGL Carbon and Others* [2006] E.C.R. I-5915 .... 16.30
C-310/04 *Spain v Council* [2006] E.C.R. I-7285 .... 2.12, 7.221
C-317/04 *European Parliament v Council*, not reported, (order of the President of
    21 September 2004).. 25.81
C-317/04 and C-318/04 *European Parliament v Council* [2006] E.C.R. I-4721 .... 12.17, 25.64
C-318/04 *European Parliament v Commission*, not reported, (order of the President of
    21 September 2004).. 25.81
C-318/04 *European Parliament v Commission* [2005] E.C.R. I-2467, (order of 17 March 2005) 25.64
C-328/04 *Vajnai* [2005] E.C.R. I-8577, (order of 6 October 2005) 6.24
C-344/04 *The Queen on the application of: International Air Transport Association and
    European Low Fares Airline Association* [2006] E.C.R. I-403......... 3.59, 3.60, 10.01, 10.08, 10.17
C-348/04 *Boehringer Ingelheim and Others* [2007] E.C.R. I-3391 .... 4.42
C-351/04 *Ikea Wholesale* [2007] E.C.R. I-7723................................. 7.205, 10.08
C-354/04 P *Gestoras Pro Amnistía and Others v Council* [2007]
    E.C.R. I-1579...7.04, 11.02, 16.20, 22.03
C-355/04 P *Segi and Others v Council* [2007] E.C.R. I-1657 .... 7.04, 11.02, 16.20, 22.03, 22.04
C-368/04 *Transalpine Ölleitung in Österreich* [2006] E.C.R. I-9957 .... 5.24

C-373/04 P *Commission v Alvarez Moreno* [2006] E.C.R. I-1*, Summ. pub. 16.30
C-380/04 P(R) *Bactria v Commission*, not reported, (order of the President of
    13 December 2004) 13.01, 13.07, 13.19, 13.29
C-392/04 and C-422/04 *i-21Germany and Arcor* [2006] E.C.R. I-8559 . . . . 4.57
C-403/04 P and C-405/04 P *Sumitomo Metal Industries and Others v Commission* [2007]
    E.C.R. I-729 . . . . 7.146, 11.20, 15.05, 15.09, 16.18, 23.87
C-404/04 P-R *Technische Glaswerke Ilmenau v Commission* [2005] E.C.R. I-3539,
    (order of the President of 29 April 2005) 13.04, 13.14, 13.31, 13.32
C-407/04 P *Dalmine v Commission* [2007] E.C.R. I-829 . . . . 15.07
C-408/04 P *Commission v Salzgitter* [2008] E.C.R. I-2767 . . . . 16.21, 16.31
C-411/04 P *Salzgitter Mannesmann v Commission* [2007] E.C.R. I-959 . . . . 7.146, 7.174, 15.07
C-413/04 *European Parliament v Council* [2006] E.C.R. I-11221 . . . . 7.177
C-414/04 *European Parliament v Council* [2006] E.C.R. I-11279 . . . . 7.177, 7.221
C-417/04 P *Regione Siciliana v Commission* [2006] E.C.R. I-3881. . . . . 7.77, 7.91, 7.96, 7.217
C-423/04 *Richards* [2006] E.C.R. I-3585 . . . . 6.34
C-432/04 *Commission v Cresson* [2006] E.C.R. I-6387 . . . . 2.10, 18.01
C-432/04 *Commission v Cresson*, not reported, (order of 9 September 2005) 23.60, 23.66
C-442/04 *Spain v Council* [2008] E.C.R. I-3517 . . . . .7.181, 7.183, 9.11, 9.15
C-446/04 *Test Claimants in the FII Group Litigation* [2006] E.C.R. I-11753 . . . . 6.11, 6.34
C-453/04 *innoventif Limited* [2006] E.C.R. I-4929 . . . . 6.20
C-466/04 *Acereda Herrera* [2006] E.C.R. I-5341 . . . . 3.36
C-470/04 *N* [2006] E.C.R. I-7409. . . . . 3.26, 4.30
C-479/04 *Laserdisken* [2006] E.C.R. I-8089 . . . . 10.15
C-480/04 *D'Antonio*, not reported, (order of 22 February 2005). 3.26
C-482/04 P *SNF v Commission*, not reported, (order of 21 November 2005). 7.100
C-489/04 *Jehle* [2006] E.C.R. I-7509. . . . . 6.21
C-490/04 *Commission v Germany* [2007] E.C.R. I-6095. . . . . 5.62
C-499/04 *Werhof* [2006] E.C.R. I-2397 . . . . 6.22
C-500/04 *Proxxon* [2006] E.C.R. I-1545. . . . . 6.18
C-502/04 *Torun* [2006] E.C.R. I-1563. . . . . 6.15
C-503/04 *Commission v Germany* [2007] E.C.R. I-6153. . . . . 5.61, 5.69, 5.78, 25.83
C-506/04 *Wilson* [2006] E.C.R. I-8613 . . . . .3.09, 4.07, 6.20
C-521/04 P(R) *Tillack v Commission* [2005] E.C.R. I-3103, (order of the President of
    19 April 2005). 13.11, 13.25
C-522/04 *Commission v Belgium* [2007] E.C.R. I-5701 . . . . 5.52
C-523/04 *Commission v Netherlands* [2007] E.C.R. I-3267. . . . . 5.62
C-524/04 *Test Claimants in the Thin Cap Litigation* [2007] E.C.R. I-2107 . . . . 6.34
C-525/04 P *Spain v Commission and Others* [2007] E.C.R. I-9947 . . . . .7.124, 7.193, 7.201
C-526/04 *Laboratoires Boiron* [2008] E.C.R. I-7529. . . . . 4.28

C-1/05 *Jia* [2007] E.C.R. I-1 . . . . 3.09
C-1/05 SA *Intek v Commission*, not reported, (order of 13 October 2005) 14.01, 14.06
C-2/05 SA *Names v Commission*, not reported, (order of 13 October 2005) 14.01, 14.06
C-3/05 SA *Statistical Agency of the Republic of Kazakhstan v Commission*, not reported,
    (order of 13 October 2005). 14.01, 14.06
C-4/05 *Güzeli* [2006] E.C.R. I-10279. . . . . 6.15
C-4/05 SA *Alt Ylmy v Commission*, not reported, (order of 13 October 2005) 14.01, 14.06
C-5/05 SA *Fil do Nascimento and Others v Commission*, not reported, (order of
    24 November 2005) 14.01, 14.03, 14.05, 14.06
C-6/05 *Medi-pac Kazantzidis* [2007] E.C.R. I-4557 . . . . 6.21, 6.22
C-11/05 *Friesland Coberco Dairy Foods* [2006] E.C.R. I-4285 . . . . 6.09, 10.06
C-12/05 *Meister v OHIM* [2007] E.C.R. I-167*, Summ. pub. 25.117, 25.119, 25.120, 26.01
C-15/05 *Kawasaki Motors Europe* [2006] E.C.R. I-3657. . . . . 10.01
C-17/05 *Cadman* [2006] E.C.R. I-9583 . . . . 6.11, 6.34
C-18/05 and C-155/05 *Casa di cura privata Salus SpA* [2006] E.C.R. I-6199, (order of
    6 July 2006). 3.23
C-19/05 *Commission v Denmark* [2007] E.C.R. I-8597 . . . . 5.09
C-24/05 P *Storck v OHIM* [2006] E.C.R. I-5677 . . . . 20.15
C-25/05 P *Storck v OHIM* [2006] I-5719. . . . . 20.15
C-29/05 P *OHIM v Kaul* [2007] E.C.R. I-2213 . . . . .7.71, 16.30, 20.03, 20.12
C-32/05 *Commission v Luxembourg* [2006] E.C.R. I-11323 . . . . 5.16, 5.52

C-35/05 *Reemtsma Cigarettenfabriken* [2007] E.C.R. I-2425 . . . . 4.24, 4.27
C-36/05 *Commission v Spain* [2006] E.C.R. I-10313 . . . . 5.09
C-45/05 *Maatschap Schonewille-Prins* [2007] E.C.R. I-3997 . . . . 10.01
C-49/05 P *Ferriere Nord v Commission* [2008] E.C.R. I-68*, Summ. pub. 9.15
C-51/05 P *Commission v Cantina sociale di Dolianova and Others* [2008] E.C.R. I-5341 . . . . 8.21,
               11.04, 11.10, 11.28, 11.30, 11.51, 11.87, 11.90, 11.91, 11.92, 11.94, 16.30
C-53/05 *Commission v Portugal* [2006] E.C.R. I-6215 . . . . 5.66, 9.11
C-61/05 *Commission v Portugal* [2006] E.C.R. I-6779 . . . . .5.09, 5.66, 9.11
C-62/05 P *Nordspedizionieri di Danielis Livio & C. and Others v Commission* [2007]
   E.C.R. I-8647 . . . . 16.20
C-64/05 P *Sweden v Commission* [2007] E.C.R. I-11389 . . . . 7.72, 16.30
C-75/05 P and C-80/05 P *Germany and Others v Kronofrance* [2008]
   E.C.R. I-6619 . . . . .7.118, 16.21, 16.24
C-76/05 *Schwarz and Gootjes-Schwarz* [2007] E.C.R. I-6849 . . . . 23.43
C-91/05 *Commission v Council* [2008] E.C.R. I-3651. . . . . 1.06, 5.66
C-91/05 *Commission v Council* [2008] E.C.R. I-3651. . . . . 7.04, 9.05
C-97/05 *Gattoussi* [2006] E.C.R. I-11917 . . . . 6.14
C-110/05 *Commission v Italy* [2009] E.C.R. I-519 . . . . 5.63, 24.14
C-113/05 P *EFfCI v European Parliament and Council* [2006] E.C.R. I-46*,
   Summ. pub., (order of 30 March 2006). 7.100, 25.42
C-119/05 *Lucchini* [2007] E.C.R. I-6911 . . . . 3.04, 3.31, 3.59, 4.31, 4.36, 4.58, 4.59, 10.11
C-132/05 *Commission v Germany* [2008] E.C.R. I-957. . . . . 5.14
C-135/05 *Commission v Italy* [2007] E.C.R. I-3475 . . . . 5.11
C-155/05 *Villa Maria Beatrice Hospital*, not reported, (order of 6 July 2006) 6.23
C-168/05 *Mostaza Claro* [2006] E.C.R. I-10421 . . . . 4.01, 4.41
C-178/05 *Commission v Greece* [2007] E.C.R. I-4185 . . . . 5.71
C-194/05 *Commission v Italy* [2007] E.C.R. I-11661 . . . . 5.53
C-199/05 *European Community v Belgium* [2006] E.C.R. I-10485 . . . . 6.04
C-201/05 *Test Claimants in the CFC and Dividend Group Litigation* [2008]
   E.C.R. I-2875, (order of 23 April 2008) 4.21, 4.22, 4.47, 4.48, 4.52
C-210/05 P *Campailla v Commission*, not reported, (order of 8 December 2005) 2.24, 7.207, 7.214
C-211/05 P *Campailla v Commission*, not reported, (order of 8 December 2005) 8.19
C-215/05 P *Papoulakos v Italy and Commission* [2006] E.C.R. I-18*, Summ. pub.,
   (order of 2 February 2006) 11.27, 11.81
C-217/05 *Confederacion Española de Empresarios de Estaciones de Servicio* [2006]
   E.C.R. I-11987 . . . . 3.26, 3.27, 3.31, 6.17
C-222/05 to C-225/05 *van der Weerd and Others* [2007] E.C.R. I-11421 . . . . 3.22, 3.27, 3.34, 4.01, 4.40
C-227/05 *Commission v Greece* [2007] E.C.R. I-8203 . . . . 5.58
C-228/05 *Stradasfalti* [2006] E.C.R. I-8391 . . . . 6.34
C-229/05 P *PKK and KNK v Council* [2007] E.C.R. I-439. . . . . .7.10, 7.84,
                   7.141, 7.207, 16.05, 16.20, 16.29
C-232/05 *Commission v France* [2006] E.C.R. I-10071 . . . . 4.31
C-238/05 *Asnef-Equifax and Others* [2006] E.C.R. I-11125 . . . . 3.29
C-239/05 *BVBA Management, Training en Consultancy* [2007] E.C.R. I-1455 . . . . 4.09
C-243/05 P *Agraz and Others v Commission* [2006] E.C.R. I-10833 . . . . .11.46, 11.58,
                   11.64, 11.75, 11.77, 16.10
C-246/05 *Häupl* [2007] E.C.R. I-4673. . . . . 3.08, 3.09
C-248/05 *Commission v Ireland* [2007] E.C.R. I-9261 . . . . 5.11
C-255/05 *Commission v Italy* [2007] E.C.R. I-5767 . . . . 5.31
C-258/05 P(R) *Makhteshim-Agan Holding and Others v Commission*, not reported, (order
   of the President of 28 October 2005). 13.10
C-259/05 *Omni Metal Service* [2007] E.C.R. I-4945 . . . . 6.23
C-260/05 P *Sniace v Commission* [2007] E.C.R. I-10005 . . . . 7.124, 16.21, 16.24
C-266/05 P *Sison v Council* [2007] E.C.R. I-1233. . . . . 7.67
C-278/05 *Robins and Others* [2007] E.C.R. I-1053 . . . . 4.47, 4.49
C-279/05 *Vonk Dairy Products* [2007] E.C.R. I-239. . . . . 4.28
C-282/05 P *Holcim v Commission* [2007] E.C.R. I-2941 .7.225, 7.226,
      11.09, 11.37, 11.38, 11.45, 11.52, 11.60, 11.61, 11.85, 11.87, 11.90, 11.94
C-284/05 *Commission v Finland* [2009] E.C.R. I-11705 . . . . 5.71
C-290/05 and C-333/05 *Nádasdi* [2006] E.C.R. I-10115. . . . . 3.23, 6.34
C-292/05 *Lechouritou* [2007] E.C.R. I-1519 . . . . 2.10

C-299/05 *Commission v Council and European Parliament* [2007] E.C.R. I-8695 . . . . 7.23, 7.221
C-301/05 P *Wilfer v OHIM*, not reported, (order of the President of 9 February 2007) 25.65
C-303/05 *Advocaten voor de Wereld* [2007] E.C.R. I-3633 . . . . 10.17
C-305/05 *Ordre des barreaux francophones et germanophone and Others* [2007] E.C.R. I-5305 . . . . . . 3.22
C-311/05 P *Naipes Heraclio Fournier* [2007] E.C.R. I-130*, Summ. pub. 20.03
C-313/05 *Brzeziński* [2007] E.C.R. I-51 . . . . 6.34
C-318/05 *Commission v Germany* [2007] E.C.R. I-6957. . . . . 23.43
C-320/05 P *Fred Olsen v Commission* [2007] E.C.R. I-131*, Summ. pub., (order of
        4 October 2007) 16.19
C-325/05 *Derin* [2007] E.C.R. I-6495 . . . . 6.15
C-326/05 P-R *Industries Quimicas del Valles v Commission*, not published, (order of the
        President of 15 December 2005). 13.14
C-326/05 P *Industrias Quimicas del Valles v Commission* [2007] E.C.R. I-6557 . . . . . . 7.201, 16.05, 16.30
C-326/05 P-DEP *Industrias Químicas del Vallés v Commission* [2009] E.C.R. I-133*,
        Summ. pub., (order of 3 September 2009). 25.93
C-328/05 P *SGL Carbon v Commission* [2007] E.C.R. I-3921 . . . . 15.07
C-330/05 P *Fredrik Granberg*, not reported, (order of the President of 24 October 2005) 24.18
C-331/05 P *Internationaler Hilfsfonds v Commission* [2007] E.C.R. I-5475. . . . .11.56, 11.78, 11.85, 25.91
C-334/05 P *OHIM v Shaker* [2007] E.C.R. I-4691 . . . . 16.05
C-337/05 *Commission v Italy* [2008] E.C.R. I-2173. . . . . 5.76
C-338/05 P *Front National v European Parliament* [2006] E.C.R. I-88*, Summ. pub.,
        (order of 13 July 2006). 7.89, 16.14
C-341/05 *Laval un Partneri* [2007] E.C.R. I-11767. . . . . 6.22, 24.18
C-342/05 *Commission v Finland* [2007] E.C.R. I-4713 . . . . 5.10
C-344/05 P *Commission v De Bry* [2006] E.C.R. I-10915. . . . . 16.30
C-346/05 *Chateignier* [2006] E.C.R. I-10951 . . . . .3.31, 6.20, 6.22
C-362/05 P *Wunenburger v Commission* [2007] E.C.R. I-4333 . . . . 7.138, 7.141, 7.142, 16.12, 26.11
C-368/05 P *Polyelectrolyte Producers Group v Council and Commission* [2006]
        E.C.R. I-130*, Summ. pub., (order of 8 December 2006). 7.89, 7.104, 9.14, 11.76
C-372/05 *Commission v Germany* [2009] E.C.R. I-11801. . . . . 5.28
C-376/05 and C-377/05 *A. Brünsteinder and Autohaus Hilgert* [2006] E.C.R. I-11383. . . . . 10.14
C-379/05 *AMURTA SGPS* [2007] E.C.R. I-9569 . . . . 3.22
C-380/05 *Centro Europa 7 Srl* [2008] E.C.R. I-349. . . . . 3.26, 3.33, 3.38, 6.24
C-385/05 *Confédération générale du travail and Others*, not reported, (order of the
        President of 21 November 2005). 24.18
C-387/05 *Commission v Italy* [2009] E.C.R. I-11831 . . . . 5.71
C-392/05 *Alevizos* [2007] E.C.R. I-3505. . . . . 6.22
C-393/05 *Commission v Austria* [2007] E.C.R. I-10195 . . . . 5.10
C-402/05 P and C-415/05 P *Kadi and Al Barakaat International Foundation v Council
        and Commission* [2008] E.C.R. I-6351 . . . . 1.03, 4.09, 7.11,
                    7.153, 7.173, 7.178, 7.221, 10.05, 16.27, 16.29, 16.30, 25.17
C-403/05 *European Parliament v Commission* [2007] E.C.R. I-9045 . . . . 7.216
C-412/05 P *Alcon v OHIM* [2007] E.C.R. I-3569. . . . . .16.21, 20.13, 20.15, 25.14
C-417/05 P *Commission v Fernández Gómez* [2006] E.C.R. I-8481 . . . . 18.04
C-420/05 P *Ricosmos v Commission* [2007] E.C.R. I-67*, Summ. pub., (order of
        15 May 2007) 16.13, 16.19
C-421/05 *City Motors Groep NV* [2007] E.C.R. I-653 . . . . 4.54
C-424/05 P *Commission v Hosman-Chevalier* [2007] E.C.R. I-5027 . . . . 16.07
C-429/05 *Rampion and Godard* [2007] E.C.R. I-8017. . . . . 4.41
C-431/05 *Merck Genéricos* [2007] E.C.R. I-7001. . . . . 6.14
C-432/05 *Unibet* [2007] E.C.R. I-2271 . . . . .4.05, 4.09, 4.11, 4.12, 4.60, 4.61
C-438/05 *International Transport Workers' Federation and The Finnish Seamen's
        Union* [2007] E.C.R. I-10779. . . . . 6.22
C-439/05 P and C-454/05 P *Land Oberösterreich and Austria v Commission* [2007]
        E.C.R. I-7141 . . . . 7.103
C-440/05 *Commission v Council* [2007] E.C.R. I-9097. . . . . 1.06, 4.42, 7.04, 22.03, 22.05
C-441/05 *Roquette Frères* [2007] E.C.R. I-1993. . . . . 9.17, 10.11
C-443/05 P *Common Market Fertilizers v Commission* [2007] E.C.R. I-7209 . . . . 7.153, 9.13
C-456/05 *Commission v Germany* [2007] E.C.R. I-10517. . . . . 5.09, 5.31, 5.58
C-462/05 *Commission v Portugal* [2008] E.C.R. I-4183 . . . . 5.76
C-467/05 *Dell'Orto* [2007] E.C.R. I-5557. . . . . 22.03

C-2/06 *Kempter* [2008] E.C.R. I-411 .... 3.22, 4.57, 6.11, 6.33
C-3/06 P *Group Danone v Commission* [2007] E.C.R. I-1331 .... 15.05, 15.07, 15.09, 16.09
C-4/06 P *Ouariachi v Commission* [2006] E.C.R. I-94*, Summ. pub. 11.21
C-6/06 P *Cofradía de pescadores de 'San Pedro' and Others v Council* [2007] E.C.R. I-164*,
    Summ. pub. 7.227, 11.37, 11.51, 11.64
C-14/06 and C-295/06 *European Parliament and Denmark v Commission* [2008]
    E.C.R. I-1649 .... 7.153, 7.221
C-15/06 P *Regione Siciliana v Commission* [2007] E.C.R. I-2591 .... 7.77, 7.91, 7.96, 16.30
C-16/06 P *Les Éditions Albert René Sàrl v OHIM* [2008] E.C.R. I-10053 .... 20.03
C-45/06 *Campina* [2007] E.C.R. I-2089 .... 3.23, 6.22
C-55/06 *Arcor* [2008] E.C.R. I-2931 .... 4.20, 6.08
C-56/06 *Euro Tex* [2007] E.C.R. I-4859 .... 6.13
C-59/06 P *Marcuccio v Commission* [2007] E.C.R. I-182*, Summ. pub. 16.31
C-62/06 *ZF Zefeser* [2007] E.C.R. I-11995 .... 3.32, 3.36
C-70/06 *Commission v Portugal* [2008] E.C.R. I-1 .... 5.78
C-80/06 *Carp* [2007] E.C.R. I-4473 .... 5.66, 6.08, 9.11
C-92/06 P *Soffass v OHIM* [2006] E.C.R. I-89*, Summ. pub., (order of 13 July 2006) 16.03
C-102/06 *Commission v Austria* [2006] E.C.R. I-111*, Summ. pub. 5.37
C-120/06 P and C-121/06 P *FIAMM and FIAMM Technologies v Council and Commission*
    [2008] E.C.R. I-6513 ....2.29, 11.01, 11.07, 11.20, 11.45, 11.51,
                  11.52, 11.69, 16.09, 16.18, 16.19, 16.27, 23.87
C-125/06 P *Infront v Commission* [2008] E.C.R. I-1451 .... 7.16, 7.91, 7.92, 7.93, 7.98
C-129/06 P *Autosalone Ispra v EAEC* [2006] E.C.R. I-131*, Summ. pub.,
    (order of 12 December 2006) 11.03, 11.81
C-150/06 P *Arizona Chemical and Others v Commission* [2007] E.C.R. I-39*, Summ. pub
    (order of 13 March 2007) 7.18, 8.10, 9.01, 9.14, 11.34
C-157/06 *Commission v Italy* [2008] E.C.R. I-7313 .... 5.76
C-161/06 *Skoma-Lux* [2007] E.C.R. I-10841 .... 6.18, 7.175
C-162/06 *International Mail Spain* [2007] E.C.R. I-9911 .... 6.19
C-167/06 P *Komninou and Others v Commission* [2007] E.C.R. I-141*, Summ. pub. 11.62, 16.02,
                        16.09, 16.30, 25.136
C-175/06 *Tedesco* [2007] E.C.R. I-7829, (order of 27 September 2007) 3.46
C-176/06 P *Stadtwerke Schwäbisch Hall and Others v Commission* [2007] E.C.R. I-170*,
    Summ. pub. 7.118, 16.22, 16.30
C-184/06 *Spain v Council* [2007] E.C.R. I-188*, Summ. pub. 7.177
C-186/06 *Commission v Spain* [2007] E.C.R. I-12093 .... 5.52
C-188/06 P *Schneider Electric v Commission* [2007] E.C.R. I-35*, Summ. pub., (order of
    9 March 2007) 7.47
C-189/06 P *TEA-CEGOS and STG v Commission* [2007] E.C.R. I-62*, Summ. pub.,
    (order of 20 April 2007) 16.21
C-193/06 P *Nestlé v OHIM* [2007] E.C.R. I-114*, Summ. pub. 16.31
C-195/06 P *Österreichischer Rundfunk* [2007] E.C.R. I-8817 .... 3.10
C-202/06 P *Cementbouw Handel & Industrie v Commission* [2007] E.C.R. I-12129 .... 7.197
C-205/06 *Commission v Austria* [2009] E.C.R. I-1301 .... 5.13, 24.14
C-210/06 *Cartesio* [2008] E.C.R. I-9641 .... 3.07, 3.08, 3.10, 3.17, 3.30, 3.34, 3.48
C-211/06 P *Adam v Commission* [2008] E.C.R. I-10*, Summ. pub. 16.19
C-212/06 *Gouvernemet de la Communauté française and Gouvernement wallon* [2008]
    E.C.R. I-1683 .... 3.17, 3.38, 5.65, 6.24
C-213/06 P *European Agency for Reconstruction v Karatzoglou* [2007] E.C.R. I-6733 .... 16.25, 16.31
C-234/06 P *Il Ponte Finanziaria v OHIM* [2007] E.C.R. I-7333 .... 26.04
C-237/06 P *Strack v Commission* [2007] E.C.R. I-33*, Summ. pub., (order of 8 March 2007) 11.10
C-239/06 *Commission v Italy* [2009] E.C.R. I-11913 .... 5.71
C-242/06 *Sahin* [2009] E.C.R. I-8465 .... 6.15
C-249/06 *Commission v Sweden* [2009] E.C.R. I-1335 .... 5.13
C-251/06 *ING. AUER* [2007] E.C.R. I-9689 .... 6.21
C-255/06 P *Yedaş Tarim ve Otomotiv Sanayi ve Ticaret v Council and Commission* [2007]
    E.C.R. I-94*, Summ. pub., (order of 5 July 2007) 11.51, 11.78
C-255/06 P-REV *Yedaş Tarim ve Otomotiv Sanayi ve Ticaret v Council and Commission* [2009]
    E.C.R. I-53*, Summ. pub. 25.119
C-266/06 P *Degussa v Commission* [2008] E.C.R. I-81*, Summ. pub. 9.08, 11.12, 15.05, 15.07
C-267/06 *Maruko* [2008] E.C.R. I-1757 .... 6.34

C-268/06 *Impact* [2008] E.C.R. I-2483 . . . . 2.01, 3.18, 4.01, 4.05, 4.07, 4.51, 6.09
C-269/06 *Commission v Translation Centre for the Bodies of the European Union*
 [2007] E.C.R. I-187*, Summ. pub., ECJ (order of 11 December 2007). 2.53, 2.54, 7.01
C-279/06 *CEPSA* [2008] E.C.R. I-6681 . . . . 6.19
C-280/06 *ETI and Others* [2007] E.C.R. I-10893 . . . . 6.16, 6.17
C-294/06 *Payir and Others* [2008] E.C.R. I-203 . . . . 6.15
C-296/06 *Telecom Italia* [2008] E.C.R. I-801 . . . . 6.22, 6.23
C-302/06 *Koval'ský* [2007] E.C.R. I-11*, Summ. pub., (order of 25 January 2007) 6.24
C-303/06 *Coleman* [2008] E.C.R. I-5603 . . . . 3.24
C-304/06 P *Eurohypo v OHIM* [2008] E.C.R. I-3297 . . . . 16.03, 16.30
C-308/06 *Intertanko and Others* [2008] E.C.R. I-4057. . . . . 6.13, 10.08
C-309/06 *Marks & Spencer* [2008] E.C.R. I-2283 . . . . 4.27
C-321/06 to C-233/06 *Jonkman and Others* [2007] E.C.R. I-5149 . . . . 6.29
C-325/06 P *Galileo International Technology and Others v Commission* [2007] E.C.R. I-44*,
 Summ. pub., (order of 20 March 2007). 11.07, 11.19, 11.34, 11.37, 11.46, 11.78, 11.84, 16.19
C-329/06 and C-343/06 *Wiedeman and Funk* [2008] E.C.R. I-4635 . . . . 6.21, 6.22
C-334/06 to C-336/06 *Zerche and Others* [2008] E.C.R. I-4691. 6.21, 6.22
C-341/06 P and C-342/06 P *Chronopost and La Poste v UFEX and Others* [2008]
 E.C.R. I-4777 . . . . .16.22, 16.29, 16.30, 16.31
C-347/06 *ASM Brescia* [2008] E.C.R. I-5641 . . . . 6.23
C-348/06 P *Commission v Girardot* [2008] E.C.R. I-833 . . . . 11.36, 11.72, 15.05, 16.09, 16.10
C-349/06 *Polat* [2007] E.C.R. I-8167. . . . . 6.15
C-353/06 *Grunkin and Paul* [2008] E.C.R. I-7639 . . . . 3.10
C-357/06 *Frigerio Luigi & C.* [2007] E.C.R. I-12311 . . . . 6.21
C-362/06 P *Sahlstedt and Others v Commission* [2009] E.C.R. I-2903 . . . . 7.99
C-372/06 *Asda Stores* [2007] E.C.R. I-11223 . . . . 6.15
C-373/06 P, C-379/06 P, and C-382/06 P *Flaherty and Others v Commission* [2008]
 E.C.R. I-2649 . . . . .7.138, 7.153, 16.30
C-383/06 to C-385/06 *Vereniging Nationaal Overlegorgaan Sociale Werkvoorziening and*
 Others [2008] E.C.R. I-1561. . . . . 4.31
C-390/06 *Nuova Agricast* [2008] E.C.R. I-2577. . . . . .3.22, 7.204, 10.15
C-393/06 *Ing. Aigner* [2008] E.C.R. I-2339 . . . . 3.08
C-399/06 P and C-403/06 P *Hassan and Ayadi v Council and Commission* [2009]
 E.C.R. I-11393 . . . . .7.11, 7.23, 16.14, 16.30
C-401/06 *Commission v Germany* [2007] E.C.R. I-609. . . . . 5.02
C-405/06 P *Miguel Torres v OHIM* [2007] E.C.R. I-115*, Summ. pub. 20.12
C-406/06 *Landtag Schleswig-Holstein v Commission*, not reported, (order of 8 February 2007) 2.54, 7.77
C-409/06 *Winner Wetten* [2010] E.C.R. I-8015 . . . . .3.35, 6.21, 7.221, 10.20
C-413/06 P *Bertelsmann and Sony Corporation of America v Impala* [2008]
 E.C.R. I-4951 .7.164, 7.197, 16.03, 16.04, 16.09, 16.21, 16.31
C-417/06 P *Italy v Commission* [2007] E.C.R. I-171*, Summ. pub. 7.223, 16.19
C-418/06 P *Belgium v Commission* [2008] E.C.R. I-3047. . . . . 2.54, 15.01
C-419/06 *Commission v Greece* [2008] E.C.R. I-27*, Summ. pub. 5.66
C-420/06 *Jager* [2008] E.C.R. I-1315. . . . . 3.23, 6.22
C-421/06 *Fratelli Martini and Cargill* [2007] E.C.R. I-152*, Summ. pub., (order of
 8 November 2007). 10.20
C-427/06 *Bartsch* [2008] E.C.R. I-7245 . . . . 6.07
C-428/06 to C-434/06 *UGT-Rioja and Others* [2006] E.C.R. I-6747 . . . . 3.32, 6.23
C-442/06 *Commission v Italy* [2008] E.C.R. I-2413. . . . . 5.41
C-443/06 *Hollmann* [2007] E.C.R. I-8491 . . . . 6.20
C-445/06 *Danske Slagterier* [2009] E.C.R. I-2119 . . . . 3.05, 4.32, 4.33, 4.46, 4.47, 4.52, 4.54, 5.31, 5.73
C-449/06 *Gysen* [2008] E.C.R. I-553 . . . . 3.23
C-450/06 *Varec* [2008] E.C.R. I-581 . . . . 23.61
C-452/06 *Synthon* [2008] E.C.R. I-7681. . . . . .4.47, 4.48, 6.26
C-454/06 *pressetext Nachrichtenagentur* [2008] E.C.R. I-4401. . . . . 3.08
C-455/06 *Heemskerk BV and Firma Schaap* [2008] E.C.R. I-8763 . . . . 4.40
C-458/06 *Gourmet Classic* [2008] E.C.R. I-4207 . . . . .3.05, 3.31, 3.34
C-459/06 P(R) *Vischim v Commission* [2007] E.C.R. I-53*, Summ. pub.,
 (order of 3 April 2007) 13.44
C-461/06 P *AEPI v Commission* [2007] E.C.R. I-97*, Summ. pub., (order of 10 July 2007). 7.18
C-468/06 to C-478/06 *Sot. Lelos kai Sia EE and Others* [2008] E.C.R. I-7139. . . . . 3.11, 6.22

C-484/06 *Commission v United Kingdom* [2006] E.C.R. I-7471 . . . . 5.52
C-487/06 P *British Aggregates v Commission* [2008] E.C.R. I-10515 . . . . 7.54, 7.104, 7.118,
7.120, 7.121, 7.124, 7.127, 7.201, 16.07, 16.31
C-489/06 *Commission v Greece* [2009] E.C.R. I-1797 . . . . 5.10, 5.11, 5.17, 5.63
C-495/06 P *Nijs v Court of Auditors* [2007] E.C.R. I-146*, Summ. pub.,
(order of 25 October 2007). 16.18
C-497/06 P *CAS Succhi di Frutta v Commission* [2009] E.C.R. I-69*,
Summ. pub. 11.38, 11.56, 11.78, 11.81, 16.27
C-500/06 *Corporación Dermoestética* [2008] E.C.R. I-5785. . . . . 6.21
C-501/06 P, C-513/06 P, C-515/06 P and C-519/06 P *GlaxoSmithKline Services and
Others v Commission and Others* [2009] E.C.R. I-9291 . . . . .7.201, 16.14, 16.27, 26.04
C-502/06 *Correia de Matos v Commission* [2007] E.C.R. I-163*, Summ. pub.,
(order of 21 November 2007). 23.17
C-502/06 P-INT *Correia de Matos v European Parliament* [2008] E.C.R. I-129*,
Summ. pub., (order of 24 September 2008). 25.125
C-503/06 R *Commission v Italy* [2006] E.C.R. I-141*, Summ. pub., (order of the
President of 19 December 2006). 13.12, 13.41
C-503/06 R *Commission v Italy* [2007] E.C.R. I-19*, Summ. pub., (order of the
President of 27 February 2007). 13.26
C-510/06 P *Archer Daniels Midland v Commission* [2009] E.C.R. I-1843 . . . . 15.07
C-511/06 P *Archer Daniels Midland v Commission* [2009] E.C.R. I-5843 . . . . 16.28, 16.30
C-514/06 P *Armacell Enterprise v OHIM* [2008] E.C.R. I-128*, Summ. pub. 16.14
C-516/06 P *Commission v Ferriere Nord* [2007] E.C.R. I-10685 . . . . .7.20, 7.42, 16.30
C-521/06 P *Athinaïki Techniki v Commission* [2008] E.C.R. I-5829 . . . . .7.16, 7.17,
7.55, 7.61, 7.208, 7.216, 16.29
C-525/06 *De Nationale Loterij NV* [2009] E.C.R. I-2197, (order of 24 March 2009). 3.30
C-531/06 *Commission v Italy* [2009] E.C.R. I-4103. . . . . 5.31
C-535/06 P *Moser Baer India v Council* [2009] E.C.R. I-7051 . . . . .7.205, 16.14, 16.19

C-11/07 *Eckelkamp and Others* [2008] E.C.R. I-6845 . . . . .3.31, 6.21
C-12/07 *Autostrada dei Fiori and AISCAT*, not reported, (order of the President of
23 March 2007). 24.18
C-17/07 P *Neirinck v Commission* [2008] E.C.R. I-36*, Summ. pub. 16.30
C-33/07 *Gheorghe Jipa*, not reported, (order of the President of 3 April 2007) 24.18
C-38/07 P *Heusen & Schrouff v Commission* [2008] E.C.R. I-8599 . . . . 16.19
C-42/07 *Liga Portuguesa de Futebol Profissional and Bwin International Ltd* [2009] E.C.R. I-7633 . . . . 6.20
C-44/07 *Les Vergers du Vieux Tauves* [2008] E.C.R. I-10627 . . . . 3.27
C-45/07 *Commission v Greece* [2009] E.C.R. I-1701 . . . . 5.18
C-47/07 P *Masdar (UK) Ltd v Commission* [2008] E.C.R. I-9761. . . . . .11.08, 11.51, 16.05, 19.10
C-48/07 *Les Vergers du Vieux Tauves* [2008] E.C.R. I-10627 . . . . .6.16, 6.17
C-54/07 *Feryn* [2008] E.C.R. I-5187 . . . . 3.23
C-71/07 P *Campoli v Commission* [2008] E.C.R. I-5887 . . . . .9.16, 16.14, 25.14
C-73/07 *Satakunnan Markkinapörssi and Satamedia* [2007] E.C.R. I-7075,
(order of the President of 12 September 2007). 24.12, 25.61
C-88/07 *Commission v Spain* [2009] E.C.R. I-1353. . . . . .5.10, 5.14
C-92/07 *Commission v Netherlands* [2010] E.C.R. I-3683. . . . . 5.05
C-95/07 and C-96/07 *Ecotrade* [2008] E.C.R. I-3457 . . . . 4.25
C-99/07 P *Smanor and Others v Commission* [2007] E.C.R. I-70*, Summ. pub.,
(order of 23 May 2007) 8.15, 13.04
C-100/07 P *É.R. and Others v Council and Commission* [2007] E.C.R. I-136*,
Summ. pub., (order of 4 October 2007) 11.07, 11.28, 11.32, 11.34,
11.38, 11.40, 11.83, 11.87, 11.92
C-101/07 P and C-110/07 P *Coop de France bétail and viande v Commission* [2008]
E.C.R. I-10193 . . . . .9.08, 15.07
C-108/07 P *Ferrero Deutschland v OHIM* [2008] E.C.R. I-61*, Summ. pub. 16.30
C-109/07 *Pilato* [2008] E.C.R. I-3503, (order of 14 May 2008). 3.09
C-113/07 P *SELEX Sistemi Integrati v Commission* [2009] E.C.R. I-2207 . . . . 16.18
C-121/07 *Commission v France* [2008] E.C.R. I-9159 . . . . .5.65, 5.74, 5.78
C-122/07 P *Eurostrategies v Commission* [2007] E.C.R. I-179*, (order of 29 November 2007) 16.13
C-125/07 P, C-133/07 P, C-135/07 P, and C-137/07 P *Erste Group Bank and
Others v Commission* [2009] E.C.R. I-8681. . . . . 15.05, 15.07, 15.09

C-127/07 *Arcelor Atlantique and Lorraine and Others* [2008] E.C.R. I-9895. . . . . 6.07, 10.18
C-138/07 *Cobelfret* [2009] E.C.R. I-731 . . . . 6.34
C-139/07 P *Commission v Technische Glaswerke Ilmenau* [2010] E.C.R. I-5885 . . . . . . 7.165, 16.28, 16.30
C-142/07 *Ecologistas en Acción-CODA* [2008] E.C.R. I-6097 . . . . 6.21
C-155/07 *European Parliament v Council* [2008] E.C.R. I-8103 . . . . 7.221
C-156/07 *Aiello and Others* [2008] E.C.R. I-5215, Summ.pub., (order of 10 July 2008) 6.23
C-157/07 *Krankenheim Ruhesitz am Wannsee-Seniorenheimstatt* [2008] E.C.R. I-8061 . . . . 6.14
C-166/07 *European Parliament v Council* [2009] E.C.R. I-7135 . . . . 7.221
C-185/07 *Allianz* [2009] E.C.R. I-663 . . . . 6.23
C-188/07 *Commune de Mesquer* [2008] E.C.R. 4501. . . . . 6.08, 6.13
C-191/07 P *Sellier v Commission* [2007] E.C.R. I-113*, Summ. pub., (order of
   18 September 2007). 7.18, 16.25
C-193/07 R *Commission v Poland*, not reported, (order of the President of 18 April 2007) 13.12
C-193/07 R *Commission v Poland*, not reported, (order of the President of 18 July 2007). 25.81
C-193/07 R-2 *Commission v Poland*, not reported, (order of the President of 25 January 2008). 13.12
C-196/07 *Commission v Spain* [2008] E.C.R. I-41*, Summ. pub. 5.66
C-198/07 P *Gordon v Commission* [2008] E.C.R. I-10701 . . . . .7.138, 16.28, 16.30, 18.07
C-199/07 *Commission v Greece* [2009] E.C.R. I-10669. . . . . 5.58
C-200/07 and C-201/07 *Marra* [2008] E.C.R. I-7929. . . . . 6.10
C-202/07 P *France Télécom v Commission* [2009] E.C.R. I-2369. . . . . 16.01, 16.19, 25.10
C-203/07 P *Greece v Commission* [2008] E.C.R. I-8161 . . . . 16.18
C-204/07 P *C.A.S. v Commission* [2008] E.C.R. I-6135. . . . . 16.30
C-204/07 P-DEP *C.A.S. v Commission* [2009] E.C.R. I-140*, Summ. pub., (order of
   10 September 2009). 25.91
C-208/07 *von Chamier-Gliszinski* [2009] E.C.R. I-6095. . . . . 6.21
C-213/07 *Michaniki* [2008] E.C.R. I-9999 . . . . 6.24
C-214/07 *Commission v France* [2008] E.C.R. I-8357 . . . . 5.22
C-236/07 P(R) *Sumitomo Chemical Agro Europe v Commission* [2008] E.C.R. I-9*,
   Summ. pub., (order of the President of 23 January 2008) 13.36
C-237/07 *Dieter Janecek v Freistaat Bayern* [2008] E.C.R. I-6221 . . . . 4.18
C-239/07 *Sabatauskas and Others* [2008] E.C.R. I-2573. . . . . 3.17
C-242/07 P *Belgium v Commission* [2007] E.C.R. I-9757, (order of 8 November 2007). 7.208
C-243/07 P *Brinkmann v OHIM* [2008] E.C.R. I-29*, Summ. pub. 20.13
C-246/07 *Commission v Sweden* [2010] E.C.R. I-3317. . . . . 5.04, 5.18
C-260/07 *Petro IV Servicios SL* [2009] E.C.R. I-2437. . . . . 3.27, 3.32, 3.53
C-265/07 *Caffaro* [2008] E.C.R. I-7085 . . . . 3.17
C-277/07 P(R) *Makhteshim-Agan Holding and Others v Commission* [2008] E.C.R. I-112*,
   Summ. pub., (order of the President of 17 July 2008). 13.10, 13.20, 13.25
C-290/07 P *Commission v Scott* [2010] E.C.R. I-7763 . . . . .7.201, 7.204, 16.29, 16.31
C-295/07 P *Commission v Départment du Loiret and Scott* [2008] E.C.R. I-9363 . . . . .7.220, 16.02,
   16.20, 16.29, 16.31
C-296/07 P(R) *Commission v Scott* [2007] E.C.R. I-166*, Summ. pub., (order of the
   President of 22 November 2007). 13.24, 13.26
C-300/07 P *Hans & Christophorus Oymanns* [2009] E.C.R. I-4779 . . . . 10.15
C-319/07 P *3F v Commission* [2009] E.C.R. I-5963. . . . . . .7.60, 7.118, 7.120, 7.127, 7.128, 7.129, 16.29
C-322/07 P, C-327/07 P, and C-338/07 P *Paperfabriek August Koehler and Others v
   Commission* [2009] E.C.R. I-7191. . . . . 16.18
C-331/07 *Commission v Greece* [2009] E.C.R. I-60*, Summ. pub. 5.11
C-333/07 *Regie Networks* [2008] E.C.R. I-10807. . . . . .3.34, 10.20, 10.23
C-334/07 P *Commission v Freistaat Sachsen* [2008] E.C.R. I-9465. . . . . 16.31
C-337/07 *Altun* [2008] E.C.R. I-10323 . . . . 6.15
C-343/07 *Bavaria NV and Bavaria Italia Srl* [2009] E.C.R. I-5491. . . . . 2.15, 10.11
C-349/07 *Sopropré* [2008] E.C.R. I-10369 . . . . 6.07, 7.161
C-350/07 *Kattner Stahlbau* [2009] E.C.R. I-1513 . . . . .3.23, 3.31, 6.20
C-361/07 *Polier* [2008] E.C.R. I-6*, Summ.pub., (order of 16 January 2008) 6.24
C-364/07 *Vassilakis and Others* [2008] E.C.R. I-90*, Summ. pub., (Order of 12 June 2008) 4.45
C-369/07 *Commission v Greece* [2009] E.C.R. I-5703 . . . . 5.61, 5.76, 5.77, 5.78
C-370/07 *Commission v Council* [2009] E.C.R. I-8917. . . . . 7.10, 7.21, 7.170, 7.172, 7.221
C-374/07 P *Mebrom v Commission* [2009] E.C.R. I-3*, Summ. pub.,
   (order of 20 January 2009) 11.65
C-378/07 to C-380/07 *Angelidaki and Others* [2009] E.C.R. I-3071. . . . . 4.01, 4.45

C-385/07 P *Der Grüne Punkt—Duales System Deutschland v Commission* [2009]
E.C.R. I-6155 . . . . 11.20, 16.09, 16.18, 23.87, 26.08
C-390/07 *Commission v United Kingdom* [2009] E.C.R. I-214*, Summ. pub. 5.63
C-393/07 *Italy v European Parliament*, not reported, (order of the President of 30 January 2008) . . . 25.65
C-393/07 and C-9/08 *Italy and Donnici v European Parliament* [2009] E.C.R. I-3679 . . . . 7.178
C-402/07 and C-423/07 *Sturgeon and Others* [2009] E.C.R. I-10923 . . . . 6.11
C-405/07 P *Netherlands v Commission* [2008] E.C.R. I-8301 . . . . 7.170, 16.30
C-416/07 *Commission v Greece* [2009] E.C.R. I-7883 . . . . 5.11, 5.63
C-423/07 *Commission v Spain* [2010] E.C.R. I-3429 . . . . 5.31, 5.32
C-424/07 *Commission v Germany* [2009] E.C.R. I-11431. . . . . 5.30
C-426/07 *Krawcyński* [2008] E.C.R. I-6021 . . . . 6.34
C-427/07 *Commission v Ireland* [2009] E.C.R. I-6277 . . . . 5.15
C-436/07 P *Commission v Efrosyni Alexiadou* [2008] E.C.R. I-152*, Summ. pub. 16.31
C-439/07 and C-499/07 *KBC Bank and Others* [2009] E.C.R. I-4409 . . . . 6.17
C-440/07 P *Commission v Schneider Electric* [2009] E.C.R. I-6413 .11.37, 11.45,
11.54, 11.61, 11.68, 11.82, 11.85, 16.03, 16.04,
16.05, 16.09, 16.10, 16.29, 16.30, 23.85, 25.88
C-441/07 P *Commission v Alrosa* [2010] E.C.R. I-5949 . . . . .7.40, 16.29, 16.30
C-443/07 P *Centeno Mediavilla and Others v Commission* [2008] E.C.R. I-10945 . . . . 9.16
C-445/07 P and C-455/07 P *Commission v Ente per le Ville Vesuviane* [2009]
E.C.R. I-7993 . . . . 7.77, 7.91, 7.96, 16.30
C-448/07 P *Ayuntamiento de Madrid and Madrid Calle 30 SA v Commission* [2008] E.C.R. I-99*,
Summ. pub., (order of 20 June 2008) 7.13
C-453/07 *Er* [2008] E.C.R. I-7299. . . . . 6.15
C-454/07 *Raulin v France* [2008] E.C.R. I-76*, Summ. pub., (order of 16 May 2008) 5.32
C-456/07 *Karol Mihal*, not reported, (order of the President of 8 November 2007) 24.18
C-457/07 *Commission v Portugal* [2009] E.C.R. I-8091 . . . . .5.02, 5.74, 5.76
C-458/07 *Commission v Portugal* [2009] E.C.R. I-29*, Summ. pub. 5.37
C-459/07 *Elshani* [2009] E.C.R. I-2759 . . . . 3.36
C-466/07 *Klarenberg* [2009] E.C.R. I-803. . . . . 3.05
C-468/07 P *Coats Holdings and J&P Coats v Commission* [2008] E.C.R. I-127*, Summ. pub.,
(order of 11 September 2008) 15.07, 16.01
C-474/07 *European Parliament v Commission*, not reported, (order of 10 July 2009) 25.133
C-475/07 *Commission v Poland* [2009] E.C.R. I-19*, Summ. pub. 5.71
C-478/07 *Budějovický Budvar* [2009] E.C.R. I-7721 . . . . 4.20
C-479/07 *France v Council* [2008] E.C.R. I-39*, Summ. pub., (order of the President of
28 February 2008) 13.31, 13.32, 13.35, 13.36, 13.40
C-481/07 P *SELEX Sistemi Integrati v Commission* [2009] E.C.R. I-127*,
Summ. pub. 11.76, 11.78, 11.85
C-483/07 P *Galileo Lebensmittel v Commission* [2009] E.C.R. I-959,
(order of 17 February 2009) 7.73, 7.85, 7.100
C-484/07 *Pehlivan* [2011] E.C.R. I-5203 . . . . 6.15
C-498/07 P-DEP *Deoleo v Aceites del Sur—Coosur*, not reported, (order of 16 May 2013) 25.93
C-500/07 P *Territorio Energia Ambiente v Commission* [2008] E.C.R. I-161*,
Summ. pub., (order of 25 November 2008). 7.210, 7.211, 7.216
C-501/07 P *S.A.BA.R. v Commission* [2008] E.C.R. I-163*, Summ. pub.,
(order of 25 November 2008) 7.210, 7.211, 7.216
C-503/07 P *Saint-Gobain Glass Deutschland and Others v Commission* [2008]
E.C.R. I-2217, (order of 8 April 2008) 7.99, 7.138, 7.141, 16.14
C-512/07 P(R) and C-15/08 P(R) *Occhetto and European Parliament v Donnici* [2009]
E.C.R. I-1, (order of the President of 13 January 2009) 13.32, 13.34, 13.40, 13.42
C-514/07 P, C-528/07 P, C-532/07 P *Sweden and Others v API and Commission* [2010]
E.C.R. I-8533 . . . . .5.40, 16.16, 16.27
C-519/07 P *Commission v Koninklijke FrieslandCampina* [2009] E.C.R. I-8495 . . . . 7.91, 7.93, 7.120,
7.122, 7.138, 7.178, 16.31
C-520/07 P *Commission v MTU Friedrichshafen* [2009] E.C.R. I-8555 . . . . 16.05
C-522/07 and C-65/08 *Dinter* [2009] E.C.R. I-10333. . . . . 10.18
C-526/07 P *Combescot v Commission* [2008] E.C.R. I-168*, Summ. pub.,
(order of 28 November 2008) 16.09, 16.10, 16.12
C-534/07 P *Prym and Prym Consumer v Commission* [2009] E.C.R. I-7415 . . . . 15.05, 15.07, 16.27
C-536/07 *Commission v Germany* [2009] E.C.R. I-10355. . . . . 5.58

C-537/07 *Gómez-Limón Sánchez-Camacho* [2009] E.C.R. I-6525 . . . . 6.22
C-546/07 *Commission v Germany* [2010] E.C.R. I-439. . . . . 5.10, 5.62
C-550/07 P *Akzo Nobel Chemicals and Akcros Chemicals v Commission* [2010]
    E.C.R. I-8301 . . . . 7.37, 16.14, 25.65, 25.69, 25.70
C-555/07 *Kücükdeveci* [2010] E.C.R. I-365. . . . . .3.20, 4.37, 6.07
C-558/07 *S.P.C.M. and Others* [2009] E.C.R. I-5783 . . . . 10.01, 10.15
C-559/07 *Commission v Greece* [2009] E.C.R. I-47*, Summ. pub. 5.71
C-562/07 *Commission v Spain* [2007] E.C.R. I-9553 . . . . 5.62
C-565/07 P *AMS Advanced Medical Services v OHIM* [2009] E.C.R. I-84*, Summ. pub.,
    (order of 19 May 2009) 16.14
C-567/07 *Woningstichting Sint Servatius* [2009] E.C.R. I-9021 . . . . .3.26, 3.36, 6.22
C-568/07 *Commission v Greece* [2009] E.C.R. I-4505 . . . . 5.78
C-570/07 and C-571/07 *Blanco Pérez and Chao Gómez* [2010] E.C.R. I-4629. . . . . 3.34, 6.24

Opinion 1/08 *Competence of the European Community to conclude agreements modifying the*
    Schedules of Specific Commitments of the Community and its Member States under the
    General Agreement on Trade in Services [2009] E.C.R. I-11129 . . . 12.01, 12.07, 12.11, 12.15, 12.19
C-2/08 *Fallimento Olimpiclub Srl* [2009] E.C.R. I-7501 . . . . .4.01, 4.59
C-3/08 *Leyman* [2009] E.C.R. I-9085 . . . . 6.22
C-6/08 P *US Steel Košice v Commission* [2008] E.C.R. I-96*, Summ. pub., (order of
    19 June 2008) 7.93
C-12/08 *Mono Car Styling SA* [2009] E.C.R. I-6653 . . . . .4.17, 4.37, 6.20
C-14/08 *Roda Golf & Beach Resort* [2009] E.C.R. I-5439 . . . . 3.08, 3.10, 3.48, 3.59, 22.02
C-19/08 *Petrosian and Others* [2009] E.C.R. I-495 . . . . 4.01
C-22/08 and C-23/08 *Vatsouras and Koupatantze* [2009] E.C.R. I-4585 . . . . 10.01
C-25/08 P *Gargani v European Parliament* [2008] E.C.R. I-154*, Summ. pub.,
    (order of 13 November 2008) 7.74
C-28/08 P *Commission v Bavarian Lager* [2010] E.C.R. I-6055. . . . . .5.40, 16.29, 16.30, 25.78
C-36/08 *Commission v Greece* [2008] E.C.R. I-35*, Summ. pub. 5.69
C-40/08 *Asturcom Telecomunicaciones* [2009] E.C.R. I-9579 . . . . 4.01, 4.02, 4.40, 4.41
C-45/08 *Spector Photo Group NV* [2009] E.C.R. I-12073 . . . . 3.31
C-46/08 *Carmen Media Group*, not reported, (order of 2 September 2010) 23.82
C-47/08 *Commission v Belgium* [2011] E.C.R. I-4105 . . . . 5.36
C-49/08 *Raulin v France* [2008] E.C.R. I-77*, Summ. pub., (order of 16 May 2008) 5.32, 7.72
C-50/08 *Commission v France* [2011] E.C.R. I-4195 . . . . 5.36, 25.59
C-51/08 *Commission v Luxembourg* [2011] E.C.R. I-4231 . . . . 5.36
C-52/08 *Commission v Portugal* [2011] E.C.R. I-4275 . . . . 5.36
C-53/08 *Commission v Austria* [2011] E.C.R. I-4309 . . . . 5.36
C-54/08 *Commission v Germany* [2011] E.C.R. I-4355. . . . . 5.36
C-58/08 *Vodafone* [2010] E.C.R. I-4999. . . . . .6.07, 10.17, 10.18
C-60/08 P(R) *Cheminova and Others v Commission* [2009] E.C.R. I-43*, Summ. pub.,
    (order of the President of 24 March 2009) 13.24, 13.25, 13.35, 13.36, 26.08
C-61/08 *Commission v Greece* [2011] E.C.R. I-4399 . . . . 5.36, 5.54
C-63/08 *Pontin* [2009] E.C.R. I-10467. . . . . 4.33, 4.34
C-69/08 *Visciano* [2009] E.C.R. I-6741 . . . . .4.23, 4.24, 4.34
C-73/08 *Bressol and Others* [2010] E.C.R. I-2735 . . . . 6.33, 6.34
C-75/08 *The Queen, on application of Christopher Mellor v Secretary of State for Communities*
    and Local Government [2009] E.C.R. I-3799 . . . . 4.09
C-76/08 R *Commission v Malta* [2008] E.C.R. I-64*, Summ. pub., (order of the President
    of 24 April 2008) 13.12, 13.16, 13.31, 13.32, 13.34, 13.40, 13.41, 13.42
C-78/08 to C-80/08 *Paint Graphos and Others* [2011] E.C.R. I-7611 . . . . 6.20, 6.23
C-84/08 P *Pitsiorlas v Council and ECB* [2008] E.C.R. I-104*, Summ. pub., (order of
    3 July 2008). 7.208, 9.08, 9.15, 11.20, 11.38, 16.25
C-89/08 P *Commission v Ireland and Others* [2009] E.C.R. I-11245 . . . 7.146, 7.219, 16.29, 16.31, 23.61
C-101/08 *Audiolux* [2009] E.C.R. I-9823 . . . . 5.06
C-105/08 *Commission v Portugal* [2010] E.C.R. I-5331 . . . . 5.63
C-109/08 *Commission v Greece* [2009] E.C.R. I-4657 . . . . .5.74, 5.77, 5.78
C-114/08 P(R) *Pellegrini v Commission* [2008] E.C.R. I-117*, Summ. pub. (order
    of the President of 17 July 2008). 11.24, 13.11, 13.34, 25.125
C-114/08 P(R)-INT *Pellegrini v Commission* [2010] E.C.R. I-48*, Summ. pub.,
    (order of the President of 20 April 2010) 25.125

C-115/08 *ČEZ* [2009] E.C.R. I-10265 . . . . .3.23, 6.07, 6.22
C-118/08 *Transportes Urbanos y Servicios Generales SAL* [2010]
    E.C.R. I-635 . . . . 4.14, 4.21, 4.46, 4.48, 4.51, 5.73, 6.23
C-120/08 *Bavaria* [2010] E.C.R. I-13393 . . . . 10.18
C-124/08 and C-125/08 *Snauwaert and Others and Deschaumes* [2009] E.C.R. I-6793 . . . . 3.26, 3.27
C-127/08 *Metock and Others* [2008] E.C.R. I-6241 . . . . 6.32, 24.18, 24.27
C-128/08 *Damseaux* [2009] E.C.R. I-6823 . . . . 6.13
C-129/08 *Carlos Cloet and Jacqueline Cloet* [2009] E.C.R. I-96*, Summ. pub. 3.30
C-133/08 *ICF* [2009] E.C.R. I-9687 . . . . 21.03
C-135/08 *Rottmann* [2010] E.C.R. I-1449 . . . . 6.04
C-137/08 *VB Pénzügyi Lízing* [2010] E.C.R. I-10847 . . . . 4.40, 4.41, 6.08, 24.10
C-141/08 P *Foshan Shunde Yongjian Housewares & Hardware v Council* [2009]
    E.C.R. I-9147 . . . . .7.166, 7.192, 16.29, 16.30
C-146/08 P *Efkon v European Parliament and Council* [2009] E.C.R. I-49*,
    Summ. pub., (order of 26 March 2009) 7.100, 16.18
C-147/08 *Römer* [2011] E.C.R. I-3591 . . . . 6.22
C-154/08 *Commission v Spain* [2009] E.C.R. I-187*, Summ. pub. 5.13, 5.38
C-159/08 P *Scippacercola and Terezakis v Commission* [2009] E.C.R. I-46*,
    Summ. pub., (order of 25 March 2009) 16.19
C-160/08 *Commission v Germany* [2010] E.C.R. I-3713 . . . . 5.10, 5.11, 5.40, 5.52
C-165/08 *Commission v Poland* [2009] E.C.R. I-6843 . . . . 5.52
C-169/08 *Presidente del Consiglio dei Minisitri v Regione Sardegna* [2009] E.C.R. I-10821 . . . . 3.17
C-171/08 *Commission v Portugal* [2010] E.C.R. I-6817 . . . . 5.52, 5.63
C-172/08 *Pontina Ambiente* [2010] E.C.R. I-1175 . . . . 6.23
C-173/08 *Kloosterboer Services* [2009] E.C.R. I-5347 . . . . 6.22
C-175/08, C-176/08, C-178/08, and C-179/08 *Abdulla and Others* [2010] E.C.R. I-1493 . . . . 6.16
C-183/08 P *Commission v Provincia di Imperia* [2009] E.C.R. I-27*, Summ. pub.,
    (order of 5 March 2009) 7.141
C-188/08 *Commission v Ireland* [2009] E.C.R. I-172*, Summ. pub. 25.83
C-189/08 *Zuid-Chemie BV* [2009] E.C.R. I-6917 . . . . 3.32
C-201/08 *Plantanol & Co*, not reported, (order of the President of 3 July 2008) 24.18
C-205/08 *Umweltanwalt voor Kärnten* [2009] E.C.R. I-11525 . . . . 3.10
C-211/08 *Commission v Spain* [2010] E.C.R. I-5267 . . . . 5.41, 5.52
C-214/08 P *Guigard v Commission* [2009] E.C.R. I-91*, Summ. pub. 11.06, 16.30, 19.11
C-216/08 RX Review of judgment T-414/06 P *Combescot v Commission*, not reported,
    (decision of 16 April 2008) 17.01
C-221/08 *Commission v Ireland* [2010] E.C.R. I-1669 . . . . 5.14
C-225/08 P *Nuova Agricast v Commission* [2009] E.C.R. I-111*, Summ. pub.,
    (order of 29 June 2009) 7.67, 16.05
C-227/08 *Martín Martín* [2009] E.C.R. I-11939 . . . . 4.41, 6.22
C-229/08 *Wolf* [2010] E.C.R. I-1 . . . . 3.23, 6.22
C-231/08 P *Giannini v Commission* [2009] E.C.R. I-11*, Summ. pub.,
    (order of 3 February 2009) 16.18
C-241/08 *Commission v France* [2010] E.C.R. I-1697 . . . . 5.53, 5.63
C-243/08 *Pannon* [2009] E.C.R. I-4713 . . . . 4.40, 4.41, 6.26
C-247/08 *Gaz de France—Berliner Investissement* [2009] E.C.R. I-9225 . . . . 10.16
C-251/08 P-R *Ayyanarsamy v Commission and Germany* [2009] E.C.R. I-37*, Summ. pub.,
    (order of the President of 17 March 2009) 13.26
C-251/08 P *Ayyanarsamy v Commission and Germany* [2009] E.C.R. I-36*, Summ. pub.,
    (order of 17 March 2009) 7.18, 26.02
C-254/08 *Futura immobiliare* [2009] E.C.R. I-6995 . . . . 6.08, 6.23
C-261/08 *Zurita García and Choque Cabrera* [2009] E.C.R. I-10143 . . . . 3.32
C-264/08 *Direct Parcel Distribution Belgium* [2010] E.C.R. I-731 . . . . 4.20
C-275/08 *Commission v Germany* [2009] E.C.R. I-168*, Summ. pub. 5.09
C-279/08 P *Commission v Netherlands* [2011] E.C.R. I-7671 . . . . .7.21, 16.29, 16.30
C-280/08 P *Deutsche Telecom v Commission* [2010] E.C.R. I-9555 . . . . 16.09, 16.19, 16.20
C-281/08 P *Landtag Schleswig-Holstein v Commission* [2009] E.C.R. I-199*,
    Summ. pub., (order of 24 November 2009) 7.83
C-287/08 *Savia and Others* [2008] E.C.R. I-136*, Summ. pub., (order of 3 October 2008) 6.24
C-295/08 P *Cofra v Commission* [2009] E.C.R. I-112*, Summ. pub., (order of 29 June 2009) 7.67
C-296/08 PPU *Santesteban Goicoechea* [2008] E.C.R. I-6307 . . . . 3.10, 22.11

C-297/08 *Commission v Italy* [2010] E.C.R. I-1749 . . . . 5.01, 5.62, 5.63, 5.65, 5.68
C-301/08 *Bogiatzi* [2009] E.C.R. I-10185. . . . . 6.13
C-303/08 *Bozkurt* [2010] E.C.R. I-13445. . . . . 6.15
C-304/08 *Plus Warenhandelsgesellschaft* [2010] E.C.R. I-217. . . . . 3.36, 3.38, 6.24
C-306/08 *Commission v Spain* [2011] E.C.R. I-4541 . . . . 5.63, 5.65
C-308/08 *Intertanko and Others* [2008] E.C.R. I-4057. . . . . 6.07
C-311/08 *SGI* [2010] E.C.R. I-487 . . . . 6.22
C-314/08 *Filipiak* [2009] E.C.R. I-11049. . . . . 3.20, 3.34
C-317/08 to C-320/08 *Alassini and Others* [2010] E.C.R. I-2213 . . . . .4.01, 6.08, 6.22
C-323/08 *Rodríguez Mayor and Others* [2009] E.C.R. I-11621 . . . . 3.23, 6.23
C-334/08 *Commission v Italy* [2010] E.C.R. I-6869 . . . . 5.37, 5.68
C-335/08 P *Transports Schiocchet—Excursions v Commission* [2009] E.C.R. I-104*,
    Summ. pub. 11.87, 11.90, 11.94, 16.21
C-336/08 *Christel Reinke* [2010] E.C.R. I-130*, Summ. pub. 3.16
C-343/08 *Commission v Czech Republic* [2010] E.C.R. I-275 . . . . 5.52
C-344/08 *Rubach* [2009] E.C.R. I-7033 . . . . 4.20
C-349/08 P-R *Kronberger v European Parliament* [2009] E.C.R. I-88*, Summ. pub.,
    (order of the President of 19 May 2009) 13.26
C-350/08 *Commission v Lithuania* [2010] E.C.R. I-10525 . . . . .5.58, 5.59, 5.62
C-355/08 P *WWF-UK v Council* [2009] E.C.R. I-73*, Summ. pub., (order of 5 May 2009) 7.100
C-362/08 P *Internationaler Hilfsfonds v Commission* [2010] E.C.R. I-669 . . . . 7.16, 7.20, 7.67, 16.29
C-372/08 P *Atlantic Dawn and Others v Commission* [2009] E.C.R. I-74*,
    Summ. pub., (order of 5 May 2009) 7.93
C-373/08 *Hoesch Metals and Alloys* [2010] E.C.R. I-951. . . . . 3.22, 10.15
C-375/08 *Pontini and Others* [2010] E.C.R. I-5767. . . . . 6.21, 6.22, 22.07, 22.19, 24.18
C-378/08 *ERG and Others* [2010] E.C.R. I-1919 . . . . .6.20, 6.22, 6.23
C-379/08 and C-380/08 *ERG and Others* [2010] E.C.R. I-2007. . . . . 3.19, 3.20, 3.27, 6.23
C-380/08 *ERA and Others* [2010] E.C.R. I-2007. . . . . 6.22
C-382/08 *Neukirchinger* [2011] E.C.R. I-139, (order of 21 April 2010) 6.22, 23.82, 24.14
C-384/08 *Attanasio Group* [2010] E.C.R. I-2055. . . . . 3.23, 3.26, 3.38, 6.22, 6.24, 24.18
C-386/08 *Brita* [2010] E.C.R. I-1289. . . . . 6.13
C-387/08 P *VDH v Commission*, not reported, (order of 3 April 2009) 7.91, 8.13
C-388/08 PPU *Leymann and Pustovarov* [2008] E.C.R. I-8983. . . . . 22.17
C-391/08 P(R) *Dow Agrosciences and Others v Commission* [2009] E.C.R. I-219*, Summ. pub.,
    (order of the President of 15 December 2009) 13.25, 13.37
C-395/08 and C-396/08 *Bruno and Pettini* [2010] E.C.R. I-5119. . . . . 3.27, 3.34
C-400/08 *Commission v Spain* [2011] E.C.R. I-1915 . . . . 5.63, 25.10
C-403/08 and C-429/08 *Football Association Premier League and Others*, not reported,
    (order of the President of 16 December 2009) 24.12, 25.61
C-407/08 P *Knauf Gips v Commission* [2010] E.C.R. I-6375 . . . . .7.36, 7.43, 16.28, 16.30
C-408/08 P *Lancôme parfums et beauté v OHIM* [2010] E.C.R. I-1347. . . . . 8.11
C-413/08 P *Lafarge v Commission* [2010] E.C.R. I-5361 . . . . 16.19
C-414/08 P *Sviluppo Italia Bailicata v Commission* [2010] E.C.R. I-2559 . . . . .11.01, 11.07, 16.27
C-419/08 P *Trubowest and Makarov v Council and Commission* [2010]
    E.C.R. I-2259 . . . . 11.01, 11.29, 11.39, 11.78, 11.81, 11.85
C-425/08 *Enviro Tech (Europe) ltd* [2009] E.C.R. I-10035. . . . . 10.18
C-436/08 and C-437/08 *Haribo and Osterreichische Salinen* [2011]
    E.C.R. I-305 . . . . 3.29, 3.33, 6.22, 6.25, 24.23
C-439/08 *VEBIC* [2010] E.C.R. I-12471 . . . . 3.11, 3.28, 6.24, 24.18
C-444/08 P *Região autónoma dos Açores v Council* [2009] E.C.R. I-200*,
    Summ. pub., (order of 26 November 2009). 7.77, 7.89, 7.97, 7.103
C-447/08 and C-448/08 *Sjöberg and Gerdin* [2010] E.C.R. I-6921. . . . . 6.21
C-454/08 *Seaport Investments*, not reported, (order of 20 May 2009). 3.26
C-455/08 *Commission v Ireland* [2009] E.C.R. I-225*, Summ. pub. 4.56
C-456/08 *Commission v Ireland* [2010] E.C.R. I-859 . . . . 5.09
C-457/08 *Commission v United Kingdom* [2009] E.C.R. I-137*, Summ. pub. 5.37
C-458/08 *Commission v Portugal* [2010] E.C.R. I-11599 . . . . 5.52, 5.63
C-467/08 *Padawan* [2010] E.C.R. I-10055. . . . . 6.21
C-472/08 *Alstom Power Hydro* [2010] E.C.R I-623 . . . . 4.25
C-475/08 *Commission v Belgium* [2009] E.C.R. I-11503 . . . . 5.52
C-476/08 P *Evropaïki Dynamiki v Commission* [2009] E.C.R. I-207*, Summ. pub. 16.04

C-483/08 *Régie communale autonome du stade Luc Varenne* [2009] E.C.R. I-121*, Summ. pub.,
(order of 9 July 2009)...4.23
C-485/08 P *Gualtieri v Commission* [2010] E.C.R. I-3009.................7.147, 9.16, 16.13, 25.14
C-486/08 *Tirols* [2010] E.C.R. I-3527 ....6.09
C-487/08 *Commission v Spain* [2010] E.C.R. I-4843.........................5.52, 5.58, 5.59
C-492/08 *Commission v France* [2010] E.C.R. I-5471 ....5.54
C-495/08 *Commission v United Kingdom* [2009] E.C.R. I-188*, Summ. pub. 5.37, 5.65
C-496/08 P *Angé Serrano and Others v European Parliament* [2010] E.C.R. I-1793 ....9.16, 11.10
C-497/08 *Amiraike Berlin* [2010] E.C.R. I-101, (order of 12 January 2010) 3.10, 3.17
C-498/08 P *Fornaci Laterizi Danesi v Commission* [2009] E.C.R. I-122*, Summ. pub.,
(order of 9 July 2009)...7.207, 7.210, 7.211, 7.216
C-501/08 P *Municipio de Gondomar v Commission* [2009] E.C.R. I-152*, Summ. pub.,
(order of 24 September 2009)...7.91, 7.96
C-506/08 P *Sweden v MyTravel and Commission* [2011] E.C.R. I-6237...................16.16
C-507/08 *Commission v Slovak Republic* [2010] E.C.R. I-13489..............4.31, 4.58, 4.59, 5.63
C-508/08 *Commission v Malta* [2010] E.C.R. I-10589............................5.58
C-515/08 *dos Santos Palhota* [2010] E.C.R. I-9133 ....3.23
C-517/08 P *Makhteshim-Agan Holding and Others v Commission* [2010] E.C.R. I-45*,
Summ. pub., (order of 15 April 2010)...........................8.10, 16.14, 16.22
C-518/08 *Fundación Gala Salvador-Dalí and VEGAP* [2010] E.C.R. I-3091 ....6.21
C-519/08 *Archontia Koukou* [2009] E.C.R. I-65*, Summ.pub., (order of 24 April 2009) 4.07
C-523/08 *Commission v Spain* [2010] E.C.R. I-19*, Summ. pub..........................5.15
C-524/08 *Barth* [2010] E.C.R. I-3189 ....4.32, 4.35
C-526/08 *Commission v Luxembourg* [2010] E.C.R. I-6151 ....5.68, 5.76, 25.37, 25.49
C-528/08 P *Marcuccio v Commission* [2009] E.C.R. I-212*, Summ. pub., (order of
9 December 2009)..18.04
C-533/08 *TNT Express Nederland* [2010] E.C.R. I-4107 ....6.13
C-535/08 *Pignataro* [2009] E.C.R. I-50*, Summ.pub., (order of 26 March 2009).............6.24
C-543/08 *Commission v Portugal* [2010] E.C.R. I-11241 ....25.11
C-551/08 *Commission v Poland* [2009] E.C.R. I-176*, Summ. pub. 5.15
C-554/08 P *Le Carbone-Lorraine v Commission* [2009] E.C.R. I-189*, Summ. pub...........15.06
C-560/08 *Commission v Spain*, not yet reported, (judgment of 15 December 2011)............5.31
C-561/08 P and C-4/09 P *Commission v Potamianos* [2009] E.C.R. I-171*, Summ. pub.,
(order of 23 October 2009)..18.04
C-565/08 *Commission v Italy* [2011] E.C.R. I-2101...............................5.63
C-568/08 *Combinatie Spijker Infrabouw-De Jonge Konstruktie and Others* [2010]
E.C.R. I-12655 ....3.36, 6.21, 6.22
C-573/08 R *Commission v Italy* [2009] E.C.R. I-217*, Summ. pub., (order of the
President of 10 December 2009)...................13.12, 13.31, 13.32, 13.34, 13.41, 13.42
C-576/08 P *People's Mojahedin Organization of Iran v Council* 7.10, 7.11
C-577/08 *Brouwer* [2010] E.C.R. I-7489 ....6.23, 6.34
C-580/08 P *Srinivasan v European Ombudsman* [2009] E.C.R. I-110*, Summ. pub.,
(order of 25 June 2009) 7.01, 7.13, 7.70, 7.219, 8.11
C-582/08 *Commission v United Kingdom* [2010] E.C.R. I-7195 ....5.20, 5.67
C-583/08 P *Gogos v Commission* [2010] E.C.R. I-4469 ....11.20, 16.18, 16.20, 18.28
C-585/08 and C-144/09 *Pammer and Alpenhof* [2010] E.C.R. I-12527 ....3.61

Opinion 1/09 *Draft Agreement Creating a Unified Patent Litigation System (European and
Community Patents Court)* [2011] E.C.R. I-1137 ....1.04, 2.02, 2.03, 2.10,
3.01, 3.14, 4.04, 7.105, 12.01, 12.08, 12.09, 12.15
C-2/09 *Kalinchev* [2010] E.C.R. I-4939 ....6.34
C-14/09 *Genc* [2010] E.C.R. I-931...6.15, 6.18
C-20/09 *Commission v Portugal* [2011] E.C.R. I-2637 ....5.48, 5.58
C-21/09 RX *Review of judgment joined cases T-90/07 P and T-99/07 P Belgium and Commission
v Genette*, not reported, (decision of 5 February 2009) 17.01
C-23/09 P *ecoblue v OHIM* [2010] E.C.R. I-7*, Summ. pub., (order of 22 January 2010) 16.18
C-27/09 P *France v People's Mojahedin Organization of Iran and Others*, not yet reported,
(judgment of 21 December 2011)............................7.161, 16.16, 16.21
C-28/09 *Commission v Austria*, not yet reported, (judgment of 21 December 2011).........5.63, 25.60
C-29/09 P *Marinova v Université Libre de Bruxelles and Commission* [2009] E.C.R. I-115*,
Summ. pub., (order of 1 July 2009)...19.13

C-32/09 P(R) *Artisjus Magyar v Commission* [2010] E.C.R. I-107*, Summ. pub.,
  (order of the President of 31 August 2010). 13.32, 13.44
C-35/09 *Speranza* [2010] E.C.R. I-6581 . . . . 4.20, 6.07
C-36/09 P *Transportes Evaristo Molina v Commission* [2010] E.C.R. I-145*, Summ. pub. 7.211, 25.65
C-38/09 P *Schrader v Community Plant Variety Office* [2010] E.C.R. I-3209 . . . . 16.21
C-39/09 P *SPM v Council and Commission* [2010] E.C.R. I-38*, Summ. pub.,
  (order of 22 March 2010) 11.13, 11.19, 11.34, 1.51
C-41/09 *Commission v Netherlands* [2011] E.C.R. I-831. . . . . 5.02
C-50/09 *Commission v Ireland* [2011] E.C.R. I-873. . . . . 5.02
C-52/09 *TeliaSonera Sverige* [2011] E.C.R. I-527 . . . . 3.28
C-56/09 *Zanotti* [2010] E.C.R. I-4517 . . . . 3.34
C-57/09 and C-101/09 *B and D* [2010] E.C.R. I-10979 . . . . 6.16
C-58/09 *Leo-Libera* [2010] E.C.R. I-5189. . . . . 23.82
C-59/09 P *Hasbro v OHIM* [2009] E.C.R. I-126*, Summ. pub., (order of 10 July 2009). 16.12
C-66/09 P *Kirin Amgen* [2010] E.C.R. I-7943 . . . . 6.22
C-68/09 P *Karatzoglou v European Ageny for Reconstruction and Commission* [2010]
  E.C.R. I-11*, Summ. pub., (order of 29 January 2010). 16.21
C-69/09 P *Makhteshim-Agan Holding and Others v Commission* [2010]
  E.C.R. I-10*, Summ. pub., (order of 22 January 2010). 7.16, 7.18, 8.10, 8.15, 25.81
C-70/09 *Hengartner and Gasser* [2010] E.C.R. I-7233 . . . . 6.14
C-71/09 P, C-73/09 P, and C-76/09 P *Comitato 'Venezia vuole vivere' v
  Commission* [2011] E.C.R. I-4727 . . . 7.122, 7.138, 7.201, 7.217, 10.11, 16.05, 16.19, 16.21, 25.44
C-75/09 *Agra* [2010] E.C.R. I-5595. . . . . 6.23
C-77/09 *Gowan Comércio Internacional e Serviços* [2010] E.C.R. I-13533 . . . . 10.01, 10.15, 10.18
C-79/09 *Commission v Netherlands* [2010] E.C.R. I-40*, Summ. pub. 5.40, 5.48, 5.51
C-81/09 *Idryma Typou* [2010] E.C.R. I-10161 . . . . 6.22
C-83/09 P *Commission v Kronoply and Kronotex* [2011] E.C.R. I-4441 . . . . 7.60, 7.118
C-85/09 P *Portela v Commission* [2009] E.C.R. I-178*, Summ. pub., (order of
  29 October 2009). 11.38, 11.69, 11.83, 16.09
C-90/09 P *General Quimica and Others v Commission* [2011] E.C.R. I-1 . . . . 16.29, 16.30
C-92/09 and C-93/09 *Volker und Schecke and Eifert* [2010]
  E.C.R. I-11063 . . . . .3.36, 6.06, 10.15, 10.18, 10.23, 24.12, 25.61
C-94/09 *Commission v France* [2010] E.C.R. I-4261 . . . . 5.63
C-96/09 P *Anheuser-Busch v Budejovvicky Budvar* [2011] E.C.R. I-2131 . . . . 16.21, 16.29, 16.31
C-98/09 *Francesca Sorge* [2010] E.C.R. I-5837 . . . . 3.31, 6.09
C-102/09 *Camar* [2010] E.C.R. I-4045 . . . . 6.13, 7.106
C-106/09 P and C-107/09 P *Commission and Spain v Government of Gibraltar and
  United Kingdom* [2011] E.C.R. I-11113. . . . . .7.165, 16.21, 16.29, 16.30
C-112/09 P *SGAE v Commission* [2010] E.C.R. I-351, (order of 14 January 2010) 7.208
C-113/09 P(R) *Ziegler v Commission* [2010] E.C.R. I-50*, Summ. pub., (order of the
  President of 30 April 2010). 13.24, 13.29, 13.36, 13.39
C-115/09 *Bund für Umwelt und Naturschutz Deutschland* [2011] E.C.R. I-36 . . . . 4.18
C-118/09 *Koller* [2010] E.C.R. I-13627 . . . . 3.10
C-128/09 to C-131/09, C-134/09 and C-135/09 *Boxus and Others* [2011]
  E.C.R. I-9711 . . . . .3.27, 3.35, 4.07
C-132/09 *Commission v Belgium* [2010] E.C.R. I-8695 . . . . 5.08
C-140/09 *Fallimento Traghetti del Mediterraneo* [2010] E.C.R. I-5243 . . . . 6.23
C-142/09 *Lahousse and Lavichy* [2010] E.C.R. I-11685 . . . . 6.22, 6.25
C-148/09 P *Belgium v Deutsche Post and Others* [2011] E.C.R. I-8573 . . . . 7.118, 16.16
C-154/09 *Commission v Portugal* [2010] E.C.R. I-127*, Summ. pub. 5.15, 5.31
C-160/09 *Iannis Katsivardas-Nikolaos Tsitsikas* [2010] E.C.R. I-4591 . . . . 6.13
C-168/09 *Flos* [2011] E.C.R. I-181 . . . . 6.25
C-173/09 *Elchinov* [2010] E.C.R. I-8889 . . . . 3.07, 3.19, 3.21, 6.27
C-177/09 to C-179/09 *Le Poumon Vert*, not yet reported, (order of 17 November 2011) 4.07
C-180/09 RX Review of judgment T-492/07 P *Sanchez Ferriz and Others v
  Commission*, not reported, (decision of 5 June 2009). 17.01
C-186/09 *Commission v United Kingdom* [2010] E.C.R. I-15*, Summ. pub. 5.37
C-189/09 *Commission v Austria* [2010] E.C.R. I-99*, Summ. pub.. . . . . .5.14, 5.66
C-191/09 P and C-200/09 P *Council and Commission v Interpipe Niko Tube and
  Interpipe NTRP*, not reported, (judgment of 16 February 2012). 7.166, 7.201,
    7.205, 16.04, 16.05, 16.09, 16.21

C-194/09 P *Alcoa Trasformazioni v Commission* [2011] E.C.R. I-6311. . . . . 16.03
C-196/09 *Miles and Others* [2011] E.C.R. I-5105 . . . . 1.04, 2.02, 3.13, 3.14
C-197/09 RX Review of judgment T-12/08 P *M v EMEA* [2009]
  E.C.R. I-12033, (decision of 24 June 2009). 17.01, 17.02
C-197/09 RX-II Review of judgment T-12/08 *M v EMEA* [2009] E.C.R. I-12033,
  (judgment of 17 December 2009) 17.01, 17.02, 17.09
C-201/09 P and C-216/09 P *ArcelorMittal Luxembourg v Commission and Commission
  v ArcelorMittal Luxembourg* [2011] E.C.R. I-2239. . . . . .7.226, 16.14, 23.58
C-203/09 *Volvo Car Germany* [2010] E.C.R. I-10721 . . . . 3.36
C-210/09 *Scott and Kimberly Clark* [2010] E.C.R. I-4613 . . . . 4.31
C-213/09 *Barsoumv Chabo* [2010] E.C.R. I-12109 . . . . 10.18
C-221/09 *AJD Tuna Ltd* [2011] E.C.R. I-1655. . . . . 10.18, 23.82
C-224/09 *Nussbaumer* [2010] E.C.R. I-9295. . . . . 6.23
C-225/09 *Jakubowska* [2010] E.C.R. I-12329 . . . . 3.27, 3.33, 3.35, 3.36
C-232/09 *Danosa* [2010] E.C.R. I-11405 . . . . 6.21
C-236/09 *Test-Achats* [2011] E.C.R. I-773 . . . . 3.20, 10.23
C-239/09 *Seydaland Vereinigte Agrarbetriebe* [2010] E.C.R. I-13083 . . . . .3.23, 6.22, 6.23
C-240/09 *Lesoochranárske zoskupenie VLK* [2011] E.C.R. I-1255 . . . . .4.18, 6.14, 24.18
C-241/09 *Fluxys* [2010] E.C.R. I-12773 . . . . 3.29, 3.35
C-242/09 *Albron Catering* [2010] E.C.R. I-10309 . . . . 6.34
C-243/09 *Fuß* [2010] E.C.R. I-9849 . . . . 6.22
C-245/09 *Omalet NV* [2010] E.C.R. I-13771. . . . . 3.38, 6.24
C-246/09 *Bulicke* [2010] E.C.R. I-7003 . . . . .4.14, 4.32, 6.22
C-250/09 and C-268/09 *Georgiev* [2010] E.C.R. I-11869 . . . . 6.23
C-251/09 *Commission v Cyprus* [2011] E.C.R. I-13*, Summ. pub. 5.46, 5.52
C-256/09 *Purrucker* [2010] E.C.R. I-7353 . . . . 22.05
C-260/09 P *Activision Blizzard Germany v Commission* [2011] E.C.R. I-419 . . . . 16.05
C-261/09 *Mantello* [2010] E.C.R. I-11477 . . . . 22.08
C-263/09 P *Edwin Co. Ltd v OHIM* [2011] E.C.R. I-5853 . . . . 16.08, 16.09, 16.13,
  16.17, 16.18, 20.03, 20.05, 26.03
C-266/09 *Stichting Natuur en Milieu and Others* [2010] E.C.R. I-13119. . . . . 23.81
C-267/09 *Commission v Portugal* [2011] E.C.R. I-3197 . . . . 25.12
C-271/09 *Commission v Poland*, not yet reported, (judgment of 21 December 2011) 5.52
C-272/09 P *KME Germany and Others v Commission*, not yet reported, (judgment of
  8 December 2011) 7.174, 7.191, 7.193, 7.194, 7.195, 15.05
C-279/09 *DEB* [2010] E.C.R. I-13849. . . . . .4.07, 6.22, 25.101
C-283/09 *Weryński* [2011] E.C.R. I-601. . . . . 3.02, 3.10, 3.33, 22.05
C-285/09 *Criminal proceedings against R.* [2010] E.C.R. I-12605 . . . . 3.33
C-291/09 *Franceso Guarnieri & Cie* [2011] E.C.R. I-2685 . . . . 6.22
C-294/09 *Commission v Ireland* [2010] E.C.R. I-46*, Summ. pub. 5.16, 5.60
C-295/09 *Hansen v Commission*, not reported, (order of 17 November 2009) 8.06
C-300/09 and C-301/09 *Toprak and Oguz* [2010] E.C.R. I-12845. . . . . 6.15
C-303/09 *Commission v Italy* [2011] E.C.R. I-102*, Summ. pub. 5.22
C-304/09 *Commission v Italy* [2010] E.C.R. I-13903 . . . . 4.31, 4.62, 5.22, 5.38
C-307/09 to C-309/09 *Vicoplus, Vermeer and Olbek* [2011] E.C.R. I-453 . . . . 3.23, 6.22
C-310/09 Accor [2011] E.C.R. I-8115, (order of the President of 19 October 2009). 6.21, 24.18
C-311/09 *Commission v Poland* [2010] E.C.R. I-55*, Summ. pub. 5.62
C-316/09 *MSD Sharp & Dohme* [2011] E.C.R. I-3249 . . . . 10.14
C-317/09 P *ArchiMEDES v Commission* [2010] E.C.R. I-150*, Summ. pub. 7.138
C-318/09 P *A2A v Commission*, not yet reported, (judgment of 21 December 2011) 16.09
C-319/09 P *ACEA v Commission*, not reported, (judgment of 21 December 2011). 7.138
C-320/09 P *A2A v Commission*, not reported, (judgment of 21 December 2011) 7.122, 7.138, 7.142
C-321/09 P *Greece v Commission* [2011] E.C.R. I-51*, Summ. pub. 15.01
C-322/09 P *NDSHT v Commission* [2010] E.C.R. I-11911 . . . . .7.16, 7.55, 7.61
C-329/09 P *Iride v Commission*, not yet reported, (judgment of 21 December 2011) 16.14
C-331/09 *Commission v Poland* [2011] E.C.R. I-2933 . . . . 5.22
C-335/09 P *Poland v Commission*, not reported, (judgment of
  26 June 2012) 7.211, 16.18, 16.19, 16.27
C-336/09 P *Poland v Commission*, not reported, (judgment of 26 June 2012) 16.29, 16.31
C-337/09 P *Council v Zhejiang Xinan Chemical Industrial Group*, not reported,
  (judgment of 19 July 2012). 16.05, 16.14, 16.19

C-337/09 P-R *Council v Zhejiang Xinan Chemical Industrial Group* [2011] E.C.R. I-77*,
  (order of the President of 18 May 2011) 13.01, 13.26, 25.84
C-338/09 *Yellow Cab Verkehrbetrieb* [2010] E.C.R. I-13927. . . . . 6.22
C-340/09 *Commission v Spain* [2010] E.C.R. I-165*, Summ. pub. 5.63, 5.64
C-343/09 *Afton Chemical* [2010] E.C.R. I-7023 . . . . 9.04, 10.09, 10.11
C-344/09 *Dan Bengtsson* [2011] E.C.R. I-1999, (order of 24 March 2011) 3.10
C-345/09 *van Delft and Others* [2010] E.C.R. I-9879 . . . . 6.21
C-347/09 *Dickinger and Ömer* [2011] E.C.R. I-8185. . . . . 6.22
C-351/09 *Commission v Malta* [2010] I-180*, Summ. pub. 25.37, 25.49
C-352/09 P *ThyssenKrupp Nirosta v Commission* [2011] E.C.R. I-2359 . . . . 16.20, 16.27
C-357/09 PPU *Kadzoev* [2010] E.C.R. I-11189. . . . . 2.12, 22.10
C-359/09 *Ebert* [2011] E.C.R. I-269 . . . . 23.14
C-361/09 P *Molder v Germany* [2010] E.C.R. I-18*, Summ. pub., (order of
  5 February 2010) 11.18
C-362/09 P *Athinaïki Techniki v Commission* [2010] E.C.R. I-13275 . . . . 7.118, 16.20, 16.29, 16.31
C-367/09 *SGS Belgium and Others* [2010] E.C.R. I-10761. . . . . 4.44
C-368/09 *Pannon Gép Centrum* [2010] E.C.R. I-7467. . . . . 6.22, 6.23
C-369/09 P *ISD Polska and Others v Commission* [2011] E.C.R. I-2011 . . . . 7.137, 7.177, 7.210,
                                                                                              7.214, 7.216, 16.20
C-372/09 *Peñarroja Fa* [2011] E.C.R. I-1785 . . . . 3.23
C-374/09 P *Hârsulescu v Romania* [2010] E.C.R. I-30*, Summ. pub., (order of
  4 March 2010). 2.02, 7.72, 8.11, 11.18
C-376/09 *Commission v Malta* [2011] E.C.R. I-4017. . . . . 5.02
C-377/09 *Hanssens-Ensch* [2010] E.C.R. I-7751 . . . . 11.01, 11.04, 19.11
C-379/09 *Casteels* [2011] E.C.R. I-1379 . . . . 3.37
C-380/09 P *Melli Bank v Council*, not reported, (judgment of 13 March 2012). 9.15
C-383/09 *Commission v France* [2011] E.C.R. I-4869 . . . . 5.59, 5.63
C-385/09 *Nidera Handelscompagnie* [2010] E.C.R. I-10385 . . . . 6.23
C-391/09 *Runevič-Vardyn and Wardyn* [2011] E.C.R. I-3787. 3.31, 3.33
C-392/09 *Uszodaépítő* [2010] E.C.R. I-8791 . . . . 6.22
C-393/09 *Bezpečnostní softwarová asociace* [2010] E.C.R. I-13971 . . . . 3.36
C-396/09 *Iteredil* [2011] E.C.R. I-9915 . . . . 3.02, 3.21
C-398/09 *Lady & Kid and Others* [2011] E.C.R. I-7375 . . . . 4.27, 4.28, 11.71
C-400/09 and C-207/10 *Orifarm and Others* [2011] E.C.R. I-7063 . . . . 6.11
C-401/09 P *Evropaïki Dynamiki v ECB* [2011] E.C.R. I-4911 . . . . 7.138, 25.87, 26.04
C-403/09 PPU *Detiček* [2009] E.C.R. I-12193 . . . . 22.11
C-407/09 *Commission v Greece* [2011] E.C.R. I-2467 . . . . 5.78
C-429/09 *Fuß* [2010] E.C.R. I-12167 . . . . 4.48, 4.52, 6.26
C-430/09 *Euro Tyre Holding* [2010] E.C.R. I-13335 . . . . 6.11
C-434/09 *McCarthy* [2011] E.C.R. I-3375 . . . . 6.22, 6.24
C-437/09 *AG2R Prévoyance* [2011] E.C.R. I-973. . . . . 6.22
C-443/09 *Grillo Star Fallimento*, not reported, (judgment of 19 April 2012) 3.10
C-444/09 and C-456/09 *Gaviero Gaviero and Iglesias Torres* [2010] E.C.R. I-14031. . . . . 5.15, 6.09
C-448/09 P *Royal Appliance International GmbH v OHIM* [2010] E.C.R. I-87*,
  Summ. pub., (order of 30 June 2010) 20.03, 20.04
C-450/09 *Schröder* [2011] E.C.R. I-2497 . . . . 3.27, 6.22
C-451/09 P *Pigasos Alieftiki Naftiki Etaireia v Council and Commission* [2010]
  E.C.R. I-62*, Summ. pub., (order of 12 May 2010). 11.07, 11.36, 11.45, 11.85
C-452/09 *Iaia and Others* [2011] E.C.R. I-4043 . . . . 4.35
C-457/09 *Chartry* [2011] E.C.R. I-819, (order of 1 March 2011). 3.39, 6.24
C-458/09 P *Italy v Commission* [2011] E.C.R. I-179*, Summ. pub., (order of the
  President of 17 August 2010) 25.86
C-459/09 P *Dominio de la Vega v OHIM* [2010] E.C.R. I-111*, Summ. pub.,
  (order of 16 September 2010). 16.05
C-460/09 P *Inalca and Cremonini v Commission*, not reported, (judgment of 28 February 2013). . . . 11.87
C-461/09 P *The Wellcome Foundation v OHIM* [2010] E.C.R I-94*, Summ. pub,
  (order of 9 July 2010). 20.03
C-465/09 P to C-470/09 P *Territorio Historico de Vizcaya and Others v Commission* [2011]
  E.C.R. I-83*, Summ. pub. 16.21, 16.24, 16.27
C-471/09 P to C-473/09 P *Territoria Historico de Vizcaya and Others v Commission* [2011]
  E.C.R. I-111*, Summ. pub. 16.05

C-474/09 P to C-476/09 P *Territorio Historico de Vizcaya and Others v Commission* [2011]
 E.C.R. I-113*, Summ. pub. 16.05
C-480/09 P *AceaElectrabel Produzione v Commission* [2010] E.C.R. I-13355 .... 16.09, 16.21
C-482/09 *Budějovický Budvar* [2011] E.C.R. I-8701 .... 3.34
C-483/09 and C-1/10 *Painer and Salmerón Sánchez* [2011] E.C.R. I-8263 .... 3.02, 3.33, 6.21, 6.22
C-489/09 *Vandoorne* [2011] E.C.R. I-225 .... 6.23
C-490/09 *Commission v Luxembourg* [2011] E.C.R. I-247 .... 5.63
C-492/09 *Agricola Esposito* [2010] E.C.R. I-167*, Summ. pub., (order of
 15 December 2010) 3.23, 3.27
C-493/09 *Commission v Portugal*, not reported, (order of the President of 15 July 2010)......... 25.63
C-494/09 *Bolton Alimentari* (judgment of 17 February 2011)............................. 10.11
C-496/09 *Commission v Italy* [2011] E.C.R. I-11483 .... 5.24, 5.78
C-496/09 INT *Italy v Commission*, not reported, (order of 11 July 2013) 25.125
C-498/09 P *Thomson Sales Europe v Commission* [2010] E.C.R. I-79*, Summ. pub., (order of
 10 June 2010) 26.02
C-503/09 *Stewart* [2011] E.C.R. I-6497 .... 3.23, 6.22
C-504/09 P *Commission v Poland*, not reported, (judgment of 29 March 2012)......7.220, 16.21, 25.14
C-505/09 P *Commission v Estonia*, not reported, (judgment of 29 March 2012)........... 7.220, 25.12
C-506/09 P *Portugal v Transnáutica*, not reported, (judgment of 22 March 2012) ... 16.16
C-507/09 P *Goldman Management Inc. v Commission and Bulgaria* [2010] E.C.R. I-57*,
 Summ. pub. 8.11, 11.47, 16.19
C-508/09 *Commission v Italy* [2011] E.C.R. I-18*, Summ. pub........................... 5.54
C-509/09 AJ *eDate*, not reported, (order of 10 December 2010)......................... 24.27
C-512/09 *Commission v Greece* [2010] E.C.R. I-96*, Summ. pub. 5.14
C-513/09 *Commission v Belgium* [2010] E.C.R. I-100*, Summ. pub. 5.37
C-514/09 P *Ségaud v Commission* [2010] E.C.R. I-71*, Summ. pub., (order of
 21 May 2010) 7.18, 11.47
C-517/09 *RTL Belgium* [2010] E.C.R. I-14093 .... 3.08, 3.09
C-520/09 P *Arkema v Commission* [2011] E.C.R. I-8901 .... 16.21
C-521/09 P *Elf Aquitaine v Commission* [2011] E.C.R. I-8947 .... 7.170, 16.20, 16.30
C-522/09 *Commission v Romania* [2011] E.C.R. I-2963 .... 5.48
C-529/09 *Commission v Spain*, not reported, (judgment of 24 January 2013)............... 5.76
C-530/09 *Inter-mark Group* [2011] E.C.R. I-10675 .... 3.23
C-532/09 P *Ivanov v Commission* [2010] E.C.R. I-123*, Summ. pub., (order of
 4 October 2010) 11.05, 11.10
C-537/09 *Bartlett and Others* [2011] E.C.R. I-3417 .... 3.23, 10.15
C-539/09 *Commission v Germany* [2011] E.C.R. I-11235 .... 5.14, 5.31, 5.64
C-542/09 *Commission v The Netherlands*, not reported, (order of the President of
 1 October 2010) 25.63
C-546/09 *Aurubis Balgaria* [2011] E.C.R. I-2531 .... 3.38
C-548/09 P *Bank Melli Iran v Council* [2011] E.C.R. I-11381 .... 9.15
C-550/09 *E and F* [2010] E.C.R. I-6213 .... 1.03, 10.11, 24.19
C-550/09 *E and F*, not reported, (order of the President of 1 March 2010).................. 24.18
C-552/09 P *Ferrero v OHIM* [2011] E.C.R. I-2063 .... 16.05, 16.14

C-2/10 *Azienda Agro-Zootecnica Franchini and Eolica di Altamura* [2011] E.C.R. I-6561 ...... 3.23, 6.23
C-3/10 *Affatato* [2010] E.C.R. I-121*, Summ. pub., (order of 1 October 2010) 4.45, 24.18
C-5/10 P-R *Torresan v OHIM* [2010] E.C.R. I-64*, Summ. pub., (order of the President
 of 12 May 2010) 13.14, 13.22, 13.35
C-14/10 *Nickel Institute* [2011] E.C.R. I-6609 .... 10.18
C-15/10 *Etimine* [2011] E.C.R I-6681 .... 6.07, 10.18
C-17/10 *Toshiba Corporation and Others*, not yet reported, (judgment of
 14 February 2012) 6.07, 7.178
C-20/10 *Cosimo Damiano Vino*, not reported, (order of the President of 16 March 2010)......... 24.18
C-25/10 *Missionswerk Werner Heukelbach* [2011] E.C.R. I-497............................ 3.23
C-26/10 P *Hansen v Commission* [2010] E.C.R. I-58*, (order of 6 May 2010)......... 8.06, 8.23, 16.19
C-28/10 P *Bayramoglu v European Parliament and Council* [2010] E.C.R. I-108*,
 (order of 2 September 2010)... 16.20, 26.02
C-29/10 *Koelzsch* [2011] E.C.R. I-1595 .... 6.05, 21.03
C-30/10 *Andersson* [2011] E.C.R. I-513 .... 3.23, 6.22
C-32/10 *Semerdzhiev* [2011] E.C.R. I-71*, Summ. pub., (order of 11 May 2011) 3.36

C-40/10 *Commission v Council* [2010] E.C.R. I-12043. . . . . 7.01, 7.178, 7.221, 25.65, 25.69, 25.81
C-42/10, C-45/10, and C-57/10 *Vlaamse Dierenartsenvereniging VZW and Janssens* [2011]
    E.C.R. I-2975 . . . . 3.22
C-47/10 P *Austria v Scheucher-Fleisch and Others* [2011]
    E.C.R. I-10707 . . . . 7.120, 16.03, 16.05, 16.09, 16.20
C-50/10 *Commission v Italy*, not reported, (order of 7 April 2011) 25.133
C-58/10 to C-68/10 *Monsanto and Others* [2011] E.C.R. I-7763 . . . . 6.22
C-69/10 *Samba Diouf* [2011] E.C.R. I-7151 . . . . 4.07
C-73/10 P *Internationale Fruchtimport Gesellschaft Weichert v Commmission* [2010]
    E.C.R. I-11535, (order of 16 November 2010) 7.207, 7.208
C-76/10 *Pohotovost* [2010] E.C.R. I-11557, (order of 16 November 2010) 3.28
C-81/10 P *France Telecom v Commission*, not yet reported, (judgment of 8 December 2011) 16.09
C-89/10 and C-96/10 *Q-Beef and Bosschaert* [2011] E.C.R. I-7819. . . . . 4.25
C-94/10 *Danfoss* [2011] E.C.R. I-9963. . . . . 4.21, 4.27
C-101/10 *Pavlov and Famira* [2011] E.C.R. I-5951. . . . . 6.13
C-104/10 *Kelly* [2011] E.C.R. I-6813. . . . . 3.22, 6.23
C-106/10 *Lidl & Companhia* [2011] E.C.R. I-7235. . . . . 3.34
C-109/10 P *Solvay v Commission* [2011] E.C.R. I-10329 . . . . 7.162, 7.163, 16.05, 16.29, 16.30
C-110/10 P *Solvay v Commission* [2011] E.C.R. I-10439 . . . . 7.36, 7.162, 7.163,
                                      16.05, 16.29, 16.30, 25.49
C-115/10 *Bábolna* [2011] E.C.R. I-5017 . . . . 3.23, 6.22
C-124/10 P *Commission v EDF*, not reported, (judgment of 5 June 2012). 16.21
C-126/10 *Foggia* [2011] E.C.R. I-10923. . . . . .3.23, 3.31, 3.38
C-128/10 and C-129/10 *Thasou and Etairia* [2011] E.C.R. I-1885. . . . . 6.21
C-130/10 *European Parliament v Council*, not reported, (order of 19 July 2012) 7.151
C-132/10 *Halley* [2011] E.C.R. I-8353. . . . . 6.22
C-134/10 *Commission v Belgium* [2011] E.C.R. I-1053 . . . . 5.52
C-135/10 *Società Consortile Fonografici*, not reported, (judgment of 15 March 2012) 3.23, 3.28
C-143/10 P *Uznański v Poland* [2010] E.C.R. I-153*, Summ. pub., (order of
    9 November 2010). 7.72
C-145/10 *Painer*, not yet reported, (judgment of 1 December 2011). 3.02, 3.36
C-145/10 REC *Painer*, not reported, (order of 7 March 2013) 3.36
C-148/10 *DHL International* [2011] E.C.R. I-9543. . . . . 3.16, 3.29
C-149/10 *Chatzi* [2010] E.C.R. I-8489 . . . . 6.09
C-151/10 *Dai Cugini* [2011] E.C.R. I-54*, Summ. pub., (order of 7 April 2011) 3.23
C-155/10 *Williams and Others* [2011] E.C.R. I-8409. . . . . 6.09
C-157/10 *Banco Bilbao Vizcaya Argentaria*, not yet reported, (judgment of 8 December 2011) 3.23
C-159/10 and C-160/10 *Fuchs and Köhler* [2011] E.C.R. I-6919 . . . . .3.23, 6.22, 6.23
C-163/10 *Patriciello* [2011] E.C.R I-7565. . . . . 6.04, 6.23
C-177/10 *Rosado Santana* [2011] E.C.R. I-7907 . . . . 4.25
C-182/10 *Solvay and Others*, not reported, (judgment of 16 February 2012) 4.07
C-183/10 RX Review of judgment T-338/07 P *Bianchi v ETF*, not reported, (decision of
    5 May 2010) 17.01
C-188/10 and C-189/10 *Melki and Abdeli* [2010] E.C.R. I-5667, (order of the President
    of 12 May 2010). 3.07, 3.20, 3.28, 3.34, 4.36, 6.21, 10.14, 22.19, 24.18, 24.19, 25.81
C-190/10 *Génesis v Boys Toys*, not reported, (judgment of 22 March 2012) 3.34
C-197/10 *Unió de Pagesos de Catalunya* [2011] E.C.R. I-8495 . . . . 3.35
C-200/10 P *Evropaiki Dynamiki v Commission* [2011] E.C.R. I-67*, Summ. pub. 16.02, 16.09, 16.31,
                                            19.10, 25.136, 26.02
C-205/10 P, C-217/10 P, and C-222/10 P *Eriksen and Others v Commission* [2011]
    E.C.R. I-1*, Summ. pub. 11.03, 11.47
C-211/10 PPU *Povse* [2010] E.C.R. I-6673. . . . . 22.11
C-212/10 *Logstor ROR Polska* [2011] E.C.R. I-5453 . . . . 6.21
C-215/10 *Pacific World Limited and FDD International Limited* [2011] E.C.R. I-7255. . . . . 10.18
C-216/10 P *Lufthansa AirPlus Servicekarten v OHIM* [2010] E.C.R. I-157*, Summ. pub. 20.12
C-221/10 P *Artegodan v Commission and Germany*, not reported, (judgment of
    19 April 2012) 7.227, 11.09, 11.11, 11.38, 11.45, 11.48, 11.52, 11.57, 11.61, 11.62, 16.27
C-228/10 *UEFA and British Sky Broadcasting*, not reported, (order of the President of
    31 August 2010) 24.18
C-240/10 *Schulz-Delzers and Schulz* [2011] E.C.R. I-8531 . . . . 6.22, 6.23
C-242/10 *Enel Produzione*, not yet reported, (judgment of 21 December 2011). 3.23

C-249/10 P *Brosmann Footwear (HK) and Others v Council*, not reported, (judgment of
  2 February 2012) 16.30
C-251/10 P *KEK Diavlos v Commission*, not reported, (order of 9 November 2010) 2.29
C-252/10 P *Evropaïki Dynamiki v European Maritime Safety Agency* [2011] E.C.R. I-107*,
  Summ. pub. 16.19
C-254/10 P *Centre de Coordination Carrefour v Commission* [2011] E.C.R. I-19*,
  Summ. pub., (order of 3 March 2011) 7.138
C-262/10 *Döhler Neuenkirchen*, not reported, (judgment of 6 September 2012) 23.81, 23.82, 24.14
C-263/10 *Nisipeanu* [2011] E.C.R. I-97*, Summ. pub. 6.34
C-264/10 *Kita*, not reported, (order of the President of 15 July 2010) 24.18
C-266/10 P *Seacid v European Parliament and Council* [2010] E.C.R. I-133*,
  Summ. pub., (order of 22 October 2010) 7.207, 7.211
C-267/10 and C-268/10 *Rossius and Collard* [2011] E.C.R. I-81*, Summ. pub.,
  (order of 23 May 2011) 3.39, 6.24
C-270/10 *Gistö* [2011] E.C.R. I-7277 . . . . 6.04
C-275/10 *Residex Capital*, not yet reported, (judgment of December 8, 2011) 7.54
C-281/10 P *PepsiCo v Grupo Promer Mon Graphic* [2011] E.C.R. I-10153 . . . . 16.05, 20.03
C-282/10 *Maribel Dominguez*, not reported, (judgment of 24 January 2012) 4.37
C-283/10 *Circul Globus Bucureşti* [2011] E.C.R. I-12031 . . . . 3.36
C-296/10 *Purrucker* [2010] E.C.R. I-11163, (order of the President of 15 July 2010) 22.19, 24.18
C-307/10 *Chartered Institute of Patent Attorneys v Register of Trade Marks*, not reported,
  (judgment of June 19, 2012) 3.33
C-309/10 *Agrana Zucker* [2011] E.C.R. I-7333 . . . . 10.01, 10.15, 10.16, 10.18
C-310/10 *Agafiţei and Others* [2011] E.C.R. I-5989 . . . . 3.36, 3.38, 6.17
C-314/10 *Pagnoul* [2011] E.C.R. I-136*, Summ. pub., (order of 22 September 2011) 3.39
C-316/10 *Danske Svineproducenter*, not yet reported, (judgment of 21 December 2011) 3.27
C-317/10 P *Union Investments Privatfonds v UniCredito Italiano and OHIM* [2011]
  E.C.R. I-5471 . . . . 16.05, 16.31
C-319/10 and C-320/10 *X and X* [2011] E.C.R. I-167*, Summ. pub. 3.23
C-338/10 *GLS*, not reported, (order of 15 June 2011) 24.23
C-338/10 *GLS*, not reported, (judgment of 22 March 2012) 10.15, 10.17, 10.18
C-339/10 *Asparuhov Estov* [2010] E.C.R. I-11465, (order of 12 November 2010) 3.39, 6.24
C-342/10 *Commission v Finland*, not reported, (judgment of 8 November 2012) 25.11
C-344/10 P and C-345/10 P *Freixenet v OHIM* [2011] E.C.R. I-10205 . . . . 16.30
C-349/10 P *Claro v OHIM* [2011] E.C.R. I-17*, Summ. pub., (order of 2 March 2011) 20.12
C-354/10 *Commission v Greece*, not reported, (judgment of 1 March 2012) 5.22, 23.05
C-355/10 *European Parliament v Council*, not reported, (judgment of 5 September 2012) 7.153
C-364/10 *Hungary v Slovak Republic*, not reported, (judgment of 16 October 2012) 5.35
C-366/10 *Air Transport Association of America and Others*, not yet reported,
  (judgment of 21 December 2011) 6.13, 10.08, 10.13, 10.14
C-367/10 P *EMC Development v Commission* [2011] E.C.R. I-46*, Summ. pub.,
  (order of 31 March 2011) 16.19
C-369/10 P *Ravensburger v OHIM* [2011] E.C.R. I-26*, Summ. pub. 16.05, 25.10
C-373/10 P(R) *Almamet v Commission* [2010] E.C.R. I-171*, Summ. pub., (order of the
  President of 16 December 2010) 13.29, 13.36, 13.39, 16.21
C-376/10 P *Tay Za v Council*, not reported, (judgment of 13 March 2012) 7.11, 16.30
C-377/10 *Adrian Băilă* [2010] E.C.R. I-161, (order of 6 December 2010) 3.36
C-379/10 *Commission v Italy* [2011] E.C.R. I-180*, Summ. pub. 4.50
C-384/10 *Voogsgeerd*, not yet reported, (judgment of 15 December 2011) 6.05, 21.03
C-386/10 P *Chalkor v Commission*, not yet reported, (judgment of
  8 December 2011) 7.193, 7.194, 15.05, 15.06, 15.07, 15.09, 16.11
C-389/10 P *KME Germany and Others v Commission*, not yet reported, (judgment of
  8 December 2011) 7.174, 7.191, 7.193, 7.194, 7.196, 15.05
C-399/10 P and C-401/10 P *Bouygues v Commission*, not reported, (judgment of
  19 March 2013) 7.27, 7.28, 7.61, 16.21
C-400/10 PPU *McB* [2010] E.C.R. I-8965 . . . . 22.11
C-404/10 P *Commission v Editions Odile Jacob*, not reported, (judgment of
  28 June 2012) 16.20, 16.29, 16.30, 26.11
C-404/10 P-R *Commission v Éditions Odile Jacob* [2011] E.C.R. I-6*, Summ. pub.,
  (order of the President of 31 January 2011) 13.01, 13.31, 13.32
C-411/10 *N.S.*, not reported, (order of the President of 1 October 2010) 24.18

C-416/10 *Križan*, not reported, (judgment of 15 January 2013) 3.19, 3.21, 3.49, 24.18
C-422/10 *Georgetown University and Others* [2011] E.C.R. I-12157 . . . . 23.45
C-426/10 P *Bell & Ross v OHIM* [2011] E.C.R. I-8849 . . . . .7.208, 23.38, 23.51
C-427/10 *Banca Antoniana Popolare Veneta*, not yet reported, (judgment of 15 December 2011) 4.25
C-431/10 *Commission v Ireland* [2011] E.C.R. I-56*, Summ. pub. 5.70
C-433/10 P *Mauerhofer v Commission* [2011] E.C.R. I-48*, Summ. pub., (order of
    31 March 2011) 11.78, 11.81, 16.03, 16.04, 16.05, 16.07, 16.20
C-441/10 *Ioan Anghel* [2010] E.C.R. I-164*, Summ. pub. 3.27
C-442/10 *Churchill Insurance Company*, not yet reported, (judgment of 1 December 2011) 3.23
C-446/10 P(R) *Alco Transformazioni v Commission*, not yet reported, (order of the President of
    14 December 2011) 13.24, 13.32, 13.36, 13.40
C-448/10 P to C-450/10 P *ThyssenKrupp and Others v Commission* [2011] E.C.R. I-147*,
    Summ. pub., (order of 6 October 2011) 16.03, 16.04, 16.05
C-451/10 P-DEP *France Télévisions v TF1*, not reported, (order of 7 June 2012) 25.93
C-452/10 P *BNP Paribas and BNL v Commission*, not reported, (judgment of
    21 June 2012) 16.28, 16.30
C-460/10 P *Marcuccio v Court of Justice of the European Union* [2011] E.C.R. I-63*, (order of
    14 April 2011) 11.64, 16.24
C-461/10 *Bonnier Audio and Others*, not reported, (judgment of 19 April 2012) 3.23
C-462/10 P *Evropaïki Dynamiki v European Environment Agency*, not reported, (order of
    13 January 2012) 16.04, 16.19, 16.24
C-463/10 P and C-475/10 P *Deutsche Post and Germany v Commission* [2011]
    E.C.R. I-9639 . . . . .7.16, 7.21, 7.28, 7.59, 16.27, 16.29
C-477/10 P *Commission v Agrofert Holding*, not reported, (judgment of 28 June 2012) 16.28, 16.30
C-478/10 RX *Review of judgment T-157/09 P Marcuccio v Commission*, not reported,
    (decision of 27 October 2010) 17.01, 18.18
C-482/10 *Cicala*, not yet reported, (judgment of 21 December 2011) 3.38, 6.17
C-484/10 *Ascafor and Asidac*, not reported, (judgment of 1 March 2012) 3.23
C-489/10 *Criminal proceedings against Łukasz Marcin Bonda*, not reported, (judgment of
    5 June 2012) 4.42
C-490/09 *Commission v Luxembourg* [2011] E.C.R. I-247 . . . . 5.63
C-491/10 PPU *Aguirre Zarraga* [2010] E.C.R. I-14247 . . . . 22.09
C-503/10 *Evroetil*, not yet reported, (judgment of 21 December 2011) 3.32
C-507/10 *Criminal proceedings against X*, not yet reported, (judgment of 21 December 2011) . . . 3.02, 6.05
C-513/10 P *Platis v Council and Greece* [2010] E.C.R. I-176*, Summ. pub., (order of
    17 December 2010) 7.72, 7.207, 7.219
C-521/10 P *Grúas Abril Assistencia v Commission* [2011] E.C.R. I-90*, Summ. pub.,
    (order of 22 June 2011) 7.18
C-525/10 P *Noko Ngele v Commission* [2011] E.C.R. I-24*, Summ. pub., (order of
    10 March 2011) 11.34, 16.25
C-526/10 P(R) *Noko Ngele v Commission* [2010] E.C.R. I-173*, Summ. pub.,
    (order of the President of 16 December 2010) 13.04, 13.07, 13.11
C-530/10 P(R) *Nencini v European Parliament* [2011] E.C.R. I-172*, Summ. pub.,
    (order of the President of 11 November 2011) 13.26, 13.29, 13.40
C-534/10 P *Brookfield New Zealand and Elaris v CPVO and Schniga*, not reported,
    (judgment of 19 December 2012) 20.15
C-538/10 *Lebrun and Howet* [2011] E.C.R. I-137*, Summ. pub., (order of 22 September 2011) 3.39
C-539/10 P and C-550/10 P *Al-Aqsa v Council and Netherlands v Al-Aqsa*, not reported,
    (judgment of 15 November 2012) 7.162, 7.170, 9.05
C-547/10 P *Swiss Confederation v Commission*, not reported, (judgment of 7 March 2013) 2.53, 7.82
C-549/10 P *Tomra Systems and Others v Commission*, not reported,
    (judgment of 19 April 2012) 16.20
C-559/10 *Deli Ostrich* [2011] E.C.R. I-10873 . . . . 3.31
C-560/10 P *Evropaïki Dynamiki v Commission* [2011] E.C.R. I-151*, Summ. pub.,
    (order of 13 October 2011) 11.35
C-561/10 P *Evropaïki Dynamiki v Commission* [2011] E.C.R. I-130*, Summ. pub.,
    (order of 20 September 2011) 11.11
C-566/10 P *Italy v Commission*, not reported, (judgment of 27 November 2012) 7.175, 7.221
C-571/10 *Servet Kamberaj*, not reported, (judgment of 24 April 2012) 3.35, 3.36, 6.24
C-573/10 *Micşa*, not reported, (order of the President of 31 January 2011) 24.18

C-581/10 and C-629/10 *Nelson and Others*, not reported, (judgment of
    23 October 2012)...6.11, 6.34, 10.08
C-583/10 *Nolan*, not reported, (judgment of 18 October 2012) 3.38, 6.17
C-584/10 P, C-593/10 P, and C-595/10 P *Commission and Others v Kadi*, not reported,
    (judgment of 18 July 2013)............7.161, 7.170, 7.173, 7.178, 23.61, 23.66, 23.81, 23.83
C-591/10 *Littlewoods Retail Ltd and Others v Her Majesty's Commissioners of Revenue and
    Customs*, not reported, (judgment of 18 July 2012)........................... 4.30
C-596/10 *Commission v Poland*, not reported, (judgment of 27 June 2013).................... 5.52
C-602/10 *SC Volksbank România*, not reported, (judgment of 12 July 2012).................. 3.31
C-605/10 P(R) *Inuit Tapiriit Kanatami v European Parliament and Council* [2011]
    E.C.R. I-164*, Summ. pub., (order of the President of 27 October 2011) 13.26, 13.45, 16.14
C-613/10 *Danilo Debiasi*, not reported, (order of 15 April 2011) 3.26, 3.33
C-617/10 *Åkerberg Fransson*, not reported, (judgment of
    26 February 2013) 3.39, 4.44, 5.06, 6.06, 6.24, 24.32
C-618/10 *Banco Español de Crédito*, not reported, (judgment of 14 June 2012) 4.41
C-626/10 P *Joséphidès v Commission and EACEA* [2011] E.C.R. I-169*,
    Summ. pub., (order of 10 November 2011)........................7.73, 7.216, 16.19
C-628/10 P and C-14/11 P *Alliance One and Others v Commission*, not reported,
    (judgment of 19 July 2012)...7.173, 7.192

C-1/11 *SA Marcuccio v Commission*, not reported, (order of
    19 November 2012)......................................14.01, 14.03, 14.05, 14.06
C-17/11 RX Review of judgment T-143/09 P *Commission v Petrilli*, not reported,
    (decision of 8 February 2011) 11.36, 17.01, 17.03
C-21/11 *Volturno Trasporti Sas di Santoro Nino*, not reported, (order of 7 June 2012) 3.27
C-24/11 P *Spain v Commission*, not reported, (judgment of 3 May 2012) 16.29, 16.30
C-25/11 *Varzim Sol—Turismo, Jogo e Animação*, not reported, (judgment of
    16 February 2012) 3.23, 3.25, 3.27
C-27/11 *Anton Vinkov*, not reported, (judgment of 7 June 2012) 3.36, 22.05
C-34/11 *Commission v Portugal*, not reported, (judgment of 15 November 2012)............ 5.52, 5.58
C-35/11 *Test Claimants in the FII Group Litigation*, not yet reported, (judgment of
    13 November 2012)...6.11, 6.28, 24.29, 24.30
C-41/11 *Inter-Environnement Wallonie and Terre wallone*, not reported, (judgment of
    28 February 2012) 3.31, 10.20
C-45/11 P *Deutsche Bahn v OHIM*, not yet reported, (order of 7 December 2011) 20.12
C-52/11 P *Victoria Sánchez v European Parliament and Commission* [2011] E.C.R. I-158*,
    Summ. pub., (order of 26 October 2011) 8.07, 8.23, 16.19
C-53/11 P *OHIM v Nike International*, not reported, (judgment of
    January 19, 2012)......................................16.29, 16.31, 20.13
C-59/11 *Association Kokopelli*, not reported, (judgment of 12 July 2012)...................... 10.11
C-61/11 *PPU El Dridi* [2011] E.C.R. I-3015 .... 22.11
C-62/11 *Feyerbacher*, not reported, (order of 4 July 2012) 23.82
C-67/11 P *DTL Corporacion v OHIM* [2011] E.C.R. I-156*, Summ. pub.,
    (order of 20 October 2011)... 16.14
C-73/11 P *Frucona Košice v Commission*, not reported, (judgment of 24 January 2013).......... 7.201
C-76/11 P *Tresplain Investments v OHIM* [2011] E.C.R. I-182*, Summ. pub.,
    (order of 29 November 2011) 16.08, 16.20
C-79/11 *Criminal proceedings against Maurizio Giovanardi*, not reported, (judgment of
    12 July 2012)..3.02, 22.05
C-84/11 *Susisalo and Others*, not reported, (judgment of 21 June 2012) 3.38
C-87/11 P *Fidelio v OHIM*, not reported, (order of 21 March 2012) 16.19
C-88/11 P *LG Electronicsv OHIM* [2011] E.C.R. I-171*, Summ. pub. 16.03, 20.15
C-89/11 P *E.ON Energie v Commission*, not reported, (judgment of 22 November 2012).......... 7.33
C-93/11 P *Verein Deutsche Sprache v Council* [2011] E.C.R. I-92*, Summ. pub., (order of
    28 June 2011) 8.04, 8.19, 11.12
C-96/11 P *August Storck v OHIM*, not reported, (judgment of 6 September 2012)............. 20.12
C-97/11 P *Amia*, not reported, (judgment of 24 May 2012) 3.18
C-100/11 P *Helena Rubinstein and L'Oréal v OHIM*, not reported, (judgment of
    12 May 2012) 16.03, 16.04, 16.09, 20.12
C-103/11 P *Commission v Systran and Systran Luxembourg*, not reported, (judgment of
    18 April 2013)..11.06, 19.10, 19.11

C-111/11 P *Ruipérez Aguirre and ATC Petition v Commission* [2011] E.C.R. I-104*,
 Summ. pub., (order of 14 July 2011). 7.18
C-118/11 *Eon Aset Menidjmunt*, not reported, (judgment of 16 February 2012) 3.23, 3.36
C-122/11 *Commission v Belgium*, not reported, (judgment of 7 February 2013). 5.62
C-135/11 P *IFAW v Commission*, not reported, (judgment of 21 June 2012). 16.31, 23.61
C-144/11 *Abdallah*, not reported, (order of 8 September 2011) 3.26
C-150/11 *Commission v Belgium*, not reported, (judgment of 6 September 2012). 25.12
C-153/11 *Klub*, not reported, (judgment of 22 March 2012) 3.23
C-155/11 *PPU Mohammad Imran* [2011] E.C.R. I-5095, (order of 10 June 2011) 22.12
C-157/11 *Sibilio*, not reported, (judgment of 15 March 2012) 3.31, 3.35
C-161/11 *Cosimo Damiano Vino* [2011] E.C.R. I-91*, Summ. pub., (order of 22 June 2011). 3.36
C-172/11 *Erny*, not reported, (judgment of 28 June 2012). 3.23
C-181/11 P *Cetarsa v Commission*, not reported, (judgment of 12 July 2012). 15.09
C-196/11 P *Formula One Licensing v OHIM*, not reported, (judgment of 24 May 2012) 16.31
C-199/11 *Europese Gemeenschap v Otis and Others*, not reported, (judgment of
 6 November 2012). 4.54, 7.174, 7.193, 7.194, 7.195
C-200/11 P *Italy v Commission*, not reported, (order of 22 March 2012). 16.19
C-208/11 P *Internationaler Hilfsfonds v Commission*, not reported, (order of
 15 February 2012) 7.67, 7.138, 16.22
C-222/11 P *Longetivity v OHIM*, not yet reported, (order of 1 December 2011) 16.18
C-226/11 P *Expedia*, not reported, (judgment of 13 December 2012) 7.25
C-235/11 P *Evropaiki Dynamiki v Commission* [2011] E.C.R. I-183*, Summ. pub.,
 (order of 29 November 2011) 11.11, 16.20
C-237/11 and C-238/11 *France v European Parliament*, not reported, (judgment of
 13 December 2012) 7.19, 7.24, 7.150
C-239/11 P *Siemens v Commission*, not reported, (order of the President of 16 April 2012). 25.63
C-240/11 P *World Wide Tobacco España v Commission*, not reported, (order of 3 May 2012) 16.19
C-241/11 *Commission v Czech Republic*, not reported, (judgment of 25 June 2013) 5.75, 5.78
C-242/11 P *Caixa Geral de Depositos v Commission*, not reported, (order of 16 May 2013) 7.96, 19.10
C-246/11 P *Portugal v Commission*, not reported, (judgment of 28 February 2013) 7.145, 7.219
C-251/11 *Huet*, not reported, (judgment of 8 March 2012) 3.19
C-256/11 *Dereci* [2011] E.C.R. I-11315. . . . . 6.24
C-262/11 *Kremikovtzi*, not reported, (judgment of 29 November 2012) 7.53
C-264/11 P *Kaimer and Others v Commission*, not reported, (judgment of 19 July 2012) 15.04
C-272/11 P *Noko Ngele v Commission and Others* [2011] E.C.R. I-145*, Summ. pub.,
 (order of 4 October 2011). 11.18, 11.38, 11.81, 26.02
C-274/11 and C-295/11 *Spain and Italy v Council*, not reported, (judgment of
 16 April 2013) 7.181, 7.183
C-277/11 *M.*, not reported, (judgment of 22 November 2012) 7.161
C-278/11 P *Dover v European Parliament*, not reported, (order of 12 July 2012) 16.18
C-279/11 *Commission v Ireland*, not reported, (judgment of 19 December 2012). 5.78
C-286/11 P *Commission v Tomkins*, not reported, (judgment of 22 January 2013) 7.86, 7.226
C-287/11 P *Commission v Aalberts Industries and Others*, not reported,
 (judgment of 4 July 2013). 15.04, 23.56, 23.62
C-288/11 P *Mitteldeutsche Flughafen and Flughafen Leipzig-Halle v Commission*, not reported,
 (judgment of 19 December 2012) 7.138
C-289/11 P *Legris Industries v Commission*, not reported, (order of 3 May 2012) 16.20
C-290/11 P *Comap v Commission*, not reported, (judgment of 3 May 2011) . . .16.03, 16.04, 16.18, 16.20
C-291/11 *TNT Freight Management*, not reported, (judgment of 12 July 2012). 6.22
C-292/11 P *Portugal v Commission*, not reported, (judgment of 15 January 2014) 5.80, 7.18
C-300/11 *ZZ*, not reported, (judgment of 4 June 2013). 7.173, 23.61
C-301/11 *REC Commission v Netherlands*, not reported, (order of 19 March 2013) 25.134
C-307/11 P *Deichmann v OHIM*, not reported, (order of 26 April 2012) 16.20
C-329/11 *Achughbabian*, not yet reported, (order of the President of 30 September 2011) . . . 22.19, 24.27
C-335/11 and C-337/11 *HK Danmark*, not reported, (judgment of 11 April 2013). 6.13
C-338/11 to C-347/11 *Santander Asset Management SGIIC*, not reported,
 (judgment of 10 May 2012) 6.34
C-348/11 *Thomson Sales Europe*, not reported, (order of 23 March 2012) 3.26, 3.33
C-363/11 *Epitropos Tou Elegktikou Synedriou*, not reported, (judgment of 19 December 2012) 3.10
C-364/11 *Mostafa Abed El Karem El Kott and Others*, not reported, (judgment of
 19 December 2012) 24.10, 24.26

C-371/11 *Punch Graphic Prepress Belgium*, not reported, (judgment of 18 October 2012)......... 6.17
C-374/11 *Commission v Ireland*, not reported, (judgment of 19 December 2012).............. 5.77
C-394/11 *Belov*, not reported, (judgment of 31 January 2013) 3.09
C-396/11 *Ciprian Vasile Radu*, not reported, (judgment of 29 January 2013) 3.35
C-399/11 *Stefano Melloni*, not reported, (judgment of 26 February 2013) 3.17, 3.32, 3.39,
                                                            5.06, 6.06, 6.24
C-404/11 P *Elf Aquitaine v Commission*, not reported, (order of 2 February 2012)......... 15.05, 15.07
C-405/11 P *Commission v Buczek Automotive*, not reported, (judgment of 21 March 2013) 7.201
C-406/11 P *Atlas Transport v OHIM*, not reported, (order of 9 March 2012) 16.19
C-411/11 P *Altner v Commission*, not yet reported, (order of 15 December 2011) 7.18, 8.06
C-413/11 *Germanwings*, not reported, (order of 18 April 2013) 6.11, 24.15
C-414/11 *Daiichi Sankyo*, not reported, (judgment of 18 July 2013)................. 6.14
C-415/11 *Aziz*, not reported, (judgment of 14 March 2013) 4.41, 6.26
C-417/11 P *Council v Bamba*, not reported, (judgment of 15 November 2012)........... 7.162, 7.170
C-418/11 *TEXDATA Software*, not reported, (judgment of 26 September 2013) 4.44
C-421/11 P *Total and Elf Aquitaine v Commission*, not reported,
   (order of 7 February 2012) 15.07, 16.09, 16.19
C-422/11 *Prezes Urzędu Komunikacji Elektronicznej and Poland v Commission*, not reported,
   (order of the President of 16 April 2012) 25.65, 25.69
C-429/11 P *Gosselin v Commission*, not reported, (judgment of 11 July 2013) 7.26
C-434/11 *Corpul Naţional al Poliţiştilor*, not yet reported, (order of 14 December 2011) 3.39
C-439/11 P *Ziegler v Commission*, not reported, (judgment of 11 July 2013)................. 25.43
C-441/11 P *Commission v Verhuizingen Coppens*, not reported, (judgment of 6 December 2012).... 7.220
C-462/11 *Cozman, not yet reported*, (order of 14 December 2011)...................... 3.39, 6.24
C-466/11 *Currà and Others*, not reported, (order of 12 July 2012) 3.39
C-469/11 P *Evropaiki Dynamiki v Commission*, not reported, (judgment of
   8 November 2012).........................11.86, 11.93, 23.26, 23.32
C-470/11 *SIA Garkalns*, not reported, (judgment of 19 July 2012)...................... 3.31, 3.38
C-474/11 P *Smanor v Commission and European Ombudsman* (order of
   1 March 2012)..8.06, 11.27, 16.19
C-478/11 to C-482/11 P *Gbagbo and Others v Council*, not reported, (judgment of
   23 April 2013)..7.208, 7.211, 23.30, 25.81
C-483/11 and C-484/11 *Boncea and Others*, not yet reported, (order of 14 December
   2011) 3.39
C-492/11 *Di Donna*, not reported, (judgment of 27 June 2013)...................... 3.35, 24.23
C-507/11 P(R) *Fapricela v Commission*, not reported, (order of the President of 20 April 2012) 13.24
C-511/11 P *Versalis v Commission*, not reported, (judgment of 13 June 2013) 7.173
C-533/11 *Commission v Belgium*, not reported, (judgment of 17 October 2013) 5.37, 5.77
C-564/11 *Consulta Regionale Ordine Ingegneri Della Lombardia and Others*, not reported,
   (order of 16 May 2013) 24.15
C-565/11 *Mariana Irimie*, not reported, (judgment of 18 April 2013)................. 4.30, 4.52
C-570/11 P(R) *Gollnisch v European Parliament*, not reported, (order of the President of
   29 March 2012).. 13.04, 13.05
C-573/11 *ClientEarth v Council*, not reported, (order of 5 September 2013) 23.19
C-581/11 P *Mugraby v Council and Commission*, not reported, (order of
   12 July 2012)...................... 8.06, 8.08, 8.23, 11.13, 11.51, 16.18
C-583/11 P *Inuit Tapiriit Kanatami and Others v Parliament and Council*, not reported,
   (judgment of 3 October 2013) 7.107, 7.108
C-584/11 P *Dow AgroSciences and Others v Commission*, not reported 9.08, 26.07
C-587/11 P-R and C-588/11 P-R *Omnicare v OHIM*, not reported, (order of the President
   of 19 July 2012)... 13.14, 13.22
C-588/11 P *Omnicare v OHIM*, not reported, (order of 18 September 2012) 25.100
C-597/11 P *Evropaiki Dynamiki v Commission*, not reported, (order of 4 October 2012) 11.34
C-602/11 P(I) *Schenker v Deutsche Lufthansa and Others*, not reported, (order of the President of
   8 June 2012) 16.12
C-615/11 P *Commission v Ryanair*, not reported, (judgment of 16 May 2013)............. 8.06, 8.13
C-617/11 P *Marcuccio v Commission*, not reported, (order of 3 October 2013)............... 18.28
C-623/11 P *Geodis Calberson GE*, not reported, (judgment of 17 January 2013) 19.05, 19.10
C-625/11 P *PPG and SNF v ECHA*, not reported, (judgment of 26 September 2013) 7.210, 23.30
C-626/11 P *PPG and SNF v ECHA*, not reported, (judgment of 26 September 2013) 7.210
C-629/11 P *Evropaiki Dynamiki v Commission*, not reported, (judgment of 4 October 2012) 11.11

C-644/11 P(R) *Qualitest FZE v Council*, not reported, (order of the President of
14 June 2012) 13.16, 13.31, 13.32, 13.36, 13.40, 13.42, 13.46, 16.12
C-652/11 P *Mindo v Commission*, not reported, (judgment of 11 April 2013) 7.86
C-656/11 R *United Kingdom v Council*, not reported, (order of the President of
18 April 2012) 13.31, 13.32, 13.35, 13.36, 13.40
C-679/11 P *Alliance One International v Commission*, not reported, (judgment of
26 September 2013) 7.194

C-6/12 P *Oy.*, not reported, (judgment of 18 July 2013) 7.53, 24.18
C-16/12 *Hermes Hitel és Faktor*, not reported, (order of 12 July 2012) 3.38
C-23/12 *Zakaria*, not reported, (judgment of 17 January 2013) 6.21
C-34/12 P *Idromacchine and Others v Commission*, not reported, (order of
3 September 2013) 11.38, 11.39, 11.64, 11.66, 11.69, 11.72
C-40/12 P *Gascogne Sack Deutschland v Commission*, not reported, (judgment of
26 November 2013) 11.20, 16.18
C-50/12 P *Kendrion v Commission*, not reported, (judgment of 26 November 2013) 11.20, 16.18
C-56/12 P *EFIM v Commission*, not reported, (judgment of 19 September 2013) 25.18
C-58/12 P *Groupe Gascogne v Commission*, not reported, (judgment of
26 November 2013) 11.20, 16.18, 23.87
C-63/12 *Commission v Council*, not reported, (judgment of 19 November 2013) 7.14, 7.20
C-66/12 *Council v Commission*, not reported, (judgment of 19 November 2013) 25.84, 25.101
C-69/12 P *Noscira v OHIM*, not reported, (order of 12 September 2012) 23.54, 25.27
C-77/12 P *Deutsche Post v Commission*, not reported, (judgment of 24 October 2013) 7.57
C-92/12 PPU *Health Service Executive*, not reported, (judgment of 26 April 2012) 24.23
C-93/12 *Agrokonsulting*, not reported, (judgment of 27 June 2013) 4.07
C-110/12 P(R) *Akhras v Council*, not reported, (order of the President of 19 July 2012) 13.24, 13.31,
13.32, 13.35, 13.40, 13.45
C-118/12 P *Enviro Tech Europe v Commission*, not reported, (order of 24 January 2013) 11.51, 25.17
C-122/12 P *Rintisch v OHIM*, not reported, (judgment of 3 October 2013) 25.12
C-134/12 *Corpul Naţional al Poliţiştilor*, not reported, (order of 10 May 2012) 3.39
C-136/12 *Consiglio nazionale dei geologi*, not reported, (judgment of 18 July 2013) 3.07, 3.19,
3.20, 3.22, 3.35, 3.50
C-138/12 *Rusedespred OOD*, not reported, (judgment of 11 April 2013) 4.37
C-149/12 P *Xeda International and Pace International v Commission*, not reported,
(judgment of 27 June 2013) 7.10, 7.141, 7.143
C-156/12 *GREP*, not reported, (order of 13 June 2012) 4.07
C-183/12 P *Ayadi v Commission*, not reported, (judgment of 6 June 2013) 7.10, 7.141, 7.143
C-184/12 *Lorenzo Ciampaglia*, not reported, (order of 3 May 2012) 3.26
C-185/12 *Ciampaglia*, not reported, (order of 3 May 2012) 3.27
C-196/12 *Commission v Council*, not reported, (judgment of 19 November 2013) 8.21
C-239/12 P *Abdulrahim v Council and Commission*, not reported, (judgment of
28 May 2013) 7.10, 7.141, 7.143
C-240/12 *Criminal proceedings against EBS*, not reported, (order of 14 March 2013) 3.26
C-272/12 P *Commission v Ireland and Others*, not reported, (judgment of
10 December 2013) 25.11, 25.14
C-274/12 P *Telefónica v Commission*, not reported, (judgment of 19 December 2013) 7.120
C-278/12 PPU *Adil*, not reported, (judgment of 19 July 2012) 22.08, 22.11
C-284/12 *Deutsche Lufthansa*, not reported, (judgment of 21 November 2013) 7.54, 7.57
C-286/12 *Commission v Hungary*, not reported, (judgment of 6 November 2012) 25.81
C-318/12 *Jean Devillers*, not reported, (order of 22 November 2012) 3.26
C-334/12 RX Review of judgment T-234/11 P *Arango Jaramillo and Others v EIB*, not
reported, (decision of 12 July 2012) 17.01, 17.02, 18.18, 18.25
C-334/12 RX-II Review of judgment T-234/11 P *Arango Jaramillo and Others v EIB*, not
reported, (judgment of 28 February 2013) 17.01, 17.02, 18.18
C-352/12 *Consiglio Nazionale degli Ingegneri*, not reported, (order of 20 June 2013) 24.15
C-368/12 *Adiamix*, not reported, (order of 18 April 2013) 3.26
C-370/12 *Thomas Pringle*, not reported, (judgment of 27 November 2012) 2.10, 2.12, 2.53, 5.09,
6.08, 6.10, 7.69, 7.75, 10.03, 11.18, 19.22, 19.24, 19.25, 19.26, 24.18, 24.19, 25.81
C-397/12 P *Transports Schiocchet—Excursions v Council and Commission*, not reported,
(order of 6 June 2013) 11.46
C-418/12 P *TME v Commission*, not reported, (order of 7 May 2013) 26.07

C-535/12 P *Faet Oltra v European Ombudsman*, not reported, (order of 6 June 2013) 23.17
C-542/12 *Fidenato*, not reported, (order of 8 May 2013) 24.15
C-551/12 P(R) *EDF v Commission*, not reported, (order of the Vice-President of
    7 March 2013) 2.18, 13.23, 13.32, 13.36, 13.40, 13.46, 16.29
C-579/12 RX Review of judgment T-268/11 P *Commission v Strack*, not reported,
    (decision of 11 December 2012) 17.01

C-73/13 *T*, not reported, (order of 8 May 2013) 24.15
C-140/13 *Altmann and Others*, not reported, (order of the President of 28 June 2013) 24.18
C-168/13 PPU *F*, not reported, (judgment of 30 May 2013) 22.11
C-278/13 P(R) *Pilkington Group v Commission*, not reported, (order of the Vice-President
    of 10 September 2013) 13.36
C-369/13 Gielen and Others, not reported, (order of the President of 24 October 2013) 24.18
C-389/13 P(R) *EMA v AbbVie*, not reported, (order of the Vice-President of
    28 November 2013) 13.36

GENERAL COURT (FORMERLY COURT OF FIRST INSTANCE)

T-1/89 *Rhône-Poulenc SA v Commission* [1991] E.C.R. II-867 . . . . 2.24, 7.179, 23.43
T-1/89 to T-4/89 and T-6/89 to T-15/89 *Rhône-Poulenc and Others v Commission* [1990]
    E.C.R. II-637, (order of 15 November 1990) 25.86
T-2/89 *Petrofina SA v Commission* [1991] E.C.R. II-1087 . . . . 2.24
T-3/89 *Atochem SA v Commission* [1991] E.C.R. II-1177 . . . . 2.24
T-4/89 *BASF AG v Commission* [1991] E.C.R. II-1523 . . . . 2.24, 7.179, 25.117
T-4/89 REV *BASF v Commission* [1992] E.C.R. II-1591, (order of 26 March 1992) 25.119
T-6/89 *Enichem Anic SpA v Commission* [1991] E.C.R. II-1623 . . . . 2.24
T-7/89 *SA Hercules Chemicals NV v Commission* [1991] E.C.R. II-1711 . . . . 2.24, 7.36, 7.161
T-8/89 *DSM NV v Commission* [1991] E.C.R. II-1833 . . . . 2.24, 7.170, 25.117
T-9/89 *Hüls AG v Commission* [1992] E.C.R. II-499 . . . . 2.24, 7.170, 7.179, 23.83
T-10/89 *Hoechst AG v Commission* [1992] E.C.R. II-629 . . . . 2.24, 23.83
T-11/89 *Shell International Chemical Co. Ltd v Commission* [1992] E.C.R. II-757 . . . . 2.24, 23.83
T-12/89 *Solvay & Cie SA v Commission* [1992] E.C.R. II-907 . . . . 2.24, 23.83
T-13/89 *Imperial Chemical Industries Plc v Commission* [1992] E.C.R. II-1021 . . . . 2.24, 15.07, 23.83
T-14/89 *Montedipe SpA v Commission* [1992] E.C.R. II-1155 . . . . 2.24, 23.83
T-14/89 REV *Montecatini v Commission* [1992] E.C.R. II-2409 . . . . 25.117
T-15/89 *Chemie Linz AG v Commission* [1992] E.C.R. II-1275 . . . . 2.24, 23.83
T-18/89 and T-24/89 *Tagaras v Court of Justice* [1992] E.C.R. II-153,
    (order of 25 February 1992) 25.93
T-20/89 RV *Moritz v Commission* [1993] E.C.R. II-1423 . . . . 16.31
T-29/89 *Moritz v Commission* [1990] E.C.R. II-787 . . . . 7.217
T-30/89 *Hilti v Commission* [1990] E.C.R. II-163, (order of 4 April 1990) 25.76, 25.86
T-33/89 and T-74/89 *Blackman v European Parliament* [1993] E.C.R. II-249 . . . . 7.208
T-33/89 and T-74/89 DEP *Blackman v European Parliament* [1993] E.C.R. II-837,
    (order of 15 July 1993) 25.92
T-35/89 TO I *Ascasibar Zubizarreta and Others v Albani and Others* [1992] E.C.R. II-1599,
    (order of 26 March 1992) 25.65, 25.108
T-35/89 TO II *Buggenhout and Others*, not reported, (order of 26 March 1992) 25.10
T-37/89 *Hanning v European Parliament* [1990] E.C.R. II-463 . . . . 7.173, 7.174, 7.223, 11.66,
    18.28, 25.14
T-38/89 *Hochbaum v Commission* [1990] E.C.R. II-43 . . . . 7.181
T-42/89 *Yorck von Wartenburg v European Parliament* [1990] E.C.R. II-31 . . . . 25.31, 25.33
T-43/89 RV *Gill v Commission* [1993] E.C.R. II-303 . . . . 16.29, 16.31, 25.13
T-46/89 *Pitrone v Commission* [1990] E.C.R. II-577 . . . . 7.181, 7.183
T-50/89 *Sparr v Commission* [1990] E.C.R. II-539, (order of 11 October 1990) 13.45, 25.137
T-51/89 *Tetra Pak v Commission* [1990] E.C.R II-309 . . . . 2.24, 2.29
T-57/89 *Alexandrakis v Commission* [1990] E.C.R. II-143 . . . . 18.13, 18.22, 18.26
T-59/89 *Yorck von Wartenburg v European Parliament*, not reported,
    (order of 6 December 1989) 23.65
T-61/89 *Dansk Pelsdyravlerforening v Commission* [1992] E.C.R. II-1931 . . . . 7.174

T-64/89 *Automec v Commission* [1990] E.C.R. II-367 . . . . .7.08, 7.28, 7.43, 8.20, 11.76, 25.12, 25.17, 25.94

T-65/89 *BPB Industries and British Gypsum v Commission* [1993] E.C.R. II-389 . . . . . .7.36, 7.161, 15.09

T-68/89, T-77/89 and T-78/89 *SIV and Others v Commission* [1992] E.C.R. II-1403 . . . . 7.179

T-73/89 *Barbi v Commission* [1990] E.C.R. II-619 . . . . 18.28

T-78/89 *DEP PPG Industries Glass v Commission* [1993] E.C.R. II-573, (order of
   9 June 1993) 25.92, 25.93

T-79/89, T-84/89 to T-86/89, T-89/89, T-91/89 to T-92/89, T-94/89, T-96/89,
   T-98/89, T-102/89, and T-104/89 *BASF and Others v Commission* [1992]
   E.C.R. II-315. . . . . .7.12, 23.56, 23.73

T-106/89 *REV Norsk Hydro v Commission* [1994] E.C.R. II-419, (order of 1 July 1994) 25.120

T-108/89 *Scheuer v Commission* [1990] E.C.R. II-411 . . . . 7.181

T-113/89 *Nefarma v Commission* [1990] E.C.R. II-797 . . . . .7.19, 7.74

T-115/89 *González Holguera v European Parliament* [1990] E.C.R. II-831. . . . . 7.174

T-119/89 *Teisonnière v Commission* [1990] E.C.R. II-7, (order of 14 December 1989). 18.07

T-120/89 *Stahlwerke Peine-Salzgitter* [1992] E.C.R. II-279. . . . . 2.24, 7.225, 11.03, 11.50, 11.57, 11.60, 11.68

T-120/89 (92) *Stahlwerke Peine-Salzgitter v Commission* [1996] E.C.R. II-1547,
   (order of 8 November 1996) 25.93

T-134/89 *Hettrich and Others v Commission* [1990] E.C.R. II-565 . . . . 18.26

T-135/89 *Pfloeschner v Commission* [1990] E.C.R. II-153. . . . . 18.05

T-138/89 *NBV and NVB v Commission* [1992] E.C.R. II-2181 . . . . .7.22, 7.139

T-139/89 *Virgili-Schettini v European Parliament* [1990] E.C.R. II-535. . . . . 18.26

T-140/89 *Della Pietra v Commission* [1990] E.C.R. II-717. . . . . 25.84

T-143/89 *Ferriere Nord v Commission* [1995] E.C.R. II-917. . . . . 7.183

T-146/89 *Williams v Court of Auditors* [1991] E.C.R. II-1293 . . . . 7.183

T-156/89 *Valverde Mordt v Court of Justice* [1991] E.C.R. II-407 . . . . 7.173

T-158/89 *Van Hecken v ESC* [1991] E.C.R. II-1341 . . . . 11.66

T-160/89 and T-161/89 *Kalavros v Court of Justice* [1990] E.C.R. II-871 . . . . 7.173

T-163/89 *Sebastiani v European Parliament* [1991] E.C.R. II-715. . . . . 18.07

T-165/89 *Plug v Commission* [1992] E.C.R. II-367 . . . . 11.66

T-169/89 *Frederiksen v European Parliament* [1991] E.C.R. II-1403 . . . . 23.68

T-1/90 *Pérez-Mínguez Casariego v Commission* [1991] E.C.R. II-143. . . . . 7.173

T-2/90 *Ferreira de Freitas v Commission* [1991] E.C.R. II-103. . . . . 18.26, 23.66

T-3/90 *Prodifarma v Commission* [1991] E.C.R. II-1, (order of 23 January 1991) 8.13

T-12/90 *Bayer v Commission* [1991] E.C.R. II-219 . . . . 23.84

T-17/90, T-28/91 and T-17/92 *Camara Alloisio and Others v Commission* [1993] E.C.R. II-841. . . . . 7.28

T-18/90 *Jongen v Commission* [1991] E.C.R. II-187. . . . . 25.12

T-21/90 *Generlich v Commission* [1991] E.C.R. II-1323. . . . . 25.10, 25.14

T-23/90 (92) and T-9/92 (92) *Peugeot v Commission* [1995] E.C.R. II-2057,
   (order of 11 July 1995). 25.92

T-24/90 *Automec v Commission* [1992] E.C.R. II-2223 . . . . .2.24, 2.29, 8.20

T-26/90 *Finsider v Commission* [1992] E.C.R. II-1789. .7.170, 7.220, 7.223

T-27/90 *Latham v Commission* [1991] E.C.R. II-35. . . . . 18.14

T-28/90 *Asia Motor France and Others v Commission* [1992] E.C.R. II-2285 . . . . 2.24, 2.29, 8.05, 8.18, 8.20, 25.16

T-44/90 *La Cinq v Commission* [1992] E.C.R. II-1 . . . . .7.170, 7.193, 13.05

T-45/90 R *Speybrouck v European Parliament* [1990] E.C.R. II-705, (order of the President of
   23 November 1990). 13.36

T-47/90 *Herremans v Commission* [1991] E.C.R. II-467, (order of 4 July 1991). 18.05

T-52/90 *Volger v European Parliament* [1992] E.C.R. II-121 . . . . .7.173, 11.66, 18.25

T-13/91 R *Harrison v Commission* [1991] E.C.R. II-179, (order of the President
   of 15 April 1991). 13.34

T-16/91 *Rendo and Others v Commission* [1992] E.C.R. II-2417. . . . . 5.33, 7.08, 7.22, 7.43

T-16/91 RV *Rendo and Others v Commission* [1996] E.C.R. II-1827. . . . . .7.170, 16.29

T-19/91 R *Vichy v Commission* [1991] E.C.R. II-265, (order of the President of 7 June 1991) 13.04

T-19/91 *Vichy v Commission* [1992] E.C.R. II-415 . . . . 7.35

T-22/91 INT *Raiola-Denti and Others v Council* [1993] E.C.R. II-817,
   (order of 14 July 1993). 25.125, 25.128, 25.131

T-23/91 *Maurissen v Court of Auditors* [1992] E.C.R. II-2377 .... 7.183
T-30/91 *Solvay v Commission* [1995] E.C.R. II-1775 .... 7.36
T-32/91 *Solvay v Commission* [1995] E.C.R. II-1825 .... 7.146, 7.169, 25.13
T-35/91 *Eurosport v Commission* [1991] E.C.R. II-1359, (order of 28 November 1991) 25.65, 25.67
T-36/91 *ICI v Commission* [1995] E.C.R. II-1847 .... 7.161
T-37/91 *ICI v Commission* [1995] E.C.R. II-1901 .... 7.161, 25.12
T-47/91 *Auzat v Commission* [1992] E.C.R. II-2536 .... 18.05
T-48/91 *Minic v Court of Auditors* [1991] E.C.R. II-479, (order of 9 July 1991) 18.13
T-51/91 R *Hoyer v Commission* [1991] E.C.R. II-679, (order of the President of 1 August 1991) ... 13.36
T-64/91 *Marcato v Commission* [1992] E.C.R. II-243, (order of 25 February 1992) 18.14
T-77/91 R *Hochbaum v Commission* [1991] E.C.R. II-1285, (order of the President of
    22 November 1991) 13.14, 16.26
T-78/91 *Moat and TAO/AFI v Commission* [1991] E.C.R. II-1387, (order of 4 December 1991) ... 18.10
T-84/91 *Meskens v European Parliament* [1992] E.C.R. II-1565 .... 18.10
T-84/91 *DEP Meskens v European Parliament* [1993] E.C.R. II-757, (order of 5 July 1993) 25.93
T-636/91 *ICI v Commission* [1995] E.C.R. II-1847 .... 7.36

T-4/92 *Vardakas v Commission* [1993] E.C.R. II-357 .... 18.26
T-6/92 and T-52/92 *Reinarz v Commission* [1993] E.C.R. II-1047 .... 9.03
T-7/92 *Asia Motor France and Others v Commission* [1993] E.C.R. II-669 .... 7.170, 7.193, 8.20
T-10/92 to T-12/92 and T-15/92 *Cimenteries CBR and Others v Commission* [1992]
    E.C.R. II 2667 .... 7.29, 7.36, 7.161
T-10/92 R to T-12/92 R and T-14/92 R to T-15/92 R *Cimenteries CBR and Others v
    Commission* [1992] E.C.R. II-1571, (order of the President of 23 March 1992) 13.25
T-13/92 *Moat v Commission* [1993] E.C.R. II-287 .... 11.66, 25.94
T-19/92 *Leclerc v Commission* [1996] E.C.R. II-1851 .... 7.112, 25.60
T-22/92 *Weissenfels v European Parliament* [1993] E.C.R. II-1095 .... 25.13, 25.49
T-24/92 R and T-28/92 R *Langnese-Iglo and Schöller Lebensmittel v Commission* [1992]
    E.C.R. II-1839, (order of the President of 16 June 1992) 13.06, 13.42
T-25/92 *Vela Palacios v ESC* [1993] E.C.R. II-201 .... 7.173
T-29/92 R *SPO v Commission* [1992] E.C.R. II-2161, (order of the President of 16 July 1992) 13.42
T-36/92 *SFEI and Others v Commission* [1992] E.C.R. II-2479 .... 7.43
T-37/92 *BEUC and NCC v Commission* [1994] E.C.R. II-285 .... 7.43, 7.86
T-39/92 and T-40/92 *CB and Europay v Commission* [1994] E.C.R. II-49 .... 7.34, 7.193
T-46/92 *Scottish Football Association v Commission* [1994] E.C.R. II-1039 .... 7.138
T-47/92 *Lenz v Commission* [1992] E.C.R. II-2523, (order of 14 December 1992) 25.86
T-55/92 *Knijff v Court of Auditors* [1993] E.C.R. II-823, (order of 14 July 1993) 18.16
T-56/92 *Koelman v Commission* [1993] E.C.R. II-1267, (order of
    29 November 1993) 8.05, 8.20, 23.51, 25.10, 25.101
T-59/92 *Caronna v Commission* [1993] E.C.R. II-1129 .... 11.66
T-64/92 *Chavane de Dalmassy and Others v Commission* [1994] E.C.R.-SC II-723 .... 9.03
T-65/92 *Arauxo-Dumay v Commission* [1993] E.C.R. II-597 .... 18.08
T-70/92 and T-71/92 *Florimex and VGB v Commission* [1997] E.C.R. II-693 .... 7.208
T-74/92 *Ladbroke v Commission* [1995] E.C.R. II-115, (order of 13 May 1993) 7.35, 8.20,
    23.03, 25.65
T-80/92 *Turner v Commission* [1993] E.C.R. II-1465 .... 7.170, 7.183
T-83/92 *Zunis Holding and Others v Commission* [1993] E.C.R. II-1169 .... 7.101
T-85/92 *De Hoe v Commission* [1993] E.C.R. II-523, (order of 28 April 1993) 25.10, 25.12
T-87/92 *Kruidvat v Commission* [1996] E.C.R. II-1931 .... 7.112, 25.65, 25.67, 25.69
T-88/92 *Leclerc v Commission* [1996] II-1961 .... 7.112
T-96/92 R *CCE de la Société Générale des Grandes Sources and Others v Commission* [1992]
    E.C.R. II-2579, (order of the President of 15 December 1992) 13.25, 13.42
T-96/92 *CCE de la Société Générale de Grandes Sources and Others v Commission* [1995]
    E.C.R. II-1213 .... 7.92, 7.114
T-97/92 and T-111/92 *Rijnoudt and Hocken v Commission* [1993] E.C.R. II-587,
    (order of 15 June 1993) 25.67
T-101/92 *Stagakis v European Parliament* [1993] E.C.R. II-63, (order of 8 February 1993) 25.27
T-106/92 *Frederiksen v European Parliament* [1995] E.C.R.-SC II-99 .... 7.184
T-109/92 *Lacruz Bassols v Court of Justice* [1994] E.C.R.-SC II-105 .... 7.183, 25.13, 25.14
T-114/92 *BEMIM v Commission* [1995] E.C.R. II-147 .... 7.86

T-115/92 R *Hogan v European Parliament* [1993] E.C.R. II-339, (order of the President of
   23 March 1993). 13.36

T-2/93 *Air France v Commission* [1994] E.C.R. II-323. . . . . 7.113, 7.200, 25.98
T-3/93 *Air France v Commission* [1994] E.C.R. II-121. . . . . 7.16
T-12/93 R *CCE de Vittel and Others v Commission* [1993] E.C.R. II-449, (order of the
   President of 2 April 1993). 13.15, 13.25
T-12/93 R *CCE de Vittel and Others v Commission* [1993] E.C.R. II-785, (order of the
   President of 6 July 1993) 13.42
T-12/93 *CCE de Vittel and Others v Commission* [1995] E.C.R. II-1247 . . . . 7.104, 7.114
T-13/93 *Cordier v Commission* [1993] E.C.R. II-1215 . . . . 5.03
T-17/93 *Matra Hachette v Commission* [1994] E.C.R. II-595 . . . . 7.43, 7.171, 7.193
T-18/93 *Marcato v Commission* [1994] E.C.R.-SC II-681. . . . . 11.66
T-21/93 *Peixoto v Commission* [1993] E.C.R. II-463, (order of the President of 5 April 1993) 13.34
T-24/93 R *CMBT v Commission* [1993] E.C.R. II-543, (order of the President of
   13 May 1993) 13.18, 13.25
T-24/93 *CMBT and Others v Commission*, not reported, (order of 19 March 1996) 25.76
T-29/93 *Calvo Alonso-Cortès v Commission* [1993] E.C.R. II-1389, (order of
   14 December 1993) 5.34, 25.42
T-32/93 *Ladbroke Racing v Commission* [1994] E.C.R. II-1015. . . . . 8.05, 8.13
T-34/93 *Société Générale v Commission* [1995] E.C.R. II-545 . . . . 7.31
T-35/93 *Cucchiara and Others v Commission* [1994] E.C.R.-SC II-413 . . . . 25.12, 25.14
T-37/93 *Stagakis v European Parliament* [1994] E.C.R.-SC I-A-137 . . . . 18.06
T-44/93 *Saby v Commission* [1995] E.C.R.-SC II-541 . . . . 18.14, 18.26
T-45/93 *Branco v Court of Auditors* [1994] E.C.R.-SC II-641, (order of 20 July 1994). 25.42
T-46/93 *Michaël-Chiou v Commission* [1994] E.C.R.-SC II-929 . . . . 7.183
T-124/93 *Werner v Commission* [1995] E.C.R. II-91, (order of 20 January 1995) 25.93
T-246/93 *Bühring v Council and Commission* [1998] E.C.R. II-171. . . . . 11.19, 11.94
T-432/93, T-433/93 and T-434/93 *Socurte and Others v Commission* [1995] E.C.R. II-503 . . . . . . 7.216
T-435/93 *ASPEC and Others v Commission* [1995] E.C.R. II-1281 . . . . 7.93, 7.124
T-443/93 *Casillo Grani v Commission* [1995] E.C.R. II-1375 . . . . 7.142
T-447/93, T-448/93 and T-449/93 *AITEC and Others v Commission* [1995]
   E.C.R. II-1971. . . . . 7.104, 7.124, 7.127, 25.60
T-447/93 DEP *AITEC v Commission* [1996] E.C.R. II-1631, (order of 28 November 1996) 25.93
T-450/93 *Lisrestal v Commission* [1994] E.C.R. II-1177. . . . . 7.157
T-452/93 and T-453/93 *Pevasa and Inpesca v Commission* [1994] E.C.R. II-229,
   (order of 28 April 1994) 7.16, 7.216
T-459/93 *Siemens v Commission* [1995] E.C.R. II-1675. . . . . 4.31, 25.60
T-460/93 *Tête and Others v EIB* [1993] E.C.R. II-1257, (order of 26 November 1993) 7.70, 25.42
T-461/93 *An Taisce and WWF UK v Commission* [1994] E.C.R. II-733 . . . . 11.76
T-462/93, T-464/93 and T-470/93 *Lenz v Commission*, not reported, (order of 14 June 1995). 18.27
T-463/93 *GUNA v Council* [1993] E.C.R. II-1206, (order of 29 October 1993) 7.94
T-465/93 *Consorzio Gruppo di Azione Locale 'Murgia Messapica' v Commission* [1994]
   E.C.R. II-361. . . . . 7.216
T-466/93, T-469/93, T-473/93, T-474/93, and T-477/93 *O'Dwyer and Others v Council*,
   not reported, (order of 15 September 1995). 25.133
T-468/93 *Frinil v Commission* [1994] E.C.R. II-33, (order of 10 February 1994). 7.216
T-472/93 *Campo Ebro Industrial and Others v Council* [1995] E.C.R. II-421 . . . . 11.50
T-473/93 *Wafer Zoo v Commission* [1995] E.C.R. II-1479 . . . . 11.35
T-480/93 and T-483/93 *Antillean RiceMills and Others v Commission* [1995]
   E.C.R. II-2305. . . . . 7.100, 7.141, 11.52, 11.74
T-481/93 and T-484/93 *Exporteurs in Levende Varkens and Others v Commission* [1995]
   E.C.R. II-2941. . . . . 7.141, 11.15, 11.50
T-482/93 *Weber v Commission* [1996] E.C.R. II-609 . . . . 7.85, 7.99, 7.108, 25.04
T-485/93 *Dreyfus v Commission* [1996] E.C.R. II-1101 . . . . 11.09, 11.10
T-485/93, T-491/93, T-494/93, and T-61/98 *Dreyfus and Others v Commission* [2000]
   E.C.R. II-3659. . . . . 7.216
T-489/93 *Unifruit Hellas v Commission* [1994] E.C.R. II-1201. . . . . 11.50
T-491/93 *Richco v Commission* [1996] E.C.R. II-1131 . . . . 11.09, 11.10
T-492/93 and T-492/93 R *Nutral v Commission* [1993] E.C.R. II-1023,
   (order of 21 October 1993). 7.93

T-497/93 R II *Hogan v Court of Justice* [1993] E.C.R. II-1005, (order of the President of
  29 September 1993).. 13.36
T-497/93 *Hogan v Court of Justice* [1995] E.C.R. II-703 .... 25.08
T-500/93 *Y v Court of Justice* [1996] E.C.R.-SC II-977 .... 18.14
T-506/93 *Moat v Commission* [1995] E.C.R.-SC II-147.............................. 18.21
T-508/93 *Mancini v Commission* [1994] E.C.R.-SC II-761........................... 25.13
T-514/93 *Cobrecaf and Others v Commission* [1995] E.C.R. II-621 ....7.23, 7.208, 11.10, 11.58
T-515/93 *B v Commission* [1994] E.C.R.-SC II-379, (order of 28 March 1994)................ 25.12
T-517/93 *Van Parijs v Council and Commission*, not reported, (order of the President of
  17 July 1995)... 25.66
T-521/93 *Atlanta and Others v EC* [1996] E.C.R. II-1707 .... 11.50, 25.13
T-528/93, T-542/93, T-543/93, and T-546/93 *Métropole Télévision and Others v
  Commission* [1996] E.C.R. II-649 .... 7.112
T-534/93 *Grynberg v Commission* [1994] E.C.R.-SC II-595 .... 7.174
T-541/93 *Connaughton and Others v Council* [1997] E.C.R. II-549.................... 7.20
T-543/93 R *Gestevisión Telecinco v Commission* [1993] E.C.R. II-1411, (order of the President of
  14 December 1993) 13.07
T-549/93 R *D v Commission* [1993] E.C.R. II-1347, (order of the President of
  30 November 1993).. 13.40
T-554/93 R *Abbott Trust v Council and Commission* [1994] E.C.R. II-1, (order of the
  President of 12 January 1994)... 13.15
T-551/93, T-231/94, T-232/94, T-233/94, and T-234/94 *Industrias Pesqueras Campos and
  Others v Commission* [1996] E.C.R. II-247.................................. 7.183
T-554/93 *Saint and Murray v Council and Commission* [1997] E.C.R. II-563.............. 7.20
T-561/93 *Tiercé Ladbroke v Commission* [1995] E.C.R. II-2755, (order of 16 October 1995)...... 25.99
T-571/93 *Lefebvre and Others v Commission* [1995] E.C.R. II-2379 .... 11.50, 11.86
T-575/93 *Koelman v Commission* [1996] E.C.R. II-1 ....5.33, 8.20, 25.10
T-584/93 *Roujansky v Council* [1994] E.C.R. II-585, (order of 14 July 1994) 7.69
T-585/93 *Greenpeace v Commission* [1995] E.C.R. II-2205, (order of 9 August 1995) 7.97
T-588/93 *G v Commission* [1994] E.C.R.-SC II-875 .... 18.26, 18.28

T-5/94 *J v Commission* [1994] E.C.R. II-391, (order of 27 May 1994) 5.34, 8.13
T-13/94 *Century Oils Hellas v Commission* [1994] E.C.R. II-431, (order of 4 July 1994) 5.34, 8.13
T-20/94 *Hartmann v Council and Commission* [1997] E.C.R. II-595............. 11.88, 11.90, 25.10
T-70/94 *Comafrica and Dole Fresh Fruit Europe v Commission* [1996] E.C.R. II-1741........... 16.16
T-76/94 *Jansma v Council and Commission* [2001] E.C.R. II-243 .... 11.68, 11.88, 11.94
T-84/94 *Bundesverband der Bilanzbuchhalter v Commission* [1995] E.C.R. II-101.............. 5.33
T-85/94 *Branco v Commission* [1995] E.C.R. II-45 .... 25.31, 25.33
T-99/94 *Asocarne v Council* [1994] E.C.R. II-871, (order of 20 October 1994) 7.94
T-107/94 *Kik v Council and Commission* [1995] E.C.R. II-1717, (order of
  19 June 1995) 7.85, 7.99, 7.108, 13.28, 25.11
T-109/94 *Windpark Groothusen v Commission* [1995] E.C.R. II-3007...................... 7.216
T-115/94 *Opel Austria v Council* [1997] E.C.R. II-39 ....7.147, 7.178, 7.210, 25.63
T-116/94 *Cassa Nazionale di Previdenza ed Assistenza a favour degli Avvocati e Procuratori*
  [1995] E.C.R. II-1, (order of 11 January 1995) 7.85, 7.99, 7.108
T-140/94 *Gutiérrez de Quijano y Llorens v European Parliament* [1996] E.C.R.-SC II-689 ... 13.28, 18.14
T-154/94 *CSF and CSME v Commission* [1996] E.C.R. II-1377..................7.18, 7.20, 7.62
T-155/94 *Climax Paper v Council* [1996] E.C.R. II-873..................7.93, 7.131, 7.205
T-156/94 *Aristrain v Commission* [1999] E.C.R. II-645............................ 15.04
T-156/94 *Siderúrgica Aristrain Madrid v Commission*, not reported, (judgment of
  14 September 2004)... 26.12
T-159/94 and T-160/94 *Ajinomoto and NutraSweet v Council* [1997] E.C.R. II-2461 .... 7.66
T-161/94 *Sinochem Heilongjiang v Council* [1996] E.C.R. II-695 ....7.83, 7.131
T-162/94 *NMB France and Others v Commission* [1996] E.C.R. II-427...................... 7.205
T-164/94 *Ferchimex v Commission* [1995] E.C.R. II-2681 .... 7.206
T-167/94 *Nölle v Council and Commission* [1995] E.C.R. II-2589..... 11.31, 11.50, 11.94, 24.26, 25.12
T-170/94 *Shanghai Bicycle v Council* [1997] E.C.R. II-1383..................7.83, 7.93, 7.131
T-175/94 *International Procurement Services v Commission* [1996] E.C.R. II-729 .... 11.78
T-177/94 *Altmann and Others v Commission* [1994] E.C.R.-SC II-969 .... 18.10
T-179/94 *Bonnamy v Council*, not reported, (order of 14 July 1994)........................ 7.69
T-182/94 *Marx Esser and Del Amo Martinez v European Parliament* [1996] E.C.R.-SC II-1197 .... 7.146

T-184/94 *ATM v Commission* [1997] E.C.R. II-2529 .... 7.138
T-185/94 *Geotronics v Commission* [1995] E.C.R. II-2795 .... 11.09
T-186/94 *Guérin Automobiles v Commission* [1995] E.C.R. II-1753........................ 8.20
T-187/94 *Rudolph v Council and Commission* [2002] E.C.R. II-367 .... 11.94
T-192/94 *Maurissen v Court of Auditors* [1996] E.C.R.-SC II-1229....................... 18.21
T-201/94 *Kustermann v Council and Commission* [2002] E.C.R. II-415.................... 11.94
T-228/94 (92) *Rusp v Council and Commission*, not reported, (order of 5 June 1996) 25.93
T-231/94 R, T-232/94 R and T-234/94 R *Transacciones Marítimas and Others v Commission*
    [1994] E.C.R. II-885, (order of the President of 26 October 1994) 13.06
T-235/94 *Galtieri v European Parliament* [1996] E.C.R.-SC II-129........................ 23.84
T-239/94 *EISA v Commission* [1997] E.C.R. II-1839.............................. 7.10, 7.217
T-243/94 *British Steel v Commission* [1997] E.C.R. II-1887 .... 25.60
T-261/94 *Schulte v Council and Commission* [2002] E.C.R. II-441 .... 11.25
T-266/94 *Skibsværftsforeningen and Others v Commission* [1996] E.C.R. II-1399............7.93, 7.118,
                                                                            7.124, 7.137, 25.60
T-271/94 (92) *Branco v Commission* [1998] E.C.R. II-3761, (order of 17 September 1998) 25.91
T-275/94 *Groupement des Cartes Bancaires 'CB' v Commission* [1995] E.C.R. II-2169............. 7.23
T-277/94 *AITEC v Commission* [1996] E.C.R. II-351 ....5.34, 8.06
T-290/94 *Kaysersberg v Commission* [1995] E.C.R. II-2247, (order of 16 August 1995) 25.73
T-290/94 (92) *Kaysersberg v Commission* [1998] E.C.R. II-4105, (order of 30 October 1998)...... 25.93
T-305/94, T-306/94, T-307/94, T-313/94 to T-316/94, T-318/94, T-325/94,
    T-328/94, T-329/94, and T-335/94 *Limburgse Vinyl Maatschappij and Others v Commission*
    [1999] E.C.R. II-931 ....7.31, 7.32, 7.36, 7.190, 7.191, 7.223
T-322/94 R *Union Carbide v Commission* [1994] E.C.R. II-1159, (order of the President of
    2 December 1994)... 13.05, 13.07
T-330/94 *Salt Union v Commission* [1996] E.C.R. II-1475.....................7.57, 7.63, 25.73
T-331/94 *IPK v Commission* [1997] E.C.R. II-1665............................. 7.23
T-331/94 *IPK-München v Commission* [2001] E.C.R. II-779 .... 7.147, 7.170
T-353/94 *Postbank v Commission* [1996] E.C.R. II-921 .... 7.38
T-358/94 *Air France v Commission* [1996] E.C.R. II-2109 .... 7.123
T-361/94 *Weir v Commission* [1996] E.C.R.-SC II-381 .... 18.26
T-367/94 *British Coal v Commission* [1997] E.C.R. II-2103, order of
    18 November 1997)................................... 23.66, 25.45
T-371/94 and T-394/94 *British Airways and Others and British Midland Airways v Commission*
    [1998] E.C.R. II-2405 .... 7.59, 7.147, 7.187, 7.202, 25.63, 25.73
T-374/94, T-375/94, T-384/94, and T-388/94 *European Night Services and Others v*
    Commission [1998] E.C.R. II-3141 .... 7.170, 7.214
T-375/94 *European Passenger Services v Commission*, not reported, (order of
    18 September 1995).. 25.67
T-380/94 *AIUFFASS and AKT v Commission* [1996] E.C.R. II-2169 ....7.26, 7.104, 7.128, 7.203
T-391/94 *Baiwir v Commission* [1996] E.C.R.-SC II-787......................... 18.14
T-394/94 *British Midland Airways v Commission*, not reported, (order of 12 June 1995).......... 25.73
T-395/94 *Atlantic Container Line and Others v Commission* [2002] E.C.R. II-875 .... 7.147
T-395/94 R II *Atlantic Container and Others v Commission* [1995] E.C.R. II-2893,
    (order of the President of 22 November 1995)............................. 13.07
T-398/94 *Kahn Scheepvaart v Commission* [1996] E.C.R. II-477 .... 7.121, 25.16

T-2/95 *Industrie des poudres sphériques v Council* [1998] E.C.R. II-3939 .... 7.133
T-2/95 (92) *Industries des Poudres Sphériques v Council* [2000] E.C.R. II-463, (order of
    7 March 2000)... 25.93
T-8/95 and T-9/95 *Pelle and Konrad v Council and Commission* [2007] E.C.R. II-4117 .....11.06, 11.68,
                                                                            23.85, 25.88
T-11/95 *BP Chemicals v Commission* [1996] E.C.R. II-599, (order of 26 June 1996) 23.05
T-11/95 *BP Chemicals v Commission* [1998] E.C.R. II-3235...............7.54, 7.118, 7.124, 7.216
T-19/95 *Adia Interim v Commission* [1996] E.C.R. II-321 .... 25.13
T-25/95, T-26/95, T-30/95, T-31/95, T-32/95, T-34/95, T-35/95, T-36/95, T-37/95,
    T-38/95, T-39/95, T-42/95, T-43/95, T-44/95, T-45/95, T-46/95, T-48/95, T-50/95,
    T-51/95, T-52/95, T-53/95, T-54/95, T-55/95, T-56/95, T-57/95, T-58/95, T-59/95,
    T-60/95, T-61/95, T-62/95, T-63/95, T-64/95, T-65/95, T-68/95, T-69/95, T-70/95,
    T-71/95, T-87/95, T-88/95, T-103/95, and T-104/95 *Cimenteries CBR and Others v*
    Commission [2000] E.C.R. II-491 ....7.36, 7.163, 7.192

T-28/95 *IECC v Commission* [1998] E.C.R. II-3597 .... 8.20
T-47/95 *Terres Rouges and Others v Commission* [1997] E.C.R. II-481 .... 7.85, 7.99, 7.108
T-73/95 *Oliveira v Commission* [1997] E.C.R. II-381 .... 7.225
T-75/95 *Günzler Aluminium v Commission* [1996] E.C.R. II-497 .... 7.223
T-77/95 *SFEI and Others v Commission* [1997] E.C.R. II-1 .... 7.147
T-77/95 DEP *Ufex and Others v Commission*, not reported, (order of 7 December 2000) 25.93
T-79 and T-80/95 *SNCF and British Railways v Commission* [1996] E.C.R. II-1491 .... 7.147
T-90/95 *Gill v Commission* [1997] E.C.R.-SC II-1231 .... 23.68
T-91/95 *De Nil and Impens v Council* [1996] E.C.R.-SC II-959 .... 7.225
T-93/95 *Laga v Commission* [1998] E.C.R. II-195 .... 7.73, 11.10, 11.25
T-94/95 *Landuyt v Commission* [1998] E.C.R. II-213 .... 7.73, 11.10, 11.25
T-97/95 *Sinochem v Council* [1998] E.C.R. II-85 .... 7.205
T-99/95 *Stott v Commission* [1996] E.C.R. II-2227 .... 11.35
T-101/95 *Zedelmaier v Council and Commission*, not reported, (order of 22 June 1995) 25.27
T-106/95 *FFSA and Others v Commission* [1997] E.C.R. II-229 .... 7.146, 7.174, 25.13
T-113/95 *Mancini v Commission* [1996] E.C.R.-SC II-543 .... 18.14
T-116/95 *Cementir v Commission* [1998] E.C.R. II-2261, (order of 10 June 1998) 7.23
T-117/95 *Corman v Commission* [1997] E.C.R. II-95 .... 7.140
T-121/95 *EFMA v Council* [1997] E.C.R. II-87, (order of 24 January 1997) 23.03
T-126/95 *Dumez v Commission* [1995] E.C.R. II-2863, (order of 13 November 1995) 5.34
T-134/95 *Dysan Magnetics and Review Magnetics v Commission* [1996] E.C.R. II-181,
 (order of 14 March 1996) 7.65
T-138/95 (92) *Engelking v Council and Commission*, not reported, (order of 13 December 1995) ... 25.93
T-140/95 *Ryanair v Commission* [1998] E.C.R. II-3327 .... 7.216
T-146/95 *Bernardi v European Parliament* [1996] E.C.R. II-769 .... 13.28, 25.49
T-149/95 *Ducros v Commission* [1997] E.C.R. II-2031 .... 7.124, 7.202
T-151/95 *INEF v Commission* [1997] E.C.R. II-1541, (order of 30 September 1997) 7.216
T-152/95 *Petrides v Commission* [1997] E.C.R. II-2427 .... 11.50
T-155/95 *LPN and GEOTA v Commission* [1998] E.C.R. II-2751 .... 7.216
T-164/95 *Kuchlenz-Winter v European Parliament* [1996] E.C.R. II-1593,
 (order of 26 November 1996) 8.06, 8.19
T-167/95 *Kuchlenz-Winter v Council* [1996] E.C.R. II-1607, (order of 26 November 1996) 8.06, 8.13
T-168/95 *Eridania Zuccherifici Nazionali and Others v Counci* [1999] E.C.R. II-2245 .... 25.10
T-174/95 *Svenska Journalistförbundet v Council* [1998] E.C.R. II-2289 .... 7.83, 7.138, 25.04,
 25.50, 25.60
T-180/95 *Nutria v Commission* [1997] E.C.R. II-1317, (order of 18 July 1997) 19.01
T-184/95 *Dorsch Consult v Council and Commission* [1998] E.C.R. II-667 .... 11.07, 25.66
T-188/95 *Waterleiding Maatschappij 'Noord-West Brabant' v Commission* [1998]
 E.C.R. II-3713 .... 7.23, 7.118
T-189/95, T-39/96, and T-123/96 *SGA v Commission* [1999] E.C.R. II-3587 .... 7.16
T-190/95 and T-45/96 *Sodima v Commission* [1999] E.C.R. II-3617 .... 7.16
T-195/95 *Guérin Automobiles v Commission* [1997] E.C.R. II-679 .... 25.10
T-196/95 *H v Commission* [1997] E.C.R.-SC II-403 .... 7.214
T-198/95, T-171/96, T-230/97, T-174/98, and T-225/99 *Comafrica and Dole Fresh Fruit Europe v
 Commission* [2001] E.C.R. II-1975 .... 7.93, 11.52, 11.58, 11.60
T-203/95 R *Connolly v Commission* [1995] E.C.R. II-2919, (order of the President of
 12 December 1995) 13.06
T-208/95 *Miwon v Commission* [1996] E.C.R. II-635, (order of 10 July 1996) 7.65
T-212/95 *Oficemen v Commission* [1997] E.C.R. II-1161 .... 7.65, 8.06, 8.21
T-213/95 and T-18/96 *SCK and FNK v Commission* [1997] E.C.R. II-1739 .... 7.22, 7.35, 11.78
T-214/95 *Vlaams Gewest v Commission* [1998] E.C.R. II-717 .... 7.26, 7.77, 7.125, 7.140, 7.203
T-216/95 *Moles García Ortúzar v Commission* [1997] E.C.R.-SC II-1083 .... 25.14
T-217/95 *Passera v Commission* [1997] E.C.R.-SC II-1109 .... 25.14
T-219/95 R *Danielsson and Others v Commission* [1995] E.C.R. II-3051, (order of the
 President of 22 December 1995) 13.25
T-224/95 *Tremblay and Others v Commission* [1997] E.C.R. II-2215 .... 7.223, 25.12
T-226/95 *Kuchlenz-Winter v Commission* [1996] E.C.R. II-1619, (order of
 26 November 1996) 8.06, 8.19
T-227/95 *AssiDomän Kraft Products and Others v Commission* [1997] E.C.R. II-1185 .... 7.226
T-228/95 R *Lehrfreund v Council* [1996] E.C.R. II-111, (order of the President of
 12 February 1996) 13.05, 13.29

T-235/95 R *Goldstein v Commission*, not reported, (order of the President of 27 February 1996). . . . 13.07
T-235/95 R II *Goldstein v Commission*, not reported, (order of the President of
11 December 1996) 13.44
T-235/95 *Goldstein v Commission* [1998] E.C.R. II-523, (order of 16 March 1998) 7.23
T-236/95 *TAT European Airlines v Commission* [2000] E.C.R. II-51, (order of 27 January 2000) 7.10

T-4/96 *S v Court of Justice* [1997] E.C.R. II-1125 . . . . 7.174
T-7/96 *Perillo v Commission* [1997] E.C.R. II-1061 . . . . 11.78
T-9/96 and T-211/96 *Européenne Automobile v Commission* [1999] E.C.R. II-3639 . . . . 25.12
T-13/96 *TEAM v Commission* [1998] E.C.R. II-4073 . . . . 11.78, 25.10
T-14/96 *BAI v Commission* [1999] E.C.R. II-139 . . . . 7.216
T-16/96 *Cityflyer Express v Commission* [1998] E.C.R. II-757 . . . . 7.141, 7.187
T-17/96 *TF1 v Commission* [1999] E.C.R. II-1757 . . . . .7.61, 7.93, 7.118, 8.06, 8.13, 8.18, 8.19
T-19/96 *Carvel and Guardian Newspapers v Council* [1996] E.C.R. II-1519,
(order of 22 October 1996) 25.99
T-22/96 *Langdon v Commission* [1996] E.C.R. II-1009, (order of 18 September 1996) 7.141
T-25/96 *Arbeitsgemeinschaft Deutscher Luftfahrt-Unternehmen and Hapag Lloyd v Commission*
[1997] E.C.R. II-363, (order of 14 March 1997) 7.141
T-30/96 *Gomes de Sá Pereira v Council* [1996] E.C.R. II-785 . . . . 18.26
T-36/96 *Gaspari v European Parliament* [1999] E.C.R.-SC I-A-135, II-729 . . . . 16.29
T-38/96 *Guérin Automobiles v Commission* [1997] E.C.R. II-1223 . . . . 25.12, 25.95
T-41/96 R *Bayer v Commission* [1996] E.C.R. II-381, (order of the President of 3 June 1996) 13.16
T-41/96 *Bayer v Commission* [2000] E.C.R. II-3383 . . . . 7.190
T-42/96 *Eyckeler & Malt v Commission* [1998] E.C.R. II-401 . . . . 7.163
T-44/96 *Oleifici Italiani v Commission* [1997] E.C.R. II-1331, (order of 18 July 1997) 19.12
T-47/96 *SDDDA v Commission* [1996] E.C.R. II-1559, (order of 12 November 1996) 8.19
T-48/96 *Acme v Council* [1999] E.C.R. II-3089 . . . . 7.206
T-50/96 *Primex Produkte Import-Export and Others v Commission* [1998] E.C.R. II-3773 . . . . 7.161
T-52/96 R *Sogecable v Commission* [1996] E.C.R. II-797, (order of the President of
12 July 1996). 13.08
T-53/96 *Syndicat des Producteurs de Viande Bovine and Others v Commission* [1996]
E.C.R. II-1579, (order of 21 November 1996). 11.76, 23.59
T-54/96 *Oleifici Italiani and Fratelli Rubino Industrie Olearie v Commission* [1998]
E.C.R. II-3377 . . . . .7.93, 11.25
T-65/96 *Kish Glass v Commission* [2000] E.C.R. II-1885 . . . . .7.43, 7.193
T-65/96 DEP *Kish Glass v Commission* [2001] E.C.R. II-3261, (order of 8 November 2001) 25.93
T-68/96 *Polyvios v Commission* [1998] E.C.R. II-153, (order of 3 February 1998) 11.10
T-69/96, *Hamburger Hafen- und Lagerhaux and Others v Commission* [2001] E.C.R. II-1037 . . . . . . 7.128
T-75/96 R *Söktas v Commission* [1996] E.C.R. II-859, (order of the President of
26 August 1996) 13.25
T-75/96 *Söktas v Commission* [1996] E.C.R. II-1689, (order of 10 December 1996) 7.65, 11.09
T-79/96, T-260/97, and T-117/98 *Camar and Tico v Commission and Council* [2000]
E.C.R. II-2193. . . . . 11.67
T-81/96 *Apostolidis and Others v Commission* [1997] E.C.R.-SC II-607 . . . . 7.225
T-82/96 *ARAP and Others v Commission* [1999] E.C.R. II-1889. . . . . .7.61, 9.03
T-84/96 *Cipeke v Commission* [1997] E.C.R. II-2081. . . . . 25.10
T-86/96 *Arbeitsgemeinschaft Deutscher Luftfahrt-Unternehmen v Commission* [1999]
E.C.R. II-179. . . . . 7.120
T-87/96 *Assicurazioni Generali and Unicredito v Commissie* [1999] E.C.R. II-203. . . . . 7.46
T-89/96 *British Steel v Commission* [1997] E.C.R. II-835, (order of 29 May 1997) 25.65, 25.76
T-89/96 *British Steel v Commission* [1999] E.C.R. II-2089 . . . . 7.216
T-95/96 *Gestevisión Telecinco v Commission* [1998] E.C.R. II-3407 . . . . .8.06, 8.13, 8.19
T-102/96 *Gencor v Commission* [1999] E.C.R. II-753 . . . . 7.138, 7.151
T-105/96 *Pharos v Commission* [1998] E.C.R. II-285. . . . . 11.50
T-106/96 *Wirtschaftsvereinigung Stahl v Commission* [1999] E.C.R. II-2155. . . . . 7.216
T-107/96 R *Pantochim v Commission* [1996] E.C.R. II-1361, (order of the President of
21 October 1996). 13.08
T-107/96 *Pantochim v Commission* [1998] E.C.R. II-311 . . . . 8.19
T-111/96 *ITT Promedia v Commission* [1998] E.C.R. II-2937 . . . . 5.33
T-113/96 *Edouard Dubois and Fils v Council and Commission* [1998] E.C.R. II-125. . . . . 11.07, 11.18

T-114/96 *Confiserie du TECH and Biscuiterie Confiserie LOR v Commission* [1999]
E.C.R. II-913, (order of 26 March 1999). 7.100
T-117/96 *Intertronic v Commission* [1997] E.C.R. II-141, (order of 19 February 1997) 5.34, 8.06
T-118/96 *Thai Bicycle v Council* [1998] E.C.R. II-2991 . . . . 7.205
T-120/96 *Lilly Industries v Commission*, not reported, (order of 28 May 1997). 25.69
T-121/96 and T-151/96 *Mutual Aid Administration Services v Commission* [1997]
E.C.R. II-1355. . . . . 7.23, 7.207
T-122/96 *Federolio v Commission* [1997] E.C.R. II-1559, (order of 30 September 1997) 7.104
T-125/96 and T-152/96 *Boehringer v Council and Commission* [1999] E.C.R. II-3427 . . . . . . 25.59, 25.60
T-132/96 and T-143/96 *Freistaat Sachsen and Others v Commission* [1999]
E.C.R. II-3663. . . . . 7.125, 7.140
T-135/96 *UEAPME v Council* [1998] E.C.R. II-2335 . . . . 6.09, 7.94, 25.69
T-136/96 *Automobiles Peugeot v Commission* [1997] E.C.R. II-663, (order of 2 May 1997). 7.38
T-137/96 R *Valio v Commission* [1996] E.C.R. II-1327, (order of the President of
14 October 1996). 13.25
T-149/96 *Coldiretti and Others v Council and Commission* [1998] E.C.R. II-3841 . . . . 11.15, 11.76
T-157/96 *Affatato v Commission* [1997] E.C.R. II-155, (order of 19 February 1997) 25.101
T-158/96 *Acciaierie di Bolzano v Commission* [1999] E.C.R. II-3927 . . . . 7.165, 25.67
T-178/96 *Eridania and Others v Council*, not reported, (order of 11 May 2001). 7.99, 25.16
T-179/96 R *Antonissen v Council and Commission* [1996] E.C.R. II-1641, (order of the
President of 29 November 1996). 13.11
T-179/96 R *Antonissen v Council and Commission* [1997] E.C.R. II-425, (order of the
President of 21 March 1997). 13.11
T-185/96, T-189/96, and T-190/96 *Riviera Auto Service and Others v Commission* [1999]
E.C.R. II-93. . . . . 7.192
T-186/96 *Mutual Aid Administration Services v Commission*, [1997] E.C.R. II-1633 (order of
3 October 1997) 7.15, 19.12
T-191/96 and T-106/97 *CAS Succhi di Frutta v Commission* [1999] E.C.R. II-3181 . . . . 7.141,
7.216, 13.45, 25.67
T-201/96 *Smanor and Others v Commission* [1997] E.C.R. II-1081, (order of 3 July 1997). 5.34
T-203/96 *Embassy Limousines & Services v European Parliament* [1998] E.C.R. II-4239 . . . . 11.66
T-220/96 *EVO v Council and Commission* [2002] E.C.R. II-2265. . . . . 11.81
T-334/96 *Smets v Commission* [1997] E.C.R. II-2333, (order of 10 December 1997). 25.45

T-4/97 *D'Orazio and Hublau v Commission* [1997] E.C.R. II-1505,
(order of 29 September 1997) 13.28
T-5/97 *Industrie des Poudres Sphériques v Commission* [2000] E.C.R. II-3755. . . . . 25.10
T-9/97 *Elf Atochem v Commission* [1997] E.C.R. II-909, (order of 9 June 1997) 7.32
T-18/97 *Atlantic Container Line and Others v Commission* [1998] E.C.R. II-589, (order of the
President of 23 March 1998). 25.69
T-22/97 *Kesko v Commission* [1999] E.C.R. II-3775 . . . . 7.10, 7.138
T-37/97 *Forges de Clabecq v Commission* [1999] E.C.R. II-859 . . . . 7.144, 25.60
T-39/97 *T. Port v Commission* [1997] E.C.R. II-2125, (order of 26 November 1997) 8.06, 8.21
T-41/97 R *Antillean Rice Mills v Council* [1997] E.C.R. II-447, (order of the President of
21 March 1997). 13.16, 13.36
T-46/97 *SIC v Commission* [2000] E.C.R. 2125 . . . . 7.54
T-74/97 and T-75/97 *Büchel v Council and Commission* [2000] E.C.R. II-3067. . . . . 7.130, 7.133
T-81/97 *Regione Toscana v Commission* [1998] E.C.R. II-2889 . . . . 25.37
T-83/97 *Sateba v Commission* [1997] E.C.R. II-1523, (order of 29 September 1997) 5.39, 7.18
T-85/97 *Horeca-Wallonie v Commission* [1997] E.C.R. II-2113, (order of 20 November 1997). 23.32
T-110/97 *Kneissl Dachstein v Commission* [1999] E.C.R. II-2881 . . . . 7.202, 7.210
T-112/97 *Monsanto v Commission* [1999] E.C.R. II-1277. . . . . 7.97
T-123/97 *Salomon v Commission* [1999] E.C.R. II-2925 . . . . 7.59, 7.187, 7.202, 7.210
T-125/97 and T-127/97 *Coca-Cola v Commission* [2000] E.C.R. II-1733 . . . . . 7.16, 7.22, 7.49, 7.51, 7.139
T-143/97 *Van den Berg v Council and Commission* [2001] E.C.R. II-277. 11.94
T-147/97 *Champion Stationery and Others v Council* [1998] E.C.R. II-4137 . . . . 7.131, 7.166
T-148/97 *Keeling v OHIM* [1998] E.C.R. II-2217, (order of 8 June 1998) 7.70
T-152/97 *Petrides v Commission* [1997] E.C.R. II-2427 . . . . 11.87
T-175/97 *Bareyt and Others v Commission* [2000] E.C.R.-SC I-A-229 and II-1053 . . . . 23.64
T-183/97 R *Micheli and Others v Commission* [1997] E.C.R. II-1473, (order of the President of
26 September 1997). 13.42

T-184/97 *BP Chemicals v Commission* [2000] E.C.R. II-3145 . . . . 7.22, 25.60

T-186/97, T-187/97, T-190/97 to T-192/97, T-210/97, T-211/97, T-216/97 to T-218/97,
    T-279/97, T-280/97, T-293/97, and T-147/99 *Kaufring and Others v Commission* [2001]
    E.C.R. II-1337 . . . . 7.146, 7.161, 7.163

T-189/97 *Comité d'entreprise de la Société francaise de production and Others v Commission*
    [1998] E.C.R. II-335, (order of 18 February 1998) 7.92, 7.123

T-194/97 and T-83/98 *Branco v Commission* [2000] E.C.R. II-69. 8.21

T-207/97 *Berthu v Council* [1998] E.C.R. II-509, (order of 12 March 1998). 7.105

T-220/97 *H & R Ecroyd v Commission* [1999] E.C.R. II-1677 . . . . 7.224, 10.21

T-222/97 *Steffens v Council and Commission* [1998] E.C.R. II-4175 . . . . 11.94

T-231/97 *New Europe Consulting and Brown v Commission* [1999] E.C.R. II-2403 . . . 11.59, 11.64, 11.65

T-238/97 *Comunidad Autónoma de Catanbria v Council* [1998] E.C.R. II-2271,
    (order of 16 June 1998) 7.77, 7.125

T-241/97 *Stork Amsterdam v Commission* [2000] E.C.R. II-309 . . . . 7.43

T-251/97 *T. Port v Commission* [2000] E.C.R. II-1775 . . . . 25.12

T-252/97 *Dürbeck v Commission* [2000] E.C.R. II-3031. . . . . 25.13

T-256/97 *BEUC v Commission* [2000] E.C.R. II-101. . . . . 7.140

T-256/97 *BEUC v Commission* [2000] E.C.R. II-169, (order of 1 February 1999) 7.141

T-260/97 *Camar v Council and Commission* [2005] E.C.R. II-2741 . . . . 11.65

T-262/97 *Goldstein v Commission* [1998] E.C.R. II-2175, (order of 14 May 1998) 25.10

T-263/97 *GAL Penisola Sorrentina v Commission* [2000] E.C.R. II-2041,
    (order of 13 April 2000) 7.208

T-267/97 *Broome & Wellington v Commission* [1998] E.C.R. II-2191, (order of 25 May 1998). 7.65

T-275/97 *Guérin Automobiles v Commission* [1998] E.C.R. II-253, (order of 13 February 1998). . . . 7.213

T-276/97 *Guérin Automobiles v Commission* [1998] E.C.R. II-261, (order of 13 February 1998). . . . 7.213

T-277/97 *Ismeri Europa v Court of Auditors* [1999] E.C.R. II-1825 . . . . 11.76, 11.78, 25.12

T-286/97 *Goldstein v Commission* [1998] E.C.R. II-2629, (order of 6 July 1998). 8.06

T-288/97 *Regione Autonoma Friuli Venezia Giulia v Commission* [1998] E.C.R. II-1871. . . . . .7.77,
    7.125, 7.140

T-296/97 *Alitalia v Commission* [2000] E.C.R. II-3871 . . . . 7.59, 7.123, 7.201, 7.210, 7.216

T-300/97 *Latino v Commission* [1999] E.C.R. II-1263 . . . . 11.35

T-309/97 *Bavarian Lager v Commission* [1999] E.C.R. II-3217. . . . . 5.40

T-310/97 R *Netherlands Antilles v Council* [1998] E.C.R. II-455, (order of the President of
    2 March 1998) 13.25

T-310/97 *Nederlandse Antillen v Council* [1998] E.C.R. II-4131, (order of 16 November 1998) 2.55

T-311/97 *Pescados Congelados Jogamar v Commission* [1999] E.C.R. II-1407,
    (order of 30 April 1999) 8.18

T-597/97 *Euromin v Council* [2000] E.C.R. II-2419 . . . . 7.131, 7.133

T-598/97 *BSC Footwear Supplies and Others v Council* [2002] E.C.R. II-1155 . . . . 7.131, 7.133

T-609/97 *Regione Puglia v Commission and Spain* [1998] E.C.R. II-4051 . . . . 7.77

T-610/97 R *Carlsen and Others v Council* [1998] E.C.R. II-485, (order of the President of
    3 March 1998) 13.04

T-613/97 *Ufex v Commission* [2000] E.C.R. II-4055 . . . . 7.61, 7.165

T-614/97 *Aduanas Pujol Rubio and Others v Council and Commission* [2000] E.C.R. II-2387,
    (order of 15 June 2000) 11.18

T-7/98 DEP, T-208/98 DEP and T-109/99 DEP *De Nicola v EIB* [2004] E.C.R.-SC II-973,
    (order of 8 July 2004). 25.93

T-9/98 *Mitteldeutsche Erdöl-Raffinerie v Commission* [2001] E.C.R. II-3367 . . . . .7.120, 7.121,
    7.122, 7.138

T-10/98 *E-Quattro v Commission* [1999] E.C.R. II-1811 . . . . 19.07

T-12/98 and T-13/98 *Argon and Others v Council and Commission* [2000] E.C.R. II-2473,
    (order of 26 June 2000) 11.18

T-14/98 *Hautala v Council* [1999] E.C.R. II-2489. . . . . 1.06

T-32/98 and T-41/98 *Nederlandse Antillen v Commission* [2000] E.C.R. II-201. . . . . 7.100

T-37/98 *FTA and Others v Council* [2000] E.C.R. II-373, (order of 24 February 2000) 23.17, 23.51

T-42/98 R *Sabbatucci v European Parliament* [1998] E.C.R. II-3043, (order of the President of
    12 August 1998) 25.82

T-43/98 *Emesa Sugar v Council* [2001] E.C.R. II-3519 . . . . .6.30, 7.100, 11.48, 11.51

T-44/98 R II *Emesa Sugar v Commission* [1999] E.C.R. II-1427, (order of the President of
30 April 1999) 13.42
T-44/98 R II *Emesa Sugar v Commission* [1999] E.C.R. II-2815, (order of the President of
29 September 1999) 13.15
T-46/98 and T-151/98 *CCRE v Commission* [2000] E.C.R. II-167 . . . . 7.11
T-60/98 R *Ecord Consortium v Commission* [1998] E.C.R. II-2205, (order of the President of
26 May 1998) 13.34
T-62/98 *Volkswagen v Commission* [2000] E.C.R. II-2707 . . . . 7.192
T-63/98 *Transpo Maastricht and Ooms v Commission* [2000] E.C.R. II-135 . . . . 7.147
T-65/98 R *Van den Bergh Foods v Commission* [1998] E.C.R. II-2641, (order of the President of
7 July 1998). 13.34
T-65/98 *Van den Bergh Foods v Commission* [2003] E.C.R. II-4653. . . . . 7.178, 25.76
T-73/98 R *Prayon-Rupel v Commission* [1998] E.C.R. II-2769, (order of the President of
15 July 1998). 25.76
T-78/98 *Unione provinciale degli agricoltori di Firenze and Others v Commission* [1999]
E.C.R. II-1377, (order of 29 April 1999) 7.140
T-81/98 *Boyes v Commission* [1999] E.C.R. II-3501. . . . . 25.84
T-94/98 *Alferink v Commission* [2008] E.C.R. II-1125 . . . . 9.15
T-110/98 *RJB Mining v Commission* [2000] E.C.R. II-2971, (order of 25 July 2000) 25.13
T-112/98 *Mannesmannröhren-Werke v Commission* [2001] E.C.R. II-729 . . . . 7.31
T-120/98 *Alce v Commission* [1999] E.C.R. II-1395, (order of 29 April 1999). 7.99
T-138/98 *ACAV and Others v Council* [2000] E.C.R. II-341 . . . . 7.106
T-145/98 *ADT Projekt v Commission* [2000] E.C.R. II-387 . . . . 23.18, 23.36, 25.12
T-154/98 *Asia Motor France and Others v Commission* [2000] E.C.R. II-3453 . . . . 7.146, 7.223
T-158/99 *Thermenhotel Stoiser Franz and Others v Commission* [2004] E.C.R. II-1 . . . . 7.118
T-163/98 *Procter & Gamble v OHIM* [1999] E.C.R. II-2383 . . . . 20.20
T-166/98 *Cantina sociale di Dolianova and Others v Commission* [2004] E.C.R. II-3991 . . . . . . 8.21, 11.10,
11.28, 11.30, 11.51
T-172/98 and T-175/98 to T-177/98 *Salamander and Others v European Parliament and Council*
[2000] E.C.R. II-2487 . . . . 7.94, 7.106, 11.12
T-173/98 *Unión de Pequeños Agricultores v Council* [1999] E.C.R. II-3357, (order of
23 November 1999) 4.11, 7.104
T-178/98 *Fresh Marine v Commission* [2000] E.C.R. II-3331 . . . . 11.09, 11.54, 11.57, 11.85
T-178/98 DEP *Fresh Marine v Commission* [2004] E.C.R. II-3127, (order of
5 September 2004) 25.92, 25.93
T-186/98 *Inpesca v Commission* [2001] E.C.R. II-557 . . . . 7.23, 11.10
T-190/98 *Gluiber v Council and Commission*, not reported, (order of 5 May 1999). 5.34
T-191/98 R II *Cho Yang Shipping v Commission* [1999] E.C.R. II-3909, (order of the
President of 15 December 1999) 13.32
T-191/98, T-212/98, T-213/98, and T-214/98 *Atlantic Container Line and Others v
Commission* [2003] E.C.R. II-3275 . . . . 7.36, 25.56, 25.95

T-1/99 *T. Port v Commission* [2001] E.C.R. II-465 . . . . 11.75
T-2/99 *T. Port v Council* [2001] E.C.R. II-2093 . . . . 11.51
T-3/99 *Banatrading v Council* [2001] E.C.R. II-2123. . . . . 11.51, 25.13
T-5/99 *Andriotis v Commission and CEDEFOP* [2000] E.C.R. II-235, (order of
10 February 2000) 7.141
T-7/99 *Medici Grimm v Council* [2000] E.C.R. II-2671 . . . . 7.133
T-9/99 *HFB and Others v Commission* [2002] E.C.R. II-1487. 23.66, 23.67
T-11/99 R *Van Parijs and Others v Commission* [1999] E.C.R. II-1355, (order of the
President of 28 April 1999). 13.25
T-11/99 *Van Parijs and Others v Commission* [1999] E.C.R. II-2653, (order of
15 September 1999) 7.99, 7.105
T-12/99 and T-63/99 *UK Coal v Commission* [2001] E.C.R. II-2153 . . . . 7.146
T-13/99 *Pfizer Animal Health v Council* [2002] E.C.R. II-3305 . . . . 7.100
T-18/99 *Cordis v Commission* [2001] E.C.R. II-913. . . . . 11.51, 11.53
T-30/99 *Bocchi Food Trade International v Commission* [2001] E.C.R. II-943. . . . . 11.51, 11.53
T-31/99 *ABB Asea Brown Boveri v Commission* [2002] E.C.R. II-1881 . . . . 7.147
T-35/99 *Keller and Keller Meccanica v Commission* [2002] E.C.R. II-261 . . . . 7.26, 7.178, 7.203

T-36/99 *Lenzing v Commission* [2004] E.C.R. II-3597 . . . . 7.124, 7.201, 25.13, 25.14, 25.17

T-38/99 to T-50/99 *Sociedade Agrícola dos Arinhos and Others v Commission* [2001]
E.C.R. II-585. . . . . 7.100

T-52/99 *T. Port v Commission* [2001] E.C.R. II-981 . . . . 11.24, 11.51

T-54/99 *max.mobil Telekommunication Service v Commission* [2002] E.C.R. II-313 . . . . 5.33, 7.44

T-55/99 *CETM v Commission* [2000] E.C.R. II-3207 . . . . 7.122, 7.127, 7.128

T-57/99 *Nardonex v Commission*, not reported, (judgment of 10 December 2008). 11.36

T-61/99 *Adriatica di Navigazione v Commission* [2003] E.C.R. II-5349. 15.09

T-62/99 *Sodima v Commission* [2001] E.C.R. II-655 . . . . 25.86

T-65/99 *Strintzis Lines Shipping v Commission* [2003] E.C.R. II-5433. 15.09

T-66/99 *Minoan Lines v Commission* [2003] E.C.R. II-5515. . . . . 15.09

T-68/99 *Toditec v Commission* [2001] E.C.R. II-1443 . . . . 2.29

T-69/99 *DSTV v Commission* [2000] E.C.R. II-4039. . . . . 7.95

T-70/99 *Alpharma v Council* [1999] E.C.R. II-3495 . . . . 7.100

T-77/99 REV *Ojha v Commission* [2002] E.C.R.-SC I-A-29 . . . . 25.117

T-78/99 (92) *Elder v Commission* [2000] E.C.R. II-3717, (order of 27 November 2000) 25.91

T-79/99 *Euro-Lex v OHIM* [1999] E.C.R. II-3555, (order of 8 December 1999). 20.21, 23.17, 23.51

T-95/99 *Satellimages TV5 v Commission* [2002] E.C.R. II-1425 . . . . 7.28

T-103/99 *Associazione delle Cantine Sociali Venete v European Ombudsman and European
Parliament* [2000] E.C.R. II-4165, (order of 22 May 2000) 8.11, 8.13, 25.84

T-107/99 R *García Retortillo v Council* [1999] E.C.R. II-1939, (order of the President of
21 June 1999) 18.27

T-112/99 *M6 and Others v Commission* [2001] E.C.R. II-2459. . . . . 7.22

T-115/99 *SEP v Commission* [2001] E.C.R. II-691 . . . . 7.192

T-120/99 *Kik v Commission* [2001] E.C.R. II-2235 . . . . 9.08, 9.16, 20.17

T-122/99 *Procter & Gamble v OHIM* [2000] E.C.R. II-265. . . . . 20.12

T-123/99 *JT's Corporation v Commission* [2000] E.C.R. II-3269 . . . . 7.27

T-127/99, T-129/99 and T-148/99 *Diputación Foral de Guipúzcoa and Others v Commission*
[2002] E.C.R. II-1275 . . . . 7.147

T-131/99 *Shaw and Falla v Commission* [2002] E.C.R. II-2023 . . . . 7.112

T-135/99 *Taurus-Film v OHIM* [2001] E.C.R. II-379 . . . . 25.91

T-136/99 *Taurus-Film v OHIM* [2001] E.C.R. II-397. . . . . 25.91

T-139/99 *AICS v European Parliament* [2000] E.C.R. II-2849 . . . . 25.13, 25.49

T-152/99 *HAMSA v Commission* [2002] E.C.R. II-3049 . . . . 7.201

T-155/99 *Dieckmann & Hansen v Commission* [2001] E.C.R. II-3143. . . . . 11.51, 11.52, 11.53

T-158/99 *Thermenhotel Stoiser Franz and Others v Commission* [2004] E.C.R. II-1 . . . . 23.51

T-171/99 *Corus UK v Commission* [2001] E.C.R. II-2967 . . . . 7.226

T-188/99 *Euroalliages v Commission* [2001] E.C.R. II-1757 . . . . 7.138

T-191/99 *Petrie and Others v Commission* [2001] E.C.R. II-3677 . . . . 5.40

T-192/99 *Dunnett and Others v EIB* [2001] E.C.R. II-813 . . . . 18.09, 18.25, 23.60, 23.66

T-196/99 *Area Cova and Others v Council and Commission* [2001] E.C.R. II-3597. . . . 11.07, 11.51, 11.78

T-204/99 *Mattila v Council and Commission* [2001] E.C.R. II-2265 . . . . 25.14

T-206/99 *Métropole Télévision v Commission* [2001] E.C.R. II-1057 . . . . 7.146, 7.170

T-210/99 *Gankema v Commission* [2004] E.C.R. II-781, (order of 1 March 2004). 25.84

T-212/99 *Intervet International v Commission* [2002] E.C.R. II-1145 . . . . 8.06, 8.19, 8.21

T-213/99 *Verheyden v Commission* [2000] E.C.R.-SC I-A-297, II-1355. . . . . 18.04

T-217/99, T-321/00 and T-222/01 *Sinaga v Commission*, not reported. 7.66

T-219/99 *British Airways v Commission* [2003] E.C.R. II-5917. . . . . 7.156

T-222/99, T-327/99 and T-329/99 *Martinez and Others v European Parliament* [2001]
E.C.R. II-2823. . . . . 7.16, 7.69, 7.92, 9.03, 9.08

T-228/99 and T-233/99 *Westdeutsche Landesbank Girozentrale v Commission* [2003]
E.C.R. II-435. . . . . 23.60, 25.86

T-231/99 *Joynson v Commission* [2002] E.C.R. II-2085 . . . . 1.03, 7.145, 7.146

T-269/99, T-271/99 and T-272/99 *Diputación Foral de Guipúzcoa and Others v
Commission* [2002] E.C.R. II-4217 . . . . 7.57, 7.125

T-326/99 *Fern Olivieri v Commission* [2000] E.C.R. II-1985 . . . . 7.140

T-331/99 *Mitsubishi HiTec Paper Bielefeld v OHIM* [2001] E.C.R. II-433. . . . . 20.20

T-332/99 *Jestädt v Council and Commission* [2001] E.C.R. II-2561, (order of
19 September 2001). 11.94

T-333/99 *X v ECB* [2001] E.C.R. II-3021,. 2.53, 18.09
T-337/99 *Henkel v OHIM* [2001] E.C.R. II-2597. . . . . 20.05
T-338/99 *Schuerer v Council* [2000] E.C.R. II-2571, E.C.R.-SC I-A-131 . . . . 25.10
T-340/99 *Arne Mathisen v Council* [2002] E.C.R. II-2905 . . . . 7.205
T-342/99 *Airtours v Commission* [2002] E.C.R. II-2585 . . . . 7.197
T-342/99 DEP *Airtours v Commission* [2004] E.C.R. II-1785, (order of 28 June 2004) 25.93
T-346/99 to T-348/99 *Diputación Foral de Álava and Others v Commission* [2002]
    E.C.R. II 4259. . . . . 7.57
T-354/99 *Kuwait Petroleum (Nederland) v Commission* [2006] E.C.R. II-1475. . . . . 7.138
T-359/99 *DKV v OHIM* [2001] E.C.R. II-1645 . . . . 20.20
T-361/99 *Meyer v Commission and European Investment Bank* [2000] E.C.R. II-2031,
    (order of 10 April 2000) 5.03, 11.27, 11.81

T-1/00 R *Hölzl and Others v Commission* [2000] E.C.R. II-251, (order of the President of
    15 February 2000) 7.99
T-3/00 and T-337/04 *Pitsiorlas v Council and ECB* [2007] E.C.R. II- 4779. . . . . 9.08, 9.15, 11.20,
    11.38, 11.81
T-5/00 R *Nederlandse Federatieve Vereniging voor de Groothandel op Elektrotechnisch Gebied v
    Commission* [2000] E.C.R. II-4121, (order of the President of 14 December 2000). 25.68
T-11/00 *Hautem v EIB* [2000] E.C.R. II-4019 . . . . 7.225, 11.64, 25.104
T-17/00 *Rothley and Others v European Parliament* [2002] E.C.R. II-579 . . . . 7.69
T-20/00 OP *Commission v Camacho-Fernandes*, not reported, (order of 21 November 2001) 23.68
T-24/00 *Sunrider v OHIM* [2001] E.C.R. II-449. . . . . 20.15, 25.16
T-26/00 *Lecureur v Commission* [2001] E.C.R. II-2623 . . . . 19.12
T-30/00 *Cartondruck v Council and Commission* [2005] E.C.R. II-27*, Summ. pub. 11.07
T-30/00 *Henkel v OHIM* [2001] E.C.R. II-2663. . . . . 20.05, 20.11
T-31/00 *BSB-Fleischimport v Commission*, not reported, (order of 31 July 2000). 7.10
T-32/00 *Messe München v OHIM* [2000] E.C.R. II-3829. . . . . 25.91
T-34/00 *Eurocool Logistik v OHIM* [2002] E.C.R. II-683. . . . . 20.12, 25.91
T-41/00 *British American Tobacco International v Commission* [2001] E.C.R. II-1301. . . . . . . 7.135, 7.140
T-44/00 *Mannesmannröhren-Werke v Commission* [2004] E.C.R. II-2223 . . . . . . 7.26, 7.146, 7.174, 7.194
T-47/00 *Rica Foods v Commission* [2002] E.C.R. II-113. . . . . 7.100
T-50/00 *Dalmine v Commission* [2004] E.C.R. II-2395 . . . . 7.22, 7.31
T-56/00 *Dole Fresh Fruit International v Council and Commission* [2003] E.C.R. II-577 . . . . 11.45,
    11.48, 11.51, 11.57, 11.60
T-67/00, T-68/00, T-71/00, and T-78/00 *JFE Engineering and Others v Commission*
    [2004] E.C.R. II-2501 . . . . 7.146, 7.190, 7.191, 7.192, 15.05, 15.09, 23.43
T-69/00 *FIAMM and FIAMM Technologies v Council and Commission* [2005]
    E.C.R. II-5393. . . . . 2.29, 11.07
T-74/00 R *Artegodan v Commission* [2000] E.C.R. II-2583, (order of the President of
    28 June 2000) 13.36
T-74/00 R *Artegodan v Commission* [2001] E.C.R. II-2367, (order of the President of
    5 September 2001). 13.44
T-79/00 *Rewe-Zentral v OHIM* [2002] E.C.R. II-705 . . . . 20.12
T-83/00 R I *Hänseler v Commission* [2000] E.C.R. II-3563, (order of the President of
    31 October 2000). 13.34
T-89/00 *Europe Chemi-Con v Council* [2002] E.C.R. II-3651. . . . . 7.138
T-94/00 R and T-110/00 R *Rica Foods and Others v Commission*, not reported, (order of the
    President of 12 July 2000) 13.36
T-97/00 *Vakalopoulou v Commission* [2001] E.C.R.-SC I-A-23, II-91 . . . . 18.04
T-106/00 *Streamserve v OHIM* [2002] E.C.R. II-723. . . . . 20.20
T-111/00 *British American Tobacco International v Commission*, not reported, (order of
    19 February 2001) 23.66
T-113/00 *Dupont Teijin Films Luxembourg and Others v Commission* [2002] E.C.R. II-3681. . . . . . . 7.16
T-123/00 DEP *Thomae v Commission*, not reported, (order of 20 December 2004) 25.92, 25.93
T-126/00 *Confindustria and Others v Commission* [2001] E.C.R. II-85, (order of
    19 January 2001) 23.32
T-129/00 *Procter & Gamble v OHIM* [2001] E.C.R. II-2793. . . . . 20.11, 20.12
T-147/00 *Laboratoires Servier v Commission* [2003] E.C.R. II-85. . . . . 7.146
T-148/00 *Panhellenic Union of Cotton Ginners and Exporters v Commission* [2003]
    E.C.R. II-4415. . . . . 5.32, 7.18

T-149/00 *Innova v Commission* [2001] E.C.R. II-1, (order of 9 January 2001). 7.15, 19.10
T-151/00 *Laboratoire du Bain v Council and Commission* [2005] E.C.R. II-23*,
    Summ. pub. 2.29, 11.07
T-158/00 *ARD v Commission*, not reported, (order of 11 December 2000) 25.70
T-170/00 *Förde-Reederei v Council and Commission* [2002] E.C.R. II-515 . . . . 11.07, 11.09, 11.53
T-174/00 *Biret International v Council* [2002] E.C.R. II-417 . . . . 11.51, 11.88
T-177/00 *Koninklijke Philips Electronics v Council*, not reported, (judgment of 13 March 2005) 7.66
T-178/00 and T-341/00 *Pflugradt v ECB* [2002] E.C.R. II-4035 . . . . 25.16
T-180/00 *Astipesca v Commission* [2002] E.C.R. II-3985 . . . . 7.170, 11.10, 23.18
T-190/00 *Regione Siciliana v Commission* [2003] E.C.R. II-5015. . . . . 7.57, 7.214, 7.216
T-198/00 *Hershey Foods v OHIM* [2002] E.C.R. II-2567 . . . . 20.12
T-202/00 *Costacurta v Commission*, not reported, (order of 7 June 2001). 25.16
T-209/00 *Lamberts v European Ombudsman* [2002] E.C.R. II-2203 . . . . 5.31, 5.34, 11.09,
                                           11.19, 11.20, 11.27, 11.53, 11.81
T-210/00 *Biret & Cie v Council* [2002] E.C.R. II-47 . . . . 11.25, 11.45, 11.51, 11.88, 25.12, 25.16
T-214/00 *X v Commission* [2001] E.C.R.-SC I-A-143 . . . . 25.92
T-224/00 *Archer Daniels Midland and Archer Daniels Midland Ingredients v Commission*
    [2003] E.C.R. II-2597 . . . . 7.185
T-228/00, T-229/00, T-242/00, T-243/00, T-245/00 to T-248/00, T-250/00, T-252/00,
    T-256/00–T-259/00, T-265/00, T-267/00, T-268/00, T-271/00, T-274/00–T-276/00,
    T-281/00, T-287/00–T-296/00 *Gruppo ormeggiatori del porto di Venezia and Others v*
    Commission [2005] E.C.R. II-787, (order of 10 March 2005) 7.122, 7.217, 10.11, 25.85
T-236/00 R *Stauner and Others v European Parliament and Commission* [2001] E.C.R. II-15,
    (order of the President of 15 January 2001) 13.29
T-236/00 *Stauner and Others v European Parliament and Commission* [2002] E.C.R. II-135
    (order of 17 January 2002) 1.03, 7.69
T-237/00 DEP *Reynolds v European Parliament*, not reported, (order of 7 December 2004) 25.92
T-238/00 *IPSO and USE v ECB* [2002] E.C.R. II-2237, (order of 18 April 2002). 7.18
T-241/00 R *Le Canne v Commission* [2001] E.C.R. II-37, (order of the President of
    15 January 2001) 13.36
T-241/00 *Le Canne v Commission* [2002] E.C.R. II-1251. . . . . 7.170, 11.09
T-251/00 *Lagardère and Canal + v Commission* [2002] E.C.R. II-4825 . . . . 7.48
T-254/00, T-270/00, and T-277/00 *Hotel Cipriani and Others v Commission* [2008]
    E.C.R. II-3269. . . . . .7.137, 7.204, 7.217
T-266/00 *Confartigianato Venezia and Others v Commission*, not reported,
    (order of 10 March 2005). 7.122
T-269/00 *Baglioni Hotels and Sagar v Commission*, not reported, (order of 10 March 2005) 7.138
T-273/00 *Unindustria and Others v Commission*, not reported, (order of
    10 March 2005). 7.120, 7.122, 7.138
T-301/00 *Groupe Fremaux and Palais Royal v Council and Commission* [2005]
    E.C.R. II-25*, Summ. pub. 2.29
T-302/00 R *Goldstein v Commission* [2001] E.C.R. II-1127, (order of the President) 23.23
T-306/00 *Conserve Italia v Commission* [2003] E.C.R. II-5705 . . . . 7.178
T-310/00 *MCI v Commission* [2004] E.C.R. II-3253 . . . . .7.138, 7.217, 13.19
T-311/00 *British American Tobacco v Commission* [2002] E.C.R. II-2781 . . . . 25.96
T-318/00 *Freistaat Thüringen v Commission* [2005] E.C.R. II-4179. . . . . 23.45
T-320/00 *CD Cartondruck v Council and Commission* [2005] E.C.R. II-27*, Summ. pub. 2.29
T-323/00 *SAT.1 v OHIM* [2002] E.C.R. II-2839 . . . . 20.05
T-334/00 *Goldstein v Court of Justice*, not reported, (order of 5 February 2001) 23.89
T-339/00 R *Bactria v Commission* [2001] E.C.R. II-1721, (order of the President of
    15 June 2001) 13.42
T-339/00 *Bactria v Commission* [2002] E.C.R. II-2287, (order of 29 April 2002). 7.106, 23.28, 25.65
T-344/00 and T-345/00 *CEVA and Pharmacia Entreprises v Commission*
    [2002] E.C.R. II-1445 . . . . 8.06, 8.19
T-350/00 R *Free Trade Foods v Commission* [2001] E.C.R. II-493, (order of the
    President of 1 February 2001). 13.08
T-353/00 R *Le Pen v European Parliament* [2001] E.C.R. II-125, (order of the
    President of 26 January 2001). 13.42
T-365/00 *AICS v European Parliament* [2002] E.C.R. II-2719 . . . . 7.23
T-366/00 R *Scott v Commission*, not reported, (order of the President of 30 March 2007). 13.24
T-372/00 *Campolargo v Commission* [2002] E.C.R.-SC I-A-49 . . . . 7.223

T-374/00 *Verband der freien Rohrwerke and Others v Commission* [2003] E.C.R. II-2275 . . . . 7.200
T-377/00, T-379/00, T-380/00, T-260/01, and T-272/01 *Philip Morris International and
    Others v Commission* [2003] E.C.R. II-1 . . . . 5.31
T-383/00 *Beamglow v European Parliament and Others* [2005] E.C.R. II-5459 . . . . 2.29, 11.07
T-387/00 *Comitato organizzatore del convegno internazionale v Commission* [2002]
    E.C.R. II-3031, (order of 10 July 2002). 25.28

T-18/01 R *Goldstein v Commission*, not reported, (order of the President of 29 March 2001) 13.07
T-19/01 *Chiquita Brands International and Others v Commission* [2005] E.C.R. II-315. . . . . 25.18
T-26/01 *Fiocchi Munizioni v Commission* [2003] E.C.R. II-3951 . . . . .5.28, 8.19, 8.21
T-30/01 to T-32/01 and T-86/02 to T-88/02 *Territorio Histórico de Álava and Others v
    Commission* [2009] E.C.R. II-2919 . . . . 7.142
T-33/01 *Infront v Commission* [2005] E.C.R. II-5897 . . . . 7.16
T-35/01 *Shanghai Teraoka Electronic v Council* [2004] E.C.R. II-3663 . . . . 7.166, 7.205
T-39/01 *Kabushiki Kaisha Fernandes v OHIM* [2002] E.C.R. II-5233. . . . . 20.20
T-40/01 *Scan Office Design v Commission* [2002] E.C.R. II-5043 . . . . 25.96
T-41/01 *Pérez Escolar v Commission* [2003] II-2157, (order of 25 June 2003) 7.118
T-45/01 *Sanders and Others v Commission* [2004] E.C.R. II-3315. . . . . 11.05, 11.68, 18.14,
                                                                                       18.18, 18.27
T-45/01 DEP *Sanders v Commission* [2009] E.C.R. II-4093, (order of 9 November 2009) 25.96
T-47/01 *Co-Frutta v Commission* [2003] E.C.R. II-4441 . . . . 7.28
T-51/01 *Fronia v Commission* [2002] E.C.R.-SC I-A-43, II-187 . . . . 18.04
T-57/01 *Solvay v Commission* [2009] E.C.R. II-4621 . . . . 7.163
T-63/01 *Procter & Gamble v OHIM* [2002] E.C.R. II-5255. . . . . 20.09
T-64/01 and T-65/01 *Afrikanische Frucht Compagnie and Others v Council and
    Commission* [2004] E.C.R. II-521 . . . . 11.07, 11.45, 11.48
T-67/01 *JCB Service v Commission* [2004] E.C.R. II-49 . . . . 7.178
T-84/01 *ACHE v European Parliament and Council* [2002] E.C.R. II-99, (order of
    14 January 2002) 7.104
T-85/01 *IAMA Consulting v Commission* [2003] E.C.R. II-4973, (order of
    25 November 2003) 2.54, 7.15, 19.10, 25.10
T-107/01 and T-175/01 *Société de Mines de Sacilor-Lormines v Commission* [2004]
    E.C.R. II-2125 . . . . 7.217
T-109/01 *Fleuren Compost v Commission* [2004] E.C.R. II-127 . . . . .7.59, 7.187, 7.204
T-110/01 *Vedial v OHIM* [2002] E.C.R. II-5275 . . . . 20.10
T-111/01 and T-133/01 *Saxonia Edelmetalle and Zemag v Commission* [2005]
    E.C.R. II-1579. . . . . 7.59, 7.187
T-116/01 and T-118/01 *P & O European Ferries and Others v Commission* [2003]
    E.C.R. II-2957. . . . . 7.227
T-120/01 and T-300/01 *De Nicola v EIB* [2004] E.C.R.-SC II-1671 . . . . 25.97
T-121/01 *Piau v Commission*, not reported, (order of 19 October 2001) 8.20
T-127/01 *Ripa di Meana v European Parliament* [2002] E.C.R. II-3005, (order of 9 July 2002) 7.23
T-129/01 DEP *Alejandro v OHIM*, not reported, (order of 15 December 2004) 25.91
T-132/01 R *Euroalliages v Commission* [2001] E.C.R. II-2307, (order of the President of
    1 August 2001) 13.36
T-133/01 *Schering-Plough v Commission and EMEA*, not reported, (order of
    5 December 2007) 7.73, 7.138
T-135/01 *Fedon & Figli and Others v Council and Commission* [2005] E.C.R. II-29*,
    Summ. pub. 2.29, 11.07
T-139/01 *Comafrica and Dole Fresh Fruit Europe v Commission* [2005] E.C.R. II-409. . . . . . . 7.100, 25.66
T-141/01 R *Entorn v Commission* [2001] E.C.R. II-3123, (order of the President of
    22 October 2001). 13.36
T-141/01 *Entorn v Commission* [2005] E.C.R. II-95 . . . . 13.36, 23.57, 23.59, 23.60, 23.63, 23.64
T-142/01 and T-283/01 *OPTUC v Commission* [2004] E.C.R. II-329 . . . . .7.207, 7.217,
                                                                                   23.34, 25.76, 25.85
T-146/01 *DLD Trading v Council* [2003] E.C.R. II-6005 .11.25, 11.78, 11.81
T-154/01 *Distilleria F. Palma v Commission* [2004] E.C.R. II-1493 . . . . 11.06
T-157/01 *Danske Busvognmænd v Commission* [2004] E.C.R. II-917 . . . . 7.104
T-167/01 *Schmitz-Gotha Fahrzeugwerke v Commission* [2003] E.C.R. II-1873, (order of
    30 April 2003) 7.141

T-172/01 *M v Court of Justice* [2004] E.C.R. II-1075 . . . . 23.67, 25.18, 25.29
T-176/01 *Ferriere Nord v Commission* [2004] E.C.R. II-3931 . . . . 7.178, 9.15
T-177/01 *Jégo-Quéré v Commission* [2002] E.C.R. II-2365 . . . . 4.11, 7.106, 7.110
T-184/01 R *IMS Health v Commission* [2001] E.C.R. II-2349, (order of the President of
    10 August 2001) 13.24
T-184/01 R *IMS Health v Commission* [2001] E.C.R. II-3193, (order of the President of
    26 October 2001). 13.05, 13.24
T-184/01 *IMS Health v Commission* [2005] E.C.R. II-817, (order of 10 March 2005) 7.10, 7.39
T-192/01 R *Lior v Commission* [2001] E.C.R. II-3657, (order of the President of
    7 December 2001) 13.36
T-194/01 *Unilever v OHIM* [2003] E.C.R. II-383. . . . . 20.15
T-195/01 and T-207/01 *Gibraltar v Commission* [2002] E.C.R. II-2309 . . . . 5.22, 7.57, 7.77, 25.81
T-196/01 R *Aristoteleio Panepistimio Thessalonikis v Commission* [2001] E.C.R. II-3107,
    (order of the President of 18 October 2001). 13.40
T-198/01 R *Technische Glaswerke Ilmenau v Commission* [2002] E.C.R. II-2153,
    (order of the President of 4 April 2002) 13.36, 13.44
T-198/01 *Technische Glaswerke Ilmenau v Commission* [2004] E.C.R. II-2717 . . . . 7.61, 7.165
T-203/01 *Michelin v Commission*, not reported, (order of the President of 15 October 2002) 25.76
T-208/01 *Volkswagen v Commission* [2003] E.C.R. II-5141 . . . . 25.46
T-209/01 *Honeywell International v Commission* [2005] E.C.R. II-5527 . . . . 25.12
T-210/01 *General Electric v Commission* 2005 E.C.R. II-5575. . . . . 7.164, 25.65
T-213/01 R *Österreichische Postsparkasse AG v Commission* [2001] E.C.R. II-3961,
    (order of the President of 20 December 2001) 7.38
T-213/01 and T-214/01 *Österreichische Postsparkasse and Bank für Arbeit und Wirtschaft v
    Commission* [2006] E.C.R. II-1601 . . . . 7.38, 7.138, 7.223
T-214/01 R *Bank für Arbeit und Wirtschaft v Commission* [2001] E.C.R. II-3993,
    (order of the President of 20 December 2001) 7.38, 13.41
T-215/01, T-220/01, and T-221/01 *Calberson v Commission* [2004] E.C.R. II-587 . . . 11.72, 19.12, 25.10
T-216/01 R *Reisebank v Commission* [2001] E.C.R. II-3481, (order of the President of
    5 December 2001) 13.08
T-216/01 *Reisebank v Commission*, not reported, (order of 9 July 2003). 7.16, 7.36
T-218/01 *Laboratoire Monique Rémy v Commission* [2002] E.C.R. II-2139, (order of
    21 March 2002). 23.38
T-219/01 R *Commerzbank v Commission* [2001] E.C.R. II-3501, (order of the President of
    5 December 2001) 13.08
T-223/01 *Japan Tobacco and JT International v European Parliament and Council* [2002]
    E.C.R. II-3259, (order of 10 September 2002). 7.94
T-226/01 *CAS Succhi di Frutta v Commission* [2006] E.C.R. II-2763 . . . . 11.56
T-227/01 to T-229/01, T-265/01, T-266/01, and T-270/01 *Territorio Histórico de Álava and
    Others v Commission* [2009] E.C.R. II-3029 . . . . 7.103, 7.126, 7.137
T-236/01, T-239/01, T-244/01, T-246/01, T-251/01, and T-252/01 *Tokai Carbon and
    Others v Commission* [2004] E.C.R. II-1181 . . . . 7.185, 15.09, 23.93
T-243/01 *Sony Computer Entertainment Europe v Commission* [2003] E.C.R. II-4189. . . . . 7.85, 7.100
T-247/01 *eCopy v OHIM* [2002] E.C.R. II-5301. . . . . 20.05, 20.12, 20.20, 25.10
T-248/01 *Papoulakos v Italy and Commission*, not reported, (order of 26 November 2001) . . . 11.27, 11.81
T-292/01 *Philips–Van Heusen v OHIM* [2003] E.C.R. II-4335. . . . . 20.04, 23.04
T-293/01 *Ineichen v Commission* [2003] E.C.R.-SC I-A-83, II-441 . . . . 25.18
T-297/01 and T-298/01 *SIC v Commission* [2004] E.C.R. II-743. . . . . 8.06, 8.19
T-301/01 *Alitalia v Commission* [2008] E.C.R. II-1753 . . . . 7.138, 7.223, 7.225
T-304/01 *Abad Péez and Others v Council and Commission* [2006] E.C.R. II-4857. . . . . 11.15, 11.34
T-306/01 *Yusuf and Al Barakaat International Foundation v Council and Commission*
    [2005] E.C.R. II-3533 . . . . 7.11, 7.153, 25.17
T-306/01 R *Aden and Others v Council and Commission* [2002] E.C.R. II-2387,
    (order of the President of 7 May 2000) 13.19, 13.26, 13.29, 13.36, 13.40, 23.66
T-307/01 *François v Commission* [2004] E.C.R. II-1669. . . . . 7.178
T-308/01 *Henkel v OHIM* [2003] E.C.R. II-3253. . . . . 20.12, 20.15
T-310/01 *Schneider Electric v Commission* [2002] E.C.R. II-4071 . . . . 25.81
T-313/01 *R v Commission*, not reported, (order of 10 July 2003) 23.68
T-315/01 *Kadi v Council and Commission* [2005] E.C.R. II-3649 . . . . 7.11
T-318/01 *Othman v Council and Commission* [2009] E.C.R. II-1627 . . . . 7.11, 7.73, 7.221

T-321/01 *Internationaler Hilfsfonds v Commission* [2003] E.C.R. II-3225. . . . . 7.23, 7.143
T-322/01 *Roquette Frères v Commission* [2006] E.C.R. II-3137 . . . . 15.04
T-329/01 *Archer Daniels Midland v Commission* [2006] E.C.R. II-3255 . . . . 15.07
T-330/01 *Akzo Nobel v Commission* [2006] E.C.R. II-3389 . . . . 15.07
T-333/01 *Meyer v Commission* [2003] E.C.R. II-117 . . . . 7.227
T-334/01 *MFE Marienfelde v OHIM* [2004] E.C.R. II-2787 . . . . 20.05

T-3/02 *Schlüsselverlag J.S.Moser and Others v Commission* [2002] E.C.R. II-1473,
(order of 11 March 2002) 8.19
T-5/02 *Tetra Laval v Commission* [2002] E.C.R. II-4381 . . . . 23.66, 25.81
T-5/02 DEP and T-80/02 DEP *Tetra Laval v Commission*, not reported,
(order of 31 March 2011) 25.93
T-10/02 *Girardot v Commission* [2004] E.C.R.-SC II-483 . . . . 15.05, 18.03
T-15/02 *BASF v Commission* [2006] E.C.R. II-497 . . . . 15.07
T-16/02 *Audi v OHIM* [2003] E.C.R. II-5167 . . . . 20.12
T-17/02 *Olsen v Commission* [2005] E.C.R. II-2031 . . . . 7.212, 7.214, 7.216
T-27/02 *Kronofrance v Commission* [2004] E.C.R. II-4177 . . . . 7.26, 7.203, 7.217,
16.16, 23.78, 25.49, 25.85
T-28/02 *First Data and Others v Commission* [2005] E.C.R. II-4119,
(order of 17 October 2005) 7.138, 7.142
T-29/02 *GEF v Commission* [2005] E.C.R. II-835 . . . . 25.85
T-38/02 *Groupe Danone v Commission* [2005] E.C.R. II-4407 . . . . 7.36, 7.192
T-43/02 *Jungbunzlauer v Commission* [2006] E.C.R. II-3435 . . . . 9.08
T-44/02 *Dresdner Bank v Commission*, not reported, (judgment of 14 October 2004) 25.31, 25.32
T-45/02 *DOW AgroSciences and Others v European Parliament and Council* [2003]
E.C.R. II-1973, (order of 6 May 2003) 7.94
T-47/02 *Danzer v Council* [2006] E.C.R. II-1779 . . . . 3.60, 11.10, 11.52
T-55/02 *Finch v Commission* [2004] E.C.R.-SC II-1621, (order of December 6, 2004) 18.25
T-64/02 *Heubach v Commission* [2005] E.C.R. II-5137 . . . . 9.08
T-76/02 *Messina v Commission* [2003] E.C.R. II-3203 . . . . 25.13, 25.49
T-77/02 DEP *Schneider Electric v Commission*, not reported, (order of 29 October 2004) 25.93
T-93/02 *Confédération nationale du Crédit mutuel v Commission* [2005] E.C.R. II-143 . . . . . . 7.170, 7.173
T-94/02 *Hugo Boss v OHIM* [2004] E.C.R. II-813, (order of 5 March 2004) 20.11
T-107/02 *GE Betz v OHIM* [2004] E.C.R. II-1845 . . . . 20.10
T-114/02 *BaByliss v Commission* [2003] E.C.R. II-1279 . . . . 7.113, 7.199, 25.60, 25.81
T-115/02 *AVEX v OHIM*, not reported, (judgment of 13 July 2004) 25.10
T-119/02 *Royal Philips Electronics v Commission* [2003] E.C.R. II-1433 . . . . 7.50, 7.116, 7.199
T-123/02 *Carrs Paper v Commission*, not reported, (order of 31 May 2006) 7.142
T-127/02 *Concept-Anlagen v OHIM* [2004] E.C.R. II-1113 . . . . 25.10
T-130/02 *Kronoply v Commission* [2003] E.C.R. II-4857, (order of 5 November 2003) 7.18
T-135/02 *Greencore v Commission* [2005] E.C.R. II-31*, Summ. pub. 8.09
T-139/02 *Institouto N. Avgerinopoulou and Others v Commission* [2004] E.C.R. II-875,
(order of 15 March 2004) 7.93, 7.101
T-143/02 *Olive v Commission and Others*, not reported, (order of 5 June 2002) 5.34, 8.06
T-144/02 *Eagle and Others v Commission* [2004] E.C.R. II-3381 . . . . 11.05, 18.14, 18.27
T-160/02 to T-162/02 *Naipes Heraclio Fournier v OHIM* [2005] E.C.R. II-1643 . . . . 20.11
T-164/02 *Kaul and Bayer v OHIM* [2004] E.C.R. II-3807 . . . . 20.12
T-165/02 *Lloris Maeso v Commission*, not reported, (order of 26 May 2004) 25.84
T-167/02 *Établissements Toulorge v European Parliament and Council* [2003] E.C.R. II-1111,
(order of 21 March 2003) 9.04
T-167/02 *Établissements Toulorge v European Parliament and Council* [2006] E.C.R. II-49*,
Summ. pub., (order of 7 July 2006) 11.76
T-171/02 *Regione autonoma della Sardegna v Commission* [2005] E.C.R. II-2123 . . . . . 7.203, 25.59, 25.60
T-177/02 *Malagutti-Vezinhet v Commission* [2004] E.C.R. II-827 . . . . 11.25
T-178/02 *WONUC and Others v Commission*, not reported, (order of 9 July 2003) 7.16
T-182/02 *Claude Ruiz-Picasso and Others v OHIM* [2004] E.C.R. II-1739 . . . . 20.15
T-185/02 *Ruiz-Picasso and Others v OHIM*, [2004] E.C.R. II-1739 . . . . 20.15, 25.04
T-189/02 *Ente per le Ville Vesuviane v Commission* [2007] E.C.R. II-89*, Summ. pub. 7.96
T-191/02 *Lebedef v Commission* [2005] E.C.R.-SC II-407 . . . . 18.05
T-193/02 *Piau v Commission* [2005] E.C.R. II-209 . . . . 7.43, 7.86
T-200/02 *Tsarnavas v Commission*, not reported, (order of 8 July 2004) 18.13

T-202/02 *Makedoniko Metro Michaniki v Commission* [2004] E.C.R. II-181,
   (order of 14 January 2004) 5.32, 7.223, 11.27, 11.47, 11.81, 15.05
T-207/02 *Falcone v Commission* [2004] E.C.R.-SC II-1393 .... 9.16
T-210/02 *British Aggregates v Commission* [2006] E.C.R. II-2789 .... 7.127
T-211/02 *Tideland Signal v Commission* [2002] E.C.R. II-3781 .... 7.141, 25.81
T-212/02 *Commune de Champagne and Others v Council and Commission* [2007]
   E.C.R. II-2017, (order of 3 July 2007). 7.17, 7.82, 7.100, 7.138, 9.15, 11.24, 11.81
T-213/02 *SNF v Commission* [2004] E.C.R. II-3047, (order of 6 September 2004) 7.100
T-216/02 *Fieldturf v OHIM* [2004] E.C.R. II-1023. .... 20.20
T-219/02 and T-337/02 *Lutz Herrera v Commission* [2004] E.C.R.-SC II-1407. .... 9.16
T-225/02 *Cámara de Comercio e Industria de Zaragoza v Commission* [2006] E.C.R. II-92*,
   Summ. pub., (order of 22 November 2006)...................................... 7.96
T-228/02 *OMPI v Council* [2006] E.C.R. II-4665. .... 7.04, 7.10, 7.11, 7.141, 11.34
T-229/02 *PKK v Council* [2008] E.C.R. II-45*, Summ. pub. 7.10, 26.12
T-229/02 *PKK and KNK v Council* [2005] E.C.R. II-539, (order of
   15 February 2005) 7.83, 7.104, 7.141, 7.218, 25.17, 25.44
T-231/02 *Gonnelli and AIFO v Commission* [2004] E.C.R. II-1051, (order of 2 April 2004)....... 7.106
T-235/02 *Strongline v OHIM* [2003] E.C.R. II-4903, (order of 17 November 2003)............ 20.21
T-236/02 *Marcuccio v Commission*, not reported, (judgment of 14 September 2011) 18.28
T-238/02 *Barbosa Goncalves v Commission* [2004] E.C.R.-SC II-473. .... 18.14, 18.26
T-242/02 *The Sunrider Corp. v OHIM* [2005] E.C.R. II-2793 .... 7.178, 20.12
T-250/02 *Autosalone Ispra v EAEC* [2005] E.C.R. II-5227 .... 11.03, 11.81
T-253/02 *Ayadi v Council* [2006] E.C.R. II-2139 .... 7.23
T-256/02 *I v Court of Justice* [2004] E.C.R. II-1307 .... 11.36
T-259/02 to T-264/02 and T-271/02 *Raiffeisen Zentralbank Österreich and Others v*
   Commission [2006] E.C.R. II-5169 .... 7.194, 15.05, 15.07, 15.09, 23.43
T-266/02 *Deutsche Post v Commission* [2008] E.C.R. II-1233 .... 7.202, 25.86
T-267/02 *Forum 187 v Commission* [2003] E.C.R. II-2075, (order of 2 June 2003)............. 7.57
T-279/02 *Degussa v Commission* [2006] E.C.R. II-897 ....9.08, 11.12, 15.05, 15.07
T-280/02 *Pikaart and Others v Commission* [2003] E.C.R. II-1621, (order of 9 April 2003) 7.18
T-282/02 *Cementbouw Handel & Industrie v Commission* [2006] E.C.R. II-319 .... 7.51
T-288/02 *AIT v Commission* [2003] E.C.R. II-2885, (order of the President of 9 July 2003) 13.26
T-289/02 *Telepharmacy Solutions v OHIM* [2004] E.C.R II-2851 .... 20.12
T-291/02 *González y Diéz v Commission*, not reported, (order of 2 September 2004) 25.99
T-296/02 *Lidl Stiftung v OHIM* [2005] E.C.R. II-563. .... 20.15
T-300/02 *AMGA v Commission* [2009] E.C.R. II-1737 .... 7.122
T-308/02 *SGL Carbon v Commission* [2004] E.C.R. II-1363, (order of
   29 April 2004)......................................7.23, 7.42, 7.217
T-310/02 *Theodorakis v Council* [2004] E.C.R.-SC II-427 .... 25.16
T-312/02 *Gussetti v Commission* [2004] E.C.R.-SC II-547 .... 18.26
T-317/02 *FICF and Others v Commission* [2004] E.C.R. II-4325 .... 7.137
T-320/02 *Esch-Leonhardt and Others v ECB* [2004] E.C.R.-SC II-79 .... 18.03
T-334/02 *Viomichania Syskevasias Typopoiisis Kai Syntirisis Agrotikon Proïonton v Commission*
   [2003] E.C.R. II-5121, (order of 2 December 2003) 8.06, 8.21
T-341/02 *Regione Siciliana v Commission* [2004] E.C.R. II-2877, (order of 8 July 2004) 7.96
T-342/02 *Metro-Goldwyn-Mayer Lion v OHIM* [2004] E.C.R. II-3191 .... 20.11
T-343/02 *Schintgen v Commission* [2004] E.C.R.-SC II-605 .... 9.07
T-346/02 and T-347/02, *Cableuropa and Others v Commission* [2003]
   E.C.R. II-4251. ....7.50, 7.93, 7.116, 25.81
T-346/02 and T-347/02 DEP *Cableuropa and Others v Commission*, not reported,
   (order of 24 January 2005) 25.93
T-351/02 *Deutsche Bahn v Commission* [2006] E.C.R. II-1047 ....7.55, 7.61, 9.15
T-356/02 *Vitakraft-Werke Wührmann & Sohn v OHIM* [2004] E.C.R. II-3445............... 23.04
T-358/02 *Deutsche Post and DHL v Commission* [2004] E.C.R. II-1565, (order of 27 May 2004) ... 7.124
T-360/02 *Yorck von Wartenburg v Commission*, not reported, (order of 14 July 2004)............ 25.04
T-370/02 *Alpenhain-Camembert-Werk and Others v Commission* [2004] E.C.R. II-2097,
   (order of 6 July 2004)..................................... 7.99, 7.100
T-381/02 *Confédération générale v Commission* [2005] E.C.R. II-5337, (order of
   13 December 2005) 7.85, 7.99, 7.100, 7.104, 7.108
T-388/02 *Kronoply and Others v Commission* [2008] E.C.R. II-305*, Summ. pub. 7.212

T-391/02 *Bundesverband der Nahrungsmittel- und Speiseresteverwertung and Kloh v European Parliament* [2004] E.C.R. II-1447, (order of 10 May 2004) 7.104
T-392/02 R *Solvay Pharmaceuticals v Council* [2003] E.C.R. II-1825, (order of the President of 11 April 2003)... 25.81
T-396/02 *Storck v OHIM* [2004] E.C.R. II-3821 .... 20.15

T-2/03 *Verein für Konsumenteninformation v Commission* [2005] II-1121.................... 25.60
T-9/03 *Coldiretti and Others v Commission*, not reported, (order of 2 July 2004) 11.15, 11.16
T-14/03 *Di Marzio v Commission* [2004] E.C.R.-SC II-167 .... 18.25
T-18/03 *CD-Contact Data v Commission* [2009] E.C.R. II-1021....................... 7.190
T-28/03 *Holcim (Deutschland) v Commission* [2005] E.C.R. II-1357 .... 7.225, 7.226, 11.60, 11.61, 11.85, 11.88, 11.94, 25.16
T-29/03 *Comunidad Autónoma de Andalucía v Commission* [2004] E.C.R. II-2923, (order of 13 July 2004)..7.13, 7.18, 7.101, 7.217
T-34/03 *Hecq v Commission* [2004] E.C.R.-SC II-1371 .... 18.05
T-45/03 *Riva Acciaio v Commission* [2007] E.C.R. II-138*, Summ. pub................ 7.148
T-46/03 R II *Leali v Commission* [2006] E.C.R. II-9*, Summ. pub., (order of the President of 24 January 2006) 13.44
T-47/03 *Sison v Council* [2007] E.C.R. II-73*, Summ. pub. 11.40, 11.49, 11.51, 11.66, 25.91
T-48/03 *Schneider Electric v Commission* [2006] E.C.R. II-111, (order of 31 January 2006) 7.47
T-49/03 *Schumann v Commission* [2004] E.C.R.-SC II-1371 .... 18.15
T-57/03 *SPAG v OHIM* [2005] E.C.R. II-287 .... 20.15
T-60/03 *Regione Siciliana v Commission* [2005] E.C.R. II-4139, (order of 18 October 2005) 7.96
T-63/03 *El Corte Inglés v OHIM*, not reported, (order of 8 May 2003) 23.37, 23.54
T-66/03 *Koffiebranderij en Theehandel 'Drie Mollen sinds 1818' v OHIM*, [2004] E.C.R. II-1765.. 20.15
T-86/03 *Holcim (France) v Commission* [2005] E.C.R. II-1539, (order of 4 May 2005) 7.226, 8.09, 11.10
T-90/03 *FICF and Others v Commission* [2007] E.C.R. II-76*, Summ. pub. 11.51
T-100/03 *Maison de l'Europe Avignon Méditerranée v Commission* [2008] E.C.R. II-43*, Summ. pub., (order of 2 April 2008)... 7.15
T-108/03 *Von Pezold v Commission* [2005] E.C.R. II-655, (order of 28 February 2005)........... 6.01
T-110/03, T-150/03 and T-405/03 *Sison v Council* [2005] E.C.R. II-1429.................... 7.67
T-115/03 *Samar v OHIM* [2004] E.C.R. II-2939 .... 20.15
T-123/03 *Pfizer v Commission* [2004] E.C.R. II-1631, (order of 2 June 2004)............... 7.27, 7.29
T-125/03 R and T-253/03 R *Akzo Nobel Chemicals and Others v Commission* [2003] E.C.R. II-4771, (order of the President of 30 October 2003) 7.32, 13.36, 13.40
T-125/03 and T-253/03 *Akzo Nobel Chemicals and Akcros Chemicals v Commission* [2007] E.C.R. II-3523..7.32, 7.37
T-133/03 *Schering-Plough v Commission and EMEA*, not reported, (order of 5 December 2007) 25.07
T-134/03 and T-135/03 *Common Market Fertilizers v Commission* [2005] E.C.R. II-3923 .... 7.146, 9.13
T-138/03 *É.R. and Others v Council and Commission* [2006] E.C.R. II-4923 .... 11.07, 11.14, 11.32, 11.34, 11.38, 11.78, 11.83, 11.87, 11.92
T-141/03 *Sniace v Commission* [2005] E.C.R. II-1197 ....7.123, 7.124, 7.139, 7.141
T-143/03 *Smit v Europol* [2005] E.C.R.-SC II-171 .... 18.09
T-144/03 *Schmit v Commission* [2005] E.C.R. II-465.................................. 18.26
T-151/03 *Nuova Agricast v Commission* [2005] E.C.R. II-1967, (order of 8 June 2005) 23.15
T-155/03, T-157/03 and T-331/03 *Cwik v Commission* [2005] E.C.R. II-1865............... 11.35
T-156/03 *Pérez-Díaz v Commission* [2006] E.C.R.-SC I-A-2-135 .... 11.35, 18.06
T-160/03 *AFCon Management Consultants and Others v Commission* [2005] E.C.R. II-981........ 11.56
T-177/03 *Strohm v Commission* [2005] E.C.R.-SC II-651................................ 25.16
T-196/03 *European Federation for Cosmetic Ingredients v European Parliament and Council* [2004] E.C.R. II-4263, (order of 10 December 2004)......................... 7.100, 7.104
T-198/03 *Bank Austria Creditanstalt v Commission* [2006] E.C.R. II-1429................. 7.138
T-203/03 *Rasmussen v Commission* [2005] E.C.R.-SC II-1287 .... 18.29, 25.97
T-212/03 *MyTravel Group v Commission* [2008] E.C.R. II-1967...... 11.34, 11.51, 11.54, 11.58, 11.62
T-217/03 R *FNCBV v Commission* [2004] E.C.R. II-239, (order of the President of 21 January 2004)... 13.36
T-217/03 and T-245/03 *FNCBV and Others v Commission* [2006] E.C.R. II-4987 .... 9.08, 15.07
T-218/03 to T-240/03 *Boyle and Others v Commission* [2006] E.C.R. II-1699............... 7.153
T-241/03 REV *Marcuccio v Commission*, not reported, (order of 11 September 2012) 25.119

T-252/03 *FNICGV v Commission* [2004] E.C.R. II-3795, (order of 9 November 2004) 15.05
T-256/03 *Bundesverband der Nahrungsmittel- und Speiseresteverwertung and Kloh v Commission,*
    not reported, (order of 2 July 2004) 25.10
T-259/03 *Nikolaou v Commission* [2007] E.C.R. II-99*, Summ. pub. 11.20, 11.21, 11.45,
                                                                    11.48, 11.49, 11.51, 11.66
T-261/03 *Euro Style 94 v OHIM,* not reported, (order of 10 December 2004) 20.21
T-264/03 R *Schmoldt and Others v Commission* [2003] E.C.R. II-5089, (order of the President of
    28 November 2003) 13.25
T-264/03 *Schmoldt and Others v Commission* [2004] E.C.R. II-1515, (order of
    25 May 2004) 7.100, 7.104, 7.106, 7.210, 7.216
T-265/03 *Helm Düngemittel v Commission* [2005] E.C.R. II-2009, (order of
    9 June 2005) 19.12, 25.16
T-266/03 *Groupement des Cartes Bancaires 'CB' v Commission,* not reported, (order of
    26 May 2004) 23.60, 23.66, 25.39
T-269/03 *Socratec v Commission* [2009] E.C.R. II-88*, Summ. pub. 7.142, 7.143
T-276/03 *Azienda Agricola « Le Canne » v Commission* [2006] E.C.R. II-10*,
    Summ. pub. 8.06, 8.19, 11.35
T-277/03 *Vlachaki v Commission* [2005] E.C.R.-SC II-243 . . . . 18.27, 25.46, 29.94
T-278/03 *Van Mannekus v Council,* not reported, (order of 27 January 2006) 7.133
T-279/03 *Galileo and Others v Commission* [2006] E.C.R. II-1291 . . . . 11.19, 11.34, 11.46, 11.69,
                                                                    11.78, 11.84
T-285/03 *Agraz and Others v Commission* [2005] E.C.R. II-1063 . . . . 11.46, 11.58, 11.72
T-289/03 *BUPA and Others v Commission* [2008] E.C.R. II-81 . . . . 7.133, 7.217, 25.76
T-294/03 *Gibault v Commission* [2005] E.C.R.-SC II-635 . . . . 18.06
T-301/03 *Canali Ireland v OHIM* [2005] E.C.R. II-2479 . . . . 20.11
T-303/03 *Lidl Stiftung v OHIM* [2005] E.C.R. II-1917 . . . . 20.14
T-309/03 *Camos Grau v Commission* [2006] E.C.R. II-1173 . . . . 7.13, 7.217, 11.04, 11.10,
                                                                    11.20, 11.44, 11.51, 11.64, 18.06
T-310/03 R *Kreuzer Medien v European Parliament and Council* [2004] E.C.R. II-3243,
    (order of the President of 21 September 2004) 13.17, 13.18
T-314/03 and T-378/03 *Musée Grévin v Commission* [2004] E.C.R. II-1421,
    (order of 10 May 2004) 7.15, 19.12
T-315/03 *Wilfer v OHIM* [2005] E.C.R. II-1981 . . . . 23.17
T-319/03 *French and Others v Council and Commission* [2004] E.C.R. II-769,
    (order of 20 February 2004) 11.44, 25.10
T-321/03 *Juchem v European Parliament and Council* [2006] E.C.R. II-50*, Summ. pub.,
    (order of 7 July 2006) 11.76
T-327/03 *Al-Aqsa v Council,* not reported, (judgment of 11 July 2007) 7.10, 7.11, 7.141
T-327/03 *Stichting Al-Aqsa v Council* [2007] E.C.R. II-79*, Summ. pub. 9.05
T-332/03 *European Service Network v Commission* [2008] E.C.R. II-32*, Summ. pub. 7.84
T-333/03 *Masdar (UK) Ltd v Commission* [2006] E.C.R. II-4377 . . . . 11.08
T-338/03 *Edidania Sadam and Others v Commission,* not reported, (order of 8 July 2004) 7.99
T-340/03 *France Télécom v Commission* [2007] E.C.R. II-107 . . . . 25.10
T-345/03 *Evropaïki Dynamiki v Commission* [2008] E.C.R. II-341 . . . . 7.219
T-346/03 *Krikorian and Others v European Parliament and Others* [2003] E.C.R. II-6037,
    (order of 17 December 2003) 11.20, 11.44, 11.78
T-349/03 *Corsica Ferries France v Commission* [2005] E.C.R. II-2197 . . . . 7.146, 7.202
T-351/03 *Schneider Electric v Commission* [2007] F.C.R. II-2237 . . . . 11.44, 11.51, 11.54,
                                                                    11.58, 11.61, 11.82, 11.85
T-354/03 *Reggimenti v European Parliament* [2005] E.C.R.-SC II-147 . . . . 18.22
T-357/03 *Gollnisch and Others v European Parliament* [2005] E.C.R. II-1, (order of
    10 January 2005) 7.102, 23.60
T-360/03 *Frischpack v OHIM* [2004] E.C.R. II-4097 . . . . 20.05, 20.15
T-363/03 *Regione Siciliana v Commission* [2008] E.C.R. II-201*, Summ. pub., (order of
    25 September 2008) 7.96
T-364/03 *Medici Grimm v Council* [2006] E.C.R. II-79 . . . . 11.09, 11.19, 11.34, 11.58, 11.60, 11.61
T-366/03 and T-235/04 *Land Oberösterreich and Austria v Commission* [2005]
    E.C.R. II-4005 . . . . 7.103, 7.125, 7.217
T-367/03 *Yedaş Tarim ve Otomotiv Sanayi ve Ticaret v Council and Commission* [2006]
    E.C.R. II-873 . . . . 11.51, 25.120, 25.121

T-369/03 *Arizona Chemical and Others v Commission* [2005] E.C.R. II-5839, (order of
14 December 2005) 9.01, 9.14, 11.34
T-369/03 R *Arizona Chemical and Others v Commission* [2004] E.C.R. II-205, (order of the
President of 16 January 2004) 13.04
T-373/03 *Solo Italia v OHIM* [2005] E.C.R. II-1881 . . . . 20.15
T-379/03 *Peek & Cloppenburg v OHIM* [2005] E.C.R. II-4633 . . . . 20.10
T-385/03 *Miles Handelsgesellschaft International v OHIM* [2005] E.C.R. II-2665 . . . . 20.10
T-388/03 *Deutsche Post and DHL International v Commission* [2009] E.C.R. II-199 . . . . 16.14
T-392/03, T-408/03 and T-435/03 *Regione Siciliana v Commission* [2008] E.C.R. II-2489,
(order of 25 September 2008) 7.09, 7.27, 7.96
T-394/03 *Angeletti v Commission* [2006] E.C.R.-SC I-A-2-95 . . . . 11.66
T-396/03 *Vanhellemont v Commission* [2005] E.C.R-SC I-A-355 . . . . 18.07
T-398/03 *Castets v Commission* [2005] E.C.R.-SC II-507 . . . . 25.97
T-406/03 *Nicolas Ravailhe v Committee of the Regions* [2005] E.C.R.-SC I-A-19, (order of
14 February 2002) 25.16
T-410/03 *Hoechst v Commission* [2008] E.C.R. II-881 . . . . 15.06, 15.07, 25.67
T-413/03 *Shandong Reipu Biochemicals v Council* [2006] E.C.R. II-2243 . . . . 7.206
T-415/03 *Cofradía de pescadores de 'San Pedro' and Others v Council* [2005]
E.C.R. II-4355 . . . . 7.227, 11.37, 11.38, 11.48, 11.49, 11.51, 11.64
T-422/03 R II *Enviro Tech Europe and Others v Commission* [2004] E.C.R. II-2003,
(order of the President of 2 July 2004) 13.07
T-433/03, T-434/03, T-367/04, and T-244/05 *Gibtelecom v Commission*, not reported,
(order of 26 June 2008) 7.142, 8.21
T-439/03 R II *Eppe v European Parliament*, not reported, (order of the President of
19 July 2004) 13.44
T-440/03, T-121/04, T-171/04, T-208/04, T-365/04, and T-484/04 *Arizmendi and
Others v Council and Commission* [2009] E.C.R. II-4883 . . . . 5.34, 11.09, 11.47, 11.81
T-443/03 *Retecal and Others v Commission* [2005] E.C.R. II-1803, (order of 25 May 2005) 7.50

T-11/04 *Werkgroep Commerciële Jachthavens Zuidelijke Randmeren and Others v Commission* [2006]
E.C.R. II-3861 . . . . 7.124
T-14/04 *Alto de Casablanca v OHIM* [2004] E.C.R. II-3077, (order of 9 September 2004) 23.17
T-16/04 *Arcelor v European Parliament and Council* [2010] E.C.R. II-211 . . . . 7.99, 7.100, 7.108
T-20/04 *Aguar Fernandez and Others v Commission*, not reported, (order of
4 February 2005) 23.59, 25.10
T-22/04 *Reemark Gesellschaft für Markenkooperation v OHIM* [2005] E.C.R. II-1559 . . . . 20.10
T-29/04 *Castellblanch v OHIM* [2005] E.C.R. II-5309 . . . . 20.15
T-30/04 *Sena v EASA* [2005] E.C.R.-SC II-519 . . . . 18.09
T-35/04 *Athinaiki Oikogeniaki Artopoiia AVEE v OHIM* [2006] E.C.R. II-785 . . . . 20.06
T-36/04 *API v Commission* [2007] E.C.R. II-3201 . . . . 16.16, 35.50
T-37/04 R *Autonomous Region of the Azores v Council* [2004] E.C.R. II-2153, (order of the
President of 7 July 2004) 13.18, 25.69
T-37/04 *Região autónoma dos Açores v Council* [2008] E.C.R. II-103*, Summ. pub. 7.97, 7.103, 25.60
T-40/04 *Bonino and Others v European Parliament and Council* [2005] E.C.R. II-2685,
(order of 11 July 2005) 7.92, 7.101, 7.104, 7.106
T-48/04 *Qualcomm v Commission* [2009] E.C.R. II-2029 . . . . 7.51, 7.214, 7.216
T-49/04 *Hassan v Council and Commission*, not reported, (judgment of 12 July 2006) 7.11, 7.73
T-65/04 *Nuova Gela Sviluppo Soc. cons. pa v Commission* [2007] E.C.R. II-68*, Summ. pub. 11.10
T-69/04 *Schunk and Schunk Kohlenstoff-Technik v Commission* [2008] E.C.R. II-2567 . . . . . . 9.08, 15.05,
15.06, 15.09
T-73/04 *Le Carbone-Lorraine v Commission* [2008] E.C.R. II-2661 . . . . 15.06
T-75/04 and T-77/04 to T-79/04 *Arch Chemicals and Others v Commission* [2011]
E.C.R. II-295*, Summ. pub. 7.100
T-76/04 R *Bactria v Commission* [2004] E.C.R. II-2025, (order of the President of
2 July 2004) 13.01, 13.19, 13.29
T-78/04 R *Sumitomo Chemical v Commission* [2004] E.C.R. II-2049, (order of 2 July 2004) 13.29
T-81/04 *Bouygues and Bouygues Télécom v Commission*, not reported, (order of 14 February 2005) 7.62
T-94/04 *EEB and Others v Commission* [2005] E.C.R. II-4919, (order of 28 November 2005) 9.04
T-100/04 *Massimo Giannini v Commission* [2008] E.C.R.-SC IA-2-9 . . . . 18.13, 18.26
T-107/04 *Aluminium Silicon Mill Products v Council* [2007] E.C.R. II-669 . . . . 7.205

T-113/04 *Atlantic Container Line and Others v Commission* [2007] E.C.R. II-171*, Summ. pub.,
(order of 12 December 2007) 7.225, 7.226, 11.38, 11.78, 11.79, 11.85
T-116/04 *Wieland-Werke v Commission* [2009] E.C.R. II-1087 . . . . 9.08, 15.05
T-117/04 *Vereniging Werkgroep Commerciële Jachthavens Zuidelijke Randmeren and Others v
Commission* [2006] E.C.R. II-3861 . . . . 7.126
T-122/04 *Outokumpu and Luvata v Commission* [2009] E.C.R. II-1135 . . . . 15.05
T-123/04 *Cargo Partner v OHIM* [2005] E.C.R. II-3979 . . . . 20.20, 25.16
T-124/04 *Ouariachi v Commission* [2005] E.C.R. II-4653, (order of 26 October 2005) 11.21
T-132/04 *Bonnet v Court of Justice*, not reported, (order of 9 July 2004) 18.15
T-136/04 *Freiherr von Cramer-Klett and Rechtlerverband Pfronten v Commission* [2006]
E.C.R. II-1805, (order of 22 June 2006) 7.93
T-137/04 *Mayer and Others v Commission* [2006] E.C.R. II-1825, (order of 22 June 2006) 7.93
T-140/04 *Adviesbureau Ehcon v Commission* [2005] E.C.R. II-3287, (order of
14 September 2005) 11.94
T-144/04 *TF1 v Commission* [2008] E.C.R. II-761, (order of 19 May 2008) 7.210, 8.10
T-148/04 R *TQ3 Travel Solutions Belgium v Commission* [2004] E.C.R. II-3027,
(order of the President of 27 July 2004) 13.24, 25.86
T-153/04 *Ferriere Nord v Commission* [2006] E.C.R. II-3889 . . . . 7.15
T-161/04 *Valero Jordana v Commission* [2011] E.C.R. II-215*, Summ. pub. 7.147
T-163/04 *Schäfer v OHIM*, not reported, (order of 12 July 2005) 25.06
T-167/04 *Asklepios Kliniken v Commission* [2007] E.C.R. II-2379 . . . . 7.118, 8.06, 8.07, 8.13, 8.19
T-175/04 *Gordon v Commission* [2007] E.C.R.-SC I-A-2-47. . . . . 18.07
T-177/04 *easyJet v Commission* [2006] E.C.R. II-1931 . . . . 7.113, 7.138
T-184/04 *Sulvida v Commission* [2005] E.C.R. II-85, (order of 13 January 2005) 23.17
T-188/04 *Freixenet v OHIM* [2006] E.C.R. II-78*, Summ. pub. 20.06
T-190/04 *Freixenet v OHIM* [2006] E.C.R. II-79*, Summ. pub. 20.06
T-191/04 *MIP Metro Group Intellectual Property GmbH & Co. KG v OHIM* [2006]
E.C.R. II-2855. . . . . 20.10
T-193/04 R *Tillack v Commission* [2004] E.C.R. II-3575. (order of the President of
15 October 2004). 13.11, 13.25, 13.34
T-193/04 *Tillack v Commission* [2006] E.C.R. II-3995. . . . . .7.13, 11.10, 11.34, 11.51
T-196/04 *Ryanair v Commission* [2008] E.C.R. II-3643 . . . . 7.201
T-199/04 *Gul Ahmed Textile Mills v Council* [2011] E.C.R. II-321*, Summ. pub. 7.206
T-201/04 R *Microsoft v Commission* [2004] E.C.R. II-2977, (order of the President of
26 July 2004). 13.18
T-201/04 *Microsoft v Commission* [2007] E.C.R. II-3601 . . . . 7.190, 7.193, 25.10, 25.60,
25.67, 25.68, 25.69, 25.76
T-209/04 *Spain v Commission* [2005] E.C.R. II-29, (order of 10 January 2005). 8.06, 25.81
T-211/04 REC and T-215/04 REC *Government of Gibraltar v Commission*, not reported,
(order of 3 June 2009) 25.133
T-213/04 *Ascione*, not reported, (order of 8 July 2004). 5.32
T-226/04 *Italy v Commission* [2006] E.C.R. II-29*, Summ. pub. 7.183
T-233/04 *Netherlands v Commission* [2008] E.C.R. II-591 . . . . 7.21
T-234/04 *Netherlands v Commission* [2007] E.C.R. II-4589 . . . . 7.18
T-236/04 and T-241/04 *EEB and Stichting* [2005] E.C.R. II-4945, (order of
28 November 2005). 7.97, 9.04
T-238/04 *Raab and Others v European Parliament and Council*, not reported, (order of
27 July 2004). 7.216
T-239/04 and T-323/04 *Italy and Brandt v Commission* [2007] E.C.R. II-3265 . . . . 7.138
T-245/04 *Commission v Lior and Others*, not reported, (order of 8 January 2008). 19.13
T-246/04 and T-71/05 *Wunenburger v Commission* [2007] E.C.R.-SC I-A-2-21 . . . . 11.66
T-247/04 *Aseprofar and Edifa v Commission* [2005] E.C.R. II-3449, (order of
19 September 2005). 5.32, 7.18
T-253/04 *KONGRA-GEL v Council* [2008] E.C.R. II-46*, Summ. pub. 7.137, 7.138, 7.219, 9.05
T-257/04 *Poland v Commission* [2009] E.C.R. II-1545. . . . . 7.207
T-260/04 *Cestas v Commission* [2008] E.C.R. II-701 . . . . 7.27
T-265/04, T-292/04 and T-504/04 *Tirrenia di Navigazione and Others v Commission*
[2009] E.C.R. II-21*, Summ. pub. 7.138
T-271/04 *Citymo v Commission* [2007] E.C.R. II-1375 . . . . 9.16, 11.06, 11.51,
11.78, 11.85, 19.07, 19.15
T-274/04 *Rounis v Commission* [2005] E.C.R.-SC I-A-407. . . . . 18.07

T-277/04 *Vitakraft-Werke Wührmann & Sohn v OHIM* [2006] E.C.R. II-2211 . . . . 20.15
T-279/04 *Éditions Jacob v Commission* [2010] E.C.R. II-185*, Summ. pub. 7.47, 7.147, 7.197, 7.200
T-281/04 *Staboli v Commission* [2006] E.C.R.-SC I-A-2-251 . . . . 11.10
T-288/04 *Van Neyghem v Committee of the Regions* [2007] E.C.R.-SC I-A-2-1 . . . . 18.04, 18.17
T-291/04 *Enviro Tech Europe and Enviro Tech International v Commission* [2011]
   E.C.R. II-8281 . . . . 7.05, 7.99, 7.100, 7.138, 7.141, 11.11, 11.51, 11.53, 25.17, 25.44
T-294/04 *Internationaler Hilfsfonds v Commission* [2005] E.C.R. II-2719,
   (order of 11 July 2005) 25.91, 25.96
T-299/04 *Selmani v Council and Commission* [2005] E.C.R. II-20*, Summ. pub.,
   (order of 18 November 2005) 7.218
T-302/04 *MEAM v Commission* [2008] E.C.R. II-61*, Summ. pub., (order of 18 April 2008) 19.10
T-303/04 R II *European Dynamics v Commission* [2004] E.C.R. II-4621, (order of the
   President of 22 December 2004) 13.16
T-309/04, T-317/04, T-329/04, and T-336/04 *TV2/Danmark and Others v Commission*
   [2008] E.C.R. II-2935 . . . . 7.76, 7.139
T-311/04 *Buendia Sierra v Commission* [2006] E.C.R. II-4137 . . . . .9.01, 9.08, 18.04, 18.06
T-312/04 *Di Bucci v Commission*, not reported, (judgment of 9 October 2008) 18.04, 18.06
T-314/04 and T-414/04 *Germany v Commission* [2006] E.C.R. II-103*, Summ. pub. 7.27
T-316/04 R *Wam v Commission* [2004] E.C.R. II-3917, (order of the President of
   10 November 2004) 13.41
T-321/04 *Air Bourbon v Commission* [2005] E.C.R. II-3469, (order of 19 September 2005) 7.212
T-325/04 *Citigroup v OHIM* [2008] E.C.R. II-29*, Summ. pub. 20.16
T-333/04 DEP and T-334/04 DEP *House of Donuts International v OHIM*, not reported,
   (order of 19 March 2009) 25.93
T-339/04 *France Télécom v Commission* [2007] E.C.R. II-521 . . . . 7.32
T-340/04 *France Télécom v Commission* [2007] E.C.R. II-573 . . . . 25.13, 25.49
T-343/04 *Tsarnavas v Commission* [2007] E.C.R.-SC II-A-2-747 . . . . 18.04
T-355/04 and T-446/04 *Co-Frutta v Commission* [2010] E.C.R. II-1 . . . . 7.138, 7.142
T-360/04 *FG Marine v Commission* [2007] E.C.R. II-92*, Summ. pub. 11.34, 11.78, 11.85
T-363/04 *Koipe Corporación v OHIM* [2007] E.C.R. II-3355 . . . . 20.06
T-375/04 *Scheucher-Fleisch and Others v Commission* [2009] E.C.R. II-4155 . . . . 7.118, 16.16
T-376/04 *Polyelectrolyte Producers Group v Council and Commission* [2005] E.C.R. II-3007,
   (order of 22 July 2005) 7.72
T-385/04 *Valero Jordana v Commission*, not reported, (judgment of 1 April 2009) 11.66
T-386/04 *Eridania Sadam and Others v Commission* [2005] E.C.R. II-2531 . . . . 4.11
T-386/04 *Eridania Sadam and Others v Commission*, not reported, (order of 28 June 2005) 7.106
T-387/04 *EnBW Energie Baden-Württemberg v Commmission* [2007] E.C.R. II-1195,
   (order of 30 April 2007) 7.138
T-394/04 *Strack v Commission* [2008] E.C.R-SC I-A-2-5 . . . . 18.04
T-395/04 *Air One v Commission* [2006] E.C.R. II-1343 . . . . 8.06, 8.13, 8.19, 8.23
T-400/04 and T-402/04 to T-404/04 *Arch Chemicals and Others v Commission*
   [2011] E.C.R. II-298*, Summ. pub. 7.101, 8.06, 8.10, 25.43
T-406/04 *Bonnet v ECJ* [2006] E.C.R.-SC I-A-2-213 . . . . 18.04
T-416/04 *Kontouli v Council* [2006] E.C.R.-SC I-A-2-181 . . . . 11.10
T-417/04 *Regione autonoma Friuli-Venezia Giulia v Commission* [2007] E.C.R. II-641,
   (order of 12 March 2007) 7.100, 7.103
T-422/04 *Lavagnoli v Commission*, not reported, (judgment of 23 November 2006) 18.07
T-423/04 *Bunker & BKR v OHIM* [2005] E.C.R. II-4035 . . . . 20.15, 25.94
T-424/04 *Angelidis v European Parliament* [2006] E.C.R-SC I-A-2-323 . . . . 18.04
T-425/04, T-444/04, T-450/04, and T-456/04 *France and Others v Commission* [2010]
   E.C.R. II-2099 . . . . .7.21, 7.76, 7.138, 7.220
T-426/04 *Tramarin v Commission* [2005] E.C.R. II-4765, (order of 21 November 2005) 7.212
T-429/04 *Trubowest Handel and Makarov v Council and Commission* [2008] E.C.R. II-128*,
   Summ. pub. 11.29, 11.85
T-431/04 R *Italy v Commission* [2007] E.C.R. II-64*, Summ. pub., (order of the President of
   18 June 2007) 13.19
T-435/04 *Dos Santos v OHIM* [2007] E.C.R.-SC I-A-2-61 . . . . 18.06
T-437/04 and T-441/04 *Standertskjöld-Nordenstam and Heyraud v Commission* [2006]
   E.C.R-SC I-1-2-29 . . . . 18.06
T-445/04 *Energy Technologies v OHIM* [2005] E.C.R. II-677, (order of 28 February 2005) 23.17

T-447/04 R *Capgemini Nederland v Commission* [2005] E.C.R. II-257, (order of the
  President of 31 January 2005) 13.01
T-448/04 *Commission v Trends* [2007] E.C.R. II-104*, Summ. pub. 19.19
T-449/04 *Commission v Trends and Others* [2006] E.C.R. II-24*, Summ. pub., (order of
  17 February 2006) 19.13, 19.19
T-451/04 *Mediocurso—Estabelecimento de Ensino Particular v Commission*, not reported,
  (order of 28 March 2006) 8.06, 8.13, 8.23
T-452/04 *Éditions Odile Jacob and Others v Commission* [2010] E.C.R. II-4713 . . . . 7.46
T-455/04 *Beyatli and Candan v Commission* [2007] E.C.R.-SC I-A-2-71, (order of
  5 March 2007) 18.06
T-457/04 and T-223/05 *Camar v Commission* [2008] E.C.R. II-215*, Summ. pub. 7.225, 11.94
T-458/04 *Au Lys de France v Commission* [2007] E.C.R. II-71*, Summ. pub. 7.83
T-465/04 *Evropaïki Dynamiki v Commission* [2008] E.C.R. II-154*, Summ. pub. 7.170, 7.219
T-466/04 and T-467/04 *Elisabetta Dami v OHIM* [2006] E.C.R. II-183 . . . . 20.10
T-472/04 *Tsarnavas v Commission* [2007] E.C.R.-SC I-A-2-5 . . . . 18.15
T-474/04 *Pergan Hilfsstoffe v Commission* [2007] E.C.R. II-4225 . . . . 7.138
T-478/04 *Campailla v Commission*, not reported, (order of 23 February 2005). 7.23
T-479/04 *Campailla v Commission*, not reported, (order of 23 February 2005). 8.19
T-485/04 *COBB v Commission*, not reported, (order of 27 May 2005) 7.216
T-486/04 *Michail v Commission* [2008] E.C.R.-SC I-A-2-25 . . . . 18.04
T-494/04 *Wineke Neirinck v Commission* [2006] E.C.R.-SC I-A-2-259 . . . . 25.16, 25.49
T-495/04 *Belfass v Council* [2008] E.C.R. II-781 . . . . .11.10, 11.64, 25.16
T-500/04 *Commission v IIC Informations-Indutrie Consulting* [2007] E.C.R. II-1443 . . . . 19.22

T-6/05 *DEF-TEC Defense Technology GmbH v OHIM* [2006] E.C.R. II-2671 . . . . 20.12, 20.15
T-7/05 *Commission v Parthenon AE Oikodomiko* [2006] E.C.R. II-100*, Summ. pub. 23.72
T-11/05 *Wieland-Werke and Others v Commission* [2010] E.C.R. II-86*, Summ. pub. 15.09
T-18/05 *IMI and Others v Commission* [2010] E.C.R. II-1769 . . . . 15.06, 15.09
T-19/05 *Boliden and Others v Commission* [2010] E.C.R. II-1843 . . . . 15.09
T-21/05 *Chalkor v Commission* [2010] E.C.R. II-1895 . . . . 15.06, 15.07, 15.09
T-27/05 *Lo Giudice v Commission* [2007] E.C.R.-SC I-A-2-197 . . . . 18.06
T-29/05 *Deltafina v Commission* [2010] E.C.R. II-4077 . . . . 15.07
T-33/05 *Cetarsa v Commission* [2011] E.C.R. II-12*, Summ. pub. 15.09
T-34/05 R *Makhteshim-Agan Holding and Others v Commission* [2005] E.C.R. II-1465,
  (order of the President of 27 April 2005) 13.10
T-35/05, T-61/05, T-107/05, T-108/05 and T-139/05 *Agne-Dapper and Others v Commission*
  [2006] E.C.R.-SC I-A-2-291 . . . . 18.05
T-38/05 *Agroexpansion v Commission* [2011] E.C.R. II-7005 . . . . 15.07
T-41/05 *Alliance One International v Commission* [2011] E.C.R. II-7101 . . . . . . .7.26, 7.194, 15.06, 15.07
T-42/05 *Williams v Commission* [2008] E.C.R. II-156*, Summ. pub. 7.170
T-47/05 *Serrano and Others v European Parliament*, not reported, (judgment of
  18 September 2008) 11.10, 18.05
T-48/05 *Franchet and Vyck v Commission* [2008] E.C.R. II-1585 . . . . . 11.20, 11.35, 11.51, 11.61, 11.64,
  11.66, 11.75, 11.76, 11.78, 11.80, 11.84, 11.85, 25.91
T-50/05 *Evropaïki Dynamiki—Proigmena Systimata v Commission* [2010] E.C.R. II-1071 . . . . 7.83
T-66/05 P *Sack v Commission* [2007] E.C.R.-SC I-A-2-229 . . . . 18.05, 18.17, 18.25
T-69/05 *Evropaïki Dynamiki v EFSA*, not reported, (order of 19 October 2007) 7.138
T-70/05 *Evropaïki Dynamiki v European Maritime Safety Agency* [2010] E.C.R. II-313 . . . . 7.70, 25.10
T-73/05 *Magone v Commission* [2006] E.C.R.-SC I-A-2-107, II-A-2-485 . . . . 11.10
T-79/05 *Gluiber v Commission*, not reported, (order of 14 July 2005) 7.217
T-87/05 *EDP v Commission* [2005] E.C.R. II-3745 . . . . 7.187, 7.196
T-89/05 *GAEC Salat v Commission* [2005] II-16*, Summ. pub., (order of 27 October 2005) 25.16
T-91/05 *Sinara Handel v Council and Commission* [2007] E.C.R. II-245, (order of
  5 February 2007) 10.11, 11.29
T-101/05 and T-111/05 *BASF and UCB v Commission* [2007] E.C.R. II-4949 . . . . 15.05
T-109/05 and T-444/05 *NLG v Commission* [2011] E.C.R. II-2479 . . . . 7.138
T-113/05 *Angelidis v European Parliament*, not reported, (judgment of 13 December 2007) 11.66
T-115/05 *Jiménez Martínez v Commission* [2006] E.C.R.-SC I-A-2-269, II-A-2-249,
  (order of 15 November 2006) 11.10, 18.06
T-122/05 *Benkö and Others v Commission* [2006] E.C.R. II-2939, (order of
  19 September 2006) 7.103, 9.04

T-128/05 *SPM v Council and Commission* [2008] E.C.R. II-260*, Summ. pub. 11.19, 11.34, 11.51
T-135/05 *Campoli v Commission* [2006] E.C.R.-SC I-A-2-297 . . . . 18.05, 18.07
T-136/05 *EARL Salvat and Others v Commission* [2007] E.C.R. II-4063 . . . . 7.122, 7.138, 7.139
T-137/05 *Gruppo La Perla SpA v OHIM* [2007] E.C.R. II-47*, Summ. pub. 20.06, 20.10
T-138/05 *Commission v Impetus Symvouloi Michanikoi* [2007] E.C.R. II-136*, Summ. pub. 2.29
T-141/05 RENV *Internationaler Hilfsfonds v Commission* [2011] E.C.R. II-6495,
   (order of 21 September 2011) 7.138, 25.84
T-148/05 *Comunidad autonoma de Madrid and Mintra v Commission*, not reported,
   (order of 5 September 2006) 7.13
T-150/05 *Sahlstedt and Others v Commission* [2006] E.C.R. II-1851, (order of 22 June 2006) . . . 7.93
T-151/05 *NVV and Others v Commission* [2009] E.C.R. II-1219 . . . . . 7.128, 7.137, 7.186, 7.197, 7.198
T-154/05 *Lo Giudice v Commission* [2007] E.C.R.-SC I-A-2-203 . . . . 18.04
T-161/05 *Hoechst v Commission* [2009] E.C.R. II-3555 . . . . 15.07
T-181/05 *Citigroupand Citibank, NA v OHIM* [2008] E.C.R. II-669 . . . . 20.10
T-185/05 *Italy v Commission* [2008] E.C.R. II-3207 . . . . 7.01, 7.17, 7.21, 7.26, 7.175, 7.208, 7.216
T-189/05 *Unisor v OHIM* [2008] E.C.R II-22*, Summ. pub. 20.15
T-198/05 *Mebrom v Commission* [2007] E.C.R. II-51*, Summ. pub. 11.65
T-209/05 *Gisti v Commission*, not reported, (order of 6 September 2005) 5.33
T-216/05 *Mebrom v Commission* [2007] E.C.R. II-1507 . . . . 7.89, 7.219, 25.46
T-237/05 *Éditions Odile Jacob v Commission* [2010] E.C.R. II-2245 . . . . 25.59
T-254/05 *European Insulation Manufacturers Association v Commission* [2007]
   E.C.R. II-124*, Summ. pub. 7.104
T-286/05 *CESD Communautaire v Commission* [2009] E.C.R. II-39*, Summ. pub. 7.15, 7.140, 7.141
T-295/05 *Document Security Systems v European Central Bank* [2007] E.C.R. II-2835,
   (order of 5 September 2007) 11.06, 11.20
T-297/05 R *IPK International—World Tourism marking Consultants v Commission*
   [2007] E.C.R. II-37*, Summ. pub., (order of the President of 2 May 2007) 13.29, 13.32
T-299/05 *Shanghai Excell M&E Enterprise and Shanghai Adeptech Precision v Council*
   [2009] E.C.R. II-565, (order of 18 March 2009) 1.03, 7.138, 7.141, 7.143, 7.205
T-306/05 *Scippacercola and Terezakis v Commission* [2008] E.C.R. II-4*, Summ. pub. 7.43, 7.137
T-308/05 *Italy v Commission* [2007] E.C.R. II-5089 . . . . 9.15, 25.12
T-319/05 *Swiss Confederation v Commission* [2010] E.C.R. II-4265. . . . . 2.53, 7.82, 7.89, 25.43
T-321/05 *Astrazeneca v Commission* [2010] E.C.R. II-2805 . . . . 7.190, 7.192, 7.193
T-324/05 *Estonia v Commission* [2009] E.C.R. II-3681 . . . . 7.156
T-329/05 *Movimondo Onlus v Commission*, not reported, (judgment of 25 April 2012) 19.15
T-345/05 R *V v European Parliament* [2007] E.C.R. II-25*, Summ. pub., (order of the
   President of 16 March 2007). 13.19, 13.25, 13.29, 13.40
T-345/05 R II *V v European Parliament* [2007] E.C.R. II-69*, Summ. pub., (order of the
   President of 27 June 2007) 13.40, 13.44
T-345/05 R III *V v European Parliament* [2007] E.C.R. II-160*, Summ. pub., (order of the
   President of 22 November 2007). 13.29, 13.34, 13.44
T-345/05 *Mote v European Parliament* [2008] E.C.R. II-2849 . . . . 7.69
T-348/05 INTP *JSC Kirovo-Chepetsky Khimichesky Kombinat v Council* [2009] E.C.R. II-116*,
   Summ. pub. 25.131, 25.132
T-376/05 R *TEA CEGOS and STG v Commission*, not reported, (order of the President of
   14 October 2005). 13.32
T-385/05 *Transnautica v Commission* [2009] E.C.R. II-163*, Summ. pub. 16.16
T-385/05 TO R *Portugal v Transnáutica—Transportes e Navegação and Commission* [2010]
   E.C.R. II-14*, Summ. pub., (order of the President of 4 February 2010) 13.04
T-396/05 R *ArchiMEDES v Commission* [2006] E.C.R. II-2*, Summ. pub., (order of the
   President of 10 January 2006) 13.25
T-396/05 and T-397/05 *ArchiMEDES v Commission* [2009] E.C.R. II-70*, Summ. pub. 7.15
T-398/05 R *Tesoka v FEACVT* [2006] E.C.R.-SC I-A-2-87, (order of the President of
   4 April 2006) 13.26, 13.45
T-403/05 *MyTravel v Commission* [2008] E.C.R. II-2027. . . . . 16.16
T-411/05 *Annemans v Commission*, not reported, (order of 12 July 2007) 7.43
T-412/05 *M v European Ombudsman* [2008] E.C.R. II-197*, Summ. pub. 11.20, 11.34, 11.51,
   11.55, 11.66, 11.80
T-415/05, T-416/05, and T-423/05 *Greece and Others v Commission* [2010]
   E.C.R. II-4749. . . . . 7.21, 7.76, 7.217

T-417/05 R *Endesa v Commission* [2006] E.C.R. II-18*, Summ. pub., (order of the
    President of 1 February 2006).. 13.35, 13.41
T-417/05 *Endesa v Commission* [2006] E.C.R. II-2533................................... 7.183
T-417/05 DEP *Endesa v Commission*, not reported, (order of 12 December 2008) 25.93
T-420/05 R *Vischim v Commission* [2006] E.C.R. II-34*, Summ. pub., (order of the
    President of 4 April 2006)....................................... 13.24, 13.25, 13.36, 13.40, 13.41
T-420/05 R II *Vischim v Commission* [2006] E.C.R. II-4085, (order of 13 October 2006) 13.44
T-420/05 *Vischim v Commission* [2009] E.C.R. II-3841 .... 7.11, 7.94, 7.141, 8.19, 11.10
T-423/05 R *Olympiaki Aeroporia Ypiresies v Commission* [2007] E.C.R. II-6*, Summ. pub.,
    (order of the President of 29 January 2007) 13.40
T-426/05 *Molliné v Commission*, not reported, (order of 16 May 2006)..................... 8.06
T-429/05 *Artegodan v Commission* [2010] E.C.R. II-491 .... 11.09, 11.37, 11.45,
                                            11.48, 11.52, 11.57, 11.60, 11.61, 11.62
T-432/05 *EMC Development v Commission* [2010] II-1629........................... 25.10, 25.12
T-437/05 R *Brink's Security Luxembourg v Commission* [2006] E.C.R. II-21*, Summ. pub.,
    (order of the President of 7 February 2006) 13.38, 13.40
T-437/05 *Brink's Security Luxembourg v Commission* [2009] E.C.R. II-3233 .... 7.14, 7.18, 7.22,
                                               7.67, 7.217, 11.09, 11.38
T-441/05 *IVG Immobilien AG v OHIM* [2007] E.C.R. II-1937 .... 20.06
T-443/05 *El Corte Inglés v OHIM* [2007] E.C.R. II-2579........................ 20.06, 20.10
T-445/05 *Associazione italiana del risparmio gestito and Others v Commission* [2009]
    E.C.R. II-289, (order of 28 February 2005) 7.126, 7.187, 23.17
T-446/05 *Amann & Sohne and Cousin Filterie v Commission* [2010] E.C.R. II-1255............. 15.05
T-447/05 *SPM v Commission* [2007] E.C.R. II-1, (order of 12 January 2007) . . .7.138, 7.223, 9.04, 11.12
T-449/05 *Dikigorikos Syllogos Ioanninon v European Parliament and Council* [2007]
    E.C.R. II-14*, Summ. pub., (order of 16 February 2007) 7.94
T-450/05 *Automobiles Peugeot and Peugeot Nederland v Commission* [2009] E.C.R. II-2533........ 15.07
T-452/05 *BST v Commission* [2010] E.C.R. II-1373, (judgment of
    28 April 2010)..11.38, 11.77, 11.78, 15.07
T-454/05 R *Sumitomo Chemical Agro Europe and Philagro France v Commission* [2006]
    E.C.R. II-131*, Summ. pub., (order of the President of 24 March 2006)........... 13.11, 13.25
T-454/05 *Sumitomo Chemical Agro Europe and Philagro France v Commission* [2007]
    E.C.R. II-131*, Summ. pub., (order of 17 October 2007)........................... 8.23
T-455/05 *Componenta Oyj v Commission* [2008] E.C.R. II-336*, Summ. pub. 7.147, 13.40, 25.91
T-456/05 and T-457/05 *Guttermann and Zwicky & Co. v Commisison* [2010] E.C.R. II-1443 ..... 15.08
T-458/05 *Tegometall International AG v OHIM* [2007] II-4721 .... 20.16

T-6/06 *Wheyco v Commission*, not reported, (order of 9 July 2007) 7.56
T-11/06 R *Romana Tabucchi v Commission* [2006] E.C.R. II-2491, (order of the President of
    13 July 2006)............................. 13.06, 13.29, 13.34, 13.39, 13.42, 13.44
T-11/06 *Romana Tabacchi v Commission* [2011] E.C.R. II-6681...........15.05, 15.06, 15.08
T-33/06 *Zenab v Commission* [2009] E.C.R. II-102*, Summ. pub........................ 11.11
T-35/06 *Honig-Verband v Commission* [2007] E.C.R. II-2865, (order of
    11 September 2007)......................................7.85, 7.99, 7.108
T-36/06 *Bundesverband v Commission* [2010] E.C.R. II-537........................... 7.89
T-39/06 *Transcatab v Commission* [2011] E.C.R. II-6831............ 7.34, 7.163, 7.185, 7.194, 15.06
T-40/06 DEP *Trioplast Industrier v Commission*, not reported, (order of 13 June 2012) 25.93
T-42/06 R *Gollnisch v European Parliament*, not reported, (order of the President of
    17 March 2006).. 13.18
T-42/06 R *Gollnisch v European Parliament* [2006] E.C.R. II-40*, Summ. pub., (order of the
    President of 12 May 2006) 13.04, 13.19
T-42/06 *Gollnisch v European Parliament* [2010] E.C.R. II-1135 .... 7.138, 7.142, 7.143,
                                         11.34, 11.38, 11.51, 11.78, 11.81
T-44/06 *Commission v Hellenic Ventures and Others* [2010] E.C.R. II-127*, Summ. pub..... 19.13, 19.15
T-45/06 *Reliance Industries v Council and Commission* [2008] E.C.R. II-2399 .... 7.66, 7.73, 7.131,
                                           7.138, 7.178, 9.01, 9.15
T-46/06 *Galileo Lebensmittel v Commission* [2007] E.C.R. II-93*, Summ. pub.,
    (order of 28 August 2007)... 7.73
T-48/06 *Astex Therapeutics Ltd v OHIM* [2008] E.C.R. II-161*, Summ. pub................ 20.16
T-50/06, T-56/06, T-60/06, T-62/06 and T-69/06 *Ireland and Others v Commission* [2007]
    E.C.R. II-172*, Summ. pub... 7.219

T-50/06 RENV, T-56/06 RENV, T-62/06 RENV and T-69/06 RENV *Ireland and Others v*
  Commission, not reported 13.45
T-59/06 *Low & Bonar and Bonar Technical Fabrics v Commission* [2011] E.C.R. II-397*,
  Summ. pub. 7.226, 15.06
T-62/06 RENV-R *Eurallumina v Commission* [2011] E.C.R. II-167*, Summ. pub., (order of the
  President of 9 June 2011) 13.14, 13.35, 13.36
T-63/06 *Evropaiki Dynamiki v European Monitoring Centre for Drugs and Drug Addiction*
  [2010] E.C.R. II-177*, Summ. pub., (judgment of 9 September 2010) 7.71, 11.11
T-68/06 *Stempher and Koninklijke Verpakkingsindustrie Stempher v Commission* [2011]
  E.C.R. II-399*, Summ. pub. 7.220
T-69/06 R *Aughinish Alumina v Commission* [2006] E.C.R. II-58*, Summ. pub., (order of the
  President of 2 August 2006) 13.32, 13.36, 13.41, 13.45
T-72/06 *Groupe Gascogne v Commission* [2011] E.C.R. II-400*, Summ. pub. 7.86
T-75/06 *Bayer CropScience and Others v Commission* [2008] E.C.R. II-2081 . . . . 7.137, 8.10
T-79/06 *Sachsa Verpackung v Commission* [2011] E.C.R. II-406*, Summ. pub. 15.05
T-80/06 and T-182/09 *Budapesti Erőmű Zrt v Commission*, not reported, (judgment of
  13 February 2012) 7.57
T-82/06 *Apple Computer International v Commission* [2008] E.C.R. II-279, (order of
  19 February 2008) 7.100
T-89/06 *Lebard v Commission* [2009] E.C.R. II-201*, Summ. pub. 7.219
T-92/06 *Lademporiki and Apostolos Parousis & Sia v Commission* [2006] E.C.R. II-66*,
  Summ. pub., (order of 8 September 2006) 11.25, 11.27, 11.47, 11.81
T-93/06 DEP *Mülhens v OHIM*, not reported, (order of 22 March 2010) 25.93
T-94/06 *Gargani v European Parliament* [2007] E.C.R. II-158*, (order of 21 November 2007) 7.74
T-95/06 DEP *Federación de Cooperativas Agrarias de la Comunidad Valenciana v CPVO*,
  not reported, (order of 6 October 2009). 25.93
T-99/06 *Phildar SA v OHIM* [2009] E.C.R. II-164*, Summ. pub. 20.06
T-109/06 *Vodafone España and Vodafone Group v Commission* [2007] E.C.R. II-5151,
  (order of 12 December 2007) 7.16
T-114/06 *Globe v Commission* [2006] E.C.R. II-2627, (order of the President of
  20 July 2006). 13.38, 13.42
T-122/06 *Helkon Media v Commission* [2008] E.C.R. II-210*, Summ. pub. 7.15, 19.12
T-125/06 *Centro Studi Antonio Manieri v Council* [2009] E.C.R. II-69 . . . . 7.68, 7.208, 11.76
T-135/06 to T-138/06 *Al-Faqih and Others v Council* [2010] E.C.R. II-208*,
  Summ. pub. 7.178, 7.221, 25.104
T-139/06 *France v Commission* [2011] E.C.R. II-7315 . . . . 5.80, 7.18, 15.01
T-143/06 *MTZ Polyfilms v Council* [2009] E.C.R. II-4133 . . . . 7.82, 7.131
T-144/06 *O'Loughlin v European Ombudsman and Ireland*, not reported, (order of
  5 September 2006) 8.11
T-145/06 *Omya v Commission* [2009] E.C.R. II-145 . . . . 7.219
T-150/06 *Smanor and Others v Commission*, not reported, (order of 14 December 2006) 8.15, 13.04
T-152/06 *NDSHT Nya Destination Stockholm Hotell & Teaterpaket v Commmission* [2009]
  E.C.R. II-1517. . . . . 7.219
T-156/06 *Regione Siciliana v Commission* [2007] E.C.R. II-168*, Summ. pub.,
  (order of 11 December 2007) 7.96
T-163/06 R *BA.L.A. di Lanciotti Vittoria & C. Sas and Others v Commission* [2006]
  E.C.R. II-59*, Summ. pub., (order of the President of 2 August 2006) 13.25, 13.29
T-165/06 *Elio Fiorucci v OHIM* [2009] E.C.R. II-1375 . . . . 20.03
T-170/06 *Alrosa v Commission* [2007] E.C.R. II-2601 . . . . 7.40, 7.112, 7.217
T-173/06 *Aisne et Nature v Commission*, not reported, (order of 16 October 2006) 7.18
T-176/06 *Sviluppo Italia Basilicata v Commission* [2008] E.C.R. II-126*, Summ. pub. 11.07
T-179/06 *Commission v Burie Onderzoek en Advies* [2009] E.C.R. II-64*, Summ. pub. 19.10, 19.13
T-186/06 *Solvay v Commission* [2011] E.C.R. II-2839 . . . . 25.49
T-191/06 *FMC Foret v Commission* [2011] E.C.R. II-2959 . . . . 7.36, 7.162, 7.163, 7.190, 7.192
T-193/06 *TF1 v Commission* [2010] E.C.R. II-4967 . . . . 7.118, 7.120
T-194/06 *SNIA v Commission* [2011] E.C.R. II-3119 . . . . 7.34, 7.163, 25.14
T-208/06 *Quinn Barlo and Others v Commission* [2011] E.C.R. II-7953 . . . . 7.220
T-209/06 R *European Association of Im- and Exporters of Birds and Live Animals and*
  Others v Commission [2006] E.C.R. II-87*, Summ. pub., (order of the President of
  26 October 2006). 13.25, 13.36

T-209/06 *Plomp and Others v Commission* [2008] E.C.R. II-86*, Summ. pub.,
(order of 11 June 2008) 7.104
T-212/06 *Bowland Dairy Products v Commission* [2009] E.C.R. II-4073 . . . . 11.25
T-214/06 *Imperial Chemical Industries v Commission*, not reported, (judgment of
5 June 2012) 11.20, 15.06, 23.87
T-216/06 *Lucite International and Lucite International UK v Commission* [2011]
E.C.R. II-284*, Summ. pub. 15.05, 15.06
T-217/06 *Arkema France and Others v Commission* [2011] E.C.R. II-2593. . . . .7.170, 15.04, 15.07, 15.09
T-223/06 P *European Parliament v Eistrup* [2007] E.C.R. II-1581 . . . . 23.51
T-225/06 RENV, T-255/06 RENV, T-257/06 RENV and T-309/06 RENV
Budejovický Budvar v OHIM, not reported 26.12
T-232/06 *Evropaiki Dynamiki v Commission* [2011] E.C.R. II-263*, Summ. pub. 11.34
T-236/06 *Landtag Schleswig-Holstein v Commission* [2008] E.C.R. II-461, (order of 3 April 2008) . . . 7.83
T-240/06 *Stewart-Smith v European Parliament*, not reported, (order of 29 January 2007) 7.207
T-249/06 *Interpipe Niko Tube and Interpipe NTRP v Council* [2009]
E.C.R. II-383. . . . . .7.166, 7.205, 7.206, 7.207
T-258/06 *Germany v Commission* [2010] E.C.R. II-2027 . . . . .5.31, 5.33, 7.17
T-263/06 *Greece v Commission* [2008] E.C.R. II-290*, Summ. pub. 7.223, 15.01
T-264/06 *DC-Hadler Networks v Commission* [2008] E.C.R. II-199*, Summ. pub. 7.138
T-269/06 *Rautaruukki Oyj v OHIM* [2008] E.C.R. II-273*, Summ. pub. 20.15
T-270/06 *Lego Juris v OHIM* [2008] E.C.R. II-3117 . . . . .20.15, 25.91, 25.98
T-270/06 DEP *Lego Juris v OHIM*, not reported, (order of 2 December 2010) 25.93
T-272/06 *Evropaiki Dynamiki v Court of Justice* [2008] E.C.R. II-169*, Summ. pub. 7.69, 7.170
T-273/06 and T-297/06 *ISD Polska and Others v Commission* [2009] E.C.R. II-2181 . . . . .7.137,
7.177, 7.210, 7.214, 7.216, 7.219
T-274/06 *Estaser El Mareny v Commission*, not reported, (order of 25 October 2007). 7.12
T-276/06 *Sellier v Commission*, not reported, (order of 15 January 2007). 7.18
T-279/06 *Evropaiki Dynamiki v European Central Bank* [2009] E.C.R. II-99*, Summ. pub.,
(order of 2 July 2009). 7.138
T-282/06 *Sun Chemical Group and Others v Commission* [2007] E.C.R. II-2149 . . . . .7.113, 7.137, 7.199
T-288/06 R *Huta Czestochowa v Commission* [2006] E.C.R. II-101*, Summ. pub.,
(order of the President of 13 December 2006) 13.29
T-289/06 *CESD-Communautaire v Commission* [2009] E.C.R. II-40*, Summ. pub. 7.15, 7.138
T-291/06 *Operator ARP v Commission* [2009] E.C.R. II-2275 . . . . 7.138, 7.217
T-301/06 *Lemaître Sécurité v Commission* [2008] E.C.R. II-261*, Summ. pub., (order of
13 November 2008). 7.66, 7.132
T-303/06 and T-337/06 *UniCredito Italiano v OHIM* [2010] E.C.R. II-62*, Summ. pub. 20.15
T-306/06 *Paul Reber GmbH & Co. KG v OHIM* [2008] II-1927 . . . . 20.16
T-310/06 R *Hungary v Commission* [2007] E.C.R. II-15*, Summ. pub., (order of the President of
16 February 2007) 13.40
T-310/06 *Hungary v Commission* [2007] E.C.R. II-4619 . . . . 7.220
T-311/06 *FMC Chemical and Arysta Life Sciences v EFSA* [2008] E.C.R. II-88*, Summ. pub. 13.22
T-311/06 R I, T-311/06 R II, T-312/06 R, and T-313/06 R *FMC Chemical and Others v
EFSA and Commission* [2007] E.C.R. II-21*, Summ. pub., (order of the President of
1 March 2007). 13.11, 13.22, 13.25
T-312/06 *FMC Chemical v EFSA* [2008] E.C.R. II-89*, Summ. pub., (order of 17 June 2008) 13.22
T-314/06 *Whirlpool Europe v Council* [2010] E.C.R. II-5005 . . . . 7.89, 23.82
T-316/06 *Commission v Premium* [2008] E.C.R. II-276*, Summ. pub. 19.19
T-324/06 R *Municipio de Gondomar v Commission* [2007] E.C.R. II-55*, Summ. pub.,
(order of the President of 11 June 2007) 13.25, 13.40
T-324/06 *Municipio de Gondomar v Commission* [2008] E.C.R. II-173*, Summ. pub.,
(order of 10 September 2008) 7.96
T-331/06 *Evropaiki Dynamiki v European Environment Agency* [2010] E.C.R. II-136*,
Summ. pub. 7.70
T-332/06 *Alcoa Transformazioni v Commission* [2009] E.C.R. II-29*, Summ. pub. 7.57, 7.217
T-346/06 R *IMS v Commission* [2007] E.C.R. II-1781, (order of the President of
7 June 2007) 13.25, 13.26, 13.29, 13.32, 13.34, 13.35, 13.36, 13.40, 13.42
T-346/06 *Industria Masetto Schio v Commission*, not reported, (order of 18 February 2009) 11.76
T-369/06 *Holland Malt v Commission* [2009] E.C.R. II-3313. . . . . 25.14
T-378/06 *IMI and Others v Commission* [2011] E.C.R. II-62*, Summ. pub. 7.217, 25.44
T-379/06 *Kaimer and Others v Commission* [2011] E.C.R. II-64*, Summ. pub. 15.04

T-380/06 *Vischim v Commission* [2009] E.C.R. II-3911 . . . . .7.94, 7.219, 7.220, 25.46
T-382/06 *Tomkins v Commission* [2011] E.C.R. II-1157 . . . . 7.86, 15.09
T-383/06 R *Icuna.Com v European Parliament* [2007] E.C.R. II-17*, Summ. pub.,
    (order of the President of 26 February 2007) 13.24, 13.26
T-384/06 R *IBP and International Building Products France v Commission* [2007] E.C.R. II-30*,
    Summ. pub., (order of the President of 28 March 2007) 13.29, 13.39
T-385/06 *Aalberts Industries and Others v Commission* [2011] E.C.R. II-1223 . . . . 15.04
T-386/06 *Pegler v Commission* [2011] E.C.R. II-1267 . . . . 15.06, 15.09
T-387/06 to T-390/06 *Inter-Ikea Systems BV v OHIM* [2008] E.C.R. II-121*, Summ. pub. 20.16
T-393/06 R, T-393/06 R II, and T-393/06 R III *Makhteshim-Agan Holding and Others v
    Commission* [2007] E.C.R. II-32*, Summ. pub., (order of the President of
    30 March 2007). 13.10, 13.25
T-393/06 *Makhteshim-Agan Holding and Others v Commission* [2008] E.C.R. II-293*,
    Summ. pub., (order of 26 November 2008) 8.10, 8.15
T-397/06 R *Dow Agrosciences v EFSA* [2007] E.C.R. II-22*, Summ. pub., (order of the
    President of 1 March 2007). 13.11, 13.25
T-406/06 *Evropaiki Dynamiki v Commission* [2008] E.C.R. II-247*, Summ. pub. 11.11, 11.34
T-411/06 R *Globe v Commission* [2006] E.C.R. II-2627, (order of the President of
    20 July 2006). 13.32
T-411/06 *Sogelma v EAR* [2008] E.C.R. II-2771 . . . . .7.68, 7.70, 7.84, 7.181, 7.208, 7.216
T-412/06 *Vitro Corporativo v OHIM* [2008] E.C.R. II-312*, Summ. pub. 20.06
T-413/06 P *Gualtieri v Commission* [2008] E.C.R.-SC I-B-1-35 . . . . 2.54
T-414/06 P *Combescot v Commission* [2008] E.C.R.-SC I-B-1-1 . . . . 11.10, 18.25

T-7/07 AJ *Neves de Silva v Commission*, not reported, (order of 7 May 2007). 8.06
T-9/07 *Grupo Promer Mon Graphic v OHIM* [2010] E.C.R. II-981. . . . . 20.15
T-11/07 *Frucona Košice v Commission* [2010] E.C.R. II-5453 . . . . .7.59, 7.187, 7.201, 7.204
T-12/07 R *Polimeri Europa v Commission* [2007] E.C.R. II-38*, Summ. pub., (order of the
    President of 3 May 2007). 13.08, 13.19, 13.29
T-18/07 R *Kronberger v European Parliament* [2007] E.C.R. II-50*, Summ. pub., (order of the
    President of 21 May 2007) 13.25
T-19/07 *Systran and Systran Luxembourg v Commission* [2010] E.C.R. II-6083. . . . . 19.10
T-22/07 *US Steel Košice v Commission* [2009] E.C.R. II-61*, Summ. pub., (order of
    14 May 2009) 7.62
T-24/07 *ThyssenKrupp Stainless v Commission* [2009] E.C.R. II-2309 . . . . 7.178
T-25/07 *Iride and Iride Energia v Commission* [2009] E.C.R. II-245 . . . . 7.123
T-31/07 R *Du Pont de Nemours (France) and Others v Commission* [2007] E.C.R. II-2767,
    (order of the President of 19 July 2007). 13.05, 13.06, 13.25, 13.34,
                                                     13.36, 13.40, 13.41, 13.42
T-33/07 *Greece v Commission* [2009] E.C.R. II-74*, Summ. pub. 15.01
T-35/07 DEP *Leche Celta v OHIM*, not reported, (order of 28 February 2011) 25.93
T-40/07 P et T-62/07 P *de Brito Sequeira Carvalho v Commission* [2009]
    E.C.R.-SC II-551 . . . . 23.83, 25.117
T-42/07 *The Dow Chemical Company and Others v Commission* [2011] E.C.R. II-4531 . . . . 15.07
T-43/07 P *Neophytos Neophytou v Commission* [2008] E.C.R-SC I-B-1-53 . . . . 18.13, 18.26
T-44/07 *Kaučuk v Commission* [2011] E.C.R. II-4601 . . . . 7.192, 15.07
T-45/07 *Unipetrol v Commission* [2011] E.C.R. II-4629. . . . . 7.192
T-49/07 *Fahas v Council* [2010] E.C.R. II-5555 . . . . .7.11, 7.181, 7.219, 11.11
T-51/07 *Agrar-Invest-Tatschl v Commission* [2008] E.C.R. II-2825 . . . . .7.219, 23.63, 25.39
T-52/07 *Movimondo Onlus v Commission*, not reported, (order of 25 April 2012). 7.142
T-53/07 *Trade-Stomil v Commission* [2011] E.C.R. II-4657 . . . . 7.192
T-54/07 *Vtesse Networks v Commission* [2011] E.C.R. II-6*, Summ. pub. 7.124
T-56/07 P *Commission v Economidis* [2008] E.C.R.-SC I-B-1-31 . . . . 18.26
T-57/07 *E.ON Ruhrgas and E.ON Földgáz v Commission* [2009] E.C.R. II-132*, Summ. pub. 7.51
T-59/07 *Polimeri Europa v Commission* [2011] E.C.R. II-4687 . . . . 7.190
T-70/07 *Cantieri Navali Termoli v Commission* [2008] E.C.R. II-250*, Summ. pub. 7.183
T-71/07 R *Icuna.Com v European Parliament* [2007] E.C.R. II-39*, Summ. pub.,
    (order of the President of 4 May 2007) 13.16, 13.25
T-85/07 *Gabel Industria Tessile SpA v OHIM* [2008] E.C.R. II-823 . . . . 20.07
T-89/07 *VIP Car Solutions v European Parliament* [2009] E.C.R. II-1403 . . . . 11.34, 25.11
T-90/07 P and T-99/07 P *Belgium and Commission v Genette* [2008] E.C.R. II-3859. . . . . 18.04

T-104/07 and T-339/08 *BVGD v Commission*, not reported, (judgment of
  11 July 2013)..7.43, 7.178, 7.192
T-108/07 *Spira v Commission*, not reported, (order of the President of 8 May 2012) 25.86
T-111/07 *Agrofert Holding v Commission* [2010] E.C.R. II-128*, Summ. pub................. 7.67
T-112/07 *Hitachi and Others v Commission* [2011] E.C.R. II-3871........................ 7.192
T-113/07 *Toshiba Corp. v Commission* [2011] E.C.R. II-3989 .... 15.07
T-117/07 and T-121/07 *Areva and Others v Commission* [2011] E.C.R. II-633 .... 15.05, 15.08
T-120/07 R *MB Immobilien Verwaltungs v Commission* [2007] E.C.R. II-130*,
  Summ. pub., (order of the President of 11 October 2007) 13.31, 13.36, 13.42
T-122/07 to T-124/07 *Siemens AG Osterreich and Others v Commission* [2011] E.C.R. II-793 ..... 15.07
T-127/07 P *Bligny v Commission* [2008] E.C.R.-SC I-B-1-19.......................... 18.19
T-132/07 *Fuji Electric v Commission* [2011] E.C.R. II-4091 .... 7.190, 7.191, 7.192, 15.05, 15.06, 15.08
T-133/07 *Mitsubishi Electric v Commission* [2011] E.C.R. II-4219 ....7.178, 15.07, 25.36
T-135/07 *Italy v Commission*, not reported, (judgment of 17 January 2012)................. 7.178
T-137/07 *Portela v Commission* [2008] E.C.R. II-329*, Summ. pub., (order of
  17 December 2008) 11.69, 11.83
T-139/07 *Pioneer Hi-Bred International v Commission*, not reported, (order of
  4 September 2009)....................................... 8.21
T-139/07 DEP *Pioneer Hi-Bred International v Commission*, not reported, (order of
  25 November 2010)....................................... 25.93
T-144/07, T-147/07, T-148/07, T-149/07, T-150/07, and T-154/07 *ThyssenKrupp*
  Liften Ascenseurs and Others v Commission [2011] E.C.R. II-5129 .... 15.06
T-152/07 *Lange Uhren v OHIM* [2009] E.C.R. II-144*, Summ. pub. 20.06
T-160/07 *Lancôme parfums et beauté v OHIM* [2008] E.C.R. II-1733................ 8.11
T-162/07 *Pigasos Alieftiki Naftiki Etaireia v Council and Commission* [2009] E.C.R. II-153*,
  Summ. pub. 11.07, 11.36
T-177/07 *Mediaset v Commission* [2010] E.C.R. II-2341 .... 25.12
T-183/07 R *Poland v Commission* [2007] E.C.R. II-152*, Summ. pub., (order of the President of
  9 November 2007)....................................... 13.41
T-190/07 *KEK Diavlos v Commission* [2010] E.C.R. II-33*, Summ. pub. 2.29, 7.89
T-214/07 *Greece v Commission* [2011] E.C.R. II-79*, Summ. pub................... 7.223
T-215/07 R *Donnici v European Parliament* [2007] E.C.R. II-4673, (order of the President of
  15 November 2007)...............................13.32, 13.34, 13.42
T-215/07 *Donnici v European Parliament* [2007] E.C.R. II-5239, (order of
  13 December 2007) 2.55, 7.01
T-215/07 R *Donnici v European Parliament* [2007] E.C.R. II-4673, (order of the President of
  15 November 2007)....................................13.04, 13.34
T-222/07 P *Kerstens v Commission*, not reported, (judgment of 8 September 2008) 2.39
T-234/07 *Koninklijke Grolsch v Commission* [2011] E.C.R. II-6169..................... 7.185
T-235/07 *Bavaria v Commission* [2011] E.C.R. II-3229 .... 7.36
T-236/07 *Germany v Commission* [2010] E.C.R. II-5253 .... 25.16, 25.49
T-238/07 R *Ristic and Others v Commission* [2007] E.C.R. II-134*, Summ. pub., (order of the
  President of 18 October 2007) 13.31, 13.42
T-238/07 *Ristic and Others* [2009] E.C.R. II-117*, Summ. pub. 7.142, 11.34, 11.48
T-252/07, T-271/07 and T-272/07 *Sungro and Others v Council and Commission* [2010]
  E.C.R. II-55, (judgment of 20 January 2010)....................11.38, 11.78, 11.82
T-256/07 *People's Mojahedin Organization of Iran v Council* [2008] E.C.R. II-3019 ....7.10, 7.11,
  7.141, 7.181, 7.183
T-257/07 R *France v Commission* [2007] E.C.R. II-4153, (order of the President of
  28 September 2007).........................13.01, 13.34, 13.40, 13.42
T-257/07 R II *France v Commission* [2008] E.C.R. II-236*, Summ. pub., (order of the
  President of 30 October 2008) 13.34, 13.42, 13.44
T-264/07 *CSL Behring v Commission and EMA* [2010] E.C.R. II-4469..................... 7.89
T-264/07 DEP *CSL Behring v Commission and EMA*, not reported, (order of 3 May 2012) 25.91
T-284/07 P *OHIM v López Teruel* [2008] E.C.R.-SC I-B-1-69...................... 18.04
T-289/07 REC *Caisse Nationale des Caisses d'Épargne et de Prévoyance v Commission*, not reported,
  (order of 14 June 2010) 25.133
T-292/07 R *Berliner Institut für Vergleichende Sozialforschung v Commission*, not reported,
  (order of the President of 13 September 2007) 13.07
T-295/07 *Vitro Corporativo v OHIM* [2008] E.C.R. II-317*, Summ. pub. 20.06
T-300/07 *Evropaiki Dynamiki v Commission* [2010] E.C.R. II-4521 ....7.170, 11.09, 11.35

T-308/07 *Tegebauer v European Parliament* [2011] E.C.R. II-279*, Summ. pub............. 7.17, 7.170

T-312/07 R *Peramatos v Commission* [2007] E.C.R. II-157*, Summ. pub., (order of the
President of 16 November 2007)....................................... 13.25, 13.41

T-312/07 R II *Peramatos v Commission*, not reported, (order of the President of
3 December 2007).. 13.04

T-316/07 *Commercy v OHIM* [2009] E.C.R. II-43 .... 25.101

T-320/07 *Jones and Others v Commission* [2011] E.C.R. II-417*, Summ. pub.............8.20, 25.20,
25.47, 25.105

T-326/07 R *Cheminova and Others v Commission* [2007] E.C.R. II-4877, (order of the
President of 4 December 2007).........................13.25, 13.29, 13.36

T-326/07 *Cheminova and Others v Commission* [2009] E.C.R. II-2685 .... 7.137, 9.15

T-332/06 *Alcoa Transformazioni v Commission* [2009] E.C.R. II-29*, Summ. pub. 7.57

T-335/07 *Volker Mergel v OHIM* [2008] E.C.R. II-324*, Summ. pub. 20.15

T-336/07 *Telefónica and Telefónica de España v Commission*, not reported, (judgment of
29 March 2012)........................... 7.190, 7.192, 7.193, 25.10, 25.12

T-338/07 P *Bianchi v ETF*, not reported, (judgment of 19 March 2010)................... 18.30

T-340/07 *Evropaïki Dynamiki v Commission* [2010] E.C.R. II-16*, Summ. pub. 19.10

T-341/07 *Sison v Council* [2011] E.C.R. II-7915.................. 11.01, 11.09, 11.38, 11.44,
11.45, 11.48, 11.51, 11.58, 11.59, 11.60, 11.61, 11.97

T-342/07 *Ryanair Holding v Commission* [2010] E.C.R. II-3457...... 7.196, 7.197, 7.198, 25.14, 25.48

T-344/07 *O2 (Germany) v OHIM* [2010] E.C.R II-153......................... 20.15

T-348/07 *Stichting Al-Aqsa v Council* [2010] E.C.R. II-4575 .... 9.05

T-349/07 R *FMC Chemical SPRL and Others v Commission* [2007] E.C.R. II-169*,
Summ. pub., (order of the President of 11 December 2007) 13.25, 13.29, 13.35, 13.36, 13.40

T-350/07 R *FMC Chemical SPRL and Others v Commission* [2007] E.C.R. II-170*,
Summ. pub., (order of the President of 11 December 2007) 13.25, 13.29, 13.35, 13.36, 13.40

T-369/07 *Latvia v Commission* [2011] E.C.R. II-1039 .... 7.12, 7.21, 7.76

T-374/07 *Pachtitis*, not reported, (order of 10 April 2011) 2.54

T-375/07 R *Pellegrini v Commission* [2008] E.C.R. II-1*, Summ. pub., (order of the
President of 7 January 2008)...................................... 13.11, 13.34

T-375/07 *Pellegrini v Commission* [2008] E.C.R. II-235*, Summ. pub..................... 11.51

T-377/07 *Evropaïki Dynamiki v Commission* [2011] E.C.R. II-442*, Summ. pub..........7.145, 7.182,
7.183, 11.11

T-380/07 *Dimitrios Kaloudis v OHIM* [2008] E.C.R. II-208*, Summ. pub., (order of
6 October 2008) 20.05

T-385/07 *FIFA v Commission* [2011] E.C.R. II-205.....................7.92, 7.141, 7.217, 9.15

T-387/07 R *Portugal v Commission* [2007] E.C.R. II-176*, Summ. pub., (order of the President of
14 December 2007) 13.41

T-387/07 *Portugal v Commission* [2011] E.C.R. II-903........................ 19.10

T-388/07 *Comune di Napoli v Commission* [2010] E.C.R. II-79*, Summ. pub. 11.07, 11.11

T-391/07 *Alfons Alber v OHIM* [2009] E.C.R. II-157*, Summ. pub. 20.15

T-395/07 *Balatsoukas v Commission*, not reported, (order of 22 April 2008)................. 11.34

T-398/07 *Spain v Commission*, not reported, (judgment of 29 March 2012) 7.86, 25.12

T-401/07 *Caixa Geral de Depositos v Commission* [2011] E.C.R. II-39*, Summ. pub......... 7.96, 19.10

T-407/07 *CMB Maschinenbau & Handels and J. Christof v Commission* [2011] E.C.R. II-286*,
Summ. pub. 7.23, 7.70, 7.207, 7.208

T-409/07 *Helbe B. Cohausz v OHIM* [2009] E.C.R. II-173*, Summ. pub. 20.15

T-410/07 R *Jurado Hermanos v OHIM* [2008] E.C.R. II-25*, Summ. pub., (order of the
President of 18 February 2008) 13.04, 13.05, 13.07, 13.19, 13.22

T-411/07 R *Aer Lingus Group v Commission* [2008] E.C.R. II-411, (order of the President of
18 March 2008)................. 13.04, 13.05, 13.15, 13.18, 13.21, 13.29, 13.36

T-411/07 *Aer Lingus Group v Commission* [2010] E.C.R. II-3691 .... 13.18

T-412/07 *Ayyanarsamy v Commission and Germany*, not reported, (order of 1 April 2008) 7.04

T-413/07 *Bayern Innovativ—Bayerische Gesellschaft für Innovation und Wissenstransfer mbH v
OHIM* [2009] II-16*, Summ. pub.................................. 20.06

T-419/07 *Okalux GmbH v OHIM* [2009] E.C.R. II-2477 .... 20.05

T-423/07 *Ryanair v Commission* [2011] E.C.R. II-2397 .... 8.06, 8.19, 8.20, 8.23

T-428/07 and T-455/07 *CEVA v Commission* [2010] E.C.R. II-2431 ....7.15, 19.12, 19.18

T-439/07 *Coats Holdings v Commission*, not reported, (judgment of 27 June 2012) ...7.190, 7.191, 7.192

T-440/07 R *Huta Buczek v Commission* [2008] E.C.R. II-39*, Summ. pub., (order of the
President of 14 March 2008)................................. 13.32, 13.40, 13.41

T-442/07 *Ryanair v Commission* [2011] E.C.R. II-333*, Summ. pub. 8.06, 8.13, 8.15,
    8.16, 8.18, 8.19, 8.20, 8.21

T-444/07 R *CPEM v Commission* [2008] E.C.R. II-27*, Summ. pub., (order of the
    President of 19 February 2008) 13.07, 13.29, 13.36, 13.41

T-444/07 *CPEM v Commission* [2009] E.C.R. II-2121 . . . . 11.15, 11.34

T-448/07 *YKK and Others v Commission*, not reported, (judgment of June 27, 2012) 7.190, 7.192

T-456/07 *Commission v Cdt* [2010] E.C.R. II-183, (order of 12 February 2010) 7.16, 7.23

T-457/07 *Evropaïki Dynamiki v EFSA*, not reported, (judgment of
    12 December 2012) 7.70, 7.141, 25.12

T-459/07 *Hangzhou Duralamp Electronics v Council*, not reported,
    (judgment of 11 July 2013) 7.89, 7.166, 7.178, 7.205, 25.50

T-460/07 *Nokia Oyj v OHIM* [2010] E.C.R. II-89 . . . . 20.19

T-461/07 *Visa Europe and Visa International Service v Commission* [2011]
    E.C.R. II-1729 . . . . .7.190, 7.192, 7.193, 25.10

T-464/07 *Korsch AG v OHIM* [2009] E.C.R. II-85*, Summ. pub. 20.16

T-466/07 *Osram v Council*, not reported, (order of the President of 5 September 2008) 25.96, 25.99

T-467/07 R *Du Pont de Nemours (France) and Others v Commission* [2008] E.C.R. II-40*,
    Summ. pub., (order of the President of 14 March 2008) 13.25, 13.36, 13.41

T-468/07 *Bönker v Germany*, not reported, (order of 2 June 2008) 2.02

T-475/07 R *Dow Agrosciences and Others v Commission* [2008] E.C.R. II-92*, Summ. pub.,
    (order of the President of 18 June 2008) 13.25, 13.36, 13.37

T-475/07 *Dow AgroSciences v Commission* [2011] E.C.R. II-5937 . . . . 7.141, 9.08

T-487/07 *Imperial Chemical Industries v OHIM* [2008] E.C.R. II-227*, Summ. pub.,
    (order of 20 October 2008) 23.17

T-502/07 *IIC—Intersport International v OHIM* [2011] E.C.R. II-138*, Summ. pub. 20.15

T-503/07 *Kulykovska-Pawlowski and Others v European Parliament and Council* [2008]
    E.C.R. II-48*, Summ. pub., (order of 4 April 2008) 7.216

T-1/08 *Buczek Automotive v Commission* [2011] E.C.R. II-2107 . . . . 7.201

T-4/08 *EMSA v Portugal*, (order of 29 January 2009) 19.14

T-5/08 and T-7/08 *Nestlé v OHIM* [2010] E.C.R. II-1177 . . . . 20.05

T-12/08 P-RENV-RX *M v EMEA* [2010] E.C.R. II-3735 . . . . 17.09

T-34/08 *Berliner Institut für Vergleichende Sozialforschung v Commission* [2011]
    E.C.R. II-305*, Summ. pub. 25.10

T-37/08 *Walton v Commission* [2011] E.C.R. II-7809 . . . . 7.15, 19.12

T-38/08 *Correia de Matos v Commission*, not reported, (order of 9 April 2008) 7.75

T-39/08 *Evropaïki Dynamiki v Commission* [2011] E.C.R. II-437*, Summ. pub. 11.65

T-40/08 *EREF v Commission* [2009] E.C.R. II-222*, Summ. pub., (order 19 November 2009) 23.17

T-41/08 R *Vakakis International v Commission* [2008] E.C.R. II-66*, Summ. pub.,
    (order of the President of 25 April 2008) 13.24, 13.25, 13.29, 13.38, 13.40

T-54/08 R, T-87/08 R, T-88/08 R, and T-91/08 R to T-93/08 R *Cyprus v Commission*,
    not reported, (order of the President of 8 April 2008) 13.25, 13.32, 13.36, 13.40

T-55/08 *UEFA v Commission* [2011] E.C.R. II-271 . . . . .7.92, 7.217, 9.15

T-64/08 *Nuova Terni Industrie Chimiche v Commission* [2010] E.C.R. II-125*, Summ. pub. 7.165

T-65/08 R *Spain v Commission* [2008] E.C.R. II-69*, Summ. pub., (order of the
    President of 30 April 2008) 13.31, 13.32, 13.34, 13.42

T-68/08 *FIFA v Commission* [2011] E.C.R. II-349 . . . . .7.92, 7.217, 9.15, 25.62

T-70/08 *Axis v OHIM* [2010] E.C.R. II-4645 . . . . 20.05

T-72/08 *Travel Service v OHIM* [2010] E.C.R. II-196*, Summ. pub. 20.08

T-76/08 *EI du Pont de Nemours and Company and Others v Commission*, not reported,
    (judgment of 2 February 2012) 15.05

T-77/08 *The Dow Chemical Company v Commission*, not reported, (judgment of
    2 February 2012) 15.05

T-83/08 *Denki Kagaku Kogyo and Denka Chemicals v Commission*, not reported,
    (judgment of 2 February 2012) 7.36, 15.05, 25.48

T-85/08 *Exalation v OHIM* [2010] E.C.R. II-3837 . . . . 20.19

T-94/08 *Centre de coordination Carrefour v Commission* [2010] E.C.R. II-1015 . . . . 7.138, 7.141

T-97/08 *KUKA Roboter v OHIM* [2010] E.C.R. II-5059 . . . . 20.15

T-102/08 P *Sundholm v Commission*, not reported, (judgment of 6 October 2009) 11.66

T-106/08 *CPEM v Commission* [2009] E.C.R. II-91*, Summ. pub., (order of
    30 June 2009) 7.23, 11.38

T-107/08 *Transnational Company 'Kazchrome' and ENRC Marketing v Council and Commission* [2011] E.C.R. II-8051 . . . . .7.66, 7.73, 7.205, 11.13, 11.38, 11.78, 11.85, 25.10

T-111/08 *MasterCard and MasterCard Europe v Commission*, not reported, (judgment of 24 May 2012) 25.47, 25.65

T-114/08 P *Marcuccio v Commission* [2009] E.C.R.-SC I-B-1-53, (order of 26 June 2009) . . . 18.17, 18.18

T-117/08 *Italy v European Economic and Social Committee* [2011] E.C.R. II-1463 . . . . 7.70, 7.175

T-118/08 *Actega Terra GmbH v OHIM* [2010] E.C.R. II-110*, Summ. pub. 20.07, 20.16

T-119/08 R *Cyprus v Commission* [2008] E.C.R. II-56*, Summ. pub., (order of the President of 11 April 2008). 13.24

T-120/08 *Arch Chemicals and Others v Commission* [2011] E.C.R. II-298*, Summ. pub. 7.99, 7.100, 25.31

T-121/08 *PC-Ware Information Technologies v Commission* [2010] E.C.R. II-1541 . . . . 7.138, 11.11

T-122/08 R *Cyprus v Commission* [2008] E.C.R. II-57*, Summ. pub., (order of the President of 11 April 2008). 13.24

T-123/08 *Spitzer v OHIM*, not reported, (order of 2 September 2010) 25.20

T-124/08 *Hurtado García v Spain*, not reported, (order of 20 May 2008) 2.02

T-135/08 *Schniga GmbH v CPVO* [2010] E.C.R. II-5089 . . . . 20.15

T-141/08 *E.ON Energie v Commission* [2010] E.C.R. II-5761 . . . . .7.33, 7.190, 7.191, 7.192

T-148/08 *Beifa Group Co. Ltd v OHIM* [2010] E.C.R. II-1681 . . . . 20.06

T-156/08 P *R v Commission* [2009] E.C.R.-SC II-B-1-51. . . . . 25.16

T-157/08 *Paroc v OHIM* [2011] E.C.R. II-137 . . . . 7.23

T-158/08 *Commune de Ne and Others v Commission*, not reported, (order of 19 June 2008) 7.208

T-165/08 *Química Atlântica and Martins de Freitas Moura v Commission*, not reported, (order of 23 July 2008). 8.19, 8.21

T-166/08 *Ivanov v Commission* [2009] E.C.R. II-190*, Summ. pub., (order of 30 September 2009) 11.05

T-167/08 *Microsoft v Commission*, (judgment of 27 June 2012) 7.41, 25.65

T-169/08 *DEI v Commission*, not reported, (judgment of 20 September 2012) 7.41

T-176/08 *infeurope v Commission* [2009] E.C.R. II-119*, Summ. pub., (order of 9 July 2009) 8.11

T-180/08 P *Tiralongo v Commission* [2009] E.C.R.-SC I-B-1-117, (order of 20 November 2009) . . . 18.18

T-181/08 *Tay Za v Council* [2010] E.C.R. II-1965 . . . . 7.11

T-182/08 *Commission v Atlantic Energy* [2009] E.C.R. II-109*, Summ. pub. 7.15, 19.12

T-185/08 *VDH Projektentwicklung and Edeka Handelsgesellschaft Rhein-Ruhr v Commission* [2008] E.C.R. II-98*, Summ. pub., (order of 25 June 2008). 8.13

T-186/08 *LPN v Commission* [2009] E.C.R. II-136*, Summ. pub. (order of 7 September 2009). 5.32, 5.33, 7.18, 11.27, 11.47, 11.81

T-187/08 *Rodd & Gunn Australia Ltd v OHIM* [2010] E.C.R. II-58*, Summ. pub. 20.15

T-189/08 *Forum 187 v Commission* [2010] E.C.R. II-1039, (judgment of 18 March 2010). 7.128, 7.138, 7.141, 25.48, 25.49

T-190/08 *CHEMK and KF v Council* [2011] E.C.R. II-7359 . . . . 7.166

T-192/08 *ENRC Marketing v Council*, not reported, (order of the President of 16 February 2009) 25.69

T-194/08 *Cattin & Cie and Cattin v Commission* [2009] E.C.R. II-242*, Summ. pub., (order of 16 December 2009) 11.91

T-195/08 R *Antwerpse Bouwwerken v Commission* [2008] E.C.R. II-141*, Summ. pub., (order of the President of 15 July 2008). 13.19, 13.37, 13.38

T-195/08 *Antwerpse Bouwwerken v Commission* [2009] E.C.R. II-4439 . . . . 7.68, 11.11

T-196/08 *Srinivasan v European Ombudsman*, not reported, (order of 3 November 2008). 7.13, 7.70, 8.11

T-199/08 R *Ziegler v Commission* [2009] E.C.R. II-2*, Summ. pub., (order of the President of 15 January 2009) 13.24

T-199/08 *Ziegler v Commission* [2011] E.C.R. II-3507. . . . . 7.36

T-202/08 R *CLL Centres de langues v Commission* [2008] E.C.R. II-143*, Summ. pub., (order of the President of 15 July 2008). 13.24, 13.34, 13.37, 13.38

T-207/08 *Habanos v OHIM* [2011] E.C.R. II-140*, Summ. pub. 20.15

T-213/08 REV *Marinova v Université de Bruxelles and Commission*, not reported, (order of 31 July 2009). 2.29, 17.01, 19.13, 23.91, 25.106

T-219/08 *İşçi Partisi (Turkish Labour Party) v Commission*, not reported, (order of 1 December 2008) 11.14

T-220/08 *İşçi Partisi (Turkish Labour Party) v Council and Commission*, not reported, (order of 1 December 2008) 7.207, 7.219

T-227/08 *Brehm v Commission*, not reported, (order of 21 July 2008) 7.208
T-228/08 *Szomborg v Commission* [2009] E.C.R. II-224*, Summ. pub., (order of
   24 November 2009) 8.19
T-238/08 *Commission v Commune de Valbonne* [2010] E.C.R. II-260*, Summ. pub. 19.19
T-239/08 DEP *Comtec Translations v Commission*, not reported, (order of 3 May 2011) 25.92
T-242/08 *Faur v Council of Europe*, not reported, (order of 11 July 2008) 11.18
T-244/08 *Konsum Nord v Commission* [2011] E.C.R. II-444*, Summ. pub. 7.201
T-246/08 R *Melli Bank v Council*, not reported, (order of the President of
   27 August 2008) 13.35, 13.36, 13.40, 13.41
T-246/08 and T-322/08 *Melli Bank v Council* [2009] E.C.R. II-2629. . . . . 9.15
T-247/08 *C-Content v Commission*, not reported, (judgment of 28 September 2010) 11.15,
                                                                                           11.56, 11.87, 11.91
T-250/08 *Batchelor v Commission* [2011] E.C.R. II-2551 . . . . 25.98
T-266/08 P-DEP *Kerstens v Commission*, not reported, (order of 23 March 2012) 25.93
T-267/08 and T-279/08 *Région Nord-Pas-de-Calais v Commission* [2011]
   E.C.R. II-1999. . . . . .7.202, 7.203, 25.17
T-271/08 P *Boudavo and Others v Commission* [2009] E.C.R.-SC I-B-1-71 . . . . 18.19, 18.20
T-282/08 *Grazer Wechselseitige Versicherung v Commission*, not reported,
   (judgment of 28 February 2012) 7.147, 7.202, 7.204
T-284/08 *People's Mojahedin Organization of Iran v Council* [2008] E.C.R. II-3487 . . . . 25.49
T-284/08 INT *People's Mojahedin Organization of Iran v Council* [2008] E.C.R. II-334*,
   Summ. pub. 25.128
T-284/08 TO *Avaessian Avaki and Others v People's Mojahedin Organization of Iran and
   Others*, not reported, (order of 17 September 2009) 25.107, 25.108, 25.110
T-293/08 *BASF Plant Science and Others v Commission*, not reported, (order of 9 June 2010) 25.101
T-299/08 *Elf Aquitaine v Commission* [2011] E.C.R. II-2149 . . . . 15.05, 25.13, 25.14
T-303/08 *Tresplain Investments Ltd v OHIM* [2010] E.C.R. II-5659. . . . . 20.19, 25.13, 25.49
T-304/08 *Smurfit Kappa Group v Commission*, not reported, (judgment of 10 July 2012) 7.118, 23.18
T-305/08 *Italy v Commission*, not reported, (order of 14 February 2012) 10.21
T-306/08 P *Braun-Neumann v European Parliament* [2009] E.C.R.-SC I-B-1-1,
   (order of 15 January 2009) 18.04, 18.23
T-312/08 R *Ellinikos Niognomon v Commission* [2008] E.C.R. II-204*, Summ. pub.,
   (order of the President of 26 September 2008) 13.04, 13.05, 13.25
T-319/08 *Grasso v Commission*, not reported, (order of 14 February 2012) 7.05
T-332/08 R *Melli Bank v Council*, not reported, (order of the President of
   17 September 2008), ... 13.24
T-335/08 *BNP Paribas and Others v Commission* [2010] E.C.R. II-3323 . . . . .7.120, 7.122,
                                                                                           7.137, 7.170, 25.48
T-338/08 *Stichting Natuur en Milieu and Pesticide Action Network Europe v Commission*, not
   reported, (judgment of 14 June 2012) 7.178, 25.15
T-343/08 *Arkema France v Commission* [2011] E.C.R. II-2287 . . . . .7.138, 15.05, 15.07
T-348/08 *Aragoneses Industrias y Energia v Commission* [2011] E.C.R. II-7583. . . . . 15.07
T-352/08 R *Pannon v Commission* [2009] E.C.R. II-9*, Summ. pub., (order of the President
   of 23 January 2009) 13.29, 13.32, 13.36
T-353/08 *vwd Vereinigte Wirtschaftsdienste v Commission*, not reported, (order of
   26 October 2009). 25.73
T-354/08 *Diamanthandel A. Spira v Commission*, not reported, (order of the President of
   11 May 2009) 25.76
T-361/08 *Peek & Cloppenburg and van Graaf v OHIM* [2010] E.C.R. II-1207 . . . . 20.11
T-365/08 *Emilio Hidalgo v OHIM*, not reported, (order of 27 September 2010) 25.84
T-367/08 *Abouchar v Commission* [2009] E.C.R. II-128*, Summ. pub., (order of
   27 August 2009) 11.64, 11.87, 11.90, 25.91
T-369/08 *EWRIA and Others v Commission* [2010] E.C.R. II-6283. . . . . 7.16, 7.65, 7.66,
                                                                                           7.188, 7.205, 7.219, 25.10
T-370/08 *Csepeli Áramtermelő v Commission*, not reported, (order of 16 December 2009). 25.65
T-373/08 *Nuova Agricast v Commission* [2011] E.C.R. II-147*, Summ. pub.,
   (order of 24 May 2011) 11.69, 11.97
T-381/08 *DAI v Commission*, not reported, (order of 4 September 2012) 25.13, 25.16, 25.49
T-386/08 *Nadine Trautwein Rolf Trautwein GbR, Research and Development v OHIM*
   [2010] E.C.R. II-139*, Summ. pub. 20.16
T-387/08 *Evropaiki Dynamiki v Commission* [2010] E.C.R. II-178*, Summ. pub. 7.181, 7.183, 11.11

T-390/08 *Melli Bank Iran v Council*, not reported, (order of the President of
   15 October 2008). 13.36, 13.40
T-390/08 *Bank Melli Iran v Council* [2009] E.C.R. II-3967 .9.01, 9.15, 25.81
T-394/08, T-408/08, T-453/08, and T-454/08 *Regione Autonoma della Sardegna v
   Commission* [2011] E.C.R. II-6255 . . . . .7.57, 7.125, 9.08, 25.60
T-398/08 R *Stowarzyszenie Autorow ZAiKS v Commission* [2008] E.C.R. II-266*,
   Summ. pub., (order of the President of 14 November 2008). 13.29
T-404/08 *Fluorsid and Minmet v Commission*, not reported, (judgment of 18 June 2013) 7.208, 23.38
T-406/08 *ICF v Commission*, not reported, (judgment of 18 June 2013) 23.51
T-412/08 *Trubion Pharmaceuticals, Inc v OHIM* [2009] E.C.R. II-239 . . . . 20.16
T-422/08 R *Sacem v Commission* [2008] E.C.R. II-271*, Summ. pub., (order of the
   President of 14 November 2008). 13.29
T-422/08 *SACEM v Commission*, not reported, (order of the President of 19 October 2009) 25.65
T-424/08 *Nexus Europe (Ireland) v Commission* [2010] E.C.R. II-96*, Summ. pub. 11.06, 19.11
T-427/08 *CEAHR v Commission* [2010] E.C.R. II-5865. .7.43, 7.192, 25.98
T-429/08 DEP *Millers v OHIM*, not reported, (order of 9 February 2011) 25.92, 25.93
T-439/08 *Joséphidès v Commission and Education, Audiovisual and Cultural Executive
   Agency (EACEA)* [2010] E.C.R. II-230*, Summ. pub. 7.73, 7.216, 9.05, 9.08, 25.07
T-441/08 *ICO Services v European Parliament and Council* [2010] E.C.R. II-100*,
   Summ. pub., (order of 21 May 2010) 7.91, 7.92, 7.218
T-442/08 *CISAC v Commission*, not reported, (judgment of 12 April 2013) 7.86
T-443/08 and T-455/08 *Freistaat Sachsen and Others v Commission* [2011]
   E.C.R. II-1311. . . . . 7.123, 7.125, 7.138
T-451/08 *Stim v Commission*, not reported, (judgment of 13 April 2013) 25.14
T-452/08 *DHL Aviation and Others v Commission* [2010] E.C.R. II-218*,
   Summ. pub. 7.137
T-457/08 R *Intel Corp. v Commission* [2009] E.C.R. II-12*, Summ. pub.,
   (order of the President of 27 January 2009) 13.25, 13.37
T-458/08 *Wilfer v OHIM* [2010] E.C.R. II-168*, Summ. pub. 20.15
T-460/08 *Commission v Acentro Turismo* [2010] E.C.R. II-6351. . . . . 19.15
T-461/08 *Evropaïki Dynamiki v European Investment Bank* [2011]
   E.C.R. II-6367. . . . . 7.05, 7.70, 7.138, 7.170, 11.20
T-463/08 *Imagion v OHIM* [2011] E.C.R. II-206*, Summ. pub. 20.15
T-468/08 R *AES-Tisza v Commission* [2008] E.C.R. II-346*, Summ. pub., (order of the
   President of 22 December 2008) 13.32, 13.36
T-474/08 *Umbach v Commission* [2010] E.C.R. II-234*, Summ. pub. 7.14
T-480/08 R *Woźniak v Poland*, not reported, (order of the President of 18 December 2008) 13.26
T-481/08 *Alisei v Commission* [2010] E.C.R. II-117, (order of 8 February 2012) 11.06, 19.12, 25.86
T-488/08 *Galileo International Technology v OHIM* [2011] E.C.R. II-350*,
   Summ. pub. 25.14
T-489/08 *Power-One Italy v Commission* [2011] E.C.R. II-149*, Summ. pub.,
   (order of 24 May 2011) 11.09, 11.10, 11.34
T-491/08 P *Bui Van v Commission*, not yet reported, (judgment of 12 May 2010) 15.05, 15.09, 16.29
T-494/08 to T-500/08 and T-509/08 *Ryanair v Commission* [2010]
   E.C.R. II-5723. . . . . 7.12, 7.14, 7.138, 7.142, 23.43
T-516/08 *Gutknecht v Commission* [2010] E.C.R. II-40*, Summ. pub. 11.81
T-526/08 P *Commission v Strack*, not reported, (judgment of 9 December 2010). 18.07
T-523/08 *Agatha Ruiz de la Prada de Sentmenat v OHIM* [2011] E.C.R. II-276*, Summ. pub. 20.06
T-528/08 *Delice and Delice v Erlangen and Commission*, not reported, (order of 19 May 2009) 11.81
T-529/08 and T-531/08 *Territorio Histórico de Álava and Others v Commission* [2010]
   E.C.R. II-53*, Summ. pub., (order of 13 April 2010) 7.55
T-532/08 *Norilsk Nickel Harjavalta and Umicore v Commission* [2010] E.C.R. II-3959,
   (order of 7 September 2010) 7.05
T-537/08 *Cixi Santai Chemical Fiber and Others v Council*, not reported, (order of the
   President of 14 December 2010) 25.65, 25.69
T-539/08 *Etimine and Etiproducts v Commission* [2010] E.C.R. II-4017 . . . . 7.05
T-549/08 *Luxembourg v Commission* [2010] E.C.R. II-2477 . . . . 7.207
T-554/08 *Evropaiki Dynamiki v Commission*, not reported, (judgment of 24 April 2012) 7.136
T-560/08 P *Commission v Meierhofer* [2010] E.C.R. II-1739 . . . . 23.57
T-561/08 *Gutknecht v Commission* [2011] E.C.R. II-364*, Summ. pub. 11.78, 25.43

T-565/08 *Corsica Ferries France v Commission*, not reported, (judgment of
 11 September 2012) 7.170, 7.187, 7.201
T-574/08 *Syndicat des thoniers méditerranéens and Others v Commission*, not reported,
 (judgment of 7 November 2012) 11.07, 25.13
T-576/08 *Germany v Commission* [2011] E.C.R. II-1578 . . . . 23.60, 25.60
T-577/08 *Proges v Commission* [2010] E.C.R. II-46*, Summ. pub. 7.138
T-582/08 *Carpent Languages SPRL v Commission* [2010] E.C.R. II-181*, Summ. pub. 1.10
T-587/08 *Fresh Del Monte Produce v Commission*, not reported, (judgment of
 14 March 2013) 7.34, 7.36, 25.10, 25.60, 25.65, 25.67
T-588/08 *Dole Food Company and Dole Food Germany v Commission*, not reported,
 (judgment of 14 March 2013) 23.63, 25.10, 25.18, 25.39, 25.48
T-589/08 *Evropaiki Dynamiki v Commission* [2011] E.C.R. II-40*, Summ. pub. 11.11

T-8/09 *Dredging International and Others v EMSA* [2011] E.C.R. II-6123 . . . . 7.138, 7.217, 11.11
T-10/09 *Formula One Licensing v OHIM* [2011] E.C.R. II-427 . . . . 20.15
T-15/09 *Européenne de traitement de l'information (Euro-Information) v OHIM*
 [2010] E.C.R. II-27*, Summ. pub. 20.06
T-17/09 *Evropaiki Dynamiki v Commission*, not reported, (judgment of 22 May 2012) 25.87
T-30/09 *Engelhorn v OHIM* [2010] E.C.R. II-3803 . . . . 25.10
T-33/09 *Portugal v Commission* [2011] E.C.R. II-1429 . . . . 5.80, 7.18
T-49/09 *Evropaiki Dynamiki v Commission*, not reported, (judgment of 19 April 2012) 25.96
T-52/09 R *Nycomed Denmark v European Medicines Agency* [2009] E.C.R. II-43*,
 Summ. pub., (order of the President of 24 April 2009) 13.22, 13.36, 13.37
T-57/09 *Alfastar Benelux v Council* [2011] E.C.R. II-368*, Summ. pub. 7.170, 11.35
T-58/09 *Schemaventotto v Commission* [2010] E.C.R. II-3863, (order of 2 September 2010) 7.46
T-59/09 *Germany v Commission*, not reported, (judgment of 14 February 2012) 7.67
T-65/09 P *Reali v Commission*, not yet reported, (judgment of 27 October 2010) 9.16
T-71/09 *Química Atlântica v Commission* [2010] E.C.R. II-1*, Summ. pub., (order of
 5 January 2010) 8.05, 8.10, 8.19, 11.34
T-82/09 *Gert-Jan Dennekamp v European Parliament*, not reported, (order of the
 President of 4 September 2009) 25.64
T-83/09 *David Chalk v OHIM* [2011] E.C.R. II-267*, Summ. pub. 20.06
T-85/09 *Kadi v Commission* [2010] E.C.R. II-5177 . . . . 7.178
T-86/09 *Evropaïki Dynamiki v Commission* [2011] E.C.R. II-309*, Summ. pub. 11.11
T-87/09 *Andersen v Commission* [2009] E.C.R. II-225*, not reported, (order of
 25 November 2009) 7.57, 7.61
T-88/09 *Idromacchine and Others v Commission* [2011] E.C.R. II-7833 . . . . 11.38, 11.39, 11.64,
  11.66, 11.69, 11.72, 11.78, 11.80
T-95/09 R *United Phosphorus v Commission*, not reported, (order of the President of
 28 April 2009) 13.06, 13.15, 13.34, 13.36, 13.40, 13.42, 13.44
T-95/09 R II *United Phosphorus v Commission*, not reported, (order of the President of
 15 January 2010) 13.15
T-95/09 R III *United Phosphorus v Commission*, not reported, (order of the President of
 25 November 2010) 13.15
T-96/09 *UCAPT v Council* [2011] E.C.R. II-328*, Summ. pub., (order of 28 September 2011) 7.99
T-101/09 AJ *Maftah v Council and Commission*, not reported, (order of the President of
 18 August 2010) 25.101
T-106/09 *adp Gauselmann v OHIM* [2010] E.C.R. II-182*, Summ. pub. 20.15
T-108/09 *Ravensburger v OHIM* [2010] E.C.R. II-99*, Summ. pub. 25.10
T-110/09 *Bayramoglu v Council and European Parliament*, not reported, (order of
 24 September 2009) 7.208, 7.219
T-112/09 *Icebreaker v OHIM* [2010] E.C.R. II-172*, Summ. pub. 20.15
T-115/09 and T-116/09 *Electrolux and Whirlpool v Commission*, not reported,
 (judgment of 14 February 2012) 7.202, 7.203
T-119/09 *Protégé International v Commission*, not reported, (order of the President of
 12 January 2010) 25.67
T-121/09 DEP *Al Shanfari v Council and Commission*, not reported, (order of
 20 November 2012) 25.93
T-122/09 *Zhejiang Xinshiji Foods Co. and Hubei Zinshiji Foods Co. v Council* [2011]
 E.C.R. II-22*, Summ. pub. 7.82, 7.207
T-123/09 *Ryanair v Commission*, not reported, (judgment of 28 March 2012) 7.118, 7.124, 7.202

T-134/09 *Basile and I Marchi Italiani v OHIM*, not reported, (judgment of 28 June 2012) 20.15
T-135/09 *Nexans France and Nexans*, not reported, (judgment of
14 November 2012) 7.32, 25.10, 25.50
T-136/09 *Commission v Gal-Or* [2010] E.C.R. II-221*, Summ. pub. 19.10, 19.19, 25.31
T-137/09 *Nike International v OHIM* [2010] E.C.R. II-5433 . . . . 7.158, 20.14
T-140/09 *Prysmian and Prysmian Cavi e Systemi Energia v Commission*, not reported
(judgment of 14 November 2012) 7.32
T-143/09 P *Commission v Petrilli*, not yet reported, (judgment of 16 December 2010) 11.36
T-149/09 *Densmore Ronald Dover v European Parliament* [2011] E.C.R. II-69*, Summ. pub. 23.60
T-149/09 R *Dover v European Parliament* [2009] E.C.R. II-66*, Summ. pub.,
(order of the President of 8 June 2009) 13.07, 13.29, 13.35, 13.40
T-152/09 *Rintisch v OHIM* [2011] E.C.R. II-460*, Summ. pub. 25.12
T-154/09 *MRI v Commission*, not reported, (judgment of 17 May 2013) 15.07
T-157/09 P *Marcuccio v Commission*, not reported, (order of 15 September 2010) 18.18
T-159/09 R *Biofrescos v Commission* [2009] E.C.R. II-63*, (order of the President of
25 May 2009) 13.29, 13.40
T-162/09 *Würth and Fasteners (Shenyang) v Council*, not reported, (judgment of
19 April 2012) 7.131, 7.133, 7.134
T-164/09 *Kitou v ECDP*, not reported, (order of 16 December 2010) 25.84, 25.96
T-170/09 *Shanghai Biaowu High-Tensile Fasteners and Shanghai Prime Machinery v
Council*, not reported, (judgment of 10 October 2012) 7.131
T-172/09 *Gem-Year Industrial and Zhejiang v Council*, not reported, (judgment of
10 October 2012) 25.87
T-173/09 *Z v Commission* [2010] E.C.R. II-105*, Summ. pub., (order of 3 June 2010) 25.42
T-176/09 *Government of Gibraltar v Commission* [2011] E.C.R. II-150*, Summ. pub.,
(order of 24 May 2011) 7.220, 25.16, 25.17
T-177/09 *Kinský v Commission*, not reported, (order of 14 July 2009) 7.18
T-181/09 *Oprea v Commission*, not reported, (order of 6 July 2009) 7.219, 11.34
T-191/09 *Hit Trading and Berkman Forwarding v Commission* [2010] E.C.R. II-283*,
Summ. pub. 7.219
T-196/09 R *TerreStar Europe v Commission* [2009] E.C.R. II-124*, Summ. pub.,
(order of the President of 10 July 2009) 13.37, 13.40
T-198/09 *UOP v Commission*, not reported, (order of 7 March 2013) 25.18, 25.48, 25.49
T-200/09 *Abertis Infraestructuras v Commission* [2010] E.C.R. II-85*, Summ. pub.,
(order of 8 May 2010) 7.216
T-207/09 *Mustapha El Jirari Bouzekri v OHIM* [2011] E.C.R. II-324*, Summ. pub. 20.07, 25.12
T-219/09 and T-326/09 *Albertini and Others v European Parliament* [2010]
E.C.R. II-5935, (order of 15 December 2010) 7.05, 7.92, 7.93, 7.100
T-223/09 *İşçi Partisi (Turkish Labour Party) v Commission*, not reported, (order of
17 December 2009) 11.14, 11.15, 11.16
T-224/09 *CEVA v Commission* [2011] E.C.R. II-277, (order of 13 September 2011) 7.27
T-229/09 *Palladino v Italy*, not reported, (order of 7 September 2009) 7.72
T-233/09 *Access Info Europe v Council* [2011] E.C.R. II-1073 . . . . .7.138, 7.213, 7.214
T-234/09 *Hârsulescu v Romania*, not reported, (order of 22 July 2009) 2.02
T-235/09 *Commission v Edificios Inteco*, not reported, (judgment of 9 March 2011) 19.19
T-236/09 *Evropaiki Dynamiki v Commission*, not reported, (judgment of 15 March 2012) 25.12
T-237/09 *Walloon Region v Commission*, not reported, (judgment of 1 February 2012) 7.22
T-238/09 R *Sniace v Commission* [2009] E.C.R. II-125*, Summ. pub., (order of the
President of 13 July 2009) 13.29, 13.40
T-239/09 *Sniace v Commission* [2011] E.C.R. II-430*, Summ. pub. 7.170
T-246/09 R *Insula v Commission* [2009] E.C.R. II-101*, Summ. pub., (order of the
President of 2 July 2009) 13.29
T-246/09 *Insula v Commission*, not reported, (judgment of 13 June 2012) 19.12, 19.18
T-247/09 *Evropaiki Dynamiki v Commission*, not reported, (judgment of 10 October 2012) 25.96
T-249/09 *Ségaud v Commission*, not reported, (order of 29 October 2009) 7.18, 11.47
T-259/09 *Commission v Archi Nuova associazione comitato di Cagliari and Gessa* [2010]
E.C.R. II-284 . . . . 2.29, 19.13
T-261/09 P *Commission v Violetti and Others*, not reported, (judgment of 20 May 2010) 11.12, 18.06
T-262/09 *Safariland v OHIM* [2011] E.C.R. II-1629 . . . . 25.12

T-264/09 *Tecnoprocess v Commission and Delegation of the EU in Morocco* [2011]
E.C.R. II-208*, Summ. pub., (order of 30 June 2011) 8.11, 8.15, 8.18,
8.21, 11.38, 11.78, 11.83
T-273/09 *Associazione 'Giùlemanidallajuve' v Commission*, not reported, (order of
19 March 2012) 25.10
T-274/09 *Deutsche Bahn v OHIM* [2011] E.C.R. II-268*, Summ. pub. 20.06
T-276/09 *Kavaklidere-Europe v OHIM*, not reported, (judgment of 21 June 2012) 20.06
T-279/09 *Antonino Aiello v OHIM*, not reported, (judgment of 12 July 2012). 20.06
T-280/09 *Morte Navarro v Parliament*, not reported, (judgment of 30 May 2013) 7.17
T-283/09 P *Aayhan v European Parliament* (order of 12 October 2009) 9.08, 9.16
T-284/09 P *Meister v OHIM*, not reported, (order of 21 June 2010) 18.25
T-285/09 *CEVA v Commission* [2011] E.C.R. II-289*, Summ. pub. 7.15, 19.12
T-289/09 *Evropaiki Dynamiki-Proigmena Systimata Tilepikoinonion Pliroforikis kai Tilematikis
v Commission* [2011] E.C.R. II-270*, Summ. pub. 8.09
T-291/09 *Carrols v OHIM* [2012] E.C.R. II 20.15
T-292/09 *Mugraby v Council and Commission* [2011] E.C.R. II-255*, Summ. pub.,
(order of 6 September 2011) 8.06, 8.08, 8.11, 8.23, 11.13, 11.51
T-295/09 R *Hansen v Commission* [2009] E.C.R. II-216*, Summ. pub., (order of the
President of 18 November 2009) 13.26
T-295/09 *Hansen v Commission*, not reported, (order of 17 November 2009) 7.219, 8.19, 8.23
T-296/09 *EFIM v Commission* [2011] E.C.R. II-425*, Summ. pub. 7.43, 25.18
T-298/09 *Evropaïki Dynamiki v Commission* [2011] E.C.R. II-300*, Summ. pub. 11.11
T-307/09 *Earle Beauty v OHIM* [2010] E.C.R. II-266*, Summ. pub. 20.06, 20.15
T-317/09 *Concord Power Nordal v Commission* [2010] E.C.R. II-253*, Summ. pub.,
(order of 24 November 2010) 7.28
T-319/09 *Pro humanum v Commission*, not reported, (order of 5 February 2010). 7.208
T-320/09 *Planet v Commission* [2011] E.C.R. II-1673, (order of 13 April 2011) 25.10, 25.11, 25.16
T-323/09 *Commission v Irish Electricity Generating Co.* [2010] E.C.R. II-254*, Summ. pub. 19.18
T-327/09 *Connefroy and Others v Commission*, not reported, (order of 27 March 2012) 7.122
T-330/09 *Rapideye v Commission* [2011] E.C.R. II-26*, Summ. pub., (order of 7 February 2011). . . . 7.55
T-332/09 *Electrabel v Commission*, not reported, (judgment of 12 December 2012) 7.46, 7.192
T-335/09 *Groupement Adriano, Jaime Ribeiro, Conduril v Commission* [2011]
E.C.R. II-7345, (order of 21 October 2011) 25.95
T-336/09 *Häfele v OHIM* [2011] E.C.R. II-4*, Summ. pub. 23.52
T-346/09 *Winzer Pharma v OHIM*, not reported, (judgment of 12 July 2012) 20.12
T-351/09 *Acetificio Marcello de Nigris v Commission* [2011] E.C.R. II-216*, Summ. pub.,
(order of 7 July 2011) 7.05
T-352/09 R *Novacke chemicke zavody v Commission* [2009] E.C.R. II-208*, Summ. pub.,
(order of the President of 29 October 2009) 13.39, 13.40
T-354/09 *Goldman Management v Commission and Bulgaria*, not reported, (order of
16 November 2009) 8.06, 8.11, 11.47
T-358/09 *Sociedad Agricola Requingua v OHIM* [2011] E.C.R. II-105*, Summ. pub. 20.15
T-359/09 *Jurašinović v Council* [2010] E.C.R. II-114*, Summ. pub., (order of 17 June 2010) 7.142
T-366/09 *Insula v Commission*, not reported, (judgment of 13 June 2012). 19.10, 19.12, 19.18
T-367/09 *Tecnoprocess v Commission* [2011] E.C.R. II-209*, Summ. pub., (order of
30 June 2011) 8.15, 8.18, 8.21, 11.06, 11.38, 11.78, 11.83
T-368/09 P *Sevenier v Commission*, not reported, (judgment of 8 July 2010) 18.17
T-372/09 *Visti Beheer v OHIM* [2011] E.C.R. II-53*, Summ. pub. 20.06
T-377/09 *Mövenpick v OHIM* [2011] E.C.R. II-455*, Summ. pub. 7.217, 20.07
T-381/09 *RWE Transgas v Commission* [2010] E.C.R. II-256*, Summ. pub., (order of
24 November 2010) 7.27
T-385/09 *Annco v OHIM* [2011] E.C.R. II-455 . . . . 20.04, 20.06
T-389/09 *Labate v Commission*, not reported, (order of 10 January 2011) 8.21, 18.27
T-390/09 R *Noko Ngele v Commission* [2009] E.C.R. II-241*, Summ. pub.,
(order of the President of 15 December 2009) 13.26
T-390/09 *Noko Ngele v Commission*, not reported, (order of 10 December 2009). 11.34
T-392/09 R *1. garantovaná v Commission* [2011] E.C.R. II-33*, Summ. pub.,
(order of 2 March 2011) 13.18, 13.34, 13.39, 13.42, 13.44
T-396/09 R *Vereniging Milieudefensie and Stichting Stop Luchtverontreiniging Utrecht v
Commission* [2009] E.C.R. II-246*, Summ. pub., (order of the President of
17 December 2009) 13.01, 13.04, 13.07, 13.29, 13.32

T-396/09 *Vereniging Milieudefensie and Stichting Stop Luchtverontreiniging Utrecht v Commission*, not reported, (judgment of 14 June 2012).............................. 9.08

T-401/09 *Marcuccio v Court of Justice of the European Union*, not reported, (order of 6 July 2010).. 11.64, 25.91

T-407/09 *Neubrandenburger Wohnungsgesellschaft v Commission*, not reported, (order of 9 January 2012).. 7.61, 8.20

T-409/09 *Evropaïki Dynamiki v Commission*, not reported, (order of 22 June 2011)..................................... 11.86, 11.87, 11.90, 11.94

T-410/09 R *Almamet v Commission* [2010] E.C.R. II-80*, Summ. pub., (order of the President of 7 May 2010).. 13.39

T-411/09 *Terezakis v Commission* [2011] E.C.R. II-1, (order of 12 January 2011)......... 7.138, 25.84

T-416/09 *Castellano v Swiss Confederation*, France and Italy, not reported, (order of 18 November 2009).. 7.72

T-419/09 *Cybergun v OHIM* [2011] E.C.R. II-73*, Summ. pub............................ 20.12

T-434/09 *Centrotherm Systemtechnik v OHIM* [2011] E.C.R. II-6227.................... 9.01

T-435/09 R *GL2006 Europe v Commission* [2010] E.C.R. II-32*, Summ. pub., (order of the President of 15 March 2010)........................... 13.09, 13.22, 13.36

T-436/09 *Dufour v European Central Bank* [2011] E.C.R. II-7727 .... 7.67, 7.170, 7.219, 11.20, 11.35, 25.12

T-442/09 *Chacón de la Torre v Spain*, not reported, (order of 17 December 2009)............... 7.72

T-442/09 REV *Chacón de la Torre v Spain*, not reported, (order of 21 June 2010)............. 25.117

T-443/09 R *Agriconsulting Europe v Commission* [2010] E.C.R. II-5*, Summ. pub., (order of the President of 20 January 2010).. 13.38

T-446/09 R *Escola Superior Agraria de Coimbra v Commission* [2010] E.C.R. II-2*, Summ. pub., (order of the President of 8 January 2010)............................. 13.41

T-455/09 *Vicente J. Jiménez Sarmiento v OHIM* [2011] E.C.R. II-50*, Summ. pub. 20.07

T-456/09 R *Bakonyi v Hungary* [2010] E.C.R. II-20*, (order of the President of 17 February 2010).. 13.04

T-458/09 and T-171/10 *Slovak Telekom v Commission*, not reported, (judgment of 22 March 2012).. 7.31

T-459/09 *Hendel v Poland*, not reported, (order of 11 February 2010) 7.72

T-461/09 *CheapFlights International v OHIM* [2011] E.C.R. II-113*, Summ. pub. 20.04

T-464/09 *Commission v New Acoustic Music Association and Hildibrandsdottir* [2011] E.C.R. II-133*, Summ. pub.................................... 19.14, 25.105

T-481/09 *ATB Norte v OHIM* [2011] E.C.R. II-199*, Summ. pub.................. 20.03, 20.06

T-492/09 *Campailla v Commission* [2011] E.C.R. II-48*, Summ. pub., (order of 14 March 2011).. 11.94

T-496/09 *Bell v Belgium*, not reported, (order of 26 February 2010)....................... 7.72

T-504/09 *Völkl v OHIM* [2011] E.C.R. II-8179 .... 20.05

T-508/09 *Cañas v Commission*, not reported, (order of 26 March 2012) 7.43

T-508/09 *Guillermo Canas v Commission*, not reported, (order of 26 March 2012).............. 23.17

T-514/09 R *De Post v Commission* [2010] E.C.R. II-15*, Summ. pub., (order of the President of 5 February 2010)........................... 13.22, 13.38, 13.45

T-514/09 *bpost v Commission* [2011] E.C.R. II-420*, Summ. pub....................... 11.64

T-520/09 *TF1 and Others v Commission*, not reported, (judgment of 10 July 2012)............. 7.118

T-530/09 *Seacid v European Parliament and Council*, not reported, (order of 16 March 2010)...... 7.208

T-1/10 R *SNF v European Chemicals Agency* [2010] E.C.R. II-47*, Summ. pub., (order of the President of 26 March 2010)........................... 13.22, 13.24, 13.29, 13.40

T-4/10 *Al Saadi v Commission*, not reported, (order of 30 June 2011).................... 25.101

T-6/10 R *Sviluppo Globale v Commission* [2010] E.C.R. II-48*, Summ. pub., (order of the President of 26 March 2010).. 13.32

T-6/10 *Sviluppo Globale v Commission*, not reported, (judgment of 22 May 2012).............. 7.23

T-6/10 R *Alisei v Commission* [2010] E.C.R. II-48*, Summ. pub., (order of the President of 26 March 2010).. 13.04, 13.38

T-7/10 *Diagnostiko kai Therapeftiko Kentro Athinon « Ygeia » AE v OHIM* [2011] E.C.R. II-136*, Summ. pub.................................... 20.06

T-15/10 R *Noko Ngele v Commission* [2010] E.C.R. II-102*, Summ. pub., (order of the President of 26 May 2010) 13.11, 13.29

T-15/10 *Noko Ngele v Commission and Others* [2011] E.C.R. II-77*, Summ. pub., (order of 25 March 2011)........................... 11.18, 11.81, 13.04

T-15/10 RII *Noko Ngele v Commission* [2010] E.C.R. II-176*, Summ. pub., (order of
  8 September 2010)...13.07, 13.11, 13.44
T-16/10 R *Alisei v Commission* [2010] E.C.R. II-50*, Summ. pub., (order of the President of
  26 March 2010)..13.19, 13.29, 13.31, 13.36
T-17/10 *Steinberg v Commission*, not reported, (order of 27 November 2012) 7.67
T-18/10 R *Inuit Tapiriit Kanatami and Others v European Parliament and Council* [2010]
  E.C.R. II-75*, Summ. pub., (order of the President of 30 April 2010)..............13.25, 13.34,
                                                                    13.35, 13.36, 13.40
T-18/10 R II *Inuit Tapiriit Kanatami and Others v European Parliament and Council*
  [2010] E.C.R. II-235*, Summ. pub., (order of the President of
  25 October 2010)............................... 13.24, 13.36, 13.40, 13.41, 13.44
T-18/10 *Inuit and Others v European Parliament and Council* [2011] E.C.R. II-5599,
  (order of 6 September 2011)............................7.05, 7.107, 7.108, 23.60
T-25/10 DEP *BASF v Commission*, not reported, (order of 14 January 2013)................. 25.93
T-28/10 *Euro-Information v OHIM* [2011] E.C.R. II-1535 .... 20.06, 20.15
T-30/10 R *Reagens v Commission* [2010] E.C.R. II-83*, Summ. pub., (order of the
  President of 12 May 2010) 13.29, 13.39
T-36/10 *Internationer Hilfsfonds v Commission* [2011] E.C.R. II-1403, (order of
  24 March 2011)... 7.138
T-37/10 P *De Nicola v EIB*, not reported, (judgment of 27 April 2012) 18.01
T-48/10 P *Meister v OHIM*, not reported, (order of 16 December 2010) 11.76
T-53/10 *Reisenthel v OHIM* [2011] E.C.R. II-7287................................. 7.146, 20.15
T-58/10 *Phoenix-Reisen and DRV v Commission*, not reported, (order of
  11 January 2012).. 7.117, 7.118
T-61/10 R *Victoria Sánchez v European Parliament and Commission* [2010] E.C.R. II-120*,
  Summ. pub., (order of the President of 30 June 2010) 13.10, 13.29, 13.31
T-61/10 *Victoria Sánchez v European Parliament and Commission* [2010] E.C.R. II-252*,
  (order of 17 November 2010) 8.07, 8.23
T-63/10 *Jurašinović v Council*, not reported, (order of 23 September 2011)................. 23.66
T-64/10 *Dorval v Commission*, not reported, (order of 5 May 2010) 7.216
T-66/10 *Zuckerfabrik Jülich v Commission*, not reported, (order of 9 April 2013) 7.142
T-71/10 R *Xeda International v Commission* [2010] E.C.R. II-77*, Summ. pub., (order of the
  President of 30 April 2010)....................................... 13.35, 13.36
T-71/10 R II *Xeda International v Commission* [2011] E.C.R. II-82*, Summ. pub.,
  (order of 8 April 2011)... 13.44
T-71/10 *Xeda International and Pace International v Commission*, not reported,
  (judgment of 19 January 2012).. 7.137
T-77/10 and T-78/10 *Certmedica International GmbH and Lehning enterprise v OHIM*,
  not reported, (judgment of 29 February 2012)............................. 20.07, 25.12
T-79/10 R *COLT Télécommunications France v Commission* [2010] E.C.R. II-107*, Summ. pub.,
  (order of the President of 9 June 2010) 13.32, 13.36
T-84/10 *Regione Puglia v Commission* [2011] E.C.R. II-282*, Summ. pub., (order of
  14 September 2011).. 7.96
T-86/10 *British Sugar v Commission*, not reported, (order of 8 April 2013) 7.142
T-93/10 *Bilbaína de Alquitranes and Others v ECHA*, not reported, (judgment of
  7 March 2013).. 7.28, 7.108
T-94/10 *Rütgers Germany and Others v ECHA*, not reported, (judgment of
  7 March 2013)..................................... 7.27, 7.28, 7.85, 7.108, 7.109
T-102/10 *Südzucker AG Mannheim v Commission*, not reported, (judgment of 9 April 2013) 7.141
T-103/10 P(R)-R *European Parliament v U*, not yet reported, (order of the President of
  28 April 2010).. 13.26
T-110/10 *Insula v Commission*, not reported, (judgment of 13 June 2012)................. 19.18
T-115/10 *United Kingdom v Commission* [2011] E.C.R. II-153*, Summ. pub.,
  (order of 24 May 2011) 7.23
T-120/10 *ClientEarth and Others v Commission*, not reported, (order of
  9 November 2011).......................................7.14, 7.138, 7.219
T-136/10 *M v EMA*, not reported, (order of 20 January 2011)...................... 2.54, 11.05
T-137/10 *CBI v Commission*, not reported, (judgment of 7 November 2012) 7.118, 7.202
T-139/10, T-280/10 to T-285/10, and T-349/10 to T-352/10 *Milux Holding v
  OHIM* [2011] II-55*, Summ. pub., (order of 11 March 2011) 23.17

T-153/10 *Schneider España de Informatica v Commission*, not reported, (order of
  28 February 2012) 7.142
T-154/10 *France v Commission*, not reported, (judgment of 20 September 2012) 7.76, 7.138, 25.13
T-160/10 *J v European Parliament*, not reported, (judgment of 27 September 2012) 7.20
T-165/10 *Grupo Osborne v OHIM*, not reported, (order of 14 July 2010) 25.101
T-166/10 *Samskip Multimodal Container Logistics v Commission*, not reported 25.84
T-170/10 *Computer Task Group Luxembourg PSF v Court of Justice of the
  EU* [2011] E.C.R. II-384*, Summ. pub. 7.69, 11.11
T-172/10 *Colas v OHIM*, not reported, (judgment of 15 March 2012) 20.12, 20.15
T-175/10 *Milux Holding v OHIM* [2011] E.C.R. II-57*, Summ. pub., (order of
  21 March 2011) 23.17
T-177/10 R *Alcoa Transformazioni v Commission* [2010] E.C.R. II-149*, Summ. pub.,
  (order of the President of 9 July 2010) 13.40
T-182/10 *Aiscat v Commission*, not reported, (judgment of 15 January 2013) 7.118
T-185/10 *Stelzer v Commission*, not reported, (order of 24 August 2010) 7.18
T-186/10 *Perret v Commission*, not reported, (order of 20 July 2010) 7.18
T-187/10 *Emram v OHIM* [2011] E.C.R. II-128*, Summ. pub. 7.170
T-190/10 *Egan and Hackett v Parliament*, not reported, (judgment of 28 March 2012) 7.67, 25.59
T-195/10 *Snemo Mars-Momchil Dobrev and Others v Commission and Bulgaria*, not reported,
  (order of 30 September 2010) 8.06, 11.47
T-201/10 *IVBN v Commission*, not reported, (order of 13 July 2012) 7.126
T-203/10 *Stichting Woonpunt and Others v Commission* [2011] E.C.R. II-462*, Summ. pub.,
  (order of 16 December 2011) 7.139
T-211/10 *Strålfors v OHIM* [2010] E.C.R. II-143*, Summ. pub., (order of 8 July 2010) 25.12
T-220/10 *Commission v EU Research Projects*, not reported, (judgment of 17 October 2012) 25.31
T-221/10 *Iberdrola v Commission*, not reported, (judgment of 8 March 2012) 7.120, 7.121, 7.122
T-224/10 *Association belge des consommateurs test-achats v Commission* [2011]
  E.C.R. II-7177 . . . . .7.50, 7.115, 7.116, 25.12
T-228/10 *Telefónica v Commission*, not reported, (order of 21 March 2012) 7.120, 7.122
T-245/10 *Verein Deutsche Sprache v Council*, not reported, (order of 17 December 2010) 8.04, 8.19
T-247/10 *medi v OHIM*, not reported, (judgment of 6 October 2011) 20.06
T-252/10 R *Cross Czech v Commission* [2010] E.C.R. II-157*, Summ. pub., (order of the
  President of 29 July 2010) 13.29
T-252/10 *Cross Czech v Commission* [2011] E.C.R. II-211*, Summ. pub., (order of
  30 June 2011) 7.15, 19.12
T-258/10 *France Télécom v Commission*, not reported, (order of the President of
  5 October 2012) 25.76
T-262/10 *Microban International and Microban (Europe) v Commission* [2011]
  E.C.R. II-7697 . . . . .7.82, 7.107, 7.108
T-264/10 and T-266/10 *Spain v Commission*, not reported, (judgment of 21 June 2012) 7.20
T-267/10 *Land Wien v Commission* [2011] E.C.R. II-303*, Summ. pub., (order of
  20 September 2011) 25.12
T-271/10 R *H v Council and Commission* [2010] E.C.R. II-154*, Summ. pub.,
  (order of the President of 22 July 2010) 13.22, 13.31
T-273/10 *Olive Line International v OHIM*, not reported, (judgment of 22 May 2012) 20.07
T-286/10 R *IDIAP v Commission* [2010] E.C.R. II-155*, Summ. pub., (order of 22 July 2010) 13.40
T-291/10 *Martin v Commission*, not reported, (order of 8 April 2011) 25.84
T-296/10 *Varga and Haliu v Council*, not reported, (order of 14 October 2010) 25.20
T-297/10 *DBV v Commission* [2011] E.C.R. II-356*, Summ. pub., (order of 11 October 2011) 7.66
T-298/10 *Gross v OHIM*, not reported, (judgment of 8 March 2012) 20.11
T-298/10 DEP *Gross v OHIM*, not reported, (order of 14 May 2013) 25.92, 25.93
T-299/10 R *Babcock Noell v The European joint undertaking for ITER and the Development of
  Fusion Energy* [2010] E.C.R. II-161*, Summ. pub., (order of the President of
  31 August 2010) 13.01, 13.29, 13.31, 13.32, 13.34, 13.38, 13.40, 13.42
T-300/10 *Internationaler Hilsfonds v Commission*, not reported, (judgment of
  22 May 2012) 7.67, 7.223
T-301/10 *Sophie in 't Veld v Commission*, not reported, (judgment of 19 March 2013) 23.61, 23.66
T-303/10 *Wam Industriale v Commission*, not reported, (judgment of 27 September 2012) . . . 25.18, 25.48
T-306/10 AJ *Yusef v Commission*, not reported, (order of the President of 22 October 2010) 25.93
T-308/10 P *Commission v Nanopoulos*, not reported, (judgment of 12 July 2012) 18.14, 18.18, 20.12
T-311/10 *Platis v Council and Greece*, not reported, (order of 30 September 2010) 7.219

T-315/10 *Groupe Partouche v Commission*, not reported, (order of 20 January 2012) 25.10
T-323/10 *Chabou v OHIM* [2011] E.C.R. II-410*, Summ. pub. 20.19
T-330/10 *M v Commission*, not reported, (order of 20 September 2011) 11.34, 25.10
T-332/10 *Viaguara v OHIM*, not reported, (judgment of 15 January 2012). 20.15
T-339/10 and T-532/10 *Cosepuri v EFSA*, not reported, (judgment of 29 January 2013) 25.10
T-341/10 *F91 Diddeléng and Others v Commission*, not reported, (order of 16 April 2012) 7.43
T-346/10 *Borax Europe v ECHA* [2011] E.C.R. II-6629, (order of 21 September 2011). 7.92
T-348/10 *Panzeri v OHIM*, not reported. 20.05, 25.86
T-353/10 R *Lito Maieftiko v Commission* [2010] E.C.R. II-238*, Summ. pub.,
    (order of the President of 25 October 2010). 13.29
T-353/10 *Lito Maieftiko Gynaikologiko kai Cheirourgiko Kentro v Commission* [2011]
    E.C.R. II-7213. . . . . 7.15, 19.12
T-357/10 *Kraft Foods Schweiz Holding GmbH v OHIM*, not reported, (judgment of
    20 June 2012) 20.15
T-363/10 *Abbott Laboratories v OHIM* [2011] E.C.R. II-387*, Summ. pub. 20.12
T-367/10 *Bloufin Touna Ellas Naftiki Etaireia and Others v Commission*, not reported,
    (judgment of 27 February 2013) 7.85, 7.108, 7.109
T-369/10 *You-Q BV v OHIM*, not reported, (order of 10 October 2011) 20.11
T-370/10 R *Rubinetterie Teorema v Commission* [2011] E.C.R. II-9*, Summ. pub.,
    (order of the President of 24 January 2011) 13.39
T-385/10 R *ArcelorMittal Wire France and Others v Commission* [2010] E.C.R. II-262*,
    Summ. pub., (order of the President of 7 December 2010) 13.39
T-393/10 R *Westfälische Drahtindustrie and Others v Commission* [2011] E.C.R. II-1697,
    (order of the President of 13 April 2011) 13.32, 13.34, 13.39, 13.44
T-395/10 R *Stichting Corporate Europe Observatory v Commission*, not reported, (order of
    12 April 2011). 7.138
T-398/10 R *Fapricela v Commission* [2011] E.C.R. II-239*, Summ. pub., (order of the
    President of 15 July 2011) 13.39
T-413/10 R *Socitrel v Commission* [2011] E.C.R. II-112*, Summ. pub., (order of the
    President of 13 April 2011). 13.39
T-414/10 R *Companhia Previdente v Commission* [2011] E.C.R. II-173*, Summ. pub.,
    (order of the President of 10 June 2011) 13.39
T-415/10 R *Nexans France v The European joint undertaking for ITER and the Development
    of fusion energy*, not reported, (order of the President of 15 October 2010) 13.19, 13.22,
                                                                                                        13.38, 13.40
T-416/10 *Yoshida Metal Industry Co. Ltd v OHIM*, not reported, (judgment of 8 May 2012) 20.07
T-421/10 *Cooperativa Vitivinícola Arousana v OHIM* [2011] E.C.R. II-347*, Summ. pub. 20.06
T-422/10 R *Emme Holding v Commission* [2011] E.C.R. II-222*, Summ. pub.,
    (order of the President of 12 July 2011). 13.39
T-433/10 P *Allen and Others v Commission*, not yet reported, (judgment of 14 December 2011). . . . 18.18
T-434/10 *Václav Hrbek v OHIM* [2011] E.C.R. II-388*, Summ. pub. 20.06, 20.08
T-437/10 *Gap granen & producten v Commission*, not reported,
    (judgment of 16 May 2013) 11.45, 11.56
T-439/10 R *Fulmen v Council* [2011] E.C.R. II-260*, Summ. pub.,
    (order of 8 September 2011) 13.32, 13.36, 13.40
T-439/10 and T-440/10 *Fulmen and Others v Council*, not reported,
    (judgment of 21 March 2012). 13.36, 25.17
T-447/10 *Evropaïki Dynamiki v Court of Justice of the European Union*, not reported,
    (judgment of 17 October 2012) 25.10
T-450/10 P *Marcuccio v Commission*, not yet reported, (order of 18 July 2011) 11.86
T-454/10 and T-482/11 *Anicav and Others v Commission*, not reported,
    (judgment of 30 May 2013) 7.93, 7.120
T-468/10 *Doherty v Commission* [2011] E.C.R. II-1497, (order of 1 April 2011) 7.208, 23.37, 23.38
T-469/10 *Padraigh Conneely v Commission*, not reported, (order of 1 April 2011). 23.37, 23.38
T-470/10 *Eileen Oglesby v Commission*, not reported, (order of 1 April 2011). 23.37, 23.38
T-478/10 *Department du Gers v Commission* [2011] E.C.R. II-83*, Summ. pub.,
    (order of 11 April 2011) 7.103
T-479/10 *Department du Gers v Commission* [2011] E.C.R. II-84*, Summ. pub.,
    (order of 11 April 2011) 7.103
T-480/10 *Department du Gers v Commission* [2011] E.C.R. II-86*, Summ. pub.,
    (order of 11 April 2011) 7.103

T-481/10 *Department du Gers v Commission* [2011] E.C.R. II-87*, Summ. pub.,
  (order of 11 April 2011) 7.103
T-482/10 *Department du Gers v Commission* [2011] E.C.R. II-89*, Summ. pub.,
  (order of 11 April 2011) 7.103
T-484/10 R *Gas Natural Fenosa SDG v Commission*, not reported, (order of
  17 February 2011) 13.18, 13.32, 13.34, 13.36, 13.42
T-486/10 R *Iberdrola v Commission*, not reported, (order of the President of
  17 February 2011) 13.04, 13.18, 13.24, 13.31, 13.32, 13.34, 13.36, 13.42
T-490/10 R *Endesa and Endesa Generacion v Commission*, not reported, (order of the
  President of 17 February 2011) 13.04, 13.18, 13.24, 13.31, 13.32, 13.34, 13.36, 13.42
T-500/10 *Dorma v OHIM* [2011] E.C.R. II-411*, Summ. pub. 20.07
T-501/10 *Ti Media Broadcasting and Ti Media v Commission*, not reported,
  (order of 21 September 2012) 7.49
T-502/10 *Department du Gers v Commission* [2011] E.C.R. II-90*, Summ. pub.,
  (order of 11 April 2011) 7.103
T-509/10 *Manufacturing Support & Procurement Kala Naft v Council*, not reported,
  (judgment of 25 April 2012) 7.173, 25.17
T-514/10 *Fruit of the Loom v OHIM*, not reported, (judgment of 21 June 2012) 20.07
T-520/10 R *Comunidad Autónoma de Galicia v Commission* [2011] E.C.R. II-27*,
  Summ. pub., (order of the President of 11 February 2011) 13.18, 13.32, 13.34,
                                                                              13.41, 13.42, 25.68
T-520/10 *Comunidad Autónoma de Galicia v Commission*, not reported, (order of the
  President of 25 October 2011) 13.18
T-526/10 *Inuit Tapiriit Kanatami and Others v Commission*, not reported, (judgment of
  25 April 2013) 7.108
T-533/10 R *DTS Distribuidora de Televisión Digital v Commission*, not reported, (order of the
  President of 24 January 2011) 25.68
T-533/10 R *DTS Distribuidora de Television Digital v Commission* [2011] E.C.R. II-168*,
  Summ. pub., (order of the President of 9 June 2011) 13.40
T-539/10 *Acino v Commission*, not reported, (judgment of 7 March 2013) 7.141
T-541/10 *Adedy and Others v Council*, not reported, (order of 27 November 2012) 7.91
T-542/10 *XXXLutz Marken v OHIM*, not reported, (judgment of 13 June 2012) 25.12
T-550/10 *FIBE v European Parliament*, not reported, (order of 26 January 2011) 7.17
T-555/10 *JBF RAK v Council*, not reported, (judgment of 24 May 2012) 7.131
T-560/10 R *Nencini v European Parliament* [2011] E.C.R. II-21*, Summ. pub., (order of the
  President of 16 February 2011) 13.32
T-562/10 *HTTS Hanseatic Trade Trust & Shipping v Council* [2011] E.C.R. II-8087 . . . . 7.221, 25.31
T-573/10 *Octapharma Pharmazeutika v EMA*, not reported, (order of 8 March 2012) 7.20, 7.23
T-587/10 *Holding kompanija Interspeed v Commission*, not reported, (judgment of 10 July 2012) . . . 23.72
T-590/10 *Thesing and Bloomberg Finance v ECB*, not reported 23.51
T-594/10 P *Marcuccio v Commission*, not reported, (judgment of 3 July 2012) 18.04

T-32/11 *Verenigde Douaneagenten v Commission*, not reported, (judgment of 10 February 2012) 7.220
T-37/11 *Hungary v Commission*, not reported, (order of 19 June 2012) 7.23
T-49/11 *NagyatádMed Egészségügyi Szolgáltató Nonprofit v Hungary*, not reported,
  (order of 4 April 2011) 7.72
T-61/11 R *Dansk Automat Brancheforening v Commission*, not reported, (order of the
  President of 13 February 2012) 13.01
T-72/11 *Sogepi Consulting y Publicidad v OHIM*, not reported, (judgment of
  13 September 2012) 20.19
T-74/11 *Omnis Group v Commission* [2010] E.C.R. II-5865 . . . . 7.192
T-79/11 *Ing. Nando Groppo and Others v European Parliament and Council*, not reported,
  (order of 3 March 2011) 7.207, 7.208
T-85/11 P *Marcuccio v Commission*, not reported, (order of 21 February 2013) 18.06
T-87/11 R *GRP Security v Court of Auditors* [2011] E.C.R. II-170*, Summ. pub.,
  (order of the President of 9 June 2011) 13.32, 13.40
T-92/11 *Andersen v Commission*, not reported, (judgment of 20 March 2013) 7.202
T-105/11 *Noko Ngele v Commission*, not reported, (order of 6 July 2011) 7.20, 11.34
T-116/11 R *EMA v Commission* [2011] E.C.R. II-412*, Summ. pub., (order of the
  President of 18 November 2011) 13.32, 13.36

T-133/11 *Fundația Pro Fondbis—1946 Semper v European Court of Human Rights*,
not reported, (order of 4 April 2011) 8.11, 11.18
T-142/11 *SIR v Council*, not reported, (order of 6 July 2011) 11.09, 13.26
T-149/11 *GS v Parliament and Council* [2011] E.C.R. II-359*, Summ. pub.,
(order of 12 October 2011) 7.92, 7.93
T-151/11 *Telefónica Móviles España v Commission*, not reported, (order of the President of
7 December 2011) 25.76
T-157/11 *Adămuț and Others v Romania*, not reported, (order of 5 May 2011) 23.51
T-160/11 R *Petroci Holding v Council*, not reported, (order of the President of 13 July 2011) 13.26
T-160/11 *Petroci Holding v Council*, not reported, (order of 6 July 2011) 11.09
T-172/11 *Polak v Austria and Austrian Constitutional Court*, not reported,
(order of 12 July 2011) 11.18
T-176/11 R *Carbunion v Commission* [2011] E.C.R. II-434*, Summ. pub.,
(order of the President of 2 December 2011) 13.07, 13.19, 13.42
T-185/11 *Smanor v Commission and European Ombudsman*, not reported,
(order of 15 July 2011) 8.06, 11.27, 11.47, 11.81
T-187/11 R *Trabelsi and Others v Council* [2011] E.C.R. II-235*, Summ. pub.,
(order of the President of 14 July 2011) 13.07, 13.11, 13.40
T-190/11 *Altner v Commission*, not reported, (order of 6 July 2011) 7.18, 8.06
T-195/11 R *Cahier v Council and Commission* [2011] E.C.R. II-132*, Summ. pub.,
(order of the President of 11 May 2011) 13.07, 13.11, 13.40
T-197/11 and T-198/11 *Commission v Strack*, not reported, (judgment of 13 December 2012) 18.27
T-203/11 *Transports Schiocchet—Excursions v Council and Commission*, not reported,
(order of 18 June 2012) 11.46
T-209/11 *MB System v Commission*, not reported, (judgment of 3 July 2013) 7.201
T-213/11 P (I) *Collège des représentants du personnel de la BEI and Others v Bömcke*, not reported,
(order of 15 July 2011) 23.32
T-215/11 *Adedy and Others v Council*, not reported, (order of 27 November 2012) 7.93
T-218/11 R *Dagher v Council and Italy* [2011] E.C.R. II-146*, Summ. pub., (order of the
President of 19 May 2011) 13.21, 13.45
T-218/11 *Dagher v Council*, not reported, (order of 17 February 2012) 7.142
T-218/11 R *Dagher v Council*, not reported, (order of the President of 27 February 2012) 13.45
T-222/11 *West Indies Pack v France*, not reported, (order of 30 June 2011) 11.18
T-228/11 *Barbin v Parliament*, not reported, (order of 17 December 2012) 25.04
T-240/11 *L'Oréal v OHIM*, not reported, (judgment of 17 July 2012) 25.91
T-243/11 *Glaxo Group v OHIM* [2011] E.C.R. II-379*, Summ. pub.,
(order of 9 November 2011) 23.17
T-245/11 *ClientEarth v ECHA*, not reported, (order of the President of 18 October 2012) 25.69
T-246/11 *Krefft v Commission*, not reported, (order of 15 July 2011) 8.06
T-264/11 P *De Nicola v EIB* 18.18
T-269/11 R *Xeda International v Commission* [2011] E.C.R. II-389*, Summ. pub.,
(order of the President of 15 November 2011) 13.35, 13.36
T-278/11 *ClientEarth and Others v Commission*, not reported, (order of 13 November 2012) 7.67
T-279/11 *T&L Sugars and Sidul Açúcares v Commission*, not reported,
(judgment of 6 June 2013) 25.88
T-285/11 *Gooré v Council*, not reported, (order of 15 December 2011) 11.40
T-289/11, T-290/11 and T-521/11 *Deutsche Bahn and Others v Commission*,
not reported, (judgment of 6 September 2013) 7.32, 25.63, 25.73
T-292/11 R *Cemex and Others v Commission* [2011] E.C.R. II-243*, Summ. pub.,
(order of the President of 29 July 2011) 13.24, 13.31, 13.32
T-296/11 R *Cementos Portland Valderrivas v Commission* [2011] E.C.R. II-246*,
Summ. pub., (order of the President of 29 July 2011) 13.40
T-301/11 *Ben Ali v Council*, not reported, (order of 11 January 2012) 7.208, 7.211,
7.223, 11.34, 15.01, 23.30, 23.38
T-316/11 *Kadio Morokro v Council* [2011] E.C.R. II-293*, Summ. pub. 7.170
T-331/11 *Besselink v Commission*, not reported, (order of 19 March 2013) 23.60, 25.86
T-333/11 *Nicolas Wessang v OHIM*, not reported, (judgment of 10 October 2012) 20.06
T-334/11 *Kauk v Germany*, not reported, (order of 8 August 2011) 7.72
T-340/11 *Régie Networks and NRJ Global v Commission*, not reported,
(order of 17 October 2012) 11.87
T-345/11 *ENISA v CEPD*, not reported, (order of 29 November 2011) 7.78, 7.208, 23.54

T-347/11 R *Gollnisch v European Parliament* [2011] E.C.R. II-341*, Summ. pub.,
(order of the President of 30 September 2011) 13.04, 13.05
T-352/11 *N'Guessan v Council* [2011] E.C.R. II-232*, Summ. pub.,
(order of 13 July 2011) 7.207, 7.208, 7.211, 7.216
T-361/11 *Hand Held Products v OHIM*, not reported, (judgment of 12 July 2012) 20.15
T-366/11 *BIAL-Portela & Cᵃ v OHIM*, not reported, (judgment of 9 October 2012) 20.06
T-369/11 *Diadikasia Symbouloi Epicheiriseon v Commission and Others*, not reported,
(judgment of 13 September 2012) 25.12
T-370/11 *Poland v Commission*, not reported, (judgment of 7 March 2013) 25.12
T-374/11 *Libyan Investment Authority and Others v Council*, not reported,
(order of 22 September 2011) 7.207, 23.34
T-375/11 *Houej v Council*, not reported, (order of 22 September 2011) 7.207
T-376/11 *CBL v Council*, not reported, (order of 22 September 2011) 7.207
T-377/11 *FDES v Council*, not reported, (order of 22 September 2011) 7.207
T-379/11 *Hüttenwerke Krupp Mannesmann and Others v Commission*, not reported,
(order of 4 June 2012) 7.108, 7.109, 7.120
T-381/11 *Eurofer v Commission*, not reported, (order of 4 June 2012) 7.108, 7.109, 7.120
T-384/11 R *Safa Nicu Sepahan Co. v Council* [2011] E.C.R. II-330*, Summ. pub.,
(order of the President of 28 September 2011) 13.36, 13.40
T-387/11 *Nitrogénmüvek Vegyipari v Commission*, not reported, (judgment of
27 February 2013) 7.201, 25.10
T-389/11 *Guccio Gucci SpA v OHIM*, not reported, (judgment of 12 July 2012) 20.12
T-395/11 R *Elti v Delegation of the European Union to Montenegro* [2011]
E.C.R. II-342*, Summ. pub., (order of the President of 30 September 2011) 13.22, 13.38, 13.40
T-395/11 *Elti v Delegation of the European Union to Montenegro*, not reported,
(order of 4 June 2012) 7.72, 13.22
T-402/11 R *Preparados Alimenticios del Sur v Commission* [2011] E.C.R. II-439*,
Summ. pub., (order of the President of 12 December 2011) 13.21, 13.40
T-415/11 *Hartman v OHIM*, not reported, (judgment of 8 November 2012) 25.12
T-418/11 P *De Nicola v EIB*, not reported, (judgment of 16 September 2013) 18.01
T-421/11 R *Qualitest v Council* [2011] E.C.R. II-344*, Summ. pub., (order of the
President of 3 October 2011) 13.41
T-421/11 *Qualitest v Council*, not reported, (judgment of 5 December 2012) 25.17
T-422/11 R *Computer Resources International (Luxembourg) v Commission* [2011]
E.C.R. II-348*, Summ. pub., (order of the President of 5 October 2011) 13.22, 13.31,
13.32, 13.35, 13.36, 13.38, 13.40
T-442/11 *Evropaïki Dynamiki v Commission*, not reported, (order of
24 October 2012) 7.23, 23.40, 25.45
T-445/11 and T-88/12 *Charron Inox and Almet v Commission and Council*, not reported,
(order of 11 January 2013) 7.66
T-460/11 *Scandic Distilleries SA v OHIM*, not reported, (judgment of 18 September 2012) 20.06
T-469/11 *Al Qadhafi v France*, not reported, (order of 11 November 2011) 7.72
T-471/11 R *Editions Odile Jacob v Commission* [2011] E.C.R. II-428*, Summ. pub.,
(order of the President of 24 November 2011) 13.31, 13.35, 13.42
T-472/11 *DMA Die Marketing Agentur and Hoffmann v Austria*, not reported,
(order of 25 October 2011) 2.02, 11.18, 13.04
T-489/11 R *Rousse Industry v Commission* [2011] E.C.R. II-362*, Summ. pub.,
(order of the President of 14 October 2011) 13.29
T-489/11 *Rousse Industry v Commission*, not reported, (judgment of 20 March 2013) 7.187
T-497/11 *Euro-Information—Européenne de traitement de l'information v OHIM*, not reported,
(judgment of 5 September 2012) 20.06
T-513/11 R *Consortium v Commission* [2011] E.C.R. II-456*, Summ. pub., (order of the
President of 15 December 2011) 13.26
T-521/11 *Deutsche Bahn and Others v Commission*, not reported, (order of 12 March 2012) 23.03
T-531/11 *Hamas v Council*, not reported, (order of 21 June 2012) 25.44
T-532/11 *Städter v European Central Bank*, not reported, (order of 16 December 2011) 7.211
T-534/11 *Schenker v Commission*, not reported, (order of 25 July 2012) 23.05
T-546/11 *Technion and Technion Research & Development Foundation v Commission*, not
reported, (order of 14 June 2012) 19.12
T-547/11 *FS Schmidt Vermögensverwaltung und Verlag v The Netherlands*, not reported,
(order of 31 January 2012) 11.18

T-551/11 *Brugola Service International v Council*, not reported,
(order of 5 February 2013) 7.109, 7.130
T-552/11 R *Lito Maieftiko Gynaikologiko kai Cheirourgiki Kentro v Commission*
[2011] E.C.R. II-453*, Summ. pub., (order of the President of 14 December 2011) 13.29
T-552/11 *Lito Maieftiko Gynaikologiko kai Cheirourgiko Kentro v Commission*, not reported,
(judgment of 9 July 2013). 19.10
T-559/11 *Bytyokd v Commission*, not reported (order of 16 May 2013) 7.104
T-572/11 R II *Hassan v Council*, not reported, (order of the President of 23 April 2012) 13.44
T-579/11 R *Akhras v Council* [2011] E.C.R. II-441*, Summ. pub., (order of the President of
12 December 2011) 13.31, 13.32, 13.40
T-589/11 DEP *Phonebook of the World v OHIM*, not reported, (order of 23 October 2013). 20.08
T-593/11 R *Al-Chihabi v Council* [2011] E.C.R. II-465*, Summ. pub.,
(order of the President of 22 December 2011) 13.31, 13.32, 13.35, 13.36, 13.40
T-601/11 R *Dansk Automat Brancheforening v Commission*, not reported,
(order of the President of 13 February 2012) 13.31, 13.32, 13.41, 13.42
T-607/11 R *Henkel and Henkel France v Commission*, not reported, (order of the
President of 23 January 2012). 13.04, 13.15, 13.16, 13.19, 13.29, 13.31, 13.32
T-609/11 *Pérez Ortega v Spain*, not reported, (order of 18 January 2012) 11.18
T-637/11 R *Euris Consult Ltd v European Parliament*, not reported, (order of the
President of 25 January 2012). 13.01, 13.31, 13.32, 13.35, 13.36, 13.38, 13.40, 13.41
T-656/11 R *MorisonMenon Chartered Accountants and Others v Council*, not reported,
(order of the President of 16 February 2012) 13.31, 13.32, 13.36, 13.40
T-656/11 RII *Morison Menon Chartered Accountants and Others v Council*, not reported,
(order of the President of 13 June 2012) 13.26
T-665/11 *Kadek v National Polish Agency for the Restructuring and Modernisation of Agriculture*,
not reported, (order of 7 February 2012) 7.72
T-671/11 *IPK International v Commission*, not reported, (judgment of 10 April 2013) 25.46
T-675/11 *Maxcom v OHIM*, not reported, (order of 8 May 2012) 23.38

T-12/12 *Laboratoires CTRS v Commission*, not reported, (judgment of 4 July 2012). 8.18, 23.83
T-15/12 *Provincie Groningen and Others v Commission*, not reported,
(order of 19 February 2013) 7.118
T-31/12 *Région Poitou-Charentes v Commission*, not reported, (order of 9 October 2012) 7.27
T-50/12 *AMC-Representações Têxteis v OHIM*, not reported, (judgment of February 7, 2013). 20.08
T-53/12 *CF Sharp Shipping Agencies v Council*, not reported, (judgment of
26 October 2012). 7.11, 7.209, 25.81
T-62/12 *ClientEarth v Council*, not reported, (order of 8 October 2012) 25.45
T-63/12 *Oil Turbo Compressor v Council*, not reported, (judgment of 26 October 2012). 25.81
T-107/12 *LTTE v Council*, not reported, (order of 15 October 2012). 25.20
T-116/12 *Tioxide Europe and Others v Council*, not reported, (order of the President of
20 September 2012). 25.99
T-134/12 R *Investigacion y Desarollo en Soluciones y Servicios IT v Commission*, not reported,
(order of the President of 8 May 2012) 13.29, 13.31, 13.32
T-163/12 R *Ternvsky v Council*, not reported, (order of the President of
23 April 2012). 13.29, 13.31, 13.32
T-213/12 R *Elitaliana v Eulex Kosovo*, not reported, (order of the President of
4 September 2012). 13.29, 13.38, 13.40
T-213/12 *Elitaliana v Eulex Kosovo*, not reported, (order of 4 June 2013) 25.07
T-227/12 *Saobraćajni institute CIP v Commission*, not reported, (order of 24 October 2012). 25.92
T-294/12 *Faet Oltra v European Ombudsman*, not reported, (order of 20 September 2012). 23.17
T-318/12 *Communicaid Group v Commission*, not reported, (order of 27 September 2012). 25.42
T-367/12 *MOL v OHIM*, not reported, (judgment of 27 June 2013) 20.15
T-400/12 *Hârsulescu v Romania*, not reported, (order of 13 November 2012) 25.20
T-418/12 *Beninca v Commission*, not reported, (order of 19 February 2013) 25.101
T-462/12 R *Pilkington Group v Commission*, not reported, (order of the President of
11 March 2013). 13.36, 25.68
T-532/12 *Morea v Commission*, not reported, (order of 17 December 2012) 25.42

T-13/13 *MasterCard International v OHIM*, not reported, (order of the President of
14 June 2013) 25.99
T-44/13 R *AbbVie v EMA*, not reported, (order of the President of 25 April 2013) 13.16, 13.36

T-120/13 *Codacons v Commission*, not reported, (order of 31 May 2013)..................... 23.17
T-213/13 *Elitaliana v Eulex Kosovo*, not reported, (order of 4 June 2013) 7.72
T-313/13 R *Codacons v Commission*, not reported, (order of the President of 3 July 2013) 13.25

CIVIL SERVICE TRIBUNAL

F-5/05 and F-7/05 *Violetti and Others and Schmit v Commission* [2009] E.C.R.-SC I-A-1-83 ...... 18.06
F-13/05 *Corvoisier and Others v ECB* [2006] E.C.R.-SC I-A-1-19........................... 18.01
F-34/05 *Lebedef and Others v Commission* [2006] E.C.R.-SC I-A-1-33, (order of 14 June 2006) 18.07
F-70/05 *Mische v Commission*, not yet reported, (judgment of 29 September 2011) 9.16
F-71/05 *Milella and Campanella v Commission* [2007] E.C.R.-SC I-A-1-321 .... 18.07
F-82/05 *Thierry v Commission* [2007] E.C.R.-SC I-A-1-93............................... 18.05
F-105/05 *Wils v European Parliament*, not reported, (judgment of 11 July 2007)............9.08, 9.16
F-114/05 *Combescot v Commission* [2006] E.C.R.-SC I-A-115 .... 18.25
F-116/05 *Cerafogli and Poloni v ECB* [2008] E.C.R.-SC I-A-1-199....................... 18.01
F-124/05 et F-96/06 *A and G v Commission*, not reported, (judgment of 13 January 2010) 23.45

F-38/06 R *Bianchi v European Training Foundation* [2006] E.C.R.-SC I-A-1-27,
   (order of the President of 31 May 2006) 13.22
F-51/06 *Tesoka v FEACVT* [2007] E.C.R.-SC I-A-1-173, (order of 20 June 2007) 18.07
F-53/06 *Gualtieri v Commission* [2006] E.C.R.-SC I-A-1-107, (order of 9 October 2006) 2.54, 7.01
F-101/06 *AJ Atanasov v Commission*, not reported, (order of the President of
   1 December 2006) 25.101
F-104/06 *Arpaillange and others v Commission* [2009] E.C.R.-SC I-A-1-57.................. 18.01
F-110/06 *Carpi Badía v Commission*, not reported, (judgment of 22 November 2007) 18.04
F-113/06 *Bouis and Others v Commission* [2008] E.C.R.-SC I-A-1-437 .... 18.06
F-120/06 R *Dálnoky v Commission* [2006] E.C.R.-SC I-A-1-187, (order of the President of
   14 December 2006) 13.28, 13.41
F-129/06 *Salvador Roldán*, not reported, (order of 26 September 2007)..................... 9.16
F-138/06 and F-37/08 *Meister v OHIM* [2009] E.C.R.-SC I-A-1-131.................. 18.15, 18.21
F-141/06 *Hartwig v Commission*, not reported, (order of 17 July 2007)................. 18.21, 18.22
F-146/06 *Speiser v European Parliament* [2007] E.C.R.-SC I-A-1-231,
   (order of 10 September 2007) 18.02

F-7/07 *Angioi v Commission*, not yet reported, (judgment of 29 June 2011)................... 9.16
F-21/07 *Marcuccio v Commission* [2007] E.C.R.-SC I-A-1-463, (order of 14 December 2007) 18.18
F-23/07 RENV-RX *M v EMEA*, not reported, (order of 31 March 2011) 17.09
F-23/07 *M v EMEA* [2007] E.C.R.-SC I-A-1-311, (order of 19 October 2007)................ 18.04
F-45/07 *Mandt v European Parliament*, not yet reported, (judgment of 1 July 2010) 18.26
F-57/06 *Hinderyckx v Council* [2007] E.C.R.-SC I-A-1-329 .... 18.28
F-60/07 *Martin Bermejo v Commission* [2007] E.C.R.-SC II-A-1-2259,
   (order of 11 December 2007) 18.26
F-64/07 R *S v European Parliament* [2008] E.C.R.-SC I-A-1-11, (order of the President of
   30 January 2008) 13.29
F-65/07 *Aayhan v European Parliament*, not reported, (judgment of 30 April 2009).......... 9.08, 9.16
F-69/07 and F-60/08 *O v Commission*, not reported, (judgment of 29 September 2009)...9.01, 9.13, 9.16
F-70/07 *Marcuccio v Commission* [2009] E.C.R.-SC I-A-1-31, (order of 18 February 2009) 18.27
F-83/07 R *Zangerl-Posselt v Commission* [2007] E.C.R.-SC I-A-1-235, (order of the President of
   10 September 2007)... 13.16, 13.32
F-94/07 *Rebizant and Others v Commission* [2009] E.C.R.-SC I-A-1-339................... 18.07
F-130/07 *Vinci v ECB* [2009] E.C.R.-SC I-A-1-307 .... 18.01
F-141/07 *Maniscalso v Commission* [2008] E.C.R.-SC I-A-1-253, (order of 10 July 2008)......... 18.02

F-20/08, F-34/08, and F-75/08 *Aparicio and Others v Commission* [2009] E.C.R.-SC I-A-1-375 ..... 9.16
F-30/08 *Nanopoulos v Commission*, not reported, (judgment of 11 May 2010) 18.18, 18.27
F-42/08 *Marcuccio v Commission* [2009] E.C.R.-SC I-A-1-35, (order of 18 February 2009) 18.18
F-46/08 *Thoss v Court of Auditors* [2008] E.C.R.-SC I-A-1-429, (order of
   10 December 2010) 2.54, 7.01, 18.08
F-53/08 *Bouillez and Others v Commission*, not reported, (judgment of 5 May 2010) 18.07
F-55/08 *De Nicola v EIB*, not reported, (judgment of 30 November 2009) 18.01

F-64/08 *Nijs v Court of Auditors* [2008] E.C.R.-SC I-A-1-493, (order of 18 December 2008) 18.06
F-80/08 R *Wenig v Commission* [2008] E.C.R.-SC I-A-1-479, (order of the President of
    17 December 2008) 13.16, 13.31, 18.07
F-82/08 *Clarke and Others v OHIM*, (judgment of 14 April 2011) 18.04

F-16/09 *de Britto Patricio-Dias v Commission* [2009] E.C.R.-SC I-A-1-497 . . . . 18.04
F-20/09 *Juvyns v Commission*, not yet reported, (judgment of 10 November 2011). 18.26
F-29/09 *Lebedef and Jones v Commission*, not yet reported, (judgment of
    30 September 2010) 9.01, 9.03, 9.14, 9.16
F-59/09 *De Nicola v EIB*, not reported, (judgment of 8 March 2011) 18.18
F-64/09 *Labate v Commission* [2009] E.C.R.-SC I-A-1-381, (order of September 2009) 8.01, 18.27
F-65/09 *Marcuccio v Commission*, not reported, (judgment of 23 November 2010) 18.06
F-92/09 R *U v European Parliament* [2009] E.C.R.-SC I-A-1-511, (order of the President of
    18 December 2009) 13.26, 13.31, 13.42
F-96/09 *Cuallado Martorell v Commission*, not reported, (judgment of 18 September 2012) 18.15
F-98/09 *Whitehead v ECB*, not yet reported, (judgment of 27 September 2011). 9.05, 9.15, 9.16
F-102/09 *Bennet and Others v OHIM*, not reported, (judgment of 15 September 2012) 18.04

F-6/10 *Munch v OHIM*, not reported, (judgment of 15 September 2011) 18.04
F-7/10 *Galan Girodit v OHIM*, not reported, (judgment of 15 September 2011) 18.04
F-13/10 *De Nicola v EIB*, not reported, (judgment of 28 September 2011) 18.18
F-41/10 R *Bermejo Garde v European Economic and Social Committee*, not reported, (order of the
    President of 14 July 2010) 13.22
F-41/10 *Bermejo Garde v EESC*, not reported, (judgment of 25 September 2012) 13.06, 18.04
F-49/10 *De Nicola v EIB*, not reported, (judgment of 28 June 2011). 18.01, 18.18
F-59/10 *Barthel and Others v Court of Justice of the European Union*, not reported,
    (order of 10 May 2011) 18.17
F-62/10 R *Esders v Commission*, not yet reported, (order of the President of 10 September 2010) . . . 13.31
F-71/10 *Cantisani v Commission*, not reported, (judgment of 5 June 2012) 18.02
F-95/10 R and F-105/10 R *Bömcke v European Investment Bank*, not yet reported,
    (order of the President of 15 December 2010) 13.31
F-114/10 *Bowles and Others v ECB*, not reported, (judgment of 29 September 2011). 18.03

F-5/11 R and F-15/11 R *Mariën v Commission and European External Action Service*, not yet
    reported, (order of the President of 27 May 2011) 13.05, 13.40
F-29/11 *BA v Commission*, not reported, (judgment of 5 December 2012). 18.04
F-31/11 *BI v European Centre for the Development of Vocational Training*, not reported,
    (order of 7 March 2012) 18.25
F-50/11 *Buxton v European Parliament*, not reported, (judgment of 18 April 2012) 18.15
F-57/11 *Eklund v Commission*, not reported, (judgment of 23 October 2012) 18.15
F-61/11 R *Possanzini v Frontex*, not yet reported, (order of the President of
    16 November 2011). 13.16, 13.22, 13.25, 13.27
F-67/11 R *Marcuccio v Commission*, not yet reported, (order of the President of
    16 November 2011). 13.16
F-83/11 *Cristina v Commission*, not reported, (judgment of 20 June 2012) 18.06
F-107/11 *Ntouvas v ECDC*, not reported, (judgment of 11 December 2012). 18.06, 18.07, 18.15
F-124/11 *Possanzini v Frontex*, not reported, (judgment of 23 October 2012) 18.06
F-129/11 R *BH v Commission*, not reported, (order of the President of 28 February 2012) . . . 13.16, 13.40
F-139/11 R *BJ v Commission*, not reported, (order of the President of 28 February 2012). . . . 13.16, 13.40
F-140/11 R *BK v Commission*, not reported, (order of the President of 28 February 2012) . . . 13.16, 13.40

F-16/12 R *Kimman v Commission*, not reported, (order of the President of 19 April 2012) 13.32
F-38/12 R *BP v EU Fundamental Rights Agency*, not reported, (order of the President of
    14 June 2012) 13.01, 13.22, 13.31
F-54/12 R *Carosi v Commission*, not reported, (order of the President of 6 June 2012) 13.31, 13.32

TABLE OF LEGISLATION, TREATIES, AND CONVENTIONS

INTERNATIONAL TREATIES AND CONVENTIONS

Act of Accession 1972 [1972] O.J., Spec. Ed. 14.....................2.05
Act of Accession 1979 [1979] O.J. L291/20 ....2.05
Act of Accession 1985 [1985] O.J. L302/26 .... 2.04, 2.05
Act of Accession 1995 [1995] O.J. L1/1 .....2.04
Act of Accession 2003 [2003] O.J. L236/33... 2.05
Act of Accession 2005 [2005] O.J. L157/203.. 2.05
Act of Accession 2012 [2012] O.J. L112/21... 2.05
AETR Agreement *See* European Agreement concerning the Work of Crews of Vehicles engaged in International Road Transport
Agreement between the European Community and the Kingdom of Denmark on jurisdiction and the recognition and enforcement of judgments in civil and commercial matters [2005] O.J. L299/62 ....21.01, 21.02
Agreement between the European Community and the Kingdom of Denmark on jurisdiction and the recognition and enforcement of judgments in civil and commercial matters [2007] O.J. L94/70....................21.02
Agreement between the European Community and the Kingdom of Denmark on the service of judicial and extrajudicial documents in civil or commercial matters [2005] O.J. L300/55....................21.01
Agreement between the European Community and the Swiss Confederation on Air Transport [2002] O.J. L114/73.......21.01
Agreement between the Federal Republic of Germany and the Republic of Austria for the avoidance of double taxation in the sphere of income and wealth tax (Deutscher Bundestag–14. Wahlperiode–Drucksache 14/7040, p.7)..........21.01
Agreement establishing an Association between the EEC and Turkey [1964] O.J. 217/3687; English text published in [1973] O.J. C113/1............... 5.05, 21.01
Agreement of 18 September 1998 concluded between the Government of the Federal Republic of Germany and the European Central Bank on the seat of that institution (BGBl. 1998 II, p. 2745) 19.05

Agreement of 19 February 2013 on a Unified Patent Court [2013] O.J. C175/1.............. 3.14, 12.20
Agreement on Implementation of Art. IV of the GATT as part of the WTO agreements [1994] O.J. L336/103 ('Anti-Dumping Agreement') 10.08
Amsterdam Treaty *See* Treaty of Amsterdam
Charter of Fundamental Rights of the European Union [2000] O.J. C364/1 proclaimed at Nice on 7 December 2000 by the European Parliament, the Council, and the Commission and adapted at Strasbourg on 12 December 2007 [2012] O.J. C326/391 ..... 1.03, 3.39, 4.07, 4.12, 4.44, 6.06, 6.24, 10.15, 11.02
  Preamble..........................1.03
  Title V 11.02
  Art. 7 ....13.36
  Art. 41 .... 11.48, 11.51
  Art. 41(1) 7.178
  Art. 41(2) 7.161
  Art. 41(3) 11.02
  Art 47......... 1.03, 4.07, 4.12, 4.54, 7.106, 7.195, 11.08, 13.36, 15.05, 16.18, 17.02, 23.87
  Art. 48 ....7.192
  Art. 51 ....6.24
  Art. 51(1) 3.39
  Art. 52(2) 11.02
Charter of the United Nations 7.178
Convention defining the Statute of the European Schools [1994] O.J. L212/3...21.01
Convention for the protection of literary and artistic works ('Berne Convention'), as revised by the Paris Act of 24 July 1971 ....5.07
Convention on access to information, public participation in decision-making, and access to justice in environmental matters ('Aarhus Convention') [2005] O.J. L124/4............... 6.14, 7.178
Convention on certain institutions common to the European Communities [1967] O.J. 152/5 (not printed in the English Special Edition of the O.J.)..........6.04
Convention on driving disqualifications [1998] O.J. C216/1 ....21.01, 21.05, 21.08, 21.09, 21.10, 21.12
Convention on international civil aviation ('Chicago Convention')............10.08

Convention on jurisdiction and the enforcement
of judgments in civil and commercial
matters of 27 September 1968 ('Brussels
Convention') [1972] O.J. L299/32 (not
printed in the English Special Edition of
the O.J.); [1998] O.J. C27/1
(consolidated version) 5.08, 21.02, 21.07
Protocol to the 1968 Convention on
jurisdiction and the enforcement of
judgments in civil and commercial
matters [1972] O.J. L299/43;
English text published in [1978]
O.J. L 304/36 . . . . 21.01, 21.02,
21.07, 21.12
Convention on jurisdiction and the recognition
and enforcement of judgments in
matrimonial matters [1998]
O.J. C221/1 . . . . 21.04, 21.05
Protocol on the interpretation by the Court of
Justice of the European Communities of
the Convention on jurisdiction and the
recognition and enforcement of judgments
in matrimonial matters [1998]
O.J. C221/19 . . . . 21.01, 21.04, 21.05
Convention on mutual assistance and
cooperation between customs
administrations [1998] O.J. C24/1 . . . 21.01,
21.05, 21.08, 21.09, 21.10, 21.12
Convention on simplified extradition procedures
between the Member States of the
European Union [1995] O.J. C78/1 . . . 21.05
Convention on the establishment of a
European Police Office ('Europol
Convention') [1995] O.J. C361/1 . . . . 21.05,
21.09
Protocol on the interpretation, by way of
preliminary rulings, by the Court of Justice
of the European Communities of the
Convention on the establishment of a
European Police Office [1996]
O.J. C299/2. . . . . 21.01, 21.08, 21.12
Protocol on the privileges and immunities
of Europol, the members of its organs, the
deputy directors and employees of Europol
[1997] O.J. C221/2 . . . . 21.05
Convention on the fight against corruption
involving officials of the European
Communities or officials of Member States
of the European Union [1997]
O.J. C195/1. . . . . 21.01, 21.05, 21.08,
21.09, 21.10, 21.12
Convention on the international recovery of
child support and other forms of family
maintenance ('Hague Convention')
[2011] O.J. L192/51 . . . . 21.04
Convention on the protection of the European
Communities' financial interests [1995]
O.J. C316/ 48 . . . . 21.05, 21.10
Protocol to the Convention on the protection of
the European Communities' financial
interests [1996] O.J. C313/1. . . . . 21.01

Second Protocol to the Convention on the
protection of the European Communities'
financial interests [1997]
O.J. C221/12. . . . . 21.08
First Protocol on the interpretation, by way of
preliminary rulings, by the Court of Justice
of the European Communities of the
Convention on the protection of the
European Communities' financial
interests [1997] O.J. C151/1. . . 21.01, 21.08,
21.09, 21.10, 21.12
Second Protocol on the interpretation, by way
of preliminary rulings, by the Court of
Justice of the European Communities of the
Convention on the protection of the
European Communities' financial
interests [1997] O.J. C221/11 . . . 21.01, 21.05,
21.10, 21.11
Convention on the service in the Member
States of the European Union of judicial
and extrajudicial documents in civil or
commercial matters [1997]
O.J. C261/1. . . . . 21.05
Protocol on the interpretation, by the Court
of Justice of the European Communities,
of the Convention on the service in the
Member States of the European Union
of judicial and extrajudicial documents
in civil or commercial matters [1997]
O.J. C261/17. . . . . 21.01, 21.04
Convention on the use of information
technology for customs purposes
[1995] O.J. C316/33 . . . 21.05, 21.09, 21.10
Protocol on the interpretation, by way of
preliminary rulings, by the Court of Justice
of the European Communities of the
Convention on the use of information
technology for customs purposes
[1997] O.J. C151/16 . . . . 21.01, 21.05,
21.08, 21.12
Convention relating to extradition between
the Member States of the European
Union [1996] O.J. C313/11 . . . . 21.05
Treaty establishing a Constitution for Europe
[2004] O.J. C310/1 . . . . . . 2.03, 6.10, 22.06
Art. I-29 . . . . 4.12
Art. III-362(3). 5.16
Art. III-365(4) 7.85, 7.107
Art. III-369, fourth para. 3.02
European Agreement concerning the Work
of Crews of Vehicles engaged in
International Road Transport
(AETR Agreement) [1978] O.J. L95/1. . . 6.14
Treaty establishing the European Atomic
Energy Community Treaty (EAEC
or Euratom) [2012]
O.J. C327/1. . . . . 1.06, 3.23, 6.03, 6.04,
6.07, 7.06, 8.01, 9.01, 9.16, 10.01,
11.03, 11.05, 11.64, 11.81, 12.06,
13.03, 14.01, 15.03, 19.04,
19.23, 19.27, 23.26

Art. 12 . . . . .15.03
Art. 46 . . . . .18.10
Art. 47 . . . . .18.10
Art. 49 . . . . .18.10
Art. 81 . . . . .26.08
Art. 83 . . . . .15.03
Art. 103 . . . . 12.06, 12.08
Art. 104 . . . . .12.06
Art. 105 . . . . .12.06
Art. 106a 5.03, 7.06
Art. 106a(1). 11.03, 13.03, 15.03,
                        19.04, 19.23, 19.27
Art. 106a(1)–(2). 6.03, 8.01,
                        9.01, 9.16, 10.01
Art. 136 . . . . .6.07
Art. 141 . . . . .11.47
Arts 141–143. . . . . .5.03
Art. 144(a). 15.03
Art. 144(b) 15.03
Art. 146 . . . . .7.06
Art. 147 . . . . .7.06
Art. 148 . . . . 8.01, 25.82
Art. 149 . . . . .7.06
Art. 150 . . . . 3.03, 6.03, 10.01
Art. 151 . . . . 11.03, 11.04, 11.05, 11.21
Art. 152 . . . . 9.15, 9.16, 11.05
Art. 153 . . . . 19.04, 19.23
Art. 154 . . . . .19.23
Art. 156 . . . . .9.01
Art. 157 . . . . 13.03, 16.12
Art. 158 . . . . .13.03
Art. 160, second para. 1.10
Art. 164 . . . . 13.04, 26.08
Art. 164, third para. 16.12
Art. 188 . . . . .11.03
Art. 188, first para. 19.04
Art. 188(2) 11.05, 11.21
Art. 189 . . . . .7.150
Art. 193 . . . . .19.27
Art. 207 . . . . 6.04, 7.177
European Convention on Human Rights
    and Fundamental Freedoms
    (ECHR) [1950] 4.12, 4.44, 6.06, 6.07,
                        6.24, 10.15
Art. 6 . . . . 4.07, 4.11, 7.106
Art. 6(1) 4.12, 16.18, 23.87
Art. 6(2) 7.192
Art. 13 . . . . 4.08, 4.11, 7.106
European Economic Area Agreement
    (EEA) [1994] O.J. L1/3 . . . . .3.15, 4.08,
        5.07, 6.14, 7.72, 12.13, 12.20, 24.07,
        24.08, 24.09, 24.28, 24.33, 25.60,
                    25.61, 25.63, 25.75
Protocol 28 on intellectual property [1994]
    O.J. L1/194, Art. 5. . . . . .5.07
Protocol 34 on the possibility for courts and
    tribunals of EFTA States to request the
    Court of Justice of the European
    Communities to decide on the interpretation
    of EEA rules corresponding to EC rules
    [1994] O.J. L1/204 . . . . . 3.15, 21.01, 24.33

General Agreement on Tariffs and
    Trade (GATT) [1947] 6.13
General Agreement on Trade in
    Services (GATS) [1994]
    O.J. L336/191 . . . . .12.07
Internal agreement between the
    representatives of the governments of the
    Member States, meeting within the
    Council, on measures to be taken and
    procedures to be followed for the
    implementation of the ACP-EC
    Partnership Agreement [2000]
    O.J. L317/376 . . . . .21.01
International Convention for the
    prevention of pollution from ships
    (Marpol 73/78) 10.08
Kyoto Protocol to the United Nations
    Framework Convention on climate
    change [2002] O.J. L130/4. . . . . .10.08
Lisbon Treaty *See* Treaty of Lisbon
Fourth ACP-EEC Convention ('Lomé
    Convention') [1991] O.J. L229/3 . . . . . .7.73
Convention on jurisdiction and the
    enforcement of judgments in civil and
    commercial matters ('Lugano
    Convention') [1988] O.J. L319/9 . . . . .21.02
Convention on jurisdiction and the enforcement
    of judgments in civil and commercial
    matters ('New Lugano convention')
    [2007] O.J. L339/3 . . . . .21.02
Maastricht Treaty *See* Treaty on European
    Union prior to 1 December 2009
    (Treaty of Maastricht)
Marpol 73/78 *See* International Convention for
    the Prevention of Pollution from Ships
Monetary Agreement between the Government
    of the French Republic, on behalf of the
    European Community, and the
    Government of His Serene Highness the
    Prince of Monaco [2002]
    O.J. L142/59 . . . . .21.01
Monetary Agreement between the European
    Union and the Principality of Monaco
    [2012] O.J. C310/1 . . . . .21.01
Nice Treaty *See* Treaty of Nice
Air Transport Agreement ('Open Skies
    Agreement') [2007] O.J. L134/4 . . . . . .10.08
Convention on the law applicable to
    contractual obligations ('Rome
    Convention') [1981] O.J. C80/1
    (consolidated version: [2005]
    O.J. C334/1) 19.16, 21.03, 21.07
First Protocol on the interpretation by the
    Court of Justice of the European
    Communities of the Convention on the
    law applicable to contractual obligations
    [1989] O.J. L48/1 (consolidated version:
    [2005] O.J. C334/1) . . . 21.01, 21.03, 21.07
Second Protocol on the interpretation by the
    Court of Justice of the European
    Communities of the Convention on the

law applicable to contractual obligations
[1989] O.J. L48/17 (consolidated
version: [2005] O.J. C334/1) 21.01, 21.12
Single European Act [1987]
O.J. L169/1 . . . . 5.28, 6.05, 11.18
Treaty establishing a Single Council and a
Single Commission of the European
Communities ('Merger Treaty') [1967]
O.J. 152/2 . . . . .6.04
Treaty establishing the European Coal and
Steel Community (ECSC)
[1951] 1.06, 3.04, 3.23, 5.03,
6.03, 7.06, 7.148, 7.161, 7.181,
7.184, 8.20, 11.03, 11.43, 11.67, 11.85,
11.87, 15.03, 19.04
Art. 14 . . . . .7.16
Arts 33–34 . . . . .7.06
Art. 34 . . . . 11.03, 11.43
Art. 36 . . . . .15.03
Arts 36–38 . . . . .7.06
Art. 38, first para. 7.76
Art. 39 . . . . .13.03
Art. 40 . . . . 11.03, 11.43, 11.48, 11.69
Art. 41 . . . . .3.04
Art. 42 . . . . .19.04
Art. 77 . . . . .7.150
Art. 88 . . . . 5.03, 15.03
Art. 89 . . . . .19.23
Art. 95 . . . . .7.10
Treaty establishing the European
Community (EC Treaty) [2006]
O.J. C321E/1 . . . . .1.06, 2.03, 2.46,
2.47, 2.48, 3.23, 4.10, 5.08, 6.04,
7.04, 7.05, 7.79, 8.11, 10.06,
12.13, 15.02, 21.04, 22.02, 22.05
Title IV 1.06, 3.02, 3.59, 6.05, 22.01,
22.02, 22.05
Art. 7 . . . . .2.46, 2.49, 2.53, 6.10
Art. 7(1) 8.02, 8.12, 11.20
Art. 12 . . . . 5.08, 11.50
Art. 14 . . . . .8.08
Art. 18 . . . . .3.31
Art. 28 . . . . .11.50
Art. 29 . . . . .11.50
Art. 32(4) 11.50
Art. 33(1) 11.50
Art. 34(3) 11.50
Art. 37(2) 11.50
Art. 61(c) 21.02, 21.03
Art. 67(1) 21.02
Art. 67(5) 21.03
Art. 68 . . . . 1.06, 1.07, 3.02, 3.48,
3.59, 6.05, 22.02, 22.05
Art. 68(1) 21.02, 21.03, 21.04, 22.02
Art. 68(2) 22.02
Art. 68(3) 22.02
Art. 81 . . . . 7.35, 7.112
Art. 81(1) 7.112, 7.139
Art. 81(3) 7.35
Art. 88(2) 5.34
Art. 88(3) 4.17

Art. 93 . . . . .5.24
Art. 95 . . . . .5.28
Art. 97 . . . . .5.34
Art. 100a(4) 5.28
Art. 107(2) 11.20
Art. 133 . . . . 1.06, 11.51
Art. 139(2) 6.09
Art. 189, fourth para. 10.10
Art. 202 . . . . .7.153
Art. 211 . . . . . . .5.34, 7.153, 8.06, 8.08, 11.51
Art. 215(2) 11.58
Art. 220 . . . . 2.03, 2.37
Arts 220–245 . . . . .22.02
Art. 220, second para. 2.03
Art. 226 . . . . .5.34
Art. 226–228 . . . . 2.46, 2.47
Art. 225 . . . . .2.47
Art. 225(1) 2.35, 2.46, 2.47, 2.48
Art. 225(1), first para. 2.47, 2.48, 2.49
Art. 225(2) 18.30, 18.31
Art. 225(3) 2.48
Art. 225a 2.03, 2.37
Art. 225a, first para. 2.48
Art. 226 . . . . .5.03
Arts 226–227 . . . . .5.04
Arts 226–228 . . . . 5.03, 5.04, 5.76
Art. 227 . . . . .5.03
Art. 228 . . . . 5.03, 5.04, 5.78
Art. 228(2) 5.75
Art. 229 . . . . .15.02
Art. 230 . . . . 1.06, 2.45, 2.48, 4.10,
4.11, 5.27, 7.03, 7.04, 7.05, 7.08,
7.69, 7.70, 7.76, 7.79, 7.85,
7.106, 7.108, 7.109, 7.112, 13.22
Art. 230, fourth para. 9.06
Art. 230, fifth para. 23.34
Art. 231 . . . . 7.06, 7.221, 10.20
Art. 232 . . . . 2.45, 2.48, 8.02, 8.11, 8.12
Art. 233 . . . . 7.06, 10.20, 11.09
Art. 234 . . . . 2.46, 3.02, 3.03, 3.11,
4.10, 6.05, 6.10, 10.06
Art. 235 . . . . . .2.45, 2.48, 11.02, 11.03, 21.11
Art. 236 . . . . 2.45, 2.48
Art. 237 . . . . 2.46, 7.70
Art. 237(b) 25.06
Art. 238 . . . . 2.45, 2.48, 19.03, 19.04
Art. 239 . . . . 2.46, 19.22
Art. 241 . . . . 4.10, 5.66, 9.02, 9.03,
9.05, 9.06, 9.11, 9.16
Art. 242 . . . . .13.02
Art. 243 . . . . .13.02
Art. 244 . . . . .23.94
Art. 245 . . . . 1.10, 2.48
Art. 245, second para. 1.10
Art. 249 . . . . 3.54, 6.08
Art. 251, second para. 2.12
Art. 253 . . . . 7.79, 7.158, 11.51
Art. 254(2) 9.11
Art. 255(1) 2.46
Art. 256 . . . . .23.94
Art. 272(4) 8.08

Art. 288 . . . . 4.46, 11.03, 11.20, 19.03
Art. 288, first para. 19.04
Art. 288, second para. . .2.45, 2.48, 11.02, 21.11
Art. 288, third para. 11.02
Art. 289 . . . . .7.150
Art. 292 . . . . .19.27
Art. 293 . . . . 5.08, 21.01, 21.02, 21.03
Art. 296 . . . . .8.19
Art. 298 . . . . .8.19
Art. 300(6) 12.04, 12.06
Art. 307 . . . . .11.51
Art. 308 . . . . .20.01
Treaty establishing the European
   Economic Community Treaty
   (EEC Treaty) [1957] 7.69, 11.18
Art. 169 . . . . .5.02
Art. 171 . . . . .5.02
Art. 173 . . . . 7.69, 7.79
Art. 108(b) 25.06
Treaty of Amsterdam [1997]
   O.J. C340/1 . . . . 1.06, 5.28
Art. 9(1) 6.04
Art. 9(2)–(7) 6.04
Art. 46 . . . . .6.05
Declaration 27 . . . . .6.09
Treaty of Lisbon [2007]
   O.J. C306/1 . . . . 1.07, 1.10, 2.02, 2.03,
              2.36, 2.47, 2.48, 2.49, 2.51, 2.53,
              3.02, 3.03, 4.12, 5.03, 5.04, 5.08,
              5.28, 5.66, 5.75, 5.76, 6.01, 6.03,
              6.04, 6.05, 6.06, 6.14, 7.03, 7.04,
       7.05, 7.06, 7.07, 7.17, 7.69, 7.70, 7.73,
    7.79, 7.81, 7.85, 7.153, 7.223, 8.01, 8.02,
        8.11, 8.13, 9.01, 9.02, 9.05, 9.16,
    10.04, 10.06, 10.11, 10.15, 11.02, 11.03,
    11.04, 11.20, 11.52, 12.01, 12.04, 12.05,
    13.02, 13.22, 14.01, 15.02, 15.03, 19.03,
    19.04, 21.01, 21.02, 21.03, 21.04, 21.05,
        21.08, 21.09, 22.01, 22.02, 22.05
Declaration (No. 38) 2.04
Declaration (No. 50) 7.04, 11.02, 22.05
Declaration (No. 56) 22.05
Declaration (No. 65) 22.05
Treaty of Nice [2001] O.J. C80/1 . . . . 1.06,
        2.36, 2.37, 2.45, 2.47, 2.48, 2.49
Art. 10 . . . . .2.35
Declaration (No. 15) 17.07
Declaration (No. 16) 2.38
Treaty establishing the European Stability
   Mechanism [2012] 5.09, 19.22, 21.01
Treaty on European Union prior to
   1 December 2009 (Treaty of
   Maastricht) [2006] O.J.
   C321E/1 . . . . . . 1.06, 3.31, 5.28, 6.05, 7.04
Art. K.3 . . . . 21.08, 21.09
Art. K.3(2) 21.05
Art. K.3(2)(c) 1.06, 21.05
Art. L 1.06, 6.05
Arts L–S 1.06
Art. 6(2) 1.06
Art. 34(2) 22.03

Art. 34(2)(d) 21.01, 22.03
Art. 35 . . . . . .1.06, 1.07, 1.09, 3.02, 3.09, 3.44,
     5.05, 6.05, 10.04, 11.02, 22.03, 22.05
Art. 35(1) 22.03, 22.04
Art. 35(2) 22.03, 22.05
Art. 35(3)(a) 22.03
Art. 35(3)(b) 22.03
Art. 35(4) 22.03
Art. 35(5) 21.08, 22.03
Art. 35(6) 7.04, 22.03, 22.04
Art. 35(7) 5.04, 5.05, 21.13, 22.03, 22.04
Art. 46 . . . . 1.06, 1.07
Arts 46–53 . . . . .6.05
Art. 47 . . . . 1.06, 1.07, 9.05
Art. 48 . . . . .4.11
Treaty on European Union post
   1 December 2009 (TEU) [2012]
   O.J. C326/13 . . . . .1.07, 3.02, 6.03,
        6.04, 6.06, 7.177, 12.01, 15.02
Title V, Ch. 2 . . . . 3.02, 6.05, 12.05
Art. 1 . . . . .6.03
Art. 1, third para. 1.07, 5.04, 6.03, 6.04,
       7.04, 7.177, 11.02, 12.04, 19.03
Art. 2 . . . . .1.03
Art. 4(3) 2.02, 3.12, 3.61, 4.04, 4.11,
       4.40, 4.43, 4.45, 4.46, 4.56, 4.57,
       5.05, 5.13, 5.14, 5.18, 5.22, 5.64,
       6.08, 6.14, 7.76, 7.152, 11.27,
                  12.08, 23.58
Art. 5(2) 1.04
Art. 6(1) 1.03, 4.07, 4.12, 6.06, 11.02
Art. 6(3) 6.06, 6.07, 6.24
Art. 7 . . . . .5.34
Art. 13 . . . . .6.10
Art. 13(1) 3.02, 7.03, 7.69, 8.02, 8.11,
        10.06, 11.02, 11.20, 12.09,
               19.14, 25.127
Art. 13(1), second para. 2.49, 6.10
Art. 13(2) 1.04
Art. 13(4) 6.12
Art. 15(1) 2.49
Art. 16(3) 1.10
Art. 17(1) 5.31, 5.64, 8.06, 8.08,
                 11.51, 13.41
Art. 19 . . . . .1.10
Art. 19(1) 2.02, 6.07, 7.178, 18.09
Art. 19(1), first para. 2.02, 12.02, 23.58
Art. 19(1), second para. . .2.02, 4.11, 4.12, 7.110
Art. 19(2), first para. 2.04
Art. 19(2), second para. 2.23
Art. 19(2), third para. 2.04, 2.23
Art. 19(3) 2.03, 3.01
Art. 19(3)(b) 6.08, 10.01, 10.06
Art. 22(1) 7.69
Art. 24(1) 1.07
Art. 24(1), second para. 2.49, 3.02, 5.05,
      6.05, 7.04, 7.69, 9.05, 10.04, 11.02,
               12.05, 19.03
Art. 25 . . . . .9.05
Art. 26(1) 7.69
Art. 31(1), first para. 2.49

Art. 35(6) 7.04
Art. 35(7) 19.22, 22.05
Art. 40 . . . . 3.02, 5.05, 6.05, 7.04, 9.05,
   10.04, 11.02, 12.05
Art. 42(3) 11.21
Art. 45. . . . . .11.21
Art. 47 . . . . 19.01, 22.04
Art. 48 . . . . 4.11, 12.04, 12.20
Art. 48(1)–(5) 7.75
Art. 48(6) 7.75, 10.03, 11.18
Art. 49 . . . . 4.52, 7.75
Art. 51 . . . . 6.04, 7.177
Art. 52 . . . . .3.13
Treaty on the Functioning of the
   European Union (TFEU) [2012]
   O.J. C326/47 . . . . . . 1.07, 3.02, 6.03, 6.04,
      6.06, 7.80, 7.177, 12.01,
      15.02, 22.05, 23.26
Pt III. 7.75
Pt III, Title V 1.07, 21.01, 22.01,
      22.07, 24.20
Pt III, Title V, Chap 2 . . . . .10.04
Pt III, Title V, Chap 3 . . . . .22.05
Pt III, Title V, Chap 4 . . . . .22.05
Pt III, Title X 6.09
Pt 4. . . . . .3.13
Art. 1 . . . . .6.03
Art. 1(2) 5.04, 6.03, 6.04, 7.177, 12.04
Art. 3(1)(e) 6.14
Art. 13(1) 8.12
Art. 15 . . . . .7.67
Art. 18 . . . . .4.08, 5.08, 6.07, 6.22, 11.50
Art. 19 . . . . .7.17
Art. 19(1), first para. 1.03
Art. 19(3(b). 6.01
Arts 20–21 .6.22, 6.24
Art. 21 . . . . .3.31
Art. 25 . . . . .6.06
Art. 26 . . . . .8.08
Art. 34 . . . . .3.26, 5.14, 5.18, 11.50
Art. 35. . . . . .11.50
Art. 36 . . . . .3.26
Art. 38(4) 11.50
Art. 39(1) 11.50
Art. 40(2), second para. 11.48
Art. 40(3) 11.50
Art. 42 . . . . .5.25
Art. 43(2) 11.50
Art. 49 . . . . .4.44
Art. 54 . . . . .4.44
Arts 67–76 . . . . .22.01
Arts 67–89 . . . . 22.01, 22.07
Art. 72 . . . . .22.05
Arts 77–80 . . . . .22.01
Art. 81 . . . . 4.02, 22.01
Art. 81(2)(f). 4.02
Arts 82–86 . . . . .22.01
Art. 85 . . . . .11.20
Arts 87–89 . . . . .22.01
Art. 88 . . . . .11.20

Art. 101 . . . . 3.12, 3.26, 4.53, 4.54, 5.32,
      7.12, 7.26, 7.30, 7.31, 7.32, 7.34,
      7.35, 7.41, 7.43, 7.86, 7.87, 7.112,
      7.143, 7.163, 7.167, 7.185, 7.190,
      7.191, 7.196, 7.226, 8.06, 8.19,
      8.20, 11.85, 16.01, 25.65, 25.67
Arts 101–109. . . . . .5.25
Art. 101(1) 7.32, 7.43, 7.112, 7.139,
      7.179, 7.226, 10.10
Art. 101(3) 7.35, 10.10
Art. 102 . . . . 3.26, 5.32, 7.26, 7.30, 7.31,
      7.32, 7.34, 7.41, 7.43, 7.44, 7.76,
      7.86, 7.87, 7.112, 7.143, 7.163,
      7.167, 7.179, 7.185, 7.190, 7.191,
      7.196, 7.226, 8.06, 8.19, 8.20,
      11.85, 16.07, 25.65, 25.67
Art. 104 . . . . .4.02
Art. 106 . . . . 5.33, 16.21
Art. 106(1) 5.26, 5.27, 5.33, 7.41, 7.44
Art. 106(2) 5.26, 5.27, 5.33, 7.76
Art. 106(3) 5.21, 5.26, 5.27, 7.44, 8.06
Art. 107 . . . . 5.22, 5.23, 5.25, 5.65, 7.52,
      7.55, 7.178, 8.13, 25.60
Arts 107–109. . . . . .5.25
Art. 107(1) 7.54, 7.55, 7.61, 7.201, 16.28
Art. 107(3) 7.26, 7.202, 7.203
Art. 108 . . . . 5.22, 5.24, 5.25, 5.27, 5.65,
      7.52, 7.204, 8.13
Art. 108(1) 7.53, 7.57, 7.63
Art. 108(2) 5.21, 5.22, 5.23, 5.24,
      5.27, 5.28, 5.34, 5.37, 5.58, 5.66,
      5.68, 5.69, 5.76, 7.53, 7.54, 7.57,
      7.61, 7.118, 7.119, 7.120, 7.124, 7.128,
      7.129, 7.142, 7.161, 7.187, 7.202, 7.210,
      8.06, 8.13, 10.20
Art. 108(2), first para. 5.24
Art. 108(2), second para. 5.22, 5.23
Art. 108(2), third para. . .2.50, 2.53, 5.22, 7.55
Art. 108(3) 4.17, 5.22, 5.24, 7.54,
      7.57, 7.118, 7.124, 7.165, 10.20
Art. 109 . . . . .7.55
Art. 110 . . . . 5.17, 5.20
Art. 114 . . . . .5.28
Arts 114–117. . . . . .4.02
Art. 114(1) 5.28
Art. 114(4) 7.170
Art. 114(4)–(8) .5.28
Art. 114(5) 7.125, 7.170
Art. 114(5)–(6) .7.18
Art. 114(9) 5.21, 5.28
Art. 126(1)–(9) .5.03
Art. 126(10) 5.03
Art. 134 . . . . .6.04
Art. 153 . . . . .6.09
Art. 154 . . . . .6.09
Art. 155 . . . . .6.09
Art. 155(2) 6.09
Art. 157 . . . . 4.34, 6.34
Art. 207 . . . . 1.06, 2.50, 2.53, 11.51
Art. 207(1) 6.14

Art. 207(2) 7.130
Arts 216–219. .6.13
Art. 216(2) 7.178
Art. 218 . . . . 10.05, 12.05, 12.08
Art. 218(1) 12.16
Art. 218(2) 6.06, 12.16
Art. 218(3) 12.05
Art. 218(6) 12.05
Art. 218(9) 12.05
Art. 218(11) 1.09, 6.05, 12.01, 12.02,
        12.03, 12.04, 12.05, 12.07, 12.08,
  12.09, 12.11, 12.12, 12.14, 12.15, 12.16,
        12.17, 12.18, 12.20, 21.02, 25.81
Art. 220(1) 7.161
Art. 223 . . . . .6.06
Art. 227 . . . . 7.17, 7.170
Art. 230 . . . . .7.69
Art. 232 . . . . .7.168
Art. 232, first para. 6.08
Art. 235(3) 6.08
Art. 240(1) 7.72
Art. 240(3) 6.08, 7.168
Art. 245(2) 18.01
Art. 249(1) 6.08, 7.168
Art. 251, first para. 2.10
Art. 251, second para. 2.10
Arts 251–281. . . . . .1.10
Art. 252 . . . . .2.04
Art. 252, first para. 2.04
Art. 252, second para. 2.15, 2.24
Art. 253, first para. 2.04
Art. 253, second para. 2.04
Art. 253, third para. 2.07
Art. 253, fourth para. 2.04
Art. 253, fifth para. 2.09
Art. 253, sixth para. 1.10
Art. 254, first para. 2.23, 2.24
Art. 254, second para. 2.23
Art. 254, third para. 2.26
Art. 254, fourth para. 2.28
Art. 254, fifth para. 1.10
Art. 254, sixth para. 2.25
Art. 255 . . . . 2.04, 2.23
Art. 256 . . . . . . .7.01, 7.82, 8.01, 11.04, 15.05
Art. 256, first para. 2.47, 2.49
Art. 256(1) 5.04, 14.02, 20.02, 26.01
Art. 256(1), first para. 19.07
Art. 256(1), second para. . . . 2.53, 16.02, 17.01
Art. 256(2) 16.01, 17.01, 17.04,
                17.07, 25.106, 26.01
Art. 256(2), first para. 2.53
Art. 256(2), second para. 2.53, 17.01
Art. 256(3) 3.01, 17.01, 17.04, 17.06,
                17.07, 25.106
Art. 256(3), first para. 17.01
Art. 256(3), third para. 2.53, 17.01, 17.06
Art. 257 . . . . 2.03, 2.37, 2.44, 8.01, 18.01,
                18.09, 26.01
Art. 257, first para. 2.03, 2.37
Art. 257, third para. 2.37, 16.01
Art. 257, fourth para. 2.39
Art. 257, fifth para. 1.10

Art. 258 . . . . 3.53, 3.56, 3.57, 5.02, 5.03,
        5.04, 5.05, 5.07, 5.08, 5.14, 5.16,
        5.22, 5.23, 5.24, 5.25, 5.26, 5.27, 5.28,
        5.29, 5.30, 5.31, 5.32, 5.34, 5.35, 5.41,
        5.42, 5.45, 5.48, 5.49, 5.52, 5.64, 5.65,
        5.70, 5.71, 5.73, 5.75, 5.76, 5.77, 5.80,
        6.11, 7.18, 7.24, 7.43, 7.50, 7.161, 8.06,
        11.27, 11.47, 11.81, 15.01, 22.03,
                22.05, 23.58
Arts 258–259 . . . . . . 5.04, 5.36, 5.38, 5.70, 5.73
Arts 258–260 . . . . 1.09, 2.53, 3.53, 5.01,
        5.03, 5.04, 5.05, 5.21, 5.45, 5.64,
        6.01, 6.29, 8.23, 9.16, 13.12, 25.109
Art. 259 . . . . 3.57, 5.02, 5.03, 5.04, 5.08,
        5.22, 5.27, 5.28, 5.35, 22.03, 23.03
Art. 260 . . . . 5.02, 5.03, 5.04, 5.69, 5.76,
        5.78, 5.80, 5.81, 7.18, 15.01, 23.94
Art. 260(1) 5.11, 5.70, 5.74
Art. 260(2) 5.02, 5.04, 5.16, 5.31, 5.70,
        5.75, 5.76, 5.77, 5.78, 5.79, 5.80
Art. 260(2), first para. 5.75
Art. 260(3) 5.02, 5.04, 5.16, 5.75, 5.78
Art. 260(3), first para. 5.15
Art. 260(3), second para. 5.15
Art. 261 . . . . .7.195, 11.20, 15.01, 15.03,
                15.05, 15.07, 15.09
Art. 261(2) 5.05
Art. 262 . . . . .6.06
Art. 263 . . . . 1.07, 1.09, 2.50, 2.53, 2.55,
        3.02, 3.59, 3.60, 4.10, 4.12, 5.27, 5.31,
        5.80, 7.01, 7.02, 7.03, 7.04, 7.05, 7.06,
        7.10, 7.11, 7.12, 7.13, 7.14, 7.15, 7.17,
        7.18, 7.21, 7.23, 7.31, 7.32, 7.40, 7.42,
        7.43, 7.59, 7.61, 7.62, 7.66, 7.67, 7.69,
  7.70, 7.71, 7.72, 7.73, 7.74, 7.76, 7.77, 7.78,
        7.79, 7.81, 7.82, 7.83, 7.85, 7.86, 7.87,
  7.88, 7.89, 7.91, 7.100, 7.103, 7.107, 7.108,
        7.109, 7.110, 7.111, 7.112, 7.118, 7.120,
        7.122, 7.124, 7.125, 7.127, 7.129, 7.136,
        7.141, 7.145, 7.175, 7.177, 7.178, 7.185,
                7.188, 7.195, 7.207, 7.208, 7.209,
        7.210, 7.211, 7.212, 7.213, 7.214, 7.216,
        7.219, 8.01, 8.02, 8.10, 8.11, 8.13, 8.14,
        9.02, 9.03, 9.06, 9.07, 9.10, 9.16, 10.04,
        10.05, 10.09, 10.10, 10.11, 10.13, 10.17,
        10.22, 11.09, 11.10, 11.12, 11.52, 11.94,
        12.03, 13.09, 13.25, 15.05, 15.09, 18.08,
        18.10, 19.12, 20.20, 21.11, 22.03, 25.82,
                25.95, 25.99
Art. 263, first para. 8.11
Art. 263, second para. 2.53, 7.86, 7.177,
                9.18, 10.14, 10.15
Art. 263, third para. 2.53
Art. 263, fourth para. 5.05, 6.05, 7.61,
        7.62, 7.77, 7.81, 7.82, 7.83, 7.85, 7.86,
  7.87, 7.88, 7.89, 7.98, 7.100, 7.103, 7.107,
        7.108, 7.109, 7.110, 7.111, 7.118, 7.120,
  7.124, 7.130, 8.10, 10.04, 10.11, 11.02, 12.05
Art. 263, sixth para. 3.23, 7.04, 7.11,
        7.12, 7.78, 7.175, 7.207, 7.208, 7.209,
        7.210, 7.211, 7.212, 7.213, 7.214, 7.216,
        9.02, 9.15, 23.26, 23.28, 23.32, 23.34

Art. 264 ...... 7.01, 7.06, 7.07, 7.141, 7.219,
7.221, 10.20, 10.21, 10.22, 11.09
Art. 264, first para. 7.219
Art. 264, second para. 7.221
Art. 265 .....1.09, 2.50, 2.53, 4.64, 5.34, 7.14,
7.226, 8.01, 8.02, 8.03, 8.04, 8.05, 8.06, 8.08,
8.09, 8.11, 8.12, 8.13, 8.14, 8.15, 8.17, 8.18,
8.19, 8.20, 8.21, 8.22, 8.23, 9.16, 10.12,
11.94, 13.10, 16.21, 25.65, 25.82
Art. 265, first para. 8.23
Art. 265, second para. 23.26
Art. 266 ..... 7.06, 7.07, 7.138, 7.143, 7.209,
7.223, 7.225, 7.226, 8.05, 8.06,
8.07, 8.09, 8.23, 10.20, 10.21, 11.09,
20.06, 23.94
Art. 266, first para. 8.06, 8.22
Art. 267 ....1.09, 2.53, 3.01, 3.02, 3.05, 3.06,
3.07, 3.08, 3.09, 3.10, 3.11, 3.12, 3.14,
3.15, 3.16, 3.19, 3.20, 3.21, 3.22, 3.23,
3.24, 3.29, 3.30, 3.31, 3.32, 3.35, 3.36,
3.40, 3.42, 3.43, 3.44, 3.45, 3.46, 3.47,
3.48, 3.50, 3.51, 3.52, 3.53, 3.55, 3.56,
3.57, 3.58, 3.59, 3.60, 3.61, 4.10, 4.40,
4.50, 4.56, 4.63, 5.13, 5.71, 6.01, 6.03,
6.08, 6.10, 6.11, 6.12, 6.13, 6.14, 6.15,
6.16, 6.17, 6.18, 6.19, 6.23, 6.27, 6.28,
6.32, 6.33, 7.02, 7.07, 9.17, 10.01,
10.03, 10.05, 10.06, 10.08, 10.09,
10.11, 10.14, 10.17, 10.19, 10.20, 10.22,
10.23, 11.28, 13.13, 21.01, 21.03,
21.04, 22.03, 22.05, 22.06, 24.15,
24.18, 24.25, 24.26, 24.29
Art. 267, first para. ...3.02, 6.08, 10.01, 10.06
Art. 267, third para............ 5.38, 24.15
Art. 267, fourth para.................24.18
Art. 268 ...... 1.09, 2.53, 7.224, 7.226, 9.16,
11.01, 11.02, 11.03, 11.04, 11.05,
11.06, 11.07, 11.08, 11.14, 11.17, 11.20,
11.28, 11.29, 11.31, 11.34, 11.69, 11.86,
11.87, 11.97, 13.11, 16.10, 18.10, 18.27,
19.10, 19.11, 21.11, 24.26, 25.08
Art. 269 .... 2.53, 3.56
Art. 270 ....2.39, 2.54, 7.01, 8.01, 9.15,
9.16, 11.05, 11.86, 18.01, 18.10, 18.27, 25.08
Art. 271 ....7.70
Art. 271(a)........................5.03
Art. 271(a)–(d) 2.53
Art. 271(b) 7.70, 25.06
Art. 271(c).........................7.70
Art. 271(d) 5.03
Art. 272 .... 2.53, 7.15, 11.04, 11.06,
13.03, 13.09, 15.01, 16.30, 19.01,
19.02, 19.03, 19.04, 19.05, 19.07, 19.08,
19.09, 19.10, 19.11, 19.12, 19.13, 19.14,
19.15, 19.17, 19.18, 19.20, 19.21,
19.22, 23.03, 25.35
Art. 273 ......2.53, 5.09, 13.03, 15.01, 19.22,
19.23, 19.24, 19.25, 19.26, 19.27, 21.01
Art 274 .... 1.04, 2.02, 11.06, 19.01,
19.11, 19.12
Art. 275 .... 1.07, 3.02, 5.05, 6.05, 7.04,
11.02, 12.05, 19.03

Art. 276 ....22.05
Art. 277 .... 1.09, 4.10, 5.66, 9.01, 9.02,
9.03, 9.04, 9.05, 9.06, 9.07, 9.08,
9.09, 9.11, 9.15, 9.16, 9.17, 9.18,
10.04, 10.10, 10.11, 25.26
Art. 278 ....11.96, 13.01, 13.02, 13.03,
13.04, 13.07, 13.11, 13.18, 13.44,
16.12, 16.26, 17.08
Art. 278, first sent 13.01
Arts 278–279............. 4.62, 4.64, 16.12
Art. 279 .... 5.70, 11.96, 13.01, 13.02,
13.03, 13.05, 13.07, 13.11, 13.12,
13.18, 13.21, 13.44, 16.26, 17.08
Art. 280 ....11.96, 13.04, 19.21, 21.15,
23.94, 26.08
Art. 281, second para. 1.10, 23.48
Art. 282(3) 11.20
Art. 286(1) 2.50
Art. 287 ....5.14
Art. 287(1)–(3) 5.14
Art. 287(4), fifth para. 6.08
Art. 288 ..... 3.54, 4.40, 4.62, 5.22, 6.08, 7.16,
7.17, 7.108, 7.178, 9.05, 10.09, 10.10, 10.11
Arts. 288–292 .... 6.08, 6.10
Art. 289 ....7.69
Arts 289–291......................9.05
Art. 289(1)–(3) 7.108
Art. 289(3) 7.108
Art. 290 ....7.73, 7.153, 11.96, 13.04
Arts 290–291.....................7.153
Art. 290(1) 7.153
Art. 290(2) 7.153
Art. 291 ....2.50
Art. 291, second para. 2.50, 2.53
Art. 291(2) 7.153
Art. 291(3) 6.08
Art. 294 .... 2.49, 10.06
Art. 296 .... 7.79, 7.158, 7.170, 7.172,
7.206, 11.48, 11.51, 20.12
Art. 297(1) 7.210
Art. 297(2) 7.210, 7.211, 7.213, 9.05
Art. 299.......... 13.04, 19.12, 19.21, 21.15,
23.94, 26.08
Art. 299, fourth para................16.12
Art. 311 ....6.06
Art. 314(3) 8.08
Art. 317 ....5.80
Art. 322 .... 5.80, 6.08
Art. 331.................... 2.50, 8.01
Art. 331, first para. 2.50, 2.53
Art. 335 .... 11.19, 19.01
Art. 339 .... 7.167, 7.170
Art. 340 .... 4.46, 7.224, 7.226, 11.03,
11.67, 11.70, 11.79, 13.11, 16.10,
18.10, 18.27, 19.04
Art. 340, first para. . 19.01, 19.03, 19.14, 19.17
Art. 340, second para. 1.09, 2.53,
9.16, 11.01, 11.04, 11.05, 11.06, 11.07,
11.08, 11.14, 11,17, 11.18, 11.20, 11.21,
11.28, 11.29, 11.31, 11.33, 11.34, 11.44,
11.51, 11.58, 11.69, 11.78, 11.86, 11.87, 11.94,
11.95, 11.97, 19.10, 21.11, 25.08, 25.13

Art. 340, third para. 2.53, 11.20
Art. 340(2) 24.26
Art. 341 . . . . .7.150
Art. 344 . . . . 5.13, 19.27
Art. 346 . . . . 5.28, 8.19
Arts 346–348. . . . . .5.28
Art. 346(1) 23.66
Art. 347 . . . . .5.28
Art. 348 . . . . 5.21, 5.28, 8.19, 23.76
Art. 351 . . . . 5.13, 11.51
Art. 352 . . . . 4.02, 20.02
Art. 355 . . . . 7.151, 21.02, 21.03
Art. 355(1) 3.13
Art. 355(2) 3.13
Art. 355(3) 3.13
Art. 355(4) 3.13
Art. 355(5)(c) 3.13
Protocols annexed to the TEU, TFEU
    and the EAEC Treaty
Protocol (No. 2) on the Application of the
    Principles of Subsidiarity and
    Proportionality [2012]
    O.J. C326/206. . . . . 3.03, 7.80
    Art. 3 . . . . .5.03
    Art. 8, first para. 7.80
    Art. 8, second para. 7.80
Protocol (No. 4) on the Statute of the
    European System of Central Banks and of
    the European Central Bank [2012]
    O.J. C326/230
    Art. 35.3 . . . . .11.20
    Art. 35.4 . . . . .19.14
    Art. 36.2 . . . . .18.09
Protocol (No. 7) on the Privileges and
    Immunities of the European Union [2012]
    O.J. C326/266. . . . . . . 6.04, 11.51, 14.01
    Art. 1 . . . .11.96, 14.01, 14.02, 14.05, 14.06
    Art. 11(a). 11.22
Protocol (No. 21) on the position of the
    UK and Ireland in respect of the AFSJ
    [2012] O.J. C326/295 . . . . .22.05
Protocol (No. 22) on the position of Denmark
    [2012] O.J. C326/299. . . . . .22.05
Protocol (No. 36) on Transitional
    Provisions [2012]
    O.J. C326/322. . . . . . . 5.05, 19.22, 21.13
    Art. 10. . . . . 3.02, 7.04, 11.02, 19.03,
                                        21.13, 22.05
    Art. 10(1) 5.05
    Art. 10(1)–(3) 7.04, 11.02, 22.05
    Art. 10(2) 5.05
    Art. 10(3) 5.05
Protocol (No. 37) on the financial
    consequences of the expiry of the
    ECSC Treaty and on the Research fund
    for Coal and Steel, [2012]
    O.J. C326/328. . . . . 3.04, 5.03
Treaty on Stability, Coordination and
    Governance in the Economic and
    Monetary Union [2012] . . . 5.09, 19.22, 21.01

Agreement on trade-related aspects of
    intellectual property rights (TRIPS)
    [1994] O.J. L336/214 . . . . .6.14
UN Convention on the Law of the Sea
    (UNCLOS) [1998] O.J. L179/3 . . . . . .10.08

UNION MEASURES

Regulations
11 Council Regulation (EEC) of 27 June 1960
    concerning the abolition of discrimination in
    transport rates and conditions, in
    implementation of Art. 79(3) of the Treaty
    establishing the European Economic
    Community (now Art. 95(3) TFEU)
    [1959–1962] O.J. English
    Spec. Ed. I, 60 . . . . .15.01
17 Council Regulation (EEC) of
    6 February 1962: First Regulation
    implementing Arts 85 and 86
    (now Arts 101 and 102) of the
    Treaty [1959–1962] O.J. English
    Spec. Ed 7.30, 7.112
    Art. 2 . . . . .7.139
    Art. 3(2) 7.43, 16.04
    Art. 15(2) 9.08
    Art. 15(6) 7.35, 25.69
    Art. 16(1) 7.31
    Art. 19(1) 8.20
    Art. 19(2) 8.20
    Art. 19(3) 7.35, 7.112
    Art. 20(2) 7.167
99/63/EEC Commission Regulation of
    25 July 1963 on the hearings provided
    for in Article 19(1° and (2) of Council
    Regulation No 17 [1963] O.J. 127/2268;
    [1963–1964] O.J. English Spec.
    Ed. I, 47 . . . . .7.30, 7.43, 8.20, 16.04
259/68 Council Regulation (EEC, Euratom,
    ECSC) of 29 February 1968 laying down the
    Staff Regulations of Officials and the
    Conditions of Employment of Other
    Servants of the European Communities and
    instituting special measures temporarily
    applicable to officials of the Commission
    [1968] O.J. English Spec. Ed. I, 30, as
    reformed by Council Regulation (EC,
    Euratom) No. 723/2004 of 22 March 2004
    amending the Staff Regulations of officials
    of the European Communities and the
    Conditions of Employment of other servants
    of the European Communities [2004]
    O.J. L124/1 ('Staff Regulations') 7.157,
                7.178, 8.06, 15.01, 18.01, 18.02,
                18.04, 18.06, 18.08, 18.14, 18.17,
                                    18.25, 18.27, 25.91
    Art. 90 . . . . .11.05, 18.10, 18.13, 18.18, 18.27
    Arts 90–91 . . . . .11.86

Art. 90c. 18.21
Art. 90(1) 18.13, 18.14, 18.17, 18.18
Art. 90(2) 11.72, 13.27, 18.05, 18.06,
18.13, 18.14, 18.15, 18.16,
18.18, 18.20, 18.21
Art. 91 . . . . .11.05, 18.08, 18.10, 18.13,
18.18, 18.27
Art. 91(1) 18.02, 18.04
Art. 91(2) 18.15
Art. 91(3) 13.27, 18.15, 18.17, 18.25
Art. 91(4) 13.27, 18.24
1408/71 Council Regulation (EEC) of
14 June 1971 on the application of social
security schemes to employed persons
and their families moving within the
Community [1971] O.J. L149/2
([1971] O.J. English Spec. Ed. I,
Vol. II, 416-463) 10.20
337/75 Council Regulation (EEC) of
10 February 1975 establishing a European
Centre for the Development of Vocational
Training [1975] O.J. L39/1 . . . . .11.20
1365/75 Council Regulation (EEC) of
26 May 1975 on the creation of a
European Foundation for the Improvement
of Living and Working Conditions
[1975] O.J. L139/1 . . . . .11.20
3245/81 Council Regulation (EEC) of
26 October 1981 setting up a European
Agency for Cooperation [1981]
O.J. L328/1 . . . . .11.20
288/82 Council Regulation (EEC) of 5 February
1982 on common rules for imports
[1982] O.J. L35/1 . . . . .7.167
857/84 Council Regulation (EEC) of
31 March 1984 adopting general
rules for the application of the levy
referred to in Article 5c of Regulation
(EEC) No. 804/68 in milk and milk
products sector [1984] O.J. L90/13. . . .11.06
2241/87 Council Regulation (EEC) of
23 July 1987 establishing certain control
measures for fishing activities [1987]
O.J. L207/1 . . . . .5.14
4064/89 Council Regulation (EEC) of
21 December 1989 on the control of
concentrations between undertakings [1990]
O.J. L257/13, as amended by Council
Regulation (EC) No. 1310/97 of
30 June 1997 [1997]
O.J. L180/1 . . . . 7.45, 7.93, 7.114, 8.06
Art. 8(5)(b) 7.93
Art. 9 . . . . .7.93
Art. 18(3) 11.51
2187/93 Council Regulation (EEC) of
22 July 1993 providing for an offer
of compensation to certain producers
of milk and milk products [1993]
O.J. L196/5 . . . . .11.06
3605/93 Council Regulation (EC) of
22 November 1993 on the application of the

Protocol on the excessive deficit procedure
annexed to the Treaty establishing the
European Community [1993]
O.J. L332/7 .7.13
40/94 Council Regulation (EC) of
20 December 1993 on the Community
trademark [1994]
O.J. L11/1. . . .2.45, 2.53, 8.11, 16.14, 20.01
2062/94 Council Regulation (EC) of
18 July 1994 establishing a European
Agency for Safety and Health at
Work [1994] O.J. L216/1. . . . . .11.20
2100/94 Council Regulation (EC)
of 27 July 1994 on Community
plant variety rights [1994]
O.J. L227/1, as amended by Council
Regulation (EC) No. 2506/95 of
25 October 1995 [1995]
O.J. L258/3 . . . . .2.45, 2.53, 11.20,
20.01, 20.02, 20.03, 20.04, 20.11,
20.12, 20.18, 20.20, 25.23
2965/94 Council Regulation (EC) of
28 November 1994 setting up a Translation
Centre for bodies of the European
Union [1994] O.J. L314/1 . . . . .11.20
384/96 Council Regulation (EC) of
22 December 1995 on protection against
dumped imports from countries
not members of the European
Community [1996] O.J. L56/1. . . . . . . .7.65
2519/97 Commission Regulation (EC) of 16
December 1997 laying down general rules
for the mobilization of products to be
supplied under Council Regulation (EC)
No. 1292/96 as Community food
aid [1997] O.J. L346/23. . . . . .19.12
447/98 Commission Regulation (EC) of
1 March 1998 on the notifications, time
limits, and hearings provided for in Council
Regulation (EEC) No. 4064/89 on
the control of concentrations between
undertakings [1998] O.J. L61/1 . . . . . .7.45
2532/98 Council Regulation (EC) of
23 November 1998 concerning the
powers of the European Central Bank to
impose sanctions [1998] O.J. L318/4 ..15.01
2842/98 Commission Regulation (EC) of
22 December 1998 on the hearing of
parties in certain proceedings under
Arts 85 and 86 of the EC Treaty
(now Arts 101 and 102 TFEU)
[1998] O.J. L354/18 . . . . 7.30, 8.20
Art. 6 . . . . 7.43, 8.20
659/1999 Council Regulation (EC)
of 22 March 1999 laying down
detailed rules for the application of
Art. 93 of the EC Treaty (now
Art. 108 TFEU) [1999]
O.J. L83/1 . . . . 5.22, 5.24, 7.52
Art. 1(b) 7.53, 7.54, 7.57
Art. 1(c) 7.54

Art. 1(h) 7.60, 7.118, 7.120, 7.123,
                     7.124, 7.129, 8.13
Art. 2(1) 7.54
Art. 3 . . . . .7.54
Art. 4 . . . . 7.55, 7.61
Art. 4(2) 7.54, 7.61
Art. 4(3) 7.54, 7.61, 7.118, 7.202
Art. 4(4) 7.54, 7.57, 7.61, 7.202
Art. 6(1) 7.54, 7.57, 7.61, 7.118,
              7.119, 7.120, 7.128, 7.129, 7.202
Art. 6(2) 7.61
Art. 7.7 . . . . 7.54, 7.55
Art. 7(2) 7.54
Art. 7(3) 7.54
Art. 7(4) 7.54
Art. 7(5) 7.54
Art. 10(1) 7.61
Art. 10(2) 7.59
Art. 10(3) 7.59
Art. 11 . . . . .5.24
Art. 11(1) 7.58
Art. 11(2) 7.58
Art. 12 . . . . .5.24
Art. 13(1) 7.61
Arts 17–19 . . . . .7.53
Art. 19(1) 7.63
Art. 20(1) 7.60
Art. 20(2) 7.60, 7.61, 7.62
Art. 25 . . . . 7.55, 7.61, 7.117
1073/1999 Regulation (EC) of the
    European Parliament and the Council
    of 25 May 1999 concerning investigations
    conducted by the European Anti-Fraud
    Office (OLAF) [1999] O.J. L136/1 . . . . .7.13
1348/2000 Council Regulation (EC) of
    29 May 2000 on the service in the
    Member States of judicial and extrajudicial
    documents in civil or commercial
    matters [2000] O.J. L160/37. . . . . .21.04
44/2001 Council Regulation (EC) of
    22 December 2000 on jurisdiction and the
    recognition and enforcement of judgments
    in civil and commercial matters
    ('Brussels I Regulation') [2001]
    O.J. L12/1 . . . . . . 5.08, 11.20, 21.02, 21.03,
                     21.04, 21.07
45/2001 Regulation (EC) of the European
    Parliament and of the Council of
    18 December 2000 on the protection
    of individuals with regard to the
    processing of personal data by the
    (Union) institutions and bodies and
    on the free movement of such data
    [2001] O.J. L8/1 . . . . .25.64
1049/2001 Regulation (EC) of the European
    Parliament and of the Council of
    30 May 2001 regarding public access to
    European Parliament, Council, and
    Commission documents, [2001]
    O.J. L145/43 . . . . .1.06, 7.14, 7.67,
                     7.135, 18.27

1206/2001 Council Regulation (EC) of
    28 May 2001 on cooperation between the
    courts of the Member States in
    the taking of evidence in civil or
    commercial matter [2001]
    O.J. L174/1 . . . . 3.10, 3.33, 21.04
2580/2001 Council Regulation (EC) of 27
    December 2001 on specific restrictive
    measures directed against certain persons
    and entities with a view to combating
    terrorism [2001] O.J. L344/70 . . . . . . .7.161
6/2002 Council Regulation (EC) of
    12 December 2001 on Community
    designs [2002] O.J. L3/1 . . . . 2.45, 2.53,
                     20.01, 20.02, 20.03, 20.04,
                  20.11, 20.12, 20.18, 20.20, 25.23
1406/2002 Regulation (EC) of the European
    Parliament and of the Council of
    27 June 2002 establishing a European
    Maritime Safety Agency [2002]
    O.J. L208/1 .11.20
1/2003 Council Regulation (EC) of
    16 December 2002 on the
    implementation of the rules laid down in
    Arts 81 and 82 of the Treaty [2003]
    O.J. L1/1 . . . . 3.11, 7.30, 7.35, 7.43,
                     8.20, 9.08, 15.01
Art. 2 . . . . .7.190
Art. 7 . . . . .7.43, 7.86
Art. 7(2) 7.43, 16.04
Art. 8 . . . . .13.05
Art. 8(1) 7.39
Art. 9 . . . . .7.35
Art. 9(1) 7.40, 7.112
Art. 10 . . . . 7.35, 7.112
Art. 11(6). 3.11
Art. 14(1) 7.159
Art. 18(1) 7.31
Art. 18(2) 7.31
Art. 18(3) 7.31
Art. 20 . . . . .7.32
Art. 20(3) 7.32
Art. 20(4) 7.32
Art. 20(7) 7.32
Art. 20(8) 7.32
Art. 21(1) 7.32
Art. 21(3) 7.32
Art. 23(1)(a) 7.31
Art. 23(1)(b) 7.31
Art. 23(1)(e) 7.33
Art. 23(2)(a) 7.194
Art. 24 . . . . .7.41
Art. 24(1) 7.31
Art. 27 . . . . 7.161, 7.167
Art. 27(2) 7.43
Art. 27(4) 7.35
Art. 28 . . . . .7.167
Art. 31 . . . . 7.195, 15.01
2004/2003 Regulation (EC) of the
    European Parliament and of the Council of
    4 November 2003 on the regulations

governing political parties at European level
and the rules regarding their funding
[2003] O.J. L297/1 . . . . .7.92
2201/2003 Council Regulation (EC) of
27 November 2003 concerning jurisdiction
and the recognition and enforcement of
judgments in matrimonial matters and the
matters of parental responsibility, repealing
Regulation (EC) No. 1347/2000
('Brussels IIbis Regulation') [2003]
O.J. L338/1 . . . . 21.04, 21.07
139/2004 Council Regulation (EC) of
20 January 2004 on the control of
concentrations between undertakings
('Merger Regulation') [2004]
O.J. L 24/1 . . . . 7.45, 7.46, 7.50, 7.93,
7.114, 7.196, 7.199, 8.06, 15.01
Art. 6(1)(c) 7.47
Art. 6(2) 7.51
Art. 8(1) 7.48
Art. 8(1)–(3) 7.46
Art. 8(2) 7.48, 7.51
Art. 9 . . . . 7.50, 7.116
Art. 9(3) 7.50, 7.116
Art. 16 . . . . .15.01
Art. 18 . . . . 7.115, 7.161
Art. 18(4) 7.114
Art. 21(4) 7.46
723/2004 Council Regulation
(EC, Euratom) of 22 March 2004
amending the Staff Regulations of officials of
the European Communities and the
Conditions of Employment of other
servants of the European Communities
[2004] OJ L124/1 . . . . .15.01
726/2004 Regulation (EC) of the European
Parliament and of the Council of
31 March 2004 laying down Community
procedures for the authorization and
supervision of medicinal products for human
and veterinary use and establishing a
European Medicines Agency [2004]
O.J. L136/1 .11.20
773/2004 Commission Regulation (EC) of
7 April 2004 relating to the conduct of
proceedings by the Commission pursuant to
Arts 81 and 82 of the EC Treaty
(now Arts 101 and 102 TFEU)
[2004] O.J. L123/18 . . . . . 7.30, 8.20, 16.04
Art. 2 . . . . .7.34
Art. 5 . . . . .7.86
Art. 7 . . . . 7.43, 8.20
Art. 7(1) 7.43
Art. 7(2) 7.43, 8.20
Art. 7(3) 8.20
Art. 8(1) 7.43
Art. 10 . . . . .7.34
Art. 15 . . . . .7.36
Form C 8.20
794/2004 Commission Regulation (EC)
of 21 April 2004 implementing

Council Regulation (EC) No. 659/1999
laying down detailed rules for the
application of Art. 93 of the EC
Treaty (now Art. 108 TFEU)
[2004] O.J. L140/1 . . . . .7.52
802/2004 Commission Regulation (EC)
of 7 April 2004 implementing Council
Regulation (EC) No. 139/2004 on the
control of concentrations between
undertakings [2004] O.J. L133/1,
as amended by Commission
Regulation (EC) No. 1033/2008
[2008] O.J. L279/3 . . . . .7.45
Art. 11(c), second indent 7.115
Art. 20 . . . . .7.51
1756/2006 Council Regulation
(EC) of 28 November 2006
amending Regulation (EC)
No. 2667/2000 on the European
Agency for Reconstruction [2006]
O.J. L332/18 .7.70
1891/2006 Council Regulation (EC) of
18 December 2006 amending Regulations
(EC) No. 6/2002 and (EC) No. 40/94 to
give effect to the accession of the European
Community to the Geneva Act of the
Hague Agreement concerning the
international registration of industrial
designs [2006] OJ L386/14 . . . . .20.01
1907/2006 Regulation (EC) of the European
Parliament and of the Council concerning the
Registration, Evaluation, Authorisation and
Restriction of Chemicals (REACH),
establishing a European Chemicals Agency,
amending Directive 1999/45/EC and
repealing Council Regulation (EEC) No.
793/93 and Commission Regulation (EC)
No. 1488/94, as well as Council
Directive 76/769/EEC and Commission
Directives 91/155/EEC, 93/67/EEC,
93/105/EC, and 2000/21/EC [2006]
O.J. L396/1 .11.20
1920/2006 Regulation (EC) of the European
Parliament and of the Council of
12 December 2006 on the European
Monitoring Centre for Drugs and Drugs
Addiction (recast) [2006] O.J. L376/1 . . . 11.20
168/2007 Council Regulation (EC) of
15 February 2007 establishing a European
Union Agency for Fundamental Rights
[2007] O.J. L53/1 . . . . .11.20
864/2007 Regulation (EC) of 11 July 2007
adopted by the European Parliament and
Council on the law applicable to
non-contractual obligations
('Rome II Regulation') [2007]
O.J. L199/40 . . . . .21.03
1393/2007 Regulation (EC) of the European
Parliament and of the Council of
13 November 2007 on the service in the
Member States of judicial and extrajudicial

documents in civil or commercial
matters, and repealing Council
Regulation (EC) No. 1348/2000
[2007] O.J. L324/79 . . . . 21.04, 21.07
15/2008 Council Regulation (EC) of
20 December 2007 amending
Regulation (EC) No. 2100/94 as
regards the entitlement to file an
application for a Community plant
variety right [2008] O.J. L8/2 . . . . .20.01
216/2008 Regulation (EC) of the European
Parliament and of the Council of
20 February 2008 on common rules
in the field of civil aviation and
establishing a European Aviation
Safety Agency, and repealing Council
Directive 91/670/EEC, Regulation (EC)
No. 1592/2002 and Directive 2004/36/EC
[2008] O.J. L79/1 . . . . .15.01
450/2008 Regulation (EC) of the European
Parliament and of the Council of
23 April 2008 laying down the
Community Customs Code [2008]
O.J. L145/1, ...11.29
593/2008 Regulation (EC) of the European
Parliament and of the Council of
17 June 2008 on the law applicable to
contractual obligations
('Rome I Regulation') [2008]
O.J. L177/6 . . . . . 19.16, 21.03, 21.04, 21.07
622/2008 Commission Regulation
(EC) of 30 June 2008 as regards
the conduct of settlement procedures in
cartel cases [2008] O.J. L171/3 . . . . .7.30
1339/2008 Regulation (EC) of the European
Parliament and of the Council of 16
December 2008 establishing a
European Training Foundation (recast)
[2008] O.J. L354/82 . . . . .11.20
4/2009 Council Regulation (EC) of
18 December 2008 on jurisdiction,
applicable law, recognition and enforcement
of decisions and cooperation in matters
relating to maintenance obligations
[2009] O.J. L7/1 . . . . .21.04
80/2009 Regulation (EC) of the European
Parliament and of the Council of 14 January
2009 on a Code of Conduct for computerised
reservation systems and repealing Council
Regulation (EEC) No. 2299/89 [2009]
OJ L35/47 . . . . .15.01
207/2009 Council Regulation (EC) of
26 February 2009 on the Community
trademark (codified version) [2009]
O.J. L78/1 . . . . .2.45, 2.53, 11.20,
20.01, 20.02, 20.03, 20.04, 20.05, 20.06,
20.07, 20.11, 20.12, 20.13, 20.14,
20.15, 20.16, 20.17, 20.18, 20.20, 25.23
391/2009 Regulation (EC) of the European
Parliament and of the Council of
23 April 2009 on common rules and

standards for ship inspection and survey
organisations [2009] O.J. L131/11 . . . .15.01
401/2009 Regulation (EC) of the
European Parliament and of the Council on
the European Environment Agency and
the European Environment Information
and Observation Network (codified
version) [2009] O.J. L126/13 . . . . .11.20
1125/2009 Commission Regulation (EC) of
23 November 2009 amending Regulation
(EC) No 794/2004 implementing
Council Regulation (EC) No 659/1999
laying down detailed rules for the application
of Article 93 of the EC Treaty, as regards
Part III.2, Part III.3 and Part III.7
of its Annex I [2009] O.J. L308/5 . . . . . .7.52
1225/2009 Council Regulation (EC) of 30
November 2009 on protection against
dumped imports from countries not
members of the European Community
[2009] O.J. L343/51 . . . . .7.65, 7.130,
7.132, 7.161, 7.166, 7.167
1080/2010 Regulation (EU, Euratom)
of the European Parliament and of
the Council of 24 November 2010
amending the Staff Regulations of
Officials of the European Communities
and the Conditions of Employment
of Other Servants of those
Communities [2010] OJ L311/1 . . . . . .18.01
182/2011 Regulation (EU) of the European
Parliament and of the Council of
16 February 2011 laying down the
rules and the general principles
concerning mechanisms for control by
Member States of the Commission's exercise of
implementing powers ('Comitology
Regulation') [2011]
O.J. L55/13 . . . . 6.08, 7.159
513/2011 Regulation (EU) of the
European Parliament and of the
Council of 11 May 2011 amending
Regulation (EC) No. 1060/2009 on credit
rating agencies [2011]
O.J. L145/30 . . . . .15.01
1173/2011 Regulation (EU) of the European
Parliament and of the Council of
16 November 2011 on the effective
enforcement of budgetary surveillance
in the euro area [2011] O.J. L306/1 . . .15.01
648/2012 Regulation (EU) of the European
Parliament and of the Council of
4 July 2012 on OTC derivatives, central
counterparties and trade repositories
[2012] O.J. L201/1 . . . . .15.01
741/2012 Regulation (EU, Euratom) of the
European Parliament and of the Council
amending the Protocol on the Statute of the
Court of Justice of the European
Union and Annex I thereto [2012]
O.J. L228/1 . . . . 2.08, 2.27

979/2012 Regulation (EU, Euratom) of the European Parliament and of the Council of 25 October 2012 relating to temporary Judges of the European Union Civil Service Tribunal [2012] O.J. L303/83 .2.38

1215/2012 Regulation (EU) of the European Parliament and of the Council of 12 December 2012 on jurisdiction and the recognition and enforcement of judgments in civil and commercial matters [2012] O.J. L351/1 . . . . 5.08, 11.20, 21.02

216/2013 Council Regulation (EU) of 7 March 2013 on the electronic publication of the Official Journal of the European Union [2013] O.J. L69/1 . . .23.30

Directives

77/388/EEC Council Directive of 17 May 1977 on the harmonization of the laws of the Member States relating to turnover taxes—Common system of value added tax: uniform basis of assessment ('Sixth VAT Directive') [1977] O.J. L145/1 . . . . 3.33, 3.36

83/189/EEC Council Directive of 28 March 1983 laying down a procedure for the provision of information in the field of technical standards and regulations [1983] O.J. L109/8 . . . 4.36, 5.41

85/337/EEC Council Directive of 27 June 1985 on the assessment of the effects of certain public and private projects on the environment [1985] O.J. L175/40 .4.18

85/577/EEC Council Directive to protect the consumer in respect of contracts negotiated away from business premises ('Doorstep Selling Directive') [1985] O.J. L372/31 . . . . .4.41

87/102/EEC Council Directive of 22 December 1986 for the approximation of the laws, regulations, and administrative provisions of the Member States concerning consumer credit ("old" Consumer Credit Directive') [1987] O.J. L42/48 . . . . .4.41

89/552/EEC Council Directive of 3 October 1989 on the coordination of certain provisions laid down by law, regulation or administrative action in the Member States concerning the pursuit of television broadcasting activities ('Television-without-frontiers directive') [1989] O.J. L298/23 . . . . . . .7.95

89/665/EEC Council Directive of 21 December 1989 on the coordination of the laws, regulations, and administrative provisions relating to the application of review procedures to the award of public supply and public works contracts [1989] O.J. L395/33 . . . . 5.29, 5.30

92/13/EEC Council Directive of 25 February 1992 coordinating the laws, regulations, and administrative provisions relating to the application of Community rules on the procurement procedures of entities operating in the water, energy, transport, and telecommunications sector [1992] O.J. L76/14 . . . . 5.29, 5.30

92/83/EEC Council Directive of 19 October 1992 on the harmonization of the structures of excise duties on alcohol and alcoholic beverages [1992] O.J. L316/21 .5.20

93/13/EEC Council Directive of 5 April 1993 on unfair terms in consumer contracts [1993] O.J. L95/29 . . . . 4.40, 4.41, 6.26

93/104/EC Council Directive of 23 November 1993 concerning certain aspects of the organization of working time ('Working Time Directive') [1993] O.J. L307/18. . .4.52

95/46/EC Directive of the European Parliament and the Council of 24 October 1995 on the protection of individuals with regard to the processing of personal data and on the free movement of such data [1995] O.J. L281/31. . . . . 21.11

96/62/EC Council Directive of 27 September 1996 on ambient air quality assessment and management, as amended by Regulation (EC) No. 1882/2003 of the European Parliament and of the Council of 29 September 2003 . . . . .4.18

96/71/EC Directive of the European Parliament and the Council of 16 December 1996 concerning the posting of workers in the framework of the provision of services [1997] O.J. L18/1 . . . . .3.32

98/34/EC Directive of the European Parliament and the Council of 22 June 1998 laying down a procedure for the provision of information in the field of technical standards and regulations [1998] O.J. L204/37 . . . . .5.41

2007/66/EC Directive of the European Parliament and the Council of 11 December 2007 amending Council Directives 89/665/EEC and 92/13/EEC with regard to improving the effectiveness of review procedures concerning the award of public contracts [2007] O.J. L335/31 .5.29

2008/48/EC Directive of the European Parliament and of the Council of 23 April 2008 on credit agreements for consumers and repealing Council Directive 87/102/EEC [2008] O.J. L133/66 .4.41

2011/83/EU Directive of the European
Parliament and of the Council of
25 October 2011 on consumer rights
('Consumer Rights Directive') [2011]
O.J. L304/64 . . . . 4.40, 4.41, 6.26

Decisions

88/591/ECSC, EEC, Euratom Council
Decision of 24 October 1988 establishing
a Court of First Instance of the European
Communities [1988]
O.J. L319/1 . . .2.35, 2.45, 2.53, 16.02, 18.09
93/350/Euratom, ECSC, EEC Council
Decision of 8 June 1993 amending Council
Decision 88/591/ECSC, EEC, Euratom
establishing a Court of First Instance
of the European Communities
[1993] O.J. L144/21 . . . . 2.35, 2.45
93/731/EC Council Decision of
20 December 1993 on public access to
Council documents [1993]
O.J. L340/43. . . . . .1.06
94/149/ECSC, EC Council Decision of 7 March
1994 amending Decision 93/350/Euratom,
ECSC, EEC amending Decision
88/591/ECSC, EEC, Euratom establishing a
Court of First Instance of the European
Communities [1994]
O.J. L66/29 . . . . 2.35, 2.45
94/810/ECSC/EC Commission
Decision of 12 December 1994 on the terms
of reference of hearing officers in competition
procedures before the Commission
[1994] O.J. L330/67 . . . . .7.38
1999/291/EC, ECSC, Euratom Council
Decision of 26 April 1999 amending Decision
88/591/ECSC, EEC, Euratom establishing a
Court of First Instance of the European
Communities to enable it to give decisions in
cases when constituted by a single judge
[1999] O.J. L114/52 . . . . .2.29
1999/352/EC, ECSC, Euratom Commission
Decision of 28 April 1999 establishing the
European Anti-fraud Office (OLAF)
[1999] O.J. L136/20 . . . . .11.20
1999/494/EC, ECSC, Euratom Council
Decision of 9 July 1999 on the referral of
the case of Mr Bangemann to the Court
of Justice [1999] O.J. L192/55 . . . . . . .18.01
2001/462/EC, ECSC Commission Decision
of 23 May 2001 on the terms of reference
of hearing officers in certain competition
proceedings [2001] O.J. L162/21 . . . . . .7.38
2002/584/JHA Council Framework Decision
of 13 June 2002 on the European arrest
warrant and the surrender procedures
between Member States [2002]
O.J. L190/1 .21.05
2002/620/EC Decision of the European
Parliament, the Council, the
Commission, the Court of Justice, the

Court of Auditors, the Economic and
Social Committee, the Committee of
the Regions, and the European Ombudsman
of 25 July 2002 establishing a European
Communities Personnel Selection
Office [2002] O.J. L197/53 . . . . 7.71, 25.08
2004/258/EC Decision of the European
Central Bank of 4 March 2004 on
public access to European Central
Bank documents [2004]
O.J. L80/42 .7.67
2004/407/EC, Euratom Council
Decision of 26 April 2004 amending
Arts 51 and 54 of the Protocol on the
Statute of the Court of Justice [2004]
O.J. L132/5 . . . . .2.36, 2.49, 2.55, 19.07
2004/752/EC, Euratom Council
Decision establishing the European
Union Civil Service Tribunal
[2004] O.J. L333/7 . . . . 2.03, 2.38,
2.39, 2.43, 18.01
2005/49/EC, Euratom Council Decision
of 18 January 2005 concerning the
operating rules of the committee
provided for in Art. 3(3) of Annex I
to the Protocol on the Statute of the
Court of Justice [2005] O.J. L21/13 . . . .2.39
2005/150/EC, Euratom Council Decision
concerning the conditions and
arrangements governing the
submission and processing of applications
for appointment as a Judge of the
European Union Civil Service
Tribunal [2005] O.J. L50/7 . . . . .2.38
2005/370/EC Council Decision of
17 February 2005 on the conclusion,
on behalf of the European Community,
of the Convention on access to information,
public participation in decision-making,
and access to justice in environmental
matters [2005] O.J. L124/1 . . . . .4.18
2005/577/EC, Euratom Council Decision
appointing Judges of the European
Union Civil Service Tribunal [2005]
O.J. L197/28 . . . . .2.38
2006/325/EC Council Decision of
27 April 2006 concerning the
conclusion of the Agreement between the
European Community and the Kingdom of
Denmark on jurisdiction and the
recognition and enforcement of judgments in
civil and commercial matters [2006]
O.J. L120/22 . . . . .21.02
2008/79/EC, Euratom Council Decision of
20 December 2007 amending the
Protocol on the Statute of the Court
of Justice [2008] O.J. L24/44 . . 22.11, 22.14
2009/26/EC Commission Decision of
22 December 2008 on the request from
the United Kingdom to accept Regulation
(EC) No. 593/2008 of the European

Parliament and the Council on the law
applicable to contractual obligations ('Rome
I Regulation') [2009] O.J. L10/22 . . . . .21.03
2009/371/JHA Council Decision of
6 April 2009 establishing the European
Police Office (Europol) [2009]
O.J. L121/37 . . . . 11.20, 21.05
2009/426/JHA Council Decision of
16 December 2008 on the strengthening of
Eurojust and amending Decision
2002/187/JHA setting up Eurojust with
a view to reinforcing the fight
against serious crime [2009]
O.J. L138/14 . . . . .11.20
2009/917/JHA Council Decision of
30 November 2009 on the use of
information technology for customs
purposes [2009] O.J. L323/20. . . . . . . .21.05
2009/937/EU Council Decision of
1 December 2009 adopting the
Council's Rules of Procedure [2009]
O.J. L325/35 . . . . .7.168
2010/124/EU Council Decision of
25 February 2010 relating to the
operating rules of the panel provided for in
Article 255 of the Treaty on the
Functioning of the European Union
[2010] O.J. L50/1 . . . . .2.04
2011/411/CFSP Council Decision of
12 July 2011 defining the statute, seat,
and operational rules of the European
Defence Agency and repealing Joint Action
2004/551/CFSP [2011]
O.J. L183/16 . . . . 6.10, 11.20
2011/695/EU Commission Decision of
13 October 2011 on the function and
terms of reference of the hearing officer in
certain competition proceedings [2011]
O.J. L275/29 . . . . .7.38
2012/671/EU Decision of the Court of
Justice of 23 October 2012 concerning the
judicial functions of the Vice-President
of the Court [2012]
O.J. L300/47 . . . . 2.08, 2.18, 13.23
2013/181/EU Council Decision drawing
up a list of three temporary Judges for
the Civil Service Tribunal [2013]
O.J. L111/49 . . . . .2.39
2013/336/EU Council Decision of
25 June 2013, increasing the number of
Advocates-General of the Court of
Justice of the European Union [2013]
O.J. L179/92 . . . . .2.04

PROCEDURAL TEXTS OF THE
UNION COURTS

Statute of the Court of Justice of the
European Union [2012] O.J. C326/210, as
amended by Regulation (EU, Euratom)
No 741/2012 of the European Parliament
and of the Council of 11 August 2012
[2012] O.J. L 228/1, and by Article 9
of the act concerning the conditions of
accession to the European Union of the
Republic of Croatia and the adjustments
to the Treaty on European Union, the
Treaty on the Functioning of the European
Union and the Treaty establishing the
European Atomic Energy Community
[2012] O.J. L 112/21 . 1.10, 2.15, 2.23, 2.48,
2.55, 14.02, 17.07, 21.12, 22.06, 22.19,
23.26, 23.87, 25.15
Art. 2 . . . . 2.06, 2.25
Arts 2–7 . . . . .2.06
Arts 2–8 . . . . .2.25
Art. 3 . . . . .2.06
Art. 4 . . . . .2.06
Art. 6 . . . . .2.06
Art. 6, first para. 2.25
Art. 7 . . . . 2.07, 2.23
Arts 7–8 . . . . .2.05
Art. 7(2) 23.01
Art. 8 . . . . .2.06
Art. 9 . . . . .2.04
Art. 9a. 2.07, 2.08, 2.27
Art. 9a, second para. 2.15
Art. 10 . . . . .2.09
Art. 16 . . . . 2.10, 2.12
Art. 16, first para. 2.10
Art. 16, first, second and third paras 2.10
Art. 16, first para. 2.10
Art. 16, second para. 2.10, 2.29
Art. 16, third para. 2.12, 2.13
Art. 16, fourth para. 2.10, 2.12
Art. 16, fifth para. 2.10
Art. 17, first para. 2.05, 2.31
Art. 17, second para. 2.31
Art. 17, fourth para. 2.11, 2.31
Art. 17, fifth para. 2.11
Art. 18 . . . . 2.12, 2.29
Art. 19 . . . . .23.17
Art. 19, first para. 23.14, 23.16
Art. 19, second para. 23.14, 23.16
Art. 19, third para. 23.14, 23.17
Art. 19, fourth para. 23.14, 23.16, 23.17
Art. 19, seventh para. 25.20
Art. 20 . . . . .23.39
Art. 20, second para. 24.09
Art. 20, fifth para. 2.15, 23.56
Art. 21 . . . . 5.52, 8.07, 23.66, 25.17
Art. 21, first para. 25.02
Art. 21, second para. 8.21, 25.21
Art. 23 . . . . 3.09, 3.16, 3.22, 3.23,
3.25, 3.26, 3.27, 3.29, 3.41, 3.55,
3.59, 6.19, 6.20, 6.21, 6.22, 6.31, 10.13,
10.15, 17.06, 17.07, 22.06, 22.13,
22.14, 22.15, 22.19, 23.39, 23.46,
23.47, 23.62, 23.74, 23.75, 23.88,
23.90, 23.91, 24.14, 24.15, 24.19,
24.23, 24.25, 24.28, 24.32

Art. 23, first para. 24.06, 24.07
Art. 23, second para. 24.09
Art. 23, second–fourth paras 24.09
Art. 23, third para. 24.07, 24.09
Art. 23, fourth para. 24.09
Art. 23a. 22.06, 22.07, 22.19
Art. 23a, first para. 24.20
Art. 23a, second para. 22.14, 24.09
Art. 23a, third para. 22.14
Art. 24 . . . . 3.55, 3.59, 10.13, 23.62,
23.64, 23.66, 24.07
Art. 25 . . . . 2.13, 23.64
Art. 28 . . . . .23.65
Art. 29 . . . . .23.71
Art. 30 . . . . .23.67
Art. 31 . . . . 5.28, 23.67, 23.76
Art. 36 . . . . .23.88
Art. 37 . . . . .23.91
Art. 39 . . . . .2.17
Art. 39, first para. 2.18, 13.23, 13.24
Art. 39, second para. 2.18
Art. 39, third para. 13.15
Art. 40 . . . . 7.82, 20.11, 24.12, 25.61
Art. 40, first para. 25.61, 25.62
Art. 40, second para. 16.15, 18.10,
25.61, 25.62, 25.63, 25.64, 25.65
Art. 40, third para. 25.61, 25.63
Art. 40, fourth para. 25.59, 25.60
Art. 41 . . . . .25.32
Arts 41–44 . . . . 6.28, 24.31
Art. 42 . . . . 25.107, 25.108, 25.127
Art. 43 . . . . 25.125, 25.126, 25.127
Art. 44 . . . . .13.44, 23.26, 25.116, 25.117,
25.119, 26.01
Art. 44, third para. 23.26, 25.121
Art. 45 . . . . .24.10
Art. 45, first para. 23.32
Art. 45, second para. 23.38
Art. 46 . . . . 11.86, 11.87, 11.94, 23.32
Art. 47, first para. 2.31
Art. 47, second para. 2.28
Art. 48 . . . . 2.23, 2.33
Art. 49 . . . . .2.24
Art. 49, third para. 2 24
Art. 50 . . . . .2.29
Art. 50, first para. 2.28, 2.29
Art. 50, second para. 2.29
Art. 50, third para. 2.29
Art. 51 . . . . 2.36, 2.50, 2.51, 2.53, 5.04,
7.01, 7.82, 8.01, 11.04, 15.05,
19.07, 20.02
Art. 52 . . . . .2.34
Art. 53 . . . . .11.34
Art. 53, first para. 23.39
Art. 54 . . .2.54, 2.55, 7.01, 23.46, 23.86, 25.112
Art. 54, first para. 2.54
Art. 54, second para. 2.54, 2.55
Art. 54, third para. 2.55
Art. 54, fourth para. 2.55
Art. 55 . . . . 16.16, 23.24
Arts 55–61 . . . . .26.01

Art. 56 . . . . 16.12, 17.01, 23.26
Art. 56, first para. 16.12, 16.25, 26.02
Art. 56, second para. 16.14, 16.15
Art. 56, third para. 16.16
Art. 57, first para. . . .2.18, 16.12, 16.15, 16.25
Art. 57, second para. 13.46, 16.12, 16.29
Art. 57, third para. 13.46
Art. 58 . . . . .16.18
Art. 58, first para. 16.02, 16.18
Art. 58, second para. 16.13
Art. 59 . . . . .26.07
Art. 59, first sent 26.01
Art. 60 . . . . 13.14, 16.26
Art. 60, first para. 11.96, 16.26, 23.93
Art. 60, second para. 16.26
Art. 61 . . . . 13.46, 16.29, 17.02
Art. 61, first para. 16.29
Art. 61, second para. 16.32
Art. 61, third para. 16.32
Art. 62 . . . . 17.04, 17.05, 17.06
Art. 62, first para. 17.01
Art. 62a. 2.38, 17.06
Art. 62a, first para. 17.07
Art. 62a, second para. 17.07
Art. 62a, third para. 17.07
Art. 62b, first para. 17.08, 17.09
Art. 62b, second para. 17.08, 17.09
Art. 62c. 2.38
Art. 62c, first para. 2.38
Art. 62c, second para. 2.38
Art. 64 . . . . 1.10, 2.48
Annex 2.38
Annex I. 2.38, 2.41, 2.43, 18.01
Annex I, Art. 1 . . . . .2.39
Annex I, Art. 2 . . . . 2.38, 2.39
Annex I, Art. 2, second para. 2.39
Annex I, Art. 3(1) 2.39
Annex I, Art. 3(3) 2.39
Annex I, Art. 3(4) 2.39
Annex I, Art. 4 . . . . .2.40
Annex I, Art. 4(1) 2.40
Annex I, Art. 4(2) 2.42
Annex I, Art. 4(3) 2.42
Annex I, Art. 5 . . . . .2.39
Annex I, Art. 6(1) 2.41
Annex I, Art. 6(2) 2.41
Annex I, Art. 7 . . . . .23.39
Annex I, Art. 7(1) 2.43
Annex I, Art. 7(3) 2.43
Annex I, Art. 7(4) 2.43
Annex I, Art. 7(5) 18.29, 25.97
Annex I, Art. 8 . . . . .2.54
Annex I, Art. 8(1) 2.54
Annex I, Art. 8(2) 2.54
Annex I, Art. 8(3) 2.55
Annex I, Art. 9 . . . . 2.44, 16.01, 18.30
Annex I, Arts 9–13. . . . . .26.01
Annex I, Art. 10. . . . . .18.30
Annex I, Art. 10(2)–(3) 13.23, 13.46
Annex I, Art. 10(3) 13.23, 13.46
Annex I, Art. 11. . . . . 2.44, 17.01

Annex I, Art. 12(1) 13.14, 23.93
Annex I, Art. 13. . . . . .2.44
Annex I, Art. 13(1) 16.29, 17.02
Rules of Procedure of the Court
  of Justice ('ECJ Rules of Procedure')
  [2012] O.J. C337/1 . . . . .1.09, 1.10,
      2.15, 2.18, 2.19, 13.07, 17.05,
    21.12, 21.13, 22.06, 22.19, 23.01,
  23.02, 23.03, 23.05, 23.24, 23.26, 23.33,
  23.43, 23.63, 23.64, 23.72, 23.77, 23.87,
  23.88, 24.15, 24.17, 24.27, 24.34, 25.03,
  25.18, 25.60, 25.80, 25.81, 25.92, 25.101,
      25.116, 25.125, 25.130, 25.134,
          26.04, 26.08, 26.09
Title II 26.08
Art. 1(2)(a) 25.127
Art. 1(2)(c) 24.09
Art. 6 . . . . .7.168
Art. 8(1) 2.07
Art. 8(2) 2.07
Art. 8(3) 2.07
Art. 8(4) 2.08
Art. 8(5) 2.08
Art. 9 . . . . .2.17
Art. 9(1) 2.18
Art. 9(3) 2.18
Art. 10(1) 2.18
Art. 10(2) 2.18
Art. 10(3) 2.08, 2.18, 13.23
Art. 11(2) 2.10
Art. 11(5) 2.10
Art. 12(1) 2.10
Art. 12(2) 2.10
Art. 12(4) 2.10
Art. 13 . . . . .2.07
Art. 14(1) 2.15, 17.01
Art. 15(1) 2.15, 2.29
Art. 16(1) 2.15
Art. 16(6) 25.26
Art. 18 . . . . .2.09
Art. 18(2) 2.09
Art. 18(4) 2.09
Art. 18(5) 2.09
Art. 18(7) 2.09
Art. 18(8) 2.09
Art. 19 . . . . .2.09
Art. 20 . . . . .2.19
Art. 20(1) 25.26
Art. 21 . . . . .2.19
Art. 21(1) 23.51
Art. 21(4) 16.15, 24.02, 25.70,
          25.108, 26.08
Art. 24(6) 23.31
Art. 25 . . . . .2.29
Art. 27 . . . . .2.10
Art. 27(5) 2.10
Art. 28 . . . . .2.10
Art. 28(2) 22.10
Art. 28(4) 2.10
Art. 29(2) 2.12

Art. 32(1) 2.13
Art. 32(2) 2.13
Art. 32(3) 2.13
Art. 32(4) 2.13
Art. 33 . . . . .2.13
Art. 36 . . . . 2.19, 23.02, 24.09
Art. 37 . . . . .23.90
Art. 37(1)(a) 23.03
Art. 37(1)(b) 23.03
Art. 37(1)(c) 23.03
Art. 37(2)(a) 23.03, 26.01
Art. 37(2)(a)–(c) 23.03
Art. 37(2)(b) 17.06, 23.03
Art. 37(2)(c) 23.03
Art. 37(3) 23.03, 24.28
Art. 37(4) 23.03
Art. 38(1) 23.05, 23.89, 24.28
Art. 38(2) 23.05
Art. 38(3) 23.05
Art. 38(4) 23.03, 23.08, 24.28, 25.73
Art. 38(4)–(5) 23.08
Art. 38(5) 23.08
Art. 38(5)–(6) 24.28
Art. 38(7) 23.02, 23.06
Art. 38(8) 23.07
Art. 39 . . . . 2.19, 23.09
Art. 40 . . . . .23.12
Art. 41 . . . . .23.10
Art. 42 . . . . .23.13
Art. 43 . . . . .23.43
Art. 43(1) 23.20
Art. 43(2) 23.21
Art. 44(1)(a) 23.16, 23.22
Art. 44(1)(b) 23.22
Art. 44(1)(b)–(c) 23.17
Art. 44(1)(c) 23.14, 23.22
Art. 45(1) 23.22
Art. 45(2) 23.22
Art. 46(1) 23.51
Art. 46(1)–(2) 23.23
Art. 46(2) 23.86
Art. 46(3) 23.23
Art. 46(4) 23.23
Art. 47(1) 23.17, 25.20
Art. 47(2) 23.14
Art. 48 . . . . 25.26, 26.02
Art. 48(1) 23.24
Art. 48(2) 23.24
Art. 48(3) 23.24
Art. 48(4) 23.25
Art. 49 . . . . .26.08
Art. 49(1)(a) 7.213, 23.29
Art. 49(1)(b) 23.33
Art. 49(1)(c) 23.33
Art. 49(1)(d) 23.31
Art. 49(1)(e) 23.31
Art. 49(2) 23.33
Art. 50 . . . . 7.210, 23.30
Art. 51 . . . . 16.25, 23.32
Art. 52 . . . . .23.26

Art. 53(1) 23.39
Art. 53(2) 3.26, 3.31, 23.40, 24.15,
           25.42, 25.45, 25.131
Art. 53(3) 23.41
Art. 53(4) 23.42
Art. 53(5) 23.42
Art. 54(1) 23.43
Art. 54(2) 23.43
Art. 55(1)(a) 23.46
Art. 55(1)(b) 23.46
Art. 55(2) 23.46
Art. 55(3) 23.46
Art. 55(4) 23.47
Art. 55(5) 23.47
Art. 55(6) 23.47
Art. 55(7) 23.47
Art. 56 . . . . .23.48
Art. 57 . . . . 23.51, 25.03, 25.31, 25.47
Art. 57(1) 23.51, 23.52, 25.03
Art. 57(2) 23.52
Art. 57(3) 23.52
Art. 57(4) 23.52, 23.53, 25.18, 25.57
Art. 57(5) 23.53
Art. 57(6) 23.36, 23.56
Art. 57(7) . . . 16.25, 23.37, 23.49, 23.50, 23.54
Art. 57(8) 23.54
Art. 58 . . . . .25.56
Arts 59–60 . . . . .2.29
Art. 58 . . . . .23.55
Art. 59(1) 23.56
Art. 59(2) 23.56
Art. 59(3) 23.56
Art. 60(1) 2.10, 2.12
Art. 60(2) 2.10, 2.12
Art. 60(3) 2.12
Art. 60(4) 23.56, 23.73
Art. 61 . . . . .23.62
Arts 61–62 . . . . 23.58, 24.23
Art. 61(1) 23.62
Art. 61(2) 23.62
Art. 62 . . . . .23.62
Art. 62(1) 23.56, 23.62
Art. 62(2) 23.62
Art. 63 . . . . .23.64
Arts 63–75 . . . . .26.09
Art. 64(1) 23.64, 23.86
Art. 64(2) 6.21, 10.17, 23.64
Art. 64(3) 23.64
Art. 65(1) 23.64
Art. 65(3) 23.64
Art. 66(1) 23.67
Art. 66(3) 23.67, 23.86
Art. 67(2)–(4) 23.67
Art. 68(2) 23.67
Art. 69 . . . . .23.67
Art. 70(1) 23.68
Art. 70(2)–(4) 23.68
Art. 71(1) 23.68
Art. 71(2) 23.68
Art. 72(1) 23.70
Art. 72(2) 23.70

Art. 73(2) 23.69
Art. 73(3) 23.69
Art. 74(1) 23.65
Art. 75 . . . . .23.73
Art. 75(1) 23.56
Art. 76 . . . . 23.39, 23.74
Art. 76(1) 23.74, 23.75, 26.06
Art. 76(2) 23.74, 24.15, 26.07
Art. 76(3) 23.74, 24.15
Art. 77 . . . . .23.43
Art. 78 . . . . .23.76
Art. 78(1) 23.76
Art. 80 . . . . .23.79
Art. 83 . . . . 23.82, 23.86, 24.13
Art. 86 . . . . .23.90
Art. 87(a)–(n) 23.88
Art. 88(1) 23.90
Art. 88(2) 23.90
Art. 89(1)(a)–(k) 23.88
Art. 89(2)(a)–(c) 23.88
Art. 90 . . . . .23.91
Art. 91(1) 23.93
Art. 91(2) 23.93
Art. 92 . . . . .23.92
Art. 94 . . . . 3.22, 3.25
Art. 94a 24.03
Art. 94b 24.03
Art. 94c 24.03
Art. 95 . . . . .26.08
Art. 95(1) 24.05
Art. 95(2) 24.05
Art. 96(1)(a)–(d) 24.09
Art. 96(1)(e) 24.09
Art. 96(1)(f) 24.09
Art. 96(2) 24.10, 24.13
Art. 97(1) 24.12
Art. 97(2) 24.12
Art. 97(3) 23.14, 24.24
Art. 98 . . . . .22.14
Art. 98(1) 24.08
Art. 98(2) 24.08
Art. 98(3) 24.09
Art. 99 . . . . 3.29, 3.32, 3.53, 6.24, 6.32,
           23.86, 24.15
Art. 100(1) 3.16, 3.29, 24.25
Art. 100(2) 3.16, 3.29, 24.25
Art. 101 . . . . 3.29, 6.21, 6.25
Art. 101(1) 24.23
Art. 102 . . . . 24.25, 24.26
Art. 103 . . . . .23.86
Art. 103(1) 24.32
Art. 103(2) 24.32
Art. 103(3) 24.32
Art. 104 . . . . 6.28, 24.30
Art. 104(1) 6.11, 24.30
Art. 104(2) 6.11, 24.29, 24.30
Art. 105 . . . . .22.19
Arts 105–106 . . . . 22.06, 23.42
Art. 105(1) 22.19, 24.17
Art. 105(2) 24.19
Art. 105(3) 22.19, 24.19

Art. 105(3)–(4) .24.09
Art. 106 . . . . 22.15, 22.19
Art. 107 . . . . .2.10
Art. 107–114. . . . . 22.06, 23.42
Art. 107(1) 22.07, 22.09, 24.20
Art. 107(2) 22.09
Art. 107(3) 22.09
Art. 108(1) 22.10
Art. 109(1)–(2) .22.14
Art. 109(2) 22.14, 24.09
Art. 109(3) 22.06, 22.14, 22.16
Art. 109(4)–(5) .22.14
Art. 109(6) 22.14
Art. 110 . . . . .24.09
Art. 110(1) 22.14
Art. 110(1)–(2) .22.14
Art. 110(3) 22.14
Art. 111 . . . . 22.14, 24.21
Art. 112 . . . . .22.18
Art. 113(1) 22.10
Art. 113(2) 22.10
Art. 114 . . . . .22.15
Art. 115(1) 24.27, 25.101
Art. 115(2) 24.27
Art. 115(3) 24.27
Art. 116(1)–(3) .24.27
Art. 116(4) 23.86, 24.27
Art. 117 . . . . .24.27
Art. 118 . . . . .24.27
Art. 119 . . . . 26.02, 26.03, 26.04
Art. 119(1) 23.14
Art. 119(2) 23.16, 25.20, 26.04
Art. 119(2)–(3) 23.17, 25.27
Art. 119(3) 25.20
Art. 119(4) 23.19, 25.20, 25.27
Art. 120 . . . . 5.52, 8.07, 23.59, 25.03
Arts 120–122. . . . 13.29, 25.113, 25.123, 25.129
Art. 120(c). 5.63, 25.09, 25.24
Art. 121 . . . . 25.03, 26.02, 26.03, 26.04
Art. 121(1) 25.05
Art. 121(1), first para. 25.05
Art. 121(2) 25.05
Art. 121(3) 25.05
Art. 122(1) 25.21, 25.27, 26.02, 26.04
Art. 122(2) 25.21, 25.27
Art. 122(3) 25.21, 26.04
Art. 123 . . . . 25.26, 25.27
Art. 123b. 17.05
Art. 124(1) 23.28, 23.59, 25.28, 25.34
Art. 124(2) 25.34, 25.35
Art. 124(3) 25.28
Art. 125 . . . . .25.26
Art. 126(1) 25.46
Art. 126(2) 25.46
Art. 127 . . . . .26.08
Art. 127(1) 7.11, 16.20, 16.29,
  23.78, 25.13, 25.37, 24.49
Art. 127(2) 25.13
Art. 128(1) 25.18, 25.39, 25.48
Art. 128(2) 23.78, 25.18
Arts 129–132. . . . . 16.15, 26.08

Art. 129(1) 25.59, 25.60
Art. 129(3) 25.60
Art. 129(4) 25.70, 25.76
Art. 130(1) 16.15, 23.28, 25.70, 26.08
Art. 130(2) 25.72
Art. 130(3) 25.72
Art. 130(4) 25.72
Art. 131(1) 25.74
Art. 131(2) 25.75, 25.76
Art. 131(3) 23.86, 25.75
Art. 131(4) 25.76
Art. 132(1) 25.78
Art. 132(2) 23.59, 25.76
Art. 132(3) 25.77, 25.78
Art. 133 . . . . .23.42
Arts 133–136. . . . . .26.08
Art. 133(1) 25.79
Art. 133(2) 25.79
Art. 133(3) 25.79
Art. 134(1) 25.81
Art. 134(2) 25.81
Art. 135(1) 23.56, 23.73
Art. 135(2) 25.81
Arts 136–146. . . . . .24.26
Art. 137 . . . . .25.89
Art. 137–146. . . . . .26.08
Art. 138(1) 25.38, 25.94
Art. 138(3) 25.95
Art. 139 . . . . 7.12, 25.96
Art. 140(1) 25.98
Art. 140(2) 25.98
Art. 140(3) 25.98
Art. 141 . . . . 25.82, 25.83
Art. 141(1) 25.99
Art. 141(2) 25.99
Art. 141(3) 25.99
Art. 141(4) 25.99
Art. 142 . . . . .13.45, 25.100
Art. 143 . . . . .25.90
Art. 144 . . . . .25.91
Art. 145(1) 23.86, 25.92
Art. 145(2) 25.92
Art. 147 . . . . 25.82, 26.08
Art. 148 . . . . 25.83, 26.08
Art. 149 . . . . 23.86, 25.84, 26.08
Art. 150 . . . . .7.08, 23.86, 25.60, 25.85, 26.08
Art. 151 . . . . 12.18, 23.27, 25.86
Art. 151(1) 25.41, 25.87
Art. 151(2) 25.87
Art. 151(3) 25.41, 25.87
Art. 151(4) 25.42
Art. 151(5) 25.42, 25.87
Art. 151(6) 25.42, 25.87
Art. 152(1) 25.31
Art. 152(2) 25.31
Art. 152(3) 25.31
Art. 152(4) 25.31
Art 153 . . . . .26.08
Art. 154 . . . . 23.86, 25.106, 25.133, 26.08
Art. 154(1) 25.134
Art. 154(2) 25.134

Art. 154(3) 25.134
Art. 154(4) 25.135
Art. 155 . . . . .25.106, 26.08
Art. 155(1) 25.136, 25.137
Art. 155(2) 25.137
Art. 155(3) 25.137
Art. 156(2) 25.32
Art. 156(3) 25.32
Art. 156(5) 25.32
Art. 157 . . . . .25.107, 26.08
Art. 157(1) 25.113
Art. 157(1)(b) 25.110
Art. 157(2) 25.114
Art. 157(3) 23.30, 25.111
Art. 157(4) 13.04
Art. 157(5) 25.115
Art. 157(6) 25.115
Art. 158 . . . . 6.11, 25.125, 26.08
Art. 158(1) 25.126, 25.127
Art. 158(2) 25.130
Art. 158(3) 25.129
Art. 158(4) 25.129
Art. 158(5) 25.131
Art. 158(6) 25.132
Art. 159 . . . . 25.116, 25.117, 26.08
Art. 159(2) 23.26, 25.121
Art. 159(3) 25.123
Art. 159(4) 25.122
Art. 159(5) 23.86, 25.123
Art. 159(6) 25.123
Art. 159(7) 25.124
Art. 160 . . . . .13.44
Arts 160–164. .26.08
Arts 160–166. . . . . 2.18, 13.23
Art. 160(1) 13.07, 13.17
Art. 160(1)–(2) 13.07, 13.26
Art. 160(2) 13.07, 13.17
Art. 160(3) 13.29, 13.31
Art. 160(4) 13.28, 13.29
Art. 160(5) 13.24
Art. 160(6) 13.24
Art. 160(7) 13.12, 13.15, 13.24
Art. 161(1) 13.23
Art. 161(3) 13.23
Art. 162(1) 13.44, 13.46, 23.86
Art. 162(2) 13.06, 13.44
Art. 162(3) 13.15, 13.44
Art. 162(4) 13.15
Art. 163 . . . . 13.15, 13.44
Art. 164 . . . . .13.44
Art. 165 . . . . 13.04, 26.08
Art. 166 . . . . .26.08
Arts 167–190. .26.01
Art. 167(1) 26.02
Art. 168(1)(a)–(c). 26.02
Art. 168(1)(d)–(e) 26.02
Art. 168(2) 26.02, 26.08
Art. 168(3) 26.02
Art. 168(4) 26.02, 26.04
Art. 169(1) 16.01, 16.23, 26.02
Art. 169(2) 16.19, 26.02

Art. 170(1) 16.01, 16.10, 16.23
Art. 170(1), last sent. 16.20
Art. 170(2) 26.02
Art. 171(1) 26.02
Art. 172 . . . . 16.17, 26.03
Art. 173(1)(a)–(b) 26.03
Art. 173(1)(c)–(d) 26.03
Art. 173(2) 26.03, 26.08
Art. 174 . . . . 16.17, 16.23, 26.03
Art. 175(1) 26.05
Art. 175(2) 26.05
Art. 176 . . . . .26.04
Art. 176–183. .16.14
Art. 176(1) 16.25
Art. 177(1) 26.04
Art. 177(2) 26.04, 26.08
Art. 178(1)–(2) 26.04
Art. 178(3) 26.04
Art. 179 . . . . .26.04
Art. 180 . . . . .26.05
Art. 181 . . . . 23.86, 26.07
Art. 182 . . . . 23.86, 26.07
Art. 183 . . . . .26.11
Art. 184 . . . . 24.26, 26.08
Art. 184(1) 26.08
Arts 185–189. .26.10
Art. 185(1) 25.101, 26.10
Art. 187 . . . . .26.10
Art. 187(3) 23.86
Art. 190 . . . . .26.08
Art. 190(2) 16.15, 26.08
Art. 190(3) 26.08
Art. 191 . . . . .17.04
Art. 192 . . . . .17.04
Art. 193(1)–(2) 17.06
Art. 193(3) 17.06
Art. 193(4) 17.06
Art. 193(5) 17.06
Art. 193(6) 17.06
Art. 194(1)–(2) 17.06
Art. 194(3) 17.06
Art. 194(5) 17.06
Art. 194(6) 17.06
Art. 194(7) 17.06
Art. 195(2) 17.07
Art. 195(3) 17.07
Art. 195(4) 17.05, 17.07
Art. 195(5) 17.05
Arts 196–200. .12.18
Art. 196(2) 12.11
Art. 196(3) 12.18
Art. 197 . . . . .12.19
Art. 198 . . . . .12.19
Art. 199 . . . . .12.19
Art. 200 . . . . .12.19
Arts 202–203. .12.06
Art. 204 . . . . .24.33
Art. 205 . . . . .22.05
Art. 205(1)–(6) 21.13
Art. 205(1)–(6) 19.22
Art. 205(7) 19.22, 21.13

Rules of Procedure—Supplementary
    Rules of the Court of Justice [2014]
      O.J. L32/37 . . . . .1.10
      Arts 1–3 and Annex I 23.71
      Arts 4–5 and Annex II 25.101
      Arts 6–7 and Annex III 23.67, 23.68
Practice Directions to Parties Concerning
    Cases Brought Before the Court
    ('ECJ Practice Directions') [2014]
      O.J. L31/1 . . . . 1.10, 23.55, 25.56
      Point 12 . . . . 25.03, 25.16, 25.56
      Point 13 . . . . 25.03, 25.24
      Point 15 . . . . 25.36, 25.56
      Point 16 . . . . .25.56
      Point 17 . . . . .25.80
      Point 20 . . . . .26.02
      Point 22 . . . . .26.03
      Point 25 . . . . 26.02, 26.05
      Point 26 . . . . .26.05
      Point 29 . . . . .25.76
      Points 34–39 . . . . .25.03
      Point 35 . . . . 25.52, 25.55
      Point 36 . . . . 25.52, 26.02
      Point 39 . . . . .25.57
      Point 41 . . . . .25.54
      Point 43 . . . . 23.37, 23.54
      Point 46 . . . . .23.75
      Point 48 . . . . 23.74, 23.76
      Point 52 . . . . .23.78
      Point 57 . . . . .23.78
Recommendations to national courts
    and tribunals in relation to the initiation
    of preliminary ruling proceedings
    ('Recommendations') [2012]
      O.J. C338/1 . . . . 1.10, 3.25
      Point 22 . . . . 3.27, 24.04
      Point 23 . . . . .24.03
      Point 24 . . . . .24.03
      Point 26 . . . . .24.04
      Point 33 . . . . .24.02
      Points 37–46 . . . . 24.19, 24.21
Rules of Procedure of the General Court
    ('EGC Rules of Procedure') [1991]
    O.J. L136/1, as last amended by
    Amendment of the Rules of Procedure
    of the General Court [2013]
      O.J. L173/66 . . . . . . 1.10, 2.24, 2.29, 13.07,
             13.46, 19.18, 20.10, 20.11, 21.13,
             23.01, 23.02, 23.03, 23.05, 23.14,
             23.22, 23.24, 23.26, 23.43, 23.55,
             23.62, 23.63, 23.64, 23.72, 23.78,
             23.88, 23.91, 23.93, 25.18, 25.60,
                  25.78, 25.92, 25.130
      Art. 2(2) 2.24
      Art. 4(1) 2.25
      Art. 5 . . . . .2.25
      Art. 7(1) 2.26
      Art. 7(2) 2.26
      Art. 7(3) 2.26
      Art. 8 . . . . .2.33
      Art. 10(1) 2.29

Art. 10(2) 2.29
Art. 11(1), first para. 2.28
Art. 11(1), second para. 2.29
Art. 11(1), third para. 2.29
Art. 12 . . . . .2.29
Art. 13(1) 2.29
Art. 13(2) 2.29
Art. 14(1) 2.30
Art. 14(2), point 1 . . . . .2.29
Art. 14(2), point 2 . . . . .2.29
Art. 15(2), first para. 2.29
Art. 15(3) 2.29
Art. 15(5) 2.29
Art. 17 . . . . .2.24
Art. 18 . . . . .2.24
Art. 19, first para. 2.24
Art. 19, second para. 2.24
Art. 20 . . . . .2.28
Arts 20–27 . . . . .2.33
Art. 24(1) 23.51
Art. 24(6) 25.26, 25.70, 25.108
Art. 24(7) 25.26
Art. 25(1) 25.26
Art. 32(1), second para. 2.24
Art. 32(3), first para. 2.31
Art. 32(3), second para. 2.31
Art. 32(4) 2.10
Art. 35(1) 23.02
Art. 35(2)(a) .23.03
Art. 35(2)(b) .23.03
Art. 35(2)(c) .23.03
Art. 35(2)(c), second para. 23.03
Art. 35(3) 23.05
Art. 35(3), first para. 23.05, 23.89
Art. 35(3), third para. 23.05
Art. 35(3), fourth para. 23.08, 25.73
Art. 35(3), fifth para. 23.08
Art. 35(4) 23.02, 23.06
Art. 35(5) 23.07
Art. 36(1) 23.09
Art. 36(2) 23.09
Art. 37 . . . . .23.10
Art. 38(1) 23.20
Art. 38(2)(a) .23.21
Art. 38(2)(c) .23.21
Art. 39(a) 23.16, 23.22
Art. 40, first para. 23.22
Art. 40, second para. 23.22
Art. 41(1) 23.23, 23.51
Art. 41(2) 23.23
Art. 41(3) 23.23
Art. 42 . . . . 23.17, 25.20
Art. 43 . . . . .13.29, 25.03, 25.31,
             25.47, 25.113, 25.123, 25.129
Art. 43(1) 23.14, 23.51, 23.52, 25.03
Art. 43(2) 23.52
Art. 43(3) 23.36, 23.49, 23.54
Art. 43(4) 23.53, 25.18
Art. 43(4)–(5) 25.57
Art. 43(5) 23.53
Art. 43(6) 23.37, 23.50, 23.54

Art. 43(7) 23.54
Art. 44 . . . . 8.07, 13.29, 25.113, 25.129
Art. 44(1) 13.44, 23.59, 25.03
Art. 44(1)(c). . . 7.09, 11.34, 11.78, 20.19, 25.09
Art. 44(2) 25.03, 25.05
Art. 44(2), first para. 25.05
Art. 44(2), second para. 25.05
Art. 44(2), third para. 25.05
Art. 44(3) 23.17, 23.22, 25.20
Art. 44(3)–(5a) .25.27
Art. 44(4) 25.21
Art. 44(5) 23.18, 23.22, 25.20
Art. 44(5a). 19.15, 25.21
Art. 44(5)(a) 25.22
Art. 44(5)(b) 23.17, 25.22
Art. 44(6) 23.19, 25.20, 25.27
Art. 45 . . . . 25.26, 25.27
Art. 46(1) 23.28, 23.59, 25.28
Art. 46(1), first para. 25.34
Art. 46(1), second para. 23.19, 25.35
Art. 46(3) 25.28
Art. 47(1) 2.43, 25.46
Art. 47(2) 25.46
Art. 48(1) 25.18, 25.39, 25.48
Art. 48(2) 7.11, 16.29, 18.26,
                    23.63, 23.78, 25.37, 25.49
Art. 48(2), first para. 25.13
Art. 48(2), second para. 25.13
Art. 50 . . . . .23.43
Art. 50(2) 23.43
Art. 51 . . . . .2.29
Art. 51(1), first para. 2.30
Art. 51(1), second para. 2.30
Art. 51(2) 2.30
Art. 52(1) 2.43, 23.56
Art. 52(2) 23.56
Art. 52(2), second para. 23.56
Art. 53 . . . . 23.56, 23.73
Art. 54 . . . . 23.56, 23.73
Art. 55(1) 23.41
Art. 55(2), first para. 23.41
Art. 55(2), second para. 23.48
Art. 56 . . . . .23.76
Art. 57 . . . . .23.76
Art. 58 . . . . .23.79
Art. 60 . . . . .23.80
Art. 61 . . . . .23.80
Art. 62 . . . . .23.82
Art. 64 . . . . 7.36, 23.58, 23.63
Art. 64(1) 23.57, 23.63
Art. 64(2) 23.57
Art. 64(3) 23.63
Art. 64(4) 23.63
Art. 64(5) 23.62, 23.63
Art. 65 . . . . 7.36, 23.64
Art. 66(1) 23.64
Art. 66(2) 23.64
Art. 67(1) 23.64
Art. 67(2) 23.64
Art. 67(3), first para. 23.66
Art. 67(3), second para. 23.66

Art. 68(1) 23.67
Art. 68(2) 23.67
Art. 68(4) 23.67
Art. 68(5) 23.67
Art. 69 . . . . .23.67
Art. 70(1) 23.68
Art. 70(5) 23.68
Art. 70(6) 23.68
Art. 71 . . . . .23.67
Art. 72 . . . . .23.68
Art. 73(1) 23.70
Art. 73(2) 23.70
Art. 74(1) 23.69
Art. 74(2) 23.69
Art. 75 . . . . .23.71
Art. 76(1) 23.65
Art. 76a. 23.42
Art. 76a(1), first para. 25.79, 25.80
Art. 76a(2). 25.81
Art. 76a(3). 25.81
Art. 77 . . . . .23.46
Art. 78 . . . . .23.46
Art. 79(1), first para. 23.47
Art. 79(1), second para. 23.47
Art. 79(2), first para. 23.47
Art. 79(2), second para. 23.47
Art. 81 . . . . .23.88
Art. 82(1) 23.90
Art. 82(2) 23.90
Art. 83 . . . . .23.93
Art. 84 . . . . .25.106
Art. 85 . . . . .25.106, 25.136
Art. 85, first para. 25.137
Art. 85, second para. 25.137
Art. 85, third para. 25.137
Art. 87(1) 13.45, 25.89
Art. 87(2) 25.94
Art. 87(2), first para. 25.38
Art. 87(3) 7.12
Art. 87(3), first para. 25.95
Art. 87(3), second para. 25.96
Art. 87(4), first para. 25.98
Art. 87(4), second para. 25.98
Art. 87(4), third para. 25.98
Art. 87(5) 25.82, 25.83
Art. 87(5), first para. 8.21, 25.99
Art. 87(5), second para. 25.99
Art. 87(5), third para. 25.99
Art. 87(6) 13.45, 25.100
Art. 90 . . . . .25.90
Art. 91 . . . . .25.91
Art. 92(1) 18.27, 25.92
Art. 94(2) 25.101
Art. 95(1) 25.101
Art. 95(2) 25.101
Art. 95(2), second para. 25.102, 25.103
Art. 96(2), first para. 25.103
Art. 96(3) 25.104
Art. 96(4) 25.102
Art. 96(5) 25.103
Art. 96(6) 25.103

Art. 97 . . . . .25.104
Art. 97(4) 25.95, 25.104
Art. 98, first para. 25.82
Art. 99 . . . . .25.83
Art. 100 . . . . .25.26
Art. 100(1) 23.24
Art. 100(2), first para.. . . . . .23.24
Art. 100(2), second para. 23.24
Art. 100(2), third para.. . . . . .23.24
Art. 100(3) 23.25
Art. 101(1)(a) 7.213, 23.29
Art. 101(1)(b) 23.33
Art. 101(1)(c) 23.33
Art. 101(1)(d) 23.31
Art. 101(1)(e) 23.31
Art. 101(2), first para. 23.33
Art. 101(2), second para. 23.31
Art. 102(1) 7.210, 23.30, 23.34
Art. 102(2) 11.86, 23.32
Art. 103 . . . . .23.26
Art. 104 . . . . .13.44
Arts 104–110.. . . . . .13.23
Art. 104(1) 13.07, 13.11, 13.25, 13.26
Art. 104(1), first para. 13.07, 13.17
Art. 104(1), second para.. . . . . .13.17
Art. 104(2) 13.29, 13.31, 13.44
Art. 104(2)–(3) 13.10
Art. 104(3) 13.28, 13.29
Art. 105(1) 13.24
Art. 105(2) 13.15, 13.24
Art. 105(2), first para. 13.24
Art. 105(2), second para. 13.24
Art. 106 . . . . .13.23
Art. 107(1) 13.44
Art. 107(2) 13.06, 13.44
Art. 107(3) 13.15, 13.44
Art. 107(4) 13.15
Art. 108 . . . . 13.04, 13.15, 13.18, 13.44
Art. 109 . . . . .13.44
Art. 110 . . . . .13.04
Art. 111 . . .23.40, 23.74, 25.42, 25.45, 25.131
Art. 113 . . . . 7.08, 23.74, 25.84, 25.85
Arts 113–149.. . . . . .18.30
Art. 114 . . . . 23.27, 23.74, 25.28, 25.86
Art. 114(1) 25.41, 25.45, 25.87
Art. 114(2) 25.41, 25.45, 25.87
Art. 114(3) 25.42
Art. 114(4), first para. 25.42, 25.87
Art. 114(4), second para. 25.42, 25.87
Art. 115(1) 23.28, 25.70
Art. 115(2) 25.72
Art. 115(2), second para. 25.72
Art. 115(3) 25.72
Art. 116(1) 25.74
Art. 116(1), third para. 25.75
Art. 116(2) 25.76
Art. 116(3) 25.60
Art. 116(4) 23.59, 25.76
Art. 116(4), first para. 25.78
Art. 116(5) 25.77, 25.78
Art. 116(6) 25.70, 25.76

Art. 117–121. . . . . .26.12
Art. 119 . . . . .16.29
Art. 119(1) 26.12
Art. 119(2) 26.12
Art. 119(3) 26.12
Art. 121 . . . . .26.12
Art. 122(1), first para. 25.31
Art. 122(1), second para. 25.31
Art. 122(2) 25.31
Art. 122(2), second para. 25.31
Art. 122(3) 25.31
Art. 122(4) 25.32
Art. 122(5) 25.32
Art. 122(6) 25.32
Art. 123 . . . . .25.107
Art. 123(1) 25.113
Art. 123(1), first para. 25.113
Art. 123(1), second para. 25.114
Art. 123(1), third para. 23.30, 25.111
Art. 123(1)(b) 25.110
Art. 123(2) 13.04
Art. 123(3), first para. 25.115
Art. 123(3), second para. 25.115
Art. 123(4) 25.112
Art. 125 . . . . 23.26, 25.116, 25.121
Arts 125–128. . . . . .25.116
Art. 126(1) 25.46, 25.123
Art. 126(2) 25.122
Art. 127(2) 25.123
Art. 127(3) 25.123
Art. 127(4) 25.124
Art. 129 . . . . .25.125, 25.126
Art. 129(1) 25.129
Art. 129(1), first para. 25.131
Art. 129(1), second para. 25.129
Art. 129(3), first para. 25.131
Art. 130(1) 20.09, 23.04
Art. 131(1) 25.26
Art. 131(2) 23.04
Art. 131(4) 20.08
Art. 131(4), second para. 25.91
Art. 132(1) 25.27
Art. 132(1), first para. 25.23
Art. 132(1), second para. 25.23
Art. 132(2) 25.27
Art. 133(1) 25.26
Art. 133(2) 20.09
Art. 134 . . . . 20.11, 20.15
Art. 134(1) 25.30, 25.71
Art. 134(2), first para. 25.71
Art. 134(2), second para. 25.71
Art. 134(4) 25.31
Art. 135(1) 25.30
Art. 135(2) 25.51
Art. 135(3) 25.30
Art. 135(4) 20.15
Art. 135a. 23.39, 23.74
Art. 136(1) 25.95
Art. 136a. 23.03
Arts 136a–149. . . . . 16.01, 26.01
Art. 136(2) 20.08, 25.91

Art. 146 . . . . 23.39, 23.74
Practice Directions to Parties Before the General
    Court ('EGC Practice Directions') [2012]
    O.J. L68/23 . . . . 1.10, 23.55, 25.56
Point 7 . . . . 23.37, 23.54
Point 9 . . . . .25.53
Point 10 . . . . .25.55
Point 11 . . . . .25.55
Point 12 . . . . .25.52
Point 14 . . . . .25.54
Point 15 . . . . 25.56, 25.76
Point 16 . . . . .25.56
Points 18–28 . . . . .25.03
Point 19 . . . . .25.03
Point 22 . . . . .25.16

Point 25 . . . . .25.24
Point 26 . . . . .25.18
Point 30 . . . . .25.34
Point 31 . . . . .25.38
Point 33 . . . . .25.36
Point 57 . . . . .25.57
Point 58 . . . . .25.57
Point 60 . . . . .25.57
Point 61 . . . . .25.57
Point 69 . . . . .25.80
Point 70 . . . . .25.80
Point 83 . . . . .13.24
Point 90 . . . . .25.76
Points 119–120 . . . . .23.78
Point 125 . . . . .23.78

1

GENERAL INTRODUCTION

A. Overview

This book generally concerns the system of judicial protection in the European Union. On **1.01** the one hand, at the European level, this concerns the role and the competences of the institution of the Court of Justice of the European Union (composed of the Court of Justice, the General Court, and the Civil Service Tribunal, which are often referred to as the 'Union courts' or the 'Union judicature' *sensu stricto*) and the various types of acts that can be brought before it by individuals, Member States, and Union institutions. On the other hand, this also includes the examination of the relationship between the national and the Union judicial and procedural frameworks more generally in terms of the relationship between the Court of Justice and the national courts through the preliminary ruling procedure, by which the national courts refer to the Court questions about the interpretation and validity of Union law, as well as through the dynamic interplay between the principle of national procedural autonomy and the Union framing principles of equivalence and effectiveness.

By way of general introduction, this chapter highlights several crucial themes underlying the system of judicial protection in the European Union and the two-fold task of the Union judicature within this system.

B. The complete and the coherent system of judicial protection in the European Union

The European Union is unique in the sense that it has a highly developed complete and **1.02** coherent system of judicial protection, such that the rights derived from Union law can be enforced in court, as opposed to international organizations, whereby enforceability is often far less certain. The 'complete' system of judicial protection means that sufficient legal remedies and procedures exist before the Union courts and the national courts to enforce Union law rights and to ensure the judicial review of Union acts, whereas the 'coherent' system of judicial protection means that there exist both direct and indirect routes by which to enforce rights based on Union law and to review the legality of Union acts, each of which implicates important, albeit differing, roles for the Union courts and the national courts as laid down by the Treaties.[1]

---

[1] K. Lenaerts, 'The Rule of Law and the Coherence of the Judicial System of the European Union' (2007) C.M.L. Rev. 1625–59. See also M. Jaeger, 'Les voies de recours sont-elles des vases communicants?', in G.C. Rodriguez Iglesias, O. Due, R. Schintgen, and C. Elsen (eds), *Mélanges en hommage à Fernand Schockweiler* (Baden Baden, Nomos, 1999), 233–53.

C. Union based on the rule of law

1.03 At the heart of the system of judicial protection in the European Union is the core principle of upholding the rule of law upon which the Union is founded.[2] The preamble to the Charter of Fundamental Rights of the European Union[3] states that the Union is based in particular on the 'principle of the rule of law'. The substance of that principle is fleshed out in the first paragraph of Art. 47 of the Charter, which provides that 'Everyone whose rights and freedoms guaranteed by the law of the Union are violated has the right to an effective remedy before a tribunal . . .'.

As proclaimed by the Court in its landmark ruling in *Les Verts*, the then European (Economic) Community, now the European Union, is 'based on the rule of law, inasmuch as neither its Member States nor its institutions can avoid a review of the question whether the measures adopted by them are in conformity with the basic constitutional charter, the Treaty'.[4] As further underscored in that judgment, the Treaties set out to establish a complete system of legal remedies, whereby any act or failure to act on the part of an institution or a Member State in violation of Union law can be subject to review by the Union judicature,[5] which must ensure that in the interpretation and application of the Treaties the law is observed.[6]

As such, the stakes are enormous in the sense that the system of judicial protection in the European Union must live up to its promise that individuals, Member States, and Union institutions are all guaranteed a route by which to enforce Union law rights. This is above all guided by the Treaties, which constitute the legal basis for the Union legal order as a whole and set down the framework for judicial protection, which combines both the judicial routes before the Union courts on the European level and before the national courts, which hold a crucial place in the Union system of judicial protection. In this way,

---

[2] Art. 2 TEU. On the rule of law in the EU, see G. De Baere, 'European Integration and the Rule of Law in Foreign Policy', in J. Dickson and P. Eleftheriadis (eds), *Philosophical Foundations of European Union Law* (Oxford, Oxford University Press, 2012), 354–383.

[3] [2000] O.J. C364/1, which was proclaimed at Nice on 7 December 2000 by the European Parliament, the Council, and the Commission and adapted at Strasbourg on 12 December 2007 ([2007] O.J. C303/1). By virtue of the first para. of Art. 6(1) TEU, the Charter has the same legal value as the Treaties.

[4] ECJ, Case 294/83 *Les Verts v European Parliament* [1986] E.C.R. 1339, para. 23. See further ECJ (order of 13 July 1990), Case C-2/88 Imm. *Zwartveld and Others* [1990] E.C.R. 3365, para. 16; ECJ, Opinion 1/91 *Draft Agreement between the Community, on the one hand, and the countries of the European Free Trade Association, on the other, relating to the creation of the European Economic Area* [1991] E.C.R. I-6079, para. 21; ECJ, Case C-314/91 *Weber v European Parliament* [1993] E.C.R. I-1093, para. 8; ECJ, Case C-15/00 *Commission v EIB* [2003] E.C.R. I-7281, para. 75; ECJ, Joined Cases C-402/05 P and C-415/05 P *Kadi and Al Barakaat International Foundation v Council and Commission* [2008] E.C.R. I-6351, para. 81; ECJ, Case C-550/09 *E and F* [2010] E.C.R. I-6213, para. 44; CFI (order of 17 January 2002), Case T-236/00 *Stauner and Others v European Parliament and Commission* [2002] E.C.R. II-135, para. 50; CFI, Case T-231/99 *Joynson v Commission* [2002] E.C.R. II-2085, para. 32; CFI, Case T-299/05 *Shanghai Excell M&E Enterprise and Shanghai Adeptech Precision v Council* [2009] E.C.R. II-565, para. 57.

[5] See further K. Lenaerts, 'Case 294/83 *Parti écologiste "Les Verts" v European Parliament*. The Basic Constitutional Charter of a Community Based on the Rule of Law', in M. Poiares Maduro and L. Azoulai (eds), *The Past and Future of EU Law: The Classics of EU Law Revisited on the 50th Anniversary of the Rome Treaty* (Oxford and Portland Oregon, Hart Publishing, 2010), 295–315.

[6] Art. 19(1), first para., TEU.

judicial protection in the European Union hinges on the interlocking system of jurisdiction of the Union courts and the national courts.[7]

D. Role of the national courts

Following on from this discussion, the national courts are in effect the 'lynchpin' of the judicial system of the European Union. They can be considered the normal Union courts in the sense that it is generally before such courts that all sorts of litigants may bring cases involving issues of Union law.[8]   **1.04**

By contrast, the 'organic' Union courts at the European level—the Court of Justice, the General Court, and the Civil Service Tribunal—are bound by the principle of conferral, whereby they exercise only the jurisdiction conferred upon them under the Treaties.[9] In other words, the Union courts do not have inherent jurisdiction just because matters of Union law are involved in a particular case. Instead, there must be a specific legal basis set down in the Treaties which delineates the extent of the Union courts' power to adjudicate a particular case or cause of action. Consequently, everything falling outside of what the Treaties confer upon the Union courts falls within the residual competences of the national courts.[10] That is to say, cases between natural and legal persons, on the one hand, and cases between natural and legal persons and national authorities, on the other, are brought before the national courts; in effect, the only occasion in which a private party may bring a case before the Union courts is under circumstances where the action is lodged against a 'Union defendant', i.e. an institution, office, body, or agency of the Union.

This serves to underscore the importance of the preliminary ruling procedure, which constitutes a mechanism by which the Court of Justice and the national courts work together so as to enable the national courts to carry out their function in deciding the various cases before them involving matters of Union law, and at the same time, allowing the Court of Justice to ensure the uniform application of Union law such that the same rules are applied in the Member States.

E. Challenges underlying the system of judicial protection of the European Union

Notwithstanding the Court of Justice's seminal proclamation in *Les Verts*, there are certain aspects of the institutional framework of the European Union that present challenges to the   **1.05**

---

[7] See K. Lenaerts, 'Interlocking Legal Orders in the European Union and Comparative Law' (2003) I.C.L.Q. 873–906; K. Lenaerts, 'La systématique des voies de recours dans l'ordre juridique de l'Union européenne', in A. De Walsche (ed.), *Mélanges en hommage à Georges Vandersanden: promenades au sein du droit européen* (Brussels, Bruylant 2008), 257–82. For an analysis in relation to the Belgian legal order, see J. T. Nowak, 'Wettigheidstoetsing van handelingen van de instellingen van de Europese Unie: complementaire rechtsbescherming in een meerlagige context' (2013) T.B.P. 195–211.

[8] ECJ (8 March 2011), Opinion 1/09 *Draft Agreement Creating a Unified Patent Litigation System (European and Community Patents Court)* [2011] E.C.R. I-1137, para. 80. See further para. 2.02.

[9] Art. 13(2) TEU; see also Art. 5(2) TEU and ECJ, Case C-196/09 *Miles and Others* [2011] E.C.R. I-5105, para. 45.

[10] See Art. 274 TFEU.

system of judicial protection in the European Union in terms of ensuring that it is both complete and coherent. This encompasses examination of the apparent gaps in the former Treaty framework comprising the EU and EC Treaties, which provides the setting for the evaluation of the extent to which such gaps have been addressed through the changes brought by the Lisbon Treaty and other institutional developments heralded by the Court of Justice of the European Union.[11]

F. Former Treaty framework and the pillar structure

1.06   The original version of Art. L of the EU Treaty limited the exercise of powers by the Court of Justice of the European Communities as it was then called, to the EC Treaty, the ECSC Treaty, the EAEC Treaty, the former third paragraph of Art. K.3(2)(c) of the EU Treaty, and former Arts L[12] to S of that Treaty. Accordingly, the jurisdiction of the Court of Justice covered Community law, certain agreements concluded by the Member States outside Community law (see Ch. 21), and the final provisions of the EU Treaty. The Amsterdam Treaty introduced a new Art. 46 into the EU Treaty (which was further amended by the Nice Treaty), replacing the former Art. L and considerably extending the jurisdiction of the Court of Justice in the field of Police and Judicial Cooperation in Criminal Matters,[13] expressly empowering the Court of Justice to review acts of the institutions in the light of fundamental rights protected by Art. 6(2) EU insofar as the Court had jurisdiction under the Community Treaties or the EU Treaty.[14]

In that regard, former Art. 46 EU did not prevent the Court of Justice itself from delimiting the scope of its jurisdiction. For instance, a measure which was purportedly adopted in connection with a pillar other than the Community pillar of the Union (for example, sanctions imposed under the Common Foreign and Security Policy) could in fact be ascribable to a Community competence (for example, the common commercial policy referred to in Art. 133 EC [now Art. 207 TFEU]), which would mean that the Court of Justice would be competent to review the measure for compatibility with the Community Treaties. In the event of a dispute, it was the task of the Court of Justice or the Court of First Instance, as it was then called, to define the pillars of the Union in relation to each other. That task could not be undertaken by any other institution, since it was a matter of interpreting and applying the Community Treaties and hence within the jurisdiction of the Court of Justice and the Court of First Instance within the Community legal order, which, by virtue of the judicially enforceable former Art. 47 EU, was not affected by any other provision of that Treaty.[15]

---

[11] K. Lenaerts, 'Le traité de Lisbonne et la protection juridictionnelle des particuliers en droit de l'Union' (2009) C.D.E. 711–45.

[12] For an application of former Art. L EU, see ECJ (order of 7 April 1995), Case C-167/94 *Grau Gomis and Others* [1995] E.C.R. I-1023, para. 6.

[13] As far as the Court's jurisdiction in this connection under the former Treaty framework was concerned, see paras 22.02–22.04.

[14] For further details, see K. Lenaerts, 'Le respect des droits fondamentaux en tant que principe constitutionnel de l'Union européenne', in M. Dony and A. De Walsche (eds), *Mélanges en hommage à Michel Waelbroeck*, Vol. I (Bruylant, Brussels, 1999), 423–57.

[15] See, e.g. ECJ, Case C-170/96 *Commission v Council* [1998] E.C.R. I-2763, paras 12–18; ECJ, Case C-176/03 *Commission v Council ('Environmental crimes')* [2005] E.C.R. I-7879, paras 38–40; ECJ, Case C-440/05 *Commission v Council ('Ship-source pollution')* [2007] E.C.R. I-9097, paras 52–53; ECJ, Case C-91/05 *Commission v Council*

Nevertheless, both in relation to the former second and third pillars of the Union and as the Community pillar, the jurisdiction of the Union judicature was curtailed to varying degrees.[16] As far as the second pillar of Common Foreign and Security Policy was concerned, generally speaking the Court of Justice was not accorded jurisdiction in this area save for certain exceptions, such as the adjudication of so-called 'inter-pillar' disputes pursuant to former Art. 47 EU, as previously mentioned. As regards the third pillar of Police and Judicial Cooperation in Criminal Matters, the Court of Justice was given some jurisdiction, although it was greatly restricted under former Art. 35 EU. Moreover, even within the Community pillar, where the Union courts' jurisdiction was in principle the strongest, there were still significant difficulties for individuals to enforce their Community law rights against certain types of Community measures due to the strict standing requirements of former Art. 230 EC. Also, for matters falling within Title IV of the EC Treaty on visas, asylum, immigration, and other policies concerning the free movement of persons, the jurisdiction of the Court of Justice was subject to special rules pursuant to former Art. 68 EC, which also curtailed that jurisdiction. As Title IV of the EC Treaty and the third pillar of Title VI of the EU Treaty comprised the Area of Freedom, Security and Justice, this had the result that measures adopted by the Union institutions in those areas often presented significant issues of judicial protection for individuals, particularly with a view to the protection of fundamental rights.[17] Altogether, the limitations placed on the Court's jurisdiction emanating from the three pillars of the Union highlighted apparent gaps in the claimed complete and coherent system of judicial protection under the former EU and EC Treaties.

G. Changes brought by the Treaty of Lisbon

The Treaty of Lisbon, which entered into force on 1 December 2009, brought significant changes to the system of judicial protection of the European Union, which are delineated in detail in the various chapters of this book.[18] With the elimination of the pillar structure by **1.07**

('*Small arms and light weapons' case*) [2008] E.C.R. I-3651, paras 31–33. In connection with litigation on access to documents of the Union institutions, it follows from the scope of Council Decision 93/731/EC of 20 December 1993 (now replaced by Regulation (EC) No. 1049/2001 of the European Parliament and of the Council of 30 May 2001 regarding public access to European Parliament, Council, and Commission documents, [2001] O.J. L145/43) that the Union judicature is competent to review the legality of any decision made pursuant to that Council decision, even if the documents to which access is sought relate to a sphere of activity of the Council which is not subject to judicial review by the Court of Justice: CFI, Case T-14/98 *Hautala v Council* [1999] E.C.R. II-2489, paras 40–42 (appeal dismissed in ECJ, Case C-353/99 P *Council v Hautala* [2001] E.C.R. I-9565).

[16] For a summary of the relevant case-law, see K. Lenaerts, 'The Rule of Law and the Coherence of the Judicial System of the European Union' (2007) C.M.L. Rev. 1625, at 1626–33.

[17] See Ch. 22.

[18] See further R. Barents, 'The Court of Justice after the Treaty of Lisbon' (2010) C.M.L. Rev. 709–28; M. Berger, 'Der Europäische Gerichtshof und der Vertrag von Lissabon', in Österreichischen Notariatskammer (eds), *Festschrift Klaus Woschnak* (Vienna, Manz, 2010), 41–54; W. Hakenberg and C. Schilhan, 'Die Architektur der EU-Gerichtsbarkeit: Aktualität und Perspektiven im Lichte von Lissabon' (2008) Zeitschrift für Europarecht, internationals Privatrecht und Rechtsvergleichung 104–112; K. Lenaerts, 'Challenges Facing the European Court of Justice After the Treaty of Lisbon' (2010) Revista Romana de Drept European 19–39; V. Skouris, 'Die Reform der Europäischen Verträge und ihre Auswirkungen auf die europäische Gerichtsbarkeit', in W. Durner and E.-J. Peine (eds), *Reform an Haupt und Gliedern—Verfassungsreform in Deutschland und Europa* (Munich, Beck, 2009), 83–102; V. Skouris, 'The Court of Justice of the European Union: A Judiciary in a Constant State of Transformation', in E. Cardonnel, A. Rosas, and N. Wahl (eds),

the Lisbon Treaty, this meant that in principle the same level of judicial protection would apply for all matters falling within the scope of the Treaties.[19] However, this is not the case wholly across the board, and the present EU Treaty as amended and the TFEU still contain vestiges of limitations placed on the Court of Justice's jurisdiction.

As regards the former Community pillar, the Treaty framers attempted to cure the apparent gap in the *locus standi* for private litigants in connection with actions for annulment under the fourth paragraph of Art. 263 TFEU, although certain questions regarding the breadth of such changes remain.[20] Also, with the consolidation of the various provisions concerning the Area of Freedom, Security and Justice in Title V of the TFEU, the constraints of former Art. 68 EC have been eliminated.[21]

As regards the former second pillar of Common Foreign and Security Policy, the Court of Justice as a general matter has still not been given jurisdiction under the Treaties, save for certain exceptions, although amendments have been made in connection with challenging the legality of restrictive measures against natural and legal persons pursuant to Art. 263 TFEU.[22]

As regards the former third pillar of Police and Judicial Cooperation in Criminal Matters, in principle the limitations of former Art. 35 EU have been deleted and the Court of Justice's jurisdiction in this area has essentially been 'mainstreamed'. Certain exceptions do remain, however, especially in relation to acts adopted within this field before the entry into force of the Lisbon Treaty.[23]

H. The two-fold task of the Union judicature

1.08   In complement to the important role played by the national courts, the Union judicature has a two-fold task in connection with the system of legal remedies set down by the Treaties. In the first place, it is responsible for enforcing all the rules of Union law. As a result, it affords protection against any act or failure to act on the part of national authorities and persons which offends against such provisions. In this respect, Union law acts as a 'sword' for safeguarding the rights deriving from that law and hence this implicates certain types of actions and procedures which ensure that the Member States comply with their obligations under the Treaties (see Part II).

In the second place, the Union judicature secures the enforcement of written and unwritten superior rules of Union law[24] and affords protection against any act or failure to act of

---

Constitutionalising The EU Judicial System. Essays in Honour of Pernilla Lindh (Oxford and Portland, Hart Publishing, 2012), 3–13.

[19] In comparison to former Art. 47 EU, Art. 1, third para., TEU now provides that the Union shall be founded on the TEU and the TFEU, both of which 'have the same legal value'.

[20] See paras 7.03 and 7.110.

[21] See para. 22.05.

[22] See Art. 24(1), second para., TEU; Art. 275 TFEU. See further para. 7.04.

[23] See para. 22.05.

[24] For a survey of the hierarchy of norms in Union law, see K. Lenaerts and P. Van Nuffel (R. Bray and N. Cambien (eds)), *European Union Law* (3rd edn, London, Sweet & Maxwell, 2011), paras 22.02–22.06. See also K. Lenaerts and M. Desomer, 'Towards a Hierarchy of Legal Acts in the European Union? Simplification of Legal Instruments and Procedures' (2005) E.L.J. 744–65.

institutions and other bodies of the Union in breach of those rules.[25] In this respect, Union law acts as a 'shield' (see Part III).

I. Structure of the book

Both the two-fold task of the Union judicature and the interlocking relationship between the Union courts and the national courts determine the structure of this book. **1.09**

Importantly, aspects concerning the relationship between the Court of Justice and the national courts through the preliminary ruling procedure permeate all five parts of the book. In Part I concerning the judicial organization of the European Union, Chapter 2 begins by highlighting the role played by both the national courts and the Union courts in the judicial system of the European Union and placing emphasis on the 'organic' Union judicature in terms of its organization, composition, and allocation of jurisdiction. Chapter 3 looks at the system of cooperation between the national courts and the Court of Justice through the reference for a preliminary ruling, thereby comprising general features of the preliminary ruling procedure, such as the framing of the questions, the obligation placed on certain national courts within a particular Member State's judicial architecture, and the division of tasks between the Court of Justice and the national courts in this context. Chapter 4 likewise examines the interaction between the national legal orders and Union law through the principle of national procedural autonomy and the Union framing principles of equivalence and effectiveness.

Part II concerns the enforcement of Union law and therefore encompasses two forms of action falling within the 'sword' function. Chapter 5 examines the action brought against a Member State for its failure to fulfil its obligations under the Treaties (commonly referred to as the 'infringement action') under Arts 258–260 TFEU. Chapter 6 proceeds to the preliminary ruling procedure in relation to the interpretation of Union law under Art. 267 TFEU, which albeit indirectly implicates matters concerning the compatibility of national law with Union law and delves further into the dialogue between the Court of Justice and the national courts in this setting.

Part III concerns the types of actions constituting protection against acts or failures to act of the Union institutions falling within the 'shield' function. These actions comprise the action for annulment under Art. 263 TFEU (Chapter 7); the action for failure to act under Art. 265 TFEU (Chapter 8); the objection of illegality under Art. 277 TFEU (Chapter 9); preliminary rulings on the validity of Union acts under Art. 267 TFEU (Chapter 10); the action for damages against the Union under Arts 268 and 340(2) TFEU (Chapter 11); and the application for an opinion on the compatibility of an international agreement to be concluded by the Union with the provisions of the Treaties under Art. 218(11) TFEU (Chapter 12). In particular, Chapter 10 includes discussion of matters concerning the interlocking system of jurisdiction between the Court of Justice and the national courts when it comes to the direct and indirect routes for assuring the review of the legality of Union acts in connection with actions for annulment and preliminary rulings on validity, respectively.

---

[25] See K. Lenaerts, 'The European Court of Justice and Process-Oriented Review' (2012) Y.E.L. 3–16.

Part IV concerns special forms of procedure before the Union courts. These include interim measures before the Union courts (Chapter 13); garnishee orders (Chapter 14); sanctions (Chapter 15); appeals (Chapter 16); the review procedure (Chapter 17); staff cases (Chapter 18); the contractual liability of the Union (the jurisdiction to give judgment pursuant to an arbitration clause or special agreement) (Chapter 19); (disputes relating to) intellectual property rights (Chapter 20); conventions concluded by the Member States (Chapter 21); and the Area of Freedom, Security and Justice (Chapter 22). To varying degrees, these subjects involve preliminary rulings given by the Court of Justice in response to references submitted by national courts, and as far as the Area of Freedom, Security and Justice is concerned, Chapter 22 covers, among other things, the urgent preliminary ruling procedure for cases falling within this area.

Part V deals with the procedure before the Union courts proper. It begins with the various common procedural rules applicable to all cases brought before the Union courts, such as those concerning service and time limits (Chapter 23). Following this, the different types of jurisdiction conferred on the Union courts generally give rise to three main sorts of procedures: first, the procedure in the case of references for a preliminary ruling pursuant to Art. 267 TFEU[26] (Chapter 24); second, the procedure in the case of direct actions (Chapter 25);[27] and third, the procedure in the case of appeals against decisions of the General Court (Chapter 26). The organization of the subjects presented in Part V reflects the structure of the new Rules of Procedure of the Court of Justice[28] and the pre-eminent position of the preliminary ruling procedure.

J. Procedural texts applicable to the procedure before the Union courts

1.10 The procedure before the Union courts is governed by a set of procedural texts. First, there are the relevant Treaty provisions conferring jurisdiction on the institution of the Court of Justice of the European Union, which are basically enshrined in Art. 19 TEU and Arts 251–281 TFEU.

Second, there is the Statute of the Court of Justice of the European Union, whose provisions have the same legal force as the Treaty provisions and which is annexed in a Protocol to the Treaties.[29] The Statute is divided into five titles with an annex concerning the Civil Service Tribunal, and generally sets down the rules governing the various types of procedures before the Court of Justice, the General Court, and the Civil Service Tribunal, as well as provisions concerning their composition and organization. Under former Art. 245 EC, the rules contained in the Statute (with the exception of those relating to the Status of Judges and Advocates General in Title 1) could only be amended by the Council acting unanimously at the request of the Court of Justice and after consulting the Commission and the European Parliament, or at the request of the Commission and after consulting the

---

[26] With respect to particular issues relating to the procedure applicable to dispute resolution under former Art. 35 EU, see paras 22.13–22.18.
[27] As far as the Civil Service Tribunal, this is dealt with in Ch. 18, concerning staff cases.
[28] See further n. 32.
[29] Protocol (No. 3), annexed to the TEU, the TFEU, and the EAEC Treaty, on the Statute of the Court of Justice of the European Union, [2012] O.J. C326/210, as amended by Regulation (EU, Euratom) No. 741/2012 of the European Parliament and of the Council of 11 August 2012, [2012] O.J. L228/1.

European Parliament and the Court of Justice.[30] However, this provision was changed by the Lisbon Treaty so as to provide that the European Parliament and the Council, acting in accordance with the ordinary legislative procedure—meaning by way of qualified majority voting in the Council and the co-decision procedure involving the European Parliament—may amend the provisions of the Statute, save for Title 1 and Art. 64 concerning the language arrangements applicable at the Court of Justice of the European Union, acting either at the request of the Court of Justice and after consultation of the Commission or on a proposal of the Commission and after consultation of the Court of Justice.[31]

Third, the rules set out in the Statute are expanded upon in the Rules of Procedure of the Court of Justice, of the General Court, and of the Civil Service Tribunal,[32] which are adopted by each respective Court in agreement with the Court of Justice as regards the latter two, and require the approval of the Council.[33]

Finally, there are various other procedural texts applicable to the procedure before the Union courts. For the Court of Justice, there are Supplementary Rules of Procedure,[34] Recommendations to national courts and tribunals in relation to the initiation of preliminary ruling proceedings,[35] and the Practice Directions to the Parties.[36] For the General Court and the Civil Service Tribunal, there are also Instructions to the Registrar[37] and Practice Directions to parties.[38] All relevant texts relating to the procedure can be found on the website of the Court of Justice of the European Union (<http://curia.europa.eu>).

---

[30] Art. 245, second para., EC; see also former Art. 160, second para., EAEC (which was repealed by the Lisbon Treaty).

[31] Art. 281, second para., TFEU.

[32] This book incorporates the recent changes made to the Rules of Procedure of the Court of Justice, done at Luxembourg on 25 September 2012 ([2012] O.J. L265/1) replacing the Rules of Procedure of the Court of Justice adopted on 19 June 1991, as last amended on 24 May 2011 ([2011] O.J. L162/17). See also the Rules of Procedure of the General Court, adopted on 2 May 1991 ([1991] O.J. L317/34), as last amended on 19 June 2013 ([2013] O.J. L173/66) and the Rules of Procedure of the Civil Service Tribunal, adopted on 25 July 2007 ([2007] O.J. L225/1; *corrigendum* [2008] O.J. L69/37) and last amended on 18 May 2011 ([2011] O.J. L162/19).

[33] As regards the Court of Justice, see Art. 253, sixth para., TFEU. As regards the General Court, see Art. 254, fifth para., TFEU. As regards the Civil Service Tribunal, see Art. 257, fifth para., TFEU. Pursuant to Art. 16(3) TEU, the Council acts by a qualified majority.

[34] Done at Luxembourg on 4 December 1974 ([1974] O.J. L350/29), last amended on 21 February 2006 ([2006] O.J. L72/1).

[35] [2012] O.J. C338/1.

[36] Available at <http://www.curia.europa.eu>.

[37] General Court: done at Luxembourg on 3 March 1994 ([1994] O.J. L78/32), last amended on 24 January 2012 ([2012] O.J. L68/20). Civil Service Tribunal: done at Luxembourg on 11 July 2012 ([2012] O.J. L260/1), replacing the Instructions to the Registrar of 19 September 2007 ([2007] O.J. L249/3)].

[38] General Court: see the Practice Directions to parties before the General Court, done at Luxembourg on 24 July 2012 ([2012] O.J. L68/23, *corrigendum* [2012] O.J. L73/23). Civil Service Tribunal: see the Practice Directions to parties on judicial proceedings before the European Union Civil Service Tribunal, done at Luxembourg on 11 July 2011 ([2012] O.J. L260/1).

PART I

THE JUDICIAL ORGANIZATION OF THE EUROPEAN UNION

2

THE EUROPEAN COURTS

I. The National Courts

(1) General

National courts and tribunals are under an obligation to apply Union law in all cases **2.01** between national authorities and natural or legal persons or between such persons[1] and to safeguard the rights conferred by Union law.[2]

(2) Primary role

The primary role played by national courts in applying Union law is connected with the **2.02** peculiar nature of that law. The Community Treaties, as were then in force before the Lisbon Treaty, created a new legal order directed at the Member States and their nationals. The relationship between the Union legal order and the national legal systems is characterized by the primacy of Union law and the direct effect of a whole series of provisions of Union law.[3] The question arises as to how individuals may assert the rights that they derive from those provisions.

The system of legal protection formulated in the Treaties does not provide for the creation of 'Union courts' in the different Member States. It starts from the premise that the national courts are the bodies to which individuals may turn whenever action or failure to act on the part of national authorities or other individuals infringes rights conferred on them by Union law.[4] The national court is therefore the normal Union court to hear and to

---

[1] See paras 4.39–4.41 with regard to the extent to which a national court is under a duty to raise a question of Union law of its own motion.

[2] See, e.g. ECJ, Case 106/77 *Simmenthal* [1978] E.C.R. 629, para. 21; ECJ, Case C-224/97 *Ciola* [1999] E.C.R. I-2517, paras 29–34; ECJ, Case C-290/00 *Duchon* [2002] E.C.R. I-3567, para. 31; ECJ, Joined Cases C-397/01 to C-403/01 *Pfeiffer and Others* [2004] E.C.R. I-8835, para. 111; ECJ, Case C-268/06 *Impact* [2008] E.C.R. I-2483, para. 42.

[3] ECJ, Opinion 1/91 *Draft Agreement between the Community, on the one hand, and the countries of the European Free Trade Association, on the other, relating to the creation of the European Economic Area* [1991] E.C.R. I-6079, para. 21 (referring to the Community as it then was); ECJ, Opinion 1/09 *Draft Agreement creating a Unified Patent Litigation System (European and Community Patents Court)* [2011] E.C.R. I-1137, para. 65. See also K. Lenaerts and P. Van Nuffel (R. Bray and N. Cambien (eds)), *European Union Law* (3rd edn, London, Sweet & Maxwell, 2011), paras 21.04–21.58.

[4] ECJ, Case 26/62 *Van Gend & Loos* [1963] E.C.R. 1, third para. Art. 19(1), second para., TEU provides: 'Member States shall provide remedies sufficient to ensure effective legal protection in the fields covered by Union law.' The Court further underlined the importance of national courts in the Union legal order in ECJ (8 March 2011), Opinion 1/09 *Draft Agreement creating a Unified Patent Litigation System (European and Community Patents Court)* [2011] E.C.R. I-1137, para. 66, stating that '[a]s is evident from Article 19(1)

determine all cases that do not fall within the jurisdiction of the Court of Justice, the General Court, or a specialized court.[5] Within the legal system of the individual's Member State, the national courts are the bridgehead of the Union legal order and secure the enforcement of Union law through dialogue with the Court of Justice.[6]

The Court of Justice has defined the task of national courts in its case-law on the operation of the preliminary ruling procedure[7] and on the application of the principle of sincere cooperation enshrined in Art. 4(3) TEU to national courts.[8]

II. The Court of Justice of the European Union

2.03 The institution known as the 'Court of Justice of the European Union' consists of the Court of Justice, the General Court, and specialized courts which, within their respective spheres of jurisdiction, ensure that in the interpretation and application of the Treaties the law is observed.[9] At present, only one specialized court has been created, namely the European

---

TEU, the guardians of that legal order and the judicial system of the European Union are the Court of Justice and the courts and tribunals of the Member States'. This provision is discussed further in para. 4.12. See also K. Lenaerts and D. Gerard, 'Decentralisation of EC Competition Law Enforcement: Judges in the Frontline' (2004) World Competition Law and Economics Review 319–49.

 [5] Art. 274 TFEU provides: 'Save where jurisdiction is conferred on the Court of Justice of the European Union by the Treaties, disputes to which the Union is a party shall not on that ground be excluded from the jurisdiction of the courts or tribunals of the Member States.' In other words, the Union judicature has been given the competence to decide those types of actions provided for in the Treaties and does not have inherent jurisdiction just because an issue of Union law is involved in a particular case. See ECJ, Case C-196/09 *Miles and Others* [2011] E.C.R. I-5105, paras 43–45. As such, the only time that a private party may bring a case before the Union judicature is when such party is bringing an action stipulated in the Treaties against an EU defendant (i.e. an institution, body, office, or agency of the Union). Conversely, cases between private parties, on the one hand, and cases between private parties and national authorities, on the other, fall within the competences of the national courts, not the Union courts. See, e.g. CFI (order of 20 May 2008), Case T-124/08 *Hurtado García v Spain*, not reported; CFI (order of 2 June 2008), Case T-468/07 *Bönker v Germany*, not reported; CFI (order of 22 July 2009), Case T-234/09 *Hârsulescu v Romania*, not reported (appeal dismissed: ECJ (order of 4 March 2010), Case C-374/09 P *Hârsulescu v Romania*, not reported); EGC (order of 25 October 2011), Case T-472/11 *DMA Die Marketing Agentur and Hoffmann v Austria*, not reported.

 [6] ECJ (Opinion 1/09 *Draft Agreement creating a Unified Patent Litigation System (European and Community Patents Court)* [2011] E.C.R. I-1137, paras 66–69. See, e.g. T. Corthaut, *EU Ordre Public* (Alphen aan de Rijn, Kluwer Law International, 2012), 436–9; T. von Danwitz, 'Sur les conditions de fonctionnement du processus jurisprudentiel à la Cour de justice de l'Union européenne' (2010) Il diritto dell'Unione europea 775–84; K. Lenaerts, 'The Rule of Law and the Coherence of the Judicial System of the European Union' (2007) C.M.L. Rev. 1625–59. For further discussion of proposed improvements in this regard, see, e.g. S. Prechal, 'National Courts in EU Judicial Structures' (2006) Y.E.L. 429–50; Resolution of the European Parliament of 9 July 2008 on the role of the national judge in the European judicial system, [2009] O.J. C294E/27.

 [7] See Ch. 3.

 [8] See Ch. 4.

 [9] Art. 19(1), first para., TEU. ECJ, Opinion 1/09 *Draft Agreement creating a Unified Patent Litigation System (European and Community Patents Court)* [2011] E.C.R. I-1137, para. 69: 'The national court, in collaboration with the Court of Justice, fulfils a duty entrusted to them both of ensuring that in the interpretation and application of the Treaties the law is observed'). See R. Barents, 'The Court of Justice After the Treaty of Lisbon' (2010) C.M.L. Rev. 709–28. The changes in appellation of the Union courts brought by the Lisbon Treaty had been anticipated to some extent by the Draft Constitutional Treaty. See further R. Barents, 'The Court of Justice in the Draft Constitution' (2004) M.J.E.C.L. 121–41.

Union Civil Service Tribunal.[10] In the future, however, new specialized courts may be attached to the General Court in order to exercise judicial competence in certain specific areas.[11] Together, there is a three-tier system of Union courts at the European Union level.[12]

Under the former Treaty framework, the institution known as the Court of Justice of the European Communities denoted the Court of Justice, the Court of First Instance, and judicial panels.[13] The changes in the names of the courts can generally be attributed, on the one hand, to the fact that the abolition of the three pillars in the Lisbon Treaty rendered any reference to the 'European Communities' obsolete and, on the other hand, to the fact that the Court of First Instance could no longer be treated merely as a court of 'first instance'. Furthermore, the reframing of judicial panels as 'specialized courts' gives expression to the fact that they constitute in reality fully fledged courts, even if they remain 'attached' to the General Court under the Lisbon Treaty, as had been the case under the former EC Treaty.[14]

As summarized by Art. 19(3) TEU, the Court of Justice of the European Union rules on actions brought by a Member State, an institution, or a natural or legal person; gives preliminary rulings on the interpretation and validity of Union law; and adjudicates other cases provided for in the Treaties.[15]

III. The Court of Justice

A. Composition

(1) Judges and Advocates-General

The Court of Justice consists of one Judge per Member State[16] and is assisted by a number **2.04** of Advocates-General.[17] Until 1 July 2013 there were only eight Advocates-General at the

---

[10] Council Decision 2004/752/EC, Euratom of 2 November 2004 establishing the European Union Civil Service Tribunal, [2004] O.J. L333/7. See H. Kanninen, 'Le Tribunal de la fonction publique de l'UE—La première juridiction specialisé dans le système juridictionnel de l'Union européenne', in M. Johansson, N. Wahl, and U. Bernitz (eds), *Liber Amicorum in Honour of Sven Norberg: A European for All Seasons* (Brussels, Bruylant, 2006), 287–99.

[11] Art. 257 TFEU. See S. Soldevila Fragoso, 'La création de juridictions spécialisées: la réponse des traités au traitement des contentieux de masse' (2011) Europe 4–7; para. 2.37. See further F. Dehousse and M. Rouland, *The Reform of the EU Courts: The Need of a Management Approach* (Brussels, Egmont Papers, 2011), 16–22.

[12] See V. Skouris, 'Vingt ans d'évolution de l'architecture juridictionelle de l'Union', in M. Arpio Santacruz *et al.* (eds), *A Man for All Treaties: Liber Amicorum en l'honneur de Jean-Claude Piris* (Brussels, Bruylant, 2011), 513–29.

[13] Art. 220 EC.

[14] Art. 257, first para., TFEU. Compare former Art. 220, second para., EC (which had provided that 'judicial panels may be attached to the Court of First Instance under the conditions laid down in Art. 225a in order to exercise, in certain specific areas, the judicial competence laid down in this Treaty').

[15] Art. 19(3) TEU.

[16] Art. 19(2), first para., TEU. See further J.-C. Bonichot, 'Le métier de juge à la Cour de justice des Communautés européennes' (2007) Revue des affairs européennes 531–7; A. Ó Caoimh, 'L'office du juge à la Cour de justice de l'Union européenne' (2010) Justice & cassation 141–9; N. Wahl, 'Quelques réflexions sur le role du juge', in *Concurrences, New Frontiers of Antitrust 2011* (Brussels, Bruylant, 2012), 151–61.

[17] Art. 252, first para., TFEU.

Court of Justice.[18] Pursuant to Council Decision 2013/336/EU of 25 June 2013 this number was increased to nine on 1 July 2013, and will be further increased to eleven by 7 October 2015.[19]

Judges and Advocates-General are chosen from persons whose independence is beyond doubt and who possess the qualifications required for appointment to the highest judicial offices in their respective countries or who are jurisconsults of recognized competence.[20] As was the case under the former Treaty framework, they are appointed for a term of six years by common accord of the governments of the Member States.[21] What is new under the Lisbon Treaty, however, is the creation of a panel to give an opinion on candidates' suitability to perform the duties of Judge and Advocate-General before the national governments take their decision.[22]

---

[18] When new Member States joined the Community in 1973, the original number of Advocates-General was increased from two to four (Art. 1 of the Decision of 1 January 1973, [1973] O.J. L2/29), which were to be shared among the four 'large' Member States. After the accession of Greece, a fifth was added (Council Decision of 30 March 1981, [1981] O.J. L100/21) for a smaller Member State and, following the accession of Spain and Portugal, a sixth (Art. 18 of the 1985 Act of Accession, [1985] O.J. L302/26). The accession of further Member States has raised the number of Advocates-General to eight, and temporarily to nine (Art. 11 of the Council Decision of 1 January 1995 amending Art. 20 of the 1994 Act of Accession, [1995] O.J. L1/1): the five 'large' Member States each put forward one person for appointment as Advocate-General, whilst the other Member States shared in turn the remaining three posts. See the Joint Declaration on Art. 31 of the Decision adjusting the instruments concerning the accession of the new Member States to the European Union, [1995] O.J. L1/221). In the case of the 2004 and 2007 accessions, the number of Advocates-General was kept at eight. The Joint Declaration on the Court of Justice of the European Communities annexed to the Acts of Accession stated that '[s]hould the Court of Justice so request, the Council, acting unanimously, may increase the number of Advocates-General' and added '[o]therwise, the new Member States will be integrated into the existing system for their appointment' ([2003] O.J. L236/971).

[19] Art. 252 TFEU states that '[s]hould the Court of Justice so request, the Council, acting unanimously, may increase the number of Advocates-General'. This is further specified in Declaration (No. 38), annexed to the Lisbon Treaty, on Article 252 of the Treaty on the Functioning of the European Union regarding the number of Advocates-General in the Court of Justice, [2012] O.J. C326/352, stating that in case of a request by the Court of Justice to increase the number of Advocates-General by three, the Council would, acting unanimously, agree on such an increase. In that case, Poland would have a permanent Advocate-General. Pursuant to Art. 252 TFEU, the Court of Justice made a request to increase the number of Advocates-General to eleven on 16 January 2013. Following Declaration (No. 38), the Council adopted Council Decision 2013/336/EU of 25 June 2013, increasing the number of Advocates-General of the Court of Justice of the European Union ([2013] O.J. L179/92).

[20] Art. 19(2), third para., TEU; Art. 253, first para., TFEU. On the independence of the Judges of the Court of Justice, see J. Malenovský, 'Les éléments constitutifs du mandat des juges de la Cour de justice à l'épreuve du temps: l'iceberg commence à fondre' (2011) Il diritto dell'Unione europea 801–36.

[21] Art. 253, first para., TFEU.

[22] Art. 253, first para., TFEU; Art. 255 TFEU. The panel comprises seven persons chosen from among former members of the Court of Justice and the General Court, members of national supreme courts, and lawyers of recognized competence, one of whom is to be proposed by the European Parliament. The Council, acting on the initiative of the President of the Court of Justice, establishes the panel's operating rules and appoints its members. This panel also applies in relation to the appointment of Judges to the General Court: see n. 82. The operating rules of this panel were set down by Council Decision 2010/124/EU of 25 February 2010, [2010] O.J. L50/18. Each year, the panel issues an activity report, which can be consulted through <http://www.curia.europa.eu>. For further discussion, see R. Barents, 'The Court of Justice in the Renewed European Treaties', in A. Ott and E. Vos (eds), *Fifty Years of European Integration: Foundations and Perspectives* (The Hague, TMC Asser Press, 2009), 57–75. A similar, though not identical, advisory panel exists in relation to the Civil Service Tribunal discussed at n. 146.

Every three years there is a partial replacement of Judges and Advocates-General. Fourteen Judges and five and four Advocates-General alternately are replaced.[23] Retiring Judges and Advocates-General may be reappointed.[24] The Treaties do not require that Judges and Advocates-General must be nationals of Member States.

(2) Uneven number of Judges

The Court must always consist of an uneven number of Judges when it takes its decisions,[25] **2.05** which is why it always had this uneven number in the past.[26] However, with the accession of Croatia, the Court now has twenty-eight judges. This poses no problems in practice, as the Grand Chamber is de facto the biggest bench, consisting of fifteen judges. When, exceptionally, the full Court will hear a case, the most junior Judge will not sit. As far as Advocates-General are concerned, at present there is a permanent one for France, Germany, Italy, Poland, Spain, and the United Kingdom; the three remaining Advocates-General come alternately from the other Member States on a rotating basis.[27]

If the office of a Judge or Advocate-General falls vacant before the expiry of its term, a successor is appointed for the remainder of the normal term of office.[28]

(3) Oath and immunity

Before taking up their duties, Judges and Advocates-General take an oath, in open court, to **2.06** perform their duties impartially and conscientiously and to preserve the secrecy of the deliberations of the Court.[29] Judges and Advocates-General are immune from legal

---

[23] Art. 253, second para., TFEU; Statute, Art. 9. Note that Council Decision 2013/336/EU of 25 June 2013 increasing the number of Advocates-General of the Court of Justice of the European Union ([2013] O.J. L179/92) has not altered the rule that every three years four Advocates-General are replaced. Such an alteration would require an adaptation of Art. 9 of the Statute of the Court of Justice of the European Union, which cannot be done by a mere Council Decision. However, it must be assumed that before 7 October 2015, the Statute will be changed so as to allow a replacement of alternately five and four Advocates-General.

[24] Art. 253, fourth para., TFEU.

[25] Statute, Art. 17, first para.

[26] The need to have an uneven number of Judges stemmed from the rule that in principle the Court of Justice met in plenary session. Accordingly, the accession of new Member States in 1973 was to have increased the original number of Judges from seven to eleven (Art. 17 of the 1972 Act of Accession, [1972] O.J. Spec. Ed. 14), but their number was reduced to nine on account of Norway's decision not to join the Community (Art. 4 of the Council Decision of 1 January 1973, [1973] O.J. L2/1). Following the accession of Greece, the Court had only ten Judges (Art. 16 of the 1979 Act of Accession, [1979] O.J. L291/20, and Council Decision of 22 December 1980 ([1980] O.J. L380/6), after which the Council raised the number to eleven by Decision of 30 March 1981 ([1981] O.J. L100/20). The number was increased to fifteen by Art. 10 of the Council Decision of 1 January 1995, adjusting the instruments concerning the accession of the new Member States to the European Union ([1995] O.J. L1/1), which amended Art. 17 of the 1985 Act of Accession ([1985] O.J. L302/26). The accession of ten Member States on 1 May 2004 brought the number to twenty-five Judges (Art. 13 of the 2003 Act of Accession, [2003] O.J. L236/33). With the accession of Bulgaria and Romania on 1 January 2007, the number was raised to twenty-seven Judges (Art. 11 of the 2005 Act of Accession, [2005] O.J. L157/203). Since the accession of Croatia on 1 July 2013, the Court of Justice consists of twenty-eight Judges (Art. 9(1) of the 2012 Act of Accession, [2012] O.J. L112/21).

[27] See para. 2.04.

[28] Statute, Arts 7–8.

[29] Statute, Art. 2. By virtue of Art. 8 of the Statute, the provisions of the Statute relating to the status of Judges (Arts 2–7) also apply to Advocates-General. As from 2007, the Court of Justice of the European Union adopted a Code of Conduct clarifying certain obligations under the relevant provisions of the Statute and Rules of Procedure for members and former members of the Court of Justice, the Court of First Instance (now the General Court), and the Civil Service Tribunal ([2007] O.J. C233/1).

proceedings. They continue to enjoy immunity after they have ceased to hold office in respect of acts performed by them in their official capacity, including words spoken or written. Their immunity may be waived only by the Court sitting in plenary session. Where immunity has been waived and criminal proceedings are instituted against a Judge or an Advocate-General, the member concerned may be tried only by the court competent to judge the members of the highest national judiciary.[30]

Judges and Advocates-General may not hold any political or administrative office or engage in any occupation unless exemption is granted by the Council. After their term of office, they must act with integrity and discretion as regards the acceptance of certain appointments or benefits.[31] A Judge or Advocate-General may be deprived of his or her office or of his or her right to a pension or other benefits in its stead only if, in the unanimous opinion of the other Judges and Advocates-General, he or she no longer fulfils the requisite conditions or meets the obligations arising from his or her office.[32]

(4) President

2.07 Immediately after their partial replacement, the Judges elect one of their number as President of the Court for a term of three years. He or she may be re-elected.[33] The rule that if an office falls vacant before the normal expiry date of its term a successor is to be elected for the remainder of the term, also applies to the President.[34]

(5) Vice-President

2.08 As part of the recent changes to the procedural texts of the Court of Justice of the European Union, it was considered that the increasing responsibilities of the President require the establishment of an office of Vice-President in order to assist the President in carrying out those responsibilities.[35] Consequently, following the election of the President, the Judges elect from among their number a Vice-President of the Court for a term of three years. He or she may be re-elected.[36] The rule that if an office falls vacant before the normal expiry

---

[30] Statute, Art. 3.

[31] Statute, Art. 4.

[32] Statute, Art. 6.

[33] Art. 253, third para., TFEU; Statute, Art. 9a; ECJ Rules of Procedure, Art. 8(1). The elections are conducted by secret ballot. The Judge obtaining the votes of more than half the Judges of the Court shall be elected; if no Judge obtains that majority, further ballots are held until that majority is attained: ECJ Rules of Procedure, Art. 8(3).

[34] ECJ Rules of Procedure, Art. 8(2). As regards circumstances in which the President and the Vice-President of the Court are prevented from acting, Art. 13 of the ECJ Rules of Procedure provides that the functions of President are to be exercised by one of the Presidents of Chambers of five Judges, or failing that, by one of the Presidents of Chambers of three Judges, or failing that, by one of the other Judges according to the order of seniority laid down in Art. 7 of the Statute.

[35] Regulation (EU, Euratom) No. 741/2012 of the European Parliament and of the Council amending the Protocol on the Statute of the Court Justice of the European Union and Annex I thereto, [2012] O.J. L228/1, third recital. According to Art. 10(3) of the ECJ Rules of procedure, the Court of Justice specifies the conditions under which the Vice-President shall take the place of the President in the performance of his judicial duties. On 23 October 2012, the Court of Justice adopted on this basis, Decision 2012/671/EU concerning the judicial functions of the Vice-President of the Court, [2012] O.J. L 300/47.

[36] Statute, Art. 9a; ECJ Rules of Procedure, Art. 8(4). Once elected, the names of the President and Vice-President are published in the *Official Journal*: ECJ Rules of Procedure, Art. 8(5). See Notice 2012/C 366/03 concerning the Election of the President of the Court and Notice 2012/C 366/04 concerning the Election of the Vice-President of the Court, [2012] O.J. C366/2.

date of its term a successor is to be elected for the remainder of the term, likewise applies to the Vice-President.[37]

(6) Registrar

An election procedure is also used to appoint the Court Registrar for a term of six years.[38] **2.09** He or she may be reappointed.[39] If the office of Registrar falls vacant before the normal expiry date, a new Registrar is to be appointed for a term of six years.[40] The Registrar takes the same oath before the Court as the Judges and Advocates-General.[41] The Court may, in accordance with the procedure laid down in respect of the Registrar, elect a Deputy Registrar to assist the Registrar and to take his or her place if he or she is prevented from acting.[42]

B. Internal organization

(1) Chambers

In principle, the Court of Justice sits in Chambers consisting of five (the most frequent **2.10** case)[43] or three Judges, or as the Grand Chamber when a Member State or an institution of the Union that is party to the proceedings so requests,[44] or when the Court considers that a case before it has an important value as a precedent.[45] For specific cases listed in the Statute or where the Court considers that a case before it is of exceptional importance, the Court may sit as a Full Court.[46]

---

[37] ECJ Rules of Procedure, Art. 8(4).

[38] Art. 253, fifth para., TFEU; ECJ Rules of Procedure, Art. 18. The name of the Registrar elected in accordance with that procedure is published in the *Official Journal*: ECJ Rules of Procedure, Art. 18(8).

[39] ECJ Rules of Procedure, Art. 18(4). As provided in this Article, the Court may decide to renew the term of office of the incumbent Registrar without availing itself of the procedure set down in Art. 18(2) of the ECJ Rules of Procedure.

[40] ECJ Rules of Procedure, Art. 18(7).

[41] Statute, Art. 10; ECJ Rules of Procedure, Art. 18(5).

[42] ECJ Rules of Procedure, Art. 19.

[43] As regards the urgent preliminary ruling procedure applicable to measures concerning the Area of Freedom, Security and Justice, the Court designates the Chambers of five Judges for a period of one year to handle such cases : ECJ Rules of Procedure, Art. 11(2) (referring to the cases of the kind referred to in Art. 107 of the ECJ Rules of Procedure). The composition and designation of such Chambers are published in the *Official Journal*: ECJ Rules of Procedure, Art. 11(5). See Notice 2013/C 336/07 concerning the Designation of the Chamber responsible for cases of the kind referred to in Article 107 of the Rules of Procedure of the Court ([2013] O.J. C336/4). This procedure is discussed further in Ch. 22.

[44] Art. 251, first para. TFEU; Statute, Art. 16, first, second, and third paras. See ECJ, Case C-292/05 *Lechouritou* [2007] E.C.R. I-1519, paras 19–20, 23, underlining that the third para. of Art. 16 of the Statute only mentions requests made by a Member State or an institution that is a party to the proceedings for the Court to sit in a Grand Chamber; individuals do not have standing to make such requests.

[45] See ECJ Rules of Procedure, Art. 60(1), which provides that 'The Court shall assign to the Chambers of five and three Judges any case brought before it insofar as the difficulty or importance of the case or particular circumstances are not such as to require that it should be assigned to the Grand Chamber.'

[46] Art. 251, second para., TFEU; Statute, Art. 16, fourth and fifth paras; ECJ Rules of Procedure, Art. 60(2). For example, see ECJ, Opinion 1/03 *Competence of the Community to conclude the new Lugano Convention on jurisdiction and the recognition and enforcement of judgments in civil and commercial matters* [2006] E.C.R. I-1145; ECJ Case C-432/04 *Commission v Cresson* [2006] E.C.R. I-6387; ECJ Opinion 1/09 *Draft Agreement creating a Unified Patent Litigation System (European and Community Patents Court)* [2011] E.C.R. I-1137; ECJ (judgment of 27 November 2012), Case C-370/12 *Pringle*, not reported. See also ECJ, Case C-292/05 *Lechouritou* [2007] E.C.R. I-1519, paras 21–23: it is the Court alone which, pursuant to the fifth para. of Art. 16 of the Statute, has the power to decide, after hearing the Advocate-General, to refer a case to the Full Court, where it considers that case to be of exceptional importance. In the proceedings at hand, the Court considered that

The Court forms Chambers consisting of three or five Judges.[47] At present, the Court has five Chambers of five Judges and five Chambers of three Judges. The Judges elect the Presidents of Chambers from among their number. The Presidents of the Chambers of five Judges are elected for three years and may be re-elected once.[48] The Presidents of the Chambers of three Judges are elected for a term of one year.[49]

The Grand Chamber consists of fifteen Judges and is presided over by the President of the Court.[50] In order to avoid the important cases assigned to that chamber being heard always by the same Judges, its composition varies. For each case, the Grand Chamber is composed of the President and the Vice-President of the Court, three Presidents of Chambers of five Judges, the Judge-Rapporteur, and the number of Judges necessary to reach fifteen. The last-mentioned Judges and three Presidents of Chambers of five Judges are designated from lists drawn up for the purpose of determining the composition of the Grand Chamber.[51] Only the President and the Vice-President of the Court are thus permanent members of the Grand Chamber, while the other Judges sit in approximately one in two Grand Chamber cases.

For each case, the Chambers of five Judges and three Judges are composed of the President of the Chamber, the Judge-Rapporteur, and the number of Judges required to attain the number of five and three Judges, respectively. The lists of Judges assigned to the Chambers of five and three Judges,[52] the order used to determine the composition of the Grand Chamber and the Chambers of five and three Judges, and the appointments of Presidents of Chambers are published in the *Official Journal of the European Union*.[53]

(2) Quorum

2.11 When the Court sits in Chambers, there is a quorum of three Judges in the case of three- or five-Judge Chambers and of eleven Judges in the case of the Grand Chamber. Decisions of the Full Court are valid if seventeen Judges are sitting.[54]

---

there were no good reasons for doing so. Accordingly, a request made by an individual for the Court to decide that the case is of exceptional importance and refer it to the Full Court must necessarily be refused.

[47] Statute, Art. 16, first para.; ECJ Rules of Procedure, Art. 28.

[48] Statute, Art. 16, first para.; ECJ Rules of Procedure, Art. 12(1).

[49] ECJ Rules of Procedure, Art. 12(2). Since in practice a rotation system is applied, they are generally not re-elected.

[50] Statute, Art. 16, second para.

[51] ECJ Rules of Procedure, Art. 27.

[52] At present, five or six Judges are assigned to each of the five Chambers of five Judges and four or five Judges are assigned to each of the five Chambers of three Judges. It falls within the Court's power of internal organization to assign the Judges from a Chamber which are to adjudicate a particular case (see ECJ, Case C-7/94 *Gaal* [1995] E.C.R. I-1031, para. 13, in which the German Government argued that the criteria determining the composition of the Chamber adjudicating a case consisting of five Judges from a Chamber to which six Judges had been appointed had not been published in the *Official Journal of the European Union*). As far as the General Court is concerned, Art. 32(4) of the EGC Rules of Procedure provides that if in a Chamber of three or five Judges the number of Judges assigned to that Chamber is higher than three or five respectively, the President of the Chamber is to decide which of the Judges will be called upon to take part in the judgment of the case.

[53] ECJ Rules of Procedure, Arts 12(4), 27(5), and 28(4). See Notice 2012/C 366/05 concerning the Election of the Presidents of the Chambers of five Judges ([2012] O.J. C366/3); Notice 2013/C 336/03 on the Election of the Presidents of the Chambers of three judges ([2013] O.J. 336/03) and Notice 2013/C 336/05 concerning the Lists for the purposes of determining the composition of the formations of the Court ([2013] O.J. C336/3).

[54] Statute, Art. 17, fourth and fifth paras.

(3) Assignment of a case to a Chamber

At the end of the written procedure, the Court may assign any case to a Chamber of five or **2.12** three Judges or to the Grand Chamber at an administrative meeting, upon consideration of the Judge-Rapporteur's preliminary report and after the Advocate-General has been heard. In principle, the Court must comply with a request from a Member State or an institution of the Union that is a party to the proceedings for a case to be assigned to the Grand Chamber.[55] The Court meets as the Full Court in very exceptional cases exhaustively listed in the Treaties (dismissal of the European Ombudsman, compulsory retirement of a Member of the Commission in breach of his or her obligations, etc.) and where the Court considers that the case before it is of exceptional importance.[56] A Chamber may, however, refer a case back to the Court at any stage in the proceedings so that it may be reassigned to a formation composed of a greater number of Judges.[57] Parties are not entitled to require that a Judge of a particular nationality sit or not sit.[58] The Court therefore constitutes a genuinely 'supranational' court vis-à-vis the Member States and specifically national procedural interests.

(4) Deliberations

The deliberations of the Court are secret.[59] The Judges are not assisted by interpreters **2.13** (as French is the working language of the Court and is used in the deliberations: see para. 23.11) or by other members of staff. The deliberations take place on the basis of a draft judgment drawn up by the Judge-Rapporteur.

The conclusions reached by a majority of Judges after final discussion determines the decision of the Court.[60] Pains are taken to reach a consensus among the Judges. It is for this reason that an uneven number of Judges always take part in the deliberations: it prevents a tied vote. Where, by reason of a Judge being absent or prevented from attending, there is an

---

[55] Art. 251, second para., TFEU; Statute, Art. 16, third para.; ECJ Rules of Procedure, Art. 60(1). However, the Court rejected a request of the Council, made pursuant to Art. 16, third para. of the Statute, to have a case reassigned to the Grand Chamber where it was made at a very advanced stage of the proceedings—after the close of the oral procedure and thus at the deliberation stage—on the grounds that such request was 'liable to cause considerable delay to the progress of the proceedings and therefore to have effects clearly contrary to the requirement of the proper administration of justice which means that the Court must be able in any case brought before it to ensure that a decision is taken following a procedure that is efficient and completed within a proper time': ECJ, Case C-310/04 *Spain v Council* [2006] E.C.R. I-7285, para. 23.

[56] Statute, Art. 16, fourth and fifth paras; ECJ Rules of Procedure, Art. 60(2). For a recent case, see ECJ (judgment of 27 November 2012), Case C-370/12 *Pringle* not reported.

[57] ECJ Rules of Procedure, Art. 60(3). See e.g. ECJ, Case C-357/09 PPU *Kadzoev* [2010] E.C.R. I-11189, para. 33. A referral back under Art. 60(3) of the ECJ Rules of Procedure constitutes a measure which the formation to which the case has been assigned in principle decides on freely and of its own motion, as opposed to Art. 16, third para. of the Statute, which requires the Court to sit as a Grand Chamber if a request is made to that effect, *inter alia*, by an institution of the Union that is party to the proceedings (see ECJ, Case C-310/04 *Spain v Council* [2006] E.C.R. I-7285, paras 21–22). As regards the composition of Chambers where cases are referred back, see ECJ Rules of Procedure, Art. 29(2).

[58] The fourth para. of Art. 18 of the Statute provides: 'A party may not apply for a change in the composition of the Court or of one of its chambers on the grounds of either the nationality of a Judge or the absence from the Court or from the chamber of a Judge of the nationality of that party.'

[59] Statute, Art. 35; ECJ Rules of Procedure, Art. 32(1). When a hearing has taken place, only those Judges who participated in that hearing and, where relevant, the Assistant Rapporteur responsible for the consideration of the case, take part in the deliberations: ECJ Rules of Procedure, Art. 32(2). Every Judge taking part in the deliberations must state his or her opinion and the reasons for it: ECJ Rules of Procedure, Art. 32(3).

[60] ECJ Rules of Procedure, Art. 32(4).

even number of Judges, the most junior Judge (where there is equal seniority in office, the younger) is to abstain from taking part in the deliberations unless he or she is the Judge-Rapporteur. In that case, the Judge immediately senior to him or her is to abstain from taking part in the deliberations.[61]

(5) Collegiate decision of the Court

2.14 For each case, there is one single judgment or order issued by the Court representing the collective decision of all the Judges participating in the case concerned. There are no dissenting or concurring opinions issued by individual Judges, as there are, for instance, in the European Court of Human Rights or the International Court of Justice.[62] Even Judges who voted against the decision ultimately adopted sign the judgment.

(6) Roles of the Judge-Rapporteur and the Advocate-General

2.15 The primary responsibility for decision-making within the Court lies with the Judge-Rapporteur, who is designated for each case by the President immediately after proceedings have been brought.[63] At the same time, the First Advocate-General[64] assigns an Advocate-General to the case.[65] The Judge-Rapporteur and the Advocate-General follow the procedural progress of the case with particular heed. The Judge-Rapporteur is responsible for drawing up the preliminary report (see para. 23.56). Finally, it falls to the Judge-Rapporteur to draw up the draft judgment and subsequently to revise it so that it reflects the consensus of the Court or the Chamber (or the majority of the bench) (see para. 2.13).

The Advocate-General, acting with complete impartiality and independence, makes, in open court, reasoned submissions (the Advocate-General's Opinion) on each case assigned to him or her in order to assist the Court in the performance of its task.[66] Unlike the Procureur-Général in some national legal systems, the Advocates-General are not entrusted with the defence of the general interest and do not form a hierarchy. As members of the institution of the Court of Justice, the Advocates-General take part in the process by which the Court reaches its judgment and in carrying out the judicial function entrusted to it.[67]

---

[61] ECJ Rules of Procedure, Art. 33.

[62] But see European Parliament legislative resolution of 5 July 2012 on the draft regulation of the European Parliament and of the Council amending the Protocol on the Statute of the Court of Justice of the European Union and Annex I thereto, point 4, in which the European Parliament 'resolves to hold a debate in Parliament in the near future on the merits of introducing the possibility of issuing dissenting opinions at the Court of Justice'. See further J. Azizi, 'Unveiling the EU Courts' Internal Decision-making Process: A Case for Dissenting Opinions?' (2011) ERA-Forum 49–68.

[63] ECJ Rules of Procedure, Art. 15(1).

[64] The First Advocate-General is appointed for one year by the Court and has the rank of a President of Chamber. He is *primus inter pares* among the Advocates-General (ECJ Rules of Procedure, Art. 14(1)). For the role of the First Advocate-General in the review procedure, see Ch. 17.

[65] ECJ Rules of Procedure, Art. 16(1).

[66] Art. 252, second para., TFEU. See further J. Kokott, *Anwältin des Rechts: zur Rolle der Generalanwälte beim Europäischen Gerichtshof* (Bonn, Zentrum für Europäisches Wirtschaftsrecht, 2006), 42; E. Sharpston, 'The Changing Role of the Advocate General', in A. Arnull, P. Eeckhout, and T. Tridimas (eds), *Continuity and Change in EU Law: Essays in Honour of Sir Francis Jacobs* (Oxford, Oxford University Press, 2008), 20–33.

[67] ECJ (order of 4 February 2000), Case C-17/98 *Emesa Sugar* [2000] E.C.R. I-665, paras 10 *et seq.* Neither the Statute nor its Rules of Procedure make provision for the parties to submit observations in response to the Advocate-General's Opinion, and therefore, applications to that effect are rejected. See ECJ, Case C-343/07 *Bavaria and Bavaria Italia* [2009] E.C.R. I-5491, para. 32 (and citations therein).

Where it considers that the case raises no new point of law, the Court may decide, after hearing the Advocate-General, that the case shall be determined without a submission from the Advocate-General.[68]

(7) Authority of the Advocate-General's Opinion

The Advocate-General's Opinion is not binding on the Court of Justice. It is merely **2.16** advisory, and in essence constitutes how the Advocate-General submits that the Court of Justice should decide the particular case before it. Thus, while the Advocate-General's Opinion is a helpful aid, there is no obligation on the Court of Justice to follow it.[69] The Court of Justice has complete discretion in this regard, and it may, for instance, wholly disregard the Advocate-General's Opinion, take up some or all of the arguments raised, or even refer explicitly to the reasoning of the Advocate-General's Opinion in the judgment itself.

Even if it is not binding on the Court of Justice, the Advocate-General's Opinion none-theless plays an important role in EU jurisprudence. This is illustrated by the fact that it was published alongside the Court's judgment in the European Court Reports. It should also be mentioned that the Advocate-General's Opinion may have significant merit for advocating necessary change or providing critical insight on matters concerning the future of the Union legal order.[70]

(8) Role of the President

The President represents the Court and directs the judicial business and the administration **2.17** of the Court. He or she presides at general meetings of the Members of the Court and at hearings before and deliberations of the Full Court and the Grand Chamber.[71] The President does not sit in the five- and three-Judge Chambers.

(9) Role of the Vice-President

The Vice-President assists the President of the Court in the performance of his duties and **2.18** takes the place of the President when the latter is prevented from acting or when the office

---

[68] Statute, Art. 20, fifth para. In this regard, see E. Sharpston, 'The Changing Role of the Advocate General', in A. Arnull, P. Eeckhout, and T. Tridimas (eds), *Continuity and Change in EU Law—Essays in Honour of Sir Francis Jacobs* (Oxford/New York, Oxford University Press, 2008), 20–33.

[69] Commentators have analysed how often the Court of Justice follows the Opinions of the Advocates-General. See, e.g. C. Ritter, 'A New Look at the Role and Impact of Advocates-General—Collectively and Generally' (2006) Col. J.E.L. 751–75. Yet, generally speaking, it is difficult to determine how much influence the particular Opinion had on the deliberations of the Court, even if the Court did not follow it; conversely, the Court may come to the same conclusions as the Advocate-General in a particular case but on the basis of very different legal reasoning.

[70] For example, as regards effective judicial protection for individuals, the Opinion of Advocate-General F. Jacobs in ECJ, Case C-50/00 P *Unión de Pequeños Agricultores v Council* [2002] E.C.R. I-6677; see further para. 7.106.

[71] ECJ Rules of Procedure, Art. 9. See also A. Tizzano and P. Iannuccelli, 'La organización y el funcionamiento del Tribunal de Justicia', in J. M. Beneyto Pérez, J. M. Gonzáles-Orús, and B. Becerril Atienza (eds), *Tratado de derecho y políticas de la Unión Europea: Sistema Jurisdiccional de la UE* (Madrid, Aranzadi, 2012), 136–8. Under Art. 39 of the Statute, the President of the Court of Justice adjudicates on applications, by way of summary procedure, to suspend execution or enforcement of acts of the Union institutions and to prescribe interim measures as provided for in the relevant provisions of the Treaties specified therein: see further Ch. 13. These functions are now performed by the Vice-President of the Court: see para. 2-18.

of President is vacant.[72] He or she may also take the President's place, at the latter's request, in performing the duties specified in Art. 9(1) and (3) of the ECJ Rules of Procedure, namely in representing the Court and ensuring the proper functioning of the services of the Court.[73] He may also take the President's place in performing some of the latter's judicial duties. The Court must, however, by decision to be published in the *Official Journal*, specify the conditions under which the Vice-President will take the place of the President in the performance of his judicial duties.[74]

(10) Role of the Registrar

2.19   The Registrar is responsible, under the authority of the President of the Court, for the acceptance, transmission, and custody of all documents and for effecting service as provided for by the ECJ Rules of Procedure. The Registrar has additional responsibilities, including assisting the Members of the Court in all their official functions; being in charge of the publications of the Court, in particular the European Court Reports; and directing the services of the Court under the authority of the President.[75]

Importantly, the Registrar is responsible for the keeping of the Registry in which all procedural documents and supporting items and documents lodged are entered in the order in which they are submitted.[76]

(11) Staff

2.20   In performing its duties, the Court of Justice has a variety of departments at its disposal. There is an interpreting service; a translation service; a research and documentation department, which also manages the Court's library; and internal administrative machinery (including personnel, finance, and technical services departments). The Registry staff assist the Registrar in the performance of his or her judicial duties. As far as his or her administrative tasks are concerned, the Registrar can have recourse to the various departments of the Court. The Judges and Advocates-General are each served by three or four law clerks, known as *référendaires*, who carry out the preparatory work for the Judges and Advocates-General, and by three secretarial staff members.

---

[72] Statute, Art. 9a, second para.; ECJ, Rules of Procedure, Art. 10(1). See also Statute, Art. 39, second para. as amended, in which it is now provided that the powers of the President under that provision may, under the conditions laid down in the Rules of Procedure, be exercised by the Vice-President of the Court.

[73] ECJ Rules of Procedure, Art. 10(2).

[74] ECJ Rules of Procedure, Art. 10(3). On this basis, on 23 October 2012, the ECJ adopted Decision 2012/671/EU concerning the judicial functions of the Vice-President of the Court, [2012] O.J. L 300/47. According to this decision, '[t]he Vice-President of the Court shall take the place of the President of the Court in the performance of the judicial duties referred to in the first paragraph of Article 39 of the Protocol on the Statute of the Court of Justice of the European Union and in Article 57 thereof and in Article 160–166 of the Rules of Procedure of the Court of Justice'. For a first application, see ECJ (order of the Vice-President of 8 March 2013), Case C-551/12 P(R), *EDF v Commission*, not reported. See further K. Lenaerts, 'Les nouvelles fonctions de vice-président de la Cour de justice de l'Union européenne' (2012) Rec. Dalloz 2880.

[75] ECJ Rules of Procedure, Art. 20. See also ECJ Rules of Procedure, Art. 39: The Registrar must, at the request of any Judge, Advocate-General, or party, arrange for anything said or written in the course of the proceedings before the Court to be translated into the languages chosen from those referred to in Art. 36 of the ECJ Rules of Procedure.

[76] ECJ Rules of Procedure, Art. 21.

C. Basic functions

(1) Constitutional and Supreme Court

The Court of Justice plays the role of the Union's constitutional court, that is to say, the **2.21** guardian of the objectives and rules of law laid down in the Treaties. The Court rules in cases in which constitutional issues come to the fore, such as the legality of Union secondary legislation, the preservation of institutional balance, the demarcation of Union and national spheres of competence, and the protection of fundamental rights.[77]

Alongside this, the Court plays the role of a supreme court where—on a request from a national court for a preliminary ruling—it ensures the uniform application of Union law.[78] In a certain sense, there is also a constitutional aspect to that function performed by the Court inasmuch as disparate application of Union law in the Member States would run counter to achievement of the objectives laid down in the Treaties.

(2) Court of last resort for constitutional issues

It is self-evident that constitutional issues of Union law may also arise in cases brought **2.22** before national courts or the General Court. Consequently, the Court of Justice is not the sole guardian of the Union legal order. But national courts may (and, in some cases, must) still bring the constitutional issue before the Court by requesting a preliminary ruling (see Ch. 3). Likewise, an appeal may be brought or, in exceptional cases, a review procedure initiated against decisions of the General Court, which means that here again the Court of Justice can have the last word in determining legal questions with constitutional implications[79] (see paras 2.45–2.55, concerning the distribution of heads of jurisdiction as between the various judicial bodies belonging to the Court of Justice of the European Union).

---

[77] J. L. da Cruz Vilaça, 'El control jurisdiccional de la constitucionalidad', in J. Vidal-Beneyto and J. Alguacil (eds), *El reto constitucional de Europa* (Madrid, Dykinson, 2005), 217–28; K. Lenaerts, *Le juge et la constitution aux Etats-Unis d'Amérique et dans l'ordre juridique européen* (Brussels, Bruylant, 1988), 817; K. Lenaerts, 'Some Thoughts About the Interaction Between Judges and Politicians' (1992) Y.E.L. 1–34; K. Lenaerts, 'La constitutionnalisation de l'ordre juridique de l'Union européenne', in R. Andersen, D. Déom, F. Leurquin-De Visscher *et al.* (eds), *En hommage à Francis Delpérée. Itinéraires d'un constitutionnaliste* (Brussels, Bruylant, 2007), 815–31; K. Lenaerts, 'The Basic Constitutional Charter of a Community Based on the Rule of Law', in M. Poiares Maduro and L. Azoulai (eds), *The Past and Future of EU Law: The Classics of EU Law Revisited on the 50th Anniversary of the Rome Treaty* (Oxford, Hart Publishing, 2010), 295–315; K. Lenaerts and T. Corthaut, 'Judicial Review as a Contribution to the Development of European Constitutionalism', in T. Tridimas and P. Nebbia (eds), *European Union Law for the Twenty-First Century: Rethinking the New Legal Order—Vol. 1: Constitutional and Public Law—External Relations* (Oxford and Portland Oregon, Hart Publishing, 2004), 17–64; E. Sharpston and G. De Baere, 'The Court of Justice as a Constitutional Adjudicator', in A. Arnull, C. Barnard, M. Dougan, and E. Spaventa (eds), *A Constitutional Order of States? Essays in EU Law in Honour of Alan Dashwood* (Oxford and Portland Oregon, Hart Publishing, 2011), 123–50; V. Skouris, 'Der Europäische Gerichtshof als Verfassungsgericht?', in D. Merten (ed.), *Verfassungsgerichtsbarkeit in Deutschland und Österreich* (Berlin, Duncker and Humblot, 2008), 43–56.

[78] The Court's *sui generis* role as both constitutional and supreme Court has been emphasized. See, e.g. B. Vesterdorf, 'A Constitutional Court for the EU?' (2006) I.J. Const. L. 607–17 (reprinted in I. Pernice, J. Kokott, and C. Saunders (eds), *The Future of the European Judicial System in a Comparative Perspective* (Baden-Baden, Nomos, 2006), 83–90); V. Skouris, 'The Position of the European Court of Justice in the EU Legal Order and its Relationship with National Constitutional Courts' (2005) Z.ö.R 323–34, at 326–7.

[79] See Chs 16 and 17.

IV. The General Court

A. Composition

(1) Judges

2.23 The General Court consists of at least one Judge per Member State[80] and, in its present composition, has twenty-eight Judges.[81] They are appointed for a term of six years by common accord of the governments of the Member States, after consultation of the panel provided for in Art. 255 TFEU.[82] They are chosen from persons whose independence is beyond doubt and who possess the ability required for appointment to high judicial office. Membership of the Court is partially renewed every three years, although retiring Judges are eligible for reappointment.[83] As in the case of the Court of Justice, there is no nationality requirement, but in practice, there is one Judge from each Member State. If a vacancy occurs during the term of office, the new Judge is appointed for the remainder of his or her predecessor's normal term.[84]

(2) Advocates-General

2.24 At present, no separate Advocates-General are attached to the General Court, on the ground that cases brought before it normally do not require the assistance of an Advocate-General. However, a Judge may be called upon to perform the task of Advocate-General in a given case.[85] In such case, he or she performs the same function as an Advocate-General in the Court of Justice and may not take part in the judgment of the case.[86] The decision to designate an Advocate-General in a particular case is taken at an administrative meeting of the General Court at the request of the Chamber dealing with the case or to which the case is assigned.[87] When the General Court sits in plenary session, it is

---

[80] Art. 19(2), second para., TEU. The number of Judges is laid down in the Statute: Art. 254, first para., TFEU.

[81] Statute, Art. 48.

[82] Art. 19(2), third para., TEU; Art. 254, second para., TFEU. As regards the panel set forth in Art. 255 TFEU, see n. 22.

[83] Art. 254, second para., TFEU.

[84] Statute, Art. 7.

[85] Statute, Art. 49. This rule is a 'compromise' between the view that the Advocate-General's role principally consists of assisting the Court of Justice in its task of ensuring uniform interpretation of Union law and that therefore there is no need for an Advocate-General in the General Court, and the view that the Advocate-General's role is an essential safeguard for the legal protection of individuals and that therefore it is important for there to be an Advocate-General in the General Court. See V. Christianos, 'Le Tribunal de première instance et la nouvelle organisation judiciaire des Communautés européennes', in *Le Tribunal de première instance des Communautés européennes* (Maastricht, European Institute for Public Administration, 1990), 17, at 23; G. Vandersanden, 'Une naissance désirée: le Tribunal de première instance des Communautés européennes' (1988) J.T. 545, at 546. Art. 254, first para., TFEU states that the Statute may provide that the General Court be assisted by Advocates-General, which leaves the possibility open to appoint permanent Advocates-General and not just Judges as ad hoc Advocates-General.

[86] Cf. the second para. of Art. 252 TFEU in conjunction with the second and fourth paras of Art. 49 of the Statute.

[87] EGC Rules of Procedure, Art. 19, first para. The third para. of Art. 49 of the Statute provides that the criteria for selecting such cases, as well as the procedures for designating the Advocates-General, are to be laid down in the EGC Rules of Procedure.

assisted by an Advocate-General.[88] In other cases, the General Court is under no obligation to have itself assisted by an Advocate-General.[89] The General Court may decide to appoint an Advocate-General when sitting in a Chamber and the Chamber considers that the legal difficulty or the factual complexity of the case requires such appointment.[90] The President of the General Court then designates the Judge called upon to perform the function of an Advocate-General.[91] The consequence is that references to the Advocate-General in the Rules of Procedure of the General Court apply only where a Judge has been designated so to act.[92]

(3) Oath and immunity

Before taking up his or her duties, each Judge takes an oath before the Court of Justice (see **2.25** para. 2.06).[93] Judges of the General Court have the same status as Judges and Advocates. General of the Court of Justice (see para. 2.06)[94] and are subject to the same constraints and obligations as regards taking up political or administrative offices and engaging in other occupations.

---

[88] EGC Rules of Procedure, Art. 17. For example, see Opinion of Judge D.A.O. Edward performing the function of Advocate-General in CFI, Case T-24/90 *Automec* [1992] E.C.R. II-2223 and CFI, Case T-28/90 *Asia Motor France* [1992] E.C.R. II-2285; and Opinion of Judge H. Kirschner performing the function of Advocate-General in CFI, Case T-51/89 *Tetra Pak* [1990] E.C.R. II-309. Where, following the designation of an Advocate-General pursuant to Art. 17 of the EGC Rules of Procedure, there is an even number of Judges in the General Court sitting in plenary session, the President is to designate, before the hearing and in accordance with a rota established in advance by the Court and published in the *Official Journal of the European Union*, the Judge who will not take part in the judgment of the case (EGC Rules of Procedure, Art. 32(1), second para.).

[89] EGC, Rules of Procedure, Art. 18. ECJ (order of 18 July 2002), Case C-136/01 P *Autosalone Ispra dei Fratelli Rossi v Commission* [2002] E.C.R. I-6565, paras 17–18; ECJ (order of 8 December 2005) Case C-210/05 P *Campailla v Commission*, not reported, paras 13–14.

[90] EGC Rules of Procedure, Art. 18. For example, see Opinion of Judge J. Biancarelli performing the function of Advocate-General in CFI, Case T-120/89 *Stahlwerke Peine-Salzgitter v Commission* [1992] E.C.R. II-279; Opinion of Judge B. Vesterdorf performing the function of Advocate-General in CFI, Case T-1/89 *Rhône-Poulenc v Commission* [1991] E.C.R. II-867; CFI, Case T-2/89 *Petrofina SA v Commission* [1991] E.C.R. II-1087; CFI, Case T-3/89 *Atochem v Commission* [1991] E.C.R. II-1177; CFI, Case T-4/89 *BASF v Commission* [1991] E.C.R. II-1523; CFI, Case T-6/89 *Enichem Anic v Commission* [1991] E.C.R. II-1623; CFI, Case T-7/89 *Hercules Chemicals v Commission* [1991] E.C.R. II-1711; CFI, Case T-8/89 *DSM v Commission* [1991] E.C.R. II-1833; CFI, Case T-9/89 *Hüls v Commission* [1992] E.C.R. II-499; CFI, Case T-10/89 *Hoechst v Commission* [1992] E.C.R. II-629; CFI, Case T-11/89 *Shell v Commission* [1992] E.C.R. II-757; CFI, Case T-12/89 *Solvay v Commission* [1992] E.C.R. II-907; CFI, Case T-13/89 *ICI v Commission* [1992] E.C.R. II-1021; CFI, Case T-14/89 *Montedipe v Commission* [1992] E.C.R. II-1155; CFI, Case T-15/89 *Chemie Linz v Commission* [1992] E.C.R. II-1275. For further discussion of Judge B. Vesterdorf's role in the latter cases, see K. Lenaerts, 'Réflexions sur la preuve et sur la procédure en droit communautaire de la concurrence', in C. Baudenbacher, C. Gulmann, K. Lenaerts, E. Coulon, and E. Barbier de La Serre (eds), *Liber Amicorum en l'honneur de Bo Vesterdorf* (Brussels, Bruylant, 2007), 475–507 (published in English in Symposium on Developments in European Union Law Dedicated To CFI President Bo Vesterdorf as K. Lenaerts, 'Some Thoughts on Evidence and Procedure in European Community Competition Law' (2007) Fordham I.L.J. 1463–95).

[91] EGC Rules of Procedure, Art. 19, second para.

[92] EGC Rules of Procedure, Art. 2(2).

[93] Statute, Art. 2; EGC Rules of Procedure, Art. 4(1).

[94] Art. 254, sixth para., TFEU; Statute, Arts 2–8.

A Judge may be removed from his or her office only by the Court of Justice, after seeking the opinion of the General Court.[95] Before that opinion—which must be reasoned—is given, the judge concerned may make representations to the General Court.[96]

(4) President

2.26 Immediately after their partial replacement, the Judges elect a President from among their number for a term of three years.[97] He or she may be re-elected.[98] If the President gives up his or her office before the expiry of its term, a successor is to be elected only for the outstanding portion of the term.[99]

(5) Vice-President

2.27 As with the Court of Justice, as part of the recent changes to the procedural texts of the Court of Justice of the European Union, it was considered that the increasing responsibilities of the President of the General Court require the establishment of an office of Vice-President in order to assist the President in carrying out those responsibilities.[100] Consequently, in addition to the election of the President, the Judges elect one of their number as Vice-President of the General Court for a term of three years. He or she may be re-elected.[101]

(6) Registrar

2.28 The Court appoints its Registrar.[102] The provisions relating to the status of the Registrar of the Court of Justice apply *mutatis mutandis* to the Registrar of the General Court.[103]

B. Internal organization

(1) Chambers

2.29 As in the case of the Court of Justice, the General Court sits as a rule in Chambers of three or five Judges.[104] The General Court has nine Chambers of five Judges and nine Chambers of three Judges. Unlike in the case of the Court of Justice, the most common formation is the three-Judge Chamber.

---

[95] Statute, Art. 6, first para.; EGC Rules of Procedure, Art. 5.

[96] For further particulars, see EGC Rules of Procedure, Art. 5.

[97] Art. 254, third para., TFEU; EGC Rules of Procedure, Art. 7(1). See Notice 2013/C 313/02 concerning the Election of the President of the General Court ([2013] O.J. C313/2).

[98] Art. 254, third para., TFEU.

[99] EGC Rules of Procedure, Art. 7(2). As with the Court of Justice, the elections are conducted by secret ballot. The Judge obtaining the votes of more than half the Judges composing the General Court shall be elected; if no Judge obtains that majority, further ballots are held until that majority is attained: EGC Rules of Procedure, Art. 7(3).

[100] Regulation (EU, Euratom) No. 741/2012 of the European Parliament and of the Council amending the Protocol on the Statute of the Court of Justice of the European Union and Annex I thereto, [2012] O.J. L228/1, third recital.

[101] Statute, Art. 9a. See Notice 2013/C 313/03 concerning the Election of the Vice-President of the General Court ([2013] O.J. C313/2).

[102] Art. 254, fourth para., TFEU; EGC Rules of Procedure, Art. 20. See Notice 2011/C 305/02 concerning the Appointment of the Registrar ([2011] O.J. C305/2).

[103] Statute, Art. 47, second para. See further E. Coulon, 'Le greffier du Tribunal de première instance des Communautés européennes' (2007–2008) Revue des affaires européennes 549–61.

[104] Statute, Art. 50, first para.; EGC Rules of Procedure, Art. 11(1), first para.

The General Court may also sit in plenary session (i.e. as a Full Court),[105] as a single Judge,[106] or as the Grand Chamber.[107] The Grand Chamber consists of thirteen Judges.[108] Under the second paragraph of Art. 50 of the Statute, the General Court is to lay down criteria by which cases are to be allocated among the Chambers.[109] As soon as the application initiating proceedings has been lodged, the President of the General Court assigns the case to one of the Chambers.[110] Each Chamber has a President of Chamber. The Presidents of

---

[105] Statute, Art. 50, second para.; EGC Rules of Procedure, Art. 11(1), second para. It has done so on three occasions: CFI, Case T-28/90 *Asia Motor France and Others v Commission* [1992] E.C.R. II-2285; CFI, Case T-24/90 *Automec v Commission* [1992] E.C.R. II-2223; and CFI Case T-51/89 *Tetra Pak v Commission* [1990] E.C.R II-309.

[106] Statute, Art. 50, second para.; EGC Rules of Procedure, Art. 11(1), third para. Under Art. 14(2), point 1, of the EGC Rules of Procedure, the Judge-Rapporteur of a Chamber of three Judges may hear and determine the sort of cases described in that Article as a single Judge (Council Decision 1999/291/EC, ECSC, Euratom, [1999] O.J. L114/5) if, having regard to the lack of difficulty of the questions of law or fact raised, to the limited importance of those cases, and to the absence of other special circumstances, they are suitable for being so heard and determined and have been delegated under the conditions laid down in Art. 51 of the EGC Rules of Procedure. However, as a result of Art. 14(2), point 2, of the EGC Rules of Procedure, it is not possible to delegate to a single Judge cases raising issues as to the legality of an act of general application or cases concerning the implementation of the rules on competition and on control of concentrations, relating to aid granted by States, relating to measures to protect trade, or relating to the common organization of the agricultural markets, with the exception of cases that form part of a series of cases in which the same relief is sought and of which one has already been finally decided. Likewise, under the EGC Rules of Procedure, a single Judge may not sit in proceedings brought against the Office for Harmonisation in the Internal Market (Trade Marks and Designs) or against the Community Plant Variety Office concerning the application of the rules relating to an intellectual property regime. For some examples of cases decided by a single Judge, see CFI, Case T-68/99 *Toditec v Commission* [2001] E.C.R. II-1443; CFI, Case T-138/05 *Commission v Impetus Symvouloi Michanikoi* [2007] E.C.R. II-136*, Summ. pub.; EGC, Case T-190/07 *KEK Diavlos v Commission* [2010] E.C.R. II-33*, Summ. pub. (appeal discontinued and removed from the register by ECJ (order of the President of the Court of 9 November 2011), Case C-251/10 P *KEK Diavlos v Commission*, not reported); EGC, Case T-259/09 *Commission v Archi Nuova associazione comitato di Cagliari and Gessa* [2010] E.C.R. II-284*, Summ. pub. See also ECJ, Case C-171/00 P *Libéros v Commission* [2002] E.C.R. 451, paras 25–39, where the judgment of the then Court of First Instance sitting as a single Judge was set aside on the ground that the case raised an issue of the legality of an act of general application and therefore could not be decided by a single Judge.

[107] Statute, Art. 50, third para.; EGC Rules of Procedure, Arts 10(1) and 11(1), second para.. The first judgments of the Court of First Instance, as it was then called, sitting as a Grand Chamber were given on 14 December 2005: see CFI, Case T-69/00 *FIAMM and FIAMM Technologies v Council and Commission* [2005] E.C.R. II-5393; CFI, Case T-151/00 *Laboratoire du Bain v Council and Commission* [2005] E.C.R. II-23*, Summ. pub.; CFI, Case T-301/00 *Groupe Fremaux and Palais Royal v Council and Commission* [2005] E. C. R. II-25*, Summ. pub.; CFI, Case T-320/00 *CD Cartondruck v Council and Commission* [2005] E. C. R. II-27*, Summ. pub.; CFI, Case T-383/00 *Beamglow v European Parliament and Others* [2005] E.C.R. II-5459; and CFI, Case T-135/01 *Fedon & Figli and Others v Council and Commission* [2005] E.C.R. II-29*, Summ. pub. Several of these judgments were appealed in ECJ, Joined Cases C-120/06 P and C-121/06 P *FIAMM and FIAMM Technologies v Council and Commission* [2008] E.C.R. I-6513): see further para. 11.07.

[108] EGC Rules of Procedure, Art. 10(1). To recall, this differs from the Grand Chamber of the Court of Justice which, as a result of the recent changes made to the Statute, has fifteen Judges. See Statute, Art. 16, second para.

[109] EGC Rules of Procedure, Art. 12.

[110] EGC Rules of Procedure, Art. 13(1). See also EGC Rules of Procedure, Art. 13(2), whereby the President of the Chamber proposes to the President of the Court, in respect of each case assigned to that Chamber, the designation of a Judge-Rapporteur; cf. ECJ Rules of Procedure, Art. 15(1) and Arts 25, 59–60 (designation of a Judge-Rapporteur by the President of the Court; at the general meeting, the Court assigns the case to a Chamber, at the proposal of the Judge-Rapporteur). The decision to assign a case to a Chamber, which is a matter for the President of the General Court, is adopted in the context of measures of administration of justice in accordance with the relevant provisions of the EGC Rules of Procedure; subject to the provisions of Art. 18 of the Statute, the parties are not entitled to formulate pleadings in that respect. Consequently, an applicant's claim to assign the application to 'an appropriate Chamber' is inadmissible: CFI

the Chambers of five Judges are elected for three years and may be reappointed once.[111] The President of the General Court him- or herself presides over the Grand Chamber and the Full Court. A President of a Chamber of five Judges is also a President of a Chamber of three Judges. Appeals against decisions of the Civil Service Tribunal are heard by a special Appeal Chamber of three Judges composed of the President of the General Court and, in rotation, two Presidents of Chambers.[112] The composition of the Chambers and appointments of Presidents of Chambers are published in the *Official Journal of the European Union*.[113]

(2) Assignment of a case to a Chamber

2.30 A case is immediately assigned to a Chamber of three Judges.[114] Whenever the legal difficulty or the importance of the case or special circumstances so justify, a case may be referred to the General Court sitting in plenary session, to the Grand Chamber, or to a Chamber consisting of a different number of Judges.[115] At any stage of the proceedings, the Chamber hearing the case may, on its own initiative or at the request of the parties, make a proposal to this effect to the Court sitting in plenary session. The Full Court then decides, after hearing the Advocate-General, whether or not to refer the case.[116] Where a Member State or an institution of the Union which is a party to the proceedings so requests, a case will be decided by a Chamber composed of at least five Judges.[117]

The decision to delegate a case to a single Judge is taken unanimously, after the parties have been heard, by the Chamber composed of three Judges before which the case is pending. Where a Member State or an institution of the Union that is a party to the proceedings objects to the case being heard by a single Judge, the case shall be maintained before or referred to the Chamber to which the Judge-Rapporteur belongs.[118]

(3) Quorum

2.31 A bench of the General Court can decide validly only when an uneven number of Judges is sitting in the deliberations.[119] A quorum consists of three Judges in the case of three- or

---

(order of 31 July 2009), Case T-213/08 REV *Marinova v Université Libre de Bruxelles and Commission*, not reported.

[111] Statute, Art. 50, first para.; EGC Rules of Procedure, Art. 15(2), first para. The President of the General Court is not subject to this limitation. By comparison, the Presidents of Chambers of three Judges shall be elected for a defined term: EGC Rules of Procedure, Art. 15(3).

[112] E. Coulon, 'Les mutations du Tribunal de première instance sous la présidence de Bo Vesterdorf: la continuité dans le changement', in C. Baudenbacher, C. Gulmann, K. Lenaerts, E. Coulon, and E. Barbier de La Serre (eds), *Liber Amicorum en l'honneur de Bo Vesterdorf* (Brussels, Bruylant, 2007), 48–9.

[113] EGC Rules of Procedure, Arts 10(2) and 15(5). See Notice 2013/C 313/07 concerning the Plenary session ([2013] O.J. C313/4); Notice 2013/C 318/08 concerning the Composition of the Grand Chamber ([2013] O.J. C318/5); Notice 2013/C 313/04 concerning Elections of Presidents of Chambers ([2013] O.J. C313/2); Notice 2013/C 313/09 concerning the Appeal Chamber ([2013] O.J. C319/09); Notice 2013/C 344/05 concerning the Assignment of Judges to Chambers ([2013] O.J. C344/2).

[114] See Notice 2013/C 313/06 concerning Criteria for assigning cases to Chambers ([2013] O.J. C313/4).

[115] EGC Rules of Procedure, Art. 14(1).

[116] EGC Rules of Procedure, Art. 51(1), first para.

[117] EGC Rules of Procedure, Art. 51(1), second para.

[118] EGC Rules of Procedure, Art. 51(2).

[119] Statute, Art. 17, first para., applicable to the General Court by virtue of Art. 47, first para., of the Statute.

five-Judge Chambers,[120] nine Judges in the case of the Grand Chamber,[121] and seventeen Judges where the Court sits in plenary session (i.e., as a Full Court).[122]

(4) Procedure

2.32 The procedure before the General Court largely parallels that before the Court of Justice in relation to direct actions (see Part V).

(5) President and Registrar

2.33 The tasks of the President,[123] the Vice-President,[124] and the Registrar[125] of the General Court are, to the extent of their powers, similar to those of their counterparts in the Court of Justice.

(6) Staff

2.34 As far as the personnel of the General Court is concerned, the Statute provides as follows: 'The President of the Court of Justice and the President of the General Court shall determine, by common accord, the conditions under which officials and other servants attached to the Court of Justice shall render their services to the General Court to enable it to function. Certain officials or other servants shall be responsible to the Registrar of the General Court under the authority of the President of the General Court.'[126]

The last sentence of that passage applies, of course, to the staff of the Registrar and the cabinets of the Judges of the General Court (Judges are assisted by, among others, three *référendaires*, who perform the same duties as the law clerks of the Judges and Advocates-General of the Court of Justice, and by secretarial staff members). The aim is to bring the staff of the General Court directly and exclusively concerned with the performance of its judicial function under the President and the Registrar, which constitutes a guarantee of independence from the Court of Justice.

C. Basic function

(1) Purpose

2.35 The purpose of establishing the Court of First Instance—as it was then called—in 1989, which was 'attached'[127] to the Court of Justice, was to maintain and improve the quality and effectiveness of judicial protection in the Union legal order. In 1988, a steadily rising tide of cases had caused proceedings before the Court of Justice to become unacceptably

---

[120] Statute, Art. 17, second para., applicable to the General Court by virtue of Art. 47, first para., of the Statute, and EGC Rules of Procedure, Art. 32(3), first para.

[121] EGC Rules of Procedure, Art. 32(3), second para. It is not the same quorum as that applicable to the Grand Chamber of the Court of Justice (providing for eleven Judges, instead of nine). Art. 47, first para., of the Statute indeed excludes the application of Art. 17, third para., of the Statute to the General Court.

[122] Statute, Art. 17, fourth para., applicable to the General Court by virtue of Art. 47, first para., of the Statute.

[123] See EGC Rules of Procedure, Art. 8.

[124] Statute, Art. 47, first para.

[125] See EGC Rules of Procedure, Arts 20–27.

[126] Statute, Art. 52.

[127] This term was employed in the pre-Nice version of Art. 225(1) EC: 'A Court of First Instance shall be attached to the Court of Justice ...'

protracted.[128] Furthermore, in cases requiring an appraisal of complex facts,[129] the Court could no longer provide the high quality of judicial protection that it was called upon to do.[130]

The transfer in stages to the Court of First Instance of jurisdiction in all cases brought by natural or legal persons against any unlawful act or failure to act on the part of the Union institutions helped to allay those shortcomings.[131] At the same time, a two-tier court system was created for such cases, which could only improve the quality of legal protection.[132]

(2) Treaty of Nice and subsequent institutional developments

2.36   As a result of the Nice Treaty, which entered into force on 1 February 2003, and the amendment of Art. 51 of the Statute on 26 April 2004,[133] the jurisdiction of the then Court of First Instance was extended to a considerable degree. It became the administrative court of general jurisdiction of the European Union (see paras 2.47–2.55, concerning the distribution of heads of jurisdiction among the various judicial bodies belonging to the Court of Justice of the European Union).[134] This was further consolidated by the Lisbon Treaty.

---

[128]   The average duration of a direct action increased from 8.5 months in 1970 to 24 months. The average time taken to complete proceedings in a reference for a preliminary ruling was 17.5 months. See B. Vesterdorf, 'The European Legal Order and the Court of First Instance' (2006) E.R.P.L./R.E.D.P. 915, at 919.

[129]   Principally, competition and anti-dumping cases.

[130]   For commentaries, see J. L. da Cruz Vilaça, 'The Court of First Instance of the European Communities. A Significant Step Towards the Consolidation of the European Community as a Community Governed by the Rule of Law' (1991) Y.E.L., 1–56; D. A. O. Edward, 'The Court of First Instance—The Beginnings', in C. Baudenbacher, C. Gulmann, K. Lenaerts, E. Coulon, and E. Barbier de la Serre (eds), *Liber Amicorum en l'honneur de Bo Vesterdorf* (Brussels, Bruylant, 2007), 1–11; K. Lenaerts, 'Het Gerecht van eerste aanleg van de Europese Gemeenschappen' (1990) S.E.W. 527–48; K. Lenaerts, 'Le Tribunal de première instance des Communautés européennes: genèse et premiers pas' (1990) J.T. 409–15. K. Lenaerts, 'The Development of the Judicial Process in the European Community After the Establishment of the Court of First Instance', in A. Claphman (ed.), *Collected Courses of the Academy of European Law*, Vol. 1 (Book 1, Florence/Dordrecht, European University Institute, Martinus Nijhoff, 1991), 53–113; K. Lenaerts, 'Le Tribunal de première instance des Communautés européennes: regard sur une décennie d'activités et sur l'apport du double degré d'instance au droit communautaire' (2000) C.D.E. 323–411; M. Van der Woude, 'Le Tribunal de première instance "Les trois premières années"' (1992) R.M.U.E. 113–57.

[131]   See Council Decision 88/591/ECSC, EEC, Euratom of 24 October 1988 establishing a Court of First Instance of the European Communities ([1988] O.J. L319/1; *corrigendum* in [1989] O.J. L241/4), as amended by Council Decision 93/350/Euratom, ECSC, EEC of 8 June 1993 ([1993] O.J. L144/21) and Council Decision 94/149/ECSC, EC of 7 March 1994 ([1994] O.J. L66/29). Art. 10 of the Nice Treaty abrogated this Decision. See on the transfer of direct actions to the then Court of First Instance: A. Tizzano, 'Le transfert des recours directs', in G. Vandersanden, U. Everling *et al.* (eds), *La réforme du système juridictionnel communautaire* (Brussels, ULB, 1994), 67–85.

[132]   K. Lenaerts, 'Le tribunal de première instance des communautés européennes:—regards sur une décennie d'activités et sur l'apport du double degré d'instance au droit communautaire' (2000) C.D.E. 323–411.

[133]   Council Decision 2004/407/EC, Euratom of 26 April 2004 amending Arts 51 and 54 of the Protocol on the Statute of the Court of Justice ([2004] O.J. L132/5; *corrigendum* in [2004] O.J. L194/3).

[134]   For the changes brought about by the Nice Treaty, see K. Lenaerts and M. Desomer, 'Het Verdrag van Nice en het "post Nice"-debat over de toekomst van de Europese Unie' (2001–2002) R.W. 73, paras 21–32. For the effects of the Nice Treaty on the judicial organization of the European Union, E. Coulon, 'L'indispensable réforme du Tribunal de première instance des Communautés européennes' (2000) R.A.E. 254–66. See E. Coulon, 'Les mutations du Tribunal de première instance sous la présidence de Bo Vesterdorf: la continuité dans le changement', in C. Baudenbacher, C. Gulmann, K. Lenaerts, E. Coulon, and E. Barbier de La Serre (eds), *Liber Amicorum en l'honneur de Bo Vesterdorf* (Brussels, Bruylant, 2007), 23–32; K. Lenaerts, 'La réorganisation de l'architecture juridictionnelle de l'Union européenne: quel angle d'approche adopter?', in

V. The European Union Civil Service Tribunal

(1) General

Under Art. 257 TFEU, the European Parliament and the Council are empowered to create **2.37** specialized courts (previously referred to as judicial panels[135]) to be attached to the General Court, which will hear and determine at first instance certain classes of action or proceeding brought in specific areas.[136]

Decisions given by specialized courts may be subject to a right of appeal before the General Court on points of law only or, when provided for in the regulation establishing the specialized court, a right of appeal also on matters of fact.[137]

(2) Creation

Declaration No. 16 annexed to the Nice Treaty called upon the Court of Justice and the **2.38** Commission 'to prepare as swiftly as possible a draft decision establishing a judicial panel which has jurisdiction to deliver judgments at first instance on disputes between the Community and its servants'.[138] On 2 November 2004, the Council adopted Decision 2004/752/EC, Euratom establishing the European Union Civil Service Tribunal.[139] This decision inserted a new Art. 62a (now Art. 62c) in the Statute which provides that the provisions relating to the jurisdiction, composition, organization, and procedure of the judicial panels are set out in an annex to the Statute.[140] Council Decision

---

M. Dony and E. Bribosia (eds), *L'avenir du système juridictionnel de l'Union européenne* (Brussels, Editions de l'Université de Bruxelles, 2002), 49–64; P. Mengozzi, 'The Judicial System of the European Community and Its Recent Evolution', in A. Del Vecchio (ed.), *New International Tribunals and New International Proceedings* (Milan, Giuffrè, 2006), 81–9; A. Tizzano, 'La Cour de Justice après Nice: le transfert des compétences au Tribunal de première instance', in A. De Walsche and G. Vandersanden (eds), *Mélanges en hommage à Jean-Victor Louis* (Brussel, ULB, 2003), 499–516.

[135] See para. 2.03.

[136] Art. 257, first para., TFEU. The European Parliament and the Council shall act, in accordance with the ordinary legislative procedure, by means of regulations either on a proposal from the Commission after consultation of the Court of Justice or at the request of the Court of Justice after consultation of the Commission. Originally, from the entry into force of the Nice Treaty, the Council was to establish judicial panels, deciding unanimously on a proposal of the Commission after consulting the European Parliament and the Court of Justice, or at the request of the Court of Justice after consulting the European Parliament and the Commission under former Arts 220 and 225a EC.

[137] Art. 257, third para., TFEU.

[138] Declaration (No. 16), annexed to the Nice Treaty, on Art. 225a of the Treaty establishing the European Community, [2001] O.J. C80/80.

[139] [2004] O.J. L333/7. On 18 January 2005, the Council adopted Decision 2005/150/EC, Euratom concerning the conditions and arrangements governing the submission and processing of applications for appointment as a Judge of the European Union Civil Service Tribunal ([2005] O.J. L50/7). On 22 July 2005, the Council adopted Decision 2005/577/EC, Euratom appointing Judges of the European Union Civil Service Tribunal ([2005] O.J. L197/28). On 2 December 2005, the President of the Court of Justice declared that the European Union Civil Service Tribunal was duly constituted ([2005] O.J. L325/1), and on 25 July 2007, the Rules of Procedure of the European Union Civil Service Tribunal were adopted ([2007] O.J. L225/1).

[140] Statute, Art. 62c, first para. In order to enable the specialized courts to continue to function satisfactorily in the absence of a Judge who, while not suffering from disablement deemed to be total, is prevented from participating in the disposal of cases for a lengthy period of time, provision has been made, as part of the recent changes to the procedural texts of the Court of Justice of the European Union, for the possibility of attaching temporary Judges to those courts (Statute, Art. 62c, second para., and Annex I, Art. 2).

2004/752 adds a new Annex I to the Statute entitled 'The European Union Civil Service Tribunal' (Civil Service Tribunal).[141]

The Civil Service Tribunal thus took over the staff cases previously falling within the jurisdiction of the Court of First Instance, as it was then called. It remains the only specialized court set up so far.

(3) Composition and jurisdiction

2.39 The Civil Service Tribunal is attached to the General Court and has its seat in Luxembourg.[142] It exercises at first instance jurisdiction in disputes between the Union and its servants referred to in Art. 270 TFEU, including disputes between all bodies and agencies and their servants in respect of which jurisdiction is conferred on the Court of Justice of the European Union.[143] It is composed of seven Judges appointed for a period of six years by the Council, acting unanimously.[144] Retiring Judges can be reappointed.[145] An advisory committee composed of former members of the Court of Justice and the General Court and lawyers of recognized competence gives an opinion on the candidates' suitability to perform the duties of Judge at the Civil Service Tribunal.[146]

The relevant rules regarding the oath, conduct, and immunity of Judges of the Court of Justice and of the General Court in the Statute generally apply to Judges of the Civil Service Tribunal.[147]

There are no Advocates-General in the Civil Service Tribunal. Moreover, there is no provision made for allowing a Judge to serve as an Advocate-General in the procedure before the Civil Service Tribunal, as is the case for the General Court (see para. 2.24).[148]

See in this respect Regulation (EU, Euratom) No. 979/2012 of the European Parliament and of the Council of 25 October 2012 relating to temporary Judges of the European Union Civil Service Tribunal ([2012] O.J. L303/83). On 22 April 2013, the Council adopted Decision 2013/181/EU drawing up a list of three temporary Judges for the Civil Service Tribunal ([2013] O.J. L111/49).

[141] For the workings of the EU Civil Service Tribunal generally, see H. Kanninen, 'Le Tribunal de la fonction publique de l'UE—la première juridiction spécialisée dans le système juridictionnel de l'Union européenne', in M. Johansson, N. Wahl, and U. Bernitz (eds), *Liber Amicorum in honour of Sven Norberg* (Brussels, Bruylant, 2006), 287–99; W. Hakenberg, 'Das Gericht für den öffentlichen Dienst der EU: eine neue Ära in der Gemeinschaftsgerichtsbarkeit' (2006) EuZW 391–3.

[142] Council Decision 2004/752, Art.1 (then referring to the Court of First Instance).

[143] Statute, Annex I, Art. 1.

[144] Art. 257, fourth para., TFEU; Statute, Annex I, Arts 2 and 3(1). The Council may, acting by a qualified majority, increase the number of Judges. The Council, when appointing Judges, will ensure a balanced composition of the Civil Service Tribunal on as broad a geographical basis as possible from among nationals of the Member States and with respect to the national legal systems represented.

[145] Statute, Annex I, Art. 2, second para. See also CST Rules of Procedure, Arts 2–4.

[146] Statute, Annex I, Art. 3(3) and (4). See Council Decision 2005/49/EC, Euratom of 18 January 2005 concerning the operating rules of the committee provided for in Art. 3(3) of Annex I to the Protocol on the Statute of the Court of Justice, [2005] O.J. L21/13. This committee is similar, though not identical, to the panel in connection with the appointment of Judges of the Court of Justice and of the General Court and Advocates-General (see para. 2.04).

[147] Statute, Annex I, Art. 5.

[148] See CFI (judgment of 8 September 2008), Case T-222/07 P *Kerstens v Commission*, not reported, paras 49–52.

(4) President

The Judges elect the President of the Civil Service Tribunal from among their number for a **2.40** term of three years.[149] He or she can be re-elected.[150] If the office of President of the Tribunal falls vacant before the usual date of expiry of his or her term, the Tribunal elects a successor for the remainder of the term.[151]

The President of the Tribunal directs the judicial business and administration of the Tribunal.[152] He or she presides over the Full Court, the chamber of five Judges, and the chamber of three Judges if assigned thereto.[153] He or she also rules on applications concerning the suspension of operation or enforcement of Union measures and interim measures.[154]

(5) Registrar and staff

The Civil Service Tribunal appoints the Registrar for a renewable term of six years.[155] As **2.41** with the General Court, the provisions relating to the status of the Registar of the Court of Justice apply to the Registrar of the Civil Service Tribunal.[156]

As provided in Annex I of the Statute, the Civil Service Tribunal is 'supported' by the departments of the Court of Justice and of the General Court.[157] As such, the President of the Court of Justice or, in appropriate cases, the President of the General Court, determines by common accord with the President of the Civil Service Tribunal the conditions under which officials and other servants attached to the Court of Justice or the General Court will render their services to the Civil Service Tribunal so as to enable it to function.[158]

(6) Chambers

The Civil Service Tribunal sits in chambers of three Judges. In certain cases determined by **2.42** its Rules of Procedure, it sits as a Full Court, as a chamber of five Judges, or as a chamber constituted by a single Judge.[159] So far, however, by its decision of 30 November 2005, the Civil Service Tribunal has decided to sit in three Chambers of three Judges or as a Full Court.[160]

---

[149] Statute, Annex I, Art. 4(1); CST Rules of Procedure, Art. 6(1).
[150] Statute, Annex I, Art. 4(1); CST Rules of Procedure, Art. 6(1).
[151] CST Rules of Procedure, Art. 6(2).
[152] CST Rules of Procedure, Art. 7(1).
[153] Statute, Annex I, Art. 4; CST Rules of Procedure, Art. 7(2).
[154] See CST Rules of Procedure, Arts 102–104.
[155] Statute, Annex I, Art. 6(2); CST Rules of Procedure, Art. 15.
[156] Statute, Annex I, Art. 6(2).
[157] Statute, Annex I, Art. 6(1).
[158] Statute, Annex I, Art. 6(1).
[159] Statute, Annex I, Art. 4(2). See CST Rules of Procedure, Arts 9–10, 12–14.
[160] Decision of the Civil Service Tribunal of 30 November 2005 on the constitution and composition of the Chambers, election of their Presidents, and assignment of the Judges to Chambers, [2005] O.J. C322/16. This has been maintained in subsequent decisions: see, e.g. Notice [2013] O.J. C313/6 on composition of the Chambers and attachment of the Judges to Chambers, [2013] O.J. C313/6.

The Judges elect from among their number the Presidents of the Chambers sitting with three Judges. They serve a term of three years and can be re-elected.[161] The criteria for the assignment of cases to Chambers,[162] as well as the composition of the Chambers and the election of their Presidents,[163] are published in the *Official Journal of the European Union*.[164]

At present, the six Judges, aside from the President of the Tribunal, comprise the first and second Chambers of three Judges, the third Chamber being composed of the President of the Tribunal and the remaining four Judges of the first and second Chambers, excluding the Presidents of those formations; of those four Judges, they sit with the President of the Tribunal on an alternating basis with a view to ensuring that a Judge from each of the first and second Chambers is represented.[165]

(7) Procedure

2.43 By and large, the procedure before the Civil Service Tribunal resembles that governing the other Union courts.[166] Yet, Council Decision 2004/752 further lightens the existing procedure in staff cases with a view to settling disputes rapidly. In particular, Annex I to the Statute provides in principle for one exchange of written submissions between the parties.[167] When the Civil Service Tribunal deems that a second exchange is necessary, it may, with the agreement of the parties, decide to proceed to judgment without an oral hearing.[168] Furthermore, at all stages of the procedure, the Civil Service Tribunal may examine the possibility for an amicable settlement and may try to facilitate such settlement.[169]

(8) Appeals

2.44 An appeal may be brought before the General Court against final decisions of the Civil Service Tribunal and decisions of the Civil Service Tribunal disposing of the substantive

---

[161] Statute, Annex I, Art. 4(3); CST Rules of Procedure, Art. 11(1).

[162] See Decision of the Civil Service Tribunal of 10 October 2011 on the criteria for the assignment of cases to Chambers, [2011] O.J. C311/4.

[163] See, for the period of 7 October 2011 to 30 September 2014, the Decision of the Civil Service Tribunal of 10 October 2011 on the composition of the Chambers and attachment of the Judges to Chambers, [2011] O.J. C311/3.

[164] CST Rules of Procedure, Arts 10(3), 11(2), and 12(3).

[165] See Decision of the Civil Service Tribunal of Civil Service Tribunal of 30 November 2005 on the constitution and composition of the Chambers, elections of their Presidents and assignment of the Judges to Chambers, [2005] O.J. C322/16. This regime has continued through to the present day. See Decision of the Civil Service Tribunal of 10 October 2011 on the criteria for the assignment of cases to Chambers, [2011] O.J. C311/4.

[166] See Statute, Annex I, Art. 7(1).

[167] Statute, Annex I, Art. 7(3).

[168] Statute, Annex I, Art 7(3); CST Rules of Procedure, Arts 41 and 48. At present, in proceedings before the General Court, a second exchange of written pleadings together with an oral hearing is the rule, with certain exceptions (see EGC Rules of Procedure, Arts 47(1) and 52(1)). See further H. Kanninen and F. Bocquillon, 'La place de la procédure devant le Tribunal de la fonction publique de l'Union européenne' (2011) RUDH 80–3.

[169] Statute, Annex I, Art. 7(4). For further particulars, see CST Rules of Procedure, Arts 68–70.

issues in part only or disposing of a procedural issue concerning a plea of lack of jurisdiction or inadmissibility (see Part V). The appeal is to be lodged within two months of the notification of the decision appealed against by any party that had been unsuccessful, in whole or in part, in its submissions.[170]

Whereas the third paragraph of Art. 257 TFEU leaves the door open for appeals on points of law and fact, Annex I of the Statute clearly opts for an appeal limited to points of law.[171] If the appeal is well-founded, the General Court will quash the decision of the Civil Service Tribunal and give final judgment in the matter. Only where the state of the proceedings does not permit the General Court to give final judgment is the case referred back to the Civil Service Tribunal, which will be bound by the decision of the General Court on points of law.[172]

VI. Allocation of Jurisdiction Among the Union Courts

A. The position before the Treaty of Nice

(1) Court of First Instance

Before the Nice Treaty, the jurisdiction of the Court of First Instance, as it was then **2.45** called, was limited as follows. The Court had jurisdiction[173] to hear and determine actions for annulment,[174] actions for failure to act,[175] and actions for compensation for non-contractual damage[176] brought by natural or legal persons against institutions and bodies of the Union and disputes between those institutions and bodies and their servants.[177] It also had jurisdiction to entertain actions brought by natural and legal persons pursuant to an arbitration clause.[178] Finally, the Court had jurisdiction in cases brought against the Office for Harmonisation in the Internal Market relating to Community trademarks[179] and designs,[180] as well as cases brought against the Community Plant Variety Office relating to Community plant variety rights.[181]

---

[170] Statute, Annex I, Art. 9.

[171] Statute, Annex I, Art. 11.

[172] Statute, Annex I, Art. 13.

[173] See Council Decision 88/591/ECSC, EEC, Euratom of 24 October 1988 establishing a Court of First Instance of the European Communities ([1988] O.J. L319/1; *corrigendum* in [1989] O.J. L241/4), as amended by Council Decision 93/350/Euratom, ECSC, EEC of 8 June 1993 ([1993] O.J. L144/21) and Council Decision 94/149/ECSC, EC of 7 March 1994 ([1994] O.J. L66/29).

[174] Art. 230 EC.

[175] Art. 232 EC.

[176] Arts 235 and 288, second para., EC.

[177] Art. 236 EC.

[178] Art. 238 EC.

[179] Council Regulation (EC) No. 40/94 of 20 December 1993 on the Community trademark, [1994] O.J. L11/1; codified version, Council Regulation (EC) No. 207/2009 of 26 February 2009 on the Community trademark, [2009] O.J. L78/1.

[180] Council Regulation (EC) No. 6/2002 of 12 December 2001 on Community designs, [2002] O.J. L3/1.

[181] Council Regulation (EC) No. 2100/94 of 27 July 1994 on Community plant variety rights, [1994] O.J. L227/1, as amended by Council Regulation (EC) No. 2506/95 of 25 October 1995, [1995] O.J. L258/3.

(2) Court of Justice

2.46   The former EC Treaty (pre-Nice) had explicitly excluded preliminary references from the potential jurisdiction of the Court of First Instance.[182] They thus came within the reserved jurisdiction of the Court of Justice. The Court of Justice also had jurisdiction to decide actions for annulment or for failure to act and actions pursuant to an arbitration clause where those actions were lodged by a Member State, a Union institution,[183] or, under certain circumstances, the European Central Bank. The Court of Justice was likewise competent to hear actions brought by the Commission or a Member State relating to the infringement of Community law by a Member State (infringement actions)[184] and actions relating to compensation for non-contractual damage brought by a Member State against the Community.[185] Finally, as regards the jurisdiction of the Court of Justice, mention should be made of appeals that could be lodged on points of law only against rulings of the Court of First Instance.[186]

B. The Treaty of Nice: a fundamental reallocation of jurisdiction in embryo

(1) Role of the Court of Justice

2.47   The Nice Treaty contained a fundamental reallocation of jurisdiction in embryo as between the Union courts.[187] It appeared from the Nice Treaty that the Court of Justice's role should be confined to the examination of questions that were of essential importance for the Union legal order. In order to achieve this objective, the EC Treaty provided that the Court of Justice was to be the competent court for infringement actions,[188] for (the great majority of) preliminary references, for appeals against rulings of the Court of First Instance,[189] and, exceptionally, for the review of preliminary rulings of the Court of First Instance or of

---

[182] The last sentence of the pre-Nice version of Art. 225(1) EC had provided: 'The Court of First Instance shall not be competent to hear and determine questions referred for a preliminary ruling under Article 234.'

[183] Former Art. 7 EC listed five institutions comprising the European Parliament, the Council, the Commission, the Court of Justice, and the Court of Auditors.

[184] Arts 226–228 EC.

[185] However, such actions have been generally lodged by natural and legal persons and not by Member States. For the sake of completeness, the following actions falling within the jurisdiction of the Court of Justice should also be mentioned: actions based on Art. 237 EC concerning the fulfilment by Member States of obligations under the Statute of the European Investment Bank (EIB), the legality of measures adopted by the Board of Governors and of the Board of Directors of the EIB, and the fulfilment by national central banks of obligations within the framework of the monetary union; and actions based on Art. 239 EC concerning any dispute between Member States relating to the subject-matter of the EC Treaty, submitted to the Court under a special agreement between the parties.

[186] Art. 225(1) EC.

[187] See in this regard A. Tizzano, 'La Cour de Justice après Nice: le transfert de compétences au Tribunal de première instance' (2002) R.D.U.E 665.

[188] Under former Art. 225(1), first para., second sent., EC, '[t]he Statute may provide for the Court of First Instance to have jurisdiction for other classes of action or proceeding'. This meant that granting the Court of First Instance jurisdiction in infringement actions (based on former Arts 226–228 EC) would not have required a Treaty amendment; an amendment of the Statute would have sufficed. The same holds true with the reframing of this provision in the Lisbon Treaty: see Art. 256(1), first para., second sent., TFEU.

[189] Art. 225 EC allowed for the introduction of a filter system for appeals insofar as Art. 225(1), second para., EC provided: 'Decisions given by the Court of First Instance [. . .] may be subject to a right of appeal to the Court of Justice on points of law only, *under the conditions and within the limits laid down by the Statute*'.

decisions taken by the Court of First Instance upon appeal in cases for which a judicial panel, as it was then called, had jurisdiction at first instance.

(2) Transfer of jurisdiction to the Court of First Instance

The Nice Treaty introduced into the EC Treaty a legal basis for the potential transfer of jurisdiction to the Court of First Instance with regard to preliminary references in specific areas, which have yet to be determined.[190] It was the intention of the Nice Treaty[191] that the Court of First Instance, regardless of the status of the applicant, should have jurisdiction to hear at first instance actions for annulment[192] and for failure to act,[193] actions relating to compensation for non-contractual damage,[194] actions pursuant to an arbitration clause,[195] and disputes between the then Community and its staff.[196] There were two exceptions. First, judicial panels could be created, which were to hear and determine at first instance certain classes of action or proceeding brought in specific areas.[197] Second, the Statute could reserve certain actions at first and last instance to the Court of Justice.[198] However, the Statute attached to the Nice Treaty confirmed the pre-Nice status quo and, as far as the direct actions mentioned above were concerned, maintained—until a later amendment of the Statute[199]—the pre-Nice division of jurisdiction *ratione personae* between the Court of Justice and the Court of First Instance.

2.48

---

[190] Art. 225(3) EC. In this regard, see K. Lenaerts, 'The Unity of European Law and the Overload of the ECJ—The System of Preliminary Rulings Revisited', in G. Ziccardi Capaldo (ed.), (2005), *The Global Community—Yearbook of International Law and Jurisprudence*, Vol. 1 (Oxford, Oceana Publications, 2006), 173–201 (and further citations therein) (reprinted in I. Pernice, J. Kokott, and C. Saunders (eds), *The Future of the European Judicial System in a Comparative Perspective* (Baden-Baden, Nomos, 2006), 211–39). See also J. Azizi, 'Opportunities and Limits for the Transfer of Preliminary Reference Proceedings to the Court of First Instance', in I. Pernice, J. Kokott, and C. Saunders (eds), *The Future of the European Judicial System in a Comparative Perspective* (Baden-Baden, Nomos, 2006), 241–56; C. Baudenbacher, 'Concentration of Preliminary References at the ECJ or Transfer to the High Court/CFI: Some Remarks on Competition Law', in I. Pernice, J. Kokott, and C. Saunders (eds), *The Future of the European Judicial System in a Comparative Perspective* (Baden-Baden, Nomos, 2006), 267–72; N. Forwood, 'The Evolving Role of the Court of First Instance of the European Communities: Some Comments on the Changes Agreed at Nice As They Affect the Judicial Architecture of the Community Courts' (2000) C.Y.E.L.S. 139–49; V. Skouris, 'Self-Conception, Challenges and Perspectives of the EU Courts', in I. Pernice, J. Kokott, and C. Saunders (eds), *The Future of the European Judicial System in a Comparative Perspective* (Baden-Baden, Nomos, 2006), 19–31; S. Wernicke, 'How to Guarantee Unity while Representing Diversity? From the Selection of Judges to the Possible Transfer of Preliminary References to the CFI', in I. Pernice, J. Kokott, and C. Saunders (eds), *The Future of the European Judicial System in a Comparative Perspective* (Baden-Baden, Nomos, 2006), 273–5.

[191] Art. 225(1) EC.

[192] Art. 230 EC.

[193] Art. 232 EC.

[194] Arts 235 and 288, second para., EC.

[195] Art. 238 EC.

[196] Art. 236 EC.

[197] Art. 225(1), first para., EC; Art. 225a, first para., EC.

[198] Art. 225(1), first para., EC.

[199] The Nice Treaty introduced a simplified procedure for amending the Statute. Whereas until the entry into force of the Nice Treaty the provisions relating to Treaty amendments generally applied, the post-Nice version of Art. 245 EC provided: 'The Council, acting unanimously at the request of the Court of Justice and after consulting the European Parliament and the Commission, or at the request of the Commission and after consulting the European Parliament and the Court of Justice, may amend the provisions of the Statute, with the exception of Title I.' The Lisbon Treaty further modified this provision. Under Art. 281, second para., TFEU, the European Parliament and the Council, acting in accordance with the ordinary legislative procedure, may amend the Statute, with the exception of Title I and Art. 64; either the Court of Justice or the Commission may take the initiative, and the other institution will be consulted. As a result, amendments

C. The present allocation of jurisdiction

(1) Present system

2.49 Council Decision 2004/407/EC, Euratom of 26 April 2004, which amended Art. 51 of the Statute,[200] (partly) implemented the principles of the Nice Treaty by transferring jurisdiction from the Court of Justice to the then Court of First Instance over direct actions, other than actions for infringement. The changes to the Statute, which aimed at leaving the Court of Justice with jurisdiction at first and last instance only in respect of basic legislative activity and in respect of the determination of inter-institutional disputes, were left relatively undisturbed by the Lisbon Treaty.[201] The Lisbon Treaty did, however, enlarge the number of Union institutions[202] and exact modifications to certain Treaty provisions governing the types of actions that may be brought before the Union courts, which introduced further nuances. Therefore, taking these developments into account, the present allocation of jurisdiction among the Union courts may be summarized as follows:

First, all actions brought by natural or legal persons that already fell within the jurisdiction of the General Court, previously the Court of First Instance, continue to be heard and determined by that Court.[203]

Second, interinstitutional disputes (including those affecting the European Central Bank[204]) are to be heard and determined at first and last instance by the Court of Justice.

Third, as regards actions brought by Member States, the Statute favours the status of the defendant as the factor determining jurisdiction. The Court of Justice has jurisdiction to hear and determine actions brought by Member States against acts and failures to act of the European Parliament and/or the Council, either in the exercise of the powers vested in each of those institutions or pursuant to the co-decision procedure, now referred to as the 'ordinary legislative procedure' in the Lisbon Treaty.[205] In principle, therefore, actions brought by Member States against the Commission, the European Council, and the

---

to the Statute no longer require unanimity in the Council; qualified majority voting suffices. Furthermore, the European Parliament is not merely consulted on amendments to the Statute, but is a co-legislator alongside the Council in this regard.

[200] Council Decision 2004/407/EC, Euratom of 26 April 2004 amending Arts 51 and 54 of the Protocol on the Statute of the Court of Justice, [2004] O.J. L132/5; *corrigendum* in [2004] O.J. L194/3.

[201] Furthermore, the general scheme of the jurisdiction allocated to the Court of First Instance, save for what was given to a judicial panel or reserved to the Court of Justice, set down in former Art. 225(1), first para., EC was retained in virtually identical terms (save for the renaming of certain of the Union courts) in Art. 256(1), first para., TFEU.

[202] Art. 13(1), second para., TEU added the European Council and the European Central Bank to the five institutions (i.e. the European Parliament, the Council, the Commission, the Court of Justice, and the Court of Auditors) that had already been listed in former Art. 7 EC (n. 183).

[203] This means that it cannot be ruled out that some cases involving basic legislative activity will be heard and determined at first instance by the General Court.

[204] The European Central Bank is now listed as an official Union institution: see n. 202.

[205] Art. 294 TFEU. For detailed discussion, see K. Lenaerts and P. Van Nuffel (R. Bray and N. Cambien (eds)), *European Union Law* (3rd edn, London, Sweet & Maxwell, 2011), paras 16.02–16-33.

European Central Bank fall within the jurisdiction of the General Court, since such cases do not normally involve review of the basic legislative activity of the Union institutions.[206]

(2) Exceptions

Art. 51 of the Statute contains two series of exceptions.[207] The first is based on the fact that **2.50** the Council sometimes adopts acts that do not concern the basic legislative activity of the Union. Reserving actions in relation to such acts to the Court of Justice would not be in conformity with the aim pursued by the changes made to the Statute. Art. 51 of the Statute therefore provides that the General Court is to have jurisdiction to hear and determine at first instance actions brought by a Member State concerning acts or failures to act of the Council in the field of State aid (Art. 108(2), third para., TFEU), with respect to implementing measures to protect trade (within the meaning of Art. 207 TFEU), as well as with respect to the Council's implementing powers reserved to itself in legally binding Union acts or which it has regained in the course of a 'committee procedure' (Art. 291, second para., TFEU).

Conversely, action by the Commission may constitute basic legislative activity. The review of the legality of such acts or of a failure on the part of the Commission to adopt such an act would therefore logically fall within the jurisdiction of the Court of Justice at first and last instance. Accordingly, Art. 51 of the Statute provides that the Court of Justice is to have jurisdiction to hear and determine actions brought by Member States against an act of or failure to act by the Commission under the first paragraph of Art. 331 TFEU relating to enhanced cooperation.

(3) Position of the European Council and the Committee of the Regions

Upon a literal reading of Art. 51 of the Statute, jurisdiction has not been reserved to the **2.51** Court of Justice for actions brought by an institution of the Union against an act or failure to act by the European Council, or a Union body, office, or agency. Likewise, the

---

[206] As regards the European Council, now listed as an official Union institution (n. 202), the Treaties explicitly state that it shall not exercise legislative functions: see Arts 15(1), 24(1), second para., 31(1), first para., TEU.

[207] Art. 51 of the Statute provides: 'By way of derogation from the rule laid down in Article 286(1) of the Treaty on the Functioning of the European Union, jurisdiction shall be reserved to the Court of Justice in the actions referred to in Articles 263 and 265 of the Treaty on the Functioning of the European Union when they are brought by a Member State against:

(a) an act of or failure to act by the European Parliament or the Council, or by both those institutions acting jointly, except for:
   – decisions taken by the Council under the third subparagraph of Article 108(2) of the Treaty on the Functioning of the European Union;
   – acts of the Council adopted pursuant to a Council regulation concerning measures to protect trade within the meaning of Article 207 of the Treaty on the Functioning of the European Union;
   – acts of the Council by which the Council exercises implementing powers in accordance with the second paragraph of Article 291 of the Treaty on the Functioning of the European Union;
(b) against an act of or failure to act by the Commission under the first paragraph of Article 331 of the Treaty on the Functioning of the European Union.

Jurisdiction shall also be reserved to the Court of Justice in the actions referred to in the same articles when they are brought by an institution of the Union against an act of or failure to act by the European Parliament, the Council, both those institutions acting jointly, or the Commission, or brought by an institution of the Union against an act of or failure to act by the European Central Bank.'

Committee of the Regions not being 'an institution of the Union', the action for annulment it brings should be decided at first instance by the General Court. All of this is the mechanical consequence of changes carried through by the Lisbon Treaty in circumstances where the wording of Art. 51 of the Statute was left untouched.

Whether that consequence was intended or not is hard to tell. It seems at least inconsistent that the jurisdiction for an action brought by an institution of the Union against an act or failure to act by the Commission is reserved to the Court of Justice, while an action brought by an institution of the Union against an act or failure to act by the European Council falls within the jurisdiction of the General Court. Along the same lines, when the Committee of the Regions brings an action against a legislative act of the European Parliament and the Council on the basis of the second paragraph of Art. 8 of Protocol (No. 2) on the application of the principles of subsidiarity and proportionality, it can be questioned whether such a matter is not of constitutional importance to the European Union and should not be decided by the Court of Justice.

The same literal reading of the Art. 51 Statute also leads to the conclusion that Member States should bring an action against an act or failure to act by the European Council in the General Court, the reason for that being that the European Council does not perform basic legislative activity. However, since the Court of Justice has accepted in its *Pringle* judgment that the legality of European Council decisions adopted in accordance with the simplified revision procedure can be reviewed,[208] it is difficult to maintain that position.

So far, however, the Union courts have not yet ruled on these matters. Therefore, for the purposes of this book, we prefer to stick as closely as possible to the text of the Treaties. That being said, the overview of the allocation of jurisdiction in para. 2.53 should be read together with the remarks made here.

(4) Infringement actions and preliminary references

2.52 Since the changes to the Statute did not bear on infringement actions or preliminary references, the Court of Justice will continue to hold exclusive jurisdiction in this respect (at first and last instance).

(5) Overview

2.53 On the basis of the Treaties, as amended by the Lisbon Treaty, and Art. 51 of the Statute, the current allocation of jurisdiction between the Court of Justice, the General Court, and the Civil Service Tribunal is as follows:

The *Court of Justice* has jurisdiction in:

– infringement actions (Arts 258–260 TFEU);
– preliminary references (Art. 267 TFEU);
– actions for annulment (Art. 263 TFEU) lodged by
  o an institution of the Union[209] against the European Parliament, the Council, both of those institutions acting jointly, the Commission, or the European Central Bank;

---

[208] ECJ (judgment of 27 November 2012), Case C-370/12 *Pringle*, not reported, paras 30–37.
[209] According to the wording of Art. 263, second para., TFEU, actions for annulment brought by the European Council and the Court of Justice appear to be excluded.

- o a Member State against the European Parliament and/or the Council, with the exception of actions relating to decisions taken by the Council in the field of State aid under Art. 108(2), third para., TFEU; acts of the Council adopted pursuant to a Council regulation concerning measures to protect trade within the meaning of Art. 207 TFEU, and acts of the Council by which the Council exercises implementing powers in accordance with Art. 291, second para., TFEU;
  - o a Member State against the Commission under Art. 331, first para., TFEU relating to enhanced cooperation;
- actions for failure to act (Art. 265 TFEU) lodged by
  - o an institution of the Union against the European Parliament, the Council, both of those institutions acting jointly, the Commission, or the European Central Bank;
  - o a Member State against the European Parliament and/or the Council, with the exception of actions relating to the Council's failure to adopt a decision in the field of State aid under Art. 108(2), third para., TFEU, the Council's failure to adopt an act pursuant to a Council regulation concerning measures to protect trade within the meaning of Art. 207 TFEU, and the Council's failure to exercise its implementing powers in accordance with Art. 291, second para., TFEU;
  - o a Member State against the Commission under Art. 331, first para., TFEU relating to enhanced cooperation;
- actions based on Art. 271(a) to (d) TFEU which concern disputes regarding the fulfilment by Member States of obligations under the Statute of the European Investment Bank ('EIB'), measures adopted by the Board of Governors and of the Board of Directors of the EIB, and the fulfilment by national central banks of obligations within the framework of the monetary Union;
- actions based on Art. 273 TFEU concerning any dispute between Member States which relates to the subject-matter of the Treaties, submitted to the Court under a special agreement between the parties;
- actions based on Art. 269 TFEU relating to the legality of acts adopted by the European Council or by the Council pursuant to Art. 7 TEU;
- appeals against rulings of the General Court (Art. 256(1), second para., TFEU);
- review of decisions which the General Court took on appeal against decisions of specialized courts (Art. 256(2), second para., TFEU).[210]

The *General Court* has jurisdiction in:

- actions for annulment (Art. 263 TFEU) lodged by
  - o natural or legal persons;[211]

---

[210] Review of preliminary rulings given by the General Court will also be possible (Art. 256(3), third para., TFEU). Yet, while one judicial panel, as it was then called, has already been created (the European Union Civil Service Tribunal), a transfer of jurisdiction to the General Court over preliminary references has not been envisaged for the time being.

[211] Regional and devolved authorities of Member States and third States fall within this category. As regards the latter, see ECJ (order of 14 July 2005), Case C-70/04 *Swiss Confederation v Commission*, not reported (reiterated in CFI (order of 7 July 2006), Case T-319/05 *Swiss Confederation v Commission* [2006] E.C.R. II-2073). Case dismissed on the merits without a ruling on the admissibility: EGC, Case T-319/05 *Swiss Confederation v Commission* [2010] E.C.R. II-4265 (confirmed on appeal: ECJ (judgment of 7 March 2013), Case C-547/10 P *Swiss Confederation v Commission*, not reported). See N. Cambien, 'Regio's en de rechtsbescherming voor de Europese Gerechtshoven' (2010) T.B.P. 622–35. See further para. 7.125.

- o the Committee of the Regions;[212]
- o a Member State against the Commission (unless the action concerns an act by the Commission under Art. 331, first para., TFEU relating to enhanced cooperation);
- o a Member State against the Council relating to decisions in the field of State aid under Art. 108(2), third para., TFEU;
- o a Member State against acts of the Council adopted pursuant to a Council regulation concerning measures to protect trade within the meaning of Art. 207 TFEU;
- o a Member State against acts of the Council by which the latter exercises implementing powers in accordance with Art. 291, second para., TFEU;
- o a Member State against the European Council, the European Central Bank, or a Union body, office, or agency;
- o an institution of the Union against acts of the European Council;
- o an institution of the Union against acts of a Union body, office, or agency;[213]
- actions for failure to act (Art. 265 TFEU) lodged by
- o natural or legal persons;[214]
- o a Member State against the Commission (unless the action concerns a failure to act by the Commission under Art. 331, first para., TFEU);
- o a Member State against the Council relating to a failure to adopt a decision in the field of State aid under Art. 108(2), third para., TFEU;
- o a Member State against the Council relating to a failure to adopt an act pursuant to a Council regulation concerning measures to protect trade within the meaning of Art. 207 TFEU;
- o a Member State against the Council relating to a failure to exercise its implementing powers in accordance with Art. 291, second para., TFEU;
- o a Member State against the European Council, the European Central Bank, or a Union body, office, or agency;
- o an institution of the Union against the European Council;
- actions relating to compensation for non-contractual damage brought against the Union (Arts 268 and 340, second and third paras, TFEU);
- actions pursuant to an arbitration clause contained in a contract concluded by or on behalf of the Union, whether that contract be governed by public or private law (Art. 272 TFEU);
- cases brought against the Office for Harmonisation in the Internal Market relating to Community trademarks[215] and designs[216] and cases brought against the Community Plant Variety Office relating to Community plant variety rights;[217]
- appeals against decisions of specialized courts (Art. 256(2), first para., TFEU).

---

[212] As introduced by the Lisbon Treaty, the Committee of the Regions, as already had been the case with regard to the European Central Bank and the Court of Auditors under the former EC Treaty, may now bring an action for annulment under Art. 263 TFEU for the purpose of protecting its prerogatives. See Art. 263, third para., TFEU. See paras 7.79–7.80.

[213] ECJ (order of 11 December 2007), Case C-269/06 *Commission v Translation Centre for the Bodies of the EU* [2007] E.C.R. I-187* Summ. pub.

[214] Regional and devolved authorities of Member States and third States fall within this category: see, by way of analogy, n. 211.

[215] Council Regulation (EC) No. 40/94 of 20 December 1993 on the Community trademark, [1994] O.J. L11/1; codified version, Council Regulation (EC) No. 207/2009 of 26 February 2009 on the Community trademark, [2009] O.J. L78/1.

[216] Council Regulation (EC) No. 6/2002 of 12 December 2001 on Community designs, [2002] O.J. L3/1.

[217] Council Regulation (EC) No. 2100/94 of 27 July 1994 on Community plant variety rights, [1994] O.J. L227/1, as amended by Council Regulation (EC) No. 2506/95 of 25 October 1995, [1995] O.J. L258/3.

The *Civil Service Tribunal* has jurisdiction in staff cases (Art. 270 TFEU).[218]

(6) Formal and substantive mistake

In addition, mention should be made of Art. 54 of the Statute, which deals with three **2.54** complications regarding the allocation of jurisdiction as between the Court of Justice and the General Court. As regards the Civil Service Tribunal, a similar regime is set forth in Art. 8 of Annex I of the Statute.

First, there is formal mistake: if an application or other procedural document addressed to the General Court is lodged by mistake with the Registrar of the Court of Justice, or vice versa, it is to be transmitted immediately from one Registrar to the other.[219]

Second, there is substantive mistake: if the General Court finds that it does not have jurisdiction to hear and determine an action in respect of which the Court of Justice has jurisdiction, it is to refer the action to the Court of Justice;[220] likewise, where the Court of Justice finds that an action falls within the jurisdiction of the General Court, it is to refer it to the General Court, whereupon that Court may not decline jurisdiction.[221] As will be appreciated, the allocation of jurisdiction as between the Court of Justice and the General Court is based on objective grounds insofar as the Court wrongly seized of a case falling within the jurisdiction of the other Court is under an obligation to refer it to that other Court. In case of doubt, the Court of Justice has the last word, since after it has referred a case to the General Court in that way, that Court cannot decline jurisdiction. This system does not detract from the right of the General Court to decline jurisdiction where a case falls outside the sphere of action of the Union judiciary regarded as a whole.

---

[218] Where the protocol establishing a Union institution or body provides that the Court of Justice should be the competent court to hear and determine disputes between that institution or body and its servants, the expression 'Court of Justice' is to 'be interpreted as referring to the Community judicature as a whole within the meaning of Art. 7 EC and thus as including the Court of First Instance' (CFI, Case T-333/99 *X v ECB* [2001] E.C.R. II-3021, IA-199, II-921, para. 41), as well as the Civil Service Tribunal. If such a provision was interpreted 'as precluding actions by certain servants against certain institutions or organs...from the improved system of legal remedies introduced by Decision 88/591 [which is characterized by a two-tier approach] for the same type of dispute, that departure from the general system of legal remedies, for which there is no objective justification, would be in breach of the principle of equal treatment and therefore of a fundamental principle of Community law' (CFI, Case T-333/99 *X v ECB*, para. 40).

[219] Statute, Art. 54, first para. As regards the Civil Service Tribunal, see Statute, Annex I, Art. 8(1).

[220] Statute, Art. 54, second para. See, e.g. CFI (order of 25 November 2003), Case T-85/01 *IAMA Consulting v Commission* [2003] E.C.R. II-4973, para. 62. As regards the Civil Service Tribunal, see Annex Art. 8(2); CST Rules of Procedure, Art. 73. See, e.g. EGC (order of 20 January 2011), Case T-136/10 *M v EMA*, not reported; EGC (order of 20 April 2012), Case T-374/07 *Pachtitis v Commission*, not reported; CST (order of 9 October 2006), Case F-53/06 *Gualtieri v Commission* [2006] E.C.R.-SC-I-A-1-107) (upheld on appeal: CFI, T-413/06 P *Gualtieri v Commission* [2008] E.C.R.-SC I-B-1-35); CST (order of 10 December 2010), Case F-46/08 *Thoss v Court of Auditors* [2008] E.C.R.-SC-I-A-1-429.

[221] Statute, Art. 54, second para. For practical examples, see ECJ (order of 23 May 1990), Case C-72/90 *Asia Motor France v Commission* [1990] E.C.R. I-2181; ECJ (order of 4 June 1991), Case C-66/90 *PTT v Commission* [1991] E.C.R. I-2723; ECJ (order of 3 May 1993), Case C-424/92 *Ladbroke Racing v Commission* [1993] E.C.R. I-2213; ECJ (order of 21 March 1997), Case C-95/97 *Région Wallonne v Commission* [1997] E.C.R. I-1787; ECJ (order of 1 October 1997), Case C-180/97 *Regione Toscana v Commission* [1997] E.C.R. I-5245, paras 9–12; ECJ (order of 14 July 2005), Case C-70/04 *Swiss Confederation v Commission*, not reported, para. 52; ECJ (order of 8 February 2007), Case C-406/06 *Landtag Schleswig-Holstein v Commission*, not reported; ECJ (order of 11 December 2007), Case C-269/06 *Commission v Translation Centre for the Bodies of the EU* [2007] E.C.R. I-187*, Summ. pub.; ECJ, Case C-418/06 P *Belgium v Commission* [2008] E.C.R. I-3047, para. 22.

(7) Identical or similar object of cases pending before different courts

2.55 Third, there is the case where the Court of Justice and the General Court are validly seized of cases in which the object is identical or similar.[222] Identity of object will occur where a natural or legal person or a Member State brings an action before the General Court against a Union institution for annulment of an act or for failure to take a decision, and another Union institution brings an action against the same act or failure to act before the Court of Justice. Similarity of object will occur where a natural or legal person or a Member State brings an action for annulment of an act—for example, of a Commission decision approving State aid—before the General Court, whilst a national court makes a reference for a preliminary ruling to the Court of Justice relating to the validity of the same act. Likewise, the same question of interpretation may be raised before both the General Court and the Court of Justice.

The third and fourth paragraphs of Art. 54 of the Statute[223] resolve the matter as follows:

> Where the Court of Justice and the General Court are seised of cases in which the same relief is sought, the same issue of interpretation is raised or the validity of the same act is called in question, the General Court may, after hearing the parties, stay the proceedings before it until such time as the Court of Justice has delivered judgment or, where the action is one brought pursuant to Article 263 of the Treaty on the Functioning of the European Union, may decline jurisdiction so as to allow the Court of Justice to rule on such actions. In the same circumstances, the Court of Justice may also decide to stay the proceedings before it; in that event, the proceedings before the General Court shall continue.
>
> Where a Member State and an institution of the Union are challenging the same act, the General Court shall decline jurisdiction so that the Court of Justice may rule on those applications.

This solution calls for a number of observations. The General Court is obliged to decline jurisdiction only in one instance, namely where a Member State (before the General Court) and an institution (before the Court of Justice) contest the same act. For the rest, the General Court cannot be compelled to decline jurisdiction (*se dessaisir*) or to stay proceedings.[224] This is a reflection of the judicial independence of the two Courts, expressed by the words 'the General Court may'. But if the General Court decides to make use of that possibility, the Court of Justice can prevent it from doing so by staying proceedings on its part, thereby causing the procedure to have to go through the General Court. In the event that the General Court has already declined jurisdiction, the Court of Justice can refer the case back to it by staying the parallel proceedings.

---

[222] R. Joliet and W. Vogel, 'Le Tribunal de première instance des Communautés européennes' (1989) R.M.C. 423, at 429. For some examples, see CFI (order of 16 November 1998), Case T-310/97 *Nederlandse Antillen v Council* [1998] E.C.R. II-4131, para. 7; CFI (order of 13 December 2007), Case T-215/07 *Donnici v European Parliament* [2007] E.C.R. II-5239.

[223] Council Decision 2004/407/EC, Euratom of 26 April 2004 amending Arts 51 and 54 of the Protocol on the Statute of the Court of Justice, [2004] O.J. L132/5; *corrigendum* in [2004] O.J. L194/3. In line with the changes made by the Lisbon Treaty regarding the names of the Union courts, further modifications were made to the Statute thereafter.

[224] The expression 'decline jurisdiction' ('*se dessaisir*' in the French version) in the third para. of Art. 54 of the Statute does not have the same meaning as it has in the second para. of Art. 54 (where the French reads '*décliner sa compétence*'). Where the General Court stays proceedings, an appeal will not lie against that decision (ECJ (order of 26 November 2003), Joined Cases C-366/03, C-368/03, C-390/03, C-391/03, and C-394/03 P *Associazione Bancaria Italiana and Others v Commission*, not reported).

A similar, though not identical, regime is set down in the Statute to deal with situations in which the Civil Service Tribunal and the General Court are validly seized of cases in which the object is identical or similar.

Art. 8(3) of Annex I of the Statute reads:

> Where the Civil Service Tribunal and the General Court are seised of cases in which the same issue of interpretation is raised or the validity of the same act is called into question, the Civil Service Tribunal, after hearing the parties, may stay the proceedings until the judgment of the General Court has been delivered.
>
> Where the Civil Service Tribunal and the General Court are seised of cases in which the same relief is sought, the Civil Service Tribunal shall decline jurisdiction so that the General Court may act on those cases.

Accordingly, this provision largely extends *mutatis mutandis* the regime set down under the third and fourth paragraphs of Art. 54 of the Statute in relation to the Court of Justice and the General Court to the Civil Service Tribunal. However, by comparison, the Civil Service Tribunal is obliged to decline jurisdiction in favour of the General Court in all cases where the same relief is sought, not just in the situation in which a Member State and Union institution are challenging the same act.

3

COOPERATION BETWEEN NATIONAL COURTS AND THE COURT OF JUSTICE: THE REFERENCE FOR A PRELIMINARY RULING

I. Introduction

A. General

3.01 The primary responsibility of national courts for the correct application of Union law is rounded off by the preliminary ruling procedure, which, in the words of the Court of Justice, is 'essential for preservation of the [Union] character of the law established by the Treaty and has the object of ensuring that in all circumstances this law is the same in all States of the [Union]'.[1]

Art. 267 TFEU empowers the Court of Justice to 'give preliminary rulings' on the interpretation of Union law[2] and on the validity of acts of the institutions, bodies, offices, or agencies of the Union.[3] Any court or tribunal of a Member State is entitled to make a reference for a preliminary ruling to the Court of Justice.[4] However, if a question regarding the validity or the interpretation of Union law is raised in a case pending before a court or tribunal of a Member State against whose decisions there is no judicial remedy under national law, that court or tribunal is obliged to bring the matter before the Court of Justice.[5]

B. Changes brought by the Treaty of Lisbon

3.02 The Lisbon Treaty brought certain changes to the preliminary ruling procedure as compared to the former EU and EC Treaties.[6]

---

[1] ECJ, Case 166/73 *Rheinmühlen-Düsseldorf* ('*Rheinmühlen I*') [1974] E.C.R. 33, para. 2; ECJ Opinion 1/09 *Draft Agreement on the European and Community Patents Court* [2011] E.C.R. I-1137, para. 83. See also Report of the Court of Justice on certain aspects of the Application of the Treaty on European Union (1995), 5, stating that 'The preliminary ruling system is the veritable cornerstone of the operation of the internal market, since it plays a fundamental role in ensuring that the law established by the Treaties retains its Community character with a view to guaranteeing that that law has the same effect in all circumstances in all the Member States of the European Union.'

[2] Ch. 6.

[3] Ch. 10. See also Art. 19(3) TEU: this provision, however, refers to 'acts adopted by the institutions' but not to acts of other Union bodies, offices, or agencies. This must be an oversight.

[4] While Art. 256(3) TFEU provides that the General Court may be conferred jurisdiction to deliver preliminary rulings in 'specific areas' as laid down by the Statute, at present this has not been done: see para. 2.53. As such, this chapter refers to the Court of Justice.

[5] See paras 3.43–3.61.

[6] See P. Van Nuffel, 'Prejudiciële vragen aan het Hof van Justitie van de Europese Unie: leidraad voor de rechtspraktijk na het Verdrag van Lissabon' (2009–2010) R.W. 1154–77.

First, as regards the reframing of Art. 234 EC as Art. 267 TFEU, minor amendments have been made by the Lisbon Treaty which reflect new realities and incorporate existing case-law. The first paragraph of Art. 267 TFEU incorporates the previous *acquis communautaire* by formally extending the Court's jurisdiction to give preliminary rulings to cover acts of 'bodies, offices or agencies of the Union'. In fact, the Court's jurisdiction to examine the validity of such acts and interpret them under the EC Treaty had not been questioned.[7] Since the European Central Bank was promoted to the status of an institution,[8] Art. 267 TFEU no longer contains an explicit reference to it.

Second, as a result of the elimination of the pillar structure by the Lisbon Treaty, Art. 267 TFEU provides that the Court of Justice of the European Union has jurisdiction to give preliminary rulings concerning the interpretation of 'the Treaties', meaning the Treaty on European Union and the Treaty on the Functioning of the European Union, and no longer just 'of this [EC] Treaty'. Consequently, the restrictions placed on the Court's preliminary ruling jurisdiction in certain areas of the former EC and EU Treaties comprising the Area of Freedom, Security and Justice by virtue of Art. 68 EC (concerning Title IV of the EC Treaty on visas, asylum, immigration, and other policies related to the free movement of persons) and Art. 35 EU (concerning the former third pillar of Police and Judicial Cooperation in Criminal Matters under Title VI of the EU Treaty), respectively, have been formally eliminated by the Lisbon Treaty.[9] However, aside from certain exceptions, the Court does not have jurisdiction with respect to the provisions relating to the former second pillar of the Common Foreign and Security Policy (CFSP) or to acts adopted on the basis of those provisions.[10] As such, the discussion of the Court's preliminary ruling jurisdiction generally concerns non-CFSP Union law.

Finally, since the preliminary ruling procedure inevitably results in national proceedings being stayed, the Treaty framers deemed it necessary to protect the interests of persons in custody. A new fourth paragraph of Art. 267 TFEU therefore provides that where a preliminary question 'is raised in a case pending before a court or tribunal of a Member State with regard to a person in custody, the Court of Justice of the European Union shall act with the minimum of delay'.[11]

---

[7] See, e.g. ECJ, Case 152/83 *Demouche and Others* [1987] E.C.R. 3833, para. 19. See further para. 6.10.

[8] Art. 13(1) TEU.

[9] ECJ (judgment of 1 December 2011), Case C-145/10 *Painer*, not reported, paras 51–55; ECJ, Case C-396/09 *Iteredil* [2011] E.C.R. I-9915, paras 18–21; ECJ, Case C-283/09 *Weryński* [2011] E.C.R. I-601, paras 26–33. That being said, complications arise especially in relation to the former third pillar governed by Art. 35 EU by virtue of the transitional provisions stipulated in Art. 10 of Protocol (No. 36), annexed to the Lisbon Treaty, on Transitional Provisions, [2012] O.J. C326/322. According to this Protocol, the regime of the former third pillar of Police and Judicial Cooperation in Criminal Matters under Art. 35 EU will hold for a five-year period from the entry into force of the Lisbon Treaty, subject to certain exceptions: see, e.g. ECJ, Joined Cases C-483/09 and C-1/10 *Painer and Salmerón Sánchez* [2011] E.C.R. I-8263, paras 30–33. ECJ (judgment of 21 December 2011), Case C-507/10 *X*, not reported, paras 18–22; ECJ (judgment of 12 July 2012), Case C-79/11 *Giovanardi and Others*, not reported, paras 30–34; See also Ch. 22.

[10] Art. 24(1), second para., TEU and Art. 275 TFEU. Art. 275 TFEU does grant certain exceptions, giving the Court jurisdiction, first, to monitor compliance with Art. 40 TEU, and second, to rule on proceedings under Art. 263 TFEU relating to the legality of decisions providing for restrictive measures against natural and legal persons adopted by the Council under Title V, Ch. 2, TEU.

[11] This provision, which had already appeared as Art. III-369, fourth para., of the Draft Constitutional Treaty, did play a role in the introduction of the urgent procedure for preliminary rulings applicable to the Area of Freedom, Security and Justice: see para. 22.06.

C. The EAEC Treaty

3.03 With the entry into force of the Lisbon Treaty, the provisions of the EAEC Treaty continue to have full effect.[12] However, many of the provisions concerning the Court of Justice were repealed, including Art. 150 EAEC, which was virtually identical to former Art. 234 EC.[13]

D. The former ECSC Treaty

3.04 The former ECSC Treaty[14] contained no provision relating to the Court's jurisdiction to give preliminary rulings on interpretation, but did provide that 'The Court shall have sole jurisdiction to give preliminary rulings on the validity of acts of the High Authority [Commission] and of the Council where such validity is in issue in proceedings brought before a national court or tribunal' (Art. 41 ECSC). Nevertheless, the Court has held that it also has jurisdiction to rule on questions relating to the interpretation of the ECSC Treaty and of measures adopted under that Treaty.[15] Furthermore, it is competent to answer questions referred for a preliminary ruling on the interpretation of the ECSC Treaty and of measures adopted under that Treaty even though such questions are referred to it after the expiry of the ECSC Treaty. The Court indeed considers that it would be contrary to the objectives and coherence of the Treaties and irreconcilable with the continuity of the Union legal order if the Court did not have jurisdiction to ensure the uniform interpretation of the rules deriving from the ECSC Treaty that continue to produce effects after the expiry of that Treaty.[16]

E. Objectives of the preliminary ruling procedure

3.05 Under established case-law, the preliminary ruling procedure enshrined in Art. 267 TFEU embodies a two-fold need: to ensure the utmost uniformity in the application of Union law and to establish for that purpose effective cooperation between the Court of Justice and national courts.[17] That cooperation requires 'the national court and the Court of Justice, both keeping within their respective jurisdiction, and with the aim of ensuring that [Union] law is applied in a uniform manner, to make direct and complementary contributions to the working out of a decision'.[18]

---

[12] See Protocol (No. 2), annexed to the Lisbon Treaty, amending the Treaty establishing the European Atomic Energy Community Treaty, [2007] O.J. C306/99.

[13] See the consolidated version of the EAEC Treaty, [2012] O.J. C327/1.

[14] The ECSC Treaty expired on 23 July 2002, and its assets and liabilities were transferred to the European Community, as it then was, on 24 July 2002. See Protocol (No. 37), annexed to the TEU and TFEU, on the financial consequences of the expiry of the ECSC Treaty and on the Research Fund for Coal and Steel, [2012] O.J. C326/328. For detailed background, see K. Lenaerts and P. Van Nuffel (R. Bray and N. Cambien (eds)), *European Union Law* (3rd edn, London, Sweet & Maxwell, 2011), para. 1.08.

[15] ECJ, Case C-221/88 *Busseni* [1990] E.C.R. I-495, para. 16.

[16] ECJ, Case C-119/05 *Lucchini* [2007] E.C.R. I-6911, para. 41.

[17] ECJ, Case C-221/88 *Busseni* [1990] E.C.R. I-495, para. 13 (referring to the relevant provisions of the E(E)C Treaty and the EAEC Treaty).

[18] ECJ, Case 16/65 *Schwarze* [1965] E.C.R. 877, at 886 (then referring to the E(E)C Treaty). See further, e.g. Case C-458/06 *Gourmet Classic* [2008] E.C.R. I-4207, paras 20–23, 32 (and further citations therein); and ECJ, Case C-466/07 *Klarenberg* [2009] E.C.R. I-803, para. 25 (and further citations therein). According

In other words, there are twin aims of the preliminary ruling procedure. First, this procedure underlies the strong relationship of judicial cooperation between the Court of Justice and the national courts. The preliminary ruling procedure constitutes an important 'judicial dialogue'[19] between the Court of Justice and the national courts that encompasses all levels of the judicial hierarchy in the various Member States, thereby ensuring 'ground level access' for citizens' assertion of Union law rights at their first point of contact with the judicial system of a particular Member State.[20] Second, the preliminary ruling procedure contributes to the uniform application of Union law, since it ensures that Union law is applied the same way throughout the Union legal order.

F. Sole power of the Court of Justice to declare a Union act invalid

The twin aims of the preliminary ruling procedure hold good no matter whether the ruling is sought on the interpretation of Union law and/or on the validity of a Union act.[21] This was the principal reason that prompted the Court in the landmark case of *Foto-Frost* to declare with regard to the application of what is now Art. 267 TFEU that it has the sole power to declare an act of a Union institution invalid.[22] This is because the uniform application of Union law is particularly necessary when the validity of a Union act is at stake. Divergences of view between courts in the Member States as to the validity of acts of Union institutions, bodies, offices, or agencies would be liable to place in jeopardy the very unity of the Union legal order and detract from the fundamental requirement of legal certainty.[23] Naturally, this does not alter the fact that reviewing the validity of acts of the

3.06

---

to the Court's oft-repeated language, the preliminary ruling procedure enshrined in what is now Art. 267 TFEU is an 'instrument of cooperation between the Court of Justice and the national courts, by means of which the Court provides the national courts with the points of interpretation of Union law which they need in order to decide the disputes before them': see, e.g. ECJ, Case C-445/06 *Danske Slagterier* [2009] E.C.R. I-2119, para. 65 and case-law cited therein. It does not install a hierarchy between the Court of Justice and the national courts: V. Skouris, 'Stellung und Bedeutung des Vorabentscheidungsverfahrens im europäischen Rechtsschutzsystem' (2008) EuGRZ 344.

[19] K. Lenaerts, 'Le dialogue des juges', in l'Institut d'études sur la Justice (ed.), *Les cahiers de l'Institut d'études sur la Justice: Le dialogue des juges* (Bruxelles, Bruylant, 2007), 121–6; A. Rosas, 'Methods of Interpretation: Judicial Dialogue', in C. Baudenbacher and E. Busek (eds), *The Role of International Courts* (Heidelberg, German Law Publishers, 2008), 185–91. See further W. Hakenberg, 'Der Dialog zwischen nationalen und europäischen Richtern: das Vorabentscheidungsverfahren zum EuGH' (2000) Deutsche Richterzeitung 345–9.

[20] Note that the judicial dialogue works in both ways and that the interpretation of Union law is also influenced by national Judges and national law: J.-C. Bonichot, 'L'influence des droits nationaux aux l'élaboration de la norme jurisprudentielle communautaire' (2009) Justice & cassation 233–43; A. Ó Caoimh, 'L'influence des droits nationaux aux l'élaboration de la norme jurisprudentielle communautaire' (2009) Justice & cassation 244–250; V. Skouris, 'L'influence du droit national et la jurisprudence des juridictions des États membres sur l'interprétation du droit communautaire' (2008) Il diritto dell'Unione europea 239–54; T. von Danwitz, 'Sur les conditions de fonctionnement du processus jurisprudential à la Cour de justice de l'Union européenne' (2010) Il diritto dell'Unione europea 775–84; T. von Danwitz, 'Der Einfluss des nationalen Rechts und der Rechtsprechung der Gerichte der Mitgliedstaaten auf die Auslegung des Gemeinschaftsrechts' (2008) ZESAR 57–64.

[21] ECJ, Case 66/80 *International Chemical* [1981] E.C.R. 1191, para. 11. It should be kept in mind, however, that this generally excludes CFSP acts: see n. 10.

[22] ECJ, Case 314/85 *Foto-Frost* [1987] E.C.R. 4199, para. 17.

[23] ECJ, Case 314/85 *Foto-Frost*, para.15. This case is discussed further at paras 3.59–3.61.

Union institutions, bodies, offices, or agencies is essentially a control of the legality of such acts, which is primarily designed to protect the rights of individuals.[24]

G. Topics to be discussed

3.07 A request for a preliminary ruling takes the form of a question put to the Court of Justice, which is subject to a number of rules. First, the *initiative* of referring the question must emanate from 'a court or tribunal [*juridiction* in French] of a Member State', either of its own motion or acting on a request made by one of the parties in proceedings pending before it, and national (procedural) law may not put impediments in the way of the right to seek a preliminary ruling (which every national court or tribunal has by virtue of Union law).[25] Second, as a consequence, the *relevance* of the question falls to be determined by the national court, albeit only within certain limits which the Court of Justice has placed upon its competence to answer questions referred for a preliminary ruling. Finally, there are issues relating to which national courts *must*, as opposed to *may*, refer questions for a preliminary ruling to the Court of Justice. Under the third paragraph of Art. 267 TFEU, a 'court or tribunal of a Member State against whose decisions there is no judicial remedy under national law' is in principle obliged to refer questions for a preliminary ruling which are raised in a case pending before it, save for certain circumstances as set forth in the case-law of the Court of Justice.

These matters will be considered in the three main sections comprising the rest of this chapter.

II. The Initiative for Requesting a Preliminary Ruling

A. What is a 'court or tribunal of a Member State'?

(1) *Vaassen* criteria

3.08 Generally, the expression 'court or tribunal of a Member State' does not raise any difficulties. Where a Member State regards a public body as a 'court or tribunal', Union law normally accepts it as such.[26] This is because in that case the body manifestly fulfils the criteria which the Court of Justice has formulated—which are known as the *Vaassen* criteria after the case in which they were first framed[27]—in order to confer on a body which is not

---

[24] Cf. ECJ, Case 294/83 *Les Verts v European Parliament* [1986] E.C.R. 1339, para. 23.

[25] ECJ, Case 166/73 *Rheinmühlen-Düsseldorf* ('*Rheinmühlen I*') [1974] E.C.R. 33, para. 2; ECJ, Case C-312/93 *Peterbroeck* [1995] E.C.R. I-4599, para. 13; ECJ, Case C-210/06 *Cartesio* [2008] E.C.R. I-9641, para. 94; ECJ, Joined Cases C-188/10 and C-189/10 *Melki and Abdeli* [2010] E.C.R. I-5667, para. 42; ECJ, Case C-173/09 *Elchinov* [2010] E.C.R. I-8889, paras 25–28; ECJ (judgment of 18 July 2013), Case C-136/12 *Consiglio nazionale dei geologi*, not reported, para. 36. Note that where a potential question of Union law arises before a court not being a court of last instance, it has to decide whether a decision on the question is necessary in order to give judgment and, if so, whether the court should order a reference to be made. Matters taken into account in the UK include, *inter alia*, the difficulty and the importance of the point of Union law concerned, as well as the question of delay and costs: see D. Anderson and M. Demetriou, *References to the European Court* (2nd edn, London, Sweet & Maxwell, 2002), paras 5.16–5.58.

[26] But see para. 3.10 *in fine*.

[27] ECJ, Case 61/65 *Vaassen (née Göbbels)* [1966] E.C.R. 261, at 273 (see R. Silva de Lapuerta, 'Organos jurisdiccionales que pueden interponer recurso prejudicial ante el Tribunal de Justicia de las Comunidades.

considered a court or tribunal under national law that capacity under Union law with a view to the application of the articles of the preliminary ruling procedure.

A 'court or tribunal' under Art. 267 TFEU is (1) a body (2) which is established by law, (3) permanent and independent;[28] and (4) charged with the settlement of disputes defined in general terms (5) which is bound by rules governing *inter partes* proceedings similar to those used by the ordinary courts of law,[29] (6) insofar as it acts as the 'proper judicial body' for the disputes in question, which means that parties must be required to apply to the court or tribunal for the settlement of their dispute and its determination must be binding,[30] and (7) is bound to apply rules of law.[31]

Sentencia de 30 de Junio de 1966' (1985) Noticias C.E.E. 4, 19–21). Given the Court's standard formula (i.e. 'The Court takes into account a number of factors, such as . . .'), these criteria may not be exhaustive, and some criteria may weigh more than others.

[28] ECJ, Case C-54/96 *Dorsch Consult* [1997] E.C.R. I-4961, para. 23; ECJ, Case C-517/09 *RTL Belgium* [2010] E.C.R. I-14093. As regards the 'independence' requirement, see further n. 36.

[29] In the case of *Dorsch Consult* (ECJ, Case C-54/96 *Dorsch Consult*, paras 22–38), the Court held that 'the requirement that the procedure before the hearing body concerned must be *inter partes* is not an absolute requirement', after which it found that the adjudicating body, the Federal German *Vergabeüberwachung-sausschuss des Bundes* (the Federal Public Procurement Awards Supervisory Board), a statutory administrative body supervising the award of procurement contracts, had to hear the parties before making any determination (see ECJ, Case C-54/96 *Dorsch Consult*, para. 31, at I-4994). The Court of Justice held on this basis that the board in question was a 'court or tribunal' within the meaning of Art. 267 TFEU; compare Opinion of Advocate-General G. Tesauro in that case, expressing doubts as to that body's compliance with the *Vaassen* criteria. The relativity of the *inter partes* requirement may potentially explain why the admissibility of a request by the investigative judge in Case C-153/00 *der Weduwe* was not challenged on this ground, as compared to Case 14/86 *Pretore di Salo v X* concerning combination of investigative judge and public prosecutor. See also in this connection ECJ, Case C-18/93 *Corsica Ferries* [1994] E.C.R. I-1783, para. 12; ECJ, Joined Cases C-110/98 to C-147/98 *Gabalfrisa and Others* [2000] E.C.R. I-1557, para. 47; ECJ, Case C-182/00 *Lutz and Others* [2002] E.C.R. I-547, para. 13; ECJ, Case C-210/06 *Cartesio* [2008] E.C.R. I-9641, para. 56; ECJ, Case C-14/08 *Roda Golf & Beach Resort* [2009] E.C.R. I-5439, para. 33. Following *Dorsch Consult*, the Court has regarded other types of public procurement bodies as satisfying the *Vaassen* criteria: see ECJ, Case C-411/00 *Felix Swoboda* [2002] E.C.R. I-10567, paras 25–28 (the Austrian *Bundesvergabeamt* [Federal Procurement Office] held to be a court or tribunal within the meaning of Art. 267 TFEU; upheld in later cases: see citations in Opinion of Advocate-General J. Kokott in ECJ, Case C-454/06 *pressetext Nachrichtenagentur* [2008] E.C.R. I-4401, points 30–31); ECJ, Case C-92/00 *HI* [2002] E.C.R. I-5553, paras 24–28 (the *Vergabekontrollsenat des Landes Wien* [Public-Procurement Review Chamber of the Vienna Region] held to be a court or tribunal within the meaning of Art. 267 TFEU; see also ECJ, Case C-393/06 *Ing. Aigner* [2008] E.C.R. I-2339).

[30] ECJ, Case C-54/96 *Dorsch Consult* [1997] E.C.R. I-4961, paras 27–29. In *Österreichischer Gewerkschaftsbund*, the Court of Justice held that the Austrian *Oberster Gerichtshof* [Supreme Court] was a court or tribunal within the meaning of Art. 267 TFEU when adjudicating in a dispute between a union for public-sector employees and the Austrian Republic, although there were features of the procedure which were less characteristic of judicial proceedings, namely the fact that the *Oberster Gerichtshof* did not rule on disputes in a specific case involving identified persons, that it must base its legal assessment on the facts alleged by the applicant without further examination, that the decision was declaratory in nature and that the right to bring proceedings was exercised collectively (ECJ, Case C-195/98 *Österreichischer Gewerkschaftsbund* [2000] E.C. R. I-10497, paras 21–32).

[31] ECJ, Case 61/65 *Vaassen (née Göbbels)* [1966] E.C.R. 261, at 273; ECJ, Joined Cases C-9/97 and C-118/97 *Jokela and Pitkäranta* [1998] E.C.R. I-6267, para.18. See also ECJ, Case C-416/96 *Eddline El-Yassini* [1999] E.C.R. I-1209, paras 17–22 (Immigration Adjudicator in the UK held to be a court or tribunal within the meaning of Art. 267 TFEU); ECJ, Case C-407/98 *Abrahamsson and Anderson* [2000] E.C.R. I-5539, paras 28–38 (the Swedish *överklagandenämnden för Högskolan*, which undertakes an independent examination of appeals lodged against decisions on appointments taken in universities and higher educational institutions, held to be a court or tribunal within the meaning of Art. 267 TFEU); ECJ, Case C-259/04 *Emanuel* [2006] E.C.R. I-3089 (the Person Appointed by the Lord Chancellor under section 76 of the Trade Marks Act 1994 held to be a court or tribunal within the meaning of Art. 267 TFEU); ECJ, Case C-246/05 *Häupl* [2007] E.C.R. I-4673 (The *Oberster Patent- und Markensenat* [Supreme Patent and Trade Mark

(2) Application of *Vaassen* criteria

3.09   In accordance with that test, the Netherlands *Commissie van Beroep Huisartsgeneeskunde* (Appeals Committee for General Medicine) was regarded as being a 'court or tribunal' even though it was part of a professional body and not considered to be a court or tribunal under Netherlands law.[32] The crucial factor appeared to be that the decisions delivered by the Appeals Committee, after an adversarial procedure, were 'in fact recognised as final', since 'in a matter involving the application of [Union] law' (registration of general practitioners) there was 'in practice [no] right of appeal to the ordinary courts', with the result that the absence of any opportunity of seeking a preliminary ruling from the Appeals Committee would constitute a threat to 'the proper functioning of [Union] law'.[33]

The position was completely different when the Court, of its own motion,[34] refused to answer a question referred for a preliminary ruling by the *Directeur des Contributions Directes et des Accises* (Director of Taxation and Excise Duties) of the Grand Duchy of Luxembourg on the grounds that he was not a 'court or tribunal'.[35] The Court emphasized that this expression, which had to be defined under Union law, referred by its nature to an authority acting as a third party in relation to the authority which adopted the decision forming the subject-matter of the proceedings.[36] This was clearly not so in the case of the

---

Adjudication Body] of Vienna, Austria held to be a court or tribunal within the meaning of Art. 267 TFEU). Compare, e.g. ECJ (order of 11 July 2003), Case C-161/03 *CAFOM and Samsung Electronics France*, not reported, paras 10–17 (the French *Commission de conciliation et d'expertise douanière* held not to be a court or tribunal within the meaning of Art. 267 TFEU).

[32] ECJ, Case 246/80 *Broekmeulen* [1981] E.C.R. 2311, para.11.

[33] ECJ, Case 246/80 *Broekmeulen*, paras 16–17.

[34] The Commission and the Luxembourg Government, which alone submitted observations to the Court pursuant to Art. 23 of the Statute, did not take issue with the competence of the body requesting the preliminary ruling in this case. Indeed, there have been cases in which, as noted by the Advocates-General, no reservations, let alone formal pleas, are put forward as regards whether the particular body can be regarded as a court or tribunal of a Member State under Art. 267 TFEU and thus the Court assesses the admissibility of such body of its own motion. See, e.g. Opinion of Advocate-General D. Ruiz-Jarabo Colomer in ECJ, Case C-259/04 *Emanuel* [2006] E.C.R. I-3089, point 24; Opinion of Advocate-General D. Ruiz-Jarabo Colomer in ECJ, Case C-246/05 *Häupl* [2007] E.C.R. I-4673, point 21. In one case, the Advocate-General surmised that by discussing the status of the Swedish *Utlänningsnämnden* (immigration appeals body) in its observations, the Swedish Government implicitly raised the question of the admissibility of the questions referred by this body, although he concluded that such body satisfied the requisite criteria; the Court of Justice did not delve into this matter in its judgment: see Opinion of Advocate-General F.G. Jacobs in ECJ, Case C-1/05 *Jia* [2007] E.C.R. I-1, points 16, 24–25.

[35] ECJ, Case C-24/92 *Corbiau* [1993] E.C.R. I-1277, para.17. Cf. ECJ, Case C-17/00 *De Coster* [2001] E.C.R. I-9445, paras 9–22, in which the Court of Justice considered that the *Rechtsprekend College van het Brussels Hoofdstedelijk Gewest/Collège juridictionnel de la Région de Bruxelles-Capitale* (Judicial Board of the Brussels-Capital region), which adjudicates disputes relating to the legality of municipal taxes, constituted a court or tribunal (Advocate-General D. Ruiz-Jarabo Colomer reached the opposite conclusion). Cf. ECJ, Joined Cases C-110/98 to C-147/98 *Gabalfrisa and Others* [2000] E.C.R. I-1577, para. 40 (relating to the Spanish *Tribunales Económico-Administrativos*).

[36] The criterion of independence implies that the authority may be held to be a court or tribunal within the meaning of Art. 267 TFEU only if it 'acts as a third party' in relation to the authority which adopted the contested decision. This assumes that there are no organizational links (e.g. in terms of its composition) or functional links which preclude this (ECJ, Case C-516/99 *Schmid* [2002] E.C.R. I-4573, paras 34–44). Therefore, the Belgian *Collège d'autorisation et de contrôle du Conseil supérieur de l'audiovisuel* (the Licensing and Control Authority of the Broadcasting Authority) could not be considered as a tribunal or court in the meaning of Art. 267 TFEU, since neither the structural organization of the Broadcasting Authority nor the tasks assigned to its various bodies guaranteed both external and internal independence. It appeared that the investigating body of the Broadcasting Authority, which brought the case against a broadcaster before the

Directeur des Contributions, who was in charge of the revenue departments which had made the contested assessment to tax. Furthermore, if the matter were to come before the Luxembourg *Conseil d'Etat* on appeal, the *Directeur des Contributions* would be the defendant, which was regarded as confirming that he was a party to proceedings and not an authority separating the parties to the proceedings as a neutral outsider.[37] In that respect, the Director should be compared with the British 'Chief Adjudication Officer', who takes the administrative decision with regard to the grant of social security benefits. That 'Officer' is not a judicial authority, but a party who, as such, defends his decision on appeal before a 'third party', namely the 'Chief Social Security Commissioner', who is entitled, as a 'court or tribunal' to make a reference to the Court for a preliminary ruling (not that there has been any dispute or doubt about this).[38]

(3) Administrative bodies

Bodies that act in an administrative capacity, but not as a judicial authority, or only submit **3.10** opinions to the public authorities with a view to their taking a decision are not entitled to refer questions for a preliminary ruling.[39] Examples are bodies of professional organizations

---

Licensing and Control Authority, was overseen by the Bureau of the Broadcasting Authority. The members of that Bureau were also sitting in the Licensing and Control Authority. Furthermore, the Bureau represented the Licensing and Control Authority in appeal proceedings against its decisions before national courts. In view of these elements, the Court decided, contrary to what the Licensing and Control Authority had stated in its order for reference, that the Licensing and Control Authority was not acting as a third party and could thus not be considered as a tribunal or court for the purposes of Art. 267 TFEU (ECJ, Case C-517/09 *RTL Belgium* [2010] E.C.R. I-14093, paras 36–49). The criterion of independence likewise implies in principle that members of the court or tribunal must be able to be challenged and that there must be circumstances in which members of the body in question must withdraw (ECJ, Case C-103/97 *Köllensperger and Atzwanger* [1999] E.C.R. I-551, paras 19–25). In *Pilato*, the Court elaborated further on this criterion, ruling that the independence of the body making a reference 'presumes that the body is protected against external intervention or pressure liable to jeopardise the independent judgment of its members as regards proceedings before them' and that the case-law requires, *inter alia*, that dismissals of members of that body should be determined by express legislative provisions: ECJ (order of 14 May 2008), Case C-109/07 *Pilato* [2008] E.C.R. I-3503, paras 23–24. As such, the Court ruled in that case that the French *prud'homie de pêche de Martigues* (Martigues Industrial Tribunal for Matters relating to Fishing) could not be regarded as meeting the requisite conditions: ECJ, Case C-109/07 *Pilato*, paras 25–31. For the application of the independence requirement of Art. 267 TFEU to a slightly different context, see ECJ, Case C-506/04 *Wilson* [2006] E.C.R. I-8613, paras 48–53.

[37] ECJ, Case C-24/92 *Corbiau* [1993] E.C.R. I-1277, para.16. See also ECJ (judgment of 31 January 2013), Case C-394/11 *Belov*, not reported, para. 49 (J. T. Nowak, case note (2013) S.E.W. 557–564).

[38] ECJ, Case 150/85 *Drake* [1986] E.C.R. 1995. See, to the same effect, ECJ, Joined Cases C-74/95 and C-129/95 *X* [1996] E.C.R. I-6609, paras 17–20, in which the Court held that the Italian *Procura della Repubblica* could not be regarded as being a court or tribunal within the meaning of Art. 267 TFEU on the grounds that its role in the main proceedings in the case in question was not to rule on an issue in complete independence but, acting as prosecutor in the proceedings, to submit that issue, if appropriate, for consideration by the competent judicial body. By contrast, a Judge in charge of preliminary inquiries in criminal proceedings acts in a judicial capacity, so that he must be regarded as a 'court or tribunal of a Member State': ECJ, Joined Cases C-54/94 and C-74/94 *Cacchiarelli and Stanghellini* [1995] E.C.R. I-391 (with respect to former 234 EC); ECJ, Case C-105/03 *Pupino* [2005] E.C.R. I-5285, para. 22 (with respect to former Art. 35 EU).

[39] Importantly, the fact that national law may deem certain functions as administrative is not decisive. For example, an indictment division of a Court of Appeal which is charged with giving opinions on requests for extradition that are deemed to constitute the exercise of administrative powers under national law constitutes a court within the meaning of Art. 267 TFEU provided the requisite criteria are satisfied: ECJ, Case C-296/08 PPU *Santesteban Goicoechea* [2008] E.C.R. I-6307, paras 39–42. For that matter, the Court has admitted references from quasi-judicial bodies situated, strictly speaking, outside the judicial system of a Member State, as in the case of Austrian independent administrative tribunals (Senate): ECJ, Case C-205/08 *Umweltanwalt voor Kärnten* [2009] E.C.R. I-11525, paras 34-39 (deeming the Austrian *Unweltsenat* (Environment Tribunal)

deciding on admission to a profession⁴⁰ or a consultative committee whose duty is to submit reasoned—but not binding—opinions to the Treasury Minister on the sanctions to be imposed by that minister on persons infringing national legislation relating to transfers of foreign exchange.⁴¹ In both cases, there was the possibility of an appeal after the final administrative decision to a judicial body that could, if necessary, make a reference for a preliminary ruling. In addition, none of the bodies concerned could be regarded as a 'third party', either because they took the first—*ex hypothesi* subsequently contested—decision themselves, or because they were directly involved in taking that decision.⁴² Judicial bodies

---

to fall within the definition of court or tribunal of a Member State); ECJ, Case C-195/06 *Österreichischer Rundfunk* [2007] E.C.R. I-8817, paras 10–13, 20–22 (deeming the Austrian *Bundeskommunikationssenat*, a body of last administrative instance set up by the Federal Chancellery to monitor the decisions of certain telecommunications and broadcasting authorities, to fall within the definition of court or tribunal of a Member State: compare Opinion of Advocate-General D. Ruiz-Jarabo Colomer, points 24–41). For an analysis, see J. T. Nowak, case note (2013) S.E.W. 557–564.

⁴⁰ ECJ, Case 65/77 *Razanatsimba* [1977] E.C.R. 2229, para.5; ECJ (order of 18 June 1980), Case 138/80 *Borker* [1980] E.C.R. 1975, para. 4. See also ECJ, Case C-178/99 *Salzmann* [2001] E.C.R. I-4421, paras 11–22, in which it was held that the Austrian *Bezirksgericht* (District Court) does not constitute a court or tribunal where, acting as an administrative body, it considers an application for registration of a contract of sale of land in the land register. This is because, in that capacity, it does not decide a dispute but merely checks that applications for registration of titles to property in the land register comply with the conditions laid down by law; and ECJ, Case C-182/00 *Lutz and Others* [2002] E.C.R. I-547, paras 11–15: when ruling on obligations to disclose annual accounts and the annual report, the Austrian *Landesgericht* [Regional Court] does not decide any dispute and therefore does not constitute a court or tribunal within the meaning of Art. 267 TFEU when acting in that capacity (see the Opinion of Advocate-General L.A. Geelhoed to the same effect). However, not all bodies deciding on the admission to a profession are considered to be administrative bodies. For example, the *Oberste Berufungs- und Disziplinarkommission* (Appeals and Disciplinary Board) of the Austrian *Oberlandesgericht* (Higher Regional Court), ruling on appeal of a decision of the *Rechtsanwaltsprüfungskommission* (Lawyers' Examination Board of the same *Oberlandesgericht*) refusing admission of an Austrian national to the aptitude test for the profession of lawyer in Austria because he had studied and practised law in another Member State, constituted a court or tribunal within the meaning of Art. 267 TFEU, since its jurisdiction was compulsory and it further exhibited all necessary features in order to be considered as a court or tribunal within the meaning of Art. 267 TFEU (ECJ, Case C-118/09 *Koller* [2010] E.C.R. I-13627, paras 21–24).

⁴¹ ECJ (order of 5 March 1986), Case 318/85 *Greis Unterweger* [1986] E.C.R. 955, para. 4. But see ECJ, Case 36/73 *Nederlandse Spoorwegen* [1973] E.C.R. 1299, together with ECJ, Joined Cases C-69/96 to C-79/96 *Garofalo and Others* [1997] E.C.R. I-5603, paras 17–27, in which the Court held that where the Italian *Consiglio di Stato* issues an opinion in relation to an extraordinary petition made to the President of the Republic for annulment of an administrative act, it constitutes a court or tribunal within the meaning of Art. 267 TFEU. The Swedish *Skatterättsnämnden* (Revenue Board), which may give a preliminary decision on matters of taxation upon application by a taxable person, is not a court or tribunal within the meaning of Art. 267 TFEU. The Court held that such board essentially performs an administrative function on the grounds that it does not have as its task to review the legality of the decisions of the tax authorities but rather to adopt a view on how a specific transaction is to be assessed to tax. It therefore acts in an administrative capacity and is not called upon to decide a dispute (ECJ, Case C-134/97 *Victoria Film* [1998] E.C.R. I-7023, paras 15–19). In contrast, the *Regeringsrätten* (Swedish Supreme Administrative Court) does constitute a court or tribunal within the meaning of Art. 267 TFEU when seized of an appeal against a ruling of the *Skatterättsnämnden* (see ECJ, Case C-200/98 *X and Y* [1999] E.C.R. I-8261, paras 13–17); ECJ (order of 26 November 1999), Case C-440/98 *RAI* [1999] E.C.R. I-8597, paras 14–15 (the *Corte dei Conti* [Italian Court of Auditors] does not perform a judicial function when it plays an administrative role consisting in the evaluation and verification of the results of administrative actions).

⁴² See also ECJ (order of 24 March 2011), Case C-344/09 *Dan Bengtsson* [2011] E.C.R. I-1999, paras 23–25 and ECJ (judgment of 19 December 2012), Case C-363/11 *Epitropos Tou Elegktikou Synedriou*, not reported, paras 24–28 (J. T. Nowak, case note (2013) S.E.W. 557–564).

that also perform non-judicial functions are likewise not entitled to make a reference for a preliminary ruling in connection with that administrative activity.[43]

(4) National competition authorities

The question arises as to whether national authorities responsible for settling disputes **3.11** relating to the application of competition law (domestic as well as European) are entitled to refer questions for a preliminary ruling. Do the authorities in question give a ruling in like manner to a court in proceedings brought by the prosecuting party (the public department responsible for ensuring that competition law is complied with) against a defendant undertaking or do they instead take an administrative decision after a procedure in which the other party is entitled to give its views which they must subsequently defend before a court or tribunal to which the undertaking, concerned has appealed? The answer to this question depends on a prior analysis of the legal position of the authorities concerned in each Member State and hence is liable to differ from one Member State to another.[44]

The Court gave a ruling, without any reservation, on the questions referred for a preliminary ruling by the Spanish *Tribunal de Defensa de la Competencia*, after Advocate-General Jacobs had pointed out that whilst, administratively, the 'Tribunal' formed part of the Ministry of Trade, it nevertheless fulfilled the *Vaassen* criteria (see para. 3.08).[45] In addition, the applicant in the proceedings was the '*Dirección General de Defensa de la Competencia*', suing a number of banks, with the result that the 'Tribunal' did in fact come across as a third party.

---

[43] ECJ, Joined Cases C-110/98 to C-147/98 *Gabalfrisa and Others* [2000] E.C.R. I-1577, para. 33; ECJ, Case C-178/99 *Salzmann* [2001] E.C.R. I-4421, paras 15–17; ECJ (order of 18 March 2004) Case C-45/03 *Dem' Yanenko*, not reported, paras 26–283; ECJ, Case C-96/04 *Standesamt Stadt Niebüll* [2006] E.C.R. I-3561, paras 13–20; compare ECJ, Case C-353/06 *Grunkin and Paul* [2008] E.C.R. I-7639, paras 9–13 (with further elaboration in the Opinion of Advocate-General E. Sharpston, points 34–36). As emphasized in recent case-law, while on the one hand, a court responsible for maintaining a register or dealing with an application for the service of judicial or extra-judicial documents under Union law makes an administrative decision without being required to resolve a legal dispute and hence cannot be regarded as exercising a judicial function, a court hearing an appeal which has been brought against that administrative decision, rejecting such an application, and which seeks the setting aside of that decision which allegedly affects the rights of the applicant is called upon to give judgment in a dispute and is considered to exercise a judicial function: ECJ, Case C-210/06 *Cartesio* [2008] E.C.R. I-9641, paras 57–62; ECJ, Case C-14/08 *Roda Golf & Beach Resort* [2009] E.C.R. I-5439, paras 35–42; ECJ (order of 12 January 2010), Case C-497/08 *Amiraike Berlin* [2010] E.C.R. I-101, paras 17–22. Furthermore, while the cooperation on the taking of evidence between courts of the Member States in the context of Regulation No. 1206/2001 ([2001] O.J. L174/1) does not necessarily lead to a judicial decision, the examining of a witness is an act clearly undertaken in the context of judicial proceedings 'intended to lead to a decision of a judicial nature', and therefore under those circumstances, a national court submitting questions to the ECJ concerning the functioning of Regulation No. 1206/2001 is acting in its judicial capacity: ECJ, Case C-283/09 *Weryński* [2011] E.C.R. I-601, paras 43–46. Conversely, an Insolvency Judge determining, on application by the creditors, which debts are to be included in the liabilities, acts in a judicial capacity where its decisions can be challenged by the administrator and other interested parties and where, in the absence of a challenge, its refusal to include a debt in the liabilities has binding legal effects: ECJ (judgment of 19 April 2012), Case C-443/09 *Grillo Star Fallimento*, not reported, para. 23.

[44] Note that some national competiton authorities may have a dual nature, exercising both administrative and judicial functions. See Opinion of Advocate-General P. Mengozzi in ECJ, Case C-439/08 *VEBIC* [2010] E.C.R. I-12471, point 82.

[45] Opinion of Advocate-General F.G. Jacobs in ECJ, Case C-67/91 *Asociación Española de Banca Privada and Others* [1992] E.C.R. I-4785, at I-4809.

In *Syfait and Others*, a case concerning a reference for a preliminary ruling made by the Greek competition authority—the *Epitropi Antagonismou*—the Court of Justice adopted a more restrictive approach.[46] According to the Court, insofar as there is an operational link between the *Epitropi Antagonismou* (a decision-making body), and its secretariat (a fact-finding body) on the basis of whose proposal it adopts decisions, the *Epitropi Antagonismou* is not a clearly distinct third party in relation to the State body which, by virtue of its role, may be akin to a party in the course of competition proceedings.[47] Moreover, the Court stressed the fact that a competition authority such as the *Epitropi Antagonismou* may, pursuant to Art. 11(6) of Council Regulation No. 1/2003,[48] be relieved of its competence by a decision of the Commission initiating its own proceedings. After having recalled its case-law according to which a body may refer a question to the Court only if that body is called upon to give judgment in proceedings intended to lead to a decision of a judicial nature,[49] the Court of Justice concluded that the *Epitropi Antagonismou* is not a court or tribunal within the meaning of Art. 234 EC (now Art. 267 TFEU) since whenever the Commission relieves a national competition authority such as the *Epitropi Antagonismou* of its competence, the proceedings initiated before that authority will not lead to a decision of a judicial nature.[50] The question was thus declared inadmissible[51] on grounds that make the admissibility of future references of national competition authorities very doubtful.

(5) Arbitrators

3.12 An arbitrator who does not fulfil all the *Vaassen* criteria cannot be regarded as a 'court or tribunal of a Member State' within the meaning of Art. 267 TFEU despite the fact that 'there are certain similarities between the activities of the arbitration tribunal in question and those of an ordinary court or tribunal in as much as the arbitration is provided for within the framework of the law, the arbitrator must decide according to law and his award has, as between the parties, the force of res judicata, and may be enforceable if leave to issue execution is obtained'.[52] Those characteristics were not sufficient to give the arbitrator the status of a 'court or tribunal of a Member State' because the parties to the contract were 'free to leave their disputes to be resolved by the ordinary courts or to opt for arbitration by inserting a clause to that effect in the contract'.[53] Consequently, the arbitrator did not act as the 'proper judicial body' designated by law, with the result that at least that *Vaassen* criterion was not fulfilled. The parties were indeed under 'no obligation, whether in law or in fact, to refer their disputes to arbitration'.[54] Moreover, the Member State in which the arbitrator operated was not involved in the decision to opt for arbitration and was not called

---

[46] ECJ, Case C-53/03 *Syfait and Others* [2005] E.C.R. I-4609.

[47] ECJ, Case C-53/03 *Syfait, and Others* para. 33.

[48] Council Regulation (EC) No. 1/2003 of 16 December 2002 on the implementation of the rules laid down in Arts 81 and 82 of the Treaty, [2003] O.J. L1/1.

[49] ECJ, Case C-134/97 *Victoria Film* [1998] E.C.R. I-7023, para.14; ECJ, Case C-195/98 *Österreichischer Gewerkschaftsbund* [2000] E.C.R. I-10497, para. 25; ECJ, Case C-53/03 *Syfait and Others* [2005] E.C.R. I-4609, para. 35.

[50] ECJ, Case C-53/03 *Syfait and Others* [2005] E.C.R. I-4609, paras 35–37.

[51] Yet, eventually the preliminary questions at issue in *Syfait* did come before the Court: ECJ, Case C-468/06 *Sot. Lélos kai Sia* [2008] E.C.R. I-7139.

[52] ECJ, Case 102/81 *Nordsee* [1982] E.C.R. 1095, para. 10.

[53] ECJ, Case 102/81 *Nordsee*, para. 11.

[54] ECJ, Case 102/81 *Nordsee*, para. 11; ECJ, Case C-125/04 *Denuit and Cordenier* [2005] E.C.R. I-923, para. 13.

upon to intervene of its own motion in the proceedings before the arbitrator.[55] If questions of Union law arise in an arbitration resorted to by agreement, the Court counts on the 'ordinary courts' examining the issues and, where necessary, requesting a preliminary ruling. The ordinary courts will have an opportunity to do so 'in the context of their collaboration' with arbitration tribunals, 'in particular in order to assist them in certain procedural matters or to interpret the law applicable', or when they are called upon to conduct a 'review of an arbitration award' in the case of 'an appeal or objection, in proceedings for leave to issue execution or by any other method of recourse available under the relevant national legislation'.[56]

In this context, it makes no difference that, in reviewing the arbitration award, the ordinary court has, pursuant to the arbitration agreement concluded between the parties, to rule *ex aequo et bono*: 'It follows from the principles of the primacy of [Union] law and of its uniform application, in conjunction with [Art. 4(3) TEU], that a court of a Member State to which an appeal against an arbitration award is made pursuant to national law must, even where it gives judgment having regard to fairness, observe the rules of [Union] law ...'.[57]

The Court of Justice likewise recognizes that the review of arbitration awards is limited in scope and that annulment of or refusal to recognize an award is possible only in exceptional circumstances. However, the limited nature of that review may not preclude reviewing the award in the light of fundamental provisions of Union law, such as Art. 101 TFEU (ex Art. 81 EC), which prohibits agreements and concerted practices in restraint of competition.[58]

By declining jurisdiction to answer questions referred for a preliminary ruling by arbitrators, the Court sought to prevent contracting parties from creating 'courts and tribunals' of their own and subsequently inducing (or obliging) them to seek preliminary rulings. Indeed, Art. 267 TFEU is intended to bring about a dialogue between courts in the Member States and the Court of Justice. National courts having the monopoly right to seek preliminary rulings submit to the Court for preliminary rulings only questions that are genuinely necessary in order to deliver a judgment with the authority of *res judicata*. In the Court's view, this mechanism would be endangered if parties to a contract could circumvent it by setting up an arbitration board whose organization is in no way based on action on the part of the public authorities and which is not regarded as the obligatory legal authority for dealing with a particular class of disputes.

---

[55] This consideration was perhaps intended to distinguish the *Broekmeulen* situation (ECJ, Case C-125/04 *Denuit and Cordenier*, para. 12); cf. n. 30, and accompanying text. See also ECJ, Case 102/81 *Nordsee* [1982] E.C.R. 1095, para. 11; ECJ, Case C-125/04 *Denuit and Cordenier* [2005] E.C.R. I-923, para. 13.

[56] ECJ, Case 102/81 *Nordsee* [1982] E.C.R. 1095, para. 14. Where a point of Union law is raised before an arbitrator and leave to appeal is sought against the award, an English Judge will normally grant leave to appeal where the point is 'capable of serious argument': *Bulk Oil (Zug) AG v Sun International Ltd and Sun Oil Trading Co.* [1984] 1 W.L.R. 147, at 154–5F, per Ackner LJ. Generally, English Judges can get involved either during arbitration proceedings to determine a point of law (Section 44 of the UK 1997 Arbitration Act) or after arbitration proceedings when a party challenges the award on the basis of the substantive jurisdiction of the arbitration tribunal (Section 67), on the basis of serious irregularity (Section 68) or by appeal on a point of law (Section 69). When deciding those issues, English courts are always at liberty to refer questions to the Court.

[57] ECJ, Case C-393/92 *Almelo* [1994] E.C.R. I-1477, para. 23.

[58] ECJ, Case C-126/97 *Eco Swiss China Time* [1999] E.C.R. I-3055, paras 33–40. This requirement is, however, subject to the proviso that it is not excessively difficult or impossible in practice for the national court to review the arbitration award in the light of the relevant provision of Union law. See further paras 4.39–4.41.

However, this does not mean that arbitral tribunals never satisfy the *Vaassen* criteria. Where there is a 'sufficiently close connection' between the arbitration and the general system of legal protection in the Member State concerned, the 'arbitrator' is deemed to be 'a court or tribunal of a Member State' within the meaning of Art. 267 TFEU (as in the case of the 'arbitration tribunal' in the *Vaassen* case itself).[59]

(6) Courts of a Member State

3.13   The court or tribunal must be 'of a Member State'.[60] Although this is generally obvious, it should be noted that the following courts qualify as such: courts and tribunals established in the Member States;[61] in several French overseas departments and territories (*départments d'outre-mer et térritoires d'outre-mer*), as well as the Azores, Madeira, and the Canary Islands;[62] in the 'overseas countries and territories' listed in Annex II to the Treaties to which the special association arrangements set out in Part Four of the TFEU apply;[63] the 'European territories for whose external relations a Member State is responsible'[64] and the Åland Islands[65] to which the Treaty applies; and finally 'the Channel Islands and the Isle of Man'[66] insofar as courts and tribunals established there refer to the Court questions concerning the interpretation of 'Protocol No. 3',[67] the interpretation and validity of the Union legislation to which that Protocol refers, and the interpretation and validity of measures adopted by the Union institutions on the basis of Protocol No. 3.

---

[59] ECJ, Case 109/88 *Danfoss* [1989] E.C.R. 3199, paras 7–9 (holding that the *Faglige Voldgiftsret*, the Danish Industrial Arbitration Board responsible for disputes concerning collective agreements, satisfied the *Vaassen* criteria, since its jurisdiction and composition was required by national law and did not depend on the parties' agreement, among other things).

[60] ECJ, Case C-196/09 *Miles and Others* [2011] E.C.R. I-5105, paras 37–43: the *Chambre de recours des écoles européennes* (the Complaints Board of the European Schools) was held not to constitute a court or tribunal of a Member State.

[61] Art. 52 TEU. In England and Wales, references may be made, e.g. by magistrates' courts, the Crown Court, the High Court, the Court of Appeal, the UK Supreme Court, and specialist courts such as the Patent Court. The Social Security Commissioner, income tax commissioners, industrial tribunals, the Employment Appeal Tribunal, and the VAT Tribunal have also made successful requests for preliminary rulings. See D. Anderson and M. Demetriou, *References to the European Court* (2nd edn, London, Sweet & Maxwell, 2002), para. 2.23.

[62] Art. 355(1) TFEU; as regards the French overseas departments, Guadeloupe, French Guiana, Martinique, Réunion, Saint-Barthélemy, and Saint-Martin are listed.

[63] Art. 355(2) TFEU; for some examples, see, e.g. ECJ, Joined Cases C-100/89 and C-101/89 *Kaefer and Procacci* [1990] E.C.R. I-4647 and ECJ, Case C-260/90 *Leplat* [1992] E.C.R. I-643, in which the *Tribunal Administratif* and the *Tribunal de Paix*, respectively, of Papeete in French Polynesia, were held to be courts or tribunals 'of a Member State'.

[64] Art. 355(3) TFEU; in practice, only Gibraltar.

[65] Art. 355(4) TFEU. The Treaty applies in accordance with the provisions set out in Protocol 2 to the Act concerning the conditions of accession of the Republic of Austria, the Republic of Finland, and the Kingdom of Sweden.

[66] Art. 355(5)(c) TFEU.

[67] Protocol No. 3 on the Channel Islands and the Isle of Man (O.J., English Special Edition of 27 March 1972, 164) annexed to the Act concerning the Conditions of Accession of the Kingdom of Denmark, Ireland and the United Kingdom of Great Britain and Northern Ireland to the European Economic Community and to the European Atomic Energy Community and the Adjustments to the Treaties (O.J., English Special Edition of 27 March 1972, 14). See ECJ, Case C-355/89 *Barr and Montrose Holdings* [1991] E.C.R. I-3479, paras 6–10; ECJ, Case C-171/96 *Pereira Roque* [1998] E.C.R. I-4607 and the Opinion of Advocate-General A. La Pergola in that case at I-4610.

(7) International courts

International courts, such as the International Court of Justice or the European Court of **3.14**
Human Rights, are not entitled to refer questions to the Court of Justice for a preliminary
ruling, even though this may be desirable in some instances. The position is different in the
case of the Benelux Court of Justice. That court has the task of ensuring that the legal rules
common to the three Benelux States are applied uniformly. The procedure before it is a
step in the proceedings before the national courts leading to definitive interpretations of
common Benelux legal rules. For those reasons, the Benelux Court of Justice is entitled—
and, as a court against whose decisions there is no judicial remedy under national law, may
be under a duty (see para. 3.47)—to refer a question to the Court of Justice for a
preliminary ruling where it is faced with the task of interpreting Union rules in the
performance of its function.[68] The same holds true for the newly created Unified Patent
Court. The initial Draft Agreement creating a Unified Patent Litigation System was
considered to be incompatible with the Treaties by the Court of Justice.[69] The Court
took issue with the fact that exclusive jurisdiction in patent litigation was transferred from
the Member States' courts to a newly designed court structure that was not common to the
legal systems of the Member States since, apart from the Member States of the European
Union, a number of third countries were also party to the Draft Agreement.[70] This was
problematic as the uniform and effective application of Union law through the preliminary
rulings mechanism could no longer be guaranteed for the matters of Union law falling in
the scope of application of the Draft Agreement. The Court of Justice based its argument
on the absence of means to enforce compliance with the obligations flowing from Art. 267
TFEU.[71] Contrary to a court that is common to the Member States, it would not be
possible to take recourse to Member State liability or infringement proceedings when the
Patent Court, a court standing outside of the legal systems of the Member States, would
breach Union law.[72] In the aftermath of Opinion 1/09, the Member States adapted the
Draft Agreement and created a court system common to the legal systems of the Member
States. In doing so, the Member States almost literally copied the relevant paragraphs of the

---

[68] ECJ, Case C-337/95 *Parfums Christian Dior* [1997] E.C.R. I-6013, paras 19–23. It would be hard to
argue that proceedings brought against a Member State in the European Court of Human Rights constitute 'a
step in the proceedings' before a national court. Proceedings before the European Court of Human Rights do
not fall within any national proceedings and hence the reasoning employed by the Court of Justice in the
Christian Dior case in order to hold that the Benelux Court of Justice constitutes a court or tribunal within the
meaning of Art. 267 TFEU cannot be used so as to allow the European Court of Human Rights to make a
reference for a preliminary ruling to the Court of Justice. The situation of the Benelux Court of Justice also
differs from the situation of the envisaged European and EU Patents Court (EPC), of which the ECJ ruled in
Opinion 1/09 that it was incompatible with the Treaties. The ECJ found that national courts were stripped of
their power to refer questions to the ECJ under Art. 267 TFEU in cases concerning patent litigation.
Furthermore, the Court considered that the full effectiveness of Union law was in danger, since the EPC
was situated outside the judicial system of the Union and its decisions in breach of Union law could not be
subject to proceedings for the infringement of Union law by the Member States: see ECJ, Opinion 1/09 *Draft
Agreement on the European and Community Patents Court* [2011] E.C.R. I-1137, paras 74–89. See also para.
2.02. See further A. Rosas, 'The National Judge as an EU Judge: Opinion 1/09', in P. Cardonnel, A. Rosas,
and N. Wahl (eds), *Constitutionalising The EU Judicial System. Essays in Honour of Pernilla Lindh* (Oxford and
Portland Oregon, Hart Publishing, 2012), 105–21.
[69] ECJ, Opinion 1/09 *Draft Agreement on the European and Community Patents Court* [2011] E.C.R.
I-1137.
[70] ECJ, Opinion 1/09 *Draft Agreement on the European and Community Patents Court*, paras 69 and 82.
[71] ECJ, Opinion 1/09 *Draft Agreement on the European and Community Patents Court*, paras 86–87.
[72] ECJ, Opinion 1/09 *Draft Agreement on the European and Community Patents Court*, para. 88.

Parfums Christian Dior judgment concerning the Benelux Court. Art. 1 of the Draft Agreement states that: 'The Unified Patent Court shall be a court common to the Contracting Member States and subject to the same obligations under Union law as any national court of the Contracting Member States.'[73] Third states that were parties to the initial Draft Agreement were left out of the amended Draft Agreement.

The judgment in *Parfums Christian Dior* and Opinion 1/09 should be contrasted with the judgment in *Miles*.[74] In *Miles*, the Court held that the Complaints Board of the European Schools was not competent to refer questions for a preliminary ruling. The judgment emphasizes that being a court common to a number of Member States alone is not sufficient to qualify as a national court within the meaning of Art. 267 TFEU. The common court should also have the necessary links to the judicial systems of the Member States concerned, meaning that it is responsible for the uniform application of legal rules common to those Member States.[75] This was not the case for the Complaints Board of the European Schools. While it was set up by the Member States of the European Union, it was not entrusted with the task of applying uniformly legal rules common to the Member States. Rather, it applied the rules governing the system of European Schools, which is a *sui generis* system of international cooperation different from the judicial systems of the Member States.[76] The fact that the system of European Schools has functional ties with the EU and applies Union law cannot alter that conclusion.[77]

(8) Third countries' courts

3.15 Of course, courts and tribunals established in non-Member States do not come under Art. 267 TFEU. In the event that it is nevertheless intended to confer on such courts and tribunals to a certain extent the right to refer questions for a preliminary ruling, that right must be enshrined in an international agreement concluded between the Union and the third countries concerned. An example is the EEA Agreement, which authorizes courts and tribunals of EFTA States to refer questions to the Court of Justice on the interpretation of an EEA rule.[78]

B. Types of proceedings in which a preliminary ruling may be requested

(1) Dispute must be pending before national court

3.16 The Court has no jurisdiction to entertain a request for a preliminary ruling when at the time when it is made the procedure before the court making it has already been terminated.[79] Art. 267 TFEU in fact restricts the right to make a reference to a court or tribunal

---

[73] Agreement of 19 February 2013 on a Unified Patent Court ([2013] O.J. C175/1), Art. 1.
[74] ECJ, Case C-196/09 *Miles and Others* [2011] E.C.R. I-5105.
[75] ECJ, Case C-196/09 *Miles and Others*, para. 41.
[76] ECJ, Case C-196/09 *Miles and Others*, para. 39.
[77] ECJ, Case C-196/09 *Miles and Others*, para. 42.
[78] EEA Agreement, Art. 107 ([1994] O.J. L1/26) and Protocol 34 annexed to the EEA Agreement on the possibility for courts and tribunals of EFTA States to request the Court of Justice of the European Communities to decide on the interpretation of EEA rules corresponding to EC rules ([1994] O.J. L1/204). See also K. Lenaerts and P. Van Nuffel (R. Bray and N. Cambien (eds)), *European Union Law* (3rd edn, London, Sweet & Maxwell, 2011), para. 25.30.
[79] ECJ, Case 338/85 *Pardini* [1988] E.C.R. 2041, para. 11, second sent.; ECJ, Case C-159/90 *Society for the Protection of Unborn Children Ireland* [1991] E.C.R. I-4685, para. 12; ECJ, Case C-148/10 *DHL International* [2011] E.C.R. I-9543, paras 29–31.

which considers that the preliminary ruling requested is necessary to enable it to give judgment.[80] A national court is empowered to bring a matter before the Court by way of reference for a preliminary ruling only if a dispute is pending before it in the context of which it is called upon to give a decision capable of taking into account the preliminary ruling.[81] The preliminary ruling must actually be intended to make a contribution to the decision that the referring court is to take.

The Court of Justice remains seized of a request for a preliminary ruling for as long as it is not withdrawn by the court or tribunal which made that request.[82]

Since this is a question of securing the very essence of the preliminary ruling procedure, the Court does not shirk from going back to seek further information about the course of the procedure before the referring court with a view to ascertaining whether the proceedings are still pending before that court.[83] In *Pardini*, the Court held—contrary to its first impressions—that, in view of the explanations which it had obtained, it had to be assumed that 'the interlocutory proceedings which gave rise to the reference to the Court must be regarded as still pending before the Pretore [Magistrate], who may take account of the preliminary ruling for the purposes of his own decision confirming, varying or discharging his original order'.[84]

(2) Types of proceedings

All sorts of proceedings may give rise to a preliminary ruling: matters of civil law, criminal **3.17** law,[85] commercial and economic law, social law, revenue law, constitutional[86] and administrative law, and so on. Neither the substantive law at issue nor the type of proceedings has any bearing. Questions may be referred by an examining magistrate[87] and in interlocutory proceedings.[88] Even *ex parte* proceedings, at which the other party is not represented, may

---

[80] ECJ, Case 338/85 *Pardini*, para. 10.

[81] ECJ, Case 338/85 *Pardini*, para. 11, first sent. Accordingly, hypothetical questions are inadmissible: see, e.g. ECJ, Case C-315/02 *Lenz* [2004] E.C.R. I-7063, paras 52–54. See further para. 3.35.

[82] ECJ Rules of Procedure, Art. 100(1). It is further provided in that para. that the withdrawal of a request may be taken into account until notice of the date of delivery of the judgment has been served on the interested persons referred to in Art. 23 of the Statute. Art. 100(2) adds, however, that the Court may at any time declare that the conditions of its jurisdiction are no longer fulfilled.

[83] For example, ECJ (order of 14 October 2010), Case C-336/08 *Reinke* [2010] E.C.R. I-130*, Summ. pub., para. 15.

[84] ECJ, Case 338/85 *Pardini*, para. 14.

[85] A request for a preliminary ruling arising in the context of an inquiry in criminal proceedings which could result in an order that no further action be taken, a summons to appear, or an acquittal is admissible (ECJ, Case 14/86 *Pretore di Salò v X* [1987] E.C.R. 2545, paras 10–11; ECJ, Case C-60/02 *X* [2004] E.C.R. I-651, para. 25).

[86] For instance, as regards the Belgian Constitutional Court, see, e.g. ECJ, Case C-212/06 *Gouvernement de la Communauté française and Gouvernement wallon* [2008] E.C.R. I-1683; as regards the Austrian Constitutional Court, see, e.g. ECJ, Joined Cases C-456/00, C-138/01, and C-139/01 *Österreichischer Rundfunk and Others* [2003] E.C.R. I-4989; as regards the Lithuanian Constitutional Court, see ECJ, Case C-239/07 *Sabatauskas and Others* [2008] E.C.R. I-2573; as regards the Italian Constitutional Court, see ECJ, Case C-169/08 *Presidente del Consiglio dei Ministri* [2009] E.C.R. I-10821; and as regards the Spanish Constitutional Court, see ECJ (judgment of 26 February 2013), Case C-399/11 *Melloni*, not reported. As regards the role played by constitutional courts in connection with the mechanism for ordinary courts to refer to them questions on the compatibility of national law with the national constitution and the preliminary ruling procedure initiated by these latter courts, see para. 3.20.

[87] ECJ, Case 65/79 *Chatain* [1980] E.C.R. 1345, para. 1.

[88] ECJ, Case 29/69 *Stauder* [1969] E.C.R. 419, at 424; ECJ, Case 107/76 *Hoffmann-La Roche* [1977] E.C.R. 957, para. 4; ECJ, Case C-176/96 *Lehtonen and Castors Braine* [2000] E.C.R. I-2681; ECJ,

result in a reference for a preliminary ruling if the body making the reference is exercising the functions of a court or tribunal.[89] Furthermore, it does not matter if the body making the reference performs other functions in addition to its functions as a court or tribunal. Accordingly, the Court held that 'the Pretori [Italian magistrates] are judges who, in proceedings such as those in which the questions referred... were raised, combine the functions of a public prosecutor and an examining magistrate'. Yet, it declared that it had jurisdiction to reply to the questions referred since the request emanated from 'a court or tribunal which has acted in the general framework of its task of judging, independently and in accordance with the law, cases coming within the jurisdiction conferred on it by law, even though certain functions of that court or tribunal in the proceedings which gave rise to the reference for a preliminary ruling are not, strictly speaking, of a judicial nature'.[90]

However, if in given proceedings the national court simply acts as an administrative authority and performs a non-judicial function, the Court of Justice considers that it has no jurisdiction to rule on questions referred for a preliminary ruling in the proceedings in question.[91]

(3) Issues concerning jurisdiction

3.18 Questions of jurisdiction that are apt to arise before national courts in connection with the classification of legal situations based on Union law cannot be determined by the Court of Justice. This is because it is for the legal system of each Member State to determine which court has jurisdiction to hear disputes involving individual rights derived from Union law.[92] In such circumstances, a national court may make a reference for a preliminary ruling to the Court of Justice with a view to obtaining an explanation of points of Union law which may help to solve the problem of jurisdiction.[93]

Case C-60/02 *X* [2004] E.C.R. I-651, para. 26 (a preliminary question raised in proceedings concerning interim measures is admissible notwithstanding the fact that the measures may be confirmed, varied or revoked).

[89] For examples, see the Italian summary proceedings for a court order in ECJ, Case 70/77 *Simmenthal* [1978] E.C.R. 1453, paras 4–11; ECJ, Case C-18/93 *Corsica Ferries* [1994] E.C.R. I-1783, para. 12 (with further citations in the Opinion of Advocate-General V. Trstenjak in ECJ, Case C-265/07 *Caffaro* [2008] E.C.R. I-7085, point 25), and the proceedings for the protective sequestration of assets in ECJ, Case 23/75 *Rey Soda* [1975] E.C.R. 1279.

[90] ECJ, Case 14/86 *Pretore di Salò v X* [1987] E.C.R. 2545, para. 7; ECJ (order of 15 January 2004), Case C-235/02 *Saetti* [2004] E.C.R. I-1005, para. 23 (a Judge investigating a criminal matter or an investigating magistrate may make a reference for a preliminary ruling).

[91] ECJ, Case C-111/94 *Job Centre* [1995] E.C.R. I-3361, paras 8–11; cf. the Opinion of Advocate-General M.B. Elmer; ECJ, Case C-447/00 *Holto* [2002] E.C.R. I-735, points 17–22; ECJ (order of 12 January 2010), Case C-497/08 *Amiraike Berlin* [2010] E.C.R. I-101. In contrast, a preliminary question raised by a national court in proceedings brought for judicial review of a decision made in such non-contentious proceedings will be admissible (ECJ, Case C-111/94 *Job Centre*, para.11; ECJ, Case C-55/96 *Job Centre* [1997] E.C.R. I-7119); see also ECJ, Case 32/74 *Haaga* [1974] E.C.R. 1201, para. 2; ECJ, Case C-210/06 *Cartesio* [2008] E.C.R. I-9641, paras 57–59. See further para. 3.10.

[92] It is not for the Court to determine whether the decision whereby a matter is brought before it was taken in conformity with the rules of domestic law governing the organisation of the courts and their procedure. As long as the questions referred to it are relevant and necessary to resolve the case before the national court, the Court of Justice will accept jurisdiction. See ECJ (judgment of 24 May 2012), Case C-97/11 *Amia*, not reported, paras 20–22.

[93] ECJ, Case 179/84 *Bozzetti v Invernizzi* [1985] E.C.R. 2301, para. 17; ECJ, Case C-446/93 *SEIM* [1996] E.C.R. I-73, paras 32–33; ECJ, Joined Cases C-10/97 to C-22/97 *IN.CO.GE. '90 and Others* [1998] E.C.R. I-6307, paras 14–17; ECJ, Case C-268/06 *Impact* [2008] E.C.R. I-2483, paras 47–48.

C. Timing and content of a request for a preliminary ruling

(1) Initiative with the national court

From the text of Art. 267 TFEU it follows that only the national court is entitled to apply to **3.19** the Court of Justice for a preliminary ruling.[94] Parties to the main proceedings, including the public prosecutor, cannot compel the national court to make a reference.[95] The national court has the right to refer questions of its own motion,[96] a right which Union law confers on every 'court or tribunal of a Member State' within the meaning of Art. 267 TFEU. National (procedural) law cannot detract from this.[97] Accordingly, the Court has held that 'the existence of a rule of domestic law whereby a court is bound on points of law by the rulings of the court superior to it cannot of itself take away the power provided for by [Art. 267 TFEU] of referring cases to the Court',[98] especially 'if it considers that the ruling on law made by the superior court could lead it to give a judgment contrary to [Union] law'.[99]

(2) Interplay between the national court's right to refer under Art. 267 TFEU and national procedural mechanisms according priority to references on the compatibility of national law with the national constitution

A particularly important issue relating to the national court's initiative to refer is that **3.20** concerning the interplay between its right to refer questions on the interpretation and/or validity of Union law, on the one hand, and national procedural mechanisms requiring references to the national constitutional court or other bodies for deciding questions relating to the compatibility of national law with the national constitution, on the other.[100]

In the landmark 1978 case of *Simmenthal*,[101] the Court of Justice was confronted with issues relating to the conflict between national law and Union law in a situation in which the national court was first required to refer the question of the incompatibility of the

---

[94] ECJ, Joined Cases 31/62 and 33/62 *Wöhrmann and Others v Commission* [1962] E.C.R. 501. See *Portsmouth City Council v Richards and Quietlynn* [1989] 1 C.M.L.R. 673, at 708, where Kerr LJ stated that '... references by consent should not creep into our practice. All references must be by the court. The court itself must be satisfied of the need for a reference...'.

[95] ECJ, Case 93/78 *Mattheus* [1978] E.C.R. 2203, paras 4–6.

[96] ECJ, Case 166/73 *Rheinmühlen-Düsseldorf* ('*Rheinmühlen I*') [1974] E.C.R. 33, para. 3; ECJ, Case 126/80 *Salonia* [1981] E.C.R. 1563, para. 7; ECJ, Case 283/81 *CILFIT* [1982] E.C.R. 3415, para. 9; ECJ, Case C-261/95 *Palmisani* [1997] E.C.R. I-4025, para. 20; ECJ (judgment of 8 March 2012), Case C-251/11 *Huet*, not reported, paras 22–26. For England and Wales, see Civil Procedure Rules, R.68.2(1): an order for reference may be made by the court of its own initiative at any stage of the proceedings.

[97] ECJ (judgment of 18 July 2013), Case C-136/12 *Consiglio nazionale dei geologi*, not reported, para. 32.

[98] ECJ, Case 166/73 '*Rheinmühlen I*', para. 5; ECJ, Case C-173/09 *Elchinov* [2010] E.C.R. I-8889, paras 25–32.

[99] ECJ Case 166/73 '*Rheinmühlen I*', para. 4. See also ECJ, Joined Cases C-379/08 and C-380/08 *ERG and Others* [2010] E.C.R. I-2007, para. 26; ECJ (judgment of 15 January 2013), Case C-416/10 *Križan and Others*, not reported, para. 68.

[100] P. Van Nuffel, 'Samenloop van prejudiciële procedures en de rechtspraak van het Hof van Justitie van de Europese Gemeenschappen', in D. Arts, I. Verougstraete, R. Andersen *et al.* (eds), *De verhouding tussen het Arbitragehof, de rechterlijke macht en de Raad van State—verslagboek van het symposium van 21 oktober 2005* (Bruges, Die Keure, 2006), 343–52.

[101] ECJ, Case 106/77 *Simmenthal* [1978] E.C.R. 629. See also S. Rodin, 'Back to Square One—the Past, the Present and the Future of the Simmenthal Mandate', in J. M. Beneyto and I. Pernice (eds), *Europe's Constitutional Challenges in the Light of the Recent Case-law of National Constitutional Courts* (Baden Baden, Nomos, 2011), 297–325.

national law concerned with the Italian constitution to the Italian Constitutional Court.[102] In response, the Court of Justice held that part and parcel of the primacy of Union law, the effectiveness of the preliminary ruling procedure would be impaired if the national court was prevented from applying Union law in accordance with the case-law of the Court of Justice, and therefore, a national court which is called upon, within the limits of its jurisdiction, to apply provisions of Union law, is under a duty to give full effect to those provisions, it not being necessary for that court to request or to await the prior setting aside of such provision by legislative or other constitutional means.[103] In 1991, *Mecanarte*[104] presented the Court of Justice with a similar scenario involving Portuguese procedural law, whereby it ruled that a national court which in a case concerning Union law takes the view that a provision of national law is unconstitutional does not lose the right or escape the obligation under Art. 267 TFEU to refer to the Court of Justice questions concerning the interpretation or validity of Union law by reason of the fact that such a declaration of unconstitutionality is subject to a mandatory reference to the constitutional court.[105] Subsequent cases reiterated such points in brief fashion.[106] Then, in the 2010 *Kücükdeveci* case,[107] situated within the context of German proceedings, the Court firmly underlined that '[t]he possibility thus given to the national court by the second paragraph of Art. 267 TFEU of asking the Court for a preliminary ruling before disapplying the national provision that is contrary to European Union law cannot, however, be transformed into an obligation because national law does not allow that court to disapply a provision it considers to be contrary to the constitution unless the provision has first been declared unconstitutional by the Constitutional Court'.[108] In other words, '[t]he optional nature of such a reference is not affected by the conditions of national law under which a court may disapply a national provision which it considers to be contrary to the constitution.'[109]

Matters came to a head in *Melki and Abdeli*,[110] involving a reference for a preliminary ruling from the French Court of Cassation (*Cour de Cassation*) as to whether a provision of French constitutional law, requiring national courts to rule, as a matter of priority, on the submission to the French Constitutional Council (*Conseil constitutionnel*) of questions of constitutionality put before them, was compatible with Art. 267 TFEU.

While it could be questioned whether the priority mechanism did effectively prevent the French Court of Cassation from making a reference for a preliminary ruling in the main proceedings, the Court of Justice considered that 'it is for the referring court to determine, in the cases before it, what the correct interpretation of national law is'.[111] After reiterating

---

102 ECJ, Case 106/77 *Simmenthal*, paras 6–7.

103 ECJ, Case 106/77 *Simmenthal*, paras 19–24.

104 ECJ, Case C-348/89 *Mecanarte—Metalúrgica da Lagoa ('Mecanarte')* [1991] E.C.R. I-3277, paras 38–40.

105 ECJ, Case C-348/89 *Mecanarte*, para. 46.

106 See, e.g. ECJ, Case C-314/08 *Filipiak* [2009] E.C.R. I-11049, para. 81 and further citations therein (relating to Polish constitutional law). See also ECJ, Case C-348/89 *Mecanarte*, para. 4; ECJ, Joined Cases C-379/08 and C-380/08 *ERG and Others* [2010] E.C.R. I-2007, para. 26.

107 ECJ, Case C-555/07 *Kücükdeveci* [2010] E.C.R. I-365, paras 52–56 (T. Roes, case note (2010) Col. Jour. Eur. L. 497–519).

108 ECJ, Case C-555/07 *Kücükdeveci*, para. 54.

109 ECJ, Case C-555/07 *Kücükdeveci*, para. 55.

110 ECJ, Joined Cases C-188/10 and C-189/10 *Melki and Abdeli* [2010] E.C.R. I-5667.

111 ECJ, Joined Cases C-188/10 and C-189/10 *Melki and Abdeli*, para. 49.

its traditional case-law on national procedural rules limiting the possibility of national courts to make use of Art. 267 TFEU, the Court of Justice provided a balanced answer, taking into account the particularities of the French constitutional system. On the one hand, as a general rule, national courts cannot be prevented from referring questions to the Court, and therefore, if an interlocutory procedure giving priority to the review of constitutionality of national law effectively prevents these courts from referring questions to the Court, such a procedure would be precluded by Art. 267 TFEU. On the other hand, such a procedure is not precluded by Art. 267 TFEU if three conditions are fulfilled. First, national courts should remain free to submit a reference for a preliminary ruling to the Court of Justice, at whatever stage of the proceedings they consider appropriate, even at the end of the interlocutory procedure for the review of constitutionality, on any question which they consider necessary. Second, national courts should remain free to adopt any measure necessary to ensure provisional judicial protection of the rights conferred under Union law. Third, national courts must have the possibility to disapply, at the end of such an interlocutory procedure, the national legislative provision at issue if they consider it to be contrary to Union law.[112]

Consequently, on the basis of *Melki and Abdeli*, national courts may be required to await the outcome of an interlocutory procedure assessing the constitutionality of the national provisions at issue, provided that the three abovementioned conditions are met. That being said, *Melki and Abdeli* does not restrict the freedom of national courts to refer questions to the Court whenever they consider it necessary, even when national provisions oblige them to do otherwise.[113]

Moreover, in its ruling in *Melki and Abdeli*, the Court of Justice added that questions concerning the validity of a Union directive take priority over questions concerning the constitutionality of national implementing measures transposing the mandatory provisions of the directive when both are challenged on the same grounds. In such a situation, the national constitutional court, being a court against whose decisions there is no judicial remedy, is obliged to refer the matter first to the Court in accordance with the third para. of Art. 267 TFEU.[114] The obligation to refer ceases to exist when the ordinary court itself has referred a question concerning the validity of the directive to the Court before or simultaneously with initiating the interlocutory procedure. Nevertheless, in both situations, the national constitutional court is under an obligation to await the outcome of the proceedings before the Court of Justice before ruling on the question of constitutionality.[115]

(3) Binding rulings of higher courts

The freedom of national courts to refer questions to the Court of Justice has an impact on   **3.21**
the hierarchical structure of the court systems in the Member States. Since any court should be free to make use of Art. 267 TFEU, a lower court cannot be bound on points of Union

---

[112] ECJ, Joined Cases C-188/10 and C-189/10 *Melki and Abdeli*, paras 52–53, 57.

[113] ECJ (judgment of 18 July 2013), Case C-136/12 *Consiglio nazionale dei geologi*, not reported, paras 32–33. See also M. Wathelet, 'Adieu, Monsieur le Professeur: de la liberté des juges nationaux de poser des questions préjudicielles à la Cour de justice de l'Union européenne' (2010) Revue de la Faculté de droit de l'Université de Liège 449–55.

[114] For an example, see ECJ, Case C-236/09 *Association belge des Consommateurs Test-Achats and Others* [2011] E.C.R. I-773 (G. De Baere and E. Goessens, case note (2012) Col. Jour. Eur. L. 339–67).

[115] ECJ, Joined Cases C-188/10 and C-189/10 *Melki and Abdeli*, paras 54–56.

law by a ruling of a higher court.[116] Accordingly, lower courts remain free to question the higher court's assessment of the point of Union law at issue, and if necessary to submit a reference for a preliminary ruling to the Court.

This line of case-law of the Court of Justice has been challenged by a number of authors in view of the hierarchy of the national legal systems and the powers of the highest national courts. In particular, a number of arguments have been advanced to limit the possibility of lower national courts to refer questions to the Court of Justice. For example, it has been asserted that while uniformity is important, not all questions of Union law need be answered by the Court of Justice. The often trivial matters that are brought before the Court through references by lower national courts could first be solved within the national legal system, and if difficulties still remain, the higher national courts can then submit a reference to the Court. Moreover, it has been contended that limiting the number of references coming from lower courts would significantly lighten the workload of the Court; alternatively, a 'European certiorari' or other mechanism of case selection could shorten the length of proceedings and provide the Court with more time to decide the cases before it and allow it to substantiate its judgments with elaborate reasoning.[117]

Arguably, while the reference for a preliminary ruling procedure has its imperfections, the amendments proposed in the literature are often the result of a misunderstanding of the functioning of the procedure and the internal functioning of the Court in particular. The possibility for a lower court to review the application of Union law by a higher court is an exceptional means to guarantee the uniform and effective application of Union law by the highest courts. If Union law is applied correctly by the higher courts, there will be no valid reason for lower courts to put that application into doubt. It has also been pointed out that some authors question the preliminary reference procedure and its implications for the national legal system merely to safeguard the position of the highest courts rather than with the aim of contributing to a more workable system of judicial protection in the European Union.[118] As such, criticism motivated by such reasons has not been considered constructive from the perspective of the system of cooperation between the European Union and the national legal orders which lies at the heart of the preliminary ruling procedure (see para. 3.05).[119] Furthermore, it should be pointed out that a number of seminal cases have been decided upon references

---

[116] ECJ, Case C-173/09 *Elchinov* [2010] E.C.R. I-8889, paras 24–32; ECJ, Case C-396/09 *Interedil* [2011] E.C.R. I-9915, paras 34–40; ECJ (judgment of 15 January 2013), Case C-416/10 *Križan and Others*, not reported, para. 68.

[117] See, e.g. J. Komarek, 'In the Court(s) We Trust? On the Need for Hierarchy and Differentiation in the Preliminary Ruling Procedure' (2007) E.L. Rev. 467–91.

[118] P. Van Nuffel, 'Technieken van doorwerking van EU-recht in het Belgische privaatrecht', in I. Samoy, V. Sagaert, and E. Terryn (eds), *Invloed van het Europese recht op het Belgische privaatrecht* (Antwerp, Antwerpen Intersentia, 2012), 10–11.

[119] M. Bossuyt and W. Verrijdt, 'The Full Effect of EU Law and of Constitutional Review in Belgium and France after the Melki Judgment' (2011) Eur. Const. L. Rev. 389, argue, inspired by Advocate-General P. Cruz Villalon, against the possibility for lower courts to review the application of Union law by higher courts and suggest that other measures such as an action for State liability or an action for infringement can effectively guarantee that higher courts act in conformity with Union law. For a critical reflection on this proposal, see M. Wathelet, 'Adieu, Monsieur le Professeur: de la liberté des juges nationaux de poser des questions préjudicielles à la Cour de justice de l'Union européenne' (2010) Revue de la Faculté de droit de l'Université de Liège 449–55.

by lower national courts. It would thus be wrong to state that their references are not important enough and that the power to refer should be limited to higher courts.[120]

(4) Content determined by the national court

It is for the national court to determine the content of the questions referred for a **3.22** preliminary ruling.[121] Certainly, the parties to the main proceedings are at liberty to make proposals, but it is the Judge alone who determines whether he or she accepts them wholly or in part or completely deviates from them.[122] In other words, the procedure is completely independent of any initiative of the parties.[123] The Court does not allow parties to the main proceedings to seek to extend the request for a preliminary ruling to cover questions that they suggested to the national court, but it did not wish to ask.[124] It is immaterial in this connection that the Commission or one or more Member States support parties in their attempt to alter the subject-matter of the preliminary ruling procedure. The Court will not go against the referring court's (express or implicit) refusal to refer a particular question because that court 'alone is competent under the system established by [Art. 267 TFEU] to assess the relevance of questions concerning the interpretation of [Union] law in order to resolve the dispute before it'.[125]

(5) Court of Justice may reformulate questions

This does not mean that the Court will refrain from giving a more precise definition of the **3.23** subject-matter of the reference for a preliminary ruling or even from altering it where this appears necessary in order to obtain a helpful answer, namely an answer which the national court can use.[126] But the adjustment of the questions referred must always be consonant

---

[120] See C. Barnard and E. Sharpston, 'The Changing Face of Article 177 References' (1997) C.M.L. Rev. 1163–4.

[121] The questions referred for a preliminary ruling are considered within the factual and legal context as set out by the referring court: see ECJ Rules of Procedure, Art. 94. The Court of Justice does not take account of observations from interested parties within the meaning of Art. 23 of the Statute which take issue with that context (ECJ, Case C-153/02 *Neri* [2003] E.C.R. I-13555, paras 33–36; see also ECJ, Case C-145/03 *Keller* [2005] E.C.R. I-2529, paras 32–34; ECJ, Case C-267/03 *Lindberg* [2005] E.C.R. I-3247, paras 40–42. But see ECJ, Case C-88/99 *Roquette Frères* [2000] E.C.R. I-10465, paras 18–19 and n. 126. The 'presumption of relevance' attached to the national court's order for reference (see further para. 3.34) is therefore not rebutted by the simple fact that one of the parties in the national proceedings contests certain facts, the accuracy of which is not a matter for the Court to determine and on which the delimitation of the subject-matter of those proceedings depends: ECJ, Joined Cases C-94/04 and C-202/04 *Cipolla and Others* [2006] E.C.R. I-11421, para. 26; ECJ, Joined Cases C-222/05 to C-225/05 *van der Weerd and Others* [2007] E.C.R. I-11421, para. 23; Case C-379/05 *AMURTA* [2007] E.C.R. I-9569, para. 65.

[122] ECJ (judgment of 18 July 2013), Case C-136/12 *Consiglio nazionale dei geologi*, not reported, paras 29–31.

[123] ECJ, Case C-2/06 *Kempter* [2008] E.C.R. I-411, para. 41 (and further citations therein); ECJ, Joined Cases C-42/10, C-45/10 and C-57/10 *Vlaamse Dierenartsvereniging and Janssens* [2011] E.C.R. I-2975, paras 41–45; ECJ, Case C-104/10 *Kelly* [2011] E.C.R. I-6813, paras 60–66.

[124] ECJ, Case 247/86 *Alsatel* [1988] E.C.R. 5987, para. 8; Case C-261/95 *Palmisani* [1997] E.C.R. I-4025, para. 31; ECJ, Case C-402/98 *ATB and Others* [2000] E.C.R. I-5501, para. 29; ECJ, Case C-236/02 *Slob* [2004] E.C.R. I-1861, paras 29–30; ECJ, Case C-373/08 *Hoesch Metals and Alloys* [2010] E.C.R. I-951, paras 57–60. The Court has made clear that this includes the grounds put forward to challenge the validity of a Union measure: see, e.g. ECJ, Case C-305/05 *Ordre des barreaux francophones et germanophone and Others* [2007] E.C.R. I-5305, paras 17–19; ECJ, Case C-390/06 *Nuova Agricast* [2008] E.C.R. I-2577, paras 42–44.

[125] ECJ, Case 247/86 *Alsatel*, para. 8.

[126] In the *Marks & Spencer* case, the Court stated that its task is to provide the referring court with an answer which will be of use to it and enable it to determine the case before it and that 'to that end, the Court may have to reformulate the question referred to it' (ECJ, Case C-62/00 *Marks & Spencer* [2002] E.C.R. I-6325, para. 32). See also ECJ, Case C-88/99 *Roquette Frères* [2000] E.C.R. I-10465, paras 18–19, where the

with the actual objective of the referring court, which precludes any change running contrary to that court's intention. In a case in which the national court had not formulated any question, but had simply referred the parties to the Court, the Court itself defined the question of interpretation of Union law, which had in fact arisen on the basis of the order for reference and the case-file directed to the Court through the Registry.[127]

A common situation requiring reformulation of the referring court's question by the Court of Justice concerns the situation in which the national court asks the Court to rule on the compatibility of national law with relevant provisions of Union law. In this regard, the Court has repeatedly held that in the context of the preliminary ruling procedure, it has no jurisdiction to rule either on the interpretation of provisions of national law or on their conformity with Union law.[128] However, while it has no jurisdiction to apply rules of

---

Court of Justice reformulated the question referred to it because it appeared from the observations submitted to the Court that the interpretation given by the referring judge to the rule of national law at issue in the proceedings did not accord with the case-law of the highest court in the Member State concerned; see also ECJ, Case C-87/97 *Consorzio per la Tutela del Formaggio Gorgonzola* [1999] E.C.R. I-1301, para. 16; ECJ (order of 18 March 2004), Case C-45/03 *Dem' Yanenko*, not reported, para. 37; ECJ, Case C-387/01 *Weigel* [2004] E.C.R. I-4981, para. 44, in which the Court of Justice held that the national court can be provided with all those elements for the interpretation of Union law, which may be of assistance in adjudicating on the case pending before it, whether or not that court has specifically referred to them in its questions. The Court of Justice can therefore take account of provisions of Union law not mentioned by the national court in formulating its questions. See also ECJ, Case C-271/01 *COPPI* [2004] E.C.R. I-1029, para. 27; ECJ, Case C-456/02 *Trojani* [2004] E.C.R. I-7573, paras 38–40; ECJ, Case C-452/03 *RAL and Others* [2005] E.C.R. I-3947, para. 25; ECJ, Case C-45/06 *Campina* [2007] E.C.R. I-2089, paras 30–31; ECJ, Case C-420/06 *Jager* [2008] E.C.R. I-1315, paras 45–46; ECJ, Case C-229/08 *Wolf* [2010] E.C.R. I-1, paras 31–46 (and further citations therein); ECJ (judgment of 21 December 2011), Case C-242/10 *Enel Produzione*, not reported, para. 37; ECJ, Case C-530/09 *Inter-mark Group* [2011] E.C.R. I-10675, para. 17; ECJ, Case C-503/09 *Stewart* [2011] E.C.R. I-6497, para. 105; ECJ, Joined Cases C-307/09 to C-309/09 *Vicoplus and Others*, [2011] E.C.R. I-453, para. 22.

[127] ECJ, Case 101/63 *Wagner* [1964] E.C.R. 195, at 199–200. In this way, the Court has declared that 'it is for the Court alone, where questions are formulated imprecisely, to extract from all the information provided by the national court and from the documents in the main proceedings the points of [Union] law which require interpretation, having regard to the subject-matter of those proceedings' (ECJ, Case C-107/98 *Teckal* [1999] E.C.R. I-8121, para. 34). See to the same effect ECJ, Case C-425/98 *Marca Mode* [2000] E.C. R. I-4861, para. 21; ECJ, Joined Cases C-223/99 and C-260/99 *Agorà and Excelsior* [2001] E.C.R. I-3605, para. 24). In particular, where a preliminary question merely refers to 'Union law' without stating which provisions are at issue, the Court finds it necessary to extract from all the factors provided by the referring court, particularly from the statement of grounds contained in the order for reference, the provisions requiring interpretation: ECJ, C-350/07 *Kattner Stahlbau* [2009] E.C.R. I-1513, paras 26–27 (and citations therein). Furthermore, it is possible that the Court of Justice will examine of its own motion a question of interpretation (not raised by the national court) 'in the context of the close cooperation which it is required to establish with national courts' (ECJ, Case C-295/97 *Piaggio* [1999] E.C.R. I-3735, para. 25). The Court may sometimes also make supplementary 'observations' with regard to questions of Union law not raised by the national court in its preliminary question to which parties have drawn attention in their observations (see, e.g. ECJ, Case C-131/97 *Carbonari and Others* [1999] E.C.R. I-1103, paras 52 *et seq.*); but see ECJ (order of 21 December 1995), Case C-307/95 *Max Mara* [1995] E.C.R. I-5083, paras 5–10, in which the Court found that the order for reference did not contain specific questions addressed to the Court and that it did not allow the questions on which the national court wished the Court to give a preliminary ruling to be discerned. The national court's order for reference also did not contain enough information to permit the Court to give a useful interpretation. Accordingly, the Court held that the national court's request was manifestly inadmissible.

[128] See, e.g. ECJ (order of 6 July 2006), Joined Cases C-18/05 and C-155/05 *Casa di cura privata Salus* [2006] E.C.R. I-6199, para. 22 (and further citations therein); ECJ, Joined Cases C-159/10 and C-160/10 *Fuchs and Köhler* [2011] E.C.R. I-6919, para. 30; ECJ (judgment of 10 November 2011), Joined Cases C-319/10 and C-320/10 *X and X*, not reported, para. 29; ECJ (judgment of 1 December 2011), Case C-442/10 *Churchill Insurance Company and Evans*, not reported, para. 22; ECJ (judgment of 16 February 2012), Case

Union law to a specific case,[129] 'there is nothing to stop the Court from reformulating the question with a view to providing the referring court with an interpretation of those provisions of Union law that would help it resolve the dispute before it'.[130]

Furthermore, the Court has not drawn the demarcation line strictly between the interpretation of Union law and the assessment of the validity of acts of the institutions.[131] Questions that ostensibly relate to the interpretation of Union law, but, having regard to the whole content of the order for reference, rather probe the validity of a Union measure, are also answered as such.[132] Accordingly, the Court has gone so far as to expand a question of interpretation to cover the validity of a Commission decision that was not mentioned in the national court's order for reference and of which the national court was probably unaware. The Court nevertheless held that the requirement for a 'useful' answer warranted its raising and answering the question of the validity of the decision in question. The Court also invoked reasons of procedural economy insofar as the question of the validity of the Commission decision in question had already been raised in an action for annulment brought by the Netherlands in relation to which proceedings had been suspended pending the Court's judgment in the preliminary ruling proceedings.[133]

The opposite situation may also arise, that is to say, the Court may consider whether the question of validity is based on a correct interpretation of the Union act at issue. It may then find—after interpreting the act in question—that it is no longer necessary to inquire into its validity inasmuch as the argument that superior Union law has been breached is founded upon a different interpretation of the relevant Union act. If it so finds, the Court will also not go into the consequences that would have ensued from a finding that the act was invalid.[134]

However, in the event that the questions referred for a preliminary ruling are concerned with the validity of an act of individual application against which no action for annulment

---

C-25/11 *Varzim Sol—Turismo, Jogo e Animação*, not reported, para. 27; ECJ (judgment of 28 June 2012), Case C-172/11 *Erny*, not reported, para. 30.

[129] ECJ, Case C-54/07 *Feryn* [2008] E.C.R. I-5187, para. 19; ECJ (judgment of 22 March 2012), Case C-153/11 *Klub*, not reported, para. 54.

[130] ECJ, Case C-350/07 *Kattner Stahlbau* [2009] E.C.R. I-1513, paras 24–25. For some examples, see ECJ, Joined Cases C-290/05 and C-333/05 *Nádasdi* [2006] E.C.R. I-10115, paras 19 and 43; ECJ, Case C-323/08 *Rodríguez Mayor and Others* [2009] E.C.R. I-11621, paras 29–32; ECJ Case C-384/08 *Attanasio Group* [2010] E.C.R. I-2055, paras 16–21; ECJ (order of 15 December 2010), Case C-492/09 *Agricola Esposito* [2010] E.C.R. I-167*, Summ. pub., para. 19; ECJ, Case C-239/09 *Seydaland Vereinigte Agrarbetriebe* [2010] E.C.R. I-13083, paras 26–27; ECJ (judgment of 1 March 2012), Case C-484/10 *Ascafor and Asidac*, not reported, para. 34; ECJ (order of 7 April 2011), Case C-151/10 *Dai Cugini* [2011] E.C.R. I-54*, Summ. pub., para. 25; ECJ, Case C-2/10 *Azienda Agro-Zootecnica Franchini and Eolica di Altamura* [2011] E.C.R. I-6561, para. 35; ECJ, Case C-126/10 *Foggia* [2011] E.C.R. I-10923, para. 29; ECJ (judgment of 16 February 2012), Case C-118/11 *Eon Aset Menidjmunt*, not reported, para. 66.

[131] For a critical appraisal, see the Opinion of Advocate-General D. Ruiz-Jarabo Colomer in ECJ, Case C-30/02 *Recheio* [2004] E.C.R. I-6053, points 23–36; ECJ (judgment of 16 February 2012), Case C-25/11 *Varzim Sol—Turismo, Jogo e Animação*, not reported, para. 28. Cf. Opinion of Advocate-General P. Mengozzi in Case C-449/06 *Gysen* [2008] E.C.R. I-553, particularly points 40–45.

[132] ECJ, Case 16/65 *Schwarze* [1965] E.C.R. 877, at 886–7.

[133] ECJ, Case C-61/98 *De Haan Beheer* [1999] E.C.R. I-5003. See also ECJ, Case C-383/98 *Polo/Lauren* [2000] E.C.R. I-2519, para. 23, in which the Court held that the question of interpretation also called the validity of the act of the institution in question and therefore ruled on its validity as well as on the question of interpretation.

[134] ECJ, Case C-334/95 *Krüger* [1997] E.C.R. I-4517, paras 21 and 35.

has been brought within the time limits prescribed in the sixth paragraph of Art. 263, TFEU, the Court of Justice will refuse to alter the substance of the questions referred insofar as the validity of the contested act can no longer be called in question (see para. 10.11). In those circumstances, to alter the substance of the questions referred would be incompatible with the Court's function under Art. 267 TFEU and with its duty to ensure that the governments of the Member States and parties concerned are given the opportunity to submit observations under Art. 23 of the Statute, bearing in mind that only the order for reference is notified to interested parties.[135] In the light of the order for reference, they may therefore confine their observations to the validity of the contested act by arguing solely that the questions raised no longer require an answer. To amend the scope of the order for reference would infringe the right conferred on them by Art. 23 of the Statute.

The Court does not hesitate to supplement the provisions of Union law of which the national courts seek an interpretation by provisions that it regards as relevant in the context of the main proceedings.[136] The Court even does so when a national court has not given any indication of the provisions of Union law of which it seeks an interpretation.[137] This is because it is the Court's duty to interpret all provisions of Union law which national courts need in order to decide the actions pending before them.[138] By the same token, the Court may limit[139] or even replace[140] the provisions indicated by the national court in its preliminary question by those provisions of Union law which are actually relevant. In one case before the expiry of the ECSC Treaty, the Court even referred to the relevant provisions of the ECSC Treaty when it found that such Treaty was applicable in the main

---

[135] ECJ, Case C-178/95 *Wiljo* [1997] E.C.R. I-585, para. 30, and the Opinion of Advocate-General F.G. Jacobs to the same effect; ECJ, Case C-239/99 *Nachi Europe* [2001] E.C.R. I-1197, paras 28–40; ECJ, Case C-241/01 *National Farmers' Union* [2002] E.C.R. I-9079, para. 34.

[136] ECJ, Case 12/82 *Trinon* [1982] E.C.R. 4089, para. 5; ECJ, Case C-241/89 *SARPP* [1990] E.C.R. I-4695, para. 8; ECJ, Case C-315/92 *Clinique Laboratoires and Estée Lauder Cosmetics* [1994] E.C.R. I-317, para. 7; ECJ, Case C-87/97 *Consorzio per la Tutela del Formaggio Gorgonzola* [1999] E.C.R. I-1301, para. 16; ECJ, Case C-190/00 *Balguerie and Others* [2001] E.C.R. I-3437, para. 22; ECJ, Case C-515/08 *dos Santos Palhota* [2010] E.C.R. I-9133, para. 22; ECJ (judgment of 15 March 2012), Case C-135/10 *Società Consortile Fonografici*, not reported, para. 62; ECJ (judgment of 19 April 2012), Case C-461/10 *Bonnier Audio and Others*, not reported, para. 47. But see ECJ, Case C-124/97 *Läuarä and Others* [1999] E.C.R. I-6067, para. 23: in its preliminary questions the national court referred not only to specific Treaty provisions but also to 'any other article of the EC Treaty' without providing any further details in that regard, either in the reasoning or in the operative part of its order. The Court was unable to rule on the question whether any provisions of that Treaty other than those specifically named precluded national legislation of the type at issue in the main proceedings.

[137] ECJ, Case C-537/09 *Bartlett and Others* [2011] E.C.R. I-3417, paras 35–36.

[138] ECJ, Case C-280/91 *Viessmann* [1993] E.C.R. I-971, para. 17; ECJ, Case C-42/96 *Società Immobiliare SIF* [1997] E.C.R. I-7089, para. 28; ECJ, Joined Cases C-228/01 and C-289/01 *Bourrasse and Perchicot* [2002] E.C.R. I-10213, para. 33 (and the case-law cited therein), in which the Court stated that, in order to provide a satisfactory answer to the national court, which has referred a question to it, it may deem it necessary to consider provisions of Union law to which the national court has not referred in its question. See also ECJ, Case C-304/00 *Strawson and Gagg & Sons* [2002] E.C.R. I-10737, para. 58; ECJ, Case C-456/02 *Trojani* [2004] E.C.R. I-7573, paras 38–40.

[139] ECJ, Case C-372/09 *Peñarroja Fa* [2011] E.C.R. I-1785, paras 23–25; ECJ, Case C-151/10 *Dai Cugini* [2011] E.C.R. I-54*, Summ. pub., para. 27.

[140] ECJ, Case 294/82 *Einberger* [1984] E.C.R. 1177, para. 6; ECJ, Case C-187/91 *Société Coopérative Belovo* [1992] E.C.R. I-4937, para. 13; ECJ, Case C-229/08 *Wolf* [2010] E.C.R. I-1, paras 31–32; ECJ, Case C-30/10 *Andersson* [2011] E.C.R. I-513, paras 20–21; ECJ, Case C-25/10 *Missionswerk Werner Heukelbach* [2011] E.C.R. I-497, paras 13–20; ECJ, Case C-115/10 *Bábolna Mezőgazdasági Termelő, Fejlesztő és Kereskedelmi* [2011] E.C.R. I-5017, para. 31; ECJ (judgment of 8 December 2011), Case C-157/10 *Banco Bilbao Vizcaya Argentaria*, not reported, paras 19–20.

proceedings and not the EC Treaty to which the national court referred in its preliminary question.[141] This can be explained in terms of the Court's concern for efficient collaboration with the national courts, whilst leaving the initiative to seek a preliminary ruling with the national courts.

(6) Timing

The decision at which stage a reference should be made for a preliminary ruling pursuant to **3.24** Art. 267 TFEU is dictated by considerations of procedural economy and efficiency to be weighed by the national court alone and not the Court of Justice.[142] The national court is 'in the best position to appreciate at which stage of the proceedings it requires a preliminary ruling from the Court of Justice'.[143] Nevertheless, the national court does not have unlimited latitude in this respect. It is only 'in the best position' to appreciate the stage at which a reference should be made. In principle, the Court of Justice goes along with its assessment, unless it is manifestly premature. This will be clear from the content of the order for reference. If the national court has not yet sufficiently ascertained the factual and legal context of the case and therefore does not say anything about it in the order for reference, it leaves the Court uncertain about the way in which the preliminary ruling sought is intended to help resolve the main action pending before the national court. In those circumstances, there is a great risk that the Court will not reach a 'helpful' determination. The upshot would be that the preliminary ruling would be ignored as a purely hypothetical 'opinion' and the collaboration between the national court and the Court of Justice would not achieve its aim.[144]

In order to avoid this the Court has gradually stepped up its requirements with regard to the content of the order for reference. As will become clear later, in order to satisfy those requirements the national court should make a request for a preliminary ruling to the Court only if it has determined the facts and non-Union law aspects of the case to such an extent that it can indicate precisely how the preliminary ruling sought is to be applied in the case before it. This inevitably restricts the national court's latitude to choose the stage at which the request for a preliminary ruling is made.

(7) Requirements for a reference

What requirements are imposed as regards the content of the order for reference? In the **3.25** 1979 judgment in *Union Laitière Normande*, the Court held in the first place that 'the need to afford a helpful interpretation of [Union] law makes it essential to define the legal

---

[141] ECJ, Case C-200/97 *Ecotrade* [1998] E.C.R. I-7907, paras 29–30. See also ECJ, Case C-115/08 *ČEZ* [2009] E.C.R. p. I-10265, paras 82–86, in which the Court examined relevant principles and provisions of the Euratom Treaty whilst the national court had referred in its order only to provisions of the EC Treaty.

[142] ECJ, Case 14/86 *Pretore di Salò v X* [1987] E.C.R. 2545, para. 11; see further ECJ, Case C-303/06 *Coleman* [2008] E.C.R. I-5603, paras 29–31 (and further citations therein) and D. Šváby, '*Festina lente*, ou le papillon et le crabe luxembourgeois', in M. T. D'Alessio, V. Kronenberger, and V. Placco (eds), *De Rome à Lisbonne: les juridictions de l'Union européenne à la croisée des chemins. Mélanges en l'honneur de Paolo Mengozzi* (Brussels, Bruylant, 2013), 245–61.

[143] ECJ, Case 14/86 *Pretore di Salò v X*, para.11; see also an earlier case: ECJ, Case 43/71 *Politi* [1971] E.C.R. 1039, para. 5, and also ECJ, Case C-176/96 *Lehtonen and Castors Braine* [2000] E.C.R. I-2681, paras 19–20. Accordingly, the choice of the most appropriate time to refer a question to the Court for a preliminary ruling lies within the exclusive jurisdiction of the national court (ECJ, Case C-60/02 *X* [2004] E.C.R. I-651, para. 28).

[144] See, e.g. ECJ, Case C-380/01 *Schneider* [2004] E.C.R. I-1389, paras 20–31.

context in which the interpretation requested should be placed'.[145] Although in that case the national court had not stated why it sought an interpretation of Union law, the reasons for the questions referred were sufficiently clear from the case-file submitted to the Court and it consequently appeared that a 'helpful interpretation of [Union] law' was possible and that the Court could give a ruling.

Two years later, in the 1981 *Irish Creamery Milk Suppliers Association* case, the Court enlarged upon that basic requirement: 'From that aspect it might be convenient, in certain circumstances, for the facts in the case to be established and for questions of purely national law to be settled at the time the reference is made to the Court of Justice so as to enable the latter to take cognisance of all the features of fact and of law which may be relevant to the interpretation of [Union] law which it is called upon to give.'[146] This sounded like encouragement to formulate the order for reference in concrete terms, yet without taking away the national court's discretion to determine at what stage in the main proceedings it needed a preliminary ruling from the Court of Justice.[147] Plainly this is a compromise: the national court was given good advice in quite strong terms, but, at the same time, failure to follow it did not make the request for a preliminary ruling inadmissible. Where the Court of Justice could fill the gaps in the order for reference by using information gleaned from the national court's case-file or adduced in the proceedings before the Court, it was still generally prepared to answer the questions referred on that basis. Nonetheless, the Court has intimated that it is not entirely happy about this on account of the risk that the quality of judicial debate will suffer if it is based on insufficiently informative orders for reference. Indeed, 'the information furnished in the decisions making the references does not serve only to enable the Court to give helpful answers but also to enable the Governments of the Member States and other interested parties to submit observations in accordance with Art. 20 [now Art. 23] of the Statute . . . It is the Court's duty to ensure that the opportunity to submit observations is safeguarded, in view of the fact that, by virtue of the above-mentioned provision, only the decisions making the references are notified to the interested parties.'[148]

Art. 94 of the ECJ Rules of Procedure now clearly indicates what is expected of national courts when submitting preliminary questions to the Court. This provision stipulates that, apart from the questions referred, an order for reference must contain: (a) a summary of the subject-matter of the dispute and the relevant findings of fact as determined by the referring court or tribunal, or at least an account of the facts on which the questions are based; (b) the tenor of any national provisions applicable in the case and, where appropriate, the relevant

---

[145] ECJ, Case 244/78 *Union Laitière Normande* [1979] E.C.R. 2663, para. 5.

[146] ECJ, Joined Cases 36/80 and 71/80 *Irish Creamery Milk Suppliers Association* [1981] E.C.R. 735, para. 6 (emphasis added).

[147] ECJ, Joined Cases 36/80 and 71/80 *Irish Creamery Milk Suppliers Association*, paras 7–9.

[148] ECJ, Joined Cases C-141/81 to C-143/81 *Holdijk* [1982] E.C.R. 1299, para. 6; ECJ (order of 20 March 1996), Case C-2/96 *Sunino and Data* [1996] E.C.R. I-1543, para. 5; ECJ (order of 25 June 1996), Case C-101/96 *Italia Testa* [1996] E.C.R. I-3081, para. 5; ECJ (order of 19 July 1996), Case C-191/96 *Modesti* [1996] E.C.R. I-3937, para. 5; ECJ (order of 19 July 1996), Case C-196/96 *Lahlou* [1996] E.C.R. I-3945, para. 5; ECJ, Case C-207/01 *Altair Chimica* [2003] E.C.R. I-8875, para. 25; ECJ, Case C-145/03 *Keller* [2005] E.C.R. I-2529, para 30; ECJ (judgment of 16 February 2012), Case C-25/11 *Varzim Sol—Turismo, Jogo e Animação*, not reported, paras 30–31. Cf. ECJ, Case C-178/95 *Wiljo* [1997] E.C.R. I-585, para. 30.

national case-law; and (c) a statement of the reasons which prompted the referring court or tribunal to inquire about the interpretation or validity of certain provisions of Union law, and the relationship between those provisions and the national legislation applicable to the main proceedings. These minimum requirements emanate from the Court's case-law and are further reflected in the Recommendations to national courts and tribunals in relation to the initiation of preliminary ruling proceedings (see para. 24.03). The main aim of this new provision appears to be to clarify the national courts' task and is not intended to serve as a benchmark for a stricter admissibility test. Nevertheless, the Court will not refrain from declaring an order for reference inadmissible when drawn up in complete disregard of the requirements laid down in Art. 94 of the ECJ Rules of Procedure.

(8) Inadmissibility of a reference

In the 1993 judgment in *Telemarsicabruzzo*, the Court converted the good advice to **3.26** national courts into a genuine requirement which, if not complied with, will cause the preliminary reference to be inadmissible. The Court held that the need to provide an interpretation of Union law that would be of use to the national court made it necessary that the national court define the factual and legislative context of the questions it was asking or, at the very least, explain the factual circumstances on which those questions were based.[149] In fact, to a limited extent the Court had previously refused to consider particular parts of preliminary references, where they were insufficiently precise, but this had never resulted in the whole of the request for a ruling being declared inadmissible.[150] The reason for this change was that the Court considered it unrealistic—particularly in the light of the complex factual and legal situations arising in competition law, which was the subject of the main proceedings—to expect it to fill the lacunae in the order for reference (which was virtually unreasoned) with sufficient certainty from the information in the file provided by the national court and the observations submitted to the Court by the parties to the main

---

[149] ECJ, Joined Cases C-320/90 to C-322/90 *Telemarsicabruzzo and Others* [1993] E.C.R. I-393, para. 5; ECJ, Case C-378/93 *La Pyramide* [1994] E.C.R. I-3999, para. 17; ECJ, Case C-217/05 *Confederacion Española de Empresarios de Estaciones de Servicio* [2006] E.C.R. I-11987, para. 26; ECJ, Joined Cases C-124/08 and C-125/08 *Snauwaert and Others and Deschaumes* [2009] E.C.R. I-6793, para. 15 (and citations therein). It is, however, enough if the order for reference 'contains the essential circumstances of the dispute in the main proceedings' (ECJ, Case C-181/97 *Van der Kooy* [1999] E.C.R. I-483, para. 29). Compare ECJ (order of 21 March 2002), Case C-447/01 *DLD Trading Company Import-Export*, not reported, paras 8–20, and ECJ (order of 21 March 2002), Case C-430/01 *Herbstrith*, not reported, paras 7–19, in which the Court declared the preliminary question inadmissible on the grounds that the national court had not given details of the legislative context of the main proceedings, had merely summarized arguments of the parties to the main proceedings which described the dispute in contradictory ways, and failed to specify the necessity for the preliminary ruling and its relevance. Moreover, the questions were formulated in general terms and did not refer to a specific provision of Union law on which an interpretation was requested. A subsequent new reference for a preliminary ruling from the national court was also declared inadmissible (ECJ (order of 1 April 2004), Case C-229/03 *Herbstrith*, not reported). See also ECJ (order of 21 April 1999), Joined Cases C-28/98 and C-29/98 *Charreire and Hirtsmann* [1999] E.C.R. I-1963, paras 12–14, in which the Court held that the order for reference contained contradictory information and that it was therefore impossible to form a clear picture of the legal situation. But see ECJ, Case C-116/02 *Gasser* [2003] E.C.R. I-14693, paras 21–27, in which the Court held that a preliminary question was admissible even though it was based on the submissions of a party to the main proceedings, the merits of which the national court had not yet assessed.

[150] ECJ, Case 52/76 *Benedetti* [1977] E.C.R. 163, paras 20–22; ECJ, Joined Cases 205/82 to 215/82 *Deutsche Milchkontor* [1983] E.C.R. 2633, para. 36; cf. ECJ, Case 222/78 *ICAP* [1979] E.C.R. 1163, paras 19–20; ECJ, Case 14/86 *Pretore di Salò v X* [1987] E.C.R. 2545, para. 16; ECJ (order of 23 March 2012), Case C-348/11 *Thomson Sales Europe*, not reported, paras 40–58.

proceedings, the Italian Government, and the Commission pursuant to what is now Art. 23 of the Statute.[151] The risk that the Court's judgment would be of no assistance to the national court was too great and hence cooperation with the referring court could not serve its purpose. The Court declined to give potentially ineffective rulings which would merely serve as an 'opinion' for a hypothetical case and not contribute towards the determination of the main proceedings. In subsequent cases, the Court has even gone so far as to decide that the preliminary reference was manifestly inadmissible for the same reasons (in orders given pursuant to Art. 53(2) of the ECJ Rules of Procedure).[152] The Court has recognized, however, that the requirement for the national court to define the factual and legislative context of the questions referred is less pressing where they relate to specific technical points and enable the Court to give a useful reply even where the national court has not given an exhaustive description of the legal and factual situation.[153]

The Court of Justice may also hold that a preliminary question is admissible in part. In *FDV*, for example, the Court accepted the admissibility of a preliminary question relating to the interpretation of Arts 34 and 36 TFEU, but observed that the national court had given no explanation of the reasons for which it raised the question of the interpretation of Arts 101 and 102 TFEU in connection with the matters of fact and law in the main proceedings. In the absence of such information the national court had failed to put the Court in a position to give an interpretation of those articles that could be of use to it. That question was therefore declared inadmissible.[154]

---

[151] ECJ, Joined Cases C-320/90 to C-322/90 *Telemarsicabruzzo and Others* [1993] E.C.R. I-393, paras 6–8. See also ECJ, Case C-134/03 *Viacom Outdoor* [2005] E.C.R. I-1167, paras 23–29; ECJ, Case C-384/08 *Attanasio Group* [2010] E.C.R. I-2055, paras 32–34 (and further citations therein). Cf. ECJ, Joined Cases C-180/98 to C-184/98 *Pavlov and Others* [2000] E.C.R. I-6451, paras 54–55, in which the Court found that the information provided in the order for reference was amplified by the case-file forwarded by the national court, by the written observations, and by the answers given to the questions asked by the Court, which were summarized in the Report for the Hearing and had been made available to the governments of the Member States and the other interested parties for the purposes of the hearing, at which they had an opportunity to amplify their observations. For those reasons, the Court rejected the argument that the preliminary question was inadmissible. See also ECJ, Case C-67/96 *Albany International* [1999] E.C.R. I-5751, para. 43; ECJ, Case C-56/99 *Gascogne Limousin Viandes* [2000] E.C.R. I-3079, para. 31; ECJ, Case C-176/96 *Lehtonen and Castors Braine* [2000] E.C.R. I-2681, para. 26; and ECJ, Case C-109/99 *ABBOI* [2000] E.C.R. I-7247, para. 43.

[152] ECJ (order of 8 July 1998), Case C-9/98 *Agostini* [1998] E.C.R. I-4261, para. 10; ECJ (order of 2 March 1999), Case C-422/98 *Colonia Versicherung and Others* [1999] E.C.R. I-1279, para. 10; ECJ, Case C-325/98 *Anssens* [1999] E.C.R. I-2969, para. 15; ECJ (order of 6 December 2000), Case C-252/00 *Vandeweerd*, not reported; ECJ, Case C-123/00 *Bellamy and English Shop Wholesale* [2001] E.C.R. I-2795, para. 52; ECJ (order of 8 October 2002), Case C-190/02 *Viacom* [2002] E.C.R. I-8287, paras 13–26; ECJ (order of 12 March 2004), Case C-54/03 *Austroplant Arzneimittel*, not reported, paras 10–22; ECJ (order of 22 February 2005), Case C-480/04 *D'Antonio*, not reported, paras 5–8; ECJ (order of 20 May 2009), Case C-454/08 *Seaport Investments*, not reported, paras 6–13; ECJ (order of 15 April 2011), Case C-613/10 *Danilo Debiasi*, not reported, paras 25–33; ECJ (order of 8 September 2011), Case C-144/11 *Abdallah*, not reported, paras 9–13; ECJ (order of 3 May 2012), Case C-185/12 *Ciampaglia*, not reported, paras 7–10; ECJ (order of 22 November 2012), Case C-318/12 *Devillers*, not reported, paras 4–9; ECJ (order of 14 March 2013), Case C-240/12 *EBS*, not reported, paras 10–23; ECJ (order of 18 April 2013), Case C-368/12 *Adiamix*, not reported, para. 35.

[153] ECJ, Case C-316/93 *Vaneetveld* [1994] E.C.R. I-763, para. 13; ECJ (order of 13 March 1996), Case C-326/95 *Banco de Fomento e Exterior* [1996] E.C.R. I-1385, para. 8.

[154] ECJ, Case C-61/97 *FDV* [1998] E.C.R. I-5171, paras 9–10; For similar situations, see, e.g. ECJ, Case C-399/98 *Ordine degli Architetti and Others* [2001] E.C.R. I-5409, paras 105–107. See also ECJ, Case C-258/98 *Carra and Others* [2000] E.C.R. I-4217, paras 19–20; ECJ, Case C-123/00 *Bellamy and English Shop Wholesale* [2001] E.C.R. I-2795, para. 52; ECJ, Case C-341/01 *Plato Plastik Robert Frank* [2004] E.C.R.

(9) Clear description of the factual and legal context

It follows from the abovementioned overview that it is essential[155] for the national court, in order to enable the Court to give a useful interpretation of Union law,[156] to provide a sufficiently clear description in its order for reference of the factual and legal context of the main proceedings.[157] In order to ascertain whether the information supplied in the order for reference satisfies such conditions, the nature and the scope of the questions raised are taken into consideration.[158] Where the Court does not have the necessary factual and legal information to enable it to give a useful answer to the question referred, it will declare

3.27

I-4883, paras 37–39; ECJ, Case C-72/03 *Carbonati Apuani* [2004] E.C.R. I-8027, paras 12–14; ECJ, Case C-380/05 *Centro Europa 7* [2008] E.C.R. I-349, paras 57–71; ECJ, Case C-567/07 *Woningstichting Sint Servatius* [2009] E.C.R. I-9021, paras 54–56; ECJ, Case C-384/08 *Attanasio Group* [2010] E.C.R. I-2055, paras 32–35. This likewise applies to additional questions that are apparent from the order for reference even though they may not have appeared, strictly speaking, in the operative part of the reference: see, e.g. ECJ, Case C-470/04 *N* [2006] E.C.R. I-7409, paras 68–72.

[155] This is also stressed in the Recommendations to national courts and tribunals in relation to the initiation of preliminary ruling proceedings, [2012] O.J. C338/1: see particularly point 22.

[156] ECJ, Case C-225/09 *Jakubowska* [2010] E.C.R. I-12329, para. 41.

[157] This must also afford the national governments and other interested parties the possibility to submit observations under Art. 23 of the Statute: ECJ, Case C-67/96 *Albany International* [1999] E.C.R. I-5751, para. 40; ECJ, Joined Cases C-480/00 to C-482/00, C-484/00, C-489/00 to C-491/00, and C-497/00 to C-499/00 *Azienda Agricola Ettore Ribaldi and Others* [2004] E.C.R. I-2943, para. 73. As stressed repeatedly in the case-law, it is the Court's duty to ensure that the opportunity to submit observations is safeguarded, bearing in mind that, by virtue of the abovementioned provision of the Statute, only the order for reference is notified to the Member States and other interested parties. See, e.g. ECJ, Joined Cases C-124/08 and C-125/08 *Snauwaerts and Others and Deschaumes* [2009] E.C.R. I-6793, para. 16 (and further citations therein). A preliminary question will be declared inadmissible if it merely refers as regards the factual context to a judgment of another court and to a decision of a national competition authority: ECJ (order of 11 February 2004), Joined Cases C-438/03, C-439/03, C-509/03, and C-2/04 *Cannito and Others* [2004] E.C.R. I-1605, paras 8–12. For the same reason, the Court will not accede to a request made by a party in its observations to reformulate the content of the questions referred: see, e.g. ECJ (judgment of 21 December 2011), Case C-316/10 *Danske Svineproducenter*, not reported, para. 33. Conversely, the fact that parties were in a position to state their views on the questions referred effectively in their observations submitted to the Court is an indication that the factual and legal context was sufficiently described in the order for reference: see, e.g. ECJ, Case C-450/09 *Schröder* [2011] E.C.R. I-2497, paras. 19–21; ECJ, Joined Cases C-128/09 to C-131/09, C-134/09 and C-135/09 *Boxus and Others* [2011] E.C.R. I-9711, para. 27; ECJ (judgment of 16 February 2012), Case C-25/11 *Varzim Sol— Turismo, Jogo e Animação*, not reported, paras 30–34.

[158] ECJ, Case C-134/03 *Viacom Outdoor* [2005] E.C.R. I-1167, para. 23. In that case, the Court distinguished the legislative context, for which the order for reference contained a sufficiently clear and full description of the relevant provisions of national law concerned, from the factual context, for which the order for reference was insufficient in that regard. ECJ, Case C-134/03 *Viacom Outdoor*, paras 24–25; ECJ, Case C-441/10 *Anghel* [2010] E.C.R. I-164*, Summ. pub., paras 8–12. While the Court can make use of the written and oral procedure in order to remedy deficiencies provided that the observations of interested parties are safeguarded under Art. 23 of the Statute, this may not suffice (see, e.g. ECJ, Case C-379/08 *ERG and Others* [2010] E.C.R. I-2007, paras 75–78; ECJ (order of 7 June 2012), Case C-21/11 *Volturno Trasporti Sas di Santoro Nino*, not reported, paras 14–16). Nevertheless, in circumstances where the order for reference lacks certain information relevant to the outcome of the case, the Court has deemed the order for reference admissible where it still allows the scope of the questions referred and the context in which they are asked to be determined. See, e.g. ECJ, Case C-217/05 *Confederacion Española de Empresarios de Estaciones de Servicio* [2006] E.C.R. I-11987, paras 29–31; ECJ, Case C-44/07 *Les Vergers du Vieux Tauves* [2008] E.C.R. I-10627, para. 19; ECJ, Case C-260/07 *Petro IV Servicios* [2009] E.C.R. I-2437, para. 30; ECJ, Joined Cases C-395/08 and C-396/08 *Bruno and Pettini* [2010] E.C.R. I-5119, para. 20; compare the Opinion of the Advocate-General in the latter case, which although coming to the same conclusion, expressed serious misgivings about the lack of adequate factual and legal material rendering the order for reference inadmissible on such grounds: see Opinion of Advocate-General E. Sharpston in ECJ, Joined Cases C-395/08 and C-396/08 *Bruno and Pettini* [2010] E.C.R. I-5119, points 42–68.

the question inadmissible.[159] This does not mean, however, that the referring court must make *all* the findings of fact and of law required by its judicial function before it may bring the matter before the Court. It is sufficient that both the subject-matter of the dispute in the main proceedings and the main issues raised for the Union legal order may be understood from the reference for a preliminary ruling.[160]

(10) National court's discretion

3.28 The *Telemarsicabruzzo* requirement as to the precision of the order for reference in terms of its content does not completely negate the national court's discretion in determining at what stage in the proceedings pending before it a reference should be made to the Court of Justice. It is sufficient for the national court to set out in the order for reference the factual and national legal premises or hypotheses underlying the questions referred, so as to enable the Court of Justice to arrive at a helpful answer. In contrast, the national court is not in principle required to have chosen between the premises or hypotheses at the time when it seeks the preliminary ruling. It may still be influenced by 'considerations of procedural organisation and efficiency'[161] and await the Court's answer to a preliminary question before making a definitive ruling on the factual and national legal aspects of the case.[162] The only condition is that the national court's order for reference should interpret the various premises or hypotheses and explain the reasons why it is seeking a preliminary ruling so as to make it clear in what way Union law is relevant in the case of each of those premises or hypotheses. It goes without saying that the national court must have fully apprized itself of the case in order to fulfil this condition. This is at the heart of the *Telemarsicabruzzo* requirement, which is designed to give rise to a genuine dialogue between courts.

In one situation, the order for reference has to contain more than an exposition of the various factual and national legal premises or hypotheses underlying the case, together with the reasons for seeking the preliminary ruling. This is where it appears that Union law is not relevant in every eventuality to the decision in the main proceedings. In such a case, it is the national court's task first to narrow down the legal debate to only those premises or hypotheses in which Union law is relevant in any event. In order to do so, it will perhaps have to make a full or partial determination of the facts and national legal aspects of the case before it makes a reference to the Court, which certainly restricts its discretion to determine at what stage the reference is made. The intention behind this restriction is to avoid a fruitless judgment from the Court in the event that the national court should subsequently

---

[159] ECJ, Case C-415/93 *Bosman* [1995] E.C.R. I-4921, paras 59–61; ECJ, Case C-36/99 *Idéal Tourisme* [2000] E.C.R. I-6049, para. 20; ECJ, Case C-137/00 *Milk Marque and National Farmers' Union* [2003] E.C.R. I-7975, para. 37; ECJ, Joined Cases C-480/00 to C-482/00, C-484/00, C-489/00 to C-491/00, C-497/00 to C-499/00 *Azienda Agricola Ettore Ribaldi and Others* [2004] E.C.R. I-2943, para. 72; ECJ, Case C-286/02 *Bellio Fratelli* [2004] E.C.R. I-3465, para. 28; ECJ, Joined Cases C-222/05 to C-225/05 *van der Weerd and Others* [2007] E.C.R. I-4233, para. 22 (and further citations therein); ECJ (order of 15 December 2010), Case C-492/09 *Agricola Esposito* [2010] E.C.R. I-167, paras 20–26; ECJ (order of 3 May 2012), Case C-185/12 *Ciampaglia*, not reported, paras 8–9.

[160] ECJ, Case C-450/09 *Schröder* [2011] E.C.R. I-2497, paras 19–21.

[161] ECJ, Joined Cases 36/80 and 71/80 *Irish Creamery Milk Suppliers Association* [1981] E.C.R. 735, para. 8.

[162] ECJ, Case C-439/08 *VEBIC* [2010] E.C.R. I-12471, paras 45–47 (P. Van Nuffel, case note (2012) T.B.P. 301–2); ECJ, Joined Cases C-188/10 and C-189/10 *Melki and Abdeli* [2010] E.C.R. I-5667, para. 41; ECJ (order of 16 November 2010), Case C-76/10 *Pohotovost'* [2010] E.C.R. I-11557, para. 33; ECJ, Case C-52/09 *TeliaSonera Sverige* [2011] E.C.R. I-527, para. 17.

find that Union law has no part to play at all, having regard to the facts or the relevant national law. The 1992 judgment in *Meilicke* illustrates this.[163] A German court had referred a long series of involved questions concerning the interpretation of the Second Company Law Directive in order to be able to rule on the compatibility with the directive of a principle of German company law enshrined in case-law. However, the parties to the main proceedings did not agree on whether that principle was applicable to the facts of the case. The national court had elected not to rule on that issue and first to submit the question of compatibility to the Court. Its rationale was that if it should become clear from the Court's interpretation of the Second Company Law Directive that the principle of German company law conflicted therewith, the question as to the applicability of that principle to the facts of the case would be of no account, given that the principle would in any event have to yield to Union law, which took precedence. The Court of Justice was unable to accept the sequence of the national court's decision-making on the grounds that if, conversely, it were to appear from the preliminary ruling that the principle of German company law was compatible with the Second Company Law Directive, the judgment of the Court of Justice would have no practical effect as a contribution to the resolution of the main proceedings, if at that stage the national court were to decide that under national law the principle laid down by case-law was not applicable to the facts of the case. The only way of eliminating the risk of a hypothetical ruling from the Court was to oblige the German court to determine the facts and to rule on the applicability of the principle of national law at issue before considering making a reference to the Court for a preliminary ruling.

It should be borne in mind that, in preliminary ruling proceedings, any assessment of the facts in the case is a matter for the national court.[164] The Court of Justice is empowered to rule on the interpretation or validity of Union law provisions only on the basis of the facts which the national court places before it.[165]

D. Annulment of a request for a preliminary ruling

(1) General

The Court considers that a request for a preliminary ruling made pursuant to Art. 267 **3.29** TFEU continues 'so long as the request of the national court has not been withdrawn by the

---

[163] ECJ, Case C-83/91 *Meilicke* [1992] E.C.R. I-4871. For some factual background on the *Meilicke* case, see S. Prechal, 'Oneigenlijk spel? Creatief gebruik van procesrecht voor het Hof van Justitie', in J.-H. Reestman, A. Schrauwen, M. van Montfrans, and J. H. Jans (eds), *De Regels & Het Spel—Opstellen over Recht, Filosofie, Literatuur en Geschiedenis aangeboden aan Tom Eijsbouts* (Den Haag, T.M.C. Asser Press, 2011), 318–19. See also ECJ, Case C-153/00 *der Weduwe* [2002] E.C.R. I-11319; ECJ, Case C-318/00 *Bacardi-Martini and Cellier des Dauphins* [2003] E.C.R. I-905.

[164] ECJ (judgment of 15 March 2012), Case C-135/10 *Società Consortile Fonografici*, not reported, para. 66.

[165] ECJ, Case C-30/93 *AC-ATEL Electronics* [1994] E.C.R. I-2305, paras 16–17; ECJ, Case C-352/95 *Phytheron International* [1997] E.C.R. I-1729, paras 11–14; ECJ, Case C-235/95 *AGS Assedic Pas-de-Calais* [1998] E.C.R. I-4531, para. 25; ECJ, Joined Cases C-175/98 and C-177/98 *Lirussi and Bizzaro* [1999] E.C.R. I-6881, paras 36–39; ECJ, Case C-9/02 *De Lasteyrie du Saillant* [2004] E.C.R. I-2409, para. 41; ECJ, Case C-267/03 *Lindberg* [2005] E.C.R. I-3247, paras 41–42.

[166] ECJ, Case 127/73 *BRT* [1974] E.C.R. 51, para. 9; ECJ, Case 106/77 *Simmenthal* [1978] E.C.R. 629, para. 10; for examples, see ECJ, Case 65/77 *Razanatsimba* [1977] E.C.R. 2229, paras 5–6; ECJ (order of 24 June 1997), Case C-184/95 *Lores Guillín*, not reported; ECJ, Case C-148/10 *DHL International* [2011] E.C.R. I-9543, para. 31. It should be mentioned that, according to Art. 100(1) of the ECJ Rules of Procedure,

court from which it emanates or has not been quashed on appeal from a superior court'.[166] Consequently, the Court refuses to go into objections to its jurisdiction raised in observations submitted pursuant to Art. 23 of the Statute claiming that the questions are no longer relevant, for example on the ground that the national legislative provisions whose compatibility with Union law the preliminary reference seeks to assess have in the meantime been declared unconstitutional,[167] or that the request for a preliminary ruling was the outcome of a decision which was not taken in accordance with the applicable national (procedural) law.[168] As explained by the Court, 'in view of the distribution of functions between itself and the national court, it is not for the Court to determine whether the decision whereby a matter is brought before it was taken in accordance with the rules of national law governing the organisation of the courts and their procedure. The Court is therefore bound by a decision of a court or tribunal of a Member State referring a matter to it, insofar as that decision has not been rescinded on the basis of a means of redress provided for by national law'.[169] However, the Court may find that the main proceedings are to no purpose and that for it to reply to the questions referred would therefore be of no avail to the national court. In those circumstances, it will hold that the reference is to no purpose and that there is no need to reply to the questions referred.[170]

---

the withdrawal of a request will, in principle, no longer be taken into account when notice of the date of delivery of the judgment has been served on the interested persons referred to in Art. 23 of the Statute. Art. 100(2) adds, however, that the Court may at any time declare that the conditions of its jurisdiction are no longer fulfilled.

[167] ECJ, Case 106/77 *Simmenthal*, paras 8–12. However, the Court can request a clarification from the national court (Art. 101 of the ECJ Rules of Procedure): see, e.g. ECJ, Joined Cases C-436/08 and C-437/08 *Haribo and Osterreichische Salinen*, not reported, para. 19.

[168] ECJ, Case 65/81 *Reina* [1982] E.C.R. 33, para. 7; cf. the Opinions of Advocate-General M. Lagrange in ECJ, Case 13/61 *Bosch and Others* [1962] E.C.R. 45, at 56, and of Advocate-General H. Mayras in ECJ, Case 127/73 *BRT* [1974] E.C.R. 51, at 68; ECJ, Joined Cases C-332/92 to C-333/92 and C-335/92 *Eurico Italia and Others* [1994] E.C.R. I-711, para. 13; ECJ, Case C-472/93 *Spano and Others* [1995] E.C.R. I-4321, para. 16; but see the Opinion of Advocate-General C. Gulmann in ECJ, Joined Cases C-320/09 to C-322/90 *Telemarsicabruzzo and Others* [1993] E.C.R. I-393, at I-410–415.

[169] ECJ, Case 65/81 *Reina*, para. 7; ECJ, Case C-39/94 *SFEI and Others* [1996] E.C.R. I-3547, para. 24; ECJ, Case C-371/97 *Gozza and Others* [2000] E.C.R. I-7881, para. 30; ECJ, Case C-309/02 *Radlberger Getränkegesellschaft and S. Spitz* [2004] E.C.R. I-11763, para. 26; ECJ, Case C-213/04 *Burtscher* [2005] E.C.R. I-10309, paras 30–32; ECJ, Case C-238/05 *Asnef-Equifax and Others* [2006] E.C.R. I-11125, para. 14. If, however, the Court of Justice finds that, after making a reference for a preliminary ruling, the national court considers that it cannot terminate the main proceedings even though the defendant has acceded to the plaintiff's claims, on the ground that Union law debars it from doing so, it considers itself entitled to inquire into the reasons given by the national court. If it appears that Union law does not preclude the national court from terminating the main proceedings under national law, the Court considers that it has no jurisdiction to answer the questions referred for a preliminary ruling as long as the national court has not found that in national law the acts of the parties have not terminated the main proceedings: ECJ, Joined Cases C-422/93 to C-424/93 *Zabala Erasun and Others* [1995] E. C.R. I-1567, paras 28–30; ECJ, Case C-343/96 *Dilexport* [1999] E.C.R. I-597, para.19.

[170] ECJ, Case C-314/96 *Djabali* [1998] E.C.R. I-1149, paras 17–23; ECJ, Case C-225/02 *Garciá Blanco*, [2005] E.C.R. I-523, paras 28–32. See also ECJ, Case C-241/09 *Fluxys* [2010] E.C.R. I-12773, paras 33–34. Where, after the national court has made a reference for a preliminary ruling, the Court of Justice gives a preliminary ruling in another case involving the same question of interpretation, the national court should consider whether it should maintain its reference. If that court subsequently makes it known that it withdraws its request, the case will be removed from the register of the Court (for an example, see ECJ (order of the President of 30 April 1999), Case C-26/97 *Giolfo and Others*, not reported). See, however, also Art. 99 of the ECJ Rules of Procedure, which allows the Court, at any time to rule by reasoned order, where a question referred to it is identical to a question on which the Court has already ruled, where the reply to such a question may be clearly deduced from existing case-law or where the answer to the question referred admits of no reasonable doubt.

(2) Appeal brought against the order for reference

In order for a request for a preliminary ruling to be admissible, it is not necessary that the **3.30** order for reference should have the force of *res judicata* under national law.[171] Union law does not in principle restrict the remedies available under national law against the order for reference.[172] However, in the 2008 case of *Cartesio*, the Court of Justice made clear that the jurisdiction of the national court to submit a preliminary reference cannot be called into question by the application of national rules that allow for the order for reference alone being subject to a limited appeal, where such rules permit the appellate court to vary the order for reference, to set aside the reference and to order the referring court to resume the domestic law proceedings.[173] At the national level, this is further illustrated by the judgment of 11 February 2010 of the Danish Supreme Court in Case no. 344/2009 *Danish Ministry of Taxation v Lady & Kid A/S and Others*.[174] In this case, the Danish Supreme Court held that an appeal brought against an order for reference of a lower court was inadmissible. The Court came to that conclusion in order to avoid an incompatibility with the Danish system of judicial hierarchy. Indeed, if an appeal were to be admissible, the lower court, as a result of the *Cartesio* judgment, would not be bound by the judgment of the higher court setting aside a decision to refer a question to the Court of Justice. Likewise, the Belgian Supreme Court declared inadmissible an appeal brought against an order for reference.[175]

The circumstances at issue in *Cartesio* should be compared with the order issued by the Court of Justice in *De Nationale Loterij*.[176] There, a preliminary reference was made by the *Rechtbank van koophandel te Hasselt* (a first instance court) in Belgium regarding the compatibility with Union law of the Belgian rules on gambling that it was required to apply in the proceedings before it. Subsequent to the reference to the Court of Justice, one of the parties brought an appeal against the order for reference before the *Hof van beroep te Antwerpen* (Court of Appeal, Antwerp), which reversed the order for reference and delivered judgment against the other party to the dispute on grounds of non-compliance with the national rules. Under such circumstances, the Court of Justice underlined that the interpretation of Art. 267 TFEU given in *Cartesio* was not relevant to this case: in *Cartesio*, the Court had to consider rules of national law, relating to the right of appeal against a decision making a reference for a preliminary ruling, 'under which the main proceedings remain pending before the referring court in their entirety, the order for reference alone

---

[171] ECJ, Case 13/61 *Bosch and Others* [1962] E.C.R. 45, at 49–50; ECJ, Joined Cases 2/82 to 4/82 *Delhaize Frères and Others* [1983] E.C.R. 2973, paras 8–9.

[172] ECJ, Case 146/73 *Rheinmühlen-Düsseldorf* ('*Rheinmühlen II*') [1974] E.C.R. 139, third subpara. of para. 3; ECJ, Case C-210/06 *Cartesio* [2008] E.C.R. I-9641, para. 89; ECJ (order of 24 March 2009), Case C-525/06 *De Nationale Loterij* [2009] E.C.R. I-2197, para. 6. Such a restriction may, however, ensue from national law itself.

[173] ECJ, Case C-210/06 *Cartesio* [2008] E.C.R. I-9641, paras 92–98.

[174] Available at <http://www.domstol.dk/>. See further *Reflets—Informations rapides sur les développements juridiques présentant un intérêt communautaire*, N° 2/2010, issued by the Court of Justice Research and Documentation Department, at 10–11, available at the website of the Court of Justice, <http://www.curia.europa.eu>.

[175] *Cour de cassation*, 30 March 2010, P.09.1592.N. Available at <http://www.cass.be>. See further *Reflets—Informations rapides sur les développements juridiques présentant un intérêt communautaire*, No. 3/2010, issued by the Court of Justice Research and Documentation Department, at 10–11, available at the website of the Court of Justice, <http://www.curia.europa.eu>.

[176] ECJ (order of 24 March 2009), Case C-525/06 *De Nationale Loterij* [2009] E.C.R. I-2197. For a similar case, see ECJ (order of 4 June 2009), Case C-129/08 *Cloet and Cloet* [2009] E.C.R. I-96*, Summ. pub.

being the subject of a limited appeal', whereas in the present proceedings the dispute is no longer pending before the referring court. In fact, the Antwerp appellate court itself adjudicated the dispute between the parties to the main proceedings, thereby assuming responsibility for ensuring compliance with Union law. Accordingly, there was no longer any dispute before the referring court, and therefore, even though such court has responsibility to draw the proper inferences from a judgment delivered on appeal against its decision to refer, and in particular, to come to the conclusion whether it is appropriate to maintain the reference, to amend it, or to withdraw it, it must be held that there is no need to reply to that reference.[177]

Where an appeal brought against the order for reference under national law has suspensory effect and the Court is officially notified of this by the national courts concerned, it will defer its ruling until it has received notification that the appeal has been decided.[178] If the appeal results in the annulment of the order for reference, the Court will order the case to be removed from the register.[179] In this way, the Court avoids giving a ruling that is no longer of any assistance for the purposes of making a determination in the main proceedings.[180]

III. Determination of the Relevance of the Request for a Preliminary Ruling

A. Task of the national court

(1) National court's responsibility for assessing relevance

3.31   Ever since the 1978 judgment in the *Pigs Marketing Board* case, it has been settled case-law that '[a]s regards the division of jurisdiction between national courts and the Court of Justice under [Art. 267 TFEU] the national court, which is alone in having a direct knowledge of the facts of the case and of the arguments put forward by the parties, and which will have to give judgment in the case, is in the best position to appreciate, with full knowledge of the matter before it, the relevance of the questions of law raised by the dispute before it and the necessity for a preliminary ruling so as to enable it to give judgment'.[181]

---

[177] ECJ (order of 4 June 2009), Case C-129/08 *Cloet and Cloet*, paras 7–11.

[178] See, by way of example, ECJ (order of the President of 8 December 1993), Case C-269/92 *Bosman*, not reported. Cf. ECJ, Case C-405/98 *Gourmet International Products* [2001] E.C.R. I-1795, para. 12, in which the Court noted the fact that an appeal against the order for reference had been rejected.

[179] See ECJ (order of 3 June 1969), Case 31/68 *Chanel* [1970] E.C.R. 403, at 403–4, and ECJ (order of 16 June 1970), Case 31/68 *Chanel* [1970] E.C.R. 404, at 405–6; ECJ (order of the President of 16 January 1996), Case C-310/94 *Garage Ardon*, not reported, paras 2–3. By an order, the President of the Court instructed a case to be struck out where an appeal against the order for reference had been blocked for seven years because one of the parties to the main proceedings had been declared insolvent. The President took the view that in the circumstances it was no longer necessary to reply to the questions set out in the order for reference (ECJ (order of the President of 20 February 1997), Case C-205/90 *Les Assurances du Crédit Namur*, not reported).

[180] Cf. the Opinion of Advocate-General K. Roemer in ECJ, Case 31/68 *Chanel*, 406, at 408–9.

[181] ECJ, Case 83/78 *Pigs Marketing Board v Redmond* [1978] E.C.R. 2347, para. 25 (emphasis added); see also, *inter alia*, ECJ, Joined Cases C-399/92, C-409/92, C-425/92, C-34/93, C-50/93, and C-78/93 *Helmig and Others* [1994] E.C.R. I-5727, para. 8; ECJ, Case C-134/94 *Esso Española* [1995] E.C.R. I-4223, para. 9; ECJ, Joined Cases C-320/94, C-328/94, C-329/94, C-337/94, C-338/94, and C-339/94 *RTI and Others* [1996] E.C.R. I-6471, para. 21; ECJ, Case C-145/03 *Keller* [2005] E.C.R. I-2529, para. 33; ECJ, Case

Consequently, the national court's responsibility for assessing the relevance of the questions referred for a preliminary ruling has a dual basis.

In the first place, that assessment falls to it as part of its jurisdiction to hear and determine the main proceedings, which is left intact by Art. 267 TFEU. This aspect of the national court's task was stressed above all during the first twenty years of preliminary rulings from the Court, when it repeatedly stated that, under what is now Art. 267 TFEU, which enshrines the principle of the mutual independence of the national and the Union courts, the Court of Justice has no jurisdiction to pronounce on the considerations which prompted the request for an interpretation or for the assessment of the validity of a Union act.[182] When the questions referred by the national court relate to the interpretation of a provision of Union law or to the validity of a Union act, 'the Court is, in principle, bound to give a ruling'.[183]

In the second place, it is for the national court to determine the relevance of the request for a preliminary ruling on account of its special ability to make the relevant assessment. This signifies that the national court's competence to determine the relevance of the preliminary questions constitutes the starting point, but is not absolute or subject to no possible correction in any circumstances (the Court is only obliged 'in principle' to reply). In exceptional circumstances, the Court must examine the conditions in which the case was referred to it by the national court in order to assess that it has jurisdiction.[184] The Court

---

C-217/05 *Confederación Española de Empresarios de Estaciones de Servicio* [2006] E.C.R. I-11987, para. 16; ECJ, Case C-119/05 *Lucchini* [2007] E.C.R. I-6199, para. 43; ECJ, Case C-11/07 *Eckelkamp and Others* [2008] E.C.R. I-6845, para. 27; ECJ, Case C-98/09 *Francesca Sorge* [2010] E.C.R. I-5837, para. 24; ECJ, Case C-391/09 *Runevič-Vardyn and Wardyn* [2011] E.C.R. I-3787, para. 30; ECJ, Case C-559/10 *Deli Ostrich* [2011] E.C.R. I-10873, para. 16; ECJ, Case C-126/10 *Foggia* [2011] E.C.R. I-10923, para. 25; ECJ (judgment of 28 February 2012), Case C-41/11 *Inter-Environnement Wallonie and Terre wallone*, not reported, para. 36; ECJ (judgment of 12 July 2012), Case C-602/10 *SC Volksbank România*, not reported, para. 48. The judgment in ECJ, Case C-193/94 *Skanavi and Chryssanthakopoulos* [1996] E.C.R. I-929, paras 17–18, affords a good example. The facts material to the main proceedings had occurred three days before the former EU Treaty (Maastricht Treaty) entered into force. The question submitted for a preliminary ruling related in part to Art. 18 EC, a new provision introduced by the former EU Treaty (now Art. 21 TFEU), which, according to the national court, might preclude application of the national rules at issue in the criminal proceedings pending before it. The Court of Justice found that the national court could apply the principle, recognized by its national law, that the more favourable rule of criminal law should take retroactive effect and, consequently, set aside national law to the extent to which it was contrary to the provisions of the Treaty. For those reasons, the Court did not contest the need for the preliminary ruling or the relevance of the questions referred. To like effect, see ECJ, Joined Cases C-163/94, C-165/94 and C-250/94 *Sanz de Lera and Others* [1995] E.C.R. I-4821, para. 14; ECJ, Case C-200/97 *Ecotrade* [1998] E.C.R. I-7907, para. 25; ECJ, Case C-167/01 *Inspire Art* [2003] E.C.R. I-10155, para. 43.

[182] ECJ, Case 13/68 *Salgoil* [1968] E.C.R. 453, at 459–60; ECJ, Case 5/77 *Tedeschi* [1977] E.C.R. 1555, paras 17–19.

[183] ECJ, Case C-231/89 *Gmurzynska-Bscher* [1990] E.C.R. I-4003, para. 20 (emphasis added); see also ECJ, Case C-231/89 *Gmurzynska-Bscher*, para. 19; ECJ, Joined Cases C-480/00 to C-482/00, C-484/00, C-489/00 to C-491/00, C-497/00 to C-499/00 *Azienda Agricola Ettore Ribaldi and Others* [2004] E.C.R. I-2943, para. 72; ECJ, Case C-458/06 *Gourmet Classic* [2008] E.C.R. I-4207, para. 24; ECJ, Case C-45/08 *Spector Photo Group and Van Raemdonck* [2009] E.C.R. I-12073, para. 25 (and further citations therein); ECJ (judgment of 15 March 2012), Case C-157/11 *Sibilio*, not reported, para. 27; ECJ (judgment of 19 July 2012), Case C-470/11 *Garkalns*, not reported, para. 17. If the request for a preliminary ruling has nothing to do with the interpretation of the Treaties or the validity or interpretation of a Union act, it will be inadmissible. The Court of Justice may then declare the request inadmissible by an order given pursuant to Art. 53(2) of the ECJ Rules of Procedure. See ECJ (order of 12 June 1996), Case C-95/96 *Clinique de la Pointe Rouge*, not reported, paras 6–7; ECJ (order of 12 June 1996), Case C-96/96 *Clinique Florens*, not reported, paras 6–7.

accordingly points out that, in the event of questions having been improperly formulated or going beyond the scope of the powers conferred on the Court of Justice by Art. 267 TFEU, it is free to extract from all the factors provided by the national court and in particular from the statement of grounds contained in the reference, the elements of Union law requiring an interpretation—or, as the case may be, an assessment of validity—having regard to the subject-matter of the dispute.[185]

(2) The ruling must contribute to resolving the dispute before the national court

3.32   In other words, the national court's jurisdiction to adjudge the relevance of the questions referred for a preliminary ruling and, in that light, to determine their content is not exclusive. The Court of Justice itself must take heed that the questions do not go beyond the scope of its powers and, where necessary, adapt the questions, 'having regard to the subject-matter of the dispute', so that the preliminary ruling achieves its aim of making an effective contribution towards resolving the dispute before the national court.[186]

Consequently, in its subsequent case-law, the Court has emphasized that the national court's power to determine the relevance of questions referred for a preliminary ruling is constrained by its aim: '[I]n the use which it makes of the facilities provided by [Art. 267 TFEU] [the national court] should have regard to the proper function of the Court of the Justice in this field',[187] which is not that of 'delivering advisory opinions on general or hypothetical questions but of assisting in the administration of justice in the Member States'.[188] The Court of Justice must always examine whether the questions raised are connected with its own task in order—just as in the case of any other court—not to exceed the limits of its jurisdiction. That limit would be exceeded if it would be impossible for the ruling requested to contribute towards the resolution of the dispute pending before the national court because of a manifest error in assessing the relevance of the questions of

---

[184] See, e.g. ECJ, Joined Cases C-295/04 to C-298/04 *Manfredi and Others* [2006] E.C.R. I-6619, para. 27; ECJ, Case C-350/07 *Kattner Stahlbau* [2009] E.C.R. I-1513, para. 29.

[185] ECJ, Case 83/78 *Pigs Marketing Board v Redmond* [1978] E.C.R. 2347, para. 26 (emphasis added). See to that effect, ECJ, Case C-346/05 *Chateignier* [2006] E.C.R. I-10951, para. 19.

[186] On those grounds, the Court may, in exceptional circumstances, examine the conditions in which the case was referred to it by the national court (ECJ, Case C-390/99 *Canal Satélite Digital* [2002] E.C.R. I-607, paras 18–20). In *Mazzoleni* (ECJ, Case C-165/98 *Mazzoleni and ISA* [2001] E.C.R. I-2189, paras 16–17), the Court held that it was 'not necessary' to give an interpretation of Directive 96/71/EC on the grounds that the period prescribed for the implementation of the directive had not expired and it had not been transposed into national law at the time of the facts of the main proceedings. Similar issues concerning the scope *ratione temporis* of Framework Decision 2002/584, however, did not stop the Court from giving judgment in ECJ (judgment of 26 February 2013), Case C-399/11 *Melloni*, not reported, paras 27–34. Furthermore, in the light of the observations submitted by the parties or the national governments, the Court may sometimes add a question which does not appear expressly in the order for reference on the grounds that it has 'jurisdiction to provide the national court with all the guidance of interpretation . . . for the purposes of deciding the case before it': ECJ, Joined Cases C-441/98 and C-442/98 *Michaïlidis* [2000] E.C.R. I-7145, paras 20–21; ECJ, Case C-387/01 *Weigel* [2004] E.C.R. I-4981, para. 44.

[187] ECJ, Case 244/80 *Foglia v Novello* ('*Foglia v Novello II*') [1981] E.C.R. 3045, para. 20 in fine; ECJ, Case C-167/01 *Inspire Art* [2003] E.C.R. I-10155, para. 45.

[188] ECJ, Case 244/80 '*Foglia v Novello II*', para. 18; ECJ, Case C-167/01 *Inspire Art*, para. 45; cf. ECJ, Case 149/82 *Robards* [1983] E.C.R. 171, para. 19; ECJ, Case C-116/02 *Gasser* [2003] E.C.R. I-14693, para. 24; ECJ, Case C-314/01 *Siemens and ARGE Telekom & Partner* [2004] E.C.R. I-2549, para. 35; ECJ, Case C-315/02 *Lenz* [2004] E.C.R. I-7063, paras 52–54; ECJ, Case C-62/06 *ZF Zefeser* [2007] E.C.R. I-11995, para. 15; ECJ, Case C-189/08 *Zuid-Chemie* [2009] E.C.R. I-6917, paras 36–41; ECJ, Case C-261/08 *Zurita García and Choque Cabrera* [2009] E.C.R. I-10143, paras 35–36.

Union law referred to the Court.[189] However, the fact that the answer to the preliminary question can be alleged to be clearly deduced from the case-law does not render the order for reference inadmissible, although the Court may deliver its ruling by way of reasoned order under Art. 99 of the ECJ Rules of Procedure.[190]

(3) The relevance of questions must appear from the order for reference

In order to enable the Court to ascertain whether it has jurisdiction, 'it is essential for national courts to explain, when the reasons do not emerge beyond any doubt from the documents, why they consider that a reply to their questions is necessary to enable them to give judgment'.[191] It is thus well settled that the order for reference must set out the precise reasons why the national court was unsure as to the interpretation of Union law[192] and why it considered it necessary to refer the questions concerned. At the very least, it is essential that the national court provides some explanation of the reasons for the choice of the provisions of Union law which it requires to be interpreted and of the link it establishes between those provisions and the national legislation applicable to the dispute in the main proceedings. It is important to underline that those reasons should be the national court's own reasons; merely taking over the arguments of the parties is not sufficient.[193] Failure to fulfil that duty to state reasons does not automatically mean that the request for a

3.33

---

[189] See, however, ECJ, Case C-343/98 *Collino and Chiappero* [2000] E.C.R. I-6659, paras 19–24, in which the Court did not question the admissibility of a preliminary question, even though it was not certain whether the provisions of the directive at issue could be invoked against one of the parties to the main proceedings; see also ECJ (order of 15 January 2004), Case C-235/02 *Saetti* [2004] E.C.R. I-1005, paras 24–30. In ECJ, Case C-315/01 *GAT* [2003] E.C.R. I-6351, paras 38–39, the Court declared inadmissible a preliminary question relating to the award of compensation for infringement of Union law—or the conditions related thereto—on the ground that the question had been referred by a court which, under national law, had no power to award damages. See further ECJ (judgment of 24 October 2013), Case C-180/12 *Stoilov i Ko*, not reported, paras 45–46.

[190] See, e.g. ECJ, Case C-260/07 *Pedro IV Servicios* [2009] E.C.R. I-2437, para. 31; Case C-428/06 *UGT-Rioja* [2006] E.C.R. I-6747, paras 42–43; ECJ (judgment of 21 December 2011), Case C-503/10 *Evroetil*, not reported, para. 36. See further para. 3.53.

[191] ECJ, Case 244/80 *Foglia v Novello* ('*Foglia v Novello II*') [1981] E.C.R. 3045, para. 17. See also Case C-325/98 *Anssens* [1999] E.C.R. I-2969, para. 14, in which the Court declared a preliminary question inadmissible, in particular because the referring court had not given reasons justifying the need for the preliminary reference, even though one of the parties to the main proceedings had drawn the national court's attention to a judgment of the Court giving a preliminary ruling on an identical question. It appears from a number of cases that the Court will declare a preliminary question inadmissible only where it is obvious that the interpretation of Union law requested is not necessary for resolving the dispute before the national court (ECJ, Case C-448/98 *Guimont* [2000] E.C.R. I-10663, para. 23; ECJ, Case C-71/02 *Herbert Karner Industrie-Auktionen* [2004] E.C.R. I-3025, para. 21; ECJ, Joined Cases C-436/08 and C-437/08 *Haribo and Salinen* [2011] E.C.R. I-305, para. 44; ECJ, Case C-391/09 *Runevič-Vardyn and Wardyn* [2011] E.C.R. I-3787, paras 33–34; ECJ, Joined Cases C-483/09 and C-1/10 *Gueye and Salmerón Sánchez* [2011] E.C.R. I-8263, para. 44 ('it is not obvious that the interpretation of the Framework Decision requested by the referring court bears no relation to the actual facts of the main proceedings or to their purpose, or that the problem raised is hypothetical').

[192] But see ECJ, Case C-285/09 *R* [2010] E.C.R. I-12605, paras 25–34, where the German *Bundesgerichtshof* (Federal Court of Justice) stated in the order for reference that it had no doubts as to the interpretation of the Sixth VAT Directive but nevertheless felt the need to make an order for reference for a preliminary ruling, since an order of a German *Finanzgericht* (Finance Court) in another case had raised doubts concerning the interpretation by the *Bundesgerichtshof* of the Sixth VAT Directive. The Court declared the reference admissible.

[193] ECJ (order of 23 March 2012), Case C-348/11 *Thomson Sales Europe*, not reported, paras 40–58.

preliminary ruling is inadmissible,[194] but it does cause the Court to adopt a more critical attitude when it makes its substantive review of the assessment of relevance that the national court is implicitly deemed to have carried out.[195]

The assessment of relevance which the Court of Justice expects the national court to carry out in order to ensure that it does not exceed the limits of its jurisdiction in answering questions referred for a preliminary ruling is very close to the description given by Lord Denning MR:

> The judge must have got to the stage when he says to himself: 'This clause of the Treaty is capable of two or more meanings. If it means this, I give judgment for the plaintiff. If it means that, I give judgment for the defendant.' In short, the point must be such that, whichever way the point is decided, it is conclusive of the case. Nothing more remains but to give judgment.'[196]

Yet, in some circumstances, a less strict approach is advisable. This might be the case for interpretation issues concerning a number of instruments providing for judicial cooperation in the context of the Area of Freedom, Security and Justice. For instance, an interpretation of Regulation No. 1206/2001 on cooperation between the courts of the Member States in the taking of evidence in civil or commercial matters is very likely to have only an indirect impact on the outcome of the case before the national court. The taking of evidence is nevertheless an important step in the outcome of a case. The requirement that an answer to a question referred should enable the national court to 'give judgment' should therefore not be interpreted too strictly, on account of the risk that an interpretation of Union law by way of a request for a preliminary ruling would not be possible in certain cases, however necessary for the national court to enable it to give judgment. Accordingly, the Court has held that in such circumstances the concept of giving judgment must be understood as 'encompassing the whole of the procedure leading to the judgment of the referring court, in order that the Court of Justice is able to interpret all procedural provisions of European Union law that the referring court is required to apply in order to give judgment'.[197] Questions regarding preliminary issues are thus not *prima facie* excluded.[198] The interpretation must, however, 'respond to an objective need inherent in the outcome of a case pending before [the national court]'.[199]

---

[194] ECJ, Joined Cases 98/85, 162/85 and 258/85 *Bertini* [1986] E.C.R. 1885, paras 6–7. There is, however, a serious risk that the question will be declared inadmissible: see, e.g. ECJ (order of 28 June 2000), Case C-116/00 *Laguillaumie* [2000] E.C.R. I-4979, paras 16–17; ECJ, Case C-380/05 *Centro Europe 7* [2008] E.C.R. I-349, paras 54–56 (and further citations therein). This risk may be even greater if the factual and legal context is not described sufficiently either: ECJ (order of 15 April 2011), Case C-613/10 *Debiasi* [2011] E.C.R. I-65*, Summ. pub., paras 19–32.

[195] When it does not appear clearly from the order for reference and the submissions of the parties why it would be necessary to answer the questions referred, the Court will, in the absence of reasons provided by the national court to the contrary, declare the order for reference manifestly inadmissible (ECJ (order of 23 March 2012), Case C-348/11 *Thomson Sales Europe*, not reported, paras 40–58). See also paras 3.31–3.33.

[196] *Bulmer v Bollinger* [1974] C.M.L.R. 91, [1974] Ch 401.

[197] ECJ, Case C-283/09 *Weryński* [2011] E.C.R. I-601, para. 42.

[198] See also ECJ, Case C-225/09 *Jakubowska* [2010] E.C.R. I-12329, para. 22.

[199] ECJ (judgment of 19 June 2012), Case C-307/10 *Chartered Institute of Patent Attorneys*, not reported, para. 33 (and further citations therein).

B. The limits set by Union law

(1) Presumption of relevance

Through the development of the jurisprudence, the Court of Justice has honed a well-known formula declaring that questions on Union law referred by a national court enjoy a 'presumption of relevance' and that the Court may refuse to rule on such questions only where it is quite obvious that the interpretation of Union law that is sought bears no relation to the actual facts of the main action or its purpose, where the problem is hypothetical, or where the Court does not have before it the factual or legal material necessary to give a useful answer to the questions submitted to it.[200] The presumption of relevance cannot be rebutted by the simple fact that one of the parties to the main proceedings contests certain facts, the accuracy of which is not a matter for the Court to determine and on which the delimitation of the subject-matter of those proceedings depends.[201] The Court will thus generally examine the questions put before it where they are not 'manifestly' or '*prima facie*' irrelevant.[202]

3.34

Of the categories elaborated by the Court, some are intertwined to some extent with the earlier discussion in connection with the timing and content of the order for reference, such as the need for a clear description of the factual and legal context in the order for reference.[203] In any event, the limits set by Union law in connection with the assessment of the relevance of an order for reference generally pertain to general or hypothetical questions, obviously irrelevant questions, and spurious or 'contrived' questions. Each will now be discussed.

(2) General or hypothetical questions

Hypothetical questions are questions referred to the Court that will result in the Court delivering an advisory opinion on certain points of Union law, rather than providing an interpretation of Union law that is useful to solve the dispute pending before the referring national court. While advisory opinions might under certain circumstances be useful, the

3.35

---

[200] See, e.g. ECJ, Case C-415/93 *Bosman* [1995] E.C.R. I-4921, para. 61; ECJ, Case C-300/01 *Salzmann* [2003] E.C.R. I-4899, para. 32; ECJ, Joined Cases C-94/04 and C-202/04 *Cipolla* [2006] E.C.R. I-11421, para. 25; ECJ, Joined Cases C-222/05 to C-225/05 *van der Weerd* [2007] E.C.R. I-4233, para. 22; Case C-333/07 *Regie Networks* [2008] E.C.R. I-10807, para.57; ECJ, Case C-458/06 *Gourmet Classic* [2008] E.C.R. I-4207, para. 25; ECJ, Case C-314/08 *Filipiak* [2009] E.C.R. I-11049, para. 42 (and further citations therein); ECJ, Case C-56/09 *Zanotti* [2010] I-4517, para. 15; ECJ, Joined Cases C-570/07 and C-571/07 *Blanco Pérez* [2010] E.C.R. I-4629, para. 36 (and further citations therein); ECJ, Joined Cases C-395/08 and C-396/08 *Bruno and Pettini* [2010] E.C.R. I-5119, para. 19; ECJ, Joined Cases C-188/10 and C-189/10 *Melki and Abdeli* [2010] E.C.R. I-5667, para. 27 (and further citations therein); ECJ, Case C-482/09 *Budějovický Budvar* [2011] E.C.R. I-8701, para. 65; ECJ (judgment of 22 March 2012), Case C-190/10 *Génesis*, not reported, paras 26–27.
[201] Joined Cases C-94/04 and C-202/04 *Cipolla* [2006] E.C.R. I-11421, para. 26; ECJ, Joined Cases C-222/05 to C-225/05 *van der Weerd* [2007] E.C.R. I-4233, para. 23.
[202] See, e.g. ECJ, Case C-152/03 *Ritter-Coulais* [2006] E.C.R. I-1711, para. 15; Case C-210/06 *Cartesio* [2008] E.C.R. I-9641, paras 72–73; see also ECJ, Joined Cases C-453/03, C-11/04, C-12/04 and C-194/04 *ABNA and Others* [2005] E.C.R. I-10423, para. 50 (finding the question not 'manifestly bereft of relevance'); ECJ, Case C-106/10 *Lidl & Companhia* [2011] E.C.R. I-7235, para. 26 (finding 'that the information provided by the referring court makes it possible for the significance of the questions referred to be determined').
[203] See para. 3.24.

Court has consistently held that the aim of the preliminary ruling procedure provided for in Art. 267 TFEU is to assist national courts in giving judgment by providing them with a ruling on the interpretation of the rules of Union law applicable to the disputes pending before them. Art. 267 TFEU does not give the Court jurisdiction to issue advisory opinions on questions of a general or hypothetical nature.[204] Questions leading the Court to answer by way of an advisory opinion will therefore be declared inadmissible.[205]

This means that the Court will have to assess the relevance and the necessity of the order for reference, in particular the reasons that motivated the national court to make an order for reference. At first sight, this seems to imply that the Court will have to trespass over the borderline between interpreting Union law and interpreting national law. Yet, this approach is in line with the division of tasks in the preliminary ruling procedure, since the Court does not pronounce upon any factual or national legal aspect of the main proceedings which is in issue between the parties (see para. 6.21). The Court regards itself as being obliged simply to supply the lacunae which the national court has left in its order, namely its omission to give reasons why it considered it needed an answer to the preliminary questions so as to decide the main action, in order not to exceed its jurisdiction.[206] In addition, it has to be borne in mind in this connection that a preliminary ruling has binding effects on national courts generally (see paras 6.27–6.34), which makes the Court—in common with all courts—careful only to decide on what is necessary in order to bring a case to a conclusion and thereby to allow the whole mosaic of case-law to build itself up incrementally.

General or hypothetical questions might be referred unknowingly or deliberately. In the latter case, a ruling of the Court may be sought by the national court in order to serve other purposes than resolving the case that gave rise to the reference for a preliminary ruling. For instance, a national court might seek an abstract ruling in order to prevent more cases of a similar nature from being brought before it.[207] Furthermore, questions might also become hypothetical in the course of proceedings before the Court due to the fact that the context of the case pending before the national court has changed.[208] The Court's case-law on hypothetical questions does not necessarily imply, however, that national courts should already have chosen between various hypotheses present in the main proceedings before submitting questions to the Court.[209] There are also cases in which the Court has expressly ruled that the questions are not of a hypothetical nature. For instance, in *Boxus*, the Court held that a national law taking away jurisdiction from the referring court to rule on the administrative acts pending in the main proceedings did not render the questions referred hypothetical, since the questions were precisely intended to determine whether, in

---

[204] ECJ, Case C-406/06 *Winner Wetten* [2010] E.C.R. I-8015, para. 38; ECJ (judgment of 24 April 2012), Case C-571/10 *Kamberaj*, not reported, paras 44–46.

[205] ECJ (judgment of 24 April 2012), Case C-571/10 *Kamberaj*, not reported, paras 44–46; ECJ (judgment of 29 January 2013), Case C-396/11 *Radu*, not reported, para. 24; ECJ (judgment of 18 July 2013), Case C-136/12 *Consiglio nazionale dei geologi*, not reported, para. 35.

[206] See, e.g. ECJ, Case C-380/01 *Schneider* [2004] E.C.R. I-1389, paras 20–31.

[207] ECJ, Case C-197/10 *Unió de Pagesos de Catalunya* [2011] E.C.R. I-8495, para. 19–25.

[208] ECJ, Case C-314/01 *Siemens and ARGE Telecom & Partner* [2004] E.C.R. I-2549, para. 37. See also ECJ, Case C-241/09 *Fluxys* [2010] E.C.R. I-12773, paras 33–34 and ECJ (judgment of 27 June 2013), Case C-492/11 *Di Donna*, not reported, paras 30–32.

[209] ECJ (judgment of 15 March 2012), Case C-157/11 *Sibilio*, not reported, paras 30–34. See also para. 3.28.

the light of Union law, such law was capable at all of taking away jurisdiction from the referring court.[210]

(3) Obviously irrelevant questions

(a) The reference bears no relation to the dispute before the national court

The Court will not follow the national court's assessment of relevance where 'it is quite **3.36** obvious that the interpretation of [Union] law or the examination of the validity of a rule of [Union] law sought by that court bears no relation to the actual nature of the case or to the subject-matter of the main action'.[211] The request for a preliminary ruling is then inadmissible and will be dismissed, wholly[212] or in part,[213] on that account.

In the words of the Court, it must be 'obvious' that the preliminary questions are irrelevant.[214] Again, the question arises, however, as to how far the Court will take its examination of the facts and national legal aspects of the main action in order to ascertain whether the preliminary ruling sought has some chance of making an actual contribution towards the decision in the case. Is it not the case that the Court must exercise a degree of restraint, given that determining the facts and the national law comes under the national court's jurisdiction? The answer to that question is yes insofar as the Court may not pronounce upon facts or aspects of national law that are in issue between the parties and on which the national court has not yet made any determination.[215] In contrast, where the

---

[210] ECJ, Joined Cases C-128/09 to C-131/09, C-134/09 and C-135/09 *Boxus and Others* [2011] E.C.R. I-9711, para. 28. See also ECJ, Case C-225/09 *Jakubowska* [2010] E.C.R. I-12329, paras 31–32.

[211] ECJ, Case 126/80 *Salonia* [1981] E.C.R. 1563, para. 6. See, e.g. ECJ, Case C-368/89 *Crispoltoni* [1991] E.C.R. I-3695, para. 11; ECJ, Case C-186/90 *Durighello* [1991] E.C.R. I-5773, para. 9; ECJ, Case C-343/90 *Lourenço Dias* [1992] E.C.R. I-4673, para. 18; ECJ, Case C-67/91 *Asociación Española de Banca Privada and Others* [1992] E.C.R. I-4785, para. 26; ECJ, Joined Cases C-332/92, C-333/92, and C-335/92 *Eurico Italia and Others* [1994] E.C.R. I-711, para. 17; ECJ, Case C-18/93 *Corsica Ferries* [1994] E.C.R. I-1783, para. 14 (and further citations therein); ECJ, Case C-62/93 *BP Supergaz* [1995] E.C.R. I-1883, para. 10; ECJ, Case C-143/94 *Furlanis* [1995] E.C.R. I-3633, para. 12; ECJ, Case C-129/94 *Bernáldez* [1996] E.C.R. I-1829, para. 7; ECJ, Joined Cases C-320/94, C-328/94, C-329/94, C-337/94, C-338/94 and C-339/94 *RTI and Others* [1996] E.C.R. I-6471, para. 23; ECJ, Case C-104/95 *Kontogeorgas* [1996] E.C.R. I-6643, paras 10–11; ECJ, Case C-261/95 *Palmisani* [1997] E.C.R. I-4025, para. 18; ECJ, Case C-373/95 *Maso and Others* [1997] E.C.R. I-4051, para. 26.

[212] See, e.g. ECJ (order of 16 May 1994), Case C-428/93 *Monin Automobiles* [1994] E.C.R. I-1707, paras 13–16; ECJ (order of 2 May 2002), Case C-129/01 *Condominio Facchinei Orsini*, not reported, paras 17–23; ECJ (order of 24 July 2003), Case C-44/03 *Horn*, not reported, paras 12–16.

[213] See, e.g. ECJ, Case C-421/97 *Tarantik* [1999] E.C.R. I-3633, paras 33–37; ECJ, Joined Cases C-430/99 and C-431/99 *Sealand Service and Nedlloyd Lijnen* [2002] E.C.R. I-5235, paras 46–47; ECJ, Case C-315/02 *Lenz* [2004] E.C.R. I-7063, paras 52–54; ECJ, Case C-466/04 *Acereda Herrera* [2006] E.C.R. I-5341, paras 47–49; ECJ, Case C-459/07 *Elshani* [2009] E.C.R. I-2759, paras 45–47.

[214] That will be the case where it is quite obvious that the questions of interpretation referred for a preliminary ruling are not necessary for the national court (ECJ, Case C-71/02 *Herbert Karner Industrie-Auktionen* [2004] E.C.R. I-3025, para. 21; ECJ, Case C-286/02 *Bellio Fratelli* [2004] E.C.R. I-3465, para. 28). A question will be regarded as relevant where the Court's answer may be of use to the national court in finding whether a provision of national law is compatible with Union law (ECJ, Case C-286/02 *Bellio Fratelli*). In *Mangold*, the Court made clear that it has no jurisdiction to give a preliminary ruling on a question raised before a national court where the interpretation of Union law has no connection whatsoever with the circumstances or purpose of the main proceedings (ECJ, Case C-144/04 *Mangold* [2005] E.C.R. I-9981, para. 37). However, such language has not precluded the admissibility of preliminary questions, particularly in cases where it is alleged that the particular Union measure, often a directive, does not apply because the facts arose before it was adopted: see, e.g. ECJ, Case C-212/04 *Adeneler and Others* [2006] E.C.R. I-6057, paras 43–53; ECJ, Case C-304/08 *Plus Warenhandelsgesellschaft* [2010] E.C.R. I-217, paras 29–30.

[215] ECJ, Case C-153/02 *Neri* [2003] E.C.R. I-13555, para. 34.

facts and national legal aspects of the case have been determined in the order for reference or are clear from the case-file submitted to the Court, there is nothing to prevent the Court from having regard to them in testing the national court's assessment of the relevance of the preliminary questions against the requirements which arise out of the aims of the Court's jurisdiction under Art. 267 TFEU. A number of examples serve to clarify the Court's approach. Notably, the distinction the Court makes between various cases is subtle and the determination of the line concerning hypothetical questions is not always easy to draw.[216]

The Court will declare an order for reference for a preliminary ruling inadmissible if the facts in the main proceedings do not warrant an answer to the questions referred.[217] Thus, in a case dealing with the Sixth VAT Directive, the Court found that questions regarding the deductibility of VAT for goods not used for an economic activity were inadmissible since it was not established in the order for reference that the goods in question were ever used for anything else but an economic activity.[218] Similarly, preliminary questions will be declared inadmissible if the facts of the case do not fall within the scope of the provisions of Union law of which an interpretation is sought[219] or within the scope of Union law at all.[220] In the same vein, the Court has declared inadmissible preliminary questions concerning facts that had occurred before the accession of the Member State of the referring court.[221]

The Court will also declare preliminary questions inadmissible when it is unclear how a national rule related to the interpretation of Union law being sought is applicable to the facts in the main proceedings.[222] For this reason, the Court held that questions referred in connection with an Italian law laying down residence and linguistic conditions for Union citizens in order to be entitled to housing benefits were inadmissible, since the national court had not explained why an interpretation of Union law could bear any relation to the main proceedings, in which a third-country national challenged the fact that his application for housing benefits was rejected on the ground that the housing benefit budget for third-country nationals was exhausted.[223]

---

[216] See, e.g. ECJ, Case C-62/06 *ZF Zefeser* [2007] E.C.R. I-11995, para. 16; ECJ, Case C-225/09 *Jakubowska* [2010] E.C.R. I-12329, paras 29–32; ECJ, Case C-203/09 *Volvo Car Germany* [2010] E.C. R. I-10721, paras 29–31; ECJ (order of 7 March 2013), Case C-145/10 *Painer*, not reported, paras 60 and 70; ECJ (judgment of 24 April 2012), Case C-571/10 *Kamberaj*, not reported, paras 44–46.

[217] ECJ, Case 132/81 *Vlaeminck* [1982] E.C.R. 2953, paras 13–14; ECJ, Case C-567/07 *Woningstichting Sint Servatius* [2009] E.C.R. I-9021, para. 43; ECJ (judgment of 24 April 2012), Case C-571/10 *Kamberaj*, not reported, paras 51–54.

[218] ECJ (judgment of 16 February 2012), Case C-118/11 *Eon Aset Menidjmunt*, not reported, paras 75–79.

[219] ECJ (order of 6 December 2010), Case C-377/10 *Băilă* [2010] E.C.R. I-161, paras 8–14; ECJ (judgment of 24 April 2012), Case C-571/10 *Kamberaj*, not reported, paras 47–50; ECJ (judgment of 7 June 2012), Case C-27/11 *Vinkov*, not reported, paras 40–45.

[220] ECJ (judgment of 7 June 2012), Case C-27/11 *Vinkov*, not reported, paras 53–54; ECJ (order of 22 June 2011), Case C-161/11 *Vino* [2011] E.C.R. I-91*, Summ. pub., para. 38. See further paras 3.38 and 3.39.

[221] ECJ (order of 11 May 2011), Case C-32/10 *Semerdzhiev* [2011] E.C.R. I-71*, Summ. pub., para. 29. See also ECJ, Case C-283/10 *Circul Globus Bucureşti* [2011] E.C.R. I-12031, paras 27–29.

[222] ECJ, Case C-393/09 *Bezpečnostní softwarová asociace* [2010] E.C.R. I-13971, para. 26.

[223] ECJ (judgment of 24 April 2012), Case C-571/10 *Kamberaj*, not reported, paras 55–58. See also ECJ, Case C-153/00 *der Weduwe* [2002] E.C.R. I-11319, in which the Court considered that the referring court had not provided the Court with all the necessary information to determine whether an interpretation of Union law would serve a useful purpose in the main proceedings. It therefore declared the request for a preliminary ruling inadmissible. In fact, the relevance of the preliminary question depended upon the

Moreover, questions will be declared inadmissible if the Court's answer is not necessary to enable the referring court to give judgment. This will be the case, for instance, when the national court refers questions concerning side-issues that are considered to have no impact on the outcome of the main proceedings,[224] or when the questions referred have a purpose other than solving the case in the main action.[225] Also, when it is clear that the questions referred are based on a false premise, the Court will declare them inadmissible,[226] even when this verges on the determination that the national court has erroneously interpreted national law.[227]

(b) The dispute concerns the legislation of another Member State

The Court will be particularly attentive where a question is referred to it in connection with proceedings between individuals that is intended to assess whether the legislation of another Member State is in conformity with Union law.[228] In those circumstances, the national court must take particular pains to explain why it considers that an answer to its questions is necessary in order to determine the dispute.[229] If it fails to do so, the preliminary question will be inadmissible. **3.37**

(c) Absence of cross-border elements in the national dispute

Questions relating to the Treaty provisions on the fundamental freedoms may be declared inadmissible where the activities in question in the main proceedings are confined in all respects within a single Member State.[230] However, the Court of Justice is rather reluctant to turn down requests for preliminary rulings simply because the main proceedings lack cross-border elements. It considers that a reply might be useful to the national court if its national law were to require that a citizen of the Member State concerned must be allowed to enjoy the same rights as those that a citizen of another Member State would derive from Union law in the same situation.[231] A further reason to accept jurisdiction in such cases is **3.38**

---

interpretation of the national law at issue in the proceedings. The Court did not rule on the relevance of the question, but found that it did not have sufficient information to be certain about its relevance.

[224] ECJ, Joined Cases C-92/09 and C-93/09 *Volker und Schecke and Eifert* [2010] E.C.R. I-11063, paras 38–42.

[225] ECJ (order of 26 January 1990), Case C-286/88 *Falciola* [1990] E.C.R. I-191. It is particular in the context of such cases that the line with hypothetical questions is very difficult to draw.

[226] ECJ, Case C-310/10 *Agafiţei and Others* [2011] E.C.R. I-5989, para. 48.

[227] ECJ, Case C-568/08 *Combinatie Spijker Infrabouw-De Jonge Konstruktie and Others* [2010] E.C.R. I-12655, paras 42–49.

[228] ECJ, Case 244/80 *Foglia v Novello* ('*Foglia v Novello II*') [1981] E.C.R. 3045, para. 31 (legality of French legislation raised by an Italian court); ECJ, Case C-150/88 *Eau de Cologne & Parfumerie-Fabrik 4711* [1989] E.C.R. 3891, para. 21 (legality of Italian legislation raised by German court); ECJ, Case C-153/00 *der Weduwe* [2002] E.C.R. I-11319 (legality of Luxembourg legislation questioned by a Belgian court); ECJ, Case C-318/00 *Bacardi-Martini and Cellier des Dauphins* [2003] E.C.R. I-905 (legality of French legislation questioned by a UK court); ECJ, Case C-379/09 *Casteels* [2011] E.C.R. I-1379 (legality of a collective agreement under German law raised by Belgian court).

[229] ECJ, Case C-318/00 *Bacardi-Martini and Cellier des Dauphins* [2003] E.C.R. I-905, paras 45–46; see also ECJ, Case C-153/00 *der Weduwe* [2002] E.C.R. I-11319, paras 31–40.

[230] See, e.g. ECJ, Case C-245/09 *Omalet* [2010] E.C.R. I-13771, paras 9–19; ECJ (order of 12 July 2012), Case C-16/12 *Hermes Hitel és Faktor*, not reported, paras 12–21.

[231] ECJ, Case C-448/98 *Guimont* [2000] E.C.R. I-10663, para. 23; ECJ, Joined Cases C-515/99, C-519/99 to C-524/99 and C-526/99 to C-540/99 *Reisch and Others* [2002] E.C.R. I-2157, para. 26 (and Opinion of Advocate-General L.A. Geelhoed in this case); ECJ (order of 17 February 2005), Case C-250/03 *Mauri*, not reported, para. 21; ECJ, Joined Cases C-94/04 and C-202/04 *Cipolla and Others* [2006] E.C.R. I-11421, paras 30–31; ECJ, Case C-380/05 *Centro Europa 7* [2008] E.C.R. I-349, paras 64–69; ECJ, Case C-384/08 *Attanasio*

that 'the legal order of the European Union clearly has an interest in ensuring that, in order to forestall future divergences of interpretation, every provision of EU law is interpreted uniformly, irrespective of the circumstances in which that provision is to apply'.[232] Moreover, in some cases, the Court even refers to the potential effect the national rule at issue might have on cross-border activities to substantiate its jurisdiction, despite the absence of a cross-border element in the main action.[233]

(d) Field of application of the Charter of Fundamental Rights of the European Union

3.39 Finally, questions relating to the Charter of Fundamental Rights of the European Union will be declared inadmissible when the national legislation in the main proceedings whose compatibility with the Charter is being questioned, is not implementing Union law in one way or another.[234] This follows from Art. 51(1) of the Charter, which provides: 'The provisions of this Charter are addressed to [. . .] the Member States only when they are implementing Union law.'[235]

(4) Spurious disputes

(a) General

3.40 The idea that the preliminary ruling should contribute towards bringing a dispute to a conclusion also underlies the Court's refusal to answer questions raised by means of spurious main proceedings. This means that the Court will refuse to give a preliminary ruling 'where it appears that the procedure of [Art. 267 TFEU] has been misused and been

---

Group [2010] E.C.R. I-2055, paras 22–31; ECJ, Case C-245/09 *Omalet* [2010] E.C.R. I-13771, paras 9–19; ECJ, Case C-126/10 *Foggia* [2011] E.C.R. I-10923, paras 20–23; ECJ (judgment of 21 June 2012), Case C-84/11 *Susisalo and Others*, not reported, paras 20–22; ECJ (judgment of 19 July 2012), Case C-470/11 *Garkalns*, not reported, para. 20. See also ECJ, Case C-212/06 *Gouvernement de la Communauté française and Gouvernement wallon* [2008] E.C.R. I-1683, para. 40. That being said, the fact that national law refers to Union law does not automatically lead the Court to accept jurisdiction: ECJ (judgment of 21 December 2011), Case C-482/10 *Cicala*, not reported, paras 13–31; ECJ (judgment of 7 November 2013), Case C-313/12 Romeo, not reported, paras 32–35. See further paras 6.16 and 6.17. It should also be pointed out that not all Union law requires a cross-border element: ECJ, Case C-304/08 *Plus Warenhandelsgesellschaft* [2010] E.C.R. I-217, paras 27–28.

[232] ECJ, Case C-546/09 *Aurubis Balgaria* [2011] E.C.R. I-2531, paras 22–24 (and references therein); ECJ, Case C-310/10 *Agafiţei and Others* [2011] E.C.R. I-5989, para. 39; ECJ (judgment of 18 October 2012), Case C-583/10 *Nolan*, not reported, paras 53–56.

[233] ECJ (judgment of 19 July 2012), Case C-470/11 *Garkalns*, not reported, para. 21 (and references therein).

[234] ECJ (order of 12 November 2010), Case C-339/10 *Asparuhov Estov and Others* [2010] E.C.R. I-11465, paras 11–15; ECJ (order of 1 March 2011), Case C-457/09 *Chartry* [2011] E.C.R. I-819, paras 25–26 (P. Van Nuffel, case note (2012) T.B.P. 303–5); ECJ (order of 23 May 2011), Joined Cases C-267/10 and C-268/10 *Rossius and Collard* [2011] E.C.R. I-81*, Summ. pub., paras 19–20; ECJ (order of 22 September 2011), Case C-314/10 *Pagnoul* [2011] E.C.R. I-136*, Summ. pub., paras 23–25; ECJ (order of 22 September 2011), Case C-538/10 *Lebrun and Howet* [2011] E.C.R. I-137*, Summ. pub., paras 19–20; ECJ (order of 14 December 2011), Joined Cases C-483/11 and C-484/11 *Boncea and Others*, not reported, paras 33–35; ECJ (order of 14 December 2011), Case C-462/11 *Cozman*, not reported, paras 14–16; ECJ (order of 14 December 2011), Case C-434/11 *Corpul Naţional al Poliţiştilor*, not reported, paras 14–16; ECJ (order of 10 May 2012), Case C-134/12 *Corpul Naţional al Poliţiştilor*, not reported, paras 12–13; ECJ (order of 12 July 2012), Case C-466/11 *Currà and Others*, not reported, paras 25–26. See also K. Lenaerts, 'Die EU-Grundrechtecharta: Anwendbarkeit und Auslegung' (2012) Europarecht 3–17.

[235] When this latter requirement is fulfilled, the Court does, of course, interpret the Charter. See ECJ (judgment of 26 February 2013), Case C-399/11 *Melloni*, not reported, paras 55–64 and ECJ (judgment of 26 February 2013), Case C-617/10 *Åkerberg Fransson*, not reported, paras 16–31. See further K. Lenaerts, 'Exploring the Limits of the EU Charter of Fundamental Rights' (2012) Eur. Const. L. Rev. 375–403; V. Skouris, 'Développements récents de la protection des droits fondamentaux dans l'Union européenne: les arrêts Melloni et Åkerberg Fransson' (2013) Il diritto dell'Unione europea 229–43.

resorted to, in fact, in order to elicit a ruling from the Court by means of a spurious dispute'.[236]

(b) Assessment

It is not, however, an easy matter for the Court to decide that it 'appears' that the main **3.41** proceedings are spurious, without in so doing exceeding the limits of its jurisdiction. It is a slippery slope from finding that preliminary questions have been raised 'within the framework of procedural devices arranged by the parties in order to induce the Court to give its views on certain problems of [Union] law which do not correspond to an objective requirement inherent in the resolution of a dispute'[237] to assessing facts and aspects of national law on which no definitive finding has yet been made by the national court, a task which falls outside the limits of the Court's jurisdiction.

In order to avoid this difficulty, the Court will decide that the preliminary reference is inadmissible only where it is manifestly apparent from the facts set out in the order for reference that the dispute is in fact fictitious.[238] In this way, the Court confines its review to a species of 'marginal review' of facts plainly set out in the order for reference, even without having regard to further particulars contained in the case-file from the national court or in observations submitted pursuant to Art. 23 of the Statute.[239]

(c) Foglia v Novello I

The only case to date in which the Court has declined jurisdiction on account of the spurious **3.42** nature of the main proceedings was one in which the parties were concerned to obtain a ruling that a tax system in one Member State was invalid by the expedient of proceedings before a court in another Member State between two private individuals who were in agreement as to the result to be obtained and had inserted a clause in their contract in order to induce a court in another Member State to give a ruling on the point.[240] The Court held that the artificial nature of this expedient was underlined by the fact that the remedies available under the law of the first Member State to contest the tax in question had not been used.[241]

This judgment has been severely criticized by commentators on the ground that the Court exceeded its powers by going too deeply into the facts of the main proceedings, specifically with the intention of making the national court respect the limits of the Court's jurisdiction insofar as it is to give only preliminary rulings which actually contribute towards resolving the main dispute. It has been argued that this puts at risk the whole relationship of trust

---

[236] ECJ, Case C-231/89 *Gmurzynska-Bscher* [1990] E.C.R. I-4003, para. 23; ECJ, Case C-118/94 *Associazione Italiana per il WWF and Others* [1996] E.C.R. I-1223, para. 15; ECJ, Case C-85/95 *Reisdorf* [1996] E.C.R. I-6257, para. 16; ECJ, Case C-28/95 *Leur-Bloem* [1997] E.C.R. I-4161, para. 26.

[237] ECJ, Case 244/80 *Foglia v Novello* ('*Foglia v Novello II*') [1981] E.C.R. 3045, para. 18. See further A. Tizzano, 'Foglia—Novello Atto II, ovvero la crisi dell' 'uso alternativo' dell' Art. 177 CEE' (1982) I foro Italiano 308–15.

[238] ECJ, Case 267/86 *Van Eycke* [1988] E.C.R. 4769, para. 12; ECJ, Case C-118/94 *Associazione Italiana per il WWF and Others* [1996] E.C.R. I-1223, para. 15; ECJ, Case C-129/94 *Bernáldez* [1996] E.C.R. I-1829, para. 7; ECJ, Case C-36/99 *Idéal Tourisme* [2000] E.C.R. I-6049, para. 22 (the documents in the case contained nothing to show that the parties to the main proceedings had colluded).

[239] Cf. ECJ, Case 267/86 *Van Eycke*, Report for the Hearing, at 4774, second column.

[240] ECJ, Case 104/79 *Foglia v Novello* ('*Foglia v Novello I*') [1980] E.C.R. 745, para.10. Where a court in one Member State makes a reference for a preliminary ruling relating to the legality of another Member State's legislation, the hurdle for admissibility will invariably be set high: see para. 3.37.

[241] ECJ, Case 104/79 *Foglia v Novello I*, para. 10.

between the Court of Justice and the national courts on which the cooperation mechanism set in place by what is now Art. 267 TFEU is founded.[242] It is therefore not surprising that subsequently the Court has done everything to reduce the scope of this case-law to a hard core of exceptional cases:[243] where it is clear from the factual data set out in the order for reference that the main proceedings are manifestly spurious, the Court will decline jurisdiction on the grounds that answering the national court's preliminary questions will not assist it in giving judgment (which is unnecessary if there is no 'dispute'). Clearly, such a situation will arise only exceptionally.[244]

IV. The Duty to Request a Preliminary Ruling

A. General

3.43 The third paragraph of Art. 267 TFEU provides that where a question concerning the interpretation of Union law or the validity of acts of Union institutions, bodies, offices, or agencies is raised in a national court and it considers that a decision on the question is necessary to enable it to give judgment, it is bound to bring the matter before the Court of Justice where 'there is no judicial remedy under national law' against the national court's decisions.

B. What national courts and tribunals are involved?

(1) Highest courts

3.44 In the first place, the highest courts in the hierarchy are under a duty to make a preliminary reference, irrespective as to whether they have general competence (for example, the UK

---

[242] K. Lenaerts, 'Toegewezen bevoegdheden en prejudiciële evenwichtsoefeningen in de rechtsorde van de Europese Gemeenschap. Een perspectiefbeeld' (1983–1984) R.W. 129, at 143–9; A. Tizzano, 'Litiges fictifs et compétence préjudicielle de la Cour de justice européenne' (1981) R.G.D.I.P. 514, at 524–5.

[243] ECJ, Case 46/80 *Vinal* [1981] E.C.R. 77, paras 5–7, and the Opinion of Advocate-General G. Reischl in that case, at 98, which refers to the exceptional nature of *Foglia v Novello I*.

[244] Consequently, the case-law on this point is in fact reverting to the Court's former stance: cf. ECJ, Case 20/64 *Albatros* [1965] E.C.R. 29, at 33–4; ECJ, Case 261/81 *Rau* [1982] E.C.R. 3961, paras 8–9; ECJ, Case 267/86 *Van Eycke* [1988] E.C.R. 4769, para. 12. But the principle that spurious proceedings are inadmissible remains: ECJ, Joined Cases C-297/88 and C-197/89 *Dzodzi* [1990] E.C.R. I-3763, para. 40; cf. ECJ, Case C-88/91 *Federconsorzi* [1992] E.C.R. I-4035, paras 6–10 (Union law applicable through a contractual provision); ECJ, Case C-412/93 *Leclerc-Siplec* [1995] E.C.R. I-179, para. 14 (the fact that the parties to the main proceedings are in agreement as to the result to be obtained makes the dispute no less real); ECJ, Case C-408/95 *Eurotunnel and Others* [1997] E.C.R. I-6315, para. 22 (the reality of the dispute may be inferred from the fact that all the arguments raised by the plaintiff in the main proceedings have been contested by the defendant in those proceedings); ECJ, Case C-451/99 *Cura Anlagen* [2002] E.C.R. I-3193, para. 27 (the preliminary question was admissible because the main proceedings related to a genuine contract the performance or annulment of which depended on a question of Union law, even if some of the information on the file might give rise to a suspicion that the situation underlying the main proceedings was contrived with a view to obtaining a decision from the Court on a question of Union law of general interest); ECJ, Case C-341/01 *Plato Plastik Robert Frank* [2004] E.C.R. I-4883, para. 30 (the fact that the parties to the main proceedings were in agreement as to the interpretation of the Union provisions in question did not affect the reality of the dispute). See further Opinion of Advocate-General A. Tizzano in ECJ, Case C-144/04 *Mangold* [2005] E.C.R. I-9981, points 22–35.

Supreme Court) or specialized jurisdiction (for example, the *Tariefcommissie voor Belas-tingzaken*, a revenue court in the Netherlands[245]).

The idea behind this is that in the national legal systems decisions of the highest courts bind lower courts (in one way or another), with the result that the most efficient way of securing the uniformity of Union law in all the Member States is to oblige courts of last resort to refer questions to the Court of Justice for a preliminary ruling.[246] If that obligation were to be extended to all courts and tribunals, the Court of Justice would be overloaded and there would be no real additional gain in terms of the uniformity of Union law, since the lower courts have to follow decisions of courts of last resort which are the outcome of collaboration with the Court of Justice. Naturally, this does not detract from the right of any court[247] to decide to refer a question to the Court of Justice of its own motion.

(2) No remedy available against the decision of a lower court

Second, courts other than those of last resort may in certain circumstances take decisions against which there is no remedy. Are those courts then under a duty to make a reference for a preliminary ruling under the third paragraph of Art. 267 TFEU? The Court of Justice appears to have answered this question in the affirmative in an *obiter dictum* in the leading case of *Costa v ENEL*, decided in 1964. It stated with regard to a request for a preliminary ruling from an Italian *Giudice Conciliatore* (magistrate) that 'By the terms of [Art. 267 TFEU] national courts against whose decisions, as in the present case, there is no judicial remedy, must refer the matter to the Court of Justice so that a preliminary ruling may be given . . . '.[248] Accordingly, where a lower court has the power to prevent an appeal from it, it must make a reference if it is minded to exercise its power not to allow an appeal. **3.45**

(3) Interim proceedings

A judge hearing an application for interim relief, where no judicial remedy is available against his order, is in a special position. In response to a preliminary question relating specifically to that situation, the Court of Justice ruled that 'a national court or tribunal is not required to refer to the Court a question of interpretation or of validity mentioned in [Art. 267 TFEU] when the question is raised in interlocutory proceedings for [interim relief], even where no judicial remedy is available against the decision to be taken in the context of those proceedings provided that each of the parties is entitled to institute proceedings or to require proceedings to be instituted on the substance of the case and that during such proceedings the question provisionally decided in the summary proceedings may be re-examined and may be the subject of a reference to the Court under [Art. 267 TFEU]'.[249] Subsequently, the Court refined this by stating that the requirements of the third paragraph of Art. 267 TFEU are observed even if only the unsuccessful party may **3.46**

---

[245] ECJ, Case 26/62 *Van Gend & Loos* [1963] E.C.R. 1; ECJ, Joined Cases 28/62 to 30/62 *Da Costa en Schaake and Others* [1963] E.C.R. 31, at 38.

[246] ECJ, Case 107/76 *Hoffmann-La Roche* [1977] E.C.R. 957, first subpara. of para. 5: '[T]he particular object of the third para. [of Art. 267 TFEU] is to prevent a body of case-law not in accord with the rules of Union law from coming into existence in any Member State.' See also ECJ, Joined Cases 35/82 and 36/82 *Morson and Jhanjan* [1982] E.C.R. 3723, para. 8.

[247] But see para. 22.05 (discussing the viability of former Art. 35 EU after the entry into force of the Lisbon Treaty).

[248] ECJ, Case 6/64 *Costa v ENEL* [1964] E.C.R. 585, third para., at 592 (emphasis added).

[249] ECJ, Case 107/76 *Hoffmann-La Roche* [1977] E.C.R. 957, para. 6.

bring proceedings as to the substance and the action is tried 'before courts or tribunals belonging to a jurisdictional system different from that under which the interlocutory proceedings are conducted, provided that it is still possible to refer to the Court under [Art. 267 TFEU] any questions of [Union] law which are raised'.[250]

(4) Benelux Court of Justice

3.47 Finally, the Benelux Court of Justice (see para. 3.14), which gives definitive rulings on questions of interpretation of uniform Benelux law, may be obliged to make a reference to the Court of Justice under the third paragraph of Art. 267 TFEU.[251] The Court of Justice has held, however, that if, before making a reference to the Benelux Court, a national court has submitted a question of (Union) law to the Court of Justice, the Benelux Court is released from its obligation to submit the question if it would be couched in 'substantially the same terms' (see para. 3.52).

C. Decisions against which there is no judicial remedy under national law

(1) Existence of a judicial remedy

3.48 The question as to against what decisions a 'judicial remedy' exists is a matter of national law, as is clear from the actual wording of the third paragraph of Art. 267 TFEU ('against whose decisions there is no judicial remedy under national law').[252] All the same, Union law does play a role, more specifically in ascertaining what type of possible 'judicial remedy' precludes the obligation to make a reference for a preliminary ruling. The starting point for any inquiry should be the aim of the third paragraph of Art. 267 TFEU, which is to avoid the most authoritative case-law in any given Member State developing contrary to Union law, thus putting all courts in that Member State at risk of going off in the same—wrong—direction.

Consequently, the obligation to make a preliminary reference arises whenever the national court finds that there is no judicial remedy available against its decisions that can normally be deployed against judicial decisions, no matter how the remedy is described. Whether the remedy is termed 'ordinary' or 'exceptional' has no bearing in this regard. The only decisive

---

[250] ECJ, Joined Cases 35/82 and 36/82 *Morson and Jhanjan* [1982] E.C.R. 3723, paras 8–9. See also Opinion of Advocate-General J. Kokott in ECJ, Case C-175/06 *Tedesco* [2007] E.C.R. I-7829, particularly points 26–28; the Court of Justice did not have the opportunity to rule on such matters as the preliminary questions became devoid of purpose and the case was therefore removed from the register: ECJ (order of 27 September 2007) Case C-175/06 *Tedesco* [2007] E.C.R. I-7829.

[251] ECJ, Case C-337/95 *Parfums Christian Dior* [1997] E.C.R. I-6013, para. 26. The first reference to be submitted by the Benelux Court of Justice (*Benelux-Gerechtshof*) was in ECJ, Case C-265/00 *Campina Melkunie* [2004] E.C.R. I-1699. The Court of Justice's ruling in that case was delivered on the same day as its ruling in ECJ, Case C-363/99 *Koninklijke KPN Nederland* [2004] E.C.R. I-1619 which involved the submission of similar preliminary questions from the *Gerechtshof te 's-Gravenhage* (Regional Court of Appeal, The Hague).

[252] See ECJ, Case C-14/08 *Roda Golf & Beach Resort* [2009] E.C.R. I-5439, paras 28–29: while there had been conflicting case-law and academic disagreement with respect to whether it was possible to appeal against a decision like the one that the referring court (*Juzgado de Primera Instancia e Instrucción No. 5, San Javier* in Spain) would deliver in the main proceedings, the Court found that it was not for it to give a ruling on that issue; it was sufficient that the referring court had indicated in its reference for a preliminary ruling that the decision it will deliver in the main proceedings will be final. The determination involved in this case was in relation to the admissibility of references from last instance courts for the purposes of former Art. 68 EC: see para. 22.02.

test is whether the legal issues that the lower court has decided may, as a matter of course, be subjected to a fresh judicial assessment. This is clearly the case with an appeal on a point of law or in cassation proceedings, which must accordingly be deemed to be a 'judicial remedy' within the meaning of the third paragraph of Art. 267 TFEU.[253] Questions of Union law are in fact legal issues that are definitively settled in the highest courts.

(2) Wholly exceptional judicial remedies

In contrast, the existence of wholly exceptional judicial remedies—even where they may be available against decisions of the highest courts—may not be invoked in order to avoid the obligation to seek a preliminary ruling.[254] Examples are applications for the revision of a judgment or tierce-opposition proceedings. The *Verfassungsbeschwerde* (constitutional appeal) which may be brought before the Federal Constitutional Court against a judgment of a court of last resort (for example, the *Bundesgerichtshof* or the *Bundesfinanzhof*) is an example from Germany. The existence of such an exceptional remedy—which, moreover, does not enable all the legal issues decided by the court of last resort to be reviewed, but relates only to the compatibility of the contested judgment with the German Basic Law— does not detract from the obligation of the ordinary German courts of last resort to request a preliminary ruling from the Court of Justice.[255] **3.49**

D. Limits placed on the duty to request a preliminary ruling

(1) Irrelevant questions

First and foremost, courts coming within the scope of the third paragraph of Art. 267 TFEU have discretion to assess the relevance of a request for a preliminary ruling (see paras 3.31–3.33). The Court of Justice enlarged upon this in the leading case of *CILFIT*, decided in 1982.[256] The mere fact that a party contends that the dispute gives rise to a question concerning the interpretation of Union law or the validity of an act of a Union institution, agency, body or office does not mean that the court concerned is compelled to request a preliminary ruling.[257] The Court takes the view that 'it follows from the relationship **3.50**

---

[253] The fact that, as in Sweden, leave is required from the highest court in order to lodge an appeal does not have the effect of depriving the parties of a judicial remedy, with the result that this must be regarded as an 'exceptional remedy'. Where appropriate, the question of Union law raised in a dispute may place the highest court under a duty to grant leave to appeal and, at a later stage, refer a question for a preliminary ruling to the Court of Justice (ECJ, Case C-99/00 *Lyckeskog* [2002] E.C.R. I-4839, paras 10–19). See further ECJ, Case C-210/06 *Cartesio* [2008] E.C.R. I-9641, paras 75–79.

[254] ECJ (judgment of 15 January 2013), Case C-416/10 *Križan and Others*, not reported, para. 72.

[255] See, e.g. BVerfG of 9 January 2001 (1 BvR 1036/99), the German Federal Constitutional Court pointing out that it is not an additional appeal jurisdiction.

[256] ECJ, Case 283/81 *CILFIT* [1982] E.C.R. 3415.

[257] Cf. ECJ, Case 283/81 *CILFIT*, para. 9. As is well-known, Advocate-General F.G. Jacobs expressed the view in his Opinion in ECJ, Case C-338/95 *Wiener* [1997] E.C.R. I-6495, points 12–20, that national courts should show self-restraint in making references where there is no question of general importance or the ruling is not likely to promote the uniform application of Union law. For discussion of other relevant Opinions of Advocates-General and additional commentary, see further K. Lenaerts, 'The Unity of European Law and the Overload of the ECJ—The System of Preliminary Rulings Revisited', in G. Ziccardi Capaldo (ed.), (2005) *The Global Community—Yearbook of International Law and Jurisprudence*, Vol. 1 (Oxford, Oceana Publications, 2006), 173–201 (reprinted in I. Pernice, J. Kokott, and C. Saunders (eds), *The Future of the European Judicial System in a Comparative Perspective* (Baden-Baden, Nomos, 2006), 211–39). For a broader view (including but not limited to, preliminary rulings) advocating more responsibility placed on the national

between the second and third paras of [Art. 267 TFEU] that the courts or tribunals referred to in the third para. have the same discretion as any other national court or tribunal to ascertain whether a decision on a question of [Union] law is necessary to enable them to give judgment. Accordingly, those courts or tribunals are not obliged to refer to the Court of Justice a question concerning the interpretation of [Union] law [or the validity of an act of a Union institution, body, office, or agency] raised before them if that question is not relevant, that is to say, if the answer to that question, regardless of what it may be, can in no way affect the outcome of the case.'[258] In such a case, the Court of Justice would moreover dismiss the request for a preliminary ruling in any event on account of the irrelevance of the question referred (see paras 3.31–3.36).

(2) Limits to the duty to refer with respect to relevant questions

3.51   Next, it falls to consider the actual exceptions to the obligation to request a preliminary ruling where the question is manifestly relevant for the purposes of reaching a decision in the main proceedings. There are three instances in which the Court of Justice has tempered the obligation to seek a preliminary ruling in the interests of more efficiently achieving the aim of the third paragraph of Art. 267 TFEU, namely 'to prevent the occurrence within the [Union] of divergences in judicial decisions on questions of [Union] law'.[259]

(a) Identical or similar question

3.52   First: in the 1963 judgment in *Da Costa en Schaake*, the Court ruled that 'the authority of an interpretation under [Art. 267 TFEU] already given by the Court may deprive the obligation [to seek a preliminary ruling] of its purpose and thus empty it of its substance. Such is the case especially when the question raised is materially identical with a question which has already been the subject of a preliminary ruling in a similar case'.[260] The national court which is obliged in principle under the third paragraph of Art. 267 TFEU to make a reference to the Court of Justice is released from its obligation provided that it follows the existing preliminary ruling. It is only the obligation to make a reference that ceases to apply, not the possibility of seeking a ruling. More specifically, where the national court would like the Court of Justice to amend, qualify, or limit its earlier preliminary ruling—for instance, in the light of the particular facts of the main action—the only solution is for the national court to make use of that possibility.[261]

(b) The answer can be clearly deduced from the case-law (acte éclairé)

3.53   Second: 'The same effect, as regards the limits set to the obligation laid down by the third para. of [Art. 267 TFEU], may be produced where previous decisions of the Court have

---

courts, see S. Prechal, 'National Courts in EU Judicial Structures' (2006) Y.E.L. 429–50. As to the importance of the assessment of relevance by national courts of last instance for the functioning of the Union system of judicial protection, see J. T. Nowak 'Wettigheidstoetsing van handelingen van de instellingen van de Europese Unie: complementaire rechtsbescherming in een meerlagige context' (2013) T.B.P. 195–211.

[258] ECJ, Case 283/81 *CILFIT* [1982] E.C.R. 3415, para. 10; ECJ (judgment of 18 July 2013), Case C-136/12 *Consiglio nazionale dei geologi*, not reported, para. 26.

[259] ECJ, Case 283/81 *CILFIT*, para. 7.

[260] ECJ, Joined Cases 28/62 to 30/62 *Da Costa en Schaake and Others* [1963] E.C.R. 31, at 38, confirmed by ECJ, Case 283/81 *CILFIT* [1982] E.C.R. 3415, para. 13 and ECJ, Case C-337/95 *Parfums Christian Dior* [1997] E.C.R. I-6013, paras 29–30 (where it was held that the question had to be in 'substantially the same terms').

[261] ECJ, Case 283/81 *CILFIT*, para. 15.

already dealt with the point of law in question, irrespective of the nature of the proceedings which led to those decisions, even though the questions at issue are not strictly identical.'[262] This is known as the *acte éclairé* doctrine and is an extension of the first exception: it is no longer a requirement for the earlier judgment of the Court to have ruled on a virtually identical preliminary question. In contrast, it is sufficient that the earlier decision should provide an answer to the question of Union law which has arisen in the main proceedings, regardless of the procedural context in which it came about. This also provides an explanation as to why the questions at issue need not be completely identical, which would appear to be out of the question where the earlier judgment was not given in answer to a request for a preliminary ruling. The only critical point is whether the decision is capable of being regarded as 'settled case-law' or one of a number of 'previous decisions' as the English translation has it, or, in other words, whether it can be definitely regarded as constituting the Court of Justice's answer to the question of Union law that has arisen. Thus, a judgment given pursuant to Arts 258 to 260 TFEU in which the Court declared that a Member State had failed to fulfil its obligations under Union law will generally contain an interpretation of provisions and principles of that law.[263] Insofar as that is so, national courts subject to the third paragraph of Art. 267 TFEU can extract from the judgment what they need in order to answer the questions concerning the interpretation of Union law that are determinative of the main proceedings pending before them. In common with any court, they are even obliged to do this,[264] unless they opt to exercise their right to bring the matter before the Court of Justice anew, perhaps with a view to an adjustment of the case-law.[265]

(c) Acte clair

Third: '[T]he correct application of [Union] law may be so obvious as to leave no scope for any reasonable doubt as to the manner in which the question raised is to be resolved. Before it comes to the conclusion that such is the case, the national court or tribunal must be convinced that the matter is equally obvious to the courts of the other Member States and to the Court of Justice.'[266] If that condition is satisfied, the national court may 'refrain from

3.54

---

[262] ECJ, Case 283/81 *CILFIT*, para. 14. Affirmed in ECJ, Case C-260/07 *Pedro IV Servicios* [2009] E.C.R. I-2437, para. 36.

[263] The fact that the Commission discontinues infringement proceedings under Art. 258 TFEU against a Member State concerning a piece of legislation has no effect on the obligation upon a court of last instance of that Member State to refer to the Court of Justice a preliminary question on the interpretation of Union law so as to be able to assess the compatibility with that law of the national legislation which was the subject of the infringement proceedings. This is because the Commission is not empowered to determine conclusively, by opinions formulated pursuant to Art. 258 TFEU or by other statements of its attitude under that procedure, the rights and duties of a Member State and hence determine the scope of Union law. The rights and duties of Member States may be determined only by a judgment of the Court of Justice: ECJ, Case C-393/98 *Gomes Valente* [2001] E.C.R. I-1327, paras 17–19.

[264] ECJ, Joined Cases 314/81 to 316/81 and 83/82 *Waterkeyn* [1982] E.C.R. 4337, paras 13–16.

[265] ECJ, Case 283/81 *CILFIT* [1982] E.C.R. 3415, para. 15. In such a case, however, the ECJ might give its ruling by reasoned order. Indeed, pursuant to Art. 99 of the ECJ Rules of Procedure, the Court may, for similar reasons, decide to give its ruling by reasoned order (i.e. where a question is identical to a question on which the Court has already ruled, where the answer to such a question may be clearly deduced from existing case-law, or where the answer to the question admits of no reasonable doubt), provided that certain requirements have been complied with.

[266] ECJ, Case 283/81 *CILFIT*, para. 16.

submitting the question to the Court of Justice and take upon itself the responsibility for resolving it'.[267] This exception is known as the *acte clair* doctrine.

The strict conditions to which implementation of the *acte clair* doctrine is subject are designed to prevent national courts from abusing the doctrine in order to evade their obligation to seek a preliminary ruling where they are disinclined to adhere to the Court's case-law. Both the French *Conseil d'Etat* and the German *Bundesfinanzhof* at one time abused the *acte clair* doctrine in this way.[268] According to those courts, the wording of the third paragraph of Art. 249 EC (now Art. 288 TFEU) was so clear that it was unnecessary to seek a preliminary ruling from the Court of Justice on the effect within a Member State's national legal system of a directive that had failed to be implemented within the prescribed period. By reference to the plain words of Art. 249 EC (now Art. 288 TFEU), however, they decided, completely contrary to the settled case-law of the Court of Justice,[269] that in the circumstances in question a directive could never have direct effect on account of its legal nature.

The *CILFIT* formulation of the *acte clair* doctrine is the expression of a particularly subtle compromise.[270] On the one hand, the Court sought to reinforce spontaneous collaboration on the part of the highest national courts by allowing them to take the responsibility upon themselves to decide questions of Union law where it is not reasonably conceivable that anyone would come to a different answer. A very limited category of extremely obvious questions of Union law is involved here. It would have been insensitive of the Court to have placed no trust in the judgment of the highest national courts with regard even to that sort of question. For other types of questions, the national courts have to place their trust in the Court of Justice once they realize that more than one answer is conceivable. On the other hand, the Court seeks to constrain the judgment of the highest national courts as to the obvious nature of the—apparently only conceivable—answer to a question of Union law as much as possible in order to preclude bona fide inadvertence. To this end, the Court has listed three factors that the highest national courts have to take into account before they are entitled to consider that they may release themselves from their obligation to seek a preliminary ruling. Those factors have to do with the 'characteristic features of [Union] law and the particular difficulties to which its interpretation gives rise'.[271] These factors are as follows: (1) the interpretation of a provision of Union law involves a comparison of the various language versions, all of which are authentic; (2) given that Union law uses terminology peculiar to it, legal concepts do not necessarily have the same meaning as they do in the different national legal systems; (3) every provision of Union law must be placed in its context and interpreted 'in the light of the provisions of [Union] law as a

---

[267] ECJ, Case 283/81 *CILFIT*, para. 16; ECJ, Case C-340/99 *TNT Traco* [2001] E.C.R. I-4109, para. 35.

[268] France: Conseil d'Etat, 22 December 1978, *Ministre de l'Intérieur v Cohn-Bendit* (1979) R.T.D. E. 168–89, translated in [1980] 1 C.M.L.R. 543; Germany: Bundesfinanzhof, 16 July 1981, (1981) EuR. 442–4. For English examples, see *R v London Boroughs Transport Committee, ex parte Freight Transport Association Ltd* [1992] 1 C.M.L.R. 5 and *Kirklees Borough Council v Wickes Building Supplies Ltd* [1992] 3 W.L.R. 170.

[269] For further discussion of the direct effect of directives, see K. Lenaerts and P. Van Nuffel (R. Bray and N. Cambien (eds)), *European Union Law* (3rd edn, London, Sweet & Maxwell, 2011), paras 22.80–22.85.

[270] Cf. the opposite view taken in the Opinion of Advocate-General F. Capotorti in ECJ, Case 283/81 *CILFIT* [1982] E.C.R. 3415, at 3442.

[271] ECJ, Case 283/81 *CILFIT* [1982] E.C.R. 3415, para. 17.

whole, regard being had to the objectives thereof and to its state of evolution at the date on which the provision in question is to be applied'.[272] It is self-evident that if these three factors were scrupulously taken into account, the number of cases in which 'the correct application of [Union] law is so obvious as to leave no scope for any reasonable doubt'[273] would be reduced to an absolute minimum.[274]

(3) Post-*CILFIT* case-law

Through the years, the Court of Justice has elaborated further on the application of **3.55** *CILFIT*. In particular, two cases delivered by the Court in 2005—*Intermodal Transports*[275] and *Gaston Schul Douane-expediteur*[276]—should be mentioned in this regard. In *Intermodal Transports*, the Court of Justice ruled that a decision of an administrative authority of one Member State that the highest court of another Member State considers contrary to Union law and thus seeks to depart from does not trigger the obligation to make a reference under the third paragraph of Art. 267 TFEU.[277] While underscoring that such national court, before coming to the conclusion that the correct application of a provision of Union law is 'so obvious that there is no scope as to the manner in which the question raised is to be resolved', must be convinced that the matter is equally obvious to the courts of the other Member States and to the Court of Justice in accordance with *CILFIT*, it found that such court cannot be required to ensure that, in addition, the matter is equally obvious to bodies of a non-judicial nature such as administrative authorities.[278]

Subsequently, the Court made clear in the *Gaston Schul* case, delivered about three months after *Intermodal Transports*, that the *CILFIT* case-law does not apply to questions relating to the validity of a Union act.[279] There, the Court of Justice was confronted with a preliminary reference concerning the question whether a last instance court could refrain from applying provisions of a Union regulation without referring a question on the validity of those provisions under circumstances where the Court of Justice had already ruled that analogous provisions of another regulation were invalid. In response, the Court held that courts of last instance are obliged to refer questions on the validity of a Union measure in accordance with the third paragraph of Art. 267 TFEU and that the *CILFIT* judgment, pertaining to questions of interpretation, could not be extended to questions relating to the validity of Union acts. The uniform application of Union law is indeed 'vital' where the validity of a Union act is in question and the Court of Justice is in the 'best position' to rule on the validity of such act in view of the participation of interested parties through Arts 23 and 24 of the Statute.[280]

---

[272] ECJ, Case 283/81 *CILFIT*, paras 18–20.

[273] ECJ, Case 283/81 *CILFIT*, para. 21.

[274] *CILFIT* may, however, also be abused: see A. Arnull, 'The Use and Abuse of Article 177 EEC [now Art. 267 TFEU]' (1989) Mod.L.Rev. 622–39, in which the author cites a number of English cases which wrongly used the *CILFIT* judgment in order not to seek a preliminary ruling.

[275] ECJ, Case C-495/03 *Intermodal Transports* [2005] E.C.R. I-8151.

[276] ECJ, Case C-461/03 *Gaston Schul Douane-expediteur* [2005] E.C.R. I-10513.

[277] ECJ, Case C-495/03 *Intermodal Transports* [2005] E.C.R. I-8151, paras 33–45.

[278] ECJ, Case C-495/03 *Intermodal Transports*, para. 39.

[279] ECJ, Case C-461/03 *Gaston Schul Douane-expediteur* [2005] E.C.R. I-10513, para. 19.

[280] ECJ, Case C-461/03 *Gaston Schul Douane-expediteur*, paras 20–24.

E. Enforcement of the obligation to request a preliminary ruling

(1) Infringement action

3.56 There is no remedy available from the Court of Justice to parties to the main proceedings against a refusal of a court of last resort to make a preliminary reference. The Commission or a Member State may, however, seek a declaration from the Court of Justice pursuant to Arts 258 or 259 TFEU that, through its national court's refusal to seek a ruling, the Member State in question has infringed the third paragraph of Art. 267 TFEU. Courts and tribunals are in fact 'institutions of the Member State concerned'.[281]

The Commission acknowledges a duty to oversee the way in which national courts subject to the obligation to seek preliminary rulings make use of the *acte clair* doctrine enshrined in the judgment in *CILFIT*.[282]

(2) Difficulties

3.57 The institution of proceedings for infringement of Union law on account of the failure of a national court to comply with its obligation under the third paragraph of Art. 267 TFEU is not, however, an efficient way of enforcing that obligation. In the first place, the parties to the main proceedings are not directly assisted thereby. Second, whilst in such proceedings it is no defence for a Member State to plead the independence under its Constitution of the State institution responsible for the infringement of Union law,[283] in a '[Union] based on the rule of law'[284] the essential principle of the constitutional independence of the judiciary from the executive and the legislature nevertheless implies that a national government which is unsuccessful in an action brought against it under Art. 258 TFEU can count on comprehension where it is not in a position to compel the offending court to change its position. Unlike other 'independent' institutions of the State (for example, legislative bodies, autonomous entities forming part of a federation, etc.), in respect of which it is felt that the Member State should, where necessary, adjust its internal structure in such a way that it is always in a position to ensure that those institutions effectively comply with Union law, even if this is at the expense of their independence, a certain reluctance is—properly—felt in advocating that idea as far as the highest national courts are concerned. Commentators are also at one in taking the view that it would be inappropriate to enforce

---

[281] ECJ, Joined Cases 314/81 to 316/81 and 83/82 *Waterkeyn* [1982] E.C.R. 4337, para. 14. See also ECJ, Case C-224/01 *Köbler* [2003] E.C.R. I-10239; ECJ, Case C-129/00 *Commission v Italy* [2003] E.C.R. I-14637.

[282] Answer given by President G. Thorn on behalf of the Commission on 25 July 1983 to a written question from A. Tyrrell MEP, [1983] O.J. C268/25. See, e.g. the reasoned opinion of the Commission concerning the failure of the Swedish Supreme Court to comply with the duty to refer under Art. 267 TFEU (2003/2161, C(2004) 3899, 13 October 2004. If a national court of last instance does not refer under circumstances where it is under an obligation to do so in accordance with the third para. of Art. 267 TFEU, then this constitutes an infringement of Union law, and often of national law as well. In Belgium, this constitutes a violation of Art. 13 of the Belgian Constitution. In Germany, the *Bundesverfassungsgericht* held that the failure of the *Bundesverwaltungsgericht* to refer a preliminary question to the Court of Justice was in breach of Art.101(1)(2) of the Basic Law: see BverfG, 9 January 2001 (2001) Eu.GR.Z. 150.

[283] See para. 5.65.

[284] ECJ, Case 294/83 *Les Verts v European Parliament* [1986] E.C.R. 1339, para. 23 (referring to the European (Economic) Community, as it then was).

the obligation laid down in the third paragraph of Art. 267 TFEU by means of proceedings under Arts 258 and 259 TFEU.[285]

The conclusion is that, in practice, the obligation to seek a preliminary ruling cannot be enforced directly. Instead, compliance with that obligation is based on the relationship of trust linking the highest national courts and the Court of Justice in a context of efficient collaboration. That being said, when the highest court of a Member State structurally fails, within its national legal system, to correct an application of national law that is in breach of Union law, the Commission has shown that it will not refrain from instituting infringement proceedings against that Member State. This was the case in *Commission v Italy*,[286] where the Italian Supreme Court did not disown a widely held judicial construction concerning rules of evidence applying to claims for reimbursement of charges paid but not due which was in breach of Union law. Although the infringement proceedings were instituted against the Member State concerned for failure to amend rules of evidence that were wrongly constructed by its judiciary, one could not escape the impression that the Commission had also taken issue with the position of the Italian Supreme Court, since it had not sought a preliminary ruling from the Court to clarify the matter although it appeared from national case-law that the application of those rules of evidence was not clear in the light of Union law. It could be argued that through this course of action, the Commission attempted, at least indirectly, to enforce the obligation enshrined in the third paragraph of Art. 267 TFEU.

(3) Claim in damages

However, Union law requires Member States to recognize the possibility of a claim in **3.58** damages against the public authorities where an infringement by a court of last resort of its obligation to make a reference for a preliminary ruling demonstrably thwarts a right conferred on individuals by Union law. The Court confirmed this in the case of *Köbler*.[287] Especially in cases where the *acte clair* doctrine is abused and the court of last resort shirks its obligation to seek a preliminary ruling in order to ignore the settled case-law of the Court of Justice on the interpretation of a particular provision on the purported ground that it is obvious, it may well be imagined that the interested individual may identify an individual right which is denied to him (loss or damage) as a result (causal link) of the national court's

---

[285] See, for instance, M. Wathelet, 'Adieu, Monsieur le Professeur: de la liberté des juges nationaux de poser des questions préjudicielles à la Cour de justice de l'Union européenne' (2010) Revue de la Faculté de droit de l'Université de Liège 449–55. However, see n. 282.

[286] ECJ, Case C-129/00, *Commission v Italy* [2003] E.C.R. I-14637.

[287] ECJ, Case C-224/01 *Köbler* [2003] E.C.R. I-10239, paras 30–50; see also ECJ, Case C-495/03 *Intermodal Transports* [2005] E.C.R. I-8151, para. 37; ECJ, Case C-173/03 *Traghetti del Mediterraneo* [2006] E.C.R. I-5177, paras 30–46. It is for the internal legal order of each Member State to designate the competent court to deal with such claims. According to the Court of Justice, the independence of the judiciary and the principle of *res judicata* do not preclude recognition of the principle of State liability stemming from a decision of a court adjudicating at last instance (ECJ, Case C-224/01 *Köbler*, paras 42, 43 and 46). See also J. Kokott, T. Henze, and C. Sobotta, 'Die Pflicht zur Vorlage an den Europäischen Gerichtshof und die Folgen ihrer Verletzung' (2006) Juristenzeitung 633–41. For a particularly critical view, see P. J. Wattel, '*Köbler, CILFIT* and *Welthgrove*: We Can't Go On Meeting Like This' (2004) C.M.L. Rev. 177–90: the author argues that the Court of Justice also ought to be able to be held liable for manifest breaches of Union law; the author, however, overlooks the fact that the Court of Justice, unlike courts of last resort in the Member States, is the highest court for the interpretation of Union law, whose decisions in this regard are, by definition, held to be correct.

refusal to comply with the third paragraph of Art. 267 TFEU (breach of Union law).[288] This development accords well with the right recognized by a number of Member States in connection with State liability in damages for loss or damage caused to individuals as a result of a breach of superior law on the part of the judiciary.[289]

F. Obligation to request a preliminary ruling *praeter legem*

(1) *Foto-Frost*

3.59   Under the landmark *Foto-Frost* case, where a court or tribunal not subject to the third paragraph of Art. 267 TFEU perceives that an act of a Union institution, body, office, or agency is invalid, it may not make such a finding itself, but must seek a preliminary ruling thereon from the Court of Justice.[290] At first sight, this obligation detracts from the national court's freedom under the second paragraph of Art. 267 TFEU to decide whether or not to make a reference to the Court of Justice. But the Court has held that, 'In enabling national courts, against whose decisions there is a judicial remedy under national law, to refer to the Court for a preliminary ruling questions on interpretation or validity, [Art. 267 TFEU] did not settle the question whether those courts themselves may declare that acts of [Union] institutions are invalid.'[291] Consequently, the relevant provision of the Treaty had a lacuna that the Court filled by answering that question in the negative.

In the Court's view, this was necessary for three reasons: first, divergences between courts in the Member States as to the validity of Union acts would be liable to place in jeopardy the unity of Union law; second, since the Court has exclusive jurisdiction to declare void an act of a Union institution (under what is now Art. 263 TFEU), the coherence of the system of judicial protection established by the Treaties requires that where the validity of a Union act

---

[288] By analogy with ECJ, Joined Cases C-6/90 and C-9/90 *Francovich and Others* [1991] E.C.R. I-5357, paras 39–40; ECJ, Joined Cases C-46/93 and C-48/93 *Brasserie du Pêcheur and Factortame* [1996] E.C. R. I-1029, para. 51. See also K. Lenaerts and P. Van Nuffel (R. Bray N. Cambien (eds)), *European Union Law* (3rd edn, London, Sweet & Mawell, 2011), paras 22.92–22.94. The Member State concerned may incur liability under Union law all the more readily inasmuch as the highest national court has no discretion in applying the third para. of Art. 267 TFEU: see para. 4.46.

[289] Belgium: Cass., 19 December 1991 (1992) J.T. 142. Netherlands: in principle there is no recognition of State liability on account of judicial conduct amounting to fault: Hoge Raad, 17 March 1978 (1979) NJ 204, but in a judgment of 11 October 1991 ((1992) NJ 62), the Hoge Raad recognized that there may be State liability for the wrong interpretation of a provision of the Code of Criminal Procedure by the public prosecutor's office.

[290] ECJ, Case 314/85 *Foto-Frost* [1987] E.C.R. 4199. Bebr identifies the autonomous nature of Union law as an additional reason for the exclusive jurisdiction of the Court of Justice to declare a Union measure invalid: see G. Bebr, 'The Reinforcement of the Constitutional Review of Community Acts under Art. 177 EEC Treaty [now Art. 267 TFEU] (cases 314/85 and 133 to 136/85)' (1988) C.M.L. Rev. 667, at 678. See also ECJ, Case C-6/99 *Greenpeace France and Others* [2000] E.C.R. I-1651, para. 55; ECJ, Case C-344/04 *IATA and ELFAA* [2006] E.C.R. I-403, para. 27 (and case-law cited therein); ECJ, Case C-119/05 *Lucchini* [2007] E.C.R. I-6199, para. 53. Under the former Treaty framework, the application of the *Foto-Frost* case-law garnered much discussion in relation to the restrictions placed on the Court's jurisdiction in the former second and third pillars, as well as former Title IV of the EC Treaty. See T. Corthaut, 'An Effective Remedy for All? Paradoxes and Controversies in Respect of Judicial Protection in the Field of the CFSP Under the European Constitution' (2005) Tilburg Foreign Law Review 110–44. As regards former Art. 68 EC, see also Opinion of Advocate-General D. Ruiz-Jarabo Colomer in ECJ, Case C-14/08 *Roda Golf & Beach Resort* [2009] E.C.R. I-5439, point 30.

[291] ECJ, Case 314/85 *Foto-Frost*, para. 13.

is challenged before a national court the power to declare the act invalid must also be reserved to the Court of Justice, since both proceedings are 'designed to permit the Court of Justice to review the legality of measures adopted by the institutions';[292] third, the Court of Justice is in the best position to decide on the validity of Union acts, since Union institutions whose acts are challenged 'are entitled [under Art. 23 of the Statute] to participate in the proceedings in order to defend the validity of the acts in question'.[293]

(2) Limits to *Foto-Frost*

What national courts not subject to the third paragraph of Art. 267 TFEU may of course do **3.60** is 'consider the validity of a [Union] act and, if they consider that the grounds put forward before them by the parties in support of invalidity are unfounded, they may reject them, concluding that the measure is completely valid.[294] By taking that action they are not calling into question the existence of the [Union] measure.'[295] It is only where the validity of a Union act is contested before a court subject to the third paragraph of Art. 267 TFEU that the court must seek a preliminary ruling from the Court of Justice, even if it itself does not share the view that the act is invalid.[296]

(3) Divergence from the case-law of the Court of Justice

According to some commentators,[297] the authority of the Court's case-law causes a second **3.61** obligation to request a preliminary ruling *praeter legem* to arise: where national courts against whose decisions a judicial remedy exists under national law are minded to diverge from the interpretation which the Court of Justice has given to a provision or a principle of Union law, they must first attempt to obtain a change in the Court's case-law by making a request for a preliminary ruling.

---

[292] ECJ, Case 314/85 *Foto-Frost*, paras 16–17.

[293] ECJ, Case 314/85 *Foto-Frost*, para. 18; in addition, under the second para. of Art. 24 of the Statute, the Court may require the Member States and Union institutions, bodies, offices, and agencies not being party to the case to supply all information which the Court considers necessary for the proceedings.

[294] One can, however, question how wide the margin of appreciation of national courts is. According to Vajda, English courts will in general only refer where it is 'more than arguable' that the Union measure is invalid. See C. Vajda, 'Access to Judicial Review in the EU and National Courts', in E. Buttigieg (ed.), *Enforcing One's Rights Under EU Law* (Hal Tarxien, Gutenberg Press, 2011), 150.

[295] ECJ, Case 314/85 *Foto-Frost* [1987] E.C.R. 4199, para. 14.

[296] ECJ, Case C-344/04 *IATA and ELFAA* [2006] E.C.R. I-403, paras 28–30; CFI, Case T-47/02 *Danzer v Council* [2006] E.C.R. II-1779, para. 37. When the addressee of a Commission decision has, within the period prescribed in the sixth para. of Art. 263 TFEU, brought an action for annulment of that decision pursuant to that article, it is for the national court to decide whether to stay proceedings until a definitive decision has been given in the action for annulment or in order to refer a question to the Court for a preliminary ruling. However, when the outcome of the dispute before the national court depends on the validity of the Commission decision, it follows from the duty of sincere cooperation that the national court should, in order to avoid reaching a decision that runs counter to that of the Commission, stay its proceedings pending final judgment in the action for annulment by the Union courts, unless it considers that, in the circumstances of the case, a reference to the Court of Justice for a preliminary ruling on the validity of the Commission decision is warranted (ECJ, Case C-344/98 *Masterfoods and HB Ice Cream* [2000] E.C.R. I-11369, paras 55 and 57).

[297] H. Kanninen, 'La marge de manoeuvre de la juridiction suprême me nationale pour procéder à un renvoi préjudiciel à la Cour de justice des Communautés européennes', in N. Colneric, J.-P. Puissochet, D. Ruiz-Jarabo Colomer, and D. A. O. Edward (eds), *Une communauté de droit: Festschrift für Gil Carlos Rodríguez Iglesias* (Berlin, Berliner Wissenschafts-Verlag, 2003), 613–14.

It is only by so doing that such courts, as institutions of a Member State, can act in accordance with Art. 4(3) TEU (principle of sincere cooperation). It would indeed be illogical if national courts of last resort were bound by the 'settled case-law' of the Court of Justice, subject to the possibility of their raising the content of the case-law afresh with the Court (see para. 3.51), yet inferior courts were completely at liberty to diverge from that case-law without having to request a preliminary ruling from the Court of Justice.[298]

The different treatment of inferior and superior courts in Art. 267 TFEU only comes into its own, therefore, where there is not as yet any case-law of the Court of Justice on a question of interpretation of Union law. In such a case, the inferior court will be at liberty to answer the question itself,[299] whilst the superior court will be under an obligation to make a reference to the Court of Justice.

---

[298] See to this effect the Opinion of Advocate-General J.-P. Warner in ECJ, Case 112/76 *Manzoni* [1977] E.C.R. 1647, second column, at 1662. Moreover, the effect of s. 3(1) of the European Communities Act 1972, as amended by European Union (Amendment) Act 2008, is that, if no reference to the Court of Justice is made, the UK courts must follow 'the principles laid down by and any relevant decision of the European Court'.

[299] See, e.g. the judgment of the Court of First Instance of Liège, Belgium (Tribunal de première instance de Liège), 1 October 2008, *R.D.C.* 2009, 610), where the national court, while acknowledging that the provision of Union law at issue had not yet been interpreted by the Court, interpreted the provision of Union law itself without referring to the Court. The same provision gave later rise to the preliminary ruling in ECJ, Joined Cases C-585/08 and C-144/09 *Pammer and Alpenhof* [2010] E.C.R I-12527.

4

NATIONAL PROCEDURAL AUTONOMY, EQUIVALENCE, AND EFFECTIVENESS

I. Introduction

A. Overview

According to settled case-law of the Court of Justice, 'in the absence of [Union] rules in the **4.01** field, it is for the domestic legal system of each Member State to designate the courts and tribunals having jurisdiction and to lay down the detailed procedural rules governing actions for safeguarding rights which individuals derive from [Union] law, provided, first, that such rules are not less favourable than those governing similar domestic actions (principle of equivalence) and, second, that they do not render virtually impossible or excessively difficult the exercise of rights conferred by [Union] law (principle of effectiveness)'.[1]

This passage is an expression of the interplay between the principle of national procedural autonomy, on the one hand, and the constraints posed by Union law through the Union principles of equivalence and effectiveness, on the other. Inside the national legal systems, there is considerable variation and diversity in the procedures and judicial organization among Member States, which now number twenty-eight. As such, there is what is referred to as the principle of national procedural autonomy,[2] whereby in the absence of Union rules on the subject, the Member States have in principle autonomy to organize their respective judicial framework and procedures, with the result that the European Union essentially 'piggybacks' on what is provided for in the national legal systems. At the same time, however, the national legal systems are under an important '*obligation de résultat*', meaning that the enforceability of Union law rights must be ensured by virtue of the Union principles of equivalence and effectiveness.

---

[1] See, e.g. ECJ, Joined Cases C-222/05 to C-225/05 *van der Weerd* [2007] E.C.R. I-4233, para. 28 (and further citations therein); ECJ, Case C-268/06 *Impact* [2008] E.C.R. I-2483, paras 44 and 46 (and further citations therein); ECJ, Joined Cases C-317/08 to C-320/08 *Alassini and Others* [2010] E.C.R. I-2213, para. 47. This well-known 'formula' can be traced back to the seminal *Rewe* and *Comet* cases: see n. 4. See also K. Lenaerts, 'National Remedies for Private Parties in the Light of the EU Law Principles of Equivalence and Effectiveness' (2011) *Irish Jurist* 13–37.

[2] See, e.g. ECJ, Case C-168/05 *Mostaza Claro* [2006] E.C.R. I-10421, para. 24; ECJ, Case C-19/08 *Petrosian and Others* [2009] E.C.R. I-495, paras 47, 52; ECJ, Joined Cases C-378/07 to C-380/07 *Angelidaki and Others* [2009] E.C.R. I-3071, para. 174; ECJ, Case C-2/08 *Fallimento Olimpiclub* [2009] E.C.R. I-7501, para. 24; ECJ, Case C-40/08 *Asturcom Telecomunicaciones* [2009] E.C.R. I-9579, para. 38. That being said, the name 'national procedural autonomy' remains a point of controversy among scholars, with some advocating different terms. See P. Craig and G. De Búrca, *EU Law—Text, Cases and Materials* (5th edn, Oxford/New York, Oxford University Press, 2011), 220 (and further references therein); see also citations listed in n. 10.

Each of these aspects is discussed further in this chapter.

B. National procedural autonomy

4.02 As has already been mentioned, Union law falls to be applied principally by national courts. Since the Union does not have procedural law or law governing sanctions of its own,[3] it is for the domestic legal system of each Member State to designate the courts and tribunals having jurisdiction and to lay down the detailed procedural rules governing actions for safeguarding rights which individuals derive from Union law.[4]

C. Judicial supervision

4.03 The full effectiveness of Union law is achieved only if individuals can assert before their national courts the rights that they derive from Union law.[5] Accordingly, the Member States are under an obligation to designate the competent court or tribunal to which individuals may apply with a view to protecting the rights which they derive from the application of Union law.

---

[3] What is meant is all those rules of law which come into play in order to apply Union law in the Member States' legal systems. They may have to do with the conduct of judicial proceedings, such as rules on admissibility, procedural time limits, and rules of evidence, or with the execution of judgments. However, concepts of civil law or other substantive law (e.g. the concept of unjust enrichment) may sometimes be relevant.

[4] See, e.g. ECJ, Case C-231/96 *Edis* [1998] E.C.R. I-4951, para. 19, which refers to the judgments in *Rewe* and *Comet* (ECJ, Case 33/76 *Rewe* [1976] E.C.R. 1989, third subpara. of para. 5; ECJ, Case 45/76 *Comet* [1976] E.C.R. 2043, para. 13). In *Rewe* and *Comet*, the Court referred to 'actions at law intended to ensure the protection of the rights which citizens have from the *direct effect* of [Union] law' (emphasis added). But the duty for Member States to ensure effective legal protection may also require access to the national courts for individuals who seek protection against acts of national authorities infringing provisions of Union law which do not have direct effect (see, e.g. ECJ, Joined Cases C-6/90 and C-9/90 *Francovich and Others* [1991] E.C.R. I-5357). The Court further pointed out in *Rewe* (fourth and fifth subparas of para. 5) and *Comet* (paras 14 and 15) that '[w]here necessary, [Arts 114–117 and 352 TFEU] enable appropriate measures to be taken to remedy differences between the provisions laid down by law, regulation or administrative action in Member States if they are likely to distort or harm the functioning of the common market', but that '[i]n the absence of such harmonisation the rights conferred by [Union] law must be exercised before the national courts in accordance with the conditions laid down by national rules'. This does not, however, preclude testing the national procedural rule against Treaty provisions relating to the four freedoms: see, e.g. ECJ, Case C-412/97 *ED* [1999] E.C.R. I-3845. Since then, additional provisions have been inserted into the Treaties which may serve as a legal basis for harmonization of national procedural rules. See Art. 81 TFEU providing for, *inter alia*, 'the elimination of obstacles to the proper functioning of civil procedure, if necessary by promoting the compatibility of the rules on civil procedure applicable in the Member States' (Art. 81(2 (f) TFEU), amplified by increasing literature on EU civil procedure (e.g. B. Allemeersch and J. T. Nowak, 'Recente ontwikkelingen op het stuk van het Europees burgerlijk procesrecht', in G. Van Calster (ed.), *Internationaal Privaatrecht* (Brugge, Die Keure, 2012), 73–103; K. Lenaerts, 'De Europese rechtsruimte in burgerlijke en handelszaken' (2011) Limburgs Rechtsleven 1–40). It should also be pointed out that various other provisions may be used to bring about harmonization of national procedural law in a particular field of Union law. For instance, it has been suggested that Art. 103 TFEU could potentially serve as a legal basis for a collective action mechanism in the area of competition law. See V. Milutinović, *The Right to Damages Under EU Competition Law: From Courage v. Crehan to the White Paper and Beyond* (Leiden, Kluwer Law International, 2010), 301–44. See also S. Prechal, 'Judge-made Harmonisation of National Procedural Rules: A Bridging Perspective', in J. Wouters and J. Stuyck (eds), *Principles of Proper Conduct for Supranational, State and Private Actors in the European Union. Towards a Ius Commune* (Antwerpen, Intersentia, 2001), 39–58.

[5] See, on this subject, K. Lenaerts, 'The Rule of Law and the Coherence of the Judicial System of the European Union' (2007) C.M.L. Rev. 1625, 1645–50.

D. Constraints

As far as the application of national rules relating to procedure and sanctions by national **4.04** courts and tribunals is concerned, two difficulties arise. First, these national rules may impede the effective application of Union law and thereby affect its primacy and direct effect.[6] Second, the uniform application of Union law may be jeopardized as a result of diverging national laws.[7]

In order to deal with these difficulties, Art. 4(3) TEU places national courts and tribunals under a duty to ensure the 'full effectiveness of Union law' (*effet utile*).[8] The Court of Justice has defined this duty by means of a number of Union constraints with which national law relating to procedure and sanctions must comply.[9] These constraints—the principles of equivalence and effectiveness—are a practical expression of the principles of the primacy and direct effect of Union law[10] and aim to enable individuals to claim before

---

[6] For example, the national law may apply very short limitation periods or deal with the burden of proof or admissible evidence in such a way that the party relying on Union law is unable or has extreme difficulty in proving his or her claims.

[7] For examples of judgments in which the Court of Justice has expressed regret at the lack of Union provisions harmonizing procedures and time limits, see ECJ, Case 130/79 *Express Dairy Foods* [1980] E.C.R. 1887, para. 12 and ECJ, Case 54/81 *Fromme* [1982] E.C.R. 1449, para. 4.

[8] ECJ, Case C-213/89 *Factortame and Others ('Factortame I')* [1990] E.C.R. I-2433, para. 21; ECJ (8 March 2011), Opinion 1/09 *Draft Agreement on the European and Community Patents Court* [2011] E.C.R. I-1137, para. 68. For a useful discussion of this topic generally, see citations in n. 13. *In R v Secretary of State for the Home Department, ex parte Gallagher* [1996] 2 C.M.L.R. 951, Lord Bingham CJ referred to the 'cardinal principle of [Union] law' that national laws should provide 'effective and adequate redress for violations' of that law. See also F. Grévisse and J.-C. Bonichot, 'Les incidences du droit communautaire sur l'organisation et l'exercice de la fonction juridictionnelle dans les États membres', in *L'Europe et le droit. Mélanges en hommage à Jean Boulouis* (Paris, Dalloz, 1991), 297; V. Skouris, 'The Principle of Procedural Autonomy and the Duty of Loyal Cooperation of National Judges under Article 10 EC', in M. Andenas and D. Fairgrieve (eds), *Tom Bingham and the Transformation of the Law: A Liber Amicorum* (Oxford, Oxford University Press, 2009), 493–507.

[9] The relevant case-law is remarkable in that the Court of Justice does not have jurisdiction to rule directly on questions of national procedural law (indeed, it systematically refuses to answer preliminary questions relating to the interpretation or the validity of national law), yet will nevertheless seize upon the basis in Union law of national courts' obligation to achieve a particular result in order to provide very concrete guidance as to how that obligation must be complied with. For a critical appraisal, see the Opinion of Advocate-General D. Ruiz-Jarabo Colomer in ECJ, Case C-30/02 *Recheio* [2004] E.C.R. I-6053, points 23–36. In fact, the need to provide concrete guidance to the national court transcends the topic of national procedural autonomy and concerns aspects of the preliminary ruling procedure generally: see K. Lenaerts, 'The Unity of European Law and the Overload of the ECJ—The System of Preliminary Rulings Revisited', in G. Ziccardi Capaldo (ed.), (2005) *The Global Community—Yearbook of International Law and Jurisprudence*, Vol. 1 (Oxford, Oceana Publications, 2006), 173–201 (reprinted in I. Pernice, J. Kokott, and C. Saunders (eds), *The Future of the European Judicial System in a Comparative Perspective* (Baden-Baden, Nomos, 2006), 211–39).

[10] F. Grévisse and J.-C. Bonichot, 'Les incidences du droit communautaire sur l'organisation et l'exercice de la fonction juridictionnelle dans les Etats membres', in *L'Europe et le droit. Mélanges en hommage à Jean Boulouis* (Paris, Dalloz, 1991), 297, at 309, observe in this connection that 'La Cour ne fixe pas les règles de procédure nationale, elle énonce les exigences du droit communautaire qu'elles doivent satisfaire' (The Court does not fix national procedural rules, it sets forth the Community-law requirements which they must fulfil). See also in this connection C. Kakouris, 'Do the Member States Possess Judicial Procedural "Autonomy"?' (1997) C.M.L. Rev. 1389–412, who argues that Member States do not possess 'procedural autonomy', but that national procedural law is an 'ancillary body of law' whose function is to 'ensure the effective application of substantive [Union] law'. He points out that where national courts apply Union law, they belong, functionally, to the Union legal order and therefore cannot be said to possess procedural autonomy. Cf. the approach taken by S. Prechal, 'Community Law in National Courts: The Lessons from

national courts the full enforcement and protection of the rights which they derive from Union law.

E. Expressions of the principle of effectiveness

4.05   In the case-law of the Court of Justice, there are several expressions of the principle of effectiveness which are intertwined.[11] Generally speaking, the principle of effectiveness can be said to be ventilated through three strands of the case-law concerning: first, the principle of effective judicial protection, which has been recognized by the Court of Justice as a general principle of Union law[12] and underpins matters concerning effective access to court, effective judicial review, and the need for judicial supervision (or control); second, the full effectiveness of Union law in relation to upholding the principle of the primacy of Union law vis-à-vis national (procedural) law; and third, the interface between national law on procedure and sanctions and the Union framing principles of equivalence and effectiveness (i.e. the principle of effectiveness *sensu stricto*).[13]

Taking a broader view, these expressions of the principle of effectiveness underpin the system of judicial protection in the European Union as a whole, including the interlocking relationship between the Union courts and the national courts, particularly through the preliminary ruling procedure and issues relating to the completeness of this system.[14] Perhaps not surprisingly, this area of the case-law of the Court of Justice has been considered to generate tensions stemming from the demands placed upon national procedural law to varying degrees by virtue of the Union requirements of equivalence and effectiveness. With a closer look, however, the course of the case-law demonstrates the extent to which the Court of Justice is attempting to find a balance between respect for the national legal orders and ensuring that Union law rights are enforced in the various Member States, both 'on the books' and 'in practice'.[15]

Van Schijndel' (1998) C.M.L. Rev. 681, at 686–7, who emphasizes that Union law is part of the national legal order and that the primacy of Union law only applies within the realm of substantive law. For detailed discussion on the principles of primacy and direct effect in the Union legal order, see K. Lenaerts and P. Van Nuffel (R. Bray and N. Cambien (eds)), *European Union Law* (3rd edn, London, Sweet & Maxwell, 2011), paras 21.02–21.59.

[11] J. L. da Cruz Vilaça, 'Le principe de l'effet utile de droit de l'Union dans la jurisprudence de la Cour', in A. Rosas, E. Levits, and Y. Bot (eds), *The Court of Justice and the Construction of Europe: Analysis and Perspectives on Sixty Years of Case-Law* (Berlin and The Hague, Springer and Asser Press, 2012), 279–301.

[12] See, e.g. ECJ, Case C-268/06 *Impact* [2008] E.C.R. I-2483, para. 43; ECJ, Case C-432/05 *Unibet* [2007] E.C.R. I-2271, para. 37 (and further citations therein).

[13] S. Prechal and R. J. G. M. Widdershoven, 'Redefining the Relationship Between "Rewe-Effectiveness" and Effective Judicial Protection' (2011) R.E.A.L. 31–50. Indeed, the various sub-categories falling within these strands of the case-law are organized differently in the literature, though invariably the same topics are discussed: see, e.g. M. Claes, *The National Courts' Mandate in the European Constitution* (Oxford/Portland, Hart Publishing, 2006), 119–43; T. Corthaut, *EU Ordre Public* (Alphen aan de Rijn, Kluwer Law International, 2012), 350–1; M. Dougan, *National Remedies Before The Court of Justice—Issues of Harmonisation and Differentiation* (Oxford/Portland, Hart Publishing, 2004), particularly 227–387; T. Tridimas, *The General Principles of EU Law* (2nd edn, Oxford/New York, Oxford University Press, 2006), 418–76.

[14] See further Ch. 1.

[15] Some scholars have viewed the balancing carried out by the Court of Justice in this area of the case-law as effectively amounting to a proportionality test: see, e.g. P. Craig and G. De Búrca, *EU Law—Text, Cases and Materials* (5th edn, Oxford/New York, Oxford University Press, 2011), 218–41 (and further citations therein).

The expressions of the principle of effectiveness infuse the structure of this chapter in the three parts that follow. First, matters relating to the principle of effective judicial protection and the need for judicial supervision in relation to both the national and Union settings are discussed. Second, the application of the Union principles of equivalence and effectiveness in connection with national law on procedure and sanctions will be examined through certain well-developed categories of the case-law, such as limitation periods, rules of evidence, and raising pleas derived from Union law of the court's own motion. Third, focus is placed on matters relating to legal protection in proceedings for interim relief at the national level.

II. The Principle of Effective Judicial Protection

A. General

As developed through the jurisprudence of the Court of Justice, the principle of effective judicial protection encompasses aspects relating to access to court and effective judicial review at both the national and European levels.   **4.06**

B. Access to a court

The full effectiveness of Union law can be attained only if claimants can assert the rights that **4.07** they derive from Union law before a national court. Consequently, the Member States must provide them actual access to a court and to judicial proceedings.[16] This may entail, among other things, extending national provisions granting legal aid to legal persons,[17] providing for specific remedies, or extending the jurisdiction of national courts to matters for which they have no competence under national law.[18] Those obligations are not only connected with the full effectiveness of Union law, but also reflect a general principle of law which underlies the constitutional traditions common to the Member States and is laid down in Arts 6 and 13 of the European Convention for the Protection of Human Rights and Fundamental Freedoms (ECHR).[19] That general principle of law is also enshrined in the first paragraph of Art. 47 of

---

[16] Provided that in any event the Member States must ensure effective protection for individual rights derived from Union law, Union law is not involved in resolving questions of jurisdiction to which the classification of certain legal situations based on Union law may give rise in the national judicial system (ECJ, Case C-446/93 *SEIM* [1996] E.C.R. I-73, para. 32; ECJ, Case C-224/01 *Köbler* [2003] E.C.R. I-10239, para. 47). See also ECJ, Case C-15/04 *Koppensteiner* [2005] E.C.R. I-4855, para. 34.

[17] ECJ, Case C-279/09 *DEB* [2010] E.C.R. I-13849; ECJ (order of 13 June 2012), Case C-156/12 *GREP*, not reported.

[18] ECJ, Case C-268/06 *Impact* [2008] E.C.R. I-2483, para. 54; ECJ (order of 24 April 2009), Case C-519/08 *Archontia Koukou* [2009] E.C.R. I-65*, Summ. pub., para. 98. In the context of access to justice in environmental matters, see ECJ, Joined Cases C-128/09 to C-131/09, C-134/09, and C-135/09 *Boxus and Others* [2011] E.C.R. I-9711, 49–57; ECJ (order of 17 November 2011), Joined Cases C-177/09 to C-179/09 *Le Poumon Vert*, not reported, paras 38–46; ECJ (judgment of 16 February 2012), Case C-182/10 *Solvay and Others*, not reported, paras 44–52.

[19] ECJ, Case 222/84 *Johnston* [1986] E.C.R. 1651, paras 17–18; ECJ, Case C-97/91 *Oleificio Borrelli v Commission* [1992] E.C.R. I-6313, paras 13–14; ECJ, Case C-226/99 *Siples* [2001] E.C.R. I-227, paras 15–20; ECJ, Case C-506/04 *Wilson* [2006] E.C.R. I-8613, para. 46 (and further citations therein); ECJ (judgment of 27 June 2013), Case C-93/12 *Agrokonsulting*, not reported, paras 59–60. As far as Art. 6 of the ECHR is concerned, see also the following judgments of the European Court of Human Rights: ECtHR, 24

the Charter of Fundamental Rights of the European Union.[20] However, the right to effective judicial protection does not afford a right to a number of levels of jurisdiction.[21]

C. Equal treatment

4.08   In addition, it is a corollary of the prohibition of discrimination enshrined in Art. 18 TFEU that nationals of a Member State carrying out an economic activity on the market of another Member State which falls within the scope of the Treaties must be able to bring actions in the courts of that Member State on the same footing as nationals of that State in order to resolve any disputes arising from their economic activities.[22] Consequently, a Member State is precluded from requiring provision of security for costs by a legal person established in another Member State or by a national of another Member State, even if the person concerned is also a national of a non-member country in which he or she is resident,[23] who has brought an action in its courts against one of its nationals or a company established in its territory where security for costs cannot be required to be provided by legal persons from the State in question[24] and the action is connected with the exercise of fundamental freedoms guaranteed by Union law.[25]

D. Statement of reasons

4.09   In addition, national law must provide for effective judicial review.[26] To that end, the court before which the case is brought should generally be empowered to require the competent

---

September 2002, Case 27824/95 *Posti and Rahko v Finland*; ECtHR, 17 January 2012, Cases 43710/07, 6023/08, 11248/08, 27668/08, 31242/08, and 52133/08 *Fetisov and Others v Russia*; ECtHR, 3 July 2012, Case 13579/09 *Razvyazkin v Russia*.

[20] The Charter of Fundamental Rights of the European Union, proclaimed at Strasbourg on 12 December 2007 by the European Parliament, the Council, and the Commission ([2007] O.J. C303/1; consolidated version, [2012] O.J. C326/391) repeats and adapts the Charter proclaimed on 7 December 2000 ([2000] O.J. C364/1) and replaces it with effect from 1 December 2009, the date of the entry into force of the Lisbon Treaty. By virtue of the first subpara. of Art. 6(1) TEU, the Charter has the same legal value as the Treaties. For detailed discussion of the Charter, see K. Lenaerts and P. Van Nuffel (R. Bray and N. Cambien (eds)), *European Union Law* (3rd edn, London, Sweet & Maxwell, 2011), paras 22.20–22.22.

[21] ECJ, Case C-69/10 *Samba Diouf* [2011] E.C.R. I-7151, para. 69. That being said, single instance appeal proceedings limited to points of law might not be sufficient: see ECJ, Case C-506/04 *Wilson* [2006] E.C.R. I-8613, paras 60–62.

[22] ECJ, Case C-43/95 *Data Delecta Aktiebolag and Forsberg* [1996] E.C.R. I-4661.

[23] ECJ, Case C-122/96 *Saldanha and MTS Securities* [1997] E.C.R. I-5325, para. 30.

[24] ECJ, Case C-323/95 *Hayes* [1997] E.C.R. I-1711, para. 22.

[25] ECJ, Case C-323/95 *Hayes*, para. 25. In *Fitzgerald v Williams* [1996] 2 QB 657, the Court of Appeal followed the emergent case-law of the Court of Justice on the grounds that to require security for costs under what was then Rules of the Supreme Court, Ord. 23, from Irish nationals resident in Ireland would be discriminatory and not justified in view of the Brussels Convention on jurisdiction and the enforcement of judgments in civil and commercial matters. See now Civil Procedure Rules, R.25.13(2)(a)(ii). See also EFTA Court, Case E-10/04 *Piazza* [2005], EFTA Court Report 2005, 76, where the EFTA Court held that a national rule limiting all means of security for costs to securities of domestic origin was in breach of the EEA Agreement.

[26] ECJ, Case 222/86 *Heylens and Others* [1987] E.C.R. 4097, paras 14–16; ECJ, Case C-340/89 *Vlassopoulou* [1991] E.C.R. I-2357, para. 22; ECJ, Case C-104/91 *Aguirre Borrell and Others* [1992] E.C.R. I-3003, para. 15; ECJ, Case C-111/97 *EvoBus Austria* [1998] E.C.R. I-5411, para. 15; ECJ, Case C-228/98 *Dounias* [2000] E.C.R. I-577, para. 63; ECJ, Case C-467/01 *Eribrand* [2003] E.C.R. I-6471, para. 61;

authority to state the reasons for any national decision which is contested on the basis of Union law.

Individuals must also be able to defend their rights in the best possible circumstances and be in a position to decide with a full knowledge of the facts whether they will benefit from going to court. The competent authority is therefore under a duty to inform them of the grounds for its decision, either in the decision itself or in a subsequent communication made at their request. The possibility of bringing legal proceedings and the duty to state reasons are designed, among other things, effectively to protect the rights conferred on individuals by Union law. These Union law requirements apply only to final decisions of national authorities, not to opinions or to measures taken at the preparatory or investigative stage.[27]

E. Deficiencies in the system of judicial protection in the European Union pre-Lisbon

The fact that Member States are under a duty to ensure effective judicial protection may **4.10** entail a national court's being obliged to hold that a particular claim based on a breach of Union law is admissible even though in normal circumstances—i.e. if it was based simply on an infringement of national law—such a claim would not be admissible[28] (for example, a claim brought against a Member State for reparation of damage caused by a breach of Union law, or a claim for interim relief in the shape of the suspension of a provision of national law which is in breach of Union law[29]).

Under the former Treaty framework, the question arose as to whether a national court had to take account of the restrictive admissibility requirements prescribed by what was then the fourth paragraph of Art. 230 EC,[30] where an individual was seeking legal protection against the application in the national legal order of allegedly unlawful provisions of Community law which were of general application.[31] The point of departure for the reasoning of the Court of Justice in this connection was that by Arts 230 and 241 (now Arts 263 and 277 TFEU), on the one hand, and Art. 234 (now Art. 267 TFEU), on the other, the EC Treaty established a complete system of legal remedies and procedures designed to ensure judicial review by the Community courts of the legality of acts of the institutions. Under that system, where natural or legal persons could not directly challenge Community measures of general application, by reason of the conditions for admissibility laid down in the fourth paragraph of Art. 230 EC, they were able, depending on the case, either indirectly to plead the invalidity of such acts before the Community courts under Art. 241 EC (now Art. 277

ECJ, C-136/03 *Dörr* [2005] E.C.R. I-4759, para. 47; ECJ, Case C-239/05 *BVBA Management, Training en Consultancy* [2007] E.C.R. I-1455, paras 36–37; ECJ, C-432/05 *Unibet* [2007] E.C.R. I-2271, para. 61; ECJ, Joined Cases C-402/05 P and C-415/05 P *Yusuf and Al Barakaat International Foundation v Council and Commission* [2008] E.C.R. I-6351, paras 336–337; ECJ, Case C-75/08 *Mellor* [2009] E.C.R. I-3799, para. 59.

[27] ECJ, Case 222/86 *Heylens and Others* [1987] E.C.R. 4097, para. 16; ECJ, Case C-75/08 *Mellor* [2009] E.C.R. I-3799, para. 59.

[28] See, e.g. ECJ, Case C-15/04 *Koppensteiner* [2005] E.C.R. I-4855, paras 30–39.

[29] ECJ, Case C-213/89 *Factortame and Others ('Factortame I')* [1990] E.C.R. I-2433; see para. 4.61.

[30] See para. 4.11.

[31] See, e.g. K. Lenaerts and T. Corthaut, 'Judicial Review as a Contribution to the Development of European Constitutionalism' (2003) Y.E.L. 1–43.

TFEU) or to do so before the national courts and ask them, since they have no jurisdiction themselves to declare those measures invalid, to make a reference to the Court of Justice for a preliminary ruling on validity.[32]

A complete system of legal remedies may not normally have any gaps. Nevertheless, the preliminary ruling procedure and the objection of illegality to which the Court of Justice referred in its case-law did not invariably afford a sufficient legal remedy for an individual who sought to contest the validity of a Community act of general application. The reason for this is that recourse to Arts 234 and 241 EC (now Arts 267 and 277 TFEU) was conditional upon the existence of a national or a Community implementing measure, respectively, which would permit the individual to contest the validity of the Community act of general application before the national court or the Community courts in an action brought against the implementing measure. Where a Community act required no implementing measures at national level, as is often the case with regulations, and national law afforded no form of declaratory relief, an individual was then faced with the prospect of first infringing the Community act before he or she could challenge its validity in the national courts. The same problem arose where there were national implementing measures—for example, where directives had to be implemented in national law—but those measures could not be challenged directly under national law.

F. Possible solutions identified in the case-law

4.11 If it is assumed that the system of legal remedies is already 'complete',[33] two solutions were conceivable. Either the Court of Justice would put a more flexible construction on what is to be understood by 'individual concern' within the meaning of the former fourth paragraph of Art. 230 EC so that individuals whose legal position was affected by a Community act of general application would be entitled to contest that act directly before the Court of First Instance, as it was then called, by means of an action for annulment, or the national courts must fill the gap.

This question was raised in the *Unión de Pequeños Agricultores*[34] and *Jégo-Quéré*[35] cases. It appeared from these cases, first, that the Court of Justice was entirely unwilling to embark upon the relaxation of the admissibility requirements set out in the former fourth paragraph of Art. 230 EC, which had been proposed by the Court of First Instance in *Jégo-Quéré*.[36] Referring to its judgment in *Plaumann*,[37] the Court of Justice held that a measure is of individual concern to natural or legal persons 'where the measure in question affects specific

---

[32] ECJ, Case 294/83 *Les Verts v European Parliament* [1986] E.C.R. I-1339, para. 23; ECJ, Case C-50/00 P *Unión de Pequeños Agricultores v Council* [2002] E.C.R. I-6677, para. 40; ECJ, Case C-167/02 P *Rothley and Others v European Parliament* [2004] E.C.R. I-3149, para. 46.

[33] ECJ, Case 294/83 *Les Verts v European Parliament*, para. 23; ECJ, Case C-50/00 P *Unión de Pequeños Agricultores v Council*, para. 40; ECJ, Case C-167/02 P *Rothley and Others v European Parliament*, para. 46.

[34] CFI (order of 23 November 1999), Case T-173/98 *Unión de Pequeños Agricultores v Council* [1999] E.C.R. II-3357; upheld on appeal in ECJ, Case C-50/00 P *Unión de Pequeños Agricultores v Council* [2002] E.C.R. I-6677.

[35] CFI, Case T-177/01 *Jégo-Quéré v Commission* [2002] E.C.R. II-2365, para. 41; overturned on appeal in ECJ, Case C-263/02 P *Commission v Jégo-Quéré* [2004] E.C.R. I-3425.

[36] See para. 7.106.

[37] ECJ, Case 25/62 *Plaumann v Commission* [1963] E.C.R. 95, at 107.

natural or legal persons by reason of certain attributes peculiar to them, or by reason of a factual situation which differentiates them from all other persons and distinguishes them individually in the same way as the addressee'.[38] No other interpretation of this admissibility condition was possible, it was held, 'without going beyond the jurisdiction conferred by the Treaty on the Community Courts'.[39] Consequently, an individual could not bring an action for annulment before the Court of First Instance against an act of general application, such as a regulation which did not distinguish him or her individually in the same way as the addressee, even where it could be shown, following an examination by that Court of the particular national procedural rules, that those rules do not allow the individual to bring proceedings before a national court to contest the validity of the Community measure at issue.[40]

As far as the second solution is concerned, the Court of Justice has repeatedly stated that the right to effective judicial protection is one of the general principles of law stemming from the constitutional traditions common to the Member States and that this right is enshrined in Arts 6 and 13 of the ECHR.[41] The Court of Justice drew the following conclusion from this: 'Thus *it is for the Member States* to establish a system of legal remedies and procedures which ensure respect for the right to effective judicial protection.'[42] Notwithstanding the wording used, what was involved here was only a commitment to make best endeavours and then it rested only on the hypothesis that there were national implementing measures for the unlawful Community act at issue. Accordingly, the Court of Justice has held that 'in accordance with the principle of sincere cooperation laid down in Art. 4(3) TEU, national courts are required, so far as possible, to interpret and apply national procedural rules governing the exercise of rights of action in a way that enables natural and legal persons to challenge before the courts the legality of any decision or other national measure relative to the application to them of a Community act of general application, by pleading the invalidity of such an act'.[43]

By virtue of this case-law, the Court of Justice thus left two loopholes open in the system of judicial protection. On the one hand, the degree of judicial protection available to an individual was made dependent on the ability and the creativity of the national judge to provide such a remedy. On the other hand, the Court provided no solution for those situations where no national implementing measures existed, despite the claim made by the

---

[38] ECJ, Case C-50/00 P *Unión de Pequeños Agricultores v Council* [2002] E.C.R. I-6677, para. 36.

[39] ECJ, Case C-50/00 P *Unión de Pequeños Agricultores v Council*, para. 44; ECJ, Case C-167/02 P *Rothley and Others v European Parliament* [2004] E.C.R. I-3149, para. 25; ECJ, Case C-263/02 P *Commission v Jégo-Quéré* [2004] E.C.R. I-3425, para. 36. Compare the well-known Opinion of Advocate-General F.G. Jacobs in ECJ, Case C-50/00 P *Unión de Pequeños Agricultores v Council* [2002] E.C.R. I-6677.

[40] ECJ, Case C-50/00 P *Unión de Pequeños Agricultores v Council* [2002] E.C.R. I-6677, para. 43; ECJ, Case C-263/02 P *Commission v Jégo-Quéré* [2004] E.C.R. I-3425, para. 33.

[41] ECJ, Case 222/84 *Johnston* [1986] E.C.R. 1651, para. 18; ECJ, Case C-424/99 *Commission v Austria* [2001] E.C.R. I-9285, para. 45; ECJ, Case C-50/00 P *Unión de Pequeños Agricultores v Council* [2002] E.C.R. I-6677, para. 39; ECJ, Case C-263/02 P *Commission v Jégo-Quéré* [2004] E.C.R. I-3425, para. 29.

[42] ECJ, Case C-263/02 P *Commission v Jégo-Quéré* [2004] E.C.R. I-3425, para. 31; ECJ, Case C-50/00 P *Unión de Pequeños Agricultores v Council* [2002] E.C.R. I-6677, para. 41. This wording is included virtually verbatim in Art. 19(1), second para. TEU.

[43] ECJ, Case C-263/02 P *Commission v Jégo-Quéré* [2004] E.C.R. I-3425, para. 32 (emphasis added); ECJ, Case C-50/00 P *Unión de Pequeños Agricultores v Council* [2002] E.C.R. I-6677, para. 42.

applicants in *Jégo-Quéré* and *Unión de Pequeños Agricultores* that they were precisely in this kind of situation.[44]

It could not therefore be inferred from this case-law alone that a national court was obliged to declare admissible an action brought against the public authority's intention to apply a regulation or to transpose a directive into the national legal order where the procedural law of the Member State in question did not provide for such a form of 'declaratory relief'.[45] On the contrary, the Court of Justice seemed resigned to the fact that in some cases an individual must first infringe a Community act before he or she could challenge its validity.[46]

However, the Court's subsequent 2007 judgment in *Unibet*[47] changed this assumption. In this case, the Court was faced with the interpretation of the principle of effective judicial protection of an individual's rights under what was then Community law in connection with an applicant seeking to contest the compatibility of Swedish betting legislation with Community law by way of a free-standing declaratory action, even though such action was not provided for under the Swedish procedural rules.[48] The Court considered that while the Treaty was not intended to create new remedies in the national courts to ensure the observance of Community law, this would be otherwise 'only if it were aparent from the overall scheme of the national legal system in question that no legal remedy existed which made it possible to ensure, even indirectly, respect for an individual's rights under Community law'.[49] This meant that the principle of effective judicial protection did not require the Swedish court to provide for a free-standing declaratory-type action that would seek primarily to challenge the compatibility of national provisions with Community law to the extent that there existed certain indirect legal remedies that would still allow an individual to challenge the compatibility of national law with Community law: first, by way of an action for damages; and second, by way of judicial review of the decision rejecting

---

[44] K. Lenaerts and T. Corthaut, 'Judicial Review as a Contribution to the Development of European Constitutionalism' (2003) Y.E.L. 1–43.

[45] In Case C-491/01 *British American Tobacco and Imperial Tobacco* [2002] E.C.R. I-11453, the Court of Justice ruled on the admissibility of a reference for a preliminary ruling made in proceedings for declaratory relief concerning the validity of a directive. The Court declared that the question was admissible on the ground that 'The opportunity open to individuals to plead the invalidity of a Community act of general application before national courts is not conditional upon that act's actually having been the subject of implementing measures adopted pursuant to national law', Case C-491/01 *British American Tobacco and Imperial Tobacco*, para. 40. Nihoul infers from this that there is an obligation for Member States to adapt their procedural rules so as to give individuals the opportunity to contest in the national courts the national authorities' intention to implement a directive. This would enable individuals to contest the legality of a directive in the national courts, which might then make a reference for a preliminary ruling to the Court of Justice (see P. Nihoul, 'Le recours des particuliers contre les actes communautaires de portée générale. Nouveaux développements dans la jurisprudence' (2003) J.T.D.E. 38–43). In the present authors' view, such an obligation cannot be inferred solely from the *British American Tobacco* judgment. See K. Lenaerts and T. Corthaut, 'Judicial Review as a Contribution to the Development of European Constitutionalism' (2003) Y.E.L. 1–43. However, the Court of Justice's 2007 judgment in *Unibet* changes this view: see text accompanying nn. 47–51. As far as declaratory relief and the validity of a regulation are concerned, see ECJ, Cases C-27/00 and C-122/00 *Omega Air and Others* [2002] E.C.R. I-2569, in which the Court of Justice did not even consider the admissibility of the reference for a preliminary ruling.

[46] ECJ, Case C-263/02 P *Commission v Jégo-Quéré* [2004] E.C.R. I-3425, para. 34; CFI (order of 28 June 2005), Case T-386/04 *Eridania Sadam and Others v Commission* [2005] E.C.R. II-2531, para. 43.

[47] ECJ, Case C-432/05 *Unibet* [2007] E.C.R. I-2271.

[48] ECJ, Case C-432/05 *Unibet*, para. 4.

[49] ECJ, Case C-432/05 *Unibet*, paras 40–41.

the individual's application for permission to engage in promoting its betting activities in Sweden.[50] That being said, the Court stressed that if an individual 'was forced to be subject to administrative or criminal proceedings and to any penalties that may result as the *sole* form of legal remedy for disputing the compatibility of the national provision at issue with Community law, that would *not* be sufficient to secure for it such effective protection'.[51]

In any event, as brought to bear in the *Unión de Pequeños Agricultores* and *Jégo-Quéré* cases, the Court of Justice posited a third solution, which, however, essentially boiled down in practice to recognition of the incompleteness of the system of legal remedies. This was because it referred to the possibility for Member States to alter the existing system of legal protection provided in the Treaties under former Art. 48 EU (now Art. 48 TEU).[52]

G. The Treaty of Lisbon

The Member States have taken up this invitation by virtue of two important changes brought by the Lisbon Treaty. In the first place, the fourth paragraph of Art. 263 TFEU relaxes the conditions for the admissibility of actions brought by individuals for the annulment of regulatory acts which are of direct concern to such individuals and do not entail implementing measures.[53]

4.12

Then, as far as judicial review by national courts is concerned, the second paragraph of Art. 19(1) TEU provides as follows: 'Member States shall provide remedies sufficient to ensure effective legal protection in the fields covered by Union law.'[54] On the one hand, it may be objected that this provision adds nothing to the *acquis*, since it amounts to a virtually verbatim repetition of a passage from the Court's judgments in *Jégo-Quéré* and *Unión de Pequeños Agricultores*,[55] from which the Court merely inferred an obligation to make best endeavours. On the other hand, it cannot be ruled out that this provision, read against the background of the Charter of Fundamental Rights of the European Union, which confers on 'everyone whose rights and freedoms guaranteed by the law of the Union are violated' the right to 'an effective remedy before a tribunal',[56] and the recent case-law of the European Court of Human Rights,[57] will prompt the Court of Justice to transform the

---

[50] ECJ, Case C-432/05 *Unibet*, paras 46–47, 55–65.

[51] ECJ, Case C-432/05 *Unibet*, para. 64 (emphasis added). See also ECJ (judgment of 3 October 2013), Case C-583/11 P *Inuit Tapiriit Kanatami and Others v Parliament and Council*, not reported, para. 104.

[52] ECJ, Case C-50/00 P *Unión de Pequeños Agricultores v Council*, para. 45.

[53] See paras 7.107–7.110.

[54] This had already appeared as Art. I-29 of the failed Draft Constitutional Treaty.

[55] See n. 52.

[56] Art. 47 of the Charter of Fundamental Rights of the European Union, which was proclaimed at Strasbourg on 12 December 2007 by the European Parliament, the Council, and the Commission ([2007] O.J. C303/1) and thereafter adapted with effect from 1 December 2009, the date of the entry into force of the Lisbon Treaty, [2010] O.J. C83/389. By virtue of the first subpara. of Art. 6(1) TEU, the Charter proclaimed in 2007 has the same legal value as the Treaties. See further S. Prechal, 'EC Requirements for an Effective Remedy', in J. Lonbay and A. Biondi (eds), *Remedies for Breach of EC Law* (New York, Wiley, 1997), 3–13.

[57] In its judgment of 24 September 2002 in Case 27824/95 *Posti and Rahko v Finland*, the European Court of Human Rights ruled that the ECHR had been violated on account of the fact that no remedy was available against a Finnish decree which curtailed the applicants' rights. The idea that one could obtain judicial review by first breaching the contested act was rejected by the European Court of Human Rights in the following terms: 'no one can be required to breach the law so as to be able to have a "civil right" determined in accordance with Article 6 §1' (para. 64). See also ECJ, Case C-432/05 *Unibet* [2007] E.C.R. I-2271, para. 64.

obligation to make best endeavours into an obligation to achieve a particular result.[58] Effective legal redress would then mean that national courts would be obliged to interpret and apply their national rules of procedural law in such a way as to give natural and legal persons the possibility to act against the national authorities' intention to apply or implement a Union measure of general application where it appears that those persons cannot attack the measure directly in the General Court by means of an action for annulment. Only then would the system of legal redress enshrined in the Treaties be complete in actual fact and not just on paper, at least as far as non-CFSP Union acts are concerned.

III. Constraints: The Principles of Equivalence and Effectiveness

A. General

(1) *Rewe/Comet* formula

4.13 The Court of Justice laid down the two most important constraints at the same time when it held that, in principle, national procedural rules and rules on sanctions are to apply, but (1) that those rules may not be less favourable than those governing similar domestic actions (principle of equivalence);[59] and (2) that they may not render virtually impossible or excessively difficult the exercise of rights conferred by Union law (principle of effectiveness).[60]

(2) Principle of equivalence

4.14 Above all, there is the requirement for 'procedural equal treatment' of claims based on Union law and those based on national law, for example as regards the effects of the expiry of a time limit for bringing proceedings or of an error in drawing up the document originating proceedings. In addition, it must be possible for every type of action provided for by national law to be available for the purpose of ensuring observance of Union provisions having direct effect.[61]

---

[58] See ECJ, Case C-432/05 *Unibet* [2007] E.C.R. I-2271, discussed in text accompanying nn. 47–51.

[59] ECJ, Case 33/76 *Rewe* [1976] E.C.R. 1989, third subpara. in fine of para. 5; ECJ, Case 45/76 *Comet* [1976] E.C.R. 2043, para. 13 in fine; ECJ, Case 811/79 *Ariete* [1980] E.C.R. 2545, para. 12; ECJ, Case 826/79 *MIRECO* [1980] E.C.R. 2559, para. 13; ECJ, Case C-338/91 *Steenhorst-Neerings* [1993] E.C.R. I-5475, para. 15; ECJ, Case C-410/92 *Johnson* [1994] E.C.R. I-5483, para. 21; ECJ, Case C-180/95 *Draehmpaehl* [1997] E.C.R. I-2195, para. 29.

[60] ECJ, Case 33/76 *Rewe*, sixth subpara. of para. 5; ECJ, Case 45/76 *Comet*, para. 16; ECJ, Case 811/79 *Ariete*, para. 12 in fine; and ECJ, Case 826/79 *MIRECO*, para. 13 in fine. See also ECJ, Case C-231/96 *Edis* [1998] E.C.R. I-4951, paras 19 and 34; ECJ, Case C-290/96 *Spac* [1998] E.C.R. I-4997, para. 18; ECJ, Joined Cases C-279/96, C-280/96, and C-281/96 *Ansaldo Energia and Others* [1998] E.C.R. I-5025, para. 27; ECJ, Joined Cases C-52/99 and C-53/99 *Camarotto and Vignone* [2001] E.C.R. I-1395, para. 21.

[61] ECJ, Case 158/80 *Rewe* [1981] E.C.R. 1805, para. 44. The Court of Justice specified in *Pasquini* that the principle of equivalence 'must be applied not only with regard to provisions of national law on limitation of actions and recovery of sums paid though not due, but also to all procedural rules governing the treatment of comparable situations, whether administrative or judicial': ECJ, Case C-34/02 *Pasquini* [2003] E.C.R. I-6515, para. 62.

In order to decide whether procedural rules relating to a claim based on national law and those relating to claims based on Union law are equivalent, the national court must verify objectively, in the abstract, whether the rules at issue are similar, taking into account the role played by those rules in the procedure as a whole, as well as the operation of that procedure and any special features of those rules.[62]

(3) Principle of effectiveness

In addition, national procedural rules and rules relating to sanctions, albeit complying with the principle of equivalence, 'may not be so framed as to render virtually impossible the exercise of rights conferred by [Union] law'.[63]   **4.15**

(4) Case-by-case approach

National procedural rules and rules relating to sanctions are assessed by the Court of Justice on a case-by-case basis in the light of the constraints they contain, which means that the categories described here must be regarded as being open to enlargement.   **4.16**

B. *Locus standi* and interest in bringing proceedings

(1) Principle

The rules of national law relating to an individual's *locus standi* and interest in bringing proceedings may not detract from the full effectiveness of Union law. In a first attempt to define the Union law requirements from the point of view of the principles of equivalence and effectiveness, the Court of Justice has held that persons who do not come within the scope *ratione personae* of a provision of Union law may nevertheless have an interest in the provision being taken into account vis-à-vis the person protected.[64] In this way, they may have sufficient *locus standi* under Union law, which must be recognized in national law.   **4.17**

Thus, an undertaking which is not a competitor of the beneficiary of unlawful State aid may have an interest in relying before the national court on the direct effect of the prohibition on implementation referred to in the last sentence of Art. 108(3) TFEU (ex Art. 88(3) EC). This will be the case, for example, where the undertaking concerned is subject to a tax that

---

[62] ECJ, Case C-78/98 *Preston and Others* [2000] E.C.R. I-3201, para. 63; ECJ, Case C-246/09 *Bulicke* [2010] E.C.R. I-7003, para. 29 (and further citations therein). As underscored by the Court, the principle of equivalence is not to be interpreted as requiring the Member States to extend their most favourable rules to all actions brought in a certain field of law: see ECJ, Case C-118/08 *Transportes Urbanos y Servicios Generales* [2010] E.C.R. I-635, para. 34 (and further citations therein).

[63] ECJ, Case 199/82 *San Giorgio* [1983] E.C.R. 3595, para. 12 (this phrase has tended to be rendered in English as 'framed in such a way as in practice to make it impossible': see, e.g. ECJ, Joined Cases C-46/93 and C-48/93 *Brasserie du Pêcheur and Factortame* [1996] E.C.R. I-1029, para. 74); in his Opinion in ECJ, Case 2/94 *Denkavit International* [1996] E.C.R. I-2829, point 75, Advocate-General F.G. Jacobs suggested 'unduly difficult'.

[64] ECJ, Joined Cases C-87/90 to C-89/90 *Verholen and Others* [1991] E.C.R. I-3757, paras 23–24 (with a case note by S. Prechal (1993) S.E.W. 163–9). Following from this judgment, the Court has underscored that while it is in principle for national law to determine an individual's *locus standi* and legal interest in bringing proceedings, Union law nevertheless requires, *in addition to observance of the principles of equivalence and effectiveness*, that the national legislation does not undermine the right to effective judicial protection: see, e.g. ECJ, Case C-12/08 *Mono Car Styling* [2009] E.C.R. I-6653, para. 49 (and further citations therein).

forms an integral part of a measure implemented in breach of the prohibition referred to in that provision.[65]

(2) Application in the field of environmental law

4.18   Traditionally, the *locus standi* of non-governmental organizations having as their object the protection of the environment is interpreted quite narrowly in a number of Member States.[66] Under the impulse of the Aarhus Convention[67] and the principles of effective judicial protection and effectiveness the Court of Justice has developed a line of case-law providing for more relaxed standing conditions for such organizations when acting within the scope of Union law. Therefore, national courts are under an obligation to interpret national procedural rules relating to the conditions to be met in order to bring administrative or judicial proceedings in such a way as to enable an environmental protection organization to challenge before a court a decision taken following administrative proceedings liable to be contrary to EU environmental law.[68] Also, concerning the application of Directive 85/337/EEC,[69] where national law only allows an applicant to bring an action conditional upon demonstrating that the contested administrative decision impairs an individual right, such condition would be at odds with the principle of effectiveness if environmental protection organizations were not allowed to rely before national courts on the impairment of rules of EU environmental law solely on the grounds that those rules protect the public interest, since it largely deprives those organizations of the possibility of having a court verify compliance with the rules of EU environmental law which, for the most part, address the public interest and not merely the protection of the interests of individuals as such.[70]

C. Limitation periods and rules of evidence

(1) General

(a) Limitation periods

4.19   It may appear from a judgment of the Court of Justice giving a preliminary ruling that the imposition of a particular charge or the refusal to grant a particular social advantage conflicts with Union law. Where a person seeks recovery of the charge or payment of the

---

[65] ECJ, Case C-174/02 *Streekgewest Westelijk Noord-Brabant* [2005] E.C.R. I-85, para. 19.

[66] See N. De Sadeleer, G. Roller, and M. Dross (eds), *Access to Justice in Environmental Matters and the Role of NGOs* (Groningen, Europa Law Publishing, 2005), 228.

[67] Council Decision 2005/370/EC of 17 February 2005 on the conclusion, on behalf of the European Community, of the Convention on access to information, public participation in decision-making, and access to justice in environmental matters, [2005] O.J. L124/1.

[68] ECJ, Case C-240/09 *Lesoochranárske zoskupenie* [2011] E.C.R. I-1255, paras 47–52 (see J. Wouters, G. De Baere, and J. T. Nowak, 'Iets over de invloed van het internationaal en Europees recht op het administratief recht', in D. D'Hooghe, K. Deketelaere, and A. M. Draye (eds), *Liber Amicorum Marc Boes* (Brugge, Die Keure, 2011), 619–34). Also, natural and legal persons which are directly concerned should, in the context of the application of Council Directive 96/62/EC of 27 September 1996 on ambient air quality assessment and management, as amended by Regulation (EC) No. 1882/2003 of the European Parliament and of the Council of 29 September 2003, have the possibility of requiring the competent authorities to draw up an action plan if limit values or alert thresholds contained in that directive are exceeded, where necessary by bringing an action before the national courts: see ECJ, Case C-237/07 *Janecek* [2008] E.C.R. I-6221, para. 39.

[69] Council Directive 85/337/EEC of 27 June 1985 on the assessment of the effects of certain public and private projects on the environment, [1985] O.J. L175/40.

[70] ECJ, Case C-115/09 *Bund für Umwelt und Naturschutz Deutschland* [2011] E.C.R. I-3673, paras 36–50.

advantage unlawfully denied before a national court, the national procedural rules should apply. Those rules may provide for limitation periods. According to a consistent line of cases, limitation periods are compatible with Union law, provided that the principles of equivalence and effectiveness are respected.[71] According to the Court of Justice, this does not amount to a temporal limitation of the effects of an interpretative judgment which falls outside the competence of a national court.[72] This is because national procedural rules providing for limitation periods do not detract from specific rights that individuals derive from Union law. It merely results in them having to bring their claim within a particular period.[73]

(b) Rules of evidence

As far as the application of rules of evidence is concerned in proceedings in which an individual asserts rights derived from Union law, the Court of Justice considers that, in the absence of Union legislation, any type of evidence admissible under the procedural law of the Member States in similar proceedings is in principle admissible, provided that the principles of equivalence and effectiveness are respected.[74] This case-law is also applicable to the use of presumptions and rules allocating the burden of proof.[75] **4.20**

The case-law on limitation periods and rules of evidence is of particular importance to the areas concerning the recovery of unlawful charges, the recovery of unlawful State aid, and claims for an advantage due under Union law. Therefore, further illustrations of the application of that case-law will be confined to these three areas.

(2) Recovery of unlawful charges

(a) Heterogeneity of national systems

The question of challenging charges unlawfully claimed or the recovery of charges unduly paid is dealt with in divergent ways in the various Member States, and even within a given Member State depending on the sort of tax or charge concerned.[76] In some cases, the law requires both complaints addressed to the tax office and appeals to comply with fairly strict requirements as to the form in which and the time limits within which such legal claims or applications may be **4.21**

---

[71] ECJ, Case 45/76 *Comet* [1976] E.C.R. 2043, paras 17–18; ECJ, Case 61/79 *Denkavit Italiana* [1980] E.C.R. 1205, para. 23; ECJ, Case C-90/94 *Haahr Petroleum* [1997] E.C.R. I-4085, para. 48; ECJ, Case C-231/96 *Edis* [1998] E.C.R. I-4951, para. 20.

[72] See para. 6.34.

[73] ECJ, Case C-231/96 *Edis* [1998] E.C.R. I-4951, paras 15–19.

[74] ECJ, Joined Cases C-310/98 and C-406/98 *Met-Trans and Sagpol* [2000] E.C.R. I-1797, para. 29; ECJ, Case C-344/08 *Rubach* [2009] E.C.R. I-7033, para. 28; ECJ, Case C-478/07 *Budějovický Budvar* [2009] E.C.R. I-7721, paras 86–89; ECJ, Case C-35/09 *Speranza* [2010] E.C.R. I-6581, paras 41–48. Accordingly, a provision of national procedural law under which, in judicial proceedings in which it is sought to establish State liability with a view to obtaining compensation for damage caused by a breach of Union law, witness evidence is admissible only in exceptional cases is permissible to the extent to which it does not infringe the principles of equivalence and effectiveness: ECJ, Case C-228/98 *Dounias* [2000] E.C.R. I-577, paras 68–72.

[75] ECJ, Case C-55/06 *Arcor* [2008] E.C.R. I-2931, paras 179–92; ECJ, Case C-264/08 *Direct Parcel Distribution Belgium* [2010] E.C.R. I-731, paras 31–36.

[76] It is for the national legal orders to classify the actions which can be used to obtain reimbursement of charges paid but not due: see ECJ (order of 23 April 2008), Case C-201/05 *Test Claimants in the CFC and Dividend Group Litigation* [2008] E.C.R. I-2875, para. 111 (and further citations therein). For instance, a claim for reimbursement can be made through an action for annulment of the decision imposing the charge (ECJ, Case C-30/02 *Recheio* [2004] E.C.R. I-6051, para. 7), an action for damages (ECJ, Case C-118/08 *Transportes Urbanos y Servicios Generales* [2010] E.C.R. I-635, para. 11), or appeal proceedings brought against an administrative decision rejecting a claim for reimbursement (ECJ, Case C-94/10 *Danfoss* [2011] E.C.R. I-9963, para. 18).

submitted. In others, actions for the recovery of unduly paid charges must be brought before the ordinary courts, for instance, in the form of an action based on an undue payment; such actions are subject to varying time limits which, in some cases, correspond to the normal limitation period laid down by the ordinary law.[77]

(b) Constraints

4.22 The heterogeneity of the national systems is the upshot in particular of the lack of Union rules on the recovery of unlawfully imposed national charges in the relevant areas.[78] As has already been observed, this is because in such a situation it is for the national law of each Member State to designate the competent court and lay down the procedural rules governing legal claims for protecting the rights which individuals derive from Union law, provided that those rules are not less favourable than those that apply to similar national claims (principle of equivalence) and do not render the exercise of rights conferred by Union law virtually impossible or excessively difficult (principle of effectiveness).[79]

(c) Limitation periods

4.23 It clearly appears from the case-law of the Court of Justice on the recovery of a charge levied under national law but undue under Union law,[80] that the setting of 'reasonable periods of limitation of actions' satisfies in principle the test of the principles of equivalence and effectiveness.[81]

(d) Principle of equivalence

4.24 In the first place, as far as the application of the principle of equivalence is concerned, a Member State may not lay down provisions for the repayment of a charge declared contrary to or incompatible with Union law by the Court of Justice which set conditions specifically relating to the charge in question that are less favourable than those otherwise laid down for repayment of charges.[82] In contrast, Union law does not prohibit a Member State from

---

[77] ECJ, Case 61/79 *Denkavit Italiana* [1980] E.C.R. 1205, paras 23–24; ECJ, Case 68/79 *Just* [1980] E.C.R. 501, paras 22–23, and Case C-231/96 *Edis* [1998] E.C.R. I-4951, para. 36.

[78] See M. Wathelet, 'La répétition des montants payés en violation du droit Communautaire', in *Scritti in onore di Giuseppe Federico Mancini*, Vol. II (Milan, Giuffrè, 1998), 1033–165.

[79] See, e.g. ECJ (order of 23 April 2008), Case C-201/05 *Test Claimants in the CFC and Dividend Group Litigation* [2008] E.C.R. I-2875, para. 113 (and further citations therein).

[80] A clear exposition of all these aspects of this doctrine is set out in ECJ, Joined Cases C-192/95 to C-218/95 *Comateb and Others* [1997] E.C.R. I-165, paras 19–34. See also ECJ, Joined Cases C-397/98 and C-410/98 *Metallgesellschaft and Others* [2001] E.C.R. I-1727, paras 82–86; ECJ, Case C-147/01 *Weber's Wine World and Others* [2003] E.C.R. I-11365, paras 93–118; Opinion of Advocate-General L. A. Geelhoed in Case C-129/00 *Commission v Italy* [2003] E.C.R. I-14640, points 68–101; Opinion of Advocate-General D. Ruiz-Jarabo Colomer in Case C-30/02 *Recheio* [2004] E.C.R. I-6053, points 23–43.

[81] ECJ, Case 33/76 *Rewe* [1976] E.C.R. 1989, seventh and eighth subparas of para. 5; ECJ, Case 45/76 *Comet* [1976] E.C.R. 2043, paras 17–18; ECJ, Case 61/79 *Denkavit Italiana* [1980] E.C.R. 1205, para. 23; ECJ, Case C-261/95 *Palmisani* [1997] E.C.R. I-4025, para. 28; ECJ, Case C-90/94 *Haahr Petroleum* [1997] E.C.R. I-4085, para. 48; ECJ, Case C-228/96 *Aprile* [1998] E.C.R. I-7141, para. 19; ECJ, Case C-343/96 *Dilexport* [1999] E.C.R. I-579, para. 26. Note that the case-law on the setting of limitation periods also concerns the point of departure of limitation periods. See, e.g. ECJ (order of 9 July 2009), Case C-483/08 *Régie communale autonome du stade Luc Varenne* [2009] E.C.R. I-121*, Summ. pub., paras 35–42; ECJ, Case C-69/08 *Visciano* [2009] E.C.R. I-6741, paras 46–50.

[82] See, e.g. ECJ, Case 309/85 *Barra* [1988] E.C.R. 355, paras 18–19, in which the Court of Justice held that a Belgian law restricting the right to repayment of an enrolment fee imposed on students from other Member States contrary to Union law made it impossible to exercise the rights guaranteed by Art. 18

resisting actions for repayment of charges levied in breach of Union law by relying on a time limit under national law of three years, by way of derogation from the ordinary rules governing actions between private individuals for the recovery of sums paid but not due, for which the period allowed is more favourable, provided that this time limit applies in the same way to actions based on Union law for repayment of such charges as to those based on national law.[83] Consequently, observance of the principle of equivalence hinges on correctly identifying what claims—based on Union law or based on national law—are of the same kind.[84] It seems appropriate to use the most precise comparative criterion, namely the recovery of charges paid but undue (undue either under Union law or under national law).[85]

Accordingly, Union law does not preclude the legislation of a Member State from laying down, alongside a limitation period applicable under the ordinary law to actions between private individuals for the recovery of sums paid but not due, special detailed rules, which are less favourable, governing claims and legal proceedings to challenge the imposition of charges and other levies. The position would be different only if those detailed rules applied solely to actions based on Union law for the repayment of such charges or levies. The same test is applied where a Member State adopts rules which retroactively restrict the right to repayment of a sum levied but not due, in order to forestall the possible effects of a judgment of the Court of Justice.[86]

(e) Principle of effectiveness

As far as the principle of effectiveness is concerned, the Court of Justice considers that it is **4.25** compatible with Union law to lay down reasonable limitation periods for bringing proceedings.[87] A reasonable limitation period finds its justification in the fundamental principle of legal certainty, which protects both the taxpayer and the administration concerned. Such time limits are not liable to render practically impossible or excessively difficult the exercise of rights conferred by Union law.[88]

TFEU. See also ECJ, Case C-343/96 *Dilexport* [1999] E.C.R. I-579, paras 37–43; ECJ, Case C-197/03 *Commission v Italy* [2006] E.C.R. I-60*, Summ. pub., paras 43–46.

[83] It is a matter of national law whether, in the case of a claim for repayment of a charge which is contrary to Union law and therefore undue, the legal relationship between the national tax authorities and companies in a Member State is regarded as a fiscal relationship or whether the rules of the ordinary law govern that legal relationship. The primacy of Union law that caused the imposition of the charge to be undue has no bearing on the classification in national law of the claim to repayment: see ECJ, Joined Cases C-10/97 to C-22/97 *IN. CO.GE. '90* [1998] E.C.R. I-6307, paras 28–29.

[84] For instance, the Court of Justice has held on the issue of the availability under national law of possible actions for reimbursement of sums paid but not due that the system of direct taxation cannot be considered similar to the system of VAT: ECJ, Case C-35/05 *Reemtsma Cigarettenfabriken* [2007] E.C.R. I-2425, paras 43–45; see also ECJ, Case C-69/08 *Visciano* [2009] E.C.R. I-6741, para. 41.

[85] ECJ, Case C-231/96 *Edis* [1998] E.C.R. I-4951, paras 36–37; ECJ, Case C-260/96 *Spac* [1998] E.C.R. I-4997, paras 20–21.

[86] ECJ, Case C-343/96 *Dilexport* [1999] E.C.R. I-579, para. 43; ECJ, Case C-147/01 *Weber's Wine World and Others* [2003] E.C.R. I-11365, para. 92.

[87] ECJ, Case C-78/98 *Preston and Others* [2000] E.C.R. I-3201, para. 43; ECJ, Case C-125/01 *Pflücke* [2003] E.C.R. I-9375, para. 36.

[88] ECJ, Case C-231/96 *Edis* [1998] E.C.R. I-4951, para. 35. The fact that the Court has given a preliminary ruling interpreting a provision of Union law without limiting the temporal effects of its judgment does not affect the right of a Member State to impose a time limit under national law within which, on penalty of being barred, proceedings for repayment of charges levied in breach of that provision must be commenced (ECJ, Case C-231/96 *Edis*, para. 26).

The Court of Justice has regarded a national limitation period of three years from the date of the contested payment as reasonable.[89] Of course, national limitation periods are assessed on a case-by-case basis.[90]

For instance, the Court of Justice has held that a Member State is not precluded from laying down, alongside a limitation period applicable under the ordinary law to actions between private individuals for the recovery of sums paid but not due, special detailed rules governing claims and legal proceedings for the recovery of sums paid but not due against the Member State, which are less favourable. When a Member State would then lay down a shorter limitation period of five years, compared to a ten-year limitation period under ordinary law, this would not in itself be precluded by the principle of effectiveness. However, that five-year limitation period does infringe the principle of effectiveness if it would result in a situation in which an intermediary who paid taxes to the Member State on behalf of another private party as a result of the interplay between the different limitation periods would not be able to have the payments made to the Member State reimbursed, so that the charges paid but not due to the Member State were solely paid by that intermediary.[91] The same logic applies when a recipient of services is not time-barred from bringing an action for reimbursement against a supplier, whereas the latter's action for reimbursement against the Member State would be time-barred as a consequence of different rules on limitation periods.[92]

(f) Reduction of a limitation period

4.26   If a Member State decides to reduce a limitation period, the new reduced period should itself be reasonable. Reducing a limitation period will infringe the principle of effectiveness where the legislation which effected the reduction does not include transitional arrangements allowing an adequate period after its enactment for lodging the claims for repayment

---

[89] ECJ, Case C-231/96 *Edis* [1998] E.C.R. I-4951, para. 35; ECJ, Case C-260/96 *Spac* [1998] E.C.R. I-4997, para. 19: ECJ, Joined Cases C-279/96, C-280/96, and C-281/96 *Ansaldo Energia and Others* [1998] E.C.R. I-5025, paras 17–18; ECJ, Case C-343/96 *Dilexport* [1999] E.C.R. I-579, para. 70; see also ECJ, Joined Cases C-216/99 and C-222/99 *Prisco and CASER* [2002] E.C.R. I-6761, para. 70. In *Roquette Frères* (ECJ, Case C-88/99 *Roquette Frères* [2000] E.C.R. I-10465), the Court of Justice considered that a national limitation period for a claim for the recovery of undue payment of up to a minimum of four years and a maximum of five years preceding the year of the judicial decision finding the rule of national law establishing the tax to be incompatible with a superior rule of law was reasonable.

[90] Assessment of the reasonableness of a limitation period is done on a case-by-case basis, taking account of each case's own factual and legal context as a whole. It is not possible to infer from such assessments a general rule which can be applied mechanically in every field (ECJ, Case C-473/00 *Cofidis* [2002] E.C.R. I-10875, para. 37). The Court of Justice has held, for example, that a short limitation period of two weeks to contest a decision to award a public procurement contract is reasonable (ECJ, Case C-470/99 *Universale-Bau and Others* [2002] E.C.R. I-11617, paras 71–78); but that a two-year limitation period for an action brought by a career civil servant challenging a decision rejecting his candidature for a competition based on the fact that the promotion procedure was contrary to clause 4 of the framework agreement on fixed-time work was precluded by the principle of effectiveness if that period was liable to render practically impossible or excessively difficult the exercise of the rights conferred by that framework agreement (ECJ, Case C-177/10 *Rosado Santana* [2011] E.C.R. I-7907, paras 96–100). As regards the question of what period is considered 'reasonable' in the context of the charges levied in the context of VAT, see ECJ, Case C-472/08 *Alstom Power Hydro* [2010] E.C.R I-623, paras 19–21 (holding a three-year limitation period in compliance with the principle of effectiveness as this period 'is, in principle, such as to permit any normally attentive taxable person validly to assert his rights derived from European Union law'); see also ECJ, Joined Cases C-95/07 and C-96/07 *Ecotrade* [2008] E.C.R. I-3457, para. 48 (finding a two-year limitation period in compliance with the principle of effectiveness).

[91] ECJ, Joined Cases C-89/10 and C-96/10 *Q-Beef and Bosschaert* [2011] E.C.R. I-7819, paras 39–45.

[92] ECJ (judgment of 15 December 2011), Case C-427/10 *Banca Antoniana Popolare Veneta*, not reported, paras 20–42.

which persons were entitled to submit under the original legislation.[93] As far as the duration of the requisite transitional period is concerned, the Court of Justice has further specified that it must be sufficient to allow taxpayers who initially thought that the old period for bringing proceedings was available to them a reasonable period of time to assert their right of recovery.

For example, in *Grundig Italia*,[94] the Court considered that a transitional period of ninety days prior to the retroactive application of a period of three years for initiating proceedings in place of a five-year period was clearly insufficient. If an initial period of five years was taken as a reference, ninety days left taxpayers whose rights accrued approximately three years earlier in a position of having to act within three months when they had thought that almost another two years were still available. Consequently, the Court of Justice considered that where a period of ten or five years for initiating proceedings is reduced to three years, the minimum transitional period required to ensure that rights conferred by Union law can be effectively exercised and that normally diligent taxpayers can familiarize themselves with the new regime and prepare and commence proceedings in circumstances which do not compromise their chances of success can be reasonably assessed at six months.[95] In contrast, in *Recheio*,[96] a limitation period of 90 days was held to be compatible with the principle of effectiveness.[97] In that case, however, there was not a longer limitation period that was subsequently reduced to ninety days.

(g) *Charge passed on to third parties*

In principle, a trader who has paid a charge that was levied unduly is entitled to recover the sum in question. The tax authorities may refuse to repay such a charge only where repayment would result in the trader being unjustly enriched.[98] Therefore, from the point of view of Union law, there is nothing to prevent national courts from taking into account in accordance with their national law the fact that it has been possible for charges unduly levied to be incorporated in the prices of the undertaking liable for the charge and to be passed on to the purchasers.[99] The direct passing on to the purchasers of the tax wrongly levied constitutes the sole exception to the right to reimbursement of tax levied in breach of Union law.[100]   **4.27**

Furthermore, it is necessary that there is a direct link between the reimbursement of the unlawful tax and the enrichment of the taxable person. Thus, the situation in which an unlawful tax is offset by the abolition of a lawful levy of an equivalent amount cannot amount

---

[93] ECJ, Case C-62/00 *Marks & Spencer* [2002] E.C.R. I-6325, paras 34–42, where the Court of Justice held that a three-year limitation period was reasonable, but that the principle of effectiveness had been infringed because the new legislation did not provide for a transitional limitation period and was applicable immediately with retroactive effect.

[94] ECJ, Case C-255/00 *Grundig Italiana* [2002] E.C.R. I-8003.

[95] ECJ, Case C-255/00 *Grundig Italiana*, paras 36–42.

[96] ECJ, Case C-30/02 *Recheio* [2004] E.C.R. I-6051.

[97] ECJ, Case C-30/02 *Recheio*, para. 21.

[98] ECJ, Joined Cases C-192/95 to C-218/95 *Comateb and Others* [1997] E.C.R. I-165, paras 20–22; ECJ, Case C-147/01 *Weber's Wine World and Others* [2003] E.C.R. I-11365, para.109. With particular regard to charges unduly levied in connection with VAT, see ECJ, Case C-309/06 *Marks & Spencer* [2008] E.C.R. I-2283.

[99] ECJ, Case 61/79 *Denkavit Italiana* [1980] E.C.R. 1205, para. 26; ECJ, Case 68/79 *Just* [1980] E.C.R. 501, para. 26; ECJ, Case 130/79 *Express Dairy Foods* [1980] E.C.R. 1887, para. 12; ECJ, Case 199/82 *San Giorgio* [1983] E.C.R. 3595, para. 13; ECJ, Joined Cases C-192/95 to C-218/95 *Comateb and Others* [1997] E.C.R. I-165, para. 12; ECJ, Case C-343/96 *Dilexport* [1999] E.C.R. I-579, para. 47. The same principle is applied in respect of a claim for repayment of an invalid Union charge: ECJ, Case 66/80 *International Chemical* [1981] E.C.R. 1191, paras 22–26.

[100] ECJ, Case C-398/09 *Lady & Kid and Others* [2011] E.C.R. I-7375, para. 20.

to the unjust enrichment of the taxable person.[101] Conversely, Member States are allowed to require a direct relationship between the tax authorities and the persons claiming reimbursement of a sum unduly paid. Accordingly, they may resist a claim made by a purchaser to whom a duty was passed on by a taxable person on the grounds that it is not the purchaser who has paid the duty to the tax authorities. Yet, this is subject to two conditions. First, it should be possible for the purchaser to bring a civil action against the taxable person for recovery of the sum unduly paid. Second, reimbursement by that taxable person of the duty unduly paid is not virtually impossible or excessively difficult.[102] In case reimbursement would not be possible, in particular in the case of the insolvency of the taxable person, the Member State has to provide the instruments necessary to enable that purchaser to recover the sum unduly paid in order to respect the principle of effectiveness.[103]

(h) Burden of proof

4.28 Rules of evidence which render it virtually impossible or excessively difficult to recover a charge levied contrary to Union law are in breach of Union law.[104] A national provision which imposes on the taxpayer the—negative—burden of proving that the charge was not passed on to third parties or embodies a presumption that the charge was passed on does not satisfy the requirements of Union law.[105] Accordingly, a national tax authority (or a national court) cannot merely state that a charge was passed on in the selling price to consumers, that the economic burden which the charge represented for the taxable person is neutralized and that, consequently, repayment would automatically entail unjust enrichment of the trader.[106]

---

[101] ECJ, Case C-398/09 *Lady & Kid and Others* paras 21–27.

[102] ECJ, Case C-94/10 *Danfoss* [2011] E.C.R. I-9963, paras 24–29.

[103] ECJ, Case C-35/05 *Reemtsma Cigarettenfabriken* [2007] E.C.R. I-2425, para. 41.

[104] Similarly, rules of evidence which render it virtually impossible or excessively difficult to demonstrate that a provision of Union law having direct effect has been breached also violate Union law: ECJ, Case C-242/95 *GT-Link* [1997] E.C.R. I-4449, para. 26.

[105] ECJ, Case 199/82 *San Giorgio* [1983] E.C.R. 3595, para. 14; ECJ, Joined Cases 331/85, 376/85, and 378/85 *Bianco and Girard* [1988] E.C.R. 1099, paras 12–13; ECJ, Case C-343/96 *Dilexport* [1999] E.C.R. I-579, para. 48; ECJ, Joined Cases C-441/98 and C-442/98 *Michaïlidis* [2000] E.C.R. I-7145, paras 40–41. See also ECJ, Case C-129/00 *Commission v Italy* [2003] E.C.R. I-14637, where the Court held that Italy had infringed Union law insofar as the case-law of the *Corte suprema di cassazione* (Supreme Court of Cassation) was in breach of the principles enshrined in the judgments in *San Giorgio* and *Dilexport*. See, with regard to the proof of the abuse of law, ECJ, Case C-110/99 *Emsland-Stärke* [2000] E.C.R. I-11569, para. 54, in which the Court of Justice held that it was necessary to prove the existence of two elements, namely a combination of objective circumstances in which, despite formal observance of the conditions laid down by the Union rules, the purpose of those rules had not been achieved, and a subjective element consisting in the intention to obtain an advantage from the Union rules by artificially creating the conditions laid down for obtaining it. It is for the national court to establish the existence of those two elements, evidence of which must be adduced in accordance with the rules of national law, provided that the effectiveness of Union law is not thereby undermined (see also ECJ, Case C-515/03 *Eichsfelder Schlachtbetrieb* [2005] E.C.R. I-7355, para. 39; ECJ, Case C-279/05 *Vonk Dairy Products* [2007] E.C.R. I-239, paras 32–34 (and further citations therein)). See with respect to national rules of evidence requiring it to be shown by the economic operator alleging an overcompensation of a company discharging public service obligations that at least one of the four so-called 'Altmark' conditions is not met in order to obtain reimbursement of the charge at issue, ECJ, Case C-526/04 *Laboratoires Boiron* [2008] E.C.R. I-7529, paras 50–57.

[106] ECJ, Case 199/82 *San Giorgio* [1983] E.C.R. 3595, para. 14; ECJ, Case C-343/96 *Dilexport* [1999] E.C.R. I-579, paras 48, 52, and 54; ECJ, Joined Cases C-441/98 and C-442/98 *Michaïlidis* [2000] E.C.R. I-7145, paras 36–37; ECJ, Case C-147/01 *Weber's Wine World and Others* [2003] E.C.R. I-11365, paras 110–111; ECJ, Case C-398/09 *Lady & Kid and Others* [2011] E.C.R. I-7375, para. 21. For an older but still valuable analysis, see the Opinion of Advocate-General L.A. Geelhoed in ECJ, Case C-129/00 *Commission v Italy* [2003] E.C.R. I-14640, points 68–100.

(i) *Payment under protest*

A Member State may not make the recovery of a sum which was paid to a public authority **4.29**
under a mistake of law and was not due under Union law depend upon the payment having
been made under protest, since such a condition is liable to prejudice effective protection of
the rights conferred by Union law on the individuals involved.[107]

(j) *Interest*

As for the question as to whether interest is payable on wrongly levied charges, case-law **4.30**
initially held that it is 'for national law to settle all ancillary questions relating to the
reimbursement of charges improperly levied, such as the payment of interest, including
the rate of interest and the date from which it must be calculated'.[108] In *Littlewoods Retail*,[109]
the Court of Justice, however, ruled that there is an obligation under Union law for Member
States to repay with interest amounts of tax levied in breach of Union law. The rate of
interest, the date from which it must be calculated as well as the question whether simple
interest, compound interest or another type of interest must be paid is left to the Member
States, provided that the principles of equivalence and effectiveness are respected.[110]

Thus, Union law does not preclude, in the event of the repayment of charges levied in breach
thereof, payment of interest calculated by methods less favourable than those applicable under
the ordinary rules governing actions for the recovery of sums paid but not due between private
individuals, provided that those methods apply in the same way to such actions brought under
Union law as to those brought under national law.[111] However, in *Irimie*, the Court has ruled
that a national rule limiting the interest to that accruing from the day following the date of the
claim for repayment of the tax unduly levied breached the principle of effectiveness.[112]

(3) Recovery of unlawful State aid

Where the Commission orders the recovery of State aid paid over unlawfully under Union **4.31**
law, applicable provisions of national law may not affect the scope and effectiveness of
Union law.[113] The decision declaring the aid incompatible with the internal market will

---

[107] ECJ, Case C 212/94 *FMC and Others* [1996] E.C.R. I-389, para. 72.

[108] ECJ, Joined Cases C-397/98 and C-410/98 *Metallgesellschaft and Others* [2001] E.C.R. I-1727,
para. 86; ECJ, Case C-470/04 *N* [2006] E.C.R. I-7409, para. 60 (and further citations therein). The same
applies for payment of interest on arrears designed to compensate for constitution of guarantees given
similarities between a restitution of taxes unduly levied and a release of guarantees demanded in breach of
Union law (ECJ, Case C-470/04 *N*, para. 61).

[109] ECJ (judgment of 18 July 2012), Case C-591/10 *Littlewoods Retail and Others*, not reported, para. 26.

[110] ECJ, Case C-591/10 *Littlewoods Retail Ltd and Others*, paras 22–34.

[111] ECJ, Joined Cases C-279/96, C-280/96, and C-281/96 *Ansaldo Energia and Others* [1998] E.C.R.
I-5025, paras 24–36. Compare ECJ, Joined Cases C-216/99 and C-222/99 *Prisco and CASER* [2002]
E.C.R. I-6761, paras 76–79.

[112] ECJ (judgment of 18 April 2013), Case C-565/11 *Irimie*, not reported, paras 26–29.

[113] ECJ, Case C-507/08 *Commission v Slovak Republic* [2010] E.C.R. I-13489, para. 51 (and further
citations therein); ECJ, Case C-119/05 *Lucchini* [2007] E.C.R. I-6199, para. 63. The same basic rules also
apply to the recovery by national authorities of Union aid which has been unduly paid: ECJ, Case C-298/96
Oelmühle Hamburg and Schmidt Söhne [1998] E.C.R. I-4767 (specification of the requirements of Union law
for the application of the principle of the loss of unjust enrichment on which the recipient of undue Union aid
may possibly rely in order to avoid having to make repayment to the national authorities). See also ECJ, Joined
Cases C-383/06 to C-385/06 *Vereniging Nationaal Overlegorgaan Sociale Werkvoorziening and Others* [2008]
E.C.R. I-1561, paras 48–50 (and further citations therein). For a general discussion on the role of national
courts and the duty to recover unlawful State aid, see J. L. da Cruz Vilaça, 'O papel dos tribunais nacionais na
aplicaçao das regras do tratado sobre auxílios de estado: até onde deve ir em virtuda da última frase do N.° 3 do
artigo 88.° TCE?', in Faculdade de Direito da Universidade de Lisboa (eds), *Estudos jurídicos e económicos em*

generally require the authority that granted the aid to recover it in accordance with the rules of national law. But the application of those rules must not make it impossible in practice to recover the sums irregularly granted or be discriminatory in relation to comparable cases that are governed solely by national legislation.[114]

Accordingly, national courts should leave unapplied a procedural rule attaching automatic suspensory effect to actions brought against demands for reimbursement of unlawful State aid.[115] Even when national courts consider a Commission decision declaring State aid unlawful to be invalid, they cannot suspend national implementing measures unless they comply with the conditions for interim relief, as laid down in the case-law (see para. 4.62).[116]

(4) Claims for an advantage due under Union law

(a) Limitation periods

4.32 An individual who claims a certain advantage on the basis of Union law from a national authority will normally also have to assert his claim within a specific time limit. Here, too, the case-law assumes that a reasonable limitation period finds its justification in the fundamental principle of legal certainty.[117]

(b) Claim based on a directive not implemented in time

4.33 It may happen that individuals base their claim to a certain social advantage on the provisions having direct effect of a directive that the Member State concerned failed to implement in time. In such a case, is the national court entitled to apply the limitation period provided for in its national procedural law?

The answer given initially by the Court of Justice was unqualifiedly in the negative. Accordingly, it held in *Emmott* that, in the light of the particular nature of directives, '[Union] law precludes the competent authorities of a Member State from relying, in proceedings brought against them by an individual before the national courts in order to protect rights directly conferred upon him by . . . [a directive], on national procedural rules relating to time-limits for bringing proceedings so long as that Member State has not properly transposed that directive into its domestic legal system'.[118] The rationale was that

---

homenagem ao prof. doutor António de Sousa Franco, Vol. 2 (Coimbra, Coimbra Editora, 2006), 698–715; K. Lenaerts, 'L'articulation entre ordres juridiques à l'oeuvre: le regime de récupération des aides d'Etat versées en violation du droit communautaire', in G. C. Rodriguez Iglesias *et al.* (ed.), *Problèmes d'interprétation: à la mémoire de Constantinos N. Kakouris* (Athens and Brussels, Bruylant and Sakkoulas, 2003), 259–83.

[114] ECJ, Joined Cases 205/82 to 215/82 *Deutsche Milchkontor* [1983] E.C.R. 2633, paras 17–24; ECJ, Case 94/87 *Commission v Germany* [1989] E.C.R. 175, para. 12; ECJ, Case C-210/09 *Scott and Kimberly Clark* [2010] I-4613, paras 20–21; CFI, Case T-459/93 *Siemens v Commission* [1995] E.C.R. II-1675, para. 82. For an example in which various principles of national law were set aside, see ECJ, Case C-24/95 *AlcanDeutschland* [1997] E.C.R. I-1591. Nevertheless, it cannot be precluded that a recipient of illegally granted aid may rely on exceptional circumstances on the basis of which it had legitimately assumed the aid to be lawful and thus declined to refund the aid (ECJ, Case C-99/02 *Commission v Italy* [2004] E.C.R. I-3353, para. 20).

[115] ECJ, Case C-232/05 *Commission v France* [2006] E.C.R. I-10071, para. 53.

[116] ECJ, Case C-304/09 *Commission v Italy* [2010] E.C.R. I-13903, para. 45.

[117] ECJ, Case C-78/98 *Preston and Others* [2000] E.C.R. I-3201, para. 33; ECJ, Case C-125/01 *Pflücke* [2003] E.C.R. I-9375, para. 36; ECJ, Case C-445/06 *Danske Slagterier* [2009] E.C.R. I-2119, para. 32 (and further citations therein); ECJ, Case C-542/08 *Barth* [2010] E.C.R. I-3189, paras 28–29; ECJ, Case C-246/09 *Bulicke* [2010] E.C.R. I-7003, para. 36 (and further citations therein).

[118] ECJ, Case C-208/90 *Emmott* [1991] E.C.R. I-4269, paras 17 and 24, at I-4298-4299.

so long as a directive has not been properly transposed into national law, individuals are unable to ascertain the full extent of their rights.[119]

Subsequently, the Court of Justice refined that case-law. It is only where it appears that, as a result of the application of a limitation period, an individual has no possibility at all of asserting the rights conferred upon him or her by a directive that the limitation period may not be applied.[120] A national rule which restricts the retroactive effect of a claim to an unpaid social security benefit is compatible with Union law, even where the claim is based on a provision with direct effect of a directive which has not been properly transposed into national law. This is because such a rule does not affect the individual's actual right to the relevant benefit. Furthermore, Union law does not preclude the application of a provision of national law whereby benefits for incapacity for work are payable not earlier than one year before the date of claim, in the case where an individual seeks to rely on rights conferred by a provision with direct effect of a directive which was not transposed into national law on time.[121]

(c) Principle of effectiveness

In contrast, a national provision that is such as to render any action by individuals relying on **4.34** Union law impossible in practice is incompatible with Union law. Thus, the Court of Justice held in *Magorrian and Cunningham* that Union law precludes the application, to a claim based on Art. 157 TFEU for recognition of the claimants' entitlement to join an occupational pension scheme, of a national rule under which such entitlement is limited to a period which starts to run from a point in time two years prior to commencement of proceedings in connection with the claim.[122] Unlike rules which in the interests of legal certainty merely limit the retroactive scope of a claim for certain benefits and do not therefore strike at the very essence of the rights conferred by the Union legal order, a rule such as the one at issue in *Magorrian and Cunningham* was such as to render any action by individuals relying on Art. 157 TFEU impossible in practice. In fact, the rule at issue meant that a large number of years

---

[119] ECJ, Case C-208/90 *Emmott*, para. 21.

[120] See, e.g. ECJ, Case C-90/94 *Haahr Petroleum* [1997] E.C.R. I-4085, para. 52; ECJ, Joined Cases C-114/95 and C-115/95 *Texaco and Olieselskabet Danmark* [1997] E.C.R. I-4263, para. 48; ECJ, Case C-188/95 *Fantask and Others* [1997] E.C.R. I-6783, para. 51; ECJ, Case C-88/99 *Roquette Frères* [2000] E.C.R. I-10465, para. 34; ECJ, Case C-445/06 *Danske Slagterier* [2009] E.C.R. I-2119, paras 53–55; ECJ, Case C-63/08 *Pontin* [2009] E.C.R. I-10467, paras 60–67.

[121] ECJ, Case C-338/91 *Steenhorst-Neerings* [1993] E.C.R. I-5475, para. 24; ECJ, Case C-410/92 *Johnson* [1994] E.C.R. I-5483, para. 36. For the application of these principles to the recovery of unlawful charges, see ECJ, Case C-231/96 *Edis* [1998] E.C.R. I-4951, paras 40–49; ECJ, Case C-260/96 *Spac* [1998] E.C.R. I-4997, paras 24–32; ECJ, Joined Cases C-279/96, C-280/96, and C-281/96 *Ansaldo Energia and Others* [1998] E.C.R. I-5025, paras 13–23. In each of those judgments, the Court of Justice held that having regard to the documents before the Court and the arguments presented at the hearing, it did not appear that the conduct of the Italian authorities, in conjunction with the existence of the contested time limit, had the effect, as it did in *Emmott* (n. 118), of depriving the claimants of any opportunity of enforcing their rights before the national courts. Union law does not preclude the application of a period of limitation or prescription laid down by a rule of national law which restricts the period prior to the bringing of the claim in the national court in respect of which reimbursement of undue payments may be obtained, where that rule is not discriminatory and does not prejudice the actual right conferred on individuals by a preliminary ruling on invalidity: ECJ, Case C-212/94 *FMC and Others* [1996] E.C.R. I-389, paras 63–64; ECJ, Case C-90/94 *Haahr Petroleum* [1997] E.C.R. I-4085, paras 45–53; ECJ, Joined Cases C-114/95 and C-115/95 *Texaco and Olieselskabet Danmark* [1997] E.C.R. I-4263, paras 44–49; ECJ, Case C-188/95 *Fantask and Others* [1997] E.C.R. I-6783.

[122] ECJ, Case C-246/96 *Magorrian and Cunningham* [1997] E.C.R. I-7153, para. 47.

of service were not taken into account in calculating the pensions to which those concerned would have been entitled in the future.[123]

(d) Deceit

4.35 Finally, the principle of effectiveness precludes the application of a national limitation period which is per se reasonable where the claim was brought out of time owing to the deceit of the other party. Accordingly, Union law precludes the application of a rule of national law which limits an employee's entitlement to arrears of remuneration or damages for breach of the principle of equal pay to a period of two years prior to the date on which the proceedings were instituted, there being no possibility of extending that period, where the delay in bringing a claim is attributable to the fact that the employer deliberately misrepresented to the employee the level of remuneration received by persons of the opposite sex performing like work.[124]

D. Assessment of the legality of national provisions in the light of Union law

(1) Inapplicability of conflicting national rules

4.36 Under *Simmenthal*, the national court's obligation to give full effect to Union law means that it must 'if necessary, [refuse] of its own motion to apply any conflicting provisions of national legislation, even if adopted subsequently, and it is not necessary for the court to request or await the prior setting aside of such provisions by legislative or other constitutional means'.[125] By that ruling, the Court of Justice debarred Member States from placing any restriction on their courts in declaring inapplicable provisions or principles of national law which conflict with Union law. If there is nevertheless such a restriction, national courts must simply set it aside on the basis of Union law, which is binding upon the Member State of which they are institutions.

(2) Avoiding conflict

4.37 This principle can be respected without any difficulty where a provision of national law conflicts with a provision of primary or secondary Union law having direct effect in proceedings between a private party and public authorities. The situation is, however, different in proceedings exclusively between private parties. Since a directive cannot of itself

---

[123] ECJ, Case C-246/96 *Magorrian and Cunningham*, paras 43–45. For other recent examples, see e.g. ECJ, Case C-63/08 *Pontin* [2009] E.C.R. I-10467, paras 55–69 (finding national rules relating to specific types of action and 15-day limitation period in respect of the dismissal of pregnant workers and workers having recently given birth or breastfeeding adopted pursuant to certain directives problematic on grounds of both principles of equivalence and effectiveness); ECJ, Case C-69/08 *Visciano* [2009] E.C.R. I-6741, paras 47–49 (finding that one-year limitation period for bringing claims pursuant to directive providing fund in event of employer insolvency without specifying when it starts to run may constitute violation of the principle of effectiveness due to the legal uncertainty caused).

[124] ECJ, Case C-326/96 *Levez* [1998] E.C.R. I-7835, para. 34. Compare ECJ, Case C-524/08 *Barth* [2010] E.C.R. I-3189, para. 36. Similar concerns are at the basis of the Court's judgment in *Emmott* (discussed in para. 4.33): see ECJ, Case C-452/09 *Iaia and Others* [2011] E.C.R. I-4043, paras 19–20.

[125] ECJ, Case 106/77 *Simmenthal* [1978] E.C.R. 629, operative part, at 645–6. See also ECJ, Case C-119/05 *Lucchini* [2007] E.C.R. I-6199, para. 61, and ECJ, Joined Cases C-188/10 and C-189/10 *Melki and Abdeli* [2010] E.C.R. I-5667, para. 43 (and further citations therein). With regard to the non-applicability of a technical provision which was not notified in accordance with Directive 83/189/EEC as then applicable in the context of a dispute between individuals relating in particular to contractual rights and obligations, national law will determine what consequences (as regards the possible nullity or unenforceability of the contract) ensue from the non-applicability of the technical provision: ECJ, Case C-159/00 *Sapod Audic* [2002] E.C.R. I-5031, para. 53.

apply in proceedings exclusively between private parties, a national court cannot be obliged simply to set aside a provision of national law conflicting with a provision of a directive, even if it concerns a clear, precise, and unconditional provision seeking to confer rights or impose obligations on individuals. Nevertheless, the national court is bound to interpret national law, so far as possible, in the light of the wording and the purpose of the directive concerned in order to achieve the result sought by it. Although the principle that national law must be interpreted in conformity with Union law concerns chiefly domestic provisions enacted in order to implement the directive in question, it does not require merely those provisions to be so interpreted but requires the national court to consider national law as a whole in order to assess to what extent it may be applied so as not to produce a result contrary to that sought by the directive. In that context, if the application of interpretative methods recognized by national law enables a provision of domestic law to be construed, in certain circumstances, in such a way as to avoid conflict with another rule of domestic law or the scope of that provision to be restricted to that end by applying it only insofar as it is compatible with the rule concerned, the national court is bound to use those methods in order to achieve the result sought by the directive. The principle of interpretation in conformity with Union law thus requires the national court to do whatever lies within its power, having regard to the whole body of rules of national law, to ensure that the directive is fully effective.[126]

(3) Time frame

The decisive point in time that the national court takes into account in order to assess the legality of an act in the light of Union law is determined by national law, provided that it does not detract from the principles of equivalence and effectiveness.[127]   **4.38**

E. Raising pleas derived from Union law of the court's own motion

(1) Principle

The principle of the full effectiveness of Union law does not require the national court to raise applicable Union law in all circumstances of its own motion ('*ex officio*'). The national court has the power to do so if it considers that Union law must be applied,[128] but it is only where the parties have failed to invoke mandatory rules of Union law having direct effect[129] that it may be obliged to raise those rules of its own motion.   **4.39**

---

[126] ECJ, Joined Cases C-397/01 to C-403/01 *Pfeiffer and Others* [2004] E.C.R. I-8835, paras 107–18 (and the case-law cited therein). See further, e.g. ECJ, Case C-212/04 *Adeneler and Others* [2006] E.C.R. I-6057, paras 108–11; ECJ, Case C-12/08 *Mono Car Styling* [2009] E.C.R. I- 6653, paras 59–63; ECJ, Case C-555/07 *Kücükdeveci* [2010] E.C.R. I-365, paras 45–47; ECJ (judgment of 24 January 2012), Case C-282/10 *Dominguez*, not reported, paras 22–44; ECJ (judgment of 11 April 2013), Case C-138/12 *Rusedespred*, not reported, para. 37. The literature involving these cases and broader issues regarding the invocability of Union law is voluminous. See generally K. Lenaerts and P. Van Nuffel (R. Bray and N. Cambien (eds)), *European Union Law* (3rd edn, London, Sweet & Maxwell, 2011), paras 22–070–22–099 for a recent selection (with further citations therein). See also K. Lenaerts and T. Corthaut, 'Towards an Internally Consistent Doctrine on Invoking Norms of EU law', in S. Prechal and Van B. van Roermund (eds), *The Coherence of EU Law—The Search for Unity in Divergent Concepts* (Oxford, Oxford University Press, 2008), 495–515; K. Lenaerts and J. A. Gutiérrez-Fons, 'The Constitutional Allocation of Powers and General Principles of EU Law' (2010) C.M.L. Rev. 1629–69.

[127] ECJ, Case C-92/00 *HI* [2002] E.C.R. I-5553, para. 67.

[128] ECJ, Joined Cases C-87-89/90 *Verholen and Others* [1991] E.C.R. I-3757, para. 13.

[129] The mandatory (or public policy) nature of a provision of Union law does not depend on criteria stemming from national law, but is determined on the basis of Union law: see ECJ, Case C-126/97 *Eco Swiss*

(2) Bases of the principle

4.40   Depending on the case, the Court of Justice has identified different bases for this principle. Where there is an obligation for the national court to raise mandatory rules of law of its own motion by virtue of domestic law, there will be the same obligation to raise Union rules of the same nature by virtue of the principle of procedural equal treatment.[130] Where domestic law merely confers on national courts a discretion to apply mandatory rules of law of their own motion, the same obligation to raise Union rules remains pursuant to the principle of sincere cooperation laid down in Art. 4(3) TEU, which requires national courts to use all the possibilities afforded by national law in order to ensure the legal protection which persons derive from the direct effect of provisions of Union law,[131] or alternatively pursuant to the duty on the courts, as authorities of the Member States, under the third paragraph of Art. 288 TFEU to take all the measures necessary to achieve the result prescribed by a directive.[132] It follows that, in the absence of any Union provision governing the matter, there will be a requirement for the national courts to raise provisions of Union law of their own motion only if there exists a requirement or a discretion to raise mandatory rules by virtue of domestic law.[133]

Furthermore, rules of national procedural law must comply with the principles of equivalence and effectiveness to which reference has already been made (see para. 4.04),[134] in particular the requirement that they must not render the exercise of rights conferred by Union law virtually impossible or excessively difficult. In addition, they must not prevent the preliminary

---

China Time [1999] E.C.R. I-3055, paras 34–39. See also T. Corthaut, *EU Ordre Public* (Alphen aan de Rijn, Kluwer Law International, 2012), 200–38; S. Prechal and N. Shelkoplyas, 'National Procedures, Public Policy and EC Law. From *Van Schijndel* to *Eco Swiss* and Beyond' (2004) Eur. Rev. Priv. L. 589–611. See further A. Ó Caimh, 'Issues of EU Law Raised by National Courts of Their Own Motion', in P. Cardonnel, A. Rosas, and N. Wahl (eds), *Constitutionalising The EU Judicial System. Essays in Honour of Pernilla Lindh* (Oxford and Portland Oregon, Hart Publishing, 2012), 123–38.

[130] Compare ECJ, Joined Cases C-222/05 to C-225/05 *van der Weerd* [2007] E.C.R. I-4233, paras 29–32, in which the Court found that provisions of a Union directive on foot-and-mouth disease did not occupy a similar position in the Union legal order to Dutch rules of public policy. This case is discussed further in n. 140 and accompanying text.

[131] ECJ, Joined Cases C-430/93 and C-431/93 *Van Schijndel and Van Veen* [1995] E.C.R. I-4705, paras 13–14.

[132] ECJ, Case C-72/95 *Kraaijeveld and Others* [1996] E.C.R. I-5403, paras 54–61. Cf. ECJ, Joined Cases C-240/98 to C-244/98 *Océano Grupo Editorial and Salvat Editores* [2000] E.C.R. I-4941, where the national court's power to declare of its own motion that it had no jurisdiction was inferred directly from Council Directive 93/13/EEC of 5 April 1993 on unfair terms in consumer contracts ([1993] O.J. L95/29), as amended by Directive 2011/83/EU of the European Parliament and of the Council of 25 October 2011 on consumer rights ([2011] O.J. L304/64), and from the objectives underlying that Directive. See S. Prechal, 'Ambtshalve toetsen van oneerlijke bedingen door middel van conforme uitleg' (2001) N.T.E.R. 104–108. In the follow-up to the *Oceano Grupo* case, see ECJ, Case C-243/08 *Pannon GSM* [2009] E.C.R. I-4713, and ECJ, Case C-40/08 *Asturcom Telecomunicaciones* [2009] E.C.R. I-9579; ECJ, Case C-137/08 *VB Pénzügyi Lízing* [2010] E.C.R. I-10847. See further para. 4.41.

[133] ECJ, Joined Cases C-430/93 and C-431/93 *Van Schijndel and Van Veen* [1995] E.C.R. I-4705, para. 15. The Court did not explain exactly why a requirement for national courts to raise of their own motion rules of Union law having direct effect exists where it is only possible to raise mandatory national rules of their own motion. In his Opinion in that case, Advocate-General F.G. Jacobs argued that if the view were taken that national procedural rules must always yield to Union law, that would unduly subvert established principles underlying the legal systems of the Member States. It could be regarded as infringing the principles of subsidiarity and proportionality. It would also give rise to widespread anomalies, since the effect would be to afford greater protection to rights which are not, by virtue of being Union rights, inherently of greater importance than rights recognized by national law: Opinion of Advocate-General F.G. Jacobs, point 27.

[134] ECJ, Joined Cases C-430/93 and C-431/93 *Van Schijndel and Van Veen*, para. 17.

ruling procedure laid down in Art. 267 TFEU from being followed.[135] A rule of national procedural law which does not satisfy those conditions must be set aside,[136] with the result that the national court in question may nevertheless be subject to the requirement to raise rules of Union law of its own motion. In this regard, the Court of Justice tests the national procedural rules against Union law having regard to their role in the procedure, its progress, and its special features, before the various national authorities. Frequently, the Court also has regard to the basic principles of the domestic legal system, such as protection of the rights of the defence, the principle of legal certainty, and the proper conduct of the procedure.[137]

Accordingly, the Court held in *Van Schijndel and Van Veen* that civil courts are not required to abandon the passive role assigned to them by raising a rule of Union law of their own motion when this would require them to go beyond the ambit of the dispute as defined by the parties and to rely upon facts and circumstances not relied upon by the parties in their application.[138] In contrast, in *Peterbroeck*, a rule of the Belgian Income Tax Code which prevented the national court from inquiring of its own motion into the compatibility of a tax assessment with a provision of Union law in proceedings relating to that assessment unless the taxpayer had raised the relevant provision within a specified time limit was held by the Court to be contrary to Union law.[139]

More recently, in *van der Weerd*,[140] the Court reiterated, in line with *Van Schijndel and Van Veen*, that Union law did not preclude national procedural rules that restricted the power of a national court to raise pleas of its own motion where that would require it to abandon the passive role assigned to it by going beyond the ambit of the dispute defined by the parties themselves.[141] Then, after distinguishing the instant proceedings from certain prior judgments,[142] the Court held that the principle of effectiveness did not impose an obligation on the national court to raise a plea based on a provision of Union law of its own motion, 'irrespective of the importance of that provision to the [Union] legal order, where the parties are given a genuine opportunity to raise a plea based on [Union] law before a national court', which had been the case here.[143]

---

[135] ECJ, Joined Cases C-430/93 and C-431/93 *Van Schijndel and Van Veen*, para.18; ECJ, Case 166/73 *Rheinmühlen-Düsseldorf* [1974] E.C.R. 33, paras 2–3 (and case-law cited therein).

[136] See para. 3.19.

[137] ECJ, Joined Cases C-430/93 and C-431/93 *Van Schijndel and Van Veen*, para. 19. The criterion whereby the Court of Justice also considers the role of the procedural rule under national law seems to go further than the criterion in Case 33/76 *Rewe* (see para. 4.01), whereby the Court of Justice considers only the effect of the relevant rule in a particular case.

[138] ECJ, Joined Cases C-430/93 and C-431/93 *Van Schijndel and Van Veen*, para. 22: Union law does not require national courts to raise of their own motion an issue concerning the breach of provisions of Union law where examination of that issue would oblige them to abandon the passive role assigned to them by going beyond the dispute defined by the parties themselves and relying on facts and circumstances other than those on which the party with an interest in application of those provisions bases his or her claim.

[139] ECJ, Case C-312/93 *Peterbroeck* [1995] E.C.R. I-4599. Characteristics and circumstances to which the Court of Justice had regard in finding that such a procedural rule was incompatible with Union law included the fact that the national court was the first judicial authority to have cognisance of the case and to be able to request a preliminary ruling, the fact that another judicial authority in a further hearing was precluded from raising the question of compatibility with Union law of its own motion, and the fact that the impossibility for national courts to raise points of Union law of their own motion did not appear to be reasonably justifiable by principles such as the requirement of legal certainty or proper conduct of the procedure.

[140] ECJ, Joined Cases C-222/05 to C-225/05 *van der Weerd* [2007] E.C.R. I-4233.

[141] ECJ, Joined Cases C-222/05 to C-225/05 *van der Weerd*, paras 34–38.

[142] ECJ, Joined Cases C-222/05 to C-225/05 *van der Weerd*, paras 39–40.

[143] ECJ, Joined Cases C-222/05 to C-225/05 *van der Weerd*, para. 41.

Likewise, in *Heemskerk and Schaap*,[144] the Court made clear that Union law cannot oblige a national court to apply Union legislation of its own motion where this would have the effect of denying the principle, enshrined in its national procedural law, of the prohibition of *reformatio in pejus* (that is to say, that an individual bringing an action must not be placed in a less favourable position than if he had not brought the action).[145] In the Court's view, such an obligation would be contrary not only to the principles of respect for the rights of the defence, legal certainty, and protection of legitimate expectations, which underlie the prohibition, but would also expose an individual who brought an action against an act adversely affecting him to the risk that such an action would place him in a less favourable position than he would have been in, had he not brought that action.[146]

(3) Application in the field of consumer protection law

4.41 The case-law of the Court on the *ex officio* application of Union law by national courts in the field of consumer protection law takes a somewhat different approach.[147] Rather than analysing national rules on *ex officio* application wholly from the standpoint of national procedural autonomy and testing their compliance with the principles of equivalence and effectiveness, the Court appears to frame this particular line of case-law primarily in the context of the full effectiveness of Union law.[148] The case-law has centred on Arts 6 and 7 of Council Directive 93/13/EEC on unfair terms in consumer contracts[149] and is based on the premise that the consumer is the weaker party to a consumer contract and should be protected.[150] Therefore, in order to restore the equality of the parties to such contract, national courts should be able to determine of their own motion whether a contractual term is unfair.[151] This case-law has been extended to other provisions of Union consumer law measures, including Art. 11(2) of Council Directive 87/102/EEC on consumer credit (the 'old' Consumer Credit Directive)[152] and Art. 4 of Council Directive 85/577/EEC to

---

[144] ECJ, Case C-455/06 *Heemskerk and Schaap* [2008] E.C.R. I-8763.

[145] ECJ, Case C-455/06 *Heemskerk and Schaap*, paras 44–46, 48.

[146] ECJ, Case C-455/06 *Heemskerk and Schaap*, para. 47.

[147] See, e.g. V. Trstenjak and E. Beysen, 'European Consumer Protection Law: *Curia semper dabit remedium*? (2011) 40 C.M.L. Rev. 95–124.

[148] See para. 4.04.

[149] Council Directive 93/13/EEC of 5 April 1993 on unfair terms in consumer contracts ([1993] O.J. L95/29). This Directive has been amended by Directive 2011/83/EU of the European Parliament and of the Council of 25 October 2011 on consumer rights, [2011] O.J. L304/64 (the so-called Consumer Rights Directive).

[150] ECJ (judgment of 14 March 2013), Case C-415/11 *Aziz*, not reported, paras 44–45. See C. Toader, 'Méthodes d'interprétation en droit de l'Union européenne en matière de protection du consommateur: une approche pratique', in V. Kronenberger, M. T. D'Alessio, and V. Placco (eds), *De Rome à Lisbonne: les juridictions de l'Union européenne à la croisée des chemins. Mélanges en l'honneur de Paolo Mengozzi* (Brussels, Bruylant, 2013), 455–7.

[151] ECJ, Joined Cases C-240/98 to C-244/98 *Océano Grupo Editorial and Salvat Editores* [2000] E.C.R. I-4941, paras 25–26 (T. Corthaut, case note (2002) Col. J. Eur. L. 293–310); ECJ, Case C-168/05 *Mostaza Claro* [2006] E.C.R. I-10421, para. 36.

[152] Council Directive 87/102/EEC of 22 December 1986 for the approximation of the laws, regulations, and administrative provisions of the Member States concerning consumer credit, [1987] O.J. L42/48; ECJ, Case C-429/05 *Rampion and Godard* [2007] E.C.R. I-8017, paras 63–69. This Directive has been replaced by Directive 2008/48/EC of the European Parliament and of the Council of 23 April 2008 on credit agreements for consumers and repealing Council Directive 87/102/EEC, [2008] O.J. L133/66.

protect the consumer in respect of contracts negotiated away from business premises (the so-called Doorstep Selling Directive).[153]

In respect of Art. 6 of Directive 93/13/EEC on unfair terms in consumer contracts, the Court of Justice has clarified in subsequent case-law that national courts, by virtue of Union law, not only have the possibility, but also the obligation to determine *ex officio* the unfairness of consumer contracts.[154] Furthermore, in *VB Pénzügyi Lízing*, the Court ruled that Directive 93/13/EEC also included an obligation for national courts to take measures of instruction *ex officio*.[155] This contrasts with the classic line of case-law on the *ex officio* application of Union law by national courts as developed in *Van Schijndel* and *Van Veen*, where the Court held that national courts should not be obliged to go beyond the ambit of the dispute as defined by the parties and to rely on facts and circumstances not relied upon by the parties in their application.[156] Another example can be found in the context of arbitration proceedings. In *Eco Swiss*, the Court of Justice relied heavily on the principle of equivalence in deciding that if it would also be possible under national law for public policy reasons, a national court must grant the application for annulment of an arbitral award even though the party challenging that arbitral award only raised for the first time before that national court the incompatibility of the arbitration agreement with Union law.[157] Yet, in *Mostaza Claro*, the Court of Justice did not rely on the principles of equivalence and effectiveness, although it referred to them in a general way, and instead ruled that 'the result sought by Art. 6 of the Directive [. . .] could not be achieved if the court seised of an action for annulment of an arbitration award was unable to determine whether that award was void solely because the consumer did not plead the invalidity of the arbitration agreement in the course of the arbitration proceedings'.[158] The emphasis in the latter judgment is thus placed on the full effectiveness of Directive 93/13/EEC, with the principle of national procedural autonomy playing a less prominent role.

In certain recent cases, the Court of Justice did, however, couch its analysis in the framework of the principle of national procedural autonomy. Yet, in doing so, the Court explicitly distinguished these cases from its general line of case-law on the *ex officio* application of Union consumer protection law. In *Asturcom*, the Court held that Art. 6 of Directive 93/13/EEC did not go as far as requiring a national court responsible for the execution of an arbitral award that had become final to assess *ex officio* the fairness of an arbitration agreement.[159] The Court took issue with the fact that the consumer had taken no action at all, either by participating in the arbitration proceedings or by bringing an action for annulment before the competent national court.[160] Therefore, in contrast with *Mostaza Claro*, the Court did not

---

[153] Council Directive 85/577/EEC of 20 December 1985 to protect the consumer in respect of contracts negotiated away from business premises, [1985] O.J. L372/31; ECJ, Case C-227/08 *Martín Martín* [2009] E.C.R. I-11939, paras 27–29. This Directive has since been repealed by the Consumer Rights Directive, cited in n. 149.

[154] ECJ, Case C-168/05 *Mostaza Claro* [2006] E.C.R. I-10421, paras 38–39; ECJ, Case C-243/08 *Pannon GSM* [2009] E.C.R. I-4713, para. 32; ECJ, Case C-137/08 *VB Pénzügyi Lízing* [2010] E.C.R. I-10847, para. 49; ECJ (judgment of 14 June 2012), Case C-618/10 *Banco Español de Crédito*, not reported, paras 42–43.

[155] ECJ, Case C-137/08 *VB Pénzügyi Lízing* [2010] E.C.R. I-10847, para. 56.

[156] See para. 4.40.

[157] See n. 129.

[158] ECJ, Case C-168/05 *Mostaza Claro* [2006] E.C.R. I-10421, para. 30.

[159] ECJ, Case C-40/08 *Asturcom Telecomunicaciones* [2009] E.C.R. I-9579.

[160] ECJ, Case C-40/08 *Asturcom Telecomunicaciones*, paras 33–34.

find that the effective application of Art. 6 of Directive 93/13/EEC required the exequatur judge to assess *ex officio* the fairness of the arbitration agreement. Instead, it analysed the principle of *res judicata* in the framework of national procedural autonomy.[161] The Court concluded that the principle of effectiveness was not breached and that by virtue of the principle of equivalence the national court was only obliged to assess the fairness of the arbitration agreement if it had the possibility to do so for similar cases under national law.[162]

In *Banco Español de Crédito*, the Court of Justice was asked in the context of the preliminary ruling procedure to clarify the obligations of the national judge in the context of an order for payment procedure where the consumer had not yet lodged an objection.[163] The Court distinguished this case from *Pannon* and *VB Pénzügyi Lízing* because in those latter cases the consumer had already objected to the order for payment.[164] As a result of that objection, the order for payment procedure had been transformed into an ordinary civil procedure, and consequently, the case-law relating to Art. 6 of Directive 93/13/EEC applied. Since in *Banco Español de Crédito*, no objection had yet been lodged by the consumer, the Court's approach was different, presumably motivated by the specificities of the order for payment procedure. The Court did not apply its case-law relating to the full effectiveness of Art. 6 of Directive 93/13/EEC, but analysed the national procedural rules concerning the order for payment procedure in the framework of national procedural autonomy.[165] The Court concluded that the prohibition under national law to determine *in limine litis* or at a later stage during the proceedings the unfairness of a consumer contract *ex officio* was contrary to the principle of effectiveness insofar as it made the application of the protection conferred by Directive 93/13/EEC on consumers impossible or excessively difficult.

F. Effects of infringements of Union law

(1) Imposition of sanctions

(a) Division of powers

4.42 The division of powers as between the Union and the Member States as regards the imposition of sanctions is a controversial question. The Union does not have a general power to impose criminal sanctions.[166] It can, however, impose other types of sanctions.[167] If it does not do so or imposes merely administrative sanctions,[168] Member States may

---

[161] ECJ, Case C-40/08 *Asturcom Telecomunicaciones*, paras 34–38.
[162] ECJ, Case C-40/08 *Asturcom Telecomunicaciones*, paras 49–56.
[163] ECJ (judgment of 14 June 2012), Case C-618/10 *Banco Español de Crédito*, not reported.
[164] ECJ, Case C-618/10 *Banco Español de Crédito*, para 45. See n. 154.
[165] ECJ, Case C-618/10 *Banco Español de Crédito SA*, paras 45–46.
[166] ECJ, Case 203/80 *Casati* [1981] E.C.R. 2595, para. 27; ECJ, Case 186/87 *Cowan* [1989] E.C.R. 195, para. 19; ECJ, Case C-226/97 *Lemmens* [1998] E.C.R. I-3711, para. 19 (though underlining that this does not mean that that branch of the law may not be affected by Union law). But see, in the specific field of EU environmental legislation, ECJ, Case C-176/03 *Commission v Council* ('*Environmental crimes*') [2005] E.C.R. I-7879; ECJ, Case C-440/05 *Commission v Council* ('*Ship-source pollution*') [2007] E.C.R. I-9097. For a more general discussion on the competences of the European Union, see K. Lenaerts and P. Van Nuffel (R. Bray and N. Cambien (eds)), *European Union Law* (3rd edn, London, Sweet & Maxwell, 2011), paras 7.08–7.25.
[167] ECJ, Case C-240/90 *Germany v Commission* [1992] E.C.R. I-5383.
[168] For an illustration, see ECJ (judgment of 5 June 2012), Case C-489/10 *Bonda*, not reported.

enforce compliance with Union law by imposing criminal sanctions or using sanctions available under other branches of national law.[169]

(b) Power of Member States

The Member States' power to impose penalties or other sanctions for infringement of **4.43** Union law must, pursuant to Art. 4(3) TEU, be exercised in order to guarantee the full effectiveness of that law.[170] This power constitutes the corollary of the Member States' obligation to impose Union law in their territory.

(c) Principles of equivalence and effectiveness

The obligation to guarantee the full effectiveness of Union law entails that the sanction **4.44** imposed by a Member State in the event of infringement of a Union provision from which individuals derive rights be such as to guarantee real and effective legal protection and have a real deterrent effect.[171] To that end, not only the imposition, but also the enforcement, of the sanction is important. For example, it would appear not to be in accordance with Union law for an obligation to pay compensation imposed upon a Member State for infringement of a Union provision to be thwarted by a general executive immunity with regard to public goods.

Infringements of Union law must be penalized under conditions, both procedural and substantive, which are analogous to those applicable to infringements of national law of a similar nature. Penalties for infringements of provisions of Union law must be effective, proportionate, and dissuasive.[172] When exercising their power to impose sanctions, Member States must comply with Union law and the general principles of law embodied therein.[173] Furthermore, control procedures must not be conceived in such a manner as

---

[169] ECJ, Joined Cases C-58/95, C-75/95, C-112/95, C-119/95, C-123/95, C-135/95, C-140/95, C-141/95, C-154/95, and C-157/95 *Gallotti and Others* [1996] E.C.R. I-4345, paras 14–15. See further ECJ, Case C-40/04 *Yonemoto* [2005] E.C.R. I-7755, paras 56–60; ECJ, Case C-212/04 *Adeneler and Others* [2006] E.C.R. I-6057, paras 93–94; ECJ, Case C-348/04 *Boehringer Ingelheim and Others* [2007] E.C.R. I-3391, paras 58–59.

[170] See, e.g. ECJ, Case 68/88 *Commission v Greece* [1989] E.C.R. 2965, para. 23; ECJ, Case C-326/88 *Hansen* [1990] E.C.R. I-2911, para. 17; ECJ, Case C-7/90 *Vandevenne* [1991] E.C.R. I-4371, para. 11; ECJ, Case C-382/92 *Commission v United Kingdom* [1994] E.C.R. I-2435, para. 55; ECJ, Case C-383/92 *Commission v United Kingdom* [1994] E.C.R. I-2479, para. 40; ECJ, Case C-230/01 *Penycoed Farming Partnership* [2004] E.C.R. I-937, para. 36 (and further citations therein).

[171] ECJ, Case 14/83 *Von Colson and Kamann* [1984] E.C.R. 1891, para. 23; ECJ, Case 79/83 *Harz* [1984] E.C.R. 1921, paras 22–23 (where a Member State chooses to penalize a breach of the prohibition of discrimination by the award of compensation, the compensation must be adequate in relation to the damage sustained). See also ECJ, Case C-177/88 *Dekker* [1990] E.C.R. I-3941, paras 23–26; ECJ, Case C-271/91 *Marshall* [1993] E.C.R. I-4367, paras 24–26; ECJ, Case C-186/98 *Nunes and De Matos* [1999] E.C.R. I-4883, paras 10–11; ECJ, Case C-354/99 *Commission v Ireland* [2001] E.C.R. I-7657, para.46.

[172] See, e.g. ECJ, Case 68/88 *Commission v Greece* [1989] E.C.R. 2965, paras 23–24; ECJ, Case C-326/88 *Hansen* [1990] E.C.R. I-2911, para. 17; ECJ, Joined Cases C-58/95, C-75/95, C-112/95, C-119/95, C-123/95, C-135/95, C-140/95, C-141/95, C-154/95, and C-157/95 *Gallotti and Others* [1996] E.C.R. I-4345, para. 14; Case C-167/01 *Inspire Art* [2003] E.C.R. I-10155, para. 62; ECJ, Case C-230/01 *Penycoed Farming Partnership* [2004] E.C.R. I-937, para. 36; ECJ, Joined Cases C-387/02, C-391/02, and C-403/02 *Berlusconi and Others* [2005] E.C.R. I-3565, para. 65; ECJ, Case C-367/09 *SGS Belgium and Others* [2010] E.C.R. I-10761, paras 40–41.

[173] ECJ, Joined Cases 201/85 and 202/85 *Klensch* [1986] E.C.R. 3477, para. 8; ECJ, Case 5/88 *Wachauf* [1989] E.C.R. 2609, para. 19; ECJ, Case C-210/91 *Commission v Greece* [1992] E.C.R. I-6735, para. 19; ECJ (judgment of 16 February 2013), Case C-617/10 *Åkerberg Fransson*, not reported, paras 17–31. It should be noted that the penalties imposed by a Member State for non-compliance with formalities lawfully required in order to establish a right conferred by Union law may not be such as to constitute an obstacle to the exercise of that right. Such penalties are disproportionate and contrary to Union law: ECJ, Case C-193/94 *Skanavi and Chryssanthakopoulos* [1996] E.C.R. I-929, paras 36–39. See also ECJ (judgment of 26 September 2013), Case

---

to restrict the freedoms required by the Treaties and must not be accompanied by a penalty that is so disproportionate to the seriousness of the infringement that it becomes an obstacle to those freedoms.[174]

(d) Examples

4.45   As illustrated by *Commission v Greece*,[175] in the field of criminal or disciplinary proceedings, the Court of Justice subscribes to the Commission's view that the Member States are required by virtue of Art. 4(3) TEU 'to penalise any persons who infringe [Union] law in the same way as they penalise those who infringe national law'.[176] In the case concerned, the Hellenic Republic was charged with having infringed Union law 'by omitting to initiate all the criminal or disciplinary proceedings provided for by national law against the perpetrators of the fraud and all those who collaborated in the commission and concealment of it'.[177] This certainly places a restriction on the public prosecutor's freedom in principle to decide whether or not to bring criminal proceedings for breaches of Union law. Yet, that freedom does not disappear altogether. The Court of Justice simply held that 'the national authorities must proceed, with respect to infringements of [Union] law, with the same diligence as that which they bring to bear in implementing corresponding national laws',[178] or, in other words, that the public prosecutor must be able to show the same strictness in respect of breaches of Union law pursued under the criminal law as he or she does in respect of similar breaches of national law. This is consistent with the general obligation for Member States to ensure that 'infringements of [Union] law are penalised under conditions, both procedural and substantive, which are analogous to those applicable to infringements of national law of a similar nature and importance and which, in any event, make the penalty effective, proportionate and dissuasive'.[179]

Another illustration can be found in the field of social policy, specifically regarding the application of clause 5(1)(a) of the framework agreement on fixed-term work, prohibiting the use of successive fixed-term employment contracts where there are no objective reasons present to justify recourse to them. In a number of references for a preliminary ruling, the Court of Justice has been asked whether that clause precludes national implementing legislation completely excluding, for the public sector, the conversion of a succession of fixed-term employment contracts into a contract of indefinite duration as a sanction for abusive use of fixed-term contracts. The Court did not object to such a national rule if other effective measures existed in the national legal order to punish the abusive use of successive

---

C-418/11 *Textdata Software,* not reported, in which the Court held that a fine of 700 euros, imposed immediately and without the possibility to make representations, to penalize companies who have not compiled and disclosed their accounts within the time period laid down in national law is compatible with, *inter alia,* Arts 49 and 54 TFEU and the Charter of Fundamental Rights of the European Union. The sanction imposed may not be contrary to provisions of the ECHR: ECJ, Case C-60/02 *X* [2004] E.C.R. I-651, paras 61–63.

[174] ECJ, Case 203/80 *Casati* [1981] E.C.R. 2595, para. 27; ECJ, Joined Cases 286/82 and 26/83 *Luisi and Carbone* [1984] E.C.R. 377, para. 34.

[175] ECJ, Case 68/88 *Commission v Greece* [1989] E.C.R. 2965.

[176] ECJ, Case 68/88 *Commission v Greece* [1989] E.C.R. 2965, para. 22, first sent.

[177] ECJ, Case 68/88 *Commission v Greece,* para. 22, second sent.

[178] ECJ, Case 68/88 *Commission v Greece,* para. 25.

[179] ECJ, Case 68/88 *Commission v Greece,* para. 24. See, to the same effect, ECJ, Case C-326/88 *Hansen* [1990] E.C.R. I-2911, para. 17; ECJ, Case C-36/94 *Siesse* [1995] E.C.R. I-3573, para. 20; ECJ, Case C-213/99 *De Andrade* [2000] E.C.R. I-11083, para. 19.

fixed-term employment contracts.[180] It was then for the national judge to verify whether those sanctions complied with the principles of equivalence and effectiveness.[181] If, however, it appeared that no other effective measures were present in the national legal order, such legislation was precluded by the framework agreement.[182]

(2) Claims for damages for an infringement of Union law by Member States

(a) Principle of State liability

Union law obliges Member States to provide for the specific 'sanction' of a right to reparation where, by their action or failure to act, national authorities infringe Union law (unlawful act or omission) and this results (causal link)[183] in damage to rights which individuals derive from Union law (loss or damage).[184] The Court of Justice takes the view that 'the principle whereby a State must be liable for loss and damage caused to individuals as a result of breaches of [Union] law for which the State can be held responsible is inherent in the system of the Treaty'.[185] The obligation of Member States to make good such loss and damage is further grounded in the principle of sincere cooperation enshrined in Art. 4(3) TEU.[186]

4.46

The basic conditions under which that liability gives rise to a right to reparation depend on the nature of the breach of Union law giving rise to the loss and damage.[187] This means that those conditions invariably have to be assessed in the light of the particular situation.[188] In determining those conditions, the Court of Justice has regard to its case-law on the non-contractual liability of the Union. First, this is because the second paragraph of Art. 340

---

[180] ECJ, Case C-53/04 *Marrosu and Sardino* [2006] E.C.R. I-7213, paras 38–57; ECJ, Case C-180/04 *Vassallo* [2006] E.C.R. I-7251, paras 31–42; ECJ, Joined Cases C-378/07 to C-380/07 *Angelidaki and Others* [2009] E.C.R. I-3071, paras 179–189.

[181] ECJ (Order of 1 October 2010), Case C-3/10 *Affatato* [2010] E.C.R. I-121*, Summ. pub., paras 52–63.

[182] ECJ, Case C-212/04 *Adeneler and Others* [2006] E.C.R. I-6057, paras 90–105; ECJ (order of 12 June 2008), Case C-364/07 *Vassilakis and Others* [2008] E.C.R. I-90*, Summ. pub., paras 118–137.

[183] The causal connection is determined in principle by the national court: see ECJ, Case C-140/97 *Rechberger and Others* [1999] E.C.R. I-3499, paras 72–73. A salient example is the case of *Brasserie de Pêcheur* itself, where the German court concluded that there was no direct causal link, since it found that the predominant cause for the damage was the prohibition of the use of additives, which did not constitute a sufficiently serious breach, and not the prohibition on the marketing of foreign beers under the German designation 'Bier', which qualified as a sufficiently serious breach: Bundesgerichtshof, 24 October 1996, III ZR 127/81, (1996) LMRR 51.

[184] ECJ, Joined Cases C-6/90 and C-9/90 *Francovich and Others* [1991] E.C.R. I-5357. See P. Mengozzi, 'La responsabilità dello Stato per danni causati a singoli da violazioni del diritto comunitario' (1994) Rivista di diritto internazionale 617–634; R. Silva de Lapuerta, 'La responsabilidad patrimonial de los Estados miembros por incumplimiento del derecho comunitario', in C. A. Garcia-Quíntana, A. Martínez-Lafuente, *et al.* (eds), *Perspectivas jurídicas actuales: homenaje a Alfredo Sánchez-Bella Carswell* (Madrid, Centro de Estudios Ramón Areces, 1995), 311–37.

[185] ECJ, Joined Cases C-6/90 and C-9/90 *Francovich*, para. 35; ECJ, Case C-63/01 *Evans* [2003] E.C.R. I-14447, para. 83; ECJ, Case C-445/06 *Danske Slagterier* [2009] E.C.R. I-2119, para. 19 (and further citations therein). With the changes brought by the Lisbon Treaty, see ECJ, Case C-118/08 *Transportes Urbanos y Servicios Generales* [2010] E.C.R. I-635, para. 29 ('inherent in the system of the Treaties on which the European Union is based'). For further discussion of the Court's grounding of the principle of State liability, see K. Lenaerts and K. Gutman, '"Federal Common Law" in the European Union: Comparative Reflections from the United States' (2006) A.J.C.L. 1–121, at 78–96.

[186] ECJ, Joined Cases C-6/90 and C-9/90 *Francovich*, para. 36.

[187] ECJ, Joined Cases C-6/90 and C-9/90 *Francovich*, para. 38.

[188] ECJ, Joined Cases C-178/94, C-179/94, C-188/94, C-189/94, and C-190/94 *Dillenkofer and Others* [1996] E.C.R. I-4845, para. 24. See also ECJ, Case C-470/03 *AGM.-COS.MET* [2007] E.C.R. I-2749, para. 78 (and further citations therein).

TFEU refers to the general principles common to the legal systems of the Member States, from which, in the absence of written rules, the Court also draws inspiration in other areas of Union law and, second, because the conditions under which the Member State may incur liability for damage caused to individuals by a breach of Union law cannot differ from those governing the liability of the Union in like circumstances.[189] Since the judgment in *Bergaderm*,[190] the conditions for the Union to incur liability have been aligned with the criteria identified by the Court of Justice for Member States to incur liability.

(b) Conditions

4.47 According to the established case-law of the Court of Justice, a Member State must make good loss or damage sustained by individuals as a result of breaches of Union law attributable to it where the following three conditions are met:[191] first, the rule of Union law infringed must be intended to confer rights on individuals;[192] second, the breach of Union law must be sufficiently serious; and third, there must be a direct causal link between the breach of the obligation resting on the Member State and the loss or damage sustained by the injured parties.[193]

As far as the second condition is concerned, namely whether the breach of Union law was sufficiently serious, all the factors which characterize the situation must be taken into account by the national court. As identified by the Court of Justice, those guiding factors include, in particular, the clarity and precision of the rule infringed, the measure of discretion left by that rule to the national or Union authorities, whether the infringement or the damage caused was intentional or involuntary, whether any error of law was excusable or inexcusable, and the fact

---

[189] ECJ, Joined Cases C-46/93 and C-48/93 *Brasserie du Pêcheur and Factortame* [1996] E.C.R. I-1029, paras 39–42. Some commentators would have preferred it if the conditions for liability on the part of the Community, as it then was, had been equated with those for liability on the part of the Member States and not the other way around, while arguing for 'clarification' of the interpretation of then Art. 288 EC (now Art. 340 TFEU) in the light of the judgment in *Francovich*: see R. Caranta, 'Judicial Protection Against Member States: A New Jus Commune Takes Shape' (1995) C.M.L. Rev. 703–26. See further C. Vajda, 'Liability for Breach of Community Law: A Survey of the ECJ Cases Post Factortame' (2006) E.B.L. Rev. 257–68.

[190] ECJ, Case C-352/98 P *Bergaderm and Goupil v Commission* [2000] E.C.R. I-5291. See T. von Danwitz, 'Die gemeinschaftsrechtliche Staatshaftung der Mitgliedstaaten: Entwicklung, Stand und Perspektiven der europäischen Haftung aus Richterhand' (1997) DVBl 1–10; M. Wathelet and S. Van Raepenbusch, 'La responsabilité des États membres en cas de violation du droit communautaire: vers un alignment de la responsabilité de l'État sur celle de la Communauté ou l'inverse' (1997) C.D.E. 13–60. See further para. 11.45.

[191] These three conditions are necessary and sufficient to found a right in individuals to obtain redress, but this does not mean that the Member State concerned cannot incur liability under less strict conditions on the basis of national law: see ECJ, Joined Cases C-46/93 and C-48/93 *Brasserie du Pêcheur and Factortame*, para. 66; ECJ, Case C-173/03 *Traghetti del Mediterraneo* [2006] E.C.R. I-5177, paras 44–45; ECJ, Case C-470/03 *AGM-COS.MET* [2007] E.C.R. I-2749, para. 85. Moreover, this does not in principle preclude specific conditions being laid down by the domestic law of a Member State in connection with State liability, provided that such rules comply with the principles of equivalence and effectiveness: see para. 4.51.

[192] S. Prechal, 'Member State Liability and Direct Effect: What's the Difference After All?' (2006) E.B.L. Rev. 299–316.

[193] ECJ, Joined Cases C-46/93 and C-48/93 *Brasserie du Pêcheur and Factortame* [1996] E.C.R. I-1029, para. 51; ECJ, Case C-424/97 *Haim* [2000] E.C.R. I-5123, para. 26; ECJ, Case C-224/01 *Köbler* [2003] E.C.R. I-10239, para. 51; ECJ, Case C-63/01 *Evans* [2003] E.C.R. I-14447, para. 83; ECJ, Case C-452/06 *Synthon* [2008] E.C.R. I-7681, para. 35; ECJ, Case C-445/06 *Danske Slagterier* [2009] E.C.R. I-2119, para. 20 (and further citations therein). For the question as to whether a directive without direct effect confers 'rights' on individuals breach of which may give rise to an obligation to make reparation, see ECJ, Case C-91/92 *Faccini Dori* [1994] E.C.R. I-3325, para. 27 and ECJ, Case C-192/94 *El Corte Inglés* [1996] E.C.R. I-1281, para. 22. The third condition (causal link) refers to a fourth condition, namely that there has been loss or damage sustained: see further (in the context of the action for damages against the Union) para. 11.63.

that the position taken by a Union institution may have contributed towards the omission, and the adoption or retention of national measures or practices contrary to Union law.[194]

(c) Margin of discretion

The decisive test for finding that a breach of Union law is sufficiently serious is whether the **4.48** Member State concerned manifestly and gravely disregarded the limits on its discretion.[195] Where an institution of a Member State acts in a matter in which it had only considerably reduced or no discretion at all at the time when it committed the infringement, the mere infringement of Union law may be sufficient to establish the existence of a sufficiently serious breach.[196] Accordingly, failure to take any measure to transpose a directive into national law within the prescribed period in order to achieve the result sought constitutes a sufficiently serious breach of Union law.[197] Where conduct has persisted in spite of a preliminary ruling, a judgment of the Court of Justice finding a failure to fulfil obligations or settled case-law of the Court on the matter from which it appears that that conduct constitutes a breach of Union law, this will also amount to a sufficiently serious breach.[198]

(d) Transposition of directives

As far as the actual transposition of the provisions of a directive is concerned, a Member **4.49** State's margin of discretion may be broader, depending on its content. In this way, improper transposition of a directive may not automatically constitute a sufficiently serious breach and give rise to liability on the part of the Member State. Accordingly, in the *British*

---

[194] ECJ, Joined Cases C-46/93 and C-48/93 *Brasserie du Pêcheur and Factortame* [1996] E.C.R. I-1029, para. 56; ECJ, Case C-424/97 *Haim* [2000] E.C.R. I-5123, para. 26; ECJ, Case C-63/01 *Evans* [2003] E.C.R. I-14447, para. 86; ECJ, C-278/05 *Robins and Others* [2007] E.C.R. I-1053, para. 77; ECJ (order of 23 April 2008), Case C-201/05 *Test Claimants in the CFC and Dividend Group Litigation* [2008] E.C.R. I-2875, para. 122 (and further citations therein). In recent cases, the Court has emphasized that the degree of the clarity and precision of the rule infringed constitutes an important criterion in determining whether there has been a sufficiently serious breach of Union law: see, e.g. ECJ, Case C-452/06 *Synthon* [2008] E.C.R. I-7681, para. 39 (and further citations therein). These factors are somewhat nuanced in relation to breaches committed by national last instance courts: see para. 4.50.

[195] ECJ, Joined Cases C-46/93 and C-48/93 *Brasserie du Pêcheur and Factortame*, para. 55. Member States are precluded from making the finding of an infringement conditional on a concept of fault, or any other other concept, which goes beyond that of a sufficiently serious breach as defined in the case-law of the Court of Justice: ECJ, Case C-429/09 *Fuß* [2010] E.C.R. I-12167, paras 64–70.

[196] For an example, see ECJ, Case C-5/94 *Hedley Lomas* [1996] E.C.R. I-2553, para. 28, where the Court of Justice held that the mere infringement of Art. 31 TFEU by the UK in refusing to grant an export licence constituted a sufficiently serious breach of Union law on the grounds that at the time of the infringement the UK had considerably reduced discretion, if any; see also ECJ, Case C-127/95 *Norbrook Laboratories* [1998] E.C.R. I-1531, para. 109; ECJ, C-150/99 *Stockholm Lindöpark* [2001] E.C.R. I-493, paras 40–42; ECJ, Case C-470/03 *AGM.-COS.MET* [2007] E.C.R. I-2749, paras 81–82; ECJ, Case C-452/06 *Synthon* [2008] E.C.R. I-7681, paras 41–45.

[197] ECJ, Joined Cases C-178/94, C-179/94, C-188/94, C-189/94, and C-190/94 *Dillenkofer and Others* [1996] E.C.R. I-4845. See, also ECJ, Case C-319/96 *Brinkmann* [1998] E.C.R. I-5255, para. 29. See, with respect to the liability of the Spanish authorities for the incorrect transposition of a directive, Tribunal Supremo (Spanish Supreme Court), Administrative Law Chamber, judgment of 12 June 2003, *Canal Satélite Digital* (Case 46/1999).

[198] ECJ, Joined Cases C-46/93 and C-48/93 *Brasserie du Pêcheur and Factortame* [1996] E.C.R. I-1029, para. 57; ECJ, Case C-118/00 *Larsy* [2001] E.C.R. I-5063, para. 44; ECJ (order of 23 April 2008), Case C-201/05 *Test Claimants in the CFC and Dividend Group Litigation* [2008] E.C.R. I-2875, para. 123. However, reparation of the damage caused by a breach of Union law by a Member State is not conditional on the requirement that the existence of such a breach must be clear from a preliminary ruling or another judgment delivered by the Court of Justice (see, e.g. ECJ, Case C-118/08 *Transportes Urbanos y Servicios Generales* [2010] E.C.R. I-635, para. 38 (and further citations therein)).

Telecommunications case, the Court of Justice held that the improper transposition of a particular directive into national law did not constitute a sufficiently serious breach of Union law on the grounds that the directive at issue was imprecisely worded and was reasonably capable of bearing the interpretation given to it by the UK in good faith and on the basis of arguments which were not entirely devoid of substance and not manifestly contrary to the wording of the directive or its objectives.[199]

Likewise, in *Robins*, the Court found that the UK's liability by reason of improper transposition of a certain provision of a directive (incidentally the very same one at issue in the *Francovich* case) by failing to ensure that the national legislation put in place adequate protection for pension schemes, was conditional on a finding of the Member State's manifest and grave disregard for the limits set on its discretion.[200] In that respect, the Court found that the clarity and the precision of the directive's provision with respect to the level of protection required was lacking, and that as far as the position of the Union institutions was concerned, there had been a report issued by the Commission indicating that the UK appeared to be in compliance with the requirements of the directive which could have served to reinforce that Member State's belief that it had transposed the directive correctly.[201]

(e) Decisions of national courts adjudicating at last instance

4.50   In *Köbler*, the Court of Justice ruled that a Member State may be held liable for a breach of Union law as a result of a decision of a national court adjudicating at last instance on the basis of the same three conditions mentioned (see para. 4.47), though it recognized that with respect to the second condition of a sufficiently serious breach 'regard must be had to the specific nature of the judicial function and to the legitimate requirements of legal certainty'.[202] Thus, State liability 'can be incurred only in the exceptional case where the court has manifestly infringed the applicable law'.[203] In order to determine whether that condition is satisfied, the national court hearing a claim for reparation must take account of all

---

[199] ECJ, Case C-392/93 *British Telecommunications* [1996] E.C.R. I-1631, para. 43. In ECJ, Joined Cases C-283/94, C-291/94, and C-292/94 *Denkavit and Others* [1996] E.C.R. I-5063, paras 51–54, the Court of Justice held that its case-law did not provide Germany with any interpretation as to how a provision of a particular directive had to be interpreted. Consequently, the erroneous interpretation which Germany had given to it, which had been adopted by almost all the other Member States following discussions within the Council, could not be regarded as a sufficiently serious breach of Union law. In contrast, in *Rechberger*, the Court of Justice held that a national implementing provision which limited the time from which a right conferred by a directive entered into effect where the directive conferred no discretion on the Member States in this respect constituted a sufficiently serious breach of Union law (ECJ, Case C-140/97 *Rechberger and Others* [1999] E.C.R. I-3499, para. 51). See also ECJ, Case C-150/99 *Stockholm Lindöpark* [2001] E.C.R. I-493, paras 40–42.

[200] ECJ, Case C-278/05 *Robins and Others* [2007] E.C.R. I-1053.

[201] ECJ, Case C-278/05 *Robins and Others*, paras 77–82.

[202] ECJ, Case C-224/01 *Köbler* [2003] E.C.R. I-10239, paras 51–53. Member States can thus neither exclude State liability nor supplement the conditions for State liability for breaches of Union law by courts of last instance on account of the specific nature of such courts: ECJ, Case C-173/03 *Traghetti del Mediterraneo* [2006] E.C.R. I-5177; ECJ (judgment of 24 November 2011), Case C-379/10 *Commission v Italy*, neither reported. See further W. Hakenberg, 'Zur Staatshaftung von Gerichten bei Verletzung von Europäischen Gemeinschaftsrecht: gleichzeitig eine Besprechung des Urteils "Köbler" des EuGH vom 30.9.2003' (2004) Deutsche Richterzeitung 113–17; V. Skouris, 'Rechtsfolgen der Verletzung des Europäischen Gemeinschaftsrechts durch oberste Gerichte der Mitgliedstaaten', in R. Hendler, M. Ibler, and J. Martinez Soria (eds), *Für Sicherheit, Für Europa: Festschrift Für Volkmar Götz Zum 70. Geburtstag* (Göttingen, Vandenhoeck and Ruprecht, 2005), 223–38.

[203] ECJ, Case C-224/01 *Köbler*, para. 53.

the factors which characterize the situation put before it. As set forth in the case-law of the Court of Justice, those guiding factors include, in particular, the degree of clarity and precision of the rule infringed, whether the infringement was intentional, whether the error of law was excusable or inexcusable, the position taken, where applicable, by a Union institution, and non-compliance by the court in question with its obligation to make a reference for a preliminary ruling under the third paragraph of Art. 267 TFEU.[204] In any event, an infringement of Union law will be sufficiently serious where the judicial decision concerned was taken in manifest breach of the case-law of the Court of Justice in the relevant matter.[205]

(f) Principles of equivalence and effectiveness

In the absence of Union rules, the procedural organization of the legal proceedings concerning State liability is left to national law, but the provisions of national law must comply with the principles of equivalence and effectiveness, that is to say, they must not be less favourable for actions for damages for breach of Union law than they are for other actions for damages, or be so framed as to make it 'virtually impossible or excessively difficult to obtain reparation'.[206] **4.51**

Moreover, traditional concepts applying in some Member States must, where appropriate, yield to State liability under Union law. Accordingly, the principle that the State cannot be held liable for an unlawful act or omission on the part of the legislature, which applies in some Member States' legal systems, cannot restrict the principle of State liability for breaches of Union law. The reason for this is that State liability holds good for any case in which a Member State breaches Union law, whatever be the organ of the State whose act or omission was responsible for the breach.[207] This applies not only to breaches of Union law by organs of the legislature or the executive, but also to judicial bodies adjudicating at last instance.[208] In addition, the acts of a federated State or a territorial authority with a

---

[204] ECJ, Case C-224/01 *Köbler*, para. 55.

[205] ECJ, Case C-224/01 *Köbler*, para. 56.

[206] ECJ, Joined Cases C-6/90 and C-9/90 *Francovich and Others* [1991] E.C.R. I-5357, para. 43; ECJ, Case C-66/95 *Sutton* [1997] E.C.R. I-2163, para. 33; ECJ, Case C-224/01 *Köbler* [2003] E.C.R. I-10239, paras 46–50; ECJ, Case C-268/06 *Impact* [2008] E.C.R. I-2483, paras 44–47; ECJ, Case C-118/08 *Transportes Urbanos y Servicios Generales* [2010] E.C.R. I-635, para. 31 (and further citations therein).

[207] ECJ, Joined Cases C-46/93 and C-48/93 *Brasserie du Pêcheur and Factortame* [1996] E.C.R. I-1029, paras 32–36, and the Opinion of Advocate-General G. Tesauro, points 35–38. It appears from the same judgment that the Court of Justice considers that the condition imposed by German law where a law is in breach of higher-ranking national provisions, which makes reparation dependent upon the legislature's act or omission being referable to an individual situation, must be set aside in the case of a breach of Union law. The reason for this is that this condition would in practice make it impossible or excessively difficult to obtain effective reparation for loss or damage resulting from a breach of Union law, since the tasks falling to the national legislature relate, in principle, to the public at large and not to identifiable persons or classes of persons (ECJ, Joined Cases C-46/93 and C-48/93 *Brasserie du Pêcheur and Factortame*, paras 71–72). The Court likewise held in *Brasserie du Pêcheur and Factortame* that any condition that may be imposed by English law on State liability requiring proof of misfeasance in public office must be set aside because such an abuse of power is inconceivable in the case of the legislature and therefore the condition makes it impossible to obtain effective reparation for loss or damage resulting from a breach of Union law (ECJ, Joined Cases C-46/93 and C-48/93 *Brasserie du Pêcheur and Factortame*, para. 73).

[208] See ECJ, Case C-224/01 *Köbler* [2003] E.C.R. I-10239: the principle of *res judicata* and the principle of the independence of the judiciary do not preclude State liability for breaches of Union law committed by courts adjudicating at last instance (paras 30–50). See also ECJ (order of 3 June 2005), Case C-396/03 P *Killinger v Germany, Council and Commission* [2005] E.C.R. I-4967, para. 28; ECJ, Case C-173/03 *Traghetti del Mediterraneo* [2006] E.C.R. I-5177.

degree of autonomy and likewise public-law bodies[209] may cause the Member State itself, as well as such authorities or bodies, to incur liability.

In Member States with a federal structure, reparation for damage caused to individuals does not necessarily have to be provided by the federal State (federal authority). It is sufficient that a party's right to reparation for loss or damage flowing from an infringement of Union law by a federated State is effectively protected. If, however, there is no effective protection, a Member State (federal authority) cannot plead the distribution of powers and responsibilities between the bodies which exist in its national legal order in order to excuse itself from liability on that basis.[210] That is also true for those Member States in which certain legislative or administrative tasks are devolved to territorial bodies with a certain degree of autonomy or to any other public-law body legally distinct from the State.[211]

(g) Compensation

4.52 The amount of the damages must be commensurate with the loss or damage sustained so as to ensure the effective protection of the rights of the injured parties.[212] In the case of late implementation of a directive, retroactive and proper application in full of the measures implementing the directive will suffice in principle, unless the beneficiaries establish the existence of complementary loss sustained on account of the fact that they were unable to benefit at the appropriate time from the financial advantages guaranteed by the directive, with the result that such loss must also be made good.[213] Limiting compensation to an upper limit or a prohibition on the national court's granting interest on that basic amount are contrary to Union law insofar as they make it impossible to make reparation in full for the damage sustained.[214] The national rules may require the injured party to show reasonable diligence in order to avoid the loss or damage or limit its extent.[215] The setting of reasonable limitation

---

[209] ECJ, Case C-424/97 *Haim* [2000] E.C.R. I-5123, para. 32.

[210] ECJ, Case C-302/97 *Konle* [1999] E.C.R. I-3099, paras 61–64.

[211] ECJ, Case C-424/97 *Haim* [2000] E.C.R. I-5123, paras 30–31.

[212] ECJ, Joined Cases C-46/93 and C-48/93 *Brasserie du Pêcheur and Factortame* [1996] E.C.R. I-1029, para. 82. See, e.g. ECJ, Case C-429/09 *Fuß* [2010] E.C.R. I-12167, paras 91–98: it is for the national court to decide, taking into account the principles of equivalence and effectiveness, whether, in order to compensate an employee for breaches of the Working Time Directive, compensation should take the form of time off in lieu or financial compensation.

[213] ECJ, Joined Cases C-94/95 and C-95/95 *Bonifaci and Others and Berto and Others* [1997] E.C.R. I-3969, para. 54; ECJ, Case C-373/95 *Maso and Others* [1997] E.C.R. I-4051, para. 41; ECJ, Case C-131/97 *Carbonari and Others* [1999] E.C.R. I-1103, para. 53.

[214] ECJ, Case C-271/91 *Marshall* [1993] E.C.R. I-4367, paras 22–32 (see S. Prechal, 'Remedies After Marshall' (1990) C.M.L. Rev. 451–73). To limit compensation to an upper limit may, where the loss or damage exceeds that upper limit, conflict with the requirement for an effective, deterrent sanction. This is also true of the prohibition on adding interest to the basic amount. If account cannot be taken of the effluxion of time, reparation will not be made for the whole of the damage. Consequently, the grant of interest under the applicable national law is essential in order to satisfy the requirement of the full effectiveness of Union law. See to the same effect ECJ, Joined Cases C-397/98 and C-410/98 *Metallgesellschaft and Others* [2001] E.C.R. I-1727, para. 4; ECJ, Case C-470/03 *AGM.-COS.MET* [2007] E.C.R. I-2749, paras 90–95 (concerning statements of a civil servant which can be attributed to the State where the persons to whom those statements are addressed can reasonably suppose, in the given context, that they are positions taken by the civil servant with authority of his office). See also ECJ (judgment of 18 April 2013), Case C-565/11 *Irimie*, not reported, paras 26–29.

[215] ECJ, Joined Cases C-46/93 and C-48/93 *Brasserie du Pêcheur and Factortame* [1996] E.C.R. I-1029, paras 84–85. However, this rule must be applied having regard to the specific circumstances of the case. In the judgment in *Metallgesellschaft* (ECJ, Joined Cases C-397/98 and C-410/98 *Metallgesellschaft and Others* [2001] E.C.R. I-1727, paras 101–107), the Court of Justice considered that rejecting or reducing reparation

periods for bringing an action for damages against a Member State is compatible with these requirements, provided that it does not make it virtually impossible or excessively difficult to obtain reparation.[216]

(3) Claims for damages for an infringement of Union law by private parties

(a) Courage

Individuals who have infringed a Union provision with direct effect may be obliged to make reparation for the loss or damage caused thereby.[217] In *Courage*,[218] the Court of Justice held that Union law (and in particular Art. 101 TFEU) precludes a rule of national law under which a party to a contract liable to restrict or distort competition is barred from claiming damages under national law for loss caused by performance of that contract on the sole ground that the claimant is a party to that contract; yet national law can deny that right to a party which bears significant responsibility for the distortion of competition.[219] The *Courage* judgment made a first approach, on the basis of the principles of equivalence and effectiveness, to define the contours of claims to damages under national law for breaches of Union law, without giving such claims a direct basis in Union law. However, the Court did state expressly that the practical effect of Art. 101 TFEU would be put at risk 'if it were not open to any individual to claim damages for loss caused to him by a contract or by conduct liable to restrict or distort competition'.[220]

4.53

(b) Subsequent case-law

Thereafter, in *Manfredi*,[221] the Court of Justice affirmed in light of the *Courage* case that any individual can rely on the invalidity of an agreement or practice prohibited under Art. 101 TFEU and, where there is a causal relationship between the latter and the harm suffered, claim compensation for that harm.[222] In the absence of Union rules governing the matter, it is for the domestic legal system of each Member State to prescribe the detailed rules governing the exercise of that right, including those on the application of the concept of 'causal relationship',

4.54

---

for a financial disadvantage sustained because the claimants had not applied for a tax advantage which national law denied them, with a view to challenging the refusal of the tax authorities by means of the legal remedies provided for that purpose, would render the exercise of rights conferred on private persons by directly applicable provisions of Union law (in that case Art. 49 TFEU) impossible or excessively difficult. See further ECJ (order of 23 April 2008), Case C-201/05 *Test Claimants in the CFC and Dividend Group Litigation* [2008] E.C.R. I-2875, paras 127–130 (and further citations therein). The interplay between reimbursement claims before national administrations, on the one hand, and damages actions before national courts, on the other hand, has been considered problematic: see P. J. Wattel, 'National Procedural Autonomy and Effectiveness of EU Law: Challenge the Charge, File for Restitution, Sue for Damages?' (2008) L.I.E.I. 109–32.

[216] ECJ, Case C-261/95 *Palmisani* [1997] E.C.R. I-4025, para. 28. See further ECJ, Case C-445/06 *Danske Slagterier* [2009] E.C.R. I-2119, para. 48.

[217] ECJ, Case C-453/99 *Courage and Crehan* [2001] E.C.R. I-6297. See also Opinion of Advocate-General W. Van Gerven in ECJ, Case C-128/92 *Banks* [1994] E.C.R. I-1209.

[218] ECJ, Case C-453/99 *Courage and Crehan* [2001] E.C.R. I-6297.

[219] ECJ, Case C-453/99 *Courage and Crehan*, paras 24–36.

[220] ECJ, Case C-453/99 *Courage and Crehan*, para. 26. For ongoing developments taking place at the European level concerning antitrust damages actions, including the Commission's Green Paper (COM (2005) 672 final) and White Paper on damages actions for breach of EC antitrust rules (COM (2008) 165 final), see the Commission's website devoted to this subject, <http://ec.europa.eu/competition/antitrust/actionsdamages/index.html>.

[221] ECJ, Joined Cases C-295/04 to C-298/04 *Manfredi and Others* [2006] E.C.R. I-6619.

[222] ECJ, Joined Cases C-295/04 to C-298/04 *Manfredi and Others*, paras 56–61, 63, 90–91. See also ECJ, Case C-421/05 *City Motors Groep* [2007] E.C.R. I-653, para. 33.

provided that the principles of equivalence and effectiveness are observed.[223] As such, national rules on the jurisdiction of courts hearing such claims, limitation periods, and damages awards (such as the prospect of punitive damages) are to be assessed in line with these principles, underscoring that injured persons must be able to seek compensation not only for actual loss (*damnum emergens*), but also for loss of profit (*lucrum cessans*) plus interest.[224]

In *Otis*,[225] the Court of Justice confirmed that the Commission can also bring an action before a national court, on behalf of the European Union, for damages in respect of loss sustained by the European Union as a result of an agreement or practice contrary to Art. 101 TFEU. The fact that national courts are bound by the Commission decision finding the infringement does not mean that the undertakings concerned do not enjoy effective judicial protection within the meaning of Art. 47 of the Charter of Fundamental Rights of the European Union. The Court pointed out in that regard that Union law provides for a system of judicial review of Commission competition decisions that affords all the safeguards required by Art. 47 of the Charter.[226]

(4) Withdrawal of a decision of a national administrative body that has become final

(a) Problem

4.55 It may appear from a judgment of the Court of Justice that earlier decisions taken by national administrative bodies are based on a wrong interpretation of Union law. The question then arises whether those national administrative bodies are obliged to reopen those decisions that have become definitive.

(b) Kühne & Heitz

4.56 *Kühne & Heitz*[227] provided an answer to this question. In its judgment, the Court underlined that the interpretation which the Court of Justice gives to a rule of Union law in a preliminary ruling clarifies and defines where necessary the meaning and scope of that rule as it must be or ought to have been understood and applied from the time of its coming into force.[228] It follows that a rule of Union law interpreted in this way must be applied by an administrative body within the sphere of its competence even to legal relationships which arose or were formed before the Court gave its ruling on the question on interpretation.[229] However, it does not follow automatically that an administrative body has to reopen an administrative decision which has become final. On the contrary, the Court, referring to the principle of legal certainty, considers that, in principle, such a body

---

[223] ECJ, Joined Cases C-295/04 to C-298/04 *Manfredi and Others*, paras 62, 64. The Court's findings in this case as regards the compliance of the limitation period at issue in the national proceedings with the principle of effectiveness was subsequently distinguished in a later case: see ECJ, Case C-445/06 *Danske Slagterier* [2009] E.C.R. I-2119, paras 50–52.

[224] ECJ, Case C-445/06 *Danske Slagterier*, paras 70–72, 77–82, 92–100.

[225] ECJ (judgment of 6 November 2012), Case C-199/11 *Otis and Others*, not reported, paras 43–44 (P.-A.Van Malleghem, case note (2013) S.E.W. 123–7).

[226] ECJ, Case C-199/11 *Otis and Others*, paras 45–67.

[227] ECJ, Case C-453/00 *Kühne & Heitz* [2004] E.C.R. I-837 (S. Prechal, case note (2004) S.E.W. 278–81; P. Van Nuffel, case note (2005) T.B.P. 44–8).

[228] ECJ, Case C-453/00 *Kühne & Heitz*, para. 21. See also ECJ, Case 61/79 *Denkavit Italiana* [1980] E.C.R. 1205, para. 16; ECJ, Case C-50/96 *Deutsche Telekom* [2000] E.C.R. I-743, para. 43; ECJ, Case C-455/08 *Commission v Ireland* [2009] E.C.R. I-225*, Summ. pub., para. 39.

[229] ECJ, Case C-453/00 *Kühne & Heitz*, para. 22.

is not required to reopen an administrative decision which has become final.[230] That being said, in very specific circumstances there may be an obligation for a national administrative body to reopen a decision. This will be the case in particular where such a body is obliged, in accordance with the principle of sincere cooperation arising from Art. 4(3) TEU, to reopen a final administrative decision where an application for such review is made to it, in order to take account of the interpretation of the relevant provision of Union law given in the meantime by the Court of Justice where the following four conditions are satisfied:

- first, under national law, the administrative body concerned has the power to reopen the decision;[231]
- second, the administrative decision in question has become final as a result of a judgment of a national court ruling at final instance;
- third, that judgment, in light of a decision given by the Court of Justice subsequent to it, was based on a misinterpretation of Union law which was adopted without a question being referred to the Court for a preliminary ruling under the third paragraph of Art. 267 TFEU; and
- fourth, the person concerned complained to the administrative body immediately after becoming aware of the decision of the Court of Justice from which it appears that the national decision is contrary to Union law.[232]

(c) Application of the Kühne & Heitz conditions

In *i-21 Germany and Arcor*,[233] the Court of Justice reiterated, in line with *Kühne & Heitz*, **4.57** that an administrative body responsible for the adoption of an administrative decision is under an obligation to review and possibly to reopen that decision if the four conditions mentioned earlier are fulfilled.[234] However, the case giving rise to the judgment in *Kühne & Heitz* was entirely different from the instant proceedings: whilst the undertaking in the former case had exhausted all legal remedies available to it, i-21 Germany and Arcor had not availed themselves of their right to appeal against the fee assessments issued to them, and therefore, the judgment in *Kühne & Heitz* was not relevant.[235] That being said, the Court proceeded to analyse the relevant national procedural rules in accordance with the principles of equivalence and effectiveness, finding that Art. 4(3) TEU, read in conjunction with the directive concerned, requires the national court to ascertain whether national legislation which is clearly incompatible with Union law, such as that on which the fee assessments at issue in the main proceedings were based, constitutes manifest unlawfulness within the meaning of the national law concerned. If that is the case, it is for the national court to draw the necessary conclusions under its national law with regard to the withdrawal

---

[230] ECJ, Case C-453/00 *Kühne & Heitz*, para. 24.

[231] See, by analogy, the question in connection with raising pleas derived from Union law of the court's own motion, para. 4.40.

[232] ECJ, Case C-453/00 *Kühne & Heitz*, paras 26–28. Given the restrictive and cumulative nature of these conditions it is very unlikely that the *Kühne & Heitz* principle will be applied broadly: V. Skouris, 'Rechtsschutz durch den Europäischen Gerichtshof', in J. Schwarze (ed.), *Rechtsschutz und Wettbewerb in der neueren europäischen Rechtsentwicklung* (Baden Baden, Nomos, 2010), 89. See also ECJ, Case C-234/04 *Kapferer* [2006] E.C.R. I-2585, paras 19–24, whereby the Court rejected the transposition of the principles laid down in *Kühne & Heitz* to the reopening of final judicial decisions and ruled that the principle of sincere cooperation under Art. 4(3) TEU does not require a national court to disapply its internal rules of procedure in order to review and set aside such a decision if it should be contrary to Union law.

[233] ECJ, Joined Cases C-392/04 and C-422/04 *i-21Germany and Arcor* [2006] E.C.R. I-8559.

[234] ECJ, Joined Cases C-392/04 and C-422/04 *i-21Germany and Arcor*, paras 51–52.

[235] ECJ, Joined Cases C-392/04 and C-422/04 *i-21Germany and Arcor*, paras 53–54.

of those assessments.[236] The Court added that where, pursuant to rules of national law, the authorities are required to withdraw an administrative decision which has become final if that decision is manifestly incompatible with domestic law, that same obligation must exist if the decision is manifestly incompatible with Union law.[237]

Thereafter, *Kempter*[238] provided the Court with the opportunity to elaborate further as regards the third and fourth conditions set forth in *Kühne & Heitz*. First, the Court explained that it could not be inferred from *Kühne & Heitz* that, for the purposes of the third condition, the parties must have raised before the national court the point of Union law in question; it is sufficient if either the point of Union law the interpretation of which proved to be incorrect in light of a subsequent judgment of the Court was considered by the national court ruling at final instance or it could have been raised by the latter of its own motion.[239] Moreover, with regard to the question of time limits for making an application for review, the fourth condition referred by the Court in *Kühne & Heitz* cannot be interpreted as an obligation to make such an application within a certain specific period after the applicant has become aware of the decision of the Court on which the application is based, and thus, the Member States remain free to set reasonable time limits for seeking remedies in a manner consistent with the principles of equivalence and effectiveness.[240]

(5) *Res judicata* effects of national judicial decisions

(a) Lucchini

4.58 In *Lucchini*,[241] the Court was presented with a conflict between a Commission decision declaring certain State aid in the Italian steel sector to be incompatible with the Treaty rules and a national judicial decision, which had become *res judicata* under Italian law, requiring the national authorities to grant the promised aid to a particular recipient. As a result, the case raised important questions concerning the obligations assumed by a national court to ensure the effectiveness of Union law.[242] In its judgment, the Court emphasized that the *res judicata* effects of the Italian judicial decision under these circumstances jeopardized the application of Union law because it made it impossible to recover State aid that was granted in breach of Union law.[243] It then pointed to the obligation placed on the national court to interpret as far as possible the provisions of national law so that they could be applied 'in a manner which contributes to the implementation of [Union] law'.[244] This meant that a national court was under the obligation to give full effect to the relevant provisions of Union law, 'if necessary refusing of its own motion to apply any conflicting provision of national law'.[245] The Court then underlined that the

---

[236] ECJ, Joined Cases C-392/04 and C-422/04 *i-21Germany and Arcor*, paras 56–72.
[237] ECJ, Joined Cases C-392/04 and C-422/04 *i-21Germany and Arcor*, para. 69.
[238] ECJ, Case C-2/06 *Kempter* [2008] E.C.R. I-411.
[239] ECJ, Case C-2/06 *Kempter*, paras 44, 46.
[240] ECJ, Case C-2/06 *Kempter*, paras 56–60.
[241] ECJ, Case C-119/05 *Lucchini* [2007] E.C.R. I-6199.
[242] See extensive analysis in the Opinion of Advocate-General Advocate-General Geelhoed in ECJ, Case C-119/05 *Lucchini* [2007] E.C.R. I-6199, points 49–86. See further T. Corthaut, *EU Ordre Public* (Alphen aan de Rijn, Kluwer Law International, 2012), 239–44; A. Tizzano and B. Gencarelli, 'Union Law and Final Decisions of National Courts in the Recent Case-Law of the Court of Justice', in A. Arnull, C. Barnard, M. Dougan, and E. Spaventa (eds), *A Constitutional Order of States? Essays in EU Law in Honour of Alan Dashwood* (Oxford and Portland Oregon, Hart Publishing, 2011), 267–80.
[243] ECJ, Case C-119/05 *Lucchini*, para. 59.
[244] ECJ, Case C-119/05 *Lucchini*, para. 60.
[245] ECJ, Case C-119/05 *Lucchini*, para. 61.

assessment of the compatibility of State aid with the internal market fell within the exclusive competence of the Commission, subject to review by the Union courts, which applied within the national legal order by virtue of the principle of primacy of Union law.[246] Accordingly, Union law precluded the application of a provision of national law laying down the principle of *res judicata* where it prevented the recovery of State aid granted in violation of Union law which had been found to be incompatible with the internal market in a final decision of the Commission.[247]

This should not be taken to mean that the Court of Justice does not heed the role played by the principle of *res judicata* in the legal systems of the Member States.[248] Yet, as illustrated by *Lucchini*, that principle should not stand in the way of recognizing the full effect of the principle of primacy of Union law in a context where the national courts do not have jurisdiction to decide the core issue of Union law at hand, i.e. the compatibility of a State aid project with the internal market which lies within the exclusive competence of the Commission.

(b) Fallimento Olimpiclub

Indeed, in *Fallimento Olimpiclub*,[249] concerning a reference for a preliminary ruling sub-   **4.59**
mitted by the Italian *Corte suprema di cassazione* (Supreme Court of Cassation) on the application of *Lucchini* to areas other than State aid, and in particular in matters relating to VAT, the Court stressed the importance, both for the Union legal order and for the national legal systems, of the principle of *res judicata*, and underlined that Union law does not require a national court to disapply domestic rules of procedure conferring finality on a decision, even if to do so would make it possible to remedy an infringement of Union law on the part of the decision in question.[250] However, it distinguished its prior judgment in *Lucchini*, which concerned a 'highly specific situation, in which the matters at issue were principles governing the division of powers between the Member States and the [Union] in the area of State aid', with the Commission having exclusive competence in such area to assess the compatibility with the internal market of a national State aid measure, from the instant proceedings in which such issues did not arise.[251] Instead, the issue here was whether it is compatible with the principle of effectiveness to interpret the principle of *res judicata* as meaning that, in tax disputes, where a final judgment in a given case concerns a

---

[246] ECJ, Case C-119/05 *Lucchini*, para. 62.

[247] ECJ, Case C-119/05 *Lucchini*, para. 63. However, *Lucchini* is not of direct relevance to a case in which the court judgment possessed of the force of *res judicata* precedes the decision whereby the Commission requires the recovery of the aid at issue: see ECJ, Case C-507/08 *Commission v Slovak Republic* [2010] E.C.R. I-13489, paras 56–58.

[248] See ECJ, Case C-224/01 *Köbler* [2003] E.C.R. I-10239, paras 37–40, discussed further at para. 4.50. But as demonstrated by that case, that principle should not stand in the way of establishing the principle of State liability for infringements of Union law committed by national courts adjudicating at last instance. See also ECJ, Case C-234/04 *Kapferer* [2006] E.C.R. I-2585, para. 21, where the Court held that Union law did not require the national court to set aside a national rule conferring *res judicata* upon a decision of a lower court, even if this would allow the national court to remedy a breach of Union law contained in that decision. See further ECJ, Case C-507/08 *Commission v Slovak Republic* [2010] E.C.R. I-13489, para. 59, in which the Court recalled 'the importance, both in the European Union legal order and in the national legal orders, of the principle of *res judicata*'. The Court added: 'In order to ensure stability of the law and legal relations, as well as the sound administration of justice, it is important that judicial decisions which have become definitive after all rights of appeal have been exhausted or after expiry of the time limits provided to exercise those rights can no longer be called into question.'

[249] ECJ, Case C-2/08 *Fallimento Olimpiclub* [2009] E.C.R. I-7501.

[250] ECJ, Case C-2/08 *Fallimento Olimpiclub*, paras 22–23. See also ECJ, Case C-507/08 *Commission v Slovak Republic* [2010] E.C.R. I-13489, paras 59–60.

[251] ECJ, Case C-2/08 *Fallimento Olimpiclub* [2009] E.C.R. I-7501, para. 25.

fundamental issue common to other cases, it has binding authority as regards that issue, even if its findings were made in relation to a different tax period.[252]

As pointed out by the national court, not only does the interpretation of the national rule in question prevent a judicial decision that has acquired the force of *res judicata* from being called into question, even if that decision entails a breach of Union law, but it also prevents any finding on a fundamental issue common to other cases contained in a judicial decision which has acquired the force of *res judicata* from being called into question in the context of judicial scrutiny of another decision taken by the relevant tax authority with respect to the same taxpayer or taxable person but relating to a different year.[253] Thus, if the principle of *res judicata* were to be applied in that manner, the effect would be that, if ever the judicial decision that had become final were based on an interpretation of the Union rules concerning abusive practice in the field of VAT which was at odds with Union law, those rules would continue to be misapplied for each new tax year, without it being possible to rectify such an interpretation.[254] Under those circumstances, 'such extensive obstacles to the effective application of the [Union] rules on VAT cannot reasonably be regarded as justified in the interests of legal certainty and must therefore be considered to be contrary to the principle of effectiveness'.[255]

IV. Legal Protection in Proceedings for Interim Relief

A. Two situations

4.60 The protracted nature of judicial proceedings may pose a threat to the actual enforcement of the rights conferred upon an individual by Union law. This explains the interest for the full effectiveness of Union law of a system of provisional legal protection which enables a real claim to those rights to be safeguarded by freezing a provision which is allegedly in conflict with (superior) Union law or by granting interim relief provisionally to settle or regulate disputed legal positions or relationships pending a judicial ruling in the main proceedings.[256]

Two situations need to be distinguished as far as interim relief before the national court is concerned.[257] First, there is the situation where the national court grants interim relief in order to freeze the effect of a national provision that is allegedly in breach of Union law. Second, the national court may grant interim relief in order to freeze the implementation of a Union measure which is allegedly in breach of higher-ranking Union law (and therefore unlawful) or provisionally to settle or regulate disputed legal positions or relationships with reference to a national measure based on a Union act whose validity is under consideration in proceedings for a preliminary ruling.

---

[252] ECJ, Case C-2/08 *Fallimento Olimpiclub*, para. 26.

[253] ECJ, Case C-2/08 *Fallimento Olimpiclub*, para. 29.

[254] ECJ, Case C-2/08 *Fallimento Olimpiclub*, para. 30.

[255] ECJ, Case C-2/08 *Fallimento Olimpiclub*, para. 31.

[256] E. Sharpston, 'Interim Relief in the National Courts', in J. Lonbay and A. Biondi (eds), *Remedies for Breach of EC Law* (New York, Wiley, 1997), 47–54.

[257] See, e.g. ECJ, Case C-432/05 *Unibet* [2007] E.C.R. I-2271, paras 79–82. For interim relief before the Union courts, see Ch. 13.

B. Allegedly illegal national measure

As far as the first situation is concerned, the Court of Justice held in the seminal *Factortame I* **4.61** case that Union law must be interpreted as meaning that 'a national court which, in a case before it concerning [Union] law, considers that the sole obstacle which precludes it from granting interim relief is a rule of national law must set aside that rule'.[258] It is only in this way that the full effectiveness of Union law can be secured by the judgment to be given on the existence of the rights claimed under Union law.[259] In other words, by virtue of this judgment, if the national court would grant interim relief to ensure the full effectiveness of rights claimed under Union law but for national law—here, all the conditions for interim relief were satisfied save for the fact that English law prohibited interim relief against the Crown—then the national court is obliged to set aside that national rule and grant interim relief in order to ensure enforcement of Union law rights. As such, while it was left to the English court to specify the conditions under which interim relief would be granted, the Court confirmed that a national rule prohibiting absolutely the granting of interim relief in this setting would contravene the principle of effectiveness.

This means that, where necessary, the national court can derive directly from Union law the power to suspend a provision of national law in interlocutory proceedings. The nature of the measure whose suspension is sought is immaterial. Furthermore, Union law embodies no special requirements for the suspension of provisions of national law, although here too the principle applies that there must be equal treatment of suspension on grounds of domestic law and suspension on Union law grounds (principle of equivalence), together with the principle that the applicable domestic law must not subject the suspension to conditions such as to make it impossible in practice to obtain (principle of effectiveness).

This leads to the discussion of the Court of Justice's judgment in *Unibet*,[260] which has already been discussed in the context of actions for annulment and gaps in the system of judicial protection for natural and legal persons,[261] but also concerned issues relating to interim relief. In this case, the applicant had submitted two applications for the granting of interim relief protection: the first was in connection with its first application seeking declaratory-type relief, thereby seeking by way of interim relief an order immediately disapplying the prohibition against its promotion of betting activities in Sweden; and the second was in connection with the applicant's second application concerning the action for damages, whereby it made a fresh application for interim relief, claiming that the national court should immediately issue an order allowing it to take specific marketing

---

[258] ECJ, Case C-213/89 *Factortame and Others ('Factortame I')* [1990] E.C.R. I-2433, operative part. After the House of Lords had held that it could not give an interim injunction in judicial review proceedings seeking to set aside an Act of Parliament because courts had no such power under the Supreme Court Act 1981 and an Act of Parliament was presumed valid until declared otherwise (*R v Secretary of State for Transport, ex parte Factortame (No. 2)* [1990] A.C. 603), the preliminary ruling in *Factortame I* was considered to give it the power to grant such an injunction (or at least to remove the common law rule that an interim injunction may not be granted against the Crown).

[259] ECJ, Case C-213/89 '*Factortame I*', para. 21. See also ECJ, Case C-226/99 *Siples* [2001] E.C.R. I-277, paras 17–20.

[260] ECJ, Case C-432/05 *Unibet* [2007] E.C.R. I-2271.

[261] See para. 4.11.

measures related to its promotion of betting activities.[262] As a result, in its reference, the Swedish Supreme Court submitted a question as to whether the principle of effective judicial protection required it to provide interim relief in these circumstances.[263] In its judgment, the Court of Justice ruled that on the one hand, the principle of effective judicial protection does not require it to be possible in the national legal order concerned to obtain interim relief in the context of an application that is inadmissible, as in the case of a declaratory-type action that is not provided for in Sweden. On the other hand, by way of the other legal remedies or avenues that must be provided in the Member States which permit the issue of the compatibility of national law with Union law to be determined as a preliminary issue—for example, in the case of Sweden, by way of judicial review of the administrative decision concerning the promotion of the applicant's betting activities or the action for damages—it must be possible to grant interim relief protection until the competent national court has given a ruling as to whether the contested national provisions are compatible with Union law, where the grant of such interim relief is necessary to ensure the full effectiveness of the judgment to be given on the existence of such Union law rights.[264]

C. Allegedly illegal Union measure

4.62 As far as the second situation is concerned, the Court of Justice has held as follows: 'In cases where national authorities are responsible for the administrative application of [Union] regulations, the legal protection guaranteed by [Union] law includes the right of individuals to challenge, as a preliminary issue, the legality of such regulations before national courts and to induce those courts to refer questions to the Court of Justice for a preliminary ruling. That right would be compromised if, pending delivery of a judgment of the Court, which alone has jurisdiction to declare that a [Union] regulation is invalid ..., individuals were not in a position, where certain conditions are satisfied, to obtain a decision granting suspension of enforcement which would make it possible for the effects of the disputed regulation to be rendered for the time being inoperative as regards them.'[265] For this reason, Art. 288 TFEU does not preclude national courts from 'granting interim relief to settle or regulate the disputed legal positions or relationships with reference to a national administrative measure based on a [Union] regulation which is the subject of a reference for a preliminary ruling on its validity'.[266]

The question arises as to what is meant by 'where certain conditions are satisfied'. The Court of Justice has held that 'the rules of procedure of the courts are determined by national law and ... those conditions differ according to the national law governing them,

---

[262] ECJ, Case C-432/05 *Unibet*, paras 18–24.

[263] ECJ, Case C-432/05 *Unibet*, paras 28–30.

[264] ECJ, Case C-432/05 *Unibet*, paras 71–77. But compare the Opinion of Advocate-General E. Sharpston in ECJ, Case C-432/05 *Unibet* [2007] E.C.R. I-2271, points 77–86 (expressing concerns about unduly stretching the action for damages in connection with the interim relief protection sought by the applicant).

[265] ECJ, Joined Cases C-143/88 and C-92/89 *Zuckerfabrik Süderdithmarschen and Zuckerfabrik Soest* [1991] E.C.R. I-415, paras 16–17.

[266] ECJ, Case C-465/93 *Atlanta Fruchthandelsgesellschaft and Others* [1995] E.C.R. I-3761, para. 30.

which may jeopardise the uniform application of [Union] law'.[267] In order to reduce this danger, the Court of Justice has held that suspension of enforcement of national administrative measures based on a Union regulation or the grant of other interim measures 'must in all the Member States be subject to conditions which are uniform'.[268] The Court identifies those 'uniform conditions' with 'the conditions which must be satisfied for the Court of Justice [itself] to allow an application to it for interim measures'.[269] The parallel between the conditions for the grant of interim relief applicable before the national court and the Court of Justice (and the General Court) is due to the fact that an assessment of validity via a request for a preliminary ruling and an action for annulment constitute two aspects of a single system of judicial review of legality. The coherence of the system demands uniformity in the procedural rules for provisional suspension or limitation of enforcement of contested Union measures until such time as the Court of Justice or the General Court has carried out its review of legality, whether by a preliminary ruling (Court of Justice) or by a judgment on an application for annulment (Court of Justice or General Court). As a result, the national court must base itself, as far as the substantive conditions for suspension or limitation of enforcement of national administrative measures based on a Union act are concerned, on the case-law of the Court of Justice concerning interim measures and no longer on national law.[270] National law governs only 'the making and examination of the application'.[271]

As set down in *Zuckerfabrik* and further elaborated in *Atlanta*, interim measures may be granted by a national court only if the following four conditions are satisfied:

1. that the court entertains serious doubts as to the validity of the Union measure and, if the validity of the contested act is not already in issue before the Court of Justice, itself refers that question to the Court;[272]
2. there is urgency, in that interim relief is necessary to avoid serious and irreparable damage to the party seeking the relief;
3. the national court takes due account of the Union interest; and
4. in its assessment of all those conditions, it respects any decisions of the Court of Justice or the General Court ruling on the lawfulness of the Union measure concerned or on an application for interim measures seeking similar interim relief at Union level.[273]

---

[267] ECJ, Joined Cases C-143/88 and C-92/89 *Zuckerfabrik Süderdithmarschen and Zuckerfabrik Soest*, para. 25.

[268] ECJ, Case C-465/93 *Atlanta Fruchthandelsgesellschaft*, paras 29 and 33.

[269] ECJ, Joined Cases C-143/88 and C-92/89 *Zuckerfabrik Süderdithmarschen and Zuckerfabrik Soest*, paras 26–27.

[270] See Arts 278–279 TFEU; for examples, see ECJ (order of the President of 25 October 1985), Case 293/85 R *Commission v Belgium* [1985] E.C.R. 3521; ECJ (order of 12 July 1990), Case C-195/90 R *Commission v Germany* [1990] E.C.R. I-3351; ECJ (order of 30 July 2003), Case C-320/03 R *Commission v Austria* [2003] E.C.R. I-7929.

[271] ECJ, Joined Cases C-143/88 and C-92/89 *Zuckerfabrik Süderdithmarschen and Zuckerfabrik Soest*, para. 26.

[272] ECJ, Joined Cases C-143/88 and C-92/89 *Zuckerfabrik Süderdithmarschen and Zuckerfabrik Soest*, para. 33. See also ECJ, Case C-334/95 *Krüger* [1997] E.C.R. I-4517, para. 47. These conditions also apply where the interim measures are directed against an authority of an overseas country or territory (OCT): ECJ, Case C-17/98 *Emesa Sugar* [2000] E.C.R. I-675, paras 69–73.

[273] ECJ, Case C-465/93 *Atlanta Fruchthandelsgesellschaft and Others* [1995] E.C.R. I-3761, para. 51.

As far as the first requirement is concerned, the Court of Justice has held that 'the national court cannot restrict itself to referring the question of the validity of the [Union measure] to the Court for a preliminary ruling, but must set out, when making the interim order, the reasons for which it considers that the Court should find the [Union measure] to be invalid. The national court must take into account here the extent of the discretion which, having regard to the Court's case-law, the [Union] institutions must be allowed in the sectors concerned.'[274] Further to this, it has to be stated that the fact that an action for annulment against a decision ordering recovery of aid has been brought before the General Court does not justify a stay of proceedings since such an action does not have suspensory effect on the obligation to implement the decision. The same holds true for appeal proceedings brought before the Court of Justice against the judgment of the General Court in such an action.[275]

The Court has clarified the second requirement as follows: 'With regard to the question of urgency, . . . damage invoked by the applicant must be liable to materialise before the Court of Justice has been able to rule on the validity of the contested [Union] measure. With regard to the nature of that damage, purely financial damage cannot, as the Court has held on numerous occasions, be regarded in principle as irreparable. However, it is for the national court hearing the application for interim relief to examine the circumstances particular to the case before it. It must in this connection consider whether immediate enforcement of the measure which is the subject of the application for interim relief would be likely to result in irreversible damage to the applicant which could not be made good if the [Union] act were to be declared invalid.'[276]

As far as the third requirement is concerned, the Court of Justice has observed that the national court 'must first examine whether the [Union] measure in question would be deprived of all effectiveness if not immediately implemented'[277] and, 'if suspension of enforcement is liable to involve a financial risk for the [Union], the national court must also be in a position to require the applicant to provide adequate guarantees, such as the deposit of money or other security'.[278] In assessing the Union interest, the national court is free to decide, in accordance with its own rules of procedure, which is the most appropriate way of obtaining all relevant information on the Union act in question.[279]

The fourth requirement signifies that if the Court of Justice has dismissed an action for annulment of the act in question or has held, in the context of a reference for a preliminary ruling on validity, that the reference disclosed nothing to affect the validity of that act, the national court can no longer order interim measures or must revoke any existing measures, unless the grounds of illegality put forward before it differ from the pleas in law or grounds of illegality rejected by the Court in its judgment. The same applies if the General Court, in

---

[274] ECJ, Case C-465/93 *Atlanta Fruchthandelsgesellschaft*, paras 36–37. See also ECJ, Case C-304/09 *Commission v Italy* [2010] E.C.R. I-13903, para. 51.

[275] ECJ, Case C-304/09 *Commission v Italy* [2010] E.C.R. I-13903, para. 52.

[276] ECJ, Joined Cases C-143/88 and C-92/89 *Zuckerfabrik Süderdithmarschen and Zuckerfabrik Soest* [1991] E.C.R. I-415, para. 29.

[277] ECJ, Joined Cases C-143/88 and C-92/89 *Zuckerfabrik Süderdithmarschen and Zuckerfabrik Soest*, para. 31.

[278] ECJ, Joined Cases C-143/88 and C-92/89 *Zuckerfabrik Süderdithmarschen and Zuckerfabrik Soest*, para. 32.

[279] ECJ, Case C-334/95 *Krüger* [1997] E.C.R. I-4517, para. 46.

a judgment which has become final and binding, has dismissed on the merits an action for annulment of the act or an objection of illegality.[280]

Following *Zuckerfabrik* and *Atlanta*, the question arose in *ABNA*[281] as to whether, provided that the requisite conditions entitling the national court of one Member State to suspend implementation of a Union measure are satisfied, the national authorities of other Member States were themselves entitled to suspend application of that same Union measure as well until such time as the Court of Justice has given its ruling on validity of that act. In response, the Court of Justice ruled that national authorities are not in a position to grant interim relief under such circumstances because they are not in the same position as national courts and that it is the national courts alone that are entitled to verify whether the requisite conditions governing interim relief have been satisfied and to grant interim relief on that basis.[282]

D. Appeal against a national decision

National procedural rules allowing an appeal to be brought against a decision granting **4.63** interim measures in the form of suspension of enforcement of a national administrative measure are compatible with Union law, provided that they do not affect the national court's obligation in such a case to make a reference for a preliminary ruling on the validity of the Union act on which the suspended national implementing measure is based, and that they do not restrict the right conferred by Art. 267 TFEU on every court or tribunal to make a reference to the Court of Justice.[283]

E. Counterpart of interim relief granted by the Union judicature

National courts' power to grant interim relief under Union law in the two situations **4.64** described above (see paras 4.61 and 4.62) is also based on the consideration that the judicial review which the Court of Justice carries out in the preliminary ruling procedure needs to retain its full effectiveness.[284] In both situations, the national court has the power, or even a duty, to make a reference to the Court of Justice for a preliminary ruling. In the first situation, it may, by referring a question on the interpretation of the applicable provision of Union law, indirectly determine whether the national provision at issue is, as alleged, contrary to Union law. In the second, it is under a duty, if the question concerning the validity of the disputed Union act has not yet been submitted to the Court, to raise that question with the Court itself. Consequently, the interim relief granted by national courts in those two situations is the precise counterpart of the interim relief which the Court of Justice or the General Court grants under Arts 278–279 TFEU in order

---

[280] ECJ, Case C-465/93 *Atlanta Fruchthandelsgesellschaft and Others* [1995] E.C.R. I-3761, para. 46.
[281] ECJ, Joined Cases C-453/03, C-11/04, C-12/04, and C-192/04 *ABNA and Others* [2005] E.C.R. I-10423.
[282] ECJ, Joined Cases C-453/03, C-11/04, C-12/04, and C-192/04 *ABNA and Others*, paras 108–111.
[283] ECJ, Case C-334/95 *Krüger* [1997] E.C.R. I-4517, paras 49–54.
[284] ECJ, Joined Cases C-143/88 and C-92/89 *Zuckerfabrik Süderdithmarschen and Zuckerfabrik Soest* [1991] E.C.R. I-415, para. 19.

to ensure the effectiveness of the judicial supervision which it carries out in direct actions.[285] The Court of Justice has held, in full accord with its concern to guarantee the coherence of the system of legal protection outlined in the Treaties, that the national courts are not empowered to grant interim relief in situations in which, by virtue of a Union act, the existence and scope of traders' rights must be established by a Commission measure which that institution has not yet adopted. This is because the Treaties make no provision for a reference for a preliminary ruling by which the national court asks the Court of Justice to rule that an institution has failed to act.[286] The Court of Justice and the General Court may only make such a ruling in a direct action brought pursuant to Art. 265 TFEU.

---

[285] For further particulars, see K. Lenaerts, 'The Legal Protection of Private Parties Under the EC Treaty: A Coherent and Complete System of Judicial Review', in *Scritti in onore di Giuseppe Federico Mancini*, Vol. II (Milan, Giuffrè, 1998), 591–623.

[286] ECJ, Case C-68/95 *T. Port v Commission* [1996] E.C.R. I-6065, paras 52–53. But see ECJ, Case C-511/03 *Ten Kate Holding Musselkanaal and Others* [2005] E.C.R. I-8979, discussed further in Ch. 8. See also K. Lenaerts, 'The Rule of Law and the Coherence of the Judicial System of the European Union' (2007) C.M.L. Rev. 1625–59.

PART II

ENFORCEMENT OF UNION LAW

5

THE ACTION FOR INFRINGEMENT OF UNION LAW BY A MEMBER STATE

I. Subject-Matter

A. General

(1) Nature of the action

The action for failure to fulfil obligations (or infringement proceedings)[1] is for the purpose of obtaining a declaration from the Court of Justice that the conduct of a Member State infringes Union law and of terminating that conduct.[2] It therefore constitutes a direct action brought before the Union judicature by which to ensure the enforcement of Union law as part of the system of judicial protection enshrined in the Treaties. The action is objective in nature and the only question raised is whether or not the defendant Member State has breached Union law.[3] The objective nature of the action for failure to fulfil obligations does not mean, however, that the Court of Justice does not subject the relevant conduct of the Member State concerned to thorough examination, from the point of view of both the law and the facts. Save for certain exceptions, any infringement of (non-CFSP) Union law may be 'found' pursuant to Arts 258–260 TFEU.[4]

5.01

(2) Purpose

The 'finding' of an infringement serves principally to enforce the actual application of Union law by the Member State in breach. In the first place, since *Francovich*,[5] a Member State may incur liability under Union law for a breach of a (non-CFSP) Union provision.

5.02

---

[1] Arts 258–260 TFEU, applicable to the EAEC Treaty. See further para. 5.03. See K. Lenaerts, 'Préface', in T. Materne (ed.), *La procédure en manquement d'État. Guide à la lumière de la jurisprudence de la Cour de justice de l'Union européenne* (Brussels, Groupe De Boeck Larcier, 2012), 13–17.

[2] ECJ, Joined Cases 15/76 and 16/76 *France v Commission* [1979] E.C.R. 321, para. 27.

[3] See, *inter alia*, ECJ, Case 7/68 *Commission v Italy* [1968] E.C.R. 423, at 428; ECJ, Case 415/85 *Commission v Ireland* [1988] E.C.R. 3097, paras 8–9; ECJ, Case 416/85 *Commission v United Kingdom* [1988] E.C.R. 3127, paras 8–9; ECJ, Case C-140/00 *Commission v United Kingdom* [2002] E.C.R. I-10372, para. 34; ECJ, Case C-297/08 *Commission v Italy* [2010] E.C.R. I-1749, para. 81. See further para. 5.65.

[4] As regards these exceptions and the specification of non-CFSP Union law, see para. 5.04.

[5] ECJ, Joined Cases C-6/90 and C-9/90 *Francovich and Others* [1991] E.C.R. I-5357 (see para. 4.46).

The judgment finding the infringement may ground such liability.[6] In addition, Art. 260 TFEU provides for options for enforcing such a judgment.[7]

The action may also be used as a means of determining the exact nature of the obligations of a Member State in the event of differences of interpretation of Union law.[8] After the Court of Justice has given judgment, the Member State concerned may no longer contest the extent of its Union obligations. If the Member State continues to be in breach of its obligations, this will constitute a sufficiently serious breach of Union law to possibly cause it to incur liability vis-à-vis injured individuals.[9]

(3) Procedure

5.03   The procedure is set forth in Arts 258, 259, and 260 TFEU.[10] With the entry into force of the Lisbon Treaty, these provisions replaced Arts 226, 227, and 228 EC, respectively, and exacted certain changes, as discussed in para. 5.04.

Former Arts 226–228 EC were identical in substance to Arts 141–143 EAEC.[11] Upon entry into force of the Lisbon Treaty, these provisions of the EAEC Treaty have been repealed, and Arts 258–260 TFEU are now applicable.[12] Art. 88 of the now-expired ECSC

---

[6] See the settled case-law since ECJ, Case 39/72 *Commission v Italy* [1973] E.C.R. 101, para. 11, in which it was held that 'a judgment by the Court under [Arts 169 and 171 EEC, now Arts 258 and 259 TFEU] may be of substantive interest as establishing the basis of a responsibility that a Member State can incur as a result of its default, as regards other Member States, the [Union] or private parties'. See also paras 4.46–4.52.

[7] The procedure provided for in Art. 260(2) TFEU may be applied only where the Court has first determined pursuant to Arts 258 or 259 TFEU that the Member State has failed to fulfil an obligation under the Union law: ECJ (order of the President of 30 May 2001), Case C-334/97 R-EX *Comune di Montorio al Vomano v Commission* [2001] E.C.R. I-4229, para. 19; ECJ, Case C-457/07 *Commission v Portugal* [2009] E.C.R. I-8091, para. 47. That being said, Art. 260(3) TFEU is also relevant in connection with pecuniary sanctions that may be imposed in proceedings brought under Art. 258 TFEU as far as a Member State's alleged failure to fulfil its obligation to notify measures transposing a legislative directive is concerned: see para. 5.16.

[8] ECJ, Case 7/71 *Commission v France* [1971] E.C.R. 1003, para. 49. For example, ECJ, Case C-50/09 *Commission v Ireland* [2011] E.C.R. I-873; ECJ, Case C-41/09 *Commission v Netherlands* [2011] E.C.R. I-831 (dealing with different language versions of a Union law text). A difference of interpretation between the Commission and a Member State can result in favour of the Member State concerned and hence the action, or certain heads of claim, brought under Art. 258 TFEU are dismissed: see, e.g. ECJ, Case C-401/06, *Commission v Germany* [2007] E.C.R. I-609; ECJ, Case C-376/09, *Commission v Malta* [2011] E.C.R. I-4017.

[9] See para. 4.48.

[10] Under Art. 271(d) TFEU, actions may be brought against a national central bank for failure to fulfil obligations under the Treaties and the Statute of the European System of Central Banks and of the European Central Bank. Proceedings are to be brought by the Governing Council of the European Central Bank, which has the same powers as the Commission has under Art. 258 TFEU. Under Art. 271(a) TFEU, the Board of Directors of the European Investment Bank may bring an action in the Court of Justice against a Member State in relation to the fulfilment of its obligations under the Bank's Statute. In this connection, the Board of Directors enjoys the powers conferred upon the Commission by Art. 258 TFEU: see CFI (order of 10 April 2000), Case T-361/99 *Meyer v Commission and EIB* [2000] E.C.R. II-2031, para. 12. Art. 126(10) TFEU rules out the possibility of bringing an action against a Member State under Arts 258 and 259 TFEU for failing to fulfil its obligations under Art. 126(1)–(9) TFEU by failing to avoid an excessive government deficit.

[11] See, e.g. ECJ, Case C-61/03 *Commission v United Kingdom* [2005] E.C.R. I-2477.

[12] See Art. 106a EAEC, consolidated version [2012] O.J. C327/1; Art. 3 of Protocol (No. 2) amending the EAEC Treaty, annexed to the Treaty of Lisbon, [2007] O.J. C306/199. Nonetheless, before the entry into force of the Lisbon Treaty, recourse to the two sets of Treaty provisions was not mutually exclusive, i.e. an action for failure to fulfil obligations could be brought on the basis of both: see, e.g. Case C-459/03 *Commission v Ireland ('Mox Plant')* [2006] E.C.R. I-4635.

Treaty had set forth a somewhat different procedure for failure to fulfil obligations under that Treaty.[13]

The action for failure to fulfil obligations is the only procedure—apart from some special procedures (see paras 5.21–5.30)—which allows the Court of Justice to measure the conduct of a Member State directly against Union law.[14]

(4) Changes brought by the Treaty of Lisbon

As already mentioned, with the entry into force of the Lisbon Treaty, former Arts 226–228 **5.04** EC were reframed as Arts 258–260 TFEU. Arts 258 and 259 TFEU reproduce former Arts 226–227 EC practically verbatim.[15] However, with respect to the Court's jurisdiction to impose a pecuniary sanction on a Member State, Art. 260 TFEU modifies the procedure of Art. 228 EC in two important respects. First, Art. 260(3) TFEU provides that where a Member State has failed to fulfil its obligation to notify measures transposing a directive adopted under a legislative procedure, the Commission may bring a case before the Court under Art. 258 TFEU, asking the latter to find an infringement and to impose a pecuniary sanction at the same time.[16] Second, in cases concerning a Member State's non-compliance with the Court's first judgment finding an infringement, Art. 260(2) TFEU does away with the need for a reasoned opinion in the pre-litigation stage of the second action; the Commission may bring the case before the Court after giving that Member State the opportunity to submit its observations.[17]

Moreover, as a general matter, since the entry into force of the Lisbon Treaty, the pillar structure has been abolished, thereby bringing both the former European Community and the non-Community pillars (i.e. Common Foreign and Security Policy (CFSP) and Police and Judicial Cooperation in Criminal Matters (PJCCM)) together as policy fields under the rubric of Union law.[18] This has the result that the Court of Justice's jurisdiction extends to

---

[13] The ECSC Treaty expired on 23 July 2002, and its assets and liabilities were transferred to the European Community, as it then was, on 24 July 2002. See Protocol (No. 37), annexed to the TEU and TFEU, on the financial consequences of the expiry of the ECSC Treaty and on the Research fund for Coal and Steel, [2012] O.J. C326/328. See further K. Lenaerts and P. Van Nuffel (R. Bray and N. Cambien (eds)), *European Union Law* (3rd edn, London, Sweet & Maxwell, 2011), paras 1.07–1.09.

[14] ECJ, Case 28/83 *Forcheri v Commission* [1984] E.C.R. 1425, para. 12; CFI, Case T-13/93 *Cordier v Commission* [1993] E.C.R. II-1215, para. 52. Since *Van Gend & Loos* (ECJ, Case 26/62 *Van Gend & Loos* [1963] E.C.R. 1, at 10–13), however, the Court of Justice has held that it can use the procedure for a preliminary ruling on interpretation in order to appraise a Member State's conduct indirectly against Union law. See further K. Lenaerts, 'The Rule of Law and the Coherence of the Judicial System of the European Union' (2007) C.M.L. Rev. 1625, 1635–45.

[15] There were adjustments made to Arts 258–259 TFEU (as well as Art. 260 TFEU) in connection with the changes brought by the Lisbon Treaty to the Treaty framework (see Art. 1, third para., TEU and Art. 1(2) TFEU) and the allocation of jurisdiction among the Union courts: the procedure set down in these provisions relates to the failure to fulfil obligations under the 'Treaties', no longer just the EC 'Treaty', and reference is made to the 'Court of Justice of the European Union', as opposed to the 'Court of Justice'. In any event, as no changes have been made to Art. 256(1) TFEU and Art. 51 of the Statute, it is the Court of Justice that will be referred to herein as the body within the Union judicature that has been conferred jurisdiction to adjudicate infringement actions. See further Ch. 2.

[16] See para. 5.16.

[17] See para. 5.75.

[18] See further K. Lenaerts and P. Van Nuffel (R. Bray and N. Cambien (eds)), *European Union Law* (3rd edn, London, Sweet & Maxwell, 2011), paras 4.12–4.15.

infringement actions in the former third pillar of PJCCM.[19] Nevertheless, as far as the CFSP is concerned, the jurisdiction of the Court of Justice remains limited and does not encompass infringement actions. There is also a special provisional regime applicable to the PJCCM, which affects the jurisdiction of the Court of Justice, as well as the competence of the Commission, in relation to infringement actions.[20]

B. Failure of a Member State to fulfil an obligation under the Treaties

(1) What rules are covered by the expression 'an obligation under the Treaties'?

(a) All rules of non-CFSP Union law

5.05   The expression 'an obligation under the Treaties' in principle covers all rules of non-CFSP Union law that are binding on the Member States. These generally comprise all the Treaty provisions,[21] binding acts of Union institutions and bodies,[22] international agreements concluded by the Union,[23] and the general principles of Union law recognized by the Court of Justice (see para. 5.06). A finding that those rules have been infringed may be made as a result of an action brought pursuant to Arts 258–260 TFEU.[24]

However, there are exceptions as far as the policy fields of the former second and third pillars are concerned. As regards the CFSP, the Court of Justice of the European Union has not been conferred jurisdiction with respect to the relevant Treaty provisions on the CFSP and the acts adopted pursuant thereto, save for monitoring compliance with Art. 40 TEU and reviewing the legality of certain decisions as provided for by that provision and the second paragraph of Art. 275 TFEU.[25] As a result, as things stand now, there is no provision under the Treaties for infringement actions to be brought against a Member State for its failure to fulfil obligations in connection with CFSP Union law. With regard to acts

---

[19] Under the former Treaty framework, there had been a somewhat similar procedure enshrined in Art. 35(7) EU as far as the third pillar of PJCCM was concerned: see Ch. 22.

[20] See para. 5.05.

[21] Violation of Art. 4(3) TEU by itself can constitute the basis of infringement proceedings against a Member State, even if no other provision of Union law has been breached: see, e.g. ECJ, Case C-246/07 *Commission v Sweden* [2010] E.C.R. I-3317 (G. De Baere, case note (2011) Eur.L. Rev. 405–19). Moreover, while the Court will consider a separate plea relating to a breach of Art. 4(3) TEU, it will not do so if ancillary or linked to another head of complaint in which such breach is subsumed therein: see, e.g. ECJ, Case C-459/03 *Commission v Ireland ('Mox Plant')* [2006] E.C.R. I-4635, paras 171–173. For further discussion of this provision, see paras 5.18 and 5.64.

[22] ECJ, Case C-205/98 *Commission v Austria* [2000] E.C.R. I-7367, para. 43. The infringement of a directive which has been annulled but whose effects the Court of Justice preserved in the judgment until such time as it had been replaced by a new directive in compliance with the Court's judgment may form the subject of an action for failure to fulfil obligations. It made no difference in the case cited here that the Council and the European Parliament did not adopt the new directive until four years had elapsed.

[23] Art. 261(2) TFEU; ECJ, Case 104/81 *Kupferberg* [1982] E.C.R. 3641, para. 11; ECJ, Case C-61/94 *Commission v Germany* [1996] E.C.R. I-3989, para. 15. See recently ECJ, Case C-92/07 *Commission v Netherlands* [2010] E.C.R. I-3683, whereby the Court ruled that the Netherlands was in breach of its obligations under the relevant provisions of the EEC–Turkey Association Agreement and measures related thereto. As regards mixed agreements, see para. 5.07. As regards a Member State's conclusion of an international agreement, see also para. 5.13.

[24] For detailed discussion of the sources of Union law, see K. Lenaerts and P. Van Nuffel (R. Bray and N. Cambien (eds)), *European Union Law* (3rd edn, London, Sweet & Maxwell, 2011), ch. 22.

[25] Art. 24(1), second para., TEU; Art. 275 TFEU. The Court of Justice's jurisdiction to review the legality of decisions providing for restrictive measures against natural and legal persons in actions brought in accordance with the conditions laid down in Art. 263, fourth para., TFEU is discussed in Ch. 7.

adopted in the field of the PJCCM prior to the entry into force of the Lisbon Treaty, Art. 10(1) of the Protocol (No. 36) on Transitional Provisions[26] provides for reduced powers of the Court of Justice of the European Union and of the Commission for a period of five years: the Commission cannot enforce the application of such acts by bringing infringement actions under Art. 258 TFEU, and the Court of Justice only has the powers that were attributed to it by Title VI of the EU Treaty before 1 December 2009, that is to say, the powers attributed to the Court of Justice under former Art. 35 EU, which excludes infringement actions.[27] Yet where such PJCCM acts are amended, the reduction in powers of both the Commission and the Court no longer applies with respect to the amended act and for those Member States to which that amended act is to apply.[28] Accordingly, with regard to the provisions of the amended act, the Commission and the Court enjoy the full scope of powers they have under the Treaties with regard to acts adopted in the field of PJCCM, which includes their respective powers in relation to infringement actions.[29] In any event, the reduced powers of these institutions will cease to apply on 1 December 2014.[30]

(b) General principles of Union law

A finding that a Member State has infringed general principles of Union law, including **5.06** fundamental rights, may be made only insofar as the national conduct falls within the scope of Union law. This will be so, in particular where the Member State justifies its conduct on one of the grounds provided for in the Treaties.[31]

(c) Mixed agreements

With respect to actions brought against a Member State pursuant to Art. 258 TFEU for **5.07** failure to fulfil obligations under an international agreement, by and large, much of the case-law centres on mixed agreements.[32] For example, in *Commission v Ireland*, the Court held that Ireland's failure to accede to the Berne Convention as required by Art. 5 of Protocol 28 to the EEA Agreement (a mixed agreement concluded by the Union, its Member States, and non-member countries and related to an area covered in large measure by the Treaties) came within the Union framework. This therefore constituted a failure to fulfil obligations within the meaning of Art. 258 TFEU.[33] Moreover, in *Commission v France*, the Court ruled that provisions of a mixed agreement come within the scope of

---

[26] Protocol (No. 36) on Transitional Provisions, annexed to the TEU, TFEU and the EAEC Treaty, [2012] O.J. C326/322.

[27] But see former Art. 35(7) EU.

[28] With respect to such an 'amended act', the Protocol does not distinguish between the parts amended and other, unamended, parts, with the result that any amendment to pre-existing PJCCM acts may result in the Commission and the Court no longer having reduced powers.

[29] Protocol (No. 36) on Transitional Provisions, Art. 10(2).

[30] Protocol (No. 36) on Transitional Provisions, Art. 10(3).

[31] See, *inter alia*, ECJ, Case C-260/89 *ERT* [1991] E.C.R. I-2925, para. 42; ECJ, Case C-159/90 *Society for the Protection of Unborn Children Ireland* [1991] E.C.R. I-4685, para. 31; ECJ, Case C-441/02 *Commission v Germany* [2006] E.C.R. I-3449, paras 107–108 (and case-law cited therein). As regards what constitutes a 'general principle' of Union law, see ECJ, Case C-101/08 *Audiolux* [2009] E.C.R. I-9823. See also ECJ (judgment of 26 February 2013), Case C-399/11 *Melloni*, not reported, paras 55–64 and ECJ (judgment of 26 February 2013), Case C-617/10 *Åkerberg Fransson*, not reported, paras 16–31.

[32] P. J. Kuijper, J. Wouters, F. Hoffmeister, G. De Baere, and T. Ramopoulos, *The Law of EU External Relations: Cases Materials, and Commentary on the EU as an International Legal Actor* (Oxford, Oxford University Press, 2013), ch. 4.

[33] ECJ, Case C-13/00 *Commission v Ireland* [2002] E.C.R. I-2943, para. 20. See also ECJ, Case C-465/01 *Commission v Austria* [2004] E.C.R. I-8291 (action upheld against Austria for failure to fulfil obligations under provisions of Union law, the EEA Agreement, and certain association agreements concluded by the Union).

Union law if they—even in the absence of specific Union legislation regarding the issue covered by these provisions (for example, discharges of fresh water and alluvia into saltwater marsh)—concern a field (for example, environmental protection) 'in large measure' covered by Union law; if this is the case, the Court of Justice has jurisdiction to assess a Member State's compliance with the provisions concerned of the mixed agreement in proceedings brought before it under Art. 258 TFEU.[34]

(d) Conventions between Member States, including those concluded pursuant to former Art. 293 EC

5.08 It remains an open question whether a Member State may be brought before the Court of Justice for infringing a convention concluded pursuant to former Art. 293 EC. Some commentators argued that this was possible on the grounds that Art. 293 EC put the Member States under a duty to enter into negotiations with each other in order to achieve clearly defined Community objectives.[35] Others contended that a distinction should be made between the obligation to conclude the convention under Art. 293 EC and the obligations ensuing out of such a convention for Member States. They maintained that the latter obligations were not part of Community law as it then was.[36] The Court of Justice has not yet had to rule on the question.[37] Since the entry into force of the Lisbon Treaty, however, the Treaties no longer mention conventions between Member States as a policy instrument of the Union, and Art. 293 EC has been repealed. Yet this does not prevent existing conventions from keeping their legal force, and thus this question may eventually arise.

In any event, in accordance with the case-law, compliance with conventions concluded by the Member States outside of what used to be Art. 293 EC cannot be enforced by proceedings under Arts 258 and 259 TFEU, even if they do contribute to the attainment of the objectives of the Treaties.[38]

---

[34] ECJ, Case C-465/01 *Commission v Austria* [2004] E.C.R. I-8291; ECJ, Case C-239/03 *Commission v France* [2004] E.C.R. I-9325, paras 22–31.

[35] See A. Dashwood and R. White, 'Enforcement Actions Under Article 169 and 170 EEC' (1989) E.L. Rev. 388, at 390.

[36] I. Schwartz, 'Voies d'uniformisation du droit dans la CEE: règlements de la Communauté ou conventions entre les États membres' (1978) J.D.I. 751, at 781.

[37] However, the Court has held in its case-law on the Brussels Convention—which has since been replaced except so far as Denmark is concerned by Council Regulation (EC) No. 44/2001 of 22 December 2000 on jurisdiction and the recognition and enforcement of judgments in civil and commercial matters ([2001] O.J. L12/1; *corrigendum* in [2001] O.J. L307/28; note that Regulation (EC) No. 44/2001 shall be replaced from 10 January 2015 onwards by Regulation (EU) No. 1215/2012 of the European Parliament and of the Council of 12 December 2012 on jurisdiction and the recognition and enforcement of judgments in civil and commercial matters, [2012] O.J. L351/1), which manifestly forms part of Union law—that the provisions of that Convention were 'linked to the E[E]C Treaty', and that this allowed the Court of Justice to assess the compatibility of those provisions with then Art. 12 EC (now Art. 18 TFEU) (prohibition of discrimination on grounds of nationality): ECJ, Case C-398/92 *Mund & Fester* [1994] E.C.R. I-467, paras 11–12. Admittedly, the Court has not provided any answer to the question whether infringements on the part of Member States of the Brussels Convention can be the subject of proceedings brought under Arts 258 and 259 TFEU. It may be considered, however, that the answer must be in the negative, given that the Court of Justice mentioned in the case cited here the Brussels Convention and the national provisions, to which it refers on an equal footing when it stated that they were linked to the then EC Treaty and therefore 'within the scope of application of this Treaty' within the meaning of Art.12 EC (now Art. 18 TFEU). As a result, the Brussels Convention came over as a joint measure of the Member States, which, in common with unilateral national measures, must be compatible with Union law, but does not form part of it.

[38] See, recently, e.g. ECJ, Case C-132/09 *Commission v Belgium* ('*European schools*') [2010] E.C.R. I-8695, paras 42–53. But an international agreement may include a clause granting jurisdiction to the Court of

(2) What is meant by 'failed to fulfil'?

(a) Any shortcoming

Since the action for failure to fulfil obligations is objective in nature (see para. 5.65), any **5.09** shortcoming by a Member State in respect of its obligations under non-CFSP Union law will ground a claim for a declaration that it is in breach. The frequency or scale of the shortcoming is irrelevant, as is the fact that the failure had no adverse effects.[39] A minimum, isolated, and negligible infringement of Union law is sufficient for the action to be declared well-founded.[40] It lies with the Commission or the applicant Member State (see paras 5.30 and 5.35) to assess whether it is appropriate to bring an action. Once the action is pending, the Court of Justice has to consider whether or not the alleged infringement was committed.[41]

(b) Administrative practice

Not only the exercise by a Member State of its regulatory powers can constitute a **5.10** failure to fulfil an obligation of the Treaties.[42] An administrative practice can also be the subject-matter of an action for failure to fulfil obligations when it is, to some degree, of a consistent and general nature.[43] The idea underlying the notion of 'administrative practice' in this regard is that while the applicable national legislation itself complies with Union law, it is the application of the relevant Union law rules by the national administrative

---

Justice pursuant to Art. 273 TFEU. See, e.g. Art. 8 of the Treaty on Stability, Coordination and Governance in the Economic and Monetary Union done at Brussels on 2 March 2012; Art. 37(3) of the Treaty on establishing the European stability mechanism done at Brussels on 2 February 2012; ECJ (judgment of 27 November 2012), Case C-370/12 *Pringle*, not reported, paras 170–177.

[39] See, e.g. ECJ, Case C-150/97 *Commission v Portugal* [1999] E.C.R. I-259, para. 22; ECJ, Case C-348/97 *Commission v Germany* [2000] E.C.R. I-4429, para. 62; ECJ, Case C-227/04 *Commission v Spain* [2004] E.C.R. I-8253, para. 58; ECJ, Case C-177/04 *Commission v France* [2006] E.C.R. I-2461, para. 52; ECJ, Case C-61/05 *Commission v Portugal* [2006] E.C.R. I-6779, para. 32; ECJ, Case C-377/03 *Commission v Belgium* [2006] E.C.R. I-9733, paras 91–97; ECJ, Case C-36/05 *Commission v Spain* [2006] E.C.R. I-10313, para. 38; ECJ, Case C-91/05 *Commission v Denmark* [2007] E.C.R. I-8597, paras 31–35; ECJ, Case C-456/05 *Commission v Germany* [2007] E.C.R. I-10517, para. 22 (underlining 'no degree of gravity' in infringement actions).

[40] Thus, the Commission may ask the Court of Justice to find that in not having achieved, in a specific case, the result intended by the directive, a Member State has failed to fulfil its obligations: ECJ, Joined Cases C-20/01 and C-28/01 *Commission v Germany* [2003] E.C.R. I-3609, para. 30; ECJ, Case C-157/03 *Commission v Spain* [2005] E.C.R. I-2911, para. 44; ECJ, Case C-275/08 *Commission v Germany* [2009] E.C.R. I-168*, Summ. pub., para. 27 (and case-law cited therein); ECJ, Case C-456/08 *Commission v Ireland* [2010] E.C.R. I-859, paras 39–41.

[41] ECJ, Case C-209/89 *Commission v Italy* [1991] E.C.R. I-1575, para. 6.

[42] ECJ, Case 8/70 *Commission v Italy* [1970] E.C.R. 961, paras 8–9; ECJ, Case 94/81 *Commission v Italy* [1982] E.C.R. 739, para. 4; ECJ, Case 41/82 *Commission v Italy* [1982] E.C.R. 4213, para.15; ECJ, Case 309/84 *Commission v Italy* [1986] E.C.R. 599, para. 9.

[43] See, *inter alia*, ECJ, Case 21/84 *Commission v France* [1985] E.C.R. 1355, paras 13, 15; ECJ, Case C-387/99 *Commission v Germany* [2004] E.C.R. I-3751, para. 42; ECJ, Case C-494/01 *Commission v Ireland* [2005] E.C.R. I-3331, para. 28; ECJ, Case C-160/08 *Commission v Germany* [2010] E.C.R I-3713, para. 107 (and case-law cited therein). The Commission does not prove the existence of an administrative practice—which must be, to some degree, of a consistent and general nature—by making reference to a single complaint: ECJ, Case C-287/03 *Commission v Belgium* [2005] E.C.R. I-3761, paras 29–30. See also ECJ, Case C-156/04, *Commission v Greece* [2007] E.C.R. I-4179, para. 51: given the large pool of EU and Greek nationals involved, the Court ruled that eight individual cases, even if established, constituted 'substantially inadequate percentage' to prove the existence of a consistent administrative practice. In some cases, the existence of an 'administrative practice' in the Member State concerned is assumed without dispute: see, e.g. ECJ, Case C-393/05 *Commission v Austria* [2007] E.C.R. I-10195; ECJ, Case C-546/07 *Commission v Germany* [2010] E.C.R. I-439.

(or other[44]) authorities that constitutes the basis for the Member State's failure to fulfil obligations.[45]

It will be easier to make a finding that there has been a failure to fulfil an obligation where it ensues from the existence of a provision of national law which infringes Union law[46] than where it ensues out of a so-called 'administrative practice' of a Member State, which assumes that a particular pattern of behaviour can be discerned on the part of the authorities of the defendant Member State.[47]

(c) General and persistent infringements

5.11   Starting with *Commission v Ireland*,[48] the Court of Justice has allowed infringement proceedings to be brought against a Member State based on the conduct of a Member State's authorities not with regard to particular specifically defined situations, but instead where the relevant provisions of Union law have not been complied with because its authorities

---

[44] Depending on the case, inquiry into the existence of an administrative practice may encompass the actions or conduct of administrative as well as judicial authorities and/or other authorities of the Member State concerned: see, e.g. ECJ, C-129/00 *Commission v Italy* [2003] E.C.R. I-14637, paras 28–29; Case C-88/07 *Commission v Spain* [2009] E.C.R. I-1353, para. 62. For further case-law bearing on the substantiation of an infringement due to case-law of national courts, see para. 5.12.

[45] See, e.g. ECJ, Case C-489/06 *Commission v Germany* [2009] E.C.R. I-1797, paras 46–47. Note that in addition to the notion of administrative practice as *the basis* for an alleged infringement, it can also be used in a different sense as *a defence* to an infringement action in terms of arguments put forward by the Member State concerned that it has remedied the alleged infringement by means of administrative practice, although such arguments usually fail.

[46] However, the scope of national laws, regulations, or administrative provisions must be assessed in the light of the interpretation given to them by national courts: see, e.g. ECJ, Case 300/95 *Commission v United Kingdom* [1997] E.C.R. I-2649, para. 37; ECJ, Case C-129/03 *Commission v Italy* [2003] E.C.R. 14637, para. 30 (and further citations therein).

[47] See, e.g. ECJ, Case 21/84 *Commission v France* [1985] E.C.R. 1355; ECJ, Case 35/84 *Commission v Italy* [1986] E.C.R. 545; ECJ, Case C-150/00 *Commission v Austria* [2004] E.C.R. I-3887; ECJ, Case C-41/02 *Commission v Netherlands* [2004] E.C.R. I-11375. Indeed, the requisite standard of proof in relation to an administrative and/or judicial practice is high: see ECJ, Case C-441/02 *Commission v Germany* [2006] E.C.R. I-3449, paras 49 and 78 (and case-law cited therein): with regard to a complaint concerning the implementation of a national provision, proof of a Member State's failure to fulfil its obligations requires production of evidence different from that usually taken into account in an action for failure to fulfil obligations concerning solely the terms of a national provision, and in those circumstances the failure to fulfil obligations can be established only by means of sufficiently documented and detailed proof of the alleged practice of the 'national administration and/or courts' for which the Member State concerned is answerable. See also ECJ, Case C-156/04 *Commission v Greece* [2007] E.C.R. I-4179, paras 50, 52–53, where the Court underscored that if the Commission intended to prove a Member State's failure to fulfil obligations on account of 'judicial practice', the criteria established in the case-law apply with particular stringency; in the instant proceedings, the Commission failed to make out such a case. For some recent examples demonstrating the Court's assessment in relation to finding the existence of an administrative practice, see ECJ, Case C-489/06 *Commission v Greece* [2009] E.C.R. I-1797, paras 46–53; ECJ, Case C-88/07 *Commission v Spain* [2009] E.C.R. I-1353. For examples in which an administrative practice was not proven, see ECJ, Case C-441/02 *Commission v Germany* [2006] E.C.R. I-3449, paras 50–56, 78–80, 98–102, 110–113, 122–125; ECJ, Case C-342/05 *Commission v Finland* [2007] E.C.R. I-4713, paras 32–39; ECJ, Case C-156/04 *Commission v Greece* [2007] E.C.R. I-4129, paras 50–53.

[48] ECJ, Case C-494/01 *Commission v Ireland* [2005] E.C.R. I-3331. Another important feature of this case concerned whether the Commission could, at the litigation stage of the procedure, submit new evidence about infringements not mentioned in the reasoned opinion but which became available at a later stage could further support the persistent nature of the breach in question. The Court ruled in this regard that the admission of fresh evidence is admissible because it does not change the subject-matter of the dispute: ECJ, Case C-494/01 *Commission v Ireland*, paras 37–39. For a detailed discussion of this case and its implications, see K. Lenaerts and J. A. Gutiérrez-Fons, 'The General Enforcement Obligation of EU Environmental Law' (2011) Y.E.L. 1–39.

have adopted a general practice thereto, which the particular situations illustrate where appropriate.[49] In holding such approach admissible in subsequent cases, the Court explained that the Treaties do not contain any rule that precludes the overall treatment of a significant number of situations on the basis of which the Commission considers that a Member State has, repeatedly and over a long period, failed to fulful its obligations under Union law.[50]

To some extent, this line of cases is interrelated with the conditions under the Court's case-law in relation to an administrative practice in the sense that specific instances of breaches of Union law are being used to substantiate the extent to which the practice of the national authorities is of a 'general' nature.[51] However, they are not the same. In the case-law that has emerged so far, an allegation of a 'general and persistent' infringement (also referred to as a 'structural and general' infringement[52]) is to be aimed at a generalized or sustained systemic failure on the part of the Member State concerned to fulfil its obligations in relation to the subject addressed by the particular Union rules. This has crucial implications for a Member State found in breach, since that Member State's obligations to take the 'necessary measures' to comply with the Court's judgment under Art. 260(1) TFEU go beyond the specific instances identified.[53]

(d) Judicial practice

A rule established by case-law in a Member State can also constitute a failure to fulfil obligations.[54] **5.12**

---

49 ECJ, Case C-494/01 *Commission v Ireland*, para. 27. See further ECJ, Case C-248/05 *Commission v Ireland* [2007] E.C.R. I-9261, paras 63–64; ECJ, Case C-331/07 *Commission v Greece* [2009] E.C.R. I-60*, Summ. pub., para. 32; ECJ, Case C-160/08 *Commission v Germany* [2010] E.C.R. I-3713, para. 106.

50 See, e.g. ECJ, Case C-135/05 *Commission v Italy* [2007] E.C.R. I-3475, paras 20–22 (and case-law cited therein); ECJ, Case C-416/07 *Commission v Greece* [2009] E.C.R. I-7883, paras 23–25 (and case-law cited therein). That said, one of the primary cases relied upon—ECJ (judgment of 6 October 2005), Case C-502/03 *Commission v Greece*, not reported—did not elaborate specifically on the Commission's overall approach in this regard.

51 See, e.g. ECJ, Case C-416/07 *Commission v Greece* [2009] E.C.R. I-7883, paras 46–50. Compare ECJ, Case C-489/06 *Commission v Greece* [2009] E.C.R. I-1797, paras 46–53, where the Court focused its relevant ruling on whether the conditions for finding an administrative practice were satisfied, with the Opinion of Advocate-General J. Mazák in the same case, points 42–76, which examined the case from the perspective of a 'general and persistent' infringement of Union law by the Member State concerned.

52 See ECJ, Case C-494/01 *Commission v Ireland*, paras 127, 136, 139, 151, 170, 171, 174, 184, and 193. The Court seems to use the two phrasings interchangeably, or at the very least, has not yet ruled as to whether there is a distinction between the two. Compare ECJ, Case C-135/05 *Commission v Italy* [2007] E.C.R. I-3475, paras 22 and 45.

53 ECJ, Case 248/05 *Commission v Ireland* [2007] E.C.R. I-9261, paras 63–69; See ECJ Case C-160/08 *Commission v Germany* [2010] E.C.R. I-3713, paras 106–111; ECJ, Case C-331/07 *Commission v Greece* [2009] E.C.R. I-60*, Summ. pub., para. 32. See also Opinion of Advocate-General L. A. Geelhoed in ECJ, Case C-494/01 *Commission v Ireland* [2005] E.C.R. I-3331, points 43–48, particularly point 48: 'a general and structural infringement may be deemed to exist where the remedy for this situation lies not merely in taking action to resolve a number of individual cases which do not comply with the [Union] obligation at issue, but where this situation of non-compliance can only be redressed by a revision of the general policy and administrative practice of the Member State in respect of the subject governed by the [Union] measure involved'.

54 ECJ, Case C-129/00 *Commission v Italy* [2003] E.C.R. I-14637, para. 32: while 'isolated or numerically insignificant judicial decisions in the context of case-law taking a different direction, or still more a construction disowned by the national supreme court, cannot be taken into account', this was 'not true of a widely-held judicial construction which has not been disowned by the supreme court, but rather confirmed by it'. Following that reasoning, the Court of Justice thereafter declared, for the first time, that a Member State had failed to fulfil

(e) International agreements

5.13 The conclusion by a Member State of an agreement with a third State constitutes a violation of the Treaties if such conclusion infringes Union law, for example, where it infringes the exclusive external competence of the Union.[55] Even the negotiation of a bilateral agreement may constitute such infringement,[56] or the recourse to dispute settlement procedures provided in the international agreement to the detriment of the exclusive jurisdiction of the Court of Justice under Art. 344 TFEU.[57]

Similarly, a Member State may not invoke as a justification for an infringement of Union law the existence of an international agreement with other Member States to which it was a party prior to its accession to the Union. Indeed, Art. 351 TFEU does not authorize Member States to exercise rights under international agreements which conflict with Union law in intra-Union relations.[58]

(f) Act or failure to act

5.14 The failure to fulfil obligations can arise both out of an act and out of a failure to act on the part of the Member State.[59] The classic example of the latter is failure by a Member State to

---

its obligations solely as a result of a decision of a national supreme court: ECJ, Case C-154/08 *Commission v Spain* [2009] E.C.R. I-187*, Summ. pub., paras 124–127. See also ECJ, Case C-289/02 *AMOK Verlags* [2003] E.C.R. I-15059, para. 41; ECJ (order of 3 June 2005), Case C-396/03 P *Killinger v Germany, Council and Commission* [2005] E.C.R. I-4967, para. 28. See also para. 5.38. As is well known, there have been proceedings initiated by the Commission against a Member State in connection with the failure of a national supreme court to comply with its obligation to refer under the third para. of what is now Art. 267 TFEU but which never came to judgment: see para. 3.56.

[55] ECJ, Case C-266/03 *Commission v Luxembourg* [2005] E.C.R. I-4805, paras 34–52.

[56] ECJ, Case C-266/03 *Commission v Luxembourg*, paras 57–67: the adoption by the Council of a decision authorizing the Commission to negotiate a multilateral agreement on behalf of the Union marks the start of a concerted Union action at international level and requires, for that purpose, if not a duty of abstention on the part of the Member States, at the very least a duty of close cooperation between the latter and the Union institutions in order to facilitate the achievement of the Union's tasks and to ensure the coherence and consistency of the action and its international representation. Therefore, if a Member State negotiates and/or concludes and ratifies a bilateral agreement in the field concerned without cooperating or consulting with the Commission, that Member State compromises the achievement of the Union's task and the attainment of the objectives of the Treaties and violates Art. 4(3) TEU. Even the willingness of the Member State concerned to denounce the contested bilateral agreement on the entry into force of a multilateral agreement binding the Union does not demonstrate compliance with the obligation of genuine cooperation laid down in Art. 4(3) TEU. See also ECJ, Case C-433/03 *Commission v Germany* [2005] E.C.R. I-6985, paras 60–74.

[57] ECJ, Case C-459/03 *Commission v Ireland ('Mox Plant')* [2006] E.C.R. I-4635, paras 123–139.

[58] ECJ, Case C-147/03 *Commission v Austria* [2005] E.C.R. I-5969, paras 71–75. Non-compliance with Art. 351 TFEU may, of course, result in a failure to fulfil obligations: see, e.g. ECJ, Case C-205/06 *Commission v Austria* [2009] E.C.R. I-1301; ECJ, Case C-249/06 *Commission v Sweden* [2009] E.C.R. I-1335.

[59] ECJ, Case 31/69 *Commission v Italy* [1970] E.C.R. 25, para. 9 (when the application of Union regulations requires a modification of certain public services or of the rules governing them, the failure of the authorities concerned to take the necessary measures constitutes a failure to fulfil obligations within the meaning of Art. 258 TFEU). In the so-called '*Spanish strawberries*' case, the French authorities' failure to adopt all necessary measures to prevent the free movement of fruit and vegetables from being obstructed by actions by private individuals constituted a failure to fulfil obligations under Art. 34 TFEU, in conjunction with Art. 4(3) TEU, and under the common organization of the markets in agricultural products (ECJ, Case C-265/95 *Commission v France* [1997] E.C.R. I-6959). The failure of the French authorities to take penal or administrative action pursuant to Regulation No. 2241/87 against those responsible in cases of infringement of Union rules on the conservation and control of fishery resources constituted a failure to fulfil obligations (ECJ, Joined Cases C-418/00 and C-419/00 *Commission v France* [2002] E.C.R. I-3969, paras 60–64). Compare ECJ, Case C-132/05 *Commission v Germany ('Parmesan')* [2008] E.C.R. I-957. The failure of the German

implement a directive in national law.[60] Failure to respond to a request from the Commission for information will also constitute a failure to fulfil obligations, namely the obligations ensuing for Member States from Art. 4(3) TEU.[61] An example of conduct contrary to Union law is the imposition of administrative formalities restricting the import of goods and therefore infringing Art. 34 TFEU.[62]

(g) Failure to transpose a directive

Each of the Member States to which a directive is addressed is obliged to adopt, within the **5.15** framework of its national legal system, all the measures necessary to ensure that the directive is fully effective, in accordance with the objective it pursues.[63] A provision of a directive that concerns only relations between a Member State and the Commission or with the other Member States need not, in principle, be transposed. However, given that the Member States are obliged to ensure that Union law is fully complied with, it is open to the Commission to demonstrate that compliance with a provision of a directive governing those relations requires the adoption of specific transposing measures in national law.[64]

For the purposes of the implementation of a directive conferring rights on individuals in a Member State, it is essential for national law to guarantee that the directive is effectively applied in full, that the legal position under national law should be sufficiently precise and clear, and that individuals are made fully aware of their rights and obligations.[65] Invariably, it is not necessary formally to incorporate the provisions of a directive in an express, specific legislative provision. Depending on the content of the directive, a general legal framework may suffice.[66] In particular, the existence of general principles of national constitutional or administrative law may render implementation by specific legislation superfluous, provided,

---

authorities to submit to an audit of the Court of Auditors constituted a failure of the Member State concerned to comply with its obligations under Art. 287 TFEU: see ECJ, Case C-539/09 *Commission v Germany* [2011] E.C.R. I-11235.

[60] For a few recent examples, see ECJ, Case C-512/09 *Commission v Greece* [2010] E.C.R. I-96*, Summ. pub.; ECJ, Case C-189/09 *Commission v Austria* [2010] E.C.R. I-99* Summ. pub. See further para. 5.15.

[61] See, e.g. ECJ, Case C-82/03 *Commission v Italy* [2004] E.C.R. I-6635; ECJ, Case C-494/01 *Commission v Ireland* [2005] E.C.R. I-3331, paras 195–200; ECJ, Case C-221/08 *Commission v Ireland* [2010] E.C.R. I-1669, paras 60–62. Likewise, the failure to cooperate with the Commission in terms of the duty placed on a Member State to engage in prior information and consultation within the framework of international agreements can result in a breach of Art. 4(3) TEU: see, e.g. ECJ, Case ECJ, Case C-459/03 *Commission v Ireland ('Mox Plant')* [2006] E.C.R. I-4653, paras 174–182. In ECJ, Case C-539/09 *Commission v Germany* [2011] E.C.R. I-11235, the ECJ found that Germany's failure to permit the Court of Auditors to review cross-border administrative cooperation in the field of VAT infringed Art. 287(1) to (3) TFEU. See further para. 5.64.

[62] See, e.g. ECJ, Case 154/85 *Commission v Italy* [1987] E.C.R. 2717, para. 12; ECJ, Case C-80/92 *Commission v Belgium* [1994] E.C.R. I-1019, para. 18; ECJ, Case C-88/07 *Commission v Spain* [2009] E.C.R. I-1353, para. 83; ECJ, Case C-432/03 *Commission v Portugal* [2005] E.C.R. I-9665, para. 41.

[63] See, e.g. ECJ, Case C-336/97 *Commission v Italy* [1999] E.C.R. I-3771, para. 19; ECJ, Case C-97/00 *Commission v France* [2001] E.C.R. I-2053, para. 9; ECJ, Case C-478/99 *Commission v Sweden* [2002] E.C.R. I-4147, para. 15.

[64] See, e.g. ECJ, Case C-296/01 *Commission v France* [2003] E.C.R. I-13909, para. 92; ECJ, Case C-429/01 *Commission v France* [2003] E.C.R. I-14355, para. 68; ECJ, Case C-410/03 *Commission v Italy* [2005] E.C.R. I-3507, paras 38–39, 52–58.

[65] See, e.g. ECJ, Case C-365/93 *Commission v Greece* [1995] E.C.R. I-499, para. 9; ECJ, Case C-429/01 *Commission v France* [2003] E.C.R. I-14355, para. 83; ECJ, Case C-154/09 *Commission v Portugal* [2010] E.C.R. I-127*, Summ. pub., para. 47 (and further citations therein).

[66] See ECJ, Case C-427/07 *Commission v Ireland* [2009] E.C.R. I-6277, paras 55–60 (and further citations therein).

however, that those principles guarantee that the national authorities will in fact apply the directive fully and that, where the directive is intended to create rights for individuals, the legal position arising from those principles is sufficiently precise and clear and the persons concerned are made fully aware of their rights and, where appropriate, afforded the possibility of relying on them before the national courts.[67] Yet the obligation to transpose directives into national law, requires a 'positive act of transposition' if the directive in question expressly requires the Member States to refer to it in adopting provisions or when officially notifying the provisions adopted.[68]

(b) Failure to notify measures transposing a legislative directive and possible financial penalties under Art. 260(3) TFEU

5.16 As mentioned earlier, a classic subject of infringement proceedings is a Member State's failure to implement a directive into national law within the time frame provided therein. As part of the changes brought by the Lisbon Treaty to render the infringement procedure more efficient, Art. 260(3) TFEU provides that where a Member State has failed to fulfil its obligation 'to notify measures transposing a directive adopted under a legislative procedure', the Commission may bring a case before the Court of Justice asking the latter to find an infringement and to impose a pecuniary sanction at the same time.[69] Under this provision, the obligation to make payment takes effect on the date set by the Court in its judgment.[70] By contrast, as far as other infringements are concerned—for example, incorrect implementation of a legislative directive, failure to transpose non-legislative directives by the requisite deadline, or other violations of Union law—the imposition of a pecuniary sanction is still conditional upon a first judgment of the Court of Justice finding against the Member State and non-compliance with the judgment by the Member State concerned.

It remains to be seen how the Commission will apply this provision.[71] Complexities may arise in cases in which the boundary line between a Member State's failure to implement a

---

[67] See, e.g. ECJ, Case C-29/84 *Commission v Germany* [1985] E.C.R. 1661, paras 22–23; ECJ, Case C-296/01 *Commission v France* [2003] E.C.R. I-13909, para. 55; ECJ, Case C-410/03 *Commission v Italy* [2005] E.C.R. I-3507, para. 60.

[68] See, e.g. ECJ, Case C-137/96 *Commission v Germany* [1997] E.C.R. I-6749, para. 8; ECJ, Case C-360/95 *Commission v Spain* [1997] E.C.R. I-7337, para. 13; ECJ, Case C-361/95 *Commission v Spain* [1997] E.C.R. I-7351, para. 15; ECJ, Case C-551/08 *Commission v Poland* [2009] E.C.R. I-176*, Summ. pub., para. 23 (and case-law cited therein); ECJ, Case C-523/08 *Commission v Spain*, E.C.R. I-19*, Summ. pub., para. 13 (and case-law cited therein). But see ECJ, Joined Cases C-444/09 and C-456/09 *Gaviero Gaviero and Iglesias Torres* [2010] E.C.R. I-14031, paras 62–67: although under these circumstances, a Member State could be found to have failed to fulfil its obligations in the context of infringement proceedings, it does not follow that a national measure which fails to refer to the directive concerned cannot be regarded as a valid measure transposing the directive.

[69] Art. 260(3), first para., TFEU. This change had already appeared in the Draft Constitutional Treaty (Art. III-362(3)), having been proposed by the Commission at the European Convention: see CONV 734/03, at 16.

[70] Art. 260(3), second para., TFEU. As far as the imposition of a pecuniary sanction is concerned, this provision states that the Court may impose a lump sum or penalty payment on the Member State 'not exceeding the amount specified by the Commission'. This limitation does not appear in Art. 260(2) TFEU: see para. 5.75.

[71] See Commission Communication—Implementation of Article 260(3) TFEU, SEC (2010) 1371 final, 11.11.2010, which explains how the Commission will make use of this new provision (para. 8). In particular, the Commission points out that Art. 260(3) TFEU covers both the total failure to notify any measures transposing a legislative directive and only partial notification of transposition measures, which may occur

legislative directive and a Member State's implementing it incorrectly or incompletely is difficult to find, for example where the Commission brings an infringement action under Art. 258 TFEU before the Court of Justice alleging a Member State's failure to notify any measures transposing a legislative directive and seeking financial penalties pursuant to Art. 260(3) TFEU, but through the course of the procedure, the dispute revolves around the extent of the Member State's alleged failure to transpose it properly within the prescribed time period.[72]

(i) Legal provision that is no longer applied

The existence of a legal provision conflicting with Union law may also be categorized as a **5.17** 'failure', even if it is not or no longer being applied by the national authorities. The fact that such a provision exists is liable to create uncertainty in those subject to the law about the possibility of relying on Union law. That uncertainty impedes the operation of Union law and is regarded as a 'failure to fulfil' an obligation.[73] Only where such a provision conflicting with Union law can have no effect at all will its mere existence be insufficient to constitute an infringement of Union law.[74]

Conversely, a failure to fulfil obligations may arise owing to the existence of an administrative practice that infringes Union law, even if the applicable national legislation itself complies with that law.[75]

---

either where the transposition measures notified do not cover the whole territory of the Member State or where the notification is incomplete with respect to the transposition measures corresponding to a part of the directive (para. 19). In line with the discretionary powers conferred on the Commission under this provision, however, there could be special cases in which the Commission would not deem it appropriate to seek financial penalties in this context (paras 16–17). The amount of the penalty payment and, where appropriate, the lump sum will be calculated by the same method used for referrals under Art. 260(2) TFEU (see para. 5.77), the sole proviso being that in cases where the Commission seeks a lump sum, the *dies a quo* should be the day after the time limit for transposition set out in the directive expires (paras 23–28).

[72] See, e.g. ECJ, Case C-456/03 *Commission v Italy* [2005] E.C.R. I-5335; ECJ, Case C-294/09 *Commission v Ireland* [2010] E.C.R. I-46*, Summ. pub. This may also be illustrated to some extent by ECJ, Case C-32/05 *Commission v Luxembourg* [2006] E.C.R. I-11323, paras 54–56, involving a situation in which the Member State concerned failed to mention any measure transposing the directive in question in the course of the pre-litigation procedure, and it was not until after the Commission brought proceedings before the Court of Justice that the Member State submitted, in its defence, that a law transposing the directive in question correctly had been adopted: see further para. 5.52.

[73] ECJ, Case 167/73 *Commission v France* [1974] E.C.R. 359, paras 41–48; ECJ, Case 159/78 *Commission v Italy* [1979] E.C.R. 3247, para. 22; ECJ, Case 168/85 *Commission v Italy* [1986] E.C.R. 2945, para. 14; Case 104/86 *Commission v Italy* [1988] E.C.R. 1799, para. 12; ECJ, Case 74/86 *Commission v Germany* [1988] E.C.R. 2139, para. 10; ECJ, Case 38/87 *Commission v Greece* [1988] E.C.R. 4415, para. 9; ECJ, Case C-197/96 *Commission v France* [1997] E.C.R. I-1489, para. 14; ECJ, Case C-358/98 *Commission v Italy* [2000] E.C.R. I-1255, para. 17; ECJ, Case C-145/99 *Commission v Italy* [2002] E.C.R. I-2235, paras 30, 37; ECJ (judgment of 7 July 2005), Case C-214/04 *Commission v Italy*, not reported, para. 13.

[74] ECJ, Case 28/69 *Commission v Italy* [1970] E.C.R. 187, paras 14–17. The excise duty that Italy imposed on cocoa shells and husks differed depending on whether they were imported or produced by the Italian processing industry. Nevertheless, they were exempt from the duty if they were used for certain specified purposes. The high level of duty made it impossible in practice to use the products for purposes other than those to which the exemption applied. The existence of differential taxation was therefore insufficient to constitute an infringement of Art. 110 TFEU.

[75] See, e.g. ECJ, Case C-212/99 *Commission v Italy* [2001] E.C.R. I-4923, para. 31; ECJ, Case C-278/03 *Commission v Italy* [2005] E.C.R. I-3747, para. 13; ECJ, Case C-489/06 *Commission v Germany* [2009] E.C.R. I-1797, paras 46–47. See para. 5.10.

(j) Non-binding acts

5.18   Even acts of a Member State that are not binding under the domestic legal system may
result in a failure to fulfil obligations under Union law insofar as their potential effects are
comparable with those resulting from binding measures. A large-scale campaign launched
by the Irish Government to promote the sale of Irish goods on the home market was
accordingly held to be a measure of equivalent effect contrary to Art. 34 TFEU.[76] Non-
binding acts in the international arena, such as proposals submitted in the context of an
international convention, may also result in a finding that a Member State has breached its
Union law obligations, for example in relation to Art. 4(3) TEU.[77]

(k) Acts affecting the jurisdiction of the Court of Justice of the European Union

5.19   Acts of a Member State that affect the jurisdiction of the Court of Justice of the European
Union will invariably contravene Union law. For instance, a Member State is prohibited
from transposing a regulation, which has direct effect, into national law, thereby concealing
its Union origin, which would be liable to jeopardize the making of preliminary references
on the interpretation or validity of the regulation.[78]

(l) National rules allegedly violating the Treaties but complying with secondary Union law

5.20   A failure to fulfil obligations under Union law will not be found under circumstances where
a national rule, which at first sight conflicts with a provision of the Treaties, expressly
complies with a provision of secondary Union law. For example, in *Commission v Greece
('Ouzo'),*[79] the Court dismissed an infringement action brought against Greece with respect
to the reduced rate of excise duty applicable in this Member State for ouzo. The Commission considered that this reduced rate was incompatible with Art. 110 TFEU, prohibiting
discriminatory internal taxes. The Court, however, found that a provision of Directive
92/83/EEC explicitly allowed Greece to apply a lower rate of excise duty for ouzo. Since
that provision had not been declared invalid or annulled by the Union courts and since it
could also not be considered to be non-existent, its legal effects were presumed to be lawful.
Greece therefore did not fail to fulfil its obligations under Union law by maintaining in
force a national measure complying with that provision of a directive.[80]

C. Relationship with special legal procedures to obtain a declaration that a Member State has failed to fulfil its obligations under Union law

(1) Overview

5.21   There are several categories of Treaty provisions that provide for special procedures
derogating from the infringement procedure of Arts 258–260 TFEU by which the

---

[76] ECJ, Case 249/81 *Commission v Ireland* [1982] E.C.R. 4005, para. 27.

[77] See ECJ, Case C-45/07 *Commission v Greece* [2009] E.C.R. I-1701; ECJ, Case C-246/07 *Commission v Sweden* [2010] E.C.R. I-3317 (with G. De Baere, case note (2011) E.L. Rev. 405–19).

[78] ECJ, Case 39/72 *Commission v Italy* [1973] E.C.R. 101, paras 16–17; ECJ, Case 34/73 *Fratelli Variola* [1973] E.C.R. 981, para. 11; ECJ, Case 50/76 *Amsterdam Bulb* [1977] E.C.R. 137, paras 4–7.

[79] ECJ, Case C-475/01 *Commission v Greece ('Ouzo')* [2004] E.C.R. I-8923.

[80] ECJ, Case C-475/01 *'Ouzo'*, paras 16–24. See also ECJ, Case C-582/08 *Commission v United Kingdom* [2010] E.C.R I-7195, paras 47–48. An individual who cannot bring an action directly against a directive before the Union judicature may, however, raise the unlawfulness of the directive before a national court, which may (or must) make a reference for a preliminary ruling to the Court of Justice: see Ch. 10.

Commission (or in certain cases a Member State) can obtain a declaration that a Member State has failed to fulfil its obligations under Union law. For the most part, the focus is placed on the following four categories of special procedures relating to: State aid (Art. 108(2) TFEU); competition rules regarding public undertakings (Art. 106(3) TFEU); misuse of derogating provisions in certain policy fields, namely that relating to internal market approximation (Art. 114(9) TFEU) and national security measures (Art. 348 TFEU); and public procurement contracts (under relevant provisions of secondary Union law). These are discussed seriatim in the sections that follow.

(2) Relationship between Arts 258 and 259 TFEU and Art. 108(2) TFEU concerning State aid

(a) Procedure under Art. 108(2) TFEU

Under Art. 108 TFEU, the Commission is empowered to rule on the compatibility of State **5.22** aid with the internal market. Both existing aid and the introduction or alteration of aid are subject to supervision by the Commission.[81] Any plans to grant or alter aid must be notified to the Commission pursuant to Art. 108(3) TFEU.[82]

The Commission may take action against aid that it considers, on the basis of Art. 107 TFEU, to be incompatible with the internal market in accordance with the procedure laid down in Art. 108(2) TFEU. It makes a finding that the aid is incompatible and orders the Member State concerned to abolish or alter the aid within a specified period.[83] If the Member State fails to comply with the decision within the prescribed period, the Commission or any other interested party may, by way of derogation from Arts 258 and 259 TFEU, refer the matter directly to the Court of Justice.[84] In these circumstances, as a general matter, the only defence available to a Member State opposing an application by the Commission under Art. 108(2) TFEU for a declaration that it has failed to fulfil its obligations is to plead that it was 'absolutely impossible' for it to properly implement the decision.[85]

---

[81] For the distinction between 'existing' and 'new' aid and an explanation of the respective powers of the Commission and the national courts in supervising aid for compatibility with the internal market, see ECJ, Case C-44/93 *Namur–Les Assurances du Crédit* [1994] E.C.R. I-3829, paras 10–17; CFI, Joined Cases T-195/01 and T-207/01 *Gibraltar v Commission* [2002] E.C.R. II-2309; see also Council Regulation (EC) No. 659/1999 of 22 March 1999 laying down detailed rules for the application of Art. 93 of the EC Treaty (now Art. 108 TFEU) ([1999] O.J. L83/1).

[82] The applicable procedural requirements are laid down in Regulation No. 659/1999 (see n. 81).

[83] See ECJ, Joined Cases C-485/03 to C-490/03 *Commission v Spain* [2006] E.C.R. I-11887, para. 53 (and case-law cited therein): since the second para. of Art. 108(2) TFEU does not provide for a pre-litigation phase in contrast to Art. 258 TFEU and hence the Commission does not issue a reasoned opinion allowing a Member State a certain time period within which to comply with its decision, the reference period can only be that provided for in the decision failure to implement which is denied or, where appropriate, that subsequently fixed by the Commission. See also ECJ (judgment of 1 March 2012), Case C-354/10 *Commission v Greece*, not reported, para. 61 (and case-law cited therein).

[84] Art. 108(2), second para., TFEU. Under settled case-law, the Member State to which the decision requiring recovery of unlawful aid is addressed is obliged under Art. 288 TFEU to take all measures necessary to ensure implementation of that decision; the Member State must actually recover the sums owed, and recovery out of time, after the deadlines set, cannot satisfy the requirements of the Treaties: see, e.g. ECJ, Case C-304/09 *Commission v Italy* [2010] E.C.R. I-13903, paras 31–32 (and further citations therein).

[85] See, e.g. ECJ, Case C-304/09 *Commission v Italy* [2010] E.C.R. I-13903, para. 35 (and further citations therein); ECJ, Case C-331/09 *Commission v Poland* [2011] E.C.R. I-2933, para. 69. In compliance with the duty of sincere cooperation imposed by Art. 4(3) TEU, the Member State must inform the Commission of the difficulties arising in applying a Union provision with a view to seeking a solution together; if a Member State

Art. 108(2) TFEU secures all interested parties the right to submit observations.[86] In addition, on application by a Member State, the Council may, acting unanimously and by way of derogation from Art. 107 TFEU, decide that the aid must be considered to be compatible with the internal market if such a decision is justified by exceptional circumstances.[87]

(b) Relationship with Art. 258 TFEU

5.23 The question arises as to whether, despite the existence of the special procedure provided for in Art. 108(2) TFEU, the general procedure set out in Art. 258 TFEU may still be used by the Commission to find infringements of Art. 107 TFEU.

In the first place, the procedure provided for in Art. 108(2) TFEU affords all interested parties guarantees commensurate with the specific problems raised by State aid for competition in the internal market; those guarantees are much more extensive than those afforded by the pre-litigation procedure under Art. 258 TFEU, in which only the Commission and the Member State concerned take part. Accordingly, if the Commission wishes to make a finding that a State aid is incompatible with the internal market, it is obliged to follow the procedure set out in Art. 108(2) TFEU.[88]

However, the existence of the procedure laid down in Art. 108(2) TFEU does not preclude an aid measure being found incompatible with rules of Union law other than Art. 107 TFEU by means of the Art. 258 TFEU procedure.[89]

Finally, in the event of an infringement of a decision made pursuant to the first paragraph of Art. 108(2) TFEU, the Commission may elect either to bring the matter directly before the Court of Justice under the second paragraph of Art. 108(2) TFEU or to initiate the Art. 258 TFEU procedure.[90]

---

does not do so, its defence will fail because the Member State will in any event be in breach of that obligation to cooperation: see ECJ, Case 52/84 *Commission v Belgium* [1986] E.C.R. 89, para. 16. See also ECJ, Case C-349/93 *Commission v Italy* [1995] E.C.R. I-343, para. 13; ECJ, Case C-348/93 *Commission v Italy* [1995] E.C.R. I-673, para. 17; ECJ, Case C-99/02 *Commission v Italy* [2004] E.C.R. I-3353, paras 16–18; ECJ, Case C-415/03 *Commission v Greece* [2005] E.C.R. I-3875, para. 43; ECJ, Case C-214/07 *Commission v France* [2008] E.C.R. I-8357, paras 44–46; ECJ, Case C-304/09 *Commission v Italy* [2010] E.C.R. I-13903, paras 35–37; ECJ, C-303/09 *Commission v Italy* [2011] E.C.R. I-102*, Summ. pub., paras 33–35; ECJ, Case C-331/09 *Commission v Poland* [2011] E.C.R. I-2933, paras 70–73: in which the Court held that the condition that it be absolutely impossible to implement a decision is not fulfilled where the defendant government merely informs the Commission of the legal, political, or practical difficulties involved in implementing the decision, without taking any real step to recover the aid from the undertakings concerned, and without proposing to the Commission any alternative arrangements for implementing the decision which could have enabled the difficulties to be overcome. As has been pointed out in the commentary, there is another defence, albeit exceptional, relating to situations in which the decision would contain such serious and manifest defects that it would be deemed non-existent: T. Materne, *La procédure en manquement d'État. Guide à la lumière de la jurisprudence de la Cour de justice de l'Union européenne* (Brussels, Groupe De Boeck Larcier, 2012), 249.

[86] ECJ, Case C-294/90 *British Aerospace and Rover v Commission* [1992] E.C.R. I-493, para. 13.

[87] Art. 108(2), third para., TFEU. For the powers of the Council under this provision, see ECJ, Case C-110/02 *Commission v Council* [2004] E.C.R. I-6333, paras 28–51.

[88] ECJ, Case 290/83 *Commission v France* [1985] E.C.R. 439, para. 17.

[89] ECJ, Case 72/79 *Commission v Italy* [1980] E.C.R. 1411, para. 12; ECJ, Case 73/79 *Commission v Italy* [1980] E.C.R. 1533, para. 9; ECJ, Case 290/83 *Commission v France* [1985] E.C.R. 439, para. 17; ECJ, Case C-35/88 *Commission v Greece* [1990] E.C.R. I-3125, para. 11.

[90] ECJ, Case 70/72 *Commission v Germany* [1973] E.C.R. 813, paras 8–13 (action based on the second para. of Art. 108(2) TFEU); ECJ, Case 130/83 *Commission v Italy* [1984] E.C.R. 2849 (action based on Art. 258 TFEU); the ECJ now considers that an application on the basis of the second para. of Art. 108(2)

(c) Violation of the obligation to notify aid

The Commission also often has a choice between the Art. 108(2) TFEU procedure and that **5.24** provided for in Art. 258 TFEU, where a Member State fails to inform the Commission in time, contrary to Art. 108(3) TFEU, of a plan to grant new aid or altered aid.[91] The fact that the duty to notify the Commission has been infringed, however, does not make the aid incompatible with the internal market. Accordingly, the Commission must initiate an examination of the compatibility of the non-notified aid with the internal market under Art. 108(2) TFEU. In that event, it may require the aid to be suspended pending the outcome of its examination and order the Member State to provide information under a procedure pursuant to Art. 108(2) TFEU.[92] If the Member State refuses to suspend the aid, the Commission may bring the matter directly before the Court of Justice pursuant to the second paragraph of Art. 108(2)[93] or bring an action against the Member State under Art. 258 TFEU.[94]

A finding by the Commission, after carrying out an examination, that the non-notified aid measure is compatible with the internal market does not retroactively remedy the infringement of the Treaties caused by the failure to notify. Since Art. 108(3) TFEU has direct effect, national courts are obliged to regard as unlawful any acts performed to implement the non-notified aid before the Commission made its finding that the aid was compatible with the internal market, and impose the appropriate sanctions.[95]

(d) Aid to agriculture

Since 'the Council is entitled to lay down, within the context of the regulations establishing **5.25** the common organisation of the markets in agricultural products, provisions prohibiting wholly or partially certain forms of national aids for the production or marketing of the products in question and . . . an infringement of such a prohibition may be dealt with within the specific framework of such an organisation', the procedure laid down by Art. 258 TFEU is to be used in order to determine the infringement.[96] Under Art. 42 TFEU, all the

---

TFEU is also an application pursuant to Art. 258 TFEU: see ECJ, Case C-99/02 *Commission v Italy* [2004] E.C.R. I-3353, para. 1; ECJ, Case C-496/09 *Commission v Italy* [2011] E.C.R. I-11483, para. 3; cf. ECJ, Case C-294/90 *British Aerospace and Rover v Commission* [1992] E.C.R. I-493, para. 12 (the Commission may also take the approach that the infringement of its decision constitutes new aid within the meaning of Art. 108(3) TFEU; if so, it must start up the special procedure under the first para. of Art. 108(2) TFEU afresh and if necessary take a fresh decision, after having put interested parties on notice to submit observations: ECJ, Case C-294/90 *British Aerospace and Rover v Commission*, para. 13); ECJ, Case C-404/00 *Commission v Spain* [2003] E.C.R. I-6695, para. 25.

[91] ECJ, Case 173/73 *Italy v Commission* [1974] E.C.R. 709, para. 9; see also A. Rosas, 'Judicial Protection in EU State Aid Law', in M. Monti *et al.* (eds), *Economic Law and Justice in Times of Globalisation: Festschrift for Carl Baudenbacher* (Baden Baden, Nomos, 2007), 586.

[92] ECJ, Case C-301/87 *France v Commission* [1990] E.C.R. I-307, paras 18–23; ECJ, Case C-142/87 *Belgium v Commission* [1990] E.C.R. I-959, paras 15–19.

[93] ECJ, Case C-301/87 *France v Commission*, para. 23. See also Council Regulation (EC) No. 659/1999 of 22 March 1999, laying down detailed rules for the application of Art. 93 of the EC Treaty (now Art. 108 TFEU) ([1999] O.J. L83/1).

[94] ECJ, Case C-301/87 *France v Commission*, para. 23. See also Arts 11 and 12 of Regulation No. 659/1999, cited in n. 93.

[95] ECJ, Case 120/73 *Lorenz* [1973] E.C.R. 1471; ECJ, Case C-354/90 *Fédération Nationale du Commerce Extérieur des Produits Alimentaires and Others* [1991] E.C.R. I-5505; ECJ, Joined Cases C-261/01 and C-262/01 *Van Calster and Cleeren* [2003] E.C.R. I-12249, para. 53; ECJ, Case C-368/04 *Transalpine Ölleitung in Österreich* [2006] E.C.R. I-9957, paras 39–41.

[96] ECJ, Case 72/79 *Commission v Italy* [1980] E.C.R. 1411, para. 12. See also ECJ, Case C-61/90 *Commission v Greece* [1992] E.C.R. I-2407.

provisions of Arts 101–109 TFEU are applicable to production of and trade in agricultural products only to the extent determined by the European Parliament and the Council within the framework of measures adopted for the organization of agricultural markets. This explains why recourse by a Member State to Arts 107–109 TFEU on State aid cannot receive priority over the provisions of a regulation on the organization of a sector of the agricultural market.[97] Consequently, the fact that there is a special procedure in Art. 108 TFEU for appraising the compatibility of State aid with the internal market cannot preclude recourse to the Art. 258 TFEU procedure in the event that the Commission considers that an aid measure of a Member State infringes the provisions of a regulation organizing a sector of the agricultural market, even though the aid measure is also open to criticism under Art. 107 TFEU.

(3) Relationship between Arts 258 and 259 TFEU and Art. 106(3) TFEU concerning public undertakings

(a) Procedure under Art. 106(3) TFEU

5.26 Art. 106(3) TFEU charges the Commission with supervising Member States' compliance with their obligations with regard to public undertakings and undertakings to which they have granted special or exclusive rights, and expressly confers on it the power to use two legal instruments to this end, namely directives and decisions.

The Commission is empowered to use directives to specify in general terms the obligations arising under Art. 106(1) TFEU. It exercises that power where, without taking into consideration the particular situation existing in the various Member States, it defines in concrete terms the obligations imposed on them under that provision of the Treaty. In view of its very nature, such a power cannot be used to make a finding that a Member State has failed to fulfil a particular obligation under the Treaties.[98]

The powers exercised by the Commission under Art. 106(3) TFEU by decision are different from those that it exercises by directive. Decisions are adopted in respect of a specific situation in one or more Member States and necessarily involve an appreciation of the situation in the light of Union law. They specify the consequences arising for the Member State concerned, regard being had to the requirements which the performance of the particular tasks assigned to an undertaking imposes on it where it is entrusted with the operation of services of general economic interest (Art. 106(1) and (2) TFEU).[99] If the power to adopt decisions conferred on the Commission by Art. 106(3) TFEU is not to be deprived of all practical effect, the Commission must be empowered to determine that a given State measure is incompatible

---

[97] ECJ, Case 177/78 *McCarren* [1979] E.C.R. 2161, paras 11 and 21.

[98] ECJ, Case C-202/88 *France v Commission* [1991] E.C.R. I-1223, para. 17; ECJ, Case C-163/99 *Portugal v Commission* [2001] E.C.R. I-2613, para. 26. In *Portugal v Commission*, the Portuguese Government argued that the Commission was wrong to commence an action for failure to fulfil obligations under Art. 258 TFEU and that it ought to have followed the procedure provided for in Art. 106(3) TFEU and adopted a harmonization directive. The Court rejected this argument, holding that, notwithstanding its other powers under the Treaties to ensure that Member States comply with Union law, the Commission enjoyed a discretion in deciding whether or not to commence an action for failure to fulfil obligations. It was not required to justify its decision, nor would the admissibility of the action be dependent upon the circumstances dictating its choice (ECJ, Case C-70/99 *Commission v Portugal* [2001] E.C.R. I-4845, para. 17).

[99] ECJ, Joined Cases C-48/90 and C-66/90 *Netherlands and Others v Commission* [1992] E.C.R. I-565, para. 27; ECJ, Case C-163/99 *Portugal v Commission* [2001] E.C.R. I-2613, para. 27.

with the rules of the Treaties and to indicate what measures the Member State to which the decision is addressed must take in order to comply with its obligations under Union law.[100] Even though there is no express provision to this effect in Art. 106(3) TFEU—unlike in Art. 258 TFEU and Art. 108(2) TFEU—the general principle of respect for the rights of the defence requires that the Member State concerned must receive an exact and complete statement of the objections that the Commission intends to raise against it. It must also be placed in a position in which it may effectively make known its views on the observations submitted by interested third parties.[101]

(b) Commission's discretion

The Commission's power to appraise, in a decision adopted pursuant to Art. 106(3) TFEU, **5.27** the conformity with the Treaties of measures adopted or applied by Member States with regard to undertakings referred to in Art. 106(1) TFEU does not run counter to the powers conferred on the Court of Justice by Art. 258 TFEU. If the Member State does not comply with the decision, this may form the basis for infringement proceedings under Art. 258 TFEU.[102]

Whether the Commission may bring an action for failure to fulfil obligations before it has adopted a decision pursuant to Art. 106(3) TFEU depends in all likelihood on the requirements of the rights of the defence. The procedure that affords the strongest guarantees for the Member State concerned should probably take precedence at the stage of the initial examination of the compatibility of a national measure with Art. 106(1) and (2) TFEU by analogy with the aforementioned case-law on Art. 108(2) TFEU (see para. 5.26).[103] In any event, it is certain that Member States may invariably bring an action under Art. 259 TFEU against a Member State for failure to fulfil its obligations under Art. 106(1) and (2) TFEU, even if the Commission has not yet exercised its powers under Art. 106(3) TFEU to address a decision to the Member State concerned.

(4) Relationship between Arts 258 and 259 TFEU and special procedures relating to the misuse of derogating provisions concerning the internal market and national security measures

Apart from Art. 108(2) TFEU, the Treaties provide for other cases in which, by way of **5.28** derogation from the procedure laid down in Arts 258 and 259 TFEU, the Commission or a Member State may bring a Member State directly before the Court of Justice, namely where the derogating provisions provided for in the Treaties are misused (Art. 114 (4)–(8) TFEU and Arts 346–348 TFEU).

---

[100] ECJ, Joined Cases C-48/90 and C-66/90 *Netherlands v Commission*, para. 28. The fact that other Member States also infringe the Treaties by granting similar exclusive rights does not oblige the Commission to bring proceedings under Art. 258 TFEU and exercise its power to address a decision to those Member States under Art. 106(3) TFEU: ECJ, Case C-163/99 *Commission v Portugal* [2001] E.C.R. I-2613, paras 31 *et seq.*

[101] ECJ, Joined Cases C-48/90 and C-66/90 *Netherlands v Commission*, paras 45–46.

[102] ECJ, Case 226/87 *Commission v Greece* [1988] E.C.R. 3611. It appears from this judgment that if the Member State to which the Commission's decision is addressed contests its legality, it must bring an action for annulment within the time limit laid down by Art. 263 TFEU (ex Art. 230 EC); thereafter, the Member State may not plead the unlawfulness of the decision as a defence in proceedings for failure to fulfil obligations.

[103] Moreover, the Court of Justice itself has strongly emphasized the parallel between Art. 106(3) TFEU and Art. 108 TFEU; see ECJ, Joined Cases C-48/90 and C-66/90 *Netherlands and Others v Commission* [1992] E.C.R. I-565, paras 31–33.

The opportunity afforded to the Commission by Art. 114(9) TFEU[104] in order to bring a matter directly before the Court of Justice without incurring the delay of a pre-litigation procedure is intended to serve the Union interest of protecting in full the establishment of the internal market. However, this does not preclude the Commission from opting to bring proceedings under Art. 258 TFEU in the interests of the defendant Member State.[105]

The action that the Commission or any Member State may bring against a Member State pursuant to the second paragraph of Art. 348 TFEU if it considers that that Member State is making improper use of the powers provided for in Arts 346 and 347 TFEU does not involve a pre-litigation stage (which is precisely the difference compared with proceedings under Arts 258 and 259 TFEU), but does afford the guarantee that the Court of Justice is to give its ruling *in camera*, this being essential in the case of a politically charged dispute.[106]

(5) Relationship between Arts 258 and 259 TFEU and special procedures relating to public procurement contracts

(a) Special procedures relating to public procurement contracts

5.29 The Commission is empowered to order the suspension of the award of a public procurement contract under Art. 3 of Directive 2007/66/EC of 11 December 2007 amending Council Directives 89/665/EEC and 92/13/EEC with regard to improving the effectiveness of review procedures concerning the award of public contracts.[107] This Directive replaces Art. 3 of Council Directive 89/665/EEC of 21 December 1989 on the coordination of the laws, regulations, and administrative provisions relating to the application of review procedures to the award of public supply and public works contracts[108] and Art. 8 of Council Directive 92/13/EEC of 25 February 1992 coordinating the laws, regulations, and administrative provisions relating to the application of Community rules on the procurement procedures of entities operating in the water, energy, transport, and telecommunications sectors.[109]

---

[104] This was formerly part of Art. 100a(4) EC introduced by the Single European Act and preserved in the Maastricht Treaty on European Union until the changes brought by the Amsterdam Treaty. With the entry into force of the Lisbon Treaty, Art. 95 EC was reframed as Art. 114 TFEU without substantial change.

[105] It is argued that proceedings should be brought under Art. 258 TFEU against a failure of a Member State to notify the Commission of the application of a national measure conflicting with a harmonizing measure adopted pursuant to Art. 114(1) TFEU. If proceedings under Art. 114(9) TFEU were to be allowed, this might also mean that a Member State would in some cases have the power not to notify the Commission of a national measure (although it is considered that this is not the case) on the grounds that such proceedings relate only to 'improper use of the powers provided for in this Article'. For the Commission's handling of a complaint on account of the grant of State aid to a manufacturer of military goods and the application of Arts 346 and 348 TFEU, see CFI, Case T-26/01 *Fiocchi Munizioni v Commission* [2003] E.C.R. II-3951.

[106] See ECJ (order of the President of 19 March 1996), Case C-120/94 *Commission v Greece* [1996] E.C.R. I-1513. A case brought under Arts 258 or 259 TFEU is heard in principle in public, although the Court of Justice may decide otherwise of its own motion or on application by the parties for serious reasons (Statute, Art. 31). See also ECJ, Case C-372/05 *Commission v Germany* [2009] E.C.R. I-11801, paras 28–30: Art. 348 TFEU is only applicable where the Commission alleges improper use of the powers provided for in Arts 346 and 347 TFEU, not to other alleged breaches of Union law.

[107] [2007] O.J. L335/31. The Member States were required to transpose the Directive by 20 December 2009 (see Art. 3).

[108] [1989] O.J. L395/33.

[109] [1992] O.J. L76/14.

(b) Commission's discretion

Even if it were preferable that the Commission should use the procedure for direct **5.30**
intervention established by that directive, such a procedure is a preventive measure which
can neither derogate from nor replace the powers of the Commission under Art. 258
TFEU.[110] The fact that the Commission used or did not use that procedure is therefore
irrelevant where it is a matter of deciding on the admissibility of infringement proceedings.
The Commission alone is competent to decide whether it is appropriate to bring proceedings under Art. 258 TFEU for failure to fulfil obligations. Thus, the choice between the two
procedures is within its discretion.[111]

II. Identity of the Parties

A. The applicant

(1) Commission

Under Art. 258 TFEU, only the Commission may bring an action against a Member **5.31**
State.[112] That power is consistent with its task of ensuring that Union law is applied.[113] The
Commission exercises its supervisory task of its own motion in the general interest of the
Union[114] and does not have to show the existence of a specific interest in bringing proceed-
ings.[115] It assesses itself whether it is appropriate to bring proceedings under Art. 258 TFEU
and has therefore no obligation to do so in the event of an alleged infringement of the
Treaties.[116] In view of the objective nature of the action (see para. 5.65), the Court must

---

[110] See, in the context of Directive 89/665/EEC, ECJ, Case C-359/93 *Commission v Netherlands* [1995]
E.C.R. I-157, para. 13; ECJ, Case C-79/94 *Commission v Greece* [1995] E.C.R. I-1071, para. 11; ECJ, Case
C-353/96 *Commission v Ireland* [1998] E.C.R. I-8565, para. 22; ECJ, Case C-328/96 *Commission v Austria*
[1999] E.C.R. I-7479, para. 57 and, in the context of Directive 92/13/EEC, ECJ, Case C-394/02 *Commission
v Greece* [2005] E.C.R. I-4713, paras 25–29. For a case in relation to a directive falling outside the public
procurement sector, see ECJ, Case C-424/07 *Commission v Germany* [2009] E.C.R. I-11431, para. 36
(concerning directives in the telecommunications sector).
[111] ECJ, Case C-394/02 *Commission v Greece* [2005] E.C.R. I-4713, paras 25–29 (and case-law cited therein).
[112] The Commission (or Member State) may bring an action for failure to fulfil obligations where a
Member State fails to submit to an audit of the Court of Auditors: see ECJ, Case C-539/09 *Commission v
Germany* [2011] E.C.R. I-11235.
[113] Art. 17(1) TEU. See, e.g. ECJ, Case C-422/92 *Commission v Germany* [1995] E.C.R. I-1097, para. 16;
ECJ, Case C-494/01 *Commission v Ireland* [2005] E.C.R. I-3331, para. 197 (and further citations therein);
ECJ, Case C-531/06 *Commission v Italy* [2009] E.C.R. I-4103, para. 23.
[114] ECJ, Case 167/73 *Commission v France* [1974] E.C.R. 359, para. 15; ECJ, Case C-191/95 *Commission
v Germany* [1998] E.C.R. I-5449, para. 35; CFI, Case T-209/00 *Lamberts v Ombudsman* [2002] E.C.R.
II-2203, para. 55 (upheld on appeal: ECJ, Case C-234/02 P *Ombudsman v Lamberts* [2004] E.C.R. I-2803).
See also generally K. Lenaerts and P. Van Nuffel (R. Bray and N. Cambien (eds)), *European Union Law*
(3rd edn, London, Sweet & Maxwell, 2011), para. 13.63.
[115] See, e.g. ECJ, Case C-422/92 *Commission v Germany* [1995] E.C.R. I-1097, para. 16; ECJ, Case
C-182/94 *Commission v Italy* [1995] E.C.R. I-1465, para. 5; ECJ, Case C-333/99 *Commission v France* [2001]
E.C.R. I-1025, para. 5; ECJ, Joined Cases C-418/00 and C-419/00 *Commission v France* [2002] E.C.R.
I-3969, para. 29; ECJ, Case C-476/98 *Commission v Germany* [2002] E.C.R. I-9855, para. 38; ECJ, Case
C-33/04 *Commission v Luxembourg* [2005] E.C.R. I-10629, para. 65; ECJ, Case C-255/05 *Commission v Italy*
[2007] E.C.R. I-5767, para. 37; ECJ, Case C-456/05 *Commission v Germany* [2007] E.C.R. I-10517, para.
25; ECJ, Case C-445/06 *Danske Slagterier* [2009] E.C.R. I-2119, para. 43 (and further citations therein).
[116] See, e.g. ECJ, Case C-87/89 *SONITO and Others v Commission* [1990] E.C.R. I-1981, paras 6–7; ECJ,
Case C-200/88 *Commission v Greece* [1990] E.C.R. I-4299, para. 9; ECJ, Case C-209/88 *Commission v Italy*

consider whether or not there has been a failure to fulfil obligations as alleged, without it being part of its role to take a view on the Commission's exercise of its discretion.[117]

The decision to apply to the Court of Justice for a declaration that a Member State has failed to fulfil its obligations cannot be described as a measure of administration or management and hence may not be delegated; it must be taken by all the members of the College of Commissioners, who should bear collective responsibility for it.[118] The formal requirements for effective compliance with that principle of collegiate responsibility are less strict in this case than in the case of the adoption of decisions affecting the legal position of individuals.[119] The reason for this is that, while the decision to commence proceedings for failure to fulfil obligations before the Court constitutes an indispensable step for the purpose of enabling the Court to give judgment by way of a binding decision on the alleged failure to fulfil obligations, it does not per se alter the legal position of the Member State in question. Consequently, it is sufficient that the decision to bring an action was the subject of collective deliberation by the college of Commissioners and that the information on which the decision was based was available to the members of the college. However, it is not necessary for the college itself formally to decide on the wording of the acts that give effect to the decision and put them in final form.[120]

The involvement of the Court is not always necessary or appropriate in order to ensure that the Member States effectively apply Union law. The Commission is therefore also free to determine the time that it brings any proceedings.[121] In contrast, the Commission is not

---

[1990] E.C.R. I-4313, para. 13; ECJ, Case C-243/89 *Commission v Denmark* [1993] E.C.R. I-3353, para. 30; ECJ, Case C-353/96 *Commission v Ireland* [1998] E.C.R. I-8565, para. 22; ECJ, Case C-333/99 *Commission v France* [2001] E.C.R. I-1025, para. 24; ECJ, Case C-383/00 *Commission v Germany* [2002] E.C.R. I-4219, para. 19; ECJ, Case C-471/98 *Commission v Belgium* [2002] E.C.R. I-9681, para. 39; ECJ, Case C-472/98 *Commission v Luxembourg* [2002] ECJ I-9741, para. 37; ECJ, Case C-33/04 *Commission v Luxembourg* [2005] E.C.R. I-10629, para. 66; Case C-445/06 *Danske Slagterier* [2009] E.C.R. I-2119, para. 44; ECJ, Case C-154/09 *Commission v Portugal* [2010] E.C.R. I-127*, Summ. pub., para. 51 (and further citations therein). See also the second para. of Art. 258 TFEU, which provides that the Commission 'may' bring the matter before the Court of Justice if the Member State concerned fails to comply with the reasoned opinion within the period laid down: ECJ, Case C-152/98 *Commission v Netherlands* [2001] E.C.R. I-3463, para. 20.

[117] See, e.g. ECJ, Case C-191/95 *Commission v Spain* [2002] E.C.R. I-5293, para. 25; ECJ, Case C-33/04 *Commission v Luxembourg* [2005] E.C.R. I-10629, para. 67; ECJ, Case 423/07 *Commission v Spain* [2010] E.C.R. I-3429, para. 78; ECJ (judgment of 15 December 2011), Case C-560/08 *Commission v Spain*, not reported, para. 72.

[118] ECJ, Case C-191/95 *Commission v Germany* [1998] E.C.R. I-5449, paras 35–37 and ECJ, Case C-272/97 *Commission v Germany* [1999] E.C.R. I-2175, paras 13–22, in which the Court justified this position in terms, *inter alia*, of 'the discretionary power of the institution', which '[i]n its role as guardian of the Treaty . . . is competent to decide whether it is appropriate to bring proceedings against a Member State for failure to fulfil its obligations'.

[119] See K. Lenaerts and P. Van Nuffel (R. Bray and N. Cambien (eds)), *European Union Law* (3rd edn, London, Sweet & Maxwell, 2011), para. 13.75.

[120] ECJ, Case C-191/95 *Commission v Germany* [1998] E.C.R. I-5449, paras 47–48. See also ECJ, Case C-272/97 *Commission v Germany* [1999] E.C.R. I-2175, paras 13–22; ECJ, Case C-198/97 *Commission v Germany* [1999] E.C.R. I-3257, paras 19–21. The decision to bring an action is therefore not a challengeable act within the meaning of Art. 263 TFEU: CFI, Joined Cases T-377/00, T-379/00, T-380/00, T-260/01, and T-272/01 *Philip Morris International and Others v Commission* [2003] E.C.R. II-1, para. 79 (upheld on appeal, ECJ, Case C-131/03 P *Reynolds Tobacco and Others v Commission* [2006] E.C.R. I-7795).

[121] ECJ, Case 7/68 *Commission v Italy* [1968] E.C.R. 423, at 428; ECJ, Case 7/71 *Commission v France* [1971] E.C.R. 1003, para. 5; ECJ, Case 324/82 *Commission v Belgium* [1984] E.C.R. 1861, para. 12. See also ECJ, Case C-422/92 *Commission v Germany* [1995] E.C.R. I-1097, paras 17–18: although the Court was surprised at the Commission's having brought an action more than six years after the national legislation at

empowered to determine conclusively whether a given conduct of a Member State is compatible with the Treaties. The rights and duties of Member States may be determined, and their conduct appraised, only by judgment of the Court of Justice.[122] Consequently, a decision by the Commission not to bring proceedings against a Member State does not mean that that Member State is not in breach of Union law.[123]

(2) No standing for individuals

Individuals may not bring actions for failure to fulfil obligations before the Court of Justice **5.32** or the General Court.[124] If the need arises, they must contest the conduct of the Member State in a national court.[125] The latter may (or must) request a preliminary ruling from the Court of Justice in order indirectly to have the conduct complained of reviewed in the light of the requirements of Union law (see Chs 3 and 6).[126] Furthermore, persons considering that a Member State is infringing Union law may lay a complaint before the Commission.[127] The Commission, however, is under no obligation to act on the complaint.[128]

---

issue had entered into force, it held that the Commission was not obliged to act within a specified period. See further para. 5.62.

[122] ECJ, Joined Cases 142/80 and 143/80 *Essevi and Salengo* [1981] E.C.R. 1413, para. 16. See further, e.g. EGC, T-258/06 *Germany v Commission* [2010] E.C.R. II-2027, para. 153 (and citations therein). For further case-law bearing on this point in connection with the role of the Commission vis-à-vis the Court of Justice in the context of the enforcement of financial sanctions imposed on a Member State under Art. 260(2) TFEU, see para. 5.78.

[123] Where it subsequently appears that the Member State is indeed infringing Union law, the fact that the Commission did not bring an action for failure to fulfil obligations may, in certain circumstances, constitute a reason for limiting the temporal effects of a judgment of the Court on a reference for a preliminary ruling which brings the infringement to light (see para. 6.34). This may also be relevant in assessing whether the breach of Union law was sufficiently serious as to cause the Member State to incur liability vis-à-vis individuals who suffered loss or damage as a result of it (see para. 4.48).

[124] See, e.g. ECJ (order of 16 May 2008), Case C-454/07 *Raulin v France* [2008] E.C.R. I-76*, Summ. pub.; ECJ (order of 16 May 2008), Case C-49/08 *Raulin v France* [2008] E.C.R. I-77*, Summ. pub.; CFI (order of 8 July 2004), Case T-213/04 *Ascione*, not reported. Individuals may also not have the General Court review the legality of national measures through an action for annulment brought against the Commission (CFI, Case T-148/00 *Panhellenic Union of Cotton Ginners and Exporters v Commission* [2003] E.C.R. II-4415, para. 66).

[125] The fact that individuals have brought proceedings before a national court cannot prevent the bringing of an action by the Commission under Art. 258 TFEU, since the two procedures have different objectives and effects: see, e.g. ECJ, Case 31/69 *Commission v Italy* [1970] E.C.R. 25, para. 9; ECJ, Case 85/85 *Commission v Belgium* [1986] E.C.R. 1149, para. 24; ECJ, Case C-87/02 *Commission v Italy* [2004] E.C.R. I-5975, para. 39; ECJ, Case C-423/07 *Commission v Spain* [2010] E.C.R. I-3429, paras 78–80 (and further citations therein).

[126] ECJ, Case 1/82 *D* [1982] E.C.R. 3709, para. 8. See also ECJ, Joined Cases C-106/90, C-317/90 and C-129/91 *Emerald Meats v Commission* [1993] E.C.R. I-209, para. 40.

[127] See the Commission's website, <http://ec.europa.eu/eu_law/your_rights/your_rights_en.htm> (providing general information on the submission of complaints and a system for the submission of complaints via the internet). See also para. 5.32.

[128] CFI (order of 14 January 2004), Case T-202/02 *Makedoniko Metro Michaniki v Commission* [2004] E.C.R. II-181, paras 42–47 (and the case-law cited therein). Consequently, the position of an individual who makes a complaint against an undertaking for infringement of Art. 101 TFEU and/or Art. 102 TFEU (see paras 7.43 and 8.07) differs fundamentally from that of an individual who brings a complaint against a Member State for infringement of Union law: see CFI (order of 19 September 2005), Case T-247/04 *Aseprofar and Edifa v Commission* [2005] E.C.R. II-3449, paras 40–61); EGC, Case T-186/08 *LPN v Commission* [2009] E.C.R. II-136*, Summ. pub., para. 56. That being said, individuals may possibly take up the matter with the European Ombudsman relating to instances of maladministration in connection with the Commission's handling of such complaints: for a recent example, see the decision in complaint 953/2009/ (JMA) MHZ, <http://www.ombudsman.europa.eu/cases/summary.faces/en/5252/html.bookmark>. See also para. 5.33.

(3) Rejection of a complaint

5.33 The Commission's decision rejecting a complaint cannot be challenged by an action for annulment,[129] since the Commission does not adopt any binding legal act in the course of the pre-litigation stage:[130] it does not determine the rights and duties of the Member State or afford any guarantee that a given line of conduct is compatible with the Treaties. An opinion of the Commission cannot release a Member State from its Treaty obligations and certainly does not give it a licence to restrict rights that individuals derive from the Treaties.[131] Consequently, the Commission's decision rejecting a complaint from individuals does not affect their legal position, since the Commission is simply refusing to take measures that in no event would have legal effects for them.

(4) Failure of the Commission to bring an infringement action

5.34 If the Commission leaves the complaint unanswered, an action for failure to act under Art. 265 TFEU will not lie, since the Commission has not infringed any duty to act.[132] The same is true where the Commission fails to bring proceedings before the Court in the event of a Member State's infringing a decision adopted pursuant to Art. 108(2) TFEU relating to State aid.[133] In addition, natural or legal persons may bring such an action against the Commission only if it failed to adopt an act addressed to them, other than a recommendation or an opinion.[134] Since in a procedure pursuant to Art. 258 TFEU the Commission addresses to the Member State concerned only a reasoned 'opinion', natural or legal persons are precluded from bringing an action for failure to deliver such an opinion.[135]

---

[129] See, e.g. ECJ, Case C-87/89 *SONITO and Others v Commission* [1990] E.C.R. I-1981, paras 5–9; CFI, Case T-16/91 *Rendo and Others v Commission* [1992] E.C.R. II-2417, para. 52; CFI, Case T-575/93 *Koelman v Commission* [1996] E.C.R. II-1, para. 71; CFI, Case T-111/96 ITT *Promedia v Commission* [1998] E.C.R. II-2937, para. 97; EGC, Case T-186/08 *LPN v Commission* [2009] E.C.R. II-136*, Summ. pub., para. 49 (and case-law cited therein). Since the Commission likewise has a broad discretion in carrying out the function conferred on it by Art. 106 TFEU of ensuring that Member States fulfil their obligations in respect of public undertakings and undertakings to which Member States grant special or exclusive rights, individuals who requested the Commission to intervene pursuant to that article may not bring an action for annulment against the decision by which the Commission refuses to act against a Member State infringing Art. 106(1) and (2) TFEU: ECJ, Case C-107/95 P *Bundesverband der Bilanzbuchhalter v Commission* [1997] E.C.R. I-947, paras 26–30 (cf., however, the Opinion of Advocate-General A. La Pergola, points 14–21, who took a different view); CFI (order of 23 January 1995), Case T-84/94 *Bundesverband der Bilanzbuchhalter v Commission* [1995] E.C.R. II-101, para. 23; ECJ, Case C-141/02 P *Commission v T-Mobile Austria* [2005] E.C.R. I-1283, para. 70 (annulling the CFI's judgment in Case T-54/99 *max.mobil Telekommunication Service v Commission* [2002] E.C.R. II-313, in which the CFI had found that the rejection of an Art. 106 TFEU complaint constituted a reviewable act).

[130] ECJ, Case 48/65 *Lütticke v Commission* [1966] E.C.R. 19, at 27: the Court held that '[n]o measure taken by the Commission during [the pre-litigation] stage has any binding force'. See further CFI (order of 6 September 2005), Case T-209/05 *Gisti v Commission*, not reported, paras 4–11; EGC, T-258/06 *Germany v Commission* [2010] E.C.R. II-2027, para. 152.

[131] ECJ, Joined Cases 142/80 and 143/80 *Essevi and Salengo* [1981] E.C.R. 1431, paras 16–18.

[132] CFI (order of 19 February 1997), Case T-117/96 *Intertronic v Commission* [1997] E.C.R. II-141, para. 32; CFI (order of 5 June 2002), Case T-143/02 *Olive v Commission and Others*, not reported, para. 11.

[133] CFI, Case T-277/94 *AITEC v Commission* [1996] E.C.R. II-351, paras 65–72.

[134] ECJ, Case 247/87 *Star Fruit v Commission* [1989] E.C.R. 291, paras 10–14; ECJ (order of 23 May 1990), Case C-72/90 *Asia Motor France v Commission* [1990] E.C.R. I-2181, para. 11; CFI (order of 14 December 1993), Case T-29/93 *Calvo Alonso-Cortès v Commission* [1993] E.C.R. II-1389, para. 55; CFI (order of 27 May 1994), Case T-5/94 *J v Commission* [1994] E.C.R. II-391, para. 16; CFI (order of 4 July 1994), Case T-13/94 *Century Oils Hellas v Commission* [1994] E.C.R. II-431, para. 13.

[135] ECJ, Case 48/65 *Lütticke and Others v Commission* [1966] E.C.R. 27, 39; CFI (order of 13 November 1995), Case T-126/95 *Dumez v Commission* [1995] E.C.R. II-2863, paras 34–37.

A failure on the part of the Commission to bring an action for failure to fulfil obligations will not ground an action for damages either.[136] The reason for this is that the Commission's inaction does not infringe Art. 258 TFEU and therefore cannot be regarded as constituting conduct amounting to a sufficiently serious breach of Union law.[137] In such a case, the source of any damage lies in the Member State's infringement of the Treaties and not in any shortcoming of the Commission.

(5) Member State

Under Art. 259 TFEU, a Member State may also bring a matter before the Court of Justice **5.35** if it considers that another Member State has failed to fulfil an obligation under Union law. The Member State must first submit a complaint to the Commission. The Commission delivers a reasoned opinion, after giving each of the States concerned the opportunity to submit its own case and its observations on the other party's case, both orally and in writing. The opinion sets out the Commission's view as to whether or not the alleged infringement of Union obligations under the Treaties is made out. If the Commission has not delivered an opinion within three months of the date of receipt of the complaint, the matter may be brought before the Court of Justice.

The Commission may also bring the matter before the Court itself pursuant to Art. 258 TFEU. If it does so, this does not prevent the Member State from also bringing an action.[138] In the event that the Commission's reasoned opinion falls short of the Member State's expectations, it may add to it in its application.

To date, very few actions have been brought under Art. 259 TFEU that have resulted in a judgment.[139]

---

[136] ECJ (order of 23 May 1990), Case C-72/90 *Asia Motor France v Commission* [1990] E.C.R. I-2181, para. 13; CFI, Case T-209/00 *Lamberts v European Ombudsman* [2002] E.C.R. II-2203, para. 53 (upheld on appeal: ECJ, Case C-234/02 P *European Ombudsman v Lamberts* [2004] E.C.R. I-2803); CFI (order of 3 July 1997), Case T-201/96 *Smanor and Others v Commission* [1997] E.C.R. II-1081, para. 30; CFI (order of 5 May 1999), Case T-190/98 *Gluiber v Council and Commission*, not reported, para. 13.

[137] However, the Commission's conduct may possibly infringe other Treaty provisions and hence potentially make it liable in damages if all the necessary conditions are fulfilled (see Ch. 11). For example, the Court of Justice has declared actions for damages for infringement of the second para. of Art. 97 EC (since repealed) and Arts 88(2), 211, and 226 EC (now Arts 108(2) TFEU, 7 TEU, and 258 TFEU), respectively, admissible but unfounded (ECJ, Case 4/69 *Lütticke v Commission* [1971] E.C.R. 325; ECJ, Case 40/75 *Produits Bertrand v Commission* [1976] E.C.R. 1). See also EGC, Joined Cases T-440/03, T-12104, T-17104, T-20804, T-36504 and T-484/04 *Arizmendi and Others v Council and Commission* [2009] E.C.R. II-4883 (not appealed): in this case, the General Court ruled as admissible an action seeking compensation for damage allegedly suffered as a result of the Commission's sending of a reasoned opinion to a Member State. On the one hand, the Commission's reasoned opinion cannot result in a sufficiently serious breach of a rule of law intended to confer rights on individuals. On the other hand, however, if the assessment set out in the reasoned opinion goes beyond the determination as to whether a Member State has failed to fulfil its obligations or if other conduct on the part of the Commission in an infringement procedure exceeds the powers conferred upon it, then those assessments or that conduct may constitute such a breach as to render the Union liable. See further K. Gutman, 'The Evolution of the Action for Damages Against the European Union and Its Place in the System of Judicial Protection', 48 C.M.L. Rev. 695–750, at 707–8.

[138] See L. Prete and B. Smulders, 'The Coming of Age of Infringement Proceedings' (2010) C.M.L. Rev. 9, at 27, finding that ECJ, Case 141/78 *France v United Kingdom* [1979] E.C.R. 2923 appears to confirm this reading of Art. 259 TFEU since in that case, France had lodged its action against the United Kingdom three months after the Commission had issued a reasoned opinion and the Commission did not raise any plea of inadmissibility in that regard.

[139] ECJ, Case 141/78 *France v United Kingdom* [1979] E.C.R. 2923; ECJ, Case C-388/95 *Belgium v Spain* [2000] E.C.R. I-3123; ECJ, Case C-145/04 *Spain v United Kingdom* [2006] E.C.R. I-7917; ECJ (judgment

B. The defendant

(1) Member State

5.36 An action under Arts 258–259 TFEU may be brought before the Court of Justice only against a Member State. Each action is directed at an individual Member State. There is no provision for such an action to be brought against more than one Member State at the same time though, depending upon the circumstances, the Commission may lodge proceedings against several Member States in successive actions for similar or identical alleged violations of Union law.[140]

(2) Notion of Member State

5.37 By 'Member State' is meant the entity under international law that acceded to the Treaties governing the European Union.[141] Any act or failure to act by any agency of the Member State or constitutionally independent bodies or institutions that are to be regarded as public bodies may potentially cause that Member State to become liable under Union law.[142] The domestic organization of a Member State may not detract from the full effect of Union law.

Consequently, it may be that a Member State is found to have infringed Union law even though the infringement was committed by a sub-entity and the national government, which represents the 'Member State' before the Court of Justice, was not at fault and has no defence under domestic law.[143] The rationale of the Court's case-law is that the Member

---

of 16 October 2012), Case C-364/10 *Hungary v Slovak Republic*, not reported. For actions that were withdrawn, see further S. Van Raepenbusch, *Droit institutionnel de l'Union européenne* (Brussels, Larcier, 2011), 596. It is often considered that the scarcity of such actions is due to political sensitivities and/or to the availability of intervention by which a Member State can submit its observations during infringement proceedings brought by the Commission (see para. 25.61).

[140] For a recent example, as regards various Member States' nationality provisions relating to notaries, see ECJ, Case C-47/08 *Commission v Belgium* [2011] E.C.R. I-4105; ECJ, Case C-50/08 *Commission v France* [2011] E.C.R. I-4195; ECJ, Case C-51/08 *Commission v Luxembourg* [2011] E.C.R. I-4231; ECJ, Case C-52/08 *Commission v Portugal* [2011] E.C.R. I-4275; ECJ, Case C-53/08 *Commission v Austria* [2011] E.C.R. I-4309; ECJ, Case C-54/08 *Commission v Germany* [2011] E.C.R. I-4355; and ECJ, Case C-61/08 *Commission v Greece* [2011] E.C.R. I-4399.

[141] Thus excluding the EFTA/EEA States, although there is provision for similar infringement proceedings brought before the EFTA Court by the EFTA Surveillance Authority against an EFTA State for infringement of the EEA Rules.

[142] ECJ, Case 77/69 *Commission v Belgium* [1970] E.C.R. 237, para. 15; ECJ, Case 169/82 *Commission v Italy* [1984] E.C.R. 1603; ECJ, Case 1/86 *Commission v Belgium* [1987] E.C.R. 2797; ECJ, Joined Cases 227/85 to 230/85 *Commission v Belgium* [1988] E.C.R. 1; ECJ, Case 45/87 *Commission v Ireland* [1988] E.C.R. 4929; ECJ, Case C-58/89 *Commission v Germany* [1991] E.C.R. I-4983; ECJ, Case C-33/90 *Commission v Italy* [1991] E.C.R. I-5987; ECJ, Case C-129/00 *Commission v Italy* [2003] E.C.R. I-14638, para. 29; ECJ, Case C-458/07 *Commission v Portugal* [2009] E.C.R. I-29*, Summ. pub., para. 20; ECJ, Case C-334/08 *Commission v Italy* [2010] E.C.R. I-6869, paras 39–44. See also the definition of the expression 'Member State' in ECJ (order of 21 March 1997), Case C-95/97 *Région Wallonne v Commission* [1997] E.C.R. I-1787, paras 16–17. The fact that a directive has been transposed in a timely manner in some, but not all, of the relevant authorities in the territories of a Member State has resulted in a finding of a failure to fulfil obligations against it: for instance, as regards the United Kingdom, see, e.g. ECJ, Case C-457/08 *Commission v United Kingdom* [2009] E.C.R. I-137*, Summ. pub.; ECJ, Case C-186/09 *Commission v United Kingdom* [2010] E.C.R. I-15*, Summ. pub.; ECJ, Case C-495/08 *Commission v United Kingdom* [2009] E.C.R. I-188*, Summ. pub.

[143] See, e.g. ECJ, Case 239/85 *Commission v Belgium* [1986] E.C.R. 3645, paras 13–14. In Belgium, there is a system of substitution whereby the federal authorities may, subject to certain conditions, invest themselves

State is under a Union law duty to construct its constitutional structure in such a way as to avoid that evil.

(3) Legislature, executive, and judiciary

An act or omission of the legislative authority of a Member State can certainly give rise to an **5.38** action for failure to fulfil obligations.[144] The same is true for shortcomings of the executive branch or of administrative authorities of the Member State. Shortcomings in the way in which national courts apply Union law may also be imputed to the Member State.[145] In all likelihood, an ordinary judicial error is not sufficient.[146] If a (supreme) national court deliberately ignored or disregarded Union law, this could certainly bring the Union liability of the relevant Member State into play.[147]

(4) Private companies controlled by public authorities

Finally, acts of legal persons governed by private law that are controlled by the public **5.39** authorities may result in an infringement of Union law on the part of the Member State concerned.[148] An example is the Irish Goods Council, which was set up to organize the 'Buy Irish' campaign in Ireland. The acts of the Irish Goods Council were imputed to the Irish State, since its membership, funding, and aims were determined by the Irish Government.[149]

---

with powers of a sub-entity in order to give effect to a judgment of the Court of Justice finding Belgium guilty of an infringement of Union law by that entity (Belgian Constitution, Art. 169 and Art. 16(3) of the Special Law on Institutional Reform). See also ECJ, Case C-87/02 *Commission v Italy* [2004] E.C.R. I-5975, para. 38; ECJ, Case C-102/06 *Commission v Austria* [2006] E.C.R. I-111*, Summ. pub., paras 7–9. For examples of actions on the part of local authorities which resulted in finding of failure to fulfil obligations, see ECJ, Case C-494/01 *Commission v Ireland* [2005] E.C.R. I-3331; ECJ, Case C-513/09 *Commission v Belgium* [2010] E.C.R. I-100*, Summ. pub., para. 7; ECJ (judgment of 17 October 2013), Case C-533/11 *Commission v Belgium*, not reported, para. 57. See also para. 5.65.

[144] ECJ, Case 8/70 *Commission v Italy* [1970] E.C.R. 961, paras 8–9; ECJ, Case 94/81 *Commission v Italy* [1982] E.C.R. 739, para. 4; Case 41/82 *Commission v Italy* [1982] E.C.R. 4213, para. 15; Case 309/84 *Commission v Italy* [1986] E.C.R. 599, para. 9.

[145] ECJ, Case C-129/00 *Commission v Italy* [2003] E.C.R. I-14637, paras 29–41: an Italian law, which in itself was not contrary to Union law, was interpreted by a large part of the Italian judiciary, including the *Corte suprema di cassazione*, in a way which was incompatible with Union law. In the context of proceedings under Art. 108(2) TFEU, see, e.g. ECJ, Case C-304/09 *Commission v Italy* [2010] E.C.R. I-13903, paras 55–56.

[146] ECJ, Case C-129/00 *Commission v Italy* [2003] E.C.R. I-14637, para. 33: where national legislation has been the subject of different relevant judicial constructions, some leading to the application of that legislation in compliance with Union law, others leading to the opposite application, it must be held that, at the very least, such legislation is not sufficiently clear to ensure its application in compliance with Union law. See also ECJ (order of 3 June 2005), Case C-396/03 P *Killinger v Germany, Council and Commission* [2005] E.C.R. I-4967, para. 28.

[147] See ECJ, Case C-154/08 *Commission v Spain* [2009] E.C.R. I-187*, Summ. pub., paras 125–127. See also paras 3.56–3.57 for the possibility of bringing proceedings under Arts 258–259 TFEU against a Member State where one of its courts infringes the obligation to seek a preliminary ruling under the third para. of Art. 267 TFEU.

[148] ECJ, Case 249/81 *Commission v Ireland* [1982] E.C.R. 4005, para. 15; ECJ, Case C-325/00 *Commission v Germany* [2002] E.C.R. I-9977, paras 14–21.

[149] ECJ, Case 249/81 *Commission v Ireland* [1982] E.C.R. 4005, para.15. See also ECJ, C-353/96 *Commission v Ireland* [1998] E.C.R. I-8565, para. 23: the Member State is liable for acts of an individual undertaking that is State-owned and acts as a contracting authority within the meaning of the directives on public contract awards. See also CFI (order of 29 September 1997), Case T-83/97 *Sateba v Commission* [1997] E.C.R. II-1523, para. 36 (and case-law cited therein) (upheld on appeal: ECJ (order of 17 July 1998), Case C-422/97 P *Sateba v Commission* [1998] E.C.R. I-4913).

III. Special Characteristics

A. The pre-litigation stage of the procedure

(1) Objective

5.40 The aim of the pre-litigation stage of the procedure is to give the Member State an opportunity (a) of remedying the infringement before the matter is brought before the Court of Justice; and (b) of putting forward its defence to the Commission's complaints.[150] Moreover, during the pre-litigation stage, the Commission and the Member State may come to an accommodation, thus rendering a court proceeding unnecessary.[151] Finally, the proper conduct of the pre-litigation procedure constitutes an essential guarantee in order not only to protect the rights of the Member State concerned, but also to ensure that any contentious procedure will have a clearly defined dispute as to its subject-matter.[152] The scope of the dispute is defined in the pre-litigation procedure. As a result, in the contentious proceedings, the Court may only judge the merits of the pleas in law put forward by the Commission in the pre-litigation procedure.[153]

(2) Letter of formal notice

(a) Content and purpose

5.41 The Art. 258 TFEU procedure formally commences with receipt of a letter before action from the Commission giving the Member State formal notice. As a rule, the letter will have been preceded by informal contacts between the Commission and the Member State by which the former starts its investigation into the possible infringements of Union law.[154]

---

[150] See, e.g. ECJ, Case 74/82 *Commission v Ireland* [1984] E.C.R. 317, para. 13; ECJ, Case C-287/00 *Commission v Germany* [2002] E.C.R. I-5811, para. 16; ECJ, Case C-79/09 *Commission v Netherlands* [2010] E.C.R. I-40*, Summ. pub., paras 21–22.

[151] Consequently, the Commission is justified to refuse to disclose a letter of formal notice and a reasoned opinion requested under the right of access to documents by an individual who lodged a complaint. This is because the Member States are entitled to expect the Commission to guarantee confidentiality during investigations that might lead to an infringement procedure and also after proceedings are brought in the Court. This enables discussions to continue between the parties even after proceedings have been brought, with a view to reaching a speedy resolution (CFI, Case T-191/99 *Petrie and Others v Commission* [2001] E.C.R. II-3677, paras 61–69). As regards disclosure of the reasoned opinion, see also CFI, Case T-309/97 *Bavarian Lager v Commission* [1999] E.C.R. II-3217 (for a related case on access to documents concerning a meeting held in the context of a procedure for failure to fulfil obligations, see ECJ, Case C-28/08 P *Commission v Bavarian Lager* [2010] E.C.R. I-6055). Compare ECJ, Joined Cases C-514/07 P, C-528/07 P, and C-532/07 P *Sweden and Others v Commission* [2010] E.C.R. I-8533, paras 118–127: access to written pleadings lodged in infringement actions for which the Court has already delivered judgment may be granted under the relevant rules regarding access to documents. See further K. Lenaerts, 'The Principle of Democracy in the Case Law of the CJEU' (2013) I.C.L.Q. 271–315.

[152] See, e.g. ECJ (order of 11 July 1995), Case C-266/94 *Commission v Spain* [1995] E.C.R. I-1975, para. 17; ECJ, Case C-362/01 *Commission v Ireland* [2003] E.C.R. I-11433, para. 18; ECJ, Case C-160/08 *Commission v Germany* [2010] E.C.R. I-3713, para. 42.

[153] ECJ, Case C-158/94 *Commission v Italy* [1997] E.C.R. I-5789, paras 59–60; ECJ, Case C-159/94 *Commission v France* [1997] E.C.R. I-5815, paras 106–107.

[154] In this context, the Commission may, for example, send a letter to a Member State requesting information by a certain deadline, but this is purely informal and does not constitute a letter of formal notice: see, e.g. ECJ, Case C-211/08 *Commission v Spain* [2010] E.C.R. I-5267, paras 21–22.

The purpose of the letter of formal notice—also referred to as the letter before action—is to delimit the subject-matter of the dispute and to provide the Member State, which is asked to submit observations, with the information necessary in order for it to prepare its defence.[155]

Consequently, the letter of formal notice must precisely specify the obligation that the Commission maintains the Member State has failed to fulfil and the grounds on which the Commission takes this view.[156] Any vagueness in the letter of formal notice depriving the Member State of the opportunity of submitting observations to good effect may be remedied by the Commission's sending a new or supplementary letter of formal notice, setting out in time additional particulars or information.[157] At that point in the pre-litigation stage, it is sufficient if the Member State receives an initial brief summary of the complaints.[158] Under the case-law, the test is whether the Member State was placed in possession of all the relevant information needed for its defence.[159]

(b) Formal notice must be complete

The Member State must be put on notice of the whole of the alleged infringement of **5.42** Union law. The complaints may not be subsequently extended in the reasoned opinion, since that would be in breach of the Commission's duty to give the Member State concerned a fair hearing.[160] The illegality cannot be regarded as cured even by the fact that the Member State put forward a defence in its observations on the reasoned opinion to the new complaints enlarging the scope of the dispute.[161]

(c) Essential procedural requirement

Because it gives the Member State concerned the opportunity to submit prior observations, **5.43** the letter of formal notice constitutes an essential procedural requirement for the legality of the procedure for a declaration that a Member State has failed to fulfil its obligations.[162]

---

[155] ECJ, Case 274/83 *Commission v Italy* [1985] E.C.R. 1077, para. 19: ECJ, Case 229/87 *Commission v Greece* [1988] E.C.R. 6347, para. 12.

[156] ECJ (order of 13 September 2000), Case C-341/97 *Commission v Netherlands* [2000] E.C.R. I-6611. A detailed opinion within the meaning of Art. 9(1) of Directive 83/189/EEC (now replaced by Directive 98/34/EC) (a procedure for the provision of information in the field of technical standards and regulations) informing a Member State that a national measure notified to the Commission did not comply with Union law cannot be regarded as a letter of formal notice within the meaning of Art. 258 TFEU. At the time when such a detailed opinion is delivered, the Member State to which it is addressed cannot have infringed Union law, since the measure exists only in draft form.

[157] ECJ, Case 211/81 *Commission v Denmark* [1982] E.C.R. 4547, paras 10–11. The Commission may also send out a supplementary letter of formal notice, which adds new complaints and provides for a new time limit, which then forms the basis for the complaints alleged in the reasoned opinion: see, e.g. ECJ, Case C-442/06 *Commission v Italy* [2008] E.C.R. I-2413, paras 23–24.

[158] ECJ, Case 274/83 *Commission v Italy* [1985] E.C.R. 1077, para. 21; ECJ, Case C-289/94 *Commission v Italy* [1996] E.C.R. I-4405, para. 16; ECJ, Case C-279/94 *Commission v Italy* [1997] E.C.R. I-4743, para. 15; ECJ, Case C-225/98 *Commission v France* [2000] E.C.R. I-7445, para. 70.

[159] ECJ, Case 229/87 *Commission v Greece* [1988] E.C.R. 6347, para. 13.

[160] ECJ, Case 51/83 *Commission v Italy* [1984] E.C.R. 2793, para. 6; ECJ, Case C-145/01 *Commission v Italy* [2003] E.C.R. I-5581, paras 17–18 (the reasoned opinion and the application made to the Court pursuant to the second para. of Art. 258 TFEU were flawed with regard to the rights of the defence (i) since they referred to rules of Union law other than those cited in the letter of formal notice; and (ii) since a change in the legal situation was likely to have affected the assessment of the compatibility of the national legislation in question with Union law).

[161] ECJ, Case 51/83 *Commission v Italy*, para. 7.

[162] ECJ, Case C-306/91 *Commission v Italy* [1993] E.C.R. I-2133, paras 22–24; ECJ, Case C-243/89 *Commission v Denmark* [1993] E.C.R. I-3353, para. 13.

Even if the Member State does not wish to make any observations, the Commission must comply with that requirement.[163]

(d) Sufficient time for lodging observations

5.44   The Member State must have a reasonable time in which to make its observations. The reasonableness of the period prescribed by the Commission has to be assessed in the light of the particular circumstances. Thus, the urgent nature of the case or the fact that the Member State was fully apprised of the Commission's position even before the letter of formal notice may warrant setting a short period.[164] However, the urgency of the case may not be brought about by the Commission itself, for instance, because it was tardy in bringing proceedings for failure to fulfil obligations. Moreover, a Member State cannot be regarded as having been fully apprised of the Commission's position before the letter of formal notice where the Commission did not make any clear view known to it.[165]

(3) Reasoned opinion

(a) Content and purpose

5.45   If the Commission is of the view that the Member State fails to remedy the failure to fulfil obligations under Union law, the Commission may issue a reasoned opinion. That document describes the infringement of Union law in detail and prescribes the time within which the Member State must put an end to it. As in the case of the letter of formal notice, delivery of a reasoned opinion is an essential procedural requirement for the purposes of the legality of the proceedings and the admissibility of any proceedings brought against the Member State in the Court of Justice.[166]

The issuance of a reasoned opinion constitutes a preliminary procedure, which does not have any binding legal effect for the addressee. It is merely a pre-litigation stage of a procedure that may lead to an action before the Court. The purpose of that pre-litigation procedure provided for by Art. 258 TFEU is to enable the Member State concerned to comply of its own accord with the requirements of the Treaties or, if appropriate, to justify its position. If that attempt at settlement is unsuccessful, the function of the reasoned opinion is to define the subject-matter of the dispute. However, the Commission is not empowered to determine conclusively, by reasoned opinions formulated pursuant to Art. 258 TFEU, the rights and duties of a Member State or to afford that State guarantees concerning the compatibility of a given line of conduct with the Treaties. According to the system embodied in Arts 258–260 TFEU, the rights and duties of Member States may be determined and their conduct appraised only by a judgment of the Court. The reasoned opinion therefore has legal effect only in relation to the commencement of proceedings

---

[163] ECJ, Case 31/69 *Commission v Italy* [1970] E.C.R. 25, paras 13–14; ECJ, Case 124/81 *Commission v United Kingdom* [1983] E.C.R. 203, para. 6; ECJ, Case 274/83 *Commission v Italy* [1985] E.C.R. 1077, para. 21.

[164] ECJ, Case C-473/93 *Commission v Luxembourg* [1996] E.C.R. I-3207, para. 22; ECJ, Case C-320/03 *Commission v Austria* [2005] E.C.R. I-9871, paras 33–34. For example, in one case involving a time limit of fifteen days in relation to the letter of formal notice and five working days in relation to the reasoned opinion, with extensions granted for both, the application was held admissible: see ECJ, Case C-1/00 *Commission v France* [2001] E.C.R. I-9989, paras 65–69, 76.

[165] ECJ, Case 293/85 *Commission v Belgium* [1988] E.C.R. 305, paras 10–20.

[166] See, e.g. ECJ, Case 325/82 *Commission v Germany* [1984] E.C.R. 777, para. 8; ECJ, Case C-152/89 *Commission v Luxembourg* [1991] E.C.R. I-3141, para. 9.

before the Court so that where a Member State does not comply with that opinion within the period allowed, the Commission has the right, but not the duty, to commence proceedings before the Court.[167]

(b) Collegiate responsibility of the Commission

A decision to issue a reasoned opinion is subject to the principle of collegiate responsibility, **5.46** since it is not a measure of administration or management and therefore may not be delegated. Yet, here too (see para. 5.31), a less stringent approach to effective compliance with the principle of collegiate responsibility applies, having regard to the legal consequences attaching to reasoned opinions in that it is not necessary for the college itself formally to decide on the wording of the act which gives effect to the decision to issue a reasoned opinion and put it in final form. It is sufficient that the decision was the subject of collective deliberation by the college of Commissioners and that the information on which the decision was based was available to the members of the college.[168]

(c) Reasoned opinion must be coherent and detailed

The reasoned opinion is sufficiently reasoned if it contains a coherent and detailed **5.47** statement of the reasons that led the Commission to believe that the Member State in question has failed to fulfil an obligation under the Treaties.[169] The opinion may only relate to shortcomings of the Member State that were mentioned in the letter of formal notice.[170]

(d) Relationship with the letter of formal notice

The reasoned opinion must be clear in itself.[171] A general reference to the letter of formal **5.48** notice is not sufficient. While the letter of formal notice, which comprises an initial succinct résumé of the alleged infringement, may be useful in construing the reasoned opinion, the Commission is nonetheless obliged to specify precisely in that opinion the grounds of complaint which it already raised more generally in the letter of formal notice and alleges against the Member State concerned, after taking cognizance of any observations submitted by it under the first paragraph of Art. 258 TFEU. That requirement is essential in order to delimit the subject-matter of the dispute prior to any initiation of the contentious procedure provided for in the second paragraph of Art. 258 TFEU and in order to ensure that the Member State in question is accurately apprised of the grounds of complaint maintained against it by the Commission and can thus bring an end to the alleged infringement or put forward its arguments in defence prior to any application to the Court by the Commission.[172]

---

[167] This summary is based on ECJ, Case C-191/95 *Commission v Germany* [1998] E.C.R. I-5449, paras 44–36 (and the case-law cited therein).

[168] ECJ, Case C-191/95 *Commission v Germany*, paras 34–36, 48. See also ECJ, Case C-251/09 *Commission v Cyprus* [2011] E.C.R. I-13*, Summ. pub., para. 17.

[169] ECJ, Case 7/61 *Commission v Italy* [1961] E.C.R. 317, at 327; ECJ, 74/82 *Commission v Ireland* [1984] E.C.R. 317, para. 20; ECJ, Case C-279/94 *Commission v Italy* [1997] E.C.R. I-4743, para. 19; ECJ, Case C-191/95 *Commission v Germany*, para. 8; ECJ, Case C-350/02 *Commission v Netherlands* [2004] E.C.R. I-6213, para. 20; ECJ, C-340/02 *Commission v France* [2004] E.C.R. I-9845, para. 27.

[170] ECJ, Case C-145/01 *Commission v Italy* [2003] E.C.R. I-5581, para. 18.

[171] In case of doubt as to the clarity of a reasoned opinion, the reply of the Member State government concerned to the opinion can be taken into account in order to assess whether the grounds of complaint raised by the Commission were comprehensible (ECJ, Case C-463/01 *Commission v Germany* [2004] E.C.R. I-11705, para. 31).

[172] ECJ, Case C-350/02 *Commission v Netherlands* [2004] E.C.R. I-6213, para. 21.

In the reasoned opinion, however, the Commission may set out the complaints contained in the letter of formal notice in more detail and refine them.[173] The Commission takes account in the reasoned opinion of the observations submitted by the Member State in response to the letter of formal notice.[174] Nevertheless, if the reasoned opinion contains new complaints, the Court of Justice will have regard in the subsequent judicial proceedings only to those contained both in the letter of formal notice and in the reasoned opinion,[175] or dismiss the action altogether.[176] This is because the Member State was in a position to submit observations only on those complaints in accordance with the first paragraph of Art. 258 TFEU before the Commission delivered its reasoned opinion.

(e) Reasoned opinion may propose measures to be taken

5.49   The Commission also may—but is not obliged to[177]—set forth the measures which need to be taken in order to bring the infringement to an end. To this extent, the Member State's freedom to determine the manner in which it terminates the relevant infringement of Union law is restricted. The fact that the Court of Justice is confined to making a 'finding' that there has been a failure to fulfil an obligation does not affect this power of the Commission. This is because the aim of Art. 258 TFEU proceedings is to achieve the practical elimination of infringements.[178] Where the Commission indicates in its reasoned opinion the measures required to this end and the Member State does not act on it, the 'finding' made by the Court of Justice refers both to the actual infringement of Union law and to the measures which could have been taken in order to bring the infringement to an end. As a result, the Member State then knows—from the reasoning of the Court's judgment finding

---

[173] ECJ, Case 274/83 *Commission v Italy* [1985] E.C.R. 1077, para. 21; ECJ, Case C-358/01 *Commission v Spain* [2003] E.C.R. I-13145, para. 29; ECJ, Case C-185/00 *Commission v Finland* [2003] E.C.R. I-14189, paras 79–81; ECJ, Case C-20/09 *Commission v Portugal* [2011] E.C.R. I-2637, paras 21–22. See further para. 5.52.

[174] If the Commission takes no account in the reasoned opinion of the observations submitted by the Member State concerned in response to the letter of formal notice, this may mean that the nature and scope of the dispute are not precisely defined at the time when the case is brought before the Court. If so, the Court will hold that the pre-litigation procedure was not properly conducted and declare the application manifestly inadmissible: ECJ (order of 11 July 1995), Case C-266/94 *Commission v Spain* [1995] E.C.R. I-1975, paras 16–26. Although, in principle, the Commission is required to state in its reasoned opinion how it assesses the Member State's observations, even if they are received late, a failure to do so will not result directly in the inadmissibility of the application if it did not make it impossible for the Member State to put an end to its infringement, did not compromise its rights of defence, and had no effect on the definition of the subject-matter of the dispute (ECJ, Case C-362/01 *Commission v Ireland* [2002] E.C.R. I-11433, paras 14–22). See also ECJ, Case C-79/09 *Commission v Netherlands* [2010] E.C.R. I-40*, Summ. pub., paras 20–25: in response to the Netherlands' objection that the Commission's failure to take account of the arguments put forward in its response to the reasoned opinion went against the fundamental objectives of the pre-litigation stage of the procedure, the Court underlined that this had no effect on the rights of defence of the Member State concerned or on the scope of the dispute, especially as the Netherlands' arguments essentially reiterated those set forth in its response to the letter of formal notice.

[175] ECJ, Case 51/83 *Commission v Italy* [1984] E.C.R. 2793, paras 6–8; ECJ, Case C-159/99 *Commission v Italy* [2001] E.C.R. I-4007, para. 54.

[176] See, e.g. ECJ, Case C-522/09 *Commission v Romania* [2011] E.C.R. I-2963, paras 15–20.

[177] ECJ, Case C-247/89 *Commission v Portugal* [1991] E.C.R. I-3659, para. 22. It is only where the Commission intends to make failure to adopt measures to enable the infringement complained of to be remedied the subject-matter of its action for failure to fulfil obligations that it has to specify those measures in the reasoned opinion (ECJ, Case C-328/96 *Commission v Austria* [1999] E.C.R. I-7479, para. 39; ECJ, Case C-394/02 *Commission v Greece* [2005] E.C.R. I-4713, para. 23).

[178] ECJ, Case 70/72 *Commission v Germany* [1973] E.C.R. 813, paras 10–13.

the infringement—what measures indicated in the reasoned opinion are capable of bringing the failure to fulfil obligations to an end.

(f) Prescribed period

The Commission must prescribe in the reasoned opinion the time within which the **5.50** Member State must comply with it. The period must be reasonable, having regard to the circumstances of the case.[179] The Court of Justice has no power to alter the period prescribed by the Commission.[180] An action for failure to fulfil obligations brought after the expiry of a period that was too short to enable the Member State to take the necessary measures or, as the case may be, to prepare its defence, will be declared inadmissible.[181] The application may be declared admissible, however, if in the actual case the aims of the pre-litigation procedure were nevertheless achieved, in spite of the unreasonably short period of time allowed to the Member State.[182]

B. The stage of the procedure held before the Court of Justice

(1) Conditions of admissibility

(a) The requirement for the pre-litigation stage of the procedure to be properly conducted

The proper conduct of the pre-litigation stage of the procedure is, as already noted, an **5.51** essential guarantee required by the Treaties in order not only to protect the rights of the Member State concerned, but also to ensure that any contentious procedure will have a clearly defined dispute as its subject-matter.[183] For those reasons, the Commission must take account in the reasoned opinion of the observations submitted by the Member State concerned in response to the letter of formal notice so that the Court may judge, when proceedings are brought, what specific obligations the Commission claims the Member State concerned has breached. If the Commission fails to satisfy this requirement, this may mean that the subject-matter of the dispute is not precisely defined. Such an irregularity in the conduct of the pre-litigation stage of the procedure may result in the application being declared manifestly inadmissible.[184]

---

[179] ECJ, Case 74/82 *Commission v Ireland* [1984] E.C.R. 317, paras 9–12; ECJ, Case 293/85 *Commission v Belgium* [1988] E.C.R. 305, para. 14; ECJ, Case C-56/90 *Commission v United Kingdom* [1993] E.C.R. I-4109, para. 18; ECJ, Case C-328/96 *Commission v Austria* [1999] E.C.R. I-7479, para. 51; ECJ, Case C-1/00 *Commission v France* [2001] E.C.R. I-9989, para. 65; ECJ, Case C-320/03 *Commission v Austria* [2005] E.C.R. I-9871, paras 33–34 (one week was deemed to be sufficient). See also para. 5.44, in relation to the time prescribed for submitting observations on the letter of formal notice.

[180] ECJ, Case 28/81 *Commission v Italy* [1981] E.C.R. 2577, para. 6; ECJ, Case 29/81 *Commission v Italy* [1981] E.C.R. 2585, para. 6.

[181] ECJ, Case 293/85 *Commission v Belgium* [1988] E.C.R. 305, para. 20.

[182] For an example, see ECJ, Case 74/82 *Commission v Ireland* [1984] E.C.R. 317, para. 13.

[183] ECJ, Case C-1/00 *Commission v France* [2001] E.C.R. I-9989, para. 53; ECJ, Case C-287/00 *Commission v Germany* [2002] E.C.R. I-5811, para. 17; ECJ, Case C-350/02 *Commission v Netherlands* [2004] E.C.R. I-6213, para. 19; ECJ, *Commission v Netherlands* [2010] E.C.R. I-40*, Summ. pub., paras 21–22.

[184] ECJ (order of 11 July 1995), Case C-266/94 *Commission v Spain* [1995] E.C.R. I-1975. Compare ECJ, Case C-362/01 *Commission v Ireland* [2002] E.C.R. I-11433, paras 19–22.

*(b)   The requirement for the letter of formal notice and the reasoned opinion to accord
with the application by which an action for failure to fulfil obligations is brought
before the Court of Justice*

(i)   Consistency between the pre-litigation stage and the application

5.52   Since the subject-matter of the proceedings is defined in the pre-litigation stage, the application by which the action for failure to fulfil obligations is brought before the Court of Justice must accord both with the reasoned opinion and with the letter of formal notice.[185] Where necessary, the Court will take up this point of its own motion.[186] This means that the alleged infringement of Union law must be defined in both the application and in the reasoned opinion in consistent, sufficiently precise terms, and that the application must be based on the same pleas and arguments as the reasoned opinion.[187] For example, in principle the Commission cannot

---

[185]   ECJ, Case C-340/96 *Commission v United Kingdom* [1999] E.C.R. I-2023, para. 36; ECJ, Case C-350/02 *Commission v Netherlands* [2004] E.C.R. I-6213, paras 19–20; ECJ, Case C-186/06 *Commission v Spain* [2007] E.C.R. I-12093, paras 16–17 (complaint in application not mentioned in either the letter of formal notice or reasoned opinion held inadmissible). Compare ECJ, Case C-475/08 *Commission v Belgium* [2009] E.C.R. I-11503, paras 20–23 (rights of defence of Member State not undermined by change of relevant Treaty provision constituting basis for complaint); ECJ, Case C-251/09 *Commission v Cyprus* [2011] E.C.R. I-13*, Summ. pub., paras 19–24 (clerical error by Commission in specifying provision of Union law allegedly infringed by the Member State concerned in its reasoned opinion does not suffice where Member State itself referred to correct provision in its response to the reasoned opinion). It goes without saying that the application must accord with the general requirements of Art. 21 of the Statute and Art. 120 of the ECJ Rules of Procedure: see, e.g. ECJ, Case C-52/90 *Commission v Denmark* [1992] E.C.R. I-2187, para.17; ECJ, Case C-141/10 *Commission v Netherlands*, not reported, para. 15. For recent examples where the application, or a complaint specified therein, failed to satisfy these requirements and was held inadmissible: see ECJ, Case C-99/04 *Commission v United Kingdom* [2006] E.C.R. I-4003, paras 17–23; ECJ, Case C-199/04 *Commission v United Kingdom* [2007] E.C.R. I-1221, paras 21–26; ECJ, Case C-195/04 *Commission v Finland* [2007] E.C.R. I-3351; ECJ, Case C-522/04 *Commission v Belgium* [2007] E.C.R. I-5701, paras 33–34; ECJ, Case C-165/08 *Commission v Poland* [2009] E.C.R. I-6843, paras 43–48; ECJ, Case C-487/08 *Commission v Spain* [2010] E.C.R. I-4843, paras 71–75. In particular, where the Commission does not include a complaint in its heads of claim, but only in the grounds of the application, the complaint has been ruled inadmissible by the Court: ECJ, Case C-255/04 *Commission v France* [2006] E.C.R. I-5251, paras 24–26. See further paras 25.03–25.27.

[186]   See, e.g. ECJ, Case C-417/02 *Commission v Greece* [2004] E.C.R. I-7973, paras 15–16; ECJ, Case C-160/08 *Commission v Germany* [2010] E.C.R. I-3713, paras 40–52 (ruling not only complaints alleged for the first time in application as compared to pre-litigation procedure inadmissible, but also those alleged for the first time in reply); ECJ (judgment of 21 December 2011), Case C-271/09 *Commission v Poland*, not reported, para. 25; ECJ (judgment of 15 November 2012), Case C-34/11 *Commission v Portugal*, not reported, para. 42. See also ECJ, Case C-580/03 *Commission v United Kingdom* [2006] E.C.R. I-3969, paras 60–64 (where the Commission failed to include a complaint in its application, even if it was mentioned in the letter of formal notice, reasoned opinion, and its reply, the complaint was held inadmissible). More generally, the Court may examine of its own motion whether the various conditions laid down by Art. 258 TFEU for bringing an action for failure to fulfil obligations are satisfied: ECJ, Case C-487/08 *Commission v Spain* [2010] E.C.R. I-4843, para. 70 (and case-law cited therein).

[187]   See, e.g. ECJ, Case C-157/91 *Commission v Netherlands* [1992] E.C.R. I-5899, para. 16; ECJ, Case 306/91 *Commission v Italy* [1993] E.C.R. I-2133, para. 22; ECJ, Case C-243/89 *Commission v Denmark* [1993] E.C.R. I-3353, para. 13; ECJ, Case C-296/92 *Commission v Italy* [1994] E.C.R. I-1, para. 11; ECJ (judgment of 7 September 2004), Case C-469/02 *Commission v Belgium*, not reported, paras 17–21; ECJ, Case C-441/02 *Commission v Germany* [2006] E.C.R. I-3449, paras 59–64 (and case-law cited therein); ECJ, Case C-211/08 *Commission v Spain* [2010] E.C.R. I-5267, paras 33–38. The fact that the Commission changes the grounds supporting a particular plea in the application as compared to the pre-litigation procedure will render that plea inadmissible: ECJ, Case C-186/06 *Commission v Spain* [2007] E.C.R. I-12093, paras 18–23. See also ECJ (judgment of 15 November 2012), Case C-34/11 *Commission v Portugal*, not reported, paras 43 and 46–51: the absence of an indispensable element from the content of the application initiating proceedings, such as the period during which the Member State concerned, according to the Commission's assertions, has infringed Union law, does not satisfy the requirements of coherence, clarity, and precision.

extend an action brought against a Member State for failing to transpose a directive in national law to cover the infringement of failing in practice to comply with provisions of the directive where that complaint was not raised during the pre-litigation stage.[188] However, the statement of the subject-matter of the proceedings in the reasoned opinion does not have to be exactly the same as the form of order sought in the application if the subject-matter of the proceedings has not been extended or altered but simply restated in greater detail[189] or if the subject-matter—compared to the pre-litigation proceedings—has been limited.[190]

Since it was, however, apparent from the documents submitted by the Member State concerned to the Commission on which the letter of formal notice had been based that the infringement related to the period 2005–2007, the application was declared admissible within these limits.

[188] ECJ, Case C-237/90 *Commission v Germany* [1992] E.C.R. I-5973, paras 20–22. But see ECJ, Case C-32/05 *Commission v Luxembourg* [2006] E.C.R. I-11323, paras 54–56: under circumstances in which the Member State concerned failed to mention any measure transposing the directive in question in the course of the pre-litigation procedure and it was not until after the Commission brought proceedings before the Court of Justice that that Member State submitted, in its defence, that a law transposing the directive in question had been adopted, the Court held that if the pre-litigation procedure attained its objective of protecting the rights of the Member State concerned, the latter could not complain that the Commission had extended or altered the subject-matter of the action as defined in the pre-litigation procedure on the grounds that the Commission, after alleging a failure to transpose a directive, has specified in its reply that the implementation pleaded for the first time by the Member State concerned in its defence is incorrect or incomplete so far as certain provisions of the directive are concerned. Where the Commission has given a Member State formal notice of a failure to transpose a directive and the Member State adopts some implementing measures after the pre-litigation stage but not all those necessary in order to transpose the directive, the Commission may restrict the form of order sought in the application made to the Court to those provisions not yet implemented at that time: ECJ, Case C-132/94 *Commission v Ireland* [1995] E.C.R. I-4789, paras 7–9; but see ECJ, Case C-274/93 *Commission v Luxembourg* [1996] E.C.R. I-2019, paras 12–13. In a case where the Commission specified that a Member State had breached 'in particular' certain provisions of an EU measure, the Court rejected the form of order sought to the extent of provisions other than those mentioned expressly therein: ECJ, Case C-343/08 *Commission v Czech Republic* [2010] E.C.R. I-275, paras 24–28. Similarly, the Commission cannot extend the subject-matter beyond the national provisions indicated in the pre-litigation procedure: ECJ (judgment of 27 June 2013), Case C-596/10 *Commission v Poland*, not reported, para. 30.

[189] See, e.g. ECJ, Case C-185/00 *Commission v Finland* [2003] E.C.R. I-14189, para. 87: the fact that in the application the Commission sets out in detail the complaints it had already made in a more general way in the letter of formal notice and the reasoned opinion has no effect on the scope of the proceedings; ECJ, Case C-279/94 *Commission v Italy* [1997] E.C.R. I-4743, para. 25; ECJ, Case C-52/00 *Commission v France* [2002] E.C.R. I-3827, para. 44; ECJ, Case C-171/08 *Commission v Portugal* [2010] E.C.R. I-6817, paras 25–29. See also ECJ, Case C-139/00 *Commission v Spain* [2002] E.C.R. I-6407, para. 19: the Commission can reword the complaints in the application to take account of additional evidence produced after notification of the reasoned opinion; ECJ, Case C-484/06 *Commission v United Kingdom* [2006] E.C.R. I-7471, paras 25–27: the fact that the Commission confined itself to criticism of certain national guidelines to substantiate a complaint of failure to implement correctly certain provisions of a directive, whereas the application was directed more generally at the lack of adequate national measures to ensure full and effective implementation of the directive, was held admissible because the subject-matter defined in the reasoned opinion had not been changed; ECJ, Case C-458/08 *Commission v Portugal* [2010] E.C.R. I-11599, paras 45–48: the fact that in its application the Commission set out in detail arguments which had already been put forward in general terms in the letter of formal notice and the reasoned opinion did not alter the subject of the infringement, and in those circumstances, 'there is no requirement that the Commission's arguments should, at the application stage, specifically relate to the details of responses given by the [Member State concerned] during the pre-litigation procedure, which the Commission has, moreover, largely reproduced in its application'. Compare ECJ, Case C-256/98 *Commission v France* [2000] E.C.R. I-2487, paras 29–33, where, in its reply, the Commission amends its grounds of complaint so as to go beyond a mere restatement, albeit in greater detail, of the initial complaints, or thereby raises submissions before the Court which were not put forward during the pre-litigation procedure or in the application initiating the proceedings, the Court will hold that the Commission must be deemed to have withdrawn its original complaints and declare the application inadmissible.

[190] See, e.g. ECJ, Case C-134/10 *Commission v Belgium* [2011] E.C.R. I-1053, para. 24 (and further citations therein). See also ECJ, Case C-117/02 *Commission v Portugal* [2004] E.C.R. I-5517, paras 52–55:

Moreover, an application will be admissible only insofar as the Commission adduces matters of fact and law which support the conclusions set out in general terms in the reasoned opinion and the application.[191]

(ii) Infringement relates to a cluster of acts

5.53 Where an action for failure to fulfil obligations relates, not to a single act, but to a cluster of acts, each involving a separate infringement, the Member State must have been given an opportunity in the pre-litigation stage to set forth its defence to each breach of which it stands accused. If the letter of formal notice referred only to certain isolated cases, the action cannot extend to the whole collection of acts categorized as infringements. In this event, the application will be admissible only to the extent to which the acts complained of in the application were also dealt with in the pre-litigation stage.[192]

(iii) Modification of national and EU legislation

5.54 If, in both the pre-litigation stage (the letter of formal notice and the reasoned opinion) and in its application, the Commission complains of a specific shortcoming on the part of the Member State, the latter cannot claim that the application is irregular on the grounds that the same shortcoming was due in the pre-litigation stage to a different national provision than the one to which it was attributable at the time when the action was brought. This is because the shortcoming with which the Member State is charged is not the existence of a specific provision incompatible with Union law, but the specific shortcoming arising as a result of such provision. As a result, a change in the national provision in the course of or after the pre-litigation procedure does not jeopardize the admissibility of the action for failure to fulfil obligations.[193] Neither does the opposite situation affect the admissibility of the application. Where Union law changes in the course of the pre-litigation procedure (after the submission of a letter of formal notice and of the reasoned opinion), the Commission may still bring, for example, an admissible application for a declaration of failure to fulfil obligations

---

the Commission can base its application on a complaint which was raised only in the alternative in the pre-litigation procedure insofar as the complaint was set out in the reasoned opinion; ECJ, Case C-203/03 *Commission v Austria* [2005] E.C.R. I-935, para. 29: to the extent that national legislation is modified during the pre-litigation procedure, the action brought by the Commission may relate to provisions of national law which are not the same as those referred to in the reasoned opinion.

[191] ECJ, Case C-429/97 *Commission v France* [2001] E.C.R. I-637, para. 56; ECJ (judgment of 15 November 2012), Case C-34/11 *Commission v Portugal*, not reported, para. 49.

[192] ECJ, Case 309/84 *Commission v Italy* [1986] E.C.R. 599, paras 15–16.

[193] ECJ, Case 45/64 *Commission v Italy* [1965] E.C.R. 857, at 864–5; ECJ, Case C-42/89 *Commission v Belgium* [1990] E.C.R. I-2821, para. 11; ECJ, Case C-105/91 *Commission v Greece* [1992] E.C.R. I-5871, para. 13; ECJ, Case C-11/95 *Commission v Belgium* [1996] E.C.R. I-4115, para. 74; ECJ, Case C-375/95 *Commission v Greece* [1997] E.C.R. I-5981, para. 38; ECJ, Case C-203/03 *Commission v Austria* [2005] E.C.R. I-935, paras 27–32; ECJ, Case C-98/03 *Commission v Germany* [2006] E.C.R. I-53, paras 24–29 (and case-law cited therein); ECJ, Case C-194/05 *Commission v Italy* [2007] E.C.R. I-11661, paras 18–23; ECJ, Case C-241/08 *Commission v France* [2010] E.C.R. I-1697, paras 12–13. However, in ECJ, Case C-177/03 *Commission v France* [2004] E.C.R. I-11671, para. 21, the Court ruled that where the relevant national provisions have fundamentally changed between the expiry of the period laid down for compliance with the reasoned opinion and the lodging of the application, that change in circumstances may render the judgment to be given by the Court otiose. According to the Court, in such situations, it may be preferable for the Commission not to bring an action (which would, however, be admissible) but to issue a new reasoned opinion precisely identifying the complaints that it intends pursuing, having regard to the changed circumstances.

in respect of an original version of a subsequently amended or withdrawn measure if the obligations are retained in the new provisions.[194]

(iv) Infringements committed after the notification of the reasoned opinion

5.55 The requirement that the reasoned opinion and the application must accord with each other does not preclude infringements committed by the Member State after notification of the reasoned opinion from nevertheless being covered by the application, provided that the conduct at issue is of the same kind as that complained of in that opinion. Accordingly, the Court of Justice is entitled to take account of administrative practices that were applied after the reasoned opinion was given but were substantively the same as those referred to in the reasoned opinion.[195] Factual circumstances referred to in the reasoned opinion that continued after it was given may unquestionably be reviewed by the Court of Justice for the whole of their duration.[196]

(v) Measures taken in order to comply with the reasoned opinion

5.56 An infringement arising where a Member State takes measures in order to eliminate an infringement complained of by the Commission may be the subject of an action for failure to fulfil obligations only if a new pre-litigation stage is held. This is because the infringement resulting from the measures in question is not the same as the breach originally complained of. It is therefore impossible to bring a new action on the basis of the original pre-litigation procedure without infringing the requirement that the subject-matter of the reasoned opinion and the application must be the same.[197]

(vi) New application may remedy defects

5.57 If the Court declares an application inadmissible on the grounds that the application does not square with the reasoned opinion, the Commission may remedy the defects by submitting a new application based on the same complaints, pleas in law, and arguments as the reasoned opinion. If it does this, it is not under a duty to start the pre-litigation stage afresh or to issue a supplementary reasoned opinion.[198]

(c) Existence of a failure to fulfil obligations

(i) Infringement no longer exists on the expiry of the period prescribed in the reasoned opinion

5.58 In principle, an action for failure to fulfil obligations is admissible only if the infringement complained of exists on the expiry of the period prescribed by the reasoned

---

[194] See, e.g. ECJ, Case C-365/97 *Commission v Italy* [1999] E.C.R. I-7773, para. 36; ECJ, Case C-492/08 *Commission v France* [2010] E.C.R. I-5471, paras 31–32; ECJ, Case C-508/09 *Commission v Italy* [2011] E.C.R. I-18*, Summ. pub., paras 19–20 (and further citations therein). As a related point, even if the Union law measure constituting the basis for the infringement has been repealed by a subsequent measure, if it was in force by the expiry of the date specified in the reasoned opinion, the action is not devoid of purpose and hence admissible: see, e.g. ECJ, Case C-61/08 *Commission v Greece* [2011] E.C.R. I-4399, paras 123–124.

[195] ECJ, Case 42/82 *Commission v France* [1983] E.C.R. 1013, para. 20; ECJ, Case 113/86 *Commission v Italy* [1988] E.C.R. 607, para. 11. See also ECJ, Case C-221/04 *Commission v Spain* [2006] E.C.R. I-4515, paras 27–29.

[196] ECJ, Case 42/82 *Commission v France*, para. 20.

[197] ECJ, Case 7/69 *Commission v Italy* [1970] E.C.R. 111, paras 4–5; for further examples, see Case 391/85 *Commission v Belgium* [1988] E.C.R. 579 and ECJ, Case C-207/97 *Commission v Belgium* [1999] E.C.R. I-275, para. 25.

[198] ECJ, Case C-57/94 *Commission v Italy* [1995] E.C.R. I-1249, para. 14.

opinion.[199] The action is to no purpose if the Member State has taken measures in time in order to eliminate the infringement at issue.[200]

Similarly, the application will be to no purpose where all the legal effects of the national conduct at issue had been exhausted on the expiry of the period prescribed by the reasoned opinion.[201] Thus, as far as concerns the award of public procurement contracts, an action for failure to fulfil obligations will be inadmissible if, when the period prescribed in the reasoned opinion expired, the contract in question had already been completely performed.[202]

(ii) Infringement ceases after the prescribed period in the reasoned opinion

5.59 If the Member State has not taken measures in time, the application will be admissible. Even if the Member State remedies the infringement after the prescribed period has expired but before the action is brought, the application will still be admissible. Under settled case-law, the question whether a Member State has failed to fulfil its obligations must be determined by reference to the situation in that Member State at the time of the deadline set down in the reasoned opinion and thus the Court cannot take account of any subsequent changes.[203] In the light of the potential liability on the part of the Member State, there remains an interest for the Union, other Member States, and individuals in the Court's making a finding that

---

[199] ECJ, Case C-166/97 *Commission v France* [1999] E.C.R. I-1719, para. 18; ECJ, Case C-384/99 *Commission v Belgium* [2000] E.C.R. I-10633, para. 16; ECJ, Case C-147/00 *Commission v France* [2001] E.C.R. I-2387, para. 26; ECJ, Case C-119/00 *Commission v Luxembourg* [2001] E.C.R. I-4795, para. 14; ECJ, Case C-29/01 *Commission v Spain* [2002] E.C.R. I-2503, para. 11; ECJ, Case C-525/03 *Commission v Italy* [2005] E.C.R. I-9405, paras 8–17; ECJ, Case C-221/04 *Commission v Spain* [2006] E.C.R. I-4515, paras 23–26; ECJ, Case C-487/08 *Commission v Spain* [2010] E.C.R. I-4843, para. 34 (and case-law cited therein). As regards matters relating to the obligations placed on Member States prior to the date of accession, compare ECJ, Case C-350/08 *Commission v Lithuania* [2010] E.C.R. I-10525, with ECJ, Case C-508/08 *Commission v Malta* [2010] E.C.R. I-10589. Where the Commission brings an action under Art. 108(2) TFEU on the grounds that the Member State concerned has not complied with a decision requiring unlawful State aid to be repaid, the reference date for determining the failure to fulfil obligations is that provided for in the decision or, where appropriate, that subsequently fixed by the Commission: ECJ, Case C-378/98 *Commission v Belgium* [2001] E.C.R. I-5107, para. 26; ECJ, Case C-99/02 *Commission v Italy* [2004] E.C.R. I-3353, para. 24.

[200] ECJ, Case 240/86 *Commission v Greece* [1988] E.C.R. 1835, para. 16; ECJ, Case C-439/99 *Commission v Italy* [2002] E.C.R. I-305, paras 16–17.

[201] See, e.g. ECJ, Case C-362/90 *Commission v Italy* [1992] E.C.R. I-2353, paras 11–13; ECJ, Case C-525/03 *Commission v Italy* [2005] E.C.R. I-9405, paras 15–17. Compare, e.g. ECJ, Case C-456/05 *Commission v Germany* [2007] E.C.R. I-10517, paras 16–20 and ECJ, Case C-20/09 *Commission v Portugal* [2011] E.C.R. I-2637, paras 31–38 (and further citations therein): finding action admissible because disputed national provisions continued to produce effects; ECJ (judgment of 15 November 2012), Case C-34/11 *Commission v Portugal*, not reported, para. 48: finding action in relation to a past situation admissible. See also ECJ, Case C-221/04 *Commission v Spain* [2006] E.C.R. I-4515, paras 24–26: finding action inadmissible in relation to a permit that expired before deadline specified in reasoned opinion.

[202] See, e.g. ECJ (judgment of 9 September 2004), Case C-125/03 *Commission v Germany*, not reported, paras 12–13 (action was admissible, since the contracts were not completely performed); ECJ, Case C-394/02 *Commission v Greece* [2005] E.C.R. I-4713 paras 18–19 (action was admissible, since only 85 per cent of the works had been completed when the period prescribed by the reasoned opinion expired); ECJ, Case C-227/05 *Commission v Greece* [2007] E.C.R. I-8203, paras 23–41 (action was inadmissible because contracts at issue were exhausted and there was inadequate proof of recurrence); ECJ, Case C-536/07 *Commission v Germany* [2009] E.C.R. I-10355, paras 23–30 (action was admissible because the contract in question, that the project at issue viewed as a whole, was not completely performed); ECJ, Case C-199/07 *Commission v Greece* [2009] E.C.R. I-10669, paras 26–27 (action was admissible, since the contract at issue had not run its full course).

[203] See, e.g. ECJ, Case C-487/08 *Commission v Spain* [2010] E.C.R. I-4843, paras 35–36 (and further citations therein); ECJ, Case C-350/08 *Commission v Lithuania* [2010] E.C.R. I-10525, para. 30 (and further citations therein); ECJ, Case C-383/09 *Commission v France* [2011] E.C.R. I-4869, para. 22 (and further citations therein).

there has been an infringement. The finding may then serve as the basis for claims for damages.[204]

(iii) Acknowledgement of the infringement by the Member State

The fact that the Member State acknowledges that it has failed to fulfil its obligations and **5.60** its resultant liability during the pre-litigation stage of the procedure or after the action has been brought before the Court of Justice does not mean that the application is to no purpose. Otherwise, the Member State would be at liberty, at any time during the proceedings, to have them brought to an end without any judicial determination of the breach of obligations and of the basis of its liability and the exclusive jurisdiction of the Court of Justice to make a determination—after an action has been brought—as to whether or not Union law has been infringed would be impaired.[205]

(d) Time limits

(i) Calculation of the expiry of the time limit laid down in the reasoned opinion

While there does not seem to have been much litigation on this issue to date, the expiry of **5.61** the time limit laid down in the reasoned opinion is calculated from the date of receipt or notification of the Member State, not the date specified in the reasoned opinion itself.[206]

(ii) Commission's discretion

In exercising its powers in connection with an action for failure to fulfil obligations, the **5.62** Commission does not have to comply with any specific time limits. Consequently, as established by the case-law, it has discretion in the sense that it is free to judge at what time it starts the pre-litigation stage and at what time after the expiry of the period prescribed by the reasoned opinion it brings an action before the Court of Justice.[207]

---

[204] ECJ, Case 39/72 *Commission v Italy* [1973] E.C.R. 101, para. 11; ECJ, Case 309/84 *Commission v Italy* [1986] E.C.R. 599, para. 18; ECJ, Case 103/84 *Commission v Italy* [1986] E.C.R. 1759, para. 8; ECJ, Case 154/85 *Commission v Italy* [1987] E.C.R. 2717, para. 6; Case 240/86 *Commission v Greece* [1988] E.C.R. 1835, para. 14; ECJ, Case 283/86 *Commission v Belgium* [1988] E.C.R. 3271, para. 6; ECJ, Case C-249/88 *Commission v Belgium* [1991] E.C.R. I-1275, para. 41; ECJ, Case C-361/88 *Commission v Germany* [1991] E.C.R. I-2567, para. 31; Case C-59/89 *Commission v Germany* [1991] E.C.R. I-2607, para. 35; ECJ, Case C-29/90 *Commission v Greece* [1992] E.C.R. I-1971, para. 12; ECJ, Case C-280/89 *Commission v Ireland* [1992] E.C.R. I-6185, para. 7; ECJ, Case C-317/92 *Commission v Germany* [1994] E.C.R. I-2039, para. 3; ECJ, Case C-289/94 *Commission v Italy* [1996] E.C.R. I-4405, para. 20; ECJ, Case C-119/00 *Commission v Luxembourg* [2001] E.C.R. I-4795, para. 17; ECJ, Case C-299/01 *Commission v Luxembourg* [2002] E.C.R. I-5899, para. 11; ECJ, Case C-209/02 *Commission v Austria* [2004] E.C.R. I-1211, paras 16–19; ECJ, Case C-168/03 *Commission v Spain* [2004] E.C.R. I-8227, para. 24.

[205] ECJ, Case C-243/89 *Commission v Denmark* [1993] E.C.R. I-3353, para. 30; ECJ (judgment of 3 March 2005), Case C-414/03 *Commission v Germany*, not reported, paras 8–9. An application from a Member State for the proceedings to be stayed in order to allow it to put an end to the infringement and hence in the expectation of a hypothetical withdrawal of the action by the Commission cannot be granted, since a failure to fulfil obligations must be determined by reference to the situation prevailing in the Member State at the end of the period prescribed in the reasoned opinion (ECJ, Case C-366/00 *Commission v Luxembourg* [2002] E.C.R. I-1749, paras 10–12; ECJ, Case C-294/09 *Commission v Ireland* [2010] E.C.R. I-46*, Summ. pub., para. 20 (and case-law cited therein)).

[206] See ECJ, Case C-503/04 *Commission v Germany* [2007] E.C.R. I-6153, paras 19–20; ECJ, Case C-369/07 *Commission v Greece* [2009] E.C.R. I-5703, paras 10, 44. For further discussion of the calculation of time limits, see paras 23.26 *et seq.*

[207] ECJ, Case 7/68 *Commission v Italy* [1968] E.C.R. 423, at 428; ECJ, Case 7/71 *Commission v France* [1971] E.C.R. 1003, paras 2–8; ECJ, Case 324/82 *Commission v Belgium* [1984] E.C.R. 1861, para. 12; ECJ, Case C-56/90 *Commission v United Kingdom* [1993] E.C.R. I-4109, para. 15; ECJ, Case C-317/92 *Commission v Germany* [1994] E.C.R. I-2039, paras 4–5; ECJ, Case C-333/99 *Commission v France* [2001] E.C.R. I-1025, para. 25 (in that case the Commission brought an action seven years after it had received the

Yet, the Commission may not abuse its discretion.[208] For instance, if the pre-litigation procedure is excessively long, the Member State may find it more difficult to refute the Commission's arguments, and this may constitute an infringement of the rights of the defence. The Member State has to prove that the unusual length of the pre-litigation procedure had adverse effects on the way in which it conducted its defence.[209] Only if it succeeds in proving this will the application be declared inadmissible. However, the burden of proof is difficult for the Member State to discharge, since there will generally be factors justifying the unusually long lapse of time between the 'infringement' and the commencement of the procedure or the unusual duration of the pre-litigation stage, causing them not to be regarded as excessive.[210] A good illustration is *Commission v Netherlands ('Open skies')*,[211] in which, despite the Netherlands' arguments that six years had elapsed before the Commission's initiation of the pre-litigation procedure and four years had elapsed between its issuance of the reasoned opinion and bringing the action before the Court of Justice, the Court found that the Netherlands failed to prove that the unusual duration of the proceedings had any effect on the way in which it organized its defence and rejected its attempt to invoke the principle of protection of legitimate expectations in this regard.[212]

(2) Aspects of the treatment given to the substantive claim

(a) Burden of proof

(i) Commission bears the burden of proof

5.63 The burden of proof as regards each head of claim constituting the failure to fulfil obligations has to be discharged by the Commission.[213] This means that it is for the

---

observations of the Member State concerned on the reasoned opinion); ECJ, Case C-40/00 *Commission v France* [2001] E.C.R. I-4539, para. 23; ECJ, Case C-297/08 *Commission v Italy* [2010] E.C.R. I-1749, para. 7; ECJ, Case C-311/09 *Commission v Poland* [2010] E.C.R. I-55*, Summ. pub., paras 13–21. Arguments concerning purported violation of the principle of legal certainty, the protection of legitimate expectations, and the principle of sound administration have been rejected, though the Court of Justice has based its rulings on the specific situations at issue, as opposed to excluding their potential applicability for rendering the action inadmissible altogether: see ECJ, Case C-508/03 *Commission v United Kingdom* [2006] E.C.R. I-3969, paras 66–69; ECJ, Case C-350/08 *Commission v Lithuania* [2010] E.C.R. I-10525, paras 36–39. See, however, ECJ (judgment of 7 February 2013), Case C-122/11 *Commission v Belgium*, not reported, para. 50, where the Court criticizes the Commission for waiting too long to bring an action before the Court.

[208] ECJ, Case C-177/03 *Commission v France* [2004] E.C.R. I-11671, para. 17.

[209] See, *inter alia*, ECJ, Case C-96/89 *Commission v Netherlands* [1991] E.C.R. I-2461, paras 14–16; ECJ, Case C-475/98 *Commission v Austria* [2002] E.C.R. I-9797, paras 34–39; ECJ, Case C-33/04 *Commission v Luxembourg* [2005] E.C.R. I-10621, paras 75–78 (and further citations therein); ECJ, Case C-490/04 *Commission v Germany* [2007] E.C.R. I-6095, paras 23–28; ECJ, Case C-562/07 *Commission v Spain* [2007] E.C.R. I-9553, paras 21–22; ECJ, Case C-546/07 *Commission v Germany* [2010] E.C.R. I-439, paras 21–28.

[210] In Case 7/71 *Commission v France* [1971] E.C.R. 1003, the Commission applied to the Court of Justice in 1971 to find an infringement which had existed since 1965. The infringement did not come to light until 1968, and the Commission formally started the procedure in April 1970 following informal contacts with the Member State. In Case 324/82 *Commission v Belgium* [1984] E.C.R. 1861, the Commission waited until the directive concerned had been implemented in all the Member States before investigating the contested Belgian measures. In Case C-96/89 *Commission v Netherlands* [1991] E.C.R. I-2461, the Commission waited for the Court of Justice to give judgment in another case and for the reaction of the Netherlands Government. See also ECJ (judgment of 2 December 2004), Case C-42/03 *Commission v Spain*, not reported, paras 21–25; ECJ, Case C-350/08 *Commission v Lithuania* [2010] E.C.R. I-10525, paras 34–35.

[211] ECJ, Case C-523/04 *Commission v Netherlands ('Open skies')* [2007] E.C.R. I-3267.

[212] ECJ, Case C-523/04 *'Open skies'*, paras 27–30.

[213] ECJ, Case 96/81 *Commission v Netherlands* [1982] E.C.R. 1791, para. 6; ECJ, Case C-249/88 *Commission v Belgium* [1991] E.C.R. I-1275, para. 6; ECJ, Case C-210/91 *Commission v Greece* [1992] E.C.R. I-6735, para. 22; ECJ, Case C-375/90 *Commission v Greece* [1993] E.C.R. I-2055, para. 33; ECJ, Case

Commission to prove the alleged failure to fulfil obligations by placing before the Court of Justice all the information needed to enable the Court to establish that the obligation has not been fulfilled.[214] It has to adduce sufficient evidence to the Court of Justice that the infringement existed at the time when the period prescribed by the reasoned opinion expired.[215] The Commission may not rely on any presumptions (of law) in this connection.[216]

It is settled case-law that the scope of national laws, regulations, or administrative provisions must be assessed in the light of the interpretation given to them by national courts. Therefore, if a national provision can be interpreted in two ways—one consistent with and another one inconsistent with Union law—the Commission will have to prove that the national courts interpret the domestic provision at issue inconsistently with Union law.[217]

C-68/99 *Commission v Germany* [2001] E.C.R. I-1865, para. 38; ECJ (judgment of 15 July 2004), Case C-419/03 *Commission v France*, not reported, paras 7–8; ECJ, Case C-297/08 *Commission v Italy* [2010] E.C.R. I-1749, paras 101–113. However, it is not sufficient for the Commission, in order to claim that the defendant Member State has not complied with a provision of Union law, merely to cite that provision in the section of the reasoned opinion or of the application which covers the legal context and which is purely descriptive and lacking of any explanatory character (ECJ, Case C-202/99 *Commission v Italy* [2001] E.C.R. I-9319, para. 21). For recent examples in which the Commission failed to carry its burden of proof, see, e.g. ECJ, Case C-580/03 *Commission v United Kingdom* [2006] E.C.R. I-3969, paras 92–94; ECJ, Case C-416/07 *Commission v Greece* [2009] E.C.R. I-7883, paras 97–101; ECJ, Case C-241/08 *Commission v France* [2010] E.C.R. I-1697, paras 22–25; ECJ, Case C-94/09 *Commission v France* [2010] E.C.R. I-4261, paras 44–47; ECJ, Case C-105/08 *Commission v Portugal* [2010] E.C.R. I-5331, paras 26–31; ECJ, Case C-490/09 *Commission v Luxembourg* [2011] E.C.R. I-247, paras 51–63. Furthermore, while the Commission may fail to carry its burden of proof as regards one of the grounds alleged to substantiate the alleged infringement, it may nonetheless carry its burden with respect to others, with the result that its action is partially well-founded: see, e.g. ECJ, Case C-383/09 *Commission v France* [2011] E.C.R. I-4869, paras 38–39.

[214] See, e.g. ECJ, Case C-490/09 *Commission v Luxembourg* [2011] E.C.R. I-247, paras 49–50 (and further citations therein, including mention of the requirements flowing from Art. 120(c) of the ECJ Rules of Procedure). See also ECJ, Case C-400/08 *Commission v Spain* [2011] E.C.R. I-1915, paras 46–50: on the one hand, with respect to certain provisions of the national law in question, the Commission's application did not achieve the requisite level of precision rendering the claims inadmissible, whereas for other provisions, despite the lack of precision, the Court had sufficient information before it to understand the scope of the infringement and the Member State was able to deploy its defence, thereby finding those claims admissible.

[215] See, e.g. ECJ, Case 121/84 *Commission v Italy* [1986] E.C.R. 107, paras 10–12; ECJ, Case 188/84 *Commission v France* [1986] E.C.R. 419, paras 38–39; ECJ, Case 298/86 *Commission v Belgium* [1988] E.C.R. 4343, para. 15; ECJ, Case C-157/91 *Commission v Netherlands* [1992] E.C.R. I-5899, para. 12; ECJ, Case C-166/97 *Commission v France* [1999] E.C.R. I-1719, para. 40; ECJ, Case C-337/98 *Commission v France* [2000] E.C.R. I-8377, para. 45; ECJ, Case C-347/98 *Commission v Belgium* [2001] E.C.R. I-3327, para. 39; ECJ, Case C-263/99 *Commission v Italy* [2001] E.C.R. I-4195, para. 27; ECJ, C-340/09 *Commission v Spain* [2010] E.C.R. I-165*, Summ. pub., para. 39; ECJ, C-306/08 *Commission v Spain* [2011] E.C.R. I-4541, paras 63–66. See also ECJ (judgment of 16 September 2004), Case C-248/02 *Commission v Italy*, not reported, para. 28 (in assessing whether or not there has been an infringement, the Court takes no account of information provided to the Commission by the Member State after the expiry of the period prescribed in the reasoned opinion).

[216] See, e.g. ECJ, Case 290/87 *Commission v Netherlands* [1989] E.C.R. 3083, para. 11; ECJ, Case C-61/94 *Commission v Germany* [1996] E.C.R. I-3989, para. 61; ECJ, Case C-214/98 *Commission v Greece* [2000] E.C.R. I-9601, para. 42; ECJ, Case C-147/00 *Commission v France* [2001] E.C.R. I-2387, para. 27; ECJ, Case C-171/08 *Commission v Portugal* [2010] E.C.R. I-6817, paras 19–23; ECJ, Case C-458/08 *Commission v Portugal* [2010] E.C.R. I-11599, para. 54 (and further citations therein).

[217] ECJ, Case C-382/92 *Commission v United Kingdom* [1994] E.C.R. I-2435, para. 36; ECJ, Case C-300/95 *Commission v United Kingdom* [1997] E.C.R. I-2649, para. 37; ECJ, Case C-287/03 *Commission v Belgium* [2005] E.C.R. I-3761, paras 28–30.

An application from the Commission for an expert's report to be commissioned by the Court will be refused, since if it were granted the Commission itself would not be providing evidence of the alleged failure to fulfil obligations.[218]

It is only when the Commission has produced sufficient evidence of the failure to fulfil obligations that the defendant Member State has to adduce its counter arguments.[219] In this regard, it is incumbent on the Member State to challenge in substance and in detail the information produced and the consequences flowing therefrom.[220]

(ii) Duty of sincere cooperation imposed on Member States

5.64 Member States are under a duty, by virtue of Art. 4(3) TEU, to facilitate the achievement of the Commission's tasks, which consist in particular, in accordance with Art. 17(1) TEU, in ensuring that the measures taken by the institutions pursuant to the Treaties are applied.[221] It follows that the Member States are required to cooperate in good faith with the inquiries of the Commission pursuant to Arts 258–260 TFEU and to provide the Commission with all the information requested for that purpose.[222] A failure to comply with this obligation may result in a finding of a failure to fulfil an obligation under the Treaties.[223]

Many directives incorporate that duty to cooperate in good faith and to provide information in a specific provision. Such a provision will require Member States to provide clear, accurate information about the legal and administrative provisions adopted in order to

---

[218] ECJ, Case 141/87 *Commission v Italy* [1989] E.C.R. 943, para. 17.

[219] ECJ, Case 272/86 *Commission v Greece* [1988] E.C.R. 4875, para. 21.

[220] See, e.g. ECJ, Case C-390/07 *Commission v United Kingdom* [2009] E.C.R. I-214*, Summ. pub., para. 45 (and case-law cited therein); ECJ, Case C-297/08 *Commission v Italy* [2010] E.C.R. I-1749, para. 102 (and case-law cited therein). Where the Member State fails to do so, then the facts alleged by the Commission can be regarded as proven (see, e.g. ECJ, Case C-489/06 *Commission v Greece* [2009] E.C.R. I-1797, paras 40–42) and the infringement sustained (see, e.g. ECJ, Case C-507/08 *Commission v Slovak Republic* [2010] E.C.R. I-13489, paras 61–65. In the context of infringement cases concerning the fundamental freedoms, while the Commission bears the burden of proof as regards a sufficient showing that a particular act or conduct of a Member State constitutes a restriction to free movement or else the action fails (e.g. ECJ, Case C-565/08 *Commission v Italy* [2011] E.C.R. I-2101, paras 52–53), a Member State carries the burden of proof in a situation where that Member State invokes an imperative requirement as justification for derogating from the free movement rules (e.g. ECJ, Case C-110/05 *Commission v Italy* ['*Motorcyle trailers*'] [2009] E.C.R. I-519, para. 66: underscoring that such burden cannot be so extensive as to require the Member State to prove, positively, that no other conceivable measures could enable the objective to be attained under the same conditions). Once the Member State has asserted a particular justification, the burden falls to the Commission to put forward sufficient proof opposing such justifications: see, e.g. ECJ, Case C-400/08 *Commission v Spain* [2011] E.C.R. I-1915, paras 100–103; see also ECJ (judgment of 21 December 2011), Case C-28/09 *Commission v Austria*, not reported, paras 118 *et seq.*

[221] See, e.g. ECJ, Case C-33/90 *Commission v Italy* [1991] E.C.R. I-5987, para. 18; ECJ, Case C-494/01 *Commission v Ireland* [2005] E.C.R. I-3331, para. 197; ECJ, Case C-340/09 *Commission v Spain* [2010] E.C.R. I-165*, Summ. pub., para. 37 (and further citations therein).

[222] ECJ, Case C-65/91 *Commission v Greece* [1992] E.C.R. I-5245, para. 14. A Member State cannot therefore claim that the Commission's application is inadmissible because the details of the national law and practice are not specific enough (ECJ, Case C-408/97 *Commission v Netherlands* [2000] E.C.R. I-6417, para. 17).

[223] ECJ, Case C-82/03 *Commission v Italy* [2004] E.C.R. I-6635, para. 15; ECJ, Case C-494/01 *Commission v Ireland* [2005] E.C.R. I-3331, paras 195–200. See further ECJ, Case C-456/03 *Commission v Italy* [2005] E.C.R. I-5335, para. 27: 'the failure of a Member State to fulfil that obligation, whether by providing no information at all or by providing insufficiently clear and precise information, may of itself justify recourse to the procedure under [Art. 258 TFEU] in order to establish the failure to fulfil the obligation'.

implement the directive in question, which enables the Commission to ascertain whether the Member State has effectively and completely implemented it.[224]

When a directive imposes upon the Member States an obligation to provide information, the information that the Member States are thus obliged to supply to the Commission must be clear and precise. It must indicate unequivocally the laws, regulations, and administrative provisions by means of which the Member State considers that it has satisfied the various requirements imposed on it by the directive. In the absence of such information, the Commission is not in a position to ascertain whether the Member State has genuinely implemented the directive completely. The failure of a Member State to fulfil that obligation, whether by providing no information at all or by providing insufficiently clear and precise information, may of itself justify recourse to the procedure under Art. 258 TFEU in order to establish the failure to fulfil the obligation.[225]

(b) Substantive defence of the Member State

(i) Objective nature of the action

The chances of success of defence pleas that a Member State wishes to raise are determined **5.65** first by the objective nature of the action for failure to fulfil obligations. As stated in para. 5.01, the action is objective in nature and the only question raised is whether or not the defendant Member State has breached Union law.[226] In determining whether the alleged infringement took place, the Court of Justice takes no account of subjective factors invoked to justify the Member State's conduct or omission, the frequency or the scale of the circumstances complained of,[227] or of the fact that there is no evidence that the infringement of Union law was intentional.[228] No reasonableness test may be applied.

---

[224] See, e.g. ECJ, Case 274/83 *Commission v Italy* [1985] E.C.R. 1077, para. 42. No infringement of Art. 4(3) TEU will be found when the Member State's duty to cooperate can be derived from a more specific provision of Union law; only the violation of the latter provision will in such case be found: see ECJ, Case C-539/09 *Commission v Germany* [2011] E.C.R. I-11235, para. 87.

[225] ECJ, Case 96/81 *Commission v Netherlands* [1982] E.C.R. 1791, para. 8; ECJ Case C-456/03 *Commission v Italy* [2005] E.C.R. I-5335, para. 27.

[226] See, e.g. ECJ, Case 7/68 *Commission v Italy* [1968] E.C.R. 423, at 428; ECJ, Case 415/85 *Commission v Ireland* [1988] E.C.R. 3097, paras 8–9; ECJ, Case 416/85 *Commission v United Kingdom* [1988] E.C.R. 3127, paras 8–9; ECJ, Case C-140/00 *Commission v United Kingdom* [2002] E.C.R. I-10372, para. 34; ECJ, Case C-297/08 *Commission v Italy* [2010] E.C.R. I-1749, paras 81–82 (and further citations therein). See also ECJ, Case 301/81 *Commission v Belgium* [1983] E.C.R. 467, para. 8: the well-foundedness of an action under Art. 258 TFEU depends only on an objective finding of a failure to fulfil obligations and not on proof of any inertia or opposition on the part of the Member State. See further ECJ (judgment of 9 September 2004), Case C-383/02 *Commission v Italy*, not reported, paras 12–20; ECJ (judgment of 16 September 2004), Case C-248/02 *Commission v Italy*, not reported, para. 25.

[227] See, e.g. ECJ, Case C-404/99 *Commission v France* [2001] E.C.R. I-2667, para. 51; ECJ, Case C-226/01 *Commission v Denmark* [2003] E.C.R. I-1219, para. 32 (and further citations therein).

[228] See, e.g. the case-law rejecting the following as pleas in justification: difficulties in the domestic decision-making process (ECJ, Case 96/81 *Commission v Netherlands* [1982] E.C.R. 1791, para. 12; ECJ, Case 97/81 *Commission v Netherlands* [1982] E.C.R. 1819, para. 12; ECJ, Case 301/81 *Commission v Belgium* [1983] E.C.R. 467, para. 6; ECJ, Joined Cases 227/85 to 230/85 *Commission v Belgium* [1988] E.C.R. 1, para. 9; ECJ, Case C-33/90 *Commission v Italy* [1991] E.C.R. I-5987, para. 24); the fact that other Member States are also guilty of the infringement (ECJ, Case 52/75 *Commission v Italy* [1976] 277, para. 11; ECJ, Case 78/76 *Steinike & Weinlig* [1977] E.C.R. 595, para. 24; ECJ, Case 232/78 *Commission v France* [1979] E.C.R. 2729, para. 9; ECJ, Case 325/82 *Commission v Germany* [1984] E.C.R. 777, para. 11; ECJ, Case C-38/89 *Blanguernon* [1990] E.C.R. I-83, para. 7); the presence of organized crime (ECJ, Case C-297/08 *Commission v Italy* [2010] E.C.R. I-1749, paras 81–82, 84).

The Court of Justice pays no regard to the underlying reasons for the breach or to circumstances that in fact limited its adverse effects or explain the breach. It is virtually certain that a defence based on such pleas will fail. Accordingly, a Member State may not plead provisions, practices, or situations existing in its internal legal system (such as those resulting from its constitutional organization)[229] in order to justify a failure to comply with its Union obligations.[230] Moreover, the fact that the failure to fulfil obligations had no adverse effects is irrelevant.[231] Neither does the fact that a directive with direct effect produces the same result in practice as if the directive had been implemented properly and in time justify a failure to fulfil the obligation to implement it.[232] What is more, a Member State cannot rely on the principle of protection of legitimate expectations—insofar as that principle can be invoked by a Member State at all—because that defence is incompatible with the objective nature of these proceedings.[233]

Second, the special nature of Union law prevents a Member State from relying on a number of common defences in international law. For instance, a Member State cannot justify its

---

[229] See, e.g. ECJ, Case C-236/99 *Commission v Belgium* [2000] E.C.R. I-5657, para. 23; ECJ, Case C-358/03 *Commission v Austria* [2004] E.C.R. I-12055, paras 12–13: the fact that Austrian constitutional law precludes the Federal State from adopting transposition measures in the place of a Land and that only censure by the Court of Justice confers the power on the Federal State to undertake the transposition cannot justify an infringement for which the Federal State bears responsibility under Union law. Although each Member State may freely allocate areas of internal legal competence as it sees fit, the fact remains that it alone is responsible to the Union under Art. 258 TFEU for compliance with obligations arising under Union law. See further ECJ, Case C-212/06 *Gouvernement de la Communauté française and Gouvernement wallon* [2008] E.C.R. I-1683, para. 58 (and citations therein); ECJ, Case C-306/08 *Commission v Spain* [2011] E.C.R. I-4541, para. 84 (noting that infringement related solely to laws adopted by the Autonomous Community of Valencia on the basis of its regional powers in area concerned).

[230] See, e.g. ECJ, Case 52/75 *Commission v Italy* [1976] E.C.R. 277, para. 14; ECJ, Case C-45/91 *Commission v Greece* [1992] E.C.R. I-2509, paras 20–21; ECJ, Case C-166/97 *Commission v France* [1999] E.C.R. I-1719, para. 13; ECJ, Case C-473/99 *Commission v Austria* [2001] E.C.R. I-4527, para. 12; ECJ, Case C-121/07 *Commission v France* [2008] E.C.R. I-9159, para. 72; ECJ, Case C-495/08 *Commission v United Kingdom* [2009] E.C.R. I-188*, Summ. pub., paras 6–7 (and case-law cited therein); ECJ, Case C-297/08 *Commission v Italy* [2010] E.C.R. I-1749, para. 83. The argument that the rule of Union law infringed is incompatible with national public policy is therefore also inadmissible (ECJ, Case C-52/00 *Commission v France* [2002] E.C.R. I-3827, para. 33).

[231] See para. 5.09.

[232] ECJ, Case 102/79 *Commission v Belgium* [1980] E.C.R. 1473, para. 12; ECJ, Case 301/81 *Commission v Belgium* [1983] E.C.R. 467, para. 13; ECJ, Case C-433/93 *Commission v Germany* [1995] E.C.R. I-2303, para. 24; ECJ, Case C-253/95 *Commission v Germany* [1996] E.C.R. I-2423, para. 13. The obligation to ensure the full effectiveness of a directive, in accordance with its objective, cannot be interpreted as meaning that the Member States are released from adopting transposition measures where they consider that their national provisions are better than the Union provisions concerned and that the national provisions are therefore more likely to ensure that the objective pursued by the directive is achieved. According to the Court's case-law, the existence of national rules may render transposition by specific legislative or regulatory measures superfluous only if those rules actually ensure the full application of the directive by the national authorities (see, e.g. ECJ, Case C-103/02 *Commission v Italy* [2004] E.C.R. I-9127, para. 33).

[233] ECJ, Case C-83/99 *Commission v Spain* [2001] E.C.R. I-445, paras 22–27; ECJ, Case C-99/02 *Commission v Italy* [2004] E.C.R. I-3353, paras 20–21, in which the Court held that a Member State whose authorities have granted aid contrary to the procedural rules laid down in Art. 108 TFEU may not plead the legitimate expectations of recipients in order to justify a failure to comply with the obligation to take the steps necessary to implement a Commission decision instructing it to recover the aid. If it could do so, Arts 107 and 108 TFEU would be deprived of all practical force, since national authorities would thus be able to rely on their own unlawful conduct in order to render decisions taken by the Commission under those Treaty provisions ineffectual.

failure to perform its obligations by reference to the shortcomings of other Member States, since the Treaties did not merely create reciprocal obligations between the Member States, but also established a new legal order governing the procedures necessary for the purposes of having any infringement of non-CFSP Union law 'declared and punished'.[234]

(ii) Illegality of the Union act

Under the former Treaty framework, it appeared from the case-law that a Member State **5.66** could plead the illegality of a regulation on the basis of Art. 241 EC in proceedings for failure to fulfil obligations.[235] In contrast, a Member State was not entitled to raise the claim that a directive or a decision addressed to it was unlawful where it was accused of breaching such a measure and the time limit for applying for its annulment had expired, or even where it had brought an action for annulment and not at the same time a (successful) application for interim measures to suspend the contested act pending the judgment in the main proceedings.[236] The Court of Justice took the view that to allow this defence would jeopardize the stability of the system of legal remedies established by the Treaty and the principle of legal certainty on which it is based.[237] Yet, in the exceptional case where the directive or decision infringed contained such serious and manifest defects that it could be deemed non-existent, the Court of Justice could be asked to declare it non-existent, thereby making the claim of an infringement to no purpose.[238]

With the changes brought by the Lisbon Treaty, however, the status of this case-law is no longer certain. Compared to the text of former Art. 241 EC, Art. 277 TFEU provides that an objection of illegality may be raised 'in proceedings in which an act of general

---

[234] ECJ, Case 52/75 *Commission v Italy* [1976] E.C.R. 277, para. 11; ECJ, Case C-11/95 *Commission v Belgium* [1996] E.C.R. I-4115, paras 36–37; ECJ, Case C-163/99 *Portugal v Commission* [2001] E.C.R. I-2613, para. 22; ECJ (judgment of 15 July 2004), Case C-118/03 *Commission v Germany*, not reported, para. 8.

[235] ECJ, Case C-11/00 *Commission v ECB* [2003] E.C.R. I-7174, paras 74–78. Former Art. 241 EC had provided, without exception, that an objection of illegality may be raised 'in proceedings in which a regulation . . . is at issue'. See further Opinion of Advocate-General P. Mengozzi in ECJ, Case C-91/05 *Commission v Council* ('*ECOWAS*') [2008] E.C.R. I-3651, points 36–54.

[236] See further para. 9.11. In ECJ, Case C-261/99 *Commission v France* [2001] E.C.R. I-2537, the Court held in connection with an action brought under Art. 108(2) TFEU that France had failed to fulfil its obligations by not implementing a Commission decision requiring it to recover unlawful State aid. That decision was deemed to be lawful despite the action for annulment already brought by France (ECJ, Case C-17/99 *France v Commission* [2001] E.C.R. I-2481).

[237] ECJ, Case 156/77 *Commission v Belgium* [1978] E.C.R. 1881, paras 15–25; ECJ, Case 52/83 *Commission v France* [1983] E.C.R. 3707, para. 10; ECJ, Case 52/84 *Commission v Belgium* [1986] E.C.R. 89, para. 13; ECJ, Case 226/87 *Commission v Greece* [1988] E.C.R. 3611, para. 14; ECJ, Case C-74/91 *Commission v Germany* [1992] E.C.R. I-5437, para. 10 (concerning a directive); ECJ, Case C-183/91 *Commission v Greece* [1993] E.C.R. I-3131, para. 10; ECJ, Case C-1/00 *Commission v France* [2001] E.C.R. I-9989, para. 101; ECJ, Case C-52/00 *Commission v France* [2001] E.C.R. I-3827, para. 28; ECJ, Case C-194/01 *Commission v Austria* [2004] E.C.R. I-4579, para. 41; ECJ (judgment of 15 July 2004), Case C-118/03 *Commission v Germany*, not reported, para. 7; ECJ, Case C-53/05 *Commission v Portugal* [2006] E.C.R. I-6215, para. 30. This also applies to an action brought on the basis of Art. 108(2) TFEU: see, e.g. ECJ, Case C-404/97 *Commission v Portugal* [2000] E.C.R. I-4897, para. 34; ECJ, Case C-419/06 *Commission v Greece* [2008] E.C.R. I-27*, Summ. pub., para. 52.

[238] ECJ, Case 226/87 *Commission v Greece*, paras 15–16; ECJ, Case C-404/97 *Commission v Portugal* [2000] E.C.R. I-4897, para. 35. The beginnings of this case-law can be found in ECJ, Joined Cases 6/69 and 11/69 *Commission v France* [1969] E.C.R. 523, paras 11–13.

application ... is at issue'. This may conceivably encompass directives and decisions, as well as regulations, to the extent that such acts are of general application.[239] In fact, in past case-law concerning Art. 241 EC, the Court had based its approach on the absence of a provision of the Treaty expressly authorizing a Member State to plead the objection of illegality in this regard.[240]

(iii) Violation of the Treaties but compliance with Union legislation

5.67 Where the Commission deems that a national rule violates a Treaty provision, the Member State concerned can justify its national legislation by referring to the fact that it expressly complies with a provision of secondary Union law. Provisions of secondary Union law are indeed presumed to be lawful (as long as they are not annulled or declared unlawful by the Union judicature).[241]

(iv) Pleas refuting the breach in an objective manner

5.68 The Member State's defence is not restricted to a limited number of pleas. Any plea, of law or fact, which refutes the alleged breach in an objective manner is admissible. In addition, the Member State may raise defences not relied upon in the pre-litigation procedure.[242] The pleas must, however, be raised timeously in the defence.[243]

Furthermore, a Member State may claim the existence of a situation constituting *force majeure*.[244] In such a case, a Member State would have to prove that there were abnormal and unforeseeable circumstances outside of its control, the consequences of which, in spite of the exercise of all due care, could not have been avoided.[245] As demonstrated by the case-law, it is difficult for a Member State to satisfy these requirements.[246] Moreover, a Member State may plead this defence only for the period necessary in order to resolve the difficulties.[247]

---

[239] For example, in the case of a legislative directive or a decision of general scope of application such as that at issue in ECJ, Case C-80/06 *Carp* [2007] E.C.R. I-4473.

[240] See ECJ, Case C-196/07 *Commission v Spain* [2008] E.C.R. I-41*, Summ. pub., para. 34; ECJ, Case C-189/09 *Commission v Austria* [2010] E..C.R. I-99*, Summ. pub., para. 15.

[241] ECJ, Case C-475/01 *Commission v Greece* ('*Ouzo*') [2004] E.C.R. I-8923, paras 18–26; ECJ, Case C-582/08 *Commission v United Kingdom* [2010] E.C.R. I-7195, paras 47–48. See para. 5.20.

[242] ECJ, Case C-414/97 *Commission v Spain* [1999] E.C.R. I-5585, paras 18–19.

[243] ECJ, Case C-519/03 *Commission v Luxembourg* [2005] E.C.R. I-3067, para. 22: plea raised for the first time in the rejoinder was inadmissible. See also ECJ, Case C-526/08 *Commission v Luxembourg* [2010] E.C.R. I-6151, paras 48–51: pleas in defence raised for the first time in rejoinder were inadmissible, even if they had been previously submitted in substance in reply to reasoned opinion.

[244] In the case of special procedures concerning State aid under Art. 108(2) TFEU, a Member State may put forward the plea of 'absolute impossibility' (see para. 5.22). Though similarly strict, the notion of *force majeure* does not presuppose absolute impossibility: see, e.g. ECJ, Case 70/86 *Commission v Greece* [1987] E.C.R. 3545, para. 8; ECJ, Case C-297/08 *Commission v Italy* [2010] E.C.R. I-1749, para. 85.

[245] ECJ, Case C-334/08 *Commission v Italy* [2010] E.C.R. I-6869, para. 46 (and further citations therein).

[246] For a selection of examples, see ECJ, Case 33/69 *Commission v Italy* [1970] E.C.R. 93, para. 9; ECJ, Case C-70/86 *Commission v Greece* [1987] E.C.R. 3545, paras 8–11; ECJ, Case C-236/99 *Commission v Belgium* [2000] E.C.R. I-5657, paras 21–22; ECJ, Case C-105/02 *Commission v Germany* [2006] E.C.R. I-9659, para. 89; ECJ, Case C-377/03 *Commission v Belgium* [2006] E.C.R. I-9733, para. 95; ECJ, Case C-297/08 *Commission v Italy* [2010] E.C.R. I-1749, paras 85–86; ECJ, Case C-334/08 *Commission v Italy* [2010] E.C.R. I-6869, paras 47–49.

[247] ECJ, Case C-1/00 *Commission v France* [2001] E.C.R. I-9989, para. 131 (and further citations therein).

IV. Consequences

A. Result of the action

The Court of Justice either finds the infringement made out or dismisses the application.[248] **5.69**
The judgment finding the failure to fulfil obligations is purely declaratory. The infringement existed before the Court made its finding. It does not have the power to require specific measures to be taken in order to give effect to the judgment.[249] At most, it may indicate such measures as it considers necessary in order to eliminate the infringement found.[250] In addition, the Court may not set a period of time for compliance with its judgment, since Art. 260 TFEU does not confer a power on it to do so.[251] Equally, the Court may not declare acts (or failures to act) on the part of a Member State unlawful, void, or not applicable. Only the national courts have the power to do so under national law.[252] The Court of Justice may find only that the act (or failure to act) was or was not contrary to Union law.

B. Legal force of the judgment declaring that a Member State has failed to fulfil its obligations

(1) Duty for the Member State to take the necessary measures

Art. 260(1) TFEU puts the Member State that has been found by the Court of Justice to **5.70**
have failed to fulfil its Treaty obligations under a duty to take the necessary measures to comply with the Court's judgment. That duty, which also arises because the judgment has the force of *res judicata*, entails a prohibition having the full force of law against applying a national rule held to be incompatible with Union law and an obligation to take every measure to enable Union law to be fully applied.[253] The duty to give effect to the Court's

---

[248] If the Court does not have sufficient information to find that the act of the Member State constitutes a failure to fulfil obligations, it may ask the parties to resume examination of the question at issue and report to it, after which the Court will give final judgment: see ECJ, Case 170/78 *Commission v United Kingdom* [1980] E.C.R. 417, para. 24.

[249] If the Commission (or a Member State) attempts to request such specific measures, this will be deemed inadmissible by the Court: see, e.g. ECJ, Case C-104/02 *Commission v Germany* [2005] E.C.R. I-2689, paras 48–51; ECJ, Case C-36/08 *Commission v Greece* [2008] E.C.R. I-35*, Summ. pub., paras 8–10.

[250] For further discussion, see Opinion of Advocate-General V. Trstenjak in ECJ, Case C-503/04 *Commission v Germany* [2007] E.C.R. I-6153, point 41. In the reasoned opinion, the Commission may prescribe the measures that it deems necessary in order to eliminate the infringement. In addition, in a procedure under Art. 108(2) TFEU, the Commission may adopt a decision finding that a measure constitutes State aid incompatible with the internal market and requiring the unlawfully granted aid to be repaid. If the Member State concerned fails to comply with that decision, the Commission may bring an action in the Court for failure to fulfil the specific obligation to obtain repayment of the aid (ECJ, Case 70/72 *Commission v Germany* [1973] E.C.R. 813, para. 13) (see para. 5.22).

[251] ECJ, Case C-473/93 *Commission v Luxembourg* [1996] E.C.R. I-3207, para. 52.

[252] Opinion of Advocate-General G. Reischl in ECJ, Case 141/78 *France v United Kingdom* [1979] E.C.R. 2923, at 2946.

[253] ECJ, Case 48/71 *Commission v Italy* [1972] E.C.R. 527, para. 7; ECJ (order of 28 March 1980), Joined Cases 24/80 and 97/80 R *Commission v France* [1980] E.C.R. 1319, para. 16; ECJ, Case C-101/91

judgment is borne by all institutions of the Member State concerned within the fields covered by their respective powers. The legislative and executive authorities have to bring the offending provisions of domestic law into conformity with the requirements of Union law. The courts of the Member State concerned have to disregard those provisions in determining cases.[254]

Because the judgment has the force of *res judicata*, the Commission may not make an application for interim measures pursuant to Art. 279 TFEU in order to require the Member State to desist from an infringement of Union law which has already been found by judgment of the Court of Justice. This is because the Member State is required to take the necessary measures under Art. 260(1) TFEU. No further decision of the Court, in interlocutory or other proceedings, is required. Where the Commission sought such interim measures in this connection, the Court held that they were not necessary within the meaning of Art. 279 TFEU.[255]

(2) Court may limit the temporal effects

5.71 Exceptionally, by virtue of the general principle of legal certainty inherent in the Union legal order, the Court may limit the effects in time of a judgment given on the basis of Art. 258 TFEU.[256] The declaratory nature of the judgment does not preclude the Court from deciding, in application of that general principle, to restrict the right to rely upon a provision it has interpreted with a view to calling into question legal relations established in good faith. The Court will only take such a step in certain specific circumstances, where there is a risk of serious economic repercussions, owing in particular to the large number of relationships entered into in good faith on the basis of rules considered to be validly in force, and where it appears that both individuals and national authorities have been led into adopting practices which did not comply with Union law by reason of objective, significant uncertainty regarding the implications of Union provisions, to which the conduct of other Member States or the Commission may even have contributed.[257] The fact that a finding of

---

Commission v Italy [1993] E.C.R. I-191, para. 24. For further discussion of the *res judicata* effects of the first judgment rendered under Art. 258 TFEU in relation to Art. 260(2) TFEU, see para. 5.76.

[254] ECJ, Joined Cases 314/81 and 316/81 and 83/82 *Waterkeyn* [1982] E.C.R. 4337, para. 14.

[255] ECJ (order of 28 March 1980), Joined Cases 24/80 and 97/80 R *Commission v France* [1980] E.C.R. 1319, para. 19. Importantly, while interim relief is deemed inadmissible in the context of ensuring compliance with a judgment already given, this is to be distinguished from the provision of interim relief pending the outcome of the Court's judgment finding the infringement pursuant to Arts 258–259 TFEU: see further para. 13.12. That said, the Court has made clear that the finding of a failure to fulfil obligations in itself precludes granting a Member State's application to suspend the proceedings pending possible withdrawal of the action by the Commission: ECJ, Case C-431/10 *Commission v Ireland* [2011] E.C.R. I-56*, Summ. pub., para. 14 (and citations therein).

[256] See, e.g. ECJ, C-35/97 *Commission v France* [1998] E.C.R. I-5325, paras 49–52; ECJ, C-359/97 *Commission v United Kingdom* [2000] E.C.R. I-6355, paras 91–96; ECJ, Case C-426/98 *Commission v Greece* [2002] E.C.R. I-2793, paras 40–43; ECJ, Case C-178/05 *Commission v Greece* [2007] E.C.R. I-4185, paras 65–68; ECJ, Case C-475/07 *Commission v Poland* [2009] E.C.R. I-19*, Summ. pub., paras 60–63; ECJ, Case C-559/07 *Commission v Greece* [2009] E.C.R. I-47*, Summ. pub., paras 75–83; ECJ, Case C-284/05 *Commission v Finland* [2009] E.C.R. I-11705, paras 56–59; ECJ, Case C-387/05 *Commission v Italy* [2009] E.C.R. I-11831, paras 57–60; ECJ, Case C-239/06 *Commission v Italy* [2009] E.C.R. I-11913, paras 57–60.

[257] See ECJ, Case C-387/05 *Commission v Italy* [2009] E.C.R. I-11831, para. 58. To the same effect: ECJ, Case C-239/06 *Commission v Italy* [2009] E.C.R. I-11913, para. 58; ECJ, Case C-284/05 *Commission v Finland* [2009] E.C.R. I-11705, para. 57.

failure to fulfil obligations (which is invariably coupled, explicitly or implicitly, with an interpretation of the applicable provision of Union law) will have serious financial consequences for the Member State concerned is not sufficient in itself to justify limiting the scope of the judgment.[258] In this regard, the Court has drawn on its case-law in the context of limiting the temporal effects of preliminary rulings,[259] but questions remain open as regards the linkage between the two.[260]

(3) Position of individuals

The judgment finding the infringement of Union law does not as such confer any rights on individuals. Individuals may not rely directly on such a judgment before the national courts, but only on the 'provision' of Union law having direct effect that the judgment finds has been infringed by the Member State.[261]   **5.72**

In the event that an individual pleads a provision of Union law in his defence which does not have direct effect but which has been found by the Court of Justice to have been infringed by the Member State concerned, the national court, as an institution of that Member State, must ensure in the exercise of its functions that it is complied with by applying national law in such a way that it is compatible with the obligations that— according to the judgment of the Court—ensue from Union law for that Member State.

(4) Judgment may constitute the basis for State liability

The finding of a failure to fulfil obligations may potentially form the basis for liability on the part of the Member State concerned.[262] However, in accordance with the case-law, a Member State may incur liability only in the case of a sufficiently serious breach of Union law.[263] A judgment finding a failure to fulfil obligations is in itself not enough, certainly not for loss or damage that arose before judgment was given.[264] The requirement for a 'sufficiently serious breach' of Union law does not square completely with the strict or objective nature of an action for failure to fulfil obligations,[265] since the Court of Justice also   **5.73**

---

[258] ECJ, Case C-35/97 *Commission v France* [1998] E.C.R. I-5325, paras 49–52; ECJ, Case C-426/98 *Commission v Greece* [2002] E.C.R. I-2793, paras 42–44.

[259] See paras 6.34 and 10.23.

[260] See, e.g. ECJ, Case C-178/05 *Commission v Greece* [2007] E.C.R. I-4185, para. 67 and ECJ, Case C-387/05 *Commission v Italy* [2009] E.C.R. I-11831, para. 59 ('Even if judgments delivered under [Art. 258 TFEU] were to have the same effects as those delivered under [Art 267 TFEU], and therefore, considerations of legal certainty might, exceptionally, make it necessary to limit their temporal effects....').

[261] ECJ, Joined Cases 314/81 to 316/81 and 83/82 *Waterkeyn* [1982] E.C.R. 4337, paras 15–16.

[262] ECJ, Case 39/72 *Commission v Italy* [1973] E.C.R. 102, para. 11; ECJ, Case 309/84 *Commission v Italy* [1986] E.C.R. 599, para. 18; ECJ, Case 240/86 *Commission v Greece* [1988] E.C.R. 1835, para. 14; ECJ, Case C-287/87 *Commission v Greece* [1990] E.C.R. I-125; ECJ, Case C-249/88 *Commission v Belgium* [1991] E.C.R. I-1275, para. 41. For a recent example, see ECJ, Case C-118/08 *Transportes Urbanos y Servicios Generales* [2010] E.C.R. I-635.

[263] See para. 4.47.

[264] See ECJ, Joined Cases C-46/93 and C-48/93 *Brasserie du Pêcheur and Factortame* [1996] E.C.R. I-1029, paras 93–96; ECJ, Joined Cases C-178/94, C-179/94, C-188/94, C-189/94, and C-190/94 *Dillenkofer and Others* [1994] E.C.R. I-28, para. 29; ECJ, Case C-445/06 *Danske Slagterier* [2009] E.C.R. I-2119, para. 37.

[265] Moreover, there is no need for the Court of Justice to have made a finding that the Member State is in breach in order for the Member State to incur liability. Indeed, the Court has consistently repeated that it is the role of the national courts to find that the Member State has infringed Union law. This is the reason for the guiding factors set down in the Court's case-law in that regard, even if in particular cases the Court may go far in 'helping' the national courts with the application of such factors, as demonstrated by *Köbler* (ECJ, Case

takes other factors into account, such as whether or not the breach was intentional and whether any mistake of law was excusable. It is self-evident that if the failure to fulfil obligations continues after delivery of the judgment declaring the Member State concerned to be in breach of its obligations, that itself will constitute a sufficiently serious breach of Union law to cause the Member State to incur liability to make good any loss or damage which occurred in that period (see para. 4.48).

In addition, it must be noted that the Union provision infringed must confer a 'right' on individuals in order for the issue of State liability to arise.[266] It follows that a finding of an infringement in proceedings under Arts 258–259 TFEU does not automatically result in the Member State concerned incurring liability under Union law. Yet, it may well be that the Member State will incur liability in damages under national law for loss or damage caused by an infringement of a Union provision, even though that provision does not directly confer any 'right' on individuals.

(5) Period within which the Member State must comply with the judgment

5.74 The Treaties themselves do not specify the period within which the judgment must be complied with, but the Court of Justice has held that the process must be initiated at once and completed as soon as possible.[267]

C. Sanctions for failure to comply with the judgment

(1) Art. 260(2) TFEU

5.75 The Commission is responsible for ensuring that the judgment finding a breach of Union law is complied with. If the Member State fails to take the necessary measures, Art. 260(2) TFEU provides for a procedure whereby the Commission may bring a case before the Court of Justice with a view to a finding that the Member State concerned has failed to comply with the original judgment (or to give effect to it in time or correctly), and in doing so, 'shall specify the amount of the lump sum or penalty payment to be paid by the Member State concerned which it considers appropriate under the circumstances'.[268]

C-224/01 *Köbler* [2003] E.C.R. I-10239). If difficulties arise in this connection, they may always enlist the help of the Court of Justice by making a reference for a preliminary ruling. This power of the national courts is important. Since the Commission has a discretion whether to bring proceedings under Art. 258 TFEU, individuals may play a major, complementary role in enforcing Union law by invoking *Francovich* liability in national courts (cf. ECJ, Case C-91/92 *Faccini Dori* [1994] E.C.R. I-3325, paras 27–29).

[266] See para. 4.47.

[267] See, e.g. ECJ, Case 69/86 *Commission v Italy* [1987] E.C.R. 773, para. 8; ECJ, Case 169/87 *Commission v France* [1988] 4093, para. 14; ECJ, Case C-345/92 *Commission v Germany* [1993] E.C.R. I-1115, para. 6; ECJ, Case C-334/94 *Commission v France* [1996] E.C.R. I-1307, para. 31; ECJ, Case C-387/97 *Commission v Greece* [2000] E.C.R. I-5047, para. 82; ECJ, Case C-478/01 *Commission v Spain* [2003] E.C.R. I-4141, para. 27; ECJ, Case C-121/07 *Commission v France* [2008] E.C.R. I-9159, para. 21; ECJ, Case C-109/08 *Commission v Greece* [2009] E.C.R. I-4657, para. 14; ECJ, Case C-457/07 *Commission v Portugal* [2009] E.C.R. I-8091, para. 38. See also ECJ, Case C-473/93 *Commission v Luxembourg* [1996] E.C.R. I-3207, paras 51–52: Art. 260(1) TFEU does not confer on the Court any power to grant a Member State a period of time for compliance with its judgments.

[268] See M. Wathelet and J. Wildemeersch, 'Double manquement et sanctions financières des États (article 228, par. 2 CE): Le point après quize ans' (2008) Revue de la Faculté de droit de l'Université de Liège 323–70. The imposition of financial penalties has had particular salience in relation to the field of EU environmental

The procedure of Art. 260(2) TFEU modifies the rather inefficient procedure that was set down in the former Art. 228(2) EC. Under the latter provision, it was only when a Member State failed to comply with a judgment of the Court of Justice finding an infringement that the Commission could initiate new proceedings before the Court—after having completed another two-stage litigation procedure (involving both a letter of formal notice and reasoned opinion)—in which it would ask the Court to impose a pecuniary sanction upon the Member State concerned. As a result, it often took years before a pecuniary sanction was imposed on a non-compliant Member State. Now, with the changes brought by the Lisbon Treaty, Art. 260(2) TFEU renders the second action somewhat less onerous by doing away with the requirement of a reasoned opinion in the pre-litigation stage. The Commission is thus able to bring an action before the Court under this provision after only having invited the Member State concerned to submit its observations.[269] This invariably means that the Commission will still need to send to the Member State a letter of formal notice which will serve to delineate the scope of the alleged non-compliance and lay down the time limit by which that Member State must take the necessary measures to comply with the first judgment or be brought before the Court of Justice.[270]

The procedure of Art. 260(2) TFEU must be distinguished from that of Art. 260(3) TFEU, which is also an innovation of the Lisbon Treaty. Whereas Art. 260(2) TFEU concerns a second action before the Court concerning a Member State's alleged non-compliance with the first judgment finding an infringement, Art. 260(3) TFEU is situated in the context of the first action brought under Art. 258 TFEU concerning a Member State's failure to notify measures transposing a legislative directive, whereby the Commission may ask the Court to find an infringement and to impose a pecuniary sanction at the same time.[271]

(2) Relationship between Art. 260(2) TFEU and Art. 258 TFEU

In proceedings under Art. 260(2) TFEU, the Court of Justice has jurisdiction to assess the suitability and effectiveness of any measures that the Member State has taken in compliance with the original judgment. Save for what has been said as regards the shortening of the pre-litigation stage (see para. 5.75), the procedure under Art. 260(2) TFEU largely resembles that of Art. 258 TFEU. It too, is based on the objective finding that a Member State has failed to fulfil its obligations.[272] The Commission must provide the Court with the information necessary to determine the extent to which a Member State has complied with a judgment declaring it to be in breach of its obligations.[273] As that judgment has the

5.76

---

law: see K. Lenaerts and J. A. Gutiérrez-Fons, 'The General Enforcement Obligation of EU Environmental Law' (2011) Y.E.L. 1–39.

[269] Art. 260(2), first para., TFEU. For an application, see ECJ (judgment of 25 June 2013), Case C-241/11 *Commission v Czech Republic*, not reported.

[270] Though Art. 260(2), first para., TFEU does not contain the language of the former Art. 228(2) EC that the Commission 'shall, after giving that [Member] State the opportunity to submit its observations, issue a reasoned opinion *specifying the points on which the Member State concerned has not complied with the judgment of the Court of Justice*' (emphasis added).

[271] See para. 5.16.

[272] See, e.g. ECJ, Case C-177/04 *Commission v France* [2006] E.C.R. I-2461, para. 43 (and case-law cited therein).

[273] See, e.g. ECJ, Case C-387/97 *Commission v Greece* [2000] E.C.R. I-5047, para. 73; ECJ, Case C-369/07 *Commission v Greece* [2009] E.C.R. I-5703, para. 74. Consequently, where the Commission does not do so, the complaint is inadmissible: see, e.g. ECJ, Case C-457/07 *Commission v Portugal* [2009] E.C.R. I-8091, paras 97–101. Conversely, where the Commission does adduce sufficient evidence to show that the breach of

force of *res judicata*, the dispute as to the original failure to fulfil obligations may not be reopened in proceedings under Art. 260(2) TFEU.[274] The only matter in issue is the alleged failure to give effect to the original judgment. Thus, matters falling outside the original judgment cannot be dealt with in Art. 260(2) TFEU proceedings and are inadmissible, as are matters that did not comprise the subject-matter delineated in the pre-litigation procedure.[275]

(3) Lump sum and/or penalty payment

5.77 The Court may impose a lump sum and/or penalty payment pursuant to the second paragraph of Art. 260(2) TFEU in the event that it finds that the original judgment rendered under Art. 258 TFEU has not been complied with.[276] In the Court's view, while the imposition of a penalty payment seems particularly suited to inducing a Member State to put an end as soon as possible to a breach of obligations which, in the absence of such a measure, would be likely to persist, the imposition of a lump sum is prompted more by the assessment of the consequences for private and public interests of the failure by the Member State concerned to comply with its obligations, in particular where the breach has persisted for a long period since the judgment which initially established it was delivered. The imposition of both types of penalty provided for in Art. 260(2) TFEU is appropriate, particularly where the breach of obligations has continued for a long period and tends to persist.[277]

---

obligations has persisted, then it is for the Member State concerned to challenge in substance and in detail the information produced and its consequences: see, e.g. ECJ, Case C-119/04 *Commission v Italy* [2006] E.C.R. I-6885, para. 41 (and case-law cited therein). In essence, this greatly resembles the case-law discussed earlier in relation to the burden of proof and submission of evidence in the context of the Art. 258 TFEU procedure.

[274] See, e.g. ECJ, Case C-462/05 *Commission v Portugal* [2008] E.C.R. I-4183, paras 23–28 (and case-law cited therein). Recently, in *Commission v Luxembourg*, the Court ruled that the principle of *res judicata* is applicable to infringement proceedings, with the result that complaints identical in fact and in law to those already settled by a judgment delivered under Art. 258 TFEU must be brought pursuant to the Art. 260 TFEU procedure and cannot be brought afresh under Art. 258 TFEU: ECJ, Case C-526/08 *Commission v Luxembourg* [2010] E.C.R. I-6151, paras 25–35. See also ECJ (judgment of 24 January 2013), Case C-529/09 *Commission v Spain*, not reported, paras 64–79 for an application of the principle of *res judicata* in relation to Art. 108(2) TFEU. Furthermore, as regards the applicability of the principle of *non bis in idem* (also referred to as the principle of 'no double jeopardy': in ECJ, Case C-337/05 *Commission v Italy* [2008] E.C.R. I-2173, paras 16, 25), the Court found that 'even if that principle could be relied on in the present case, its application is in any event precluded because the matters of fact and law involved in this case and the case which gave rise to the [previous] judgment in *Commission v Luxembourg* are not identical': ECJ, Case C-337/05 *Commission v Italy*, para. 36. See already ECJ, Case C-127/99 *Commission v Italy* [2001] E.C.R. I-8305, paras 27–29 (where the Court held that the principle *non bis in idem* had not been violated as regards the question whether the Member State concerned had implemented the directive within the prescribed period, since the earlier judgment of the Court related to provisions other than those at issue in the new proceedings); ECJ, Case C-157/06 *Commission v Italy* [2008] E.C.R. I-7313, paras 20–21.

[275] ECJ, Case C-457/07 *Commission v Portugal* [2009] E.C.R. I-8091, paras 66–68. This case dealt with the former Treaty framework enshrined in Arts 226–228 EC, and thus it remains to be seen to what extent the Court will incorporate its ruling within the context of the changes brought by the Lisbon Treaty, i.e. the elimination of the reasoned opinion, in relation to the delineation of the subject-matter in Art. 260(2) TFEU proceedings. Nevertheless, the judgment underscored the parallelism between the pre-litigation procedures of Art. 260 TFEU and Art. 258 TFEU.

[276] As for the use of 'and/or' instead of 'or' appearing in the text of the Treaties, see ECJ, Case C-369/07 *Commission v Greece* [2009] E.C.R. I-5703, para. 58.

[277] ECJ, Case C-304/02 *Commission v France* [2005] E.C.R. I-6263, paras 80–86, 89–95. According to the Court (para. 83), the conjunction 'or' in Art. 260(2) TFEU to link the financial penalties capable of being imposed may, linguistically, have an alternative or a cumulative sense and must therefore be read in the context

(4) Court's discretion

In proceedings under Art. 260(2) TFEU, it is for the Court to assess, in light of the **5.78** circumstances of each case, the financial penalties to be imposed on a Member State. Thus, the Commission's suggestions cannot bind the Court, but merely constitute a useful point of reference. Likewise, guidelines such as those laid down in Commission Communications are not binding on the Court, but contribute to ensuring that the action is transparent, foreseeable, and consistent with legal certainty.[278] Indeed, by providing in the second paragraph of Art. 260(2) TFEU that the Court 'may' impose a lump sum or penalty payment on the defaulting Member State, that provision is deemed to confer a wide discretion upon the Court in deciding whether it is necessary to impose such sanctions.[279] As a result, the fact that the Commission may take the view, at a certain stage of the procedure before the Court, that the imposition of a particular penalty is no longer necessary does not render the action inadmissible, as the Court has jurisdiction to impose a financial penalty not suggested by the Commission.[280]

If the Court decides to impose a penalty payment and/or lump sum payment, it must do so, in exercising its discretion, in a manner that is appropriate to the circumstances and proportionate both to the breach that has been established and the ability to pay of the Member State concerned.[281] The Court has made clear that an order imposing a periodic penalty payment and/or lump sum is intended to place the defaulting Member State under economic pressure, which induces it to put an end to the infringement established.[282]

Thus, as far as the imposition of a penalty payment is concerned, it is justified only so far as the failure to comply with an earlier judgment of the Court continues up to the time of the Court's examination of the facts.[283] Where the Court imposes a penalty payment, its

---

in which it is used. In the light of the objective pursued by Art. 260 TFEU, the conjunction 'or' in Art. 260(2) TFEU must be understood as being used in a cumulative sense. For subsequent cases in which both penalties have been imposed by the Court, see, e.g. ECJ, Case C-304/02 *Commission v France* [2005] E.C.R. I-6263; ECJ, Case C-109/08 *Commission v Greece* [2009] E.C.R. I-4657; ECJ, Case C-369/07 *Commission v Greece* [2009] E.C.R. I-5703; ECJ (judgment of 19 December 2012), Case C-374/11 *Commission v Ireland*, not reported; ECJ (judgment of 17 October 2013), Case C-533/11 *Commission v Belgium*, not reported.

[278] See, e.g. ECJ, Case C-369/07 *Commission v Greece* [2009] E.C.R. I-5703, paras 111–112 (and case-law cited therein); ECJ (judgment of 25 June 2013), Case C-241/11 *Commission v Czech Republic*, not reported, paras 42–43. In early cases, only a penalty payment was sought by the Commission and imposed by the Court: see ECJ, Case C-387/97 *Commission v Greece* [2000] E.C.R. I-5047; ECJ, Case C-278/01 *Commission v Spain* [2003] E.C.R. I-14141. However, in the aftermath of ECJ, Case C-304/02 *Commission v France* [2005] E.C.R. I-6263, discussed in n. 277, the Commission issued a Communication on the 'Application of Article 228 of the EC Treaty' (SEC (2005) 1658, amended by SEC (2010) 923/3), replacing the previous 1996 and 1997 Communications, which stated that as from 1 January 2006, the Commission would generally include in its applications under Art. 260 TFEU the specification of both a lump sum and penalty payment and set down a predetermined and objective approach for the calculation of both types of pecuniary sanctions.

[279] ECJ, Case C-121/07 *Commission v France* [2009] E.C.R. I-9159, para. 63. Compare Art. 260(3) TFEU, which explicitly limits the Court's imposition of a lump sum or penalty payment on the Member State concerned 'not exceeding the amount specified by the Commission'. For further discussion of Art. 260(3) TFEU, see para. 5.16.

[280] ECJ, Case C-503/04 *Commission v Germany* [2007] E.C.R. I-6153, para. 22.

[281] See, e.g. ECJ, Case C-109/08 *Commission v Greece* [2009] E.C.R. I-4657, para. 52; ECJ (judgment of 19 December 2012), Case C-279/11 *Commission v Ireland*, not reported, para. 76.

[282] ECJ, Case C-109/08 *Commission v Greece* [2009] E.C.R. I-4657, para. 28.

[283] ECJ, Case C-369/07 *Commission v Greece* [2009] E.C.R. I-5703, para. 59 (and case-law cited therein); see also ECJ, Case C-70/06 *Commission v Portugal* [2008] E.C.R. I-1, para. 37; ECJ, Case C-109/08 *Commission v Greece* [2009] E.C.R. I-4657, para. 30; ECJ (judgment of 17 October 2013), *Commission v*

amount (which must ensure that penalty payments have coercive force and that Union law is applied uniformly and effectively) must be determined having regard to the duration of the infringement, its degree of seriousness, and the ability of the Member State to pay. Regard should also be had to the effects of failure to comply on private and public interests and to the urgency of getting the Member State concerned to fulfil its obligations.[284] Where a Member State has taken certain measures—but not all that are needed—to comply with the Court's judgment finding that it has failed to fulfil its obligations, the amount of the penalty payment will take account of the progress that it has made in complying with its obligations.[285]

As regards the imposition of a lump sum payment, the decision depends, in each individual case, on all the relevant factors pertaining to both the specific nature of the infringement established and the individual conduct of the Member State involved in the procedure instigated pursuant to Art. 260 TFEU. These relevant factors include, in particular, how long the breach of obligations has persisted since the judgment that initially established it was delivered and the public and private interests involved.[286] Notably, in its

---

Belgium, not reported, paras 64–66. For judgments in which this was not the case, see ECJ, Case C-503/04 *Commission v Germany* [2007] E.C.R. I-6153, para. 40; ECJ, Case C-121/07 *Commission v France* [2008] E.C.R. I-9159, paras 27–28; ECJ, Case C-568/07 *Commission v Greece* [2009] E.C.R. I-4505, paras 42–43; ECJ, Case C-496/09 *Commission v Italy* [2011] E.C.R. I-11483, para. 42. The imposition of a periodic penalty payment can also be deemed not justified under circumstances where the Court does not have sufficient information to permit it to find that, on the date of the Court's examination of the facts, the breach persisted: ECJ, Case C-119/04 *Commission v Italy* [2006] E.C.R. I-6885, paras 45–46. This is interrelated to some extent with the evidence burden placed on the Commission in Art. 260 TFEU proceedings.

[284] ECJ, Case C-369/07 *Commission v Greece* [2009] E.C.R. I-5703, para. 115 (and case-law cited therein).

[285] See, e.g. ECJ, Case C-278/01 *Commission v Spain* [2003] E.C.R. I-14141, para. 50. When a Member State has failed to adopt all the measures necessary to comply with a judgment of the Court of Justice finding an infringement for non-recovery of aid which had been found by Commission decision to be unlawful and incompatible with the internal market, the Court acknowledges that—when a general aid scheme is concerned—the Member State concerned will normally not manage to implement the Commission decision fully in the short term. If the amount of the penalty payment were invariable, it would continue to be due in its entirety for as long as the Member State concerned had not achieved complete implementation of the decision. In those circumstances, a penalty which takes account of the progress that the Member State may have made in complying with its obligations appears appropriate and proportionate to the infringement that has been found (ECJ, Case C-496/09 *Commission v Italy* [2011] E.C.R. I-11483, para. 49). See also ECJ, Case C-369/07 *Commission v Greece* [2009] E.C.R. I-5703, para. 125: the Court considered it appropriate to defer the point at which the penalty payment took effect until one month after the judgment was delivered in the present case so as to enable the Member State concerned to demonstrate that it had brought the infringement to an end. To be clear, this is to be distinguished from a request from the defendant Member State to suspend the application of a penalty payment until after the entry into force of a legislative enactment that would render it in compliance, which the Court will not do: ECJ, Case C-70/06 *Commission v Portugal* [2008] E.C.R. I-1, paras 29, 53.

[286] ECJ, Case C-121/07 *Commission v France* [2008] E.C.R. I-9159, paras 62 and 64 (and further case-law cited therein); ECJ, Case C-109/08 *Commission v Greece* [2009] E.C.R. I-4657, paras 51–52; ECJ, Case C-369/07 *Commission v Greece* [2009] E.C.R. I-5703, paras 144, 147. For illustrations of the Court's assessment, see ECJ, Case C-304/02 *Commission v France* [2005] E.C.R. I-6263, paras 114–116; ECJ, Case C-121/07 *Commission v France* [2008] E.C.R. I-9159, paras 65–88; ECJ, Case C-568/07 *Commission v Greece* [2009] E.C.R. I-4505, paras 49–62; ECJ, Case C-109/08 *Commission v Greece* [2009] E.C.R. I-4657, paras 53–55; ECJ, Case C-369/07 *Commission v Greece* [2009] E.C.R. I-5703, paras 145–150; ECJ, Case C-568/07 *Commission v Greece* [2009] E.C.R. I-4505, paras 49–62; ECJ, Case C-407/09 *Commission v Greece* [2011] E.C.R. I-2467, paras 33–44. There seems to be some overlap in relation to the Court's emphasis on taking account of all the factual and legal circumstances in the individual case, especially those relating to the conduct of the Member State, and the duration and seriousness of the infringement: see ECJ, Case C-568/07 *Commission v Greece* [2009] E.C.R. I-4505, para. 48; ECJ, Case C-369/07 *Commission v Greece* [2009]

Communication on the application of Art. 260 TFEU, the Commission considers the possibility of recourse only to the lump sum payment in specific cases. In cases where a Member State has remedied the infringement after the referral of the case to the Court of Justice but before the judgment has been delivered, it will no longer withdraw its action for that reason alone, since the Court of Justice can still impose a lump sum payment penalizing the duration of the infringement up to the time that the situation was rectified.[287] As mentioned earlier, however, such guidelines are not binding on the Court, and by the terms of Art. 260(2) TFEU, that provision confers a wide discretion on the Court in deciding whether it is necessary to impose such a sanction.[288]

(5) Retroactive pecuniary sanctions

5.79 In the events culminating in the entry into force of the Lisbon Treaty, the Treaty framers did not consider it necessary to grant jurisdiction to the Court of Justice explicitly to impose pecuniary sanctions retroactively (as from the first day of the infringement). A provision in that regard was not necessary, since Art. 260(2) TFEU allows the Court to impose not only a penalty payment to be paid per day of infringement as from the day the judgment is given, but also a lump sum, which can be determined having regard to the gravity of the infringement in the period preceding the judgment.[289]

(6) Enforcement of the Court's judgment imposing pecuniary sanctions

5.80 The Treaties do not lay down detailed rules for the enforcement of the judgment delivered by the Court of Justice at the conclusion of the Art. 260 TFEU procedure imposing pecuniary sanctions on a Member State or make any specific provision regarding the settlement of disputes between a Member State and the Commission in this regard.[290] Until recently, there had been minimal scrutiny of the means by which the Commission enforces the Court's judgment imposing a pecuniary sanction on a Member State, at least as far as the case-law of the Union courts was concerned. However, case-law devoted to such matters is steadily emerging.

In *Portugal v Commission*,[291] the General Court made clear that where a judgment delivered pursuant to Art. 260(2) TFEU orders a Member State to pay a financial penalty to the Commission into the European Union's 'own resources' account and since under Art. 317 TFEU the Commission implements the budget, the latter is responsible for recovering the amounts that would be due to the budget pursuant to the judgment in accordance with the provisions of the regulations made under Art. 322 TFEU and consequently, the decision by

---

E.C.R. I-5703, para. 148; ECJ, Case C-496/09 *Commission v Italy* [2011] E.C.R. I-11483, para. 94; ECJ (judgment of 25 June 2013), Case C-241/11 *Commission v Czech Republic*, not reported, para. 40.

[287] Communication from the Commission—Application of Article 228 of the EC Treaty, n. 278, points 10.5 and 11. For examples, see ECJ, Case C-121/07 *Commission v France* [2008] E.C.R. I-9159; ECJ, Case C-568/07 *Commission v Greece* [2009] E.C.R. I-4505; ECJ, Case C-407/09 *Commission v Greece* [2011] E.C.R. I-2467.

[288] ECJ, Case C-121/07 *Commission v France* [2009] E.C.R. I-9159, paras 61, 63; ECJ (judgment of 19 December 2012), Case C-279/11 *Commission v Ireland*, not reported, paras 65–81.

[289] CONV 734/03, cited at n. 69; see also the Opinion of Advocate-General L.A. Geelhoed in ECJ, Case C-304/02 *Commission v France* [2005] E.C.R. I-6263, points 81–108.

[290] See EGC, Case T-33/09 *Portugal v Commission* [2011] E.C.R. II-1429, paras 61, 63.

[291] EGC, Case T-33/09 *Portugal v Commission* [2011] E.C.R. II-1429 (confirmed on appeal: ECJ (judgment of 15 January 2014), Case C-292/11 P *Commission v Portugal*, not reported). See also EGC, Case T-139/06 *France v Commission* [2011] E.C.R. II-7315.

which the Commission determines the amount due from the Member State can be the subject of an action for annulment under Art. 263 TFEU. However, in exercising its jurisdiction to adjudicate annulment actions, the General Court cannot impinge on the exclusive jurisdiction reserved to the Court of Justice under Arts 258 and 260 TFEU and therefore cannot rule, in the context of annulment proceedings, on a question relating to the infringement by the Member State that has not been previously decided by the Court of Justice.[292] Then turning to the instant proceedings concerning the Commission's enforcement of the Court's judgment imposing a periodic penalty payment on Portugal, it annulled the Commission's decision on the grounds that it failed to take into account the operative part of the Court's judgment rendered pursuant to Art. 260(2) TFEU in the sense that it was sufficient to comply with that judgment by repealing the offending national law, which Portugal did with the adoption of a Decree Law issued in 2007. The fact that the Commission considered that it was only with a Decree Law issued in 2008 that the Member State had complied with the Court's judgment amounted to an assessment of the compatibility of the 2007 Law with Union law going far beyond the formal review determining whether the offending national law had been repealed. The rights and duties of the Member States may be determined, and their conduct appraised, only by a judgment of the Court of Justice, and thus the Commission was not entitled to decide, within the context of the enforcement of the Court's judgment, that the 2007 Law did not comply with Union law and then draw conclusions from this for the calculation of the penalty payment determined by the Court of Justice; insofar as it considered that such law infringed Union law, the Commission should have initiated the procedure provided in Art. 258 TFEU.[293]

(7) New failure to comply with the judgment

5.81 Failure to comply with a judgment constitutes an infringement of Art. 260 TFEU and may therefore give rise in itself to a finding of liability on the part of the Member State concerned.

---

[292] EGC, Case T-33/09 *Portugal v Commission*, paras 62, 64–67.

[293] EGC, Case T-33/09 *Portugal v Commission*, paras 69–91. By contrast, in EGC, Case T-139/06 *France v Commission* [2011] E.C.R. II-7315, the Member State's action was dismissed. In the latter case, the Commission had not exceeded its competence since it only found in the contested decision that the Member State's infringement persisted. See also J. T. Nowak, case note (2012) S.E.W. 163–8.

6

PRELIMINARY RULINGS ON THE INTERPRETATION OF UNION LAW

I. Introduction

A. General

Under Art. 267 TFEU, the Court of Justice has been conferred jurisdiction to give **6.01** preliminary rulings on the interpretation of Union law, as well as on the validity of acts adopted by the Union institutions, bodies, offices, or agencies.[1] Art. 267 TFEU is the only form of action provided for in the Treaties that allows the Union judicature to rule on the interpretation of a Union act.[2] Moreover, in the system of judicial protection in the European Union, preliminary rulings on the interpretation of Union law constitute an indirect route for ensuring the compatibility of acts of the Member States with Union law, alongside the direct route of infringement actions under Arts 258–260 TFEU.[3]

B. Topics to be discussed

The request for a preliminary ruling on the interpretation of Union law raises three main **6.02** issues. The first relates to the subject-matter of the preliminary ruling on interpretation, in other words, what provisions and principles may be interpreted by the Court of Justice. The second relates to the content of the preliminary ruling on interpretation and the related limits placed on the jurisdiction of the Court of Justice. Third, there is the question of the consequences of a preliminary ruling on interpretation.

These three issues will be considered in turn in the main parts of this chapter.

---

[1] See also Art. 19(3)(b) TEU. For an overview of the preliminary ruling procedure, including discussion of the changes brought by the Lisbon Treaty and the general requirements that requests for preliminary rulings have to satisfy, see Ch. 3. As regards preliminary rulings on validity, see Ch. 10. At present, the preliminary ruling jurisdiction is vested with the Court of Justice; although envisaged by the Treaties, no preliminary ruling jurisdiction has been conferred on the General Court: see para. 2.53. See further K. Lenaerts, 'Interpretation and the Court of Justice: A Basis for Comparative Reflection' (2007) International Lawyer 1011–32.

[2] See, e.g. EGC (order of 28 February 2005), Case T-108/03 *Von Pezold v Commission* [2005] E.C.R. II-655, paras 56–58.

[3] See generally K. Lenaerts, 'The Rule of Law and the Coherence of the Judicial System of the European Union' (2007) C.M.L. Rev. 1625–2659. See further para. 6.23.

II. Subject-Matter of a Preliminary Ruling on Interpretation

A. Overview

6.03 According to Art. 267 TFEU, the jurisdiction of the Court of Justice to give preliminary rulings on interpretation extends to 'the Treaties' and 'acts of the institutions, bodies, offices or agencies of the Union'.

Under Art. 1 of the TEU and of the TFEU, the TEU and the TFEU are referred to as 'the Treaties'.[4] Moreover, with the entry into force of the Lisbon Treaty, Art. 267 TFEU applies to preliminary rulings in connection with the EAEC Treaty, as Art. 150 EAEC, the counterpart to the former Art. 234 EC, has been repealed and references to, *inter alia*, the 'Treaties' are taken as references to the EAEC Treaty in this regard.[5]

The upshot is that, as far as the subject-matter of a reference for a preliminary ruling is concerned, the Court of Justice has jurisdiction to give preliminary rulings on interpretation under the three Treaties (the TEU, the TFEU, and the EAEC Treaty). This generally covers the following four main categories: (1) the Treaties themselves and other Union instruments and principles having the status of primary Union law; (2) acts of the Union institutions, bodies, offices, or agencies; (3) international agreements concluded by the Union and acts of bodies set up by such agreements; and (4) provisions of Union law to which national law refers.

B. The Treaties

(1) Notion of the Treaties

6.04 As successor to the Treaty establishing the European Community, the TFEU, together with the TEU and the EAEC Treaty, constitute the 'basic constitutional charter' of the Union.[6] They are the written constitution at the apex of the hierarchy of Union norms, i.e. primary Union law, and consequently, are the first instruments whose interpretation may form the subject-matter of preliminary rulings by the Court of Justice.

The notion of the Treaties generally encompasses the TEU, the TFEU, and the EAEC Treaty and all amendments thereto; the Treaties and Acts relating to the accession of new Member States; 'complementary' Treaties, such as the former (1957) Convention on certain institutions common to the European Communities[7] and the former (1965) Treaty

---

[4] Art. 1, third para., TEU; Art. 1(2) TFEU.

[5] Art. 106a(1)–(2) EAEC of the consolidated version of the EAEC Treaty, [2012] O.J. C327/1: see further para. 3.03. Despite the expiry of the ECSC Treaty whose provisions were taken over by what was then the EC Treaty, the Court of Justice considers that it has jurisdiction pursuant to Art. 267 TFEU to give preliminary rulings on the interpretation of the ECSC Treaty and measures adopted pursuant thereto which continue to produce effects after the expiry of that Treaty: see para. 3.04.

[6] ECJ, Case 294/83 *'Les Verts' v European Parliament* [1986] E.C.R. 1339, para. 23. See Art. 1, third para., TEU; Art. 1(2) TFEU, specifying that the TEU and the TFEU constitute the Treaties upon which the Union is founded.

[7] See [1967] O.J. 152/5. Not printed in the English Special Edition of the O.J.; for the English text, see <http://www.cvce.lu>.

establishing a Single Council and a Single Commission of the European Communities (the Merger Treaty);[8] and all of the Annexes and Protocols to those Treaties and Acts of Accession, which are deemed to have the same legal force as the Treaties themselves.[9] In contrast, the Declarations of intergovernmental conferences accompanying the Treaties do not have Treaty status, although their content may be taken into account in interpreting the Treaty provisions to which they relate.[10]

(2) Former second and third pillars of the Union

Under the former Treaty framework, not all provisions of the Treaties concerned the European Communities.[11] Consequently, only those parts relating to what was then Community law fell within the Court's jurisdiction to give preliminary rulings on interpretation under Art. 234 EC.[12] With the entry into force of the Lisbon Treaty, however, this has changed. **6.05**

The Court of Justice's preliminary ruling jurisdiction in connection with the interpretation of the provisions of the Treaties relating to the former third pillar of Police and Judicial Cooperation in Criminal Matters (PJCCM) and the interpretation (and validity) of acts adopted thereunder has been streamlined, subject to a five-year provisional period in which former Art. 35 EU holds for PJCCM acts adopted before the entry into force of the Lisbon Treaty until such acts are amended.[13]

With respect to the former second pillar of the Common Foreign and Security Policy (CFSP), as a general matter, the Court of Justice has still not been conferred preliminary

---

[8] See [1967] O.J. 152/2. Not printed in the English Special Edition of the O.J.; for the English text, see <http://www.cvce.lu>. This Treaty and the Convention cited in n. 7 have been repealed by Art. 9(1) of the Treaty of Amsterdam ([1997] O.J. C340/76-77). Most of their provisions had been incorporated into the Community Treaties. As for the remainder, Art. 9(2) to (7) of the Amsterdam Treaty set out to retain their essential elements. See further K. Lenaerts and P. Van Nuffel (R. Bray and N. Cambien (eds)), *European Union Law* (3rd edn, London, Sweet & Maxwell, 2011), para. 1.16.

[9] Art. 51 TEU; Art. 207 EAEC. The principal Protocols annexed to the TEU, TFEU, and/or EAEC Treaty can be found at [2012] O.J. C326/201, and the Annexes at [2012] O.J. C326/331. For a practical example, see ECJ, Case C-147/95 *Evrenopoulos* [1997] E.C.R. I-2057, in which the Court of Justice gave a ruling on the interpretation of the Protocol on what is now Art. 134 TFEU. Other examples arise with respect to questions concerning the interpretation of provisions of what is now Protocol (No. 7), annexed to the TEU, TFEU, and EAEC Treaty, on the Privileges and Immunities of the European Union ([2012] O.J. C326/266): see, e.g. ECJ, Case C-199/05 *European Community v Belgium* [2006] E.C.R. I-10485; ECJ, Case C-270/10 *Gistö* [2011] E.C.R. I-7277; ECJ, Case C-163/10 *Patriciello* [2011] E.C.R I-7565.

[10] See, e.g. ECJ, Case C-135/08 *Rottman* [2010] E.C.R. I-1449, para. 40. This applies at least insofar as they do not conflict with those provisions: see ECJ, Case C-233/97 *KappAhl Oy* [1998] E.C.R. I-8068, paras 22–23; see further K. Lenaerts and P. Van Nuffel (R. Bray and N. Cambien (eds)), *European Union Law* (3rd edn, London, Sweet & Maxwell, 2011), para. 22.14. The set of Declarations annexed to the Final Act of the Intergovernmental Conference which adopted the Lisbon Treaty, Declarations concerning Protocols annexed to the Treaties, and Declarations by Member States can be found starting at [2012] O.J. C326/337.

[11] See Single European Act ([1987] O.J. C169/1), Art. 31; Maastricht Treaty on European Union ([1992] O.J. C224/1), Art. L; Treaty of Amsterdam ([1997] O.J. C340/2), Art. 46.

[12] Arts 46–53 EU. Even with respect to the EC Treaty itself, there were limitations placed on the jurisdiction of the Court of Justice under Art. 68 EC in connection with matters relating to Title IV concerning visas, asylum, immigration, and other policies relating to the free movement of persons. Within this setting, several conventions were concluded between the Member States for which the protocols annexed thereto set forth the scope of the preliminary ruling jurisdiction of the Court of Justice in this regard; even though these conventions were progressively reframed as EU regulations, these protocols have not lost their salience: see, e.g. ECJ, Case C-29/10 *Koelzsch* [2011] E.C.R. I-1595, and ECJ (judgment of 15 December 2011), Case C-384/10 *Voogsgeerd*, not reported (concerning the Rome Convention). See para. 22.02.

[13] See para. 22.05. See also ECJ (judgment of 21 December 2011), Case C-507/10 *X*, not reported, paras 18–22.

ruling jurisdiction, although there are potential outlets in the Treaties that could allow for preliminary rulings on the interpretation of the provisions of the Treaties and the acts adopted on the basis of those provisions.[14] Under Art. 275 TFEU, the Court of Justice of the European Union does 'not have jurisdiction with respect to the provisions relating to the common foreign and security policy nor with respect to the acts adopted on the basis of those provisions', subject to two exceptions: (1) it has jurisdiction to monitor compliance with Art. 40 TEU; and (2) it has jurisdiction to rule on proceedings brought under the fourth paragraph of Art. 263 TFEU reviewing the legality of decisions providing for restrictive measures against natural or legal persons adopted by the Council on the basis of Chapter 2 of Title V of the TEU (concerning specific provisions on the CFSP).[15]

As regards the first exception, the Court's assessment pursuant to Art. 40 TEU as to whether the implementation of the CFSP affects the application of the procedures and the extent of the powers of the institutions in the other policy fields of the Treaties, or vice versa, could arguably arise within the context of a preliminary ruling on interpretation, for instance, with respect to questions on the interpretation of the provisions of the Treaties concerning the CFSP or Treaty provisions falling outside the sphere of the CFSP but which raise issues relating thereto.[16] The second exception pertains, in view of the reference to the requirements of the fourth paragraph of Art. 263 TFEU, to actions for annulment and, therefore, does not in principle encompass the Court's preliminary ruling jurisdiction, at least as far as the interpretation of CFSP acts are concerned.[17] Nevertheless, the Court of Justice has full jurisdiction to give preliminary rulings on the interpretation of international agreements concluded by the Union even where such agreements encompass CFSP matters.[18] The Court of Justice's preliminary ruling jurisdiction on interpretation vis-à-vis the CFSP thus remains limited but not wholly excluded, and issues regarding the extent of such jurisdiction await clarification in the case-law.

(3) Other Union instruments having Treaty status

6.06 Treaty status also has to be given to such provisions, adopted by the Council by means of a special procedure, which enter into force after their approval by the Member States 'in accordance with their respective constitutional requirements' (i.e. by act of parliament and/or after a referendum, depending upon the 'constitutional requirements' of the Member State concerned).[19] Once they have been so adopted, they obtain the status of primary Union law.[20]

---

[14] See further para. 3.02.   [15] See also Art. 24(1), second para., TEU.

[16] For example, as one commentator surmises, on the basis of Art. 40 TEU, the Court of Justice could be asked to interpret the exclusion of legislative acts in the field of the CFSP: P. Eeckhout, *EU External Relations Law* (2nd edn, Oxford, Oxford University Press, 2011), 183–4. Likewise, another commentator has posited that questions of interpretation could arise with respect to the primacy of Union law vis-à-vis CFSP matters: see M.-G. Garbagnati Ketvel, 'The Jurisdiction of the European Court of Justice in Respect of the Common Foreign and Security Policy' (2006) 55 I.C.L.Q. 77–120, at 101.

[17] As regards preliminary rulings on validity: see para. 10.04.

[18] See, e.g. P. Eeckhout, *EU External Relations Law* (Oxford, Oxford University Press, 2011), 498. For the Court of Justice's jurisdiction over CFSP agreements in the context of Opinions delivered pursuant to Art. 218 (11) TFEU, see para. 12.05.

[19] See Art. 223 TFEU (determining a uniform procedure for elections to the European Parliament); see the so-called '1976 Act' concerning the election of the representatives of the Assembly by direct universal suffrage, annexed to the Council Decision of 20 September 1976, [1976] O.J. L278/1, as amended by Council Decision of 1 February 1993, [1993] O.J. L33/15) and by Council Decision of 25 June 2002 and 23 September 2002, [2002] O.J. L283/1; and Art. 311 TFEU (determining the system of the Union's own resources).

[20] This should be distinguished from those Treaty provisions setting down means by which amendments may be made to the Treaties without necessitating an intergovernmental conference, which do not obtain such

Likewise, with the entry into force of the Lisbon Treaty, the rights, freedoms, and principles set out in the Charter of Fundamental Rights of the European Union of 7 December 2000, as adapted at Strasbourg on 12 December 2007 and published alongside the TEU and TFEU,[21] have 'the same legal value as the Treaties'.[22] Yet, while the Court of Justice's preliminary ruling jurisdiction covers the interpretation of the provisions of the Charter,[23] certain limits are placed on such jurisdiction in relation to action taken by the Member States that must fall within the scope of Union law.[24]

(4) General principles of Union law

The unwritten general principles of Union law, including fundamental rights, may also be the subject of a reference for a preliminary ruling on interpretation. Those principles form part of the 'law' which the Court of Justice of the European Union has to ensure is observed in the interpretation and application of the Treaties.[25]   **6.07**

Examples include the principles of equal treatment, proportionality, and *ne bis in idem* and the rights of the defence prior to the adoption of an individual decision having adverse effect.[26] Naturally, a preliminary ruling on the interpretation of those principles may be

---

Treaty status, e.g. Art. 25 TFEU (rights related to Union citizenship); Art. 262 TFEU (jurisdiction of the Court of Justice of the European Union in disputes relating to the application of acts creating European intellectual property rights); Art. 218(2) TFEU (accession to the European Convention for the Protection of Human Rights and Fundamental Freedoms (ECHR)): see further K. Lenaerts and P. Van Nuffel (R. Bray and N. Cambien (eds)), *European Union Law* (3rd edn, London, Sweet & Maxwell, 2011), paras 5.08 and 22.15.

[21] [2012] O.J. C326/391.

[22] Art. 6(1) and (3) TEU. Although the Charter of Fundamental Rights of the European Union was given legally binding force with the entry into force of the Lisbon Treaty on 1 December 2009, it constituted an important instrument, alongside other sources, in connection with the protection of fundamental rights in the EU prior to this date, particularly where the Union measure concerned contained express reference to it. See further K. Lenaerts and P. Van Nuffel (R. Bray and N. Cambien (eds)), *European Union Law* (3rd edn, London, Sweet & Maxwell, 2011), para. 22.22.

[23] For preliminary rulings dealing with the assessment of the validity of Union measures vis-à-vis the Charter, see ECJ, Joined Cases C-92/09 and C-93/09 *Volker und Markus Schecke and Eifert* [2010] E.C.R. I-11063, paras 44–46.

[24] ECJ (judgment of 26 February 2013), Case C-399/11 *Melloni*, not reported, paras 55–64 and ECJ (judgment of 26 February 2013), Case C-617/10 *Åkerberg Fransson*, not reported, paras 16–31. See A. Rosas, '"Implementing" EU Law in the Member States: Some Observations on the Applicability of the Charter of Fundamental Rights', in L. Weitzel, *Mélanges en hommage à Albert Weitzel. L'Europe des droits fondamentaux* (Paris, Pedone, 2013), 185–200. See further para. 6.24. Of course, this also includes action taken by the Union, as in the case of measures adopted by the Union institutions: see, e.g. ECJ, Case C-403/09 PPU *Detiček* [2009] E.C.R. I-12193; ECJ, Case C-400/10 PPU *McB.* [2010] E.C.R. I-8965.

[25] Art. 19(1) TEU (applicable to the EAEC Treaty with repeal of Art. 136 EAEC). See, e.g. ECJ, Case C-115/08 *ČEZ* [2009] E.C.R. I-10265, paras 88–91: extending the principle of prohibition of discrimination on grounds of nationality under Art. 18 TFEU to the EAEC Treaty. Under Art. 6(3) TEU, fundamental rights, as guaranteed by the ECHR and as they result from the 'constitutional traditions common to the Member States' constitute general principles of Union law.

[26] For a general survey, see K. Lenaerts and P. Van Nuffel (R. Bray and N. Cambien (eds)), *European Union Law* (3rd edn, London, Sweet & Maxwell, 2011), paras 22.16–22.42. See, e.g. ECJ (judgment of 14 February 2012), Case C-17/10 *Toshiba Corporation and Others*, not reported (*ne bis in idem*). The 'interpretation' of the principle concerned is often concealed behind the appraisal of the 'validity' of a provision of secondary Union law: see, e.g. ECJ, Case C-308/08 *Intertanko and Others* [2008] E.C.R. I-4057, paras 69–71 (principles of legal certainty and of legality of criminal offences and penalties); ECJ, Case C-127/07 *Arcelor Atlantique and Lorraine and Others* [2008] E.C.R. I-9895, paras 23, 25–26 (principle of equal treatment); ECJ, Case C-58/08 *Vodafone and Others* [2010] E.C.R. I-4999, paras 51–71 (principle of proportionality); ECJ, Case C-15/10 *Etimine* [2011] E.C.R I-6681, paras 124–125 (principle of proportionality).

sought only in connection with the application of substantive Union law, that is to say, in connection with main proceedings relating (at least to some extent) to Union law.[27]

C. Acts of Union institutions, bodies, offices, or agencies

(1) All acts of Union institutions, bodies, offices, or agencies

6.08   Art. 267 TFEU explicitly envisages preliminary rulings to be sought on the interpretation of acts of Union institutions, bodies, offices, or agencies.[28] Subject to the limitations placed on the Court of Justice's preliminary ruling jurisdiction in the former second and third pillars (see para. 6.05), all acts of Union institutions, bodies, offices, or agencies may be the subject of a request for a preliminary ruling on their interpretation,[29] irrespective of whether the act is specifically mentioned in the Treaties[30] or not,[31] whether it is binding or non-binding,[32] or whether or not it has direct effect.[33]

---

[27] See, e.g. ECJ, Case C-349/07 *Sopropré* [2008] E.C.R. I-10369, paras 33–36 (principle of respect for the rights of defence); ECJ, Case C-427/06 *Bartsch* [2008] E.C.R. I-7245, para. 15; ECJ, Case C-555/07 *Kücükdeveci* [2010] E.C.R. I-365, paras 53–55 (principle of equal treatment); ECJ, Case C-35/09 *Speranza* [2010] E.C.R. I-6581, paras 28–30 (principle of proportionality). See further para. 6.24 and n. 24.

[28] Art. 267, first para., indent (b), TFEU. Art. 19(3)(b) TEU merely refers to preliminary rulings on the interpretation and validity of acts adopted by 'the institutions' in more abbreviated fashion.

[29] See, e.g. ECJ, Case C-137/08 *VB Pénzügyi Lízing* [2010] E.C.R. I-10847, para. 38 (and further citations therein): 'As regards the provisions of European Union law which may be the subject of a ruling of the Court of Justice under Article 267 TFEU, it must be recalled that the Court of Justice has jurisdiction to give a preliminary ruling on the validity and interpretation of all acts of the institutions of the European Union without exception.'

[30] In Arts 288–292 TFEU or elsewhere in the Treaties, such as the Rules of Procedure of the Union institutions (e.g. Arts 232, first para., 235(3), 240(3), 249(1), 287(4), fifth para., TFEU), the Financial Regulation (Art. 322 TFEU) or the measures provided for in Art. 291(3) TFEU, i.e. the so-called 'Comitology Regulation' (Regulation No. 182/2011 of the European Parliament and of the Council of 16 February 2011 laying down the rules and the general principles concerning mechanisms for control by Member States of the Commission's exercise of implementing powers, [2011] O.J. L55/13). Yet, to be clear, the conclusions of the 'comitology' committees arguably would not by themselves—that is to say, apart from the resulting act adopted through this process—be subject to a preliminary ruling on interpretation: see further para. 6.12.

[31] For example, a Council resolution: ECJ, Case 9/73 *Schlüter* [1973] E.C.R. 1135, para. 40. See also ECJ, Case C-80/06 *Carp* [2007] E.C.R. I-4473 (a Commission decision of general, as opposed to individual, scope of application which, before the entry into force, was not explicitly mentioned in what was then Art. 249 EC). For a list of 'atypical' Union instruments, see K. Lenaerts and P. Van Nuffel (R. Bray and N. Cambien (eds)), *European Union Law* (3rd edn, London, Sweet & Maxwell, 2011), para. 22.102.

[32] For example, a recommendation (or opinion) within the meaning of Art. 288 TFEU: see, e.g. ECJ, Case 113/75 *Frecassetti* [1976] E.C.R. 983, paras 8–9; ECJ, Case C-322/88 *Grimaldi* [1989] E.C.R. 4407, paras 7–9; ECJ, Case C-207/01 *Altair Chimica* [2003] E.C.R. I-8875, paras 41–43. Under established case-law, national courts are bound to take recommendations into consideration in order to decide disputes referred to them, in particular where they cast light on the interpretation of national measures adopted in order to implement them or where they are designed to supplement binding Union provisions: see, e.g. ECJ, Case C-55/06 *Arcor* [2008] E.C.R. I-293, para. 94; ECJ, Joined Cases C-317/08 to C-320/08 *Alassini and Others* [2010] E.C.R. I-2213, para. 40 (and further citations therein).

[33] For example, ECJ, Case 14/83 *Von Colson and Kamann* [1984] E.C.R. 1891, para. 27; ECJ, Case C-373/95 *Maso and Others* [1997] E.C.R. I-4051, para. 28; ECJ, Case C-254/08 *Futura immobiliare* [2009] E.C.R. I-6995, para. 34 (and further citations therein). Irrespective of whether the Union measure has direct effect, its interpretation will be useful to the national court, which, as a public body, is required under Art. 4(3) TEU to apply its domestic legislation in conformity with the requirements of Union law: see, e.g. ECJ, Case C-188/07 *Commune de Mesquer* [2008] E.C.R. 4501, paras 83–84 (and further citations therein). See also ECJ (judgment of 27 November 2012), Case C-370/12 *Pringle*, not reported, para. 89. For detailed discussion, see K. Lenaerts and P. Van Nuffel (R. Bray and N. Cambien (eds)), *European Union Law* (3rd edn, London, Sweet & Maxwell, 2011), paras 22.87–22.88.

(a) Act must be attributable to Union institution, body, office, or agency

The key criterion is whether the act may be ascribed to a Union institution, body, office, or agency.[34] The test that a Union institution, body, office, or agency must have 'taken part' in the conclusion of the act in order for it to be amenable to interpretation by the Court of Justice in preliminary ruling proceedings is, in all likelihood, open to flexible application. There are many ways in which a Union institution, body, office, or agency might conceivably 'take part' in the conclusion of an act. Thus, the test is satisfied in the case of international agreements concluded by the Union and of (binding and non-binding) acts adopted by bodies set up by such agreements (since the Union participates in the operation of such bodies). Moreover, while acts of the governments of the Member States that do, or do not, have their legal basis in the Treaties—for example, acts adopted by the representatives of the Member State governments meeting within the Council—probably would not fall within the Court of Justice's preliminary ruling jurisdiction, since they are acts of the Member States and not of the Council as a Union institution, arguably there could be exceptions to the extent that such acts are taken by the Council and the Member State governments jointly when the matter concerned falls partly within the Member States' jurisdiction and partly within the Union's jurisdiction.[35]

6.09

New forms of regulatory activity within the Union will also make it necessary to take a creative approach to this test. A prominent example can be found in the Title of the TFEU concerning social policy (Title X of Part Three). Under Art. 155 TFEU, management and labour may conclude agreements at Union level. The question is whether, in certain circumstances, such agreements may also be the subject of a reference for a preliminary ruling. Such agreements are intended to be an alternative to the Union legislation contemplated by Art. 153 TFEU. In addition, before submitting proposals for legislation, the Commission has to consult management and labour and, if they express a wish to that effect, must give them the opportunity to conclude an agreement on the content of the proposal (Art. 154 TFEU). Lastly, '[a]greements concluded at Union level shall be implemented . . . in matters covered by Art. 153, at the joint request of the signatory parties, by a Council decision on a proposal from the Commission' (Art.155(2) TFEU). Although, strictly speaking, Union institutions, bodies, offices, or agencies do not play any part in drawing up the agreements to be concluded by management and labour at Union level, it can be considered, in the light of the contribution they make, that they 'take part' to a sufficient extent in the conferral of legal force on the agreements, as a result of the Council decisions implementing them, as to make them qualify for preliminary rulings by the Court of Justice.[36] The position will be different, of course, where the agreements are

---

[34] For example, ECJ, Case 152/83 *Demouche and Others* [1987] E.C.R. 3833, paras 15–21; ECJ, Case C-193/98 *Pfennigmann* [1999] E.C.R. I-7747, paras 16–20; ECJ, Case C-11/05 *Friesland Coberco Dairy Foods* [2006] E.C.R. I-4285, para. 37.

[35] For further discussion of such acts, see K. Lenaerts and P. Van Nuffel (R. Bray and N. Cambien (eds)), *European Union Law* (3rd edn, London, Sweet & Maxwell, 2011), paras 22.109–22.111.

[36] See, e.g. ECJ, Case C-149/10 *Chatzi* [2010] E.C.R. I-8489, paras 25-26: such a framework agreement 'is admittedly the product of a dialogue . . . between management and labour at European level, but it has been implemented . . . by a Council directive, of which it is thus an integral component', and consequently, the Court of Justice's jurisdiction to interpret such a framework agreement within the context of the preliminary ruling procedure 'does not differ from its general jurisdiction to interpret other provisions contained in directives'. On similar grounds, the Court has applied its case-law on the assessment of the direct effect of provisions of a directive to framework agreements: see, e.g. ECJ, Case C-98/09 *Sorge* [2010] E.C.R. I-5837, para. 51; ECJ, Joined Cases C-444/09 and C-456/09 *Gavieiro Gavieiro and Iglesias Torres* [2010] E.C.R. I-14031, para. 77; ECJ, Case C-486/08 *Tirols* [2010] E.C.R. I-3527, para. 23 (and further citations therein); ECJ, Case C-268/06 *Impact* [2008] E.C.R. I-2483, para. 58; ECJ, Case C-155/10 *Williams and Others*

implemented, not by Council decision, but 'in accordance with the procedures and practices specific to management and labour and the Member States' (the other alternative set out in Art. 155(2) TFEU). The main reason for taking this view is that it is stated in Declaration No. 27 annexed to the Treaty of Amsterdam that 'the content of [such] agreements' is to be developed 'by collective bargaining according to the rules of each Member State' and that there is therefore 'no obligation on the Member States to apply the agreements directly or to work out rules for their transposition, nor any obligation to amend national legislation in force to facilitate their implementation'.[37] Precisely the opposite situation obtains where the agreements are implemented by Council decision, which means that the aim of the procedure of preliminary rulings on interpretation may be achieved in full in that case.

(b) Notion of Union institution, body, office, or agency

6.10 First, as regards the notion of Union 'institution', Art. 13 TEU—as compared to former Art. 7 EC—lists seven, and no longer just five, institutions, adding the European Council and the European Central Bank alongside the European Parliament, the Council, the Commission, the Court of Justice of the European Union, and the Court of Auditors.[38] This explains why there is no longer need for a separate reference to the European Central Bank in Art. 267 TFEU as had been the case with the former Art. 234 EC.[39] Likewise, the promotion of the European Council to the status of Union institution makes clear that preliminary rulings can be sought on the interpretation and validity of acts adopted by the European Council and has settled the controversy concerning the extent to which acts of the European Council could have fallen within the Court of Justice's preliminary ruling jurisdiction under former Art. 234 EC.[40]

It is self-evident that all measures adopted by the Council, the Commission, the European Parliament, or the European Parliament and the Council jointly may be the subject of a reference for a preliminary ruling on their interpretation. In the overwhelming majority of cases, Union decision-making results in such an act in one form or another (see Arts 288–292 TFEU). Certainly, acts of the European Parliament and the Court of Auditors also come under the jurisdiction of the Court of Justice to give preliminary rulings on interpretation, albeit it is more exceptional for the interpretation of such acts to be relevant to the determination of main proceedings before a national court.[41]

[2011] E.C.R. I-8409, para. 16. With respect to framework agreements concluded at Union level, the Council's implementing 'decision' normally takes the form of a 'directive': see further K. Lenaerts and P. Van Nuffel (R. Bray and N. Cambien (eds)), *European Union Law* (3rd edn, London, Sweet & Maxwell, 2011), paras 16.44 and 17.04. An action for annulment may lie against such a Council 'decision' (i.e. a directive): see EGC, Case T-135/96 *UEAPME v Council* [1998] E.C.R. II-2335.

[37] Declaration (No. 27), annexed by the Amsterdam Treaty, on Art. 118b (later Art. 139(2) EC, now Art. 155 TFEU), [1997] O.J. C340/136.

[38] Art. 13(1), second para., TEU.

[39] Similarly, indent (c) of the first para. of former Art. 234 EC, referring to 'the interpretation of the statutes of bodies established by an act of the Council', was also deleted with the entry into force of the Lisbon Treaty on the view that whatever distinction with indent (b) of the same provision had been intended by the Treaty framers, it had been rendered superfluous with the Court's broad interpretation of indent (b) and in any event had not been resorted to: see M. Broberg and N. Fenger, *Preliminary References to the European Court of Justice* (Oxford, Oxford University Press, 2010), 139.

[40] ECJ (judgment of 27 November 2012), Case C-370/12 *Pringle*, not reported, paras 34–36. See para. 10.03.

[41] For example, with respect to the interpretation of the Rules of Procedure of the European Parliament, see ECJ, Joined Cases C-200/07 and C-201/07 *Marra* [2008] E.C.R. I-7929.

Second, as regards the notion of Union 'bodies, offices or agencies', this language essentially incorporates the case-law on former Art. 234 EC in which the Court had already interpreted the expression 'institutions of the Community' broadly by referring to a 'Community institution or agency' which must have taken part in the conclusion of the relevant act,[42] thereby covering any Community body, in addition to the Community institutions mentioned in former Art. 7 EC. As was pointed out in the preceding section, the Court of Justice requires a Union institution, body, office, or agency to have taken part in the adoption of an act for it to be capable of being the subject of an Art. 267 TFEU reference on its interpretation. That requirement can certainly be fulfilled in the case of offices, agencies, foundations, centres, and other 'bodies' established by Union institutions.[43] Accordingly, subject to the limitations placed on the Court's preliminary ruling jurisdiction under the former second and third pillars,[44] acts of bodies, offices, or agencies established by Union institutions in the exercise of their powers and given specific executive tasks (and the associated power to take decisions) can constitute the subject of a request for a preliminary ruling.

(2) Judgments of the Court of Justice of the European Union

Preliminary rulings may also be sought on the interpretation of judgments of the Court of Justice of the European Union. For instance, an interpretation of a previous judgment may be sought in the event that the national court (including other courts dealing with the case[45]) has difficulty in understanding or applying it.[46] The judgment to be interpreted does

6.11

---

[42] ECJ, Case 152/83 *Demouche and Others* [1987] E.C.R. 3833, para. 19.

[43] Nowhere in the Treaties is the distinction between Union 'bodies', 'offices', and 'agencies' explained. It does not appear that the words 'Union bodies, offices and agencies' are exhaustive; they can in principle cover acts of Union 'bodies' in the general sense, e.g. centres, foundations, supervisory authorities, and the like. In the European Convention documents and the subsequent provisions of the Draft Constitutional Treaty on the Court of Justice, reference was made to Union 'bodies and agencies', despite the widespread recognition of various kinds of bodies, offices, agencies, monitoring centres, foundations, etc. See further para. 7.70.

[44] For example, a Union body, office, or agency created pursuant to the Treaty provisions on the CFSP, for which the Court of Justice's preliminary ruling jurisdiction is generally excluded save for certain exceptions (see para. 6.05), as illustrated by the European Defence Agency (see Council Decision 2011/411/CFSP of 12 July 2011 defining the statute, seat, and operational rules of the European Defence Agency and repealing Joint Action 2004/551/CFSP, [2011] O.J. L183/16).

[45] See, e.g. ECJ, Case C-206/94 *Brennet* [1996] E.C.R. I-2357; ECJ (judgment of 13 November 2012), Case C-35/11 *Test Claimants in the FII Group Litigation*, not reported: submission of preliminary question regarding Court's ruling in ECJ, Case C-446/04 *Test Claimants in the FII Group Litigation* [2006] E.C.R. I-11753.

[46] ECJ (order of 5 March 1986), Case 69/85 *Wünsche* [1986] E.C.R. 947, para. 15 (albeit making clear that it would not be permissible to contest the validity of a previous judgment: see para. 6.28); ECJ, Case 14/86 *Pretore di Salò v X* [1987] E.C.R. 2545, para. 12. For examples, see ECJ, Case C-377/89 *Cotter and Others* [1991] E.C.R. I-1155; ECJ, Joined Cases C-363/93 and C-407/93 to C-411/93 *Lancry and Others* [1994] E.C.R. I-3957; ECJ, Case C-280/94 *Posthuma-van Damme and Oztürk* [1996] E.C.R. I-179, para. 13; ECJ, Case C-5/97 *Ballast Nedam Groep* [1997] E.C.R. I-7549, para. 1; ECJ, Case C-219/98 *Anastasiou and Others* [2000] E.C.R. I-5241, paras 13–14; ECJ, Case C-466/00 *Kaba* [2003] E.C.R. I-2219; ECJ, Case C-224/01 *Köbler* [2003] E.C.R. I-10239; ECJ, Case C-17/05 *Cadman* [2006] E.C.R. I-9583; ECJ, Case 2/06 *Kempter* [2008] E.C.R. I-411; ECJ, Case C-430/09 *Euro Tyre Holding* [2010] E.C.R. I-13335, para. 21. See also ECJ (judgment of 23 October 2012), Joined Cases C-581/10 and C-629/10 *Nelson and Others*, not reported: submission of preliminary question regarding Court's ruling in Joined Cases C-402/07 and C-423/07 *Sturgeon and Others* [2009] E.C.R. I-10923. This does not necessarily mean only one judgment; a reference can be made in relation to a line of case-law related to the interpretation of a Union measure: see, e.g. ECJ, Joined Cases C-400/09 and C-207/10 *Orifarm and Others* [2011] E.C.R. I-7063, para. 1.

not have to be a preliminary ruling; it may have been given in any sort of proceedings before the Union judicature.[47]

Commentators have long been divided on this issue. Those arguing that judgments of the Court of Justice of the European Union could be the subject of a reference for a preliminary ruling did so chiefly on the basis of the wording of what is now Art. 267 TFEU: the Court of Justice is an 'institution' of the Union and so its 'acts' (judgments/orders) may be interpreted by way of a preliminary ruling.[48] Those taking the opposite view contended that the subject-matter of a reference for a preliminary ruling on the interpretation of an earlier judgment was in fact not the judgment as such but the provisions and principles of Union law applied or interpreted therein.[49]

The distinction is perhaps not as clear-cut as it seems. The Court of Justice allows national courts and tribunals to refer questions to it on the interpretation of its previous judgments, but in answering them, it inevitably falls back on the provisions and principles of Union law underlying those judgments. This is also true where national courts apply to the Court of Justice for an interpretation of a judgment of the General Court or of the Civil Service Tribunal. The possibility of making such a reference is of great practical importance for national courts where they query whether a judgment of the General Court against which no appeal has been brought before the Court of Justice or a judgment of the Civil Service Tribunal against which no appeal has been brought before the General Court correctly interprets the principles and provisions of Union law with which it deals.

(3) Acts of committees established under Union law

6.12   The European Economic and Social Committee and the Committee of the Regions, which assist the European Parliament, the Council, and the Commission in an advisory capacity (Art. 13(4) TEU), are not formally speaking Union institutions or bodies, offices, or agencies whose acts are amenable to interpretation by the Court of Justice pursuant to Art. 267 TFEU. The Opinions which they deliver as envisaged by the various Treaty provisions or on their own initiative form part of the decision-making process carried out between the Commission, the Council, and (generally) the European Parliament. They

---

[47] See, e.g. ECJ, Joined Cases 314/81 to 316/81 and 83/82 *Waterkeyn* [1982] E.C.R. 4337 (concerning the interpretation of the scope and legal effects of a judgment given pursuant to what is now Art. 258 TFEU). It should, however, be stressed that pursuant to Art. 104(1) of the ECJ Rules of Procedure, 'Article 158 of these Rules relating to the interpretation of judgments and orders shall not apply to decisions given in reply to a request for a preliminary ruling.' Art. 104(2) adds: 'It shall be for the national courts or tribunals to assess whether they consider that sufficient guidance is given by a preliminary ruling, or whether it appears to them that a further reference to the Court is required.' See also para. 6.28.

[48] G. Vandersanden, *La procédure préjudicielle devant la Cour de justice de l'Union européenne* (Brussels, Bruylant, 2011), para. 34, at 39.

[49] Broberg and Fenger take the view that judgments of the Court of Justice are not open to review in the context of preliminary ruling proceedings: M. Broberg and N. Fenger, *Preliminary References to the European Court of Justice* (Oxford, Oxford University Press, 2010), 122. They refer to ECJ (order of 5 March 1986), Case 69/85 *Wünsche* [1986] E.C.R. 947, paras 10–16. Further evidence for this view may be found in ECJ, Case 135/77 *Bosch* [1978] E.C.R. 855 and ECJ, Joined Cases 87/79, 112/79 and 113/79 *Bagusat and Others* [1980] E.C.R. 1159; see also the Opinion of Advocate-General J.-P. Warner in ECJ, Case 8/78 *Milac* [1978] E.C.R. 1721, at 1740–1. However, albeit drafted as a question of interpretation of provisions and principles of Union law, the reference in ECJ (order of 18 April 2013), Case C-413/11 *Germanwings*, not reported, directly challenged the Court's judgment in Joined Cases C-402/07 and C-423/07 *Sturgeon and Others* [2009] E.C.R. I-10923.

have no independent existence and could, at the most, be used to help interpret Union acts where they took part in the process of their adoption.[50] Similar remarks could be made for other committees established under Union law, for example, the various scientific, consultative, and advisory committees in the relevant field.[51]

D. International agreements concluded by the Union and acts of bodies established by such agreements

(1) Agreements concluded by the Union

Not only acts adopted by Union institutions autonomously, but also 'contractual' acts are **6.13** covered by indent (b) of the first paragraph of Art. 267 TFEU. Thus, the Court of Justice has held that it has jurisdiction to give preliminary rulings on the interpretation of international agreements concluded by the Union with third countries or international organizations (see Arts 216–219 TFEU).[52]

Under established case-law, international agreements concluded by the Union form an integral part of its legal order and can therefore be the subject of a request for a preliminary ruling on their interpretation; however, the Court of Justice does not in principle have jurisdiction to interpret in preliminary ruling proceedings international agreements concluded between Member States and non-member countries outside the confines of Union law,[53] subject to the following exception: 'only where and insofar as the European Union has assumed the powers previously exercised by the Member States in the field to which the international convention not concluded by the European Union applies, and therefore, the provisions of the convention have the effect of binding the European Union'.[54] In this way, international

---

[50] K. Lenaerts and P. Van Nuffel (R. Bray and N. Cambien (eds)), *European Union Law* (3rd edn, London, Sweet & Maxwell, 2011), paras 13.107–13.113.

[51] For a survey, see K. Lenaerts and P. Van Nuffel (R. Bray and N. Cambien (eds)), *European Union Law* (3rd edn, London, Sweet & Maxwell, 2011), paras 13.114–13.115.

[52] ECJ, Case 181/73 *Haegeman* [1974] E.C.R. 449, paras 1–6; for examples, see, e.g. ECJ, Case 87/75 *Bresciani* [1976] E.C.R. 129; ECJ, Case 65/77 *Razanatsimba* [1977] E.C.R. 2229; ECJ, Case C-18/90 *Kziber* [1991] E.C.R. I-199; ECJ, Case C-113/97 *Babahenini* [1998] E.C.R. I-183; ECJ, Case C-265/03 *Simutenkov* [2005] E.C.R. I-2579; ECJ, Case C-102/09 *Camar* [2010] E.C.R. I-4045; ECJ, Case C-160/09 *Iannis Katsivardas-Nikolaos Tsitsikas* [2010] E.C.R. I-4591; ECJ (judgment of 11 April 2013), Joined Cases C-335/11 and C-337/11 *HK Danmark*, not reported. Sometimes, the Court of Justice's interpretation of international agreements concluded by the Union can implicate sensitive political issues in international relations: for example, as regards the Israel–Palestinian conflict, see ECJ, Case C-386/08 *Brita* [2010] E.C.R. I-1289. Questions concerning the interpretation of such agreements have sometimes involved third countries which since acceded to the European Union: in addition to ECJ, Case 181/73 *Haegeman*, see, e.g. ECJ, Case C-432/92 *Anastasiou and Others* [1994] E.C.R. I-3087; ECJ, Joined Cases C-23/04 to C-25/04 *Sfakianakis* [2006] E.C.R. I-1265; ECJ, Case C-56/06 *Euro Tex* [2007] E.C.R. I-4859; ECJ, Case C-101/10 *Pavlov and Famira* [2011] E.C.R. I-5951.

[53] ECJ, Case 130/73 *Vandeweghe and Others* [1973] E.C.R. 1329, para. 2; ECJ, Case 44/84 *Hurd* [1986] E.C.R. 26, para. 20. For example, as regards bilateral tax conventions, see ECJ, Case C-128/08 *Damseaux* [2009] E.C.R. I-6823, paras 20–22 (and further citations therein). Likewise, the Court considers that it has no jurisdiction under Art. 267 TFEU to interpret a provision of an agreement concluded between a number of Member States, even if the agreement was concluded pursuant to an EU directive: ECJ (order of 12 November 1998), Case C-162/98 *Hartmann* [1998] E.C.R. I-7083, paras 8–10.

[54] ECJ, Case C-533/08 *TNT Express Nederland* [2010] E.C.R. I-4107, paras 59–62 (and further citations therein). See also ECJ, Case C-188/07 *Commune de Mesquer* [2008] E.C.R. I-4501, para. 85; ECJ, Case C-301/08 *Bogiatzi* [2009] E.C.R. I-10185, paras 24–34, and ECJ (judgment of 21 December 2011), Case C-366/10 *Air Transport Association of America and Others*, not reported, para. 62 (see G. De Baere and

agreements by which the Union is bound by way of substitution for the Member States are treated in the same way as international agreements concluded by the Union.

(2) Agreements concluded by the Union and the Member States

6.14 Sometimes, in preliminary ruling proceedings, when the Court of Justice determines that an international agreement falls within its jurisdiction, it does not explain whether what is involved is an international agreement concluded by the Union and the Member States jointly with third countries, commonly referred to as a mixed agreement.[55]

Yet a key question has arisen in the case-law as to whether in the case of a mixed agreement concluded by the Union and the Member States jointly with a third country the jurisdiction of the Court of Justice extends to rulings interpreting provisions of the agreement by which the Member States enter into commitments vis-à-vis that country by virtue of their own powers.[56] The Court of Justice first left this question expressly open.[57] It was able to do so because it could take the view that the provisions whose interpretation was sought fell partly within the Union's powers to guarantee commitments towards the non-member country concerned. The fact that the Member States had to carry out the commitments was irrelevant because in doing so they were simply fulfilling an obligation in relation to the Union and did not assume, vis-à-vis the non-member country, the Union's responsibility for the due performance of the agreement.[58]

C. Ryngaert, case note (2013) E.F.A. Rev. 389–410). As illustrated by the foregoing cases, the Court of Justice takes a strict approach with respect to the evaluation of the Union's functional succession to obligations entered into by the Member States. Yet, as noted by the Court (ECJ, Case C-308/06 *Intertanko and Others* [2008] E.C.R. I-4057, para. 48), functional succession has been found in the context of the GATT. See also ECJ, Joined Cases 267/81 to 269/81 *SPI and SAMI* [1983] E.C.R. 801, paras 14–19 (and citations therein): the Court of Justice took quite an expansive approach, holding that it had jurisdiction to give preliminary rulings on the interpretation of the 1947 GATT (General Agreement on Tariffs and Trade) on the grounds that, since the Common Customs Tariff entered into effect, the then Community had been substituted for the Member States as regards the fulfillment of the commitments laid down in the GATT, thereby assuming jurisdiction to give preliminary rulings simply by referring to the aim of that jurisdiction, namely 'to ensure the uniform interpretation of Community [now Union] law'. This case is relied upon for establishing the rationale for requiring uniform application of international law that is an integral part of Union law in other contexts.

[55] For example, as regards the EEA Agreement, see ECJ, Case C-321/97 *Andersson and Wåkerås-Andersson* [1999] E.C.R. I-3551, paras 23–33. It is clear from this judgment that the Court of Justice has jurisdiction to interpret the EEA Agreement; however, the interpretation is binding only on the Union, and not on the EFTA States. The EFTA Court is empowered to give rulings on the interpretation of the EEA Agreement which are applicable in the EFTA States. See more recently, ECJ, Case C-157/07 *Krankenheim Ruhesitz am Wannsee-Seniorenheimstatt* [2008] E.C.R. I-8061 and further citations therein. For examples concerning other agreements, see, e.g. ECJ, Case C-213/03 *Syndicat professionnel coordination des pêcheurs de l'étang de Berre et de la région* [2004] E.C.R. I-7357 (the Court of Justice has been forthcoming in the context of an infringement action concerning the same agreement: ECJ, Case C-239/03 *Commission v France* [2004] E.C.R. I-9325, paras 22–31); ECJ, Case C-97/05 *Gattoussi* [2006] E.C.R. I-11917; ECJ, Case C-70/09 *Hengartner and Gasser* [2010] E.C.R. I-7233, paras 35–43 (and further citations therein). See further A. Rosas, 'The Status in EU Law of International Agreements Concluded by EU Member States' (2011) Fordham Int'l L.J. 1304–45.

[56] See also M. Wathelet and S. Van Raepenbusch, 'Quelques considérations sur l'interprétation par la Cour de justice des accords externes conclus par la Communauté européenne', in G. C. Rodriguez Iglesias (ed.), *Problèmes d'interprétation: à la mémoire de Constantinos N. Kakouris* (Athens and Brussels, Bruylant and Sakkoulas, 2003), 471–502.

[57] ECJ, Case 12/86 *Demirel* [1987] E.C.R. 3719, para. 9; ECJ, Case C-53/96 *Hermès International* [1998] E.C.R. I-3603, paras 24–33.

[58] Art. 4(3) TEU; ECJ, Case 104/81 *Kupferberg* [1982] E.C.R. 3641. See also ECJ, Case C-439/01 *Cipra and Kvasnicka* [2003] E.C.R. I-745, paras 23–24 with respect to the AETR Agreement (European Agreement concerning the Work of Crews of Vehicles engaged in International Road Transport). The Court held, after

In *Parfums Christian Dior*,[59] the Court held, however, that it had jurisdiction to interpret Art. 50 of TRIPs[60] (a procedural provision conferring on the judicial authorities of the Contracting Parties the authority to order prompt and effective provisional measures to prevent a threatened or suspected infringement of any intellectual property right from occurring) both in situations falling within the scope of the national law of the Member States and in those coming under Union law. The Court inferred its interpretative jurisdiction from the finding that Art. 50 of TRIPs constitutes a procedural provision which should be applied in the same way in every situation falling within its scope (both situations covered by national law and situations covered by Union law) and that this obligation requires the judicial bodies of the Member States and the Union, to give it a uniform interpretation, for practical and legal reasons.

Lately, the Court of Justice seems to consider itself competent to interpret provisions of a mixed agreement if the agreement concerns a field in large measure covered by Union law. In *Merck Genéricos*,[61] concerning questions on the interpretation of Art. 33 of TRIPs (a provision on the term of protection for patents), the Court of Justice held that it has jurisdiction under Art. 267 TFEU to interpret the provisions of the TRIPs Agreement in order to define the obligations that the Union has thereby assumed and to determine whether the relevant sphere covering the provision of the TRIPs Agreement at issue in the main proceedings is one in which the Union has, or has not, legislated, which 'calls for a uniform reply at [Union] level that the Court alone is capable of supplying'. In the case at hand, the sphere concerned (patent law) was not covered sufficiently by Union legislation to lead to the conclusion that it fell within the scope of Union law.[62]

With respect to the WTO Agreement, including TRIPs, the foregoing case-law might be affected by the changes brought by the Lisbon Treaty, since the Union's exclusive competence now explicitly covers the common commercial policy, including 'the commercial aspects of intellectual property',[63] which refers to TRIPs.[64] Nonetheless, the approach taken by the Court of Justice remains relevant in assessing its jurisdiction to interpret the provisions of other mixed agreements. For example, in *Lesoochranárske zoskupenie VLK*,[65] the Court declared that it has 'jurisdiction to define the obligations

having recalled that in ratifying or acceding to that agreement, the Member States had acted in the interest and on behalf of the Union (then Community), that it forms part of Union law and hence that it has jurisdiction to interpret it.

[59] ECJ, Joined Cases C-300/98 and C-392/98 *Parfums Christian Dior and Others* [2000] E.C.R. I-11307, paras 32–40. See also ECJ, Case C-89/99 *Schieving-Nijstad and Others* [2001] E.C.R. I-5851, para. 30; ECJ, Case C-245/02 *Anheuser-Busch* [2004] E.C.R. I-10989, paras 40–46.

[60] On the WTO and the competence of the Union and the Member States for matters falling within the scope of the WTO, see generally K. Lenaerts and P. Van Nuffel (R. Bray and N. Cambien (eds)), *European Union Law* (3rd edn, London, Sweet & Maxwell, 2011), paras 25.03–25.15.

[61] ECJ, Case C-431/05 *Merck Genéricos* [2007] E.C.R. I-7001, paras 31–37. Compare Opinion of AG D. Ruiz-Jarabo Colomer in ECJ, Case C-431/05 *Merck Genéricos*, particularly points 54–61 (advocating that the Court of Justice should have unlimited jurisdiction to interpret the TRIPs Agreement, irrespective of whether the Union has legislated in the field concerned).

[62] ECJ, Case C-431/05 *Merck Genéricos*, para. 46.

[63] Arts 3(1)(e), 207(1) TFEU.

[64] ECJ (judgment of 18 July 2013), Case C-414/11 *Daiichi Sankyo*, not reported, paras 45–48.

[65] ECJ, Case C-240/09 *Lesoochranárske zoskupenie* [2011] E.C.R. I-1255, paras 30–31. See also the accompanying Opinion of Advocate-General E. Sharpston, points 43–62 (providing a neat summary of the case-law to date praising the approach taken in *Merck Genéricos*).

which the [Union] has assumed and those which remain the sole responsibility of the Member States in order to interpret the Aarhus Convention'. Specifically, the Court ruled that it has jurisdiction to interpret Art. 9(3) of the Aarhus Convention (concerning the right of access to procedures to challenge acts contravening national law provisions relating to the environment), stressing that where a provision can apply both to situations falling within the scope of national and of Union law, it is in the interests of Union law that the provision is interpreted uniformly, whatever the circumstances in which it is to apply.[66]

(3) Acts of bodies established by international agreements

6.15 That same aim of the Court of Justice's jurisdiction to give preliminary rulings on interpretation (that is, of ensuring the uniform application of Union law) has prompted it to hold that it may give preliminary rulings on the interpretation of binding and non-binding acts of bodies established by international agreements concluded by the Union. Thus, the Court has held that decisions of an Association Council form an integral part of Union law on account of their direct connection with the agreement itself.[67] Since the function of Art. 267 TFEU is to ensure the uniform application throughout the Union of all provisions forming part of the Union legal system and to ensure that their effects do not vary according to the interpretation accorded to them in the various Member States, the Court of Justice must have jurisdiction to give preliminary rulings on the interpretation not only of the agreement itself, but also of decisions of the body established by the agreement and entrusted with responsibility for its implementation.[68]

E. Provisions of Union law to which national law refers

(1) The *Dzodzi* case-law

6.16 In *Dzodzi*,[69] the Court of Justice considerably extended its jurisdiction to give preliminary rulings on interpretation (after Advocate-General M. Darmon had delivered an Opinion

---

[66] ECJ, Case C-240/09 *Lesoochranárske zoskupenie*, paras 40–43.

[67] ECJ, Case 30/88 *Greece v Commission* [1989] E.C.R. 3711, para. 13.

[68] ECJ, Case C-192/89 *Sevince* [1990] E.C.R. I-3461, paras 9–11; for further examples, see ECJ, Case C-237/91 *Kus* [1992] E.C.R. I-6781; ECJ, Case C-188/91 *Deutsche Shell* [1993] E.C.R. I-363 (the latter case was concerned with the interpretation of a non-binding act, which was of interest to the national court because it wanted to apply its national law as consistently as possible with that act on account of the obligation of cooperation in good faith borne by the Member State of which that court was a body); ECJ, Case C-277/94 *Taflan-Met and Others* [1996] E.C.R. I-4085; ECJ, Case C-171/95 *Tetik* [1997] E.C.R. I-329; ECJ, Case C-351/95 *Kadiman* [1997] E.C.R. I-2133; ECJ, Case C-386/95 *Eker* [1997] E.C.R. I-2697; ECJ, Case C-285/95 *Kol* [1997] E.C.R. I-3069; ECJ, Case C-36/96 *Günaydin* [1997] E.C.R. I-5143; ECJ, Case C-98/96 *Ertanir* [1997] E.C.R. I-5179; ECJ, Case C-210/97 *Akman* [1998] E.C.R. I-7519; ECJ, Case C-1/97 *Birden* [1998] E.C.R. I-7747; ECJ, Case C-329/97 *Ergat* [2000] E.C.R. I-1487; ECJ, Case C-275/02 *Ayaz* [2004] E.C.R. I-8765; ECJ, Case C-230/03 *Sedef* [2006] E.C.R. I-157; ECJ, Case C-502/04 *Torun* [2006] E.C.R. I-1563; ECJ, Case C-4/05 *Güzeli* [2006] E.C.R. I-10279; ECJ, Case C-325/05 *Derin* [2007] E.C.R. I-6495; ECJ, Case C-349/06 *Polat* [2007] E.C.R. I-8167; ECJ, Case C-372/06 *Asda Stores* [2007] E.C.R. I-11223; ECJ, Case C-294/06 *Payir and Others* [2008] E.C.R. I-203; ECJ, Case C-453/07 *Er* [2008] E.C.R. I-7299; ECJ, Case C-337/07 *Altun* [2008] E.C.R. I-10323; ECJ, Case C-242/06 *Sahin* [2009] E.C.R. I-8465; ECJ, Case C-14/09 *Genc* [2010] E.C.R. I-931; ECJ, Joined Cases C-300/09 and C-301/09 *Toprak and Oguz* [2010] E.C.R. I-12845; ECJ, Case C-303/08 *Bozkurt* [2010] E.C.R. I-13445; and ECJ, Case C-484/07 *Pehlivan* [2011] E.C.R. I-5203.

[69] ECJ, Joined Cases C-297/88 and C-197/89 *Dzodzi* [1990] E.C.R. I-3763. Although the Court of Justice has drawn attention to some earlier case-law in which it took a similar approach (namely, ECJ, Case

proposing that it should not do so), finding that it did not appear either from the wording of what is now Art. 267 TFEU or from the aim of the procedure introduced by that provision that the authors of the Treaties intended to exclude from the jurisdiction of the Court requests for a preliminary ruling on a provision of Union law 'in the specific case where the national law of a Member State refers to the content of that provision in order to determine rules applicable to a situation which is purely internal to that State'.[70] The Court considered that it was 'manifestly in the interest of the [Union] legal order that, in order to forestall future differences of interpretation, every Union provision should be given a uniform interpretation irrespective of the circumstances in which it is to be applied'.[71]

Dzodzi remains within the confines of the interpretation of Union law, although it breaks new ground because it accepts that Union law is being applied, not by virtue of its own authority, but by virtue of that of national law, and that this does not prevent the Court from ruling on its interpretation.[72] By recognizing its interpretative jurisdiction, the Court avoids the provisions of Union law in issue taking on a life of their own. Moreover, if the Court of Justice refused—in a case like *Dzodzi*—to accede to a request from the national court to provide the correct interpretation of the provisions in question, a national court could, in a future case in which—by contrast to *Dzodzi*—Union law is applicable in its own right, be more easily inclined to come to the (possibly wrong) conclusion that the answer to the question of interpretation is obvious (or already in existence) and that it is therefore under no obligation to seek a preliminary ruling. This would in turn put the uniform interpretation of Union law at risk.[73]

166/84 *Thomasdünger* [1985] E.C.R. 3001, paras 11–12), it has given the label of the '*Dzodzi* line of cases' to the established line of judgments in which the Court has held that it has jurisdiction to give preliminary rulings on questions concerning Union law provisions in situations where the facts of the cases being considered by the national courts are outside the scope of Union law but where those provisions have been rendered applicable by domestic law: ECJ, Case C-28/95 *Leur-Bloem* [1997] E.C.R. I-4161, para. 27; ECJ, Case C-130/95 *Giloy* [1997] E.C.R. I-4291, para. 23; see also ECJ, Case C-48/07 *Les Vergers du Vieux Tauves* [2008] E.C.R. I-10627, para. 21.

[70] ECJ, Joined Cases C-297/88 and C-197/89 *Dzodzi*, para. 36. See also, e.g. ECJ, Case C-231/89 *Gmurzynska-Bscher* [1990] E.C.R. I-4003, para. 25; ECJ (order of 26 April 2002), Case C-454/00 *Vis Farmaceutici Istituto Scientifico delle Venezie,* not reported, paras 21–24; ECJ, Case C-222/01 *British American Tobacco Manufacturing* [2004] E.C.R. I-4683, paras 40–41; ECJ, Case C-280/06 *ETI and Others* [2007] E.C.R. I-10893, para. 22 (and further citations therein).

[71] ECJ, Joined Cases C-297/88 and C-197/89 *Dzodzi*, para. 37. See also, e.g. ECJ, Case C-43/00 *Andersen og Jensen* [2002] E.C.R. I-379, para. 18; ECJ, Case C-267/99 *Adam* [2001] E.C.R. I-7467, paras 27–28 (stressing that this reasoning applies all the more when the national legislation which uses a concept of a provision of Union law has been adopted with a view to the transposition into internal law of a directive of which the said provision forms part); ECJ, Joined Cases C-175/08, C-176/08, C-178/08, and C-179/08 *Abdulla and Others* [2010] E.C.R. I-1493, para. 48 (and further citations therein). Reasoning by analogy with the latter judgment (involving a situation where national law refers to the provisions of a directive in order to determine the rules applicable to a situation which is purely internal to that Member State), the Court of Justice held that this also applied to the specific case where national law refers to the content of provisions of an international agreement which have been re-stated in a directive in order to determine the rules applicable to a situation that is purely internal to that Member State: 'In such a case, it is clearly in the interests of the European Union that, in order to forestall future differences of interpretation, the provisions of that international agreement which have been taken over by national law and by EU law should be given a uniform interpretation, irrespective of the circumstances in which they are to apply': ECJ, Joined Cases C-57/09 and C-101/09 *B and D* [2010] E.C.R. I-10979, para. 71.

[72] For some applications, see, e.g. ECJ, Case C-231/89 *Gmurzynska-Bscher* [1990] E.C.R. I-4003, paras 24–26; ECJ, Case C-384/89 *Tomatis and Fulchiron* [1991] E.C.R. I-127, Summ. pub., para. 9; ECJ, Case C-170/03 *Feron* [2005] E.C.R. I-2299, paras 10–12.

[73] For an extensive discussion, see K. Lenaerts, 'Prejudiciële uitlegging van het gemeenschapsrecht met het oog op toepassing van nationaal recht', in D. C. Buijs (ed.), *Mok-aria: opstellen aangeboden aan prof.*

The Court of Justice also accepts jurisdiction to give preliminary rulings on interpretation on the same terms where provisions of Union law are applicable for the resolution of a dispute by virtue of a contractual relationship between the parties.[74]

(2) Limits of the *Dzodzi* case-law

6.17 In *Kleinwort Benson*,[75] the Court of Justice established some important limits to the *Dzodzi* case-law. In that case, the Court held that it had no jurisdiction to give a preliminary ruling on a provision of the Brussels Convention on the grounds that the dispute in the main proceedings was not concerned with the interpretation of this provision as such, but of a provision of domestic law modelled on the Convention and partially reproducing its terms and, moreover, that the domestic law provided for the national authorities to adopt modifications designed to produce divergence between the provisions of that law and the corresponding provisions of the Convention. The Court properly inferred from this that the provisions of the Convention could not be regarded as having been rendered applicable as such in cases outwith the scope of the Convention by the law of the Contracting State concerned. The Court also emphasized that, in applying the provisions of national law modelled on the Brussels Convention, the national courts were not bound by its case-law, but were required only to have regard to it.

In subsequent cases, the Court of Justice has taken pains to distinguish, albeit loosely, the factors identified in *Kleinwort Benson* from those situations in which the *Dzodzi* case-law applies. Recently, for example, in *Les Vergers du Vieux Tauves*,[76] the Court pointed out that the national legislation was expressly intended, as was clear from its title, to transpose an EU directive and, even though it was not stated explicitly, the fact that the referring court had referred a question for a preliminary ruling and that it established a connection between the

---

mr. M.R. Mok ter gelegenheid van zijn 70ste verjaardag (Deventer, Kluwer, 2002), at 173–86. That said, the *Dzodzi* case-law has received its fair share of criticism: see, e.g. A. Arnull, *The European Union and Its Court of Justice* (2nd edn, Oxford, Oxford University Press, 2006), 107–14; A. Barav, 'Une anomalie préjudicielle', in *50 ans de droit communautaire–Mélanges en hommage de Guy Isaac* (Presses de l'Université des Sciences sociales de Toulouse, Toulouse, 2004), 773–801; S. Lefevre, 'The Interpretation of Community Law by the Court of Justice in Areas of National Competence' (2004) E.L. Rev. 501–16. The *Dzodzi* case-law is equally well known for differences in approach between the Court of Justice and the Advocates-General, though at present, this seems to be dying down; see further K. Lenaerts, 'The Unity of European Law and the Overload of the ECJ: The System of Preliminary Rulings Revisited', in G. Ziccardi Capaldo (ed.), *The Global Community: Yearbook of International Law and Jurisprudence 2005* (New York, Oceana Publications, 2006), 173–201.

[74] ECJ, Case C-88/91 *Federconsorzi* [1992] E.C.R. I-4035, paras 6–9. Yet, in doing so, the Court emphasized that its jurisdiction concerned only the interpretation of Union law, not matters relating to the contract or provisions of national law which may determine the scope of the contractual obligations: ECJ, Case C-88/91 *Federconsorzi*, para. 10. See also ECJ, Case C-73/89 *Fournier* [1992] E.C.R. I-5621, paras 22–24.

[75] ECJ, Case C-346/93 *Kleinwort Benson* [1995] E.C.R. I-615. Prior to this case, the Court of Justice was known for a somewhat lax approach: see, e.g. ECJ, Case C-73/89 *Fournier* [1992] E.C.R. I-5621, paras 22–23.

[76] ECJ, Case C-48/07 *Les Vergers du Vieux Tauves* [2008] E.C.R. I-10627, paras 22–25. In ECJ (judgment of 18 October 2012), Case C-371/11 *Punch Graphic Prepress Belgium*, not reported, para. 27, the Court held that 'where domestic legislation adopts for purely internal situations the same solutions as those adopted by European Union law, it is for the national court alone, in the context of the division of judicial functions between national courts and the Court of Justice under Art. 267 TFEU, to assess the precise scope of that reference to European Union law, the jurisdiction of the Court of Justice being confined to the examination of provisions of that law'. For some earlier examples, see, e.g. ECJ, Case C-28/95 *Leur-Bloem* [1997] E.C.R. I-4161, paras 28–31; ECJ, Case C-130/95 *Giloy* [1997] E.C.R. I-4291, paras 24–28; ECJ, Case C-1/99 *Kofisa Italia* [2001] E.C.R. I-207, paras 29–32; ECJ, Case C-306/99 *BIAO* [2003] E.C.R. I-1, paras 91–93.

national legislation and the directive concerned led to the conclusion that the judgment was binding on the national court. In another case, involving EU competition law, the Court ruled that, although the national legislation expressly referred to the EU regulation concerned only in order to determine the rules in domestic situations, the national legislature nonetheless decided to apply the same treatment to domestic and to Union law situations, which justified its providing a preliminary ruling in the instant case.[77]

Conversely, the Court of Justice has not shied away from deeming inadmissible questions for a preliminary ruling when the provisions of Union law of which interpretation is sought clearly cannot be applied, either directly or indirectly, to the circumstances of the main proceedings[78] and thus fall outside the scope of the *Dzodzi* case-law altogether.[79]

Furthermore, as made clear starting in *Dzodzi,* the Court has jurisdiction only to interpret Union law; it cannot 'take account of the general scheme of the provisions of domestic law which, while referring to [Union] law, define the extent of that reference'.[80] The Court has therefore drawn the boundary between its own jurisdiction and that of the national court in the following terms: '[C]onsideration of the limits which the national legislature may have placed on the application of [Union] law to purely internal situations is a matter for domestic law and consequently falls within the exclusive jurisdiction of the courts of the Member States.'[81]

III. Content of a Preliminary Ruling on Interpretation and Limits Placed on the Jurisdiction of the Court of Justice

A. Interpretation versus application

The Treaties do not define precisely what is meant by 'interpretation' of Union law in the **6.18** context of the preliminary ruling procedure.[82] Initially, the Court of Justice strongly

---

[77] ECJ, Case C-217/05 *Confederación Española de Empresarios de Estaciones de Servicio* [2006] E.C.R. I-11987, paras 21–22. For other examples which do not identify *Kleinwort Benson* explicitly, see, e.g. ECJ, Case C-3/04 *Poseidon Chartering* [2006] E.C.R. I-2505, paras 16–19; ECJ, Case C-280/06 *ETI and Others* [2007] E.C.R. I-10893, paras 23–26 (also concerning EU competition law).

[78] See, e.g. ECJ, Case C-2/97 *IP* [1998] E.C.R. I-8597, paras 59–62; ECJ, Case C-310/10 *Agafiţei and Others* [2011] E.C.R. I-5989, paras 38–48; ECJ (judgment of 18 October 2012), Case C-583/10 *Nolan*, not reported, paras 47–52.

[79] See also ECJ (judgment of 21 December 2011), Case C-482/10 *Cicala*, not reported, paras 17–30; ECJ (judgment of 7 November 2013), Case C-313/12 *Romeo*, not reported, paras 32–35.

[80] ECJ, Joined Cases C-297/88 and C-197/89 *Dzodzi* [1990] E.C.R. I-3763, para. 42.

[81] See, e.g. ECJ, Case C-48/07 *Les Vergers du Vieux Tauves* [2008] E.C.R. I-10627, para. 27 (and further citations therein, though stressing that, with regard to Union law, the referring court may not diverge within the limits of the reference of domestic law back to Union law, from the interpretation provided by the Court). See also ECJ (order of 4 June 2009), Joined Cases C-439/07 and C-499/07 *KBC Bank and Others* [2009] E.C.R. I-4409, paras 58–60. In *Leur-Bloem* and *Giloy,* the Court held, however, that in every case where it had held that it had jurisdiction to give preliminary rulings on questions concerning Union provisions in situations where the facts of the cases being considered by the national courts were outside the scope of Union law, the application of the provisions of Union law was manifestly not limited by provisions of domestic law or contractual provisions incorporating those Union provisions (ECJ, Case C-28/95 *Leur-Bloem* [1997] E.C.R. I-4161, para. 27, and ECJ, Case C-130/95 *Giloy* [1997] E.C.R. I-4291, para. 23).

[82] See ECJ, Case 13/61 *Bosch and Others* [1962] E.C.R. 45, at 50, where the Court of Justice held that since the question as to what is meant in what is now Art. 267 TFEU by 'the interpretation of [Union] law' may itself be a matter of interpretation, it is permissible for the national court to formulate its request in a simple and direct way.

emphasized the distinction between interpretation and application, which was also to demarcate the respective functions of the Court of Justice and the national courts.[83] At the same time, however, it referred to 'the special field of judicial cooperation' under what is now Art. 267 TFEU, which requires that the national court and the Court of Justice, both keeping within their respective jurisdiction and with the aim of ensuring that Union law is applied in a unified manner, 'make direct and complementary contributions to the working out of a decision'.[84]

B. Judicial cooperation

6.19   As the case-law has evolved, the idea of 'judicial cooperation' has got the upper hand over the distinction between interpretation and application,[85] the aim being to ensure that the main proceedings are determined in a way which secures the uniform 'application' of Union law. This is not to discount the Court of Justice's repeated admonition that the application of Union law falls within the exclusive jurisdiction of the national court.[86] Nonetheless, the idea is that this does not preclude the Court from ensuring that it can give an answer that will be of use to the national court to enable it to determine the case before it.[87]

This is why the Court of Justice regularly refers to 'the need to afford a helpful interpretation of [Union] law'.[88] Such an interpretation can be confined specifically to the facts and points of national law underlying the national proceedings as they emerge from the 'documents before the Court'.[89] The documents in the case from which the Court derives the relevant facts and points of national law include not only the order for reference and the file submitted by the national court, but also the written and oral observations of the parties

---

Recently, the Court received such a question, holding that the enforceability against an individual of a Union regulation which is not published in the language of a Member State is a question of the interpretation, not validity, of Union law: ECJ, Case C-161/06 *Skoma-Lux* [2007] E.C.R. I-10841, paras 57–61.

[83] ECJ (order of 3 June 1964), Case 6/64 *Costa v ENEL* [1964] E.C.R. 614, at 614–15; ECJ, Case 20/64 *Albatros* [1965] E.C.R. 29, at 34; ECJ, Case 13/68 *Salgoil* [1968] E.C.R. 453, at 459–60.

[84] ECJ, Case 16/65 *Schwarze* [1965] E.C.R. 877, at 886; see also ECJ, Joined Cases C-260/00 to C-263/00 *Lohmann and Medi Bayreuth* [2002] E.C.R. I-10045, para. 27 (referring to the 'close cooperation' between the national courts and the Court of Justice in this context) and para. 26 (where the Court stated in connection with a preliminary question concerning a tariff classification in the Combined Nomenclature that 'its task is to provide the national court with guidance on the criteria which will enable the latter to classify the products at issue correctly in the [Combined Nomenclature], rather than to effect that classification itself'); ECJ, Case C-500/04 *Proxxon* [2006] E.C.R. I-1545, para. 24 (and citations therein); ECJ, C-14/09 *Genc* [2010] E.C.R. I-931, para. 30 (and citations therein).

[85] In ECJ, Case C-162/06 *International Mail Spain* [2007] E.C.R. I-9911, para. 24, the Court opined: 'It is one of the essential characteristics of the system of judicial cooperation established under Article [267 TFEU] that the Court replies in rather abstract and general terms to a question on the interpretation of [Union] law referred to it, while it is for the referring court to give a ruling in the dispute before it, taking into account the Court's reply.' Despite the sensitivities that this distinction continues to engender, there seems to be widespread recognition of the inherent tensions placed on the Court in terms of ensuring that the answer given by the Court is sufficiently concrete to be of service to the national court, on the one hand, and providing a general answer as part of ensuring the uniform interpretation of Union law in the various legal orders, on the other.

[86] See, e.g. ECJ, Case C-451/03 *Servizi Ausiliari Dottori Commercialisti* [2006] E.C.R. I-2941, para. 69 (and citations therein).

[87] See, e.g. ECJ, Case C-279/06 *CEPSA* [2008] E.C.R. I-6681, para. 31 (and citations therein).

[88] ECJ, Case 244/78 *Union Laitière Normande* [1979] E.C.R. 2663, para. 5.

[89] ECJ, Case 311/85 *VVR* [1987] E.C.R. 3801, para. 11.

to the main proceedings, the Member States, the Commission, and the Union institution, body, office, or agency which adopted the act at issue in the proceedings under Art. 23 of the Statute.

C. Limits placed on the jurisdiction of the Court of Justice

As developed in the case-law, certain limits are placed on the jurisdiction of the Court of **6.20**
Justice to deliver preliminary rulings on the interpretation of Union law.[90] These limits are primarily gauged, first, at precluding the Court from ruling on facts and points of national law and on the compatibility of national rules with Union law. Where the referring court's questions are framed in such a manner, however, there is the possibility for the Court of Justice to reformulate such questions. Consequently, attempts by 'interested parties' within the meaning of Art. 23 of the Statute to challenge the admissibility of the questions submitted by the referring court on these grounds alone routinely fail.[91] Moreover, the Court of Justice in principle does not have jurisdiction to deliver preliminary rulings involving situations in the main proceedings which have no factor linking them to Union law, as illustrated by case-law concerning the free movement provisions and fundamental rights, although some exceptions have been carved out in the case-law as discussed in the sections that follow.

D. The Court of Justice does not rule on facts and points of national law

Under settled case-law, in the context of preliminary ruling proceedings, the Court of **6.21**
Justice is not entitled to rule on facts or points of national law, or to verify whether they are correct.[92] Likewise, it is not for the Court to identify the provisions of national law relevant to the dispute, to give a ruling on their interpretation, or to decide whether the referring

---

[90] Note that such limits are in addition to those placed on the preliminary ruling jurisdiction of the Court of Justice generally in relation to the assessment of questions which implicate the material, personal, territorial, and temporal scope of Union law.

[91] For some recent examples, see ECJ, Case C-453/04 *innoventif* [2006] E.C.R. I-4929, paras 28–31; ECJ, Case C-506/04 *Wilson* [2006] E.C.R. I-8613, paras 33–36; ECJ, Case C-346/05 *Chateignier* [2006] E.C.R. I-10951, paras 17–18; ECJ, Case C-443/06 *Hollmann* [2007] E.C.R. I-8491, paras 20–22; ECJ, Case C-12/08 *Mono Car Styling* [2009] E.C.R. I-6653, paras 30–31; ECJ, Case C-42/07 *Liga Portuguesa de Futebol Profissional and Bwin International* [2009] E.C.R. I-7633, paras 36–38; ECJ, Case C-350/07 *Kattner Stahlbau* [2009] E.C.R. I-1513, para. 25; ECJ, Case C-378/08 *ERG and Others* [2010] E.C.R. I-1919, paras 30–33; ECJ, Joined Cases C-78/08 to C-80/08 *Paint Graphos and Others* [2011] E.C.R. I-7611, para. 36.

[92] ECJ, Case 104/77 *Oehlschläger* [1978] E.C.R. 791, para. 4. More recently, see, e.g. ECJ, Case C-253/03 *CLT-UFA* [2006] E.C.R. I-1831, paras 35–37; ECJ, Case C-489/04 *Jehle* [2006] E.C.R. I-7509, para. 36; ECJ, Case C-251/06 *ING. AUER* [2007] E.C.R. I-9689, paras 18–19; ECJ, Case C-357/06 *Frigerio Luigi & C.* [2007] E.C.R. I-12311, para. 16; ECJ, Case C-11/07 *Eckelkamp* [2008] E.C.R. I-6845, paras 31–32, 51–53; ECJ, Case C-142/07 *Ecologistas en Acción-CODA* [2008] E.C.R. I-6097, paras 48–50; ECJ, Case C-345/09 *van Delft and Others* [2010] E.C.R. I-9879, paras 114–115. In particular, it is not for the Court of Justice, but for the national court to ascertain the facts that have given rise to the dispute and to establish the consequences which they have for the judgment which it is required to deliver: see, e.g. ECJ, Case C-232/09 *Danosa* [2010] E.C.R. I-11405, paras 31–36; ECJ, Case C-310/09 *Accor* [2011] E.C.R. I-8115, para. 37 (and further citations therein); ECJ (judgment of 17 January 2013), Case C-23/12 *Zakaria*, not reported, para. 29.

court's interpretation is correct.[93] These matters fall within the exclusive jurisdiction of the national court.[94]

That said, there is nothing to prevent the Court from spelling out its understanding of the facts and points of national law as its starting point for its 'useful' (i.e. specific) interpretation of the applicable provisions and principles of Union law.[95] The Court of Justice may also ask the national court or the government concerned to elucidate certain facts and/or points of national law and take account of them in the judgment giving a preliminary ruling.[96] A request to the national court will be based on Art. 101 of the ECJ Rules of Procedure. Generally, a request to the national government will be informal in the shape of a letter from the Registrar, but it may if necessary be made in the form of an order of the Court prescribing measures of inquiry within the meaning of Art. 64(2) of the ECJ Rules of Procedure (request for information and production of documents).[97] Other measures of inquiry, such as taking oral testimony, commissioning an expert's report, and inspections of a place or thing, are not formally precluded in proceedings for a preliminary ruling on the interpretation of Union law, but probably go too far in practice because they are intrinsically intended to determine or verify contested facts and points of national law, and the Court of Justice has indeed no jurisdiction to do this.[98]

---

[93] See, e.g. ECJ, Case C-222/04 *di Firenze and Others* [2006] E.C.R. I-289, para. 63; ECJ, Case C-500/06 *Corporación Dermoestética* [2008] E.C.R. I-5785, paras 20–22; ECJ, Case C-518/08 *Fundación Gala Salvador-Dalí and VEGAP* [2010] E.C.R. I-3091, para. 21; ECJ, Case C-375/08 *Pontini and Others* [2010] E.C.R. I-5767, para. 51; ECJ, Joined Cases C-447/08 and C-448/08 *Sjöberg and Gerdin* [2010] E.C.R. I-6921, para. 54; ECJ, Case C-409/06 *Winner Wetten* [2010] E.C.R. I-8015, para. 35; ECJ, Case C-467/08 *Padawan* [2010] E.C.R. I-10055, para. 2; ECJ, Joined Cases C-483/09 and C-1/10 *Gueye and Salmerón Sánchez* [2011] E.C.R. I-8263, para. 42.

[94] For this reason, the Court bases its consideration on the description given in the order for reference and disregards observations of interested parties within the meaning of Art. 23 of the Statute (including the 'defendant' government) which contradict information in the order for reference: see, e.g. ECJ, Case C-153/02 *Neri* [2003] E.C.R. I-13555, paras 33–36; ECJ, Joined Cases C-482/01 and C-493/01 *Orfano-poulous and Others* [2004] E.C.R. I-5257, paras 41–43; ECJ, Case C-267/03 *Lindberg* [2005] E.C.R. I-3247, paras 41–42; ECJ, Joined Cases C-128/10 and C-129/10 *Thasou and Etairia* [2011] E.C.R. I-1885, paras 37–41; ECJ, Case C-212/10 *Logstor ROR Polska* [2011] E.C.R. I-5453, paras 27–31.

[95] For a very explicit example, see ECJ, Joined Cases C-188/10 and C-189/10 *Melki and Abdeli* [2010] E.C.R. I-5667, paras 46–50 involving a delicate situation in which the provisions of national law concerned could be considered to yield more than one interpretation, whereby the Court of Justice took as its starting point the alternative readings of the national provisions concerned, whilst holding fast to the presentation of national law in the order for reference.

[96] See, e.g. ECJ, Case C-343/90 *Lourenço Dias* [1992] E.C.R. I-4673, para. 52; ECJ (order of 12 March 2004), Case C-54/03 *Austroplant-Arzneimittel*, not reported, para. 14; ECJ, Case C-235/03 *QDQ Media* [2005] E.C.R. I-1937, paras 11–12, 14–15; ECJ, Case C-208/07 *von Chamier-Gliszinski* [2009] E.C.R. I-6095, paras 21–22, 71–73, 76; ECJ, Case C-568/08 *Combinatie Spijker Infrabouw-De Jonge Konstruktie and Others* [2010] E.C.R. I-12655, paras 39–41.

[97] See ECJ, Case 148/77 *Hansen* [1978] E.C.R. 1787, at 1790, from which it appears that the Court decided 'to open the procedure without any preparatory inquiry', but requested the German and French Governments and the Commission 'to provide written answers to a certain number of questions before the opening of the oral procedure'. Germany had submitted observations to the Court pursuant to Art. 23 of the Statute, but France had not, so that the questions were intended to involve the latter Member State in the proceedings, which is what happened: see ECJ, Case 148/77 *Hansen* [1978], at 1798–9. See also ECJ, Case C-6/05 *Medi-pac Kazantzidis* [2007] E.C.R. I-4557, para. 31 (on account of procedural reasons, the national court could not respond to the Court of Justice's request for clarification, so the Court decided to hold a hearing at which the 'defendant' government provided the requisite information which was taken up as part of the ruling); ECJ, Joined Cases C-334/06 to C-336/06 *Zerche and Others* [2008] E.C.R. I-4691, paras 40–41 (submission of a series of written questions to the government concerned); ECJ, Joined Cases C-329/06 and C-343/06 *Wiedeman and Funk* [2008] E.C.R. I-4635, paras 42–43 (same).

[98] When ruling on the interpretation or validity of Union law provisions, the Court of Justice is empowered to do so only on the basis of the facts which the national court puts before it: see, e.g. ECJ,

E. Reformulation of questions

In order to arrive at a 'useful interpretation', the Court of Justice often has to rework the **6.22** questions to some extent before answering them (see, generally para. 3.23). It will do this where the questions referred are too vague, for instance, where they do not refer specifically to any provision or principle of Union law,[99] or are deficient in other respects.[100] In such cases, the Court will specify and flesh out the questions in the light of the particulars set out in the order for reference and in the national case-file. Sometimes, too, a great many questions are referred and the Court prunes them back somewhat[101] or the questions are put in a very complicated way (for example, divided into propositions and sub-propositions), and the Court has first to identify the core issue(s) raised.[102] This exercise often makes it unnecessary to answer some of the questions referred.[103]

Case C-378/08 *ERG and Others* [2010] E.C.R. I-1919, para. 42; ECJ, Joined Cases C-379/08 and C-380/08 *ERA and Others* [2010] E.C.R. I-2007, para. 35; ECJ, Case C-375/08 *Pontini and Others* [2010] E.C.R. I-5767, para. 48 (and further citations therein).

[99] See, e.g. ECJ, Case 10/71 *Muller* [1971] E.C.R. 723, para. 8; ECJ, Case 251/83 *Haug-Adrion* [1984] E.C.R. 4277, paras 6–11; ECJ Case C-384/08 *Attanasio Group* [2010] E.C.R. I-2055, paras 20–21; ECJ, Joined Cases C-436/08 and C-437/08 *Haribo Lakritzen Hans Riegel* [2011] E.C.R. I-305, paras 31–38.

[100] For example, this can involve considering additional points or issues (see, e.g. ECJ, Case C-513/03 *van Hilten-van der Heijden* [2006] E.C.R. I-957, paras 24–27; ECJ, Case C-420/06 *Jager* [2008] E.C.R. I-1315, paras 45–58; ECJ, Case C-142/09 *Lahousse and Lavichy* [2010] E.C.R. I-11685, paras 35–48; ECJ, Case C-307/09 to C-309/09 *Vicoplus and Others* [2011] E.C.R. I-453, paras 22–25); 'tightening up' the question(s) referred (see, e.g. ECJ, Case C-210/04 *FCE Bank* [2006] E.C.R. I-2803, paras 21–24; ECJ, Case C-227/08 *Martín Martín* [2009] E.C.R. I-11939, paras 17–18); 'knocking out' certain points of Union law (see, e.g. ECJ, Case C-338/09 *Yellow Cab Verkehrbetrieb* [2010] E.C.R. I-13927, paras 24-27; ECJ, Joined Cases C-58/10 to C-68/10 *Monsanto and Others* [2011] E.C.R. I-7763, paras 57–58); spotlighting the relevant Union law rule or principle at issue (see, e.g. ECJ, Case C-341/05 *Laval un Partneri* [2007] E.C.R. I-11767, paras 51–53 (identifying specific provisions of the Treaties and the directive concerned); ECJ, Case C-246/09 *Bulicke* [2010] E.C.R. I-7003, paras 21–23 (reframing as matter of principles of equivalence and of effectiveness); ECJ, Case C-279/09 *DEB* [2010] E.C.R. I-13849, paras 27–33 (reframing principle of effectiveness as principle of effective judicial protection)). See also ECJ (judgment of 12 July 2012), Case C-291/11 *TNT Freight Management*, not reported, paras 24-27, where the Court held it was not necessary to interpret the International Convention on the Harmonised Commodity Description and Coding System, since that convention applied at Union level only via the Combined Nomenclature.

[101] See, e.g. ECJ, Case C-115/10 *Bábolna* [2011] E.C.R. I-5017, para. 32.

[102] See, e.g. ECJ, Joined Cases C-297/88 and C-197/89 *Dzodzi* [1990] E.C.R. I-3763, paras 11–15 (containing, under the heading 'The object of the questions submitted to the Court', a meticulous analysis of the orders for reference and the associated case-files showing which provisions and principles of Union [then Community] law raise difficulty for the referring courts). For some recent examples, see ECJ, Case C-402/03 *Skov and Bilka* [2006] E.C.R. I-199, paras 17–18, 31, 46; ECJ, Case C-438/05 *International Transport Workers' Federation and The Finnish Seamen's Union* [2007] E.C.R. I-10779, paras 27, 32, 56, 67; ECJ, Joined Cases C-468/06 to C-478/06 *Sot. Lelos kai Sia and Others* [2008] E.C.R. I-7139, paras 23, 28; ECJ, Case C-567/07 *Woningstichting Sint Servatius* [2009] E.C.R. I-9021, paras 18–19, 40; ECJ, Case C-115/08 *ČEZ* [2009] E.C.R. I-10265, paras 54, 109, 137; ECJ, Case C-229/08 *Wolf* [2010] E.C.R. I-1, paras 23–24; ECJ, Joined Cases C-159/10 and C-160/10 *Fuchs and Köhler* [2011] E.C.R. I-6919, paras 28, 32, 76, 84; ECJ, Case C-347/09 *Dickinger and Ömer* [2011] E.C.R. I-8185, paras 29–30, 33, 39–40. This may also involve the Court having to reshuffle the order of the questions: see, e.g. ECJ, Case C-537/07 *Gómez-Limón Sánchez-Camacho* [2009] E.C.R. I-6525, paras 30–31.

[103] See, e.g. ECJ, Case C-229/08 *Wolf* [2010] E.C.R. I-1, para. 47; ECJ, Case C-147/08 *Römer* [2011] E.C.R. I-3591, para. 65.

Under established case-law, the Court of Justice has a duty to interpret all provisions of Union law which the national court needs to decide the case pending before it, even if those provisions are not expressly indicated in the questions.[104] This arises on the Court's own motion, sometimes on the basis of the written or oral submissions of the interested parties within the meaning of Art. 23 of the Statute.[105] Such a situation typically involves the interpretation of additional[106] or different[107] provisions of the Union instrument concerned,[108] or the interpretation of additional rules of either secondary or primary Union law (including general principles of Union law) altogether.[109] It bears emphasis in this regard that the Court of Justice's inclusion of provisions of Union law not mentioned by the national court does not alter the terms of the order for reference but is intended to be of help to the national court in deciding the case before it.

A classic scenario arising in the case-law is where the referring court has framed its question in relation to certain Treaty provisions (usually in connection with free movement and/or Union citizenship), and the Court of Justice hones in on the particular provision(s) applicable in the main proceedings.[110] Invariably, the Court 'knocks out' Art. 18 TFEU, which lays down a general prohibition of discrimination on grounds of nationality, since it only applies independently in the absence of specific provisions on non-discrimination, so once the applicable free movement provision(s) is identified which contains specific rules on discrimination, that provision does not apply.[111] Another classic scenario is when the Union law provision or measure whose interpretation is sought has been replaced by

---

[104] See, e.g. ECJ, Case C-115/08 *ČEZ* [2009] E.C.R. I-10265, para. 81 (and further citations therein).

[105] See, e.g. ECJ, Case C-392/05 *Alevizos* [2007] E.C.R. I-3505, paras 63–65 (on the basis of Commission observations at hearing). This is so, despite protestations by such parties that the Court may not of its own motion raise a question which was not touched on by the referring court: see, e.g. ECJ, Case C-321/03 *Dyson* [2007] E.C.R. I-687, paras 21–26.

[106] See, e.g. ECJ, Case C-296/06 *Telecom Italia* [2008] E.C.R. I-801, paras 18–19; ECJ, Joined Cases C-329/06 and C-343/06 *Wiedeman and Funk* [2008] E.C.R. I-4635, paras 45–46; ECJ, Joined Cases C-334/06 to C-336/06 *Zerche and Others* [2008] E.C.R. I-4691, paras 42–43; ECJ, Case C-243/09 *Fuß* [2010] E.C.R. I-9849, paras 38–43; ECJ, Joined Cases C-483/09 and C-1/10 *Gueye and Salmerón Sánchez* [2011] E.C.R. I-8263, paras 47–49.

[107] See, e.g. ECJ, Case C-66/09 *Kirin Amgen* [2010] E.C.R. I-7943, paras 21–28.

[108] This can also involve consideration of additional provisions of national law at issue in the main proceedings: see, e.g. ECJ, Case C-239/09 *Seydaland Vereingte Agrarbetriebe* [2010] E.C.R. I-13083, para. 29.

[109] See e.g. ECJ, Case C-196/04 *Cadbury Schweppes and Cadbury Schweppes Overseas* [2006] E.C.R. I-7995, paras 29–30; ECJ, Case C-346/05 *Chateignier* [2006] E.C.R. I-10951, paras 24–26; ECJ, Case C-45/06 *Campina* [2007] E.C.R. I-2089, paras 31–35; ECJ, Case C-6/05 *Medipac—Kazantzidis* [2007] E.C.R. I-4557, paras 32–34; ECJ, Case C-115/08 *ČEZ* [2009] E.C.R. I-10265, paras 84–86; ECJ, Case C-81/09 *Idryma Typou* [2010] E.C.R. I-10161, paras 30–32; ECJ, Case C-437/09 *AG2R Prévoyance* [2011] E.C.R. I-973, paras 23–27. In particular, this occurs in connection with Union citizenship provisions (Arts 20–21 TFEU): e.g. ECJ, Case C-434/09 *McCarthy* [2011] E.C.R. I-3375, paras 24–26; ECJ, Case C-503/09 *Stewart* [2011] E.C.R. I-6497, paras 78–79.

[110] See, e.g. ECJ, Case C-311/08 *SGI* [2010] E.C.R. I-487, paras 23–37; ECJ, Case C-291/09 *Franceso Guarnieri & Cie* [2011] E.C.R. I-2685, para. 11; ECJ, Case C-132/10 *Halley* [2011] E.C.R. I-8353, paras 16–21. The Court may also have to reframe the reference to the Treaty provisions on Union citizenship as those relating to the free movement of workers: see, e.g. ECJ, Case C-3/08 *Leyman* [2009] E.C.R. I-9085, paras 18–21.

[111] See, e.g. ECJ, Case C-450/09 *Schröder* [2011] E.C.R. I-2497, paras 23–29 (and citations therein); ECJ, Case C-240/10 *Schulz-Delzers and Schulz* [2011] E.C.R. I-8531, para. 29; ECJ, Case C-384/08 *Attanasio Group* [2010] E.C.R. I-2055, para. 37 (and further citations therein). Conversely, despite the reference to the free movement provisions in the question, the Court may find such provisions inapplicable and that Art. 18 TFEU applies instead, even if not mentioned explicitly in the reference: see, e.g. ECJ, Case C-382/08 *Neukirchinger* [2011] E.C.R. I-139, para. 30.

another provision or measure, or there is a previous Union law measure found to be applicable instead, so that the relevant measure is substituted or added, depending on the relevant time frame.[112]

In this way, as a practical matter, the Court's reformulation of the questions is sometimes linked to its assessment of the substance of the case, even if it is precluded from interpreting facts and points of national law. For example, this can occur when the facts of the case demonstrate that certain Union law rules are inapplicable to the main proceedings,[113] or that the hypothesis upon which the questions are posed does not obtain in the main proceedings,[114] which then necessitates the reformulation of the questions posed. This may also relate to the temporal application of the Union law rules to be interpreted, since in the Court's evaluation of the question, it may find that the events at issue in the main proceedings somehow rule out the interpretation of certain provisions of Union law, for instance, that the interpretation of a particular directive is not necessary in view of the fact that the period of transposition had not yet expired on the date of the events at issue in the main proceedings.[115]

F. No jurisdiction to rule on the compatibility of national rules with Union law

Moreover, the Court sometimes reworks the wording of the questions referred on account of **6.23** the limits placed by the Treaties on its jurisdiction to give preliminary rulings. It has to do so because the Treaties do not expressly or by implication prescribe a particular form in which a national court must present its request for a preliminary ruling, and therefore, it falls to the Court of Justice itself to decide 'on that request only insofar as it has jurisdiction to do so, that is to say, only insofar as the decision relates to the interpretation' of Union law.[116]

This has occurred where questions were referred by which the national court sought a preliminary ruling on whether or not national provisions were compatible with Union law.[117] Commonly, the national court puts the question of compatibility with Union law

---

[112] See, e.g. ECJ, Case C-173/08 *Kloosterboer Services* [2009] E.C.R. I-5347, paras 20–23; ECJ, Case C-368/09 *Pannon Gép Centrum* [2010] E.C.R. I-7467, paras 30–35; ECJ, Case C-392/09 *Uszodaépítő* [2010] E.C.R. I-8791, paras 27–32; ECJ, Case C-30/10 *Andersson* [2011] E.C.R. I-513, paras 20–21; ECJ, Case C-115/10 *Bábolna* [2011] E.C.R. I-5017, paras 29–31.

[113] See, e.g. ECJ, Joined Cases C-317/08 to C-320/08 *Alassini and Others* [2010] E.C.R. I-2213, paras 31–37.

[114] See, e.g. ECJ, Case C-568/08 *Combinatie Spijker Infrabouw-De Jonge Konstruktie and Others* [2010] E.C.R. I-12655, paras 73–74.

[115] See, e.g. ECJ, Case C-499/04 *Werhof* [2006] E.C.R. I-2397, paras 14–16.

[116] ECJ, Case 13/61 *Bosch and Others* [1962] E.C.R. 45. With particular regard to the field of State aid, see, e.g. ECJ, Case C-237/04 *Enirisorse* [2006] E.C.R. I-2843, paras 23–24; ECJ, Joined Cases C-428/06 to C-434/06 *UGT-Rioja and Others* [2008] E.C.R. I-6747, paras 77–78; ECJ, Case C-140/09 *Fallimento Traghetti del Mediterraneo* [2010] E.C.R. I-5243, paras 22–24 (and citations therein).

[117] Though, of course, this also occurs in connection with other limits placed on the jurisdiction of the Court of Justice, for instance, with respect to not ruling on the interpretation of national law (see, e.g. ECJ, Case C-104/10 *Kelly* [2011] E.C.R. I-6813, paras 49–50; ECJ, Joined Cases C-159/10 and C-160/10 *Fuchs and Köhler* [2011] E.C.R. I-6919, paras 30–31), or not applying Union law to a particular case (see, e.g. ECJ, Case C-259/05 *Omni Metal Service* [2007] E.C.R. I-4945, paras 15–18; ECJ, Case C-163/10 *Patriciello* [2011] E.C.R. I-7565, paras 20–24). Compare ECJ, Joined Cases C-250/09 and C-268/09 *Georgiev* [2010] E.C.R. I-11869, paras 74–78: despite the possibility to rework the question on interpretation of national law to that concerning Union law, there is no need to answer the question concerned, since it was not distinct from previous questions.

directly to the Court of Justice, as indeed is its right precisely because of the lack of any requirements as to the form in which questions are to be referred. Furthermore, formulating questions directly in this way affords the advantage that there is no doubt as to the scope of the request for a preliminary ruling. Consequently, the referring court should not be concerned if the Court of Justice, referring to its settled case-law,[118] prefaces its judgment with a standard formula to the effect that 'although the Court may not, in proceedings brought under Art. 267 TFEU, rule on the compatibility of a provision of domestic law with European Union law, it may nevertheless provide the national court with an interpretation of European Union law on all such points so as to enable that court to determine the issue of compatibility for the purposes of the case before it'.[119]

That caveat, which the Court enters as regards the limits placed on its jurisdiction, however, does not lead it to give an interpretation of the Union law at issue that is too abstract. On the contrary, the Court will reformulate the national court's questions in a somewhat concrete manner, usually as to whether the rules or principles of Union law to be interpreted preclude a provision 'such as' that at issue in the main proceedings,[120] or even more to the point, whether they preclude national legislation of the kind concerned[121] (or words of similar effect[122]). As a result, although the questions are primarily based on the interpretation of provisions or principles of Union law, the answers given will nevertheless at the same time be determinative of the outcome of the question of compatibility.[123]

G. The issues raised must fall within the scope of Union law

6.24 Where the question of interpretation referred by the national court is intended to test the compatibility of a national measure with provisions of secondary or primary Union law

---

[118] For the first of those cases, see ECJ, Case 6/64 *Costa v ENEL* [1964] E.C.R. 585, at 592–3.

[119] ECJ, Joined Cases C-78/08 to C-80/08 *Paint Graphos and Others* [2011] E.C.R. I-7611, para. 34 (and citations therein). For similar formulations, see, e.g. ECJ, Case C-323/08 *Rodríguez Mayor and Others* [2009] E.C.R. I-11621, para. 30 (and citations therein); ECJ, Case C-118/08 *Transportes Urbanos y Servicios Generales* [2010] E.C.R. I-635, para. 23 (and citations therein); ECJ, Case C-127/08 *Pontina Ambiente* [2010] E.C.R. I-1175, para. 24; ECJ, Case C-378/08 *ERG and Others* [2010] E.C.R. I-1919, para. 31 (and citations therein); ECJ, Joined Cases C-379/08 and C-380/08 *ERG and Others* [2010] E.C.R. I-2007, para. 25 (and citations therein).

[120] See, e.g. ECJ, Case C-347/06 *ASM Brescia* [2008] E.C.R. I-5641, paras 24–25, 31, 42; ECJ, Case C-368/09 *Pannon Gép Centrum* [2010] E.C.R. I-7467, paras 27–29, 36; ECJ, Case C-75/09 *Agra* [2010] E.C.R. I-5595, paras 27–29; ECJ, Case C-239/09 *Seydaland Vereingte Agrarbetriebe* [2010] E.C.R. I-13083, paras 25–28; ECJ, Case C-489/09 *Vandoorne* [2011] E.C.R. I-225, paras 25–26; ECJ, Case C-240/10 *Schulz-Delzers and Schulz* [2011] E.C.R. I-8531, para. 33.

[121] See, e.g. ECJ, Case C-254/08 *Futura Immobiliare and Others* [2009] E.C.R. I-6995, paras 25, 36; ECJ, Case C-323/08 *Rodríguez Mayor and Others* [2009] E.C.R. I-11621, paras 29–32; ECJ, Case C-577/08 *Brouwer* [2010] E.C.R. I-7489, para. 27; ECJ, Case C-224/09 *Nussbaumer* [2010] E.C.R. I-9295, paras 17–18; ECJ, Case C-385/09 *Nidera Handelscompagnie* [2010] E.C.R. I-10385, paras 32–33; ECJ, Case C-2/10 *Azienda Agro-ZootechnicaFranchini and Eolica di Altamura* [2011] E.C.R. I-6561, paras 35–36.

[122] See, e.g. ECJ, Case C-296/06 *Telecom Italia* [2008] E.C.R. I-801, paras 16–17, 20; ECJ (order of 6 July 2006), Case C-155/05 *Villa Maria Beatrice Hospital*, not reported, paras 22–25; ECJ (order of 10 July 2008), Case C-156/07 *Aiello and Others* [2008] E.C.R. I-5215, Summ. pub., paras 41–43.

[123] It happened in the past that the Court did not formulate the operative part neutrally and referred expressly to the provisions of national law as being compatible or incompatible with Union law: see, e.g. ECJ, Case C-130/92 *OTO* [1994] E.C.R. I-3281, para. 21; for a critical appraisal, see the Opinion of Advocate-General D. Ruiz-Jarabo Colomer in ECJ, Case C-30/02 *Recheio* [2004] E.C.R. I-6051, points 23–36, at I-6053. Yet this is rare nowadays (see, e.g. ECJ, Case C-185/07 *Allianz* [2009] E.C.R. I-663, para. 34).

(including general principles of Union law, such as fundamental rights), the Court must verify whether the issues raised in the main proceedings are linked to a situation falling within the scope of Union law. This is because, as a general matter, the Court of Justice has no jurisdiction with regard to national provisions falling outside the scope of Union law and when the subject-matter of the dispute is not connected in any way with any of the situations contemplated by the Treaties.[124]

This finds specific expression in relation to questions concerning the interpretation of Union law in connection with free movement and fundamental rights.[125] In particular, where the question referred by the national court concerns the interpretation of the Treaty provisions on the free movement of persons, goods, services, and capital,[126] the Court ascertains that the issues raised in the main proceedings have some link to one of the situations envisaged by the Treaties in relation to the fundamental freedom concerned.[127] This is because if the issues raised in the main proceedings do not do so and relate to activities which are confined in all respects within a single Member State (a so-called purely 'internal situation'), the Treaty provisions on free movement are not applicable to the main proceedings,[128] and the Court will in principle leave the preliminary question without a substantive answer,[129] or rule that it

---

[124] See, e.g. ECJ, Case C-299/95 *Kremzow* [1997] E.C.R. I-2629, paras 18–19; ECJ (order of 6 October 2005), Case C-328/04 *Vajnai* [2005] E.C.R. I-8577, para. 13; ECJ (order of 14 December 2011), Case C-462/11 *Cozman*, not reported, para. 12.

[125] As highlighted by Advocate-General P. Mengozzi's Opinion in ECJ, Case C-439/08 *VEBIC* [2010] E.C.R. I-12471, point 36 n. 5 (although not dealt with by the Court of Justice in its judgment), there are several lines of case-law that overlap or co-exist in this regard.

[126] While perhaps obvious, this should be distinguished from preliminary rulings concerning the interpretation of measures of secondary Union law, which need not have an actual link to free movement: for a few recent examples, see ECJ, Case C-213/07 *Michaniki* [2008] E.C.R. I-9999, paras 28–29; ECJ, Case C-304/08 *Plus Warenhandelsgesellschaft* [2010] E.C.R. I-217, paras 27–28.

[127] Under the case-law, national legislation which applies without distinction to nationals of that Member State and to those of other Member States alike is generally capable of falling within the scope of the provisions on the fundamental freedoms only to the extent that it applies to situations related to intra-EU trade. Nevertheless, this appears to be fulfilled if it is possible (or not inconceivable) that entities from other Member States have been or would be interested in taking up the transactions at issue in the main proceedings: see, e.g. ECJ, Case C-380/05 *Centro Europa 7* [2008] E.C.R. I-349, paras 65–67 (further noting that the finding of a link to intra-EU trade will be presumed if the market in question has a certain cross-border element); ECJ, Case C-384/08 *Attanasio Group* [2010] E.C.R. I-2055, paras 23–24 (and citations therein); ECJ, Joined Cases C-570/07 and C-571/07 *Blanco Pérez and Chao Gómez* [2010] E.C.R. I-4629, paras 40–41.

[128] As emphasized by the Court of Justice, it is not possible to raise against this conclusion the Treaties provisions on Union citizenship (Arts 20–21 TFEU) because Union citizenship is not intended to expand the material scope of the Treaties to internal situations which have no link to Union law: see, e.g. ECJ, Case C-212/06 *Gouvernement de la Communauté française and Gouvernement wallon* [2008] E.C.R. I-1683, para. 39 (and citations therein); see also ECJ (order of 26 March 2009), Case C-535/08 *Pignataro* [2009] E.C.R. I-50*, Summ. pub., paras 15–16. For the purposes of interpreting the Union citizenship provisions, the Treaty rules governing free movement of persons and the measures adopted to implement them cannot be applied to situations which have no factor linking them to any of the situations governed by Union law and are confined in all relevant respects within a single Member State, provided, however, that the situation of the Union citizen concerned does not include national measures which have the effect of depriving Union citizens of the genuine enjoyment of the substance of those rights: see ECJ, Case C-434/09 *McCarthy* [2011] E.C.R. I-3375, paras 44–57 (and citations therein).

[129] See, e.g. ECJ, Joined Cases C-54/88, C-91/88 and C-14/89 *Nino and Others* [1990] E.C.R. I-3537, paras 11–12; ECJ, Joined Cases C-29/94 to C-35/94 *Aubertin and Others* [1995] E.C.R. I-301, paras 9–11; ECJ, Case C-134/95 *USSL No. 47 di Biella* [1997] E.C.R. I-195, paras 19–23; ECJ, Case C-108/98 *RI.SAN.* [1999] E.C.R. I-5219, paras 21–23; ECJ, Case C-97/98 *Jägerskiöld* [1999] E.C.R. I-7319, paras 42–44; ECJ,

has no jurisdiction to answer the questions referred.[130] Yet an exception has been carved out in the case-law in which the Court of Justice has held that even in such a purely internal situation, the Court's answer may nevertheless be useful to the referring court, in particular if its national law requires it to grant the same rights to a national of a given Member State as those which a national of another Member State in the same situation would derive from Union law, in short, if the national law concerned were to prohibit reverse discrimination.[131] Consequently, if these circumstances are applicable, the Court finds that it has jurisdiction to answer the questions referred.[132]

Similarly, where the question concerns the interpretation of provisions of the Charter of Fundamental Rights of the European Union or other sources relating to the EU regime for the protection of fundamental rights (see Art. 6(3) TEU), the Court of Justice examines whether the subject-matter of the main proceedings is situated within the field of application of Union law. Specifically, with respect to the Charter, Art. 51 states that the provisions of the Charter are addressed to the Member States 'only when they are

---

Case C-212/06 *Gouvernement de la Communauté française and Gouvernement wallon* [2008] E.C.R. I-1683, paras 32–42.

[130] See, e.g. ECJ, Case C-245/09 *Omalet* [2010] E.C.R. I-13771, paras 9–18. While such issues have been dealt with by the Court of Justice as part of the substance of the ruling on the question referred, the Court has (increasingly) emphasized that where a reference is sought on the interpretation of the free movement provisions in a situation where all the relevant facts of the dispute in the main proceedings are confined within a single Member State, the Court must assess whether it has jurisdiction to rule on the interpretation of those provisions: see, e.g. ECJ, Case C-380/05 *Centro Europa 7* [2008] E.C.R. I-349, para. 64; ECJ, Case C-384/08 *Attanasio Group* [2010] E.C.R. I-2055, para. 22; ECJ, Case C-245/09 *Omalet* [2010] E.C.R. I-13771, paras 9–10.

[131] See, e.g. ECJ, Case C-448/98 *Guimont* [2000] E.C.R. I-10663, para. 23; ECJ, Case C-6/01 *Anomar and Others* [2003] E.C.R. I-8621, para. 41; ECJ, Case C-451/03 *Servizi Ausiliari Dottori Commercialisti* [2006] E.C.R. I-2941, para. 29; ECJ, ECJ, Joined Cases C-94/04 and C-202/04 *Cipolla and Others* [2006] E.C.R. I-11421, para. 30; ECJ, ECJ, Joined Cases C-570/07 and C-571/07 *Blanco Pérez and Chao Gómez* [2010] E.C.R. I-4629, para. 36; ECJ, Case C-245/09 *Omalet* [2010] E.C.R. I-13771, para. 15.

[132] See, e.g. ECJ, Joined Cases C-515/99, C-519/99 to C-524/99, and C-524/99 to C-540/99 *Reisch and Others* [2002] E.C.R. I-2157, paras 24, 26; ECJ, Case C-300/01 *Salzmann* [2003] E.C.R. I-4899, paras 32–35; ECJ, Case C-6/01 *Anomar and Others* [2003] E.C.R. I-8621, paras 39, 41; ECJ (order of 17 February 2005), Case C-250/03 *Mauri* [2005] E.C.R. I-1267, para. 21; ECJ, Case C-380/05 *Centro Europa 7* [2008] E.C.R. I-349, paras 69–70. For cases in which this exception has been held not to apply, see, e.g. ECJ, Case C-245/09 *Omalet* [2010] E.C.R. I-13771, paras 16–17. There are other cases in which, as a matter of substance, the Court has stressed that its interpretation of the relevant Union law rules may be helpful to the national court under these conditions (i.e. whether national law requires nationals of that Member State to be accorded the same rights as nationals of other Member States in comparable situations), without providing a basis for the Court's preliminary rulings jurisdiction as such: see, e.g. ECJ, Case C-238/02 *Douwe Egberts* [2004] E.C.R. I-7007, para. 58; ECJ, Case C-212/06 *Gouvernement de la Communauté française and Gouvernement wallon* [2008] E.C.R. I-1683, para. 40. As noted by commentators, there is some connection between this exception and the *Dzodzi* case-law: see, e.g. C. Ritter, 'Purely Internal Situations, Reverse Discrimination, *Guimont, Dzodzi* and Article 234' (2006) E.L. Rev. 690–710 (advocating that the so-called '*Guimont* principle' be abandoned and subsumed under the *Dzodzi* case-law, with established limits). Indeed, the rationale for this exception, as with the *Dzodzi* case-law, goes back to the emphasis placed on the system of judicial cooperation in the preliminary ruling procedure, in the sense that the preliminary ruling given by the Court of Justice can be of help to the national court in adjudicating the case before it under circumstances where it may be confronted with questions concerning the rights derived from Union law afforded to nationals of other Member States in order to grant the same rights to nationals of the Member State concerned, thereby justifying the approach in the case-law to extend the Court of Justice's preliminary ruling jurisdiction. Moreover, in comparison to past judgments in this regard, lately the case-law finds the Court of Justice verifying whether these circumstances actually hold (see n. 127).

implementing Union law',[133] that is to say, only when they are acting within the scope of Union law.[134] Therefore, the Court has ruled—often by way of reasoned order under Art. 99 of the ECJ Rules of Procedure—that it has no jurisdiction to answer questions referred by the national court relating to situations that fall outside the scope of Union law.[135] The same goes for questions on the interpretation of provisions of other sources of fundamental rights protection, such as the European Convention for the Protection of Human Rights and Fundamental Freedoms (ECHR).[136]

H. Reference back to the national court

When the Court of Justice interprets Union law in a case where certain relevant facts or points of national law have not yet been established in the main proceedings, it will indicate precisely what findings the national court has to make in order to resolve the case in accordance with its interpretation.[137] However, the Court of Justice may not abuse this sort of reference back to the national court by evading its responsibility for making the necessary appraisals in interpreting Union law, especially the fundamental provisions and principles. The Court is under a duty to give the national court an answer which, in principle, will lead directly to the resolution of the case (at least as far as Union law is concerned). Only where, in the concrete context of the main proceedings, some specific facts or points of national law require clarification in order to make a 'useful interpretation' of Union law work will that clarification have to be made by the national court after the Court of Justice has clearly identified which facts and points of national law must be elucidated.[138] Where, by contrast, the Court of Justice is itself apprised of the uncontested facts and points of national law which are necessary in order to reach a decision in the main proceedings, then it has to have

6.25

---

[133] Art. 51(1) of the Charter of Fundemental Rights of the European Union, [2012] O.J. C326/391. See also Art. 6(1), second para., TEU: 'The provisions of the Charter shall not extend in any way the competences of the Union as defined in the Treaties.'

[134] For detailed discussion, see K. Lenaerts and P. Van Nuffel (R. Bray and N. Cambien (eds)), *European Union Law* (3rd edn, London, Sweet & Maxwell, 2011), paras 22.25–22.27. See also ECJ (judgment of 15 November 2011), Case C-256/11 *Dereci*, not reported, paras 71–72; ECJ (judgment of 26 February 2013), Case C-399/11 *Melloni*, not reported, paras 55–64; ECJ (judgment of 26 February 2013), Case C-617/10 *Åkerberg Fransson*, not reported, paras 16–31. See further K. Lenaerts, 'The EU Charter of Fundamental Rights: Scope of Application and Methods of Interpretation', in V. Kronenberger, M. T. D'Alessio, and V. Placco (eds), *De Rome à Lisbonne: les juridictions de l'Union européenne à la croisée des chemins. Mélanges en l'honneur de Paolo Mengozzi* (Brussels, Bruylant, 2013), 107–43.

[135] See, e.g. ECJ (order of 12 November 2010), Case C-339/10 *Estov and Others* [2010] E.C.R. I-11465; ECJ (order of 1 March 2011), Case C-457/09 *Chartry* [2011] E.C.R. I-819; ECJ (order of 23 May 2011), Joined Cases C-267/10 and C-268/10 *Rossius and Collard* [2011] E.C.R. I-81* Summ. pub.

[136] See, e.g. ECJ, Case C-299/95 *Kremzow* [1997] E.C.R. I-2629; ECJ (order of 25 January 2007), Case C-302/06 *Koval'ský* [2007] E.C.R. I-11*, Summ. pub.; ECJ (order of 16 January 2008), Case C-361/07 *Polier* [2008] E.C.R. I-6*, Summ. pub.; ECJ (order of 3 October 2008), Case C-287/08 *Savia and Others* [2008] E.C.R. I-136*, Summ. pub.; ECJ (order of 26 March 2009), Case C-535/08 *Pignataro* [2009] E.C.R. I-50*, Summ. pub., paras 19–24; ECJ (judgment of 24 April 2012), Case C-571/10 *Servet Kamberaj*, not reported, paras 47–58.

[137] For some recent examples, see ECJ, Joined Cases C-482/01 and C-493/01 *Orfanopoulous and Others* [2004] E.C.R. I-5257, paras 52–54; ECJ, Case C-142/09 *Lahousse and Lavichy* [2010] E.C.R. I-11685, para. 47; ECJ, Case C-168/09 *Flos* [2011] E.C.R. I-181, para. 31.

[138] However, the Court may, after hearing the Advocate-General, request clarification from the national court (ECJ Rules of Procedure, Art. 101). For an illustration, see ECJ (order of 12 March 2004), Case C-54/03 *Austroplant-Arzneimittel*, not reported, para. 14. See also ECJ, Joined Cases C-436/08 and C-437/08 *Haribo Lakritzen Hans Riegel* [2011] E.C.R. I-305, para. 19.

regard to those facts and points of law as such in making the 'useful interpretation' of Union law expected by the national court.[139]

I. Jurisdiction of the national court

6.26   Naturally, it falls in any event to the national court to dispose of the case. In that sense, the judgment giving a ruling on interpretation, no matter to what extent it determines the outcome of the main proceedings, is always 'preliminary', that is to say, given before the national court gives final judgment in the main proceedings.[140] However, the Court of Justice does not shrink from giving guidance based on the case-file and the written and oral observations which have been submitted to it, with a view to enabling the national court to give judgment on the application of Union law in the specific case which it has to adjudicate.[141]

In some cases, the Court of Justice has trodden a fine line with respect to leaving the case in the hands of the national court. In particular,[142] the Court has gone a step further when dealing with requests for preliminary rulings in certain cases on the principle of State liability for an alleged breach of Union law by a Member State. While recognizing that it was in principle for the national courts to verify whether or not the conditions governing State liability for a breach of Union law are fulfilled, the Court held that in the case in question it had all the necessary information to assess the conduct of the Member State concerned itself.[143] Given that these cases largely concern factually complex scenarios or particularly flagrant examples of violations of Union law by the Member State concerned, they appear to represent exceptional circumstances in which the Court seeks to ensure, as much as possible, judicial protection for individuals, and therefore, while cognizant of the division of tasks between the Court and the national courts in the

---

[139] See also K. Lenaerts, 'Form and Substance of the Preliminary Rulings Procedure', in D. Curtin and T. Heukels (eds), *Institutional Dynamics of European Integration. Essays in Honour of H.G. Schermers* (Martinus Nijhoff, Dordrecht, 1994), Vol. II, 355–80, at 364–70.

[140] Cf. ECJ, Case 1/80 *Salmon* [1980] E.C.R. 1937, para. 6.

[141] ECJ, Case C-328/91 *Thomas and Others* [1993] E.C.R. I-1247, para. 13; ECJ, Case C-278/93 *Freers and Speckmann* [1996] E.C.R. I-1165, para. 24; ECJ, Joined Cases C-4/02 and C-5/02 *Schönheit and Becker* [2003] E.C.R. I-12575, para. 83 (and further citations therein); see also the more cautious terms employed in ECJ, Joined Cases C-46/93 and C-48/93 *Brasserie du Pêcheur and Factortame* [1996] E.C.R. I-1029, para. 58; ECJ, Case C-319/96 *Brinkmann* [1998] E.C.R. I-5255, para. 29; ECJ, Case C-381/99 *Brunnhofer* [2001] E.C.R. I-4961, para. 53.

[142] Conceivably, one could also contemplate as another example some previous case-law of the Court of Justice on the interpretation of Council Directive 93/13/EEC of 5 April 1993 on unfair terms in consumer contracts ([1993] O.J. L95/29), now amended by Directive 2011/83/EU of the European Parliament and of the Council of 25 October 2011 on consumer rights ([2011] O.J. L304/64), in which the Court ruled that it had all the criteria before it to determine that a particular contract term was unfair (see, e.g. in ECJ, Joined Cases C-240/98 to C-244/98 *Océano Grupo Editorial and Salvat Editores* [2000] E.C.R. I-4941, paras 21–23), although it has essentially 'backed away' from this approach in subsequent case-law: see, e.g. ECJ, Case C-243/08 *Pannon GSM* [2009] E.C.R. I-4713, paras 40–43 (and citations therein); ECJ (judgment of 14 March 2013), Case C-415/11 *Aziz*, not reported, para. 72.

[143] See, e.g. ECJ, Case C-392/93 *British Telecommunications* [1996] E.C.R. I-1631, para. 41; ECJ, Joined Cases C-283/94, C-291/94, and C-292/94 *Denkavit and Others* [1996] E.C.R. I-5063, para. 49; ECJ, Case C-302/97 *Konle* [1999] E.C.R. I-3099, para. 59; ECJ, Case C-140/97 *Rechberger and Others* [1999] E.C.R. I-3499, paras 72–73; ECJ, Case C-452/06 *Synthon* [2008] E.C.R. I-7681, paras 36–46; ECJ, Case C-429/09 *Fuß* [2010] E.C.R. I-12167, paras 53–58.

preliminary ruling procedure, these cases find the Court mindful to ensure that the rights derived from Union law are upheld as the cases proceed to adjudication before the national court.

IV. Consequences of a Preliminary Ruling on Interpretation

A. As regards the national court deciding the case at issue in the main proceedings

(1) Binding effect

A judgment given by the Court under Art. 267 TFEU is binding on the national court **6.27** hearing the case in which the decision is given.[144] This is to be understood as meaning that all courts and tribunals dealing with the case, also at a later stage of the proceedings, on appeal or upon an appeal on a point of law, are obliged to comply with the substance of the judgment giving the preliminary ruling.[145]

The binding effect attaches to the whole of the operative part and main body of the judgment, since the operative part has to be understood in the light of the reasoning on which it is based.[146]

Naturally, the fact that the judgment given by way of preliminary ruling is binding does not mean that the national court has invariably to apply the provisions or principles of Union law elucidated thereby in reaching its decision in the main proceedings. It may be that this judgment specifically indicates why those provisions or principles are not applicable.[147]

(2) New reference possible

The fact that a judgment given by way of a preliminary ruling is binding does not preclude **6.28** the court to which the judgment is addressed, or another court involved in deciding the case, from making a further reference for a preliminary ruling to the Court of Justice if it considers such a step to be necessary in order to give judgment in the main proceedings.[148] Such a request will be justified 'when the national court encounters difficulties in understanding or applying the judgment, when it refers a fresh question of law to the Court, or

---

[144] For example, ECJ, Case 29/68 *Milch-, Fett-, und Eierkontor* [1969] E.C.R. 165, para. 2; ECJ (order of 5 March 1986), Case 68/85 *Wünsche* [1986] E.C.R. 947, para. 13; ECJ, Case C-446/98 *Fazenda Pública* [2000] E.C.R. I-11435, para. 49; ECJ, Case C-173/09 *Elchinov* [2010] E.C.R. I-8889, para. 29.

[145] Cf. ECJ, Case 52/76 *Benedetti* [1977] E.C.R. 163, para. 26.

[146] ECJ, Case 135/77 *Bosch* [1978] E.C.R. 855, para. 4. Commentators have noted that issues concerning the binding effect of a preliminary ruling particularly arise with respect to rulings that have, in the referring court's view, gone beyond the questions submitted in the order for reference or have diverged from the facts presented therein: see, e.g. M. Broberg and N. Fenger, *Preliminary References to the European Court of Justice* (Oxford, Oxford University Press, 2010), 434–8 (highlighting issues arising in national legal orders on account of the Court's different reading of the facts, which then makes binding effect problematic on account of national procedural rules).

[147] ECJ, Case 222/78 *ICAP* [1979] E.C.R. 1163, paras 7–12.

[148] See ECJ, Case 29/68 *Milch-, Fett-, und Eierkontor* [1969] E.C.R. 165, para. 3; ECJ (judgment of 13 November 2012), Case C-35/11 *Test Claimants in the FII Group Litigation*, not reported, para. 2. See further para. 6.11.

again when it submits new considerations which might lead the Court to give a different answer to a question submitted earlier'.[149]

The validity of the judgment delivered previously cannot be contested by means of a further reference for a preliminary ruling 'as this would call in question the allocation of jurisdiction as between national courts and the Court of Justice' under Art. 267 TFEU.[150]

Furthermore, the initiative for making a fresh request for a preliminary ruling lies with the national court dealing with the main proceedings alone. The parties to those proceedings are not entitled to ask the Court of Justice to interpret an earlier preliminary ruling.[151] Moreover, the Court has held that Arts 41–44 of the Statute 'list exhaustively the exceptional review procedures available for challenging the authority of the Court's judgments; however, since there are no parties to such proceedings in which the Court gives judgment by way of a preliminary ruling, the aforementioned articles do not apply to such a judgment'.[152]

(3) Sanctions for non-compliance

6.29 In the event that the national court fails to comply with its obligation to follow the judgment giving the preliminary ruling, that court, as an institution of its Member State, will be in breach of Union law. This means that in principle, infringement proceedings may be brought against that Member State under Arts 258–260 TFEU.[153] This may also result in domestic remedies being taken with a view to reversing the infringement of Union law, or at least its consequences (including potential recourse to State liability).[154]

B. As regards national courts generally

(1) Binding on all national courts

6.30 The binding effect of a judgment by way of preliminary ruling extends further than to merely what is necessary to determine the main proceedings. It also applies outside the specific dispute in respect of which it was given to all national courts and tribunals, subject, of course, to their right to make a further reference on interpretation to the Court of Justice.[155] In other words, the judgment of a preliminary ruling on interpretation (as well as on validity: see para. 10.18) is said to have *erga omnes*, as opposed to merely *inter partes*, effect.[156]

---

[149] ECJ, Case 14/86 *Pretore di Salò v X* [1987] E.C.R. 2545, para. 12.

[150] ECJ (order of 5 March 1986), Case 69/85 *Wünsche* [1986] E.C.R. 947, para. 15.

[151] ECJ (order of 16 May 1968), Case 13/67 *Becher* [1968] E.C.R. 196; ECJ (order of 18 October 1979), Case 40/70 *Sirena* [1979] E.C.R. 3169, at 3170–1. See also Art. 104 of the ECJ Rules of Procedure and para. 6.11.

[152] ECJ (order of 5 March 1986), Case 69/85 *Wünsche* [1986] E.C.R. 947, para. 14.

[153] See also para. 5.38.

[154] As regards the obligations on a Member State stemming from a judgment given on an order for reference from which it is apparent that national legislation is incompatible with Union law, see ECJ, Joined Cases C-321/06 to C-233/06 *Jonkman and Others* [2007] E.C.R. I-5149, paras 36–41.

[155] For an example, see ECJ, Case 68/74 *Alaimo* [1975] E.C.R. 109. The General Court is bound by a preliminary ruling of the Court of Justice, unless it appears that the latter court 'based its assessment on inaccurate or incomplete information' (CFI, Case T-43/98 *Emesa Sugar v Council* [2001] E.C.R. II-3519, para. 73).

[156] That being said, this is an area that has been the subject of a long-running academic debate, which has been complicated by the fact that some of the terms used, such as *erga omnes*, have varying connotations in the national legal orders: D. Anderson and M. Demetriou, *References to the European Court* (London, Sweet & Maxwell, 2002), 331–2 (and citations therein).

There are two arguments in favour of the generalization of the binding effect of judgments on the interpretation of Union law given by way of preliminary ruling: the first relates to the declaratory nature of the interpretation, and the second concerns the aim of ensuring uniformity in the application of Union law.

(2) Declaratory nature of the interpretation

First, there is the fact that the interpretation is declaratory; it does not lay down any new rule, **6.31** but is incorporated into the body of provisions and principles of Union law on which it is based. Consequently, the binding effect of the interpretation coincides with the binding effect of the provisions and principles on which it is based and which all national courts must respect. It is, moreover, precisely because the interpretation has, by its very nature, such effect *erga omnes* that there are no 'parties to proceedings',[157] but in contrast a system in which, alongside the parties to the main proceedings, all the Member States, the Commission and the Union institution, body, office, or agency which adopted the act which is in dispute are entitled to submit observations pursuant to Art. 23 of the Statute (and to take part in the oral procedure before the Court). The compass of the legal discussion which takes place before the Court accordingly corresponds with the scope of the judgment to be given.[158] It would therefore be wrong to seize on the idea that a judgment given in preliminary ruling proceedings has effects only *inter partes* on the ground that it is designed primarily to help the national court reach its decision in the main proceedings in which the question referred for a preliminary ruling arose. The *inter partes* aspect attaches only to the judicial decision in the main proceedings, including the way in which that decision deals with the judgment given by way of preliminary ruling, but it does not extend to that judgment itself.

(3) Uniformity in the application of Union law

Second, the purpose for which the preliminary ruling procedure exists, which is to secure **6.32** uniformity in the application of Union law throughout the Member States, would be defeated if it were to be considered that a ruling under Art. 267 TFEU had 'no binding effect at all except in the case in which it was given'.[159] The Court of Justice assumes that, with the exception of any new feature necessitating a refinement or even a reversal of the existing case-law, the preliminary ruling provides all national courts and tribunals with an answer to the question of Union law which gave rise to the interpretation given.[160] This is underscored by Art. 99 of the ECJ Rules of Procedure: 'Where a question referred to the Court for a preliminary ruling is identical to a question on which the Court has already ruled ... the Court may at any time, on a proposal from the Judge Rapporteur and after

---

[157] ECJ (order of 5 March 1986), Case 69/85 *Wünsche* [1986] E.C.R. 947, para. 14.

[158] It would appear from ECJ, Joined Cases 141/81 to 143/81 *Holdijk and Others* [1982] E.C.R. 1299, para. 6, that the Court of Justice takes the same view.

[159] Opinion of Advocate-General J.-P. Warner in ECJ, Case 112/76 *Manzoni* [1977] E.C.R. 1647, at 1662–3, where he went on to say as follows: 'This, it seems to me, is where the doctrine of *stare decisis* must come into play. ... It means that all Courts throughout the Community [now Union], with the exception of the Court itself, are bound by the ratio decidendi of a Judgment of this Court.' He then referred to German legislation and the UK European Communities Act 1972, which confirm this binding effect.

[160] ECJ, Joined Cases 76/87, 86/87 to 89/87 and 149/87 *Seguela and Others* [1988] E.C.R. 2397, paras 11–14. For some examples of an express reversal of the case-law prompted by a new reference for a preliminary ruling, see ECJ, Case C-10/89 *CNL-SUCAL* [1990] E.C.R. I-3711, para. 10; ECJ, Joined Cases C-267/91 and C-268/91 *Keck and Mithouard* [1993] E.C.R. I-6097, para. 14; ECJ, Case C-127/08 *Metock and Others* [2008] E.C.R. I-6241, para. 58.

hearing the Advocate General, decide to rule by reasoned order.' That provision combines with the practice of many years standing by which the Court informs the national court by letter from the Registrar that an earlier judgment has answered its question and requests it to inform it whether in the circumstances it still wishes to pursue its request for a preliminary ruling. (Often the national court will then withdraw its request.)

Moreover, the binding effect *erga omnes* of the judgment given by way of preliminary rulings on interpretation is reinforced by the approach taken in the case-law concerning the temporal effects of such preliminary rulings, namely with respect to limiting such temporal effects as seen in the remainder of the chapter (see para. 6.34).

C. Temporal effects

(1) *Ex tunc* effect

6.33 In principle, the interpretation simply expresses what was contained *ab initio* in the provisions and principles of Union law to which it relates. Consequently, its temporal effects are the same as the effects of those provisions and principles; in other words, it is effective as from their entry into force or *ex tunc*. This is the starting point for the Court's case-law: 'The interpretation which, in the exercise of the jurisdiction conferred upon it by [Art. 267 TFEU], the Court of Justice gives to a rule of [Union] law clarifies and defines where necessary the meaning and scope of that rule as it must be or ought to have been understood and applied from the time of its entry into force. It follows that the rule as thus interpreted may, and must, be applied by the courts even to legal relationships arising and established before the judgment ruling on the request for interpretation, provided that in other respects the conditions enabling an action relating to the application of that rule to be brought before the courts having jurisdiction, are satisfied.'[161]

The proviso set out in the last sentence of that passage refers to the national procedural rules which continue to govern the conditions in which such a dispute may be brought before the courts (for example, time limits and other procedural requirements). Admittedly, the procedural rules must accord with Union law (see para. 4.04), but their relevance—and hence the fact that they may prevent the dispute from being brought back before the courts—is not necessarily defeated by the effects *ex tunc* of the preliminary ruling on interpretation.[162]

---

[161] ECJ, Case 61/79 *Denkavit Italiana* [1980] E.C.R. 1205, para. 16; ECJ, Joined Cases 66/79, 127/79, and 128/79 *Salumi* [1980] E.C.R. 1237, para. 9; see further, e.g. ECJ, Case C-137/94 *Richardson* [1995] E.C.R. I-3407, para. 31; ECJ, Case C-209/03 *Bidar* [2005] E.C.R. I-2119, para. 66; ECJ, Case C-402/03 *Skov and Bilka* [2006] E.C.R. I-199, para. 50; ECJ, Case C-292/04 *Meilicke and Others* [2007] E.C.R. I-1835, para. 34; ECJ, Case C-2/06 *Kempter* [2008] E.C.R. I-411, para. 35; ECJ, Case C-73/08 *Bressol and Others* [2010] E.C.R. I-2735, para. 90 (and further citations therein). See further E. Sharpston, 'The Shock Troops Arrive in Force: Horizontal Direct Effect of a Treaty Provision and Temporal Limitation of Judgments Join the Armoury of EC Law', in M. Poiares Maduro and L. Azoulai (eds), *The Past and Future of EU Law* (Oxford and Portland Oregon, Hart Publishing, 2010), 251–64.

[162] The fact that the Court has given a preliminary ruling interpreting a provision of Union law without limiting the temporal effects of its judgment does not affect the right of a Member State to impose a time limit under national law within which, on penalty of being barred, proceedings for repayment of charges levied in breach of that provision must be commenced (ECJ, Case C-88/99 *Roquette Frères* [2000] E.C.R. I-10465, para. 36).

(2) Exceptional limitation of temporal effects

It is only exceptionally that the Court may, in application of the general principle of legal **6.34** certainty which is inherent in the Union legal order, be moved to restrict for any person concerned the opportunity of relying on a provision which it has interpreted with a view to calling into question legal relationships established in good faith; however, two essential criteria must be fulfilled before such a limitation can be imposed, namely that those concerned should have acted in good faith, and that there should be a risk of serious difficulties. More specifically, the Court has taken that step only in quite specific circumstances, where (1) there was a risk of serious economic consequences owing in particular to the large number of legal relationships entered into in good faith on the basis of the rules considered to be validly in force; and (2) where it appeared that individuals and national authorities had been led to adopt practices which did not comply with Union legislation, to which the conduct of other Member States or the Commission may even have contributed.[163] In other words, taking into account the serious difficulties which the Court's judgment may create as regards events in the past, the Court limits the effects of its preliminary rulings in time, subject to compliance with strict requirements.[164] Accordingly, on the basis of these two main components or 'factors',[165] the Court determines whether limiting the temporal effects of its preliminary ruling is justified on a case-by-case basis.

It is settled case-law that the financial consequences which might ensue for a Member State from a preliminary ruling do not in themselves justify limiting the temporal effect of the ruling.[166] The Court reasons that, if it were otherwise, the most serious infringements would receive more lenient treatment insofar as it is those infringements that are likely to have the most significant financial implications for Member States.[167]

Furthermore, as the Court has consistently held, such a limitation on the temporal effects of a preliminary ruling may be allowed only in the actual judgment ruling upon the interpretation sought.[168] In *Meilicke*,[169] the Court of Justice refused to grant a Member State's request to limit the temporal effects of its ruling on these grounds, emphasizing that there

---

[163] See, e.g. ECJ, Case C-73/08 *Bressol and Others* [2010] E.C.R. I-2735, paras 91, 93 (and citations therein); ECJ, Case C-242/09 *Albron Catering* [2010] E.C.R. I-10309, paras 36–37 (and citations therein); ECJ (judgment of 10 May 2012), Joined Cases C-338/11 to C-347/11 *Santander Asset Management SGIIC*, not reported, paras 59–60. Compare the approach taken with respect to limiting the temporal effects of preliminary rulings on validity: see para. 10.23.

[164] See the wording used in ECJ, Case C-267/06 *Maruko* [2008] E.C.R. I-1757, para. 77.

[165] ECJ, Case C-577/08 *Brouwer* [2010] E.C.R. I-7489, para. 36.

[166] See, e.g. ECJ, Case C-104/98 *Buchner and Others* [2000] E.C.R. I-3625, para. 41; ECJ, Case C-184/99 *Grzelczyk* [2001] E.C.R. I-6193, paras 52–53; ECJ, Case C-209/03 *Bidar* [2005] E.C.R. I-2119, paras 68–69; ECJ, Case C-73/08 *Bressol and Others* [2010] E.C.R. I-2735, para. 92; ECJ, Case C-577/08 *Brouwer* [2010] E.C.R. I-7489, paras 34–35 (and further citations therein); ECJ (judgment of 10 May 2012), Joined Cases C-338/11 to C-347/11 *Santander Asset Management SGIIC*, not reported, para. 62. The fact that the interpretative judgment could result in the re-examination of numerous files and give rise to administrative and practical difficulties did not suffice in order to limit the temporal effect of the interpretative judgment: ECJ, Case C-372/98 *Cooke* [2000] E.C.R. I-8683, para. 43.

[167] See, e.g. ECJ, Case C-294/99 *Athinaïki Zythoppoïïa* [2001] E.C.R. I-6797, para. 39 (and citations therein).

[168] See, e.g. ECJ, Case C-292/04 *Meilicke and Others* [2007] E.C.R. I-1835, para. 36 (and citations therein); ECJ, Case C-267/06 *Maruko* [2008] E.C.R. I-1757, para. 77; ECJ (judgment of 23 October 2012), Joined Cases C-581/10 and C-629/10 *Nelson and Others*, not reported, paras 92–94.

[169] ECJ, Case C-292/04 *Meilicke and Others* [2007] E.C.R. I-1835, paras 37–41 (P. Van Nuffel, case note (2007) T.B.P. 422–3). See also ECJ, Case C-426/07 *Krawczyński* [2008] E.C.R. I-6021, paras 43–47.

must necessarily be a single occasion when a decision is made on the temporal effects of the requested interpretation. The principle that a restriction may be allowed only in the actual judgment ruling upon that interpretation guarantees the equal treatment of the Member States and other persons subject to Union law, under that law, while fulfilling at the same time the requirements arising from the principle of legal certainty. In the instant case, as there were prior judgments which had clarified the Union law provisions at issue for which no temporal limitation had been granted, the Court held that it was therefore not appropriate to limit the temporal effects of the present judgment.[170] In this way, the Court's approach taken to the temporal effects of preliminary rulings further underscores the *erga omnes* effect of preliminary rulings in terms of constituting an important 'precedential' value for courts in other Member States.

Generally speaking, only the Court of Justice can limit the temporal effects of its preliminary rulings; the national legislature or the domestic courts have no power to restrict the effects *ratione temporis* of a judgment given by way of preliminary ruling if the Court of Justice itself has not done so.[171]

The burden of proof is on the party requesting the limitation of the temporal effects of the Court's judgment to demonstrate with specific evidence that all of the requirements have been fulfilled; otherwise, the request is rejected.[172] As mentioned earlier, the Court takes account of the conduct of the Commission[173] and the other Member States in the period

---

[170] Compare the Opinion of Advocate-General C. Stix-Hackl in ECJ, Case C-292/04 *Meilicke and Others* [2007] E.C.R. I-1835: while coming to the similar conclusion that the Member State's request must be rejected, she accepted the premise that a temporal limitation could be obtained in a later judgment, i.e. one coming after the actual judgment ruling on the interpretation of the provision of Union law concerned. This case should be viewed in tandem with another case, ECJ, Case C-475/03 *Banco popolare di Cremona* [2006] E.C.R. I-9273, which also invited significant attention on the approach taken in the case-law to the limiting of temporal effects of preliminary rulings in the accompanying Opinions of Advocate-General F. Jacobs and Advocate-General C. Stix-Hackl, even though the Court's judgment never got to the issue.

[171] ECJ, Case 309/85 *Barra* [1988] E.C.R. 355, para. 13, at 375: 'The fundamental need for a general and uniform application of [Union] law implies that it is for the Court of Justice alone to decide upon the temporal restrictions to be placed on the interpretation which it lays down.' However, the Union legislator or the Member States as the Treaty-framers can change the interpreted provisions (e.g. the Barber Protocol).

[172] For recent examples (in which the standard of proof was not met), see ECJ, Case C-481/99 *Heininger* [2001] E.C.R. I-9945, paras 52–54; ECJ, Case C-209/03 *Bidar* [2005] E.C.R. I-2119, paras 70–71; ECJ, Joined Cases C-290/05 and C-333/05 *Nádasdi* [2006] E.C.R. I-10115, paras 61–72; ECJ, Case C-313/05 *Brzeziński* [2007] E.C.R. I-513, paras 59–60; ECJ, Case C-73/08 *Bressol and Others* [2008] E.C.R. I-2735, paras 94–96; ECJ, Case C-2/09 *Kalinchev* [2010] E.C.R. I-4939, paras 54–55; ECJ, Case C-263/10 *Nisipeanu* [2011] E.C.R. I-97*, Summ. pub., paras 34–38. While typically it is the Member State whose national legislation is at issue in the main proceedings which requests the limitation of the temporal effects of the Court's preliminary ruling, such a request can also be made by other 'interested parties' within the meaning of Art. 23 of the Statute, such as the Commission (see, e.g. Case C-262/88 *Barber* [1990] E.C.R. I-1889, para. 40), other Member States submitting observations in the preliminary ruling proceedings (see, e.g. ECJ, Case C-209/03 *Bidar* [2005] E.C.R. I-2119, para. 65; ECJ, Joined Cases C-290/05 and C-333/05 *Nádasdi* [2006] E.C.R. I-10115, para. 61), or a party to the main proceedings (see, e.g. ECJ, Case C-481/99 *Heininger* [2001] E.C.R. I-9945, paras 49–54; ECJ, Case C-242/09 *Albron Catering* [2010] E.C.R. I-10309, paras 33–34). In certain cases, the Court of Justice has entertained a request put forward by the 'defendant' Member State for the first time at the oral hearing, although it ultimately rejected the requests concerned: see ECJ, Case C-366/99 *Griesmar* [2001] E.C.R. I-9383, paras 70–78; ECJ, Case C-446/04 *Test Claimants in the FII Group Litigation* [2006] E.C.R. I-11753, paras 221–225; ECJ, Case C-524/04 *Test Claimants iin the Thin Cap Litigation* [2007] E.C.R. I-2107, paras 129–133.

[173] See, e.g. ECJ, Case 43/75 *Defrenne* [1976] E.C.R. 455, paras 72–73; ECJ, Case 24/86 *Blaizot* [1988] E.C.R. 379, paras 32–33; ECJ, Case C-163/90 *Legros and Others* [1992] E.C.R. I-4625, para. 32. See also ECJ, Case C-437/97 *EKW and Wein & Co.* [2000] E.C.R. I-1157, para. 58. Compare, e.g. ECJ, Case C-228/05

prior to the judgment, as well as the Court's earlier case-law,[174] any measures of other Union institutions, offices, bodies, or agencies,[175] and the acts or conduct of the Member State concerned.[176] Notwithstanding these considerations, the Court may be apt to reject a request where it is clear that the party concerned has not put forward sufficient evidence that all of the requirements have been satisfied.[177]

In practice, the Court of Justice weighs on a case-by-case basis the principle of legal certainty—which is applied to obviate the serious effects which its judgment might have, as regards the past, on legal relationships entered into in good faith—against the principle of the uniform application of Union law. Where the scales tip in favour of the principle of legal certainty, the Court declares that no reliance may be placed in the provision as interpreted in order to support claims concerning periods prior to the date of its judgment, except in the case of persons who have before that date initiated legal proceedings or raised an equivalent claim under national law.[178]

Finally, it should be noted that the precise scope of the temporal limitation of the effects of a preliminary ruling may be the subject of a further request for an interpretation by way of preliminary ruling (see para. 6.11).[179]

Stradasfalti [2006] E.C.R. I-8391, paras 71–77 (the fact that the Commission supported the national authorities during the years at issue in the main proceedings is not sufficient); ECJ, Case C-577/08 *Brouwer* [2010] E.C.R. I-7489, para. 39 (the fact that the Commission had not initiated infringement proceedings against the Member State concerned cannot be interpreted as the Commission's tacit consent to the national rules concerned).

[174] Cited in favour of restricting the temporal effects of the preliminary ruling, see, e.g. ECJ, Case 24/86 *Blaizot* [1988] E.C.R. 379, para. 31, and ECJ, Case C-262/96 *Sürül* [1999] E.C.R. I-2685, paras 106–113, and against ECJ, Case 61/79 *Denkavit Italiana* [1980] E.C.R. 1205, paras 19–21; ECJ, Case C-366/99 *Griesmar* [2001] E.C.R. I-9383, paras 70–78. The Court has not foreclosed the possibility of granting a request for limiting the temporal effects of a preliminary ruling under circumstances where the Court would depart from established case-law, albeit in the instant proceedings the Court dismissed the request on the grounds that the judgment contained a clarification of the case-law in the field: see ECJ, Case C-17/05 *Cadman* [2006] E.C.R. I-9583, paras 42–43.

[175] See, e.g. ECJ, Case C-262/88 *Barber* [1990] E.C.R. I-1889, para. 42; ECJ, Case C-163/90 *Legros and Others* [1992] E.C.R. I-4625, para. 32; ECJ, Joined Cases C-197/94 and C-252/94 *Société Bautiaa and Société Française Maritime* [1996] E.C.R. I-505, paras 44–56; ECJ, Case C-347/00 *Barreira Pérez* [2002] E.C.R. I-8191, paras 43–47.

[176] See, e.g. ECJ, Case C-184/04 *Uudenkaupungin kaupunki* [2006] E.C.R. I-3039, para. 57 (stressing that the very fact that the Member State seeking the limitation on temporal effects invoked a derogation in the measure concerned which was predicated on the adjustments being 'insignificant' casts doubt on the claim that the judgment would have any significant economic repercussions); ECJ, Case C-423/04 *Richards* [2006] E.C.R. I-3585, para. 43 (placing emphasis on the adoption of legislation and the Member State's withdrawal of its request to limit the temporal effects of the Court's preliminary ruling).

[177] See, e.g. ECJ, Case C-138/07 *Cobelfret* [2009] E.C.R.-731, paras 67–70.

[178] See, e.g. ECJ, Case 43/75 *Defrenne* [1976] E.C.R. 455, paras 69–75; ECJ, Case 24/86 *Blaizot* [1988] E.C.R. 379, para. 35; ECJ, Case C-262/88 *Barber* [1990] E.C.R. I-1889, paras 44–45; ECJ, Case C-163/90 *Legros and Others* [1992] E.C.R. I-4625, paras 34–35; ECJ, Joined Cases C-485/93 and C-486/93 *Simitzi* [1995] E.C.R. I-2655, para. 34; ECJ, Case C-126/94 *Société Cadi Surgelés and Others* [1996] E.C.R. I-5647, paras 32–34; ECJ, Case C-72/03 *Carbonati Apuani* [2004] E.C.R. I-8027, paras 37–42.

[179] See, e.g. ECJ, Case C-109/91 *Ten Oever* [1993] E.C.R. I-4879; ECJ, Case C-110/91 *Moroni* [1993] E.C.R. I-6591 (these two judgments interpret the restriction of the temporal effects of the judgment in *Barber*, which the Court of Justice associated with its interpretation of Art. 157 TFEU); see also ECJ, Joined Cases C-363/93 and C-407/93 to C-411/93 *Lancry and Others* [1994] E.C.R. I-3957, paras 42–43.

PART III

PROTECTION AGAINST ACTS
OF THE INSTITUTIONS

7

THE ACTION FOR ANNULMENT

I. Introduction

A. General

The action for annulment set forth in Art. 263 TFEU enables Union institutions, Member **7.01**
States, and natural and legal persons to protect themselves against unlawful binding acts
of Union institutions, bodies, offices, or agencies, provided that specific conditions as to
admissibility are fulfilled. By this procedure, the Court of Justice or the General Court[1]
reviews the contested act in the light of higher-ranking rules of—written and unwritten—
Union law. In the event that a violation of such rules is found, the action will result in
the annulment of the contested act (i.e. a declaration that the act is void pursuant to
Art. 264 TFEU).[2]

---

[1] The allocation of jurisdiction between the Court of Justice and the General Court with respect to actions for annulment is determined by Art. 256 TFEU and Art. 51 of the Statute. See para. 2.53. For an example, see ECJ (order of 11 December 2007), Case C-269/06 *Commission v Translation Centre for the Bodies of the EU* [2007] E.C.R. I-187*, Summ. pub., paras 2–7. When the same Union act is challenged before the Court of Justice and the General Court, see Art. 54 of the Statute. See further para. 2.55. For an example, see CFI, Case T-215/07 *Donnici v European Parliament* [2007] E.C.R. II-5239, paras 4–12. The EU Civil Service Tribunal has first instance jurisdiction to hear 'staff disputes' brought on the basis of Art. 270 TFEU; thus, where it determines that the action before it falls within the scope of Art. 263 TFEU, it is not competent to adjudicate it and will refer it to the General Court. See, e.g. CST (order of 9 October 2006), Case F-53/06 *Gualtieri v Commission* [2006] E.C.R. II-A-1-399, paras 20–27; CST (order of 10 December 2008), Case F-46/08 *Thoss v Court of Auditors* [2008] E.C.R. II-A-1-337, paras 19–48. Yet, Art. 270 TFEU covers only disputes between the Union and its officials or servants; actions seeking the annulment of a Union act falling outside those confines come within the first instance jurisdiction of the General Court, e.g. an action brought by a Member State seeking the annulment of acts relating to the European Civil Service (see CFI, Case T-185/05 *Italy v Commission* [2008] E.C.R. II-3207, paras 23–32) or of the Court of Justice where, e.g. an action for annulment is brought by the Commission against an act of the Council on grounds of its infringement of provisions of the Staff Regulations (see ECJ, Case C-40/10 *Commission v Council* [2010] E.C.R. I-12043; the admissibility was not examined in this case).

[2] The jurisdiction of the Union courts under Art. 263 TFEU is confined to the review of the legality of Union acts. Applications asking the Union courts, *inter alia*, to make declarations or to issue directions or injunctions to the Union institutions are inadmissible: see para. 7.219. It also bears noting that the jurisdiction of the Union courts concerning the review of the legality of Union acts is determined and governed by Art. 263 TFEU, not by national rules and case-law: see ECJ (order of 25 June 2009), Case C-580/08 P *Srinivasan v European Ombudsman* [2009] E.C.R. I-110*, Summ. pub., paras 44–47.

B. Role in the complete and coherent system of judicial protection in the European Union

7.02   The action for annulment is at the core of the complete system of EU judicial protection by allowing direct review of the legality of binding Union measures before the Union courts. By virtue of Art. 263 TFEU, the Court of Justice of the European Union has exclusive jurisdiction to declare a particular Union act void.

Moreover, the action for annulment has interplay with other types of actions which may be brought before the Union courts and the national courts as part of the coherent system of EU judicial protection, which provides for both direct and indirect routes for the review of the legality of Union acts, for example as regards the relationship between the direct route of annulment and the indirect route of preliminary rulings on the validity of Union acts under Art. 267 TFEU (see para. 10.11), as well as complementary means by which to compensate parties for damage caused by unlawful acts and conduct of Union institutions and bodies through the action for damages against the Union (see para. 11.09).

C. Overview of the changes brought by the Treaty of Lisbon

7.03   There are three main changes brought by the Lisbon Treaty to the action for annulment enshrined in Art. 263 TFEU as compared to the wording found in the former Art. 230 EC.[3] First, under the first paragraph of Art. 263 TFEU, the category of defendants against which annulment proceedings may be brought has been enlarged so as to cover acts of the European Council (now a Union institution under Art. 13(1) TEU)[4] and of Union bodies, offices, or agencies intended to produce legal effects vis-à-vis third parties.[5] Second, under the third paragraph of Art. 263 TFEU, the Committee of the Regions is now included in the category of 'semi-privileged' applicants which are entitled to challenge a Union act where the action is brought for the purposes of protecting its prerogatives.[6] Third, in efforts to improve judicial protection for individuals, the fourth paragraph of Art. 263 TFEU relaxes the standing requirements for actions for annulment brought by natural and legal persons by removing the condition of individual concern for the category of regulatory acts which are of direct concern to such persons and do not entail implementing measures.[7]

---

[3] For more a general discussion, see, e.g. R. Barents, 'The Court of Justice After the Treaty of Lisbon' (2010) C.M.L. Rev. 709–28; J. Kokott, I. Dervisopoulos and T. Henze, 'Aktuelle Fragen des effektiven Rechtsschutzes durch die Gemeinschaftsgerichte' (2008) EuGRZ 13–15; K. Lenaerts, 'Le traité de Lisbonne et la protection juridictionnelle des particuliers en droit de l'Union' (2009) C.D.E. 725–8.

[4] See further para. 7.69.

[5] See further para. 7.70.

[6] See further para. 7.80. Pursuant to Art. 8 of Protocol (No. 2) on the application of the principles of subsidiarity and proportionality, the Committee of the Regions may also bring an action for annulment in accordance with the conditions set out in Art. 263 TFEU against legislative acts on grounds of infringement of the principle of subsidiarity, provided that it had to be consulted in the course of the legislative process.

[7] See further paras 7.105 *et seq.* As regards when such changes brought by the Lisbon Treaty take effect, see para. 7.05.

D. The former second and third pillars of the Union

Furthermore, certain changes brought by the Lisbon Treaty to the institutional framework **7.04** of the Union generally have a crucial impact on the action for annulment. Under former Art. 230 EC, the jurisdiction of the Union courts was confined to the review of acts adopted within the sphere of the EC Treaty and generally did not extend to acts adopted in the second pillar of Common Foreign and Security Policy (CFSP) or the third pillar of Police and Judicial Cooperation in Criminal Matters (PJCCM).[8] However, with respect to the latter pillar, former Art. 35(6) EU provided for a comparable, but not identical, procedure to Art. 230 EC, which conferred jurisdiction on the Court of Justice to review the legality of framework decisions and decisions in actions brought by Member States or the Commission (see Ch. 22).[9]

By virtue of the elimination of the pillar structure and the replacement of the European Community with the Union upon the entry into force of the Lisbon Treaty,[10] certain restrictions placed on the Union courts' jurisdiction in this regard have been removed. With respect to the former third pillar of PJCCM, the Union courts' jurisdiction is no longer precluded for actions for annulment challenging acts adopted in this field. Yet, where such an action is brought against a pre-existing PJCCM act adopted before the entry into force of the Lisbon Treaty, the Union courts' jurisdiction is subject to the five-year provisional period set forth in Art. 10 of Protocol No. 36 on transitional provisions.[11]

With respect to the former second pillar of the CFSP, the Union judicature still has not been conferred jurisdiction in this field as a general matter, although there are exceptions laid down in the Treaties which implicate the Union courts' jurisdiction over actions for annulment in relation to, first, monitoring compliance with Art. 40 TEU and, second, reviewing the legality of restrictive measures against natural and legal persons in proceedings brought in accordance with the fourth paragraph of Art. 263 TFEU.[12]

---

[8] See ECJ, Case C-160/03 *Spain v Eurojust* [2005] E.C.R. I-2077, paras 35–44. However, this was subject to the exception that an act adopted in the former second and third pillars said to encroach on the competences of the then Community could be annulled under former Art. 230 EC. As regards the former second pillar, see ECJ, Case C-91/05 *Commission v Council* (*'ECOWAS'*) [2005] E.C.R. I-3651, paras 29–34; CFI, Case T-228/02 *PMOI v Council* [2006] E.C.R. II-4665, paras 56–59. As regards the former third pillar, see ECJ, Case C-176/03 *Commission v Council* (*'Environmental crimes'*) [2005] E.C.R. I-7879, paras 38–40; ECJ, Case C-440/05 *Commission v Council* (*'Ship-source pollution'*) [2007] E.C.R. I-9097, paras 52–54.

[9] See CFI (order of 1 April 2008), Case T-412/07 *Ayyanarsamy v Commission and Germany*, not reported, paras 17–18 (underlining that former Art. 35(6) EU allowed for a means of recourse similar to the action for annulment provided by Art. 230 EC but may only be brought by a Member State or by the Commission). But see ECJ, Case C-354/04 P *Gestoras Pro Amnistía and Others v Council* [2007] E.C.R. I-1579, para. 55; and ECJ, Case C-355/04 P *Segi and Others v Council* [2007] E.C.R. I-1657, para. 55, in which the Court of Justice held that it has jurisdiction to review the lawfulness of common positions intended to produce legal effects vis-à-vis third parties, *inter alia*, when an action has been brought by a Member State or the Commission under the conditions fixed by Art. 35(6) EU.

[10] See Art. 1(3) TEU.

[11] Given the two-month time limit prescribed by the sixth para. of Art. 263 TFEU, this provision is no longer relevant for annulment actions. Where a pre-existing PJCCM act is amended, the jurisdiction of the Union courts reverts to the regime of the Lisbon Treaty (i.e. former Art. 35 EU is not applicable). See Art. 10 (1)–(3) of Protocol (No. 36), annexed to the TEU, TFEU and the EAEC Treaty, on transitional provisions, [2012] O.J. C326/322. See also Declaration No. 50, annexed to the Lisbon Treaty, concerning Art. 10 of the Protocol on transitional provisions, [2012] O.J. C326/356.

[12] Art. 24(1), second para., TEU; Art. 275 TFEU.

E. Temporal effect of the Treaty of Lisbon

7.05 Given the crucial impact that the changes brought by the Lisbon Treaty have for the admissibility of actions for annulment, especially those brought by natural and legal persons, an important question arises as to when such changes take effect.

Under the case-law, the question of the temporal application of the rules laying down the conditions of admissibility of an action is resolved on the basis of the rules in force at the date on which it was brought, and the conditions of admissibility of an action are judged at the time of bringing the action, that is to say, the lodging of the application.[13] Therefore, the admissibility of an action for annulment lodged after the date of the entry into force of the Lisbon Treaty (i.e. 1 December 2009) is adjudicated on the basis of Art. 263 TFEU,[14] whereas an action for annulment lodged before that date is adjudicated on the basis of Art. 230 EC, even though a Union court delivers its judgment after that date.[15]

F. EAEC and former ECSC Treaties

7.06 Comparable provisions concerning an action for annulment in the context of the EAEC Treaty used to be found in Art. 146 EAEC. However, in tandem with the entry into force of the Lisbon Treaty, there is a new consolidated version of the EAEC Treaty, in which Art. 146 EAEC has been repealed and replaced by Art. 263 TFEU.[16]

There was a somewhat different regime for actions for annulment brought in connection with acts of the High Authority, the Council, and the Assembly, which was set forth in the now-expired ECSC Treaty.[17]

---

[13] EGC (order of 7 September 2010), Case T-532/08 *Norilsk Nickel Harjavalta and Umicore v Commission* [2010] E.C.R. II-3959, paras 68–75; EGC (order of 7 September 2010), Case T-539/08 *Etimine and Etiproducts v Commission* [2010] E.C.R. II-4017, paras 74–81. See further, e.g. EGC (order of 15 December 2010), Joined Cases T-219/09 and T-326/09 *Albertini and Others v European Parliament* [2010] E.C.R. II-5935, paras 39–40; EGC, Case T-461/08 *Evropaiki Dynamiki v EIB* [2011] E.C.R. II-6367, paras 28–29; EGC, Case T-291/04 *Enviro Tech Europe and Enviro Tech International v Commission* [2011] E.C.R. II-8281, para. 98; EGC (order of 7 July 2011), Case T-351/09 *Acetificio Marcello de Nigris v Commission* [2011] E.C.R. II-216*, Summ. pub., paras 56–58; EGC (order of 6 September 2011), Case T-18/10 *Inuit Tapiriit Kanatami and Others v European Parliament and Council* [2011] E.C.R. II-5599, para. 34; EGC (order of 14 February 2012), Case T-319/08 *Grasso v Commission*, not reported, paras 16–17.

[14] This is so, even if the contested measure was adopted on the basis of the former EC Treaty: see, e.g. EGC (order of 6 September 2011), Case T-18/10 *Inuit Tapriit Kanatami and Others v European Parliament and Council* [2011] E.C.R. II-5599, paras 32–35.

[15] See further M. Jaeger, 'L'accès des personnes physiques ou morales à la justice: les premières interprétations par le Tribunal des nouvelles dispositions de l'Article 263, quatrième alinéa, TFUE', in L. Weitzel (ed.), *L' Europe des droit fondamentaux: mélanges en hommage à Albert Weitzel* (Zutphen, Paris Legal Publishers, 2013), 102–6.

[16] See Art. 106a of the consolidated version of the EAEC Treaty, [2012] O.J. C327/1. The same applies for Arts 147 and 149 EAEC, which were comparable to former Arts 231 and 233 EC and have now been replaced by Arts 264 and 266 TFEU, respectively.

[17] See Arts 33–34, 36–38 of the former ECSC Treaty.

G. Overview of the chapter

The action for annulment has several components and characteristics for which all six **7.07**
paragraphs of Art. 267 TFEU, as well as Arts 264 and 266 TFEU, come into play. First, the
subject-matter of the action for annulment implicates the type of Union act being
challenged and requires there to be a reviewable act within the meaning of the case-law.
Second, as mentioned in connection with the changes brought by the Lisbon Treaty, the
standing of the parties in annulment proceedings must be evaluated, as regards both the
potential applicants and defendants, in which context certain admissibility conditions
placed on applications for annulment brought by natural and legal persons arise. The
grounds on which the action for annulment may be based, compliance with the applicable
time limits, and other procedural aspects comprise special characteristics of the action for
annulment that must also be taken into account. This is followed by the consequences of an
action for annulment.

II. Subject-Matter

A. The concept of a reviewable act

(1) The requirement for there to be a contested act

(a) Existing act

An application for annulment is admissible only if it is directed against an existing act.[18] **7.08**
A non-existent act may not be declared void.

(b) Identification of the act

Consequently, the applicant must identify precisely the act which it is seeking to have **7.09**
annulled. If it fails to do so, the application will be inadmissible on the grounds that its
subject-matter is unknown.[19] However, it may be that an application for annulment which
is formally directed against a particular act is in fact directed against other acts which are
linked with the contested act in such a way that they constitute a single whole.[20]

---

[18] ECJ, Case C-27/04 *Commission v Council* [2004] E.C.R. I-6649, para. 34 (failure by the Council to
adopt acts that are recommended by the Commission cannot be regarded as giving rise to acts open to
challenge for the purposes of Art. 230 of the EC Treaty); CFI, Case T-64/89 *Automec v Commission* [1990]
E.C.R. II-367, para. 41; CFI, Case T-16/91 *Rendo v Commission* [1992] E.C.R. II-2417, para. 39. The Court
of Justice (under Art. 150 of the ECJ Rules of Procedure) and the General Court (under Art. 113 of the EGC
Rules of Procedure) may declare of its own motion that an act is non-existent.
[19] ECJ, Case 30/68 *Lacroix v Commission* [1970] E.C.R. 301, paras 20–27; ECJ, Case 247/87 *Star Fruit v
Commission* [1989] E.C.R. 291, para. 9. See, e.g. CFI (order of 25 September 2008), Joined Cases T-392/03,
T-408/03, and T-435/03 *Regione Siciliana v Commission* [2008] E.C.R. II-2489, para. 48 (and citations
therein, finding that subject-matter of applications for annulment of all 'preceding and subsequent acts' is
insufficiently specific and thus must be dismissed under Art. 44(1)(c) of the EGC Rules of Procedure).
[20] ECJ, Joined Cases 25/65 and 26/65 *SIMET and FERAM v High Authority* [1967] E.C.R. 33, at 43–4.
See also ECJ, Case 34/77 *Oslizlok v Commission* [1978] E.C.R. 1099, paras 5 and 6, where an application for
annulment which was not expressly directed against a specific Commission decision was nevertheless regarded
as being directed against that decision in view of the arguments put forward in one of the applicant's pleas
raised against other decisions related to the first decision, which were expressly mentioned as being the subject-
matter of the application for annulment.

(c) Act no longer in force

7.10 An application for annulment of an act which is no longer in force is not necessarily devoid of purpose. If the applicant has an interest in the annulment of an act which is no longer in force and it is within the time limit prescribed by the sixth paragraph of Art. 263 TFEU, the application will be admissible (at least from this point of view).[21] This also applies where the contested act has already been implemented at the time when the action is brought.[22]

(d) Act replacing a withdrawn act

7.11 In the interests of the due administration of justice and the requirements of procedural economy, an action for annulment of an act which is withdrawn in the course of the proceedings may also be redirected against a new, closely related act which replaces or simply revokes the contested act.[23] In such case, the new act is regarded as a new matter

---

[21] For an example of a case where the applicant had an interest, see ECJ, Case 207/86 *APESCO v Commission* [1988] E.C.R. 2151, paras 15–16: the interest which the Court of Justice considered sufficient was in preventing a repetition of the alleged illegality in similar future acts; ECJ (judgment of 27 June 2013), Case C-149/12 P *Xeda International and Pace International v Commission*, not reported, paras 32 and 33: the applicant has an interest since a declaration of illegality of the withdrawn act can constitute the basis for an action for damages. For examples of cases in which the applicant was held not to have an interest, see ECJ, Joined Cases 294/86 and 77/87 *Technointorg v Commission and Council* [1988] E.C.R. 6077, paras 11–14 (the application for annulment of a regulation imposing a provisional anti-dumping duty became devoid of purpose where, in the course of the proceedings, it was replaced by a definitive regulation, against which a new action for annulment had been brought); ECJ, Joined Cases C-305/86 and C-160/87 *Neotype Techmashexport v Commission and Council* [1990] E.C.R. I-2945, paras 14–15; CFI, Case T-239/94 *EISA v Commission* [1997] E.C.R. II-1839, paras 34–35 (an action brought against a Commission decision authorizing the grant of aid by a Member State pursuant to Art. 95 of the ECSC Treaty which was withdrawn in the course of the procedure was held to be devoid of purpose because the contested decision had become 'inapplicable'); CFI (order of 31 July 2000), Case T-31/00 *BSB-Fleischimport v Commission*, not reported, para. 11 (application to no purpose following the withdrawal of the contested act); CFI (order of 10 March 2005), Case T-184/01 *IMS Health v Commission* [2005] E.C.R. II-817, paras 34–49 (the Court of First Instance held that there was no need to give a judgment in this case, since no legal effect of the contested decision remained following its withdrawal). An action brought against a Commission decision implementing a 'basic decision' of that institution will have no subject-matter if the decision which it implements has been declared void. If, pursuant to the judgment annulling the basic decision, the Commission adopts a new basic decision incorporating the original implementing decision, the applicant will lose any interest in continuing an action to obtain annulment of the original implementing decision. This is because the annulment of the original basic decision causes the implementing decision to lose its *raison d'être*, with the result that the new decision cannot be regarded as a confirmatory act but as an 'autonomous act creating or altering legal rights', which takes the place of the original implementing act: CFI (order of 27 January 2000), Case T-236/95 *TAT European Airlines v Commission* [2000] E.C.R. II-51. In the case of restrictive measures against individuals, the applicant has been found to retain an interest in securing the annulment of a measure imposing restrictive measures which has been repealed and replaced: see, e.g. CFI, Case T-228/02 *PMOI v Council* [2006] E.C.R. II-4665, paras 34–35; CFI (judgment of 11 July 2007), Case T-327/03 *Al-Aqsa v Council*, not reported, paras 38–39; CFI (judgment of 3 April 2008), Case T-229/02 *PKK v Council* [2008] E.C.R. II-45*, Summ. pub., paras 49–51; CFI, Case T-256/07 *PMOI v Council* [2008] E.C.R. II-3019, para. 48 (appeal withdrawn in ECJ (order of 3 June 2009), Case C-576/08 P *PMOI v Council*, not reported). The same also applies where the applicant's name is removed from the list of persons whose funds had been frozen by the challenged act: see ECJ (judgment of 28 May 2013), Case C-239/12 P *Abdulrahim v Council and Commission*, not reported, paras 61–81; ECJ (judgment of 6 June 2013), Case C-183/12 P *Ayadi v Commission*, not reported, paras 59–81. See also para. 7.141.

[22] ECJ, Case 53/85 *AKZO Chemie v Commission* [1986] E.C.R. 1965, para. 21; CFI, Case T-22/97 *Kesko v Commission* [1999] E.C.R. II-3775, para. 59. See also ECJ, Case C-370/07 *Commission v Council* [2009] E.C.R. I-8917, paras 14–18 (holding admissible an action for annulment against contested measure, even though the Community position contained in that measure was already expressed at the conference of the parties to the international convention).

[23] ECJ, Case 14/81 *Alpha Steel v Commission* [1982] E.C.R. 749, para. 8 (the withdrawal of an unlawful measure is permissible, provided that the withdrawal occurs within a reasonable time and that the Commission

which has arisen in the course of the proceedings and the applicant may put forward new pleas in law.[24] Naturally, it is also possible to bring a new action for annulment. The new act is regarded as being of the same kind as the act that was withdrawn.

(e) Non-existent act

The requirement that the contested measure must exist is applied in the special case of the **7.12** doctrine of the non-existent act. Such a measure exhibits such particularly serious and manifest defects that it must be regarded as non-existent. If a measure is found to be non-existent, it loses the benefit of the normal presumption that an act is valid in so far as it has

---

has had sufficient regard to how the applicant might have been led to rely on the lawfulness of the measure); CFI, Joined Cases T-46/98 and T-151/98 *CCRE v Commission* [2000] E.C.R. II-167, para. 33. But see CFI, Case T-420/05 *Vischim v Commission* [2009] E.C.R. II-3841, paras 53–55 (this does not cover the situation where the applicant puts forward a new claim, not directed at the later measure, but rather seeks from another angle the partial or entire annulment of the original measure already the subject of the claim set out in the application). With particular regard to restrictive measures in relation to individuals, see, e.g. CFI, Case T-306/01 *Yusuf and Al Barakaat International Foundation v Council and Commission* [2005] E.C.R. II-3533, paras 71–77; and CFI, Case T-315/01 *Kadi v Council and Commission* [2005] E.C.R. II-3649, paras 52–58 (judgments set aside on other grounds in ECJ, Joined Cases C-402/05 P and C-415/05 P *Kadi and Al Barakaat International Foundation v Council* [2008] E.C.R. I-6351); CFI, Case T-228/02 *PMOI v Council* [2006] E.C.R. II-4665, paras 27–30; CFI (judgment of 11 July 2007), Case T-327/03 *Al-Aqsa v Council*, not reported, paras 32–35; CFI, Case T-256/07 *PMOI v Council* [2008] E.C.R. II-3019, paras 45–47 (appeal withdrawn in ECJ (order of 3 June 2009), Case C-576/08 P *People's Mojahedin Organization of Iran v Council*, not reported). But see, e.g. CFI, Case T-228/02 *PMOI v Council* [2006] E.C.R. II-4665, paras 32–33; and CFI (judgment of 11 July 2007), Case T-327/03 *Al-Aqsa v Council*, not reported, paras 36–37: although the applicant may be permitted to reformulate its claims so as to seek annulment of acts which have, during the proceedings, replaced the acts initially challenged, that solution cannot authorize the speculative review of the lawfulfulness of hypothetical acts which have not yet been adopted; EGC (judgment of 26 October 2012), Case T-53/12 *CF Sharp Shipping Agencies v Council*, not reported paras 26–30. As regards the time period during which an adaptation of claims may be made, the EGC considers that the two-month time period provided for in the sixth para. of Art. 263 TFEU is, in principle, applicable when the action for annulment of a measure is brought by application as when, in the course of a pending case, it is made through an adaptation of the claims for annulment of an earlier measure which has been repealed and replaced by the measure in question. This outcome is justified by the fact that rules concerning time limits for bringing proceedings are mandatory and must be applied by the court in question in such a way as to safeguard legal certainty and equality of persons before the law. However, by way of an exception to that rule, the EGC considers that this period is not applicable in proceedings in which, first, the act in question and the measure which that act repeals and replaces have, with regard to the person concerned, the same subject-matter, are essentially based on the same grounds, and have essentially the same content, and therefore differ only by reason of their respective scopes of application *ratione temporis* and, second, the adaptation of the claim is not based on any new plea, fact, or evidence apart from the actual adoption of the act in question repealing and replacing that earlier act. In such circumstances, since the subject-matter and context of the dispute as established by the original action have not undergone any alteration except as regards its temporal dimension, legal certainty is in no way affected by the fact that the adaptation of the claim was made after the two-month period in question had expired. It follows that, in such circumstances, an applicant may adapt its claims and pleas in law, even if the adaptation is made after the two-month period provided for in the sixth para. of Art. 263 TFEU has expired.) Notably this line of case-law has been held to apply to a situation in which a measure of direct and individual concern to a person is replaced by another measure, during the proceedings, having the same subject-matter: CFI, Case T-318/01 *Othman v Council and Commission* [2009] E.C.R. II-1627, paras 53–54; see also EGC, Case T-49/07 *Fahas v Council* [2010] E.C.R. II-5555, paras 33–36. This should be distinguished from the situation in which a particular act has been amended by a subsequent act, in which case annulment proceedings may be brought against a restrictive ('basic'/legislative) measure as amended by a subsequent (delegated/implementing) measure or against that subsequent measure alone: see CFI (judgment of 12 July 2006), Case T-49/04 *Hassan v Council and Commission*, not reported, paras 53–56, and on appeal, ECJ, Joined Cases C-399/06 P and C-403/06 P *Hassan and Ayadi v Council and Commission* [2009] E.C.R. I-11393, paras 23–24, 67; EGC, Case T-181/08 *Tay Za v Council* [2010] E.C.R. II-1965, paras 37–41 (set aside on other grounds in ECJ (judgment of 13 March 2012), Case C-376/10 P *Tay Za v Council*, not reported).

[24] ECJ Rules of Procedure, Art. 127(1); EGC Rules of Procedure, Art. 48(2).

not been annulled, or the institution which adopted it has not properly repealed or withdrawn it.[25] Moreover, the non-existent act cannot produce any legal effects at all. Consequently, an application for annulment of a non-existent act will invariably be declared inadmissible.[26] Furthermore, an act may be declared non-existent after the period prescribed for bringing an action for annulment has run out. To date, the case-law, which shows every sign of reluctance,[27] affords only two instances in which a measure was actually declared non-existent (one of them being a case heard by the now General Court, the judgment ultimately being set aside by the Court of Justice).[28]

(2) The requirement for a binding act

(a) Definition

7.13 It follows from the wording of the first paragraph of Art. 263 TFEU, which precludes the annulment of opinions and recommendations, that acts whose annulment is sought must be binding.[29] Binding acts are the outcome of 'the exercise, upon the conclusion of an

---

[25] ECJ, Joined Cases 7/56 and 3/57 to 7/57 *Algera and Others v Common Assembly* [1957 and 1958] E.C.R. 39, at 60–1; ECJ, Case 15/85 *Consorzio Cooperative d'Abruzzo v Commission* [1987] E.C.R. 1005, para. 10. The purpose of this exception to the principle that acts are presumed to be lawful is to 'maintain a balance between two fundamental, but sometimes conflicting, requirements with which a legal order must comply, namely stability of legal relations and respect for legality': see, e.g. ECJ, Case C-199/92 P *Hüls v Commission* [1999] E.C.R. I-4287, para. 85; ECJ, Case C-200/92 P *ICI v Commission* [1999] E.C.R. I-4399, para. 70; ECJ, Case C-235/92 P *Montecatini v Commission* [1999] E.C.R. I-4539, para. 97; ECJ, Case C-475/01 *Commission v Greece* [2004] E.C.R. I-8923, para. 19 (and citations therein).

[26] In view of the non-existence of the contested measure, the Court of Justice and the General Court may make an order for costs against the defendant and in favour of the applicant while declaring that the application is inadmissible (ECJ Rules of Procedure, Art. 139; EGC Rules of Procedure, Art. 87(3), second para.).

[27] See, e.g. ECJ, Joined Cases 7/56 and 3/57 to 7/57 *Algera and Others v Common Assembly* [1957 and 1958] E.C.R. 39, at 60–1; ECJ, Joined Cases 15/73 to 33/73, 52/73 to 53/73, 57/73 to 109/73, 116/73 to 117/73, 123/73, 132/73 and 135/73 to 137/73 *Schots (née Kortner) and Others v Council and Others* [1974] E.C.R. 177, para. 33; ECJ, Case 15/85 *Consorzio Cooperative d'Abruzzo v Commission* [1987] E.C.R. 1005, para. 10; ECJ, Case 226/87 *Commission v Greece* [1988] E.C.R. 3611, para. 16; EGC, Joined Cases T-494/08 to T-500/08 and T-509/08 *Ryanair v Commission* [2010] E.C.R. II-5723, paras 49–51; EGC, Case T-369/07 *Latvia v Commission* [2011] E.C.R. II-1039, para. 61 (and citations therein); ECJ, Case C-245/92 P *Chemie Linz v Commission* [1999] E.C.R. I-4643, paras 95–97; ECJ, Case C-475/01 *Commission v Greece* [2004] E.C.R. I-8923, paras 20–21. See further CFI (order of 25 October 2007), Case T-274/06 *Estaser El Mareny v Commission*, not reported, para. 41: in the context of rejecting various arguments of the applicant in relation to a finding that the application was lodged out of time, the Court ruled that even if the contested measure was manifestly contrary to what is now Art. 101 TFEU, it was not of such gravity to render it a non-existent act and thus evade the time limit set down in the sixth para. of Art. 263 TFEU.

[28] ECJ, Joined Cases 1/57 and 14/57 *Société des Usines à Tubes de la Sarre v High Authority* [1957 and 1958] E.C.R. 105, at 112–13. It must be noted, however, that that judgment was not so much concerned with the non-existence of the measure in question, but to fathom its nature (P. Mathijsen, 'Nullité et annulabilité des actes des institutions européennes', in *Miscellanea W.J. Ganshof van der Meersch* (Brussels, Bruylant, 1972), Vol. II, 272–6); CFI, Joined Cases T-79/89, T-84/89 to T-86/89, T-89/89, T-91/89 to T-92/89, T-94/89, T-96/89, T-98/89, T-102/89, and T-104/89 *BASF and Others v Commission* [1992] E.C.R. II-315, set aside by ECJ, Case C-137/92 P *Commission v BASF and Others* [1994] E.C.R. I-2555, paras 66–102.

[29] ECJ, Joined Cases 1/57 and 14/57 *Société des Usines à Tubes de la Sarre v High Authority*, at 114; ECJ, Case 133/79 *Sucrimex v Commission* [1980] E.C.R. 1299, paras 12–19. Under the case-law, the European Ombudsman does not have the power to take binding measures, and therefore, a decision by the Ombudsman concluding the substantive examination of a complaint by deciding to take no further action does not constitute a challengeable act for the purposes of Art. 263 TFEU, since it does not produce binding legal effects on third parties: CFI (order of 3 November 2008), Case T-196/08 *Srinivasan v European Ombudsman*, not reported, paras 11–12 (appeal dismissed in ECJ (order of 25 June 2009), Case C-580/08 P *Srinivasan v European Ombudsman* [2009] E.C.R. I-110*, Summ. pub.). A report drawn up by OLAF pursuant to Art. 9 of

internal procedure laid down by law, of a power provided for by law which is intended to produce legal effects'.[30] They must therefore have a legitimate legal basis, reflect the definitive position of a Union institution, body, office, or agency, and be intended to have legal effects.

(b) Silence on the part of an institution

When a party makes a request to a Union institution, mere silence on the part of that institution cannot be placed on the same footing as an implied refusal, except where that result is expressly provided for by a provision of Union law.[31] So, for example, where in a legislative procedure, the Council does not act upon measures proposed by the Commission, that failure cannot be regarded as giving rise to a challengeable act within the meaning of Art. 263 TFEU.[32] The position would be different if, under Union law, the Council were deemed, after the expiry of a specific period of time, to have taken an implied decision whose content is determined by Union law[33] or if the Council adopted a decision rejecting explicitly the proposal of the Commission.[34]

7.14

Regulation No. 1073/1999 contains only recommendations and is therefore not a challengeable act within the meaning of Art. 263 TFEU: see, e.g. CFI (order of 13 July 2004), Case T-29/03 *Comunidad Autónoma de Andalucía v Commission* [2004] E.C.R. II-2923, paras 33–40; CFI, Case T-309/03 *Camos Grau v Commission* [2006] E.C.R. II-1173, paras 46–58; see also CFI, Case T-193/04 *Tillack v Commission* [2006] E.C.R. II-3995, paras 66–82: act by which OLAF, on the basis of Art. 10(2) of Regulation No. 1073/1999 forwards information to national authorities held not challengeable under Art. 263 TFEU. In the context of the procedure concerning excessive deficits under Regulation No. 3605/93, a letter issued by Eurostat as regards the classification of a certain undertaking in the 'general government' sector within the European System of Accounts has been considered merely a measure of voluntary cooperation within which the Commission simply plays a consultative role and therefore not a challengeable act for the purposes of Art. 263 TFEU: CFI (order of 5 September 2006), Case T-148/05 *Comunidad autonoma de Madrid and Mintra v Commission*, not reported, paras 39–64. Likewise, a press release issued by the Commission (Eurostat) publishing data relating to government debt and deficit procedures of the Member States was held not to contain an implicit decision concerning classification of a particular undertaking in the 'general government' sector within the European System of Accounts: ECJ (order of 20 June 2008), Case C-448/07 P *Ayuntamiento de Madrid and Madrid Calle 30 v Commission* [2008] E.C.R. I-99*, Summ. pub., paras 44–53.

[30] ECJ, Case 182/80 *Gauff v Commission* [1982] E.C.R. 799, para. 18. Since the case was brought by a non-privileged applicant, the ECJ added with respect to the legal effects that they are 'of such a nature as to affect adversely the interests of the applicant by modifying its legal position' (see paras 7.20 and 7.21). Under Union law, there is no general obligation on the administrative or judicial authorities to inform the addressees of measures of the judicial remedies available or of the conditions for availing themselves thereof (ECJ (order of 5 March 1999), Case C-154/98 P *Guérin Automobiles v Commission* [1999] E.C.R. I-1451, para. 15) and hence a Union institution, body, office, or agency is not obliged to indicate whether one of its acts is binding.

[31] ECJ, Case C-123/03 P *Commission v Greencore* [2004] E.C.R. I-11647, para. 45. For example, as regards the rules concerning access to documents, failure to abide by the requisite time limits may render the contested measure an implicit decision to refuse access within the meaning of Art. 8(3) of Regulation No. 1049/2001: see, e.g. EGC, Joined Cases T-494/08 and T-500/08 to T-509/08 *Ryanair v Commission* [2010] E.C.R. II-5723, paras 38–40; EGC (order of 9 November 2011), Case T-120/10 *ClientEarth and Others v Commission*, not reported, paras 38–40. The EGC, however, ruled that the applicants had no interest in challenging the implied decisions concerned by reason of subsequently adopted express decision. Compare in the context of public procurement, CFI, Case T-437/05 *Brink's Security Luxembourg v Commission* [2009] E.C.R. II-3233, paras 57–59. See also EGC, Case T-474/08 *Umbach v Commission* [2010] E.C.R. II-234*, Summ. pub., paras 35–41, where the Court held that the express rejection of a request made pursuant to Regulation No. 1049/2001 does not constitute an implicit refusal insofar as the request was based on primary law.

[32] ECJ, Case C-27/04 *Commission v Council* [2004] E.C.R. I-6649, para. 34. In the event of an unlawful failure to act, an action for failure to act may be brought under Art. 265 TFEU (see Ch. 8).

[33] ECJ, Case C-27/04 *Commission v Council* [2004] E.C.R. I-6649, para. 32. See in this connection, ECJ, C-76/01 P *Eurocoton and Others v Council* [2003] E.C.R. I-10091, paras 54–65.

[34] ECJ (judgment of 19 November 2013), Case C-63/12 *Commission v Council*, not reported, paras 28–34.

(c) Acts of a contractual nature

7.15   Mere contractual acts of an institution, body, office, or agency cannot be regarded as acts exercising prerogatives of a public authority and, as a result, such acts cannot be the subject of an action for annulment.[35]

For instance, an application for the annulment of a letter by which the Commission demanded a party to a contract with it to repay certain sums on account of improper performance of the contract will therefore be inadmissible.[36] In the absence of an arbitration clause within the meaning of Art. 272 TFEU,[37] the national courts have jurisdiction (see Ch. 19).

---

[35] See, e.g. CFI (order of 3 October 1997), Case T-186/96 *Mutual Aid Administration Services v Commission* [1997] E.C.R. II-1633, paras 50–51; CFI (order of 9 January 2001), Case T-149/00 *Innova v Commission* [2001] E.C.R. II-1, para. 28; CFI (order of 25 November 2003), Case T-85/01 *IAMA Consulting v Commission* [2003] E.C.R. II-4973, paras 51–53; CFI (order of 10 May 2004), Joined Cases T-314/03 and T-378/03 *Musée Grévin v Commission* [2004] E.C.R. II-1421, paras 80–85; CFI (order of 2 April 2008), Case T-100/03 *Maison de l'Europe Avignon Méditerranée v Commission* [2008] E.C.R. II-43*, Summ. pub., paras 21–24; CFI, Joined Cases T-396/05 and T-397/05 *ArchiMEDES v Commission* [2009] E.C.R. II-70*, Summ. pub., para. 54–58; EGC, Joined Cases T-428/07 and T-455/07 *CEVA v Commission* [2010] E.C.R. II-2431, paras 52–55; EGC (order of 30 June 2011), Case T-252/10 *Cross Czech v Commission* [2011] E.C.R. II-211*, Summ. pub., paras 38–60; EGC, Case T-285/09 *CEVA v Commission* [2011] E.C.R. II-289*, Summ. pub., paras 45–48. But see CFI, Case T-153/04 *Ferriere Nord v Commission* [2006] E.C.R. II-3889, paras 38–43 (rejecting Commission arguments that the present case is not a dispute of a contractual nature). See also CFI, Case T-286/05 *CESD-Communautaire v Commission* [2009] E.C.R. II-39*, Summ. pub., paras 60–62 and CFI, Case T-289/06 *CESD-Communautaire v Commission* [2009] E.C.R. II-40*, Summ. pub., paras 58–60, in which the Court rejected the Commission's assumption that the action concerned the interpretation of contracts concluded between it and the applicant and hence in the absence of an 'arbitration clause' within the meaning of Art. 272 TFEU, the Court did not have jurisdiction. The Court held that the action sought annulment of a decision adopted by the Commission under the Treaties and was properly brought under Art. 263 TFEU.

[36] CFI (order of 10 May 2004), Joined Cases T-314/03 and T-378/03 *Musée Grévin v Commission* [2004] E.C.R. II-1421, paras 62–89. See also EGC, Case T-285/09 *CEVA v Commission* [2011] E.C.R. II-289*, Summ. pub., paras 45–48; EGC (order of 30 June 2011), Case T-252/10 *Cross Czech v Commission* [2011] E.C.R. II-211*, Summ. pub., paras 39–60 (action for annulment of a Commission letter confirming the findings of a financial audit report of financial statements declared by the applicant over a certain period in connection with three contracts concluded between the applicant and the Commission held to be part of a purely contractual framework and thus inadmissible). See also EGC (order of 12 October 2011), Case T-353/10 *Lito Maieftiko Gynaikologiko kai Cheirourgiko Kentro v Commission* [2011] E.C.R. II-7213, paras 22–32 (action for annulment of a debit note declared inadmissible, since it is part of the contractual framework and thus not an exercise of the prerogatives of public authority).

[37] Under the case-law, when hearing an action for annulment in which the dispute is found to be contractual in nature, the Union judicature has consented to the reclassification of the action, provided that the conditions for such reclassification are satisfied. The Union judicature considers itself unable to reclassify an action for annulment where the applicant's express intention is not to base its application on Art. 272 TFEU or where the action is not based on any plea alleging infringement of the rules governing the contractual relationship in question. For a case in which a reclassification was done, see EGC, Joined Cases T-428/07 and T-455/07 *CEVA v Commission* [2010] E.C.R. II-2431, paras 59–64 (rejecting the Commission's submission that reclassification is made subject to the condition that the law applicable to the contract is relied upon in the application). Compare EGC (order of 30 June 2011), Case T-252/10 *Cross Czech v Commission* [2011] E.C.R. II-211*, Summ. pub., paras 62–64 and EGC, Case T-285/09 *CEVA v Commission* [2011] E.C.R. II-289*, Summ. pub., paras 29–35. Conversely, an act by which the Commission effects an out-of-court set-off between debts and claims resulting from different legal relationships with the same person is a challengeable act for the purposes of Art. 263 TFEU (see, e.g. ECJ, Case C-87/01 P *Commission v CCRE* [2003] E.C.R. I-7617, para. 45; EGC, Case T-37/08 *Walton v Commission* [2011] E.C.R. II-7809, paras 25–26), and it is not for the Court to assess the legality of an act of offsetting in the context of an action under Art. 272 TFEU (see, e.g. CFI, Case T-122/06 *Helkon Media v Commission* [2008] E.C.R. II-210*, Summ. pub., paras 46–53; CFI, Case T-182/08 *Commission v Atlantic Energy* [2009] E.C.R. II-109*, Summ. pub., para. 70 and citations therein).

(3) Content determines whether the act is binding

(a) Content

The binding nature of an act is inferred from its content.[38] Where an act is cast in one of the **7.16** forms of binding acts of Art. 288 TFEU, its binding nature will not be brought into question.[39] However, with respect to other acts, the form in which it is cast is in principle irrelevant as regards the right to challenge such act in an action for annulment.[40] Consequently, an act which does not satisfy the relevant requirements as to form does not cease to be binding as a result.[41]

---

[38] See, e.g. ECJ, Case C-322/09 P *NDSHT v Commission* [2010] E.C.R. I-11911, para. 46 (and citations therein). In this regard, the Union judicature looks to the content of the act concerned, as well as to the intention of the author of the act challenged (see, e.g. ECJ, Case C-521/06 P *Athinaïki Techniki v Commission* [2008] E.C.R. I-5829, para. 42; ECJ (order of 22 January 2010), Case C-69/09 P *Makhteshim-Agan Holding and Others v Commission* [2010] E.C.R. I-10*, Summ. pub., para. 38; ECJ, Case C-362/08 P *Internationaler Hilfsfonds v Commission* [2010] E.C.R. I-669, para. 52) and to the context in which it was adopted (see, e.g. ECJ, Case 362/08 P *Internationaler Hilfsfonds v Commission* [2010] E.C.R. I-669, para. 58; CFI, Case T-33/01 *Infront v Commission* [2005] E.C.R. II-5897, para. 90; EGC, Case T-369/08 *EWRIA and Others v Commission* [2010] E.C.R. II-6283, para. 34). In *Infront v Commission*, the Court of First Instance held that the contested measure produced binding legal effects: CFI, Case T-33/01 *Infront v Commission*, paras 91–111 (the Court rejected in para. 110 the Commission's argument that it was not legally bound by the measure concerned, based on the fact that it was published in the 'C' as opposed to the 'L' series of the *Official Journal*) (appeal dismissed in ECJ, Case C-125/06 P *Commission v Infront WM* [2008] E.C.R. I-1451); compare CFI (order of 12 December 2007), Case T-109/06 *Vodafone España and Vodafone Group v Commission* [2007] E.C.R. II-5151, paras 70 *et seq.*: looking at the context in which the contested act was adopted and its content, the Court of First Instance ruled that the contested act did not produce binding legal effects, distinguishing the measure concerned from that in CFI, Case T-33/01 *Infront v Commission*, paras 109–112. For some examples, see ECJ, Case C-57/95 *France v Commission* [1997] E.C.R. I-1627, para. 9; CFI, Joined Cases T-125/97 and T-127/97 *Coca-Cola v Commission* [2000] E.C.R. II-1733, para. 78; CFI, Joined Cases T-222/99, T-327/99, and T-329/99 *Martinez and Others v European Parliament* [2001] E.C.R. II-2823, para. 26; CFI, Case T-113/00 *Dupont Teijin Films Luxembourg and Others v Commission* [2002] E.C.R. II-3681, para. 45; CFI (order of 9 July 2003), Case T-216/01 *Reisebank v Commission*, not reported, para. 45.

[39] ECJ, Joined Cases C-463/10 P and C-475/10 P *Deutsche Post and Germany v Commission* [2011] E.C.R. I-9639, paras 43–45.

[40] See, e.g. CFI (order of 28 April 1994), Joined Cases T-452/93 and T-453/93 *Pevasa and Inpesca v Commission* [1994] E.C.R. II-229, para. 29; ECJ, Case 101/76 *Koninklijke Scholten Honig v Council and Commission* [1977] E.C.R. 797, para. 7; ECJ, Case C-521/06 P *Athinaïki Techniki v Commission* [2008] E.C.R. I-5829, para. 43; ECJ, Case C-322/09 P *NDSHT v Commission* [2010] E.C.R. I-11911, para. 47; see also EGC (order of 12 February 2010), Case T-456/07 *Commission v Cdt* [2010] E.C.R. II-183, para. 58 (and citations therein): although the form in which an act is adopted cannot change its nature and is thus not decisive, the Union judicature may nonetheless take into consideration the form in which acts, the annulment of which is sought, are adopted inasmuch as it could help enable their nature to be identified. In this case, the mere fact that the contested act is entitled 'opinion' cannot lead to the conclusion, for that reason alone, that the action is inadmissible; yet, that title has to be taken into account for the purposes of interpreting the content of the act: EGC, Case T-456/07 *Commission v Cdt*, para. 62.

[41] Thus, the Court of Justice held that it did not follow from non-compliance with the formal requirements prescribed by the High Authority 'as a matter of obligation' for decisions within the meaning of Art. 14 of the former ECSC Treaty that a measure should not be considered a decision if it did not comply with those formal requirements, provided that it satisfied the substantive requirements which decisions had to fulfil under that Treaty (ECJ, Joined Cases 23/63, 24/63, and 52/63 *Usines Emile Henricot and Others v High Authority* [1963] E.C.R. 217, at 222). See also ECJ, Joined Cases 53/63 and 54/63 *Lemmerz-Werke and Others v High Authority* [1963] E.C.R. 239, at 247–248; ECJ, Case C-521/06 P *Athinaïki Techniki v Commission* [2008] E.C.R. I-5829, para. 44; ECJ, Case C-322/09 P *NDSHT v Commission* [2010] E.C.R. I-11911, para. 47. Once the Court has established that a measure contained in a letter satisfies the substantive requirements of a binding act, the application cannot be declared inadmissible on that basis: ECJ, Joined Cases 15/59 and 29/59 *Société Métallurgique de Knutange v High Authority* [1960] E.C.R. 1, at 7; ECJ, Joined Cases 8/66 to 11/66 *Cimenteries CBR Cementbedrijven and Others v Commission* [1967] E.C.R. 75, at 90–1; ECJ, Case C-135/92 *Fiskano v Commission* [1994] E.C.R. I-2885, paras 21–26 (Commission letter to Sweden constituting a binding act);

To take a well-known example, the General Court has held that an action will lie against an act made simply orally—by means of a statement by the spokesman for the Commissioner responsible for competition matters, also reported by the press agency *Agence Europe*—on the grounds that its contents were not contested by the parties and had subsequently been confirmed by the Commission itself, and that hence the General Court was in a position to investigate whether it had produced legal effects.[42] However, an action for annulment will not lie against a 'practice' of the Commission.[43] Silence on the part of an institution cannot produce legal effects unless this is expressly provided for in a provision of Union law.[44]

(b) Acts not listed in Art. 288 TFEU

7.17 The class of measures against which an action for annulment will lie is not confined to the binding acts mentioned in Art. 288 TFEU.[45] The Court of Justice has held that to confine that class of measures in that way would conflict with the obligation under what is now the first paragraph of Art. 19(1) TEU to ensure that the law is observed in the interpretation and application of the Treaties and that an action for annulment, as a means of fulfilling that obligation, 'must therefore be available in the case of all measures adopted by the institutions, whatever their nature or form, which are intended to have legal effects'.[46]

ECJ, Case C-249/02 *Portugal v Commission* [2004] E.C.R. I-10717, paras 35–43 (letter from a Commission official to the Portuguese authorities constituting a binding act).

[42] CFI, Case T-3/93 *Air France v Commission* [1994] E.C.R. II-121, paras 55–60. In a staff case, the Court of Justice likewise accepted that a binding act could be communicated orally (ECJ, Joined Cases 316/82 and 40/83 *Kohler v Court of Auditors* [1984] E.C.R. 641, paras 8–13). See also ECJ, Case C-208/03 *Le Pen v European Parliament* [2005] E.C.R. I-6051, para. 47. But see CFI (order of 9 July 2003), Case T-178/02 *WONUC and Others v Commission*, not reported, para. 7, in which the Court of First Instance held that statements made by a Member of the Commission, Ms Loyola de Palacio, at a press conference did not have legal effects and therefore did not constitute an act which could be challenged before the Court.

[43] ECJ, Case C-159/96 *Portugal v Commission* [1998] E.C.R. I-7379, paras 23–24. In this case, Portugal brought an action for annulment of the 'practice' of exceptional flexibility allegedly followed by the Commission in the administration of quantitative limits on the importation into the Union of textile products originating in various non-member countries. The Court of Justice held that the application was inadmissible insofar as it was brought against this practice.

[44] CFI, Joined Cases T-189/95, T-39/96, and T-123/96 *SGA v Commission* [1999] E.C.R. II-3587, paras 26–27; CFI, Joined Cases T-190/95 and T-45/96 *Sodima v Commission* [1999] E.C.R. II-3617, paras 31–36. Cf., however, ECJ, Case C-19/93 P *Rendo and Others v Commission* [1995] E.C.R. I-3319, para. 29, where the Court of Justice held that where the Commission gives a ruling on only a part of a complaint, that act may be regarded as a partial, implicit dismissal of the part of the complaint to which it has not responded. Silence on the part of an institution which is obliged to act may constitute the subject-matter of an action for failure to act (see para. 8.05).

[45] There is a line of case-law indicating that the category of acts not producing binding legal effects include 'purely implementing acts' as measures not giving rise to any rights or obligations for third parties: see CFI, Case T-185/05 *Italy v Commission* [2008] E.C.R. II-3207, paras 51–53 (and citations therein, providing a list of examples in well-known case-law). This case-law must be distinguished from what may be considered non-legislative acts—implementing or delegated acts—following the changes brought by the Lisbon Treaty reforms to the regime of legal instruments which may be capable of producing binding legal effects. See para. 7.153.

[46] ECJ, Case 22/70 *Commission v Council* (the 'AETR' case) [1971] E.C.R. 263, para. 42. See also ECJ, Case 60/81 *IBM v Commission* [1981] E.C.R. 2639, para. 8; ECJ, Case C-25/94 *Commission v Council* [1996] E.C.R. I-1469, para. 29; ECJ, Case C-27/04 *Commission v Council* [2004] E.C.R. I-6649, para. 44; see also ECJ, Case C-521/06 P *Athinaiki Techniki v Commission* [2008] E.C.R. I-5829, paras 44–45 (underscoring that the form in which an act is adopted is in principle irrelevant to the right to challenge such act under Art. 263 TFEU; if it were otherwise, the Union institutions could avoid judicial review simply by failing to comply with procedural requirements, and as the Union is based on the rule of law, the procedural rules governing actions before the Union courts must be interpreted in such a way as to ensure, wherever possible, that those rules contribute to the attainment of the objective of ensuring effective judicial protection of an individual's rights under Union law).

In the judgment in the *AETR* case, the Court of Justice found that the Council's decision establishing a common negotiating position on the part of the Member States with a view to the conclusion of an international agreement fell within the competence of the Union and therefore laid down a course of action binding on the institutions as well as on the Member States. Accordingly, the Court held that the decision constituted a binding act and hence one against which an action would lie, even though it could not be brought within one of the classes of binding acts listed in what is now Art. 288 TFEU.[47] However, in *Commune de Champagne and Others v Council and Commission*, the now General Court held that an act of an institution adopted pursuant to the Treaties cannot create rights and obligations outside the territory of the Union and thus the scope of the contested act—by which the Council and Commission concluded an international agreement on behalf of now the Union with Switzerland—was limited to that territory and has no legal effect in the territory of Switzerland. Consequently, that act did not produce any binding legal effect such as to bring about a distinct change in the applicants' legal position in Switzerland, such position being governed only by the provisions adopted in that third State in the exercise of its sovereign power, and thus the application for annulment of the contested act was held inadmissible so far as concerns the territory of Switzerland.[48]

Council conclusions holding the excessive deficit procedure brought against France and Germany in abeyance have been held to be challengeable because they have legal effects, even though such conclusions are not provided for as an instrument in the Treaties.[49] Moreover, a decision of the Committee on Petitions of the European Parliament by which the petition submitted by the applicant pursuant to Art. 227 TFEU was put on the file without further action being taken was held to constitute a challengeable act for the purposes of Art. 263 TFEU, on the basis that the actions taken by the European Parliament in this context must be subject to judicial review, given that such a decision affects the very essence of the right of Union citizens to submit a petition as guaranteed by the Treaties.[50]

---

[47] An action for annulment will even lie against an act by which the Commission concludes an international agreement on behalf of the Union (formerly the Community): see, e.g. ECJ, Case C-327/91 *France v Commission* [1994] E.C.R. I-3641, paras 14–17. See also CFI (order of 3 July 2007), Case T-212/02 *Commune de Champagne and Others v Council and Commission* [2007] E.C.R. II-2017, para. 87 (and citations therein), underlining that although an agreement between the Union and a non-Member State or international oganization, as an instrument expressing the joint intention of those bodies, cannot be regarded as an act of an institution and is hence not reviewable pursuant to Art. 263 TFEU, it is settled case-law that the act whereby the competent institution sought to conclude the agreement is an act of an institution within the meaning of that Article and thus susceptible to an action for annulment.

[48] CFI (order of 3 July 2007), Case T-212/02 *Commune de Champagne and Others v Council and Commission* [2007] E.C.R. II-2017, paras 90–96.

[49] ECJ, Case C-27/04 *Commission v Council* [2004] E.C.R. I-6649, paras 44–51.

[50] EGC, Case T-308/07 *Tegebauer v European Parliament* [2011] E.C.R. II-279*, Summ. pub., para. 21. But see EGC (order of 26 January 2011), Case T-550/10 *FIBE v European Parliament*, not reported (holding the working document of the Commission of the Petitions of the European Parliament in connection with a mission conducted in a certain region of the Member State concerned (attributing responsibility for certain problems to the applicant) did not constitute a challengeable act for the purposes of Art. 263 TFEU; it merely contained conclusions and recommendations to remedy the problems identified and did not produce any binding legal effects). See also EGC (judgment of 30 May 2013), Case T-280/09 *Morte Navarro v European Parliament*, not reported, para. 25: the assessment of the admissibility of a petition addressed to the European Parliament (in contrast to the action taken by the European Parliament upon a petition declared admissible) may be subject to judicial review. See also n. 66.

In contrast, the Court of Justice did not find that a decision of the representatives of the governments of the Member States meeting in the Council, made at the Commission's proposal, to grant special aid to Bangladesh was a binding act of the Council. The Court did not come to that view because of the name of the act in question ('Council conclusions'),[51] but based its assessment on the precise content of the act and the context in which it was adopted.[52] Likewise, the General Court held that a Commission interpretative communication on the Union law applicable to contract awards not or not fully subject to the provisions of the Public Procurement Directives did not contain new rules for the award of public contracts going beyond the obligations under Union law as it currently stood and hence did not constitute a challengeable act for the purposes of Art. 263 TFEU.[53]

(c) Refusal

7.18 An act of an institution amounting to a rejection must be appraised in the light of the nature of the request to which it constitutes a reply.[54] The refusal by a Union institution to withdraw or amend an act may constitute an act whose legality may be reviewed under Art. 263 TFEU only if the act which the Union institution refuses to withdraw or amend could itself have been contested under that provision.[55] Accordingly, the fact that a letter is sent by a Union institution to its addressee in response to a request from the addressee is not sufficient to make that letter a challengeable act within the meaning of Art. 263 TFEU.[56]

---

[51] Press release entitled 'Aid for Bangladesh–Council conclusions' (reference 6004/91, Press 60-c).

[52] ECJ, Joined Cases C-181/91 and C-248/91 *European Parliament v Council and Commission* [1993] E.C.R. I-3685, para. 14.

[53] EGC, Case T-258/06 *Germany v Commission* [2010] E.C.R. II-2027, paras 100, 131, and 162.

[54] See, e.g. ECJ (order of 13 March 2007), Case C-150/06 P *Arizona Chemical and Others v Commission* [2007] E.C.R. I-39*, Summ. pub., para. 22 (and citations therein).

[55] See, e.g. ECJ, Case 42/71 *Nordgetreide v Commission* [1972] E.C.R. 105, para. 5; CFI (order of 18 April 2002), Case T-238/00 *IPSO and USE v ECB* [2002] E.C.R. II-2237, para. 45; CFI (order of 13 July 2004), Case T-29/03 *Comunidad Autónoma de Andalucía v Commission* [2004] E.C.R. II-2923, para. 30. See also CFI, Case T-154/94 *CSF and CSME v Commission* [1996] E.C.R. II-1377, paras 37 *et seq.*

[56] See, e.g. ECJ (order of 13 March 2007), Case C-150/06 P *Arizona Chemical and Others v Commission* [2007] E.C.R. I-39*, Summ. pub., paras 21–25: the act that the Commission refused to withdraw or amend in response to request of applicants must itself have been open to challenge, in case draft amendment does not constitute a measure open to challenge under Art. 263 TFEU because merely provisional and preparatory in nature; CFI (order of 9 April 2003), Case T-280/02 *Pikaart and Others v Commission* [2003] E.C.R. II-1621, para. 23; CFI (order of 5 November 2003), Case T-130/02 *Kronoply v Commission* [2003] E.C.R. II-4857, para. 42; CFI (order of 13 July 2004), Case T-29/03 *Comunidad Autónoma de Andalucía v Commission* [2004] E.C.R. II-2923, para. 29; CFI, Case T-234/04 *Netherlands v Commission* [2007] E.C.R. II-4589, paras 48 *et seq.* (Commission decision rendered in connection with the procedure set down in now Art. 114(5)–(6) TFEU is not a challengeable act); CFI, Case T-437/05 *Brink's Security Luxembourg v Commission* [2009] E.C.R. II-3233, para. 63 (and further citations therein, the contested measure rejecting the applicant's tender was deemed to be a challengeable act, but the contested measure merely conveying information to the applicant was not: CFI, Case T-437/05 *Brink's Security Luxembourg v Commission*, paras 64–66); EGC (order of 15 December 2009), Case T-107/06 *Inet Hellas v Commission* [2009] E.C.R. II-4591, paras 55 *et seq.* (holding a Commission letter in connection with EURid's rejection of applicant's request for registration of a certain domain name was not a challengeable act for the purposes of Art. 263 TFEU). See also ECJ (order of 17 March 2009), Case C-251/08 P *Ayyanarsamy v Commission and Germany* [2009] E.C.R. I-36*, Summ. pub., paras 15–20 (where the applicant sent the Commission several letters complaining about actions of national authorities, the Commission response indicating that it is not able to intervene in matters within the competences of the Member State concerned held not to be a challengeable act for the purposes of Art. 263 TFEU); ECJ (order of 22 January 2010), Case C-69/09 P *Makhteshim-Agan Holding and Others v Commission* [2010] E.C.R. I-10*, Summ. pub., paras 40–47 (upholding a Court of First Instance decision declaring action for annulment against a letter of the Commission (not addressed to the applicant) expressing intention not to submit to the Council proposal inadmissible, since it was the Council, not the Commission, which had the

A Commission decision to shelve a complaint from an individual in the course of a procedure brought pursuant to Art. 258 TFEU does not have any legal effects as regards the complainant. This is because the act sought by the complainant, a decision to commence infringement proceedings against a Member State before the Court of Justice, is not per se a challengeable act.[57] In any event, the complainant has no entitlement to a Commission decision, since the rationale underlying the case-law is also based on the fact that the Commission has a discretion whether or not to bring proceedings for a particular Member State's failure to fulfil obligations under the Treaties.[58]

(d) Legitimate legal basis

Finally, an institution may adopt a binding act only in so far as it has a legitimate legal basis **7.19** which empowers the institution to adopt a binding act.[59] No such power may be presumed to exist in the absence of a specific Union provision.[60] As a result of that requirement, the Court of Justice and the General Court often take the view that they have to consider whether the application for annulment is admissible together with the substance.[61]

---

power to authorize the inclusion of the particular substance in the annex to the directive and hence it was the Council's position that produced binding legal effects capable of affecting the applicant's interests).

[57] See, e.g. ECJ (order of 10 July 2007), Case C-461/06 P *AEPI v Commission* [2007] E.C.R. I-97*, Summ. pub., para. 23; ECJ (order of 22 June 2011), Case C-521/10 P *Grúas Abril Assistencia v Commission* [2011] E.C.R. I-90*, Summ. pub., para. 29; ECJ (order of 14 July 2011), Case C-111/11 P *Ruipérez Aguirre and ATC Petition v Commission* [2011] E.C.R. I-104*, Summ. pub., paras 11–12; CFI (order of 16 October 2006), Case T-173/06 *Aisne et Nature v Commission*, not reported, paras 23–29; CFI (order of 15 January 2007), Case T-276/06 *Sellier v Commission*, not reported, paras 10–12 (appeal dismissed on other grounds in ECJ (order of 18 September 2007), Case C-191/07 P *Sellier v Commission* [2007] E.C.R. I-113*, Summ. pub.; appeal lodged out of time); CFI (order of 7 September 2009), Case T-186/08 *LPN v Commission* [2009] E.C.R. II-136*, Summ. pub., paras 49–57; CFI (order of 29 October 2009), Case T-249/09 *Ségaud v Commission*, not reported, paras 5–10, appeal dismissed in ECJ (order of 21 May 2010), Case C-514/09 P *Ségaud v Commission* [2010] E.C.R. I-71*, Summ. pub.; CFI (order of 14 July 2009), Case T-177/09 *Kinský v Commission*, not reported, paras 7–8; EGC (order of 20 July 2010), Case T-186/10 *Perret v Commission*, not reported, paras 8–9; EGC (order of 24 August 2010), Case T-185/10 *Stelzer v Commission*, not reported, paras 6–10; EGC (order of 6 July 2011), Case T-190/11 *Altner v Commission*, not reported, paras 6–10, appeal dismissed in ECJ (order of 15 December 2011), Case C-411/11 P *Altner v Commission*, not reported. See also ECJ, Case C-131/03 P *Reynolds Tobacco and Others v Commission* [2006] E.C.R. I-7795, paras 54–68: a Commission decision to bring legal proceedings—in the particular case before a US court—cannot be considered per se to be a decision which is open to challenge. See further paras 7.26 and 7.27. That being said, the decision by which the Commission determines the amount due from the Member State in terms of the penalty payment which it has been ordered to make can be the subject of an action for annulment pursuant to Art. 263 TFEU, though in adjudicating such a case, the General Court cannot impinge on the exclusive jurisdiction reserved to the Court of Justice under Arts 258 and 260 TFEU: EGC, Case T-33/09 *Portugal v Commission* [2011] E.C.R. II-1429, paras 64–67 (confirmed on appeal: ECJ (judgment of 15 January 2014), Case C-292/11 P *Commission v Portugal*, not reported); see also EGC, Case T-139/06 *France v Commission* [2011] E.C.R. II-7315, para. 33 (J. T. Nowak, case note (2012) S.E.W. 163–8).

[58] See, e.g. CFI (order of 29 September 1997), Case T-83/97 *Sateba v Commission* [1997] E.C.R. II-1523, paras 32–40 (appeal dismissed in ECJ (order of 17 July 1998), Case C-422/97 P *Sateba v Commission* [1998] E.C.R. I-4913); CFI, Case T-148/00 *Panhellenic Union of Cotton Ginners and Exporters v Commission* [2003] E.C.R. II-4415, para. 66; CFI (order of 19 September 2005), T-247/04 *Aseprofar and Edifa v Commission* [2005] E.C.R. II-3449, paras 40–61. Moreover, the complainant has no procedural rights on the basis of which it can require the Commission to inform it and give it a hearing.

[59] CFI, Case T-113/89 *Nefarma v Commission* [1990] E.C.R. II-797, paras 68 *et seq.* (see para. 7.150).

[60] ECJ (order of 30 September 1987), Case 229/86 *Brother Industries v Commission* [1987] E.C.R. 3757, at 3763; CFI, Case T-113/89 *Nefarma v Commission*, para. 69.

[61] See ECJ, Case C-233/02 *France v Commission* [2004] E.C.R. I-2759, para. 26, where the Court of Justice did not rule on the admissibility of an action for annulment of the decision by which the Commission concluded an agreement with the United States on Guidelines on Regulatory Cooperation and Transparency

(4) The act is intended to produce legal effects

(a) Legal effects

7.20 Acts of a Union institution are binding in so far as they produce legal effects.[62] If the applicant is a natural or legal person, the case-law further requires that the acts must be 'capable of affecting the interests of the applicant by bringing about a distinct change in his legal position'[63] or adversely affect his legal position by restricting his rights.[64] A proposal lacks binding legal effect and will therefore, in principle, not constitute a challengeable act.[65] Similarly, an institution's written response to Parliamentary questions has also been considered not to constitute a challengeable act.[66]

(b) Standard applicable to privileged and non-privileged applicants

7.21 The question has arisen as to whether the standard for a binding act elaborated above for the purposes of an admissible action under Art. 263 TEU applies to privileged applicants (i.e. Member States and Union institutions) in the same way as to non-privileged applicants (i.e. natural and legal persons), that is to say, whether a privileged applicant such as a Member State must only demonstrate that the contested measure is intended to have binding legal effects in general without having to prove that such measure gives rise to

---

since the 'form of order sought by the French Republic must in any event be dismissed on the substance'. The question whether the contested act has a legitimate legal basis coincides with the question whether the institution was empowered to adopt it: ECJ, Joined Cases 358/85 and 51/86 *France v European Parliament* [1988] E.C.R. 4821, paras 13–15; ECJ, Case C-366/88 *France v Commission* [1990] E.C.R. I-3571; ECJ, Case C-303/90 *France v Commission* [1991] E.C.R. I-5315, para. 12, with a case note by M. Van der Woude (1993) S.E.W. 522–7; ECJ, Case C-325/91 *France v Commission* [1993] E.C.R. I-3283, paras 8–11. See also ECJ (judgment of 13 December 2012), Joined Cases C-237/11 and C-238/11 *France v European Parliament*, not reported, para. 20.

[62] ECJ, Joined Cases 8/66 to 11/66 *Cimenteries CBR Cementbedrijven and Others v Commission* [1967] ECJ 75, at 91; ECJ, Case 22/70 *Commission v Council* (the *'AETR'* case) [1971] E.C.R. 263, para. 39; ECJ, Case C-312/90 *Spain v Commission* [1992] E.C.R. I-4117, paras 11–26, and ECJ, Case C-327/91 *France v Commission* [1994] E.C.R. I-3641, paras 14–15 (the application for annulment of an act by which the Commission purported to conclude an international agreement 'between the Commission of the [then] European Communities and the Government of the United States of America regarding the application of their competition laws' was declared admissible on the grounds that, 'as is apparent from its actual wording, the Agreement is intended to produce legal effects'); ECJ (judgment of 19 November 2013), Case C-63/12 *Commission v Council*, not reported, para. 28; CFI, Case T-154/94 *CSF and CSME v Commission* [1996] E.C.R. II-1377, paras 37 *et seq.* (the binding nature of a letter from the Commission was considered in the light of a letter from the applicants to which the Commission's letter answered). See also EGC (order of 8 March 2012), Case T-573/10 *Octapharma Pharmazeutika v EMA*, not reported, para. 29; EGC (judgment of 21 June 2012), Joined Cases T-264/10 and T-266/10 *Spain v Commission*, not reported, paras 9–29.

[63] See, e.g. ECJ, Case 60/81 *IBM v Commission* [1981] E.C.R. 2639, para. 9; ECJ, Case 53/85 *AKZO Chemie v Commission* [1986] E.C.R. 1965, para. 16; ECJ, Case C-131/03 P *Reynolds Tobacco and Others v Commission* [2006] E.C.R. I-7795, para. 51; ECJ, Case C-516/06 P *Commission v Ferriere Nord* [2007] E.C.R. I-10685, para. 27; ECJ, Case C-362/08 P *Internationaler Hilfsfonds v Commission* [2010] E.C.R. I-669, para. 51.

[64] For cases in which this was held not to be the case, see CFI, Case T-541/93 *Connaughton and Others v Council* [1997] E.C.R. II-549, para. 35 and CFI, Case T-554/93 *Saint and Murray v Council and Commission* [1997] E.C.R. II-563, para. 41.

[65] ECJ, Case C-301/03 *Italy v Commission* [2005] E.C.R. I-10217, paras 21–24.

[66] EGC (order of 6 July 2011), Case T-105/11 *Noko Ngele v Commission*, not reported, paras 5–7. By contrast, a decision of the Petitions Committee to take no action on the applicant's petition is a reviewable act: see EGC (judgment of 27 September 2012), Case T-160/10 *J v European Parliament*, not reported.

binding legal effects capable of adversely affecting the interests of that privileged applicant specifically by bringing about a distinct change to its legal position.[67]

Under the case-law, it seems that privileged applicants only have to prove that the challenged act produces binding legal effects.[68] The Union courts have, moreover, emphasized that, contrary to a non-privileged applicant, a privileged applicant is not required to prove a legal interest to bring the action (see further para. 7.76) and thus a Member State is not required to show that the contested act produces legal effects with regard to it.[69]

In its 2011 judgment in *Deutsche Post and Germany v Commission*, the Court of Justice underlined that according to case-law developed in the context of actions for annulment brought by Member States or institutions, any measures adopted by the institutions, whatever their form, which are intended to have binding legal effects are regarded as acts open to challenge within the meaning of Art. 263 TFEU.[70] Where an action for annulment is brought by a natural or legal person, the action lies only if the binding legal effects of the contested act are capable of affecting the interests of the applicant by bringing about a distinct change in its legal position.[71]

(c) Operative part and recitals

Whether an act is capable of having binding (and adverse) effect as far as non-privileged **7.22** applicants are concerned must be determined in the first place from its operative part.[72]

---

[67] See Opinion of Advocate-General E. Sharpston in ECJ, Case C-131/03 P *Reynolds Tobacco and Others v Commission* [2006] E.C.R. I-7795, points 94–108 (and citations therein).

[68] ECJ, Case 22/70 *Commission v Council* (the *'AETR'* case) [1971] E.C.R. 263, para. 42; ECJ, Case C-316/91 *European Parliament v Council* [1994] E.C.R. I-625, para. 8; ECJ, Case C-443/97 *Spain v Commission* [2000] E.C.R. I-2415, para. 27; ECJ, Joined Cases C-138/03, C-324/03 and C-431/03 *Italy v Commission* [2005] E.C.R. I-10043, para. 32; ECJ, Case C-301/03 *Italy v Commission* [2005] E.C.R. I-10217, para. 19; ECJ, Case C-370/07 *Commission v Council* [2009] E.C.R. I-8917, para. 42; CFI, Case T-233/04 *Netherlands v Commission* [2008] E.C.R. II-591, para. 42; CFI, Case T-185/05 *Italy v Commission* [2008] E.C.R. II-3207, particularly paras 46, 49. There exist some examples to the contrary with respect to State aid decisions favourable to the Member State concerned: see ECJ, Case C-242/00 *Germany v Commission* [2002] E.C.R. I-5603, paras 39–46; ECJ (order of 28 January 2004), Case C-164/02 *Netherlands v Commission* [2004] E.C.R. I-1177, para. 18.

[69] See, e.g. ECJ (order of 27 November 2001), Case C-208/99 *Portugal v Commission* [2001] E.C.R. I-9183, paras 22–24 (noting that under the case-law the contested measure must be intended to produce legal effects, 'even where, in the event that it is a Member State which intends to bring such an action, those effects are not to deploy with regard to the Member State itself'); CFI, Case T-233/04 *Netherlands v Commission* [2008] E.C.R. II-591, paras 37–42, appeal dismissed in ECJ, Case C-279/08 P *Commission v Netherlands* [2011] E.C.R. I-7671, paras 39–43; EGC, Joined Cases T-415/05, T-416/05, and T-423/05 *Greece and Others v Commission* [2010] E.C.R. II-4749, paras 57–60 (underlining that a Member State need not prove that the contested measure produces legal effects with regard to that Member State in order for its action to be admissible and concluding action admissible on the basis that the contested act has binding legal effects and thus constitutes a challengeable act); EGC, Joined Cases T-425/04, T-444/04, T-450/04, and T-456/04 *France and Others v Commission* [2010] E.C.R. II-2099, paras 118–119; EGC, Case T-369/07 *Latvia v Commission* [2011] E.C.R. II-1039, paras 33–34.

[70] ECJ, Joined Cases C-463/10 P and C-475/10 P *Deutsche Post and Germany v Commission* [2011] E.C.R. I-9639, para. 36.

[71] ECJ, Joined Cases C-463/10 P and C-475/10 P *Deutsche Post and Germany v Commission*, paras 37–38.

[72] CFI, Case T-138/89 *NBV and NVB v Commission* [1992] E.C.R. II-2181, para. 31; CFI, Joined Cases T-125/97 and T-127/97 *Coca-Cola v Commission* [2000] E.C.R. II-1733, paras 77–92. See, e.g. CFI, Case T-112/99 *M6 and Others v Commission* [2001] E.C.R. I-2459, paras 39–41, in which the Court found from the operative part of the Commission decision to grant clearance for a period shorter than that of the whole agreement was held to be a challengeable act, as it produced binding legal effects capable of affecting the applicants' interests.

But the explanations and recitals contained in the act in support of the operative part[73] as well as the context in which the act is adopted[74] may also mean that the act has adverse effect and is amenable to review.[75] Where a measure against which an action for annulment has been brought comprises essentially distinct parts, only those parts of that measure which produce binding legal effects capable of bringing about a significant change in the (non-privileged) applicant's legal situation can be challenged.[76]

(5) Confirmatory acts

7.23 An application for annulment of an act which merely confirms an irrevocable act which was previously adopted is inadmissible.[77] The confirmatory act does not produce any new legal

---

[73] This is because the operative part of an act is indissociably linked to the statement of reasons for it, so that when it has to be interpreted, account must be taken of the reasons which led to its adoption: ECJ, Case C-355/95 P *TWD Textilwerke Deggendorf v Commission* [1997] E.C.R. I-2549, para. 21; CFI, Joined Cases T-213/95 and T-18/96 *SCK and FNK v Commission* [1997] E.C.R. II-1739, para. 104 and the case-law cited therein). Whether the operative part has adverse effect consequently extends to the recitals, which constitute the necessary support for the operative part. The assessments made in the recitals to an act can be subject to judicial review by the Union judicature to the extent that, as grounds of an act adversely affecting the applicant's interests, they constitute the essential basis for the operative part of that act: CFI, Case T-16/91 *Rendo and Others v Commission* [1992] E.C.R. II-2417, paras 40–41 and 55; ECJ (order of 28 January 2004), Case C-164/02 *Netherlands v Commission* [2004] E.C.R. I-1177, para. 21.

[74] ECJ, Case C-301/03 *Italy v Commission* [2005] E.C.R. I-10217, paras 21–24.

[75] See, e.g. EGC (judgment of 1 February 2012), Case T-237/09 *Walloon Region v Commission*, not reported, paras 42–48.

[76] See, e.g. CFI, Case T-184/97 *BP Chemicals v Commission* [2000] E.C.R. II-3145, para. 34. In this case, BP Chemicals contested a Commission decision whereby aid was approved for two groups of bio-fuels which differed in point of their composition, use, and the market for which they were of interest. The applicant had shown that it had locus standi only in so far as it was a producer of synthetic ethyl alcohol, a product which competes with bio-ethanol, but not with regard to the measures for the esters sector. The Court of First Instance therefore held that the applicants had not suffered a significant change in their legal situation as a result of the decision approving aid for esters and declared the application inadmissible in that regard. See also CFI, Case T-50/00 *Dalmine v Commission* [2004] E.C.R. II-2395, paras 134–135; CFI, Case T-437/05 *Brink's Security Luxembourg v Commission* [2009] E.C.R. II-3233, paras 67, 76–77.

[77] See, e.g. ECJ, Case 56/72 *Goeth v Commission* [1973] E.C.R. 181, para. 15; ECJ, Case 1/76 *Wack v Commission* [1976] E.C.R. 1017, para. 7; ECJ, Case 26/76 *Metro v Commission* [1977] E.C.R. 1875, para. 4; ECJ, Joined Cases 166/86 and 220/86 *Irish Cement v Commission* [1988] E.C.R. 6473, paras 1–16; ECJ (order of 21 November 1990), Case C-12/90 *Infortec v Commission* [1990] E.C.R. I-4265, para. 10; ECJ, Case C-199/91 *Foyer Culturel du Sart-Tilman v Commission* [1993] E.C.R. I-2667, paras 20–24; ECJ, Case C-480/93 P *Zunis Holding and Others v Commission* [1996] E.C.R. I-1, para. 14; CFI, Case T-514/93 *Cobrecaf and Others v Commission* [1995] E.C.R. II-621, para. 44; CFI, Case T-275/94 *Groupement des Cartes Bancaires 'CB' v Commission* [1995] E.C.R. II-2169, para. 27; CFI (order of 16 March 1998), Case T-235/95 *Goldstein v Commission* [1998] E.C.R. II-523, paras 36–48; CFI (order of 10 June 1998), Case T-116/95 *Cementir v Commission* [1998] E.C.R. II-2261, paras 19–25; CFI, Case T-188/95 *Waterleiding Maatschappij 'Noord-West Brabant' v Commission* [1998] E.C.R. II-3713, paras 88–141 (a complaint made against State aid which the Commission had already declared to be compatible with the internal market does not, where the decision has become definitive, cause time to start running afresh in order to bring an action for annulment of the decision by which the Commission rejects the complaint while confirming its earlier decision); CFI (order of 9 July 2002), Case T-127/01 *Ripa di Meana v European Parliament* [2002] E.C.R. II-3005, para. 25; CFI (order of 23 February 2005), Case T-478/04 *Campailla v Commission*, not reported, paras 21–22; EGC (order of 30 June 2009), Case T-106/08 *CPEM v Commission* [2009] E.C.R. II-91*, Summ. pub., paras 32–37; EGC, Case T-157/08 *Paroc v OHIM* [2011] E.C.R. II-137, paras 28–41; EGC (order of 24 May 2011), Case T-115/10 *United Kingdom v Commission* [2011] E.C.R. II-153*, Summ. pub., paras 25–43; EGC (order of 19 June 2012), Case T-37/11 *Hungary v Commission*, not reported, paras 35–43 (Commission debit note confirmatory act and hence not challengeable act for the purposes of Art. 263 TFEU). In contrast, where a provision in a Union measure is amended, a fresh right of action arises not only with respect to that provision alone, but also against all provisions which, even if not amended, form a whole with it, and thus the time limits are calculated from the

effects. If the Court of Justice or the General Court were to hold that an application for annulment of a confirmatory act was admissible despite the fact that the time limit for bringing an action against the original act had run out, this would make it possible to circumvent that time limit. An applicant who was out of time would then be able to reactivate the possibility of bringing proceedings by provoking the adoption of a confirmatory act, thereby jeopardizing legal certainty.[78] Consequently, as long as the time limit for bringing an action against the original act has not expired, an action for annulment may be brought against the original act, the confirmatory act, or both concurrently.[79]

An action against a confirmatory act will be inadmissible only in so far as it is a genuinely confirmatory act.[80] Thus, from the point of view of procedural law, a measure will be regarded as confirmatory of an earlier measure only if the latter is or was amenable to appeal.[81] Furthermore, a new fact which is of such a character as to alter the essential circumstances and conditions which governed the adoption of the original act causes the new act no longer to be confirmatory, even though it has the same content as the original act. An action brought against such an ostensibly confirmatory act will be admissible.[82] On those grounds, an act by which an institution, body, office, or agency refuses to amend an earlier act—in spite of the new facts presented by the applicant—may be the subject of an action for annulment.[83]

---

date of the amended act: see ECJ, Case C-299/05 *Commission v Council and European Parliament* [2007] E.C.R. I-8695, paras 29–34.

[78] See, e.g. ECJ, Joined Cases 166/86 and 220/86 *Irish Cement v Commission* [1988] E.C.R. 6473, para. 16; ECJ, Case C-199/91 *Foyer Culturel du Sart-Tilman v Commission* [1993] E.C.R. I-2667, paras 23–24; CFI, Joined Cases T-121/96 and T-151/96 *Mutual Aid Administration Services v Commission* [1997] E.C.R. II-1355, para. 50; EGC (order of 12 February 2010), Case T-456/07 *Commission v Cdt* [2010] E.C.R. II-183, paras 54, 67. But see EGC, Case T-407/07 *CMB and Christof v Commission* [2011] E.C.R. II-286*, Summ. pub., paras 90–105: although the measure concerned did not contain any new fact capable of conferring on it the character of a new decision having adverse effects and hence in principle the applicant should not be allowed to evade time limits for bringing action for annulment against the initial decision, the General Court considered that the Union agency concerned acted in such a way as to give rise to pardonable confusion in the mind of the applicants as regards the procedure to be followed and as such the applicant should not be deprived of its right to bring action for annulment in these circumstances. See also EGC (order of 8 March 2012), Case T-573/10 *Octapharma Pharmazeutika v EMA*, not reported, para. 59.

[79] ECJ, Joined Cases 193/87 and 194/87 *Maurissen and European Public Service Union v Court of Auditors* [1989] E.C.R. 1045, para. 26. See also EGC (order of 24 October 2012), Case T-442/11 *Evropaïki Dynamiki v Commission*, not reported, para. 66.

[80] See, e.g. ECJ, Case 9/81 *Williams v Court of Auditors* [1982] E.C.R. 3301, para. 15; ECJ (order of 7 December 2004), Case C-521/03 *Internationaler Hilfsfonds v Commission*, not reported, para. 47 (and further citations therein); CFI, Case T-321/01 *Internationaler Hilfsfonds v Commission* [2003] E.C.R. II-3225, para. 31; CFI, Case T-253/02 *Ayadi v Council* [2006] E.C.R. II-2139, para. 70 (and citations therein, set aside on other grounds in ECJ, Joined Cases C-399/06 P and C-403/06 P *Hassan and Ayadi v Council and Commission* [2009] E.C.R. I-11393); EGC (judgment of 22 May 2012), Case T-6/10 *Sviluppo Globale v Commission*, not reported, paras 22–23.

[81] ECJ, Joined Cases 193/87 and 194/87 *Maurissen and European Public Service Union v Court of Auditors* [1989] E.C.R. 1045, para. 23.

[82] ECJ, Joined Cases 42/59 and 49/59 *SNUPAT v High Authority* [1961] E.C.R. 53, at 75–76; CFI, Case T-331/94 *IPK v Commission* [1997] E.C.R. II-1665, para. 26; CFI, Case T-365/00 *AICS v European Parliament* [2002] E.C.R. II-2719, paras 28–40.

[83] ECJ, Case C-514/99 *France v Commission* [2000] E.C.R. I-4705, para. 45, in which the Court of Justice declared an action brought by France inadmissible on the grounds that the Commission had not taken any decision on the application to amend a former decision. France argued that the Commission had refused to amend or withdraw an earlier decision. The Court of Justice suggested that the applicant could have brought an

(6) Resolutions

7.24 Resolutions often express a political declaration of intent which embodies no binding commitments and therefore produces no legal effects. Accordingly, an action will not lie against a resolution,[84] unless it appears from its content that it produces binding legal effects.[85]

(7) Internal instructions and guidelines

(a) No legal effects vis-à-vis *third parties*

7.25 Internal instructions are usually simply guidelines for the adoption of acts of institutions. Generally, they do not produce legal effects.[86] Consequently, for example, the Court of Justice held that an internal instruction of the Commission indicating the manner in which it intended to exercise its provisional power to compile a list of candidates for service contracts concluded within the framework of the Lomé Convention was not an act producing legal effects. It was not the line of conduct set out in the internal instruction which produced legal effects and reflected the Commission's definitive position, but the drawing up of the list itself.[87]

Even where internal instructions do have legal effects, they must create rights or obligations outside the institution concerned before third parties may bring an admissible application for their annulment.[88]

---

action for failure to act. See also CFI, Case T-186/98 *Inpesca v Commission* [2001] E.C.R. II-557, paras 45–51, and CFI (order of 29 April 2004), Case T-308/02 *SGL Carbon v Commission* [2004] E.C.R. II-1363, paras 51–53, in which the Court of First Instance emphasized that the confirmatory nature of a decision cannot be assessed solely in the light of its content as compared with the previous decision, which it purportedly confirms. The confirmatory nature of the decision must also be assessed having regard to the application to which the decision constitutes an answer. If the application in question is based on significant new facts of which neither the applicant nor the administration was aware when the earlier decision was taken and which are liable to bring about a significant change in the applicant's position which was the starting point for the original—now definitive—decision, the new decision cannot in that respect be regarded as merely confirmatory, since it makes a determination on the new facts and so contains a new factor as compared with the earlier decision. See also ECJ, Joined Cases C-138/03, C-324/03 and C-431/03 *Italy v Commission* [2005] E.C.R. I-10043, paras 36–37; ECJ, Case C-46/03 *United Kingdom v Commission* [2005] E.C.R. I-10167, paras 23–26.

[84] ECJ, Joined Cases 90/63 and 91/63 *Commission v Luxembourg and Belgium* [1964] E.C.R. 625, at 631 (in that judgment, given pursuant to what is now Art. 258 TFEU, the Court of Justice held that a Council resolution was not a binding measure); ECJ, Case 9/73 *Schlüter* [1973] E.C.R. 1135, para. 40 (in that judgment, given in response to a request for a preliminary ruling, the Court of Justice held that the resolution in question was 'primarily an expression of the policy favoured by the Council and Government Representatives of the Member States' and could not, 'by reason of its content, create legal consequences of which parties might avail themselves in court').

[85] ECJ, Case 108/83 *Luxembourg v European Parliament* [1984] E.C.R. 1945, paras 19–23; ECJ, Joined Cases C-213/88 and C-39/89 *Luxembourg v European Parliament* [1991] E.C.R. I-5643, paras 24–28; ECJ (judgment of 13 December 2012), Joined Cases C-237/11 and C-238/11 *France v European Parliament*, not reported, paras 19–20.

[86] See, e.g. ECJ, Case C-233/02 *France v Commission* [2004] E.C.R. I-2759, paras 24–26.

[87] ECJ, Case 114/86 *United Kingdom v Commission* [1988] E.C.R. 5289, paras 12-15; ECJ, Case C-443/97 *Spain v Commission* [2000] E.C.R. I-2415, para. 34. The same applies to notices in the field of competition law: ECJ (judgment of 13 December 2012), Case C-226/11 *Expedia*, not reported, paras 29–30.

[88] For examples of cases in which the internal instruction produced only internal effects, see ECJ, Case 20/58 *Phoenix-Rheinrohr v High Authority* [1959] E.C.R. 75, at 82; ECJ, Case 190/84 *Les Verts v European Parliament* [1988] E.C.R. 1017, para. 8. For a case in which the internal instruction had effects outside the institution and could therefore be challenged before the Court of Justice, see Case C-366/88 *France v Commission* [1990] E.C.R. I-3571, paras 9–12 and 25.

(b) Binding on the institution concerned

Where the Commission notifies guidelines for the exercise of its discretion (for example, **7.26** for the assessment of State aid under Art. 107(3) TFEU or the determination of a fine on account of infringement of Art. 101 and/or Art. 102 TFEU), this entails a self-imposed limitation of that discretion in so far as it must comply with the indicative rules which it has itself laid down.[89] Such guidelines may be relied upon as against the Commission. In an action for annulment (brought, for instance, against a decision relating to State aid or a decision based on Art. 101 and/or Art. 102 TFEU), parties may therefore argue before the Union judicature that the Commission has wrongly failed to apply the guidelines.[90]

(8) Preparatory acts and measures laying down a definitive position

(a) Definitive statement of position

An action will lie against an act only if it definitively lays down the position of the **7.27** institution that adopted it.[91]

(b) Measure concluding an internal procedure

Some acts of institutions are adopted by means of a procedure comprising different stages. **7.28** Only the measure which concludes the procedure expresses the definitive position of the institution. Measures paving the way for the final measure do not determine a definitive

---

[89] For guidelines in connection with State aid, see: CFI, Case T-380/94 *AIUFFASS and AKT v Commission* [1996] E.C.R. II-2169, para. 57; CFI, Case T-214/95 *Vlaams Gewest v Commission* [1998] E.C.R. II-717, para. 89; CFI, Case T-27/02 *Kronofrance v Commission* [2004] E.C.R. II-4177, para. 79. For guidelines with regard to the amount of fines which may be imposed on account of infringement of Arts 101 and 102 TFEU, see CFI, Case T-44/00 *Mannesmannröhren-Werke v Commission* [2004] E.C.R. II-2223, paras 212 and 232; EGC, Case T-41/05 *Alliance One International v Commission* [2011] E.C.R. II-7101, para. 190. With respect to staff regulations, see CFI, Case T-185/05 *Italy v Commission* [2008] E.C.R. II-3207, paras 41–57. For guidelines on the effect on trade concept in Arts 101 TFEU and 102 TFEU, see ECJ (judgment of 11 July 2013), Case C-429/11 P *Gosselin v Commission*, not reported, para. 64.

[90] CFI, Case T-35/99 *Keller and Keller Meccanica v Commission* [2002] E.C.R. II-261, para. 77; CFI, Case T-27/02 *Kronofrance v Commission* [2004] E.C.R. II-4177, para. 79.

[91] ECJ, Joined Cases 23/63, 24/63 and 52/63 *Usines Emile Henricot and Others v High Authority* [1963] E.C.R. 217, at 223–4; ECJ, Case 60/81 *IBM v Commission* [1981] E.C.R. 2639, para. 10; EGC (judgment of 7 March 2013), Case T-94/10 *Rütgers Germany and Others v ECHA*, not reported, para. 29. For some examples in which the contested act did not definitively lay down a position and therefore had no legal effects, see ECJ (order of 28 June 1993), Case C-64/93 *Danotab and Others v Commission* [1993] E.C.R. I-3595, paras 13–14; ECJ (judgment of 19 March 2013), Case C-401/10 P *Bouygues and Others v Commission*, not reported, paras 76–78; CFI, Joined Cases T-314/04 and T-414/04 *Germany v Commission* [2006] E.C.R. II-103*, Summ. pub., paras 38 *et seq.*; CFI, Case T-260/04 *Cestas v Commission* [2008] E.C.R. II-701, paras 70–77; EGC (order of 24 November 2010), Case T-381/09 *RWE Transgas v Commission* [2010] E.C.R. II-256*, Summ. pub., paras 37–47; EGC (order of 9 October 2012), Case T-31/12 *Région Poitou-Charentes v Commission*, not reported, para. 33. It was possible to infer from additional questions put by the Commission with regard to a request for access to documents that the contested act was not a definitive decision and therefore produced no legal effects: CFI, Case T-123/99 *JT's Corporation v Commission* [2000] E.C.R. II-3269, para. 25. See also CFI (order of 2 June 2004), Case T-123/03 *Pfizer v Commission* [2004] E.C.R. II-1631, paras 25–27. This issue often arises in the context of annulment proceedings brought against Commission measures involving payment/reimbursement of money: see, e.g. CFI (order of 25 September 2008), Joined Cases T-392/03, T-408/03, T-414/03, and T-435/03 *Regione Siciliana v Commission* [2008] E.C.R. II-2489, paras 37–38 (the contested measure does not in itself constitute a claim for payment of default interest or calculate the actual amount of such interest, but merely sets out the relevant Union law rules for the calculation of such interest over a certain period); EGC (order of 13 September 2011), Case T-224/09 *CEVA v Commission* [2011] E.C.R. II-277*, Summ. pub., paras 52 *et seq.* (letter of Commission inviting the applicant to pay certain sums and informing it of the consequences of non-payment was held not to constitute a challengeable act).

position. Consequently, preparatory acts may not be the subject of an action for annulment.[92] This is because an action brought against such a measure would make it necessary for the Court of Justice or the General Court to 'arrive at a decision on questions on which the [institution] has not yet had an opportunity to state its position and would as a result anticipate the arguments on the substance of the case, confusing different procedural stages both administrative and judicial'.[93]

(c) Irregularities in preparatory acts

7.29   Where an action for annulment is brought against the measure concluding the procedure, any irregularities in the preparatory acts may be raised in challenging the final act.[94]

B. The concept of a reviewable act: some fields of application

(1) Enforcement of Arts 101 and 102 TFEU

(a) Regulatory framework

7.30   The processing of complaints relating to, inquiries into, and the prosecution of infringements of Arts 101 and 102 TFEU is governed by Regulation No. 1/2003[95] and Regulation No. 773/2004,[96] which determine an administrative procedure in which the Commission and/or the national competition authorities adopt various acts. The acts adopted by the national authorities may be challenged only before the courts of the Member State concerned, which may—and in some cases must—refer a question for a preliminary ruling to the Court of Justice. Acts adopted by the Commission on the basis of Regulations Nos 1/2003 and 773/2004 can be challenged before the General Court,[97] provided that they produce binding legal effects.

---

[92] See, e.g. ECJ, Case 346/87 *Bossi v Commission* [1989] 303, para. 23; ECJ, Case C-147/96 *Netherlands v Commission* [2000] E.C.R. I-4723, para. 35; CFI, Case T-64/89 *Automec v Commission* [1990] E.C.R. II-367, para. 42; CFI, Joined Cases T-17/90, T-28/91 and T-17/92 *Camara Alloisio and Others v Commission* [1993] E.C.R. II-841, para. 39; CFI, Case T-95/99 *Satellimages TV5 v Commission* [2002] E.C.R. II-1425, paras 32–41; CFI, Case T-47/01 *Co-Frutta v Commission* [2003] E.C.R. II-4441, paras 28–33 (in connection with access to documents); EGC (order of 24 November 2010), Case T-317/09 *Concord Power Nordal v Commission* [2010] E.C.R. II-253*, Summ. pub., para. 44; EGC (judgment of 7 March 2013), Case T-93/10 *Bilbaína de Alquitranes and Others v ECHA*, not reported, para. 28; EGC (judgment of 7 March 2013), Case T-94/10 *Rütgers Germany and Others v ECHA*, not reported, para. 29.

[93] ECJ, Case 60/81 *IBM v Commission* [1981] E.C.R. 2639, para. 20; ECJ (judgment of 19 March 2013), Case C-401/10 P *Bouygues and Others v Commission*, not reported, para. 78. But see ECJ, Joined Cases C-463/10 P and C-475/10 P *Deutsche Post and Germany v Commission* [2011] E.C.R. I-9639, paras 49–60 (and citations therein).

[94] ECJ, Joined Cases 12/64 and 29/64 *Ley v Commission* [1965] E.C.R. 107, at 118; CFI, Joined Cases T-10/92 to T-12/92, and T-15/92 *Cimenteries CBR and Others v Commission* [1992] E.C.R. II-2667, para. 31; CFI (order of 2 June 2004), Case T-123/03 *Pfizer v Commission* [2004] E.C.R. II-1631, para. 24. The unlawful act in the preparatory phase may even affect an institution other than the one against which the action for annulment is brought (ECJ, Case C-445/00 *Austria v Council* [2003] E.C.R. I-8549, paras 31–35: in an action for annulment of a Council regulation, it was argued that the Commission proposal was unlawful).

[95] Council Regulation (EC) No. 1/2003 of 16 December 2002 on the implementation of the rules on competition laid down in Arts 81 and 82 (now Arts 101 and 102 TFEU) of the Treaty ([2003] O.J. L1/1).

[96] Commission Regulation (EC) No. 773/2004 of 7 April 2004 relating to the conduct of proceedings by the Commission pursuant to Arts 81 and 82 of the EC Treaty (now Arts 101 and 102 TFEU) ([2004] O.J. L123/18) as amended by Commission Regulation (EC) No 622/2008 of 30 June 2008 as regards the conduct of settlement procedures in cartel cases ([2008] O.J. L171/3).

[97] In the unlikely event that a Union institution would challenge such act, proceedings would have to be brought before the Court of Justice (see para. 2.53).

Until 30 April 2004, Regulation No. 17[98] and Regulation No. 2842/98[99] were in force. It may be assumed that the case-law which has been built up with regard to acts adopted by the Commission on the basis of those regulations will apply *mutatis mutandis* to similar acts adopted on the basis of the new Regulations Nos 1/2003 and 773/2004.

(b) Requests for information

Whenever the Commission becomes aware that an infringement of Art. 101 and/or Art. 102 **7.31** TFEU may have been committed, it may decide to address a request for information to the undertakings or associations of undertakings concerned in order to obtain 'all necessary information'.[100] A distinction has to be drawn between 'simple requests' for information on the basis of Art. 18(2) of Regulation No. 1/2003 and requests 'by decision' on the basis of Art. 18(3) of that Regulation. The addressees of a simple request are free to reply or not to reply to the questions put to them. Such requests for information do not bring about a distinct change in the legal position of the undertakings and associations concerned and cannot be challenged before the General Court.[101] By contrast, the addressees of a Commission decision based on Art. 18(3) of Regulation No. 1/2003 requiring them to supply information are obliged, on pain of penalties, to comply with such a request.[102] Such a decision is a reviewable act.[103] If the party to which such a decision is addressed wishes to challenge its legality, it will have to bring its action within the two-month time limit imposed by the sixth paragraph of Art. 263 TFEU. Indeed, an undertaking or association concerned which has not sought the annulment of such a decision within this two-month time limit will be foreclosed from pleading the illegality of the decision requiring information in an action for annulment brought against the Commission decision finding an infringement.[104]

The decision by which, in a first stage, the Commission, acting on the basis of Art. 24(1) of Regulation No. 1/2003,[105] fixes a deadline by which an undertaking which has provided what the Commission considers to be an incomplete response to a decision requesting information[106] is required to give a full response and at the same time imposes a penalty

---

[98] Regulation No. 17: First Regulation implementing Arts 85 and 86 (now Arts 101 and 102 TFEU) of the Treaty, O.J., English Special Edition 1959–1962, 87.

[99] Commission Regulation (EC) No. 2842/98 of 22 December 1998 on the hearing of parties in certain proceedings under Arts 85 and 86 of the EC Treaty (now Arts 101 and 102 TFEU) ([1998] O.J. L354/18). That regulation replaced the earlier Regulation No. 99/63 (English Special Edition, Series I, Chapter 1963–1964, 47).

[100] Regulation No. 1/2003, Art. 18(1).

[101] Regulation No. 1/2003, Arts 18(2) and 23(1)(a). A penalty may only be imposed where, having agreed to reply, the undertaking or association concerned provides incorrect or misleading information.

[102] Regulation No. 1/2003, Arts 18(3) and 23(1)(b). The Commission may not, however, compel an undertaking or an association to provide answers which might involve an admission on its part of the existence of an infringement which it is incumbent on the Commission to prove (ECJ, Case 374/87 *Orkem v Commission* [1989] E.C.R. I-3283, para. 35; CFI, Case T-34/93 *Société Générale v Commission* [1995] E.C.R. II-545, para. 74; CFI, Case T-112/98 *Mannesmannröhren-Werke v Commission* [2001] E.C.R. II-729, para. 67).

[103] Under Art. 18(3) of Regulation No. 1/2003 the Commission is even obliged to indicate in a request by decision the right of the parties concerned to have the decision reviewed by the Union courts. See also ECJ, Case 374/87 *Orkem v Commission* [1989] E.C.R. 3282, para. 34; CFI, Case T-34/93 *Société Générale v Commission* [1995] E.C.R. II-545, para. 74; CFI, Case T-112/98 *Mannesmannröhren-Werke v Commission* [2001] E.C.R. II-729, para. 65; CFI, Case T-50/00 *Dalmine v Commission* [2004] E.C.R. II-2395, para. 47; EGC (judgment of 22 March 2012), Joined Cases T-458/09 and T-171/10 *Slovak Telekom v Commission*, not reported, para. 41.

[104] CFI, Joined Cases T-305/94, T-306/94, T-307/94, T-313/94 to T-316/94, T-318/94, T-325/94, T-328/94, T-329/94, and T-335/94 *Limburgse Vinyl Maatschappij and Others v Commission* [1999] E.C.R. II-931, paras 441 and 442.

[105] Formerly Art. 16(1) of Regulation No. 17.   [106] Regulation No. 1/2003, Art. 18(3).

payment is, however, not a challengeable act as regards the imposition of the penalty payment. This is because such a decision does not produce binding legal effects in so far as it only fixes a periodical penalty in terms of a specific amount for each day by which the deadline is exceeded. It is not enforceable because it does not fix the total amount of the penalty payable. The total amount is fixed in a second stage by a new decision when it is found that the undertaking has not provided the information in good time.[107]

(c) Inspections

7.32   Art. 20 of Regulation No. 1/2003 draws a distinction between two forms of inspections, namely inspections carried out upon production of an authorization in writing[108] ('inspections under authorisation') and inspections formally ordered by a decision of the Commission.[109] The former type of inspection may be carried out only on the premises, land, and means of transport of the undertakings and associations concerned and only if the undertakings and associations concerned are prepared to cooperate. No fine may be imposed where an undertaking or association of undertakings refuses to submit to an inspection under authorization. Where the Commission wishes to search other premises, land, and means of transport, including the homes of directors, managers, and other members of staff of the undertakings and associations concerned, or where it expects the parties concerned not to adopt a cooperative attitude, it will order an inspection by a formal decision.[110] It should be stressed that the Commission may carry out such an inspection without first attempting an inspection by authorization.[111] There is a legal obligation to submit to an inspection ordered by a decision.

Given its binding character, a decision ordering an inspection can be the subject of an action for annulment brought under Art. 263 TFEU.[112] However, all persons subject to Union law are under an obligation to acknowledge that measures adopted by the institutions are fully effective as long as they have not been declared invalid by the Court of Justice or the General Court and to recognize their enforceability unless one of those Courts has decided to suspend the legal effects of the said measures.[113] Practically speaking, this means that an undertaking or association of undertakings will not be in a position to prevent an inspection ordered by a decision of the Commission from taking place. The party concerned will only be able to seek judicial redress before the General Court after the event by lodging an

---

[107] CFI (order of 24 June 1998), Case T-596/97 *Dalmine v Commission* [1998] E.C.R. II-2383, paras 27–34.

[108] Regulation No. 1/2003, Art. 20(3).

[109] Regulation No. 1/2003 Arts 20(4) and 21(1).

[110] Regulation No. 1/2003, Arts 20(4) and 21(1).

[111] ECJ, Case 136/79 *National Panasonic v Commission* [1980] E.C.R. 2033, paras 10–12.

[112] EGC (judgment of 14 November 2012), Case T-135/09 *Nexans France and Nexans*, not reported; EGC (judgment of 14 November 2012), Case T-140/09 *Prysmian and Prysmian Cavi e Systemi Energia v Commission*, not reported; EGC (judgment of 6 September 2013), Joined Cases T-289/11, T-290/11 and T-521/11 *Deutsche Bahn and Others v Commission*, not reported. Art. 20(4) of Regulation No. 1/2003 requires the Commission to specify in such a decision that the right exists to have it reviewed by the Court of Justice/ General Court. It should be noted, however, that reports, drawn up by the Commission's officials during an investigation into an undertaking and containing a summary of what was said by that undertaking's representatives in the course of the investigation, are not actionable measures: CFI (order of 9 June 1997), Case T-9/97 *Elf Atochem v Commission* [1997] E.C.R. II-909, paras 18–27. Similarly, the copying of documents and the asking of questions during an inspection are not to be regarded as acts separable from the decision under which the inspection was ordered: see EGC (judgment of 14 November 2012), Case T-135/09 *Nexans France and Nexans*, not reported, para. 125; EGC (judgment of 14 November 2012), Case T-140/09 *Prysmian and Prysmian Cavi e Systemi Energia v Commission*, not reported, para. 102.

[113] ECJ, Joined Cases 46/87 and 227/88 *Hoechst v Commission* [1989] E.C.R. I-2859, para. 64.

action for annulment against the decision ordering an inspection.[114] If such action were to be lodged within the two-month time limit laid down by the sixth paragraph of Art. 263 TFEU and the General Court were to find that the inspection had been unlawful, the evidence obtained in the course of such inspection would also be unlawful. The Commission could then no longer find an infringement on the basis of that evidence.[115]

When the Union judicature examines the lawfulness of an inspection decision, it will do so in the light of the matters of law and fact existing at the time when the decision was adopted. The way the Commission implements the inspection decision therefore has no effect on the lawfulness of that decision.[116] However, arguments relating to the implementation of the inspection decision may be raised in the action for annulment brought against the final decision of the Commission finding the infringement.[117]

An addressee of a decision ordering an inspection who does not seek the annulment of that decision within the two-month time limit laid down by the sixth paragraph of Art. 263 TFEU will be foreclosed from pleading the illegality of the decision (as well as of the evidence obtained in the course of such inspection) in any subsequent action for annulment of the Commission decision finding an infringement of Art. 101(1) and/or Art. 102 TFEU.[118]

Before an inspection takes place, a national judicial authority will generally be asked to carry out a limited review of the Commission decision ordering the inspection.[119] This will be the case where the Commission requests the assistance of the police in order to compel the undertaking or association concerned to submit to an inspection, or where the Commission seeks to conduct an inspection in the homes of members of staff of the undertaking or

---

[114] There remains the theoretical possibility of bringing an application for interim relief. However, it would be hard to prove irreparable damage as a result of an inspection. See CFI (order of the President of 30 October 2003), Joined Cases T-125/03 R and T-253/03 R *Akzo Nobel Chemicals and Others v Commission* [2003] E.C.R. II-4771, paras 159–178.

[115] Opinion of Advocate-General J.-P. Warner in Case 136/79 *National Panasonic v Commission* [1980] E.C.R. 2033, at 2069: '[The fact that the remedy can only be invoked] after the investigation has taken place, [. . .] does not make it an ineffective remedy. The Court may [. . .] if it holds the decision to have been unlawful, order the Commission to return to the undertaking any copies of documents obtained as a result of the investigation and to refrain from using any information so obtained.' See also ECJ (order of the President of 26 March 1987), Case 46/87 R *Hoechst v Commission* [1987] E.C.R. 1549, para. 34 and ECJ (order of the President of 26 March 1987), Case 85/87 R *Dow Chemical Nederland v Commission* [1987] E.C.R. 4367, para. 17.

[116] ECJ, Case 85/87 *Dow Benelux v Commission* [1989] E.C.R. 3137, para. 49; CFI, Joined Cases T-305/94 to T-307/94, T-313/94 to T-316/94, T-318/94, T-325/94, T-328/94, T-329/94, and T-335/94 *Limburgse Vinyl Maatschappij and Others v Commission* [1999] E.C.R. II-931, para. 413; CFI, Case T-339/04 *France Télécom v Commission* [2007] E.C.R. II-521, para. 54; CFI, Joined Cases T-125/03 and T-253/03 *Akzo Nobel Chemicals and Akcros Chemicals v Commission* [2007] II-3523, paras 55–56 (in this case the applicant sought the annulment of the inspection decision in so far as it had been interpreted by the Commission as legitimizing the basis of its action of seizing and/or reviewing documents protected by the legal professional privilege; this action was inadmissible, since the disputed acts of the Commission occurred after the adoption of the inspection decision, which merely authorized the Commission's agents to enter the applicant's premises and to take copies of the relevant business records, and which did not refer to the issue of legal professional privilege).

[117] ECJ, Case 85/87 *Dow Benelux v Commission* [1989] E.C.R. I-3137, para. 49; CFI, Joined Cases T-305/94, T-306/94, T-307/94, T-313/94, T-316/94, T-318/94, T-325/94, T-328/94, T-329/94, and T-335/94 *Limburgse Vinyl Maatschappij v Commission* [1999] E.C.R. II-931, para 413; EGC (judgment of 14 November 2012), Case T-135/09 *Nexans France and Nexans*, not reported, para. 132; EGC (judgment of 14 November 2012), Case T-140/09 *Prysmian and Prysmian Cavi e Systemi Energia v Commission*, not reported, para. 108.

[118] CFI, Joined Cases T-305/94, T-306/94, T-307/94, T-313/94, T-316/94, T-318/94, T-325/94, T-328/94, T-329/94, and T-335/94 *Limburgse Vinyl Maatschappij v Commission* [1999] E.C.R. II-931, paras 408–410.

[119] Regulation No. 1/2003, Art. 20(7) and (8) and Art. 21(3).

association concerned. The national judicial authority will check whether the Commission decision is authentic. It will verify that the coercive measures envisaged are neither arbitrary nor excessive having regard to the subject-matter of the inspection. In reviewing the proportionality of the coercive measures, the national judicial authority may ask the Commission, directly or through the Member State competition authority, for detailed explanations, in particular of the grounds the Commission has for suspecting an infringement of Arts 101 and 102 TFEU, as well as of the seriousness of the suspected infringement and the nature of the involvement of the undertaking concerned. However, the national judicial authority may not call into question the necessity for the inspection or demand that it be provided with the information in the Commission's file. Only the General Court and the Court of Justice on appeal can review the legality of the Commission's decision.[120]

(d) Decision imposing a fine for breaking of seals

7.33 Under Art. 23(1)(e) of Regulation No. 1/2003, the Commission may by decision impose on undertakings and associations of undertakings fines not exceeding 1 per cent of the total turnover in the preceding business year where, intentionally or negligently, seals affixed during the investigation by officials or other accompanying persons authorized by the Commission have been broken. Such a decision is a reviewable act.[121]

(e) Initiation of infringement proceedings and statement of objections

7.34 If the Commission considers, on the basis of the information obtained during its investigation, that certain undertakings and/or associations of undertakings have infringed the EU competition rules, it may open a formal procedure against the parties concerned pursuant to Art. 2 of Regulation No. 773/2004. Shortly after the initiation of proceedings, it will send a statement of objections to these parties pursuant to Art. 10 of Regulation No. 773/2004. The initiation of an administrative procedure[122] and the communication of a statement of objections[123] are not acts against which an application for annulment may be brought. This is because they are preparatory acts. Any irregularities in such acts may be raised in an action brought against the decision concluding the procedure.[124] Thus, if the final decision alleges that the undertakings concerned have committed infringements other than those referred to in the statement of objections or takes into consideration different facts, there will be an infringement of the rights of the defence.[125]

---

[120] Regulation No. 1/2003, Art. 20(7) and (8) and Art. 21(3). See in particular ECJ, Case C-94/00 *Roquette Frères* [2002] E.C.R. I-9011, para. 51.

[121] EGC, Case T-141/08 *E.ON Energie v Commission* [2010] E.C.R. II-5761 (confirmed on appeal: ECJ (judgment of 22 November 2012), Case C-89/11 P *E.ON Energie v Commission*, not reported).

[122] Regulation No. 773/2004, Art. 2. The initiation of the administrative procedure requires 'an authoritative act of the Commission, evidencing its intention of taking a decision [on the matter]' (ECJ, Case 48/72 *Brasserie de Haecht v Wilkin-Janssen* [1973] E.C.R. 77, para. 16). The undertaking addressed is aware of the fact that an administrative procedure is underway against it and knows its procedural position. Such notification does not constitute a definitive adoption of a position.

[123] Regulation No. 773/2004, Art. 10. See in this connection ECJ, Case 60/81 *IBM v Commission* [1981] E.C.R. 2639, para. 21. The Commission is obliged to apprize the undertaking charged with an infringement of Art. 101 or Art. 102 TFEU of the facts and arguments underlying its charges. That statement secures the right of the undertaking concerned to a fair hearing.

[124] See e.g. EGC, Case T-194/06 *SNIA v Commission* [2011] E.C.R. II-3119, paras 78–92; EGC, Case T-39/06 *Transcatab v Commission* [2011] E.C.R. II-6831, paras 115–118 (and case-law cited therein).

[125] ECJ, Case 41/69 *ACF Chemiefarma v Commission* [1970] E.C.R. 661, para. 94; CFI, Joined Cases T-39/92 and T-40/92 *CB and Europay v Commission* [1994] E.C.R. II-49, paras 49 to 52; EGC (judgment of 14 March 2013), Case T-587/08 *Fresh Del Monte Produce v Commission*, not reported, para. 706.

Accordingly, in its judgment in the '*Woodpulp*' cases, the Court of Justice annulled a number of paragraphs of the operative part of the Commission's final decision after finding that the infringements found in those paragraphs had not been clearly set out in the statement of objections. The parties concerned had therefore not been given an opportunity to defend themselves effectively during the administrative procedure against the objections raised against them.[126]

(f) Notice pursuant to Art. 27(4) of Regulation No. 1/2003

It may be assumed that a Commission notice pursuant to Art. 27(4) of Regulation No. 1/2003 **7.35** in which the Commission informs interested third parties either of its intention to adopt a decision making the commitments offered by the undertakings concerned binding on them or of its intention to adopt a decision finding the inapplicability of Art. 101 TFEU to an agreement, a decision of an association of undertakings, or a concerted practice, and invites third parties to submit their observations within a fixed time limit, does not constitute a challengeable act.[127] The reason is that such notice is a preparatory act in a procedure which will normally result in the adoption of a challengeable act based on Art. 9 or Art. 10 of Regulation No. 1/2003.

(g) Commission's refusal to give access to its file to the parties under investigation

In the course of the administrative procedure, the Commission has to give the parties under **7.36** investigation access to its file. The right of access to the Commission's file is a corollary of the principle of respect for the rights of the defence.[128] The Commission's obligation extends to all the documents in its investigation file[129] which may be relevant for the

---

[126] ECJ, Joined Cases C-89/85, C-104/85, C-114/85, C-116/85, C-117/85, and C-125/85, C-129/85 *Ahlström and Others v Commission* [1993] E.C.R. I-1307, paras 52 and 154; see also CFI, Joined Cases T-39/92 and T-40/92 *CB and Europay International v Commission* [1994] E.C.R. II-49, paras 49–61.

[127] See, by analogy, CFI, Case T-74/92 *Ladbroke v Commission* [1995] E.C.R. II-115, para. 72, with regard to the notice given by the Commission pursuant to Art. 19(3) of Regulation No. 17 (notice indicating that the Commission intended to adopt a favourable position with regard to a notified agreement; under Regulation No. 1/2003 agreements can no longer be notified to the Commission with a view to obtaining an exemption under Art. 101(3) TFEU). By contrast, a communication pursuant to Art. 15(6) of Regulation No. 17 by which the Commission withdrew exemption from a fine from an undertaking which had notified an agreement was held to be an act against which an annulment action could be brought. The Commission took that decision where, after conducting a preliminary examination, it considered that the agreement notified was prohibited by Art. 81 EC (now Art. 101 TFEU) and that a declaration under Art. 81(3) EC (now Art. 101(3) TFEU) that the first para. of that Article was inapplicable was unjustified. The Court of Justice ruled that if such a 'preliminary measure' were excluded from all (direct) judicial review, there would be no alternative for the undertakings concerned than to 'take the risk of a serious threat of a fine or to terminate against their own interests an agreement which, if proceedings had been instituted, might have had a chance of escaping the prohibition' (ECJ, Joined Cases 8/66 to 11/66 *SA Cimenteries CBR Cementbedrijven and Others v Commission* [1967] E.C.R. 75 at 92–3; CFI, Case T-19/91 *Vichy v Commission* [1992] E.C.R. II-415, para. 5; CFI, Joined Cases T-213/95 and T-18/96 *SCK and FNK v Commission* [1997] E.C.R. II-1739, para. 68). That dilemma for the undertakings concerned generally led to the termination of the notified agreement, with the result that the Commission often did not have to take a final decision in order to impose its views on the merits. If no action had been possible against a communication pursuant to Art. 15(6) of Regulation No. 17, the Commission could have effectively avoided any judicial review of its action.

[128] ECJ, Joined Cases C-204/00 P, C-205/00 P, C-211/00 P, C-213/00 P, C-217/00 P, and C-219/00 P *Aalborg Portland and Others v Commission* [2004] E.C.R. I-123, para. 68; ECJ, Case C-407/08 P *Knauf Gips v Commission* [2010] E.C.R. I-6375, para. 22.

[129] Access has to be given only to documents which are part of the investigation file. Replies given by the other undertakings concerned to the statement of objections are not part of the investigation file proper. Accordingly, since they are documents which are not part of the file compiled at the time of notification of the statement of objections, the Commission is required to disclose those replies to the other undertakings

defence of the undertaking(s) concerned. Those documents include both incriminating and exculpatory evidence, save where the business secrets of other undertakings, the internal documents of the Commission, or other confidential information are involved.[130] A refusal on the part of the Commission to accede to a request of a party under investigation to disclose some documents in its file does not constitute a challengeable act.[131] The possible illegality of such refusal may be raised in an application brought against the final decision of the Commission finding an infringement (and possibly imposing fines).[132]

If a party demonstrates in the context of an action for annulment brought against the final Commission decision that it was not in a position to express its views with regard to one or more inculpatory documents in the course of the administrative procedure, the General Court will find that there has been a violation of the rights of the defence. The inculpatory documents will be excluded as evidence. Far from leading inevitably to the annulment of the decision in its entirety, the exclusion of such documents will lead to the annulment in whole or in part of the decision only in so far as the corresponding objection raised by the Commission can only be proved by reference to them.[133] In other words, if the General Court considers that the infringement has been sufficiently made out on the basis of other

concerned only if it transpires that they contain new incriminating or exculpatory evidence: EGC, Case T-191/06 *FMC Foret v Commission* [2011] E.C.R. II-2959, paras 266–267.

[130] CFI, Case T-7/89 *Hercules Chemicals v Commission* [1991] E.C.R. II-1711, para. 54; CFI, Case T-65/89 *BPB Industries and British Gypsum v Commission* [1993] E.C.R. II-389, para. 29; CFI, Joined Cases T-25/95, T-26/95, T-30/95, T-31/95, T-32/95, T-34/95, T-35/95, T-36/95, T-37/95, T-38/95, T-39/95, T-42/95, T-43/95, T-44/95, T-45/95, T-46/95, T-48/95, T-50/95, T-51/95, T-52/95, T-53/95, T-54/95, T-55/95, T-56/95, T-57/95, T-58/95, T-59/95, T-60/95, T-61/95, T-62/95, T-63/95, T-64/95, T-65/95, T-68/95, T-69/95, T-70/95, T-71/95, T-87/95, T-88/95, T-103/95, and T-104/95 *Cimenteries CBR and Others v Commission* [2000] E.C.R. II-491, para. 144; CFI, Case T-38/02 *Groupe Danone v Commission* [2005] E.C.R. II-4407, para. 34; EGC, Case T-191/06 *FMC Foret v Commission* [2011] E.C.R. II-2959, paras 262–263. See also ECJ, Joined Cases C-204/00 P, C-205/00 P, C-211/00 P, C-213/00 P, C-217/00 P, and C-219/00 P *Aalborg Portland and Others v Commission* [2004] E.C.R. I-123, para. 68; ECJ, Case C-407/08 P *Knauf Gips v Commission* [2010] E.C.R. I-6375, para. 22; ECJ, Case C-110/10 P *Solvay v Commission* [2011] E.C.R. I-10439, para. 49. This rule, which was first developed in the case-law, is now incorporated into Art. 15 of Regulation No. 773/2004, which adds that the right of access does not also extend to internal documents of the national competition authorities, to correspondence between the Commission and such authorities, and to correspondence between national competition authorities where that correspondence is contained in the Commission's file.

[131] CFI, Joined Cases T-10/92 to T-12/92, and T-15/92 *CBR Cementbedrijven and Others v Commission* [1992] E.C.R. II-2667, para. 42; CFI (order of 9 July 2003), Case T-216/01 *Reisebank v Commission*, not reported, paras 49–51.

[132] Infringement of the right of access to the Commission's file during the procedure prior to adoption of a decision can, in principle, cause the decision to be annulled if the rights of defence of the undertaking concerned have been infringed: see ECJ, Case C-110/10 P *Solvay v Commission* [2011] E.C.R. I-10439, para. 50.

[133] ECJ, Case 107/82 *AEG v Commission* [1983] E.C.R. 3151, paras 24–30; ECJ, Joined Cases C-204/00 P, C-205/00 P, C-211/00 P, C-213/00 P, C-217/00 P, and C-219/00 P *Aalborg Portland and Others v Commission* [2004] E.C.R. I-123, para. 68; ECJ, Case C-407/08 P *Knauf Gips v Commission* [2010] E.C.R. I-6375, para. 13; CFI, Case T-30/91 *Solvay v Commission* [1995] E.C.R. II-1775, para. 58; CFI, Joined Cases T-25/95, T-26/95, T-30/95, T-31/95, T-32/95, T-34/95, T-35/95, T-36/95, T-37/95, T-38/95, T-39/95, T-42/95, T-43/95, T-44/95, T-45/95, T-46/95, T-48/95, T-50/95, T-51/95, T-52/95, T-53/95, T-54/95, T-55/95, T-56/95, T-57/95, T-58/95, T-59/95, T-60/95, T-61/95, T-62/95, T-63/95, T-64/95, T-65/95, T-68/95, T-69/95, T-70/95, T-71/95, T-87/95, T-88/95, T-103/95, and T-104/95 *Cimenteries CBR and Others v Commission* [2000] E.C.R. II-491, para. 364; CFI, Case T-38/02 *Groupe Danone v Commission* [2005] E.C.R. II-4407, para. 35; EGC, Case T-191/06, *FMC Foret v Commission* [2011] E.C.R. II-2959, paras 264 and 271; EGC, Case T-199/08 *Ziegler v Commission* [2011] E.C.R. II-3507, para. 123; EGC (judgment of 2 February 2012),

inculpatory documents which were made available to the applicant in the course of the administrative procedure and in respect of which the applicant was able to express its views, the violation of the rights of the defence will not affect the legality of the decision.[134]

If a party claims in the context of an action for annulment brought against the final Commission decision that a document in the Commission's file which might contain exculpatory evidence was not available to it during the administrative procedure, the General Court will find a violation of that party's rights of defence and annul the contested decision in whole or in part if the party concerned can show that there is even a small chance that the outcome of the administrative procedure might have been different if it had been able to rely on that document during that procedure.[135] It is thus sufficient for the undertaking to show that it would have been able to use the exculpatory documents for its defence, in the sense that, had it been able to rely on them during the administrative procedure, it would have been able to invoke evidence which was not consistent with the inferences made at that stage by the Commission and therefore could have had an influence, in any way at all, on the assessments made by the Commission in its decision, as regards the conduct in which the undertaking was found to have engaged.[136]

Consequently, when, in the context of an action seeking annulment of the Commission's final decision, an applicant challenges the Commission's refusal to disclose one or more

---

Case T-83/08 *Denki Kagaku Kogyo and Denka Chemicals v Commission*, not reported, para. 84; EGC (judgment of 14 March 2013), Case T-587/08 *Fresh Del Monte Produce v Commission*, not reported, paras 664–668.

[134] It is therefore only exceptionally that the non-communication of incriminating documents during the administrative procedure will lead to the partial or total annulment of the decision finding the infringement. For an example, see ECJ, Joined Cases C-89/85, C-104/85, C-114/85, C-116/85, C-117/85, and C-125/85, C-129/85 *Ahlström and Others v Commission* [1993] E.C.R. I-1307, para. 138, where the Court of Justice held that 'in establishing the infringement relating to transaction prices, the Commission must have relied essentially on documents gathered after the statement of objections was drawn up. Since the members of KEA had no opportunity to make their views known on those documents, Art. 1(3) of the contested decision must be annulled for disregard of the rights of the defence in so far as it concerns that infringement.'

[135] See CFI, Case T-7/89 *Hercules Chemicals v Commission* [1991] E.C.R. II-1711, para. 56; CFI, Case T-30/91 *Solvay v Commission* [1995] E.C.R. II-1775, para. 68; CFI, Case T-636/91 *ICI v Commission* [1995] E.C.R. II-1847, para. 78; CFI, Joined Cases T-25/95, T-26/95, T-30/95, T-31/95, T-32/95, T-34/95, T-35/95, T-36/95, T-37/95, T-38/95, T-39/95, T-42/95, T-43/95, T-44/95, T-45/95, T-46/95, T-48/95, T-50/95, T-51/95, T-52/95, T-53/95, T-54/95, T-55/95, T-56/95, T-57/95, T-58/95, T-59/95, T-60/95, T-61/95, T-62/95, T-63/95, T-64/95, T-65/95, T-68/95, T-69/95, T-70/95, T-71/95, T-87/95, T-88/95, T-103/95, and T-104/95 *Cimenteries CBR and Others v Commission* [2000] E.C.R. II-491, paras 241 and 247; CFI, Joined Cases T-191/98, T-212/98, T-213/98, and T-214/98 *Atlantic Container Line and Others v Commission* [2003] E.C.R. II-3275, para. 340; EGC, Case T-235/07 *Bavaria v Commission* [2011] E.C.R. II-3229, para. 239; EGC (judgment of 2 February 2012), Case T-83/08 *Denki Kagaku Kogyo and Denka Chemicals v Commission*, not reported, para. 84. The test applied by the Court of First Instance (now the General Court) with respect to the non-disclosure of potentially exculpatory documents is fully in line with the case-law which the Court of Justice developed in *Distillers* (ECJ, Case 30/78 *Distillers v Commission* [1980] E.C.R. 2229, para. 26) with respect to procedural defects, according to which an alleged procedural defect cannot be relied upon to annul a decision where that defect could not in any event have affected the content of the decision. The applicant does not have to show that, if it had had access to certain documents in the administrative proceedings, the Commission decision would have been different in content, merely that it would have been able to use those documents in its defence (ECJ, Case C-51/92 P *Hercules Chemicals v Commission* [1999] E.C.R. I-4235, para. 81).

[136] ECJ, Joined Cases C-204/00 P, C-205/00 P, C-211/00 P, C-213/00 P, C-217/00 P, and C-219/00 P *Aalborg Portland and Others v Commission* [2004] E.C.R. I-123, paras 74–75; ECJ, Case C-407/08 P *Knauf Gips v Commission* [2010] E.C.R. I-6375, para. 23; ECJ, Case C-110/10 P *Solvay v Commission* [2011] E.C.R. I-10439, para. 52.

documents during the administrative procedure, the General Court will require their disclosure in the proceedings before it.[137] The applicant will then be invited to inspect the
documents and to substantiate its plea alleging infringement of its rights of defence.[138] If the
General Court did not order such disclosure, it would be impossible for an applicant, which
alleges that its rights of defence have been infringed during the administrative procedure
because of the failure to disclose certain documents to it, to demonstrate that the outcome of
the administrative procedure might have been different had such access been granted.[139]

(h) Commission's rejection of a request for protection of a document under the legal professional privilege

7.37 Where an undertaking relies on the legal professional privilege (LPP) for the purpose of
opposing the seizure of a document in the course of an inspection pursuant to Art. 20 of
Regulation No. 1/2003, the decision whereby the Commission rejects that request produces
legal effects for that undertaking by bringing about a distinct change in its legal position. That
decision in effect withholds from the undertaking the protection provided by Union law and
is definitive in nature and independent of any final decision making a finding of an
infringement of the competition rules. Indeed, the opportunity which the undertaking has
to bring an action against a final decision establishing that the competition rules have been
infringed does not provide it with an adequate degree of protection of its rights. First, it is
possible that the administrative procedure will not result in a decision finding that an
infringement has been committed. Secondly, if an action is brought against that decision,
it will not in any event provide the undertaking with the means of preventing the irreversible
consequences which would result from improper disclosure of documents protected under
legal professional privilege. It follows that the Commission's decision rejecting a request for
protection of a specific document under LPP—and ordering, where appropriate, the production of the document in question—brings to an end a special procedure distinct from that
enabling the Commission to rule on the existence of an infringement of the competition rules
and thus constitutes an act capable of being challenged by an action for annulment.[140]

---

[137] By way of a measure of organization of procedure within the meaning of Art. 64 or a measure of inquiry within the meaning of Art. 65 of the EGC Rules of Procedure.

[138] CFI, Joined Cases T-305/94, T-306/94, T-307/94, T-313/94, T-316/94, T-318/94, T-325/94, T-328/94, T-329/94, and T-335/94 *Limburgse Vinyl Maatschappij and Others v Commission* [1999] E.C.R. II-931, para. 1023; CFI, Joined Cases T-25/95, T-26/95, T-30/95, T-31/95, T-32/95, T-34/95, T-35/95, T-36/95, T-37/95, T-38/95, T-39/95, T-42/95, T-43/95, T-44/95, T-45/95, T-46/95, T-48/95, T-50/95, T-51/95, T-52/95, T-53/95, T-54/95, T-55/95, T-56/95, T-57/95, T-58/95, T-59/95, T-60/95, T-61/95, T-62/95, T-63/95, T-64/95, T-65/95, T-68/95, T-69/95, T-70/95, T-71/95, T-87/95, T-88/95, T-103/95, and T-104/95 *Cimenteries CBR and Others v Commission* [2000] E.C.R. II-491, paras 158 to 162, and 241.

[139] In CFI, Joined Cases T-25/95, T-26/95, T-30/95, T-31/95, T-32/95, T-34/95, T-35/95, T-36/95, T-37/95, T-38/95, T-39/95, T-42/95, T-43/95, T-44/95, T-45/95, T-46/95, T-48/95, T-50/95, T-51/95, T-52/95, T-53/95, T-54/95, T-55/95, T-56/95, T-57/95, T-58/95, T-59/95, T-60/95, T-61/95, T-62/95, T-63/95, T-64/95, T-65/95, T-68/95, T-69/95, T-70/95, T-71/95, T-87/95, T-88/95, T-103/95, and T-104/95 *Cimenteries CBR and Others v Commission* [2000] E.C.R. II-491, para 161, the Court of First Instance held that 'Applicants who have raised a plea alleging infringement of their rights of defence cannot be required to set out in their application detailed arguments or a consistent body of evidence to show that the outcome of the administrative procedure might have been different if they had had access to certain documents which were in fact never disclosed to them. Such an approach would in effect amount to requiring a *probatio diabolica . . . .'*. See also ECJ, Case C-110/10 P *Solvay v Commission* [2011] E.C.R. I-10439, paras 59–62 and 72: the loss of part of the Commission's file to which the applicant had not had access during the administrative proceedings led inevitably to the annulment of the contested decision.

[140] ECJ, Case 155/79 *AM & S Europe v Commission* [1982] E.C.R. 1575; CFI, Joined Cases T-125/03 and T-253/03 *Akzo Nobel Chemicals and Akcros Chemicals v Commission* [2007] E.C.R. II-3523, paras 46–48

Similarly, where the Commission, during an inspection, seizes a document in respect of which LPP is claimed and places it on the administrative file without putting it in a sealed envelope and without having taken a formal rejection decision, that physical act necessarily entails a tacit decision by the Commission to reject the protection claimed by the undertaking and allows the Commission to examine the document in question immediately. That tacit decision is also open to challenge by an action for annulment.[141]

(i) Commission's disclosure of documents to third parties

For the same reasons as those indicated under paragraph 7.37, a decision by the Commission not to treat certain documents as confidential during the administrative procedure and to disclose them to third parties may form the subject-matter of an action for annulment.[142] Such a decision is independent of the final decision bringing the administrative procedure to an end. Moreover, the possibility of bringing an action for annulment of the final decision does not afford adequate protection. **7.38**

(j) Interim measures

The Commission has the power to impose interim measures[143] in the course of the administrative procedure in order to avoid serious and irreparable damage to competition which could not be remedied by its final decision. The decision imposing interim measures must be 'made in such a form that an action may be brought upon them ... by any party who considers it has been injured'.[144] However, it will have to be assessed whether an applicant still retains an interest in having the decision imposing interim measures annulled **7.39**

(appeal dismissed: see ECJ, Case C-550/07 P *Akzo Nobel Chemicals and Akcros Chemicals v Commission* [2010] E.C.R. I-8301).

[141] CFI, Joined Cases T-125/03 and T-253/03 *Akzo Nobel Chemicals and Akcros Chemicals v Commission* [2007] E.C.R. II-3523, para. 49. See also by analogy, ECJ, Case 53/85 *AKZO Chemie v Commission* [1986] E.C.R. 1965, para. 17.

[142] CFI, Case T-353/94 *Postbank v Commission* [1996] E.C.R. II-921, paras 33–39: a letter by which the Commission removes the prohibition—mentioned when the statement of objections was sent to undertakings which were participating, but were not formal complainants, in a proceeding before the Commission—on using the statement of objections in national legal proceedings and by which it also gives its view as to the lack of any obstacle to production, in the national court, of that statement of objections and the minutes of the subsequent hearing, is in the nature of a challengeable decision. But see CFI (order of 2 May 1997), Case T-136/96 *Automobiles Peugeot v Commission* [1997] E.C.R. II-663: an action will not lie against a letter addressed by the Commission to an undertaking in which it expresses its intention to communicate purported business secrets of that undertaking and fixing a time limit within which it may submit written comments pursuant to Art. 8 of Commission Decision No. 2011/695/EU of 13 October 2011 on the function and terms of reference of the hearing officer in certain competition proceedings ([2011] O.J. L275/29). Such an act is only a preparatory act forming part of the first stage of the procedure set out in Art. 8 of Decision No. 2001/462 (the order refers to the similarly worded Art. 5 of Decision No. 94/810, which was replaced first by Decision No. 2001/462, then by Decision No. 2011/695). A decision to transmit a non-confidential version of the statement of objections to the complainant is *prima facie* a challengeable act: CFI (order of the President of 20 December 2001), Case T-213/01 R *Österreichische Postsparkasse AG v Commission* [2001] E.C.R. II-3961, paras 49–52; CFI (order of the President of 20 December 2001), Case T-214/01 R *Bank für Arbeit und Wirtschaft v Commission* [2001] E.C.R. II-3993, paras 43–46. See also CFI, Joined Cases T-213/01 and T-214/01 *Österreichische Postsparkasse and Bank für Arbeit und Wirtschaft v Commission* [2006] E.C.R. II-1601, paras 64–73.

[143] The Commission will adopt interim measures only on its own initiative and not at the request of a party. Indeed, Art. 8(1) of Regulation No. 1/2003 provides: 'In cases of urgency due to the risk of serious and irreparable damage to competition, the Commission, acting on its own initiative may by decision, on the basis of a *prima facie* finding of infringement, order interim measures.'

[144] ECJ, Case 792/79 R *Camera Care v Commission* [1980] E.C.R. 119, para. 19; ECJ, Joined Cases 228/82 and 229/82 *Ford v Commission* [1984] E.C.R. 1129, para. 10.

where the Commission has adopted a final decision withdrawing the decision imposing interim measures.[145]

(k) Commitments

7.40 Where the Commission intends to adopt a decision requiring that an infringement be brought to an end and the undertakings concerned offer commitments to meet the concerns expressed to them by the Commission in its preliminary assessment, the Commission may by decision make those commitments binding on the undertakings.[146] Such a decision is a challengeable act within the meaning of Art. 263 TFEU.[147]

(l) Finding of infringement and imposition of fines

7.41 The decision by which the Commission finds an infringement of Art. 101 and/or Art. 102 TFEU and, possibly, imposing a fine produces obligatory legal effects and is a challengeable act.[148] The same applies to a decision finding an infringement of Art. 106(1) TFEU read in combination with Art. 102 TFEU.[149]

(m) Acts relating to the execution of a decision imposing a fine

7.42 An action for annulment will not lie against the Commission's refusal to accede to a request from one of the addressees of the decision to agree to their paying the fine in a particular way.[150] This is because such an act must be regarded as confirming the initial decision. The obligatory legal effects therefore arise out of the initial decision and not out of the refusal.[151]

Similarly, an action for annulment will not lie against an act by which the Commission demands the payment of the outstanding balance of a fine to its debtor and threatens to take steps to enforce the bank guarantee provided for by the latter.[152] Indeed, such acts must be regarded as giving notice of enforcement of a decision taken previously. They cannot be regarded as producing legal effects binding on, and capable of affecting the interests of, their addressee. In reality, they merely constitute acts purely preparatory to enforcement. Neither the former nor the latter acts constitute acts open to challenge under Art. 263 TFEU.[153]

---

[145] CFI (order of 10 March 2005), Case T-184/01 *IMS Health v Commission* [2005] E.C.R. II-817, paras 34–49.

[146] Regulation No. 1/2003, Art. 9(1).

[147] CFI, Case T-170/06 *Alrosa v Commission* [2007] E.C.R. II-2601, paras 36–41 (appeal granted on the merits; case dismissed at first instance by the Court of Justice: ECJ, Case C-441/07 P *Commission v Alrosa* [2010] E.C.R. I-5949).

[148] A decision of the Commission fixing, pursuant to Art. 24 of Regulation No. 1/2003, the definitive amount of the periodic penalty payment imposed on an undertaking on the ground that it has not complied with the obligations imposed upon it by the decision finding an infringement, is also a reviewable act: see EGC (judgment of 27 June 2012), Case T-167/08 *Microsoft v Commission*, not reported.

[149] EGC (judgment of 20 September 2012), Case T-169/08 *DEI v Commission*, not reported.

[150] CFI (order of 29 April 2004), Case T-308/02 *SGL Carbon v Commission* [2004] E.C.R. II-1363, paras 39–73.

[151] There is a possibility of securing the suspension of the decision finding the infringement and imposing a fine, provided that the conditions for the grant of interim measures are satisfied (see Ch. 13).

[152] ECJ, Case C-516/06 P *Commission v Ferriere Nord* [2007] E.C.R. I-10685, paras 28–29. The Court of Justice set aside the Court of First Instance's judgment in which the latter court had held such act to be a challengeable act under what is now Art. 263 TFEU.

[153] ECJ, Case C-516/06 P *Commission v Ferriere Nord* [2007] E.C.R. I-10685, para. 29; see, to that effect, also ECJ, Case C-46/03 *United Kingdom v Commission* [2005] E.C.R. I-10167, para. 25; ECJ, Case C-131/03 P *Reynolds Tobacco and Others v Commission* [2006] E.C.R. I-7795, para. 55.

(n) Position of complainant

According to settled case-law, it is in the interests of a satisfactory administration of justice and **7.43** of the proper application of Arts 101 and 102 TFEU that natural or legal persons who are entitled, pursuant to Art. 7(2) of Regulation No. 1/2003,[154] to request the Commission to find an infringement of Arts 101 and 102 TFEU should be able, if their request is not complied with either wholly or in part, to institute proceedings in order to protect their legitimate interests.[155] However, acts adopted by the Commission during the administrative procedure vis-à-vis persons who have lodged complaints alleging breaches of Art. 101 and/or Art. 102 TFEU are not all capable of forming the subject-matter of an action for annulment.

Acts containing a provisional assessment of the complaint cannot be challenged under Art. 263 TFEU. Accordingly, an action will not lie against the notification to be served on the complainants under Art. 7 of Regulation No. 773/2004[156] informing them that the Commission is not going to take up the complaint, and fixes a time limit for them to submit any further comments, following which it will take its final decision.[157] The notification must make it clear that the complainant is entitled to submit comments on the proposed rejection of its complaint. If the letter addressed to the complainant does not contain such an invitation to submit comments, the rejection of the complaint is final and, according to established case-law,[158] may be the subject of judicial proceedings.[159]

---

[154] Formerly Art. 3(2) of Regulation No. 17.

[155] ECJ, Case 26/76 *Metro v Commission* [1977] E.C.R. 1875, para. 13; ECJ, Case 210/81 *Schmidt v Commission* [1983] E.C.R. 3045, para. 14; CFI, Case T-37/92 *BEUC and NCC v Commission* [1994] E.C.R. II-285, para. 36; CFI, Case T-193/02 *Piau v Commission* [2005] E.C.R. II-209, para. 38; CFI, Case T-306/05 *Scippacercola and Terezakis v Commission* [2008] E.C.R. II-4*, Summ. pub., para. 66. The interest of the applicant to seek the annulment of the Commission decision may, however, disappear: see, e.g. EGC (order of 26 March 2012), Case T-508/09 *Cañas v Commission*, not reported, paras 44–70.

[156] Formerly Art. 6 of Regulation No. 99/63 and Art. 6 of Regulation No. 2842/98.

[157] ECJ, Case C-282/95 P *Guérin automobiles v Commission* [1997] E.C.R. I-1503, para. 34; CFI, Case T-64/89 *Automec v Commission* [1990] E.C.R. II-367, para. 46. See also CFI (order of 12 July 2007), Case T-411/05 *Annemans v Commission*, not reported, paras 31–45.

[158] ECJ, Case 210/81 *Demo Studio Schmidt v Commission* [1983] E.C.R. 3045, paras 10–16; ECJ, Case 298/83 *CICCE v Commission* [1985] E.C.R. 1105, paras 15–20; ECJ, Joined Cases 142/84 and 156/84 *BAT and Reynolds v Commission* [1987] E.C.R. 4487, paras 11– 13.

[159] See ECJ, Case C-39/93 P *SFEI and Others v Commission* [1994] E.C.R. I-2681, paras 24–33, in which the Court of Justice set aside the order of the CFI in Case T-36/92 *SFEI and Others v Commission* [1992] E.C.R. II-2479. The judgment given on appeal by the Court of Justice links up with the analysis carried out by the CFI in Case T-64/89 *Automec v Commission* [1990] E.C.R. II-367 of the procedure to be applied where the Commission deals with a complaint alleging infringement of the EU competition rules. The CFI distinguished between three stages (CFI, Case T-64/89 *Automec v Commission* [1990] E.C.R. II-367, paras 45–47). During the first of those stages, the Commission collects the information needed to decide what action to take on the complaint. That stage may include an informal exchange of views and information between the Commission and the complainant. In the view of the CFI, preliminary observations made by Commission officials in the context of those informal contacts cannot be regarded as measures open to challenge. In the second stage, the Commission *either* informs the complainant, in accordance with Art. 7(1) of Regulation No. 773/2004, that it does not intend to take up the complaint and sets a time limit within which the complainant is to submit its observations, *or* serves on the undertaking allegedly in breach of the competition rules a statement of objections if it considers that the infringement raised in the complaint should be pursued. As already mentioned, neither of those acts may be challenged because they do not amount to a definitive position on the part of the Commission. If the Commission intends to reject the complaint, the Commission takes cognizance of the complainant's comments in the third stage. That stage may end with a final decision by which the Commission rejects the complaint (Regulation No. 773/2004, Art. 7(2)). The complainant may bring an action to annul that decision. In its order in *SFEI and Others v Commission*, the CFI took the view that the contested act formed part of the first stage of the investigation and was therefore not

If the complainant makes known its views within the time limit set by the Commission and the written submissions made by the complainant do not lead to a different assessment of the complaint, the Commission is to reject the complaint by decision. An action for annulment will lie against that act.[160] If the complainant fails to make known its views within the time limit set by the Commission, the complaint is deemed to have been withdrawn.[161]

An action will also lie against a decision of the Commission suspending an administrative procedure under Regulation No. 1/2003 pending delivery of judgment in proceedings pursuant to Art. 258 TFEU.[162] This is because such a decision affects the procedural rights of persons who have submitted a complaint pursuant to Art. 7 of Regulation No. 1/2003, in particular the right to be informed beforehand of the Commission's intention not to uphold their complaint and to submit observations in that connection and the right to bring an action for annulment against the rejection of the complaint. In the case of proceedings under Art. 258 TFEU, persons who have lodged a complaint do not have those rights. If some of the questions raised in the complaint pursuant to Regulation No. 1/2003 are going to form the subject of infringement proceedings and the Commission therefore suspends judgment on the complaint as far as those questions are concerned, this deprives the complainant of its procedural rights. An action may consequently be brought against the decision suspending the administrative procedure.[163]

As far as access to the file is concerned, the principle that there must be full disclosure applies only to undertakings and associations on which a penalty may be imposed by a Commission decision finding an infringement of Art. 101(1) or Art. 102 TFEU.[164] Such access ensures that those parties can effectively exercise their rights of defence.[165] Thus, complainants cannot claim to have a right of access to the file on the same basis as the parties under investigation.[166] In any event, the Commission's refusal to grant (partial)

---

amenable to an action for annulment. On appeal, however, the Court of Justice held that the act constituted a final decision definitively rejecting the complaint, and set aside the order of the CFI. That judgment does not detract from the analysis of the CFI in *Automec*. It merely indicates—as also emerges from the judgment of the CFI in *Automec* (para. 48)—that the breakdown of the processing of a complaint into three stages for analytical purposes does not mean that an action will lie against the rejection of a complaint only if all three stages of the procedure have been completed; see also CFI, Case T-37/92 *BEUC and NCC v Commission* [1994] E.C.R. II-285, paras 27–36; CFI, Case T-241/97 *Stork Amsterdam v Commission* [2000] E.C.R. II-309, paras 49–69); CFI (order of 12 July 2007), Case T-411/05 *Annemans v Commission*, not reported, paras 40–45.

[160] See, e.g. EGC, Case T-427/08 *CEAHR v Commission* [2010] E.C.R. II-5865; EGC, Case T-296/09 *EFIM v Commission* [2011] E.C.R. II-425*, Summ. pub.

[161] Regulation No. 773/2004, Art. 7.

[162] However, the initiation of Art. 258 TFEU proceedings does not automatically imply that the complaint regarding a violation of Arts 101 or 102 TFEU has been suspended or dismissed: see ECJ (order of 17 July 1998) Case C-422/97 P *Sateba v Commission* [1998] E.C.R. I-4913, paras 36 and 37; EGC (order of 16 April 2012), Case T-341/10 *F91 Diddeléng and Others v Commission*, not reported, para. 43.

[163] CFI, Case T-16/91 *Rendo and Others v Commission* [1992] E.C.R. II-2417, paras 51–55 (those paras are not affected by the fact that the Court of Justice partially set aside that judgment in ECJ, Case C-19/93 P *Rendo and Others v Commission* [1995] E.C.R. II-3319).

[164] Regulation No. 1/2003, Art. 27(2). CFI, Case T-17/93 *Matra Hachette v Commission* [1994] E.C.R. II-595, para. 34; CFI, Case T-65/96 *Kish Glass v Commission* [2000] E.C.R. II-1885, para 34; EGC (judgment of 11 July 2013), Joined Cases T-104/07 and T-339/08 *BVGD v Commission*, not reported, para. 89.

[165] ECJ, Joined Cases C-204/00 P, C-205/00 P, C-211/00 P, C-213/00 P, C-217/00 P, and C-219/00 P *Aalborg Portland and Others v Commission* [2004] E.C.R. I-123, para. 68; ECJ, Case C-407/08 P *Knauf Gips v Commission* [2010] E.C.R. I-6375, para. 22.

[166] CFI, Case T-17/93 *Matra Hachette v Commission* [1994] E.C.R. II-595, para. 34; CFI, Case T-65/96 *Kish Glass v Commission* [2000] E.C.R. II-1885, para. 34; EGC (judgment of 11 July 2013), Joined Cases T-104/07 and T-339/08 *BVGD v Commission*, not reported, para. 89.

access to its file to a complainant cannot be held to be a challengeable act. However, when the Commission rejects the complaint, the complainant may challenge the Commission's final decision on the grounds that it had insufficient access to the Commission's file during the administrative procedure. In this connection it must be borne in mind that Art. 8(1) of Regulation No. 773/2004 provides that the complainant may request access to the documents on which the Commission bases its provisional assessment that the complaint should be rejected.

(o) Complaint relating to a violation of Art. 106(3) TFEU

Art. 106(3) TFEU requires the Commission to ensure that the Member States comply with **7.44** the obligations imposed on them in regard to the undertakings mentioned in Art. 106(1) TFEU, and expressly confers on it the power to take action for that purpose by way of directives and decisions. The Commission is empowered to determine that a given State measure is incompatible with the rules of the Treaties and to indicate what measures the Member State to which a decision is addressed must adopt in order to comply with its obligations under Union law.[167] This constitutes a reviewable act.[168]

If an undertaking requests the Commission to find that a Member State has infringed the combined provisions of Arts 102 and 106(1) TFEU, an action will not lie against the Commission's rejection of that request. The Union judicature considers that a letter to that effect cannot be regarded as producing binding legal effects.[169] As a result, complaints based on Arts 102 and 106(1) TFEU are treated in the same way as complaints that a Member State has infringed other provisions of Union law.[170]

(2) Merger control

(a) Regulatory framework

Until 1 May 2004, the Commission's supervisory competence with regard to mergers **7.45** (or concentrations) and the administrative procedure which it had to follow in that area was laid down in Council Regulation No. 4064/89[171] and Commission Regulation No. 447/98.[172] The applicable regulations now in force are Council Regulation No. 139/2004[173] and Commission Regulation No. 802/2004.[174]

---

[167] ECJ, Case C-107/95 P *Bundesverband der Bilanzbuchhalter v Commission* [1997] E.C.R. I-947, para. 23.
[168] See, e.g. ECJ, Case C-163/99 *Portugal v Commission* [2001] E.C.R. I-2613.
[169] ECJ, Case C-141/02 P *Commission v max.mobil* [2005] E.C.R. I-1283, para. 70, setting aside CFI, Case T-54/99 *max.mobil v Commission* [2002] E.C.R. II-313, in which the CFI had categorized the Commission's rejection of such a complaint as a formal decision addressed to the complainant.
[170] See para. 7.18.
[171] Council Regulation (EEC) No. 4064/89 of 21 December 1989 on the control of concentrations between undertakings ([1990] O.J. L257/13) as amended by Council Regulation (EC) No. 1310/97 of 30 June 1997 ([1997] O.J. L180/1).
[172] Commission Regulation (EC) No. 447/98 of 1 March 1998 on the notifications, time limits, and hearings provided for in Council Regulation (EEC) No. 4064/89 on the control of concentrations between undertakings ([1998] O.J. L61/1; *corrigendum* in [1998] O.J. L66/25).
[173] Council Regulation (EC) No. 139/2004 of 20 January 2004 on the control of concentrations between undertakings (the Merger Regulation) ([2004] O.J. L24/1).
[174] Commission Regulation (EC) No. 802/2004 of 7 April 2004 implementing Council Regulation (EC) No. 139/2004 on the control of concentrations between undertakings ([2004] O.J. L133/1), as amended by Commission Regulation (EC) No. 1033/2008 ([2008] O.J. L279/3).

(b) Final decisions on notification

7.46 An action will lie against a decision by which the Commission declares a merger compatible or incompatible with the internal market[175] or by which the Commission imposes a fine for not notifying or putting into effect without prior authorization a merger falling within the scope of Regulation No. 139/2004.[176] An action will also lie against a Commission decision finding that a joint venture does not constitute a concentration within the meaning of Regulation No. 139/2004 and therefore does not fall within the scope of that regulation.[177]

(c) Initiation of the procedure

7.47 The initiation of the formal investigation procedure provided for in Art. 6(1)(c) of Regulation No. 139/2004 is a preparatory measure and cannot be challenged before the Union courts.[178]

(d) Ancillary restrictions

7.48 The assessment made by the Commission which is contained in the grounds of a concentration decision on whether ancillary restrictions mentioned by the notifying undertakings are permitted or not permitted is likewise a challengeable act.[179] This is because a decision declaring a concentration compatible with the internal market is to be deemed to cover restrictions directly related and necessary to the implementation of the concentration.[180]

(e) Finding of a dominant position

7.49 The mere finding in a concentration decision that an undertaking occupies a dominant position cannot be challenged. The reason for this is that such a finding does not produce binding legal effects.[181]

---

[175] Regulation No. 139/2004, Art. 8(1)–(3). A decision pursuant to Art. 21 (4) of Regulation No. 139/2004 also constitutes a challengeable act: see ECJ, Case C-42/01 *Commission v Portugal* [2004] E.C.R. I-6079, paras 50–60. However, where the proposed merger has been abandoned the Commission is no longer competent to terminate the procedure initiated pursuant to Art. 21(4) of Regulation No. 139/2004 by a decision relating to the recognition of a public interest protected by the national measures at issue. The Commission's decision to discontinue the procedure under such circumstances does not constitute a challengeable act: see EGC (order of 2 September 2010), Case T-58/09 *Schemaventotto v Commission* [2010] E.C.R. II-3863, paras 117–120.

[176] EGC (judgment of 12 December 2012), Case T-332/09 *Electrabel v Commission*, not reported. The Commission decision approving the sale of assets resulting from the decision declaring a merger compatible with the internal market is also a reviewable act: see EGC, Case T-452/04 *Éditions Odile Jacob and Others v Commission* [2010] E.C.R. II-4713.

[177] CFI, Case T-87/96 *Assicurazioni Generali and Unicredito v Commissie* [1999] E.C.R. II-203, paras 37–44.

[178] CFI (order of 31 January 2006), Case T-48/03 *Schneider Electric v Commission* [2006] E.C.R. II-111, para. 79 (appeal dismissed in ECJ (order of 9 March 2007), Case C-188/06 P *Schneider Electric v Commission* [2007] E.C.R. I-35*, Summ. pub.); EGC, Case T-279/04 *Éditions Jacob v Commission* [2010] E.C.R. II-185*, Summ. pub., paras 89–93.

[179] CFI, Case T-251/00 *Lagardère and Canal+ v Commission* [2002] E.C.R. II-4825, paras 63–118.

[180] Regulation No. 139/2004, Art. 8(1) and (2).

[181] CFI, Joined Cases T-125/97 and T-127/97 *Coca-Cola v Commission* [2000] E.C.R. II-1733, para. 92; EGC (order of 21 September 2012), Case T-501/10 *Ti Media Broadcasting and Ti Media v Commission*, not reported, paras 55–56.

(f) Referral to national authorities

An action will lie against the referral of a merger falling within the scope of Regulation No. **7.50**
139/2004 to the competition authorities of a Member State pursuant to Art. 9 of that
Regulation.[182]

(g) Commitments

Commitments submitted by the undertakings concerned in the administrative procedure **7.51**
are as such not challengeable acts.[183] However, the conditions which the Commission
imposes in its decision with a view to ensuring that the undertakings concerned comply
with the commitments they have entered into vis-à-vis the Commission produce binding
legal effects and may be reviewed by the Union courts.[184]

(3) State aid cases

(a) Regulatory framework

The Commission's supervisory competence and the administrative procedure which it **7.52**
must comply with in relation to State aid are laid down in Arts 107 and 108 TFEU and
in Regulation Nos 659/99[185] and 794/2004.[186] This legal framework makes provision for
separate procedures, depending on whether the aid concerned is existing aid or new aid.

(b) Existing aid

As far as existing aid[187] is concerned, Art. 108(1) TFEU and Arts 17–19 of Regulation **7.53**
No. 659/99 empower the Commission, in cooperation with the Member States, to keep aid
under constant review. Where the Commission considers that existing aid is not, or is no
longer, compatible with the internal market, it informs the Member State concerned of its

---

[182] CFI, Case T-119/02 *Royal Philips Electronics v Commission* [2003] E.C.R. II-1433, paras 267–300;
CFI, Joined Cases T-346/02 and T-347/02 *Cableuropa and Others v Commission* [2003] E.C.R. II-4251, paras
47–82. A decision taken by such national authorities following a referral may be contested only before the
national courts, although they may refer a question to the Court of Justice for a preliminary ruling on
the interpretation of Regulation No. 139/2004. A complaint made to the Commission about the handling of
the case after referral is a complaint under Art. 258 TFEU and the rejection of such a complaint is not a
challengeable act: see CFI (order of 25 May 2005), Case T-443/03 *Retecal and Others v Commission* [2005]
E.C.R. II-1803, paras 34–46. An action brought by a third party against a decision of the Commission
rejecting a request from a national competition authority for partial referral of the case under Art. 9(3) of
Regulation No. 139/2004 will be declared inadmissible, not because of the fact that such decision would not
constitute a reviewable act, but because a third party is considered not to be directly and individually
concerned by such decision: see EGC, Case T-224/10 *Association belge des consommateurs test-achats v
Commission* [2011] E.C.R. II-7177, paras 70–85.
[183] See Regulation No. 139/2004, Arts 6(2) and 8(2); Regulation No. 802/2004, Art. 20. See ECJ, Joined
Cases C-68/94 and C-30/95 *France and Others v Commission ('Kali & Salz')* [1998] E.C.R. I-1375, paras
64–67; CFI (order of 2 September 2009), Case T-57/07 *E.ON Ruhrgas and E.ON Földgáz v Commission*
[2009] E.C.R. II-132*, Summ. pub., paras 30–52.
[184] See in this regard CFI, Joined Cases T-125/97 and T-127/97 *Coca-Cola v Commission* [2000]
E.C.R. II-1733, paras 94–106. See also CFI, Case T-282/02 *Cementbouw Handel & Industrie v Commission*
[2006] E.C.R. II-319, paras 294 and 307–311; CFI, Case T-48/04 *Qualcomm v Commission* [2009]
E.C.R. II-2029, paras 89–90, and 112.
[185] Council Regulation (EC) No. 659/1999 of 22 March 1999 laying down detailed rules for the
application of Art. 93 of the EC Treaty (now Art. 108 TFEU) ([1999] O.J. L83/1).
[186] Commission Regulation (EC) No. 794/2004 of 21 April 2004 implementing Council Regulation (EC)
No. 659/1999 laying down detailed rules for the application of Art. 93 of the EC Treaty (now Art. 108
TFEU) ([2004] O.J. L140/1; *corrigendum* in [2005] O.J. L25/74), as amended by Commission Regulation
(EC) No. 1125/2009 of 23 November 2009 ([2009] O.J. L308/5).
[187] For this concept, see Regulation No. 659/1999, Art. 1(b).

preliminary view and gives the Member State concerned the opportunity to submit its comments. Where the Commission, in the light of the information submitted by the Member State, concludes that the existing aid scheme is not, or is no longer, compatible with the internal market, it will propose to the Member State concerned any appropriate measures required by the progressive development or by the functioning of the internal market. Where the Member State concerned does not accept the proposed measures and the Commission, having taken into account the arguments of the Member State concerned, still considers that those measures are necessary, it will initiate the procedure provided for in Art. 108(2) TFEU.

Therefore, as far as existing aid is concerned, the initiative lies with the Commission.[188] If the Commission considers that there is existing aid whose compatibility with the internal market it wishes to re-examine, it cannot require the Member State concerned to suspend that aid before it has taken a final decision holding it incompatible with the internal market. For its part, the Member State is not under any obligation to suspend existing aid before such final decision.[189]

(c) New aid

7.54 As far as new aid is concerned,[190] Art. 108(3) TFEU and Art. 2(1) of Regulation No. 659/1999 provide that the Commission is to be informed, in sufficient time, of any plans to grant or alter aid. The Commission then proceeds to an initial examination of the planned aid. If, at the end of that examination, it considers that the notified measure does not constitute aid, it will make such finding in a decision pursuant to Art. 4(2) of Regulation No. 659/1999. Where the Commission, after a preliminary examination, finds that no doubts are raised as to the compatibility with the internal market of a notified measure, it will decide that the measure is compatible with the internal market in a 'decision not to raise objections' pursuant to Art. 4(3) of Regulation No. 659/1999. If the Commission has doubts as to the compatibility with the internal market of the measure concerned, it will adopt a decision pursuant to Art. 4(4) of Regulation No. 659/1999 to initiate the formal investigation procedure provided for in Art. 108(2) TFEU.[191] Such a decision is to call upon the Member State concerned and upon other interested parties to submit comments within a prescribed period, which must

---

[188] ECJ, Case C-44/93 *Namur-Les assurances du crédit* [1994] E.C.R. I-3829, para. 11; ECJ (judgment of 18 July 2013), Case C-6/12 P *Oy*, not reported, paras 40–41.

[189] ECJ, Case C-400/99 *Italy v Commission* [2001] E.C.R. I-7303, para. 48; ECJ (judgment of 29 November 2012), Case C-262/11 *Kremikovtzi*, not reported, para. 49; ECJ (judgment of 18 July 2013), Case C-6/12 P, not reported, paras 40–41.

[190] ECJ, Case C-295/97 *Piaggio* [1999] E.C.R. I-3735, paras 47–48: the answer to the question whether aid is new cannot depend on a subjective assessment by the Commission. According to Art. 1(c) of Regulation No. 659/1999, new aid is aid which is not existing. Art. 1(b) of Regulation No. 659/1999 provides a list of all aid which must be regarded as existing aid.

[191] See Art. 4(4) of Regulation No. 659/1999. Proceedings must also be initiated where the Commission has doubts whether the measure should be categorized as aid unless, in the course of the initial examination, the Commission is able to satisfy itself that the measure at issue is in any event compatible with the internal market, even if it is aid (CFI, Case T-11/95 *BP Chemicals v Commission* [1998] E.C.R. II-3235, para. 166; CFI, Case T-46/97 *SIC v Commission* [2000] E.C.R. 2125, para. 72). This case-law was confirmed by ECJ, Case C-400/99 *Italy v Commission* [2005] E.C.R. I-3657, para. 47 and ECJ, Case C-487/06 P *British Aggregates v Commission* [2008] E.C.R. I-10515, para. 113. The fact that the time spent on an initial examination under Art. 108(3) TFEU considerably exceeds the time usually taken may, in addition to other factors, justify the conclusion that the Commission encountered serious difficulties of assessment necessitating initiation of the procedure under Art. 108(2) TFEU (CFI, Case T-46/97 *SIC v Commission* [2000] E.C.R. II-2125, para. 102).

not, as a rule, exceed one month.[192] This formal investigation procedure will be closed by one of the decisions mentioned in Art. 7 of Regulation No. 659/1999, namely: (a) a decision pursuant to Art. 7(2) of Regulation No. 659/1999 by which the Commission finds that no aid within the meaning of Art. 107(1) TFEU is being granted; (b) a decision pursuant to Art. 7(3) or (4) of Regulation No. 659/1999 (to which conditions may be attached) by which the Commission finds that the aid is compatible with the internal market; or (c) a decision pursuant to Art. 7(5) of Regulation No. 659/1999 in which the Commission finds that the aid is incompatible with the internal market.

The last sentence of Art. 108(3) TFEU prohibits the Member State concerned from putting the proposed measures into effect until the procedure has resulted in a final decision.[193] New aid is therefore subject to preventive review by the Commission, and in principle cannot be put into effect as long as that institution has not declared it compatible with the Treaties.[194]

(d) Final decisions

Irrespective of whether existing aid or new aid is involved, Commission decisions by which **7.55** national measures are held to be aid and compatible or incompatible with the internal market produce binding legal effects and constitute challengeable acts.[195] The same is true of decisions by which the Commission determines that a measure of a Member State does not constitute aid within the meaning of Art. 107(1) TFEU.[196]

It is irrelevant for the classification of an act as a reviewable act whether or not it satisfies certain formal requirements, in particular that it is duly identified by its author and that it mentions the provisions providing the legal basis for it. It is therefore irrelevant that the act may not be described as a 'decision' or that it does not refer to Art. 4 or Art. 7 of Regulation No. 659/1999. It is also of no importance that the Member State concerned was not notified of the act at issue by the Commission, infringing Art. 25 of that Regulation, as such an error is not capable of altering the substance of that act.[197]

---

[192] Art. 6(1) of Regulation No. 659/1999.

[193] See also Regulation No. 659/1999, Art. 3.

[194] ECJ, Case C-44/93 *Namur-Les Assurances du Crédit* [1994] E.C.R. I-3829, para. 12; ECJ (judgment of 21 November 2011), Case C-284/12 *Deutsche Lufthansa*, not reported, paras 25–26 (and case-law cited). While assessment of the compatibility of aid measures with the internal market falls within the exclusive competence of the Commission, subject to review by the Union courts, it is for the national courts to ensure that the rights of individuals are safeguarded where the obligation to give prior notification of state aid to the Commission pursuant to Art. 108(3) TFEU has been infringed: see ECJ (judgment of December 8, 2011), Case C-275/10 *Residex Capital*, not reported, para. 27 (and case-law cited therein).

[195] A decision of the Council pursuant to Art. 108(2), third para. TFEU by which aid is considered to be compatible with the internal market by way of derogation from the provisions of Art. 107 TFEU or from the regulations provided for in Art. 109 TFEU is also a challengeable act (see ECJ, Case C-110/02 *Commission v Council* [2004] E.C.R. I-6333). By contrast, a letter confirming the content of an earlier decision does not constitute a reviewable act: see EGC (order of 13 April 2010), Joined Cases T-529/08 and T-531/08 *Territorio Histórico de Álava and Others v Commission* [2010] E.C.R. II-53*, Summ. pub., paras 29–31; EGC (order of 7 February 2011), Case T-330/09 *Rapideye v Commission* [2011] E.C.R. II-26*, Summ. pub., paras 28–29.

[196] ECJ, Case C-367/95 P *Commission v Sytraval and Brink's France* [1998] E.C.R. I-1719, paras 45–48; CFI, Case T-351/02 *Deutsche Bahn v Commission* [2006] E.C.R. II-1047, paras 34–62.

[197] See ECJ, Case C-521/06 P *Athinaiki Techniki v Commission* [2008] E.C.R. I-5829, paras 43–44 (and case-law cited therein); ECJ, Case C-322/09 P *NDSHT v Commission* [2010] E.C.R. I-11911, para. 47.

(e) *Undertakings by the Member State concerned*

7.56 An undertaking entered into by a Member State during the course of the administrative proceedings and mentioned only in the recitals of the Commission decision has to be considered to be a voluntary modification of the notification and is not as such a reviewable act.[198] Indeed, regardless of the grounds on which such a decision is based, only the operative part thereof is capable of producing legal effects and, as a consequence, of adversely affecting the interests of the applicant.[199]

(f) *Initiation of the procedure*

7.57 Another question is whether the initiation of the formal investigation procedure provided for in Art. 108(2) TFEU and Art. 6(1) of Regulation No. 659/1999[200] constitutes a challengeable act in itself. Under these provisions, the Commission has to give notice to the 'interested parties' to submit their comments before it decides whether aid is compatible with the internal market.

It is settled case-law that the initiation of that procedure produces no legal effects and therefore cannot be challenged before the Union courts where it relates to existing aid,[201] since the Member State concerned may maintain the aid at that stage of the procedure.[202] Where, in contrast, the procedure initiated relates to a measure which the Commission considers to constitute new aid, the decision to initiate the formal investigation procedure, which will be based on Art. 4(4) of Regulation No. 659/1999, will constitute a challengeable act.[203] Such a decision entails independent legal effects,[204] particularly in relation to the suspension of the measure under consideration since, according to Art. 108(3) TFEU, a proposed aid measure must not be put into effect until the investigation procedure has resulted in a final decision.[205] The initiation decision will be challengeable not only where a

---

[198] CFI (order of 9 July 2007), Case T-6/06 *Wheyco v Commission*, not reported, paras 95–96.

[199] CFI (order of 9 July 2007), Case T-6/06 *Wheyco v Commission*, not reported, para. 94 (and case-law cited therein): the assessments made in the recitals to a decision are not in themselves capable of forming the subject of an application for annulment. They can be subject to judicial review by the Union judicature only to the extent that, as grounds of an act adversely affecting a person's interests, they constitute the essential basis for the operative part of that act.

[200] Such decision will be grounded on Art. 4(4) of Regulation No. 659/1999.

[201] ECJ (order of the President of 26 June 2003), Joined Cases C-182/03 R and C-217/03 R *Belgium and Forum 187 v Commission* [2003] E.C.R. I-6887, para. 119; CFI (order of 2 June 2003), Case T-267/02 *Forum 187 v Commission* [2003] E.C.R. II-2075. For a list of all measures to be regarded as being existing aid, see Art. 1(b) of Regulation No. 659/1999 ([1999] O.J. L83/1).

[202] As far as existing aid is concerned, the Commission's proposal of appropriate measures under Art. 108(1) TFEU is also not a reviewable act. See CFI, Case T-330/94 *Salt Union v Commission* [1996] E.C.R. II-1475, paras 31–38.

[203] ECJ, Case C-312/90 *Spain v Commission* [1992] E.C.R. I-4117, paras 11–26; ECJ, Case C-47/91 *Italy v Commission* [1992] E.C.R. I-4145, paras 19–32; ECJ, Case C-400/99 *Italy v Commission* [2001] E.C.R. I-7303, paras 45–70; CFI, Joined Cases T-269/99, T-271/99 and T-272/99 *Diputación Foral de Guipúzcoa and Others v Commission* [2002] II-4217, paras 37–40; CFI, Case T-332/06 *Alcoa Transformazioni v Commission* [2009] E.C.R. II-29*, Summ. pub., paras 35–36; EGC, Joined Cases T-394/08, T-408/08, T-453/08, and T-454/08 *Regione Autonoma della Sardegna v Commission* [2011] E.C.R. II-6255, para. 77.

[204] As a result, an action to annul the decision to initiate the formal procedure does not become devoid of purpose where the Commission adopts a final decision and that decision is not contested by the party which challenged the decision initiating the procedure: see ECJ, Case C-400/99 *Italy v Commission* [2005] E.C.R. I-3657, paras 15–18.

[205] ECJ, Case C-400/99 *Italy v Commission* [2001] E.C.R. I-7303, para. 62; CFI, Joined Cases T-346/99 to T-348/99 *Diputación Foral de Álava and Others v Commission* [2002] E.C.R. II-4259, para. 33; CFI, Case T-332/06 *Alcoa Transformazioni v Commission* [2009] E.C.R. II-29*, Summ. pub., para. 35.

measure in the course of implementation is regarded by the authorities of the Member State concerned as existing aid, but also where these authorities take the view that the measure to be formally investigated does not fall within the scope of Art. 107(1) TFEU.[206]

Indeed, a decision to initiate the formal investigation procedure pursuant to Art. 4(4) of Regulation No. 659/1999 in relation to a measure in the course of implementation and classified by the Commission as new aid necessarily alters the legal implications of the measure under consideration and the legal position of the recipient firms, particularly as regards the continued implementation of the measure. Until the adoption of such a decision, the Member State, the recipient firms, and other economic operators may think that the measure is being lawfully implemented as a general measure not falling within the scope of Art. 107(1) TFEU or as existing aid. After the adoption of the decision to initiate the procedure, there is at the very least a significant element of doubt as to the legality of the measure which, without prejudice to the possibility of seeking interim relief from the Court, must lead the Member State to suspend its application, since the initiation of the formal investigation procedure excludes the possibility of an immediate decision that the measure is compatible with the internal market, which would enable it to continue to be lawfully implemented. Such a decision might also be invoked before a national court called upon to draw all the consequences arising from infringement of the last sentence of Art. 108(3) TFEU. Finally, it is capable of leading the firms which are beneficiaries of the measure to refuse in any event new payments or new advantages or to hold the necessary sums as provision for possible subsequent financial compensations. Businesses will also take account, in their relations with those beneficiaries, of the uncertainty cast on the legal and financial situation of the latter.[207] An action for annulment will therefore lie against a decision to initiate the formal investigation procedure pursuant to Art. 4(4) of Regulation No. 659/199, where the action is brought by a Member State or by a beneficiary of the measure.[208] Such a decision is, however, considered not to alter the legal position of a competitor of the beneficiary of the measure. Accordingly, an action for annulment of a

---

[206] ECJ, Case C-400/99 *Italy v Commission* [2001] E.C.R. I-7303, paras 59, 60, and 69; ECJ (judgment of 24 October 2013), Case C-77/12 P *Deutsche Post v Commission*, not reported, para. 53; CFI, Joined Cases T-346/99 to T-348/99 *Diputación Foral de Álava and Others v Commission* [2002] E.C.R. II-4259, para. 33; CFI, Case T-332/06 *Alcoa Transformazioni v Commission* [2009] E.C.R. II-29*, Summ. pub., para. 35. See further EGC (judgment of 13 February 2012), Joined Cases T-80/06 and T-182/09 *Budapesti Erőmű Zrt v Commission*, not reported, para. 37.

[207] ECJ, Case C-400/99 *Italy v Commission* [2001] E.C.R. I-7303, paras 59 and 69; ECJ (judgment of 24 October 2013), Case C-77/12 P *Deutsche Post v Commission*, not reported, para. 52; CFI, Joined Cases T-195/01 and T-207/01 *Government of Gibraltar v Commission* [2002] E.C.R. II-2309, para. 85; CFI, Joined Cases T-346/99 to T-348/99 *Diputación Foral de Álava and Others v Commission* [2002] E.C.R. II-4259, para. 34; CFI, Case T-332/06 *Alcoa Transformazioni v Commission* [2009] E.C.R. II-29*, Summ. pub., para. 36; EGC (judgment of 13 February 2012), Joined Cases T-80/06 and T-182/09 *Budapesti Erőmű v Commission*, not reported, paras 38–40 (the fact that the Member State concerned did not raise objections during the preliminary procedure as regards the measure at issue being classified as new aid is not relevant to categoriza-tion of that measure as a challengeable act with regard to the applicant). With respect to the binding character of a decision to initiate proceedings before a national court, see ECJ (judgment of 21 November 2011), Case C-284/12 *Deutsche Lufthansa*, not reported, paras 36–44.

[208] ECJ (judgment of 24 October 2013), Case C-77/12 P *Deutsche Post v Commission*, not reported, para. 55; EGC (judgment of 13 February 2012), Joined Cases T-80/06 and T-182/09 *Budapesti Erőmű v Commission*, not reported, paras 41–42.

decision adopted pursuant to Art. 4(4) of Regulation No. 659/1999 brought by a competitor will be declared inadmissible.[209]

It should be stressed that classification of a measure as State aid in a decision to initiate the formal investigation procedure is provisional.[210] The very aim of initiating the procedure is to enable the Commission to obtain all the views it needs in order to be able to adopt a definitive decision on that point (as well as—if the measure constitutes aid—on the compatibility of the measure with the internal market).[211] In order to avoid confusion between the administrative and judicial proceedings and to preserve the division of powers between the Commission and the Union courts, any review by the General Court of the legality of a decision to initiate the formal investigation procedure must necessarily be limited. The Union judicature must in fact avoid giving a final ruling on questions on which the Commission has merely formed a provisional view.[212] Thus, where in an action against a decision to initiate the formal investigation procedure the applicants challenge the Commission's assessment of a measure as constituting State aid, review by the Union judicature is limited to ascertaining whether or not the Commission has made a manifest error of assessment in forming the view that it was unable to resolve all the difficulties on that point during its initial examination of the measure concerned.[213]

(g) Suspension and recovery injunctions

7.58   An action will also lie against an injunction to suspend or recover aid that the Commission may address to a Member State by separate decision (before taking a final decision with regard to the compatibility of the aid with the internal market) under Art. 11(1) and (2) of Regulation No. 659/1999.[214]

---

[209] CFI (order of 25 November 2009), Case T-87/09 *Andersen v Commission* [2009] E.C.R. II-225*, not reported, paras 49–63.

[210] For this reason, the right to contest a decision to initiate the procedure provided for in Art. 108(2) TFEU does not affect the procedural rights of interested parties to challenge the final decision. The latter decision can indeed not be held to be confirmatory of the decision to initiate the procedure. See in that respect CFI, Case T-190/00 *Regione Siciliana v Commission* [2003] E.C.R. II-5015 paras 42–53; EGC, Joined Cases T-394/08, T-408/08, T-453/08, and T-454/08 *Regione Autonoma della Sardegna v Commission* [2011] E.C.R. II-6255, para. 78.

[211] CFI, Joined Cases T-346/99 to T-348/99 *Diputación Foral de Álava and Others v Commission* [2002] E.C.R. II-4259, para 43; CFI, Case T-332/06 *Alcoa Transformazioni v Commission* [2009] E.C.R. II-29*, Summ. pub., para. 60.

[212] CFI, Joined Cases T-346/99 to T-348/99 *Diputación Foral de Álava and Others v Commission* [2002] E.C.R. II-4259, para 44; CFI, Case T-332/06 *Alcoa Transformazioni v Commission* [2009] E.C.R. II-29*, Summ. pub., para. 61. See also ECJ, Case 60/81 *IBM v Commission* [1981] E.C.R. 1857, para. 20.

[213] CFI, Joined Cases T-346/99 to T-348/99 *Diputación Foral de Álava and Others v Commission* [2002] E.C.R. II-4259, para 45; CFI, Case T-332/06 *Alcoa Transformazioni v Commission* [2009] E.C.R. II-29*, Summ. pub., para. 62. By contrast, the Court's review of the question whether the measure is 'new' as opposed to 'existing' is complete. The Commission is indeed not entitled to open the formal investigation procedure of Art. 108(2) TFEU with respect to existing aid if it did not first propose appropriate measures under Art. 108(1) TFEU (see in this respect CFI, Joined Cases T-195/01 and T-207/01 *Government of Gibraltar v Commission* [2002] E.C.R. II-2309, paras 105–116). In Case C-400/99 *Italy v Commission* [2005] E.C.R. I-3657, the ECJ partially annulled the decision to initiate the procedure on procedural grounds: the Commission had infringed the Member State's right to submit observations before adopting the contested decision (paras 29–34).

[214] The Commission's power to issue such injunctions was already recognized by case-law: ECJ, Case C-301/87 *France v Commission* [1990] E.C.R. I-307, paras 19 and 22; ECJ, C-39/94 *SFEI and Others* [1996] E.C.R. I-3547, para. 34. See also ECJ, Case C-400/99 *Italy v Commission* [2001] E.C.R. I-7303, para. 51.

(h) Information injunction

In the course of the administrative procedure, the Commission may address a request for **7.59** information to the Member State concerned.[215] Where, despite a reminder, the Member State does not provide the information requested within the period prescribed by the Commission, or where it provides incomplete information, the Commission may by decision require the information to be provided. Such 'information injunction' is a reviewable act.[216] In the event of non-compliance with an information injunction, the Commission will decide on the basis of the information available.[217]

(i) Right to file a complaint

As regards the position of complainants, Art. 20(2) of Regulation No. 659/1999 provides **7.60** that '[a]ny interested party may inform the Commission of any alleged unlawful aid and any alleged misuse of aid'.[218] It follows from Art. 20(1) and (2) of Regulation No. 659/1999 that the interested parties entitled to file a complaint are those which may submit comments following a Commission decision to initiate the formal investigation procedure. They include, according to Art. 1(h) of Regulation No. 659/1999, '[...] any person, undertaking or association of undertakings whose interests might be affected by the granting of aid, in particular [...] competing undertakings and trade associations [...]'.[219]

(j) Decisions pursuant to a complaint

In so far as the Commission has exclusive jurisdiction to assess the compatibility of a grant **7.61** of State aid with the internal market, in the interests of the sound administration of the fundamental rules of the Treaties relating to State aid, it is required to conduct a diligent and impartial examination of complaints reporting the grant of aid which is incompatible with the internal market.[220] After examining the complaint, the Commission takes one of

---

[215] Regulation No. 659/1999, Art. 10(2).

[216] Regulation No. 659/1999, Art. 10(3). ECJ, Joined Cases C-463/10 P and C-475/10 P *Deutsche Post and Germany v Commission* [2011] E.C.R. I-9639, para. 45.

[217] In the context of an action for annulment under Art. 263 TFEU, the legality of a Union measure must be assessed on the basis of the elements of fact and of law existing at the time when the measure was adopted. In particular, the complex assessments made by the Commission must be examined solely on the basis of the information available to the Commission at the time when those assessments were made (ECJ, Joined Cases 15/76 and 16/76 *France v Commission* [1979] E.C.R. 321, para. 7; ECJ, Case C-288/96 *Germany v Commission* [2000] E.C.R. I-8237, para. 34; CFI, Joined Cases T-371/94 and T-394/94 *British Airways and Others and British Midland Airways v Commission* [1998] E.C.R. II-2405, para. 81; CFI, Case T-123/97 *Salomon v Commission* [1999] E.C.R. II-2925, para. 42; CFI, Case T-296/97 *Alitalia v Commission* [2000] E.C.R. II-3871, para. 86; CFI, Case T-109/01 *Fleuren Compost v Commission* [2004] E.C.R. II-127, para. 50; CFI, Joined Cases T-111/01 and T-133/01 *Saxonia Edelmetalle and Zemag v Commission* [2005] E.C.R. II-1579, para. 67; EGC, Case T-11/07 *Frucona Košice v Commission* [2010] E.C.R. II-5453, para. 48.

[218] For the form to be used for filing a complaint, see [2003] O.J. C116/3.

[219] That provision does not rule out the possibility that an undertaking which is not a direct competitor of the beneficiary of the aid can be categorized as an interested party, provided that undertaking demonstrates that its interests could be adversely affected by the grant of the aid: see ECJ, Case C-83/09 P *Commission v Kronoply and Kronotex* [2011] E.C.R. I-4441, paras 64–65. For that purpose, it is necessary for that undertaking to establish, to the requisite legal standard, that the aid is likely to have a specific effect on its situation: see ECJ, Case C-319/07 P *3F v Commission* [2009] E.C.R. I-5963, para. 33.

[220] CFI, Case T-17/96 *TF1 v Commission* [1999] E.C.R. II-1757, para. 73. See also Art. 10(1) of Regulation No. 659/1999, which obliges the Commission to examine: '[...] information from whatever source regarding alleged unlawful aid'. Diligent and impartial examination of the complaint may make it necessary for the Commission to examine matters not expressly raised by the complainant. The Commission may therefore be obliged to extend its investigation beyond a mere examination of the facts and the points of

the following decisions—unless it considers on the basis of the information in its possession that there are insufficient grounds for taking a view on the case[221]—all of which will be addressed to the Member State concerned:[222] (a) a decision pursuant to Art. 4(2) of Regulation No. 659/1999 by which the Commission finds that no aid within the meaning of Art. 107(1) TFEU is being granted; (b) a decision pursuant to Art. 4(3) of Regulation No. 659/1999 by which the Commission finds that the aid is compatible with the internal market; or (c) if it has doubts as to the compatibility with the internal market of a notified measure, a decision pursuant to Art. 4(4) of Regulation No. 659/1999 to initiate proceedings pursuant to Art. 108(2) TFEU and Art. 6(1) of Regulation No. 659/1999, in which case all interested parties, in particular the complainant and the Member States, may submit comments.[223] The first two decisions, which are to be addressed to the Member State concerned,[224] may be contested by the complainant, if it demonstrates that they are of direct and individual concern to it within the meaning of the fourth paragraph of Art. 263 TFEU.[225] The complainant will have no interest in challenging the initiation of proceedings under Art. 108(2) TFEU and Art. 6(1) of Regulation No. 659/1999.[226] This is because the complaint will normally aim to have the aid declared incompatible with the internal market and this can only happen after the Commission has gone through the procedure prescribed by Art. 108(2) TFEU and Art. 6(1) of Regulation No. 659/1999.[227]

---

law brought to its notice by the complainant (see ECJ, Case C-367/95 *Commission v Sytraval and Brink's France* [1998] E.C.R. I-1719, para. 62).

[221] See Regulation No. 659/1999, Art. 20(2). It follows from Art. 10(1) of Regulation No. 659/1999, according to which the Commission has to examine any possible unlawful aid, read in conjunction with Art. 13(1), according to which 'the examination of possible unlawful aid shall result in a decision pursuant to Art. 4(2), (3) or (4) [i.e. a decision finding that the measure does not constitute aid, a decision finding that no doubts are raised as to the compatibility with the internal market, or a decision initiating proceedings pursuant to Art. 108(2)]' that the Commission has not much scope for responding to a complainant that there are no grounds for taking a view on the case.

[222] Regulation No. 659/1999, Art. 25. See also ECJ, Case C-367/95 *Commission v Sytraval and Brink's France* [1998] E.C.R. I-1719, para. 45.

[223] Regulation No. 659/1999, Art. 4. See also CFI, Case T-17/96 *TF1 v Commission* [1999] E.C.R. II-1757, para. 78; ECJ (judgment of 19 March 2013), Case C-401/10 P *Bouygues and Others v Commission*, not reported, paras 76–78.

[224] Regulation No. 659/1999, Art. 25. An action will not lie against a letter from the Commission informing the complainant about its decision addressed to a Member State with regard to State aid (CFI, Case T-82/96 *ARAP and Others v Commission* [1999] E.C.R. II-1889, para. 28). As a result, the complainant should challenge the decision addressed to the Member State. The latter action will be admissible only if the decision is of direct and individual concern to the complainant within the meaning of the fourth para. of Art. 263 TFEU. But see, however, CFI, Case T-351/02 *Deutsche Bahn v Commission* [2006] E.C.R. II-1047, paras 34–62, in which the CFI found that a Commission letter addressed to the complainant in which the alleged measure was held not to constitute aid, was in substance a decision pursuant to Art. 4(2) of Regulation No. 659/1999, which was addressed to the complainant and not, as it was incumbent on the Commission under Art. 25 of said Regulation, to the Member State concerned. In that particular case, there was therefore no need to examine whether the complainant was directly and individually concerned by the 'no aid' decision adopted pursuant to Art. 4(2) of Regulation No. 659/1999.

[225] ECJ, Case C-322/09 P *NDSHT v Commission* [2010] E.C.R. I-11911, paras 51, 53, and 54. See also paras 7.90–7.100. However, preparatory acts before reaching such a decision are not reviewable: see EGC (order of 9 January 2012), Case T-407/09 *Neubrandenburger Wohnungsgesellschaft v Commission*, not reported, paras 28–35.

[226] See CFI (order of 25 November 2009), Case T-87/09 *Andersen v Commission* [2009] E.C.R. II-225*, Summ. pub., paras 49–63.

[227] The formal investigation procedure does not lead to an *inter partes* debate involving the complainant, or even the recipient, of the aid. The comments received in the course of the formal investigation will only be submitted to the Member State concerned (Regulation No. 659/1999, Art. 6 (2)). See also CFI, Case T-613/97

If the Commission considers, after having received a complaint, that on the basis of the information in its possession there are insufficient grounds for taking a view on the case, it will inform the complainant thereof.[228] Such act based on Art. 20(2) of Regulation No. 659/1999 also constitutes a reviewable act within the meaning of Art. 263 TFEU.[229] Indeed, by such act, the Commission states that the review it initiated has not enabled it to establish the existence of State aid within the meaning of Art. 107(1) TFEU and it implicitly refuses to initiate the formal investigation procedure provided for in Art. 108(2) TFEU and Art. 6(1) of Regulation No. 659/1999. In such a situation, the persons to whom the procedural guarantees under the latter provision apply may ensure that they are observed only if they are able to challenge that decision before the Union judicature. Furthermore, a dismissal of a complaint on the ground of Art. 20(2) of Regulation No. 659/1999 cannot be classified as a preliminary or a preparatory act, since it cannot be followed, in the context of the administrative procedure which has been initiated, by any other decision amenable to annulment proceedings.[230]

A decision pursuant to Art. 20(2) of Regulation No. 659/1999 may be challenged independently of whether or not the Commission finds in this decision that the aid complained of constitutes new or existing aid. Indeed, where it receives a complaint relating to allegedly unlawful aid, the Commission, in classifying the measure as existing aid, subjects it to the procedure provided for by Art. 108(1) TFEU and thus refuses by implication to initiate the procedure provided for by Art. 108(2) TFEU.[231]

(k) Mere correspondence with complainants

Any letters which the Commission may address to complainants are not acts amenable to judicial review. In principle,[232] only the formal decision addressed to the Member State concerned can be challenged.[233] Thus, an action for annulment lodged by a complainant against a letter from the Commission informing the complainant that a specific aid measure   **7.62**

Ufex v Commission [2000] E.C.R. II-4055, paras 85–90; CFI, Case T-198/01 *Technische Glaswerke Ilmenau v Commission* [2004] E.C.R. II-2717, paras 193–198.

[228] See Regulation No. 659/1999, Art. 20(2).

[229] ECJ, Case C-521/06 P *Athinaïki Techniki v Commission* [2008] E.C.R. I-5829, para. 62. See also ECJ, Case C-322/09 P *NDSHT v Commission* [2010] E.C.R. I-11911, paras 58–60.

[230] ECJ, Case C-521/06 P *Athinaïki Techniki v Commission* [2008] E.C.R. I-5829, paras 52–54. The ECJ added that it is not relevant, in that regard, that the interested party may still provide the Commission with additional information which might oblige the Commission to review its position on the State measure at issue. Indeed, the lawfulness of a decision taken at the end of the preliminary examination stage is examined only on the basis of the information which the Commission had at its disposal at the time the contested act was adopted. If an interested party provides additional information after the closing of the file, the Commission can be obliged to open a new administrative procedure, if appropriate. By contrast, that information has no effect on the fact that the first preliminary examination procedure is already closed (ECJ, Case C-521/06 P *Athinaïki Techniki v Commission*, paras 55–57). See also ECJ, Case C-322/09 P *NDSHT v Commission* [2010] E.C.R. I-11911, paras 51–55.

[231] ECJ, Case C-313/90 *CIRFS and Others v Commission* [1993] E.C.R. I-1125, paras 25–27; ECJ, Case C-321/99 P *ARAP and Others v Commission* [2002] E.C.R. I-4287, paras 61–62; ECJ, Case C-322/09 P *NDSHT v Commission* [2010] E.C.R. I-11911, paras 52–54.

[232] However, the decision based on Art. 20(2) of Regulation No. 659/1999 is addressed to the complainant. See para. 7.61.

[233] See ECJ, Case C-367/95 *Commission v Sytraval and Brink's France* [1998] E.C.R. I-1719, para. 45; CFI (order of 14 February 2005), Case T-81/04 *Bouygues and Bouygues Télécom v Commission*, not reported, para. 23; CFI (order of 14 May 2009), Case T-22/07 *US Steel Košice v Commission* [2009] E.C.R. II-61*, Summ. pub., paras 42 *et seq.*

is covered by an approved general aid scheme will be inadmissible.[234] By contrast, a similar action brought against a decision addressed to a Member State in which the Commission raises no objections to an aid measure on the grounds that it falls within the scope of an approved aid scheme will be admissible insofar as the complainant demonstrates that the contested act is of direct and individual concern to it within the meaning of the fourth paragraph of Art. 263 TFEU.[235]

(l) Refusal to take appropriate measures

7.63   Finally, as regards existing aid, an action will not lie against the Commission's refusal to take appropriate measures within the meaning of Art. 108(1) TFEU.[236] It should be borne in mind that when the Court is considering whether an action for the annulment of a negative decision of an institution is admissible, the decision must be appraised in the light of the nature of the request to which it constitutes a reply. Since, according to the wording of Art. 108(1) TFEU, appropriate measures are merely proposals, which the Member State concerned is not bound to respect,[237] the Commission's refusal to take such measures does not constitute an act producing binding legal effects.

(4) Anti-dumping cases

(a) General

7.64   The final decision in an anti-dumping procedure normally lies with the Council. It imposes definitive anti-dumping duties or decides to terminate the anti-dumping procedure without imposing such duties. It also decides on the definitive imposition of provisional anti-dumping duties. Such regulations and decisions produce legal effects and constitute challengeable acts.[238]

(b) Preparatory measures

7.65   Regulation No. 1225/2009[239] confers extensive duties on the Commission in connection with the investigation of dumping and the provisional control thereof. It receives complaints, initiates investigations, and decides whether or not protective measures are needed. Various acts adopted by the Commission pursuant to that Regulation are preparatory and hence cannot be the subject of an application for annulment, the reason being that sufficient protection is afforded by bringing an action for annulment against the final decision. Examples of acts against which an action will not lie are: a decision to

---

[234]   CFI, Case T-154/94 *CSF and CSME v Commission* [1996] E.C.R. II-1377, paras 37–54; but see ECJ, Case C-313/90 *CIRFS and Others v Commission* [1993] E.C.R. I-1125, paras 25–27.

[235]   ECJ, Case C-321/99 *ARAP and Others v Commission* [2002] E.C.R. I-4287, paras 60 and 61.

[236]   CFI, Case T-330/94 *Salt Union v Commission* [1996] E.C.R. II-1475, paras 31–38.

[237]   ECJ (order of the President of 26 June 2003), Joined Cases C-182/03 R and C-217/03 R *Belgium and Forum 187 v Commission* [2003] E.C.R. I-6887, para. 119. However, where the Member State concerned accepts the proposed measures and informs the Commission thereof, it will be bound by its acceptance to implement the appropriate measures (see in this respect Regulation No. 659/1999, Art. 19(1)).

[238]   ECJ, Case C-121/86 *Epicheiriseon Metalleftikon Viomichanikon kai Naftiliakon and Others v Council* [1989] E.C.R. I-3919; ECJ, Case C-76/01 *Eurocoton and Others v Council* [2003] E.C.R. I-10091, para. 72.

[239]   Council Regulation (EC) No. 1225/2009 of 30 November 2009 on protection against dumped imports from countries not members of the European Community ([2009] O.J. L343/51) repealed Council Regulation (EC) No. 384/96 of 22 December 1995 on protection against dumped imports from countries not members of the European Community ([1996] O.J. L56/1). The new Regulation is basically a codified version of the old one. The existing case-law still refers to the old Regulation No. 384/96.

initiate an anti-dumping procedure;[240] the initiation of an interim review of anti-dumping measures;[241] a proposal submitted by the Commission to the Council, following an objection raised in the Advisory Committee, to terminate the procedure without imposing protective measures;[242] a decision of the Commission rejecting an undertaking offered by the company concerned in return for the termination of the anti-dumping investigation;[243] and a Commission decision terminating an undertaking breached by an exporter.[244]

(c) Definitive measures

Some acts adopted by the Commission in anti-dumping procedures have definitive **7.66** legal effects and may be challenged by means of an action for annulment. Examples of such acts include:[245] a Commission decision rejecting a request for initiation of a partial interim review of anti-dumping measures;[246] a Commission decision to terminate the anti-dumping procedure without imposing anti-dumping duties;[247] and a Commission regulation imposing provisional anti-dumping duties.[248]

Similarly, a Commission notice of initiation of an expiry review of anti-dumping or countervailing measures applicable to imports of certain goods is a reviewable act, since such notice has the effect that the measures concerned by the review remain in force until the conclusion of that review, whereas they would have expired if the review had not taken place.[249]

As far as Commission regulations imposing provisional anti-dumping duties are concerned, an action for the annulment of such a regulation will become devoid of purpose when the

---

[240] CFI (order of 14 March 1996), Case T-134/95 *Dysan Magnetics and Review Magnetics v Commission* [1996] E.C.R. II-181, para. 23 and CFI (order of 10 December 1996), Case T-75/96 *Söktas v Commission* [1996] E.C.R. II-1689, paras 26–43.

[241] CFI (order of 25 May 1998), Case T-267/97 *Broome & Wellington v Commission* [1998] E.C.R. II-2191, para. 29; EGC, Case T-369/08 *EWRIA and Others v Commission* [2010] E.C.R. II-6283, para. 37. By contrast, a Commission decision rejecting a request for initiation of a partial interim review of anti-dumping measures is a reviewable act, since it cannot be followed by any other measure amenable to annulment proceedings: see EGC, Case T-369/08 *EWRIA and Others v Commission* [2010] E.C.R. II-6283, para. 37.

[242] CFI, Case T-212/95 *Oficemen v Commission* [1997] E.C.R. II-1161, paras 45–54.

[243] ECJ, Joined Cases C-133/87 and C-150/87 *Nashua Corporation and Others v Commission and Council* [1990] E.C.R. I-719, paras 8–11; ECJ, Case C-156/87 *Gestetner Holdings v Council and Commission* [1990] E.C.R. I-781, para. 8.

[244] CFI (order of 10 July 1996), Case T-208/95 *Miwon v Commission* [1996] E.C.R. II-635, para. 31.

[245] Note that an action will also lie against a decision of the Commission denying a third party access to the non-confidential file: ECJ, Case C-170/89 *BEUC v Commission* [1991] E.C.R. I-5709, para. 11.

[246] EGC, Case T-369/08 *EWRIA and Others v Commission* [2010] E.C.R. II-6283, paras 30–43.

[247] ECJ, Case C-315/90 *Gimelec and Others v Commission* [1991] E.C.R. I-5589; ECJ, Case C-76/01 *Eurocoton and Others v Council* [2003] E.C.R. I-10091, para. 72; CFI (order of 13 November 2008), Case T-301/06 *Lemaître Sécurité v Commission* [2008] E.C.R. II-261*, Summ. pub., para. 19.

[248] In EGC (order of 11 October 2011), Case T-297/10 *DBV v Commission* [2011] E.C.R. II-356*, Summ. pub., the General Court examined the substance of the case without examining the plea of inadmissibility raised by the Commission. The General Court referred to that effect to the '*Boehringer* case-law' (ECG, Case T-297/10 *DBV v Commission*, para. 12): see ECJ, Case C-23/00 P *Council v Boehringer* [2002] E.C.R. I-1873, paras 51–52; see also CFI, Joined Cases T-217/99, T-321/00, and T-222/01 *Sinaga v Commission*, not reported, para. 68.

[249] CFI, Case T-45/06 *Reliance Industries v Council and Commission* [2008] E.C.R. II-2399, para. 37. The fact that the applicant did not challenge the regulation which concluded the review does not cause the applicant to lose its interest in seeking annulment of the review notice (CFI, Case T-45/06 *Reliance Industries v Council and Commission*, paras 33–44).

Council takes a decision with regard to the imposition of definitive anti-dumping duties.[250] This does not prevent irregularities committed by the Commission in the course of the procedure leading to the imposition of provisional anti-dumping duties from being raised in order to claim that the Council regulation imposing definitive anti-dumping duties should be annulled, provided that the Council regulation takes the place of the Commission regulation. If, however, the defects are remedied in the course of the procedure resulting in the imposition of definitive anti-dumping duties, the unlawfulness of the Commission regulation will no longer affect the legality of the Council regulation.[251]

Not only the Council regulation imposing definitive anti-dumping duties may be contested in judicial proceedings.[252] The tacit rejection by the Council (on account of failure to achieve the requisite majority in the Council) of the Commission's proposal for a regulation imposing definitive anti-dumping duties also constitutes a reviewable act.[253]

(5) Access to documents pursuant to Regulation No. 1049/2001

7.67 Regulation No. 1049/2001[254] defines the principles, conditions, and limits governing the right of access by the public to European Parliament, Council, and Commission documents laid down by what is now Art. 15 TFEU.[255] A two-stage administrative procedure applies.[256] If an initial application for access to documents is refused,[257] the person

---

[250] ECJ, Case 56/85 *Brother v Commission* [1988] E.C.R. 5655, paras 3–7; ECJ, Joined Cases 294/86 and 77/87 *Technointorg v Commission and Council* [1988] E.C.R. 6077, paras 10–14; EGC (order of 11 January 2013), Joined Cases T-445/11 and T-88/12 *Charron Inox and Almet v Commission and Council*, not reported, para. 31.

[251] CFI, Joined Cases T-159/94 and T-160/94 *Ajinomoto and NutraSweet v Council* [1997] E.C.R. II-2461, para. 87, upheld by ECJ, Joined Cases C-76/98 P and C-77/98 P *Ajinomoto and NutraSweet v Council and Commission* [2001] E.C.R. I-3223, paras 65–72.

[252] An application brought against the Council and the Commission seeking the annulment of a Council regulation imposing definitive anti-dumping duties will be declared inadmissible in so far as it is brought against the Commission: see EGC, Case T-107/08 *Transnational Company 'Kazchrome' and ENRC Marketing v Council and Commission* [2011] E.C.R. II-8051, para. 26 (and case-law cited therein).

[253] ECJ, Case C-76/01 P *Eurocoton and Others v Council* [2003] I-10091, paras 54–65 (see also CFI (judgment of 13 March 2005), Case T-177/00 *Koninklijke Philips Electronics v Council*, not reported, paras 29–33). In a subsequent judgment, given in relation to an excessive-deficit procedure, the Court of Justice held that the Council's failure to adopt acts recommended by the Commission could not be regarded as giving rise to acts open to challenge for the purposes of Art. 263 TFEU. The Court stressed, however, that in an excessive-deficit procedure—unlike in the case of an anti-dumping procedure—there is no provision of Union law prescribing a period on the expiry of which the Council is no longer empowered to adopt the measure proposed by the Commission: ECJ, Case C-27/04 *Commission v Council* [2004] E.C.R. I-6649, paras 32–34.

[254] Regulation (EC) No. 1049/2001 of the European Parliament and of the Council of 30 May 2001 regarding public access to European Parliament, Council and Commission documents ([2001] O.J. L145/43). Access to documents to other Union institutions and bodies is regulated by other measures of Union secondary law. For example, as regards the European Central Bank (ECB), see, e.g. EGC, Case T-436/09 *Dufour v ECB* [2011] E.C.R. II-7727, concerning the access to documents of the ECB under Decision 2004/258/EC ([2004] O.J. L80/42).

[255] With respect to the interplay between Regulation No. 1049/2001 on access to documents and the specific regulations in the field of competition law, see K. Lenaerts, 'Due Process in Competition Cases', NZKart, Vol. 1, No. 5 (2013).

[256] See Arts 7–8 of Regulation No. 1049/2001, on access to documents and the specific regulations in the field of competition law.

[257] A decision to grant access to certain documents also constitutes a reviewable act: see, e.g. EGC (judgment of 14 February 2012), Case T-59/09 *Germany v Commission*, not reported, paras 1–13 in which Germany objected to the disclosure of the requested documents.

concerned may make a confirmatory application asking the institution to reconsider its position. In principle, therefore, only the institution's decision to reject a confirmatory application is a reviewable act for the purposes of Art. 263 TFEU.[258] The general rules on confirmatory acts (see para. 7.23) therefore do not apply to the confirmatory refusal decision taken at the end of the two-stage administrative procedure. These rules do, however, in principle apply to any further refusal decisions taken with respect to the same request for access to the same documents.[259]

However, in its 2010 judgment in *Internationaler Hilfsfonds v Commission*, the Court of Justice held in essence that a derogation could be made under certain circumstances.[260] In these proceedings, the applicant had submitted both an initial application and a confirmatory application in response to the Commission's refusal to grant it access to certain documents. Following the applicant's submission of a complaint to the European Ombudsman, the Commission reconsidered the applicant's request, disclosing some, but still not all, documents to which it had been previously refused access. Thereafter, acting on the basis of the conclusions of the European Ombudman's definitive decision, the applicant submitted an application to the Commission for full access to the documents to which access had been to date refused. By virtue of the contested measure, the Commission responded to the applicant's request, deciding not to grant access to the documents requested save for what had already been disclosed. In an action for annulment of the contested measure, the Court of First Instance held that the action was inadmissible on the grounds that the contested measure was merely a confirmatory act.[261] On appeal, the Court of Justice considered that the contested measure constituted, in light of its content and the context in which it was adopted, a definitive refusal by the Commission to disclose all of the documents requested, which brought to an end a long series of successive steps taken by the

---

[258] See, e.g. ECJ, Case C-362/08 P *Internationaler Hilfsfonds v Commission* [2010] E.C.R. I-669, paras 53–54; ECJ (order of 15 February 2012), Case C-208/11 P *Internationaler Hilfsfonds v Commission*, not reported, paras 30–31; EGC (order of 27 November 2012), Case T-17/10 *Steinberg v Commission*, not reported, paras 47–49; EGC, Case T-111/07 *Agrofert Holding v Commission* [2010] E.C.R. II-128*, Summ. pub., paras 33–38. But see CFI, Case T-437/05 *Brink's Security Luxembourg v Commission* [2009] E.C.R. II 3233, paras 73–75: although the applicant failed to make a confirmatory application, the institution's response to the initial application was vitiated by a procedural flaw in that it omitted to inform the applicant, as it is required to do under Art. 7(1) of Regulation No. 1049/2001, of its right to make a confirmatory application. That irregularity has the consequence of rendering admissible, exceptionally, an action for annulment of the initial application. The Court reasoned that if it were otherwise, the institution concerned could avoid review by the Union judicature of a breach of procedure attributable to it. Moreover, as the EU is based on the rule of law, the procedural rules governing actions before the Union courts must be interpreted so as to ensure, as far as possible, that those rules are implemented in such a way as to contribute to the attainment of the objective of ensuring effective judicial protection of an individual's rights under Union law (see also EGC (judgment of 28 March 2012), Case T-190/10 *Egan and Hackett v Parliament*, not reported, paras 42–46). Procedural time limits should also be respected when bringing an action against an implied confirmatory decision: see EGC (order of 13 November 2012), Case T-278/11 *ClientEarth and Others v Commission*, not reported, paras 29–47.

[259] An action for annulment against a decision of an institution refusing access which is merely confirmatory of one or more previous decisions refusing access will therefore generally be deemed inadmissible: see, e.g. ECJ (order of 29 June 2009), Case C-225/08 P *Nuova Agricast v Commission* [2009] E.C.R. I-111*, Summ. pub., paras 35–48; ECJ (order of 29 June 2009), Case C-295/08 P *Cofra v Commission* [2009] E.C.R. I-112*, Summ. pub., paras 32–44; CFI, Joined Cases T-110/03, T-150/03 and T-405/03 *Sison v Council* [2005] E.C.R. II-1429, para. 26 (appeal dismissed on other grounds in ECJ, Case C-266/05 P *Sison v Council* [2007] E.C.R. I-1233).

[260] ECJ, Case C-362/08 P *Internationaler Hilfsfonds v Commission* [2010] E.C.R. I-669; EGC (judgment of 22 May 2012), Case T-300/10 *Internationaler Hilsfonds v Commission*, not reported, para. 80.

[261] See ECJ, Case C-362/08 P *Internationaler Hilfsfonds v Commission* [2010] E.C.R. I-669, paras 27–39.

applicant to gain access to such documents. It was open to the applicant to submit a new application for access to those documents without the Commission being able to oppose them on the basis of the earlier refusals to grant access. Equally, the Commission could not reasonably claim that the applicant should have made a new confirmatory application and waited until that institution refused its application again before it could be regarded as a definitive measure open to challenge, since this could not have led to the desired result in light of the fact that the Commission had clearly and definitively adopted its position with regard to the refusal of access to the documents sought. To require such a step would also have been contrary to the objective of the procedure established by Regulation No. 1049/2001 to guarantee swift and straightforward access to the documents of the institutions concerned. On this basis, the Court set aside the Court of First Instance's judgment that the action was inadmissible on the grounds that the contested measure could not be the subject of an action for annulment under Art. 263 TFEU.[262]

(6) Public procurement

7.68 In the context of public procurement, provisional measures intended to pave the way for the decision awarding a public procurement contract, which is a decision drawn up under an internal procedure involving several stages, cannot themselves be contested in an action for annulment; such an action can only be brought against measures which definitively lay down the position of the Union institution concerned upon the conclusion of that internal procedure.[263] Moreover, as a general rule, a decision to organize a tender procedure has no adverse effects, since it does no more than give to interested parties the possibility of taking part in the procedure and submitting a tender.[264]

III. Identity of the Parties

A. Defendants

(1) Acts of Union institutions

7.69 The first paragraph of Art. 263 TFEU enables actions for annulment to be brought against legislative acts,[265] acts of the Council, of the Commission, and of the European Central

---

[262] ECJ, Case C-362/08 P *Internationaler Hilfsfonds v Commission*, paras 58–63.

[263] See, e.g. EGC, Case T-195/08 *Antwerpse Bouwwerken v Commission* [2009] E.C.R. II-4439, paras 26–30 (and citations therein).

[264] See, e.g. CFI, Case T-411/06 *Sogelma v EAR* [2008] E.C.R. II-2771, paras 86–90 (accepting that an applicant may demonstrate with sufficient proof that such a decision could nonetheless be regarded as adversely affecting its legal position, but this was not fulfilled in the instant proceedings). In this context, see also CFI, Case T-125/06 *Centro Studi Antonio Manieri v Council* [2009] E.C.R. II-69, paras 92–94: as an internal act unconnected with the tendering procedure, the Council's favourable evaluation of the proposal of the Office for Infrastructure and Logistics (OIB) which preceded the decision to entrust the services in question to that office was held not to constitute an act against which an action for annulment can be brought.

[265] In contrast to the first para. of former Art. 230 EC, which had specified 'acts adopted jointly by the European Parliament and the Council', the wording of the first para. of Art. 263 TFEU has been modified to 'legislative acts' in line with the changes brought by the Lisbon Treaty to the regime of legal instruments. This category of legislative acts comprises acts adopted jointly by the European Parliament and the Council under the ordinary legislative procedure (i.e. co-decision), as well as acts adopted by the European Parliament or the Council alone, with the participation of the other, under a special legislative procedure and acts that are

Bank. Acts of the European Parliament may also be reviewed if they are intended to produce legal effects vis-à-vis third parties.[266] This confirms the case-law on the EEC Treaty with regard to the admissibility of applications for annulment of acts of the European Parliament.[267]

Under former Art. 230 EC, an action to annul an act of the European Council was held inadmissible on the grounds that such act did not fall within the jurisdiction of the Union judicature.[268] However, with the changes brought by the Lisbon Treaty, the first paragraph of Art. 263 TFEU now provides that the Union judicature can review the legality of acts of the European Council intended to produce legal effects vis-à-vis third parties.[269] Since, under the Treaties, the European Council is one of the Union institutions[270] which adopts acts intended to produce legal effects,[271] it is only logical to include its acts among those

---

adopted on the initiative of certain Union institutions and bodies or a group of Member States in the specific cases provided for in the Treaties. See Art. 289 TFEU. For detailed discussion, see K. Lenaerts and P. Van Nuffel (R. Bray and N. Cambien (eds)), *European Union Law* (London, Sweet & Maxwell, 2011), para. 16.03.

[266] For example, a decision by which the European Parliament deprived some of its Members of the possibility of forming a political group affects the conditions under which the parliamentary mandate of the Members concerned is exercised, and thus produces legal effects in their regard and goes beyond an act confined to the internal organization of the work of the Parliament: CFI, Joined Cases T-222/99, T-327/99 and T-329/99 *Martinez and Others v European Parliament* [2001] E.C.R. II-2823, paras 56–62, appeal dismissed in ECJ, Case C-488/01 P *Jean-Claude Martinez v European Parliament* [2003] E.C.R. I-13355, but judgment set aside on other grounds in so far as the Court of First Instance had declared the action brought by Front National admissible (in connection with the requirement of direct concern) in ECJ, Case C-486/01 P *Front National v European Parliament* [2004] E.C.R. I-6289, para. 43. Moreover, a decision of the European Parliament laying down the conditions in which OLAF can conduct an investigation in the Parliament goes beyond the internal organisation of the work of the Parliament, in both its object and its effects, and may therefore be the subject of an action for annulment: CFI, Case T-17/00 *Rothley and Others v European Parliament* [2002] E.C.R. II-579, paras 56–67, upheld on appeal by ECJ, Case C-167/02 P *Rothley and Others v European Parliament* [2004] E.C.R. I-3149. Likewise, a decision by which the European Parliament waives the immunity of one of its Member States has legal effects going beyond the internal organization of the Parliament, since it makes it possible for proceedings to be brought against that Member in respect of the matters identified, and therefore constitutes an act which produces legal effects vis-à-vis third parties: CFI, Case T-345/05 *Mote v European Parliament* [2008] E.C.R. II-2849, paras 22–31. In contrast, a framework agreement concluded by the European Parliament with the Commission which applied a code of conduct governing relations between the two institutions is not an act affecting the legal position of individual Members of Parliament, in particular the right to put questions to the Commission under Art. 230 TFEU. Consequently, an action brought by a number of Members of Parliament against that framework agreement was dismissed as inadmissible: CFI (order of 17 January 2002), Case T-236/00 *Stauner and Others v European Parliament and Commission* [2002] E.C.R. II-135, para. 62.

[267] The first para. of the former Art. 173 of the EEC Treaty confined actions for annulment to acts of the Council or the Commission. That limitation stemmed from the original institutional structure of the former Community in which only the Council and the Commission were empowered to adopt binding acts. The gradual expansion of the European Parliament's competence which enabled it to adopt binding acts prompted the Court of Justice to give a broad interpretation to the first para. of the former Art. 173 of the EEC Treaty in order to avoid acts of the European Parliament not being subject to judicial review with regard to their compatibility with the EEC Treaty (now Treaties): ECJ, Case 294/83 *Les Verts v European Parliament* [1986] E.C.R. 1339, paras 20–26, confirmed by ECJ, Case 34/86 *Council v European Parliament* [1986] E.C.R. 2155, para. 5.

[268] See CFI (order of 14 July 1994), Case T-179/94 *Bonnamy v Council*, not reported, para. 10; CFI (order of 14 July 1994), Case T-584/93 *Roujansky v Council* [1994] E.C.R. II-585, para. 12.

[269] ECJ (judgment of 27 November 2012), Case C-370/12 *Pringle*, not reported, paras 34–36.

[270] Art. 13(1), second para., TEU.

[271] See, e.g. Art. 22(1) TEU; Art. 24(1), second para., TEU; Art. 26(1) TEU.

against which an action for annulment will lie insofar as they are intended to produce legal effects vis-à-vis third parties.

Noticeably, although the Court of Justice of the European Union and the Court of Auditors are Union institutions listed in Art. 13(1) TEU, acts adopted by them are not expressly mentioned in the first paragraph of Art. 263 TFEU. Nevertheless, there have been actions for annulment brought against acts of the Court of Justice of the European Union[272] and of the Court of Auditors[273] having effects on third parties which have not been declared inadmissible on these grounds.

(2) Acts of Union bodies, offices, or agencies

(a) Express provision

7.70 As mentioned earlier, as part of the changes brought by the Lisbon Treaty, the first paragraph of Art. 263 TFEU expressly provides that the Union judicature may review the legality of acts of Union bodies, offices, or agencies intended to produce legal effects vis-à-vis third parties.

The inclusion of acts of Union bodies, offices, and agencies among the acts that may be challenged in an action for annulment under Art. 263 TFEU was anticipated to some extent by the approach taken in certain case-law under former Art. 230 EC, insofar as the Community act establishing the Community body, office, or agency in question did not provide for an effective procedure organizing supervision of the legality of acts of that body.[274] Following from the judgment in *Les Verts*, the General Court held in several cases that the general principle to be elicited from that judgment is that any act adopted by a body of the Union which is intended to have legal effects vis-à-vis third parties must be amenable to review by the Union courts and therefore held admissible actions brought against several bodies, offices, and agencies notwithstanding the lack of reference to such bodies, offices, or agencies in the first paragraph of former Art. 230 EC.[275] Yet, matters did

---

[272] In the context of the award of public service contracts, see, e.g. CFI, Case T-272/06 *Evropaiki Dynamiki v Court of Justice* [2008] E.C.R. II-169*, Summ. pub.; EGC, Joined Cases T-170/10 and T-340/10 *Computer Task Group Luxembourg PSF v Court of Justice* [2011] E.C.R. II-384*, Summ. pub.

[273] See, e.g. ECJ, Joined Cases 193/87 and 194/87 *Maurissen and European Public Service Union v Court of Auditors* [1989] E.C.R. 1045, paras 29–49 (in so far as the admissibility inquiry concerned the action brought under then Art. 173 of the EEC Treaty by the applicant trade union concerned).

[274] See, e.g. CFI (order of 8 June 1998), Case T-148/97 *Keeling v OHIM* [1998] E.C.R. II-2217, paras 31–34.

[275] See, e.g. CFI, Case T-411/06 *Sogelma v EAR* [2008] E.C.R. II-2771, paras 33–57; EGC, Case T-70/05 *Evropaiki Dynamiki v EMSA* [2010] E.C.R. II-313, paras 61–75 (noting that this solution is confirmed by the first para. of Art. 263 TFEU); EGC, Case T-331/06 *Evropaiki Dynamiki v EEA* [2010] E.C.R. II-136*, Summ. pub., paras 31–39 (noting that this solution is confirmed by the first para. of Art. 263 TFEU); EGC, Case T-117/08 *Italy v EESC* [2011] E.C.R. II-1463, paras 29–35; EGC (judgment of 12 December 2012), Case T-457/07 *Evropaiki Dynamiki v EFSA*, not reported, para. 24. As far as the European Agency for Reconstruction (EAR) is concerned, it should be noted that according to Council Regulation (EC) No. 1756/2006 of 28 November 2006 ([2006] O.J. L332/18), its mandate was renewed for the final time until 31 December 2008. Therefore, the Commission has since appeared before the Union courts as the legal successor to the EAR in actions for annulment, among others, lodged thereafter: see, e.g. EGC, Case T-407/07 *CMB and Christof v Commission* [2011] E.C.R. II-286*, Summ. pub., paras 55–64. In particular, as regards actions for annulment brought against the European Investment Bank (EIB), the jurisdiction of the Union courts is governed in the first place by Art. 271 TFEU (ex Art. 237 EC). In an order of 26 November 1993, the Court of First Instance held that now Art. 271(c) TFEU did not afford a legal basis for individuals to bring an action for annulment of decisions of the Board of Directors of the EIB. The Court took this view because the EIB, unlike the European Parliament, had

not appear to be fully settled.[276] Even so, the procedure of former Art. 230 EC was confined to Community bodies and could not be used against bodies established on the basis of provisions of the EU Treaty (pertaining to the second or third pillars).[277] Consequently, the express wording introduced by the Lisbon Treaty ensures that acts of Union bodies, offices, or agencies producing effects in relation to third parties do not escape judicial review, subject to the limits placed on the Union courts' jurisdiction under the Treaties with respect to the former second pillar of the CFSP and the former third pillar of PJCCM (see para. 7.04).

(b) Specific arrangements in secondary Union law

As had already been the case under the former Treaty framework, acts of secondary Union **7.71** law establishing the Union body, office, or agency in question may have specific arrangements concerning the review of the legality of the acts of that body, office, or agency.[278] Therefore, the fifth paragraph of Art. 263 TFEU provides that acts setting up Union

---

not increased its original powers and because acts of the EIB did not have legal effects vis-à-vis third parties. Consequently, there was no need to give a broad interpretation to former Art. 230 EC as the Court of Justice had done in the judgment in *Les Verts*: CFI (order of 26 November 1993), Case T-460/93 *Tête and Others v EIB* [1993] E.C.R. II-1257, paras 16–24. An action for annulment of a decision of the Management Committee of the European Investment Bank brought by the Commission now under Art. 271(b) TFEU has been declared admissible (and well-founded) by the Court of Justice: ECJ, Case C-15/00 *Commission v EIB* [2003] E.C.R. I-7281. Recently, on the basis of ensuring full judicial review in line with *Les Verts*, the General Court held admissible an action for annulment brought by an individual under former Art. 230 EC against an act of the EIB producing legal effects vis-à-vis third parties which was not covered by what was then Art. 237 EC (now Art. 271 TFEU): EGC, Case T-461/08 *Evropaiki Dynamiki v EIB* [2011] E.C.R. II-6367, paras 44–52. Commentators consider the European Investment Bank to be included among the Union bodies, offices, or agencies against which a natural and legal person may bring an action for annulment under Art. 263 TFEU to the extent that the contested act is intended to produce legal effects vis-à-vis those persons.

[276] See, e.g. CFI (order of 3 November 2008), Case T-196/08 *Srinivasan v European Ombudsman*, not reported, para. 13, in which the Court of First Instance ruled that the European Ombudsman is not a Community institution and is not among the institutions and bodies whose acts are referred to by the first para. of Art. 230 EC and therefore according to the case-law he does not have the capacity to be made defendant in an action for annulment. Yet, this language followed from discussion of the lack of binding measures adopted by the European Ombudsman for the purposes of satisfying the challengeable act requirement, and there was no objection to the admissibility of the action for annulment brought against the European Ombudsman on grounds of the first para. of Art. 230 EC as such. Therefore, it is difficult to determine the impact of this language taken alone. Appeal of this order was dismissed in ECJ (order of 25 June 2009), Case C-580/08 P *Srinivasan v European Ombudsman* [2008] E.C.R. I-110*, Summ. pub., although this aspect of the order was not challenged.

[277] As regards the provisions of Title VI of the EU Treaty concerning the former third pillar, see ECJ, Case C-160/03, *Spain v Eurojust* [2005] E.C.R. I-2077, paras 35–40.

[278] Art. 4 of Decision 2002/620/EC of the European Parliament, the Council, the Commission, the Court of Justice, the Court of Auditors, the Economic and Social Committee, the Committee of the Regions, and the European Ombudsman of 25 July 2002 establishing a European Communities Personnel Selection Office ([2002] O.J. L197/53) provides that any appeal in the area of competence of EPSO shall be made against the Commission. As regards the Office of Harmonisation in the Internal Market (Trademarks and Designs) (OHIM), see, e.g. ECJ, Case C-29/05 *Kaul v OHIM* [2007] E.C.R. I-2213, paras 51–54. As regards litigation concerning intellectual property rights generally, see Ch. 20. For another example, see EGC, Case T-63/06 *Evropaiki Dynamiki v EMCDDA* [2010] E.C.R. II-177*, Summ. pub., paras 31–33 (finding that the reference to 'Court of Justice' in the relevant provision is meant to denote the institution encompassing the Court of Justice and the General Court and thus in accordance with the regime for allocating jurisdiction between the two Courts set down in primary Union law, the General Court has jurisdiction to rule on the applicant's action for annulment) brought against an act of the European Monitoring Centre for Drugs and Drugs Addiction.

bodies, offices, or agencies may lay down specific conditions and arrangements concerning actions brought by natural and legal persons against acts of these bodies, offices, or agencies intended to produce legal effects in relation to them.

(c) Other bodies

7.72 Acts of entities that do not constitute Union institutions, bodies, offices, or agencies fall outside the scope of the jurisdiction of the Court of Justice and the General Court under Art. 263 TFEU.[279] For example, this includes acts of bodies established on the basis of provisions of the EEA Agreement (the EEA Joint Committee)[280] or decisions of the European Court of Human Rights.[281] This also includes acts of Member State authorities.[282]

Similarly, it has become clear from the case-law[283] that Coreper is not a Union institution but an auxiliary body of the Council which carries out the preparatory work and tasks assigned to it by the Council[284] and does not have the power to take decisions, which belongs, under the Treaties, to the Council. As such, acts adopted by Coreper cannot be regarded as binding acts of the Council that are challengeable in annulment proceedings under Art. 263 TFEU.[285]

(3) What acts may be imputed to a Union institution, body, office, or agency?

(a) Outcome of the institution, body, office, or agency's decision-making power

7.73 An action for annulment will lie only against acts which may be imputed to a Union institution, body, office, or agency.[286] It is not enough that an institution was involved

---

[279] Action for annulment brought against Eulex Kosovo (a temporary mission of the Union) was inadmissible: see EGC (order of 4 June 2013), Case T-213/13 *Elitaliana v Eulex Kosovo*, not reported, paras 19–35. The action should have been brought against the Commission instead.

[280] CFI (order of 22 July 2005), Case T-376/04 *Polyelectrolyte Producers Group v Council and Commission* [2005] E.C.R. II-3007, para. 31.

[281] CFI (order of 18 November 2009), Case T-416/09 *Castellano v Swiss Confederation, France, and Italy*, not reported, paras 3–8.

[282] See, e.g. ECJ (order of 16 May 2008), Case C-49/08 *Raulin v France* [2008] E.C.R. I-77*, Summ. pub.; ECJ (order of 9 November 2010), Case C-143/10 P *Uznański v Poland* [2010] E.C.R. I-153*, Summ. pub.; ECJ (order of 4 March 2010), Case C-374/09 P *Hârsulescu v Romania* [2010] E.C.R. I-30*, Summ. pub.; ECJ (order of 17 December 2010), Case C-513/10 P *Platis v Council and Greece* [2010] E.C.R. I-176*, Summ. pub., paras 11–16; CFI (order of 7 September 2009), Case T-229/09 *Palladino v Italy*, not reported; EGC (order of 17 December 2009), Case T-442/09 *Chacón de la Torre v Spain*, not reported; EGC (order of 26 February 2010), Case T-496/09 *Bell v Belgium*, not reported; EGC (order of 11 February 2010), Case T-459/09 *Hendel v Poland*, not reported; EGC (order of 4 April 2011), Case T-49/11 *NagyatádMed Egészségügyi Szolgáltató Nonprofit v Hungary*, not reported; EGC (order of 8 August 2011), Case T-334/11 *Kauk v Germany*, not reported; EGC (order of 11 November 2011), Case T-469/11 *Al Qadhafi v France*, not reported; EGC (order of 7 February 2012), Case T-665/11 *Kadek v National Polish Agency for the Restructuring and Modernisation of Agriculture*, not reported. As regards the regime of access to documents, see also ECJ, Case C-64/05 P *Sweden v Commission* [2007] E.C.R. I-11389, paras 91–94.

[283] ECJ, Case C-25/94 *Commission v Council* [1996] E.C.R. I-1469, paras 21–28.

[284] See Art. 240(1) TFEU.

[285] Similarly, the Delegation of the EU to a third country does not have the legal capacity required to act as a defendant: see EGC (order of 4 June 2012), Case T-395/11 *Elti v Delegation of the European Union to Montenegro*, not reported, paras 25–75.

[286] See, e.g. ECJ, Case C-201/89 *Le Pen and Front National* [1990] E.C.R. I-1183, para. 14: acts of a political group of the European Parliament cannot be imputed to the Parliament *qua* institution; ECJ, Case C-97/91 *Oleificio Borelli v Commission* [1992] E.C.R. I-6313, paras 9–10; ECJ, Joined Cases C-181/91 and C-248/91 *European Parliament v Council and Commission* [1993] E.C.R. I-3685, para. 25: acts adopted by representatives of the Member States' governments meeting in the Council cannot be imputed to the Council, a Union institution. As regards a Union body, office, or agency, see EGC, Case T-439/08 *Joséphidès v*

in bringing the act about in order for it to be imputed to that institution. The act must be the outcome of the institution's decision-making power.[287] Under the case-law, a Union act is generally imputable to the institution or body which is the author of the act concerned.[288]

A classic example is a decision to award a tender in a public tendering procedure for works in the ACP States which are financed by the Union. The decision to award the tender is a sovereign decision of the ACP State concerned.[289] The Commission's involvement, which

---

Commission and EACEA [2010] E.C.R. II-230*, Summ. pub., paras 34–38 (holding that the contested act was imputable to the Education, Audiovisual and Cultural Executive Agency (EACEA) and thus the application for annulment directed at the Commission was inadmissible, which was upheld on appeal in ECJ (order of 10 November 2011), Case C-626/10 P *Agapiou Joséphidès v Commission and EACEA* [2011] E.C.R. I-169*, Summ. pub.). Compare, e.g. CFI (order of 28 August 2007), Case T-46/06 *Galileo Lebensmittel v Commission* [2007] E.C.R. II-93*, Summ. pub., paras 31–33 (appeal dismissed on other grounds in ECJ (order of 17 February 2009), Case C-483/07 P *Galileo Lebensmittel v Commission* [2009] E.C.R. I-959) (holding action properly directed at the Commission as regards the challenge of the Commission decision reserving use of a certain domain name and rejecting the defendant's argument that an action should have been brought against EURid, a non-profit association incorporated under Belgian law appointed by the Commission under Union law to manage the '.eu' domain name registration). See, e.g. CFI (order of 5 December 2007), Case T-133/01 *Schering-Plough v Commission and EMEA*, not reported, paras 16–23 (holding contested measure imputed to the Commission, not to the EMEA—the European Agency for the Evaluation of Medicinal Products).

[287] For instance, in the context of anti-dumping, compare CFI, Case T-45/06 *Reliance Industries v Council and Commission* [2008] E.C.R. II-2399, paras 50–51 (finding that pursuant to the basic regulations in the field, the contested notices were adopted by the Commission and thus the application for annulment of those notices is admissible only against the Commission, not the Council), with EGC, Case T-107/08 *Transnational Company 'Kazchrome' and ENRC Marketing v Council and Commission* [2011] E.C.R. II-8051, para. 26 (and citations therein) (finding the application for annulment of the contested regulation inadmissible in so far as it concerns the Commission, since that regulation was adopted solely by the Council; the Commission's role in anti-dumping proceedings forms an integral part of the Council's decision-making process, but the power of decision belongs to the Council). Under the former Treaty framework, the case-law recognized the principle that acts adopted on the basis of a delegation of powers are normally imputable to the delegating institution, with the result that the action against the act of the body to which the power has been delegated is admissible as being brought against the delegating institution. Such case-law normally concerned Community bodies to whom tasks had been delegated by the institutions within the Community sphere. As witnessed by more recent case-law, this may also be applicable in relation to the delegation of powers made by the Council to the Commission in connection with anti-terrorism measures. See CFI (judgment of 12 July 2006), Case T-49/04 *Hassan v Council and Commission*, not reported, para. 59 (and citations therein). However, by virtue of the changes brought to the regime of Union legal instruments by the Lisbon Treaty, there is now a category of delegated acts, involving situations in which a legislative act delegates to the Commission the power to adopt non-legislative acts of general application to supplement or amend certain non-essential elements of the legislative act: see Art. 290 TFEU. An action for annulment against such a delegated act would therefore have to be brought against the Commission as the author of the act, not the European Parliament and/or the Council as the delegating institutions pursuant to the legislative act concerned.

[288] Particularly in the context of restrictive measures against individuals in the fight against terrorism, which typically involve measures adopted by the Council and the Commission, many of which are repealed and replaced by new measures, the application for annulment may be dropped against one of the institutions depending upon the author of the replacement measures, or may be maintained against the two on account of the amendments made to the measures concerned. See, e.g. CFI (judgment of 12 July 2006), Case T-49/04 *Hassan v Council and Commission*, not reported, paras 53–60 (maintaining admissibility of action against the Commission, as author of one of the contested regulations, and the Council, as author of the other contested regulation so amended); CFI, Case T-318/01 *Othman v Council and Commission* [2009] E.C.R. II-1627, paras 56–58 (where on account of the repeal of a contested measure adopted by the Commission and the replacement with one adopted by the Council, the action must be directed at the Council alone).

[289] See, e.g. the former Lomé Convention, [1991] O.J. L229/3.

is governed by EU legislation, in preparing the decision does not mean that that decision may be imputed to it.[290]

Moreover, in the so-called *'Family reunification'* case,[291] the Court of Justice ruled that the fact that the contested provisions of a directive afford the Member States a certain margin of discretion and allow them in certain circumstances to apply national legislation derogating from the basic rules imposed by the directive cannot have the effect of excluding those provisions from review by the Court of their legality as envisaged by Art. 263 TFEU. For that matter, a provision of a Union act could not in itself respect fundamental rights if it required, or expressly or implicitly authorized, the Member States to adopt or retain national legislation not respecting those rights. On this basis, the Court dismissed the plea of inadmissibility, alleging that the action for annulment brought by the European Parliament did not actually concern an act of the institutions.[292]

(b) Act of a Member or staff member of an institution

7.74   An act of a Member or of a staff member of an institution is not necessarily to be imputed to the institution.[293] It will be so imputable only if the person who adopts the act makes it clear that he or she does so pursuant to his or her power to act in the name of the institution.[294] Furthermore, it must transpire from the content of the act that the person in question intended to express the position or the decision of the institution.[295]

---

[290] ECJ, Case 126/83 *STS v Commission* [1984] E.C.R. 2769, paras 16–18; ECJ, Case 118/83 *CMC v Commission* [1985] E.C.R. 2325, paras 28–29; ECJ, Case C-257/90 *Italsolar v Commission* [1993] E.C.R. I-9, paras 17–27. For an application of this principle in the agricultural sector, see CFI, Case T-93/95 *Laga v Commission* [1998] E.C.R. II-195, paras 33–42; CFI, Case T-94/95 *Landuyt v Commission* [1998] E.C.R. II-213, paras 33–42 (in which the Court of First Instance held that the claim for annulment was essentially directed against the act of a national authority and not against an act of a Union institution). But see ECJ, Case C-395/95 P *Geotronics v Commission* [1997] E.C.R. I-2271, paras 9–16.

[291] ECJ, Case C-540/03 *European Parliament v Council* (*'Family reunification'* case) [2006] E.C.R. I-5769.

[292] ECJ, Case C-540/03 *'Family reunification'*, paras 21–24.

[293] ECJ, Joined Cases 42/59 and 49/59 *SNUPAT v High Authority* [1961] E.C.R. 53, at 72. See also CFI (order of 21 November 2007), Case T-94/06 *Gargani v European Parliament* [2007] E.C.R. II-158*, in which the Court of First Instance held inadmissible an action for annulment brought by Mr Gargani, the President of the Committee of Legal Affairs of the European Parliament against Mr Borrell Fontelles, the President of the European Parliament, in his individual capacity pursuant to the fourth para. of Art. 263 TFEU. It based its decision on the grounds that Art. 263 TFEU did not allow an action for annulment brought by one natural or legal person against another, that this provision did not provide for the form of order sought by the applicant (that is, a declaration that the contested 'decision' of the President of European Parliament was in violation of the relevant internal rules), and that the action was lodged out of time. On appeal, the Court of Justice only examined the plea concerning time limits and did not find it necessary to examine the plea as regards whether an action brought on this basis fell within the scope of the Union courts' competence under Art. 263 TFEU: ECJ (order of 13 November 2008), Case C-25/08 P *Gargani v European Parliament* [2008] E.C.R. I-154*, Summ. pub., paras 15, 16, and 25.

[294] ECJ, Case 34/86 *Council v European Parliament* [1986] E.C.R. 2155, paras 7–8. A report commissioned by an institution from a private consultancy firm cannot be imputed to the institution. This is because such a report does not contain any act adopted by the institution itself (ECJ (order of 26 March 1980), Case 51/79 *Buttner v Commission* [1980] E.C.R. 1201, at 1202–03).

[295] CFI, Case T-113/89 *Nefarma v Commission* [1990] E.C.R. II-797, para. 81 (a letter from the Member of the Commission responsible for competition to the Netherlands Government appeared to have been written in his own name and in the context of an exchange of views between politicians, and could therefore not be regarded as an act of the Commission).

(c) Treaty amendments

Treaty amendments adopted pursuant to the ordinary revision procedure laid down in Art.   **7.75**
48 (1) to (5) TEU and Acts relating to the accession of new Member States (adopted
pursuant to Art. 49 TEU) are not acts of Union institutions.[296] They are provisions of
primary Union law which are not subject to the system of judicial review provided for in the
Treaties. Even if modifications of acts of the institutions, bodies, offices, or agencies ensue
out of those provisions, they still do not constitute acts of the institutions and are therefore
not amenable to judicial review.[297]

However, under the simplified revision procedures prescribed in Art. 48(6) TEU, the
European Council may adopt a decision amending all or part of the provisions of Part
Three of the TFEU, which does not enter into force until it is approved by the Member
States in accordance with their respective constitutional requirements. The European
Council decision constitutes a challengeable act as it is an act of a Union institution.[298]

B. Applicants

(1) The European Parliament, the Council, the Commission, and the Member States

(a) Privileged applicants

The European Parliament, the Council, the Commission, and the Member States derive   **7.76**
from the second paragraph of Art. 263 TFEU the right to bring actions for annulment.
They are privileged applicants.[299] They may, without proving that they have an interest in
bringing proceedings,[300] bring an action for annulment against any binding act of a Union
institution, body, office, or agency, whether general or individual, and may also rely on any
plea in law permitted under Art. 263 TFEU.[301] The right to bring an action for annulment

---

[296] ECJ, Case C-313/89 *Commission v Spain* [1991] E.C.R. I-5231, para. 10.
[297] ECJ, Joined Cases 31/86 and 35/86 *LAISA and Others v Council* [1988] E.C.R. 2285, paras 1–18; CFI
(order of 9 April 2008), Case T-38/08 *Correia de Matos v Commission*, not reported, para. 13 (underscoring
that the Commission has no competence to modify provisions of the Treaties).
[298] ECJ (judgment of 27 November 2012), Case C-370/12 *Pringle*, not reported, paras 30–37.
[299] For the first case brought by the European Parliament as a privileged applicant, see ECJ, Case C-540/03
European Parliament v Council ('Family reunification') [2006] E.C.R. I-5769.
[300] ECJ, Case 45/86 *Commission v Council* [1987] E.C.R. 1493, para. 3. See also e.g. CFI, Joined Cases
T-309/04, T-317/04, T-329/04, and T-336/04 *TV2/Danmark and Others v Commission* [2008]
E.C.R. II-2935, paras 63–66; EGC, Joined Cases T-425/04, T-444/04, T-450/04, and T-456/04 *France
and Others v Commission* [2010] E.C.R. II-2099, paras 118–120; EGC, Joined Cases T-415/05, T-416/05,
and T-423/05 *Greece and Others v Commission* [2010] E.C.R. II-4749, para. 57; EGC, Case T-369/07 *Latvia
v Commission* [2011] E.C.R. II-1039, para. 33; EGC (judgment of 20 September 2012), Case T-154/10
France v Commission, not reported, paras 36–38.
[301] ECJ, Case 41/83 *Italy v Commission* [1985] E.C.R. 873, para. 30. One of the questions raised in that
case was whether Italy could bring an action for annulment against a Commission decision finding that British
Telecommunications, at that time a nationalized undertaking having a statutory monopoly in the UK over the
running of telecommunications services, had infringed Art. 102 TFEU. Italy argued, amongst other things,
that the Commission had disregarded Art. 106(2) TFEU and that undertakings entrusted with the operation
of services of general economic interest were subject to EU competition law only in so far as its application did
not impede the performance of their particular tasks. The Court of Justice allowed Italy to raise that plea,
despite the fact that what was involved was a balancing of interests—described by the Commission as
difficult—which affected only the UK. See further K. Lenaerts and J. A. Gutiérrez-Fons, 'Le rôle du juge de
l'Union dans l'interprétation des articles 14 et 106, paragraphe 2, TFUE' (2011) Concurrences: revue des
droits de la concurrence (4) 4–7.

is not dependent upon the position which they took up when the act at issue was adopted. Thus, the fact that an act was voted for in the Council by the representative of a Member State does not preclude that Member State from bringing an application for its annulment.[302] Any Member State has a right to bring an action for annulment, and that right is not dependent upon other Member States, the Council, or the Commission participating in the proceedings before the Union judicature.[303]

(b) Constitutionally autonomous regions and devolved authorities

7.77 Regional and devolved authorities (municipalities, federated States, etc.) are not equated to a Member State and are therefore not privileged applicants. If they have legal personality under national law, they may be regarded as legal persons within the meaning of the fourth paragraph of Art. 263 TFEU[304] and bring an action for annulment, provided that the admissibility requirements laid down in that Treaty provision are satisfied.[305]

---

[302] ECJ, Case 166/78 *Italy v Council* [1979] E.C.R. 2575, paras 5–6.

[303] ECJ, Case 230/81 *Luxembourg v European Parliament* [1983] E.C.R. 255, paras 22–26 (interpretation of Art. 38, first para., of the ECSC Treaty, which also held good for what was then the second para. of Art. 230 EC [now Art. 263 TFEU]). Union law does not impose any obligation on a Member State to bring an action for annulment for the benefit of one of its citizens. As to the question whether national law may impose such an obligation, the Court of Justice ruled that such obligation would not, in principle, infringe Union law, but added that a Member State could, however, breach the obligation of sincere cooperation laid down in Art. 4(3) TEU if it did not retain a degree of discretion as to the appropriateness of bringing an action, thereby giving rise to a risk that the Union courts might be inundated with actions, some of which would be patently unfounded, thus jeopardizing the proper functioning of the Court of Justice of the European Union: ECJ, Case C-511/03 *Ten Kate Holding Musselkanaal and Others* [2005] E.C.R. I-8979, paras 30–31.

[304] See ECJ (order of 8 February 2007), Case C-406/06 *Landtag Schleswig-Holstein v Commission*, not reported, paras 6–11: for the purposes of jurisdiction, since an action brought by a regional or sub-national entity is not assimilated to a Member State or an institution but falls within the category of legal person for the purposes of the fourth para. of Art. 263 TFEU, the action must be lodged in the General Court, not the Court of Justice.

[305] See, e.g. ECJ, Case 222/83 *Municipality of Differdange and Others v Commission* [1984] E.C.R. 2889, para. 9; see also the Opinion of Advocate-General C.O. Lenz in ECJ, Joined Cases 62/87 and 72/87 *Exécutif Régional Wallon and Glaverbel v Commission* [1988] E.C.R. 1573, at 1582; ECJ, Case C-298/89 *Gibraltar v Council* [1993] E.C.R. I-3605, para. 14; ECJ (order of 21 March 1997), Case C-95/97 *Région Wallonne v Commission* [1997] E.C.R. I-1787, para. 6; ECJ (order of 1 October 1997), Case C-180/97 *Regione Toscana v Commission* [1997] E.C.R. I-5245, paras 6–8; ECJ, Case C-417/04 P *Regione Siciliana v Commission* [2006] E.C.R. I-3881, para. 24; ECJ, Case C-15/06 P *Regione Siciliana v Commission* [2007] E.C.R. I-2591, para. 29; ECJ, Joined Cases C-445/07 P and C-455/07 P *Commission v Ente per le Ville Vesuviane* [2009] E.C.R. I-7993, para. 42; ECJ (order of 26 November 2009), Case C-444/08 P *Região autónoma dos Açores v Council* [2009] E.C.R. I-200*, Summ. pub., paras 30–33; CFI, Case T-214/95 *Vlaams Gewest v Commission* [1998] E.C.R. II-717, para. 28; CFI (order of 16 June 1998), Case T-238/97 *Comunidad Autónoma de Catanbria v Council* [1998] E.C.R. II-2271, para. 43; CFI, Case T-288/97 *Regione Autonoma Friuli Venezia Giulia v Commission* [1998] E.C.R. II-1871, paras 28 *et seq.*, in particular paras 46–48, in which the Court of First Instance held that the fact that a Member State is responsible in an action for failure to fulfil obligations for the acts of devolved bodies and cannot rely in its defence on the division of powers in effect nationally does not mean that the devolved body cannot bring an action for annulment where a decision addressed to a Member State is of direct and individual concern to it. This is because the two actions (action for failure to fulfil obligations and action for annulment) are autonomous procedures and, as a result, the admissibility of an action brought under what is now Art. 263 TFEU must be decided only in the light of 'the objectives specific to that provision and of the principle of judicial protection according to which it must be open to every natural or legal person to apply to the courts on his own initiative, that is to say in the exercise of his own judgment, in order to obtain review of an act which adversely affects that person'; CFI, Case T-609/97 *Regione Puglia v Commission and Spain* [1998] E.C.R. II-4051, para. 17; CFI, Joined Cases T-195/01 and T-207/01 *Gibraltar v Commission* [2002] E.C.R. II-2309, paras 52–55. For an extended discussion, see P. Van Nuffel, 'What's in a Member State? Central and Decentralised Authorities before the Community Courts' (2001) C.M.L. Rev. 871–901; see also K. Lenaerts and N. Cambien,

(c) Union bodies, offices, or agencies

Given the express wording of the second and fourth paragraphs of Art. 263 TFEU, which **7.78**
refers to actions brought by Member States, certain Union institutions and natural
and legal persons, the question arises whether actions for annulment brought by a Union
body, office, or agency are precluded. Although so far such an action has not been ruled out
on such grounds,[306] the definitive answer to this question awaits development in the case-
law.[307]

(2) The European Central Bank, the Court of Auditors, and the Committee of the Regions

(a) Semi-privileged applicants

In the judgment in the *Chernobyl* case, the Court of Justice granted the European Parlia- **7.79**
ment a right not conferred by the former Art. 173 EEC (now Art. 263 TFEU) to bring an
action for annulment against acts of the Council or the Commission 'provided that the
action seeks only to safeguard its prerogatives and that it is founded only on submissions
alleging their infringement'.[308] The primary intention of the Court in so ruling was to
maintain the balance between the institutions laid down by the Treaties.[309] The Treaty of
Nice since raised the European Parliament to the status of a privileged applicant.

The former EC Treaty already included a category of 'semi-privileged applicants' which
were entitled to challenge a Community act where the action was brought for the purpose
of protecting their prerogatives within the meaning of the *Chernobyl* judgment. Under the
third paragraph of former Art. 230 EC, this category comprised the European Central Bank
and the Court of Auditors.

With the entry into force of the Lisbon Treaty, this category has been extended to the
Committee of the Regions. Accordingly, under the third paragraph of Art. 263 TFEU, the
European Central Bank, the Court of Auditors, and the Committee of the Regions must
clearly show which of their prerogatives should have been respected and in what way

---

'Regions and the European Courts: Giving Shape to the Regional Dimension of Member States', (2010)
E.L. Rev. 609–635. For discussion of the standing requirements in the context of actions brought by
regional and devolved authorities, see further para. 7.103.

[306] See EGC (order of 29 November 2011), Case T-345/11 *ENISA v CEPD*, not reported, paras 10–25, in
which the General Court held inadmissible an action for annulment brought by the European Network and
Information Security Agency (ENISA) on the grounds that it was lodged out of time under the sixth para. of
Art. 263 TFEU and did not pronounce on the admissibility of this action on other grounds.

[307] As regards the European Investment Bank, one commentator noted that although literal interpretation
of Art. 263 TFEU would preclude it from having the right to bring an action for annulment as compared to
the ECB as semi-privileged applicant, there are possible arguments that could support a contrary reading: see
G. Marchegiani, 'The European Investment Bank after the Treaty of Lisbon' (2012) E.L. Rev. 70–78, at 77.

[308] ECJ, Case C-70/88 *European Parliament v Council* [1990] E.C.R. I-2041, para. 27. In the judgment on
the substance of the case, moreover, the Court of Justice declared the European Parliament's second and third
pleas inadmissible in that they did not allege any infringement of its prerogatives: ECJ, Case C-70/88 *European
Parliament v Council* [1991] E.C.R. I-4529, paras 19–20. That condition for admissibility has been confirmed
in, for example, ECJ, Case C-295/90 *European Parliament v Council* [1992] E.C.R. I-4193, paras 8–10; ECJ,
Case C-316/91 *European Parliament v Council* [1994] E.C.R. I-625, para. 19; ECJ, Case C-187/93 *European
Parliament v Council* [1994] E.C.R. I-2857, paras 14–16; ECJ, Case C-189/97 *European Parliament v Council*
[1999] E.C.R. I-4741, paras 13–17.

[309] Cf. K. Bradley, 'The Variable Evolution of the Standing of the European Parliament in Proceedings
before the Court of Justice' (1988) Y.E.L. 27–57.

the prerogative in question has been infringed. The former case-law developed when the European Parliament was still only a semi-privileged applicant will have a bearing on the assessment of the admissibility of future actions brought by the Committee of the Regions, as well as by the European Central Bank and the Court of Auditors.[310]

(b) Violation of the principle of subsidiarity

7.80   However, in one specific situation, namely where the Committee of the Regions considers that a legislative act infringes the principle of subsidiarity, it will be entitled to bring an action for annulment even if the action is not brought for the purpose of protecting the Committee's prerogatives. Under Protocol (No. 2) on the application of the principles of subsidiarity and proportionality,[311] the Union judicature is to have jurisdiction in actions for annulment brought by the Committee of the Regions on grounds of infringement of the principle of subsidiarity by a legislative act for the adoption of which the TFEU provides that it be consulted.[312] The action for annulment will be admissible regardless of whether the Committee was actually consulted.[313]

(3) Natural and legal persons

7.81   Under the fourth paragraph of Art. 263 TFEU, any natural or legal person[314] has the right to institute annulment proceedings against an act addressed to that person or which is of direct and individual concern to him, and against a regulatory act which is of direct concern to him and does not entail implementing measures. For the sake of discussion, the requirements relating to the admissibility of actions for annulment brought by natural and legal persons are divided into four parts concerning those relating to the person; those relating to the type of act, which include a general survey of the requirements of direct and individual concern and the changes brought by the Lisbon Treaty (i.e. the concept of regulatory act and restrictive measures against individuals in the field of CFSP); specific fields of application in connection with the individual concern requirement; and interest.

---

[310] ECJ, Case C-316/91 *European Parliament v Council* [1994] E.C.R. I-625, para. 16; ECJ, Case C-21/94 *European Parliament v Council* [1995] E.C.R. I-1827, para. 8; ECJ, Case C-156/93 *European Parliament v Commission* [1995] E.C.R. I-2019, para. 11 (infringement of the requirement laid down in Art. 253 EC (now Art. 296 TFEU) to state the reasons on which acts are based cannot be relied upon by the European Parliament on the ground that it is not clear how that breaches its prerogatives); ECJ, Case C-360/93 *European Parliament v Council* [1996] E.C.R. I-1195, para. 18 (an action contesting the legal basis on which the contested act is founded has a bearing on the protection of the Parliament's prerogatives); ECJ, Case C-392/95 *European Parliament v Council* [1997] E.C.R. I-3213, paras 14–15; ECJ, Case C-259/95 *European Parliament v Council* [1997] E.C.R. I-5303, para. 9.

[311] Protocol (No. 2), annexed to the TEU and the TFEU, on the application of the principles of subsidiarity and proportionality, [2012] O.J. C326/206, Art. 8, second para.

[312] If, in the context of one and the same action, the Committee of the Regions raises a plea relating to the infringement of the principle of subsidiarity as well as other pleas, it may be argued that the latter pleas will be admissible only if it can be shown that they are raised for the purpose of protecting the Committee's prerogatives.

[313] An action on the same grounds may also be brought by a Member State or notified to them in accordance with their legal order on behalf of their national Parliament or a chamber of it: Protocol (No. 2) on the application of the principles of subsidiarity and proportionality, Art. 8, first para.

[314] In this book 'natural and legal persons' are also referred to as 'individuals' or 'individual applicants'.

(4) Requirements as to admissibility relating to the person

(a) Nationality of natural or legal person is irrelevant

Any natural or legal person may bring an action for annulment under the fourth paragraph **7.82**
of Art. 263 TFEU.[315] The applicant's nationality is irrelevant as far as the admissibility of
the application is concerned.[316]

(b) Notion of legal personality

In principle, national law determines whether the applicant has legal personality.[317] **7.83**
Sometimes lack of legal personality precludes access to the General Court (or to the
Court of Justice on appeal).[318] Often, however, entities without legal personality may
nevertheless be admitted to bring an action for annulment.[319] In order for them to bring an
action, they must be entitled and in a position to act as a responsible body in legal

---

[315] In all probability this includes third countries, although the Court of Justice has not yet definitively
opined on the matter. See ECJ (order of 14 July 2005), Case C-70/04 *Swiss Confederation v Commission*, not
reported, paras 17–24, in which the Court ruled that supposing that the Swiss Confederation could be
assimilated to a Member State, the instant action challenging the contested act of the Commission must be
heard by the now General Court as determined by Art. 256 TFEU and Art. 51 of the Statute. Even if the Swiss
Confederation would, on the contrary, not be assimilated to a Member State but to a natural and legal person
under the fourth para. of Art. 263 TFEU, the action must still be heard by the General Court. Consequently,
the action was referred to the now General Court for adjudication, which dismissed the case on the merits
without ruling on the admissibility: EGC, Case T-319/05 *Swiss Confederation v Commission* [2010]
E.C.R. II-4265, para. 55 (appeal dismissed without ruling on the question of admissibility at first instance:
ECJ (judgment of 7 March 2013), Case C-547/10 P *Swiss Confederation v Commission*, not reported). Cf. ECJ
(order of 23 February 1983), Joined Cases 91/82 and 200/82 *Chris International Foods v Commission* [1983]
E.C.R. 417, at 419, in which the Court of Justice gave a third country leave to intervene in the proceedings on
the grounds that it was an interested 'person' within the meaning of the second para. of Art. 40 of the Statute
of the Court of Justice. Needless to say, actions brought by sub-national entities of third States fall within the
fourth para. of Art. 263 TFEU: see, e.g. CFI (order of 3 July 2007), Case T-212/02 *Commune de Champagne
and Others v Council and Commission* [2007] E.C.R. II-2017, paras 178–179.

[316] For some examples of successful actions for annulment brought by natural and legal persons from a
non-Member State, see CFI, Case T-143/06 *MTZ Polyfilms v Council* [2009] E.C.R. II-4133 (applicant
established in India); EGC, Case T-122/09 *Zhejiang Xinshiji Foods Co. and Hubei Zinshiji Foods Co. v Council*
[2011] E.C.R. II-22*, Summ. pub. (applicants established in China); EGC, Case T-262/10 *Microban
International and Microban (Europe) v Commission* [2011] E.C.R. II-7697 (one of the applicants established
in the United States).

[317] ECJ, Case 18/57 *Nold v High Authority* [1959] E.C.R. 41, at 48–9; ECJ, Case 50/84 *Bensider v
Commission* [1984] E.C.R. 3991, para. 7; CFI, Case T-174/95 *Svenska Journalistförbundet v Council* [1998]
E.C.R. II-2289, para. 43; cf. ECJ, Case 294/83 *Les Verts v European Parliament* [1986] E.C.R. 1339, paras
13–18, in regard to merging associations and the assignment of a pending legal action to the new association.
See also CFI, Case T-458/04 *Au Lys de France v Commission* [2007] E.C.R. II-71*, Summ. pub., paras 34–39
(as regards legal capacity in connection with bankruptcy of the entity concerned). As regards sub-national
territorial bodies, see, e.g. CFI (order of 3 April 2008), Case T-236/06 *Landtag Schleswig-Holstein v Commission* [2008] E.C.R. II-461, para. 22 (holding that the applicant, the Parliament of the *Land* of Schleswig-
Holstein, did not have legal capacity under German law and thus did not have the capacity to be a party to
legal proceedings before the Union courts) (appeal dismissed in ECJ (order of 24 November 2009), Case
C-281/08 P *Landtag Schleswig-Holstein v Commission* [2009] E.C.R. I-199*, Summ. pub.).

[318] ECJ, Case 50/84 *Bensider v Commission* [1984] E.C.R. 3991, para. 9; CFI (order of 15 February 2005),
Case T-229/02 *PKK and Others v Council* [2005] E.C.R. II-539, para. 37.

[319] See, however EGC, Case T-50/05 *Evropaiki Dynamiki—Proigmena Systimata v Commission* [2010]
E.C.R. II-1071, para. 40 (finding that although formally the contested decision was addressed to the tenderer
consortium, that consortium never had legal personality and hence from the point of view of Art. 263 TFEU,
given that its members remain visible in that ad hoc structure, the two undertakings at issue must both be
considered the addressees of the contested decision and entitled to challenge that decision under Art. 263
TFEU).

matters.[320] As a result, the expression 'legal person' has been given an independent Union law meaning which is not necessarily the same one it has in national law. The fact that the applicant was recognized by the defendant as a negotiating partner before the proceedings arose[321] and the fact that an ad hoc association was allowed to take part in a tendering procedure organized by the Commission[322] have helped applicants to be recognized as legal persons within the meaning of the fourth paragraph of Art. 263 TFEU.

(c) Capacity to bring action on behalf of another

7.84   A natural or legal person is entitled to demonstrate by sufficient evidence that he is bringing annulment proceedings acting on behalf of another party.[323] In the '*PKK*' case, the Court of Justice, finding that the PKK could not be considered to have been dissolved on the evidence submitted, set aside the Court of First Instance's decision in which the action brought for annulment by Mr Osman Ocalan on behalf of the Kurdistan Workers' Party (PKK) was held to be inadmissible.[324] In order to ensure effective judicial protection, the Court considered that since by virtue of the contested measure the Union legislator took the view that the PKK retains an existence sufficient for it to be subject to restrictive measures, it must be accepted on grounds of consistency and justice that this entity continues to have an existence sufficient to contest that measure before the Union courts. Consequently, although the relevant procedural rules of the Union courts were not devised with a view to actions being brought by organizations lacking legal personality, such as the PKK, these rules must be adapted to the extent necessary to the circumstances of the case. On this basis, the Court found that there was sufficient evidence to establish that Mr Ocalan was qualified to act on behalf of the PKK.[325]

(5) Requirements as to admissibility based on the type of act

(a) Threshold determination: what type of act?

7.85   Under the fourth paragraph of former Art. 230 EC, the only Community acts that could in principle be challenged by natural and legal persons in an action for annulment were decisions addressed to them, addressed to another person, or adopted in the form of a regulation. In the last two cases, an action for annulment of the 'decision' would lie only if it

---

[320] ECJ, Case 175/73 *Union Syndicale and Others v Council* [1974] E.C.R. 917, paras 7–17, at 924–5; ECJ, Case 18/74 *Syndicat Général du Personnel des Organismes Européens v Commission* [1974] E.C.R. 933, paras 3–11.

[321] ECJ, Case 175/73 *Union Syndicale and Others v Council*, para. 12; ECJ, Case 18/74 *Syndicat Général du Personnel des Organismes Européens v Commission*, para. 9,; CFI, Case T-161/94 *Sinochem Heilongjiang v Council* [1996] E.C.R. II-695, para. 34; CFI, Case T-170/94 *Shanghai Bicycle v Council* [1997] E.C.R. II-1383, para. 26.

[322] ECJ, Case 135/81 *Groupement des Agences de Voyage v Commission* [1982] E.C.R. 3799, paras 10–11.

[323] See, e.g. CFI, Case T-411/06 *Sogelma v EAR* [2008] E.C.R. II-2771, paras 95–105: where the applicant does not claim that an undertaking has assigned its rights to the applicant, the Court held that the applicant failed to submit sufficient proof that it was able to assert the rights of that undertaking in the instant proceedings, finding that it is not acceptable for a company to assert in legal proceedings the rights of another company where it has not been unequivocally instructed to do so. See also Case T-332/03 *European Service Network v Commission* [2008] E.C.R. II-32*, Summ. pub., paras 53–58 (applicant declared expressly that it was bringing the action in its own name, but the question arose in the proceedings as to whether the applicant was also bringing the action on behalf of a certain consortium of which it was part).

[324] ECJ, Case C-229/05 P *PKK and KNK v Council* [2007] E.C.R. I-439, paras 38–54.

[325] ECJ, Case C-229/05 P *PKK and KNK v Council*, paras 107–122 (discounting the Council's objection based on the lack of headed notepaper for the power of attorney for the PKK).

was of direct and individual concern to the applicant. The expression 'decision addressed to another person' also covered decisions addressed to a Member State.[326]

Consequently, the fourth paragraph of former Art. 230 EC seems to preclude individuals from bringing an action for annulment against measures of general application. The reason is that, in accordance with a literal reading of this provision, an individual may bring an action for annulment only against 'genuine' decisions and 'disguised' decisions, that is to say, decisions adopted in the form of regulations.[327] However, the case-law has evolved so that the only question to be determined in relation to the admissibility of proceedings brought by an individual against an act which is not addressed to that person is whether the act is of direct and individual concern to that person.[328] If this is the case, the action will be admissible even if the annulment of a measure of general application is sought.[329]

With the entry into force of the Lisbon Treaty, the fourth paragraph of Art. 263 TFEU codifies this development in the case-law by providing that 'any natural and legal person may ... institute proceedings against an act addressed to that person or which is of direct and individual concern to them'.[330]

Despite the change in wording, the case-law on the former fourth paragraph of Art. 230 EC does not lose any of its salience as regards the type of act involved. Although no longer framed in the old nomenclature of decisions and regulations, the fourth paragraph of Art. 263 TFEU nonetheless centres on the threshold question on the type of act involved and whether such act is, or is not, addressed to the applicant.[331] The answer to this question determines the standing requirements that must be fulfilled by the natural or legal person bringing the action for annulment.

---

[326] ECJ, Case 25/62 *Plaumann v Commission* [1963] E.C.R. 95, at 106–7.

[327] ECJ, Case 101/76 *Koninklijke Scholten Honig* [1977] E.C.R. 797, at 805.

[328] ECJ, Case C-309/89 *Codorníu v Council* [1994] E.C.R. I-1853, para. 19; ECJ, Case C-452/98 *Nederlandse Antillen v Council* [2001] E.C.R. I-8973, para. 55.

[329] ECJ, Case C-309/89 *Codorníu v Council* [1994] E.C.R. I-1853; CFI, Case T-243/01 *Sony Computer Entertainment Europe v Commission* [2003] E.C.R. II-4189, paras 58–76. Anti-dumping cases afford striking illustrations. Undertakings which can prove that their identity is apparent from the contested regulation or that the investigation which resulted in the imposition of anti-dumping duties related to them may bring an action for annulment of the regulation or of the provisions of the regulation which imposed anti-dumping duties on them (ECJ, Case 113/77 NTN *Toyo Bearing v Council* [1979] E.C.R. 1185, paras 10–11; ECJ, Case 118/77 *ISO v Council* [1979] E.C.R. 1277, paras 17–27; ECJ, Case 119/77 *Nippon Seiko v Council and Commission* [1979] E.C.R. 1303, paras 12–15; ECJ, Case 121/77 *Nachi Fujikoshi v Council* [1979] E.C.R. 1363, paras 7–13; ECJ, Joined Cases 239/82 and 275/82 *Allied Corporation v Commission* [1984] E.C.R. 1005, paras 7–16; ECJ, Case 53/83 *Allied Corporation v Council* [1985] E.C.R. 1621, paras 2–5; ECJ, Case 240/84 NTN *Toyo Bearing v Council* [1987] E.C.R. 1809, paras 4–7; ECJ, Joined Cases C-133/87 and C-150/87 *Nashua and Others v Commission and Council* [1990] E.C.R. I-719, paras 12–21; ECJ, Joined Cases C-305/86 and C-160/87 *Neotype Techmashexport v Commission and Council* [1990] E.C.R. I-2945, para. 19; ECJ, Case C-358/89 *Extramet Industrie v Council* [1991] E.C.R. I-2501, paras 13–14).

[330] This was already the case in Art. III-365(4) of the Draft Constitution Treaty in almost identical form ('against an act addressed to that person or which is of direct and individual concern to him or her').

[331] See, e.g. ECJ (order of 17 February 2009), Case C-483/07 P *Galileo Lebensmittel v Commission* [2009] E.C.R. I-959, para. 29 ('The essential distinguishing factor lies in whether or not the applicant for annulment is the addressee of the [measure] being challenged').

There are in essence four possible scenarios:

- If the act is addressed to the individual applicant, in principle such applicant has standing (i.e. that applicant does not have to satisfy the conditions of direct and individual concern).
- If the act is one of individual application not addressed to the individual applicant but addressed to a third party, the applicant must satisfy the conditions of direct and individual concern.
- If the act is an act of general application,[332] other than a regulatory act, the individual applicant must, here too, satisfy the conditions of direct and individual concern.
- Finally, as introduced by the Lisbon Treaty, if the act is an act of general application falling within the category of regulatory act and that act does not entail implementing measures, the individual applicant only needs to satisfy the condition of direct concern (not individual concern). The question of what types of acts fall within the concept of regulatory act is gradually being answered in the case-law (see para. 7.108).

(b) Contested act is addressed to applicant

(i) Decisions finding a violation of Art. 101 and/or Art. 102 TFEU or rejecting a complaint

7.86 Where the Commission finds that certain undertakings or associations of undertakings have infringed Art. 101 and/or Art. 102 TFEU and possibly imposes fines on them, the undertakings or associations of undertakings concerned may bring an action for the annulment of the decision in question.[333] As addressees of the decision, they derive that right from the fourth paragraph of Art. 263 TFEU.[334] Similarly, when a natural or legal

---

[332] If a measure lays down generally applicable principles, applies to objectively defined situations, and produces legal effects for categories of persons determined in an abstract manner, the measure will be regarded as an act of general application (see, e.g. ECJ, Joined Cases 36/58 to 38/58 and 40/58 to 41/58 *SIMET and Others v High Authority* [1959] E.C.R. 157, at 166; ECJ, Case 147/83 *Binderer v Commission* [1985] E.C.R. 257, paras 11–15; ECJ, Case C-244/88 *Usines Coopératives de Déshydratation du Vexin and Others v Commission* [1989] E.C.R. 3811, para. 13; ECJ, Case C-229/88 *Cargill and Others v Commission* [1990] E.C.R. I-1303, paras 13–19; CFI (order of 11 January 1995), Case T-116/94 *Cassa Nazionale di Previdenza ed Assistenza a favore degli Avvocati e Procuratori* [1995] E.C.R. II-1, paras 21–25; CFI (order of 19 June 1995), Case T-107/94 *Kik v Council and Commission* [1995] E.C.R. II-1717, para. 35; CFI, Case T-482/93 *Weber v Commission* [1996] E.C.R. II-609, para. 55; CFI, Case T-47/95 *Terres Rouges and Others v Commission* [1997] E.C.R. II-481, paras 40–41; CFI (order of 13 December 2005), Case T-381/02 *Confederation generale v Commission* [2005] E.C.R. II-5337, para. 49; CFI (order of 11 September 2007), Case T-35/06 *Honig-Verband v Commission* [2007] E.C.R. II-2865, paras 39–42; EGC (judgment of 27 February 2013), Case T-367/10 *Bloufin Touna Ellas Naftiki Etaireia and Others v Commission*, not reported, para. 19; EGC (judgment of 7 March 2013), Case T-94/10 *Rütgers Germany and Others v ECHA*, not reported, para. 57).

[333] A jointly and severally liable debtor may not attack the decision imposing a fine (for which he is jointly and severally liable) on another undertaking (since the Commission decision finding the infringement and imposing fines constitutes a bundle of individual decisions which can each be attacked by its own addressee) but such a debtor may put into question the validity of the determination of the fine imposed on the latter undertaking: see EGC, Case T-72/06 *Groupe Gascogne v Commission* [2011] E.C.R. II-400*, Summ. pub., paras 20–22. See also EGC, Case T-382/06 *Tomkins v Commission* [2011] E.C.R. II-1157, paras 35–46 (appeal dismissed: ECJ (judgment of 22 January 2013), Case C-286/11 P *Commission v Tomkins*, not reported). See also ECJ (judgment of 11 April 2013), Case C-652/11 P *Mindo v Commission*, not reported, paras 29–57.

[334] It goes without saying that a Member State, as a privileged applicant under the second paragraph of Art. 263 TFEU, can also bring an action seeking the annulment of a decision finding an infringement of Arts 101 and/or 102 TFEU: see EGC (judgment of 29 March 2012), Case T-398/07 *Spain v Commission*, not reported. A third party may also bring an action if he is directly and individually concerned by the challenged decision: see EGC (judgment of 12 April 2013), Case T-442/08 *CISAC v Commission*, not reported, paras 63–79.

person showing a legitimate interest lodges a complaint with the Commission on account of an alleged infringement of Art. 101 and/or Art. 102 TFEU,[335] such persons will be entitled—as addressees of the Commission decision—to bring an action for annulment against the full or partial rejection of their complaint.[336]

(ii) Addressees of merger decision

Where the Commission finds that a concentration is incompatible with the internal **7.87** market, the addressees of the relevant decision have standing, pursuant to the fourth paragraph of Art. 263 TFEU, to bring an action for annulment of that decision.

(c) The contested (non-regulatory) act is not addressed to the individual applicant: requirement of direct and individual concern to him

(i) General

Avoiding the risk of an actio popularis - Under the fourth paragraph of Art. 263 TFEU, an **7.88** application brought by natural or legal persons against acts not addressed to them will be admissible only insofar as such acts are of direct and individual concern to them, save for those acts falling within the concept of regulatory act (see para. 7.108).

The justification for the restriction lies in the far-reaching consequences of the annulment of a Union act. Annulment applies *erga omnes* and is retroactive. To make the action for annulment generally available might mean permanent litigation on Union measures of general application and open the way to an *actio popularis*.[337]

Cumulative requirements - Following from the text of the fourth paragraph of Art. 263 **7.89** TFEU, under circumstances in which the individual applicant is challenging an act not addressed to him, which falls outside the scope of a regulatory act (see para. 7.108), that applicant must fulfil the requirements of direct concern and individual concern within the meaning of the case-law. These two requirements are cumulative, meaning that both must be satisfied or the application for annulment is inadmissible.[338]

Accordingly, the Union judicature may find it appropriate to examine either the requirement of direct concern or that of individual concern first, and then, if necessary, proceed to examine the other. Depending on the particular circumstances of the case, the Union judicature may proceed to the substantive merits of the application for annulment

---

[335] Regulation No. 1/2003, Art. 7, and Regulation No. 773/2004, Art. 5.

[336] ECJ, Case 26/76 *Metro v Commission* [1977] E.C.R. 1875, para. 13; ECJ, Case 210/81 *Demo-Studio Schmidt v Commission* [1983] E.C.R. 3045, paras 10–16; CFI, Case T-37/92 *BEUC and NCC v Commission* [1994] E.C.R. II-285, para. 36; CFI, Case T-114/92 *BEMIM v Commission* [1995] E.C.R. II-147, para. 27; CFI, Case T-193/02 *Piau v Commission* [2005] E.C.R. II-209, para. 38.

[337] Opinion of Advocate General A. Dutheillet de Lamothe in ECJ, Joined Cases 9/71 and 11/71 *Compagnie d'Approvisionnement, de Transport et Crédit and Others v Commission* [1972] E.C.R. 391, at 411; Opinion of Advocate-General H. Mayras in ECJ, Case 43/72 *Merkur Aussenhandels v Commission* [1973] E.C.R. 1055, at 1078.

[338] See, e.g. ECJ (order of 13 July 2006), Case C-338/05 P *Front National v European Parliament* [2006] E.C.R. I-88*, Summ. pub., para. 32; ECJ (order of 8 December 2006), Case C-368/05 P *Polyelectrolyte Producers Group v Council and Commission* [2006] E.C.R. I-130*, Summ. pub., para. 63; ECJ (order of 26 November 2009), Case C-444/08 P *Azores v Council* [2009] E.C.R. I-200*, Summ. pub., para. 75, rejecting the applicant's contention that the Union judicature may consider the cumulative effect of the various factors relied upon by the applicant in order to demonstrate that one of those requirements (*in casu*, individual concern) has been met.

without first deciding on the objections raised by the defendant institution, body, office, or agency as regards the alleged inadmissibility of the action based upon the individual applicant's *locus standi*, in particular where it finds that the application must in any event be dismissed.[339]

(ii) Direct concern

7.90 *Definition* - The requirement that the contested measure not addressed to the applicant must be of direct concern to it expresses the rule that an applicant may bring an action for annulment only against acts of Union institutions, bodies, offices, or agencies which, as such, have legal effects on it.[340] By contrast, Union acts which are to be implemented by national authorities and in respect of which the latter have a discretion do not obtain their precise scope until they have been implemented. Interested individuals are entitled to challenge the implementing measures before the national courts when they have been adopted. If it is argued that the implementing measures are unlawful on the ground that the Union act purported to be implemented is invalid, the national court may (or must) make a reference to the Court of Justice for a preliminary ruling (see Ch. 10). In this way, the system of EU judicial protection reflects the structure of Union law-making.

7.91 *Criteria* - Under the case-law, in order for an individual to be regarded as directly concerned by a Union measure for the purposes of Art. 263 TFEU, that measure must first directly affect the legal situation of the person concerned;[341] and second, there must be no discretion left to the persons to whom that measure is addressed and who are responsible for its implementation, such implementation being purely automatic and resulting from Union rules without the application of other intermediate rules.[342] These two criteria are cumulative,[343] meaning that both must be satisfied or the application for annulment brought by the individual applicant is inadmissible.

---

[339] See, e.g. ECJ, Case C-23/00 P *Council v Boehringer* [2002] E.C.R. I-1873, paras 51–52; EGC, Case T-314/06 *Whirlpool Europe v Council* [2010] E.C.R. II-5005, para. 66; EGC, Case T-264/07 *CSL Behring v Commission and EMA* [2010] E.C.R. II-4469, para. 23; EGC, Case T-319/05 *Swiss Confederation v Commission* [2010] E.C.R. II-4265, paras 54–55; EGC, Case T-190/07 *KEK Diavlos v Commission* [2010] E.C.R. II-33*, Summ. pub., paras 32–33; EGC, Case T-36/06 *Bundesverband v Commission* [2010] E.C.R. II-537, paras 32–33; EGC (judgment of 11 July 2013), Case T-459/07 *Hangzhou Duralamp Electronics v Council*, not reported, paras 60–61. See also CFI, Case T-216/05 *Mebrom v Commission* [2007] E.C.R. II-1507, paras 60, 111.

[340] ECJ, Case 294/83 *Les Verts v European Parliament* [1986] E.C.R. 1339, para. 31: the contested measures are of direct concern to the applicant because they 'constitute a complete set of rules which are sufficient in themselves and . . . require no implementing provisions'. See also the Opinion of Advocate-General K. Roemer in ECJ, Case 25/62 *Plaumann v Commission* [1963] E.C.R. 95, at 114–15.

[341] If this requirement is not satisfied, the contested act may as regards the applicant be viewed not to constitute a challengeable act within the meaning of Art. 263 TFEU. See para. 7.21.

[342] See, e.g. ECJ, Case C-386/96 P *Dreyfus v Commission* [1998] E.C.R. I-2309, para. 43; ECJ, Case C-486/01 P *Front National v European Parliament* [2004] E.C.R. I-6289, para. 34; ECJ, Case C-417/04 P *Regione Siciliana v Commission* [2006] E.C.R. I-3881, para. 28; ECJ, Case C-15/06 P *Regione Siciliana v Commission* [2007] E.C.R. I-2591, para. 31; ECJ, Case C-125/06 P *Commission v Infront WM* [2008] E.C.R. I-1451, para. 47; ECJ, Case C-519/07 P *Commission v Koninklijke FrieslandCampina* [2009] E.C.R. I-8495, para. 48. The Court of Justice has further specified that the same applies where the possibility for addressees not to give effect to the Union measure is purely theoretical and their intention to act in conformity with it is not in doubt: see, e.g. ECJ, Case C-386/96 P *Dreyfus v Commission* [1998] E.C.R. I-2309, para. 44 (and citations therein). See also EGC (order of 27 November 2012), Case T-541/10 *Adedy and Others v Council*, not reported, para. 64 (and case-law cited therein).

[343] See, e.g. ECJ, Joined Cases C-445/07 and C-455/07 *Commission v Ente per le Ville Vesuviane* [2009] E.C.R. I-7993, para. 45; ECJ (order of 3 April 2009), Case C-387/08 P *VDH v Commission*, not reported,

Contested measure must directly affect the applicant's legal situation - As regards the first **7.92**
criterion, the requirement that the contested measure must be of direct concern will be
satisfied only if that measure is capable of directly producing effects on the applicant's legal
situation.[344]

A notable example is *Front National v European Parliament*, where the Court held that
an interpretative note, adopted in plenary session on 13 September 1999, to Rule 29(1) of
the Rules of Procedure of the European Parliament[345] which no longer permitted a political
group to be formed where the group openly rejected any political character and all
political affiliation between its Members did not directly affect the Front National as a
political party. As a result, the '*Groupe technique des députés indépendants*', to which the
Members of the Front National belonged, could no longer function as a political group.
Since, in accordance with the wording of Rule 29 of the Rules of Procedure, only Members
of the European Parliament could form political groups, the Front National as a political
party was affected only indirectly, with the result that the application brought by that party
for annulment of the interpretative note was declared inadmissible.[346] By contrast, a measure
relating to the funding of European political parties[347] was of direct concern only to the
political parties in question and not to individual Members of the European Parliament.[348]

Contested measure must leave no discretion to addressees entrusted with implementation - As regards **7.93**
the second criterion, in order for it to be found that a Union act is of direct concern to the
applicant, the question whether the contested measure confers a discretion on the national

---

para. 21; ECJ (order of 24 September 2009), Case C-501/08 P *Municipio de Gondomar v Commission* [2009]
E.C.R. I-152*, Summ. pub., para. 25; EGC (order of 21 May 2010), Case T-441/08 *ICO Services v European
Parliament and Council* [2010] E.C.R. II-100*, Summ. pub., para. 56 (and citations therein). The Union
judicature may mention only one of the criteria where the other one is obviously satisfied: see, e.g. EGC (order
of 15 December 2010), Joined Cases T-219/09 and T-326/09 *Albertini and Donnelly v European Parliament*
[2010] E.C.R. II-5935, para. 44.

[344] For examples in which this condition was not met, see ECJ, Case C-486/01 P *Front National v
European Parliament* [2004] E.C.R. I-6289, paras 34–43; CFI, Case T-96/92 *CCE de la Société Générale de
Grandes Sources and Others v Commission* [1995] E.C.R. II-1213, paras 38–46; CFI (order of 18 February
1998), Case T-189/97 *Comité d'entreprise de la Société française de production and Others v Commission* [1998]
E.C.R. II-335, paras 46–52; EGC (order of 21 May 2010), Case T-441/08 *ICO Services v European
Parliament and Council* [2010] E.C.R. II-100*, Summ. pub., paras 57 *et seq.* For examples in which this
condition was met, see ECJ, Case C-125/06 P *Commission v Infront WM* [2008] E.C.R. I-1451, paras 48–58;
EGC, Case T-385/07 *FIFA v Commission* [2011] E.C.R. II-205, paras 36–42; EGC, Case T-55/08 *UEFA v
Commission* [2011] E.C.R. II-271, paras 29–35; EGC, Case T-68/08 *FIFA v Commission* [2011]
E.C.R. II-349, paras 32–38; EGC (order of 21 September 2011), Case T-346/10 *Borax Europe v ECHA*
[2011] E.C.R. II-6629, paras 20–48. The fact that a regulation is directly applicable in the Member States
does not automatically mean that all legal or natural persons are directly concerned by that regulation: EGC
(order of 12 October 2011), Case T-149/11 *GS v European Parliament and Council* [2011] E.C.R. II-359*,
Summ. pub., para. 24.

[345] [1999] O.J. L202/1.

[346] ECJ, Case C-486/01 P *Front National v European Parliament* [2004] E.C.R. I-6289, paras 34–43 and
47. In contrast, the interpretative note did have a direct effect on Members of the European Parliament; see
CFI, Joined Cases T-222/99, T-327/99, and T-329/99 *Martinez and Others v European Parliament* [2001]
E.C.R. II-2823, para. 65, upheld on appeal in ECJ (order of 11 November 2003), Case C-488/01 P *Martinez
v European Parliament* [2003] E.C.R. I-3355.

[347] Regulation (EC) No. 2004/2003 of the European Parliament and of the Council of 4 November 2003
on the regulations governing political parties at European level and the rules regarding their funding ([2003]
O.J. L297/1).

[348] CFI (order of 11 July 2005), Case T-40/04 *Bonino and Others v European Parliament and Council*
[2005] E.C.R. II-2685, paras 39–59.

authorities or on its addressee[349] with regard to its implementation must be answered in the negative.[350] The idea is that there are no further national or Union acts required, the implementation of the contested measure being 'purely automatic' without the application of other intermediate rules, and hence the effects on the applicant's legal position are the direct consequence of the contested measure itself.[351] Conversely, the contested act will not be of direct concern to the applicant where, in implementing the act, the authorities entrusted with the task of implementation have a genuine discretion.[352]

Accordingly, an undertaking was found to be directly concerned by a Commission decision on State aid where there was no doubt as to the national authorities' intention to put the aid measure into effect.[353] An interested third party will also be directly affected by a

---

[349] The fact that the Commission declares a concentration notified to it pursuant to Regulation No. 4064/89 (now Regulation No. 139/2004—see para. 7.45) compatible with the internal market on condition that the notifying parties implement 'commitments' set forth in the notification does not prevent a third undertaking, which is affected by the implementation of those commitments, from being directly concerned by the Commission's decision. This is because there is no doubt that parties to the concentration have undertaken to implement those commitments, given that the Commission declared it compatible with the internal market in return for compliance with those commitments and the Commission may always revoke its decision under Art. 8 (5)(b) of Regulation No. 4064/89 if the undertakings concerned commit a breach of an obligation attached thereto (ECJ, Joined Cases C-68/94 and C-30/95 *France and Others and EMC v Commission* [1998] E.C.R. I-1375, para. 51).

[350] For examples where this criterion of direct concern was found, see, e.g. ECJ, Joined Cases 41/70 to 44/70 *International Fruit and Others v Commission* [1971] E.C.R. 411, paras 23–28; ECJ, Case 113/77 *NTN Toyo Bearing v Council* [1979] E.C.R. 1185, paras 11–12; ECJ, Case 118/77 *ISO v Council* [1979] E.C.R. 1277, paras 26–27; ECJ, Case 119/77 *Nippon Seiko v Council and Commission* [1979] E.C.R. 1303, paras 14–15; ECJ, Case 120/77 *Koyo Seiko v Council and Commission* [1979] E.C.R. 1337, paras 25–26; ECJ, Case 121/77 *Nachi Fujikoshi v Council* [1979] E.C.R. 1363, paras 11–12; ECJ, Joined Cases 87/77 and 130/77, 22/83, 9/84 and 10/84 *Salerno and Others v Commission* [1985] E.C.R. 2523, paras 31–32; ECJ, Case 207/86 *APESCO v Commission* [1988] E.C.R. 2151, para. 12; ECJ, Case C-386/96 P *Dreyfus v Commission* [1998] E.C.R. I-2309, paras 43 *et seq*; ECJ, Case C-125/06 P *Commission v Infront WM* [2008] E.C.R. I-1451, paras 59–63; CFI, Case T-155/94 *Climax Paper v Council* [1996] E.C.R. II-873, para. 53; CFI, Case T-170/94 *Shanghai Bicycle v Council* [1997] E.C.R. II-1383, para. 41; CFI, Joined Cases T-198/95, T-171/96, T-230/97, T-174/98, and T-225/99 *Comafrica and Dole Fresh Fruit Europe v Commission* [2001] E.C.R. II-1975, paras 96–98; EGC (order of 15 December 2010), Case T-219/09 and T-326/09 *Albertini and Donnelly v European Parliament* [2010] E.C.R. II-5935, para. 44. With respect to State aid, see, e.g. ECJ, Case C-519/07 P *Commission v Koninklijke FrieslandCampina* [2009] E.C.R. I-8495, paras 49–50.

[351] See CFI (order of 22 June 2006), Case T-150/05 *Sahlstedt and Others v Commission* [2006] E.C.R. II-1851, para. 53.

[352] See, e.g. ECJ, Case 123/77 *UNICME v Council* [1978] E.C.R. 845, para. 11; ECJ, Case 55/86 *ARPOSOL v Council* [1988] E.C.R. 13, paras 11–13; ECJ (order of 5 May 2009), Case C-372/08 P *Atlantic Dawn and Others v Commission* [2009] E.C.R. I-74*, Summ. pub., paras 35–41; ECJ (order of 19 June 2008), Case C-6/08 P *US Steel Košice v Commission* [2008] E.C.R. I-96*, Summ. pub., para. 60; CFI (order of 21 October 1993), Joined Cases T-492/93 and T-492/93 R *Nutral v Commission* [1993] E.C.R. II-1023, paras 26–29; CFI, Case T-54/96 *Oleifici Italiani and Fratelli Rubino Industrie Olearie v Commission* [1998] E.C.R. II-3377, para. 56; CFI (order of 15 March 2004), Case T-139/02 *Instituto N. Avgerinopoulou and Others v Commission* [2004] E.C.R. II-875, paras 62–70; CFI (order of 22 June 2006), Case T-136/04 *Freiherr von Cramer-Klett and Rechtlerverband Pfronten v Commission* [2006] E.C.R. II-1805, paras 47 *et seq.*; CFI (order of 22 June 2006), Case T-137/04 *Mayer and Others v Commission* [2006] E.C.R. II-1825, paras 60 *et seq.*; EGC (order of 12 October 2011), Case T-149/11 *GS v European Parliament and Council* [2011] E.C.R. II-359*, Summ. pub., paras 20–23; EGC (order of 27 November 2012), Case T-215/11 *Adedy and Others v Council*, not reported, paras 80–85.

[353] CFI, Case T-435/93 *ASPEC and Others v Commission* [1995] E.C.R. I-1281, para. 60; CFI, Case T-17/96 *TF1 v Commission* [1999] E.C.R. II-1757, para. 30; CFI, Case T-266/94 *Skibsværftsforeningen and Others v Commission* [1996] E.C.R. II-1399, para. 49; EGC (judgment of 30 May 2013), Joined Cases T-454/10 and T-482/11 *Anicav and Others v Commission*, not reported, para. 41.

Commission decision referring the examination of a concentration to the authorities of a Member State pursuant to Art. 9 of Regulation No. 4064/89 (now Regulation No. 139/2004). This is because the effect of the contested decision is to deprive the applicant of a review of the concentration by the Commission on the basis of Regulation No. 4064/89, of the procedural rights provided therein for third parties and of the judicial protection provided for by the Treaties. That effect is direct because the contested decision requires no additional implementing measure in order to render the referral effective.[354]

Directives - Although an application brought by a natural or legal person for annulment of a **7.94** directive is not inadmissible per se, nonetheless a directive is generally not likely to be of direct concern to such persons. This is because at least in principle, in transposing the directive, the Member States remain free to choose the form and method of implementing it in national law and achieving the result to be attained. In that context, a directive cannot in itself impose obligations on individuals. For those reasons, a directive is not capable in itself, independently of the adoption of implementing measures, of affecting the legal position of market participants.[355] That being said, there are circumstances in the case-law where a directive may be found to be of direct (and individual) concern to an individual applicant.[356]

Authorization by the Commission of an act of a Member State - A decision by which the **7.95** Commission authorizes Member States in some areas of Union law to diverge from the applicable general provisions may be of direct concern to individuals, depending on the circumstances. This will be so where, before they were given authorization, the national

---

[354] CFI, Joined Cases T-346/02 and T-347/02 *Cableuropa and Others v Commission* [2003] E.C.R. II-4251, paras 64–65.

[355] CFI (order of 10 September 2002), Case T-223/01 *Japan Tobacco and JT International v European Parliament and Council* [2002] E.C.R. II-3259, paras 45–50; CFI, Joined Cases T-172/98 and T-175/98 to T-177/98 *Salamander and Others v European Parliament and Council* [2000] E.C.R. II-2487, para. 54; CFI (order of 6 May 2003) Case T-45/02 *DOW AgroSciences and Others v European Parliament and Council* [2003] E.C.R. II-1973, paras 35–40. See also ECJ (order of 7 December 1988), Case 138/88 *Flourez v Council* [1988] E.C.R. 6393, paras 10–12; ECJ (order of 7 December 1988) Case 160/88 *Fédération Européenne de la Santé Animale and Others v Council* [1988] E.C.R. 6399, paras 12–14; ECJ, Case C-298/89 *Gibraltar v Council* [1993] E.C.R. I-3605, paras 14–24; CFI (order of 29 October 1993), Case T-463/93 *GUNA v Council* [1993] E.C.R. II-1206, para. 13; CFI (order of 20 October 1994), Case T-99/94 *Asocarne v Council* [1994] E.C.R. II-871, paras 17–19; ECJ (order of 23 November 1995), Case C-10/95 P *Asocarne v Council* [1995] E.C.R. I-4149, paras 29–34; CFI (order of 16 February 2007), Case T-449/05 *Dikigorikos Syllogos Ioanninon v European Parliament and Council* [2007] E.C.R. II-14*, Summ. pub., paras 60, 67–68.

[356] See, e.g. CFI, Case T-135/96 *UEAPME v Council* [1998] E.C.R. II-2335, para. 90, from which it appears that, exceptionally, it is possible that an applicant may be directly and individually concerned by a directive if it can prove that it has a right which the Union institutions should have taken into account when they adopted the directive. This is because the mere existence of such a right means that its holder should be afforded legal protection. See also CFI, Case T-420/05 *Vischim v Commission* [2009] E.C.R. II-3841, paras 69–79 (finding that contested directive was of direct and individual concern to the applicant; as regards direct concern (paras 74–78), the Court of First Instance considered, first, that in laying down the conditions for placing the substance at issue on the EU market, the contested directive directly affected the applicant's legal situation, as a company manufacturing that substance; and second, the action which the Member States had to take pursuant to the contested directive was purely automatic, without any discretion in the matter concerned); CFI, Case T-380/06 *Vischim v Commission* [2009] E.C.R. II-3911, paras 57–59, where the Court of First Instance held, first, that the applicant, as a notifier and a holder of existing authorizations for plant protection products containing the substance at issue, is directly and individually concerned by the inclusion of that substance in certain provisions of Union law and thus by the contested directive amending the conditions of its inclusion; and second, the contested directive was adopted following an assessment requested by the applicant and relating, *inter alia*, to its product. Consequently, the applicant was entitled to seek the annulment of the contested directive as regards the temporal effects defined by a certain provision therein.

authorities limited their discretion themselves. The Court of Justice has therefore held that where the Member State concerned makes it known beforehand that it will implement an authorizing decision, that decision will be of direct concern to individuals.[357] The Member State's position does not have to be express; it may be inferred from all relevant factors.[358] If a Member State does not make its position known beforehand with regard to an authorizing decision, it reserves its power of discretion and the decision is not of direct concern to individuals.[359]

If an application from a Member State for authorization is refused and this adversely affects an individual's interests, the requirement that the contested act must be of direct concern to the applicant is assessed just as if the authorization had been granted.[360] Authorization from the Commission of a protective measure already adopted by a Member State is of direct concern to individuals.[361]

7.96 *Aid programmes financed by the Commission* - In the context of aid programmes financed by the Union or the grant of Union loans to non-member countries, one and the same division of powers is generally instituted between the authorities of the beneficiary State and the Union institutions. The authorities of the beneficiary State have the power to select a contractual partner to carry out a particular project, to negotiate the contractual conditions, and to conclude the agreement. The Commission is given the task only of examining whether the conditions for Union financing are met. Entities competing for the grant of a particular project are in a legal relationship only with the authorities of the beneficiary State. For its part, the Commission has legal relations only with the authorities of the beneficiary State. This pattern of legal relations means that the decision by which the Commission approves the financing of a contract concluded by the beneficiary State is not of direct concern to natural and legal persons to which the contract is not granted.[362] This is because the Commission's decision to finance the project does not take the place of the decision of the beneficiary State granting the contract in question.[363] However, it is possible for

---

[357] ECJ, Case 62/70 *Bock v Commission* [1971] E.C.R. 897, paras 6–8; contra: ECJ, Joined Cases 10/68 and 18/68 '*Eridania' Zuccherifici Nationali and Others v Commission* [1969] E.C.R. 459, para. 11. A decision by which the Commission declares, pursuant to Directive 89/552/EEC ('television-without-frontiers' directive), that an autonomous decision by a Member State to impede reception of a television broadcaster established in a another Member State on the grounds that it is likely to impair the development of minors is compatible with Union law is not of direct concern to the broadcaster. The reason for this is that the Commission decision does not replace the national measure and cannot be regarded as a prior authorization, with the result that the national measure does not implement the Commission decision (CFI, Case T-69/99 *DSTV v Commission* [2000] E.C.R. II-4039, paras 24–32).

[358] ECJ, Case 11/82 *Piraiki-Patraiki v Commission* [1985] E.C.R. 207, paras 7–10.

[359] Cf. ECJ, Case 123/77 *UNICME v Council* [1978] E.C.R. 845, paras 8–20 (where derogating rules were provided for a Member State in a Council regulation).

[360] ECJ, Case 69/69 *Alcan v Commission* [1970] E.C.R. 385, para. 15: 'The decision rejecting the request does not . . . concern the applicants in any other way than would the positive decision which they wish to obtain.'

[361] ECJ, Joined Cases 106/63 and 107/63 *Toepfer and Getreide-Import v Commission* [1965] E.C.R. 405, at 411.

[362] ECJ, Case 126/83 *STS v Commission* [1984] E.C.R. 2769, para. 18; ECJ, Case 118/83 *CMC v Commission* [1985] E.C.R. 2325, para. 28.

[363] However, a Commission act which, by reason of its context, may be isolated from the procedure for the conclusion of a contract between the beneficiary State and an undertaking inasmuch as the Commission adopted it in the exercise of its own powers and specifically directed it to an individual undertaking, which loses any chance of actually being awarded the contract simply because that act is adopted, does give rise to

the natural or legal person, including sub-national or regional entities to which the beneficiary State awarded a contract, to be directly concerned by the Commission decision refusing financing. This depends on the circumstances in which the Commission decision was adopted.[364] If it appears that the Commission decision refusing Union financing deprived the applicant of any real possibility of performing the transaction entered into with the beneficiary State or of obtaining payment of the goods supplied on the agreed terms, the applicant's 'legal situation' will be directly concerned. This will be the case where the contract with the beneficiary State was concluded on account of the commitments which the Commission would enter into in its capacity as 'financing authority' once it found that the contract was in conformity with the Union rules.[365]

(iii) Individual concern

Definition - An act not addressed to natural or legal persons will be of individual concern to them if it 'affects them by reason of certain attributes which are peculiar to them or by reason of circumstances in which they are differentiated from all other persons and by virtue of these factors distinguishes them individually just as in the case of the person addressed   **7.97**

---

binding legal effects as regards the undertaking in question and may therefore be regarded as an act adversely affecting it against which the undertaking concerned may bring an action for annulment: ECJ, Case C-395/95 P *Geotronics v Commission* [1997] E.C.R. I-2271, paras 12–15.

[364] The assessment is not always easy to make. Compare, in particular, CFI (order of 8 July 2004), Case T-341/02 *Regione Siciliana v Commission* [2004] E.C.R. II-2877, paras 47–80 (no direct concern), appeal dismissed in ECJ, Case C-417/04 P *Regione Siciliana v Commission* [2006] E.C.R. I-3881; CFI (order of 18 October 2005), Case T-60/03 *Regione Siciliana v Commission* [2005] E.C.R. II-4139, paras 44–68 (direct concern), set aside in ECJ, Case C-15/06 P *Regione Siciliana v Commission* [2007] E.C.R. I-2591; and CFI, Case T-189/02 *Ente per le Ville Vesuviane v Commission* [2007] E.C.R. II-89*, Summ. pub., paras 37–53 (direct concern), set aside in ECJ, Joined Cases C-445/07 P and C-455/07 P *Commission v Ente per le Ville Vesuviane* [2009] E.C.R. I-7993. See further CFI (order of 22 November 2006), Case T-225/02 *Cámara de Comercio e Industria de Zaragoza v Commission* [2006] E.C.R. II-92*, Summ. pub., paras 41–51 (no direct concern); CFI (order of 11 December 2007), Case T-156/06 *Regione Siciliana v Commission* [2007] E.C.R. II-168*, Summ. pub., paras 39–55 (no direct concern); CFI (order of 10 September 2008), Case T-324/06 *Municipio de Gondomar v Commission* [2008] E.C.R. II-173*, Summ. pub., paras 37–44 (no direct concern), upheld on appeal in ECJ, C-501/08 P *Municipio de Gondomar v Commission* [2009] E.C.R. I-152*, Summ. pub.; CFI (order of 25 September 2008), Joined Cases T-392/03, T-408/03, T-414/03, and T-435/03 *Regione Siciliana v Commission* [2008] E.C.R. II-2489, paras 24–28 (no direct concern); CFI (order of 25 September 2008), Case T-363/03 *Regione Siciliana v Commission* [2008] E.C.R. II-201*, Summ. pub., paras 19–26 (no direct concern); EGC, Case T-401/07 *Caixa Geral de Depositos v Commission* [2011] E.C.R. II-39*, Summ. pub., pars 58–85 (no direct concern), upheld on appeal in ECJ (order of 16 May 2013), Case C-242/11 P *Caixa Geral de Depositos v Commission*, not reported; EGC (order of 14 September 2011), Case T-84/10 *Regione Puglia v Commission* [2011] E.C.R. II-282*, Summ. pub., paras 42–44 (no direct concern). For broader discussion, with particular regard to the *Regione Siciliana* litigation, see J. L. da Cruz Vilaça, 'La protection juridictionnelle des particuliers en matière de fonds communautaire. Peut-on être "directement concerné" par une décision adressée à un État membre?', in C. Boutayeb, J. C. Masclet, S. Rodrigues, and H. Ruiz Fabri (eds), *L'Union européenne: union de droit, union des droits. Mélanges en l'honneur de Philippe Manin* (Paris, Pedone, 2010), 851–64.

[365] ECJ, Case C-386/96 P *Dreyfus v Commission* [1998] E.C.R. I-2309, paras 40–56; ECJ, Case C-391/96 P *Compagnie Continentale v Commission* [1998] E.C.R. I-2377, paras 38–54; ECJ, Case C-403/96 P *Glencore Grain v Commission* [1998] E.C.R. I-2405, paras 40–56; ECJ, Case C-404/96 P *Glencore Grain v Commission* [1998] E.C.R. I-2435, paras 38–54: the Court of Justice set aside the judgments given by the Court of First Instance in these cases in which the latter court held that the applicants were not directly concerned. In comparison with the approach taken by the Court of Justice, the Court of First Instance made a formal juridical analysis of the question whether the applicants' 'legal situation' was affected, whereas the Court of Justice based its reasoning more on the 'objective economic' finding that the third country could not execute the contracts concluded with the applicant for the supply of grain in the absence of EU aid.

[by the act]'.[366] This means that the applicant must prove that the contested act, which, in terms of form, is not addressed to him, affects him substantively as if the act were addressed to him.[367] This is a particularly strict requirement, and it extensively curtails the ability of natural or legal persons to bring actions for annulment.[368]

7.98 *Contested act is a measure of individual application* - Where the contested measure is an act of individual application, it is sufficient for the applicant to show that, at the time when that act was adopted, he or she was part of a closed class of persons concerned by that act.[369] In other words, where the contested measure (formerly a 'decision' under the nomenclature of what was then the fourth paragraph of Art. 230 EC) affects a group of persons who were identified or identifiable when that measure was adopted by reason of criteria specific to the members of the group, those persons may be individually concerned by that measure inasmuch as they form part of a limited class of traders.[370] This is so particularly when the contested measure alters rights acquired by the individual prior to its adoption.[371]

It makes no difference whether the class is large or small or whether its members are known by name. Various sets of circumstances may bring about a closed class. Accordingly, a closed class is involved where the contested decision affects only persons who satisfied certain conditions before it was adopted.[372] This is a situation in which the contested act has completely retroactive effect. Because the number of persons who satisfied the conditions laid down for the application of the decision in the past can no longer change, the act

---

[366] ECJ, Case 25/62 *Plaumann v Commission* [1963] E.C.R. 95, at 107.

[367] ECJ (order of 12 December 2003), Case C-258/02 P *Bactria Industriehygiene-Service v Commission* [2003] E.C.R. I-15105, paras 34, 36, and 50: the time for assessing whether the individual was individually concerned is the date of adoption of the contested act; CFI, Case T-112/97 *Monsanto v Commission* [1999] E.C.R. II-1277, paras 48–60: a parent company is individually concerned by a decision addressed to its wholly owned subsidiary.

[368] An attempt by Greenpeace to have the individual concern requirement less strictly interpreted in environmental cases was rejected by both the now General Court and the Court of Justice (sitting as the Full Court): CFI (order of 9 August 1995), Case T-585/93 *Greenpeace v Commission* [1995] E.C.R. II-2205, paras 59–65 and ECJ, Case C-321/95 P *Greenpeace and Others v Commission* [1998] E.C.R. I-1651, paras 27–35. See also CFI (order of 28 November 2005), Joined Cases T-236/04 and T-241/04 *EEB and Stichting Natuur en Milieu v Commission* [2005] E.C.R. II-4945, para. 63, in which the CFI, in finding that these two environmental entities did not satisfy the requirement of individual concern, made clear that Union law, 'as it stands now, does not provide for a right to bring a class action' before the Union courts as envisaged by the applicants in relation to environmental protection. It also made clear that notwithstanding the adoption of a Union measure on the Aarhus Convention, this did not remove the requirement that the applicant must be individually concerned by the contested measure, thereby declaring the action inadmissible. CFI, Joined Cases T-236/04 and T-241/04 *EEB and Stichting Natuur en Milieu v Commission*, paras 70–73. In the latter regard, see also CFI, Case T-37/04 *Região autónoma dos Açores v Council* [2008] E.C.R. II-103*, Summ. pub., para. 93 (appeal dismissed in ECJ (order of 26 November 2009), Case C-444/08 P *Região autónoma dos Açores v Council* [2009] E.C.R. I-200*, Summ. pub.).

[369] ECJ, Case 97/85 *Deutsche Lebensmittelwerke v Commission* [1987] E.C.R. 2265, para. 11 (using the expression 'closed circle', albeit such circumstances were not present in those proceedings); See also ECJ (order of 24 May 1993), Case C-131/92 *Arnaud and Others v Council* [1993] E.C.R. I-2573, para. 8 (where the applicant used the expression 'closed class').

[370] See, e.g. ECJ, Case 11/82 *Piraiki-Patraiki and Others v Commission* [1985] E.C.R. 207, para. 31; ECJ, Case C-152/88 *Sofrimport v Commission* [1990] E.C.R. I-2477, para. 11; ECJ, Joined Cases C-182/03 and C-217/03 *Belgium and Forum 187 v Commission* [2006] E.C.R. I-5479, para. 60; ECJ, Case C-125/06 P *Commission v Infront WM* [2008] E.C.R. I-1451, para. 71.

[371] ECJ, Case C-125/06 P *Commission v Infront WM* [2008] E.C.R. I-1451, para. 72 (and citations therein).

[372] See, e.g. ECJ, Joined Cases C-182/03 and C-217/03 *Belgium and Forum 187 v Commission* [2006] E.C.R. I-5479, paras 60–64; ECJ, Case C-125/06 P *Commission v Infront WM* [2008] E.C.R. I-1451, paras 71–78.

is applicable to a closed class. For example, a Commission decision approving a national decision refusing to grant import licences concerns the closed class of importers who were refused an import licence before the Commission decision was taken. That group was known (or at least ascertainable) when the decision was adopted.[373]

More recently, in its judgment in *Commission v Infront WM*, the Court of Justice considered that the applicant held pre-existing exclusive broadcasting rights for certain designated events approved by the contested decision and at the time of its adoption, there were only six companies who had made substantial investments in the acquisition of television broadcasting rights to events on the list set forth in the decision. On that basis, it found that the contested decision affected the members of the group formed of those six companies, including the applicant, by reason of an attribute peculiar to them, namely as holders of the exclusive television broadcasting rights to designed events, and thus the applicant was individually concerned by the contested decision.[374]

Contested act is a measure of general application - Where, in contrast, the contested act is a **7.99** measure of general application,[375] it is not enough for the applicant to show that it belongs to a closed class in order to show that it is individually concerned by it.[376]

The fact that the persons to whom such a measure is applicable are identifiable (meaning the possibility of determining more or less precisely the number, or even the identity, of the persons to whom a measure applies) is not determinative in itself.[377] Also, the fact that an

---

373 ECJ, Joined Cases 106/63 and 107/63 *Toepfer and Getreide-Import v Commission* [1965] E.C.R. 405, at 411–12. See also ECJ, Case 62/70 *Bock v Commission* [1971] E.C.R. 897, paras 2–5.

374 ECJ, Case C-125/06 P *Commission v Infront WM* [2008] E.C.R. I-1451, paras 71–78.

375 If a measure lays down generally applicable principles, applies to objectively defined situations, and produces legal effects for categories of persons determined in an abstract manner, the measure will be regarded as an act of general application (see, e.g. ECJ, Joined Cases 36/58 to 38/58 and 40/58 to 41/58 *SIMET and Others v High Authority* [1959] E.C.R. 157, at 166; ECJ, Case 147/83 *Binderer v Commission* [1985] E.C.R. 257, paras 11–15; ECJ, Case C-244/88 *Usines Coopératives de Déshydratation du Vexin and Others v Commission* [1989] E.C.R. 3811, para. 13; ECJ, Case C-229/88 *Cargill and Others v Commission* [1990] E.C.R. I-1303, paras 13–19; CFI (order of 11 January 1995), Case T-116/94 *Cassa Nazionale di Previdenza ed Assistenza a favore degli Avvocati e Procuratori* [1995] E.C.R. II-1, paras 21–25; CFI (order of 19 June 1995), Case T-107/94 *Kik v Council and Commission* [1995] E.C.R. II-1717, para. 35; CFI, Case T-482/93 *Weber v Commission* [1996] E.C.R. II-609, para. 55; CFI, Case T-47/95 *Terres Rouges and Others v Commission* [1997] E.C.R. II-481, paras 40–41; CFI (order of 13 December 2005), Case T-381/02 *Confederation generale v Commission* [2005] E.C.R. II-5337, para. 49; CFI (order of 11 September 2007), Case T-35/06 *Honig-Verband v Commission* [2007] E.C.R. II-2865, paras 39–42).

376 CFI, Case T-482/93 *Weber v Commission* [1996] E.C.R. II-609, paras 65 *et seq.*; EGC, Case T-291/04 *Enviro Tech Europe and Enviro Tech International v Commission* [2011] E.C.R. II-8281, paras 103–104; EGC, Case T-120/08 *Arch Chemicals, Inc. and Others v Commission* [2011] E.C.R. II-298*, Summ. pub., paras 38–47. See also EGC, Case T-16/04 *Arcelor v European Parliament and Council* [2010] E.C.R. II-211, paras 76–81, 106–109, 112–117 (rejecting the applicant's argument that it was part of a 'closed category' of companies particularly affected by the contested measure of general application, especially on account of the allegedly 'unique lock-in situation' of that group of producers); EGC (order of 28 September 2011), Case T-96/09 *UCAPT v Council* [2011] E.C.R. II-328*, Summ. pub., paras 32–33.

377 See, e.g. ECJ, Case 6/68 *Zuckerfabrik Watenstedt v Council* [1968] E.C.R. 409; ECJ, Case 63/69 *Compagnie Française Commerciale et Financière v Commission* [1970] E.C.R. 221, para. 11; ECJ, Case 123/77 *UNICME v Council* [1978] E.C.R. 845, para. 16; ECJ, Case 242/81 *Roquette Frères v Council* [1982] E.C.R. 3213, para. 7; ECJ, Case 26/86 *Deutz and Geldermann v Council* [1987] E.C.R. 941, para. 8; ECJ, Joined Cases 97/86, 193/86, 99/86, and 215/86 *Asteris v Commission* [1988] E.C.R. 2181, para. 13; ECJ (order of the President of 13 July 1988), Case 160/88 R *Fédération Européenne de la Santé Animale and Others v Council* [1988] E.C.R. 4121, para. 29; ECJ, Joined Cases C-15/91 and C-108/91 *Buckl and Others v Commission* [1992] E.C.R. I-6061, para. 25; ECJ (order of 24 May 1993), Case C-131/92 *Arnaud v Council* [1993]

act of general application is applicable only to a small number of individuals,[378] that certain market participants are affected more harshly in economic terms than their competitors,[379] or that different specific consequences may ensue for the various persons to whom the contested measure applies[380] is not sufficient to show that the persons in question are individually concerned by the measure.[381]

If the situation to be regulated is such that, in order to attain its aim, the contested measure must be held to be applicable without distinction to facts which existed at the time when it entered into effect and to similar facts which arose thereafter, an applicant cannot rely on its partial retroactive effect in order to claim that it is individually concerned by that measure.[382]

7.100 *Exceptional circumstances in which the applicant is individually concerned by a measure of general application* - An applicant can show in only limited ways that it is individually concerned by a measure of general application.[383]

E.C.R. I-2573, paras 13–17; ECJ, Case C-213/91 *Abertal v Commission* [1993] E.C.R. I-3177, paras 17–24; ECJ (orders of 21 June 1993), Case C-257/93 *Van Parijs and Others v Council and Commission* [1993] E.C.R. I-3335, para. 8, and ECJ, Case C-276/93 *Chiquita Banana and Others v Council* [1993] E.C.R. I-3345, para. 8; ECJ, Case C-298/89 *Gibraltar v Council* [1993] E.C.R. I-3605, para. 17; ECJ (order of 8 April 2008), Case C-503/07 P *Saint-Gobain Glass Deutschland and Others v Commission* [2008] E.C.R. I-2217, para. 70; ECJ, Case C-362/06 P *Sahlstedt and Others v Commission* [2009] E.C.R. I-2903, para. 31; EGC, Case T-16/04 *Arcelor v European Parliament and Council* [2010] E.C.R. II-211, para. 106; EGC, Case T-291/04 *Enviro Tech Europe and Enviro Tech International v Commission* [2011] E.C.R. II-8281, paras 104, 110. For the possibility that the contested act is also applicable to situations in the future, see ECJ, Case 231/82 *Spijker v Commission* [1983] E.C.R. 2559, paras 8–11; CFI (order of 11 May 2001), Case T-178/96 *Eridania and Others v Council*, not reported, para. 53.

[378] ECJ, Case C-263/02 P *Commission v Jégo-Quéré* [2004] E.C.R. I-3425, para. 46. For the possibility that the contested measure is also applicable to individuals established in another Member State, see ECJ, Case 1/64 *Glucoseries Réunies v Commission* [1964] E.C.R. 413, at 417.

[379] ECJ, Case C-312/00 P *Commission v Camar and Tico* [2002] E.C.R. I-11355, paras 69–83: the chief importer of Somalian bananas was not individually concerned by the Commission's refusal to adjust the tariff quota for such bananas; CFI (order of 15 September 1999), Case T-11/99 *Van Parijs and Others v Commission* [1999] E.C.R. II-2653, para. 50; CFI (order of 8 July 2004), Case T-338/03 *Edidania Sadam and Others v Commission*, not reported, para. 35; EGC, Case T-16/04 *Arcelor v European Parliament and Council* [2010] E.C.R. II-211, para. 106 (and citations therein). The fact that the applicant may lose a major source of revenue as a result of new legislation does not prove that he is in a specific situation and is not sufficient to establish that that legislation applies to him individually, the applicant having to adduce proof of circumstances which make it possible to consider that the harm allegedly suffered is such as to distinguish him individually from all other economic operators concerned by that legislation in the same way as he is: see, e.g. EGC, Case T-291/04 *Enviro Tech Europe and Enviro Tech International v Commission* [2011] E.C.R. II-8281, para. 110 (and citations therein). Also, the fact that the applicant is the largest undertaking in the sector in question does not individualize its position sufficiently: see, e.g. CFI (order of 29 April 1999), Case T-120/98 *Alce v Commission* [1999] E.C.R. I-1395, paras 21–23.

[380] ECJ (order of 18 December 1997), Case C-409/96 P *Sveriges Betodlares Centralförening and Henrikson v Commission* [1997] E.C.R. I-7531, para. 37; CFI (order of the President of 15 February 2000), Case T-1/00 R *Hölzl and Others v Commission* [2000] E.C.R. II-251, para. 21; CFI (order of 6 July 2004), Case T-370/02 *Alpenhain-Camembert-Werk and Others v Commission* [2004] E.C.R. II-2097, para. 62.

[381] ECJ, Case 38/64 *Getreide-Import v Commission* [1965] E.C.R. 203, at 208. In that case, the contested act was a decision addressed to all Member States valid for one day and laying down the basis for an import levy. The applicant was the only individual who had applied for an import certificate.

[382] ECJ, Case C-244/88 *Usines Coopératives de Déshydratation du Vexin and Others v Commission* [1989] E.C.R. 3811, paras 11–14; ECJ, Case C-229/88 *Cargill and Others v Commission* [1990] E.C.R. I-1303, paras 13–18.

[383] This is so, in particular in the case of actions for annulment brought by individual applicants against tariff classification regulations. Generally, natural and legal persons may not, as a rule, bring actions under the

In the first place, an applicant will be individually concerned where the act adversely affected specific rights of the applicant or its members.[384] This is exceptional, and there is only one instance to be found in the case-law to date. In *Codorníu*,[385] the Court of Justice held that a provision of a Council regulation which reserved the use of the term 'crémant' to sparkling wine produced in France and Luxembourg prevented the Spanish undertaking concerned from continuing to sell its wine under the trade mark '*Gran Cremant de Codorníu*'. It had registered this trade mark in Spain as long ago as 1924. It was therefore in a position which differentiated it, from the point of view of the provision concerned, from all other market participants.

---

fourth para. of Art. 263 TFEU for annulment of such measures, since in spite of the apparent specificity of the descriptions they contain, they are nonetheless entirely of general application. Although such measures may be, in certain circumstances, of direct and individual concern to some operators, here too, the assessment of the individual concern requirement is strict, save for some exceptional circumstances carved out in the case-law, namely, CFI, Case T-243/01 *Sony Computer Entertainment Europe v Commission* [2003] E.C.R. II-4189, paras 58–78. Compare CFI (order of 19 February 2008), Case T-82/06 *Apple Computer International v Commission* [2008] E.C.R. II-279, paras 44–60 (distinguishing the present proceedings from the *Sony* case).

[384] ECJ, Case C-309/89 *Codorníu v Council* [1994] E.C.R. I-1853, paras 19–22. For some examples in which *Codorníu* was distinguished from the instant proceedings, see ECJ (order of 23 November 1995), Case C-10/95 P *Asocarne v Council* [1995] E.C.R. I-4149, para. 49 (no specific right infringed); ECJ (order of 21 November 2005), Case C-482/04 P *SNF v Commission*, not reported, paras 40–42 (upholding the CFI's decision that the applicant did not hold a right exclusively to market products identical to that at issue in *Codorníu*); ECJ (order of 30 March 2006), Case C-113/05 P *EFfCI v European Parliament and Council* [2006] E.C.R. I-46*, Summ. pub., paras 45–47 (no specific right infringed, despite the fact that the applicant complained that its intellectual property rights had been impaired by the contested general measure); ECJ (order of 17 February 2009), Case C-483/07 P *Galileo Lebensmittel v Commission* [2009] E.C.R. I-959, para. 45 (no specific right infringed, despite the fact that the applicant complained that its intellectual property rights had been impaired by the contested general measure); ECJ (order of 26 March 2009), Case C-146/08 P *Efkon v European Parliament and Council* [2009] E.C.R. I-49*, Summ. pub., paras 39–42 (no specific right infringed, despite alleged interference with intellectual property rights); CFI (order of 26 March 1999), Case T-114/96 *Confiserie du TECH and Biscuiterie Confiserie LOR v Commission* [1999] E.C.R. II-913, para. 33 (no specific right infringed); CFI (order of 6 July 2004), Case T-370/02 *Alpenhain-Camembert-Werk and Others v Commission* [2004] E.C.R. II-2097, paras 65–66 (no specific right infringed; an application for annulment brought by manufacturers of Feta cheese established in Denmark against a regulation that made it impossible for them to go on making cheese under that denomination was declared inadmissible); CFI (order of 6 September 2004), Case T-213/02 *SNF v Commission* [2004] E.C.R. II-3047, paras 65–71 (no specific right infringed, despite the fact that the applicant complained that its intellectual property rights had been impaired by the contested general measure); CFI (order of 10 December 2004), Case T-196/03 *European Federation for Cosmetic Ingredients v European Parliament and Council* [2004] E.C.R. II-4263, paras 56–62 (no specific rights infringed, despite the fact that the applicant complained that its intellectual property rights had been impaired by the contested general measure); CFI (order of 13 December 2005), Case T-381/02 *Confederation generale des producteurs v Commission* [2005] E.C.R. II-5337, paras 79–80 (no specific right affected in context of action for annulment brought by association established in France against regulation concerning the registration of 'feta' as designation of origin); CFI (order of 12 March 2007), Case T-417/04 *Regione autonoma Friuli-Venezia Giulia v Commission* [2007] E.C.R. II-paras 59–60 (no sufficient proof that any industrial and commercial property rights or intellectual property rights have been affected); CFI (order of 3 July 2007), Case T-212/02 *Commune de Champagne and Others v Council and Commission* [2007] E.C.R. II-2017, paras 186–189 (distinguishing the applicants' right to use the Swiss designation 'Champagne' under Swiss law from situation in *Codorníu*). Indeed, as recognized in the case-law, the existence of an actual or individual right, including a right of ownership, whose scope or exercise is potentially affected by the contested measure is not as such capable of distinguishing the rightholder individually, especially where other operators may enjoy similar rights and hence be in the same situation as the rightholder: see EGC, Case T-291/04 *Enviro Tech Europe and Enviro Tech International v Commission* [2011] E.C.R. II-8281, para. 116 (and citations therein); see also EGC, Case T-120/08 *Arch Chemicals, Inc. and Others v Commission* [2011] E.C.R. II-298*, Summ. pub., paras 54–56.

[385] ECJ, Case C-309/89 *Codorníu v Council* [1994] E.C.R. I-1853 paras 19–22.

Second, the applicant may argue that, in adopting the contested measure of general application, the Union institution was under a duty to take account of its specific circumstances. Such specific protection distinguishes it sufficiently from other market participants to which the act applies. In addition, there is the fact that such a market participant must be able to assert that specific protection and therefore to bring an action.[386] However, the fact that a natural or legal person intervenes in some way in the procedure leading to the adoption of a Union act can only cause that person to be individually concerned with regard to that act within the meaning of the fourth paragraph of Art. 263 TFEU if the applicable Union rules confer on that person specific procedural guarantees,[387] such as the right to be heard.[388] Even then, a natural or legal person enjoying a procedural right will not, as a rule, where there is any type of procedural guarantee, have standing to bring proceedings contesting the legality of a Union act in terms of its substantive content; the precise scope of an individual's right of action against a Union act depends on his legal position as defined by Union law with a view to protecting the legitimate interests thus afforded to him.[389]

---

[386] ECJ, Case 11/82 *Piraiki-Patraiki v Commission* [1985] E.C.R. 207, paras 17–32; ECJ, Case C-209/94 P *Buralux and Others v Council* [1996] E.C.R. I-615, paras 30–35; ECJ, Case C-152/88 *Sofrimport v Commission* [1990] E.C.R. I-2477, paras 8–13; ECJ, Case C-390/95 P *Antillean Rice Mills v Council* [1999] E.C.R. I-769, paras 25–30; ECJ, Case C-167/02 P *Rothley and Others v European Parliament* [2004] E.C.R. I-3149, paras 32–38. Compare, e.g. EGC (order of 15 December 2010), Joined Cases T-219/09 and T-326/09 *Albertini and Donnelly v European Parliament* [2010] E.C.R. II-5935, paras 47–51 (rejecting applicant' arguments, on the basis of this line of case-law, finding no obligation by virtue of the provisions of Union law concerned, to take account of the applicants' situation). Cf., however, ECJ, Case C-451/98 *Antillean Rice Mills v Council* [2001] E.C.R. I-8949, paras 56–68 and ECJ, Case C-452/98 *Nederlandse Antillen v Council* [2001] E.C.R. I-8973, paras 54–77, in which the Court of Justice stated in relatively strong terms that the requirement for the Council to take account of the effects of an intended safeguard measure based on the OCT Decision (Decision on the association of the overseas countries and territories) on the OCTs concerned was not sufficient to individualize the OCT in question. In CFI, Joined Cases T-32/98 and T-41/98 *Nederlandse Antillen v Commission* [2000] E.C.R. II-201, the Court of First Instance declared an action brought by the Netherlands Antilles for annulment of a safeguard measure relating to the import of sugar from OCTs admissible and well-founded. It considered that the Commission was required to take account of the adverse effects for the Netherlands Antilles of a safeguard measure adopted pursuant to Art. 109(2) of the OCT Decision. However, that judgment was set aside by the Court of Justice on the grounds that the factual situation of the Netherlands Antilles did not differentiate them from all other OCTs. Other OCTs, too, suffered the effects of the safeguard measure. Consequently, the Netherlands Antilles were not individually concerned by the safeguard measure and the Court of First Instance should have declared the claim inadmissible (ECJ, Case C-142/00 P *Commission v Nederlandse Antillen* [2003] E.C.R. I-3483). See also CFI, Joined Cases T-480/93 and T-483/93 *Antillean Rice Mills and Others v Commission* [1995] E.C.R. II-2305, paras 67–78; CFI, Case T-47/00 *Rica Foods v Commission* [2002] E.C.R. II-113, para. 41. But see CFI, Joined Cases T-38/99 to T-50/99 *Sociedade Agrícola dos Arinhos and Others v Commission* [2001] E.C.R. II-585, paras 49–51; CFI, Case T-43/98 *Emesa Sugar v Council* [2001] E.C.R. II-3519, paras 54–56.

[387] See, e.g. CFI, Joined Cases T-38/99 to T-50/99 *Sociedade Agrícola dos Arinhos v Commission* [2001] II-585, para. 48; CFI, Case T-47/00 *Rica Foods v Commission* [2002] E.C.R. II-113, para. 55; CFI, Case T-70/99 *Alpharma v Council* [1999] E.C.R. II-3495, paras 73–98; CFI, Case T-13/99 *Pfizer Animal Health v Council* [2002] E.C.R. II-3305, paras 81–106; CFI (order of 25 May 2004), Case T-264/03 *Schmoldt and Others v Commission* [2004] E.C.R. II-1515, para. 100; CFI (order of 6 July 2004), Case T-370/02 *Alpenhain-Camembert-Werk and Others v Commission* [2004] E.C.R. II-2097, paras 67–68; EGC, Case T-16/04 *Arcelor v European Parliament and Council* [2010] E.C.R. II-211, paras 119–120; EGC, Case T-291/04 *Enviro Tech Europe and Enviro Tech International v Commission* [2011] E.C.R. II-8281, para. 106; EGC, Case T-120/08 *Arch Chemicals, Inc. and Others v Commission* [2011] E.C.R. II-298*, paras 48–53.

[388] ECJ, Case C-263/02 P *Commission v Jégo-Quéré* [2004] E.C.R. I-3425, para. 47.

[389] See, e.g. ECJ (order of 5 May 2009), Case C-355/08 P *WWF-UK v Council* [2009] E.C.R. I-73*, Summ. pub., para. 44 (and citations therein). As the Court held in that case (para. 47), 'the mere fact of relying on the existence of a procedural guarantee before the [Union] judicature does not mean that an action will be admissible

Third, an applicant will be individually concerned when the contested act mentions it by name (although it is not the addressee of the act), and a situation specific to it is directly governed by the act.[390] What is involved, therefore, is a situation in which the Union authority adopts an act with the aim of obtaining a specific result in favour of,[391] or to the disadvantage of,[392] specific persons.

Refusal of an institution - An action for annulment may be brought by a natural or legal **7.101** person against an institution's refusal to adopt an act only if an application brought against the act refused would have been admissible.[393]

Judgment in Les Verts - In very exceptional circumstances, the requirement that the contested **7.102** act must be of individual concern to the applicant has been found to discriminate against persons who find themselves in a similar position. In such a case, the Court of Justice, applying the principle of equal treatment—part of superior general principles of Union law— will, if necessary, lower the hurdle of admissibility. The judgment in *Les Verts v European Parliament*[394] provides the only illustration to date. The decision of the Bureau of the European Parliament determining the allocation of financial assistance to political parties with a view to preparing for the European elections applied both to political parties which were represented in the Parliament at the time when the decision was adopted, which were therefore identifiable, and to parties which were not so represented at that time and therefore were not identifiable, but which would be taking part in the elections. According to the wording of the judgment, there was no doubt that parties represented in the Parliament, which were identifiable, were individually concerned. The question arose whether this was also true of parties not represented in the Parliament, who were therefore not identifiable. The Court of Justice held that the fact that the decision applied to all parties taking part in the elections placed the second class of parties in a similar position to the first, with the result that both classes had to be regarded as individually concerned by the decision in the same way.[395]

---

where it is based on pleas alleging infringement of substantive rules of law'. In the instant proceedings, even though the applicable provisons of Union law afforded to regional advisory councils ('RACs'), of which the applicant was a member, the right to be heard, it was not apparent from those provisions that a RAC may be recognized as having the right to challenge the validity of the contested measure in terms of its content. Accordingly, the Court upheld the Court of First Instance's decision finding the applicant's action inadmissible on this ground. ECJ, Case C-355/08 P *WWF-UK v Council*, paras 45–49.

[390] ECJ, Case 138/79 *Roquette Frères v Council* [1980] E.C.R. 3333, paras 13–16; ECJ, Case 139/79 *Maizena v Council* [1980] E.C.R. 3393, paras 13–16; ECJ, Joined Cases 239/82 and 275/82 *Allied Corporation v Commission* [1984] E.C.R. 1005, paras 4 and 12. But see EGC, Joined Cases T-75/04 and T-77/04 to T-79/04 *Arch Chemicals and Others v Commission* [2011] E.C.R. II-295*, Summ. pub., para. 60.

[391] CFI, Case T-139/01 *Comafrica and Dole Fresh Fruit Europe v Commission* [2005] E.C.R. II-409, para. 110.

[392] ECJ, Case 100/74 *CAM v Commission* [1975] E.C.R. 1393, para. 16.

[393] See, e.g. ECJ, Case 42/71 *Nordgetreide v Commission* [1972] E.C.R. 105, para. 5; ECJ, Joined Cases 97/86, 193/86, 99/86 and 215/86 *Asteris and Others v Commission* [1988] E.C.R. 2181, paras 17–18; ECJ, Case C-87/89 *SONITO and Others v Commission* [1990] E.C.R. I-1981, para. 8; ECJ, Joined Cases C-15/91 and C-108/91 *Buckl and Others v Commission* [1992] E.C.R. I-6061, para. 22; CFI, Case T-83/92 *Zunis Holding and Others v Commission* [1993] E.C.R. II-1169, para. 31; CFI (order of 15 March 2004), Case T-139/02 *Instituto N. Avgerinopoulou and Others v Commission* [2004] E.C.R. II-875, paras 56–57; CFI (order of 13 July 2004), Case T-29/03 *Comunidad Autónoma de Andalucía v Commission* [2004] E.C.R. II-2923, para. 30; EGC, Joined Cases T-400/04 and T-402/04 to T-404/04 *Arch Chemicals, Inc. and Others v Commission* [2011] E.C.R. II-298*, Summ. pub., paras 79 *et seq.* See further para. 7.18.

[394] ECJ, Case 294/83 *Les Verts v European Parliament* [1986] E.C.R. 1339, paras 35–37.

[395] See, however, CFI (order of 10 January 2005), Case T-357/03 *Gollnisch and Others v European Parliament* [2005] E.C.R. II-1, paras 69–70; CFI (order of 11 July 2005), Case T-40/04 *Bonino and Others v European Parliament and Council* [2005] E.C.R. II-2685, paras 73–74.

7.103 *Standing of constitutionally autonomous regions and devolved authorities* - Where the contested measure is not addressed to a particular region or devolved authority of a Member State, such entity must demonstrate that it is individually concerned by such measure within the meaning of the case-law.[396] It should be borne in mind that the general interest that a region or devolved authority may have, as the body competent for economic, social, or environmental matters in its territory, in obtaining an outcome conducive to the prosperity of that territory cannot, of itself, be sufficient for that region or devolved authority to be regarded as individually concerned within the meaning of the fourth paragraph of Art. 263 TFEU.[397] That said, the Union judicature has recognized that where the contested measure affects a measure of which the entity concerned is the author and prevents it from exercising, as it sees fit, its own powers conferred on it under the particular national constitutional system, that entity is individually concerned for the purposes of the fourth paragraph of Art. 263 TFEU.[398]

7.104 *Associations* - The question whether trade associations are individually concerned is arising increasingly frequently. It appears from the case-law that trade associations may be deemed to be sufficiently individually concerned in three types of situation.[399] First, a trade

---

[396] See paras 7.97 *et seq.* For detailed discussion, see K. Lenaerts and N. Cambien, 'Regions and the European Courts: Giving Shape to the Regional Dimension of Member States' (2010) E.L. Rev. 607.

[397] See, e.g. CFI, Case T-37/04 *Região autónoma dos Açores v Council* [2008] E.C.R. II-103*, Summ. pub., para. 53; orders of 11 April 2011 in EGC, Case T-478/10 *Department du Gers v Commission* [2011] E.C.R. II-83*, Summ. pub., paras 25–26; EGC, Case T-479/10 *Department du Gers v Commission* [2011] E.C.R. II-84*, Summ. pub., paras 25–26; EGC, Case T-480/10 *Department du Gers v Commission* [2011] E.C.R. II-86*, Summ. pub., paras 25–26; EGC, Case T-481/10 *Department du Gers v Commission* [2011] E.C.R. II-87*, Summ. pub., paras 25–26; EGC, Case T-482/10 *Department du Gers v Commission* [2011] E.C.R. II-89*, Summ. pub., paras 25–26; EGC, Case T-502/10 *Department du Gers v Commission* [2011] E.C.R. II-90*, Summ. pub., paras 25–26.

[398] See, e.g. CFI, Joined Cases T-366/03 and T-235/04 *Land Oberösterreich and Austria v Commission* [2005] E.C.R. II-4005, para. 28 (and citations therein) (appeal dismissed in ECJ, Joined Cases C-439/05 P and C-454/05 P *Land Oberösterreich v Commission* [2007] E.C.R. I-7141); CFI, Joined Cases T-227/01 to T-229/01, T-265/01, T-266/01, and T-270/01 *Territorio Histórico de Álava and Others v Commission* [2009] E.C.R. II-3029, para. 76. Compare, e.g. CFI (order of 19 September 2006), Case T-122/05 *Benkö and Others v Commission* [2006] E.C.R. II-2939, paras 58–64, particularly para. 60 (local authority applicants held not individually concerned because not generally competent under national constitutional system for the implementation of the directive concerned); CFI (order of 12 March 2007), Case T-417/04 *Regione autonoma Friuli-Venezia Giulia v Commission* [2007] E.C.R. II-641, paras 61–66, particularly para. 63: 'the legislative and regulatory prerogatives which may be conferred on a public law legal person of a Member State, other than the State, are not in themselves of such a nature as to give an individual interest in applying for the annulment of any measure of substantive [Union] law which does not affect the scope of its powers, as long as, in principle, such prerogatives are not exercised in its own interest by the person on whom they have been conferred'); CFI, Case T-37/04 *Região autónoma dos Açores v Council* [2008] E.C.R. II-103*, Summ. pub., paras 82–88, upheld on appeal in ECJ (order of 26 November 2009), Case C-444/08 P *Região autónoma dos Açores v Council* [2009] E.C.R. I-200*, Summ. pub., paras 62–67. As regards the context of State aid, see further para. 7.125.

[399] For a clear survey of the case-law, see CFI (order of 30 September 1997), Case T-122/96 *Federolio v Commission* [1997] E.C.R. II-1559, paras 60 *et seq.*; CFI (order of 23 November 1999), Case T-173/98 *Unión de Pequeños Agricultores v Council* [1999] E.C.R. II-3357, para. 62; CFI, Case T-157/01 *Danske Busvognmænd v Commission* [2004] E.C.R. II-917, paras 40–41; CFI (order of 10 May 2004), Case T-391/02 *Bundesverband der Nahrungsmittel- und Speiseresteverwertung and Kloh v European Parliament* [2004] E.C.R. II-1447, paras 44–59; CFI (order of 10 December 2004), Case T-196/03 *European Federation for Cosmetic Ingredients v European Parliament and Council* [2004] E.C.R. II-4263, paras 41–42; CFI (order of 13 December 2005), Case T-381/02 *Confederation générale des producteurs v Commission* [2005] E.C.R. II-5337, paras 54 *et seq.*; CFI, Case T-254/05 *European Insulation Manufacturers Association v Commission* [2007] E.C.R. II-124*, Summ. pub., paras. 36; CFI (order of 11 June 2008), Case T-209/06 *Plomp and Others v*

association may be individually concerned if it can show that a provision of Union law expressly grants it a series of procedural rights.[400] Second, this may be so where the association represents the interests of natural or legal persons who would be entitled to bring proceedings in their own right.[401] Third, a trade association will be sufficiently individually concerned where it is differentiated because its own interests as an association are affected by the contested measure, especially where its position as negotiator of the act in question is affected.[402] In those three situations, the Court of Justice and the General Court also take account of the participation of the association in question in the decision-making procedure.

(d) The contested act is a regulatory act not entailing implementing measures:
   individual applicant needs to prove only direct concern

(i) Problem of effective judicial protection

In the years leading up to the entry into force of the Lisbon Treaty, the Court of Justice was **7.105** not prepared to relax the criteria developed in its case-law for individual concern depending on the legal protection enjoyed by individuals before their national courts.[403] The Court pointed out that, in the complete system of legal remedies and procedures established by the EC Treaty with a view to ensuring judicial review of the legality of acts of the

---

Commission [2008] E.C.R. II-86*, Summ. pub., paras 36 *et seq.*; EGC (order of 16 May 2013), Case T-559/11 *Bytyokd v Commission*, not reported, para. 29. As regards the context of State aid (in which these three situations are parsed down to two), see further para. 7.126.

[400] See, e.g. ECJ, Case 191/82 *Fediol v Commission* [1983] E.C.R. 2913, paras 28–29; CFI, Case T-12/93 *CCE de Vittel and Others v Commission* [1995] E.C.R. II-1247, paras 40–41.

[401] See, e.g. ECJ, Case 487/06 P *British Aggregates Association v Commission* [2008] E.C.R. I-10515, para. 39; CFI, Joined Cases T-447/93, T-448/93 and T-449/93 *AITEC and Others v Commission* [1995] E.C.R. II-1971, paras 58–62; CFI, Case T-380/94 *AIUFASS and AKT v Commission* [1996] E.C.R. II-2169, para. 50; CFI (order of 15 February 2005), Case T-229/02 *PKK and KNK v Council* [2005] E.C.R. II-539, para. 45.

[402] See, e.g. ECJ, Joined Cases 67/85, 68/85 and 70/85 *Van der Kooy and Others v Commission* [1988] E.C.R. 219, para. 21; ECJ, Case C-313/90 *CIRFS and Others v Commission* [1993] E.C.R. I-1125, paras 29–30; CFI (order of 14 January 2002), Case T-84/01 *ACHE v European Parliament and Council* [2002] E.C.R. II-99, para. 25. The test is that the position as negotiator is clearly defined and must be related to the subject-matter of the contested act and that this position must have been affected by the adoption of the contested act (CFI (order of 10 May 2004), Case T-391/02 *Bundesverband der Nahrungsmittel- und Speiseresteverwertung and Kloh v European Parliament* [2004] E.C.R. II-1447, para. 48; CFI (order of 25 May 2004), Case T-264/03 *Schmoldt and Others v Commission* [2004] E.C.R. II-1515, paras 131–143). See also ECJ (order of 8 December 2006), Case C-368/05 P P *Polyelectrolyte Producers Group v Council and Commission* [2006] E.C.R. I-130*, Summ. pub., paras 59–61 (affirming the Court of First Instance's decision that the applicant association was not individually concerned, observing that the association had not demonstrated that its role as negotiator had been affected by the decision of the Council). The fact that an association has communicated information to the Union institutions or has tried to influence the position adopted by the national authorities in the Union decision-making procedure does not suffice in itself to show that the act adopted at the end of that procedure affects the association in its position as negotiator: CFI (order of 10 May 2004), Case T-391/02 *Bundesverband der Nahrungsmittel- und Speiseresteverwertung and Kloh v European Parliament* [2004] E.C.R. II-1447, paras 48–50; see also CFI (order of 25 May 2004), Case T-264/03 *Schmoldt and Others v Commission* [2004] E.C.R. II-1515, paras 137–143; CFI (order of 11 July 2005), Case T-40/04 *Bonino and Others v European Parliament and Council* [2005] E.C.R. II-2685, para. 70.

[403] ECJ, Case C-321/95 P *Greenpeace and Others v Commission* [1998] E.C.R. I-1651, paras 33–34; see also CFI (order of 12 March 1998), Case T-207/97 *Berthu v Council* [1998] E.C.R. II-509, para. 29; CFI (order of 15 September 1999), Case T-11/99 *Van Parijs and Others v Commission* [1999] E.C.R. II-2653, para. 54. See further T. von Danwitz, 'Die Garantie effektiven Rechtsschutzes im Recht der Europäischen Gemeinschaften: zur Verbesserung des Individualrechtsschutzes vor dem EuGH' (1993) NjW 1108–15; M. Jaeger, 'L'accès des personnes physiques ou morales à la justice: les premières interprétations par le Tribunal des nouvelles dispositions de l'Article 263, quatrième alinéa, TFUE', in L. Weitzel (ed.), *L'Europe des droit fondamentaux: mélanges en hommage à Albert Weitzel* (Zutphen, Paris Legal Publishers, 2013), 94–9.

institutions, where natural or legal persons cannot, by reason of the conditions for admissibility laid down in the fourth paragraph of what was then Art. 230 EC, directly challenge measures of general application, they were able, depending on the case, either indirectly to raise an objection of illegality against such measures before the Union judicature or to plead the invalidity of such measures before the national courts and ask them, since they have no jurisdiction themselves to declare those measures invalid, to make a reference to the Court of Justice for a preliminary ruling.[404]

(ii) Acts which do not entail implementing measures

7.106 In some cases, it happened that an individual had no remedy to challenge the legality of a provision of what was then Community law before a national court.[405] This occurred in particular where the contested measure did not require Member States to adopt any implementing measures. The question thus arose as to whether the Community courts would take a more flexible approach to the admissibility requirements laid down in the former fourth paragraph of Art. 230 EC in such circumstances.[406]

In its judgment of 3 May 2002 in *Jégo-Quéré*,[407] the Court of First Instance recalled that the EC Treaty established a complete system of legal remedies and procedures designed to permit the Court of Justice to review the legality of acts of the institutions.[408] The right to an effective remedy before a court of competent jurisdiction is based on the constitutional traditions common to the Member States, Arts 6 and 13 of the European Convention for the Protection of Human Rights and Fundamental Freedoms (ECHR), and Art. 47 of the Charter of Fundamental Rights of the European Union.[409] The Court of First Instance therefore considered that the strict interpretation of the notion of a person individually concerned according to the former fourth paragraph of Art. 230 EC had to be reconsidered

---

[404] ECJ, Case C-491/01 *British American Tobacco and Imperial Tobacco* [2002] E.C.R. I-11453, paras 39–40; ECJ, Case C-167/02 P *Rothley and Others v European Parliament* [2004] E.C.R. I-3149, para. 46. See also ECJ, Opinion 1/09 *Draft Agreement on the European and Community Patents Court* [2011] E.C.R. I-1137, para. 70.

[405] CFI, Case T-138/98 *ACAV and Others v Council* [2000] E.C.R. II-341, para. 68: the Court of First Instance held that the lack of a legal remedy at national level or the fact that such remedies are in any event ineffective do not enable an action for annulment to be declared admissible where it does not satisfy the conditions laid down in the fourth para. of Art. 230 of the EC Treaty. To declare such an application admissible would result in a wrongful amendment by judicial interpretation of the system of remedies and procedures laid down in the Treaty; CFI, Joined Cases T-172/98 and T-175/98 to T-177/98 *Salamander and Others v European Parliament and Council* [2000] E.C.R. II-2487, para. 75; CFI (order of 29 April 2002), Case T-339/00 *Bactria v Commission* [2002] E.C.R. II-2287, para. 54: the Court of First Instance held that the possible absence of remedies cannot justify an amendment by way of judicial interpretation of the system of remedies and procedures laid down in the Treaty (upheld on appeal in ECJ (order of 12 December 2003), Case C-258/02 P *Bactria Industriehygiene-Service v Commission* [2003] E.C.R. I-15105, paras 57–60); CFI (order of 28 June 2005), Case T-386/04 *Eridania Sadam and Others v Commission*, not reported, paras 42–43; CFI (order of 11 July 2005), Case T-40/04 *Bonino and Others v European Parliament and Council* [2005] E.C.R. II-2685, para. 77. See also K. Lenaerts, 'The Legal Protection of Private Parties under the EC Treaty: a Coherent and Complete System of Judicial Review', in *Scritti in onore di Giuseppe Federico Mancini* (Milan, Guiffrè, 1998), Vol. II, at 591–623.

[406] N. Forwood, '*Locus standi* in Direct Actions—A Case for Treaty Reinterpretation?' in *Problèmes d'interprétation: à la mémoire de Constantinos N. Kakouris* (Brussels, Bruylant, 2004), 135–41.

[407] See, e.g. CFI, Case T-177/01 *Jégo-Quéré v Commission* [2002] E.C.R. II-2365, para. 41; set aside on appeal by ECJ, Case C-263/02 P *Commission v Jégo-Quéré* [2004] E.C.R. I-3425.

[408] CFI, Case T-177/01 *Jégo-Quéré v Commission*, para. 41; ECJ, Case 294/83 *Les Verts v European Parliament* [1986] E.C.R. 1339, para. 23.

[409] CFI, Case T-177/01 *Jégo-Quéré v Commission* [2002] E.C.R. II-2365, paras 41–42; ECJ, Case 222/84 *Johnston* [1986] E.C.R. 1651, para. 18.

in order to ensure effective judicial protection for individuals.[410] It took the view in the *Jégo-Quéré* case that 'a natural or legal person is to be regarded as individually concerned by a Community measure of general application that concerns him directly if the measure in question affects his legal position, in a manner which is both definite and immediate, by restricting his rights or by imposing obligations on him'.[411]

Less than three months later, the Court of Justice made it very clear in its judgment in the *Unión de Pequeños Agricultores* case[412] that it would not follow the approach of the Court of First Instance.[413] Referring to the *Plaumann* case,[414] the Court of Justice declared that natural or legal persons may be individually concerned by a measure where 'the measure in question affects [them] by reason of certain attributes peculiar to them, or by reason of a factual situation which differentiates them from all other persons and distinguishes them individually in the same way as the addressee'.[415] The Court considered that no other interpretation of this condition for admissibility was possible 'without going beyond the jurisdiction conferred by the Treaty on the Community Courts'.[416] As a result, only a Treaty amendment could make the admissibility requirements set out in the former fourth paragraph of Art. 230 EC more flexible.[417] At the same time, the Court of Justice called on national courts 'so far as possible, to interpret and apply national procedural rules governing the exercise of rights of action in a way that enables natural and legal persons to challenge before the courts the legality of any decision or other national measure relative to the application to them of a Community act of general application, by pleading the invalidity of such an act'[418] (see also paras 4.10 and 4.12).

(iii) Opening for regulatory acts
It is in this context that the new fourth paragraph of Art. 263 TFEU should be **7.107** understood.[419] This provision states that '[a]ny natural or legal person may [. . .] institute

---

[410] CFI, Case T-177/01 *Jégo-Quéré v Commission* [2002] E.C.R. II-2365, paras 50 and 51.

[411] CFI, Case T-177/01 *Jégo-Quéré v Commission*, para. 51.

[412] ECJ, Case C-50/00 P *Unión de Pequeños Agricultores v Council* [2002] E.C.R. I-6677.

[413] The Opinion of Advocate-General F.G. Jacobs in Case C-50/00 P *Unión de Pequeños Agricultores v Council* [2002] E.C.R. I-6681 was closer to the view taken by the Court of First Instance in *Jégo-Quéré*.

[414] ECJ, Case 25/62 *Plaumann v Commission* [1963] E.C.R. 95, at 107.

[415] ECJ, Case C-50/00 P *Unión de Pequeños Agricultores v Council* [2002] E.C.R. I-6677, para. 36.

[416] ECJ, Case C-50/00 P *Unión de Pequeños Agricultores v Council*, para. 44; ECJ, Case C-167/02 P *Rothley and Others v European Parliament* [2004] E.C.R. I-3149, para. 25; ECJ, Case C-263/02 P *Commission v Jégo-Quéré* [2004] E.C.R. I-3425, para. 36; CFI (order of 2 April 2004), Case T-231/02 *Gonnelli and AIFO v Commission* [2004] E.C.R. II-1051, paras 53–54; CFI (order of 25 May 2004), Case T-264/03 *Schmoldt and Others v Commission* [2004] E.C.R. II-1515, paras 151–159. In ECJ, Case C-312/00 P *Commission v Camar and Tico* [2002] E.C.R. I-11355, para. 78, the Court of Justice declared that 'the condition that natural or legal persons may bring an action challenging a regulation only if they are concerned individually must be interpreted in the light of the principle of effective judicial protection by taking account of the various circumstances that may distinguish an applicant individually'. See in this connection K. Lenaerts and T. Corthaut, 'Judicial Review as a Contribution to the Development of European Constitutionalism' [2003] Y.E.L. 1–43, point 39: a measure of flexibility in the actual assessment whether the *Plaumann* test is satisfied may make a great difference. Nevertheless, it is not clear whether the Court of Justice sought to create an opening by that dictum in the *Camar* case: see, e.g. ECJ, Case C-263/02 P *Commission v Jégo-Quéré* [2004] E.C.R. I-3425, paras 43–48.

[417] ECJ, Case C-50/00 P *Unión de Pequeños Agricultores v Council* [2002] E.C.R. I-6677, para. 45.

[418] ECJ, Case C-50/00 P *Unión de Pequeños Agricultores v Council* [2002] E.C.R. I-6677, para. 42; ECJ, Case C-263/02 P *Commission v Jégo-Quéré* [2004] E.C.R. I-3425, para. 32.

[419] See EGC, Case T-262/10 *Microban International and Microban (Europe) v Commission* [2011] E.C.R. II-7697, para. 32. Such an opening had already appeared as Art. III-365(4) of the Draft Constitutional Treaty, which also forms the background to what is now the fourth para. of Art. 263 TFEU. See EGC, Case

proceedings against an act addressed to that person or which is of direct and individual concern to them, and against a regulatory act which is of direct concern to them and does not entail implementing measures'. The fourth paragraph of Art. 263 TFEU relaxes the standing requirements for individuals by removing the requirement of individual concern for regulatory acts which do not require implementing measures.

(iv) Concept of 'regulatory act'

7.108 The concept of a 'regulatory act' is not defined among the legal instruments referred to in Art. 288 TFEU.[420] In the first decision on this issue, *Inuit Tapiriit Kanatami and Others v European Parliament and Council*, the General Court— later confirmed on appeal by the Court of Justice —held, on the basis of a literal, historical, and teleological analysis, that the meaning of 'regulatory act' for the purposes of the fourth paragraph of Art. 263 TFEU must be understood as 'covering all acts of general application apart from legislative acts'.[421] Consequently, a legislative act may form the subject of an action for annulment brought by a natural and legal person only if it is of direct and individual concern to them.[422] Thereafter, in *Microban International and Microban (Europe) v Commission*, the General Court ruled that an action for annulment brought against a Commission decision constituting a measure of general application adopted by the Commission in the exercise of implementing powers should be considered a regulatory act within the meaning of the fourth paragraph of Art. 263 TFEU.[423] A regulatory act is indeed an act of general

---

T-18/10 *Inuit Tapiriit Kanatami and Others v European Parliament and Council* [2011] E.C.R. II-5599, para. 49 (confirmed on appeal, ECJ (judgment of 3 October 2013), Case C-583/11 P *Inuit Tapiriit Kanatami and Others v European Parliament and Council*, not reported, paras 57–61). See further T. Corthaut and F. Vanneste, 'Waves Between Strasbourg and Luxembourg: The Right of Access to a Court to Contest the Validity of Legislative or Administrative Measures', Y.E.L. (2006), 475–514.

[420] In EGC, Case T-16/04 *Arcelor v European Parliament and Council* [2010] E.C.R. II-211, para. 123, although the instant proceedings were conducted under the regime of the former fourth para. of Art. 230 EC, the General Court observed that 'the Member States have a broad discretion with regard to implementation of the contested directive. For that reason, . . . the directive cannot, in any event, be regarded as being a regulatory act which does not entail implementing measures' within the terms of the fourth para. of Art. 263 TFEU. This appears to indicate that it will be difficult to find circumstances in a which a (non-legislative) directive will fall within the category of regulatory acts for the purposes of the fourth para. of Art. 263 TFEU.

[421] EGC (order of 6 September 2011), Case T-18/10 *Inuit Tapiriit Kanatami and Others v European Parliament and Council* [2011] E.C.R. II-5599, paras 41–56 (confirmed on appeal, ECJ (judgment of 3 October 2013), Case C-583/11 P *Inuit Tapiriit Kanatami and Others v European Parliament and Council*, not reported, para. 60). In the instant proceedings, the General Court therefore held that the contested measure— a 'legislative' regulation adopted under co-decision (which would fall within the concept of legislative acts under Art. 289(3) TFEU, only it had been adopted before the entry into force of the Lisbon Treaty)—was not a regulatory act (EGC, Case T-18/10 *Inuit Tapiriit Kanatami and Others v European Parliament and Council*, para. 66). In *Inuit*, the Commission's implementing measure was also challenged. This action was admissible but ill-founded: EGC (judgment of 25 April 2013), Case T-526/10 *Inuit Tapiriit Kanatami and Others v Commission*, not reported. See also EGC (order of 4 June 2012), Case T-379/11 *Hüttenwerke Krupp Mannesmann and Others v Commission*, not reported, para. 34. For critical discussion of the initial case-law on this issue, see also M. Wathelet and J. Wildemeersch, 'Recours en annulation: une première interpretation restrictive du droit d'action élargi des particuliers?' (2012) J.D.E. 75.

[422] EGC (order of 6 September 2011), Case T-18/10 *Inuit Tapiriit Kanatami and Others v European Parliament and Council* [2011] E.C.R. II-5599, para. 57 (confirmed on appeal, ECJ (judgment of 3 October 2013), Case C-583/11 P *Inuit Tapiriit Kanatami and Others v Parliament and Council*, not reported, para. 70).

[423] EGC, Case T-262/10 *Microban International and Microban (Europe) v Commission* [2011] E.C.R. II-7697, paras 22–25. However, not only the Commission has the power to adopt a regulatory act within the meaning of the fourth para. of Art. 263 TFEU: see EGC (judgment of 7 March 2013), Case T-93/10 *Bilbaína de Alquitranes and Others v ECHA*, not reported, paras 55–59.

application[424] which has not been adopted in accordance with either the ordinary legislative procedure or the special legislative procedure within the meaning of paragraphs 1 to 3 of Art. 289 TFEU.[425]

(v) Requirements of direct concern and no implementing measures
Furthermore, in its judgment in *Microban International and Microban (Europe) v Commission*, the General Court elaborated on the requirements of direct concern and no implementing measures for the purposes of an individual's standing to challenge a regulatory act under the fourth paragraph of Art. 263 TFEU.

7.109

As regards the concept of direct concern as introduced in the fourth paragraph of Art. 263 TFEU in connection with a regulatory act, the General Court raised the question whether it should be subject to a different interpretation from the notion of direct concern already found in the former fourth paragraph of Art. 230 EC. It held that, in line with the objective of this provision to open up the conditions for bringing direct actions, this concept cannot be subject to a more restrictive interpretation than that already developed in the case-law. Accordingly, since it had already been established that the applicants were directly concerned by the contested measure within the meaning of the case-law regarding the former fourth paragraph of Art. 230 EC, they were also directly concerned for the purposes of the regulatory act prong.[426]

As regards the question whether the contested decision entails implementing measures, the General Court considered that the subject of the contested measure is the non-inclusion of the substance at issue in the positive list of additives pursuant to Union law, which required no implementing measures on the part of the Member States. Although the transitional provision, allowing the possibility of marketing that substance to be extended to a specified date, may give rise to implementing measures on the part of the Member States, it is

---

[424] If a measure lays down generally applicable principles, applies to objectively defined situations, and produces legal effects for categories of persons determined in an abstract manner, the measure will be regarded as an act of general application (see, e.g. ECJ, Joined Cases 36/58 to 38/58 and 40/58 to 41/58 *SIMET and Others v High Authority* [1959] E.C.R. 157, at 166; ECJ, Case 147/83 *Binderer v Commission* [1985] E.C.R. 257, paras 11–15; ECJ, Case C-244/88 *Usines Coopératives de Déshydratation du Vexin and Others v Commission* [1989] E.C.R. 3811, para. 13; ECJ, Case C-229/88 *Cargill and Others v Commission* [1990] E.C.R. I-1303, paras 13–19; CFI (order of 11 January 1995), Case T-116/94 *Cassa Nazionale di Previdenza ed Assistenza a favore degli Avvocati e Procuratori* [1995] E.C.R. II-1, paras 21–25; CFI (order of 19 June 1995), Case T-107/94 *Kik v Council and Commission* [1995] E.C.R. II-1717, para. 35; CFI, Case T-482/93 *Weber v Commission* [1996] E.C.R. II-609, para. 55; CFI, Case T-47/95 *Terres Rouges and Others v Commission* [1997] E.C.R. II-481, paras 40–41; CFI (order of 13 December 2005), Case T-381/02 *Confederation generale v Commission* [2005] E.C.R. II-5337, para. 49; CFI (order of 11 September 2007), Case T-35/06 *Honig-Verband v Commission* [2007] E.C.R. II-2865, paras 39–42).

[425] EGC (order of 4 June 2012), Case T-379/11 *Hüttenwerke Krupp Mannesmann and Others v Commission*, not reported, para. 36; EGC (order of 4 June 2012), Case T-381/11 *Eurofer v Commission*, not reported, para. 44. See also EGC (judgment of 27 February 2013), Case T-367/10 *Bloufin Touna Ellas Naftiki Etaireia and Others v Commission*, not reported, para. 18; EGC (judgment of 7 March 2013), Case T-94/10 *Rütgers Germany and Others v ECHA*, not reported, paras 56–59. See further M. Jaeger, 'L'accès des personnes physiques ou morales à la justice: les premières interprétations par le Tribunal des nouvelles dispositions de l'Article 263, quatrième alinéa, TFUE', in L. Weitzel (ed.), *L' Europe des droit fondamentaux: mélanges en hommage à Albert Weitzel* (Zutphen, Paris Legal Publishers, 2013), 107–14.

[426] See EGC (judgment of 7 March 2013), Case T-94/10 *Rütgers Germany and Others v ECHA*, not reported, paras 38 and 59. See further M. Jaeger, 'L'accès des personnes physiques ou morales à la justice: les premières interprétations par le Tribunal des nouvelles dispositions de l'Article 263, quatrième alinéa, TFUE', in L. Weitzel (ed.), *L' Europe des droit fondamentaux: mélanges en hommage à Albert Weitzel* (Zutphen, Paris Legal Publishers, 2013), 114–16.

intended to facilitate the implementation of the contested decision, in that its effect is to prohibit the marketing of that substance so that natural and legal persons affected by that prohibition may make the necessary arrangements, and therefore is ancillary to the main purpose of the contested decision. Accordingly, the General Court ruled that the contested decision does not entail implementing measures.[427]

(vi) Extent of the opening

7.110 As matters stand now, the opening created by the fourth paragraph of Art. 263 TFEU is not as large as the one envisaged by the Court of First Instance in its judgment in *Jégo-Quéré*.[428] This is because the relaxation of the admissibility conditions in *Jégo-Quéré* would have covered both legislative and non-legislative acts of general application. In contrast, the opening created by the fourth paragraph of Art. 263 TFEU only covers non-legislative acts of general application. In other words, an action for annulment brought by an individual applicant against legislative acts will be admissible only if that applicant successfully demonstrates that the act is of direct and individual (within the meaning of the *Plaumann* case-law[429]) concern to him, irrespective of whether the act in question requires further implementation at national level. By contrast, in cases concerning non-legislative acts of general application, the applicant need only demonstrate direct—not individual—concern and that the act does not entail implementing measures.[430]

This has the anomalous result that the level of judicial protection depends on the procedure by which the contested measure is adopted and leads to different outcomes in situations resembling *Jégo-Quéré* (involving a non-legislative act of general application for which the opening of the fourth paragraph of Art. 263 TFEU is available) versus situations resembling *Union Pequeños Agricultores* (involving a legislative act of general application for which the opening of the fourth paragraph of Art. 263 TFEU would not be available). Consequently, under such an interpretation of regulatory act, the fourth paragraph of Art. 263 TFEU would not appear to be able by itself to remedy the gap in the system of EU judicial

---

[427] EGC, Case T-94/10 *Rütgers Germany and Others*, paras 33–38. In EGC (order of 4 June 2012), Case T-379/11 *Hüttenwerke Krupp Mannesmann and Others v Commission*, not reported, paras 48–53, the General Court pointed out that the question of whether or not the contested regulatory act leaves a degree of discretion to the authorities responsible for the implementing measures is irrelevant. The lack of discretion is a criterion which must be examined in order to determine whether the applicant is directly concerned. However, the requirement of an act which does not entail implementing measures laid down in the fourth para. of Art. 263 TFEU constitutes a different condition than the requirement that the act be of direct concern to the applicant. See also EGC (order of 4 June 2012), Case T-381/11 *Eurofer v Commission*, not reported, para. 59; EGC (order of 5 February 2013), Case T-551/11 *Brugola Service International v Council*, not reported, para. 56; EGC (judgment of 27 February 2013), Case T-367/10 *Bloufin Touna Ellas Naftiki Etaireia and Others v Commission*, not reported, paras 18–28; EGC (judgment of 7 March 2013), Case T-94/10 *Rütgers Germany and Others v ECHA*, not reported, paras 64–67. According to Advocate-General M. Wathelet, however, the requirement of an act which does not entail implementing measures laid down in the fourth para. of Art. 263 TFEU is the same as the one requiring that the act be of direct concern to the applicant: see Opinion of Advocate-General M. Wathelet of 29 May 2013 in Case C-132/12 P *Stichting Woonpunt and Others v Commission*, not reported, point 76. But see ECJ (judgment of 19 December 2013), Case C-274/12 P *Telefónica v Commission*, not reported, paras 27–39. See further M. Jaeger, 'L'accès des personnes physiques ou morales à la justice: les premières interprétations par le Tribunal des nouvelles dispositions de l'Article 263, quatrième alinéa, TFUE', in L. Weitzel (ed.), *L'Europe des droit fondamentaux: mélanges en hommage à Albert Weitzel* (Zutphen, Paris Legal Publishers, 2013), 117–24.

[428] CFI, Case T-177/01 *Jégo-Quéré v Commission* [2002] E.C.R. II-2365, paras 49–53.

[429] ECJ, Case 25/62 *Plaumann v Commission* [1963] E.C.R. 95, 107.

[430] Likewise, for acts of individual application not addressed to the individual applicant, that applicant will need to satisfy the requirements of direct and individual concern.

protection insofar as actions for annulment brought by natural and legal persons against legislative acts of general application entailing no implementing measures are concerned.

Importantly, however, even if the concept of regulatory act is limited to non-legislative acts of general application, there is not necessarily a gap, provided that the second paragraph of Art. 19(1) TEU assumes a complementary role at national level. The second paragraph of Art. 19(1) TEU provides that 'Member States shall provide remedies sufficient to ensure effective legal protection in the fields covered by Union law'. This provision, taken in combination with the fourth paragraph of Art. 263 TFEU, may lead to a desirable outcome after all in terms of ensuring effective judicial protection for individuals.[431]

(6) The concept of individual concern: some fields of application

(a) The individual applicant is not the addressee of the contested act

As has been indicated in paragraphs 7.86 and 7.87, the addressee of a reviewable Union act **7.111** derives a right under the fourth paragraph of Art. 263 TFEU to bring an action for the annulment of the act concerned. An individual applicant who is not the addressee of an act of individual application will only have standing if he can demonstrate that he is directly and individually concerned by such act. The following sections will examine the condition of 'individually concerned' in some fields of application.

(b) Application of Arts 101 and 102 TFEU

Under the rules of Regulation No. 17, under which the Commission had exclusive competence to declare that Art. 81(1) EC (now Art. 101(1) TFEU) was inapplicable, persons who submitted objections in writing to the Commission during the investigation in regard to a proposed declaration that Art. 81(1) EC (now Art. 101(1) TFEU) was not applicable to the practices of a competitor or supplier, or persons who participated in the hearing organized by the Commission, were individually concerned by such declaration.[432] The Court of Justice and the General Court considered that those classes of person had been sufficiently involved in the procedure whereby the contested decision was adopted in order to constitute a closed class in the light of the act.[433] A similar reasoning is now

---

[431] See ECJ (judgment of 3 October 2013), Case C-583/11 P *Inuit Tapiriit Kanatami and Others v Parliament and Council*, not reported, paras 89–107.

[432] ECJ, Case 75/84 *Metro v Commission* [1986] E.C.R. 3021, paras 18–23; CFI, Case T-19/92 *Leclerc v Commission* [1996] E.C.R. II-1851, paras 53–63, and Case T-88/92 *Leclerc v Commission* [1996] II-1961, paras 49–50. In these judgments, the CFI based its finding that the applicant—a cooperative society—was individually concerned also on the fact that it had taken part in the administrative procedure as a representative of its members, who, as potential competitors of the traders belonging to the selective distribution system to which Art. 81(1) EC (now Art. 101(1) TFEU) had been declared inapplicable, could have taken part in the administrative procedure, and been individually concerned thereby, as 'interested third parties' under Art. 19(3) of Regulation No. 17.

[433] In CFI, Joined Cases T-528/93, T-542/93, T-543/93, and T-546/93 *Métropole Télévision and Others v Commission* [1996] E.C.R. II-649, para. 62, the Court of First Instance held that it is sufficient for the applicant to be an interested third party within the meaning of the first sentence of Art. 19(3) of Regulation No. 17. The Court considered it irrelevant that the applicant had not availed itself of its procedural rights under Art. 19(3) of Regulation No. 17. It considered that to make the capacity to bring proceedings of such interested third parties subject to their actually taking part in the administrative procedure would be tantamount to introducing an additional condition of admissibility in the form of a compulsory pre-litigation procedure not provided for in Art. 230 EC (now Art. 263 TFEU). Cf., however, CFI, Case T-87/92 *Kruidvat v Commission* [1996] E.C.R. II-1931, paras 61–67: the fact that a trade organization participated in the administrative procedure before the Commission cannot relieve their members of the need to establish a link between their individual situation and the action of the organization. In other words, the organization's

followed when third parties bring an action for annulment against a decision making commitments binding on undertakings or finding that there are no longer grounds for action by the Commission (Regulation No. 1/2003, Art. 9(1)).[434] This case-law will also likely be relevant for the purpose of assessing the admissibility of actions for annulment brought by third parties against decisions in which the Commission finds that Art. 101 and/or Art. 102 TFEU are inapplicable to a certain practice or agreement (Regulation No. 1/2003, Art. 10).

(c) Merger control

(i) Competitors

7.113   A competitor of undertakings involved in the concentration which has actively participated in the administrative procedure (by submitting observations and criticisms, clarifying, among other things, the effects of the concentration on its competitive position) will be individually concerned by a Commission decision declaring the concentration compatible with the internal market, at least where the contested decision has an appreciable effect on the applicant's position on the market.[435] It would appear to be sufficient that the applicant is a potential competitor on most of the markets affected.[436]

(ii) Representatives of employees

7.114   The General Court has held in connection with Regulation No. 4064/89 (now Regulation No. 139/2004) that recognized employees' representatives of an undertaking involved in a concentration were individually concerned by a Commission decision adopted pursuant to that Regulation on the ground that that Regulation mentioned them expressly and specifically among the third persons showing a 'sufficient interest' to submit observations to the Commission during the administrative investigation of the concentration's

---

participation was not sufficient to individualize one of its members which had not participated in the administrative procedure (confirmed on appeal in ECJ, Case C-70/97 P *Kruidvat v Commission* [1998] E.C.R. I-7183, para. 23). An undertaking which participated in the administrative procedure before the Commission and which started proceedings in the national courts for compensation for having had obligations contrary to Art. 81 EC (now Art. 101 TFEU) imposed on it under an agreement to which Art. 81(1) EC (now Art. 101(1) TFEU) was declared inapplicable was held to be individually concerned by the decision exempting the agreement (CFI, Case T-13/99 *Shaw and Falla v Commission* [2002] E.C.R. II-2023, paras 25–27).

[434]   CFI, Case T-170/06 *Alrosa v Commission* [2007] E.C.R. II-2601, paras 36–41: however, it is not clear whether the participation of the applicant in the administrative proceedings is as such sufficient to find that the applicant is individually concerned by the contested decision. The CFI indeed also refers to the fact that the contested decision, which refers to the applicant expressly, is liable to have an appreciable effect on the applicant's competitive position on the market.

[435]   ECJ, Joined Cases C-68/94 and C-30/95 *France and Others v Commission* ('Kali & Salz') [1998] E.C.R. I-1375, paras 54–58 (the Court of Justice took account in this case of the participation in the administrative procedure and of the fact that the conditions attached to the declaration by which the concentration was stated to be compatible with the internal market primarily touched the applicant's interests); CFI, Case T-2/93 *Air France v Commission* [1994] E.C.R. II-323, paras 40–48 (the CFI also took account in this case of the fact that the Commission had judged the competitive structure of the market in question above all in the light of the applicant's competitive position and that some months before the concentration came about, the applicant undertaking had given up its interest in one of the undertakings concerned pursuant to an agreement concluded with the Commission); CFI, Case T-114/02 *BaByliss v Commission* [2003] E.C.R. II-1279, paras 87–117. It follows, however, from CFI, Case T-282/06 *Sun Chemical Group and Others v Commission* [2007] E.C.R. II-2149, para. 49 that an active participation in the administrative procedure is sufficient for a third party to be individually concerned by the contested decision. But see CFI, Case T-177/04 *easyJet v Commission* [2006] E.C.R. II-1931, para. 35, in which the CFI held that active participation in the administrative procedure is a factor taken into account to establish, *in conjunction with other specific circumstances*, the admissibility of the action.

[436]   CFI, Case T-114/02 *BaByliss v Commission* [2003] E.C.R. II-1279, paras 99–100.

compatibility with the internal market.[437] The General Court regarded it as irrelevant whether the employees' representatives of the undertaking had actually taken part in the administrative procedure.[438]

(iii) Consumer associations
Under Art. 11(c), second indent, of Regulation No. 802/2004, consumer associations are **7.115** entitled to the right to be heard, pursuant to Art. 18 of Regulation No. 139/2004, subject to compliance with two conditions: first, that the merger concerns products or services used by final consumers; and, second, that an application to be heard by the Commission during the investigation procedure is made in writing. Provided that those two conditions are fulfilled, a consumer organization is entitled to challenge the clearance decision on the grounds of infringement of its procedural right to be heard.[439] The action will be declared admissible only to the extent to which its purpose is to ensure protection of procedural rights.[440]

(iv) Referral to national authorities
An undertaking is individually concerned by a decision to refer the matter to the national **7.116** competition authorities pursuant to Art. 9 of Regulation No. 139/2004 if the undertaking would have been individually concerned by the Commission's final decision had the Commission not referred the case to the national authorities.[441]

(d) *State aid cases*
(i) Position of beneficiaries of State aid and their competitors
Decisions addressed to Member States - State aid decisions are addressed to the Member State **7.117** concerned.[442] It is settled case-law that persons other than those to whom a decision is addressed may claim to be individually concerned only if the decision affects them by reason of certain attributes peculiar to them or by reason of circumstances in which they are

---

[437] Representatives of employees and representatives of management enjoy the same right under Art. 18(4) of Regulation No. 139/2004.

[438] CFI, Case T-96/92 *CCE de la Société générale des Grandes Sources and Others v Commission* [1995] E.C.R. II-1213, para. 37; CFI, Case T-12/93 *CCE de Vittel and Others v Commission* [1995] E.C.R. II-1247, para. 48. In those cases, the CFI subsequently held that the applicants were directly affected by the contested decision only in so far as their procedural rights during the administrative procedure had been affected. Consequently, it considered only the plea alleging that those rights had been breached.

[439] EGC, Case T-224/10 *Association belge des consommateurs test-achats v Commission* [2011] E.C.R. II-7177, paras 36–38. In this case, the action was declared inadmissible since, following the notification of the merger to the Commision, the consumer organization in question had not submitted an application to be heard (EGC, Case T-224/10 *Association belge des consommateurs test-achats v Commission*, paras 46–64).

[440] EGC, Case T-224/10 *Association belge des consommateurs test-achats v Commission* [2011] E.C.R. II-7177, paras 30–31 (drawing a parallelism with state aid cases).

[441] CFI, Case T-119/02 *Royal Philips Electronics v Commission* [2003] E.C.R. II-1433, paras 291–298; CFI, Joined Cases T-346/02 and T-347/02 *Cableuropa and Others v Commission* [2003] E.C.R. II-4251, paras 78–79. By contrast, a third party will not be directly and individually concerned by a decision of the Commission rejecting a request from a national competition authority for partial referral of the case under Art. 9(3) of Regulation No. 139/2004: see EGC, Case T-224/10 *Association belge des consommateurs test-achats v Commission* [2011] E.C.R. II-7177, paras 70–85 (the admissibility of an action against the non-referral decision cannot result from the fact that the national law in question may confer on the applicant more extensive procedural rights and/or judicial protection than provided for under Union law).

[442] Regulation No. 659/1999, Art. 25. See also ECJ, Case C-367/95 P *Commission v Sytraval and Brink's France* [1998] E.C.R. I-1719, para. 45; EGC (order of 11 January 2012), Case T-58/10 *Phoenix-Reisen and DRV v Commission*, not reported, para. 25.

differentiated from all other persons and if, by virtue of those factors, it distinguishes them individually in the same way as the person addressed.[443]

7.118 *Decisions taken on the basis of the preliminary procedure provided for in Art. 108(3) TFEU* - As far as new aid[444] is concerned, the Commission is empowered to take decisions at two stages of its investigation into its compatibility with the internal market.

First, there is the preliminary stage for reviewing aid pursuant to Art. 108(3) TFEU. Where, at the conclusion of its investigation, the Commission decides to initiate the procedure under Art. 108(2) TFEU, that decision is of individual concern to undertakings which are the envisaged beneficiaries of the proposed aid.[445] Where, in contrast, the Commission considers at the end of the preliminary stage that the proposed aid is compatible with the internal market and therefore decides not to initiate a procedure pursuant to Art. 108(2) TFEU and Art. 6(1) of Regulation No. 659/1999,[446] the lawfulness of such decision not to raise objections will depend on whether there are doubts as to the compatibility of the aid with the internal market. Since such doubts must trigger the initiation of a formal investigation procedure in which the interested parties referred to in Art. 1(h) of Regulation No. 659/1999 can participate, any interested party within the meaning of the latter provision is directly and individually concerned by such a decision.[447] If the beneficiaries of the procedural guarantees provided for in Art. 108(2) TFEU and Art. 6(1) of Regulation No. 659/1999 are to be able to ensure that those guarantees are respected, it must indeed be possible for them to challenge before the Union judicature the decision not to raise objections.[448] Accordingly, the specific status of 'interested party'

---

[443] ECJ, Case 25/62 *Plaumann v Commission* [1963] E.C.R. 197; ECJ Case C-321/95 P *Greenpeace and Others v Commission* [1998] E.C.R. I-1651, paras 7 and 28; ECJ, Joined Cases C-15/98 and C-105/99 *Italy and Sardegna Lines v Commission* [2000] E.C.R. I-8855, para. 32. See further K. Jürimäe, 'Standing in State Aid Cases: What's the State of Play?' (2010) European State Aid Law Quarterly 303–21.

[444] For a definition, see para. 7.54.

[445] The Member State concerned may not put the measure into effect before the procedure has resulted in a final decision.

[446] Where the Commission adopts a decision not to raise objections, it declares not only that the measure is compatible with the internal market, but also—by implication—that it refuses to initiate the formal investigation procedure laid down under Art. 108(2) TFEU and Art. 6(1) of Regulation No. 659/1999: see ECJ, Case C-83/09 P *Commission v Kronoply and Kronotex* [2011] E.C.R. I-4441, para. 45; ECJ, Case C-148/09 P *Belgium v Deutsche Post and Others* [2011] E.C.R. I-8573, para. 54. Such decision may only be withdrawn by the Commission in order to remedy an illegality affecting the decision. After such withdrawal, the Commission cannot pick up the procedure again at a stage earlier than the exact point at which the illegality had occurred: ECJ, Case C-362/09 P *Athinaïki Techniki v Commission* [2010] E.C.R. I-13275, para. 70.

[447] ECJ, Case C-198/91 *Cook v Commission* [1993] E.C.R. I-2487, paras 13–26; ECJ, Case C-225/91 *Matra v Commission* [1993] E.C.R. I-3203, paras 15–20; ECJ, Joined Cases C-75/05 P and C-80/05 P *Germany and Others v Kronofrance* [2008] E.C.R. I-6619, paras 37–41; ECJ, Case C-83/09 P *Commission v Kronoply and Kronotex* [2011] E.C.R. I-4441, para. 48; CFI, Case T-167/04 *Asklepios Kliniken v Commission* [2007] E.C.R. II-2379, paras 47–51; CFI, Case T-375/04 *Scheucher-Fleisch and Others v Commission* [2009] E.C.R. II-4155, para. 64; EGC (judgment of 28 March 2012), Case T-123/09 *Ryanair v Commission*, not reported, para. 64. The same applies where the Commission considers that there is no question of State aid, with the result that competing undertakings which have submitted complaints about it are deprived in any event of their procedural rights under Art. 108(2) TFEU. They are directly and individually concerned by such a Commission decision and may enforce their procedural rights before the Union judicature: ECJ, Case C-367/95 P *Commission v Sytraval and Brink's France* [1998] E.C.R. I-1719, para. 47; CFI, Case T-11/95 *BP Chemicals v Commission* [1998] E.C.R. II-3232, paras 164–166.

[448] ECJ, Case C-78/03 P *Commission v Aktionsgemeinschaft Recht und Eigentum* [2005] E.C.R. I-10737, para. 35; ECJ, Case C-487/06 P *British Aggregates v Commission* [2008] E.C.R. I-10515, para. 28; ECJ, Case

within the meaning of Art. 1(h) of Regulation No. 659/1999, in conjunction with the specific subject-matter of the action—i.e. an action seeking to safeguard the applicant's procedural rights—[449] is sufficient to distinguish individually, for the purposes of the fourth paragraph of Art. 263 TFEU, an applicant contesting a decision not to raise objections.[450]

'Interested parties' within the meaning of Art. 1(h) of Regulation No. 659/1999 comprise not only the undertaking or undertakings in receipt of aid (which in this event naturally have no interest in bringing an action for annulment),[451] but also such persons, undertakings, or associations whose interests might be affected by the grant of the aid, for instance, competing undertakings and trade associations.[452]

C-319/07 P *3F v Commission* [2009] E.C.R. I-5963, para. 31; ECJ, Case C-83/09 P *Commission v Kronoply and Kronotex* [2011] E.C.R. I-4441, para. 47; EGC (judgment of 28 March 2012), Case T-123/09 *Ryanair v Commission*, not reported, para. 63.

[449] It matters little whether the application initiating proceedings states that it is seeking the annulment of 'a decision not to raise objections'—the term used in Art. 4(3) of Regulation No. 659/1999—or of a decision not to initiate the formal investigation procedure, since the Commission takes a position on both aspects of the question by means of a single decision (ECJ, Case C-83/09 P *Commission v Kronoply and Kronotex* [2011] E.C.R. I-4441, para. 52). However, where an applicant does not seek the annulment of a decision taken on the basis of the preliminary procedure laid down by Art. 108(3) TFEU on the grounds that the Commission was in breach of the obligation to initiate the procedure provided for in Art. 108(2) or on the grounds that the procedural safeguards provided for by Art. 108(2) were infringed, the mere fact that the applicant may be considered to be an interested party concerned within the meaning of Art. 108(2) TFEU and Art. 1(h) of Regulation No. 659/1999 does not render it individually concerned for the purposes of the fourth para. of Art. 263 TFEU. In such a case, the action will be admissible only if the applicant is affected by the contested decision by reason of other circumstances distinguishing it individually in like manner to the person addressed, in accordance with the *Plaumann* test: see CFI, Case T-266/94 *Skibsværftsforeningen and Others v Commission* [1996] E.C.R. II-1399, para. 45; CFI, Case T-188/95 *Waterleiding Maatschappij 'Noord-West Brabant' v Commission* [1998] E.C.R. II-3713, para. 54; EGC, Case T-193/06 *TF1 v Commission* [2010] E.C.R. II-4967, paras 76–77; EGC (order of 11 January 2012), Case T-58/10 *Phoenix-Reisen and DRV v Commission*, not reported, para. 33. See also ECJ, Case C-176/06 P *Stadtwerke Schwäbisch Hall and Others v Commission* [2007] E.C.R. I-170, para. 25; ECJ, Case C-83/09 P *Commission v Kronoply and Kronotex* [2011] E.C.R. I-4441, para. 55; ECJ, Case C-148/09 P *Belgium v Deutsche Post and Others* [2011] E.C.R. I-8573, para. 58; EGC (judgment of 15 January 2013), Case T-182/10 *Aiscat v Commission*, not reported, paras 42–43.

[450] ECJ, Case C-83/09 P *Commission v Kronoply and Kronotex* [2011] E.C.R. I-4441, para. 48; EGC (judgment of 28 March 2012), Case T-123/09 *Ryanair v Commission*, not reported, para. 64.

[451] EGC (order of 19 February 2013), Case T-15/12 *Provincie Groningen and Others v Commission*, not reported, paras 39–59 (application by beneficiary of aid held inadmissible).

[452] ECJ, Case 323/82 *Intermills v Commission* [1984] E.C.R. 3809, para. 16; CFI, Case T-17/96 *TF1 v Commission* [1999] E.C.R. II-1757, para. 31; CFI, Case T-158/99 *Thermenhotel Stoiser Franz and Others v Commission* [2004] E.C.R. II-1, para. 69; EGC (judgment of 28 March 2012), Case T-123/09 *Ryanair v Commission*, not reported, para. 65. That provision does not rule out the possibility that an undertaking which is not a direct competitor of the beneficiary of the aid can be categorized as an interested party, provided that undertaking demonstrates that its interests could be adversely affected by the grant of the aid: see ECJ, Case C-83/09 P *Commission v Kronoply and Kronotex* [2011] E.C.R. I-4441, para. 64 (applicant which requires the same raw material for its production process as the beneficiary of the aid is an interested party). For that purpose, it is necessary for the applicant to establish, to the requisite legal standard, that the aid is likely to have a specific effect on its situation: see ECJ, Case C-319/07 P *3F v Commission* [2009] E.C.R. I-5963, paras 33 and 98–108 (a trade union may be regarded as 'interested' within the meaning of Art. 1(h) of Regulation No. 659/1999 if it shows that its interests or those of its members might be affected by the granting of aid); ECJ, Case C-83/09 P *Commission v Kronoply and Kronotex* [2011] E.C.R. I-4441, para. 65. See also CFI, Case T-188/95 *Waterleiding Maatschappij 'Noord-West Brabant' v Commission* [1998] E.C.R. II-3713, paras 79–81 and 85–86. A taxpayer per se is not an interested party within the meaning of Artice 1(h) of Regulation No. 659/1999. This is because if this were admitted to be the case it would deprive the notion of a person individually concerned within the meaning of the fourth para. of Art. 263 TFEU of any legal meaning in the context of actions for annulment brought against decisions taken on the basis of Art. 108(3) TFEU by making that remedy into a species of *actio popularis*.

Where an 'interested party' seeks the annulment of a decision not to raise objections, the applicant may invoke any plea to show that the assessment of the information and evidence which the Commission had at its disposal during the preliminary investigation examination phase of the measure notified should have raised doubts as to the compatibility of that measure with the internal market.[453]

7.119 *Decision taken upon completion of the procedure provided for in Art. 108(2) TFEU* - In addition, the Commission may also take a decision after the procedure provided for in Art. 108(2) TFEU and Art. 6(1) of Regulation No. 659/1999 has been completed. Such a decision is likewise addressed to the Member State concerned. As regards the position of beneficiaries of State aid and their competitors, a distinction has to be drawn between decisions relating to general aid regimes and decisions relating to individual aid measures.

(ii) Decisions relating to general aid regimes

7.120 *Measures of general application* - Commission decisions which declare general aid regimes compatible or incompatible with the internal market upon completion of the procedure provided for in Art. 108(2) TFEU and Art. 6(1) of Regulation No. 659/1999 are considered to be measures of general application. They may generally be assumed to constitute regulatory acts[454] which *do* entail implementing measures (by the Member States),[455] so that the requirement of 'individual concern' still applies under the fourth paragraph of Art. 263 TFEU.[456] By and large, actions brought by undertakings against such

---

The fact that a person has submitted a complaint to the Commission is not sufficient in itself for that person to be regarded as an interested party within the meaning of Art. 1(h) of Regulation No. 659/1999. A complainant has to show that it has a legitimate interest, consisting, for instance, in the protection of its competitive position on the market vis-à-vis the measures complained of (CFI (order of 25 June 2003), Case T-41/01 *Pérez Escolar v Commission* [2003] II-2157, paras 36–40; see also CFI, Case T-188/95 *Waterleiding Maatschappij 'Noord-West Brabant' v Commission* [1998] E.C.R. II-3713, para. 68 (and case-law cited therein)).

[453] The use of arguments relating to the incompatibility of the aid measure with the internal market does nothing to bring about a change in the subject-matter of the action (seeking to safeguard the procedural rights of an interested party) or in the conditions for its admissibility. On the contrary, the existence of doubts concerning that compatibility is precisely the evidence which must be adduced in order to show that the Commission was required to initiate the formal investigation procedure under Art. 108(2) TFEU and Art. 6(1) of Regulation No. 659/1999: see ECJ, Case C-319/07 P *3F v Commission* [2009] E.C.R. I-5963, para. 35; ECJ, Case C-83/09 P *Commission v Kronoply and Kronotex* [2011] E.C.R. I-4441, para. 59; ECJ, Case C-148/09 P *Belgium v Deutsche Post and Others* [2011] E.C.R. I-8573, paras 64–66; EGC (judgment of 10 July 2012), Case T-520/09 *TF1 and Others v Commission*, not reported, para. 48; EGC (judgment of 10 July 2012), Case T-304/08 *Smurfit Kappa Group v Commission*, not reported, paras 51–52, and 68; EGC (judgment of 7 November 2012), Case T-137/10 *CBI v Commission*, not reported, paras 66–67.

[454] See Opinion of Advocate-General J. Kokott of 21 March 2013 in Case C-274/12 P *Telefónica v Commission*, not reported, points 17–29. Such acts are generally of direct concern to the applicant within the meaning of the fourth para. of Art. 263 TFEU. In EGC (order of 4 June 2012), Case T-379/11 *Hüttenwerke Krupp Mannesmann and Others v Commission*, not reported, paras 48–53, the General Court pointed out that the question of whether or not the contested regulatory act leaves a degree of discretion to the authorities responsible for the implementing measures is irrelevant. The requirement of an act which does not entail implementing measures laid down in the fourth para. of Art. 263 TFEU constitutes indeed a different condition than the requirement that the act be of direct concern to the applicant. See also EGC (order of 4 June 2012), Case T-381/11 *Eurofer v Commission*, not reported, para. 59.

[455] See ECJ (judgment of 19 December 2013), Case C-274/12 P *Telefónica v Commission*, not reported, paras 27–39 and the points 30–57.

[456] EGC (judgment of 8 March 2012), Case T-221/10 *Iberdrola v Commission*, not reported, para. 46; EGC (order of 21 March 2012), Case T-228/10 *Telefónica v Commission*, not reported, paras 42–43. But see, however, with respect to aid granted by the Union: EGC (judgment of 30 May 2013), Joined Cases T-454/10 and T-482/11 *Anicav and Others v Commission*, not reported, paras 42–43.

acts will be inadmissible, since they will generally fail to satisfy the condition of individual concern laid down in the fourth paragraph of Art. 263 TFEU.[457] By contrast, the general nature of the aid measure does not prevent an interested party within the meaning of Art. 1(h) of Regulation No. 659/1999 from being individually concerned by the decision not to raise objections.[458]

Competitors of potential beneficiaries of the aid - An undertaking which is a competitor of a **7.121** potential beneficiary of aid authorized under a general aid scheme will only exceptionally have *locus standi* to challenge a Commission decision authorizing that scheme.[459] This is because the contested decision generally affects such an undertaking only by virtue of its objective capacity in the same manner as any other undertaking which is, or might be in the future, in the same situation.[460] The fact that the applicant is a competitor of the beneficiaries of the aid[461] and/or made a complaint to the Commission (and in that connection corresponded and even had meetings with the Commission) does not constitute sufficient circumstances peculiar to the applicant by which it can be distinguished individually from all other persons, thus conferring on it standing to bring proceedings against a decision of the Commission relating to a general aid scheme.[462]

Beneficiaries of the aid - Similarly, potential beneficiaries of a general aid scheme are not **7.122** individually concerned by a Commission decision relating to that scheme. The Union courts have therefore consistently held that an undertaking cannot, in principle, contest a Commission decision prohibiting a sectoral aid scheme if it is concerned by that decision solely by virtue of belonging to the sector in question and being a *potential beneficiary* of the scheme. Such a decision is, vis-à-vis that undertaking, a measure of general application covering situations which are determined objectively and entails legal effects for a class of persons envisaged in a general and abstract manner.[463]

---

[457] ECJ, Cases 67/85 to 68/85, and 70/85 *Van der Kooy v Commission* [1988] E.C.R. 219, paras 13–16; ECJ, Joined Cases C-15/98 and C-105/99 *Italy and Sardegna Lines v Commission* [2000] E.C.R. I-8855, para. 33; ECJ, Case C-298/00 P *Italy v Commission* [2004] E.C.R. I-4087, para 37; CFI, Case T-86/96 *Arbeitsgemeinschaft Deutscher Luftfahrt-Unternehmen v Commission* [1999] E.C.R. II-179, paras 45–46; CFI, Case T-9/98 *Mitteldeutsche Erdöl-Raffinerie v Commission* [2001] E.C.R. II-3367, para. 77; ECJ, Case C-519/07 P *Commission v Koninklijke FrieslandCampina* [2009] E.C.R. I-8495, para. 53; CFI (order of 10 March 2005), Case T-273/00 *Unindustria and Others v Commission*, not reported, para. 25; EGC, Case T-335/08 *BNP Paribas and Others v Commission* [2010] E.C.R. II-3323, para. 65.
[458] ECJ, Case C-487/06 P *British Aggregates* v *Commission* [2008] E.C.R. I-10515, para. 31; ECJ, Case C-319/07 P *3F v Commission* [2009] E.C.R. I-5963; ECJ, Case C-47/10 P *Austria v Scheucher-Fleisch and Others* [2011] E.C.R. I-10707; EGC, Case T-193/06 *TF1 v Commission* [2010] E.C.R. II-4967, para. 73.
[459] ECJ, Case 169/84 *Cofaz and Others v Commission* [1986] E.C.R. 391, paras 22–25.
[460] See, per analogy, CFI, Case T-9/98 *Mitteldeutsche Erdöl-Raffinerie v Commission* [2001] E.C.R. II-3367, paras 78–85; EGC (judgment of 8 March 2012), Case T-221/10 *Iberdrola v Commission*, not reported, para. 37.
[461] ECJ, Case C-487/06 P *British Aggregates v Commission* [2008] E.C.R. I-10515, para. 48.
[462] CFI, Case T-398/94 *Kahn Scheepvaart v Commission* [1996] E.C.R. II-477, para. 42.
[463] ECJ, Cases 67/85, 68/85 and 70/85 *Van der Kooy and Others v Commission* [1988] E.C.R. 219, para. 15; ECJ, Case C-6/92 *Federmineraria and Others v Commission* [1993] E.C.R. I-6357, para. 14; ECJ, Joined Cases C-15/98 and C-105/99 *Italy and Sardegna Lines v Commission* [2000] E.C.R. I-8855, para. 33; ECJ, Case C-519/07 P *Commission v Koninklijke FrieslandCampina* [2009] E.C.R. I-8495, para. 53; CFI (order of 10 March 2005), Case T-273/00 *Unindustria and Others v Commission*, not reported, para. 25; EGC, Case T-335/08 *BNP Paribas and Others v Commission* [2010] E.C.R. II-3323, para. 65. See also A. Rosas, 'Judicial Protection in EU State Aid Law' in *Economic Law and Justice in Times of Globalisation—Festschrift for Carl Baudenbacher* (Nomos Verlagsgesellschaft, Baden-Baden, 2007), 579–91.

Where, however, the applicant undertaking is concerned by the contested decision not only by virtue of its being potential beneficiary of the aid scheme in question, but also by virtue of its being an actual recipient of individual aid granted under that scheme, the recovery of which has been ordered by the Commission, the Union judicature will find that the *Plaumann* test[464] is satisfied. Thus, an *actual beneficiary* of individual aid granted under a general scheme is individually concerned by the Commission decision declaring the aid incompatible with the internal market in the case of a decision ordering the recovery of the aid.[465] The Commission's (lack of) knowledge of the situation of such undertakings has no bearing on the fact that those undertakings may be individually concerned by the contested decision.[466] It should further be recalled that as a result of the *Deggendorf* line of case-law (see para. 10.11), a person who undoubtedly has the right under Art. 263 TFEU to seek the annulment of a Union act may not plead the illegality of that act in subsequent proceedings before the national courts.[467] That case-law, however, only applies where there is absolutely no doubt that the recovery order applies to the undertaking concerned.[468]

---

[464] See para. 7.97. In absence of such recovery order, this test can also, exceptionally, be satisfied where the contested decision takes into account particular features of the applicant's situation: see CFI, Case T-9/98 *Mitteldeutsche Erdöl-Raffinerie v Commission* [2001] E.C.R. II-3367, paras 78–85; EGC (judgment of 8 March 2012), Case T-221/10 *Iberdrola v Commission*, not reported, para. 37.

[465] ECJ, Joined Cases C-15/98 and C-105/99 *Italy and Sardegna Lines v Commission* [2000] E.C.R. I-8855, para. 34; ECJ, Case C-298/00 P *Italy v Commission* [2004] E.C.R. I-4087, paras 37–39; ECJ, Joined Cases C-71/09 P, C-73/09 P and C-76/09 P *Comitato 'Venezia vuole vivere' v Commission* [2011] E.C.R. I-4727, para. 53; ECJ (judgment of 21 December 2011), Case C-320/09 P *A2A v Commission*, not reported, paras 57–60; CFI, Case T-136/05 *Salvat and Others v Commission* [2007] E.C.R. II-4063, para. 69; CFI, Case T-55/99 *CETM v Commission* [2000] E.C.R. II-3207, para. 25; CFI, Case T-300/02 *AMGA v Commission* [2009] E.C.R. II-1737, para. 50 (as regards a tax exemption, a company which made losses during the period concerned is not an actual recipient of the aid and will therefore not be individually concerned by the decision concerning the aid scheme); EGC, Case T-335/08 *BNP Paribas and Others v Commission* [2010] E.C.R. II-3323, para. 66; EGC (judgment of 8 March 2012), Case T-221/10 *Iberdrola v Commission*, not reported, para. 26; EGC (order of 27 March 2012), Case T-327/09 *Connefroy and Others v Commission*, not reported, para. 22: the applicant has to provide sufficient proof in its application that it was effectively granted State aid under the general aid scheme (EGC, Case T-327/09 *Connefroy and Others v Commission*, paras 33–33). The *Plaumann* test may also be satisfied where the contested measure affects a group of persons who were identified or identifiable when that measure was adopted by reason of criteria—other than being the actual beneficiaries of the aid—specific to the members of the group: see ECJ, Joined Cases C-182/03 and C-217/03 *Belgium and Forum 187 v Commission* [2006] E.C.R. I-5479, paras 60–64; ECJ, Case C-519/07 P *Commission v Koninklijke FrieslandCampina* [2009] E.C.R. I-8495, paras 53–58. However if recovery of the aid is not ordered: see ECJ (judgment of 19 December 2013), Case C-274/12 P *Telefónica v Commission*, not reported, paras 44–51.

[466] ECJ, Case C-519/07 P *Commission v Koninklijke Friesland Campina* [2009] E.C.R. I-8495, para. 59; EGC (order of 21 March 2012), Case T-228/10 *Telefónica v Commission*, not reported, paras 28–33.

[467] ECJ, Case C-188/92 *TWD Textilwerke Deggendorf* [1994] E.C.R. I-833, paras 24–26; ECJ, Case C-241/95 *Accrington Beef* [1996] E.C.R. I-6699, paras 15–16; ECJ, Joined Cases C-71/09 P, C-73/09 P and C-76/09 P *Comitato 'Venezia vuole vivere' v Commission* [2011] E.C.R. I-4727, paras 58–59.

[468] When the national authorities consider that the recovery order does not apply to the undertaking having brought an action for annulment before the General Court, that court will declare the action inadmissible and the *Deggendorf* line of case-law will not apply: see CFI (order of 10 March 2005), Joined Cases T-228/00, T-229/00, T-242/00, T-243/00, T-245/00 to T-248/00, T-250/00, T-252/00, T-256/00 to T-259/00, T-265/00, T-267/00, T-268/00, T-271/00, T-274/00 to T-276/00, T-281/00, T-287/00 to T-296/00 *Gruppo ormeggiatori del porto di Venezia and Others v Commission* [2005] E.C.R. II-787, paras 24 and 30–32; CFI (order of 10 March 2005), Case T-266/00 *Confartigianato Venezia and Others v Commission*, not reported, paras 21–23; CFI (order of 10 March 2005), Case T-273/00 *Unindustria and Others v Commission*, not reported, paras 21–23. See also Opinion of Advocate-General D. Ruiz-Jarabo Colomer in Joined Cases C-346/03 and C-529/03 *Atzeni and Others* [2006] E.C.R. I-1875, points 86–90 and 98.

(iii) Decisions relating to individual aid measures

Recipient of aid - If the Commission declares the aid incompatible with the internal market, **7.123**
the undertaking for which the aid was intended will be individually concerned.[469] Furthermore, a recipient of aid will likewise be individually concerned by a Commission decision
declaring aid compatible with the internal market subject to the express condition that the
recipient of the aid fulfils a number of obligations. It will also have an interest in the
annulment of such a decision.[470] In contrast, it will have no interest such as to claim
annulment of a decision which simply declares a specific aid measure compatible with the
internal market. Accordingly, it cannot contest the classification of a measure as aid where
the aid is declared unconditionally compatible with the internal market.[471]

Competitors of recipient - As regards an undertaking which is *not the beneficiary of the aid* **7.124**
measure, the Court has consistently held that a decision closing a procedure under Art. 108(2)
TFEU is of individual concern to those competitors of the beneficiary which have played a
significant role in the investigation procedure, provided that their position on the market is
significantly affected by the aid which is the subject of the decision at issue.[472] The Court of
Justice has thus held that the fact that an undertaking was at the origin of the complaint
which led to the opening of the formal examination procedure, the fact that its views were
heard, and the fact that the conduct of that procedure was largely determined by its
observations are factors which are relevant to the assessment of the *locus standi* of that
undertaking.[473] However, that does not preclude the possibility that an undertaking may be
in a position to demonstrate by other means—by reference to specific circumstances

---

[469] ECJ, Case 730/79 *Philip Morris v Commission* [1980] E.C.R. 2671, para. 5; ECJ, Case 323/82
Intermills v Commission [1984] E.C.R. 3809, para. 5; ECJ, Joined Cases 296/82 and 318/82 *Netherlands
and Leeuwarder Papierwarenfabriek v Commission* [1985] E.C.R. 809, para. 13; CFI, Case T-358/94 *Air
France v Commission* [1996] E.C.R. II-2109, para. 31. Works councils and trade unions of undertakings in
receipt of aid were, however, not held to be individually concerned by a Commission decision declaring the aid
incompatible with the internal market. Such works councils and trade unions are interested parties within the
meaning of Art. 1(h) of Regulation No. 659/1999, but that is not sufficient to render them individually
concerned, not even if they submitted comments during the administrative procedure: CFI (order of 18
February 1998), Case T-189/97 *Comité d'entreprise de la Société française de production and Others v Commission* [1998] E.C.R. II-335, paras 42–44, upheld by ECJ, Case C-106/98 P *Comité d'entreprise de la Société
française de production and Others v Commission* [2000] E.C.R. I-3659, paras 47–55.
[470] CFI, Case T-296/97 *Alitalia v Commission* [2000] E.C.R. II-3871; CFI, Case T-25/07 *Iride and Iride
Energia v Commission* [2009] E.C.R. II-245.
[471] CFI, Case T-141/03 *Sniace v Commission* [2005] E.C.R. II-1197, paras 20–41. See also EGC, Joined
Cases T-443/08 and T-455/08 *Freistaat Sachsen and Others v Commission* [2011] E.C.R. II-1311, paras
46–69.
[472] See in this respect ECJ, Case 169/84 *Cofaz v Commission* [1986] E.C.R. 391, paras 22–25; ECJ, Case
C-260/05 P *Sniace v Commission* [2007] E.C.R. I-10005, para. 55; CFI, Joined Cases T-447/93, T-448/93
and T-449/93 *AITEC and Others v Commission* [1995] E.C.R. II-1971, paras 33–42 and 75–80; CFI, Case
T-149/95 *Ducros v Commission* [1997] E.C.R. II-2031, paras 30–43; CFI, Case T-36/99 *Lenzing v Commission* [2004] E.C.R. II-3597, para. 90: the fact that the position on the market of the person concerned is
substantially affected does not necessarily mean that its profitability falls, that its market share is reduced, or
that operating losses are incurred. The question in that connection is whether the person concerned would be
in a more favourable situation in the absence of the decision which it seeks to have annulled. That may validly
cover the situation in which the applicant loses the opportunity to make a profit because the public authorities
confer an advantage on one of its competitors.
[473] ECJ, Case 169/84 *Cofaz v Commission* [1986] E.C.R. 391, paras 24–25; ECJ, Case C-260/05 P *Sniace
v Commission* [2007] E.C.R. I-10005, para. 56; CFI, Case T-11/04 *Werkgroep Commerciële Jachthavens
Zuidelijke Randmeren and Others v Commission* [2006] E.C.R. II-3861, para. 52.

distinguishing it individually, as in the case of the person addressed—that it is individually concerned.[474]

Indeed, recent case-law indicates that participation in the administrative procedure is neither a sufficient nor a necessary condition to be individually concerned by the Commission decision within the meaning of the fourth paragraph of Art. 263 TFEU. The determining factor is whether the market position of the applicant is substantially affected by the measure.[475] Unlike in the case of an action for annulment of a decision taken on the basis of the preliminary procedure provided for in Art. 108(3) TFEU, an undertaking cannot simply rely on its status as 'interested party' within the meaning of Art. 1(h) of Regulation No. 659/1999 in order to demonstrate that it is individually concerned by the Commission's decision.[476] The applicant must prove that it is in a distinct competitive position which differentiates it, as regards the State aid in question, from any other trader.[477] Accordingly, the General Court has accepted that undertakings which had not taken part in the formal investigation pursuant to Art. 108(2) TFEU could be individually concerned on the ground that the market in which the aid was granted was characterized by a limited number of producers (the applicants had a market share of 95 per cent) and by the significant increase in production capacity involved in the investments planned by the company in receipt of the aid in question. That special situation distinguished them from every other market participant as far as the aid in issue was concerned.[478]

---

[474] Case C-260/05 P *Sniace v Commission* [2007] E.C.R. I-10005, para. 57; CFI, Case T-435/93, *ASPEC and Others v Commission* [1995] E.C.R. II-1281, para. 64; CFI, Case T-11/95 *BP Chemicals v Commission* [1998] E.C.R. II-3235, para. 72.

[475] The mere fact that a measure may exercise an influence on the competitive relationships existing on the relevant market and that the applicant was in a competitive relationship with the addressee of that measure cannot in any event suffice for the applicant to be regarded as being individually concerned by that measure: see ECJ, Case C-525/04 P *Spain v Lenzing* [2007] E.C.R. I-9947, para. 32; ECJ, Case C-487/06 P *British Aggregates v Commission* [2008] E.C.R. I-10515, para. 47. See also ECJ, Case C-260/05 P *Sniace v Commission* [2007] E.C.R. I-10005, paras 57–60; see also CFI, Case T-11/04 *Werkgroep Commerciële Jachthavens Zuidelijke Randmeren and Others v Commission* [2006] E.C.R. II-3861, para. 53; EGC, Case T-54/07 *Vtesse Networks v Commission* [2011] E.C.R. II-6*, Summ. pub., paras 92–93 (and case-law cited therein); EGC (judgment of 28 March 2012), Case T-123/09 *Ryanair v Commission*, not reported, paras 196–197.

[476] ECJ, Case C-106/98 P *Comité d'entreprise de la Société française de production and Others v Commission* [2000] E.C.R. I-3659, para. 41; CFI, Case T-141/03 *Sniace v Commission* [2005] E.C.R. II-1197, para. 70.

[477] ECJ, Case C-525/04 P *Spain v Lenzing* [2007] E.C.R. I-9947, para. 33; ECJ, Case C-487/06 P *British Aggregates v Commission* [2008] E.C.R. I-10515, para. 48. See also CFI, Case T-435/93 *ASPEC and Others v Commission* [1995] E.C.R. II-1281, para. 70; CFI, Case T-266/94 *Skibsvaerftsforeningen and Others v Commission* [1996] E.C.R. II-1399, para. 47; CFI Case T-11/95 *BP Chemicals v Commission* [1998] E.C.R. II-3235, para. 77; CFI (order of 27 May 2004) Case T-358/02 *Deutsche Post and DHL v Commission* [2004] E.C.R. II-1565, para. 36.

[478] CFI, Case T-435/93 *ASPEC and Others v Commission* [1995] E.C.R. II-1281, para. 70. See also ECJ, Case C-487/06 P *British Aggregates v Commission* [2008] E.C.R. I-10515, para. 53, in which the ECJ held that 'it does not follow from the Court's case-law that a special status of this kind, which distinguishes a "person other than the persons addressed", within the meaning of *Plaumann* v Commission, from any other economic operator, must necessarily be inferred from factors such as a significant decline in turnover, appreciable financial losses or a significant reduction in market share following the grant of the aid in question. The grant of State aid can have an adverse effect on the competitive situation of an operator in other ways too, in particular by causing the loss of an opportunity to make a profit or a less favourable development than would have been the case without such aid. Similarly, the seriousness of such an effect may vary according to a large number of factors such as, in particular, the structure of the market concerned or the nature of the aid in question. Demonstrating a substantial adverse effect on a competitor's position on the market cannot, therefore, simply be a matter of the existence of certain factors indicating a decline in its commercial or financial performance.'

(iv) Position of constitutionally autonomous regions and devolved authorities

Individually concerned if the authority concerned is the author of the aid measure - It must be **7.125**
recalled that regions and other devolved authorities are not entitled to bring proceedings
pursuant to the second paragraph of Art. 263 TFEU (see paras 7.77 and 7.103).[479] By contrast,
where devolved authorities have legal personality under national law they must, on that basis, be
treated as legal persons within the meaning of the fourth paragraph of Art. 263 TFEU.[480]

A constitutionally autonomous region or other devolved authority will be deemed to be
individually concerned by a Commission decision declaring a general aid scheme[481] or an
individual aid measure[482] adopted by the region or authority concerned incompatible with
the internal market. Indeed, under such circumstances, the contested decision directly
prevents the region or authority concerned from exercising its own powers as it sees fit.[483]
However, where the applicant is not the author of the aid scheme, reliance by a regional or
other devolved authority of a Member State on the fact that the application or implementation of the contested Union measure is capable generally of affecting socio-economic
conditions within its territorial jurisdiction is not sufficient to render an action brought
by that authority admissible.[484]

(v) Position of associations

General - An action for annulment brought by an association of undertakings against a **7.126**
Commission decision relating to State aid will be admissible in two[485] sets of circumstances.
The first is where the association, by bringing its action, has substituted itself for one or

---

[479] ECJ (order of 21 March 1997), Case C-95/97 *Région Wallonne v Commission* [1997] E.C.R. I-1787,
para. 6; ECJ (order of 1 October 1997), C-180/97 *Regione Toscana v Commission* [1997] E.C.R. I-5245,
para. 6; CFI, Case T-214/95 *Vlaams Gewest v Commission* [1998] E.C.R. II-717, para. 28.
[480] ECJ (order of 21 March 1997), Case C-95/97 *Région Wallonne v Commission* [1997] E.C.R. I-1787,
para. 11; ECJ (order of 1 October 1997), C-180/97 *Regione Toscana v Commission* [1997] E.C.R. I-5245,
para. 11; CFI, Case T-214/95 *Vlaams Gewest v Commission* [1998] E.C.R. II-717, para. 28; CFI, Joined Cases
T-366/03 and T-235/04 *Land Oberösterreich and Austria v Commission* [2005] E.C.R. II-4005, paras 25–30
(with respect to Art. 114(5) TFEU decision).
[481] CFI, Case T-288/97 *Regione autonoma Friuli-Venezia Giulia v Commission* [1999] E.C.R. II-1871,
para. 31; CFI, Joined Cases T-269/99, T-271/99 and T-272/99 *Diputación Foral de Guipúzcoa and Others v
Commission* [2002] E.C.R. II-4217, para. 41; EGC, Joined Cases T-394/08, T-408/08, T-453/08, and
T-454/08 *Regione Autonoma della Sardegna v Commission* [2011] E.C.R. II-6255 (admissibility no longer
examined by the GC).
[482] CFI, Case T-214/95 *Vlaams Gewest v Commission* [1998] E.C.R. II-717, para. 29; CFI, Joined Cases
T-132/96 and T-143/96 *Freistaat Sachsen and Others v Commission* [1999] E.C.R. II-3663, para. 84.
[483] CFI, Case T-214/95 *Vlaams Gewest v Commission* [1998] E.C.R. II-717, para. 29; CFI, Joined Cases
T-132/96 and T-143/96 *Freistaat Sachsen and Others v Commission* [1999] E.C.R. II-3663, para. 84; CFI,
Case T-288/97 *Regione autonoma Friuli-Venezia Giulia v Commission* [1999] E.C.R. II-1871, para. 31; CFI,
Joined Cases T-269/99, T-271/99, and T-272/99 *Diputación Foral de Guipúzcoa and Others v Commission*
[2002] E.C.R. II-4217, para. 41. When the aid scheme is declared compatible, the action will in principle be
inadmissible: see EGC, Joined Cases T-443/08 and T-455/08 *Freistaat Sachsen and Others v Commission*
[2011] E.C.R. II-1311, paras 46–69.
[484] CFI, Case T-238/97 *Comunidad Autónoma de Cantabria v Council* [1998] E.C.R. II-2271, para. 50.
[485] In the case-law within the context of State aid, the three situations mentioned in para. 7.104 are indeed
parsed down to two. This could be explained by the fact that, depending on the way these three situations are
framed, the first (procedural rights affected) and third situations (own interests affected) could be subsumed
into one general category. See, e.g. CFI, Joined Cases T-227/01 to T-229/01, T-265/01, T-266/01, and
T-270/01 *Territorio Histórico de Álava and Others v Commission* [2009] E.C.R. II-3029, para. 108 (and further
citations therein); CFI, Case T-117/04 *Vereniging Werkgroep Commerciële Jachthavens Zuidelijke Randmeren
and Others v Commission* [2006] E.C.R. II-3861, para. 65; CFI, Case T-445/05 *Associazione italiana del
risparmio gestito and Others v Commission* [2009] E.C.R. II-289, para. 55.

more of the members whom it represents, on condition that those members were them-selves in a position to bring an admissible action. The second is where the association can prove an interest of its own for bringing an action for annulment, for example where its negotiating position is affected by the measure which it seeks to have annulled.[486]

7.127 *Association representing the interests of undertakings which are directly and individually concerned* - The defence of common interests is not enough to establish the admissibility of an action for annulment brought by an association. An association will, however, be able to bring an action where it defends the individual interests of certain of its members before the General Court in accordance with the powers conferred on it by its statutes if it can be demonstrated that these members are directly and individually concerned by the contested decision. Such collective action brought by the association presents procedural advantages, since it obviates the institution of numerous separate actions against the same decision, whilst avoiding any risk of Art. 263 TFEU being circumvented by means of such a collective action.[487]

7.128 *The association can prove an interest of its own* - An association will be considered to be individually concerned by a Commission decision relating to State aid if it is capable of demonstrating that its position as a negotiator is affected by that decision.[488]

A trade organization which was closely involved in the development of the Commission's policy on aid in a particular sector will be individually concerned by a Commission decision which is allegedly at odds with the policy outlined. This is because such a decision affects the trade organization in its capacity as a negotiator of the policy.[489]

Thus, in the *CIRFS* case, the Court of Justice held that the *Comité International de la Rayonne et des Fibres Synthétiques* (International Rayon and Synthetic Fibres Committee) was individually concerned by a Commission decision which allegedly violated the Com-mission's 'discipline' with respect to aid to the synthetic fibre industry, after noting that the association concerned had been the Commission's interlocutor with regard to the adoption of this 'discipline' and to its later extension and adaptation and had actively pursued negotiations with the Commission during the pre-litigation procedure, in particular by

[486] ECJ, Joined Cases C-182/03 and C-217/03 *Belgium and Forum 187 v Commission* [2006] E.C.R. I-5479, para. 56 (and case-law cited therein); EGC (order of 13 July 2012), Case T-201/10 *IVBN v Commission*, not reported, point 32.

[487] ECJ, Case 282/85 *DEFI v Commission* [1986] E.C.R. 2469, para. 16; ECJ, Case C-6/92 *Federminer-aria and Others v Commission* [1993] E.C.R. I-6357, para. 17; ECJ, Case C-319/07 P *3F v Commission* [2009] E.C.R. I-5963, paras 87–94; CFI, Joined Cases T-447/93, T-448/93, and T-449/93 *AITEC and Others v Commission* [1995] E.C.R. II-1971, paras 60 and 62; CFI, Case T-55/99 *CETM v Commission* [2000] E.C.R. II-3207, para. 23; CFI, Case T-210/02 *British Aggregates v Commission* [2006] E.C.R. II-2789, para. 47 (this part of judgment is not affected by ECJ, Case C-487/06 P *British Aggregates* v *Commission* [2008] E.C.R. I-10515). With respect to merger control, see CFI, Case T-151/05 *NVV and Others v Commission* [2009] E.C.R. II-1219, para 44.

[488] ECJ, Joined Cases 67/85, 68/85 and 70/85 *Van der Kooy and Others v Commission* [1988] E.C.R. 219, paras 19–25; ECJ, Case C-313/90 *CIRFS and Others v Commission* [1993] E.C.R. I-1125, paras 29 and 30; ECJ, Case C-319/07 P *3F v Commission* [2009] E.C.R. I-5963, paras 87–94; CFI, Case T-380/94 *AIUFFASS and AKT v Commission* [1996] E.C.R. II-2169, para. 50; CFI, Case T-55/99 *CETM v Commission* [2000] E.C.R. II-3207, para. 23.

[489] ECJ, Case C-313/90 *CIRFS and Others v Commission* [1993] E.C.R. I-1125, paras 28–31; CFI, Case T-380/94 *AIUFASS and AKT v Commission* [1996] E.C.R. I-2169, para. 51.

submitting written observations to it and by keeping in close contact with the responsible departments.[490]

Similarly, in the *Van der Kooy* case, the *Landbouwschap* (a body established under public law of the Netherlands to protect the common interests of agricultural undertakings) had negotiated with a public undertaking a preferential gas tariff which was considered by the Commission to constitute State aid. It was also one of the signatories of the agreement establishing that tariff. The Court of Justice held that the *Landbouwschap* was individually concerned by the Commission decision declaring the preferential gas tariff incompatible with the internal market. The Court stressed that the association's position as negotiator of gas tariffs in the interests of the growers concerned was affected by the contested decision and that in this capacity the association had taken an active part in the procedure under Art. 108(2) TFEU by submitting written comments to the Commission and by keeping in close contact with the responsible officials throughout the procedure.[491] Accordingly, the *Van der Kooy* and *CIRFS* cases concerned particular situations in which the applicants occupied a clearly circumscribed position as negotiators which was closely linked to the actual subject-matter of the Commission decision, thus placing them in a factual situation which distinguished them from all other persons.[492]

An association will also prove an interest of its own to bring the action—and will be considered to be individually concerned by a Commission decision relating to State aid— where that decision violates rights of a procedural nature expressly conferred on such association by a legal provision.[493]

Trade unions - A trade union will not normally be individually concerned by a decision of **7.129** the Commission declaring an aid measure incompatible with the internal market. The status of negotiator with regard to the social aspects constitutes only a tenuous link with the actual subject-matter of the decision. Whereas, when determining whether or not State aid is compatible with the internal market, social aspects are liable to be taken into account by the Commission, this will be done only as part of an overall assessment which includes a large number of considerations of various kinds, linked in particular to the protection of competition, regional development, the promotion of culture, or again to the protection of the environment.[494] By contrast, where the Commission declares an aid measure compatible with the internal market without opening the formal procedure provided for in Art. 108(2) TFEU and Art. 6(1) of Regulation No. 659/1999, a trade union may be regarded as 'interested' within the meaning of Art. 1(h) of Regulation No. 659/1999 and thus

---

[490] ECJ, Case C-313/90 *CIRFS and Others v Commission* [1993] E.C.R. I-1125, paras 24–31.

[491] ECJ, Joined Cases 67/85 to 68/85, and 70/85 *Van der Kooy v Commission* [1988] E.C.R. 219, paras 20–24. The position of the association as a negotiator at both national and EU level is taken into account.

[492] ECJ, Case C-106/98 P *Comité d'entreprise de la Société française de production and Others v Commission* [2000] E.C.R. I-3659, para. 45. See also CFI, Case T-69/96, *Hamburger Hafen- und Lagerhaux and Others v Commission* [2001] E.C.R. II-1037, para. 50.

[493] EGC (judgment of 18 March 2010), Case T-189/08 *Forum 187 v Commission* [2010] E.C.R. II-1039, para. 58 (and case-law cited therein). As regards the procedural rights conferred by Art. 108(2) TFEU and Art. 6(1) of Regulation No. 659/1999, the association which brings the action will generally represent the interests of undertakings which are 'interested parties' within the meaning of these provisions, as a result of which the association will not have to prove an interest of its own to bring the action.

[494] ECJ, Case C-106/98 P *Comité d'entreprise de la Société française de production and Others v Commission* [2000] E.C.R. I-3659, paras 52–53.

individually concerned by such decision if it shows that its interests or those of its members might be affected by the granting of aid.[495]

(e) Anti-dumping cases

(i) Measures of general application

7.130 Provisional and definitive anti-dumping duties are imposed by regulation pursuant to Art. 14(1) of Regulation No. 1225/2009.[496] What is involved is essentially a provision of general application, which applies to all economic entities concerned. Here as well it may be assumed that anti-dumping regulations constitute regulatory acts[497] which *do* entail implementing measures (by the Member States), so that the requirement of 'individual concern' still applies under the fourth paragraph of Art. 263 TFEU.[498] It is apparent from the case-law that some parts of such an anti-dumping regulation or the extension of existing anti-dumping duties to like products or parts thereof are of individual concern to some persons.[499]

(ii) Producers and exporters

7.131 Producers or exporters established outside the EU of products on which anti-dumping duties are imposed are individually concerned where information about their trading activities is used with a view to determining the duties. Generally speaking, this will be the case where manufacturing and exporting undertakings can establish that they were identified in measures adopted by the Commission or the Council or concerned by the preliminary investigation.[500] Such a factor should have in some way prompted the intervention of the institutions or to

---

[495] ECJ, Case C-319/07 P *3F v Commission* [2009] E.C.R. I-5963, paras 33 and 98–108: this was the case since the measure at issue could affect the position of the trade union and that of its members in collective negotiations, and since the Community guidelines acknowledge the part played by trade unions such as the appellant in those negotiations.

[496] See n. 239.

[497] They are not legislative acts. Under Art. 207(2) TFEU, only measures defining the framework for implementing the common commercial policy are legislative acts.

[498] See EGC (order of 5 February 2013), Case T-551/11 *Brugola Service International v Council*, not reported, paras 42–66.

[499] For a survey, see G. Ress and J. Ukrow, 'Direct Actions Before the EC Court of Justice. The Case of EEC Anti-Dumping Law', in *Adjudication of International Trade Disputes in International and National Economic Law*, Pupil, Vol. 7 (Freiburg, Freiburg, University Press, 1992), 159–260. See also CFI, Joined Cases T-74/97 and T-75/97 *Büchel v Council and Commission* [2000] E.C.R. I-3067.

[500] ECJ, Joined Cases 239 and 275/82 *Allied Corporation v Commission* [1984] 1005, para. 12; ECJ, Case C-156/87 *Gestetner Holdings v Council and Commission* [1990] E.C.R. I-781, para. 17; CFI, Case T-598/97, *BSC Footwear Supplies and Others v Council* [2002] E.C.R. II-1155, para. 45. See, however, CFI, Case T-161/94 *Sinochem Heilongjiang v Council* [1996] E.C.R. II-695, paras 45–48, where the CFI held that the preliminary investigation had concerned the applicant undertaking, even though the Commission had decided not to make use of the information which it had provided; CFI, Case T-155/94 *Climax Paper v Council* [1996] E.C.R. II-873, paras 46–51; CFI, Case T-170/94 *Shanghai Bicycle v Council* [1997] E.C.R. II-1383, para. 39; CFI, Case T-147/97 *Champion Stationery and Others v Council* [1998] E.C.R. II-4137, paras 30–38; CFI, Case T-597/97 *Euromin v Council* [2000] E.C.R. II-2419, para. 45; CFI, Case T-598/97 *BSC Footwear Supplies and Others v Council* [2002] E.C.R. II-1155, para. 45; ECJ, Case C-239/99 *Nachi Europe* [2001] E.C.R. I-1197, para. 21; EGC (judgment of 19 April 2012), Case T-162/09 *Würth and Fasteners (Shenyang) v Council*, not reported, para. 23. See with respect to regulation imposing countervailing duties, EGC (judgment of 24 May 2012), Case T-555/10 *JBF RAK v Council*, not reported. The same test is applied in order to determine whether a producer and exporter is individually concerned by a Commission review notice: see CFI, Case T-45/06 *Reliance Industries v Council and Commission* [2008] E.C.R. II-2399, para. 47 (a company which was identified in the regulation imposing anti-dumping or countervailing duties as a producer and exporter which had offered an undertaking during the administrative proceeding which was accepted by the Commission is individually concerned by the review notice).

have formed part of the *raison d'être* of the regulation itself.[501] An action for annulment is often the only legal remedy available to them against the imposition of such duties.[502] This argument provides support for the Union judicature in finding that such an action is admissible.

Where a regulation which introduces an anti-dumping duty imposes different duties on a series of undertakings, an undertaking is individually concerned only by those provisions which impose on it a specific anti-dumping duty and determine the amount thereof, and not by those provisions which impose anti-dumping duties on other undertakings. Manufacturing and exporting undertakings are thus not individually concerned by an anti-dumping duty which is imposed on other undertakings by the same regulation. Consequently, an action brought by such undertakings will be admissible only insofar as they seek the annulment of those provisions of the regulation that exclusively concern them.[503]

(iii) Complainants

Natural or legal persons or associations without legal personality acting on behalf of the EU **7.132** industry which lodge a complaint leading to a preliminary administrative procedure[504] are entitled to bring an action for annulment against a refusal by the Commission to initiate the actual anti-dumping procedure on the grounds that there is insufficient evidence.[505] Their particular legal position founded upon the procedural guarantees conferred by Regulation No. 1225/2009[506] must be protected by the Union judicature. A decision refusing to initiate a procedure may not undermine those procedural safeguards.

An action brought against the regulation imposing a definitive anti-dumping duty is available only to a complainant whose involvement in the adoption of the regulation extends further than simply lodging the complaint which initiated the anti-dumping procedure. Only where the complainant's observations were determinative of the course of the investigation or where its specific position on the market was taken into account, will the complainant be individually concerned by the regulation imposing a definitive anti-dumping duty.[507] The fact that the complaint was lodged by a trade association of which the applicant is a member does not detract from the undertaking's right to bring an

---

[501] ECJ, Case C-75/92 *Gao Yao v Council* [1994] E.C.R. I-3141, paras 26–32; CFI, Case T-597/97 *Euromin v Council* [2000] E.C.R. II-2419, para. 45.
[502] ECJ, Joined Cases 239/82 and 275/82 *Allied Corporation v Commission* [1984] 1005, para. 13.
[503] ECJ, Case 240/84 *Toyo v Council* [1987] E.C.R. 1809, paras 4–7; ECJ, Case 258/84 *Nippon Seiko v Council* [1987] E.C.R. 1923, para. 7; ECJ, Case C-156/87 *Gestetner Holdings v Council and Commission* [1990] E.C.R. I-781, para. 12; ECJ, Case C-174/87 *Ricoh v Council* [1992] E.C.R. I-1335, paras 6–8; ECJ, Case C-239/99 *Nachi Europe* [2001] E.C.R. I-1197, para. 22; CFI, Case T-143/06 *MTZ Polyfilms v Council and Commission* [2009] E.C.R. II-4133, para. 27; EGC (judgment of 10 October 2012), Case T-170/09 *Shanghai Biaowu High-Tensile Fasteners and Shanghai Prime Machinery v Council*, not reported, paras 38–43.
[504] The 'investigation' provided for by Art. 6 of Regulation No. 1225/2009.
[505] ECJ, Case 191/82 *Fediol v Commission* [1983] E.C.R. 2913, paras 15–33. The simple fact that an EU producer was entitled to file a complaint but did not do so is not sufficient to consider that this producer is individually concerned, even if the undertaking concerned is considerably affected by the refusal to adopt anti-dumping measures: see CFI (order of 13 November 2008), Case T-301/06 *Lemaître Sécurité v Commission* [2008] E.C.R. II-261*, Summ. pub., paras 23–30.
[506] The procedural guarantees conferred by Regulation No. 1225/2009 are the right to lodge a complaint, the associated right that the complaint should be investigated with due care in accordance with the procedure laid down by the Commission and the right, upon written request, to inspect all information made available by any party to an investigation which is not confidential (Art. 6(7)).
[507] ECJ, Case 264/82 *Timex v Council and Commission* [1985] E.C.R. 849, paras 8–17.

action.[508] If the aforementioned conditions are fulfilled by both the trade association and the undertaking, both of them can bring an action for annulment.

(iv) Importers

7.133 Importers associated with an exporter are individually concerned by a regulation imposing an anti-dumping duty where their resale prices, and not their export prices, of the products in question are considered in order to determine whether dumping is taking place[509] or the level of the anti-dumping duty.[510] Where an importer brings an action for annulment against a regulation which, following circumvention, was extended to cover like products or parts thereof, an 'importer' which is affected by the extension of the anti-dumping duty will be individually concerned only if the Commission took account of the undertaking's commercial activities in its investigation carried out following circumvention of the original anti-dumping duty or if the undertaking concerned participated in good time in the investigation.[511]

Generally speaking, *importers not associated with an exporter* are not individually concerned by a regulation imposing an anti-dumping duty.[512] The reason for this is that the imposition of the duty affects them in their objective capacity as importers of the product subjected to an anti-dumping duty. Consequently, the regulation remains a regulation, even if independent importers were involved in the procedure which led to its adoption[513] or if their identity emerges from the regulation.[514] The existence of dumping is not normally determined by reference to importers' resale prices, but by reference to the actual prices paid or payable on export.[515]

---

[508] ECJ, Case 264/82 *Timex v Council and Commission*, paras 8–17.

[509] ECJ, Case 118/77 *ISO v Council* [1979] E.C.R. 1277, paras 10–16; ECJ, Joined Cases 239/82 and 275/82 *Allied Corporation v Commission* [1984] E.C.R. 1005, para. 15; ECJ, Case C-156/87 *Gestetner Holdings v Council and Commission* [1990] E.C.R. I-781, para. 17; ECJ, Case C-239/99 *Nachi Europe* [2001] E.C.R. I-1197, para. 21; CFI, Case T-598/97 *BSC Footwear Supplies and Others v Council* [2002] E.C.R. II-1155, para. 45; EGC (judgment of 19 April 2012), Case T-162/09 *Würth and Fasteners (Shenyang) v Council*, not reported, para. 25.

[510] ECJ (order of 11 November 1987), Case 205/87 *Nuova Ceam v Commission* [1987] E.C.R. 4427, para. 13; ECJ, Joined Cases C-305/86 and C-160/87 *Neotype Techmashexport v Commission and Council* [1990] E.C.R. I-2945, paras 20–21. See also ECJ, Case 113/77 *NTN Toyo Bearing and Others v Council* [1979] E.C.R. 1185, para. 9; CFI (order of 27 January 2006), Case T-278/03 *Van Mannekus v Council*, not reported, para. 119; EGC (judgment of 19 April 2012), Case T-162/09 *Würth and Fasteners (Shenyang) v Council*, not reported, para. 25.

[511] CFI, Joined Cases T-74/97 and T-75/97 *Büchel v Council and Commission* [2000] E.C.R. II-3067, paras 50–68.

[512] ECJ, Case 307/81 *Alusuisse v Council and Commission* [1982] E.C.R. 3463, paras 7–14; ECJ (order of 8 July 1987), Case 279/86 *Sermes v Commission* [1987] E.C.R. 3109, paras 14–22; ECJ (order of 8 July 1987), Case 301/86 *Frimodt Pedersen v Commission* [1987] E.C.R. 3123, paras 14–22. A regulation which is confined to accepting price undertakings offered by an exporter in an anti-dumping investigation in relation to products imported by the applicant is of individual concern only to the exporter in question. The importer—even if he is the sole importer—is necessarily not party to the undertakings given: ECJ (order of 8 July 1987), Case 295/86 *Garelly v Commission* [1987] E.C.R. 3117, para. 14; CFI, Case T-598/97 *BSC Footwear Supplies and Others v Council* [2002] E.C.R. II-1155, paras 49–52. For a critical discussion, see E. Van Ginderachter, 'Recevabilité des recours en matière de dumping' (1987) C.D. E. 635–66; see also ECJ (order of 11 November 1987), Case 205/87 *Nuova Ceam v Commission* [1987] E.C.R. 4427, para. 14.

[513] ECJ, Case 307/81 *Alusuisse v Council and Commission*, para. 13.

[514] ECJ (order of 8 July 1987), Case 301/86 *Frimodt Pedersen v Commission* [1987] E.C.R. 3123, para. 3.

[515] ECJ, Case 301/86 *Frimodt Pedersen v Commission*, para. 17. However, non related importers will have *locus standi* to bring an action for annulment against a regulation imposing anti-dumping duties where their resale prices were used in order to construct export prices: see ECJ, Joined Cases C-133/87 and C-150/87

The restrictive scope of the case-law relating to independent importers is mitigated by the fact that they can challenge the imposition of an anti-dumping duty in the national courts, which, in turn, may (or must) make a reference to the Court of Justice for a preliminary ruling on the validity of the regulation (see Ch. 10).

In exceptional circumstances, the Court of Justice has recognized the particular economic situation of an independent importer as a specific circumstance causing the importer to be individually concerned by a regulation imposing an anti-dumping duty.[516] The Court pointed out that the applicant was the largest importer of the product and that its business activities depended to a very large extent on imports, given that there was only one producer within the Union of the product, which, moreover, was its direct competitor and had strengthened its position considerably vis-à-vis the applicant as a result of the restriction of imports. It made no difference that its resale price was not taken into account in adopting the regulation.[517]

(v) Original equipment manufacturers
An original equipment manufacturer (OEM)—an undertaking selling goods produced by **7.134** other manufacturers under its own brand name[518]—will be individually concerned by a regulation imposing an anti-dumping duty where, in calculating the dumping margin, account was taken of the particular features of its business dealings with the manufacturers in respect of which anti-dumping duties are imposed by the regulation. An application by an OEM will be admissible only insofar as it seeks annulment of the specific anti-dumping duty imposed by the regulation on the producer from which the OEM obtains the goods which it sells.[519]

(f) Access to documents pursuant to Regulation No. 1049/2001
A legal person seeking the annulment of a decision addressed to another person refusing **7.135** that person access to documents does not have standing before the Union judicature. In such a case, the applicant cannot be considered to have an interest in seeking the annulment of such a decision, since it does not affect its own rights.[520]

Nashua Corporation and Others v Commission and Council [1990] E.C.R. I-719, paras 12 and 15; CFI, Case T-7/99 *Medici Grimm v Council* [2000] E.C.R. II-2671, para. 65; EGC (judgment of 19 April 2012), Case T-162/09 *Würth and Fasteners (Shenyang) v Council*, not reported, para. 24.

[516] ECJ, Case C-358/89 *Extramet Industry v Council* [1991] E.C.R. I-2501, para. 17. See also CFI, Case T-2/95 *Industrie des poudres sphériques v Council* [1998] E.C.R. II-3939, paras 49–54; CFI, Case T-597/97 *Euromin v Council* [2000] E.C.R. II-2419, paras 46 and 49–50; CFI, Case T-598/97 *BSC Footwear Supplies and Others v Council* [2002] E.C.R. II-1155, para. 48. CFI (order of 27 January 2006), Case T-278/03 *Van Mannekus v Council*, not reported, para. 122; EGC (judgment of 19 April 2012), Case T-162/09 *Würth and Fasteners (Shenyang) v Council*, not reported, para. 28. For an extensive commentary, see O. Brouwer and F. Carlin, 'Qualité pour agir dans les procédures anti-dumping après Extramet' (1981) D.P.C.I. 243–67. For a critical note, see A. Arnull, 'Challenging EC Anti-dumping Regulations: The Problem of Admissibility' (1992) E.C.L.R. 73, at 79.

[517] This case-law was applied by analogy in the field of State aid: see CFI, Case T-289/03 *BUPA and Others v Commission* [2008] E.C.R. II-81, para. 79.

[518] Consequently, an OEM falls somewhere between a producer/exporter, on the one hand, and an importer, on the other.

[519] ECJ, Joined Cases C-133/87 and C-150/87 *Nashua Corporation and Others v Commission and Council* [1990] E.C.R. I-719, paras 16–21; ECJ, Case C-156/87 *Gestetner Holdings v Council and Commission* [1990] E.C.R. I-781, paras 19–24; EGC (judgment of 19 April 2012), *Würth and Fasteners (Shenyang) v Council*, not yet reported, para. 26.

[520] CFI, Case T-41/00 *British American Tobacco International v Commission* [2001] E.C.R. II-1301, paras 18–24.

(g) Public contracts

7.136 Natural or legal persons who participate in a public tender procedure organized by the Union belong to a closed class. Each of them is individually concerned by a decision awarding the contract to one of their number.[521] The withdrawal or modification of a definitive decision awarding the contract is also of individual concern to the persons who participated in the public tender procedure.[522]

(7) Assessment of admissibility where different individual applicants

7.137 Where more than one applicant has brought one and the same action, a finding of admissibility in relation to one applicant means that there is no need to consider whether the other applicants are entitled to bring proceedings.[523]

(8) The requirement that there should be an interest in the annulment of the contested act

(a) Concept

7.138 In contrast to privileged applicants (see para. 7.76),[524] natural or legal persons may bring an action for annulment only insofar as they can establish that they have an interest.[525] This means

---

[521] ECJ, Case 135/81 *Groupement des Agences de Voyages v Commission* [1982] E.C.R. 3799, para. 11; ECJ, Case C-496/99 P *Commission v CAS Succhi di Frutta* [2004] E.C.R. I-3801, paras 58–59; EGC (judgment of 24 April 2012), Case T-554/08 *Evropaïki Dynamiki v Commission*, not reported, paras 30–34 (a member of a consortium, which is the addressee of the contested decision, is entitled to challenge that decision in accordance with the conditions laid down by Art. 263 TFEU).

[522] ECJ, Case 232/81 *Agricola Commerciale Olio and Others v Commission* [1984] E.C.R. 3881, para. 11; ECJ, Case C-496/99 P *Commission v CAS Succhi di Frutta* [2004] E.C.R. I-3801, paras 58–61.

[523] See, e.g. ECJ, Case C-313/90 *CIRFS and Others v Commission* [1993] E.C.R. I-1125 paras 30–31; CFI, Case T-266/94 *Skibsvaerftsforeningen and Others v Commission* [1996] E.C.R. II-1399, para. 51; CFI, Case T-317/02 *FICF and Others v Commission* [2004] E.C.R. II-4325, paras 40–42; CFI, Joined Cases T-254/00, T-270/00, and T-277/00 *Hotel Cipriani and Others v Commission* [2008] E.C.R. II-3269, para. 114; CFI, Case T-253/04 *KONGRA-GEL v Council* [2008] E.C.R. II-46*, Summ. pub., para. 79; CFI, Case T-306/05 *Scippacercola and Terezakis v Commission* [2008] E.C.R. II-4*, Summ. pub., paras 71–72; CFI, Case T-75/06 *Bayer CropScience and Others v Commission* [2008] E.C.R. II-2081, paras 68–70; CFI, Joined Cases T-227/01 to T-229/01, T-265/01, T-266/01, and T-270/01 *Territorio Histórico de Álava and Others v Commission* [2009] E.C.R. II-3029, paras 75–77; CFI, Joined Cases T-273/06 and T-297/06 *ISD Polska and Others v Commission* [2009] E.C.R. II-2181, paras 47–48 (appeal dismissed on other grounds in ECJ, Case C-369/09 P *ISD Polska and Others v Commission* [2011] E.C.R. I-2011); CFI, Case T-326/07 *Cheminova and Others v Commission* [2009] E.C.R. II-2685, paras 68–69; EGC, Case T-335/08 *BNP Paribas and Others v Commission* [2010] E.C.R. II-3323, para. 77; EGC, Case T-452/08 *DHL Aviation and Others v Commission* [2010] E.C.R. II-218*, Summ. pub., paras 26–27. For discussion of the rationale underlying this case-law, see CFI, Case T-151/05 *NVV and Others v Commission* [2009] E.C.R. II-1219, paras 45–48; EGC (judgment of 19 January 2012), Case T-71/10 *Xeda International and Pace International v Commission*, not reported, paras 60–61. See also CFI, Case T-282/06 *Sun Chemical Group and Others v Commission* [2007] E.C.R. II-2149, paras 50–53, rejecting Commission's argument to depart from this line of case-law and finding that for reasons of economy of procedure, it is not appropriate to consider the admissibility of the actions brought by the applicants concerned separately.

[524] EGC (judgment of 20 September 2012), Case T-154/10 *France v Commission*, not reported, paras 36–38 (and case-law cited).

[525] See, in general, S. Van Raepenbusch, 'L'intérêt à agir dans le contentieux communautaire', in A. De Walsche (ed.), *Mélanges en hommage à Georges Vandersanden: promenades au sein du droit européen* (Brussels, Bruylant, 2008), 381–97.

that they must benefit from the annulment of the contested act.[526] That benefit consists in the elimination of the adverse repercussions on their legal position.[527] In other words, the action must be liable, if successful, to procure an advantage to the party bringing it.[528]

---

[526] It suffices if the applicant has an interest in the annulment of the part of the act which is unfavourable to it (CFI, Case T-89/00 *Europe Chemi-Con v Council* [2002] E.C.R. II-3651, para. 35). Conversely, an applicant can be held not to have an interest only in relation to certain, not all, of the contested portions of the measure concerned: see, e.g. EGC, Case T-136/05 *EARL Salvat and Others v Commission* [2007] E.C.R. II-4063, paras 35–48. The legal sphere of an association of beneficiaries of a mutual provident association was held not to have been affected by a decision to close the file on its complaint. This was because it could derive no benefit from the annulment of the contested act (CFI, Case T-184/94 *ATM v Commission* [1997] E.C.R. II-2529, paras 62–63, upheld on appeal in ECJ (order of 5 May 1999), Case C-57/98 P *ATM v Commission*, not reported, para. 41).

[527] For example, in the context of a 'staff case', see ECJ, Case C-198/07 P *Gordon v Commission* [2008] E.C.R. I-10701, paras 41–53, in which the Court of Justice ruled that the permanent invalidity of a former official does not preclude his possible re-employment and thus he has an interest in challenging a 'career development report' (CDR), thereby setting aside the decision of the Court of First Instance in so far as it had ruled that there was no need to rule on the application for annulment brought by the applicant. Similarly, in ECJ, Joined Cases C-373/06 P, C-379/06 P, and C-382/06 P *Flaherty and Others v Commission* [2008] E.C.R. I-2649, paras 27–35, the Court of Justice found that the Court of First Instance had committed an error in holding that the applicants did not have an interest in bringing an action on the grounds that at the date of the contested decision they had not had the vessels referred to in that decision built, so that at the date of that decision they were not owners of the vessels. The Court considered, first, that the authorization procedure concerned did not require the necessary works to be carried out, or at least initiated, before the authorization in question is granted. Moreover, it underlined that anyone who, in compliance with the applicable rules, has sought an increase in capacity on the grounds of safety improvements by having a replacement vessel built clearly has an interest in seeking the annulment of a decision refusing the corresponding authorization; while the interest is more urgent for those who had already, at the time of the decision, committed expenditure to the building of a vessel, those who have not yet commenced such building nevertheless have such an interest. On that basis, the Court held that all of the applicants at first instance had an interest in bringing an action against the contested decision. See also CFI, Case T-188/99 *Euroalliages v Commission* [2001] E.C.R. II-1757, paras 26–30: an undertaking which had lodged a complaint against dumping prices of products imported into the Union was held to have an interest in the annulment of a decision by which the Commission terminated a review procedure carried out at the time when existing anti-dumping measures were to expire, without introducing new measures. This was because in the event of the annulment of that decision, the existing anti-dumping measures would have remained in force until such time as the Commission had taken a new decision completing the review procedure. Moreover, in the event of annulment, the Commission is obliged under Art. 266 TFEU to take the necessary measures to comply with the judgment. For an example in the context of the common organization of bananas, see CFI (order of 12 January 2007), Case T-447/05 *SPM v Commission* [2007] E.C.R. II-1, paras 52–60, where the Court of First Instance rejected the Commission's argument that the applicant did not have an interest in bringing proceedings inasmuch as the contested measure is not applicable to producers like the applicant, underlining that the applicant was challenging the contested measure precisely because it did not take into account the situation of producers like itself and thus deprives it of the opportunity to export its products to the EU market. As such, the annulment of an act on the grounds that it does not take account of a specific category of economic operators, which requires the institution which adopted the act to adopt the measures necessary to give effect to the judgment, can affect the applicant's legal position.

[528] See, e.g. ECJ, Case C-362/05 P *Wunenburger v Commission* [2007] E.C.R. I-4333, para. 42; ECJ, Joined Cases C-373/06, C-379/06 and C-382/06 P *Flaherty and Others* [2008] E.C.R. I-2649, para. 25; ECJ (order of 8 April 2008), Case C-503/07 P *Saint-Gobain Glass Deutschland and Others v Commission* [2008] E.C.R. I-2217, para. 48; CFI (order of 17 October 2005), Case T-28/02 *First Data and Others v Commission* [2005] E.C.R. II-4119, para. 34; CFI (order of 30 April 2007), Case T-387/04 *EnBW Energie Baden-Württemberg v Commmission* [2007] E.C.R. II-1195, para. 96; CFI, Case T-212/02 *Commune de Champagne and Others v Commission* [2007] E.C.R. II-2017, para. 39; CFI, Case T-299/05 *Shanghai Excell M&E Enterprise and Others v Council* [2009] E.C.R. II-565, para. 43; EGC, Case T-189/08 *Forum 187 v Commission* [2010] E.C.R. II-1039, para. 62; EGC, Case T-343/08 *Arkema France v Commission* [2011] E.C.R. II-2287, paras 39–49; EGC, Case T-291/04 *Enviro Tech Europe and Enviro Tech International v Commission* [2011] E.C.R. II-8281, para. 77. The Union judicature may also resort to other formulations. See, e.g. CFI (order of 5 December 2007), Case T-133/01 *Schering-Plough v Commission and EMEA*, not reported,

If an interest cannot be shown at the stage of lodging the action, the action is held inadmissible.[529]

An interest will have to be shown by the individual applicant, whether he brings an action for annulment of a *decision finding an infringement on Arts 101 or 102 TFEU*,[530] an *anti-dumping regulation*,[531] a decision relating to *public contracts*[532] or any other reviewable Union act.

As far as *State aid* is concerned, the conduct of the Member State to which the Commission decision is addressed does not have any bearing on the applicant's interest in the annulment of the Commission decision declaring the aid granted to the applicant unlawful and

---

para. 31 (and citations therein): 'In other words, the annulment of that measure must be capable, in itself, of producing legal effects which may consist in redressing any harmful consequences arising from the measure annulled, or in preventing future repetition of the alleged illegality.' In that case, the Court of First Instance found that the applicant failed to demonstrate either of those criteria. CFI, Case T-133/01 *Schering-Plough v Commission and EMEA*, paras 32–36; compare, e.g. CFI, Case T-264/06 *DC-Hadler Networks v Commission* [2008] E.C.R. II-199*, Summ. pub., paras 18–21. However, sometimes, the latter line of case-law on the interest requirement appears to blur with the challengeable act requirement: see, e.g. CFI, Case T-212/02 *Commune de Champagne and Others v Commission* [2007] E.C.R. II-2017, paras 39 *et seq.*; see also CFI, Case T-253/04 *KONGRA-GEL v Council* [2008] E.C.R. II-46*, Summ. pub., paras 82–85 (finding that the contested act produced binding legal effects capable of bringing about a distinct change in the applicants' legal position and this change in their legal position had real effects on the applicant); CFI (order of 30 April 2007), Case T-387/04 *EnBW Energie Baden-Württemberg v Commission* [2007] E.C.R. II-1195, paras 96–130 (when examining the interest requirement, the Court of First Instance emphasizes the absence of a legally binding decision).

[529] See, e.g. EGC, Joined Cases T-355/04 and T-446/04 *Co-Frutta v Commission* [2010] E.C.R. II-1, paras 40–41; EGC, Joined Cases T-494/08 to T-400/08 and T-509/08 *Ryanair v Commission* [2010] E.C.R. II-5723, paras 41–42.

[530] See CFI, Joined Cases T-213/01 and T-214/01 *Österreichische Postsparkasse and Bank für Arbeit und Wirtschaft v Commission* [2006] E.C.R. II-1601, paras 55–56; CFI, Case T-198/03 *Bank Austria Creditanstalt v Commission* [2006] E.C.R. II-1429, paras 42–46; CFI, Case T-474/04 *Pergan Hilfsstoffe v Commission* [2007] E.C.R. II-4225, paras 37–42.

[531] See, particularly, CFI, Case T-45/06 *Reliance Industries v Council and Commission* [2008] E.C.R. II-2399, paras 33–44: in an action for annulment challenging certain Notices of Initiation of the Commission, the Council argued that the applicant lost its interest in bringing annulment proceedings, since it failed to bring an action for annulment against certain regulations imposing definitive anti-dumping duties adopted by the Council after the lodging of the action. The Court rejected this argument, and held that the applicant had an interest in bringing proceedings on the grounds that the contested Notices adversely affected it, had not been formally withdrawn and their legal effects were not eradicated by the regulations adopted by the Council, and such proceedings may prevent the alleged unlawfulness of the contested Notices fom recurring in the future.

[532] See CFI (order of 19 October 2007), Case T-69/05 *Evropaiki Dynamiki v EFSA*, not reported, paras 53–64; CFI, Case T-289/06 *CESD-Communautaire v Commission* [2009] E.C.R. II-40*, Summ. pub., paras 67–72; EGC, Case T-8/09 *Dredging International and Others v EMSA* [2011] E.C.R. II-6123, paras 133–137; EGC, Case T-461/08 *Evropaiki Dynamiki v EIB* [2011] E.C.R. II-6367, paras 63–68; EGC, Case T-577/08 *Proges v Commission* [2010] E.C.R. II-46*, Summ. pub., paras 14–18; see particularly EGC, Case T-121/08 *PC-Ware Information Technologies v Commission* [2010] E.C.R. II-1541, para. 40 (applying '*Wunenburger*-like' reasoning [see n. 551] to public contract context). See also EGC (order of 2 July 2009), Case T-279/06 *Evropaiki Dynamiki v ECB* [2009] E.C.R. II-99*, Summ. pub., paras 95–100 (upheld in ECJ, Case C-401/09 P *Evropaiki Dynamiki v ECB* [2011] E.C.R. I-4911, para. 49), where as regards to applicant's eighth plea, the General Court rejected the ECB's plea of inadmissibility based on applicant's alleged lack of interest in bringing proceedings, but as regards seven remaining pleas, it found that the applicant lacked interest in bringing proceedings, observing that an applicant cannot have a legitimate interest in annulment of a decision where it is already certain that that decision which concerns it cannot be other than reconfirmed; it also observed that a plea for annulment is inadmissible on account of an applicant's lack of interest in bringing proceedings where, even if the plea is well-founded, annulment of the contested act on the basis of that plea would not give the applicant satisfaction.

requiring the Member State to recover the aid, even though the Member State has fully complied with the contested decision and does not intend to reintroduce the aid scheme in question if the decision is annulled. The rationale is that the applicant may be able to put forward certain claims before the national authorities if the contested decision is found to be unlawful.[533]

As far as *merger control* is concerned, an applicant has an interest in challenging a contested measure authorizing a concentration between its competitors, since that may affect its commercial situation.[534] The fact that the addressees have complied with the Commission decision does not affect their interest in bringing proceedings. Where the Commission declares a concentration incompatible with the internal market and orders it to be reversed, the undertakings involved in the concentration do not lose their interest in the annulment of the decision if they have complied with it and thereby brought the concentration irreversibly to an end.[535] Where a concentration has not been effectuated before the Commission takes its decision declaring it to be incompatible with the internal market, an undertaking party to the intended concentration retains an interest in the annulment of the Commission decision also where the concentration can no longer take place, even in the event that the judgment of the General Court is in the applicant's favour, as a result of the disappearance of its contractual basis. The General Court takes account in particular of the existing and future legal consequences of annulment of such a decision by virtue of Art. 266 TFEU and of the requirements of judicial review of the legality of Commission acts under the concentration regulation.[536]

---

[533] See, e.g. ECJ, Case C-519/07 P *Commission v Koninklijke FrieslandCampina* [2009] E.C.R. I-8495, paras 64–68 (upholding the Court of First Instance's decision that the applicant had an interest in bringing proceedings, since contrary to the Commission's argument, it cannot be ruled out that the Netherlands' authorities will be prompted to allow the applicant to benefit from the tax scheme in question); ECJ, Joined Cases C-71/09 P, C-73/09 P, and C-76/09 P *Comitato 'Venezia vuole vivere' v Commission* [2011] E.C.R. I-4727, paras 76–77 (rejecting the Commission's argument that the actions were inadmissible for lack of interest, since as from the time of the adoption of the contested decision, the applicant undertakings had to expect, in principle, to be obliged to repay the aid already received, thereby giving them an interest in bringing an action); see also ECJ (judgment of 21 December 2011), Case C-320/09 P *A2A v Commission*, not reported, paras 68–71; ECJ (judgment of 21 December 2011), Case C-319/09 P *ACEA v Commission*, not reported, paras 67–70; CFI, Case T-9/98 *Mitteldeutsche Erdöl-Raffinerie v Commission* [2001] E.C.R. II-3367, paras 32–38; CFI, Case T-354/99 *Kuwait Petroleum (Nederland) v Commission* [2006] E.C.R. II-1475, paras 34–35; CFI, Joined Cases T-239/04 and T-323/04 *Italy and Brandt v Commission* [2007] E.C.R. II-3265, para. 43; CFI, Case T-301/01 *Alitalia v Commission* [2008] E.C.R. II-1753, paras 38–47; CFI, Case T-291/06 *Operator ARP v Commission* [2009] E.C.R. II-2275, para. 27; CFI, Joined Cases T-265/04, T-292/04 and T-504/04 *Tirrenia di Navigazione and Others v Commission* [2009] E.C.R. II-21*, Summ. pub., paras 63–82; EGC, Case T-189/08 *Forum 187 v Commission* [2010] E.C.R. II-1039; EGC, Joined Cases T-425/04, T-444/04, T-450/04, and T-456/04 *France and Others v Commission* [2010] E.C.R. II-2099, paras 121–124; EGC, Joined Cases T-443/08 and T-455/08 *Freistaat Sachsen and Others v Commission* [2011] E.C.R. II-1311, paras 46–69 (upheld on appeal in ECJ (judgment of 19 December 2012), Case C-288/11 P *Mitteldeutsche Flughafen and Flughafen Leipzig v Commission*, not reported).

[534] See, e.g. CFI, Case T-177/04 *easyJet v Commission* [2006] E.C.R. II-1931, para. 41. In this case, the Commission attempted to argue that the applicant lacks interest in bringing proceedings in respect of specific pleas. In response, the Court of First Instance held: 'Even assuming that the concept of inadmissibility for lack of interest in bringing proceedings can apply independently to an individual plea, the third and fifth pleas in the present case constitute criticisms of various aspects of the Commission's reasoning which led it to adopt the operative part of the contested decision, which does in fact adversely affect the applicant.'

[535] CFI, Case T-22/97 *Kesko v Commission* [1999] E.C.R. II-3775, paras 55–65.

[536] CFI, Case T-102/96 *Gencor v Commission* [1999] E.C.R. II-753, paras 41–45. The same applies where the parties concerned withdraw from the merger before the Commission takes its decision, but the Commission nonetheless adopts a decision: CFI, Case T-310/00 *MCI v Commission* [2004] E.C.R. II-3253, paras 49–61.

Along the same lines, in litigation concerning *access to documents* of Union institutions, a natural or legal person who has been refused access to all or part of a document requested has an interest in the annulment of the (confirmatory) decision of refusal.[537] The General Court has held that it was irrelevant that the documents to which access had been refused were already in the public domain. A person who is refused access to a document has a sufficient interest in the annulment of the decision refusing such access.[538]

Where necessary, the Court of Justice and the General Court will consider of their own motion whether the requirement to have an interest in bringing proceedings is satisfied and whether that interest has ceased to exist in the course of the proceedings.[539] They may have regard to the effect of the law of a Member State when they consider the applicant's legal position in assessing the applicant's interest in bringing annulment proceedings.[540]

(b) No interest in challenging the act the adoption of which was sought by applicant

7.139 Where a natural or legal person receives from the Commission an act which that person sought, the person in question has no interest in applying for the annulment of that act (or of certain grounds of that act), even if the grounds of the act contain a number of unfavourable passages. Accordingly, an undertaking which has notified a concentration

---

[537] See, e.g. EGC, Joined Cases T-109/05 and T-444/05 *NLG v Commission* [2011] E.C.R. II-2479, paras 62–63 (the fact that the requested documents relate to a measure concerning State aid which has been annulled does not remove such interest).

[538] See, e.g. CFI, Case T-46/92 *Scottish Football Association v Commission* [1994] E.C.R. II-1039, paras 13–14; CFI, Case T-174/95 *Svenska Journalistenförbundet v Council* [1998] E.C.R. II-2289, paras 66–69; EGC, Case T-233/09 *Access Info Europe v Council* [2011] E.C.R. II-1073, paras 34–37. But where the defendant institution subsequently withdraws and replaces the contested measure refusing access with a measure granting access, the action may become devoid of purpose: EGC (order of 12 January 2011), Case T-411/09 *Terezakis v Commission* [2011] E.C.R. II-1, paras 14–21. See also EGC (order of 24 March 2011), Case T-36/10 *International Hilfsfonds v Commission* [2011] E.C.R. II-1403, paras 44–51 (appeal dismissed in ECJ (order of 15 February 2012), Case C-208/11 P *Internationaler Hilfsfonds v Commission*, not reported), in which the applicant's interest in challenging implicit decision of the Commission refusing access was held to have disappeared by reason of the subsequent adoption by that institution of an express decision responding to the applicant's confirmatory application against which an action for annulment had been brought; and to the same effect, EGC (order of 9 November 2011), Case T-120/10 *ClientEarth and Others v Commission*, not reported, paras 51–52. See also EGC (order of 12 April 2011), Case T-395/10 *Stichting Corporate Europe Observatory v Commission*, not reported, paras 11–14.

[539] See, e.g. ECJ, Case 108/86 *D.M. v Council* [1987] E.C.R. 3933, para. 10; CFI (order of 10 March 2005), Case T-273/00 *Unione degli industriali della provincia di Venezia v Commission*, not reported, para. 15; CFI (order of 10 March 2005), Case T-269/00 *Baglioni Hotels and Sagar v Commission*, not reported, para. 16; CFI, Case T-299/05 *Shanghai Excell M&E Enterprise and Others v Council* [2009] E.C.R. II-565, para. 42; CFI, Case T-291/06 *Operator ARP v Commission* [2009] E.C.R. II-2275, para. 26; EGC, Case T-461/08 *Evropaiki Dynamiki v EIB* [2011] E.C.R. II-6367, para. 62; EGC (order of 21 September 2011), Case T-141/05 RENV *Internationaler Hilfsfonds v Commission* [2011] E.C.R. II-6495, para. 22.

[540] See, e.g. EGC, Case T-42/06 *Gollnisch v European Parliament* [2010] E.C.R. II-1135, paras 63–66 (ruling, in relevant part on the basis of a judgment given by the *Cour de cassation*, that the applicant no longer has any legal interest in obtaining the annulment of the contested decision); ECJ, Case C-317/09 P *ArchiMEDES v Commission* [2010] E.C.R. I-150*, Summ. pub., paras 102 and 107–112 (analysing the requirement of interest in the context of annulment proceedings brought against Commission decision seeking recovery of payment on the basis of French civil law); EGC, Case T-291/04 *Enviro Tech Europe and Enviro Tech International v Commission* [2011] E.C.R. II-8281, paras 86–91 (ruling the applicants retained interest in proceedings on account of, *inter alia*, enforcement measures and sanctions adopted in respect of the applicants by the national rules intended to implement the contested measure). See also EGC, Case T-94/08 *Centre de coordination Carrefour v Commission* [2010] E.C.R. II-1015, paras 50 *et seq.* (appeal dismissed in ECJ (order of 3 March 2011), Case C-254/10 P *Centre de coordination Carrefour v Commission* [2011] E.C.R. I-19*, Summ. pub.).

has no interest in having the decision declaring it compatible with the internal market annulled, even if the decision finds that the undertaking concerned has a dominant position on a particular market.[541] Likewise, a recipient of aid generally has no interest in obtaining the annulment of a decision declaring this aid compatible with the internal market.[542]

(c) Personal interest

The interest must be personal to the applicant itself.[543] An applicant to which the contested general act is not applicable cannot claim that it has a personal interest.[544] Accordingly, an undertaking was held to have no legal interest in bringing proceedings for the annulment of a measure which did not concern the product which it manufactured.[545]   **7.140**

As far as federated Member States are concerned, the regions and other devolved authorities often have autonomous policy-making powers which are not subject to the control of the federal State. Consequently, such regions and other devolved authorities have an interest of their own, distinct from the interest of the federal or central authorities, in challenging a Union act which restricts their policy-making powers.[546]

---

[541] CFI, Joined Cases T-125/97 and T-127/97 *Coca-Cola v Commission* [2000] E.C.R. II-1733, paras 77–92. See also in this connection CFI, Case T-138/89 *NBV and NVB v Commission* [1992] E.C.R. II-2181, paras 32–34: undertakings which obtained at their request a declaration from the Commission pursuant to Art. 2 of the former Regulation No. 17 that their agreement was not in breach of Art. 81(1) EC (now Art. 101(1) TFEU) had no interest in having that declaration annulled, even though they considered that the decision contained considerations capable of damaging their interests. Since the undertakings had ended up in the legal position which they had requested of the Commission, they had no interest in having the decision annulled.

[542] CFI, Case T-141/03 *Sniace v Commission* [2005] E.C.R. II-1197, paras 20–41; EGC (order of 16 December 2011), Case T-203/10 *Stichting Woonpunt and Others v Commission* [2011] E.C.R. II-462*, Summ. pub., paras 56–64 (appeal pending in ECJ, Case C-132/12 P *Stichting Woonpunt and Others v Commission*). Compare EGC, Case T-136/05 *EARL Salvat and Others v Commission* [2007] E.C.R. II-4063, paras 35–48 (finding that although the portion of contested decision concerned related to compatible aid, this did not dispense from examining whether that part of the decision affects the applicants' interests, concluding that it did not). Notably, where the contested decision classifies aid as partly compatible and partly incompatible with the internal market, the recipient of the aid may have an interest in bringing proceedings against the contested decision, and such a situation must be distinguished from the situation in which the aid is classified as entirely compatible with the internal market: see CFI, Joined Cases T-309/04, T-317/04, T-329/04, and T-336/04 *TV2/Danmark and Others v Commission* [2008] E.C.R. II-2935, paras 69–83, particularly 71–75.

[543] See, e.g. ECJ, Case 282/85 *DEFI v Commission* [1986] E.C.R. 2469, para. 18; ECJ, Case 204/85 *Stroghili v Court of Auditors* [1987] E.C.R. 389, para. 9; CFI, Case T-256/97 *BEUC v Commission* [2000] E.C.R. II-101, para. 33; CFI (order of 30 April 2001), Case T-41/00 *British American Tobacco International v Commission* [2001] E.C.R. II-1301, para. 19 CFI, Case T-286/05 *CESD-Communautaire v Commission* [2009] E.C.R. II-39*, Summ. pub., para. 68. See also CFI, Case T-326/99 *Fern Olivieri v Commission* [2000] E.C.R. II-1985, paras 66–100, in which the Court of First Instance held that a specialist of worldwide repute in a particular illness had no locus standi to claim that a Commission decision granting a licence for the marketing of a medicinal product should be annulled on the grounds that the product was ineffective for treating that illness.

[544] ECJ, Case 88/76 *Société pour l'Exportation des Sucres v Commission* [1977] E.C.R. 709, paras 18–19.

[545] CFI, Case T-117/95 *Corman v Commission* [1997] E.C.R. II-95, paras 82–84. A Commission regulation protecting a geographical domination of origin which the applicant did not use was held not to affect its legal sphere, with the result that it had no legal interest in obtaining its annulment (CFI (order of 29 April 1999), Case T-78/98 *Unione provinciale degli agricoltori di Firenze and Others v Commission* [1999] E.C.R. II-1377, paras 30–34).

[546] CFI, Case T-214/95 *Vlaams Gewest v Commission* [1998] E.C.R. II-717, para. 30; CFI (order of 29 April 1999), Case T-78/98 *Unione provinciale degli agricoltori di Firenze and Others v Commission* [1999] E.C.R. II-1377, para. 39; CFI, Case T-288/97 *Regione Autonoma Friuli Venezia Giulia v Commission* [1999] E.C.R. II-1871, para. 34; CFI, Joined Cases T-132/96 and T-143/96 *Freistaat Sachsen and Others v Commission* [1999] E.C.R. II-3663, para. 92.

(d) Vested and present interest

7.141 The interest must be vested and present.[547] A hypothetical interest is therefore insufficient to ground an action for annulment.[548] Moreover, if the interest pleaded by the applicant concerns a future legal situation, that applicant must demonstrate that the prejudice to that situation is already certain; in other words, an applicant cannot plead future uncertain circumstances to establish his interest in seeking annulment of the contested measure.[549]

An applicant may have an interest in the annulment of *a measure which has expired*.[550] The annulment of such a measure has the effect of preventing its author from adopting a similar act in the future.[551] The applicant may also have an interest in bringing an action against a *measure which has been implemented in full*, the intention being for the defendant institution to do justice to the applicant, possibly by way of the payment of damages,[552] or for it to

---

[547] See, e.g. ECJ (order of 5 March 2009), Case C-183/08 P *Commission v Provincia di Imperia* [2009] E.C.R. I-27*, para. 26; CFI, Case T-141/03 *Sniace v Commission* [2004] E.C.R. II-1197, para. 25 (and citations therein); CFI, Case T-286/05 *CESD-Communautaire v Commission* [2009] E.C.R. II-39*, Summ. pub., para. 66; EGC, Case T-94/08 *Centre de coordination Carrefour v Commission* [2010] E.C.R. II-1015, para. 49; EGC, Case T-189/08 *Forum 187 v Commission* [2010] E.C.R. II-1039, para. 63. For example, in EGC, Case T-385/07 *FIFA v Commission* [2011] E.C.R. II-205, paras 48–49: as regards Germany's argument that at the time of the adoption of the contested decision, FIFA had already sold the broadcasting rights for the years 2006, 2010, and 2014 World Cups, the General Court held that the Commission declared the measures adopted by Belgium, as reproduced in the annex to the contested decision, to be compatible with Union law and those measures refer to the World Cup without specifying any temporal limitation, with the result that they are covered by the contested decision for as long as they remain in force. As such, the applicant's legal interest cannot be called into question by such argument. Compare CFI (order of 10 February 2000), Case T-5/99 *Andriotis v Commission and CEDEFOP* [2000] E.C.R. II-235, para. 39: the Court of First Instance held that since the applicant had already achieved the result which he was pursuing, he had no legal interest in bringing proceedings.

[548] ECJ, Case 204/85 *Stroghili v Court of Auditors* [1987] E.C.R. 389, para. 11; CFI (order of 30 April 2003), Case T-167/01 *Schmitz-Gotha Fahrzeugwerke v Commission* [2003] E.C.R. II-1873, para. 58.

[549] See, e.g. CFI, Case T-16/96 *Cityflyer Express v Commission* [1998] E.C.R. II-757, para. 30; CFI, Case T-141/03 *Sniace v Commission* [2005] E.C.R. II-1197, para. 26.

[550] See, e.g. ECJ, Case 53/85 *AKZO Chemie v Commission* [1986] E.C.R. 1965, para. 21; ECJ, Case 207/86 *APESCO v Commission* [1988] E.C.R. 2151, para.16; ECJ, Case C-362/05 P *Wunenburger v Commission* [2007] E.C.R. I-4333, para. 47; CFI, Joined Cases T-191/96 and T-106/97 *CAS Succhi di Frutta v Commission* [1999] E.C.R. II-3181, paras 62–63; CFI, T-299/05 *Shanghai Excell M&E Enterprise and Others v Council* [2009] E.C.R. II-565, paras 46, 56–57 (underlining that to accept Council's argument would be tantamount to admitting that acts adopted by institutions whose temporal effects are limited and which will expire after an action for annulment has been lodged but before the judgment would be excluded from review, which is incompatible with the spirit of Art. 263 TFEU and the fact that the Union is based on the rule of law along the lines of *Les Verts*—see para. 7.102). See also para. 7.10.

[551] See ECJ, Case C-362/05 P *Wunenburger v Commission* [2007] E.C.R. I-4333, paras 50–60: in the context of a 'staff case', where the Court of Justice upheld the Court of First Instance's decision that notwithstanding the fact that the contested measures were obsolete by the date of the delivery of that decision, the applicant retained an interest in obtaining a judgment concerning the unlawfulness of the selection procedure at issue so that the alleged unlawfulness might not recur in the future in a similar procedure to that of the instant proceedings. See also ECJ (judgment of 28 May 2013), Case C-239/12 P *Abdulrahim v Council and Commission*, not reported, para. 63; ECJ (judgment of 6 June 2013), Case C-183/12 P *Ayadi v Commission*, not reported, para. 61; CFI, Case T-299/05 *Shanghai Excell M&E Enterprise and Others v Council* [2009] E.C.R. II-565, paras 48–52; EGC, Case T-291/04 *Enviro Tech Europe and Enviro Tech International v Commission* [2011] E.C.R. II-8281, paras 86–91.

[552] ECJ, Case C-496/99 P *Commission v CAS Succhi di Frutta* [2004] E.C.R. I-3801, para. 83; ECJ (judgment of 27 June 2013), Case-149/12 P *Xeda International and Pace International v Commission*, not reported, paras 32 and 33. See also EGC (judgment of 7 March 2013), Case T-539/10 *Acino v Commission*, not reported, paras 41–46.

make the necessary amendments for the future to the legal system in the context of which the act was adopted.[553]

Furthermore, an applicant may have an interest in the annulment of *a measure which has been replaced*[554] *or repealed*.[555] The reason for this is that the repeal of a measure cannot invariably be equated with annulment by the Union judicature since, by definition, it does not amount to recognition of the decision's illegality.[556] Moreover, repeal generally takes effect *ex nunc*, whereas annulment within the meaning of Art. 264 TFEU takes effect *ex tunc*. Accordingly, the judgment annulling a measure which has been withdrawn may put the author of the act under an obligation to remove the effects of the illegal conduct found

---

[553] ECJ, Case 92/78 *Simmenthal v Commission* [1979] E.C.R. 777, para. 32; ECJ (judgment of 28 May 2013), Case C-239/12 P *Abdulrahim v Council and Commission*, not reported, para. 63; ECJ (judgment of 6 June 2013), Case C-183/12 P *Ayadi v Commission*, not reported, para. 61; CFI, Joined Cases T-480/93 and T-483/93 *Antillean Rice Mills v Commission* [1995] E.C.R. II-2305, para. 60; CFI (order of 1 February 1999), Case T-256/97 *BEUC v Commission* [1999] E.C.R. II-169, para. 18; EGC (judgment of 12 December 2012), Case T-457/07 *Evropaïki Dynamiki v EFSA*, not reported, para. 27.

[554] See CFI, Case T-420/05 *Vischim v Commission* [2009] E.C.R. II-3841, paras 58–63: despite the fact that the specification envisaged by the contested directive was replaced by the amended specification, which had to be transposed retroactively by the Member States, that retroactive effect did not extend to the date upon which the contested directive entered into force, with the result that that retroactive effect was not capable of eliminating the legal consequences produced by the contested directive and hence the applicant retained an interest in bringing proceedings. See also ECJ (order of 8 April 2008), Case C-503/07 P *Saint-Gobain Glass Deutschland and Others v Commission* [2008] E.C.R. I-2217, paras 46–52: the Court of Justice rejected the Commission's argument that the applicant no longer had an interest in bringing proceedings on account of the adoption of a subsequent Commission decision, since the latter decision does not replace the contested decision and the applicants were challenging the legality of other provisions of the contested decision unaffected by the subsequent decision. In those circumstances, the Court considered it was not in a position to hold that the applicant has no interest in bringing the present proceedings.

[555] In the case of restrictive measures against individuals, the applicant has been found to retain an interest in securing the annulment of a measure imposing restrictive measures which has been repealed and replaced: see, e.g. CFI, Case T-228/02 *PMOI v Council* [2006] E.C.R. II-4665, paras 34–35; CFI (judgment of 11 July 2007), Case T-327/03 *Al-Aqsa v Council*, not reported, paras 38–39; CFI (judgment of 3 April 2008), Case T-229/02 *PKK v Council* [2008] E.C.R. I-45*, Summ. pub., paras 49–51 (appealed on other grounds in ECJ, Case C-229/05 P *PKK and KNK v Council* [2007] E.C.R. I-439); CFI, Case T-256/07 *PMOI v Council* [2008] E.C.R. II-3019, para. 48. The same also applies where the applicant's name is removed from the list of persons whose funds had been frozen by the challenged act: see ECJ (judgment of 28 May 2013), Case C-239/12 P *Abdulrahim v Council and Commission*, not reported, paras 61–81. In the latter case, the ECJ explained that restrictive measures have substantial negative consequences and a considerable impact on the rights and freedoms of the persons covered. Apart from the freezing of funds as such which, through its broad scope, seriously disrupts both the working and the family life of the persons covered and impedes the conclusion of numerous legal acts, account must be taken of the opprobrium and suspicion that accompany the public designation of the persons covered as being associated with a terrorist organisation. The interest of an applicant in bringing proceedings is retained, despite the removal of his name from the list at issue, for the purpose of having the Union Courts recognize that he should never have been included on the list or that he should not have been included under the procedure which was adopted by the institutions. Indeed, whilst recognition of the illegality of the contested act cannot, as such, compensate for material harm or for interference with one's private life, it is nevertheless capable of rehabilitating him or constituting a form of reparation for the non-material harm which he has suffered by reason of that illegality, and of thereby establishing that he retains his interest in bringing proceedings (ECJ, Case C-239/12 P *Abdulrahim v Council and Commission*, paras 70–72). See also ECJ (judgment of 6 June 2013), Case C-183/12 P *Ayadi v Commission*, not reported, paras 68–70.

[556] If the challenged act has been declared invalid by the ECJ in the context of a reference for a preliminary ruling, the action for annulment will become devoid of purpose: see EGC (judgment of 9 April 2013), Case T-102/10 *Südzucker AG Mannheim v Commission*, not reported, paras 26–32.

in the judgment by taking adequate steps to restore the applicant to its original position or to avoid the adoption of an identical measure.[557]

(e) Interest may disappear

7.142 In order to obtain judgment on the substance, it is not enough that the applicant had an interest at the time when it brought its action. The applicant's interest must continue until a Union court's final judgment.[558] Consequently, the interest may disappear in the course of the proceedings, with the result that there is no longer any need to adjudicate on the claim for annulment, since a decision of a Union court on the merits cannot bring the applicant any benefit.[559]

For instance, an undertaking which was declared bankrupt after bringing an application for annulment against a Commission decision authorizing national aid to a competitor ceased to have any interest in bringing the proceedings, since the competitive situation no longer existed as a result of the applicant's having been declared bankrupt and that situation could

---

[557] See, e.g. CFI, Joined Cases T-481/93 and T-484/93 *Exporteurs in Levende Varkens and Others v Commission* [1995] E.C.R. II-2941, paras 46–48; CFI, Case T-211/02 *Tideland Signal v Commission* [2002] E.C.R. II-3781, paras 48–49; EGC, Case T-475/07 *Dow AgroSciences v Commission* [2011] E.C.R. II-5937, paras 68–69 (finding that the applicants retained an interest since the contested measure was repealed, and not withdrawn, by the Commission, with the result that its annulment may therefore have, itself, consequences for the legal position of the applicants). However, the withdrawal of the contested decision may take effect *ex tunc* and also have the same consequences as a declaration of nullity. In such case, the Court of Justice or the General Court, as the case may be, may decide in an order that the action for annulment is devoid of purpose and that there is no need to proceed to judgment: ECJ (order of 4 March 1997), Case C-46/96 *Germany v Commission* [1997] E.C.R. I-1189, paras 3–6; CFI (order of 18 September 1996), Case T-22/96 *Langdon v Commission* [1996] E.C.R. II-1009, paras 12–14; CFI (order of 14 March 1997), Case T-25/96 *Arbeitsgemeinschaft Deutscher Luftfahrt-Unternehmen and Hapag Lloyd v Commission* [1997] E.C.R. II-363, paras 16–20.

[558] ECJ (judgment of 21 December 2011), Case C-320/09 P *A2A v Commission*, not reported, para. 68.

[559] See, e.g. ECJ, Case C-362/05 P *Wunenburger v Commission* [2007] E.C.R. I-4333, paras 42–43; EGC, Case T-42/06 *Gollnisch v European Parliament* [2010] E.C.R. II-1135, paras 60–61; CFI (order of 17 October 2005), Case T-28/02 *First Data and Others v Commission* [2005] E.C.R. II-4119, paras 36–53; CFI, Case T-238/07 *Ristic and Others* [2009] E.C.R. II-117*, Summ. pub., paras 39–40; EGC, Joined Cases T-355/04 and T-446/04 *Co-Frutta v Commission* [2010] E.C.R. II-1, paras 43–44; EGC, Joined Cases T-494/08 to T-500/08 and T-509/08 *Ryanair v Commission* [2010] E.C.R. II-5723, paras 43–48 (holding that interest of applicant to challenge contested implied decision disappeared with the adoption of express decision by the Commission); EGC (order of 17 June 2010), Case T-359/09 *Jurašinović v Council* [2010] E.C.R. II-114*, Summ. pub., paras 36–41; EGC (order of 9 April 2013), Case T-66/10 *Zuckerfabrik Jülich v Commission*, not reported, paras 24–30; EGC (order of 8 April 2013), Case T-86/10 *British Sugar v Commission*, not reported, paras 27–33. It should be noted that it is only the action for annulment which becomes to no purpose if the applicant's interest disappears in the course of the proceedings. This does not mean, however, that an action for damages cannot subsequently be brought against the defendant institution which was late in giving satisfaction to the applicant: ECJ, Case 66/76 *CFDT v Council* [1977] E.C.R. 305, paras 9–10. See EGC (order of 28 February 2012), Case T-153/10 *Schneider España de Informatica v Commission*, not reported, paras 17–23; CFI, Joined Cases T-30/01 to T-32/01 and T-86/02 to T-88/02 *Territorio Histórico de Álava and Others v Commission* [2009] E.C.R. II-2919, paras 345 *et seq*. For some examples to elucidate the latter, see CFI (order of 31 May 2006), Case T-123/02 *Carrs Paper v Commission*, not reported, paras 4–15; CFI (order of 26 June 2008), Joined Cases T-433/03, T-434/03, T-367/04, and T-244/05 *Gibtelecom v Commission*, not reported, paras 44–48. See in this respect also ECJ, Case C-400/99 *Italy v Commission* [2005] E.C.R. I-3657, paras 15–18: an action brought by a Member against a decision to initiate the formal procedure under Art. 108(2) TFEU is not devoid of purpose, even if the Commission has already adopted a final decision declaring the aid incompatible with the internal market and the Member State concerned has not sought annulment of the final decision.

not have been affected by the aid since the applicant had been declared bankrupt before the aid was paid.[560]

If the interest for bringing an action disappears in the course of the proceedings (for example, if the defendant institution revokes the contested act in all its aspects), it is for the applicant to discontinue the proceedings. If it fails to do so, it may be ordered to pay the costs.[561]

In a judgment given on appeal, the Court of Justice held that the Commission and a party which had intervened in the proceedings before the General Court still had an 'interest' in bringing a cross-appeal against the judgment of the General Court declaring part of a Commission decision void, even though that part of the decision would no longer have been applicable if the General Court had not annulled it. That Court had annulled the provision of the Commission decision by which the addressee of the decision was prohibited from concluding exclusive purchasing agreements up until 31 December 1997. Since the Court of Justice had not adjudicated on the cross-appeal by that date, the addressee of the decision, who had appealed, claimed that there was no need to adjudicate on the cross-appeal on the grounds that it was to no purpose. The Court of Justice held, however, that the fact that the end-date for the prohibition had expired did 'not make it any less desirable to settle definitively the dispute as to the legality and scope of [the relevant provision] of the contested decision with a view to determining its legal effects in the period up to the abovementioned date'.[562] In all likelihood, the same reasoning would hold good in the case of an application for annulment of an act whose validity has expired.

(f) Balanced approach taken by the Union judicature

By and large, the Court of Justice and the General Court take a balanced approach about the requirement to establish an interest.   **7.143**

Even if the contested decision finding an infringement of Art. 101 and/or Art. 102 TFEU does not impose a fine on the applicant, it nevertheless has an interest in having its legality reviewed.[563] In the event that, owing to the fact that bringing an action for annulment does not have suspensory effect, the applicant tailors its conduct to comply with the contested measure, that will not destroy its interest.[564]

---

[560] CFI, Case T-443/93 *Casillo Grani v Commission* [1995] E.C.R. II-1375, paras 5–9; EGC (order of 25 April 2012), Case T-52/07 *Movimondo Onlus v Commission*, not reported, paras 21–29. For similar circumstances in the context of proceedings relating to merger control, see CFI, Case T-269/03 *Socratec v Commission* [2009] E.C.R. II-88*, Summ. pub., paras 40–49.

[561] ECJ, Case 243/78 *Simmenthal v Commission* [1980] E.C.R. 593, para. 9 (where the Court of Justice dismissed the application); ECJ, Case 179/80 *Roquette Frères v Commission* [1982] E.C.R. 3623, paras 8–12 (where the Court of Justice declared that there was no need to proceed to judgment). However, where the defendant institution repeals the contested measure and replaces it with a subsequent measure after the action has been brought, which leads the Union judicature to find that the applicant's interest in challenging the repealed measure has disappeared, the defendant institution may expose itself to an order requiring it to pay the costs of the applicant. See, e.g. EGC, Joined Cases T-494/08 to T-500/08, and T-509/08 *Ryanair v Commission* [2010] E.C.R. II-5723, para. 106; EGC (order of 17 February 2012), Case T-218/11 *Dagher v Council*, not reported, para. 51.

[562] ECJ, Case C-279/95 P *Langnese-Iglo v Commission* [1998] E.C.R. I-5609, para. 71.

[563] ECJ, Case 77/77 *BP v Commission* [1978] E.C.R. 1513, para. 13.

[564] ECJ, Joined Cases 172/83 and 226/83 *Hoogovens Groep v Commission* [1985] E.C.R. 2831, paras 18–19.

Neither does it have any effect on the applicant's interest that, in the event of annulment of the contested act, it will be impossible for the defendant institution to take all the measures necessary to comply with the judgment of the Court of Justice or the General Court.[565] The declaration of nullity can always constitute the basis for a damages claim.[566]

(g) Pleas solely in the interest of the law

7.144   The applicant may adduce only pleas in law against the contested act which raise breaches of the law adversely affecting it—no matter how indirectly. Pleas solely raised in the interests of the law or of the institutions are inadmissible.[567] However, this does not prevent a party from raising a plea in an application for annulment which was not raised in any administrative proceedings prior to the adoption of the contested act.[568]

IV. Special Characteristics

A. Grounds for annulment

(1) Pleas which may be raised by the applicant

7.145   Under the second paragraph of Art. 263 TFEU, an act of a Union institution, body, office, or agency may be annulled on grounds of lack of competence, infringement of an essential

---

[565] ECJ, Case 76/79 *Könecke v Commission* [1980] E.C.R. 665, paras 8–9; ECJ (judgment of 28 May 2013), Case C-239/12 P *Abdulrahim v Council and Commission*, not reported, paras 64 and 80: the interest in securing the annulment of the contested act is retained where its annulment is such as to procure an advantage for the applicant, irrespective of whether it will be unnecessary or in practice impossible for the defendant institution to adopt measures under Art. 266 TFEU to comply with the judgment annulling that act. See also ECJ (judgment of 6 June 2013), Case C-183/12 P *Ayadi v Commission*, not reported, para. 77.

[566] See, e.g. ECJ, Joined Cases C-68/94 and C-30/95 *France and Others v Commission* [1998] E.C.R. I-1375, para. 74; ECJ (judgment of 27 June 2013), Case-149/12 P *Xeda International and Pace International v Commission*, not reported, paras 32 and 33; CFI, Case T-321/01 *Internationaler Hilfsfonds v Commission* [2003] E.C.R. II-3225, paras 36–37; CFI (order of 18 March 2009), Case T-299/05 *Shanghai Excell M&E Enterprise and Others v Council* [2009] E.C.R. II-565, paras 53–55. But the possibility of demonstrating an interest in bringing an action as the basis for a possible damages claim is not watertight. For some examples, see CFI, Case T-269/03 *Socratec v Commission* [2009] E.C.R. II-88*, Summ. pub., paras 42–49 (in circumstances in which the possibility of bringing such a damages claim was found to be purely hypothetical); EGC, Case T-42/06 *Gollnisch v European Parliament* [2010] E.C.R. II-1135, paras 71–72 (holding the applicant not able to rely on this line of case-law to establish a legal interest since in the instant proceedings, the applicant claimed damages concurrently with his claim for annulment and the Court can therefore determine the existence of an unlawful act possibly committed by the European Parliament without any need to adjudicate on the claim for annulment).

[567] ECJ, Case 85/82 *Schloh v Council* [1983] E.C.R. 2105, paras 13–14. This will arise only in extremely rare cases. Thus, even where an individual raises, as applicant, a breach of the division of powers as between the institutions or as between the Union and the Member States, or a breach of any procedural requirement in the course of the adoption of the contested act, he or she will never do so exclusively in the interests of the law or of the institutions, since all the higher-ranking rules of law in that connection are intended, *inter alia*, generally to protect individuals affected by acts of the institutions. See ECJ, Case 138/79 *Roquette Frères v Council* [1980] E.C.R. 3333, para. 2; ECJ, Case 139/79 *Maizena v Council* [1980] E.C.R. 3393, para. 2. A likely example of an inadmissible plea is where the applicant argues that the contested measure is discriminatory, while admitting that the discrimination operates only in his or her favour. Something somewhat similar arose, moreover, in *Schloh*: the applicant relied on the fact that the vacancy for the post for which his candidature had been rejected (which he was contesting) had not been brought to the notice of staff of the institutions other than his own. Although that constituted a breach of the Staff Regulations, this had operated in the event only to the applicant's advantage, since there had been less competition for the post as a result.

[568] CFI, Case T-37/97 *Forges de Clabecq v Commission* [1999] E.C.R. II-859, para. 94.

procedural requirement, infringement of the Treaties or of any rule of law relating to their application, or misuse of powers. Consequently, the review exercised under this provision must be limited to the legality of the contested measure and the Court of Justice and the General Court will not consider its expediency[569] or substitute their own reasoning for that of the author of the contested act.[570]

(2) Pleas which may be raised by the Union judicature of its own motion

It appears from the case-law that the first three grounds for annulment may be subsumed under the heading of breach of higher-ranking Union law, since the rules on competence and essential procedural requirements form part of the Treaties or of general rules adopted pursuant thereto. This blurs the distinction between the different grounds for annulment. Yet the distinction is not without importance.[571] The Court of Justice and the General Court are bound to raise of their own motion[572] pleas alleging lack of competence[573] and infringement of an essential procedural requirement[574] in relation to the adoption of the act

7.146

---

[569] ECJ, Case C-84/94 *United Kingdom v Council* [1996] E.C.R. I-5755, para. 23.

[570] ECJ, Case C-164/98 P *DIR International Film and Others v Commission* [2000] E.C.R. I-447, para. 38; ECJ (judgment of 28 February 2013), Case C-246/11 P *Portugal v Commission*, not reported, paras 90–91. Where the Union courts review the legality of a complicated economic assessment made by the Commission or another institution and the institution concerned has a broad discretion, the review will be confined to whether the procedural requirements were complied with, whether the statement of reasons is sufficient, whether the facts are correctly reproduced, and whether there was a manifestly wrong assessment or a misuse of power: see, e.g. ECJ, Joined Cases 142/84 and 156/84 *British American Tobacco and Reynolds v Commission* [1987] E.C.R. 4487, para. 62; ECJ, Joined Cases C-204/00 P, C-205/00 P, C-211/00 P, C-213/00 P, C-217/00 P, and C-219/00 P *Aalborg Portland and Others v Commission* [2004] E.C.R. I-123, para. 249; ECJ, Case C-12/03 P *Commission v Tetra Laval* [2005] E.C.R. I-987, paras 102–105; CFI, Case T-231/99 *Joynson v Commission* [2002] E.C.R. II-2085, para. 36; EGC, Case T-377/07 *Evropaïki Dynamiki v Commission* [2011] E.C.R. II-442*, Summ. pub., para. 22 (and further citations therein).

[571] Opinion of Advocate-General M. Lagrange in ECJ, Case 66/63 *Netherlands v High Authority* [1964] E.C.R. 533, at 553–4. Compare Opinion of Advocate-General F.G. Jacobs in ECJ, Case C-210/98 P *Salzgitter v Commission and Germany* [2000] E.C.R. I-5843, points 125–150.

[572] ECJ, Case C-166/95 P *Commission v Daffix* [1997] E.C.R. I-983, para. 24; ECJ, Case C-367/95 P *Commission v Sytraval and Brink's France* [1998] E.C.R. I-1719, para. 67; ECJ, Case C-286/95 P *Commission v ICI* [2000] E.C.R. I-2341, para. 55; ECJ, Case C-210/98 P *Salzgitter v Commission* [2000] E.C.R. I-5843, para. 56. For further details, see K. Lenaerts, 'Rechter en partijen in de rechtspleging voor Hof en Gerecht' (2002) S.E.W. 231–7.

[573] ECJ, Case 14/59 *Société des Fonderies de Pont-à-Mousson v High Authority* [1959] E.C.R. 215, at 229; CFI, Case T-182/94 *Marx Esser and Del Amo Martinez v European Parliament* [1996] E.C.R.-SC II-1197, para. 44 (English abstract at I-A-411); CFI, Joined Cases T-12/99 and T-63/99 *UK Coal v Commission* [2001] E.C.R. II-2153, para. 199; CFI, Case T-147/00 *Laboratoires Servier v Commission* [2003] E.C.R. II-85, paras 45–46; CFI, Joined Cases T-134/03 and T-135/03 *Common Market Fertilizers v Commission* [2005] E.C.R. II-3923, para. 52; EGC, Case T-53/10 *Reisenthel v OHIM* [2011] E.C.R. II-7287, para. 27.

[574] ECJ, Case 1/54 *France v High Authority* [1954 to 1956] E.C.R. 1, at 15; ECJ, Case 6/54 *Netherlands v High Authority* [1954 to 1956] E.C.R. 103, at 112; ECJ, Case 18/57 *Nold v High Authority* [1959] E.C.R. 41, at 51–2; ECJ, Case C-291/89 *Interhotel v Commission* [1991] E.C.R. I-2257, para. 14; ECJ, Case 304/89 *Oliveira v Commission* [1991] E.C.R. I-2283, para. 18; ECJ, Case C-265/97 P *VBA v Florimex and Others* [2000] E.C.R. I-2061, para. 114; CFI, Case T-32/91 *Solvay v Commission* [1995] E.C.R. II-1825, para. 43; CFI, Case T-106/95 *FFSA and Others v Commission* [1997] E.C.R. II-229, para. 62; CFI, Case T-206/99 *Métropole Télévision v Commission* [2001] E.C.R. II-1057, para. 43; CFI, Case T-231/99 *Joynson v Commission* [2002] E.C.R. II-2085, para. 163; CFI, Case T-44/00 *Mannesmannröhren-Werke v Commission* [2004] E.C.R. II-2223, paras 126 and 210 (appeal dismissed in ECJ, Case C-411/04 P *Salzgitter Mannesmann v Commission* [2007] E.C.R. I-959) (defective statement of reasons). The General Court may inquire of its own motion into whether essential procedural requirements, especially procedural safeguards conferred by Union law, have been infringed (CFI, Case T-154/98 *Asia Motor France and Others v Commission* [2000] E.C.R. II-3453, para. 46). But see ECJ, Case C-89/08 P *Commission v Ireland and Others* [2009] E.C.R. I-11245, paras 50–62 and 70–85: this appeal concerned a judgment of the Court of First Instance

(*la légalité externe*) in the light of the facts adduced.[575] In contrast, pleas alleging infringement of the Treaties or of any rules of law relating to their application and misuse of powers, which relate to the content of the contested act (*la légalité interne*), may only be considered by the Court of Justice or the General Court if they are raised by the applicant.[576] Furthermore, it should be pointed out that a Union court can never base its decision on a plea raised of its own motion without having first invited the parties to the case to submit observations.[577]

(3) Time frame

7.147 The legality of the contested act is reviewed in the light of the facts and the state of the law at the time it was adopted.[578] The content of the act being reviewed is determined as at that time also. Addenda and improvements effected by the institution subsequently are not

---

in which that Court, notwithstanding a total of 23 pleas raised by the applicants, had considered it appropriate to raise of its own motion a plea relating to the defective statement of reasons on which the contested decision was based. On appeal, the Court of Justice held that the Court of First Instance had not gone beyond the scope of the dispute by doing so, but as the plea raised on the Court of First Instance's own motion had not been debated or even touched upon in the course of the procedure, it considered that the Court of First Instance had failed to have regard to the rule that the parties should be heard on pleas which adversely affected the interests of the Commission. The Court of Justice further ruled that the Court of First Instance had erred in deciding that the Commission had failed to fulfil the obligation to state reasons and set aside its judgment in so far as it had annulled the contested measure on such ground, thereby referring the case back to the now General Court. The General Court has considered of its own motion whether rights of the defence have been infringed during the administrative procedure (CFI, Joined Cases T-186/97, T-187/97, T-190/97 to T-192/97, T-210/97, T-211/97, T-216/97 to T-218/97, T-279/97, T-280/97, T-293/97, and T-147/99 *Kaufring and Others v Commission* [2001] E.C.R. II-1337, para. 134), but in another case it refused to do so: see CFI, Joined Cases T-67/00, T-68/00, T-71/00, and T-78/00 *JFE Engineering and Others v Commission* [2004] E.C.R. II-2501, para. 425, in which the Court of First Instance held that a breach of the rights of the defence, which by its nature is subjective, does not fall within the scope of an infringement of essential procedural requirements and therefore does not have to be raised by the Court of its own motion (appeal dismissed in ECJ, Joined Cases C-403/04 P and C-405/04 P *Sumitomo Metal Industries and Nippon Steel v Commission* [2007] E.C.R. I-729).

[575] ECJ, Case C-235/92 P *Montecatini v Commission* [1999] E.C.R. I-4539, para. 107.

[576] ECJ, Case C-367/95 P *Commission v Sytraval and Brink's France* [1998] E.C.R. I-1719, para. 67; ECJ, Case C-265/97 P *VBA v Florimex and Others* [2000] E.C.R. I-2061, para. 114; EGC, Case T-349/03 *Corsica Ferries France v Commission* [2005] E.C.R. II-2197, para. 52. It is 'sufficient for the grounds for instituting the proceedings to be expressed in terms of their substance rather than the legal classification provided[;] however, [it must be] sufficiently clear from the application which of the grounds referred to in the [Treaties] is being invoked': ECJ, Joined Cases 19/60, 21/60, 2/61 and 3/61 *Société Fives Lille Cail and Others v High Authority* [1961] E.C.R. 281, at 295.

[577] ECJ, Case C-89/08 P *Commission v Ireland and Others* [2009] E.C.R. I-11245, para. 57; ECJ (judgment of 17 December 2009), Case C-197/09 RX-II Review of Judgment T-12/08 *MvEMEA* [2009] E.C.R. I-12033, para. 57.

[578] See, e.g. ECJ, Joined Cases 9/71 and 11/71 *Compagnie d'Approvisionnement, de Transport et de Crédit and Others v Commission* [1972] E.C.R. 391, para. 39; ECJ, Case 40/72 *Schroeder* [1973] E.C.R. 125, para. 14; ECJ, Joined Cases 15/76 and 16/76 *France v Commission* [1979] E.C.R. 321, para. 7; ECJ, Case C-449/98 P *IECC v Commission* [2001] E.C.R. I-3875, para. 87; ECJ, Case C-277/00 *Germany v Commission* [2004] E.C.R. I-3925, para. 39; ECJ, Case C-485/08 P *Gualtieri v Commission* [2010] E.C.R. I-3009, paras 25–27; CFI, Joined Cases T-79/95 and T-80/95 *SNCF and British Railways v Commission* [1996] E.C.R. II-1491, para. 48; CFI, Case T-77/95 *SFEI and Others v Commission* [1997] E.C.R. II-1, para. 74; CFI, Case T-115/94 *Opel Austria v Council* [1997] E.C.R. II-39, para. 87; CFI, Joined Cases T-371/94 and T-394/94 *British Airways and Others v Commission* [1998] E.C.R. II-2405, para. 81; CFI, Case T-63/98 *Transpo Maastricht and Ooms v Commission* [2000] E.C.R. II-135, para. 55; CFI, Case T-395/94 *Atlantic Container Line and Others v Commission* [2002] E.C.R. II-875, para. 252; CFI, Joined Cases T-127/99, T-129/99, and T-148/99 *Diputación Foral de Guipúzcoa and Others v Commission* [2002] E.C.R. II-1275, para. 212; CFI, Case T-455/05 *Componenta v Commission* [2008] E.C.R. II-336*, Summ. pub., para. 60 (and further citations therein); EGC, Case T-279/04 *Éditions Odile Jacob v Commission* [2010] E.C.R. II-185*, Summ. pub., para. 338; EGC (judgment of 28 February 2012), Case T-282/08 *Grazer Wechselseitige Versicherung v Commission*, not reported, para. 49.

capable of regularizing the act and will not be taken into account.[579] Acts adopted after the adoption of the contested act cannot affect the validity of that act.[580]

(4) Grounds

(a) Lack of competence

As a ground for annulment, lack of competence on the part of the defendant institution, body, **7.148** office, or agency has several aspects, namely substantive, territorial, and personal aspects.[581]

(i) Substantive competence

Concept - The Union is empowered only to act in policy areas assigned to it by the Treaties. A **7.149** Union act which falls outside those areas may be annulled.[582] That 'external' lack of competence results, in some commentators' view, in the act's being non-existent, and consequently not within the compass of the grounds for annulment under discussion in this section.[583]

Division of powers - The next question to be considered is the division of powers in the **7.150** context of Union decision-making. An example may be found in the case-law on the seat of the European Parliament: the scope of the Parliament's powers of internal organization had to be delimited as against the powers of the national governments under then Art. 77 ECSC, Art. 289 EC (now Art. 341 TFEU) and Art.189 EAEC to determine the seats of the institutions.[584]

Where an application for annulment is based on an alleged 'lack of competence' of a Union institution, body, office, or agency which has acted, the case will generally consist of a dispute about the legal basis of the contested act.[585] If the provision of higher-ranking Union law which is stated as being the legal basis for the act is substantively insufficient to support its content, at the same time the mode of decision-making laid down in that provision (including the powers provided for therein for the institutions and bodies, offices, and agencies concerned), together with the permitted legal instruments (regulations, directives, decisions or still other—albeit unspecified— instruments), will clearly have been used unlawfully. In that sense,

---

[579] ECJ, Case 195/80 *Michel v European Parliament* [1981] E.C.R. 2861, para. 22 (it seems from para. 27 that addenda or improvements effected by the defendant institution before the period prescribed for bringing proceedings has expired may indeed regularize the act); ECJ, Case C-343/87 *Culin v Commission* [1990] E.C.R. I-225, para. 15; CFI, Case T-331/94 *IPK-München v Commission* [2001] E.C.R. II-779, para. 91; EGC, Case T-161/04 *Valero Jordana v Commission* [2011] E.C.R. II-215*, Summ. pub., para. 107.

[580] CFI, Case T-31/99 *ABB Asea Brown Boveri v Commission* [2002] E.C.R. II-1881, para. 103.

[581] There may also be temporal aspects. See, e.g. CFI, Case T-45/03 *Riva Acciaio v Commission* [2007] E.C.R. II-138*, Summ. pub., para. 96 (annulment of Commission decision on grounds taken after the expiry of the ECSC Treaty).

[582] Cf. ECJ, Case 294/83 *Les Verts v European Parliament* [1986] E.C.R. 1339, paras 51–55.

[583] See M.-C. Bergerès, *Contentieux communautaire* (3rd edn, Presses Universitaires de France, Paris, 1998), 204, at 226.

[584] ECJ, Case 230/81 *Luxembourg v European Parliament* [1983] E.C.R. 255, paras 34–59; ECJ, Case 108/83 *Luxembourg v European Parliament* [1984] E.C.R. 1945, 28–32; ECJ, Joined Cases 358/85 and 51/86 *France v European Parliament* [1988] E.C.R. 4821, 29–42. For a different example, see ECJ, Joined Cases 281/85, 283/85 to 285/85, and 287/85 *Germany and Others v Commission* [1987] E.C.R. 3203, paras 28–32; ECJ, Case C-57/95 *France v Commission* [1997] E.C.R. I-1627, para. 24. See also ECJ (judgment of 13 December 2012), Joined Cases C-237/11 and C-238/11 *France v European Parliament*, not reported, paras 36–72.

[585] See, e.g. ECJ, Case C-376/98 *Germany v European Parliament and Council* ('*Tobacco Advertising I*') [2000] E.C.R. I-8419, paras 76–116; ECJ, Case C-380/03 *Germany v European Parliament and Council* ('*Tobacco Advertising II*') [2006] E.C.R. I-11573; ECJ (order of 19 July 2012), Case C-130/10 *European Parliament v Council*, not reported, paras 79–86.

the institution, body, office, or agency which adopted the contested measure will have exceeded its powers (even if it could have adopted the same measure on the basis of some other provision of higher-ranking Union law).[586] Thus, it would seem that in such cases the ground for nullity of lack of competence fuses almost entirely with the ground of infringement of the Treaties or of any rules of law relating to their application. From the procedural viewpoint, however, it is more a question of the correct application of the rules invoked as the legal basis for adopting a given act than a question purely of competence (or lack of it).[587]

(ii) Territorial competence

7.151 A Union act may apply to natural or legal persons established in areas outside the territorial scope of the Treaties.[588] It must, however, be applied in conformity with international law.[589] As far as competition law is concerned, it is enough that agreements concluded outside the Union are implemented in the territory of the Union.[590]

(iii) Delegation of powers

7.152 *Concept* - In the Union legal order, an institution may, subject to certain conditions, delegate powers to itself or to other institutions,[591] to Member States,[592] to international organizations,[593] or to agencies governed by public or private law not mentioned in the Treaties.[594]

7.153 *Delegation and implementation in Union decision-making* - Following the reform of legal instruments by the Lisbon Treaty, the terms 'delegation' and 'implementation' are associated with certain types of acts as provided for in Arts 290–291 TFEU.[595]

On the one hand, it is sufficient for the institution charged with a legislative task to determine the 'general objectives' of the policy in compliance with the applicable mode of decision-making.[596] The execution of those general objectives may be delegated to the institution itself (using a simplified manner of decision-making), to another institution or

---

[586] In this way, the Court of Justice held in ECJ, Case C-110/02 *Commission v Council* [2004] E.C.R. I-6333, paras 28–51, that where the Commission has declared in a decision that State aid is incompatible with the internal market, the Council may no longer decide that this aid must be regarded as being compatible with the internal market under the third para. of Art. 108(2) TFEU. By adopting a decision to that effect, the Council exceeded its powers.

[587] For an analysis of the concept of legal basis and its function in Union law, see K. Lenaerts and P. Van Nuffel (R. Bray and N. Cambien (eds)), *European Union Law* (London, Sweet & Maxwell, 2011), paras 7.09 *et seq.*

[588] See Art. 355 TFEU.

[589] ECJ, Case C-286/90 *Poulsen and Diva Navigation and Others* [1992] E.C.R. I-6019, paras 21–29.

[590] ECJ, Joined Cases 89/85, 104/85, 114/85, 116/85 to 117/85, and 125/85 to 129/85 *Ahlström and Others v Commission* [1988] E.C.R. 5193, paras 11–18. As far as merger control is concerned, see CFI, Case T-102/96 *Gencor v Commission* [1999] E.C.R. II-753, paras 78–111.

[591] ECJ, Case 25/70 *Köster* [1970] E.C.R. 1161, para. 9.

[592] As a result of the principle of sincere cooperation now enshrined in Art. 4(3) TEU, it is implicit in every Union act that the Member States are under a duty to implement it, although the extent of the obligation and the detailed rules relating to it may also be expressly defined in the act itself (see ECJ, Case 5/77 *Tedeschi* [1977] E.C.R. 1555, para. 49; ECJ, Joined Cases 213/81 to 215/81 *Norddeutsches Vieh- und Fleischkontor and Others* [1982] E.C.R. 3583, para. 10).

[593] ECJ, Opinion 1/76 *Draft Agreement establishing a European laying-up fund for inland waterway vessels* [1977] E.C.R. 741, para. 5.

[594] ECJ, Case 9/56 *Meroni v High Authority* [1957 and 1958] E.C.R. 133, at 151.

[595] See generally K. Lenaerts and P. Van Nuffel (R. Bray and N. Cambien (eds)), *European Union Law* (London, Sweet & Maxwell, 2011), at paras 17.08 *et seq.*

[596] ECJ, Case 23/75 *Rey Soda* [1975] E.C.R. 1279, para. 14.

to the Member States, even if a measure of discretion is involved. The delegating institution, however, must always be able to supervise and, if necessary, correct the exercise of the discretion. In particular, as provided in Art. 290 TFEU, a legislative act may delegate to the Commission the power to adopt non-legislative acts of general application to supplement or amend certain non-essential elements of the legislative act, which are now referred to as 'delegated acts'.[597] This is subject to the explicit conditions set down in the legislative act to which the delegation is subject.[598]

Moreover, pursuant to Art. 291(2) TFEU, where uniform conditions for implementing legally binding Union acts are needed, such acts will confer implementing powers on the Commission, or in 'duly justified specific cases' (as well as in the cases provided for in Arts 24 and 26 TEU) on the Council.[599] For this purpose, the European Parliament and the Council have adopted a regulation laying down in advance the rules and general principles concerning mechanisms for control by Member States of the Commission's exercise of implementing powers (so-called 'comitology'). This is generally subject to the requirement that specific committees must be involved.[600] Yet, as with the former EC Treaty framework, in the 'implementing acts', the Commission must remain within the limits of the implementing powers conferred upon it. If it does not respect those limits, its decisions may be annulled for want of competence.[601]

Delegation to international bodies - The Union is also empowered to assign 'powers of decision' to an international body.[602] Such a delegation of powers, however, may not detract from the requirement for the objectives of the Union to be attained by common action on the part of the institutions, each one acting within the limits of the powers conferred on it. If they did otherwise, it would constitute a surrender of the independence of Union action in its external relations and a change in the internal constitution of the Union as regards both the prerogatives of the institutions and the position of the Member

7.154

---

[597] As provided in the second para. of Art. 290(1) TFEU, '[t]he objectives, content, scope and duration of the delegation of power shall be explicitly defined in the legislative acts. The essential elements of an area shall be reserved for the legislative act and accordingly shall not be the subject of a delegation of power.'

[598] See Art. 290(2) TFEU.

[599] Art. 291(2) TFEU. As regards the similar previous regime provided by the third indent of Art. 202 EC and the last indent of Art. 211 EC, see ECJ, Case C-240/90 *Germany v Commission* [1992] E.C.R. I-5383, paras 30–43. In cases in which implementing powers are conferred on the Council, the Union legislator must state in detail the grounds for its decision: see ECJ, Case 16/88 *Commission v Council* [1989] E.C.R. 3457, para. 10; ECJ, Case C-257/01 *Commission v Council* [2005] E.C.R. I-345, paras 49–61.

[600] See, e.g. ECJ, Case C-443/05 P *Common Market Fertilizers v Commission* [2007] E.C.R. I-7209, paras 111–139 (in customs context).

[601] Cf. ECJ, Case 22/88 *Vreugdenhil and Others* [1989] E.C.R. 2049, para. 20; ECJ, Joined Cases C-14/06 and C-295/06 *European Parliament and Denmark v Commission* [2008] E.C.R. I-1649, paras 50–78; ECJ (judgment of 5 September 2012), Case C-355/10, *European Parliament v Council*, not reported, paras 63–85; CFI, Case T-306/01 *Yusuf and Al Barakaat International Foundation v Council and Commission* [2005] E.C.R. II-3533, paras 172–176 (set aside on other grounds in ECJ, Joined Cases C-402/05 P and C-415/05 P *Kadi and Al Barakaat International Foundation v Council and Commission* [2008] E.C.R. I-6351); CFI, Joined Cases T-218/03 to T-240/03 *Boyle and Others v Commission* [2006] E.C.R. II-1699, paras 101–134 (appealed on other grounds in ECJ, Joined Cases C-373/06 P, C-379/03 P, and C-382/06 P *Flaherty and Others v Commission* [2008] E.C.R. I-2649, paras 46–47).

[602] ECJ, Opinion 1/76 *Draft Agreement establishing a European laying-up fund for inland waterway vessels* [1977] E.C.R. 741, para. 5.

States vis-à-vis one another.[603] Consequently, the possibility of delegating 'powers of decision' is confined to implementing powers.

7.155 *Delegation to agencies* - Finally, agencies governed by public or private law may exceptionally be set up to carry out support tasks.[604] Such agencies must help to attain the objectives underlying the substantive Union competence pursuant to which they are set up.[605] In addition, the delegation of powers to such agencies may not detract from the balance of powers as between the institutions, which constitutes a safeguard against institutions exceeding their powers.[606] Consequently, no discretionary power may be delegated. Moreover, an institution may not delegate powers broader than those which it itself derives from the Treaties.[607] In exercising their powers, such agencies are subject to the same conditions as the delegating institution (in particular, as regards the duty to state reasons and judicial supervision of their acts). They carry out mainly preparatory or strictly executive work.[608]

7.156 *Delegation to a Member of the Commission* - The Commission may—provided that it does not detract from the principle of collegiate responsibility[609]—empower one or more of its Members to take, on its behalf and under its responsibility, clearly defined management or administrative measures.[610] Measures adopted pursuant to such a delegation of authority are still ascribed to the Commission, which, as a collegiate body, has the last word.[611] Members of the Commission who voluntarily resign retain their full powers until they are replaced.[612]

7.157 *Delegation to members of staff* - Insofar as it is compatible with the intention behind the provision conferring a power on the Commission,[613] that institution may also delegate powers to its officials. In exceptional cases, a delegation of powers properly so called is involved where officials take decisions in the name of the Commission.[614] Usually, however, what is involved is a delegation of signature, which, as a matter of the internal organization of the institution, authorizes an official to notify a decision taken by the

---

[603] ECJ, Opinion 1/76 *Draft Agreement establishing a European laying-up fund for inland waterway vessels*, para. 12.

[604] ECJ, Case 9/56 *Meroni v High Authority* [1957 and 1958] E.C.R. 133.

[605] ECJ, Case 9/56 *Meroni v High Authority*, at 151.

[606] ECJ, Case 9/56 *Meroni v High Authority*, at 152.

[607] ECJ, Case 9/56 *Meroni v High Authority*, at 150.

[608] For a survey of these agencies, see K. Lenaerts and P. Van Nuffel (R. Bray and N. Cambien (eds)), *European Union Law* (London, Sweet & Maxwell, 2011), para. 13.123.

[609] See, e.g. CFI, Case T-324/05 *Estonia v Commission* [2009] E.C.R. II-3681, paras 65–68.

[610] Art. 1 of the Rules of Procedure of the Commission of 29 November 2000 ([2000] O.J. L308/26), as amended by Commission Decision of 24 February 2010 ([2010] O.J. L55/60).

[611] ECJ, Case 5/85 *AKZO Chemie v Commission* [1986] E.C.R. 2585, paras 28–40; ECJ, Joined Cases 97/87 to 99/87 *Dow Chemical Ibérica and Others v Commission* [1989] E.C.R. 3165, paras 58–59.

[612] This is also the case when all the Members of the Commission voluntarily resign. The Commission retains its full powers until the new Members take office (CFI, Case T-219/99 *British Airways v Commission* [2003] E.C.R. II-5917, paras 46–58).

[613] ECJ, Case 35/67 *Van Eick v Commission* [1968] E.C.R. 329, at 344–5. In that case, the point at issue was whether the appointing authority was entitled to delegate to an official its duty under the third para. of Art. 7 of Annex IX to the Staff Regulations to hear an official concerned by disciplinary proceedings before taking its decision in those proceedings. The Court of Justice held that the Article in question constituted a peremptory legal requirement which did not authorize any delegation of powers. See also ECJ, Case C-249/02 *Portugal v Commission* [2004] E.C.R. I-10717, paras 44–47.

[614] ECJ, Case 48/70 *Bernardi v European Parliament* [1971] E.C.R. 175, paras 30–36. This arises in all institutions as far as decisions in staff matters are concerned.

Commission;[615] sometimes both aspects arise in the same case.[616] Where a delegation of powers properly so called is involved, the limits imposed on the Commission's ability to delegate powers to its Members apply *a fortiori* (see para. 7.156).

(b) Infringement of an essential procedural requirement

(i) Concept

An essential procedural requirement is a procedural rule intended to ensure that measures are formulated with due care, compliance with which may influence the content of the measure.[617] Essential procedural requirements enable the legality of an act to be reviewed, or may express a fundamental institutional rule. **7.158**

The fact that such a rule has been breached in the preparation or adoption of a measure will constitute a ground for its annulment only if the Court of Justice or the General Court finds that in the absence of the irregularity in question the contested measure might have been substantively different,[618] that the irregularity makes judicial review impossible,[619] or that, on account of the irregularity which it contains, the act in question breaches a fundamental institutional rule.[620] If a procedural provision is infringed but this does not prevent the aims of the provision from being achieved, no 'substantial procedural defect' will be involved.[621]

An express obligation to comply with certain procedural requirements when carrying out a particular act may not be extended to other acts by way of interpretation.[622] As has already been mentioned, the Court of Justice or the General Court will raise the issue of an infringement of an essential procedural requirement of its own motion (see para. 7.146).[623]

---

[615] ECJ, Case 48/69 *ICI v Commission* [1972] E.C.R. 619, paras 11–15; ECJ, Case 8/72 *Vereeniging van Cementhandelaren v Commission* [1972] E.C.R. 977, paras 10–14; ECJ, Joined Cases 43/82 and 63/82 *VBVB and VBBB v Commission* [1984] E.C.R. 19, para. 14; ECJ, Case C-220/89 *FUNOC v Commission* [1990] E.C.R. I-3669, para. 14; CFI, Case T-450/93 *Lisrestal v Commission* [1994] E.C.R. II-1177, para. 34.

[616] ECJ, Case C-200/89 *FUNOC v Commission* [1990] E.C.R. I-3669, paras 13–14.

[617] ECJ, Case 6/54 *Netherlands v High Authority* [1954 to 1956] E.C.R. 103, at 111–12.

[618] ECJ, Joined Cases 209/78 to 215/78, and 218/78 *Van Landewyck v Commission* [1980] E.C.R. 3125, para. 47; ECJ, Case 150/84 *Bernardi v European Parliament* [1986] E.C.R. 1375, para. 28; EGC, Case T-137/09 *Nike International v OHIM* [2010] E.C.R. II-5433, para. 30. See also the Opinion of Advocate-General G. Reischl in Joined Cases 275/80 and 24/81 *Krupp v Commission* [1981] E.C.R. 2489, at 2524.

[619] This is why the duty to give a statement of reasons is strictly enforced (paras 7.170–7.174). See also ECJ, Case C-137/92 P *Commission v BASF and Others* [1994] E.C.R. I-2555, paras 75–76, in which the Court of Justice held that authentication of a Commission decision is intended to guarantee legal certainty by ensuring that the text adopted by the college of Commissioners becomes fixed in the languages in which it is binding. Thus, in the event of a dispute, it can be verified that the texts notified or published correspond precisely to the text adopted by the college and so with the intention of the author. On those grounds, the Court held that authentication was an essential procedural requirement because failure to comply therewith makes judicial review impossible.

[620] ECJ, Case 138/79 *Roquette Frères v Council* [1980] E.C.R. 3333, para. 33; ECJ, Case 139/79 *Maizena v Council* [1980] E.C.R. 3393, para. 34.

[621] ECJ, Case 282/81 *Ragusa v Commission* [1983] E.C.R. 1245, para. 22; ECJ, Case 207/81 *Ditterich v Commission* [1983] E.C.R. 1359, para. 19.

[622] ECJ, Case 21/64 *Macchiorlati Dalmas v Commission* [1965] E.C.R. 175, at 190–1; ECJ, Case 22/70 *Commission v Council* [1971] E.C.R. 263, para. 98.

[623] See, e.g. ECJ, Case 1/54 *France v High Authority* [1954 to 1956] E.C.R. 1, at 15; ECJ, Case 2/54 *Italy v High Authority* [1954 to 1956] E.C.R. 37, at 52; ECJ, Case 18/57 *Nold v High Authority* [1959] E.C.R. 41, at 51–2; ECJ, Joined Cases 73/63 to 74/63 *Handelsvereniging Rotterdam v Minister van Landbouw* [1964] E.C.R. 1, at 13–14; ECJ, Case 185/85 *Usinor v Commission* [1986] E.C.R. 2079, para. 19; ECJ, Case C-166/95 P *Commission v Daffix* [1997] E.C.R. I-983, para. 24.

The ground of infringement of an essential procedural requirement encompasses five main aspects: the requirement to consult; the requirement to hear the addressee (the right to be heard and infringement of the rights of the defence); the duty of confidentiality; compliance with internal procedural rules; and the requirement to provide a statement of reasons under Art. 296 TFEU.

(ii) Requirement to consult

7.159 *Duty to seek an opinion* - In the Union decision-making process, the institution, body, office, or agency adopting or implementing an act is sometimes under a duty (imposed by higher-ranking Union law) to seek the opinion of another institution or committee before acting.[624] The requirement to consult constitutes an essential procedural requirement.[625] This is because consultation may affect the substance of the measure adopted.[626]

Furthermore, the Court of Justice has held that the consultation of the European Parliament required by the Treaties in certain cases constitutes a fundamental rule designed to guarantee the institutional balance intended by the Treaties, which reflects the fundamental democratic principle that the peoples should take part in the exercise of power through a representative assembly.[627]

7.160 *Time frame and scope* - It is not sufficient merely to ask the Union institution or committee having to be consulted for its opinion; that institution or committee must have made its views known before the act was adopted,[628] unless a derogating provision provides otherwise[629] or the institution, body, office, or agency requesting the advice exhausted all possibilities of obtaining a preliminary opinion.[630] In addition, the draft instrument submitted to the consultative institution or committee must basically correspond to the instrument ultimately adopted, unless the amendments made to the draft are specifically intended to comply with the wishes expressed by the consultative institution or committee in its opinion.[631]

---

[624] In the case, for instance, of legislative action, the committees concerned are often the Economic and Social Committee and the Committee of the Regions; in the case of implementing action, they are the Advisory Committee on Restrictive Practices and Dominant Positions (Regulation No. 1/2003, Art. 14(1) and the committees involved in the various procedures prescribed by the Comitology Regulation.

[625] ECJ, Case 1/54 *France v High Authority* [1954 to 1956] E.C.R. 1, at 15; ECJ, Case 2/54 *Italy v High Authority* [1954 to 1956] E.C.R. 37, at 52.

[626] ECJ, Case 165/87 *Commission v Council* [1988] E.C.R. 5545, para. 20.

[627] ECJ, Case 138/79 *Roquette Frères v Council* [1980] E.C.R. 3333, para. 33; ECJ, Case 139/79 *Maizena v Council* [1980] E.C.R. 3393, para. 34; ECJ, Case 1253/79 *Battaglia v Commission* [1982] E.C.R. 297, para. 17; ECJ, Case C-417/93 *European Parliament v Council* [1995] E.C.R. I-1185, para. 9; ECJ, Case C-21/94 *European Parliament v Council* [1995] E.C.R. I-1827, para. 17.

[628] ECJ, Case 138/79 *Roquette Frères v Council*, para. 34; ECJ, Case 139/79 *Maizena v Council*, para. 35.

[629] ECJ, Case 128/86 *Spain v Commission* [1987] E.C.R. 4171, paras 22–26.

[630] ECJ, Case 138/79 *Roquette Frères v Council* [1980] E.C.R. 3333, para. 36; ECJ, Case 139/79 *Maizena v Council* [1980] E.C.R. 3393, para. 37.

[631] ECJ, Case 41/69 *ACF Chemiefarma v Commission* [1970] E.C.R. 661, paras 68–69; ECJ, Case 817/79 *Buyl v Commission* [1982] E.C.R. 245, paras 14–24; ECJ, Case 828/79 *Adam v Commission* [1982] E.C.R. 269, paras 18–25; ECJ, Case C-65/90 *European Parliament v Council* [1992] E.C.R. I-4593, paras 16–21, whereby the Court of Justice annulled a Council Regulation on the grounds that the Council had not reconsulted the European Parliament, whereas the Regulation ultimately adopted by the Council departed substantially from the text on which the Parliament had originally been consulted; ECJ, Joined Cases C-13/92 to C-16/92 *Driessen and Others* [1993] E.C.R. I-4751, para. 23; ECJ, Case C-388/92 *European Parliament v Council* [1994] E.C.R. I-2067, para. 10; ECJ, Case C-280/93 *Germany v Council* [1994] E.C.R. I-4973, para. 38.

It is sufficient, however, that the opinion be delivered before the act is adopted. The institution, body, office, or agency seeking the opinion is not obliged to allow a certain period of time to elapse between receipt of the opinion and adoption of the act in order to be able better to consider the opinion. Consequently, a measure which is adopted only a matter of days after the European Parliament delivered its opinion was held to have been validly adopted.[632]

(iii) Requirement to hear the addressee

The right to be heard - Before an act adversely affecting a person is adopted, the addressee 7.161
of the act or interested third parties must be heard by the institution, body, office, or
agency concerned.[633] That obligation is prescribed either by the Treaties[634] or by secondary
Union law[635] or arises out of the general legal principle that 'a person whose interests
are perceptibly affected by a decision taken by a public authority must be given the
opportunity to make his point of view known'.[636] This obligation is an essential procedural
requirement.[637]

The person concerned must be informed in time,[638] effectively,[639] and personally[640] of all
the information in the file which might be useful for his or her defence[641] and of the

---

[632] ECJ, Case 114/81 *Tunnel Refineries v Council* [1982] E.C.R. 3189, para. 18.

[633] ECJ, Case 17/74 *Transocean Marine Paint v Commission* [1974] E.C.R. 1063, para. 15; ECJ, Joined Cases 209/78 to 215/78, and 218/78 *Van Landewyck v Commission* [1980] E.C.R. 3125, para. 17. But see ECJ, Case C-111/92 P *European Parliament v Reynolds* [2004] E.C.R. I-5475, paras 57–60.

[634] See, e.g. Art. 108(2) TFEU. The rights of defence are also affirmed in Art. 41(2) of the Charter of Fundamental Rights of the European Union and include the right to be heard and the right to have access to the file, while respecting legitimate interests of confidentiality: see ECJ (judgment of 18 July 2013), Joined Cases C-584/10 P, C-593/10 P, and C-595/10 P *Commission and Others v Kadi*, not reported, para. 99.

[635] See, e.g. Art. 27 of Regulation No. 1/2003, Art. 6(7) of Regulation No. 1225/2009 (anti-dumping); and Art. 18 of Regulation No. 139/2004 (control of concentrations).

[636] ECJ, Case 17/74 *Transocean Marine Paint v Commission* [1974] E.C.R. 1063, para. 15. See to the same effect ECJ, Case 85/76 *Hoffmann-La Roche v Commission* [1979] E.C.R. 461, para. 9; ECJ, Case C-462/98 P *Mediocurso v Commission* [2000] E.C.R. I-7183, para. 36; CFI, Case T-50/96 *Primex Produkte Import-Export and Others v Commission* [1998] E.C.R. II-3773, para. 59. The purpose of the rule that the addressee of a decision affecting him adversely must be placed in a position to submit his observations before that decision is adopted is to enable the authority concerned effectively to take into account all relevant information. In order to ensure that the addressee is in fact protected, the object of that rule is, in particular, to enable him to correct an error or produce such information relating to his personal circumstances as will tell in favour of the decision's being adopted or not, or of its having this content or that (see, to this effect, ECJ, Case C-349/07 *Sopropé* [2008] E.C.R. I-10369, para. 49; ECJ (judgment of 21 December 2011), Case C-27/09 P *France v People's Mojahedin Organization of Iran and Others*, not yet reported, para. 65).

[637] ECJ, Case 31/69 *Commission v Italy* [1970] E.C.R. 25, para. 13 (proceedings brought pursuant to Art. 258 TFEU); CFI, Joined Cases T-186/97, T-187/97, T-190/97 to T-192/97, T-210/97, T-211/97, T-216/97 to T-218/97, T-279/97, T-280/97, T-293/97, and T-147/99 *Kaufring and Others v Commission* [2001] E.C.R. II-1337, para. 134.

[638] ECJ, Case 55/69 *Cassella v Commission* [1972] E.C.R. 887, paras 13–15 (12 days' notice of the hearing did not jeopardize the defence).

[639] ECJ, Joined Cases 56/64 and 58/64 *Consten and Grundig v Commission* [1964] E.C.R. 299, at 338; CFI, Case T-7/89 *Hercules Chemicals v Commission* [1991] E.C.R. II-1711, paras 51–54; CFI, Joined Cases T-10/12 to T-12/12 and T-15/92 *Cimenteries CBR and Others v Commission* [1992] E.C.R. II-2667, para. 38; CFI, Case T-65/89 *BPB Industries and British Gypsum v Commission* [1993] E.C.R. II-389, paras 29–30.

[640] ECJ, Case C-176/99 P *ARBED v Commission* [2003] I-10687, paras 19–25 (a decision addressed to the parent company finding that it had committed an infringement of the competition rules of the ECSC Treaty was annulled on the ground that the statement of objections was addressed only to a subsidiary).

[641] CFI, Case T-36/91 *ICI v Commission* [1995] E.C.R. II-1847, paras 69–70; CFI, Case T-37/91 *ICI v Commission* [1995] E.C.R. II-1901, paras 49–50.

grounds of the proposed act so that he or she is in a position to challenge it with full knowledge of the facts.[642]

7.162 *Infringement of the rights of the defence* - The rights of the defence are infringed where it is possible that the outcome of the administrative procedure conducted by the Commission may have been different as a result of an error committed by it.[643] An applicant undertaking establishes that there has been such an infringement where it adequately demonstrates, not that the Commission's decision would have been different in content, but rather that it would have been better able to ensure its defence had there been no error.[644]

7.163 *Application of Arts 101 and 102 TFEU* - The question whether the Commission has infringed the rights of the defence in competition proceedings through the non-disclosure of certain items in the file compiled during the administrative investigation has to be

---

[642] ECJ, Case 121/76 *Milo v Commission* [1977] E.C.R. 1971, paras 19–20; ECJ, Case 75/77 *Mollet v Commission* [1978] E.C.R. 897, paras 18–21; ECJ, Case C-32/95 P *Commission v Lisrestal and Others* [1996] E.C.R. I-5373, para. 21; ECJ, Case C-462/98 P *Mediocurso v Commission* [2000] E.C.R. I-7183, para. 36; ECJ (judgment of 22 November 2012), Case C-277/11 *M.*, not reported, para. 87; ECJ (judgment of 18 July 2013), Joined Cases C-584/10 P, C-593/10 P, and C-595/10 P *Commission and Others v Kadi*, not reported, para. 112. With respect to restrictive measures, see ECJ (judgment of 21 December 2011), Case C-27/09 P *France v People's Mojahedin Organization of Iran*, not reported, paras 61–62: in the case of an initial decision to freeze funds, the Council is not obliged to inform the person or entity concerned beforehand of the grounds on which that institution intends to rely in order to include that person or entity's name in the list referred to in Art. 2(3) of Regulation No. 2580/2001. So that its effectiveness may not be jeopardized, such a measure must be able to take advantage of a surprise effect and to apply immediately. In such a case, it is as a rule enough if the institution notifies the person or entity concerned of the grounds and affords it the right to be heard at the same time as, or immediately after, the decision is adopted. In contrast, in the case of a subsequent decision to freeze funds by which the inclusion of the name of a person or entity already appearing in the list referred to in Art. 2(3) of Regulation No. 2580/2001 is maintained, that surprise effect is no longer necessary in order to ensure that the measure is effective, with the result that the adoption of such a decision must, in principle, be preceded by notification of the incriminating evidence and by allowing the person or entity concerned an opportunity of being heard. In ECJ (judgment of 18 July 2013), Joined Cases C-584/10 P, C-593/10 P, and C-595/10 P *Commission and Others v Kadi*, not reported, paras 114 and 115, the ECJ further held that when comments are made by the individual concerned on the summary of reasons, the competent Union authority is under an obligation to examine, carefully and impartially, whether the alleged reasons are well-founded, in the light of those comments and any exculpatory evidence provided with those comments. In that context, it is for that authority to assess, having regard, *inter alia*, to the content of any such comments, whether it is necessary to seek the assistance of the Sanctions Committee and, through that committee, the Member of the United Nations which proposed the listing of the individual concerned on that committee's Consolidated List, in order to obtain, in that ambience of appropriate cooperation which, under Art. 220(1) TFEU, must prevail in relations between the Union and the organs of the United Nations in the area of combating international terrorism, the disclosure of information or evidence, confidential or not, to enable it to discharge its duty of careful and impartial examination.

[643] ECJ, Case 30/78 *Distillers Company v Commission* [1980] E.C.R. 2229, para. 26; ECJ, Case C-194/99 P *Thyssen Stahl v Commission* [2003] E.C.R. I-10821, para. 31. However, the question whether there is an infringement of the rights of the defence must be examined in relation to the specific circumstances of each particular case, *inter alia*, the nature of the act at issue, the context of its adoption, and the legal rules governing the matter in question: see ECJ, Case C-110/10 P *Solvay v Commission* [2011] E.C.R. I-10439, para. 63; ECJ (judgment of 15 November 2012), Joined Cases C-539/10 P and C-550/10 P *Al-Aqsa v Council and Netherlands v Al-Aqsa*, not reported, paras 139 and 140; ECJ (judgment of 15 November 2012), Case C-417/11 P *Council v Bamba*, not reported, para. 53; ECJ (judgment of 18 July 2013), Joined Cases C-584/10 P, C-593/10 P, and C-595/10 P *Commission and Others v Kadi*, not reported, para. 102.

[644] ECJ, Case C-51/92 P *Hercules Chemicals v Commission* [1999] E.C.R. I-4235, para. 81; ECJ, Case C-194/99 P *Thyssen Stahl v Commission* [2003] E.C.R. I-10821, para. 31; EGC, Case T-191/06, *FMC Foret v Commission* [2011] E.C.R. II-2959, para. 265. See also ECJ, Case C-109/10 P *Solvay v Commission* [2011] E.C.R. I-10329, paras 51–73, and ECJ, Case C-110/10 P *Solvay v Commission* [2011] E.C.R. I-10439, paras 46–70: loss by Commission of part of its investigation file led to the annulment of the Commission decision.

considered in the light of the specific circumstances of each particular case, since such an infringement depends chiefly on the objections raised by the Commission in order to determine the breach of competition law alleged against the undertaking concerned.[645] The Commission infringes the rights of the defence if it appears that certain documents to which the undertaking concerned had no access could have been used in its defence having regard to the alleged breach of competition law (see also para. 7.36).[646]

The infringement is not remedied by the mere fact that access was made possible during the judicial proceedings. As the examination undertaken by the General Court is limited to review of the pleas in law put forward, it has neither the object nor the effect of replacing a full investigation of the case in the context of an administrative procedure. Moreover, belated disclosure of documents in the file at the stage of the judicial proceedings does not return the undertaking which has brought the action against the Commission decision to the situation in which it would have been if it had been able to rely on those documents in presenting its written and oral observations to the Commission.[647]

Merger control - Similarly, compliance with the rights of the defence prior to the adoption **7.164** of any decision which may impact adversely on the undertakings concerned is imperative in procedures for the control of concentrations.[648] However, the rights of the defence are infringed by reason of a procedural irregularity only insofar as the irregularity has a concrete effect on the ability of the undertakings to defend themselves. Consequently, non-compliance with rules in force whose purpose is to protect the rights of the defence can vitiate the administrative procedure only if it is shown that the latter could have had a different outcome if the rules had been followed.[649]

State aid cases - As far as State aid is concerned, the formal investigation procedure is **7.165** initiated in respect of the Member State responsible, in light of its Treaty obligations, for

---

[645] With respect to the parallelism between statement of objections and the final decision, see e.g. EGC, Case T-194/06 *SNIA v Commission* [2011] E.C.R. II-3119, paras 78–92; EGC, Case T-39/06 *Transcatab v Commission* [2011] E.C.R. II-6831, paras 115–118 (and case-law cited therein).

[646] CFI, Joined Cases T-25/95, T-26/95, T-30/95, T-31/95, T-32/95, T-34/95, T-35/95, T-36/95, T-37/95, T-38/95, T-39/95, T-42/95, T-43/95, T-44/95, T-45/95, T-46/95, T-48/95, T-50/95, T-51/95, T-52/95, T-53/95, T-54/95, T-55/95, T-56/95, T-57/95, T-58/95, T-59/95, T-60/95, T-61/95, T-62/95, T-63/95, T-64/95, T-65/95, T-68/95, T-69/95, T-70/95, T-71/95, T-87/95, T-88/95, T-103/95, and T-104/95 *Cimenteries CBR and Others v Commission* [2000] E.C.R. II-491, paras 142–148, 156, 240, 241, 248, 284, 318, 323 and 364; ECJ, Case C-109/10 P, *Solvay v Commission* [2011] E.C.R. I-10329, para. 57, and ECJ, Case C-110/10 P *Solvay v Commission* [2011] E.C.R. I-10439, para. 52; for customs cases, see CFI, Case T-42/96 *Eyckeler & Malt v Commission* [1998] E.C.R. II-401, para. 80; CFI, Joined Cases T-186/97, T-187/97, T-190/97 to T-192/97, T-210/97, T-211/97, T-216/97 to T-218/97, T-279/97, T-280/97, T-293/97, and T-147/99 *Kaufring and Others v Commission* [2001] E.C.R. II-1337, paras 151 and 179. EGC, Case T-191/06, *FMC Foret v Commission* [2011] E.C.R. II-2959, paras 265. See also K. Lenaerts and J. Vanhamme, 'Procedural Rights of Private Parties in the Community Administrative Process' (1997) C. M.L. Rev. 531–69.

[647] ECJ, Case C-109/10 P, *Solvay v Commission* [2011] E.C.R. I-10329, para. 56; ECJ, Case C-110/10 P *Solvay v Commission* [2011] E.C.R. I-10439, para. 51.

[648] ECJ, Case C-413/06 P *Bertelsmann and Sony Corporation of America v Impala* [2008] E.C.R. I-4951, para. 88.

[649] CFI, Case T-210/01 *General Electric v Commission* 2005 E.C.R. II-5575, para. 632 (and case-law cited therein).

granting the aid.[650] Although all interested parties are invited to submit observations in the course of the formal investigation procedure, this procedure does not lead to an *inter partes* debate with the complainant, or even with the recipient of the aid. Indeed, the comments received in the course of the formal investigation will be submitted only to the Member State concerned.[651] Only the Member State concerned can successfully raise a plea relating to a violation of its rights of defence in an annulment procedure before the Union courts.[652]

7.166   *Anti-dumping* - Compliance with defence rights must be observed not only in the course of proceedings which may result in the imposition of penalties, but also in investigative proceedings prior to the adoption of anti-dumping regulations which may directly and individually affect the undertakings concerned and entail adverse consequences for them. Respect for the rights of the defence is indeed of crucial importance in anti-dumping investigations[653] In particular, the undertakings concerned should have been placed in a position during the administrative procedure in which they could effectively make known their views on the correctness and relevance of the facts and circumstances alleged and on the evidence presented by the Commission in support of its allegation concerning the existence of dumping and the resultant injury.[654] In addition, the parties concerned must be informed on a date which still allows them effectively to make their point of view known before the adoption of the contested regulation.[655]

---

[650] ECJ, Case 234/84 *Belgium v Commission (Meura)* [1986] E.C.R. 2263, para. 29, and CFI, Case T-158/96 *Acciaierie di Bolzano v Commission* [1999] E.C.R. II-3927, para. 81.

[651] ECJ, Case C-367/95 P *Commission v Sytraval and Brink's France* [1998] E.C.R. I-1719, para. 59; CFI, Case T-613/97 *Ufex v Commission* [2000] E.C.R. II-4055, paras 85–90; CFI, Case T-198/01 *Technische Glaswerke Ilmenau v Commission* [2004] E.C.R. II-2717, paras 193–198.

[652] ECJ, Case 234/84 *Belgium v Commission* [1986] E.C.R. 2263, para. 30; ECJ, Joined Cases C-106/09 P and C-107/09 P *Commission v Government of Gibraltar and United Kingdom* [2011] E.C.R. I-11113, para. 165 (and case-law cited therein); ECJ, Case C-139/07 P *Commission v Technische Glaswerke Ilmenau* [2010] E.C.R. I-5885, paras 57–58; EGC, T-64/08 *Nuova Terni Industrie Chimiche v Commission* [2010] E.C.R. II-125*, Summ. pub., paras 161–178. Similarly, in the initial stage of the examination of a State aid measure under Art. 108(3) TFEU, the Commission is not under an obligation to exchange views and arguments with interested parties other than the Member State concerned (see ECJ, Case C-367/95 P *Commission v Sytraval and Brink's France* [1998] E.C.R. I-1719, para. 58). Even as regards the Member State concerned, the Court of Justice is reluctant to refer to a right to be heard during the initial stage of the investigation (see ECJ, Case C-400/99 *Italy v Commission* [2005] E.C.R. I-3657, paras 29–35).

[653] ECJ (judgment of 16 February 2012), Joined Cases C-191/09 P and C-200/09 P *Council and Commission v Interpipe Niko Tube and Interpipe NTRP*, not reported, para. 77 (and case-law cited therein).

[654] ECJ, Case C-49/88 *Al-Jubail Fertilizer v Council* [1991] E.C.R. I-3187, paras 15 and 17; ECJ (judgment of 16 February 2012), Joined Cases C-191/09 P and C-200/09 P *Council and Commission v Interpipe Niko Tube and Interpipe NTRP*, not reported, para. 76; EGC, Case T-35/01 *Shanghai Teraoka Electronic v Council* [2004] E.C.R. II-3663, paras 287–290; EGC (judgment of 11 July 2013), Case T-459/07 *Hangzhou Duralamp Electronics v Council*, not reported, para. 110. Those requirements have also been set out in Art. 20 of Regulation No. 1225/2009, para. 2 of which provides that complainants, importers, and exporters and their representative associations, and representatives of the exporting country 'may request final disclosure of the essential facts and considerations on the basis of which it is intended to recommend the imposition of definitive measures'. See also CFI, Case T-249/06 *Interpipe Niko Tube and Interpipe NTRP v Council* [2009] E.C.R. II-383, para. 64; EGC, Case T-190/08 *CHEMK and KF v Council* [2011] E.C.R. II-7359, para. 224.

[655] CFI, Case T-249/06 *Interpipe Niko Tube and Interpipe NTRP v Council* [2009] E.C.R. II-383, para. 200 (the CFI found an infringement of defence rights and partially annulled the anti-dumping regulation); see also CFI, Case T-147/97 *Champion Stationery and Others v Council* [1998] E.C.R. II-4137, para. 83; CFI, Case T-35/01 *Shanghai Teraoka Electronic v Council* [2004] E.C.R. II-3663, para. 330.

However, the existence of an irregularity relating to the rights of the defence can result in annulment of the contested regulation only where there is a possibility that, due to that irregularity, the administrative procedure could have resulted in a different outcome.[656]

(iv) Duty of confidentiality

Art. 339 TFEU imposes an obligation not to disclose information of the kind covered by **7.167** the obligation of professional secrecy, in particular information about undertakings, their business relations, or their cost components.[657] The question often arises in the Commission's administrative procedure for investigating infringements of competition law[658] or for determining dumping practices.[659] It is the institution to which the purportedly confidential information is made available itself which has to judge whether or not the duty of confidentiality is applicable after giving the party concerned the opportunity to state its views. In addition, before implementing its decision, the institution must give that party the opportunity of bringing an action before the Union judicature with a view to having its assessments reviewed and to preventing disclosure.[660] Unlawful disclosure of confidential information in the course of the administrative procedure which leads to the adoption of a decision finding an infringement of Art. 101 and/or 102 TFEU will be regarded as an infringement of an essential procedural requirement only if it were shown that in the absence of such irregularity the contested decision might have been different. Consequently, it does not inevitably result in the act being declared void.[661]

(v) Compliance with internal procedural rules

Concept and scope - The institutions adopt internal procedural rules in their Rules of **7.168** Procedure[662] and thereafter are obliged to comply with them.[663] Such rules may be categorized as essential procedural requirements. For instance, in one case the Court of Justice annulled a Council directive which was adopted in breach of Art. 6 of its Rules of Procedure.[664] The directive was adopted by the so-called written procedure, even though

---

[656] ECJ, Case C-141/08 P *Foshan Shunde Yongjian Housewares & Hardware* v *Council* [2009] E.C.R. I-9147, para. 107; ECJ (judgment of 16 February 2012), Joined Cases C-191/09 P and C-200/09 P *Council and Commission v Interpipe Niko Tube and Interpipe NTRP*, not reported, para. 79; EGC (judgment of 11 July 2013), Case T-459/07 *Hangzhou Duralamp Electronics v Council*, not reported, para. 111.

[657] There are specific applications of this duty of confidentiality in regulations and directives: see, e.g. Art. 8(2) of Council Regulation No. 288/82 on common rules for imports ([1982] O.J. L35/1).

[658] See Art. 20(2) of Regulation No. 17 in connection with the specific duty of confidentiality in competition cases, replaced by Arts 27 and 28 of Council Regulation (EC) No. 1/2003 of 16 December 2002 on the implementation of the rules on competition laid down in Arts 81 and 82 (now Arts 101 and 102 TFEU) of the Treaty ([2003] O.J. L1/1).

[659] See Art. 19 of Regulation No. 1225/2009 in relation to the duty of confidentiality in the investigation procedure for determining dumping practices; ECJ, Case C-36/92 P *SEP v Commission* [1994] E.C.R. I-1911, paras 36–38.

[660] ECJ, Case 53/85 *AKZO Chemie v Commission* [1986] E.C.R. 1965, para. 29. See also paras 7.37 and 7.38.

[661] Cf. ECJ, Joined Cases 209/78 to 215/78 and 218/78 *Van Landewyck v Commission* [1980] E.C.R. 3125, para. 47. Naturally, this does not preclude the person who has been disadvantaged by disclosure from bringing an action for damages against the institution responsible: ECJ, Case 145/83 *Adams v Commission* [1985] E.C.R. 3539, paras 34–44.

[662] See Art. 232 TFEU (European Parliament), Art. 240(3) TFEU (Council), and Art. 249(1) TFEU (Commission).

[663] Sometimes internal procedural rules are adopted in a different connection, e.g. in regard to staff matters, see ECJ, Case 282/81 *Ragusa v Commission* [1983] E.C.R. 1245, para. 18.

[664] [1979] O.J. L268/1, now replaced by Council Decision 2009/937/EU of 1 December 2009 adopting the Council's Rules of Procedure ([2009] O.J. L325/35).

two Member States had expressed objections to its use. Art. 6 provides that recourse to a written vote on an urgent matter may be had only if all members of the Council agree.[665]

7.169 *Protection for individuals* - Natural or legal persons may plead infringement of internal procedural rules which guarantee legal certainty.[666] This qualifies the view that internal procedural rules are intended to guarantee the sound functioning of internal decision-making while respecting the prerogatives of each of the Members of the Union institution, and that they are therefore not intended to ensure protection for individuals.[667]

(vi) Requirement to provide a statement of reasons

7.170 *Concept and scope* - The statement of reasons required by Art. 296 TFEU[668] must disclose in a clear and unequivocal fashion the reasoning followed by the Union institution, body, office, or agency which adopted the measure in question in such a way as to make the persons concerned aware of the reasons for the measure and thus enable them to defend their rights and the Union judicature to exercise its supervisory jurisdiction.[669]

---

[665] ECJ, Case 68/86 *United Kingdom v Council* [1988] E.C.R. 855, paras 40–49. For a case in which the Rules of Procedure of the Economic and Social Committee were invoked, but no infringement was found, see ECJ, Case 307/85 *Gavanas v ESC and Council* [1987] E.C.R. 2435. For a case in which a Commission decision was annulled because a prior opinion was adopted in breach of the Rules of Procedure of the Standing Committee on Construction which assists the Commission in implementing a regulation in that a draft document was not sent to two addressees within the time limit laid down and the vote was not postponed despite the request made to that effect by a Member State, see ECJ, Case C-263/95 *Germany v Commission* [1998] E.C.R. I-441, para. 32. The Court of Justice declared void a Commission decision which was adopted without being authenticated as provided for in its Rules of Procedure (instruments adopted by the Commission in the course of a meeting have to be attached, in the authentic language or languages, in such a way that they cannot be separated, to the minutes of the meeting at which they were adopted and are to be authenticated by the signatures of the President and the Secretary-General on the first page of the minutes): ECJ, Case C-107/99 *Italy v Commission* [2002] E.C.R. I-1091, paras 47–48.

[666] ECJ, Case C-137/92 P *BASF and Others v Commission* [1994] E.C.R. I-2555, paras 72–78, in which the Court of Justice annulled a Commission decision on the grounds that it infringed Art. 12 of the Commission's Rules of Procedure (failure to authenticate a decision in the way provided for by said provision); cf. CFI, Case T-32/91 *Solvay v Commission* [1995] E.C.R. II-1825, paras 46–54; see also ECJ, Case C-280/93 *Germany v Council* [1994] E.C.R. I-4973, para. 36, from which it appears that in adopting acts which directly affect individuals, the procedural requirements applicable to such acts must be strictly complied with.

[667] ECJ, Case C-69/89 *Nakajima v Council* [1991] E.C.R. I-2069, paras 48–51.

[668] The second para. of Art. 296 TFEU provides: 'Legal acts shall state the reasons on which they are based and shall refer to any proposals, initiatives, recommendations, requests or opinions required by the Treaties.'

[669] See, e.g. ECJ, Case C-350/88 *Delacre and Others v Commission* [1990] E.C.R. I-395, para. 15; ECJ, Case C-370/07 *Commission v Council* [2009] E.C.R. I-8917, para. 37; CFI, Case T-93/02 *Confédération nationale du Crédit mutuel v Commission* [2005] E.C.R. II-143, para. 68 (see also the case-law cited in those judgments). Cf. ECJ, Case 18/57 *Nold v High Authority* [1959] E.C.R. 41, at 51–2; ECJ, Case 24/62 *Germany v Commission* [1963] E.C.R. 63, at 68–9; ECJ, Case 294/81 *Control Data v Commission* [1983] E.C.R. 911, para. 14; EGC, Case T-217/06 *Arkema France and Others v Commission* [2011] E.C.R. II-2593, para. 133; EGC, Case T-308/07 *Tegebauer v European Parliament* [2011] E.C.R. II-279*, Summ. pub., paras 22–30 (action for annulment of European Parliament decision rejecting an individual's petition pursuant to Art. 227 TFEU upheld for infringement of the requirement to provide a statement of reasons). With respect to *access to documents*, see, e.g. CFI, Case T-42/05 *Williams v Commission* [2008] E.C.R. II-156*, Summ. pub., para. 94; EGC, Case T-436/09 *Dufour v ECB* [2011] E.C.R. II-7727, para. 47; with respect to *public contracts*, the contested measure was annulled on account of the infringement to state reasons in e.g. CFI, Case T-465/04 *Evropaïki Dynamiki v Commission* [2008] E.C.R. II-154*, Summ. pub., para. 80; EGC, Case T-272/06 *Evropaïki Dynamiki v Court of Justice* [2008] E.C.R. II-169*, Summ. pub., paras 44–45; EGC, Case T-300/07 *Evropaïki Dynamiki v Commission* [2010] E.C.R. II-4521, paras 44–75; EGC, Case T-461/08 *Evropaïki Dynamiki v EIB* [2011] E.C.R. II-6367, paras 105–116; EGC, Case T-57/09 *Alfastar Benelux v Council* [2011] E.C.R. II-368*, Summ. pub., paras 21–43; with respect to *restrictive measures*, see ECJ (judgment of 18 July 2013), Joined Cases C-584/10 P, C-593/10 P, and C-595/10 P *Commission and Others v Kadi*, not reported, para. 116, in which the ECJ held that the obligation to state reasons laid down in Art.

The reasoning must be logically compatible with the content of the measure.[670] A minimal, merely formal statement of reasons is not enough because it does not effectively enable interested parties[671] and the Union judicature to verify the legality of the act.[672] However, the Union institution, body, office, or agency is not under a duty to go into all the arguments raised by interested parties during the administrative procedure which led to the adoption of the act.[673] It is sufficient if it sets out the facts and legal considerations having decisive importance in the context of the decision so as to enable its reasoning to be clearly understood.[674] It is therefore unnecessary to have a specific statement of reasons for each technical choice made.[675]

In principle, the various relevant factual and legal aspects should be set out in the statement of reasons. There is a consistent line of cases, however, to the effect that this is not always necessary on the grounds that, in considering whether the statement of reasons of an act

---

296 TFEU entails in all circumstances, not least when the reasons stated for the Union measure represent reasons stated by an international body, that this statement of reasons identifies the individual, specific, and concrete reasons why the competent authorities consider that the individual concerned must be subject to restrictive measures. See alo ECJ (judgment of 15 November 2012), Joined Cases C-539/10 P and C-550/10 P *Al-Aqsa v Council* and *Netherlands v Al-Aqsa*, not reported, paras 140 and 142; ECJ (judgment of 15 November 2012), Case C-417/11 P *Council v Bamba*, not reported, paras 49 to 53; EGC, Case T-316/11 *Kadio Morokro v Council* [2011] E.C.R. II-293*, Summ. pub., paras 20–23; with respect to *decisions on the basis of Art. 114(4) and (5) TFEU*, see ECJ, Case C-405/07 P *Netherlands v Commission* [2008] E.C.R. I-8301, paras 51–72, where the observance of procedural guarantees is even more important, since the right to be heard does not apply in the procedure under those provisions.

[670] ECJ, Case 2/56 *Geitling v High Authority* [1957] E.C.R. 3, at 16. With respect to the balancing between the obligation to state reasons and the obligation not to disclose information covered by professional secrecy (Art. 339 TFEU) see EGC (judgment of 11 September 2012), Case T-565/08 *Corsica Ferries France v Commission*, not reported, para. 43.

[671] Interested parties comprise not only the addressee of an act, but also persons to whom the act is of direct and individual concern. The latters' interest in obtaining an explanation of the act should therefore be taken into account in determining the extent of the obligation to provide a statement of reasons: ECJ, Case 41/83 *Italy v Commission* [1985] E.C.R. 873, para. 46; ECJ, Case C-367/95 P *Commission v Sytraval and Brink's France* [1998] E.C.R. I-1719, para. 63; CFI, Case T-16/91 RV *Rendo and Others v Commission* [1996] E.C.R. II-1827, para. 43; CFI, Case T-93/02 *Confédération nationale du Crédit mutuel v Commission* [2005] E.C.R. II-143, para. 68.

[672] ECJ, Case C-269/90 *Technische Universität München* [1991] E.C.R. I-5469, paras 26–27; cf., however, the case of a decision ordering the repayment of unlawfully paid State aid: ECJ, Case C-75/97 *Belgium v Commission* [1999] E.C.R. I-3671, para. 83.

[673] ECJ, Case 55/69 *Cassella v Commission* [1972] E.C.R. 887, para. 22; ECJ, Case 56/69 *Hoechst v Commission* [1972] E.C.R. 927, para. 22; ECJ, Joined Cases 209/78 to 215/78 and 218/78 *Van Landewyck v Commission* [1980] E.C.R. 3125, para. 66; ECJ, Joined Cases 43/82 and 63/82 *VBVB and VBBB v Commission* [1984] E.C.R. 19, para. 19; ECJ, Case 42/84 *Remia v Commission* [1985] E.C.R. 2545, para. 26; ECJ, Joined Cases 240/82 to 242/82, 261/82, 262/82, 268/82 and 269/82 *Stichting Sigarettenindustrie v Commission* [1985] E.C.R. 3831, para. 88; ECJ, Case C-41/93 *France v Commission* [1994] E.C.R. I-1829, para. 36; CFI, Case T-8/89 *DSM v Commission* [1991] E.C.R. II-1833, para. 257; CFI, Case T-9/89 *Hüls v Commission* [1992] E.C.R. II-499, para. 332.

[674] CFI, Case T-44/90 *La Cinq v Commission* [1992] E.C.R. II-1, paras 40–44; CFI, Case T-7/92 *Asia Motor France and Others v Commission* [1993] E.C.R. II-669, para. 31; CFI, Joined Cases T-374/94, T-375/94, T-384/94, and T-388/94 *European Night Services and Others v Commission* [1998] E.C.R. II-3141, para. 95; EGC, Case T-335/08 *BNP Paribas and Others v Commission* [2010] E.C.R. II-3323, para. 94; EGC, Case T-239/09 *Sniace v Commission* [2011] E.C.R. II-430*, Summ. pub., paras 37–38.

[675] ECJ, Case C-168/98 *Luxembourg v European Parliament and Council* [2000] E.C.R. I-9131, para. 62; ECJ, Case C-100/99 *Italy v Council and Commission* [2001] E.C.R. I-5217, paras 63–64; ECJ, Joined Cases C-27/00 and C-122/00 *Omega Air* [2002] E.C.R. I-2569, para. 47; ECJ, Case C-340/98 *Italy v Council* [2002] E.C.R. I-2663, para. 59.

satisfies the requirements of Art. 296 TFEU, regard must be had not only to its wording but also to its context and to all the legal rules governing the matter in question.[676]

The nature of the contested measure is one aspect of its context which goes to determine the extent of the obligation to provide a statement of reasons.[677] In the case of an act of general application it is enough for the circumstances which led to its adoption, together with its general objectives, to be mentioned.[678] If the need for the act is obvious from its content, additional reasoning is unnecessary.[679]

The degree of precision of the statement of reasons of a measure of individual application depends on the practical realities and the time and technical facilities available for drawing it up.[680] Furthermore, a measure of individual application which fits into a well-established line of decisions may be reasoned in a summary manner, for instance, by reference to the practice in question. If, in contrast, the measure deviates from previous practice, for example, by going appreciably further than previous decisions, the Union authority which adopted the measure must expressly explain why this is so.[681]

Finally, the degree to which the addressee was involved in the process by which an act was drawn up has a bearing on the extent of the duty to provide a statement of reasons.[682] In

---

[676] ECJ, Case C-350/88 *Delacre and Others v Commission* [1990] E.C.R. I-395, para. 16 (and the case-law cited in that judgment); see also ECJ, Case 25/68 *Schertzer v European Parliament* [1977] E.C.R. 1729, para. 39; ECJ, Case 35/80 *Denkavit v Produktschap voor Zuivel* [1981] E.C.R. 45, para. 33; ECJ, Case C-120/99 *Italy v Council* [2001] E.C.R. I-7997, paras 28–29; ECJ, Case C-310/99 *Italy v Commission* [2002] E.C.R. I-2289, para. 48; EGC, Case T-335/08 *BNP Paribas and Others v Commission* [2010] E.C.R. II-3323, para. 93; ECJ, Case C-521/09 P *Elf Aquitaine v Commission* [2011] E.C.R. I-8947, para. 150; ECJ (judgment of 15 November 2012), Case C-417/11 P *Council v Nadiany Bamba*, not reported, para. 53; EGC, Case T-187/10 *Emram v OHIM* [2011] E.C.R. II-128*, Summ. pub., para. 26.

[677] CFI, Case T-26/90 *Finsider v Commission* [1992] E.C.R. II-1789, para. 70. In the case of a decision reducing EU financial aid for a project not carried out as specified, the statement of the reasons for such a measure must include an indication of the reasons for which the alterations taken into account have been judged to be unacceptable (CFI, Case T-241/00 *Le Canne v Commission* [2002] E.C.R. II-1251, para. 55; CFI, Case T-180/00 *Astipesca v Commission* [2002] E.C.R. I-3985, para. 126).

[678] ECJ, Case 5/67 *Beus* [1968] E.C.R. 83, at 95; ECJ, Case 244/81 *Klöckner-Werke v Commission* [1983] E.C.R. 1451, para. 33.

[679] ECJ, Case 57/72 *Westzucker* [1973] E.C.R. 321, para. 19.

[680] Settled case-law ever since ECJ, Case 16/65 *Schwarze* [1965] E.C.R. 877, at 888. For examples of the influence of 'practical realities' on the obligation to provide a statement of reasons, see ECJ, Case 89/79 *Bonu v Council* [1980] E.C.R. 553, para. 6; ECJ, Case 64/82 *Tradax v Commission* [1984] E.C.R. 1359, para. 21.

[681] ECJ, Case 73/74 *Papiers peints v Commission* [1975] E.C.R. 1491, para. 31. A substantial change as compared with a previously adopted position of the institution concerned must be justified in the statement of reasons of the new decision containing the change (CFI, Case T-206/99 *Métropole télévision v Commission* [2001] E.C.R. II-1057, para. 53). The same stricter requirement to state reasons applies where an act derogates from a more general rule (ECJ, Case C-120/99 *Italy v Council* [2001] E.C.R. I-7997, para. 53).

[682] ECJ, Case 13/72 *Netherlands v Commission* [1973] E.C.R. 27, paras 11–13; ECJ, Case 819/79 *Germany v Commission* [1981] E.C.R. 21, paras 15–21; ECJ, Case 347/85 *United Kingdom v Commission* [1988] E.C.R. 1749, para. 60; ECJ, Case 14/88 *Italy v Commission* [1989] E.C.R. 3677, para. 11. For decisions clearing EAGGF accounts, see ECJ, Case C-278/99 *Netherlands v Commission* [2001] E.C.R. I-1501, para. 19. In staff cases, previous memoranda and staff notices influence the duty to provide a statement of reasons in the same way: ECJ, Case 61/76 *Geist v Commission* [1977] E.C.R. 1419, paras 21–26; ECJ, Case 86/77 *Ditterich v Commission* [1978] E.C.R. 1855, paras 34–42; ECJ, Joined Cases 36/81, 37/81 and 218/81 *Seton v Commission* [1983] E.C.R. 1789, paras 47–49; CFI, Case T-80/92 *Turner v Commission* [1993] E.C.R. II-1465, paras 62–63. The fact that an official was involved in the reorganization of his department may justify a decision adversely affecting him or her having a summary statement of reasons: ECJ, Case 125/80 *Arning v Commission* [1981] E.C.R. 2539, para. 14.

addition, persons concerned by a measure may be expected to make a certain effort to interpret the reasons if the meaning of the text is not immediately clear. The duty to give a statement of reasons is not infringed if it is possible to resolve ambiguities in the statement of reasons by means of such interpretation.[683]

Material inaccuracy - A shortcoming in the material accuracy of the statement of reasons, such as a factual inaccuracy or a wrong legal categorization, is considered an infringement of the Treaties or of a rule relating to its application.[684]   **7.171**

Failure to specify legal basis of contested act - The obligation to indicate the legal basis for a measure is related to the requirement under Art. 296 TFEU to state reasons.[685] The failure to refer to a precise provision of the Treaties need not necessarily constitute an infringement of an essential procedural requirement if the legal basis for a measure may be determined from other parts of the measure; however, such an explicit reference is indispensable where, in its absence, the parties concerned and the Union courts are left uncertain as to the precise legal basis.[686] Accordingly, for example, the Court of Justice has held that where the legal basis cannot clearly be deduced and the fact that no legal basis is indicated can be explained by disagreement within the institution concerned, the failure to indicate any legal basis in the contested measure cannot be regarded as a purely formal defect, and consequently the contested measure must be annulled for this reason.[687]   **7.172**

Time frame - A sufficient statement of reasons should be notified at the same time as the person concerned has notice of the act.[688] The absence of such a statement of reasons cannot be regularized after proceedings have been brought.[689]   **7.173**

---

[683] CFI, Case T-16/91 RV *Rendo and Others v Commission* [1996] E.C.R. II-1827, para. 46. Cf. CFI, Case T-331/94 *IPK-München v Commission* [2001] E.C.R. II-779, para. 90.

[684] ECJ, Case 8/65 *Acciaierie e Ferriere Pugliesi v High Authority* [1966] E.C.R. 1, at 7–8; CFI, Case T-17/93 *Matra Hachette v Commission* [1994] E.C.R. II-595, para. 57; cf. ECJ, Case 119/86 *Spain v Council and Commission* [1987] E.C.R. 4121, para. 51. It is not always easy to draw a clear distinction in this connection, as can be seen from ECJ, Case C-360/92 *Publishers Association v Commission* [1995] E.C.R. I-23, paras 39–48; ECJ, Joined Cases C-329/93, C-62/95, and C-63/95 *Germany and Others v Commission* [1996] E.C.R. I-5151, paras 23–58; ECJ, Case C-367/95 P, *Commission v Sytraval and Brink's France* [1998] E.C.R. I-1719, paras 65–78; ECJ, Case C-172/01 P *International Power and Others v Commission* [2003] I-11421, paras 134–139.

[685] This should be distinguished from the ground of lack of competence involving disputes about the legal basis for a contested measure: see para. 7.150.

[686] See, e.g. ECJ, Case C-370/07 *Commission v Council* [2009] E.C.R. I-8917, paras 37–38 and 56 (and citations therein). See also ECJ, Case 45/86 *Commission v Council* [1987] E.C.R. 1493, para. 9; ECJ, Case 203/86 *Spain v Council* [1988] E.C.R. 4563, para. 37. Failure to indicate the legal basis also infringes the principle of legal certainty (ECJ, Case C-325/91 *France v Commission* [1993] E.C.R. I-3283, para. 30).

[687] ECJ, Case C-370/07 *Commission v Council*, paras 60–62.

[688] ECJ, Case 195/80 *Michel v European Parliament* [1981] E.C.R. 2861, para. 22; ECJ, Case C-353/01 P *Mattila v Council and Commission* [2004] I-1073, para. 32. The person concerned must be able to ascertain the reasons upon which the decision taken in relation to him is based. At the very least these reasons should be communicated as swiftly as possible after the adoption of the decision, in order to enable that person to exercise, within the periods prescribed, his right to bring an action. See, to this effect, ECJ, Case 222/86 *Heylens and Others* [1987] E.C.R. 4097, para. 15; ECJ, Joined Cases C-402/05 P and C-415/05 P *Kadi and Al Barakaat International Foundation v Council and Commission* [2008] E.C.R. I-6351, para. 337; ECJ (judgment of 4 June 2013), Case C-300/11 *ZZ*, not reported, para. 53; ECJ (judgment of 18 July 2013), Joined Cases C-584/10 P, C-593/10 P, and C-595/10 P *Commission and Others v Kadi*, not reported, para. 100; EGC (judgment of 25 April 2012), Case T-509/10 *Manufacturing Support & Procurement Kala Naft v Council*, not reported, paras 92–93.

[689] ECJ, Case C-343/87 *Culin v Commission* [1990] E.C.R. I-225, para. 15 (staff case); ECJ, Case C-353/01 P *Mattila v Council and Commission* [2004] I-1073, para. 32 (access to documents); CFI, Case T-52/90 *Volger v*

7.174 *Plea raised by the Union judicature of its own motion* - The Union judicature must raise of its own motion[690] the question as to whether the requirement for a statement of reasons has been fulfilled (see para. 7.146).[691]

(vii) Publication and notification of the contested act

7.175 Irregularities in the publication or notification of the contested act are not regarded as infringements of an essential procedural requirement because they do not affect the act itself.[692] Such irregularities may at most prevent time from beginning to run for the purposes of bringing proceedings as provided in the sixth paragraph of Art. 263 TFEU.[693]

(c) Infringement of the Treaties or of any rule of law relating to their application

7.176 This ground for annulment encompasses any infringement of any provision of higher-ranking Union law.[694]

(i) Treaties

7.177 The reference to 'Treaties' in the second paragraph of Art. 263 TFEU denotes the TEU and the TFEU,[695] the Protocols annexed thereto,[696] the Charter of Fundamental Rights of the

---

European Parliament [1992] E.C.R. II-121, paras 40–42, upheld by ECJ, Case C-115/92 P *European Parliament v Volger* [1993] E.C.R. I-6549, para. 23; CFI, Case T-93/02 *Confédération nationale du Crédit mutuel v Commission* [2005] E.C.R. II-143, paras 123–126 (State aid); ECJ (judgment of 19 July 2012), Joined Cases C-628/10 P and C-14/11 P *Alliance One and Others v Commission*, not reported, paras 73–74; ECJ (judgment of 13 June 2013), Case C-511/11 P *Versalis v Commission*, not reported, para. 141. At most, in staff cases the Court allows a concise statement of reasons to be completed in the course of the proceedings: ECJ, Case 111/83 *Picciolo v European Parliament* [1984] E.C.R. 2323, para. 22; ECJ, Joined Cases 64/86, 71/86 to 73/86 and 78/86 *Sergio v Commission* [1988] E.C.R. 1399, para. 52; CFI, Case T-37/89 *Hanning v European Parliament* [1990] E.C.R. II-463, para. 42; CFI, Joined Cases T-160 and T-161/89 *Kalavros v Court of Justice* [1990] E.C.R. II-871, para. 72; CFI, Case T-1/90 *Pérez-Mínguez Casariego v Commission* [1991] E.C.R. II-143, para. 87; CFI, Case T-156/89 *Valverde Mordt v Court of Justice* [1991] E.C.R. II-407, paras 130–133; CFI, Case T-25/92 *Vela Palacios v ESC* [1993] E.C.R. II-201, para. 26; ECJ, Case C-150/03 *Hectors v European Parliament* [2004] E.C.R. I-8691, para. 50.

[690] ECJ, Case C-166/95 P *Commission v Daffix* [1997] E.C.R. I-983, para. 24; ECJ, Case C-367/95 P, *Commission v Sytraval and Brink's France* [1998] E.C.R. I-1719, para. 67; ECJ (judgment of 8 December 2011), Case C-272/09 P *KME Germany and Others v Commission*, not reported, para. 101; ECJ (judgment of 8 December 2011), Case C-389/10 P *KME Germany and Others v Commission*, not reported, para. 128; ECJ (judgment of 6 November 2012), Case C-199/11 *Otis*, not reported, para. 60.

[691] ECJ, Case 18/57 *Nold v High Authority* [1959] E.C.R. 41, at 52; ECJ, Case 185/85 *Usinor v Commission* [1986] E.C.R. 2079, para. 19; CFI, Case T-37/89 *Hanning v European Parliament* [1990] E.C.R. II-463, para. 38; CFI, Case T-115/89 *González Holguera v European Parliament* [1990] E.C.R. II-831, para. 37; CFI, Case T-61/89 *Dansk Pelsdyravlerforening v Commission* [1992] E.C.R. II-1931, para. 129; CFI, Case T-534/93 *Grynberg v Commission* [1994] E.C.R.-SC II-595, para. 59 (English abstract at [1994] E.C.R.-SC I-A-179); CFI, Case T-106/95 *FFSA and Others v Commission* [1997] E.C.R. II-229, para. 62; CFI, Case T-4/96 *S. v Court of Justice* [1997] E.C.R. II-1125, para. 53; CFI, Case T-44/00 *Mannesmannröhren-Werke v Commission* [2004] E.C.R. II-2223, paras 126 and 210 (dismissed on appeal, see ECJ, Case C-411/04 P *Salzgitter Mannesmann v Commission* [2007] E.C.R. I-959).

[692] This is apart from substantive issues regarding how the particularly contested measure was published; see, e.g. cases on publication of vacancy notices in only specific languages (CFI, Case T-185/05 *Italy v Commission* [2008] E.C.R. II-3207, paras 114–153; EGC, Case T-117/08 *Italy v EESC* [2011] E.C.R. II-1463, paras 69–88 (held violation of discrimination on grounds of language); see also ECJ (judgment of 27 November 2012), Case C-566/10 P *Italy v Commission*, not reported, paras 61–100).

[693] ECJ, Case 48/69 *ICI v Commission* [1972] E.C.R. 619, para. 40; ECJ, Case 185/73 *König* [1974] E.C.R. 607, para. 6; ECJ, Case C-161/06 *Skoma-Lux* [2007] E.C.R. I-10841 paras 57–61.

[694] See, by way of example, ECJ, Case 92/78 *Simmenthal v Commission* [1979] E.C.R. 777, para. 106.

[695] Art. 1, third para., TEU; Art. 1(2) TFEU.

[696] Art. 51 TEU; Art. 207 EAEC.

European Union, and the Accession Treaties and Acts.[697] The pleas raised by the applicant do not necessarily have to be confined to infringements of the Treaties on the basis of which the action is brought. An action for annulment based on Art. 263 TFEU may embody admissible pleas referring to infringements of provisions of the EAEC Treaty.[698]

(ii) Rule of law relating to the application of the Treaties

The wording 'any rule of law relating to [the Treaties'] application' covers all other binding provisions of the Union legal order.   **7.178**

These include in the first place provisions of international law, in particular provisions originating in conventions concluded by Member States before the former E(E)C Treaty was concluded,[699] agreements concluded by the Union itself,[700] and customary international law.[701]

---

[697] ECJ, Case C-91/03 *Spain v Council* [2005] E.C.R. 2267, paras 19–31; ECJ, Case C-413/04 *European Parliament v Council* [2006] E.C.R. I-11221, paras 30–61; ECJ, Case C-414/04 *European Parliament v Council* [2006] E.C.R. I-11279, paras 28–54 (annulling contested measures on grounds that could not be validly adopted on the basis of the Accession Treaty concerned). See also ECJ, Joined Cases C-87/03 and C-100/03 *Spain v Council* [2006] E.C.R. I-2915, paras 64–68 (no violation of Accession Treaty); ECJ, Case C-184/06 *Spain v Council* [2007] I-188*, Summ. pub., paras 44–49 (no violation of Accession Treaty); CFI, Joined Cases T-273/06 and T-297/06 *ISD Polska and Others v Commission* [2009] E.C.R. II-2181, paras 89–104 (appeal dismissed in ECJ, Case C-369/09 P *ISD Polska and Others v Commission* [2011] E.C.R. I-2011) (no violation of Accession Treaty).

[698] ECJ, Case C-62/88 *Greece v Council* [1990] E.C.R. I-1527, para. 8.

[699] ECJ, Joined Cases 21/72 to 24/72 *International Fruit Company* [1972] E.C.R. 1219, paras 6–7.

[700] Art. 216(2) TFEU; ECJ, Case 181/73 *Haegeman* [1974] E.C.R. 449, para. 5. For an example arising in connection with an action for annulment, see ECJ, Case 30/88 *Greece v Commission* [1989] E.C.R. 3711, para. 12. The Court of Justice will review the legality of a Union measure under Art. 263 TFEU in the light of the WTO rules only where the EU intended by means of that measure to implement a particular obligation assumed in the context of the WTO or where the measure refers expressly to the precise provisions of the WTO agreements: see, e.g. ECJ, Case C-149/96 *Portugal v Council* [1999] E.C.R. I-8395, paras 47–49 (P. Van Nuffel, case note (2001) T.B.P. 38–9); see also P. Mengozzi, 'La Cour de justice et l'applicabilité des règles de l'OMC en droit communautaire à la lumière de l'affaire Portugal c. Conseil' (2000) R.D.U.E. 509–??); CFI, Case T-45/06 *Reliance Industries v Council and Commission* [2008] E.C.R. II-2399, paras 87–88; EGC (judgment of 11 July 2013), Case T-459/07 *Hangzhou Duralamp Electronics v Council*, not reported, paras 76–79. See also J. Kokott, 'International Law—A Neglected "Integral" Part of the EU Legal Order?—Newer Tendencies in the European Court of Justice's Case-Law on the Relationship Between EU law and Public International Law', in V. Kronenberger, M. T. D'Alessio, and V. Placco (eds), *De Rome à Lisbonne: les juridictions de l'Union européenne à la croisée des chemins. Mélanges en l'honneur de Paolo Mengozzi* (Brussels, Bruylant, 2013), 72–5; K. Lenaerts, 'Droit international et autonomie constitutionnelle de l'ordre juridique de l'Union' (2010) Il Diritto dell'Unione Europea 555–70. With regard to the Aarhus Convention, see EGC (judgment of 14 June 2012), Case T-338/08 *Stichting Natuur en Milieu and Pesticide Action Network Europe v Commission*, not reported, paras 52–59 (appeal pending, Joined Cases C-404/12 P and C-405/12 P *Stichting Natuur en Milieu and Pesticide Action Network Europe v Commission*). See also para. 10.08.

[701] ECJ, Joined Cases 89/85, 104/85, 114/85, 116/85 to 117/85, and 125/85 to 129/85 *Åhlström Osakeyhtiö v Commission* [1988] E.C.R. 5193, paras 11–23; CFI, Case T-115/94 *Opel Austria v Council* [1997] E.C.R. II-39, paras 87–95. But see ECJ, Joined Cases C-402/05 P and C-415/05 P *Kadi and Al Barakaat International Foundation v Council* [2008] E.C.R. I-6351, paras 280–330, particularly para. 287 ('With more particular regard to a [Union] act which, like the contested regulation, is intended to give effect to a resolution adopted by the Security Council under Chapter VII of the Charter of the United Nations, it is not, therefore, for the [Union] judicature, under the exclusive jurisdiction provided for by [Art. 19(1) TEU], to review the lawfulness of such a resolution adopted by an international body, even if that review were to be limited to examination of the compatibility of that resolution with jus cogens'). However, the Union courts review the lawfulness of *all* Union measures, including those which implement a measure of international law, in the light of the fundamental rights guaranteed by the EU. Thus, Union measures implementing restrictive measures decided at international level do not enjoy immunity from jurisdiction. See, in that respect, ECJ (judgment of 18 July 2013), Joined Cases C-584/10 P, C-593/10 P, and C-595/10 P *Commission and Others v*

Second, there is the category made up of the general principles of Union law,[702] such as the principle of proportionality,[703] the principle of protection of legitimate expectations,[704] the principle of equal treatment,[705] the principle of effective judicial protection,[706] the principle *ne bis in idem*,[707] and the principle of reasonable time in administrative procedures.[708]

Kadi, not reported, paras 66–67 (and case-law cited therein). See also J. Kokott, 'International Law—A Neglected "Integral" Part of the EU Legal Order?—Newer Tendencies in the European Court of Justice's Case-Law on the Relationship Between EU law and Public International Law', in V. Kronenberger, M. T. D'Alessio, and V. Placco (eds), *De Rome à Lisbonne: les juridictions de l'Union européenne à la croisée des chemins. Mélanges en l'honneur de Paolo Mengozzi* (Brussels, Bruylant, 2013), 63–72; K. Lenaerts, 'Droit international et monisme de l'ordre juridique de l'Union' (2010) Revue de la Faculté de Droit de l'Université de Liège 505–19.

[702] ECJ, Case 4/73 *Nold v Commission* [1974] E.C.R. 491, para. 13; ECJ, Case 114/76 *Bela-Mühle v Grows-Farm* [1977] E.C.R. 1211, paras 5–7; ECJ, Case 224/82 *Meiko-Konservenfabrik v Germany* [1983] E.C.R. 2539, para. 11; ECJ, Case C-325/91 *France v Commission* [1993] E.C.R. I-3283, para. 30; CFI, Case T-65/98 *Van den Bergh Foods v Commission* [2003] II-4653, paras 197–198 (pleas based on infringement of the principles of subsidiarity, loyal cooperation, and legal certainty dismissed). For general discussion of the general principles of Union law, see K. Lenaerts and P. Van Nuffel (R. Bray and N. Cambien (eds)), *European Union Law* (London, Sweet & Maxwell, 2011), at paras 22.36 *et seq.*

[703] See, e.g. CFI, Case T-306/00 *Conserve Italia v Commission* [2003] E.C.R. II-5705, paras 127–151 (annulment of a Commission decision for infringing the principle of proportionality).

[704] See, e.g. ECJ, Joined Cases C-182/03 and C-217/03 *Belgium and Forum 187 v Commmission* [2006] E.C.R. I-5479, paras 147–167; ECJ, Case C-519/07 P *Commission v Koninklijke FrieslandCampina* [2009] E.C.R. I-8495, paras 84–96.

[705] See, e.g. ECJ, Joined Cases C-182/03 and 217/03 *Belgium and Forum 187 v Commmission* [2006] E.C.R. I-5479, paras 170–173 (finding that the Commission infringed the principle of equal treatment); EGC, Case T-133/07 *Mitsubishi Electric v Commission* [2011] E.C.R. II-4219, paras 264–280 (violation of this principle led to the annulment of the fine imposed); EGC (judgment of 17 January 2012), Case T-135/07 *Italy v Commission*, not reported, paras 46–100 (violation of the principle of equal treatment).

[706] See, e.g. Joined Cases C-402/05 P and C-415/05 P *Kadi and Others v Council and Commission* [2008] E.C.R. I-6351, para. 353; ECJ (judgment of 18 July 2013), Joined Cases C-584/10 P, C-593/10 P, and C-595/10 P *Commission and Others v Kadi*, not reported, paras 100, 102, 199–122 (The effectiveness of the judicial review requires that the Union courts are to ensure that a restrictive measure, which affects the applicant individually, is taken on a sufficiently solid factual basis. That entails a verification of the allegations as to fact in the summary of reasons underpinning that measure, with the consequence that judicial review cannot be restricted to an assessment of the abstract probability of the reasons relied on, but must concern whether those reasons, or, at the very least, one of those reasons, deemed sufficient in itself to support that measure, is substantiated); EGC, Case T-85/09 *Kadi v Commission* [2010] E.C.R. II-5177, paras 171–188; EGC, Joined Cases T-135/06 to T-138/06 *Al-Faqih and Others v Council* [2010] E.C.R. II-208*, Summ. pub., paras 32–39.

[707] See, e.g. ECJ (order of 22 March 2004), Case C-455/02 P *Sgaravatti Mediterranea v Commission*, not reported, paras 45–46; ECJ (judgment of 14 February 2012), Case C-17/10 *Toshiba Corporation and Others*, not reported, para. 94; CFI, Case T-24/07 *ThyssenKrupp Stainless v Commission* [2009] E.C.R. II- 2309, paras 178–192.

[708] Observation of a reasonable time in conducting administrative procedures in the sphere of competition policy is a general principle of Union law which the Union judicature ensures is respected (ECJ, Case C-282/95 P *Guérin automobiles v Commission* [1997] E.C.R. I-1503, paras 36–37; ECJ, Joined Cases C-238/99 P, C-244/99 P, C-245/99 P, C-247/99 P, C-250/99 P, C-252/99 P, and C-254/99 P *Limburgse Vinyl Maatschappij and Others v Commission* [2002] E.C.R. I-8375, paras 167 and 171; CFI, Case T-67/01 *JCB Service v Commission* [2004] E.C.R. II-49, para. 36; EGC (judgment of 11 July 2013), Joined Cases T-104/07 and T-339/08 *BVGD v Commission*, not reported, para. 127). It is set out, as part of the right to good administration, in Art. 41(1) of the Charter of Fundamental Rights of the European Union. An infringement of the reasonable-time principle justifies the annulment of a decision adopted at the end of the administrative procedure only when it also entails an infringement of the right of defence of the under-taking concerned. In the event that it is not proved that the undertaking could defend itself less effectively as a result of the excessively long period of time taken, the Commission's failure to respect the principle of reasonable time will have no effects on the validity of the administrative procedure in a competition case (CFI, Case T-67/01 *JCB Service v Commission* [2004] E.C.R. II-49, para. 40, and the case-law cited therein); see also

Finally, there are all valid, binding acts of Union institutions, bodies, offices, or agencies (including but not limited to the acts listed in Art. 288 TFEU).[709]

(iii) Infringement

The 'infringement' of Union law for which annulment is imposed under this head may **7.179** consist equally of a misapplication of the law (including an erroneous legal categorization of the facts in question or a misinterpretation of the applicable rule) or of an error in determining the factual basis on which the application of Union law is founded.[710]

(iv) Margin of discretion

It is only in areas in which the institutions have a broad discretion that the Court of Justice **7.180** and the General Court show reluctance in reviewing the assessment of economic facts and circumstances which played a determinative role in the adoption of the contested act.[711] In such a case, there will have to be a manifestly wrong assessment or a misuse of power if the act is to be annulled (apart, of course, from any misapplication of Union law in some other respect).[712]

CFI, Case T-307/01 *François v Commission* [2004] E.C.R. II-1669, para. 54, in which the plea—raised in a staff case—was declared well-founded and the administrative procedure was held to be unlawful; CFI, Case T-242/02 *Sunrider v OHIM* [2005] E.C.R. II-2793, paras 51–55, in which the plea—raised in a trademark case—was rejected.

[709] For example, this includes provisions of the Staff Regulations: see, e.g. ECJ, Case C-40/10 *Commission v Council* [2010] E.C.R. I-12043, para. 25. This also includes provisions of the 1976 Act concerning the election of the representatives to the European Parliament by direct, universal suffrage: see, e.g. ECJ, Joined Cases C-393/07 and C-9/08 *Italy and Donnici v European Parliament* [2009] E.C.R. I-3679, paras 31–32. As far as State aid cases are concerned, the Union judicature may consider whether, in adopting the contested decision, the Commission complied with the rules which it laid down itself in guidelines and notices (see CFI, Case T-35/99 *Keller and Keller Meccanica v Commission* [2002] E.C.R. II-261, paras 74 and 77; CFI, Case T-176/01 *Ferriere Nord v Commission* [2004] E.C.R. II-3931, para. 134). This is because the compatibility with the internal market of planned aid has to be assessed in accordance with the provisions of Art. 107 TFEU and by reference to the EU guidelines which the Commission has previously adopted for the purposes of such an examination. The Commission is in principle bound by the guidelines and notices that it issues in the area of supervision of State aid.

[710] ECJ, Case 18/62 *Barge v High Authority* [1963] E.C.R. 259, at 279–81. For an analytical breakdown of those two aspects, see CFI, Case T-1/89 *Rhône-Poulenc v Commission* [1991] E.C.R. II-867, paras 31–128; CFI, Case T-4/89 *BASF v Commission* [1991] E.C.R. II-1523, paras 54–258; CFI, Case T-9/89 *Hüls v Commission* [1992] E.C.R. II-499, paras 90–328. It also transpires from these judgments that the General Court thoroughly reviews the findings of fact which the Commission regards as constituting an infringement of Art. 101(1) or Art. 102 TFEU. See also CFI, Joined Cases T-68/89, T-77/89 and T-78/89 *SIV and Others v Commission* [1992] E.C.R. II-1403, paras 172–369. The Court effects its review by inquiring into the correctness of the factual claims set out in the Commission decision by testing it against the admissible evidence from the parties to the proceedings.

[711] In *agricultural cases*: ECJ, Case 138/79 *Roquette Frères v Council* [1980] E.C.R. 3333, para. 25, and ECJ, Case C-301/97 *Netherlands v Council* [2001] E.C.R. I-8853, para. 105 (reluctance shown even with regard to determining the facts); in *transport cases*: ECJ, Case C-354/89 *Schiocchet v Commission* [1991] E.C.R. I-1775, para. 14; in *competition cases*, paras 7.190–7.206.

[712] ECJ, Case 29/77 *Roquette Frères v France* [1977] E.C.R. 1835, paras 19–20. In his opinion of 17 February 2005 in ECJ, Case C-40/03 P *Rica Foods v Commission* [2005] E.C.R. I-6811, points 45 to 50, Advocate-General P. Léger draws a distinction between discretion of a political nature (which corresponds to the political responsibilities which a Union provision confers on an institution) and discretion of a technical nature (discretion of an administrative authority justified by the technical, economic, and legal complexity of the situations which it has to consider). The intensity of judicial review will be stronger where the act is the outcome of the exercise of discretion of a technical nature (e.g. in competition cases) than it is where the act is the result of the exercise of political discretion (e.g. in agricultural cases). See with respect with the standard of review in competition cases, paras 7.190–7.206.

(d) Misuse of powers

(i) Concept

7.181 An institution is said to misuse its powers when it uses them for a purpose other than that for which they were conferred *(détournement de pouvoir)*.[713] An act may be annulled on those grounds. The Court of Justice has evolved from a subjective approach to an objective approach, principally in the context of the ECSC Treaty, of the concept of misuse of powers. It is not always necessary to know the actual grounds which motivated the institution (subjective approach). When the outcome of the contested act diverges from the objectives for which the power was conferred, this can afford a sufficient basis for annulling the contested act for misuse of powers (objective approach).[714] Thus, the Court of Justice has equated with 'disregard for the lawful aim' pursuing 'objectively', through a serious lack of care or attention in the exercise of a power, purposes other than those for which the power was conferred.[715] An unlawful choice of a decision-making procedure in order to evade other procedures which would normally be applicable also constitutes a misuse of powers.[716] That being said, the use of enhanced cooperation in areas of competence that must, according to the Treaties, be exercised by unanimity does not constitute a misuse of powers.[717]

(ii) Act pursuing authorized and unauthorized aims

7.182 An act which pursues both unauthorized and authorized aims may be annulled only if this detracts from the main aim for which the power was conferred[718] or if the unauthorized aim constitutes the main reason for exercising the power.[719]

---

[713] See, e.g. ECJ, Case 8/55 *Fédération Charbonnière de Belgique v High Authority* [1954 to 1956] E.C.R. 292, at 303; ECJ, Case 15/57 *Compagnie des Hauts Fourneaux de Chasse v High Authority* [1957 and 1958] E.C.R. 211, at 230; ECJ, Case 92/78 *Simmenthal v Commission* [1979] E.C.R. 777, para. 106; ECJ, Case 817/79 *Buyl v Commission* [1982] E.C.R. 245, para. 28; ECJ, Case C-400/99 *Italy v Commission* [2005] E.C.R. I-3657, para. 38; ECJ, Case C-442/04 *Spain v Council* [2008] E.C.R. I-3517, para. 49; CFI, Case T-38/89 *Hochbaum v Commission* [1990] E.C.R. II-43, para. 22; CFI, Case T-108/89 *Scheuer v Commission* [1990] E.C.R. II-411, para. 49; CFI, Case T-46/89 *Pitrone v Commission* [1990] E.C.R. II-577, para. 70; CFI, Case T-411/06 *Sogelma v EAR* [2008] E.C.R. II-2771, para. 139; CFI, Case T-256/07 *PMOI v Council* [2008] E.C.R. II-3019, para. 151; EGC, Case T-49/07 *Fahas v Council* [2010] E.C.R. II-5555, para. 88; EGC, Case T-387/08 *Evropaïki Dynamiki v Commission* [2010] E.C.R. II-178*, Summ. pub., para. 159.

[714] ECJ, Joined Cases 351/85 and 360/85 *Fabrique de Fer de Charleroi v Commission* [1987] E.C.R. 3639, paras 19 and 20; ECJ, Joined Cases 32/87, 52/87 and 57/87 *ISA v Commission* [1988] E.C.R. 3305, para. 19; ECJ, Joined Cases 33/86, 44/86, 110/86, 226/86 and 285/86 *Stahlwerke Peine-Salzgitter and Others v Commission* [1988] E.C.R. 4309, paras 27–28.

[715] ECJ, Case 8/55 *Fédération Charbonnière de Belgique v High Authority* [1954 to 1956] E.C.R. 292, at 303; ECJ, Case 13/57 *Wirtschaftsvereinigung Eisen- und Stahlindustrie and Others v High Authority* [1957 and 1958] E.C.R. 265, at 282.

[716] ECJ, Case 2/57 *Compagnie des Hauts Fourneaux de Chasse v High Authority* [1957 and 1958] E.C.R. 199, at 207; ECJ, Joined Cases 140/82, 146/82, 221/82 and 226/82 *Walzstahl-Vereinigung and Thyssen v Commission* [1984] E.C.R. 951, paras 27 *et seq.*; ECJ, Joined Cases 32/87, 52/87 and 57/87 *ISA v Commission* [1988] E.C.R. 3305, para. 19; ECJ, Joined Cases 33/86, 44/86, 110/86, 226/86 and 285/86 *Stahlwerke Peine-Salzgitter and Others v Commission* [1988] E.C.R. 4309, paras 27–28.

[717] ECJ (judgment of 16 April 2013), Joined Cases C-274/11 and C-295/11 *Spain and Italy v Council*, not reported, paras 33–41.

[718] ECJ, Case 1/54 *France v High Authority* [1954 to 1956] E.C.R. 1, at 16; ECJ, Case 8/55 *Fédération Charbonnière de Belgique v High Authority* [1954 to 1956] E.C.R. 292, at 301; EGC, Case T-377/07 *Evropaïki Dynamiki v Commission* [2011] E.C.R. II-442*, Summ. pub., para. 109 (and further citations therein).

[719] ECJ, Case 2/57 *Compagnie des Hauts Fourneaux de Chasse v High Authority* [1957 and 1958] E.C.R. 199, at 232.

(iii) Proof

The Union judicature subjects claims alleging misuse of powers to strict requirements as to   **7.183**
proof. Only if the applicant proves, on the basis of objective, relevant and consistent facts,
that the act was adopted for unauthorized purposes, will the Court of Justice or the General
Court entertain a claim of misuse of powers.[720] A misuse of powers cannot be presumed.[721]

(iv) Exceptional ground

In spite of the prominent role which this ground of nullity played in the now-expired   **7.184**
ECSC Treaty, it is only seldom that the Court of Justice and the General Court declare an
act void for misuse of powers.[722]

B. Conduct during the administrative procedure and admissibility of pleas in judicial proceedings

(1) Acknowledgement of the facts in Arts 101 and 102 TFEU proceedings

An undertaking involved in an alleged infringement of Arts 101 and 102 TFEU may raise   **7.185**
in its application any ground for annulment mentioned in Art. 263 TFEU. Where the
undertaking does not expressly acknowledge the facts, the Commission must prove the
facts in its decision, and the undertaking is free to put forward in the proceedings before the
Court any plea in its defence which it deems appropriate, even if such plea has not been
raised during the administrative proceedings.[723] However, where the undertaking explicitly

---

[720] See, e.g. ECJ, Joined Cases 18/65 and 35/65 *Gutmann v Commission* [1966] E.C.R. 103, at 117; ECJ, Case 69/83 *Lux v Court of Auditors* [1984] E.C.R. 2447, para. 30; ECJ, Case 52/86 *Banner v European Parliament* [1987] E.C.R. 979, para. 6; ECJ, Joined Cases 361/87 and 362/87 *Caturla-Poch and De la Fuente Pascual v European Parliament* [1989] E.C.R. 2471, para. 21; ECJ, Case C-323/88 *Sermes* [1990] E.C.R. I-3027, para. 33; ECJ, Case C-331/88 *Fedesa and Others* [1990] E.C.R. I-4023, para. 24; ECJ, Case C-400/99 *Italy v Commission* [2005] E.C.R. I-3657, para. 38; ECJ, Case C-442/04 *Spain v Council* [2008] E.C.R. I-3517, para. 49; CFI, Case T-46/89 *Pitrone v Commission* [1990] E.C.R. II-577, para. 71; CFI, Case T-23/91 *Maurissen v Court of Auditors* [1992] E.C.R. II-2377, para. 28; CFI, Case T-80/92 *Turner v Commission* [1993] E.C.R. II-1465, para. 70; CFI, Case T-109/92 *Lacruz Bassols v Court of Justice* [1994] E.C.R.-SC II-105, para. 52 (English abstract at [1994] E.C.R.-SC I-A-31); CFI, Case T-46/93 *Michaël-Chiou v Commission* [1994] E.C.R.-SC II-929, para. 35 (English abstract at [1994] E.C.R.-SC I-A-297); CFI, Case T-143/89 *Ferriere Nord v Commission* [1995] E.C.R. II-917, para. 68; CFI, Joined Cases T-551/93 and T-231/94 to T-234/94 *Industrias Pesqueras Campos and Others v Commission* [1996] E.C.R. II-247, para. 168; CFI, Case T-226/04 *Italy v Commission* [2006] E.C.R. II-29*, Summ. pub., para. 92; CFI, Case T-417/05 *Endesa v Commission* [2006] E.C.R. II-2533, para. 258; CFI, Case T-70/07 *Cantieri Navali Termoli v Commission* [2008] E.C.R. II-250*, Summ. pub., paras 93–95; CFI, Case T-256/07 *PMOI v Council* [2008] E.C.R. II-3019, paras 152–153; EGC, Case T-387/08 *Evropaïki Dynamiki v Commission* [2010] E.C.R. II-178*, Summ. pub., paras 160–161; EGC, Case T-377/07 *Evropaïki Dynamiki v Commission* [2011] E.C.R. II-442*, Summ. pub., paras 109–117; ECJ (judgment of 16 April 2013), Joined Cases C-274/11 and C-295/11 *Spain and Italy v Council*, not reported, para. 33.

[721] ECJ, Case 23/76 *Pellegrini and Others v Commission* [1976] E.C.R. 1807, para. 30, and the Opinion of Advocate-General H. Mayras, at 1829–1830; CFI, Case T-146/89 *Williams v Court of Auditors* [1991] E.C.R. II-1293, para. 89.

[722] ECJ, Joined Cases 18/65 and 35/65 *Gutmann v Commission* [1966] E.C.R. 103, at 117; ECJ, Case 105/75 *Giuffrida v Council* [1976] E.C.R. 1395, para. 18; ECJ, Case 92/78 *Simmenthal v Commission* [1979] E.C.R. 777, para. 106, at 811; ECJ, Joined Cases 59/80 and 129/80 *Turner v Commission* [1981] E.C.R. 1883, para. 71, at 1920; ECJ, Joined Cases 33/86, 44/86, 110/86, 226/86, and 285/86 *Stahlwerke Peine-Salzitter and Others v Commission* [1988] E.C.R. 4309, para. 28; CFI, Case T-106/92 *Frederiksen v European Parliament* [1995] E.C.R.-SC II-99, paras 46–60 (English abstract at [1995] E.C.R.-SC I-A-29).

[723] EGC, Case T-234/07 *Koninklijke Grolsch v Commission* [2011] E.C.R. II-6169, paras 37–41.

admits during the administrative procedure the substantive truth of the Commission's allegations made against it in the statement of objections, those facts must thereafter be regarded as established and the undertaking will be in principle estopped from disputing them during the proceedings before the Union courts.[724]

(2) Merger control

7.186   The assessments made by the Commission will be examined by the Union courts on the basis of the information available to the Commission at the time when those assessments were made. The applicant should thus not alter, during the proceedings before these courts, the legal and factual framework previously submitted to the Commission for the purposes of the adoption of the contested decision.[725]

(3) State aid proceedings

7.187   The legality of a Union measure is assessed on the basis of the elements of fact and of law existing at the time when the measure was adopted. In particular, the assessments made by the Commission are examined by the Union judicature solely on the basis of the information available to the Commission at the time when those assessments were made.[726] It follows that an applicant which took part in the investigation procedure provided for in Art. 108(2) TFEU cannot rely on factual arguments which were not known to the Commission and of which it did not inform the Commission during the investigation procedure.[727] However, there is nothing to prevent a recipient of State aid or any other interested party from raising against the final decision a plea in law not raised at the stage of the administrative procedure.[728]

---

[724] ECJ, Case C-297/98 P *SCA Holding v Commission* [2000] E.C.R. I-10101, para. 37; CFI, Case T-224/00 *Archer Daniels Midland and Archer Daniels Midland Ingredients v Commission* [2003] E.C.R. II-2597, para. 227; CFI, Joined Cases T-236/01, T-239/01, T-244/01, T-246/01, T-251/01, and T-252/01 *Tokai Carbon and Others v Commission* [2004] E.C.R. II-1181, para. 108. Only where the acknowledgement of the facts leaves no room for doubt will the applicant be barred from contesting such facts beforte the General Court: see EGC, Case T-39/06 *Transcatab v Commission* [2011] E.C.R. II-6831, paras 400–404. Moreover, inferences made by the Commission on the basis of declarations made during the administrative procedure may still be challenged before the General Court (CFI, Joined Cases T-236/01, T-239/01, T-244/01, T-246/01, T-251/01, and T-252/01 *Tokai Carbon and Others v Commission* [2004] E.C.R. II-1181, para. 109).

[725] CFI, Case T-87/05 *EDP v Commission* [2005] E.C.R. II-3745, para. 158; CFI, Case T-151/05 *NVV and Others v Commission* [2009] E.C.R. II-1219, paras 58 and 63.

[726] ECJ, Joined Cases 15/76 and 16/76 *France v Commission* [1979] E.C.R. 321, para. 7; CFI, Joined Cases T-371/94 and T-394/94 *British Airways and Others v Commission* [1998] E.C.R. II-2405, para. 81; CFI, Case T-109/01 *Fleuren Compost v Commission* [2004] E.C.R. II-127, para. 50; CFI, Joined Cases T-111/01 and T-133/01 *Saxonia Edelmetalle and Zemag v Commission* [2005] E.C.R. II-1579, para. 67; EGC, Case T-11/07 *Frucona Košice v Commission* [2010] E.C.R. II-5453, para. 48; EGC (judgment of 20 March 2013), Case T-489/11 *Rousse Industry v Commission*, not reported, para. 33.

[727] CFI, Joined Cases T-111/01 and T-133/01 *Saxonia Edelmetalle and Zemag v Commission* [2005] E.C.R. II-1579, para. 68; CFI, Case T-445/05 *Associazione italiana del risparmio gestito and Fineco Asset Management v Commission* [2009] E.C.R. II-289, para. 177. See also EGC (judgment of 11 September 2012), Case T-565/08 *Corsica Ferries France v Commission*, not reported, para. 64.

[728] CFI, Case T-16/96 *Cityflyer Express v Commission* [1998] E.C.R. II-757, para. 39; CFI, Case T-123/97 *Salomon v Commission* [1999] E.C.R. II-2925, para. 55; CFI, Joined Cases T-111/01 and T-133/01 *Saxonia Edelmetalle and Zemag v Commission* [2005] E.C.R. II-1579, para. 68; CFI, Case T-445/05 *Associazione italiana del risparmio gestito and Fineco Asset Management v Commission* [2009] E.C.R. II-289, para. 177.

(4) Anti-dumping proceedings

In principle, nothing prevents an applicant from raising in its application any ground for **7.188**
annulment mentioned in Art. 263 TFEU, including a plea which was not raised during the
administrative proceedings.[729]

(5) *Nemo auditur*

In proceedings before the General Court, a party cannot rely on its own wrongful conduct **7.189**
in the administrative procedure.[730] Similarly, a party cannot rely on the unlawful conduct
of a person authorized to act on its behalf in order to evade its own liability as a result of
actions performed by that person.[731]

C. Standard of review in competition cases

In competition cases, too, the Union judicature only inquires into the legality of the
contested act.

(1) Enforcement of Arts 101 and 102 TFEU

(a) *Comprehensive review as a general rule*

The burden of proof of the existence of the circumstances that constitute an infringement **7.190**
of Arts 101 TFEU or 102 TFEU is borne by the Commission.[732] The General Court will
therefore consider whether the evidence and other information relied on by the Commission in its decision is sufficient to prove the existence of the alleged infringement.[733] As a

---

[729] However, EGC, Case T-369/08 *EWRIA and Others v Commission* [2010] E.C.R. II-6283, paras
105–109, seems to suggest that only a plea raised during the administrative proceedings is admissible.

[730] CFI, Case T-141/01 *Entorn v Commission* [2005] E.C.R. II-95, para. 121; see, by analogy, ECJ, Case
39/72 *Commission v Italy* [1973] E.C.R. 101, para. 10, and the Opinion of Advocate-General J. Mischo in
Case C-453/99 *Courage and Crehan* [2001] E.C.R. I-6297, I-6300, point 39.

[731] CFI, Case T-141/01 *Entorn v Commission* [2005] E.C.R. II-95, para. 121. In that case, a letter from the
Commission intended to ensure the recipient its right to be heard was sent to the wrong address. The CFI
dismissed a plea alleging infringement of the rights of the defence on the grounds that the management of the
undertaking concerned deliberately misled the Commission as to its correct address.

[732] Art. 2 of Regulation 1/2003. See also ECJ, Case C-185/95 P *Baustahlgewebe v Commission* [1998]
E.C.R. I-8417, para. 58; ECJ, Case C-49/92 P *Commission v Anic Partecipazioni* [1999] E.C.R. I-4125, para. 86;
CFI, Case T-201/04 *Microsoft v Commission* [2007] E.C.R. II-3601, para. 688; CFI, Case T-321/05 *Astrazeneca
v Commission* [2010] E.C.R. II-2805, para. 474; EGC, Case T-141/08 *E.ON Energie v Commission* [2010]
E.C.R. II-5761, para. 48 (and case-law cited therein); EGC, Case T-59/07 *Polimeri Europa v Commission* [2011]
E.C.R. II-4687, para. 50; EGC (judgment of 27 June 2012), Case T-439/07 *Coats Holdings v Commission*, not
reported, para. 38. Although the burden of proof of the existence of the circumstances that constitute an
infringement of Art. 102 TFEU is borne by the Commission, it is for the dominant undertaking concerned, and
not for the Commission, before the end of the administrative procedure, to raise any plea of objective justification
and to support it with arguments and evidence. It then falls to the Commission, where it proposes to make a
finding of an abuse of a dominant position, to show that the arguments and evidence relied on by the
undertaking cannot prevail and, accordingly, that the justification put forward cannot be accepted (CFI, Case
T-201/04 *Microsoft v Commission* [2007] E.C.R. II-3601, para. 688). See further K. Lenaerts, 'Some Thoughts
on Evidence and Procedure in European Competition Law' (2006) Fordham Int'l L.J. 1463–95; A. Ó Caoimh,
'Standard of Proof, Burden of Proof, Standards of Review and Evaluation of Evidence in Antitrust and Merger
Cases', in D. Ehlermann and M. Marquis (eds), *European Competition Law Annual 2009* (Oxford and Portland
Oregon, Hart Publishing, 2011), 271–83.

[733] CFI, Joined Cases T-305/94, T-306/94, T-307/94, T-313/94 to T-316/94, T-318/94, T-325/94,
T-328/94, T-329/94, and T-335/94 *Limburgse Vinyl Maatschappij and Others v Commission* [1999]
E.C.R. II-931, para. 891; CFI, Joined Cases T-67/00, T-68/00, T-71/00, and T-78/00 *JFE Engineering
and Others v Commission* [2004] E.C.R. II-2501, paras 174–175; EGC, Case T-141/08 *E.ON Energie v*

general rule, the Union courts undertake a comprehensive review of the question as to whether or not the conditions for the application of the competition rules are met.[734]

(b) Role of applicant

7.191   It is for the applicant to raise pleas in law against the Commission decision and to adduce evidence in support of those pleas. That requirement, which is procedural in nature, does not conflict with the rule that, in regard to infringements of the competition rules, it is for the Commission to prove the infringement found by it and to adduce evidence capable of demonstrating to the requisite legal standard the existence of the circumstances constituting an infringement. What the applicant is required to do in the context of a legal challenge is to identify the impugned elements of the contested decision, to formulate grounds of challenge in that regard, and to adduce evidence—direct or circumstantial—to demonstrate that its objections are well-founded.[735]

Accordingly, when the Commission found an infringement on Arts 101 TFEU or 102 TFEU on the basis of the mere conduct of the undertakings concerned, the Union courts will annul such finding if the applicants prove circumstances which cast the facts established by the Commission in a different light and which thus allow another explanation of the facts to be substituted for the one adopted by the contested decision.[736] However, if the Commission relies on documentary evidence in support of its finding of the existence of an infringement on Arts 101 TFEU or 102 TFEU, the General Court will only annul such finding when the applicant demonstrates that the evidence relied on in the contested decision to establish the existence of the infringement is insufficient.[737]

Commission [2010] E.C.R. II-5761, para. 50; EGC, Case T-132/07 *Fuji Electric v Commission* [2011] E.C.R. II-4091, para. 89; EGC (judgment of 27 June 2012), Case T-439/07 *Coats Holdings v Commission*, not reported, para. 38.

[734] ECJ, Case 42/84 *Remia v Commission* [1985] E.C.R. 2545, para. 34; ECJ, Joined Cases 142/84 and 156/84 *BAT and Reynolds v Commission* [1987] E.C.R. 4487, para. 62; CFI, Case T-41/96 *Bayer v Commission* [2000] E.C.R. II-3383, para. 62; CFI, Case T-201/04 *Microsoft v Commission* [2007] E.C.R. II-3601, para. 87; CFI, Case T-18/03 *CD-Contact Data v Commission* [2009] E.C.R. II-1021, para. 50; EGC, Case T-321/05, *Astrazeneca v Commission* [2010] E.C.R. II-2805, para 32; EGC, Case 461/07 *Visa Europe and Visa International Service v Commission* [2011] E.C.R. II-1729, para. 70; EGC, Case T-191/06, *FMC Foret v Commission* [2011] E.C.R. II-2959, para. 110; EGC (judgment of 29 March 2012), Case T-336/07 *Telefónica and Telefónica de España v Commission*, not reported, paras 68–69. However, in their review, the ECJ and the EGC take account of the fact that anti-competitive activities take place clandestinely, and accordingly, in most cases, the existence of an anti-competitive practice or agreement must be inferred from a number of coincidences and indicia which, taken together, may, in the absence of another plausible explanation, constitute evidence of an infringement of the competition rules: see Joined Cases C-204/00 P, C-205/00 P, C-211/00 P, C-213/00 P, C-217/00 P, and C-219/00 P *Aalborg Portland and Others v Commission* [2004] E.C.R. I-123, paras 55–57; EGC (judgment of 27 June 2012), Case T-448/07 *YKK and Others v Commission*, not reported, para. 80. See further N. Wahl, 'Standard of Review: Comprehensive or Limited?', in D. Ehlermann and M. Marquis (eds), *European Competition Law Annual 2009* (Oxford and Portland Oregon, Hart Publishing, 2011), 285–94.

[735] ECJ (judgment of 8 December 2011), Case C-272/09 P *KME Germany and Others v Commission*, not yet reported, paras 104–105; ECJ (judgment of 8 December 2011), Case C-389/10 P *KME Germany and Others v Commission*, not yet reported, paras 131–132. See further EGC, Case T-132/07 *Fuji Electric v Commission* [2011] E.C.R. II-4091, para. 84 (and case-law cited therein).

[736] ECJ, Joined Cases 29/83 and 30/83 *CRAM and Rheinzink v Commission* [1984] E.C.R. 1679, para. 16; ECJ, Joined Cases C-89/85, C-104/85, C-114/85, C-116/85, C-117/85, and C-125/85 to C-129/85 *Ahlström Osakeyhtiö and Others v Commission* [1993] E.C.R. I-1307, paras 126–127; EGC, Case T-141/08 *E.ON Energie v Commission* [2010] E.C.R. II-5761, para. 54.

[737] In such case, it is not sufficient for the applicant to put forward a plausible alternative to the Commission's view. See CFI, Joined Cases T-305/94, T-306/94, T-307/94, T-313/94 to T-316/94,

(c) Doubt benefits to applicant

In the proceedings before the General Court, the Commission may not adduce new **7.192**
inculpatory evidence in support of the contested decision which is not contained in that
decision.[738] The existence of an infringement must be assessed by reference solely to the
evidence gathered by the Commission in the decision finding that infringement and the
only relevant question is therefore to ascertain, on the merits, whether or not the infringement has been proved by that evidence.[739] The Commission must thus in its decision
produce sufficiently precise and consistent evidence to support the firm conviction that the
alleged infringement took place.[740] Where there is doubt as regards the existence of the
infringement, the General Court must give the benefit of that doubt to the applicant.[741] As
a result, the General Court will conclude that the Commission has not established the
existence of the infringement at issue to the requisite legal standard if it still entertains
doubts on that point.[742] This is because, given the nature of the infringements in question

T-318/94, T-325/94, T-328/94, T-329/94, and T-335/94 *Limburgse Vinyl Maatschappij and Others v Commission* [1999] E.C.R. II-931, paras 725–728; CFI, Joined Cases T-67/00, T-68/00, T-71/00, and T-78/00 *JFE Engineering and Others v Commission* [2004] E.C.R. II-2501, para. 187; EGC, Case T-141/08 *E.ON Energie v Commission* [2010] E.C.R. II-5761, para. 55; EGC (judgment of 27 June 2012), Case T-439/07 *Coats Holdings v Commission*, not reported, para. 39.

[738] See, e.g. ECJ (judgment of 19 July 2012), Joined Cases C-628/10 P and C-14/11 P *Alliance One and Others v Commission*, not reported, para. 79. In so far as the applicants seek to establish, on the basis of 'new documents' produced to the General Court, that the Commission's position is based on inaccurate facts, the Commission is entitled to respond to their arguments by referring to the documents in question (CFI, Joined Cases T-67/00, T-68/00, T-71/00, and T-78/00 *JFE Engineering and Others v Commission* [2004] E.C.R. II-2501, paras 177–178).

[739] CFI, Joined Cases T-25/95, T-26/95, T-30/95, T-31/95, T-32/95, T-34/95, T-35/95, T-36/95, T-37/95, T-38/95, T-39/95, T-42/95, T-43/95, T-44/95, T-45/95, T-46/95, T-48/95, T-50/95, T-51/95, T-52/95, T-53/95, T-54/95, T-55/95, T-56/95, T-57/95, T-58/95, T-59/95, T-60/95, T-61/95, T-62/95, T-63/95, T-64/95, T-65/95, T-68/95, T-69/95, T-70/95, T-71/95, T-87/95, T-88/95, T-103/95, and T-104/95 *Cimenteries CBR and Others v Commission* [2000] E.C.R. II-491, para. 726; EGC, Case T-132/07 *Fuji Electric v Commission* [2011] E.C.R. II-4091, para. 90.

[740] CFI, Joined Cases T 185/96, T-189/96, and T-190/96 *Riviera Auto Service and Others v Commission* [1999] E.C.R. II-93, para. 47; CFI, Case T-62/98 *Volkswagen v Commission* [2000] E.C.R. II-2707, para. 43; EGC, Case T-112/07 *Hitachi and Others v Commission* [2011] E.C.R. II-3871, para. 265; EGC, Case T-132/07 *Fuji Electric v Commission* [2011] E.C.R. II-4091, para. 87. However, it is not necessary for every item of evidence produced by the Commission to satisfy those criteria in relation to every aspect of the infringement. It is sufficient if the body of evidence relied on by the institution, viewed as a whole, meets that requirement: see EGC, Case T-132/07 *Fuji Electric v Commission* [2011] E.C.R. II-4091, para. 87 (and case-law cited therein); EGC (judgment of 27 June 2012), Case T-439/07 *Coats Holdings v Commission*, not reported, paras 40–41. With respect to the probative value which should be attached to freely adduced evidence (such as statements of other incriminated undertakings), see EGC (judgment of 27 June 2012), Case T-439/07 *Coats Holdings v Commission*, not reported, paras 45–50 (and case-law cited therein).

[741] ECJ, Case 27/76 *United Brands and United Brands Continentaal v Commission* [1978] E.C.R. 207, para. 265; ECJ, Case C-199/92 P *Hüls v Commission* [1999] E.C.R. I-4287, paras 149–150; EGC, Case T-141/08 *E.ON Energie v Commission* [2010] E.C.R. II-5761, para. 50; EGC, Case 461/07 *Visa Europe and Visa International Service v Commission* [2011] E.C.R. II-1729, para. 70; EGC, Case T-191/06 *FMC Foret v Commission* [2011] E.C.R. II-2959, para. 111; EGC, Case T-44/07 *Kaučuk v Commission* [2011] E.C.R. II-4601, para. 48; EGC, Case T-53/07 *Trade-Stomil v Commission* [2011] E.C.R. II-4657, para. 63 (proof of infringement deemed insufficient—doubt benefited to the applicant); EGC (judgment of 29 March 2012), Case T-336/07 *Telefónica and Telefónica de España v Commission*, not reported, para. 72; EGC (judgment of 27 June 2012), Case T-448/07 *YKK and Others v Commission*, not reported, para. 48; EGC (judgment of 12 December 2012), Case T-332/09 *Electrabel v Commission*, not reported, para. 106.

[742] CFI, Case T-38/02 *Groupe Danone v Commission* [2005] E.C.R. II-4407, para. 63; EGC, Case T-53/07 *Trade-Stomil v Commission* [2011] E.C.R. II-4657, para. 63; EGC, Case T-132/07 *Fuji Electric v Commission* [2011] E.C.R. II-4091, para. 89.

and the nature and degree of severity of the ensuing penalties, the principle of the presumption of innocence (resulting in particular from Art. 6(2) of the ECHR and Art. 48 of the Charter of Fundamental Rights of the European Union) applies to competition procedures.[743]

(d) Review takes into account the complex nature of economic and technical appraisals

7.193 Although as a general rule the Union courts undertake a comprehensive review of the question as to whether or not the conditions for the application of the competition rules are met, their review of complex economic appraisals made by the Commission is limited to checking whether the relevant rules on procedure and on stating reasons have been complied with, whether the facts have been accurately stated, and whether there has been any manifest error of assessment or a misuse of powers.[744]

Likewise, insofar as the Commission's decision is the result of complex technical appraisals, those appraisals are in principle subject to only limited review by the Union courts, which means that they cannot substitute their own assessment of matters of fact for that of the Commission.[745]

---

[743] ECJ, Case C-199/92 P *Hüls v Commission* [1999] E.C.R. I-4287, paras 149–150; ECJ, Case C-235/92 P *Montecatini v Commission* [1999] E.C.R. I-4539, paras 175–176; CFI, Joined Cases T-67/00, T-68/00, T-71/00, and T-78/00 *JFE Engineering and Others v Commission* [2004] E.C.R. II-2501, paras 177–178; EGC, Case T-321/05, *Astrazeneca v Commission* [2010] E.C.R. II-2805, paras 475–476; EGC, Case T-141/08 *E.ON Energie v Commission* [2010] E.C.R. II-5761, para. 52; EGC, Case T-132/07 *Fuji Electric v Commission* [2011] E.C.R. II-4091, para. 89; EGC, Case T-45/07 *Unipetrol v Commission* [2011] E.C.R. II-4629, para. 48; EGC (judgment of 29 March 2012), Case T-336/07 *Telefónica and Telefónica de España v Commission*, not reported, para. 73. The review of the Commission's assessment of the Union interest of a complaint in a decision rejecting the complaint is also limited. Review by the Union courts of the Commission's exercise of the discretion conferred on it in this regard must not lead them to substitute their own assessment of the Union interest for that of the Commission, but focuses on whether the contested decision is based on materially incorrect facts, or is vitiated by an error of law, manifest error of appraisal, or misuse of powers: see CFI, Case T-115/99 *SEP v Commission* [2001] E.C.R. II-691, para. 34; EGC, Case T-427/08 *CEAHR v Commission* [2010] E.C.R. II-5865, para. 65; EGC, Case T-74/11 *Omnis Group v Commission* [2010] E.C.R. II-5865, para. 50; EGC (judgment of 11 July 2013), Joined Cases T-104/07 and T-339/08 *BVGD v Commission*, not reported, para. 219.

[744] ECJ, Case 42/84 *Remia v Commission* [1985] E.C.R. 2545, para. 34; ECJ, Joined Cases 142/84 and 156/84 *BAT and Reynolds v Commission* [1987] E.C.R. 4487, para. 62; ECJ, Joined Cases C-204/00 P, C-205/00 P, C-211/02 P, C-213/00 P, C-217/00 P, and C-219/00 P *Aalborg Portland and Others v Commission* [2004] E.C.R. I-123, para. 279; CFI, Case T-44/90 *La Cinq v Commission* [1992] E.C.R. II-1, para. 85; CFI, Case T-7/92 *Asia Motor France and Others v Commission* [1993] E.C.R. II-669, para. 33; CFI, Joined Cases T-39/92 and T-40/92 *CB and Europay v Commission* [1994] E.C.R. II-49, para. 109; CFI, Case T-17/93 *Matra Hachette v Commission* [1994] E.C.R. II-595, para. 104; Case T-65/96 *Kish Glass v Commission* [2000] E.C.R. II-1885, para. 64; CFI, Case T-201/04 *Microsoft v Commission* [2007] E.C.R. II-3601, para. 87; EGC, Case 461/07 *Visa Europe and Visa International Service v Commission* [2011] E.C.R. II-1729, para. 70; EGC, Case T-321/05, *Astrazeneca v Commission* [2010] E.C.R. II-2805, para 32; EGC (judgment of 29 March 2012), Case T-336/07 *Telefónica and Telefónica de España v Commission*, not reported, para. 69. See further M. Jaeger, 'Standard of Review in Competition Cases: Can the General Court Increase Coherence in the European Judicial System?', in T. Baumé, E. Oude Elferink, P. Phoa, and D. Thiaville (eds), *Today's Multilayered Legal Order: Current Issues and Perspectives, Liber Amicorum Arjen Meij* (Zutphen, Paris Legal Publishers, 2011), 115–40; M. Jaeger, 'The Standard of Review in Competition Cases Involving Complex Economic Assessments' (2011) J.E.C.L. & Pract. 295–314. For a critical analysis, see R. Wesseling and M. van der Woude, 'Over de rechtmatigheid en aanvaardbaarheid van de handhaving van het Europese kartelrecht' (2012) S.E.W. 174–86.

[745] ECJ, Case C-12/03 P *Commission v Tetra Laval* [2005] E.C.R. I-987, para. 39; ECJ, Case C-525/04 P *Spain v Lenzing* [2007] E.C.R. I-9947, paras 56–57; ECJ (judgment of 8 December 2011), Case C-272/09 P *KME Germany and Others v Commission*, not reported, para. 94; ECJ (judgment of 8 December 2011), Case C-389/10 P *KME Germany and Others v Commission*, not reported, para. 121 (note: the case-law of the ECJ— contrary to the *Microsoft* judgment of the CFI, refers only to economic assessments and not to technical ones); CFI, Case T-201/04 *Microsoft v Commission* [2007] E.C.R. II-3601, paras 88 and 379 (the assessment

However, while the Union courts recognize that the Commission has a margin of discretion in economic or technical matters, that does not mean that they must decline to review the Commission's interpretation of economic or technical data. The Union courts must not only establish whether the evidence put forward is factually accurate, reliable, and consistent but must also determine whether that evidence contains all the information which must be taken into account in order to assess a complex situation, and whether it is capable of substantiating the conclusions drawn from it.[746]

The Union courts must also establish of their own motion that the Commission has stated reasons for its decision and, among other things, that it has explained the weighting and assessment of the factors taken into account.[747]

(e) Review of compliance with the Commission Guidelines

In its Guidelines on the method of setting fines imposed pursuant to Art. 23(2)(a) of **7.194** Regulation No. 1/2003,[748] the Commission indicates the basis on which it will take account of one or other aspect of the infringement and what this will imply as regards the amount of the fine. The Union courts will examine whether the Commission decision complies with the Guidelines. Indeed, the Guidelines form rules of practice from which the administration may not depart in an individual case without giving reasons compatible with the principle of equal treatment.[749]

The Union courts carry out the review of legality of the Commission decision on the basis of the evidence adduced by the applicant in support of the pleas in law put forward. In carrying out such a review, the Union judicature cannot use the Commission's margin of discretion—either as regards the choice of factors taken into account in the application of

---

(or lack) of interoperability of Windows and non-Windows operating systems is a complex technical appraisal); EGC (judgment of 29 March 2012), Case T-336/07 *Telefónica and Telefónica de España v Commission*, not reported, para. 70.

[746] ECJ (judgment of 8 December 2011), Case C-272/09 P *KME Germany and Others v Commission*, not reported, para. 94; ECJ (judgment of 8 December 2011), Case C-389/10 P *KME Germany and Others v Commission*, not reported, para. 121; ECJ (judgment of 8 December 2011), Case C-386/10 P *Chalkor v Commission*, not reported, para. 54; CFI, Case T-201/04 *Microsoft v Commission* [2007] E.C.R. II-3601, para. 89 (and case-law cited therein); EGC, Case T-321/05 *Astrazeneca v Commission* [2010] E.C.R. II-2805, para. 33.

[747] ECJ (judgment of 8 December 2011), Case C-386/10 P *Chalkor v Commission*, not reported, para. 61; ECJ (judgment of 6 November 2012), Case C-199/11 *Otis*, not reported, para. 60. See also para. 7.174.

[748] [2006] O.J. C210/2.

[749] ECJ, Case C-397/03 P *Archer Daniels Midland and Archer Daniels Midland Ingredients v Commission* [2006] E.C.R. I-4429, para. 91; ECJ (judgment of 8 December 2011), Case C-272/09 P *KME Germany and Others v Commission*, not reported, paras 99–100; ECJ (judgment of 8 December 2011), Case C-389/10 P *KME Germany and Others v Commission*, not reported, paras 126–127; ECJ (judgment of 8 December 2011), Case C-386/10 P *Chalkor v Commission*, not reported, para. 60; CFI, Case T- 44/00 *Mannesmannröhren-Werke v Commission* [2004] E.C.R. II-2223, paras 212 and 232; EGC, Case T-39/06 *Transcatab v Commission* [2011] E.C.R. II-6831, paras 142–143. See, however, EGC, Case T-41/05 *Alliance One International v Commission* [2011] E.C.R. II-7101, para. 190 (appeal pending in Case C-679/11 P *Alliance One International v Commission*), in which the EGC held that in the Guidelines, there was no binding indication regarding the attenuating circumstances that may be taken into account; the Commission therefore retains a degree of latitude in making an overall assessment of the extent to which a reduction of fines may be made in respect of attenuating circumstances (see also EGC, Joined Cases T-259/02 to T-264/02 and T-271/02 *Raiffeisen Zentralbank Österreich and Others v Commission* [2006] E.C.R. II-5169, para. 473).

the criteria mentioned in the Guidelines or as regards the assessment of those factors—as a basis for dispensing with the conduct of an in-depth review of the law and of the facts.[750]

(f) Review of legality supplemented by unlimited jurisdiction as regards the fines satisfies the requirements of effective judicial protection

7.195 The review of legality is supplemented by the unlimited jurisdiction which the Union courts enjoy pursuant to Art. 31 of Regulation No. 1/2003 in accordance with Art. 261 TFEU. That jurisdiction empowers the Union courts, in addition to carrying out a mere review of the lawfulness of the penalty, to substitute their own appraisal for the Commission's and, consequently, to cancel, reduce, or increase the fine or penalty payment imposed.[751] The review provided by the Treaties thus involves review by the Union courts of both the law and the facts. The review of legality provided for under Art. 263 TFEU, supplemented by the unlimited jurisdiction in respect of the amount of the fine, satisfies the requirements of the principle of effective judicial protection in Art. 47 of the Charter of Fundamental Rights of the European Union.[752]

(2) Merger control

(a) Decision based on prospective analysis

7.196 In contrast to the adoption of a decision finding an infringement on Arts 101 and/or 102 TFEU, which entails the examination of past events for which different items of evidence may be available, the adoption of a decision pursuant to Regulation No. 139/2004 concerning a concentration requires a prospective analysis of future events.[753] That prospective analysis consists of an examination of how the notified concentration might alter the factors determining the state of competition on a given market in order to establish whether it would give rise to a serious impediment to effective competition.[754]

(b) Review takes account of margin of discretion of Commission

7.197 The Commission has a margin of discretion with respect to assessments of an economic nature. The review by the Union courts of decisions in the field of merger control must take

---

[750] ECJ (judgment of 8 December 2011), Case C-272/09 P *KME Germany and Others v Commission*, not reported, para. 102; ECJ (judgment of 8 December 2011), Case C-389/10 P *KME Germany and Others v Commission*, not reported, para. 129; ECJ (judgment of 8 December 2011), Case C-386/10 P *Chalkor v Commission*, not reported, para. 62; ECJ (judgment of 6 November 2012), Case C-199/11 *Otis*, not reported, para. 59.

[751] ECJ (judgment of 8 December 2011), Case C-272/09 P *KME Germany and Others v Commission*, not reported, para. 103; ECJ (judgment of 8 December 2011), Case C-389/10 P *KME Germany and Others v Commission*, not reported, para. 130. The exercise of unlimited jurisdiction does not amount to a review of the Court's own motion. The proceedings before the Union courts are indeed *inter partes*.

[752] ECJ (judgment of 8 December 2011), Case C-272/09 P *KME Germany and Others v Commission*, not reported, para. 106; ECJ (judgment of 8 December 2011), Case C-389/10 P *KME Germany and Others v Commission*, not reported, para. 133; ECJ (judgment of 6 November 2012), Case C-199/11 *Otis*, not reported, paras 62–63.

[753] ECJ, Case C-12/03 P *Commission v Tetra Laval* [2005] E.C.R. I-987, para. 42; EGC, Case T-342/07 *Ryanair v Commission* [2010] E.C.R. II-3457, para. 27.

[754] ECJ, Case C-12/03 P *Commission v Tetra Laval* [2005] E.C.R. I-987, para. 43; EGC, Case T-342/07 *Ryanair v Commission* [2010] E.C.R. II-3457, para. 27. Where commitments have been validly proposed by the parties to the concentration during the administrative procedure in order to obtain a decision that the concentration is compatible with the internal market, the Commission is required to examine the concentration as modified by those commitments. It is then for the Commission to demonstrate that those commitments do not render the concentration, as modified by the commitments, compatible with the internal market (CFI, Case T-87/05 *EDP v Commission* [2005] E.C.R. II-3745, paras 63–65; EGC, Case T-342/07 *Ryanair v Commission* [2010] E.C.R. II-3457, para. 28).

account of that margin of discretion.[755] It follows that the review by the Union courts of a Commission decision relating to concentrations is confined to ascertaining that the facts have been accurately stated and that there has been no manifest error of assessment.[756] That does not mean, however, that the Union courts must refrain from reviewing the Commission's interpretation of information of an economic nature. Not only must they verify, in particular, whether the evidence relied on is factually accurate, reliable, and consistent, but also whether that evidence contains all the information which must be taken into account in order to assess a complex situation and whether it is capable of substantiating the conclusions drawn from it.[757] The evidence relied upon by the Commission to find that a concentration is (in)compatible with the internal market must indeed be convincing.[758]

(c) Observance of procedural guarantees

In addition, according to settled case-law, where the institutions have a power of appraisal, **7.198** respect for the rights guaranteed by the Union legal order in administrative procedures is of even more fundamental importance. Those guarantees include, in particular, the duty of the Commission to examine carefully and impartially all the relevant aspects of the individual case, the right of the person concerned to make his views known, and also his right to have an adequately reasoned decision.[759]

(d) Review of compliance with Commission Guidelines and Notices

The Commission is bound by guidelines and notices which it issues in the area of super- **7.199** vision of concentrations, provided they do not depart from the rules in the Treaties and from Regulation No. 139/2004.[760] The Union courts will examine whether the Commission decision complies with such guidelines and notices.

(e) Lawfulness assessed on the basis of fact and law existing at time of notification

The appraisal by the Commission of the compatibility of a concentration with the internal **7.200** market must be carried out solely on the basis of matters of fact and law existing at the time of

---

[755] ECJ, Joined Cases C-68/94 and C-30/95 *France and Others v Commission ('Kali & Salz')* [1998] E.C.R. I-1375, paras 223–224; ECJ, Case C-12/03 P *Commission v Tetra Laval* [2005] E.C.R. I-987, para. 38; ECJ, Case C-202/06 P *Cementbouw Handel & Industrie v Commission* [2007] E.C.R. I-12129, para. 53; CFI, Case T-151/05 *NVV and Others v Commission* [2009] E.C.R. II-1219, para. 53; EGC, Case T-342/07 *Ryanair v Commission* [2010] E.C.R. II-3457, para. 29; EGC, Case T-279/04 *Éditions Odile Jacob v Commission* [2010] E.C.R. II-185*, Summ. pub., para. 248.

[756] ECJ, Joined Cases C-68/94 and C-30/95 *France and Others v Commission ('Kali & Salz')* [1998] E.C.R. I-1375, paras 223–224; ECJ, Case C-413/06 P *Bertelsmann and Sony Corporation of America v Impala* [2008] E.C.R. I-4951, para. 144; ECJ, Case C-12/03 P *Commission v Tetra Laval* [2005] E.C.R. I-987, para. 38.

[757] ECJ, Case C-12/03 P *Commission v Tetra Laval* [2005] E.C.R. I-987, para. 29; Case C-413/03 P *Bertelsmann and Sony Corporation of America v Impala* [2008] E.C.R. I-4951, para. 69; CFI, Case T-151/05 *NVV and Others v Commission* [2009] E.C.R. II-1219, para 54; EGC, Case T-342/07 *Ryanair v Commission* [2010] E.C.R. II-3457, para. 30; EGC, Case T-279/04 *Éditions Odile Jacob v Commission* [2010] E.C.R. II-185*, Summ. pub., para. 249.

[758] That evidence was held not to be convincing and, consequently, the contested act was annulled in CFI, Case T-342/99 *Airtours v Commission* [2002] E.C.R. II-2585, paras 63, 294–295.

[759] ECJ, C-269/90 *Technische Universität München* [1991] E.C.R. I-5469, para. 14; Case T-151/05 *NVV and Others v Commission* [2009] E.C.R. II-1219, para. 163; CFI, Case T-342/07 *Ryanair v Commission* [2010] E.C.R. II-3457, para. 31.

[760] CFI, Case T-114/02 *BaByliss v Commission* [2003] E.C.R. II-1279, para. 143; CFI, Case T-119/02 *Royal Philips Electronics v Commission* [2003] E.C.R. II-1433, para. 242; CFI, Case T-282/06 *Sun Chemical Group and Others v Commission* [2007] E.C.R. II-2149, para. 55.

notification of that transaction, and not on the basis of hypothetical factors, the economic implications of which cannot be assessed at the time when the decision is adopted.[761]

(3) State aid cases

(a) Legal characterization of measure as aid

7.201 State aid, as defined in the Treaties, is a legal concept which must be interpreted on the basis of objective factors. For that reason, the Union courts must in principle, having regard both to the specific features of the case before them and to the technical or complex nature of the Commission's assessments, carry out a comprehensive review as to whether a measure falls within the scope of Art. 107(1) TFEU.[762]

The General Court will thus comprehensively review whether the alleged aid measure is selective or whether it is financed through State resources, since these issues do not involve complex economic assessments. The question whether the measure confers an advantage on its recipient may, on the other hand, involve complex economic assessments. For instance, this will be the case when the Commission examines whether a particular measure satisfies the 'private investor test', or in other words whether a public authority acted in the same way as a private investor would have done.[763] The General Court's review of such assessments is limited and confined to verifying whether the rules on procedure and on the statement of reasons have been complied with, whether the facts have been accurately stated and whether there has been any manifest error of assessment or misuse of powers.[764]

However, that does not mean that the Union judicature will refrain from reviewing the Commission's interpretation of information of an economic nature.[765] According to the

---

[761] CFI, Case T-2/93 *Air France v Commission* [1994] E.C.R. II-323, para. 70; CFI, Case T-374/00 *Verband der freien Rohrwerke and Others v Commission* [2003] E.C.R. II-2275, para 170; EGC, Case T-279/04 *Éditions Jacob v Commission* [2010] E.C.R. II-185*, Summ. pub., para. 338.

[762] ECJ, Case C-83/98 P *France v Ladbroke Racing and Commission* [2000] E.C.R. I-3271, para. 25; ECJ, Case C-487/06 P *British Aggregates* v *Commission* [2008] E.C.R. I-10515, paras 111–112; ECJ, Joined Cases C-71/09 P, C-73/09 P, and C-76/09 P *Comitato 'Venezia vuole vivere' v Commission* [2011] E.C.R. I-4727, para. 132; CFI, Case T-296/97 *Alitalia v Commission* [2000] E.C.R. II-3871, para. 95; EGC, Case T-244/08 *Konsum Nord v Commission* [2011] E.C.R. II-444*, Summ. pub., para. 37; EGC (judgment of 11 September 2012), Case T-565/08 *Corsica Ferries France v Commission*, not reported, para. 88.

[763] ECJ, Case C-525/04 P *Spain v Lenzing* [2007] E.C.R. I-9947, para. 59; EGC, Case T-11/07 *Frucona Košice v Commission* [2010] E.C.R. II-5453, para. 108; EGC, Case T-1/08 *Buczek Automotive v Commission* [2011] E.C.R. II-2107, para. 82.

[764] ECJ, Joined Cases C-501/06 P, C-513/06 P, C-515/06 P, and C-519/06 P *GlaxoSmithKline Services and Others v Commission and Others* [2009] E.C.R. I-9291, para. 163; ECJ, Case C-290/07 P *Commission v Scott* [2010] E.C.R. I-7763, para. 66; CFI, Case T-152/99 *HAMSA v Commission* [2002] E.C.R. II-3049, para. 127; CFI, Case T-196/04 *Ryanair v Commission* [2008] II-3643, para 41; EGC, Case T-11/07 *Frucona Košice v Commission* [2010] E.C.R. II-5453, para. 108; EGC, Case T-1/08 *Buczek Automotive v Commission* [2011] E.C.R. II-2107, para. 82; EGC (judgment of 3 July 2013), Case T-209/11 *MB System v Commission*, not reported, para. 25 (a plea which refers to an error of assessment and not to a manifest error of assessment will be admissible; the Court will, however, only examine whether the Commission made a manifest error). It should be stressed that the Commission bears the burden to prove that a measure constitutes state aid and therefore does not satisfy the private investor test: see in this respect, ECJ (judgment of 21 March 2013), Case C-405/11 P *Commission v Buczek Automotive*, not reported, paras 27–36.

[765] ECJ, Case C-525/04 P *Spain v Lenzing* [2007] E.C.R. I-9947, para. 56, in which the ECJ refers to ECJ, Case C-12/03 P *Commission v Tetra Laval* [2005] E.C.R. I-987, para. 39; EGC, Case T-11/07 *Frucona Košice v Commission* [2010] E.C.R. II-5453, para. 109. In order to establish that the Commission committed a manifest error in assessing the facts such as to justify the annulment of the contested decision, the evidence adduced by the applicant must be sufficient to make the factual assessments used in the decision at issue

case-law, not only must the Union judicature verify whether the evidence relied on is factually accurate, reliable, and consistent, but also whether that evidence contains all the information which must be taken into account in order to assess a complex situation and whether it is capable of substantiating the conclusions drawn from it.[766] When conducting such a review, the Union judicature must not substitute its own economic assessment for that of the Commission.[767] The case-law thus draws a distinction between what the Union courts are prohibited from doing, namely substituting their own economic assessment for that of the institutions, and what they are allowed to do, that is to say, checking the legal classification that the institutions have placed on economic factors. The issue is therefore the dichotomy between, first, the assessment of facts of an economic nature carried out by the institutions, the judicial review of which precludes a new independent assessment by the Union courts and must be confined to establishing a manifest error and, second, the legal classification of the facts which is subject, as a point of law, to full review by the Union courts.[768]

As in all cases in which the Union institution has a wide discretion, the review of observance of certain procedural guarantees is of fundamental importance. Those guarantees include the obligation for the competent institution to examine carefully and impartially all the relevant elements of the individual case and to give an adequate statement of the reasons for its decision.[769]

(b) Assessment of compatibility of aid measure

It is settled case-law that, in the application of Art. 107(3) TFEU, the Commission has a wide discretion, the exercise of which involves complex economic and social assessments **7.202**

---

implausible (EGC (judgment of 27 February 2013), Case T-387/11 *Nitrogénmüvek Vegyipari v Commission*, not reported, para. 25, and case-law cited).

[766] ECJ, Case C-290/07 P *Commission v Scott* [2010] E.C.R. I-7763, para. 65. See also ECJ, Case C-525/04 P *Spain v Lenzing* [2007] E.C.R. I-9947, para. 57, in which the ECJ refers to ECJ, Case 98/78 *Racke* [1979] E.C.R. 69, para. 5; ECJ, Case C-16/90 *Nölle* [1991] E.C.R. I-5163, para. 12; ECJ, Case C-12/03 P *Commission v Tetra Laval* [2005] E.C.R. I-987, para. 39; and ECJ, Case C-326/05 P *Industrias Químicas del Vallés v Commission* [2007] E.C.R. I-6557, paras 75–77 In CFI, Case T-36/99 *Lenzing v Commission* [2004] E.C.R. II-3597, paras 127–162, the Commission's assessment was held not to satisfy these criteria. See also EGC, Case T-1/08 *Buczek Automotive v Commission* [2011] E.C.R. II-2107, paras 82–97; EGC, Case T-244/08 *Konsum Nord v Commission* [2011] E.C.R. II-444*, Summ. pub., paras 38 and 40–76.

[767] ECJ, Case C-323/00 P *DSG Dradenauer Stahlgesellschaft v Commission* [2002] E.C.R. I-3919, para. 43; ECJ, Case C-525/04 P *Spain v Lenzing* [2007] E.C.R. I-9947, para. 57; ECJ, Case C-290/07 P *Commission v Scott* [2010] E.C.R. I-7763, para. 66; CFI, Case T-152/99 *HAMSA v Commission* [2002] E.C.R. II-3049, para. 127; CFI, Case T-196/04 *Ryanair v Commission* [2008] II-3643, para 41; EGC, Case T-11/07 *Frucona Košice v Commission* [2010] E.C.R. II-5453, para. 110; EGC, Case T-1/08 *Buczek Automotive v Commission* [2011] E.C.R. II-2107, para. 82; EGC, Case T-244/08 *Konsum Nord v Commission* [2011] E.C.R. II-444*, Summ. pub., para. 38.

[768] See in this respect also the Opinion of Advocate-General P. Mengozzi of 14 April 2011 in Joined Cases C-191/09 P and C-200/09 P *Council and Commission v Interpipe Niko Tube and Interpipe NTRP*, not reported, point 107. See also ECJ (judgment of 24 January 2013), Case C-73/11 P *Frucona Košice v Commission*, not reported, paras 89–91, in which the ECJ set aside the judgment of the EGC, since the latter court had filled a gap in the reasoning in the Commission decision, by means of its own reasoning.

[769] ECJ, Case C-525/04 P *Spain v Lenzing* [2007] E.C.R. I-9947, para. 58. See also Case C-269/90 *Technische Universität München* [1991] E.C.R. I-5469, para. 14, and Joined Cases C-258/90 and C-259/90 *Pesquerias De Bermeo and Naviera Laida v Commission* [1992] E.C.R. I-2901, para. 26; EGC, Case T-11/07 *Frucona Košice v Commission* [2010] E.C.R. II-5453, para. 111. With respect to the obligation to give an adequate statement of the reasons, see ECJ, Case C-367/95 P *Commission v Sytraval and Brink's France* [1998] E.C.R. I-1719, para. 63; ECJ, Case C-487/06 P *British Aggregates v Commission* [2008] E.C.R. I-10515, paras 172–179.

which must be made in an EU context. Judicial review of the manner in which that discretion is exercised is restricted.[770] It is indeed confined to establishing that the rules of procedure and the rules relating to the duty to give reasons have been complied with and to verifying the accuracy of the facts relied on and that there has been no error of law, manifest error of assessment in regard to the facts or misuse of powers.[771] In particular, it is not for the Union judicature to substitute its own economic assessment for that of the author of the decision.[772]

However, when the Commission, after a preliminary examination, finds that no doubts are raised as to the compatibility with the internal market of a notified measure and decides that the measure is compatible with the internal market in a 'decision not to raise objections' pursuant to Art. 4(3) of Regulation No. 659/1999, the review by the Union courts of the assessment of the inexistence of doubts will not be restricted to the examination whether the Commission made a manifest error in that regard.[773]

(c) Review of compliance with Commission Guidelines

7.203 The Commission has a wide discretion to assess the compatibility of an aid measure with the internal market under Art. 107(3) TFEU. In order to exercise that discretion, it may adopt rules of guidance, so long as those rules do not depart from the provisions of the Treaties. Where such guidelines have been adopted, the Commission is bound by

---

[770] ECJ, Case 310/85 *Deufil v Commission* [1987] E.C.R. 901, para. 18; ECJ, Case C-225/91 *Matra v Commission* [1993] E.C.R. I-3203, paras 24–25; ECJ, Case C-372/97 *Italy v Commission* [2004] E.C.R. I-3679, para. 83; CFI, Case T-349/03 *Corsica Ferries v Commission* [2005] E.C.R. II-2197, paras 137–138; EGC, Joined Cases T-267/08 and T-279/08 *Région Nord-Pas-de-Calais v Commission* [2011] E.C.R. II-1999, para. 129; EGC (judgment of 14 February 2012), Joined Cases T-115/09 and T-116/09 *Electrolux and Whirlpool v Commission*, not reported, para. 37; EGC (judgment of 20 March 2013), Case T-92/11 *Andersen v Commission*, not reported, para. 58. However, it should be stressed that if, after the preliminary examination, the Commission finds that the notified measure raises doubts as to its compatibility with the internal market, it is required to adopt, on the basis of Art. 4(4) of Regulation No. 659/1999, a decision to open the formal investigation procedure provided for under Art.108(2) TFEU and Art. 6(1) of the said regulation. Although it has no discretion in relation to the decision to initiate the formal investigation procedure, where it finds that such doubts exist, the Commission nevertheless enjoys a certain margin of discretion in identifying and evaluating the circumstances of the case in order to determine whether or not they present doubts. The applicant bears the burden of proving the existence of doubts and may discharge that burden of proof by reference to a body of consistent evidence, concerning, first, the circumstances and the length of the preliminary examination procedure and, second, the content of the contested decision: see EGC (judgment of 28 March 2012), Case T-123/09 *Ryanair v Commission*, not reported, paras 77–78 (and case-law cited).

[771] ECJ, Case C-409/00 *Spain v Commission* [2003] E.C.R. I-1487, para. 93; ECJ, Case C-372/97 *Italy v Commission* [2004] E.C.R. I-3679, para. 83; CFI, Case T-149/95 *Ducros v Commission* [1997] E.C.R. II-2031, para. 63; CFI, Case T-123/97 *Salomon v Commission* [1999] E.C.R. II-2925, para. 47; CFI, Case T-110/97 *Kneissl Dachstein v Commission* [1999] E.C.R. II-2881, para. 46; CFI, Case T-349/03 *Corsica Ferries v Commission* [2005] E.C.R. II-2197, para. 138; EGC (judgment of 14 February 2012), Joined Cases T-115/09 and T-116/09 *Electrolux and Whirlpool v Commission*, not reported, para. 40.

[772] CFI, Joined Cases T-371/94 and T-394/94 *British Airways and Others v Commission* [1998] E.C.R. II-2405, para. 79; CFI, Case T-349/03 *Corsica Ferries v Commission* [2005] E.C.R. II-2197, para. 138; EGC (judgment of 14 February 2012), Joined Cases T-115/09 and T-116/09 *Electrolux and Whirlpool v Commission*, not reported, para. 40. It is thus not for the Union judicature to replace the Commission by carrying out in its stead an examination it never carried out and drawing the conclusions which it would have drawn (CFI, Case T-266/02 *Deutsche Post v Commission* [2008] E.C.R. II-1233, para. 95; EGC (judgment of 14 February 2012), Joined Cases T-115/09 and T-116/09 *Electrolux and Whirlpool v Commission*, not reported, para. 42; EGC (judgment of 28 February 2012), Case T-282/08 *Grazer Wechselseitige Versicherung v Commission*, not reported, para. 48).

[773] EGC (judgment of 7 November 2012), Case T-137/10 *CBI v Commission*, not reported, paras 76–77 (and case-law cited therein).

them.[774] The General Court will thus verify whether the Commission has observed such guidelines in the contested decision.[775]

(d) *Lawfulness assessed in light of information available when the decision was adopted*

The lawfulness of a decision concerning State aid is to be assessed in the light of the **7.204** information available to the Commission when the decision was adopted.[776] An applicant cannot therefore rely, before the Union judicature, on matters of fact which were not put forward in the course of the pre-litigation procedure laid down in Art. 108 TFEU.[777]

(4) Anti-dumping cases

(a) *Limited review of complex economic situations*

In the sphere of measures to protect trade, the Union institutions enjoy a wide discretion by **7.205** reason of the complexity of the economic, political, and legal situations which they have to examine.[778] The determination of normal value, the choice between the different methods of calculating the dumping margin, and the existence of harm to the EU industry require an appraisal of complex economic situations, and the judicial review of such appraisals must therefore be limited to establishing whether the relevant procedural rules have been complied with, whether the facts on which the contested choice is based have been accurately stated, and whether there has been a manifest error of assessment of the facts

---

[774] Guidelines in connection with the assessment of State aid: see CFI, Case T-380/94 *AIUFFASS and AKT v Commission* [1996] E.C.R. II-2169, para. 57; CFI, Case T-214/95 *Vlaams Gewest v Commission* [1998] E.C.R. II-717, para. 89; CFI, Case T-27/02 *Kronofrance v Commission* [2004] E.C.R. II-4177, para. 79.

[775] CFI, Case T-35/99 *Keller and Keller Meccanica v Commission* [2002] E.C.R. II-261, para. 77; CFI, Case T-27/02 *Kronofrance v Commission* [2004] E.C.R. II-4177, para. 79; CFI, Case T-171/02 *Regione autonoma della Sardegna v Commission* [2005] E.C.R. II-2123, paras 95–97; CFI, Case T-349/03 *Corsica Ferries v Commission* [2005] E.C.R. II-2197, para. 141; EGC, Joined Cases T-267/08 and T-279/08 *Région Nord-Pas-de-Calais v Commission* [2011] E.C.R. II-1999, paras 129–131; EGC (judgment of 14 February 2012), Joined Cases T-115/09 and T-116/09 *Electrolux and Whirlpool v Commission*, not reported, para. 41.

[776] ECJ, Case 234/84 *Belgium v Commission* [1986] E.C.R. 2263, para. 16; ECJ, Case C-241/94 *France v Commission* [1996] E.C.R. I-4551, para. 33; ECJ, Case C-276/02 *Spain v Commission* [2004] E.C.R. I-8091, para. 31; ECJ, Case C-390/06 *Nuova Agricast* [2008] E.C.R. I-2577, para. 54; ECJ, Case C-290/07 P *Commission v Scott* [2010] E.C.R. I-7763, para 91; CFI, Joined Cases T-254/00, T-270/00 and T-277/00 *Hotel Cipriani and Others v Commission* E.C.R. [2008] II-3269, para. 238; EGC, Case T-11/07 *Frucona Košice v Commission* [2010] E.C.R. II-5453, para. 49; EGC (judgment of 28 February 2012), Case T-282/08 *Grazer Wechselseitige Versicherung v Commission*, not reported, para. 49.

[777] ECJ, Joined Cases C-278/92 to C-280/92 *Spain v Commission* [1994] E.C.R. I-4103, para. 31; ECJ, Case C-382/99 *Netherlands v Commission* [2002] E.C.R. I-5163, paras 49 and 76; CFI, Case T-109/01 *Fleuren Compost v Commission* [2004] E.C.R. II-127, para. 51; CFI, Joined Cases T-254/00, T-270/00 and T-277/00 *Hotel Cipriani and Others v Commission* E.C.R. [2008] II-3269, para. 326; EGC, Case T-11/07 *Frucona Košice v Commission* [2010] E.C.R. II-5453, para. 50.

[778] ECJ, Case C-351/04 *Ikea Wholesale* [2007] E.C.R. I-7723, para. 40; ECJ, Case C-535/06 P *Moser Baer India v Council* [2009] E.C.R. I-7051, para 85; ECJ (judgment of 16 February 2012), Joined Cases C-191/09 P and C-200/09 P *Council and Commission v Interpipe Niko Tube and Interpipe NTRP*, not reported, para. 63; CFI, Case T-162/94 *NMB France and Others v Commission* [1996] E.C.R. II-427, para. 72; CFI, Case T-97/95 *Sinochem v Council* [1998] E.C.R. II-85, para. 51; CFI, Case T-118/96 *Thai Bicycle v Council* [1998] E.C.R. II-2991, para. 32; CFI, Case T-340/99 *Arne Mathisen v Council* [2002] E.C.R. II-2905, para. 53; CFI, Case T-35/01 *Shanghai Teraoka Electronic v Council* [2004] E.C.R. II-3663, para. 48; CFI, Case T-249/06 *Interpipe Niko Tube and Interpipe NTRP v Council* [2009] E.C.R. II-383, para. 38; CFI, Case T-299/05 *Shanghai Excell M&E Enterprise and Shanghai Adeptech Precision v Council* [2009] E.C.R. II-565, para. 79; EGC, Case T-369/08 *EWRIA and Others v Commission* [2010] E.C.R. II-6283, para. 77; EGC (judgment of 11 July 2013), Case T-459/07 *Hangzhou Duralamp Electronics v Council*, not reported, para. 71.

or a misuse of power.[779] The same applies to factual situations of a legal and political nature in the country concerned which the institutions must assess in order to determine whether an exporter operates in market conditions without significant State interference and can, accordingly, be granted market economy status.[780]

(b) Obligation to carefully and impartially examine all the relevant aspects
of the case and to state reasons

7.206 Whilst in the area of commercial defence measures, and anti-dumping measures in particular, the Union courts cannot intervene in the assessment reserved for the Union institutions, it is nevertheless for them to satisfy themselves that the institution concerned took account of all the relevant circumstances and appraised the facts of the matter with all due care, so that the institution's findings, for example with respect to normal value and injury, may be regarded as having been determined in a reasonable manner.[781] Indeed, given the wide discretion the Union institutions enjoy in the sphere of commercial defence measures, respect of the rights guaranteed by the Union legal order in administrative procedures is of a fundamental importance. Those guarantees include, in particular, the duty of the competent institution to examine carefully and impartially all the relevant aspects of the individual case[782] and to give an adequate statement of reasons.[783]

---

[779] ECJ, Case 240/84 *NTN Toyo Bearing v Council* [1987] E.C.R. 1809, para. 19; ECJ, Case 187/85 *Fediol v Commission* [1988] E.C.R. 4155, para. 6; ECJ, Case C-156/87 *Gestetner Holdings v Council and Commission* [1990] E.C.R. I-781, para. 63; ECJ, Case C-174/87 *Ricoh v Council* [1992] E.C.R. I-1335, para. 68; ECJ, Case C-351/04 *Ikea Wholesale* [2007] E.C.R. I-7723, para. 41; ECJ, Case C-535/06 P *Moser Baer India v Council* [2009] E.C.R. I-7051, para 86; CFI, Case T-118/96 *Thai Bicycle v Council* [1998] II-2991, para. 33; CFI, Case T-35/01 *Shanghai Teraoka Electronic v Council* [2004] E.C.R. II-3663, para. 49; CFI, Case T-299/05 *Shanghai Excell M&E Enterprise and Shanghai Adeptech Precision v Council* [2009] E.C.R. II-565, para. 80; EGC (judgment of 11 July 2013), Case T-459/07 *Hangzhou Duralamp Electronics v Council*, not reported, para 71. A manifest error of assessment was found in EGC, Case T-107/08 *Transnational Company 'Kazchrome' and ENRC Marketing v Council and Commission* [2011] E.C.R. II-8051, para. 69; an error of fact led to the annulment of the anti-dumping regulation in CFI, Case T-107/04 *Aluminium Silicon Mill Products v Council* [2007] E.C.R. II-669, para. 66: as a result of the error of fact, the Council had based its finding of the existence of injury on a manifestly incorrect ground.

[780] CFI, Case T-155/94 *Climax Paper v Council* [1996] E.C.R. II-873, para. 98; CFI, Case T-35/01 *Shanghai Teraoka Electronic v Council* [2004] E.C.R. II-3663, paras 48–49; CFI, Case T-299/05 *Shanghai Excell M&E Enterprise and Shanghai Adeptech Precision v Council* [2009] E.C.R. II-565, para. 81. See in this respect also Opinion of Advocate-General P. Mengozzi in Joined Cases C-191/09 P and C-200/09 P *Council and Commission v Interpipe Niko Tube and Interpipe NTRP*, not reported, points 90–126.

[781] CFI, Case T-48/96 *Acme v Council* [1999] E.C.R. II-3089, para. 39; 64; CFI, Case T-249/06 *Interpipe Niko Tube and Interpipe NTRP v Council* [2009] E.C.R. II-383, para. 41; EGC, Case T-199/04 *Gul Ahmed Textile Mills v Council* [2011] E.C.R. II-321*, Summ. pub., paras 60 and 85.

[782] ECJ, Case C-269/90 *Technische Universität München* [1991] E.C.R. I-5469, para. 14; CFI, Case T-413/03 *Shandong Reipu Biochemicals v Council* [2006] E.C.R. II-2243, para. 63; CFI, Case T-249/06 *Interpipe Niko Tube and Interpipe NTRP v Council* [2009] E.C.R. II-383, para. 40.

[783] The statement of reasons required by Art. 296 TFEU must show clearly and unequivocally the reasoning of the Union authority which adopted the contested measure, so as to inform the persons concerned of the justification for the measure adopted and thus to enable them to defend their rights and the Union judicature to exercise its powers of review. On the other hand, in the statement of reasons for the regulation, the Council is not required to reply to all the points of fact and law raised by the persons concerned during the administrative procedure. Nor is there a requirement that the statement of reasons give details of all relevant factual or legal aspects, the question whether it fulfils the applicable requirements having to be assessed with particular regard to the context of the act and to all the legal rules governing the matter in question (see CFI, Case T-48/96 *Acme Industry v Council* [1999] E.C.R. II-3089, para. 141; CFI, Case T-164/94 *Ferchimex v Commission* [1995] E.C.R. II-2681, para. 118; CFI, Case T-249/06 *Interpipe Niko Tube and Interpipe NTRP v Council* [2009] E.C.R. II-383, para. 65). The Council is thus not required to reply, in the statement of reasons for the anti-dumping regulation, to all the points of fact and law raised by the undertakings concerned during

D. Time limits

(1) Time limit

Under the sixth paragraph of Art. 263 TFEU, annulment proceedings 'shall be instituted   **7.207** within two months of the publication of the measure, or its notification to the plaintiff, or, in the absence thereof, of the day on which it came to the knowledge of the latter, as the case may be'.[784]

It is settled case-law that the time limit prescribed for bringing actions under Art. 263 TFEU is a matter of public policy and not subject to the discretion of the parties or the Union courts, since it was established in order to ensure that legal positions are clear and certain and to avoid any discrimination or arbitrary treatment in the administration of justice.[785] The Union courts will therefore consider of their own motion whether the time limit for bringing an action for annulment has been respected.[786]

---

the administrative procedure (see CFI, Case T-249/06 *Interpipe Niko Tube and Interpipe NTRP v Council* [2009] E.C.R. II-383, para. 154). But see Case T-122/09 *Zhejiang Xinshiji Foods Co. and Hubei Zinshiji Foods v Council* [2011] E.C.R. II-22*, Summ. pub., paras 75–93, in which an infringement of the rights of the defence and the duty to state reasons was upheld.

[784] For the method of calculating time limits in general, see paras 23.28–23.38. This section deals only with factors determining the onset of the period for bringing an action for annulment. Some examples of applications lodged out of time may be found in ECJ (order of 11 January 2000), Case C-295/98 *Italy v Commission* [2000] E.C.R. I-111, paras 3–6 (concerning notification); EGC (order of 22 September 2011), Case T-374/11 *Libyan Investment Authority and Others v Council*, not reported, paras 11–19 (concerning publication); EGC (order of 22 September 2011), Case T-375/11 *Houej v Council*, not reported, paras 11–19 (concerning publication); EGC (order of 22 September 2011), Case T-376/11 *CBL v Council*, not reported, paras 11–19 (concerning publication); EGC (order of 22 September 2011), Case T-377/11 *FDES v Council*, not reported, paras 12–20 (concerning publication); EGC, Case T-549/08 *Luxembourg v Commission* [2010] E.C.R. II-2477, paras 35–37 (concerning notification; out of time for one measure but not for another).

[785] ECJ, Case 152/85 *Misset v Council* [1987] E.C.R. 223, para. 11; ECJ, Case C-246/95 *Coen* [1997] E.C.R. I-403, para. 21; ECJ (order of 8 December 2005), Case C-210/05 P *Campailla v Commission*, not reported, para. 28; ECJ (order of 17 December 2010), Case C-513/10 P *Platis v Council and Greece* [2010] E.C.R. I-176*, Summ. pub., para. 9; CFI, Joined Cases T-121/96 and T-151/96 *Mutual Aid Administration Services v Commission* [1997] E.C.R. II-1355, paras 38–39; CFI (order of 1 December 2008), Case T-220/08 *İşçi Partisi (Turkish Labour Party) v Council and Commission*, not reported, para. 9; CFI, Case T-257/04 *Poland v Commission* [2009] E.C.R. II-1545, para. 33 (and citations therein); EGC (order of 3 March 2011), Case T-79/11 *Ing. Nando Groppo and Others v European Parliament and Council*, not reported, para. 6; EGC (order of 13 July 2011), Case T-352/11 *N'Guessan v Council* [2011] E.C.R. II-232*, Summ. pub., para. 12. On the basis of these precepts, the rules on time limits do not permit derogations based on the fact that fundamental rights or other general principles of Union law are at stake: see ECJ, Case C-229/05 P *PKK and KNK v Council* [2007] E.C.R. I-439, para. 101; ECJ (order of 16 November 2010), Case C-73/10 P *Internationale Fruchtimport Gesellschaft Weichert v Commmission* [2010] E.C.R. I-11535, paras 48–59. Likewise, the right to effective judicial protection is in no way undermined by the strict application of Union rules concerning procedural time limits in the context of annulment proceeding: see ECJ (order of 22 October 2010), Case C-266/10 P *Seacid v European Parliament and Council* [2010] E.C.R. I-133*, Summ. pub., para. 30 (and citations therein).

[786] See, e.g. ECJ (order of 9 July 2009), Case C-498/08 P *Fornaci Laterizi Danesi v Commission* [2009] E.C.R. I-122*, Summ. pub., para. 19 (and citations therein); ECJ (order of 22 October 2010), Case C-266/10 P *Seacid v European Parliament and Council* [2010] E.C.R. I-133*, Summ. pub., para. 21; CFI, Joined Cases T-142/01 and T-283/01 *OPTUC v Commission* [2004] E.C.R. II-329, para. 30; CFI, Case T-257/04 *Poland v Commission* [2009] E.C.R. II-1545, para. 33; EGC, Case T-407/07 *CMB and Christof v Commission* [2011] E.C.R. II-286*, Summ. pub., para. 74. See also CFI (order of 29 January 2007), Case T-240/06 *Stewart-Smith v European Parliament*, not reported, para. 1; CFI (order of 1 December 2008), Case T-220/08 *İşçi Partisi (Turkish Labour Party) v Council and Commission*, not reported, para. 9; CFI (order of 19 June 2008), Case T-158/08

(2) Burden of proof

7.208 The party alleging that the time limit for bringing proceedings has run out has to prove the date on which time started running.[787] When the time limit for instituting proceedings is exceeded, the applicant will bear the burden of proving the existence of unforeseeable circumstances, *force majeure*, or excusable error.[788] However, in order for legal certainty not to suffer too much, these exceptions are strictly interpreted.[789]

Commune de Ne and Others v Commission, not reported, para. 7; CFI (order of 21 July 2008), Case T-227/08 *Brehm v Commission*, not reported, para. 7; CFI (order of 24 September 2009), Case T-110/09 *Bayramoglu v Council and European Parliament*, not reported, para. 7; EGC (order of 16 March 2010), Case T-530/09 *Seacid v European Parliament and Council*, not reported, para. 6; EGC (order of 3 March 2011), Case T-79/11 *Ing. Nando Groppo and Others v European Parliament and Council*, not reported, para. 6; EGC (order of 13 July 2011), Case T-352/11 *N'Guessan v Council* [2011] E.C.R. II-232*, Summ. pub., para. 12. See also para. 7.217.

[787] This holds generally, whether the time limit is calculated from the date of publication of the act in the *Official Journal*, the date of notification, or the date on which the applicant had knowledge of the contested act. See, e.g. ECJ, Case C-521/06 P *Athinaiki Techniki v Commission* [2008] E.C.R. I-5829, paras 70–78; CFI, Joined Cases T-70/92 and T-71/92 *Florimex and VGB v Commission* [1997] E.C.R. II-693, para. 74; CFI (order of 13 April 2000), Case T-263/97 *GAL Penisola Sorrentina v Commission* [2000] E.C.R. II-2041, paras 47–48; CFI, Case T-411/06 *Sogelma v EAR* [2008] E.C.R. II-2771, para. 76/paras 76–81; CFI, Case T-185/05 *Italy v Commission* [2008] E.C.R. II-3207, paras 70–82.

[788] As regards the concepts of unforeseeable circumstances and *force majeure*, the Court of Justice has pointed out that they contain both an objective element relating to abnormal circumstances unconnected with the person in question and a subjective element involving the obligation, on that person's part, to guard against the consequences of the abnormal event by taking appropriate steps without making unreasonable sacrifices. In particular, the person concerned must pay close attention to the course of the procedure set in motion and demonstrate diligence in order to comply with the prescribed time limits. See, e.g. ECJ, Case C-195/91 P *Bayer v Commission* [1994] E.C.R. I-5619, para. 32; ECJ (order of 8 November 2007), Case C-242/07 P *Belgium v Commission* [2007] E.C.R. I-9757, para. 17; ECJ, Case C-426/10 P *Bell & Ross v OHIM* [2011] E.C.R. I-8849, para. 48. As a consequence, the concept of *force majeure* has been held not to apply to a situation in which, objectively, a diligent and prudent person would have been able to take the necessary steps before the expiry of the period prescribed for instituting proceedings. See, e.g. CFI, Case T-125/06 *Centro Studi Antonio Manieri v Council* [2009] E.C.R. II-69, para. 28 (and citations therein). Similarly, the concept of excusable error justifying a derogation from Union rules on time limits for instituting proceedings can concern only exceptional circumstances in which, in particular, the conduct of the institution concerned has been, either alone or to a decisive extent, such as to give rise to a pardonable confusion in the mind of the party acting in good faith and displaying all the diligence required of a normally well-informed person. See, e.g. ECJ (order of 14 January 2010), Case C-112/09 P *SGAE v Commission* [2010] E.C.R. I-351, para. 20; ECJ (order of 16 November 2010), Case C-73/10 P *Internationale Fruchtimport Gesellschaft Weichert v Commmission* [2010] E.C.R. I-11535, para. 42; ECJ (judgment of 23 April 2013), Joined Cases C-478/11 to C-482/11 P *Laurent Gbagbo and Others*, not reported, paras 68–75; EGC (judgment of 18 June 2013), Case T-404/08 *Fluorsid and Minmet v Commission*, not reported, paras 60–61.

[789] See, e.g. ECJ, Case 284/82 *Busseni v Commission* [1984] E.C.R. 557, paras 11–12; ECJ, Case 224/83 *Ferriera Vittoria v Commission* [1984] E.C.R. 2349, para. 13; ECJ, Case 209/83 *Valsabbia v Commission* [1984] E.C.R. 3089, paras 21–22; ECJ, Case C-195/91 P *Bayer v Commission* [1994] E.C.R. I-5619, paras 30–34; ECJ (order of 8 November 2007), Case 242/07 P *Belgium v Commission* [2007] E.C.R. I-9757, paras 29–30; ECJ (order of 3 July 2008), Case C-84/08 P *Pitsiorlas v Council and ECB* [2008] E.C.R. I-104*, Summ. pub., paras 14–18; ECJ (order of 14 January 2010), Case C-112/09 P *SGAE v Commission* [2010] E.C.R. I-351, paras 19–30; ECJ (order of 16 November 2010), Case C-73/10 P *Internationale Fruchtimport Gesellschaft Weichert v Commmission* [2010] E.C.R. I-11535, paras 41–42; ECJ, Case C-426/10 P *Bell & Ross v OHIM* [2011] E.C.R. I-8849, paras 47–50; CFI, Joined Cases T-33/89 and T-74/89 *Blackman v European Parliament* [1993] E.C.R. II-249, paras 32–36; CFI, Case T-514/93 *Cobrecaf and Others v Commission* [1995] E.C.R. II-621, para. 40; EGC (order of 5 February 2010), Case T-319/09 *Pro humanum v Commission*, not reported, paras 11–13; EGC (order of 11 January 2012), Case T-301/11 *Ben Ali v Council*, not reported, paras 28–56; EGC (order of 1 April 2011), Case T-468/10 *Doherty v Commission* II-1497, paras 17–30; EGC (order of 29 November 2011), Case T-345/11 *ENISA v CEPD*, not reported, paras 19–24. Occasionally, however, there are situations in which such exceptional circumstances are found. See, e.g. CFI, Case T-125/06 *Centro Studi Antonio Manieri v Council* [2009] E.C.R. II-69, paras 23–30: the Court of First Instance found a

(3) Subsequent act repealing earlier contested act

Especially in the case of restrictive measures against individuals, there are situations in **7.209**
which the contested measure is repealed during the proceedings and thus applications for
the annulment against those subsequent measures are allowed (see further para. 7.11). In
principle, the time limit laid down in the sixth paragraph of Art. 263 TFEU applies both
where an action for annulment of an act is brought by means of an application and where it is
brought in the course of the proceedings by means of a request to adapt a claim for annulment
of an earlier act that has been repealed and replaced by the act in question. However, by way
of exception to that rule, that period is not applicable in proceedings in which, first, the act in
question and the measure which that act repeals and replaces have, with respect to the person
concerned, the same subject-matter, are essentially based on the same grounds, and have
essentially the same content, and therefore differ only by reason of their respective scopes of
application *ratione temporis*; and second, the request to adapt a claim is not based on any new
plea, fact, or evidence apart from the actual adoption of the act in question repealing and
replacing the earlier act. Since the subject-matter and context of the dispute as established by
the original action have not undergone any alteration except as for its temporal dimension,
legal certainty is not affected. This exception is also justified in light of the measures that a
Union institution, body, office, or agency is obliged to take under Art. 266 TFEU.[790]

(4) Publication

(a) *Effects of publication*

Under the third paragraph of Art. 297(1) TFEU and the second paragraph of Art. 297(2) **7.210**
TFEU, legislative acts and non-legislative acts adopted in the form of regulations and
directives addressed to all Member States, as well as decisions which do not specify to whom
they are addressed, must be published in the *Official Journal of the European Union*. Time
for bringing proceedings against such acts starts to run from the end of the fourteenth day
after their publication in the *Official Journal*.[791] There is a rebuttable presumption that the

---

case of *force majeure* under circumstances where the package containing the original signed application was
kept by the Luxembourg postal service for a period of 42 days, which was considered to constitute abnormal
circumstances unconnected with the applicant, which for its part demonstrated diligence in order to comply
with the prescribed time limit under the sixth para. of Art. 263 TFEU; EGC, Case T-407/07 *CMB and
Christof v Commission* [2011] E.C.R. II-286*, Summ. pub., paras 99–105: the General Court found a case of
excusable error under circumstances in which the author of the contested measure acted in such a way as to
give rise to a pardonable confusion in the mind of the applicants by including a provision in the tender file
setting out the appeals available to the unsuccessful candidates in an unclear way.

[790] EGC (judgment of 26 October 2012), Case T-53/12 *CF Sharp Shipping Agencies v Council*, not
reported, paras 26–30.

[791] ECJ Rules of Procedure, Art. 50; EGC Rules of Procedure, Art. 102(1). This rule applies to all Union
acts published in the *Official Journal of the European Union* and not only to those which enter into effect only
after publication therein: see CFI (order of 25 May 2004), Case T-264/03 *Schmoldt and Others v Commission*
[2004] E.C.R. II-1515, paras 51–62. However, the sixth para. of Art. 263 TFEU does not give any indication
as to the method of publication envisaged by that provision and does not restrict the publication within the
meaning of that provision to specified methods of publication. Publication within the meaning of that provision
cannot, therefore, consist of a publication in the *Official Journal of the European Union* only. If an act is published
by other means (such as on the website of a Union body, office, or agency), the 14-day extension of the period for
bringing the action also applies: see ECJ (judgment of 26 September 2013), Case C-625/11 P *PPG and SNF v
ECHA*, not reported, paras 30–37. An action against an act can, however, be brought prior to its publication if
the applicant has knowledge of the existence of such act at such an earlier date: ECJ (judgment of 26 September
2013), Case C-626/11 P *PPG and SNF v ECHA*, not reported, para. 41.

date of publication is the date borne by the issue of the *Official Journal* containing the contested act.[792] Since publication is necessary in order for such acts to enter into effect,[793] time for bringing proceedings cannot start to run until they have been published in the *Official Journal*.[794] It makes no difference if the applicant became aware of the content of such acts also in some other way.

The same is true of acts which do not have to be published in order to enter into force where there is a consistent practice of publishing them. In those circumstances, the applicant is entitled to see such an act published in the *Official Journal* and the starting point of the period for instituting proceedings is the date of publication, regardless of whether the applicant had earlier or later notice by some other means of the existence and content of the act in question.[795]

(b) Date of publication, if applicable, is in principle decisive

7.211 Where the applicant is not the addressee of the contested act which, pursuant to the third paragraph of Art. 297(2) TFEU, should receive formal notification of such act, the date of publication, if there is one, is the decisive criterion for determining the starting point of the period prescribed for initiating annulment proceedings under the sixth paragraph of Art. 263 TFEU.[796] Consequently, an applicant cannot invoke the date on which he gained

---

[792] ECJ, Case 98/78 *Racke* [1979] E.C.R. 69, paras 15–17; CFI, Case T-115/94 *Opel Austria v Council* [1997] E.C.R. II-39, para. 127.

[793] ECJ, Case 185/73 *König* [1974] E.C.R. 607, para. 6.

[794] Cf. Opinion of Advocate-General K. Roemer in ECJ, Joined Cases 10/68 and 18/68 '*Eridania' Zuccherifici Nazionali and Others v Commission* [1969] E.C.R. 459, at 488–9.

[795] See, e.g. ECJ, Case C-122/95 *Germany v Council* [1998] E.C.R. I-973, paras 34–39, in which the Court of Justice held that there was a consistent practice for Council decisions embodying the conclusion of international agreements binding the Union to be published in the *Official Journal*; compare ECJ, Case C-309/95 *Commission v Council* [1998] E.C.R. I-655 for acts which are not published. See also CFI, Case T-110/97 *Kneissl Dachstein v Commission* [1999] E.C.R. II-2881, paras 40–44; CFI, Case T-123/97 *Salomon v Commission* [1999] E.C.R. II-2925, paras 40–45, in which the Court of First Instance held that the Commission has committed itself to publishing the complete text of decisions granting conditional authorization for State aid taken at the end of the procedure provided for in Art. 108(2) TFEU and that, for an undertaking to which the relevant decision was not notified, the period for commencing proceedings began to run from the day on which it was published in the *Official Journal*. For annulment proceedings against measures taken in the field of State aid, see also ECJ (order of 25 November 2008), Case C-500/07 P *Territorio Energia Ambiente v Commission* [2008] E.C.R. I-161*, Summ. pub., para. 24; ECJ (order of 25 November 2008), Case C-501/07 P *S.A.B.A.R. v Commission* [2008] E.C.R. I-163*, Summ. pub., para. 23; ECJ (order of 9 July 2009), Case C-498/08 P *Fornaci Laterizi Danesi v Commission* [2009] E.C.R. I-122*, Summ. pub., paras 23–25; CFI, Case T-296/97 *Alitalia v Commission* [2000] E.C.R. II-3871, paras 59–63; CFI (order of 19 May 2008) Case T-144/04 *TF1 v Commission* [2008] E.C.R. II-761, paras 20–23. Compare in the context of State aid, CFI, Joined Cases T-273/06 and T-297/06 *ISD Polska and Others v Commission* [2009] E.C.R. II-2181, paras 56–59 (appeal dismissed on other grounds in ECJ, Case C-369/09 P *SD Polska and Others v Commission* [2011] E.C.R. I-2011): the Court of First Instance underlined that it is consistent practice for Commission decisions closing a State aid investigation procedure to be published in the *Official Journal* and that since the applicants were not the addressees of the contested decision, the criterion of notification was not applicable; however, the Court opined that even on the assumption that a decision may be notified to a person who is not the addressee thereof and that the communication of the decision to the applicants could be considered to constitute a notification, the actions were still brought within the requisite period. In recent case-law, it is not even considered whether there is an established practice of publication. Time for beginning proceedings begins to run on notification or on the day of publication in the *Official Journal*. The subsidiary criterion of having knowledge of the act is relevant only where the act is neither notified nor published in the *Official Journal*: see CFI (order of 25 May 2004), Case T-264/03 *Schmoldt and Others v Commission* [2004] E.C.R. II-1515, paras 51–61.

[796] See, e.g. ECJ (order of 25 November 2008), Case C-500/07 P *Territorio Energia Ambiente v Commission* [2008] E.C.R. I-161*, Summ. pub., para. 23; ECJ (order of 25 November 2008), Case C-501/07 P *S.A.B.A.R. v*

knowledge of the contested act subsequent to its publication in order to extend this starting point.[797] However, under circumstances where the contested act which is published imposes restrictive measures against the applicant, the Union institutions are under an obligation to communicate as soon as possible after the publication of the act in the *Official Journal of the European Union* the grounds on which that measure is based. Time limits do not start to run in respect of the affected natural or legal person as long as the measure has not been notified or otherwise communicated to him (which can be done by way of publication of a notice in the C series of the *Official Journal of the European Union*).[798]

As regards new Member States, the Court of Justice stresses that compliance with the rule of law implies that they are treated on the basis of equality with the old Member States. Therefore, according to the Court, the new Member States must enjoy, in relation to all measures which are adopted on the basis of the Accession Treaty and which affect them in their capacity as Member States, a right of action as applicants pursuant to the second paragraph of Art. 263 TFEU. Independently of the date of publication of such measure, the two-month period laid down in the sixth paragraph of Art. 263 TFEU begins to run on the day of accession of the Member State concerned to the Union.[799]

(c) Summary publication and Internet link
The fact that the Commission gave third parties full access to the text of a decision on its **7.212** Internet site, combined with the publication of a succinct notice in the *Official Journal of the European Union* which enabled interested parties to identify the decision in question and brought their attention to the possibility of accessing it over the Internet must be regarded as constituting publication within the meaning of the sixth paragraph of Art. 263 TFEU.[800] Such publication constitutes the starting point of the period for instituting proceedings.

Commission [2008] E.C.R. I-163*, Summ. pub., para. 22; ECJ (order of 9 July 2009), Case C-498/08 P *Fornaci Laterizi Danesi v Commission* [2009] E.C.R. I-122*, Summ. pub., para. 22; ECJ, Case C-36/09 P *Transportes Evaristo Molina v Commission* [2010] E.C.R. I-145*, Summ. pub., para. 37; ECJ (order of 22 October 2010), Case C-266/10 P *Seacid v European Parliament and Council* [2010] E.C.R. I-133*, Summ. pub., para. 25; EGC (order of 13 July 2011), Case T-352/11 *N'Guessan v Council* [2011] E.C.R. II-232*, Summ. pub., para. 16; EGC (order of 16 December 2011), Case T-532/11 *Städter v ECB*, not reported, para. 10.

[797] See, e.g. ECJ (order of 25 November 2008), Case C-500/07 P *Territorio Energia Ambiente v Commission* [2008] E.C.R. I-161*, Summ. pub., para. 23; ECJ (order of 25 November 2008), Case C-501/07 P *S.A.B.A.R. v Commission* [2008] E.C.R. I-163*, Summ. pub., para. 22; ECJ (order of 9 July 2009), Case C-498/08 P *Fornaci Laterizi Danesi v Commission* [2009] E.C.R. I-122*, Summ. pub., para. 22; EGC (order of 13 July 2011), Case T-352/11 *N'Guessan v Council* [2011] E.C.R. II-232*, Summ. pub., para. 16 (underscoring that where the contested act is published, the calculation of the time limit for commencing annulment proceedings starts from that date even if such act is not notified to the applicant; in that case, the contested measure was not formally addressed to the applicant).

[798] EGC (order of 11 January 2012), Case T-301/11 *Ben Ali v Council*, not reported, paras 18–20. See in this respect also ECJ (judgment of 23 April 2013), Joined Cases C-478/11 to C-482/11 *Gbagbo and Others v Council*, not reported, paras 53–64.

[799] ECJ (judgment of 26 June 2012), Case-335/09 P *Poland v Commission*, not reported, paras 48–51. Such reasoning does not apply to individuals: see ECJ (order of 22 October 2010), Case C-266/10 P *Seacid v European Parliament and Council* [2010] E.C.R. I- I-133*, Summ. pub., paras 26–27.

[800] CFI, Case T-17/02 *Olsen v Commission* [2005] E.C.R. II-2031, para. 80; CFI (order of 19 September 2005), Case T-321/04 *Air Bourbon v Commission* [2005] E.C.R. II-3469, paras 34 and 37; CFI (order of 21 November 2005), Case T-426/04 *Tramarin v Commission* [2005] E.C.R. II-4765, paras 53–56 (noting that the fact that access to the text of the contested measure is not immediate cannot invalidate this conclusion); CFI, Case T-388/02 *Kronoply and Others v Commission* [2008] E.C.R. II-305*, Summ. pub., paras 32–34.

(5) Notification

(a) Effects of notification

7.213 Under the third paragraph of Art. 297(2) TFEU, all other directives and decisions which specify to whom they are addressed must be notified to those to whom they are addressed and take effect upon such notification. Therefore, the period of time for commencing proceedings against such acts runs from the day following the receipt by the person concerned of due notification,[801] where any delay in notification is not attributable to that person.[802] The person to whom the act is addressed cannot prevent time from starting to run by refusing to take cognisance of a properly notified act.[803]

Publication in the *Official Journal* of an act which takes effect upon notification to the addressee or the fact that the addressee has knowledge of its existence before or after notification has no effect on when time starts running.[804]

(b) Due notification

7.214 Due notification requires that the act be communicated to the person to whom it is addressed[805] and should put that person in a position to take cognizance of its content and of the grounds on which it is based.[806] Registered mail with an acknowledgement slip is

---

[801] However, a purely formal error in the notification (e.g. a mistake in the name of the addressee) does not prevent the time limits laid down in the Treaties from applying, provided that the act in question actually reached the addressee and the latter realized that he or she actually was the addressee: ECJ (order of 4 July 1984), Case 82/84 *Metalgoi v Commission* [1984] E.C.R. 2585, at 2586; CFI (order of 13 February 1998), Case T-275/97 *Guérin Automobiles v Commission* [1998] E.C.R. II-253, para. 14; CFI (order of 13 February 1998), Case T-276/97 *Guérin Automobiles v Commission* [1998] E.C.R. II-261, para. 18.

[802] ECJ, Case 5/76 *Jänsch v Commission* [1976] E.C.R. 1027, para. 9. ECJ Rules of Procedure, Art. 49(1)(a); EGC Rules of Procedure, Art. 101(1)(a). This rule is applicable to all acts of Union institutions which enter into force upon notification.

[803] ECJ, Case 6/72 *Europemballage and Continental Can v Commission* [1973] E.C.R. 215, para. 10.

[804] ECJ, Case 31/76 *Hebrant (née Macevicius) v European Parliament* [1977] E.C.R. 883, para. 13. See, e.g. EGC, Case T-233/09 *Access Info Europe v Council* [2011] E.C.R. II-1073, para. 28: where the addressee has been notified of the contested measure, it is the date of notification which is to be taken into consideration for the purposes of calculating the time limit under the sixth para. of Art. 263 TFEU, not the date on which knowledge of the measure was taken, which comes into play only as an alternative in cases where there is no notification.

[805] The notification to the Member State concerned of a decision declaring aid granted by a region incompatible with the internal market has no effect on the period within which the region concerned has to bring an action for annulment (CFI, Case T-190/00 *Regione Siciliana v Commission* [2003] E.C.R. II-5015, paras 29–33). Moreover, notification causes time to run within the meaning of the sixth para. of Art. 263 TFEU only where the act is notified to the person to whom the decision is addressed. If the Commission sends a copy of a State aid decision (addressed to the Member State) by e-mail to the undertaking which had lodged a complaint relating to the aid concerned, that communication does not start time running, but rather the subsequent publication of that act does: see CFI, Case T-17/02 *Olsen v Commission* [2005] E.C.R. II-2031, paras 72–87. See also CFI, Joined Cases T-273/06 and T-297/06 *ISD Polska and Others v Commission* [2009] E.C.R. II-2181, paras 56–59 (appeal dismissed on other grounds in ECJ, Case C-369/09 P *ISD Polska and Others v Commission* [2011] E.C.R. I-2011) (noting that since the applicants were not the addressees of the contested decision, the criterion of notification was not applicable; however, it surmised that even on the assumption that a decision may be notified to a person who is not the addressee thereof and that the communication of the decision to the applicants could be considered to constitute a notification, the actions were still brought within the requisite period); CFI, Case T-48/04 *Qualcomm Wireless Business Solutions Europe v Commission* [2009] E.C.R. II-2029, paras 46–54 (dealing with merger control).

[806] ECJ, Case 6/72 *Europemballage and Continental Can v Commission* [1973] E.C.R. 215, para. 10; CFI, Case T-196/95 *H v Commission* [1997] E.C.R.-SC II-403, para. 31 (English abstract at I-A-133). Consequently, to send only a brief summary of the contents of the act is not sufficient and will not start time running for the purposes of bringing proceedings: ECJ, Case C-143/95 P *Commission v Socurte and Others* [1997] E.C.R. I-1, para. 32.

accepted as an appropriate means of notification, provided that the rules applicable to the delivery of mail are complied with,[807] since it enables the Union judicature to determine with certainty when time started to run.[808] In such case, only unforeseen circumstances, *force majeure*, or excusable error which prevented the applicant from actually taking cognizance of the act notified may justify exceeding the time limit for instituting proceedings (see para. 7.208).[809]

(c) Notification to a legal person

If the act is addressed to a legal person, notification to the registered office suffices. **7.215** Companies have no right to require the Commission to give notice at a place other than the registered office or to a particular person.[810] In the case of companies, the rule is that measures addressed to the parent company may not be validly notified to subsidiaries.[811]

(6) Knowledge

By virtue of the wording of the sixth paragraph of Art. 263 TFEU ('or in the absence thereof, **7.216** of the day on which [the measure] came to the knowledge' of the plaintiff), the criterion of the day on which a measure came to the knowledge of an applicant is subsidiary to the criteria of publication or notification of the measure.[812] In other words, it is only relevant where the

---

[807] CFI, Joined Cases T-374/94, T-375/94, T-384/94, and T-388/94 *European Night Services and Others v Commission* [1998] E.C.R. II-3141, paras 75–79. In that case, the Court of First Instance found that the first notification had been made to a person not authorized to take delivery of mail under the French postal rules, and so this did not cause time to start running.

[808] ECJ, Joined Cases 32/58 and 33/58 *SNUPAT v High Authority* [1959] E.C.R. 127, at 136; ECJ, Case 224/83 *Ferriera Vittoria v Commission* [1984] E.C.R. 2349, para. 9. Compare EGC, Case T-233/09 *Access Info Europe v Council* [2011] E.C.R. II-1073, para. 27 (noting that in the absence of a registered letter with acknowledgment of receipt or an email or fax followed by acknowledgment of receipt—*in casu*, the Council sent the contested measure by unregistered post—the institution's contention of an earlier date of notification than that submitted by the applicant remains unsubstantiated). In a situation in which the exact date of notification of the contested decision to the applicant is not known, the date on which the applicant responded to this decision has been considered to constitute the day which starts the time running (the *dies a quo*), which resulted in a finding, upheld on appeal, that the action was lodged out of time: ECJ (order of 8 December 2005), Case C-210/05 P *Campailla v Commission*, not reported, paras 30–31.

[809] ECJ, Joined Cases 220/78 and 221/78 *ALA and ALFER v Commission* [1979] E.C.R. 1693, para. 9; ECJ (order of 27 April 1988), Case 352/87 *Farzoo and Kortmann v Commission* [1988] E.C.R. 2281, para. 7; ECJ (order of 5 February 1992), Case C-59/91 *France v Commission* [1992] E.C.R. I-525, para. 8. An excusable error can occur 'when the conduct of the institution concerned has been, either alone or to a decisive extent, such as to give rise to pardonable confusion in the mind of a party acting in good faith and exercising all the diligence required of a normally well-informed person' (ECJ, Case C-193/01 P *Pitsiorlas v Council* [2003] E.C.R. I-48037, para. 24).

[810] ECJ, Case 42/85 *Cockerill-Sambre v Commission* [1985] E.C.R. 3749, paras 10–11.

[811] ECJ, Case 48/69 *ICI v Commission* [1972] E.C.R. 619, paras 34–38. In that case, however, the parent company had had full knowledge of the contested act and exercised the right to bring proceedings within the prescribed period. Consequently, the finding that notification might not have been properly effected had no bearing on the case: ECJ, Case 48/69 *ICI v Commission*, paras 39–44.

[812] See, e.g. ECJ, Case C-122/95 *Germany v Council* [1998] E.C.R. I-973, para. 35; ECJ (order of 25 November 2008), Case C-500/07 P *Territorio Energia Ambiente v Commission* [2008] E.C.R. I-161*, Summ. pub., para. 22; ECJ (order of 25 November 2008), Case C-501/07 P *S.A.B.A.R. v Commission* [2008] E.C.R. I-163*, Summ. pub., para. 21; CFI, Case T-296/97 *Alitalia v Commission* [2000] E.C.R. II-3871, para. 61; CFI, Case T-190/00 *Regione Siciliana v Commission* [2003] E.C.R. II-5015, para. 30; CFI (order of 4 April 2008), Case T-503/07 *Kulykovska-Pawlowski and Others v European Parliament and Council* [2008] E.C.R. II-48*, Summ. pub., para. 8; CFI, Case T-185/05 *Italy v Commission* [2008] E.C.R. II-3207, para. 66; CFI, Joined Cases T-273/06 and T-297/06 ISD *Polska and Others v Commission* [2009] E.C.R. II-2181, para. 55 (appeal dismissed on other grounds in ECJ, Case C-369/09 P *ISD Polska and Others v Commission* [2011] E.C.R. I-2011); EGC (order of 5 May 2010), Case T-64/10 *Dorval v Commission*, not reported, para. 8.

contested act is neither published in the *Official Journal* nor notified to the applicant.[813] This means that an individual who already has knowledge of the content of an act before it is published in the *Official Journal* is not obliged to bring proceedings within two months of the date when it came to his or her knowledge, but may wait until it is published.[814] The same applies where an act comes to the addressee's knowledge before it is officially notified to it.[815]

The period for commencing proceedings in the case of interested third parties seeking annulment of an act addressed to another person begins—except in the case of publication in the *Official Journal*—on the day on which that person acquired knowledge of the existence and the precise contents of the measure and of the reasons on which it is based in such a way as to enable him or her profitably to exercise his or her right of action.[816] If the act is published in an official publication of a Member State[817] or if it is brought to the notice of interested third parties, this will constitute sufficient notice, with the result that time will start running.[818] However, whether an action for annulment brought by an interested third party against an act directed to another person is admissible does not depend on the fact of publication or notification. An application lodged before publication or notification will be admissible.[819]

---

[813] CFI (order of 25 May 2004), Case T-264/03 *Schmoldt and Others v Commission* [2004] E.C.R. II-1515, paras 51–61. See, e.g. ECJ, Case C-403/05 *European Parliament v Commission* [2007] E.C.R. I-9045, paras 28–29 (the contested act was neither published in the *Official Journal* nor notified to the European Parliament as an addressee, thereby making it necessary to determine on what date the applicant acquired knowledge of that decision). See also ECJ, Case C-521/06 P *Athinaiki Techniki v Commission* [2008] E.C.R. I-5829, para. 69.

[814] See, e.g. CFI, Case T-140/95 *Ryanair v Commission* [1998] E.C.R. II-3327, para. 25; CFI, Case T-11/95 *B.P. v Commission* [1998] E.C.R. II-3235, paras 47–48; CFI, Case T-106/96 *Wirtschaftsvereinigung Stahl v Commission* [1999] E.C.R. II-2155, paras 28–31; CFI, Case T-89/96 *British Steel v Commission* [1999] E.C.R. II-2089, paras 33–36; CFI, Case T-14/96 *BAI v Commission* [1999] E.C.R. II-139, paras 33–37; CFI, Case T-48/04 *Qualcomm Wireless Business Solutions Europe v Commission* [2009] E.C.R. II-2029, paras 55–57 (dealing with merger control).

[815] CFI, Case T-11/95 *B.P. v Commission* [1998] E.C.R. II-3235, paras 38, 52.

[816] See, e.g. ECJ, Case 236/86 *Dillinger Hüttenwerke v Commission* [1988] E.C.R. 3761, para. 14; ECJ, Case 378/87 *Top Hit Holzvertrieb v Commission* [1989] E.C.R. 1359, para. 15; ECJ (order of 10 November 2011), Case C-626/10 P *Joséphidès v Commission and EACEA*, not reported, para. 127 (and citations therein); CFI, Case T-185/05 *Italy v Commission* [2008] E.C.R. II-3207, para. 68 (and citations therein); EGC (order of 8 May 2010), Case T-200/09 *Abertis Infraestructuras v Commission* [2010] E.C.R. II-85*, Summ. pub., para. 47. See also ECJ, Case C-403/05 *European Parliament v Commission* [2007] E.C.R. I-9045, paras 29–38, in which the Court of Justice determined that the European Parliament acquired precise knowledge of the content of the contested decision and of the reasons on which it was based only on the date when the Commission sent the full text of that decision to it, noting that the Commission failed to adduce proof that the European Parliament received a copy of that decision before that date and failed to refute the Parliament's argument that the information derived from previous informal exchanges between the institutions was not sufficiently precise to enable it to acquire full knowledge of the content of and reasons for that decision.

[817] ECJ, Joined Cases 31/62 and 33/62 *Wöhrmann and Others v Commission* [1962] E.C.R. 501, at 508.

[818] Time will start running irrespective as to whether or not the applicant had actual knowledge of the contested act which is published in the *Official Journal*. See CFI (order of 27 July 2004), Case T-238/04 *Raab and Others v European Parliament and Council*, not reported, paras 9–10. Indeed, as underlined by the Union judicature, since the date of publication, if there is one, is the decisive element for determining the starting point for the time limit prescribed by the sixth para. of Art. 263 TFEU, an applicant is not able to invoke the date on which he gained knowledge of the contested act subsequent to its publication in order to extend this starting point: see, e.g. ECJ (order of 25 November 2008), Case C-500/07 P *Territorio Energia Ambiente v Commission* [2008] E.C.R. I-161*, Summ. pub., para. 23; and ECJ (order of 25 November 2008), Case C-501/07 P *S.A.B. A.R. v Commission* [2008] E.C.R. I-163*, Summ. pub., para. 22; ECJ (order of 9 July 2009), Case C-498/08 P *Fornaci Laterizi Danesi v Commission* [2009] E.C.R. I-122*, Summ. pub., para. 22; EGC (order of 13 July 2011), Case T-352/11 *N'Guessan v Council* [2011] E.C.R. II-232*, Summ. pub., para. 16.

[819] ECJ, Joined Cases 172/83 and 226/83 *Hoogovens Groep v Commission* [1985] E.C.R. 2831, para. 8; CFI, Case T-17/02 *Olsen v Commission* [2005] E.C.R. II-2031, para. 83.

A third party who acquires precise knowledge of the content of an act (not published in the *Official Journal*) must bring proceedings within two months of the moment at which it acquired that precise knowledge.[820] The expression 'precise knowledge of the content of an act' does not mean knowledge of every aspect of the decision, but of its essential contents and the reasons on which it was based.[821] It has been held that where the applicant had knowledge of the contested act from a letter of which the date of receipt could not be definitely established, the period for commencing proceedings began on the date on which the applicant itself referred to the act in a letter.[822]

However, a third party may not remain idle indefinitely until it acquires precise knowledge of the content of an act. Indeed, if interested parties are put on notice of the existence of an act, they are under an obligation to request the complete text of the act within a reasonable period.[823] Thus, where the applicant fails to ask for the full text of the act after it had had

---

[820] ECJ, Case C-309/95 *Commission v Council* [1998] E.C.R. I-655, paras 18–22. It could be inferred from the wording of this judgment that interested third parties invariably have to comply with this time limit, irrespective as to whether or not the contested act has entered into force. But the objection to this interpretation is that if the act does not enter into force within two months of the time at which the third party acquired knowledge of it, the action would have to be brought against an act which does not yet produce any legal effects.

[821] CFI, Joined Cases T-485/93, T-491/93, T-494/93, and T-61/98 *Dreyfus and Others v Commission* [2000] E.C.R. II-3659, para. 49.

[822] CFI (order of 28 April 1994), Joined Cases T-452/93 and T-453/93 *Pevasa and Inpesca v Commission* [1994] E.C.R. II-229, paras 33–36. See also CFI, Case T-411/06 *Sogelma v EAR* [2008] E.C.R. II-2771, paras 75–76: in light of case-law regarding notification, the Court of First Instance surmised that if the date on which the applicant gained knowledge of the contested act cannot be established, the applicant is accorded a benefit of the doubt, which results in his application for annulment being regarded as having been lodged within the requisite time period if, in light of the facts, it does not appear absolutely impossible that the letter by which the applicant gained knowledge arrived so late that the time limit was complied with; see further CFI, Case T-185/05 *Italy v Commission* [2008] E.C.R. II-3207, paras 70–82: under the case-law, where it is not possible to ascertain with any certainty the date on which the applicant first knew exactly what was in the contested measure and what were the reasons on which it was based, the period prescribed for initiating proceedings must be considered to have begun to run, at the latest, from the date on which it can be established that the plaintiff had such knowledge. Consequently, in the instant proceedings, since the Commission did not provide sufficient proof to the contrary, the Court of First Instance found that the application was brought within the two-month time limit.

[823] ECJ, Case 59/84 *Tezi Textiel v Commission* [1986] E.C.R. 887, paras 9–11 (period of 14 months held to be reasonable); ECJ, Case C-180/88 *Wirtschaftsvereinigung Eisen- und Stahlindustrie v Commission* [1990] E.C.R. I-4413, para. 22 (two years held to be unreasonable); ECJ (order of 5 March 1993), Case C-102/92 *Ferriere Acciaierie Sarde v Commission* [1993] E.C.R. I-801, paras 18–19 (two months held to be unreasonable); CFI (order of 10 February 1994), Case T-468/93 *Frinil v Commission* [1994] E.C.R. II-33, paras 33–34 (one year and 10 months held to be unreasonable); CFI, Case T-465/93 *Consorzio Gruppo di Azione Locale 'Murgia Messapica' v Commission* [1994] E.C.R. II-361 (7.5 months held to be reasonable); CFI, Joined Cases T-432/93, T-433/93, and T-434/93 *Socurte and Others v Commission* [1995] E.C.R. II-503, para. 49 (two weeks held to be reasonable); CFI, Case T-109/94 *Windpark Groothusen v Commission* [1995] E.C.R. II-3007, paras 24–28 (7 months held to be unreasonable); CFI (order of 30 September 1997), Case T-151/95 *INEF v Commission* [1997] E.C.R. II-1541, para. 48 (18 months held to be unreasonable); CFI (order of 15 July 1998), Case T-155/95 *LPN and GEOTA v Commission* [1998] E.C.R. I-2751, para. 44 (6 months held to be unreasonable); CFI (order of 27 May 2005), Case T-485/04 *COBB v Commission*, not reported, paras 17–22 (4.5 months held to be unreasonable); CFI, Case T-439/08 *Joséphidès v Commission and EACEA* [2010] E.C.R. II-230*, Summ. pub., paras 160–161 (period of more than four months held to be unreasonable), upheld on appeal in ECJ (order of 10 November 2011), Case C-626/10 P *Joséphidès v Commission and EACEA*, not reported, paras 130–132. Notably, in its judgment in the previous case, the Court of Justice made clear that the time limit of two months set down in the sixth para. of Art. 263 TFEU starting from the date on which the applicant had knowledge of the contested act should not be confused with the reasonable period within which the applicant must request the complete text of the contested act after gaining such knowledge: ECJ, Case C-626/10 P *Joséphidès v Commission and EACEA*, paras 128–129.

knowledge of its existence, its application will be held to be inadmissible if, at the time when it had cognizance of the content of the act, the reasonable time had expired.[824]

E. Examination *ex officio* of the conditions governing the admissibility of an action for annulment

(1) *Ex officio* examination

7.217 The conditions governing the admissibility of an action are a matter of public policy. The Union courts therefore examine of their own motion (*ex officio*) absolute bars to proceedings, which include, for example,[825] bars relating to the time limit for bringing an action,[826] to whether the contested measure is of a challengeable nature,[827] to the interest of the applicant in obtaining the annulment of the contested measure,[828] and to the applicant's standing to bring proceedings.[829] The *lis pendens* objection may also be raised by the Union courts of their own motion.[830]

---

[824] ECJ (order of 10 November 2011), Case C-626/10 P *Joséphidès v Commission and EACEA*, not reported, paras 130–132; CFI, Joined Cases T-191/96 and T-106/97 *CAS Succhi di Frutta v Commission* [1999] E.C.R. II-3181, paras 93–103; CFI (order of 27 May 2005), Case T-485/04 *COBB v Commission*, not reported, paras 17–22.

[825] See, e.g. EGC, Case T-8/09 *Dredging International and Ondernemingen Jan de Nul v EMSA* [2011] E.C.R. II-6123, para. 129 (the lack of a right of action constitutes an absolute bar to proceedings, which a Union court may raise of its own motion). See also EGC, Case T-377/09 *Mövenpick v OHIM* [2011] E.C.R. II-455*, Summ. pub., para. 10.

[826] See, e.g. ECJ, Case 4/67 *Collignon v Commission* [1967] E.C.R. 365, at 372; ECJ, Case 108/79 *Belfiore v Commission* [1980] E.C.R. 1769, para. 3; ECJ, Case 227/83 *Moussis v Commission* [1984] E.C.R. 3133, para. 12; CFI, Case T-29/89 *Moritz v Commission* [1990] E.C.R. II-787, para. 13; CFI, Joined Cases T-142/01 and T-283/01 *OPTUC v Commission* [2004] E.C.R. II-329, para. 30.

[827] See, e.g. CFI (order of 29 April 2004), Case T-308/02 SGL *Carbon v Commission* [2004] E.C.R. II-1363, paras 39–73; CFI (order of 13 July 2004), Case T-29/03 *Comunidad Autónoma de Andalucía v Commission* [2004] E.C.R. II-2923, paras 28–40; CFI, Case T-437/05 *Brink's Security Luxembourg v Commission* [2009] E.C.R. II-3233, paras 55–78.

[828] See, e.g. CFI, Case T-310/00 *MCI v Commission* [2004] E.C.R. II-3253, paras 44–45; CFI, Case T-291/06 *ARP v Commission* [2009] E.C.R. II-2275, para. 26 (and citations therein). See also para. 7.138.

[829] See, e.g. ECJ, Case C-298/00 P *Italy v Commission* [2004] E.C.R. I-4087, para. 35; ECJ, Case C-417/04 P *Regione Siciliana* [2006] E.C.R. I-3881, para. 36; CFI, Case T-239/94 *EISA v Commission* [1997] E.C.R. II-1839, para. 27; CFI (judgment of 7 July 2004), Joined Cases T-107/01 and T-175/01 *Société de Mines de Sacilor-Lormines v Commission* [2004] E.C.R. II-2125, paras 51–52; CFI, Case T-27/02 *Kronofrance v Commission* [2004] E.C.R. II-4177, para. 30; CFI, Joined Cases T-366/03 and T-235/04 *Land Oberösterreich and Austria v Commission* [2005] E.C.R. II-4005, para. 25; CFI, Case T-170/06 *Alrosa Company v Commission* [2007] E.C.R. II-2601, paras 36–37; CFI, Case T-289/03 *British United Provident Association and Others v Commission* [2008] E.C.R. II-81, para. 69. Sometimes, different bars to proceedings are examined *ex officio* in the same judgment: see, e.g. EGC, Case T-68/08 *FIFA v Commission* [2011] E.C.R. II-349, para. 31; EGC, Case T-55/08 *UEFA v Commission* [2011] E.C.R. II-271, para. 28; and EGC, Case T-385/07 *FIFA v Commission* [2011] E.C.R. II-205, para. 35 (assessing grounds of inadmissibility relating to applicant's interest, legal standing, compliance with the time limit and the Court's jurisdiction; in doing so, the Court made clear that it was examining such pleas of its own motion, since these pleas put forward by interveners were not allowed); EGC, Joined Cases T-415/05, T-416/05, and T-423/05 *Greece and Others v Commission* [2010] E.C.R. II-4749, paras 56–63 (assessing of its own motion admissibility conditions relating to challengeable act and applicant's interest); CFI, Case T-332/06 *Alcoa Transformazioni v Commission* [2009] E.C.R. II-29*, Summ. pub., paras 33–44 (verifying the challengeable act requirement and that the applicant is directly and individually concerned by the contested act).

[830] See, e.g. ECJ, Joined Cases 45/70 and 49/70 *Bode v Commission* [1971] E.C.R. 465, para. 11; ECJ, Case 75/72 *Perinciolo v Council* [1973] E.C.R. 511, para. 5; CFI (order of 10 March 2005), Joined Cases T-228/00, T-229/00, T-242/00, T-243/00, T-245/00 to T-248/00, T-250/00, T-252/00, T-256/00 to T-259/00,

(2) Time frame

The admissibility of an action for annulment is judged by reference to the situation   **7.218**
prevailing when the application was lodged.[831]

V. Consequences

A. Result of an application for annulment

(1) Power of the Union courts limited to annulment

Under the first paragraph of Art. 264 TFEU, if the action for annulment is well-founded,   **7.219**
the Court of Justice or the General Court will declare the contested act void (declaration of
nullity). The power of the Union judicature under Art. 263 TEU is limited to the
annulment of the contested act.[832] Accordingly, applications seeking, for example, the
Court of Justice or the General Court to make declarations or statements of law,[833] or to

---

T-265/00, T-267/00, T-268/00, T-271/00, T-274/00 to T-276/00, T-281/00, T-281/00, T-287/00, and
T-296/00 *Gruppo ormeggiatori del porto di Venezia and Others v Commission* [2005] E.C.R. II-787, para. 38;
CFI (order of 14 July 2005), Case T-79/05 *Gluiber v Commission*, not reported, para. 7; CFI, Case T-309/03
Camos Grau v Commission [2006] E.C.R. II-1173, para. 41 (and further citations therein). This objection will be
raised when more than one action is brought between the same parties seeking the annulment of the same act on
the basis of the same submissions: see ECJ, Joined Cases 172/83 and 226/83 *Hoogovens Groep v Commission*
[1985] E.C.R. 2831, para. 9; ECJ, Joined Cases 358/85 and 51/86 *France v European Parliament* [1988]
E.C.R. 4821, para. 12; ECJ, Joined Cases C-138/03, C-324/03, and C-431/03 *Italy v Commission* [2005]
E.C.R. I-10043, paras 64–68; CFI (order of 10 March 2005), Joined Cases T-228/00, T-229/00, T-242/00,
T-243/00, T-245/00 to T-248/00, T-250/00, T-252/00, T-256/00 to T-259/00, T-265/00, T-267/00, T-268/00,
T-271/00, T-274/00 to T-276/00, T-281/00, T-287/00 to T-296/00 *Gruppo ormeggiatori del porto di Venezia
and Others v Commission* [2005] E.C.R. II-787, para. 40; CFI (order of 14 July 2005), Case T-79/05 *Gluiber v
Commission*, not reported, para. 11; EGC, Case T-378/06 *IMI and Others v Commission* [2011] E.C.R. II-62*,
Summ. pub., paras 29–32. Compare CFI, Joined Cases T-254/00, T-270/00, and T-277/00 *Hotel Cipriani
and Others v Commission* [2008] E.C.R. II-3269, paras 43–47 (rejecting the objection of inadmissibility based
on *lis pendens*), upheld on appeal in ECJ, Joined Cases C-71/09 P, C-73/09 P, and C-76/09 P *Comitato
'Venezia vuole vivere' and Others v Commission* [2011] E.C.R. I-4727, paras 30–43.

[831] ECJ, Case 50/84 *Bensider and Others v Commission* [1984] E.C.R. 3991, para. 8; ECJ, Joined Cases
C-61/96, C-45/98, C-27/99, C-81/00, and C-22/01 *Spain v Council* [2002] E.C.R. I-3439, para. 23; CFI
(order of 15 February 2005), Case T-229/02 *PKK and Others v Council* [2005] E.C.R. II-539, para. 30; CFI
(order of 18 November 2005), Case T-299/04 *Selmani v Council and Commission* [2005] E.C.R. II-20*,
Summ. pub., para. 69 (and further citations therein); EGC (order of 21 May 2010), Case T-441/08 *ICO
Services v European Parliament and Council* [2010] E.C.R. II-100*, Summ. pub., para. 60.

[832] Art. 264, first para., TFEU. The Union courts cannot substitute their own reasoning for that of the
author of the contested act: see, e.g. ECJ, Case C-164/98 P *DIR International Film and Others v Commission*
[2000] E.C.R. I-447, para. 38; ECJ (judgment of 28 February 2013), Case C-246/11 P *Portugal v Commission*, not reported, paras 90–91.

[833] See, e.g. ECJ (order of 9 December 2003), Case C-224/03 *Italy v Commission* [2003] E.C.R. I-14751,
paras 20–22; CFI, Joined Cases T-50/06, T-56/06, T-60/06, T-62/06 and T-69/06 *Ireland and Others v
Commission* [2007] E.C.R. II-172*, Summ. pub., paras 42–44 (set aside on other grounds in ECJ, Case C-89/08 P
Commission v Ireland and Others [2009] E.C.R. I-11245); CFI (order of 1 December 2008), Case T-220/08 *Işçi
Partisi (Turkish Labour Party) v Council and Commission*, not reported, para. 13; CFI, Case T-145/06 *Omya
v Commission* [2009] E.C.R. II-145, para. 23; CFI, Joined Cases T-273/06 and T-297/06 *ISD Polska and Others
v Commission* [2009] E.C.R. II-2181, para. 78; EGC (order of 30 September 2010), Case T-311/10 *Platis v
Council and Greece*, not reported, para. 13 (appeal dismissed in ECJ, Case C-513/10 P *Platis v Council and Greece*
[2010] E.C.R. I-176*, Summ. pub.); EGC, Case T-439/09 *Purvis v European Parliament* [2011]
E.C.R. II-7231, paras 26–27; EGC (order of 9 November 2011), Case T-120/10 *ClientEarth and BirdLife
International v Commission*, not reported, paras 28–29.

issue orders, directions, or injunctions to Union institutions, bodies, offices, or agencies[834] are inadmissible.

If the application for annulment is not well-founded, it will be dismissed.

(2) Partial annulment

7.220   The Court of Justice and the General Court may also declare part of the contested act void, either by annulling some of its provisions or by confining the declaration of nullity to some substantive or personal aspect.[835] The applicant may have sought partial annulment[836] or the Court of Justice or the General Court may itself take the view that only some provisions of the contested act must be annulled.[837]

---

[834] See, e.g. ECJ (order of 25 June 2009), Case C-580/08 P *Srinivasan v European Ombudsman* [2009] E.C.R. I-110*, Summ. pub., paras 12–18; CFI, Case T-216/05 *Mebrom v Commission* [2007] E.C.R. II-1507, para. 56; CFI, Case T-345/03 *Evropaiki Dynamiki v Commission* [2008] E.C.R. II-341, paras 46–47; CFI, Case T-253/04 *KONGRA-GEL v Council* [2008] E.C.R. II-46*, Summ. pub., paras 47–48; CFI, Case T-465/04 *Evropaïki Dynamiki v Commission* [2008] E.C.R. II-154*, Summ. pub., paras 35–36; CFI, Case T-51/07 *Agrar-Invest-Tatschl v Commission* [2008] E.C.R. II-2825, paras 25–29 (rejecting the applicant's claim that the Commission did not enjoy any discretion and thus there was no reason precluding the Court, once the contested decision was declared unlawful, from enjoining the Commission to adopt a decision in accordance with its claims); CFI, Case T-89/06 *Lebard v Commission* [2009] E.C.R. II-201*, Summ. pub., paras 53–56; CFI, Case T-152/06 *NDSHT Nya Destination Stockholm Hotell & Teaterpaket v Commmission* [2009] E.C.R. II-1517, para. 73; CFI (order of 6 July 2009), Case T-181/09 *Oprea v Commission*, not reported, paras 5–6; CFI, Case T-380/06 *Vischim v Commission* [2009] E.C.R. II-3911, paras 46–47; CFI (order of 24 September 2009), Case T-110/09 *Bayramoglu v Council and European Parliament*, not reported, para. 10; CFI (order of 17 November 2009), Case T-295/09 *Hansen v Commission*, not reported, paras 14–16; EGC, Case T-191/09 *Hit Trading and Berkman Forwarding v Commission* [2010] E.C.R. II-283*, Summ. pub., paras 20–21; EGC, Case T-49/07 *Fahas v Council* [2010] E.C.R. II-5555, paras 28–30; EGC, Case T-369/08 *EWRIA and Others v Commission* [2010] E.C.R. II-6283, paras 45–46; EGC (order of 9 November 2011), Case T-120/10 *ClientEarth and BirdLife International v Commission*, not reported, paras 28–29; EGC, Case T-436/09 *Dufour v ECB* [2011] E.C.R. II-7727, paras 39–40.

[835] See, e.g. ECJ, Joined Cases 33/86, 44/86, 110/86, 226/86 and 285/86 *Stahlwerke Peine-Salzgitter and Others v Commission* [1988] E.C.R. 4309, point 1 of the operative part; CFI, Case T-26/90 *Finsider v Commission* [1992] E.C.R. II-1789, paras 52–57; EGC, Case T-68/06 *Stempher and Koninklijke Verpakking-sindustrie Stempher v Commission* [2011] E.C.R. II-399*, Summ. pub., paras 42–44; EGC, Case T-208/06 *Quinn Barlo and Others v Commission* [2011] E.C.R. II-7953, para. 151. The mere fact that the General Court finds that a plea relied on in support of an action for annulment is well-founded does not automatically enable it to annul the contested measure in its entirety. Annulment of the measure in its entirety is not acceptable where it is obvious that, being directed only at a specific part of the contested measure, that plea can provide a basis only for partial annulment: see ECJ (judgment of 6 December 2012), Case C-441/11 P *Commission v Verhuizingen Coppens*, not reported, para. 37.

[836] If the applicant seeks only partial annulment of an act and the Court of Justice or the General Court considers that the contested provisions are not severable, it may not rule *ultra petita* (ECJ, Case 37/71 *Jamet v Commission* [1972] E.C.R. 483, para. 12), but would have to declare the application inadmissible (see, e.g. ECJ, Case C-36/04 *Spain v Council* [2006] E.C.R. I-2981, para. 21; EGC (order of 24 May 2011), Case T-176/09 *Government of Gibraltar v Commission* [2011] E.C.R. II-150*, Summ. pub., paras 38–52).

[837] ECJ, Case 27/76 *United Brands v Commission* [1978] E.C.R. 207, para. 268. But see ECJ, Case C-295/07 P *Commission v Département du Loiret and Scott* [2008] E.C.R. I-9363, paras 103–110, in which the Court of Justice set aside the judgment of the Court of First Instance in part on the grounds that it annulled the contested decision in its entirety, finding that the General Court may not, merely because it considers a plea well-founded in support of the action for annulment, annul automatically the contested act in its entirety where it is obvious that the plea is directed at only a specific part of the contested act and is as such to provide a basis only for partial annulment, the requirements of which were fulfilled.

However, partial annulment of a Union act is possible only if the elements to be annulled may be severed from the remainder of the act.[838] The requirement of severability is not satisfied where partial annulment of an act would have the effect of altering its substance.[839] This is because the Court of Justice and the General Court cannot 'revise' the contested act in annulment proceedings.

(3) *Ex tunc* effect

The annulment of a Union act causes it to disappear from the Union legal order from the **7.221** date on which that act entered into force (*ex tunc*), so that the parties to the proceedings are restored to the situation they were in before it entered into force.[840]

The retroactive force of a declaration of nullity may be attenuated, pursuant to the second paragraph of Art. 264 TFEU, in the light of the aim behind the action or on grounds of legal certainty.[841] Thus, the Court of Justice or the General Court may—either on request

---

[838] ECJ, Case 17/74 *Transocean Marine Paint Association v Commission* [1974] E.C.R. 1063, para. 21; ECJ, Joined Cases C-68/94 and C-30/95 *France and Others v Commission* [1998] E.C.R. I-1375, paras 251–259; ECJ, Case C-29/99 *Commission v Council* [2002] E.C.R. I-11221, paras 45 and 46; ECJ, Case C-378/00 *Commission v European Parliament and Council* [2003] E.C.R. I-937, para. 30; ECJ, Case C-239/01 *Germany v Commission* [2003] E.C.R. I-10333, para. 33; ECJ, Case C-244/03 *France v European Parliament and Council* [2005] E.C.R. I-4021, para. 12; ECJ, Case C-36/04 *Spain v Council* [2006] E.C.R. I-2981, para. 12; ECJ, Case C-540/03 *European Parliament v Council* ('*Family reunification*' case) [2006] E.C.R. I-5769, para. 27; ECJ, Case C-295/07 P *Commission v Département du Loiret and Scott* [2008] E.C.R. I-9363, para. 105; CFI, Case T-310/06 *Hungary v Commission* [2007] E.C.R. II-4619, paras 39–45; CFI, Case T-380/06 *Vischim v Commission* [2009] E.C.R. II-3911, paras 54–56; EGC, Joined Cases T-425/04, T-444/04, T-450/04, and T-456/04 *France and Others v Commission* [2010] E.C.R. II-2099, paras 112–115; EGC, Case T-32/11 *Verenigde Douaneagenten v Commission*, not reported, para. 56.

[839] ECJ, Case 34/86 *Council v European Parliament* [1986] E.C.R. 2155, paras 40–42; ECJ, Joined Cases C-68/94 and C-30/95 *France and Others v Commission* [1998] E.C.R. I-1375, para. 257; ECJ, Case C-376/98 *Germany v European Parliament and Council* [2000] E.C.R. I-8419, para. 117; ECJ, Case C-29/99 *Commission v Council* [2002] E.C.R. I-11221, para. 46; ECJ, Case C-239/01 *Germany v Commission* [2003] E.C.R. I-10333, para. 34; ECJ, Case C-244/03 *France v European Parliament and Council* [2004] E.C.R. I-4021, para. 13; ECJ, Case C-36/04 *Spain v Council* [2006] E.C.R. I-2981, paras 13–21; ECJ, Case C-540/03 *European Parliament v Council* ('*Family reunification*' case) [2006] E.C.R. I-5769, para. 28; ECJ, Case C-295/07 P *Commission v Département du Loiret and Scott* [2008] E.C.R. I-9363, para. 106; ECJ (judgment of 29 March 2012), Case C-504/09 P *Commission v Poland*, not reported, paras 98–109; ECJ (judgment of 29 March 2012), C-505/09 P *Commission v Estonia*, not reported, para. 111. Whether the partial annulment of a measure would cause the substance of that measure to be altered is a point which must be determined on the basis of an objective criterion and not of a subjective criterion linked to the political intention of the authority which adopted the measure at issue: see ECJ (judgment of 6 December 2012), Case C-441/11 P *Commission v Verhuizingen Coppens*, not reported, para. 38 (and case-law cited therein).

[840] ECJ, Case 22/70 *Commission v Council* (the '*AETR*' case) [1971] E.C.R. 263, paras 59–60; ECJ, Joined Cases 97/86, 193/86, 99/86 and 215/86 *Asteris and Others v Commission* [1988] E.C.R. 2181, para. 30.

[841] See, e.g. ECJ, Case C-409/06 *Winner Wetten* [2010] E.C.R. I-8015, paras 64–66, underscoring that the purpose of the maintenance of the effects of a Union measure which has been annulled (or declared invalid since Art. 264, second para., TFEU is applied by analogy: see para. 10.20) is 'to prevent a legal vacuum from arising before a new measure replaces the measure thus annulled or declared invalid' and 'may be justified where overriding considerations of legal certainty involving all the interests, public as well as private, are at stake and during the period of time necessary in order to allow such illegality to be remedied') (citations omitted). The second para. of Art. 264 TFEU provides that the Court of Justice of the European Union, 'if it considers this necessary, states which of the effects of the act which it has declared void shall be considered as definitive'. In contrast, the wording of the former second para. of Art. 231 EC had been limited to 'the case of a regulation'. Nonetheless, the power of the Union courts to state which effects of the annulled regulation were to be considered as definitive had already been exercised with regard to other types of acts: see, e.g. ECJ, Case 92/78 *Simmenthal v Commission* [1979] E.C.R. 777, para. 107 (annulment of a decision); ECJ, Case 34/86 *Council v European Parliament* [1986] E.C.R. 2155, para. 48 (annulment of the act by which the President of

413

of a party or of its own motion[842]—maintain the effects of the annulled act as definitive[843] or for a particular period of time until the competent institution, body, office, or agency has taken the necessary measures to give effect to the judgment annulling the act.[844]

B. Authority of the judgment

(1) Declaration of nullity

(a) Erga omnes *effect*

7.222 The declaration of nullity applies *erga omnes*, meaning that it extends beyond the parties involved in the particular case (*inter partes*) and has general effect throughout the Union legal order. Consequently, an action for annulment of a Union measure which has already

---

the European Parliament declares the budget finally adopted); ECJ, Case C-295/90 *European Parliament v Council* [1992] E.C.R. I-4193, paras 22–27 (annulment of a directive); ECJ, Case C-106/96 *United Kingdom v Commission* [1998] E.C.R. I-2729, paras 39–42 (annulment of a decision pursuant to which contracts had been concluded under a Union action programme); ECJ, Case C-211/01 *Commission v Council* [2003] E.C.R. I-8913, paras 54–57 (annulment of a Council decision concluding an international agreement between the former EC and Bulgaria (before it was a Member State)); ECJ, Case C-155/07 *European Parliament v Council* [2008] E.C.R. I-8103, paras 87–89 (annulment of a Council decision granting what was then a Community guarantee to the EIB against losses under loans and loan guarantees for projects outside the former Community); ECJ, Case C-370/07 *Commission v Council* [2009] E.C.R. I-8917, paras 64–66 (annulment of a Council decision establishing the position to be adopted on behalf of the former EC with regard to certain proposals submitted at a meeting of the contracting parties of an international convention).

[842] See, e.g. ECJ, Joined Cases C-14/06 and C-295/06 *European Parliament and Denmark v Commission* [2008] E.C.R. I-1649, para. 85.

[843] See, e.g. ECJ, Case 45/86 *Commission v Council* [1987] E.C.R. 1493, para. 23; ECJ, Case 51/87 *Commission v Council* [1988] E.C.R. 5459, para. 22; ECJ, Case C-360/93 *European Parliament v Council* [1996] E.C.R. I-1195, paras 32–36; ECJ, Case C-22/96 *European Parliament v Council* [1998] E.C.R. I-3231, para. 42; ECJ, Case C-166/07 *European Parliament v Council* [2009] E.C.R. I-7135, paras 73–75.

[844] See, e.g. ECJ, Case 81/72 *Commission v Council* [1973] E.C.R. 575, para. 15; ECJ, Case 264/82 *Timex v Council and Commission* [1985] E.C.R. 849, para. 32; ECJ, Case 275/87 *Commission v Council* [1989] E.C.R. 259, at 261; ECJ, Case C-295/90 *European Parliament v Council* [1992] E.C.R. I-4193, paras 22–27; ECJ, Case C-65/90 *European Parliament v Council* [1992] E.C.R. I-4593, paras 22–24; ECJ, Case C-271/94 *European Parliament v Council* [1996] E.C.R. I-1689, para. 40; ECJ, Joined Cases C-164/97 and C-165/97 *European Parliament v Council* [1999] E.C.R. I-1139, paras 22–24; ECJ, Case C-211/01 *Commission v Council* [2003] E.C.R. I-8913, paras 54–57; ECJ, Case C-178/03 *Commission v European Parliament* [2006] E.C.R. I-107, paras 64–65; ECJ, Case C-310/04 *Spain v Council* [2006] E.C.R. I-7285, paras 140–141; ECJ, Case C-414/04 *European Parliament v Council* [2006] E.C.R. I-11279, paras 58–59; ECJ, Case C-299/05 *Commission v European Parliament and Council* [2007] E.C.R. I-8695, paras 74–75; ECJ, Joined Cases C-402/05 P and C-415/05 P *Kadi and Al Barakaat International Foundation v Council and Commission* [2008] E.C.R. I-6351, paras 373–376; ECJ, Joined Cases C-14/06 and C-295/06 *European Parliament and Denmark v Commission* [2008] E.C.R. I-1649, para. 86; ECJ, Case C-155/07 *European Parliament v Council* [2008] E.C.R. I-8103, paras 87–89; ECJ, Case C-166/07 *European Parliament v Council* [2009] E.C.R. I-7135, paras 73–75; ECJ, Case C-370/07 *Commission v Council* [2009] E.C.R. I-8917, paras 64–66; ECJ, Case C-40/10 *Commission v Council* [2010] E.C.R. I-12043, para. 95; EGC, Case T-562/10 *HTTS Hanseatic Trade Trust & Shipping v Council* [2011] E.C.R. II-8087, paras 41–43. Compare, e.g. CFI, Case T-318/01 *Othman v Council and Commission* [2009] E.C.R. II-1627, paras 95–99; and EGC, Joined Cases T-135/06 to T-238/06 *Al-Faqih and Others v Council* [2010] E.C.R. II-208*, Summ. pub., paras 44–47, in which the instant proceedings were distinguished from the circumstances at issue in ECJ, Joined Cases C-402/05 P and C-415/05 P *Kadi and Al Barakaat International Foundation v Council and Commission*. See also ECJ (judgment of 27 November 2012), Case C-566/10 P *Italy v Commission*, not reported, para. 103.

been declared void is to no purpose.[845] This is because the annulled act can no longer compromise the applicant's rights or interests.[846] In exceptional cases, the Court of Justice or the General Court may be prompted to curtail the general effect of the declaration of nullity on grounds of legal certainty.[847]

(b) Obligations for the institutions concerned

The Union institution, body, office, or agency whose act has been declared void is required **7.223** by the first paragraph of Art. 266 TFEU to take the necessary measures to comply with the judgment.[848] The Court of Justice and the General Court have no power to indicate what measures should be taken.[849] The extent of the obligation to comply with the judgment is determined both by the operative part and by the grounds underlying the operative part.[850] The institution, body, office, or agency must comply with the judgment in good faith and may not take any measures liable to circumvent correct implementation of the judgment.[851] However, the institution, body, office, or agency concerned is not required to consider

---

[845] ECJ, Case C-372/97 *Italy v Commission* [2004] E.C.R. I-3679, paras 33–38: where what is now the General Court has annulled a decision and an appeal against its judgment is dismissed, an action brought before the Court of Justice for the annulment of the same decision will be held to be to no purpose.

[846] ECJ, Case 3/54 *ASSIDER v High Authority* [1954 to 1956] E.C.R. 63, at 70.

[847] ECJ, Case 92/78 *Simmenthal v Commission* [1979] E.C.R. 777, para. 107.

[848] As regards the distinction between the declaration of nullity and the measures taken under Art. 266 TFEU, as those 'concerned in particular with eradicating the consequences of the act in question which are affected by the illegalities found to have been committed', see, e.g. CFI, Joined Cases T-213/01 and T-214/01 *Österreichische Postsparkasse and Bank für Arbeit und Wirtschaft v Commission* [2006] E.C.R. II-1601, para. 54; CFI (order of 12 January 2007), Case T-447/05 *SPM v Commission* [2007] E.C.R. II-1, para. 57. Art. 266 TFEU mentions only '[t]he institution whose act has been declared void' but presumably, with the language added by the Lisbon Treaty as regards annulment actions brought against acts of Union bodies, offices, or agencies intended to produce legal effects vis-à-vis third parties, similar obligations are placed on a Union body, office, or agency whose act has been annulled by the Union judicature.

[849] ECJ, Case 53/85 *AKZO Chemie v Commission* [1986] E.C.R. 1965, para. 23; ECJ, Case C-199/91 *Foyer Culturel du Sart-Tilman v Commission* [1993] E.C.R. I-2667, para. 7; CFI, Case T-37/89 *Hanning v European Parliament* [1990] E.C.R. II-463, para. 79; CFI, Case T-26/90 *Finsider v Commission* [1992] E.C.R. II-1789, para. 65; CFI, Case T-75/95 *Günzler Aluminium v Commission* [1996] E.C.R. II-497, para. 18; CFI (order of 14 January 2004), Case T-202/02 *Makedoniko Metro and Michaniki v Commission* [2004] E.C.R. II-181, para. 53. Likewise, the Union courts have no power to substitute another act for the annulled act or to amend that act in the context of annulment proceedings: see, e.g. CFI, Case T-263/06 *Greece v Commission* [2008] E.C.R. II-290*, Summ. pub., para. 209; EGC, Case T-214/07 *Greece v Commission* [2011] E.C.R. II-79*, Summ. pub., para. 136; EGC (order of 11 January 2012), Case T-301/11 *Ben Ali v Council*, not reported, para. 62 (and further citations therein). That being said, the Union courts may provide additional guidance so as to enable the defendant institution, body, office, or agency to draw all useful consequences from its judgment: see, e.g. EGC (judgment of 22 May 2012), Case T-300/10 *Internationaler Hilfsfonds v Commission*, not reported, para. 151 (concerning access to documents).

[850] ECJ, Joined Cases 97/86, 193/86, 99/86, and 215/86 *Asteris and Others v Commission* [1988] E.C.R. 2181, para. 27; see also, e.g. ECJ (order of 13 July 2000), Case C-8/99 P *Gòmez de Enterría y Sanchez v European Parliament* [2000] E.C.R. I-6031, paras 19–20; ECJ, Case C-458/98 P *Industrie des Poudres Sphériques v Council* [2000] E.C.R. I-8147, para. 21; ECJ, Case C-417/06 P *Italy v Commission* [2007] E.C.R. I-171*, Summ. pub., paras 50–53; CFI, Case T-224/95 *Tremblay and Others v Commission* [1997] E.C.R. II-2215, para. 72; CFI, Case T-154/98 *Asia Motor France and Others v Commission* [2000] E.C.R. II-3453, para. 101; CFI, Case T-301/01 *Alitalia v Commission* [2008] E.C.R. II-1753, paras 97–98; CFI (order of 12 January 2007), Case T-447/05 *SPM v Commission* [2007] E.C.R. II-1, paras 58–59 (further specifying that the institution concerned is required to ensure that any act intended to replace the annulled act is not affected by the same irregularities as those identified in the judgment which annulled the original act).

[851] See in a staff case: ECJ, Case C-153/99 P *Commission v Giannini* [2000] E.C.R. I-2891, paras 14–15.

whether, in the light of the reasoning of the judgment annulling the contested act, it needs to take measures in relation to persons for whom the partly annulled act remains in place.[852]

In addition, an institution, body, office, or agency which wishes to replace an annulled act may take up the decision-making procedure at the precise point where the illegality arose. This is because the annulment of the final decision does not necessarily affect the validity of the preparatory acts. The grounds of the judgment annulling the act set out precisely what the reasons are for the annulment pronounced in the operative part and the institution, body, office, or agency concerned must take account of them in replacing the annulled act.[853]

(c) Compensation

7.224 The institution, body, office, or agency whose act is annulled may in addition be obliged, in complying with the judgment, to pay compensation for the damage originating in the illegality of the act annulled, provided that all the requirements for liability set out in the second paragraph of Art. 340 TFEU are satisfied.[854]

(d) Time limit

7.225 The institution, body, office, or agency has a reasonable time in which to comply with the judgment.[855] What constitutes a reasonable time depends on the nature of the measures having to be taken in order to carry out the judgment declaring the contested act void and on the attendant circumstances.[856] In the event that there are special difficulties in giving effect to the judgment annulling the contested act, the institution, body, office, or agency may comply with its obligation to give effect to the judgment by adopting any measure which fairly compensates for the disadvantage suffered by the applicant as a result of the unlawful conduct found.[857] Failure to comply with the judgment constitutes an infringement of Art. 266 TFEU, which may cause the Union to incur liability.[858]

---

[852] ECJ, Case C-310/97 P *Commission v AssiDomän Kraft Products and Others* [1999] E.C.R. I-5363, paras 53–71; CFI, Case T-372/00 *Campolargo v Commission* [2002] E.C.R.-SC I-A-49, II-223, para. 109 (as regards the duty to give effect to a judgment annulling an act which had already been carried out). See also ECJ, Case C-239/99 *Nachi Europe* [2001] E.C.R. I-1197, paras 24–26.

[853] ECJ, Case C-415/96 *Spain v Commission* [1998] E.C.R. I-6993, paras 30–32; CFI, Joined Cases T-305/94, T-306/94, T-307/94, T-313/94 to T-316/94, T-318/94, T-325/94, T-328/94, T-329/94, and T-335/94 *Limburgse Vinyl Maatschappij and Others v Commission* [1999] E.C.R. II-931, paras 183–193; CFI, Case T-301/01 *Alitalia v Commission* [2008] E.C.R. II-1753, paras 99–100 (and further citations therein).

[854] CFI, Case T-220/97 *H & R Ecroyd v Commission* [1999] E.C.R. II-1677, para. 56. Indeed, the action for damages against the Union pursuant to Art. 268 TFEU and the second para. of Art. 340 TFEU is an autonomous action vis-à-vis the action for annulment with a different set of requirements to fulfil: see para. 11.09.

[855] ECJ, Case 266/82 *Turner v Commission* [1984] E.C.R. 1, para. 5; CFI, Case T-120/89 *Stahlwerke Peine-Salzgitter v Commission* [1991] E.C.R. II-279, para. 66; CFI, Case T-81/96 *Apostolidis and Others v Commission* [1997] E.C.R.-SC II-607, para. 37 (English abstract at I-A-207).

[856] CFI, Case T-73/95 *Oliveira v Commission* [1997] E.C.R. II-381, para. 41. See, e.g. CFI, Case T-301/01 *Alitalia v Commission* [2008] E.C.R. II-1753, paras 155–156 (finding a period of a little over seven months cannot be regarded as excessive in the context of State aid).

[857] CFI, Case T-91/95 *De Nil and Impens v Council* [1996] E.C.R.-SC II-959, para. 34 (English abstract at I-A-327).

[858] CFI, Case T-11/00 *Hautem v EIB* [2000] E.C.R. II-4019, para. 45; CFI, Joined Cases T-457/04 and T-223/05 *Camar v Commission* [2008] E.C.R. II-215*, Summ. pub., paras 39–43. Art. 266 TFEU does not, however, constitute an autonomous remedy: see CFI, Case T-28/03 *Holcim v Commission* [2005] E.C.R. II-1357, paras 27–40 (appeal dismissed in ECJ, Case C-282/05 P *Holcim v Commission* [2007] E.C.R. I-2941). See also CFI (order of 12 December 2007), Case T-113/04 *Atlantic Container Line and Others v Commission* [2007] E.C.R. II-171*, Summ. pub., para. 23.

(e) Reimbursement of fines

If the Court of Justice or the General Court annuls a decision finding an infringement of **7.226**
Art. 101 and/or Art. 102 TFEU and the undertakings concerned have already paid the fines
imposed by the decision, the Commission is obliged, pursuant to Art. 266 TFEU, to repay
the fines plus interest to the undertakings which successfully brought the action for
annulment.[859] If the Commission does not comply with this obligation, the undertaking
concerned has the choice to either introduce an action for failure to act under Art. 265
TFEU or an action for damages under Art. 268 TFEU and the second paragraph of Art.
340 TFEU.[860] An explicit refusal on the part of the Commission to pay interest on the
principal sum is itself a challengeable act.[861] The undertaking concerned may decide not to
introduce an action for annulment of the Commission's refusal to pay interest, but bring a
damages claim instead.[862]

Where, in contrast, the undertakings concerned have not paid the fine but furnished a bank
guarantee, they are not entitled to claim the costs of that guarantee from the Commission.
This is owing to the absence of any causal link between those costs and the unlawful act.[863]

Where the Court of Justice or the General Court annuls a decision finding an infringement
of Art. 101 and/or Art. 102 TFEU, the Commission is not obliged to repay fines imposed
by that decision to undertakings which did not bring an action for annulment. In the
AssiDomän case, a number of Swedish woodpulp producers which had not brought an
action for annulment of a Commission decision finding an infringement of Art. 101(1)
TFEU on account of concerted practices and imposing fines brought an action for
annulment of a Commission decision rejecting their claim for repayment of the fines.
The undertakings concerned had lodged a request for repayment with the Commission
after the Court of Justice had annulled the original decision, finding an infringement of
Art. 101(1) TFEU as far as the undertakings which had brought an action against it were
concerned. The Court of First Instance had held that it would be inconsistent with the
principle of legality for the Commission not to have a duty to examine its initial position in
relation to undertakings which had not brought an action for annulment of the original

---

[859] CFI, Case T-171/99 *Corus UK v Commission* [2001] E.C.R. I-2967, paras 54–58. See further EGC,
Case T-59/06 *Low & Bonar and Bonar Technical Fabrics v Commission* [2011] E.C.R. II-397*, Summ. pub.,
paras 21–26, in which the General Court held inadmissible an application seeking an order that the
Commission pay default interest incurred by one or more of the applicants, with respect to all or part of
the fine imposed by the Commission in the contested decision under Art. 101 TFEU. It made clear that
annulment proceedings concern only the contested measure and do not relate to acts that the institution may
carry out after its adoption. The Union courts may not decide on the measures that the Commission must take
in order to comply with its judgments.

[860] CFI (order of 4 May 2005), Case T-86/03 *Holcim v Commission* [2005] E.C.R. II-1539, paras 33–34.

[861] ECJ, Case C-123/03 P *Commission v Greencore* [2004] E.C.R. I-11647, para. 47; CFI (order of 4 May
2005), Case T-86/03 *Holcim v Commission* [2005] E.C.R. II-1539, para. 44. The mere fact that the fine has
been repaid without interest cannot be regarded as a refusal to pay as far as the interest is concerned.
Accordingly, the Commission's express refusal to pay interest in subsequent correspondence cannot be
regarded as a confirmatory act against which an action for annulment will not lie (ECJ, Case C-123/03 P
Commission v Greencore [2004] E.C.R. I-11647, paras 39–47).

[862] See to that effect, CFI (order of 4 May 2005), Case T-86/03 *Holcim v Commission* [2005]
E.C.R. II-1539, paras 32–33.

[863] CFI, Case T-28/03 *Holcim v Commission* [2005] E.C.R. II-1357, paras 119–132 (appeal dismissed in
ECJ, Case C-282/05 P *Holcim v Commission* [2007] E.C.R. I-2941); CFI (order of 12 December 2007), Case
T-113/04 *Atlantic Container Line and Others v Commission* [2007] E.C.R. II-171*, Summ. pub., paras 61–63.

decision after the Court of Justice had held that the alleged concerted practice was not proved.[864] On appeal, however, the Court of Justice did not follow the Court of First Instance, but relied on the principle that where the contested act is not challenged by its addressees within the time limit prescribed by Art. 263 TFEU, it becomes definitive vis-à-vis those addressees. Moreover, it held that the authority of a judgment annulling a decision finding an infringement of Art. 101 and/or Art. 102 TFEU cannot apply to the situation of persons who were not parties to the proceedings and with regard to whom the judgment cannot therefore have decided anything whatsoever.[865]

(2) Dismissal of an application for annulment

7.227   After a judgment has been given dismissing an application for annulment (in all or in part), the applicant may not raise the same pleas in another action brought against the same act and the same defendant.[866] An action for annulment which is brought after a judgment dismissing an action brought between the same parties, has the same purpose, and is based on the same submissions as the application which led to the first judgment will be inadmissible on the grounds that the first judgment has the authority of *res judicata*.[867] Yet, the principle of *res judicata* extends only to matters of fact and law actually or necessarily settled in the judicial decision in question.[868]

---

[864] CFI, Case T-227/95 *AssiDomän Kraft Products and Others v Commission* [1997] E.C.R. II-1185, para. 72.

[865] ECJ, Case C-310/97 P *Commission v AssiDomän Kraft Products and Others* [1999] E.C.R. I-5363, paras 53–71. See also ECJ, Joined Cases C-201/09 P and C-216/09 P *ArcelorMittal Luxembourg v Commission and Commission v ArcelorMittal Luxembourg* [2011] E.C.R. I-2239, para. 142. In ECJ (judgment of 22 January 2013), Case C-286/11 P *Commission v Tomkins*, not reported, paras 32–51, the ECJ, however, ruled that where the liability of the parent company is derived exclusively from that of its subsidiary and where the parent company and its subsidiary have brought parallel actions having the same object, the General Court is entitled, without ruling *ultra petita*, to take account of the outcome of the action brought by the subsidiary (*in casu* the reduction of the duration of the infringement) in the action brought by the parent company.

[866] ECJ, Case 62/82 *Italy v Commission* [1983] E.C.R. 687, paras 17–18. It seems that any person is barred from raising the same pleas in another action for annulment or action for damages relating to the same act of general application: CFI, Case T-415/03 *Cofradía de pescadores 'San Pedro' de Bermeo and Others v Council* [2005] E.C.R. II-4355, paras 66–67 (appeal dismissed in ECJ, Case C-6/06 P *Cofradía de pescadores 'San Pedro' de Bermeo and Others v Council* [2007] E.C.R. I-164*, Summ. pub.).

[867] ECJ (order of 1 April 1987), Joined Cases 159/84 and 267/84, 12/85 and 264/85 *Ainsworth v Commission* [1987] E.C.R. 1579, para. 1; ECJ (judgment of 19 April 2012), Case C-221/10 P *Artegodan v Commission and Germany*, not reported, paras 86–93; CFI, Joined Cases T-116/01 and T-118/01 P & O *European Ferries and Others v Commission* [2003] E.C.R. II-2957, paras 75–82, in which the Court of First Instance held that *res judicata* could not be pleaded in respect of an earlier judgment pronouncing annulment in new proceedings seeking to annul the decision taken to comply with that judgment. The reason was that the proceedings did not have the same subject-matter. See also para. 23.94.

[868] ECJ (order of 28 November 1996), Case C-277/95 P *Lenz v Commission* [1996] E.C.R. I-6109, para. 50. CFI, Case T-333/01 *Meyer v Commission* [2003] E.C.R. II-117, paras 22–27: *res judicata* did not mean that a first judgment in which the application was held inadmissible caused a second application between the same parties and having the same subject-matter to be inadmissible. This was because, in the first judgment, the Court of First Instance decided no point of fact or law by which it could be bound in the second proceedings.

8

THE ACTION FOR FAILURE TO ACT

I. Subject-Matter

A. General

(1) Judicial review covers both action and inaction

The action for failure to act is provided for in Art. 265 TFEU.[1] Its object is a declaration on **8.01** the part of the Court of Justice or the General Court[2] that the defendant institution, body, office, or agency of the Union acted unlawfully by failing to take a decision or other sort of action requested in the particular case.[3] Accordingly, the action for failure to act forms part of the complete and coherent system of judicial review, which covers both action and inaction on the part of Union institutions, bodies, offices, or agencies.

Conceivably, the action for failure to act may not garner as much attention as other actions brought before the Union courts, such as the action for annulment, but it is not any less important in the system of remedies set down in the Treaties. As illustrated by the

---

[1] With the entry into force of the Lisbon Treaty, Art. 265 TFEU applies to actions for failure to act in connection with the EAEC Treaty, as Art. 148 EAEC has been repealed: see Art. 106a(1)–(2) EAEC of the consolidated version of the EAEC Treaty, [2012] O.J. C 327/1.

[2] Under Art. 256 TFEU, the General Court has jurisdiction to hear and determine at first instance actions or proceedings referred to in, *inter alia*, Art. 265 TFEU, with the exception of those assigned to a specialized court set up under Art. 257 TFEU (to date, the Civil Service Tribunal) and those reserved in the Statute to the Court of Justice. The jurisdiction of the Civil Service Tribunal derives from Art. 270 TFEU as regards disputes between the Union and its servants within the limits and under the conditions laid down in the Staff Regulations and the Conditions of Employment of other servants of the Union: see Ch. 18. In a situation in which the dispute between the applicant and a Union institution falls within the scope of Art. 270 TFEU but the applicant has brought an action for failure to act under Art. 265 TFEU, the Civil Service Tribunal has given precedence to the jurisdiction of the General Court under the latter: see CST (order of September 2009), Case F-64/09 *Labate v Commission* [2009] E.C.R.-SC I-A-1-381. Moreover, under Art. 51 of the Statute, jurisdiction is reserved to the Court of Justice as regards actions brought under Art. 265 TFEU (as well as Art. 263 TFEU) when they are brought by a Member State against (a) a failure to act by the European Parliament, the Council, or by those institutions acting jointly, save for three exceptions listed therein (involving the Council, of which the General Court retains jurisdiction); and (b) a failure to act by the Commission under the first para. of Art. 331 TFEU. Under this provision, jurisdiction is also reserved to the Court of Justice as regards actions brought under Art. 265 TFEU when they are brought by a Union institution against a failure to act by the European Parliament, the Council, both those institutions acting jointly, the Commission, or the ECB. In other words, save for failures to act brought by a Member State or inter-institutional litigation as mentioned above which fall within the jurisdiction of the Court of Justice, the General Court has first instance jurisdiction over actions for failure to act, including all such actions brought by natural and legal persons. See further para. 2.53. This explains why this chapter refers generally to the Court of Justice or the General Court.

[3] ECJ, Case 377/87 *European Parliament v Council* [1988] E.C.R. 4017, para. 9; ECJ, Case 383/87 *Commission v Council* [1988] E.C.R. 4051, para. 9.

development of the case-law so far, the action for failure to act may be relied upon by individual applicants in a variety of contexts, such as EU competition law and State aid or the EU decision-making process (for example, as regards the authorization procedures laid down for the marketing of products under the applicable rules of Union law), and thus plays an important role in the judicial protection of individuals.

(2) Changes brought by the Treaty of Lisbon

8.02 With the entry into force of the Lisbon Treaty, certain changes were made to the wording of Art. 265 TFEU as compared to its predecessor, former Art. 232 EC, which mainly relate to the parties against which an action for failure to act may be brought.[4] In view of the list of Union institutions set forth in Art. 13(1) TEU,[5] the first paragraph of Art. 265 TFEU provides that an action for failure to act may be brought not only against the European Parliament, Council, and Commission, as already mentioned in former Art. 232 EC, but also against the European Council, the European Central Bank, and bodies, offices, and agencies of the Union. With the recognition of the European Central Bank as a Union institution under the Lisbon Treaty,[6] this accounts for the streamlining of Art. 265 TFEU into three paragraphs and the deletion of what was the fourth paragraph of former Art. 232 EC.[7]

(3) Overview of basic elements of the action for failure to act

8.03 Taking account of the three paragraphs of Art. 265 TFEU, the basic elements of an action for failure to act are:

1. the Union institution, body, office, or agency must have failed to act, meaning that it failed to take a decision or to adopt a given measure;
2. the Union institution, body, office, or agency was under a duty to act;
3. the Union institution, body, office, or agency was first called upon to act by the applicant;
4. if within two months of being called upon to act, the Union institution, body, office, or agency does not define its position or otherwise fails to act;
5. then, an action for failure to act may be brought by the applicant within a further period of two months to the Court of Justice or the General Court asking for a declaration that the Union institution, body, office, or agency concerned acted unlawfully by failing to act and putting that institution, body, office, or agency under the obligation to take the requested act.

---

[4] There were also certain modifications made to the text of Art. 265 TFEU stemming from the changes brought by the Lisbon Treaty to the constitutional framework of the EU generally, including the substitution of 'Treaties' for 'Treaty' and 'Union' for 'Community', as well as certain adjustments with reference to the 'Court of Justice of the European Union' in the first para. of Art. 265 TFEU and the 'Court' in the third para. of Art. 265 TFEU in light of the allocation of jurisdiction between the Union courts as regards the action for failure to act: see further n. 2. As regards the potential impact of changes brought by the Lisbon Treaty concerning the standing for natural and legal persons under the fourth para. of Art. 263 TFEU on the admissibility requirements of the third para. of Art. 265 TFEU, see para. 8.13.

[5] Art. 13(1) TEU states that the Union's institutions shall be the European Parliament, the European Council, the Council, the Commission, the Court of Justice of the European Union, the European Central Bank, and the Court of Auditors.

[6] Compare former Art. 7(1) EC, which listed the following five then Community institutions: the European Parliament, the Council, the Commission, the Court of Justice, and the Court of Auditors.

[7] The fourth para. of former Art. 232 EC had provided: 'The Court of Justice shall have jurisdiction, under the same conditions, in actions or proceedings brought by the ECB in the areas falling within the latter's field of competence and in actions or proceedings brought against the latter.'

The first two elements are discussed in the sections of Part I. The standing of the parties, meaning which parties may bring an action for failure to act (applicants) and against which parties the action for failure to act may be brought (defendants), is dealt with in Part II. The third, fourth, and fifth elements relate to the special characteristics of the action for failure to act involving the pre-litigation and litigation stages of the procedure addressed in Part III. Finally, the consequences of a successful action for failure to act are evaluated in Part IV of this chapter.

B. Subject-matter of an action for failure to act

(1) Subject-matter

The subject-matter of the action for failure to act is confined to an inquiry into whether the **8.04** omission on the part of the Union institution, body, office, or agency to take a given decision or to adopt a given measure was unlawful.[8]

(2) Omission to take a decision or other sort of action

In the first place, the Union institution, body, office, or agency against which the **8.05** proceedings are brought must have failed to act, meaning it must have failed to take a decision or to adopt a given measure.[9] Under the express terms of the second paragraph of Art. 265 TFEU, an action for failure to act will be admissible only if the institution, body, office, or agency concerned has first been called upon to act.[10] Under the second paragraph of Art. 265 TFEU, if, within two months of being so called upon, the institution, body, office, or agency concerned has not defined its position, the action may be brought within a further period of two months.

The subject-matter of the action will cease to exist (i.e. it loses its object or is no longer to any purpose) if the act to which it relates is adopted after the action was brought but before judgment, since in these circumstances a declaration by the Court of Justice or the General Court that the initial failure to act was unlawful can no longer bring about the consequences prescribed by Art. 266 TFEU.[11]

---

[8] In a case where the applicant failed to indicate on what basis of jurisdiction it was bringing an action against the Council for failing to make the Internet websites of the Council Presidency available in the German language, the General Court classified such action as a failure to act under Art. 265 TFEU (which was dismissed as inadmissible): EGC (order of 17 December 2010), Case T-245/10 *Verein Deutsche Sprache v Council*, not reported, paras 12–14 (upheld on appeal in ECJ (order of 28 June 2011), Case C-93/11 P *Verein Deutsche Sprache v Council* [2011] E.C.R. I-92*, Summ. pub., para. 21).

[9] See, e.g. ECJ, Case 8/71 *Komponistenverband v Commission* [1971] E.C.R. 705, para. 2 ('failure to take a decision or to define a position'); Opinion of Advocate-General J. Mischo in ECJ, Case 377/87 *European Parliament v Council* [1988] E.C.R. 4017, para. 12 at 4027 ('failed to adopt an act or take a given measure').

[10] See, e.g. EGC (order of 5 January 2010), Case T-71/09 *Química Atlântica v Commission* [2010] E.C.R. II-1*, Summ. pub., para. 28. See further para. 8.15.

[11] See, e.g. ECJ, Case 377/87 *European Parliament v Council* [1988] E.C.R. 4017, para. 10; ECJ, Case 383/87 *Commission v Council* [1988] E.C.R. 4051, para. 10; ECJ, Joined Cases C-15/91 and C-108/91 *Buckl and Others v Commission* [1992] E.C.R. I-6061, paras 13–18; ECJ, Case C-25/91 *Pesqueras Echebastar v Commission* [1993] E.C.R. I-1719, paras 11–12; ECJ (order of 10 June 1993), Case C-41/92 *Liberal Democrats v European Parliament* [1993] E.C.R. I-3153, para. 4; ECJ (order of 13 December 2000), Case C-44/00 P *Sodima v Commission* [2000] E.C.R. I-11231, paras 83–85; CFI, Case T-28/90 *Asia Motor France and Others v Commission* [1992] E.C.R. II-2285, paras 34–38; CFI (order of 29 November 1993), Case T-56/92 *Koelman v Commission* [1993] E.C.R. II-1267, para. 28; CFI, Case T-32/93 *Ladbroke Racing v Commission*

(3) Duty to act

8.06   Furthermore, a failure to take a decision or another kind of act is unlawful only if the defendant institution, body, office, or agency was under a duty to act.[12] The duty to act must derive from superior Union law.[13] The reference in the first paragraph of Art. 265

[1994] E.C.R. II-1015, para. 22; CFI (order of 26 November 1996), Case T-164/95 *Kuchlenz-Winter v European Parliament* [1996] E.C.R. II-1593, para. 36; CFI (order of 26 November 1996), Case T-226/95 *Kuchlenz-Winter v Commission* [1996] E.C.R. II-1619, para. 30; CFI, Case T-212/95 *Oficemen v Commission* [1997] E.C.R. II-1161, paras 65–68; CFI (order of 26 November 1997), Case T-39/97 *T. Port v Commission* [1997] E.C.R. II-2125, para. 22; CFI, Case T-212/99 *Intervet International v Commission* [2002] E.C.R. II-1145, para. 67; CFI, Joined Cases T-344/00 and T-345/00 *CEVA and Pharmacia Entreprises v Commission* [2002] E.C.R. II-1445, para. 85; CFI, Joined Cases T-297/01 and T-298/01 *SIC v Commission* [2004] E.C.R. II-743, paras 57–58 (this also applies where the act concerned was not submitted within a reasonable time); CFI, Case T-276/03 *Azienda Agricola « Le Canne » v Commission* [2006] E.C.R. II-10*, Summ. pub., para. 36; CFI (order of 28 March 2006), Case T-451/04 *Mediocurso—Estabelecimento de Ensino Particular v Commission*, not reported, para. 19; EGC, Case T-423/07 *Ryanair v Commission* [2011] E.C.R. II-2397, paras 26, 30–33. In these circumstances, however, the Union institution, body, office, or agency may be subject to an order of costs made against it: see para. 8.21.

[12] See, e.g. EGC, Joined Cases T-400/04 and T-402/04 to T-404/04 *Arch Chemicals and Others v Commission* [2011] E.C.R. II-296*, Summ. pub., para. 57 (and citations therein). For some examples, see ECJ, Case 64/82 *Tradax v Commission* [1984] E.C.R. 1359, paras 22–23; CFI, Case T-334/02 *Viomichania Syskevasias Typopoiisis Kai Syntirisis Agrotikon Proïonton v Commission* [2003] E.C.R. II-5121, paras 42–48. With particular regard to alleged failures to act in a situation in which the defendant institution has a discretion under Union law, see, e.g. CFI, Case T-277/94 *AITEC v Commission* [1996] E.C.R. II-351, paras 65–72 (as for the question whether an action should be brought either under Art. 258 TFEU (concerning the action for infringement) or under Art. 108(2) TFEU (concerning State aid), this depends on how the Commission uses its discretion; it does not entail any obligation which may be invoked by the applicant for the purposes of establishing a failure to act on the part of the Commission and such a claim will be inadmissible); CFI (order of 26 November 1996), Case T-167/95 *Kuchlenz-Winter v Council* [1996] E.C.R. II-1607, paras 24–26 (where an action is brought by a natural or legal person for a declaration that, by failing to request the Commission to submit to it proposals for the amendment of the Staff Regulations, the Council has unlawfully failed to act, such action is inadmissible, since the Council enjoys a wide discretion in that context); EGC (order of 6 September 2011), Case T-292/09 *Mugraby v Council and Commission* [2011] E.C.R. II-255*, Summ. pub., paras 35–39 and 43–5 (underlining in relevant part that the failure by an institution to exercise its discretion cannot be the subject of an action for failure to act, thereby dismissing on such ground claims based on the Commission's failure to address a proposal to the Council and the Council's failure to act in not requesting the Commission to submit to it a proposal for the adoption of measures in the area concerned) (appeal dismissed: ECJ (order of 12 July 2012), Case C-581/11 P *Mugraby v Council and Commission*, not reported). But see CFI, Case T-17/96 *TF1 v Commission* [1999] E.C.R. II-1757, in which the CFI held that the applicant found itself in exceptional circumstances which allowed it to bring an action against the Commission for failure to adopt a decision under what is now Art. 106(3) TFEU, even though the Commission has a wide discretion in this regard. However, it remains to be seen whether this case-law is still good law in the light of ECJ, Case C-141/02 P *Commission v T-Mobile Austria* [2005] E.C.R. I-1283 (see para. 7.44).

[13] Such a duty can arise, for example, out of Art. 266 TFEU. An action for failure to act is the appropriate means for obtaining a declaration that the failure by an institution to take the necessary measures to comply with a judgment of the Court of Justice or the General Court is unlawful: CFI, Joined Cases T-297/01 and T-298/01 *SIC v Commission* [2004] E.C.R. II-743, para. 32. But again, such action loses its object once such institution takes a decision in response to the applicant's invitation to act after the action has been brought but before judgment: CFI (order of 28 March 2006), Case T-451/04 *Mediocurso—Estabelecimento de Ensino Particular v Commission*, not reported (rejecting the applicant's arguments that such action has not lost its object on account of putting in peril the principle of effective judicial protection in the delay in taking the necessary measures pursuant to Art. 266 TFEU and in obtaining the 'public condemnation' of the institution concerned). See also EGC, Joined Cases T-400/04 and T-402/04 to T-404/04 *Arch Chemicals and Others v Commission* [2011] E.C.R. II-296*, Summ. pub., para. 60: Art. 17(1) TEU (ex Art. 211 EC) cannot form the basis of an obligation on the Commission to withdraw or amend a measure of general application, such as a regulation, or in the event of its not acting, a ground to bring an action before the Court to have that lack of action declared unlawful; this provision refers to the power conferred on the Commission to ensure that the institutions, Member States, and third parties comply with Union law ('It shall ensure the application of the

TFEU to 'infringement of the Treaties'[14] does not mean that only a duty to act enshrined in an article of the Treaties may be enforced by means of an action for failure to act. An action will lie on the basis of any rule of Union law which is as such binding on the defendant institution, body, office, or agency and contains a duty to act.[15]

In particular, the Commission has no duty to institute infringement proceedings under Art. 258 TFEU against a Member State that violates Union law. If the Commission leaves a complaint filed for that purpose unanswered, an action for failure to act brought by natural or legal persons is deemed inadmissible on the grounds that the Commission has discretion as to whether to initiate such proceedings and that such persons are seeking the adoption of acts of which they are neither the potential addressees nor directly or individually concerned, as required under the third paragraph of Art. 265 TFEU (see para. 8.13).[16] However, the Commission is under a duty to act upon a complaint regarding a violation of the competition rules.[17] But the earliest moment at which the Commission may be under

---

Treaties and of measures adopted by the institutions pursuant to them') and not to the power to amend an existing regulation, a prerogative which falls within the power to take decisions that stems directly from either the relevant provisions of the Treaties or as regards the Commission the measures that confer such power upon it. On similar reasoning, the General Court underlined that the principles of sound administration, legitimate expectations, and legal certainty constitute standards against which the allegedly unlawful failure to act of the Union institutions are examined, but they cannot themselves form the basis of an obligation on the part of the institution concerned (*in casu*, the Commission) to act when a request for amendment of a regulation, which is a measure of general application, is made to it, since as stated earlier, the power to amend such a measure, which falls within the decision-making power of the institutions, stems directly from the relevant provisions of the Treaties or, as regards the Commission, from the measures which confer such power upon it: EGC, Joined Cases T-400/04 and T-402/04 to T-404/04 *Arch Chemicals and Others v Commission*, paras 64–67.

[14] See also Art. 266, first para., TFEU ('contrary to the Treaties').

[15] ECJ, Joined Cases 10/68 and 18/68 *'Eridania' Zuccherifici Nazionali and Others v Commission* [1969] E.C.R. 459, para. 16, where the Court of Justice used the expression 'provision of Community [now Union] law'.

[16] See, e.g. ECJ, Case C-247/97 *Star Fruit v Commission* [1989] E.C.R. I-291, paras 10–14; CFI (order of 19 February 1997), Case T-117/96 *Intertronic v Commission* [1997] E.C.R. II-141, para. 32; CFI (order of 5 June 2002), Case T-143/02 *Olive v Commission and Others*, not reported, para. 11; CFI, Case T-334/02 *Viomichania Syskevasias Typopoiisis Kai Syntirisis Agrotikon Proionton v Commission* [2003] E.C.R. II-5121, paras 43–44; CFI (order of 16 May 2006), Case T-426/05 *Molliné v Commission*, not reported, paras 7–10; CFI (order of 16 November 2009), Case T-354/09 *Goldman Management v Commission and Bulgaria*, not reported, paras 6–8; CFI (order of 17 November 2009), Case C-295/09 *Hansen v Commission*, not reported, paras 6–8 (appeal dismissed: ECJ (order of 6 May 2010), Case C-26/10 P *Hansen v Commission* [2010] E.C.R. I-58*, Summ. pub.); EGC (order of 30 September 2010), Case T-195/10 *Snemo Mars-Momchil Dobrev and Others v Commission and Bulgaria*, not reported, paras 6–7; EGC (order of 6 July 2011), Case T-190/11 *Altner v Commission*, not reported, paras 11–12 (appeal dismissed: ECJ (order of 15 December 2011), Case C-411/11 P *Altner v Commission*, not reported); EGC (order of 15 July 2011), Case T-185/11 *Smanor v Commission and European Ombudsman*, not reported, paras 12–14 (appeal dismissed: ECJ (order of 1 March 2012), Case C-474/11 P *Smanor v Commission and Mediator*, not reported); EGC (order of 15 July 2011), Case T-246/11 *Krefft v Commission*, not reported. See also CFI (order of 7 May 2007), Case T-7/07 AJ *Neves de Silva v Commission*, not reported: although it was not apparent from the application for legal aid as to whether the applicant wanted the Commission to engage infringement proceedings against the Member State in question or if the applicant sought to imply that the Commission had failed to conduct inspections in accordance with the relevant Union law rules, the General Court ruled the action manifestly inadmissible on the ground that the possible measures to be taken by the Commission would neither be addressed to the applicant nor would they concern him directly and individually.

[17] For complaints alleging violation of Art. 101 and/or Art. 102 TFEU, see the case-law cited in para. 8.20. The Commission is likewise under an obligation to act where an undertaking lodges a complaint to the effect that a competitor is involved in a non-notified concentration falling within the scope of Regulation No. 4064/89 (now Regulation No. 139/2004): ECJ, Case C-170/02 P *Schlüsselverlag J.S. Moser and Others v Commission* [2003] E.C.R. I-9889, paras 27–30.

an obligation to take a decision on a complaint is when it has been able to examine all the considerations of fact and law brought to its notice by the complainant.[18]

The Commission is also under a duty to act on a complaint regarding a violation of the State aid rules in similar circumstances. Recently, in *Ryanair v Commission*, the General Court evaluated five separate pleas in law alleging a failure to act on the part of the Commission in relation to the applicant's complaint alleging unlawful State aid, finding that the Commission was under a duty to act under the applicable rules of Union law by setting in motion the preliminary stage and examining the information without delay, which should have led the Commission either to inform the applicant that there were insufficient grounds for taking a view on the case or to adopt a decision.[19] The Commission is under a duty to conduct a diligent and impartial examination of the applicant's complaint alleging the existence of non-notified State aid within a reasonable period, which is determined in relation to the particular circumstances of each case and especially its context, the various procedural stages to be followed by the Commission, and the complexity of the case.[20]

(4) Identification of the act to be taken

8.07 The applicant must state what act the defendant institution, body, office, or agency has failed to adopt, or its application will be inadmissible.[21] The applicant must also describe the act sufficiently precisely in order that the Court of Justice or the General Court may give a judgment which will enable the defendant institution, body, office, or agency to take the necessary measures to comply with it in accordance with Art. 266 TFEU.[22]

---

[18] CFI (order of 6 July 1998), Case T-286/97 *Goldstein v Commission* [1998] E.C.R. II-2629, paras 26–28; see also CFI (order of 10 January 2005), Case T-209/04 *Spain v Commission* [2005] E.C.R. II-29, paras 41–44.

[19] EGC, Case T-442/07 *Ryanair v Commission* [2011] E.C.R. II-333*, Summ. pub., paras 28–38, 49–53, 65–8, 78 (confirmed on appeal: ECJ (judgment of 16 May 2013), Case C-615/11 P *Commission v Ryanair*, not reported, para. 39). The Commission was under no duty to act in relation to certain pleas for which no complaint existed: EGC, Case T-442/07 *Ryanair v Commission*, paras 44–47, 58–64, 74–77. Compare EGC, Case T-423/07 *Ryanair v Commission* [2011] E.C.R. II-2397, paras 27–33 (finding that there was no need to decide whether the Commission was under a duty to act in relation to the complaint of the applicant concerning alleged unlawful State aid, since after the action was brought, but before judgment, the Commission initiated the formal investigation procedure laid down in Art. 108(2) TFEU) and paras 34–41 (ruling that the Commission was under no duty to act in relation to the applicant's plea for which no complaint existed).

[20] Provided the other conditions for the action are satisfied, where such period is held unreasonable and no exceptional circumstances can be shown, an action for failure to act against the Commission is made out: see, e.g. CFI, Case T-95/96 *Gestevisión Telecinco v Commission* [1998] E.C.R. II-3407, paras 71–86, 90 (47 months for first complaint and 26 months for second complaint deemed unreasonable). See also CFI, Case T-17/96 *TF1 v Commission* [1999] E.C.R. II-1757, paras 72–81 (period of 31 months deemed unreasonable). For examples in which the duration of the Commission's investigation has been held reasonable, see CFI, Case T-395/04 *Air One v Commission* [2006] E.C.R. II-1343, paras 60–67 (when the applicant sent the letter of formal notice, the duration of the preliminary investigation of the complaint which had been ongoing for less than six months held not unreasonable); CFI, Case T-167/04 *Asklepios Kliniken v Commission* [2007] E.C.R. II-2379, paras 80–91 (on the date of the applicant's letter of formal notice, the duration of the Commission's preliminary examination of the complaint, which had been going on for 12 months, held not to have exceeded the limits of what was reasonable).

[21] ECJ (order of 7 May 1980), Joined Cases 114/79 to 117/79 *Fournier v Commission* [1980] E.C.R. 1529, at 1531.

[22] ECJ, Case 13/83 *European Parliament v Council* [1985] E.C.R. 1513, paras 35–37. This is linked to the requirements of the letter before action: see paras 8.15 and 8.16. This is also linked to some extent with the requirements of clarity and precision of applications more generally pursuant to Art. 21 of the Statute and

(5) The act must be capable of having legal effects

The duty to take a decision or other sort of action requested must give rise to an act that is **8.08** capable of having legal effects.[23] The nature of the legal effects required, however, is not always the same. It depends on the status of the party bringing the action.

If the action for failure to act is brought by a natural or legal person, the defendant institution, body, office, or agency must have failed to 'address to that person any act other than a recommendation or an opinion' under the third paragraph of Art. 265 TFEU. It follows that where an action for failure to act is brought by a natural or legal person, it will be admissible only if it relates to the failure on the part of the defendant institution, body, office, or agency to adopt a binding act.[24]

In contrast, if the action for failure to act is brought by a Member State or a Union institution,[25] the act which was not taken does not necessarily have to be binding in order to have legal effects, and thus, an action may be brought in this case too. For instance, an action may be brought against the Commission if it fails to submit a proposal to the Union legislator relating to a matter on which the Union is under an obligation to legislate.[26] The rationale is that the Commission proposal is necessary in order to enable the Council and the European Parliament to play their respective roles in the legislative process.[27]

Art. 120 and Art. 44, respectively of the ECJ and EGC Rules of Procedure: see, e.g. CFI, Case C-167/04 *Asklepios Kliniken v Commission* [2007] E.C.R. II-2379, paras 41, 44; CFI (order of 17 November 2010), Case T-61/10 *Victoria Sánchez v European Parliament and Commission* [2010] E.C.R. II-252*, Summ. pub., paras 27–39 (upheld on appeal: ECJ (order of 26 October 2011), Case C-52/11 P *Victoria Sánchez v European Parliament and Commission* [2011] E.C.R. I-158*, Summ. pub., paras 20–26).

[23] Opinion of Advocate General J. Mischo in ECJ, Case 377/87 *European Parliament v Council* [1988] E.C.R. 4017, para. 30, at 4029 ('The decisive criterion is therefore that of legal effects. Thus, a "failure to act" within the meaning of [now Art. 265 TFEU] may be constituted by the non-adoption . . . of an act or a measure, of whatever nature, form or description, which is capable of producing legal effects vis-à-vis third parties.').

[24] Consequently, individuals cannot challenge an institution's failure to adopt a non-binding act, not even where the failure to act takes the form of an express refusal: see ECJ, Case 15/70 *Chevalley v Commission* [1970] E.C.R. 975. In recent case-law, in relation to the applicant's claims based on the Commission's failure to adopt a recommendation and the Council's failure in not requesting the Commission to submit to it a proposal for Union measures in the area concerned, the General Court based its ruling dismissing such claims on the fact that the failure of an institution to exercise a discretion cannot be the subject of an action for failure to act: EGC (order of 6 September 2011), Case T-292/09 *Mugraby v Council and Commission* [2011] E.C.R. II-255*, Summ. pub., paras 49–50 and 55 (appeal dismissed: ECJ (order of 12 July 2012), Case C-581/11 P *Mugraby v Council and Commission*, not reported).

[25] By virtue of the express wording of Art. 265 TFEU, an action for failure to act may be brought against bodies, offices, and agencies of the Union, but they cannot bring such an action: see para. 8.12.

[26] ECJ (order of 11 July 1996), Case C-445/93 *European Parliament v Commission*, not reported (failure of the Commission to submit the necessary proposals pursuant to Arts 14 and 211 EC [now Arts 26 TFEU and 17(1) TEU, respectively] for the liberalization of the movement of persons; on an application from the European Parliament, an order was given declaring that there was no need to proceed to judgment following the submission of the relevant proposal by the Commission). If the Council and European Parliament are not under a duty to legislate, but instead merely have a discretion to do so, then the Commission cannot be obliged to submit a proposal for a legislative measure to the Council and the European Parliament: there is simply no duty to act under such circumstances. See also by analogy, e.g. EGC (order of 6 September 2011), Case T-292/09 *Mugraby v Council and Commission*, paras 49–50 and 55 (appeal dismissed: ECJ (order of 12 July 2012), Case C-581/11 P *Mugraby v Council and Commission*, not reported). For a case in which the Council was under a duty to legislate, see ECJ, Case 13/83 *European Parliament v Council* [1985] E.C.R. 1513, paras 54–71.

[27] The same reasoning applies to decision-making in connection with the Union budget: ECJ, Case 377/87 *European Parliament v Council* [1988] E.C.R. 4017 (action brought against the Council for failure to act on the grounds that it had failed to place before the European Parliament, in accordance with former Art. 272(4) EC

C. Relationship between the action for annulment and the action for failure to act

(1) No necessary link between the two forms of action

8.09   The action for annulment and the action for failure to act provide for one and the same means of recourse. Indeed, the possibility for individuals to assert their rights should not depend upon whether the Union has acted or failed to act.[28] Accordingly, the action for failure to act and the action for annulment are meant to be 'two sides of the same coin' for the most part in the sense that the two actions often follow each other: where the institution, body, office, or agency has not acted, the action for failure to act urges it to do so; and when the institution, body, office, or agency acts and the act taken is not what the party wanted, then the action for annulment comes to the fore as a means to challenge such act.

There is, however, no necessary link between the action for annulment and the action for failure to act,[29] since the action for failure to act does not always enable the applicant to induce the adoption of a measure that can be the subject of an action for annulment.[30]

First, Member States or Union institutions may compel an institution, body, office, or agency to adopt a measure by means of an action for failure to act, even though no action for annulment would be available against the act in question. For example, the European Parliament is entitled to a declaration from the Court of Justice that the Council's failure to lay before it a draft budget is unlawful. Yet, once the draft budget has been adopted, no action for annulment will lie against it, since it is a preparatory act.[31]

Second, even if the applicant seeks the adoption of a binding act,[32] the defendant institution, body, office, or agency may, under certain circumstances, put an end to its failure to

---

[now Art. 314(3) TFEU], a draft general budget of the then Community for the following financial year by no later than 5 October).

[28] ECJ, Case 15/70 *Chevalley v Commission* [1970] E.C.R. 975, para. 6; ECJ, Case C-68/95 *T. Port v Commission* [1996] E.C.R. I-6065, para. 59.

[29] This is apart from issues concerning the admissibility of an action for annulment vis-à-vis the action for failure to act. See ECJ, Case C-123/03 P *Commission v Greencore* [2004] E.C.R. I-11647, para. 46 (ruling that the fact that the applicant had not used the procedure provided for in Art. 265 TFEU had no bearing on the admissibility of the action for annulment subsequently brought in connection with the Commission's alleged disregard of its obligations under Art. 266 TFEU concerning compliance with a judgment annulling or reducing the fine imposed on an undertaking for infringement of the competition rules requiring repayment not only of the principal amount of the fine overpaid, but also the default interest on that amount to the undertaking concerned); see further CFI, Case T-135/02 *Greencore v Commission* [2005] E.C.R. II-31*, Summ. pub., paras 59–60; CFI (order of 4 May 2005), Case T-86/03 *Holcim (France) v Commission* [2005] E.C.R. II-1539, paras 33–36, 42–45. In another case, an objection of inadmissibility of an action for annulment, advanced by the Commission on the grounds that the applicant should have brought an action for failure to act which was out of time, was not dealt with by the General Court on the grounds that the applicant's plea in law in the context of annulment was unfounded in any event: EGC, Case T-289/09 *Evropaïki Dynamiki-Proigmena Systimata Tilepikoinonion Pliroforikis kai Tilematikis v Commission* [2011] E.C.R. II-270*, Summ. pub., paras 55–58.

[30] ECJ, Case 302/87 *European Parliament v Council* [1988] E.C.R. 5615, para. 16.

[31] ECJ, Case 302/87 *European Parliament v Council*, para. 16.

[32] As mentioned earlier, unlike Member States and Union institutions, a natural or legal person can seek only the adoption of a binding act by virtue of the third para. of Art. 265 TFEU: see para. 8.08.

act by adopting a non-binding act against which an action for annulment will not lie. Since the failure to act has been terminated, an action for failure to act will no longer be admissible, unless at a later stage a further failure to act on the part of the defendant institution, body, office, or agency can be established in the light of new circumstances (see paras 8.19 and 8.20).

(2) Annulment action will lie only against a binding act

Once the institution, body, office, or agency adopts a binding act, an action for annulment **8.10** will lie against it. The act in question may be a refusal to adopt the act sought[33] or the adoption of an act different from the one requested.[34] If, however, the failure to act is terminated by a definition of a position not constituting a binding act (see paras 8.19 and 8.20), no action for annulment may be brought against it.[35] That said, an act which is not open to an action for annulment may constitute a definition of a position terminating the failure to act if it is the prerequisite for the next step in a procedure which is to culminate in a legal act which is itself open to an action for annulment.[36]

The Court of Justice and the General Court will not tolerate any improper use of the action for failure to act.[37] In the event that an institution, body, office, or agency has adopted a binding act, only an action for annulment will be available to challenge it. If the applicant has allowed the period for bringing an action to expire, it cannot provoke a failure to act by addressing a request to the institution, body, office, or agency concerned to revoke the measure adversely affecting it.[38] Moreover, if the institution, body, office, or agency does not comply with such a request, it is not in breach of any duty to act.

---

[33] ECJ, Case 42/71 *Nordgetreide v Commission* [1972] E.C.R. 105, para. 4 (an action for annulment brought by an individual applicant will then be admissible if the measure sought, constituting the subject-matter of the refusal, satisfies the conditions laid down in the fourth para. of what is now Art. 263 TFEU); ECJ, Case 44/81 *Germany v Commission* [1982] E.C.R. 1855, para. 6; EGC (order of 5 January 2010), Case T-71/09 *Química Atlântica v Commission* [2010] E.C.R. II-1*, Summ. pub., paras 30, 32.

[34] ECJ, Case 8/71 *Komponistenverband v Commission* [1971] E.C.R. 705, para. 2. For some examples, see CFI, Case T-75/06 *Bayer CropScience and Others v Commission* [2008] E.C.R. II-2081, particularly paras 40–43 (action for annulment dismissed) (upheld on appeal: ECJ (order of 15 April 2010), Case C-517/08 P *Makhteshim-Agan Holding and Others v Commission* [2010] E.C.R. I-45*, Summ. pub.); CFI (order of 19 May 2008) Case T-144/04 *TF1 v Commission* [2008] E.C.R. II-761, particularly paras 1–5 (action for annulment dismissed).

[35] ECJ, Case 48/65 *Lütticke v Commission* [1966] E.C.R. 19, at 27; ECJ, Case 42/71 *Nordgetreide v Commission* [1972] E.C.R. 105. For an example, see ECJ, Case C-150/06 P *Arizona Chemical and Others v Commission* [2007] E.C.R. I-39*, Summ. pub., paras 21–25: under the case-law, an act of the Commission amounting to a rejection must be appraised in the light of the nature of the request to which it constituted a reply, *in casu* a proposal to amend a Union measure which is not a challengeable act for the purposes of Art. 263, fourth para., TFEU.

[36] See, e.g. CFI (order of 26 November 2008), Case T-393/06 *Makhteshim-Agan Holding and Others v Commission* [2008] E.C.R. II-293*, Summ. pub., paras 51–52 (and case-law cited therein) (appeal dismissed in ECJ (order of 22 January 2010), Case C-69/09 P *Makhteshim-Agan Holding and Others v Commission* [2010] E.C.R. I-10*, Summ. pub.): in these proceedings, the Commission defined its position by the submission of a proposal which is not open to an action for annulment, but resulted in the adoption of a legal act by the Council which is open to an action for annulment.

[37] See, e.g. EGC, Joined Cases T-400/04 and T-402/04 to T-404/04 *Arch Chemicals and Others v Commission* [2011] E.C.R. II-296*, Summ. pub., para. 63 (finding that the applicants' argument exceeds the actual scope of an action for failure to act and is in reality seeking a declaration that the provisions of an existing EU regulation are unlawful, against which the remedy of the action for annulment is available).

[38] ECJ, Joined Cases 10/68 and 18/68 'Eridania' *Zurcherifici Nationali and Others v Commission* [1969] E.C.R. 459, para. 17.

II. Identity of the Parties

A. Defendants

8.11 In the first place, as regards Union institutions, the first paragraph of Art. 265 TFEU provides that an action for failure to act may be brought against the European Parliament, the European Council, the Council, the Commission,[39] or the European Central Bank. Noticeably, of the seven Union institutions enumerated in Art. 13(1) TEU, the Court of Justice of the European Union and the Court of Auditors are not mentioned among the list of potential defendant institutions in the first paragraph of Art. 265 TFEU. This can be taken to mean that no action for failure to act may be brought against these two Union institutions.

Moreover, pursuant to the changes introduced by the Lisbon Treaty as mentioned in para. 8.02, the first paragraph of Art. 265 TFEU further provides: 'This Article shall apply, under the same conditions, to bodies, offices and agencies of the Union which fail to act.' Since the action for annulment and the action for failure to act are envisaged to provide for one and the same means of recourse,[40] the wording of Art. 265 TFEU has been brought in line with that of Art. 263 TFEU.[41]

As a consequence, case-law decided under the former Art. 232 EC in which only 'institutions of the Community' were mentioned may merit some refinement. For example, this provision was deemed inapplicable to the Office for Harmonisation in the Internal Market (Trade Marks and Designs) (OHIM) on the grounds that it concerned omissions of only those institutions listed in the EC Treaty, which did not include the OHIM.[42] Likewise, an action for failure to act brought by an individual applicant against the European Ombudsman was held inadmissible before the entry into force of the Lisbon Treaty because it was not considered a Community institution within the meaning of Art. 232 EC.[43] Yet, as part

---

[39] EU delegations are attached to the Commission, and thus, an action for failure to act is inadmissible insofar as such action is brought against a delegation separately: EGC (order of 30 June 2011), Case T-264/09 *Tecnoprocess v Commission and Delegation of the EU in Morocco* [2011] E.C.R. II-208*, Summ. pub., paras 70–71.

[40] ECJ, Case 15/70 *Chevalley v Commission* [1970] E.C.R. 975, para. 6; ECJ, Case C-68/95 *T. Port v Commission* [1996] E.C.R. I-6065, para. 59.

[41] However, Art. 265 TFEU does not specify that the acts of Union bodies, offices, and agencies must be 'intended to produce legal effects vis-à-vis third parties', as is the case in Art. 263, first para., TFEU. Art. 265 TFEU has been interpreted as pertaining to acts capable of having legal effects in any event: see para. 8.08.

[42] CFI, Case T-160/07 *Lancôme parfums et beauté v OHIM* [2008] E.C.R. II-1733, para. 31 (appealed on other grounds: ECJ, Case C-408/08 P *Lancôme v OHIM* [2010] E.C.R. I-1347). But see CFI (order of 9 July 2009), Case T-176/08 *infeurope v Commission* [2009] E.C.R. II-119*, Summ. pub., paras 36–39, in which the CFI ruled that as regards Art. 118 of Regulation No. 40/94, which lays down a system for control by the Commission of the legality of some acts of the President of the OHIM, an action for failure to act seeking a declaration that the Commission has been guilty of inaction is not admissible in the context of a system such as that laid down by this provision, in which it is expressly provided that the Commission's inaction results in an implied dismissal; any declaration that the Commission acted unlawfully is possible only in the context of an action for annulment brought against a final decision of the institution in which it decides, either expressly or impliedly, on the merits of the applicant's complaint.

[43] CFI (order of 22 May 2000), Case T-103/99 *Associazione delle Cantine Sociali Venete v European Ombudsman and European Parliament* [2000] E.C.R. II-4165, para. 46. See also CFI (order of 5 September 2006), Case T-144/06 *O'Loughlin v European Ombudsman and Ireland*, not reported, para. 15; CFI (order of

---

of its reasoning, the CFI also considered that the only act which the applicant could have obtained in the proceedings concerned was the report issued by the European Ombudsman to the European Parliament finding a case of maladministration of the Commission, which was not capable of having legal effects for the purposes of the action for failure to act (see para. 8.08).[44] Consequently, such an approach may not necessarily be disturbed by the changes brought by the entry into force of the Lisbon Treaty.

In any event, an action for failure to act can only be brought against a Union institution, body, office, or agency. Since the Union (or former Community) itself is not referred to in Art. 265 TFEU, a failure to act brought against it would be inadmissible.[45] Likewise, an action for failure to act under Art. 265 TFEU cannot be brought against a Member State[46] or the European Court of Human Rights.[47]

B. Applicants

(1) Union institutions and Member States

The first paragraph of Art. 265 TFEU authorizes 'the Member States and the other **8.12** institutions of the Union' to bring an action for failure to act. It confers that right of action on all the Union institutions.[48] This includes the European Council and the European Central Bank, now recognized as Union institutions under Art. 13(1) TEU, as well as the European Parliament, the Council, the Commission, and the Court of Auditors, which had already been mentioned in former Art. 7(1) EC.[49] Accordingly, under Art. 265 TFEU, the European Central Bank is no longer limited to bringing an action for failure to act 'in the areas falling within the latter's field of competence', as was the case under the fourth paragraph of former Art. 232 EC. Only the Court of Justice of the European Union has no such right of action. This is because it is responsible for legal protection and does not itself seek it.[50]

By virtue of the reference in the first paragraph of Art. 265 TFEU to Union bodies, offices, and agencies 'which fail to act', the Treaties indicate that although such bodies, offices, and agencies may be defendants to an action for failure to act, they cannot as applicants bring such an action.

---

3 November 2008), Case T-196/08 *Srinivasan v European Ombudsman*, not reported, para 13 (appeal dismissed on other grounds: ECJ (order of 25 June 2009), Case C-580/08 P *Srinivasan v European Ombudsman* [2009] E.C.R. I-110*, Summ. pub.).

[44] CFI (order of 22 May 2000), Case T-103/99 *Associazione delle Cantine Sociali Venete v European Ombudsman and European Parliament* [2000] E.C.R. II-4165, paras 47–55.

[45] EGC (order of 6 September 2011), Case T-292/09 *Mugraby v Council and Commission* [2011] E.C.R. II-255*, Summ. pub., para. 23.

[46] ECJ (order of 4 March 2010), Case C-374/09 P *Hârsulescu v Romania* [2010] E.C.R. I-30*, Summ. pub., para. 12; CFI (order of 16 November 2009), Case T-354/09 *Goldman Management Inc. v Commission and Bulgaria*, not reported, paras 13, 15–16 (appeal dismissed: ECJ, Case C-507/09 P *Goldman Management Inc. v Commission and Bulgaria* [2010] E.C.R. I-57*, Summ. pub.).

[47] EGC (order of 4 April 2011), Case T-133/11 *Fundația Pro Fondbis—1946 Semper v European Court of Human Rights*, not reported.

[48] ECJ, Case 13/83 *European Parliament v Council* [1985] E.C.R. 1513, paras 17–18 (albeit concerning the phrasing of the first para. of the former Art. 232 EC).

[49] See n. 6.

[50] Opinion of Advocate-General C.O. Lenz in ECJ, Case 13/83 *European Parliament v Council* [1985] E.C.R. 1513, at 1519.

(2) Natural and legal persons

8.13 Under the third paragraph of Art. 265 TFEU, a natural or legal person may complain to the General Court that 'an institution, body, office, or agency of the Union has failed to address to that person any act other than a recommendation or an opinion'. An action brought by a natural or legal person can therefore relate only to a failure to adopt an act that has a direct influence on that person's legal position.[51]

As had been the case before the entry into force of the Lisbon Treaty, although a literal reading of the text of Art. 265 TFEU could appear to indicate that an action for failure to act can be brought by a natural or legal person only in relation to binding acts addressed 'to that person', under the case-law, it is enough for a natural or legal person to be directly and individually concerned by the act which the institution, body, office, or agency failed to adopt and which formally ought to have been addressed to another person (for example, a Member State).[52] This is because the Court of Justice has held that what are now Arts 263 and 265 TFEU merely prescribe one and the same method of recourse.[53] It follows that just as the fourth paragraph of what is now Art. 263 TFEU allows individuals to bring an action for annulment against a measure not addressed to them provided that the measure is of direct and individual concern to them, the third paragraph of Art. 265 TFEU must be interpreted as also entitling them to bring an action for failure to act against an institution, body, office, or agency which they claim has failed to adopt a measure which would have concerned them in the same way.[54]

Consequently, in spite of the more stringent wording of the third paragraph of Art. 265 TFEU as compared to the fourth paragraph of Art. 263 TFEU, the subject-matter of the right of action of a natural or legal person is not confined to the defendant institution, body, office, or agency's failure expressly to address a particular act to the applicant and extends to

---

[51] ECJ, Case 6/70 *Borromeo v Commission* [1970] E.C.R. 815; ECJ, Case 15/70 *Chevalley v Commission* [1970] E.C.R. 975; ECJ (order of 17 October 1984), Joined Cases 83/84 and 84/84 *NM v Commission and Council* [1984] E.C.R. 3571, para. 10; ECJ (order of 30 March 1990), Case C-371/89 *Emrich v Commission* [1990] E.C.R. I-1555, para. 6; CFI (order of 27 May 1994), Case T-5/94 *J v Commission* [1994] E.C.R. II-391, para. 16; CFI (order of 4 July 1994), Case T-13/94 *Century Oils Hellas v Commission* [1994] E.C.R. II-431, para. 13.

[52] As recognized in past case-law, an 'indirect interest' which a natural or legal person might have in the adoption of the act requested is completely insufficient for him to be regarded as a potential addressee of the act for the purposes of direct and individual concern: ECJ, Case 246/81 *Lord Bethell v Commission* [1982] E.C.R. 2277, para. 16; cf. CFI (order of 23 January 1991), Case T-3/90 *Prodifarma v Commission* [1991] E.C.R. II-1, paras 35–45; CFI, Case T-32/93 *Ladbroke Racing v Commission* [1994] E.C.R. II-1015, paras 40–43.

[53] ECJ, Case 15/70 *Chevalley v Commission* [1970] E.C.R. 975, para. 6; ECJ, Case C-68/95 *T. Port v Commission* [1996] E.C.R. I-6065, para. 59; CFI, Case T-17/96 *TF1 v Commission* [1999] E.C.R. II-1757, para. 27; CFI (order of 22 May 2000), Case T-103/99 *Associazione delle Cantine Sociali Venete v European Ombudsman and European Parliament* [2000] E.C.R. II-4165, para. 47; CFI, Case T-395/04 *Air One v Commission* [2006] E.C.R. II-1343, para. 25; CFI (order of 28 March 2006), Case T-451/04 *Mediocurso—Estabelecimento de Ensino Particular v Commission*, not reported, para. 26; CFI, Case T-167/04 *Asklepios Kliniken v Commission* [2007] E.C.R. II-2379, para. 45; CFI (order of 25 June 2008), Case T-185/08 *VDH Projektentwicklung and Edeka Handelsgesellschaft Rhein-Ruhr v Commission* [2008] E.C.R. II-98*, Summ. pub.

[54] See, e.g. ECJ, Case C-68/95 *T. Port v Commission* [1996] E.C.R. I-6065, para. 59; CFI, Case T-395/04 *Air One v Commission* [2006] E.C.R. II-1343, para. 25; CFI, Case T-167/04 *Asklepios Kliniken v Commission* [2007] E.C.R. II-2379, para. 45; CFI (order of 25 June 2008), Case T-185/08 *VDH Projektentwicklung and Edeka Handelsgesellschaft Rhein-Ruhr v Commission* [2008] E.C.R. II-98*, Summ. pub., para. 9 (ruling action inadmissible because parties not directly concerned by Union measure in question) (upheld on appeal in ECJ (order of 3 April 2009), Case C-387/08 P *VDH Projektentwicklung and Edeka Rhein-Ruhr v Commission* [2009] E.C.R. I-56*, Summ. pub.).

other acts provided that the standing requirements of direct and individual concern are satisfied. The idea behind this is to underscore the parallelism between the action for annulment and the action for failure to act as far as the measure at issue is concerned,[55] on the grounds that the possibility for individuals to assert their rights should not depend upon whether the institution, body, office, or agency concerned has acted or failed to act.[56]

As such, the case-law on the requirements for direct and individual concern under the fourth paragraph of Art. 263 TFEU has been brought to bear on the admissibility of actions brought by natural and legal persons under the third paragraph of Art. 265 TFEU.[57] Moreover, with the changes brought by the Lisbon Treaty as regards the standing requirements for individual applicants under the fourth paragraph of Art. 263 TFEU, namely the introduction of the category of regulatory acts which do not entail implementing measures and for which individual applicants must demonstrate only direct concern (see para. 7.108), it will have to be seen whether in the future the Union courts will read a similar development into the third paragraph of Art. 265 TFEU in light of the apparent parallelism between the two provisions as far as the standing of natural and legal persons is concerned.

(3) The action for failure to act and the indirect and direct routes of judicial review

8.14 The said parallelism of the standing requirements for natural and legal persons under the third paragraph of Art. 265 TFEU and the fourth paragraph of Art. 263 TFEU brings into play related aspects in the case-law concerning the interplay between direct and indirect

---

[55] ECJ, Case 247/87 *Star Fruit v Commission* [1989] E.C.R. 291, para. 13. As regards the State aid context, see ECJ (order of 1 October 2004), Case C-379/03 P *Pérez Escolar v Commission*, not reported, paras 15–26 (the fact that an individual lodged a complaint with the Commission with respect to an alleged violation of Arts 107 and 108 TFEU is as such—not sufficient for that individual to have the standing to bring an action under Art. 265 TFEU before the General Court. The person concerned will have to demonstrate that he or she is directly and individually concerned by the decision which the Commission failed to adopt). If pursuant to the filing of the complaint, the Commission has not taken any decision, the fact that the complainant is an 'interested party' within the meaning of Art. 1(h) of Regulation No. 659/1999 will be sufficient to satisfy the requirement of individual concern in order to challenge a failure to act on the part of the Commission to take a decision on State aid addressed to a Member State: see CFI, Case T-95/96 *Gestevisión Telecinco v Commission* [1998] E.C.R. II-3407, paras 64–69; CFI, Case T-395/04 *Air One v Commission* [2006] E.C.R. II-1343, paras 25–42; CFI, Case T-167/04 *Asklepios Kliniken v Commission* [2007] E.C.R. II-2379, paras 45–57; see also implicitly EGC, Case T-442/07 *Ryanair v Commission* [2011] E.C.R. II-333*, Summ. pub. (appeal dismissed: ECJ (judgment of 16 May 2013), Case C-615/11 P *Commission v Ryanair*, not reported). If, however, the action concerns the Commission's failure to act subsequent to its opening of the formal procedure of Art. 108 (2) TFEU, or in other words the Commission's failure to adopt a final decision, the applicant will in principle have to demonstrate that its position on the market is significantly affected by the aid concerned in order to satisfy the requirement of individual concern. Under such circumstances, it will not be sufficient to demonstrate that it is an 'interested party' within the meaning of Art. 1(h) of Regulation No. 659/1999. See para. 7.124.

[56] ECJ, Case C-68/95 *T. Port v Commission* [1996] E.C.R. I-6065, para. 59.

[57] This may be seen in the approach taken in earlier case-law, in which the words 'address to' in what is now Art. 265 TFEU were read to preclude an applicant who is a natural or legal person from bringing an action for failure to adopt an act of general application. See, e.g. ECJ, Case 15/71 *Mackprang v Commission* [1971] E.C.R. 797, para. 4; ECJ, Case 134/73 *Holtz & Willemsen v Council* [1974] E.C.R. 1, para. 5; ECJ, Case 90/78 *Granaria v Council and Commission* [1979] E.C.R. 1081, paras 12–15; ECJ (order of 11 July 1979), Case 60/79 *Fédération Nationale des Producteurs de Vins de Table et Vins de Pays v Commission* [1979] E.C.R. 2429, at 2433; CFI (order of 26 November 1996), Case T-167/95 *Kuchlenz-Winter v Council* [1996] E.C.R. II-1607, para. 21. Yet, this approach should arguably be read against subsequent developments in the case-law concerning the admissibility requirements for natural and legal persons in the context of the action for annulment in which it has been recognized that depending on the particular case it cannot be automatically foreclosed that a Union act of general application may be of direct and individual concern to the applicant (see para. 7.85).

routes of judicial review when it comes to failures to act on the part of Union institutions, offices, bodies, and agencies.

As discussed in para. 10.12, in *T. Port*, the Court ruled that the Treaties make no provision for a reference for a preliminary ruling in which the national court asks the Court to rule that a Union institution, office, body, or agency has failed to act.[58] At the same time, the Court emphasized several routes to ensure judicial protection for the persons concerned, including the fact that the German undertaking or the Member State concerned could bring an action for failure to act before the Union courts under what is now Art. 265 TFEU, thereby making clear that the direct route of an action for failure to act is available when the indirect route of a preliminary ruling procedure is not.

Thereafter, in *Ten Kate*, the Court was confronted with a question for a preliminary ruling from a national court about the possibility of Member State liability arising out of the fact that the Member State concerned had refrained from bringing an action for failure to act (or an action for annulment) against the Commission in circumstances where the natural and legal persons involved in the main proceedings could not bring such an action themselves because they were not individually concerned and hence such a direct route was unavailable.[59] In response, the Court ruled that Union law did not impose any obligation on a Member State to bring an action for failure to act (or an action for annulment), but emphasized that just as natural and legal persons should be able to challenge before a national court the legality of any decision or other national measure relative to the application to him or her of a Union act of general application by pleading the invalidity of that act, 'the same holds true where a natural and legal person invokes a failure to take a decision, within the meaning of Article [265 TFEU], which it considers to be contrary to [Union] law'.[60] Accordingly, the approach taken by the Court of Justice ensures that the indirect route of a preliminary ruling on the validity of a failure to act remains open in circumstances where the direct route of an action for failure to act is not available.

III. Special Characteristics

A. Pre-litigation procedure

8.15 (1) **The Union institution, body, office, or agency must first have been called upon to act**

Under the second paragraph of Art. 265 TFEU, an action for failure to act is admissible only if, before proceedings are brought, the defendant institution, body, office, or agency has first been called upon to act by the applicant.[61] This means that the applicant (a Member

---

[58] ECJ, Case C-68/95 *T. Port v Commission* [1996] E.C.R. I-6065, para. 53.

[59] ECJ, Case C-511/03 *Ten Kate Musselkanaal and Others* [2005] E.C.R. I-8979, para. 17 (also indicating that an action for damages would not have sufficed).

[60] ECJ, Case C-511/03 *Ten Kate Musselkanaal and Others*, para. 29.

[61] See, e.g. EGC, Case T-442/07 *Ryanair v Commission* [2011] E.C.R. II-333*, Summ. pub., para. 22; EGC (order of 30 June 2011), Case T-264/09 *Tecnoprocess v Commission and Delegation of the EU to Morocco* [2011] E.C.R. II-208*, Summ. pub., para. 84; EGC (order of 30 June 2011), Case T-367/09 *Tecnoprocess v Commission* [2011] E.C.R. II-209*, Summ. pub., para. 47. Art. 265 TFEU does not provide any derogation from the requirement of formal notice: see CFI (order of 26 November 2008), Case T-393/06 *Makhteshim-Agan Holding and Others v Commission* [2008] E.C.R. II-297*, Summ. pub., paras 46–50 (appeal dismissed on

State, Union institution, or a natural or legal person) has a duty to raise the matter with the Union institution, body, office, or agency by means of some sort of communication, which is often referred to as a letter before action or letter of formal notice. The idea behind raising the matter with the institution, body, office, or agency in this way is to prompt it to adopt the measure requested within two months, or at least to define its position in regard to the alleged failure to act.[62]

(2) Letter of formal notice is an essential procedural requirement

The letter of formal notice calling upon the defendant institution, body, office, or agency to act is an essential procedural requirement, the effects of which are, first, to cause the two-month period within which the institution, body, office, or agency is required to define its position to begin to run, and second, to delimit any action that might be brought should that institution, body, office, or agency fail to define its position.[63] **8.16**

(3) The Union institution, body, office, or agency must be called upon to act within a reasonable time

There is no specific time limit set forth in Art. 265 TFEU for calling upon the institution, body, office, or agency to act.[64] Conceivably, this is because the precise moment when a failure to act becomes reproachable is difficult to establish. But this does not mean that the applicant can wait for an indefinite period of time after finding that there has been a failure to act on the part of a Union institution, body, office, or agency. **8.17**

Under the case-law, the Union institution, body, office, or agency must be called upon to act within a reasonable time after the applicant initially finds that there has been a failure to act. What constitutes a reasonable time is determined by the Union courts on a case-by-case basis. An eighteen-month period was held to be unreasonable.[65]

(4) Content of the letter of formal notice

There is no particular requirement as to form, but the letter of formal notice must be sufficiently clear and precise to enable the institution, body, office, or agency concerned to ascertain in specific terms the content of the act which it is being asked to adopt and must make clear that its purpose is to compel such institution, body, office, or agency to define its **8.18**

---

other grounds: ECJ (order of 22 January 2012), Case C-69/09 P *Makhteshim-Agan Holding and Others v Commission* [2010] E.C.R. I-10*, Summ. pub.) (rejecting applicants' argument that it was not necessary to formally call upon the institution concerned to act because the 'prior notice' was already contained in the applicable EU legislation). For another example in which the action was held inadmissible on the grounds that the applicant failed to call upon the defendant institution concerned to act, see, e.g. CFI (order of 14 December 2006), Case T-150/06 *Smanor and Others v Commission*, not reported, paras 13–16 (appeal dismissed: ECJ (order of 23 May 2007), Case C-99/07 P *Smanor and Others v Commission* [2007] E.C.R. I-70*, Summ. pub.).

[62] ECJ, Case 17/57 *De Gezamenlijke Steenkolenmijnen in Limburg v High Authority* [1959] E.C.R. 1, at 8; ECJ (order of 18 November 1999), Case C-249/99 P *Pescados Congelados Jogamar v Commission* [1999] E.C.R. I-8333, para. 18.

[63] EGC, Case T-442/07 *Ryanair v Commission* [2011] E.C.R. II-333*, Summ. pub., para. 22.

[64] This should be distinguished from the explicit time limits set down in Art. 265 TFEU once the letter before action has been sent to the Union institution, body, office, or agency as discussed in para. 8.21.

[65] ECJ, Case 59/70 *Netherlands v Commission* [1971] E.C.R. 639, paras 12–24. See also ECJ, Case C-170/02 P *Schlüsselverlag J.S. Moser and Others v Commission* [2003] E.C.R. I-9889, paras 36–38 (where an action for failure to act in respect of the Commission's failure to respond to a complaint to the effect that an unnotified merger had a Union dimension was declared inadmissible. The Court of Justice held that as four months had elapsed since the national authorities' decision approving the merger, it was no longer possible to call on the Commission to act within a reasonable time.)

position.[66] As indicated by the case-law so far, the letter of formal notice calling upon the defendant institution, body, office, or agency to act must essentially do four crucial things.

First, it must call upon the Union institution, body, office, or agency to act.[67] Second, it must make it clear that it is made pursuant to Art. 265 TFEU.[68] Third, it must indicate precisely what measure(s) of Union law the applicant expects the defendant to adopt.[69] Fourth, it must make clear the identity of the person or entity making the request, since only that person or entity calling upon the institution, body, office, or agency to act is entitled to bring an action for failure to act before the Court of Justice or the General Court.

(5) Reaction of the institution, body, office, or agency put on notice

8.19   In order to have the failure to act in question brought to an end, the defendant institution, body, office, or agency must have 'defined its position' within two months of its having been called upon to act under the second paragraph of Art. 265 TFEU. Once the defendant institution, body, office, or agency has defined its position, an action for failure to act will be inadmissible.[70]

The reaction of the institution, body, office, or agency that has been called upon to act will be deemed to be a definition of a position within the meaning of the second paragraph of Art. 265 TFEU only insofar as it explains the institution, body, office, or agency's stance with regard to the measure requested. It is the content and not the form of the definition of a position which determines whether this condition has been met. Accordingly, the institution, body, office, or agency called upon to act may reject a request to adopt a particular measure by letter,[71] by telex,[72] or impliedly by adopting a measure other than the one requested. Importantly, however, a letter emanating from an institution, body, office, or agency, stating that examination of the questions raised is in progress, does not constitute a definition of position that brings to an end a failure to act.[73]

---

[66] See, e.g. EGC, Case T-442/07 *Ryanair v Commission* [2011] E.C.R. II-333*, Summ. pub., para. 22 (and citations therein). This case provides an example in which the General Court found the requisite conditions of the letter of formal notice were fulfilled over the objection of the Commission as regards some of the applicant's claims. Compare, e.g. EGC (order of 30 June 2011), Case T-367/09 *Tecnoprocess v Commission* [2011] E.C.R. II-209*, Summ. pub., para. 48 (and citations therein); and EGC (order of 30 June 2011), Case T-264/09 *Tecnoprocess v Commission and Delegation of the EU to Morocco* [2011] E.C.R. II-208*, Summ. pub., para. 85 (holding the actions brought by the applicant in both sets of proceedings inadmissible on these grounds).

[67] ECJ, Case 13/83 *European Parliament v Council* [1985] E.C.R. 1513, para. 24; ECJ, Case 84/82 *Germany v Commission* [1984] E.C.R. 1451, para. 23; CFI (order of 30 April 1999), Case T-311/97 *Pescados Congelados Jogamar v Commission* [1999] E.C.R. II-1407, para. 37.

[68] This should transpire from the content of the letter. An express reference to Art. 265 TFEU is helpful, but not necessary: EGC (judgment of 4 July 2012), Case T-12/12 *Laboratoires CTRS v Commission*, not reported, para. 40.

[69] ECJ, Case 25/85 *Nuovo Campsider v Commission* [1986] E.C.R. 1531, para. 8; CFI, Case T-28/90 *Asia Motor France and Others v Commission* [1992] E.C.R. II-2285, para. 28; CFI (order of 30 April 1999), Case T-311/97 *Pescados Congelados Jogamar v Commission* [1999] E.C.R. II-1407 (appeal dismissed: ECJ (order of 18 November 1999), Case C-249/99 P *Pescados Congelados Jogamar v Commission* [1999] I-8333). For an instance in which the action was declared admissible only in part, see CFI, Case T-17/96 *TF1 v Commision* [1999] E.C.R. II-1757, paras 41–44.

[70] See, however, CFI (order of 23 February 2005), Case T-479/04, *Campailla v Commission*, not reported, in which the CFI found that such an action was manifestly lacking any foundation in law (appeal dismissed: ECJ (order of 8 December 2005), Case C-211/05 P *Campailla v Commission*, not reported).

[71] ECJ, Case 125/78 *GEMA v Commission* [1979] E.C.R. 3173, paras 14–23.

[72] ECJ, Case 42/71 *Nordgetreide v Commission* [1972] E.C.R. 105, para. 4.

[73] See, e.g. CFI, Case T-95/96 *Gestevisión Telecinco v Commission* [1998] E.C.R. II-3407, para. 88; CFI, Case T-212/99 *Intervet International v Commission* [2002] E.C.R. II-1445, para. 61 (and citations therein); CFI, Joined Cases T-344/00 and T-345/00 *CEVA and Pharmacia Entreprises v Commission* [2003] E.C.R. II-229, para. 80; CFI (order of 23 July 2008), Case T-165/08 *Química Atlântica and Martins de Freitas Moura v Commission*, not reported, para. 11 (and citations therein).

Under settled case-law, if the position defined by the institution, body, office, or agency concerned does not come up to the expectations of the person who requested the institution to act, that person may no longer challenge the position defined by means of an action for failure to act. This is because Art. 265 TFEU refers to the failure to take a decision or to define a position, and not to the adoption of a measure different from that desired or considered necessary by the person concerned.[74]

Although a definition of a position brings the failure to act to an end, thereby making it impossible to bring an action for failure to act any more, it is not always in the nature of a binding act against which an action for annulment will lie.[75] This will, of course, be the case where the invitation to act is made by a Union institution or a Member State with a view to the adoption of a preparatory act needed for the purpose of the Union's decision-making procedure (see paras 7.27–7.29 and 8.08). The only way in which the Court of Justice or the General Court can secure legal protection for the applicant in such a situation is to be relatively exacting in adjudging whether the content of the definition of a position is such as to bring the failure to act to an end. The reason is that, since an action for annulment is ruled out in any event as a potential means of recourse, the only avenue remaining is an action for failure to act if the defendant institution, body, office, or agency is not fulfilling its obligations and so blocking the Union's decision-making process.[76]

Even where the invitation to act comes from a natural or legal person who, in principle, has in mind the adoption of a binding act against which an action for annulment will lie (see para. 8.08), it is possible for the failure to act to be brought to an end by a non-binding definition of a position. This will be the case when the defendant institution, body, office, or agency adopts a preparatory act which is a prerequisite in the procedure leading to a definitive and legally binding act.[77] The procedure for the investigation of complaints relating to infringements of Art. 101 and Art. 102 TFEU affords an illustration.[78]

---

[74] See, e.g. ECJ, Case 8/71 *Komponistenverband v Commission* [1971] E.C.R. 705, para. 2; ECJ, Joined Cases 166/86 and 220/86 *Irish Cement v Commission* [1988] E.C.R. 6473, para. 17; ECJ, Joined Cases C-15/91 and C-108/91 *Buckl and Others v Commission* [1992] E.C.R. I-6061, paras 16–17; ECJ (order of 13 December 2000), Case C-44/00 P *Sodima v Commission* [2000] E.C.R. I-11231, para. 83; CFI (order of 12 November 1996), Case T-47/96 *SDDDA v Commission* [1996] E.C.R. II-1559, para. 40; CFI (order of 26 November 1996), Case T-164/95 *Kuchlenz-Winter v European Parliament* [1996] E.C.R. II-1593, para. 37; CFI (order of 26 November 1996), Case T-226/95 *Kuchlenz-Winter v Commission* [1996] E.C.R. II-1619, para. 31; CFI, Case T-107/96 *Pantochim v Commission* [1998] E.C.R. II-311, para. 30; CFI (order of 11 March 2002), Case T-3/02 *Schlüsselverlag J.S. Moser and Others v Commission* [2002] E.C.R. II-1473, para. 27; CFI, Case T-276/03 *Azienda Agricola «Le Canne» v Commission* [2006] E.C.R. II-10*, Summ. pub., paras 37–38; CFI, Case T-420/05 *Vischim v Commission* [2009] E.C.R. II-3841, para. 255; CFI (order of 17 November 2009), Case T-295/09 *Hansen v Commission*, not reported, para. 11; EGC (order of 5 January 2010), Case T-71/09 *Química Atlântica v Commission* [2010] E.C.R. I-1*, Summ. pub., paras 28, 31; EGC (order of 17 December 2010), Case T-245/10 *Verein Deutsche Sprache v Council*, not reported, para. 15 (appeal dismissed in ECJ (order of 28 June 2011), Case C-93/11 P *Verein Deutsche Sprache v Council* [2011] E.C.R. I-92*, Summ. pub.); EGC, Case T-423/07 *Ryanair v Commission* [2011] E.C.R. II-2397, para. 26.

[75] See para. 8.10.

[76] ECJ, Case 13/83 *European Parliament v Council* [1985] E.C.R. 1513, para. 25; moreover, it was in an inter-institutional context that the Court of Justice held—in all likelihood for these reasons—that an express refusal to act does not put an end to a failure to act: ECJ, Case 302/87 *European Parliament v Council* [1988] E.C.R. 5615, para. 17.

[77] See CFI (order of 24 November 2009), Case T-228/08 *Szomborg v Commission* [2009] E.C.R. II-224*, Summ. pub., para. 19 (and case-law cited therein). See also EGC, Case T-423/07 *Ryanair v Commission* [2011] E.C.R. II-2397, paras 27–33.

[78] For the Commission's handling of complaints relating to State aid, see, e.g. CFI, Case T-95/96 *Gestevisión Telecinco v Commission* [1998] E.C.R. II-3407; CFI, Case T-17/96 *TF1 v Commission* [1999]

(6) Complaint regarding infringement of Art. 101 or Art. 102 TFEU

8.20 A complaint is lodged in the hope that the Commission will find that there has been an infringement of Art. 101 or Art. 102 TFEU.[79] But the complainant is not entitled to a definitive decision from the Commission on the existence of the alleged infringement.[80] Yet, it does have the right to a decision on the outcome which the Commission is to give to its complaint, so that, in the event that the complaint is rejected, it can be ensured of being able to bring an action against the decision rejecting the complaint and hence of securing judicial review by the General Court (and the Court of Justice on appeal).[81] Before the complaint is rejected, the Commission should send a letter to the complainant pursuant to Art. 7 of Regulation No. 773/2004 (formerly Art. 6 of Regulation No. 2842/98)[82] informing it of the reasons why it considers that on the basis of the information in its possession there are insufficient grounds for upholding the complaint and fixing a time limit within which the complainant may make its views known in writing. Such a letter constitutes a definition of a position within the meaning of the second paragraph of Art. 265 TFEU,[83] even though it is not a binding act against which an action for annulment will lie.[84]

E.C.R. II-1757; CFI, Joined Cases T-297/01 and T-298/01 *SIC v Commission* [2004] E.C.R. II-743; EGC, Case T-395/04 *Air One v Commission* [2006] E.C.R. II-1343; CFI, Case C-167/04 *Asklepios Kliniken v Commission* [2007] E.C.R. II-2379; EGC, Case T-423/07 *Ryanair v Commission* [2011] E.C.R. II-2397; EGC, Case T-442/07 *Ryanair v Commission* [2011] E.C.R. II-333*, Summ. pub. For the Commission's handling of a complaint relating to the grant of State aid to a producer of military goods and the application of what are now Arts 346 and 348 TFEU (ex Arts 296 and 298 EC), see CFI, Case T-26/01 *Fiocchi Munizioni v Commission* [2003] E.C.R. II-3951.

[79] Importantly, the complaint submitted by the applicant must comply with the applicable rules of Regulation Nos 1/2003 and 773/2004, including the information required by Form C annexed to Regulation No. 773/2004 to be supplied by the complainants in support of their complaint. Where the complaint fails to provide sufficient information to be classified as a complaint, the Commission cannot be held to be under a duty to act in relation to the alleged violations of the competition rules: see EGC, Case T-423/07 *Ryanair v Commission* [2011] E.C.R. II-2397, paras 52–63 (rejecting the complainant's action seeking a declaration that the Commission failed to act in relation to a complaint alleging abuse of a dominant position on such grounds).

[80] ECJ, Case 125/78 *GEMA v Commission* [1979] E.C.R. 3173, paras 17–18.

[81] CFI, Case T-7/92 *Asia Motor France and Others v Commission* [1993] E.C.R. II-669; cf. CFI (order of 29 November 1993), Case T-56/92 *Koelman v Commission* [1993] E.C.R. II-1267, paras 26–28 (action for failure to act held to be to no purpose because the Commission had definitively rejected the complaint) and CFI, Case T-575/93 *Koelman v Commission* [1996] E.C.R. II-1, in which the applicant sought the annulment of the definitive rejection of its complaint. For an application in relation to the ECSC Treaty, see EGC, Case T-320/07 *Jones and Others v Commission* [2011] E.C.R. II-417*, Summ. pub.

[82] Commission Regulation (EC) No. 773/2004 of 7 April 2004 relating to the conduct of proceedings by the Commission pursuant to Arts 81 and 82 of the EC Treaty (now Arts 101 and 102 TFEU), [2004] O.J. L123/18, repealing Commission Regulation (EC) No. 2842/98 of 22 December 1998 on the hearing of parties in certain proceedings under Arts 85 and 86 of the EC Treaty, [1998] O.J. L354/18. Before the entry into force of Regulation No. 2842/98, a similar obligation was imposed by Art. 6 of (Commission) Regulation No. 99/63/EEC (of 25 July 1963 on the hearings provided for in Art. 19(1) and (2) of Council Regulation No. 17, O.J. English Spec. Ed., Series I, Ch. 1963–1964, p. 47).

[83] ECJ, Case 125/78 *GEMA v Commission* [1979] E.C.R. 3173, para. 21; ECJ, Case C-282/95 P *Guérin Automobiles v Commission* [1997] E.C.R. I-1503, para. 30 (cf. the Opinion of Advocate-General G. Tesauro in that case); CFI, Case T-186/94 *Guérin Automobiles v Commission* [1995] E.C.R. II-1753, para. 26; CFI (order of 19 October 2001), Case T-121/01 *Piau v Commission*, not reported, para. 14.

[84] CFI, Case T-64/89 *Automec v Commission* [1990] E.C.R. II-367, para. 46; CFI, Case T-186/94 *Guérin Automobiles v Commission*, para. 41; CFI, Case T-38/96 *Guérin Automobiles v Commission* [1997] E.C.R. II-1223, para. 31.

If the complainant wishes to avail itself of the procedure provided for in Art. 265 TFEU in order to induce the Commission to take a decision on the outcome of its complaint, it will call on the Commission to take that decision (which, moreover, the complainant hopes will be favourable to it).[85] Only if the Commission is planning to reject its complaint will the complainant receive (under the normal procedure in such a case) a letter pursuant to Art. 7 of Regulation No. 773/2004, i.e. a definition of a position that is not a binding act.[86] This provisionally exhausts the complainant's possibilities of recourse, but not necessarily for long. This is because the initiative reverts to the complainant. If it submits written observations within the prescribed period, the Commission must take, within a reasonable time,[87] a final decision on the outcome of the complaint in the light of those observations.[88] If necessary, the complainant can call on the Commission pursuant to Art. 265 TFEU to take the decision.[89] If the Commission rejects the complaint, the complainant may bring an action for annulment; if the Commission does nothing at all, an action for failure to act will lie.[90]

B. Procedure before the Court

(1) Conditions for admissibility

The applicant must bring its action within the applicable time limits prescribed in Art. 265 **8.21**
TFEU. The letter before action marks the starting point of the two-month period which the institution, body, office, or agency has in order to bring the failure to act to an end.[91]

---

[85] CFI, Case T-28/90 *Asia Motor France and Others v Commission* [1992] E.C.R. II-2285, para. 28.

[86] EGC (order of 9 January 2012), Case T-407/09 *Neubrandenburger Wohnungsgesellschaft v Commission*, not reported, para. 40. The fact that a complainant which requests that a decision be taken has to be satisfied in the first instance with a definition of a position which is not a decision, has to do with the Commission's obligation to take the intermediate step—designed to protect the complainant's interests—of notifying the draft decision, following which the complainant is entitled to submit observations. Sometimes, however, the decision is taken directly, whereupon an action for annulment will lie against it: see ECJ, Case C-39/93 P *SFEI and Others v Commission* [1994] E.C.R. I-2681, paras 24–33.

[87] ECJ, Case C-282/95 P *Guérin Automobiles v Commission* [1997] E.C.R. I-1503, para. 37. The call to act may not, however, be made at the same time as the observations to a letter under Art. 7 of Regulation No. 773/2004. This is because the Commission must be given a reasonable period within which to examine the complainant's observations before being required to define its final position on the complaint (this can be inferred from the order for costs in a case where it was held that the action for failure to act was to no purpose at the time of the judgment: CFI, Case T-28/95 *IECC v Commission* [1998] E.C.R. II-3597, para. 15). See also para. 8.06.

[88] Art. 7(2) of Regulation No. 773/2004 provides: 'If the complainant makes known its views within the time limit set by the Commission and the written submissions made by the complainant do not lead to a different assessment of the complaint, the Commission shall reject the complaint by decision.' According to Art. 7(3), '[i]f the complainant fails to make known its views within the time-limit set by the Commission, the complaint shall be deemed to have been withdrawn'.

[89] Cf. Opinion of Judge D. A. O. Edward, appointed to act as Advocate-General, in CFI, Case T-24/90 *Automec v Commission* [1992] E.C.R. II-2223, para. 23.

[90] An action for failure to act will not be held to have lost its purpose merely because the restriction of competition referred to in the complaint has been terminated following the intervention of the Commission, since that did not dispense the Commission from defining its position on the applicant's complaint. If, therefore, the Commission has failed to define its position on the complaint, the action does not lose its purpose in those circumstances: CFI, Case T-74/92 *Ladbroke Racing v Commission* [1995] E.C.R. II-115, paras 66–67.

[91] See, e.g. EGC, Case T-442/07 *Ryanair v Commission* [2011] E.C.R. II-333*, Summ. pub., para. 22. As a consequence, an action brought during this period of two months will be deemed premature and hence

The case-law indicates that the Court looks at the day on which the letter before action reached the defendant institution, body, office, or agency, not the date of the letter before action itself, to mark the starting point of this two-month period.[92] Similarly, the failure to act comes to an end not on the day on which the institution, body, office, or agency concerned actually defines its position, but instead on the day on which the party which called on it to act receives the document by which the institution defined its position.[93]

If, during the two-month period after being called upon to act, the institution, body, office, or agency persists in its failure to act, Member States, Union institutions or natural or legal persons who have called upon it to act may bring an action before the Court of Justice or the General Court 'within a further period of two months', as prescribed in the second paragraph of Art. 265 TFEU (plus ten days for distance). Actions brought out of time are inadmissible.[94]

In the event that the institution, body, office, or agency concerned defines its position before the action is brought before the Court of Justice or the General Court, the action for failure to act will be inadmissible.[95] If the act in question is adopted after the action for failure to act has been brought but before judgment is given, the application becomes to no purpose (see para. 8.05). However, in such a case, the defendant institution, body, office, or agency exposes itself to having an order for costs made against it.[96]

---

inadmissible: see, e.g. EGC (order of 30 June 2011), Case T-367/09 *Tecnoprocess v Commission* [2011] E.C.R. II-209*, Summ. pub., paras 51–55.

[92] See, e.g. EGC, Case T-166/98 *Cantina sociale di Dolianova and Others v Commission* [2004] E.C.R. I-3991, para. 81 (appealed to the ECJ on other grounds: ECJ, Case C-51/05 P *Commission v Cantina sociale di Dolianova and Others* [2008] E.C.R. I-5341). In this case, the applicant's letter before action dated 23 January 1998 was received by the Commission on 5 February 1998. The Court calculated that the Commission should have defined its position by 5 April 1998, and if it did not do so, the applicant had a further period of two months to lodge its action, i.e. by 15 June 1998 (5 June 1998 plus ten days for distance as mentioned later). The applicant lodged its action on 12 October 1998, which was therefore ruled out of time. In order to facilitate the calculation of time limits regarding actions for failure to act, Art. 21, second para. of the Statute provides that for actions based on Art. 265 TFEU, the application must be accompanied by documentary evidence of the date on which the institution was requested to act.

[93] CFI, Joined Cases T-194/97 and T-83/98 *Branco v Commission* [2000] E.C.R. II-69, paras 23, 55–56. In this case, the applicant's letter before action dated 27 February 1997 was received by the Commission on 3 March 1997; however, the Commission's definition of its position reached the applicant on 5 May 1997 and thus was deemed out of time (presumably, it should have reached the applicant by 3 May 1997).

[94] For some examples of an action which was brought out of time, see CFI (order of 2 December 2003), Case T-334/02 *Viomichania Syskevasias Typopoiisis Kai Syntirisis Agrotikon Proïonton v Commission* [2003] E.C.R. II-5121, paras 31–34 (the applicant's attempt to justify such lateness on the existence of an excusable error was denied: CFI, Case T-334/02 *Viomichania Syskevasias Typopoiisis Kai Syntirisis Agrotikon Proïonton v Commission*, paras 35–41); CFI (order of 23 July 2008), Case T-165/08 *Química Atlântica and Martins de Freitas Moura v Commission*, not reported, paras 9–12; EGC (order of 30 June 2011), Case T-264/09 *Tecnoprocess v Commission and Delegation of the EU in Morocco* [2011] E.C.R. II-208*, Summ. pub., paras 91–94.

[95] See, eg ECJ (judgment of 19 November 2013), Case C-196/12 *Commission v Council*, not reported, paras 22–31. The Court will raise this question of inadmissibility of its own motion: see, e.g. CFI, Case T-26/01 *Fiocchi Munizioni v Commission* [2003] E.C.R. II-3951, paras 92–93. This also applies in the case of an action that has become devoid of purpose in light of circumstances occurring after the action has been brought: see, e.g. CFI (order of 26 June 2008), Joined Cases T-433/03, T-434/03, T-367/04, and T-244/05 *Gibtelecom v Commission*, not reported.

[96] See, e.g. ECJ, Case 377/87 *European Parliament v Council* [1988] E.C.R. 4017, para. 12; CFI, Case T-212/95 *Oficemen v Commission* [1997] E.C.R. II-1161, paras 72–75; CFI, Case T-212/99 *Intervet International v Commission* [2002] E.C.R. II-1445, paras 69–71 (because the applicant's action for annulment failed, but the Commission did not define its position until after the action for failure to act had been brought, the General Court 'split the difference' and ordered the Commission to pay half of the applicant's costs); CFI

Moreover, the letter before action determines the subject-matter of the action.[97] The action can relate only to a failure to act that has been previously so raised with the defendant institution, body, office, or agency.[98]

(2) Pleas in law

Under the first paragraph of Art. 265 TFEU, the only plea open to the applicant is that the **8.22** failure to act constitutes an 'infringement of the Treaties'.[99] As has already been mentioned, the expression 'infringement of the Treaties' covers any Union law provision under which an obligation to act arises for the defendant institution, body, office, or agency (see para. 8.06).

IV. Consequences

If the Court of Justice or the General Court finds pursuant to Art. 265 TFEU that a Union **8.23** institution, body, office, or agency has infringed the Treaties by failing to act, that institution, body, office, or agency is required under Art. 266 TFEU to take the necessary measures to comply with the judgment.

The scope of the judgment is limited. It merely declares that the institution, body, office, or agency's failure to act is illegal[100] and reinforces the duty on that institution, body, office, or agency to act, but it does not take the place of the act which the institution, body,

---

(order of 4 September 2009) Case T-139/07 *Pioneer Hi-Bred International v Commission*, not reported. See also EGC (order of 10 January 2011), Case T-389/09 *Labate v Commission*, not reported: in circumstances where the applicant withdrew its action for failure to act following the adoption by the Commission of the act requested after proceedings had been lodged before the General Court but the Commission requested that the applicant be ordered to bear its own costs and those incurred by it on the grounds that the action for failure to act in the proceedings concerned was inadmissible, the Court ruled that under Art. 87(5), first para., of the Rules of Procedure, it is bound to order the other party to pay the costs if this appears justified by the conduct of that party, and it is not entitled to take into account aspects other than those referring to that party's conduct, including the possible inadmissibility of the applicant's action for failure to act. Accordingly, by reason of its conduct, the Commission was ordered to bear the costs. Compare CFI (order of 26 November 1997), Case T-39/97 *T. Port v Commission* [1997] E.C.R. II-2125, para. 29. As for what costs can be recovered, see para. 25.91.

[97] See, e.g. EGC, Case T-442/07 *Ryanair v Commission* [2011] E.C.R. II-333*, Summ. pub., para. 22.

[98] ECJ, Joined Cases 24/58 and 34/58 *Chambre Syndicale de la Sidérurgie de l'Est de la France and Others v High Authority* [1960] E.C.R. 281, at 299; ECJ, Joined Cases 41/59 and 50/59 *Hamborner Bergbau and Others v High Authority* [1960] E.C.R. 493; ECJ, Case 75/69 *Hake v Commission* [1970] E.C.R. 535, paras 8–9; CFI, Case T-334/02 *Viomichania Syskevasias Typopoiisis Kai Syntirisis Agrotikon Proïonton v Commission* [2003] E.C.R. II-5121, paras 46–47 (as regards applicant's request for a declaration that the defendant institution failed to act by not adopting a decision to withdraw the assistance granted, the invitation to act did not contain a request to act in that way and was thus inadmissible, though the Court went on to find no duty to act in any event).

[99] See also Art. 266, first para., TFEU ('contrary to the Treaties').

[100] See Art. 265, first para., TFEU ('may bring an action before the Court of Justice of the European Union *to have the infringement established*') (emphasis added). The action for failure to act must be distinguished from the action for infringement (Arts 258–260 TFEU) in the sense that there is no 'public condemnation' involved: see CFI (order of 28 March 2006), Case T-451/04 *Mediocurso—Estabelecimento de Ensino Particular v Commission*, not reported, para. 25; see also EGC, Case T-423/07 *Ryanair v Commission* [2011] E.C.R. II-2397, para. 26.

office, or agency failed to adopt.[101] The Union courts cannot issue directions or tell the institution, body, office, or agency concerned what act to take in an action based on Art. 265 TFEU, and thus, requests for them to do so are inadmissible.[102] The actual discretion as to the type, content, and form of the act required lies with the institution, body, office, or agency concerned. Still, as a practical matter, sometimes in circumstances where an institution, body, office, or agency has an obligation to take a specific act, it may in fact have very little discretion following the judgment of the Court of Justice or the General Court.

Therefore, unlike the action for annulment in which the judgment of the Court of Justice or the General Court brings about a legal change—the act is retroactively annulled and ceases to exist in the Union legal order—no such similar change in legal status occurs in the context of the action for failure to act, in the sense that the Union courts cannot adopt the act that should have been taken.

---

[101] See, e.g. CFI, Case T-395/04 *Air One v Commission* [2006] E.C.R. II-1343, para. 24 (and citations therein) ('All that the [EGC] can do is determine whether there has been a failure to act. It is then for the institution[, body, office, or agency], pursuant to Article [266 TFEU], to take the measures necessary to comply with the order of the Court.').

[102] See, e.g. EGC (order of 6 September 2011), Case T-292/09 *Mugraby v Council and Commission* [2011] E.C.R. II-255*, Summ. pub., paras 47–48 (appeal dismissed: ECJ (order of 12 July 2012), Case C-581/11 P *Mugraby v Council and Commission*, not reported); EGC (order of 17 November 2010), Case T-61/10 *Victoria Sánchez v European Parliament and Commission* [2010] E.C.R. II-252*, Summ. pub., paras 41–42 (upheld on appeal: ECJ (order of 26 October 2011), Case C-52/11 P *Victoria Sánchez v European Parliament and Commission* [2011] E.C.R. I-158*, Summ. pub., paras 38–40); CFI (order of 17 November 2009), Case T-295/09 *Hansen v Commission*, not reported, paras 14–16 (appeal dismissed: ECJ (order of 6 May 2010), Case C-26/10 P *Hansen v Commission* [2010] E.C.R. I-58*, Summ. pub.); CFI (order of 17 October 2007), Case T-454/05 *Sumitomo Chemical Agro Europe and Philagro France v Commission* [2007] E.C.R. II-131*, Summ. pub., para. 53; CFI, Case T-395/04 *Air One v Commission* [2006] E.C.R. II-1343, para. 24.

9

THE OBJECTION OF ILLEGALITY

I. Subject-Matter

A. General

(1) Not an independent right of action

The objection of illegality enshrined in Art. 277 TFEU[1] does not constitute an indepen- **9.01**
dent right of action.[2] It is an incidental plea in law[3] intended to avoid the application of
unlawful Union acts of general application to the detriment of parties who are not—or are
no longer[4]—entitled to challenge them.[5] In other words, the objection of illegality does not
stand alone, but may only be raised in the context of one or more direct actions lodged
before the Union courts (see para. 9.16).[6] This may explain why it is often called a plea of
illegality, since it is not a separate cause of action in and of itself, as, for example, in the case
of the action for annulment or the action for failure to act.

(2) Changes brought by the Treaty of Lisbon

With the entry into force of the Lisbon Treaty, former Art. 241 EC was reframed as Art. **9.02**
277 TFEU, which provides: 'Notwithstanding the expiry of the period laid down in Art.
263, sixth paragraph, any party may, in proceedings in which an act of general application

---

[1] With the entry into force of the Lisbon Treaty, Art. 277 TFEU applies to objections of illegality in
connection with the EAEC Treaty, as Art. 156 EAEC has been repealed: see Art. 106a(1)–(2) EAEC of the
consolidated version of the EAEC Treaty, [2012] O.J. C327/1.
[2] See, e.g. ECJ, Case 33/80 *Albini v Council and Commission* [1981] E.C.R. 2141, para. 17; ECJ, Joined
Cases 87/77 and 130/77, 22/83, 9/84 and 10/84 *Salerno and Others v Commission and Council* [1985] E.C.R.
2523, para. 36; CFI (order of 14 December 2005), Case T-369/03 *Arizona Chemical and Others v Commission*
[2005] E.C.R. II-5839, para. 129 (appeal dismissed on other grounds: ECJ (order of 13 March 2007), Case
C-150/06 P *Arizona Chemical and Others v Commission* [2007] E.C.R. I-39*, Summ. pub.); CST (judgment
of 30 September 2010), Case F-29/09 *Lebedef and Jones v Commission*, not reported, para. 30.
[3] See, e.g. CFI (order of 14 December 2005), Case T-369/03 *Arizona Chemical and Others v Commission*
[2005] E.C.R. II-5839, para. 129 (appeal dismissed on other grounds: ECJ (order of 13 March 2007), Case
C-150/06 P *Arizona Chemical and Others v Commission* [2007] E.C.R. I-39*, Summ. pub.); CST (judgment
of 30 September 2010), Case F-29/09 *Lebedef and Jones v Commission*, not reported, para. 30
[4] For the parties entitled to raise an objection of illegality, see paras 9.09 to 9.13.
[5] ECJ, Joined Cases 31/62 and 33/62 *Wöhrmann and Others v Commission* [1962] E.C.R. 501, at 507.
[6] The objection of illegality may be brought as a subsidiary plea: see, e.g. CFI, Case T-45/06 *Reliance
Industries v Council and Commission* [2008] E.C.R. II-2399, para. 26; CFI, Case T-390/08 *Bank Melli Iran v
Council* [2009] E.C.R. II-3967, para. 21; EGC, Case T-434/09 *Centrotherm Systemtechnik v OHIM* [2011]
E.C.R. II-6227, para. 17; CST (judgment of 29 September 2009), Joined Cases F-69/07 and F-60/08 *O v
Commission*, not reported, para. 67. An applicant may raise a number of objections of illegality in the same
case: see, e.g. CFI, Case T-311/04 *Sierra v Commission* [2006] E.C.R. II-4137 (raising five pleas of illegality).

adopted by an institution, body, office, or agency of the Union is at issue, plead the grounds specified in Art. 263, second paragraph, in order to invoke before the Court of Justice of the European Union the inapplicability of that act.'

Art. 277 TFEU thus refers to 'an act of general application' and no longer to 'a regulation adopted jointly by the European Parliament and the Council, or a regulation of the Council, of the Commission, or of the ECB' as former Art. 241 EC had done. Art. 277 TFEU also mentions acts of general application adopted by the institutions, as well as by bodies, offices, and agencies of the Union in line with adjustments made to the provisions of the Treaties concerning other actions that may be brought before the Union courts (for example, the action for annulment under Art. 263 TFEU). Accordingly, the Lisbon Treaty introduced important changes as regards the scope of the objection of illegality. Moreover, in referring to the 'Court of Justice of the European Union', as opposed to the 'Court of Justice', as former Art. 241 EC had done, Art. 277 TFEU recognizes that an objection of illegality may be brought before any of the Union courts (thereby including the General Court and the Civil Service Tribunal) in line with the allocation of jurisdiction governing the Union courts generally under the Treaties.[7]

(3) Essential function

9.03 The purpose of the objection of illegality is two-fold. First, the right to bring an action for annulment is limited, since it must be brought within a short period of time, as prescribed by the sixth paragraph of Art. 263 TFEU, and the illegality of acts of general application may not yet become apparent. Thus, there needed to be an indirect possibility so as to allow for a declaration of inapplicability of such measures, as provided by Art. 277 TFEU.

Second, with particular regard to natural and legal persons, the idea going back to the former Treaty framework was that in situations where such persons were bringing proceedings to obtain the annulment of acts addressed to them or acts that were not addressed to them but were of direct and individual concern to them, such acts may be based on illegal Union measures which such persons had no standing to challenge directly in view of the standing requirements under what is now the fourth paragraph of Art. 263 TFEU. The objection of illegality therefore affords an indirect means by which the illegality of such measures could be raised incidentally in such proceedings. Under well-settled case-law, the remedy enshrined in what is now Art. 277 TFEU 'gives expression to a general principle conferring upon any party to proceedings the right to challenge, for the purpose of obtaining the annulment of a decision of direct and individual concern to that party, the validity of previous acts of the institutions which form the legal basis of the decision which is being attacked, if that party was not entitled under [Art. 263 TFEU] to bring a direct action challenging those acts by which it was thus affected without having been in a position to ask that they be declared void'.[8]

---

[7] See para. 2.53.

[8] ECJ, Case 92/78 *Simmenthal v Commission* [1979] E.C.R. 777, para. 39. See also ECJ, Case 9/56 *Meroni v High Authority* [1957 and 1958] E.C.R. 133, at 140; ECJ, Case 10/56 *Meroni v High Authority* [1957 and 1958] E.C.R. 156, at 162–3; ECJ, Case 15/57 *Compagnie des Hauts Fourneaux de Chasse v High Authority* [1957 and 1958] E.C.R. 211, at 224–5; ECJ, Case 262/80 *Andersen v European Parliament* [1984] E.C.R. 195, para. 6; CFI, Joined Cases T-6/92 and T-52/92 *Reinarz v Commission* [1993] E.C.R. II-1047, para. 56; CFI, Case T-64/92 *Chavane de Dalmassy and Others v Commission* [1994] E.C.R.-SC II-723, para. 41 (English abstract at I-A-227); CFI, Case T-82/96 *ARAP and Others v Commission* [1999] E.C.R. II-1889, paras 46–48

It followed that even under the former Treaty framework, the field of application of the objection of illegality extended to acts of the institutions of a general nature which were not in the form of a regulation as prescribed in what was then Art. 241 EC, but produced similar effects, and on those grounds could not be challenged in an action for annulment brought by national and legal persons.[9] In so deciding, the Court of Justice intimated that the essential function of the objection of illegality is to enable natural and legal persons to have set aside an act against which they cannot bring an action for annulment under the fourth paragraph of what is now Art. 263 TFEU, in a case where they are seeking the annulment of a measure adopted by the Union on the basis of that act.

(4) Part of the complete and coherent system of judicial protection

The objection of illegality under Art. 277 TFEU provides an indirect means of challenging   **9.04** the legality of Union acts and thus ensures protection for individuals against unlawful acts of the Union institutions, bodies, offices, and agencies. As famously proclaimed by the Court of Justice starting in *Les Verts*, the objection of illegality is part of the complete system of legal remedies and procedures, alongside the action for annulment and the preliminary ruling procedure on the validity of Union law, designed to permit the Union judicature to review the legality of Union acts.[10]

That being said, natural and legal persons are not the only parties to have recourse to the objection of illegality. According to Art. 277 TFEU, the objection of illegality can indeed be raised by 'any party'.

B. Acts against which an objection of illegality may be raised

(1) 'An act of general application'

Art. 277 TFEU provides that an objection of illegality may be brought against 'an act of   **9.05** general application'.[11] This undoubtedly covers the category of regulations, as former Art. 241 EC had done, as well as directives and decisions to the extent that such acts are found

---

(an applicant who has brought an action for annulment against a decision approving an individual aid measure may raise an objection of illegality against the measure approving the general aid measure pursuant to which the individual aid was granted); CST (judgment of 30 September 2010), Case F-29/09 *Lebedef and Jones v Commission*, not reported, para. 29 (and further citations therein) ('that remedy is the expression of a general principle which ensures that every person has or will have had the opportunity to challenge a legal act deriving from the Union which forms the basis of a[n] act adversely affecting him').

  [9] ECJ, Case 92/78 *Simmenthal v Commission*, para. 40; CFI, Joined Cases T-222/99, T-327/99, and T-329/99 *Martinez and Others v European Parliament* [2001] E.C.R. II-2823, para. 134.

  [10] ECJ, Case 294/03 *Parti écologiste 'Les Verts' v European Parliament* [1986] E.C.R. I-1339, para. 23. See further ECJ, Case C-50/00 P *Union de Pequeños Agricultores v Council* [2002] E.C.R. I-6677, para. 40; ECJ, Case C-263/02 P *Commission v Jégo-Quére* [2004] E.C.R. I-3425, para. 30; ECJ, Case C-343/09 *Afton Chemical* [2010] E.C.R. I-7023, para. 18; CFI (order of 21 March 2003), Case T-167/02 *Établissements Toulorge v European Parliament and Council* [2003] E.C.R. II-1111, para. 65; CFI (order of 28 November 2005), Case T-94/04 *EEB and Others v Commission* [2005] E.C.R. II-4919, para. 62; CFI (order of 28 November 2005), Joined Cases T-236/04 and T-241/04 *EIB and Stichting Natuur en Milieu v Commission* [2005] E.C.R. II-4945, para. 66; CFI (order of 19 September 2006), Case T-122/05 *Benkö and Others v Commission* [2006] E.C.R. II-2939, para. 49; CFI, Case T-447/05 *SPM v Commission* [2007] E.C.R. II-1, para. 81.

  [11] For discussion of what is meant by an act of general as opposed to individual application, see para. 7.85.

to be acts of general application.[12] With the reform of the system of legal instruments brought by the Lisbon Treaty, regulations, directives, and decisions may be legislative or non-legislative (delegated or implementing) acts.[13] The fact that the act of general application invoked in an objection of illegality may be classified as a legislative as opposed to a non-legislative act does not render the objection of illegality inadmissible.[14]

Furthermore, in *ECOWAS,* the Court of Justice confirmed that it has jurisdiction to consider an objection of illegality raised in relation to an act of general application falling within the former second pillar of the Common Foreign and Security Policy (CFSP), *in casu* a CFSP joint action,[15] in the context of an action for annulment brought against a decision implementing that joint action, insofar as the objection alleges an infringement of what is now Art. 40 TEU (ex Art. 47 EU).[16]

(2) Linkage between the type of act and the status of the party invoking the objection of illegality

9.06   As mentioned earlier, it had already been the case for the purposes of the application of former Art. 241 EC that any measure having similar effects to a regulation would be treated as if it were a regulation, provided that natural or legal persons could not bring an action for annulment against it pursuant to the fourth paragraph of what was then Art. 230 EC, now Art. 263 TFEU (see para 9.03). This meant that acts of general application were covered under the case-law concerning former Art. 241 EC as far as natural and legal persons were concerned.

---

[12] See Art. 288 TFEU. Under this provision, recognition has been given to decisions with and without addressees. See also Art. 297(2) TFEU, which provides that regulations, directives addressed to all Member States, and decisions which do not specify to whom they are addressed are to be published in the same way in the *Official Journal.* See also EGC, Case T-439/08 *Agapiou Joséphidès v Commission and EACEA* [2010] E.C.R. II-230*, Summ. pub., para. 50.

[13] See Arts 289–291 TFEU. See further K. Lenaerts and P. Van Nuffel (R. Bray and N. Cambien (eds)), *European Union Law* (3rd edn, London, Sweet & Maxwell, 2011), paras 22.62–22.63.

[14] CST (judgment of 27 September 2011), Case F-98/09 *Whitehead v ECB*, not reported, paras 71, 73 (rejecting the ECB's objection of inadmissibility based on the fact that the objection of illegality was invoked in relation to a Union measure that was legislative, not administrative, in nature).

[15] With the changes brought by the Lisbon Treaty, the regime of Union legal instruments has been streamlined, and there is no longer a separate set of instruments applicable to the former second pillar of the CFSP. The adoption of legislative instruments is excluded, and the Union is to conduct the CFSP by adopting general guidelines and decisions defining actions and positions to be taken by the Union, as well as decisions implementing the foregoing decisions: see Art. 24(1), second para., TEU and Art. 25 TEU. As such, although there is no longer recourse to the instrument of the joint action, such instrument may be equated with decisions envisaged to be taken in this field under the aforementioned provisions. See further K. Lenaerts and P. Van Nuffel (R. Bray and N. Cambien (eds)), *European Union Law* (3rd edn, London, Sweet & Maxwell, 2011), para. 25.42.

[16] ECJ, Case C-91/05 *Commission v Council ('ECOWAS')* [2008] E.C.R. I-3651, paras 29–34. However, the Court ultimately found that since the contested decision was to be annulled because of its own defects, it was not necessary to examine the objection of illegality as regards the alleged unlawfulness of the contested joint action: ECJ, Case C-91/05 *ECOWAS*, ibid., para 111. Indeed, as brought to light by other case-law in the context of the CFSP, the Union judicature may find that on account of the fact that certain pleas are well-founded, resulting in the annulment of the contested measure, there is no need to examine the applicant's other pleas and arguments, including an objection of illegality based on Art. 277 TFEU: see, e.g. CFI, Case T-327/03 *Stichting Al-Aqsa v Council* [2007] E.C.R. II-79*, Summ. pub., paras 66–67; CFI, Case T-253/04 *KONGRA-GEL v Council* [2008] E.C.R. II-46*, Summ. pub., paras 104–105 (the objection of illegality was pleaded in the alternative); EGC, Case T-348/07 *Stichting Al-Aqsa v Council* [2010] E.C.R. II-4575, paras 183–184 (judgment of EGC set aside on appeal and action and appeal dismissed on other grounds in ECJ (judgment of 15 November 2012), Joined Cases C-539/10 P and C-550/10 P *Al Aqsa v Council and the Netherlands*, not reported).

That being said, Member States and Union institutions, unlike natural and legal persons, are privileged applicants and thus may bring an action for annulment against all sorts of binding acts, whether general or individual in nature (see para. 7.76). As a result, there was a distinction made in the case-law concerning former Art. 241 EC as regards the types of acts that could be the subject of an objection of illegality as far as Member States and Union institutions were concerned. In large part, this is intertwined with the standing of the parties in terms of who can invoke the objection of illegality addressed in Part II (see para. 9.11). The bottom line is that as compared with the approach taken by the Union courts to the interpretation of former Art. 241 EC in which a Member State or a Union institution could only invoke an objection of illegality against acts of general application in the form of a regulation, but not against those in the form of a directive or a decision in line with the wording of that provision, the explicit reference to 'an act of general application' in Art. 277 TFEU means that such approach will have to be refined in the case-law.

(3) Exclusion of acts of individual application of which annulment could have been sought

As had been the case under the former Treaty framework, under the case-law, a party may **9.07** not rely on Art. 277 TFEU in order to challenge the legality of an act of individual application, such as a decision, addressed to it where it could have applied for that act to be annulled under Art. 263 TFEU.[17] This is because legal certainty would be affected if a party could still challenge such an act by means of an objection of illegality after the time limit for bringing an action against it had expired.[18] The only exceptions are where the party concerned was entitled to entertain reasonable doubt as to the admissibility of an action for annulment[19] or in the exceptional case where the contested act contained such particularly serious and manifest defects that it could be deemed non-existent.[20]

In this regard, it is not sufficient that the act invoked in an objection of illegality should have the 'label' of a general act. According to the Court of Justice, the general principle, to which Art. 277 TFEU gives expression and which has the effect of ensuring that every person has or will have had the opportunity to challenge a Union measure which forms the basis of a measure adversely affecting him, does not in any way preclude a regulation from becoming definitive as against an individual in regard to whom it must be considered to be an act of individual application. In this connection, the Court referred to regulations imposing anti-dumping duties by virtue of their dual nature as acts of a legislative nature and acts liable to be of direct and individual concern to certain traders.[21]

(4) An act of general application must be 'at issue'

Art. 277 TFEU requires the act of general application in respect of which the objection of **9.08** illegality is raised to be 'at issue'. This alludes to the fact that the general act which is the subject of the objection of illegality must form the basis of the act in dispute, failing which

---

[17] ECJ, Case 156/77 *Commission v Belgium* [1978] E.C.R. 1881, para. 20. See also paras 9.10 and 9.11.
[18] ECJ, Case 156/77 *Commission v Belgium*, para. 21.
[19] CFI, Case T-343/02 *Schintgen v Commission* [2004] E.C.R.-SC II-605, para. 26.
[20] ECJ, Case 223/87 *Commission v Greece* [1988] E.C.R. 3611, para. 16.
[21] See, e.g. ECJ, Case C-239/99 *Nachi Europe* [2001] E.C.R. I-1197, para. 37; ECJ, Case C-11/00 *Commission v ECB* [2003] E.C.R. I-7147, para. 75. This latter case is discussed in further detail in para. 9.11.

the objection of illegality is rejected.[22] As the Court of Justice explained early on, the intention of what is now Art. 277 TFEU is not to allow a party to contest at will the applicability of any general measure in support of an application; the measure of which the legality is called into question must be 'applicable, directly or indirectly, to the issue with which the application is concerned'.[23] There must be a direct or sufficiently close legal connection between the contested measure and the general measure invoked by means of the objection of illegality.[24]

Consequently, in the light of the essential function of the objection of illegality (see para. 9.03), the case-law has interpreted that requirement as meaning that the general measure against which the objection is raised must constitute the legal basis of the individual measure which is being directly challenged.[25] The upshot is that, in principle, an objection of illegality may be raised only against the provisions of a general act which the individual act implements.[26] Nevertheless, other provisions of the general act may be affected by the objection if they are applicable to 'the issue with which the application is concerned'.[27]

With the same concern to guarantee the essential function of the objection of illegality, the case-law has also accepted that such an objection may be raised against any act which cannot be contested for one reason or another, but whose content was nevertheless determinative in the adoption of individual acts which may be directly challenged. Thus, for example,[28] an objection of illegality may be raised against the Commission's Guidelines on the method of

---

[22] See, e.g. EGC (judgment of 7 May 2013), Case T-475/07 *Dow AgroSciences v Commission* [2011] E.C.R. II-5937, paras 183–184 (appeal dismissed: ECJ (order of 7 May 2013), Case C-584/11 P *Dow AgroSciences and Others v Commission*, not reported); CFI, Joined Cases T-3/00 and T-337/04 *Pitsiorlas v Council and ECB* [2007] E.C.R. II- 4779, paras 175–177 (appeal dismissed: ECJ (order of 3 July 2008), Case C-84/08 P *Pitsiorlas v Council and ECB* [2008] E.C.R. I-104*, Summ. pub.).

[23] ECJ, Case 32/65 *Italy v Council and Commission* [1966] E.C.R. 389, at 409.

[24] ECJ, Case 32/65 *Italy v Council and Commission* [1966] E.C.R. 389, at 409 (finding 'no necessary connexion' between the contested measure and the general measures invoked by means of the objection of illegality). See, e.g. CFI, Case T-311/04 *Buendía Sierra v Commission* [2006] E.C.R. II-4137, para. 233 (and citations therein) (underscoring that there must be a 'direct legal connection' between the contested individual measure and the general measure raised via the objection of illegality); CST (judgment of 30 April 2009), Case F-65/07 *Aayhan v European Parliament*, not reported, para. 87 (and citations therein) ('there must be a sufficiently close connection between the contested individual measure at issue and the measure against which the plea is raised, so that the inapplicability of the one will necessarily have an effect on the lawfulness of the other') (appeal dismissed on other grounds: CFI (order of 12 October 2009), Case T-283/09 P *Aayhan and Others v Parliament* [2009] E.C.R.-SC I-B-1–113). See also EGC, Case T-439/08 *Agapiou Joséphidès v Commission and EACEA* [2010] E.C.R. II-230*, Summ. pub., para. 51 and EGC, Case T-439/09 *Purvis v Parliament* [2011] E.C.R. II-7231, para. 35.

[25] ECJ, Case 21/64 *Macchiorlati Dalmas & Figli v High Authority* [1965] E.C.R. 175, at 187–8 (where the Court of Justice referred to a 'direct legal connection between the contested measure and the ... general decisions'); CFI, Joined Cases T-222/99, T-327/99, and T-329/99 *Martinez and Others v European Parliament* [2001] E.C.R. II-2823, para.136.

[26] ECJ, Joined Cases 275/80 and 24/81 *Krupp v Commission* [1981] E.C.R. 2489, para. 32; CFI, Case T-120/99 *Kik v OHIM* [2001] E.C.R. II-2235, para. 25; CST (judgment of 11 July 2007), Case F-105/05 *Wils v European Parliament*, not reported, para. 36 ('the individual measure being challenged was adopted in direct implementation of the measure of general application'). See in this connection also ECJ, Joined Cases C-432/98 P and C-433/98 P *Council v Chvatal and Others* [2000] E.C.R. I-8535.

[27] ECJ, Case 32/65 *Italy v Council and Commission* [1966] E.C.R. 389, at 409; cf. ECJ, Case 18/62 *Barge v High Authority* [1963] E.C.R. 259, at 279–80; ECJ, Joined Cases 140/82, 146/82, 221/82 and 226/82 *Walzstahl-Vereinigung and Thyssen v Commission* [1984] E.C.R. 951, para. 20. See also EGC (judgment of 14 June 2012), Case T-396/09 *Vereniging Milieudefensie and Stichting Stop Luchtverontreiniging Utrecht v Commission*, not reported, para. 77 (appeal pending: ECJ, Joined Cases C-401/12 P, C-402/12 P, and C-403/12 P).

[28] For another example, see ECJ, Joined Cases 32 and 33/58 *SNUPAT v High Authority* [1959] E.C.R. 127, at 141 (concerning the assessment, via an objection of illegality, of the lawfulness of a letter in which the High Authority gave directions for interpretation to a body which had to apply only articles of the [now-

---

setting fines for violations of the competition rules in an action for annulment brought against a decision imposing fines, since although the Guidelines do not constitute the legal basis of the contested decision, they nonetheless determine, generally and abstractly, the method which the Commission has bound itself to use in assessing the fines imposed by that decision.[29] Similarly, under the case-law, Art. 277 TFEU has been held to extend to the internal rules of an institution on the grounds that although they do not constitute the legal basis of the contested decision, they determine the essential procedural requirements for adopting that decision.[30]

II. Identity of the Parties

Under Art. 277 TFEU, 'any party' may raise an objection of illegality. **9.09**

A. Natural or legal persons

'Any party' covers, first, natural or legal persons who are unable to challenge before the **9.10** Union judicature the act against which the objection of illegality is raised (see para. 9.07). Natural or legal persons may therefore raise an objection against acts of general application which they could not reasonably challenge in an action for annulment before the General Court, provided, of course, that the act concerned applies to the issue with which the application is concerned.[31]

---

expired] ECSC Treaty and secondary [then Community] legislation, after finding that the letter did not constitute an act against which an action would lie).

[29] ECJ, Joined Cases C-189/02 P, C-202/02 P, C-205/02 P to C-208/02 P, and C-213/02 P *Dansk Røyrindustrl and Others v Commission* [2005] E.C.R. I-5425, paras 212–213; CFI, Case T-64/02 *Heubach v Commission* [2005] E.C.R. II-5137, para. 35; CFI, Joined Cases T-217/03 and T-245/03 *FNCBV and Others v Commission* [2006] E.C.R. II-4987, para. 250 (and citations therein) (appeal dismissed on other grounds: ECJ (judgment of 18 December 2008), Joined Cases C-101/07 P and C-110/07 P *FNSEA and Others v Commission*, not reported). As a related point, in principle an objection of illegality may be raised in relation to Art. 15(2) of Regulation No. 17 (now replaced by Regulation No. 1/2003), authorizing the Commission to impose fines for infringements of competition law, but in practice, such a plea has not been successful: see, e.g. CFI, Case T-43/02 *Jungbunzlauer v Commission* [2006] E.C.R. II-3435, paras 69–92; CFI, Case T-279/02 *Degussa v Commission* [2006] E.C.R. II-897, paras 66–88 (appeal dismissed in ECJ, Case C-266/06 P *Evonik Degussa v Commission and Council* [2008] E.C.R. I-81*, Summ. pub.); CFI, Case T-69/04 *Schunk and Schunk Kohlenstoff-Technik v Commission* [2008] E.C.R. II-2567, paras 27–50; CFI, Case T-116/04 *Wieland-Werke v Commission* [2009] E.C.R. II-1087, paras 49–50; EGC, Joined Cases T-394/08, T-408/08, T-453/08, and T-454/08 *Regione autonoma della Sardegna and Others v Commission* [2011] E.C.R. II-6255, paras 206–211.

[30] See, e.g. CFI, Joined Cases T-3/00 and T-337/04 *Pitsiorlas v Council and ECB* [2007] E.C.R. II- 4779, paras 178–257 (dismissed on appeal in ECJ (order of 3 July 2008), Case C-84/08 P *Pitsiorlas v Council and European Central Bank* [2008] E.C.R. I-104*, Summ. pub.) (objection of illegality raised in relation to ECB Rules of Procedure).

[31] However, as already mentioned, an objection of illegality cannot be raised by a natural or legal person against a regulation in the exceptional case where the regulation has a dual nature and should be considered to constitute an individual measure as regards the natural or legal person concerned, with the result that such person could undoubtedly have sought the annulment of the regulation under the fourth para. of Art 263 TFEU: see para. 9.07. In ECJ, Case C-11/00 *Commission v ECB* [2003] E.C.R. I-7147, para. 75, the Court of Justice cited by way of example regulations imposing anti-dumping duties. They have the dual nature of acts of a legislative nature and acts liable to be of direct and individual concern to certain traders.

In this regard, it remains to be seen how the changes brought by the Lisbon Treaty to the standing requirements for natural and legal persons under the fourth paragraph of Art. 263 TFEU—namely, the introduction of the category of regulatory acts which do not entail implementing measures and for which only direct concern has to be demonstrated (see para. 7.108)—will have a bearing on the assessment of the admissibility of an objection of illegality raised by a natural or legal person against such act.

B. Member States and Union institutions

9.11 In order to ascertain the types of acts of general application that may be raised by Member States and Union institutions under Art. 277 TFEU, it is important to understand the situation concerning the approach taken by the Union courts to this issue under the former Treaty framework.

By way of background, there was much debate in the academic literature concerning former Art. 241 EC and the kinds of acts that may be raised by the Member States and the then Community institutions. There was a school of thought to the effect that the fact that they could bring an action for annulment against any binding Community act precluded them from making use of the objection of illegality on the grounds that, if they were authorized to do so, they would effectually be able to start time running again in breach of the principle of legal certainty.[32] But this view was not shared by all commentators. Some argued that the Member States and Community institutions could have recourse to the objection of illegality to challenge the legality of regulations and similar acts, even though they had not taken advantage of their right to bring an action for annulment against the acts in question within the requisite time limits, relying on the wording of what was then Art. 241 EC ('any party') and the ancillary function of the objection of illegality of avoiding the application of regulations and similar acts whose deficiencies and possible illegality became apparent to Member States or Community institutions after the time limit for bringing proceedings had passed.[33] The unlawful nature of an act may indeed not appear so much on its face as from the manner in which it is interpreted and applied.[34]

Consequently, as regards the interpretation of former Art. 241 EC, the Union courts took the following approach. On the one hand, under the case-law, a Member State or Community institution could raise an objection of illegality against a regulation which it could have challenged directly via an action for annulment.[35] This was expressly confirmed in the

---

[32] See, e.g. G. Bebr, 'Judicial Remedy of Private Parties Against Normative Acts of the European Communities: The Role of the Exception of Illegality' (1966) C.M.L. Rev. 11–13; J. Usher, 'The Inter-relationship of Arts 173, 177 and 184 EEC [now Arts 263, 267, and 277 TFEU]' (1979) E.L. Rev. 37.

[33] See, e.g. R. H. Lauwaars, *Lawfulness and Legal Force of Community Decisions* (Leiden, Sijthoff, 1973), 277–9, who systematically refutes Bebr's arguments (n. 32). See also T. Van Rijn, *Exceptie van onwettigheid en prejudiciële procedure inzake geldigheid van Gemeenschapshandelingen* (Deventer, Kluwer, 1978), 160; P. Dubois, "L'exception d'illégalité devant la Cour de Justice des Communautés européennes" (1978) C.D.E. 407, at 411–13.

[34] See, e.g. ECJ, Case C-11/00 *Commission v ECB* [2003] E.C.R. I-7147, para. 73, in which the ECB contended that it had not brought an action for the annulment of the regulation in respect of which it subsequently raised an objection of illegality because it believed that the regulation did not apply to it.

[35] As long ago as 1966, the Court of Justice had implicitly accepted that Member States could raise an objection of illegality against provisions of a Council regulation and a Commission regulation in an action for the annulment of another Council regulation. Although it did not consider whether Member States were

Court of Justice's 2003 judgment in *Commission v ECB*.[36] The case involved an action for annulment brought by the Commission against an act adopted by the ECB on fraud prevention[37] in which the ECB raised an objection of illegality against a regulation previously adopted by the European Parliament and the Council concerning investigations conducted by the European Anti-Fraud Office (OLAF).[38] The Court of Justice held that the ECB's objection of illegality was admissible.[39] It based its ruling on the text of then Art. 241 EC which expressly provided that 'any party'—hence also privileged applicants—may raise an objection of illegality against 'regulations'.[40] It also made clear that the regulation concerned was of a general or legislative character, to be distinguished from regulations of a dual nature and decisions, pointing to its case-law to the effect that a decision which has not been challenged by its addressee within the time limit for bringing an action for annulment became definitive against that person.[41] The Court's ruling in this case was confirmed in subsequent case-law.[42]

On the other hand, however, under the case-law on former Art. 241 EC, privileged applicants were not entitled to raise an objection of illegality against directives or decisions, since that possibility was not provided for in any Treaty provision. As regards directives, this was so, even though there were good arguments to opine that what was good for regulations of general legislative character also held good for directives of genuinely legislative or general character as far as the objection of illegality was concerned (and even for decisions of genuinely legislative character [43]), especially since regulations and directives addressed to all Member States were published in the same way as regulations in the *Official Journal* as stipulated in former Art. 254(2) EC, and their illegality often became apparent years later after the time for bringing an action for annulment had expired, for example when the Commission informed the Member States of the precise content of their obligations. Thus, in the context of an action for infringement, a Member State was precluded from challenging the legality of a directive in its defence to an action brought by the Commission on the

---

entitled to invoke what is now Art. 277 TFEU, it did reject the objection on the ground that it was directed against provisions of regulations which were not applicable to the issue with which the application was concerned: see ECJ, Case 32/65 *Italy v Council and Commission* [1966] E.C.R. 389.

[36] ECJ, Case C-11/00 *Commission v ECB* [2003] E.C.R. I-7147. Notably, a number of Advocates General of the Court of Justice had earlier expressed the view in Opinions that the wording of former Art. 241 EC did not preclude Member States and Community institutions from raising an objection of illegality (Opinion of Advocate-General K. Roemer in ECJ, Case 32/65 *Italy v Council and Commission* [1966] E.C.R. 389, at 414; Opinion of Advocate-General Sir Gordon Slynn in ECJ, Case 181/85 *France v Commission* [1987] E.C.R. 689, at 702–3; Opinion of Advocate-General G. F. Mancini in ECJ, Case 204/86 *Greece v Council* [1988] E.C.R. 5323, at 5343–5). On this view, the possibility of Member States' or Community institutions' raising such an objection was not even subject to any limitation, because Art. 241 EC did not so provide. Thus, a Member State did not have to show that there was a good reason why it had not acted in time in bringing an action for annulment against the regulation or similar act at issue or that it had been taken by surprise—after the time limit for bringing an action for annulment had passed—by the interpretation given to the act, which raised doubts as to its legality (Opinion of Advocate-General Sir Gordon Slynn in ECJ, Case 181/85 *France v Commission* [1987] E.C.R. 689, at 703).

[37] [1999] O.J. L291/36.
[38] [1999] O.J. L136/1.
[39] ECJ, Case C-11/00 *Commission v ECB* [2003] E.C.R. I-7147, para. 78.
[40] ECJ, Case C-11/00 *Commission v ECB*, para. 76.
[41] ECJ, Case C-11/00 *Commission v ECB*, paras 74–75, 77 (and citations therein).
[42] See ECJ, Case C-442/04 *Spain v Council* [2008] E.C.R. I-3517, para. 22.
[43] For an example of such a decision, see ECJ, Case C-80/06 *Carp* [2007] E.C.R. I-4473.

grounds that it failed to fulfil its obligations in relation to that directive.[44] Moreover, the case-law did not make any distinction between directives addressed only to certain Member States and those addressed to all Member States, and thus, directives shared the same fate as decisions as far as an objection of illegality raised by a privileged applicant was concerned.[45]

The foregoing approach of the Union courts under the former Treaty framework is now subject to revision in light of the changes brought by the Lisbon Treaty, in which Art. 277 TFEU now expressly refers to acts of general application and no longer solely to regulations as Art. 241 EC had done. The wording of Art. 277 TFEU is manifestly broader than that of the former Art. 241 EC and undoubtedly covers directives and decisions to the extent that they constitute acts of general application. It remains to be seen, however, how the Union courts will reconcile Art. 277 TFEU with the requirement of legal certainty. The fact that the objection of illegality has in principle *inter partes* effects may help to 'soften the blow' (see para. 9.19).

C. Union bodies, offices, and agencies

9.12 Although there is no case-law as of yet, the reference to 'any party' presumably encompasses an objection of illegality invoked by a Union body, office, or agency.

D. Objection raised by the parties and exceptionally by the Union courts

9.13 Both applicants and defendants in a direct action before the Union courts are entitled to raise an objection of illegality with a view to having such action decided in their favour.[46]

In principle, an objection of illegality must be raised by one of the parties. Nevertheless, exceptionally, the Union courts may consider whether a general act constituting the basis for the measure contested in the proceedings is unlawful of their own motion.[47] The Court

---

[44] See, e.g. ECJ (judgment of 15 July 2004), Case C-118/03 *Commission v Germany*, not reported, para. 7; ECJ (judgment of 15 July 2004), Case C-139/03 *Commission v Germany*, not reported, para. 7; ECJ, Joined Cases C-53/05 and C-61/05 *Commission v Portugal* [2006] E.C.R. I-6215, para. 30 (and further citations therein). Likewise, the Commission cannot, in infringement proceedings, claim that a directive, the provisions of which were complied with by the Member State concerned, is unlawful with a view to demonstrating the existence of an infringement by that Member State of a Treaty provision: ECJ, Case C-475/01 *Commission v Greece ('Ouzo')* [2004] E.C.R. I-8923, paras 17, 18, 24, and 25. Such an issue arose also in other contexts, such as in an action for annulment. See, e.g. ECJ, Case C-86/03 *Greece v Commission* [2005] E.C.R. I-10979, para. 86 ('even assuming that a Member State were authorized, in the context of an annulment action before the Community judicature, to plead the illegality of a Community directive addressed to it and against which it had not brought an annulment action within the period prescribed for that purpose . . . , that plea is, in any case, unfounded').

[45] See, e.g. ECJ, Case C-74/91 *Commission v Germany* [1992] E.C.R. I-5437, para. 10; ECJ, Joined Cases C-53/05 and C-61/05 *Commission v Portugal* [2006] E.C.R. I-6215, para. 30; see also ECJ, Case C-241/01 *National Farmers' Union* [2002] E.C.R. I-9079, para. 39, in which the Court held that a Member State which was an addressee of a Commission decision addressed to all Member States and, despite its title, was legislative in nature, but which had not challenged the legality of that decision within the requisite time limits for an action for annulment did not have standing subsequently before a national court to invoke its unlawfulness in order to dispute the merits of an action brought against it.

[46] See ECJ, Case C-475/01 *Commission v Greece ('Ouzo')* [2004] E.C.R. I-8923, para. 17.

[47] ECJ, Case 14/59 *Société des Fonderies de Pont-à-Mousson v High Authority* [1959] E.C.R. 215, at 230; CFI, Joined Cases T-134/03 and T-135/03 *Common Market Fertilizers v Commission* [2005] E.C.R. II-3923,

may do so in particular where the general act may possibly be unlawful for lack of competence or infringement of an essential procedural requirement (see para. 7.146).[48]

III. Special Characteristics

A. Requirements for admissibility

(1) Action in connection with which the objection is raised must be admissible

An objection of illegality will be admissible only insofar as the direct action in connection **9.14** with which it is raised is admissible.[49] The applicant's interest in successfully raising an objection of illegality against the general act on which the contested individual measure is based coincides with its interest in its succeeding with its application for the annulment of that measure. If the general act is declared inapplicable, the individual measure loses its legal basis and the action for annulment of that measure will succeed. If the objection is raised by the defendant, its interest in obtaining a declaration that a Union act which it has allegedly infringed is inapplicable is likewise self-evident.

(2) Other conditions

As already noted, an objection of illegality may be raised only in respect of an act of general **9.15** application which is applicable to the issue with which the application is concerned (see para. 9.08).[50]

---

paras 51–52; on appeal in ECJ, Case C-443/05 P *Common Market Fertilizers v Commission* [2007] E.C.R. I-7029, paras 111–139, the Court of Justice rejected the applicant's ground of appeal based on the CFI's failure to take account of the public policy nature of the illegality invoked as an objection, finding that although the CFI did hold that the possible illegality of the general measure in question was not a matter of public policy and that it did not follow from the case-law that it must of its own motion consider whether the Commission exceeded its powers by adopting the content of that measure which is the legal basis for the contested decisions of which annulment was sought, this argument was directed against a ground which was included in the judgment purely for the sake of completeness and thus, being nugatory, could not lead to the judgment being set aside. In any event, whether a possible illegality is a matter of public policy is irrelevant where the CFI correctly holds that the measure at issue is untainted by illegality and consequently does not raise the issue of illegality of its own motion.

[48] See, e.g. CST (judgment of 29 September 2009), Joined Cases F-69/07 and F-60/08 *O v Commission*, not reported, para. 71 (holding admissible an objection of illegality directed against a provision of the Conditions of Employment on the basis that such provision does not state the reasons on which it is based. Even though the objection was not mentioned by the applicant in its application but only at a later stage of the proceedings, it was admissible, since it concerned a matter of public policy which may be raised at any stage of the proceedings and in any event may be examined by the Union judicature of its own motion.)

[49] See, e.g. ECJ (order of 8 December 2006), Case C-368/05 P *Polyelectrolyte Producers Group v Council and Commission* [2006] E.C.R. I-130*, Summ. pub., para. 72; CFI (order of 14 December 2005), Case T-369/03 *Arizona Chemical and Others v Commission* [2005] E.C.R. II-5839, paras 129–130 (appeal dismissed on other grounds: ECJ (order of 13 March 2007), Case C-150/06 P *Arizona Chemical and Others v Commission* [2007] E.C.R. I-39*, Summ. pub.); CST (judgment of 30 September 2010), Case F-29/09 *Lebedef and Jones v Commission*, not reported, para. 30 (and citations therein) ('when there is no right to bring the main action or where the main action is inadmissible [the objection of illegality] must also be declared inadmissible').

[50] By its nature, the objection of illegality must be invoked in order to challenge the legality of the act of general application concerned; where an applicant does not challenge the legality of the general measure as such, but instead the allegedly illegal application of that measure, an objection of illegality cannot succeed: see CFI, Case T-326/07 *Cheminova and Others v Commission* [2009] E.C.R. II-2685, paras 76–77.

Furthermore, the objection of illegality must be raised in time, in principle in the application or the defence.[51]

To be clear, however, the possibility of raising an objection of illegality in relation to an act of general application is as such not restricted to a period of time.[52] An objection of illegality may be raised against acts of general application outside the time limit for bringing an action for annulment against them. This follows from the essential nature of the objection[53]; it is also confirmed by Art. 277 TFEU ('Notwithstanding the expiry of the period laid down in Article 263, sixth paragraph' TFEU).

Finally, an objection of illegality may be held inadmissible if it infringes the principle of *res judicata*, but as illustrated by the case-law so far, several requirements must be fulfilled for that to be the case.[54]

---

[51] See, e.g. ECJ, Case C-86/03 *Greece v Commission* [2005] E.C.R. I-10979, paras 80–85 (finding that the objection of illegality raised by the applicant was raised with sufficient clarity in the application, thereby rejecting challenge to its admissibility). An objection of illegality expressly raised for the first time in the reply is admissible if it constitutes the amplification of a plea raised by implication in the application: see, e.g. ECJ, Case C-442/04 *Spain v Council* [2008] E.C.R. I-3517, paras 23–24; CFI, Case T-176/01 *Ferriere Nord v Commission* [2004] E.C.R. II-3931, para. 136 (appeal dismissed on other grounds in ECJ, Case C-49/05 P *Ferriere Nord v Commission* [2008] E.C.R. I-68*, Summ. pub.); CFI, Joined Cases T-3/00 and T-337/04 *Pitsiorlas v Council and ECB* [2007] E.C.R. II-4779, paras 179–183 (appealed on other grounds: ECJ, Case C-193/01 P and C-84/08 P *Pitsiorlas v Council and European Central Bank* [2003] E.C.R. I-4837); CFI, Case T-45/06 *Reliance Industries v Council and Commission* [2008] E.C.R. II-2399, paras 62–66. Otherwise, it is inadmissible: see, e.g. CFI, Case T-94/98 *Alferink v Commission* [2008] E.C.R. II-1125, paras 38–39. In a batch of related cases, such an issue was put before the General Court, but it found it unnecessary to rule on the question whether the applicant could legitimately put forward an objection of illegality pursuant to Art. 277 TFEU in its reply or whether it must be regarded as having been put forward implicitly in the application on the grounds that any discussion of the lawfulness of the general act concerned was purposeless: see EGC, Case T-68/08 *FIFA v Commission* [2011] E.C.R. II-349, para. 115; EGC, Case T-55/08 *UEFA v Commission* [2011] E.C.R. II-271, para.122; EGC, Case T-385/07 *FIFA v Commission* [2011] E.C.R. II-205, para. 97. In some cases, the Union courts delve into the substance of the objection of illegality invoked by a party, even where such an objection may be deemed inadmissible or without ruling on its admissibility. See, e.g. CFI, Case T-351/02 *Deutsche Bahn v Commission* [2006] E.C.R. II-1047, paras 108–112 (noting that even if the applicant intended to raise an objection of illegality, such objection was not clear from its pleadings, but in any event such objection could not be upheld); CFI, Case T-212/02 *Commune de Champagne and Others v Council and Commission* [2007] E.C.R. II-2017, paras 157–162 (holding objection of illegality inadmissible because it was raised out of time, but in any event rejecting applicant's arguments regarding alleged unlawfulness of the general measure concerned); CFI, Case T-308/05 *Italy v Commission* [2007] E.C.R. II-5089, paras 83, 92 (finding no need to rule on the admissibility of the objection of illegality on account of the fact that the objection must be rejected in any event). See also CFI, Case T-390/08 *Bank Melli Iran v Council* [2009] E.C.R. II-3967, paras 21–22 (appeal dismissed in ECJ, Case C-548/09 P *Bank Melli Iran v Council* [2011] E.C.R. I-11381) (at the hearing, the applicant withdrew its objection of illegality stating that it must be considered to be a claim seeking annulment of the contested measure for want of a legal basis; nevertheless, the Court was willing to assume that certain arguments of the applicant could be understood as an objection of illegality, but in any event were rejected).

[52] See, e.g. CST (judgment of 27 September 2011), Case F-98/09 *Whitehead v ECB*, not reported, para. 74 (finding no reason not to apply this interpretation of Art. 277 TFEU to actions based on Art. 270 TFEU, Art. 152 EAEC, or Art. 36.2 of the Statute of the European System of Central Banks).

[53] ECJ, Case 185/85 *Usinor v Commission* [1986] E.C.R. 2079, para. 11.

[54] See ECJ, Case C-442/04 *Spain v Council* [2008] E.C.R. I-3517, para. 25: the principle of *res judicata* extends only to matters of fact and law actually or necessarily settled by the judicial decision in question; in the proceedings concerned, this was not the case. In the CFI's previous judgment involving the same parties, the Court did not rule on the legality of those provisions of the general measure covered by the objection of illegality raised before the ECJ, but rejected the pleas on the basis of which annulment of those provisions was sought on the grounds that the pleas were inadmissible. See also CFI, Joined Cases T-246/08 and T-322/08 *Melli Bank v Council* [2009] E.C.R. II-2629, paras 31–37 (rejecting the Commission's challenge to the admissibility of an objection of illegality on the basis of *lis pendens*, i.e. pending before another competent court) (appeal dismissed in ECJ (judgment of 13 March 2012), Case C-380/09 P *Melli Bank v Council*, not reported).

B. Actions in which an objection of illegality may be raised

(1) Any direct action

An objection of illegality may be raised in any direct action that has been brought before the **9.16** Union courts. Objections of illegality are raised most often in the context of an action for annulment under Art. 263 TFEU.[55]

Such an objection may also be raised, however, in an action for failure to act under Art. 265 TFEU, either by the defendant Union institution, body, office, or agency where it asserts that the act of general application which—the applicant claims—gives rise to an obligation for it to act is unlawful, or by the applicant, where it argues that an act of general application which the defendant institution, body, office, or agency invokes in order to deny the existence of any obligation to act is unlawful.[56] That being said, it is not as easy to raise an objection of illegality in proceedings for failure to act. Where the institution, body, office, or agency concerned has failed to act, the applicant can sometimes only presume on what general measure the failure to act is based. Once the institution indicates the general act on which its failure to act is based, it has defined its position and the action for failure to act becomes inadmissible.

In addition, it should be possible for a Member State to defend itself against an action for infringement under Arts 258–260 TFEU by raising an objection of illegality against an act of general application pursuant to Art. 277 TFEU. Under the former Treaty framework, it appeared from the case-law that a Member State could plead the illegality of a regulation on the basis of Art. 241 EC in proceedings for failure to fulfil obligations, but was not entitled to do so in relation to a directive or a decision addressed to it (save for exceptional circumstances where the act concerned could be deemed non-existent) (see para. 9.11). However, with the changes brought by the Lisbon Treaty, this case-law is no longer certain, since the express reference in Art. 277 TFEU to an 'act of general application' encompasses directives and decisions, as well as regulations, to the extent that such acts are of general application (see para. 5.66).

In principle, it is also possible to raise an objection of illegality in the context of an action for damages against the Union under Arts 268 and 340, second para., TFEU.[57] In practice, however, recourse to such an objection in this connection will be of little utility. The illegality of the general act against which the objection is raised admittedly results in the act being declared inapplicable, but it does not as such result in a determination that the Union has incurred extra-contractual liability, irrespective of whether the general act allegedly caused damage directly or because it served as the legal basis for the individual measure which caused the damage incurred by the applicant; there are other requisite conditions that must be satisfied.

Finally, an objection of illegality assumes importance in staff cases under Art. 270 TFEU.[58] Indeed, in this context, an objection of illegality may be invoked against provisions of

---

[55] For an example in an action for annulment based on Regulation No. 40/94, see CFI, Case T-120/99 *Kik v Commission* [2001] E.C.R. I-2235 (appeal dismissed in ECJ, Case C-361/01 P *Kik v OHIM* [2003] E.C.R. I-8283).

[56] ECJ, Joined Cases 32/58 and 33/58 *SNUPAT v High Authority* [1959] E.C.R. 127, at 139 (in that case under the now-expired ECSC Treaty, the action for failure to act was in fact an action to annul a tacit refusal).

[57] For an example, see CFI, Case T-271/04 *Citymo v Commission* [2007] E.C.R. II-1375, para. 118 (objection of illegality against provisions of the Financial Regulation dismissed).

[58] Art. 277 TFEU is applicable to acts based on Art. 270 TFEU: see, e.g. CST (judgment of 30 September 2010), Case F-29/09 *Lebedef and Jones v Commission*, not reported, para. 29. With the entry into force of the

various types of acts of general application, such as the Staff Regulations,[59] the Conditions of Employment,[60] a call for expression of interest published by the EPSO,[61] a competition notice,[62] the Commission Decision laying down the rules applicable to national experts on secondment to the Commission (the so-called SNE decision),[63] or an ECB budgetary envelope allocated to a particular year.[64] Importantly, though, an objection of illegality is subject to certain admissibility requirements according to the applicable rules governing staff disputes (see Ch. 18).[65]

(2) Objection cannot be raised in proceedings for a preliminary ruling

9.17   An objection of illegality cannot be raised before the Court of Justice in proceedings for a preliminary ruling on the interpretation or validity of Union law under Art. 267 TFEU. Proceedings for a preliminary ruling are not direct actions brought before the Union courts. Instead, the preliminary ruling procedure embodies a relationship of co-operation between the national courts and the Court of Justice. The national court determines the question(s) to be brought before the Court of Justice and the parties to the main proceedings are not entitled to alter their scope.[66]

Lisbon Treaty, Art. 270 TFEU applies to staff cases in connection with the EAEC Treaty, as Art. 152 EAEC has been repealed: see Art. 106a(1)–(2) EAEC of the consolidated version of the EAEC Treaty, [2012] O.J. C327/1.

[59] See, e.g. ECJ, Case C-443/07 P *Centeno Mediavilla and Others v Commission* [2008] E.C.R. I-10945, paras 43–55; ECJ, Case C-71/07 P *Campoli v Commission* [2008] E.C.R. I-5887; ECJ, Case C-496/08 P *Angé Serrano and Others v European Parliament* [2010] E.C.R. I-1793, paras 78–88; CST (judgment of 11 July 2007), Case F-105/05 *Wils v European Parliament*, not reported; CST (order of 26 September 2007), Case F-129/06 *Salvador Roldán*, not reported, paras 71–74; CST (judgment of 29 September 2011), Case F-70/05 *Mische v Commission*, not reported. For an example of a successful objection of illegality in this regard, see ECJ, Joined Cases 75/82 and 117/82 *Razzouk and Beydoun v Commission* [1984] E.C.R. 1509, paras 15–18.

[60] See, e.g. CST (judgment of 30 April 2009), Case F-65/07 *Aayhan v European Parliament*, not reported, paras 84–122 (appeal dismissed on other grounds: CFI (order of 12 October 2009), Case T-283/09 P *Aayhan and Others v Parliament* [2009] E.C.R.-SC I-B-1-113); CST (judgment of 29 September 2009), Joined Cases F-69/07 and F-60/08 *O v Commission*, not reported, paras 68–138.

[61] See, e.g. CST (judgment of 29 June 2011), Case F-7/07 *Angioi v Commission*, not reported, paras 57, 67–75, 89–114.

[62] See, e.g. CFI, Case T-207/02 *Falcone v Commission* [2004] E.C.R.-SC II-1393, paras 18–25; CFI, Joined Cases T-219/02 and T-337/02 *Lutz Herrera v Commission* [2004] E.C.R.-SC II-1407, paras 38–50.

[63] See, e.g. ECJ, Case C-485/08 P *Gualtieri v Commission* [2010] E.C.R. I-3009, paras 103–106.

[64] See CST (judgment of 27 September 2011), Case F-98/09 *Whitehead v ECB*, not reported, paras 73–77 (though held in part inadmissible and in part lacking any legal basis on account of the applicant's failure to substantiate the objection).

[65] In particular, under the case-law, in order for an objection of illegality not to be inadmissible, the forms of order sought by the applicant may be based only on grounds of challenge having the same legal basis as those raised in the complaint and that a plea raised before the Union courts must have already been raised in the pre-litigation procedure with a view to clearly informing the appointing authority of the complaints raised and thus allowing for a possible amicable settlement. Although the rule that the complaint must be consistent with the action brought before the Union judicature (the so-called correspondence rule) is applied with an open mind, so that the heads of claim raised in the complaint may be developed by submissions and arguments which do not necessarily appear in the complaint but which are closely linked to it, where an applicant raises an objection of illegality in his application which had not been raised in the complaint, such an objection is inadmissible. See, e.g. EGC (judgment of 27 October 2010), Case T-65/09 P *Reali v Commission*, not reported, paras 42–49; CST, Joined Cases F-20/08, F-34/08, and F-75/08 *Aparicio and Others v Commission* [2009] E.C.R.-SC I-A-1-375, paras 48–50. But see CST (judgment of 30 September 2010), Case F-29/09 *Lebedef and Jones v Council*, not reported, paras 28–43 (holding that it is appropriate in the circumstances of that case to accept that officials may challenge their pay slips by raising against a provision of the Staff Regulations fixing their pecuniary rights a plea of illegality alleging, in particular, a breach of the principle of equal treatment notwithstanding the restrictions arising under the case-law).

[66] ECJ, Case 44/65 *Singer* [1965] E.C.R. 965, at 970.

Nevertheless, in accordance with well-settled case-law, Art. 277 TFEU 'expresses a general principle of law under which the applicant must, in proceedings brought under national law against the rejection of his application, be able to plead the illegality of a [Union] measure on which the national decision adopted in his regard is based, and the question of the validity of that [Union] measure may thus be referred to the Court in proceedings for a preliminary ruling'.[67] In this way, similar results are achieved in the sense that through the preliminary ruling on validity, a party is able to challenge the legality of Union acts of general application.

C. Pleas in law

By virtue of Art. 277 TFEU, any party may plead the grounds specified in Art. 263, second para., TFEU in order to claim that an allegedly unlawful act of general application is inapplicable. The pleas of lack of competence, infringement of an essential procedural requirement, infringement of the Treaties or of any rule of law relating to its application, or misuse of powers (see paras 7.145 *et seq.*) are therefore potentially available in support of an objection of illegality. **9.18**

IV. Consequences

If an objection of illegality is successfully raised, the act of general application to which it relates is declared inapplicable for the purposes of the proceedings in which the objection was raised. It is inapplicable only in relation to the parties involved in those proceedings, i.e. in principle it has *inter partes* effects.[68] The act of general application subsists as far as third parties are concerned.[69] Nevertheless, the Union institution, body, office, or agency which adopted the act declared inapplicable may be under a duty to withdraw or adjust the act in order to eliminate the illegality found.[70] **9.19**

---

[67] See, e.g. ECJ, Case C-441/05 *Roquette Frères* [2007] E.C.R. I-1993, para. 39.

[68] See, e.g. ECJ, Joined Cases 15/73 to 33/73, 52/73 to 53/73, 57/73 to 109/73, 116/73 to 117/73, 123/73, 132/73 and 135/73 to 137/73 *Schots (née Kortner) and Others v Council and Others* [1974] E.C.R. 177, para. 36; ECJ, Case C-434/98 P *Council v Busacca and Others* [2000] E.C.R. I-8577, para. 26.

[69] Nevertheless, the declaration that the act is inapplicable may have indirect effects on third parties. For instance, if the implementation of the general act was determined by an individual act which was addressed to a number of persons, the annulment of the implementing measure on account of the non-applicability of the general act might also alter the legal position of persons to whom the implementing measure was addressed but who did not bring proceedings against it. In such an event, the Court of Justice or the General Court may, of course, restrict the effects of the declaration of nullity if such a step is necessary to protect the interests of third parties (see para. 7.222); for an example, see ECJ, Case C-242/90 P *Commission v Albani and Others* [1993] E.C.R. I-3839, paras 13–16.

[70] Opinion of Advocate-General M. Lagrange in ECJ, Case 14/59 *Société des Fonderies de Pont-à-Mousson v High Authority* [1959] E.C.R. 215, at 242, who refers to 'the need—moral if not legal—to adopt a new decision', and in ECJ, Joined Cases 14/60, 16/60 to 17/60, 20/60, 24/60, 26/60 to 27/60, and 1/61 *Meroni and Others v High Authority* [1961] E.C.R. 161, at 174; Opinion of Advocate-General K. Roemer in ECJ, Joined Cases 9/60 and 12/60 *Vloeberghs v High Authority* [1961] E.C.R. 197, at 227. Cf. ECJ, Joined Cases 75/82 and 117/82 *Razzouk and Beydoun v Commission* [1984] E.C.R. 1509, para. 19.

10

PRELIMINARY RULINGS ON THE VALIDITY OF UNION LAW

I. Introduction

A. General

10.01 Art. 267 TFEU confers jurisdiction on the Court of Justice of the European Union[1] to give preliminary rulings on the validity of Union law, namely, 'acts of the institutions, bodies, offices or agencies of the Union'.[2] What this involves is a review of the validity of a given Union act as a step in proceedings before a national court in which the validity of that act is at issue, but the national court does not resolve that question itself, referring it instead to the Court of Justice for its assessment. Preliminary rulings on the validity of Union law are, like those concerning the interpretation of Union law, subject to the requirements placed on orders for reference[3] (see Ch. 3) and invariably, the Court of Justice may be presented with questions concerning both the validity and the interpretation of Union law in orders for reference submitted by national courts.[4]

Importantly, Art. 267 TFEU contains no obligation for national courts and tribunals to make a reference for a preliminary ruling in the case of courts and tribunals against whose decisions there is a 'judicial remedy under national law' (see paras 3.48–3.49) but, as already mentioned, the Court of Justice has decided that even these courts and tribunals have no jurisdiction themselves to declare that Union acts are invalid (see paras 3.59–3.60).

---

[1] At present, the preliminary ruling jurisdiction is vested with the Court of Justice: see further para. 2.53.
[2] Art. 267, first para., indent (b), TFEU. See also Art. 19(3)(b) TEU, which refers in more succinct language to 'acts adopted by the institutions'. With the entry into force of the Lisbon Treaty, Art. 267 TFEU applies to preliminary rulings in connection with the EAEC Treaty, as Art. 150 EAEC has been repealed: see Art. 106a (1)–(2) EAEC of the consolidated version of the EAEC Treaty, [2012] O.J. C327/1: see further para. 3.03.
[3] See, e.g. ECJ, Case C-77/09 *Gowan Comércio Internacional e Serviços* [2010] E.C.R. I-13533, paras 24–27.
[4] See, e.g. ECJ, Case C-15/05 *Kawasaki Motors Europe* [2006] E.C.R. I-3657; ECJ, Case C-45/05 *Maatschap Schonewille-Prins* [2007] E.C.R. I-3997; ECJ, Case C-558/07 *S.P.C.M. and Others* [2009] E.C.R. I-5783; ECJ, Joined Cases C-22/08 and C-23/08 *Vatsouras and Koupatantze* [2009] E.C.R. I-4585; ECJ, Case C-309/10 *Agrana Zucker* [2011] E.C.R. I-7333. See further ECJ, Case C-344/04 *IATA and ELFAA* [2006] E.C.R. I-403, para. 25: in the main proceedings, the claimants contested the validity of an EU regulation. This led the referring court to submit a question on the interpretation of what is now Art. 267 TFEU in connection with the obligation placed on national courts to refer questions on the validity of Union law. In response to a challenge to the admissibility of that reference, the Court of Justice ruled that the fact that the referring court has at the same time referred questions on the validity of that regulation and that the answers provided to them may dispose of the main proceedings 'cannot call into question the relevance which the question on the interpretation of Art. 267 TFEU possesses in itself'.

Consequently, they too are under an obligation to submit the question of validity to the Court of Justice whenever they regard a Union act as invalid.[5]

B. Topics to be discussed

Similar to the treatment of preliminary rulings on the interpretation of Union law (see **10.02** Ch. 6), the request for a preliminary ruling on the validity of Union law raises three main issues. The first relates to the subject-matter of the preliminary ruling on validity (what acts may be subject to such a ruling and what acts—for example, international agreements—can be used to assess the validity of Union acts), as well as broader issues relating to the interplay between the indirect route of a preliminary ruling on validity and the direct route provided in the Treaties for challenging the legality of Union acts, namely the action for annulment. The second relates to the substance of the review of validity of a Union act in preliminary ruling proceedings, which invites discussion of the differences between a preliminary ruling on validity and the action for annulment. The third relates to the consequences of a preliminary ruling on validity, examining the effects *erga omnes* and *ex tunc* of a declaration of invalidity and comparing them with the declaration of nullity in the context of an action for annulment. In this way, a common theme running through the topics discussed in this chapter is the place of preliminary rulings on validity in the context of a complete and coherent system of judicial protection in the European Union, especially when it comes to its relationship with the action for annulment.[6]

II. Subject-Matter of Preliminary Ruling Proceedings Relating to the Validity of a Union Act

A. Acts excluded from review

The Treaties themselves and all Union rules of constitutional rank generally fall outside the **10.03** ambit of preliminary rulings on the validity of Union acts. Those rules constitute in fact the yardstick against which the validity of such acts is reviewed.[7]

In addition, the Court of Justice has held that 'a preliminary ruling of the Court does not rank among the acts of the [Union] institutions whose validity is open to review in

---

[5] ECJ, Case 314/85 *Foto-Frost* [1987] E.C.R. 4199, paras 12–20.

[6] See K. Lenaerts, 'The Rule of Law and the Coherence of the Judicial System of the European Union' (2007) C.M.L. Rev. 1625–59; J. T. Nowak, 'Wettigheidstoetsing van handelingen van de instellingen van de Europese Unie: complementaire rechtsbescherming in een meerlagige context' (2013) T.B.P. 195–211.

[7] As provided by the Treaties, some acts of the European Council and the Council can be regarded as 'constitutional' acts having the status of primary Union law because their entry into force depends upon their being adopted by the Member States in accordance with their constitutional requirements. See further K. Lenaerts and P. Van Nuffel (R. Bray and N. Cambien (eds)), *European Union Law* (3rd edn, London, Sweet & Maxwell, 2011), para. 22.15. However, to the extent that these acts are acts of a Union institution, they may be the subject of references for preliminary rulings on their validity. See ECJ (judgment of 27 November 2012), Case C-370/12 *Pringle*, not reported, paras 34–36, relating to a decision adopted by the European Council pursuant to Art. 48(6) TEU.

proceedings under [Art. 267 TFEU]'.[8] Undoubtedly, that ruling must be extended to cover any judgment of the Court of Justice of the European Union, which, as a result, remains outside the scope of review by way of preliminary rulings on validity. However, the fact that the Court of Justice has already given a preliminary ruling on the interpretation of a Union act does not preclude the Court from ruling on the validity of the same act in a later judgment.[9]

B. Union acts in the former second and third pillars of the Union

10.04 Under the former Treaty framework, there were limitations placed on the Court of Justice's preliminary ruling jurisdiction in relation to the former third pillar of Police and Judicial Cooperation in Criminal Matters (PJCCM) and the former second pillar of Common Foreign and Security Policy (CFSP). With the entry into force of the Lisbon Treaty, however, this has changed.

The limitations on the Court of Justice's jurisdiction to give preliminary rulings on the validity (and interpretation) of Union law adopted in the field of PJCCM have been abolished, subject to a five-year provisional period under which the limitations of former Art. 35 EU hold for PJCCM acts adopted before the entry into force of the Lisbon Treaty until such acts are amended (see further paras 3.02 and 22.05).

With respect to the former second pillar of the CFSP, the Court of Justice has generally not been conferred jurisdiction, subject to two exceptions: it has jurisdiction to monitor compliance with Art. 40 TEU and to rule on proceedings brought under the fourth paragraph of Art. 263 TFEU reviewing the legality of decisions providing for restrictive measures against natural and legal persons adopted by the Council on the basis of Chapter Two of Title V of Part Three of the TFEU (concerning specific provisions on the CFSP).[10] Nevertheless, it cannot be wholly excluded that the exceptions set down in the Treaties may afford possibilities for the Court to deliver preliminary rulings on the validity of Union acts adopted on the basis of the provisions relating to the CFSP.[11] For instance, the latter exception mentions only actions for annulment under Art. 263 TFEU, that is to say, the direct route of legality control for CFSP acts entailing restrictive measures against individuals. However, it remains to be seen in the case-law whether the complete and coherent system of judicial protection set up by the Treaties implies that the indirect route of legality control via preliminary rulings on validity should also be available as regards such measures.

---

[8] ECJ (order of 5 March 1986), Case 69/85 *Wünsche* [1986] E.C.R. 947, para. 16.

[9] ECJ, Joined Cases C-393/99 and C-394/99 *Hervein and Others* [2002] E.C.R. I-2829, para. 27. Consequently, a judgment giving a preliminary ruling on interpretation does not therefore implicitly rule on the validity of the act interpreted.

[10] See Art. 24(1), second para., TEU; Art. 275 TFEU.

[11] As regards possibilities in relation to preliminary rulings on the interpretation of Union law, see para. 6.05.

C. Review of the validity of international agreements concluded by the Union

A trickier question is whether the validity of international agreements concluded by the **10.05** Union may be reviewed in preliminary ruling proceedings.[12] Textbook writers have long voiced great reservations,[13] chiefly on the grounds that, in the event that it failed to give effect to such agreements, the Union might stand to incur liability at international level. Moreover, it was for that reason that the Treaties introduced a procedure whereby the Court of Justice gives a prior opinion on the compatibility of proposed international agreements with the provisions of the Treaties (which means in practice primary Union law as a whole) (see Ch. 12). However, it is no simple matter to exclude international agreements concluded by the Union from the scope of the review of validity under the preliminary ruling procedure.

In the first place, this is because the Court of Justice has held that it has jurisdiction to give preliminary rulings on the interpretation of international agreements concluded by the Union (see para. 6.13). Since indent (b) of the first paragraph of Art. 267 TFEU draws no distinction between preliminary rulings on the validity of acts of the institutions as opposed to preliminary rulings on their interpretation, if the Court of Justice holds that it has jurisdiction to interpret international agreements by preliminary ruling, it creates the impression that it also has jurisdiction to review their validity.

What is more, a statement of the Court of Justice issued early on further reinforced this impression: 'The question whether the conclusion of a given agreement is within the power of the [Union] and whether, in a given case, such power has been exercised in conformity with the provisions of the [Treaties] is, in principle, a question which may be submitted to the Court of Justice . . . in accordance with the preliminary procedure.'[14] This passage has been understood to mean that the Court of Justice should review the validity of the act whereby the Union purported to conclude the agreement, but not the validity of the agreement itself.[15] But that reading of the Court's case-law does not resolve the question of the possible liability of the Union at international level, since if the act by which the Union purported to conclude an international agreement is declared invalid, it will lose all binding force in the Union legal order, just as if the agreement itself was to be declared invalid.[16]

Yet, this did not stop the Court of Justice in its 1994 judgment in *France v Commission* from declaring void the act whereby the Commission sought to conclude the Agreement

---

[12] To be distinguished from this is the assessment of the validity of Union acts in the light of international agreements (see para. 10.08).

[13] See, e.g. R. Joliet, *Le droit institutionnel des Communautés européennes—Le contentieux* (Faculté de Droit, d'Économie et de Sciences sociales de Liège, Liège, 1981), 198; M. Waelbroeck, D. Waelbroeck, and G. Vandersanden, 'La Cour de Justice', in M. Waelbroeck, J.-V. Louis, D. Vignes *et al.* (eds), *Commentaire Mégret* (2nd edn, Éditions de l'Université de Bruxelles, Brussels, 1993), 214–15.

[14] ECJ, Opinion 1/75 *Draft Understanding on a Local Cost Standard drawn up under the auspices of the OECD* [1975] E.C.R. 1355, at 1361.

[15] R. Joliet, *Le droit institutionnel des Communautés européennes—Le contentieux* (Faculté de Droit, d'Économie et de Sciences sociales de Liège, Liège, 1981), 59–60 and 198.

[16] Cf. ECJ, Joined Cases C-402/05 P and C-415/05 P *Kadi and Al Barakaat International Foundation v Council and Commission* [2008] E.C.R. I-6351.

with the United States regarding the application of the competition laws of the EU and the United States, which was signed and entered into force on 23 September 1991[17] (essentially on the grounds that the Commission had disregarded the Council's powers under what is now Art. 218 TFEU). Although '[i]n the event of non-performance of the Agreement by the Commission . . . the Community could incur liability at international level',[18] the Court of Justice held that the action for annulment of the act whereby the Commission sought to conclude the agreement was admissible, on the grounds that, 'as is apparent from its actual wording, the Agreement [on which that act was based was] intended to produce legal effects'[19] within the meaning of the *AETR* case-law.[20] In addition, it held that '[e]xercise of the powers delegated to the [Union] institutions in international matters cannot escape judicial review, under [Art. 263 TFEU], of the legality of the acts adopted'.[21]

Finally, given that the Court of Justice considers the action for annulment and the preliminary ruling on validity to be two mechanisms in the same system of judicial review at Union level,[22] it would seem probable that the Court would not assess the legality of an act by which the Union sought to conclude an international agreement any differently if this question were to be raised by a national court in a reference for a preliminary ruling on the validity of that act.

D. Acts of Union institutions, bodies, offices, or agencies

10.06   Art. 267 TFEU explicitly envisages preliminary rulings to be sought on the validity of acts of Union institutions, bodies, offices, or agencies,[23] subject to the limitations placed on the Court of Justice's preliminary ruling jurisdiction in the former second and third pillars as discussed earlier.

In the first place, this means that the validity of acts of the European Parliament, the European Council, the Council, the Commission, the European Central Bank, and the Court of Auditors, all institutions of the Union within the meaning of the second paragraph of Art. 13(1) TEU, may be reviewed under the preliminary ruling procedure.[24] It goes without saying that this also applies to acts adopted jointly by the European Parliament and the Council under the ordinary legislative procedure provided for in Art. 294 TFEU.

---

[17] ECJ, Case C-327/91 *France v Commission* [1994] E.C.R. I-3641.
[18] ECJ, Case C-327/91 *France v Commission*, para. 25.
[19] ECJ, Case C-327/91 *France v Commission*, paras 14-15.
[20] ECJ, Case 22/70 *Commission v Council* (the *'AETR'* case) [1971] E.C.R. 263.
[21] ECJ, Case C-327/91 *France v Commission* [1994] E.C.R. I-3641, para. 16.
[22] ECJ, Case 112/83 *Société des Produits de Maïs* [1985] E.C.R. 719, para. 17; ECJ, Case 294/83 *Les Verts v European Parliament* [1986] E.C.R. 1339, para. 23; ECJ, Case 314/85 *Foto-Frost* [1987] E.C.R. 4199, para. 16.
[23] Art. 267, first para., indent (b), TFEU. Art. 19(3)(b) TEU merely refers to preliminary rulings on the validity (and interpretation) of acts adopted by 'the institutions' in more abbreviated fashion.
[24] As regards the Court of Justice of the European Union, see para. 10.03. See also ECJ, Case C-11/05 *Friesland Coberco Dairy Foods* [2006] E.C.R. I-4285, paras 34–41, in which the Court ruled that the validity of conclusions of the Customs Code Committee cannot be examined within the framework of what is now Art. 267 TFEU on the grounds that the Committee's conclusions cannot be regarded as constituting an act of the Union institutions and, like the opinions of a similar kind issued by other Committees in the field, are not binding on national customs authorities in taking final decisions which are subject to judicial review before the national courts.

In the second place, as introduced by the Lisbon Treaty, acts of Union 'bodies, offices or agencies' also come within the jurisdiction of the Court of Justice to give preliminary rulings on validity, again subject to the limitations placed on the preliminary ruling jurisdiction of the Court of Justice discussed earlier. This additional language essentially reflects existing case-law and underscores the importance of ensuring that the system of judicial protection is complete. Already under former Art. 234 EC, when it came to reviewing the validity of 'acts of the institutions' in preliminary ruling proceedings, the Court gave this expression a broad interpretation, encompassing acts of bodies or agencies set up by the Union institutions to which powers of executive decision had been delegated by those institutions. This was because the Court of Justice had made the compatibility with the former EC Treaty of such a delegation of powers dependent upon its complying with the Treaty provisions to which the exercise of the powers by the delegating institution would have been subject, including the Treaty provisions on judicial supervision, had it exercised the powers itself.[25]

E. Acts of bodies established by international agreements concluded by the Union

The question whether acts of a body established by an international agreement concluded **10.07** by the Union may be subjected to a review of their validity under the preliminary ruling procedure is difficult to answer. In this context, the Court of Justice has emphasized the need for a system of judicial supervision which provides effective legal protection for all individuals,[26] but so far has left it undecided whether the Court of Justice itself ought to provide the judicial protection insofar as the international agreement in question provides for no (or an insufficient) system of judicial supervision of the bodies which it establishes. Here too, the possibility of the Union incurring liability at international level counsels caution, but even so, the requirement for a complete system of judicial protection is an argument in favour of allowing validity to be tested by references for preliminary rulings, especially since the Union institutions contributed, within the framework of the bodies concerned, towards the adoption of the acts in question.[27]

F. Review of the validity of Union acts in the light of international agreements

Apart from the issue of whether the validity of international agreements can be reviewed in **10.08** the context of preliminary ruling proceedings (see para. 10.05), the question arises as to what extent the Court of Justice may review the validity of Union acts in the light of international agreements. Under the case-law, the validity of a Union act may be affected by the fact that it is incompatible with rules of international law, and where such invalidity is

---

[25] ECJ, Case 9/56 *Meroni v High Authority* [1957 and 1958] E.C.R. 133. See further K. Lenaerts and P. Van Nuffel (R. Bray and N. Cambien (eds)), *European Union Law* (3rd edn, London, Sweet & Maxwell, 2011), paras 17.20–17.24.

[26] ECJ, Opinion 1/76 *Draft Agreement establishing a European laying-up fund for inland waterway vessels* [1977] E.C.R. 741, para. 21.

[27] Cf. ECJ, Case C-192/89 *Sevince* [1990] E.C.R. I-3461, para. 3.

pleaded before a national court, the Court of Justice ascertains, as is requested of it by questions submitted by the referring court, whether certain conditions are satisfied in the case before it in order to determine whether, pursuant to Art. 267 TFEU, the validity of a particular act may be assessed in the light of the rules of international law relied upon to this effect: first, the EU must be bound by those rules; second, the Court can examine the validity of a Union act in light of an international treaty only where the nature and the broad logic of the latter do not preclude this; third, where the nature and the broad logic of the treaty in question permit the validity of the Union act to be reviewed in the light of the provisions of that treaty, it is also necessary that the provision of that treaty which is relied upon for the purpose of examining the validity of the Union act appears, as regards its content, to be unconditional and sufficiently precise. The latter condition will be fulfilled where the provision relied upon contains a clear and precise obligation that is not subject, in its implementation or its effects, to the adoption of any subsequent measure.[28] Moreover, when the EU adopts an act, it is bound to observe international law in its entirety, including customary international law, and to the extent that the invalidity of a Union act is alleged to violate customary international law within the context of a preliminary ruling on validity, the Court proceeds by first verifying whether the principles to which the referring court makes reference are recognized as forming part of customary international law; and if so, second, determining whether and to what extent they may be relied upon by individuals to call into question the validity of a Union act.[29] Consequently, the Court of Justice proceeds on a case-by-case basis in determining whether these conditions are fulfilled.

Recently, for example, in *Air Transport Association of America and Others*, the Court was confronted with questions concerning the validity of a Union act in the light of several international agreements (the Chicago Convention, the Kyoto Protocol, and the so-called Open Skies Agreement between the United States, of the one part, and the then European Community and its Member States, of the other) and certain principles of customary international law. Since the EU is not bound by the Chicago Convention and the relevant provisions of the Kyoto Protocol cannot be considered unconditional and sufficiently precise so as to confer on individuals the right to rely on them in legal proceedings to contest the validity of a Union act, these international agreements could not be used as a yardstick for assessing the validity of the Union act concerned.[30] In contrast, the relevant provisions of the Open Skies Agreement fulfilled the abovementioned conditions and could be relied upon for the purposes of assessing the validity of the Union act concerned,[31] although ultimately, the Court found that the Union act at issue was not invalid in the light of those provisions.[32] Moreover, the three principles of customary international law identified by the referring court were regarded as embodying customary international law and could be relied upon by an individual for the purpose of the Court's examination of the validity of a Union act insofar as, first, those principles are capable of calling into question

---

[28] ECJ (judgment of 21 December 2011), Case C-366/10 *Air Transport Association of America and Others*, not reported, paras 51–55 (and citations therein). See G. De Baere and C. Ryngaert, 'The ECJ's Judgment in *Air Transport Association of America* and the International Legal Context of the EU's Climate Change Policy' (2013) E.F.A. Rev. 389–410.

[29] ECJ, Case C-366/10 *Air Transport Association of America and Others*, paras 101–102.

[30] ECJ, Case C-366/10 *Air Transport Association of America and Others*, paras 57–78.

[31] ECJ, Case C-366/10 *Air Transport Association of America and Others*, paras 79–100.

[32] ECJ, Case C-366/10 *Air Transport Association of America and Others*, paras 135, 147, 156.

the EU's competence to adopt that act, and second, that act is liable to affect rights which the individual derives from Union law or to create obligations under Union law in his or her regard, both of which conditions were satisfied in the proceedings at issue.[33] However, in the Court's view, since a principle of customary international law does not have the same degree of precision as a provision of an international agreement, judicial review must necessarily be limited to the question whether, in adopting the Union act in question, the Union institutions made 'manifest errors of assessment concerning the conditions for applying those principles'.[34] On that basis, the Court determined that the Union act in question was not invalid in the light of the principles of customary international law concerned.[35]

As illustrated by further case-law, there are difficulties in satisfying all of the conditions elaborated here. In *Ikea Wholesale*, the Court held that the validity of an EU anti-dumping regulation could not be reviewed in the light of the Agreement on Implementation of Art. IV of the GATT as part of the WTO agreements (the so-called Anti-Dumping Agreement), as subsequently interpreted by the Dispute Settlement Body (DSB)'s recommendations, since it was clear from the subsequent regulations that the Union did not in any way intend to give effect to a specific obligation assumed in the context of the WTO.[36] Thereafter, in *Intertanko and Others*, the Court ruled that the validity of certain provisions of an EU directive on ship-source pollution could not be assessed in the light of either the UN Convention on the Law of the Sea (UNCLOS) or the International Convention for the Prevention of Pollution from Ships (Marpol 73/78).[37] As regards the former, UNCLOS does not establish rules intended to apply directly and immediately to individuals and to confer upon them rights or freedoms capable of being relied upon,[38] and as regards the latter, the EU is not bound by Marpol 73/78, and the relevant provisions could not be regarded as the expression of principles of customary international law.[39]

The Court's approach has come in for criticism.[40] Yet, again, it depends upon the particular international rule or agreement concerned. For instance, in *IATA and ELFAA*, the Court held that certain provisions of the Montreal Convention were among the rules in the light of which the Court reviews the legality of Union acts in accordance with the conditions elaborated in the case-law.[41] The Court ultimately determined, however, that the Union act in question was not inconsistent with those provisions.[42]

---

[33] ECJ, Case C-366/10 *Air Transport Association of America and Others*, paras 103–109 (and citations therein).
[34] ECJ, Case C-366/10 *Air Transport Association of America and Others*, para. 110.
[35] ECJ, Case C-366/10 *Air Transport Association of America and Others*, para. 130.
[36] ECJ, Case C-351/04 *Ikea Wholesale* [2007] E.C.R. I-7723, para. 35.
[37] ECJ, Case C-308/06 *Intertanko and Others* [2008] E.C.R. I-4057, para. 66.
[38] ECJ, Case C-308/06 *Intertanko and Others*, paras 53–65.
[39] ECJ, Case C-308/06 *Intertanko and Others*, paras 47–52.
[40] M. Mendez, 'The Legal Effect of Community Agreements: Maximalist Treaty Enforcement and Judicial Avoidance Techniques', 21 EJIL 83–104.
[41] ECJ, Case C-344/04 *IATA and ELFAA* [2006] E.C.R. I-403, paras 36, 39.
[42] ECJ, Case C-344/04 *IATA and ELFAA*, para. 48; see also ECJ (judgment of 23 October 2012), Joined Cases C-581/10 and C-629/10 *Nelson and Others*, not reported, paras 41–60.

G. Binding and non-binding Union acts

10.09 The validity of acts of Union institutions, bodies, offices, or agencies may be reviewed in the context of a reference for a preliminary ruling irrespective as to what they are called[43] and whether or not they have direct effect.[44] The Union acts may be non-binding.[45] Reviewing the validity of non-binding Union acts in preliminary rulings can be of considerable interest: in the Court's words, such acts 'cannot . . . be regarded as having no legal effect. The national courts are bound to take recommendations[46] into consideration in order to decide disputes submitted to them, in particular where they cast light on the interpretation of national measures adopted in order to implement them or where they are designed to supplement binding [Union] provisions.'[47] Sometimes, it will be sufficient for the Court to interpret a non-binding act (for example, a communication), thereby appraising its compatibility with the Union provisions that it is intended to elucidate.[48]

H. Acts of general application

10.10 Since the review of validity effected by means of a reference for a preliminary ruling is a species of review incidental to the main proceedings, some commentators in the past argued—by analogy with the objection of illegality (enshrined in what is now Art. 277 TFEU)—that only acts of general application could be so reviewed.[49] The Court of Justice also gave the impression of acceding to that view by referring to the 'complete system' of judicial protection of acts of the institutions early on in its landmark judgment in *Les Verts* in the context of the former EC Treaty, in which it declared that natural and legal persons are protected against the application against them of general measures which they could not contest directly before the Union judicature by reason of the admissibility requirements for actions for annulment: 'Where the Community [now Union] institutions are responsible for the administrative implementation of . . . measures [of general application], natural or legal persons may bring a direct action before the Court against administrative measures which are addressed to them or which are of direct and individual concern to them and, in support of such an action, plead the illegality of the general measure on which they are based. Where implementation is a matter for the national authorities, such persons may plead the invalidity of general measures before the national courts and cause the latter to

---

[43] For the indirect review in a preliminary ruling of the validity of a Council resolution, see ECJ, Case 59/75 *Manghera and Others* [1976] E.C.R. 91, paras 19–22.

[44] The Court has jurisdiction to give preliminary rulings concerning the validity of a directive, regardless of whether it is directly applicable, even though the period for its implementation has not yet expired, provided that the question referred for a preliminary ruling is connected with a real dispute: see, e.g. ECJ, Case C-491/01 *British American Tobacco (Investments) and Imperial Tobacco* [2002] E.C.R. I-11453, paras 32–38; ECJ, Case C-343/09 *Afton Chemical* [2010] E.C.R. I-7023, paras 15–17.

[45] ECJ, Case C-322/88 *Grimaldi* [1989] E.C.R. 4407, para. 8, where the Court of Justice compared the wording of what is now Arts 263 and 267 TFEU, reaching the conclusion that the Court has jurisdiction to give a preliminary ruling on the validity and interpretation of all acts of the institutions 'without exception'.

[46] Recommendations are not binding pursuant to Art. 288 TFEU.

[47] ECJ, Case C-322/88 *Grimaldi* [1989] E.C.R. 4407, para. 18. This is so, even though in the cited case, the Court of Justice was confronted with a preliminary ruling on the interpretation (not validity) of what is now Union law.

[48] ECJ, Case C-94/91 *Wagner* [1992] E.C.R. I-2765, paras 16–17.

[49] As regards the distinction between acts of general and individual application, see para. 7.85.

request the Court of Justice for a preliminary ruling.'[50] It is clear, however, that while that passage correctly reproduces the rationale of judicial review of validity by means of the preliminary ruling procedure, it does not necessarily mean that such a review may in no circumstances be carried out in respect of an individual act.[51]

I. Individual acts and the *Deggendorf* line of case-law

What is typically behind the question whether it is possible to review by way of preliminary **10.11** ruling the validity of an individual act of a Union institution, office, body, or agency concerns a different aspect relating to the coherent system of judicial protection, namely, whether it is still possible for a party to the main proceedings to have recourse to the indirect route of a preliminary ruling on the validity of a Union act which that party could have challenged via the direct route of an action for annulment, but neglected to do so within the prescribed time limit under the sixth paragraph of Art. 263 TFEU.[52] Under the so-called *Deggendorf* line of case-law, the Court of Justice has answered this question in the negative: a natural or legal person who undoubtedly[53] has the right under Art. 263 TFEU to seek the annulment of a Union act may not plead the illegality of that act in subsequent proceedings before the national courts by way of a preliminary ruling on validity under Art. 267 TFEU.

In *TWD Textilwerke Deggendorf*, the Court held that the applicant, a beneficiary of an individual aid measure, who could 'without any doubt' have brought an action for annulment against the Commission decision addressed to the Member State concerned and declaring the aid incompatible with the internal market, and who allowed the mandatory time limit set down in the Treaties to expire was precluded from calling into question the lawfulness of that decision before the national courts in an action brought against measures taken by the national authorities in implementation of that decision.[54]

---

[50] ECJ, Case 294/83 *Les Verts v European Parliament* [1986] E.C.R. 1339, para. 23.

[51] See ECJ, Joined Cases 133/85 to 136/85 *Rau and Others* [1987] E.C.R. 2289, point 1 of the operative part: 'The possibility of bringing a direct action under the [fourth] para. of [Art. 263 TFEU] against a decision adopted by a [Union] institution does not preclude the possibility of bringing an action in a national court against a measure adopted by a national authority for the implementation of that decision on the ground that the latter decision is unlawful.' That case was concerned with a Commission decision addressed to the Federal Republic of Germany within the meaning of the fourth para. of Art. 189 EC (now Art. 288 TFEU); that is, an individual act which a German authority had implemented with respect to the plaintiffs in the main proceedings, whereupon the plaintiffs brought an action for annulment of the Commission decision in the Court of Justice and an action for annulment of the German implementing decision in a national court referring the question of the validity of the Commission decision to the Court. It was in this context that the Court of Justice held that it had jurisdiction to conduct judicial review of an individual act of a Union institution in a preliminary ruling procedure on the basis of the rationale of that jurisdiction set out earlier. See, to the same effect, ECJ, Case C-70/97 P *Kruidvat v Commission* [1998] E.C.R. I-7183, paras 47–49 (relating to a Commission decision declaring now Art. 101(1) TFEU inapplicable to a selective distribution system pursuant to now Art. 101(3) TFEU).

[52] See K. Lenaerts, 'The Rule of Law and the Coherence of the Judicial System of the European Union' (2007) C.M.L. Rev. 1625–59.

[53] The case-law uses a variety of terms, e.g. 'beyond doubt' or 'indisputably': see, e.g. ECJ, Case C-550/09 *E and F* [2010] E.C.R. I-6209, paras 48, 50, 52. This involves a situation where a Union act is addressed to a natural or legal person or a Union act is not addressed to that person but such person is manifestly deemed to satisfy the standing requirements for an action for annulment under the fourth para. of Art. 263 TFEU.

[54] ECJ, Case C-188/92 *TWD Textilwerke Deggendorf* [1994] E.C.R. I-833, paras 17, 24: the Commission's decision addressed to the Member State concerned made explicit reference to the recipient of the individual aid in question and that State had communicated the decision to the recipient, stating that it could

In subsequent cases, the Court ruled that the same principle applies for other kinds of Union acts.[55] The Court also ruled that the same principle applies with regard to Member States and decisions addressed to them.[56] To have decided otherwise would have detracted excessively from the legal certainty which the time limit prescribed by what is now the sixth paragraph of Art. 263 TFEU is intended to secure. In a case where a party who undoubtedly fulfils the standing requirement of the fourth paragraph of Art. 263 TFEU to bring an annulment action against a Union act before the Union judicature and who allows the mandatory time limit set down in the sixth paragraph of that Article to expire, the national courts must regard the act in question as valid vis-à-vis such party and therefore apply it in any event. As a result, there is no point in making a reference to the Court of Justice for a preliminary ruling, or at least not with a view to protecting a party to the main proceedings who is no longer entitled to plead that the act is unlawful.

---

bring an action for annulment thereof. For further cases in which the Court precluded the indirect route of preliminary rulings on validity in relation to decisions of individual application, see ECJ, Case C-178/95 *Wiljo* [1997] E.C.R. I-585, paras 19–24; ECJ, Case C-119/05 *Lucchini* [2007] E.C.R. I-6199, paras 54–56. Compare ECJ, Case C-390/98 *Banks* [2001] E.C.R. I-6117, paras 111–113 (distinguishing *Deggendorf* case-law from circumstances of instant case); ECJ, Joined Cases C-346/03 and C-529/03 *Atzeni and Others* [2006] E.C.R. I-1875, paras 30–34 (although the applicants' direct action for annulment against the contested decision was dismissed as inadmissible by the CFI because it was brought after expiry of the time limit, this did not preclude the applicants from challenging the decision indirectly by way of a preliminary ruling on validity, since the proceedings concerned were distinguished from *Deggendorf* as involving a Commission decision addressed to a Member State concerning a general aid scheme applicable to categories of persons defined in a general manner and were not communicated by the Member State concerned to the applicants or any other aid recipient).

[55] See, e.g. ECJ, Case C-239/99 *Nachi Europe* [2001] E.C.R. I-1197, paras 28–40: the Court held that the applicant was precluded from challenging the validity of a regulation imposing a definitive anti-dumping levy, for which it could undoubtedly have brought an annulment action before the CFI but failed to do so, even where the regulation has been declared null vis-à-vis other undertakings which did bring actions for annulment, underscoring the 'dual nature' of such regulations as acts of a legislative nature (applying to objectively defined situations and of general scope of application), on the one hand, and acts liable to be of direct and individual concern to certain traders, on the other. But compare, e.g. ECJ, Case C-241/95 *Accrington Beef* [1996] E.C.R. I-6699, para. 15 (involving regulation of general scope of application); and for a similar ruling relating to a directive, ECJ, Case C-408/95 *Eurotunnel and Others* [1997] E.C.R. I-6315, paras 29–30 and ECJ (judgment of 12 July 2012), Case C-59/11 *Association Kokopelli*, not reported, paras 34–36. See also CFI (order of 5 February 2007), Case T-91/05 *Sinara Handel v Council and Commission* [2007] E.C.R. II-245, paras 61–63 (distinguishing circumstances of instant proceedings from those of *Nachi Europe*).

[56] ECJ, Case C-241/01 *National Farmers' Union* [2002] E.C.R. I-9079, paras 34–39, in which the Court held that a Member State which was an addressee of the contested Commission decisions and which had not challenged the legality of those decisions within the time limit laid down in what is now the sixth para. of Art. 263 TFEU did not have standing subsequently before a national court to invoke its unlawfulness in order to dispute the merits of an action brought against it. This judgment has been confirmed in subsequent case-law: see, e.g. ECJ, Case C-11/00 *Commission v ECB* [2003] E.C.R. I-7147. With the reform of the system of legal instruments brought by the Lisbon Treaty, recognition has been given to decisions with and without addressees; directives are addressed to the Member States, whereas regulations are not: see Art. 288 TFEU. Post-Lisbon, a Member State is entitled to raise an objection of illegality under Art. 277 TFEU in respect of 'an act of general application' (no longer expressly mentioning only regulations) which it failed to challenge within the time limit prescribed by the sixth para. of Art. 263 TFEU (see para. 9.11). Consequently, it remains to be seen in the case-law as to whether a Member State may challenge the legality of decisions (without addressees) and regulations and directives (to the extent they are of general application) before a national court, even if it did not bring an action for annulment against such measures.

Conversely, however, if there remains doubt on the admissibility of the action for annulment, then access to the indirect route of a preliminary ruling on validity is not foreclosed.[57] This typically involves the situation where the applicant cannot be deemed to be manifestly, directly, and individually concerned by the contested act of which it is not the addressee.[58] With the changes brought by the Lisbon Treaty in relation to the standing requirements for natural and legal persons under the fourth paragraph of Art. 263 TFEU, i.e. the introduction of the category of regulatory acts that do not entail implementing measures for which such persons must demonstrate only to be directly concerned (see para. 7.108), it remains to be seen how the Court's approach in the *Deggendorf* line of case-law will be affected by this development.[59]

Another party to the main proceedings that was not entitled to challenge the act in question pursuant to Art. 263 TFEU may persuade the national court to make a reference for a preliminary ruling on the validity of the act. There is nothing to prevent the national court from inquiring into this question or from raising it with the Court of Justice of its own motion.[60] If the Court then finds that the act is invalid, it will be for it to determine what consequences that finding should have for the party to the main proceedings for whom the act has become unappealable because of its failure to bring an action for annulment.

J. Failure to act

In proceedings for a preliminary ruling, the Court of Justice has no power to rule that a **10.12** Union institution, office, body, or agency has failed to act,[61] when an action brought on the basis of Art. 265 TFEU (see Ch. 8) would be admissible to challenge an unlawful failure to act on the part of such institution, office, body, or agency.

That being said, in *Ten Kate*, the Court emphasized that just as natural and legal persons should be able to challenge before a national court the legality of any decision or other national measure relative to the application to him or her of a Union act of general application by pleading the invalidity of that act, 'the same holds true where a natural and legal person invokes a failure to take a [Union act of general application], within the

---

See, e.g. ECJ (judgment of 17 February 2011), Case C-494/04 *Bolton Alimentari*, not reported, para. 23 (and citations therein) ('such a direct action [for annulment] must be beyond any doubt'); ECJ, Joined Cases C-71/09 P, C-73/09 P, and C-76/09 P *Comitato 'Venezia vuole vivere' and Others v Commission* [2011] E.C.R. I-4727, paras 58–59. See also CFI (order of 10 March 2005), Joined Cases T-228/00, T-229/00, T-242/00, T-243/00, T-245/00 to T-248/00, T-250/00, T-252/00, T-256/00 to T-259/00, T-265/00, T-267/00, T-268/00, T-271/00, T-274/00 to T-276/00, T-281/00, and T-287/00 to T-296/00 *Gruppo ormeggiatori del porto di Venezia and Others v Commission* [2005] E.C.R. II-787, para. 30.

[58] For recent examples, see, e.g. ECJ, Case C-441/05 *Roquette Frères* [2007] E.C.R. I-1993, paras 35–48 (applicant held not directly concerned by contested regulation); ECJ, Case C-343/07 *Bavaria and Bavaria Italia* [2009] E.C.R. I-5491, paras 40–46 (applicant held not directly and individually concerned by contested regulation); ECJ, Case C-343/09 *Afton Chemical* [2010] E.C.R. I-7023, paras 19–26 (applicant held not individually concerned by contested provisions of directive); ECJ, Case C-550/09 *E and F* [2010] E.C.R. I-6209, paras 48–52 (applicants held not directly and individually concerned by contested decisions).

[59] J. Kokott, I. Dervisopoulos, and T. Henze, 'Aktuelle Fragen des effektiven Rechtsschutzes durch die Gemeinschaftsgerichte' (2008) EuGRZ 14.

[60] Where such a question is referred by a national court of its own motion, it cannot be declared inadmissible by virtue of the *Deggendorf* line of case-law: ECJ, Case C-222/04 *Cassa di Risparmio di Firenze* [2006] E.C.R. I-289, paras 72–74.

[61] ECJ, Case C-68/95 *T. Port v Commission* [1996] E.C.R. I-6065, para. 53.

meaning of Article [265 TFEU], which it considers to be contrary to [Union] law'.[62] The Court's approach thus ensures that recourse to a preliminary ruling on the validity of a failure to act remains open to such persons under circumstances where, as in the instant proceedings, an action for failure to act is not available.

III. Substance of the Review of the Validity of a Union Act in Preliminary Ruling Proceedings

A. Review of legality of Union acts reserved to the Court of Justice under *Foto-Frost*

10.13 Following on from *Foto-Frost*, the review of the validity of a Union act by preliminary ruling, in common with the action for annulment, is a form of judicial review of the legality of acts of Union institutions, offices, bodies, or agencies:[63] since Art. 263 TFEU gives the Court of Justice of the European Union exclusive jurisdiction to declare void an act of a Union institution, office, body, or agency, the coherence of the system requires that where the validity of a Union act is challenged before a national court, the power to declare the act invalid must also be reserved to the Court of Justice.[64] Moreover, the Court is 'in the best position' to decide on the validity of Union acts, since under Art. 23 of the Statute, Union institutions, offices, bodies, or agencies whose acts are challenged are entitled to participate in the proceedings in order to defend the validity of the acts in question.[65]

B. Differences compared with an action for annulment

10.14 The most important differences between the action for annulment and the preliminary ruling on the validity of Union law are that the latter is not subject to any time limit, is not limited to the grounds specified for the action for annulment (Art. 263, second para., TFEU),[66] and the initiative for seeking a preliminary ruling on validity comes from the

---

[62] ECJ, Case C-511/03 *Ten Kate Musselkanaal and Others* [2005] E.C.R. I-8979, para. 29.

[63] See ECJ, Case 314/85 *Foto-Frost* [1987] E.C.R. 4199, para. 16.

[64] ECJ, Case 314/85 *Foto-Frost*, para. 17. See further, e.g. ECJ (judgment of 21 December 2011), Case C-366/10 *Air Transport Association of America and Others*, not reported, paras 47–48 (and citations therein).

[65] ECJ, Case 314/85 *Foto-Frost* [1987] E.C.R. 4199, para. 18. The wording of this passage of the judgment is more consonant with the procedure in the case of a direct action (see Ch. 25), than with the formally non-contentious procedure of a reference for a preliminary ruling. The Court of Justice added that under the second para. of Art. 24 of the Statute the Court may require the Member States and 'institutions which are not participating in the proceedings' to supply all information which it considers necessary for the purposes of the case before it. It did so on one occasion in order to enable the European Parliament, which was (then) formerly not entitled to submit observations to the Court under Art. 23 of the Statute, to defend its prerogatives in proceedings for a preliminary ruling on validity: ECJ, Case 20/85 *Roviello* [1988] E.C.R. 2805, at 2816.

[66] ECJ, Joined Cases 21/72 to 24/72 *International Fruit and Others* [1972] E.C.R. 1219, para. 5; ECJ, Case C-162/96 *Racke* [1998] E.C.R. I-3655, para. 26 (where the Court reviewed the validity of a Union act in the light of customary international law). For another example in which the Court reviewed the validity of a Union act in the light of customary international law, see ECJ (judgment of 21 December 2011), Case C-366/10 *Air Transport Association of America and Others*, not reported. See also para. 10.08.

national court and not from interested parties.[67] In the main proceedings, the parties may try to move the national court to make a reference to the Court of Justice, but they cannot compel the Court to rule on the validity of a Union act if the national court has not put a question to that effect.[68] Under settled case-law, Art. 267 TFEU does not make available a means of redress to the parties in a case pending before a national court, such that the Court cannot be compelled to evaluate the validity of a Union act on the sole ground that the question has been put before it by one of the parties in its written observations in situations where the referring court has not put such a question to the Court.[69]

C. Grounds on which validity may be contested

The parties to the main proceedings, the Union institutions, offices, bodies, or agencies whose act is at issue, and the Member States submitting observations pursuant to Art. 23 of the Statute cannot oblige the Court of Justice to appraise the validity of a Union act in the light of 'submissions' or 'grounds' of illegality not raised in the order for reference.[70] This does not mean, however, that the Court has no latitude at all in the matter.

10.15

First, the national court may request the Court of Justice merely to interpret a Union act, but the Court, having regard to the whole of the content of the order for reference, may consider the reference to be concerned with the validity of the act with a view to promoting the efficiency of judicial cooperation.[71] It is important in such a case that the order for reference may be construed as a request for a ruling on validity, even though it is couched as a request for a ruling on interpretation. The reason for this is that only in such a case may the 'interested parties' within the meaning of Art. 23 of the Statute correctly assess what the Court's ruling may cover and formulate their views thereon.[72]

Second, the Court of Justice may supplement the 'submissions' or 'grounds' of illegality of the Union act at issue, as set forth in the order for reference in the light of matters that come to light in the course of legal argument before the Court itself.

---

[67] As such, a party to the national proceedings cannot compel the national court to submit a question on the validity (or interpretation) of the Union act concerned, as it is solely for the national court before which the dispute is brought to determine the need for a preliminary ruling in order to enable it to deliver judgment and the relevance of the questions it submits to the Court of Justice: see further para. 3.19.

[68] ECJ, Case 44/65 *Singer* [1965] E.C.R. 965, at 970.

[69] See, e.g. ECJ, Joined Cases C-276/05 and C-377/05 *A. Brünsteinder and Autohaus Hilgert* [2006] E.C.R. I-11383, paras 25–28 (and citations therein); ECJ, Joined Cases C-188/10 and C-189/10 *Melki and Abdeli* [2010] E.C.R. I-5665, para. 63; ECJ, Case C-316/09 *MSD Sharp & Dohme* [2011] E.C.R. I-3249, paras 20–24 (and case-law cited therein).

[70] ECJ, Joined Cases 50/82 to 58/82 *Dorca Marina and Others* [1982] E.C.R. 3949, para. 13. See further, e,g. ECJ, Case C-390/06 *Nuova Agricast* [2008] E.C.R. I-2577, paras 42–44; ECJ, Case C-373/08 *Hoesch Metals and Alloys* [2010] E.C.R. I-951, paras 57–60.

[71] ECJ, Case 16/65 *Schwarze* [1965] E.C.R. 877, at 886. For a recent example, see ECJ, Case C-300/07 *Hans & Christophorus Oymanns* [2009] E.C.R. I-4779, paras 40–47. For matters relating to the Court of Justice's reformulation of questions in connection with references for preliminary rulings on interpretation and validity generally, see para. 3.23.

[72] Cf. ECJ, Case 62/76 *Strehl* [1977] E.C.R. 211, at 217, where the Court of Justice held of its own motion that a provision of a regulation, of which only the interpretation had been sought, was invalid having regard to a decided case. See also ECJ (judgment of 22 March 2012), Case C-338/10 *GLS*, not reported, paras 14 and 17.

One situation occurs where the national court raises the question of the validity of an act in general terms only. In such a case, the Court of Justice will answer that question in the light of an assessment of the submissions which are set out by the claimant or other 'interested parties' in their observations before the Court concerning the validity of the act[73] or which emerge from the statement of reasons of the order for reference.[74] Similarly, the national court may refer a question on the validity of a Union act in relation to only certain pleas, but the Court may find it necessary in the light of the order for reference and the observations lodged before it to examine the validity of such a measure in relation to additional pleas in order to give a useful answer to the referring court.[75]

Another situation occurs by virtue of the fact that the Court of Justice has held that it is empowered to find of its own motion infringements of essential procedural requirements by which an act is vitiated, thereby, if necessary, supplementing the submissions set out in the order for reference alleging that the act is invalid.[76] The case-law to this effect is related to the rule applicable to actions for annulment that the Court of Justice or the General Court will find infringements of essential procedural requirements of its own motion.[77] Lack of competence on the part of the Union institution, body, office, or agency which adopted the contested act is also (at least insofar as the parallelism with the action for annulment is concerned) regarded as a peremptory plea, with the result that, as in the case of an infringement of an essential procedural requirement, it may be raised by the Court of its own motion in conducting judicial review of a contested act in preliminary ruling proceedings.[78]

---

[73] ECJ, Joined Cases 103/77 and 145/77 *Royal Scholten Honig* [1978] E.C.R. 2037, paras 16–17. See also ECJ (judgment of 22 March 2012), Case C-338/10 *GLS*, not reported, in which the assessment of the validity of the contested measure prompted the Court to adopt a measure of inquiry.

[74] ECJ, Case 41/72 *Getreide-Import* [1973] E.C.R. 1, para. 2. For recent examples, see, e.g. ECJ, Case C-479/04 *Laserdisken* [2006] E.C.R. I-8089; ECJ, Case C-537/09 *Bartlett and Others* [2011] E.C.R. I-3417, paras 34–36.

[75] See, e.g. ECJ, Case C-309/10 *Agrana Zucker* [2011] E.C.R. I-7333, para. 23; ECJ, Case C-77/09 *Gowan Comércio Internacional e Serviços* [2010] E.C.R. I-13533, paras 29–30. In the light of its latitude for the reformulation of questions submitted by national courts in orders for reference generally (see para. 3.23), the Court may adjust certain questions presented to it: see, e.g. ECJ, Case C-558/07 *S.P.C.M. and Others* [2009] E.C.R. I-5783, paras 17, 39–40 (finding that the complaint concerning the irrationality of a certain provision of a Union measure must be regarded as relating to the infringement of the principle of proportionality). With regard to the changes brought by the Lisbon Treaty in connection with the binding force of the Charter of Fundamental Rights of the European Union (in a situation in which the referring court had only referred to the European Convention for the Protection of Human Rights and Fundamental Freedoms), see ECJ, Joined Cases C-92/09 and C-93/09 *Volker und Markus Schecke and Eifert* [2010] E.C.R. I-11063, paras 44–46.

[76] ECJ, Joined Cases 73/63 and 74/63 *Internationale Crediet- en Handelsvereniging Rotterdam and Others* [1964] E.C.R. 1, at 14.

[77] See ECJ, Case C-291/89 *Interhotel v Commission* [1991] E.C.R. I-2257, para. 14; ECJ, Case C-304/89 *Oliveira v Commission* [1991] E.C.R. I-2283, para. 18.

[78] See, to this effect, the Opinion of Advocate-General J. Gand in ECJ, Case 5/67 *Beus* [1968] E.C.R. 83, at 108–9, who added that, in his view, the Court would not raise the question of misuse of powers of its own motion and that 'there is doubt about the situation where there is a question of a breach of the Treaty or a rule of law'. But taking account of the parallelism with the action for annulment, see the Opinion of Advocate-General F. Jacobs in ECJ, Case C-210/98 P *Salzgitter v Commission and Germany* [2000] E.C.R. I-5843, questioning the distinction between the first two grounds listed in what is now Art. 263, second para., TFEU that the Union courts may raise of their own motion (i.e. lack of competence and infringements of essential procedural requirements or so-called '*legalité externe*'), as opposed to the latter two grounds (i.e. infringement of the Treaties or any rule of law relating to their application and misuse of powers or so-called '*legalité interne*'), which the Union courts may not raise of their own motion.

D. Assessment of validity normally based on the situation existing when Union measure adopted

Under the case-law, the assessment of the validity of a Union measure which the Court of **10.16** Justice is called upon to undertake on a reference for a preliminary ruling must normally be based on the facts and law as they stood at the time that measure was adopted, and cannot in particular depend on retrospective considerations relating to its efficacy.[79] However, in certain cases, the validity of the particular Union measure can be assessed by reference to new factors arising after that measure was adopted, depending on the determination of the Court.[80]

E. Finding of facts necessary to assess the legality of a given Union act

In arriving at its preliminary ruling on the validity of a given Union act, the Court of Justice **10.17** may go no deeper into the facts of the main proceedings than it may in the case of a preliminary ruling on interpretation (see para. 6.21). There is a slight difference, however, in that the Court may make all the findings of fact necessary to assess the legality of the contested act.[81] In this respect, the Court's powers are no different if it reviews the legality of an act under Art. 263 TFEU or Art. 267 TFEU.[82] In this connection, it would be perfectly possible for measures of inquiry to be ordered pursuant to Art. 64(2) of the ECJ Rules of Procedure.[83]

IV. Consequences of the Review of the Validity of a Union Act in Preliminary Ruling Proceedings

A. Ruling of the Court of Justice

Where the Court of Justice comes to the conclusion that the contested Union act or certain **10.18** provisions thereof should not be declared invalid, the answer which it generally gives to the national court is not that the act is valid, but that the examination of the question raised has disclosed no factor of such a kind as to affect the validity of that act.[84] That answer does not

---

[79] See, e.g. ECJ, Case C-309/10 *Agrana Zucker* [2011] E.C.R. I-7333, para. 31 (and case-law cited therein) (adding in para. 45 that where the Union legislature is obliged to assess the future effects of rules to be adopted and those effects cannot be accurately foreseen, its assessment is open to criticism only if it appears manifestly incorrect in the light of the information available to it at the time when the rules in question were adopted).

[80] ECJ, Case C-247/08 *Gaz de France—Berliner Investissement* [2009] E.C.R. I-9225, paras 49–50 (ruling that the assessment of the validity of the Union measure concerned by reference to new factors arising after its adoption did not need to be made in the present proceedings).

[81] For some recent examples, see, e.g. ECJ, Case C-344/04 *IATA and ELFAA* [2006] E.C.R. I-403; ECJ, Case C-303/05 *Advocaten voor de Wereld* [2007] E.C.R. I-3633; ECJ, Case C-58/08 *Vodafone and Others* [2010] E.C.R. I-4999; ECJ (judgment of 22 March 2012), Case C-338/10 *GLS*, not reported.

[82] The parallel between the two procedures as adverted to by the Court in ECJ, Case 314/85 *Foto-Frost* [1987] E.C.R. 4199 emerges clearly here; for an example, see ECJ, Case C-16/90 *Nölle* [1991] E.C.R. I-5163, paras 17, 23, and 24.

[83] ECJ, Case 5/67 *Beus* [1968] E.C.R. 83, at 86; ECJ (judgment of 22 March 2012), Case C-338/10 *GLS*, not reported, para. 15.

[84] For some recent examples, see, e.g. ECJ, Case C-127/07 *Société Arcelor Atlantique et Lorraine and Others* [2008] E.C.R. I-9895, para. 74; ECJ, Case C-425/08 *Enviro Tech (Europe) ltd* [2009] E.C.R. I-10035, para. 78; ECJ, C-58/08 *Vodafone and Others* [2010] E.C.R. I-4999, paras 49, 80; ECJ, Case C-213/09 *Barsoum*

preclude the national court to which the preliminary ruling is addressed, or other national courts, from referring other questions to the Court of Justice which might call into question the validity of the same act.[85]

Where, in contrast, the Court of Justice declares the Union act in question or certain provisions thereof[86] invalid (declaration of invalidity),[87] its answer is binding on the national court to which it is made. It may no longer apply the act. The same applies to 'any other national court', since the declaration of invalidity constitutes 'sufficient reason [for it] to regard that act as void for the purposes of a judgment which it has to give'.[88] The effect *erga omnes* of the preliminary ruling on validity is justified as being the inevitable corollary of 'particularly imperative requirements concerning legal certainty in addition to those concerning the uniform application of Union law. It follows from the very nature of such a declaration that a national court may not apply the act declared to be void without once more creating serious uncertainty as to the Union law applicable.'[89]

B. Definitive effect of a declaration of invalidity

10.19 The declaration that an act is invalid is definitive, as in the case of a declaration of nullity in relation to an action for annulment (hence the Court's exclusive jurisdiction to declare an act void results in it also having exclusive jurisdiction to declare an act invalid[90]).

Chabo [2010] E.C.R. I-12109, para. 35; ECJ, Case C-77/09 *Gowan Comércio Internacional e Serviços* [2010] E.C.R. I-13533, para. 88; ECJ, Case C-14/10 *Nickel Institute* [2011] E.C.R. I-6609, para. 120; ECJ, C-15/10 *Etimine* [2011] E.C.R. I-6681, paras 131, 145; ECJ, Case C-309/10 *Agrana Zucker* [2011] E.C.R. I-7333, para. 55. Depending on the circumstances, the Court may declare that the examination of certain grounds did not disclose factors of such a kind as to affect the validity of a Union act, whereas for others, it may declare such act partially invalid: see, e.g. ECJ, Case C-221/09 *AJD Tuna* [2011] E.C.R. I-1655. The Court may also exceptionally diverge from its usual framing of its response and declare that the Union act is valid, though only insofar as the question presented to it is concerned: see, e.g. ECJ, Case C-215/10 *Pacific World and FDD International* [2011] E.C.R. I-7255, para. 52.

[85] ECJ, Case 8/78 *Milac* [1978] E.C.R. 1721, paras 4–9. For example, as regards references for preliminary rulings on the validity of different provisions of the same Union act, see ECJ, Case C-491/01 *British American Tobacco (Investments) and Imperial Tobacco* [2002] E.C.R. I-11453; and ECJ, Case C-434/02 *Arnold André* [2004] E.C.R. I-11825, and ECJ, Case C-210/03 *Swedish Match* [2004] E.C.R. I-11893. That being said, if faced with a subsequent reference in which the question regarding the validity of a Union act is the same as that decided by the Court in a previous case, the Court may find it unnecessary to answer such question: see, e.g ECJ, Case C-120/08 *Bavaria* [2010] E.C.R. I-13393, paras 32–34.

[86] For example, the Court may find certain provisions of a Union measure invalid in relation to the question raised, but not others: see, e.g. ECJ, Joined Cases C-454/03, C-11/04, C-12/04, and C-194/04 *ABNA and Others* [2005] E.C.R. I-10423, para. 85.

[87] Depending on the case, the Court's declaration of invalidity may be framed in relation to the question raised by the national court, namely that the Union act concerned is invalid 'in so far as' or 'to the extent' that such act falls foul of the rules of Union law raised in the question submitted: see, e.g. ECJ, Joined Cases C-92/09 and C-93/09 *Volker und Markus Schecke and Eifert* [2010] E.C.R. I-11063, para. 92; ECJ, Joined Cases C-522/07 and C-65/08 *Dinter* [2009] E.C.R. I-10333, para. 42. The declaration of invalidity may also be framed in general terms: see ECJ (judgment of 22 March 2012), Case C-338/10 *GLS*, not reported, para. 31.

[88] ECJ, Case 66/80 *International Chemical* [1981] E.C.R. 1191, point 1 of the operative part.

[89] ECJ, Case 66/80 *International Chemical*, para. 12. See further J. Kokott and T. Henze, 'Das Zusammenwirken von EuGH und nationalem Richter bei der Herstellung eines europarechtskonformen Zustands', in R. Mellinghoff, W. Schön, and H.-U. Viskorf (eds), *Steuerrecht im Rechtsstaat: Festschrift für Wolfgang Spindler* (Cologne, Verlag Dr Otto Schmidt, 2011), 281–8.

[90] ECJ, Case 314/85 *Foto-Frost* [1987] E.C.R. 4199, para. 16.

Nevertheless, the Court of Justice endeavours to reconcile the absolute effect of the declaration that a given act is invalid with the requirements of the preliminary ruling procedure as laid down by Art. 267 TFEU. Consequently, it acknowledges that the declaration of invalidity 'does not mean... that national courts are deprived of the power given to them by [Art. 267 TFEU] and it rests with those courts to decide whether there is a need to raise once again a question which has already been settled by the Court where the Court has previously declared an act of a [Union] institution [invalid]'.[91] The Court does not mean that the declaration of invalidity may be reversed, but that any national court (including the one which obtained the ruling that the act in question was invalid) may possibly have an interest in referring further questions for a preliminary ruling 'if questions arise as to the grounds, the scope and possibly the consequences of the invalidity established earlier'.[92]

C. Consequences of the declaration of invalidity in the national legal order

It is for the national court to decide disputes concerning the consequences of the declaration by the Court of Justice that a Union act is invalid in accordance with its national law insofar as Union law does not provide otherwise. For instance, national law in principle governs the formal and substantive requirements for the refund of amounts collected on behalf of the Union—on the basis of a regulation subsequently declared invalid—unless a rule of Union law specifically deals with such refunds.[93]

10.20

More generally, all national authorities have to draw the necessary conclusions from the Court's declaration that a Union measure is invalid. Action by the national authorities may no longer be based on that measure and any action previously taken on the basis of that measure must be withdrawn (and, where necessary, its consequences rectified).[94] However, the consequences which may be drawn in the national legal systems from such a ruling of invalidity depend directly on Union law as it stands in the light of that ruling.[95]

Sometimes, the Court of Justice spells out the consequences of the declaration that an act is invalid in the national legal system, either in the judgment ruling that it is invalid or in a subsequent judgment following a request for an interpretation of the consequences of the declaration of invalidity.

The first scenario presented itself in *Van Landschoot*, when an agricultural regulation which denied the benefit of exemption from a levy to a particular group of traders, thereby discriminating against them, was declared invalid. As far as the 'scope of the preliminary ruling' was concerned, the Court of Justice inferred from that declaration that the Union legislature had to act upon the judgment by adopting such measures as might be appropriate in order to establish equal treatment for the traders concerned as regards the rules governing exemption from the levy.[96] In so doing, the Court implicitly applied what is now

---

[91] ECJ, Case 66/80 *International Chemical* [1981] E.C.R. 1191, para. 14.
[92] ECJ, Case 66/80 *International Chemical*, para. 14.
[93] ECJ, Case 199/86 *Raiffeisen* [1988] E.C.R. 1169, paras 12–19.
[94] ECJ, Case 23/75 *Rey Soda* [1975] E.C.R. 1279, paras 50–51.
[95] ECJ, Case C-127/94 *H. & R. Ecroyd and Rupert Ecroyd* [1996] E.C.R. I-2731, para. 58.
[96] ECJ, Case 300/86 *Van Landschoot* [1988] E.C.R. 3443, para. 22.

Art. 266 TFEU[97] (governing the consequences of a declaration of nullity in the context of an action for annulment) by analogy to a declaration of invalidity. Next, the Court noted that, in the particular circumstances of the case, in which the discrimination did not arise from what the offending provision provided but from what it did not provide, a straightforward declaration that it was invalid would have had the result that, pending the adoption of new provisions, all exemptions would be precluded.[98] In order to avoid such a situation, the Court expressly held that the second paragraph of what is now Art. 264 TFEU[99] had to be applied 'by analogy' for the same reasons of legal certainty which underlay that provision. Specifically, this meant that, pending such new provisions, 'the competent authorities must continue to apply the exemption provided for in the provision declared invalid but they must also grant it to the operators affected by the discrimination found to exist'.[100]

Recently, in *Société Regie Networks*, involving a declaration of invalidity of a Commission decision in the field of State aid in which the Commission had asked the Court to preserve the effects of the invalid decision,[101] the Court underlined that where it is justified by overriding considerations of legal certainty, the second paragraph of Art. 264 TFEU, applicable by analogy to a reference for a preliminary ruling on the validity of a Union measure under Art. 267 TFEU, confers on the Court a discretion to decide in each particular case which specific effects of such measure must be regarded as definitive. Where the Court rules in proceedings under Art. 267 TFEU that such a measure is invalid, its decision has the legal effect of requiring the competent Union institutions to take the necessary measures to remedy that illegality, as the obligation laid down in Art. 266 TFEU in the case of a judgment annulling a measure applies in such a situation by analogy. On this basis, the Court ruled that the effects of the declaration that the contested decision is invalid must be suspended until a new decision is adopted by the Commission to remedy the illegality established in the judgment, laying down a period of no more than two months from the date of delivery of its judgment if the Commission decides to adopt a new decision under Art. 108(3) TFEU and for a reasonable further period if the Commission decides to initiate the procedure under Art. 108(2) TFEU.[102]

---

[97] The first para. of Art. 266 TFEU (ex Art. 233 EC) provides: 'The institution whose act has been declared void or whose failure to act has been declared contrary to the Treaties shall be required to take the necessary measures to comply with the judgment of the Court of Justice of the European Union.'

[98] ECJ, Case 300/86 *Van Landschoot* [1988] E.C.R. 3443, para. 23.

[99] The second para. of Art. 264 TFEU (ex Art. 231 EC) provides in relevant part that, 'the Court shall, if it considers this necessary, state which of the effects of the act which it has declared void shall be considered as definitive'.

[100] ECJ, Case 300/86 *Van Landschoot* [1988] E.C.R. 3443, para. 24; cf. ECJ, Case 264/82 *Timex v Council and Commission* [1985] E.C.R. 849, para. 32.

[101] This case also presented issues relating to the limitation of the temporal effects of the Court's declaration of invalidity: see para. 10.23.

[102] ECJ, Case C-333/07 *Société Regie Networks* [2007] E.C.R. I-10807, paras 119–121, 124, 126. Compare ECJ, Case C-409/06 *Winner Wetten* [2010] E.C.R. I-8015, paras 63–67, where the Court ruled that although under the second para. of Art. 264 TFEU, applicable by analogy to preliminary rulings on validity, the Court has a discretion to indicate in each case which effects of a Union measure which it annuls or declares invalid must be regarded as definitive (using the aforementioned case as an example), such reasoning could not be extended to the national context as regards the recognition of a principle authorizing, in exceptional circumstances, the provisional maintenance of the effects of a national rule held contrary to a directly applicable rule of Union law. But see, however, ECJ (judgment of 28 February 2012), Case C-41/11 *Inter-Environnement Wallonie et Terre wallonne*, not reported, para. 63, in which the Court allowed, under certain conditions, a national court to make use of its national provision empowering it to maintain certain

The second scenario concerns the case where the national court comes back to the Court of Justice with a new request for a preliminary ruling for guidance on how it should react to the declaration of invalidity in deciding the case before it in the main proceedings. Such a request gives the Court of Justice an opportunity to give a precise indication of the consequences of its declaration of invalidity.[103]

D. Declaration of invalidity comparable to declaration of nullity

The Court of Justice attaches similar consequences to the declaration of invalidity and the declaration of nullity,[104] especially as far as the application of the second paragraph of Art. 264 TFEU and Art. 266 TFEU[105] is concerned. The act which has been declared invalid may no longer be applied by a national court or a national authority, the institution, office, body, or agency which adopted the offending act must take appropriate steps to cure the illegality and, if necessary, adopt a new measure, and the Court of Justice is prepared in certain circumstances to maintain certain aspects of the act which has been declared invalid in force until another measure is adopted.   **10.21**

That being said, although both the review of Union acts by way of preliminary ruling and the action for annulment constitute forms of judicial review of the legality of acts of the Union institutions, there is a distinction between a declaration of invalidity and a declaration of nullity. The action for annulment constitutes a direct attack on a Union act (i.e. it is aimed at its total elimination), and therefore, a declaration of nullity means that the Union act concerned never existed in the Union legal order. In contrast, as regards a preliminary ruling on the validity of a Union act, a declaration of invalidity does not formally result in nullity, but only prevents the invalid Union act from being applied. In other words, the Court's declaration of invalidity means that the national court which requested the preliminary ruling must treat the act as inoperative in that case. However, as discussed earlier, the declaration of invalidity has effects not just *inter partes* but also *erga omnes*. It is thus binding in relation to the national court which made the reference, as well as to other national courts outside the specific dispute in the various Member States, subject to the right to make further references.

---

effects of a national measure adopted in breach of a procedural obligation laid down in a Union directive where that national measure constituted the correct substantive transposition of another Union directive.

[103] ECJ, Case 359/87 *Pinna* [1989] E.C.R. 585, at 612–16, where the Court explained the consequences of its declaration that Art. 73(2) of Regulation No. 1408/71 was invalid for 'those authorities [which were obliged] to draw the inferences in their legal system from a declaration of invalidity' given in the context of (what is now) Art. 267 TFEU 'so long as the Council has failed, following the judgment of the Court, to lay down new rules', ECJ, Case 359/87 *Pinna*, para. 13; the earlier judgment containing the declaration of invalidity is reported at ECJ, Case 41/84 *Pinna* [1986] E.C.R. 1. For a more recent example, see ECJ (order of 8 November 2007), Case C-421/06 *Fratelli Martini and Cargill* [2007] E.C.R. I-152*, Summ. pub., concerning the consequences of the Court's declaration of invalidity in ECJ, Joined Cases C-453/03, C-11/04, C-12/04, and C-194/04 *ABNA and Others* [2005] E.C.R. I-10423 (which also led the Court to respond to questions concerning the obligations of the Union institutions under Art. 266 TFEU following the declaration of invalidity delivered in *ABNA and Others*: ECJ, Case C-421/06 *Fratelli Martini and Cargill*, paras 52–63).

[104] EGC (order of 14 February 2012), Case T-305/08 *Italy v Commission*, not reported, paras 22–23. See also ECJ, Case C-475/01 *Commission v Greece* [2004] E.C.R. I-8923, para. 18.

[105] CFI, Case T-220/97 *H & R Ecroyd v Commission* [1999] E.C.R. II-1677, para. 49.

E. Temporal effects

10.22 As far as temporal effects are concerned, the declaration of invalidity and the declaration of nullity also run on parallel lines. The Court of Justice has held that a preliminary ruling declaring a Union act invalid in principle has retroactive effect, just like a judgment annulling a Union act, meaning that in principle it has *ex tunc* effect going back to the date on which the act took effect.[106] However, a problem may arise as a result of the fact that there is no temporal restriction on a national court's requesting the Court of Justice to declare a Union act invalid, in contrast to an action for annulment, which has to be brought within the time limit laid down in the sixth paragraph of Art. 263 TFEU. Consequently, the idea that the legal uncertainty resulting from the effect *ex tunc* of a declaration of nullity (i.e. from the date on which the measure declared void took effect) is mitigated by the relatively short period within which an action for annulment must be brought has no relevance to a declaration of invalidity.

This may explain why under the case-law the Court of Justice has inferred from Art. 267 TFEU the power to modulate the temporal effects of preliminary rulings declaring Union acts invalid on a case-by-case basis.[107] In order to justify that power, the Court reasons that the declaration of nullity and the declaration of invalidity are 'two mechanisms' provided under the Treaties for reviewing the legality of Union acts and that the 'necessary consistency' between the two mechanisms warrants interpreting the second paragraph of what is now Art. 264 TFEU as enabling the Court to impose temporal limits on the invalidity of a Union act, whether under Art. 263 TFEU or Art. 267 TFEU in the interests of ensuring the uniform application of Union law. (In the event of the declaration's having full effect *ex tunc*, it would perhaps be impossible under the procedural law of some Member States to undo all the effects which the act declared invalid had already had, which would be at the expense of the uniform non-application of the act as far as the past was concerned.)[108]

F. Exceptional limitation of temporal effects

10.23 Under the case-law, the Court has limited the temporal effect of a declaration that a Union measure is invalid where overriding considerations of legal certainty involving all the

---

[106] ECJ, Case C-228/92 *Roquette Frères* [1994] E.C.R. I-1445, para. 17, from which it follows that the national authorities must ensure the repayment of sums unduly charged on the basis of EU regulations which are subsequently declared invalid by the Court, ECJ, Case C-228/92 *Roquette Frères*, para. 18; see also ECJ, Case 130/79 *Express Dairy Foods* [1980] E.C.R. 1887, para. 14.

[107] ECJ, Case 112/83 *Société des Produits de Maïs* [1985] E.C.R. 719; for a case in which the Court of Justice refused to restrict the effect *ex tunc* of a declaration of invalidity, see Joined Cases C-363/93 and C-407/93 to C-411/93 *Lancry and Others* [1994] E.C.R. I-3957, paras 40–45. See also ECJ, Joined Cases C-177/99 and C-181/99 *Ampafrance and Sanofi Synthelabo* [2000] E.C.R. I-7013, para. 67 (in this case a Member State invoked for the first time the principle of protection of legitimate expectations with a view to limiting the temporal effects of a judgment declaring a decision invalid. The Court of Justice held that this was not possible on the grounds that to allow a Member State to do so would jeopardize the possibility for individuals to be protected against conduct of the public authorities based on unlawful rules); ECJ, Case C-228/99 *Silos e Mangimi Martini* [2001] E.C.R. I-8401, paras 35–38.

[108] ECJ, Case 112/83 *Société des Produits de Maïs* [1985] E.C.R. 719, para. 17.

interests, public as well as private, at stake in the cases concerned precluded calling into question the charging or payment of sums of money effected on the basis of that measure in respect of the period prior to the date of the judgment.[109] For example, in *Société Regie Networks*, concerning the declaration that a Commission decision in the field of State aid is invalid, as mentioned earlier (see para. 10.20), the Court granted the French Government's request to limit the temporal effects of its judgment, excluding only those undertakings which prior to the date of delivery of the judgment concerned had brought legal proceedings or made an equivalent complaint regarding the levying of the charge on advertising companies which was related to the aid scheme at issue. The Court justified the imposition of a limitation on the temporal effects of the declaration that the contested decision is invalid on the grounds that, first, the aid scheme in question was applicable for a period of five years and a great deal of aid was paid under that scheme, affecting a large number of operators, and second, the overriding considerations of legal certainty invoked by the French Government and the Commission and in particular the fact that the aid scheme at issue was not challenged before the Union judicature.[110] Noticeably, as illustrated by this case, the Court's approach diverges somewhat from the strict conditions applied by the Court for limiting the temporal effects of preliminary rulings on interpretation (see para. 6.34). While future case-law aligning these two sets of conditions cannot be ruled out, the approach taken so far in the case-law may be explained in part by the particular consequences of the retroactive application of a declaration of invalidity on account of the lack of time limits placed on the submission of references by national courts for preliminary rulings on validity.

As far as limiting the temporal effects of its judgments declaring a Union act invalid is concerned, the Court of Justice will decide in each particular case whether an exception to that temporal limitation may be granted in favour of the party who brought the action before the national court or of any other party which took similar steps before the declaration of invalidity, or conversely, whether a declaration of invalidity applicable only to the future constitutes an adequate remedy for the party concerned.[111]

In earlier case-law, the Court had in fact considered that the parties which took the initiative of challenging in the national courts the act ultimately declared invalid are sufficiently rewarded for their efforts by seeing the act eliminated from the legal system for the future.[112] That approach has been criticized on the grounds that it effectively deprives the party who successfully pleaded the invalidity of the Union act of the benefit of its success, since that party only shares in the general benefit which anyone may have in an invalid Union act which is detrimental to his or her interests being no longer applied.[113]

---

[109] See, e.g. ECJ, Case C-333/07 *Société Regie Networks* [2007] E.C.R. I-10807, para. 122 (and citations therein).

[110] ECJ, Case C-333/07 *Société Regie Networks*, paras 123, 127.

[111] ECJ, Case 112/83 *Société des Produits de Maïs* [1985] E.C.R. 719, para. 18.

[112] ECJ, Case 4/79 *Providence Agricole de la Champagne* [1980] E.C.R. 2823, paras 42–46; ECJ, Case 109/79 *Maïseries de Beauce* [1980] E.C.R. 2883, paras 42–46; ECJ, Case 145/79 *Roquette Frères* [1980] E.C.R. 2917, paras 50–53.

[113] See, among others, P. Vanavermaete, case note (1982) S.E.W. 469; H. Labayle, 'La Cour de justice des Communautés et les effets d'une déclaration d'invalidité' (1982) R.T.D.E. 484–510; D. Waelbroeck, 'Le principe de la non-rétroactivité en droit communautaire à la lumière des arrêts "isoglucose"'(1983) R.T.D.E. 363.

The Court of Justice recognized this when it was faced with this question on a subsequent occasion and had to consider whether 'an importer who, like the plaintiff in the main proceedings, has brought an administrative complaint followed by judicial proceedings, challenging a notice to pay MCAs [monetary compensatory amounts] on the ground that the [Union] regulation on the basis of which the notice was adopted was invalid, is entitled to rely for the purposes of those proceedings on the invalidity of a regulation declared by the Court of Justice in the same proceedings'.[114] If the Court were to have held that 'a declaration of invalidity applicable only to the future is an adequate remedy even for that party', this would have meant that 'the national court would dismiss the action brought against the notice in question, even though the regulation on the basis of which that notice was adopted had been declared invalid by the Court in the same proceedings'.[115] The Court found that this outcome would be unacceptable: 'An economic agent such as the plaintiff in the main proceedings would thereby be deprived of its right to effective judicial protection in the event of a breach of [Union] law by the institutions, and the practical effect of [Art. 267 TFEU] would thereby be jeopardised.'[116] Consequently, it concluded that 'a trader who before the date of the present judgment has brought an action in a national court challenging a notice to pay MCAs adopted on the basis of a [Union] regulation declared invalid by the present judgment is entitled to rely on that invalidity in the national proceedings'.[117] This meant not only the applicant in the main proceedings which had resulted in the reference to the Court of Justice, but also anyone who had brought judicial proceedings or 'submitted an administrative complaint' before the date of the declaration of invalidity.[118]

That being said, since as already mentioned the Court determines on a case-by-case basis whether a limitation on the temporal effects of a declaration that a particular Union measure is invalid is justified, there may be circumstances that may lead the Court to hold that a declaration of invalidity is only applicable for the future. For example, in *Volker und Markus Schecke and Eifert*, the Court ruled that, in view of the large number of publications which had taken place in the Member States on the basis of provisions of EU regulations in connection with the publication of personal data relating to natural persons who are beneficiaries of agricultural aid, the declaration of invalidity of these provisions did not allow any action to be brought to challenge the effects of the publication of the lists of beneficiaries of such aid carried out by the national authorities on the basis of those provisions during the period prior to the date on which the judgment was delivered.[119] Moreover, in *Association belge de Consommateurs Test-Achats and Others*, the Court declared invalid a certain provision of an EU directive relating to the treatment of sex-specific risk assessments in insurance contracts upon the expiry of an appropriate

---

[114] ECJ, Case C-228/92 *Roquette Frères* [1994] E.C.R. I-1445, para. 24, with R. Silva de Lapuerta, case note (1995) Noticias de la Unión Europea 69–72.

[115] ECJ, Case C-228/92 *Roquette Frères*, paras 25 and 26.

[116] ECJ, Case C-228/92 *Roquette Frères*, para. 27.

[117] ECJ, Case C-228/92 *Roquette Frères*, para. 30.

[118] ECJ, Case C-228/92 *Roquette Frères*; see also the earlier case ECJ, Case 41/84 *Pinna* [1986] E.C.R. 1, paras 29–30.

[119] ECJ, Joined Cases C-92/09 and C-93/09 *Volker und Markus Schecke and Eifert* [2010] E.C.R. I-11063, para. 94.

transitional period in the future (i.e. with effect from 21 December 2012), which in contrast to the accompanying Opinion of the Advocate-General, did not carve out as an exception to that temporal limitation those persons who had initiated legal proceedings or equivalent claims under the applicable national law prior to the date of delivery of the Court's judgment.[120]

---

[120] ECJ, Case C-236/09 *Association belge des Consommateurs Test-Achats and Others* [2011] E.C.R. I-773, paras 33–34. The transitional period declared by the Court coincided with a five-year period provided under the provision of Union law in question for review of the option afforded to the Member States to permit sex-specific risk assessments of insurance contracts: see ECJ, Case C-236/09 *Association belge des Consommateurs Test-Achats and Others*, para. 26. Compare the Opinion of Advocate-General J. Kokott, paras 73–82.

11

THE ACTION FOR DAMAGES

I. Subject-Matter

A. General

(1) Objective and conditions

11.01   An action for damages against the Union brought on the basis of Art. 268 TFEU and the second paragraph of Art. 340 TFEU seeks to have the Union held non-contractually liable to make good any damage caused by its institutions or by its servants in the performance of their duties.[1]

The conditions for the Union's incurring non-contractual liability are determined by the Court of Justice and the General Court 'in accordance with the general principles common to the laws of the Member States' as set forth in the second paragraph of Art. 340 TFEU.[2] The Union courts have drawn on those general principles—insofar as they could be identified—only as a source of inspiration with a view to developing an independent Union law on non-contractual liability. Consequently, starting early on in the case-law, the Court of Justice proclaimed that the non-contractual liability of what is now the Union 'presupposes the existence of a set of circumstances comprising actual damage, a causal link between the damage claimed and conduct alleged against the institution, and the illegality of such conduct'.[3]

(2) Changes brought by the Treaty of Lisbon

11.02   The Lisbon Treaty did not substantially change the wording of Art. 268 TFEU and the second paragraph of Art. 340 TFEU as compared to the former Art. 235 EC and the second paragraph of Art. 288 EC, respectively. Art. 268 TFEU states: 'The Court of Justice of the European Union shall have jurisdiction in disputes relating to compensation for damage

---

[1] For an extensive discussion, see K. Gutman, 'The Evolution of the Action for Damages Against the European Union and Its Place in the System of Judicial Protection' (2011) 48 C.M.L. Rev. 695–750.

[2] See ECJ, Case C-377/09 *Hanssens-Ensch* [2010] E.C.R. I-7751, para. 21 ('The purpose of that particular reference [in the second para. of Art. 340 TFEU to the general principles common to the laws of the Member States] is to determine the conditions which must be met if the [Union] is to be required to make good such damage').

[3] ECJ, Case 4/69 *Lütticke v Commission* [1971] E.C.R. 325, para. 10. More recently, see, e.g. ECJ, Joined Cases C-120/06 P and C-121/06 P *FIAMM and Others v Council and Commission* [2008] E.C.R. I-6513, para. 106 (and citations therein); ECJ, Case C-414/08 P *Sviluppo Italia Basilicata v Commission* [2010] E.C.R. I-2559, para. 138; ECJ, Case C-419/08 P *Trubowest Handle and Others v Council and Commission* [2010] E.C.R. I-2559, para. 40; EGC, Case T-341/07 *Sison v Council* [2011] E.C.R. II-7915, para. 28.

provided for in the second and third paragraphs of Article 340.' Former Art. 235 EC had referred to 'the Court of Justice'. Accordingly, Art. 268 TFEU makes clear that it is the institution of the Court of Justice of the European Union, as opposed to the Court of Justice as the highest judicial body within that institution, which has (exclusive) jurisdiction over this action (see further para. 11.04). Moreover, while former Art. 235 EC mentioned only the second paragraph and not the third paragraph of former Art. 288 EC concerning the non-contractual liability of the European Central Bank (ECB), Art. 268 TFEU refers to both. This dovetails with changes made to the language of the third paragraph of Art. 340 TFEU, making clear that it is the ECB, as opposed to the Union itself, which makes good any damage caused by it or by its servants in the performance of their duties on account of its separate legal personality (see further para. 11.20). In any case, apart from issues related to the substitution of the 'Union' for the 'Community' discussed later, the second paragraph of Art. 340 TFEU was left untouched.

Going beyond the text of Art. 268 TFEU and the second paragraph of Art. 340 TFEU, however, the changes brought by the Lisbon Treaty to the constitutional and institutional framework of the European Union impact the Union's non-contractual liability regime. First, with the elimination of the pillar structure and the replacement of the EC with the Union,[4] certain restrictions placed on the Union judicature's jurisdiction in relation to the action for damages have been removed. With respect to the former third pillar of Police and Judicial Cooperation in Criminal Matters (PJCCM), the action for damages is in principle no longer precluded for acts adopted in this field, as had been the case under the former Treaty framework.[5] However, where an action for damages is brought on the basis of a PJCCM act adopted before the entry into force of the Lisbon Treaty, it is subject to the five-year provisional period set forth in Art. 10 of Protocol No. 36 on transitional provisions.[6] With respect to the former second pillar of the Common Foreign and Security Policy (CFSP), the Union judicature as a general matter has not been conferred jurisdiction in this field, save for the exceptions laid down in the Treaties relating to monitoring compliance with Art. 40 TEU and reviewing the legality of restrictive measures against natural and legal persons in proceedings brought in accordance with the fourth paragraph of Art. 263 TFEU.[7] Thus, in principle the Union judicature still does not have jurisdiction over an action for damages against the Union brought on the basis of an act or conduct taken in the field of the CFSP.

Second, as far as the institutions whose acts or conduct may constitute the basis for an action for damages against the Union are concerned, the Lisbon Treaty's recognition of the European Council as a Union institution in Art. 13(1) TEU has widened the scope of potential defendants against which such an action may be directed, as compared to the previous Treaty framework (see further para. 11.20). It may be regretted, however, that the second paragraph of Art. 340 TFEU contains no express reference to bodies, offices, or

---

[4] See Art. 1(3) TEU.

[5] See ECJ, Case C-354/04 P *Gestoras Pro Amnistía and Others v Council* [2007] E.C.R. I-1579; ECJ, Case C-355/04 P *Segi and Others v Council* [2007] E.C.R. I-1657.

[6] Though where such a pre-existing PJCCM act has been amended, the jurisdiction of the Union courts is everts to the regime of the Lisbon Treaty (i.e. former Art. 35 EU is not applicable). See Art. 10(1)–(3) of Protocol (No. 36), annexed to the TEU, TFEU, and the EAEC Treaty, on transitional provisions, [2012] O.J. C326/322. See also Declaration No. 50, annexed to the Lisbon Treaty, concerning Art. 10 of the Protocol on transitional provisions, [2012] O.J. C326/356.

[7] Art. 24(1), second para., TEU; Art. 275 TFEU.

agencies of the Union, even though the principle that the Union is responsible for acts committed by such bodies, offices, or agencies is clearly established in the case-law (see para. 11.20).

Finally, since 2000, the action for damages against the Union has been given concrete expression in Art. 41(3) of the Charter of Fundamental Rights of the European Union[8] concerning the right to good administration as part of Title V on Citizens' Rights. With the entry into force of the Lisbon Treaty, the Charter has the same legal value as the Treaties, meaning it has the status of binding primary Union law.[9] Art. 41(3) of the Charter states: 'Every person has the right to have the Union make good any damage caused by its institutions or by its servants in the performance of their duties, in accordance with the general principles common to the laws of the Member States.' This provision reiterates the wording of the second paragraph of Art. 340 TFEU and as such does not modify the regime governing the Union's non-contractual liability under the Treaties (i.e. the requisite conditions under the case-law must be fulfilled).[10] Nevertheless, its inclusion in the Charter reflects the central role played by the action for damages as part of ensuring the right to good administration on the part of the Union.

(3) EAEC and former ECSC Treaties

11.03 Comparable provisions concerning an action for damages against the European Atomic Energy Community used to be found in Art. 151[11] and the second paragraph of Art. 188 of the EAEC Treaty.[12] In tandem with the entry into force of the Lisbon Treaty, however, there is a new consolidated version of the EAEC Treaty, whereby the second paragraph of Art. 188 EAEC remains applicable, but Art. 151 has been repealed and replaced by Art. 268 TFEU.[13]

There was a different non-contractual liability regime governing the European Coal and Steel Community set forth in Arts 34 and 40 of the now-expired ECSC Treaty (see further para. 11.43).[14]

---

[8] Charter of Fundamental Rights of the European Union, proclaimed in Nice on 7 December 2000, [2000] O.J. C364/1, re-enacted by the European Parliament, the Council, and the Commission on the day that the Lisbon Treaty was signed: Charter of Fundamental Rights of the European Union, proclaimed at Strasbourg on 12 December 2007, [2007] O.J. C303/1, reprinted alongside the consolidated versions of the TEU and the TFEU, [2012] O.J. C326/391.

[9] Art. 6(1) TEU.

[10] See Art. 52(2) Charter of Fundamental Rights.

[11] Akin to former Art. 235 EC, Art. 151 EAEC states: 'The Court of Justice shall have jurisdiction in disputes relating to compensation for damage provided for in the second paragraph of Article 188.'

[12] Identical to the second para. of former Art. 288 EC, the second para. of Art. 188 EAEC provides: 'In the case of non-contractual liability, the Community shall, in accordance with the general principles common to the laws of the Member States, make good any damage caused by its institutions or by its servants in the performance of their duties.' For a case concerning the non-contractual liability of the EAEC, see CFI, Case T-250/02 *Autosalone Ispra v EAEC* [2005] E.C.R. II-5227 (appeal dismissed: ECJ (order of 12 December 2006), Case C-129/06 P *Autosalone Ispra v EAEC* [2006] E.C.R. I-131*, Summ. pub.).

[13] See Art. 106a(1) of the consolidated version of the EAEC Treaty, [2012] O.J. C327/1. For an example of an action for damages brought on the basis of the second para. of what is now Art. 340 TFEU and Art. 188 EAEC, see ECJ (order of 12 January 2011), Joined Cases C-205/10 P, C-217/10 P, and C-222/10 P *Eriksen and Others v Commission* [2011] E.C.R. I-1*, Summ. pub.

[14] The ECSC Treaty expired on 23 July 2002. See, as regards the ECSC Treaty, CFI, Case T-120/89 *Stahlwerke Peine-Salzgitter v Commission* [1991] E.C.R. II-279, which should be compared with ECJ, Case C-220/91 P *Commission v Stahlwerke Peine-Salzgitter* [1993] E.C.R. I-2393.

(4) Exclusive jurisdiction

Though not stated expressly, Art. 268 TFEU has been interpreted as conferring on the **11.04** Court of Justice of the European Union exclusive jurisdiction to find the Union non-contractually liable.[15] This jurisdiction is now vested in the General Court by virtue of Art. 256 TFEU.[16] The exclusive jurisdiction of the General Court at first instance—and of the Court of Justice on appeal—to find the Union non-contractually liable guarantees the Union's independence insofar as its acts are not reviewed in the light of national law by national courts. It also has the advantage of ensuring that there are uniform rules governing the Union's non-contractual liability.[17]

(5) Staff disputes

Yet, a dispute between an official and the institution to which he or she is answerable **11.05** concerning compensation for damage, where it originates in the relationship of employment between the person concerned and the institution, falls within the first instance jurisdiction of the Civil Service Tribunal on the basis of Art. 270 TFEU and Arts 90 and 91 of the Staff Regulations and lies outside the sphere of application of Arts 268 and 340 TFEU for which the General Court has first instance jurisdiction.[18] Therefore, in order to determine its jurisdiction, the General Court (or the Civil Service Tribunal as the case may be) will assess whether the claim for compensation brought before it may be classified as litigation concerning the Union's non-contractual liability under Art. 268 TFEU and the second paragraph of Art. 340 TFEU, or as litigation concerning relations between the Union and its servants under Art. 270 TFEU.[19]

---

[15] See, e.g. ECJ, Case C-51/05 P *Commission v Cantina sociale di Dolianova and Others* [2008] E.C.R. I-5341, para. 68 (and citations therein). See also ECJ, Case C-377/09 *Hanssens-Ensch* [2010] E.C.R. I-7751, in which the Court ruled that an action for damages against the Union on the basis of non-contractual liability, even if it is brought under national legislation establishing special statutory rules which differ from the ordinary rules of law governing civil liability in the Member State concerned, does not—pursuant to Art. 268 TFEU, read in conjunction with the second para. of Art. 340 TFEU—fall within the jurisdiction of the national courts. As regards non-contractual liability of the EAEC, the Union judicature used to have the same exclusive jurisdiction pursuant to Art. 151 EAEC; with the entry into force of the Lisbon Treaty, Art. 151 EAEC has been repealed and Art. 268 TFEU is now applicable: see n. 13. The fact that the Union judicature has exclusive jurisdiction also means that a national court has no competence to order proceedings, with respect to one of the institutions of the Union, for an expert report whose purpose is to determine the role of that institution in events alleged to have caused damage, for the purposes of subsequent proceedings against the Union to establish its non-contractual liability: ECJ, Case C-275/00 *First and Franex* [2002] E.C.R. I-10943, para. 48.

[16] For which there are no exceptions carved out for the Court of Justice: see Statute, Art. 51.

[17] The same approach was not taken with regard to jurisdiction over the contractual liability of the Union (under Art. 272 TFEU): see Ch. 19.

[18] See, e.g. EGC (order of 20 January 2011), Case T-136/10 *M v European Medicines Agency*, not reported, para. 12 (and citations therein).

[19] See, e.g. CFI, Case T-309/03 *Camós Grau v Commission* [2006] E.C.R. II-1173, paras 65–74; CFI (order of 30 September 2009), Case T-166/08 *Ivanov v Commission* [2009] E.C.R. II-190*, Summ. pub., paras 37–47 (appeal dismissed in ECJ (order of 4 October 2010), Case C-532/09 P *Ivanov v Commission*, not reported); EGC (order of 20 January 2011), Case T-136/10 *M v European Medicines Agency*, not reported, paras 13–15. Likewise, for cases brought on the basis of the EAEC Treaty warranting a classification of the dispute as either general litigation on non-contractual liability under Arts 151 and 188(2) EAEC or as 'staff' litigation under Art. 152 EAEC, see, e.g. CFI, Case T-45/01 *Sanders and Others v Commission* [2004] E.C.R. II-3315, paras 41–54; CFI, Case T-144/02 *Eagle and Others v Commission* [2004] E.C.R. II-3381, paras 39–52.

B. Union 'non-contractual' liability

(1) Non-contractual versus contractual liability

11.06   The action for damages brought pursuant to Art. 268 and the second paragraph of Art. 340 TFEU only pertains to the 'non-contractual liability' of the Union, meaning that it concerns unlawful acts or conduct on the part of the Union institutions that have allegedly caused damage to the applicant.[20] This should be distinguished from an action for damages on account of the contractual liability of the Union, meaning liability arising out of a contract entered into on behalf of the Union and the applicant which is governed by Art. 272 TFEU (see Ch. 19).[21]

The Union judicature's jurisdiction to hear and to determine an action for damages differs according to the contractual or non-contractual nature of the liability involved. On the one hand, with respect to the contractual liability of the Union, it is only in the presence of an 'arbitration clause' within the meaning of Art. 272 TFEU that the Union judicature has jurisdiction, and thus, in the absence of such a clause, it cannot on the basis of Art. 268 TFEU adjudicate on the basis of what is in reality an action for contractual damages, since to do so would extend its jurisdiction beyond the limits of Art. 274 TFEU, which specifically gives national courts general jurisdiction over disputes to which the Union is a party. On the other hand, as regards the non-contractual liability of the Union, the Union judicature has jurisdiction without there being any need for the parties to the dispute to express their consent; the jurisdiction of the Court of Justice and the General Court flows directly from Art. 268 TFEU and the second paragraph of Art. 340 TFEU.[22] Consequently, to determine its jurisdiction under Art. 268 TFEU, the Union judicature must assess whether the applicant's claim for compensation is contractual or non-contractual in nature.[23] Specifically, the Union courts 'must examine, on an analysis of the various matters

---

[20] In CFI (order of 5 September 2007), Case T-295/05 *Document Security Systems, Inc. v ECB* [2007] E.C.R. II-2835, the then Court of First Instance held that it did not have jurisdiction to adjudicate on an action for patent infringement in the context of an action for damages against the Union under Art. 268 TFEU and the second para. of Art 340 TFEU.

[21] See, e.g. EGC (order of 30 June 2011), Case T-367/09 *Tecnoprocess v Commission* [2011] E.C.R. II-209*, Summ. pub., para. 73 (underscoring that under Art. 268 TFEU and the second para. of Art. 340 TFEU, the competence of the General Court in an action for damages is limited to matters of non-contractual, as opposed to contractual, liability).

[22] ECJ (judgment of 18 April 2013), Case C-103/11 P *Commission v Systran and Systran Luxembourg*, not reported, paras 56–60.

[23] For some recent examples, see ECJ, Case C-214/08 P *Guigard v Commission* [2009] E.C.R. I-91*, Summ. pub., paras 35–44 (and further citations therein); ECJ (judgment of 18 April 2013), Case C-103/11 P *Commission v Systran and Systran Luxembourg*, not reported, paras 56–84; EGC, Case T-424/08 *Nexus Europe (Ireland) v Commission* [2010] E.C.R. II-96*, Summ. pub., paras 58–60. Case-law stemming from the so-called *Mulder* litigation is also illustrative: on the one hand, it was clear from the Court of Justice's judgment in *Mulder II* that the Union (then Community) was liable to every producer who had suffered a reparable loss owing to the fact that he was prevented from delivering milk by Regulation No. 857/84, save where such claim were time-barred: see, e.g. CFI, Joined Cases T-8/95 and T-9/95 *Pelle and Konrad v Council and Commission* [2007] E.C.R. II-4117, para. 57 (and citations therein). But compare ECJ, Joined Cases C-80/99 to C-82/99 *Flemmer and Others* [2001] E.C.R. I-7211: the terms of a contract for compensation concluded with an individual in the name and on behalf of the Council and the Commission by the competent national authority pursuant to Regulation No. 2187/93, which gave so-called SLOM producers the possibility of obtaining flat-rate compensation following the judgment in *Mulder II*, were not categorized as non-contractual liability. They constituted contractual terms, which in the absence of an arbitration clause within the meaning of what

in the file, such as, for example, the rule of law allegedly infringed, the nature of the damage claimed, the conduct complained of and the legal relations between the parties in question, whether there exists between them a genuine contractual context, linked to the subject-matter of the dispute, the in-depth examination of which proves to be indispensable for the resolution of the said action. If a preliminary analysis of those matters shows that it is necessary to interpret one or more contracts concluded between the parties in question in order to establish whether the applicant's claims are well-founded, the [Union courts] are required at that point to halt their examination of the dispute and declare that they have no jurisdiction to rule thereon in the absence of an arbitration clause in the said contracts within the meaning of Article 272 TFEU'.[24] The mere reference to legal rules or principles which do not stem from the contract between the parties but which are binding on them cannot have the effect of changing the contractual nature of the dispute, since otherwise, the nature of the dispute and hence the jurisdiction of the Union courts would depend on the types of rules invoked by the parties.[25]

(2) Non-contractual liability in the absence of unlawful action or conduct: the Court of Justice's judgment in *FIAMM*

In considering the action for damages, the unlawfulness of the action or conduct on the part of the institutions has been a central feature of the Union's non-contractual liability regime under Art. 268 TFEU and the second paragraph of Art. 340 TFEU. However, the question arises as to the potential non-contractual liability of the Union on the basis of lawful action or conduct of the institutions (which has sometimes been referred to as a regime of 'no-fault' liability).   **11.07**

In past case-law, the Court of Justice and the General Court left matters open, taking the approach that 'in the event of the principle of [Union] liability for a lawful act being recognised in [Union] law, a precondition for such liability would in any event be the existence of "unusual" and "special" damage'.[26] Thus, it remained unclear to what extent

---

is now Art. 272 TFEU fell to be adjudicated by the national courts. Depending on the case, the Union judicature may find that some alleged infringements may incur the Union's contractual liability, whereas others may incur the Union's non-contractual liability: see, e.g. CFI, Case T-154/01 *Distilleria F. Palma v Commission* [2004] E.C.R. II-1493, paras 37–51. Likewise, an applicant may lodge an action in contractual liability and an action for non-contractual liability in the alternative: see, e.g. CFI, Case T-271/04 *Citymo v Commission* [2007] E.C.R. II-1375, in which the Court of First Instance held the action inadmissible insofar as it had been brought under Art. 272 TFEU, but upheld the action on the basis of the Union's non-contractual liability under Art. 268 TFEU and the second para. of Art. 340 TFEU with respect to certain claims grounded in pre-contract negotiations between the parties.

[24] ECJ (judgment of 18 April 2013), Case C-103/11 P *Commission v Systran and Systran Luxembourg*, not reported, paras 66–67. In this case, the Court of Justice held that the General Court had erred in classifying the dispute as non-contractual in nature and that the Union courts did not have jurisdiction to hear the action for compensation brought by the applicants. ECJ, Case C-103/11 P *Commission v Systran and Systran Luxembourg*, paras 75–86.

[25] ECJ, Case C-214/08 P *Guigard v Commission* [2009] E.C.R. I-91*, Summ. pub., para. 43. See also, e.g., ECJ (judgment of 18 April 2013), Case C-103/11 P *Commission v Systran and Systran Luxembourg*, not reported, paras 64–65; EGC (order of 8 February 2012), Case T-481/08 *Alisei v Commission* [2010] E.C.R. II-117, para. 94.

[26] ECJ, Case C-237/98 P *Dorsch Consult v Council and Commission* [2000] E.C.R. I-4549, para. 18 (and citations therein); see further ECJ, Joined Cases 9/71 and 11/71 *Compagnie d'Approvisionnement, de Transport et de Crédit and Others v Commission* [1972] E.C.R. 391, para. 46; ECJ, Case 59/83 *Biovilac v EEC* [1984] E.C.R. 4057, para. 28; ECJ, Case 267/82 *Développement and Clemessy v Commission* [1986] E.C.R. 1907, para. 33; ECJ (order of 20 March 2007), Case C-325/06 P *Galileo International Technology and Others v*

such a principle was recognized in Union law until 14 December 2005, when the Court of First Instance delivered five related judgments, which affirmatively established this principle for the first time.[27] Two of these judgments were appealed to the Court of Justice in *FIAMM and Others v Council and Commission*.[28] In a judgment of 9 September 2008, the Court of Justice ruled that the Court of First Instance had erred in law by affirming the existence of a Union regime of 'no-fault' liability.[29] In its view, the regime concerning the Union's non-contractual liability for unlawful conduct was firmly established, but this was not the case with respect to that for lawful conduct, which could not be deduced from previous case-law framing the matter in merely hypothetical terms.[30] Moreover, although comparative examination of the Member States' legal systems had enabled the Court to make at a very early stage the finding of a principle of liability in the case of an unlawful act or omission, that was in no way the position as regards the possible existence of a principle of liability in the case of a lawful act or omission of the public authorities, in particular where it is of a legislative nature.[31] On that basis, the Court of Justice declared that 'as [Union] law currently stands, no liability regime exists under which the [Union] can incur liability for conduct falling within the sphere of its legislative competence in a situation where any failure of such conduct to comply with the WTO agreements cannot be relied upon before the [Union] courts'.[32]

Commission [2007] E.C.R. I-44*, Summ. pub., para. 76; CFI, Case T-113/96 *Edouard Dubois et Fils v Council and Commission* [1998] E.C.R. II-125, para. 42; CFI, Case T-184/95 *Dorsch Consult v Council and Commission* [1998] E.C.R. II-667, para. 80; CFI, Case T-196/99 *Area Cova and Others v Council and Commission* [2001] E.C.R. II-3597, para. 171; CFI, Case T-170/00 *Förde-Reederei v Council and Commission* [2002] E.C.R. II-515, paras 56–57; CFI, Joined Cases T-64/01 and T-65/01 *Afrikanische Frucht Compagnie and Others v Council and Commission* [2004] E.C.R. II-521, paras 150–156.

[27] CFI, Case T-69/00 *FIAMM and FIAMM Technologies v Council and Commission* [2005] E.C.R. II-5393; CFI, Case T-151/00 *La Laboratoire du Bain v Council and Commission* [2005] E.C.R. II-23*, Summ. pub.; CFI, Case T-30/00 *Cartondruck v Council and Commission* [2005] E.C.R. II-27*, Summ. pub.; CFI, Case T-383/00 *Beamglow v European Parliament, Council and Commission* [2005] E.C.R. II-5459; and CFI, Case T-135/01 *Fedon & Figli and Others v Council and Commission* [2005] E.C.R. II-29*, Summ. pub. On the same basis, see also CFI, Case T-138/03 *É.R. and Others v Council and Commission* [2006] E.C.R. II-4923, para. 153 (appeal dismissed in ECJ (order of 4 October 2007), Case C-100/07 P *É.R. and Others v Council and Commission* [2007] E.C.R. I-136*, Summ. pub.).

[28] ECJ, Joined Cases C-120/06 P and C-121/06 P *FIAMM and Others v Council and Commission* [2008] E.C.R. I-6513, dismissing appeal against the decisions in CFI, Case T-69/00 *FIAMM and FIAMM Technologies v Council and Commission* [2005] E.C.R. II-5393 and CFI, Case T-135/01 *Fedon & Figli and Others v Council and Commission* [2005] E.C.R. II-29*, Summ. pub. Apart from ruling on the issue of Union no-fault liability, this judgment merits detailed discussion in connection with the applicant's attempt to rely on the WTO rules for the purposes of establishing unlawful conduct on the part of the institutions concerned: see further para. 11.51.

[29] ECJ, Joined Cases C-120/06 P and C-121/06 P *FIAMM and Others v Council and Commission*, para. 179. Yet, the Court of Justice ultimately dismissed this ground of the appeal on the basis that the Court of First Instance rejected the applicants' claims in any event: ECJ, Joined Cases C-120/06 P and C-121/06 P *FIAMM and Others v Council and Commission*, paras 187–189.

[30] ECJ, Joined Cases C-120/06 P and C-121/06 P *FIAMM and Others v Council and Commission*, paras 167–169.

[31] ECJ, Joined Cases C-120/06 P and C-121/06 P *FIAMM and Others v Council and Commission*, para. 175.

[32] ECJ, Joined Cases C-120/06 P and C-121/06 P *FIAMM and Others v Council and Commission*, paras 176, 188. That being said, the Court of Justice pointed out that, first, its judgment was without prejudice to the Union legislator's discretion to assess whether the adoption of a given legislative measure justifies the provision of certain forms of compensation 'when account is taken of certain harmful effects that are to result from its adoption'; and, second, a Union legislative measure restricting a party's fundamental rights to property and the freedom to pursue a trade or profession could give rise to a non-contractual liability claim, though

Although the Court of Justice's judgment in *FIAMM* appears to preclude Union non-contractual liability for lawful acts or conduct,[33] it was premised by the caveat 'as [Union] law currently stands' and was framed to a large extent within the context of the particular circumstances of the proceedings before it which involved the institutions' (lack of) compliance with the WTO agreements and their 'legislative' activity. Therefore, it remains to be seen to what extent the Union judicature may refine its position in future case-law.[34]

(3) Recognition of an action for unjust enrichment: the Court of Justice's judgment in *Masdar*

However, the Court of Justice has not ruled out completely the possibility for the Union to **11.08** incur non-contractual liability in the absence of unlawful conduct. In *Masdar (UK) Ltd v Commission*,[35] the Court of Justice held that Union non-contractual liability may be grounded in an action for unjust enrichment, given that the principle of unjust enrichment is a source of non-contractual obligation common to the laws of the Member States,[36] and hence the Union cannot be dispensed from the application to itself of the same principles where a natural or legal person alleges that the Union has been unjustly enriched to the detriment of that person.[37] Moreover, since any obligation arising out of unjust enrichment

---

noting certain limitations with respect to the present proceedings: ECJ, Joined Cases C-120/06 P and C-121/06 P *FIAMM and Others v Council and Commission*, paras 180–186. Compare the approach taken by the Advocate-General, who advocated the recognition of a principle of Union no-fault liability: see Opinion of Advocate-General M. Poaires Maduro in ECJ, Joined Cases C-120/06 P and C-121/06 P *FIAMM and Others v Council and Commission* [2008] E.C.R. I-6513, points 54–63 (and for its field of application, points 64–83).

[33] See, e.g. EGC, Case T-162/07 *Pigasos Alieftiki Naftiki Etaireia v Council and Commission* [2009] E.C.R. II-153*, Summ. pub., para 74–77 (rejecting the applicant's claim for compensation based on Union non-contractual liability for a lawful act in line with the Court of Justice's reasoning in *FIAMM*, though without citing that judgment explicitly) (appeal dismissed on other grounds: ECJ (order of 12 May 2010), Case C-451/09 P *Pigasos Alieftiki Naftiki Etaireia v Council and Commission* [2010] E.C.R. I-62*, Summ. pub.); EGC, Case T-388/07 *Comune di Napoli v Commission* [2010] E.C.R. II-79*, Summ. pub., paras 184–190 (rejecting the applicant's claim for compensation based on Union non-contractual liability for a lawful act, expressly referring to the Court of Justice's judgment in *FIAMM*).

[34] See ECJ, Case C-414/08 P *Sviluppo Italia Bailicata v Commission* [2010] E.C.R. I-2559, paras 140–141, where the Court ruled, without any explicit reference to *FIAMM*, that there was no need to adjudicate on the possibility of the Union's no-fault liability in connection with the Commission's non-legislative activity and that it was sufficient to state that the General Court was entitled to reject that claim on the grounds that the damage alleged was neither special nor unusual (the General Court's decision under appeal (Case T-176/06) was delivered on 8 July 2008, i.e. about a month before *FIAMM*). See also EGC (judgment of 7 November 2012), Case T-574/08 *Syndicat des thoniers méditerranéens and Others v Commission*, not reported, paras 67–89, where the General Court reached the conclusion that the damage suffered was not unusual without rejecting in principle the concept of liability for lawful act (appeals pending in ECJ, Case C-12/13 P and ECJ, Case C-13/13 P).

[35] ECJ, Case C-47/07 P *Masdar (UK) Ltd v Commission* [2008] E.C.R. I-9761. For further discussion reconciling the Court of Justice's judgments in *Masdar* and *FIAMM*, see Gutman, n. 1, 740–7.

[36] As the Court declared, on the basis of the general principles common to the laws of the Member States, 'a person who has suffered a loss which increases the wealth of another person without there being any legal basis for that enrichment has the right, as a general rule, to restitution from the person enriched, up to the amount of the loss' and 'legal redress for undue enrichment, as provided for in the majority of national legal systems, is not necessarily conditional upon unlawfulness or fault with regard to the defendant's conduct'. However, in order for such an action to be upheld, 'it is essential that there be no valid legal basis for the enrichment. That condition is not satisfied, in particular, where the enrichment derives from contractual obligations.' (ECJ, Case C-47/07 P *Masdar (UK) Ltd v Commission*, paras 44–46.)

[37] ECJ, Case C-47/07 P *Masdar (UK) Ltd v Commission*, para. 47.

is by definition non-contractual in nature, it is necessary to allow it to be invoked pursuant to Art. 268 TFEU and the second paragraph of Art. 340 TFEU.[38] The Court noted that actions for unjust enrichment do not fall within the rules governing non-contractual liability in the strict sense, i.e. they differ from actions brought under those rules in that they do not require proof of unlawful conduct—indeed, of any form of conduct at all—on the part of the defendant, but merely proof of enrichment on the part of the defendant for which there is no valid legal basis and of impoverishment on the part of the applicant which is linked to that enrichment.[39] Despite these characteristics, however, the Court ruled that the possibility of bringing an action for unjust enrichment against the Union could not be denied to a person solely on the grounds that the Treaties did not make express provision for a means of pursuing that type of action and if Art. 268 TFEU and the second paragraph of Art. 340 TFEU were construed as excluding such a possibility, the result would be contrary to the principle of effective judicial protection laid down in the case-law and confirmed in Art. 47 of the Charter of Fundamental Rights of the European Union.[40]

Also, in *Masdar*, the applicant attempted to bring a claim for compensation under Art. 268 TFEU and the second paragraph of Art. 340 TFEU, based on the principle of *negotiorum gestio*. In its judgment, the Court of First Instance ruled, similar to its treatment of the action for unjust enrichment brought by the applicant, that an action based on *negotiorum gestio* could in principle be brought within the context of an action for damages against the Union even though the condition relating to the unlawfulness of the act or conduct of the institution concerned was not satisfied; however, it considered that the conditions governing this action were not satisfied in the present proceedings.[41] On appeal, the Court of Justice found it unnecessary to determine whether the Court of First Instance made a correct classification of the legal nature of actions based on *negotiorum gestio*, since the arguments put forward by the applicant could not in any case be upheld.[42] Therefore, this issue awaits further clarification in the case-law.

C. The relationship between the action for damages and other actions in the Treaties

(1) Independent form of action

11.09 The question arises as to the extent to which the independent nature of the action for damages is influenced by the existence of other procedures that are available to an applicant in order to have the legality of an act causing damage reviewed by the Union courts. More specifically, the question is whether the action for damages is an independent form of action or whether the applicant may bring such proceedings only after it has been determined in some other proceedings that the act in question is unlawful.

---

[38] ECJ, Case C-47/07 P *Masdar (UK) Ltd v Commission*, para. 48.
[39] ECJ, Case C-47/07 P *Masdar (UK) Ltd v Commission*, para. 49.
[40] ECJ, Case C-47/07 P *Masdar (UK) Ltd v Commission*, para. 50. In the present proceedings, the Court of Justice upheld the Court of First Instance's rejection of the unjust enrichment claim: see ECJ, Case C-47/07 P *Masdar (UK) Ltd v Commission*, paras 51–61.
[41] CFI, Case T-333/03 *Masdar (UK) Ltd v Commission* [2006] E.C.R. II-4377, paras 91–104.
[42] ECJ, Case C-47/07 P *Masdar (UK) Ltd v Commission* [2008] E.C.R. I-9761, paras 66–69.

Originally, the case-law seemed to take the second of these two approaches in that actions for damages seemed to be regarded as admissible only if an action for the annulment of the contested act had been brought.[43] Shortly thereafter, however, matters took a different turn when the Court of Justice described the action for damages as 'an independent form of action with a particular purpose to fulfil within the system of actions and subject to conditions for its use, conceived with a view to its specific purpose'.[44]

Consequently, an action for damages will be admissible even if no prior action for annulment[45] or for failure to act[46] has been brought and if no preliminary ruling declaring the offending act invalid has been obtained. The purpose of an action for damages is solely to obtain financial compensation and, on that ground, differs from that of other forms of action.[47] What is more, the requirements in order for liability to be incurred are

---

[43] ECJ, Case 25/62 *Plaumann v Commission* [1963] E.C.R. 95, at 108: 'An administrative measure which has not been annulled cannot of itself constitute a wrongful act on the part of the administration inflicting damage on those whom it affects.' On this view, a finding of an unlawful failure to act or a declaration by way of preliminary ruling that a measure was invalid was to be equated with a declaration that the measure was void.

[44] ECJ, Case 4/69 *Lütticke v Commission* [1971] E.C.R. 325, at 336. See also, e.g. ECJ (order of 21 June 1993), Case C-257/93 *Van Parijs and Others v Council and Commission* [1993] E.C.R. I-3335, para. 14; ECJ, Case C-234/02 P *European Ombudsman v Lamberts* [2004] E.C.R. I-2803, para. 59; CFI, Case T-170/00 *Förde-Reederei v Council and Commission* [2002] E.C.R. II-515, para. 35; CFI, Case T-437/05 *Brink's Security Luxembourg v Commission* [2009] E.C.R. II-3233, para. 231; EGC, Joined Cases T-440/03, T-121/04, T-171/04, T-208/04, T-365/04, and T-484/04 *Arizmendi and Others v Council and Commission* [2009] E.C.R. II-4883, para. 64; EGC, Case T-429/05 *Artegodan v Commission* [2010] E.C.R. II-491, paras 50–51 (appeal dismissed in ECJ (judgment of 19 April 2012), Case C-221/10 P *Artegodan v Commission*, not reported); EGC (order of 24 May 2011), Case T-489/08 *Power-One Italy v Commission* [2011] E.C.R. II-149*, Summ. pub., para. 42; EGC, Case T-341/07 *Sison v Council* [2011] E.C.R. II-7915, para. 32 (and further citations therein). In his Opinion in ECJ, Joined Cases 9/71 and 11/71 *Compagnie d'Approvisionnement, de Transport et de Crédit and Others v Commission* [1972] E.C.R. 391, at 411, Advocate-General A. Dutheillet de Lamothe argued cogently that the action for damages should be independent of any action for annulment. He pointed out that a declaration of nullity applies *erga omnes* and is retroactive. In his view, those far-reaching consequences explained why the authors of the Treaty had restricted individuals' access to the Court of Justice (now the General Court) on the basis of what is now Art. 263 TFEU, and why the second para. of what is now Art. 264 TFEU had conferred on the Court of Justice the power to restrict the retroactive effect of a declaration of nullity. In contrast, the action for damages was an action for a declaration of subjective rights (i.e. rights pertaining to the applicant personally) and did not have the same far-reaching results. Consequently, the same stringent conditions as to admissibility ought not to apply. The argument that the authors of the Treaty had sought—irrespective of the type of dispute— to prevent the Court of Justice from ruling on the legality of a general act on an application from individuals was therefore misconceived. For staff cases, see Ch. 18.

[45] ECJ, Case 5/71 *Zuckerfabrik Schöppenstedt v Council* [1971] E.C.R. 975, para. 3. A party may bring a claim for damages without there being any provision requiring it also to claim annulment of the unlawful act which gave rise to the damage: CFI, Case T-178/98 *Fresh Marine v Commission* [2000] E.C.R. II-3331, para. 49; see further, e.g. EGC (order of 6 July 2011), Case T-160/11 *Petroci Holding v Council*, not reported, para. 25; EGC (order of 6 July 2011), Case T-142/11 *SIR v Council*, not reported, para. 28. There is also no requirement for the act that gave rise to the damage to be legally binding: CFI, Case T-209/00 *Lamberts v European Ombudsman* [2002] E.C.R. II-2203, para. 58; see also EGC, Joined Cases T-440/03, T-121/04, T-171/04, T-208/04, T-365/04, and T-484/04 *Arizmendi and Others v Council and Commission* [2009] E.C.R. II-4883, para. 65 (and citations therein) ('irrespective of whether it constitutes a challengeable act apt to lead to an action for annulment . . . any act of an institution . . . is in principle capable of forming the subject-matter of an action for compensation'). The annulment of a decision does not have any effect on the limitation period for bringing an action for damages. Indeed, the infringement of Union law, which allegedly causes harm, exists before the annulment of the decision by a Union court: ECJ, Case C-282/05 P *Holcim (Deutschland) v Commission* [2007] E.C.R. I-2941, para. 31.

[46] ECJ, Case 4/69 *Lütticke v Commission* [1971] E.C.R. 325.

[47] See, e.g. CFI, Case T-437/05 *Brink's Security Luxembourg v Commission* [2009] E.C.R. II-3233, para. 231 (and citations therein) ('It differs from an action for annulment in that its end is not the abolition of a particular measure, but compensation for damage caused by an institution'); EGC, Case T-341/07 *Sison v*

substantively different from the criteria for reviewing the legality of an action or an alleged failure to act on the part of the Union. Therefore, a finding that an act is unlawful or that the Union has failed to act does not suffice to establish the requisite conditions for the Union's non-contractual liability.[48] Furthermore, the fact that an action for annulment of an act of a Union institution which at the same time is the subject of an action for damages is inadmissible does not necessarily make the claim for damages inadmissible.[49]

(2) Improper use of an action for damages

11.10 However, an action for damages will be inadmissible where it is used improperly as an action for annulment or for failure to act. An applicant who seeks to use an action for damages in order to obtain the specific outcome sought by one of those forms of action will be denied access to the Union judicature. To use an action for damages for that purpose would amount to an abuse of process.

Accordingly, an action for damages may not be brought in order to avoid the consequences of time having run out for bringing an action for annulment against an act against which the applicant could have brought such an action. The improper use of the action for damages will be inferred from the fact that the reparation sought coincides with the benefit which the applicant would have obtained as a result of the annulment of the contested

---

Council [2011] E.C.R. II-7915, para. 32 (and citations therein) ('Whereas actions for annulment and for failure to act seek a declaration that a legally binding measure is unlawful or that such a measure has not been taken, an action for damages seeks compensation for damage resulting from a measure or from unlawful conduct, attributable to an institution'). See also the Opinion of Advocate-General F. Capotorti in ECJ, Case 68/77 *IFG v Commission* [1978] E.C.R. 353, at 375.

[48] See, e.g. CFI, Case T-364/03 *Medici Grimm v Council* [2006] E.C.R. II-79, paras 61–62 (unlawfulness established in previous annulment action not sufficient to justify the condition relating to unlawfulness for the purposes of an action for damages, since it required the showing of a sufficiently serious breach of a rule of law intended to confer rights on individuals under *Bergaderm*); EGC, Case T-300/07 *Evropaïki Dynamiki v Commission* [2010] E.C.R. II-4521, paras 143–145 (with respect to claim for damages based on the same pleas that were considered in the context of the claim for annulment; the fact that the contested decision was vitiated by defective reasoning and was therefore annulled did not mean that wrongful conduct or a direct causal link was established in the context of the claim for damages) (appeal dismissed in ECJ (order of 13 October 2011), Case C-560/10 P *Evropaïki Dynamiki v Commission* [2011] E.C.R. I-151*, Summ. pub.); EGC, Case T-429/05 *Artegodan v Commission* [2010] E.C.R. II-491, para. 49 (the fact that a provision of a Union measure was annulled in a previous action was not sufficient for it to be held that the condition for the incurring of the Union's non-contractual liability relating to the unlawfulness of the institutions' alleged conduct was satisfied) (appeal dismissed in ECJ (judgment of 19 April 2012), Case C-221/10 P *Artegodan v Commission*, not reported); EGC, Case T-341/07 *Sison v Council* [2011] E.C.R. II-7915, para. 31 (the fact that certain provisions of a Union measure were annulled in a previous action was not sufficient for it to be held that the condition for the incurring of the Union's non-contractual liability relating to unlawfulness of the institutions' alleged conduct was satisfied).

[49] See, e.g. ECJ, Case 175/84 *Krohn v Commission* [1986] E.C.R. 735, para. 32; CFI, Case T-185/94 *Geotronics v Commission* [1995] E.C.R. II-2795, para. 38; CFI, Case T-485/93 *Dreyfus v Commission* [1996] E.C.R. II-1101, para. 67; CFI, Case T-491/93 *Richco v Commission* [1996] E.C.R. II-1131, para. 64; CFI, Case T-437/05 *Brink's Security Luxembourg v Commission* [2009] E.C.R. II-3233, paras 229, 231–233. But an action for damages which is brought together with an action for annulment and seeks compensation for damage allegedly caused solely by the unlawfulness of an act of an institution will be inadmissible if it appears from examination of the application for annulment that the act has no legal effects: ECJ (order of 13 June 1991), Case C-50/90 *Sunzest v Commission* [1991] E.C.R. I-2917, para. 19; ECJ (order of 4 October 1991), Case C-117/91 *Bosman v Commission* [1991] E.C.R. I-4837, para. 20; CFI (order of 10 October 1996), Case T-75/96 *Söktas v Commission* [1996] E.C.R. II-1689, para. 49. The Court of First Instance also dismissed a damages claim after annulling the act that had allegedly caused the damage, stating that it could not rule on that claim without prejudging the substance of any new decision to be taken by the Commission to comply with its judgment pursuant to Art. 266 TFEU (ex Art. 233 EC): CFI, Case T-241/00 *Le Canne v Commission* [2002] E.C.R. II-1251, paras 61–64.

Union act[50] or from the close connection between the damage which arose and the applicant's own failure to have recourse to another form of action.[51]

No matter how comprehensible this case-law may be, it cannot help but detract from the autonomous nature of the action for damages.[52] Yet it must be stressed that the Union

---

[50] ECJ, Case 59/65 *Schreckenberg v Commission* [1966] E.C.R. 543, at 550; ECJ, Case 175/84 *Krohn v Commission*, para. 33; ECJ, Joined Cases C-199/94 and C-200/94 P *Pevasa and Inpesca v Commission* [1995] E.C.R. I-3709, para. 28; CFI, Case T-514/93 *Cobrecaf and Others v Commission* [1995] E.C.R. II-621, paras 59–60; CFI, Case T-485/93 *Dreyfus v Commission*, para. 68; CFI, Case T-491/93 *Richco v Commission*, para. 65; CFI (order of 3 February 1998), Case T-68/96 *Polyvios v Commission* [1998] E.C.R. II-153, paras 32–45; CFI, Case T-93/95 *Laga v Commission* [1997] E.C.R. II-195, paras 48–49; CFI, Case T-94/95 *Landuyt v Commission* [1997] E.C.R. II-213, paras 48–49; CFI, Case T-186/98 *Inpesca v Commission* [2001] E.C.R. II-557, paras 76–77; CFI, Case T-180/00 *Astipesca v Commission* [2002] E.C.R. II-3985, paras 139–147; CFI, Case T-47/02 *Danzer and Danzer v Council* [2006] E.C.R. II-1779, paras 28–30.

[51] ECJ, Case 4/67 *Muller (née Collignon) v Commission* [1967] E.C.R. 365, at 373; see further ECJ, Case 346/87 *Bossi v Commission* [1989] E.C.R. 303, paras 31–35; ECJ (order of 8 March 2007), Case C-237/06 P *Strack v Commission* [2007] E.C.R. I-33*, Summ. pub., para. 98; ECJ (order of 4 October 2010), Case C-532/09 P *Ivanov v Commission*, not reported, paras 23–25; CFI (judgment of 5 March 2008), Case T-414/06 P *Combescot v Commission*, not reported, para. 49. Compare CFI, Case T-309/03 *Camós Grau v Commission* [2006] E.C.R. II-1173, paras 59, 75–80 (rejecting the defendant's argument based on the *Bossi* case-law). There appears to be a related line of case-law holding that an application for damages must be dismissed where there is a close connection between it and an application for annulment which itself has been dismissed. See, e.g. CFI, Case T-65/04 *Nuova Gela Sviluppo Soc. cons. pa v Commission* [2007] E.C.R. II-68*, Summ. pub., paras 100–102; CFI, Case T-495/04 *Belfass v Council* [2008] E.C.R. II-781, paras 122–123; CFI, Case T-420/05 *Vischim v Commission* [2009] E.C.R. II-3841, paras 260–262; EGC, Case T-582/08 *Carpent Languages SPRL v Commission* [2010] E.C.R. II-181*, Summ. pub., paras 84–86. Compare CFI, Case T-193/04 *Tillack v Commission* [2006] E.C.R. II-3995, paras 96–99 (rejecting the Commission's argument that a certain claim for compensation put forward by the applicant is inadmissible because it is closely linked to an action for annulment which itself is inadmissible, underscoring the autonomous nature of the action for damages). Sometimes *Bossi* is cited in this context: see, e.g. CFI (order of 15 November 2006), Case T-115/05 *Jiménez Martínez v Commission* [2006] E.C.R.-SC I-A-2-269, paras 35–36. Yet, this line of case-law appears not so much focused on the abuse of the action for damages, but on the fact that the same pleas and arguments which have been put forth by the applicant in the context of the annulment action have been rejected, and hence action for damages is also rejected. See also with regard to staff disputes, e.g. CFI, Case T-281/04 *Staboli v Commission* [2006] E.C.R.-SC I-A-2-251, paras 61–62; CFI, Case T-73/05 *Magone v Commission* [2006] E.C.R.-SC I-A-2-107, paras 103–105; CFI (judgment of 18 September 2008), Case T-47/05 *Serrano and Others v European Parliament*, not reported, paras 178–179 (appeal dismissed in ECJ, Case C-496/08 P *Angé Serrano and Others v Parliament* [2010] E.C.R. I-1793). But to avoid confusion, note further that in staff cases, under the system of remedies established by Arts 90–91 of the Staff Regulations, an action for damages, which constitutes an autonomous remedy separate from annulment, is admissible only if it has been preceded by a pre-litigation procedure which differs according to whether the reparation sought results from an act adversely affecting the applicant within the meaning of Art. 90(2) of the Staff Regulations or from conduct on the part of the administration which contains nothing in the nature of a decision: in the first case, it is for the person concerned to submit a complaint directed against the act in question, whereas in the second case, the administrative procedure must commence with the submission of a request within the meaning of Art. 90(1) of the Staff Regulations for compensation and continue with a complaint against the decision rejecting that complaint. Thus, where there is a direct link between an action for annulment and an action for damages, the latter is admissible as being ancillary to the action for annulment, without necessarily having to be preceded by a request from the person concerned to the appointing authority for compensation for the damage allegedly suffered and by a complaint challenging the correctness of the implied or express rejection of that request. So, where the applicant does not submit a request for compensation to the authority during the administrative procedure, the question of whether there is a direct link between the claim and the annulment action arises, i.e. where the claim for damage is found to be ancillary to the annulment claim, it is admissible if the latter claim is admissible. See, e.g. CFI, Case T-416/04 *Kontouli v Council* [2006] E.C.R.-SC I-A-2-181, paras 181–186.

[52] See, e.g. ECJ, Case 153/73 *Holtz & Willemsen v Council and Commission* [1974] E.C.R. 675, paras 3–5; ECJ, Joined Cases 197/80 to 200/80, 243/80, 245/80, and 247/80 *Ludwigshafener Walzmühle and Others v Council and Commission* [1981] E.C.R. 3211, paras 4–5; ECJ, Case C-87/89 *SONITO and Others v Commission* [1990] E.C.R. I-1981, paras 13–15; CFI, Case T-309/03 *Camós Grau v Commission* [2006] E.C.R. II-1173, paras 75–80.

courts take a strict approach to the application of this case-law so as to preserve as much as possible the autonomy of the action for damages. For example, in *Cantina sociale di Dolianova v Commission*, the Court of First Instance emphasized that '[i]t is only where the action for damages is actually aimed at securing the withdrawal of an individual decision addressed to the applicants which has become definitive—so that it has the same purpose and the same effect as an action for annulment—that the action for damages could be considered to be an abuse of process'.[53] In *Holcim (France) v Commission*, the Court of First Instance considered that the case-law by virtue of which an action for damages must be declared inadmissible where it is in fact aimed at securing the withdrawal of an individual decision which has become definitive and would, if successful, cause the legal effects of that decision to be nullified is, 'in very exceptional circumstances, having regard to the principle of the autonomy of an action for damages vis-à-vis other remedies, supported by the consideration that the applicant would have standing under [Article 263 TFEU], to bring an action for annulment of the very act which he claims causes him damage, after the time limit for bringing an action for annulment of that act has expired' and 'therefore applicable only where the alleged damage flows exclusively from an individual administrative measure which has become definitive, which the party concerned could have challenged by means of an action for annulment'.[54]

(3) Relevance of annulment action for damages action

11.11   Notwithstanding the autonomous nature of the action for damages in terms of its admissibility vis-à-vis the action for annulment, there is some linkage between the two in practice. Under the case-law, where an applicant brings an action for annulment against an allegedly unlawful Union act at the same time as an action for damages for the damage allegedly suffered on account of such act which are based on the same grounds, the General Court may utilize its reasoning relative to the annulment action to find that the applicant has failed to prove one or more of the requisite conditions for the damages action, typically the unlawfulness of the act or conduct on the part of the institution concerned, at least insofar as the applicant puts forth no further arguments in the context of the latter action.[55]

---

[53] CFI, Case T-166/98 *Cantina sociale di Dolianova and Others v Commission* [2004] E.C.R. II-3991, para. 122 (finding that this was not so in the present proceedings: CFI, Case T-166/98 *Cantina sociale di Dolianova and Others v Commission*, paras 123–124) (judgment set aside on other grounds in ECJ, Case C-51/05 P); EGC (order of 24 May 2011), Case T-489/08 *Power-One Italy v Commission* [2011] E.C.R. II-149*, Summ. pub., paras 43–48.

[54] CFI (order of 4 May 2005), Case T-86/03 *Holcim (France) v Commission* [2005] E.C.R. II-1357, paras 49–50 (referring to ECJ, Case 175/84 *Krohn v Commission*, n. 49, finding such circumstances not relevant to the instant proceedings: ECJ, Case 175/84 *Krohn v Commission*, para. 51).

[55] See, e.g. CFI, Case T-406/06 *Evropaïki Dynamiki v Commission* [2008] E.C.R. II-247*, Summ. pub., paras 134–135; CFI, Case T-33/06 *Zenab v Commission* [2009] E.C.R. II-102*, Summ. pub., para. 166; EGC, Case T-195/08 *Antwerpse Bouwwerken v Commission* [2009] E.C.R. II-4439, paras 92–93; EGC (judgment of 9 September 2010), Case T-63/06 *Evropaïki Dynamiki v Commission*, not reported, para. 127; EGC, Case T-49/07 *Fahas v Council* [2010] E.C.R. II-5555, paras 94–95; EGC, Case T-388/07 *Comune di Napoli v Commission* [2010] E.C.R. II-79*, Summ. pub., paras 177–179; EGC, Case T-121/08 *PC-Ware Information Technologies v Commission* [2010] E.C.R. II-1541, paras 107–108; EGC (judgment of 9 September 2010), Case T-387/08 *Evropaïki Dynamiki v Commission*, not reported, paras 171–172 (appeal dismissed in ECJ (order of 20 September 2011), Case C-561/10 P *Evropaïki Dynamiki v Commission* [2011] E.C.R. I-130*, Summ. pub.); EGC, Case T-589/08 *Evropaïki Dynamiki v Commission* [2011] E.C.R. II-40*, Summ. pub., para. 113 (appeal dismissed in ECJ (order of 29 November 2011), Case C-235/11 P *Evropaïki Dynamiki v Commission* [2011] E.C.R. I-183*, Summ. pub.); EGC, Case T-8/09 *Dredging International and Ondernemingen Jan de Nul v European Maritime Safety Agency* [2011] E.C.R. II-6123, paras 144–147; EGC, Case T-298/09 *Evropaïki Dynamiki v Commission* [2011] E.C.R. II-300*, Summ. pub., paras 102–103 (appeal dismissed in

Moreover, where there has been a previous judgment of a Union court in which the validity of a Union act is examined and confirmed, that previous judgment may be deemed to have *res judicata* effects precluding a Union court from re-examining, in an action for damages, the same matters of fact and law previously raised by the same parties.[56]

(4) Part of the complete system of judicial protection in the European Union

Notwithstanding its autonomous nature, the action for damages has a complementary **11.12** relationship to the other actions set forth in the Treaties as part of the complete system of judicial protection in the European Union.[57] In the case-law, the Union courts have referred to the availability of the action for damages where the applicant failed to satisfy the standing requirements for natural and legal persons under the fourth paragraph of what is now Art. 263 TFEU. The action for damages thus guarantees that such applicant is not deprived of effective judicial protection.[58] In particular, in *R.J. Reynolds Tobacco Holdings, Inc. and Others v Commission*, the Court of Justice explained that 'such an action is not part of the system of review of the legality of [Union] acts with legal effects which are binding on, and capable of affecting the interests of the applicant, but it is available where a party has suffered harm on account of unlawful conduct by an institution'.[59]

II. Identity of the Parties

A. Applicants

(1) Any natural or legal person

Any natural or legal person who claims to have been injured by acts or conduct of a Union **11.13** institution or its officials or servants may bring an action for damages in the General Court.[60]

ECJ, Case C-629/11 P *Evropaïki Dynamiki v Commission*, not reported); EGC, Case T-86/09 *Evropaïki Dynamiki v Commission* [2011] E.C.R. II-309*, Summ. pub., paras 164–165; EGC, Joined Cases T-170/10 and T-340/10 *CTG Luxembourg PSF v Court of Justice* [2011] E.C.R. II-384*, Summ. pub., para. 59; EGC, Case T-377/07 *Evropaïki Dynamiki v Commission* [2011] E.C.R. II-442*, Summ. pub., para. 122.

[56] See EGC, Case T-291/04 *Enviro Tech Europe and Enviro Tech International v Commission* [2011] E.C.R. II-8281, para 137–138 (appeal dismissed in ECJ (order of 24 January 2013), Case C-118/12 P *Enviro Tech Europe v Commission*, not reported). But compare ECJ (judgment of 19 April 2012), Case C-221/10 P *Artegodan v Commission*, not reported, paras 86–94.

[57] The action for damages has been given particular focus within the context of the EU system of judicial protection and judicial review before the Union courts: see, e.g. K. Gutman, 'The Evolution of the Action for Damages Against the European Union and Its Place in the System of Judicial Protection' (2011) 48 C.M.L. Rev. 695–750, at 706–7.

[58] See, e.g. ECJ, Case C-131/03 *Reynolds Tobacco and Others v Commission* [2006] E.C.R. I-779, paras 82–84; ECJ (order of 28 June 2011), Case C-93/11 P *Verein Deutsche Sprache v Council* [2011] E.C.R. I-92*, Summ. pub., para. 30; CFI (order of 12 January 2007), Case T-447/05 *SPM v Commission* [2007] E.C.R. II-1, para. 83; CFI, Case T-279/02 *Degussa v Commission* [2006] E.C.R. II-897, para. 424 (appeal dismissed in ECJ, Case C-266/06 P *Evonik Degussa v Commission and Council* [2008] E.C.R. I-81*, Summ. pub.); CFI, Joined Cases T-172 and T-175 to T-177/98 *Salamander and Others v European Parliament and Council* [2000] E.C.R. II-2487, para. 77 (undisturbed by separate orders of 23 October 2001 in Case C-281/00 P and in Case C-313/00 P). See also, in the context of a staff dispute, EGC (judgment of 20 May 2010), Case T-261/09 P *Commission v Violetti and Others*, not reported, para. 69 (and citations therein).

[59] ECJ, Case C-131/03 *Reynolds Tobacco and Others v Commission*, para. 83; see also Opinion of Advocate-General E. Sharpston in ECJ, Case C-131/03 *Reynolds Tobacco and Others v Commission* [2006] E.C.R. I-779, points 73–76.

[60] ECJ, Case 118/83 *CMC v Commission* [1985] E.C.R. 2325, para. 31.

There is no requirement as to the applicant's nationality in the case of such an action.[61]

(a) Interest must be shown

11.14 Under settled case-law, a natural or legal person has the right to bring an action for damages against the Union only where that person is able to assert in law either a particular interest of his or her own or a right to compensation which has been assigned to him or her by others; otherwise, the applicant has not established that he or she has any interest in bringing proceedings and the action for damages fails.[62]

(b) Injury must be personal

11.15 The injury for which the applicant seeks reparation must affect his or her own personal assets.[63] Legal persons (including trade associations) in particular must show that the damage sustained affected their own separate assets and not (exclusively) the personal assets of their members.[64] They may also not claim compensation for the collective damage suffered by their members.[65]

(c) Assignment

11.16 Nevertheless, a person who suffers injury may assign his or her right, which was infringed, together with his or her claim to damages, to another person who will consequently be entitled to bring an action by subrogation.[66] Once the injured party has assigned his or her

---

[61] For some recent examples, see, e.g. ECJ, Case C-39/09 P *SPM v Council and Commission* [2010] E.C.R. I-38*, Summ. pub.; EGC (order of 6 September 2011), Case T-292/09 *Mugraby v Council and Commission* [2011] E.C.R. II-255*, Summ. pub. (appeal dismissed in ECJ (order of 12 July 2012), Case C-581/11 P *Mugraby v Council and Commission*, not reported); EGC, Case T-107/08 *Transnational Company 'Kazchrome' AO and ENRC Marketing v Council and Commission* [2011] E.C.R. II-8051.

[62] See, e.g. CFI (order of 1 December 2008), Case T-219/08 *İşçi Partisi (Turkish Labour Party) v Commission*, not reported; EGC (order of 17 December 2009), Case T-223/09 *İşçi Partisi (Turkish Labour Party) v Commission*, not reported (with further citations therein). In a recent action for damages brought pursuant to Art. 268 TFEU and the second para. of Art. 340 TFEU arising out of the rejection of a public tender contract, the Commission asserted that since the applicant was not a tenderer but a proposed sub-contractor, it had no direct interest in obtaining the contract, and hence it lacked standing; the General Court did not expressly deal with these arguments, finding certain claims of the action inadmissible on grounds of expiry of the limitation period: see EGC (judgment of 28 September 2010), Case T-247/08 *C-Content v Commission*, not reported, paras 50–51.

[63] See, e.g. EGC (order of 17 December 2009), Case T-223/09 *İşçi Partisi (Turkish Labour Party) v Commission*, not reported, para. 12 (and further citations therein) (underscoring that an interest in seeing that the person who suffered damage obtains compensation is not sufficient to establish a particular interest within the meaning of the case-law).

[64] ECJ, Case 114/83 *Société d'Initiatives et de Coopération Agricoles v Commission* [1984] E.C.R. 2589, paras 3–5; ECJ, Case 289/83 *GAARM v Commission* [1984] E.C.R. 4295, paras 4–5; CFI, Joined Cases T-481 and T-484/93 *Exporteurs in Levende Varkens and Others v Commission* [1995] E.C.R. II-2941, para. 76; CFI, Case T-149/96 *Coldiretti and Others v Council and Commission* [1998] E.C.R. II-3841, paras 57–60; CFI (order of 2 July 2004), Case T-9/03 *Coldiretti and Others v Commission*, not reported, para. 47; CFI, Case T-304/01 *Abad Pérez and Others v Council and Commission* [2006] E.C.R. II-4857, paras 52–55. Compare, e.g. CFI, Case T-444/07 *CPEM v Commission* [2009] E.C.R. II-2121, paras 39–40 (application for damages brought on behalf of applicant's staff rejected as inadmissible on the grounds of absence of any interest in bringing proceedings under circumstances where the applicant neither indicated nor proved that it was authorized by its staff to bring an action for damages in their name).

[65] ECJ, Case 72/74 *Union Syndicale and Others v Council* [1975] E.C.R. 401, para. 21.

[66] See, e.g. ECJ, Case 238/78 *Ireks-Arkady v Council and Commission* [1979] E.C.R. 2955, para. 5; ECJ, Joined Cases 256/80 to 257/80, 265/80, 267/80, 5/81, 51/81, and 282/82 *Birra Würrer and Others v Council and Commission* [1984] E.C.R. 3693, para. 12; CFI (order of 2 July 2004), Case T-9/03 *Coldiretti and Others v Commission*, not reported, para. 47; EGC (order of 17 December 2009), Case T-223/09 *İşçi Partisi (Turkish Labour Party) v Commission*, not reported, para. 13 (and further citations therein).

claim, that party ceases to have the right to bring an action.[67] If the assignment is of a fraudulent nature—if the assignor and/or the assignee does not act in good faith—it may not be relied upon as against the defendant.[68]

(2) Member States

Art. 268 TFEU and the second paragraph of Art. 340 TFEU do not preclude Member **11.17** States from bringing an action for damages. To date, no Member State has done so, and hence there is no case-law concerning the conditions that such an action has to satisfy.

B. Defendants

(1) General

(a) Overview

The Union may incur non-contractual liability under the second paragraph of Art. 340 TFEU **11.18** as a result of damage caused by its institutions (see para. 11.20) or by its servants in the performance of their duties (see paras 11.11–11.23). Union liability may also arise in conjunction with liability on the part of the Member States (see paras 11.24–11.32). However, the Union cannot incur non-contractual liability for an act of primary Union law (such as amendments to the Treaties), since such an act cannot be imputed to a Union institution.[69]

Similarly, acts or conduct of the Member States,[70] of institutions outside the Union (such as the Council of Europe[71] or the European Court of Human Rights[72]) or of natural and legal persons[73] cannot cause the Union to incur non-contractual liability.

---

[67] ECJ, Joined Cases 256/80 to 257/80, 265/80, 267/80, 5/81, 51/81, and 282/82 *Birra Wührer and Others v Council and Commission*, para. 7.

[68] ECJ, Case 250/78 *DEKA v EEC* [1983] E.C.R. 421.

[69] ECJ, Case 169/73 *Compagnie Continentale v Council* [1975] E.C.R. 117, para. 16; ECJ, Joined Cases 31/86 and 35/86 *LAISA and Others v Council* [1988] E.C.R. 2285, paras 19–22; ECJ (order of 8 July 1999), Case C-95/98 P *Edouard Dubois and Fils v Council and Commission* [1999] E.C.R. I-4835; CFI, Case T-113/96 *Edouard Dubois and Fils v Council and Commission* [1998] E.C.R. II-125, para. 47; CFI (order of 26 June 2000), Joined Cases T-12/98 and T-13/98 *Argon and Others v Council and Commission* [2000] E.C.R. II-2473. The adoption (signature and ratification) of the Single European Act (or of any other Treaty amending the original EC Treaty) is an act of the Member States and cannot be imputed to the Union: CFI (order of 15 June 2000), Case T-614/97 *Aduanas Pujol Rubio and Others v Council and Commission* [2000] E.C.R. II-2387. But see ECJ (judgment of 27 November 2012), Case C-370/12 *Pringle*, not reported, paras 30–37, where a Treaty amendment was adopted by the European Council under a simplified revision procedure laid down in Art. 48(6) TEU.

[70] For some recent examples, see ECJ (order of 5 February 2010), Case C-361/09 P *Molder v Germany* [2010] E.C.R. I-18*, Summ. pub.; ECJ (order of 4 March 2010), Case C-374/09 P *Hârsulescu v Romania* [2010] E.C.R. I-30*, Summ. pub.; EGC (order of 25 March 2011), Case T-15/10 *Noko Ngele v Commission and Others* [2011] E.C.R. II-77*, Summ. pub., paras 40–41 (and citations therein) (appeal dismissed in ECJ (order of 4 October 2011), Case C-272/11 P *Noko Ngele v Commission and Others* [2011] E.C.R. I-145*, Summ. pub.); EGC (order of 30 June 2011), Case T-222/11 *West Indies Pack v France*, not reported; EGC (order of 12 July 2011), Case T-172/11 *Polak v Austria and Austrian Constitutional Court*, not reported; EGC (order of 25 October 2011), Case T-472/11 *DME Die Marketing Agentur and Hofmann v Austria*, not reported; EGC (order of 31 January 2012), Case T-547/11 *FS Schmidt Vermögensverwaltung und Verlag v The Netherlands*, not reported; EGC (order of 18 January 2012), Case T-609/11 *Pérez Ortega v Spain*, not reported.

[71] See EGC (order of 11 July 2008), Case T-242/08 *Faur v Council of Europe*, not reported.

[72] See EGC (order of 4 April 2011), Case T-133/11 *Fundaţia Pro Fondbis—1946 Semper v European Court of Human Rights*, not reported.

[73] See, e.g. EGC (order of 25 March 2011), Case T-15/10 *Noko Ngele v Commission and Others* [2011] E.C.R. II-77*, Summ. pub., paras 38–39 (and citations therein) (appeal dismissed: ECJ (order of 4 October 2011), Case C-272/11 P *Noko Ngele v Commission and Others* [2011] E.C.R. I-145*, Summ. pub.).

(b) Institution to which the harmful act or conduct is attributable

11.19 Substantively, it is the Union which has to be regarded as being the defendant and not the institutions, since they have no legal personality.[74] Yet, it is the Union institution to which the harmful act is attributable[75] which has to be summoned before the General Court at first instance or the Court of Justice on appeal as representing the Union.[76] The Commission has no general right to represent the Union.[77] It is advisable for the applicant to specify the institution against which its action is brought in its application, even though the Union judicature takes a flexible, non-formalistic approach in this regard.[78] If the damage was allegedly caused by more than one institution, they must all be brought into the proceedings.[79]

(2) Damage caused by institutions

11.20 First, the 'institutions' that may cause the Union to incur liability under the second paragraph of Art. 340 TFEU are those listed in Art. 13(1) TEU: the European Parliament, the European Council, the Council, the Commission, the Court of Justice of the European Union,[80] the

---

[74] ECJ, Case 302/87 *European Parliament v Council* [1988] E.C.R. 5615, para. 9. It does not follow that because an action was brought directly against a Union body, office, or agency that it is inadmissible. Such an action must be deemed to be directed against the Union represented by that body: see, e.g. ECJ, Case 353/88 *Briantex and Di Domenico v Commission* [1989] E.C.R. 3623, para. 7; CFI, Case T-209/00 *Lamberts v European Ombudsman* [2002] E.C.R. II-2203, para. 48.

[75] See, e.g. CFI, Case T-279/03 *Galileo and Others v Commission* [2006] E.C.R. II-1291, para. 129 (and citations therein) (appeal dismissed in ECJ (order of 20 March 2007), Case 325/06 P *Galileo and Others v Commission* [2007] E.C.R. I-44*, Summ. pub.) (including acts or conduct attributable to what is now a Union body: see para. 11.20). See further para. 11.80.

[76] ECJ, Joined Cases 63/72 to 69/72 *Werhahn Hansamühle and Others v Council* [1973] E.C.R. 1229, para. 7; see also Opinion of Advocate-General C.O. Lenz in ECJ, Case 62/83 *Eximo v Commission* [1984] E.C.R. 2295, at 2317–18 ('the correct defendant is that institution to which the action of the Community [now Union] giving rise to liability is to be attributed. An action against the Community [now Union] must accordingly in principle be directed against those institutions which in the applicant's view have caused the damage') (citations omitted).

[77] Art. 335 TFEU is concerned only with the Union's power to act and its representation in the various Member States.

[78] ECJ, Case 106/81 *Kind v EEC* [1982] E.C.R. 2885; compare, e.g. ECJ, Joined Cases 63/72 to 69/72 *Werhahn Hansamuhle and Others v Council* [1973] E.C.R. 1229, para. 8; CFI, Case T-246/93 *Bühring v Council and Commission* [1998] E.C.R. II-171, para. 26, in which the defendant institutions argued that the application was inadmissible on the grounds that it designated the Council and the Commission as defendants and not the Union (then Community). The Court of First Instance held that this could not render the application inadmissible where it did not affect the rights of the defence; CFI, Case T-364/03 *Medici Grimm v Council* [2006] E.C.R. II-79, para. 47 (and citations therein), in which the Court of First Instance noted as a preliminary point that although the action was formally brought against the Council and not against the Union, under settled case-law, the fact of bringing, against the institution itself, an action seeking, to establish the non-contractual liability of the Union on account of damage allegedly caused by an institution cannot render the application inadmissible; such an application must be deemed to be directed against the Union represented by that institution.

[79] Conversely, where an applicant directs its action against several institutions, but the act or conduct forming the basis for the action cannot be attributed to one of those institutions, the Union judicature will find the action inadmissible insofar as it is directed at that institution: see, e.g. CFI, Case T-128/05 *SPM v Council and Commission* [2008] E.C.R. II-260*, Summ. pub., para. 61 (appeal dismissed in ECJ (order of 22 March 2010), Case C-39/09 P *SPM v Council and Commission* [2010] E.C.R. I-38*, Summ. pub.).

[80] The failure on the part of the General Court to adjudicate a case within a reasonable time may give rise to an action for damages against the Union pursuant to Art. 268 TFEU and the second para. of Art. 340 TFEU: see ECJ, Case C-385/07 P *Der Grüne Punkt—Duales System Deutschland v Commission* [2009] E.C.R. I-6155, para. 195. See also ECJ (judgment of 26 November 2013), Case C-40/12 P *Gascogne Sack Deutschland v Commission*, not reported, paras 89–96; ECJ (judgment of 26 November 2013), Case C-50/12 P *Kendrion v Commission*, not reported, paras 94–101; ECJ (judgment of 26 November 2013), Case C-58/12 P *Groupe*

European Central Bank, and the Court of Auditors. Under the former Treaty framework, the European Council had been excluded on the grounds that only the act or conduct of a Community institution per Art. 7(1) EC[81] could give rise to non-contractual liability of the then European Community.[82] However, with the changes brought by the Lisbon Treaty, an action for damages may be brought in relation to acts or conduct on the part of the European Council, although to the extent that it is a primary actor (alongside the Council) in the field of the Common Foreign and Security Policy (CFSP), its acts or conduct in this field in principle fall outside the jurisdiction of the Union courts under the Treaties.[83]

As far as the European Central Bank is concerned, it has also been elevated to an 'official' Union institution under Art. 13(1) TEU as compared to former Art. 7(1) EC,[84] but its non-contractual liability is governed by the third paragraph of Art. 340 TFEU. As already mentioned (see para. 11.02), certain adjustments were made to Art. 268 TFEU and the third paragraph of Art. 340 TFEU with the entry into force of the Lisbon Treaty. Under the former EC Treaty, the third paragraph of Art. 288 EC provided that the Community

---

Gascogne v Commission, not reported, paras 83–90. To date, no compensation on this basis has been granted. In that regard, the reasonableness of a period must be appraised in the light of the circumstances specific to each case and, in particular, the importance of the case for the person concerned, its complexity and the conduct of the applicant and of the competent authorities: see, e.g. ECJ, Joined Cases C-403/04 P and C-405/04 P *Sumitomo Metal Industries Ltd and Nippon Steel Corp. v Commission* [2007] E.C.R. I-729, paras 116–117 (finding duration of procedure justified: paras 118–123); ECJ, Joined Cases C-120/06 P and C-121/06 P *FIAMM and Others v Council and Commission* [2008] E.C.R. I-6513, para. 212 (and citations therein) (finding duration of the period justified: paras 213–214). Moreover, where there is no indication that the length of the proceedings affected their outcome in any way, a plea that the proceedings before the General Court did not satisfy the requirements concerning completion within a reasonable time cannot as a general rule lead to the setting aside of the judgment delivered by that Court, and must therefore be declared inadmissible: see, e.g. ECJ, Case C-583/08 P *Gogos v Commission* [2010] E.C.R. I-4469, paras 56–59. See further ECJ, Joined Cases C-120/06 P and C-121/06 P *FIAMM and Others v Council and Commission* [2008] E.C.R. I-6513, paras 203–211: in the context of an appeal challenging a judgment of the General Court dismissing an action for damages against the Union, the setting aside of such a judgment cannot lead to the grant of reasonable satisfaction for the excessive duration of the proceedings before the General Court, since in such proceedings, the General Court is not, in any event any more than the Court of Justice on appeal, called upon to order the applicants to pay a sum from which that reasonable satisfaction could, where appropriate, be subtracted. The Court of Justice thus held that the applicants' claim seeking reasonable satisfaction for the allegedly excessive duration of the proceedings before the General Court must be dismissed as inadmissible. However, when the General Court or the Court of Justice exercises its unlimited jurisdiction pursuant to Art. 261 TFEU, it can reduce a fine imposed by the Commission on the applicant undertaking for infringement of the competition rules, as a means of immediate compensation for the excessive duration of proceedings before the General Court: ECJ, Case C-185/95 P *Baustahlgewebe v Commission* [1998] E.C.R. I-8417, paras 47, 48, and 141; ECJ, Joined Cases C-120/06 P and C-121/06 P *FIAMM and Others v Council and Commission* [2008] E.C.R. I-6513, paras 206–208; EGC (judgment of 5 June 2012), Case T-214/06 *Imperial Chemical Industries v Commission*, not reported, paras 278–291; Opinion of Advocate-General E. Sharpston of 30 May 2013 in Case C-58/12 P *Groupe Gascogne v Commission*, not reported, points 70–150; see further ch. 16. It is, however, apparent from the *Gascogne* and *Kendrion* judgments that the Court of Justice has reconsidered its *Baustahlgewebe* case-law: see ECJ, Case C-40/12 P *Gascogne Sack Deutschland v Commission*, paras 88–89; ECJ, Case C-50/12 P *Kendrion v Commission*, paras 93-94; ECJ, Case C-58/12 P *Groupe Gascogne v Commission*, paras 82–83.

[81] Former Art. 7(1) EC had listed the following five institutions: the European Parliament, the Council, the Commission, the Court of Justice, and the Court of Auditors.

[82] CFI (order of 17 December 2003), Case T-346/03 *Krikorian and Others v European Parliament and Others* [2003] E.C.R. II-6037, para. 17 (appeal dismissed in ECJ (order of 29 October 2004), Case C-18/04 P *Krikorian and Others v European Parliament and Others*, not reported).

[83] See para. 11.02.

[84] See n. 81.

was to make good any damage caused by the ECB,[85] even though the ECB has separate legal personality.[86] Accordingly, the wording of the third paragraph of Art. 340 TFEU now stipulates that it is the ECB, and not the Union itself, which is responsible for making good any damage caused by it or by its servants in the performance of their duties.[87] Likewise, as compared to former Art. 235 EC, Art. 268 TFEU provides that the Court of Justice of the European Union has jurisdiction over an action for damages brought against the Union and the ECB under the second and third paragraphs of Art. 340 TFEU, respectively. In any case, the non-contractual liability of the ECB under the third paragraph of Art. 340 TFEU is evaluated under the same conditions as those applicable to the Union under the second paragraph of Art. 340 TFEU.[88]

Second, as had been the case under the former Treaty framework, Union non-contractual liability under Art. 268 TFEU and the second paragraph of Art. 340 TFEU may be incurred on account of acts or conduct committed by Union bodies, offices, or agencies[89] (subject to the limits placed on the Union courts' jurisdiction under the Treaties with respect to the former second pillar of the CFSP and the former third pillar of PJCCM: see para. 11.02), such as the European Investment Bank[90] and the European Ombudsman.[91] This broad interpretation is designed to prevent the Union from escaping possible liability where it acts through bodies, offices, and agencies that are not institutions within the meaning of Art. 13(1) TEU, since national courts have no jurisdiction to find the Union non-contractually liable.

Some Union bodies, offices, and agencies have legal personality. Thus, the Court of Justice or the General Court may hold that these bodies have incurred non-contractual liability pursuant to a specific provision in the measures establishing them.[92] As regards certain 'bodies'

---

[85] The former third para. of Art. 288 EC stated: 'The preceding paragraph shall apply under the same conditions to damage caused by the ECB or by its servants in the performance of their duties.' See CFI (order of 5 September 2007), Case T-295/05 *Document Security Systems, Inc. v ECB* [2007] E.C.R. II-2835, para. 76.

[86] See Art. 282(3) TFEU (ex Art. 107(2) EC). See further EGC, Case T-436/09 *Dufour ECB* [2011] E.C.R. II-7727, para. 188.

[87] The third para. of Art. 340 TFEU states: 'Notwithstanding the second paragraph, the European Central Bank shall, in accordance with the general principles common to the laws of the Member States, make good any damage caused by it or by its servants in the performance of their duties.' This is confirmed in Art. 35.3 of Protocol (No. 4), annexed to the TEU and the TFEU, on the Statute of the European System of Central Banks and of the European Central Bank [2012] O.J. C326/230.

[88] See, e.g. CFI, Joined Cases T-3/00 and T-337/04 *Pitsiorlas v Council and ECB* [2007] E.C.R. II-4779 (appeal dismissed in ECJ (order of 3 July 2008), Case C-84/08 P *Pitsiorlas v Council and ECB* [2008] E.C.R. I-104*, Summ. pub.).

[89] Notwithstanding the extension of Union non-contractual liability to Union bodies, offices, and agencies under the case-law, reference is generally made to a (Union) institution in this chapter for purposes of brevity.

[90] See ECJ, Case C-370/89 *SGEEM and Etroy v EIB* [1992] E.C.R. I-6211, paras 12–16. See also EGC, Case T-461/08 *Evropaïki Dynamiki v EIB* [2011] E.C.R. II-6367.

[91] CFI, Case T-209/00 *Lamberts v European Ombudsman* [2002] E.C.R. II-2203, para. 49: the Court of First Instance declared admissible an action for compensation for the damage that Mr Lamberts allegedly sustained as a result of negligence on the part of the European Ombudsman in the performance of his duties. The judgment was upheld on appeal: ECJ, Case C-234/02 *European Ombudsman v Lamberts* [2004] E.C.R. I-2803. See also CFI, Case T-412/05 *M v European Ombudsman* [2008] E.C.R. II-197*, Summ. pub.

[92] See, e.g. Community [now Union] Plant Variety Office: Art.33(3) and (4) of Council Regulation (EC) No. 2100/94 of 27 July 1994 on Community (now Union) plant variety rights, [1994] O.J. L227/1; European Agency for Cooperation: Art. 18(2), first and second subparas, of Council Regulation (EEC) No. 3245/81 of 26 October 1981 setting up a European Agency for Cooperation, [1981] O.J. L328/1; European Medicines Agency: Art. 72(2) of Regulation (EC) No. 726/2004 of the European Parliament and of the

with legal personality established pursuant to measures falling within the former second and third pillars of the CFSP and PJCCM, different arrangements may be worked out.[93]

Council of 31 March 2004 laying down Community procedures for the authorization and supervision of medicinal products for human and veterinary use and establishing a European Medicines Agency, [2004] O.J. L136/1; European Agency for Safety and Health at Work: Art. 21(2), first and second subparas, of Council Regulation (EC) No. 2062/94 of 18 July 1994 establishing a European Agency for Safety and Health at Work, [1994] O.J. L216/1; European Centre for the Development of Vocational Training: Art. 17(2), first and second subparas, of Council Regulation (EEC) No. 337/75 of 10 February 1975 establishing a European Centre for the Development of Vocational Training, [1975] O.J. L39/1; European Chemicals Agency: Arts 100 and 101 of Regulation (EC) No. 1907/2006 of the European Parliament and of the Council concerning the Registration, Evaluation, Authorisation and Restriction of Chemicals (REACH), establishing a European Chemicals Agency, amending Directive 1999/45/EC and repealing Council Regulation (EEC) No. 793/93 and Commission Regulation (EC) No. 1488/94, as well as Council Directive 76/769/EEC and Commission Directives 91/155/EEC, 93/67/EEC, 93/105/EC, and 2000/21/EC, [2006] O.J. L396/1; European Environment Agency: Art. 18 of Regulation (EC) No. 401/2009 of the European Parliament and of the Council on the European Environment Agency and the European Environment Information and Observation Network (codified version), [2009] O.J. L126/13; European Foundation for the Improvement of Living and Working Conditions: Art. 21(2), first and second subparas, of Council Regulation (EEC) No. 1365/75 of 26 May 1975 on the creation of a European Foundation for the Improvement of Living and Working Conditions, [1975] O.J. L139/1; European Maritime Safety Agency: Art. 8(3)–(4) of Regulation (EC) No. 1406/2002 of the European Parliament and of the Council of 27 June 2002 establishing a European Maritime Safety Agency, [2002] O.J. L208/1; European Monitoring Centre for Drugs and Drug Addiction: Art. 19(2) of Regulation (EC) No. 1920/2006 of the European Parliament and of the Council of 12 December 2006 on the European Monitoring Centre for Drugs and Drugs Addiction (recast), [2006] O.J. L376/1; European Training Foundation: Art. 22(2) of Regulation (EC) No. 1339/2008 of the European Parliament and of the Council of 16 December 2008 establishing a European Training Foundation (recast), [2008] O.J. L354/82; European Union Agency for Fundamental Rights: Art. 27(2) of Council Regulation (EC) No. 168/2007 of 15 February 2007 establishing a European Union Agency for Fundamental Rights, [2007] O.J. L53/1; Office for Harmonisation in the Internal Market (Trade Marks and Designs) (OHIM): Art. 118(3)–(4) of Council Regulation (EC) No. 207/2009 of 26 February 2009 on the Community [now Union] trade mark (codified version), [2009] O.J. L78/1; Translation Centre for Bodies of the European Union: Art. 18(2), first and second subparas, of Council Regulation (EC) No. 2965/94 of 28 November 1994 setting up a Translation Centre for bodies of the European Union, [1994] O.J. L314/1. By contrast, the European Anti-Fraud Office (OLAF), established by Commission Decision 1999/352/EC, ECSC, Euratom of 28 April 1999, [1999] O.J. L136/20, is under the helm of the Commission (see Art. 2(1) of that Decision providing that OLAF 'shall exercise the Commission's powers to carry out external administrative investigations for the purposes of strengthening the fight against fraud, corruption and any other illegal activity adversely affecting the [Union's] financial interests'). Consequently, a claim for compensation in connection with allegedly unlawful acts or conduct committed by OLAF is directed at the Commission for the purposes of an action for damages brought pursuant to Art. 268 TFEU and the second para. of Art. 340 TFEU: see, e.g. CFI, Case T-259/03 *Nikolaou v Commission* [2007] E.C.R. II-99*, Summ. pub.; CFI, Case T-309/03 *Camós Grau v Commission* [2006] E.C.R. II-1173; CFI, Case T-48/05 *Franchet and Vyck v Commission* [2008] E.C.R. II-1585.

[93] With respect to the PJCCM, for example, as regards Europol (Art. 88 TFEU), see Art. 53(2) of Council Decision 2009/371/JHA of 6 April 2009 establishing the European Police Office (Europol), [2009] O.J. L121/37 stating: 'In the case of non-contractual liability, Europol shall be obliged, independently of any liability under Article 52 [concerning liability for unauthorized or incorrect data processing], to make good any damage caused by the fault of its organs, or its staff in the performance of their duties, in so far as it may be imputed to them and regardless of the different procedures for claiming damages which exist under the law of the Member States', and under Art. 53(4), the national courts of the Member States competent to deal with disputes involving Europol's liability as referred to in Art. 53 are to be determined under the Brussels I Regulation (Council Regulation (EC) No. 44/2001 of 22 December 2000 on jurisdiction and the recognition and enforcement of judgments in civil and commercial matters, [2001] O.J. L12/1, from 10 January 2015 replaced by Regulation (EU) No. 1215/2012 of the European Parliament and of the Council of 12 December 2012 on jurisdiction and the recognition and enforcement of judgments in civil and commercial matters, [2012] O.J. L351/1); there are similar provisions with respect to the non-contractual liability of Eurojust (Art. 85 TFEU): see Art. 27c(2), (3) and (5) of Council Decision 2009/426/JHA of 16 December 2008 on the strengthening of Eurojust and amending Decision 2002/187/JHA setting up Eurojust with a view to reinforcing the fight against serious crime, [2009] O.J. L138/14. With respect to the CFSP, for

(3) Damage caused by servants of institutions in the performance of their duties

(a) Acts carried out in performance of the servant's duties

11.21 The Union courts have regarded only a limited class of acts of servants of the institutions as acts carried out 'in the performance of their duties' which are potentially capable of causing the Union to incur liability for the purposes of the second paragraph of Art. 340 TFEU. The Union may be held liable only for damage caused by acts that are the 'necessary extension' of the tasks entrusted to the institution to which the staff member belongs.[94]

For example, under the case-law, where a servant drives his or her own car pursuant to a travel order, this does not satisfy that test, except in the case of *force majeure* or in exceptional circumstances of such overriding importance that the Union would otherwise have been unable to carry out the tasks entrusted to it. A servant who causes a road accident with his or her own car pursuant to a travel order issued by his or her institution therefore does not cause his or her institution to incur liability for the ensuing damage in the absence of *force majeure* or exceptional circumstances.[95]

(b) Other acts

11.22 Servants are liable for acts not performed in pursuance of their duties. They are not immune from legal proceedings in respect of such acts under Art. 11(a) of the Protocol on the Privileges and Immunities of the European Union, since such immunity is limited to 'acts performed by them in their official capacity, including their words spoken or written'.[96]

(c) Immunity of the servant and liability of the Union

11.23 There is no parallel between the possible liability of the Union and the staff member's immunity from legal proceedings.[97] If the staff member's immunity is waived, this does not prevent the unlawful act from causing the Union to incur liability. Consequently, an act which cannot be regarded as having been performed by the staff member in an 'official capacity' within the meaning of Art. 11(a) of the Protocol may nevertheless be deemed an act carried out 'in the performance of his duties' and imputed to the Union. The idea behind this case-law is to avoid the Union getting out of a claim all too easily by simply waiving the immunity of the staff member concerned, which would ultimately result in the injured party's risking coming up against an insolvent debtor—the staff member as

---

example, as regards the European Defence Agency (Arts 42(3) and 45 TEU), there are no provisions concerning its non-contractual liability, as compared to its contractual liability and the personal liability of staff: see Art. 27 of Council Decision 2011/411/CFSP of 12 July 2011 defining the statute, the seat, and operational rules of the European Defence Agency and repealing Joint Action 2004/551/CFSP, [2011] O.J. L183/16.

[94] ECJ, Case 9/69 *Sayag and Others* [1969] E.C.R. 329, para. 7. See, e.g. CFI (order of 26 October 2005), Case T-124/04 *Ouariachi v Commission* [2005] E.C.R. II-4653, paras 18–23 (appeal dismissed in ECJ (order of 20 September 2006), Case C-4/06 P *Ouariachi v Commission* [2006] E.C.R. I-94*, Summ. pub.); CFI, Case T-259/03 *Nikolaou v Commission* [2007] E.C.R. II-99*, Summ. pub., paras 193–199. The staff members concerned are the servants of any 'institution' within the meaning of the second para. of Art. 340 TFEU.

[95] ECJ, Case 9/69 *Sayag and Others* [1969] E.C.R. 329, paras 8–13. Note that this judgment refers to Art.151 and the second para. of Art. 188 of the EAEC Treaty, the provisions corresponding to Art. 268 TFEU and the second para. of Art. 340 TFEU, although as discussed earlier, Art. 151 of the EAEC Treaty has now been repealed and replaced by Art. 268 TFEU: see para. 11.03.

[96] Art. 11(a) of Protocol (No. 7), annexed to the TEU, the TFEU, and the EAEC Treaty, on the Privileges and Immunities of the European Union, [2012] O.J. C326/266.

[97] ECJ, Case 5/68 *Sayag and Others* [1968] E.C.R. 395, at 402.

opposed to the Union. As a result, concurrent claims against the Union (before the General Court) and against the staff member himself or herself (before the national courts) are not ruled out either.

(4) Liability concurrent with that of Member States

(a) General

(i) Principle

The Member States make an extensive contribution to the implementation of Union law. **11.24** If they act unlawfully in this connection, this may affect the assets of individuals. First, sometimes the financial loss is exclusively attributable to the Member State's infringing Union law in performing its executive task. Second, the loss may also arise because of the illegality of a Union act which was still regarded as valid at the time when it was implemented by the Member State. Finally, the pecuniary loss may be the result of unlawful joint action on the part of the Union and a Member State.

In principle, the financial loss must be made good by the authority that caused it through its unlawful action. Accordingly, the Union must make good the financial loss caused by its institutions or by servants of its institutions in the performance of their duties, whereas the Member State will be liable for the financial loss caused by national authorities.[98]

(ii) Grounds on which an act may be attributed to the Union or a Member State

Having stated this principle, however, the central question remains as to the grounds on **11.25** which an unlawful act may be attributed to a Union institution or a national authority. The answer determines the extent to which the Union may be held liable for financial loss arising as a result of illegality vitiating the application of a Union measure by a national authority.[99]

The decisive criterion appears to be the respective decision-making powers of the Union and the Member States. For example, in *Mulder*,[100] the Court of Justice held that, on the basis of Union law in force, the Member States did not have the power to carry out the act that individuals had claimed, namely allocation of a milk quota. The refusal to perform the act sought could not therefore be attributed to them. The ensuing financial loss was in fact the result of the illegality of the underlying Union act that had not provided for the grant of

---

[98] ECJ, Case 175/84 *Krohn v Commission* [1986] E.C.R. 753, para. 18; ECJ, Joined Cases 89/86 and 91/86 *L'Étoile Commerciale and CNTA v Commission* [1987] E.C.R. 3005, paras 16–21; ECJ (order of the President of the Court of 17 July 2008), Case C-114/08 P(R) *Pellegrini v Commission* [2008] E.C.R. I-117*, Summ. pub., paras 17–18 (referring to cited case in relation to holding that the damage caused by national institutions must be assessed by national courts, not via an action for damages). The same principle applies in the event of financial loss arising where a non-member country (e.g. an ACP country) and the Union act jointly. The non-member country is liable for the financial loss attributable to its acts and the Union for the loss attributable to its acts: ECJ, Case 118/83 *CMC v Commission* [1985] E.C.R. 2325, para. 31; ECJ, Case 33/82 *Murri Frères v Commission* [1985] E.C.R. 2759, paras 4–8; ECJ, Case 267/82 *Développement and Clemessy v Commission* [1986] E.C.R. 1907, paras 16–17; ECJ, Case C-370/89 *SGEEM and Etroy v EIB* [1993] E.C.R. I-2583, paras 29–31; CFI, Case T-52/99 *T. Port v Commission* [2001] E.C.R. II-981, para. 26; CFI (order of 3 July 2007), Case T-212/02 *Commune de Champagne and Others v Council and Commission* [2007] E.C.R. II-2017, paras 207–213 (as regards alleged damage that the applicants might have suffered in the territory of Switzerland, the conduct was held attributable to the national authorities of that State, for which the General Court lacks jurisdiction; but as regards the damage alleged within the territory of the Union, the requirement of causal link was lacking).
[99] See, e.g. CFI, Case T-177/02 *Malagutti-Vezinhet v Commission* [2004] E.C.R. II-827, paras 26–31.
[100] ECJ, Joined Cases C-104/89 and C-37/90 *Mulder and Others v Council and Commission* [1992] E.C.R. I-3061, para. 9; CFI, Case T-210/00 *Biret & Cie v Council* [2002] E.C.R. II-47, para. 36 (appeal dismissed in ECJ, Case C-94/02 P *Biret & Cie v Council* [2003] E.C.R. I-10565).

milk quota, even though the mere instrumental application of the act was entrusted to the Member States. The conclusion reached was that the loss of earnings had to be made good by the Union.

In *Étoile Commerciale*,[101] in contrast, the Court of Justice considered that the sole cause of the damage was a decision taken by a national authority pursuant to a general obligation imposed upon it by a Union regulation which did not, however, instruct it to take the specific decision that gave rise to the damage. Consequently, the national authority had in fact a genuine discretion in carrying out the general obligation imposed by the Union regulation and hence could have taken a different decision. The financial loss incurred therefore had to be made good by the Member State.[102] Moreover, the underlying Union regulation as a whole was not unlawful.

A Member State that follows an opinion given by the Commission at its request remains liable for any damage that may nevertheless ensue from any infringement of Union law. This is because opinions are not binding and hence do not restrict the Member State's discretion. Such cooperation cannot make the Union liable.[103]

The position will be different only where, acting on the basis of a power conferred on it by Union law, the Commission imposes a requirement or a prohibition on a Member State, which has no choice other than to comply. Although, on the face of it, the financial loss results from the national 'decision', it is really the outcome of the Commission's binding direction. The illegality on which the action for damages is based regards that direction alone and must therefore be attributed to the Commission, making an action for damages admissible.[104]

(iii) Genuine discretion of a Member State

11.26 Consequently, an infringement of Union law committed by a Member State which has a genuine discretion in implementing that law must be distinguished from a merely instrumental application by a Member State of an unlawful Union act where the Member State has no real discretion.

(b) Pecuniary loss resulting from an infringement of Union law by a Member State

11.27 The principle that a Member State will be liable for damage caused to individuals as a result of a breach of Union law for which that State can be held responsible is inherent in the system of the Treaties. A further basis for the obligation of Member States to make good such loss and damage is grounded in the principle of sincere cooperation enshrined in what is now Art. 4(3) TEU, under which the Member States are required to take all appropriate

---

[101] ECJ, Joined Cases 89/86 and 91/86 *L'Étoile Commerciale and CNTA v Commission* [1987] E.C.R. 3005, paras 16–21. See also CFI, Case T-261/94 *Schulte v Council and Commission* [2002] E.C.R. II-441, para. 52.

[102] CFI, T-93/95 *Laga v Commission* [1998] E.C.R. II-195, para. 47; CFI, Case T-94/95 *Landuyt v Commission* [1998] E.C.R. II-213, para. 47; see also CFI, Case T-146/01 *DLD Trading v Council* [2003] E.C.R. II-6005, paras 80–82 and 91–97: after pointing out that the Member State had a genuine discretion in implementing the Union legislation in issue, the Court of First Instance held that there was no direct causal link between the Council's conduct and the damage allegedly sustained by the applicant.

[103] See, e.g. ECJ, Case 133/79 *Sucrimex v Commission* [1980] E.C.R. 1299, para. 22; ECJ, Case 217/81 *Interagra v Commission* [1982] E.C.R. 2233, paras 8–9; CFI, Case T-54/96 *Oleifici Italiani and Fratelli Rubino Industrie Olearie v Commission* [1998] E.C.R. II-3377, paras 66–67; CFI (order of 8 September 2006), Case T-92/06 *Lademporiki and Apostolos Parousis & Sia v Commission* [2006] E.C.R. II-66*, Summ. pub., paras 26–27; CFI, Case T-212/06 *Bowland Dairy Products v Commission* [2009] E.C.R. II-4073, paras 41–43.

[104] ECJ, Case 175/84 *Krohn v Commission* [1986] E.C.R. 753, paras 19–23.

measures, whether general or particular, to ensure fulfilment of their obligations under Union law. Among these is the obligation to nullify the unlawful consequences of a breach of Union law.[105]

For those reasons, the Court of Justice has held that 'it is a principle of [Union] law that the Member States are obliged to make good loss and damage caused to individuals by breaches of [Union] law for which they can be held responsible'.[106] The action for damages against a Member State must be brought in the national courts.[107] The conditions on which a Member State's liability under Union law will give rise to a right to damages are to be determined by national law, unless they have already been prescribed by Union law.[108] The applicable national law must result in effective legal redress and the rules on liability for loss or damage ensuing from breaches of Union law must be at least equivalent to the rules governing liability for loss or damage resulting from breaches of domestic law (see paras 4.46–4.52).

Obviously, the Union cannot incur liability for damage resulting from breaches of Union law that are attributable exclusively to a Member State.[109]

(c) Pecuniary loss resulting from the unlawfulness of the Union measure implemented

(i) Claim before the national court secures full compensation

Where a Member State carries out an allegedly unlawful Union act,[110] an action for **11.28** damages brought pursuant to Art. 268 TFEU and the second paragraph of Art. 340 TFEU will be inadmissible where the alleged damage can be made good by bringing a claim before the national courts. The Court of Justice has described the circumstances in which this is most likely to occur as follows: 'Where an individual considers that he has been injured by the application of a [Union] legislative measure that he considers illegal, he may, when the implementation of the measure is left to the national authorities, contest the

---

[105] ECJ, Joined Cases C-6/90 and C-9/90 *Francovich and Others* [1991] E.C.R. I-5357, paras 35–36.

[106] ECJ, Joined Cases C-6/90 and C-9/90 *Francovich and Others*, para. 37.

[107] ECJ (order of 23 May 1990), Case C-72/90 *Asia Motor France v Commission* [1990] E.C.R. I-2181, paras 14–15.

[108] For the procedural conditions, see ECJ, Joined Cases C-6/90 and C-9/90 *Francovich and Others* [1991] E.C.R. I-5357, para. 42; the basic conditions 'depend on the nature of the breach of [Union] law giving rise to the loss and damage', ECJ, Joined Cases C-6/90 and C-9/90 *Francovich and Others*, para. 38, and the Court of Justice has specified them accordingly. They are designed to secure the full effect of the principle of State liability and hence the applicable national law must always satisfy them, cf. ECJ, Case 101/78 *Granaria* [1979] E.C.R. 623, paras 12–14.

[109] The Commission's failure to bring an action under Art. 258 TFEU against a Member State for failure to fulfil obligations under Union law cannot cause the Union to incur liability. Liability attaches only to the Member State: see, e.g. ECJ (order of 23 May 1990), Case C-72/90 *Asia Motor France v Commission* [1990] E.C.R. I-2181, para. 13; CFI (order of 10 April 2000), Case T-361/99 *Meyer v Commission* [2000] E.C.R. II-2031, para. 13; CFI (order of 26 November 2001), Case T-248/01 *Papoulakos v Italy and Commission*, not reported, para. 27 (appeal dismissed in ECJ (order of 2 February 2006), Case C-215/05 P *Papoulakos v Italy and Commission* [2006] E.C.R. I-18*, Summ. pub.); CFI, Case T-209/00 *Lamberts v European Ombudsman* [2002] E.C.R. II-2203, para. 53; CFI (order of 14 January 2004), Case T-202/02 *Makedoniko Metro and Michaniki v Commission* [2004] E.C.R. II-181, paras 42–47; CFI (order of 8 September 2006), Case T-92/06 *Lademporiki and Apostolos Parousis & Sia v Commission* [2006] E.C.R. II-66*, Summ. pub., paras 29–30; CFI (order of 7 September 2009), Case T-186/08 *LPN v Commission* [2009] E.C.R. II-136*, Summ. pub., paras 65–66; EGC (order of 15 July 2011), Case T-185/11 *Smanor v Commission and European Ombudsman*, not reported, para.16 (appeal dismissed in ECJ (order of 1 March 2012), Case C-474/11 P *Smanor v Commission and Mediator*, not reported).

[110] If the Union act has already been annulled or declared invalid at the time when it is implemented by the Member State, the latter will be guilty of a breach of Union law and the question of compensation for any pecuniary loss will be dealt with in accordance with para. 11.27).

validity of the measure, when it is implemented, before a national court in an action against the national authorities. That court may, or even must, as provided for in Art. 267 TFEU, refer the question of the validity of the Union measure in dispute to the Court of Justice.'[111] This means that, in order to decide on the admissibility of an action for damages brought before it, the General Court has to consider whether bringing a claim before the national courts would be capable of securing full compensation for the alleged damage. This will depend first on the type of pecuniary loss that purportedly constitutes the damage, together with the possibility that the declaration of the invalidity of the Union act in question by preliminary ruling will constitute a direct basis for the national courts to remedy the pecuniary loss suffered. This has to be considered in the light of the particular circumstances of the case concerned. Only if, on account of the type of the alleged damage or of the limited extent of the consequences of any declaration of invalidity by way of preliminary ruling, compensation cannot be obtained from the national courts, will an action for damages lie against the Union institution from which the act implemented by the Member State originated.[112]

(ii) Undue payment to a national authority

11.29 First, it may be that the pecuniary loss simply stems from a payment that the individual concerned made to a national authority pursuant to what he or she considers to be an unlawful Union act. In order to recover the undue amount paid over, together with the applicable interest at the legal rate, the individual concerned must apply to the national courts.[113] Union law obliges the Member States to provide for legal proceedings enabling undue amounts paid to be recovered.[114] The national courts have no jurisdiction themselves to declare that the Union act on the basis of which payment was made is invalid, but if they consider that there are grounds for doubting whether the act is lawful, they must make a reference to the Court of Justice for a preliminary ruling on its validity.[115] If the Court of Justice declares the Union act at issue invalid, it provides the national court in principle with a sufficient basis for ordering restitution of the undue amount. Hence, it is

---

[111] ECJ, Case 281/82 *Unifrex v Commission and Council* [1984] E.C.R. 1969, para. 11; see also ECJ, Case 175/84 *Krohn v Commission* [1986] E.C.R. 753, para. 27; ECJ, Case 81/86 *De Boer Buizen v Council and Commission* [1987] E.C.R. 3677, para. 9.

[112] CFI, Case T-166/98 *Cantina sociale di Dolianova and Others v Commission* [2004] E.C.R. II-3991, paras 115–116 (appeal dismissed on other grounds: ECJ, Case C-51/05 P *Commission v Cantina sociale di Dolianova and Others* [2008] E.C.R. I-5341). See further CFI, Case T-138/03 *É.R. and Others v Council and Commission* [2006] E.C.R. II-4923, paras 38, 40–41 (and citations therein) (finding remedies available under national law could not automatically guarantee effective judicial protection of the applicants' rights in present proceedings, i.e. compensation for all the damage alleged by them, since compensation for the damage alleged cannot be obtained even in part through the annulment of one or more specific measures of a national authority) (appeal dismissed on other grounds: ECJ (order of 4 October 2007), Case C-100/07 P *É.R. and Others v Council and Commission* [2007] E.C.R. I-136*, Summ. pub.)

[113] ECJ, Case 26/74 *Roquette Frères v Commission* [1976] E.C.R. 677, paras 11–12. See also ECJ, Case 96/71 *Haegeman v Commission* [1972] E.C.R. 1005, paras 15–16, and Regulation (EC) No. 450/2008 of the European Parliament and of the Council of 23 April 2008 laying down the Community Customs Code (Modernised Customs Code), [2008] O.J. L145/1, in connection with the recovery of overpaid import and export levies. As regards a claim for the repayment of anti-dumping duties (which an applicant alleges to have wrongfully paid to the national authorities), it too falls within the jurisdiction of the national courts: see CFI, Case T-429/04 *Trubowest Handel and Makarov v Council and Commission* [2008] E.C.R. II-128*, Summ. pub., paras 41–74 (and citations therein) (upheld on appeal: ECJ, Case C-419/08 P *Trubowest and Makarov v Council and Commission* [2010] E.C.R. I-2259, paras 20–26); CFI (order of 5 February 2007), Case T-91/05 *Sinara Handle v Council and Commission* [2007] E.C.R. II-245, para. 64.

[114] See paras 4.21 *et seq.*

[115] ECJ, Case 314/85 *Foto-Frost* [1987] E.C.R. 4199; see also paras 3.59 to 3.61.

not possible to bring an action for damages under Art. 268 TFEU and the second paragraph of Art. 340 TFEU in respect of this kind of pecuniary loss.[116] An action for damages under those provisions will lie only in the exceptional case where the Court of Justice limits the effects as regards the past of a preliminary ruling declaring an act invalid. In such case, the national court cannot order restitution of the undue payment. Since in such a case compensation for the alleged damage cannot be secured by bringing proceedings in the national courts, an action for damages may unquestionably be brought in the General Court against the institution in which the act in question originated.[117]

(iii) National authority's unlawful refusal to effect a payment or to perform an act

Second, the pecuniary loss may possibly be caused by a national authority's refusal to effect a **11.30** payment or to perform some other act, whereby the individual concerned takes the view that the refusal is based on an unlawful Union act. Insofar as individuals seek only reparation for the pecuniary loss resulting from the refusal, namely payment of what they maintain they are owed, or adoption of the act to which they consider they are entitled (i.e. compensation in kind), the only question arising in principle is whether the declaration by preliminary ruling of the Court of Justice that the Union act on which the refusal is based is invalid affords in itself the legal basis needed by the national court for ordering the payment requested or, as the case may be, the adoption of the act requested. If the answer to that question is in the affirmative, an action for damages brought in the General Court against the institution from which the act originated will be inadmissible.[118] If, in contrast, the answer to that question is in the negative, such an action for damages will be admissible.[119]

It should not come as a surprise in the light of the above that the admissibility of an action for damages should turn on a close analysis of the individual case. A degree of unpredictability of the outcome is therefore inevitable. For example, the importance of the time factor should not be underestimated. Even if a declaration of invalidity in preliminary ruling proceedings results in the national court's annulling the refusal to adopt the act

---

[116] Naturally, this does not mean that the Union does not have to bear the financial burden of repayment. Repayment occurs as a result of a preliminary ruling by the Court of Justice declaring the Union act in question invalid, which is binding on all Union institutions.

[117] ECJ, Case 20/88 *Roquette Frères v Commission* [1989] E.C.R. 1553, paras 18–20.

[118] For examples, see ECJ, Case 99/74 *Société des Grands Moulins des Antilles v Commission* [1975] E.C.R. 1531; ECJ, Case 12/79 *Hans-Otto Wagner v Commission* [1979] E.C.R. 3657, paras 11–14; ECJ, Case C-119/88 *AERPO and Others v Commission* [1990] E.C.R. I-2189, paras 12–14.

[119] The examples in the case-law are generally concerned with cases in which the Union act was unlawful because it exhibited a lacuna which could be filled only by the necessary political decisions; on the basis of the mere finding that the act is invalid, the national court cannot order compensation to be paid for the 'alleged damage', and hence the injured party will be entitled to bring proceedings in the Union courts: see, e.g. ECJ, Joined Cases 9/71 and 11/71 *Compagnie d'Approvisionnement, de Transport et de Crédit and Others v Commission* [1972] E.C.R. 391; ECJ, Case 43/72 *Merkur Aussenhandels v Commission* [1973] E.C.R. 1055; ECJ, Case 153/73 *Holtz & Willemsen v Council and Commission* [1974] E.C.R. 675; ECJ, Case 281/82 *Unifrex v Council and Commission* [1984] E.C.R. 1969, para. 12; ECJ, Case 81/86 *De Boer Buizen v Council and Commission* [1987] E.C.R. 3677, para. 10; CFI, Case T-166/98 *Cantina sociale di Dolianova and Others v Commission* [2004] E.C.R. II-3991, paras 112–113 and 115–116 (appealed on other grounds: ECJ, Case C-51/05 P *Commission v Cantina sociale di Dolianova and Others* [2008] E.C.R. I-5341). More exceptionally, the Court itself will limit the effects of the declaration of invalidity by way of preliminary ruling, with the result that this ruling no longer constitutes a legal basis justifying the national court ordering reparation of the financial loss: see ECJ, Case 238/78 *Ireks-Arkady v Council and Commission* [1979] E.C.R. 2955, para. 6; ECJ, Joined Cases 241/78 to 242/78, 245/78 to 250/78 *DGV v Council and Commission* [1979] E.C.R. 3017, para. 6; ECJ, Joined Cases 261/78 and 262/78 *Interquell Stärke-Chemie and Diamalt v Council and Commission* [1979] E.C.R. 3045, para. 6.

requested (for example, the grant of import licences), the loss of a number of years can no longer be made good. Consequently, an action for damages brought against the Union institution from which the act declared invalid originated will be admissible.[120]

(iv) Actual injury

11.31 Third, the pecuniary loss may take the form of actual 'injury', possibly alongside the financial loss resulting from an undue payment or from the fact that a payment or an act was unlawfully withheld. Examples include an undertaking becoming the subject of insolvency proceedings, a weakening of the undertaking's competitive position, or the price of having to obtain credit at short notice. Compensation for such injury may be obtained only by bringing an action for damages in the Union courts.[121]

The General Court and the Court of Justice have exclusive jurisdiction to find the Union liable to make good actual injury pursuant to an action brought under Art. 268 TFEU and the second paragraph of Art. 340 TFEU.[122] If the Union judicature finds that the illegality of the Union measure at issue does not cause the Union to incur liability because the relevant requirements are not satisfied, that finding makes it impossible to bring a claim before the national courts for a declaration that the Member State which implemented that provision is liable on account of the same illegality.[123] The judgment of the Union judicature does not preclude 'an action on grounds other than the unlawfulness of the [Union] measure in issue in that judgment brought against the competent national authorities for damage caused to individuals by the national authorities, even where they were acting within the framework of [Union] law'.[124]

(d) Pecuniary loss resulting from unlawful joint action on the part of the Union and a Member State

11.32 The Union and a Member State act jointly where they both contribute to the adoption of a measure through the exercise of their own discretion. An example is where Member States adopt protective measures with the agreement of the Union.[125] If such action is unlawful, here again a distinction has to be drawn between the three types of pecuniary loss mentioned above (see paras 11.29–11.31). As far as the first two types of pecuniary loss are concerned (that is to say recovery of an undue payment or a claim for a payment or for an act which was wrongfully refused), proceedings must in principle be brought before the national courts.[126] In contrast, where actual 'injury' is involved, although an action brought against the Union will be admissible before national remedies have been exhausted, the extent of the Union's liability will not be determined until the national courts have determined the proportion of the liability to be borne by the Member State under national law. The Court of

---

[120] ECJ, Case 62/83 *Eximo v Commission* [1984] E.C.R. 2295, paras 15–17; ECJ, Case 175/84 *Krohn v Commission* [1986] E.C.R. 753, paras 27–28.

[121] For examples, see ECJ, Case 26/74 *Roquette Frères v Commission* [1976] E.C.R. 677, paras 15–25; ECJ, Joined Cases 116/77 and 124/77 *Amylum and Others v Council and Commission* [1979] E.C.R. 3479, para. 9; CFI, Case T-167/94 *Nölle v Council and Commission* [1995] E.C.R. II-2589, paras 41–42.

[122] ECJ, Case 101/78 *Granaria* [1979] E.C.R. 623, para. 10.

[123] ECJ, Joined Cases 106/87 to 120/87 *Asteris and Others v Greece and EEC* [1988] E.C.R. 5515, paras 17–18.

[124] ECJ, Joined Cases 106/87 to 120/87 *Asteris and Others v Greece and EEC*, para. 19.

[125] ECJ, Joined Cases 5/66, 7/66, and 13/66 to 24/66 *Kampffmeyer and Others v Commission* [1967] E.C.R. 245.

[126] ECJ, Joined Cases 5/66, 7/66, and 13/66 to 24/66 *Kampffmeyer and Others v Commission*, at 263–4.

Justice has held in that connection that '[i]t is necessary to avoid the applicants' being insufficiently or excessively compensated for the same damage by the different assessment of two different courts applying different rules of law'.[127]

III. Special Characteristics

A. General

(1) Overview of requirements

Under the current case-law, the incurring of the Union's non-contractual liability on the **11.33** basis of the second paragraph of Art. 340 TFEU depends on the fulfilment of a set of conditions relating to the unlawfulness of the act or conduct on the part of a Union institution or body, the reality of damage, and a (direct) causal link between such act or conduct and the damage alleged (see section B).

There are some additional procedural-type requirements bearing on the admissibility of an action for damages against the Union which include rules concerning the specificity and content of the application (see para. 11.34), the non-premature character of the claim (see para. 11.35) and compliance with the applicable limitation period (see section C).

(2) Application for damages must be sufficiently detailed

Under the first paragraph of Art. 21 of the Statute[128] and Art. 44(1)(c) of the Rules of Procedure **11.34** of the General Court, every application must state the subject-matter of the proceedings and contain a summary of the pleas in law on which the application is based. That statement must be sufficiently clear and precise to enable the defendant to prepare its defence and the Court to rule on the application, if necessary, without any further information.[129] In order to satisfy those requirements, an application seeking compensation for damages pursuant to Art. 268 TFEU and the second paragraph of Art. 340 TFEU must state the evidence from which the unlawful act or conduct alleged against the institution(s) can be identified, the reasons for which the applicant considers there to be a direct causal link between that act or conduct and the damage it claims to have suffered, and the nature and the extent of that damage,[130] failing which

---

[127] ECJ, Joined Cases 5/66, 7/66 and 13/66 to 24/66 *Kampffmeyer and Others v Commission*, at 226. See further CFI, Case T-138/03 *É.R. and Others v Council and Commission* [2006] E.C.R. II-4923, para. 42 (and citations therein) (pointing out in this regard that this question does not concern the admissibility of the action for damages brought before the Union judicature but merely, where relevant, the final decision on the amount of the compensation that it should grant) (appeal dismissed in ECJ (order of 4 October 2007), Case C-100/07 P *É.R. and Others v Council and Commission* [2007] E.C.R. I-136*, Summ. pub.).

[128] Applicable to the General Court by virtue of Art. 53 of the Statute.

[129] See further para. 25.10.

[130] For examples in which these requirements have been declared satisfied, see, e.g. CFI, Case T-138/03 *É.R. and Others v Council and Commission* [2006] E.C.R. II-4923, paras 34–37 (appeal dismissed in ECJ (order of 4 October 2007), Case C-100/07 P *É.R. and Others v Council and Commission* [2007] E.C.R. I-136*, Summ. pub.); CFI, Case T-364/03 *Medici Grimm v Council* [2006] E.C.R. II-79, paras 51–57; CFI, Case T-304/01 *Abad Pérez and Others v Council and Commission* [2006] E.C.R. II-4857, paras 44–46; CFI, Case T-193/04 *Tillack v Commission* [2006] E.C.R. II-3995, paras 89–95; CFI, Case T-360/04 FG *Marine v Commission* [2007] E.C.R. II-92*, Summ. pub., paras 33–39; CFI, Case T-212/03 *MyTravel Group v Commission* [2008] E.C.R. II-1967, paras 100–104; CFI, Case T-128/05 *SPM v Council and Commission* [2008] E.C.R. II-260*, Summ. pub., paras 62–68 (appeal dismissed in ECJ (order of 22 March 2010), Case C-39/09 P *SPM v Council and*

the application for damages[131] (or certain heads of claim therein[132]) will be declared inadmissible.

(3) Premature claim

11.35 Under the case-law, the General Court may reject as premature a claim for damages where it is unable to determine at the time that such claim is brought before it whether the conditions to incur Union non-contractual liability have been made out.[133]

B. Substantive requirements for liability

(1) General

(a) Three conditions

11.36 The classic conditions for Union non-contractual liability—an unlawful Union act or conduct, loss or actual damage, and a causal link between that act and the loss

---

Commission [2010] E.C.R. I-38*, Summ. pub.); CFI, Case T-238/07 *Ristic and Others v Commission* [2009] E.C.R. II-117*, Summ. pub., paras 51–54; EGC, Case T-42/06 *Gollnisch v European Parliament* [2010] E.C.R. II-1135, paras 77–81. For further particulars in relation to rules on sufficient proof of the alleged damage, see further para. 11.75–11.76.

[131] See, e.g. CFI, Case T-369/03 *Arizona Chemical and Others v Commission* [2005] E.C.R. II-5839, para. 124 (upheld on appeal: ECJ (order of 13 March 2007), Case C-150/06 P *Arizona Chemical and Others v Commission* [2007] E.C.R. II-39*, Summ. pub., paras 45–46); CFI, Case T-228/02 *Organisation des Modjahedines du people d'Iran v Council* [2006] E.C.R. II-4665, paras 176–180; CFI (order of 22 April 2008), Case T-395/07 *Balatsoukas v Commission*, not reported; CFI (order of 6 July 2009), Case T-181/09 *Oprea v Commission*, not reported; CFI, Case T-89/07 *VIP Car Solutions v European Parliament* [2009] E.C.R. II-1403, paras 103–108; EGC (order of 10 December 2009), Case T-390/09 *Noko Ngele v Commission*, not reported (appeal dismissed in ECJ (order of 10 March 2011), Case C-525/10 P *Noko Ngele v Commission* [2011] E.C.R. I-24*); EGC (order of 5 January 2010), Case T-71/09 *Química Atlàntica v Commission* [2010] E.C.R. II-1*, Summ. pub., paras 35–40; EGC (order of 6 July 2011), Case T-105/11 *Noko Ngele v Commission*, not reported; EGC, Case T-232/06 *Evropaïki Dynamiki v Commission* [2011] E.C.R. II-263*, Summ. pub., paras 30–32 (appeal dismissed: ECJ (order of 4 October 2012), Case C-597/11 P *Evropaïki Dynamiki v Commission*, not reported); EGC (order of 20 September 2011), Case T-330/10 *M v Commission*, not reported; EGC (order of 24 May 2011), Case T-489/08 *Power-One Italy v Commission* [2011] E.C.R. II-149*, Summ. pub., para. 62; EGC (order of 11 January 2012), Case T-301/11 *Ben Ali v Council*, not reported, paras 69–77. Depending on the circumstances, the General Court may find that there is no need to rule on an objection of inadmissibility based on lack of compliance with Art. 21 of the Statute and Art. 44(1)(c) EGC Rules of Procedure, since the forms of order sought by the applicant must in any event be rejected on their merits and thus dismiss the application for damages on that basis: see, e.g. CFI, Case T-406/06 *Evropaïki Dynamiki v Commission* [2008] E.C.R. II-247*, Summ. pub., paras 131–135.

[132] See, e.g. CFI, Case T-279/03 *Galileo International Technology and Others v Commission* [2006] E.C.R. II-1291, paras 36–59 (appeal dismissed on other grounds: ECJ (order of 20 March 2007), Case C-325/06 P *Galileo International Technology and Others v Commission* [2007] E.C.R. I-44*, Summ. pub.); CFI, Case T-412/05 *M v European Ombudsman* [2008] E.C.R. II-197*, Summ. pub., paras 44–50; CFI, Case T-444/07 *CPEM v Commission* [2009] E.C.R. II-2121, paras 32–38.

[133] See, e.g. CFI, Case T-473/93 *Wafer Zoo v Commission* [1995] E.C.R. II-1479, paras 49–50; CFI, Case T-276/03 *Azienda Agricola « Le Canne » v Commission* [2006] E.C.R. II-10*, Summ. pub., paras 44–48; EGC, Case T-300/07 *Evropaïki Dynamiki v Commission* [2010] E.C.R. II-4521, para. 146 (appeal dismissed in ECJ (order of 13 October 2011), Case C-560/10 P *Evropaïki Dynamiki v Commission* [2011] E.C.R. I-151*, Summ. pub.); EGC, Case T-57/09 *Alfastar Benelux v Council* [2011] E.C.R. II-368*, Summ. pub., paras 51–52; EGC, Case T-436/09 *Dufour ECB* [2011] E.C.R. II-7727, paras 197–199. In the context of staff disputes, see, e.g. CFI, Case T-99/95 *Stott v Commission* [1996] E.C.R. II-2227, paras 72–73; CFI, Case T-300/97 *Latino v Commission* [1999] E.C.R. II-1263, paras 95, 100–101; CFI, Joined Cases T-155/03, T-157/03 and T-331/03 *Cwik v Commission* [2005] E.C.R. II-1865, para. 199; CFI, Case T-156/03 *Pérez-Díaz v Commission* [2006] E.C.R.-SC I-A-2-135, paras 75–77. But compare CFI, Case T-48/05 *Franchet and Byk v Commission* [2008] E.C.R. II-1585, paras 90–92 (holding that claim for compensation cannot be rejected as premature on grounds that national proceedings are still pending, since alleged damage in present proceedings is distinct from the damage that might be confirmed by the decision of national judicial authority).

or damage[134] alleged—must be fulfilled if the Union is to be held non-contractually liable.[135]

(b) Development in the case-law

These three conditions have been refined through the course of the case-law. In particular, **11.37** with the alignment of the conditions governing the non-contractual liability of the Union with those governing the principle of State liability in *Bergaderm* (see further para. 11.45), the following three main conditions must be satisfied: (1) a sufficiently serious breach of a rule of law which is intended to confer rights on individuals; (2) actual damage is shown to have occurred; and (3) a direct causal link between the unlawful act or conduct on the part of the institution or body concerned and the damage sustained by the injured party.[136] The unlawfulness requirement encompasses the components relating to a sufficiently serious breach and a rule of law intended to confer rights on individuals.[137]

---

[134] As the case-law has developed, reference has been made to the 'loss'or 'damage' allegedly suffered by the claimant; as such, it appears that there is not meant to be a distinction between the two, i.e. the case-law merely uses such terms synonymously, with damage perhaps getting the upper hand in the more recent case-law.

[135] ECJ, Case 153/73 *Holz & Willemsen v Council and Commission* [1974] E.C.R. 675, para. 7; see further, e.g. EGC, Case T-162/07 *Pigasos Alieftiki Naftiki Etairrea v Council and Commission* [2009] E.C.R. II-153*, Summ. pub., para. 45 (and citations therein) (appeal dismissed in ECJ (order of 12 May 2010), Case C-451/09 P *Pigasos Alieftiki Naftiki Etaireia v Council and Commission* [2010] E.C.R. I-62*, Summ. pub.). As regards the non-contractual liability of the Union in staff cases, these same three classic conditions apply: see, e.g. ECJ, Case C-348/06 P *Commission v Girardot* [2008] E.C.R. I-833, para. 52 (and citations therein); CFI, Case T-256/02 *I v Court of Justice* [2004] E.C.R. II-1307, paras 48–49 (and citations therein). Recently, the Court of Justice ruled that it was not necessary to review the General Court's judgment in EGC (judgment of 16 December 2010), Case T-143/09 P *Commission v Petrilli*, not reported, on the grounds that it diverged from the approach taken in other cases, namely CFI (judgment of 10 December 2008), Case T-57/99 *Nardone v Commission*, not reported, particularly as regards the condition relating to the existence of a sufficiently serious breach of Union law, finding that 'it is now solely for the Civil Service Tribunal and the General Court of the European Union to develop the case-law in matters relating to the civil service': see ECJ (Decision of 8 February 2011), Case C-17/11 *RX Commission v Petrilli*, not reported. Notably, in *Nardone*, the General Court considered that there was no reason why the conditions set down in *Bergaderm* could not apply to staff cases, and thus applied the conditions of a sufficiently serious breach of a rule of law that must be intended to confer rights on individuals, specifically verifying the extent of the discretion of the institution concerned: see paras 162–173. In *Petrilli*, the General Court stressed the special regime of Union non-contractual liability in staff cases and ruled that the Civil Service Tribunal correctly considered in substance that in view of the total absence of the exercise of a margin of discretion, the Commission's conduct constituted an infringement of Union law engaging the non-contractual liability of the Union: see paras 45–49 (thus rejecting the Commission's arguments that it disposed of a large margin of discretion necessitating the finding that it must have manifestly and gravely disregarded the limits on that discretion to engage such liability). Therefore, while further case-law is needed to elucidate the extent to which the General Court and the Civil Service Tribunal will further elaborate on whether the specific nature of litigation in the staff context justifies making the non-contractual liability of the Union subject to special conditions or if the *Bergaderm* conditions apply in the same way, the position in those two cases is not necessarily divergent, in the sense that in accordance with the case-law since *Bergaderm*, where the institution concerned does not have a discretion, the mere infringement of Union law may be sufficient to establish a sufficiently serious breach.

[136] Depending on the particular formulation chosen by the Union courts, sometimes these three conditions are parsed out into four, e.g. the requirements concerning a sufficiently serious breach and the rule of law intended to confer rights on individuals may be presented separately, or the damage requirement may or may not be mentioned expressly. Compare, e.g. ECJ, Case C-472/00 P *Fresh Marine v Commission* [2003] E.C.R. I-7541, para. 25, ECJ, Case C-325/06 P *Galileo International Technology and Others v Commission* [2007] E.C.R. I-44*, Summ. pub., para. 49; CFI, Case T-415/03 *Confradia de pescadores de 'San Pedro' de Bermeo v Council* [2005] E.C.R. II-4355, para. 34 (appeal dismissed in ECJ, Case C-6/06 P *Confradia de pescadores de 'San Pedro' de Bermeo v Council* [2007] E.C.R. I-164*, Summ. pub.).

[137] See, e.g. ECJ, Case C-440/07 P *Commission v Schneider Electric* [2009] E.C.R. I-6413, para. 160; ECJ, Case C-282/05 P *Holcim (Deutschland) v Commission* [2007] E.C.R. I-2941, para. 47: specifying that a sufficiently serious breach of a rule of law intended to confer rights on individuals applies 'where the unlawfulness of a legal measure is at issue'; EGC, Case T-429/05 *Artegodan v Commission* [2010]

(c) Cumulative conditions

11.38   These three main conditions relating to unlawfulness, damage, and causation are cumulative, meaning that they must all be fulfilled or the action for damages against the Union fails.[138] If one of the requirements is not satisfied, the action for damages may be dismissed in its entirety without it being necessary for the General Court (or the Court of Justice on appeal) to undertake assessment of the others.[139]

(d) No particular order of assessment

11.39   Under the case-law, there is no requirement that these three conditions governing the Union's non-contractual liability be examined in any particular order.[140] The Court of Justice confirmed this in *Trubowest Handel and Others v Council and Commission*,[141] where it rejected the applicants' argument challenging the order by which the Court of First Instance had examined the conditions (contending that the examination of the causal link

---

E.C.R. II-491, para. 52 ('In order to accept that the condition for the non-contractual liability of the [Union] relating to the unlawfulness of the conduct of the institutions complained of is satisfied, the case-law requires that a sufficiently serious breach of a rule of law intended to confer rights on individuals is established') (appeal dismissed in ECJ (judgment of 19 April 2012), Case C-221/10 P *Artegodan v Commission*, not reported). See also CFI, Case T-415/03 *Confradía de pescadores de 'San Pedro' de Bermeo v Council* [2005] E.C.R. II-4355, paras 61–62: breaking down the inquiry even further to determine whether there has been a breach of a rule of law by a Union institution, and if so, whether that rule is intended to confer rights on individuals and whether the breach is sufficiently serious.

[138] See, e.g. EGC, Case T-437/05 *Brink's Security Luxembourg v Commission* [2009] E.C.R. II-3233, para. 241; EGC, Case T-42/06 *Gollnisch v European Parliament* [2010] E.C.R. II-1135, para. 91 (and citations therein).

[139] See, e.g. ECJ, Case C-282/05 P *Holcim (Deutschland) v Commission* [2007] E.C.R. I-2941, para. 57; ECJ (order of 29 October 2009), Case C-85/09 P *Portela v Commission* [2009] E.C.R. II-178*, Summ. pub., paras 34–35; ECJ, Case C-497/06 P *CAS Succhi di Frutta v Commission* [2009] E.C.R. I-69*, Summ. pub., para. 40; ECJ (order of 4 October 2011), Case C-272/11 P *Noko Ngele v Commission and Others* [2011] E.C.R. I-145*, Summ. pub., paras 15–16; EGC, Joined Cases T-252/07, T-271/07, and T-272/07 *Sungro and Others v Council and Commission* [2010] E.C.R. II-55, para. 36; EGC (order of 30 June 2011), Case T-367/09 *Tecnoprocess v Commission* [2011] E.C.R. II-209*, para. 75; EGC (order of 30 June 2011), Case T-264/09 *Tecnoprocess v Commission* [2011] E.C.R. II-208*, Summ. pub., para. 118; EGC, Case T-88/09 *Idromacchine and Others v Commission* [2011] E.C.R. II-7833, para. 27 (appeal dismissed: ECJ (order of 3 September 2013), Case C-34/12 P *Idromacchine and Others v Commission*, not reported); EGC, Case T-341/07 *Sison v Council* [2011] E.C.R. II-7915, para. 29. For some recent examples, see CFI, Joined Cases T-3/00 and T-337/04 *Pitsiorlas v Council and ECB* [2007] E.C.R. II-4779, para. 326 (no causal link or actual damage) (appeal dismissed in ECJ (order of 3 July 2008), Case C-84/08 P *Pitsiorlas v Council and ECB* [2008] E.C.R. I-104*, Summ. pub.); CFI, Case T-138/03 *É.R. and Others v Council and Commission* [2006] E.C.R. II-4923, paras 147–148 (no causal link) (appeal dismissed in ECJ (order of 4 October 2007), Case C-100/07 P *É.R. and Others v Council and Commission* [2007] E.C.R. I-136*, Summ. pub.); CFI (order of 30 June 2009), Case T-106/08 *CPEM v Commission* [2009] E.C.R. II-91*, Summ. pub., paras 42–43 (no causal link); EGC, Case T-452/05 *BST v Commission* [2010] E.C.R. II-1373, paras 179–180 (no causal link); EGC, Case T-107/08 *Transnational Company 'Kazchrome' and ENRC Marketing v Council and Commission* [2011] E.C.R. II-8051, para. 84 (no causal link). See also CFI (order of 12 December 2007), Case T-113/04 *Atlantic Container Line and Others v Commission* [2007] E.C.R. II-171*, Summ. pub., paras 51–53 (failure to prove a direct causal link resulted in rejection of the action without any need to examine whether the other conditions of unlawfulness and damage were satisfied or any need to determine whether that action was time-barred under Art. 46 of the Statute). However, depending on the circumstances, even where one of the conditions is found lacking, the Union courts may proceed to assess the others: see, e.g. CFI, Case T-415/03 *Confradía de pescadores de 'San Pedro' de Bermeo v Council* [2005] E.C.R. II-4355 (appeal dismissed in ECJ, Case C-6/06 P *Confradía de pescadores de 'San Pedro' de Bermeo v Council* [2007] E.C.R. I-164*, Summ. pub.).

[140] See, e.g. ECJ (order of 22 June 2004), Case C-51/03 P *Meyer v Commission*, not reported, para. 68; EGC, Case T-88/09 *Idromacchine and Others v Commission* [2011] E.C.R. II-7833, para. 27 (and further citations therein) (appeal dismissed: ECJ (order of 3 September 2013), Case C-34/12 P *Idromacchine and Others v Commission*, not reported).

[141] ECJ, Case C-419/08 P *Trubowest Handel and Makarov v Council and Commission* [2010] E.C.R. I-2559.

requirement presupposes the assessment of the other two conditions) and underlined that the causal link requirement is independent of the requirement relating to the unlawfulness of the act in question.[142]

(e) Burden of proof is on the applicant

The applicant bears the burden of proof that all of the conditions for incurring Union non-contractual liability are fulfilled.[143] **11.40**

(2) The unlawful act or conduct

The requirement of an unlawful act or conduct of a Union institution or body is the first pillar on which Union non-contractual liability is based.[144] **11.41**

(a) What test for unlawfulness?

(i) Unlawfulness and fault

In the past, the case-law was not always clear as to whether the unlawfulness of the act or conduct constituting the basis for the action for damages was based simply on the breach of a rule of Union law (objective liability) or whether 'fault' was also required on the part of the institution or body responsible for the act or conduct concerned (subjective liability).[145] **11.42**

(ii) Former ECSC Treaty

In the case of the now-expired ECSC Treaty, 'fault' or 'a wrongful act or omission on the part of the Community in the performance of its functions' (*faute de service* or in English, maladministration) was required in order for the Community to incur liability under Arts 34 and 40 ECSC. Such a requirement to show fault meant that actual 'blame' had to attach to the act. The criterion for determining blame was derived on an individual basis from the whole of the particular facts.[146] The complexity of the situations with which the institution had to deal, the difficulties in applying the Treaty provisions, and the discretion that the institution had under those provisions were taken into account.[147] In addition, the fault had to be of a particular nature. Thus, only 'unjustifiably bad administration'[148] or 'a lack of adequate supervision'[149] might be regarded as constituting fault capable of causing the Community to incur liability. Consequently, the fact that a Community act was unlawful did not necessarily mean that it had to be regarded as constituting 'fault' giving rise to Community liability. **11.43**

---

[142] ECJ, Case C-419/08 P *Trubowest Handel and Makarov v Council and Commission*, paras 37, 41–50.

[143] See, e.g. ECJ (order of 4 October 2007), Case C-100/07 P *É.R. and Others v Council and Commission* [2007] E.C.R. I-136*, Summ. pub., paras 27, 37; EGC (order of 15 December 2011), Case T-285/11 *Goorév Council*, not reported, para. 25; CFI, Case T-47/03 *Sison v Council* [2007] E.C.R. II-73*, Summ. pub., para. 244 (and citations therein).

[144] This is not to discount recourse to certain actions within the scope of non-contractual liability in which no unlawful act or conduct need be demonstrated, including an action for unjust enrichment: see para. 11.08.

[145] J. Hermann-Rodeville, 'Un exemple de contentieux économique: le recours en indemnité devant la Cour de justice des Communautés européennes'(1986) R.T.D.E. 5, at 13–27.

[146] ECJ, Case C-220/91 P *Commission v Stahlwerke Peine-Salzgitter* [1993] E.C.R. I-2393, para. 37.

[147] ECJ, Joined Cases C-363 and C-364/88 *Finsider and Others v Commission* [1992] E.C.R. I-359, para. 24 (these criteria for determining the type of fault which must have been committed in order for the Community to incur liability applied in connection with both Art. 34 and Art. 40 of the ECSC Treaty).

[148] ECJ, Joined Cases 14/60, 16/60, 17/60, 20/60, 24/60, 26/60, 27/60, and 1/61 *Meroni and Others v High Authority* [1961] E.C.R. 161, at 169.

[149] ECJ, Joined Cases 19/60 and 21/60, 2/61, and 3/61 *Société Fives Lille Cail and Others v High Authority* [1961] E.C.R. 281, at 297. See, to the same effect, ECJ, Joined Cases 29/63, 31/63, 36/63, 39/63, 47/63, 50/63, and 51/63 *SA des Laminoirs, Hauts Fourneaux, Forges, Fonderies et Usines de la Providence and Others v High Authority* [1965] E.C.R. 911, at 937.

(iii) **The TEU and the TFEU**

11.44   The second paragraph of Art. 340 TFEU puts the Court of Justice and the General Court under a duty to determine any non-contractual liability incurred by the Union 'in accordance with the general principles common to the laws of the Member States'. In theory, that provision provides an opportunity for formulating a system of objective liability, in which a generally applicable criterion of unlawfulness is determined in advance, without having regard to the particular circumstances surrounding the Union act or conduct at issue. In that case, a breach of a rule of Union law would be sufficient in itself to cause the act or conduct to be regarded as unlawful and hence to cause the Union to incur liability, regardless of whether the act or conduct was actually blameworthy and hence vitiated by fault.[150]

In practice, however, this is not exactly what was worked out in the case-law.[151] The concept of fault has not disappeared entirely from the system of Union non-contractual liability founded upon the second paragraph of Art. 340 TFEU. Over the years, the case-law has swung between mentioning fault[152] and not mentioning it,[153] but it is of course in the background whenever the mere unlawfulness of a Union act is insufficient to render the Union liable.

(iv) *Bergaderm* **judgment**

11.45   The relevance of the question whether the test as to unlawfulness is objective or subjective seems to have been blurred following the judgment of the Court of Justice in *Bergaderm*.[154] In that case, the Court of Justice aligned the conditions that must be met in order for the Union to incur liability on the conditions prescribed by Union law for a Member State to incur liability for damage sustained by individuals as a result of an infringement of Union law (i.e. the principle of State liability).[155]

By virtue of *Bergaderm*, the case-law now requires there to have been a sufficiently serious breach of a rule of law intended to confer rights on individuals.[156] Where the Union institution concerned has a discretion, a sufficiently serious breach will be involved where

---

[150] ECJ, Case C-352/98 P *Bergaderm and Goupil v Commission* [2000] E.C.R. I-5291, paras 43–44.

[151] See, e.g. EGC, Case T-341/07 *Sison v Council* [2011] E.C.R. II-7915, para. 31 (and citations therein): 'a finding of unlawfulness of a legal measure... is not enough, however regrettable that unlawfulness may be, for it to be held that the condition for the incurring of the [Union's] non-contractual liability relating to the unlawfulness of the institutions' alleged conduct has been satisfied'.

[152] See, e.g. ECJ, Case 25/62 *Plaumann v Commission* [1963] 95, at 108; ECJ, Joined Cases 5/66, 7/66, and 13/66 to 24/66 *Kampffmeyer and Others v Commission* [1967] E.C.R. 245, at 262; ECJ, Case 30/66 *Becher v Commission* [1967] E.C.R. 285, at 296; ECJ, Case 16/67 *Labeyrie v Commission* [1968] E.C.R. 293, at 304; ECJ, Joined Cases 19/69 to 20/69, 25/69, and 30/69 *Richez-Parise and Others v Commission* [1970] E.C.R. 325, para. 31; ECJ, Case 257/78 *Devred v Commission* [1979] E.C.R. 3767, para. 22; ECJ, Case 137/79 *Kohl v Commission* [1980] E.C.R. 2601, para. 14; CFI (order of 17 December 2003), Case T-346/03 *Krikorian and Others v European Parliament and Others* [2003] E.C.R. II-6037, para. 23; CFI (order of 20 February 2004), Case T-319/03 *French and Others v Council and Commission* [2004] E.C.R. II-769, para. 23; CFI, Case T-309/03 *Camós Grau v Commission* [2006] E.C.R. II-1173, para. 141; CFI, Case T-351/03 *Schneider Electric v Commission* [2007] E.C.R. II-2237, paras 154, 157, and 263.

[153] ECJ, Case 5/71 *Zuckerfabrik Schöppenstedt v Council* [1971] E.C.R. 975; ECJ, Case C-352/98 P *Bergaderm and Goupil v Commission* [2000] E.C.R. I-5291.

[154] ECJ, Case C-352/98 P *Bergaderm and Goupil v Commission* [2000] E.C.R. I-5291.

[155] ECJ, Case C-352/98 P *Bergaderm and Goupil v Commission*, paras 41–42.

[156] ECJ, Case C-352/98 P *Bergaderm and Goupil v Commission*, paras 41–42, 55, 62. See further, e.g. ECJ, Case C-440/07 P *Commission v Schneider Electric* [2009] E.C.R. I-6413, para. 160; ECJ, Case C-282/05 P *Holcim (Deutschland) v Commission* [2007] E.C.R. I-2941, para. 47: specifying that a sufficiently serious breach of a rule of law intended to confer rights on individuals applies 'where the unlawfulness of a legal measure is at issue'.

that institution 'manifestly and gravely' disregarded the limits on its discretion. Where the Union institution in question has only considerably reduced—or even no—discretion, the mere infringement of Union law may be sufficient to establish the existence of a sufficiently serious breach.[157]

As regards the determination of a sufficiently serious breach, the general or individual nature of the measure taken by an institution is not a decisive criterion. As made clear starting with *Bergaderm*, it is the extent of the discretion enjoyed by the institution concerned which is a decisive criterion and not the nature of the act at issue (general or individual),[158] as had been the case under the previous case-law emanating from *Lütticke* and *Schöppenstedt*.[159] Furthermore, account must be taken of certain 'justifications' developed in the case-law concerning, *inter alia*, the complexity of the situations to be regulated

---

[157] ECJ, Case C-352/98 P *Bergaderm and Goupil v Commission* [2000] E.C.R. I-5291, paras 43–44. See also, e.g. ECJ, Case C-312/00 P *Commission v Camar and Tico* [2002] E.C.R. I-11355, para. 54; ECJ, Case C-440/07 P *Commission v Schneider Electric* [2009] E.C.R. I-6413, para. 160; ECJ, Case C-282/05 P *Holcim (Deutschland) v Commission* [2007] E.C.R. I-2941 para. 47; CFI, Case T-210/00 *Biret & Cie v Council* [2002] E.C.R. II-47, para. 52 (appeal dismissed in ECJ, Case C-94/02 P *Biret & Cie v Council* [2003] E.C.R. I-10565); CFI, Case T-56/00 *Dole Fresh Fruit International v Council and Commission* [2003] E.C.R. II-577, para. 71; CFI, Joined Cases T-64/01 and T-65/01 *Afrikanische Frucht-Compagnie and Others v Council and Commission* [2004] E.C.R. II-521, para. 71; EGC, Case T-341/07 *Sison v Council* [2011] E.C.R. II-7915, para. 35 (and further citations therein); EGC (judgment of 16 May 2013), Case T-437/10 *Gap granen & producten v Commission*, not reported, para. 41.

[158] ECJ, Case C-352/98 P *Bergaderm and Goupil v Commission*, para. 46. See, e.g. ECJ, Case C-472/00 P *Commission v Fresh Marine* [2003] E.C.R. I-7541, para. 27; ECJ, Case C-282/05 P *Holcim (Deutschland) v Commission* [2007] E.C.R. I-2941, paras 48–49; CFI, Case T-429/05 *Artegodan v Commission* [2010] E.C.R. II-491, paras 53–54 (appeal dismissed in ECJ (judgment of 19 April 2012), Case C-221/10 P *Artegodan v Commission*, not reported). See further CFI, Case T-259/03 *Nikolaou v Commission* [2007] E.C.R. II-99*, Summ. pub., paras 40–42 (rejecting the Commission's argument that the *Bergaderm* judgment only pertains to the context of the adoption of normative (legislative) acts).

[159] The rules on liability set out in the judgment in *Bergaderm*, which formerly applied to a comparable degree for legislative acts involving an economic policy choice, largely correspond to the rules set forth in the *Schöppenstedt* judgment on liability for legislative acts according to which, '[w]here legislative action involving measures of economic policy is concerned', the Community will be liable only for damage suffered by individuals as a consequence of that action where there has been 'a sufficiently flagrant violation of a superior rule of law for the protection of the individual' (ECJ, Case 5/71 *Zuckerfabrik Schöppenstedt v Council* [1971] E.C.R. 975, para. 11). That rule reflected the reluctance of the Court of Justice and the Court of First Instance to assess the legality of acts that inevitably involve choices made on the basis of considerations of expediency. The particular nature of the role played by the Union courts means that they have to accept such choices. On those grounds, moreover, the Member States have sharply curtailed or even ruled out altogether liability for legislative acts. See ECJ, Joined Cases 83/76 and 94/76, 4/77, 15/77, and 40/77 *HNL and Others v Council and Commission* [1978] E.C.R. 1209, paras 5 and 6: 'This restrictive view is explained by the consideration that the legislative authority, even where the validity of its measures is subject to judicial review, cannot always be hindered in making its decisions by the prospect of applications for damages whenever it has occasion to adopt legislative measures in the public interest which may adversely affect the interests of individuals. It follows from these considerations that individuals may be required, in the sectors coming within the economic policy of the Community, to accept within reasonable limits certain harmful effects on their economic interests as a result of a legislative measure without being able to obtain compensation from public funds even if that measure has been declared null and void.' On the other hand, the existence of rules governing such liability—no matter how restrictive they may be—expresses a genuine concern to afford individuals the widest possible legal protection in the absence of effective parliamentary control. See also the Opinion of Advocate-General K. Roemer in ECJ, Case 5/71 *Zuckerfabrik Schöppenstedt v Council* [1971] E.C.R. 975, at 989. Such considerations carry over to the rationale for the requirements of a sufficiently serious breach of a rule of law intended to confer rights post-*Bergaderm* in relation to the restrictive approach towards Union liability in the exercise of its legislative activities: see ECJ, Joined Cases C-120/06 P and C-121/06 P *FIAMM and Others v Council and Commission* [2008] E.C.R. I-6513, paras 172–174; see also, e.g. ECJ (order of 12 May 2010), Case C-451/09 P *Pigasos Aliefiki Naftiki Etaireia v Council and Commission* [2010] E.C.R. I-62*, Summ. pub., para. 23.

and of difficulties in the application or interpretation of the texts concerned.[160] Indeed, although perhaps not expressly stated in *Bergaderm*, subsequent case-law has indicated that these so-called justifications may be considered in order to determine whether the institution is found to have a discretion or not.[161]

Consequently, it appears that the test for liability applied by the Union courts will invariably contain a major 'subjective' element, which is related to the discretion available to the institution concerned as well as to the consideration of the abovementioned 'justifications', as the case may be. The liability test starting with *Bergaderm* requires a finding to be made that the rule of law which has been breached is intended to confer rights on individuals and that the infringement in question constitutes a sufficiently serious breach of Union law, whereby the discretion of the institution concerned must first be identified and then the justifications elaborated in the case-law may be considered.

(v) Non-contractual liability on account of a failure to act

11.46   Non-contractual liability of the Union on account of an alleged unlawful failure to act must also be determined on the basis of the same criteria as those for unlawful acts or conduct. Thus, the inaction of an institution may give rise to liability where it constitutes a manifest and grave disregard of the limits imposed on the institution's discretion, or where the institution concerned has little or no discretion, that unlawful failure to act may be sufficient to establish the existence of a sufficiently serious breach.[162] Yet, at base, omissions by Union institutions can only give rise to liability on the part of the Union where the institutions have infringed a legal obligation to act under a provision of Union law.[163]

(vi) Infringement proceedings

11.47   Accordingly, there is a well-established body of case-law that an action for damages based on the Commission's failure to initiate proceedings for failure to fulfil obligations (or infringement proceedings) against a Member State under Art. 258 TFEU is inadmissible, since the Commission is under no obligation to initiate such proceedings, so its failure to do so cannot give rise to non-contractual liability on the part of the Union.[164] However, in

---

[160] ECJ, Case C-352/98 P *Bergaderm and Goupil v Commission* [2000] E.C.R. I-5291, para. 40.

[161] See, e.g. EGC, Case T-341/07 *Sison v Council* [2011] E.C.R. II-7915, paras 37–40 (and citations therein). See further para. 11.52.

[162] See, e.g. ECJ, Case 50/86 *Grands Moulins de Paris v Council and Commission* [1987] E.C.R. 4833, para. 9; ECJ, Case C-198/03 P *Commission v CEVA Santé Animale and Pfizer Enterprises* [2005] E.C.R. I-6357, paras 63–69 and 73; CFI, Case T-285/03 *Agraz and Others v Commission* [2005] E.C.R. II-1063, paras 39–40, 47–54 (judgment set aside on other grounds in ECJ, Case C-243/05 P).

[163] CFI, Case T-279/03 *Galileo International Technology and Others v Commission* [2006] E.C.R. II-1291, para. 137 (and citations therein) (appeal dismissed in ECJ (order of 20 March 2007), Case C-325/06 P *Galileo International Technology and Others v Commission* [2007] E.C.R. I-44*, Summ. pub.); EGC (order of 18 June 2012), Case T-203/11 *Transports Schiocchet—Excursions v Council and Commission*, not reported, para. 37 (appeal dismissed in ECJ, Case C-397/12 P).

[164] See, e.g. ECJ (order of 23 May 1990), Case C-72/90 *Asia Motor France v Commission* [1990] E.C.R. I-2181, para. 13; CFI (order of 14 January 2004), Case T-202/02 *Makedoniko Metro and Michaniki v Commission* [2004] E.C.R. II-181, paras 42–47; CFI (order of 8 September 2006), Case T-92/06 *Lademporiki and Apostolos Parousis & Sia v Commission* [2006] E.C.R. II-66*, Summ. pub., paras 29–30; CFI (order of 7 September 2009), Case T-186/08 *LPN v Commission* [2009] E.C.R. II-136*, Summ. pub., paras 65–66; CFI (order of 29 October 2009), Case T-249/09 *Ségaud v Commission*, not reported, paras 11–12 (appeal dismissed in ECJ (order of 21 May 2010), Case C-514/09 P *Ségaud v Commission* [2010] E.C.R. I-71*, Summ. pub.); CFI (order of 16 November 2009), Case T-354/09 *Goldman Management v Commission and Bulgaria*, not reported, para 10–11 (appeal dismissed in ECJ (order of 6 May 2010), Case C-507/09 P *Goldman Management v Commission and Bulgaria* [2010] E.C.R. I-57*, Summ. pub.); EGC (order of 30 September 2010), Case

Arizmendi and Others v Council and Commission, the General Court held that it cannot be inferred from that absence of liability for failure to initiate infringement proceedings that the institution of such proceedings by the Commission also precludes any liability on the part of the Union.[165] In light of the autonomous nature of the action for damages, any act of an institution, even though it was adopted by that institution in the exercise of a discretion, is in principle capable of forming the subject-matter of an action for damages, reasoning that a contrary approach would run counter to a Union based on the rule of law.[166] Consequently, even though within the framework of its powers under Art. 258 TFEU, the Commission enjoys a discretion in deciding whether to send a reasoned opinion to a Member State, it cannot be precluded that in very exceptional circumstances a person may be able to demonstrate that such a reasoned opinion is vitiated with illegality constituting a sufficiently serious breach of a rule of law that is likely to cause damage to him, and thus the action was held admissible.[167] In proceeding to the assessment of the sufficiently serious breach requirement, the General Court held that, on the one hand, provided that the Commission confines itself in the reasoned opinion to adopting a position on the existence of a failure by a Member State to fulfil its obligations under Union law, the Commission's adoption of that opinion—even where it takes an incorrect position on the scope of Union law—cannot constitute a sufficiently serious breach capable of rendering the Union non-contractually liable.[168] On the other hand, however, if the assessments made in a reasoned opinion 'go beyond the determination of the existence of a breach by a Member State or if other action taken by the Commission on the occasion of infringement proceedings exceeds the powers conferred on it, for example, if it wrongfully discloses business secrets or information that harms a person's reputation, those assessments or actions are capable of constituting a breach of such a kind as to render the Union liable'.[169]

(vii) Intended to confer rights on individuals

As mentioned earlier, since the judgment in *Bergaderm*, an infringement of a rule of law is capable of causing the Union to incur liability only where the rule of law is intended to confer rights on individuals.[170] Sometimes other formulations are used in the case-law[171]— **11.48**

T-195/10 *Snemo Mars-Momchil Dobrev and Others v Commission and Bulgaria*, not reported, paras 8–9; EGC (order of 15 July 2011), Case T-185/11 *Smanor v Commission and European Ombudsman*, not reported, para. 16 (appeal dismissed in ECJ (order of 12 January 2011), Joined Cases C-205/10 P, C-217/10 P, and C-222/10 P *Eriksen and Others v Commission* [2011] E.C.R. I-1*, Summ. pub., paras 37–45 (upholding the General Court's reference to ECJ, Case C-72/90 *Asia Motor France v Commission* and CFI, Case T-202/02 *Makedoniko Metro and Michaniki v Commission*, as part of its ruling that the Commission's decision not to bring infringement procedings under Art. 258 TFEU or Art. 141 EAEC was not unlawful so that it could not give rise to non-contractual liability, underlining that the Commission's discretionary power whether to bring infringement proceedings against a Member State is not conditional on its power to grant exemptions).

[165] EGC, Joined Cases T-440/03, T-121/04, T-171/04, T-208/04, T-365/04, and T-484/04 *Arizmendi and Others v Council and Commission* [2009] E.C.R. II-4883, paras 61–63.
[166] EGC, Joined Cases T-440/03, T-121/04, T-171/04, T-208/04, T-365/04, and T-484/04 *Arizmendi and Others v Council and Commission*, paras 64–67.
[167] EGC, Joined Cases T-440/03, T-121/04, T-171/04, T-208/04, T-365/04, and T-484/04 *Arizmendi and Others v Council and Commission*, paras 68–71.
[168] EGC, Joined Cases T-440/03, T-121/04, T-171/04, T-208/04, T-365/04, and T-484/04 *Arizmendi and Others v Council and Commission*, paras 76–77.
[169] EGC, Joined Cases T-440/03, T-121/04, T-171/04, T-208/04, T-365/04, and T-484/04 *Arizmendi and Others v Council and Commission*, para. 78.
[170] ECJ, Case C-352/98 P *Bergaderm and Goupil v Commission* [2000] E.C.R. I-5291, paras 55, 62.
[171] See also CFI, Case T-56/00 *Dole Fresh Fruit International v Council and Commission* [2003] E.C.R. II-577, para. 71 ('a sufficiently serious breach of *a rule of law protecting individuals*') (emphasis added).

such as a rule of law 'for the protection of the individual' (the *Schöppenstedt* test discussed later) or a rule of law 'intended to protect individuals'—but these are, in the view of the General Court, 'mere variations on a single legal concept which is expressed by the formula 'intended to confer rights on individuals'.[172] The rule of law concerned does not have to have 'direct effect' for it to be considered to be intended to confer rights on individuals.[173] As noted in the case-law, this requirement includes situations where a provision of Union law gives rise to rights which have 'direct effect',[174] but the two are not necessarily the same.[175]

The requirement of a rule of law intended to confer rights on individuals appears to be based closely on the requirement laid down in the *Schöppenstedt* test that a superior rule of law intended to protect an interest peculiar to the person concerned must be involved.[176] This doctrine of the *Schutznorm*,[177] which originates in German law and may be found also in some other jurisdictions, has the aim of limiting liability. Under the traditional *Schöppenstedt* test, it was applied flexibly, and such an approach appears to have been carried through to some extent in current case-law following the *Bergaderm* formulation. The Union judicature does not rule out the possibility of rules of law protecting both general and individual interests.[178] Accordingly, for example, the prohibition of discrimination laid

---

[172] EGC, Case T-341/07 *Sison v Council* [2011] E.C.R. II-7915, para. 33. See further CFI, Case T-259/03 *Nikolaou v Commission* [2007] E.C.R. II-99*, Summ. pub., para. 42: 'Si la Cour a certes voulu modifier cette condition afin d'harmoniser la jurisprudence, cela ne signifie pas pour autant qu'elle ait considéré que la notion de protection des particuliers et la jurisprudence antérieure qui s'y réfère sont denuées de pertinence aux fins d'apprécier dans quelles situations des règles de droit confèrent des droits aux particuliers. *En effet, les règles de droit qui visent à protéger les particuliers sont, dans la plupart des cas, également des règles qui leur confèrent des droits.*'

[173] See ECJ, Joined Cases C-6/90 and C-9/90 *Francovich and Others* [1991] E.C.R. I-5357, in which the applicant could not rely on the provision of the unimplemented directive because it did not have direct effect, but the directive was nevertheless regarded as a rule of law which conferred rights on individuals.

[174] See CFI, Case T-415/03 *Cofradía de pescadores 'San Pedro' de Bermeo and Others v Council* [2005] E.C.R. II-4355, para. 86: 'a rule of law is intended to confer rights on individuals where the infringement concerns a provision which gives rise to rights for individuals which national courts must protect, so that it has direct effect, a provision which creates an advantage which could be defined as a vested right, a provision which is designed for the protection of the interests of the individual, or a provision which entails the grant of rights to individuals, the content of which being sufficiently identifiable'.

[175] See S. Prechal, *Directives in EC Law* (2nd edn, Oxford, Oxford University Press, 2005), para. 10.4.2, at 283–4.

[176] See Opinion of Advocate-General M. Léger in ECJ, Case C-5/94 *Hedley Lomas* [1996] E.C.R. I-2553, point 133. In ECJ, Case 5/71 *Zuckerfabrik Schöppenstedt v Council* [1971] E.C.R. 975, para. 11, the ECJ held: 'Where legislative action involving measures of economic policy is concerned, the Community does not incur non[-]contractual liability for damage suffered by individuals as a consequence of that action ... unless a sufficiently flagrant violation of a *superior rule of law for the protection of the individual has occurred*' (emphasis added). This requirement was expressed for the first time in ECJ, Joined Cases 9/60 and 12/60 *Vloebergbs v High Authority* [1961] E.C.R. 197, at 217, where the Court of Justice dismissed a claim for damages brought under Art. 40 of the ECSC Treaty on the grounds that the article of that Treaty which the Commission had allegedly infringed had been adopted only in the interests of the Community.

[177] Under German law, the public authorities are liable only if they cause damage and breach a 'Schutznorm' protecting an individual right, not of individuals in general, but of a specific group to which the interested party belongs: see Opinion of Advocate-General M. Léger in ECJ, Case C-5/94 *Hedley Lomas* [1996] E.C.R. I-2553, point 133.

[178] ECJ, Joined Cases 5/66, 7/66, and 13/66 to 24/66 *Kampffmeyer and Others v Commission* [1967] E.C.R. 245, at 262–3. See, more recently, EGC, Case T-429/05 *Artegodan v Commission* [2010] E.C.R. II-491, para. 89 ('that condition is satisfied where the rule of law breached, while referring essentially to interests of a general nature, also ensures the protection of the individual interests of the undertakings concerned', citing ECJ, Joined Cases 5/66, 7/66, and 13/66 to 24/66 *Kampffmeyer and Others v Commission*); see also to the same effect, EGC, Case T-341/07 *Sison v Council* [2011] E.C.R. II-7915, para. 47 (see further paras 48–52: holding that the rules of law concerned were not designed to delimit the respective competences of the Union and the Member States, but intended essentially to protect the interests of the individuals concerned).

down in what is now the second paragraph of Art. 40(2) TFEU assists the common organization of the agricultural markets and, at the same time, protects the interests of individual market participants.[179]

In contrast, this requirement is not satisfied where the rule of law at issue is not found to protect any individual interests. For example, the requirement laid down by Art. 296 TFEU for a statement of reasons is intended only to enable the Court of Justice or the General Court to review the legality of acts and does not serve any individual interest, with the result that an infringement of that requirement cannot make the Union non-contractually liable.[180] The same is true of the system of rules governing the division of powers between the Union institutions which is designed to 'ensure that the balance between the institutions ... is maintained, and not to protect individuals'; however, the position is different if a Union measure were to be adopted which not only disregarded the division of powers between the institutions, but also, in its substantive provisions, disregarded a rule of law intended to confer rights on individuals. Consequently, as the Court of Justice recently held in *Artegodan v Commission*, although an infringement by the Commission of the rules governing the division of powers between the Commission and the Member States resulting from a particular Union measure is not of such a kind to cause the Union to incur non-contractual liability on the grounds that those rules are intended to confer rights on individuals, such an infringement, when it is accompanied by an infringement of a substantive provision which has such intention, is capable of giving rise to that liability.[181]

Likewise, in order to ensure the practical effect of the condition relating to the breach of a rule of law intended to confer rights on individuals, it is necessary for the protection offered by the rule invoked to be effective in relation to the person who invokes it, and hence that person must be among those upon whom the rule concerned confers rights; conversely, a rule not protecting the person against the unlawfulness he invokes but protecting another person cannot be accepted as the source of the obligation to provide compensation on the part of the Union.[182]

(viii) Any rule of Union law

Following *Bergaderm*, it is not important whether or not the rule of law infringed constitutes a 'superior' or 'higher-ranking' rule of law,[183] as had been the case under the *Schöppenstedt* formula. **11.49**

---

[179] ECJ, Joined Cases 83/76 and 94/76, 4/77, 15/77, and 40/77 *HNL and Others v Council and Commission* [1978] E.C.R. 1209, para. 5; ECJ, Case 238/78 *Ireks-Arkady v Council and Commission* [1979] E.C.R. 2955, para. 11; ECJ, Joined Cases 241/78 to 242/78, and 245/78 to 250/78 *DGV v Council and Commission* [1979] E.C.R. 3017, para. 11; ECJ, Joined Cases 261/78 and 262/78 *Interquell Stärke-Chemie and Diamalt v Council and Commission* [1979] E.C.R. 3045, para. 14.

[180] ECJ, Case 106/81 *Kind v EEC* [1982] E.C.R. 2885, para. 14; ECJ, Case C-119/88 *AERPO and Others v Commission* [1990] E.C.R. I-2189, para. 20; ECJ, Case C-76/01 P *Eurocoton and Others v Council* [2003] E.C.R. I-10091, para. 98; CFI, Case T-43/98 *Emesa Sugar v Council* [2001] E.C.R. II-3519, para. 63; CFI, Joined Cases T-64/01 and T-65/01 *Afrikanische Frucht-Compagnie and Others v Council and Commission* [2004] E.C.R. II-521, para. 128. But see para 11.51 with respect to the right to good administration (Art. 41 of Charter of Fundamental Rights).

[181] ECJ (judgment of 19 April 2012), Case C-221/10 P *Artegodan v Commission*, not reported, paras 81–82.

[182] See, e.g. CFI, Case T-259/03 *Nikolaou v Commission* [2007] E.C.R. II-99*, Summ. pub., paras 43–44; CFI, Case T-238/07 *Ristic and Others v Commission* [2009] E.C.R. II-117*, Summ. pub., para. 60.

[183] See, e.g. CFI, Case T-415/03 *Cofradía de pescadores 'San Pedro' de Bermeo and Others v Council* [2005] E.C.R. II-4355, para. 85; CFI, Case T-259/03 *Nikolaou v Commission* [2007] E.C.R. II-99*, Summ. pub., para. 41; CFI, Case T-47/03 *Sison v Council* [2007] E.C.R. II-73*, Summ. pub., para. 234.

The rules of law that may constitute the basis for Union non-contractual liability include the provisions of the Treaties, the general principles of Union law, and the Union measures on which the alleged unlawful act or conduct is based. In other words, a rule of law intended to confer rights on individuals may constitute a provision of primary or secondary Union law (legislative as well as non-legislative acts).[184]

(ix) Case-law prior to the *Bergaderm* judgment

11.50 Since a *Schutznorm* under the *Schöppenstedt* case-law necessarily constitutes a rule of law intended to confer rights on individuals, the case-law prior to the *Bergaderm* judgment retains relevance in the assessment of this requirement and, moreover, continues to be taken into account by the Union courts.

The Treaty provisions which were already used before the judgment in *Bergaderm* to test the legality of an act in the context of an action for damages include what are now Art. 18 TFEU (ex Art. 12 EC);[185] Arts 34 and 35 TFEU (ex Arts 28 and 29 EC),[186] Art. 39(1) TFEU (ex Art. 33(1) EC)[187] and Art. 40(3) TFEU (ex Art. 34(3) EC).[188]

The general rules of law which operated as superior rules of law for the protection of individuals included the principle of protection of legitimate expectation,[189] the principle of proportionality,[190] the principle of equal treatment (also known as the principle of equality or the prohibition of discrimination),[191] the principle of

---

[184] For this distinction, see further K. Lenaerts and P. Van Nuffel (R. Bray and N. Cambien (eds)), *European Union Law* (3rd edn, London, Sweet & Maxwell, 2011), paras 22.62 and 22.63.

[185] ECJ, Joined Cases 71/84 and 72/84 *Surcouf and Vidou v EEC* [1985] E.C.R. 2925.

[186] ECJ, Case 265/85 *Van den Bergh and Jurgens v Commission* [1987] E.C.R. 1155.

[187] ECJ, Case 27/85 *Vandemoortele v Commission* [1987] E.C.R. 1129.

[188] ECJ, Case 281/82 *Unifrex v Council and Commission* [1984] E.C.R. 1969. Art. 38(4) TFEU [(ex Art. 32(4) EC)) and Art. 43(2) TFEU [(ex Art. 37(2) EC)) were, however, held not to constitute superior rules of law for the protection of individuals: see CFI, Case T-571/93 *Lefebvre and Others v Commission* [1995] E.C.R. II-2379, para. 41.

[189] ECJ, Case 74/74 *CNTA v Commission* [1975] E.C.R. 533, at 548–50 (manifest infringement of the principle of protection of legitimate expectation); ECJ, Case C-152/88 *Sofrimport v Commission* [1990] E.C.R. I-2477, para. 26 (manifest infringement of that principle); ECJ, Joined Cases C-104/89 and C-37/90 *Mulder and Others v Council and Commission* [1992] E.C.R. I-3061, para. 15 (manifest infringement of that principle); CFI, Case T-472/93 *Campo Ebro Industrial and Others v Council* [1995] E.C.R. II-421, para. 52 (no infringement of the principle of protection of legitimate expectation); CFI, Joined Cases T-481/93 and T-484/93 *Exporteurs in Levende Varkens and Others v Commission* [1995] E.C.R. II-2941, paras 148–150 (no infringement of the principle of protection of legitimate expectation); CFI, Case T-521/93 *Atlanta and Others v EC* [1996] E.C.R. II-1707, paras 55–58 (no infringement of the principle of protection of legitimate expectation); CFI, Case T-105/96 *Pharos v Commission* [1998] E.C.R. II-285, paras 63–72 (no infringement of the principle of protection of legitimate expectation).

[190] ECJ, Joined Cases 63/72 to 69/72 *Werhahn Hansamühle and Others v Council* [1973] E.C.R. 1229, paras 18–20; ECJ, Joined Cases 279/84 to 280/84, 285/84, and 286/84 *Rau v Commission* [1987] E.C.R. 1069, paras 33–37; ECJ, Case 27/85 *Vandemoortele v Commission* [1987] E.C.R. 1129, paras 30–34; ECJ, Case 265/85 *Van den Bergh and Jurgens v Commission* [1987] E.C.R. 1155, paras 30–34; CFI, Case T-152/95 *Petrides v Commission* [1997] E.C.R. II-2427, paras 48–53 (no infringement of the principle of proportionality).

[191] ECJ, Joined Cases 83/76 and 94/76, 4/77, 15/77, and 40/77 *HNL and Others v Council and Commission* [1978] E.C.R. 1209, para. 5; ECJ, Joined Cases 64/76 and 113/76, 167/78 and 239/78, 27/79 to 28/79 and 45/79 *Dumortier Frères v Council* [1979] E.C.R. 3091, para. 11; ECJ, Case 238/78 *Ireks-Arkady v Council and Commission* [1979] E.C.R. 2955, para. 11; ECJ, Joined Cases 241/78 to 242/78, and 245/78 to 250/78 *DGV v Council and Commission* [1979] E.C.R. 3017, para. 11; ECJ, Joined Cases 261/78 and 262/78 *Interquell Stärke-Chemie and Diamalt v Council and Commission* [1979] E.C.R. 3045, para. 14; ECJ, Case 106/81 *Kind v EEC* [1982] E.C.R. 2885, paras 22–25 (no infringement of the principle of equal treatment); ECJ, Case C-63/89 *Assurances du Crédit v Council and Commission* [1991] E.C.R. I-1799, paras 14–23 (no infringement of the principle of equal treatment); CFI, Case T-120/89 *Stahlwerke Peine-Salzgitter v Commission* [1991]

care,[192] the principle of proper administration,[193] and the prohibition of misuse of powers.[194] Fundamental rights, such as the right to property,[195] the right to be heard (*audi alteram partem*),[196] and freedom to pursue an economic activity,[197] were also recognized as being superior rules of law for the protection of individuals.

(x) Further examples of rules of law intended to confer rights on individuals following *Bergaderm*

Since the judgment in *Bergaderm*, the Union judicature has expressly (or sometimes **11.51** indirectly) recognized the following general principles of Union law as being rules of law conferring rights on individuals: the principle of non-discrimination;[198] the principle of proportionality;[199] the principle of protection of legitimate expectations;[200] the principle of good faith and rule against abuse of rights;[201] and the prohibition of unjust enrichment.[202]

Notably, as far as the principle of sound administration is concerned, it does not in itself confer rights on individuals,[203] except where it constitutes the expression of specific rights, such as the right to have affairs handled impartially, fairly, and within a reasonable time, the

---

E.C.R. II-279, para. 92 (manifest infringement of the principle of equal treatment); CFI, Case T-489/93 *Unifruit Hellas v Commission* [1994] E.C.R. II-1201, paras 76–80 (no infringement of the principle of equal treatment); CFI, Case T-472/93 *Campo Ebro Industrial and Others v Commission* [1995] E.C.R. II-421, para. 52; CFI, Joined Cases T-481 and T-484/93 *Exporteurs in Levende Varkens and Others v Commission* [1995] E.C.R. II-2941, para. 102 (no infringement of the principle of equal treatment); CFI, Case T-152/95 *Petrides v Commission* [1997] E.C.R. II-2427, paras 54–60 (no infringement of the principle of equal treatment).

[192] CFI, Case T-167/94 *Nölle v Council and Commission* [1995] E.C.R. II-2589, para. 76 (no infringement of the principle of care).

[193] CFI, Case T-105/96 *Pharos v Commission* [1998] E.C.R. II-285, paras 73–78 (no infringement of the principle of proper administration).

[194] ECJ, Case C-119/88 *AERPO and Others v Commission* [1990] E.C.R. I-2189, para. 19; CFI, Joined Cases T-481/93 and T-484/93 *Exporteurs in Levende Varkens and Others v Commission* [1995] E.C.R. II-2941, paras 134–135 (no infringement of the prohibition of misuse of powers).

[195] ECJ, Case 59/83 *Biovilac v EEC* [1984] E.C.R. 4057, paras 21–22; ECJ, Case 281/84 *Zuckerfabrik Bedburg v Council and Commission* [1987] E.C.R. 49, paras 25–28.

[196] CFI, Joined Cases T-481/93 and T-484/93 *Exporteurs in Levende Varkens and Others v Commission* [1995] E.C.R. II-2941, para. 154 (no infringement of the right to be heard).

[197] CFI, Case T-521/93 *Atlanta and Others v EC* [1996] E.C.R. II-1707, paras 62–64 (no infringement of the freedom to pursue an economic activity).

[198] See, e.g. CFI, Case T-56/00 *Dole Fresh Fruit International v Council and Commission* [2003] E.C.R. II-577, para. 73; CFI, Case T-166/98 *Cantina Sociale di Dolianova and Others v Commission* [2004] E.C.R. II-3991, para. 176 (and citations therein) (judgment set aside on other grounds: ECJ, Case C-51/05 P).

[199] See, e.g. CFI, Case T-43/98 *Emesa Sugar v Council* [2001] E.C.R. II-3519, para. 64; CFI, Case T-412/05 *M v European Ombudsman* [2008] E.C.R. II-197*, Summ. pub., para. 125.

[200] See, e.g. CFI, Case T-43/98 *Emesa Sugar v Council* [2001] E.C.R. II-3519, para. 64; CFI, Case T-155/99 *Dieckmann & Hansen v Commission* [2001] E.C.R. II-3143, para. 77 (no express recognition); CFI, Case T-210/00 *Biret & Cie v Council* [2002] E.C.R. II-47, para. 57 (appeal dismissed in ECJ, Case C-94/02 P *Biret & Cie v Council* [2003] E.C.R. I-10565); CFI, Case T-128/05 *SPM v Commission* [2008] E.C.R. II-260*, Summ. pub., para. 146 (and citations therein) (appeal dismissed in ECJ (order of 22 March 2010), Case C-39/09 P *SPM v Council and Commission* [2010] E.C.R. I-38*, Summ. pub.). See further CFI, Case T-271/04 *Citymo v Commission* [2007] E.C.R. II-1375, para. 108 (and citations therein) (underscoring that in a public procurement procedure, that principle confers rights on any tenderer who is in a situation in which it is apparent that, in giving him specific assurances, the Union administration has led him to entertain reasonable expectations).

[201] For a finding of a sufficiently serious breach, but not dealing explicitly with the question whether the principle confers rights: CFI, Case T-271/04 *Citymo v Commission* [2007] E.C.R. II-1375, para. 137.

[202] See, e.g. CFI, Case T-166/98 *Cantina Sociale di Dolianova and Others v Commission* [2004] E.C.R. II-3991, paras 160–162 (judgment set aside on other grounds: ECJ, Case C-51/05 P).

[203] CFI, Case T-196/99 *Area Cova and Others v Council and Commission* [2001] E.C.R. II-3597, para. 43.

right to be heard, the right to have access to files, or the obligation to give reasons for decisions for the purposes of Art. 41 of the Charter of Fundamental Rights of the European Union.[204]

Various fundamental rights (enshrined in the Charter), including the right to freely exercise a trade or profession,[205] the principle of the protection of property,[206] the right of protection of private and family life,[207] the right of freedom of the press, the principle of the presumption of innocence,[208] the right to a fair trial, and the principle of observance of the rights of defence[209] have been held by the Union courts to confer rights on individuals.[210]

Furthermore, the Union courts have found provisions of the Protocol on Privileges and Immunities,[211] rules laid down in secondary Union law in connection with the conduct of investigations by OLAF[212] and the opening of disciplinary proceedings by the Commission,[213] and provisions of secondary law on the control of concentrations[214] to confer rights on individuals.

---

[204] See, e.g. CFI, Case T-128/05 *SPM v Council and Commission* [2008] E.C.R. II-260*, Summ. pub., para. 127 (appeal dismissed in ECJ (order of 22 March 2010), Case C-39/09 P *SPM v Council and Commission* [2010] E.C.R. I-38*, Summ. pub.); CFI, Case T-193/04 *Tillack v Commission* [2006] E.C.R. II-3995, para. 127. See also ECJ, Case C-47/07 P *Masdar v Commission* [2008] E.C.R. I-9761, paras 90–95 (reframing the claim of 'negligence' as a breach of duty of care, which is inherent in the principle of sound administration and upholding the judgment of the General Court that the Commission was not under a duty alleged by the applicant that would incur Union non-contractual liability); CFI, Case T-309/03 *Camós Grau v Commission* [2006] E.C.R. II-1173, paras 102–103 (right of impartiality); CFI, Case T-412/05 *M v European Ombudsman* [2008] E.C.R. II-197*, Summ. pub., para. 125 (referring to the '*principe du contradictoire*'); CFI, Case T-48/05 *Franchet and Byk v Commission* [2008] E.C.R. II-1585, para. 218 (ruling that the applicants are entitled to rely on the principle of sound administration in that it entails the right to have their cases dealt with in such a way that confidentiality is maintained). See also CFI, Case T-212/03 *MyTravel Group v Commission* [2008] E.C.R. II-1967, paras 49–50 (framing the 'duty of diligence' in relation to individuals, which imposes on the competent institution the obligation to examine carefully and impartially all of the relevant elements of the individual cases as have been recognized in the case-law relating to the principle of sound administration); EGC, Case T-291/04 *Enviro Tech Europe and Enviro Tech International v Commission* [2011] E.C.R. II-8281, paras 155–157 (referring to rights of defence, the duty to act with care, and procedural rights relating to assessing each case individually, impartially, and diligently as part of claim of infringement of the principle of 'sound administration' but not dealing specifically with conferral of rights) (appeal dismissed in ECJ (order of 24 January 2013), Case C-118/12 P *Enviro Tech Europe v Commission*, not reported).
[205] See, e.g. CFI, Case T-30/99 *Bocchi Food Trade International v Commission* [2001] E.C.R. II-943, paras 79–83; CFI, Case T-52/99 *T. Port v Commission* [2001] E.C.R. II-981, para. 81.
[206] See, e.g. CFI, Case T-52/99 *T. Port v Commission* [2001] E.C.R. II- 981, para. 99; EGC, Case T-341/07 *Sison v Council* [2011] E.C.R. II-7915, paras 41, 75.
[207] See also CFI, Case T-412/05 *M v European Ombudsman* [2007] E.C.R. II-197*, Summ. pub., para. 125; EGC, Case T-341/07 *Sison v Council* [2011] E.C.R. II-7915, paras 41, 75.
[208] See also CFI, Case T-48/05 *Franchet and Byk v Commission* [2008] E.C.R. II-1585, para. 209 (also finding that this principle has its corollary in the obligation to maintain confidentiality in relation to an OLAF investigation).
[209] See, e.g. CFI, Case T-47/03 *Sison v Council* [2007] E.C.R. II-73*, Summ. pub., para. 213 (and citations therein).
[210] CFI, Case T-193/04 *Tillack v Commission* [2006] E.C.R. II-3995, para. 121.
[211] See, e.g. EGC, Case T-42/06 *Gollnisch v European Parliament* [2010] E.C.R. II-1135, paras 94, 108.
[212] See, e.g. CFI, Case T-259/03 *Nikolaou v Commission* [2007] E.C.R. II-99*, Summ. pub., para. 210; CFI, Case T-48/05 *Franchet and Byk v Commission* [2008] E.C.R. II-1585, paras 152–153, 166–169.
[213] See, e.g. CFI, Case T-48/05 *Franchet and Byk v Commission* [2008] E.C.R. II-1585, paras 351–352.
[214] See, e.g. CFI, Case T-351/03 *Schneider Electric v Commission* [2007] E.C.R. II-2237, paras 149–151 (relates to the respect of the rights of defence in administrative procedures of which Art. 18(3) of the Regulation then applicable to control of concentrations—Regulation (EEC) No. 4064/89—constituted an expression); CFI, Case T-212/03 *MyTravel Group v Commission* [2008] E.C.R. II-1967, para. 44–48.

In contrast, the principle of relative stability and respect for traditional fisheries rights governs only relations between the Member States and does not confer on individuals rights whose infringement would ground a claim in damages.[215] The same applies to the competences of the Commission enshrined in Art. 17(1) TEU (formerly Art. 211 EC),[216] the duty to state reasons in Art. 296 TFEU (ex Art. 253 EC),[217] Art. 207 TFEU (ex Art. 133 EC)[218] concerning the common commercial policy, and Art. 351 TFEU (ex Art. 307 EC) concerning agreements concluded between the Member States and third countries before 1 January 1958 or their date of accession.[219]

In principle, the WTO agreements do not constitute—under Union law—rules of law which confer rights for individuals.[220] Likewise, to the extent that an applicant seeks to rely on provisions of other international agreements concluded by the Union (and the Member States as the case may be) with third countries in order to establish unlawful conduct on the part of the institutions for the purposes of an action for damages, those provisions are deemed not to confer rights on individuals where they cannot be held to be directly applicable.[221]

---

[215] See CFI, Case T-196/99 *Area Cova and Others v Council and Commission* [2001] E.C.R. II-3597, para. 152; CFI, Case T-415/03 *Cofradía de pescadores de 'San Pedro' and Others v Council* [2005] E.C.R. II-4355, paras 86–93 (upheld on appeal: see ECJ, Case C-6/06 P *Cofradía de pescadores de 'San Pedro' and Others v Council* [2007] E.C.R. I-164*, Summ. pub., paras 48–62).

[216] See, e.g. CFI, Case T-90/03 *FICF and Others v Commission* [2007] E.C.R. II-76*, Summ. pub., para. 61; CFI (order of 27 October 2008), Case T-375/07 *Pellegrini v Commission* [2008] E.C.R. II-235*, Summ. pub., para. 19 (and citations therein).

[217] See, e.g. ECJ, Case C-76/01 P *Eurocoton and Others v Council* [2003] E.C.R. I-10091, paras 98–99; CFI, Case T-43/98 *Emesa Sugar v Council* [2001] E.C.R. II-3519, para. 63; CFI, Case T-48/05 *Franchet and Byk v Commission* [2008] E.C.R. II-1585, para. 243 (and further citations therein); CFI, Case T-47/03 *Sison v Council* [2007] E.C.R. II-73*, Summ. pub., para. 238.

[218] See, e.g. CFI, Case T-90/03 *FICF and Others v Commission* [2007] E.C.R. II-76*, Summ. pub., para. 61.

[219] CFI, Case T-2/99 *T. Port v Council* [2001] E.C.R. II-2093, para. 83; CFI, Case T-3/99 *Banatrading v Council* [2001] E.C.R. II-2123, para. 78.

[220] See, e.g. CFI, Case T-52/99 *T. Port v Commission* [2001] E.C.R. II-981, para. 51; CFI, Case T-2/99 *T. Port v Council* [2001] E.C.R. II-2093, para. 51; CFI, Case T-18/99 *Cordis v Commission* [2001] E.C.R. II-913, para. 46; CFI, Case T-30/99 *Bocchi Food Trade International v Commission* [2001] E.C.R. II-943, para. 56; CFI, Case T-174/00 *Biret International v Council* [2002] E.C.R. II-417, para. 61; ECJ, Case C-93/02 P *Biret International v Council* [2003] E.C.R. I-10497, para. 52 (however, the Court of Justice did not rule out the possibility of reviewing the legality of Union acts in the light of the WTO rules in the event of a recommendation or ruling of the WTO Dispute Settlement Body (DSB) against the Union (paras 57–64)). Yet, this appears to have been superseded by the Court of Justice's judgment in *FIAMM*, in which it ruled that there was no basis for a distinction between the 'direct effect' of the WTO rules imposing substantive obligations and that of a decision of the DSB and that a recommendation or a ruling of the DSB, finding that the substantive rules contained in the WTO agreements have not been complied with, is 'no more capable than those rules of conferring upon individuals a right to rely thereupon before the [Union] courts for the purpose of having the legality of the conduct of the [Union] institutions reviewed': ECJ, Joined Cases C-120/06 P and C-121/06 P *FIAMM and Others v Council and Commission* [2008] E.C.R. I-6513, paras 125–129. The Court also ruled that the established case-law, according to which the WTO agreements are not in principle among the rules in the light of which the Court reviews the legality of Union measures, save for certain exceptions, is applicable to the context of an action for damages and that there was no reason for drawing a distinction according to whether the legality of the Union action is to be reviewed in annulment proceedings or for the purpose of deciding an action for damages (paras 111–124). See also Opinion of Advocate-General M. Poiares Maduro in ECJ, Joined Cases C-120/06 P and C-121/06 P *FIAMM and Others v Council and Commission* [2008] E.C.R. I-6513, points 18–52 for a summary of the various issues and relevant case-law.

[221] See, e.g. CFI, Case T-128/05 *SPM v Commission* [2008] E.C.R. II-260*, Summ. pub., paras 96–106, 119, 131 (appeal dismissed in ECJ (order of 22 March 2010), Case C-39/09 P *SPM v Council and Commission* [2010] E.C.R. I-38*, Summ. pub.). For some other examples, see CFI, Case T-367/03 *Yedas Tarim ve*

(b) The requirement of a sufficiently serious breach

(i) The discretion of the Union institution

11.52 *General or individual, legislative or non-legislative nature of the act is irrelevant* - The General Court at first instance and the Court of Justice on appeal have to determine the extent of the institution's discretion in the light of the legal context in which the Union act at issue was adopted. The nature of the act in itself[222]—whether it is general or individual, legislative or non-legislative—is, as such, irrelevant.[223]

11.53 *Discretion involves policy choices* - It is critical whether the institution had a discretion when it adopted the measure. There will be a discretion where the provision of the Treaties or of secondary Union law on which the measure is based requires the institution to make a policy choice.

This is what the Court of First Instance held in *Dieckmann*,[224] which was concerned with a Commission decision excluding a State from the list of third counties from which importation of fishery products was authorized and placing that act in the context of the common agricultural policy, a policy area for which it had already been established that the Union

---

Otomotiv Sanayi ve Ticaret v Council and Commission [2006] E.C.R. II-873, paras 36–49 (upheld in ECJ (order of 5 July 2007), Case C-255/06 P *Yedas Tarim ve Otomotiv Sanayi ve Ticaret v Council and Commission* [2007] E.C.R. I-94*, Summ. pub., paras 35–39 (Association Agreement with Turkey)); EGC (order of 6 September 2011), Case T-292/09 *Mugraby v Council and Commission*, not reported, paras 61–69 (Association Agreement with Lebanon) (appeal dismissed in ECJ (order of 12 July 2012), Case C-581/11 P *Mugraby v Council and Commission*, not reported).

[222] This is not to say that elements of the *Schöppenstedt* test do not creep back in. The Union legislator often enjoys a broad discretion. This explains the rationale for the restrictive nature of the action for damages in relation to its 'legislative' activity; see, e.g. ECJ, Joined Cases C-120/06 P and C-121/06 P *FIAMM and Others v Council and Commission* [2008] E.C.R. I-6513, paras 172, 174; CFI, Case T-47/02 *Danzer and Danzer v Council* [2006] E.C.R. II-1779, para. 52 ('with regard to the [Union's] *liability in respect of legislative acts involving choices of economic policy*, in the drafting of which the [Union] institutions likewise have a wide discretionary power, the unlawfulness of a coordinating directive is not in itself sufficient to establish the [Union's] non-contractual liability, as there is no non-contractual liability on the part of the [Union] unless there has been a sufficiently serious breach of a rule of law designed to confer rights on individuals') (citations omitted).

[223] See, e.g. ECJ, Case C-352/98 P *Bergaderm and Goupil v Commission* [2000] E.C.R. I-5291, para. 46; ECJ, Case C-472/00 P *Commission v Fresh Marine* [2003] E.C.R. I-7541, para. 27; ECJ, Case C-282/05 P *Holcim (Deutschland) v Commission* [2007] E.C.R. I-2941, paras 48–49; CFI, Case T-155/99 *Dieckmann & Hansen v Commission* [2001] E.C.R. II-3143, paras 45–46; ECJ, Joined Cases T-198/95, T-171/96, T-230/97, T-174/98, and T-225/99 *Comafrica and Dole Fresh Fruit Europe v Commission* [2001] E.C.R. II-1975, paras 135–136; EGC, Case T-429/05 *Artegodan v Commission* [2010] E.C.R. II-491, para. 54 (appeal dismissed in ECJ (judgment of 19 April 2012), Case C-221/10 P *Artegodan v Commission*, not reported). With the changes brought by the Lisbon Treaty, the regime of legal instruments has been reformed, with the result that there is now a distinction between legislative and non-legislative (delegated/implementing) acts: see K. Lenaerts and P. Van Nuffel (R. Bray and N. Cambien (eds)), *European Union Law* (3rd edn, London, Sweet & Maxwell, 2011), paras 22.62 and 22.63. The fact that a regulation is of direct and individual concern to a particular person within the meaning of the fourth para. of Art. 263 TFEU does not mean that it loses its legislative nature for the purposes of an action for damages brought pursuant to the second para. of Art. 340 TFEU: see ECJ, Case C-152/88 *Sofrimport v Commission* [1990] E.C.R. I-2477, at I-2510. See also CFI, Joined Cases T-480/93 and T-483/93 *Antillean Rice Mills and Others v Commission* [1995] E.C.R. II-2305, paras 180–186, where the *Schöppenstedt* test was applied. This approach was confirmed by the Court of Justice in ECJ, Case C-390/95 P *Antillean Rice Mills and Others v Commission* [1999] E.C.R. I-769, paras 56–59, and remains applicable in the context of the *Bergaderm* case-law. For directives, see ECJ, Case C-63/89 *Assurances du Crédit v Council and Commission* [1991] E.C.R. I-1799, para. 12.

[224] CFI, Case T-155/99 *Dieckmann & Hansen v Commission* [2001] E.C.R. II-3143, paras 48–56.

institutions had a discretion. Moreover, it appeared from the legislative acts on which the Commission decision was based that the legislator had expressly conferred a broad discretion on the Commission as regards controlling the import of fisheries products.[225]

Also, the fact that the institution has to reconcile divergent interests and thus select options within the context of the policy choices which are its own responsibility obviously points to the existence of a discretion.[226]

Case-by-case assessment - However, the fact that an act was adopted in a policy area that **11.54** frequently involves (economic) policy choices does not automatically lead to a finding that a discretion exists. The Union judicature will always assess the margin of discretion in the light of the specific circumstances.

Thus, in the *Fresh Marine* case, the Court of First Instance held that an act of the Commission by which an undertaking on the part of the applicant (offer to avoid the imposition of anti-dumping duties) was said to have been breached and anti-dumping duties were imposed 'did not involve any choices of economic policy'. In that connection, the Commission had 'only very little or no discretion'.[227]

Likewise, for example, in *Commission v Schneider Electric*, the Court of Justice affirmed the General Court's decision holding that the Commission had committed a sufficiently serious breach of the rules of law relating to the applicant's rights of defence in connection with the procedure for assessing the compatibility of a concentration with the internal market, which resulted from the mere application of the relevant procedural rules. In relation to the applicant's right to be heard, the margin of discretion was therefore considerably reduced, or even non-existent.[228] By comparison, as regards defects committed by the Commission in the analysis of a proposed concentration under the competition rules, the General Court's judgments in *Schneider Electric v Commission* and *MyTravel Group v Commission* attest that although the possibility cannot be ruled out that manifest and serious defects affecting the economic analysis underlying competition policy decisions may constitute a sufficiently serious breach of a rule of law to cause the Union to incur non-contractual liability, for such a finding to be made, several considerations must be taken into account which include '[t]he complexity of the situations to be regulated in the control of concentrations, difficulties in the application connected with the time constraints

---

[225] See also CFI, Case T-18/99 *Cordis v Commission* [2001] E.C.R. II-913, para. 75 (the Commission has a margin of discretion in the area of the common organization of markets, which involves constant adjustments to meet changes in the economic situation); CFI, Case T-170/00 *Förde-Reederei v Council and Commission* [2002] E.C.R. II-515, para. 46; CFI, Case T-209/00 *Lamberts v European Ombudsman* [2002] E.C.R. II-2203, para. 79.

[226] See, e.g. CFI, Case T-30/99 *Bocchi Food Trade International v Commission* [2001] E.C.R. II-943, paras 91–93; EGC, Case T-291/04 *Enviro Tech Europe and Enviro Tech International v Commission* [2011] E.C.R. II-8281, para. 125 (finding that 'the contested classification, which the applicants consider to be unlawful, was adopted by the Commission in the form of a directive relating to the protection of consumer health and in the exercise of the broad discretion which is conferred upon it in this complex technical and legal context which is essentially in a state of flux') (appeal dismissed in ECJ (order of 24 January 2013), Case C-118/12 P *Enviro Tech Europe v Commission*, not reported).

[227] CFI, Case T-178/98 *Fresh Marine v Commission* [2000] E.C.R. II-3331, para. 57 (upheld on appeal: ECJ, Case C-472/00 P *Commission v Fresh Marine* [2003] E.C.R. I-7541).

[228] CFI, Case T-351/03 *Schneider Electric v Commission* [2007] E.C.R. II-2237, paras 122, 152–156; ECJ, Case C-440/07 P *Commission v Schneider Electric* [2009] E.C.R. I-6413, para. 166.

imposed on the administration in that regard and the margin of discretion available to the Commission'.[229]

11.55 *European Ombudsman* - In order to determine whether there has been a sufficiently serious breach of Union law rendering the Union non-contractually liable owing to the conduct of the European Ombudsman, regard must be had to the specific nature of the latter's function. In that context, it should be borne in mind that the European Ombudsman is merely under an obligation to use his or her best endeavours and that he or she enjoys wide discretion.[230]

11.56 *Institution has a discretion* - The requirement for there to have been a sufficiently serious breach reflects once again the Union judiciary's reluctance to find the Union liable for loss or damage caused by acts involving policy choices.[231] In these circumstances in which a Union institution or body has a discretion, there can have been a sufficiently serious breach only in the event that the Union institution in question manifestly and gravely disregarded the limits on the exercise of its discretion.[232]

11.57 *Extent of the loss or damage* - The Court of Justice and the General Court have also tackled the question as to whether the Union institution concerned manifestly and gravely

---

[229] CFI, Case T-212/03 *MyTravel Group v Commission* [2008] E.C.R. II-1967, paras 80–84; see also CFI, Case T-351/03 *Schneider Electric v Commission* [2007] E.C.R. II-2227, paras 131–132 (set aside in part on other grounds in ECJ, Case C-440/07 P *Commission v Schneider Electric* [2009] E.C.R. I-6413: see further para. 11.82). In the latter case, the General Court found it unnecessary to apply these considerations, since the defects in the Commission's analysis could not have had any effect on the finding ultimately reached by the Commission that the transaction was incompatible with the internal market: CFI, Case T-351/03 *Schneider Electric v Commission*, paras 133–138. In the former case, however, the General Court ruled, on the basis of those considerations, that the line of reasoning adopted by the Commission, however incorrect it may be in the light of the review of the lawfulness of the decision, did not constitute a sufficiently serious error considered to be incompatible with 'the normal conduct of an institution responsible for ensuring that the competition rules are applied', and hence the Commission did not commit a sufficiently serious breach giving rise to the Union's non-contractual liability: CFI, Case T-212/03 *MyTravel Group v Commission*, paras 85–93.

[230] ECJ, Case C-234/02 P *European Ombudsman v Lamberts* [2004] E.C.R. I-2803, para. 50. See further CFI, Case T-412/05 *M v European Ombudsman* [2008] E.C.R. II-197*, Summ. pub., para. 123 (finding that the European Ombudsman manifestly and gravely exceeded the limits on his discretion and thus committed a sufficiently serious breach of a rule of law conferring rights on individuals (para. 145), which resulted in an award of compensation for moral damage suffered by the applicant (para. 158)).

[231] See also EGC, Case T-341/07 *Sison v Council* [2011] E.C.R. II-7915, para. 34 (and citations therein) ('This requirement of a sufficiently serious breach of [Union] law, within the meaning of *Bergaderm*... is intended, whatever the nature of the unlawful act at issue, to avoid the risk of having to bear the losses claimed by the persons concerned obstructing the institution's ability to exercise to the full its powers in the general interest, whether that be in its legislative activity, or in that involving choices of economic policy or in the sphere of its administrative competence, without however thereby leaving individuals to bear the consequences of flagrant and inexcusable misconduct.'). See also EGC (judgment of 16 May 2013), Case T-437/10 *Gap granen & producten v Commission*, not reported, para. 41.

[232] For legislative acts, see ECJ, Joined Cases 83/76 and 94/76, 4/77, 15/77, and 40/77 *HNL and Others v Council and Commission* [1978] E.C.R. 1209, para. 6; ECJ, Case 50/86 *Grands Moulins de Paris v Council and Commission* [1987] E.C.R. 4833, para. 8; ECJ, Case 20/88 *Roquette Frères v Commission* [1989] E.C.R. 1553, paras 23–26; ECJ, Case C-352/98 P *Bergaderm and Goupil v Commission* [2000] E.C.R. I-5291, para. 43. For public tender procedures, see CFI, Case T-160/03 *AFCon Management Consultants and Others v Commission* [2005] E.C.R. II-981, para. 93. For some recent examples in which the Court has clarified the extent of this ruling, see, e.g. CFI, Case T-226/01 *CAS Succhi di Frutta v Commission* [2006] E.C.R. II-2763, paras 68–71 (appeal dismissed in ECJ, Case C-497/06 P *CAS Succhi di Frutta v Commission* [2009] E.C.R. I-69*, Summ. pub., paras 71–76); EGC (judgment of 28 September 2010), Case T-247/08 *C-Content v Commission*, not reported, paras 86–87 (see also ECJ, Case C-331/05 P *Internationaler Hilfsfonds v Commission* [2007] E.C.R. I-5475, para. 31).

disregarded its powers in the light of an appraisal of the loss or damage caused thereby.[233] The particular intensity of the damage and the fact that a limited or ascertainable number of persons were affected determine the matter.[234] Notably, in previous case-law, account was taken of the specific situation of a clearly defined group of individuals and required that the damage must go beyond the normal economic risks inherent in the sector concerned, but these elements are not mentioned as requirements for liability in *Bergaderm*.[235]

Institution does not have a discretion - Where the institution has only considerably reduced **11.58** or no discretion, a sufficiently serious breach will be involved where there is a mere infringement of Union law, in particular a finding of an error which an administrative authority exercising ordinary care and diligence would not have committed in analogous circumstances.[236]

---

[233] ECJ, Joined Cases 83/76 and 94/76, 4, 15, and 40/77 *HNL and Others v Council and Commission* [1978] E.C.R. 1209, para. 7; CFI, Case T-56/00 *Dole Fresh Fruit International v Council and Commission* [2003] E.C.R. II-577, para. 79.

[234] ECJ, Joined Cases 83/76 and 94/76, 4, 15, and 40/77 *HNL and Others v Council and Commission*, para. 7; CFI, Case T-56/00 *Dole Fresh Fruit International v Council and Commission*, para 79; cf. CFI, Case T-120/89 *Stahlwerke Peine-Salzgitter v Commission* [1991] E.C.R. II-279, para. 131 (ruling under the ECSC Treaty); see also ECJ, Case 50/86 *Grands Moulins de Paris v Council and Commission* [1987] E.C.R. 4833, para. 21.

[235] See, e.g. ECJ, Case 278/78 *Ireks-Arkady v Council and Commission* [1979] E.C.R. 2955, para. 11; ECJ, Joined Cases C-104/89 and C-37/90 *Mulder and Others v Council and Commission* [1992] E.C.R. I-3061, paras 13, 16. See also CFI, Case T-429/05 *Artegodan v Commission* [2010] E.C.R. II-491, para. 56 (finding applicant's argument based on ECJ, Case 278/78 *Ireks-Arkady v Council and Commission*, that the Union measure concerned was confined to a closed group of interested parties and that the damage alleged exceeds the limits of the economic risks inherent in the sector concerned 'irrelevant' for determining whether the alleged breaches of Union law are sufficiently serious for the purposes of the *Bergaderm* judgment) (appeal dismissed in ECJ (judgment of 19 April 2012), Case C-221/10 P *Artegodan v Commission*, not reported). However, there have been cases decided after *Bergaderm* where liability has been denied at least in part on the grounds that the alleged damage did not go beyond the bounds of the economic risks inherent in the sector concerned: see P. Craig, *EU Administrative Law* (2nd edn, Oxford, Oxford University Press, 2012), 688 (and citations therein).

[236] See, e.g. CFI, Case T-178/98 *Fresh Marine v Commission* [2000] E.C.R. II-3331, para. 61; CFI, Joined Cases T-198/95, T-171/96, T-230/97, T-174/98, and T-225/99 *Comafrica and Dole Fresh Fruit Europe v Commission* [2001] E.C.R. II-1975, para. 144; CFI, Case T-285/03 *Agraz v Commission* [2005] E.C.R. II-1063, para. 40 (set aside on other grounds in ECJ, Case C-243/05 P); CFI, Case T-364/03 *Medici Grimm v Council* [2006] E.C.R. II-79, para. 79; EGC, Case T-341/07 *Sison v Council* [2011] E.C.R. II-7915, para. 39. See also CFI, Case T-351/03 *Schneider Electric v Commission* [2007] E.C.R. II-2237, para. 118 (noting after the 'mere infringement' language that '[t]he same applies where the defendant institution breaches a general obligation of diligence or misapplies relevant substantive or procedural rules'); CFI, Case T-212/03 *MyTravel Group v Commission* [2008] E.C.R. II-1967, para. 39 (noting after the 'mere infringement' language, '[t]he same applies where the defendant institution improperly applies the relevant substantive or procedural rules'). Various shortcomings in the performance of administrative acts were held to constitute serious breaches (before the judgment in *Bergaderm*). See M. Van der Woude, 'Liability for Administrative Acts Under Art. 215(2) EC [now Art. 340(2) TFEU]', in T. Heukels and A. McDonnell (eds), *The Action for Damages in Community Law* (The Hague, Kluwer, Law International, 1997), 109–28. The shortcomings in question included lack of care in exercising implementing powers: ECJ, Case 169/73 *Compagnie Continentale v Council* [1975] E.C.R. 117, para. 21; CFI, Case T-514/93 *Cobrecaf and Others v Commission* [1995] E.C.R. II-621, paras 63–70 (by waiting fifteen months before rectifying a manifest error in paying a promised Community subsidy, the Commission exhibited an obvious lack of care); misuse of powers: ECJ, Joined Cases 5/66, 7/66, and 13/66 to 24/66 *Kampffmeyer and Others v Commission* [1967] E.C.R. 245, at 262; failure to adopt a required act: ECJ, Joined Cases 9/60 and 12/60 *Vloeberghs v High Authority* [1961] E.C.R. 197, at 213; a defective system adopted by an authority which can be attributed to the Union: ECJ, Case 23/59 *FERAM v High Authority* [1959] E.C.R. 245, at 251–2 (system adopted held not defective); ECJ, Case 33/59 *Compagnie des Hauts Forneaux de Chasse v High Authority* [1962] E.C.R. 381, at 389 (system held not defective); ECJ, Joined Cases 46/59 and 47/59 *Meroni and Others v High Authority* [1962] E.C.R. 411, at 422–3; lack of supervision: ECJ, Joined Cases 19/60 and 21/60, 2/61 and 3/61 *Société Fives Lille Cail and Others v High Authority* [1961] E.C.R. 281, at 297; failure to rectify

(ii) Consideration of justifications

11.59 *Discretion is a decisive but not sole criterion* - The extent of the discretion enjoyed by the institution concerned is a decisive criterion but it is not the only criterion taken into account by the Union judicature. After the Union judicature has determined whether the institution concerned enjoys any discretion, it may take into consideration certain justifications elaborated in the case-law in its determination whether the requirement of a sufficiently serious breach has been satisfied.[237]

11.60 *Justifications* - According to the well-known formula in the case-law, the system of rules which the Court of Justice has worked out in relation to the non-contractual liability of the Union 'takes into account, *inter alia*, the complexity of the situations to be regulated, difficulties in the application or interpretation of the legislation, and more particularly, the margin of discretion available to the author of the act in question'.[238] Other justifications are inspired by the case-law on the principle of State liability, such as the inexcusable or intentional character of the error.[239]

Accordingly, the 'breach' of a rule of law is sometimes justified, *inter alia*, on the ground that an important general interest takes precedence over the individual interest of the injured party[240] or that the breach was the result of an erroneous, but excusable, approach

---

information in time once it became clear that the information provided was incorrect: ECJ, Joined Cases 19/69 to 20/69, 25/69, and 30/69 *Richez-Parise and Others v Commission* [1970] E.C.R. 325, paras 38–42; failure to comply with internal rules: ECJ, Joined Cases 10/72 and 47/72 *Di Pillo v Commission* [1973] E.C.R. 763, para. 24; breach of the duty of confidentiality: ECJ, Case 145/83 *Adams v Commission* [1985] E.C.R. 3539, paras 28–44; principle of sound administration: the Commission infringed that principle by sending a fax to the persons responsible nationally for a PHARE programme funded by the Commission, in which it cast doubt on the financial reliability of an undertaking which had managed several PHARE projects, without checking the data on which the fax was based or giving the undertaking concerned the opportunity to put over its views (CFI, Case T-231/97 *New Europe Consulting and Brown v Commission* [1999] E.C.R. II-2403, paras 38–45).

[237] See, e.g. EGC, Case T-341/07 *Sison v Council* [2011] E.C.R. II-7915, para. 40 (and citations therein).

[238] See, e.g. ECJ, Case C-282/05 P *Holcim (Deutschland) v Commission* [2007] E.C.R. I-2941, para. 50 (and citations therein).

[239] See, e.g. CFI, Case T-364/03 *Medici Grimm v Council* [2006] E.C.R. II-79, para. 87; CFI, Case T-429/05 *Artegodan v Commission* [2010] E.C.R. I-491, para. 62. With the alignment of the conditions governing the non-contractual liability of the Union with those of State liability in *Bergaderm*, these justifications inspired a special set of factors elaborated by the Court of Justice in *Brasserie du Pecheur and Factortame* in order to guide the national courts' assessment of the sufficiently serious breach requirement, which include: 'the clarity and precision of the rule breached, the measure of discretion left by that rule to the national or [Union] authorities, whether the infringement and the damage caused was intentional or involuntary, whether any error of law was excusable or inexcusable, the fact that the position taken by a [Union] institution may have contributed towards the omission, and the adoption or retention of national measures or practices contrary to [Union] law': ECJ, Joined Cases C-46/93 and C-48/93 *Brasserie du Pêcheur and Secretary of State for Transport, ex parte: Factortame and Others* [1996] E.C.R. I-1029, para. 56. This list of factors diverges to some extent from the factors elaborated in *Köbler* on account of the nature of the breach concerned in that latter case, namely, breaches or infringements of Union law committed by national courts adjudicating at last instance: see ECJ, Case C-224/01 *Köbler* [2003] E.C.R. I-10239, para. 55. See also EGC, Case T-341/07 *Sison v Council* [2011] E.C.R. II-7915, para. 40, noting by analogy to case-law on State liability that '[o]n any view, an infringement of Union law is sufficiently serious if it has persisted despite a judgment finding the infringement in question to be established, or a preliminary ruling or settled case-law of the Court on the matter from which it is clear that the conduct in question constituted an infringement'.

[240] See, e.g. ECJ, Case 97/76 *Merkur v Commission* [1977] E.C.R. 1063, para. 5; ECJ, Case 281/84 *Zuckerfabrik Bedburg v Council and Commission* [1987] E.C.R. 49, para. 38; ECJ, Case 50/86 *Grands Moulins de Paris v Council and Commission* [1987] E.C.R. 4833, para. 21; CFI, Case T-56/00 *Dole Fresh Fruit International v Council and Commission* [2003] E.C.R. II-577, para. 76.

to an unresolved legal question[241] or of the complexity of the situations to be regulated and the difficulties in the application or interpretation of the texts.[242] The absence of such a justification raises a presumption that the Union institution acted 'arbitrarily', as a result of which the breach of the relevant rule of law is deemed to be sufficiently serious.[243]

Justifications may be taken into account irrespective of the extent of the discretion - The **11.61** case-law indicates that the Union courts may take into consideration justifications irrespective of the extent of the discretion enjoyed by the institution, that is to say, in situations where the institution has a discretion within the context of the 'manifest and grave disregard' prong,[244] as well as in cases involving little or no discretion on the part of the institution concerned within the context of the 'mere infringement' prong.[245] This harkens back to the Court's formulation that in situations in which the institution concerned has only considerably reduced or even no discretion, the mere infringement of Union law *may* be sufficient to establish the existence of a sufficiently serious breach, but this is not automatic.[246] That being said, in some circumstances, where the institution concerned

---

[241] See, e.g. CFI, Case T-120/89 *Stahlwerke Peine-Salzgitter v Commission* [1991] E.C.R. II-279, paras 108–118.

[242] See, e.g. CFI, Joined Cases T-198/95, T-171/96, T-230/97, T-174/98, and T-225/99 *Comafrica and Dole Fresh Fruit Europe v Commission* [2001] E.C.R. II-1975, para. 149; CFI, Case T-28/03 *Holcim (Deutschland) v Commission* [2005] E.C.R. II-1357, paras 100–101 (upheld on appeal: ECJ, Case C-282/05 P *Holcim (Deutschland) v Commission* [2007] E.C.R. I-2941, paras 50–51).

[243] ECJ, Joined Cases 116/77 and 124/77 *Amylum and Others v Council and Commission* [1979] E.C.R. 3497, para. 19; ECJ, Case 106/81 *Kind v Commission* [1982] E.C.R. 2885, para. 22.

[244] See, e.g. ECJ, Case C-198/03 P *Commission v Ceva Santé Animale and Others* [2005] E.C.R. I-6357, paras 74–93: on the basis of the margin of discretion available to the Commission and all of the factual circumstances, particularly the complexity of the matter concerned, the Court of Justice held that the Commission did not disregard in a clear and serious manner the limits on its discretion, and thus did not breach Union law in a sufficiently serious way to give rise to non-contractual liability on the part of the Union.

[245] See, e.g. CFI, Case T-28/03 *Holcim (Deutschland) v Commission* [2005] E.C.R. II-1357, paras 98–118 (upheld on appeal: ECJ, Case C-282/05 *Holcim (Deutschland) v Commission* [2007] E.C.R. I-2941, paras 41, 50–51); CFI, Case T-364/03 *Medici Grimm v Council* [2006] E.C.R. II-79, paras 82–98; CFI, Case T-429/05 *Artegodan v Commission* [2010] E.C.R. II-491, paras 104–112 (appeal dismissed in ECJ (judgment of 19 April 2012), Case C-221/10 P *Artegodan v Commission*, not reported), EGC, Case T-341/07 *Sison v Council* [2011] E.C.R. II-7915, paras 57–74. See also ECJ, Case C-440/07 P *Commission v Schneider Electric* [2009] E.C.R. I-6413, paras 166–170: the Court of Justice affirmed that the Commission's breach of the applicant's rights of defence resulted from the mere application of the relevant procedural rules and thus in relation to Schneider's right to be heard the Commission's margin of discretion was considerably reduced, or even non-existent (this was so, despite the General Court's framing of such breach in its decision as 'a manifest and serious disregard by the Commission of the limits to which it is subject': CFI, Case T-351/03 *Schneider Electric v Commission* [2007] E.C.R. II-2237, para. 156) and upheld the General Court's declaration of a sufficiently serious breach in those circumstances after considering, and discounting, the Commission's arguments concerning the purported complexity of the situation to be regulated and the time constraints involved in doing so (see CFI, Case T-351/03 *Schneider Electric v Commission*, para. 155 finding the defendant's argument as to the difficulty inherent in undertaking a complex market analysis under a very rigid time constraint 'irrelevant', since the fact giving rise to the damage here 'did not involve any particular technical difficulty'), thereby rejecting the Commission's arguments on appeal that the General Court did not take account of the complexity of the situation to be regulated in order to exclude the existence of a sufficiently serious breach.

[246] See, e.g. CFI, Case T-429/05 *Artegodan v Commission* [2010] E.C.R. II-491, paras 59–62 (referring by analogy to relevant paras of ECJ, Case C-424/97 *Haim* [2000] E.C.R. I-5123, para. 41, in which the Court of Justice ruled, in the context of proceedings concerning the principle of State liability, that a mere infringement of Union law by a Member State 'may, but does not necessarily, constitute a sufficiently serious breach') (appeal dismissed in ECJ (judgment of 19 April 2012), Case C-221/10 P *Artegodan v Commission*, not reported); EGC, Case T-341/07 *Sison v Council* [2011] E.C.R. II-7915, paras 36–40.

has no discretion, the mere infringement of Union law will be sufficient for finding a sufficiently serious breach without consideration of justifications.[247]

11.62 *No cumulative effects to establish a sufficiently serious breach* - Under the case-law, where taken individually, the alleged infringements of Union law relied on by the applicant are not of such a kind to establish a sufficiently serious breach, the action is dismissed, and this cannot be remedied by arguments that the cumulative effects of the alleged errors committed by the institution concerned taken together suffice to constitute a sufficiently serious breach.[248]

(3) The reality of the loss or damage

11.63 The requirement relating to the reality of the loss or damage is the second pillar on which Union non-contractual liability is based.

The requirement is satisfied when the existence and the extent of the damage have been proved. In practice, the determination as to the existence and the extent of the damage that the applicant claims to have suffered is merged with that concerning the proof of such damage put forward by the applicant. For the purposes of the following survey, they will be considered separately.

(a) Existence and extent of the damage

(i) Damage must be actual and certain

11.64 The condition relating to the damage requires that the damage for which compensation is sought be actual and certain.[249] By contrast, damage that is purely hypothetical and indeterminate does not confer an entitlement to compensation.[250] The damage claimed by the applicant may include material[251] damage in the form of a reduction in a person's

---

[247] See, e.g. CFI, Case T-48/05 *Franchet and Byk v Commission* [2008] E.C.R. II-1585, para. 314 (finding that in the circumstances of the present case, the Commission's breach of the principle of the presumption of innocence must be considered sufficiently serious, since the Commission has no discretion with respect to its obligation to respect that principle).

[248] See, e.g. CFI, Case T-212/03 *MyTravel v Commission* [2008] E.C.R. II-1967, paras 94–95; EGC, Case T-429/05 *Artegodan v Commission* [2010] E.C.R. II-491, paras 140–143 (appeal dismissed in ECJ (judgment of 19 April 2012), Case C-221/10 P *Artegodan v Commission*, not reported). See also ECJ, Case C-167/06 P *Komninou and Others v Commission* [2007] E.C.R. I-141*, Summ. pub., para. 73 (upholding the Court of First Instance's rejection of the applicants' argument that even though the various events taken in isolation did not constitute infringements, such events appreciated in a global manner were of such a nature as to incur non-contractual liability).

[249] See, e.g. ECJ, Case C-243/05 P *Agraz and Others v Commission* [2006] E.C.R. I-10833, para. 27 (and citations therein). As illustrated by this case, the requirement that the existence of the damage must be certain should be distinguished from that concerning the extent of the damage: see further para. 11.77.

[250] See, e.g. CFI, Case T-415/03 *Cofradía de pescadores 'San Pedro' de Bermeo and Others v Council* [2005] E.C.R. II-4355, paras 110–148 (appeal dismissed in ECJ, Case C-6/06 P *Cofradía de pescadores 'San Pedro' de Bermeo and Others v Council* [2007] E.C.R. I–164*, Summ. pub.); CFI, Case T-495/04 *Belfass v Council* [2008] E.C.R. II-781, para. 127.

[251] Costs incurred by the parties for the purposes of the judicial proceedings before the Union courts are not regarded as constituting damage distinct from the burden of costs: see, e.g CFI, Case T-48/05 *Franchet and Byk v Commission* [2008] E.C.R. II-1585, para. 414 (and citations therein); CFI (order of 27 August 2009), Case T-367/08 *Abouchar v Commission* [2009] E.C.R. II-128*, Summ. pub., para. 42; EGC (order of 6 July 2010), Case T-401/09 *Marcuccio v Court of Justice of the EU*, not reported, para. 31 (appeal dismissed in ECJ (order of 14 April 2011), Case C-460/10 P *Cofradía de pescadores 'San Pedro' de Bermeo and Others v Council* [2007] E.C.R. I–164*, Summ. pub.). See further para. 11.85. Moreover, under the case-law, charges and expenses incurred by a tenderer in connection with his participation in a tendering procedure cannot in principle constitute damage which is capable of being remedied by an award of damages: see, e.g. EGC, Case T-514/09 *bpost NV van publiek recht v Commission* [2011] E.C.R. II-420*, Summ. pub., para. 173 (and citations therein).

assets (*damnum emergens*) or loss of profit (*lucrum cessans*),[252] non-material damage,[253] and future damage.[254]

(ii) Loss of profit

As has already been mentioned, there are no objections in principle to an award of damages for **11.65**
loss of profit.[255] The applicant must show that it was legitimately entitled in all the circumstances
to make the profit and was only frustrated by the unlawful act of the Union institution.[256]

(iii) Non-material damage

Where non-material damage is found, equitable damages (rendered *ex aequo et bono*)[257] or **11.66**
sometimes symbolic damages[258] may be awarded.[259]

---

[252] Opinion of Advocate-General F. Capotorti in ECJ, Case 238/78 *Ireks-Arkady v Council and Commission* [1979] E.C.R. 2955, at 2998–9.

[253] Non-material or non-pecuniary damage is not an actual reduction in assets, but may be, for example the 'reflection' of unreasonable inconvenience caused to an individual on account of an unlawful act or failure to act of a Union institution: see, e.g. CFI, Case T-231/97 *New Europe Consulting and Brown v Commission* [1999] E.C.R. II-2403, paras 53–55; CFI, Case T-11/00 *Hautem v EIB* [2000] E.C.R. II-4019, para. 52, in which the Court of First Instance held that the unlawful conduct at issue (failure to comply with a judgment) had placed the applicant in a prolonged state of uncertainty and anxiety with regard to the recognition of his rights and his professional future, while the indeterminate nature of his work status had caused him difficulties in finding employment, which constituted non-material damage. Non-material damage may also consist of impairment of the applicant's image, honour, and reputation: see, e.g. CFI, Case T-309/03 *Camós Grau v Commission* [2006] E.C.R. II-1173, para. 162; EGC, Case T-88/09 *Idromacchine and Others v Commission* [2011] E.C.R. II-7833, para. 63 (appeal dismissed in ECJ (order of 3 September 2013), Case C-34/12 P *Idromacchine and Others v Commission*, not reported). In the context of the EAEC Treaty, see ECJ, Case C-308/87 *Grifoni v EAEC* [1994] E.C.R. I-341, para. 37 ('The victim of an accident must be compensated, irrespective of any financial loss, for any personal damage which may cover physical or mental suffering').

[254] Damage not yet sustained at the time it is being appraised.

[255] ECJ, Joined Cases 5/66, 7/66, and 13/66 to 24/66 *Kampffmeyer and Others v Commission* [1967] E.C.R. 245, at 266: the alleged loss must not be essentially speculative in nature; consequently, the Court of Justice held in that case that the intended transaction must at least have been begun to be performed. See also CFI, Case T-260/97 *Camar v Council and Commission* [2005] E.C.R. II-2741 (award of damages for loss of profit); compare CFI, Case T-198/05 *Mebrom v Commission* [2007] E.C.R. II-51*, Summ. pub. (action for damages held inadmissible on the grounds that the applicant failed to prove it actually incurred the loss of profit alleged) (appeal dismissed in ECJ (order of 11 February 2008), Case 347/07 P *Commission v Italy*, not reported) and EGC, Case T-39/08 *Evropaiki Dynamiki v Commission* [2011] E.C.R. II-437*, Summ. pub., paras 46–49 (loss of profit following the award of a contract to another tenderer was not actual and certain).

[256] ECJ, Case 74/74 *CNTA v Commission* [1975] E.C.R. 533, para. 45; CFI, Case T-231//97 *New Europe Consulting and Brown v Commission* [1999] E.C.R. II-2403, paras 51–52.

[257] See, e.g. ECJ, Joined Cases 7/56 and 3/57 to 7/57 *Algera and Others v Common Assembly* [1957 and 1958] E.C.R. 39, at 66–7; ECJ, Case 110/63 *Willame v Commission* [1965] E.C.R. 649, at 667; ECJ, Joined Cases 10/72 and 47/72 *Di Pillo v Commission* [1973] E.C.R. 763, paras 23–25; ECJ, Case 75/77 *Mollet v Commission* [1978] E.C.R. 897, paras 27–29; ECJ, Case 207/81 *Ditterich v Commission* [1983] E.C.R. 1359, paras 28–29; ECJ, Joined Cases 169/83 and 136/84 *Leussink-Brummelhuis v Commission* [1986] E.C.R. 2801, para. 18; CFI, Case T-13/92 *Moat v Commission* [1993] E.C.R. II-287, para. 49; CFI, Case T-59/92 *Caronna v Commission* [1993] E.C.R. II-1129, para. 107; CFI, Case T-203/96 *Embassy Limousines & Services v European Parliament* [1998] E.C.R. II-4239, para. 109; CFI, Case T-394/03 *Angeletti v Commission* [2006] E.C.R.-SC I-A-2-95, para. 167; Case T-48/05 *Franchet and Byk v Commission* [2008] E.C.R. II-1585, para. 411; CFI, Case T-412/05 *M v European Ombudsman* [2008] E.C.R. II-197*, Summ. pub., para. 158; EGC, Case T-88/09 *Idromacchine and Others v Commission* [2011] E.C.R. II-7833, para. 76 (appeal dismissed in ECJ (order of 3 September 2013), Case C-34/12 P *Idromacchine and Others v Commission*, not reported).

[258] See, e.g. CFI, Case T-18/93 *Marcato v Commission* [1994] E.C.R.-SC II-681, para. 80 (English abstract at [1994] E.C.R.-SC I-A-215); CFI, Joined Cases T-246/04 and T-71/05 *Wunenburger v Commission* [2007] E.C.R.-SC I-A-2-21, para. 168; CFI, Case T-259/03 *Nikolaou v Commission* [2007] E.C.R. II-99*, Summ. pub., para. 333 (finding award of sum fixed *ex aequo et bono* of 3000 euro sufficient to compensate the claimant for non-material damage, including purely symbolic damage).

[259] In the context of staff cases, the Union judicature sometimes considers that the judgment itself, together with its reasoning annulling the contested decision, affords adequate and in principle sufficient

(iv) Future loss or damage

11.67 There has been a change as far as recovery of future loss or damage is concerned. Originally, the Court of Justice held, with regard to the ECSC Treaty, that a claim for compensation for damage that had not yet materialized was inadmissible.[260] It moderated its stance under the second paragraph of what is now Art. 340 TFEU when it held that a claim for compensation for damage that was to materialize only in the future, yet was foreseeable with sufficient certainty, was admissible.[261] It reached this view on the grounds that it might prove necessary to prevent even greater damage to bring the matter before the Court as soon as the cause of damage was certain, and that most Member States recognized an action for declaration of liability based on future damage which was sufficiently certain.

(v) Determination of the quantum

11.68 The award of damages is intended to restore the injured party's financial situation to what it would have been in the absence of the unlawful act or as close as possible thereto.[262] The quantum of the damage is therefore generally determined by comparing the actual assets of the person concerned with his notional assets in the event that he had not been affected by the wrongful act. An 'exact assessment' of the damage sustained is needed, but an approximate determination based on sufficiently reliable facts, preferably collected by an expert, will suffice if it is not possible to make an exact assessment.[263]

The question of the determination of the amount of the damages will be reserved in the event that the necessary information is not available at the time when the finding of liability

---

redress for the typically non-material damage sustained (ECJ, Joined Cases 59/80 and 129/80 *Turner v Commission* [1981] E.C.R. 1883, at 1921). See also ECJ, Joined Cases 44/85, 77/85, 294/85, and 295/85 *Hochbaum and Rawes v Commission* [1987] E.C.R. 3259, para. 22; CFI, Case T-37/89 *Hanning v European Parliament* [1990] E.C.R. II-463, para. 83 (concerning symbolic damage); CFI, Case T-158/89 *Van Hecken v ESC* [1991] E.C.R. II-1341, para. 37; CFI, Case T-52/90 *Volger v European Parliament* [1992] E.C.R. II-121, paras 44–46 (concerning symbolic damage); CFI (judgment of 13 December 2007), Case T-113/05 *Angelidis v European Parliament*, not reported, paras 85–86; CFI (judgment of 1 April 2009), Case T-385/04 *Valero Jordana v Commission*, not reported, para. 159 (considering the annulment of the contested decision adequate and sufficient reparation for the non-material damage and the loss of the career chances suffered by the applicant); CFI (judgment of 6 October 2009), Case T-102/08 P *Sundholm v Commission*, not reported, paras 46–48 (concerning symbolic damage). See also CFI, Case T-47/03 *Sison v Council* [2007] E.C.R. II-73*, Summ. pub., para. 241 (outside of staff dispute, holding that since the fundamental principle of observance of the rights of defence constitutes essentially a procedural guarantee, in the circumstances of the case, annulment of the contested act was deemed to constitute adequate compensation for the damage caused by the sufficiently serious breach of that rule of law). However, depending on the circumstances, a Union court may find that annulment of the contested decision cannot in itself constitute appropriate and sufficient reparation for the non-material damage sustained: see, e.g. ECJ, Case C-343/87 *Culin v Commission* [1990] E.C.R. I-225, paras 26–29 (concerning symbolic damage); CFI, Case T-165/89 *Plug v Commission* [1992] E.C.R. II-367, para. 118.

[260] ECJ, Joined Cases 9/64 and 25/64 *FERAM and Others v High Authority* [1965] E.C.R. 311, at 320–1.

[261] ECJ, Joined Cases 56/74 to 60/74 *Kampffmeyer and Others v Commission and Council* [1976] E.C.R. 711, paras 6–8. See further CFI, Joined Cases T-79/96, T-260/97, and T-117/98 *Camar and Tico v Commission and Council* [2000] E.C.R. II-2193, paras 192, 207 (set aside in part on other grounds in ECJ, Case C-312/00 P).

[262] See, e.g. ECJ, Case C-304/89 and C-37/90 *Mulder and Others v Council and Commission* [2000] E.C.R. I-203, para. 216 (referring to 'the principle, universally applied in all the Member States . . . that full restitution is to be made for the damage suffered'); see also Opinion of Advocate-General F. Capotorti in ECJ, Case 238/78 *Ireks-Arkady v Council and Commission* [1979] E.C.R. 2955, at 2999. It is not clear whether punitive damages could be asked for in the context of an action for damages. No case-law exists on this issue.

[263] ECJ, Joined Cases 29/63, 31/63, 36/63, 39/63 to 47/63, 50/63, and 51/63 *SA des Laminoirs, Hauts Fourneaux, Forges, Fonderies et Usines de la Providence and Others v High Authority* [1965] E.C.R. 911, at 939.

is made.[264] In that event, the Union judicature will indicate as far as possible a number of calculation criteria and invite the parties to reach agreement on the amount of the damages within a specified period and to submit the result to it. If the parties fail to reach agreement, the Union judicature will itself determine the amount of the damages.

(vi) Compensation in kind

There has been a change in the case-law as far as the requirement that there must be **11.69** quantifiable damage is concerned. Until recent case-law, it had generally been considered that the Court of Justice and the General Court were empowered only to make an award of money. In *Galileo International Technology v Commission*, the General Court held, however, that Art. 268 TFEU and the second paragraph of Art. 340 TFEU (in contrast to Art. 40 of the former ECSC Treaty, which only envisaged monetary compensation) do not preclude the grant of compensation in kind and that the Union courts have the power to impose on the Union 'any form of reparation that accords with the general principles of non-contractual liability common to the laws of the Member States, including, if it accords with those principles, compensation in kind, if necessary in the form of an injunction to do or not to do something'.[265] In the instant proceedings, the Court reasoned that for the damage alleged to be fully compensated, the right of the proprietor of the trade mark must be re-established intact which, irrespective of any damages to be assessed, requires at the very least the immediate cessation of the infringement of his right and that it is precisely by means of the injunction applied for that the applicants are seeking to ensure that the Commission's alleged infringement of the applicants' trade mark rights should cease.[266] Furthermore, the Court noted that as the Commission itself stated in response to a question from the Court, if it were ordered to pay damages it was inconceivable that it would disregard that decision by continuing with actions that the Court had declared unlawful and hence such a decision is tantamount to an implied injunction against the Commission.[267] Consequently, the applicants' application for an injunction prohibiting the Commission from using the word 'Galileo' in connection with the Union satellite radio navigation system project was held admissible,[268] though

---

[264] ECJ, Joined Cases 95/74 to 98/74, 15/75, and 100/75 *Coopératives Agricoles de Céréales and Others v Commission and Council* [1975] E.C.R. 1615, para. 5. The Court may find that liability exists in principle, indicating the wrongful unlawful conduct, the existence of actual damage, and the causal link between them, while deferring only the determination of the amount of damages: ECJ, Joined Cases 29/63, 31/63, 36/63, 39/63 to 47/63, 50/63, and 51/63 *SA des Laminoirs, Hauts Fourneaux, Forges, Fonderies et Usines de la Providence and Others v High Authority*, at 940–1; see also, e.g. ECJ, Case C-152/88 *Sofrimport v Commission* [1990] E.C.R. I-2477, para. 30; ECJ, Joined Cases C-104/89 and C-37/90 *Mulder and Others v Council and Commission* [1992] E.C.R. I-3061, paras 37–38; ECJ, Case C-440/07 P *Commission v Schneider Electric* [2009] E.C.R. I-6413, paras 214–217; CFI, Case T-120/89 *Stahlwerke Peine-Salzgitter v Commission* [1991] E.C.R. II-279, para. 137; CFI, Case T-76/94 *Jansma v Council and Commission* [2001] E.C.R. II-243, paras 101–103; CFI, Case T-45/01 *Sanders and Others v Commission* [2004] E.C.R. II-3315, paras 170–177; CFI, Joined Cases T-8/95 and T-9/95 *Pelle and Konrad v Council and Commission* [2007] E.C.R. II-4117, paras 98–99. Exceptionally, depending on the circumstances of the case concerned, the Court may confine itself to the unlawful nature of the act at issue and defer finding the causal link and the damage: see ECJ, Case 90/78 *Granaria v Council and Commission* [1979] E.C.R. 1081, paras 4–6.

[265] CFI, Case T-279/03 *Galileo International Technology and Others v Commission* [2006] E.C.R. II-1291, para. 63 (appeal dismissed on other grounds: ECJ (order of 20 March 2007), Case C-325/06 P *Galileo International Technology and Others v Commission* [2007] E.C.R. I-44*, Summ. pub.).

[266] CFI, Case T-279/03 *Galileo International Technology and Others v Commission*, para. 71.

[267] CFI, Case T-279/03 *Galileo International Technology and Others v Commission*, para. 72.

[268] CFI, Case T-279/03 *Galileo International Technology and Others v Commission*, para. 73. In doing so, the Court was cognizant of the Commission's arguments challenging the admissibility of the application for an injunction on the basis of settled case-law, according to which the Union courts cannot make orders against

ultimately was not granted.[269] Subsequent case-law may indicate other kinds of compensation in kind which may be awarded in the context of an action for damages.[270]

11.70   (vii) **Damage in case of the unlawful collection of a charge or the withholding of a payment**

If the damage originated in the unlawful collection of a charge or the unlawful withholding of a payment, the amount of the charge or payment in question will form the basis for calculating the damages.[271] The fact that the amount of the damages coincides precisely with the charge or payment at issue does not detract from the autonomous nature of the action for damages. The payment of compensation is founded upon a legal basis—the second paragraph of Art. 340 TFEU—different from that of the contested charge or payment.

(viii) **Damage passed on to others**

11.71   Loss or damage which the individual passes or could pass on to others is not eligible for an award of damages.[272] So, if financial aid is withdrawn, a producer may recover his or her loss by increasing the price of his or her products. Insofar as that price increase offsets the loss, it must be taken into account when quantifying the damage. However, it must be certain that the producer concerned did pass on the loss, or could have done so.[273]

Union institutions even in proceedings for compensation, and that the second para. of Art. 340 TFEU permits compensation only in respect of past damage and does not confer the right to issue injunctions aimed at preventing future unlawfulness: CFI, Case T-279/03 *Galileo International Technology and Others v Commission*, paras 60–61. In rejecting those contentions in the instant case, the Court's reasoning was arguably premised on ensuring that the applicant was 'fully compensated' for the damage sustained by virtue of the institutions' unlawful action. Arguably therefore, this position does not conflict with case-law (decided both before and after this case) outside of these confines in which the General Court has rejected demands made by applicants requesting the Union courts to addresss an injunction to a Union institution ordering it to take a particular form of action: see, e.g. CFI (order of 17 December 2008), Case T-137/07 *Portela v Commission* [2008] E.C.R. II-329*, Summ. pub., paras 44–46 (appeal dismissed on other grounds: ECJ (order of 29 October 2009), Case C-85/09 P *Portela v Commission* [2009] E.C.R. I-178*, Summ. pub.). See also EGC (order of 24 May 2011), Case T-373/08 *Nuova Agricast v Commission* [2011] E.C.R. II-147*, Summ. pub., para. 46 (rejecting the applicant's demand for a declaratory judgment).

[269] The Court held that the conditions concerning the unlawfulness of the conduct alleged against the Commission and a direct causal link were not fulfilled, and thus dismissed the action on that basis: CFI, Case T-279/03 *Galileo International Technology and Others v Commission*, paras 141–142. The Court also dismissed the claim for Union liability on account of a lawful act for failure to satisfy the condition of 'unusual' damage (CFI, Case T-279/03 *Galileo International Technology and Others v Commission*, paras 151–152), as this case was decided before the Court of Justice's decision in *FIAMM*: see further para. 11.07.

[270] See, e.g. EGC, Case T-88/09 *Idromacchine and Others v Commission* [2011] E.C.R. II-7833, paras 81–83: the Court rejected the demand of the applicant for rehabilitating his image and reputation (appeal dismissed in ECJ (order of 3 September 2013), Case C-34/12 P *Idromacchine and Others v Commission*, not reported).

[271] ECJ, Case 238/78 *Ireks-Arkady v Council and Commission* [1979] E.C.R. 2955, para. 13; ECJ, Joined Cases 64/76, 113/76, 167/78, 239/78, 27/79 to 28/79, and 45/79 *Dumortier Frères v Council* [1982] E.C.R. 1733, paras 9–10.

[272] ECJ, Case 238/78 *Ireks-Arkady v Council and Commission*, para. 14; ECJ, Case 256/81 *Pauls Agriculture v Council and Commission* [1983] E.C.R. 1707, paras 8–10; ECJ, Joined Cases 256/80 to 257/80, 265/80, 267/80, and 51/81, and 282/82 *Birra Wührer and Others v Council and Commission* [1984] E.C.R. 3693, paras 26–30. However, in the context of case-law on the repayment of charges levied by Member States in breach of Union law, the Court of Justice has interpreted the 'defence' of passing on strictly: see, recently, ECJ, Case C-398/09 *Lady & Kid and Others* [2011] E.C.R. I-7375. See further para. 4.27.

[273] Seemingly, there is an obligation on a prudent vendor to pass on the loss brought about by an unlawful act of a public authority in his or her selling prices if market conditions so permit.

(ix) Default and compensatory interest

Default interest, calculated at the normal legal rate as from the date of judgment until full   **11.72**
payment,[274] may be awarded.[275] Interest is not due until the date of judgment, since the
extent of the damage is also determined at that date, which means that any increase in the
damage from the time at which it arose until the date of judgment is therefore taken
into account.[276] In staff cases, interest is generally due from the date on which the staff
member lodged his or her complaint with the administration concerned pursuant to
Art. 90(2) of the Staff Regulations or from the date on which a debt not paid by the
administration became payable if that date occurred after the day on which the complaint
was lodged.[277]

Compensatory interest may also be awarded for the period prior to the date of judgment. It
is different from default interest, and one may be awarded without the other.[278] That form
of interest is intended to make up for the adverse consequences resulting from the lapse of
time between the occurrence of the event causing the damage and the date of payment of
the compensation, thereby taking into account the fall of money.[279]

---

[274] In early case-law, the rate of interest applied was that held proper in the circumstances of the case,
provided that it did not exceed the rate claimed in the application: see, e.g. ECJ, Joined Cases C-104/89 and
C-37/90 *Mulder and Others v Council and Commission* [1992] E.C.R. I-3061, paras 35–36. More recently, the
rate of interest to be applied has been calculated on the basis of the rates set by the European Central Bank for
principal refinancing operations, applicable during the period concerned plus two points: see, e.g. EGC, Case
T-88/09 *Idromacchine and Others v Commission* [2011] E.C.R. II-7833, para. 79 (and citations therein)
(appeal dismissed in ECJ (order of 3 September 2013), Case C-34/12 P *Idromacchine and Others v Commission*, not reported).
[275] See, e.g. ECJ, Joined Cases 64/76, 113/76, 167/78, 239/78, 27/79 to 28/79, and 45/79 *Dumortier
Frères v Council* [1979] E.C.R. 3091, para. 25; ECJ, Case 238/78 *Ireks-Arkady v Council and Commission*
[1979] E.C.R. 2955, para. 20. As noted by these cases, the fact that a claim for interest is generally admissible
in an action for damages follows from the general principles common to the laws of the Member States.
A claim for default interest does not have to be supported by specific reasons: see CFI, Joined Cases T-215/01,
T-220/01, and T-221/01 *Calberson v Commission* [2004] E.C.R. II-587, paras 90–91.
[276] ECJ, Joined Cases 64/76, 113/76, 167/78, 239/78, 27/79 to 28/79, and 45/79 *Dumortier Frères v
Council* [1982] E.C.R. 1733, para. 11; Opinion of Advocate-General G.F. Mancini in ECJ, Case 256/81
Pauls Agriculture v Council and Commission [1983] E.C.R. 1707, at 1723–9; ECJ, Joined Cases 256/80, 257/80,
265/80, 267/80, and 51/81, and 282/82 *Birra Wührer and Others v Council and Commission* [1984] E.C.R. 3693,
para. 37; ECJ, Case C-152/88 *Sofrimport v Commission* [1990] E.C.R. I-2477, para. 32; ECJ, Joined Cases
C-104/89 and C-37/90 *Mulder and Others v Council and Commission* [1992] E.C.R. I-3061, para. 35. The award
of interest, however, may be a means of assessing the total amount of the damage at the date of judgment. In that
case, it is due from the day on which the damage materialized: ECJ, Case 185/80 *Garganese v Commission* [1981]
E.C.R. 1785, paras 19–21.
[277] ECJ, Joined Cases 75/82 and 117/82 *Razzouk and Beydoun v Commission* [1984] E.C.R. 1509, para.
19; ECJ, Case 158/79 *Roumengous Carpentier v Commission* [1985] E.C.R. 39, para. 11; ECJ, Joined Cases
532/79, 534/79, 567/79, 600/79, 618/79, 660/79, and 543/79 *Amesz and Others v Commission* [1985]
E.C.R. 55, para. 14; ECJ, Case 737/79 *Battaglia v Commission* [1985] E.C.R. 71, para. 10. Compare ECJ,
Case C-348/06 P *Commission v Girardot* [2008] E.C.R I-833, paras 20, 23: set interest as from the date the
parties sent their submissions on the quantum of damages to the CFI.
[278] See ECJ, Case C-304/89 and C-37/90 *Mulder and Others v Council and Commission* [2000]
E.C.R. I-203, para. 55 (and citations therein) (noting the line of cases in the context of staff disputes).
[279] See, e.g. EGC, Case T-88/09 *Idromacchine and Others v Commission* [2011] E.C.R. II-7833, para. 77
(and citations therein) (appeal dismissed in ECJ (order of 3 September 2013), Case C-34/12 P *Idromacchine
and Others v Commission*, not reported): as noted in that case, the rate of interest to be applied may also be
calculated on the basis of the rates set by the European Central Bank for principal refinancing operations,
applicable during the period concerned plus two points; compare CFI, Case T-285/03 *Agraz and Others v
Commission* [2008] E.C.R. II-1063 (applying in relation to certain applicants the annual inflation rate for the
period concerned by Eurostat in the Member State where they are established).

(x) Exchange rate

11.73 The currency exchange rate for an award of damages to the extent applicable is that prevailing on the date of judgment.[280]

(xi) Effect of other '*Bergaderm*' conditions

11.74 The extent of the compensation awarded also depends on the manner in which the requirement for there to be a causal link between the unlawful Union act and the loss or damage is fulfilled (see paras 11.78–11.85).

Furthermore, as has already been mentioned, in the case of an act involving discretion the extent and the specific characteristics of the damage suffered play a particular role with a view to determining whether the relevant breach of a rule of law was sufficiently serious (see para. 11.57).[281]

(b) *Proof of damage*

(i) Applicant bears the burden of proof

11.75 The burden of proof has to be discharged by the applicant.[282] This means that the applicant has to convince the Union judicature of the existence of the damage and of its extent. The defendant may adduce factual evidence that casts doubt on the existence and extent of the damage.[283] As a public authority, the defendant may sometimes be compelled to disclose information to which it alone has access.[284]

(ii) Factual evidence

11.76 If the applicant does not succeed in proving that damage occurred and its extent, the application will be inadmissible[285] or, albeit declared admissible, will be

---

[280] ECJ, Joined Cases 64/76, 113/76, 167/78, 239/78, 27/79 to 28/79, and 45/79 *Dumortier Frères v Council* [1982] E.C.R. 1733, para. 12. To date, most judgments for damages are awarded in euro, but this conversion rate has relevance for applicants from Member States whose currency is not the euro.

[281] For an application, see CFI, Joined Cases T-480/93 and T-483/93 *Antillean Rice Mills and Others v Commission* [1995] E.C.R. II-2305, paras 200–208.

[282] See, e.g. ECJ, Case 26/74 *Roquette Frères v Commission* [1976] E.C.R. 677, paras 22–24; ECJ, Case C-243/05 P *Agraz and Others v Commission* [2006] E.C.R. I-10833, para. 27 (and citations therein). A head of damage (such as the payment of bank interest), which is incidental in relation to another head of damage and is not sufficiently proved, does not qualify for compensation: CFI, Case T-1/99 *T. Port v Commission* [2001] E.C.R. II-465, para. 74.

[283] See, e.g. the cases on passing on the loss (see para. 11.71). The defendant has to show that the loss was actually passed on. The applicant may counter the defendant's evidence by showing that the loss was not passed on, or that a price increase was attributable to other factors.

[284] See CFI, Case T-48/05 *Franchet and Byk v Commission* [2008] E.C.R. II-1585, para. 183 (and citations therein), holding that 'where a harmful event may have been the result of a number of different causes and where the [Union] institution has adduced no evidence enabling it to be established to which of those causes the event was imputable, although it was best placed to provide evidence in that respect, so that the uncertainty which remains must be construed against it'.

[285] See, e.g. ECJ, Case 68/63 *Luhleich v Commission* [1965] E.C.R. 581, at 605; CFI, Case T-64/89 *Automec v Commission* [1990] E.C.R. II-367, paras 72–75; CFI, Case T-461/93 *An Taisce and WWF UK v Commission* [1994] E.C.R. II-733, paras 42–43; ECJ (order of 8 December 2006), Case C-368/05 P *Polyelectrolyte Producers Group v Council and Commission* [2008] E.C.R. I-130*, Summ. pub., paras 77–78 (upholding the Court of First Instance's ruling declaring the action for damages inadmissible on the grounds that neither the nature nor the extent of the loss had been clearly established). Although a claim for any unspecified form of damages is insufficiently concrete and thus regarded as inadmissible, the Union judicature has accepted that in special circumstances it is not essential to specify the exact extent of the damage in the application and to state the amount of compensation sought, although the applicant has to establish, or at least indicate, the existence of any such circumstances in the application, or the claim for damages is inadmissible:

dismissed.[286] The application must indicate the nature and extent of the damage sufficiently precisely.[287] For example, it is not sufficient for the applicant to allege that he or she suffered 'serious damage'.[288] He or she must at least adduce factual evidence on the basis of which the nature and the extent of the damage may be assessed. The Union judicature recognizes that to hold an action inadmissible on this ground requires an assessment of the facts, in particular of whether the appellant has sufficiently proved the amount of compensation claimed by it in the application and the reply. It lies beyond the jurisdiction of the Court of Justice on appeal to rule on whether the factual assessment made by the General Court was well-founded.[289]

(iii) Uncertainty about the extent of the damage

Uncertainty about the extent of the damage does not mean that the application will be declared inadmissible, provided that the case discloses a real possibility that damage has been suffered.[290] This has recently been confirmed by *Agraz and Others v Commission*,[291] concerning an action for damages brought by nearly 100 companies from various Member States on account of the Commission's failure to consider the Chinese tomato prices before adopting a measure establishing the production aid allotted to that sector. The General Court held that the damage alleged by the applicants was uncertain, taking the view that

11.77

---

see, e.g. CFI, Case T-125/06 *Centro Studi Antonio Manieri v Council* [2009] E.C.R. II-69, paras 99–103 (and citations therein); CFI (order of 18 February 2009), Case T-346/06 *Industria Masetto Schio v Commission*, not reported, paras 35–38 (and citations therein) (further noting that the elements furnished by the applicant in the reply were insufficient to remedy the inadmissibility of the action: paras 39–47). With respect to staff cases, see e.g. EGC (order of 16 December 2010), Case T-48/10 P *Meister v OHIM*, not reported, paras 49–50.

[286] See, e.g. ECJ, Case 10/55 *Mirossevich v High Authority* [1954 to 1956] E.C.R. 333, at 344–5; ECJ, Joined Cases 14/60, 16/60 to 17/60, 20/60, 24/60, 26/60 to 27/60, and 1/61 *Meroni and Others v High Authority* [1961] E.C.R. 161, at 171; ECJ, Case 15/63 *Lassalle v European Parliament* [1964] E.C.R. 31, at 39; ECJ, Case 26/74 *Roquette Frères v Commission* [1976] E.C.R. 677; ECJ, Case 49/79 *Pool v Council* [1980] E.C.R. 569, para. 12; CFI (order of 7 July 2006), Case T-321/03 *Juchem v European Parliament and Council* [2006] E.C.R. II-50*, Summ. pub., paras 29–35; CFI (order of 7 July 2006), Case T-167/02 *Établissements Toulorge v European Parliament and Council* [2006] E.C.R. II-49*, Summ. pub., paras 29–32; ECJ Case C-481/07 P *SELEX Sistemi Integrati v Commission* [2009] E.C.R. I-127*, Summ. pub., paras 36–46 (upholding the Court of First Instance's ruling declaring action manifestly lacking all foundation in law for failure on the part of the applicant to submit proof of the existence and the reality of the damage claimed).

[287] See, e.g. ECJ, Case 5/71 *Zuckerfabrik Schöppenstedt v Council* [1971] E.C.R. 975, para. 9; CFI, Case T-64/89 *Automec v Commission* [1990] E.C.R. II-367, para. 73; CFI (order of 21 November 1996), Case T-53/96 *Syndicat des Producteurs de Viande Bovine and Others v Commission* [1996] E.C.R. II-1579, paras 22–23; CFI, Case T-149/96 *Coldiretti v Council and Commission* [1998] E.C.R. II-3841, paras 47–51; CFI, Case T-277/97 *Ismeri Europa v Court of Auditors* [1999] E.C.R. II-1825, paras 65 and 81.

[288] Nor is it sufficient for the applicant to state that at the Court's request, the applicant is prepared to provide details of the constituent elements of the alleged damage: see CFI, Case T-48/04 *Franchet and Byk v Commission* [2008] E.C.R. II-1385, para. 413.

[289] ECJ, Case C-209/94 P *Buralux and Others v Council* [1996] E.C.R. I-615, para. 21.

[290] ECJ, Case 74/74 *CNTA v Commission* [1975] E.C.R. 533; ECJ, Case 90/78 *Granaria v Council and Commission* [1979] E.C.R. 1081, paras 4–6. See also EGC, Case T-452/05 *BST v Commission* [2010] E.C.R. II-1373, para. 168: 'Where it is necessary to determine the value of a lost opportunity to make money and therefore, of necessity, the value of hypothetical economic transactions, it can be difficult, if not impossible, for the claimant to put an exact figure on the loss which it claims to have sustained. In such cases, the Court can rely on mean statistical values. However, that does not relieve [the claimant] entirely of the obligation to adduce evidence of the loss claimed. Although the value of a lost opportunity to make money is necessarily a hypothetical fact which must be estimated, since it cannot be calculated with certainty, the fact remains that the data on which that estimate is based can—and must, in so far as is possible—be proved by the party relying on it.' (citations omitted).

[291] ECJ, Case C-243/05 P *Agraz and Others v Commission* [2006] E.C.R. I-10833.

given the discretion conferred on the Commission by the basic regulation to fix the amount of the aid, it was impossible to determine with certainty what the impact on the amount of the aid would have been had the price paid to the Chinese tomato producers been taken into account.[292] On appeal, the ECJ held that the fact that the institution enjoys a wide discretion in the matter concerned cannot as such lead to the damage alleged being regarded as uncertain. To hold otherwise would deprive the action for damages of all useful effect.[293] In the present proceedings, even though, taking account of the Commission's discretion, it was not certain that the applicants were entitled to the exact amount at which they valued their damage, this authorized the General Court only to find that there was uncertainty as regards the exact extent of the damage claimed, but not to find that the very existence of the damage was uncertain.[294]

Mention has already been made (see para. 11.68) of the fact that where the Union judicature finds the Union liable in an interlocutory judgment, it can set a time within which the parties are to agree on the amount of damages. If they do not succeed and, in addition, the applicant does not adduce sufficiently precise evidence of the extent of the damage within the prescribed period, the application will be dismissed.[295]

(4) The causal link

(a) The causal link must be direct

11.78   The third main requirement governing Union non-contractual liability is that there must be a direct causal link between the unlawful act or conduct on the part of the institution or body concerned and the damage alleged.[296] The causal link requirement is the third pillar on which Union non-contractual liability is based.

At present, there is not one standard or uniform formulation of this requirement in the case-law. Instead, it is articulated by the Union courts in various ways (sometimes in the very same case)[297] and may be accompanied by other language, for example, that the alleged loss or damage must be a 'sufficiently direct consequence' of the conduct complained of and thus the act or conduct complained of must be the 'determining'[298] or

---

[292] ECJ, Case C-243/05 P *Agraz and Others v Commission*, paras 28–29.

[293] ECJ, Case C-243/05 P *Agraz and Others v Commission*, paras 30–31.

[294] ECJ, Case C-243/05 P *Agraz and Others v Commission*, paras 35–36. The Court set aside the General Court's decision insofar as it dismissed the applicants' claim on the grounds that the alleged loss was not certain, and referred the case back to the General Court so that it could give final judgment on the amount of compensation for that damage: ECJ, Case C-243/05 P *Agraz and Others v Commission*, paras 48–50.

[295] ECJ, Case 74/74 *CNTA v Commission* [1976] E.C.R. 797.

[296] See ECJ (order of 5 July 2007), Case C-255/06 P *Yedas Tarim ve Otomotiv Sanayi ve Ticaret v Council and Commission* [2007] E.C.R. I-94*, Summ. pub., paras 60–62 (underscoring settled case-law requiring a direct causal link and thus rejecting applicant's contention that the case-law does not require a direct causal link and that it is sufficient to establish that the unlawful act concerned contributed to the alleged damage).

[297] See, e.g. ECJ, Case C-497/06 P CAS *Succhi di Frutta v Commission* [2009] E.C.R. I-69*, Summ. pub., para. 60 ('un lien direct de cause à effet'); ECJ, Case C-419/08 P *Trubowest Handel and Makarov v Council and Commission* [2010] E.C.R. I-2259, para. 53 ('a sufficiently direct causal nexus') and para. 58 ('a direct link of cause and effect'); CFI, Case T-138/03 *É.R. and Others v Council and Commission* [2006] E.C.R. II-4923, para. 103 ('a definite and direct causal nexus'); EGC (order of 30 June 2011), Case T-367/09 *Tecnoprocess v Commission* [2011] E.C.R. II-209*, Summ. pub., para. 76 ('un lien suffisament direct de cause à effet'); EGC (order of 30 June 2011), Case T-264/09 *Tecnoprocess v Commission* [2011] E.C.R. II-208*, Summ. pub., para. 120 ('un lien suffisament direct de cause à effet').

[298] See, e.g. ECJ (order of 31 March 2011), Case C-433/10 P *Mauerhofer v Commission* [2011] E.C.R. I-48*, Summ. pub., para. 127; CFI, Case T-279/03 *Galileo and Others v Commission* [2006] E.C.R. II-1291, para. 130 (appeal dismissed in ECJ (order of 20 March 2007), Case C-325/06 P *Galileo and Others v Commission* [2007]

'immediate'[299] cause of the damage sustained. Nevertheless, the core idea underlying the case-law is that the Union is liable only for damage which is the direct consequence of the unlawful acts or conduct of its institutions and bodies.[300] By contrast, if the damage alleged does not flow directly from such act or conduct but is too indirect and remote, this is not sufficient because there is no obligation on the part of the Union to make good every harmful consequence, even a remote one, of the unlawful act or conduct alleged.[301] This requirement of a direct causal link is reflected in the Treaties[302] and is grounded in the general principles common to the laws of the Member States.[303]

As with the other conditions (see para. 11.40), the burden of proof is on the applicant.[304]

E.C.R. I-44*, Summ. pub.); CFI, Case T-360/04 FG *Marine v Commission* [2007] E.C.R. II-92*, Summ.pub., para. 50; EGC, Joined Cases T-252/07, T-271/07, and T-272/07 *Sungro and Others v Council and Commission* [2010] E.C.R. II-55, para. 47, as well as para. 49 (the Court must consider whether the unlawful act is 'the immediate cause of the damage alleged to establish the existence of a direct relationship of cause and effect') (citations omitted); EGC, Case T-42/06 *Gollnisch v European Parliament* [2010] E.C.R. II-1135, para. 110; EGC, Case T-88/09 *Idromacchine and Others v Commission* [2011] E.C.R. II-7833, para. 26.

[299] See, e.g. CFI (order of 12 December 2007) Case T-113/04 *Atlantic Container Line AB and Others v Commission* [2007] E.C.R. II-171*, Summ. pub., para. 31.

[300] See, e.g. ECJ, Case 18/60 *Worms v High Authority* [1962] E.C.R. 195, at 206; ECJ, Joined Cases 64/76, 113/76, 167/78, 239/78, 27/79 to 28/79, and 45/79 *Dumortier Frères v Council* [1979] E.C.R. 3091, para. 21; ECJ, Case C-331/05 P *Internationaler Hilfsfonds v Commission* [2007] E.C.R. I-5475, para. 23; ECJ, Case C-481/07 P *SELEX Sistemi Integrati* [2009] E.C.R. I-127*, Summ. pub., para. 22; ECJ, Case C-497/06 P *CAS Succhi di Frutta v Commission* [2009] E.C.R. I-69*, Summ. pub., para. 59; CFI, Case T-175/94 *International Procurement Services v Commission* [1996] E.C.R. II-729, para. 55; CFI, Case T-7/96 *Perillo v Commission* [1997] E.C.R. II-1061, para. 41; CFI, Joined Cases T-213/95 and T-18/96 *SCK and FNK v Commission* [1997] E.C.R. II-1739, paras 94–98; CFI, Case T-13/96 *TEAM v Commission* [1998] E.C.R. II-4073, paras 68 and 74; CFI, Case T-196/99 *Area Cova and Others v Council and Commission* [2001] E.C.R. II-3597, para. 152; CFI (order of 17 December 2003), Case T-346/03 *Krikorian and Others v European Parliament and Others* [2003] E.C.R. II-6037, para. 23; EGC, Case T-561/08 *Gutknecht v Commission* [2011] E.C.R. II-364*, Summ. pub., para. 30.

[301] See ECJ, Joined Cases 64/76, 113/76, 167/78, 239/78, 27/79 to 28/79, and 45/79 *Dumortier Frères v Council* [1979] E.C.R. 3091, para. 21; see also/further CFI, Case T-279/03 *Galileo and Others v Commission* [2006] E.C.R. II-1291, para. 130 (appeal dismissed in ECJ (order of 20 March 2007), Case C-325/06 P *Galileo and Others v Commission* [2007] E.C.R. I-44*, Summ. pub.); EGC, Case T-42/06 *Gollnisch v European Parliament* [2010] E.C.R. II-1135, para. 110.

[302] The second para. of Art. 340 TFEU provides that the Union is liable to 'make good any damage *caused* by its institutions or by its servants in the performance of their duties' (emphasis added); CFI, Case T-277/97 *Ismeri Europa v Court of Auditors* [1999] E.C.R. II-1825, para. 100.

[303] See, e.g. ECJ (order of 31 March 2011), Case C-433/10 P *Mauerhofer v Commission* [2011] E.C.R. I-48*, Summ. pub., para. 127 (and citations therein) ('it must be recalled that the principles common to the laws of the Member States to which the second paragraph of Article 340 TFEU refers cannot be relied upon to found an obligation on the Union to make good every harmful consequence, even a remote one, of its institutions').

[304] See, e.g. ECJ, Joined Cases 197/80 to 200/80, 243/80, 245/80, and 247/80 *Ludwigshafener Walzmühle and Others v Council and Commission* [1981] E.C.R. 3211, paras 51–56; ECJ, Case 310/81 *EISS v Commission* [1984] E.C.R. 1341, paras 16–17; ECJ (order of 31 March 2011), Case C-433/10 P *Mauerhofer v Commission* [2011] E.C.R. I-48*, Summ. pub., para. 127; CFI, Case T-146/01 *DLD Trading v Council* [2003] E.C.R. II-6005, para. 73; CFI (order of 17 December 2003), Case T-346/03 *Krikorian and Others v European Parliament and Others* [2003] E.C.R. II-6037, para. 23; CFI, Case T-138/03 *É.R. and Others v Council and Commission* [2006] E.C.R. II-4923, para. 103; CFI (order of 12 December 2007), Case T-113/04 *Atlantic Container Line AB and Others v Commission* [2007] E.C.R. II-171*, Summ. pub., para. 34; EGC, Joined Cases T-252/07, T-271/07, and T-272/07 *Sungro and Others v Council and Commission* [2010] E.C.R. II-55, para. 47; EGC, Case T-452/05 *BST v Commission* [2010] E.C.R. II-1373, para. 166. Furthermore, it is for the applicant to adduce sufficient proof to establish a sufficiently direct causal link: see, e.g. CFI, Case T-271/04 *Citymo v Commission* [2007] E.C.R. II-1375, paras 159, 162–163, 166; EGC, Case T-452/05 *BST v Commission* [2010] E.C.R. II-1373, paras 167 and 176–179 (and citations therein); CFI, Case T-48/05 *Franchet and Byk v Commission* [2008] E.C.R. II-1585, para. 397; see also EGC, Case T-107/08 *Transnational*

(b) Rejection of broad definition of the causal link requirement

(i) Strict interpretation

11.79 According to the case-law, the directness of the causal link requirement is interpreted strictly by the Union courts. For example, in *Atlantic Container Line and Others v Commission*,[305] the Court of First Instance rejected the applicants' argument that for a direct causal link to exist, it is enough if the unlawful conduct constituted a necessary condition (a *sine qua non*) for the damage in the sense that it would not have occurred without (or 'but for') such conduct and declared that such a broad definition of the causal link is not supported by the case-law on the second paragraph of (now) Art. 340 TFEU, which limits Union liability to 'damage flowing directly, or sufficiently directly, from the conduct of the institution concerned which is complained of, which, in particular, precludes that liability from covering damage which arises only as a remote consequence of that conduct'.

(ii) Case-by-case assessment

11.80 Whether or not there is found to be a direct causal link between the damage alleged and the act or conduct complained of on the part of the Union institution or body is assessed by the Union judicature on a case-by-case basis and thus will depend on various circumstances.[306]

(c) Damage must be attributable to a Union institution or body

11.81 For a direct causal link to be established, it is necessary that the damage alleged was actually caused by the act or conduct of the institution or body and therefore, even in the case of a possible contribution by the institution or body concerned to the damage for which compensation is sought, that contribution might be too remote because of some responsibility resting on others (whether it be the applicant himself or a third party).[307] Where the alleged damage is not shown to be attributable to a Union institution or body, the action for damages against the Union fails.[308] Accordingly, the Union will not be liable for damage which is attributable

---

Company 'Kazchrome' and ENRC Marketing v Council and Commission [2011] E.C.R. II-8051, para. 76 (noting that 'a mere reference to the reduction in the volume of sales cannot suffice as evidence of the causal link required for the [Union] to incur non-contractual liability') and para. 85 (where no reference made by the applicant to alleged injury in their arguments on the causal link, claim dismissed as inadmissible pursuant to the requirements of Art. 21 of the Statute and Art. 44(1)(c) EGC Rules of Procedure).

[305] CFI (order of 12 December 2007) Case T-113/04 *Atlantic Container Line AB and Others v Commission* [2007] E.C.R. II-171*, Summ. pub., paras 39–40.

[306] It may be the case that a direct causal link will be assessed separately with respect to the types of damage alleged by the applicant, finding the requirement of a causal link satisfied for certain claims but not for others: see, e.g. CFI, Case T-48/05 *Franchet and Byk v Commission* [2008] E.C.R. II-1585, paras 399–411 (concerning certain but not all claims of non-material damage); CFI, Case T-412/05 *M v European Ombudsman* [2008] E.C.R. II-197*, Summ. pub., paras 107, 112, 119–120; EGC, Case T-88/09 *Idromacchine and Others v Commission* [2011] E.C.R. II-7833, paras 65–68 (as regards the applicants' demand for immaterial damage), but this was not the case in respect of the applicants' demand for material damage (paras 106–107, 110–115).

[307] See, e.g. ECJ, Case C-419/08 P *Trubowest Handel and Makarov v Council and Commission* [2010] E.C.R. I-2259, para. 59; ECJ (order of 31 March 2011), Case C-433/10 P *Mauerhofer v Commission* [2011] E.C.R. I-48*, Summ. pub., paras 131–132.

[308] See, e.g. CFI (order of 19 May 2009), Case T-528/08 *Delice and Delice v Erlangen and Commission*, not reported, paras 18–19 (action held inadmissible on account of, *inter alia*, applicant's failure to demonstrate that act or conduct attributable to the Commission). The same requirement of attribution applies in the context of the EAEC Treaty: see CFI, Case T-250/02 *Autosalone Ispra v EAEC* [2005] E.C.R. II-5227 (upheld on appeal: ECJ (order of 12 December 2006), Case C-129/06 P *Autosalone Ispra v EAEC* [2006] E.C.R. I-131*, Summ. pub.).

exclusively to action by a Member State (including various kinds of national authorities),[309] by an institution of a third country,[310] by the applicant himself,[311] or by any other third party.[312]

In particular, the Commission's failure to bring an action against a Member State for failure to fulfil obligations under Union law under Art. 258 TFEU cannot cause the Union to incur non-contractual liability. The reason for this is that the damage caused by the infringement of Union law is attributable only to the Member State concerned.[313]

---

[309] See, e.g. ECJ, Case 132/77 *Société pour l'Exportation des Sucres v Commission* [1978] E.C.R. 1061, para. 27; EGC, Case T-42/06 *Gollnisch v European Parliament* [2010] E.C.R. II-1135, paras 112–113: finding that the applicant himself identified his prosecution by the French authorities as the cause of that damage or part of it, and thus the Parliament's alleged unlawful act is not the direct and determining cause of the damage alleged, or at least part of it. But in any event, the General Court found that the illegality vitiating the Parliament's decision on the grounds that it was adopted on an incorrect legal basis was not the direct and determining cause of the damage alleged (paras 114–117); CFI, Case T-146/01 *DLD Trading v Council* [2003] E.C.R. II-6005, paras 80–82 and 91–97.

[310] See, e.g. CFI, Case T-220/96 *EVO v Council and Commission* [2002] E.C.R. II-2265, paras 41–48; CFI (order of 3 July 2007), Case T-212/02 *Commune de Champagne and Others v Council and Commission* [2007] E.C.R. II-2017, paras 206–213 (any damage that applicants may suffer in the territory of a third State (Switzerland) deemed to be the result of action taken by the authorities of that State and cannot be regarded as attributable to the Union; the General Court lacks jurisdiction to hear and determine such a claim).

[311] See, e.g CFI, Joined Cases T-3/00 and T-337/04 *Pitsiorlas v Council and ECB* [2007] E.C.R. II-4779, paras 315–322; EGC (order of 25 March 2011), Case T-15/10 *Noko Ngele v Commission and Others* [2011] E.C.R. II-77*, Summ. pub., paras 55–57 (upheld on appeal in ECJ (order of 4 October 2011), Case C-272/11 P *Noko Ngele v Commission and Others* [2011] E.C.R. I-145*, Summ. pub., paras 17–19).

[312] For some recent examples, see ECJ, Case C-497/06 P *CAS Succhi di Frutta v Commission* [2009] E.C.R. I-69*, Summ. pub., paras 61–67; ECJ (order of 31 March 2011), Case C-433/10 P *Mauerhofer v Commission* [2011] E.C.R. I-48*, Summ. pub., paras 129–131; EGC, Case T-516/08 *Gutknecht v Commission* [2010] E.C.R. II-40*, Summ. pub., paras 31–40.

[313] See, e.g. ECJ (order of 23 May 1990), Case C-72/90 *Asia Motor France v Commission* [1990] E.C.R. I-2181, para. 13; CFI, Case T-361/99 *Meyer v Commission and EIB* [2000] E.C.R. II-2031, para. 13; CFI (order of 26 November 2001), Case T-248/01 *Papoulakos v Italy and Commission*, not reported, para. 27 (appeal dismissed in ECJ (order of 2 February 2006), Case C-215/05 P *Papoulakos v Italy and Commission* [2006] E.C.R. I-18*, Summ. pub.); CFI, Case T-209/00 *Lamberts v European Ombudsman* [2002] E.C.R. II-2203, para. 53; CFI (order of 14 January 2004), Case T-202/02 *Makedoniko Metro and Michaniki v Commission* [2004] E.C.R. II-181, paras 42–47; CFI (order of 8 September 2006), Case T-92/06 *Lademporiki and Apostolos Parousis & Sia v Commission* [2006] E.C.R. II-66*, Summ. pub., paras 29–30; CFI (order of 7 September 2009), Case T-186/08 *LPN v Commission* [2009] E.C.R. II-136*, Summ. pub., paras 65–66; EGC (order of 15 July 2011), Case T-185/11 *Smanor v Commission and European Ombudsman*, not reported, para. 16. Yet, it cannot be inferred from the absence of liability for the Commission's failure to initiate infringement proceedings that the Union cannot be held non-contractually liable for action or conduct of the Commmission in the context of infringement proceedings against a Member State under Art. 258 TFEU: see EGC, Joined Cases T-440/03, T-121/04, T-171/04, T-208/04, T-365/04, and T-484/04 *Arizmendi and Others v Council and Commission* [2009] E.C.R. II-4883, paras 61–71, 76–77, holding that it could not be precluded that in very exceptional circumstances a person may be able to demonstrate that a reasoned opinion is vitiated with illegality constituting a sufficiently serious breach of a rule of law that is likely to cause damage to him. However, as far as the existence of a direct causal link was concerned, the General Court ruled in the present proceedings that the fact that in the Commission's reasoned opinion it considered certain provisions of French law to be incompatible with Union law and that it may have been mistaken in that regard was 'immaterial', since that reasoned opinion did not require the Member State concerned to amend its legislation; only a judgment of the Court can have such a binding effect. As such, the reasoned opinion could not be regarded as the decisive cause of the loss alleged by the applicants, and the causal link requirement was not established (EGC, Joined Cases T-440/03, T-121/04, T-171/04, T-208/04, T-365/04, and T-484/04 *Arizmendi and Others v Council and Commission*, paras 92–93). See further para. 11.47.

However, express Union approval of a national measure that is in breach of Union law may be regarded as the direct cause of any damage flowing from that measure.[314]

(d) Damage attributable to unlawful act

11.82 Under the case-law, in order to determine the harm attributable to an unlawful act of an institution, account must be taken of the effects of the failure which caused liability to be incurred and not of those of the measure of which it forms part, provided that the institution could or should have adopted an act having the same effect without breaching any rule of law. In other words, the analysis of the causal link requirement cannot start from the incorrect premise that, in the absence of the unlawful act, the institution would have refrained from acting or would have adopted a contrary measure which could also amount to unlawful conduct on its part, but rather, must be based on a comparison between the situation arising, for the third party concerned, from the unlawful measure and the situation that would have arisen for that party if the institution's conduct had been in conformity with the law.[315]

For example, in *Schneider Electric v Commission*,[316] involving an unlawful Commission decision declaring a concentration between the applicant, Schneider, and another undertaking, Legrand, incompatible with the internal market, the General Court considered that it could not be presumed that in the absence of the breach committed by the Commission, the applicant would necessarily have been granted what it sought, namely that the transaction would have been declared compatible with the internal market.[317] Consequently, the General Court ruled that the breach of the applicant's rights of defence did not deprive Schneider from any right to a decision that the transaction was compatible with the internal market so as to justify treating all of the financial consequences of the loss of that right and, in particular, those deriving from the obligation to dispose of the assets of Legrand as attributable to the Union.[318] It thereby rejected the applicant's claim for damages equal to the entire loss of value of the assets of Legrand, as well as those stemming from the prospect of achieving synergies from the transaction and the adverse effects on its image and reputation.[319] However, the General Court found that there was a direct causal link with respect to two types of damage alleged by the applicant: first, certain consultancy fees and administrative expenses incurred by Schneider by virtue of its participation in the resumed investigation of the transaction pursuant to the annulment of the incompatibility decision,[320] and second, the reduction in the transfer price which Schneider granted to the purchaser of the assets in Legrand in order to secure a deferral of the final date for the transfer of assets ordered by the incompatibility decision (in order to avoid the annulment

---

[314] ECJ, Joined Cases 5/66, 7/66, and 13/66 to 24/66 *Kampffmeyer and Others v Commission* [1967] E.C.R. 245, at 260 *et seq.*

[315] See CFI, Case T-351/03 *Schneider Electric v Commission* [2007] E.C.R. II-2237, paras 263–264; EGC Joined Cases T-252/07, T-271/07, and T-272/07 *Sungro and Others v Council and Commission* [2010] E.C.R. II-55, paras 48, 59.

[316] CFI, Case T-351/03 *Schneider Electric v Commission*, paras 263–264. For further discussion of this case, see para. 11.54.

[317] CFI, Case T-351/03 *Schneider Electric v Commission*, paras 265–267.

[318] CFI, Case T-351/03 *Schneider Electric v Commission*, para. 278.

[319] CFI, Case T-351/03 *Schneider Electric v Commission*, paras 279, 286–287.

[320] CFI, Case T-351/03 *Schneider Electric v Commission*, paras 298–302 (compare paras 289–297).

action to become devoid of purpose).[321] On appeal, it was this latter aspect of the General Court's decision that was set aside by the Court of Justice in *Commission v Schneider Electric*.[322] The Court of Justice pointed out that the normal consequences of annulling the incompatibility decision was that Schneider would have participated in the resumed investigation until its conclusion, at which point there would have been either a decision finding the concentration compatible or a further incompatibility (and divestiture) decision, in which case the transfer would not have been the cause of the damage, since it was among the risks normally assumed by an undertaking such as the applicant which implemented a concentration before the Commission had given its decision on the transaction.[323] It followed that the direct cause of the damage was Schneider's decision, which it was not obliged to take, to defer the transfer date and the fact that in making that choice Schneider was at risk of having to pay a penalty derived from the agreement that it had entered into with the purchaser.[324] The Court held that there was no direct causal link between the price reduction at issue and the illegality vitiating the Commission's incompatibility decision on the transaction and dismissed the action insofar as it concerned that claim.[325]

(e) Damage attributable to omission to act

In cases where the conduct of an institution which allegedly caused the damage pleaded **11.83** consists in refraining from taking action, the Union judicature has held that 'it is particularly necessary to be certain that that damage was actually caused by the inaction complained of and could not have been caused by conduct separate from that alleged against the defendant institutions'.[326] For example, in *É.R. and Others v Council and Commission*, concerning an action for damage allegedly suffered by the applicants as a consequence of the infection and subsequent death of family members from Jakob-Creutzfeldt ('mad cow') disease on account of the alleged failure of the Council and the Commission to take the appropriate measures to avoid the risks linked to the spread of this disease, the General Court ruled that there was no such certainty[327] and dismissed all of the applicants' claims for failure to establish a direct causal link.[328]

(f) Too remote in the chain of causation

Damage that is found to be too remote from the unlawful act or conduct of the institution **11.84** will not satisfy the causal link requirement. Accordingly, for example,[329] loss suffered by

---

[321] CFI, Case T-351/03 *Schneider Electric v Commission*, paras 288, 316–317.

[322] ECJ, Case C-440/07 P *Commission v Schneider Electric* [2009] E.C.R. I-6413, paras 207–208.

[323] ECJ, Case C-440/07 P *Commission v Schneider Electric*, para. 204.

[324] ECJ, Case C-440/07 P *Commission v Schneider Electric*, paras 205–206.

[325] ECJ, Case C-440/07 P *Commission v Schneider Electric*, paras 221–222.

[326] CFI, Case T-138/03 *É.R. and Others v Council and Commission* [2006] E.C.R. II-4923, para. 134.

[327] CFI, Case T-138/03 *É.R. and Others v Council and Commission*, paras 135–140.

[328] CFI, Case T-138/03 *É.R. and Others v Council and Commission*, paras 127, 145–148. This ruling was upheld on appeal in ECJ (order of 4 October 2007), Case C-100/07 P *É.R. and Others v Council and Commission* [2007] E.C.R. I-136*, Summ. pub. See further, e.g. CFI (order of 17 December 2008), Case T-137/07 *Portela v Commission* [2008] E.C.R. II-329*, Summ. pub., paras 80–101 (appeal dismissed in ECJ (order of 29 October 2009), Case C-85/09 P *Portela v Commission* [2009] E.C.R I-178*, Summ. pub.); EGC (order of 30 June 2011), Case T-367/09 *Tecnoprocess v Commission* [2011] E.C.R. II-209*, Summ. pub., paras 77–85; EGC (order of 30 June 2011), Case T-264/09 *Tecnoprocess v Commission* [2011] E.C.R. II-208*, Summ. pub., paras 121–135.

[329] See, e.g. CFI, Case T-48/05 *Franchet and Byk v Commission* [2008] E.C.R. II-1585, para. 410: the Court rejects non-material damage linked to serious consequences for the close relatives of the applicants but without

members of the family of a member of the Commission's staff on account of the personal injuries and psychological sequelae suffered by that person as a result of a road accident attributable to careless maintenance of the car on the part of the Commission could not be indemnified.[330]

(g) Reasonable diligence of the applicant

11.85   Under established case-law, the Court of Justice held that in light of the general principles common to the laws of the Member States, the injured party must show reasonable diligence in avoiding or limiting the extent of his damage or else risk having to bear that damage himself. Thus, even if the conduct alleged against the Union institution or body contributed to bringing about the damage, that causal link may be broken by negligence on the part of the person adversely affected where that negligence proves to be the immediate or determinant cause of the damage.[331]

If the applicant does not show reasonable diligence, the Union will either not be liable[332] or liable only for part of the damage suffered.[333] This attests to the fact that the applicant's reasonable diligence bears on both the causal link and damage requirements as regards the determination of the extent to which the damage is a sufficiently direct consequence of the unlawful act or conduct of the institution, as well as the extent of the damage for which the Union is liable. As such, although under the case-law, the assessment of the applicant's reasonable diligence in connection with the causal link requirement—i.e. whether the chain of causation is broken by the applicant's conduct—may be evaluated separately from that of the applicant's contributory negligence in connection with the quantification of the

---

ample reasoning; CFI, Case T-279/03 *Galileo and Others v Commission* [2006] E.C.R. II-1291, paras 131–135 (finding that the third party undertakings' use of the word 'Galileo' in connection with their economic activities was based on a choice which they made independently (without any demonstrable connection to the Commission) and must be regarded as the direct and determining cause of the applicants' alleged damage, since the Commission's possible contribution to that damage was too remote for the relevant undertakings' liability to fall back on to the Commission) (upheld on appeal: ECJ (order of 20 March 2007), Case C-325/06 P *Galileo International Technology and Others v Commission* [2007] E.C.R. I-44*, Summ. pub., paras 69–71).

[330] ECJ, Joined Cases 169/83 and 136/84 *Leussink-Brummelhuis v Commission* [1986] E.C.R. 2801, para. 22; see also the Opinion of Advocate-General Sir Gordon Slynn, at 2819.

[331] See, e.g. CFI (order of 12 December 2007), Case T-113/04 *Atlantic Container Line and Others v Commission* [2007] E.C.R. II-171*, Summ. pub., paras 32–33 (and citations therein). See in the context of the ECSC Treaty, ECJ, Case 36/62 *Société des Aciéries du Temple v High Authority* [1963] E.C.R. 289, at 296. See also ECJ (order of 12 May 2010), Case C-451/09 P *Pigasos Alieftiki Naftiki Etaireia v Council and Commission* [2010] E.C.R. I-62*, Summ. pub., para. 39.

[332] See, e.g. ECJ, Joined Cases 14/60, 16/60 to 17/60, 20/60, 24/60, 26/60 to 27/60 and 1/61 *Meroni and Others v High Authority* [1961] E.C.R. 161, at 171; ECJ, Case 4/67 *Muller (née Collignon) v Commission* [1967] E.C.R. 365, at 373 (application inadmissible); ECJ, Case 169/73 *Compagnie Continentale v Council* [1975] E.C.R. 117, paras 22–32; ECJ, Case 58/75 *Sergy v Commission* [1976] E.C.R. 1139, paras 46–47; ECJ, Case 26/81 *Oleifici Mediterranei v EEC* [1982] E.C.R. 3057, para. 24; ECJ, Joined Cases C-104/89 and C-37/90 *Mulder and Others v Council and Commission* [1992] E.C.R. I-3061, para. 33, and the Opinion of Advocate-General W. Van Gerven, at I-3122-3123; CFI, Case T-360/04 *FG Marine v Commission* [2007] E.C.R. II-92*, Summ. pub., paras 75–77; CFI, Case T-429/04 *Trubowest Handel and Makarov v Council and Commission* [2008] E.C.R. II-128*, Summ. pub., paras 133–135 (appeal dismissed in ECJ, Case C-419/08 P *Trubowest Handel and Makarov v Council and Commission* [2010] E.C.R. I-2259, para. 61).

[333] ECJ, Case 145/83 *Adams v Commission* [1985] E.C.R. 3539, paras 53–55; ECJ, Case C-308/87 *Grifoni v Commission* [1990] E.C.R. I-1203, paras 16–17; CFI, Case T-178/98 *Fresh Marine v Commission* [2000] E.C.R. II-3331, paras 84–92 (upheld in ECJ, Case C-472/00 P *Fresh Marine v Commission* [2003] E.C.R. I-7541).

compensation claimed in the context of the damages requirement, these two aspects are nevertheless linked.[334]

The requisite causal link will not be found under circumstances where the alleged damage is the direct consequence of the applicant's own decision or free choice.[335] For example, in *Holcim (Deutschland) v Commission*,[336] the Court of First Instance ruled that an undertaking cannot claim compensation for the costs it incurred relating to the provision of a bank guarantee when the Court subsequently annuls the decision in which the Commission found that the undertaking concerned had infringed Arts 101 and/or 102 TFEU. This is because the damage suffered is the consequence of the undertaking's own decision not to comply with its obligation to pay the fine. Moreover, in *Internationaler Hilfsfonds v Commission*,[337] the Court of Justice upheld the Court of First Instance's finding of no causal link in connection with a claim for compensation based on, first, costs incurred in seeking legal advice at the pre-litigation stage of the procedure, and second, costs incurred in submitting complaints to the European Ombudsman (as opposed to costs incurred in contentious proceedings before the Union courts which are subject to different rules[338]) on

---

[334] K. Gutman, 'The Evolution of the Action for Damages Against the European Union and Its Place in the System of Judicial Protection' (2011) 48 C.M.L. Rev. at 730–1. In *Schneider*, for example, after affirming that a direct causal link existed with respect to two heads of damage—certain costs in participating in the resumed investigation of the transaction and the reduction of the Legrand transfer price granted to the purchaser to secure the deferral of the final date of the transfer—the Court of First Instance proceeded to the quantification of such damage, holding that Schneider had contributed to its own loss in relation to the second head of damage and thus held that the applicant was responsible for one-third of that damage: CFI, Case T-351/03 *Schneider Electric v Commmission* [2007] E.C.R. II-2237, paras 332–334. On appeal, the Court of Justice decided that there was no direct causal link in respect of that second head of damage and set aside the General Court's ruling insofar as it held the Union liable for two-thirds of that damage; then, in light of the reasoning which led to that judgment being set aside in part, it dismissed the action insofar as it concerned compensation for that damage: ECJ, Case C-440/07 P *Commission v Schneider Electric* [2009] E.C.R. I-6413, paras 218–223.

[335] See, e.g. EGC, Case T-107/08 *Transnational Company 'Kazchrome' and ENRC Marketing v Council and Commission* [2011] E.C.R. II-8051, para. 80 (the injury must result directly from the alleged illegality and not from the applicant's choice as to how to react to the allegedly unlawful act—thereby rejecting a claim for damages based on procedural expenses as the applicants are not required to participate in anti-dumping proceedings and are free to assess whether and the extent to which they should do so). But compare CFI, Case T-271/04 *Citymo v Commission* [2007] E.C.R. II-1375, paras 179–180: although the Court of First Instance found that the loss of opportunity to let the property in question for the duration of the pre-contract negotiations was the result of the applicant's own decision, it nevertheless held that the Commission, by not notifying the applicant of its decision not to lease the property, deprived the applicant of the opportunity to let the property to a third party for a period of two months.

[336] CFI, Case T-28/03 *Holcim (Deutschland) v Commission* [2005] E.C.R. II-1357, paras 119–131 (this finding was not dealt with on appeal because the requirement relating to a sufficiently serious breach of Union law was not satisfied: ECJ, Case C-282/05 P *Holcim (Deutschland) v Commission* [2007] E.C.R. I-2941, para. 57). See also CFI (order of 12 December 2007), Case T-113/04 *Atlantic Container Line AB and Others v Commission* [2007] E.C.R. II-171*, Summ. pub., paras 38, 41–45.

[337] ECJ, Case C-331/05 P *Internationaler Hilfsfonds v Commission* [2007] E.C.R. I-5475, paras 24–32. See also, e.g. ECJ, Case C-481/07 P *SELEX Sistemi Integrati v Commission* [2009] E.C.R. I-127*, Summ. pub., paras 20–23; CFI, Case T-48/05 *Franchet and Byk v Commission* [2008] E.C.R. II-1585, paras 415–417 (reasoning in light of *Internationaler Hilfsfonds*, the applicants cannot claim in an action for compensation reparation for the damage resulting from costs which they alleged to have incurred during the administrative stage of the procedure before the Commission. The same solution applies with respect to lawyers' fees linked to the procedure before OLAF. Likewise, costs incurred in proceedings before the national courts cannot be recovered in the absence of a causal link. In any event, recovery of such costs falls within the exclusive jurisdiction of the national courts which, in the absence of EU harmonization measures, must be settled in accordance with the applicable national law).

the grounds that they are attributed to the applicant's own decision for which an institution cannot be held liable.

C. Limitation period

(1) Commencement and duration

(a) Period of five years

11.86 Under Art. 46 of the Statute, a claim against the Union for non-contractual liability pursuant to Art. 268 TFEU and the second paragraph of Art. 340 TFEU[339] becomes time-barred after a period of five years from the occurrence of the event giving rise thereto. The general approach taken in the case-law appears to indicate that this five-year period is not extended by 10 days for distance under Art. 102(2) of the Rules of Procedure of the General Court.[340]

(b) Materialization of the damage causes time to start running

11.87 The five-year limitation period referred to in Art. 46 of the Statute does not begin to run until all of the requirements governing the obligation to provide compensation for damage are satisfied, and in particular, until the damage to be made good has materialized.[341] It is then that time starts running.

---

[338] For further particulars on costs, see paras 25.89 *et seq.*

[339] A different approach is taken with respect to claims for compensation within the context of staff disputes brought on the basis of Art. 270 TFEU and Arts 90–91 of the Staff Regulations: see, e.g. EGC (order of 18 July 2011), Case T-450/10 P *Marcuccio v Commission*, not reported, paras 24–35, particularly paras 29–30.

[340] See EGC (order of 22 June 2011), Case T-409/09 *Evropaïki Dynamiki v Commission*, not reported, paras 73–80 (upheld on appeal: ECJ (judgment of 8 November 2012), Case C-469/11 P *Evropaïki Dynamiki v Commission*, not reported). In particular, the General Court noted that the fact that there exists an isolated case decided in 1995 (CFI, Case T-571/93 *Lefebvre and Others v Commission* [1995] E.C.R. II-2379, para. 26) taking into account this period of distance, does not as such change its conclusion.

[341] See, e.g. ECJ, Case C-51/05 P *Commission v Cantina sociale di Dolianova and Others* [2008] E.C.R. I-5341, para. 54 (and citations therein); EGC (judgment of 28 September 2010), Case T-247/08 *C-Content v Commission*, not reported, para. 53 (and citations therein). For some recent applications, see ECJ, Case C-335/08 P *Transports Schiocchet—Excursions v Commission* [2009] E.C.R. I-104*, Summ. pub., paras 34–36; CFI (order of 27 August 2009), Case T-367/08 *Abouchar v Commission* [2009] E.C.R. II-128*, Summ. pub., paras 26–41; EGC (order of 22 June 2011), Case T-409/09 *Evropaïki Dynamiki v Commission*, not reported, paras 52–55; EGC (order of 17 October 2012), Case T-340/11 *Régie Networks and NRJ Global v Commission*, not reported, paras 39–40. Compare the approach taken in CFI, Case T-138/03 *É.R. and Others v Council and Commission* [2006] E.C.R. II-4923, para. 50 (upheld on appeal: ECJ (order of 4 October 2007), Case C-100/07 P *É.R. and Others v Council and Commission* [2007] E.C.R. I-136*, Summ. pub., paras 30–31): In an action for damages against the Union in connection with the damage allegedly suffered by the applicants as the result of the infection and subsequent death of members of their families from Jakob-Creuzfeldt disease ('mad cow disease'), the Court of First Instance found, contrary to the defendants' arguments, that it was not appropriate to rely on the moment when the first clinical symptoms of the disease suffered by the applicants' relatives appeared as the beginning of the limitation period and instead held that the limitation period in the present proceedings is not to begin before the respective dates of the death of each of the victims, or if it is later, of the establishment of a definite diagnosis of that disease (on the grounds that, first, before the victims' deaths, the alleged damage cannot be regarded as having been fully materialized, and second, it was undisputed that at the material time in this case a diagnosis of that disease was particularly difficult to establish and could often not be fully confirmed until after death). As regards the now-expired ECSC Treaty, see ECJ, Joined Cases 46/59 and 47/59 *Meroni and Others v High Authority* [1962] E.C.R. 411, at 420. See further CFI, Case T-152/97 *Petrides v Commission* [1997] E.C.R. II-2427, paras 25–31: the applicant has to show that there is a link between the allegedly unlawful act and time when the damage arose; if it fails to do so, the claim will be inadmissible in any event insofar as it is based on an act which took place more than five years before the application was lodged.

A recent example is illustrated by the Court of Justice's judgment in *Holcim (Deuschland) v Commission*.[342] In appeal proceedings concerning a claim for compensation brought on the basis of Art. 268 TFEU and the second paragraph of Art. 340 TFEU for bank guarantee charges incurred by the applicant's predecessor in order to avoid paying a fine imposed on it by a Commission decision for infringement of the competition rules, the Court of Justice underscored that with respect to the starting point of the limitation period for bringing an action for damages related to the harm caused by that decision, it is the alleged infringement of Union law in the contested decision which causes the damaging effects on the applicant and not the finding of such infringement by the General Court in its judgment annulling the decision.[343] Thus, it was not necessary for the contested decision to be annulled in order for the limitation period for the action for compensation to begin. Yet, the Court of Justice considered that the Court of First Instance had erred in law by holding that the limitation period started running as soon as the bank guarantees were provided: 'Whilst the claim for damages could no doubt have been brought as soon as the guarantees were provided, since at that time the damage caused by the contested Commission decision was certain as to the grounds and could be determined as to the scope, the period of limitation could not, for its part, begin until the financial loss had in fact materialised, that is, until the bank guarantee charges had begun to run.'[344]

(c) Continuous damage

If the full extent of the damage does not materialize immediately but only over a period of   **11.88**
time, the damages claim will be admissible only for compensation for the damage which arose during the period starting five years before the date on which the action was brought.[345]

(d) Future damage

The possibility of bringing a claim for compensation for future damage or damage which   **11.89**
has not yet been assessed does not influence when time starts to run. Time under the limitation period always starts to run when the damage materializes and not from the time when it became possible to bring an action for damages. If that were not the case, the claim for damages could be time-barred before the damage had actually materialized.[346]

(e) Legislative and individual acts

In cases where the liability of the Union has its origin in a legislative or normative act, the   **11.90**
limitation period does not begin to run until the resulting damage materializes, that is to say, the limitation period does not begin to run until the damaging effects of that act have arisen and hence until the time at which the persons concerned were bound to have suffered

---

[342] ECJ, Case C-282/05 P *Holcim (Deutschland) v Commission* [2007] E.C.R. I-2941.

[343] ECJ, Case C-282/05 P *Holcim (Deutschland) v Commission*, para. 31.

[344] ECJ, Case C-282/05 P *Holcim (Deutschland) v Commission*, para. 33. See also ECJ (judgment of 28 February 2013), Case C-460/09 P *Inalca and Cremonini v Commission*, not reported, para. 59.

[345] See, e.g. CFI, Case T-20/94 *Hartmann v Council and Commission* [1997] E.C.R. II-595, para. 132; CFI, Case T-76/94 *Jansma v Council and Commission* [2001] E.C.R. I-243, paras 78–79; CFI, Case T-210/00 *Biret & Cie v Council* [2002] E.C.R. II-47, paras 44–45 (appeal dismissed in ECJ, Case C-94/02 P *Biret & Cie v Council* [2003] E.C.R. I-10565); CFI, Case T-174/00 *Biret International v Council* [2002] E.C.R. II-417, CFI, para. 41; Case T-28/03 *Holcim (Deutschland) v Commission* [2005] E.C.R. II-1357, paras 69–70 (and citations therein) (undisturbed on appeal: ECJ, Case C-282/05 P *Holcim (Deutschland) v Commission* [2007] E.C.R. I-2941).

[346] ECJ, Joined Cases 56/74 to 60/74 *Kampffmeyer and Others v Commission and Council* [1976] E.C.R. 711.

certain damage.[347] This solution is likewise applied to disputes arising from individual acts, such that the limitation period begins to run as soon as the decision has produced its effects vis-à-vis the persons concerned by it.[348] Neither notification of the act concerned nor its entry into force as such causes the limitation period to begin running.[349] As such, for the purposes of calculating the limitation period, the case-law does not take a different approach according to the nature of the act.

(f) Objective, not subjective, inquiry

11.91 In *Commission v Cantina sociale di Dolianova*,[350] the Court of Justice set aside the Court of First Instance's ruling which had taken a subjective approach according to which the damage caused by an unlawful legislative act could not be regarded as certain as long as the allegedly injured party did not perceive it as such (*in casu* it made the assessment of whether the damage caused to the applicants was certain contingent on their becoming aware that they would not obtain compensation for their damage before the national courts).[351] The Court underlined that the rules on limitation periods which govern actions for damages must be based only on strictly objective criteria, since if it were otherwise, there would be a risk of undermining the principle of legal certainty on which the rules on limitations periods specifically rely and the point in time in which such actions become time-barred would vary according to the individual perception that each party may have as to the reality of damage.[352] Accordingly, the start of the limitation period for actions for damages is linked to the objective loss actually caused to the assets of the party which claims to have suffered harm (and hence in the present proceedings, the Court of First Instance should have made the five-year limitation period for the action for compensation brought before it start to run from the date on which the damage caused by the Union act concerned objectively materialized in the form of an adverse impact on the applicants' assets).[353]

---

[347] See, e.g. ECJ, Joined Cases 256/80 to 257/80, 265/80, 267/80, and 5/81 *Birra Wührer and Others v Council and Commission* [1982] E.C.R. 85, paras 9–12; ECJ, Case 51/81 *De Franceschi v Council and Commission* [1982] E.C.R. 117, paras 9–11; ECJ, Joined Cases 256/80 to 257/80, 265/80, 267/80, 5/81, and 51/81 and 282/82 *Birra Wührer and Others v Council and Commission* [1984] E.C.R. 3693, para. 15; ECJ, Case C-51/05 P *Commission v Cantina sociale di Dolianova* [2008] E.C.R. I-5341, para. 54. For an example of how to calculate the limitation period, see how it was done for each of the applicants in ECJ, Joined Cases 256/80 to 257/80, 265/80, 267/80, 5/81, and 51/81 and 282/82 *Birra Wührer and Others v Council and Commission*, paras 16–24; CFI, Case T-20/94 *Hartmann v Council and Commission* [1997] E.C.R. II-595, para. 107.

[348] ECJ, Case C-282/05 P *Holcim (Deutschland) v Commission* [2007] E.C.R. I-2941, paras 29–30; see further, e.g. ECJ, Case C-335/08 P *Transports Schiocchet—Excursions v Commission* [2009] E.C.R. I-104*, Summ. pub., para. 33; CFI, (order of 27 August 2009), Case T-367/08 *Abouchar v Commission* [2009] E.C.R. II-128*, Summ. pub., para. 23.

[349] See also EGC (order of 22 June 2011), Case T-409/09 *Evropaïki Dynamiki v Commission*, not reported, paras 69–70: The General Court underlined that the applicant's damage materialized on the date on which the applicant was personally informed of the rejection of its offer and not on the date of publication in the Official Journal of the award notice.

[350] ECJ, Case C-51/05 P *Commission v Cantina sociale di Dolianova v Commission* [2008] E.C.R. I-5341.

[351] ECJ, Case C-51/05 P *Commission v Cantina sociale di Dolianova v Commission*, paras 58, 70.

[352] ECJ, Case C-51/05 P *Commission v Cantina sociale di Dolianova v Commission*, paras 59–60.

[353] ECJ, Case C-51/05 P *Commission v Cantina sociale di Dolianova v Commission*, paras 63–64. In the present proceedings, the Court of Justice ultimately ruled that the action was time-barred and thus had to be dismissed as inadmissible: see ECJ, Case C-51/05 P *Commission v Cantina sociale di Dolianova v Commission*, paras 71–74. Cf. Opinion of Advocate-General E. Sharpston in ECJ, Case C-51/05 P *Commission v Cantina sociale di Dolianova Soc. coop.* [2008] E.C.R. I-5341, points 98–114. See further EGC (order of 16 December 2009), Case T-194/08 *Cattin & Cie and Cattin v Commission* [2009] E.C.R. II-242*, Summ. pub.; EGC (judgment of 28 September 2010), Case T-247/08 *C-Content v Commission*, not reported, paras 55–58.

(g) Unawareness of the event giving rise to the damage

Nevertheless, expiry of the limitation period cannot be pleaded against an applicant who **11.92** was not aware in time of the event which gave rise to the damage and therefore did not have a reasonable time before the limitation period ran out in order to bring a claim.[354] The fact that the applicant was unaware must be excusable.[355] This means that a normally prudent person who had done everything possible to become apprised of the facts which resulted in the damage would not have been in a position in the same circumstances to have been aware of the event which led to the damage.

(h) Expiry of the limitation period must be raised by the defendant

As in most Member States, expiry of the limitation period cannot be raised by the Union **11.93** judicature of its own motion.[356]

(2) Interruption of the limitation period

Art. 46 of the Statute of the Court of Justice provides that the period of limitation is to be **11.94** interrupted if proceedings are instituted before the General Court[357] or if prior to such proceedings an application is made by the aggrieved party to the relevant Union institution. In the latter event, proceedings must be instituted within the two-month period provided for in Art. 263 TFEU; the provisions of the second paragraph of Art. 265 TFEU apply where appropriate.

---

[354] ECJ, Case 145/83 *Adams v Commission* [1985] E.C.R. 3539, para. 50. See further, e.g. CFI, Case T-138/03 CFI, Case T-138/03 *É.R. and Others v Council and Commission* [2006] E.C.R. II-4923, para. 49 (appeal dismissed in ECJ (order of 4 October 2007), Case C-100/07 P *É.R. and Others v Council and Commission* [2007] E.C.R. I-136*, Summ.pub.). Compare ECJ (order of 18 July 2002), Case C-136/01 P *Autosalone Ispra dei Fratelli Rossi v Commission* [2002] E.C.R. I-6565, paras 30–31 (the fact that the person who sustained the damage was not aware at that time of the precise cause of the damage was held to be irrelevant for the purposes of establishing the moment when time started to run). This case-law does not conflict with the exclusively objective approach in the case-law. See further ECJ, Case C-51/05 P *Commission v Cantina sociale di Dolianova* [2008] E.C.R. I-5341, para. 61 (considering that the Court rejected the argument that the limitation period in Art. 46 of the Statute cannot begin to run until the victim has specific and detailed knowledge of the facts of the case, since knowledge of the facts is not one of the conditions which must be met in order for the limitation period to begin running, citing the order in ECJ (order of 18 July 2002), Case C-136/01 P *Autosalone Ispra dei Fratelli Rossi v Commission*) and para. 67 (rejecting the applicants' argument based on ECJ, Case 145/83 *Adams v Commission*, since unlike that case, the applicants in the present proceedings cannot claim that they were not aware of the event giving rise to their damage).

[355] Opinion of Advocate-General G.F. Mancini in ECJ, Case 145/83 *Adams v Commission* [1985] E.C.R. 3539, at 3550.

[356] ECJ, Case 20/88 *Roquette Frères v Commission* [1989] E.C.R. 1553, para. 12. This is because procedural time limits, such as time limits to bring an action, are rules of public policy laid down with a view to ensuring due administration of justice, clarity, and legal certainty and are not subject to the discretion of the parties. The limitation period for an action for damages, however, is a matter of substantive law that affects the enforceability of a subjective right. It protects both the aggrieved person and the person responsible for the harm and is not a rule of public policy. See ECJ (judgment of 8 November 2012), Case C-469/11 P *Evropaïki Dynamiki*, not reported, paras 48–59.

[357] The institution of proceedings before the national courts does not constitute an act interrupting the limitation period under Art. 46 of the Statute: see, e.g. ECJ (order of 18 July 2002), Case C-136/01 P *Autosalone Ispra dei Fratelli Rossi v Commission* [2002] E.C.R. I-6565, para. 57; CFI, Case T-246/93 *Bühring v Council and Commission* [1998] E.C.R. II-171, para. 72; ECJ, Case C-51/05 P *Commission v Cantine sociale di Dolianova and Others* [2008] E.C.R. I-5341, para. 69; ECJ, Case C-335/08 P *Transports Schiocchet— Excursions v Commission* [2009] E.C.R. I-104*, Summ. pub., para. 30. As regards the interruption of the limitation period in connection with the lodging of an action for damages: see CFI, Joined Cases T-457/04 and T-223/05 *Camar v Commission* [2008] E.C.R. II-215*, Summ. pub.

Reference to Arts 263 and 265 TFEU is made solely in connection with the possibility of interrupting the five-year limitation period prescribed by the first sentence of Art. 46 of the Statute. This reference is not intended to shorten the five-year limitation period, but simply to protect interested parties by preventing certain periods from being taken into account in calculating that limitation period. Its aim is merely 'to postpone the expiration of the period of five years when proceedings instituted or a prior application made within this period start time to run in respect of the periods provided for in Art. [263 TFEU] or Art. [265 TFEU]'.[358]

If a prior application is addressed by the aggrieved party to the institution concerned, interruption will occur only if that application is followed by an application to the General Court within the time limits determined by reference to Arts 263 and 265 TFEU.[359] If the aggrieved party does not bring proceedings within those time limits, the initial five-year limitation period continues to run in spite of the application made to the defendant institution. On the other hand, the limitation period is not reduced as a result.[360]

IV. Consequences

A. Judgment holding the Union liable

(1) Obligation to pay compensation

11.95 If the Court of Justice or the General Court finds the Union liable, the Union will be obliged under the second paragraph of Art. 340 TFEU to pay the necessary damages to the person concerned.

---

[358] ECJ, Joined Cases 5/66, 7/66, and 13/66 to 24/66 *Kampffmeyer and Others v Commission* [1967] E.C.R. 245, at 260. See also ECJ, Case C-282/05 P *Holcim (Deutschland) v Commission* [2007] E.C.R. I-2941, para. 36 (holding that since Art. 46 of the Statute relates to actions against the Union in respect of non-contractual liability, the 'proceedings' which fall within that provision, which, moreover, are treated as interrupting the limitation period, are those which seek to put that liability in issue in accordance with the second para. of Art. 340 TFEU; an action for annulment cannot therefore be deemed to be 'proceedings' which will interrupt the limitation period for the purposes of Art. 46 of the Statute); EGC (order of 14 March 2011), Case T-249/09 *Campailla v Commission* [2011] E.C.R. II-48*, Summ. pub., para. 43.

[359] ECJ, Case 11/72 *Giordano v Commission* [1973] E.C.R. 417, para. 6; CFI, Case T-222/97 *Steffens v Council and Commission* [1998] E.C.R. II-4175, paras 35–41; CFI, Case T-76/94 *Jansma v Council and Commission* [2001] E.C.R. II-243, para. 81; CFI (order of 19 September 2001), Case T-332/99 *Jestädt v Council and Commission* [2001] E.C.R. II-2561, para. 47; CFI (order of 14 September 2005), Case T-140/04 *Adviesbureau Ehcon v Commission* [2005] E.C.R. II-3287, paras 46–47; CFI, Case T-28/03 *Holcim (Deutschland) v Commission* [2005] E.C.R. II-1357, paras 72–73, (appealed on other grounds: ECJ, Case C-282/05 P *Holcim (Deutschland) v Commission* [2007] E.C.R. I-2941); EGC (order of 22 June 2011), Case T-409/09 *Evropaïki Dynamiki v Commission*, not reported, paras 57–58. For an exhaustively reasoned, specific application in the context of the *Mulder* cases, see, *inter alia*, CFI, Case T-143/97 *Van den Berg v Council and Commission* [2001] E.C.R. II-277, paras 58–74; CFI, Case T-187/94 *Rudolph v Council and Commission* [2002] E.C.R. II-367, paras 49–65; CFI, Case T-201/94 *Kustermann v Council and Commission* [2002] E.C.R. II-415, paras 61–77.

[360] ECJ, Case 11/72 *Giordano v Commission* [1973] E.C.R. 417, para. 7; CFI, Case T-167/94 *Nölle v Council and Commission* [1995] E.C.R. II-2589, para. 30.

(2) Judgment is enforceable

By virtue of Arts 280 and 299 TFEU, judgments of the Court of Justice and of the General **11.96**
Court are enforceable.[361] Enforcement is carried out in accordance with the law of the
Member State on whose territory it takes place. However, the property and assets of the
Union shall not be the subject of any administrative or legal measure of constraint without
the authorization of the Court of Justice.[362]

B. Judgment dismissing the action for damages

A judgment dismissing an application for damages does not have *erga omnes* effects. Its force **11.97**
as *res judicata* extends only to the parties to the proceedings: they are no longer entitled to
bring the same claim before the Union judicature on the basis of the same facts.[363] Other
parties wishing to bring an action for damages on the basis of the same facts may indeed
do so.

---

[361] Judgments of the General Court are enforceable even if an appeal has been brought before the Court of Justice. Appeals do not have suspensory effect (Statute, Art. 60, first para.). Yet, the Court of Justice may order application of the judgment of the General Court to be suspended for the duration of the appeal proceedings pursuant to Arts 278 and 279 TFEU.

[362] Art. 1 of the Protocol on the Privileges and Immunities of the European Union (cited in n. 96). See Ch.14.

[363] See EGC, Case T-341/07 *Sison v Council* [2011] E.C.R. II-7915, paras 17–25: The General Court ruled that the principle of *res judicata* attaching to a previous judgment ('*Sison I*') means that the applicant cannot claim afresh, pursuant to Art. 268 TFEU and the second para. of Art. 340 TFEU, compensation for damage corresponding to the damage in respect of which a claim for compensation on the same grounds has already been rejected by that judgment and therefore dismissed the applicant's action for damages as inadmissible insofar as it sought compensation for damage allegedly caused by the acts challenged in the case giving rise to that judgment. To the extent that the same party brings a subsequent action for damages based on the same arguments but on the basis of different facts (e.g. the period in which the alleged damage was sustained or proof and quantification of new damage for which compensation is sought), the General Court has not deemed such action inadmissible, but has dismissed such action in light of its findings in the previous action: see EGC (order of 24 May 2011), Case T-373/08 *Nuova Agricast v Commission* [2011] E.C.R. II-147*, Summ. pub., paras 49, 93.

12

APPLICATION FOR AN OPINION ON THE COMPATIBILITY WITH THE TREATIES OF AN INTERNATIONAL AGREEMENT TO BE CONCLUDED BY THE UNION

I. Subject-Matter

A. General

(1) Objective

12.01 Art. 218(11) TFEU provides: 'A Member State, the European Parliament, the Council or the Commission may obtain the opinion of the Court of Justice as to whether an agreement envisaged is compatible with the Treaties. Where the opinion of the Court is adverse, the agreement envisaged may not enter into force unless it is amended or the Treaties are revised.' Under established case-law, the purpose of Art. 218(11) TFEU is to forestall complications which would result from legal disputes concerning the compatibility with the Treaties of international agreements binding on the Union.[1] The Court has described such complications in the following terms: 'A possible decision of the Court, after the conclusion of an international agreement binding upon the European Union, to the effect that such an agreement is, by reason either of its content, or the procedure adopted for its conclusion, incompatible with the provisions of the Treaties could not fail to provoke, not only in the internal Union context, but also in that of international relations, serious difficulties and might give rise to adverse consequences for all interested parties, including third countries.'[2] To avoid such complications, the Treaties provide for recourse to the procedure set forth in Art. 218(11) TFEU of a prior reference to the Court

---

[1] See, e.g. ECJ, Opinion 1/75 *Draft Understanding on a Local Cost Standard drawn up under the auspices of the OECD* [1975] E.C.R. 1355, at 1360; ECJ, Opinion 3/94 *GATT-WTO-Framework Agreement on Bananas* [1995] E.C.R. I-4577, para. 16; ECJ, Opinion 2/94 *Accession by the Communities to the Convention for the Protection of Human Rights and Fundamental Freedoms* [1996] E.C.R. I-1759, para. 3; ECJ, Opinion 1/08 *Competence of the European Community to conclude agreements modifying the Schedules of Specific Commitments of the Community and its Member States under the General Agreement on Trade in Services* [2009] E.C.R. I-11129, para. 107; ECJ, Opinion 1/09 *Draft Agreement creating a Unified Patent Litigation System (European and Community Patents Court)* [2011] E.C.R. I-1137, para. 47.

[2] See, e.g. ECJ, Opinion 1/75 *Draft Understanding on a Local Cost Standard drawn up under the auspices of the OECD* [1975] E.C.R. 1355, at 1360–1; ECJ, Opinion 1/09 *Draft Agreement creating a Unified Patent Litigation System (European and Community Patents Court)* [2011] E.C.R. I-1137, para. 48 (and further citations therein).

of Justice for the purpose of elucidating, before the conclusion of an agreement, whether that agreement is compatible with the Treaties.[3] To date, the Court has given a limited number of opinions.[4]

(2) *Ex ante* judicial control

Consequently, opinions delivered by the Court of Justice pursuant to Art. 218(11) TFEU **12.02** perform an *ex ante* function. In the words of the Court of Justice, Art. 218(11) TFEU embodies 'a special procedure of collaboration between the Court of Justice on the one hand and the other [Union] institutions and the Member States on the other whereby, at a stage prior to conclusion of an agreement which is capable of giving rise to a dispute concerning the legality of a [Union] act which concludes, implements or applies it, the Court is called upon to ensure, in accordance with [Art. 19(1), first para., TEU], that in the interpretation and application of the Treaties the law is observed'.[5]

(3) Relationship with other remedies in the Treaties

The existence of the procedure under Art. 218(11) TFEU, however, does not mean that the **12.03** Court of Justice will not conduct judicial review *ex post* of the act by which a Union

---

[3] See, e.g. ECJ, Opinion 1/75 *Draft Understanding on a Local Cost Standard drawn up under the auspices of the OECD* [1975] E.C.R. 1355; ECJ, Opinion 3/94 *GATT–WTO-Framework Agreement on Bananas* [1995] E.C.R. I-4577, para. 18; ECJ, Opinion 2/94 *Accession by the Communities to the Convention for the Protection of Human Rights and Fundamental Freedoms* [1996] E.C.R. I-1759, para. 5. See also ECJ, Opinion 1/08 *Competence of the European Community to conclude agreements modifying the Schedules of Specific Commitments of the Community and its Member States under the General Agreement on Trade in Services* [2009] E.C.R. I-11129, para. 107: 'It must be borne in mind that the procedure laid down in [Art. 218(11) TFEU] is intended to make it possible to settle the question—prior to the conclusion of an agreement—as to whether the agreement is compatible with the [Treaties].'

[4] See ECJ, Opinion 1/75 *Draft Understanding on a Local Cost Standard drawn up under the auspices of the OECD* [1975] E.C.R. 1355; ECJ, Opinion 1/76 *Draft Agreement establishing a European laying-up fund for inland waterway vessels* [1977] E.C.R. 741; ECJ, Opinion 1/78 *International Agreement on Natural Rubber* [1979] E.C.R. 2871; ECJ, Opinion 1/91 *Draft Agreement between the Community, on the one hand, and the countries of the European Free Trade Association, on the other, relating to the creation of the European Economic Area* [1991] E.C.R. I-6079; ECJ, Opinion 1/92 *Draft Agreement between the Community, on the one hand, and the countries of the European Free Trade Association, on the other, relating to the creation of the European Economic Area* [1992] E.C.R. I-2821; ECJ, Opinion 2/91 *Convention No 170 of the International Labour Organisation concerning safety in the use of chemicals at work* [1993] E.C.R. I-1061; ECJ, Opinion 1/94 *Agreement establishing the World Trade Organisation* [1994] E.C.R. I-5267; ECJ, Opinion 2/92 *Competence of the Community or one of its institutions to participate in the Third Revised Decision of the OECD on national treatment* [1995] E.C.R. I-521; ECJ, Opinion 3/94 *GATT–WTO–Framework Agreement on Bananas* [1995] E.C.R. I-4577; ECJ, Opinion 2/94 *Accession by the Communities to the Convention for the Protection of Human Rights and Fundamental Freedoms* [1996] E.C.R. I-1759; ECJ, Opinion 2/00 *Cartagena Protocol* [2001] E.C.R. I-9713; ECJ, Opinion 1/00 *Proposed Agreement between the European Community and non-Member States on the establishment of a European Common Aviation Area* [2002] E.C.R. I-3493; ECJ, Opinion 1/03 *New Lugano Convention* [2006] E.C.R. I-1145; ECJ, Opinion 1/08 *Competence of the European Community to conclude agreements modifying the Schedules of Specific Commitments of the Community and its Member States under the General Agreement on Trade in Services* [2009] E.C.R. I-11129; ECJ, Opinion 1/09 *Draft Agreement creating a Unified Patent Litigation System (European and Community Patents Court)* [2011] E.C.R. I-1137. Notably, Opinion 1/09 is the first opinion of the Court of Justice delivered on the basis of the TEU and TFEU; this is so, even though the request was lodged before the entry into force of the Lisbon Treaty: see Opinion 1/09, para. 58. In contrast, the Court delivered Opinion 1/08 the day before the entry into force of the Lisbon Treaty and thus was rendered on the basis of the former Treaty framework.

[5] ECJ, Opinion 2/94 *Accession by the Communities to the Convention for the Protection of Human Rights and Fundamental Freedoms* [1996] E.C.R. I-1759, para. 6.

institution intended to conclude an international agreement.[6] In other words, while the procedure for obtaining the opinion of the Court of Justice is intended to obviate the adoption of unlawful acts, if it does not succeed in this, the usual channels for judicial review of the acts in question remain open.[7]

Moreover, the fact that certain questions may be dealt with by means of other remedies in the Treaties, in particular by bringing an action for annulment under Art. 263 TFEU, does not constitute an argument which precludes the Court from being asked for an opinion on those questions under Art. 218(11) TFEU.[8]

(4) Changes brought by the Treaty of Lisbon

12.04 The Lisbon Treaty introduced several changes to the wording of Art. 218(11) TFEU as compared with former Art. 300(6) EC. Adjustments have been made to the first sentence as regards the order of listing of the parties which may obtain an opinion from the Court of Justice[9] and the reference to the 'Treaties' and no longer 'provisions of this Treaty', in line with the changes introduced by the Lisbon Treaty to the institutional framework of the Union generally (as regards the elimination of the pillar structure, see further para. 12.05).[10]

Moreover, with respect to the second sentence, Art. 218(11) TFEU states that where the opinion of the Court of Justice is adverse, 'the agreement envisaged may not enter into force unless it is amended or the Treaties are revised', as compared with former Art. 300(6) EC, which had stipulated that in such circumstances, 'the agreement may enter into force only in accordance with Article 48 of the Treaty on European Union'. These changes reflect, on the one hand, the possibility already under the former Treaty framework of amending an envisaged agreement as a consequence of an adverse opinion by the Court of Justice,[11] and on the other hand, the fact that with the entry into force of the Lisbon Treaty, there is more than one means—including both ordinary and simplified revision procedures—of amending the Treaties, as set forth in the amended Art. 48 TEU.

(5) International agreements concerning the former second and third pillars

12.05 As mentioned in previous chapters, with the elimination of the pillar structure and the Union's replacement of and succession to the European Community brought by the entry into force of the Lisbon Treaty, the jurisdiction of the Court of Justice of the European Union has as a general matter been 'mainstreamed' in relation to the former third pillar of Police and Judicial Cooperation in Criminal Matters (PJCCM), although certain limitations remain; however, this was not the case with respect to the former second

---

[6] See, e.g. ECJ, Case C-327/91 *France v Commission* [1994] E.C.R. I-3641, paras 15–17; ECJ, Opinion 3/94 *GATT-WTO-Framework Agreement on Bananas* [1995] E.C.R. I-4577, para. 22; ECJ, Case C-122/95 *Germany v Council* [1998] E.C.R. I-973, paras 41–42.

[7] For the action for annulment, see Ch. 7; for preliminary rulings on validity, see Ch. 10.

[8] ECJ, Opinion 2/00 *Cartagena Protocol* [2001] E.C.R. I-9713, para. 12 (and citations therein).

[9] In comparison to former Art. 300(6) EC ('The European Parliament, the Council, the Commission or a Member State'), Art. 218(11) TFEU puts the reference to a Member State first ('A Member State, the European Parliament, the Council or the Commission').

[10] See Art. 1, third para., TEU; Art. 1(2) TFEU.

[11] See para. 12.20.

pillar of the Common Foreign and Security Policy (CFSP).[12] As explicitly provided in the Treaties, the Court of Justice of the European Union does not have jurisdiction with respect to the provisions relating to the CFSP or acts adopted on the basis of those provisions save for certain exceptions with respect to monitoring compliance with Art. 40 TEU and ruling on proceedings brought under the fourth paragraph of Art. 263 TFEU reviewing the legality of decisions providing for restrictive measures against natural and legal persons adopted by the Council on the basis of Chapter 2 of Title V of the TEU.[13]

That being said, there is no express reference in the Treaties to any limitations placed on the jurisdiction of the Court of Justice to deliver opinions under Art. 218(11) TFEU with respect to international agreements concerning CFSP matters. In fact, several other paragraphs of Art. 218 TFEU make provision for the conclusion of an envisaged agreement relating to the CFSP and the role to be played in that regard by the High Representative of the Union for Foreign Affairs and Security Policy.[14]

As such, although further case-law is awaited to address this point, it appears that a request for an opinion of the Court of Justice under Art. 218(11) TFEU may encompass an envisaged agreement concerning the PJCCM as well as the CFSP (provided that the other requisite conditions for the admissibility of such a request are satisfied) and thus may constitute an exception to the otherwise general exclusion of the Union courts' jurisdiction over CFSP matters.[15]

(6) Comparable provisions of the EAEC Treaty

The Court of Justice also has the power to give opinions under Art. 103 of the EAEC Treaty.[16] As highlighted in the case-law, this provision is comparable to Art. 218(11) TFEU,[17] but it is not exactly the same, since it concerns an application for an opinion of the Court submitted by a Member State in relation to the compatibility with the provisions of the EAEC Treaty of proposed clauses of draft agreements or contracts between that Member State and third parties in the context of communications about such agreements or contracts with the Commission.[18] Moreover, Arts 104 and 105 of the EAEC Treaty

12.06

---

[12] See para. 1.06.

[13] See Art. 24(1), second para., TEU; Art. 275 TFEU.

[14] See Art. 218(3), (6), (9) TFEU.

[15] See P. Eeckhout, *EU External Relations Law* (2nd edn, Oxford, Oxford University Press, 2011), 274.

[16] See ECJ, Ruling 1/78 *Draft Convention of the International Energy Agency on the Physical Protection of Nuclear Materials, Facilities and Transports* [1978] E.C.R. 2151, particularly paras 1–4.

[17] See, e.g. ECJ, Opinion 1/78 *International Agreement on Natural Rubber* [1979] E.C.R 2871, para. 30; ECJ, Opinion 2/91 *Convention No. 170 of the International Labour Organisation concerning safety in the use of chemicals at work* [1993] E.C.R. I-1061, para. 3.

[18] See ECJ, Case C-29/99 *Commission v Council* [2002] E.C.R. I-11221, paras 52–55: in an action for annulment brought by the Commission against a Council decision approving the accession of the EAEC to the Nuclear Safety Convention, the Court had the occasion to note that 'the Euratom Treaty does not provide that the Court may rule by way of an opinion on the compatibility with that Treaty of international agreements which the Community is planning to conclude' in the course of rejecting the Council's argument that the action was inadmissible on the grounds that the Commission was not really seeking the annulment of the act concerned but instead was seeking to obtain from the Court an opinion on the extent of the EAEC's competence in the context of its accession to this Convention which was not provided for under the EAEC Treaty as compared to what is now Art. 218(11) TFEU (then Art. 300(6) EC).

allow the Court of Justice to give opinions, on an application of the Commission, generally relating to agreements or contracts between a person or undertaking and third parties.[19]

B. The expression 'agreement envisaged'

(1) Agreement

12.07 The term 'agreement' in Art. 218(11) TFEU has been interpreted by the Court of Justice as referring to any undertaking entered into by entities subject to international law which has binding force, whatever its formal designation.[20] Provided that it is a ' "standard", that is to say a rule of conduct, covering a specific field, determined by precise provisions, which is binding upon the participants', the Court of Justice has jurisdiction to give an opinion on its compatibility with the Treaties.[21]

(2) Participation of the Union

12.08 Since the Court's jurisdiction to give opinions is provided for in Art. 218 TFEU, which lays down in general the decision-making procedure to be followed with regard to the conclusion of international agreements, that jurisdiction extends only to agreements in which the Union (as opposed to just the Member States) seeks to participate.[22] This relates to the aim of the procedure set forth in Art. 218(11) TFEU, which is to forestall legal disputes concerning the compatibility with the Treaties of international agreements binding on the Union.[23] By the same token, the Court of Justice is entitled to give opinions on the compatibility with the Treaties of mixed agreements to which both the Union and some or all Member States are parties.[24]

---

[19] See ECJ Rules of Procedure, Arts 202–203.

[20] ECJ, Opinion 1/75 *Draft Understanding on a Local Cost Standard drawn up under the auspices of the OECD* [1975] E.C.R. 1355, at 1359–60.

[21] ECJ, Opinion 1/75 *Draft Understanding on a Local Cost Standard drawn up under the auspices of the OECD*, at 1360. In Opinion 1/08, the Court found for the purposes of assessing the subject-matter of an 'envisaged agreement', here involving agreements modifying the schedules of specific commitments of the then Community and its Member States under the General Agreement on Trade in Services (GATS) that even though the modification and withdrawal of commitments annexed to the GATS could be implemented unilaterally by the then Community and its Member States, they constituted an 'indissociable whole' with the compensatory adjustments, all of which were binding on the parties to the agreements at issue and on the other WTO members as well, and thus formed the content of the agreements at issue: see ECJ, Opinion 1/08 *Competence of the European Community to conclude agreements modifying the Schedules of Specific Commitments of the Community and its Member States under the General Agreement on Trade in Services* [2009] E.C.R. I-11129, paras 96–105.

[22] Although in the past it has been argued that the term 'agreement' in what is now Art. 218(11) TFEU included agreements concluded by Member States, this possibility has to be ruled out. Unlike Art. 103 of the EAEC Treaty (see para. 12.06), Art. 218(11) TFEU affords no textual basis for such a reading. Furthermore, such agreements are not binding on the Union and thus, if they are subsequently found to be incompatible with the Treaties, there will be no likelihood of the Union incurring liability under international law. In contrast, in the case of mixed agreements, the Court of Justice is entitled to test Member States' obligations against the requirements of what is now Art. 4(3) TEU concerning the principle of sincere cooperation.

[23] See, e.g. ECJ, Opinion 1/75 *Draft Understanding on a Local Cost Standard drawn up under the auspices of the OECD* [1975] E.C.R. 1355, at 1360; ECJ, Opinion 1/09 *Draft Agreement creating a Unified Patent Litigation System (European and Community Patents Court)* [2011] E.C.R. I-1137, para. 47 (and further citations therein).

[24] See, e.g. ECJ, Opinion 1/76 *Draft Agreement establishing a European laying-up fund for inland waterway vessels* [1977] E.C.R. 741; ECJ, Opinion 1/09 *Draft Agreement creating a Unified Patent Litigation System (European and Community Patents Court)* [2011] E.C.R. I-1137.

II. Identity of the Parties

A. Applicants

Under Art. 218(11) TFEU, only a Member State, the European Parliament,[25] the Council, **12.09**
or the Commission may request the Court of Justice to deliver an opinion.[26] Accordingly,
this does not include all the Union institutions as listed in Art. 13(1) TEU.

B. No obligation

It is optional whether a request for an opinion is made. The Union can validly conclude an **12.10**
international agreement without seeking the opinion of the Court.

III. Special Characteristics

A. Extent of the jurisdiction to give opinions

(1) Scope of review

The Court of Justice has interpreted its jurisdiction to review 'whether an agreement **12.11**
envisaged is compatible with the Treaties' within the meaning of Art. 218(11) TFEU in
the sense that its judgment may depend not only on provisions of substantive law, but also
on those concerning the powers, procedure, or organization of the institutions of the
Union.[27] This approach is also expressed in Art. 196(2) of the ECJ Rules of Procedure.[28]
In particular, the Court's opinion may be obtained on questions concerning the division of
competence between the Union and the Member States to conclude a given agreement

---

[25] The European Parliament has had this power since the entry into force of the Nice Treaty. For the former
position of the European Parliament, see R. Barents, 'The Court of Justice and the EEA Agreement: Between
Constitutional Values and Political Realities', in J. Stuyck and A. Looijestijn-Clearie (eds), *The European
Economic Area EC-EFTA: Institutional Aspects and Financial Services* (Kluwer, Deventer, 1994), 57, at 58.

[26] To date, all requests for opinions have been made by the Commission with the exception of: 1) ECJ, Opinion
2/92 *Competence of the Community or one of its institutions to participate in the Third Revised Decision of the OECD on
national treatment* [1995] E.C.R. I-521 (Belgium); 2) ECJ, Opinion 2/94 *Accession by the Communities to the Convention
for the Protection of Human Rights and Fundamental Freedoms* [1996] E.C.R. I-1759 (the Council); 3) ECJ, Opinion
3/94 *GATT–WTO–Framework Agreement on Bananas* [1995] E.C.R. I-4577 (Germany); 4) ECJ, Opinion 1/03 *New
Lugano Convention* [2006] E.C.R. I-1145 (the Council); and 5) ECJ, Opinion 1/09 *Draft Agreement creating a Unified
Patent Litigation System (European and Community Patents Court)* [2011] E.C.R. I-1137 (the Council).

[27] ECJ, Opinion 1/75 *Draft Understanding on a Local Cost Standard drawn up under the auspices of the OECD*
[1975] E.C.R. 1355; ECJ, Opinion 1/76 *Draft Agreement establishing a European laying-up fund for inland waterway
vessels* [1977] E.C.R. 741; ECJ, Opinion 1/78 *International Agreement on Natural Rubber* [1979] E.C.R. 2871, para.
30; ECJ, Opinion 2/91 *Convention No. 170 of the International Labour Organisation concerning safety in the use of
chemicals at work* [1993] E.C.R. I-1061, para. 3; ECJ, *Opinion 2/94 Accession by the Communities to the Convention for
the Protection of Human Rights and Fundamental Freedoms* [1996] E.C.R. I-1759, para. 9; ECJ, Opinion 1/08
*Competence of the European Community to conclude agreements modifying the Schedules of Specific Commitments of the
Community and its Member States under the General Agreement on Trade in Services* [2009] E.C.R. I-11129, para. 108.

[28] Art. 196(2) of the ECJ Rules of Procedure provides as follows: 'A request for an opinion may relate both
to whether the envisaged agreement is compatible with the provisions of the Treaties and to whether the
European Union or any institution of the European Union has the power to enter into that agreement.'

with non-member countries.[29] This includes questions concerning the choice of the proper legal basis for the envisaged agreement.[30]

(2) Review limited to the compatibility of the agreement with the Treaties

12.12 The Court's review is limited, however, to the envisaged agreement's compatibility with the Treaties. The requirements imposed upon the Union by international law are not covered. Thus, in Opinion 2/91, the Court did not inquire into the provisions establishing the International Labour Organisation to see whether what was then the Community was entitled to join that organization.[31] The procedure under Art. 218(11) TFEU is also not intended to solve difficulties associated with implementation of an envisaged agreement which falls within shared Union and Member State competence.[32] In addition, the review as to compatibility covers only the legal aspects of the envisaged agreement. Judicial review does not extend to political expediency. As a result of the broad compass of the Court's review, conflicting powers often form the basis of requests for opinions.

(3) Review may be limited to parts of the agreement

12.13 As illustrated by the case-law, the Court may examine the whole agreement, or as the case may be, only part of it. In Opinion 1/91, the Court, at the Commission's request, considered only the provisions of the envisaged EEA Agreement which related to the system of judicial supervision provided for therein.[33] In Opinion 1/92, the Court confined its review to those provisions of the EEA Agreement which had been amended following Opinion 1/91 finding the Agreement incompatible with the former EC Treaty, despite the request made by the European Parliament in its observations submitted to the Court that it should consider the influence of the EEA Agreement on the role and powers of the Parliament.[34] In Opinion 1/00, the Court assessed the compatibility with the EC Treaty of the system of judicial supervision established by an agreement on a European Common

---

[29] See, e.g. ECJ, Opinion 2/00 *Cartagena Protocol* [2001] E.C.R. I-9713, para. 3 (and citations therein); ECJ, Opinion 1/03 *New Lugano Convention*, para. 112; ECJ, Opinion 1/08 *Competence of the European Community to conclude agreements modifying the Schedules of Specific Commitments of the Community and its Member States under the General Agreement on Trade in Services* [2009] E.C.R. I-11129, para. 109.

[30] See ECJ, Opinion 2/00 *Cartagena Protocol* [2001] E.C.R. I-9713, paras 1, 5–6, 9. For other examples, see ECJ, Opinion 1/94 *Agreement establishing the World Trade Organisation* [1994] E.C.R. I-5267; ECJ, Opinion 2/92 *Competence of the Community or one of its institutions to participate in the Third Revised Decision of the OECD on national treatment* [1995] E.C.R. I-521; ECJ, Opinion 2/94 *Accession by the Communities to the Convention for the Protection of Human Rights and Fundamental Freedoms* [1996] E.C.R. I-1759; ECJ, Opinion 1/08 *Competence of the European Community to conclude agreements modifying the Schedules of Specific Commitments of the Community and its Member States under the General Agreement on Trade in Services* [2009] E.C.R. I-1112. As acknowledged by the Court in the latter opinion (paras 111–113), the question concerning the character, exclusive or not, of Union competence to conclude the agreements in issue and the question of what is the proper legal basis for that purpose are closely linked and it was thus found appropriate to consider the two together.

[31] ECJ, Opinion 2/91 *Convention No. 170 of the International Labour Organisation concerning safety in the use of chemicals at work* [1993] E.C.R. I-1061, para. 4.

[32] ECJ, Opinion 2/00 *Cartagena Protocol* [2001] E.C.R. I-9713, para. 17.

[33] ECJ, Opinion 1/91 *Draft Agreement between the Community, on the one hand, and the countries of the European Free Trade Association, on the other, relating to the creation of the European Economic Area* [1991] E.C.R. I-6079, para. 1.

[34] ECJ, Opinion 1/92 *Draft Agreement between the Community, on the one hand, and the countries of the European Free Trade Association, on the other, relating to the creation of the European Economic Area* [1992] E.C.R. I-2821, para. 1.

Aviation Area. In determining the scope of the assessment requested, the Court considered all the language versions in which the request had been made.[35]

B. Time limit

(1) *Ex ante* nature

Art. 218(11) TFEU sets no time limit. Nevertheless, the *ex ante* nature of the procedure **12.14** and the extent of the Court's jurisdiction to give opinions place restrictions on the time within which a request may be made to the Court.

(2) Subject-matter of the envisaged agreement must be known

First, a request for an opinion may be made to the Court only as from the time when the **12.15** subject-matter of the envisaged agreement is known.[36] It is hard to conceive that the Court would be requested to give an opinion at a time when the subject-matter of the envisaged agreement was still uncertain. But as soon as the subject-matter is known, the Court's opinion may be sought, even before the negotiations have started.[37] From that time, the Court is in a position to adjudge whether the Union is competent to conclude the agreement in question. Indeed, in the event of any conflicts of jurisdiction, it is of essential importance for the Union, the Member States, and third countries or international organizations concerned to be certain about the precise powers of the parties at the beginning of the negotiations. As a result, it is not a prerequisite condition of being able to submit a request for an opinion pursuant to Art. 218(11) TFEU that the institutions concerned have reached final agreement; the right afforded to the Council, the Parliament, the Commission, and the Member States to request such an opinion can be exercised individually, without any coordinated action and without waiting for the final outcome of any related legislative procedure. The fact that the adoption of the agreement concerned cannot occur until after consulting or obtaining the approval of an institution and that the adoption of related legislative measures will be subject to a legislative procedure involving that institution has no effect on another institution's power to request an opinion from the Court.[38]

That being said, the Court will not be in a position to give its opinion on the compatibility of an envisaged agreement so long as it does not have sufficient information about the

---

[35] ECJ, Opinion 1/00 *Proposed Agreement between the European Community and non-Member States on the establishment of a European Common Aviation Area* [2002] E.C.R. I-3493, para. 1.

[36] ECJ, Opinion 1/78 *International Agreement on Natural Rubber* [1979] E.C.R. 2871, paras 32–34.

[37] See ECJ, Opinion 2/94 *Accession by the Communities to the Convention for the Protection of Human Rights and Fundamental Freedoms* [1996] E.C.R. I-1759, paras 11–17; ECJ, Opinion 1/09 *Draft Agreement creating a Unified Patent Litigation System (European and Community Patents Court)* [2011] E.C.R. I-1137, paras 53–54 (underscoring that the fact that draft agreement or related legislative measures linked to it do not currently enjoy unanimous support in the Council cannot by itself affect the admissibility of a request for an opinion under Art. 218(11) TFEU).

[38] ECJ, Opinion 1/09 *Draft Agreement creating a Unified Patent Litigation System (European and Community Patents Court)* [2011] E.C.R. I-1137, paras 55–56 (rejecting the Parliament's arguments concerning the admissibility of the request for an opinion submitted by the Council on the grounds that the principle of institutional balance had been compromised).

content and institutional machinery of the agreement.[39] Consequently, a request for an opinion raising the question of the compatibility of an envisaged agreement with the Treaties will be admissible only insofar as the Court can have access to such information.[40]

(3) Union must not yet be bound by the agreement

12.16 Second, a request may be made to the Court only insofar as the Union is not yet bound by the agreement. Failing this, the opinion would not play its preventive role.[41] It makes no difference in this connection at what stage in the process of concluding the international agreement the opinion is sought, provided that the Union is not yet bound by it. Accordingly, an opinion may be obtained from the Court before the Commission (or the High Representative, as the case may be) has made any recommendations to the Council pursuant to Art. 218(1) TFEU with a view to opening negotiations and before the Council has given it the necessary authorisation. The Court's opinion may also be sought after the negotiations have closed, but before the Council concludes the agreement pursuant to Art. 218(2) TFEU.[42]

If, however, the envisaged agreement is concluded after the request for an opinion was submitted, but before the Court has given its opinion, the request becomes devoid of purpose. The *ex ante* nature of the procedure provided for in Art. 218(11) TFEU requires the 'envisaged' agreement to be still only envisaged at the time when the Court gives its opinion. Moreover, if the Court were to give an adverse opinion on the compatibility with the Treaties of an agreement which had already been concluded, that opinion would not be capable of having the legal effect prescribed by the second sentence of Art. 218(11) TFEU, namely that, if the Court has given an adverse opinion, the agreement may not enter into force unless it is amended or the Treaties are revised (see para. 12.20). In those circumstances, the Court will not respond to the request for an opinion.[43]

---

[39] See ECJ, Opinion 2/94 *Accession by the Communities to the Convention for the Protection of Human Rights and Fundamental Freedoms* [1996] E.C.R. I-1759, paras 20–22.

[40] For some recent examples, see ECJ, Opinion 1/03 *New Lugano Convention* [2006] E.C.R. I-1145, para. 111; ECJ, Opinion 1/09 *Draft Agreement creating a Unified Patent Litigation System (European and Community Patents Court)* [2011] E.C.R. I-1137, paras 49–52. In Opinion 1/08, the Court of Justice delivered an opinion on the compatibility of seventeen agreements, even though only one of those agreements had been produced to the Court on the grounds that they were confirmed by the requesting institution (the Commission) as well as the Council to be substantially the same: see ECJ, Opinion 1/08 *Competence of the European Community to conclude agreements modifying the Schedules of Specific Commitments of the Community and its Member States under the General Agreement on Trade in Services* [2009] E.C.R. I-11129, paras 21, 29.

[41] An opinion dealing with the compatibility with the Treaties of an international agreement which has already entered into force may be given where the Union is not yet bound by it, but is considering acceding to it.

[42] ECJ, Opinion 1/94 *Agreement establishing the World Trade Organisation* [1994] E.C.R. I-5267, para. 12. The Commission requested Opinion 2/00 (ECJ, Opinion 2/00 *Cartagena Protocol* [2001] E.C.R. I-9713) after the Protocol had been signed by the Council, but before the Commission had submitted a proposal to the Council for the conclusion of the Protocol.

[43] ECJ, Opinion 3/94 *GATT–WTO–Framework Agreement on Bananas* [1995] E.C.R. I-4577. As a consequence, the Member State which had requested an opinion (Germany) in that case brought an action for annulment against the Council decision approving the international agreement concerned on behalf of the Community, resulting in the annulment of a certain provision of that decision: see ECJ, Case C-122/95 *Germany v Council* [1998] E.C.R. I-973.

(4) No suspensory effect of the request

A request for an opinion under Art. 218(11) TFEU does not suspend the procedure for **12.17** adopting the international agreement in question. This is illustrated, for example,[44] by the saga concerning the proposed agreement between what was then the European Community and the United States of America on the processing and transfer of Passenger Name Record (PNR) data, in which the European Parliament lodged a request for an opinion concerning this envisaged agreement, but before the Court delivered its opinion the Council adopted a decision on the conclusion of the agreement, with the result that the Parliament withdrew its request and subsequently brought a successful action for annulment against this decision and a related measure.[45]

C. Procedure before the Court

(1) Non-contentious nature of the procedure

Since a request for an opinion pursuant to Art. 218(11) TFEU does not introduce normal **12.18** contentious proceedings, the decision is reached in the Court of Justice in accordance with a special procedure. It is further elaborated in Arts 196–200 of the ECJ Rules of Procedure.

The request for an opinion has to be lodged with the Registry. It is served on the Member States, the European Parliament, the Council, and the Commission.[46]

The President of the Court of Justice prescribes a period within which the Member States and the institutions which have been served with the request may submit written observations.[47] On account of the special or non-contentious nature of the procedure, it is not possible to apply the expedited procedure (applicable to direct actions before the Union courts) in the case of a request for an opinion made pursuant to Art. 218(11) TFEU.[48]

(2) Opinion

The Court delivers its opinion in open court as soon as possible after hearing the appointed **12.19** Advocate-General.[49] The Court may decide that the procedure before it shall also include a hearing.[50] The opinion is signed by the President, by the Judges who took part in the

---

[44] See ECJ, Case C-122/95 *Germany v Council.*

[45] ECJ, Joined Cases C-317/04 and C-318/04 *European Parliament v Council* [2006] E.C.R. I-4721.

[46] ECJ Rules of Procedure, Art. 196(3).

[47] ECJ Rules of Procedure, Art. 196(3).

[48] ECJ (order of the President of 29 April 2004), Opinion 1/04 *Proposed Agreement between the European Community and the United States of America on the processing and transfer of Passenger Name Record data,* not reported. For the expedited procedure, see paras 25.79 *et seq.* Likewise, Art. 151 of the ECJ Rules of Procedure cannot be relied upon for raising a preliminary objection to the admissibility of a request for an opinion under Art. 218(11) TFEU: ECJ, Opinion 2/92 *Competence of the Community or one of its institutions to participate in the Third Revised Decision of the OECD on national treatment* [1995] E.C.R. I-521, para. 11.

[49] ECJ Rules of Procedure, Arts. 197, 199, and 200. Under the former ECJ Rules of Procedure, Art. 108(2) provided that all the Advocates-General were heard.

[50] ECJ, Rules of Procedure, Art. 198. See, e.g. ECJ, Opinion 1/08 *Competence of the European Community to conclude agreements modifying the Schedules of Specific Commitments of the Community and its Member States under the General Agreement on Trade in Services* [2009] E.C.R. I-11129.

deliberations, and by the Registrar, following which it is served on the European Parliament, the Council, the Commission, and the Member States.[51]

IV. Consequences

A. Adverse opinion

12.20 Under Art. 218(11) TFEU, an agreement on which the Court of Justice has given an adverse opinion may not enter into force unless it is amended or the Treaties are revised. This means, first, that the Treaties may be amended in accordance with the applicable procedure (see Art. 48 TEU).[52]

As had been the case under the former Treaty framework, this also means that it is possible for the envisaged agreement to be amended by the Union institutions in consultation with the third countries and international organizations concerned in order to meet the objections raised by the Court.[53] As such, this provision implicitly confirms the binding effects of the Court's opinion under Art. 218(11) TFEU.

B. Favourable opinion

12.21 A favourable opinion leaves the way free for the Union to enter into the agreement, but naturally does not compel it to do so. However, the opinion does not prevent the legality of the act by which the Union concludes the agreement from being raised in some other judicial proceedings, especially where the Court's review was limited to only certain parts of the agreement (see para. 12.13).

---

[51] ECJ Rules of Procedure, Art. 200.
[52] For further discussion of the ordinary and special revision procedures laid down in Art. 48 TEU, see K. Lenaerts and P. Van Nuffel (R. Bray and N. Cambien (eds)), *European Union Law* (3rd edn, London, Sweet & Maxwell, 2011), paras 5.02–5.09.
[53] See, e.g. the EEA Agreement: the proposed system of judicial supervision was amended following Opinion 1/91: cf. Opinions 1/91 and 1/92 (see para. 12.13). See also the Agreement on a Unified Patent Court: the proposed court system was altered following Opinion 1/09 (see para. 3.14).

PART IV

SPECIAL FORMS OF PROCEDURE

13

PROCEEDINGS FOR INTERIM MEASURES BEFORE THE UNION COURTS

I. Subject-Matter

A. Introduction

(1) Objective

Proceedings for interim measures before the Union courts essentially constitute provisional **13.01** legal protection granted in favour of a party before the main action is decided. Art. 278 TFEU lays down the principle that actions brought before the Court of Justice or the General Court do not have suspensory effect.[1] As a result of the time which elapses between the bringing of proceedings and judgment, this principle may detract from the effectiveness of legal protection. Consequently, interim measures that the respective Court may impose as necessary in interlocutory proceedings are intended, *inter alia*, to secure full effect for the application in the event that the dispute is decided in the applicant's favour.[2] In other words, the provision of interim relief in proceedings before the Union courts pursuant to Arts 278 and 279 TFEU enables a claimant to safeguard its rights under Union law because the passage of time would undo the benefits of the judgment to be given on the merits.

The principle just mentioned that actions brought before the Union courts do not have suspensory effect can be explained by the fact that measures adopted by Union institutions, bodies, and agencies are presumed to be lawful. Therefore, as has been emphasized in the case-law, it is only exceptionally that the Judge hearing the application may order suspension of the operation of such a measure or other interim relief pursuant to Arts 278 and 279 TFEU.[3]

---

[1] Art. 278 TFEU, first sent.

[2] See, e.g. ECJ (order of the President of 3 May 1996), Case C-399/95 R *Germany v Commission* [1996] E.C.R. I-2441, para. 46; ECJ (order of the President of 31 January 2011), Case C-404/10 P-R *Commission v Éditions Odile Jacob* [2011] E.C.R. I-6*, Summ. pub., para. 22; ECJ (order of the President of 18 May 2011), Case C-337/09 P-R *Council v Zhejiang Xinan Chemical Industrial Group* [2011] E.C.R. I-77*, Summ. pub., para. 45; CFI (order of the President of 31 January 2005), Case T-447/04 R *Capgemini Nederland v Commission* [2005] E.C.R. II-257, para. 89; CFI (order of the President of 2 July 2004), Case T-76/04 R *Bactria v Commission* [2004] E.C.R. II-2025, para. 44 (and citations therein) (appeal dismissed in ECJ (order of the President of 13 December 2004), Case C-380/04 P(R) *Bactria v Commission*, not reported); CFI (order of the President of 28 September 2007), Case T-257/07 R *France v Commission* [2007] E.C.R. II-4153, para. 122; CST (order of the President of 14 June 2012), Case F-38/12 R *BP v EU Fundamental Rights Agency*, not reported, para. 22. With particular regard to the Civil Service Tribunal, see para. 13.27.

[3] See, e.g. EGC (order of the President of 17 December 2009), Case T-396/09 R *Vereniging Milieudefensie and Stichting Stop Luchtverontreiniging Utrecht v Commission* [2009] E.C.R. II-246*, Summ. pub., para. 31 (and

(2) Changes brought by the Treaty of Lisbon

13.02   Art. 278 TFEU reproduces verbatim former Art. 242 EC, save for the replacement of 'Court of Justice' with the 'Court of Justice of the European Union' and the 'Court' in the two sentences of this provision, respectively. Similarly, Art. 279 TFEU reproduces verbatim former Art. 243 EC, save for the replacement of 'Court of Justice' with the 'Court of Justice of the European Union'. These changes brought by the entry into force of the Lisbon Treaty merely give expression to the fact that proceedings for interim measures may be brought before each of the Union courts (the Court of Justice, the General Court, and the Civil Service Tribunal).

(3) EAEC and now-expired ECSC Treaties

13.03   A comparable provision to Art. 278 TFEU is set forth in Art. 157 EAEC.[4] There used to be a comparable provision to Art. 279 TFEU set forth in Art. 158 EAEC,[5] but with the entry into force of the new consolidated version of the EAEC Treaty in tandem with that of the Lisbon Treaty, Art. 158 EAEC has been repealed and Art. 279 TFEU is now applicable.[6]

Furthermore, Art. 39 of the now-expired ECSC Treaty was comparable to Arts 272 and 273 TFEU.

B. Types of measure

(1) Suspension of the operation of the contested act

13.04   First, under Art. 278 TFEU, the Court may order that application of the contested act be suspended.

Only the operation of 'enforceable' measures may be suspended.[7] On that ground, an administrative authority's refusal to grant a request made to it may not be suspended,

---

citations therein); EGC (order of the President of 31 August 2010), Case T-299/10 R *Babcock Noell v The European joint undertaking for ITER and the Development of Fusion Energy* [2010] E.C.R. II-161*, Summ. pub., paras 14, 57; EGC (order of the President of 25 January 2012), Case T-637/11 R *Euris Consult Ltd v European Parliament*, not reported, para. 9; EGC (order of the President of 13 February 2012), Case T-61/11 R *Dansk Automat Brancheforening v Commission*, not reported, para. 16.

   [4] Art. 157 EAEC states: '*Save as otherwise provided in this Treaty,* actions brought before the Court of Justice of the European Union shall not have suspensory effect. The *Court of Justice of the European Union* may, however, if it considers that circumstances so require, order that application of the contested act be suspended.' (emphasis added). Except as indicated by the italicized language, this provision reproduces verbatim Art. 278 TFEU.

   [5] Former Art. 158 EAEC provided: 'The Court of Justice may in any cases before it prescribe any necessary interim measures.'

   [6] See Art. 106a(1) of the consolidated version of the EAEC Treaty, [2012] O.J. C327/1.

   [7] CFI (order of the President of 7 June 1991), Case T-19/91 R *Vichy v Commission* [1991] E.C.R. II-265, para. 20. See also EGC (order of the President of 8 September 2010), Case T-15/10 R II *Ngele v Commission* [2010] E.C.R. II-176*, Summ. pub., para. 8 (request that the President of the Court 'declare illegal and irregular' an act of the Commission held inadmissible as beyond the scope of Art. 278 TFEU) (appeal dismissed in ECJ (order of the President of 16 December 2010), Case C-526/10 P(R) *Ngele v Commission* [2010] E.C.R. I-173*, Summ. pub.). The chapter devoted to suspension of operation or enforcement and other interim measures in the Rules of Procedure of the respective Courts applies to applications to suspend the enforcement of a decision of the Court or of any measure adopted by the Council, the Commission, or the European Central Bank pursuant to Arts 280 and 299 TFEU or Art. 164 EAEC. See ECJ Rules of Procedure, Art. 165; EGC Rules of Procedure, Art. 110; CST Rules of Procedure, Art. 108. However, the Judge hearing

generally speaking, unless, as such, it alters the applicant's legal position.[8] The Judge dealing with applications for interim relief must not encroach upon the domain of the 'executive'.[9] If he or she did so, suspension of the operation of the rejection of a request would be tantamount to performing the act requested, which would entail the Judge acting in place of the administrative authority. At the same time, the purpose of the main action would disappear.[10]

---

an application for interim measures is not competent to order interim relief in relation to measures taken at the national level related to enforcement under Art. 299 TFEU: see CFI (order of the President of 3 December 2007), Case T-312/07 R II *Peramatos v Commission*, not reported, paras 13–18. Moreover, in the context of third-party proceedings, the Court may, on application of the third party, order a stay of execution of the contested judgment and in that case, the respective chapter on interim relief is to apply: see ECJ Rules of Procedure, Art. 157(4); EGC Rules of Procedure, Art. 123(2); CST Rules of Procedure, Art. 117(5). For an example, see EGC (order of the President of 4 February 2010), Case T-385/05 TO R *Third-party proceedings Portugal v Transnáutica—Transportes e Navegação and Commission* [2010] E.C.R. II-14*, Summ. pub.

[8] For example, ECJ (order of the President of 23 March 1988), Case 76/88 R *La Terza v Court of Justice* [1988] E.C.R. 1741, in which the decision rejecting the applicant's request for an extension of her authorization to work part-time was suspended. The decision rejecting her request meant that she had to start working full-time with immediate effect, which altered her legal position as an official. In principle, suspension of the operation of a negative administrative decision is impossible, however, since suspension would not be capable of effecting any change in the applicant's situation: see, e.g. ECJ (order of the President of 30 April 1997), Case C-89/97 P(R) *Moccia Irme v Commission* [1997] E.C.R. I-2327, para. 45; ECJ (order of the President of 29 April 2005), Case C-404/04 P-R *Technische Glaswerke v Commission* [2005] E.C.R. I-3539, para.13; CFI (order of the President of 16 January 2004), Case T-369/03 R *Arizona Chemical and Others v Commission* [2004] E.C.R. II-205, para. 62; CFI (order of the President of 12 May 2006), Case T-42/06 R *Gollnisch v European Parliament* [2006] E.C.R. II-40*, Summ. pub., para. 30; CFI (order of the President of 18 February 2008), Case T-410/07 R *Jurado Hermanos v OHIM* [2008] E.C.R. II-25*, Summ. pub., para. 31; CFI (order of the President of 18 March 2008), Case T-411/07 R *Aer Lingus Group v Commission* [2008] E.C.R. II-411, para. 46; CFI (order of the President of 26 September 2008), Case T-312/08 R *Ellinikos Niognomon v Commission* [2008] E.C.R. II-204*, Summ. pub., para. 26; EGC (order of 30 September 2011), Case T-347/11 R *Gollnisch v European Parliament* [2011] E.C.R. II-341*, Summ. pub., para. 17. As a consequence, generally an application for suspension of a negative administrative decision is found to be of no practical use to the applicant and hence dismissed for lack of an interest (see further para. 13.16), save insofar as suspension of the operation of such decision may be necessary in order to prescribe one of the other interim measures sought by the applicants, which the Judge hearing the application for interim measures may consider to be admissible and well-founded: see, e.g. CFI (order of the President of 18 March 2008), Case T-411/07 R *Aer Lingus Group v Commission* [2008] E.C.R. II-411, paras 47–48; EGC (order of the President of 17 December 2009), Case T-396/09 R *Vereniging Milieudefensie and Stichting Stop Luchtverontreiniging Utrecht v Commission* [2009] E.C.R. II-246*, Summ. pub., paras 34–35; EGC (order of the President of 26 March 2010), Case T-6/10 R *Alisei v Commission* [2010] E.C.R. II-48*, Summ. pub., paras 25–26; EGC (order of the President of 23 January 2012), Case T-607/11 R *Henkel and Henkel France v Commission*, not reported, para. 21. But see CFI (order of the President of 15 November 2007), Case T-215/07 R *Donnici v European Parliament* [2007] E.C.R. II-4673, paras 33–37 (rejecting the European Parliament's argument that the contested measure, insofar as it concerned the applicant, constituted a negative administrative decision and holding that the applicant had proven to the requisite legal standard that he had an interest in the suspension of operation requested and hence the application was admissible).

[9] See, e.g. ECJ (order of the President of 5 October 1969), Case C-50/69 R *Germany v Commission* [1969] E.C.R. 449, at 451; CFI (order of the President of 18 February 2008), Case T-410/07 R *Jurado Hermanos v OHIM* [2008] E.C.R. II-25*, Summ. pub., paras 33–34; CFI (order of the President of 26 September 2008), Case T-312/08 R *Ellinikos Niognomon v Commission* [2008] E.C.R. II-204*, Summ. pub., paras 28–29; EGC (order of the President of 30 September 2011), Case T-347/11 R *Gollnisch v European Parliament* [2011] E.C.R. II-341*, Summ. pub., para. 19 (appeal dismissed in ECJ (order of the President of 29 March 2012), Case C-570/11 P(R) *Gollnisch v European Parliament*, not reported).

[10] ECJ (order of the President of 15 October 1976), Case 91/76 R *De Lacroix v Court of Justice* [1976] E.C.R. 1561, para. 2; in general, the Judge hearing an application for interim relief may not grant measures which cause the main action to become nugatory: see, e.g. ECJ (order of the President of 26 September 1986), Case 231/86 R *Breda-Geomineraria v Commission* [1986] E.C.R. 2639, para. 18; CFI (order of the President of 3 March 1998), Case T-610/97 R *Carlsen and Others v Council* [1998] E.C.R. II-485, para. 56; EGC (order

Moreover, the Treaties do not provide for any means of recourse allowing parties to demand the suspension of the execution of measures adopted by national authorities, including decisions of national courts and tribunals, before the Union courts, and therefore, applications to this effect are inadmissible.[11]

(2) Other interim measures

13.05   In some cases, suspension of the operation of the contested act does not suffice in order to prevent irreparable damage from occurring. Consequently, under Art. 279 TFEU, the Court may prescribe 'any necessary interim measures'.[12] The range of possible measures is not predetermined,[13] but the Judge who imposes them may not exercise a power that is vested in another institution, as this would jeopardize the balance between the institutions.[14]

---

of the President of 23 January 2012), Case T-607/11 R *Henkel and Henkel France v Commission*, not reported, para. 24. See also para. 13.07.

[11] See, e.g. CFI (order of 14 December 2006), Case T-150/06 *Smanor and Others v Commission*, not reported, paras 17–18 (appeal dismissed in ECJ (order of 23 May 2007), Case C-99/07 P *Smanor and Others v Commission* [2007] E.C.R. I-70*, Summ. pub.); EGC (order of the President of 25 October 2011), Case T-472/11 R *DMA Die Marketing Agentur and Hofmann v Austria* [2011] E.C.R. II-374*, Summ. pub. That being said, this does not prevent interim measures being directed at national authorities: see para. 13.21. Moreover, as the Treaties do not provide means by which natural and legal persons can lodge an action against a Member State in the Union courts (see further para. 13.04), interim measures brought pursuant to such an action will fail because the main action is inadmissible: see, e.g. EGC (order of the President of 17 February 2010), Case T-456/09 R *Bakonyi v Hungary* [2010] E.C.R. II-20*. As regards interim measures in the context of preliminary ruling proceedings, see para. 13.13. See also EGC (order of the President of 17 February 2011), Case T-486/10 R *Iberdrola v Commission*, not reported; and EGC (order of the President of 17 February 2011), Case T-490/10 R *Endesa and Endesa Generacion v Commission*, not reported, paras 21–24, 30–31: following its admission to intervene in the proceedings for interim measures, Spain submitted a demand, pursuant to Art. 108 of the EGC Rules of Procedure, to rescind the order of the President of the Court temporarily suspending the contested Union act on account of measures that had been taken at the national level; in response, by letter, the Registrar informed Spain that the President of the General Court did not envisage, at that stage, the revocation of its order, which was in any event not dependent on a decision of a national judge or measures producing similar effects at the national level.

[12] By virtue of this broad wording, interim measures may even be directed at third parties not party to the proceedings: see para. 13.21. Nevertheless, the provision of any such interim measures must be compatible with Union law, including the specific nature of interim proceedings and the system of remedies of which it forms a part: see CFI (order of the President of 12 February 1996), Case T-228/95 R *S. Lehrfreund v Council* [1996] E.C.R. II-111, paras 60–61 (holding request for a declaration as to the interpretation of the contested measure inadmissible).

[13] This may even include the issuance, on a provisional basis, of appropriate injunctions to a Union institution or body: see, e.g. CFI (order of the President of 19 July 2007), Case T-31/07 R *Du Pont de Nemours (France) and Others v Commission* [2007] E.C.R. II-2767, para. 53 (and citations therein) (in relation to the Commission). Compare the approach taken in the case-law in connection with direct actions, namely the action for annulment: see para. 7.219. In context of staff cases, the case-law makes clear that claims requesting the CST to issue a direction to an administrative authority are declared inadmissible (see, e.g. CST (order of the President of 27 May 2011), Joined Cases F-5/11 R and F-15/11 R *Mariën v Commission and European External Action Service*, not reported, para. 43).

[14] See, e.g. ECJ (order of the President of 5 October 1969), Case C-50/69 R *Germany v Commission* [1969] E.C.R. 449, at 451; ECJ (order of the President of 22 October 1975), Case 109/75 R *National Carbonising v Commission* [1975] E.C.R. 1193, para. 8; CFI (order of the President of 18 February 2008), Case T-410/07 R *Jurado Hermanos v OHIM* [2008] E.C.R. II-25*, Summ. pub., paras 33–34; CFI (order of the President of 18 March 2008), Case T-411/07 R *Aer Lingus Group v Commission* [2008] E.C.R. II-411, paras 49–51, 54; CFI (order of the President of 26 September 2008), Case T-312/08 R *Ellinikos Niognomon v Commission* [2008] E.C.R. II-204*, Summ. pub., paras 28–29; EGC (order of the President of 30 September 2011), Case T-347/11 R *Gollnisch v European Parliament* [2011] E.C.R. II-341*, Summ. pub., para. 19 (appeal dismissed in ECJ (order of the President of 29 March 2012), Case C-570/11 P(R) *Gollnisch v European Parliament*, not

(3) Interim relief is tailored to the case

The interim relief imposed by the Court is tailored to the case. Consequently, suspension of **13.06** operation may be ordered of only part of the contested act or other such relief granted may be made subject to specific conditions.[15] Sometimes, security may be required to be lodged.[16] The Judge hearing an application for interim relief may also remind a party to comply with existing provisions where this may provisionally ensure appropriate protection of the applicant's rights.[17]

C. The ancillary nature of proceedings for interim measures

(1) Ancillary to the main proceedings

The ancillary nature of proceedings for interim measures clearly emerges from Art. 278 **13.07** TFEU, which merely permits application of the 'contested act' to be suspended, and from Art. 279 TFEU, which provides only for interim measures in cases before the Court of Justice or the General Court.[18]

---

reported). For the Commission's power to impose interim measures during an investigation into infringements of the competition rules, see Art. 8 of Regulation No. 1/2003; see also ECJ (order of 17 January 1980), Case 792/79 R *Camera Care v Commission* [1980] E.C.R. 119; CFI, Case T-44/90 *La Cinq v Commission* [1992] E.C.R. II-1; CFI (order of the President of 2 December 1994), Case T-322/94 R *Union Carbide v Commission* [1994] E.C.R. II-1159, paras 26–27; CFI (order of the President of 26 October 2001), Case T-184/01 R *IMS Health v Commission* [2001] E.C.R. II-3193.

[15] For some examples, see ECJ (order of the President of 15 October 1974), Cases 71/74 R and RR *Fruiten Groentenimporthandel and Frubo v Commission* [1974] E.C.R. 1031, para. 8 (order subject to conditions); ECJ (order of the President of 31 March 1982), Joined Cases 43/82 R and 63/82 R *VBVB and VBBB v Commission* [1982] E.C.R. 1241, paras 9–11 (order suspending part of act and subject to conditions); CFI (order of the President of 16 June 1992), Joined Cases T-24/92 R and T-28/92 R *Langnese-Iglo and Schöller Lebensmittel v Commission* [1992] E.C.R. II-1839 (order suspending part of act and subject to conditions); CFI (order of the President of 13 July 2006), Case T-11/06 R *Romana Tabacchi v Commission* [2006] E.C.R. II-2491, para. 146 (obligation to provide bank guarantee suspended subject to conditions); CFI (order of the President of 19 July 2007), Case T-31/07 R *Du Pont de Nemours (France) and Others v Commission* [2007] E.C.R. II-2767 (order concerning only certain provisions of contested act); EGC (order of the President of 28 April 2009), Case T-95/09 R *United Phosphorus v Commission*, not reported, para. 89; EGC (order of the President of 13 April 2011), Case T-393/10 R *Westfälische Drahtindustrie and Others v Commission* [2011] E.C.R. II-1697, para. 69 (obligation to provide bank guarantee suspended subject to conditions).

[16] ECJ Rules of Procedure, Art. 162(2); EGC Rules of Procedure, Art. 107(2); for applications, see, e.g. ECJ (order of the President of 7 May 1982), Case 86/82 R *Hasselblad v Commission* [1982] E.C.R. 1555; CFI (order of the President of 26 October 1994), Joined Cases T-231/94 R, T-232/94 R, and T-234/94 R *Transacciones Marítimas and Others v Commission* [1994] E.C.R. II-885, para. 46. Compare, e.g. ECJ (order of the President of 12 July 1990), Case C-195/90 R *Commission v Germany* [1990] E.C.R. I-3351, paras 48–50 (rejecting request of Member State concerned for making the grant of the interim measure subject to the lodging of security by the Commission).

[17] CFI (order of the President of 12 December 1995), Case T-203/95 R *Connolly v Commission* [1995] E.C.R. II-2919, para. 25; EGC (order of the President of 28 April 2009), Case T-95/09 R *United Phosphorus v Commission*, not reported, paras 91–92 (ordering the Commission to take, should the applicant so request, the measures necessary to ensure that the present order is fully effective in regard to the Member States). See further CST (order of the President of 14 July 2010), Case F-41/10 R *Bermejo Garde v European Economic and Social Committee*, not reported, paras 44–46.

[18] See also ECJ Rules of Procedure, Art. 160(1)–(2); EGC Rules of Procedure, Art. 104(1). See further J.L. da Cruz Vilaça, 'La procédure en référé comme instrument de protection juridictionnelle des particuliers en droit communautaire', in *Scritti in onore di Giuseppe Federico Mancini* (Milan, Giuffrè, 1998), Vol. II, 257, at 265–9.

Accordingly, the Rules of Procedure of the two Courts provide that an application to suspend the operation of a measure shall be admissible only if the applicant is challenging it in main proceedings[19] and that an application for any other interim measures must be made by a party to a pending case and must relate to that case.[20]

---

[19] ECJ Rules of Procedure, Art. 160(1); EGC Rules of Procedure, Art.104(1), first para. See, e.g. CFI (order of the President of 13 September 2007), Case T-292/07 R *Berliner Institut für Vergleichende Sozialforschung v Commission*, not reported (application held inadmissible because the applicant has not challenged the contested measures before the General Court); CFI (order of the President of 8 June 2009), Case T-149/09 R *Dover v European Parliament* [2009] E.C.R. II-66*, Summ. pub., para. 17 (application inadmissible insofar as it seeks to suspend measures that are not the subject of the action in the main proceedings); EGC (order of the President of 2 December 2011), Case T-176/11 R *Carbunion v Commission* [2011] E.C.R. II-434*, Summ. pub., para. 23 (where main action seeks annulment of only specific provisions of contested measure, application to suspend contested measure in its entirety held inadmissible for lack of concordance with main action). As underlined in this case, the case-law concerning the allowance for partial annulment holds in the context of proceedings for interim measures, with the result that where the requirement of severability is not satisfied, the applicant may not seek suspension of only certain provisions of the contested measure: EGC, Case T-176/11 R *Carbunion v Commission*, paras 26–34. See CFI (order of the the President of 19 February 2008), Case T-444/07 R *CPEM v Commission* [2008] E.C.R. II-27*, Summ. pub., para. 23 (Judge hearing the application for interim measures may also 'interpret' the application so that it is concordant with the main action). See also EGC (order of 8 September 2010), Case T-15/10 RII *Ngele v Commission* [2010] E.C.R. II-176*, Summ. pub., para. 9 (appeal dismissed in ECJ (order of the President of 16 December 2010), Case C-526/10 P(R) *Ngele v Commission* [2010] E.C.R. I-173*, Summ. pub.) (order for suspension of contested act inadmissible on account of the fact that the main proceedings concern action for damages, not action for annulment); EGC (order of the President of 11 May 2011), Case T-195/11 R *Cahier v Council and Commission* [2011] E.C.R. II-132*, Summ. pub., para. 13 (order for suspension of contested act inadmissible on account of the fact that the main proceedings concern action for damages, not action for annulment). These requirements are not always interpreted in a strictly formalistic manner. For instance, the applicant may seek suspension of the operation of an act which is not the immediate subject-matter of the main proceedings, but the consequence of the act challenged in those proceedings: ECJ (order of the President of 8 April 1965), Case 18/65 R *Gutmann v Commission* [1966] E.C.R. 135, at 136–7 ('it would be excessively formalistic in an application for the adoption of an interim measure to compel the parties to enter multiple pleadings when the facts of the case show that the subject-matter of the main application and of the application for the adoption of the interim measure are so linked as cause and effect that the second appears as the inevitable consequence of the first'). But as noted in the latter order, the subject-matter of the main action and that of the application for interim relief must nonetheless be linked: see, e.g. ECJ (order of the President of 16 July 1963), Joined Cases 35/62 and 16/63 R *Leroy v High Authority* [1963] E.C.R. 213, at 215; CFI (order of the President of 18 February 2008), Case T-410/07 R *Jurado Hermanos v OHIM* [2008] E.C.R. II-25*, Summ. pub., paras 37–39. CFI (order of the President of 22 November 1995), Case T-395/94 R II *Atlantic Container and Others v Commission* [1995] E.C.R. II-2893, para. 39. See also CFI (order of the President of 2 July 2004), Case T-422/03 R II *Enviro Tech Europe and Others v Commission* [2004] E.C.R. II-2003, paras 48 and 56 (the President raised this requirement of admissibility of his own motion).

[20] ECJ Rules of Procedure, Art. 160(2); EGC Rules of Procedure, Art. 104(1), second para. For examples of applications for interim measures held not to be related to the relevant case before the Court, see ECJ (order of the President of 19 October 1976), Case 88/76 R *Société pour l'Exportation des Sucres* [1976] E.C.R. 1585, at 1587; ECJ (order of the President of 3 November 1980), Case 186/80 R *Suss v Commission* [1980] E.C.R. 3501, paras 15–16; ECJ (order of the President of 16 December 1980), Case 258/80 R *Rumi v Commission* [1980] E.C.R. 3867, paras 20–22; ECJ (order of the President of 17 May 1991), Case C-313/90 R *CIRFS and Others v Commission* [1991] E.C.R. I-2557, para. 23; CFI (order of the President of 14 December 1993), Case T-543/93 R *Gestevisión Telecinco v Commission* [1993] E.C.R. II-1411, para. 25; CFI (order of the President of 2 December 1994), Case T-322/94 R *Union Carbide v Commission* [1994] E.C.R. II-1159, para. 28; CFI (order of the President of 27 February 1996), Case T-235/95 R *Goldstein v Commission*, not reported, para. 38; CFI (order of the President of 29 March 2001), Case T-18/01 R *Goldstein v Commission*, not reported, para. 32; EGC (order of 17 December 2009), Case T-396/09 R *Vereniging Milieudefensie and Stichting Stop Luchtverontreiniging Utrecht v Commission* [2009] E.C.R. II-246*, Summ. pub., paras 39–42; EGC (order of 8 September 2010), Case T-15/10 RII *Ngele v Commission* [2010] E.C.R. II-176*, Summ. pub., paras 10–12 (appeal dismissed in ECJ (order of the President of 16 December 2010), Case C-526/10 P(R) *Ngele v Commission* [2010] E.C.R. I-173*, Summ. pub.); EGC (order of the President of 14 July 2011), Case T-187/11 R *Trabelsi and Others v Council* [2011] E.C.R. II-235*, Summ. pub., paras 46–49.

Where an applicant seeks, pursuant to Art. 279 TFEU, an interim measure that essentially seeks the same result as an application for suspension of operation under Art. 278 TFEU, the application will be declared admissible only if the applicant is challenging the same act in the main proceedings.[21] Moreover, in the light of the ancillary nature of interim measures, where the main action falls, so does the application for interim relief.

In principle, an application for interim measures may be made after any direct action has been brought. However, the interim relief sought may not make the claim in the main proceedings nugatory.[22]

(2) Judge may not assume the role of the defendant institution

If the application aims at the adoption of a measure that would be contrary to Union law, **13.08** the application will be dismissed.[23] Consequently, an application for a measure amounting to the Judge's assuming the role of the defendant institution, not merely reviewing its activity, may not be granted unless the application contains evidence from which the Judge hearing the interim application can find that there are exceptional circumstances justifying the adoption of the measure requested.[24]

(3) Interim relief possible in relation to all direct actions before the Union courts

In principle, interim relief is possible in relation to all types of direct actions that may be **13.09** brought before the Union courts (as regards the preliminary ruling procedure, see para. 13.13).[25] So far, in the case-law to date, one of the most common contexts in which interim relief is sought is in connection with the action for annulment under Art. 263 TFEU. Nonetheless, there are particular aspects related to the provision of interim relief in relation to certain other types of direct actions.

(4) Interim relief in the context of an action for failure to act

As just alluded to, in principle, the grant of interim relief in the context of an action for **13.10** failure to act under Art. 265 TFEU is possible,[26] but in practice, it is more exceptional. This is because there would seem to be little chance of successfully applying for suspension of operation in connection with an action for failure to act under Art. 265 TFEU, since the very object of that action is to procure the adoption of a measure. An application for other

---

[21] ECJ (order of the President of 13 December 2004), Case C-380/04 *Bactria v Commission*, not reported, paras 13–18.

[22] See citations in n. 10.

[23] CFI (order of the President of 21 October 1996), Case T-107/96 R *Pantochim v Commission* [1996] E.C.R. II-1361, paras 37–42. See also CFI (order of the President of 3 May 2007), Case T-12/07 R *Polimeri Europa v Commission* [2007] E.C.R. II-38*, Summ. pub., paras 50–55.

[24] CFI (order of the President of 12 July 1996), Case T-52/96 R *Sogecable v Commission* [1996] E.C.R. II-797, paras 38–41 (and case-law cited therein); CFI (order of the President of 1 February 2001), Case T-350/00 R *Free Trade Foods v Commission* [2001] E.C.R. II-493, para. 48; CFI (order of the President of 5 December 2001), Case T-216/01 R *Reisebank v Commission* [2001] E.C.R. II-3481, para. 52; CFI (order of the President of 5 December 2001), Case T-219/01 R *Commerzbank v Commission* [2001] E.C.R. II-3501, para. 42.

[25] This includes all of the actions to be discussed, as well as others, such as an action based on an arbitration clause within the meaning of Art. 272 TFEU: see, e.g. EGC (order of the President of 15 March 2010), Case T-435/09 R *GL2006 Europe v Commission* [2010] E.C.R. II-32*, Summ. pub. (dismissed for lack of urgency).

[26] See, e.g. ECJ, Case C-319/97 *Kortas* [1999] E.C.R. I-3143, para. 37.

interim measures would normally make the action in the main proceedings devoid of purpose and would therefore be inadmissible.[27]

(5) Interim relief in the context of an action for damages against the Union

13.11　The question whether, in connection with an action for damages against the Union under Art. 268 TFEU and the second paragraph of Art. 340 TFEU, suspension of the operation of the act that allegedly caused the damage may be sought still remains to some extent open.[28] Nevertheless, as highlighted in recent case-law, such an application generally falls foul of the admissibility requirements related to, *inter alia*,[29] the concordance between the interim relief sought and the main action, since as far as Art. 278 TFEU is concerned, by virtue of the fact that the main action is an action for damages and not an action for annulment, it does not satisfy the requirement that in order to be admissible, the applicant has challenged that measure in proceedings before the General Court pursuant to EGC Rules of Procedure Art. 104(1), and as far as Art. 279 TFEU is concerned, there must be a sufficient link between the contested measure and damage invoked by the applicant in its main action (see further para. 13.07).[30]

In any event, it is now clear that it is not possible 'to rule out in advance, in a general and abstract manner, that payment, by way of advance, even of an amount corresponding to

---

[27] Certainly, an application may be dismissed on other grounds, for instance, where the action for failure to act in the main proceedings is inadmissible: see, e.g. CFI (order of the President of 27 April 2005), Case T-34/05 R *Makhteshim-Agan Holding and Others v Commission* [2005] E.C.R. II-1465 (appeal dismissed in ECJ (order of the President of 28 October 2005), Case C-258/05 P(R) *Makhteshim-Agan Holding and Others v Commission*, not reported); CFI (order of the President of 30 March 2007), Joined Cases T-393/06 R, T-393/06 RII, and T-393/06 RIII *Makhteshim-Agan Holding and Others v Commission* [2007] E.C.R. II-32*, Summ. pub., paras 51–59 (appeal dismissed in ECJ (order of the President of 17 July 2008), Case C-277/07 P(R) *Makhteshim-Agan Holding and Others v Commission* [2008] E.C.R. I-112*, Summ. pub.). See also EGC (order of the President of 30 June 2010), Case T-61/10 R *Victoria Sánchez v European Parliament and Commission* [2010] E.C.R. II-120*, Summ. pub. (rejection of application for interim relief in the context of action for failure to act on account of failure to satisfy the requirements of EGC Rules of Procedure, Art. 104(2)–(3) in relation to the *fumus boni juris* requirement).

[28] ECJ (order of the President of 23 May 1990), Joined Cases C-51/90 R and C-59/90 R *Comos-Tank and Others v Commission* [1990] E.C.R. I-2167, para. 33. See also CFI (order of the President of 15 October 2004), Case T-193/04 R *Tillack v Commission* [2004] E.C.R. II-3575, paras 52–63 (no *prima facie* case) (appeal dismissed in ECJ (order of the President of 19 April 2005), Case C-521/04 P(R) *Tillack v Commission* [2005] E.C.R. I-3103). In cases where the main action concerns an action for damages as well as another type of action, such as an action for annulment, an application for interim measures may be attached only to that latter action: see, e.g. CFI (order of the President of 24 March 2006), Case T-454/05 R *Sumitomo Chemical Agro Europe and Philagro France v Commission* [2006] E.C.R. II-131*, Summ. pub., para. 44; CFI (order of the President of 1 March 2007), Joined Cases T-311/06 R I, T-311/06 R II, T-312/06 R, and T-313/06 R *FMC Chemical and Others v European Food Safety Authority (EFSA) and Commission* [2007] E.C.R. II-21*, Summ. pub., para. 49; CFI (order of the President of 1 March 2007), Case T-397/06 R *Dow Agrosciences v EFSA* [2007] E.C.R. II-22*, Summ. pub., para. 32. As a result, issues related to the grant of interim relief in connection with the action for damages as the subject of the main proceedings do not arise.

[29] Certainly, an application submitted in this context may be deemed inadmissible for other reasons, for example by virtue of the fact that it is directed against entities other than the Union institutions: see, e.g. CFI (order of the President of 7 January 2008), Case T-375/07 R *Pellegrini v Commission* [2008] E.C.R. II-1*, Summ. pub., para. 19 (appeal dismissed in ECJ (order of the President of 17 July 2008), Case C-114/08 P(R) *Pellegrini v Commission* [2008] E.C.R. I-117*, Summ. pub.); EGC (order of the President of 26 May 2010), Case T-15/10 R *Ngele v Commission* [2010] E.C.R. II-102*, Summ. pub., paras 10–12.

[30] See, e.g. EGC (order of 8 September 2010), Case T-15/10 R II *Ngele v Commission* [2010] E.C.R. II-176*, Summ. pub., paras 9–13 (appeal dismissed in ECJ (order of the President of 16 December 2010), Case C-526/10 P(R) *Ngele v Commission* [2010] E.C.R. I-173*, Summ. pub.); EGC (order of the President of 11 May 2011), Case T-195/11 R *Cahier v Council and Commission* [2011] E.C.R. II-132*, Summ. pub., para. 13.

that sought in the main application, may be necessary in order to ensure the practical effect of the judgment in the main action and may, in certain cases, appear justified with regard to the interests involved'.[31]

(6) Interim relief in the context of an action for infringement

The Court of Justice may order the adoption of interim measures under Art. 279 TFEU in **13.12** the context of an action for infringement under Arts 258–260 TFEU.[32] The interim relief most often sought is—full or partial, conditional or unconditional—suspension of the operation of a contested national measure.[33] The fact that the judgment finding the failure to fulfil obligations is declaratory in nature does not preclude the imposition of interim measures.[34] The Court's interlocutory order does not derive its binding force from the Court's power to give judgment in the main proceedings. If a contested national measure threatens to cause irreparable damage to one of the parties, the Judge hearing the application for interim relief must be able to order the necessary measures to secure the full

---

[31] ECJ (order of the President of 29 January 1997), Case C-393/96P(R) *Antonissen v Council and Commission* [1997] E.C.R. I-441, para. 37, thereby setting aside the opposite view; see CFI (order of the President of 29 November 1996), Case T-179/96 R *Antonissen v Council and Commission* [1996] E.C.R. II-1641, para. 30; on referral of the case back to the then Court of First Instance, the President dismissed the application on the grounds that the requirement of a *prima facie* case was not satisfied: CFI (order of the President of 21 March 1997), Case T-179/96 R *Antonissen v Council and Commission* [1997] E.C.R. II-425, paras 52–54. But see EGC (order of the President of 14 July 2011), Case T-187/11 R *Trabelsi and Others v Council* [2011] E.C.R. II-235*, Summ. pub., para. 50 (underlining that grant of interim measures in context of an action for damages remains exceptional).

[32] See, e.g. ECJ (order of 21 May 1977), Cases 31/77 R and 53/77 R *Commission v United Kingdom* [1977] E.C.R. 921; ECJ (order of 22 May 1977), Case 61/77 R *Commission v Ireland* [1977] E.C.R. 937 and ECJ (order of 13 July 1977), Case 61/77 R II *Commission v Ireland* [1977] E.C.R. 1411; ECJ (order of the President of 2 October 2003), Case C-320/03 R *Commission v Austria* [2003] E.C.R. I-11665 and ECJ (order of the President of 27 April 2004), Case C-320/03 R *Commission v Austria* [2004] E.C.R. I-3593; ECJ, Case C-459/03 *Commission v Ireland* ('Mox Plant') [2006] E.C.R. I-4635, para. 138; ECJ (order of the President of 24 April 2008), Case C-76/08 R *Commission v Malta* [2008] E.C.R. I-64*, Summ. pub. In this context, depending on the particular circumstances of the case, the interim relief may sometimes be granted on a temporary basis, even before the observations of the opposing party (*in casu*, the Member State concerned) have been submitted pursuant to Art. 160(7) of the ECJ Rules of Procedure. See, e.g. ECJ (order of 30 July 2003), Case C-320/03 R *Commission v Austria* [2003] E.C.R. I-7929; ECJ (order of the President of 19 December 2006), Case C-503/06 R *Commission v Italy* [2006] E.C.R. I-141*, Summ. pub.; ECJ (order of the President of 18 April 2007), Case C-193/07 R *Commission v Poland*, not reported. Other more informal arrangements may also be made in this regard: see, e.g. ECJ (order of the President of 24 April 2008), Case C-76/08 R *Commission v Malta* [2008] E.C.R. I-64*, Summ. pub., para. 7 (Member State concerned confirmed to the Court that no national decision would be made before the Court had given its decision in the proceedings for interim measures); note that the Commission's application pursuant to ECJ Rules of Procedure Art. 160(7) seems to have been rejected on account of the fact that Malta was invited to submit its observations on the application (ECJ, Case C-76/08 R *Commission v Malta*, paras 2, 4). Depending on the assurances given by the Member State concerned, such arrangements may even cause the Commission to withdraw its application: see ECJ (order of the President of 18 July 2007), Case C-193/07 R *Commission v Poland*, not reported; and ECJ (order of the President of 25 January 2008), Case C-193/07 R-2 *Commission v Poland*, not reported.

[33] See, e.g. ECJ (order of the President of 25 October 1985), Case 293/85 R *Commission v Belgium* [1985] E.C.R. 3521; ECJ (order of the President of 2 October 2003), Case C-320/03 R *Commission v Austria* [2003] E.C.R. I-11665 and ECJ (order of the President of 27 April 2004), Case C-320/03 R *Commission v Austria* [2004] E.C.R. I-3593; ECJ (order of the President of 10 December 2009), Case C-573/08 R *Commission v Italy* [2009] E.C.R. I-217*, Summ. pub.

[34] Although in principle interim relief is possible in respect of the grant of an order that the Member State concerned should do what the Commission is requesting, most often by suspending the allegedly infringing national measure, it is nonetheless awkward because the Commission is asking for a direct order at the interlocutory stage to do what the main action cannot do because it is merely declaratory.

effectiveness of the action in the main proceedings. This view is firmly established in the case-law.[35]

(7) Interim relief in the context of preliminary ruling proceedings

13.13 The Court of Justice takes the view that it is not empowered to order interim measures in preliminary ruling proceedings under Art. 267 TFEU.[36] However, in the seminal judgments in *Factortame I*,[37] *Zuckerfabrik*,[38] and *Atlanta Fruchthandelsgesellschaft*,[39] and subsequent case-law, it provided indications as to the interim relief which the national courts are under a duty to provide following the bringing of proceedings relating to the application of Union law (see paras 4.60–4.64).

(8) Interim relief in the context of appeals

13.14 A party who has brought an appeal may apply for interim measures in the form of suspension of the operation of the judgment of the General Court or other interim relief. The application must be made to the Court of Justice under Art. 60 of the Statute.[40]

When the General Court has dismissed an application to annul an act of a Union institution, body, office, or agency, an order of the President of the Court of Justice to suspend the judgment of the General Court would be to no avail to the applicant.[41] In order to grant effective judicial protection to such an applicant, the President of the Court of Justice may, in the context of an appeal, suspend the application of the act that had been challenged before the General Court.[42]

---

[35] See in this regard ECJ (order of the President of 24 April 2008), Case C-76/08 R *Commission v Malta* [2008] E.C.R. I-64*, Summ. pub., paras 16–20: in upholding the admissibility of the application for interim measures, the Court rejected the argument that the present application for interim measures sought to anticipate the decision of the Court on the merits, pointing out that while it was in line with established case-law that the interim measures applied for must be provisional, in the instant proceedings, such measures do no more than guard against a deterioration in the conservation status of certain wild birds during two spring hunting seasons. Moreover, as the Commission was seeking an order that the Member State concerned refrain from adopting any measures (as opposed to the suspension of a national measure), the Court underlined that under Art. 279 TFEU, the Judge hearing an application for interim measures may issue on a provisional basis appropriate directions to the other party.

[36] For a criticism, see C. Vajda, 'Access to Judicial Review in the EU and National Courts', in E. Buttigieg (ed.), *Enforcing One's Rights Under EU Law* (Hal Tarxien, Gutenberg Press, 2011), 154.

[37] ECJ, Case C-213/89 *Factortame and Others ('Factortame I')* [1990] E.C.R. I-2433.

[38] ECJ, Joined Cases C-143/88 and C-92/89 *Zuckerfabrik Süderdithmarschen and Zuckerfabrik Soest* [1991] E.C.R. I-415.

[39] ECJ, Case C-465/93 *Atlanta Fruchthandelsgesellschaft and Others* [1995] E.C.R. I-3761.

[40] See, e.g. ECJ (order of the President of 8 May 2003), Case C-39/03 P-R *Commission v Artegodan and Others* [2003] E.C.R. I-4485, para. 36; CFI (order of the President of 22 November 1991), Case T-77/91 R *Hochbaum v Commission* [1991] E.C.R. II-1285, paras 19–22. Similar provisions apply in the context of appeals of decisions of the Civil Service Tribunal to the General Court: see Statute, Annex, Art. 12(1). Moreover, it is possible that where on appeal the Court of Justice sets aside the judgment of the General Court and refers the case back to the General Court, a party may submit an application for interim measures before the General Court: see, e.g. EGC (order of the President of 9 June 2011), Case T-62/06 RENV-R *Eurallumina v Commission* [2011] E.C.R. II-167*, Summ. pub. (dismissing application for lack of urgency).

[41] Nevertheless, in the case-law, there are examples in which the President of the Court still 'goes through the motions' and assesses whether the requisite conditions are fulfilled: see, e.g. ECJ (order of the President of 12 May 2010), C-5/10 P-R *Torresan v OHIM* [2010] E.C.R. I-64*, Summ. pub. See also ECJ (order of the President of 19 July 2012), Joined Cases C-587/11 P-R and C-588/11 P-R *Omnicare v OHIM*, not reported, para. 29.

[42] ECJ (order of the President of 29 April 2005), Case C-404/04 P-R *Technische Glaswerke v Commission* [2005] E.C.R. I-3539, paras 13–14. The fact that the Court of Justice may find (on appeal) that interim relief

D. The provisional nature of interim measures

(1) Interim measures apply for a limited period of time

Interim measures are only provisional. There are two aspects to this:[43] first, the interim **13.15** measures are valid only for a limited period; and second, they may not prejudice the judgment in the main proceedings.

As regards the first aspect, the period of time for which the interim measures are to apply may be expressly specified in the order.[44] Otherwise, the order will expire when judgment is given in the main proceedings.[45] At the request of one of the parties[46] or by order given by the Court of its own motion,[47] interim measures may at any time be varied, extended,[48] or cancelled on account of a change in circumstances.[49]

---

is warranted in the form of the suspension of the contested measure in the context of proceedings before the General Court may not necessarily lead to the same result in the context of an application to suspend such measure in the context of an appeal of the General Court's judgment before the Court of Justice. See ECJ (order of the President of 15 December 2005), Case C-326/05 P-R *Industries Quimicas del Valles v Commission*, not published.

[43] Statute, Art. 39, third para.; see also ECJ Rules of Procedure, Art. 162(4); EGC Rules of Procedure, Art. 107(4). These two aspects of the provisional nature of interim relief have been recognized in the case-law: see, e.g. EGC (order of the President of 23 January 2012), Case T-607/11 R *Henkel and Henkel France v Commission*, not reported, para. 23.

[44] See, e.g. ECJ (order of the President of 8 April 1965), Case 18/65 R *Gutmann v Commission* [1966] 135, at 138; ECJ (order of the President of 5 July 1983), Case 78/83 R *Usinor v Commission* [1983] E.C.R. 2183, para. 9; ECJ (order of the President of 16 July 1984), Case 160/84 R *Oryzomyli Kavallas v Commission* [1984] E.C.R. 3217, para. 9; ECJ (order of the President of 17 March 1986), Case 23/86 R *United Kingdom v European Parliament* [1986] E.C.R. 1085, operative part; CFI (order of the President of 2 April 1993), Case T-12/93 R *CCE de Vittel and Others v Commission* [1993] E.C.R. II-449, para. 33; CFI (order of the President of 12 January 1994), Case T-554/93 R *Abbott Trust v Council and Commission* [1994] E.C.R. II-1, para. 19; CFI (order of the President of 28 April 2009), Case T-95/09 R *United Phosphorus v Commission*, not reported, para. 88.

[45] ECJ Rules of Procedure, Art. 162(3); EGC Rules of Procedure Art. 107(3). Consequently, the applicant's request cannot extend beyond the date when judgment is given in the main action: see CFI (order of the President of 18 March 2008), Case T-411/07 R *Aer Lingus Group v Commission* [2008] E.C.R. II-411, para. 45 (rejecting applicant's request for interim measures until the judgment in the main application or in another related case, 'whichever is later', insofar as it involves the application of interim measures beyond the date of judgment in the main application, since in principle the duration of such measures cannot extend beyond that of the main proceedings to which they relate).

[46] ECJ Rules of Procedure, Art. 163; EGC Rules of Procedure, Art. 108.

[47] ECJ Rules of Procedure, Art. 160(7); EGC Rules of Procedure, Art. 105(2). These provisions, however, deal only with applications for interim relief granted before observations of other party are submitted (so-called *ex parte* orders).

[48] See, e.g. ECJ (order of the President of 8 July 1974), Case 20/74 R II *Kali-Chemie v Commission* [1974] E.C.R. 787; ECJ (order of the President of 2 October 2003), Case C-320/03 R *Commission v Austria* [2003] E.C.R. I-11665; ECJ (order of the President of 27 April 2004), Case C-320/03 R *Commission v Austria* [2004] E.C.R. I-3593; CFI (order of the President of 29 September 1999), Case T-44/98 R II *Emesa Sugar v Commission* [1999] E.C.R. II-2815; EGC (order of the President of 15 January 2010), Case T-95/09 R II *United Phosphorus v Commission*, not reported; EGC (order of the President of 25 November 2010), Case T-95/09 R III *United Phosphorus v Commission*, not reported. As highlighted by the latter case, in the process of examining whether the interim relief granted may be extended, the President of the Court may find it necessary to revise his or her findings providing the basis for such extension: see EGC, Case T-95/09 R II *United Phosphorus v Commission*, para. 19.

[49] See para. 13.44.

(2) Interim measures may not prejudge the decision to be given in the main proceedings

13.16   As regards the second aspect, the order giving interim relief may not prejudge the decision to be given in the main proceedings.[50] It may not decide disputed points of law or fact or neutralize in advance the consequences of the decision to be taken subsequently on the substance.[51] The Judge hearing applications for interim relief may not order measures which are irrevocable and would confront the Judges responsible for the substantive decision with an irreversible situation[52] or which would make the main application devoid of purpose.[53] Indeed, proceedings for interim relief do not lend themselves to an in-depth investigation of the facts and the parties' pleas. In addition, an excessively far-reaching pronouncement would completely reverse the relationship between interim measures and the main proceedings, which is not the intention behind interim relief.[54] Exceptionally, however, the proceedings for interim measures may create an irreversible situation, which the Judges hearing the main case have to accept.[55]

---

[50] See, e.g. ECJ (order of the President of 25 June 1963), Case 65/63 R *Prakash v Commission* [1965] E.C.R. 576, at 579; ECJ (order of the President of 7 July 1981), Joined Cases 60/81 and 190/81 R *IBM v Commission* [1981] E.C.R. 1857, para. 4; ECJ (order of the President of 17 March 1986), Case 23/86 R *United Kingdom v European Parliament* [1986] E.C.R. 1085, paras 32 *et seq.*; ECJ (order of the President of 30 April 1986), Case 62/86 R *AKZO Chemie v Commission* [1986] E.C.R. 1503, para.18; ECJ (order of the President of 26 March 1987), Case 46/87 R *Hoechst v Commission* [1987] E.C.R. 1549, paras 29–31; CFI (order of the President of 3 June 1996), Case T-41/96 R *Bayer v Commission* [1996] E.C.R. II-381, para. 13; CFI (order of the President of 4 May 2007), Case T-71/07 R *Icuna.Com v European Parliament* [2007] E.C.R. II-39*, Summ. pub., para. 48; EGC (order of the President of 23 January 2012), Case T-607/11 R *Henkel France and Henkel v Commission*, not reported, paras 23–25; EGC (order of the President of 25 April 2013), Case T-44/13 R *AbbVie v EMA*, not reported, para. 41. As far as staff cases are concerned, see CST (order of the President of 28 February 2012), Case F-129/11 R *BH v Commission*, not reported, paras 29–30; CST (order of the President of 28 February 2012), Case F-139/11 R *BJ v Commission*, not reported, paras 28–29; CST (order of the President of 28 February 2012), Case F-140/11 R *BK v Commission*, not reported, paras 30–31.

[51] See, e.g. ECJ (order of the President of 26 February 1981), Case 20/81 R *Arbed v Commission* [1981] E.C.R. 721, para. 13; ECJ (order of the President of 20 July 1981), Case 206/81 R *Alvarez v European Parliament* [1981] E.C.R. 2187, para. 6; ECJ (order of the President of 19 July 1995), Case C-149/95 P(R) *Commission v Atlantic Container Line and Others* [1995] E.C.R. I-2165, para. 22; ECJ (order of the President of 29 January 1997), Case C-393/96 P(R) *Antonissen v Council and Commission* [1997] E.C.R. I-441, para. 27; ECJ (order of the President of 24 April 2008), Case C-76/08 R *Commission v Malta* [2008] E.C.R. I-64*, Summ. pub., para. 17; ECJ (order of the President of 14 June 2012), Case C-644/11 P(R) *Qualitest FZE v Council*, not reported, para. 77; CFI (order of the President of 22 December 2004), Case T-303/04 R II *European Dynamics v Commission* [2004] E.C.R. II-4621, para. 30.

[52] See, e.g. ECJ (order of the President of 28 May 1975), Case 44/75 R *Könecke v Commission* [1975] E.C.R. 637, para. 4; CST (order of the President of 17 December 2008), Case F-80/08 *Wenig v Commission* [2008] E.C.R.-SC I-A-1-479, paras 27–36 (citing CFI, Case T-41/97 R *Antillean Rice Mills*, para. 46).

[53] See, e.g. ECJ (order of the President of 15 October 1976), Case 91/76 R *De Lacroix v Court of Justice* [1976] E.C.R. 1561, para. 2; CST (order of the President of 10 September 2007), Case F-83/07 R *Zangerl-Posselt v Commission* [2007] E.C.R.-SC I-A-1-235, para. 20 (and citations therein); CST (order of the President of 16 November 2011), Case F-61/11 R *Possanzini v Frontex*, not reported, paras 54–56 (and citations therein); CST (order of the President of 16 November 2011), Case F-67/11 R *Marcuccio v Commission*, not reported, paras 27–28.

[54] Opinion of Advocate-General F. Capotorti in ECJ (order of 28 March 1988), Joined Cases 24/80 and 97/80 R *Commission v France* [1980] E.C.R. 1319, at 1338–9.

[55] See, e.g. ECJ (order of 17 January 1980), Case 792/79 R *Camera Care v Commission* [1980] E.C.R. 119, in which the Court of Justice recognized the Commission's power to adopt interim measures.

II. Identity of the Parties

A. The applicant

(1) General

The ancillary nature of interim measures also determines the identity of the parties who **13.17** may apply to the Court for such relief. An application for suspension of the operation of an act may be made only by the party that is challenging that act in proceedings before the Court.[56] Other interim measures may be sought by any party to the main proceedings.[57]

(2) Interveners

Textbook writers are divided over the question of whether a party intervening in the main **13.18** proceedings is entitled to apply for interim measures regardless of the stance taken by the party in support of whose submissions it has intervened.[58] It is arguably preferable not to grant interveners a right of their own to apply for interim measures, since if they were given such a right they might obtain the initiative in the litigation, something which Art. 40 of the Statute sought specifically to avoid by allowing them only to intervene in support of the submissions of one of the parties.

However, interveners may join in proceedings for interim measures provided that they show a sufficient interest.[59] If they satisfy that requirement, it appears even to be unnecessary for them to have already intervened in the main proceedings.[60] In such a case, the view

---

[56] ECJ Rules of Procedure, Art. 160(1); EGC Rules of Procedure, Art. 104(1), first para. See CFI (order of the President of 21 September 2004), Case T-310/03 R *Kreuzer Medien v European Parliament and Council* [2004] E.C.R. II-3243, paras 15–22 (application by intervener held to be inadmissible).

[57] ECJ Rules of Procedure, Art. 160(2); EGC Rules of Procedure, Art. 104(1), second para.

[58] See in this connection CFI (order of the President of 21 September 2004), Case T-310/03 R *Kreuzer Medien v European Parliament and Council* [2004] E.C.R. II-3243, paras 15–22: the Court did not have to rule on this question, since the application based on Art. 279 TFEU had to be regarded as an application for the suspension of the operation of a Union act based on Art. 278 TFEU. Since the intervener had not brought an action for the annulment of the act in question, the application for interim measures was inadmissible. On intervention generally, see para. 25.58.

[59] For some examples in which applications for intervention in interim proceedings have been granted, see EGC (order of the President of 17 February 2011), Case T-490/10 R *Endesa and Endesa Generación v Commission*, not reported, paras 32–42; EGC (order of 17 February 2010), Case T-520/10 R *Comunidad Autónoma de Galicia v Commission* [2011] E.C.R. II-27*, Summ. pub., paras 27–37. For some examples in which applications for intervention in interim proceedings have been rejected, see CFI (order of the President of 17 March 2006), Case T-42/06 R *Gollnisch v European Parliament*, not reported; EGC (order of the President of 2 March 2011), Case T-392/09 R *1.garantovaná v Commission* [2011] E.C.R. II-33*, Summ. pub., paras 11–19 (finding that a small shareholding in the applicant's capital cannot on its own and in the absence of other factors confer on the prospective interveners a sufficient interest). For some examples in which some applications have been granted and others rejected, see CFI (order of the President of 7 July 2004), Case T-37/04 R *Autonomous Region of the Azores v Council* [2004] E.C.R. II-2153, paras 57–71; CFI (order of the President of 26 July 2004), T-201/04 R *Microsoft v Commission* [2004] E.C.R. II-2977; EGC (order of the President of 17 February 2011), Case T-484/10 R *Gas Natural Fenosa SDG v Commission*, not reported, paras 35–49.

[60] See, by implication, CFI (order of the President of 13 May 1993), Case T-24/93 R *CMBT v Commission* [1993] E.C.R. II-543, paras 14–16. See also EGC (order of the President of 17 February 2010), Case T-520/10 R *Comunidad Autónoma de Galicia v Commission* [2011] E.C.R. II-27*, Summ. pub., para. 26 (noting that the party already granted admission to intervene in the main action automatically becomes the intervening party for the purposes of proceedings for interim measures). But as mentioned earlier, the opposite does not hold, in that a party granted admission to intervene in the proceedings for interim measures (see, e.g. CFI (order of the

of the Judge hearing the application for interim relief as to whether leave should be granted to intervene in those proceedings would not be binding on the Judges hearing the main application.[61]

(3) Interest

13.19 In order to obtain interim measures, an applicant must establish an interest in obtaining the measures sought.[62] As such, an application for interim measures is dismissed where the relief sought could not have the effect of changing the applicant's position and thus could not be of any practical use to the applicant.[63]

As compared to the interest that must be shown by natural and legal persons for the admissibility of an action for annulment (see para. 7.138),[64] the interest requirement for

---

President of 18 March 2008), Case T-411/07 R *Aer Lingus Group v Commission* [2008] E.C.R. II-411, para. 27; CFI, Case T-411/07 R *Aer Lingus Group v Commission*, paras 27–37) has to apply separately to intervene in the main action (see, e.g. EGC, Case T-411/07 *Aer Lingus Group v Commission* [2010] E.C.R. II-3691, para. 36; EGC (order of the President of 25 October 2011), Case T-520/10 *Comunidad Autónoma de Galicia v Commission*, not reported).

[61] But see EGC (order of the President of 17 February 2011), Case T-490/10 R *Endesa and Endesa Generacion v Commission*, not reported, paras 21–24, 30–31: following its admission to intervene in the proceedings for interim measures, Spain submitted a demand, pursuant to Art. 108 of the EGC Rules of Procedure, to rescind the order of the President of the Court temporarily suspending the contested act on account of measures that had been taken at the national level; in response, by letter, the Registrar informed Spain that the President of the General Court did not envisage, at that stage, the revocation of the order, which was in any event not dependent on a decision of a national judge or measures producing similar effects at the national level. Nonetheless, in light of Spain's request and the fact that the parties intended to withdraw their application for interim measures, the President of the Court examined whether the suspension ordered should be maintained and held that it should be withdrawn.

[62] See, e.g. CFI (order of the President of 7 May 2002), Case T-306/01 R *Aden and Others v Council and Commission* [2002] E.C.R. II-2387, para. 57; CFI (order of the President of 2 July 2004), Case T-76/04 R *Bactria v Commission* [2004] E.C.R. II-2025, para. 52 (appeal dismissed in ECJ (order of the President of 13 December 2004), Case C-380/04 P(R) *Bactria v Commission*, not reported); CFI (order of the President of 12 May 2006), Case T-42/06 R *Gollnisch v European Parliament* [2006] E.C.R. II-40*, Summ. pub., para. 28; CFI (order of the President of 16 March 2007), Case T-345/05 R *V v European Parliament* [2007] E.C.R. II-25*, Summ. pub., para. 55 (and further citations therein).

[63] See, e.g. CFI (order of the President of 2 July 2004), Case T-76/04 R *Bactria v Commission* [2004] E.C.R. II-2025, paras 52–56 (appeal dismissed in ECJ (order of the President of 13 December 2004), Case C-380/04 P(R) *Bactria v Commission*, not reported); CFI (order of the President of 3 May 2007), Case T-12/07 R *Polimeri Europa v Commission* [2007] E.C.R. II-38*, Summ. pub., paras 59–63); EGC (order of the President of 26 March 2010), Case T-16/10 R *Alisei v Commission* [2010] E.C.R. II-50*, Summ. pub., paras 28–32; CFI (order of the President of 18 February 2008), Case T-410/07 R *Jurado Hermanos v OHIM* [2008] E.C.R. II-25*, Summ. pub., paras 29–30. For some recent examples in which interest has been found, see, e.g. CFI (order of the President of 16 March 2007), Case T-345/05 R *V v European Parliament* [2007] E.C.R. II-25*, Summ. pub., paras 56–60; EGC (order of the President of 15 October 2010), Case T-415/10 R *Nexans France v The European joint undertaking for ITER and the Development of fusion energy*, not reported, para. 24 (in the context of a public contract, the applicant still has interest in relation to urgency, even though the defendant body did not proceed to enter into a contract with a competitor as foreseen by the contested act).

[64] However, in some cases, the discussion of the interest requirement in the context of proceedings for interim measures seems to blur with that for the action for annulment. See, e.g. CFI (order of the President of 15 July 2008), Case T-195/08 R *Antwerpse Bouwwerken v Commission* [2008] E.C.R. II-141*, Summ. pub., paras 21–25, citing case-law dealing with interest in context of both interim measures and annulment and framing the discussion as to whether the applicant would procure a benefit by the interim measures sought, which it determined that it would, and thus held the application admissible; EGC (order of the President of 2 December 2011), Case T-176/11 R *Carbunion v Council* [2011] E.C.R. II-434*, Summ. pub., paras 18–21, framing in context of annulment and citing CFI, Case T-310/00 *MCI v Commission* [2004] E.C.R. II-3253, para. 44 concerning action for annulment, though concluding that the interim measure sought (suspension of measure in entirety) was of no practical use to the applicant; EGC (order of the President of 23 January 2012),

the purposes of the admissibility of proceedings for interim relief appears to apply to all types of applicants, including Member States.[65]

B. The defendant

(1) Opponent in the main proceedings

The defendant in proceedings for interim measures is the opponent in the main proceedings of the party that lodged the application for interim relief. By virtue of the ancillary nature of proceedings for interim measures, the jurisdiction of the Judge hearing an application for interim measures may not in principle be exercised unless the acts at issue in the main action and interim proceedings emanate from the same institution and that institution is a party to the proceedings.[66] Consequently, if the relief sought by the applicant relates to an act of a Union institution, body, office, or agency which is not a named defendant in the interim proceedings, the application for such relief is generally inadmissible.[67]

13.20

(2) Third parties

That being said, the case-law does allow for the application of interim measures to third parties. There has been one exceptional case so far with respect to the Union institutions in which the Commission was obliged to comply with an interim measure addressed to it in the context of proceedings concerning the Union budget that were brought by the United Kingdom against the European Parliament.[68] Moreover, interim measures addressed to an intervener have been held admissible.[69] Relying on the broad wording of what is now Art. 279 TFEU ('any necessary interim measures'), the President of the General Court considered that in order to ensure the full effectiveness of this provision, it cannot be excluded that the Judge hearing the application for interim measures may in exceptional circumstances impose orders directly on third parties if necessary, though such broad discretion

13.21

Case T-607/11 R *Henkel and Henkel France v Commission*, not reported, para. 19, again citing case-law dealing with interest in the context of both interim measures and annulment and framing the discussion as to whether the applicant would procure a benefit by the interim measures sought.

[65] See, e.g. CFI (order of the President of 18 June 2007), Case T-431/04 R *Italy v Commission* [2007] E.C.R. II-64*, Summ. pub., paras 25–35.

[66] See, e.g. ECJ (order of the President of 25 June 1987), Case 133/87 R *Nashua v Commission* [1987] E.C.R. 2883, paras 7–8; ECJ (order of the President of 17 July 2008), Case C-277/07 P(R) *Makteshim-Agan Holding and Others v Commission* [2008] E.C.R. II-112*, Summ. pub., paras 28–31.

[67] ECJ, Case 133/87 R *Nashua v Commission*, concerned a situation in which the decision under challenge in the main proceedings was adopted by the Commission, whereas the regulation establishing definitive anti-dumping duties, the operation of which the applicant sought to have suspended by way of an interim measure, was adopted by the Council. It followed that the Judge hearing the application for interim measures was not empowered to allow such an application, since to do so would have the effect of suspending an act emanating from an institution that was not a party to the proceedings. Likewise, ECJ, Case C-277/07 P(R) *Makteshim-Agan Holding and Others v Commission* concerned a situation in which the act challenged in the main proceedings was adopted by the Commission, whereas the interim relief sought related to the suspension of a certain provision of an act adopted by the Council. As the Council was not a party to the proceedings, the application for such suspension was rejected as inadmissible.

[68] ECJ (order of the President of 17 March 1986), Case 23/86 R *United Kingdom v European Parliament* [1986] E.C.R. 1085, paras 22–24.

[69] CFI (order of the President of 18 March 2008), Case T-411/07 R *Aer Lingus v Commission* [2008] E.C.R. II-411, paras 55–59.

should be exercised with due regard to the procedural rights, particularly the right to be heard, of the addressees of interim measures and of parties directly affected by such measures.[70] On this basis, interim measures directed at national authorities have also been held admissible, even though the Union courts do not have jurisdiction to hear actions brought by natural and legal persons against national authorities.[71]

(3) Union bodies, offices, and agencies

13.22 A Union body, office, or agency may be a defendant in proceedings for interim relief,[72] provided that it has been accorded the status of an independent body and has legal personality under Union law.[73] By contrast, a Union body, office,

---

[70] CFI, Case T-411/07 R *Aer Lingus v Commission*, para. 56.

[71] See, e.g. EGC (order of the President of 19 May 2011), Case T-218/11 R *Dagher v Council and Italy* [2011] E.C.R. II-146*, Summ. pub., paras 5–7; EGC (order of the President of 12 December 2011), Case T-402/11 R *Preparados Alimenticios del Sur v Commission* [2011] E.C.R. II-439*, Summ. pub., paras 14–15.

[72] In particular, before the entry into force of the Lisbon Treaty, the issue of the extent to which actions for annulment could be brought against a Union body, office, or agency had not yet been settled: see para. 7.70. As a consequence, the Judge hearing an application for interim measures against the body, office, or agency in question was invariably faced with such an issue and thus exhibited caution so as not to prejudge the position of the Court in the main action. For example, as regards the European Food Safety Authority (EFSA), compare CFI (order of the President of 1 March 2007), Joined Cases T-311/06 R I, T-311/06 R II, T-312/06 R, and T-313/06 R *FMC Chemical SPRL and Others v EFSA* [2007] E.C.R. II-21*, Summ. pub., particularly paras 54–56 (finding that the applicants did not *prima facie* put forward evidence to establish the Court's jurisdiction over actions for annulment against the EFSA), with CFI (order of 17 June 2008), Case T-311/06 *FMC Chemical and Arysta Life Sciences v EFSA* [2008] E.C.R. II-88*, Summ. pub., paras 67–68; CFI (order of 17 June 2008), Case T-312/06 *FMC Chemical v EFSA* [2008] E.C.R. II-89*, Summ. pub., paras 67–68 (Case T-313/06 was discontinued) (holding that the contested act was not a challengeable act for the purposes of then Art. 230 EC and thus there was no need to rule on the EFSA's contention that the then Court of First Instance did not have jurisdiction to rule on an application brought pursuant to the fourth para. of Art. 230 EC to annul an act of the EFSA). For some recent examples of interim proceedings brought against Union bodies, offices, and agencies, see CFI (order of the President of 24 April 2009), Case T-52/09 R *Nycomed Denmark v European Medicines Agency* [2009] E.C.R. II-43*, Summ. pub.; EGC (order of the President of 26 March 2010), Case T-1/10 R *SNF v European Chemicals Agency* [2010] E.C.R. II-47*, Summ. pub., para. 11; EGC (order of the President of 15 October 2010), Case T-415/10 *R Nexans France v The European joint undertaking for ITER and the Development of fusion energy*, not reported, para. 1. For some examples of interim proceedings brought against the OHIM, see, e.g. ECJ (order of the President of 12 May 2010), Case C-5/10 P-R *Torresan v OHIM* [2010] E.C.R. I-64*, Summ. pub.; ECJ (order of the President of 19 July 2012), Joined Cases C-587/11 P-R and C-588/11 P-R *Omnicare v OHIM*, not reported; CFI (order of the President of 18 February 2008), Case T-410/07 R *Jurado Hermanos v OHIM* [2008] E.C.R. II-25*, Summ. pub. Actions, including applications for interim measures, relating to measures of the Publications Office of the European Union are brought against the Commission as provided under the relevant provisions of Union law: see, e.g. EGC (order of the President of 5 February 2010), Case T-514/09 R *De Post v Commission* [2010] E.C.R. II-15*, Summ. pub., para. 7; EGC (order of the President of 5 October 2011), Case T-422/11 R *Computer Resources International (Luxembourg) v Commission* [2011] E.C.R. II-348*, Summ. pub., para. 12. The same holds with respect to OLAF—such actions must be directed against the Commission alone: see, e.g. EGC (order of the President of 15 March 2010), Case T-435/09 R *GL2006 Europe v Commission* [2010] E.C.R. II-32*, Summ. pub., paras 13–17.

[73] See, e.g. EGC (order of the President of 22 July 2010), Case T-271/10 R *H v Council and Commission* [2010] E.C.R. II-154*, Summ. pub., paras 18–21, in which the General Court held that the application for suspension could not be brought against the Head of the European Union Police Mission (EUPM) in Bosnia and Herzegovina and that the Council and the Commission were considered to be the only defendants. On the basis of the relevant Union measure establishing it, the Court found that the EUPM does not have legal personality and there is no provision for it to be a party to proceedings before the Union courts and therefore has not been accorded the legal status of an agency of the Union but instead is a 'mission', despite the fact that the EUPM seems to have some legal capacity to enter into contracts concerning the recruitment of staff and concluding technical arrangements regarding the provision of equipment, services, and premises. Moreover, the Court also ruled that the application was admissible even though the contested acts were made in the area

or agency, whether having separate legal personality under Union law or not, may of course be involved in proceedings for interim measures in the staff context.[74]

III. Special Characteristics

A. Competent Judge

Until 1 November 2012, the President of the Court of Justice was empowered to rule on applications for interim measures brought before that Court. However, by a decision taken by the Court on 23 October 2012, pursuant to Art. 10(3) of the ECJ Rules of Procedure, these judicial functions of the President have been transferred to the Vice-President of the Court of Justice.[75] At the General Court, it is the President who is empowered to rule on applications for interim measures.[76]

13.23

---

of the CFSP, finding that it could not be ruled out that the contested acts were attributable to the Council or to the Commission and that it should be ensured that these institutions do not evade review by the Union judicature in respect of purely administrative decisions which are taken in relation to staff management within the EUPM, which are separable from the 'political' measures taken as part of the CFSP: see paras 23–25. Invariably, given the nature of interim relief, the issue of the capacity of a particular entity to act as a defendant in legal proceedings before the Union judicature may be dealt with in the main action, as opposed to the proceedings for interim measures: compare, e.g. EGC (order of the President of 30 September 2011), Case T-395/11 R *Elti v Delegation of the European Union to Montenegro* [2011] E.C.R. II-342*, Summ. pub. (dismissing application for interim measures for lack of urgency), with EGC (order of 4 June 2012), Case T-395/11 *Elti v Delegation of the European Union to Montenegro*, not reported (dismissing action on grounds that the Delegation of the European Union to Montenegro cannot be considered to be a body, office, or agency of the Union and be recognized as having capacity to act as a defendant in legal proceedings).

[74] For some recent examples of staff cases involving Union bodies, offices, and agencies, see CST (order of the President of 31 May 2006), Case F-38/06 R *Bianchi v European Training Foundation* [2006] E.C.R.-SC I-A-1-27; CST (order of the President of 14 July 2010), Case F-41/10 R *Bermejo Garde v European Economic and Social Committee*, not reported; CST (order of the President of 16 November 2011), Case F-61/11 R *Possanzini v Frontex*, not reported; CST (order of the President of 14 June 2012), Case F-38/12 R *BP v EU Fundamental Rights Agency*, not reported.

[75] See Decision 2012/671/EU concerning the judicial functions of the Vice-President of the Court, [2012] O.J. L300/47. According to this decision, '[t]he Vice-President of the Court shall take the place of the President of the Court in the performance of the judicial duties referred to in the first paragraph of Article 39 of the Protocol on the Statute of the Court of Justice of the European Union and in Article 57 thereof and in Articles 160 to 166 of the Rules of Procedure of the Court of Justice.' It follows from this decision that the Vice-President of the Court of Justice is also empowered to rule on appeals brought against orders given by the President of the General Court on applications for interim relief. See ECJ (order of the Vice-President of 7 March 2013), Case C-551/12 P(R) *EDF v Commission*, not reported; ECJ (order of the Vice-President of 28 November 2013), Case C-390/13 P(R) *European Medicines Agency v InterMune UK and Others*, not reported.

[76] Statute, Art.39, first para. and EGC Rules of Procedure, Arts 104–110. See also Notice 2013/C 313/10 concerning Designation of the Judge replacing the President as the Judge hearing application for interim measures ([2013] O.J. C313/5). With respect to the Civil Service Tribunal, its President is empowered to rule on applications for interim measures: CST Rules of Procedure, Art. 103(1). See also Notice 2012/C 303/02 concerning Designation of the Judge replacing the President of the Tribunal as the Judge hearing applications for interim measures ([2012] O.J. C303/2). Moreover, the President of the General Court is empowered to rule on appeals brought against orders given by the President of the Civil Service Tribunal on applications for interim relief: see Statute, Annex I, Arts 10(2)–(3). As provided in Art. 10(3), such summary procedure 'may, in so far as necessary, differ from some of the rules contained in this Annex and which shall be laid down in the [R]ules of [P]rocedure of the General Court'. See further M. Jaeger, 'Le référé devant le président du Tribunal de l'Union européenne depuis septembre 2007' (2010) J.D.E. 197–213.

The Vice-President of the Court of Justice may refer the application to the Court for decision.[77] Such a reference will generally be made on the grounds of the difficulty or exceptional interest of the case. If the application is so referred, the Court of Justice has to give a decision immediately, after hearing the Advocate-General.[78] By contrast, before the General Court, only the President will hear applications for interim relief. However, when the latter is absent or prevented from dealing with such applications, the Judge specifically designated for this purpose[79] will hear applications for interim relief.[80]

B. Procedure before the Union courts

13.24 An application for interim relief is adjudicated upon 'by way of summary procedure'.[81] The application is served on the opposing party; and the Vice-President of the Court of Justice or the President of the General Court, as the case may be, prescribes a short period within which that party may submit written or oral observations.[82] The (Vice-) President may grant the application even before the observations of the opposing party have been submitted, which has been referred to by way of a so-called *ex parte* order.[83]

---

[77] ECJ Rules of Procedure, Art. 161(1).

[78] ECJ Rules of Procedure, Art. 161(3).

[79] See, e.g. [2012] O.J. C235/2.

[80] EGC Rules of Procedure, Art. 106 . See also, with respect to the Civil Service Tribunal, CST Rules of Procedure, Art. 103(2).

[81] Statute, Art. 39, first para. See also Point 83 of the EGC Practice Directions.

[82] ECJ Rules of Procedure, Art. 160(5); EGC Rules of Procedure, Art. 105(1). The applicant does not have the right to submit a rejoinder; if the President of the General Court refuses to give the applicant the possibility to submit a rejoinder or to take measures of inquiry as requested, no infringement of the rights of the defence ensues: see, e.g. ECJ (order of 30 September 2003), Case C-348/03 P(R) *Asian Institute of Technology v Commission*, not reported, paras 23–24.

[83] ECJ Rules of Procedure, Art. 160(7); EGC Rules of Procedure, Art. 105(2), second para.; under those provisions, this decision may be varied, extended, or cancelled even without any application being made by any party. For some examples, see ECJ (order of the President of 28 June 1990), Case C-195/90 R *Commission v Germany* [1990] E.C.R. I-2715, extended by ECJ (order of the President of 12 July 1990), Case C-195/90 R *Commission v Germany* [1990] E.C.R. I-3351; ECJ (order of the President of 30 July 2003), Case C-320/03 R *Commission v Austria* [2003] E.C.R. I-7929, extended by ECJ (order of the President of 2 October 2003), Case C-320/03 R *Commission v Austria* [2003] E.C.R. I-11665, and ECJ (order of the President of 27 April 2004), Case C-320/03 R *Commission v Austria* [2004] E.C.R. I-3593; CFI (order of the President of 10 August 2001), Case T-184/01 R *IMS Health v Commission* [2001] E.C.R. II-2349, extended by CFI (order of the President of 26 October 2001), Case T-184/01 R *IMS Health v Commission* [2001] E.C.R. II-3193; CFI (order of the President of 4 April 2006), Case T-420/05 R *Vischim v Commission* [2006] E.C.R. II-34*, Summ. pub., paras 33–34 (cancelled); CFI (order of the President of 26 February 2007), Case T-383/06 R *Icuna.Com v European Parliament* [2007] E.C.R. II-17*, Summ. pub., paras 3, 11 (cancelled—application became devoid of purpose); EGC (order of the President of 25 October 2010), Case T-18/10 R II *Inuit Tapiriit Kanatami and Others v European Parliament and Council* [2010] E.C.R. II-235*, Summ. pub. (cancelled); EGC (order of the President of 17 February 2011), Case T-486/10 R *Iberdrola v Commission*, not reported (cancelled); EGC (order of the President of 17 February 2011), Case T-490/10 R *Endesa and Endesa Generacion v Commission*, not reported (cancelled). There are several examples in the case-law in which the President acknowledges the provisional order granted under Art. 105(2) of the EGC Rules of Procedure, but in dismissing the application for interim measures does not say explicitly that this order is cancelled. See CFI (order of the President of 30 March 2007), Case T-366/00 R *Scott v Commission*, not reported, para. 12 (though this application was found to be devoid of purpose, not rejected on merits) (appeal dismissed in ECJ (order of the President of 22 November 2007), Case C-296/07 P(R) *Commission v Scott* [2007] E.C.R. I-166*, Summ. pub.); CFI (order of the President of 15 July 2008), Case T-202/08 R *CLL Centres de langues v Commission* [2008] E.C.R. II-143*, Summ. pub., para. 12; CFI (order of the President of 15 January 2009), Case T-199/08 R *Ziegler v Commission* [2009] E.C.R. II-2*, Summ. pub., para. 7 (appeal dismissed in ECJ (order of the President of 30 April 2010), Case C-113/09 P(R) *Ziegler v Commission* [2010] E.C.R. I-50*, Summ. pub.); EGC (order of 5 February 2010), Case T-514/09 R *De Post v Commission* [2010] E.C.R. II-15*,

Depending on the circumstances of the particular case, an oral hearing may be held at which the parties put their case and the (Vice-)President puts his or her questions.[84] If necessary, a preparatory inquiry may be ordered insofar as this is compatible with the objectives of the interim proceedings.[85]

In addition, under circumstances where the application for interim measures is based on essentially identical arguments to a previous application that has already been rejected by reasoned order, the Judge hearing the application may reject such arguments on the same grounds by reference to what was decided in that order.[86]

C. Other requirements for admissibility

(1) Admissibility of the application in the main proceedings

Again, on account of the ancillary nature of proceedings for interim relief, whether an application for interim measures is admissible will be contingent upon the admissibility of the application in the main proceedings.[87] Proceedings for interim relief would acquire an **13.25**

Summ. pub., para. 9; EGC (order of the President of 26 March 2010), Case T-1/10 R *SNF SAS v European Chemicals Agency* [2010] E.C.R. II-47*, Summ. pub., para. 18.

[84] If the Judge hearing applications for interim relief considers that the case-file contains all the information which is required to make a pronouncement, he or she may lawfully dispense with oral argument from the parties. As a consequence, a request by a party for an oral hearing may be rejected: see, e.g. EGC (order of the President of 29 July 2011), Case T-292/11 R *Cemex and Others v Commission* [2011] E.C.R. II-243*, Summ. pub., para. 19. The decision as to whether to hold an oral hearing is considered to fall within the broad discretion of the Judge hearing the application for interim measures; save for situations in which there would be evidence in the file to support the conclusion that he or she exceeded the limits of that discretion, pleas challenging the decision of the President of the General Court not to hold a hearing fail on appeal: see, e.g. ECJ (order of the President of 24 March 2009), Case C-60/08 P(R) *Cheminova and Others v Commission* [2009] E.C.R. I-43*, Summ. pub., paras 81–83; ECJ (order of the President of 14 December 2011), Case C-446/10 P(R) *Alco Transformazioni v Commission*, not reported, paras 72–74; ECJ (order of the President of 20 April 2012), Case C-507/11 P(R) *Fapricela v Commission*, not reported, paras 48–57; ECJ (order of the President of 19 July 2012), Case C-110/12 P(R) *Akhras v Council*, not reported, paras 54–64.

[85] ECJ Rules of Procedure, Art. 160(6); EGC Rules of Procedure, Art. 105(2), first para. See, e.g. CFI (order of the President of 27 July 2004), Case T-148/04 R *TQ3 Travel Solutions Belgium v Commission* [2004] E.C.R. II-3027, paras 60–63; CFI (order of the President of 25 April 2008), Case T-41/08 R *Vakakis International v Commission* [2008] E.C.R. II-66*, Summ. pub., paras 76–78. As with the decision on an oral hearing (see n. 84), the decision to hold a preparatory inquiry also falls within the broad discretion of the Judge hearing the application for interim measures: see, e.g. ECJ (order of the President of 20 April 2012), Case C-507/11 P(R) *Fapricela v Commission*, not reported, paras 50–51; ECJ (order of the President of 19 July 2012), Case C-110/12 *Akhras v Council*, not reported, paras 58–59.

[86] See, e.g. CFI (order of the President of 11 April 2008), Case T-119/08 R *Cyprus v Commission* [2008] E.C.R. II-56*, Summ. pub., paras 6–7; CFI (order of the President of 11 April 2008), Case T-122/08 R *Cyprus v Commission* [2008] E.C.R. II-57*, Summ. pub., paras 6–7; CFI (order of the President of 17 September 2008), Case T-332/08 R *Melli Bank v Council*, not reported, para. 17.

[87] See, e.g. ECJ (order of the President of 23 May 1990), Case C-68/90 R *Blot and Front National v European Parliament* [1990] E.C.R. I-2177, paras 4–5; ECJ (order of the President of 27 June 1991), Case C-117/91 R *Bosman v Commission* [1991] E.C.R. I-3353, para. 6; ECJ (order of the President of 6 July 1993), Case C-257/93 R *Van Parijs and Others v Council and Commission* [1993] E.C.R. I-3917, para. 4; ECJ (order of the President of 9 July 1993), Case C-64/93 R *Donatab and Others v Commission* [1993] E.C.R. I-3955, para. 4; ECJ (order of the President of 16 July 1993), Case C-107/93 R *AEFMA v Commission* [1993] E.C.R. I-4177, para. 4. Indeed, it has been consistently held that the rule, provided under Art. 104(1) of the EGC Rules of Procedure, that an application for interim measures is admissible only if it is made by a party to a case that is before the Court, implies that the main action to which the application for interim measures relates can in fact be examined by the Court: see, e.g. CFI (order of the President of 16 November 2007), Case T-312/07 R

impermissible degree of autonomy if interim measures could be ordered in connection with an inadmissible application in the main proceedings. This requirement confronts the Judge hearing the application for interim relief with a dilemma: because of the provisional nature of such relief he or she may not prejudge in any way the final judgment, but in order to determine the admissibility of the application for interim relief, he or she must make a reasonably accurate determination of whether the main application will be declared admissible.

Consequently, the Judge hearing the application for interim relief takes a cautious approach to this question. It has been consistently held that the issue of the admissibility of the main application should not as a rule be examined in proceedings relating to an application for interim measures so as not to prejudice the substantive proceedings.[88] Yet, where the opposing party contends that the main application is manifestly inadmissible,[89]

Dimos Peramatos v Commission [2007] E.C.R. II-157*, Summ. pub., para. 21; CFI (order of the President of 4 December 2007), Case T-326/07 R *Cheminova and Others v Commission* [2007] E.C.R. II-4877, para. 42; CFI (order of the President of 11 December 2007), Case T-349/07 R *FMC Chemical SPRL and Others v Commission* [2007] E.C.R. II-169*, Summ. pub., para. 44; CFI (order of the President of 11 December 2007), Case T-350/07 R *FMC Chemical SPRL and Others v Commission* [2007] E.C.R. II-170*, Summ. pub., para. 45; CFI (order of the President of 25 April 2008), Case T-41/08 R *Vakakis International v Commission* [2008] E.C.R. II-66*, Summ. pub., para. 33; CFI (order of the President of 14 March 2008), Case T-467/07 R *Du Pont de Nemours (France) and Others v Commission* [2008] E.C.R. II-40*, Summ. pub., para. 25; CFI (order of the President of 18 June 2008), Case T-475/07 R *Dow Agrosciences and Others v Commission* [2008] E.C.R. II-92*, Summ. pub., para. 25; CFI (order of the President of 27 January 2009), Case T-457/08 R *Intel Corp. v Commission* [2009] E.C.R. II-12*, Summ. pub., para. 45; EGC (order of the President of 30 April 2010), Case T-18/10 R *Inuit Tapiriit Kanatami and Others v European Parliament and Council* [2010] E.C.R. II-75*, Summ. pub., para. 37; EGC (order of the President of 3 July 2013), Case T-313/13 R *Codacons v Commission*, not reported, para. 4.

[88] See, e.g. ECJ (order of the President of 16 October 1986), Case 221/86 R *Group of the European Right and National Front Party v European Parliament* [1986] E.C.R. 2969, para. 19; ECJ (order of the President of 8 April 1987), Case 65/87 R *Pfizer v Commission* [1987] E.C.R. 1691, para. 15; CFI (order of the President of 16 March 2007), Case T-345/05 R *V v European Parliament* [2007] E.C.R. II-25*, Summ. pub., para. 42; CFI (order of the President of 21 May 2007), Case T-18/07 R *Kronberger v European Parliament* [2007] E.C.R. II-50*, Summ. pub., para. 27; CFI (order of the President of 16 November 2007), Case T-312/07 R *Dimos Peramatos v Commission* [2007] E.C.R. II-157*, Summ. pub., para. 22; CFI (order of the President of 4 December 2007), Case T-326/07 R *Cheminova and Others v Commission* [2007] E.C.R. II-4877, para. 43; CFI (order of the President of 11 December 2007), Case T-349/07 R *FMC Chemical SPRL and Others v Commission* [2007] E.C.R. II-169*, Summ. pub., para. 45; CFI (order of the President of 11 December 2007), Case T-350/07 R *FMC Chemical SPRL and Others v Commission* [2007] E.C.R. II-170*, Summ. pub., para. 46; CFI (order of the President of 14 March 2008), Case T-467/07 R *Du Pont de Nemours (France) and Others v Commission* [2008] E.C.R. II-40*, Summ. pub., para. 26; CFI (order of the President of 8 April 2008), Joined Cases T-54/08 R, T-87/08 R, T-88/08 R, and T-91/08 R to T-93/08 R *Cyprus v Commission*, not reported, para. 50; CFI (order of the President of 25 April 2008), Case T-41/08 R *Vakakis International v Commission* [2008] E.C.R. II-66*, Summ. pub., para. 34; CFI (order of the President of 18 June 2008), Case T-475/07 R *Dow Agrosciences and Others v Commission* [2008] E.C.R. II-92*, Summ. pub., para. 26; CFI (order of the President of 27 January 2009), Case T-457/08 R *Intel Corp. v Commission* [2009] E.C.R. II-12*, Summ. pub., para. 46; EGC (order of the President of 30 April 2010), Case T-18/10 R *Inuit Tapiriit Kanatami and Others v European Parliament and Council* [2010] E.C.R. II-75*, Summ. pub., para. 38.

[89] The fact that the opposing party does not plead the manifest inadmissibility of the main action in proceedings for interim relief has been held not to preclude the Judge hearing the application for interim measures from undertaking this assessment, since the inadmissibility of an action (for lack of *locus standi* in proceedings seeking review of a Union measure) involves a question of public policy which may, and even must, be raised by the Union judicature of its own motion: see ECJ (order of the President of 24 March 2009), Case C-60/08 P(R) *Cheminova and Others v Commission* [2009] E.C.R. I-43*, Summ. pub., para. 31; CFI (order of the President of 18 June 2008), Case T-475/07 R *Dow Agrosciences and Others v Commission* [2008] E.C.R. II-92*, Summ. pub., para. 30, upheld on appeal in ECJ (order of the President of 15 December 2009), Case C-391/08 P(R) *Dow Agrosciences and Others v Commission* [2009] E.C.R. I-219*, Summ. pub., para. 39. See also CST (order of the President of 16 November 2011), Case F-61/11 R *Possanzini v Frontex*, not reported, para. 18.

it may[90] nevertheless be necessary for the Judge hearing the application for interim relief to establish whether there are any grounds for concluding *prima facie* that the main application is admissible.[91] In doing so, he or she will take care that the Judges hearing

---

[90] The Judge hearing the application for interim measures may base its order on other grounds and find that it is not necessary to consider the question of the possible inadmissibility of the main proceedings: see, e.g. CFI (order of the President of 10 January 2006), Case T-396/05 R *ArchiMEDES v Commission* [2006] E.C.R. II-2*, Summ. pub., paras 49, 57; CFI (order of the President of 4 April 2006), Case T-420/05 R *Vischim v Commission* [2006] E.C.R. II-34*, Summ. pub., para. 65; CFI (order of the President of 2 August 2006), Case T-163/06 R *BA.L.A. di Lanciotti Vittoria & C. Sas and Others v Commission* [2006] E.C.R. II-59*, Summ. pub., paras 33–34; CFI (order of the President of 26 October 2006), Case T-209/06 R *European Association of Im- and Exporters of Birds and Live Animals and Others v Commission* [2006] E.C.R. II-87*, Summ. pub., para. 29 (also including the question of the admissibility of the application for interim measures); CFI (order of the President of 4 March 2007), Case T-71/07 R *Icuna.Com SCRL v European Parliament* [2007] E.C.R. II-39*, Summ. pub., para. 36 (also including the question of the admissibility of the application for interim measures); CFI (order of the President of 26 September 2008), Case T-312/08 R *Ellinikos Niognomon v Commission* [2008] E.C.R. II-204*, Summ. pub., para. 30.

[91] See, e.g. ECJ (order of the President of 13 July 1988), Case 160/88 R *Fédération Européenne de la Santé Animale and Others v Council* [1988] E.C.R. 4121, para. 22; ECJ (order of the President of 27 June 1991), Case C-117/91 R *Bosman v Commission* [1991] E.C.R. I-3353, para. 7; ECJ (order of the President of 12 October 1992), Case C-295/92 R *Landbouwschap v Commission* [1992] E.C.R. I-5069; CFI (order of the President of 23 March 1992), Joined Cases T-10/92 to T-12/92 R and T-14/92 to T-15/92 R *Cimenteries CBR and Others v Commission* [1992] E.C.R. II-1571, para. 44; CFI (order of the President of 15 December 1992), Case T-96/92 R *CCE de la Société Générale des Grandes Sources and Others v Commission* [1992] E.C.R. II-2579, para. 31; CFI (order of the President of 2 March 1998), Case T-310/97 R *Netherlands Antilles v Council* [1998] E.C.R. II-455, paras 30–38; CFI (order of the President of 28 November 2003), Case T-264/03 R *Schmoldt and Others v Commission* [2003] E.C.R. II-5089, para. 55; CFI (order of the President of 10 January 2006), Case T-396/05 R *ArchiMEDES v Commission* [2006] E.C.R. II-2*, Summ. pub., para. 44; CFI (order of the President of 24 March 2006), Case T-454/05 R *Sumitomo Chemical Agro Europe and Philagro France v Commission* [2006] E.C.R. II-131*, Summ. pub., para. 46; CFI (order of the President of 2 August 2006), Case T-163/06 R *BA.L.A. di Lanciotti Vittoria & C. Sas and Others v Commission* [2006] E.C.R. II-59*, Summ. pub., para. 16; CFI (order of the President of 1 March 2007), Joined Cases T-311/06 R, T-311/06 R II, T-312/06 R and T-313/06 R *FMC Chemical SPRL and Others v EFSA* [2007] E.C.R. II-21*, Summ. pub., para. 50; CFI (order of the President of 1 March 2007), Case T-397/06 R *Dow Agrosciences v EFSA* [2007] E.C.R. II-22*, Summ. pub., para. 33; CFI (order of the President of 16 March 2007), Case T-345/05 R *V v European Parliament* [2007] E.C.R. II-25*, Summ. pub., para. 42; CFI (order of the President of 21 May 2007), Case T-18/07 R *Kronberger v European Parliament* [2007] E.C.R. II-50*, Summ. pub., para. 27; CFI (order of the President of 7 June 2007), Case T-346/06 R *IMS v Commission* [2007] E.C.R. II-1781, para. 31; CFI (order of the President of 11 June 2007), Case T-324/06 R *Municipio de Gondomar v Commission* [2007] E.C.R. II-55*, Summ. pub., para. 27; CFI (order of the President of 19 July 2007), Case T-31/07 R *Du Pont de Nemours (France) and Others v Commission* [2007] E.C.R. II-2767, para. 106; CFI (order of the President of 16 November 2007), Case T-312/07 R *Dimos Peramatos v Commission* [2007] E.C.R. II-157*, Summ. pub., para. 22; CFI (order of the President of 4 December 2007), Case T-326/07 R *Cheminova and Others v Commission* [2007] E.C.R. II-4877, para. 43; CFI (order of the President of 11 December 2007), Case T-349/07 R *FMC Chemical SPRL and Others v Commission* [2007] E.C.R. II-169*, Summ. pub., para. 45; CFI (order of the President of 11 December 2007), Case T-350/07 R *FMC Chemical SPRL and Others v Commission* [2007] E.C.R. II-170*, Summ. pub., para. 46; CFI (order of the President of 14 March 2008), Case T-467/07 R *Du Pont de Nemours (France) and Others v Commission* [2008] E.C.R. II-40*, Summ. pub., para. 26; CFI (order of the President of 8 April 2008), Joined Cases T-54/08 R, T-87/08 R, T-88/08 R, and T-91/08 R to T-93/08 R *Cyprus v Commission*, not reported, para. 50; CFI (order of the President of 25 April 2008), Case T-41/08 R *Vakakis International v Commission* [2008] E.C.R. II-66*, Summ. pub., para. 34; CFI (order of the President of 18 June 2008), Case T-475/07 R *Dow Agrosciences and Others v Commission* [2008] E.C.R. II-92*, Summ. pub., para. 26; CFI (order of the President of 27 January 2009), Case T-457/08 R *Intel Corp. v Commission* [2009] E.C.R. II-12*, Summ. pub., para. 46; EGC (order of the President of 30 April 2010), Case T-18/10 R *Inuit Tapiriit Kanatami and Others v European Parliament and Council* [2010] E.C.R. II-75*, Summ. pub., para. 38.

the main case retain their latitude. The assessment made by the Judge hearing the application for interim relief does not preclude interim measures being granted following the bringing of an action which is subsequently declared inadmissible,[92] but it does avoid an application which is manifestly inadmissible giving rise to proceedings for interim relief which enable the application or effects of a Union act to be temporarily averted.[93]

The Judge hearing the application for interim measures takes the view that the application is admissible where he or she finds that the application in the main proceedings discloses *prima facie* grounds for concluding that there is a certain probability that it is admissible[94] or, framed another way in more recent case-law, that the admissibility of the main application cannot be excluded.[95] Such grounds will be lacking where, in the light of settled case-law, the main application is manifestly inadmissible.

For instance, an application for annulment of the Commission's refusal to initiate proceedings for failure to fulfil obligations is manifestly inadmissible (see para. 8.06). Accordingly, an application for interim measures brought in connection with such an action will also be inadmissible.[96] Likewise, an application for an institution's failure to act is manifestly inadmissible where the requisite conditions under the case-law, including calling upon the institution concerned to act or where the institution concerned has defined its position (see paras 8.15 *et seq.*), are not satisfied. Other examples of manifest inadmissibility of the main application include where the applicant has failed to comply with certain formal

---

[92] See, e.g. ECJ (order of the President of 25 October 1985), Case 293/85 R *Commission v Belgium* [1985] E.C.R. 3521, followed by ECJ, Case 293/85 *Commission v Belgium* [1988] E.C.R. 305.

[93] ECJ (order of the President of 27 January 1988), Case 376/87 R *Distrivet v Council* [1988] E.C.R. 209, para. 22; CFI (order of the President of 28 April 1999), Case T-11/99 R *Van Parijs and Others v Commission* [1999] E.C.R. II-1355, para. 51. This also applies to the requirement for a *prima facie* case (see paras 13.33 and 13.34).

[94] See, e.g. ECJ (order of the President of 1 February 1984), Case 1/84 R *Ilford v Commission* [1984] E.C.R. 423, paras 6–7; CFI (order of the President of 2 April 1993), Case T-12/93 R *CCE de Vittel and Others v Commission* [1993] E.C.R. II-449, paras 20–26; CFI (order of the President of 13 May 1993), Case T-24/93 R *CMBT v Commission* [1993] E.C.R. II-543, paras 27–30; EGC (order of the President of 30 April 2010), Case T-18/10 R *Inuit Tapiriit Kanatami and Others v European Parliament and Council* [2010] E.C.R. II-75*, Summ. pub., para. 41. For staff cases, see, e.g. CST (order of the President of 28 February 2012), Case F-140/11 R *BK v Commission*, not reported, para. 34.

[95] See, e.g. CFI (order of the President of 7 June 2007), Case T-346/06 R *IMS v Commission* [2007] E.C.R. II-1781, para. 33; CFI (order of the President of 19 July 2007), Case T-31/07 R *Du Pont de Nemours (France) and Others v Commission* [2007] E.C.R. II-2767, paras 108, 117; CFI (order of the President of 16 November 2007), Case T-312/07 R *Dimos Peramatos v Commission* [2007] E.C.R. II-157*, Summ. pub., para. 24; CFI (order of the President of 4 December 2007), Case T-326/07 R *Cheminova and Others v Commission* [2007] E.C.R. II-4877, para. 45; CFI (order of the President of 11 December 2007), Case T-349/07 R *FMC Chemical SPRL and Others v Commission* [2007] E.C.R. II-169*, Summ. pub., para. 47; CFI (order of the President of 11 December 2007), Case T-350/07 R *FMC Chemical SPRL and Others v Commission* [2007] E.C.R. II-170*, Summ. pub., para. 48; CFI (order of the President of 14 March 2008), Case T-467/07 R *Du Pont de Nemours (France) and Others v Commission* [2008] E.C.R. II-40*, Summ. pub., para. 28; CFI (order of the President of 8 April 2008), Joined Cases T-54/08 R, T-87/08 R, T-88/08 R, and T-91/08 R to T-93/08 R *Cyprus v Commission*, not reported, para. 51; CFI (order of the President of 18 June 2008), Case T-475/07 R *Dow Agrosciences and Others v Commission* [2008] E.C.R. II-92*, Summ. pub., para. 28; CFI (order of the President of 27 January 2009), Case T-457/08 R *Intel Corp. v Commission* [2009] E.C.R. II-12*, Summ. pub., para. 48; EGC (order of the President of 30 April 2010), Case T-18/10 R *Inuit Tapiriit Kanatami and Others v European Parliament and Council* [2010] E.C.R. II-75*, Summ. pub., para. 40.

[96] See, e.g. ECJ (order of the President of 5 May 1994), Case C-97/94 P-R *Schulz v Commission* [1994] E.C.R. I-1701, paras 12–15.

requirements[97] or to lodge the application within the prescribed time limit[98] and where natural or legal persons have brought an action for annulment against an act for which they fail to satisfy the requirements of direct and/or individual concern under the fourth paragraph of Art. 263 TFEU[99] or against an act which is not challengeable within the meaning of the case-law.[100]

In particular, it has been held that the case-law in the context of the action for annulment, to the effect that where one and the same application is involved and one of the applicants satisfies the standing requirements, there is no need to consider whether the other applicants are entitled to bring proceedings (see para. 7.137), does not apply in the context of

---

[97] See, e.g. ECJ (order of the President of 26 February 1981), Case 10/81 *Farrall v Commission* [1981] E.C.R. 717 (application not lodged by a lawyer).

[98] See, e.g. ECJ (order of the President of 23 May 1984), Case 50/84 R *Bensider v Commission* [1984] E.C.R. 2247, para. 24; CFI (order of the President of 21 May 2007), Case T-18/07 R *Kronberger v European Parliament* [2007] E.C.R. II-50*, Summ. pub., paras 33–34. Compare, e.g. CFI (order of the President of 16 November 2007), Case T-312/07 R *Dimos Peramatos v Commission* [2007] E.C.R. II-157*, Summ. pub., paras 25–33 (concluding that the admissibility of the main action cannot be wholly excluded on account of the time limits prescribed by what is now the sixth para. of Art. 263 TFEU).

[99] See, e.g. ECJ (order of the President of 13 July 1988), Case 160/88 R *Fédération Européenne de la Santé Animale and Others v Council* [1988] E.C.R. 4121, paras 23–30; CFI (order of the President of 22 December 1995), Case T-219/95 R *Danielsson and Others v Commission* [1995] E.C.R. II-3051, paras 66–76; CFI (order of the President of 11 June 2007), Case T-324/06 R *Municipio de Gondomar v Commission* [2007] E.C.R. II-55*, Summ. pub., paras 29–48. Compare, e.g. CFI (order of the President of 16 March 2007), Case T-345/05 R *V v European Parliament* [2007] E.C.R. II-25*, Summ. pub., paras 50–52 (concluding that the possibility *prima facie* remains that applicant is directly concerned by contested act); CFI (order of the President of 7 June 2007), Case T-346/06 R *IMS v Commission* [2007] E.C.R. II-1781, paras 48–60 (concluding that the possibility *prima facie* remains that the applicant is directly and individually concerned by the contested measure and consequently that the main action is admissible; there was further, on the basis of material available, no reason to believe that the main action for damages was inadmissible); CFI (order of the President of 25 April 2008), Case T-41/08 R *Vakakis International v Commission* [2008] E.C.R. II-66*, Summ. pub., paras 35–39 (as far as the *locus standi* of the applicant is concerned, *prima facie* the application for annulment is not manifestly inadmissible; EGC (order of the President of 30 April 2010), Case T-18/10 R *Inuit Tapiriit Kanatami and Others v European Parliament and Council* [2010] E.C.R. II-75*, Summ. pub., paras 42–48 (where the main action for annulment implicated several issues related to the application of the new wording of the fourth para. of Art. 263 TFEU, the Judge hearing the application for interim measures concluded that the admissibility of the main action could not be excluded).

[100] See, e.g. CFI (order of the President of 26 August 1996), Case T-75/96 R *Söktas v Commission* [1996] E.C.R. II-859, paras 16–30; CFI (order of the President of 14 October 1996), Case T-137/96 R *Valio v Commission* [1996] E.C.R. II-1327, paras 27–37; CFI (order of the President of 15 October 2004), Case T-193/04 R *Tillack v Commission* [2004] E.C.R. II-3575, paras 38–48, confirmed on appeal in ECJ (order of the President of 19 April 2005), Case C-521/04P(R) *Tillack v Commission* [2005] E.C.R. I-3103, paras 35–41 (the finding of the manifest inadmissibility of the main action in an order regarding an application for interim measures does not violate the principle of effective judicial protection); CFI (order of the President of 24 March 2006), Case T-454/05 R *Sumitomo Chemical Agro Europe and Philagro France v Commission* [2006] E.C.R. II-131*, Summ. pub., paras 50–63; CFI (order of the President of 30 March 2007), Joined Cases T-393/06 R, T-393/06 R II and T-393/06 R III *Makhteshim-Agan Holding and Others v Commission* [2007] E.C.R. II-32*, Summ. pub., paras 34–50 (appeal dismissed in ECJ (order of the President of 17 July 2008), Case C-277/07 P(R) *Makhteshim-Agan Holding and Others v Commission* [2008] E.C.R. I-112*, Summ. pub.); CFI (order of the President of 27 January 2009), Case T-457/08 R *Intel Corp. v Commission* [2009] E.C.R. II-12*, Summ. pub., paras 50–81. Compare, e.g. CFI (order of the President of 16 March 2007), Case T-345/05 R *V v European Parliament* [2007] E.C.R. II-25*, Summ. pub., paras 44–49 (concluding that it cannot be excluded that the action for annulment is admissible in so far as it is conceivable that the contested act affects the applicant's personal interests and brings about a distinct change in his legal position); CFI (order of the President of 7 June 2007), Case T-346/06 R *IMS v Commission* [2007] E.C.R. II-1781, paras 34–42, 47 (concluding that the possibility remains *prima facie* that the Commission's measure may give rise to binding legal effects).

proceedings for interim relief as far as the issue of assessing urgency is concerned, with the result that those applicants that fail to satisfy the requirements of direct and/or individual concern under the fourth paragraph of Art. 263 TFEU are not entitled to bring an application for interim measures or to put forward their own individual situation in order to establish urgency.[101]

(2) Time limits

(a) General

13.26 An application for interim measures will be admissible only as from the time when the application in the main proceedings has been brought.[102] As long as the main action is pending, an application for interim measures can in principle be made.[103] Nevertheless, the

---

[101] See, e.g. CFI (order of the President of 4 December 2007), Case T-326/07 R *Cheminova and Others v Commission* [2007] E.C.R. II-4877, paras 48–64, confirmed on appeal in ECJ (order of the President of 24 March 2009), Case C-60/08 P(R) *Cheminova and Others v Commission* [2009] E.C.R. I-43*, Summ. pub., paras 32–51; CFI (order of the President of 11 December 2007), Case T-349/07 R *FMC Chemical SPRL and Others v Commission* [2007] E.C.R. II-169*, Summ. pub., paras 50–65; CFI (order of the President of 11 December 2007), Case T-350/07 R *FMC Chemical SPRL and Others v Commission* [2007] E.C.R. II-170*, Summ. pub., paras 51–67; CFI (order of the President of 14 March 2008), Case T-467/07 R *Du Pont de Nemours (France) and Others v Commission* [2008] E.C.R. II-40*, Summ. pub., paras 31–63; CFI (order of the President of 18 June 2008), Case T-475/07 R *Dow Agrosciences and Others v Commission* [2008] E.C.R. II-92*, Summ. pub., paras 33–67, confirmed on appeal in ECJ (order of the President of 15 December 2009), Case C-391/08 P(R) *Dow Agrosciences and Others v Commission* [2009] E.C.R. I-219*, Summ. pub., paras 40–63.

[102] This may be implied from ECJ Rules of Procedure, Art. 160(1)–(2). EGC Rules of Procedure, Art. 104(1).

[103] An application for interim relief is to no purpose once the Court of Justice or the General Court has given judgment in the main proceedings: see, e.g. ECJ (order of the President of 13 September 2004), Case C-18/04 P(R) *Krikorian v European Parliament, Council and Commission*, not reported, paras 6–7; ECJ (order of the President of 17 March 2009), Case C-251/08 P(R) *Ayyanarsamy v Commission and Germany* [2009] E.C.R. I-37*, Summ. pub.; ECJ (order of the President of 19 May 2009), Case C-349/08 P(R) *Kronberger v European Parliament* [2009] E.C.R. I-88*, Summ. pub.; ECJ (order of the President of 27 October 2011), Case C-605/10 P(R) *Inuit Tapiriit Kanatami v European Parliament and Council* [2011] E.C.R. I-164*, Summ. pub. (finding no need to adjudicate on the appeal of General Court's order dismissing application for interim relief where main action dismissed as inadmissible); ECJ (order of the President of 22 November 2007), Case C-296/07 P(R) *Commission v Scott* [2007] E.C.R. I-166*, Summ. pub., para. 22; CFI (order of the President of 18 December 2008), Case T-480/08 R *Woźniak v Poland*, not reported; CFI (order of the President of 18 November 2009), Case T-295/09 R *Hansen v Commission* [2009] E.C.R. II-216*, Summ. pub.; EGC (order of the President of 15 December 2009), Case T-390/09 R *Ngele v Commission* [2009] E.C.R. II-241*, Summ. pub.; EGC (order of the President of 15 December 2011), Case T-513/11 R *Consortium v Commission* [2011] E.C.R. II-456*, Summ. pub., paras 3–4. With particular regard to cases dealing with restrictive measures, where the Union legislator has withdrawn the applicant's name from the contested measure, the Judge hearing the application to suspend the contested measure finds that there is no need to adjudicate the application: see, e.g. EGC (order of the President of 13 July 2011), Case T-142/11 R *SIR v Council*, not reported, paras 5–6; EGC (order of the President of 13 July 2011), Case T-160/11 R *Petroci Holding v Council*, not reported, paras 5–6; EGC (order of the President of 13 June 2012), Case T-656/11 RII *Morison Menon Chartered Accountants and Others v Council*, not reported. An application for interim measures may also become devoid of purpose in other circumstances: see, e.g. ECJ (order of the President of 27 February 2007), Case C-503/06 R *Commission v Italy* [2007] E.C.R. I-19*, Summ. pub.; CFI (order of the President of 4 April 2006), Case T-398/05 R *Tesoka v FEACVT* [2006] E.C.R.-SC I-A-2-87; CFI (order of the President of 26 February 2007), Case T-383/06 R *Icuna.Com v European Parliament* [2007] E.C.R. II-17*, Summ. pub. For an example in which the Court proclaimed that the application was held not to have lost its object, see ECJ (order of the President of 11 November 2011), Case C-530/10 P(R) *Nencini v European Parliament* [2011] E.C.R. I-172*, Summ. pub., paras 14–19. With respect to interim measures in the context of appeals, see ECJ (order of the President of 18 May 2011), Case C-337/09 P-R *Council v Zhejiang Xinan Chemical Industrial Group* [2011] E.C.R. I-77*, Summ. pub., para. 44 (no longer need to adjudicate on the application requesting an order that the effects of the General Court judgment are not suspended pending the outcome of the appeal

Judge hearing applications for interim relief will not hold an application admissible if it is lodged after the written and oral procedures in the main case have been concluded and only a matter of weeks before final judgment is given.[104] In addition, the applicant should take care that its decision as to the time when it submits an application for interim measures does not prejudice its chance of the measures being granted. If the applicant delays too long, there is a danger that the Judge hearing the application for interim relief will draw inferences detracting from the urgency of the measures sought.[105]

(b) Staff cases

Generally speaking, the relevant provisions of the CST Rules of Procedure concerning proceedings for interim measures in the context of staff cases are comparable to those before the Court of Justice and the General Court.[106] Yet, with regard to the issue of time limits, it should be noted that in staff cases, an application may be made for interim measures from the time when the applicant lodges his or her complaint with the appointing authority.[107] At the same time, the main action must have been brought before the Civil Service Tribunal.[108] The proceedings in the main action are then suspended until such time as an express or implied decision rejecting the complaint is taken.[109]

13.27

---

where anti-dumping procedure applicable to the applicants has been terminated and the anti-dumping duties concerned have been repealed; the President held that considerations of a general nature or even the interest in the resolution of legal questions that might be raised in the future in similar cases cannot suffice to justify the maintenance of the application); EGC (order of the President of 28 April 2010), Case T-103/10 P(R)-R *European Parliament v U*, not reported (contested judgment annulled, so application seeking suspension of that judgment is to no purpose).

[104] ECJ (order of the President of 11 April 1960), Joined Cases 3/58 to 16/58, 18/58, and 25/85 to 26/58 R *Barbara Erzbergbau and Others v High Authority* [1960] E.C.R. 220, at 223–4.

[105] See, e.g. ECJ (order of the President of 22 April 1994), Case C-87/94 R *Commission v Belgium* [1994] E.C.R. I-1395, paras 38 and 42; CFI (order of the President of 9 July 2003), Case T-288/02 *AIT v Commission* [2003] E.C.R. II-2885, para. 17. But see CFI (order of the President of 7 May 2002), Case T-306/01 R *Aden and Others v Council and Commission* [2002] E.C.R. II-2387, para. 90 (finding that it cannot be inferred from the mere fact that the application for interim measures was lodged more than three months after the action for annulment was brought that there is no urgency as regards ordering the interim relief sought); CFI (order of the President of 7 June 2007), Case T-346/06 R *IMS v Commission* [2007] E.C.R. II-1781, paras 155–158 (rejecting Commission's argument that not lodging the present application more quickly demonstrated lack of urgency). With respect to staff cases, see, e.g. CST (order of the President of 18 December 2009), Case F-92/09 R *U v European Parliament* [2009] E.C.R.-SC I-A-1-511, para. 65 (the fact that the applicant requested suspension of the contested measures three months after their adoption does not lead to the conclusion of a lack of serious and irreparable damage).

[106] See CST Rules of Procedure, Arts 102–107. Thus, the case-law of the Civil Service Tribunal on proceedings for interim measures generally follows that of the Court of Justice and the General Court, although sometimes, given the nature of staff cases, some slight nuances in approach may be detected. See CST Rules of Procedure, Art. 68(2), expressly providing that measures possibly leading to the amicable settlement of disputes apply to interim measures.

[107] See CST Rules of Procedure, Art. 102(1), third para. ('Those applications may be presented as soon as the complaint provided for in Article 90(2) of the Staff Regulations has been submitted, in the conditions fixed in Article 91(4) of those Regulations.')

[108] In principle, an application to the Civil Service Tribunal will be admissible only after the administrative phase has run its course: the official lodges a complaint with his or her appointing authority, which then has four months to take a decision. If no decision is taken within that four-month period, the complaint is deemed to have been impliedly refused (Staff Regulations, Art. 90(2)).

[109] Staff Regulations, Art. 91(4). See CST (order of the President of 16 November 2011), Case F-61/11 R *Possanzini v Frontex*, not reported, para. 31; for an example where in the context of proceedings for interim relief the main action was held manifestly inadmissible for failure to observe the requisite time limits (*in casu*, under Art. 91(3) of the Staff Regulations providing appeal to the CST must be brought within three months of

(3) Sufficiency of separate application

(a) Separate document

13.28 Under Art. 160(4) of the ECJ Rules of Procedure and Art. 104(3) of the EGC Rules of Procedure, an application for interim measures must be made by a separate document. Accordingly, a request for interim relief contained in the application initiating the main proceedings will be inadmissible.[110]

(b) Sufficiency of the application

13.29 As further provided under Art. 160(4) of the ECJ Rules of Procedure and Art. 104(3) of the EGC Rules of Procedure, an application for interim measures must be in accordance with the formal requirements applying to procedural documents in general and applications in particular.[111] Moreover, under Art. 160(3) of the ECJ Rules of Procedure and Art. 104(2) of the EGC Rules of Procedure, applications for interim measures must state the subject-matter of the proceedings, the circumstances giving rise to urgency, and the pleas of fact and law establishing a *prima facie* case for the interim measures applied for.[112]

On the basis of the foregoing provisions, an application for interim measures must be sufficient in itself to enable the opposing party to prepare its observations and the Judge hearing the application to rule on it, where appropriate, without other supporting information, the essential elements of fact and law on which it is founded having to be set out in a coherent and comprehensible fashion in the application for interim measures itself.[113] An

---

the decision of the appointing authority taken in response to the complaint), see CST (order of the President of 14 December 2006), Case F-120/06 R *Dálnoky v Commission* [2006] E.C.R.-SC I-A-1-187, paras 44–50.

[110] See, e.g. ECJ, Case 108/63 *Merlini v High Authority* [1965] E.C.R. 1, at 9; ECJ, Case 32/64 *Italy v Commission* [1965] E.C.R. 365, at 372; CFI (order of 19 June 1995), Case T-107/94 *Kik v Council and Commission* [1995] E.C.R. II-1717; CFI, Case T-140/94 *Gutiérrez de Quijano y Llorens v European Parliament* [1996] E.C.R.-SC II-689, para. 32 (English abstract at I-A-241); CFI, Case T-146/95 *Bernardi v European Parliament* [1996] E.C.R. II-769, para. 30; CFI (order of 29 September 1997), Case T-4/97 *D'Orazio and Hublau v Commission* [1997] E.C.R. II-1505, para.14.

[111] See ECJ Rules of Procedure, Arts 120–122; EGC Rules of Procedure, Arts 43 and 44.

[112] Since failure to comply with these provisions of the Rules of Procedure constitutes an absolute bar to proceedings, the Judge hearing the application for interim measures may consider of his or her own motion whether they have been complied with: see, e.g. CFI (order of the President of 7 May 2002), Case T-306/01 R *Aden and Others v Council and Commission* [2002] E.C.R. II-2387, para. 49; CFI (order of the President of 25 April 2008), Case T-41/08 R *Vakakis International v Commission* [2008] E.C.R. II-66*, Summ. pub., para. 41; CFI (order of the President of 25 May 2009), Case T-159/09 R *Biofrescos v Commission* [2009] E.C.R. II-63, para. 15; CFI (order of the President of 2 July 2009), Case T-246/09 R *Insula v Commission* [2009] E.C.R. II-101*, Summ. pub., para. 6.

[113] See, e.g. ECJ (order of the President of 30 April 2010), Case C-113/09 P(R) *Zeigler v Commission* [2010] E.C.R. I-50*, Summ. pub., para. 13; ECJ (order of the President of 11 November 2011), Case C-530/10 P(R) *Nencini v European Parliament* [2011] E.C.R. I-172*, Summ. pub., para. 28; CFI (order of the President of 15 January 2001), Case T-236/00 R *Stauner and Others v European Parliament and Commission* [2001] E.C.R. II-15, para. 34; CFI (order of the President of 7 May 2002), Case T-306/01 R *Aden and Others v Council and Commission* [2002] E.C.R. II-2387, paras 52–53: the same goes with respect to the presentation of observations on an application for interim relief which are lodged by the defendant; CFI (order of the President of 13 December 2006), Case T-288/06 R *Huta Czestochowa v Commission* [2006] E.C.R. II-101*, Summ. pub., para. 12; CFI (order of the President of 4 December 2007), Case T-326/07 R *Cheminova and Others v Commission* [2007] E.C.R. II-4877, para. 66; EGC (order of the President of 12 May 2010), Case T-30/10 R *Reagens v Commission* [2010] E.C.R. II-83*, Summ. pub., para. 50; EGC (order of the President of 26 May 2010), Case T-15/10 R *Ngele v Commission* [2010] E.C.R. II-102*, Summ. pub., para. 16; EGC (order of the President of 25 October 2010), Case T-353/10 R *Lito Maieftiko v Commission* [2010] E.C.R. II-238*, Summ. pub., para. 11; EGC

application for interim measures that fails to satisfy these requirements will be deemed inadmissible.[114]

(order of the President of 14 October 2011), Case T-489/11 R *Rousse Industry v Commmission* [2011] E.C.R. II-362*, Summ. pub., para. 17 (concerning urgency); EGC (order of the President of 14 December 2011), Case T-552/11 R *Lito Maieftiko Gynaikologiko kai Cheirourgiki Kentro v Commission* [2011] E.C.R. II-453*, Summ. pub., para. 11; EGC (order of the President of 23 April 2012), Case T-163/12 R *Ternvsky v Council*, not reported, para. 10; EGC (order of the President of 8 May 2012), Case T-134/12 R *Investigacion y Desarollo en Soluciones y Servicios IT v Commission*, not reported, para. 10. It follows that it is not for the Judge hearing the application for interim measures to seek, in the place of the party concerned, those matters contained in, *inter alia*, the annexes or the main application which would support the application for interim measures: see, e.g. EGC (order of the President of 29 July 2010), Case T-252/10 R *Cross Czech v Commission* [2010] E.C.R. II-157*, Summ. pub., paras 14–15; EGC (order of the President of 31 August 2010), Case T-299/10 R *Babcock Noell v The European joint undertaking for ITER and the Development of Fusion Energy* [2010] E.C.R. II-161*, Summ. pub., para. 30 (and citations therein). It also follows that an application for interim measures may not validly be supplemented by a document lodged subsequently by the party seeking interim relief, possibly in response to observations from the opposing party to the proceedings, in order to remedy any deficiencies: see, e.g. ECJ (order of the President of 10 April 2010), Case C-113/09 P(R) *Zeigler v Commission* [2010] E.C.R. I-50*, Summ. pub., paras 14–21; ECJ (order of the President of 16 December 2010), Case C-373/10 P(R) *Almamet v Commission* [2010] E.C.R. I-171*, Summ. pub., para. 21; ECJ (order of the President of 11 November 2011), Case C-530/10 P(R) *Nencini v European Parliament* [2011] E.C.R. I-172*, Summ. pub., paras 31–39; CFI (order of the President of 23 January 2009), Case T-352/08 R *Pannon v Commission* [2009] E.C.R. II-9*, Summ. pub., paras 31–32; EGC (order of the President of 12 May 2010), Case T-30/10 R *Reagens v Commission* [2010] E.C.R. II-83*, Summ. pub., para. 51.

[114] See, e.g. CFI (order of the President of 2 August 2006), Case T-163/06 R *BA.L.A. di Lanciotti Vittoria & C. Sas and Others v Commission* [2006] E.C.R. II-59*, Summ. pub., paras 40–42; CFI (order of the President of 13 December 2006), Case T-288/06 R *Huta Czestochowa v Commission* [2006] E.C.R. II-101*, Summ. pub., paras 14–21 (concerning urgency); CFI (order of the President of 19 February 2008), Case C-444/07 R *CPEM v Commission* [2008] E.C.R. II-27*, Summ. pub., paras 26–33 (concerning *prima facie* case); CFI (order of the President of 14 November 2008), Case T-398/08 R *Stowarzyszenie Autorow ZAiKS v Commission* [2008] E.C.R. II-266*, Summ. pub., paras 30–43 (concerning urgency); CFI (order of the President of 25 May 2009), Case T-159/09 R *Biofrescos v Commission* [2009] E.C.R. II-63*, Summ. pub., paras 16–20 (concerning *prima facie* case); CFI (order of the President of 8 June 2009), Case T-149/09 R *Dover v European Parliament* [2009] E.C.R. II-66*, Summ. pub., paras 20–22 (concerning urgency); CFI (order of the President of 2 July 2009), Case T-246/09 R *Insula v Commission* [2009] E.C.R. II-101*, Summ. pub., paras 11–15 (concerning *prima facie* case); CFI (order of the President of 13 July 2009), Case T-238/09 R *Sniace v Commission* [2009] E.C.R. II-125*, Summ. pub., paras 19–22; EGC (order of the President of 26 May 2010), Case T-15/10 R *Ngele v Commission* [2010] E.C.R. II-102*, Summ. pub., paras 17–22 (concerning *prima facie* case and urgency); EGC (order of the President of 30 June 2010), Case T-61/10 R *Sanchez v European Parliament and Commission* [2010] E.C.R. II-120*, Summ. pub., paras 16–19 (concerning *prima facie* case); EGC (order of the President of 29 July 2010), Case T-252/10 R *Cross Czech v Commission* [2010] E.C.R. II-157*, Summ. pub., paras 12–16 (concerning *prima facie* case); EGC (order of the President of 25 October 2010), Case T-353/10 R *Lito Maieftiko v Commission* [2010] E.C.R. II-238*, Summ. pub., paras 12–19 (concerning urgency); EGC (order of the President of 14 December 2011), Case T-552/11 R *Lito Maieftiko Gynaikologiko kai Cheirourgiki Kentro v Commission* [2011] E.C.R. II-453*, Summ. pub., paras 13–20 (concerning urgency); EGC (order of the President of 23 April 2012), Case T-163/12 R *Ternvsky v Council*, not reported, paras 11–20 (concerning urgency); EGC (order of the President of 8 May 2012), Case T-134/12 R *Investigacion y Desarollo en Soluciones y Servicios IT v Commission*, not reported, paras 11–19 (concerning urgency); EGC (order of the President of 4 September 2012), Case T-213/12 R *Elitaliana v Eulex Kosovo*, not reported, paras 7–14, 16 (concerning urgency). For some examples in which an application for interim measures has been held to comply with these requirements, see CFI (order of the President of 13 July 2006), Case T-11/06 R *Romana Tabacchi v Commission* [2006] E.C.R. II-2491, paras 47–50, 61; CFI (order of the President of 2 May 2007), Case T-297/05 R *IPK International—World Tourism marking Consultants v Commission* [2007] E.C.R. II-37*, Summ. pub., paras 34–40; CFI (order of the President of 7 June 2007), Case T-346/06 R *IMS v Commission* [2007] E.C.R. II-1781, paras 64–69; CFI (order of the President of 28 March 2007), Case T-384/06 R *IBP and International Building Products France v Commission* [2007] E.C.R. II-30*, Summ. pub., paras 36–37; CFI (order of the President of 4 December 2007), Case T-326/07 R *Cheminova and Others v Commission*

This means that it is not sufficient for the application for interim measures merely to refer to the pleas and arguments set out in the pleadings in the main proceedings, and where some of the grounds contained in the application for interim measures (as well as the observations submitted in response to the application by the defendant) are not set out in a manner consistent with these requirements, they will not be taken into consideration in order to establish the points of fact and law to which they relate.[115] It should also be pointed out that a head of claim in an application for interim measures inviting the Judge hearing the application to adopt any other measures considered appropriate without providing further details has generally been held vague and imprecise in character, and thus is inadmissible.[116]

(c) 'Variation' of the subject of the application

13.30 The application may be 'varied' in the course of the oral procedure if the variation falls within the framework of the measures requested in the application for interim relief and has less of an effect on the defendant.[117] If those requirements are not fulfilled and the varied

---

[2007] E.C.R. II-4877, paras 67–68; CFI (order of the President of 11 December 2007), Case T-349/07 R *FMC Chemical SPRL and Others v Commission* [2007] E.C.R. II-169*, Summ. pub., paras 66–69; CFI (order of the President of 11 December 2007), Case T-350/07 R *FMC Chemical SPRL and Others v Commission* [2007] E.C.R. II-170*, Summ. pub., paras 68–71.

[115] See, e.g. CFI (order of the President of 15 January 2001), Case T-236/00 R *Stauner and Others v European Parliament and Commission* [2001] E.C.R. II-15, paras 36–38 (and citations therein); CFI (order of the President of 7 May 2002), Case T-306/01 R *Aden and Others v Council and Commission* [2002] E.C.R. II-2387, paras 48, 54–55; CFI (order of the President of 25 April 2008), Case T-41/08 R *Vakakis International v Commission* [2008] E.C.R. II-66*, Summ. pub., paras 40, 45–46. See also CFI (order of the President of 14 November 2008), Case T-422/08 R *Sacem v Commission* [2008] E.C.R. II-271*, Summ. pub., paras 27–28: where the applicant in the formal conclusions of the application seeks the suspension of the contested measure in its entirety but the arguments contained therein as regards urgency are limited to certain provisions of the contested measure, the President of the Court held the application inadmissible insofar as the applicant invokes urgency in relation to other provisions of the contested measure for which the essential elements of fact and law in relation to that requirement are lacking.

[116] See, e.g. CFI (order of the President of 12 February 1996), Case T-228/95 R *S. Lehrfreund v Council and Commission* [1996] E.C.R. II-111, para. 58; CFI (order of the President of 2 July 2004), Case T-76/04 R *Bactria v Commission* [2004] E.C.R. II-2025, paras 49–50, confirmed on appeal in ECJ (order of the President of 13 December 2004), Case C-380/04 P(R) *Bactria v Commission,* not reported, paras 19–21; CFI (order of 2 July 2004), Case T-78/04 R *Sumitomo Chemical v Commission* [2004] E.C.R. II-2049, paras 49–50, confirmed on appeal in ECJ (order of the President of 13 December 2004), Case C-380/04 P(R) *Sumitomo Chemical v Commission,* not reported, paras 19–21; CFI (order of the President of 16 March 2007), Case T-345/05 R *V v European Parliament* [2007] E.C.R. II-25*, Summ. pub., paras 61–63; CFI (order of the President of 3 May 2007), Case T-12/07 R *Polimeri Europa v Commission* [2007] E.C.R. II-38*, Summ. pub., paras 56–58; CFI (order of the President of 22 November 2007), Case T-345/05 R III *V v European Parliament* [2007] E.C.R. II-160*, Summ. pub., para. 34; EGC (order of the President of 17 December 2009), Case T-396/09 R *Vereniging Milieudefensie and Stichting Stop Luchtverontreiniging Utrecht v Commission* [2009] E.C.R. II-246*, Summ. pub., para. 36; EGC (order of the President of 26 March 2010), Case T-16/10 R *Alisei v Commission* [2010] E.C.R. II-50*, Summ. pub., para. 27; EGC (order of the President of 23 January 2012), Case T-607/11 R *Henkel and Henkel France v Commission,* not reported, para. 22; EGC (order of the President of 4 September 2012), Case T-213/12 R *Elitaliana v Eulex Kosovo,* not reported, para. 15. Compare CFI (order of the President of 18 March 2008), Case T-411/07 R *Aer Lingus Group v Commission* [2008] E.C.R. II-411, paras 52–53 (finding that where the content of the measures sought by the applicant is sufficiently clear from the rest of the application, the Judge hearing the application may conclude that the request is not vague and imprecise in nature and thus consider it admissible). In some cases, the applicant will request such relief, but the Judge hearing the application for interim measures does not appear to deal with this claim in the reasoned order: see, e.g. EGC (order of the President of 26 March 2010), Case T-1/10 R *SNF SAS v ECHA* [2010] E.C.R. II-47*, Summ. pub., para. 17. See also CST (order of the President of 30 January 2008), Case F-64/07 R *S v European Parliament* [2008] E.C.R.-SC I-A-1-11, paras 39–40 (holding inadmissible the applicant's head of claim requesting suspension of acts subsequent, precedent, concomitant, or otherwise connected to the contested act as vague and imprecise).

[117] ECJ (order of 29 June 1993), Case C-280/93 R *Germany v Council* [1993] E.C.R. I-3667, para.15.

application substantially differs in kind from the original application, the application to vary the initial request for interim measures will be inadmissible.[118]

D. Substantive requirements

(1) General

(a) Three conditions

Three substantive requirements have to be met if the application for interim measures is to be granted: (1) the application must establish a *prima facie* case, which means that the application in the main proceedings with which it is associated must, at first sight, have a reasonable chance of succeeding (*fumus boni juris*); (2) the application must be urgent; and (3) the applicant's interest in the imposition of interim measures must outweigh the other interests at stake in the proceedings.

13.31

The first two requirements are set forth in Art. 160(3) of the ECJ Rules of Procedure and Art. 104(2) of the EGC Rules of Procedure. The third emerged from the case-law, sometimes in connection with the determination whether the application in the main proceedings is potentially well-founded or with the urgency of the application for interim relief. Accordingly, there is often language found in the case-law to the effect that the Judge hearing the application for interim measures must, where appropriate, balance the interests concerned.[119] Noticeably, in some cases, no explicit reference is made to the balance of

---

[118] ECJ (order of 29 June 1993), Case C-280/93 R *Germany v Council* [1993] E.C.R. I-3667, para. 16.

[119] For some examples, see ECJ (order of the President of 29 April 2005), Case C-404/04 P(R) *Technische Glaswerke Ilmenau v Commission* [2005] E.C.R. I-3539, para. 11; ECJ (order of the President of 28 February 2008), Case C-479/07 *France v Council* [2008] E.C.R. I-39*, Summ. pub., para. 16; ECJ (order of the President of 24 April 2008), Case C-76/08 R *Commission v Malta* [2008] E.C.R. I-64*, Summ. pub., para. 21; ECJ (order of the President of 10 December 2009), Case C-573/08 R *Commission v Italy* [2009] E.C.R. I-217*, Summ. pub., para. 11; ECJ (order of the President of 31 January 2011), Case C-404/10 P-R *Commission v Editions Odile Jacob* [2011] E.C.R. I-6*, Summ. pub., para. 19; ECJ (order of the President of 18 April 2012), Case C-656/11 R *United Kingdom v Council*, not reported, para. 27; ECJ (order of the President of 14 June 2012), Case C-644/11 P(R) *Qualitest v Council*, not reported, para.61 (and further citations therein); EGC (order of the President of 29 July 2011), Case T-292/11 R *Cemex SAB de CV and Others v Commission* [2011] E.C.R. II-243*, Summ. pub., para. 16; EGC (order of the President of 5 October 2011), Case T-422/11 R *Computer Resources International (Luxembourg) v Commission* [2011] E.C.R. II-348*, Summ. pub., para. 15; EGC (order of the President of 12 December 2011), Case T-579/11 R *Akhras v Council* [2011] E.C.R. II-441*, Summ. pub., para. 16; EGC (order of the President of 22 December 2011), Case T-593/11 R *Al-Chihabi v Council* [2011] E.C.R. II-465*, Summ. pub., para. 15; EGC (order of the President of 25 January 2012), Case T-637/11 R *Euris Consult v European Parliament*, not reported, para. 11; EGC (order of the President of 13 February 2012), Case T-601/11 R *Dansk Automat Brancheforening v Commission*, not reported, para. 18; EGC (order of the President of 16 February 2012), Case T-656/11 R *Morison Menon Chartered Accountants and Others v Council*, not reported, para. 14. In the case-law on proceedings for interim relief before the Civil Service Tribunal, the approach to the balance of interests requirement is similar, either mentioned as being applied 'where appropriate' (see, e.g. CST (order of the President of 10 September 2010), Case F-62/10 R *Esders v Commission*, not reported, para.42; CST (order of the President of 15 December 2010), Joined Cases F-95/10 R and F-105/10 R *Bömcke v EIB* not reported, para. 45), or not mentioned in the recitation of the main requirements to be fulfilled for an application for interim measures to succeed (see, e.g. CST (order of the President of 17 December 2008), Case F-80/08 R *Wenig v Commission* [2008] E.C.R.-SC I-A-1-479, paras 20–21; CST (order of the President of 18 December 2009), Case F-92/09 R *U v European Parliament* [2009] E.C.R.-SC I-A-1-2771, paras 41–42, but note that in this latter case, the President of the CST still undertook assessment of the balance of interests (see paras 96–101). Noticeably, in recent case-law, the 'where appropriate' language is even dropped, making clear it is incumbent on the Judge hearing the application to carry out a balance of interests (see, e.g. CST (order of the President of 6 June 2012), Case F-54/12 R *Carosi v Commission*, not reported, para. 19; CST (order of the President of 14 June 2012), Case F-38/12 R *BP v EU Fundamental Rights Agency*, not reported, para.19.)

interests as part of the recitation of the main requirements that must be satisfied for the grant of interim relief.[120] Yet, even where it is not mentioned in this regard, the Judge hearing the application for interim measures may proceed to examine whether it is satisfied.[121]

(b) Overall assessment

13.32   In the context of the overall assessment of these requirements, the Judge hearing the application for interim measures enjoys a broad discretion and is free to determine, having regard to the particular circumstances of the case, the manner and the order in which these requirements are to be examined, there being no rule of Union law imposing a pre-established scheme of analysis within which the need to order interim measures must be analysed and assessed.[122]

Furthermore, these requirements are cumulative, with the result that if one of them is not satisfied, the application for interim measures is dismissed.[123] In practice, the determination

---

[120] For some examples, see ECJ (order of the President of 19 July 2012), Case C-110/12 P(R) *Akhras v Council*, not reported, para. 21; EGC (order of the President of 26 March 2010), Case T-16/10 R *Alisei v Commission* [2010] E.C.R. II-50*, Summ. pub., para. 12; EGC (order of the President of 30 June 2010), Case T-61/10 R *Sanchez v European Parliament and Commission* [2010] E.C.R. II-120*, Summ. pub., para. 13; EGC (order of the President of 22 July 2010), Case T-271/10 R *H v Council and Commission* [2010] E.C.R. II-154*, Summ. pub., para.14; EGC (order of the President of 17 February 2011), Case T-486/10 R *Iberdrola v Commission*, not reported, para. 45; EGC (order of the President of 17 February 2011), Case T-490/10 R *Endesa and Endesa Generacion v Commission*, not reported, para. 44; EGC (order of the President of 23 April 2012), Case T-163/12 R *Ternavsky v Council*, not reported, para. 8; EGC (order of the President of 23 January 2012), Case T-607/11 R *Henkel and Henkel France v Commission*, not reported, para. 14; EGC (order of the President of 8 May 2012), Case T-134/12 R *Investigacion y Desarrollo en Soluciones y Servicios IT v Commission*, not reported, para. 8.

[121] See, e.g. CFI (order of the President of 11 October 2007), Case T-120/07 R *MB Immobilien Verwaltungs v Commission* [2007] E.C.R. II-130*, Summ. pub., paras 20, 23, 44–49. Moreover, in cases where the balance of interests is mentioned, the President of the Court has emphasized that even supposing certain heads of claim could be deemed urgent, the interim relief sought may only be granted if a balance of interests weighs in the applicant's favour: see, e.g. CFI (order of the President of 18 October 2007), Case T-238/07 R *Ristic and Others v Commission* [2007] E.C.R. II-134*, Summ. pub., para. 71; CFI (order of the President of 30 April 2008), Case T-65/08 R *Spain v Commission* [2008] E.C.R. II-69*, Summ. pub., para. 81; EGC (order of the President of 31 August 2010), Case T-299/10 R *Babcock Noell v The European joint undertaking for ITER and the Development of Fusion Energy* [2010] E.C.R. II-161*, Summ. pub., para. 63; EGC (order of the President of 24 November 2011), Case T-471/11 R *Editions Odile Jacob v Commission* [2011] E.C.R. II-428*, Summ. pub., para. 73.

[122] See, e.g. ECJ (order of the President of 19 July 1995), Case C-149/95 P (R) *Commission v Atlantic Container Line and Others* [1995] E.C.R. I-2165, para. 23; ECJ (order of the President of 17 December 1998), Case C-364/98 P (R) *Emesa Sugar v Commission* [1998] E.C.R. I-8815, para. 44; ECJ (order of the President of 31 January 2011), Case C-404/10 P-R *Commission v Editions Odile Jacob* [2011] E.C.R. I-6*, Summ. pub., para. 21; ECJ (order of the President of 14 June 2012), Case C-644/11 P(R) *Qualitest v Council*, not reported, para. 63; ECJ (order of the President of ECJ (order of the President of 19 July 2012), Case C-110/12 P(R) *Akhras v Council*, not reported, para. 23 (and citations therein); EGC (order of the President of 29 July 2011), Case T-292/11 R *Cemex SAB de CV and Others v Commission* [2011] E.C.R. II-243*, Summ. pub., para. 17; EGC (order of the President of 5 October 2011), Case T-422/11 R *Computer Resources International (Luxembourg) v Commission* [2011] E.C.R. II-348*, Summ. pub., para. 15; EGC (order of the President of 12 December 2011), Case T-579/11 R *Akhras v Council* [2011] E.C.R. II-441*, Summ. pub., para. 16; EGC (order of the President of 22 December 2011), Case T-593/11 R *Al-Chihabi v Council* [2011] E.C.R. II-465*, Summ. pub., para. 15; EGC (order of the President of 23 January 2012), Case T-607/11 R *Henkel and Henkel France v Commission*, not reported, para. 14; EGC (order of the President of 25 January 2012), Case T-637/11 R *Euris Consult v European Parliament*, not reported, para. 11; EGC (order of the President of 13 February 2012), Case T-601/11 R *Dansk Automat Brancheforening v Commission*, not reported, para. 18; EGC (order of the President of 16 February 2012), Case T-656/11 R *Morison Menon Chartered Accountants and Others v Council*, not reported, para. 15; CST (order of the President of 19 April 2012), Case F-16/12 R *Kimman v Commission*, not reported, para.16; CST (order of the President of 6 June 2012), Case F-54/12 R *Carosi v Commission*, not reported, para. 20.

[123] See, e.g. EGC (order of the President of 12 December 2011), Case T-579/11 R *Akhras v Council* [2011] E.C.R. II-441*, Summ. pub., paras 40–43 (the existence of a *prima facie* case by itself is not sufficient

of the urgency of the interim measures sought is often decisive and the other requirements do not have to be considered[124] or are merely considered on a subsidiary basis.[125]

for the grant of the interim relief requested). See also CST (order of the President of 10 September 2007), Case F-83/07 R *Zangerl-Posselt v Commission* [2007] E.C.R.-SC I-A-1-235, paras 29–30. There are two approaches taken in recent case-law. The first is where reference is made only to the two requirements of *prima facie* case and urgency, after which it is stated that these two conditions are cumulative such that if either of them is absent, the application for interim measures is dismissed. This is so even where mention is made of the balance of interests 'where appropriate' thereafter (see the first group of cases). The second is where all three requirements are listed, after which it is stated that the requirements are cumulative, which implicitly includes balance of interests (see the second group of cases). The first approach may be due more to clerical oversight or judicial economy of language, than to being intended to exclude the importance of the balance of interests, especially since even if the balance of interests is not mentioned by the President of the Court, it is nonetheless mentioned in the arguments of the parties (see, e.g. EGC (order of the President of 17 December 2009), Case T-396/09 R *Vereniging Milieudefensie and Stichting Stop Luchtverontreiniging Utrecht v Commission* [2009] E.C.R. II-246*, Summ. pub.), and even where it is mentioned that the balance of interests is only assessed 'where appropriate', the President of the Court has stressed that it must be fulfilled (see, e.g. EGC (order of the President of 31 August 2010), Case T-299/10 R *Babcock Noell v The European joint undertaking for ITER and the Development of Fusion Energy* [2010] E.C.R. II-161*, Summ. pub., para. 63). For some citations mentioning cumulative only in relation to first two requirements: see, e.g. ECJ (order of the President of 17 December 1998), Case C-364/98 P (R) *Emesa Sugar v Commission* [1998] E.C.R. I-8815, para. 47; ECJ (order of the Vice-President of 7 March 2013), Case C-551/12 P(R) *EDF v Commission*, not reported, para. 21; EGC (order of the President of 29 July 2011), Case T-292/11 R *Cemex SAB de CV and Others v Commission* [2011] E.C.R. II-243*, Summ. pub., para. 16; EGC (order of the President of 5 October 2011), Case T-422/11 R *Computer Resources International (Luxembourg) v Commission* [2011] E.C.R. II-348*, Summ. pub., para. 14; EGC (order of the President of 12 December 2011), Case T-579/11 R *Akhras v Council* [2011] E.C.R. II-441*, Summ. pub., para. 15; EGC (order of the President of 22 December 2011), Case T-593/11 R *Al-Chihabi v Council* [2011] E.C.R. II-465*, Summ. pub., para. 14; EGC (order of the President of 25 January 2012), Case T-637/11 R *Euris Consult v European Parliament*, not reported, para. 10; EGC (order of the President of 13 February 2012), Case T-601/11 R *Dansk Automat Brancheforening v Commission*, not reported, para. 17; EGC (order of the President of 16 February 2012), Case T-656/11 R *Morison Menon Chartered Accountants and Others v Council*, not reported, para. 14; EGC (order of the President of 23 April 2012), Case T-163/12 R *Ternavsky v Council*, not reported, para. 8; EGC (order of the President of 8 May 2012), Case T-134/12 R *Investigacion y Desarrollo en Soluciones y Servicios IT v Commission*, not reported, para. 8. For some citations listing all three requirements and then stating that they are cumulative: see, e.g. ECJ (order of the President of 29 April 2005), Case C-404/04 P(R) *Technsche Glaswerke Ilmenau v Commission* [2005] E.C.R. I-3539, para. 11; ECJ (order of the President of 28 February 2008), Case C-479/07 *France v Council* [2008] E.C.R. I-39*, Summ. pub., para. 17; ECJ (order of the President of 24 April 2008), Case C-76/08 R *Commission v Malta* [2008] E.C.R. I-64*, Summ. pub., para. 22; ECJ (order of the President of 10 December 2009), Case C-573/08 R *Commission v Italy* [2009] E.C.R. I-217*, Summ. pub., para. 12; ECJ (order of the President of 31 January 2011), Case C-404/10 P-R *Commission v Editions Odile Jacob* [2011] E.C.R. I-6*, Summ. pub., para. 20; ECJ (order of the President of 18 April 2012), Case C-656/11 R *United Kingdom v Council*, not reported, para. 28; ECJ (order of the President of 14 June 2012), Case C-644/11 P(R) *Qualitest v Council*, not reported, para. 62 (and further citations therein).

[124] See, e.g. ECJ (order of the President of 28 February 2008), Case C-479/07 R *France v Council* [2008] E.C.R. I-39*, Summ. pub., para. 31; ECJ (order of the President of 18 April 2012), Case C-656/11 R *United Kingdom v Council*, not reported, para.48; EGC (order of the President of 26 March 2010), Case T-6/10 R *Sviluppo Globale v Commission* [2010] E.C.R. II-48*, Summ. pub., para. 34; EGC (order of the President of 9 June 2010), Case T-79/10 R *COLT Télécommunications France v Commission* [2010] E.C.R. II-107*, Summ. pub., para. 46; EGC (order of the President of 16 February 2011), Case T-560/10 R *Nencini v European Parliament* [2011] E.C.R. II-21*, Summ. pub., para. 18; EGC (order of the President of 9 June 2011), Case T-87/11 R *GRP Security v Court of Auditors* [2011] E.C.R. II-170*, Summ. pub., para. 41; EGC (order of the President of 8 September 2011), Case T-439/10 R *Fulmen v Council* [2011] E.C.R. II-260*, Summ. pub., para. 35; EGC (order of the President of 5 October 2011), Case T-422/11 R *Computer Resources International (Luxembourg) v Commission* [2011] E.C.R. II-348*, Summ. pub., para. 43; EGC (order of the President of 18 November 2011), Case T-116/11 R *EMA v Commission* [2011] E.C.R. II-412*, Summ. pub., para. 23; EGC (order of the President of 12 December 2011), Case T-579/11 R *Akhras v Council* [2011] E.C.R. II-441*, Summ. pub., paras 39–43.

[125] See, e.g. EGC (order of the President of 17 February 2011), Case T-484/10 R *Gas Natural Fenosa SDG v Commission*, not reported, para. 94; EGC (order of the President of 17 February 2011), Case T-486/10 R

As noted in the case-law, there is some linkage between the three substantive requirements,[126] for instance, as regards the effect of the relative strength or weakness of the *prima facie* case on the assessment of urgency and, if appropriate, of the balance of interests,[127] or the fact that one of the criteria for establishing urgency also constitutes the first element in the comparison carried out in assessing the balance of interests.[128] Nevertheless, it remains the case that each requirement is distinct and must be sufficiently demonstrated by the applicant.[129]

Iberdrola v Commission, not reported, para. 91; EGC (order of the President of 17 February 2011), Case T-490/10 R *Endesa and Endesa Generacion v Commission*, not reported, para. 87; EGC (order of the President of 17 February 2010), Case T-520/10 R *Comunidad Autónoma de Galicia v Commission* [2011] E.C.R. II-27*, Summ. pub., para. 79; ECJ (order of the President of 14 June 2012), Case C-644/11 P(R) *Qualitest FZE v Council*, not reported, para. 71.

[126] Likewise, it is sometimes found that the dismissal of the application for interim measures by reason of the failure to satisfy one of the requirements (typically urgency) is corroborated or supported by analysis of another (namely, balance of interests): see, e.g. CFI (order of the President of 14 March 2008), Case T-440/07 R *Huta Buczek v Commission* [2008] E.C.R. II-39*, Summ. pub., para.74; CFI (order of the President of 8 April 2008), Joined Cases T-54/08 R, T-87/08 R, T-88/08 R, and T-91/08 to T-93/08 R *Cyprus v Commission*, not reported, para. 79; CFI (order of the President of 22 December 2008), Case T-468/08 R *AES-Tisza v Commission* [2008] E.C.R. II-346*, Summ. pub., para. 60; CFI (order of the President of 23 January 2009), Case T-352/08 R *Pannon v Commission* [2009] E.C.R. II-9*, Summ. pub., para. 57; EGC (order of the President of 13 February 2012), Case T-601/11 R *Dansk Automat v Commission*, not reported, para. 46.

[127] See, e.g. ECJ (order of the President of 23 February 2001), Case C-445/00 R *Austria v Council* [2001] E.C.R. I-1461, para. 110; ECJ (order of the President of 31 July 2003), Case C-208/03 R *Le Pen v European Parliament* [2003] E.C.R. I-7939, para. 110 (and citations therein); CFI (order of the President of 20 July 2006), Case T-411/06 R *Globe v Commission* [2006] E.C.R. II-2627, para. 140; CFI (order of the President of 7 June 2007), Case T-346/06 R *IMS v Commission* [2007] E.C.R. II-1781, para.147; CFI (order of the President of 15 November 2007), Case T-215/07 *Donnici v European Parliament* [2007] E.C.R. II-4673, para. 111 (appeal dismissed in ECJ (order of the President of 13 January 2009), Joined Cases C-512/07 P(R) and C-15/08 P(R) *Occhetto and European Parliament v Donnici* [2009] E.C.R. I-1).

[128] See, e.g. ECJ (order of the President of 31 July 2003), Case C-208/03 *Le Pen v European Parliament* [2003] E.C.R. I-7939, para. 106 (and citations therein); CFI (order of the President of 15 November 2007), Case T-215/07 R *Donnici v European Parliament* [2007] E.C.R. II-4673, para. 106 (appeal dismissed in ECJ (order of the President of 13 January 2009), Joined Cases C-512/07 P(R) and C-15/08 P(R) *Occhetto and European Parliament v Donnici* [2009] E.C.R. I-1); EGC (order of the President of 13 April 2011), Case T-393/10 R *Westfälische Drahtindustrie and Others v Commission* [2011] E.C.R. II-1697, para. 63. Findings as regards urgency have an impact on the scope of assessment of the balance of interests requirement: see, e.g. EGC (order of the President of 31 August 2010), Case T-299/10 R *Babcock Noell v The European joint undertaking for ITER and the Development of Fusion Energy* [2010] E.C.R. II-161*, Summ. pub., para. 66. In the context of control of concentrations, see CFI (order of the President of 30 April 2008), Case T-65/08 R *Spain v Commission* [2008] E.C.R. II-69*, Summ. pub., paras 82–89, particularly 87–88 (linking balance of interest assessment to showing of urgency and *fumus boni juris*).

[129] See, e.g. ECJ (order of the President of 31 January 2011), Case C-404/10 P-R *Commission v Editions Odile Jacob* [2011] E.C.R. I-6*, Summ. pub., para. 27; ECJ (order of the President of 14 December 2011), Case C-446/10 P(R) *Alcoa Transformazioni v Commission*, not reported, para. 66; ECJ (order of the President of 19 July 2012), Case C-110/12 P(R) *Akhras v Council*, not reported, para. 26; ECJ (order of the Vice-President of 7 March 2013), Case C-551/12 P(R) *EDF v Commission*, not reported, paras 24–25; CFI (order of the President of 2 August 2006), Case T-69/06 R *Aughinish Alumina v Commission* [2006] E.C.R. II-58*, Summ. pub., para. 84; CFI (order of the President of 2 May 2007), Case T-297/05 R *IPK International— World Tourism marking Consultants v Commission* [2007] E.C.R. II-37*, Summ. pub., para. 52; EGC (order of the President of 17 February 2011), Case T-484/10 R *Gas Natural Fenosa SDG v Commission*, not reported, para. 93; EGC (order of the President of 17 February 2011), Case T-486/10 R *Iberdrola v Commission*, not reported, para. 90; EGC (order of the President of 17 February 2011), Case T-490/10 R *Endesa and Endesa Generacion v Commission*, not reported, para. 86; EGC (order of the President of 22 December 2011), Case T-593/11 R *Al-Chihabi v Council* [2011] E.C.R. II-465*, Summ. pub., para. 41.

The Judge hearing applications for interim relief must proceed with the necessary care, in particular where the institution, body, office, or agency concerned has a discretion. According to the Court of Justice, the mere fact that a discretionary power is vested in the institution which adopted the contested act cannot in itself, in the absence of any consideration whether there is a *prima facie* case and of any balancing of the interests involved, determine requirements relating to the condition of urgency. To take a different approach would mean excluding, or at least restricting, legal protection in proceedings for interim relief where the act at issue was adopted pursuant to a broad discretionary power. The result could, in particular, be that provisional measures necessary to secure the effectiveness of the judgment in the main proceedings would be refused on the sole ground that the urgency was not indisputable in cases where there was a particularly strong *prima facie* case and the balance of interests was in favour of the party applying for the interim measures.[130]

It may be noted in this connection that the Judge hearing the application for interim relief is not required to reply explicitly to all the points of law and fact raised in the course of the interlocutory proceedings. It is sufficient that the reasons given validly justify the order given in the light of the circumstances of the case.[131]

(2) *Prima facie* case

(a) *Objective*

The requirement for a *prima facie* case to be made out (also referred to as *fumus boni juris*) is designed—just as in the case of the determination that the main application is not manifestly inadmissible—to prevent improper use being made of applications for interim relief (see para. 13.25).   **13.33**

(b) *Evolution towards* fumus non mali juris

The main case must have a reasonable chance of succeeding. According to the standard elaborated in recent case-law, in order to determine whether the condition for establishing a *prima facie* case is satisfied, it is necessary to carry out a *prima facie* examination of the substance of the pleas in law advanced by the applicant in support of the main action and to ascertain whether at least one of them is so weighty that it cannot be discounted, or cannot be discounted without a detailed examination, which is reserved for the decision on the merits.[132]   **13.34**

---

[130] ECJ (order of the President of 17 December 1998), Case C-364/98 P (R) *Emesa Sugar v Commission* [1998] E.C.R. I-8815, paras 50–51.

[131] See, e.g. ECJ (order of the President of 10 September 1997), Case C-248/97 P(R) *Chaves Fonseca Ferrão v Office for Harmonisation in the Internal Market (Trade Marks and Designs)* [1997] E.C.R. I-4729, para. 20; ECJ (order of the President of 31 August 2010), Case C-32/09 P(R) *Artisjus Magyar v Commission* [2010] E.C.R. I-107*, Summ. pub., para. 17 (and further citations therein). In exceptional circumstances, the Judge hearing applications for interim relief may order the suspension of the contested act or part of it pending additional information, which will enable him or her to assess the basic requirements for the grant of interim measures. Such suspension by way of 'intermediate order' is valid until such time as a decision is given terminating the proceedings for interim relief: see, e.g. CFI (order of the President of 15 December 1999), Case T-191/98 R II *Cho Yang Shipping v Commission* [1999] E.C.R. II-3909; CFI (order of the President of 14 October 2005), Case T-376/05 R *TEA CEGOS and STG v Commission*, not reported, paras 1–3.

[132] See, e.g. CFI (order of the President of 28 September 2007), Case T-257/07 R *France v Commission* [2007] E.C.R. II-4153, para. 59; CFI (order of the President of 15 November 2007), Case T-215/07 R *Donnici v European Parliament* [2007] E.C.R. II-4673, para. 39; CFI (order of the President of 28 April 2009), Case T-95/09 R *United Phosphorus v Commission*, not reported, para. 21; EGC (order of the President of 31 August 2010), Case T-299/10 R *Babcock Noell v The European joint undertaking for ITER and the Development of Fusion Energy* [2010] E.C.R. II-161*, Summ. pub., para. 16; EGC (order of the President of

Since the Judge hearing the application for interim relief may not prejudge the decision to be given in the main proceedings, his or her assessment in this regard will essentially be confined to whether the arguments put forward by the applicant in the main proceedings are, *prima facie*, basically sound or are clearly doomed to fail.[133] The application for interim measures must describe the pleas raised in the main proceedings sufficiently precisely to enable the Judge hearing the application to assess whether there is a *prima facie* case.[134]

The case-law, which is influenced greatly by the particular circumstances of the case concerned, exhibits in practice quite considerable subtle differences in the interpretation of this requirement. Sometimes, the Judge hearing the application for interim relief holds that there should be 'a strong presumption that the application in the main action is well founded'.[135] In other cases, it is found that there is substantial *prima facie* evidence that the applicant is in the right,[136] or that the legality of the contested act is, to say the least, doubtful.[137] In other—more recent—cases, the Judge hearing the applications for interim relief takes the opposite approach and finds that there are no grounds for holding that the substantive application is manifestly without foundation.[138] That formula expresses the

---

17 February 2011), Case T-484/10 *Gas Natural Fenosa SDG v Commission*, not reported, para. 55; EGC (order of the President of 17 February 2011), Case T-486/10 R *Iberdrola v Commission*, not reported, para. 49; EGC (order of the President of 17 February 2011), Case T-490/10 R *Endesa and Endesa Generacion v Commission*, not reported, para. 48; EGC (order of the President of 17 February 2010), Case T-520/10 R *Comunidad Autonoma de Galicia v Commission* [2011] E.C.R. II-27*, Summ. pub., para. 43; EGC (order of the President of 13 April 2011), Case T-393/10 R *Westfälische Drahtindustrie and Others v Commission* [2011] E.C.R. II-1697, para. 54 (and citations therein).

[133] See, e.g. CFI (order of the President of 5 April 1993), Case T-21/93 *Peixoto v Commission* [1993] E.C.R. II-463, para. 27, where it was found that the arguments advanced provided a 'firm basis' for the applicant's claims in the main proceedings. Cf. CFI (order of the President of 26 May 1998), Case T-60/98 R *Ecord Consortium v Commission* [1998] E.C.R. II-2205 (where the President held that the plea alleging infringement of the principle of protection of legitimate expectation appeared unfounded); CFI (order of the President of 22 November 2007), Case T-345/05 R III *V v European Parliament* [2007] E.C.R. II-160*, Summ. pub., paras 51, 56, 57, 63–65; CFI (order of the President of 15 July 2008), Case T-202/08 R *CLL Centres de langues v Commission* [2008] E.C.R. II-143*, Summ. pub., paras 31–53 (concluding, without prejudice to the appreciation of the Court in the main proceedings, that none of the pleas advanced by the applicant establish the existence of a *fumus boni juris*); CFI (order of the President of 7 January 2008), Case T-375/07 R *Pellegrini v Commission* [2008] E.C.R. II-1*, Summ. pub., para. 28 (where the President held that the applicant's arguments were not of a nature, *prima facie*, to prove that the institution concerned had committed a sufficiently serious violation of Union law so as to trigger an action for damages against the Union) (appeal dismissed in ECJ (order of the President of 17 July 2008), Case C-114/08 P(R) *Pellegrini v Commission* [2008] E.C.R. I-117*, Summ. pub.).

[134] If this is not done, the application for interim relief will be inadmissible.

[135] See, e.g. ECJ (order of the President of 20 October 1959), Joined Cases 43/59, 44/59, and 45/59 R *Von Lachmüller and Others v Commission* [1960] E.C.R. 489, at 492. See, to the same effect, ECJ (order of the President of 25 June 1963), Case 65/63 R *Prakash v Commission* [1965] E.C.R. 576, at 578, in which the President dismissed the application for interim measures on the ground that he did not have sufficient information to assess whether the main application was *prima facie* well-founded.

[136] See, e.g. ECJ (order of 4 March 1982), Case 42/82 R *Commission v France* [1982] E.C.R. 841, paras 13–14.

[137] See, e.g. ECJ (order of the President of 21 August 1981), Case 232/81 R *Agricola Commerciale Olio and Others v Commission* [1981] E.C.R. 2193, para. 5; CFI (order of the President of 7 June 2007), Case T-346/06 R *IMS v Commission* [2007] E.C.R. II-1781, para. 93 ('the factual and legal arguments put forward by the applicant in its first plea give rise . . . to very serious doubts as to the lawfulness of the contested measure' and thus application cannot be dismissed for failure to make a *prima facie* case).

[138] See, e.g. ECJ (order of the President of 16 January 1975), Case 3/75 R *Johnson & Firth Brown v Commission* [1975] E.C.R. 1, para. 1; ECJ (order of the President of 24 April 2008), Case C-76/08 R *Commission v Malta* [2008] E.C.R. I-64*, Summ. pub., para. 30 ('it cannot be ruled out from the outset that

view of the Judge hearing the application that the arguments put forward by the party seeking the interim measures cannot be rejected at that stage of the proceedings in the absence of an in-depth consideration of the case.[139] Consequently, *fumus boni juris* (i.e. the

---

the main action is well founded', even though the arguments relied upon by the Member State concerned in defending itself could not be disregarded); ECJ (order of the President of 10 December 2009), Case C-573/08 R *Commission v Italy* [2009] E.C.R. I-217*, Summ. pub., para. 15 ('les arguments présentés par la Commission ne paraissent pas, à première vue, dénués de fondement'); CFI (order of the President of 7 July 1998), Case T-65/98 R *Van den Bergh Foods v Commission* [1998] E.C.R. II-2641, para. 61 ('the pleas in law put forward by the applicants cannot be held *prima facie* to lack any foundation'); CFI (order of the President of 31 October 2000), Case T-83/00 R I *Hänseler v Commission* [2000] E.C.R. II-3563, para. 32 ('the pleas raised by the applicant do not *prima facie* appear to be entirely unfounded'); CFI (order of the President of 15 October 2004), Case T-193/04 R *Tillack v Commission* [2004] E.C.R. II-3575, paras 52–63 (the applicant had not shown that his application in the main proceedings was not manifestly unfounded); CFI (order of the President of 30 April 2008), Case T-65/08 R *Spain v Commission* [2008] E.C.R. II-69*, Summ. pub., paras 62–63; EGC (order of the President of 17 February 2011), Case T-484/10 *Gas Natural Fenosa SDG v Commission*, not reported, paras 69–70 (considering plea invoked by applicant *prima facie* not manifestly lacking all foundation); EGC (order of the President of 17 February 2011), Case T-486/10 R *Iberdrola v Commission*, not reported, paras 63–64 (considering plea invoked by applicant *prima facie* not manifestly lacking all foundation); EGC (order of the President of 17 February 2011), Case T-490/10 R *Endesa and Endesa Generacion v Commission*, not reported, paras 62–63 (considering plea invoked by applicant *prima facie* not manifestly lacking all foundation); EGC (order of the President of 17 February 2010), Case T-520/10 R *Comunidad Autónoma de Galicia v Commission* [2011] E.C.R. II-27*, Summ. pub., paras 57–58 (considering plea invoked by applicant *prima facie* not manifestly lacking all foundation); EGC (order of the President of 13 April 2011), Case T-393/10 R *Westfälische Drahtindustrie and Others v Commission* [2011] E.C.R. II-1697, paras 58–61 ('the plea in question does not appear at first sight to be totally without foundation').

[139] See, e.g. ECJ (order of the President of 13 June 1989), Case 56/89 R *Publishers Association v Commission* [1989] E.C.R. 1693, para. 33; ECJ (order of the President of 10 October 1989), Case 246/89 R *Commission v United Kingdom* [1989] E.C.R. 3125, para. 33; ECJ (order of the President of 28 June 1990), Case C-195/90 R *Commission v Germany* [1990] E.C.R. I-2715, para. 19; ECJ (order of the President of 31 January 1992), Case C-272/91 R *Commission v Italy* [1992] E.C.R. I-457, para. 24; ECJ (order of the President of 29 June 1993), Case C-280/93 R *Germany v Council* [1993] E.C.R. I-3667, para. 21; ECJ (order of the President of 19 July 1995), Case C-149/95 P(R) *Commission v Atlantic Container Line and Others* [1995] E.C.R. I-2165, para. 26; CFI (order of the President of 13 July 2006), Case T-11/06 R *Romana Tabacchi v Commission* [2006] E.C.R. II-2491, para. 68 ('foregoing considerations are sufficient for it to be concluded that at least some of the pleas put forward by the applicant are relevant *prima facie* and are, in any event, not entirely without merit'); CFI (order of the President of 19 July 2007), Case T-31/07 R *Du Pont de Nemours (France) and Others v Commission* [2007] E.C.R. II-2767, para. 143 ('applicants' two pleas—[...]which, because of their complexity, require an in-depth examination which cannot be conducted by the [J]udge hearing the application for interim relief—cannot, at first sight, be considered to be wholly unfounded'); CFI (order of the President of 28 September 2007), Case T-257/07 R *France v Commission* [2007] E.C.R. II-4153, para. 116 (finding applicant's claim 'does not seem, at least *prima facie*, irrelevant' and 'requires an in-depth examination which falls to be carried out by the [C]ourt adjudicating on the merits'); CFI (order of the President of 30 October 2008), Case T-257/07 R II *France v Commission* [2008] E.C.R. II-236*, Summ. pub., paras 75, 120; CFI (order of the President of 15 November 2007), Case T-215/07 R *Donnici v European Parliament* [2007] E.C.R. II-4673, para. 95 (appeal dismissed in ECJ (order of the President of 13 January 2009), Joined Cases C-512/07 P(R) and C-15/08 P(R) *Occhetto and European Parliament v Donnici* [2009] E.C.R. I-1); CFI (order of the President of 28 April 2009), Case T-95/09 R *United Phosphorus v Commission*, not reported, para. 31 (concluding that at the present stage the President cannot regard the heads of complaint invoked by the applicant as being '*prima facie* manifestly lacking in any merit' and thus 'appear, at first view, to be sufficiently relevant and serious as to constitute a *prima facie* case'); EGC (order of the President of 30 April 2010), Case T-18/10 R *Inuit Tapiriit Kanatami v European Parliament and Council* [2010] E.C.R. II-75*, Summ. pub., para. 95 (in light of 'complex and delicate issues calling for a detailed examination' raised by the action in the main proceedings, the President of the General Court 'cannot therefore, at the present stage, regard the heads of complaint invoked by the applicants as being manifestly lacking in any merit'); EGC (order of the President of 2 March 2011), Case T-392/09 R *l. garantovaná v Commission* [2011] E.C.R. II-33*, Summ. pub., paras 26–28 (finding plea concerned requires examination which cannot be resolved in

applicant must demonstrate that the allegations in the main action are *prima facie* well founded) has gradually evolved into *fumus non mali juris* (i.e. the applicant must demonstrate that the allegations in the main action are not obviously or manifestly unfounded). It would therefore seem that the Judge hearing interim applications is no longer required to be of the opinion that the main action will succeed in order to grant the measures requested, but merely has to be persuaded that the main application is reasonable.[140]

If the application in the main proceedings raises questions of legal principle which the Court has not yet had occasion to determine and the pleas adduced relate to those questions, the application will be regarded as not being manifestly unfounded, and the Judge hearing the application for interim relief will hold that the requirement of a *prima facie* case has been made out.[141]

(3) Urgency

(a) Urgency relates to damage liable to arise

13.35 An application for interim relief is urgent where the absence of the judgment in the main proceedings threatens to cause the person seeking the relief serious and irreparable damage. Under settled case-law, the urgency of an application for interim measures must be assessed in relation to the necessity for an interlocutory order to avoid serious and irreparable damage being caused to the party applying for those measures.[142] The urgent nature of the interim application is therefore determined by the nature of the damage that is liable to arise as a result of the duration of the main proceedings.[143] Accordingly, it was not by

---

interlocutory proceedings and appears at first sight to be sufficiently pertinent and serious to establish a *prima facie* case).

[140] See ECJ (order of the President of 31 January 1992), Case C-272/91 R *Commission v Italy* [1992] E.C.R. I-457, paras 19–24 (the President of the Court of Justice set forth the Commission's and Italy's arguments alongside each other before holding that the Commission's application did not appear to be without substance); CFI (order of the President of 15 April 1991), Case T-13/91 R *Harrison v Commission* [1991] E.C.R. II-179, para. 26: the President found first that the pleas adduced in support of the application in the main proceedings did not bear out the applicant's claims, before going on to hold that 'the applicant has failed to make out a *prima facie* case suggesting that his main application is well founded'.

[141] See, e.g. ECJ (order of the President of 31 January 1991), Case C-345/90 P-R *European Parliament v Hanning* [1991] E.C.R. I-231, paras 29–30; EGC (order of the President of 2 March 2011), Case T-392/09 R *l. garantovaná v Commission* [2011] E.C.R. II-33*, Summ. pub., paras 26–28, particularly para. 27.

[142] See, e.g. ECJ (order of the President of 24 March 2009), Case C-60/08 P(R) *Cheminova and Others v Commission* [2009] E.C.R. I-43*, Summ. pub., para. 62; ECJ (order of the President of 18 April 2012), Case C-656/11 R *United Kingdom v Council*, not reported, para. 31; CFI (order of the President of 27 August 2008), Case T-246/08 R *Melli Bank v Council*, not reported, para. 32; EGC (order of the President of 30 April 2010), Case T-18/10 R *Inuit Tapiriit Kanatami v European Parliament and Council* [2010] E.C.R. II-75*, Summ. pub., para. 105; EGC (order of the President of 5 October 2011), Case T-422/11 R *Computer Resources International (Luxembourg) v Commission* [2011] E.C.R. II-348*, Summ. pub., para. 19; EGC (order of the President of 25 January 2012), Case T-637/11 R *Euris Consult v European Parliament*, not reported, para. 15.

[143] ECJ (order of the President of 25 July 2000), Case C-377/98 R *Netherlands v European Parliament and Council* [2000] E.C.R. I-6229, para.45: it is not enough to allege infringement of fundamental rights in the abstract for the purposes of establishing that the harm which could result would necessarily be irreparable; CFI (order of the President of 1 February 2006), Case T-417/05 R *Endesa v Commission* [2006] E.C.R. II-18*, Summ. pub., paras 59–60 (allegation of damage to legal order insufficient to establish urgency); EGC (order of the President of 24 November 2011), Case T-471/11 R *Editions Odile Jacob v Commission* [2011] E.C.R. II-428*, Summ. pub., paras 37–39 (damage occasioned by the duration of proceedings before the Union courts not taken into account); EGC (order of the President of 22 December 2011), Case T-593/11 R *Al-Chihabi v Council* [2011] E.C.R. II-465*, Summ. pub., paras 42–43 (concluding that applicant unable to demonstrate urgency in relation to the harm linked to the violation of his fundamental rights).

chance that the serious and irreparable nature of the damage has emerged in the case-law as the yardstick for determining the urgency of an application for interim measures. This two-fold criterion of serious and irreparable damage is intended to restrict the grant of interim measures to cases in which the judgment in the main proceedings would not afford any legal redress in the absence of the interim relief sought.[144]

At present, the case-law does not provide any conclusive definitions of the two terms. Moreover, the seriousness and the irreparable nature of the alleged damage are not always considered separately.[145] Although the damage must be both serious and irreparable,[146] where one of the two criterion is found lacking, the Judge hearing the application for interim measures may consider that it is not necessary to examine the other.[147] The burden of proof is on the applicant to establish the existence of serious and irreparable damage and adduce the facts that are considered to found the prospect of such damage.[148]

(b) Serious and irreparable damage

First, the damage is irreparable where it will not be eliminated by a judgment in the main proceedings in favour of the applicant.[149] Save for exceptional circumstances, damage that is   **13.36**

---

[144] ECJ (order of the President of 28 November 1966), Case 29/66 R *Gutmann v Commission* [1967] E.C.R. 241, at 242.

[145] See the Opinion of Advocate-General F. Capotorti in ECJ (order of 28 March 1980), Joined Cases 24/80 and 97/80 R *Commission v France* [1980] E.C.R. 1319, at 1341–2, who equated irreparable with serious. In ECJ (order of the President of 26 June 1959), Case 31/59 R *Acciaieria e Tubificio di Brescia v High Authority* [1960] E.C.R. 98, at 99, the requirement for urgency was defined in terms of the applicant's having to show that the implementation of the contested measure would cause 'irreparable or at least serious damage'. But see, e.g. EGC (order of the President of 15 November 2011), Case T-269/11 R *Xeda International v Commission* [2011] E.C.R. II-389*, Summ. pub., para. 41 (pointing out that the applicant's arguments concerning whether alleged damage is reparable are irrelevant in the context of the examination of seriousness).

[146] See, e.g. ECJ (order of the President of 13 January 1978), Case 4/78 R *Salerno v Commission* [1978] E.C.R. 1, para. 11.

[147] See, e.g. EGC (order of the President of 30 April 2010), Case T-71/10 R *Xeda International v Commission* [2010] E.C.R. II-77*, Summ. pub., para. 59 (no seriousness); EGC (order of the President of 15 November 2011), Case T-269/11 R *Xeda International v Commission* [2011] E.C.R. II-389*, Summ. pub., para. 54 (no seriousness).

[148] See, e.g. ECJ (order of the President of 28 February 2008), Case C-479/07 R *France v Council* [2008] E.C.R. I-39*, Summ. pub., para. 19; ECJ (order of the President of 12 May 2010), Case C-5/10 P-R *Torresan v OHIM* [2010] E.C.R. I-64*, Summ. pub., para. 17; ECJ (order of the President of 19 July 2012), Case C-110/12 P(R) *Akhras v Council*, not reported, paras 42–43; CFI (order of the President of 7 June 2007), Case T-346/06 R *IMS v Commission* [2006] E.C.R. II-1781, para. 123; CFI (order of the President of 11 December 2007), Case T-349/07 R *FMC Chemical and Others v Commission* [2007] E.C.R. II-169*, Summ. pub., para. 98; CFI (order of the President of 11 December 2007), Case T-350/07 R *FMC Chemical v Commission* [2007] E.C.R. II-170*, Summ. pub., para. 109; CFI (order of the President of 27 August 2008), Case T-246/08 R *Melli Bank v Council*, not reported, para. 32; CFI (order of the President of 8 June 2009), Case T-149/09 R *Dover v European Parliament* [2009] E.C.R. II-66*, Summ. pub., paras 25–26; EGC (order of the President of 30 April 2010), Case T-18/10 R *Inuit Tapiriit Kanatami v European Parliament and Council* [2010] E.C.R. II-75*, Summ. pub., paras 105–106; EGC (order of the President of 25 January 2012), Case T-637/11 R *Euris Consult v European Parliament*, not reported, para. 15. With particular regard to the burden of proof in the context of financial damage, see also, e.g. EGC (order of the President of 9 June 2011), Case T-62/06 RENV-R *Eurallumina v Commission* [2011] E.C.R. II-167*, Summ. pub., para. 22; EGC (order of the President of 5 October 2011), Case T-422/11 R *Computer Resources International (Luxembourg) v Commission* [2011] E.C.R. II-348*, Summ. pub., paras 21–22; EGC (order of the President of 22 December 2011), Case T-593/11 R *Al-Chihabi v Council* [2011] E.C.R. II-465*, Summ. pub., para. 23; EGC (order of the President of 25 January 2012), Case T-637/11 R *Euris Consult v European Parliament*, not reported, para. 17.

[149] See, e.g. CFI (order of the President of 8 April 2008), Joined Cases T-54/08 R, T-87/08 R, T-88/08 R, and T-91/08 R to T-93/08 R *Cyprus v Commission*, not reported, para. 78 (finding non-material damage was not irreparable, since the eventual annulment of the contested acts constitutes sufficient compensation).

purely financial cannot be regarded as irreparable, or even as reparable only with difficulty, since normally it may be the subject of subsequent financial compensation.[150] Such exceptional circumstances may exist, for instance, where the alleged damage threatens the existence of the undertaking concerned or where the damage, even when it occurs, cannot be quantified.[151] Nevertheless, the principle remains that pure financial loss which may be

---

[150] See, e.g. ECJ (order of the President of 28 February 2008), Case C-479/07 R *France v Council* [2008] E.C.R. I-39*, Summ. pub., para. 24; ECJ (order of the President of 24 March 2009), Case C-60/08 P(R) *Cheminova and Others v Commission* [2009] E.C.R. I-43*, Summ. pub., para. 63; ECJ (order of the President of 18 April 2012), Case C-656/11 R *United Kingdom v Council*, not reported, paras 42–43; CFI (order of the President of 4 April 2006), Case T-420/05 R *Vischim v Commission* [2006] E.C.R. II-34*, Summ. pub., para. 89; CFI (order of the President of 26 October 2006), Case T-209/06 R *European Association of Im- and Exporters of Birds and Live Animals and Others v Commission* [2006] E.C.R. II-87*, Summ. pub., paras 34–35 (applicants failed to demonstrate that they could not obtain compensation by eventual recourse to action for damages against the Union); CFI (order of the President of 7 June 2007), Case T-346/06 R *IMS v Commission* [2007] E.C.R. II-1781, para. 122; CFI (order of the President of 11 December 2007), Case T-349/07 R *FMC Chemical and Others v Commission* [2007] E.C.R. II-169*, Summ. pub., para. 99; CFI (order of the President of 11 December 2007), Case T-350/07 R *FMC Chemical v Commission* [2007] E.C.R. II-170*, Summ. pub., para. 110; CFI (order of the President of 27 August 2008), Case T-246/08 R *Melli Bank v Council*, not reported, para. 33; CFI (order of the President of 15 October 2008), Case T-390/08 *Melli Bank Iran v Council*, not reported, para. 22; EGC (order of the President of 30 April 2010), Case T-18/10 R *Inuit Tapiriit Kanatami v European Parliament and Council* [2010] E.C.R. II-75*, Summ. pub., para. 107; EGC (order of the President of 8 September 2011), Case T-439/10 R *Fulmen v Council* [2011] E.C.R. II-260*, Summ. pub., paras 23–24; EGC (order of the President of 28 September 2011), Case T-384/11 R *Safa Nicu Sepahan Co. v Council* [2011] E.C.R. II-330*, Summ. pub., paras 21–22; EGC (order of the President of 25 January 2012), Case T-637/11 R *Euris Consult v European Parliament*, not reported, para. 16. In CFI (order of the President of 1 August 2001), Case T-132/01 R *Euroalliages v Commission* [2001] E.C.R. II-2307, it was held that the high liability threshold which applies in the context of an action for damages against the Union (see Ch.11) may have the result that the financial loss sustained by the applicant on account of a possibly unlawful act of a Union institution could be regarded as constituting irreparable damage in proceedings for interim relief. However, this order was set aside on appeal in ECJ (order of 14 December 2001), Case C-404/01 P(R) *Commission v Euroalliages and Others* [2001] E.C.R. I-10367, paras 70–75, ruling out the possibility that the uncertainty in obtaining compensation for financial damage through an action for damages might in itself be regarded as a factor capable of establishing that such damage is irreparable. See further CFI (order of the President of 24 April 2009), Case T-52/09 R *Nycomed Denmark v EMEA* [2009] E.C.R. II-43*, Summ. pub., paras 71–73; EGC (order of the President of 9 June 2011), Case T-62/06 RENV-R *Eurallumina v Commission* [2011] E.C.R. II-167*, Summ. pub., para. 46. See also ECJ (order of the President of 14 December 2011), Case C-446/10 P(R) *Alcoa Transformazioni v Commission*, not reported, paras 54–58; EGC (order of the President of 28 April 2009), Case T-95/09 R *United Phosphorus v Commission*, not reported, paras 73–75 (finding that notwithstanding the mere possibility of bringing an action for damages is sufficient to show that such financial harm is 'in principle reparable', the Judge hearing the application for interim measures must take account of the factual and legal circumstances specific to each case in order to establish the finding, notwithstanding the 'in principle reparable' nature of the damage alleged, with a view to preventing that harm from actually arising); EGC (order of the President of 17 February 2011), Case T-484/10 R *Gas Natural Fenosa SDG v Commission*, not reported, para. 75; EGC (order of the President of 17 February 2011), Case T-486/10 R *Iberdrola v Commission*, not reported, para. 70; EGC (order of the President of 17 February 2011), Case T-490/10 R *Endesa and Endesa Generacion v Commission*, not reported, para. 69.

[151] See, e.g. ECJ (order of the President of 23 May 1990), Joined Cases C-51/90 R and C-59/90 R *Comos-Tank and Others v Commission* [1990] E.C.R. I-2167, para. 24; CFI (order of the President of 21 March 1997), Case T-41/97 R *Antillean Rice Mills v Council* [1997] E.C.R. II-447, para. 47; CFI (order of the President of 28 June 2000), Case T-74/00 R *Artegodan v Commission* [2000] E.C.R. II-2583, para. 46; CFI (order of the President of 4 April 2002), Case T-198/01 R *Technische Glaswerke Ilmenau v Commission* [2002] E.C.R. II-2153, paras 96–109 (appeal dismissed on other grounds in ECJ (order of the President of 18 October 2002), Case C-232/02 P(R) *Commission v Technische Glaswerke Ilmenau* [2002] E.C.R. I-8977). As emphasized in recent case-law, if the risk of damage is purely financial, the interim measure sought is justified only if it appears that, without such a measure, the applicant would be in a position that would imperil its existence before final judgment in the main action or irremediably alter its position in the market: see, e.g. ECJ (order of the Vice-President of 7 March 2013), Case C-551/12 P(R) *EDF v Commission*, not reported, para.

awarded in full pursuant to the judgment in the main proceedings (for example, recovery of an unlawfully imposed levy or grant of a subsidy) cannot be regarded as irreparable.[152]

54; CFI (order of the President of 2 August 2006), Case T-69/06 R *Aughinish Alumina v Commission* [2006] E.C.R. II-58*, Summ. pub., para. 67; CFI (order of the President of 19 July 2007), Case T-31/07 R *Du Pont de Nemours (France) and Others v Commission* [2007] E.C.R. II-2767, paras 175, 199; CFI (order of the President of 11 December 2007), Case T-349/07 R *FMC Chemical and Others v Commission* [2007] E.C.R. II-169*, Summ. pub., para. 100; CFI (order of the President of 11 December 2007), Case T-350/07 R *FMC Chemical v Commission* [2007] E.C.R. II-170*, Summ. pub., para. 111; CFI (order of the President of 14 March 2008), Case T-467/07 R *Du Pont de Nemours (France) and Others* [2008] E.C.R. II-40*, Summ. pub., para. 90; CFI (order of the President of 18 March 2008), Case T-411/07 R *Aer Lingus Group v Commission* [2008] E.C.R. II-411, para. 131; CFI (order of the President of 27 August 2008), Case T-246/08 R *Melli Bank v Council*, not reported, para. 34; CFI (order of the President of 15 October 2008), Case T-390/08 *Melli Bank Iran v Council*, not reported, para. 23; CFI (order of the President of 28 April 2009), Case T-95/09 R *United Phosphorus v Commission*, not reported, para. 34; EGC (order of the President of 9 June 2010), Case T-79/10 R *COLT Telecommunications France v Commission* [2010] E.C.R. II-107*, Summ. pub., para. 37; EGC (order of the President of 9 June 2011), Case T-62/06 RENV-R *Eurallumina v Commission* [2011] E.C.R. II-167*, Summ. pub., para. 21; EGC (order of the President of 8 September 2011), Case T-439/10 R *Fulmen v Council* [2011] E.C.R. II-260*, Summ. pub., para. 25; EGC (order of the President of 28 September 2011), Case T-384/11 R *Safa Nicu Sepahan Co. v Council* [2011] E.C.R. II-330*, Summ. pub., para. 23; EGC (order of the President of 5 October 2011), Case T-422/11 R *Computer Resources International (Luxembourg) v Commission* [2011] E.C.R. II-348*, Summ. pub., para. 20; EGC (order of the President of 22 December 2011), Case T-593/11 R *Al-Chihabi v Council* [2011] E.C.R. II-465*, Summ. pub., para. 22; EGC (order of the President of 16 February 2012), Case T-656/11 R *Morison Menon Chartered Accountants and Others v Council*, not reported, para. 20; EGC (order of the President of 25 January 2012), Case T-637/11 R *Euris Consult v European Parliament*, not reported, para. 16. In that regard, it is settled case-law that the claim that the applicant's market share would be irremediably (or irreparably) affected has been placed on the same footing as that of the risk of disappearance from the market, provided that the irremediable effect on market share is also of a serious nature. It is therefore not sufficient that a market share, however, minimal, may be irremediably lost; it is necessary for that market share to be sufficiently large and that regaining a significant proportion of that market share is impossible by reason of obstacles of a structural or legal nature: see, e.g. CFI (order of the President of 4 April 2006), Case T-420/05 R *Vischim v Commission* [2006] E.C.R. II-34*, Summ. pub., para. 76; CFI (order of the President of 4 December 2007), Case T-326/07 R *Cheminova and Others v Commission* [2007] E.C.R. II-4877, paras 100, 130–131 and citations therein (finding that while recapture of market share lost on account of the contested measure may be financially and economically onerous, such a return to the market does not appear impossible and hence alleged damage could not be regarded as irreparable), confirmed on appeal in ECJ (order of the President of 24 March 2009), Case C-60/08 P(R) *Cheminova and Others v Commission* [2009] E.C.R. I-43*, Summ. pub., paras 64–76; CFI (order of the President of 11 December 2007), Case T-349/07 R *FMC Chemical and Others v Commission* [2007] E.C.R. II-169*, Summ. pub., paras 101, 120–128; CFI (order of the President of 11 December 2007), Case T-350/07 R *FMC Chemical v Commission* [2007] E.C.R. II-170*, Summ. pub., paras 112, 143–151; CFI (order of the President of 14 March 2008), Case T-467/07 R *Du Pont de Nemours (France) and Others* [2008] E.C.R. II-40*, Summ. pub., paras 91, 120–123; CFI (order of the President of 27 August 2008), Case T-246/08 R *Melli Bank v Council*, not reported, para. 35; CFI (order of the President of 28 April 2009), Case T-95/09 R *United Phosphorus v Commission*, not reported, para. 35; EGC (order of the President of 16 February 2012), Case T-656/11 R *Morison Menon Chartered Accountants and Others v Council*, not reported, paras 28–29. See also ECJ (order of the President of 23 January 2008), Case C-236/07 P(R) *Sumitomo Chemical Agro Europe v Commission* [2008] E.C.R. I-9*, Summ. pub., paras 19–27 (rejecting arguments on appeal that the use of the word 'impossible' in relation to analysis of harm due to loss of market share imposes standard of proof incompatible with Union law). For an example in which the President concluded that the contested measure would irremediably affect the applicant's market share and that risk of loss of market share constitutes serious and irreparable damage, see CFI (order of the President of 19 July 2007), Case T-31/07 R *Du Pont de Nemours (France) and Others v Commission* [2007] E.C.R. II-2767, paras 176–205; EGC (order of the President of 28 April 2009), Case T-95/09 R *United Phosphorus v Commission*, not reported, paras 63–82.

[152] See, e.g. ECJ (order of the President of 19 July 1983), Case 120/83 R *Raznoimport v Commission* [1983] E.C.R. 2573, para. 15; CFI (order of the President of 23 November 1990), Case T-45/90 R *Speybrouck v European Parliament* [1990] E.C.R. II-705, para. 23; CFI (order of the President of 1 August 1991), Case T-51/91 R *Hoyer v Commission* [1991] E.C.R. II-679, para. 19; CFI (order of the President of 23 March 1993), Case T-115/92 R *Hogan v European Parliament* [1993] E.C.R. II-339, para. 17; CFI (order of

When assessing the risk of serious as well as irreparable damage to the applicants, account may be taken of the group to which the applicant belongs, since the objective interests of the undertaking concerned cannot be regarded in isolation from the interests of the persons who control the undertaking.[153] This applies not only to legal persons, but also to natural persons who control the undertaking and shareholders of the undertaking concerned.[154] As such, by taking account of the group to which the applicant belongs, it follows that the fact that an undertaking may become insolvent does not necessarily mean that the condition as to urgency is fulfilled.[155]

---

the President of 29 September 1993), Case T-497/93 R II *Hogan v Court of Justice* [1993] E.C.R. II-1005, para. 17; EGC (order of the President of 25 April 2013), Case T-44/13 R *AbbVie v EMA*, not reported, para. 51 set aside on appeal on other grounds: ECJ (order of the Vice-President of 28 November 2013), Case C-389/13 P(R) *EMA v AbbVie*, not reported.

[153] See, e.g. ECJ (order of the President of 7 March 1995), Case C-12/95 P *Transacciones Maritimas and Others v Commission* [1995] E.C.R. I-467, para. 12; ECJ, Case C-268/96 P(R) *SCK and FNK v Commission* [1996] E.C.R. I-4971, paras 35–38 (concerning association of undertakings); ECJ (order of the President of 14 December 1999), Case C-364/99 P(R) *DSR-Senator Lines v Commission* [1999] E.C.R. I-8733, para. 49; ECJ (order of the President of 30 April 2010), Case C-113/09 P(R) *Zeigler v Commission* [2010] E.C.R. I-50*, Summ. pub., paras 44–47; ECJ (order of the President of 16 December 2010), Case C-373/10 P(R) *Almamet v Commission* [2010] E.C.R. I-171*, Summ. pub., paras 17–18; ECJ (order of the President of 14 December 2011), Case C-446/10 P(R) *Alcoa Transformazioni v Commission*, not reported, paras 17–18; ECJ (order of the Vice-President of 7 March 2013), Case C-551/12 P(R) *EDF v Commission*, not reported, paras 57–58; CFI (order of the President of 22 October 2001), Case T-141/01 R *Entorn v Commission* [2001] E.C.R. II-3123, paras 51–52; CFI (order of the President of 7 December 2001), Case T-192/01 R *Lior v Commission* [2001] E.C.R. II-3657, para. 54 (and the case-law cited therein); CFI (order of the President of 4 April 006), Case T-420/05 R *Vischim v Commission* [2006] E.C.R. II-34*, Summ. pub., para. 81; CFI (order of the President of 2 August 2006), Case T-69/06 R *Aughinish Alumina v Commission* [2006] E.C.R. II-58*, Summ. pub., para. 69. As for associations, account is taken of the financial situation of the members: see, e.g. CFI (order of the President of 21 January 2004), Case T-217/03 R *FNCBV v Commission* [2004] E.C.R. II-239, para. 78. The same holds with respect to a European Economic Interest Grouping (EEIG): CFI (order of the President of 7 December 2001), Case T-192/01 R *Lior v Commission* [2001] E.C.R. II-3657, paras 54–56. That being said, the fact that an association is non-profit-making cuts against arguments as to the seriousness of the damage to its operation: see, e.g. CFI (order of the President of 7 May 2002), Case T-306/01 R *Aden and Others v Council and Commission* [2002] E.C.R. II-2387, para. 118; CFI (order of the President of 19 February 2008), Case T-444/07 R *CPEM v Commission* [2008] E.C.R. II-27*, Summ. pub., para. 50; EGC (order of the President of 26 March 2010), Case T-16/10 R *Alisei v Commission* [2010] E.C.R. II-50*, Summ. pub., para. 41; EGC (order of the President of 25 October 2010), Case T-18/10 R II *Inuit Tapiriit Kanatami v European Parliament and Council* [2010] E.C.R. II-235*, Summ. pub., para. 70; EGC (order of the President of 18 November 2011), Case T-116/11 R *EMA v Commission* [2011] E.C.R. II-412*, Summ. pub., para. 20.

[154] See, e.g. ECJ (order of the President of 7 March 1995), Case C-12/95 P *Transacciones Maritimas and Others v Commission* [1995] E.C.R. I-467, para. 12; ECJ (order of the President of 14 December 1999), Case C-335/99 P(R) *HFB and Others v Commission* [1999] E.C.R. I-8705, para. 64; See, e.g. CFI (order of the President of 15 January 2001), Case T-241/00 R *Le Canne v Commission* [2001] E.C.R. II-37, paras 41–42; CFI (order of the President of 11 October 2007), Case T-120/07 R *MB Immobilien Verwaltungs v Commission* [2007] E.C.R. II-130*, Summ. pub., para. 38 (and further citations therein); EGC (order of the President of 15 March 2010), Case T-435/09 R *GL2006 Europe v Commission* [2010] E.C.R. II-32*, Summ. pub., paras 35–37.

[155] See, e.g. CFI (order of the President of 22 December 2008), Case T-468/08 R *AES-Tisza v Commission* [2008] E.C.R. II-346*, Summ. pub., para. 37; CFI (order of the President of 23 January 2009), Case T-352/08 R *Pannon v Commission* [2009] E.C.R. II-9*, Summ. pub., para. 42. Yet, the Court of Justice has underlined that the financial situation of the group to which an undertaking belongs or that of its shareholders cannot be taken into consideration in the same way in the particular situation of restrictive measures that are aimed at freezing funds or economic resources. See ECJ (order of the President of 14 June 2012), Case C-644/11 P(R) *Qualitest FZE v Council*, not reported, para. 39: the President of the Court held that the Judge hearing the application for interim measures was not entitled to conclude that the application should be dismissed without taking into consideration the specific circumstances associated with the nature of the restrictive measures of freezing funds or economic resources and set aside the order under appeal (ECJ (order of the

Second, the damage must be serious, which gives a relative aspect to the urgency of an application for interim relief. In the case of financial damage alleged by an applicant having the status of natural person, an interim measure is justified if it appears that in the absence of that measure, the applicant would find himself in a position which is likely to jeopardize his financial viability, since he would not have an amount of money which under normal circumstances should enable him to meet all the expenditure necessary for satisfying his own basic needs and those of his family until judgment is given in the main action.[156] In the case of financial damage alleged by a legal person, the seriousness of the damage may be assessed in the light, in particular, of its size and turnover and, where relevant, the characteristics of the group to which it belongs.[157] Thus, save where account is taken of the group to which it belongs, a small undertaking has less of an ability to bear financial or economic burdens than a multinational or a Member State.[158] Importantly, however, although the assessment of the concept of seriousness is generally comparative, meaning that the amount of any financial harm is compared with the size of the undertaking which would sustain the harm in the absence of the adoption of the interim measures sought, this is not the case with regard to an application for interim measures which is based not on the applicant undertaking's financial situation but on the obligation to make a commercial choice within a period alleged to be disadvantageous, with the result that it cannot be excluded that financial harm to a legal person which is objectively significant and which

---

President of 14 June 2012), Case C-644/11 P(R) *Qualitest FZE v Council*, paras 46–47, 57). The President of the Court concluded that the application did not satisfy the condition of urgency: see ECJ (order of the President of 14 June 2012), Case C-644/11 P(R) *Qualitest FZE v Council*, paras 64–70.

[156] EGC (order of the President of 25 October 2010), Case T-18/10 R II *Inuit Tapiriit Kanatami v European Parliament and Council* [2010] E.C.R. II-235*, Summ. pub., para. 59 (and citations therein).

[157] See, e.g. CFI (order of the President of 4 December 2007), Case T-326/07 R *Cheminova and Others v Commission* [2007] E.C.R. II-4877, para. 102; CFI (order of the President of 11 December 2007), Case T-349/07 R *FMC Chemical and Others v Commission* [2007] E.C.R. II-169*, Summ. pub., para. 103; CFI (order of the President of 11 December 2007), Case T-350/07 R *FMC Chemical v Commission* [2007] E.C.R. II-170*, Summ. pub., para. 114; CFI (order of the President of 14 March 2008), Case T-467/07 R *Du Pont de Nemours (France) and Others* [2008] E.C.R. II-40*, Summ. pub., paras 93; CFI (order of the President of 18 June 2008), Case T-475/07 R *Dow AgroSciences and Others v Commission* [2008] E.C.R. II-92*, Summ. pub., para. 77; CFI (order of the President of 27 August 2008), Case T-246/08 R *Melli Bank v Council*, not reported, paras 36–38; CFI (order of the President of 22 December 2008), Case T-468/08 R *AES-Tisza v Commission* [2008] E.C.R. II-346*, Summ. pub., paras 38–39; CFI (order of the President of 24 April 2009), Case T-52/09 R *Nycomed Denmark v Commission* [2009] E.C.R. II-43*, Summ. pub., paras 77–78; EGC (order of the President of 25 October 2010), Case T-18/10 R II *Inuit Tapiriit Kanatami v European Parliament and Council* [2010] E.C.R. II-235*, Summ. pub., para. 68; EGC (order of the President of 9 June 2011), Case T-62/06 RENV-R *Eurallumina v Commission* [2011] E.C.R. II-167*, Summ. pub., paras 29–31, particularly paras 32–45 (rejecting the applicant's argument that case-law is not applicable to the present proceedings, since it is essentially a 'shell operation' which generates no income for the parent company) and paras 48–56 (rejecting the applicant's argument to reconsider this line of case-law because it is excessively onerous and breaches its fundamental right to an effective judicial remedy); EGC (order of the President of 5 October 2011), Case T-422/11 R *Computer Resources International (Luxembourg) v Commission* [2011] E.C.R. II-348*, Summ. pub., paras 29–30; EGC (order of the President of 15 November 2011), Case T-269/11 R *Xeda International v Commission* [2011] E.C.R. II-389*, Summ. pub., para. 20.

[158] See, e.g. ECJ (order of the President of 26 February 1981), Case 20/81 R *Arbed v Commission* [1981] E.C.R. 721, para. 14; ECJ (order of the President of 24 September 1986), Case 214/86 R *Greece v Commission* [1986] E.C.R. 2631, para. 20; ECJ (order of the President of 17 December 1986), Case 294/86 R *Technointorg v Commission* [1986] E.C.R. 3979, para. 28; ECJ (order of the President of 10 August 1987), Case 223/87 R *ASSIDER v Commission* [1987] E.C.R. 3473, para. 22; ECJ (order of the President of 6 May 1988), Case 111/88 R *Greece v Commission* [1988] E.C.R. 2591, para. 18; ECJ (order of the President of 10 June 1988), Case 152/88 R *Sofrimport v Commission* [1988] E.C.R. 2931, paras 31–32; CFI (order of the President of 12 July 2000), Joined Cases T-94/00 R and T-110/00 R *Rica Foods and Others v Commission*, not reported, para. 115.

allegedly results from the obligation to make a final commercial choice of some magnitude within a disadvantageous time-scale may be considered serious, even in the absence of information concerning the size of the undertaking concerned.[159] In the evaluation of the seriousness of the damage, the Judge hearing the application for interim measures is not confined to having recourse in a mechanical and rigid manner solely to the relevant turnover of the applicant, but must also examine the particular circumstances of each case.[160]

In addition, the requirement for the damage to be serious prevents interim measures being imposed in order to avert irreparable but negligible damage.[161] The impending damage does not necessarily have to be financial.[162] For example, the excessive burden caused by the increasing number of heavy goods vehicles transiting through a country was held to constitute irreparable damage.[163]

(c) Reasonable diligence of applicant

13.37 In assessing the seriousness of the damage and the related urgency of the measures requested, the Judge hearing the application for interim relief may take account of the reasonable diligence on the part of the applicant in causing or limiting the extent of the

---

[159] ECJ (order of the Vice-President of 7 March 2013), Case C-551/12 P(R) *EDF v Commission*, not reported, paras 31–33. The Vice-President also made clear that the requirements for the applicant to establish that it would be in a position, in the absence of the interim measures requested, that could imperil its very existence or substantially affect its market share relate, by their very nature, to the concept of the irreparable nature of the alleged damage, rather than to the seriousness thereof. ECJ, Case C-551/12 P(R) *EDF v Commission*, para 34.

[160] See, e.g. EGC (order of the President of 28 April 2009), Case T-95/09 R *United Phosphorus v Commission*, not reported, paras 69–71, in which the President of the General Court held that the specific circumstances of the instant case, involving the significance of the world economic and financial crisis that at the time affected the group to which the applicant belonged, should be taken into account, concluding that the applicant has established the gravity (seriousness) of the harm which it will suffer if the interim measures sought are not granted; distinguished in EGC (order of the President of 30 April 2010), Case T-71/10 R *Xeda International v Commission* [2010] E.C.R. II-77*, Summ. pub., paras 45–48; EGC (order of the President of 15 November 2011), Case T-269/11 R *Xeda International v Commission* [2011] E.C.R. II-389*, Summ. pub., paras 22–53, particularly para. 27.

[161] See, in this regard, CFI (order of the President of 8 April 2008), Joined Cases T-54/08 R, T-87/08 R, T-88/08 R, and T-91/08 R to T-93/08 R *Cyprus v Commission*, not reported, paras 64–76 (holding that alleged violations of international and Union law in relation to Cyprus are not qualified as serious). This concern is very much to the fore in the case of the third substantive requirement that the applicant's interest must outweigh the interest of the opposing party/third parties (see paras 13.42 and 13.43).

[162] CFI (order of the President of 30 October 2003), Joined Cases T-125/03 R and T-253/03 R *Akzo Nobel and Others v Commission* [2003] E.C.R. II-4771, paras 162–169: a breach of professional confidentiality may result in irreparable damage. In that case, the Commission wished to have cognizance of documents containing notes made by a member of staff of an undertaking following a meeting with a lawyer. The President of the Court of Justice annulled the relevant paragraphs of this order (ECJ (order of the President of 29 September 2004), Case C-7/04 P (R) *Commission v Akzo Nobel and Others* [2004] E.C.R. I-8739) and considered that the breach of professional confidentiality did not in itself establish the urgency of the application for interim measures, since the Commission had undertaken not to disclose the relevant documents to third parties (CFI, Joined Cases T-125/03 R and T-253/03 R *Akzo Nobel and Others v Commission*, paras 41–42). But see EGC (order of the President of 11 March 2013), Case T-462/12 R *Pilkington Group v Commission*, not reported, para. 53 and EGC (order of the President of 25 April 2013), Case T-44/13 R *AbbVie v EMA*, not reported, para. 52 stating that 'an imminent risk of a serious and irreparable breach of the fundamental rights conferred by Articles 7 and 47 of the Charter [. . .] in that field has had to be regarded, in itself, as harm justifying the grant of the interim protection requested'. This line of reasoning was not followed by the Vice-President of the Court of Justice in ECJ (order of the Vice-President of 10 September 2013), Case C-278/13 P(R) *Commission v Pilkington Group*, not reported, paras 40–42; and ECJ (order of the Vice-President of 28 November 2013), Case C-389/13 P(R) *EMA v AbbVie*, not reported, paras 41–43.

[163] ECJ (order of 23 February 2001), Case C-445/00 R *Austria v Council* [2001] E.C.R. I-1461, para. 106.

damage alleged.[164] Accordingly, in one case, for instance, the European Parliament was held not to be entitled to maintain that to give immediate effect to a judgment of what is now the General Court annulling the appointment of an official would cause it serious damage, since it had left the post vacant for some six months.[165] In another case, the situation giving rise to the application for interim measures was found to have resulted from a free choice on the part of the applicant in the implementation of its commercial strategy and thus the damage alleged could not establish the urgency of the interim relief sought.[166]

(d) Public contracts

In the context of proceedings for interim relief concerning tenders for public contracts **13.38** under Union law, it is not easy to use financial damage linked to the loss of the opportunity to obtain the contract at issue to satisfy the standard elaborated in the case-law for urgency. As consistently repeated in the case-law, an undertaking taking part in a tendering procedure never has an absolute guarantee that it will be awarded the contract and therefore the adverse consequences which the applicant may suffer as a result of the rejection of its tender have generally been considered part of the normal commercial risks that each undertaking in the market must face, with the result that the loss of an opportunity to be awarded and to perform a public contract forms an integral part of the exclusion from the tendering procedure, and cannot be regarded as constituting in itself serious damage; the applicant undertaking must show that it would have been able to derive sufficiently sizeable benefits from the award and performance of that contract in order to establish that the loss of opportunity would cause it serious damage.[167] Moreover, should the applicant be

---

[164] See, e.g. CFI (order of the President of 18 June 2008), Case T-475/07 R *Dow Agrosciences and Others v Commission* [2008] E.C.R. II-92*, Summ. pub., paras 111–113 (appeal dismissed in ECJ (order of the President of 15 December 2009), Case C-391/08 P(R) *Dow Agrosciences and Others v Commission* [2009] E.C.R. I-219*); CFI (order of the President of 15 July 2008), Case T-195/08 R *Antwerpse Bouwwerken v Commission* [2008] E.C.R. II-141*, Summ. pub., paras 47–48 (finding damage alleged a result of lack of diligence on the part of the applicant); CFI (order of the President of 15 July 2008), Case T-202/08 R *CLL Centres de langues v Commission* [2008] E.C.R. II-143*, Summ. pub., paras 73–77 (finding that the damage alleged is a result of lack of diligence on the part of the applicant); CFI (order of the President of 27 January 2009), Case T-457/08 R *Intel v Commission* [2009] E.C.R. II-12*, Summ. pub., paras 88–89; CFI (order of the President of 10 July 2009), Case T-196/09 R *TerreStar Europe v Commission* [2009] E.C.R. II-124*, Summ. pub., paras 85–88 (holding that the situation giving rise to application for interim measures resulted from the lack of diligence of the applicant).

[165] ECJ (order of the President of 3 April 1992), Case C-35/92 P-R *European Parliament v Frederiksen* [1992] E.C.R. I-2399, para. 20.

[166] CFI (order of the President of 24 April 2009), Case T-52/09 R *Nycomed Denmark v Commission* [2009] E.C.R. II-43*, Summ. pub., paras 83–93.

[167] See, e.g. CFI (order of the President of 7 February 2006), Case T-437/05 R *Brink's Security Luxembourg v Commission* [2006] E.C.R. II-21*, Summ. pub., paras 50–58; CFI (order of the President of 15 July 2008), Case T-195/08 R *Antwerpse Bouwwerken v Commission* [2008] E.C.R. II-141*, Summ. pub., paras 41–44; EGC (order of the President of 20 January 2010), Case T-443/09 R *Agriconsulting Europe v Commission* [2010] E.C.R. II-5*, Summ. pub., paras 28–30; EGC (order of the President of 5 February 2010), Case T-514/09 R *De Post v Commission* [2010] E.C.R. II-15*, Summ. pub., paras 27–28; EGC (order of the President of 26 March 2010), Case T-6/10 R *Sviluppo Globale GEIE v Commission* [2010] E.C.R. II-48*, Summ. pub., paras 25–28; EGC (order of the President of 31 August 2010), Case T-299/10 R *Babcock Noell v The European joint undertaking for ITER and the Development of Fusion Energy* [2010] E.C.R. II-161*, Summ. pub., para. 52; EGC (order of the President of 15 October 2010), Case T-415/10 R *Nexans France v The European joint undertaking for ITER and the Development of fusion energy*, not reported, para. 37; EGC (order of the President of 30 September 2011), Case T-395/11 R *Elti v Delegation of the European Union to Montenegro* [2011] E.C.R. II-342*, Summ. pub., paras 13–14; EGC (order of the President of 5 October 2011), Case T-422/11 R *Computer Resources International (Luxembourg) v Commission* [2011] E.C.R. II-348* paras 25, 28; EGC (order of the President of 25 January 2012), Case T-637/11 R *Euris Consult v European*

successful in the main action, an economic value can be assigned to the damage owing to the loss of opportunity to be awarded the contract. The individual loss actually suffered can therefore in principle be fully remedied in the main action. Thus, save where the applicant is able to demonstrate that it would be prevented from obtaining subsequent financial compensation by means of an action for damages against the Union, such damage is generally not considered irreparable.[168]

(e) Competition law (bank guarantees)

13.39   In the situation where the applicant is seeking suspension of the operation of a Commission decision imposing a fine on the applicant pursuant to the Union competition rules, it may be the case that the Judge hearing the application for interim relief will make clear that the subject-matter of the application—and thus also the investigation of urgency—relates to the question whether to release the applicant from the obligation to provide a bank guarantee as a precondition for not immediately collecting the fine imposed on it.[169] In that regard, an application for an exemption from the obligation to provide a bank guarantee as a condition for the fine not being recovered immediately will only be granted

---

Parliament, not reported, paras 19–20; EGC (order of the President of 4 September 2012), Case T-213/12 R *Elitaliana v Eulex Kosovo*, not reported, para. 12. In this regard, the amount of that loss is assessed having regard to the size of the company and the characteristics of the group to which it belongs: see n. 157.

[168] See, e.g. CFI (order of the President of 25 April 2008), Case T-41/08 R *Vakakis International v Commission* [2008] E.C.R. II-66*, Summ. pub., paras 66–68; CFI (order of the President of 15 July 2008), Case T-195/08 R *Antwerpse Bouwwerken v Commission* [2008] E.C.R. II-141*, Summ. pub., paras 49–51; CFI (order of the President of 15 July 2008), Case T-202/08 R *CLL Centres de langues v Commission* [2008] E.C.R. II-143*, Summ. pub., paras 78–80; EGC (order of the President of 20 January 2010), Case T-443/09 R *Agriconsulting Europe v Commission* [2010] E.C.R. II-5*, Summ. pub., paras 32–35; EGC (order of the President of 26 March 2010), Case T-6/10 R *Sviluppo Globale GEIE v Commission* [2010] E.C.R. II-48*, Summ. pub., paras 29–32; EGC (order of the President of 31 August 2010), Case T-299/10 R *Babcock Noell v The European joint undertaking for ITER and the Development of Fusion Energy* [2010] E.C.R. II-161*, Summ. pub., paras 48–51; EGC (order of the President of 30 September 2011), Case T-395/11 R *Elti v Delegation of the European Union to Montenegro* [2011] E.C.R. II-342*, Summ. pub., para. 12; EGC (order of the President of 15 October 2010), Case T-415/10 R *Nexans France v The European joint undertaking for ITER and the Development of fusion energy*, not reported, paras 32–33; EGC (order of the President of 5 October 2011), Case T-422/11 R *Computer Resources International (Luxembourg) v Commission* [2011] E.C.R. II-348*, Summ. pub., paras 26–27; EGC (order of the President of 25 January 2012), Case T-637/11 R *Euris Consult v European Parliament*, not reported, paras 24–25; EGC (order of the President of 4 September 2012), Case T-213/12 R *Elitaliana v Eulex Kosovo*, not reported, para. 13. In this regard, it should be pointed out that previous case-law, such as the order in *Globe v Commission* (CFI (order of the President of 20 July 2006), Case T-114/06 *Globe v Commission* [2006] E.C.R. II-2627, paras 117–118, 127), holding that the loss of opportunity to be awarded a public contract was very difficult, if not impossible, to quantify with the result that such loss could be held to be irreparable, has been superseded by more recent case-law: see, e.g. EGC (order of the President of 20 January 2010), Case T-443/09 R *Agriconsulting Europe v Commission* [2010] E.C.R. II-5*, Summ. pub., para. 34; EGC (order of the President of 26 March 2010), Case T-6/10 R *Sviluppo Globale GEIE v Commission* [2010] E.C.R. II-48*, Summ. pub., para. 31; EGC (order of the President of 31 August 2010), Case T-299/10 R *Babcock Noell v The European joint undertaking for ITER and the Development of Fusion Energy* [2010] E.C.R. II-161*, Summ. pub., para. 50; EGC (order of the President of 15 October 2010), Case T-415/10 R *Nexans France v The European joint undertaking for ITER and the Development of fusion energy*, not reported, para. 34.

[169] See, e.g. EGC (order of the President of 13 April 2011), Case T-393/10 R *Westfälische Drahtindustrie and Others v Commission* [2011] E.C.R. II-1697, paras 15–20; ECJ (order of the President of 30 April 2010), Case C-113/09 P(R) *Zeigler v Commission* [2010] E.C.R. I-50*, Summ. pub., paras 23–25; CFI (order of the President of 13 July 2006), Case T-11/06 R *Romana Tabacchi v Commission* [2006] E.C.R. II-2491, paras 23–26; CFI (order of the President of 28 March 2007), Case T-384/06 R *IBP and International Building Products France v Commission* [2007] E.C.R. II-30*, Summ. pub., paras 24–27; EGC (order of the President of 7 December 2010), Case T-385/10 R *ArcelorMittal Wire France and Others v Commission* [2010] E.C.R. II-262*, Summ. pub., paras 18–19; EGC (order of the President of 24 January 2011), Case T-370/10 R *Rubinetterie Teorema v Commission* [2011] E.C.R. II-9*, Summ. pub., paras 13–15.

in exceptional circumstances, which are regarded as being established where the applicant adduces evidence that it is objectively impossible for it to provide such guarantee or that such provision would imperil its existence.[170]

(f) Objective is to avoid damage from arising

As already mentioned, the purpose of interim proceedings is not to secure reparation of **13.40** damage but to guarantee the full effectiveness of the judgment on the substance.[171] Thus, as far as urgency is concerned, interim measures serve only to avoid the serious and irreparable damage pleaded by the applicant from arising. This requirement relating to the imminence of the damage alleged is considered separately.[172] If the Judge hearing the application for interim relief finds that the contested act has been completely implemented and produced all its effects, damage can no longer be averted by imposing interim measures. If that is so, the

---

[170] See, e.g. ECJ (order of the President of 30 April 2010), Case C-113/09 P(R) *Zeigler v Commission* [2010] E.C.R. I-50*, Summ. pub., para. 48; CFI (order of the President of 13 July 2006), Case T-11/06 R *Romana Tabacchi v Commission* [2006] E.C.R. II-2491, paras 97–98; CFI (order of the President of 28 March 2007), Case T-384/06 R *IBP and International Building Products France v Commission* [2007] E.C.R. II-30*, Summ. pub., paras 56–58; CFI (order of the President of 29 October 2009), Case T-352/09 R *Novacke chemicke zavody v Commission* [2009] E.C.R. II-208*, Summ. pub., para. 52; EGC (order of the President of 7 May 2010), Case T-410/09 R *Almamet v Commission* [2010] E.C.R. II-80*, Summ. pub., paras 34–36 (appeal dismissed in ECJ (order of the President of 16 December 2010), Case C-373/10 P(R) *Almamet v Commission* [2010] E.C.R. I-171*); EGC (order of the President of 12 May 2010), Case T-30/10 R *Reagens v Commission* [2010] E.C.R. II-83*, Summ. pub., paras 42–43; EGC (order of the President of 7 December 2010), Case T-385/10 R *ArcelorMittal Wire France and Others v Commission* [2010] E.C.R. II-262*, Summ. pub., paras 36–37; EGC (order of the President of 24 January 2011), Case T-370/10 R *Rubinetterie Teorema v Commission* [2011] E.C.R. II-9*, Summ. pub., paras 31–33; EGC (order of the President of 2 March 2011), Case T-392/09 R *l. garantovaná v Commission* [2011] E.C.R. II-33*, Summ. pub., paras 41–42; EGC (order of the President of 13 April 2011), Case T-393/10 R *Westfälische Drahtindustrie and Others v Commission* [2011] E.C.R. II-1697, paras 22–24; EGC (order of the President of 13 April 2011), Case T-413/10 R *Socitrel v Commission* [2011] E.C.R. II-112*, Summ. pub., paras 21–22; EGC (order of the President of 10 June 2011), Case T-414/10 R *Companhia Previdente v Commission* [2011] E.C.R. II-173*, Summ. pub., paras 21–22; EGC (order of the President of 12 July 2011), Case T-422/10 R *Emme Holding v Commission* [2011] E.C.R. II-222*, Summ. pub., paras 22–23; EGC (order of the President of 15 July 2011), Case T-398/10 R *Fapricela v Commission* [2011] E.C.R. II-239*, Summ. pub., paras 22–23. In this context, in order to assess whether a company is in the position to provide a bank guarantee, account may be taken of the group of undertakings to which it belongs and, in particular, of the resources of the group as a whole: see, e.g. ECJ (order of the President of 30 April 2010), Case C-113/09 P(R) *Zeigler v Commission* [2010] E.C.R. I-50*, Summ. pub., paras 50–54; EGC (order of the President of 7 December 2010), Case T-385/10 R *ArcelorMittal Wire France and Others v Commission* [2010] E.C.R. II-262*, Summ. pub., paras 39–40; EGC (order of the President of 24 January 2011), Case T-370/10 R *Rubinetterie Teorema v Commission* [2011] E.C.R. II-9*, Summ. pub., paras 37–38, 41; EGC (order of the President of 12 July 2011), Case T-422/10 R *Emme Holding v Commission* [2011] E.C.R. II-222*, Summ. pub., paras 26–28 (and citations therein). In this regard, arguments to the effect that this line of case-law should not be applied on the grounds that it is contrary to fundamental principles of Union law has been rejected: see CFI (order of the President of 28 March 2007), Case T-384/06 R *IBP and International Building Products France v Commission* [2007] E.C.R. II-30*, Summ. pub., paras 80–95. For some recent examples in which urgency has been established on the grounds that it was objectively impossible for the applicants concerned (including the group of undertakings to which it belongs or its shareholders, as the case may be) to constitute a bank guarantee, see CFI (order of the President of 13 July 2006), Case T-11/06 R *Romana Tabacchi v Commission* [2006] E.C.R. II-2491, paras 100–124; EGC (order of the President of 2 March 2011), Case T-392/09 R *l. garantovaná v Commission* [2011] E.C.R. II-33*, Summ. pub., paras 43–92; EGC (order of the President of 13 April 2011), Case T-393/10 R *Westfälische Drahtindustrie and Others v Commission* [2011] E.C.R. II-1697, paras 25–53.

[171] See citations in n. 2.

[172] See, e.g. ECJ (order of the President of 28 August 1978), Case 166/78 R *Italy v Council* [1978] E.C.R. 1745, para. 14; CFI (order of the President of 11 June 2007), Case T-324/06 R *Municipio de Gondomar v Commission* [2007] E.C.R. II-55*, Summ. pub., para. 55 (and citations therein); CFI (order of the President of 8 April 2008), Joined Cases T-54/08 R, T-87/08 R, T-88/08 R, and T-91/08 R to T-93/08 R *Cyprus v Commission*, not reported, para. 61 (and citations therein).

application for interim measures is to no purpose.[173] However, it may happen that a measure which had already produced damage before the application for interim measures was brought is continuing to cause damage, in which case interim measures may be imposed to prevent any increase in the damage.[174]

Furthermore, the threat of damage must be a real one, which means that it does not have to be established with absolute certainty that damage is imminent; it is sufficient that the damage, particularly when it depends on a number of factors, is foreseeable with a sufficient degree of probability.[175] Hypothetical or indefinite potential damage does not suffice.[176]

---

[173] See, e.g. CFI (order of the President of 30 October 2003), Joined Cases T-125/03 R and T-253/03 R *Akzo Nobel and Others v Commission* [2003] E.C.R. II-4771, paras 170–178 (order set aside in relevant part on other grounds in ECJ (order of the President of 27 September 2004), Case C-7/04 P(R) *Commission v Akzo Nobel and Others* [2004] E.C.R. I-8739). As illustrated by case-law in the staff context, this issue as to whether the contested measure has exhausted its effects may be assessed in relation to the object of the proceedings for interim relief, as opposed to the context of urgency: see CST (order of the President of 27 May 2011), Joined Cases F-5/11 R and F-15/11 R *Mariën v Commission and European External Action Service*, not reported, para. 39; CST (order of the President of 28 February 2012), Case F-129/11 R *BH v Commission*, not reported, para. 28; CST (order of the President of 28 February 2012), Case F-139/11 R *BJ v Commission*, not reported, para. 27; CST (order of the President of 28 February 2012), Case F-140/11 R *BK v Commission*, not reported, para. 29. For cases relating to damage that already occurred, see CFI (order of the President of 27 August 2008), Case T-246/08 R *Melli Bank v Council*, not reported, paras 52–53; CFI (order of the President of 29 October 2009), Case T-352/09 R *Novacke chemicke zavody v Commission* [2009] E.C.R. II-208*, Summ. pub., paras 39–43 (in which the President of the Court underlined that the urgency must continue until the time when the Judge hearing the application for interim measures makes his final decision; in the instant proceedings, as the applicant itself applied for the opening of national (insolvency) proceedings endangering its existence, the granting of the interim relief sought could not dispel that danger, and therefore, it cannot be maintained that such relief is still necessary, since that harm to be avoided has already occurred); EGC (order of the President of 29 July 2011), Case T-296/11 R *Cementos Portland Valderrivas v Commission* [2011] E.C.R. II-246*, Summ. pub., para. 28. See also ECJ (order of the President of 18 April 2012), Case C-656/11 R *United Kingdom v Council*, not reported, paras 23–26: this case involved the situation where the UK sought the suspension of the operation of a Council decision on the position to be taken by the Union in the Joint Committee established under the EU–Swiss Agreement, but the decision of the Joint Committee had been adopted and entered into force during the proceedings, which led the UK to request the Court to find that this decision had not entered into force; despite the Council's doubts as to whether it was possible for the UK to bring an application for interim relief, the Court considered (finding it unnecessary to rule on the consequences of notification of the official position of the Union to the Swiss authorities and the question whether the decision of the Joint Committee entered into force) that since the UK had requested in the alternative that the Council be ordered to engage in urgent consultations with those authorities with a view to securing suspension of the implementation of the decision of the Joint Committee, the present application for interm relief should be examined from that angle.

[174] See, e.g. CFI (order of the President of 28 September 2007), Case T-257/07 R *France v Commission* [2007] E.C.R. II-4153, para. 131 (although the risk to public health represented by the presence on the market of meat infected by BSE was already present before the adoption of the contested provisions, that risk objectively increased following the entry into force of those provisions owing to the placing on the market of a range of infected meat, which under the previous system would have been destroyed).

[175] See, e.g. ECJ (order of the President of 19 July 1995), Case C-129/95 P(R) *Commission v Atlantic Container Line and Others* [1995] E.C.R. I-2165, para. 38; ECJ (order of the President of 24 April 2008), Case C-76/08 R *Commission v Malta* [2008] E.C.R. I-64*, Summ. pub., para. 32; CFI (order of the President of 7 June 2007), Case T-346/06 R *IMS v Commission* [2006] E.C.R. II-1781, para. 123; CFI (order of the President of 11 December 2007), Case T-349/07 R *FMC Chemical and Others v Commission* [2007] E.C.R. II-169*, Summ. pub., para. 98; CFI (order of the President of 11 December 2007), Case T-350/07 R *FMC Chemical v Commission* [2007] E.C.R. II-170*, Summ. pub., para. 109; CFI (order of the President of 27 August 2008), Case T-246/08 R *Melli Bank v Council*, not reported, para. 32; EGC (order of the President of 5 October 2011), Case T-422/11 R *Computer Resources International (Luxembourg) v Commission* [2011] E.C.R. II-348*, Summ. pub., para. 19; EGC (order of the President of 25 January 2012), Case T-637/11 R *Euris Consult v European Parliament*, not reported, para. 15.

[176] See, e.g. ECJ (order of the President of 15 June 1987), Case 142/87 R *Belgium v Commission* [1987] E.C.R. 2589, para. 25; ECJ (order of the President of 16 July 1993), Case C-296/93 R *France v Commission*

Likewise, where it is determined that the decisive cause of the damage alleged is not the contested measure at issue, the interim relief sought cannot be granted on the basis of the claims put forward by the applicant or the damage alleged is deemed irrelevant to the assessment of urgency.[177]

The Judge hearing the application for interim measures may have regard, in assessing the seriousness and irreparability of damage, whether or not effective relief is available from the national courts.[178]

[1993] E.C.R. I-4181, para. 26; ECJ (order of the President of 24 April 2008), Case C-76/08 R *Commission v Malta* [2008] E.C.R. I-64*, Summ. pub., para. 43 (finding that urgency made out in the application as regards the current year, but not the future year); CFI (order of the President of 4 April 2006), Case T-420/05 R *Vischim v Commission* [2006] E.C.R. II-34*, Summ. pub., paras 71, 75, 77 (finding alleged damage not sufficiently probable); CFI (order of the President of 16 February 2007), Case T-310/06 R *Hungary v Commission* [2007] E.C.R. II-15*, Summ. pub., para. 50; CFI (order of the President of 16 March 2007), Case T-345/05 R *V v European Parliament* [2007] E.C.R. II-25*, Summ. pub., paras 90, 92; CFI (order of the President of 27 June 2007), Case T-345/05 R II *V v European Parliament* [2007] E.C.R. II-69*, Summ. pub., paras 39–44; CFI (order of the President of 8 April 2008), Joined Cases T-54/08 R, T-87/08 R, T-88/08 R, and T-91/08 R to T-93/08 R *Cyprus v Commission*, not reported, para. 63; CFI (order of the President of 25 April 2008), Case T-41/08 R *Vakakis International v Commission* [2008] E.C.R. II-66*, Summ. pub., paras 71–73 (holding that the applicant's claims do not satisfy the condition of foreseeability of harm to the requisite degree of probability); CFI (order of the President of 10 July 2009), Case T-196/09 R *TerreStar Europe v Commission* [2009] E.C.R. II-124*, Summ. pub., paras 54, 68 (a simple allegation that damage is impossible to quantify is not sufficient); EGC (order of the President of 30 April 2010), Case T-18/10 R *Inuit Tapiriit Kanatami v European Parliament and Council* [2010] E.C.R. II-75*, Summ. pub., paras 106, 111–114 (urgency not established in relation to the measure not yet adopted); EGC (order of 22 July 2010), Case T-286/10 R *IDIAP v Commission* [2010] E.C.R. II-155*, Summ. pub., para. 22; EGC (order of the President of 25 October 2010), Case T-18/10 R II *Inuit Tapiriit Kanatami v European Parliament and Council* [2010] E.C.R. II-235*, Summ. pub., para. 90; EGC (order of the President of 9 June 2011), Case T-87/11 R *GRP Security v Court of Auditors* [2011] E.C.R. II-170*, Summ. pub., para. 40; EGC (order of the President of 9 June 2011), Case T-533/10 R *DTS Distribuidora de Television Digital v Commission* [2011] E.C.R. II-168*, Summ. pub., para. 55. But see CFI (order of the President of 19 July 2007), Case T-31/07 R *Du Pont de Nemours (France) and Others v Commission* [2007] E.C.R. II-2767, paras 150–161 (rejecting the argument that alleged damage is not dependent on a hypothetical amendment which might be proposed by the Commission and concluding that it cannot be ruled out that damage is imminent).

[177] See, e.g. CFI (order of the President of 11 December 2007), Case T-349/07 R *FMC Chemical and Others v Commission* [2007] E.C.R. II-169*, Summ. pub., paras 109–113 (finding damage alleged would not be the direct consequence of the contested measure); CFI (order of the President of 28 April 2009), Case T-95/09 R *United Phosphorus v Commission*, not reported, paras 55–58/62; EGC (order of the President of 26 March 2010), Case T-1/10 R *SNF v ECHA* [2010] E.C.R. II-47*, Summ. pub., para. 66; EGC (order of the President of 30 April 2010), Case T-18/10 R *Inuit Tapiriit Kanatami v European Parliament and Council* [2010] E.C.R. II-75*, Summ. pub., para. 115; Case EGC (order of the President of 25 October 2010), Case T-18/10 R II *Inuit Tapiriit Kanatami v European Parliament and Council* [2010] E.C.R. II-235*, Summ. pub., paras 91–92; EGC (order of the President of 12 December 2011) Case T-579/11 R *Akhras v Council* [2011] E.C.R. II-441*, Summ. pub., paras 36–37; EGC (order of the President of 16 February 2012), Case T-656/11 R *Morison Menon Chartered Accountants and Others v Council*, not reported, paras 22–26 (and citations therein). As emphasized in recent case-law, when suspension of the operation of a measure is sought, the grant of the interim measure requested is justified only where the measure at issue constitutes the 'decisive cause' of the alleged serious and irreparable damage: see, e.g. ECJ (order of the President of 19 July 2012), Case C-110/12 P(R) *Akhras v Council*, not reported, para. 44; EGC (order of the President of 22 December 2011), Case T-593/11 R *Al-Chihabi v Council* [2011] E.C.R. II-465*, Summ. pub., para. 16 (and further citations therein). See also ECJ (order of the Vice-President of 7 March 2013), Case C-551/12 P(R) *EDF v Commission*, not reported, para. 41.

[178] See, e.g. ECJ (order of the President of 6 February 1986) 310/85 R *Deufil v Commission* [1986] E.C.R. 537, para. 22; ECJ (order of the President of 15 June 1987), Case 142/87 R *Belgium v Commission* [1987] E.C.R. 2589, para. 26; ECJ (order of the President of 28 February 2008), Case C-479/07 R *France v Council* [2008] E.C.R. I-39*, Summ. pub., para. 29; ECJ (order of the President of 11 November 2011), Case C-530/10 P(R) *Nencini v European Parliament* [2011] E.C.R. I-172*, Summ. pub., para. 53; EGC (order of the

The fact that both material and non-material damage is imminent may result in the grant of interim measures.[179] Nevertheless, as far as non-material damage is concerned, urgency cannot be established where the interim measure would not remedy the damage any more than any judgment in the main proceedings.[180]

President of 11 May 2011), Case T-195/11R *Cahier v Council and Commission* [2011] E.C.R. II-132*, Summ. pub., para. 21. With respect to an application for interim measures seeking to suspend a restrictive measure, the Judge hearing the application may account for the provision in the contested measure of the applicant's ability to request from the national authority in question sufficient funds to support the applicant's daily needs: see, e.g. EGC (order of the President of 14 July 2011), Case T-187/11 R *Trabelsi and Others v Council* [2011] E.C.R. II-235*, Summ. pub., paras 37–43; EGC (order of the President of 22 December 2011), Case T-593/11 R *Al-Chihabi v Council* [2011] E.C.R. II-465*, Summ. pub., paras 28–29. With respect to an application for interim measures in the field of State aid, it is for the applicant to show that the domestic remedies available to him under national law to oppose recovery of State aid do not enable him to avoid serious and irreparable damage: see, e.g. CFI (order of the President of 29 January 2007), Case T-423/05 R *Olympiaki Aeroporia Ypiresies v Commission* [2007] E.C.R. II-6*, Summ. pub., para. 112; CFI (order of the President of 14 March 2008), Case T-440/07 R *Huta Buczek v Commission* [2008] E.C.R. II-39*, Summ. pub., para. 68; CFI (order of 13 July 2009), Case T-238/09 R *Sniace v Commission* [2009] E.C.R. II-125*, Summ. pub., para. 27; EGC (order of the President of 9 July 2010), Case T-177/10 R *Alcoa Transformazioni v Commission* [2010] E.C.R. II-149*, Summ. pub., para. 57 (upheld on appeal in ECJ (order of the President of 14 December 2011), Case C-446/10 P(R) *Alcoa Transformazioni v Commission*, not reported, paras 43, 46–51). This case-law has been held to apply in other contexts: see, e.g. CFI (order of the President of 25 May 2009), Case T-159/09 R *Biofrescos v Commission* [2009] E.C.R. II-63*, Summ. pub., paras 29–31; CFI (order of the President of 8 June 2009), Case T-149/09 R *Dover v European Parliament* [2009] E.C.R. II-66*, Summ. pub., paras 31–32; EGC (order of the President of 12 December 2011), Case T-402/11 R *Preparados Alimenticios del Sur v Commission* [2011] E.C.R. II-439*, Summ. pub., paras 23–24.

[179] This may be inferred from ECJ (order of the President of 26 June 1959), Case 31/59 R *Acciaieria e Tubificio di Brescia v High Authority* [1960] E.C.R. 98, at 100, and CFI (order of the President of 30 November 1993), Case T-549/93 R *D v Commission* [1993] E.C.R. II-1347, para. 44. For an example of serious and irreparable damage to the applicant's commercial reputation, see CFI (order of the President of 7 June 2007), Case T-346/06 R *IMS v Commission* [2007] E.C.R. II-1781, paras 133–160. In this case, the President of the now General Court distinguished the present proceedings from the line of case-law relating to the harm to the reputation of an undertaking eliminated from a tender for a public contract and rejected the argument that such harm constitutes serious and irreparable damage: CFI, Case T-346/06 R *IMS v Commission*, para. 134 (and citations therein). In this latter context (concerning rejection of alleged non-material damage in the context of tenders for public contracts), see, e.g. CFI (order of the President of 7 February 2006), Case T-437/05 R *Brink's Security Luxembourg v Commission* [2006] E.C.R. II-21*, Summ. pub., paras 67–68; CFI (order of the President of 25 April 2008), Case T-41/08 R *Vakakis International v Commission* [2008] E.C.R. II-66*, Summ. pub., para. 34; EGC (order of the President of 31 August 2010), Case T-299/10 R *Babcock Noell v The European joint undertaking for ITER and the Development of Fusion Energy* [2010] E.C.R. II-161*, Summ. pub., paras 59–62; EGC (order of the President of 15 October 2010), Case T-415/10 R *Nexans France v The European joint undertaking for ITER and the Development of fusion energy*, not reported, paras 44–48; EGC (order of the President of 30 September 2011), Case T-395/11 R *Elti v Delegation of the European Union to Montenegro* [2011] E.C.R. II-342*, Summ. pub., para.16; EGC (order of the President of 5 October 2011), Case T-422/11 R *Computer Resources International (Luxembourg) v Commission* [2011] E.C.R. II-348*, Summ. pub., paras 37–42; EGC (order of the President of 4 September 2012), Case T-213/12 R *Elitaliana v Eulex Kosovo*, not reported, para. 14.

[180] See, e.g. ECJ (order of the President of 13 January 2009), Joined Cases C-512/07 P(R) and C-15/08 P(R) *Occhetto and European Parliament v Donnici* [2009] E.C.R. I-1, para. 58; CFI (order of the President of 7 May 2002), Case T-306/01 R *Aden and Others v Council and Commission* [2002] E.C.R. II-2387, paras 116–117; CFI (order of the President of 18 October 2001), Case T-196/01 R *Aristoteleio Panepistimio Thessalonikis v Commission* [2001] E.C.R. II-3107, para 36 (and the case-law cited therein); CFI (order of the President of 27 August 2008), Case T-246/08 R *Melli Bank v Council*, not reported, para. 53; CFI (order of the President of 15 October 2008), Case T-390/08 *Melli Bank Iran v Council*, not reported, para. 41; CFI (order of the President of 8 June 2009), Case T-149/09 R *Dover v European Parliament* [2009] E.C.R. II-66*, Summ. pub., para. 37; EGC (order of the President of 8 September 2011), Case T-439/10 R *Fulmen v Council* [2011] E.C.R. II-260*, Summ. pub., para. 33; EGC (order of the President of 14 July 2011), Case T-187/11 R *Trabelsi and others v Council* [2011] E.C.R. II-235*, Summ. pub., para. 32; EGC (order of the President of

(g) Serious and irreparable damage must affect the applicant personally

For the condition of urgency to be met, the applicant must demonstrate that the serious **13.41** and irreparable damage alleged affects him or her personally.[181] In particular, damage to the applicant's employees or related third parties is generally not taken into consideration.[182]

A Member State may rely on damage allegedly suffered by a domestic industrial sector[183] on the grounds that it is the guardian of national economic and social interests.[184]

---

28 September 2011), Case T-384/11 R *Safa Nicu Sepahan Co. v Council* [2011] E.C.R. II-330*, Summ. pub., para. 27; EGC (order of the President of 3 October 2011), Case T-421/11 R *Qualitest v Council* [2011]E.C.R. II-344*, Summ. pub., para. 29 (appeal upheld on other grounds in ECJ (order of the President of 14 June 2012), Case C-644/11 P(R) *Qualitest v Council*, not reported, paras 54–56); EGC (order of the President of 22 December 2011), Case T-593/11 R *Al-Chihabi v Council* [2011] E.C.R. II-465*, Summ. pub., para. 33.

[181] See, e.g. ECJ (order of the President of 6 May 1988), Case 111/88 R *Greece v Commission* [1988] E.C.R. 2591, para. 15; ECJ (order of the President of 6 May 1988), Case 112/88 R *Crete Citron Producers Association v Commission* [1988] E.C.R. 2597, para. 20; CFI (order of the President of 10 November 2004), Case T-316/04 R *Wam v Commission* [2004] E.C.R. II-3917, para. 28; CFI (order of the President of 1 February 2006), Case T-417/05 R *Endesa v Commission* [2006] E.C.R. II-18*, Summ. pub., paras 59–60; CFI (order of the President of 25 April 2006), Case T-455/05 R *Componenta Oyj v Commission* [2006] E.C.R. II-336*, Summ. pub., para. 41; CFI (order of the President of 2 August 2006), Case T-69/06 R *Aughinish Alumina v Commission* [2006] E.C.R. II-58*, Summ. pub., para. 80; CFI (order of the President of 4 April 2006), Case T-420/05 R *Vischim v Commission* [2006] E.C.R. II-34*, Summ. pub., paras 73–74; CFI (order of the President of 14 March 2008), Case T-440/07 R *Buczek v Commission* [2008] E.C.R. II-39*, Summ. pub., paras 23–25. The damage caused to parties other than the applicant may be taken into account, if appropriate, only in the context of the balance of interests requirement: see, e.g. CFI (order of the President of 2 August 2006), Case T-69/06 R *Aughinish Alumina v Commission* [2006] E.C.R. II-58*, Summ. pub., para. 80; CFI (order of the President of 4 April 2006), Case T-420/05 R *Vischim v Commission* [2006] E.C.R. II-34*, Summ. pub., para. 73; CFI (order of the President of 19 July 2007), Case T-31/07 R *Du Pont de Nemours (France) and Others v Commission* [2007] E.C.R. II-2767, paras 147–148, 168.

[182] See, e.g. CFI (order of the President of 2 August 2006), Case T-69/06 R *Aughinish Alumina v Commission* [2006] E.C.R. II-58*, Summ. pub., para. 81; CFI (order of the President of 19 February 2008), Case T-444/07 R *CPEM v Commission* [2008] E.C.R. II-27*, Summ. pub., para. 51; CFI (order of the President of 14 March 2008), Case T-467/07 R *Du Pont de Nemours (France) and Others* [2008] E.C.R. II-40*, Summ. pub., para. 104; CFI (order of the President of 27 August 2008), Case T-246/08 R *Melli Bank v Council*, not reported, para. 50 (and further citations therein); EGC (order of the President of 25 January 2012), Case T-637/11 R *Euris Consult v European Parliament*, not reported, para. 26. But see CFI (order of the President of 20 December 2001), Case T-214/01 R *Bank für Arbeit und Wirtschaft v Commission* [2001] E.C.R. II-3993, para. 69: damage to the personal reputation of employees and members of the board of directors of the applicant not taken into consideration in proceedings for interim relief unless the applicant succeeds in showing that such damage is likely to cause serious harm to its own reputation. In the context of staff cases, see, e.g. CST (order of the President of 14 December 2006), Case F-120/06 R *Dalnoky v Commission* [2006] E.C.R.-SC I-A-1-187, para. 56 (arguments relating to interests of potential applicants, the Union institution concerned, and other related parties deemed not personal to the applicant and hence incapable of establishing the urgency requirement).

[183] ECJ (order of the President of 28 August 1978), Case 166/78 R *Italy v Council* [1978] E.C.R. 1745: Italy sought to protect the interests of its domestic cereal starch industry. The application for interim measures was dismissed on the grounds that Italy had not established the imminence of damage. No objection of admissibility was raised on account of the fact that the alleged damage was not imminent for the Italian State as such. See, to the same effect, ECJ (order of the President of 16 July 1993), Case C-296/93 R *France v Commission* [1993] E.C.R. I-4181; ECJ (order of the President of 16 July 1993), Case C-307/93 R *Ireland v Commission* [1993] E.C.R. I-4191.

[184] See, e.g. ECJ (order of the President of 29 June 1993), Case C-280/93 R *Germany v Council* [1993] E.C.R. I-3667, para. 27; CFI (order of the President of 9 November 2007), Case T-183/07 R *Poland v Commission* [2007] E.C.R. II-152*, Summ. pub., para. 39 (and citations therein); CFI (order of the President of 14 December 2007), Case T-387/07 R *Portugal v Commission* [2007] E.C.R. II-176*, Summ. pub., paras 34–38 (and further citations therein). This similarly applies to other entities of public law responsible for protecting the economic, social, and cultural interests at national, regional, or local level: see, e.g. CFI (order of the President of 16 November 2007), Case T-312/07 R *Dimos Peramatos v Commission* [2007] E.C.R. II-157*, Summ. pub., paras 36–44; EGC (order of the

Furthermore, by virtue of its participation in the exercise of legislative and budgetary powers and contribution to the Union budget, a Member State may rely on the damage which would arise from expenditure being incurred contrary to the rules governing the powers of the Union and its institutions.[185] All the same, it does not appear sufficient for a Member State to refer to damage specifically suffered by an individual undertaking.[186]

In connection with an action for infringement, the Commission is entitled to adduce evidence of damage to the Union as the promoter of its general interest,[187] to the interests of nationals of other Member States,[188] or even of the Member State concerned.[189]

(4) Balance of interests

(a) Concept

13.42 The balance of interests constitutes the third requirement that must be fulfilled for an application for interim measures to be granted. According to settled case-law with regard to interim measures seeking suspension of the execution of a Union act, the balance of interests requires the Judge hearing the application for interim measures to determine, in particular, whether or not the interest of the applicant in obtaining the interim measures sought outweighs the interest in the immediate application of the contested act by examining specifically whether the possible annulment of that act by the Court giving judgment in the main action would make it possible to reverse the situation that would be brought about by its immediate implementation and, conversely, whether the suspension of operation of that act would be such as to prevent its being fully effective in the event of the main application being dismissed.[190]

Consequently, even where the Judge hearing the application for interim relief has found that the application in the main proceedings is *prima facie* not unreasonable and that the interim measures sought are urgent, he or she is not obliged to give an order imposing those measures. He or she will withhold consent if the applicant's interest does not outweigh the

---

President of 8 January 2010), Case T-446/09 R *Escola Superior Agraria de Coimbra v Commission* [2010] E.C.R. II-2*, Summ. pub., paras 26–33; EGC (order of the President of 25 October 2010), Case T-18/10 R II *Inuit Tapiriit Kanatami v European Parliament and Council* [2010] E.C.R. II-235*, Summ. pub., paras 52–54; EGC (order of the President of 17 February 2010), Case T-520/10 R *Comunidad Autonoma de Galicia v Commission* [2011] E.C.R. II-27*, Summ. pub., paras 62–78; EGC (order of the President of 13 February 2012), Case T-601/11 R *Dansk Automat Brancheforening v Commission*, not reported, paras 25–27.

[185] ECJ (order of the President of 24 September 1996), Joined Cases C-239 and C-240/96 R *United Kingdom v Commission* [1996] E.C.R. I-4475, para. 66.

[186] ECJ (order of the President of 15 June 1987), Case 142/87 R *Belgium v Commission* [1987] E.C.R. 2589, paras 23–24; ECJ (order of the President of 8 May 1991), Case C-356/90 R *Belgium v Commission* [1991] E.C.R. I-2423, para. 23.

[187] Art. 17(1) TEU. For example, as regards ecological damage to the common heritage of the Union, see, e.g. ECJ (order of the President of 19 December 2006), Case C-503/06 R *Commission v Italy* [2006] E.C.R. I-141*, Summ. pub., paras 16–18; ECJ (order of the President of 24 April 2008), Case C-76/08 R *Commission v Malta* [2008] E.C.R. I-64*, Summ. pub., paras 33–43; ECJ (order of the President of 10 December 2009), Case C-573/08 R *Commission v Italy* [2009] E.C.R. I-217*, Summ. pub., paras 19–26.

[188] ECJ (order of the President of 13 July 1977), Case 61/77 R II *Commission v Ireland* [1977] E.C.R. 1411, para.14; ECJ (order of the President of 25 October 1985), Case 293/85 R *Commission v Belgium* [1985] E.C.R. 3521.

[189] ECJ (order of 7 June 1985), Case 154/85 R *Commission v Italy* [1985] E.C.R. 1753, para. 19.

[190] See, e.g. ECJ (order of the President of 14 June 2012), Case C-644/11 P(R) *Qualitest v Council*, not reported, para. 72 (and citations therein); EGC (order of the President of 2 March 2011), Case T-392/09 R *l garantovaná v Commission* [2011] E.C.R. II-33*, Summ. pub., para. 101 (and citations therein); EGC (order of the President of 23 February 2012), Case T-601/11 R *Dansk Automat v Commission*, not reported, para. 46 and citations therein.

possible effects of the measures on the interests of the opposing party,[191] third parties,[192] or the public (Union)[193] interest.[194]

[191] See, e.g. CFI (order of the President of 30 April 2008), Case T-65/08 R *Spain v Commission* [2008] E.C.R. II-69*, Summ. pub., para. 86. In staff cases, the interests of the institution concerned are weighed against the applicant's interests. See, e.g. ECJ (order of the President of 11 July 1988), Case 176/88 R *Hanning v European Parliament* [1988] E.C.R. 3915, para. 14. For a recent example (finding in favour of the applicant and that the suspension of the contested measure did not carry a risk of serious financial damage for the Union institution concerned), see CST (order of the President of 18 December 2009), Case F-92/09 R *U v European Parliament* [2009] E.C.R.-SC I-A-1-511, paras 96–101.

[192] See, e.g. ECJ (order of the President of 16 January 1975), Case 3/75 R *Johnson & Firth Brown v Commission* [1975] E.C.R. 1; ECJ (order of the President of 22 May 1978), Case 92/78 R *Simmenthal v Commission* [1978] E.C.R. 1129, para. 18; ECJ (order of the President of 13 June 1989), Case 56/89 R *Publishers Association v Commission* [1989] E.C.R. 1693, para. 35; CFI (order of the President of 6 July 1993), Case T-12/93 R *CCE de Vittel and Others v Commission* [1993] E.C.R. II-785, paras 19–20; EGC (order of the President of 24 November 2011), Case T-471/11 R *Editions Odile Jacob v Commission* [2011] E.C.R. II-428*, Summ. pub., paras 76–77. The balance of interests may, of course, also be used to reinforce other arguments on the basis of which the application for interim measures is rejected: see CFI (order of the President of 26 September 1997), Case T-183/97 R *Micheli and Others v Commission* [1997] E.C.R. II-1473, para. 75; CFI (order of the President of 30 April 1999), Case T-44/98 RII *Emesa Sugar v Commission* [1999] E.C.R. II-1427, paras 137–146. In principle, the interest of protection of public health takes precedence over economic interests: see, e.g. ECJ (order of the President of 11 April 2001), Case C-471/00 P(R) *Cambridge Healthcare Supplies v Commission* [2001] E.C.R. I-2865, para. 121; CFI (order of the President of 15 June 2001), Case T-339/00 R *Bactria v Commission* [2001] E.C.R. II-1721, paras 112–113; CFI (order of the President of 19 July 2007), Case T-31/07 R *Du Pont de Nemours (France) and Others v Commission* [2007] E.C.R. II-2767, para. 207; CFI (order of the President of 28 September 2007), Case T-257/07 R *France v Commission* [2007] E.C.R. II-4153, para. 141; CFI (order of the President of 30 October 2008), Case T-257/07 R II *France v Comission* [2008] E.C.R. II-236*, Summ. pub., para. 125; CFI (order of the President of 18 October 2007), Case T-238/07 R *Ristic and Others v Commission* [2007] E.C.R. II-134*, Summ. pub., para. 73 (and citations therein). Compare, e.g. CFI (order of the President of 28 April 2009), Case T-95/09 R *United Phosphorus v Commission*, not reported, paras 84–87 (finding that several elements indicated that the suspension of the implementation of the contested measure would not involve any risk to public health or to the environment, as argued by the opposing party; interim relief sought by the applicant granted for a particular period of time).

[193] See, e.g. ECJ (order of the President of 14 June 2012), Case C-644/11 P(R) *Qualitest v Council*, not reported, para. 72–79 (applicant's interest in obtaining interim relief sought did not outweigh public interest in immediate application of the contested measure involving restrictive measures in the fight against terrorism); CFI (order of the President of 7 June 2007), Case T-346/06 R *IMS v Commission* [2007] E.C.R. II-1781, paras 161–169 (rejecting the opposing party's arguments based on Union interest in ensuring an equivalent degree of protection of health and safety and finding the balance of interests weighed in favour of the applicant); EGC (order of the President of 31 August 2010), Case T-299/10 R *Babcock Noell v The European joint undertaking for ITER and the Development of Fusion Energy* [2010] E.C.R. II-161*, Summ. pub., paras 64–68 (applicant's interest in obtaining the interim measure sought did not outweigh the general interest of the Union, including that of its citizens, in seeking prompt completion of the project concerned). In the field of State aid, it is difficult for the applicant to demonstrate that its interest outweighs the public interest or other interests involved in seeing the particular State aid decision implemented: for some recent examples, see, e.g. CFI (order of the President of 11 October 2007), Case T-120/07 R *MB Immobilien Verwaltungs v Commission* [2007] E.C.R. II-130*, Summ. pub., paras 45–49; EGC (order of the President of 17 February 2011), Case T-484/10 R *Gas Natural Fenosa SDG v Commission*, not reported, paras 95–113; EGC (order of the President of 17 February 2011), Case T-486/10 R *Iberdrola v Commission*, not reported, paras 92–110; EGC (order of the President of 17 February 2011), Case T-490/10 R *Endesa and Endesa Generacion v Commission*, not reported, paras 88–106; EGC (order of the President of 17 February 2010), Case T-520/10 R *Comunidad Autonoma de Galicia v Commission* [2011] E.C.R. II-27*, Summ. pub., paras 80–97; EGC (order of the President of 2 December 2011), Case T-176/11 R *Carbunion v Council* [2011] E.C.R. II-434*, Summ. pub., paras 36–43. As regards the balance of interests involving an applicant seeking release from the obligation to provide a bank guarantee under Union competition rules, see, e.g. CFI (order of the President of 13 July 2006), Case T-11/06 R *Romana Tabacchi v Commission* [2006] E.C.R. II-2491, paras 135–144 (application granted subject to conditions); EGC (order of the President of 2 March 2011), Case T-392/09 R *l. garantovaná v Commission* [2011] E.C.R. II-33*, Summ. pub., paras 103–119 (application granted subject to conditions). In the context of ecological justifications in protecting the common heritage of the Union, see, e.g. ECJ (order of the President of 24 April 2008), Case C-76/08 R *Commission v Malta* [2008] E.C.R. I-64*, Summ. pub., para. 48; ECJ (order of the President of 10 December 2009), Case C-573/08 R *Commission v Italy* [2009] E.C.R. I-217*, Summ. pub., paras 29–30.

[194] See, e.g. CFI (order of the President of 15 December 1992), Case T-96/92 R *CCE de la Société des Grandes Sources and Others v Commission* [1992] E.C.R. II-2579, para.39; CFI (order of the President of

The exercise of weighing the various interests against each other may sometimes result in interim measures different from those sought being imposed.[195] This exercise provides yet another illustration of the cautious approach taken by the Judge hearing the application for interim relief. Since he or she conducts only a 'marginal review' of the application in the main proceedings, it is not certain that the applicant will win his or her case and therefore not unreasonable to have regard to the possible impact of the interim measures sought on others' interests.

(b) Applications

13.43   The interest of the opposing party or of a third party sometimes weighs so heavily in the balance that interim measures are not granted even though there has been a manifest infringement of Union law. For example, in *Commission v Ireland*, the President of the Court of Justice considered that the interests of the inhabitants of Dundalk in having sound water supplies as soon as possible outweighed the Commission's interest in having the relevant Union rules applied to the grant of a public contract for the construction of a water main to carry water from the river to the treatment plant. Notwithstanding the manifest infringement of Union law and the urgency of the interim measures sought, the Commission's application for the suspension of the award of any construction contract until judgment had been given in the main proceedings was rejected.[196]

An interest originating in an omission or shortcoming on the part of a party in principle carries little weight.[197] Yet, it does not prevent the Judge hearing the application for interim relief from recognizing the parallel interest of third parties and allowing the balance to be

---

20 July 2006), Case T-114/06 R *Globe v Commission* [2006] E.C.R. II-2627, para. 148 (taking account of the interests of the applicant, a third party, the opposing party, and of the public interest in the context of an application seeking to suspend the operation of a Commission decision rejecting the applicant's bid in a tendering procedure). The individual interest of a Member of the European Parliament (MEP) in being able to continue to exercise his or her mandate prevails over the general interest of the European Parliament in the maintenance of the application of the applicant's disqualification from holding office (pursuant to national law): CFI (order of the President of 26 January 2001), Case T-353/00 R *Le Pen v European Parliament* [2001] E.C.R. II-125, paras 101–103. See ECJ (order of the President of 31 July 2003), Case C-208/03 P-R *Le Pen v European Parliament* [2003] E.C.R. I-7939, paras 107–111. Compare CFI (order of the President of 15 November 2007), Case T-215/07 *Donnici v European Parliament* [2007] E.C.R. II-4673, paras 107–115, distinguishing the aforementioned case from the situation in the present proceedings, where account must also be taken of the interests of the candidate who was appointed in the applicant's place to be a MEP. Since the specific interests of the applicant and this appointed candidate were evenly matched, the President considered that the more general interests involved—the interest of the Member State in question in having its electoral legislation respected by the European Parliament, and the interest of the European Parliament in the maintenance in force of its decisions—to find that neither of those interests could prevail in balancing the interests involved. As a result, the President took into consideration the strength of the applicant's pleas to establish a *prima facie* case and the fact that the MEP concerned had already been able to exercise his mandate for a period of more than one year to rule that the balance of interests weighed in favour of the applicant's interest to suspend the contested measure. This approach was confirmed on appeal: ECJ (order of the President of 13 January 2009), Joined Cases C-512/07 P(R) and C-15/08 P(R) *Occhetto and European Parliament v Donnici* [2009] E.C.R. I-1, paras 65–71.

[195] See, e.g. ECJ (order of the President of 16 January 1975), Case 3/75 R *Johnson & Firth Brown v Commission* [1975] E.C.R. 1, para. 7; CFI (order of the President of 16 June 1992), Joined Cases T-24 and T-28/92 R *Langnese-Iglo and Schöller Lebensmittel v Commission* [1992] E.C.R. II-1839; CFI (order of the President of 16 July 1992), Case T-29/92 R *SPO v Commission* [1992] E.C.R. II-2161.

[196] ECJ (order of the President of 13 March 1987), Case 45/87 R *Commission v Ireland* [1987] E.C.R. 1369, para.33.

[197] ECJ (order of the President of 27 September 1988), Case 194/88 R *Commission v Italy* [1988] E.C.R. 5647, para.16.

tilted in favour of the party that showed negligence in that way. In *Commission v Belgium*,[198] Belgium invoked its interest in the speedy replacement of a very old bus fleet as a defence against an application from the Commission for suspension, by way of interim measure, of the implementation of contracts for the supply of new buses. The President of the Court of Justice found that Belgium (more specifically the Walloon regional transport company) had been guilty of a gross failure to replace the bus fleet in due time, but nevertheless caused the balance of interests to tip in Belgium's favour on the grounds that the dilapidated state of the vehicles constituted a danger to the safety of staff and customers. The decision of the Judge hearing the application for interim relief could not perpetuate that situation.

IV. Consequences

A. Provisional nature

The decision on the application for interim measures takes the form of a reasoned order, **13.44** which is served on the parties[199] and is enforceable.[200] The interim measure lapses when final judgment is delivered or on the date fixed by the order.[201] On application by a party, the order may at any time be varied or cancelled on account of a change in circumstances.[202]

---

[198] ECJ (order of the President of 22 April 1994), Case C-87/94 R *Commission v Belgium* [1994] E.C.R. I-1395, paras 39–42.

[199] ECJ Rules of Procedure, Art. 162(1); EGC Rules of Procedure, Art. 107(1). See ECJ (order of the President of 31 August 2010), Case C-32/09 P(R) *Artisjus Magyar Szerzői Jogvédő Iroda Egyesület v Commission* [2010] E.C.R. I-107*, Summ. pub., paras 17–22, in which the President of the Court of Justice rejected the appellant's allegation of a breach of Art. 107(1) of the EGC Rules of Procedure, on the grounds that the Judge hearing an application for interim measures cannot be required to reply explicitly to all of the points of fact and law raised in the course of the interlocutory proceedings and it is sufficient that the reasons given validly justify his order in the light of the circumstances of the case and enable the Court of Justice to exercise its power of review (ECJ (order of the President of 31 August 2010), Case C-32/09 P(R) *Artisjus Magyar Szerzői Jogvédő Iroda Egyesület v Commission*, para. 17 and citations therein).

[200] Enforcement of the order may be made conditional on the applicant's lodging security, of an amount and nature to be fixed in the light of the circumstances: ECJ Rules of Procedure, Art. 162(2); EGC Rules of Procedure, Art.107(2). See also para. 13.06. In *R v Secretary of State for Transport, ex parte Factortame Ltd* [1997] Eu L.R. 475, at 523G, the English Divisional Court stated that an order of the Court of Justice is an order 'which is expressed in mandatory terms and which takes immediate effect. Under [Union] law, the Order of the President has the same force and direct effect as any other order of the court or provision of [Union] law. It must immediately be complied with by the party to which it is addressed . . . and failure to do so is a breach of [Union] law.'

[201] ECJ Rules of Procedure, Art. 162(3); EGC Rules of Procedure, Art. 107(3).

[202] ECJ Rules of Procedure, Art. 163; EGC Rules of Procedure, Art. 108. See ECJ (order of 14 February 2002), Case C-440/01 P(R) *Commission v Artegodan* [2002] E.C.R. I-1489, paras 61–64, underlining that the term 'change in circumstances' for the purposes of the foregoing provisions 'is to be interpreted as covering the occurrence of any factual or legal matter such as to call into question the assessment by the judge who heard the application with regard to the conditions . . . which are to be met if the operation of an act is to be suspended or other interim relief is to be granted' and thus the scope of this term 'cannot be limited to the coming to light of circumstances of a factual nature or of new facts, as is provided, with regard to applications for revision, by the second para. of [Article 44 of the Statute] or, in relation to the making of a fresh application for interim relief following the dismissal of the previous application, by [Article 164] of the Rules of Procedure of the Court of Justice or Article 109 of the Rules of Procedure of the [General Court]'. In this case, the President of the General Court had considered that the expression 'change in circumstances' had to be interpreted restrictively (CFI (order of the President of 5 September 2001), Case T-74/00 R *Artegodan v Commission* [2001] E.C.R. II-2367, paras 77–99). He decided that the annulment on appeal of the orders given in parallel cases could not be regarded as a change in circumstances, especially since the Commission had

Rejection of an application for an interim measure does not bar the party who made it from making a fresh application on the basis of new facts.²⁰³ The Judge hearing the application for interim relief will then consider whether the new facts justify the grant of the measures sought.²⁰⁴

---

failed to appeal against the order whose cancellation was sought. In those circumstances, the cancellation or variation of the earlier order would be in breach of the principle of legal certainty. However, the President of the Court of Justice annulled the order, referring to the difference between the legal force of an order given in proceedings for interim relief and that of a final judgment or of an order bringing proceedings to an end. Accordingly, the annulment on appeal of an order given by the President of the General Court could constitute a circumstance warranting the variation of an earlier order that had not been the subject of appeal. See also CFI (order of the President of 4 April 2002), Case T-198/01 R *Technische Glaswerke Ilmenau v Commission* [2002] E.C.R. II-2153, para. 123 (appeal dismissed on other grounds in ECJ (order of the President of 18 October 2002), Case C-232/02 P(R) *Commission v Technische Glaswerke Ilmenau* [2002] E.C.R. I-8977); CFI (order of the President of 30 October 2008), Case T-257/07 R II *France v Commission* [2008] E.C.R. II-236*, Summ. pub., paras 75–81 (holding that the approach taken with respect to the assessment of the *fumus boni juris* requirement was consistent with Art. 108 of the EGC Rules of Procedure, even though the latter provision did not formally apply to the case, in view of the particular circumstances of the instant proceedings); EGC (order of the President of 2 March 2011), Case T-392/09 R *l. garantovaná v Commission* [2011] E.C.R. II-33*, Summ. pub., para. 121; EGC (order of the President of 13 April 2011), Case T-393/10 R *Westfälische Drahtindustrie and Others v Commission* [2011] E.C.R. II-1697, para. 70. It may be the case that the President of the Court may make the order granting the interim relief subject to the proviso that it is up to the parties to petition the Court in the event that a change of circumstances, within the meaning of Art. 108 of the EGC Rules of Procedure, arises: see, e.g. EGC (order of the President of 28 April 2009), Case T-95/09 R *United Phosphorus v Commission*, not reported, para. 90; and with particular regard to applications seeking suspension of the obligation to provide a bank guarantee in the context of competition law, see, e.g. CFI (order of the President of 13 July 2006), Case T-11/06 R *Romana Tabucchi v Commission* [2006] E.C.R. II-2491, paras 147–148; EGC (order of the President of 13 April 2011), Case T-393/10 R *Westfälische Drahtindustrie and Others v Commission* [2011] E.C.R. II-1697, para. 70.

²⁰³ ECJ Rules of Procedure, Art. 164; EGC Rules of Procedure, Art. 109. The term 'new facts' for the purposes of the foregoing provisions 'should be taken to mean facts which appear after the order dismissing the first application for interim measures was made or which the applicant was not capable of invoking in the first application or during the proceedings leading to the first order and which are relevant to the assessment of the case in question': see, e.g. CFI (order of 13 October 2006), Case T-420/05 R II *Vischim v Commission* [2006] E.C.R. II-4085, para. 54 (and citations therein) (appeal dismissed in ECJ (order of 3 April 2007), Case C-459/06 P(R) *Vischim v Commission* [2007] E.C.R. I-53*, Summ. pub., paras 24–28). See also CFI (order of the President of 27 June 2007), Case T-345/05 R II *V v European Parliament* [2007] E.C.R. II-69*, Summ. pub., paras 21–25, 35 (and citations therein) (underlining, on the basis of the ECJ's order in CFI, Case T-420/05 R II *Vischim v Commission*, that the Judge hearing the application for interim measures is entitled to begin his examination of an application based on new facts by assessing whether the condition of urgency is satisfied and that he may take the first order as the basis for examining the second application and consider the new facts in the light of his first assessment); EGC (order of the President of 25 October 2010), Case T-18/10 R II *Inuit Tapiriit Kanatami and Others v European Parliament and Council* [2010] E.C.R. II-235*, Summ. pub., paras 22–23 (ruling that the applicants were authorized to base their further application on the draft measure concerned without waiting for the formal entry into force of the measure considered and thus the application was admissible, further noting that the examination of the fresh application would be limited to the requirement of urgency (on which basis the first application had been dismissed) and that the arguments of the parties relating to the admissibility of the main proceedings and the *prima facie* case went beyond the scope of Art. 109 of the EGC Rules of Procedure). In contrast, where a further application seeks the grant of interim measures other than those sought in the previous application, Art. 109 of the EGC Rules of Procedure does not apply; instead, such application is examined on the basis of the general provisions of Arts 278 and 279 TFEU and Art. 160 of ECJ Rules of Procedure and Art. 104 of the EGC Rules of Procedure: see, e.g. EGC (order of the President of 8 September 2010), Case T-15/10 R II *Ngele v Commission* [2010] E.C.R. II-176*, Summ. pub., para. 7.

²⁰⁴ For some examples resulting in dismissal of the application, see ECJ (order of the President of 10 July 1979), Case 51/79 R II *Buttner v Commission* [1979] E.C.R. 2387; CFI (order of the President of 11 December 1996), Case T-235/95 R II *Goldstein v Commission*, not reported (confirmed on appeal in ECJ (order of the President of 10 March 1997), Case C-78/97 P(R) *Goldstein v Commission*, not reported);

B. Costs

In general, the costs in proceedings for interim measures are reserved for the decision on the **13.45** substance.[205] Usually, costs follow the event in the main proceedings,[206] even if the successful party did not obtain the interim relief that it sought.[207] Unless one of the parties raises the issue of the distribution of costs as between the proceedings for interim relief and the main proceedings (in which case, the Court of Justice or the General Court, as the case

---

CFI (order of the President of 19 July 2004), Case T-439/03 R II *Eppe v European Parliament*, not reported; CFI (order of the President of 24 January 2006), Case T-46/03 R II *Leali v Commission* [2006] E.C.R. II-9*, Summ. pub.; CFI (order of 13 October 2006), Case T-420/05 R II *Vischim v Commission* [2006] E.C.R. II-4085, paras 55 *et seq.* (appeal dismissed in ECJ (order of 3 April 2007), Case C-459/06 P(R) *Vischim v Commission* [2007] E.C.R. I-53*); CFI (order of the President of 22 November 2007), Case T-345/05 R III *V v European Parliament* [2007] E.C.R. II-160*, Summ. pub.; EGC (order of 8 April 2011), Case T-71/10 R II *Xeda International v Commission* [2011] E.C.R. II-82*, Summ. pub.; EGC (order of the President of 25 October 2010), Case T-18/10 R II *Inuit Tapiriit Kanatami and Others v European Parliament and Council* [2010] E.C.R. II-235*, Summ. pub.; EGC (order of the President of 23 April 2012), Case T-572/11 R II *Hassan v Council*, not reported. See also CFI (order of the President of 22 November 2007), Case T-345/05 R III *V v European Parliament* [2007] E.C.R. II-160*, Summ. pub., paras 31–32: the President rejected the defendant's argument that the applicant's third application was inadmissible in not containing sufficient pleas of fact and law establishing a *prima facie* case, ruling that this third application forms part of the 'same overall framework and thus constitutes an extension of the first and second applications for interim measures' and as the first application had contained a series of pleas and arguments seeking to establish the requirement of a *prima facie* case which allowed the defendant usefully to submit its observations, the application cannot be dismissed as failing to fulfil the conditions laid down by Art. 104(2) and 44(1) of the EGC Rules of Procedure as regards the head of claim seeking suspension of the contested measure.

[205] See, e.g. EGC (order of the President of 5 February 2010), Case T-514/09 R *De Post v Commission* [2010] E.C.R. II-15*, Summ. pub., para. 36, in which the President of the General Court ruled that, in accordance with Art. 87(1) of the EGC Rules of Procedure, a decision as to costs is to be given in the final judgment or in the order which closes the proceedings. Since it is the decision in the applicant's main action that corresponds to such a judgment, the costs relating to the proceedings for interim relief are reserved. However, exceptionally, depending on the circumstances of the particular case, there may be an award on costs in the context of proceedings for interim relief before the President of the General Court (see, e.g. CFI (order of the President of 4 April 2006), Case T-398/05 R *Tesoka v FEACVT* [2006] E.C.R.-SC I-A-2-87, paras 15–17; EGC (order of the President of 19 May 2011), Case T-218/11 R *Dagher v Council and Italy* [2011] E.C.R. II-146*, Summ. pub., para. 8), or on appeal before the President of the Court of Justice (see, e.g. ECJ (order of the President of 19 July 2012), Case C-110/12 P(R) *Akhras v Council*, not reported, para. 66). Moreover, in line with the general rules on costs (see para. 25.89), where a case does not proceed to judgment, in accordance with Art. 142 of the ECJ Rules of Procedure, Art. 87(6) of the EGC Rules of Procedure, and Art. 89(6) of the CST Rules of Procedure, the costs of the interim proceedings are in the discretion of the respective Court: see, e.g. ECJ (order of the President of 27 October 2011), Case C-605/10 P(R) *Inuit Tapiriit Kanatami and Others v European Parliament and Council* [2011] E.C.R. I-164*, Summ. pub., paras 19–21 (ordering the parties to bear their own costs); EGC (order of the President of 27 February 2012), Case T-218/11 R *Dagher v Council*, not reported, paras 9–10 (ordering the Council to pay its own costs and the applicant's costs).

[206] CFI, Joined Cases T-191/96 and T-106/97 *CAS Succhi di Frutta v Commission* [1999] E.C.R. II-3181, provides an example of a case in which a party which was successful in the main proceedings nevertheless was ordered to pay its own costs in relation to the proceedings for interim relief, in which its application for interim measures was refused for want of urgency.

[207] See, e.g. EGC, Joined Cases T-50/06 RENV, T-56/06 RENV, T-62/06 RENV and T-69/06 RENV *Ireland and Others v Commission*, not reported, para. 112, in which the President of the General Court ordered the Commission, which was unsuccessful in the main action, to pay the costs of the applicants, including the costs of the application for interim measures in CFI (order of the President of 2 August 2006), Case T-69/06 R *Aughinish Alumina v Commission* [2006] E.C.R. II-58*, Summ. pub., which was dismissed for lack of urgency.

may be, will have to rule thereon), the order to pay the costs covers both the costs of the proceedings for interim measures and of the main proceedings.[208]

C. Appeal

13.46   An appeal will lie to the Court of Justice against interim orders of the General Court within two months of their notification. Appeals are dealt with by way of summary procedure.[209] The same applies with respect to an appeal to the General Court against interim orders of the Civil Service Tribunal.[210] There is no appeal against the decision on the application for interim measures before the Court of Justice.[211]

---

[208] CFI (order of 11 October 1990), Case T-50/89 *Sparr v Commission* [1990] E.C.R. II-539, para. 9.

[209] Statute, Art. 57, second and third paras. Art. 61 of the Statute, providing that if the Court of Justice quashes the decision of the General Court, it may itself give judgment in the matter, where the state of the proceedings so permits, or refer the case back to the General Court for judgment, applies also to appeals brought in the context of proceedings for interim relief: see, e.g. ECJ (order of the President of 14 June 2012), Case C-644/11 P(R) *Qualitest FZE v Council*, not reported, para. 59 (and citations therein); ECJ (order of the Vice-President of 7 March 2013), Case C-551/12 P(R) *EDF v Commission*, not reported, para. 37.

[210] Statute, Annex I, Art. 10(2)–(3). As provided in Art. 10(3), such summary procedure 'may, in so far as necessary, differ from some of the rules contained in this Annex and which shall be laid down in the [R]ules of [P]rocedure of the General Court'.

[211] See ECJ Rules of Procedure, Art. 162(1).

14

PROCEEDINGS FOR AUTHORIZATION
TO SERVE A GARNISHEE ORDER
ON THE UNION

I. Subject-Matter

A. Principle and purpose

Where a debtor fails to pay the sums owed, the creditor may seek to claim the funds owed **14.01** by a third party to its debtor. However, where that third party is the European Union,[1] account should be taken of Art. 1 of the Protocol on the Privileges and Immunities of the European Union (the 'Protocol') which provides in relevant part: 'The property and assets of the Union shall not be the subject of any administrative or legal measure of constraint without the authorisation of the Court of Justice.'[2] The purpose of this provision is to ensure that there is no interference with the functioning and independence of the Union.[3] Therefore, a garnishee order can be served on the Union only after prior authorization of the Court of Justice.[4]

---

[1] Under the former Treaty framework, proceedings for authorization to serve a garnishee order concerned the European Communities. With the entry into force of the Lisbon Treaty, such proceedings are generally effected against the European Union. Even with the replacement of the European Community with that of the Union, the EAEC Treaty still stands, and as such, such proceedings may equally be brought against the European Atomic Energy Community.

[2] Protocol (No. 7) on the Privileges and Immunities of the European Union, annexed to the TEU, the TFEU, and the EAEC Treaty, [2012] O.J. C326/266, Art. 1.

[3] See, e.g. ECJ (order of 11 May 1971), Case C-1/71 SA *X v Commission* [1971] E.C.R. 363, para. 4; ECJ (order of 17 June 1987), Case 1/87 SA *Universe Tankship v Commission* [1987] E.C.R. 2807, para. 2; ECJ (order of 11 April 1989), Case 1/88 SA *Générale de Banque v Commission* [1989] E.C.R. 857, para. 2; ECJ (order of 29 May 2001), Case C-1/00 SA *Cotecna Inspection v Commission* [2001] E.C.R. I-4219, para. 9; ECJ (order of 27 March 2003), Case 1/02 SA *Antippas v Commission* [2003] E.C.R. I-2893, para. 12; ECJ (order of 14 December 2004), Case C-1/04 SA *Tertir-Terminais de Portugal v Commission* [2004] E.C.R. I-11931, para. 10; ECJ (order of 13 October 2005), Case C-1/05 SA *Intek v Commission*, not reported, para. 13; ECJ (order of 13 October 2005), Case C-2/05 SA *Names v Commission*, not reported, para. 13; ECJ (order of 13 October 2005), Case C-3/05 SA *Statistical Agency of the Republic of Kazakhstan v Commission*, not reported, para. 13; ECJ (order of 13 October 2005), Case C-4/05 SA *Alt Ylmy v Commission*, not reported, para. 13; ECJ (order of 24 November 2005), Case C-5/05 SA *Fil do Nascimento and Others v Commission*, not reported, para. 11; ECJ (order of 19 November 2012), Case C-1/11 SA *Marcuccio v Commission*, not reported, para. 22.

[4] In certain older judgments, the Court has referred to 'attachment order' instead of 'garnishee order', though no difference in meaning appears to be intended. See, e.g. ECJ (order of 11 May 1971), Case C-1/71 SA *X v Commission* [1971] E.C.R. 363.

B. Competent court

14.02 The Court of Justice has exclusive jurisdiction over these proceedings, since Art. 256(1) TFEU and the Statute do not confer jurisdiction on the General Court with respect to actions brought under Art. 1 of the Protocol.

II. Identity of the Parties

A. Applicants

14.03 Proceedings for authorization to serve a garnishee order on a Union institution, body, office, or agency[5] are brought by a natural or legal person in relation to the amounts owed by the institution to the party's debtor.

Nothing precludes a Member State from bringing an application for authorization to serve a garnishee order on the Union. However, to date, no Member State has done so.

B. Defendants

14.04 It is the Union institution, body, office, or agency that owes sums to the applicant's debtor which will be summoned before the Court of Justice. To date, all applications have been brought against the Commission.

III. Special Characteristics

A. Automatic immunity

14.05 The immunity provided for in Art. 1 of the Protocol is automatic. There is no need for the Union institution concerned to rely expressly on Art. 1 of the Protocol, in particular by giving notice to the person who caused the order to be issued. Under those circumstances, it is for the latter to seek authorization from the Court to waive the immunity. However, if the institution concerned states that it has no objection to the measure of constraint, the application for authorization is devoid of purpose and need not be considered by the Court.[6]

---

[5] However, so far there is no case-law as regards proceedings for a garnishee order lodged against a Union body, office, or agency. Recent case-law refers generally to a Union institution (see, e.g. ECJ (order of 24 November 2005), Case C-5/05 SA *Gil do Nascimento and Others v Commission*, not reported, paras 11–15; ECJ (order of 19 November 2012), Case C-1/11 SA *Marcuccio v Commission*, not reported, para. 22). Nevertheless, in all likelihood, a Union body, office, or agency may be a defendant to proceedings for authorization to serve a garnishee order on the Union.

[6] See, e.g. ECJ (order of 11 May 1971), Case C-1/71 SA *X v Commission* [1971] E.C.R. 363, paras 7, 9; ECJ (order of 17 June 1987), Case 1/87 SA *Universe Tankship v Commission* [1987] E.C.R. 2807, paras 4–7; ECJ, Case C-182/91 *Forafrique Burkinabe v Commission* [1993] E.C.R. I-2161, para. 12; ECJ (order of 10 January 1995), Case C-1/94 SA *Dupret v Commission* [1995] E.C.R. I-1, paras 3–5; ECJ (order of 24 November 2005), Case C-5/05 SA *Fil do Nascimento and Others v Commission*, not reported, paras 15–17; ECJ (order of 19 November 2012), Case C-1/11 SA *Marcuccio v Commission*, not reported, para. 22.

B. Limited jurisdiction

It is neither the object nor the effect of Art. 1 of the Protocol to substitute review by the Court **14.06** of Justice for that exercised by the national court having jurisdiction to determine whether all the conditions for a garnishee order are actually satisfied. Thus, the determination of the question of the garnishee's indebtedness to the debtor does not fall within the jurisdiction of the Court of Justice, but within that of the competent national court.[7] Consequently, the Court of Justice's competence with respect to garnishee orders is confined to considering whether such measures are likely, in view of the effects which they have under the applicable national law, to interfere with the proper functioning and the independence of the European Union.[8] However, the Court can make such an assessment only if the indebtedness is not contested by the institution concerned, or has been found in a prior judgment of a national court.[9]

C. Applications

The Court has repeatedly held that the functioning of the Union may be hampered by **14.07** measures of constraint affecting the financing of common policies or the implementation of the action programmes established by the Union.[10] Since an application for authorization to serve a garnishee order on the Union normally concerns funds that the Commission decided to allocate to the financing of a common policy[11] or the implementation of a specific action programme,[12] such application will rarely be successful.[13]

---

[7] See, e.g. ECJ (order of 27 March 2003), Case 1/02 SA *Antippas v Commission* [2003] E.C.R. I-2893, para. 13; ECJ (order of 13 October 2005), Case C-1/05 SA *Intek v Commission*, not reported, para. 15; ECJ (order of 13 October 2005), Case C-2/05 SA *Names v Commission*, not reported, para. 15; ECJ (order of 13 October 2005), Case C-3/05 SA *Statistical Agency of the Republic of Kazakhstan v Commission*, not reported, para. 15; ECJ (order of 13 October 2005), Case C-4/05 SA *Alt Ylmy v Commission*, not reported, para. 15; ECJ (order of 24 November 2005), Case C-5/05 SA *Fil do Nascimento and Others v Commission*, not reported, para. 13. See, however, ECJ (order of 19 November 2012), Case C-1/11 SA *Marcuccio v Commission*, not reported, paras 23–31.

[8] See, e.g. ECJ (order of 17 June 1987), Case 1/87 SA *Universe Tankship v Commission* [1987] E.C.R. 2807, para. 3; ECJ (order of 29 May 2001), Case 1/00 SA *Cotecna Inspection v Commission* [2001] E.C.R. I-4219, para. 10; ECJ (order of 27 March 2003), Case 1/02 SA *Antippas v Commission* [2003] E.C.R. I-2893, para. 14; ECJ (order of 13 October 2005), Case C-1/05 SA *Intek v Commission*, not reported, para. 14; ECJ (order of 13 October 2005), Case C-2/05 SA *Names v Commission*, not reported, para. 14; ECJ (order of 13 October 2005), Case C-3/05 SA *Statistical Agency of the Republic of Kazakhstan v Commission*, not reported, para. 14; ECJ (order of 13 October 2005), Case C-4/05 SA *Alt Ylmy v Commission*, not reported, para. 14; ECJ (order of 24 November 2005), Case C-5/05 SA *Fil do Nascimento and Others v Commission*, not reported, para. 12.

[9] ECJ (order of 13 October 2005), Case C-1/05 SA *Intek v Commission*, not reported, paras 16–22; ECJ (order of 13 October 2005), Case C-2/05 SA *Names v Commission*, not reported, paras 16–22; ECJ (order of 13 October 2005), Case C-3/05 SA *Statistical Agency of the Republic of Kazakhstan v Commission*, not reported, paras 16–22; ECJ (order of 13 October 2005), Case C-4/05 SA *Alt Ylmy v Commission*, not reported, paras 16–22; ECJ (order of 24 November 2005), Case C-5/05 SA *Fil do Nascimento and Others v Commission*, not reported, paras 18–21.

[10] ECJ (order of 11 April 1989), Case 1/88 SA *Générale de Banque v Commission* [1989] E.C.R. 857, para. 13; ECJ (order of 29 May 2001), Case C-1/00 SA *Cotecna Inspection v Commission* [2001] E.C.R. I-4219, para. 12; ECJ (order of 27 March 2003), Case C-1/02 SA *Antippas v Commission* [2003] E.C.R. I-2893, para. 15; ECJ (order of 14 December 2004), Case C-1/04 SA *Tertir-Terminais de Portugal v Commission* [2004] E.C.R. I-11931, para. 14.

[11] ECJ (order of 14 December 2004), Case C-1/04 SA *Tertir-Terminais de Portugal v Commission* [2004] E.C.R. I-11931 (fisheries).

[12] ECJ (order of 29 May 2001), Case C-1/00 SA *Cotecna Inspection v Commission* [2001] E.C.R. I-4219; ECJ (order of 27 March 2003), Case C-1/02 SA *Antippas v Commission* [2003] E.C.R. I-2893. Both cases concerned the financing of action programmes in the field of development aid.

[13] For a successful application, see ECJ (order of 11 April 1989), Case 1/88 SA *Générale de Banque v Commission* [1989] E.C.R. 857.

15

UNLIMITED JURISDICTION OF THE UNION COURTS IN RESPECT OF ACTIONS RELATING TO SANCTIONS

I. General

A. Legal basis

15.01 Under Art. 261 TFEU, regulations adopted jointly by the European Parliament and the Council and by the Council, pursuant to the provisions of the Treaties, may give the Court of Justice of the European Union unlimited jurisdiction with regard to penalties provided for in such regulations.[1] Accordingly, there must be a legal basis for the Union courts'

---

[1] The relevant regulations are as follows:

(1) Regulation No. 11 of 27 June 1960 concerning the abolition of discrimination in transport rates and conditions, in implementation of Art. 79(3) of the Treaty establishing the European Economic Community (now Art. 95(3) TFEU) ([1959–1962] O.J. English Spec. Ed. I, 60), Art. 25;

(2) Council Regulation (EC) No. 2532/98 of 23 November 1998 concerning the powers of the European Central Bank to impose sanctions ([1998] O.J. L318/4), Art. 5;

(3) Council Regulation (EC) No. 1/2003 of 16 December 2002 on the implementation of the rules on competition laid down in Arts 81 and 82 of the Treaty (now Arts 101 and 102 TFEU) ([2003] O.J. L1/1), Art. 31;

(4) Council Regulation (EC) No. 139/2004 of 20 January 2004 on the control of concentrations between undertakings (the EC Merger Regulation) ([2004] O.J. L1/1), Art. 16;

(5) Regulation (EC) No. 216/2008 of the European Parliament and of the Council of 20 February 2008 on common rules in the field of civil aviation and establishing a European Aviation Safety Agency, and repealing Council Directive 91/670/EEC, Regulation (EC) No. 1592/2002 and Directive 2004/36/EC ([2008] O.J. L79/1), Art. 25(4);

(6) Regulation (EC) No. 80/2009 of the European Parliament and of the Council of 14 January 2009 on a Code of Conduct for computerised reservation systems and repealing Council Regulation (EEC) No. 2299/89 ([2009] O.J. L35/47), Art. 15(5);

(7) Regulation (EC) No. 391/2009 of the European Parliament and of the Council of 23 April 2009 on common rules and standards for ship inspection and survey organsations ([2009] O.J. L131/11), Art. 6(4);

(8) Regulation (EU) No. 513/2011 of the European Parliament and of the Council of 11 May 2011 amending Regulation (EC) No. 1060/2009 on credit rating agencies ([2011] O.J. L145/30), Art. 36e;

(9) Regulation (EU) No. 1173/2011 of the European Parliament and of the Council of 16 November 2011 on the effective enforcement of budgetary surveillance in the euro area ([2011] O.J. L306/1), Art. 8(5);

(10) Regulation (EU) No. 648/2012 of the European Parliament and of the Council of 4 July 2012 on OTC derivatives, central counterparties and trade repositories ([2012] O.J. L201/1), Art. 69

(11) Regulation (EEC, Euratom, ECSC) No. 259/68 of the Council of 29 February 1968 laying down the Staff Regulations of Officials and the Conditions of Employment of Other Servants of the European Communities and instituting special measures temporarily applicable to officials of the Commission, ([1968] O.J. Spec. Ed. I, 30), as reformed by Council Regulation (EC, Euratom) No. 723/2004 of 22 March 2004 amending the Staff Regulations of officials of the European Communities and the

unlimited jurisdiction, and where a particular regulation does not confer such jurisdiction, a claim submitted on this basis is inadmissible.[2]

In addition, the Union courts may have unlimited jurisdiction under an arbitration clause (Art. 272 TFEU) or a special agreement (Art. 273 TFEU).

B. Changes brought by the Treaty of Lisbon

Art. 261 TFEU reproduces verbatim former Art. 229 EC, except for the replacement of 'this Treaty' with 'Treaties' and 'Court of Justice' with 'Court of Justice of the European Union', which merely gives expression to, on the one hand, changes made to the constitutional framework of the EU following the entry into force of the Lisbon Treaty (i.e. the replacement of the EC Treaty with the TEU and the TFEU) and, on the other hand, the fact that such unlimited jurisdiction may be exercised by not only the Court of Justice, but also by the General Court and the Civil Service Tribunal pursuant to the allocation of jurisdiction between them as set down in the Treaties. **15.02**

C. EAEC Treaty and former ECSC Treaty

As far as the EAEC Treaty is concerned, the Commission is empowered to impose sanctions by virtue of Art. 83 EAEC. Art. 144(b) EAEC confers on the Court of Justice of the European Union unlimited jurisdiction in proceedings instituted against such sanctions.[3] With the entry into force of the new consolidated version of the EAEC Treaty in tandem with that of the Lisbon Treaty, Art. 261 TFEU now applies to this Treaty.[4] **15.03**

Furthermore, there used to be legal bases setting forth the Court of Justice's unlimited jurisdiction under the now-expired ECSC Treaty.[5]

D. Objective

Sometimes, an action for annulment is too narrow to be used in order to contest an act of Union law imposing a fine. This is because, in annulment proceedings, a Union court has **15.04**

Conditions of Employment of other servants of the European Communities, [2004] O.J. L124/1; *corrigendum* in [2005] l51/28, Arts 22 and 91(1). See further para. 18.01.

[2] For example, as regards the European Agricultural Guidance and Guarantee Fund (EAGGF), see ECJ, Case C-418/06 P *Belgium v Commission* [2008] E.C.R. I-3047, paras 153–156; CFI, Case T-263/06 *Greece v Commission* [2008] E.C.R. II-290*, Summ. pub., para. 209; CFI, Case T-33/07 *Greece v Commission* [2009] E.C.R. II-74*, Summ. pub., para. 381 (appeal dismissed on other grounds in ECJ, Case C-321/09 P *Greece v Commission* [2011] E.C.R. I-51*, Summ. pub.); as regards restrictive measures adopted on the basis of the provisions on the Common Foreign and Security Policy (CFSP), see EGC (order of 11 January 2012), Case T-301/11 *Ben Ali v Council*, not reported, para. 62. Furthermore, the Union courts' unlimited jurisdiction under Art. 261 TFEU cannot be inferred from the wording of Art. 258 TFEU or Art. 260 TFEU in the context of a judgment for failure to fulfil obligations: EGC, Case T-139/06 *France v Commission* [2011] E.C.R. II-7315, para. 81.

[3] Art. 144(a) EAEC also confers unlimited jurisdiction on the Court of Justice of the European Union in proceedings instituted under Art. 12 EAEC to have the appropriate terms fixed for the granting by the Commission of licences or sub-licences.

[4] See Art. 106a(1) of the consolidated version of the EAEC Treaty, [2012] O.J. C327/1.

[5] See Arts 36 and 88 ECSC.

jurisdiction only to review the legality of the act in the light of pleas raised in the application or of its own motion. If the act is found to be unlawful, it may only be annulled entirely or in part. In the event that the act is partly annulled, the sanction imposed may become unreasonable having regard to the breach of Union law remaining extant.[6] Moreover, a 'lawful' act may possibly impose a sanction not consonant with what is considered to be just for reasons peculiar to the person on whom the sanction is imposed or relating to the particular circumstances of the case which may not be taken into account in the judicial review of the legality of the act. Accordingly, for example, the amount of a fine imposed by the Commission for infringement of the competition rules may be reduced by the Court on the grounds that the calculation was based on defective data provided by the relevant undertaking, without any blame attaching to the Commission.[7]

E. Notion of unlimited jurisdiction

15.05   The precise extent of the Court's 'unlimited jurisdiction' in actions brought against sanctions has not yet been definitively determined. The case-law has provided some clarification.

On the one hand, the Union judicature has proclaimed that unlimited jurisdiction under Art. 261 TFEU does not constitute an autonomous remedy; rather, its sole effect is to enlarge the extent of the powers the Union courts have in the context of an action for annulment under Art. 263 TFEU, and thus, an action in which the Union courts are asked to exercise their unlimited jurisdiction with respect to a decision imposing a penalty includes a request for the annulment, in whole or in part, of that decision.[8] On the other hand, it has been consistently held that more than a simple review of legality within an action for annulment, which only permits dismissal of the action for annulment or annulment of the contested measure, the unlimited jurisdiction conferred on the Union judicature authorizes it to vary the contested measure, even without annulling it, by taking into account all of the factual circumstances, so as to amend, for example, the amount of the fine.[9] The Union judicature is therefore empowered, in addition to carrying out a mere

---

[6] See, e.g. EGC, Case T-379/06 *Kaimer and Others v Commission* [2011] E.C.R. II-64*, Summ. pub. (appeal dismissed: ECJ, Case C-264/11 P *Kaimer and Others v Commission*, not reported). However, the Court may also annul the provision imposing the sanction altogether: EGC, Case T-385/06 *Aalberts Industries and Others v Commission* [2011] E.C.R. II-1223, para. 122 (appeal dismissed: ECJ (judgment of 4 July 2013), Case C-287/11 P *Commission v Aalberts Industries and Others*, not reported).

[7] See, e.g. CFI, Case T-156/94 *Aristrain v Commission* [1999] E.C.R. II-645, para. 586 (set aside in part on other grounds in ECJ, Case C-196/99 P *Aristrain v Commission* [2003] E.C.R. I-11005); EGC, Case T-322/01 *Roquette Frères v Commission* [2006] E.C.R. II-3137, paras 293–316; EGC, Case T-217/06 *Arkema France and Others v Commission* [2011] E.C.R. II-2593, paras 247–280.

[8] See, e.g. CFI (order of 9 November 2004), Case T-252/03 *FNICGV v Commission* [2004] E.C.R. II-3795, paras 20–26; CFI, T-69/04 *Schunk and Schunk Kohlenstoff-Technik v Commission* [2008] E.C.R. II-2567, para. 246; EGC, Case T-132/07 *Fuji Electric Co. v Commission* [2011] E.C.R. II-4091, para. 207. In particular, as underlined in CFI, Case T-252/03 *FNICGV v Commission*, as far as the allocation of jurisdiction between the Court of Justice and the General Court is concerned, neither Art. 256 TFEU nor Art. 51 of the Statute refers to Art. 261 TFEU, which indicates that a separate legal procedure is not involved. On this basis, the Court held that, since unlimited jurisdiction is not an autonomous form of action, the time limits laid down by the sixth para. of Art. 263 TFEU apply to an action in which recourse is made to Art. 261 TFEU.

[9] See, e.g. ECJ, Joined Cases C-238/99 P, C-244/99 P, C-245/99 P, C-247/99 P, C-250/99 P to C-252/99 P, and C-254/99 P *Limburgse Vinyl Maatschappij and Others v Commission* [2002] E.C.R. I-8375, para. 692; ECJ, Case C-534/07 P *Prym and Prym Consumer v Commission* [2009] E.C.R. I-7415, para. 86; CFI, Joined Cases T-67/00, T-68/00, T-71/00, and T-78/00 *JFE Engineering and Others v Commission* [2004]

review of the lawfulness of the penalty, to substitute its own appraisal for the Commission and, consequently, to cancel, reduce, or increase the fine or penalty payment imposed.[10] Furthermore, the Court has pointed out that the discretion enjoyed by the Commission and the limits which it has imposed in that regard do not prejudge the exercise by the Union judicature of its unlimited jurisdiction.[11]

In the context of Union competition rules, commentators have advocated a broader view of unlimited jurisdiction so as to encompass the review of decisions adopted by the Commission, not just the amount of the fines imposed, thus ensuring full appellate jurisdiction at Union level.[12] Going one step further, it is even claimed that unlimited jurisdiction embraces all the sanctions which are available to the Court in other procedures.[13] However, the Court has no power to issue directions, for instance, to order repayment of a fine which has been paid.[14]

E.C.R. II-2501, para. 577 (appeal dismissed in ECJ, Joined Cases C-403/04 P and C-405/04 P *Sumitomo Metal Industries v Commission* [2007] E.C.R. I-729*, Summ. pub.); EGC, Case T-11/06 *Romana Tabacchi v Commission* [2011] E.C.R. II-6681, para. 265; EGC, Joined Cases T-117/07 and T-121/07 *Areva and Others v Commission* [2011] E.C.R. II-633, para. 227; EGC, Case T-132/07 *Fuji Electric Co. v Commission* [2011] E.C. R. II-4091, para. 208; EGC, Case T-299/08 *Elf Aquitaine v Commission* [2011] E.C.R. II-2149, para. 379 (appeal dismissed: ECJ (order of 2 February 2012), Case C-404/11 P *Elf Aquitaine v Commission*, not reported); EGC, Case T-343/08 *Arkema France v Commission* [2011] E.C.R. II-2287, para. 203; EGC (judgment of 2 February 2012), Case T-76/08 *EI du Pont de Nemours and Company and Others v Commission*, not reported, para. 164; EGC (judgment of 2 February 2012), Case T-77/08 *The Dow Chemical Company v Commission*, not reported, para. 181; EGC (judgment of 2 February 2012), Case T-83/08 *Denki Kagaku Kogyo Kabushiki Kaisha and Denka Chemicals v Commission*, not reported, para. 264. See also EGC, Case T-79/06 *Sachsa Verpackung v Commission* [2011] E.C.R. II-406*, Summ. pub., paras 179–182: in rejecting the claim by the Commission that the applicant's plea was inadmissible because it was not submitted in the context of pleas seeking annulment of the contested measure and that it was only under circumstances that there was an illegality vitiating the contested measure that the Court exercises its unlimited jurisdiction, the Court underscored that the exercise of its unlimited jurisdiction was not subordinated to the finding of an illegality and thus may amend the contested act even in the absence of annulment.

[10] See, e.g. ECJ, Case C-3/06 P *Group Danone v Commission* [2007] E.C.R. I-1331, para. 61; CFI, T-69/04 *Schunk and Schunk Kohlenstoff-Technik v Commission* [2008] E.C.R. II-2567, para. 243; EGC, Case T-79/06 *Sachsa Verpackung v Commission* [2011] E.C.R. II-406*, Summ. pub., para. 180. See also EGC, Case T-11/06 *Romana Tabacchi v Commission* [2011] E.C.R. II-6681, para. 266 (and citations therein) ('Furthermore, the Court is not bound by the Commission's calculations or by its Guidelines when it adjudicates in the exercise of its unlimited jurisdiction, but must make its own appraisal, taking account all of the circumstances of the case'). See in this respect also CFI, Joined Cases T-101/05 and T-111/05 *BASF and UCB v Commission* [2007] E.C.R. II-4949, para. 213 (and citations therein).

[11] See, e.g. CFI, Joined Cases T-259/02 to T-264/02 and T-271/02 *Raiffeisen Zentralbank Osterreich and Others v Commission* [2006] E.C.R. II-5169, para. 227 (appeals dismissed on other grounds in ECJ, Joined Cases C-125/07 P, C-133/07 P, and C-137/07 P *Erste Group Bank and Others v Commission* [2009] E.C.R. I-8681); CFI, Case T-116/04 *Wieland-Werke v Commission* [2009] E.C.R. II-1087, para. 33; CFI, Case T-122/04 *Outokumpu and Luvata v Commission* [2009] E.C.R. II-1135, para. 36; EGC, Case T-216/06 *Lucite International and Lucite International UK v Commission* [2011] E.C.R. II-284*, Summ. pub., para. 120.

[12] See, e.g. A. Arabadjiev, 'Unlimited Jurisdiction: What Does It Mean Today?', in P. Cardonnel, A. Rosas and N. Wahl (eds), *Constitutionalising the EU Judicial System—Essays in Honour of Pernilla Lindh* (Oxford and Portland Oregon, Hart Publishing, 2012), 383–402.

[13] Thus, in staff cases, it has been held that the Union judicature, exercising its unlimited jurisdiction, may annul an act or award damages, as well as order any other form of redress: see, e.g. CFI, Case T-10/02 *Girardot v Commission* [2004] E.C.R.-SC II-483, para. 89 (appeal dismissed: ECJ, Case C-348/06 P *Commission v Girardot* [2008] E.C.R.-SC I-B-2-5); see also EGC (judgment of 12 May 2010), Case T-491/08 P *Bui Van v Commission*, not reported, para. 88.

[14] See, e.g. ECJ, Case C-5/93 P *DSM v Commission* [1999] E.C.R. I-4695, paras 36–37; CFI (order of 14 January 2004), Case T-202/02 *Makedoniko Metro and Michaniki v Commission* [2004] E.C.R. II-181, para. 53. Moreover, the Union judicature has no power, either in the context of an action for annulment or in the exercise of its unlimited jurisdiction, to amend the decision of a Union institution by replacing the addressee thereof by another natural or legal person when that addressee still exists; that power belongs only to

While it remains to be seen the extent to which the scope of the Union courts' unlimited jurisdiction may be further refined by the case-law, the action for annulment in combination with unlimited jurisdiction in respect of the amount of the fine has withstood challenge in the light of the requirements of the principle of effective judicial protection in Article 47 of the Charter of Fundamental Rights of the European Union.[15]

II. Scope of Review

A. Review of the sanction

15.06 The Court is empowered to review the sanction imposed by the contested act.[16] The applicant[17] may adduce submissions which are targeted exclusively against the sanction,[18] alleging, for instance, that the amount of the sanction is such that it is in breach of the principle of equal treatment or proportionality, or that the reasoning for the sanction is insufficient or erroneous.[19]

---

the institution that adopted the measure concerned, and it is not for the Court to substitute another person for the identity of the person to whom that measure is addressed: see CFI, Joined Cases T-259/02 to T-264/02 and T-271/02 *Raiffeisen Zentralbank Osterreich and Others v Commission* [2006] E.C.R. II-5169, para. 72 (and citations therein) (appeals dismissed on other grounds in ECJ, Joined Cases C-125/07 P, C-133/07 P, C-135/07 P, and C-137/07 P *Erste Group Bank and Others v Commission* [2009] E.C.R. I-8681).

[15] See, e.g. ECJ (judgment of 8 December 2011), Case C-272/09 P *KME Germany and Others*, not reported, paras 91–106; ECJ (judgment of 8 December 2011), Case C-386/10 P *Chalkor v Commission*, not reported, paras 45–67; ECJ (judgment of 8 December 2011), Case C-389/10 P *KME Germany and Others v Commission*, not reported, paras 118–134. Moreover, in the context of arguments challenging the imposition of a fine based on alleged breach of the principle *nulla poena sine lege*, the Court emphasized that by virtue of the exercise of its unlimited jurisdiction, allowing it not only to annul the contested decision but also to cancel, reduce, or increase the fine imposed, the Commission's administrative practice is subject to 'full' or 'unlimited review' by the Union judicature: see, e.g. CFI, Case T-279/02 *Degussa v Commission* [2006] E.C.R. II-897, para. 79 (appeal dismissed in ECJ, Case C-266/06 P *Degussa v Commission* [2008] E.C.R. I-81*, Summ. pub.); EGC, Case T-446/05 *Amann & Sohne and Cousin Filterie v Commission* [2010] E.C.R. II- 1255, para. 144.

[16] The Commission has asked the Court, in the exercise of its unlimited jurisdiction, to withdraw the immunity granted to an undertaking in the context of the application of Union competition rules; the Court rejected this request, holding that there were no grounds for doing so in the instant proceedings and finding it unnecessary to consider whether such a request is admissible: see EGC, Case T-216/06 *Lucite International and Lucite International UK v Commission* [2011] E.C.R. II-284*, Summ. pub., paras 180–184.

[17] Note that also the Commission is allowed to request an alteration of a fine. For example, it may in the course of proceedings ask for an increase of a fine if new facts have come to light in the pleas of the applicant. See, e.g. EGC, Case T-41/05 *Alliance One International v Commission* [2011] E.C.R. II-7101, para. 197. Conversely, the Commission may also request the Court to reduce a fine by way of a counterclaim: EGC, Case T-39/06 *Transcatab v Commission* [2011] E.C.R. II-6831, paras 398–403.

[18] Where an application pursues two objectives—that is to say, principally an action for annulment and in the alternative, an application for the annulment or reduction of the fine—it may be the case that the pleas in law submitted by the applicant do not distinguish between the two; under these circumstances, the Court may have to inquire into the scope of application of certain arguments and determine how they must be examined: see, e.g. CFI, Case T-69/04 *Schunk and Schunk Kohlenstoff-Technik v Commission* [2008] E.C.R. II-2567, paras 24–26; CFI, Case T-73/04 *Le Carbone-Lorraine v Commission* [2008] E.C.R. II-2661, paras 31–32 (appeal dismissed in ECJ, Case C-554/08 P *Le Carbone-Lorraine v Commission* [2009] E.C.R. I-189*, Summ. pub.).

[19] For some examples, see EGC, Case T-18/05 *IMI and Others v Commission* [2010] E.C.R. II-1769, paras 166–174 (breach of equal treatment); EGC, Case T-21/05 *Chalkor v Commission* [2010] E.C.R. II-1895, paras 104–113 (breach of principle of equal treatment) (appeal dismissed in ECJ (judgment of 8 December 2011), Case C-386/10 P *Chalkor v Commission*, not yet reported); EGC, Case T-59/06 *Low & Bonar and Bonar Technical Fabrics v Commission* [2011] E.C.R. II-397*, Summ. pub., paras 70–71 and 84–87 (erroneous assessment of sanction); EGC, Case T-11/06 *Romana Tabacchi v Commission* [2011] E.C.R.

Moreover, the Court has held that it may take into account the excessive length of the administrative and judicial proceedings in the exercise of its unlimited jurisdiction and reduce the fine on that ground.[20]

B. Reasonableness of the sanction

In previous case-law it had been held that '[i]t is possible for the Court to exercise its **15.07** unlimited jurisdiction under [Article 261 TFEU] only where it has made a finding of illegality affecting the decision, of which the undertaking concerned has complained in its action, and in order to remedy the consequences which that illegality has for determination of the amount of the fine imposed, by annulling or adjusting that fine if necessary'.[21] Yet, this narrow view has been superseded. Indeed, it is now generally held that the Court is entitled to assess the reasonableness of the sanction even where the act imposing it is not tainted by any illegality.[22]

II-6681, para. 267 (erroneous assessment of sanction and breach of equal treatment); EGC, Case T-386/06 *Pegler v Commission* [2011] E.C.R. II-1267, para. 142 (insufficient reasoning for sanction); EGC, Case T-132/07 *Fuji Electric Co. v Commission* [2011] E.C.R. II-4091, paras 259–269 (erroneous assessment of sanction). See further CFI, Case T-410/03 *Hoechst v Commission* [2008] E.C.R. II-881, paras 433–438 (defective reasoning and violation of rights of defence); EGC, Joined Cases T-144/07, T-147/07, T-148/07, T-149/07, T-150/07, and T-154/07 *ThyssenKrupp Liften Ascenseurs and Others v Commission* [2011] E.C.R. II-5129, paras 303–323 (defective reasoning and breach of proportionality and rights of defence).

[20] See EGC (judgment of 5 June 2012), Case T-214/06 *Imperial Chemical Industries v Commission*, not reported, paras 278–297 (and case-law cited therein). However, it ruled that there were no grounds in the instant proceedings for doing so: EGC, Case T-214/06 *Imperial Chemical Industries v Commission*, paras 298–319. By comparison, when it comes to the annulment of the contested measure, the fact that a reasonable time is exceeded does not necessarily constitute a ground for the annulment of the measure, and for the purposes of the application of the Union competition rules, exceeding a reasonable time can constitute a ground for annulment only in the case of a decision finding an infringement, provided that it is established that the breach of that principle adversely affected the rights of defence of the undertakings concerned: see, e.g. CFI, Case T-410/03 *Hoechst v Commission* [2008] E.C.R. II-881, para. 227 (and case-law therein). See further para. 7.178 (n. 711).

[21] See CFI, Case T-15/02 *BASF v Commission* [2006] E.C.R. II-497, para. 582. As such, where none of the pleas raised against the legality of the contested measure has been upheld, the Court has found that the fine imposed on the applicant in such measure should therefore not be reduced pursuant to its unlimited jurisdiction: see, e.g. CFI, Case T-329/01 *Archer Daniels Midland v Commission* [2006] E.C.R. II-3255, para. 382 (appeal dismissed on other grounds in ECJ, Case C-510/06 P *Archer Daniels Midland v Commission* [2009] E.C.R. I-1843); CFI, Case T-330/01 *Akzo Nobel v Commission* [2006] E.C.R. II-3389, para. 130.

[22] See, e.g. ECJ, Joined Cases 6/73 and 7/73 *Instituto Chemioterapico Italiano and Commercial Solvents v Commission* [1974] E.C.R. 223, paras 51–52; CFI, Case T-13/89 *ICI v Commission* [1992] E.C.R. II-1021, paras 389–394; ECJ, Case C-3/06 P *Group Danone v Commission* [2007] E.C.R. I-1331 (upholding an EGC judgment in which the fine was reduced on account of the fact that the Commission was wrong to find against the applicant in relation to aggravating circumstances); ECJ, Case C-534/07 P *Prym and Prym Consumer v Commission* [2009] E.C.R. I-7415 (upholding EGC judgment in which fine reduced on the ground that the applicants had been been wrongfully refused the benefit of the provisions of the Commission Notice on the non-imposition or reduction of fines in cartel cases); CFI, Case T-15/02 *BASF v Commission* [2006] E.C.R. II-497, particularly paras 337–338, 405–407, 419–420, 440–441, 462–463, 541–542, 612–613 (finding various instances of erroneous reasoning such that the decision was 'vitiated by illegality' but did not annul the measure, only reduced the fine); CFI, Joined Cases T-259/02 to T-264/02 and T-271/02 *Raiffesen Zentralbank Osterreich and Others v Commission* [2006] E.C.R. II-5169, para. 570 (inaccuracy of Commission findings concerning joint market share of particular undertakings) (appeals dismissed on other grounds in ECJ, Joined Cases C-125/07 P, C-133/07 P, C-135/07 P, and C-137/07 P *Erste Group Bank and Others v Commission* [2009] E.C.R. I-8681); CFI, Case T-279/02 *Degussa v Commission* [2006] E.C.R. II-897, paras 245–254 (holding the Commission fully entitled to classify infringement as serious but only partly demonstrated the actual effects of infringement, resulting in a reduction of the fine) (appeal dismissed: ECJ, Case C-266/06 P *Degussa v Commission* [2008] E.C.R. I-81*, Summ. pub.); CFI, Joined Cases T-217/03 and

Alternatively, the Court may find, taking into account the particular circumstances of the case, that it is not appropriate, in the context of its unlimited jurisdiction, to vary the amount of the fine imposed on an undertaking.[23] The fact that the examination of the pleas

---

T-245/03 *FNCBV and Others v Commission* [2006] E.C.R. II-4987, paras 357–364 (appeal dismissed in ECJ, Joined Cases C-101/07 P and C-110/07 P *Coop de France bétail et viande and Others v Commission* [2008] E.C.R. I-10193) (finding that the Commission breached a duty to state reasons, but Commission calculation, although justified, did not take due account of all the exceptional circumstances, with the result that breach should not entail annulment but modification of the fine); CFI, Case T-410/03 *Hoechst v Commission* [2008] E.C.R. II-881, particularly paras 581–582 (after observing that certain procedural irregularities can sometimes justify reduction in the fine, even though they cannot lead to an annulment of the decision, the Court took account of the Commission's breach of principles of sound administration and equal treatment to reduce the fine); CFI, Case T-450/05 *Automobiles Peugeot and Peugeot Nederland v Commission* [2009] E.C.R. II-2533, paras 327–329; EGC, Case T-161/05 *Hoechst v Commission* [2009] E.C.R. II-3555, paras 98–102 (finding that appraisal of non-contestation of the facts by the applicant should have been included in the recitals relating to cooperation and hence the applicant wrongfully denied reduction of its fine for not contesting the facts in line with the relevant provisions of the Leniency Notice); EGC, Case T-21/05 *Chalkor v Commission* [2010] E.C.R. II-1895, paras 104–113 (finding the Commission infringed the principle of equal treatment but as for consequences to be drawn from that finding, the Commission was not to blame in certain respects, leading to the conclusion that it was appropriate merely to amend the fine imposed on the applicant to reflect the fact that it did not participate in the SANCO arrangements) (appeal dismissed in ECJ (judgment of 8 December 2011), Case C-386/10 P *Chalkor v Commission*, not yet reported); EGC, Case T-29/05 *Deltafina v Commission* [2010] E.C.R. II-4077, para. 437 (the Commission did not sufficiently prove in the decision that the applicant acted as the leader of a cartel and thus was not justified in taking into account as part of the calculation of the fine); EGC, Case T-452/05 *BST v Commission* [2010] E.C.R. II-1373, paras 150–153 (finding that the Commission made a manifest error of assessment in relation to the applicant's cooperation); EGC, Case T-38/05 *Agroexpansion v Commission* [2011] E.C.R. II-7005, paras 270–272 (erroneous reasoning on the part of the Commission); EGC, Case T-217/06 *Arkema France and Others v Commission* [2011] E.C.R. II-2593, para. 274; EGC (judgment of 17 May 2013), Case T-154/09 *MRI v Commission*, not reported, paras 345–360 (fine imposed in the decision was considered to be reasonable and appropriate, notwithstanding the fact that the Commission committed an error in the calculation of the fine and insufficiently reasoned a step in its calculations). If an undertaking asks the Court of Justice on appeal to vary the amount of a fine imposed by the Commission on the basis of arguments put forward on appeal, the Court, without also setting aside the judgment of the General Court for infringing the law, has no jurisdiction to reconsider this matter. This is because it is not for the Court of Justice, where it is deciding questions of law in the context of an appeal, to substitute, on grounds of fairness, its own appraisal for that of the General Court adjudicating, in the exercise of its unlimited jurisdiction, on the amount of a fine imposed on an undertaking by reason of its infringement of Union law: ECJ, Case C-320/92 P *Finsider v Commission* [1994] E.C.R. I-5697, paras 45–46; see further, e.g. ECJ, Joined Cases C-189/02 P, C-202/02 P, C-205/02 P to C-208/02 P, and C-213/02 P *Dansk Rørindustri and Others v Commission* [2005] E.C.R. I-5425, paras 145–146; ECJ, Case C-397/03 P *Archer Daniels Midland and Archer Daniels Midland Ingredients v Commission* [2006] E.C.R. I-4429, para. 152; ECJ, Case C-113/04 P *Technische Unie v Commission* [2006] E.C.R. I-8831, paras 210–213; ECJ, Case C-328/05 P SGL *Carbon v Commission* [2007] E.C.R. I-3921, para. 98; ECJ (order of 11 September 2008), Case C-468/07 P *Coats Holdings and J&P Coats v Commission* [2008] E.C.R. I-127*, Summ. pub., para. 24; ECJ, Case C-534/07 P *William Prym and Prym Consumer v Commission* [2009] E.C.R. I-7415, para. 112; ECJ (order of 2 February 2012), Case C-404/11 P *Elf Aquitaine v Commission*, not reported, para. 90; ECJ (order of 7 February 2012), Case C-421/11 P *Total and Elf Aquitaine v Commission*, not reported, para. 87. Yet, the Court of Justice has made clear that the exercise of that jurisdiction cannot result in a breach of the principle of equal treatment between undertakings which have participated in an agreement or concerted practice contrary to Union competition rules and thus the Court of Justice may entertain pleas on that basis: see, e.g. ECJ, Case C-407/04 P *Dalmine v Commission* [2007] E.C.R. I-829, paras 153–155; ECJ, Case C-411/04 P *Salzgitter Mannesmann v Commission* [2007] E.C.R. I-959, paras 69–74; ECJ, Case C-266/06 P *Degussa v Commission* [2008] E.C.R. I-81*, Summ. pub., paras 95, 114.

[23] See, e.g. EGC, Case T-343/08 *Arkema France v Commission* [2011] E.C.R. II-2287, paras 204–206; EGC, Case T-41/05 *Alliance One International v Commission* [2011] E.C.R. II-7101, para. 197. See also EGC, Case T-113/07 *Toshiba Corp. v Commission* [2011] E.C.R. II-3989, para. 297: given that the illegality vitiating the contested measure concerned the choice itself of the basis on which to calculate the fine imposed on the applicant, the Court was not able to calculate the fine and thus found that it was not appropriate to exercise its unlimited jurisdiction in this regard.

challenging the lawfulness of a Commission decision imposing a fine for infringement of Union competition rules has revealed an illegality does not dispense the Court from examining whether it is necessary to amend the contested decision.[24] Depending on the circumstances of the case, the Court may determine, for example, that despite the fact that the contested measure is vitiated by an illegality, it is not necessary to modify the amount of the fine set by the Commission.[25] It may also be the case that the annulment of the contested measure, either in all or in part, may make it unnecessary for the Court to exercise its unlimited jurisdiction.[26]

C. Criteria

Generally, the gravity and the duration of the infringement of Union law are the most **15.08** important criteria which are used to determine the amount of the sanction. In addition, consideration is given to the particular circumstances of the case and to the context in which the infringement took place.[27]

In the context of unlimited jurisdiction in connection with Union competition rules, the Court's assessment of the appropriateness of the fine imposed by the Commission may justify the production and taking into account of additional information which is not mentioned in the contested decision.[28]

III. Force of Unlimited Jurisdiction

Under Art. 261 TFEU, the substance of the Court's unlimited jurisdiction is determined **15.09** by the regulations which provide for such jurisdiction: the Court may cancel, reduce, or

---

[24] See, e.g. EGC, Joined Cases T-122/07 to T-124/07 *Siemens AG Osterreich and Others v Commission* [2011] E.C.R. II-793, para. 238; EGC, Case T-348/08 *Aragoneses Industrias y Energia v Commission* [2011] E.C.R. II-7583, para. 306.

[25] See, e.g. EGC, Case T-42/07 *The Dow Chemical Company and Others v Commission* [2011] E.C.R. II-4531, para. 167: notwithstanding the fact that a plea challenging the legality of the contested measure was upheld resulting in its partial annulment, the Court considered it unnecessary to adjust the amount of the relevant fine, since the Commission's error could not have any effect on the increase applied for the duration of the infringement.

[26] See, e.g. EGC, Case T-133/07 *Mitsubishi Electric Corp. v Commission* [2011] E.C.R. II-4219, paras 280–282; EGC, Case T-348/08 *Aragoneses Industrias y Energia v Commission* [2011] E.C.R. II-7583, paras 307–308; EGC, Case T-44/07 *Kaucuk v Commission* [2011] E.C.R. II-4601, paras 67–68.

[27] See, e.g. EGC, Case T-11/06 *Romana Tabacchi v Commission* [2011] E.C.R. II-6681, paras 266–286, in which the Court took account of the particular circumstances of the instant case, including the cumulative effect of the illegalities found in the contested measure and of the applicant's weak financial capacity, to make an 'equitable assessment' of how the fine should be reduced so as to make it possible to penalize the applicant's unlawful conduct effectively, which was not disproportionate to the infringement found against the applicant appraised as a whole; EGC, Joined Cases T-117/07 and T-121/07 *Areva and Others v Commission* [2011] E.C.R. II-633, paras 319–323, in which the Court took account of all of the particular circumstances of the case to make a fair assessment of the role of leader in the infringement played by the undertaking in question in the calculation of certain increases in the basic fine to be imposed.

[28] See, e.g. EGC, Joined Cases T-456/05 and T-457/05 *Guttermann and Zwicky & Co. v Commision* [2010] E.C.R. II-1443, para. 106; EGC, Case T-132/07 *Fuji Electric Co. v Commission* [2011] E.C.R. II-4091, para. 209 (and citations therein).

increase the fine or penalty payment imposed.[29] Generally, a reduction of the fine is commonly requested by the applicant. Even if the applicant has not expressly claimed that the fine should be cancelled or reduced, the Court may do so of its own motion if it can infer such a claim indirectly from another claim.[30]

As for the possibility of increasing the amount of a fine or penalty payment, it must be considered not whether this would be *ultra petita*,[31] but rather whether it respects the rights of defence.[32] Where the General Court finds that an undertaking has had a fine imposed on it which infringes the principle of equal treatment on the grounds that the fines imposed on

---

[29] For the references of the relevant regulations, see n.1.

[30] ECJ, Case 8/56 *ALMA v High Authority* [1957 and 1958] E.C.R. 95, at 99–100; CFI, Case T-65/89 *BPB Industries and British Gypsum v Commission* [1993] E.C.R. II-389, para. 162 (appeal dismissed in ECJ, Case C-310/93 P *BPB Industries and British Gypsum v Commission* [1995] E.C.R. I-865). But see EGC, Case T-382/06 *Tomkins v Commission* [2011] E.C.R. II-1157, paras 55–59: in the context of the exercise of its unlimited jurisdiction to vary the fine imposed, the General Court considered that since the applicant withdrew its complaint alleging error of assessment with regard to the increase in the amount of the fine for the purpose of deterrence, it could not rule on that point without going beyond the bounds of the dispute, although it found in another judgment issued on the same day concerning the same cartel that the Commission had erred in applying a multiplier of 1.25 for deterrence (EGC, Case T-386/06 *Pegler v Commission* [2011] E.C.R. II-1267).

[31] See ECJ, Case C-3/06 P *Group Danone v Commission* [2007] E.C.R. I-1331, paras 56–64: on appeal, the applicant argued, *inter alia*, that the General Court had adjudicated *ultra petita* by essentially calculating the amount of the fine based on certain factors not raised at first instance. In response, the Court underlined that it is empowered to exercise its unlimited jurisdiction where the question of the amount of the fine is before it and that 'that jurisdiction may be exercised to reduce that amount as well as to increase it'. The Commission may request the Court, in the exercise of its unlimited jurisdiction, to increase the amount of the fine imposed on an undertaking. In various cases, the Court has dismissed such a request, not on the grounds that it had no power to make such an increase, but because there were no grounds in the case in question for granting it. See, e.g. CFI, Case T-61/99 *Adriatica di Navigazione v Commission* [2003] E.C.R. II-5349, paras 208–209 (upheld on appeal in ECJ, Case C-111/04 P *Adriatica di Navigazione v Commission* [2006] E.C.R. I-22*, Summ. pub., paras 90–93); CFI, Case T-65/99 *Strintzis Lines Shipping v Commission* [2003] E.C.R. II-5433, para. 30 (upheld on appeal in ECJ, Case C-110/04 P *Strintzis Lines Shipping v Commission* [2006] E.C.R. I-44*, Summ. pub., paras 62–64); CFI, Case T-66/99 *Minoan Lines v Commission* [2003] E.C.R. II-5515, paras 356–359 (appeal dismissed in ECJ (order of 17 November 2005), Case C-121/04 P *Minoan Lines v Commission*, not reported, paras 65–67); CFI, Joined Cases T-259/02 to T-264/02 and T-271/02 *Raiffeisen Zentralbank Österreich and Others v Commission* [2006] E.C.R. II-5169, paras 572–576 (appeals dismissed on other grounds in ECJ, Joined Cases C-125/07 P, C-133/07 P, C-135/07 P, and C-137/07 P *Erste Group Bank and Others v Commission* [2009] E.C.R. I-8681; EGC, Case T-11/05 *Wieland-Werke and Others v Commission* [2010] E.C.R. II-86*, Summ. pub., paras 248–250; EGC, Case T-19/05 *Boliden and Others v Commission* [2010] E.C.R. II-1843, paras 115–117; EGC, Case T-33/05 *Cetarsa v Commission* [2011] E.C.R. II-12*, Summ. pub., para. 127 (appeal dismissed in ECJ (judgment of 12 July 2012), Case C-181/11 P *Cetarsa v Commission*, not reported). In CFI, Joined Cases T-236/01, T-239/01, T-244/01 to T-246/01, T-251/01, and T-252/01 *Tokai Carbon and Others v Commission* [2004] E.C.R. II-1181, paras 107–113, the Court granted for the first time an increase of a fine requested by the Commission. The Court considered that the undertaking had called into question facts which it had conceded during the administrative procedure on the grounds of which the Commission had granted it a reduction of the fine. Thereafter, in CFI, Case T-69/04 *Schunk and Schunk Kohlenstoff-Technik v Commission* [2008] E.C.R. II-2567 paras 239–250, the Court confronted the admissibility of the Commission's counter claim to increase the amount of the fine, emphasizing that although the exercise of unlimited jurisdiction is most often requested by applicants in the sense of a reduction of the fine, there is nothing preventing the Commission from also referring to the Union judicature the question of the amount of the fine and from applying to have that fine increased. Moreover, such a possibility is expressly provided for in the relevant provisions of the Leniency Notice in the context of Union competition rules, and as the sole effect of Art. 261 TFEU is to enlarge the scope of the powers of the Union judicature in the context of the action for annulment under Art. 263 TFEU, the applicant's arguments that the application to increase the fine is incompatible with Art. 263 TFEU and fails to have regard to the subject-matter of the action defined in the application must be rejected. Ultimately, however, the Court held that there were no grounds to justify an increase of the fine in the instant proceedings (CFI, Case T-69/04 *Schunk and Schunk Kohlenstoff-Technik v Commission*, paras 251–262).

[32] See cases cited in n. 31. Moreover, in the context of staff cases, concern for the rights of defence has also been evident: see EGC (judgment of 12 May 2010), Case T-491/08 P *Bui Van v Commission*, not reported.

other undertakings which participated in the same way in the same infringement were lower, the Court logically has two ways of bringing the infringement of that principle to an end. It can either reduce the fine imposed on the first undertaking or increase the fines imposed on the other undertakings. The latter eventuality is contingent on the other undertakings also having brought an application before the Court.[33] In the *JFE Engineering* case, the Court opted, reluctantly, for the first option, that is to say, of reducing the fine. In the Court's view, the fines imposed on the other undertakings could not be increased because the Commission had not claimed such an increase and the other undertakings had therefore not been given the possibility to express their views on this question in the proceedings before the Court.[34]

---

[33] See, in that regard, EGC, Case T-217/06 *Arkema France and Others v Commission* [2011] E.C.R. II-2593, para. 342.

[34] CFI, Joined Cases T-67/00, T-68/00, T-71/00, and T-78/00 *JFE Engineering and Others v Commission* [2004] E.C.R. I-2501, paras 566–579 (appeal dismissed in ECJ, Joined Cases C-403/04 P and C-405/04 P *Sumitomo Metal Industries v Commission* [2007] E.C.R. I-729). Compare, e.g. EGC, Case T-18/05 *IMI and Others v Commission* [2010] E.C.R. II-1769, paras 166–174, and EGC, Case T-21/05 *Chalkor v Commission* [2010] E.C.R. II-1895, paras 104–113 (appeal dismissed in ECJ (judgment of 8 December 2011), Case C-386/10 P *Chalkor v Commission*, not reported), in which the Court held that the Commission infringed the principle of equal treatment with respect to imposing a fine on certain undertakings that should have been lower than those imposed on other undertakings, but it rejected the Commission's argument that the Court should increase the amounts of the fines imposed on those other undertakings, the 'SANCO producers', rather than reducing the fine imposed on the applicants.

16

APPEALS

I. Subject-Matter

A. General

16.01 The fact that an appeal is possible against judicial decisions in the Union legal order means that they have to be scrupulously reasoned. A system of two-tier legal protection in the EU enhances the legitimacy of judicial decisions and the quality of legal protection.[1]

Under Art. 169(1) of the ECJ Rules of Procedure, an appeal before the Court of Justice must seek to set aside, in whole or in part, the decision of the General Court as set out in the operative part of that decision. Moreover, under Art. 170(1) of the ECJ Rules of Procedure, an appeal must seek the same form of order, in whole or in part, as that sought at first instance and cannot seek a different form of order. As far as decisions of the European Union Civil Service Tribunal are concerned, an appeal may be brought before the General Court.[2]

In the context of an appeal, the purpose of review by the Court of Justice is primarily to examine to what extent the General Court took into consideration, in a legally correct manner, all of the arguments that the appellant relied on.[3]

This chapter addresses the main characteristics of appeals against decisions of the General Court before the Court of Justice. It should, however, be stressed that all of the observations set out below are equally applicable to appeals brought before the General Court against decisions of the Civil Service Tribunal. For specific aspects dealing with procedure in relation to appeals, see Chapter 26.

---

[1] K. Lenaerts, 'Le tribunal de première instance des communautés européennes: regards sur une décennie d'activités et sur l'apport du double degré d'instance au droit communautaire' (2000) C.D.E. 323–411.

[2] Statute, Annex I, Art. 9; Art. 256(2) TFEU; Art. 257, third para., TFEU; EGC Rules of Procedure, Arts 136a–149. On this subject, see also paras 2.37 and 18.30.

[3] See, e.g. ECJ, Case C-202/07 P *France Telecom v Commission* [2009] E.C.R. I-2369, para. 41 and citations therein. With regard to the review of a judgment of the General Court pronouncing on the legality of a Commission decision in relation to the application of Art. 101 TFEU, see, e.g. ECJ (order of 11 September 2008), Case C-468/07 P *Coats Holdings and J&P Coats v Commission* [2008] E.C.R. I-127*, Summ. pub., para. 23 and citations therein.

B. Appeals are confined to points of law

(1) Errors of law

An appeal brought before the Court of Justice against a decision of the General Court is not **16.02** an appeal on the facts and the law. Appeals are confined to points of law,[4] irrespective of the type of decision of the General Court against which they are brought.[5] The Court of Justice's jurisdiction to hear appeals is thus confined to reviewing the legality of decisions of the General Court in order to remedy errors of law and hence guarantee the necessary coherence of the Union legal order[6] and the uniform interpretation of Union law.[7] This avoids the Court of Justice having to inquire into findings of fact already made by the General Court, which satisfies the dual aim of alleviating the workload of the Court of Justice and improving the legal protection of individuals in direct actions.

An error of law may have been committed by the General Court in its appraisal of a particular plea or argument raised before it. The omission of the General Court to examine a plea of law raised before it or a form of order sought by the applicant also constitutes an error of law which may lead to the annulment of the decision of the General Court.[8]

(2) The Court of Justice has no jurisdiction to make findings of fact

The fact that appeals are confined to points of law means that the General Court has **16.03** exclusive jurisdiction to make findings as to the facts underlying the proceedings at first instance, save where the substantive inaccuracy of its findings are apparent from the documents submitted to it.[9] Parties are not entitled on appeal to contest the factual findings

---

[4] Art. 256(1), second para., TFEU; Statute, Art. 58, first para. See also ECJ, Case C-136/92 P *Commission v Brazzelli Lualdi and Others* [1994] E.C.R. I-1981, para. 29; ECJ, Case C-295/07 P *Commission v Departement du Loiret and Scott* [2008] E.C.R. I-9363, para. 95.

[5] ECJ (order of the President of 11 July 1996), Case C-148/96 P(R) *Goldstein v Commission* [1996] E.C.R. I-3883, para. 22. Consequently, an appeal against an interim order or an order dismissing an application to intervene may be based only on the pleas listed in Art. 58, first para., of the Statute: ECJ (order of the President of 19 July 1995), Case C-149/95 P(R) *Commission v Atlantic Container Line and Others* [1995] E.C.R. I-2165, paras 17–18.

[6] Opinion of Advocate–General G. Tesauro in ECJ, Case C-132/90 P *Schwedler v European Parliament* [1991] E.C.R. I-5745, at I-5757; ECJ, Case C-49/92 P *Commission v Anic Partecipazioni* [1999] E.C.R. I-4125, paras 70–71.

[7] Fifth recital in the preamble to Council Decision 88/591 (cited in para. 2.35, n. 131).

[8] See, e.g. ECJ, Case C-123/03 P *Commission v Greencore* [2004] E.C.R. I-11647, paras 40–41; see also ECJ (order of 3 June 2005), Case C-396/03 P *Killinger v Germany, Council and Commission* [2005] E.C.R. I-4967, paras 11–13; ECJ, Case C-167/06 P *Komninou and Others v Commission* [2007] E.C.R. I-141*, Summ. pub., paras 22,26–28; ECJ, Case C-200/10 P *Evropaïki Dynamiki v Commission* [2011] E.C.R. I-67*, Summ. pub., paras 30–43.

[9] See, e.g. ECJ, Case C-413/06 P *Bertelsmann and Sony Corporation of America—Impala v Commission* [2008] E.C.R. I-4951, para. 29; ECJ, Case C-440/07 P *Commission v Schneider Electric* [2009] E.C.R. I-6413, para. 103; ECJ, Case C-47/10 P *Austria—Scheucher-Fleisch and Others v Commission* [2011] E.C.R. I-10707, paras 57, 102–103; ECJ (order of 31 March 2011), Case C-433/10 P *Mauerhofer v Commission* [2011] E.C.R. I-48*, Summ. pub., para. 69; ECJ, Case C-194/09 P *Alcoa Trasformazioni v Commission* [2011] E.C.R. I-6311, paras 39–43; ECJ (order of 6 October 2011), Case C-448/10 P to C-450/10 P *ThyssenKrupp and Others v Commission* [2011] E.C.R. I-147*, Summ. pub., para. 32; ECJ, Case C-88/11 P *LG Electronics v OHIM* [2011] E.C.R. I-171*, Summ. pub., para. 36; ECJ (judgment of 10 May 2012), Case C-100/11 P *Helena Rubinstein and L'Oreal v OHIM*, not reported, para. 84; ECJ (judgment of 3 May 2011), Case C-290/11 P *Comap v Commission*, not reported, para. 70.

of the General Court[10] or to offer to adduce evidence of facts which were not found by the General Court.[11] This is because, if they were so entitled, it would oblige the Court of Justice to make a determination of the facts, which it is not competent to do on appeal.[12] Consequently, the Court of Justice must leave out of account in reviewing the decision of the General Court any new facts raised.

(3) Appraisal of evidence by the General Court

16.04 Finding certain facts may be straightforward. For example, parties may agree that a particular event occurred on a particular date or that an uncontested fact appears from a measure contested (on other grounds) before the General Court. However, often the finding of facts by the General Court has to be preceded by an appraisal of the evidence. On appeal, the Court of Justice has no jurisdiction to make findings of fact or, in principle, to inquire into the evidence on the basis of which the General Court made its findings of fact.[13] It is thus not for the Court of Justice to substitute its assessment of the evidence or to criticise the choices made by the General Court in that regard, particularly where it decides to rely on certain items of evidence and reject others.[14] Where the evidence has been properly obtained and the general principles of law and the rules of procedure in relation to the burden of proof and the taking of evidence have been observed, it is for the General Court alone to assess the value which should be attached to the evidence produced to it.[15]

---

[10] See, e.g. ECJ, Case C-378/90 P *Pitrone v Commission* [1992] E.C.R. I-2375, paras 12–13; ECJ, Case C-326/91 P *De Compte v European Parliament* [1994] E.C.R. I-2091, para. 29; ECJ, Case C-1/98 P *British Steel v Commission* [2000] E.C.R. I-10349, para. 53; ECJ (order of 13 July 2006), Case C-92/06 P *Soffass v OHIM* [2006] E.C.R. I-89*, Summ. pub.; ECJ, Case C-304/06 P *Eurohypo v OHIM* [2008] E.C.R. I-3297, paras 32–36; ECJ (judgment of 10 May 2012), Case C-100/11 P *Helena Rubinstein and L'Oreal v OHIM*, not reported, paras 73–77, 83–90, 98.

[11] ECJ, Case C-396/93 P *Henrichs v Commission* [1995] E.C.R. I-2611, para. 14.

[12] See case-law cited in n. 4.

[13] See, e.g. ECJ, Case C-53/92 P *Hilti v Commission* [1994] E.C.R. I-667, para. 42; ECJ, Case C-7/95 P *John Deere v Commission* [1998] E.C.R. I-3111, paras 21–22; ECJ, Case C-185/95 P *Baustahlgewebe v Commission* [1998] E.C.R. I-8417, para. 24; ECJ, Joined Cases C-24/01 P and C-25/01 P *Glencore and Compagnie Continentale v Commission* [2002] E.C.R. I-10119, para. 65; ECJ, Joined Cases C-204/00 P, C-205/00 P, C-211/00 P, C-213/00 P, C-217/00, P and C-219/00 P *Aalborg Portland and Others v Commission* [2004] E.C.R. I-123, paras 48–49. But see ECJ, Case C-32/95 P *Commission v Lisrestal and Others* [1996] E.C.R. I-5373, para. 40, in which the Court held that 'the assessment made by the [General Court] of the tenor and wording' of letters produced as evidence could be considered on appeal. The Court cited in support of this view of the scope of its power of review on appeal the judgment in ECJ, Case C-39/93 P *SFEI and Others v Commission* [1994] E.C.R. I-2681, para. 26, in which it held that, where the General Court not only assessed the facts but also assigned a classification to them, that categorisation could be reviewed on appeal. This is logical, since the categorisation of a letter which the Commission sent as the response to a complaint pursuant to Art. 3(2) of Regulation (EEC) No. 17 [now Art. 7(2) of (EC) Regulation No. 1/2003] is nothing other than a legal categorisation of a fact in the light of Regulation (EEC) No. 99/63 [now Regulation (EC) No. 773/2004], which determines the applicant's procedural rights. It is plain that such a legal categorisation of a fact can be reviewed by the Court of Justice on appeal. Yet, in *Lisrestal*, no legal categorisation of facts was involved, but merely the question as to whether the General Court had correctly assessed the evidence adduced, which is an entirely different matter.

[14] See, e.g. ECJ (judgment of 16 February 2012), Joined Cases C-191/09 P and C-200/09 P *Council and Commission v Interpipe Niko Tube and Interpipe NTRP*, not reported, para. 160.

[15] See, e.g. ECJ, Case C-413/06 P *Bertelsmann and Sony Corporation of America—Impala v Commission* [2008] E.C.R. I-4951, para. 29; ECJ, Case C-440/07 P *Commission v Schneider Electric* [2009] E.C.R. I-6413, para. 103; ECJ, Case C-476/08 P *Evropaïki Dynamiki v Commission* [2009] E.C.R. I-207*, Summ. pub., paras 16–17; ECJ (order of 31 March 2011), Case C-433/10 P *Mauerhofer v Commission* [2011] E.C.R. I-48*, Summ. pub., para. 70; ECJ (order of 6 October 2011), Case C-448/10 P to C-450/10 P *ThyssenKrupp and Others v Commission* [2011] E.C.R. I-147*, Summ. pub., para. 32; ECJ (order of 13 January 2012), Case

Consequently, on the one hand, an appeal brought against decisions of the General Court concerning the assessment of evidence adduced before it will be inadmissible, unless the General Court has committed an error of law.[16] On the other hand, the party bringing the appeal—the appellant[17]—may argue that evidence was not lawfully obtained or that the General Court failed to respect the legal rules and general principles relating to the burden of proof or the procedural rules of evidence.[18] As a result, the General Court must respect the parties' right to be heard.[19] Yet, this does not mean that the General Court (and the Union judicature generally) has to incorporate in full in its decision all the submissions put forward by each party. The Court, after listening to the submissions of the parties and assessing the evidence, has to decide whether or not to grant the relief sought in the application and give reasons for its decision.[20]

(4) Distortion of the evidence or of the content of the contested act

It is not always straightforward to distinguish between 'points of law' in relation to the interpretation and application of Union law which come within the scope of the Court of Justice's jurisdiction on appeal and questions of fact which fall solely within the purview of the General Court.[21]

16.05

C-462/10 P *Evropaiki Dynamiki v European Environment Agency*, not reported, para. 57; ECJ (judgment of 10 May 2012), Case C-100/11 P *Helena Rubinstein and L'Oreal v OHIM*, not reported, para. 74; ECJ (judgment of 3 May 2012), Case C-290/11 P *Comap v Commission*, not reported, para. 71.

[16] ECJ (order of 30 September 1992), Case C-294/91 P *Sebastiani v European Parliament* [1992] E.C.R. I-4997, para. 13; ECJ, Case C-53/92 P *Hilti v Commission* [1994] E.C.R. I-667, para. 42; ECJ, Case C-143/95 P *Commission v Socurte and Others* [1997] E.C.R. I-1, para. 36; ECJ (order of 11 November 2003), Case C-488/01 P *Martinez v European Parliament* [2003] E.C.R. I-13355, para. 53.

[17] ECJ Rules of Procedure, Art. 168(1)(a).

[18] ECJ (order of 11 January 1996), Case C-89/95 P *D v Commission* [1996] E.C.R. I-53, para. 14; ECJ (order of 17 September 1996), Case C-19/95 P *San Marco v Commission* [1997] E.C.R. I-4435, para. 39; ECJ (order of 6 October 1997), Case C-55/97 P *AIUFFASS and AKT v Commission* [1997] E.C.R. I-5383, para. 25; ECJ (order of 16 October 1997), Case C-140/96 P *Dimitriadis v Court of Auditors* [1997] E.C.R. I-5635, para. 27; ECJ, Case C-401/96 P *Somaco v Commission* [1998] E.C.R. I-2587, para. 54.

[19] Whether the General Court acted in breach of the rights of the defence is a question of law (ECJ, Case C-82/01 P *Aéroports de Paris v Commission* [2002] E.C.R. I-9297, para. 38). See also para. 16.09.

[20] ECJ, Case C-221/97 P *Schröder and Others v Commission* [1998] E.C.R. I-8255, para. 24. If the appellant can show that the failure by the General Court to consider certain parts of its arguments affected the outcome of the proceedings and so adversely affected its interests, this may possibly constitute a breach of the right to be heard. Cf. ECJ, Case C-237/98 P *Dorsch Consult v Council and Commission* [2000] E.C.R. I-4549, para. 51, in which the Court of Justice held that the General Court cannot be required to give express reasons for its assessment of the value of each piece of evidence presented to it, in particular where it considers that that evidence is unimportant or irrelevant to the outcome of the dispute. See also ECJ, Case C-330/00 P *AICS v European Parliament* [2001] E.C.R. I-4805, para. 37.

[21] For some applications finding points of law, not questions of fact, see, e.g. ECJ, Case C-113/04 P *Technische Unie v Commission* [2006] E.C.R. I-8831, paras 111–113, 161; ECJ, Case C-334/05 P *OHIM v Shaker* [2007] E.C.R. I-4691, paras 28–30; ECJ, Case C-47/07 P *Masdar v Commission* [2008] E.C.R. I-9761, para. 77; ECJ (order of 26 June 2009), Case C-225/08 P *Nuova Agricast v Commission* [2009] E.C.R. I-111*, Summ. pub., paras 36–37; ECJ (order of 16 September 2010), Case C-459/09 P *Dominio de la Vega v OHIM* [2010] E.C.R. I-111*, Summ. pub., paras 26–27; ECJ, Joined Cases C-471/09 P to C-473/09 P *Territoria Historico de Vizcaya and Others v Commission* [2011] E.C.R. I-111*, Summ. pub., paras 54–62; ECJ, Joined Cases C-474/09 P to C-476/09 P *Territorio Historico de Vizcaya and Others v Commission* [2011] E.C.R. I-113*, Summ. pub., paras 56–64; ECJ, Case C-552/09 P *Ferrero v OHIM* [2011] E.C.R. I-2063, paras 73–76, 95–96; ECJ, Case C-109/10 P *Solvay v Commission* [2011] E.C.R. I-10329, para. 51; ECJ, Case C-110/10 P *Solvay v Commission* [2011] E.C.R. I-10439, para. 46; ECJ, Case C-317/10 P *Union Investments Privatfonds—Uni-Credito Italiano v OHIM* [2011] E.C.R. I-5471, paras 44–47; ECJ (order of 14 March 2011), Case C-369/10 P *Ravensburger v OHIM* [2011] E.C.R. I-26*, Summ. pub., para. 68; ECJ (judgment of 19 July 2012), Case

It appears from the case-law that in exceptional circumstances a wrong finding of fact by the General Court may nevertheless produce a point of law which can be reviewed by the Court of Justice on appeal.[22] This will be the case where it is manifest from the documents in the case remitted to the General Court that the findings of fact are substantially incorrect or that the General Court has distorted the clear sense of the evidence,[23] which must be obvious from the documents in the Court's file without any need to carry out a new assessment of the facts or evidence.[24]

It may indeed happen that the General Court makes a wrong reading of the contested measure.[25] According to the Court of Justice, this error constitutes a question of law because the General Court read something into the contested measure which was not there and thereby infringed the law by substituting its own reasoning for that set out in the contested measure.[26]

Similarly, it may be apparent from the presentation of evidence in the decision of the General Court that the General Court interpreted the evidence adduced in a way that is at

---

C-337/09 P *Council v Zhejiang Xinan Chemical Industrial Group*, not reported, paras 54–57. For an application finding some points of law and others questions of fact falling outside the jurisdiction of the Court of Justice on appeal, see, e.g. ECJ, Case C-520/07 P *Commission v MTU Friedrichshafen* [2009] E.C.R. I-8555, paras 46–50.

[22] The national courts to which jurisdiction in cassation has been conferred consider that they have a general power to quash decisions of inferior courts where it appears that their assessment of the facts does not square with reality as perceived by a normal observer. Such a manifestly wrong assessment of the facts is regarded as an infringement of the law (case-law or statute law). If the Court of Justice were to put itself in a position in which findings of fact could be reviewed, this would undermine the objectives of setting up the General Court because the former power of the Court of Justice to take cognisance of certain categories of cases necessitating an inquiry into complicated facts was transferred to the General Court. In this way, the Court of Justice can concentrate on its essential task, which is guaranteeing uniformity in the interpretation of Union law, and can maintain efficient and effective legal protection in the Union legal order.

[23] As underlined by the case-law, there is a distortion of the clear sense of the evidence where, without recourse to new evidence, the assessment of the existing evidence appears to be clearly or manifestly incorrect. See, e.g. ECJ, Case C-229/05 P *PKK and KNK v Council* [2007] E.C.R I-439, para. 37; ECJ, Case C-326/05 P *Industrias Quimicas del Valles v Commission* [2007] E.C.R. I-6557, para. 60; ECJ, Joined Case C-71/09 P, Case C-73/09 P and C-76/09 P *Comitato 'Venezia voule vivere' and Others v Commission* [2011] E.C.R. I-4727, para. 153.

[24] See, e.g. ECJ, Case C-229/05 P *PKK and KNK v Council* [2007] E.C.R. I-439, para. 35; ECJ, Case C-326/05 P *Industrias Quimicas del Valles v Commission* [2007] E.C.R. I-6557, para. 57; ECJ, Case C-440/07 P *Commission v Schneider Electric* [2009] E.C.R. I-6413, para. 104; ECJ, Case C-47/10 P *Austria—Scheucher-Fleisch and Others v Commission* [2011] E.C.R. I-10707, paras 58–59; ECJ (order of 31 March 2011), Case C-433/10 P *Mauerhofer v Commission* [2011] E.C.R. I-48*, Summ. pub., paras 70–71; ECJ (order of 6 October 2011), Case C-448/10 P to C-450/10 P *ThyssenKrupp and Others v Commission* [2011] E.C.R. I-147*, Summ. pub., paras 32–34 (and further citations therein); ECJ, Case C-281/10 P *PepsiCo v Grupo Promer Mon Graphic* [2011] E.C.R. I-10153, paras 78–81. For an application of the obvious requirement, see ECJ (judgment of 16 February 2012), Joined Cases C-191/09 P and C-200/09 P *Council and Commission v Interpipe Niko Tube and Interpipe NTRP*, not reported, paras 116–117.

[25] ECJ, Case C-164/98 P *DIR International Film and Others v Commission* [2000] E.C.R. I-447, paras 44–48; ECJ, Case C-197/99 P *Belgium v Commission* [2003] E.C.R. I-8461, paras 58–67; ECJ, Joined Cases C-172/01 P, C-175/01 P, C-176/01 P, and C-180/01 P *International Power v Commission* [2003] E.C.R. I-11421, para. 156; ECJ, Joined Cases C-204/00 P, C-205/00 P, C-211/00 P, C-213/00 P, C-217/00 P, and C-219/00 P *Aalborg Portland and Others v Commission* [2004] E.C.R. I-123, paras 381–385.

[26] ECJ, Case C-164/98 P *DIR International Film and Others v Commission* [2000] E.C.R. I-447, paras 43–48. But see ECJ, Joined Cases C-204/00 P, C-205/00 P, C-211/00 P, C-213/00 P, C-217/00 P, and C-219/00 P *Aalborg Portland and Others v Commission* [2004] E.C.R. I-123, paras 381–385: in its '*Cement*' judgment, the General Court found that it was uncontested that an undertaking formed part of a particular group at the time of the infringement, whereas it was clear from the contested decision itself that that was not the case. The Court of Justice held that the General Court 'made a *manifest error* which could be detected upon reading a document such as the Cement Decision' (para. 383, emphasis added).

odds with its wording.[27] Where the General Court thus wrongly presents the evidence adduced or distorts it, this will constitute a question of law which the Court of Justice may review.[28] It should, however, be stressed that the actual assessment of the evidence by the General Court is to be regarded as definitive (see para. 16.04).

(5) Evidence on which the parties were not heard at first instance

The question whether the General Court can base its dismissal of the appellant's case on **16.06** factual evidence on which the appellant was not heard is a question of law on appeal. Furthermore, under these circumstances, the Court of Justice may also examine whether the contested decision of the General Court is in fact based on such evidence. This is because that examination is directed at the procedure followed before the General Court and is not an examination of the facts relating to the substance of the case.[29]

(6) Legal categorization of facts

In addition, the fact that appeals are confined to points of law does not preclude the Court **16.07** of Justice from reviewing the legal categorization of facts found by the General Court.[30] This is because infringements of Union law not only occur in the form of a wrong interpretation of the Union rule which has been applied or not applied, but also in that

---

[27] See in this connection the Opinion of Advocate–General J. Mischo in ECJ, Case C-433/97 P *IPK v Commission* [1999] E.C.R. I-6795, point 36, at I-6797, where he stated as follows: 'According to settled case-law, a finding of fact by the [General Court] cannot, *prima facie*, be reopened on appeal. There is, however, an exception to this principle where the finding is vitiated by a manifest error of assessment. This occurs, in particular, where a finding of fact by the [General Court] is contradicted by the case documents.'

[28] For some successful applications, see, e.g. ECJ, Case C-229/05 P *PKK and KNK v Council* [2007] E.C.R. I-439, paras 37–54; ECJ, Case C-326/05 P *Industrias Quimicas del Valles v Commission* [2007] E.C.R. I-6557, paras 60–69. For some counterexamples, see, e.g. ECJ, Case C-440/07 P *Commission v Schneider Electric* [2009] E.C.R. I-6413, paras 105–133; ECJ, Case C-260/09 P *Activision Blizzard Germany v Commission* [2011] E.C.R. I-419, paras 51–58. See also ECJ (order of 11 November 2003), Case C-488/01 P *Martinez v European Parliament* [2003] E.C.R. I-13355, para. 53; ECJ, Joined Cases C-204/00 P, C-205/00 P, C-211/00 P, C-213/00 P, C-217/00 P, and C-219/00 P *Aalborg Portland and Others v Commission* [2004] E.C.R. I-123, para. 49; ECJ, Joined Cases C-2/01 P and C-3/01 P *BAI and Commission* [2004] E.C.R. I-23, para. 47. Compare Opinion of Advocate General P. Léger in ECJ, Case C-197/99 P *Belgium v Commission* [2003] E.C.R. I-8461, points 105–120: the General Court had given a distorted picture of the evidence in so far as it had left some evidence out of account in assessing the facts. The Court of Justice did not follow its Advocate–General in this respect (see paras 121–124 of the judgment) because the evidence that the General Court had left out of account had not been brought to the Commission's attention during the administrative procedure.

[29] ECJ, Case C-480/99 P *Plant and Others v Commission and South Wales Small Mines Association* [2002] E.C.R. I-265, para. 20; ECJ (order of 27 September 2004), Case C-470/02P *UER v Commission*, not reported, para. 75.

[30] See, e.g. ECJ (order of 11 July 1996), Case C-325/94 P *An Taisce and WWF UK v Commission* [1996] E.C.R. I-3727, paras 28 and 30; ECJ (order of 17 September 1996), Case C-19/95 P *San Marco v Commission* [1996] E.C.R. I-4435, para. 39; ECJ, Case C-278/95 P *Siemens v Commission* [1997] E.C.R. I-2507, para. 44; ECJ, Case C-154/99 P *Politi v European Training Foundation* [2000] E.C.R. I-5019, para. 11; ECJ, Joined Cases C-2/01 P and C-3/01 P *BAI and Commission* [2004] E.C.R. I-23, para. 47; ECJ, Case C-424/05 P *Commission v Hosman-Chevalier* [2007] E.C.R. I-5027, paras 30–33 (finding appeal relating not to assessment of facts but their legal characterisation, thereby rejecting plea of inadmissibility); ECJ, Case C-487/06 P *British Aggregates v Commission* [2008] E.C.R. I-10515, para. 96; ECJ (order of 31 March 2011), Case C-433/10 P *Mauerhofer v Commission* [2011] E.C.R. I-48*, Summ. pub., para. 69 (and further citations therein). The question whether a 'fact' on which an application for revision can be regarded as a 'new fact' within the meaning of Art. 44 of the Statute is a question of law which is amenable to appeal (ECJ, Case C-2/98 P *De Compte v European Parliament* [1999] E.C.R. I-1787, paras 15–23; ECJ, Case C-5/93 P *DSM v Commission* [1999] E.C.R. I-4695, paras 30–33).

of a wrong categorization of a given situation of fact, as a result of which the rule at issue is wrongly applied—or, conversely, not applied—in a particular case.[31]

For example, the identification of the relevant product market for the purpose of determining whether a given undertaking is in a dominant position within the meaning of Art. 102 TFEU is a conclusion of law. Accordingly, the Court of Justice is entitled to examine whether the General Court took account of all the relevant factors. If relevant factors were not taken into consideration, the General Court will have erred in law by basing its conclusions on insufficient reasoning.[32]

(7) Error with respect to the interpretation of national law

16.08 The distinction between fact and Union law is also not straightforward when an error with respect to the interpretation of national law is alleged. As regards the examination, in the context of an appeal, of findings made by the General Court with regard to national law, the Court of Justice has jurisdiction to determine, first of all, whether the General Court, on the basis of the documents and other evidence submitted to it, distorted the wording of the national provisions at issue or of the national case-law relating to them, or of the academic writings concerning them; second, whether the General Court, as regards those particulars, made findings that were manifestly inconsistent with their content; and, lastly, whether the General Court, in examining all the particulars, attributed to one of them, for the purpose of establishing the content of the national law at issue, a significance which is not appropriate in the light of the other particulars, where that is manifestly apparent from the documentation in the case-file.[33]

(8) Extent of the duty to provide a statement of reasons

16.09 The extent of the duty to provide a statement of reasons is a point of law.[34] The judgment of the General Court must be sufficiently reasoned to enable the Court of Justice to review it.[35]

---

[31] Opinion of Advocate–General W. Van Gerven in ECJ, Case C-145/90 P *Costacurta v Commission* [1991] E.C.R. I-5449, at I-5459; ECJ, Case C-132/90 P *Schwedler v European Parliament* [1991] E.C.R. I-5745, paras 13–25; ECJ, Case C-255/90 P *Burban v European Parliament* [1992] E.C.R. I-2253, para. 5; ECJ, Case C-322/93 P *Peugeot v Commission* [1994] E.C.R. I-2727, para. 34; ECJ (order of 21 January 1997), Case C-156/96 P *Williams v Court of Auditors* [1997] E.C.R. I-239, para. 27.

[32] For an application, see ECJ, Case C-82/01 P *Aéroports de Paris v Commission* [2002] E.C.R. I-9297, paras 84–97 (with regard to the correct delimitation of the relevant market) and paras 98–102 (with the regard to the existence of a dominant position). See also the Opinion of Advocate–General F.G. Jacobs in ECJ, Case C-53/92 P *Hilti v Commission* [1994] E.C.R. I-667, point 28. Compare, e.g. ECJ, Case C-95/04 P *British Airways v Commission* [2007] E.C.R. I-2331, paras 78–79, 88, 101, 114, 122, 136–137 (finding various elements, such as assessment of market data and competitive position constitute questions of fact, not law).

[33] ECJ, Case C-263/09 P *Edwin v OHIM* [2011] E.C.R. I-5853, para. 53; ECJ (order of 29 November 2011), Case C-76/11 P *Tresplain Investments v OHIM* [2011] E.C.R. I-182*, Summ. pub., para. 66.

[34] ECJ, Case C-166/95 P *Commission v Daffix* [1997] E.C.R. I-983; ECJ, Case C-188/96 P *Commission v V.* [1997] E.C.R. I-6561, para. 24; ECJ, Case C-413/06 P *Bertelsmann and Sony Corporation of American— Impala v Commission* [2008] E.C.R. I-4951, para. 30 (and further citations therein).

[35] See, e.g. ECJ, Case C-259/96 P *Council v De Nil and Impens* [1998] E.C.R. I-2915, para. 32; ECJ, Case C-197/99 P *Belgium v Commission* [2003] E.C.R. I-8461, paras 80–83 and 126–130; ECJ, Case C-480/09 P *AceaElectrabel Produzione v Commission* [2010] E.C.R. I-13355, paras 77, 107; ECJ, Case C-280/08 P *Deutsche Telecom v Commission* [2010] E.C.R. I-9555, para. 136; ECJ (order of 7 February 2012), Case C-421/11 P *Total and Elf Aquitaine*, not reported, para. 41. If the General Court refers in its judgment to one of its earlier judgments, it necessarily integrates the grounds of that earlier judgment into the contested judgment (ECJ, Case C-248/99 P *France v Monsanto and Commission* [2002] E.C.R. I-1, para. 35).

The obligation on the General Court to give reasons for its decisions does not go so far as to require it to respond in detail to every single argument advanced by a party,[36] particularly if the argument was not sufficiently clear and precise and was not adequately supported by evidence.[37] However, the General Court is obliged to respond to all pleas raised by an applicant.[38]

The General Court must have taken account of the requirement to state reasons also in assessing purely factual matters (for instance, in determining the amount of damage sustained[39]) because the Court of Justice must be in a position to check that the General Court has not breached the law in assessing the facts.[40]

The question whether the grounds of a judgment of the General Court (or of any other decision amenable to appeal) are contradictory is a question of law.[41]

(9) Assessment of damages

In an appeal against a judgment given in an action for damages against the Union brought **16.10** pursuant to Art. 268 TFEU and the second paragraph of Art. 340 TFEU, the General Court has the last word on whether there has been loss or damage or an event causing damage, except where there is a wrong presentation or a distortion (*'dénaturation'*) of evidence.[42] The question

---

[36] See, e.g. ECJ (order of 29 October 2009), Case C-85/09 P *Portela v Commission* [2009] E.C.R. I-178*, Summ. pub., paras 31–33; ECJ (judgment of 10 May 2012), Case C-100/11 P *Helena Rubinstein and L'Oreal v OHIM*, not reported, paras 111–112.

[37] See, e.g. ECJ, Case C-274/99 P *Connolly v Commission* [2001] E.C.R. I-1611, para. 121; ECJ, Case C-197/99 P *Belgium v Commission* [2003] E.C.R. I-8461, para. 81.

[38] See, e.g. ECJ, Joined Cases C-238/99 P, C-244/99 P, C-245/99 P, C-247/99 P, C-250/99 P, C-251/99 P, C-252/99 P and C-254/99 P *Limburgse Vinyl Maatschappij and Others v Commission* [2002] E.C.R. I-8375, paras 416–428; ECJ, Case C-197/99 P *Belgium v Commission* [2003] E.C.R. I-8461, para. 82; ECJ, Case C-167/06 P *Komninou and Others v Commission* [2007] E.C.R. I-141*, Summ. pub., paras 22, 26–28; ECJ, Case C-200/10 P *Evropaïki Dynamiki v Commission* [2011] E.C.R. I-67*, Summ. pub., paras 30–43. An implicit statement of reasons may be sufficient: see, e.g. ECJ, Joined Cases C-204/00 P, C-205/00 P, C-211/00 P, C-213/00 P, C-217/00 P and C-219/00 P *Aalborg Portland and Others v Commission* [2004] E.C.R. I-123, para. 372; ECJ, Case C-397/03 P *Archer Daniel Midlands v Commission* [2006] E.C.R. I-4429, para. 60; ECJ, Case C-3/06 P *Group Danone v Commission* [2007] E.C.R. I-1331, para. 46; ECJ, Joined Cases C-120/06 P and C-121/06 P *FIAMM and Others v Council and Commission* [2008] E.C.R. I-6513, para. 96; ECJ, Case C-440/07 P *Commission v Schneider Electric* [2009] E.C.R. I-6413, para. 135; ECJ, Case C-263/09 P *Edwin v OHIM* [2011] E.C.R. I-5853, para. 64; ECJ, Case C-47/10 P *Austria—Scheucher-Fleisch v Commission* [2011] E.C.R. I-10707, para. 104; ECJ (judgment of 8 December 2011), Case C-81/10 P *France Telecom v Commission*, not reported, para. 88; ECJ (judgment of 21 December 2011), Case C-318/09 P *A2A v Commission*, not reported, para. 97; ECJ (judgment of 16 February 2012), Joined Cases C-191/09 P and C-200/09 P *Council and Commission v Interpipe Niko Tube and Interpipe NTRB*, not reported, para. 105; ECJ (order of 22 March 2012), Case C-200/11 P *Italy v Commission*, not reported, para. 57 (and further citations therein). Where the General Court incorrectly presents the undertaking's pleas, the judgment will contain an incorrect statement of reasons and be annulled (ECJ, Case C-57/02 P *Acerinox v Commission* [2005] E.C.R. I-6689, paras 33–39).

[39] See, e.g. ECJ, Case C-348/06 P *Commission v Giradot* [2008] E.C.R. I-833, para. 45; ECJ (order of 28 November 2008), Case C-526/07 P *Combescot v Commission* [2008] E.C.R. I-168*, Summ. pub., para. 48.

[40] See, e.g. ECJ, Case C-200/10 P *Evropaïki Dynamiki v Commission* [2011] E.C.R. I-67*, Summ. pub., paras 30–43.

[41] See, e.g. ECJ, Case C-401/96 P *Somaco v Commission* [1998] E.C.R. I-2587, para. 53; ECJ, Case C-446/00 P *Cubero Vermurie v Commission* [2001] E.C.R. I-10315, para. 20; ECJ (order of 5 June 2002), Case C-217/00 P *Buzzi Unicem v Commission*, not reported, para. 125; ECJ, Case C-3/06 P *Group Danone v Commission* [2007] E.C.R. I-1331, para. 45; ECJ, Case C-385/07 P *Der Grune Punkt v Commission* [2009] E.C.R. I-6155, para. 71 and citations therein.

[42] See, e.g. ECJ, Case C-348/06 P *Commission v Giradot* [2008] E.C.R. I-833, para. 45; ECJ (order of 28 November 2008), Case C-526/07 P *Combescot v Commission* [2008] E.C.R. I-168*, Summ. pub., para. 48; ECJ, Case C-362/95 P *Blackspur DIY and Others v Council and Commission* [1997] E.C.R. I-4775, paras 28–29; ECJ, Case C-62/01 P *Campogrande v Commission* [2002] E.C.R. I-3793, para. 24; ECJ, Case C-243/05 P

whether, in an action for damages, the amount of compensation has been sufficiently proven in the application and the reply is exclusively part of the assessment of the facts[43] and cannot be raised on appeal.

(10) Exercise by General Court of its unlimited jurisdiction

16.11 On appeal, the Court of Justice is not empowered to substitute, on grounds of fairness, its own assessment for that of the General Court exercising its unlimited jurisdiction to rule on the amount of fines imposed on undertakings for infringements of Union law.[44] The only review which the Court of Justice may conduct in this connection consists of considering whether the General Court responded to a sufficient legal standard[45] or in accordance with the principle of equal treatment[46] to all the arguments raised with a view to having the fine abolished or reduced.

C. Against what decisions of the General Court will an appeal lie?

(1) Final decisions

16.12 Under the first paragraph of Art. 56 of the Statute, an appeal may be brought against final decisions of the General Court and against decisions of that Court disposing of substantive issues in part only or disposing of a procedural issue concerning a plea of lack of competence or inadmissibility.[47] An appeal will not lie against the part of a judgment of the General

---

Agraz and Others v Commission [2006] E.C.R. I-10833, paras 26–47 (set aside judgment under appeal on account of error of law as regards classification of damage as uncertain); ECJ, Case C-440/07 P *Commission v Schneider Electric* [2009] E.C.R. I-6413, paras 197–208, 210–223 (set aside judgment under appeal on account of wrong legal characterisation of facts in relation to assessment of direct causal link).

[43] ECJ, Case C-209/94 P *Buralux and Others v Council* [1996] E.C.R. I-615, para. 21.

[44] ECJ, Case C-310/93 P *BPB Industries and British Gypsum v Commission* [1995] E.C.R. I-865, para. 34; ECJ, Case C-199/92 P *Hüls v Commission* [1999] E.C.R. I-428, para. 197. In the context of reviewing a judgment of the General Court imposing a fine in the exercise of its unlimited jurisdiction, the Court of Justice ruled that in so far as the appellant calls into question the General Court's fairness, a decision based solely on fairness cannot be reviewed by the Court of Justice in the context of an appeal: ECJ (judgment of 8 December 2011), Case C-386/10 P *Chalkor v Commission*, not reported, para. 101.

[45] ECJ, Case C-219/95 P *Ferriere Nord v Commission* [1997] E.C.R. I-4411, para. 31; ECJ, Case C-185/95 P *Baustahlgewebe v Commission* [1998] E.C.R. I-8417, para. 128; ECJ, Case C-283/98 P *Mooch Domsjö v Commission* [2000] E.C.R. I-9855, para. 24.

[46] ECJ, Case C-291/98 P *Sarrió v Commission* [2000] E.C.R. I-9991, paras 96–97.

[47] The Court may examine of its own motion whether the claim submitted by the appellant is directed against a decision open to appeal: see, e.g. ECJ, Case C-23/00 P *Council v Boehringer* [2002] E.C.R. I-1873, para. 46. An appeal seeking to have an order made by the General Court set aside is inadmissible where the order under appeal instructs a party to produce documents (ECJ (order of 4 October 1999), Case C-349/99 P *Commission v ADT Projekt* [1999] E.C.R. I-6467). If the General Court stays proceedings on the ground that a case pending before the Court of Justice concerns the same subject-matter, no appeal will lie against that decision: ECJ (order of 26 November 2003), Joined Cases C-366/03 P to C-368/03 P, C-390/03 P, C-391/03 P and C-394/03 P *Associazione Bancaria Italiana and Others v Commission*, not reported. See also ECJ (order of 28 November 2008), Case C-526/07 P *Combescot v Commission* [2008] E.C.R. I-168*, Summ. pub., para. 36 and citations therein (decision of General Court concerning joinder of cases does not fall within category of decisions which may be subject to appeal within the terms of Art. 56 of the Statute); ECJ (order of 10 July 2009), Case C-59/09 P *Hasbro—Enercon v OHIM* [2009] E.C.R. I-126*, Summ. pub., paras 7–9 (a letter from the Registry rejecting appellant's request to be represented at the hearing by a 'Trade Mark and Design Litigator' does not fall within the categories of decisions which may be the subject of an appeal within the terms of Art. 56 of the Statute).

Court in which that Court considers that it is unnecessary to rule on an objection of inadmissibility since the claims have in any event to be dismissed on the merits. This is because that decision makes the objection to no purpose.[48]

An appeal will also lie against decisions of the General Court dismissing an application to intervene.[49] Decisions of the General Court relating to applications for interim relief may also be the subject of an appeal (Arts 278–279 TFEU),[50] together with decisions suspending the operation of Council, Commission or European Central Bank acts imposing a financial obligation on natural or legal persons (Art. 299, fourth para., TFEU).[51]

(2) Appeal regarding costs

Under the second paragraph of Art. 58 of the Statute, no appeal shall lie regarding only the **16.13** amount of the costs or the party ordered to pay them.[52] In addition, where all the other pleas put forward in an appeal have been rejected, any plea challenging the decision of the General Court on costs must be rejected as inadmissible by virtue of that provision.[53]

II. Identity of the Parties

A. Appellant

An appeal may be brought by any party which has been unsuccessful, in **16.14** whole or in part, in its submissions made before the General Court,[54] provided

---

[48] ECJ, Case C-23/00 P *Council v Boehringer* [2002] E.C.R. I-1973, para. 51. However, this position is different in the case of a judgment where the main application is rejected as unfounded after the General Court has also rejected an objection of inadmissibility. An appeal directed only against the rejection of the objection of inadmissibility will lie in that event: see, e.g. ECJ, Case C-73/97 P *France v Comafrica and Others* [1999] E.C.R. I-185; ECJ, Case C-362/05 P *Wunenburger v Commission* [2007] E.C.R. I-4333, paras 37–40 (and further citations therein).

[49] Statute, Art. 57, first para. For an application, see ECJ (order of the President of 8 June 2012), Case C-602/11 P(I) *Schenker—Deutsche Lufthansa and Others v Commission*, not reported.

[50] For a recent example, see ECJ (order of the President of 14 June 2012), Case C-644/11 P(R) *Qualitest v Council*, not reported.

[51] Statute, Art. 57, second para. (also referring to appeals against decisions of the General Court made pursuant to Art. 157 EAEC or the third para. of Art. 164 EAEC, which correspond to Art. 278 TFEU and the fourth para. of Art. 299 TFEU, respectively).

[52] See, e.g. ECJ (order of 29 November 2007), Case C-122/07 P *Eurostrategies v Commission* [2007] E.C.R. I-179*.

[53] See, e.g. ECJ (order of 13 January 1995), Case C-253/94 P *Roujansky* [1995] E.C.R. I-7, paras 12–14; ECJ (order of 13 January 1995), Case C-264/94 P *Bonnamy* [1995] E.C.R. I-15, paras 12–14; ECJ, Case C-396/93 P *Henrichs v Commission* [1995] E.C.R. I-2611, paras 65–66; ECJ (order of 6 March 1997), Case C-303/96 P *Bernardi v European Parliament* [1997] E.C.R. I-1239, para. 49; ECJ, Case C-301/02 P *Tralli v ECB* [2005] E.C.R. I-4071, para. 88; ECJ (order of 15 May 2007), Case C-420/05 P *Ricosmos v Commission* [2007] E.C.R. I-67*, Summ. pub., para. 174 ; ECJ, Case C-485/08 P *Gualteri v Commission* [2010] E.C.R. I-3009, para. 111; ECJ, Case C-263/09 P *Edwin—OHIM v Fiorucci* [2011] E.C.R. I-5853, para. 78 (and further citations therein).

[54] Statute, Art. 56, second para. See, e.g. ECJ (order of 15 April 2010), Case C-517/08 P *Makhteshim-Agan Holding and Others v Commission* [2010] E.C.R. I-45*, Summ. pub., paras 50–53; ECJ, Case C-383/99 P *Procter & Gamble v OHIM* [2001] E.C.R. I-6251, paras 16–27, in which the Court of Justice held that the appellant had an interest in appealing notwithstanding the fact that the General Court had (partially) annulled the decision contested by it (a refusal by the OHIM to register a trade mark pursuant to Art. 7(3) of Regulation (EC) No. 40/94). The Court of Justice held that the General Court had refused to uphold the claim to annul the OHIM's decision to refuse registration in so far as it was based on Art. 7(1)(b) and (c) of Regulation (EC) No. 40/94.

that the appeal, if successful, is likely to procure an advantage to the party bringing it.[55]

A cross-appeal may therefore be brought only if both parties have been unsuccessful—at least in part—before the General Court.[56] The Court of Justice may of its own motion raise the objection that a party has no interest in bringing or maintaining an appeal on the ground that an event subsequent to the judgment of the General Court removes its prejudicial effect as regards the appellant.[57]

See also ECJ (order of 28 June 2004), Case C-445/02 P *Glaverbel v OHIM* [2004] E.C.R. I-6267; ECJ, Case C-514/06 P *Armacell Enterprise v OHIM* [2008] E.C.R. I-128*, Summ. pub., para. 51 (holding that since the General Court rejected, in the judgment under appeal, the appellant's submissions seeking annulment of the contested decision, the appellant has established that it has an interest in entering an appeal against that judgment, regardless of whether that prevents it from requesting the conversion of its Union trade mark application into a national trade mark application); ECJ, Case C-552/09 P *Ferrero v OHIM* [2011] E.C.R. I-2063, paras 39–44 (finding appellant had an interest in the appeal notwithstanding surrender of the contested trade mark). It remains an open question whether a party to the proceedings before the Board of Appeal of the OHIM may lodge an appeal against a judgment of the General Court if that party has not intervened in the proceedings before the General Court (see, however, implicitly ECJ (order of 18 January 2005), Case C-325/03 P *Zuazaga Meabe v OHIM* [2005] E.C.R. I-403).

[55] See, e.g. ECJ, Case C-19/93 P *Rendo and Others v Commission* [1995] E.C.R. I-3319, para. 13; ECJ, Case C-40/03 P *Comunita Montana della Valnerina v Commission* [2006] E.C.R. I-6811, para. 115; ECJ (order of 13 July 2006), Case C-338/05 P *Front National and Others v European Parliament and Council* [2006] E.C.R. I-88*, Summ. pub., para. 29; ECJ (order of 8 April 2008), Case C-503/07 P *Saint-Gobain Glass Deutschland v Commission* [2008] E.C.R. I-2217, para. 48; ECJ, Joined Cases C-501/06 P, C-513/06 P, C-515/06 P and C-519/06 P *GlaxoSmithKline Services Unlimited v Commission* [2009] E.C.R. I-9291, para. 23; ECJ, Case C-535/06 P *Moser Baer India v Council* [2009] E.C.R. I-7051, para. 24; ECJ, Case C-550/07 P *Akzo Nobel Chemicals and Akcros Chemicals v Commission* [2010] E.C.R. I-8301, paras 22-23; ECJ (judgment of 21 December 2011), Case C-329/09 P *Iride v Commission*, not reported, paras 47–51. Consequently, an appellant cannot raise a ground of appeal for the benefit of another party to the proceedings: see, e.g. ECJ, Joined Cases C-201/09 P and C-216/09 P *ArcelorMittal Luxembourg v Commission and Commission v ArcelorMittal Luxembourg and Others* [2011] E.C.R. I-2239, para. 83. Moreover, depending on the circumstances of the case, the appeal may become devoid of purpose. See, e.g. ECJ (order of 19 January 2006), Case C-82/04 P *Audi v OHIM*, not reported, paras 20–24; ECJ (order of 19 May 2009), Case C-565/07 P *AMS Advanced Medical Services v OHIM* [2009] E.C.R. I-84*, Summ. pub., paras 13–16; ECJ (order of 20 October 2011), Case C-67/11 P *DTL Corporacion v OHIM* [2011] E.C.R. I-156*, Summ. pub., paras 24–26; ECJ (judgment of 19 July 2012), Case C-337/09 P *Council v Zhejiang Xinan Chemical Industrial Group*, not reported, paras 44–53.

[56] See, e.g. ECJ, Case C-71/07 P *Franco Campoli v Commission and Council* [2008] E.C.R. I-5887, paras 39–43, in which the Court of Justice held the Commission's cross-appeal inadmissible on the grounds that the judgment under appeal granted the form of order it sought before the General Court and the cross-appeal did not seek to have the judgment under appeal set aside but rather a declaration that the principal appeal lodged by the appellant is inadmissible. Cross-appeals are possible as provided under Arts 176–183 of the ECJ Rules of Procedure. See further para. 26.04. The Court of Justice may examine the cross-appeal even if the main appeal is dismissed (see, e.g. ECJ, Case C-234/02 P *European Ombudsman v Lamberts* [2004] E.C.R. I-2803). It also happens that the Court of Justice first examines the cross-appeal and then decides that there is no longer any need to adjudicate on the main appeal (see, e.g. ECJ, Case C-486/01 P *Front National v European Parliament* [2004] E.C.R. I-6289: the General Court had dismissed the application of the Front National on the merits and the Front National appealed against that judgment; the European Parliament, in its cross-appeal, successfully alleged that the action brought before the General Court should have been declared inadmissible. In these circumstances, there was no longer need to adjudicate on the main appeal).

[57] See, e.g. ECJ, Case C-19/93 P *Rendo and Others v Commission* [1995] E.C.R. I-3319, para. 23; ECJ, Case C-535/06 P *Moser Baer India v Council* [2009] E.C.R. I-7051, para. 24; ECJ, Joined Cases C-399/06 P and C-403/06 P *Hassan and Ayadi v Council* [2009] E.C.R. I-11393, para. 58 (the withdrawal of the contested regulation and its retroactive replacement by another regulation did not render appeal devoid of purpose); ECJ (order of the President of 27 October 2011), Case C-605/10 P(R) *Inuit Tapiriit Kanatami and Others v European Parliament and Council* [2011] E.C.R. I-164*, Summ. pub., para. 15 and citations therein.

B. Interveners

Persons who have been refused leave to intervene may appeal against that decision of the **16.15**
General Court.[58]

A separate issue is whether persons who have intervened before the General Court may
appeal against that Court's final decision.

With respect to interveners other than Member States or Union institutions, an appeal will lie
only if their situation is directly affected by the decision of the General Court.[59] The interest
which such an intervener, including bodies, offices, and agencies of the Union as well as any
other person, must establish in order to be able to bring an appeal is, in principle, the same as
it had to establish in order to obtain leave to intervene at first instance (Statute, Art. 40,
second para.),[60] but the Court of Justice has, in the decision of the General Court, a more
concrete basis for testing that interest than the General Court has when appraising the interest
of a would-be intervener before any decision on the substance has been taken. It is therefore
possible that the intervener at first instance may be refused leave to appeal.

C. Union institutions and Member States

In contrast, Union institutions and Member States may invariably appeal,[61] even if the **16.16**
decision of the General Court does not affect them directly[62] and they did not intervene in
the proceedings at first instance,[63] with the exception, in the latter case, of staff cases.[64]

---

[58] Statute, Art. 57, first para.

[59] Statute, Art. 56, second para. See, e.g. ECJ, Case C-200/92 P *ICI v Commission* [1999] E.C.R. I-4399,
paras 22–33; ECJ, Joined Cases C-172/01 P, C-175/01 P, C-176/01 P and C-180/01 P *International Power v
Commission* [2003] E.C.R. I-11421, paras 49–53.

[60] Note, however, that while Arts 129–132 of the ECJ Rules of Procedure concerning intervention apply to
the procedure before the Court of Justice on an appeal against decisions of the General Court, by way of
derogation from Art. 130(1), an application to intervene must, according to Art. 190(2) of the ECJ Rules of
Procedure, be made within one month, as opposed to six weeks, of the publication of the notice of appeal as
referred to in Art. 21(4).

[61] Statute, Art. 56, third para. For an example, see ECJ, Case C-73/97 P *France v Comafrica and Others*
[1999] E.C.R. I-185.

[62] See, e.g. ECJ (judgment of 21 December 2011), Case C-27/09 P *France v People's Mojahedin
Organization of Iran*, not reported, paras 43–45 (further underlining that Member States, whether or not
they were parties to the case at first instance, do not have to show an interest in order to bring an appeal against
a decision of the General Court).

[63] Statute, Art. 56, third para. See, by way of example, the appeal brought by France against CFI, Case T-
70/94 *Comafrica and Dole Fresh Fruit Europe v Commission* [1996] E.C.R. II-1741 (Case C-73/97 P); the
appeal brought by Germany against CFI, Case T-27/02 *Kronofrance v Commission* [2004] E.C.R. II-4177
(Case C-75/05 P); the appeal brought by Sweden against CFI, Case T-36/04 *API v Commission* [2007]
E.C.R. II-3201 (Case C-514/07 P); the appeal brought by Sweden against CFI, Case T-403/05 *MyTravel v
Commission* [2008] E.C.R. II-2027 (Case C-506/08 P); the appeal brought by Belgium against CFI, Case
T-388/03 *Deutsche Post and DHL International v Commission* [2009] E.C.R. II-199 (Case C-148/09 P); the
appeal brought Portugal against CFI, Case T-385/05 *Transnautica v Commission* [2009] E.C.R. I-163*,
Summ. pub. (Case C-506/09 P); the appeal brought by Austria against CFI, Case T-375/04 *Scheucher-Fleisch
and Others v Commission* [2009] E.C.R. II-4155 (Case C-47/10 P).

[64] Statute, Art.56, third para. See, e.g. ECJ, Case C-434/98 P *Council v Busacca and Others* [2000]
E.C.R. I-8577, para. 21. As regards to how Member States and Union institutions would become aware of
decisions of the General Court to be appealed against if they were not parties to those proceedings, see Art. 55 of the
Statute.

D. Other parties to the proceedings

16.17 Any party to the relevant case before the General Court 'having an interest in the appeal being allowed or dismissed' may submit a response to the appeal.[65]

III. Special Characteristics

A. Pleas

16.18 Appeals must be based on pleas alleging lack of competence of the General Court, a breach of procedure before it which adversely affects the interests of the appellant,[66] or

---

[65] ECJ Rules of Procedure, Art. 172. A response that does not seek to have the appeal allowed or dismissed, in whole or in part, as provided under Art. 174 of the ECJ Rules of Procedure, is inadmissible: see, e.g. ECJ, Case C-263/09 P *Edwin—OHIM v Fiorucci* [2011] E.C.R. I-5853, paras 83–85 (dismissing claim for amendment of judgment under appeal).

[66] See, e.g. ECJ, Case C-113/07 P *SELEX Sistemi Integrati v Commission* [2009] E.C.R. I-2207, paras 39–41 (plea rejected on the grounds that although the General Court's decision is vitiated on account of a defect, the appellant failed to demonstrate that the breach on which it relied adversely affected its interests; moreover, there was 'absolutely no indication' that that breach could have had any effect whatsoever on the outcome of the proceedings'). For instance, the General Court is bound by the general principle of Union law derived from Art. 6 § 1 of the ECHR, now enshrined in Art. 47 of the Charter of Fundamental Rights, that everyone is entitled to legal process within a reasonable period in the context of proceedings brought against a Commission decision imposing fines on an undertaking for infringement of competition law. In *Baustahlgewebe* (ECJ, Case C-185/95 P *Baustahlgewebe v Commission* [1998] E.C.R. I-8417), the Court of Justice held (three years after the appeal had been brought) that the General Court had not respected that requirement on the ground that 32 months had elapsed between the end of the written procedure and the decision to open the oral procedure and 22 months had elapsed between the close of the oral procedure and the delivery of the judgment of the General Court. That amount of time was not reasonable in the light of the circumstances of the case, not even having regard to the particular attention that the General Court must pay to investigating actions calling for a close examination of complex facts. See further ECJ, Case C-199/99 P *Corus UK v Commission* [2003] E.C.R. I-11177, paras 41–56 (duration of proceedings justified); ECJ, Joined Cases C-403/04 P and C-405/04 P *Sumitomo Metal Industries and Nippon Steel—JFE Engineering and Others v Commission* [2007] E.C.R. I-729, paras 115–123 (duration of proceedings justified); ECJ, Joined Cases C-322/07 P, C-327/07 P and C-338/07 P *Paperfabriek August Koehler and Others v Commission* [2009] E.C.R. I-7191, paras 143–149 (duration of proceedings satisfied requirements concerning completion within reasonable time); ECJ, Case C-385/07 P *Der Grüne Punkt v Commission* [2009] E.C.R. I-6155, paras 176–197 (though the Court determined that there was a failure to adjudicate the case within a reasonable time, it held that, having regard to the need to ensure that Union competition law is complied with, this cannot allow the appellant to reopen the question of the existence of an infringement on this sole ground where all of its pleas against the findings made by the General Court concerning that infringement and the administrative procedure relating to it have been rejected as unfounded and thus cannot lead to the judgment under appeal being set aside). See also ECJ, Joined Cases C-120/06 P and C-121/06 P *FIAMM and Others v Council and Commission* [2008] E.C.R. I-6513, paras 203–214; ECJ (order of 3 February 2009), Case C-231/08 P *Giannini v Commission* [2009] E.C.R. I-11*, Summ. pub., paras 30–36; ECJ (order of 26 March 2009), Case C-146/08 P *Efkon v European Parliament and Council* [2009] E.C.R. I-49*, Summ. pub., paras 51–57; ECJ, Case C-583/08 P *Gogos v Commission* [2010] E.C.R. I-4469, paras 56–59; ECJ (judgment of 26 November 2013), Case C-40/12 P *Gascogne Sack Deutschland v Commission*, not reported, paras 74-103; ECJ (judgment of 26 November 2013), Case C-50/12 P *Kendrion v Commission*, not reported, paras 7-107; ECJ (judgment of 26 November 2013), Case C-58/12 P *Groupe Gascogne v Commission*, not reported, paras 66–103.

infringement of Union law by the General Court.[67] A plea which merely takes issue with a factual appraisal made by the General Court will be inadmissible.[68]

B. Appeal must clearly indicate errors of law

Following from Art. 169(2) of the ECJ Rules of Procedure, which requires that the pleas in law and legal arguments relied on must identify precisely those points in the grounds of the decision of the General Court which are contested, the appellant must clearly state which aspects of the contested decision of the General Court it is criticising and indicate the contested parts of the judgment,[69] together with the legal arguments supporting those complaints.[70]   **16.19**

---

[67] Statute, Art. 58, first para.; see, e.g. ECJ, Joined Cases C-204/00 P, C-205/00 P, C-211/00 P, C-213/00 P, C-217/00 P, and C-219/00 P *Aalborg Portland and Others v Commission* [2004] E.C.R. I-123, para. 47; ECJ (judgment of 26 June 2012), Case C-335/09 P *Poland v Commission*, not reported, para. 23; ECJ (order of 12 July 2012), Case C-278/11 P *Dover v European Parliament*, not reported, para. 23; ECJ (order of 12 July 2012), Case C-581/11 P *Mugraby v Council and Commission*, not reported, para. 42 and citations therein. See also ECJ, Case C-203/07 P *Greece v Commission* [2008] E.C.R. I-8161, paras 40–41 (holding that it is not contrary to Art. 58 of the Statute for the pleas put forward in support of the application to have the judgment of the General Court set aside to entail an analysis of the scope of legal acts which cannot themselves be contested before the General Court; for the purposes of determining whether the contested act is well-founded, it is necessary to interpret those legal acts, but such an analysis does not necessarily give rise to an action in respect of those legal acts); ECJ, Case C-263/09 P *Edwin Co.—OHIM v Fiorucci* [2011] E.C.R. I-5853, paras 46–47 (involving alleged infringement of a rule of national law made applicable to the dispute by the reference made in a provision of Union law).

[68] See, e.g. ECJ, Case C-326/91 P *De Compte v European Parliament* [1994] E.C.R. I-2091, para. 29; ECJ, Case C-1/98 P *British Steel v Commission* [2000] E.C.R. I-10349, para. 53; ECJ (order of 1 December 2011), Case C-222/11 P *Longetivity—OHIM v Performing Science*, not reported, paras 28–30; ECJ (judgment of 3 May 2012), Case C-290/11 P *Comap v Commission*, not reported, paras 73–78, 82–84. See further para. 16.03. See ECJ (order of 25 October 2007), Case C-495/06 P *Nijs v Court of Auditors* [2007] E.C.R. I-146*, Summ. pub., paras 54–56 (holding appellant's claim inadmissible as constituting a *venire contra factum propium*); ECJ (order of 22 January 2010), Case C-23/09 P *ecoblue v OHIM* [2010] E.C.R. I-7*, Summ. pub., paras 55–56 (rejecting appellant's claims that contested decision should be annulled and that opposition (in context of trade mark) should be dismissed, underscoring that the Court of Justice does not have jurisdiction in the context of the review of legality carried out in an appeal to issue directions to Union institutions and administrative authorities).

[69] If the appellant fails to do so, the plea will be declared inadmissible (ECJ, Case C-248/99 P *France v Monsanto and Commission* [2002] E.C.R. I-1, para. 69). However, an appeal, or a plea in support of an appeal, does not have to refer to all the points of the contested judgment containing all the reasons which led the General Court to adopt a position on a question. The fact that an appeal, or a plea in support of an appeal, takes up some points containing only some of the reasons given by the General Court will not result in its being declared inadmissible (ECJ, Case C-458/98 P *Industrie des Poudres Sphériques v Council* [2000] E.C.R. I-8147, para. 67).

[70] See, e.g. ECJ (order of 26 April 1993), Case C-244/92 P *Kupka-Floridi v ESC* [1993] E.C.R. I-2041, para. 9; ECJ (order of 13 January 2012), Case C-462/10 P *Evropaiki Dynmaiki v European Environment Agency*, not reported, para. 19 and citations therein. The Court of Justice will sometimes particularise the pleas adduced by the appellant (ECJ, Case C-283/90 P *Vidrányi v Commission* [1991] E.C.R. I-4339, para. 29; ECJ, Case C-255/90 P *Burban v European Parliament* [1992] E.C.R. I-2253, paras 4–5; ECJ (order of 17 October 1995), Case C-62/94 P *Turner v Commission* [1995] E.C.R. I-3177, para. 16; ECJ (order of 6 March 1997), Case C-303/96 P *Bernardi v European Parliament* [1997] E.C.R. I-1239, paras 37–40; ECJ, Case C-138/95 P *Campo Ebro Industrial and Others v Council* [1997] E.C.R. I-2027, paras 60–61.) Moreover, the Court may take a 'global' reading of the pleas to deduce that they are sufficiently detailed: see, e.g. ECJ, Case C-240/03 P *Comunita Montana della Valnerina v Commission* [2006] E.C.R. I-731, paras 109–110; ECJ (order of 20 March 2007), Case C-325/06 P *Galileo International Technology and Others v Commission* [2007] E.C.R. I-44*, Summ. pub., paras 36–39; ECJ, Case C-280/08 P *Deutsche Telecom v Commission* [2010] E.C.R. I-9555, paras 26–27; ECJ, Case C-369/09 P *ISD Polska and Others v Commission* [2011] E.C.R. I-2011, para. 67; for further examples where plea held sufficiently detailed, see, e.g. ECJ, Case C-417/06 P *Italy v Commission* [2007]

A head of complaint which is not sufficiently explained will be inadmissible and rejected.[71]

It is not enough for the appellant to support a plea by merely referring back to arguments raised in connection with another plea.[72] It is also not permitted in an appeal simply to repeat pleas already raised in the General Court, since to interpret an appeal in that way would be no more than an attempt to have the case retried and no provision is made for retrials by the Court of Justice.[73] Consequently, a plea declared inadmissible by the General

---

E.C.R. I-171*, Summ. pub., paras 25–29; ECJ, Case C-211/06 P *Herta Adam v Commission* [2008] E.C.R. I-10*, Summ. pub., paras 33–36; ECJ, Case C-535/06 P *Moser Baer India v Council* [2009] E.C.R. I-7051, paras 78–80. For cases in which the Court of Justice took a plea-by-plea approach, see, e.g. ECJ (order of 15 May 2007), Case C-420/05 P *Ricosmos v Commission* [2007] E.C.R. I-67*, Summ. pub., paras 64–67; ECJ (order of 4 October 2007), Case C-320/05 P *Fred Olsen v Commission* [2007] E.C.R. I-131*, Summ. pub., paras 47–53; ECJ (order of 25 March 2009), Case C-159/08 P *Scippacercola and Terezakis v Commission* [2009] E.C.R. I-46*, Summ. pub., paras 34–39; ECJ (order of 31 March 2011), Case C-367/10 P *EMC Development v Commission* [2011] E.C.R. I-46*, Summ. pub., paras 39–43; ECJ (judgment of 26 June 2012), Case C-335/09 P *Poland v Commission*, not reported, paras 25–29. Where the appellant alleges a wrong presentation or distortion of the evidence by the General Court, that party must indicate precisely the evidence alleged to have been distorted by that Court and show the errors of appraisal which led to that distortion: see, e.g. ECJ, Joined Cases C-204/00 P, C-205/00 P, C-211/00 P, C-213/00 P, C-217/00 P, and C-219/00 P *Aalborg Portland and Others v Commission* [2004] E.C.R. I-123, para. 50; ECJ (order of 16 December 2004), Case C-222/03P *APOL and AIPO v Commission*, not reported, para. 40; ECJ, Case C-413/08 *Lafarge v Commission* [2010] E.C.R. I-5361, para. 10; ECJ, Joined Case C-71/09 P, Case C-73/09 P and C-76/09 P *Comitato 'Venezia vuole vivere' and Others v Commission* [2011] E.C.R. I-4727, para. 152. In this regard, the pleas and legal arguments relied on are distinguished from the form of order sought in the action; where an appeal set out a claim in the form of order sought but does not contain such pleas and legal arguments, the claim will be inadmissible: see, e.g. ECJ, Joined Cases C-120/06 P and C-121/06 P *FIAMM and Others v Council and Commission* [2008] E.C.R. I-6513, paras 201–202.

[71] See, e.g. ECJ (order of 12 December 1996), Case C-49/96 P *Progoulis v Commission* [1996] E.C.R. I-6803, para. 24; ECJ, Joined Cases C-280/99 P, C-281/99 P and C-282/99 P *Moccia Irme and Others v Commission* [2001] E.C.R. I-4717, paras 35–36; ECJ, Case C-202/07 P *France Telecom v Commission* [2009] E.C.R. I-2369, paras 55–56; ECJ (order of 26 October 2011), Case C-52/11 P *Victoria Sanchez v European Parliament and Commission* [2011] E.C.R. I-158*, Summ. pub., paras 34–35; ECJ (order of 10 November 2011), Case C-626/10 P *Josephides v Commission* [2011] E.C.R. I-169*, Summ. pub., paras 60–61, 114–115, 118–119; ECJ (order of 21 March 2012), Case C-87/11 P *Fidelio v OHIM*, not reported, para. 47; ECJ (order of 7 February 2012), Case C-421/11 P *Total and Elf Aquitaine v Commission*, not reported, paras 18–19, 68; ECJ (order of 1 March 2012), Case C-474/11 P *Smanor v Commission and European Ombudsman*, not reported; ECJ (order of 22 March 2012), Case C-200/11 P *Italy v Commission*, not reported, paras 52–55; ECJ (order of 3 May 2012), Case C-240/11 P *World Wide Tobacco Espana v Commission*, not reported, paras 40–42, 52–54.

[72] ECJ (order of 5 February 1997), Case C-51/95 P *Unifruit Hellas v Commission* [1997] E.C.R. I-727, para. 33.

[73] See, e.g. ECJ (order of 28 June 2001), Case C-351/99 P *Eridania and Others v Council* [2001] E.C.R. I-5007, para. 36; ECJ, Joined Cases C-204/00 P, C-205/00 P, C-211/00 P, C-213/00 P, C-217/00 P and C-219/00 P *Aalborg Portland and Others v Commission* [2004] E.C.R. I-123, para. 51; ECJ, Case C-499/03 P *Biegi Nahrungsmittel and Commonfood v Commission* [2005] E.C.R. I-1751, paras 37–38; ECJ, Case C-202/07 P *France Telecom v Commission* [2009] E.C.R. I-2369, paras 69–73; ECJ, Case C-535/06 P *Moser Baer India v Council* [2009] E.C.R. I-7051, paras 50–54; ECJ (order of 6 May 2010), Case C-507/09 P *Goldman Managemen In. v Commission and Bulgaria* [2010] E.C.R. I-57*, Summ. pub.; ECJ (order of 6 May 2010), Case C-26/10 P *Hansen v Commission* [2010] E.C.R. I-58*, Summ. pub.; ECJ (order of 26 October 2011), Case C-52/11 P *Victoria Sanchez v European Parliament and Commission* [2011] E.C.R. I-158*, Summ. pub., paras 29–31; ECJ, Case C-252/10 P *Evropaiki Dynamiki v European Maritime Safety Agency* [2011] E.C.R. I-107*, Summ. pub., para. 54; ECJ (order of 9 March 2012), Case C-406/11 P *Atlas Transport — OHIM v Atlas Air*, not reported, para. 32 (and further citations therein). However, a point of law examined at first instance may be discussed again in the course of an appeal, provided that the appellant challenges the interpretation or application of Union law by the General Court: ECJ (judgment of 19 July 2012), Case C-337/09 P *Council v Zhejiang Xinan Chemical Industrial Group*, not reported, para. 61 (and further citations therein).

Court cannot be raised afresh by the appellant, although the latter may challenge on specific grounds the lower court's finding that the plea is inadmissible.[74] The appellant must raise arguments in this connection establishing that the General Court has erred in law.[75] However, where an appellant submits that the General Court did not respond to a plea, its submission cannot be challenged, in terms of the admissibility of the ground of appeal, on the basis that it does not cite any passage or part of the contested judgment as the specific object of its complaint. Such submission can also not be challenged on the ground that it simply repeats or reproduces the plea raised at first instance.[76]

C. No change in the subject-matter of the proceedings

The limited range of pleas which may be raised on appeal against a decision of the General **16.20**
Court precludes any change in the subject-matter of the proceedings as compared with the proceedings before the General Court.[77] As already mentioned in para. 16.01, parties are not entitled to seek a new form of order—i.e. relating to pleas not raised before the General Court.[78] The reason for this is that such a plea would involve the Court of Justice, not in

---

[74] This may be inferred from ECJ, Case C-354/92 P *Eppe v Commission* [1993] E.C.R. I-7027, para. 13. See further, e.g. ECJ, Case C-202/07 P *France Telecom v Commission* [2009] E.C.R. I-2369, para. 93. See further ECJ, Case C-38/07 P *Heusen & Schrouff v Commission* [2008] E.C.R. I-8599, paras 33–37.

[75] ECJ (order of 5 February 1998), Case C-30/96 P *Abello and Others v Commission* [1998] E.C.R. I-377, para. 45.

[76] ECJ, Joined Cases C-238/99 P, C-244/99 P, C-245/99 P, C-247/99 P, C-250/99 P and C-251/99 P, C-252/99 P and C-254/99 P *Limburgse Vinyl Maatschappij and Others v Commission* [2002] E.C.R. I-8375, paras 416–428.

[77] ECJ Rules of Procedure, Art. 170(1), last sent.: 'The subject-matter of the proceedings before the General Court may not be changed in the appeal'.

[78] ECJ Rules of Procedure, Art. 170(1). See, e.g. ECJ, Case C-1/98 P *British Steel v Commission* [2000] E.C.R. I-10349, para. 47; ECJ, Case C-450/98 P *IECC v Commission* [2001] E.C.R. I-3947, para. 36; ECJ, Joined Cases C-24/01 P and C-25/01 P *Glencore and Compagnie Continentale v Commission* [2002] E.C.R. I-10119, para. 62; ECJ (order of 2 September 2010), Case C-28/10 P *Bayramoglu v Parliament and Council* [2010] E.C.R. I-108*, Summ. pub., paras 15–16; ECJ (order of 31 March 2011), Case C-433/10 P *Mauerhofer v Commission* [2011] E.C.R. I-48*, Summ. pub., paras 88–89, 104–105; ECJ (order of 29 November 2011), Case C-76/11 P *Tresplain Investments v OHIM* [2011] E.C.R. I-182*, Summ. pub., paras 51–57; ECJ (order of 29 November 2011), Case C-235/11 P *Evropaïki Dynamiki v Commission* [2011] E.C.R. I-183*, Summ. pub., para. 61; ECJ (judgment of 19 April 2012), Case C-549/10 P *Tomra Systems and Others v Commission*, not reported, paras 97–100; ECJ (order of 26 April 2012), Case C-307/11 P *Deichmann v OHIM*, not reported, paras 65–66; ECJ (order of 3 May 2012), Case C-289/11 P *Legris Industries v Commission*, not reported, paras 33–37; ECJ (order of 3 May 2012), Case C-290/11 P *Comap v Commission*, not reported, paras 42–46. For an extensive discussion, see ECJ, Case C-280/08 P *Deutsche Telecom v Commission* [2010] E.C.R. I-9555, paras 34–52; for an example in the customs context in which although parties challenged the exact amount of the customs debt, they never raised any argument before the General Court regarding the very existence of that debt and thus that plea was rejected as inadmissible: ECJ, Case C-62/05 P *Nordspedizionieri di Danielis Livio & C. and Others v Commission* [2007] E.C.R. I-8647, paras 27–31; in the context of restrictive measures against individuals to combat terrorism, see ECJ, Case C-354/04 P *Gestoras Pro Amnistia and Others v Council* [2007] E.C.R. I-1579, paras 29–32; and ECJ, Case C-355/04 P *Segi and Others v Council* [2007] E.C.R. I-1657, paras 29–32. Compare, e.g. ECJ, Case C-362/09 P *Athinaiki Techniki v Commission* [2010] E.C.R. I-13275, para. 55; ECJ, Case C-583/08 P *Gogos v Commission* [2010] E.C.R. I-4469, paras 23–28, 41–43; ECJ, Case C-369/09 P ISD *Polska and Others v Commission* [2011] E.C.R. I-2011, paras 83–87; ECJ, Case C-521/09 P *Elf Aquitaine v Commission* [2011] E.C.R. I-8947, para. 36; ECJ, Case C-352/09 P *ThyssenKrupp Nirosta v Commission* [2011] E.C.R. I-2359, paras 109–113; ECJ, Case C-47/10 P *Austria—Scheucher-Fleisch and Others v Commission* [2011] E.C.R. I-10707, paras 122–125; ECJ (judgment of 28 June 2012), Case C-404/10 P *Commission v Editions Odile Jacob*, not reported, paras 104–106.

reviewing the decision of the General Court, but in carrying out an additional substantive inquiry, thereby changing the subject-matter of the proceedings.[79] However, there is no requirement that each argument put forward on appeal must previously have been discussed at first instance; otherwise, an appeal would be deprived of much of its purpose.[80] Moreover, the Court of Justice has held that if the appeal is not to be rendered meaningless, it must have jurisdiction to review the findings of law on the pleas argued before the General Court, as well as the legal conclusions drawn by the General Court from those findings, since such conclusions may not necessarily be anticipated by the parties during the proceedings at first instance and thus should not be regarded as changing the subject-matter of the proceedings.[81]

Pleas withdrawn by a party in the proceedings before the General Court are also inadmissible on appeal.[82] This is because the Court of Justice's jurisdiction is confined to a review of the findings of law on the pleas argued at first instance[83] (and of the legal conclusions drawn by the General Court from those findings).[84] Moreover, a party who tolerates the rejection of a plea raised at first instance before the General Court by not contesting the point in question of the decision of the General Court in the pleas set out in its appeal cannot contest the General Court's decision on this point for the first time in the reply. It cannot rely on a new plea based on a new matter of fact or law within the meaning of Art. 127(1) of the ECJ Rules of Procedure which is inescapably and directly linked to a plea which the General Court rejected. If such a plea were admissible, this would be tantamount to allowing the appellant to challenge for the first time at the stage of the reply the dismissal by the General Court of a plea which it had raised before that Court, whereas nothing prevented it from submitting such a plea at the time of its application to the Court of Justice.[85]

D. Inoperative or ineffective pleas

16.21 A plea alleging that the grounds of a judgment are unlawful is inoperative or ineffective and will therefore be rejected where those grounds had no effect on the judgment.[86] Thus, a

---

[79] Cf. the Opinion of Advocate–General C.O. Lenz in ECJ, Case C-348/90 P *European Parliament v Virgili-Schettini* [1991] E.C.R. I-5211, at I-5222; ECJ, Case C-279/95 P *Langnese-Iglo v Commission* [1998] E.C.R. I-5609, para. 55.

[80] ECJ, Case C-229/05 P *PKK and KNK v Council* [2007] E.C.R. I-439, paras 66–67.

[81] ECJ, Case C-295/07 P *Commission v Departement du Loiret and Scott* [2008] E.C.R. I-9363, paras 97–102.

[82] ECJ, Case C-354/92 P *Eppe v Commission* [1993] E.C.R. I-7027, para. 13.

[83] See, e.g. ECJ (order of 12 December 1996), Case C-49/96 P *Progoulis v Commission* [1996] E.C.R. I-6803, para. 32; ECJ, Case C-153/96 P *De Rijk v Commission* [1997] E.C.R. I-2901, para. 18; ECJ, Case C-450/98 P *IECC v Commission* [2001] E.C.R. I-3947, para. 36.

[84] See n. 81.

[85] ECJ, Case C-104/97 P *Atlanta v EC* [1999] E.C.R. I-6983, paras 17–23.

[86] ECJ, Joined Cases C-302/99 P and C-308/99 P *Commission and France v TF1* [2001] E.C.R. I-5603, paras 26–29. In this case (decided by the Full Court), the Commission had appealed against a judgment of the General Court in which an action for failure to act under Art. 265 TFEU in so far as it was directed against the Commission's failure to act pursuant to Art. 106 TFEU was declared admissible in the grounds of the judgment. In the operative part of the judgment, the General Court decided, however, that it did not have to adjudicate on the claim because, as it pointed out elsewhere in the grounds, the Commission had defined its position and for that reason the action was to no purpose. See also, e.g. ECJ (order of 28 October 2004), Case

plea directed against a superabundant ground of the decision of the General Court, i.e. a ground given in a judgment of the General Court merely for the sake of completeness, will be nugatory and cannot lead to the setting aside of that decision and is therefore ineffective.[87]

E. Pleas of public interest (*moyens d'ordre public*)

The bar on raising new pleas on appeal and hence on changing the subject-matter of the **16.22** proceedings does not prevent pleas relating to a matter of public interest (*moyens d'ordre public*) from being raised for the first time on appeal if the General Court has failed to raise such pleas, since the Court of Justice can do so of its own motion. It is, however, difficult to distinguish admissible pleas relating to a matter of public interest from ordinary inadmissible new pleas.[88]

C-236/03 P *Commission v CMA CGM and Others*, not reported, paras 25–27; ECJ (order of 28 September 2006), Case C-552/03 P *Unilever Bestfoods (Ireland) v Commission* [2006] E.C.R. I-9091, paras 148–151; ECJ, Case C-260/05 P *Sniace v Commission* [2007] E.C.R. I-10005, paras 59–60; ECJ, Case C-412/05 P *Alcon v OHIM* [2007] E.C.R. I-3569, paras 98–101; ECJ (order of 20 April 2007), Case C-189/06 P *TEA-CEGOS and STG v Commission* [2007] E.C.R. I-62*, Summ. pub., para. 65; ECJ, Case C-408/04 P *Commission v Salzgitter* [2008] E.C.R. I-2767, paras 47–48; ECJ, Joined Cases C-75/05 P and C-80/05 P *Germany and Others v Commission* [2008] E.C.R. I-6619, paras 52–53; ECJ, Case C-335/08 P *Transports-Schiocchet-Excursions v Commission* [2009] E.C.R. I-104*, Summ. pub., para. 38; ECJ, Case C-480/09 P *AceaElectrabel v Commission* [2010] E.C.R. I-13355, para. 69; ECJ (order of the President of 16 December 2010), Case C-373/10 P(R) *Almamet v Commission* [2010] E.C.R. I-171*, Summ. pub., paras 31–35; ECJ, Joined Cases C-465/09 P to C-470/09 P *Territorio Historico de Vizcaya—Diputación Foral de Vizcaya and Others v Commission* [2011] E.C.R. I-83*, Summ. pub., paras 115–116; ECJ, Joined Cases C-71/09 P, Case C-73/09 P and C-73/09 P *Comitato 'Venezia vuole vivere' and Others v Commission* [2011] E.C.R. I-4727, paras 65, 73–74; ECJ, Joined Cases C-106/09 P and C-107/09 P *Commission and Spain v Government of Gibraltar and United Kingdom* [2011] E.C.R. I-11113, paras 68–69; ECJ (judgment of 16 February 2012), Joined Cases C-191/09 P and C-200/09 P *Council and Commission v Interpipe Niko Tube and Interpipe NTRP*, not reported, para. 158; ECJ (judgment of 5 June 2012), Case C-124/10 P *Commission v EDF*, not reported, para. 109. See also ECJ, Case C-413/06 P *Bertelsmann and Sony Corporation of America v Commission* [2008] E.C.R. I-4951, paras 76–77, 95–96, 103, 133–134, 149–150, 182–183 (various instances of inoperative pleas; another plea was successful and judgment was set aside); ECJ, Case C-167/04 P *JCB Service v Commission* [2006] E.C.R. I-8935, paras 142–143; ECJ, Joined Cases C-75/05 P and C-80/05 P *Germany and Others v Commission* [2008] E.C.R. I-6619, para. 89 (grounds on appeal were deemed irrelevant); ECJ (judgment of 19 March 2013), Joined Cases C-399/10 P and C-401/10 P *Bouygues v Commission*, not reported, paras 67–79 (grounds on appeal deemed ineffective since brought against the General Court's assessment of questions on which the Commission had not yet stated a position). For a contrary example, see, e.g. ECJ, Case C-520/09 P *Arkema v Commission* [2011] E.C.R. I-8901, paras 30–36 (holding ground of appeal could not be rejected as ineffective; the Court underlined in para. 31 that an objection that a ground of appeal is ineffective concerns its ability successfully to found an appeal and does not affect its admissibility).

[87] See, e.g. ECJ (order of 25 March 1996), Case C-137/95 P *SPO and Others v Commission* [1996] E.C.R. I-1611, para. 47; ECJ, Case C-264/95 P *Commission v UIC* [1997] E.C.R. I-1287, para. 48; ECJ, Case C-395/95 P *Geotronics v Commission* [1997] E.C.R. I-2271, para. 23; ECJ, Case C-38/09 P *Schrader v Community Plant Variety Office* [2010] E.C.R. I-3209, para. 122; ECJ (order of 29 January 2010), Case C-68/09 P *Karatzoglou v European Agency for Reconstruction and Commission* [2010] E.C.R. I-11*, Summ. pub., para. 49; ECJ (judgment of 21 December 2011), Case C-27/09 P *France v People's Mojahedin Organization of Iran*, not reported, para. 79; ECJ, Case C-96/09 P *Anheuser-Busch v Budejovicky Budvar* [2011] E.C.R. I-2131, para. 211; ECJ (judgment of 29 March 2012), Case C-504/09 P *Commission v Poland*, not reported, para. 90 (and further citations therein).

[88] K. Lenaerts, 'Le Tribunal de première instance des Communautés européennes: genèse et premiers pas' (1990) J.T. 409, at 414. See the grounds for annulling a measure which the Court of Justice and the General Court may raise of their own motion and certain requirements for admissibility which the Court of Justice and the General Court may inquire into of their own motion, such as whether the time limits prescribed for

F. Injury suffered as a result of the bringing of the appeal

16.23 In the response, the respondent may not claim damages for injury allegedly suffered as a result of the bringing of the appeal. This may be inferred from Art. 174 of the ECJ Rules of Procedure, stipulating that a response must 'seek to have the appeal allowed or dismissed, in whole or in part', read together with the rules concerning the form of order sought in the appeal.[89]

G. Measures of inquiry

16.24 The limitation of appeals to questions of law also means that the Court of Justice cannot order measures of inquiry in order to determine in what way the Union institution, body, office, or agency adopted the act contested before the General Court. Such measures of inquiry would necessarily lead the Court of Justice to decide questions of fact and, as a result, to go beyond its competence in appeals.[90] The General Court is the sole judge of any need for the information available to it concerning the cases before it to be supplemented through measures of inquiry (as is generally the case for measures of organization of procedure save where there is a distortion of the evidence or an inaccuracy in its findings apparent from the case-file).[91] In these circumstances, a plea relating to the refusal of the General Court to order the production of a document, which had been explicitly requested

---

bringing certain actions have been complied with (see paras 7.146 and 7.217). In the context of appeals, see also, e.g. ECJ, Joined Cases C-442/03 P and C-471/03 P *P&O European Ferries (Vizcaya) and Diputacion Foral de Vizcaya* [2006] E.C.R. I-4845, para. 45 (*res judicata*); ECJ, Case C-176/06 P *Stadtwerke Schwabisch and Others v Commission* [2007] E.C.R. I-170*, Summ. pub., para. 18 (admissibility of annulment action); ECJ (order of 15 April 2010), Case C-517/08 P *Makhteshim-Agan and Others v Commission* [2010] E.C.R. I-45*, Summ. pub., para. 54 (admissibility of annulment action); ECJ (order of 15 February 2012), Case C-208/11 P *Internationaler Hilfsfonds v Commission*, not reported, para. 34 (and citations therein) (admissibility of annulment action). But see ECJ, Case C-121/01 P *O'Hannrachain v European Parliament* [2003] E.C.R. I-5539, para. 9, in which the Court of Justice held that a plea relating to the insufficient reasoning of the decision contested before the General Court was inadmissible on the ground that it had not been raised at first instance (notwithstanding the fact that such a plea may—or even must—be raised by the General Court of its own motion: see ECJ, Case C-367/95 P *Commission v Sytraval and Brink's France* [1998] E.C.R. I-1719, para. 67). See further, as regards a ground of appeal alleging an irregularity in the composition of the General Court, ECJ, Joined Cases C-341/06 P and C-342/06 P *Chronopost and La Poste v Commission* [2008] E.C.R. I-4777, paras 46–48.

[89] See Art. 169(1) and Art. 170(1) of the ECJ Rules of Procedure. Under former Art. 116(1) and (2) of the ECJ Rules of Procedure, this was spelled out specifically in relation to the response: see ECJ, Case C-35/92 P *European Parliament v Frederiksen* [1993] E.C.R. I-991, paras 33–36.

[90] ECJ, Case C-234/92 P *Shell v Commission* [1999] E.C.R. I-4501, paras 70–73.

[91] See, e.g. ECJ, Case C-315/99 P *Ismeri v Court of Auditors* [2001] E.C.R. I-5281, para. 19; ECJ, Joined Cases C-24/01 P and C-25/01 P *Glencore and Compagnie Continentale v Commission* [2002] E.C.R. I-10119, para. 77; ECJ (judgment of 14 October 2004), Case C-279/02 P *Antas de Campos v European Parliament*, not reported, paras 34 and 35; ECJ (order of 7 December 2004), Case C-521/03 P *Internationaler Hilfsfonds v Commission*, not reported, paras 37–38; ECJ (order of 13 January 2012), Case C-462/10 P *Evropaiki Dynamiki v European Environment Agency*, not reported, para. 21 (and further citations therein). With respect to measures of organisation of procedure, see, e.g. ECJ, Case C-260/05 P *Sniace v Commission* [2007] E.C.R. I-10005, paras 77–79; ECJ, Joined Cases C-75/05 and C-80/05 P *Germany and Others—Kronofrance v Commission* [2008] E.C.R. I-6619, paras 78–80; ECJ (order of 14 April 2011), Case C-460/10 P *Marcuccio v Court of Justice* [2011] E.C.R. I-63*, Summ. pub., para. 49. The question of the allocation of the burden of proof is a question of law, although it may have an impact on the findings of fact by the General Court (ECJ, Joined Cases C-2/01 P and C-3/01 P *BAI and Commission* [2004] E.C.R. I-23, para. 61).

by a party, will only be successful if it is apparent that the General Court was not in a position to rule on the correctness of the allegations made by that party without ordering the measure of inquiry concerned.[92]

H. Time limits

An appeal must be lodged within two months of notification of the decision appealed **16.25** against.[93] Time starts to run on the date of reception of the notification of the contested decision by the appellant.[94] By virtue of Art. 51 of the ECJ Rules of Procedure, ten days for distance are added.[95]

Appeals against decisions of the General Court refusing leave to intervene must be brought within two weeks of notification of the decision dismissing the application.[96] Cross-appeals must be brought within two months after service on the respondent of the appeal, that is to say, within the time limit for lodging the response.[97]

IV. Consequences

A. No suspensory effect

Appeals do not have suspensory effect, but the parties are entitled under Arts 278 and 279 **16.26** TFEU to apply for suspension of the operation of the decision of the General Court and for interim measures.[98] If, however, the contested decision of the General Court declares a

---

[92] See ECJ, Case C-119/97 P *Ufex and Others v Commission* [1999] E.C.R. I-1341, paras 107–112; ECJ (judgment of 14 October 2004), Case C-279/02 P *Antas de Campos v European Parliament*, not reported, paras 34–35; ECJ (judgment of 14 April 2005), Case C-243/04 P *Gaki-Kakouri v Court of Justice*, not reported, paras 52–55; ECJ, Joined Cases C-465/09 P to C-470/09 P *Territorio Historico de Vizcaya— Diputación Foral de Vizcaya and Others v Commission* [2011] E.C.R. I-83*, Summ. pub., paras 108–110. Compare ECJ (order of 13 January 2012), Case C-462/10 P *Evropaiki Dynamiki v European Environment Agency*, not reported, paras 22–23 (while the Court of Justice must examine the question whether the General Court committed an error of law in refusing to order those measures at the request of the appellant, in the instant proceedings, the appellant made no request).

[93] Statute, Art. 56, first para.

[94] ECJ (order of 30 April 1999), Case C-7/99 P *Campoli v Commission* [1999] E.C.R. I-2679, paras 5–7.

[95] ECJ Rules of Procedure, Art. 51. For some examples of calculating the time limit for submission of the appeal, see ECJ (order of 18 September 2007), Case C-191/07 P *Sellier v Commission* [2007] E.C.R. I-113*, Summ. pub., paras 3–5 (appeal out of time); ECJ (order of 3 July 2008), Case C-84/08 P *Pitsiorlas v Council and ECB* [2008] E.C.R. I-104*, Summ. pub., paras 8–11 (appeal out of time); ECJ (order of 10 March 2011), Case C-525/10 P *Ngele v Commission* [2011] E.C.R. I-24*, Summ. pub., paras 4–6 (appeal out of time). For a successful example involving submission of the appeal by electronic means, in compliance with Art. 57(7) of the ECJ Rules of Procedure, see ECJ, Case C-213/06 P *European Agency for Reconstruction v Karatzoglou* [2007] E.C.R. I-6733, paras 27–29. For a general discussion of calculating time limits, see paras 23.26 *et seq.*

[96] Statute, Art. 57, first para. By virtue of Art. 51 of the ECJ Rules of Procedure, ten days for distance are added.

[97] ECJ Rules of Procedure, Art. 176(1). In contrast to former Art. 115(1), this provision now explicitly makes clear that the submission of a cross-appeal is subject to the 'same time-limit as that prescribed for the submission of a response'. Nonetheless, as regards the former rule, see ECJ, Case C-136/92 P *Commission v Brazzelli Lualdi and Others* [1994] E.C.R. I-1981, paras 70–73.

[98] Statute, Art. 60, first para. See further para. 13.14. For examples, see ECJ (order of the President of 27 November 1990), Case C-242/90 P-R *Commission v Albani and Others* [1990] E.C.R. I-4329, para. 3; ECJ (order of the President of 31 January 1991), Case C-345/90 P-R *European Parliament v Hanning* [1991]

regulation void, the decision takes effect only as from the date of expiry of the period for lodging an appeal or, if an appeal is brought within that period, as from the date of the dismissal of the appeal.[99]

B. Dismissal of the appeal

16.27 If the appeal is unfounded, it will be dismissed. In the event that the reasoning of the contested decision of the General Court contains an infringement of Union law, but its operative part is nevertheless lawful, the appeal will likewise be dismissed.[100] In that event, the Court of Justice sets out the 'correct' grounds in its judgment, but does not set aside the judgment of the General Court (substitution of grounds[101]).[102] The Court of Justice may also find that the operative part of the judgment of the General Court is correct in law and dismiss the appeal on a legal ground different from the ground or grounds put forward by

---

E.C.R. I-231, paras 24–26; ECJ (order of the President of 3 April 1992), Case C-35/92 P-R *European Parliament v Frederiksen* [1992] E.C.R. I-2399, paras 17–18; ECJ (order of the President of 6 July 1995), Case C-166/95 P-R *Commission v Daffix* [1995] E.C.R. I-1955, para. 17; ECJ (order of the President of 15 September 1995), Case C-254/95 P-R *European Parliament v Innamorati* [1995] E.C.R. I-2707, paras 14–19. An application for suspension of the operation of the decision of the General Court against which an appeal has been brought must be made to the Court of Justice as indicated in Art. 60 of the Statute: CFI (order of the President of 22 November 1991), Case T-77/91 R *Hochbaum v Commission* [1991] E.C.R. II-1285, paras 21–22.

[99] Statute, Art. 60, second para. Under Arts 278 and 279 TFEU, a party may also request the Court of Justice to suspend the operation of the regulation declared void or to grant any other interim measures.

[100] See ECJ, Case C-534/07 P *William Prym and Prym Consumer v Commission* [2009] E.C.R. I-7415, paras 72–84 (rejecting the Commission's request for substitution of grounds, though declining to affirm whether such a request could be granted in the circumstances outlined by the Commission).

[101] Such a substitution may also be relevant in the context where an appeal is successful. See, e.g. ECJ, Joined Cases C-463/10 P and C-475/10 P *Deutsche Post and Germany v Commission* [2011], E.C.R. I-9639, para. 64 in which the Commission requested substitution of grounds if the Court were to set aside ruling of General Court in relation to challengeable act, so as to indicate action inadmissible since no direct and individual concern; the Court found there was no need to carry out the substitution because the appellant was held to be directly and individually concerned (paras 64–75).

[102] See, e.g. ECJ (order of 3 June 2005), Case C-396/03 *Killinger v Germany, Council and Commission* [2005] E.C.R. I-4967, para. 12; ECJ, Case C-167/04 P *JCB Service v Commission* [2006] E.C.R. I-8935, para. 186; ECJ, Joined Cases C-402/05 P and C-415/05 P *Kadi and Al Barakaat International Foundation v Council and Commission* [2008] E.C.R. I-6351, para. 233; ECJ, Joined Cases C-120/06 P and C-121/06 P *FIAMM and Others v Council and Commission* [2008] E.C.R. I-6513, para. 187; ECJ, Case C-497/06 P *CAS Succhi di Frutta v Commission* [2009] E.C.R. I-69*, Summ. pub., para. 32; ECJ, Joined Cases C-501/06 P, C-513/06 P, C-515/06 P, and C-519/06 P *GlaxoSmithKline Services and Others v Commission and Others* [2009] E.C.R. I-9291, para. 65; ECJ, Case C-352/09 P *ThyssenKrupp Nirosta v Commission* [2011] E.C.R. I-2359, paras 136, 157; ECJ, Joined Cases C-465/09 P to C-470/09 P *Territorio Historico de Vizcaya—Diputación Foral de Vizcaya and Others v Commission* [2011] E.C.R. I-83*, Summ. pub., para. 171; ECJ (judgment of 19 April 2012), Case C-221/10 P *Artegodan v Commission*, not reported, para. 94. See also ECJ, Case C-414/08 P *Sviluppo Italia Basilicata v Commission* [2010] E.C.R. I-2559, paras 130–131; ECJ, Joined Cases C-514/07 P, C-528/07 P, and C-532/07 P *Sweden and Others v API and Commission* [2010] E.C.R. I-8533, paras 104–106; ECJ (judgment of 26 June 2012), Case C-335/09 P *Poland v Commission*, not reported, paras 54–55. Where, in contrast, a fresh appraisal of the facts of the case is required by reason of the adoption of other legal grounds, the Court of Justice may carry out that appraisal only after setting aside the decision of the General Court. It then gives final judgment on the ground that the state of the proceedings permits it to do so. In this way, the Court of Justice may set aside a judgment of the General Court and then produce an operative part identical to that set out in the judgment at first instance after making its own assessment of the law and the facts. See ECJ, Case C-298/93 P *Klinke v Court of Justice* [1994] E.C.R. I-3009, in which the Court of Justice set aside a decision of the General Court and then set out an identical operative part.

the General Court, without pronouncing on the 'legality' of the grounds of the General Court's judgment. In such case, the pleas put forward on appeal will not be considered.[103]

C. Successful appeal

An appeal will be well-founded if at least one of the appellant's pleas succeeds. In that event, **16.28** the Court of Justice will set aside the contested decision. The decision may be set aside in its entirety or only in part.

A decision may be set aside in part not only if the contested decision determines a number of claims made in a single action—the decision on one claim being quashed, for example, and the appeal dismissed as regards the others[104]—but also if the decision of the General Court relates only to a single claim. In that case, the Court of Justice will confine itself to quashing one or more grounds of the decision.[105]

D. Consequences of a successful appeal

In the event that it sets aside a decision of the General Court, the Court of Justice may itself **16.29** give final judgment in the matter if the state of the proceedings so permits, or refer the case back to the General Court for judgment.[106] Depending on the circumstances of the case,

---

[103] See, e.g. ECJ (order of 3 December 1992), Case C-32/92 P *Moat v Commission* [1992] E.C.R. I-6379, para. 11; ECJ, Case C-480/93 P *Zunis Holding and Others v Commission* [1996] E.C.R. I-1, paras 15-16; ECJ, Case C-170/02 P *Schlüsselverlag J.S. Moser and Others v Commission* [2003] E.C.R. I-9889, paras 25–39.

[104] See, e.g. ECJ, Case C-18/91 P *V v European Parliament* [1992] E.C.R. I-3997; ECJ, Case C-19/93 P *Rendo and Others v Commission* [1995] E.C.R. I-3319; ECJ, Case C-198/07 P *Gordon v Commission* [2008] E.C.R. I-10701, paras 53, 63–64 (setting aside judgment under appeal in so far as the application for annulment is concerned, but finding appeal against application for damages inadmissible); ECJ, Case C-511/06 P *Archer Daniels Midland v Commission* [2009] E.C.R. I-5843, para. 130 (setting aside judgment in so far as assessment of certain pleas related to appellant's infringement of competition rules); ECJ, Case C-139/07 P *Commission v Technische Glaswerke Ilmenau* [2010] E.C.R. I-5885, para. 64 (setting aside judgment annulling contested decision in so far as it refused access to documents); ECJ, Case C-407/08 P *Knauf v Commission* [2010] E.C.R. I-6375, paras 92–93 (setting aside judgment in relation to General Court's reasoning in specific para. on infringement of competition rules); ECJ (judgment of 21 June 2012), Case C-452/10 P *BNP Paribas and BNL v Commission*, not reported, para. 105 (setting aside judgment to the extent that it infringed Art. 107(1) TFEU); ECJ (judgment of 28 June 2012), Case C-477/10 P *Commission v Agrofert Holding*, not reported, para. 81 (setting aside part of judgment under appeal concerning refusal of access to documents).

[105] See, e.g. ECJ, Case C-294/95 P *Ojha v Commission* [1996] E.C.R. I-5863, para. 62; see also the Opinion of Advocate–General P. Léger in that case, points 178–91.

[106] Statute, Art. 61, first para. For some examples, see ECJ, Joined Cases C-402/05 P and C-415/05 P *Kadi and Al Barakaat International Foundation v Council and Commission* [2008] E.C.R. I-6351, para. 332 (case disposed of by Court of Justice); ECJ, Case C-440/07 P *Commission v Schneider Electric* [2009] E.C.R. I-6413, para. 211 (case disposed of by the Court of Justice); ECJ, Case C-441/07 P *Commission v Alrosa Company* [2010] E.C.R. I-5949, para. 99 (case disposed of by the Court of Justice); ECJ, Case C-89/08 P *Commission v Ireland and Others* [2009] E.C.R. I-11245, para. 89 (referred back to the General Court); ECJ, Case C-28/08 P *Commission v Bavarian Lager* [2010] E.C.R. I-6055, paras 82–83 (case disposed of by Court of Justice); ECJ, Case C-362/09 P *Athinaiki Techniki v Commission* [2010] E.C.R. I-13275, para. 80 (referred back to the General Court); ECJ, Case C-96/09 P *Anheuser-Busch v Budejoviky Budvar* [2011] E.C.R. I-2131, para. 220 (referred back to the General Court); ECJ, Joined Cases C-106/09 P and C-107/09 P *Commission and Spain v Government of Gibraltar and United Kingdom* [2011] E.C.R. I-11113, para. 112 (case disposed of by the Court of Justice); ECJ, C-109/10 P *Solvay v Commission* [2011] E.C.R. I-10329, para. 74 (case disposed of by the Court of Justice); ECJ, Case C-110/10 P *Solvay v Commission* [2011] E.C.R. I-10439, para. 71 (case disposed

the Court of Justice may decide to give final judgment on a plea of inadmissibility raised during the proceedings at first instance, while referring the case back to the General Court to rule on the substance of the action.[107]

The subject-matter of the proceedings concluded by the Court of Justice after a judgment setting aside a decision of the General Court depends on various factors. It appears from the wording of the first paragraph of Art. 61 of the Statute and Art. 119 of the EGC Rules of Procedure that the judgment setting aside the decision of the General Court does not extend to the written and/or oral procedure which preceded that decision. What is annulled is therefore determined in the first place by the form of order sought and the pleas put forward by the parties in the pleadings which they originally lodged with the General Court. Consequently, the judgment setting aside the original decision does not enable them to seek a new form of order or to raise new pleas and to have completely new proceedings determined by the Court of Justice or the General Court, as the case may be, except where a new plea is based on a new matter of law or of fact within the meaning of Art. 127(1) of the ECJ Rules of Procedure or Art. 48(2) of the EGC Rules of Procedure.[108]

In the second place, regard must be had to the extent to which the judgment of the Court of Justice annulled the decision of the General Court. This can be determined from close consideration of the judgment on appeal. It is clear from earlier case-law that in order to comply with a judgment and to implement it fully, regard must be had not only to the operative part, but also to the grounds which led to the judgment and constitute its essential basis, in so far as they are necessary to determine the exact meaning of what is stated in the operative part.[109] Depending on the reasoning of the judgment of the Court of Justice, the assessment made by the General Court of all the pleas submitted may be rejected or the Court of Justice may reject the assessment of one or more pleas and accept the remainder of the lower court's reasoning.[110]

---

of by the Court of Justice); ECJ (judgment of 26 June 2012), Case C-336/09 P *Poland v Commission*, not reported, para. 43 (referred back to the General Court); ECJ (judgment of 28 June 2012), Case C-404/10 P *Commission v Editions Odile Jacob*, not reported, para. 139 (case disposed of by the Court of Justice); ECJ (judgment of 3 May 2012), Case C-24/11 P *Spain v Commission*, not reported, para. 50 (case disposed of by the Court of Justice). The first para. of Art. 61 of the Statute is also applicable to appeals brought under the second para. of Art. 57 of the Statute (see n. 51 and accompanying text): ECJ (order of the President of 29 January 1997), Case C-393/96 P(R) *Antonissen v Council and Commission* [1997] E.C.R. I-441, para. 45; ECJ (order of the Vice-President of 7 March 2013), Case C-551/12 P(R) *EDF v Commission*, not reported, para. 36. A similar provision applies when the General Court sets aside a decision of the Civil Service Tribunal. See Annex I of the Statute, Art. 13(1). For an application, see EGC (judgment of 12 May 2010), Case T- 491/08 P *Bui Van v Commission*, not reported, paras 93–95.

[107] See, e.g. ECJ, Case C-229/05 P *PKK and KNK v Council* [2007] E.C.R. I-439, paras 91, 123; ECJ, Case C-521/06 P *Athinaiki Techniki v Commission* [2008] E.C.R. I-5829, para. 66; ECJ, Case C-319/07 P *3F v Commission* [2009] E.C.R. I-5963, para. 98; ECJ, Case C-362/08 P *Internationaler Hilfsfonds v Commission* [2010] E.C.R. I-669, paras 65–67; ECJ, Joined Cases C-463/10 P and C-475/10 P *Deutsche Post and Germany v Commission* [2011] E.C.R. I-9639, paras 77–82.

[108] Where a case is referred back to the General Court after the latter's judgment has been set aside, the parties may not present any facts which were not brought before that Court when it first considered the case (CFI, Case T- 36/96 *Gaspari v European Parliament* [1999] E.C.R.-SC I-A-135, para. 77).

[109] ECJ, Joined Cases 97/86, 99/86, 193/86, and 215/86 *Asteris and Others v Commission* [1988] E.C.R. 2181, para. 27.

[110] For examples, see CFI, Case T-16/91 RV *Rendo and Others v Commission* [1996] E.C.R. II-1827, para. 28; ECJ, Joined Cases C-341/06 P and C-342/06 P *Chronopost and La Poste—UFEX and Others v Commission* [2008] E.C.R. I-4777, paras 134–140 (delimiting subject-matter of the dispute remaining before

Thirdly, the content of the decision of the General Court which is set aside influences the way in which the case is finally dispatched. Where the General Court dismisses an application, having considered all the pleas raised, and the Court of Justice then sets aside the decision on account of an error of law in assessing one of the pleas, it will be unlikely that in order to wind up the case, the Court of Justice or the General Court will pronounce (again) on the assessment of the pleas that the decision on appeal leaves unaffected. The proceedings will be confined in that event to a re-examination of the plea which the General Court wrongly rejected, having regard to the determination made by the Court of Justice of the point of law at issue.[111] Where, in contrast, the General Court grants the application—for instance, in the case of an action for annulment of an act of an institution—on the basis of a plea without considering the other pleas raised and the Court of Justice sets aside its decision on appeal, it would appear that, in order to wind up the case, not only the plea which wrongly succeeded will have to be re-examined, but consideration will also have to be given to those pleas which the General Court did not examine in its original decision,[112] although it is possible that the case may be able to be dispatched by upholding only one of the pleas raised.

E. Court of Justice gives final judgment

The Court of Justice will give final judgment where it has all of the necessary information before it to adjudicate the case.[113] For example, it may find that all the appellant's claims can be rejected because the Union act in issue was lawfully adopted,[114] or that the action   **16.30**

---

the Court of Justice following the setting aside of the judgment under appeal, such that arguments rejected by the General Court at first instance not affected).

[111] See the Opinion of Advocate–General P. Léger in ECJ, Case C-294/95 P *Ojha v Commission* [1996] E.C.R. I-5863, points 184–189. For some examples, see ECJ, Case C-141/08 P *Foshan Shunde Yongjian Housewares & Hardware Co. v Council* [2009] E.C.R. I-9147, paras 106–115; ECJ, Case C-90/09 P *General Quimica and Others v Commission* [2011] E.C.R. I-1, paras 92–111.

[112] See, e.g. CFI, Case T-43/89 RV *Gill v Commission* [1993] E.C.R. II-303; ECJ, Case C-295/07 P *Commission v Department du Loiret* [2008] E.C.R. I-9363, para. 112; ECJ, Case C-290/07 P *Commission v Scott* [2010] E.C.R. I-7763, para. 102; ECJ, Case C-279/08 P *Commission v The Netherlands* [2011] E.C.R. I-7671, paras 115–120; ECJ (judgment of 19 January 2012), Case C-53/11 P *OHIM v Nike International*, not reported, para. 60 (referred case back to General Court to decide plea that it had not previously examined).

[113] See, e.g. ECJ, Joined Cases C-341/06 P and C-342/06 P *Chronopost and La Poste—UFEX and Others v Commission* [2008] E.C.R. I-4777, para. 134. It may happen that the Court of Justice gives final judgment even when the General Court has not examined every plea of the application: see, e.g. ECJ, Joined Cases C-106/09 P and C-107/09 P *Commission and Spain v Government of Gibraltar and United Kingdom*, E.C.R. I-11113, paras 111–188; ECJ (judgment of 8 September 2011), Case C-279/08 P *Commission v Netherlands* [2011] E.C.R. I-7671, paras 116–134.

[114] See, e.g. ECJ, Case C-373/04 P *Commission v Alvarez Moreno* [2006] E.C.R. I-1, paras 47–52; ECJ, Case C-344/05 P *Commission v De Bry* [2006] E.C.R. I-10915, paras 50–58; ECJ, Case C-304/06 P *Eurohypo v OHIM* [2008] E.C.R. I-3297, paras 65–70; ECJ, Joined Cases C-341/06 P and C-342/06 P *Chronopost and La Poste—UFEX and Others v Commission* [2008] E.C.R. I-4777, paras 134–164; ECJ, Case C-139/07 P *Commission v Technische Glaswerke Ilmenau* [2010] E.C.R. I-5885, paras 65–71; ECJ, Case C-441/07 P *Commission v Alrosa Company* [2010] E.C.R. I-5949, paras 99–100, 118–121; ECJ, Case C-28/08 P *Commission v Bavarian Lager* [2010] E.C.R. I-6055, paras 82–85; ECJ, Case C-407/08 P *Knauf v Commission* [2010] E.C.R. I-6375, paras 94–111; ECJ, Case C-279/08 P *Commission v The Netherlands* [2011] E.C.R. I-7671, paras 116–120, 125–134; ECJ, Case C-90/09 P *General Quimica and Others v Commission* [2011] E.C.R. I-1, paras 94–111; ECJ, Joined Cases C-106/09 P and C-107/09 P *Commission and Spain v Government of Gibraltar and United Kingdom* [2011] E.C.R. I-11113, paras 112–188; ECJ (judgment of 28

should be dismissed, in all or in part, on other grounds.[115] Alternatively, the Court of Justice may determine that the contested Union act must be annulled in all or in part[116] or otherwise dispose of the matter before it.[117]

June 2012), Case C-404/10 P *Commission v Editions Odile Jacob*, not reported, paras 139–147; ECJ (judgment of 21 June 2012), Case C-452/10 P *BNP Paribas and BNL v Commission*, not reported, paras 107–139; ECJ (judgment of 28 June 2012), Case C-477/10 P *Commission v Agrofert Holding*, not reported, paras 81–90.

[115] See, e.g. ECJ, Case C-78/03 P *Commission v Aktionsgemeinschaft Recht und Eigentum* [2005] E.C.R. I-10737, paras 63–74 (dismissing action as inadmissible because appellant not individually concerned); ECJ, Case C-105/04 P *Technische Unie v Commission* [2006] E.C.R. I-3*, Summ. pub., paras 54–62; and ECJ, Case C-113/04 P *Technische Unie v Commission* [2006] E.C.R. I-8831, paras 59–72 (rejecting action for annulment in so far it is based on plea relating to application of 'reasonable time' principle); ECJ, Case C-373/04 P *Commission v Alvarez Moreno* [2006] E.C.R. I-1, paras 47–52 (dismissing action for annulment as inadmissible because contested acts not challengeable); ECJ, Case C-15/06 P *Regione Siciliana v Commission* [2007] E.C.R. I-2591, paras 41–43 (dismissing action for annulment as inadmissible because appellant cannot be considered to be directly concerned); ECJ, Case C-167/06 P *Komninou and Others v Commission* [2007] E.C.R. I-141*, Summ. pub., paras 30–74 (dismissing application for damages); ECJ, Case C-176/06 P *Stadtwerke Schwabisch Hall and Others v Commission* [2007] E.C.R. I-170*, Summ. pub., paras 28–32 (dismissing action for annulment as inadmissible because appellants not individually concerned); ECJ, Case C-516/06 P *Commission v Ferriere Nord* [2007] E.C.R. I-10685, para. 34 (dismissing action for annulment as inadmissible because contested act not challengeable); ECJ, Case C-51/05 P *Commission v Cantina sociale di Dolianova and Others* [2008] E.C.R. I-5341, paras 71–74 (dismissing application for damages); ECJ, Case C-440/07 P *Commission v Schneider Electric* [2009] E.C.R. I-6413, paras 211–223 (assessing alleged losses in appellant's application for damages); ECJ, Joined Cases C-445/07 P and C-455/07 P *Commission v Ente per le Ville Vesuviane* [2009] E.C.R. I-7993, paras 69–71 (holding action must be dismissed as inadmissible because appellant not directly concerned); ECJ, Case C-214/08 P *Guigard v Commission* [2009] E.C.R. I-91*, Summ. pub., paras 47–49 (finding that appellant's action is in reality seeking damages arising out of a contract for which there is no 'arbitration clause' for the purposes of Art. 272 TFEU).

[116] See, e.g. ECJ, Case C-227/04 P *Lindorfer v Council* [2007] E.C.R. I-6767, paras 87–90; ECJ, Case C-29/05 *OHIM v Kaul* [2007] E.C.R. I-2213, paras 66–70; ECJ, Case C-64/05 P *Sweden —IFAW Internationaler Tierschutz-Fonds v Commission* [2007] E.C.R. I-11389, paras 96–100; ECJ, Case C-326/05 P *Industrias Quimicas del Valles v Commission* [2007] E.C.R. I-6557, paras 71–89; ECJ, Joined Cases C-402/05 P and C-415/05 P *Kadi and Al Barakaat International Foundation v Council and Commission* [2008] E.C.R. I-6351, paras 332–376; ECJ, Joined Cases C-373/06 P, C-379/06 P and C-382/06 P *Flaherty and Others v Commission* [2008] E.C.R. I-2649, paras 44–47; ECJ, Case C-17/07 P *Neirinck v Commission* [2008] E.C.R. I-36*, Summ. pub., paras 94–98 (rejected claim for damages finding annulment adequate compensation); ECJ, Case C-108/07 P *Ferrero Deutschland v OHIM* [2008] E.C.R. I-61*, Summ. pub., paras 40–60; ECJ, Case C-198/07 P *Gordon v Commission* [2008] E.C.R. I-10701, paras 64, 71–75; ECJ, Case C-204/07 P *C.A.S. v Commission* [2008] E.C.R. I-6135, paras 135–136; ECJ, Case C-405/07 P *The Netherlands v Commission* [2008] E.C.R. I-8301, paras 76–78; ECJ, Joined Cases C-399/06 P and C-403/06 P *Hassan and Ayadi v Council and Commission* [2009] E.C.R. I-11393, paras 79–96; ECJ, Case C-511/06 P *Archer Daniels Midland v Commission* [2009] E.C.R. I-5843, paras 131–164; ECJ, Case C-141/08 P *Foshan Shunde Yongjian Housewares & Hardware Co. v Council* [2009] E.C.R. I-9147, paras 106–115; ECJ, Case C-521/09 P *Elf Aquitaine v Commission* [2011] E.C.R. I-8947, paras 177–180; ECJ, C-109/10 P *Solvay v Commission* [2011] E.C.R. I-10329, paras 74–75; ECJ, Case C-110/10 P *Solvay v Commission* [2011] E.C.R. I-10439, paras 71–72; ECJ (judgment of 20 October 2011), Joined Cases C-344/10 P and C-345/10 P *Freixenet v OHIM*, not reported, paras 54–56; ECJ (judgment of 2 February 2012), Case C-249/10 P *Brosmann Footwear (HK) and Others v Council*, not reported, paras 41–43; ECJ (judgment of 13 March 2012), Case C-376/10 P *Tay Za v Council*, not reported, paras 75–76; ECJ (judgment of 3 May 2012), Case C-24/11 P *Spain v Commission*, paras 50–59.

[117] See, e.g. ECJ, Case C-167/04 P *JCB Service v Commission* [2006] E.C.R. I-8935, para. 244 (fixing amount of fine imposed on appellants for infringement of competition rules); ECJ, Case C-301/04 P *Commission v SGL Carbon and Others* [2006] E.C.R. I-5915, paras 72–77 (setting fine imposed on appellants for infringement of competition rules).

F. Referral back to the General Court

The Court of Justice will refer the case back to the General Court for final judgment where **16.31** it is not in a position to rule on the substance of the action, the case has not been completely decided and additional findings of fact are needed, or a fresh look has to be taken at those already made.[118] Where a case is referred back to the General Court, that Court is bound by the decision of the Court of Justice on points of law.[119]

G. Effects of a successful appeal brought by a Member State or a Union institution

Where an appeal brought by a Member State or a Union institution which did not **16.32** intervene in the proceedings before the General Court is well-founded, the Court of Justice may, if it considers it necessary, state which of the effects of the decision of the General Court which has been set aside are to be considered definitive in respect of the other parties to the litigation.[120]

---

[118] See, e.g. ECJ, Case C-59/06 P *Marcuccio v Commission* [2007] E.C.R. I-182*, Summ. pub., para. 76; ECJ, Case C-193/06 P *Societe des Produits Nestle v OHIM* [2007] E.C.R. I-114*, Summ. pub., para. 78; ECJ, Case C-213/06 P *European Agency for Reconstruction v Karatzoglou* [2007] E.C.R. I-6733, para. 47; ECJ, Case C-408/04 P *Commission v Salzgitter* [2008] E.C.R. I-2767, paras 109–112; ECJ, Case C-413/06 P *Bertelsmann and Sony Corporation of America v Commission* [2008] E.C.R. I-4951, para. 190; ECJ, Case C-487/06 P *British Aggregates Association v Commission* [2008] E.C.R. I-10515, para. 197; ECJ, Case C-295/07 P *Commission v Department du Loiret* [2008] E.C.R. I-9363, para. 112; ECJ, Case C-334/07 P *Commission v Freistaat Sachsen* [2008] E.C.R. I-9465, paras 61–63; ECJ, Case C-436/07 P *Commission v Efrosyni Alexiadou* [2008] E.C.R. I-152*, Summ. pub., paras 28–29; ECJ, Case C-519/07 P *Commission v Koninklijke FrieslandCampina* [2009] E.C.R. I-8495, paras 107–109; ECJ, Case C-89/08 P *Commission v Ireland and Others* [2009] E.C.R. I-11245, para. 89; ECJ, Case C-290/07 P *Commission v Scott* [2010] E.C.R. I-7763, para. 102; ECJ, Case C-362/09 P *Athinaiki Techniki v Commission* [2010] E.C.R. I-13275, paras 79–80; ECJ, Case C-96/09 P *Anheuser-Busch v Budejoviky Budvar* [2011] E.C.R. I-2131, paras 217–220; ECJ, Case C-317/10 P *Union Investment Privatfonds—UnitCredito Italiano v OHIM* [2011] E.C.R. I-5471, para. 64; ECJ (judgment of 26 June 2012), Case C-336/09 P *Poland v Commission*, not reported, para. 43; ECJ (judgment of 19 January 2012), Case C-53/11 P *OHIM v Nike International*, not reported, para. 60; ECJ (judgment of 21 June 2012), Case C-135/11 P *IFAW Internationaler Tierschutz-Fonds v Commission*, not reported, para. 79; ECJ (judgment of 24 May 2012), Case C-196/11 P *Formula One Licensing v OHIM*, not reported, paras 56–58. The Court may refer the case back to the General Court, depending on the circumstances of the proceedings, despite a request submitted by the appellant for the Court of Justice to rule itself on the action: see, e.g. ECJ, Case C-200/10 P *Evropaiki Dynamiki v Commission* [2011] E.C.R. I-67*, Summ. pub., paras 98–102.

[119] Statute, Art. 61, second para. For examples, see CFI, Case T- 43/89 RV *Gill v Commission* [1993] E.C.R. II-303; CFI, Case T- 20/89 RV *Moritz v Commission* [1993] E.C.R. II-1423. Upon referral of the case back to the General Court, that Court's ruling may be subject to appeal: see, e.g. ECJ, Joined Cases C-341/06 P and C-342/06 P *Chronopost and La Poste—UFEX and Others v Commission* [2008] E.C.R. I-4777.

[120] Statute, Art. 61, third para.

17

THE REVIEW PROCEDURE

I. Subject-Matter

17.01 From the point of view of the parties concerned, the Member States, and the Union institutions, bodies, offices, and agencies, neither decisions of the General Court in appeals brought against decisions of specialized courts[1] nor its decisions on preliminary references (when such jurisdiction would be conferred on it)[2] are open to be challenged. Exceptionally, however, by virtue of the review procedure provided in Arts 256(2) and (3) TFEU,[3] such decisions may be subject to review by the Court of Justice where there is a serious risk of the unity or consistency of Union law being affected.[4]

Only the First Advocate-General of the Court of Justice[5] can take the initiative for a review of decisions of the General Court when he or she considers that such a risk exists.[6] The

---

[1] At present, only one such specialized court has been created: the EU Civil Service Tribunal. See further para. 2.03.

[2] A transfer of jurisdiction to the General Court over preliminary references pursuant to Art. 256(3), first para., TFEU has not been put into effect: see further para. 2.53.

[3] This review procedure should be distinguished from applications for revision of a judgment, which constitutes 'an exceptional review procedure that allows an applicant to call in question the authority of *res judicata* attaching to a judgment bringing the proceedings to an end on the basis of the findings of fact relied upon by the Court' and 'presupposes the discovery of elements of a factual nature which existed prior to the judgment and which were unknown at that time to the court which delivered it as well as to the party applying for revision and which, had the court been able to take them into consideration, could have led it to a different determination of the proceedings': CFI (order of 31 July 2009), Case T-213/08 REV *Marinova v Université Libre de Bruxelles and Commission*, not reported, para. 34 (and case-law therein). See further paras 25.116 *et seq.*

[4] Art. 256(2), second para., TFEU; Art. 256(3), third para., TFEU. In preliminary ruling proceedings, the General Court may avoid a review by referring a case which falls under its jurisdiction to the Court of Justice. This is because Art. 256(3), second para., TFEU provides: 'Where the General Court considers that the case requires a decision of principle likely to affect the unity or consistency of Union law, it may refer the case to the Court of Justice for a ruling,' See A. Tizzano and P. Iannuccelli, 'Premières applications de la procedure de "réexamen" devant la Cour de Justice de l'Union européenne', in N. Parisi, M. Fumagalli Meraviglia, A. Santini, and D.G. Rinoldo (eds), *Scritti in onore di Ugo Draetta* (Naples, Editoriale scientifica, 2011), 733–54.

[5] The First Advocate-General is appointed for one year by the Court and has the rank of a President of Chamber. See ECJ Rules of Procedure, Art. 14(1).

[6] Statute, Art. 62, first para. This provision specifies that where the First Advocate-General considers that there is a serious risk of the unity or consistency of Union law being affected, he 'may' propose that the Court of Justice reviews the decision of the General Court. In other words, the initiative to propose a review is at the First Advocate-General's discretion.

review should therefore be distinguished from an appeal, which, in principle, is brought by one of the parties to the case[7] and may be based on any error of law which the General Court or specialized court may have committed in the judgment under appeal.[8]

Given its exceptional nature, the review procedure has been employed in a small number of cases. To date, there have been few occasions in which the Court of Justice has decided that there should be a review of a decision of the General Court pursuant to the second paragraph of Art. 256(2) TFEU.[9] In the majority of cases, the First Advocate-General's proposal has not led to a review by the Court of Justice.[10]

II. Special Characteristics

A. Determination whether there is a serious risk of the unity or consistency of Union law being affected

(1) Circumstances justifying a review

As the case-law on the review procedure develops, the Court of Justice has clarified the circumstances in which a review is necessary where there is a serious risk of the unity or consistency of Union law being affected. **17.02**

In its decision concerning the review of the judgment of the General Court in Case T-197/09 P *M v EMEA*,[11] the Court of Justice observed that in the judgment concerned, the General Court had upheld in part, as to the substance, the application for compensation for the damage alleged by the applicant even though the preliminary issue which arose before the Civil Service Tribunal (plea of inadmissibility) did not permit a written or oral exchange of arguments on the substance before that Tribunal, and it appears that no such exchange of arguments took place before the General Court either. In those circumstances, the Court found that there is a serious risk of the unity or consistency of Union law being affected in

---

[7] With the exception of cases relating to disputes between the Union and its servants, an appeal may also be brought by Member States and Union institutions which did not intervene in the proceedings before the General Court (Statute, Art. 56).

[8] Art. 256(1), second para., TFEU; Statute, Annex I, Art. 11.

[9] See ECJ (decision of 24 June 2009), Case C-197/09 RX Review of Judgment T-12/08 P *M v EMEA* [2009] E.C.R. I-12033 (followed by the review of the judgment itself in ECJ (judgment of 17 December 2009), Case C-197/09 RX-II Review of Judgment T-12/08 *M v EMEA* [2009] E.C.R. I-12033); ECJ (decision of 12 July 2012), Case C-334/12 RX Review of Judgment T-234/11 P *Arango Jaramillo and Others v EIB*, not reported (followed by the review of the judgment itself in ECJ (judgment of 28 February 2013), Case C-334/12 RX-II Review of Judgment T-234/11 P *Arango Jaramillo and Others v EIB*, not reported); ECJ (decision of 11 December 2012), Case C-579/12 RX Review of Judgment T-268/11 P *Commission v Strack*, not reported (followed by the review of the judgment itself in ECJ (judgment of 19 September 2013), Case C-579/12 RX-II *Commission v Strack*, not reported, para. 61).

[10] See, e.g. ECJ (decision of 16 April 2008), Case C-216/08 RX Review of judgment T-414/06 P *Combescot v Commission*, not reported; ECJ (decision of 5 February 2009), Case C-21/09 RX Review of Judgment T-90/07 P and T-99/07 P *Belgium and Commission v Genette*, not reported; ECJ (decision of 5 June 2009), Case C-180/09 RX Review of judgment T-492/07 P *Sanchez Ferriz and Others v Commission*, not reported; ECJ (decision of 5 May 2010), Case C-183/10 RX Review of Judgment T-338/07 P *Bianchi v ETF*, not reported; ECJ (decision of 27 October 2010), Case C-478/10 RX Review of Judgment T-157/09 P *Marcuccio v Commission*, not reported; ECJ (decision of 8 February 2011), Case C-17/11 RX Review of Judgment T-143/09 P *Commission v Petrilli*, not reported.

[11] ECJ (decision of 24 June 2009), Case C-197/09 RX Review of Judgment T-12/08 P *M v EMEA* [2009] E.C.R. I-12033.

that the judgment of the General Court ruled on the application for compensation for non-material damage alleged by the applicant as regards the substance.[12] Accordingly, the Court held that there should be a review of that judgment and the review should cover the question whether that judgment affects the unity or consistency of Union law in that the General Court, as an appeal court, interpreted the expression 'where the state of the proceedings... permits' in Art. 61 of the Statute and Art. 13(1) of the Annex to the Statute as permitting it to dispose of a case and rule on the substance, despite the fact that the appeal before it concerned the examination of the treatment given at first instance to a plea of inadmissibility and that, as regards the aspect of the case which was disposed of, there had been no exchange of arguments before it or before the Civil Service Tribunal as the court seized at first instance.[13]

Likewise, in its decision concerning the review of the judgment of the General Court in Case T-234/11 P *Arango Jaramillo and Others v EIB*,[14] the Court of Justice considered that there is a serious risk that the unity or consistency of Union law might be affected in that it is apparent from the General Court's judgment in that case that the period of three months and ten days, which in the absence of any provision laying down time limits for bringing proceedings applicable to disputes between the European Investment Bank (EIB) and its staff, must in principle be deemed a reasonable period within which an EIB staff member is required to bring an action for annulment of an EIB measure adversely affecting that staff member, is a period which, if exceeded, has the effect of making the action out of time and hence inadmissible, without the Union courts being required to take account of the particular circumstances of the individual case. As a result, that serious risk arises for two reasons which justified a review of the judgment concerned. First, it is necessary to determine whether, by taking the view that the Civil Service Tribunal is not required, when assessing whether the period for bringing an action for annulment of an EIB measure is reasonable, to take account of the particular circumstances of the case, the General Court adopted, by *a contrario* reasoning, an interpretation that is consistent with the case-law to the effect that the reasonableness of a period which is not laid down by primary or secondary Union law must be assessed by

---

[12] ECJ, Case C-197/09 RX Review of Judgment T-12/08 P *M v EMEA*, paras 16–17.

[13] In its subsequent judgment on the substance of the case, the Court of Justice ruled, *inter alia*, that in view of several circumstances taken as a whole—(1) the judgment concerned could constitute a precedent for future cases; (2) the General Court departed from established case-law in interpreting the expression 'where the state of the proceedings... permits'; (3) the errors of the General Court relate to two rules of procedure which do not pertain solely to the law relating to the employment of Union officials but are applicable regardless of the matter at issue; and (4) the rules which the General Court failed to comply with occupy an important position in the Union legal order and in particular the Statute and the Annex to the Statute constitute primary Union law—the judgment concerned did affect the unity and consistency of Union law: ECJ (judgment of 17 December 2009), Case C-197/09 RX-II Review of Judgment T-12/08 *M v EMEA* [2009] E.C.R. I-12033, paras 60–66. Particularly viewing the two decisions together—the decision to review and the decision on the substance—provides insight into certain considerations that the Court takes into account in deciding to review a judgment of the General Court on account of the serious risk of the unity or consistency of Union law being affected: the precedent value of the case, the departure from settled case-law, and the significance of the Union law rules that the General Court failed to comply with in the Union legal order. Notably, the Court of Justice did not follow Advocate-General J. Mazák's submission that an incorrect decision of the General Court can affect the unity or consistency of Union law only if it is inconsistent with a general principle of Union law. See Opinion of Advocate-General J. Mazák in ECJ, Case C-197/09 RX Review of Judgment T-12/08 P *M v EMEA* [2009] E.C.R. I-12033, points 6, 31.

[14] ECJ (decision of 12 July 2012), Case C-334/12 RX Review of Judgment T-234/11 P *Arango Jaramillo and Others v EIB*, not reported.

reference to the circumstances specific to each case. Second, it is necessary to ascertain whether, by finding that, where a period for bringing an action not provided for by primary or secondary Union law is exceeded, the action is time-barred, the interpretation of the General Court might not interfere with the right to an effective judicial remedy enshrined in Art. 47 of the Charter of Fundamental Rights of the European Union.[15]

(2) Circumstances where no review is necessary

By comparison, in its decision concerning the review of the judgment of the General Court **17.03** in Case T-143/09 P *Commission v Petrilli*,[16] the Court of Justice considered that the circumstances involved—that the judgment concerned allegedly showed a divergence in the case-law of the General Court concerning the conditions governing the non-contractual liability of the Union in staff cases and that the Court of Justice had not yet ruled on whether the specific nature of litigation in staff cases justifies making the non-contractual liability of the Union in this area subject to special conditions—did not justify the proposed review.[17] This was based on two grounds. First, it was not for the Court of Justice, in the context of the review procedure, to rule on the merits of the General Court's development of its own case-law when acting in its appellate capacity. Second, the fact that the Court of Justice has not yet ruled on a point of law is not in itself sufficient to justify a review 'in so far as it is now solely for the Civil Service Tribunal and the General Court of the European Union to develop the case-law in matters relating to the civil service, since the Court of Justice has jurisdiction only to prevent the decisions of the General Court affecting the unity or consistency of European Union law', which was not the case here.[18]

B. Procedure

(1) Initiation of the review

The proposal of the First Advocate-General must be made within one month of delivery of **17.04** the decision of the General Court, and the Court of Justice must decide within one month of receiving the proposal whether or not the decision should be reviewed.[19]

---

[15] ECJ, Case C-334/12 RX Review of Judgment T-234/11 P *Arango Jaramillo and Others v EIB*, paras 13–16. See also ECJ (judgment of 28 February 2013), Case C-334/12 RX-II Review of Judgment T-234/11 P *Arango Jaramillo and Others v EIB*, not reported. The Court set aside the judgment of the General Court because it affected the consistency of Union law inso ar as it interpreted the concept of a 'reasonable period', in the context of an action brought by members of staff of the European Investment Bank for annulment of a measure adopted by that bank adversely affecting those members, as a period of three months, which, if exceeded, entailed automatically that the action was out of time and, therefore, inadmissible, without the Union courts being required to take into consideration the circumstances of the case. The Court came to this conclusion after assessing the circumstances of the case, namely that (1) the judgment concerned could constitute a precedent for future cases; (2) the General Court departed from established case-law in interpreting the concept of 'reasonable period'; (3) the errors of the General Court relate to a procedural concept which does not pertain solely to the law relating to the employment of Union officials are applicable regardless of the matter at issue; and (4) the rules which the General Court failed to comply with occupy an important position in the Union legal order and in particular the right to an effective remedy before a tribunal guaranteed by Art. 47 of the Charter.
[16] ECJ (decision of 8 February 2011), Case C-17/11 RX Review of Judgment T-143/09 P *Commission v Petrilli*, not reported.
[17] ECJ, Case C-17/11 RX Review of Judgment T-143/09 P *Commission v Petrilli*, paras 2–4.
[18] ECJ, Case C-17/11 RX Review of Judgment T-143/09 P *Commission v Petrilli*, paras 4–5.
[19] Statute, Art. 62.

As soon as the date for the delivery or signature of a decision to be given under Art. 256(2) or (3) TFEU is fixed, the Registry of the General Court is required to inform the Registry of the Court of Justice, whereby that decision and the file in the case is made available to the First Advocate-General.[20]

(2) Reviewing Chamber

17.05 As part of the recent changes to the Rules of Procedure of the Court of Justice, a Chamber of five Judges, referred to as the reviewing Chamber, is designated for a period of one year to handle review proposals made by the First Advocate-General pursuant to Art. 62 of the Statute.[21] This Chamber is responsible both for the decision on whether to follow the proposal made by the First Advocate-General and for the final decision if the review procedure is launched.[22] In contrast, under the former Rules of Procedure of the Court of Justice, there had been a special Chamber set up for the purposes of deciding whether a decision of the General Court was to be reviewed, which had been composed of the President and the Presidents of the then four Chambers of five Judges.[23]

(3) Decision whether to review

17.06 The proposal of the First Advocate-General to review a decision of the General Court under Art. 256(2) or (3) TFEU is forwarded to the President of the Court of Justice and to the President of the reviewing Chamber; notice of that transmission is also given to the Registrar at the same time, whereby he or she communicates the file in the case before the General Court to the members of the reviewing Chamber.[24] As soon as the proposal to review has been received, the President of the Court designates the Judge-Rapporteur from among the Judges of the reviewing Chamber on a proposal from the President of that Chamber.[25] That Chamber, acting on a proposal from the Judge-Rapporteur, then decides whether the decision of the General Court is to be reviewed, and the decision to review indicates only the questions which are to be reviewed.[26]

The General Court, the national court or tribunal in the case of preliminary rulings, those referred to in Article 23 of the Statute and, in the cases provided for in Article 256(2) TFEU, the parties to the proceedings before the General Court are informed as to whether or not the decision of the General Court is to be reviewed.[27] Notice of the date of the decision to

---

[20] ECJ Rules of Procedure, Art. 192.

[21] ECJ Rules of Procedure, Art. 191. See Notice 2013/C 336/08 concerning the Designation of the Chamber responsible for cases of the kind referred to in Article 193 of the Rules of Procedure of the Court ([2013] O.J. C336/4).

[22] ECJ Rules of Procedure, Art. 191; Art. 195(4). However, as regards the judgment on the substance of the case after a decision to review, the reviewing Chamber may request the Court of Justice to assign the case to a formation of the Court composed of a greater number of Judges: ECJ Rules of Procedure, Art. 195(5).

[23] Ex ECJ Rules of Procedure, Art. 123b.

[24] ECJ Rules of Procedure, Art. 193(1)–(2); Art. 194(1)–(2). With particular regard to the review of preliminary rulings of the General Court, it is further provided that the Registrar informs the General Court, the referring court or tribunal, the parties to the main proceedings, and other interested persons referred to in the second para. of Art. 62a of the Statute of the existence of a proposal to review: ECJ Rules of Procedure, Art. 194(3).

[25] ECJ Rules of Procedure, Art. 193(3); Art. 194(4).

[26] ECJ Rules of Procedure, Art. 193(4); Art. 194(5). As far as the language of the procedure is concerned, see ECJ Rules of Procedure, Art. 37(2)(b), which provides that 'where, in accordance with the second paragraph of Article 62 of the Statute, the Court decides to review a decision of the General Court, the language of the case shall be the language of the decision of the General Court which is the subject of review'.

[27] ECJ Rules of Procedure, Art. 193(5); Art. 194(6) and Statute, Art. 62a.

review the decision of the General Court and of the questions which are to be reviewed is published in the *Official Journal.*[28]

(4) Judgment on the substance of the case after a decision to review

The Court of Justice will give a ruling on the questions which are subject to review by means of an urgent procedure on the basis of the file forwarded to it by the General Court.[29] **17.07**

The review procedure does not constitute a mere appeal in the interest of the law.[30] Indeed, the parties to the decision under review and, in the case of a preliminary ruling, all interested parties within the meaning of Art. 23 of the Statute, are entitled to lodge statements or written observations with the Court of Justice relating to the questions which are subject to review.[31] The Court of Justice may decide to open the oral procedure before giving a ruling.[32]

As soon as a decision to review a decision of the General Court has been taken, the First Advocate-General assigns the review to an Advocate-General.[33] The reviewing Chamber rules on the substance of the case, after hearing the Advocate-General.[34]

(5) Suspensory effect

If the review concerns a decision given upon appeal by the General Court, the procedure will not in principle have suspensory effect.[35] By contrast, a preliminary ruling of the General Court takes effect only as from the date of expiry of the period for opening a review procedure or, if a review procedure is initiated within that period, as from the end of such review procedure, unless the Court of Justice decides otherwise.[36] The review procedure concerning a preliminary ruling of the General Court will thus in principle have suspensory effect. **17.08**

---

[28] ECJ Rules of Procedure, Art. 193(6); Art. 194(7).

[29] Statute, Art. 62a, first para. Provision for the urgent procedure had been envisaged with particular regard to the review of preliminary rulings by Declaration (No. 15), annexed to the Nice Treaty, on Article 225(3) of the Treaty establishing the European Community, [2001] O.J. C80/80, which stated: 'The Conference considers that in exceptional cases in which the Court of Justice decides to review a decision of the Court of First Instance (now General Court) on a question referred for a preliminary ruling, it should act under an emergency procedure.'

[30] It was already apparent from Declaration (No. 13), annexed to the Nice Treaty, on Article 225(2) and (3) of the Treaty establishing the European Community, [2001] O.J. C80/80, that the parties concerned were to be involved in the review procedure. This Declaration stated: 'The Conference considers that the essential provisions of the review procedure in Article 225(2) and (3) (now Art. 256(2) and (3) TFEU) should be defined in the Statute of the Court of Justice. Those provisions should in particular specify:

– the role of the parties in proceedings before the Court of Justice, in order to safeguard their rights;
– the effect of the review procedure on the enforceability of the decision of the Court of First Instance (now General Court);
– the effect of the Court of Justice decision on the dispute between the parties.'

[31] Statute, Art. 62a, second para. This must be done within one month of the date of service of the decision to review: see ECJ Rules of Procedure, Art. 195(2).

[32] Statute, Art. 62a, third para.

[33] ECJ Rules of Procedure, Art. 195(3).

[34] ECJ Rules of Procedure, Art. 195(4).

[35] Statute, Art. 62b, first para., though this is 'without prejudice to Arts 278 and 279 TFEU'. Thus, interim relief can be granted.

[36] Statute, Art. 62b, second para.

III. Consequences

17.09   If the decision of the General Court is reviewed, the effects of such review will be as follows.

As regards a decision given upon appeal by the General Court which has been reviewed by the Court of Justice and the Court of Justice finds that this decision affects the unity or consistency of Union law, the Court will, after having given a correct interpretation of the law, refer the case back to the General Court. The General Court will be bound by the decision of the Court of Justice on points of law. If necessary, the Court of Justice will state which of the effects of the decision of the General Court are to be considered as definitive in respect of the parties to the litigation.[37] Alternatively,[38] the Court of Justice may itself give final judgment where, having regard to the result of the review, the outcome of the case is obvious from the facts on which the decision of the General Court was based.[39]

In the case of the review of a preliminary ruling of the General Court where the Court of Justice finds that the decision of the General Court affects the unity or consistency of Union law, the answer given by the Court to the questions subject to review will be substituted for that given by the General Court.[40] The 'new' interpretation of the Court of Justice will thus be binding on the national court.

---

[37] Statute, Art. 62b, first para. See, e.g. ECJ, Case C-197/09 RX-II Review of Judgment T-12/08 *M v EMEA* [2009] E.C.R. I-12033, paras 67–71, in which the Court noted that it follows from the first para. of Art. 62b of the Statute that the Court cannot confine itself to finding that the unity or consistency of Union law is affected without drawing the necessary inferences from that finding as regards the dispute in question. In these proceedings, the judgment of the General Court was set aside as regards certain points of the operative part and as the Court could not itself give final judgment pursuant to the last sentence of that provision, it referred the case back to the General Court as regards those aspects. In turn, the General Court referred the case back to the Civil Service Tribunal: see EGC, Case T-12/08 P-RENV-RX *M v EMEA* [2010] E.C.R. II-3735. Before the Civil Service Tribunal, the dispute was amicably settled for the very sum that had been incorrectly awarded by the General Court and the case was removed from the register: see CST (order of 31 March 2011), Case F-23/07 RENV-RX *M v EMEA*, not reported.

[38] This alternative has been framed by the Court of Justice as more exceptional: see ECJ (judgment of 17 December 2009), Case C-197/09 RX-II Review of Judgment T-12/08 *M v EMEA* [2009] E.C.R. I-12033, para. 68; ECJ (judgment of 19 September 2013), Case C-579/12 RX-II *Commission v Strack*, not reported, para. 61.

[39] ECJ, Case C-197/09 RX-II Review of Judgment T-12/08 *M v EMEA*, para. 68. When the appeal before the General Court is limited to points of law (as is the case with respect to decisions of the Civil Service Tribunal), the facts on which the decision of the General Court is based will necessarily be the facts on which the decision of the specialized court was based.

[40] Statute, Art. 62b, second para.

18

PROCEEDINGS BROUGHT BY OFFICIALS AND OTHER SERVANTS OF THE UNION (STAFF CASES)

I. Subject-Matter

A. General

(1) Disputes between the Union and its staff

The relationship between the Union and its servants is governed by the 'Staff Regulations of officials of the European Communities' (Staff Regulations) and the 'Conditions of employment of other servants of the European Communities' (Conditions of Employment).[1] Every Union act regarding staff policy must comply with the provisions of the Staff Regulations or Conditions of Employment. Disputes between the Union and its staff within the limits of and under the conditions set down in the Staff Regulations or Conditions of Employment are brought before the European Union Civil

18.01

---

[1] Regulation (EEC, Euratom, ECSC) No. 259/68 of the Council of 29 February 1968 laying down the Staff Regulations of Officials and the Conditions of Employment of Other Servants of the European Communities and instituting special measures temporarily applicable to officials of the Commission, [1968] O.J. Spec. Ed. I, 30, as reformed by Council Regulation (EC, Euratom) No. 723/2004 of 22 March 2004 amending the Staff Regulations of Officials of the European Communities and the Conditions of Employment of Other Servants of the European Communities, [2004] O.J. L124/1; *corrigendum* in [2005] L51/28. The latest substantial amendment to the Staff Regulations concerned its application to the staff members of the European Union External Action Service (Regulation (EU, Euratom) No. 1080/2010 of the European Parliament and of the Council of 24 November 2010 amending the Staff Regulations of Officials of the European Communities and the Conditions of Employment of Other Servants of those Communities, [2010] O.J. L311/1). The Conditions of Employment indicate the provisions of the Staff Regulations which apply to categories of Union staff other than officials (temporary staff, auxiliary staff, contract staff, local staff, and special advisers). These staff members are engaged by contract. The fact that different provisions apply to different categories of staff does not breach the principle of equality. The Union legislator is free to create different categories of officials corresponding to the legitimate needs of the Union's civil service and to the nature of the tasks that need to be performed (CST, Case F-104/06 *Arpaillange and Others v Commission* [2009] E.C.R.-SC I-A-1-57, paras 60–61).

Service Tribunal (Civil Service Tribunal).[2] Until 12 December 2005,[3] this jurisdiction was exercised by what is now the General Court.

It should be pointed out, however, that the Staff Regulations and Conditions of Employment do not apply to all officials employed by the Union. For instance, the European Central Bank (ECB) and the European Investment Bank (EIB) have their own set of staff regulations.[4] These regulations contain provisions regulating disputes between the officials and those bodies similar to the Staff Regulations and Conditions of Employment. The Union courts apply their case-law concerning the Staff Regulations and Conditions of Employment by way of analogy.[5]

(2) Art. 91(1) of the Staff Regulations

18.02 The jurisdiction of the Union judicature is delineated in Art. 91(1) of the Staff Regulations.[6] It has jurisdiction in any dispute between the Union and any person to whom the Staff Regulations apply regarding the legality of an act adversely affecting such a person either because the appointing authority has taken a decision or because it has not adopted a measure which it was under a duty to adopt under the Staff Regulations. In the case of disputes of a financial nature, the Union judicature has unlimited jurisdiction.[7]

---

[2] Art. 257 TFEU in conjunction with Art. 270 TFEU and Annex I to the Statute of the Court of Justice. The Civil Service Tribunal was established by Council Decision 2004/752/EC, Euratom of 2 November 2004 ([2004] O.J. L333/7). The Court of Justice has special jurisdiction with regard to members of some institutions. For instance, the second para. of Art. 245 TFEU provides that the Council or the Commission may apply to the Court of Justice where Members or former Members of the Commission have breached their obligation not to engage in any other occupation, whether gainful or not, or their undertaking that, both during and after their term of office, they will respect the obligations arising therefrom and in particular their duty to behave with integrity and discretion as regards the acceptance, after they have ceased to hold office, of certain appointments or benefits. For an application, see Council Decision 1999/494/EC, ECSC, Euratom of 9 July 1999 on the referral of the case of Mr Bangemann to the Court of Justice ([1999] O.J. L192/55). See also ECJ, Case C-432/04 *Commission v Cresson* [2006] E.C.R. I-6387.

[3] This is the date of publication in the *Official Journal of the European Union* of the Decision of the President of the Court of Justice recording that the Civil Service Tribunal has been constituted in accordance with the law ([2005] O.J. L325/1).

[4] Conditions for Employment for Staff of the European Central Bank of 9 June 1988, as subsequently amended. Latest amendments entered into force on 2 January 2013 (to be consulted at <http://www.ecb. int>); Staff Regulations of the European Investment Bank of 20 April 1960, as subsequently amended. Latest version is of 1 January 2009 (to be consulted at <http://www.eib.europa.eu>).

[5] CST, Case F-13/05 *Corvoisier and Others v ECB* [2006] E.C.R.-SC I-A-1-19, para. 25; CST, Case F-116/05 *Cerafogli and Poloni v ECB* [2008] E.C.R.-SC I-A-1-199, para. 43; CST, Case F-130/07 *Vinci v ECB* [2009] E.C.R.-SC I-A-1-307, para. 52. This will, however, not be the case when the staff regulations of those bodies clearly deviate from the provisions of the Staff Regulations or Conditions for Employment: see, e.g. EGC (judgment of 27 April 2012), Case T-37/10 P *De Nicola v EIB*, not reported, paras 74–81, overturning an application by analogy in CST (judgment of 30 November 2009), Case F-55/08 *De Nicola v EIB*, not reported, paras 80–90. See also EGC (judgment of 16 September 2013), Case T-418/11 P *De Nicola v EIB*, not reported, overturning CST (judgment of 28 June 2011), Case F-49/10 *De Nicola v EIB*, not reported, para. 64 on similar grounds.

[6] Note that Art. 91(1) of the Staff Regulations is applied by analogy to temporary staff (Art. 46 of the Conditions of Employment), auxiliary staff (Art. 73 of the Conditions of Employment), contract staff (Art. 117 of the Conditions of Employment), special advisers (Art. 124 of the Conditions of Employment), and parliamentary assistants (Art. 138 of the Conditions of Employment). See, for instance, CST (order of 10 September 2007), Case F-146/06 *Speiser v European Parliament* [2007] E.C.R.-SC I-A-1-231, paras 21–23; CST (order of 10 July 2008), Case F-141/07 *Maniscalso v Commision* [2008] E.C.R.-SC I-A-1-253; CST (judgment of 5 June 2012), Case F-71/10 *Cantisani v Commission*, not reported, paras 58–62.

[7] Accordingly, the Civil Service Tribunal can award damages to the applicant of its own motion where the applicant seeks the annulment of a particular decision yet protecting the interests of third

B. Against what measures will an action lie?

An action will lie only against an act adversely affecting the person concerned.[8] The **18.03**
expression 'act having adverse effect' has two aspects: (1) the act must have legal effects as
far the applicant is concerned; and (2) those legal effects must be unfavourable to the staff
member, with the result that he or she can establish a personal interest in a judgment
granting his or her claims.[9]

(1) What measures constitute acts having adverse effect?

(a) Binding act

An act having adverse effect is one which directly affects the applicant's legal position.[10] **18.04**
No strict conditions exist as to the form in which a binding act should be adopted. The
Union courts will take into account the substance of the act to determine its binding nature.[11]
A mere letter or email replying to a request made by an official might thus constitute a
binding act.[12] On that same account, it is not required that a binding act contains an express
decision. Implicit decisions can also have an adverse effect which directly affects an applicant's
legal position.[13] The concept is thus very similar to the expression 'binding act', which has
been discussed in connection with actions for annulment (see para. 7.13).[14]

In the context of staff litigation, the Union courts have held that the following acts constitute binding acts within the meaning of Art. 91(1) of the Staff Regulations: staff reports;[15]
career development reports;[16] a decision refusing to convoke the invalidity committee;[17]

---

parties precludes the annulment of the decision (CFI, Case T-10/02 *Girardot v Commission* [2004]
E.C.R.-SC II-483, para. 89).

[8] This also applies to proceedings brought against the ECB: see CFI, Case T-320/02 *Esch-Leonhardt and Others v ECB* [2004] E.C.R.-SC II-79, paras 36–37; CST (judgment of 29 September 2011), Case F-114/10 *Bowles and Others v ECB*, not reported, paras 48–51.

[9] The fact that a decision adversely affects an official and he or she can bring an action against it does not automatically mean that the appointing authority was under an obligation to give him or her a proper hearing before adopting the decision at issue (ECJ, Case C-111/02 P *European Parliament v Reynolds* [2004] E.C.R. I-5475, para. 57).

[10] ECJ, Case 26/63 *Pistoj v Commission* [1964] E.C.R. 341, at 352; ECJ, Case 32/68 *Graselli v Commission* [1969] E.C.R. 505, para. 4; CFI, Case T-213/99 *Verheyden v Commission* [2000] E.C.R.-SC IA-297, II-1355, para. 20. For some recent cases see, ECJ (order of 9 December 2009), Case C-528/08 P *Marcuccio v Commission* [2009] E.C.R. I-212*, Summ. pub., paras 40–47; CFI (order of 2 February 2001), Case T-97/00 *Vakalopoulou v Commission* [2001] E.C.R.-SC I-A-23, II-91, para.13; CFI, Case T-51/01 *Fronia v Commission* [2002] E.C.R.-SC I-A-43, II-187, paras 24–35.

[11] CFI (order of 15 January 2009), Case T-306/08 P *Braun-Neumann v European Parliament* [2009] E.C.R.-SC I-B-1-1, para. 39.

[12] CFI (order of 15 January 2009), Case T-306/08 P *Braun-Neumann v European Parliament* [2009] E.C.R.-SC I-B-1-1, paras 31–32.

[13] CFI, Case T-154/05 *Lo Giudice v Commission* [2007] E.C.R.-SC I-A-2-203, paras 41–44; CFI, Case T-486/04 *Michail v Commission* [2008] E.C.R.-SC I-A-2-25, para. 49; EGC (judgment of 3 July 2012), Case T-594/10 P *Marcuccio v Commission*, not reported, paras 19–25.

[14] See, e.g. ECJ, Case 346/87 *Bossi v Commission* [1989] E.C.R. I-303, para. 23; ECJ (order of 9 March 2004), Case C-159/03 *Pflugradt v ECB*, not reported, para. 17.

[15] CFI, Case T-343/04 *Tsarnavas v Commission* [2007] E.C.R.-SC II-A-2-747.

[16] CST, Case F-16/09 *de Britto Patricio-Dias v Commission* [2009] E.C.R.-SC I-A-1-497.

[17] CST (order of 19 October 2007), Case F-23/07 *M v EMEA* [2007] E.C.R.-SC I-A-1-311, para. 41.

a decision refusing assistance to an official pursuant to Art. 24 of the Staff Regulations;[18] a decision fixing the total number of points awarded to a staff member in the context of a promotion exercise;[19] a decision adopting the list of promoted officials;[20] a decision not to promote an official;[21] salary statements;[22] a vacancy note containing conditions that exclude the applicant from taking part in the recruitment procedure;[23] a contractual clause providing for the resiliation of a contract upon the occurrence of a determined but uncertain future event at the moment the determined event occurs;[24] and a modification of contractual clauses.[25]

Conversely, an action for annulment brought against an act not directly affecting an applicant's legal position will be declared inadmissible. Examples of such acts are a delay in the establishment of a staff report;[26] the rejection of a spontaneous application for the position of legal secretary at the Court of Justice of the European Union;[27] and the decision of a hierarchical superior not to pass on information notified to him by a lower–ranking official to OLAF.[28]

Likewise, acts of a purely confirmatory[29] or declaratory nature do not constitute binding acts within the meaning of Art. 91(1) of the Staff Regulations, since they do not alter the legal position of the applicant. On that account, an action for annulment brought against a decision not to renew the contract of a contractual agent was held to be inadmissible.[30]

---

[18] CFI, Case T-154/05 *Lo Giudice v Commission* [2007] E.C.R.-SC-I-A-2-203, paras 41–44; CFI, Case T-486/04 *Michail v Commission* [2008] E.C.R.-SC I-A-2-25, para. 49. Only in exceptional circumstances is an institution required to act without a request made by one of its officials. See, for instance, CFI, Joined cases T-90/07 P and T-99/07 P *Belgium and Commission v Genette* [2008] E.C.R. II-3859, paras 98–103.

[19] CFI, Case T-311/04 *Buendía Sierra v Commission* [2006] E.C.R. II-4137, paras 87–94; CFI (judgment of 9 October 2008), Case T-312/04 *Di Bucci v Commission*, not reported, para. 64–66; CST (judgment of 22 November 2007), Case F-110/06 *Carpi Badía v Commission*, not reported, paras 31–34.

[20] CFI, Case T-311/04 *Buendía Sierra v Commission* [2006] E.C.R. II-4137, paras 87–94; CFI (judgment of 9 October 2008), Case T-312/04 *Di Bucci v Commission*, not reported, para. 64–66; CST (judgment of 22 November 2007), Case F-110/06 *Carpi Badía v Commission*, not reported, paras 31–34.

[21] CFI, Case T-394/04 *Strack v Commission* [2008] E.C.R-SC I-A-2-5, para. 28.

[22] CFI, Case T-288/04 *Van Neyghem v Committee of the Regions* [2007] E.C.R.-SC I-A-2-1, paras 39–41. The Court seems to limit this possibility to salary statements clearly reflecting a decision of a pecuniary nature. See also para. 18.05.

[23] CST (judgment of 14 April 2011), Case F-82/08 *Clarke and Others v OHIM*, para. 79; CST (judgment of 5 December 2012), Case F-29/11 *BA v Commission*, not reported, para. 42.

[24] CST (judgment of 15 September 2011), Case F-6/10 *Munch v OHIM*, not reported, paras 32–38; CST (judgment of 15 September 2011), Case F-7/10 *Galan Girodit v OHIM*, not reported, paras 41–47.

[25] CST (judgment of 15 September 2011), Case F-102/09 *Bennet and Others v OHIM*, not reported, para. 59; CST (judgment of 15 September 2011), Case F-6/10 *Munch v OHIM*, not reported, para. 53.

[26] CFI, Case T-424/04 *Angelidis v European Parliament* [2006] E.C.R-SC I-A-2-323, para. 145.

[27] CFI, Case T-406/04 *Bonnet v ECJ* [2006] E.C.R.-SC I-A-2-213, para. 33.

[28] CST (judgment of 25 September 2012), Case F-41/10 *Bermejo Garde v EESC*, not reported, paras. 59–540 (appeal pending: EGC, Case T-530/12 P *Bermejo Garde v EESC*).

[29] See, for instance, ECJ, Case C-417/05 P *Commission v Fernández Gómez* [2006] E.C.R. I-8481, paras 42–46; CFI, Case T-154/05 *Lo Giudice v Commission* [2007] E.C.R.-SC I-A-2-203, paras 52–53; CFI, Case T-284/07 P *OHIM v López Teruel* [2008] E.C.R.-SC I-B-1-69, para. 40; CFI (order of 15 January 2009), Case T-306/08 P *Braun-Neumann v European Parliament* [2009] E.C.R.-SC I-B-1-1, para. 40.

[30] ECJ, Case C-417/05 P *Commission v Fernández Gómez* [2006] E.C.R. I-8481, paras 42–46. However, under certain particular circumstances, for instance, when the decision not to renew a contract somehow alters the provisions of the initial contract, such a decision can constitute a binding act within the meaning of Art. 91(1) of the Staff Regulations: see ECJ (order of 23 October 2009), Joined Cases C-561/08 P and C-4/09 P *Commission v Potamianos* [2009] E.C.R. I-171*, Summ. pub., paras 43–49; CST (judgment of 15 September 2011), Case F-102/09 *Bennet and Others v OHIM*, not reported, para. 58; CST (judgment of 15 September 2011), Case F-6/10 *Munch v OHIM*, not reported, para. 52.

(b) Measures of a general nature

Where an applicant challenges a 'measure of a general nature' (Staff Regulations, Art. 90(2), **18.05** first indent), the application will be admissible only insofar as he or she shows that the act adversely affects him or her.[31] This means that the measure of a general nature must directly affect his or her legal position.[32] If this is not the case, no action will lie against the measure in question, but subsequently an objection of illegality may be raised against it if that measure is used as the basis for an act adversely affecting the applicant.[33] For instance, an official was allowed to challenge new pension rules through its individual pension state-ments, since they constituted a first concretization of the new pension scheme in regard of that official.[34] The same goes for salary statements when refusing for the first time a financial advantage to an official on account of new general measures affecting the remuneration of officials.[35] Subsequent statements, however, cannot be challenged, since they constitute purely confirmatory acts.[36] The objection of illegality can thus only be raised in the context of proceedings against the binding act of individual application, which is the first concretization of the contested general measure.

(c) Preparatory measures

Frequently, decisions of the appointing authority are prepared by a lower-ranking official or **18.06** in an advisory body. Such preparatory measures are not acts having adverse effect because they do not affect the applicant's legal position.[37] For instance, the Union courts have held that an end of probationary period report does not constitute a binding act, since it is only a preparatory measure in the lead–up to a final decision, namely the decision to appoint the probationer as an established official or not.[38] The same goes for interim probationary reports, reaffectation measures during the probationary period, or decisions to extend the probationary period, as they allow the appointing authority to appreciate the capacities of the probationer before taking a final decision.[39] Further to this, the Union courts have, *inter alia*, held the following acts to be preparatory measures: a decision of an invalidity

---

[31] See also ECJ, Case 125/87 *Brown v Court of Justice* [1988] E.C.R. 1619, para.17; CFI, Case T-191/02 *Lebedef v Commission* [2005] E.C.R.-SC II-407, paras 49–54 and 90–95.

[32] See, *inter alia*, ECJ, Case 78/63 *Huber v Commission* [1964] E.C.R. 367, at 375; CFI, Case T-135/89 *Pfloeschner v Commission* [1990] E.C.R. II-153, para. 11; CFI (order of 4 July 1991), Case T-47/90 *Herremans v Commission* [1991] E.C.R. II-467, para. 22. Insofar as the conditions set out in a notice of vacancy exclude a person from applying for the post in question, that person will be adversely affected by the notice. See, by way of example, ECJ, Case 79/74 *Küster v European Parliament* [1975] E.C.R. 725, para. 6; ECJ, Case 25/77 *De Roubaix v Commission* [1978] E.C.R. 1081, para. 8.

[33] See CFI, Case T-47/91 *Auzat v Commission* [1992] E.C.R. II-2536, para. 11; CFI (order of 6 May 2004), Case T-34/03 *Hecq v Commission* [2004] E.C.R.-SC II-1371, paras 32–39; CFI, Case T-47/05 *Serrano and Others v European Parliament* [2008] E.C.R.-SC I-A-2-55, 92-156; CST, Case F-82/05 *Thierry v Commission* [2007] E.C.R.-SC I-A-1-93, para. 48.

[34] CFI, Case T-135/05 *Campoli v Commission* [2006] E.C.R.-SC I-A-2-297, paras 39–40; CFI, Joined Cases T-35/05, T-61/05, T-107/05, T-108/05 and T-139/05 *Agne-Dapper and Others v Commission* [2006] E.C.R.-SC I-A-2-291, para. 32.

[35] CFI, Joined Cases T-35/05, T-61/05, T-107/05, T-108/05 and T-139/05 *Agne-Dapper and Others v Commission* [2006] E.C.R.-SC I-A-2-291, para. 32; CFI, Case T-66/05 P *Sack v Commission* [2007] E.C.R.-SC I-A-2-229, para. 31.

[36] CFI, Case T-66/05 P *Sack v Commision* [2007] E.C.R.-SC I-A-2-229, para. 32.

[37] CST (judgment of 23 October 2012), *Possanzini v Frontex*, not reported, paras 42–43.

[38] CFI (judgment of 16 March 2009), Case T-156/08 P *R v Commission*, not reported, para. 50.

[39] CFI (judgment of 16 March 2009), Case T-156/08 P *R v Commission*, not reported, para. 50.

committee finding that an official is not suffering from invalidity;[40] intermediary evaluations in preparation of a career development report;[41] a decision to award priority points;[42] a decision not to include an official on the merit list;[43] an initial staff appraisal report;[44] the opinion of an institution's medical officer;[45] and the nomination of a reporting officer.[46]

The legality of a preparatory measure can nevertheless be challenged by bringing an action for annulment against the decision adopted at the end of the decision-making procedure in the context of which the preparatory measure was taken.[47]

In some cases, however, preparatory acts actually do have adverse effect. A recurring example in the case-law is a selection board's decision, taken in the course of a recruitment competition, to eliminate the applicant from the further stages of the competition.[48]

It should be pointed out also that the appointing authority itself can perform preparatory measures. The Union courts will declare an action for annulment against such measures inadmissible, since they do not directly affect the applicant's legal position. Exceptionally, a preparatory measure performed by an appointing authority can constitute a binding act. For instance, the decision to exclude an applicant from the list of most deserving officials in the context of a second stage promotion ('*promotion de deuxième filière*') was considered to constitute a binding act, since the non-inclusion effectively precluded the applicant from obtaining a possible promotion.[49]

Finally, the notion of preparatory measures is not confined to acts taken in the course of a decision-making process within a single institution, body, or agency. For instance, the final report by OLAF concluding an investigation conducted in respect of an official is considered to be a preparatory measure in the lead-up to a final decision either taken by the

---

[40] CFI (order of 15 November 2006), Case T-115/05 *Jiménez Martínez v Commission* [2006] E.C.R.-SC I-A-2-269, paras 28–30.

[41] CFI, Case T-27/05 *Lo Giudice v Commission* [2007] E.C.R.-SC I-A-2-197, paras 27–30.

[42] CFI, Case T-311/04 *Buendía Sierra v Commission* [2006] E.C.R. II-4137, paras 96–98; CFI (judgment of 9 October 2008), Case T-312/04 *Di Bucci v Commision*, not reported, paras 67–68.

[43] CFI, Case T-311/04 *Buendía Sierra v Commission* [2006] E.C.R.-SC II-4137, paras 96–98; CFI (judgment of 9 October 2008), Case T-312/04 *Di Bucci v Commision*, not reported, para. 67–68.

[44] CST (judgment of 11 December 2012), Case F-107/11 *Ntouvas v ECDC*, not reported, para. 44.

[45] CST (judgment of 23 November 2010), Case F-65/09 *Marcuccio v Commission*, not reported, para. 44 (upheld on appeal: EGC (order of 21 February 2013), Case T-85/11 P *Marcuccio v Commission*, not reported).

[46] CST (order of 18 December 2008), Case F-64/08 *Nijs v Court of Auditors* [2008] E.C.R.-SC I-A-1-493, para. 17.

[47] CFI, Case T-435/04 *Dos Santos v OHIM* [2007] E.C.R.-SC I-A-2-61, para. 51.

[48] CFI, Case T-37/93 *Stagakis v European Parliament* [1994] E.C.R.-SC I-A-137, at I-A-138-139; CFI, Case T-294/03 *Gibault v Commission* [2005] E.C.R.-SC II-635, para. 22; CFI (order of 5 March 2007), Case T-455/04 *Beyatli and Candan v Commision* [2007] E.C.R.-SC I-A-2-71, para. 38; CFI, Case T-156/03 *Pérez-Díaz v Commission* [2006] E.C.R.-SC I-A-2-135, para. 23; CST (judgment of 20 June 2012), Case F-83/11 *Cristina v Commission*, not reported, para. 36.

[49] CFI, Joined Cases T-437/04 and T-441/04 *Standertskjöld-Nordenstam and Heyraud v Commission* [2006] E.C.R-SC I-1-2-29, paras 31–34. Note that this situation is no longer possible since the 2004 amendements to the Staff Regulations. While second-stage promotions allowed officials to be promoted without changing their position, Art. 2 of the current Staff Regulations provides that no appointment or promotion shall be made for any purpose other than that of filling a vacant post. In principle, the decision to exclude an applicant from the list of most deserving officials is thus considered to constitute a preparatory measure not amenable to judicial review. See, e.g. CST, Case F-113/06 *Bouis and Others v Commission* [2008] E.C.R.-SC I-A-1-437, paras 31–33 (and case-law cited therein).

institution concerned or the national judicial authorities.[50] Such decision cannot be challenged independently, even though it constitutes the end of a decision-making process within OLAF. Similarly, a decision by OLAF to pass on information concerning an official to the competent national authorities is not considered to be a binding act.[51]

(2) The requirement for an interest

Applicants are entitled to challenge a decision which has implications for their legal position only insofar as that decision adversely affects that legal position. In other words, there must be an advantage for the applicant personally in a judgment granting his or her claims. Accordingly, no interest is present when the annulment of the contested decision will lead to the adoption of the same decision in respect of the applicant.[52] Equally, an applicant has no interest in the annulment of an appointment to a post to which he or she personally is ineligible for appointment.[53] Conversely, officials eligible for promotion to a particular grade in principle have a personal interest in challenging the decisions promoting other officials to that grade.[54] An official may also establish an interest when an act, while not affecting the grade or the material situation of the official, causes prejudice to his morale and future prospects.[55] The same goes for measures affecting an official's reputation.[56] Therefore, an official will be allowed to bring an action for annulment against a staff appraisal report, even after having retired from the service.[57] However, in principle staff reports will not generate an interest allowing an official to bring an action for annulment.[58] A particular issue in the context of staff report litigation is the situation in which an official has been automatically retired on the grounds of total permanent invalidity. As long as it cannot be ruled out that the official will be reinstated in the institutions at some point in the future, he or she retains an interest in the annulment of a career development report, since the official might need the report at that point to further his or her career.[59]

18.07

Consequently, the applicant is entitled only to adduce grievances which affect him or her personally. He or she may not bring an action in the interests of the law or of the

---

[50] CFI, Case T-309/03 *Camós Grau v Commission* [2006] E.C.R.-SC II-1173, paras 46–58.

[51] EGC (judgment of 20 May 2010), Case T-261/09 P *Commission v Violetti and Others*, not reported, para. 73 (overturning CST, Joined Cases F-5/05 and F-7/05 *Violetti and Others v Commission* [2009] E.C.R.-SC I-A-1-83, paras 71-83, in which the Civil Service Tribunal held that a decision by OLAF to pass on information concerning an official to the competent national authorities constituted a binding act within the meaning of Art. 90(2) of the Staff Regulations). The fact that the information has been passed on in breach of the rights of defence has no influence on the binding nature of the act: see EGC, Case T-261/09 P *Commission v Violetti and Others*, para. 48.

[52] CST, Case F-94/07 *Rebizant and Others v Commission* [2009] E.C.R.-SC I-A-1-339, para. 62.

[53] ECJ, Case 126/87 *Plato v Commission* [1989] E.C.R. 643, paras 18–20.

[54] CST (judgment of 5 May 2010), Case F-53/08 *Bouillez and Others v Commission*, not reported, para. 80.

[55] CST (order of 20 June 2007), Case F-51/06 *Tesoka v FEACVT* [2007] E.C.R.-SC I-A-1-173, para. 40.

[56] CST, Case F-80/08 *Wenig v Commission* [2009] E.C.R.-SC I-A-1-479, paras 33–36.

[57] CST (judgment of 11 December 2012), Case F-107/11 *Ntouvas v ECDC*, not reported, paras 33–37 (appeal pending: EGC, Case T-94/13 P *Ntouvas v ECDC*).

[58] CFI, Case T-274/04 *Rounis v Commission* [2005] E.C.R.-SC I-A-407, paras 17–31.

[59] ECJ, Case C-198/07 P *Gordon v Commission* [2008] E.C.R. I-10701, paras 41–53 (overturning CFI, Case T-175/04 *Gordon v Commission* [2007] E.C.R.-SC I-A-2-47, paras 27–39). See also EGC (judgment of 9 December 2010), Case T-526/08 P *Commission v Strack*, not reported, paras 69–75.

institutions.[60] That being said, in the context of staff representation elections, officials entitled to vote establish an interest in the annulment of binding acts adopted in connection with such elections solely on the basis of their objective capacity as voter.[61] Furthermore, the applicant's interest must be legitimate, present, and vested.[62] In addition, the applicant may only make submissions which genuinely serve his or her interest.[63] A plea criticizing a defect in the contested act will therefore be inadmissible if the defect was incapable of disadvantaging the applicant.[64]

II. Identity of the Parties

A. Applicants

(1) Any member of staff

18.08   Any person whose relationship with the Union is determined by the Staff Regulations or the Conditions of Employment may bring a dispute concerning the application of the Staff Regulations or the Conditions of Employment before the Civil Service Tribunal.[65] Only 'local staff'—staff engaged in places outside the European Union according to local practice for manual or service duties—must, under Art. 122 of the Conditions of Employment, bring any dispute between them and the institution concerned before the arbitral body indicated in their contract for employment.

Persons taking part in recruitment procedures are also among those deriving rights under the Staff Regulations or the Conditions of Employment,[66] together with the legal successors of persons whose relationship with the Union was governed by the Staff Regulations or the Conditions of Employment.[67]

---

[60] ECJ, Case 85/82 *Schloh v Council* [1983] E.C.R. 2105, para. 14; CFI, Case T-163/89 *Sebastiani v European Parliament* [1991] E.C.R. II-715, para. 24; CFI (judgment of 23 November 2006), Case T-422/04 *Lavagnoli v Commision*, not reported, para. 31; CST (order of 14 June 2006), Case F-34/05 *Lebedef and Others v Commission* [2006] E.C.R.-SC I-A-1-33, paras 21–29.

[61] CFI, Case T-396/03 *Vanhellemont v Commission* [2005] E.C.R-SC I-A-355, paras 26–32; CST, Case F-71/05 *Milella and Campanella v Commission* [2007] E.C.R.-SC I-A-1-321, paras 47–49.

[62] ECJ, Case 17/78 *Deshormes v Commission* [1979] E.C.R. 189, para. 9; CFI (order of 14 December 1989), Case T-119/89 *Teisonnière v Commission* [1990] E.C.R. II-7, para. 19; CFI, Case T-135/05 *Campoli v Commision* [2006] E.C.R.-SC I-A-2-297, para. 42.

[63] ECJ, Case 90/74 *Deboeck v Commission* [1975] E.C.R. 1123, para. 12.

[64] ECJ, Case 90/74 *Deboeck v Commission*, paras 13–16. The plea must also be able to be inferred from the content of the complaint (see para. 18.26).

[65] Staff Regulations, Art. 91(1); Conditions of Employment, Art. 46 (temporary staff), Art. 73 (auxiliaries), Art. 117 (contract staff), and Art. 124 (special advisers). See, however, as regards 'local staff' and the application of national law to their employment relationship, ECJ, Case C-165/01 *Betriebsrat der Vertretung der Europäischen Kommission in Österreich* [2003] E.C.R. I-7683. Further to this, members of an institution are not considered to be members of staff. Accordingly, an action brought against a decision taken in connection with a member of the Court of Auditors was declared inadmissible: CST (order of 20 December 2008), Case F-46/08 *Thoss v Court of Auditors* [2008] E.C.R.-SC I-A-1-429, paras 19–44. The action for annulment should have been brought in accordance with what is now Art. 263 TFEU.

[66] ECJ, Case 23/64 *Vandevyvere v European Parliament* [1965] E.C.R. 157, at 163–4.

[67] ECJ, Case 18/70 *Duraffour v Council* [1971] E.C.R. 515; ECJ, Case 24/71 *Meinhardt (née Forderung) v Commission* [1972] E.C.R. 269, para. 2; CFI, Case T-65/92 *Arauxo-Dumay v Commission* [1993] E.C.R. II-597.

(2) Staff of bodies and agencies

Members of staff of Union bodies and agencies with legal personality may also bring actions in the Civil Service Tribunal where it appears from the regulation establishing the relevant body or agency that its staff are in a legal position equivalent to that of servants of Union institutions.[68]   **18.09**

(3) Trade unions and staff associations of employees

Trade unions and staff associations of employees of the Union which have legal personality are not entitled to bring proceedings pursuant to Art. 270 TFEU because the procedure for complaint and appeal established by Arts 90 and 91 of the Staff Regulations is designed to deal exclusively with individual disputes.[69] Consequently, they must satisfy the requirements of the fourth paragraph of Art. 263 TFEU in order to bring an action for annulment and of Art. 268 TFEU and the second paragraph of Art. 340 TFEU in order to bring an action for damages. In addition, they may intervene in support of the form of order sought by a party in proceedings instituted under Art. 270 TFEU.[70]   **18.10**

B. Defendants

(1) Institution

Actions are brought against the institution from which the act at issue emanated.[71]   **18.11**

---

[68] The Union judicature has jurisdiction to hear and determine disputes between the EIB and its servants: see ECJ, Case 110/75 *Mills v EIB* [1976] E.C.R. 955, para. 14; CFI, Case T-192/99 *Dunnett and Others v EIB* [2001] E.C.R. II-813, para. 46. As far as the ECB is concerned, Art. 36.2 of the Protocol on the Statute of the European System of Central Banks and of the European Central Bank provides that 'The Court of Justice shall have jurisdiction in any dispute between the ECB and its servants within the limits and under the conditions laid down in the conditions of employment.' The ECB argued that, under that provision, not the Court of First Instance (now the Civil Service Tribunal), but the Court of Justice was the competent court to hear and determine disputes between the ECB and its staff. The Court of First Instance held, however, that the interpretation of that provision should not conflict with the general and uniform system of legal remedies for servants of the Union laid down by Decision 88/591 and based on what is now Art. 257 TFEU. The term 'the Court of Justice' was therefore to be interpreted as referring to the Union judicature as a whole within the meaning of what is now Art. 19(1) TEU and thus as including the Court of First Instance (now the Civil Service Tribunal). Consequently, the Court of First Instance (now the Civil Service Tribunal) had jurisdiction to hear the dispute (CFI, Case C-333/99 *X v ECB* [2001] E.C.R.-SC I-A 199, II-921, paras 36–44). See concerning the European Aviation Safety Agency, CFI, Case T-30/04 *Sena v EASA* [2005] E.C.R.-SC II-519. The jurisdiction of the Civil Service Tribunal may also extend to a former 'third pillar' body: see ECJ, Case C-160/03 *Spain v Eurojust* [2005] E.C.R. I-2077, para. 42; CFI, Case T-143/03 *Smit v Europol* [2005] E.C.R.-SC II-171.

[69] ECJ, Case 175/73 *Union Syndicale and Others v Council* [1974] E.C.R. 917, para. 19; ECJ, Case 18/74 *Syndicat Général du Personnel des Organismes Européens v Commission* [1974] E.C.R. 933, para. 15; ECJ, Joined Cases 193/87 and 194/87 *Maurissen and European Public Service Union v Court of Auditors* [1989] E.C.R. 1045, para. 29; CFI (order of 4 December 1991), Case T-78/91 *Moat and TAO/AFI v Commission* [1991] E.C.R. II-1387, para. 7.

[70] In accordance with the second para. of Art. 40 of the Statute. See, by way of example, CFI, Case T-84/91 *Meskens v European Parliament* [1992] E.C.R. II-1565, para. 9: trade-union organizations are widely allowed to intervene in staff cases where the decision is likely to affect a collective interest.

[71] ECJ, Case 18/63 *Wollast (née Schmitz) v EEC* [1964] E.C.R. 85, at 96. Cf. CFI, Case T-177/94 *Altmann and Others v Commission* [1994] E.C.R.-SC II-969, paras 32–45 (action held inadmissible insofar as it was brought against JET, a joint undertaking within the meaning of Arts 46, 47, and 49 of the EAEC Treaty, and the JET Council).

(2) Body or agency

18.12 A staff member employed by a body or agency with legal personality in its own right has to bring his or her claim against that body or agency, not against a Union institution.

III. Special Characteristics

A. The requirement for a pre-litigation procedure

(1) General

18.13 Litigation before the Union courts is considered to be the ultimate way to settle disputes between staff members and their appointing authority. A mandatory pre-litigation procedure has thus been provided for in Art. 90 of the Staff Regulations, the purpose of which is to come to an amicable settlement.[72]

The procedure consists of one or two phases, depending on whether the appointing authority has already adopted an act adversely affecting the staff member. In case such an act has been adopted, the staff member has to file a complaint with the appointing authority.[73] In the absence of an act having an adverse effect, the staff member should first request a decision from the appointing authority in relation to him. An unfavourable reply to that request will then constitute an act having adverse consequences against which a complaint can be filed.[74]

Upon the rejection of the complaint, an action will lie before the Civil Service Tribunal against the act adversely affecting the legal position of the staff member. The action will be declared inadmissible if the pre-litigation procedure was not lawfully conducted.

The question whether the pre-litigation procedure was lawfully conducted may be inquired into by the Civil Service Tribunal of its own motion in considering whether the application made to it is admissible.[75] The Tribunal will further examine whether the time limits prescribed by Arts 90 and 91 of the Staff Regulations were complied with in the course of the pre-litigation procedure and whether the complaint and the application to the Tribunal are consistent with each other.[76]

---

[72] CFI, Case T-43/07 P *Neophytos Neophytou v Commission* [2008] E.C.R-SC I-B-1-53, para. 89; CFI, Case T-100/04 *Massimo Giannini v Commission* [2008] E.C.R.-SC I-A-2-9, para. 39. See also Art. 68 of the CST Rules of Procedure, by which the Civil Service Tribunal is allowed to examine at all stages of the procedure the possibility of an amicable settlement. See further H. Kreppel, 'The Mediating Function of Judges: The Amicable Settlement of Cases before the Civil Service Tribunal of the EU', in G. Palmieri (ed.), *New Developments in the Legal Protection of International and European Civil Servants* (Bruylant, Brussels, 2012), 145–65; S. Van Raepenbusch, 'L'apport jurisprudentiel du Tribunal de la fonction publique de l'Union européenne', in I. Govaere and G. Vandersanden (eds), *La fonction publique communautaire* (Brussels, Bruylant, 2008), 144–8.

[73] Staff Regulations, Art. 90(2).

[74] Staff Regulations, Art. 90(1).

[75] CFI, Case T-57/89 *Alexandrakis v Commission* [1990] E.C.R. II-143, para. 8; CFI (order of 8 July 2004), Case T-200/02 *Tsarnavas v Commission*, not reported, para. 41.

[76] For an example relating to time limits, see CFI (order of 9 July 1991), Case T-48/91 *Minic v Court of Auditors* [1991] E.C.R. II-479; as for whether the complaint and the application are consistent with each other, see CFI, Case T-57/89 *Alexandrakis v Commission* [1990] E.C.R. II-143, para. 8.

(2) Course

(a) Requests

If a person to whom the Staff Regulations apply seeks to challenge an omission to take a **18.14** decision relating to him or her, he or she must first submit a request to the appointing authority pursuant to Art. 90(1) of the Staff Regulations for the decision in question to be taken.[77] The appointing authority then has four months, starting from the date on which the request was made, to notify the person concerned of its reasoned decision. If at the end of that period no reply to the request has been received, this will be deemed to constitute an implied decision rejecting the request. A complaint may be submitted against such a decision, just as in the case of a decision whose content is unfavourable to the person concerned.[78]

The same holds true for non-contractual liability disputes. When a civil servant seeks compensation from the appointing authority for damages not originating in a decision adversely affecting him or her, he or she is required to submit a request for compensation via the pre-litigation procedure first.[79] The decision not to award the requested compensation will then constitute a decision adversely affecting him or her, which can subsequently be challenged by submitting a complaint to the appointing authority.[80] If, in contrast, the damage is caused directly by a decision adversely affecting the civil servant, he or she is required to submit a complaint pursuant to Art. 90(2) of the Staff Regulations.

(b) Complaints

Under Art. 91(2) of the Staff Regulations, an appeal to the Civil Service Tribunal will **18.15** lie only if the applicant has previously submitted a complaint within the prescribed period to the appointing authority about the act allegedly adversely affecting him or her, and the complaint has been rejected by express or implied decision.[81] A complaint is

---

[77] If he or she submits a 'complaint' at the same time and then brings an action before the Court of First Instance (now the Civil Service Tribunal) when it is rejected, that action will be inadmissible for infringing Art. 90(1) and (2) of the Staff Regulations: see CFI (order of 25 February 1992), Case T-64/91 *Marcato v Commission* [1992] E.C.R. II-243, paras 31–46.

[78] If the appointing authority has already taken a decision adversely affecting the official concerned, that official may no longer commence the pre-litigation procedure by submitting a request for a decision under Art. 90(1) of the Staff Regulations, but must directly submit a complaint pursuant to Art. 90(2): CFI, Case T-113/95 *Mancini v Commission* [1996] E.C.R.-SC II-543, para. 28 (English abstract at I-A-239).

[79] CFI, Case T-391/94 *Baiwir v Commission* [1996] E.C.R.-SC II-787, paras 45–48 (English abstract at I-A-269); CFI, Case T-500/93 *Y v Court of Justice* [1996] E.C.R.-SC II-977, paras 64–70 (English abstract at I-A-355). The request must be lodged within a reasonable time (see, in this connection, CFI, Case T-45/01 *Sanders v Commission* [2004] E.C.R.-SC II-1183, paras 59–85, and CFI, Case T-144/02 *Eagle and Others v Commission* [2004] E.C.R.-SC II-1231, paras 57–84). See also EGC (judgment of 12 July 2012), Case T-308/10 P *Commission v Nanopoulos*, not reported, para. 61.

[80] If there is a close link between an action for annulment and a claim for compensation, the compensation claim will be admissible as ancillary to the action for annulment and does not have to be preceded by a request to the appointing authority to make good the alleged damage, followed by a complaint directed against the implied or express rejection of that complaint: CFI, Case T-27/90 *Latham v Commission* [1991] E.C.R. II-35; CFI, Case T-44/93 *Saby v Commission* [1995] E.C.R.-SC II-541, para. 31 (English abstract at I-A-175); CFI, Case T-140/94 *Gutiérrez de Quijano y Llorens v European Parliament* [1996] E.C.R.-SC II-689, para. 54 (English abstract at I-A-241); CFI, Case T-238/02 *Barbosa Goncalves v Commission* [2004] E.C.R.-SC II-473, para. 26.

[81] See, e.g. CFI (order of 9 July 2004), Case T-132/04 *Bonnet v Court of Justice*, not reported, paras 11–17. An action against an act which is connected to another act against which the applicant lodged a complaint is

defined as an act by which a civil servant protests in a specific manner against an act that adversely affects him or her.[82]

The appeal should be brought against the act in respect of which the official has filed a complaint pursuant to Art. 90(2) of the Staff Regulations and not against the reply of the institution, body, or agency to the complaint, for this will only constitute a decision of a purely confirmatory nature. That being said, as long as an action was brought within the appropriate time limits, the Union courts will interpret an action for annulment brought against the rejection of a complaint as an action for annulment against the decision against which the complaint was filed.[83] Exceptionally, the Union courts may hold that a decision rejecting a complaint contains new elements and can itself be the object of an action for annulment.[84]

An exception to the requirement that a complaint should be submitted to the appointing authority exists in relation to decisions of a jury. Since the appointing authority has no power to alter the decision of a jury, an action for annulment lies directly against a decision of a jury without the requirement to conduct a pre-litigation procedure.[85] However, if an official chooses to launch the pre-litigation procedure, it has to be conducted in a lawful way before an admissible action for annulment can be brought before the Civil Service Tribunal.[86]

(3) Time limits

(a) General

18.16 The complaint must be submitted to the appointing authority within three months. When time starts to run depends on the type of measure against which the complaint is brought.[87] The appointing authority then has four months from the date on which the complaint was lodged to notify its reasoned decision to the person concerned. If at the end of that period no reply to the complaint has been received, this will be deemed to constitute a decision rejecting the complaint.

(b) Point of departure

18.17 A civil servant is obliged to request the appointing authority to communicate to him or her a decision adversely affecting him or her within a reasonable time after he or she gained

---

admissible, even though the applicant did not submit a prior complaint in respect of the related act (ECJ, Case 806/79 *Gerin v Commission* [1980] E.C.R. 3515, at 3524).

[82] CST, Joined Cases F-138/06 and F-37/08 *Meister v OHIM* [2009] E.C.R.-SC I-A-1-131, para. 189.

[83] CFI, Case T-472/04 *Tsarnavas v Commission* [2007] E.C.R.-SC I-A-2-5, para. 53; CST (judgment of 18 April 2012), Case F-50/11 *Buxton v European Parliament*, not reported, para. 21; CST (judgment of 11 December 2012), Case F-107/11 *Ntouvas v ECDC*, not reported, paras 45–47.

[84] CST (judgment of 14 October 2010), Case F-86/09 *W v Commission*, not reported, paras 29–31; CST (judgment of 23 October 2012), Case F-57/11 *Eklund v Commission*, not reported, para. 34.

[85] See, e.g. ECJ, Case 44/71 *Marcato v Commission* [1972] E.C.R. 427, paras 4–9; CFI, Case T-49/03 *Schumann v Commission* [2004] E.C.R.-SC II-1371, para. 25. If the applicant nevertheless submits a prior complaint against such a decision, it cannot be objected that his application is inadmissible for being out of time.

[86] CST (judgment of 18 September 2012), Case F-96/09 *Cuallado Martorell v Commission*, not reported, paras 53–58.

[87] Art. 90(2) of the Staff Regulations determines when time starts running in each case. Failure to comply with the time limit for submitting a complaint will inevitably result in a subsequent action being declared inadmissible: CFI (order of 14 July 1993), Case T-55/92 *Knijff v Court of Auditors* [1993] E.C.R. II-823.

knowledge of that decision. It is only upon receiving the decision that the period in which the civil servant can submit a complaint starts to run. Failure to request the communication of the decision within a reasonable period of time will cause the three-month period in which a complaint can be submitted to run from the moment the civil servant became aware of the existence of the decision adversely affecting him or her.[88]

When a request is rejected by means of an implicit decision pursuant to Art. 90(1) of the Staff Regulations and later on followed by a decision expressly rejecting that same request, an admissible complaint can only be brought against the implicit decision. The express decision confirming the implicit decision is considered to be an act of a purely confirmatory nature against which no admissible complaint can be brought.[89] Time limits thus start to run from the moment of the implicit rejection of a request.

In case of multiple requests with the same object in relation to a single omission, only the first request is relevant for the calculation of time limits. All subsequent writings addressed to the appointing authority will be considered to be merely reiterating the civil servant's position and cannot have the effect of prolonging the time limits of the pre-litigation procedure.[90]

The time limit for a request for compensation starts to run from the point in time the civil servant became aware of the situation complained of.[91]

(c) Absence of a time limit in staff regulations

Art. 90(1) of the Staff Regulations does not specify a time limit by which a civil servant has **18.18** to submit to the appointing authority a request that a decision should be taken relating to him or her. However, this does not mean that civil servants have an unlimited period of time to submit such requests.[92] The Court has held that, in the absence of specific time limits set out in the applicable regulations, a reasonable period should be taken into account. The 'reasonableness' of the period in which a civil servant has submitted a request is to be appraised in the light of all the circumstances specific to the case and, in particular, the importance of the dispute for the person concerned, its complexity, and the conduct of the parties to the dispute.[93]

---

[88] CFI, Case T-288/04 *Van Neyghem v Committee of the Regions* [2007] E.C.R.-SC I-A-2-1, paras 39–54.
[89] EGC (judgment of 8 July 2010), Case T-368/09P *Sevenier v Commission*, not reported, paras 24–37. Note that a different solution is applied in the situation where the implicit rejection of a complaint is followed by the notification of an express rejection within the three-month period for bringing the action before the Civil Service Tribunal. That situation is different, since Art. 91(3) of the Staff Regulations expressly states that a new time limit starts to run upon notification of such express decision: CFI, Case T-66/05 *Sack v Commission* [2007] E.C.R.-SC I-A-2-229, para. 48. In the absence of any specific provision in the Staff Regulations, this solution is, however, not transposable to the situation in which an implied rejection of a request is followed by an express rejection of a request. See CST (order of 10 May 2011), Case F-59/10 *Barthel and Others v Court of Justice of the European Union*, not reported, paras 25–26.
[90] CFI, Case T-66/05 *Sack v Commission* [2007] E.C.R.-SC I-A-2-229, para. 37.
[91] CFI (order of 26 June 2009), Case T-114/08 P *Marcuccio v Commission* [2009] E.C.R.-SC I-B-1-53, para. 22.
[92] EGC (judgment of 14 December 2011), Case T-433/10 P *Allen and Others v Commission*, not reported, para. 26.
[93] ECJ (judgment of 28 February 2013), Case C-334/12 RX-II *Arango Jaramillo and Others v EIB*, not reported, para. 28.

This issue is of particular importance in the context of compensation claims submitted by civil servants when the alleged damage does not originate in a decision adversely affecting him or her. In the absence of a specific time limit, the Union courts have drawn inspiration from the action for damages to consider a period of five years as reasonable.[94] However, since the time limit is to be appraised in the light of all the circumstances specific to the case, it should not be applied rigidly[95] and a separate assessment should be made in each individual case.[96] This implies that a request for compensation submitted more than five years after the point in time the civil servant became aware of the situation complained of cannot be held inadmissible only on that account.[97] Conversely, it may happen that, taking into account the circumstances of the dispute, a request submitted within five years after the point in time the civil servant became aware of the damage, will be declared inadmissible.[98] That being said, as soon as a decision adversely affecting the civil servant has been taken, the time limits spelled out in Art. 90(2) of the Staff Regulations apply.[99]

Further to this, the Civil Service Tribunal has, in the absence of specific time limits laid down in the staff regulations of the European Investment Bank, applied by way of analogy the time limits laid down in Arts 90 and 91 of the Staff Regulations to the opposition procedure in sickness insurance matters[100] and the conciliation procedure,[101] as provided for in the staff regulations of the European Investment Bank, holding that a three-month period was considered to be reasonable. This approach has been invalidated by the General Court, holding that the Civil Service Tribunal should have applied the notion of 'reasonable delay'.[102]

(d) Excusable errors

18.19 Only excusable errors will allow a civil servant to bring a complaint out of time. Being an exception to the general rule, the concept of excusable error is interpreted strictly and can

---

[94] CFI, Case T-45/01 *Sanders and Others v Commission* [2004] E.C.R. II-3315, para. 69; CST (order of 14 December 2007), Case F-21/07 *Marcuccio v Commission* [2007] E.C.R.-SC I-A-1-463, para. 21.

[95] CST (order of 18 February 2009), Case F-42/08 *Marcuccio v Commission* [2009] E.C.R.-SC I-A-1-35, para 22.

[96] See, e.g. CST (judgment of 11 May 2010), Case F-30/08 *Nanopoulos v Commission*, not reported, paras 116–120 (confirmed on appeal in EGC (judgment of 12 July 2012), Case T-308/10 P *Commission v Nanopoulos*, not reported, paras 74–80).

[97] See by analogy, ECJ (judgment of 28 February 2013), Case C-334/12 RX-II *Arango Jaramillo and Others v EIB*, not reported, paras 25–46.

[98] See, for instance, CST (order of 14 December 2007), Case F-21/07 *Marcuccio v Commission* [2007] E.C.R.-SC I-A-1-463, paras 19–23 (confirmed on appeal in EGC (order of 26 June 2009), Case T-114/08 P *Marcuccio v Commission* [2009] E.C.R.-SC I-B-1-53, paras 27–30); CST (order of 19 February 2009), Case F-42/08 *Marcuccio v Commission* [2009] E.C.R.-SC I-A-1-35, paras 19–28 (confirmed on appeal in EGC (order of 15 September 2010), Case T-157/09 P *Marcuccio v Commission*, not reported, paras 40–50; no need to proceed to a review: ECJ (decision of 27 October 2010), Case C-478/10 RX Review of Judgment T-157/09 P *Marcuccio v Commission*, not reported).

[99] CFI (order of 20 November 2009), Case T-180/08 P *Tiralongo v Commission* [2009] E.C.R.-SC I-B-1-117, paras 45–47.

[100] CST (judgment of 28 June 2011), Case F-49/10 *De Nicola v EIB*, not reported, para. 70.

[101] CST (judgment of 28 September 2011), Case F-13/10 *De Nicola v EIB*, not reported, paras 61–65; CST (judgment of 8 March 2011), Case F-59/09 *De Nicola v EIB*, not reported, para. 140. But see ECJ (decision of 12 July 2012), Case C-334/12 RX Review of Judgment T-234/11 P *Arango Jaramillo and Others v EIB*, not reported.

[102] The Civil Service Tribunal is, however, not authorized to draw the *a contrario* conclusion from this. See ECJ (judgment of 28 February 2013), Case C-334/12 RX-II *Arango Jaramillo and Others v EIB*, not reported, paras 25–46. EGC (judgment of 16 September 2013), Case T-148/11 P *De Nicola v EIB*, not reported, paras 29–31; EGC (judgment of 16 September 2013), Case T-264/11 P *De Nicola v EIB*, not reported, paras 49–52.

only concern 'exceptional circumstances in which, in particular, the conduct of the institution concerned has been, either alone or to a decisive extent, such as to give rise to a pardonable confusion in the mind of a party acting in good faith and exercising all the diligence required of a normally experienced civil servant. In such an event, the administration may not relay on its own failure to observe the principles of legal certainty and the protection of legitimate expectations out of which the civil servant's error arose.'[103]

(e) New facts

The presence of new and substantial facts may justify a request to have a decision that has become definitive as a result of the expiry of the time limits set out in Art. 90(2) of the Staff Regulations reviewed.[104]   **18.20**

(4) Formal requirements

Requests for decisions and complaints are not subject to any requirement as to form.[105]   **18.21**
A mere e-mail may suffice.[106] Art. 90c of the Staff Regulations provides that requests and complaints must be lodged with the appointing authority entrusted with the exercise of powers. The institutions themselves may lay down procedures for the submission and processing of requests and complaints. Internal procedures, however, may not lay down conditions that affect a civil servant's possibility to bring an admissible complaint pursuant to Art. 90(2) of the Staff Regulations.[107]

(5) Substantive requirements

(a) Content of a complaint

The aim of the pre-litigation procedure is to enable the dispute to be settled amicably.   **18.22**
Consequently, the complaint must put the appointing authority in a position to know in sufficient detail the applicant's criticisms of the contested act.[108] Therefore, a complaint should spell out in a clear and precise manner the reasons why the civil servant contests the decision taken in relation to him.[109]

(b) Content of a decision rejecting a complaint

There is no obligation incumbent upon the appointing authority to inform the civil servant   **18.23**
about the possibility of bringing judicial proceedings against the act adversely affecting him,

---

[103] CFI, Case T-271/08 P *Boudavo and Others v Commission* [2009] E.C.R.-SC I-B-1-71, paras 71–72; CFI, Case T-127/07 P *Bligny v Commission* [2008] E.C.R.-SC I-B-1-19, paras 40–41.
[104] CFI, Case T-271/08 P *Boudavo and Others v Commission* [2009] E.C.R.-SC I-B-1-71, para. 38.
[105] ECJ, Case 54/77 *Herpels v Commission* [1978] E.C.R. 585, para. 47; CFI, Case T-506/93 *Moat v Commission* [1995] E.C.R.-SC II-147, para.18; CFI, Case T-192/94 *Maurissen v Court of Auditors* [1996] E.C.R.-SC II-1229, para. 31 (English abstract at I-A-425).
[106] CST (order of 17 July 2007), Case F-141/06 *Hartwig v Commission*, not reported, para. 27.
[107] CST, Joined Cases F-138/06 and F-37/08 *Meister v OHIM* [2009] E.C.R.-SC I-A-1-131, paras 136–142.
[108] See, e.g. ECJ, Case 58/75 *Sergy v Commission* [1976] E.C.R. 1139, para. 32; ECJ, Case 133/88 *Del Amo Martinez v European Parliament* [1989] E.C.R. 689, para. 9; CFI, Case T-57/89 *Alexandrakis v Commission* [1990] E.C.R. II-143, para. 8. A 'complaint' is an act whereby an official or servant specifically challenges an administrative measure which adversely affects him or her. It is necessary to give priority to the content of the document rather than its form or title (ECJ, Case C-154/99 P *Politi v European Training Foundation* [2000] E.C.R. I-5019, para. 17). See also CFI, Case T-354/03 *Reggimenti v European Parliament* [2005] E.C.R.-SC II-147, paras 43 and 44. See also para. 18.26.
[109] CST (order of 17 July 2007), Case F-141/06 *Hartwig v Commission*, not reported, para. 26.

or about the time limits by which such proceedings should be brought.[110] The appointing authority is also not required to indicate that the reclamation was inadmissible and that further judicial proceedings will thus be inadmissible.[111]

(6) Action before the Civil Service Tribunal

(a) General

18.24 If the pre-litigation procedure does not bring the dispute to an end, an action may be brought before the Civil Service Tribunal.[112]

(b) Time limits

18.25 The action must be brought within three months.[113] Time starts running on the date of notification of the decision taken in response to the complaint or, in the case of an implied decision rejecting the complaint, on the date of expiry of the period of four months after the complaint was lodged.[114]

Furthermore, when an implicit decision rejecting a complaint is followed by the notification of an express rejection within the three-month period for bringing an action before the Civil Service Tribunal, time only starts to run from the moment of

---

[110] CFI, Case T-306/08 P *Braun-Neumann v European Parliament* [2009] E.C.R.-SC I-B-1-1, paras 34–36.

[111] CFI, Case T-306/08 P *Braun-Neumann v European Parliament* [2009] E.C.R.-SC I-B-1-1, para. 37.

[112] Under Art. 91(4) of the Staff Regulations, an applicant may bring an action before the Civil Service Tribunal without awaiting the reply from the appointing authority, provided that he or she applies for interim measures at the same time. The proceedings in the principal action are then suspended until such time as the appointing authority has responded to the complaint.

[113] The question of admissibility will be raised by the Union judicature of its own motion (CFI, Case T-14/03 *Di Marzio v Commission* [2004] E.C.R.-SC II-167, para. 37).

[114] Art. 91(3) of the Staff Regulations provides as follows: where a complaint is rejected by express decision after being rejected by implied decision but before the period for lodging an appeal to the Civil Service Tribunal has expired, time for bringing court proceedings starts to run afresh (the date of adoption of the decision is relevant in this respect, not the date of its notification: CFI (order of December 6, 2004), Case T-55/02 *Finch v Commission* [2004] E.C.R.-SC II-1621, paras 46–49). That provision may not be invoked to the detriment of an applicant where the latter has already brought an action and the defendant institution seeks to remedy, by means of a late, reasoned rejection of the complaint, the fact that the act adversely affecting the applicant entirely lacked any statement of reasons: see CFI, Case T-52/90 *Volger v European Parliament* [1992] E.C.R. II-121, paras 31–42, upheld by ECJ, Case C-115/92 P *European Parliament v Volger* [1993] E.C.R. I-6549, paras 22–24. Where an express decision rejecting a complaint is taken after the period for lodging an appeal has run out, time does not start running afresh; although the express decision makes it clear why the complaint was rejected, it constitutes merely confirmation of the implied decision rejecting the complaint: ECJ (order of 25 June 1998), Case C-312/97 P *Fichtner v Commission* [1998] E.C.R. I-4135, paras 16–17, dismissing an appeal against CFI (order of 9 July 1997), Case T-63/96 *Fichtner v Commission* [1997] E.C.R. II-563 (English abstract at I-A-189). Where the applicable rules of a functionally autonomous body—such as the EIB—lay down no time limit for bringing actions relating to disputes between staff and that body, the Civil Service Tribunal has decided that actions must be brought within a reasonable time having regard to the rules laid down in the Staff Regulations. In reaching this conclusion, the Civil Service Tribunal weighed the entitlement of those subject to its jurisdiction to effective protection by the courts, which implies that such persons must have a sufficient period of time available to them, against the need for legal certainty which requires that, after a certain time, measures taken by Union bodies become definitive (CFI, Case T-192/99 *Dunnett and Others v EIB* [2001] E.C.R. II-813, paras 44–58). But see ECJ (decision of 12 July 2012), Case C-334/12 RX Review of judgment T-234/11 P *Arango Jaramillo and Others v EIB*, not reported.

notification of the express decision.[115] An express rejection decision notified after the expiry of that period does not give rise to a new period for lodging the appeal.[116]

Also, in case a civil servant has submitted multiple complaints with the same object in relation to one act adversely affecting him, only the first complaint will be taken into account. All subsequent writings addressed to the appointing authority will be considered to be merely reiterating the civil servant's position and cannot have the effect of prolonging the time limits of the pre-litigation procedure.[117] An action for annulment will thus lie against the decision rejecting the first complaint, and time limits should be calculated accordingly.

When the decision rejecting the complaint is drafted in a language which is neither the mother tongue of the civil servant nor the language in which the complaint was drawn up, a translation might be requested. Provided that such a request was made within a reasonable period, the time limit to bring an action before the Civil Service Tribunal will only start to run from the moment the translation is notified to the civil servant.[118]

(c) Parallelism between the complaint and the application

The prior complaint defines the subject-matter of the action to a negative extent only. The **18.26** action may not extend the purpose or the subject-matter of the complaint, but may curtail them. Consequently, the subject-matter of the action is defined solely by the application, provided that it remains within the limits laid down by the complaint.[119] That being said, Art. 48(2) of the EGC Rules of Procedure on the introduction of new pleas based on matters which come to light in the course of the judicial procedure does not cease to apply in the context of staff litigation.[120] Further to this, the Tribunal can always raise public policy pleas of its own motion, even if not raised in the complaint.[121]

Generally, the complaint will not be drawn up by a lawyer and will be very informal, since it aims at achieving an amicable settlement of the dispute.[122] Consequently, it is sufficient if the pleas set out in the application emerge implicitly from the complaint[123] or are closely linked thereto if they do not appear as such in the complaint.[124] The Tribunal takes a

---

[115] Art. 91(3) of the Staff Regulations. CFI, Case T-66/05 *Sack v Commission* [2007] E.C.R.-SC I-A-2-229, para. 48; EGC (order of 21 June 2010), Case T-284/09 P *Meister v OHIM*, not reported, para. 28.

[116] CST, Case F-114/05 *Combescot v Commission* [2006] E.C.R.-SC I-A-115, paras 39–42 (confirmed on appeal in CFI, Case T-414/06 *Combescot v Commission* [2008] E.C.R.-SC I-B-1-1, paras 36–47).

[117] CFI, Case T-66/05 *Sack v Commission* [2007] E.C.R.-SC I-A-2-229, para. 37.

[118] CST (order of 7 March 2012) Case F-31/11 *BI v European Centre for the Development of Vocational Training*, not reported, para. 20.

[119] CFI, Case T-134/89 *Hettrich and Others v Commission* [1990] E.C.R. II-565, para. 16; CFI, Case T-144/03 *Schmit v Commission* [2005] E.C.R. II-465, paras 90–93.

[120] CFI, Case T-43/07 P *Neophytos Neophytou v Commission* [2008] E.C.R.-SC I-B-1-53, para. 90.

[121] CST (judgment of 10 November 2011), Case F-20/09 *Juvyns v Commission*, not reported, para. 65.

[122] However, the complaint may be lodged by a lawyer acting on behalf of his or her client: see CFI, Case T-139/89 *Virgili-Schettini v European Parliament* [1990] E.C.R. II-535.

[123] ECJ, Case 184/80 *Van Zaanen v Court of Auditors* [1981] E.C.R. 1951, para. 13.

[124] See, e.g. ECJ, Case 133/88 *Del Amo Martinez v European Parliament* [1989] E.C.R. 689, para. 10; CFI, Case T-57/89 *Alexandrakis v Commission* [1990] E.C.R. II-143, para. 9; CFI, Case T-2/90 *Ferreira de Freitas v Commission* [1991] E.C.R. II-103, para. 41; CFI, Case T-312/02 *Gussetti v Commission* [2004] E.C.R.-SC II-547, para. 47; CFI, Case T-56/07 P *Commission v Economidis* [2008] E.C.R.-SC I-B-1-31, para. 94.

flexible approach in this regard.[125] It is not the purpose of the complaint to fix rigorously and definitively the scope of the judicial proceedings in relation to its content.[126] Provided that the subject-matter and the grounds of the complaint are not altered, the application and the pleas adduced in support of it will be admissible.[127] The test is whether an open-minded assessment of the complaint carried out by the appointing authority would have enabled it to know the heads of complaint set out in the application to the Tribunal in order to reach an amicable settlement of the dispute.[128] If the heads of complaint, from the point of view of their subject-matter and purpose, remain the same in the complaint and the application, the application will be admissible, even if those heads of complaint are given a more legal character in pleas and arguments which were not raised as such in the complaint.[129]

Furthermore, according to the case-law, a claim for compensation for damage arising out of the contested act may be made even if no mention was made of it in the complaint. This flexible approach is attributable to the close link between such a claim and the complaint made against the contested act.[130]

B. Priority of an action brought under Art. 270 TFEU

18.27 Any dispute arising out of the employment relationship between a person and the Union must if necessary be brought before the Union judicature in accordance with the conditions prescribed by Art. 270 TFEU and Arts 90 and 91 of the Staff Regulations. No other judicial procedure may be used for this purpose.[131] The subject-matter of the application

---

[125] CST (judgment of 1 July 2010), Case F-45/07 *Mandt v European Parliament*, not reported, para. 112.
[126] CST (order of 11 December 2007), Case F-60/07 *Martin Bermejo v Commission* [2007] E.C.R.-SC II-A-1-2259, para. 35.
[127] ECJ, Joined Cases 75/82 and 117/82 *Razzouk and Beydoun v Commission* [1984] E.C.R. 1509, para. 9.
[128] See, e.g. CFI, Case T-312/02 *Gussetti v Commission* [2004] E.C.R.-SC II-547, para. 47; CFI, Case T-43/07 P *Neophytos Neophytou v Commission* [2008] E.C.R-SC I-B-1-53, para. 89; CFI, Case T-100/04 *Giannini v Commission* [2008] E.C.R.-SC I-A-2-9, para. 39.
[129] For a case in which this condition was not satisfied, at least as regards one of the pleas raised, see CFI, Case T-4/92 *Vardakas v Commission* [1993] E.C.R. II-357, paras 16–17. See also CFI, Case T-588/93 *G v Commission* [1994] E.C.R.-SC II-875, paras 27–30 (English abstract at I-A-277); CFI, Case T-361/94 *Weir v Commission* [1996] E.C.R.-SC II-381, para. 32 (English abstract at I-A-121).
[130] ECJ, Case 126/87 *Del Plato v Commission* [1987] E.C.R. 643, para. 12; ECJ, Case 224/87 *Koutchoumoff v Commission* [1989] E.C.R. 99, para. 10; CFI, Case T-44/93 *Saby v Commission* [1995] E.C.R.-SC II-541, para. 28 (English abstract at I-A-175); CFI, Case T-238/02 *Barbosa Gonçalves v Commission* [2004] E.C.R.-SC II-473, para. 26.
[131] ECJ, Case 9/75 *Meyer-Burckhardt v Commission* [1975] E.C.R. 1171, para. 7; CFI (order of 11 July 1996), Case T-30/96 *Gomes de Sá Pereira v Council* [1996] E.C.R. II-785, paras 24–26. Even if the legality of a recruitment procedure initiated by a Union institution may depend on whether certain acts of the national authorities, to which that institution has turned, are themselves lawful (where, for instance, the Union institution asks the Member State concerned to present suitable candidates for appointment as members of the temporary staff), it is for the person aggrieved to exercise, within the time limits laid down by the Staff Regulations, the remedies provided for in the Staff Regulations, even if only as a precautionary measure: ECJ, Case C-246/95 *Coen* [1997] E.C.R. I-403, para. 22. Cf. CFI (order of the President of 21 June 1999), Case T-107/99 R *García Retortillo v Council* [1999] E.C.R. II-1939, para. 45. See also CST (judgment of 11 May 2010), Case F-30/08 *Nanopoulos v Commission*, not reported, paras 70–74.

determines whether it has to be regarded as a 'staff case'.[132] Accordingly, an action brought by members of an official's family pursuant to Arts 268 and 340 TFEU for compensation for damage suffered by them personally as a result of effects of 'the conduct of an institution' on the career of the official in question will be inadmissible on the ground that the official himself was 'in a position to avail himself of the opportunities afforded by the [Treaties] to challenge any decision of the institution concerned'.[133]

However, the Civil Service Tribunal is not competent to hear an action for annulment brought by a Commission civil servant against a decision of the Commission rejecting a request for access to documents on the basis of Regulation No. 1049/2001. Such a rejection does not constitute an act adversely affecting the civil servant within the meaning of Articles 90 and 91 of the Staff Regulations and thus does not fall within the jurisdiction of the Civil Service Tribunal.[134] Also, disputes relating to costs between a civil servant and an institution following legal proceedings before the General Court should be brought on the basis of Art. 92(1) of the EGC Rules of Procedure and not be settled in the context of Arts 90 and 91 of the Staff Regulations.[135] Further to this, the Civil Service Tribunal once held that 'the eventuality cannot be excluded, first, of a "person to whom [the] Staff Regulations apply" pursuing at the same time an action for failure to act and the dispute procedure provided for in the Staff Regulations, thereby provoking procedural difficulties as to the determination of both the court having jurisdiction and the applicable rules on admissibility, and, second, even of a "person to whom [the] Staff Regulations apply" giving, through pursuit of an action for failure to act, precedence to the jurisdiction of the [General Court] over that of the Tribunal, despite the Tribunal's being the ordinary court for [Union] staff cases'.[136] The question was never answered though, since after referring the case to the General Court the applicants decided to discontinue the proceedings.[137]

IV. Consequences

A. Decision of the Civil Service Tribunal

Depending upon the purpose and outcome of the proceedings, the Civil Service Tribunal may dismiss the application, annul the contested act, award damages— together, in a proper case, with default interest—and, in disputes of a financial nature, impose such measures as it may grant in the exercise of its unlimited jurisdiction.[138]

18.28

---

[132] See, in this connection, CFI, Case T-45/01 *Sanders v Commission* [2004] E.C.R.-SC II-1183, paras 42–54; CFI, Case T-144/02 *Eagle and Others v Commission* [2004] E.C.R.-SC II-1231, paras 40–52; CFI, Case T-277/03 *Vlachaki v Commission* [2005] E.C.R.-SC II-243, paras 29–39.

[133] ECJ (order of 7 May 1980), Joined Cases 114/79 to 117/79 *Fournier v Commission* [1980] E.C.R. 1529, at 1531. See also CFI (order of 14 June 1995), Joined Cases T-462/93, T-464/93 and T-470/93 *Lenz v Commission*, not reported, paras 55–59.

[134] EGC (judgment of 13 December 2012), Joined Cases T-197/11 and T-198/11 *Commission v Strack*, not reported, paras 43–60.

[135] CST (order of 18 February 2009), Case F-70/07 *Marcuccio v Commission* [2009] E.C.R.-SC I-A-1-31, paras 15–20.

[136] CST (order of 29 September 2009), Case F-64/09 *Labate v Commission* [2009] E.C.R.-SC I-A-1-381, para. 22.

[137] EGC (order of 10 January 2011), Case T-389/09 *Labate v Commission*, not reported.

[138] ECJ, Case C-583/08 P *Gogos v Commission* [2010] E.C.R. I-4469, paras 44–50.

However, the Tribunal may not substitute itself for the institution party to the proceedings;[139] at the most, it may provide 'guidance' as to the measures to be taken in order to comply with its judgment.[140] At the same time, it must make sure that the scope of the operative part of its judgment emerges clearly from the grounds in conjunction with which it must be read. This is a corollary of the obligation weighing on the Union judicature to state reasons for its decisions.[141]

B. Costs

18.29   The Civil Service Tribunal rules on the costs. Subject to the specific provisions of the Rules of Procedure, the unsuccessful party will be ordered to pay the costs.[142] However, if equity so requires, the Tribunal may decide that an unsuccessful party is to pay only part of the costs, or even that he is not to be ordered to pay any.[143] Where there are several unsuccessful parties, the Tribunal will decide how the costs are to be shared.[144]

C. Appeal

18.30   An appeal, limited to points of law,[145] may be brought before the General Court, within two months of notification of the decision appealed against, against final decisions of the Civil Service Tribunal and decisions of that Tribunal disposing of the substantive issues in part only or disposing of a procedural issue concerning a plea of lack of jurisdiction or inadmissibility. Such an appeal may be brought by any party which has been unsuccessful, in whole or in part, in its submissions. However, interveners other than the Member States and the institutions may bring such an appeal only where the decision of the Civil Service Tribunal directly affects them.[146]

---

[139] CST, Case F-57/06 *Hinderyckx v Council* [2007] E.C.R.-SC I-A-1-329, para. 65.

[140] ECJ, Case 225/82 *Verzyck v Commission* [1983] E.C.R. 1991, paras 19–20; CFI, Case T-37/89 *Hanning v European Parliament* [1990] E.C.R. II-463, para. 79; CFI, Case T-588/93 *G v Commission* [1994] E.C.R.-SC II-875, para. 26; cf. CFI, Case T-73/89 *Barbi v Commission* [1990] E.C.R. II-619, para. 38; EGC (judgment of 14 September 2011), Case T-236/02 *Marcuccio v Commission*, not reported, para. 163 (appeal dismissed: ECJ (order of 3 October 2013), Case C-617/11 P *Marcuccio v Commission*, not reported).

[141] Opinion of Advocate-General W. Van Gerven in ECJ, Case C-242/90 P *Commission v Albani and Others* [1993] E.C.R. I-3839, at I-3861-3862.

[142] Statute, Annex I, Art. 7(5). CST Rules of Procedure, Art. 87(1).

[143] CST Rules of Procedure, Art. 87(2).

[144] CST Rules of Procedure, Art. 89(1). However, pursuant to Art. 88 of the CST Rules of Procedure, an applicant, even if successful, may be ordered to pay the institution's costs which he or she unreasonably or vexatiously caused it to incur: see for an example prior to the creation of the Civil Service Tribunal, CFI, Case T-203/03 *Rasmussen v Commission* [2005] E.C.R.-SC II-1287, paras 88–89.

[145] EGC (judgment of 19 March 2010), Case T-338/07 P *Bianchi v ETF*, not reported, para. 58.

[146] Art. 256(2), first para., TFEU; Statute, Annex I, Arts 9 and 10; EGC Rules of Procedure, Arts 113–149.

D. Review

Decisions taken by the General Court upon appeal in cases for which the Civil Service **18.31**
Tribunal has jurisdiction at first instance may, exceptionally, be reviewed by the Court of
Justice where there is a serious risk of the unity or consistency of Union law being
affected.[147]

---

[147] Art. 256(2), second para., TFEU; see Ch. 17.

19

JURISDICTION OF THE UNION COURTS TO GIVE JUDGMENT PURSUANT TO AN ARBITRATION CLAUSE OR A SPECIAL AGREEMENT

I. Art. 272 TFEU

A. Subject-Matter

(1) General

(a) Arbitration clause

19.01 Under Art. 335 TFEU, the Union, which has legal personality,[1] enjoys in each of the Member States the most extensive legal capacity accorded to legal persons under national law. The Union's participation in legal transactions may give rise to contractual disputes having to be decided judicially.

Art. 272 TFEU authorizes the Union and parties contracting with it to confer jurisdiction over such disputes on the Court of Justice of the European Union pursuant to an arbitration clause contained in a contract governed by private or public law concluded by or on behalf of the Union.[2] In the absence of such a clause, the national courts have jurisdiction under national law to settle any such disputes under Art. 274 TFEU.[3]

Pursuant to the first paragraph of Art. 340 TFEU, '[t]he contractual liability of the Union shall be governed by the law applicable to the contract in question'.

---

[1] Art. 47 TEU.

[2] Art. 272 TFEU states: 'The Court of Justice of the European Union shall have jurisdiction to give judgment pursuant to any arbitration clause contained in a contract concluded by or on behalf of the Union, whether that contract be governed by public or private law.'

[3] Art. 274 TFEU provides: 'Save where jurisdiction is conferred on the Court of Justice of the European Union by the Treaties, disputes to which the Union is a party shall not on that ground be excluded from the jurisdiction of the courts or tribunals of the Member States.' In the absence of an arbitration clause within the meaning of Art. 272 TFEU, the Court of Justice or the General Court lacks jurisdiction to rule on any liability in contract where one of the parties brings an action for non-contractual liability. As regards the Union courts' jurisdiction in relation to contractual versus non-contractual liability claims, see further para. 19.11. In that event, the fact that the parties have brought their dispute before the Court of Justice or the General Court cannot be regarded as an expression of their intention to confer on the Union judicature jurisdiction over disputes arising out of an agreement: CFI (order of 18 July 1997), Case T-180/95 *Nutria v Commission* [1997] E.C.R. II-1317, paras 37–40.

As from 1 June 2004, all actions brought under Art. 272 TFEU are to be lodged at first instance before the General Court, with appeal to the Court of Justice (see para. 19.07).

(b) Objective

There are a number of grounds which may prompt the conclusion of an arbitration clause **19.02** that confers jurisdiction on the Union judicature within the meaning of Art. 272 TFEU. The Union judicature constitutes the meeting place of a number of legal cultures, as a result of which it may be regarded as a suitable forum for deciding a dispute relating to an international contract. Moreover, an arbitration clause is a means of avoiding a national court's adjudicating a contractual dispute in which important Union interests are at stake. The Union through its institutions, bodies, offices, or agencies may also want to bring any contractual disputes before its natural court under a procedure with which it is familiar.

(c) Changes brought by the Treaty of Lisbon

Art. 272 TFEU reproduces virtually verbatim former Art. 238 EC. The changes to the text **19.03** of the latter provision brought by the Lisbon Treaty concern the substitution of 'Court of Justice of the European Union' for 'Court of Justice', and of 'Union' for 'Community'. Similarly, the wording of the first paragraph of Art. 340 TFEU and former Art. 288 EC are the same, save for the substitution of 'Union' for 'Community'. These changes correspond to the allocation of jurisdiction between the Court of Justice and the General Court in this context (see para. 19.07) and the elimination of the pillar structure and the replacement of the European Community with the Union upon the entry into force of the Lisbon Treaty.[4]

So far in the case-law, a claim brought before the Union judicature pursuant to Art. 272 TFEU and the first paragraph of Art. 340 TFEU implicates a contract concluded between the Union and a third party falling within the former Community—now Union—sphere. As far as the contracts concluded by Union bodies, offices, or agencies falling within the former second pillar of the Common Foreign and Security Policy (CFSP) and the former third pillar of Police and Judicial Cooperation in Criminal Matters (PJCCM) are concerned, there does not yet appear to be relevant case-law. One could, however, take the view that the changes brought by the Lisbon Treaty to the constitutional and institutional framework of the Union may impact the Union's contractual liability for the purposes of Art. 272 TFEU and the first paragraph of Art. 340 TFEU, since after the elimination of the pillar structure, the Union courts' jurisdiction may extend to subjects falling within the field of PJCCM, and thus is no longer limited to the former Community sphere, provided, of course, that there is an arbitration clause within the meaning of Art. 272 TFEU. Furthermore, the Union's contractual liability is rooted in a (public or private) contract between the parties concerned, as opposed to an act adopted under the Treaties pursuant to the provisions concerning the PJCCM and the CFSP and hence the Union courts' jurisdiction pursuant to an arbitration clause within the meaning of Art. 272 TFEU may not be precluded by rules restricting the Union courts' jurisdiction in these fields (as regards the PJCCM, Art. 10 of Protocol (No. 36) on Transitional Provisions, and as regards the CFSP, Art. 24(1), second para., TEU and Art. 275 TFEU).

---

[4] See Art. 1(3) TEU.

(d) EAEC and former ECSC Treaties

19.04 Comparable provisions concerning the Union courts' jurisdiction to give judgment pursuant to an arbitration clause in relation to the European Atomic Energy Community's contractual liability used to be found in Art. 153 EAEC[5] and the first paragraph of Art. 188 EAEC.[6] In tandem with the entry into force of the Lisbon Treaty, however, there is a new consolidated version of the EAEC Treaty, whereby the first paragraph of Art. 188 EAEC remains applicable, but Art. 153 EAEC has been repealed and Art. 272 TFEU is now applicable.[7]

There was also a provision comparable to Art. 272 TFEU in the now-expired ECSC Treaty as regards the Court of Justice's jurisdiction to give judgment pursuant to an arbitration clause set forth in Art. 42 ECSC.[8]

(2) What contracts are concerned?

(a) Contract concluded by or on behalf of the Union

19.05 As has already been noted, under Art. 272 TFEU, the Union judicature may have jurisdiction to give judgment pursuant to an arbitration clause 'contained in a contract concluded by or on behalf of the Union, whether that contract be governed by public or private law'. The case-law so far has not yet made it clear what is meant by a public-law contract in this context. What may be meant is agreements concluded by the Union (or its Union institutions, bodies, offices, or agencies) with Member States, third countries, or international organizations (whether or not in the form of a convention) and administrative agreements concluded with individuals.[9] Private-law contracts presumably denote all contracts into which the Union enters as a party to normal legal transactions.

However, an arbitration clause is not always contained in a contract. A Union Regulation can refer a whole class of pre-defined contractual disputes to the Union judicature.[10]

(b) Union institutions, bodies, offices, agencies, or other entities

19.06 The stipulation that the contract may be concluded 'on behalf of the Union' undoubtedly indicates that entities which are not institutions, bodies, offices, or agencies may nevertheless include an arbitration clause in a contract concluded by them on behalf of the Union.

---

[5] Akin to former Art. 238 EC (now Art. 272 TFEU), Art. 153 EAEC provided: 'The Court of Justice shall have jurisdiction to give judgment pursuant to any arbitration clause contained in a contract concluded by or on behalf of the Community, whether that contract be governed by public or private law.'

[6] Akin to the first para. of Art. 288 EC (now Art. 340 TFEU), the first para. of Art. 188 EAEC stated: 'The contractual liability of the Community shall be governed by the law applicable to the contract in question.'

[7] See Art. 106a(1) of the consolidated version of the EAEC Treaty, [2012] O.J. C327/1.

[8] Art. 42 ECSC provided: 'The Court shall have such jurisdiction as may be provided under any clause to such effect in a public or private contract to which the Community is a party or which is undertaken for its account.'

[9] See, e.g. ECJ, Case C-220/03 *ECB v Germany* [2005] E.C.R. I-10595, paras 22–27, in which the Court upheld its jurisdiction involving an arbitration clause contained in the Agreement of 18 September 1998 concluded between the Government of the Federal Republic of Germany and the European Central Bank on the seat of that institution.

[10] ECJ (judgment of 17 January 2013), Case C-623/11 *Geodis Calberson GE*, not reported, para. 33.

(3) Nature and extent of the Union courts' jurisdiction pursuant to an arbitration clause

(a) Allocation of jurisdiction between the Court of Justice and the General Court

Before 1 June 2004, the situation was that, in the case of a contract concluded between what was then the Community (now the Union) and a natural or legal person, disputes could be brought before either the Court of Justice or the former Court of First Instance (now General Court), depending on whether the applicant was the Community or an individual. The Court of Justice had jurisdiction if the Community initiated the proceedings,[11] whereas the Court of First Instance had jurisdiction if they were brought by a natural or legal person.[12] This split jurisdiction had the result that a private party which was a defendant in proceedings brought before the Court of Justice by the Community pursuant to an arbitration clause had only one chance of putting over its defence, whereas if the Community was the defendant in proceedings brought by a natural or legal person, it might have a second chance, if it lost, by appealing the decision of the Court of First Instance to the Court of Justice.

19.07

This lack of symmetry in the contracting parties' position as litigants was brought to an end by the entry into force of Council Decision 2004/407/EC, Euratom of 26 April 2004, which amended Art. 51 of the Statute.[13] Consequently, as from 1 June 2004, all claims brought under Art. 272 TFEU are to be brought before the General Court at first instance, with appeal to the Court of Justice.[14]

(b) Expression 'arbitration clause' is misleading

The expression 'arbitration clause' employed in Art. 272 TFEU is misleading. Where the General Court gives judgment pursuant to an 'arbitration clause', it acts not as an arbitrator, but as a court giving judgments which may be directly enforced.

19.08

(c) Jurisdiction of national courts

The arbitration clause may or may not give the Court of Justice of the European Union exclusive jurisdiction. If the clause confers an exclusive right on the Court of Justice of the

19.09

---

[11] ECJ, Case C-356/99 *Commission v Hitesys* [2000] E.C.R. I-9517.

[12] An application brought before the Court of Justice by an individual pursuant to an arbitration clause was referred by that Court to the former Court of First Instance (now the General Court): see CFI, Case T-10/98 *E-Quattro v Commission* [1999] E.C.R. II-1811, paras 8–9. Where, with regard to the same contract, the Community (now Union) brought proceedings in the Court of Justice and the individual concerned brought proceedings in the then Court of First Instance, the Court of Justice referred the case before it to the Court of First Instance as a counterclaim. See, however, ECJ (order of 21 November 2003), Case C-280/03 *Commission v Lior and Others*, not reported, para. 9, in which the Court of Justice did not regard the Commission's claim as a counterclaim, on the grounds that it had been lodged two years after the proceedings had been initiated in the Court of First Instance and that the claim brought before the Court of Justice was directed not only against the applicant in the proceedings before the Court of First Instance, but also against other undertakings.

[13] Council Decision 2004/407/EC, Euratom of 26 April 2004 amending Arts 51 and 54 of the Protocol on the Statute of the Court of Justice, [2004] O.J. L132/5; *corrigendum* in [2004] O.J. L194/3. See para. 2.49.

[14] Art. 256(1), first para., TFEU; Statute, Art. 51. This is so even if a Member State may be a party to the dispute; under the aforementioned Articles, there is no provision for the Court of Justice to have jurisdiction at first instance in claims brought under Art. 272 TFEU. In cases where an arbitration clause stipulates the jurisdiction of the 'Court of Justice', these words have been interpreted as designating the institution of the Court of Justice of the European Union referred to in Art. 272 TFEU, which comprises the General Court as the competent court at first instance: see, e.g. CFI, Case T-271/04 *Citymo v Commission* [2007] E.C.R. II-1375, para. 57 (and citations therein).

European Union (namely, the General Court at first instance and the Court of Justice on appeal) to hear and determine disputes concerning a contract, courts in Member States must decline jurisdiction by reason of the primacy of Union law (i.e. compliance with the arbitration clause concluded pursuant to Art. 272 TFEU). If a number of courts, including the General Court, are entitled to determine disputes under the arbitration clause, a problem of *lis alibi pendens* may arise. No specific rules are set forth in the Treaties (or the procedural texts of the Union courts) for resolving this problem.

(d) Extent of jurisdiction of the General Court

19.10   The extent of the General Court's jurisdiction emerges from the arbitration clause itself.[15] Because that jurisdiction is conferred by derogation from the ordinary rules of law, it must be construed narrowly, so that only claims and pleas arising from the contract containing the arbitration clause or directly connected therewith may be entertained.[16] Claims falling outside the scope of the arbitration clause will be dismissed.[17] Consequently, for example, a claim based on the other party's having been unjustly enriched inevitably falls outside the scope of the contractual relations between the parties.[18] This means that the General Court

---

[15] See, e.g. ECJ, Case 1/56 *Bourgaux v Common Assembly* [1954 to 1956] E.C.R. 361, at 367; EGC, Case T-401/07 *Caixa Geral de Depósitos v Commission* [2011] E.C.R. II-39*, Summ. pub., para. 99 (and further citations therein) (appeal dismissed: ECJ (order of 16 May 2013), Case C-242/11 P *Caixa Geral de Depósitos v Commission*, not reported). The Union judicature may inquire into whether the contract incorporating the arbitration clause has been rescinded under the law applicable to the contract (ECJ, Case C-274/97 *Commission v Coal Products* [2000] E.C.R. I-3175, paras 17–18).

[16] ECJ, Case 426/85 *Commission v Zoubek* [1986] E.C.R. 4057, para. 11; ECJ, Case C-114/94 *IDE v Commission* [1997] E.C.R. I-803, para. 82; ECJ, Case C-337/96 *Commission v IRACO* [1998] E.C.R. I-7943, para. 49; ECJ (judgment of 17 January 2013), Case C-623/11 *Geodis Calberson GE*, not reported, para. 30. See further, e.g. EGC, Case T-19/07 *Systran and Systran Luxembourg v Commission* [2010] E.C.R. II-6083, para. 61 (overturned on appeal: ECJ (judgment of 18 April 2013), Case C-103/11 P *Commission v Systran and Systran Luxembourg*, not reported); EGC, Case T-401/07 *Caixa Geral de Depósitos v Commission* [2011] E.C.R. II-39*, Summ. pub., para. 99 (appeal dismissed: ECJ (order of 16 May 2013), Case C-242/11 P *Caixa Geral de Depósitos v Commission*, not reported). It is possible that the Union judicature would take cognizance of a cluster of contracts concluded by the parties on the basis of an arbitration clause contained in only one (or some) of the contracts. In *Porta v Commission*, the applicant had concluded contracts, each for a term of one year, over a number of years with the director of the then Community's research centre in Ispra to teach at the centre's school. Initially, the contract was only oral, but subsequently was put down in writing, whereupon an arbitration clause was added. The Court of Justice held that this arbitration clause entitled it to have regard to all the contracts entered into between Mrs Porta and the Commission: see ECJ, Case 109/81 *Porta v Commission* [1982] E.C.R. 2469, para. 10. The Union judicature may adjudicate under an arbitration clause on a claim for damages for non-performance of the contract based on the law applicable to the contract that provides for such compensation (ECJ, Case C-69/97 *Commission v SNUA* [1999] E.C.R. I-2363, paras 35–36).

[17] See, e.g. CFI (order of 18 April 2008), Case T-302/04 *MEAM v Commission* [2008] E.C.R. II-61*, Summ. pub., paras 27–29; EGC, Case T-136/09 *Commission v Gal-Or* [2010] E.C.R. II-221*, Summ. pub., paras 34–35; EGC, Case T-387/07 *Portugal v Commission* [2011] E.C.R. II-903, para. 115; EGC, Case T-401/07 *Caixa Geral de Depósitos v Commission* [2011] E.C.R. II-39*, Summ. pub., para. 101 (appeal dismissed: ECJ (order of 16 May 2013), Case C-242/11 P *Caixa Geral de Depósitos v Commission*, not reported). In particular, claims concerning alleged violation of certain general principles of Union law are rejected on the grounds that the Union institutions are subject to obligations arising under the general principles raised in relation to individuals exclusively within the framework of the exercise of their administrative responsibilities; as the relationship between the parties within the context of a claim brought under Art. 272 TFEU is contractual in nature, the applicant can allege only that the Union institution, body, office, or agency concerned breached contractual terms or the law applicable to the contract in question. See, e.g. CFI, Case T-179/06 *Commission v Burie Onderzoek en Advies* [2009] E.C.R. II-64*, Summ. pub., paras 117–118; EGC, Case T-340/07 *Evropaïki Dynamiki v Commission* [2010] E.C.R. II-16*, Summ. pub., para. 124 (set aside on other grounds in ECJ, Case C-200/10 P *Evropaïki Dynamiki v Commission* [2011] E.C.R. I-67*, Summ. pub.); EGC (judgment of 13 June 2012), Case T-366/09 *Insula v Commission*, not reported, paras 227 and 250.

[18] This may be inferred from ECJ, Case C-47/07 P *Masdar (UK) Ltd v Commission* [2008] E.C.R. I-9761, paras 44–61, in which the Court of Justice sustained the possibility of bringing an action for unjust

has no jurisdiction to entertain such a claim pursuant to an arbitration clause.[19] In contrast, counterclaims made by the defendant which are directly based on the contract are admissible.[20]

(e) Contractual versus non-contractual liability claims

The Union courts' jurisdiction to hear and determine an action for damages differs **19.11** according to the contractual or non-contractual nature of the liability involved. For the purposes of the Union's contractual liability under the first paragraph of Art. 340 TFEU, the Union courts have jurisdiction only if there is an arbitration clause within the meaning of Art. 272 TFEU; otherwise, pursuant to Art. 274 TFEU, jurisdiction to adjudicate an action based on the Union's contractual liability falls within the jurisdiction of the national courts. In contrast, the Union courts have exclusive jurisdiction to adjudicate actions concerning the Union's non-contractual liability under Art. 268 TFEU and the second paragraph of Art. 340 TFEU, without the need for the parties concerned to express their consent (see para. 11.04).[21]

Consequently, the Union courts may have to determine the nature (contractual or non-contractual) of the dispute in order to assess their jurisdiction.[22] In that regard, they must examine, by reference to the various relevant matters in the file, such as, for example, the rule of law allegedly infringed, the nature of the damage claimed, the conduct complained

---

enrichment against the Union in the context of an action for damages under Art. 268 TFEU and the second para. of Art. 340 TFEU, distinguishing between enrichment that is 'unjust' and enrichment that derives from contractual obligations. For further discussion of this case, see para. 11.08.

[19] ECJ, Case C-330/88 *Grifoni v EAEC* [1991] E.C.R. I-1045, para. 20. The President of the General Court held that that Court had no jurisdiction to adjudicate proceedings relating to the termination by the Commission of a contract concluded with an organization that included a term conferring jurisdiction over disputes relating to the performance of the contract on the courts of Brussels. The applicant argued that the jurisdiction of the courts of Brussels concerned only disputes relating to the performance of the contract, not the Commission's decision to terminate the contract itself. The President of the General Court dismissed this argument on the grounds that there was a direct connection between the contract and the dispute: CFI (order of the President of 20 July 2000), Case T-149/00 R *Innova v Commission* [2000] E.C.R. II-2941, para. 21.

[20] ECJ, Case C-114/94 *IDE v Commission* [1997] E.C.R. I-803, paras 82–83; EGC (judgment of 9 July 2013), Case T-552/11 *Lito Maieftiko Gynaikologiko kai Cheirourgiko Kentro v Commission*, not reported, paras 33–41. In CFI (order of 25 November 2003), Case T-85/01 *IAMA Consulting v Commission* [2003] E.C.R. II-4973, para. 62, the then Court of First Instance (which at that time could only hear actions brought by natural and legal persons) referred a counterclaim brought by the Commission to the Court of Justice after it had determined that the applicant's main claim was inadmissible. However, the Court of Justice referred the case back to the Court of First Instance (ECJ (order of 27 May 2004), Case C-517/03 *IAMA Consulting v Commission*, not reported). It did this on the grounds that it is implicit in the jurisdiction of the Court of First Instance to entertain the main claim, with the result that it also has jurisdiction to entertain a counterclaim.

[21] See, e.g. ECJ (judgment of 18 April 2013), Case C-103/11 P *Commission v Systran and Systran Luxembourg*, not reported, paras 56–60.

[22] For example, in one case, although the application was brought pursuant to the second para. of Art. 340 TFEU governing the Union's non-contractual liability, the General Court determined that the dispute was contractual in nature but that this finding did not have the effect of excluding its jurisdiction, since the contracts in question contained an arbitration clause within the meaning of Art. 272 TFEU: EGC, Case T-424/08 *Nexus Europe (Ireland) v Commission* [2010] E.C.R. II-96*, Summ. pub., paras 59–61. See also ECJ, Case C-377/09 *Hanssens-Ensch v European Community* [2010] E.C.R. I-7751, paras 16–20, rejecting the assertion that in addition to contractual liability and non-contractual liability within the meaning of the second para. of Art. 340 TFEU, there is a third category of liability which, pursuant to Art. 274 TFEU, falls within the jurisdiction of the national courts (paras 22–25). See further P. Van Nuffel, 'De contractuele aansprakelijkheid van de Europese Gemeenschap: een bevoegdheidskluwen ontward' (2000) Algemeen Juridisch Tijdschrift 157–62.

of, and the legal relations between the parties in question, whether there exists between them a genuine contractual context, linked to the subject-matter of the dispute, the in-depth examination of which proves to be indispensable for the resolution of the said action; if a preliminary analysis of those matters shows that it is necessary to interpret one or more contracts concluded between the parties in question in order to establish whether the applicant's claims are well-founded, the Union courts are required at that point to halt their examination of the dispute and declare that they have no jurisdiction to rule thereon in the absence of an arbitration clause in the said contracts within the meaning of Article 272 TFEU.[23] Importantly, the Court of Justice has held that the mere reliance on legal rules which did not follow from the contract in question but which were binding on the parties cannot have the consequence of altering the contractual nature of the dispute and removing it from the court with jurisdiction to determine it, since otherwise this would make the nature of the dispute and the court with jurisdiction susceptible to change depending on the norms invoked by the parties.[24]

(f) Contractual liability versus annulment claims

19.12 Contractual acts of an institution, body, office, or agency are not regarded as acts exercising prerogatives of a public authority and hence cannot be the subject of an action for annulment under Art. 263 TFEU (see para. 7.15).[25] Instead, claims related to such acts may be brought before the Union judicature pursuant to an arbitration clause within the meaning of Art. 272 TFEU, failing which the national courts have jurisdiction under Art. 274 TFEU. Moreover, a party cannot unilaterally circumvent the division of jurisdiction between the Union courts and the national courts by causing the Union institution concerned to reject its request for compensation relating to a contract for the purposes of

---

[23] See, e.g. ECJ (judgment of 18 April 2013), Case C-103/11 P *Commission v Systran and Systran Luxembourg*, not reported, paras 66–67. In this case, the Court of Justice held that the General Court had erred in classifying the dispute as non-contractual in nature and that the Union courts did not have jurisdiction to hear the action for compensation brought by the applicants: ECJ, Case C-103/11 P *Commission v Systran and Systran Luxembourg*, paras 75–86.

[24] ECJ, Case C-214/08 P *Guigard v Commission* [2009] E.C.R. I-91*, Summ. pub., para. 43. See also ECJ (judgment of 18 April 2013), Case C-103/11 P *Commission v Systran and Systran Luxembourg*, not reported, paras 64–65.

[25] EGC (order of 14 June 2012), Case T-546/11 *Technion and Technion Research & Development Foundation v Commission*, not reported, paras 30–55. In contrast to contractual acts, there are certain kinds of acts that may be the subject of an action for annulment under Art. 263 TFEU. For example, acts of execution, in the sense of Art. 299 TFEU, including those which are adopted in relation to the recovery of a debt emanating from a contract concluded by a Union party, as may be envisaged in the contract itself, are among those which may be challenged by way of an action for annulment (see, e.g. EGC (judgment of 13 June 2012), Case T-246/09 *Insula v Commission*, not reported, paras 91–99). Likewise, an act by which the Commission effects out-of-court set-off between debts and claims resulting from different legal relationships with the same person is a challengeable act for the purposes of Art. 263 TFEU (see, e.g. ECJ, Case C-87/01 P *Commission v CCRE* [2003] E.C.R. I-7617, para. 45; EGC, Case T-37/08 *Walton v Commission* [2011] E.C.R. II-7809, paras 25–26), and it is not for the General Court to assess the legality of an act of offsetting in the context of an action under Art. 272 TFEU (see, e.g. CFI, Case T-122/06 *Helkon Media v Commission* [2008] E.C.R. II-201*, Summ. pub., paras 46–53; CFI, Case T-182/08 *Commission v Atlantic Energy* [2009] E.C.R. II-109*, Summ. pub., para. 70 and citations therein). See further V. Pelikanova, 'La protection juridictionnelle des particuliers par le Tribunal de première instance des Communautés européennes', in X (eds), *Le droit à la mesure de l'homme: En l'honneur de Philippe Léger* (Paris, Pedone, 2006), 246–52.

Art. 272 TFEU and then describing that rejection as a decision within the meaning of Art. 263 TFEU.[26]

Nevertheless, when hearing an action for annulment[27] in which the dispute is found to be contractual in nature (or vice versa), the Union judicature has consented to the requalification of the action for annulment as an action brought pursuant to Art. 272 TFEU, provided that the conditions for such requalification are satisfied. In this regard, the Union judicature considers itself unable to reclassify an action for annulment where the applicant's express intention is not to base its application on Art. 272 TFEU or where the action is not based on any plea alleging infringement of the rules governing the contractual relationship in question, whether they are contractual clauses or provisions of the national law designated in the contract.[28]

B. Identity of the parties

(1) Any party to the contract

Any party bound by the contract embodying the arbitration clause has the right to bring a **19.13** dispute before the Union judicature.[29] However, if a person bringing or defending against a

---

[26] CFI (order of 18 July 1997), Case T-44/96 *Oleifici Italiani v Commission* [1997] E.C.R. II-1331, para. 44; CFI (order of 3 October 1997), Case T-186/96 *Mutual Aid Administration Services v Commission* [1997] E.C.R. II-1633, para. 44; CFI (order of 10 May 2004), Joined Cases T-314/03 and T-378/03 *Musée Grévin v Commission* [2004] E.C.R. II-1421, paras 79–89. Cf., however, CFI, Case T-26/00 *Lecureur v Commission* [2001] E.C.R. II-2623, paras 37–39, in which the General Court held that Art. 24 of Commission Regulation (EC) No. 2519/97 of 16 December 1997 laying down general rules for the mobilization of products to be supplied under Council Regulation (EC) No. 1292/96 as Community food aid, [1997] O.J. L346/23, which provides that the Court of Justice is to be competent to resolve any dispute resulting from the implementation or the non-implementation or from the interpretation of the rules governing supply operations carried out in accordance with that Regulation, formed an integral part of the supply contract concluded on the basis of that Regulation and therefore had to be regarded as an arbitration clause. See to the same effect CFI, Joined Cases T-215/01, T-220/01, and T-221/01 *Calberson v Commission* [2004] E.C.R. II-587, paras 11 and 81–88; CFI (order of 9 June 2005), Case T-265/03 *Helm Düngemittel v Commission* [2005] E.C.R. II-2009, para. 46.

[27] Just because the applicant may use the term 'annul' does not necessarily mean that an action for annulment is being meant, as it may be determined to be situated within the context of a claim brought on the basis of Art. 272 TFEU: see EGC (judgment of 13 June 2012), Case T-366/09 *Insula v Commission*, not reported, paras 85–86.

[28] For some examples in which requalification was granted, see EGC, Joined Cases T-428/07 and T-455/07 *CEVA v Commission* [2010] E.C.R. II-2431, paras 57–64 (rejecting the Commission's submission that requalification is made subject to the condition that the law applicable to the contract is relied on in the application). For some examples in which the actions for annulment could not be requalified as applications based on Art. 272 TFEU, see, e.g. EGC (order of 30 June 2011), Case T-252/10 *Cross Czech v Commission* [2011] E.C.R. II-211*, Summ. pub., paras 62–64; EGC (order of 12 October 2011), Case T-353/10 *Lito Maieftiko Gynaikologiko kai Cheirourgiko Kentro v Commission* [2011] E.C.R. II-7213, paras 33–39; EGC, Case T-285/09 *CEVA v Commission* [2011] E.C.R. II-289*, Summ. pub., paras 29–35. Requalification will also not be granted where there is no arbitration clause within the meaning of Art. 272 TFEU: see, e.g. EGC (order of 8 February 2010), Case T-481/08 *Alisei v Commission* [2010] E.C.R. II-117, paras 56–59; EGC (order of 14 June 2012), Case T-546/11 *Technion and Technion Research & Development Foundation v Commission*, not reported, paras 56–67. The case-law certainly does not preclude the requalification of an action founded on Art. 272 TFEU as one brought under Art. 263 TFEU, but the Union courts may find that even supposing such qualification could be effected, the action is inadmissible as being brought out of time: CFI, Case T-122/06 *Helkon Media v Commission* [2008] E.C.R. II-201*, Summ. pub., paras 54–55.

[29] There is nothing to prevent a party to a contract from assigning his or her rights to a successor. For an example, see ECJ, Case C-209/90 *Commission v Feilhauer* [1992] E.C.R. I-2613, para. 5.

claim brought on the basis of Art. 272 TFEU is not a party to the contract containing the arbitration clause, the claim in relation to that person will be rejected.[30]

(2) Legal capacity of the parties

19.14 An action against a legal person, such as a company or partnership, is inadmissible if, when the action is brought, that entity had neither the legal capacity nor the standing to be a party to legal proceedings.[31] An action brought against a dissolved company will thus be inadmissible. Similarly, an action brought against a party against which insolvency proceedings have been instituted will also be inadmissible.[32]

As mentioned earlier, the reference in Art. 272 TFEU to 'a contract concluded by or on behalf of the Union' encompasses contracts concluded by Union institutions, bodies, offices, and agencies, as well as other entities acting on behalf of the Union (see para. 19.06).

So far, much of the case-law concerning Art. 272 TFEU and the first paragraph of Art. 340 TFEU involves a contract concluded by a Union institution (typically, the Commission) on behalf of the Union with a third party. With particular regard to the European Central Bank, although it is now listed as a Union institution in the second paragraph of Art. 13(1) TEU, it has separate legal personality, and as such, there can be found a provision comparable to Art. 272 TFEU in Art. 35.4 of Protocol (No. 4) on the Statute of the European System of Central Banks and of the European Central Bank.[33] Certainly, a claim involving a contract concluded

---

[30] See, e.g. CFI (order of 8 January 2008), Case T-245/04 *Commission v Lior and Others*, not reported; CFI (order of 5 November 2008), Joined Cases T-213/08 and T-213/08 AJ *Marinova v Université Libre de Bruxelles and Commission*, not reported, paras 14–17 (appeal dismissed in ECJ (order of 1 July 2009), Case C-29/09 P *Marinova v Université Libre de Bruxelles and Commission* [2009] E.C.R. I-115*, Summ. pub.); CFI, Case T-179/06 *Commission v Burie Onderzoek en Advies* [2009] E.C.R. II-64*, Summ. pub., paras 60–69. In particular, where a natural person signs the contract merely on behalf of the entity concerned and not in his or her own name, that person is not deemed to be party to the contract: see, e.g. CFI (order of 17 February 2006), Case T-449/04 *Commission v Trends and Others* [2006] E.C.R. II-24*, Summ. pub.; EGC, Case T-44/06 *Commission v Hellenic Ventures and Others* [2010] E.C.R. II-127*, Summ. pub., paras 48–55; EGC, Case T-259/09 *Commission v Arci Nuova associazione comitato di Cagliari and Gessa* [2010] E.C.R. II-284*, Summ. pub., paras 40–45. In this case, the General Court ruled that since the natural person concerned signed the agreement in the name of the association as president and the contract referred solely to the Commission and the association as parties to the contract, that natural person was not a party to the contract and the action brought against that person must be dismissed. The Court emphasized that its holding was not affected by the fact that the association concerned was not recognized under the applicable national law and that such law provided that persons who act in the name of such an association are personally responsible for its obligations, since that provision of national law cannot serve to circumvent the rules on jurisdiction of the Union courts under Art. 272 TFEU.

[31] See, e.g. EGC, Case T-464/09 *Commission v New Acoustic Music Association and Hildibrandsdottir* [2011] E.C.R. II-133*, Summ. pub., paras 43–53, in which the General Court, looking to the applicable national law in which the partnership concerned was established, found that legal proceedings could be instituted against the partners only, in the name of the partnership, and not against the partnership as such, and thus declared the action inadmissible insofar as it was brought against the partnership concerned.

[32] ECJ, Case C-294/02 *Commission v AMI Semiconductor Belgium and Others* [2005] E.C.R. I-2175, paras 60, 66–72.

[33] Art. 35.4 of the Protocol (No. 4), annexed to the TEU and the TFEU, on the Statute of the European System of Central Banks and of the European Central Bank ([2012] O.J. C326/230) states: 'The Court of Justice of the European Union shall have jurisdiction to give judgment pursuant to any arbitration clause contained in a contract concluded by or on behalf of the ECB, whether that contract be governed by public or private law.' For an example of an action brought by the ECB on the basis of Art. 272 TFEU, see ECJ, Case C-220/03 *ECB v Germany* [2005] E.C.R. I-10595 (involving an arbitration clause contained in the Agreement of 18 September 1998 concluded between Germany and the ECB on the seat of that institution).

by a Union body, office, or agency is not precluded by the terms of Art. 272 TFEU, although so far there is not a considerable body of case-law in this regard.[34]

C. Special characteristics

(1) Requirements relating to validity of arbitration clause

The Treaties do not lay down any particular wording to be used in an arbitration clause. Accordingly, any wording indicating that the parties intend to remove any dispute between them from the purview of the national courts and to submit it to the Union courts must be regarded as sufficient to give the latter jurisdiction under Art. 272 TFEU.[35]   **19.15**

The validity of the arbitration clause is determined exclusively on the basis of Art. 272 TFEU and Art. 44(5a) of the EGC Rules of Procedure, under which the application must be accompanied by a copy of the contract containing that clause.[36] The Union judicature pays no regard to special requirements laid down by the national law applicable to the contract.[37] For the same reason, a court or an administrative authority in a Member State cannot refuse to give effect to the judgment of the General Court on the ground that that Court's jurisdiction is based on an arbitration clause which is invalid under national law.

(2) Applicable law

(a) Choice of the parties

In the absence of applicable Union law, a Union court must identify the applicable law of its own authority. The Court respects the parties' choice of applicable law, whether express or implied,[38] provided that this does not detract from the scope and effectiveness of Union   **19.16**

---

[34] For example, there was an action brought by the European Agency for Maritime Security on the basis of an arbitration clause in the Seat Agreement concluded between it and Portugal, but it was subsequently withdrawn: CFI (order of 29 January 2009), Case T-4/08 *European Agency for Maritime Security v Portugal*, removed from the register.

[35] ECJ, Case C-294/02 *Commission v AMI Semiconductor Belgium and Others* [2005] E.C.R. I-2175, para. 50. As highlighted in the case-law, the parties may stipulate means by which to reach amicable settlement before bringing the dispute before the General Court. However, where such means fail and the parties do not elaborate more detailed provisions as to how to proceed in such circumstances, the General Court has held that it has jurisdiction to adjudicate the contractual dispute before it. See, e.g. EGC, Case T-44/06 *Commission v Hellenic Ventures and Others* [2010] E.C.R. II-127*, Summ. pub., paras 68–71; EGC (judgment of 25 April 2012), Case T-329/05 *Movimondo Onlus v Commission*, not reported, paras 17–18.

[36] See CFI, Case T-271/04 *Citymo v Commission* [2007] E.C.R. II-1375, paras 54–65 (ruling that since the applicant failed to demonstrate the existence of an arbitration clause validly concluded by the parties and to comply with the provisions of Art. 44(5a) of the EGC Rules of Procedure, its action based on Art. 272 TFEU is inadmissible. In doing so, the Court noted that although Art. 272 TFEU does not state what form the arbitration clause is to take, it is clear from Art. 44(5a) of the EGC Rules of Procedure that the clause must in principle be stipulated in writing).

[37] See, e.g. ECJ, Case 23/76 *Pellegrini and Others v Commission* [1976] E.C.R. 1807, paras 8–10; ECJ, Case C-209/90 *Commission v Feilhauer* [1992] E.C.R. I-2613, paras 12–14; ECJ, Case C-299/93 *Bauer v Commission* [1995] E.C.R. I-839, para. 11 (Art. 153 EAEC applied in the same way); EGC, Case T-460/08 *Commission v Acentro Turismo* [2010] E.C.R. II-6351, paras 33–38 (ruling that this case-law applies in circumstances where the contract stipulates specific approval in writing).

[38] ECJ, Case 318/81 *Commission v CO.DE.MI.* [1985] E.C.R. 3693, paras 18–22; ECJ, Case 220/85 *Fadex v Commission* [1986] E.C.R. 3387, para. 10; ECJ, Case C-209/90 *Commission v Feilhauer*, paras 3, 16.

law.[39] In the absence of such a choice, the Rome Convention of 19 June 1980 on the law applicable to contractual obligations,[40] now converted into the 'Rome I' Regulation,[41] is a possible source of inspiration, apart from the general private international law of the Member States.

(b) Formulation of rules of contract law based on general principles common to the Member States

19.17   In a case in which neither the contracts in question nor the applicable Union law specified the applicable law, the Court of Justice held that the first paragraph of Art. 340 TFEU 'refers, as regards the law applicable to a contract, to the Member States' own laws and not to the general principles common to the legal systems of the Member States'.[42] Consequently, the Union judicature has so far declined to formulate a Union law on contractual liability. However, depending upon the circumstances, the Union judicature has had occasion to formulate rules of contract law in the context of adjudicating cases implicating its jurisdiction, *inter alia*, pursuant to an arbitration clause under Art. 272 TFEU.[43] It remains to be seen in the context of the ongoing debate concerning European contract law to what extent a Union instrument of substantive contract law may be chosen by parties to contracts concluded by or on behalf of the Union and impact the jurisprudence of the Union courts in this setting.[44]

(c) Distinction between substantive law and rules of procedure

19.18   Under an arbitration clause within the meaning of Art. 272 TFEU, a Union court is called upon to resolve a dispute in accordance with the substantive national law governing the contract. However, in accordance with the principle that each court applies its own procedural rules, the Union judicature assesses its jurisdiction and the admissibility of claims put forward by the applicant or defendant solely under Union law.[45]

---

[39] ECJ, Joined Cases C-80/99 to C-82/99 *Flemmer and Others* [2001] E.C.R. I-7211, para. 57.

[40] Rome Convention of 19 June 1980 on the law applicable to contractual obligations, [1998] O.J. C27/34 (consolidated version).

[41] Regulation (EC) No. 593/2008 of the European Parliament and of the Council of 17 June 2008 on the law applicable to contractual obligations (Rome I), [2008] O.J. L177/6. The 'Rome I' Regulation does not apply to all Member States, namely Denmark.

[42] ECJ, Joined Cases C-80/99 to C-82/99 *Flemmer and Others* [2001] E.C.R. I-7211, para. 54.

[43] For further discussion, see K. Lenaerts and K. Gutman, '"Federal Common Law" in the European Union: A Comparative Perspective from the United States', (2006) 26 A.J.C.L. 1-121, at 102–9.

[44] For detailed discussion of the debate on European contract law and the role of the Union courts in this context, see K. Gutman, *The Constitutional Foundations of European Contract Law: A Comparative Analysis* (Oxford, Oxford University Press, 2014), chs 2, 4–6.

[45] See, e.g. EGC (judgment of 13 June 2012), Case T-246/09 *Insula v Commission*, not reported, paras 87–88; EGC (judgment of 13 June 2012), Case T-366/09 *Insula v Commission*, not reported, paras 81–82; EGC (judgment of 13 June 2012), Case T-110/10 *Insula v Commission*, not reported, paras 29–30 (and citations therein). See also EGC, Joined Cases T-428/07 and T-455/07 *CEVA v Commission* [2010] E.C.R. II-2431, para. 108 (ruling that the alternative claims put forward by the applicant seeking the appointment of an expert must be examined in the light of the relevant EGC Rules of Procedure concerning measures of inquiry, and therefore, the applicant cannot be accused of not having based such claims on the applicable law of the contracts). Compare EGC, Case T-323/09 *Commission v Irish Electricity Generating Co.* [2010] E.C.R. II-254*, Summ. pub., paras 63–66, in which the General Court examined the question whether in the present case the right to reimbursement claimed by the Commission was time-barred under Irish law, ruling that since the coordinator did not invoke the statute of limitations in its defence in line with the applicable law, the claim for reimbursement must be upheld.

(d) Determination based primarily on contractual provisions

According to the case-law, disputes arising from the performance of a contract must be resolved in principle on the basis of the contractual provisions. A Union court's interpretation of the contract in light of provisions of the applicable national law is justified only where there is doubt on the content of the contract or on the meaning of some of its provisions, or where the contract alone does not enable all aspects of the dispute to be resolved. Thus, the assessment of the merits of the application must be carried out in the light of the contractual provisions alone, and recourse is had to the applicable national law only if those provisions do not enable the dispute to be resolved.[46]   **19.19**

(3) Procedure before Union courts

The procedure ordinarily applied to direct actions before the Union courts is used for the determination of disputes under an arbitration clause pursuant to Art. 272 TFEU.   **19.20**

D. Consequences

A judgment given by the General Court pursuant to Art. 272 TFEU is enforceable under Arts 280 and 299 TFEU in the same way as any other judgment.[47] An appeal may be brought before the Court of Justice (see Ch. 16).   **19.21**

II. Art. 273 TFEU

A. Disputes between Member States

Art. 273 TFEU[48] provides that the Court of Justice has 'jurisdiction in any dispute between Member States that relates to the subject matter of the Treaties if the dispute is submitted to it under a special agreement between the parties'.[49] This provision thereby allows Member States to conclude a special agreement to refer any dispute between them relating   **19.22**

---

[46] See, e.g. CFI, Case T-448/04 *Commission v Trends* [2007] E.C.R. II-104*, Summ. pub., paras 63–64; CFI, Case T-449/04 *Commission v Trends* [2007] E.C.R. II-106*, Summ. pub., paras 72–73; CFI, Case T-316/06 *Commission v Premium* [2008] E.C.R. II-276*, Summ. pub., para. 53; EGC, Case T-136/09 *Commission v Gal-Or* [2010] E.C.R. II-221*, Summ. pub., paras 45–46; EGC, Case T-238/08 *Commission v Commune de Valbonne* [2010] E.C.R. II-260*, Summ. pub., paras 52–53; EGC (judgment of 9 March 2011), Case T-235/09 *Commission v Edificios Inteco*, not reported, para. 49 (and further citations therein).

[47] See, in this regard, CFI, Case T-500/04 *Commission v IIC Informations-Indutrie Consulting* [2007] E.C.R. II-1443, paras 187–191.

[48] Save for the replacement of 'Treaty' with 'Treaties', Art. 273 TFEU reproduces verbatim former Art. 239 EC. Notably, as compared to Art. 272 TFEU, no change was made to the reference to 'Court of Justice' enshrined in former Art. 239 EC, since the Court of Justice retains jurisdiction to adjudicate such proceedings, not the General Court.

[49] ECJ Rules of Procedure, Art. 205(7) provides that the same procedure as that laid down for the settlement of disputes between Member States or between Member States and the Commission as referred to in Art. 35(7) EU as maintained in force by Protocol No. 36 on Transitional Provisions (which is laid down in Arts 205(1)–(6)) applies where an agreement concluded between Member States confers jurisdiction on the Court of Justice to rule on a dispute between Member States or between Member States and an institution.

to the subject-matter of the Treaties to the Court of Justice. To date, the Court of Justice was only asked once to interpret this provision.[50]

B. EAEC and now-expired ECSC Treaties

19.23   A comparable provision concerning the Court of Justice's jurisdiction to give judgment pursuant to a special agreement in relation to the European Atomic Energy Community used to be found in Art. 154 EAEC.[51] In tandem with the entry into force of the Lisbon Treaty, however, there is a new consolidated version of the EAEC Treaty, whereby Art. 154 EAEC has been repealed and Art. 273 TFEU is now applicable.[52]

There was also a provision similar to Art. 273 TFEU in Art. 89 of the now-expired ECSC Treaty.[53]

C. Special agreement

19.24   While it is true that the jurisdiction of the Court of Justice under Art. 273 TFEU is subject to the existence of a special agreement, there is no reason, given the objective pursued by that provision, why such agreement should not be given in advance, with reference to a whole class of pre-defined disputes.[54]

D. Dispute related to the subject-matter of the Treaties

19.25   Only disputes related to the subject-matter of the Treaties can be submitted to the jurisdiction of the Court of Justice pursuant to Art. 273 TFEU. In *Pringle*, it was held that a dispute linked to the interpretation or application of the Treaty establishing the European Stability Mechanism fulfilled that condition, since the conditions to be attached to the grant of support to a Member State under that Treaty are, at least in part, determined by Union law.[55]

---

[50] See ECJ (judgment of 27 November 2012), Case C-370/12 *Pringle*, not reported, paras 170–176 (concerning the Treaty establishing the European Stability Mechanism concluded on 2 February 2012 between the Eurogroup Member States: pursuant to Art. 37 of the ESM Treaty, as further explained in recital 16, disputes concerning the interpretation and application of this Treaty arising between the Contracting Parties or between the Contracting Parties and the ESM are submitted to the jurisdiction of the Court of Justice of the European Union, in accordance with Art. 273 TFEU). It should be noted that Art. 8 of the Treaty on Stability, Coordination and Governance in the Economic and Monetary Union of 2 March 2012 also contains a special agreement within the meaning of Art. 273 TFEU.
[51] Art. 153 EAEC provided: 'The Court of Justice shall have jurisdiction in any dispute between the Member States which relates to the subject matter of this Treaty if the dispute is submitted to it under a special agreement between the parties.'
[52] See Art. 106a(1) of the consolidated version of the EAEC Treaty, [2012] O.J. C327/1.
[53] The second para. of Art. 89 ECSC stipulated: 'The Court shall also have jurisdiction to settle any dispute among [M]ember States related to the purpose of the present Treaty, if such dispute is submitted to it by virtue of an agreement to arbitrate.'
[54] See ECJ (judgment of 27 November 2012), Case C-370/12 *Pringle*, not reported, para. 172.
[55] See ECJ (judgment of 27 November 2012), Case C-370/12 *Pringle*, not reported, para. 174.

E. Only between Member States

The jurisdiction of the Court of Justice under Art. 273 TFEU is subject to the condition   **19.26**
that only Member States are parties to the dispute submitted to it.[56]

F. Art. 273 TEU *juncto* Art. 344 TFEU

Read in the light of Art. 344 TFEU,[57] which puts Member States under an obligation not   **19.27**
to submit a dispute concerning the interpretation or application of the Treaties to any
method of settlement other than those provided for therein,[58] Art. 273 TFEU is not an
optional provision. Once a dispute arises relating to 'the interpretation or application' of the
Treaties, which the Member States have no other way of bringing before the Court of
Justice, Art. 344 TFEU obliges them to conclude a special agreement within the meaning
of Art. 273 TFEU, which confers jurisdiction on the Court of Justice to resolve the
dispute.[59]

---

[56] See ECJ (judgment of 27 November 2012), Case C-370/12 *Pringle*, not reported, para. 175, in which
the Court stated that since the membership of the European Stability Mechanism consists solely of Member
States, a dispute to which that Mechanism is party may be considered to be a dispute between Member States
within the meaning of Art. 273 TFEU.

[57] Save for the replacement of 'Treaty' with 'Treaties', Art. 344 TFEU reproduces verbatim former Art. 292
EC. A comparable provision is set forth in Art. 193 EAEC. However, Art. 106a(1) of the consolidated version of
the EAEC Treaty ([2012] O.J. C327/1) provides that Art. 344 TFEU is applicable to the EAEC Treaty.

[58] The only example to date is ECJ, Case C-459/03 *Commission v Ireland ('Mox Plant')* [2006] E.C.R.
I-4635, in which the Court of Justice held that Ireland, by submitting a dispute with the United Kingdom to
an arbitrator outside the Union legal order, was in breach of the exclusive jurisdiction of the Court of Justice
laid down in Art. 344 TFEU.

[59] In the Opinion of Advocate-General M. Poiares Maduro in ECJ, Case C-459/03 *Commission v Ireland
('Mox Plant')* [2006] E.C.R. I-4635, point 14 n. 9, he surmised: 'This does not necessarily mean that
Member States should always carefully isolate the [Union] elements from a dispute between them in order to
bring only those elements before the Court of Justice, while submitting the rest of the dispute to another
method of settlement. In theory, such a solution would be in line with [Art. 344 TFEU]. Yet, in practice it
may be preferable to bring "hybrid disputes" between Member States—concerning both matters falling within
and matters falling outside the scope of the Court's jurisdiction—in their entirety before the Court under
[Art. 273 TFEU].'

20

JURISDICTION OF THE UNION COURTS OVER DISPUTES RELATING TO INTELLECTUAL PROPERTY RIGHTS

I. Subject-Matter

20.01 To date, Union intellectual property rights have been created by three regulations adopted on the basis of former Art. 308 EC (now Art. 352 TFEU). First, the Community trade mark was introduced by Council Regulation (EC) No. 40/94 of 20 December 1993.[1] Currently, the Community trade mark is regulated by Council Regulation (EC) No. 207/2009 of 26 February 2009, which repealed and codified Council Regulation (EC) No. 40/94 and its subsequent amendments.[2] Second, Community plant variety rights were introduced by Council Regulation (EC) No. 2100/94 of 27 July 1994,[3] as amended by Council Regulation (EC) No. 15/2008 of 20 December 2007.[4] Third, Community designs were introduced by Council Regulation (EC) No. 6/2002 of 12 December 2001,[5] as amended by Council Regulation (EC) No. 1891/2006 of 18 December 2006.[6]

These intellectual property rights are granted by Union bodies especially set up for the purpose. Community trademarks are granted by the Office for Harmonisation in the Internal Market (Trade Marks and Designs) (OHIM), whereas Community plant variety rights are conferred by the Community Plant Variety Office. The two Offices may also declare intellectual property rights falling within their jurisdiction null and void or cancel them, and take decisions on observations or objections submitted by third parties.

---

[1] Council Regulation (EC) No. 40/94 of 20 December 1993 on the Community trade mark ([1994] O.J. L11/1).
[2] Council Regulation (EC) No. 207/2009 of 26 February 2009 on the Community trade mark (codified version, [2009] O.J. L78/24).
[3] Council Regulation (EC) No. 2100/94 of 27 July 1994 on Community plant variety rights ([1994] O.J. L227/1).
[4] Council Regulation (EC) No. 15/2008 of 20 December 2007 amending Regulation (EC) No. 2100/94 as regards the entitlement to file an application for a Community plant variety right ([2008] O.J. L8/2).
[5] Council Regulation (EC) No. 6/2002 of 12 December 2001 on Community designs ([2002] O.J. L3/1).
[6] Council Regulation (EC) No. 1891/2006 of 18 December 2006 amending Regulations (EC) No. 6/2002 and (EC) No. 40/94 to give effect to the accession of the European Community to the Geneva Act of the Hague Agreement concerning the international registration of industrial designs ([2006] O.J. L386/14).

II. System of Legal Protection

A. Boards of Appeal

Each of the three regulations introduces a specific system of legal protection which safe-guards the rights of parties affected by the Offices' decisions and takes account of the specific characteristics of intellectual property rights. One or more Boards of Appeal have been set up at the two Offices to which appeals may be brought against the decisions of other authorities of the relevant Office.[7] Accordingly, as far as the Community trade mark is concerned, an appeal may be brought before the Boards of Appeal[8] against decisions of the examiners (who are responsible for taking decisions in relation to an application for registration of a Community trade mark),[9] decisions of the Opposition Divisions (which are responsible for taking decisions on an opposition to an application to register a Community trade mark),[10] decisions of the Administration of Trade Marks and Legal Division (which is responsible for matters not attributed to other divisions, in particular relating to the particulars to be included in the registry of Community trade marks[11]), and decisions of the Cancellation Divisions (which are responsible for taking decisions in relation to an application for the revocation or declaration of invalidity of a Community trade mark[12]). An appeal may be lodged against decisions of the Boards of Appeal in the General Court.[13]

20.02

---

[7] Under Art. 67 of Regulation No. 2100/94, appeals will lie against a declaration that a Community plant variety right is null and void (Art. 20), the cancellation of such a right (Art. 21), decisions concerning objections lodged against the grant of such a right (Art. 59), the refusal of applications for a right (Art. 61), the grant of a Community plant variety right (Art. 62), the approval and amendment of a variety denomination (Arts 63 and 66), decisions concerning the fees payable under Art. 83 and costs under Art. 85, the registration and deregistration of particulars in the registers under Art. 87, and public inspection under Art. 88. The Office may grant compulsory exploitation rights under Art. 29 and may in certain circumstances grant exploitation rights to a person not being the holder of the relevant plant variety right under Art. 100(2). Decisions under Arts 29 and 100(2) may also be challenged before the Boards of Appeal or be the subject of a direct appeal to the General Court under Art. 74(1). Under Arts 55 and 106 of Regulation No. 6/2002, an appeal will lie from decisions of the examiners (Art. 103 empowers the examiners to take decisions in relation to an application for registration of a Community design), the Administration of Trade Marks and Designs and Legal Division (responsible under Art. 104(2) for taking those decisions which do not fall within the competence of an examiner or an Invalidity Division), and Invalidity Divisions (responsible under Art. 105 for taking decisions in relation to applications for declarations of invalidity of registered Community designs).

[8] Regulation No. 207/2009, Art. 58.

[9] Regulation No. 207/2009, Art. 131.

[10] Regulation No. 207/2009, Art. 132.

[11] Regulation No. 207/2009, Art. 133.

[12] Regulation No. 207/2009, Art. 134.

[13] Art. 65 of Regulation No. 207/2009, Art. 73 of Regulation No. 2100/94, and Art. 61 of Regulation No. 6/2002. Those provisions confer jurisdiction on the 'Court of Justice'. By virtue of Art. 256(1) TFEU and Art. 51 of the Statute, this jurisdiction is to be exercised by the General Court. See P. Mengozzi, 'Le contrôle des décisions de l'OHMI par le Tribunal de première instance et la Cour de justice dans le contentieux rélatif aux droits de la propriété' (2002) R.D.U.E. 315–33.

B. The General Court

(1) Jurisdiction of the General Court

(a) Legality control

20.03 The purpose of an action before the General Court is to review the legality of a decision of the Board of Appeal on grounds of lack of competence, infringement of an essential procedural requirement, infringement of the Treaties, of the applicable Regulations, or of any rule of law relating to their application, or misuse of power.[14] This entails a full review[15] of the legality of the decision of a Board of Appeal.[16] It implies, *inter alia*, examining whether a Board of Appeal has made a correct legal classification of the facts of the dispute[17] and evaluating whether its assessment of the facts submitted to it was erroneous.[18] Therefore, judicial review before the General Court cannot consist of a mere repetition of a review previously carried out by a Board of Appeal.[19] Conversely, the General Court cannot go beyond the context of the dispute as presented before a Board of Appeal. It can only exercise its power within the limits of Regulation No. 207/2009 (Art. 65(2)), Regulation No. 2100/94 (Art. 73(2)), or Regulation No. 6/2002 (Art. 61(2)).

(b) Jurisdiction to annul or alter the contested decision

20.04 The General Court has jurisdiction to annul or alter a contested decision.[20] In addition to its power to annul a decision of a Board of Appeal, the General Court is vested with a form of unlimited jurisdiction to alter the Board's decision and replace it with its own.[21]

(2) Limits to the General Court's jurisdiction

(a) General

20.05 The General Court may exercise its jurisdiction to annul or alter only where the Office has taken a decision.[22] Where the Office has not processed a claim or an application, the

---

[14] Art. 65(2) of Regulation No. 207/2009, Art. 73(2) of Regulation No. 2100/94, and Art. 61(2) of Regulation No. 6/2002. See also ECJ (order of 30 June 2010), Case C-448/09 P *Royal Appliance International v OHIM* [2010] E.C.R. I-87*, Summ. pub., para. 43; EGC, Case T-481/09 *ATB Norte v OHIM* [2011] E.C.R. II-199*, Summ. pub., para. 16.

[15] ECJ, Case C-281/10 P *PepsiCo v Grupo Promer Mon Graphic* [2011] E.C.R. I-10153, para. 66; ECJ, Case C-263/09 P *Edwin v OHIM* [2011] E.C.R. I-5853, para. 52.

[16] ECJ (order of 9 July 2010), Case C-461/09 P *The Wellcome Foundation v OHIM* [2010] E.C.R I-94*, Summ. pub., para. 25; CFI, Case T-165/06 *Fiorucci v OHIM* [2009] E.C.R. II-1375, para. 21.

[17] ECJ, Case C-311/05 P *Naipes Heraclio Fournier SA* [2007] E.C.R. I-130*, Summ. pub., para. 39.

[18] ECJ, Case C-16/06 P *Les Éditions Albert René* [2008] E.C.R. I-10053, para. 39.

[19] ECJ, Case C-29/05 P *OHIM v Kaul* [2007] I-2213, para. 55.

[20] Art. 65(2) of Regulation No. 207/2009, Art. 73(2) of Regulation No. 2100/94, and Art. 61(2) of Regulation No. 6/2002. See also ECJ (order of 30 June 2010), Case C-448/09 P *Royal Appliance International v OHIM* [2010] E.C.R. I-87*, Summ. pub., para. 43 and EGC, Case T-385/09 *Annco v OHIM* [2011] E.C.R. II-455, para. 52. The Court will not alter a decision when the applicant's interests are sufficiently safeguarded by the annulment of it: EGC, Case T-461/09 *CheapFlights International v OHIM* [2011] E.C.R. II-113*, Summ. pub., para. 51.

[21] For a case in which the contested decision was altered, see CFI, Case T-292/01 *Philips–Van Heusen v OHIM* [2003] E.C.R. II-4335. When exercising its power to amend a decision of the OHIM, the General Court may annul not only the contested decision, but also the decision of the Opposition Division (see CFI, Case T-334/01 *MFE Marienfelde v OHIM* [2004] E.C.R. II-2787).

[22] Decisions may be annulled or altered only where they contain a substantive or procedural irregularity: see CFI, Case T-247/01 *eCopy v OHIM* [2002] E.C.R. II-5301, para. 46; CFI, Case T-360/03 *Frischpack v OHIM* [2004] E.C.R II-4097, para. 25. In the absence of an irregularity, the Court cannot dismiss the action

General Court is not empowered to consider whether the claim is well-founded for the first time.[23] Accordingly, the General Court is not empowered to consider whether a trade mark applied for has distinctive character in consequence of the use which has been made of it[24] where that argument was not raised before the Board of Appeal.[25] However, exceptionally, the Court may take a decision without a prior decision of the Office. That possibility is limited to situations 'in which the case has reached a stage appropriate for judicial adjudication',[26] when the Court is in a position to determine, on the basis of elements of law and fact as established, what decision the Board of Appeal was required to take.[27] This is not the case when the Court is deciding for the first time on the substance of the claims on which a Board of Appeal has failed to rule.[28] Therefore, an application for partial revocation of a Community trade mark should be rejected when a Board of Appeal did not consider the facts and the evidence at issue with regard to the partial revocation.[29]

(b) No power to issue an injunction to the Office

Since the Office itself has to draw the appropriate inferences from the operative part and grounds of the Court's judgment, it is not for the General Court to issue injunctions to the Office.[30] This is a consequence of Art. 266 TFEU[31] and the obligation laid down in Art. 65(6) of Regulation No. 207/2009 that the Office has to take the necessary measures to comply with a judgment of the Court.[32] Therefore, the General Court cannot order the Office to register[33]

20.06

---

while substituting its own reasoning for that of the Office: EGC, Case T-70/08 *Axis v OHIM* [2010] E.C.R. II-4645, para. 29.

[23] CFI, Case T-323/00 *SAT.1 v OHIM (SAT.2)* [2002] E.C.R. II-2839, para. 18; EGC, Case T-504/09 *Völkl v OHIM* [2011] E.C.R. II-8179, para. 121. See also paras 20.06 and 20.15.

[24] Regulation No. 207/2009, Art. 7(3).

[25] CFI, Case T-30/00 *Henkel v OHIM* [2001] E.C.R. II-2663, para. 66; CFI, Case T-337/99 *Henkel v OHIM* [2001] E.C.R. II-2597, para. 62.

[26] CFI, Case T-419/07 *Okalux v OHIM* [2009] E.C.R. II-2477, para. 20.

[27] ECJ, Case C-263/09 P *Edwin v OHIM* [2011] E.C.R. I-5853, para. 72; EGC, Joined Cases T-5/08 and T-7/08 *Nestlé v OHIM* [2010] E.C.R. II-1177, para. 77; EGC (judgment of 8 May 2012), Case T-348/10 *Panzeri v OHIM*, not reported, para. 44.

[28] CFI, Case T-419/07 *Okalux v OHIM* [2009] E.C.R. II-2477, para. 20; see also CFI (order of 6 October 2008), Case T-380/07 *Kaloudis v OHIM* [2008] E.C.R. II-208*, Summ. pub., paras 37–40, where the Court rejected a head of claim dealing with the substance of the case as inadmissible, since the Board of Appeal had only ruled on the admissibility of the appeal before it.

[29] CFI, Case T-419/07 *Okalux v OHIM* [2009] E.C.R. II-2477, paras 19–20.

[30] CFI, Case T-35/04 *Athinaiki Oikogeniaki Artopoiia v OHIM* [2006] E.C.R. II-785, para. 15 (and references therein); EGC, Case T-421/10 *Cooperativa Vitivinicola Arousana v OHIM* [2011] E.C.R. II-347*, Summ. pub., para. 15; CFI, Case T-443/05 *El Corte Inglés v OHIM* [2007] E.C.R. II-2579, para. 20; EGC (judgment of 6 October 2011), Case T-247/10 *medi v OHIM*, not reported, para. 13; EGC, Case T-434/10 *Hrbek v OHIM* [2011] E.C.R. II-388*, Summ. pub., para. 15.

[31] CFI, Case T-441/05 *IVG Immobilien v OHIM* [2007] E.C.R. II-1937, para. 12.

[32] Art. 65(6) Regulation No. 207/2009.

[33] CFI, Case T-35/04 *Athinaiki Oikogeniaki Artopoiia v OHIM* [2006] E.C.R. II-785, para. 16; CFI, Case T-413/07 *Bayern Innovativ v OHIM* [2009] II-16*, Summ. pub., para. 17; EGC, Case T-481/09 *ATB Norte v OHIM* [2011] E.C.R. II-199*, Summ. pub., para 18; EGC, Case T-385/09 *Annco v OHIM* [2011] E.C.R. II-455, para. 52; EGC, Case T-7/10 *Diagnostiko kai Therapeftiko Kentro Athinon « Ygeia » v OHIM* [2011] E.C.R. II-136*, Summ. pub., paras 12–14; EGC, Case T-523/08 *Agatha Ruiz de la Prada de Sentmenat v OHIM* [2011] E.C.R. II-276*, Summ. pub., paras 17–19; EGC (judgment of 21 June 2012), Case T-276/09 *Kavaklidere-Europe v OHIM*, not reported, para 17; EGC (judgment of 18 September 2012), Case T-460/11 *Scandic Distilleries v OHIM*, not reported, paras. 14–15; EGC, Case T-307/09 *Earle Beauty v OHIM* [2010] E.C.R. II-266*, Summ. pub., para. 13. However, a claim requesting the Court to declare possible the registration of a Community trade mark may be declared admissible when it can be interpreted as a request for annulment. This is the case when it appears clearly from the submissions of the applicant that the

or to refuse registration of[34] a Community trade mark. It also cannot compel the Office to remove an intervener's name from the register as the proprietor of a Community trade mark and replace it by the applicant's name[35] or to declare a trade mark invalid.[36] It should be pointed out, however, that a specific claim may often be interpreted both as an injunction and an alteration.[37] Since the Court is competent to alter a decision of a Board of Appeal, it is therefore necessary to distinguish between a claim seeking an injunction and a claim seeking an alteration. The decisive criterion to distinguish between those two types of claims is whether the Court is compelling the Office to take action or to refrain from doing so.[38] Consequently, when the Court takes a decision 'which the Board of Appeal ought to have taken or could have taken'[39] rather than compelling the Office to follow a certain course of action, such a decision constitutes an alteration within the meaning of Art. 65(2) of Regulation No. 207/2009.[40]

(c) No declaratory or confirmatory judgments

20.07   The General Court's jurisdiction is limited to the review of the legality of decisions of the Boards of Appeal. Claims which seek, in reality, to obtain from the Court statements of law and a ruling on the merits of certain of the submissions put forward in support of the claims for annulment are inadmissible.[41] Therefore, the Court cannot give declaratory or confirmatory judgments.[42] A claim requesting the Court to confirm the validity of a registration of a

---

actual form of order sought was the annulment of the decision of the Board of Appeal. See CFI, Case T-412/06 *Vitro Corporativo v OHIM* [2008] E.C.R. II-312*, Summ. pub., para. 16; CFI, Case T-295/07 *Vitro Corporativo, v OHIM* [2008] E.C.R. II-317*, Summ. pub., para. 17.

[34] EGC (judgment of 9 October 2012), Case T-366/11 *BIAL-Portela v OHIM*, not reported, para. 14; EGC (judgment of 10 October 2012), Case T-333/11 *Wessang v OHIM*, not reported, paras 15–16.

[35] EGC, Case T-83/09 *Chalk v OHIM* [2011] E.C.R. II-267*, Summ. pub., para. 18.

[36] CFI, Case T-137/05 *La Perla v OHIM* [2007] E.C.R. II-47*, Summ. pub., paras 17–18. For other examples, see EGC (judgment of 12 July 2012), Case T-279/09 *Aiello v OHIM*, not reported, para. 17 (claim that the Court should direct the OHIM to declare an opposition inadmissible).

[37] ECG, Case T-15/09 *Euro-Information v OHIM* [2010] E.C.R. II-27*, Summ. pub., paras 13–14; EGC, Case T-28/10 *Euro-Information v OHIM* [2011] E.C.R. II-1535, paras 12–13; EGC, Case T-372/09 *Visti Beheer v OHIM* [2011] E.C.R. II-53*, Summ. pub., para. 14; EGC (judgment of 5 September 2012), Case T-497/11 *Euro-Information v OHIM*, not reported, paras 11–13. For instance, a claim requesting the Court to refer the case back to the lower adjudicating body—an opposition division—whose decision was challenged before a Board of Appeal was considered to be an alteration in *Beifa Group* (EGC, Case T-148/08 *Beifa Group v OHIM* [2010] E.C.R. II-1681, para. 42), but a request for an injunction in *Phildar* (EGC, Case T-99/06 *Phildar v OHIM* [2009] E.C.R. II-164*, Summ. pub., paras 15–17).

[38] CFI, Case T-152/07 *Lange Uhren v OHIM* [2009] E.C.R. II-144*, Summ. pub., para. 39.

[39] EGC, Case T-148/08 *Beifa Group v OHIM* [2010] E.C.R. II-1681, para. 43; EGC, Case T-274/09 *Deutsche Bahn v OHIM* [2011] E.C.R. II-268*, Summ. pub., paras 20–24.

[40] CFI, Case T-190/04 *Freixenet v OHIM* [2006] E.C.R. II-79*, Summ. pub., paras 16–18 and CFI, Case T-188/04 *Freixenet v OHIM* [2006] E.C.R. II-78*, Summ. pub., paras 16–18 (decision that the conditions for publication of the requested trade mark are fulfilled); CFI, Case T-363/04 *Koipe Corporación v OHIM* [2007] E.C.R. II-3355, paras 29–30 (decision that conditions for opposition have been fulfilled); CFI, Case T-152/07 *Lange Uhren v OHIM* [2009] E.C.R. II-144*, Summ. pub., para. 39 (decision that a trade mark could be registered under certain conditions). See also CFI, Case T-413/07 *Bayern Innovativ v OHIM* [2009] II-16*, Summ. pub., para. 14–16 (decision finding that the conditions for allowing an opposition had not been fulfilled).

[41] EGC, Case T-207/09 *El Jirari Bouzekri v OHIM* [2011] E.C.R. II-324*, Summ. pub., para. 17.

[42] CFI, Case T-85/07 *Gabel Industria Tessile v OHIM* [2008] E.C.R. II-823, paras 16–18; EGC (judgment of 21 June 2012), Case T-514/10 *Fruit of the Loom v OHIM*, not reported, para. 12.

contested Community trade mark is thus inadmissible on that account.[43] For the same reason, a claim requesting the Court to declare that a decision does not comply with Regulation No. 207/2009 has been declared inadmissible.[44] An application for a declaratory judgment may nevertheless be declared admissible[45] if, despite the wording of the form of order sought in the application, it is clear from the application that the applicant seeks, in substance, the annulment of the contested decision.[46]

(d) Decision concerning the costs of proceedings before the Office

Often, parties may claim that the Court should order the OHIM to reimburse them for **20.08** certain costs they have incurred in the course of the proceedings before the Office. However, the Court is only competent to rule on recoverable costs as defined by Art. 136(2) of the EGC Rules of Procedure, meaning 'costs necessarily incurred by the parties for the purposes of the proceedings before the Board of Appeal and costs incurred for the purposes of the production, prescribed by the second subparagraph of Article 131(4), of translations of pleadings or other documents into the language of the case'.[47] Therefore, a claim for reimbursement of costs incurred in the course of opposition proceedings is inadmissible.[48]

III. Identity of the Parties

A. The defendant

(1) The Office is the defendant

As has already been mentioned, an appeal will lie to the General Court against decisions **20.09** of the Offices' Boards of Appeal. Nevertheless, the Boards of Appeal of these Union agencies are not the defendants in proceedings before the Court, but rather the Offices themselves. It should be noted in this connection that although the members of the Boards of Appeal are independent and not bound by any instructions, they constitute an integral part of the relevant Office and hence a decision of a Board of Appeal is ascribed

---

[43] EGC (judgment of 8 May 2012), Case T-416/10 *Yoshida Metal Industry v OHIM*, not reported, paras 12–13. See also EGC (judgment of 29 February 2012), Joined Cases T-77/10 and T-78/10 *Certmedica International and Lehning entreprise v OHIM*, not reported, paras 30–33.

[44] EGC, Case T-118/08 *Actega Terra v OHIM* [2010] E.C.R. II-110*, Summ. pub., para. 10; EGC, Case T-377/09 *Mövenpick v OHIM* [2011] E.C.R. II-455*, Summ. pub., para. 12; EGC, Case T-455/09 *Jiménez Sarmiento v OHIM* [2011] E.C.R. II-50*, Summ. pub., paras 17–18; EGC, Case T-500/10 *Dorma v OHIM* [2011] E.C.R. II-411*, Summ. pub., paras 16–17.

[45] EGC, Case T-500/10 *Dorma v OHIM* [2011] E.C.R. II-411*, Summ. pub., para. 18.

[46] EGC (judgment of 22 May 2012), Case T-273/10 *Olive Line International, SL v OHIM*, not reported, para. 22.

[47] See, e.g. EGC (judgment of 7 February 2013), Case T-50/12 *AMC-Representações Têxteis v OHIM*, not reported, para. 64; EGC (order of 23 October 2013), Case T-589/11 DEP *Phonebook of the World v OHIM*, not reported, para. 9.

[48] EGC, Case T-72/08 *Travel Service v OHIM* [2010] E.C.R. II-196*, Summ. pub., paras 21–23; EGC, Case T-434/10 *Hrbek v OHIM* [2011] E.C.R. II-388*, Summ. pub., paras 16–18.

to the Office to which it belongs in the course of proceedings before the Court.[49] A Board of Appeal therefore cannot be regarded as being a 'court or tribunal'.[50]

(2) Forms of order that may be sought by the Office

20.10 In its judgment of 12 December 2002 in *Vedial*, the Court held that the Office was not entitled to ask the Court to alter or annul a contested decision of a Board of Appeal.[51] The Court referred in this connection to the fact that the Boards of Appeal formed an integral part of the Office and that the Office did not have the right to appeal against a decision of one of the Boards. In addition, the EGC Rules of Procedure designated the Office as sole defendant.[52] In its subsequent judgment of 30 June 2004 in the *GE Betz* case, the Court specified that there was nothing to prevent the Office from endorsing a head of claim of an applicant or from simply leaving the decision to the discretion of the Court, while putting forward all the arguments that it considered appropriate for giving guidance to the Court.[53] The difference between these two judgments lies in the fact that in *Vedial* the Office asked for the annulment of the decision of the Board of Appeal independently from the applicant. In *GE Betz*, the Office had claimed that the Court should 'grant the applicant's claim for annulment of the contested decision'.[54] The distinction between an admissible claim by which the Office asks the Court to grant the applicant's claim for annulment of the contested decision and an inadmissible claim by which the Office asks the Court to annul the contested decision does not seem convincing. Nevertheless, it is now established case-law that the Office may claim that the form of order sought by the applicant or another party be granted and put forward arguments in support of the pleas in law advanced by that party.[55] The Office cannot be required to defend systematically every contested decision of a Board of Appeal or to claim automatically that every action challenging such a decision should be dismissed.[56] However, it cannot independently seek an order for annulment or alteration of the decision of a Board of Appeal or put forward pleas in law that have not been raised by other parties.[57]

---

[49] See Art. 130(1) of the EGC Rules of Procedure, under which '[s]ubject to the special provisions of this Title the provisions of these Rules of Procedure shall apply to proceedings brought against the Office for Harmonisation in the Internal Market (Trade Marks and Designs) and against the Community Plant Variety Office', and Art. 133(2) of the same Rules, which provides that the application initiating the proceedings is to be served on the Office 'as defendant'. See P. Mengozzi, 'Le contrôle des décisions de l'OHMI par le Tribunal de première instance et la Cour de justice dans le contentieux relatif aux droits de la propriété industrielle' (2002) R.D.U.E. 315–33.

[50] CFI, Case T-63/01 *Procter & Gamble v OHIM* [2002] E.C.R. II-5255, para. 20.

[51] CFI, Case T-110/01 *Vedial v OHIM* [2002] E.C.R. II-5275, paras 16–25.

[52] CFI, Case T-110/01 *Vedial v OHIM*, paras 16–25.

[53] CFI, Case T-107/02 *GE Betz v OHIM* [2004] E.C.R. II-1845, paras 29–37.

[54] CFI, Case T-107/02 *GE Betz v OHIM*, para. 27.

[55] CFI, Joined Cases T-466/04 and T-467/04 *Dami v OHIM* [2006] E.C.R. II-183, paras 27–33; CFI, Case T-191/04 *MIP Metro v OHIM* [2006] E.C.R. II-2855, para. 14.

[56] CFI, Case T-181/05 *Citigroup, and Citibank v OHIM* [2008] E.C.R. II-669, para. 18.

[57] CFI, Case T-379/03 *Peek & Cloppenburg v OHIM* [2005] E.C.R. II-4633, paras 22–29; CFI Case T-22/04 *Reemark v OHIM* [2005] E.C.R. II-1559, paras 16–18; CFI, Case T-137/05 *La Perla v OHIM* [2007] E.C.R. II-47*, Summ. pub., paras 19–20; CFI, Case T-443/05 *El Corte Inglés v OHIM* [2007] E.C.R. II-2579, para. 21. See also ECJ, C-106/03 P *Vedial v OHIM* [2004] E.C.R. I-9573, para. 34. Where the OHIM requests the General Court to dismiss the application, its pleas and arguments should support this request. Where the pleas and arguments of the OHIM seek in reality the annulment of the decision of the

B. The applicant

Art. 65(4) of Regulation No. 207/2009, Art. 73(4) of Regulation No. 2100/94, and Art. 61(4)   **20.11**
of Regulation No. 6/2002 provide that an action may be brought by any party to
proceedings before the Board of Appeal adversely affected by its decision in whole or in
part.[58] The other parties to the proceedings before the Board of Appeal may participate, as
interveners, in the proceedings before the General Court and have the same procedural rights
as the main parties.[59] This means that, unlike 'ordinary' interveners in direct actions,[60] they
can present an autonomous form of order sought and autonomous pleas in law.

An application will be admissible only insofar as the applicant has an interest in annulment.
This means that annulment of the measure of itself must be capable of having legal
consequences.[61] A decision may therefore only be the subject of an application for annulment insofar as it denies the applicant's claims.[62]

A particular issue concerns the transfer of ownership of the contested Community trade
mark in the course of proceedings and the right to act before the General Court. Where the
transfer takes place before the Board of Appeal has adopted a final decision, the transfer has
to be registered at the Office. The new proprietor will then be allowed to act before the
General Court pursuant to Art. 134 of the EGC Rules of Procedure.[63] Where the trade
mark is transferred after the decision of the Board of Appeal but before proceedings were
brought before the Court, the new owners of an earlier trade mark may bring an action
before the Court and should be accepted as a party to the proceedings once they have
proven ownership of the right invoked before the Office.[64] The situation is different when
proceedings have already been brought before the General Court. Neither the Statute nor

---

Board of Appeal, the request to dismiss the application will be inadmissible in the absence of pleas and
arguments in support of the request (CFI, Case T-385/03 *Miles International v OHIM* [2005] E.C.R. II-2665,
paras 11–13).

[58] The identity of parties to proceedings before a Board of Appeal depends on the type of decision against
which an appeal has been brought before the Board. Art. 58 of Regulation No. 40/94 provides that any party
to proceedings adversely affected by a decision may appeal to a Board. Any other parties to the proceedings are
parties to the appeal by operation of law.

[59] EGC Rules of Procedure, Art. 134(1) and (2). See, e.g. CFI, Joined Cases T-160/02 to T-162/02 to
Naipes Heraclio Fournier v OHIM [2005] E.C.R. II-1643, paras 17–18. Under the present EGC Rules of
Procedure, such parties only acquire the status of intervener after lodging their responses to the application. It
may, however, be desirable that they can already intervene in the proceedings before the General Court by
other acts of procedure before they lodge their responses to the application.

[60] Statute, Art. 40. See paras 25.59–25.60.

[61] CFI, Case T-129/00 *Procter & Gamble v OHIM* [2001] E.C.R. II-2793, para. 12.

[62] CFI, Case T-30/00 *Henkel v OHIM* [2001] E.C.R. II-2663, para. 15; CFI, Case T-342/02 *Metro-
Goldwyn-Mayer Lion v OHIM* [2004] E.C.R. II-3191, paras 36–50.

[63] EGC (judgment of 8 March 2012), Case T-298/10 *Arrieta D. Gross v OHIM*, not reported, paras
33–39. Therefore, a person who is according to the applicable provisions of the law of succession of the
Member State referred to in Art. 16(1) of Regulation No. 207/2009 the lawful successor to a deceased
applicant is, pursuant to Art. 134(1) of the EGC Rules of Procedure, allowed to participate as an intervener in
proceedings before the General Court when the original applicant has died before the Board of Appeal adopted
a decision.

[64] EGC, Case T-361/08 *Peek & Cloppenburg and van Graaf v OHIM* [2010] E.C.R. II-1207, para. 31.

the present EGC Rules of Procedure provide for specific rules on the substitution of parties in such cases.[65] In *Canali Ireland,* the General Court stated that the new trade mark holder can take the place of the former holder in the proceedings before it.[66] In case the original trade mark holder agrees to this substitution, the new trade mark holder will be regarded as an intervener within the meaning of Art. 134 of the EGC Rules of Procedure. If the original trade mark holder objects, the new holder can be admitted to the proceedings only as an 'ordinary' intervener pursuant to Art. 40 of the Statute.[67]

IV. Special Characteristics

A. Pleas in law

(1) Parallelism with Art. 263 TFEU

20.12   An action for annulment or alteration brought under Regulation No. 207/2009 (Art. 65(2)), Regulation No. 2100/94 (Art. 73(2)), or Regulation No. 6/2002 (Art. 61(2)) may be brought on grounds of lack of competence,[68] infringement of an essential procedural requirement,[69] infringement of the Treaty, of the relevant regulation, or of any rule of law relating to their application, or misuse of power.[70] These grounds are approximate to the pleas which may be raised in an action for annulment brought under Art. 263 TFEU (see para. 7.145 *et seq.*). Likewise, the Court's case-law on raising pleas of its own motion applies to proceedings brought in the General Court against decisions of the Board of Appeal.

---

[65] EGC (order of 10 October 2011), Case T-369/10 *You-Q v OHIM,* not reported, para. 9.

[66] CFI, Case T-301/03 *Canali Ireland v OHIM* [2005] E.C.R. II-2479, paras 18–20.

[67] CFI (order of 5 March 2004), Case T-94/02 *Hugo Boss v OHIM* [2004] E.C.R. II-813, para. 29.

[68] By virtue of the principle of continuity of functions between the examiners and the Boards of Appeal, the Boards can re-examine the application without limiting themselves to the reasoning of the examiner (CFI, Case T-122/99 *Procter & Gamble v OHIM* [2000] E.C.R. II-265, para. 17; CFI, Case T-198/00 *Hershey Foods v OHIM* [2002] E.C.R. II-2567, para. 25). This case-law may also be applied to relations between the other authorities of the OHIM which can give rulings at first instance, such as the Opposition and Cancellation Divisions, and the Boards of Appeal EGC, Case T-419/09 *Cybergun v OHIM* [2011] E.C.R. II-73*, Summ. pub., paras 13–29; CFI, Case T-308/01 *Henkel v OHIM* [2003] E.C.R. II-3253, para. 25; ECJ (order of 2 March 2011), Case C-349/10 *Claro v OHIM* [2011] E.C.R. II-17*, Summ. pub., para. 44; ECJ, Case C-308/10 P *Union Investment Privatfonds v OHIM* [2011] E.C.R. II-79*, Summ. pub., para. 40. If, in taking his or her decision, the examiner infringes the right to be heard, that defect may be remedied by the Board of Appeal given the continuity that exists in terms of their functions (CFI, Case T-16/02 *Audi v OHIM* [2003] E.C.R. II-5167, paras 80–82). That being said, while the Board of Appeal cannot automatically leave out a particular fact merely because it was raised before it for the first time and not raised before the authority which ruled at first instance, the Board of Appeal cannot be obliged either to admit facts or evidence not submitted in due time. Article 76(2) of Regulation No. 207/2009 grants the OHIM a wide discretion to decide, while giving reasons for its decision in that regard, whether or not to take such information into account (ECJ, Case C-29/05 P *OHIM v Kaul* [2007] I-2213, paras 41–43, setting aside CFI, Case T-164/02 *Kaul v OHIM* [2004] E.C.R. II-38/07, paras 25–30).

[69] ECJ (judgment of 6 September 2012), Case C-96/11 P *August Storck v OHIM,* not reported, paras 85–91; the duty to state reasons is an essential procedural requirement (see, e.g. EGC (judgment of 12 July 2012), Case T-389/11 *Guccio Gucci v OHIM,* not reported, para. 17). It has been laid down in Art. 75 of Regulation No. 207/2009 and has the same scope as that which derives from Art. 296 TFEU (ECJ, Case C-216/10 P *Lufthansa AirPlus Servicekarten v OHIM* [2010] E.C.R. I-157*, Summ. pub., para. 39). See also fn. 71.

[70] EGC, Case T-363/10 *Abbott Laboratories v OHIM* [2011] E.C.R. II-387*, Summ. pub., para. 15; EGC (judgment of 15 March 2012), Case T-172/10 *Colas v OHIM,* not reported, para. 22.

On that account, pleas relating to a lack of competence or the infringement of an essential procedural requirement[71] should be invoked by the General Court *ex officio*, since they concern the external legality of the decisions and are thus of public order. Conversely, substantive defects of decisions of the Board of Appeal cannot be raised by the Court of its own motion and should be raised by the applicant. However, absolute grounds for refusal[72] may always be invoked *ex officio*.[73] The corollary of the General Court's power to invoke certain pleas of its own motion is that parties are allowed to put such pleas forward for the first time before the Court.[74]

(2) Review of the contested decision

The legality of the contested decision falls to be assessed on the basis of the elements of fact **20.13** and of law existing at the time when that decision was adopted.[75] Since decisions concerning the registration of a sign as a Community trade mark which the Boards of Appeal of the OHIM take under Regulation No. 207/2009 are adopted in the exercise of circumscribed powers, that assessment must be made solely on the basis of that regulation as interpreted by the Union judicature, and not on the basis of a previous decision-making practice by the Boards of Appeal[76] or the OHIM Guidelines.[77]

(3) Pleas must relate to a decision of a Board of Appeal

Since by virtue of Art. 65(1) of Regulation No. 207/2009, actions may be brought before **20.14** the Union courts only against decisions of the Boards of Appeal, only pleas directed against the decision of the Board of Appeal itself are admissible. As a result, pleas relating to a decision of the Opposition Division will be inadmissible.[78]

---

[71] Infringement of the requirement to state reasons is a matter of public policy and must be raised by the Court of its own motion (ECJ (order of 7 December 2011), Case C-45/11 P *Deutsche Bahn v OHIM*, not reported, para. 57; CFI, Case T-129/00 *Procter & Gamble v OHIM* [2001] E.C.R. II-2793, para. 72). The Board of Appeal will infringe an essential procedural requirement if it applies absolute grounds of refusal of its own motion without according the applicant an opportunity to express its view thereon (CFI, Case T-122/99 *Procter & Gamble v OHIM* [2000] E.C.R. II-265, para. 47; CFI, Case T-34/00 *Eurocool Logistik v OHIM* [2002] E.C.R. II-683, para. 22; CFI, Case T-79/00 *Rewe-Zentral v OHIM* [2002] E.C.R. II-705, paras 16–19; CFI, Case T-289/02 *Telepharmacy Solutions v OHIM* [2004] E.C.R I-2851, paras 22–30). It should be pointed out, however, that mere procedural defects that have no impact on the final decision will not lead to the annulment of the decision of the Board of Appeal (ECJ, Case C-405/06 P *Miguel Torres v OHIM* [2007] E.C.R. I-115*, Summ. pub., para. 29). A violation of the rules governing the language of proceedings will lead to the annulment of the decision of the Board of Appeal only if the procedural irregularities violated the applicant's rights of the defence (CFI, Case T-242/02 *Sunrider v OHIM* [2005] E.C.R. II-2793, paras 39–45; see also ECJ (judgment of 12 May 2012), Case C-100/11 P *Helena Rubinstein and L'Oréal v OHIM*, not reported, paras 100–105) and EGC (judgment of 12 July 2012), Case T-346/09 *Winzer Pharma v OHIM*, not reported, paras 21–40.

[72] Regulation No. 207/2009, Art. 7.

[73] Regulation No. 207/2009, Art. 76.

[74] CFI, Case T-6/05 *DEF-TEC Defense Technology v OHIM* [2006] E.C.R. II-2671, paras 21–24.

[75] CFI, Case T-247/01 *eCopy v OHIM* [2002] E.C.R. II-5301, para. 46.

[76] ECJ, Case C-412/05 P *Alcon v OHIM* [2007] E.C.R. I-3569, para. 65; ECJ, Case C-243/07 P *Brinkmann v OHIM* [2008] E.C.R. I-29*, Summ. pub., para. 39.

[77] ECJ (judgment of 19 January 2012), Case C-53/11 P *OHIM v Nike International*, not reported, para. 57.

[78] CFI, Case T-303/03 *Lidl Stiftung v OHIM* [2005] E.C.R. II-1917, paras 59–60; EGC, Case T-137/09 *Nike International v OHIM* [2010] E.C.R. II-5433, para. 13.

(4) Pleas must not change the subject-matter of the proceedings

20.15   Art. 135(4) of the EGC Rules of Procedure provides that the parties' pleadings may not change the subject-matter of the proceedings before the Board of Appeal.[79] On that ground, claims not put forward by a party before the Board of Appeal, but in its application (or at a later stage) in the proceedings before the General Court will be inadmissible.[80] Consequently, the review by the General Court must not exceed the factual and legal context of the dispute as it was brought before the Office.[81] In accordance with Art. 65 of Regulation No. 207/2009, it will only assess the legality of the contested measure on the basis of the elements of fact and law existing at the time the measure was adopted.[82]

Therefore, arguments raised for the first time before the General Court will be inadmissible where their assessment (such as the assessment of the reputation of an older mark) would be based on factual data not adduced in the course of the proceedings before the Office,[83] or when the Office was not required to raise those arguments of its own motion.[84]

Similarly, facts raised for the first time before the General Court cannot affect the legality of the Office's decision, unless the Office should have taken them into account of its own motion.[85] It must be stressed in this connection that in proceedings concerning relative

---

[79] Case C-534/10 P *Brookfield New Zealand and Elaris v CPVO and Schniga*, not reported; EGC, Case T-135/08 *Schniga v CPVO* [2010] E.C.R. II-5089, para. 34 (appeal dismissed: ECJ judgment of 19 December 2012); CFI, Case T-373/03 *Solo Italia v OHIM* [2005] E.C.R. II-1881, paras 25–26; CFI, Case T-360/03 *Frischpack v OHIM* [2004] E.C.R. II-4097, paras 30–35; EGC, Case T-53/10 *Reisenthel v OHIM* [2011] E.C.R. II-7287, para. 21; EGC (judgment of 28 June 2012), Case T-134/09 *Basile and I Marchi Italiani v OHIM*, not reported, para. 15.

[80] CFI, Case T-24/00 *Sunrider v OHIM* [2001] E.C.R. II-449, para. 13; CFI, Case T-423/04 *Bunker & BKR v OHIM* [2005] E.C.R. II-4035, paras 17–22; EGC, Case T-53/10 *Reisenthel v OHIM* [2011] E.C.R. II-7287, paras 24–26. But it should be noted that the party bringing an appeal before a Board of Appeal has to determine only the subject-matter and not the extent of the examination which the Board of Appeal must conduct. The extent of the examination which the Board of Appeal must conduct is not determined by the grounds relied on by the party who has brought the appeal. Even if the party who has brought the appeal has not raised a specific ground of appeal, the Board of Appeal is nonetheless bound to examine whether or not, in the light of all the relevant matters of fact and of law, a new decision with the same operative part as the decision under appeal may be lawfully adopted at the time of the appeal ruling (CFI, Case T-308/01 *Henkel v OHIM* [2003] E.C.R. II-3253, paras 29–30 and 34).

[81] CFI, Case T-194/01 *Unilever v OHIM* [2003] E.C.R. II-383, para. 16; CFI, Case T-66/03 *Koffiebranderij en Theehandel 'Drie Mollen sinds 1818' v OHIM* [2004] E.C.R. II-1765, paras 40–49.

[82] EGC (judgment of 27 June 2013), Case T-367/12 *MOL v OHIM*, not reported, para. 22. This also means that the Court cannot take into account documents the Board of Appeal should not have examined: EGC, Case T-53/10 *Reisenthel v OHIM* [2011] E.C.R. II-7287, paras 52–56.

[83] CFI, Case T-66/03 *Koffiebranderij en Theehandel 'Drie Mollen sinds 1818' v OHIM* [2004] E.C.R. II-1765, para. 46; CFI, Case T-57/03 *SPAG v OHIM* [2005] E.C.R. II-287, paras 30–32: an argument concerning the reputation of an older mark which is raised for the first time before the General Court will be inadmissible. In contrast, the assessment of the intrinsically distinctive character does not presuppose any matter of fact which is up to the parties to establish. Accordingly, an argument in that regard raised for the first time in the General Court will be admissible. Similarly, arguments that consist of a mere amplification of arguments raised before the Board of Appeal will also be admissible: ECJ, Case C-412/05 P *Alcon v OHIM* [2007] E.C.R. I-3569, para. 40; EGC (judgment of 28 June 2012), Case T-134/09 *Basile and I Marchi Italiani v OHIM*, not reported, para. 16.

[84] CFI, Case T-189/05 *Unisor v OHIM* [2008] E.C.R II-22*, Summ. pub., para. 20; CFI, Case T-6/05 *DEF-TEC Defense Technology v OHIM* [2006] E.C.R. II-2671, paras 21–24. See also para. 20.08.

[85] CFI, Case T-396/02 *Storck v OHIM* [2004] E.C.R. II-3821, para. 24 (it is not the function of the General Court to re-examine the facts in the light of documents submitted for the first time before it), confirmed on appeal by ECJ, Case C-24/05 P *Storck v OHIM* [2006] E.C.R. I-5677, paras 45–50; CFI, Case T-185/02 *Ruiz-Picasso and Others v OHIM* [2004] E.C.R. II-1739, paras 27–32; CFI, Case T-115/03 *Samar*

grounds for refusal, the Office is not obliged to review facts of its own motion. This is because Art. 76 of Regulation No. 207/2009 confines review by the Office as regards relative grounds for refusal to the facts, evidence, and arguments adduced by the parties.[86] However, since that rule constitutes a restriction to the general rule that the Office examines the facts *ex officio*, it should be interpreted restrictively.[87] Therefore, the Board of Appeal is allowed to take well-known facts into account. These are facts which are likely to be known by anyone or which may be learned from generally accessible sources.[88] The Court has clarified this exception by stating that the restriction laid down in Art. 76 of Regulation No. 207/2009 cannot have as its purpose to compel the Office to adopt a decision based on facts that are manifestly incomplete or contrary to reality.[89] However, the Office is not obliged to establish the accuracy of well-known facts.[90] Conversely, parties are allowed to challenge the accuracy of those well-known facts before the General Court, even when they have not put them forward in proceedings before the Office.[91] Thus, in *LG Electronics*, the Court of Justice held that a party could submit documents for the first time before the General Court, challenging the accuracy of the well-known fact established by the Board of Appeal that hoovers can be used as compressors in a certain configuration.[92]

Since it is not the Court's function to re-examine the facts in the light of documents produced for the first time before it, evidence sought to be adduced for the first time before the General Court will also be inadmissible,[93] independently of whether it was adduced in support of admissible facts and arguments[94] or merely to substantiate arguments submitted before the Board of Appeal.[95] The Court has thus held that annexes containing extracts of archived internet pages were inadmissible, even though they showed how those pages

---

v OHIM [2004] E.C.R. II-2939, paras 13–15; EGC, Case T-97/08 *KUKA Roboter v OHIM* [2010] E.C.R. II-5059, para. 11; EGC, Case T-207/08 *Habanos v OHIM* [2011] E.C.R. II-140*, Summ. pub., para. 18; EGC (judgment of 15 January 2012), Case T-332/10 *Viaguara v OHIM*, not reported, para. 15.

[86] CFI, Case T-115/03 *Samar v OHIM* [2004] E.C.R. II-2939, paras 13–15; CFI, Case T-185/02 *Ruiz-Picasso and Others v OHIM* [2004] E.C.R. II-1739, paras 27–32; CFI, Case T-396/02 *Storck v OHIM* [2004] E.C.R. II-3821, para. 24; CFI, Case T-57/03 *SPAG v OHIM* [2005] E.C.R. II-287, paras 17–35 (extensive survey of the applicable case-law).

[87] CFI, Case T-185/02 *Ruiz-Picasso and Others v OHIM* [2004] E.C.R. II-1739, para. 30.

[88] CFI, Case T-185/02 *Ruiz-Picasso and Others v OHIM*, para. 29.

[89] CFI, Case T-185/02 *Ruiz-Picasso and Others v OHIM*, para. 32.

[90] ECJ, Case C-88/11 P *LG Electronics v OHIM* [2011] E.C.R. I-171*, Summ. pub., para. 27.

[91] ECJ, Case C-88/11 P *LG Electronics v OHIM*, para. 29; ECJ, Case C-25/05 P *August Storck KG v OHIM* [2006] I-5719, para. 52; EGC (judgment of 9 March 2012), Case T-172/10 *Colas v OHIM*, not reported, para. 27; EGC (judgment of 20 June 2012), Case T-357/10 *Kraft Foods Schweiz Holding GmbH v OHIM*, not reported, para. 16; EGC (judgment of 12 July 2012), Case T-361/11 *Hand Held Products v OHIM*, not reported, paras 25–26.

[92] ECJ, Case C-88/11 P *LG Electronics v OHIM*, paras 31–32.

[93] EGC, Case T-307/09 *Earle Beauty v OHIM* [2010] E.C.R. II-266*, Summ. pub., para. 12; EGC, Case T-112/09 *Icebreaker v OHIM* [2010] E.C.R. II-172*, Summ. pub., para. 15; EGC, Case T-106/09 adp *Gauselmann v OHIM* [2010] E.C.R. II-182*, Summ. pub., para. 16; EGC, Case T-458/08 *Wilfer v OHIM* [2010] E.C.R. II-168*, Summ. pub., para. 10; EGC, Case T-463/08 *Imagion v OHIM* [2011] E.C.R. II-206*, Summ. pub., para. 10; EGC, Case T-28/10 *Euro-Information v OHIM* [2011] E.C.R. II-1535, paras 17–18; EGC, Case T-10/09 *Formula One Licensing v OHIM* [2011] E.C.R. II-427, paras 18–19; EGC (judgment of 28 June 2012), Case T-134/09 *Basile and I Marchi Italiani v OHIM*, not reported, para. 18.

[94] CFI, Case T-296/02 *Lidl Stiftung v OHIM* [2005] E.C.R. II-563, paras 36–38.

[95] EGC, Case T-358/09 *Sociedad Agricola Requingua v OHIM* [2011] E.C.R. II-105*, Summ. pub., paras 14–17.

appeared at the time of proceedings before the Office.[96] Also, documents submitted in support of answers to questions asked by the Court were inadmissible.[97] In a similar vein, the Court declared inadmissible a document containing the international registration of a mark,[98] a decision of a national patent office,[99] extracts from national registers,[100] and witness statements.[101] However, depending on the circumstances of a case, documents produced for the first time before the Court may not be declared inadmissible if they do not change the subject-matter of the proceedings before the Board of Appeal.[102] Further to this, parties are allowed to refer to national judicial decisions for the first time before the General Court where the plea is not that the Board of Appeal failed to take the factual aspects of a specific national judgment into account. This is because neither the parties nor the General Court are precluded from relying on national or international case-law to interpret Union law.[103]

As far as the inadmissibility of new facts, evidence, and arguments is concerned, the same rules apply for the applicant, the Office, and the interveners participating in the proceedings before the Court pursuant to Art. 134 of the EGC Rules of Procedure. The principle of equality of arms requires that all parties before the General Court have the same means at their disposal.[104]

(5) Change of the subject-matter of the proceedings

20.16 According to Art. 43(1) of Regulation No. 207/2009, an applicant may at any time withdraw his Community trade mark application or restrict the lists of goods or services contained therein. A withdrawal or a restriction subsequent to the start of the proceedings might be taken into account by the Court when it does not change the subject-matter of the proceedings. A mere withdrawal of categories of goods or services from the list in respect of which the trade mark application is filed is in principle not capable of changing the factual context of the examination carried out by the Board of Appeal.[105] Such type of restriction will be considered as a request for partial annulment of the decision of the Board of Appeal

---

[96] CFI, Case T-409/07 *Cohausz v OHIM* [2009] E.C.R. II-173*, Summ. pub., para. 19. The General Court has consistently declared documents containing extracts of websites inadmissible if submitted for the first time before it (see, e.g. CFI, Case T-335/07 *Mergel and Others v OHIM* [2008] E.C.R. II-324*, Summ. pub., para. 9; CFI, Case T-391/07 *Alber v OHIM* [2009] E.C.R. II-157*, Summ. pub., paras 10–11; EGC, Case T-502/07 *IIC v OHIM* [2011] E.C.R. II-138*, Summ. pub., para. 18), even when it concerned extracts from the OHIM website (EGC, Case T-9/07 *Grupo Promer Mon Graphic v OHIM* [2010] E.C.R. II-981, paras 22–25).

[97] EGC, Case T-344/07 *O2 (Germany) v OHIM* [2010] E.C.R II-153, para. 11.

[98] EGC, Case T-502/07 *IIC v OHIM* [2011] E.C.R. II-138*, Summ. pub., para. 19.

[99] EGC, Case T-269/06 *Rautaruukki v OHIM* [2008] E.C.R. II-273*, Summ. pub., paras 19–23.

[100] EGC, Joined Cases T-303/06 and T-337/06 *UniCredito Italiano v OHIM* [2010] E.C.R. II-62*, Summ. pub., para. 21.

[101] EGC, Case T-187/08 *Rodd & Gunn Australia v OHIM* [2010] E.C.R. II-58*, Summ. pub., paras 22–24.

[102] EGC, Case T-187/08 *Rodd & Gunn Australia v OHIM* [2010] E.C.R. II-58*, Summ. pub., para. 24.

[103] CFI, Case T-29/04 *Castellblanch v OHIM* [2005] E.C.R. II-5309, para. 16; CFI, Case T-277/04 *Vitakraft-Werke Wührmann & Sohn v OHIM* [2006] E.C.R. II-2211, para. 71; CFI, Case T-270/06 *Lego Juris v OHIM* [2008] E.C.R. II-3117, paras 24–25; EGC, (judgment of 1 February 2012), Case T-291/09 *Carrols v OHIM*, not reported, paras 33–36.

[104] CFI, Case T-57/03 *SPAG v OHIM* [2005] E.C.R. II-287, para. 23.

[105] CFI, Case T-325/04 *Citigroup v OHIM* [2008] E.C.R. II-29*, Summ. pub., para. 26; CFI, Joined Cases T-387/06 to T-390/06 *Inter-Ikea Systems BV v OHIM* [2008] E.C.R. II-121*, Summ. pub., para. 25; EGC, Case T-386/08 *Trautwein v OHIM* [2010] E.C.R. II-139*, Summ. pub., para. 12.

and taken into account by the General Court.[106] Conversely, a restriction will in principle not be allowed when it leads to the introduction of new elements not taken into account during the Board of Appeal's examination of the trade mark application. For instance, this is the case when the object of the restriction is to change the description or characteristics of goods included in the application in such a way that it influences the assessment of the similarity of goods or the determination of the target audience.[107] Such restriction would change the factual context presented before the Board of Appeal and cannot be taken into account by the General Court.

(6) Objection of illegality

When seeking the annulment or alteration of a decision of the Office, a party may raise an objection of illegality notwithstanding the fact that Regulation No. 207/2009 does not expressly mention such a plea as a collateral legal remedy that persons bringing actions may use before the General Court.[108]   **20.17**

B. Time limits

An action has to be brought within two months of the date of notification of the decision of the Board of Appeal.[109]   **20.18**

C. Content of the application

According to Art. 44(1)(c) of the EGC Rules of Procedure, an application shall state the subject-matter of the proceedings and a summary of the pleas in law on which the application is based.[110] That summary must be sufficiently clear and precise as to enable the Court to rule on the action without any other supporting information.[111] Although specific points in the text of the application may be supported and supplemented by references to specific passages in attached documents, a general reference to other documents, even those annexed to the application, cannot compensate for the lack of sufficiently detailed legal arguments in the application.[112] Consequently, arguments based on a general   **20.19**

---

[106] CFI, Case T-458/05 *Tegometall International v OHIM* [2007] II-4721, para. 24; CFI, Case T-464/07 *Korsch v OHIM* [2009] E.C.R. II-85*, Summ. pub., paras 12–13.

[107] CFI, Case T-458/05 *Tegometall International v OHIM* [2007] E.C.R. II-4721, para. 25; CFI, Case T-48/06 *Astex Therapeutics v OHIM* [2008] E.C.R. II-161*, Summ. pub., para. 21; CFI, Case T-325/04 *Citigroup v OHIM* [2008] E.C.R. II-29*, Summ. pub., para. 27; CFI, Case T-304/06 *Reber v OHIM* [2008] E.C.R. II-1927, para. 29; EGC, Case T-118/08 *Actega Terra v OHIM* [2010] E.C.R. II-110*, Summ. pub., paras 12–13; EGC, Case T-412/08 *Trubion Pharmaceuticals v OHIM* [2009] E.C.R. II-239*, Summ. pub., paras 19–25.

[108] CFI, Case T-120/99 *Kik v OHIM* [2001] E.C.R. II-2235, para. 21.

[109] Art. 65(5) of Regulation No. 207/2009, Art. 73(5) of Regulation No. 2100/94, and Art. 61(5) of Regulation No. 6/2002.

[110] EGC, Case T-323/10 *Chabou v OHIM* [2011] E.C.R. II-410* Summ. pub., paras 13–20.

[111] EGC, Case T-460/07 *Nokia v OHIM* [2010] E.C.R. II-89, para. 26.

[112] EGC, Case T-85/08 *Exalation v OHIM* [2010] E.C.R. II-3837, para. 34; EGC, Case T-303/08 *Tresplain Investments v OHIM* [2010] E.C.R. II-5659, para. 38.

reference to the case-file before the Board of Appeal, whether or not annexed to the application, will be declared inadmissible.[113] The Court cannot be expected to identify the relevant facts and legal arguments in the file.[114]

V. Consequences

(1) Successful action

20.20 If the General Court upholds the claim, it may annul or alter the decision of the Board of Appeal. Annulment has the same characteristics as a declaration of nullity made pursuant to Art. 263 TFEU. If the Court alters the Board's decision, the Court's decision replaces that of the Board. In either case, the Office is required to take the necessary steps to comply with the Court's judgment.[115] The General Court is not entitled to issue directions to the Office in relation thereto,[116] although the Office is obliged to draw the necessary conclusions from the operative part and the grounds of the judgment.[117] However, the Court does consider that it is competent to remit the case back to the examiner.[118] The reason for this is that, by remitting the case to the examiner, the Court would not be imposing on the Office any obligation to take action or refrain from doing so and would not therefore be issuing directions to the Office.[119]

(2) Action dismissed

20.21 If the appeal is dismissed,[120] the Board's decision stands.

(3) Appeal

20.22 An appeal will lie against the decision of the General Court to the Court of Justice (see Ch. 16).[121]

---

[113] EGC (judgment of 13 September 2012), Case T-72/11 *Sogepi Consulting y Publicidad v OHIM*, not reported, para. 18.

[114] EGC, Case T-303/08 *Tresplain Investments v OHIM* [2010] E.C.R. II-5659, para. 38.

[115] Art. 65(6) of Regulation No. 207/2009, Art. 73(6) of Regulation No. 2100/94, and Art. 61(6) of Regulation No. 6/2002.

[116] CFI, Case T-247/01 *eCopy v OHIM* [2002] E.C.R. II-5301, para. 13; CFI, Case T-39/01 *Kabushiki Kaisha Fernandes v OHIM* [2002] E.C.R. II-5233, para. 18; CFI, Case T-216/02 *Fieldturf v OHIM* [2004] E.C.R. II-1023, para. 15. See also para 20.06.

[117] CFI, Case T-163/98 *Procter & Gamble v OHIM* [1999] E.C.R. II-2383, para. 53; CFI, Case T-331/99 *Mitsubishi HiTec Paper Bielefeld v OHIM* [2001] E.C.R. II-433, para. 33; CFI, Case T-359/99 *DKV v OHIM* [2001] E.C.R. II-1645; CFI, Case T-123/04 *Cargo Partner v OHIM* [2005] E.C.R. II-3979, para. 32.

[118] CFI, Case T-106/00 *Streamserve v OHIM* [2002] E.C.R. II-723, paras 17–19. In the case in question, the Court considered that the applicant's interests were sufficiently secured by annulment of the contested decision.

[119] The Court refers in this connection to the fact that remission of the case to the examiner may be ordered by the Board of Appeal under Art. 64(1) of Regulation No. 207/2009. It therefore falls within the measures which may be taken by the General Court in the exercise of its power to amend decisions, as provided for in Art. 65(3) of Regulation No. 207/2009 (CFI, Case T-106/00 *Streamserve v OHIM* [2002] E.C.R. II-723, para. 19).

[120] The General Court may declare in a reasoned order that an application is manifestly inadmissible (see CFI (order of 8 December 1999), Case T-79/99 *Euro-Lex v OHIM* [1999] E.C.R. II-3555) or manifestly lacks any foundation in law (CFI (order of 17 November 2003), Case T-235/02 *Strongline v OHIM* [2003] E.C.R. II-4903; CFI (order of 10 December 2004), Case T-261/03 *Euro Style 94 v OHIM*, not reported).

[121] See K. Lenaerts, 'De hogere voorziening voor het Hof van Justitie in merkzaken', in B. Dauwe, E. De Gryse, B. De Gryse, B. Maes, and K. Van Lint (eds), *Liber Amicorum Ludovic De Gryse* (Brussel, Larcier, 2010) 195–208.

21

JURISDICTION OF THE COURT OF JUSTICE UNDER CONVENTIONS CONCLUDED BY THE MEMBER STATES

I. Subject-Matter

A. General

Formerly, both the EC Treaty and the EU Treaty expressly empowered the Member States **21.01** to conclude agreements with each other in certain areas. In the resulting conventions or in protocols annexed thereto, additional jurisdiction was often conferred on the Court of Justice.[1] That jurisdiction generally involved a special power to give preliminary rulings not based on what is now Art. 267 TFEU. In addition, conventions which the Member States

---

[1] The following conventions and protocols are involved:

1. Agreement establishing an Association between the EEC and Turkey, Art. 25 (O.J. 3687/64; English text published in [1973] O.J. C113/1).
2. Protocol of 3 June 1971 on the interpretation by the Court of Justice of the Brussels Convention of 27 September 1968 on jurisdiction and the enforcement of judgments in civil and commercial matters (consolidated version in [1998] O.J. C27/1).
3. First Protocol of 19 December 1988 on the interpretation by the Court of Justice of the European Communities of the Convention on the law applicable to contractual obligations (consolidated version in [1998] O.J. C27/47).
4. Second Protocol of 19 December 1988 on the interpretation by the Court of Justice of the European Communities of the Convention on the law applicable to contractual obligations (consolidated version in [1998] O.J. C27/52).
5. Agreement on the European Economic Area–Protocol 34 on the possibility for courts and tribunals of EFTA States to request the Court of Justice of the European Communities to decide on the interpretation of EEA rules corresponding to EC rules ([1994] O.J. L1/204).
6. Convention defining the Statute of the European Schools, Art. 26 ([1994] O.J. L212/3).
7. Council Act of 24 July 1996 drawing up the Protocol on the interpretation, by way of preliminary rulings, by the Court of Justice of the European Communities of the Convention on the establishment of a European Police Office ([1996] O.J. C299/1).
8. Council Act of 27 September 1996 drawing up a Protocol to the Convention on the protection of the European Communities' financial interests, Art. 8 ([1996] O.J. C313/1).
9. Council Act of 29 November 1996 drawing up the First Protocol on the interpretation, by way of preliminary rulings, by the Court of Justice of the European Communities of the Convention on the protection of the European Communities' financial interests ([1997] O.J. C151/1).
10. Council Act of 29 November 1996 drawing up the Protocol on the interpretation, by way of preliminary rulings, by the Court of Justice of the European Communities of the Convention on the use of information technology for customs purposes ([1997] O.J. C151/15).

concluded in the area of cooperation in the field of justice and home affairs (i.e. the original 'third pillar' of the Union) often provided for a direct action which may be brought before the Court of Justice in order to resolve disputes relating to the application or interpretation of the relevant convention which arise as between Member States or one or more Member States and the Commission.

With the entry into force of the Lisbon Treaty, the pillar structure has been eliminated and the provisions of the former Title VI of the EU Treaty concerning Police and Judicial Cooperation in Criminal Matters (PJCCM), or the so-called third pillar, have been reformulated and consolidated in Title V of Part Three of the TFEU on the Area of Freedom, Security and Justice (see Ch. 22). Moreover, by virtue of the changes brought by this Treaty, Art. 293 EC has been repealed, and the instrument of the convention in the former third pillar (under former Art. 34(2)(d) EU) has been eliminated. Nevertheless, to the extent that such conventions have not been superseded by Union instruments (see para. 21.02), the special features of the jurisdiction of the Court of Justice under the conventions

---

11. Council Act of 26 May 1997 drawing up the Convention on the fight against corruption involving officials of the European Communities or officials of Member States of the European Union, Art. 12 ([1997] O.J. C195/1).
12. Council Act of 26 May 1997 drawing up the Protocol on the interpretation, by the Court of Justice of the European Communities, of the Convention on the service in the Member States of the European Union of judicial and extrajudicial documents in civil or commercial matters ([1997] O.J. C261/17).
13. Council Act of 19 June 1997 drawing up the Second Protocol on the interpretation, by way of preliminary rulings, by the Court of Justice of the European Communities of the Convention on the protection of the European Communities' financial interests, Arts 13–15 ([1997] O.J. C221/11).
14. Council Act of 18 December 1997 drawing up the Convention on mutual assistance and cooperation between customs administrations, Art. 26 ([1998] O.J. C24/1).
15. Council Act of 17 June 1998 drawing up the Convention on Driving Disqualifications, Art. 14 ([1998] O.J. C216/1).
16. Council Act of 28 May 1998 drawing up the Protocol on the interpretation by the Court of Justice of the European Communities of the Convention on jurisdiction and the recognition and enforcement of judgments in matrimonial matters ([1998] O.J. C221/19).
17. Internal agreement between the representatives of the governments of the Member States, meeting within the Council, on measures to be taken and procedures to be followed for the implementation of the ACP-EC Partnership Agreement, Art. 6 ([2000] O.J. L317/376).
18. Agreement between the Federal Republic of Germany and the Republic of Austria for the avoidance of double taxation in the sphere of income and wealth tax, Art. 25 (Deutscher Bundestag–14. Wahlperiode–Drucksache 14/7040, p. 7).
19. Agreement between the European Community and the Swiss Confederation on Air Transport, Art. 20 ([2002] O.J. L114/73). See ECJ (order of 14 July 2005), Case C-70/04 *Swiss Confederation v Commission*, not reported, on the question as to whether an action for annulment should be brought before the Court of Justice or the then Court of First Instance. Upon referral to the General Court, the action was dismissed: EGC, Case T-319/05 *Swiss Confederation v Commission* [2010] E.C.R. II-4265. The action before the Court of Justice was also dismissed on the substance without entering into questions of jurisdiction: ECJ (judgment of 7 March 2013), Case C-547/10 P *Swiss Confederation v Commission*, not reported.
20. Monetary Agreement between the Government of the French Republic, on behalf of the European Community, and the Government of His Serene Highness the Prince of Monaco, Art. 13 ([2002] O.J. L142/59) (repealed by the Monetary Agreement between the European Union and the Principality of Monaco, [2012] O.J. C310/1).
21. Agreement between the European Community and the Kingdom of Denmark on jurisdiction and the recognition and enforcement of judgments in civil and commercial matters, Art. 6 ([2005] O.J. L299/62).
22. Agreement between the European Community and the Kingdom of Denmark on the service of judicial and extrajudicial documents in civil or commercial matters, Art. 7 ([2005] O.J. L300/55).

concluded by the Member States (and the Union as the case may be) that are still in force remain relevant.

However, since the entry into force of the Lisbon Treaty, conventions concluded between Member States conferring jurisdiction on the Court of Justice do so, in the absence of any other provision in the Treaties, on the basis of Art. 273 TFEU (see Ch. 19).[2]

B. What conventions are involved?

(1) The Brussels Convention

Former Art. 293 EC (now repealed with the entry into force of the Lisbon Treaty) required **21.02** Member States, as far as is necessary, to enter into negotiations with each other with a view to removing barriers in certain areas related to the sound functioning of what was then the common (now internal) market. It was pursuant to that provision that the Convention of 27 September 1968 on jurisdiction and the enforcement of judgments in civil and commercial matters came about ('the Brussels Convention').[3] Since the Brussels Convention contributed towards the attainment of the internal market, it was essential that, just like Union law in the ordinary sense,[4] it was applied uniformly in the Member States. To that end, the Protocol of 3 June 1971 conferred on the Court of Justice jurisdiction to interpret the Brussels Convention by preliminary ruling at the request of certain national courts.[5]

In the meantime, the Council adopted Regulation (EC) No. 44/2001 of 22 December 2000 on jurisdiction and the recognition and enforcement of judgments in civil and commercial

---

[2] Art. 37 of the Treaty establishing the European Stability Mechanism concluded on 2 February 2012 between the Eurogroup Member States as well as Art. 8 of the Treaty on Stability, Coordination and Governance in the Economic and Monetary Union of 2 March 2012, concluded between 25 Member States, confer jurisdiction on the Court of Justice on the basis of Art. 273 TFEU. See for another example, Art. 12 of the Monetary Agreement between the European Union and the Principality of Monaco, [2012] O.J. C310/1.

[3] On 16 September 1988, the Member States of the Community concluded with the member countries of the European Free Trade Association (EFTA) the Lugano Convention on jurisdiction and the enforcement of judgments in civil and commercial matters, which contains rules on jurisdiction and enforcement similar to those of the Brussels Convention ([1988] O.J. L319/9). The Court of Justice had no power to interpret that convention. Yet, the Contracting Parties did sign a Protocol setting up an information-exchange system providing for the centralization of judgments of the Court of Justice and courts of last instance in the Contracting Parties with a view to uniform interpretation. That convention has now been replaced by the 'new' Lugano Convention ([2007] O.J. L339/3; corrigenda in [2009] O.J. L147/44). The information-exchange system has been retained (see <http://curia.europa.eu>). As is well known, this latter convention was the subject of an Opinion of the Court of Justice under now Art. 218(11) TFEU: see ECJ, Opinion 1/03 *New Lugano Convention* [2006] E.C.R. I-1145.

[4] The Court of Justice observed that the Brussels Convention was concluded on the basis of the fourth indent of former Art. 293 EC, whose purpose was to facilitate the working of the common (now internal) market through the adoption of rules of jurisdiction and through the elimination, as far as possible, of difficulties concerning the enforcement of judgments in the territory of the Contracting States. It is for these reasons that the provisions of the Brussels Convention and also the national provisions to which the Convention refers were linked to the former EC Treaty: ECJ, Case C-398/92 *Mund & Fester* [1994] E.C.R. I-467, paras 11–12.

[5] Protocol on the interpretation by the Court of Justice of the Convention of 27 September 1968 on jurisdiction and the enforcement of judgments in civil and commercial matters, which entered into force on 1 September 1975. The original protocol has been adjusted each time new Member States have acceded to the Union (a consolidated version of the Brussels Convention and the Protocol is to be found in [1998] O.J. C27/1, which lists the publication references of the successive official versions of the Convention and the Protocol).

matters (the 'Brussels I' Regulation).[6] This Regulation was based on former Art. 61(c) and Art. 67(1) EC. As a result, the jurisdiction of the Court of Justice to give preliminary rulings was based on Art. 68(1) EC (and no longer on the Protocol); with the entry into force of the Lisbon Treaty, however, this provision was repealed and the Court of Justice's preliminary ruling jurisdiction is no longer subject to the restrictions placed on it thereunder.[7]

The Brussels I Regulation entered into force on 1 March 2002.[8] Under Art. 68 of this Regulation, as between the Member States, the Regulation supersedes the Brussels Convention, except as regards the territories of the Member States which fall within the territorial scope of that Convention and which are excluded from the Regulation pursuant to Art. 355 TFEU. Initially, the Brussels I Regulation did not apply to relations between Denmark and the other Member States, to which the Brussels Convention and the Protocol continued to apply. However, with the entry into force on 1 July 2007[9] of the Agreement between the European Community and the Kingdom of Denmark on jurisdiction and the recognition and enforcement of judgments in civil and commercial matters,[10] the Brussels I Regulation applies to Denmark as well.[11]

From 10 January 2015 onwards, Regulation (EC) No. 44/2001 will be replaced by Regulation (EU) No. 1215/2012 of the European Parliament and of the Council of 12 December 2012 on jurisdiction and the recognition and enforcement of judgments in civil and commercial matters.[12] Regulation (EU) No. 1215/2012 will not apply to relations between Denmark and the other Member States. However, it has the possibility of applying the amendments to Regulation (EC) No. 44/2001 pursuant to Article 3 of the Agreement on jurisdiction and the recognition and enforcement of judgments in civil and commercial matters.

(2) The Rome Convention

21.03 Furthermore, the Member States concluded the Convention of 19 June 1980 on the law applicable to contractual obligations ('the Rome Convention'), even though this subject was not specifically mentioned in former Art. 293 EC. Yet it did link up with the aims underlying that provision. It was probably for that reason that the First Protocol of 19 December 1988[13] conferred on the Court of Justice jurisdiction to interpret the Rome Convention by preliminary ruling at the request of certain national courts.[14]

---

[6] [2001] O.J. L12/1; *corrigendum* in [2001] O.J. L307/38.

[7] See para 22.05.

[8] Brussels I Regulation, cited in n. 6, Art. 76.

[9] Information concerning the date of entry into force of the Agreement between the European Community and the Kingdom of Denmark on jurisdiction and the recognition and enforcement of judgments in civil and commercial matters, [2007] O.J. L94/70.

[10] Agreement between the European Community and the Kingdom of Denmark on jurisdiction and the recognition and enforcement of judgments in civil and commercial matters, [2005] O.J. L299/62; Council Decision 2006/325/EC of 27 April 2006 concerning the conclusion of the Agreement between the European Community and the Kingdom of Denmark on jurisdiction and the recognition and enforcement of judgments in civil and commercial matters, [2006] O.J. L120/22.

[11] Albeit in a slightly different version: see Art. 2 of the Agreement between the European Community and the Kingdom of Denmark on jurisdiction and the recognition and enforcement of judgments in civil and commercial matters.

[12] [2012] O.J. L351/1.

[13] The First Protocol entered into effect on 1 August 2004. For a consolidated version of the Rome Convention and the First Protocol (incorporating all changes consequential upon the accession of new Member States), see [1998] O.J. C27/34.

[14] ECJ, Case C-133/08 *ICF* [2009] E.C.R. I-9687; ECJ, Case C-29/10 *Heiko Koelzsch* [2011] E.C.R. I-1595; ECJ (judgment of 15 December 2011), Case C-384/10 *Jans Voogsgeerd*, not reported.

Thereafter, the European Parliament and Council adopted Regulation (EC) No. 593/2008 of 17 June 2008 on the law applicable to contractual obligations (the 'Rome I' Regulation).[15] This Regulation was based on former Art. 61(c) EC and the second indent of Art. 67(5) EC, which meant that, similar to the Brussels I Regulation, the Court of Justice's preliminary ruling jurisdiction was based on former Art. 68(1) EC until the entry into force of the Lisbon Treaty, when such jurisdiction was mainstreamed to the ordinary procedure set down in Art. 267 TFEU. The Rome I Regulation entered into force on 17 December 2009 (save for Art. 26, which applied from 17 July 2009) and applies to contracts entered into after that date.[16] Under Art. 24 of this Regulation, it supersedes the Rome Convention as between the Member States, except as regards the territories of the Member States, which fall within the territorial scope of that Convention and which are excluded from the Regulation pursuant to Art. 355 TFEU. Moreover, while Ireland and the United Kingdom have opted in, the Rome I Regulation does not apply to relations between Denmark and the other Member States, to which the Rome Convention and its accompanying Protocol continue to apply.[17]

(3) Further conversion of conventions concluded by the Member States into Union instruments

Similar to what occurred with the Brussels I Regulation and the Rome I Regulation, several **21.04** other conventions that had been concluded between the Member States concerning private international law and other aspects of judicial cooperation in civil matters were gradually transformed into Union (formerly Community) instruments.[18] For example, this occurred with the Convention on the service in the Member States of the European Union of judicial and extrajudicial documents in civil or commercial matters, for which there was an accompanying Protocol on the interpretation by the Court of Justice of this Convention,[19] by virtue of the adoption of Council Regulation (EC) No. 1348/2000,[20] which has now been replaced by Regulation (EC) No. 1393/2007,[21] applicable to Denmark[22] as well as the other Member States of the EU. Similarly, the Convention on the jurisdiction and the recognition and enforcement of judgments in matrimonial matters and its accompanying

---

[15] [2008] O.J. L177/6; *corrigendum* in [2009 O.J. L309/87. Previously, the European Parliament and Council had adopted Regulation (EC) No. 864/2007 of 11 July 2007 on the law applicable to non-contractual obligations (the 'Rome II' Regulation), [2007] O.J. L199/40. Like the Rome I Regulation, the UK and Ireland decided to take part in this Regulation, but Denmark did not.

[16] Rome I Regulation, cited in n. 15, Arts 28–29.

[17] Rome I Regulation, recitals 44–46 and Commission Decision of 22 December 2008 on the request from the United Kingdom to accept Regulation (EC) No. 593/2008 of the European Parliament and the Council on the law applicable to contractual obligations (Rome I), [2009] O.J. L10/22.

[18] There was also adoption of Union (formerly Community) instruments in this area which emanated from international conventions between Member States which had not entered into force (e.g. Regulation (EC) No. 1206/2001 on taking of evidence) or involved international conventions to which both the Union and Member States were parties (e.g. 2007 Hague Convention, which was taken into account in adoption of Regulation (EC) No. 4/2009 on maintenance obligations).

[19] See n. 3 (Council Act of 26 May 1997 drawing up the Protocol on the interpretation, by the Court of Justice of the European Communities, of the Convention on the service in the Member States of the European Union of judicial and extrajudicial documents in civil or commercial matters ([1997] O.J. C261/17).

[20] [2000] O.J. L160/37.

[21] [2007] O.J. L324/79.

[22] [2008] O.J. L331/21.

Protocol on the interpretation of the Court of Justice of this Convention[23] was replaced by Council Regulation (EC) No. 2201/2003 (the so-called 'Brussels IIbis' Regulation).[24] Yet this Regulation does not apply to Denmark, to which the Convention and accompanying Protocol remain applicable.[25] Similar to what was said earlier, as these former Community instruments had been based on the provisions of the former EC Treaty concerning judicial cooperation in civil matters, Art. 68(1) EC placed restrictions on the Court of Justice's preliminary ruling jurisdiction until the entry into force of the Lisbon Treaty, when this provision was repealed and the Court of Justice's preliminary ruling jurisdiction was mainstreamed to the ordinary procedure set down in Art. 267 TFEU (see para. 22.05).

(4) Conventions based on the EU Treaty in the version in force before the Treaty of Lisbon

21.05   Furthermore, the Member States concluded conventions under the first and third subsubparagraphs of former Art. K.3(2)(c) of the EU Treaty in the version in force before the Lisbon Treaty, which conferred on the Court of Justice, in some cases by separate protocols, jurisdiction to interpret them and sometimes to rule on disputes between Member States or between one or more Member States and the Commission regarding their application and interpretation in a direct action brought by a Member State or the Commission.[26]

---

[23] See n. 2 (Council Act of 28 May 1998 drawing up the Protocol on the interpretation by the Court of Justice of the European Communities of the Convention on jurisdiction and the recognition and enforcement of judgments in matrimonial matters ([1998] O.J. C221/19).

[24] [2003] O.J. L338/1.

[25] Brussels IIbis Regulation, cited n. 24, recital 31.

[26] The following conventions were concluded pursuant to the former Art. K.3(2) of the fomer EU Treaty:

– Convention on simplified extradition procedures between the Member States of the European Union, drawn up by Council Act of 10 March 1995 ([1995] O.J. C78/1; no jurisdiction conferred on the Court of Justice; replaced by Council Framework Decision 2002/584/JHA of 13 June 2002 on the European arrest warrant and the surrender procedures between Member States [2002] O.J. L190/1);

– Convention relating to extradition between the Member States of the European Union, drawn up by Council Act of 27 September 1996 ([1996] O.J. C313/11; replaced by Council Framework Decision 2002/584/JHA of 13 June 2002 on the European arrest warrant and the surrender procedures between Member States [2002] O.J. L190/1). This Convention did not confer jurisdiction on the Court of Justice, but in a declaration appended to the Convention on the follow-up thereto the Council stated that it would consider, one year after the entry into force of the Convention, whether jurisdiction should be given to the Court of Justice;

– Convention on the establishment of a European Police Office (Europol Convention), drawn up by Council Act of 26 July 1995 ([1995] O.J. C361/1; as far as dispute settlement is concerned, see Art. 40 of the Declaration made by all the Member States with the exception of the United Kingdom [1995] O.J. C316/32). By Council Act of 23 July 1996 drawn up on the basis of the former Art. K.3 of the EU Treaty, a Protocol was added on the interpretation, by way of preliminary rulings, by the Court of Justice of the European Communities of the Convention on the establishment of a European Police Office ([1996] O.J. C299/1). It was signed on 24 July 1996. By Council Act of 19 June 1997, a protocol was drawn up on the privileges and immunities of Europol, the members of its organs, the Deputy Directors and employees of Europol pursuant to the former Art. K.3 of the EU Treaty and Art. 41(3) of the Europol Convention ([1997] O.J. C221/1, for dispute settlement, see Art. 13). The Europol Convention entered into force on 1 October 1998. Both the Convention and the Protocol on the privileges and immunities have been replaced by Council Decision 2009/371/JHA of 6 April 2009 establishing the European Police Office ([2009] O.J. L121/37);

– Convention on the use of information technology for customs purposes, drawn up by Council Act of 26 July 1995 ([1995] O.J. C316/33; for the powers of the Court of Justice, see Art. 27; replaced by Council Decision 2009/917/JHA of 30 November 2009 on the use of information technology for customs purposes [2009] O.J. L323/20). By Council Act of 29 November 1996, a Protocol, drawn up on the basis of the former Art. K.3 of the EU Treaty, was annexed to the Convention on the interpretation, by way of

II. Survey of the Court's Powers

A. Jurisdiction to give preliminary rulings

(1) Different rules

Different rules govern the jurisdiction of the Court of Justice to give preliminary rulings **21.06** on the interpretation of these Conventions and Protocols. The differences have to do with limiting the number of courts which are entitled to make references to the Court of Justice.

(2) The Brussels and Rome Conventions

Under the Protocols annexed to the Brussels Convention[27] and the Rome Convention,[28] **21.07** which are at present only relevant within the confines set out in paragraphs 21.02 and

---

preliminary rulings, by the Court of Justice of the European Communities of the Convention on the use of information technology for customs purposes ([1997] O.J. C151/15);

– Convention on the protection of the European Communities' financial interests, drawn up by Council Act of 26 July 1995 ([1995] O.J. C316/ 48; for the jurisdiction of the Court of Justice, see Art. 8). By Council Act of 27 September 1996, a First Protocol was adopted to that convention ([1996] O.J. C313/1; for the jurisdiction of the Court of Justice, see Art. 8). Subsequently, by Council Act of 29 November 1996, a Protocol was drawn up, on the basis of the former Art. K.3 of the EU Treaty, on the interpretation by way of preliminary rulings, by the Court of Justice of the European Communities of the Convention on the protection of the European Communities' financial interests (under Art. 2(1) the Court's powers extend to interpreting both the Convention and the First Protocol) ([1997] O.J. C151/1). By Council Act of 19 June 1997, a Second Protocol was annexed to the Convention ([1997] O.J. C221/11; for the jurisdiction of the Court of Justice, see Arts 13, 14, and 15).

– Convention on the fight against corruption involving officials of the European Communities or officials of Member States of the European Union, drawn up by Council Act of 26 May 1997 ([1997] O.J. C195/1; for the jurisdiction of the Court of Justice, see Art. 12);

– Convention on the service in the Member States of the European Union of judicial and extrajudicial documents in civil or commercial matters, drawn up by Council Act of 26 May 1997 ([1997] O.J. C261/1; for the interpretative jurisdiction of the Court of Justice, see Art. 17). Also by Council Act of 26 May 1997, a Protocol was drawn up on the interpretation, by the Court of Justice of the European Communities of the Convention on the service in the Member States of the European Union of judicial and extrajudicial documents in civil or commercial matters ([1997] O.J. C261/17, including explanatory reports at pp. 26 and 38).

– Convention on mutual assistance and cooperation between customs administrations, drawn up by Council Act of 18 December 1997 ([1998] O.J. C24/1; with an explanatory report in [1998] O.J. C189/1; for the jurisdiction of the Court of Justice, see Art. 26);

– Convention on Jurisdiction and the Recognition and Enforcement of Judgments in Matrimonial Matters, drawn up by Council Act of 28 May 1998 ([1998] O.J. C221/1; for the interpretative jurisdiction of the Court of Justice, see Art. 45). A Protocol on the interpretation, by the Court of Justice of the European Communities of the Convention on Jurisdiction and the Recognition and Enforcement of Judgments in Matrimonial Matters was appended to this Convention by Council Act of the same date ([1998] O.J. C221/19, with explanatory reports at pp. 27 and 65).

– Convention on Driving Disqualifications, drawn up by Council Act of 17 June 1998 ([1998] O.J. C216/1; for the jurisdiction of the Court of Justice, see Art. 14).

[27] Now replaced as between the Member States by Council Regulation (EC) No. 44/2001 of 22 December 2000 on jurisdiction and the recognition and enforcement of judgments in civil and commercial matters (the 'Brussels I' Regulation), [2001] O.J. L21/1; *corrigendum* in [2004] O.J. L307/28. See para. 21.02.

[28] Now replaced as between the Member States by Regulation (EC) No. 593/2008 of 17 June 2008 on the law applicable to contractual obligations (the 'Rome I' Regulation), [2008] O.J. L177/6; *corrigendum* in [2009] O.J. L309/87. See para. 21.03.

21.03, only a limited number of courts are entitled to make a reference to the Court of Justice for a preliminary ruling. Only those mentioned in Art. 2(1) of the Protocol of 3 June 1971 and in Art. 2(a) of the First Protocol of 19 December 1988 and appellate courts may request a ruling.[29] A similar restriction is contained in Art. 2(1)(a) (the 'highest courts') and Art. 2(1)(b) (courts sitting in an appellate capacity)[30] of the Protocol of 26 May 1997 (service of judicial and extrajudicial documents in civil or commercial matters)[31] and Art. 2(2)(a) (the 'highest courts') and Art. 2(2)(b) (courts sitting in an appellate capacity) of the Protocol of 28 May 1998 (jurisdiction and the recognition and enforcement of judgments in matrimonial matters).[32] This restriction was introduced out of concern that too many questions might be referred in all sorts of private-law disputes. In addition, it was thought that no more heed should be given to differences of interpretation of these Conventions by inferior courts in applying them than was paid to differences as between decided cases of lower courts in a given Member State. Finally, there was a concern that the Court of Justice should only be required to give preliminary rulings where it was 'fully informed', so as to allow stable case-law to develop.[33]

Art. 2(1) of the Protocol of 28 May 1998 was novel, in comparison with the 1971, 1988, and 1997 Protocols, in that it allowed each Member State to restrict by declaration the courts empowered to make references for preliminary rulings to the highest courts. The reason for this is that judgments on matters covered by the Convention (divorce, legal separation, marriage annulment, parental responsibility for children of a marriage) needed to be given as promptly as possible in order not to prejudice the interests of individuals.[34]

A court which, under Art. 37 of the Brussels Convention, has to decide on an appeal against a decision authorizing enforcement of a judicial decision given in another Member State[35] may, under Art. 2(3) of the Protocol of 3 June 1971, also refer questions to the Court of Justice for a preliminary ruling. A court which, pursuant to Art. 40 of the Brussels Convention, has to give judgment on an appeal against a refusal to grant an application for enforcement may make a reference for a preliminary ruling under the general provision contained in Art. 2(2) of the Protocol of 3 June 1971.[36]

---

[29] ECJ (order of 9 November 1983), Case 80/83 *Habourdin International and Others* [1983] E.C.R. 3639; ECJ (order of 18 March 1984), Case 56/84 *Von Gallera* [1984] E.C.R. 1769; ECJ, Case C-69/02 *Reichling* [2002] E.C.R. I-3393; ECJ, Case C-24/02 *Marseille Fret* [2002] E.C.R. I-3383.

[30] For an application, see ECJ, Case C-38/98 *Renault* [2000] E.C.R. I-2973, paras 17–23.

[31] Now replaced as between all Member States, including Denmark, by Regulation (EC) No. 1393/2007 of the European Parliament and of the Council of 13 November 2007 on the service in the Member States of judicial and extrajudicial documents in civil or commercial matters (service of documents), and repealing Council Regulation (EC) No. 1348/2000, [2007] O.J. L324/79: see para. 21.04.

[32] Now replaced by Council Regulation (EC) No. 2201/2003 of 27 November 2003 concerning jurisdiction and the recognition and enforcement of judgments in matrimonial matters and the matters of parental responsibility, repealing Regulation (EC) No. 1347/2000, [2003] O.J. L338/1. See para. 21.04.

[33] See the Jenard Report ([1979] O.J. C59/68).

[34] Explanatory report ([1998] O.J. C221/66, point 4).

[35] Art. 37 of the Brussels Convention sets out the courts in which an appeal may be brought against a decision authorizing enforcement of a judgment given in another Member State. The court granting an enforcement order does so in the absence of the person against whom enforcement is sought (Brussels Convention, Art. 34).

[36] ECJ, Case 178/83 *Firma P.* [1984] E.C.R. 3033.

(3) Conventions based on the EU Treaty in the version in force before the Treaty of Lisbon

Member States have to accept the Court's jurisdiction to give preliminary rulings pursuant **21.08** to other Conventions[37] and Protocols[38] drawn up on the basis of the Art. K.3 of the EU Treaty in the version in force before the Lisbon Treaty (see para. 21.05) by means of a declaration, either that any national court or tribunal against whose decisions there is no judicial remedy under national law may make a reference for a preliminary ruling if the court or tribunal in question considers it to be necessary in order to give judgment, or that any national court or tribunal may request a preliminary ruling.[39] Courts or tribunals which may request a preliminary ruling are not obliged to do so, even if they consider such a ruling to be necessary in order to give judgment.

---

[37] Art. 12(3) to (5) of the Convention of 26 May 1997 on the fight against corruption involving officials of the European Communities or officials of Member States of the European Union; Art. 26(3) to (8) of the Convention of 18 December 1997 on mutual assistance and cooperation between customs administrations (Art. 26(8) limits the Court's jurisdiction in precisely the same way as former Art. 35(5) EU did: see para. 22.04): the Court 'shall not have jurisdiction to check the validity or proportionality of operations carried out by competent law enforcement agencies under this Convention nor to rule on the exercise of responsibilities which devolve upon Member States for maintaining law and order and for safeguarding internal security'); Art. 14(2–(4) of the Convention of 17 June 1998 on Driving Disqualifications.

[38] Protocol of 24 July 1996 (Europol); Protocol of 29 November 1996 (use of information technology for customs purposes); Protocol of 29 November 1996 (protection of the Communities' financial interests), the applicability of which was extended by Art. 13(2) of the Second Protocol of 19 June 1997.

[39] The following Member States have declared in respect of the Protocol indicated that only national courts or tribunals against whose decisions there is no judicial remedy under national law may make a reference for a preliminary ruling (for the O.J. references of the Protocols, see n. 1):

– Protocol of 24 July 1996 (Europol): France and Ireland;
– Protocol of 29 November 1996 (use of information technology for customs purposes): Ireland and Portugal;
– Protocol of 29 November 1996 (protection of financial interests): France, Ireland, and Portugal (a Member State may declare that a declaration made under the Protocol of 29 November 1996 does not apply to the Second Protocol of 19 June 1997; see Art. 13(3) of the Second Protocol).

The following Member States have declared that any national court or tribunal may seek a preliminary ruling from the Court of Justice (for the O.J. references of the Protocols, see n. 1):

– Protocol of 24 July 1996 (Europol): Austria, Belgium, Finland, Germany, Greece, Italy, Luxembourg, the Netherlands, Portugal, and Sweden (as far as Sweden is concerned, see [1997] O.J. C100/1). In addition, Austria, Belgium, Germany, Greece, Italy, Luxembourg, the Netherlands, and Portugal reserved the right to make provision in their national law to the effect that, where a question relating to the interpretation of the Convention or the Protocol is raised in a case pending before a national court or tribunal against whose decision there is no judicial remedy under national law, that court or tribunal will be required to refer the matter to the Court of Justice.
– Protocol of 29 November 1996 (use of information technology for customs purposes): Austria, Finland, France, Germany, Greece, the Netherlands, and Sweden. In addition, Austria, Germany, Greece, and the Netherlands reserved the right to make provision in their national law to the effect that, where a question relating to the interpretation of the Convention or the Protocol is raised in a case pending before a national court or tribunal against whose decision there is no judicial remedy under national law, that court or tribunal will be required to refer the matter to the Court of Justice.
– Protocol of 29 November 1996 (protection of financial interests): Austria, Finland, Germany, Greece, the Netherlands, and Sweden (a Member State may declare that a declaration made under the Protocol of 29 November 1996 does not apply to the Second Protocol of 19 June 1997; see Art. 13(3) of the Second Protocol). In addition, Austria, Germany, Greece, and the Netherlands reserved the right to make provision in their national law to the effect that, where a question relating to the interpretation of the Convention or the First Protocol is raised in a case pending before a national court or tribunal against whose decision there is no judicial remedy under national law, that court or tribunal will be required to refer the matter to the Court of Justice.

B. Direct actions

(1) Disputes between Member States

21.09   A direct action under Conventions concluded on the basis of Art. K.3 of the EU Treaty in the version in force before the Lisbon Treaty may be brought in the Court of Justice in the event of a dispute on the 'interpretation or application' of the Convention in question.

In an initial stage, such disputes are to be discussed by the Council with the aim of finding a settlement. If the dispute is not settled within six months, one of the parties may submit it to the Court of Justice.[40]

(2) Disputes between the Commission and Member States

21.10   The Commission or one or more Member States may bring a dispute between that institution and one or more Member States on the 'application' of a Convention directly before the Court of Justice if it cannot be settled through negotiation.[41]

(3) Convention on the Protection of the European Communities' Financial Interests

21.11   Finally, Art. 14 of the Second Protocol to the Convention on the protection of the European Communities' financial interests declared Art. 235 EC and the second paragraph of Art. 288 EC (now Art. 268 TFEU and Art. 340, second para., TFEU, respectively) concerning an application for damages against the Union to be applicable. Art. 15 of that Protocol gives the now General Court (and, on appeal, the Court of Justice) jurisdiction in proceedings instituted by any natural or legal person for annulment of a decision of the Commission which is addressed to that person or of direct and/or individual concern to that person under what is now the fourth paragraph of Art. 263 TFEU, or for interim measures, on the grounds of infringement of Art. 8 of the Protocol (infringement of the duty to provide a level of protection of personal data equivalent to that set out in Directive 95/46/EC) or any rule adopted pursuant thereto or misuse of powers in connection with

---

[40] Art. 27(1) of the Convention on the use of information technology for customs purposes; Art. 8(1) of the Convention on the protection of the European Communities' financial interests (see also Art. 8(1) of the First Protocol and Art. 13(1) of the Second Protocol); Art. 12(1) of the Convention on the fight against corruption involving officials of the European Communities or officials of Member States of the European Union; Art. 26(1) of the Convention on mutual assistance and cooperation between customs administrations; Art. 14(1) of the Convention on Driving Disqualifications. Art. 40(2) of the Europol Convention provides that if such disputes are not settled within six months, the Member States party to the dispute are to decide, by agreement amongst themselves, the modalities according to which they are to be settled. It appears from a declaration on Art. 40(2) annexed to the Convention that all the Member States, with the exception of the United Kingdom, agree that in such cases they will systematically submit the dispute to the Court of Justice.

[41] Art. 27(2) of the Convention on the use of information technology for customs purposes; Art. 8(2) of the Convention on the protection of the European Communities' financial interests (see also Art. 8(2) of the First Protocol and Art. 13(2) of the Second Protocol); Art. 12(2) of the Convention on the fight against corruption involving officials of the European Communities or officials of Member States of the European Union (this Article restricts the bringing of disputes directly before the Court of Justice to a few articles of the Convention and then only insofar as they concern a question of Union law or the Union's financial interests or involve members or officials of Union institutions or bodies set up in accordance with the Treaties); Art. 26(2) of the Convention on mutual assistance and cooperation between customs administrations; Art. 14(1) of the Convention on Driving Disqualifications.

the exchange of information between the Member States and the Commission in connection with combating fraud, active and passive corruption, and money laundering.[42]

III. Procedure before the Court of Justice

A. Preliminary references

The Statute and the Rules of Procedure of the Court of Justice are applicable insofar as the relevant Convention or Protocol do not provide otherwise.[43] Consequently, the procedure applicable to requests for preliminary rulings generally applies.

21.12

B. Direct actions

Art. 205(7) of the ECJ Rules of Procedure provides that the same procedure as that laid down for the settlement of disputes between Member States or between Member States and the Commission referred to in Art. 35(7) EU as maintained in force by Protocol No. 36 on Transitional Provisions[44]—which is laid down in Arts 205(1)–(6) of those Rules—applies where an agreement concluded between Member States confers jurisdiction on the Court of Justice to rule on a dispute between Member States or between Member States and an institution. In the absence of specific provisions in the Rules of Procedure of the ECJ or of the EGC, as the case may be, the rules applicable to direct actions generally would presumably be applicable.

21.13

IV. Consequences

A. Preliminary references

Judgments given by the Court of Justice pursuant to the Conventions and Protocols discussed earlier have the same consequences as preliminary rulings generally (see paras 6.27–6.34).

21.14

B. Direct actions

Judgments given in direct actions are enforceable under Arts 280 and 299 TFEU in the same way as any other judgment.

21.15

---

[42] Second Protocol, Art. 7(2).

[43] Art. 5 of the Protocol of 3 June 1971; Art. 1(1) of the Second Protocol conferring on the Court of Justice of the European Communities certain powers to interpret the Convention on the law applicable to contractual obligations ([1989] O.J. L48/18); Art. 3 of the Protocol of 24 July 1996; Art. 3 of the two Protocols of 29 November 1996; Art. 5 of the Protocol of 26 May 1997; Arts 5 and 7 of the Protocol of 28 May 1998; Art. 12(6) of the Convention on the fight against corruption involving officials of the European Communities or officials of Member States of the European Union; Art. 26(6) and (7) of the Convention on mutual assistance and cooperation between customs administrations; Art. 14(4) of the Convention on Driving Disqualifications.

[44] Protocol (No. 36), annexed to the TEU, the TFEU, and the EAEC Treaty, on Transitional Provisions, Art. 10.

22

JURISDICTION OF THE COURT OF JUSTICE OF THE EUROPEAN UNION WITH REGARD TO THE AREA OF FREEDOM, SECURITY, AND JUSTICE

22.01 The Area of Freedom, Security, and Justice (AFSJ) comprises the provisions falling within what used to be Title IV of the former EC Treaty on visas, asylum, immigration, and other policies related to free movement of persons, on the one hand, and Title VI of the former EU Treaty concerning Police and Judicial Cooperation in Criminal Matters (PJCCM) or the former third pillar, on the other.[1] With the entry into force of the Lisbon Treaty, these provisions have been consolidated in Title V of Part III of the TFEU (Arts 67–89 TFEU).[2] At the same time, by virtue of this Treaty, many of the restrictions placed on the jurisdiction of the Court of Justice of the European Union in the AFSJ have been removed. Moreover, the urgent preliminary ruling procedure is designed to enable the Court of Justice to give preliminary rulings more speedily on questions arising in the areas covered by the AFSJ. These subjects are discussed respectively in the two parts of this chapter which follow.

I. Removal of Restrictions Placed on Jurisdiction of the Court of Justice of the European Union in the AFSJ

A. Former Treaty framework

(1) Former Art. 68 EC

22.02 Before the entry into force of the Lisbon Treaty, although measures based on the former Title IV of the EC Treaty were in principle subject to the normal judicial supervision

---

[1] For detailed discussion, see K. Lenaerts and P. Van Nuffel (R. Bray and N. Cambien (eds)), *European Union Law* (3rd edn, London, Sweet & Maxwell, 2011), paras 10.01 to 10.27. See further Y. Bot, 'La creation de l'espace penal européen—les réalisations d'auhourd'hui et les espoirs de demain', in A. Frąckowiak-Adamska and R. Grzeszczak (eds), *L'espace judiciaire européen* (Wroclaw, Willy Brandt Zentrum, 2010), 241–50; K. Lenaerts, 'The Contribution of the European Court of Justice to the Area of Freedom, Security and Justice' (2010) International and Comparative Law Quarterly 255–301; E. Sharpston, 'The Future of the Areas of Freedom, Security and Justice', in M. Dougan and S. Currie (eds), *50 Years of the European Treaties* (Oxford and Portland Oregon, Hart Publishing, 2009), 219–28.

[2] Title V on the AFSJ contains five chapters concerning; (1) general provisions (Arts 67–76 TFEU); (2) policies on border checks, asylum, and immigration (Arts 77–80 TFEU); (3) judicial cooperation in civil matters (Art. 81 TFEU); (4) judicial cooperation in criminal matters (Arts 82–86 TFEU); and (5) police cooperation (Arts 87–89 TFEU).

provided for in what was then Arts 220–245 EC, Art. 68 EC laid down a number of specific provisions with regard to preliminary rulings. In particular, former Art. 68(1) EC restricted the possibility of making references for preliminary rulings to the Court of Justice to courts and tribunals 'against whose decisions there is no judicial remedy under national law'.[3] As a consequence, this provision eliminated the possibility of referring a question to the Court of Justice for a preliminary ruling for courts other than those of last instance. Moreover, as already mentioned in Chapter 21 (see paras 21.02–21.04), a number of conventions in the AFSJ dealing mainly with judicial cooperation in civil matters were transformed into what were then Community, now Union, instruments, which were adopted under the provisions falling within Title IV of the EC Treaty. Until the entry into force of the Lisbon Treaty, the competence of the Court of Justice to give preliminary rulings was founded on Art. 68(1) EC, and no longer on the Protocols attached to those conventions. This constituted a step backwards as compared to the former Protocols, which had afforded the possibility to submit references to lower instance courts as well.

Second, Art. 68(3) EC provided for a species of preliminary ruling procedure to be brought, not by a national court, but by the Council, the Commission, or a Member State insofar as it stated that 'the Council, the Commission or a Member State may request the Court of Justice to give a ruling on a question of interpretation of [Title IV of the EC Treaty] or of acts of the institutions of the [then] Community based on this title'.

Finally, Art. 68(2) EC further limited the jurisdiction of the Union judicature by providing that with respect to measures taken with a view to ensuring the absence of any controls on persons when crossing internal borders,[4] the Court of Justice did not have jurisdiction to rule on any measure relating to the maintenance of law and order and the safeguarding of internal security. This restriction seemed to be aimed at all the judicial procedures provided for in the EC Treaty, and not only at the preliminary ruling procedure.

(2) Former Art. 35 EU

Former Art. 35 EU governed the jurisdiction of the Court of Justice in the field of the former third pillar concerning the PJCCM. **22.03**

Under Art. 35(1) EU, the Court of Justice was empowered to give preliminary rulings on the validity and interpretation of framework decisions and decisions on the interpretation of conventions established under Title VI, and on the validity and interpretation of the measures implementing them.[5] That jurisdiction had to be expressly accepted by Member

---

[3] See, e.g. ECJ (order of 18 March 2004), Case C-45/03 *Dem'Yanenko*, not reported, paras 41–43; ECJ (order of 31 March 2004), Case C-51/03 *Georgescu* [2004] E.C.R. I-3203, para. 29; ECJ (order of 10 June 2004), Case C-555/03 *Warbecq* [2004] E.C.R. I-6041, paras 11–16 (reference for a preliminary ruling from a lower court declared inadmissible); ECJ, Case C-14/08 *Roda Golf & Beach Resort* [2009] E.C.R. I-5439, paras 27–29. For background on former Art. 68 EC, see Opinion of Advocate-General D. Ruiz-Jarabo Colomer in ECJ, Case C-14/08 *Roda Golf & Beach Resort* [2009] E.C.R. I-5439, points 21–37 (advocating a restrictive interpretation to the limitation placed on the Court of Justice's preliminary ruling jurisdiction under former Art. 68(1) EC).

[4] Measures taken pursuant to former Art. 62(1) EC.

[5] For examples of references for a preliminary ruling on the interpretation of a framework decision, see ECJ, Case C-105/03 *Pupino* [2005] E.C.R. I-5285; ECJ, Case C-354/04 P *Gestoras Pro Amnistia and Others v Council* [2007] E.C.R. I-1579; ECJ, C-355/04 P *Segi and Others v Council* [2007] E.C.R. I-1657 (in which the Court of Justice held that its preliminary ruling jurisdiction under Art. 35 EU could extend to the validity or interpretation of common positions adopted under Art. 34 EU); ECJ, Case C-467/05 *Dell'Orto* [2007] E.C.R. I-5557 (in which the Court of Justice ruled that references for preliminary rulings submitted under

States by declaration.[6] In such a declaration, the Member State could elect to allow either any court or tribunal against whose decisions there is no judicial remedy under national law[7] or any court or tribunal to request a preliminary ruling from the Court of Justice.[8] Yet, under Art. 35(5) EU, the Court of Justice had no jurisdiction to review the 'validity or proportionality of operations carried out by the police or other law enforcement services of a Member State or the exercise of the responsibilities incumbent upon Member States with regard to the maintenance of law and order and the safeguarding of internal security'.

In addition to that specific power to give preliminary rulings, the Court was given jurisdiction in direct actions brought under Art. 35(6) EU to review the legality of framework decisions and decisions.[9] This procedure resembled in some respects the action for annulment provided for in Art. 263 TFEU (see Ch. 7), except that an action could be brought only by a Member State or the Commission, and not by any other institution or natural or legal person. The pleas which could be raised and the requisite time limit for bringing such an action were the same. Moreover, under Art. 35(7) EU, the Court of Justice had jurisdiction to rule on any dispute between Member States regarding the interpretation or the application of acts adopted under Art. 34(2) EU whenever such dispute could not be settled by the Council within six months of its being referred to that institution by one of its members. This procedure bore a resemblance to the action which a Member State may bring before the Court against another Member State under Art. 259 TFEU for failure to fulfil an obligation (see para. 5.35). Art. 35(7) EU also conferred jurisdiction on the Court of Justice to 'rule on any dispute between Member States and the Commission regarding the interpretation or the application of conventions established under Art. 34(2)(d) EU'. This procedure resembled the action for failure to fulfil obligations which the Commission may bring against a Member State under Art. 258 TFEU (see para. 5.31).

Art. 35 EU are subject to the condition that the national court considers that a decision on the question is necessary to enable it to give judgment, with the result that the case-law of the Court of Justice on the admissibility of references under Art. 267 TFEU (see Ch. 3) was transposable to references for a preliminary ruling submitted to the Court under Art. 35 EU). See further L. Bay Larsen, 'From Palma de Mallorca, via Schengen, to Luxembourg: Some Notes on the Case-Law of the European Court of Justice in the Field of Police and Judicial Cooperation in Criminal Matters', in C. Baudenbacher, C. Gulmann, K. Lenaerts, E. Coulon, and E. Barbier de La Serre (eds), *Liber Amicorum en l'honneur de/in honour of Bo Vesterdorf* (Brussels, Bruylant, 2007), 723–44; T. von Danwitz, 'Aktuelle Fragen der Grundrechte, des Umwelt- und Rechtsschutzes in der Europäischen Union' (2008) DVBl. 543–4.

[6] Former Art. 35(2) EU. However, irrespective as to whether a Member State had or had not accepted the Court's jurisdiction under Art. 35(1) EU, it was entitled to submit statements of case or written observations to the Court in cases arising under that provision (see former Art. 35(4) EU).

[7] Art. 35(3)(a) EU. Spain and Hungary accepted the Court's jurisdiction on these terms, see [2005] O.J. L327/19; [2005] O.J. C318/1 (and further citations therein). However, Hungary has later withdrawn its declaration and has declared that it accepts the jurisdiction of the Court of Justice in accordance with Art. 35(3)(b) EU ([2008] O.J. L70/23; [2008] O.J. C69/1).

[8] Art. 35(3)(b) EU. A declaration to this effect has been lodged by Austria, Belgium, the Czech Republic, Cyprus, Finland, France, Germany, Greece, Hungary, Italy, Latvia, Lithuania, Luxembourg, the Netherlands, Portugal, Romania, Slovenia, and Sweden: see [2010] O.J. L56/14; [2010] O.J. C56/1 (and further citations therein). Upon lodging such a declaration, Member States may reserve the right to make provision in their national law to the effect that a national court or tribunal against whose decisions there is no remedy under national law is required to make a reference to the Court of Justice: Declaration (No. 10) and Art. 35 of the EU Treaty, [1997] O.J. C340/133. In their declarations, Austria, Belgium, the Czech Republic, France, Germany, Italy, Luxembourg, the Netherlands, Romania, Slovenia, and Spain reserved that right: see [2010] O.J. L56/14; [2010] O.J. C56/1 (and further citations therein).

[9] See ECJ, Case C-176/03 *Commission v Council ('Environmental crimes')* [2005] E.C.R. I-7879; ECJ, Case C-440/05 *Commission v Council ('Ship-source pollution')* [2007] E.C.R. I-9097.

(3) No other jurisdiction for the Court of Justice of the European Union in the former third pillar

Apart from the actions provided for in Arts 35(1), (6), and (7) EU, the Court of Justice of **22.04** the European Union had no jurisdiction to review acts of the institutions of the Union in the field of the PJCCM.[10] This meant, for example, that actions for damages brought by natural and legal persons alleging that they sustained damage as a result of such action on the part of the Union were declared inadmissible.[11] Nevertheless, in order to obviate the choice of an incorrect legal basis wrongly resulting in the exclusion of any legal redress, the Union judicature was conferred competence to closely monitor whether the Union was justified in basing its action on a provision of Title VI of the EU Treaty.[12]

B. Changes brought by the Treaty of Lisbon

With the entry into force of the Lisbon Treaty, the pillar structure has been abolished, and **22.05** as already mentioned, the provisions of the AFSJ were consolidated into a specific title of the TFEU. The restrictions placed on the Court of Justice's jurisdiction in former Title IV of the EC Treaty and the former third pillar of Title VI of the EU Treaty have for the most part been removed, which in principle constitutes an improvement in the system of judicial protection in the EU. In practice, however, certain exceptions still remain.[13]

As regards the area covered by former Title IV EC, Art. 68 EC has been repealed, and references on questions falling within this area are now governed by the ordinary procedure for preliminary rulings set down in Art. 267 TFEU.[14]

As regards the former third pillar of PJCCM, the jurisdiction of the Court of Justice of the European Union has, too, been mainstreamed. This means that the power of national courts to refer preliminary questions no longer depends on a declaration of the Member States to that effect; all national courts (without restriction) are now empowered to make a reference. Similarly, actions for annulment and infringement actions are no longer subject to the restrictions laid down in Art. 35 EU.

However, with respect to Union acts in the field of PJCCM which have been adopted before the entry into force of the Lisbon Treaty, the powers of the Commission under

---

[10] See ECJ, Case C-160/03 *Spain v Eurojust* [2005] E.C.R. I-2077, paras 35–44.

[11] ECJ, Case C-354/04 P *Gestoras Pro Amnistía and Others v Council* [2007] E.C.R. I-1579; ECJ, Case C-355/04 P *Segi and Others v Council* [2007] E.C.R. I-1657.

[12] See former Art. 47 TEU.

[13] Aside from the remaining restrictions placed on the jurisdiction of the Court of Justice of the European Union laid down in the Treaties in this regard, there are complexities arising from the fact that certain Member States are allowed to opt out of measures adopted in the AFSJ: see Protocol (No. 21), annexed to the TEU, TFEU, and the EAEC Treaty, on the position of the UK and Ireland in respect of the AFSJ, [2012] O.J. C326/295; Protocol (No. 22), annexed to the TEU, TFEU, and the EAEC Treaty, on the position of Denmark, [2012] O.J. C326/299. But see Declaration (No. 56), annexed to the Lisbon Treaty, by Ireland on Art. 3 of the Protocol on the position of the UK and Ireland in respect of the AFSJ, [2012] O.J. C326/358, and Declaration (No. 65), annexed to the Lisbon Treaty, by the UK on Art. 75 TFEU, [2012] O.J. C326/361.

[14] See, in this regard, ECJ, Case C-283/09 *Weryński* [2011] E.C.R. I-601, paras 26–33. See also the Opinion of Advocate-General E. Sharpston in ECJ, Case C-256/09 *Purrucker* [2010] E.C.R. I-7353, point 27.

Art. 258 TFEU are not applicable and the powers of the Court of Justice shall remain the same, including where they have been accepted under former Art. 35(2) EU, for a period of five years after the date of entry into force of that Treaty (1 December 2009); however, the amendment of such an act will entail the applicability of the powers of the institutions as set out in the Treaties with respect to the amended act for those Member States to which the amended act applies.[15] Consequently, insofar as pre-Lisbon PJCCM acts are concerned, the restrictions which had been placed on the Court of Justice's jurisdiction under Art. 35 EU continue to apply until 1 December 2014. In other words, the Court of Justice's preliminary ruling jurisdiction is contingent upon a declaration submitted by the Member State concerned.[16] Also during this period, an action for failure to fulfil obligations brought by the Commission against a Member State is precluded.

Moreover, Art. 276 TFEU provides that the Court of Justice of the European Union, in exercising its powers regarding the provisions of Chapters 4 and 5 of Title V of Part III of the TFEU (concerning Judicial Cooperation in Criminal Matters and Police Cooperation, respectively), does not have 'jurisdiction to review the validity or proportionality of operations carried out by the police or law enforcement services of a Member State or the exercise of the responsibilities incumbent upon Member States with regard to the maintenance of law and order and the safeguarding of internal security'.[17]

II. Urgent Preliminary Ruling Procedure in the AFSJ

A. General

22.06 As of 1 March 2008, a reference for a preliminary ruling which raises one or more questions concerning the AFSJ may, at the request of the referring court or tribunal, or exceptionally, of the Court's own motion, be dealt with under the urgent preliminary ruling procedure derogating from certain provisions of the Statute and ECJ Rules of Procedure.[18] The urgent preliminary ruling procedure is laid down in Art. 23a of the Statute and Arts 107–114 of the ECJ Rules of Procedure.

The urgent procedure was introduced in response to the Presidency Conclusions of the European Council, which invited the Commission to submit, after consultation with the

---

[15] See Art. 10(1)–(3) of Protocol (No. 36), annexed to the TEU, TFEU, and the EAEC Treaty, on transitional provisions, [2012] O.J. C326/356. See also Declaration No. 50, annexed to the Lisbon Treaty, concerning Art. 10 of the Protocol on transitional provisions, [2012] O.J. C326/356. With respect to the procedure to be followed in the case of disputes between Member States or between Member States and the Commission as referred to in Art. 35(7) TEU as maintained in force by this Protocol, see ECJ Rules of Procedure, Art. 205.

[16] See, in this regard, ECJ (judgment of 7 June 2012), Case C-27/11 *Vinkov*, not reported, paras 46–51; ECJ (judgment of 12 July 2012), Case C-79/11 *Giovanardi and Others*, not reported, paras 30–34.

[17] See also Art. 72 TFEU: 'This Title shall not affect the exercise of the responsibilities incumbent upon Member States with regard to the maintenance of law and order and the safeguarding of internal security.'

[18] The first reference to be dealt with under the urgent preliminary ruling procedure was ECJ, Case C-195/08 PPU *Rinau* [2008] E.C.R. I-5271 (with case note M. Rofes i Puyol (2009) Cuardernos Europeas de Deusto (2009) 227–31). See further R. Barents, 'De prejudiciële spoedprocedure' (2009) Delikt en delinkwent 454–64; A. Tizzano and P. Iannuccelli, 'La procedure préjudicielle d'urgence devant la Cour de Justice: premier bilan et nouvelles questions', in A. Weitzel (ed.), *Mélanges en hommage à Albert Weitzel. L'Europe des droits fondamentaux* (Paris, Pedone, 2013), 201–24.

Court of Justice, a proposal 'for the speedy and appropriate handling of requests for preliminary rulings concerning the area of freedom, security and justice'.[19] The idea for such a procedure emerged in 2004 amidst activities surrounding the failed Draft Constitutional Treaty, which contained a provision now inscribed in the fourth paragraph of Art. 267 TFEU requiring the Court of Justice, in the context of its preliminary ruling jurisdiction, to 'act with the minimum of delay' where questions were raised in a case pending before a national court or tribunal with regard to a person in custody. Moreover, while there was already provision for an expedited (formerly called accelerated) procedure for preliminary rulings of exceptional urgency,[20] this procedure was granted sparingly and appeared to be ill-equipped to deal with preliminary references in the AFSJ, since it followed the ordinary procedure for preliminary rulings, while significantly accelerating it.

Consequently, the urgent preliminary ruling procedure has three key features that distinguish it from the ordinary preliminary ruling procedure and from the expedited procedure applicable to preliminary rulings with a view to achieving substantial savings in the duration of the proceedings: (1) only the parties to the main proceedings, the Member State of the referring court or tribunal, the Commission, and the other Union institutions if one of their measures is at issue may participate in the written procedure;[21] (2) references dealt with under the urgent procedure are referred to a five-Judge Chamber specifically designated for that purpose, which gives its ruling without first going through the General Meeting of the Court; and (3) communications in the urgent procedure (both internal and those involving the parties and interested persons within the meaning of Art. 23 of the Statute) are, as far as possible, electronic.[22]

B. Scope

(1) Questions concerning the AFSJ

The urgent preliminary ruling procedure is limited to references which raise 'one or more questions in the areas covered by Title V of Part Three' of the TFEU,[23] which is the specific title in the Treaties devoted to the AFSJ (Arts 67–89 TFEU).[24] Consequently, a request for the application of the urgent preliminary ruling procedure which concerns a reference for a preliminary ruling which falls outside this field will be rejected.[25]   **22.07**

(2) Request by national court

To request the application of the urgent preliminary ruling procedure, the referring court or tribunal must set out the matters of fact and law which establish the urgency and justify the application of that exceptional procedure and, insofar as possible, indicate the answer   **22.08**

---

[19] Presidency Conclusions, European Council, 4–5 November 2004, Brussels, 14292/1/04, para. 3.1.

[20] Statute, Art. 23a; ECJ Rules of Procedure, Art. 105–106 (formerly Art. 104a). See further paras 24.17 *et seq*. For its usage in relation to the urgent preliminary ruling procedure, see para. 22.19.

[21] But see Art. 109(3) of ECJ Rules of Procedure and para 22.14.

[22] Report on the use of the urgent preliminary ruling procedure by the Court of Justice, 31 January 2012, available on the website of the Court of Justice, <http://curia.europa.eu>.

[23] ECJ Rules of Procedure, Art. 107(1). See also Art. 23a of Statute.

[24] See para. 22.01.

[25] See, e.g. ECJ, Case C-375/08 *Pontini and Others* [2010] E.C.R. I-5767, paras 42–43 (further noting that in any event the degree of urgency was not such as to warrant application of the urgent procedure).

that it proposes to the questions referred.[26] A request that does not satisfy these conditions will be rejected.[27]

(3) Request by Court of its own motion

22.09   Exceptionally, the Court may decide of its own motion that a reference for a preliminary ruling be dealt with under the urgent preliminary ruling procedure.[28] In this regard, Art. 107(3) of the ECJ Rules of Procedure provides that the President of the Court may, if the application of that procedure appears, *prima facie*, to be required, ask the designated Chamber to consider whether it is necessary to deal with the reference under that procedure.[29]

(4) Decision to apply urgent preliminary procedure taken by designated Chamber

22.10   The decision to deal with a reference for a preliminary ruling under the urgent procedure is taken by the designated Chamber of five Judges, acting on a proposal from the Judge-Rapporteur and after hearing the Advocate-General.[30] So far, the Court has, each judicial year, designated only one Chamber of five Judges for that purpose. However, the designated Chamber may decide to sit in a formation of three Judges[31] or may request the Court to assign the case to a formation composed of a greater number of Judges.[32]

(5) Circumstances warranting application of urgent procedure

22.11   Given that the urgent preliminary ruling procedure imposes considerable constraints on those concerned, the application of the urgent preliminary ruling procedure should therefore be requested 'only where it is absolutely necessary for the Court to give its ruling very quickly on the questions submitted by the referring court or tribunal'.[33] For example, the large number of persons or legal situations potentially affected by the decision that the referring court has to deliver after bringing the matter before the Court for a preliminary ruling does not, in itself, constitute an exceptional circumstance that would justify the use of the urgent preliminary ruling procedure.[34] Also, the fact that a national judge is required

---

[26] ECJ Rules of Procedure, Art. 107(2). See also Recommendations to national courts and tribunals in relation to the initiation of preliminary ruling proceedings ([2012] O.J. C 338/1), points 41–44, particularly point 43, which provides that the referring court's request 'must be included in a clearly identifiable place in its order for reference (for example, at the head of the page or in a separate judicial document)'. Therefore, there appears to be no requirement that such a request must be made by separate application, although the national court is free to do so. See, e.g. ECJ (judgment of 28 June 2012), Case C-192/12 PPU *West*, not reported, para. 32. As part of the Court of Justice's preliminary ruling in a particular case, generally there is a section devoted to the decision for the use of the urgent preliminary ruling procedure: see e.g. ECJ (judgment of 19 July 2012), Case C-278/12 PPU *Adil*, not reported, paras 33–35.

[27] See e.g. ECJ, Case C-261/09 *Mantello* [2010] E.C.R.I-11477, para. 31.

[28] ECJ Rules of Procedure, Art. 107(1).

[29] See ECJ, Case C-491/10 PPU *Aguirre Zarraga* [2010] E.C.R. I-14247.

[30] ECJ Rules of Procedure, Art. 108(1). As indicated therein, the composition of that Chamber is determined in accordance with ECJ Rules of Procedure, Art. 28(2) either on the date on which the case is assigned to the Judge-Rapporteur if the application of the urgent procedure is requested by the referring court or, if the application of that procedure is considered at the request of the President of the Court, on the day on which that request is made.

[31] ECJ Rules of Procedure, Art. 113(1).

[32] ECJ Rules of Procedure, Art. 113(2). See, e.g. ECJ, Case C-357/09 PPU *Kadzoev (Huchbarov)* [2009] E.C.R. I-11189 (decided by the Grand Chamber).

[33] Recommendations to national courts and tribunals in relation to the initiation of preliminary ruling proceedings, cited in n. 26, point 39. See also the View of Advocate-General E. Sharpston in ECJ (judgment of 19 July 2012), Case C-278/12 PPU *Adil*, not reported, points 32–33.

[34] Recommendations to national courts and tribunals in relation to the initiation of preliminary ruling proceedings, cited in n. 26, points 38–39.

to decide the case pending before it within a specific time limit has so far not justified recourse to the urgent preliminary ruling procedure.[35] Conversely, the urgent procedure was applied in proceedings relating to detention in the context of extradition proceedings[36] or criminal proceedings.[37]

While the decision to apply the urgent preliminary ruling procedure depends upon the particular case, the Court of Justice's Recommendations to national courts and tribunals in relation to the initiation of preliminary ruling proceedings provides a non-exhaustive list of circumstances in which the referring court or tribunal may consider submitting a request for the urgent procedure to be applied in proceedings in which a person is in custody or deprived of his or her liberty, 'where the answer to the question raised is decisive as to the assessment of that person's legal situation, or in proceedings concerning parental authority or custody of children, where the identity of the court having jurisdiction under European Union law depends on the answer to the question referred for a preliminary ruling'.[38]

(6) Reference may become devoid of purpose

It may be the case that even where the request for the application of the urgent preliminary **22.12** ruling procedure has been granted, subsequent proceedings before the national court make the request for a preliminary ruling to no purpose and thus the Court of Justice will find it unnecessary to give a ruling where, for instance, the ruling would entail an advisory opinion or be on general or hypothetical questions (see paras 3.35 *et seq.*).[39]

C. Procedure

(1) General

The procedure in the case of references for preliminary ruling involving the application of **22.13** the urgent procedure generally contains both a written and oral stage. In essence, the idea underlying the procedure is that the written stage is confined to the parties to the main

---

[35] See, for instance, ECJ (judgment of 30 May 2013), Case C-168/13 PPU *F*, not reported, paras 28–32, in which the Court did not take into account the fact that under national procedural law the referring court had to give a decision within a three-month period. See, by contrast, in relation to the expedited procedure, para. 24.18.

[36] ECJ, Case C-296/08 PPU *Santesteban Goicoechea* [2008] E.C.R. I-6307, paras 32–34.

[37] ECJ, Case C-61/11 PPU *El Dridi* [2011] E.C.R. I-3015, paras 26–28.

[38] Recommendations to national courts and tribunals in relation to the initiation of preliminary ruling proceedings, cited in n. 26, point 40. See also Statement of the Council annexed to Council Decision 2008/79/EC, Euratom of 20 December 2007 amending the Protocol on the Statute of the Court of Justice, [2008] O.J. L24/44, first para.: 'The Council calls upon the Court to apply the urgent preliminary ruling procedure in situations involving deprivation of liberty.' Moreover, under the third para., the Council requests the Court to submit, no later than three years following the entry into force of the urgent procedure, a report—the content of which will be updated annually—on its use and 'in particular, the Court's practice for deciding whether or not to launch it'. See further Report on the use of the urgent preliminary ruling procedure by the Court of Justice, n. 22, particularly point 5, at 6 (identifying two types of situations which have resulted in the Court delivering a ruling in the shortest possible time in the context of the urgent procedure: a risk of irreparable damage in the parent/child relationship and where a person is being detained and further detention depends on the ruling to be given by the Court). For an application of the risk of irreparable harm in the parent/child relationship, see ECJ, Case C-403/99 PPU *Detiček* [2009] E.C.R. I-12193, paras 29–31; ECJ, Case, C-211/10 PPU *Povse* [2010] E.C.R. I-6673, paras 36–36; ECJ, Case C-400/10 PPU *McB* [2010] E.C.R. I-8965, paras 26–29.

[39] See, e.g. ECJ (order of 10 June 2011), Case C-155/11 PPU *Mohammad Imran* [2011] E.C.R. I-5095.

proceedings, the Member State from which the reference is made, the Commission, and the Union institution which adopted the act whose validity or interpretation is in dispute. The other Member States and interested parties referred to in Art. 23 of the Statute are allowed to participate in the proceedings but are in principle limited to the oral stage.

(2) Written stage

22.14   The request for a preliminary ruling and the decision as to whether or not to deal with the reference under the urgent procedure are first served on the parties to the main proceedings, the Member State from which the reference is made, the Commission, and the Union institution which adopted the act whose validity or interpretation is in dispute.[40] If granted, the decision to deal with the reference under the urgent procedure prescribes the time limit within which those parties or entities may lodge statements of case or written observations,[41] and that decision may specify the matters of law to which such statements of case or written observations must relate and the maximum length of those documents.[42] As soon as service is effected, these documents are also communicated to the other interested parties referred to in to Art. 23 of the Statute, who are also informed as soon as possible of the likely date of the hearing.[43]

Where a request for a preliminary ruling refers to an administrative procedure or judicial proceedings conducted in a Member State other than that from which the reference is made—which is regularly the case in child custody proceedings—the Court may invite that first Member State to provide all relevant information in writing or at the hearing.[44]

Where the reference is dealt with under the urgent procedure,[45] the statements of case or written observations which have been lodged are served on the parties to the main proceedings, the Member State from which the reference is made, the Commission, and the Union institution which adopted the act whose validity or interpretation is in dispute, as well as the other interested parties under Art. 23 of the Statute.[46] The date of the hearing is communicated at the same time as these documents are served.[47]

In cases of extreme urgency, the designated Chamber may decide to omit the written part of the procedure altogether.[48] So far, however, this has not been done.

---

[40]   ECJ Rules of Procedure, Art. 109(1)–(2).

[41]   Statute, Art. 23a, second para.

[42]   ECJ Rules of Procedure, Art. 109(2). See also Statement of the Council annexed to Council Decision 2008/79/EC, Euratom of 20 December 2007 amending the Protocol on the Statute of the Court of Justice, [2008] O.J. L24/44, second para., in which the Council calls upon the Court 'to ensure that deadlines in this regard are not, in principle, less than 10 working days, and to adapt the oral procedure to the requirements of the urgent procdure'. It further states that 'the urgent preliminary ruling procedure should be concluded within three months'.

[43]   ECJ Rules of Procedure, Art. 109(4)–(5).

[44]   ECJ Rules of Procedure, Art. 109(3).

[45]   Where the reference is not to be dealt with under the urgent procedure, the proceedings continue in accordance with Art. 23 of the Statute and the applicable provisions of the ECJ Rules of Procedure (ECJ Rules of Procedure, Art. 109(6)).

[46]   ECJ Rules of Procedure, Arts 110(1)–(2). For other interested parties referred to in Art. 23 of the Statute, the order for reference may be accompanied by a translation, where appropropriate, of a summary, in accordance with Art. 98 of the ECJ Rules of Procedure (ECJ Rules of Procedure, Art. 110(1)).

[47]   ECJ Rules of Procedure, Art. 110(3).

[48]   Statute, Art. 23a, third para.; ECJ Rules of Procedure, Art. 111.

(3) Electronic transmission of procedural documents

Procedural documents submitted in the context of the urgent preliminary ruling procedure **22.15** (for example, statements of case or written observations) are generally transmitted electronically.[49] In practice, documents, both internal and those of interested parties within the meaning of Art. 23 of the Statute, have been communicated through the creation of 'functional mailboxes' specifically dedicated to communication in relation to the urgent procedure.[50]

(4) Oral stage

The focus in urgent preliminary proceedings lies with the oral stage of the procedure. **22.16** Member States—other than the Member State from which the reference is made—can only submit their observations during that stage of the procedure.[51]

(5) View of the Advocate-General

After the close of the written and oral stages, the Advocate-General delivers his or her 'View' **22.17** (as opposed to 'Opinion') on how the particular reference for a preliminary ruling should be determined. Generally, the View of the Advocate-General is published alongside the ruling given by the Court of Justice,[52] unless the formation of the Court decides otherwise after hearing the Advocate-General.[53]

(6) Decision on the substance

The designated Chamber (or another formation of the Court as the case may be) delivers its **22.18** preliminary ruling after hearing the Advocate-General.[54]

D. Relationship to expedited procedure

As already mentioned (see para. 22.06), in addition to the urgent preliminary ruling procedure, **22.19** there is also provision for the expedited preliminary ruling procedure in the Statute and ECJ Rules of Procedure.[55] This procedure may be used, for example, where a reference needs to be dealt with within a short period of time but falls outside the field of the AFSJ.

Moreover, depending on the circumstances of the case, a national court or tribunal may request that a reference concerning questions falling within the field of the AFSJ be decided under the expedited procedure, notwithstanding the existence of the urgent procedure.[56]

---

[49] ECJ Rules of Procedure, Art. 106, applicable by virtue of Art. 114.

[50] See Report on the use of the urgent preliminary ruling procedure by the Court of Justice, n. 22, point 6.

[51] See, however, ECJ Rules of Procedure, Art. 109(3) and para. 22.14.

[52] See Report on the use of the urgent preliminary ruling procedure by the Court of Justice, n. 22, point 3, at 5.

[53] See, e.g. ECJ, Case C-388/08 PPU *Leymann and Pustovarov* [2008] E.C.R. I-8983.

[54] ECJ Rules of Procedure, Art. 112.

[55] Statute, Art. 23a; ECJ Rules of Procedure, Arts 105 and 106. On the difference between the expedited procedure and the urgent procedure, see V. Skouris, 'De nouveaux défis pour la Cour de justice dans une Europe élargie' ERA Forum (2008) 106.

[56] See, e.g. ECJ (order of the President of 12 May 2010), Joined Cases C-188/10 and C-189/10 *Melki and Abdeli* [2010] E.C.R. I-5667; ECJ (order of the President of 15 July 2010), Case C-296/10 *Purrucker* [2010] E.C.R. I-11163; ECJ (order of the President of 30 September 2011), Case C-329/11 *Achughbabian*, not reported.

That being said, a request submitted by the referring court for the application of the expedited procedure may not be likely to succeed where its request for the application of the urgent procedure has been refused for failure to satisfy the requisite conditions, particularly that concerning urgency.[57]

Finally, when the referring national court requests the urgent procedure, the President of the ECJ can still of his or her own motion decide that the reference is to be determined pursuant to the expedited procedure.[58] Such course of action may be indicated when, given the importance of the questions raised, it is considered necessary to invite all interested parties within the meaning of Art. 23 of the Statute to submit written observations.[59]

---

[57] See, e.g. ECJ, Case C-375/08 *Pontini and Others* [2010] E.C.R. I-5767, paras 42–45. But compare, e.g. ECJ (judgment of 6 December 2011), Case C-329/11 *Achughbabian*, not reported, para. 27 (noting that the referring court had submitted a request for the application of the urgent procedure which was refused by the designated Chamber); and ECJ (order of the President of 30 September 2011), Case C-329/11 *Achughbabian*, not reported (granting the referring court's request to apply the accelerated procedure). See further V. Skouris, 'L'urgence dans la procédure applicable aux renvois préjudiciels', in C. Baudenbacher, C. Gulmann, K. Lenaerts, E. Coulon, and E. Barbier de La Serre (eds), *Liber amicorum en l'honneur de Bo Vesterdorf* (Brussels, Bruylant, 2007), 59–78.

[58] ECJ Rules of Procedure, Art. 105(1).

[59] Contrary to the urgent procedure, all interested parties within the meaning of Art. 23 of the Statute have the right to submit written observations in the context of an expedited procedure: see ECJ Rules of Procedure, Art. 105(3).

PART V

PROCEDURE BEFORE THE UNION COURTS

23

COMMON PROCEDURAL RULES APPLICABLE TO CASES BEFORE THE UNION COURTS

In the recently revised ECJ Rules of Procedure,[1] a distinction has been drawn between the **23.01** procedural rules common to all cases and those that are specific to a particular type of case, each of which are contained in separate titles.[2] As mentioned in the General Introduction (see para. 1.09), the former is the subject of the present chapter,[3] whereas the specific procedural rules applicable to the main types of actions—preliminary rulings, direct actions, and appeals—are taken up in the next three chapters of Part V of this book.

I. Language Arrangements

A. Language of a case

(1) Official languages of the Union

At present, a case before the Union courts may be conducted in any of the following **23.02** twenty-four languages: Bulgarian, Croatian, Czech, Danish, Dutch, English, Estonian, Finnish, French, German, Greek, Hungarian, Irish, Italian, Latvian, Lithuanian, Maltese, Polish, Portuguese, Romanian, Slovak, Slovenian, Spanish, and Swedish.[4] In other words, a

---

[1] On the recently revised ECJ Rules of Procedure, see N. Cariat and J. T. Nowak, 'Le nouveau règlement de procédure de la Cour de Justice de l'Union européenne *anno* 2012' (2013) J.T. 185–9; M. A. Gaudissart, 'La refonte du règlement de procedure de la Cour de justice' (2012) C.D.E. 605–69; J. T. Nowak and N. Cariat, 'Het nieuwe Reglement voor de procesvoering van het Hof van Justitie: een overzicht' (2013) NtEr 36–44.

[2] General procedural rules similar to the ones applicable to proceedings before the General Court apply to proceedings before the Civil Service Tribunal. The specific rules applicable to such proceedings are set out in Ch. 18, and in some instances, in the present chapter.

[3] This chapter includes the discussion of the procedural rules on language arrangements, since they are common to the procedure before the Union courts, even though such rules do not as a formal matter appear in the specific title devoted to common procedural rules; they are instead found in the initial title of the ECJ and EGC Rules of Procedure concerning the organization of the respective Court. According to Art. 7(2) of the Statute, the provisions concerning the General Court's language arrangements apply to the Civil Service Tribunal.

[4] ECJ Rules of Procedure, Art. 36; EGC Rules of Procedure, Art. 35(1). Accordingly, a language not listed in the foregoing provisions of the ECJ and EGC Rules of Procedure (e.g. Welsh, Luxembourgish, or Turkish) cannot serve as the language of a case. However, witnesses and experts may be authorized to use a language not capable of being a language of the case: ECJ Rules of Procedure, Art. 38(7); EGC Rules of Procedure, Art. 35(4). For further discussion of the language regime at the Court of Justice of the European Union, see M. A. Gaudissart, 'Le régime et la pratique linguistiques à la Cour de Justice', in D. Hanf, K. Malacek, and E. Muir (eds), *Langues et construction européenne* (Peter Lang, Brussels, 2010), 137–60; E. Levits, 'Probleme der Sprachenvielfalt am Europäischen Gerichtshof', in Fischer (ed.), *Herausforderungen des Sprachenvielfalt in der Europäischen Union* (Baden Baden, Nomos, 2007), 44–50.

language listed among the foregoing twenty-four official languages of the European Union may constitute the language of the case.

(2) Determination of the language of a case

23.03 In direct actions, in principle, the applicant chooses the language of the case, subject to the following exceptions:

– Where the defendant is a Member State[5] or a natural or legal person having the nationality of a Member State,[6] the language of the case will be the official language of that State; where the State has more than one official language, the applicant may choose between them.[7]

– At the joint request of the parties, the President of the Court of Justice or the General Court may authorize another Union language to be used for all or part of the proceedings.[8]

– At the request of only one of the parties (which cannot be a Union institution), the use of another official Union language may be authorized as the language of the case for all or part of the proceedings, but only after the opposing party and the Advocate-General have been heard.[9] Although requests for the use of another language are generally decided upon by the President of the Court of Justice or of the General Court, where the President wishes to give such authorization but the parties do not agree, he or she must refer the request to the Court of Justice or the General Court, as the case may be.[10]

Although not expressly mentioned in the text of the ECJ and EGC Rules of Procedure, a request for leave to derogate from the rule on the use of the language of the case must be accompanied by a detailed and specific statement of reasons, especially where the request is made by the applicant in the course of the proceedings.[11]

In preliminary ruling proceedings, the language of the case is the language of the referring court or tribunal. A derogation can exceptionally be authorized, but only as regards the oral part of the procedure (see para. 24.28).[12]

For certain types of proceedings, namely appeals against decisions of the General Court and of the Civil Service Tribunal (see Ch. 26),[13] the review procedure by which the Court decides to review a decision of the General Court in accordance with Art. 62 of the

---

[5] A Member State is also entitled to use its official language when it is bringing a matter before the Court of Justice pursuant to Art. 259 TFEU concerning an action for infringement against another Member State for its failure to fulfil its obligations under the Treaties: ECJ Rules of Procedure, Art. 38(4).

[6] This may occur where a Union institution brings proceedings against a natural or legal person pursuant to an arbitration clause within the meaning of Art. 272 TFEU.

[7] ECJ Rules of Procedure, Art. 37(1)(a); EGC Rules of Procedure, Art. 35(2)(a).

[8] ECJ Rules of Procedure, Art. 37(1)(b); EGC Rules of Procedure, Art. 35(2)(b).

[9] ECJ Rules of Procedure, Art. 37(1)(c); EGC Rules of Procedure, Art. 35(2)(c).

[10] ECJ Rules of Procedure, Art. 37(4); EGC Rules of Procedure, Art. 35(2)(c), second para.

[11] CFI (order of 13 May 1993), Case T-74/92 *Ladbroke Racing v Commission* [1993] E.C.R. II-535, para. 14; CFI (order of 24 January 1997), Case T-121/95 *EFMA v Council* [1997] E.C.R. II-87, para. 10; EGC (order of 12 March 2012), Case T-521/11 *Deutsche Bahn and Others v Commission*, not reported.

[12] ECJ Rules of Procedure, Art. 37(3).

[13] ECJ Rules of Procedure, Art. 37(2)(a); EGC, Rules of Procedure, Art. 136a.

Statute (Ch. 17)[14] and in the case of challenges concerning the costs to be recovered, applications to set aside judgments by default, third-party proceedings, and applications for interpretation or revision of a judgment or for the Court of Justice or General Court to remedy a failure to adjudicate (see Ch. 25),[15] the language of the case is the language of the decision of the lower Court or of the decision to which the particular application is brought.[16]

(3) Disputes relating to intellectual property rights

The language of the case in disputes relating to intellectual property rights is determined in accordance with a special procedure laid down in Art. 131(2) of the EGC Rules of Procedure on account of the fact that the dispute concerned involves individuals. Under this provision, the language of the case is the language, chosen from among the twenty-four official Union languages, in which the application is drafted where the applicant was the only party to the proceedings before the Board of Appeal or if no other party objects. If, within a period following the lodgment of the application determined by the Registrar, the parties agree to use an official Union language other than the one used in the application, that language will become the language of the case. However, if a party objects to the language used in the application being the language of the case and the parties cannot agree on the choice of language, the language in which the application for registration in question was filed at the Office (i.e. either the OHIM or the Community Plant Variety Office (EGC Rules of Procedure, Art. 130(1)) becomes the language of the case,[17] unless the President or the General Court, on the matter being referred to it, finds that the use of that language would not enable all parties to the proceedings before the Board of Appeal to follow the proceedings and defend their interests and that only the use of another language would make it possible to remedy that situation. In that case, the President of the General Court may designate another official language as the language of the case after receipt of a reasoned request by any party and after hearing the other parties; he or she may also refer the matter to the General Court.

23.04

(4) Use of the language of a case

The language of the case is used in the written and oral pleadings of the parties, including supporting documents, i.e. the items and documents produced or annexed to such pleadings, and also in the minutes and decisions of the respective Court.[18]

23.05

---

[14] ECJ Rules of Procedure Art. 37(2)(b); see, e.g. ECJ (order of 20 May 2010), Case C-64/98 P-REV *Petrides v Commission* [2010] E.C.R. I-65*, Summ. pub., paras 14–16.

[15] ECJ Rules of Procedure, Art. 37(2)(c); there is at present no similar provision in the EGC Rules of Procedure.

[16] ECJ Rules of Procedure, Art. 37(2)(a)–(c); there is at present no similar provision in the EGC Rules of Procedure.

[17] See, e.g. CFI, Case T-292/01 *Philips-Van Heusen v OHIM* [2003] E.C.R. I-4335, paras 15–17; CFI, Case T-356/02 *Vitakraft-Werke Wührmann v OHIM* [2004] E.C.R. II-3445, para. 13.

[18] ECJ Rules of Procedure, Art. 38(1); EGC Rules of Procedure, Art. 35(3), first para. As regards written pleadings, see also Art. 7(5), first para., of the Instructions to the Registrar of the General Court, which states that except for the cases expressly provided for in the Rules of Procedure, the Registrar refuses to accept procedural documents of the parties drawn up in a language other than the language of the case.

Any supporting documents expressed in another language must be accompanied by a translation into the language of the case.[19] This means that if an intervener is not a Member State (see para. 25.73), it must in principle produce a translation in the language of the case of all documents and annexes which it produces.[20] If, however, substantial items or lengthy documents are involved, translations may be confined to extracts, unless the Court of Justice or the General Court, as the case may be, calls for a complete or fuller translation of its own motion or at the request of a party.[21]

(5) Witnesses and experts

23.06   A witness or expert who is unable adequately to express himself or herself in the language of the case may be authorized to use another language, even a language not included among the list of possible languages which may be used before the Court of Justice or the General Court.[22] The Registrar arranges for translation into the language of the case.[23]

(6) Members of the Court

23.07   The President, the Vice-President, and also the Presidents of Chambers in conducting oral proceedings, Judges and Advocates-General in putting questions, and Advocates-General in delivering their opinions are entitled to use a language other than the language of the case.[24] Here, too, the Registrar is responsible for arranging for translation into the language of the case.[25]

(7) Intervening States

23.08   A Member State intervening in a case is entitled to use its official language (or one of its official languages at its election) during both the written and oral part of the procedure.[26]

Likewise, EEA States not being Member States of the European Union (i.e. Iceland, Liechtenstein, and Norway) and the EFTA Surveillance Authority may be authorized to use an official Union language other than the language of the case where they intervene in proceedings before the Court of Justice or the General Court for the purposes of both the written and oral part of the procedure.[27]

In these instances, again, it is the Registrar who arranges for translation into the language of the case.[28]

---

[19] ECJ Rules of Procedure, Art. 38(2); EGC Rules of Procedure, Art. 35(3), second para. See also Art. 7(5), second para., of the Instructions to the Registrar of the General Court, which provides that where documents annexed to a procedural document are not accompanied by a translation into the language of the case, the Registrar will require the party concerned to make good the irregularity if such a translation appears necessary for the purposes of the efficient conduct of the proceedings. The translation of supporting documents may be lodged at the stage of the reply: ECJ (judgment of 1 March 2012), Case C-354/10 *Commission v Greece*, not reported, paras 31–35.

[20] See, e.g. CFI (order of 26 June 1996), Case T-11/95 *BP Chemicals v Commission* [1996] E.C.R. II-599; EGC (order of 25 July 2012), Case T-534/11 *Schenker v Commission*, not reported.

[21] ECJ Rules of Procedure, Art. 38(3); EGC Rules of Procedure, Art. 35(3), third para.

[22] ECJ Rules of Procedure, Art. 38(7); EGC Rules of Procedure, Art. 35(4).

[23] ECJ Rules of Procedure, Art. 38(7); EGC Rules of Procedure, Art. 35(4).

[24] ECJ Rules of Procedure, Art. 38(8); EGC Rules of Procedure, Art. 35(5).

[25] ECJ Rules of Procedure, Art. 38(8); EGC Rules of Procedure, Art. 35(5).

[26] ECJ Rules of Procedure, Art. 38(4); EGC Rules of Procedure, Art. 35(3), fourth para.

[27] ECJ Rules of Procedure, Art. 38(5); EGC Rules of Procedure, Art. 35(3), fifth para.

[28] ECJ Rules of Procedure, Arts 38(4)–(5); EGC Rules of Procedure, Art. 35(3), fourth and fifth paras.

(8) Responsibility of the Registrar

Furthermore, at the request of any Judge, Advocate-General, or party, the Registrar is **23.09** responsible for arranging for anything said or written in the course of the proceedings before the Court of Justice or the General Court to be translated into the languages chosen from the list of official Union languages which may serve as the language of a case.[29]

(9) Authentic text

The texts of documents drawn up in the language of the case or, where applicable, in **23.10** another language authorized by the Court of Justice or the General Court, as the case may be, are authentic.[30]

B. Internal language arrangements at the Court of Justice of the European Union

(1) Working language

The working language of the Court of Justice of the European Union is French. This **23.11** should not to be confused with the language of the case in which the proceedings before the respective Union court are conducted. This means that the respective Union court uses French for the purposes of its internal workings, for example, in its deliberations and for drafting preliminary reports, judgments, and orders.

(2) Publications

Publications of the Union courts are issued in the languages referred to in Art. 1 of Council **23.12** Regulation No. 1,[31] that is to say, the twenty-four official languages of the European Union.[32]

(3) Language service

The Court of Justice of the European Union has a language service staffed by experts with **23.13** adequate legal training and a thorough knowledge of several official languages of the European Union.[33]

II. Parties' Representation

A. General

(1) Distinction between direct actions and preliminary ruling proceedings

There is a distinction to be drawn between direct actions and preliminary ruling proceed- **23.14** ings as regards the representation of the parties. In direct actions before the Union courts,

---

[29] ECJ Rules of Procedure, Art. 39; EGC Rules of Procedure, Art. 36(1).
[30] ECJ Rules of Procedure, Art. 41; EGC Rules of Procedure, Art. 37.
[31] ECJ Rules of Procedure, Art. 40; EGC Rules of Procedure, Art. 36(2).
[32] Art. 1 of Council Regulation No. 1 stipulates that the official languages and the working languages of the Union institutions are Bulgarian, Croatian, Czech, Danish, Dutch, English, Estonian, Finnish, French, German, Greek, Hungarian, Irish, Italian, Latvian, Lithuanian, Maltese, Polish, Portuguese, Romanian, Slovak, Slovenian, Spanish, and Swedish.
[33] ECJ Rules of Procedure, Art. 42.

generally speaking, a party must be represented either by an agent or a lawyer, depending on its status,[34] and in turn, either a party or an agent may be assisted by an adviser.[35]

In preliminary ruling proceedings, the Court of Justice has regard to the rules of procedure applicable to the referring court or tribunal as far as the representation of the parties to the main proceedings (and their attendance at the Court) is concerned.[36] Consequently, parties to preliminary ruling proceedings do not necessarily have to be represented by a lawyer, in contrast to direct actions. This is the case where, in accordance with the applicable national rules of procedure, such a party may validly be otherwise represented before the national court (for example, by a representative of a trade union in employment disputes in some jurisdictions) or where a party is entitled to represent himself.[37]

(2) Intermediaries

23.15 The agents, advisers, and lawyers are intermediaries representing the parties. Only the person, Member State, or institution represented are parties to the proceedings before the Union courts.[38]

(3) Agents

23.16 Union institutions, bodies, offices, and agencies, Member States, EEA States which are not Member States of the European Union, and the EFTA Surveillance Authority are represented by an agent,[39] who has to lodge an authority to act with the Registry of the Court of Justice or the General Court, as the case may be.[40] An agent may be assisted by an adviser or by a lawyer entitled to practise before a court of a Member State.[41]

(4) Lawyers

23.17 All other parties (for the purposes of direct actions) must be represented either by a lawyer who is entitled to practise before a court of a Member State or of an EEA State or by a university teacher who is a national of a Member State whose law accords him or her a right of audience[42] (that is to say, as a university teacher and not as, say, a member of the Bar),

---

[34] Statute, Art. 19, first, second, and third paras; ECJ Rules of Procedure, Art. 119(1); EGC Rules of Procedure, Art. 43(1).

[35] Statute, Art. 19, first and fourth paras; ECJ Rules of Procedure, Art. 44(1)(c); at present, the EGC Rules of Procedure do not contain a similar provision.

[36] ECJ Rules of Procedure, Art. 97(3).

[37] ECJ Rules of Procedure, Art. 47(2). For an example, see ECJ, Case C-293/93 *Houtwipper* [1994] E.C.R. I-4249, at I-4262; ECJ, Case C-359/09 *Ebert* [2011] E.C.R. I-269, at I-272.

[38] CFI (order of 8 June 2005), Case T-151/03 *Nuova Agricast v Commission* [2005] E.C.R. II-1967, para. 29.

[39] Statute, Art. 19, first and second paras.

[40] ECJ Rules of Procedure, Arts 44(1)(a) and 119(2); EGC Rules of Procedure, Art. 39(a).

[41] Statute, Art. 19, first and fourth paras.

[42] Statute, Art. 19, third, fourth, and seventh paras; ECJ Rules of Procedure, Art. 47(1); EGC Rules of Procedure, Art. 42. It does not suffice that the person who signs the application is entitled to plead before a national court of a Member State; he or she has to be a member of the Bar (see, e.g. CFI (order of 28 February 2005), Case T-445/04 *Energy Technologies v OHIM* [2005] E.C.R. II-677, paras 1–3). The lawyer who signs the original of each pleading must be entitled to practise before a court of a Member State, even where he or she signs a pleading 'on behalf of' another lawyer who satisfies this requirement and represents the party concerned (CFI (order of 24 February 2000), Case T-37/98 *FTA and Others v Council* [2000] E.C.R. II-373, paras 26–32: the then Court of First Instance declared the application inadmissible on the grounds that the lawyer who had signed the pleading on behalf of his colleague was not entitled to practise before a court of a Member State); CFI (order of 9 September 2004), Case T-14/04 *Alto de Casablanca v OHIM* [2004] E.C.R. II-3077, para. 11, and CFI, Case T-315/03 *Wilfer v OHIM* [2005] E.C.R. II-1981, paras 10–11 (patent and

even if the applicant is a lawyer with rights of audience before a national court or tribunal.[43] Note that these are two cumulative conditions.[44] Therefore, a person—other than a university teacher—having a right of audience before the courts of a Member State without being a lawyer cannot validly represent a party before the Union courts.[45]

The lawyer representing the party cannot be an officer of the applicant (for example, the director of the applicant company).[46] The requirement to use a 'third party' as one's lawyer is based on a conception of the lawyer's role as collaborating in the administration of justice and as being required to provide, in full independence and in the overriding interests of justice, such legal assistance as his client needs.[47]

The lawyer must lodge a certificate that he or she is entitled to practise before a court of a Member State or of a non-EU EEA State and an authority from the party which he or she represents.[48]

(5) Representation of legal persons

If, in a case brought before the General Court, the applicant is a legal person governed by **23.18** private law, the lawyer must ensure that the application contains proof that the authority granted to him or her has been properly conferred on him or her by someone authorized for that purpose.[49]

---

trade mark agents are not authorized to represent parties in proceedings before the General Court, even if they are entitled to represent parties in certain actions before national courts); EGC (order of 26 March 2012), Case T-508/09 *Guillermo Canas v Commission*, not reported, paras 21–43 (a Swiss lawyer with right of audience in France was entitled to represent a party before the General Court).

[43] See, e.g. ECJ (order of 5 December 1996), Case C-174/96 P *Lopes v Court of Justice* [1996] E.C.R. I-6401, para. 10; ECJ, (order of 5 December 1996), Case C-175/96 P *Lopes v Court of Justice* [1996] E.C.R. I-6409, para. 10; ECJ (order of 21 November 2007), Case C-502/06 *Correia de Matos v Commission* [2007] E.C.R. I-163*, Summ. pub., para. 12; EGC (order of 20 September 2012), Case T-294/12 *Faet Oltra v European Ombudsman*, not reported, para. 7 (upheld on appeal in ECJ (order of 6 June 2013), Case C-535/12 P *Faet Oltra v European Ombudsman*, not reported).

[44] CFI (order of 20 October 2008), Case T-487/07 *Imperial Chemical Industries v OHIM* [2008] E.C.R. II-227*, Summ. pub., para. 13.

[45] CFI (order of 20 October 2008), Case T-487/07 *Imperial Chemical Industries v OHIM* [2008] E.C.R. II-227*, Summ. pub., paras 8–22 (although having a right to audience before the courts of a Member State, a Patent Attorney Litigator is not a lawyer within the meaning of Art. 19 of the Statute and therefore cannot represent a party validly before the Union courts).

[46] CFI (order of 8 December 1999), Case T-79/99 *Euro-Lex v OHIM* [1999] E.C.R. II-3555, paras 23–31; CFI (order of 13 January 2005), Case T-184/04 *Sulvida v Commission* [2005] E.C.R. II-85, paras 8–9; EGC (order of 11 March 2011), Joined Cases T-139/10, T-280/10 to T-285/10, and T-349/10 to T-352/10 *Milux v OHIM* [2011] II-55*, Summ. pub., para. 22; EGC (order of 21 March 2011), Case T-175/10 *Milux v OHIM* [2011] E.C.R. II-57*, Summ. pub., para. 20. More controversially, in EGC (order of 9 November 2011), Case T-243/11 *Glaxo Group v OHIM* [2011] E.C.R. II-379*, Summ. pub., paras 13–20, the General Court held that an in-house lawyer for a company which is part of the same group of companies as the applicant cannot be considered a third person within the meaning of Art. 19 of the Statute. See also EGC (order of 31 May 2013), Case T-120/13 *Codacons v Commission*, not reported, paras 7–14.

[47] CFI (order of 28 February 2005), Case T-445/04 *Energy Technologies v OHIM* [2005] E.C.R. II-677, para. 9; EGC (order 19 November 2009), Case T-40/08 *EREF v Commission* [2009] E.C.R. II-222*, Summ. pub., para. 26; EGC (order of 21 March 2011), Joined Cases T-139/10, T-280/10 to T-285/10 and T-349/10 to T-352/10 *Milux v OHIM* [2011] E.C.R. II-55*, para. 21.

[48] ECJ Rules of Procedure, Arts 44(1)(b)–(c) and 119(2)–(3); EGC Rules of Procedure, Art. 44(3) and (5)(b).

[49] EGC Rules of Procedure, Art. 44(5). See, e.g. CFI, Case T-145/98 *ADT Projekt v Commission* [2000] E.C.R. II-387, paras 50–54; CFI, Case T-180/00 *Astipesca v Commission* [2002] E.C.R. II-3985, paras 41–46; EGC (judgment of 10 July 2012), Case T-304/08 *Smurfit Kappa Group v Commission*, not reported, paras 29–39.

(6) Regularization

23.19 If necessary, the authority and proof of the status of the agent, lawyer, or adviser in question may be furnished within a 'reasonable time' to be prescribed by the Registrar. The sanction for failing to produce them within the time prescribed is that the Court of Justice or the General Court will decide, after hearing the Advocate-General (only in the case of the Court of Justice), whether non-compliance renders the application/defence formally inadmissible.[50]

B. Rights and obligations

(1) Immunity

23.20 Agents, advisers, and lawyers who appear before the Union courts or before any judicial authority to which the Court of Justice or the General Court has addressed letters rogatory[51] enjoy immunity in respect of words spoken or written by them concerning the case or the parties.[52]

(2) Privileges and facilities

23.21 Agents, advisers, and lawyers also enjoy certain privileges and immunities, mainly concerning the exemption from search and seizure of papers and documents relating to the proceedings and being able to travel without hindrance.[53]

(3) Qualification and waiver

23.22 To qualify for such privileges, immunities, and facilities, agents must produce an official document issued by the party for whom they act, with a copy immediately sent to the Registrar,[54] whereas lawyers must produce a certificate that they are authorized to practice before a court of a Member State or non-EU EEA State and, where the party they represent is a legal person governed by private law, an authority to act issued by that person.[55] Advisers must produce an authority to act issued by the party to whom they are assisting.[56]

These privileges, immunities, and facilities are granted exclusively in the interest of the proper conduct of the proceedings.[57] The Court of Justice or General Court, as the case may be, may waive immunity where it considers that the proper conduct of the proceedings will not be hindered thereby.[58]

---

[50] ECJ Rules of Procedure, Art. 119(4); EGC Rules of Procedure, Arts 44(6) and 46(1), second para. The regularization does, however, not concern the designation of a new lawyer where the lawyer mentioned in the application did not satisfy the 'third party' requirement: see ECJ (order of 5 September 2013), C-573/11 *ClientEarth v Council*, not reported, para. 23.

[51] See para. 23.71.

[52] ECJ Rules of Procedure, Art. 43(1); EGC Rules of Procedure, Art. 38(1).

[53] ECJ Rules of Procedure, Art. 43(2); EGC Rules of Procedure, Art. 38(2)(a) and (c).

[54] ECJ Rules of Procedure, Art. 44(1)(a); EGC Rules of Procedure, Art. 39(a).

[55] ECJ Rules of Procedure, Art. 44(1)(b); EGC Rules of Procedure, Art. 44 (3) and (5).

[56] ECJ Rules of Procedure, Art. 44(1)(c); at present the EGC Rules of Procedure do not contain a similar provision.

[57] ECJ Rules of Procedure, Art. 45(1); EGC Rules of Procedure, Art. 40, first para.

[58] ECJ Rules of Procedure, Art. 45(2); EGC Rules of Procedure, Art. 40, second para.

(4) Exclusion from the proceedings

Any agent, adviser, or lawyer whose conduct towards the Court of Justice or the General **23.23**
Court is incompatible with the dignity of the respective Court or with the requirements of
the proper administration of justice, or who uses his rights for purposes other than those for
which they were granted, may be excluded from the proceedings by way of reasoned order
with immediate effect.[59] Where an agent, lawyer, or adviser is excluded from the proceedings, the proceedings will be suspended for a period fixed by the President of the respective
Court so that the party concerned can appoint another agent, lawyer, or adviser.[60]

III. Service

A. Methods of service

Generally, there are two main methods of service dealing with either physical service at the **23.24**
particular addressee's address or via electronic means.

First, where the ECJ or EGC Rules of Procedure require that a document be served on a
person, such service is effected by the Registar at that person's address for service (see
further para. 25.05), which may be either by dispatch of the copy of the document
concerned by registered mail with a form of acknowledgment of receipt, or by personal
delivery of the copy of the document concerned against a receipt.[61]

Second, where the addressee has agreed that service is to be effected by telefax or any other
technical means of communication, any procedural document, including a judgment or
order of the Court of Justice or the General Court, may be served by transmission of a copy
of that document by such means.[62]

Yet, there is an exception where for technical reasons or on account of the length of the
document, transmission by telefax or any other technical means is impossible or impractic-
able, in which case the procedural document must be served, if the addressee has not
specified an address for service, at his address essentially in accordance with the same
procedures used for effecting service at the person's address for service, i.e. either by
registered post with acknowledgment of receipt or by personal delivery against a receipt,
and the addressee is so informed via telefax or other technical means of communication.[63]
Under these circumstances, service is then deemed to have been effected on the addressee
by registered post on the tenth day following the lodging of the registered letter at the post

---

[59] ECJ Rules of Procedure, Art. 46(1)–(2); EGC Rules of Procedure, Art. 41(1). Such decisions may be
rescinded: ECJ Rules of Procedure, Art. 46(4); EGC Rules of Procedure, Art. 41(3). See also CFI (order of the
President of 29 March 2001), Case T-302/00 R *Goldstein v Commission* [2001] E.C.R. II-1127, paras 40–42.
[60] ECJ Rules of Procedure, Art. 46(3); EGC Rules of Procedure, Art. 41(2).
[61] ECJ Rules of Procedure, Art. 48(1); EGC Rules of Procedure, Art. 100(1). As further specified in the
foregoing provision, the Registrar prepares and certifies the copies of the documents to be served, unless the
parties themselves supply the copies.
[62] ECJ Rules of Procedure, Art. 48(2); EGC Rules of Procedure, Art. 100(2), first para. In addition, with
particular regard to judgments and orders notified to Member States and Union institutions not parties to the
proceedings pursuant to Art. 55 of the Statute, these are sent by telefax or any other technical means of
communication: EGC Rules of Procedure, Art. 100(2), second para.
[63] ECJ Rules of Procedure, Art. 48(3); EGC Rules of Procedure, Art. 100(2), third para.

office of the place in which the respective Court has its seat, unless it is shown by the acknowledgment of receipt that the letter was received on a different date or the addressee informs the Registrar within three weeks of being informed by telefax or any other technical means of communication that the document to be served has not reached him or her.[64]

B. Service by e-Curia

23.25   As instructed by the relevant Rules of Procedure,[65] the Union courts have set down by decision published in the *Official Journal* the criteria for a procedural document to be served by means of e-Curia (see further para. 23.50).[66]

IV. The Calculation of Time Limits

A. Distinction between procedural time limits and limitation periods

23.26   The procedural time limits prescribed by the TFEU, the EAEC Treaty, the Statute, and the Rules of Procedure of the Court of Justice and the General Court are calculated in a uniform manner.[67] Procedural time limits, such as the time limit for bringing an annulment action[68] or an appeal,[69] are intended to ensure legal certainty, clarity, and due administration of justice. They guarantee that an administrative or court decision becomes final after a certain period of time and thus serve the public interest. Therefore, procedural time limits are a matter of public policy, compliance of which can be examined by the Union courts of their own motion.[70]

---

[64] ECJ Rules of Procedure, Art. 48(3); EGC Rules of Procedure, Art. 100(2), third para.

[65] ECJ Rules of Procedure, Art. 48(4); EGC Rules of Procedure, Art. 100(3); CST Rules of Procedure, Art. 99(3).

[66] For the Court of Justice, see the Decision [of the Court of Justice] of 13 September 2011 on the lodging and service of procedural documents by means of e-Curia ([2011] O.J. C289/11), Arts 6–7. For the General Court, see the Decision [of the General Court] of 14 September 2011 on the lodging and service of procedural documents by means of e-Curia ([2011] O.J. C289/9), Arts 6–7. For the Civil Service Tribunal, see the Decision [of the Civil Service Tribunal] No. 3/2011 taken at the Plenary Meeting on 20 September 2011 on the lodging and service of procedural documents by means of e-Curia ([2011] O.J. C289/11), Arts 6–7. See also the documents available on the website of the Court of Justice of the European Union on e-Curia applicable to the Union courts (the Court of Justice, the General Court, and the Civil Service Tribunal): e-Curia: conditions of use applicable to parties' representatives, done at Luxembourg on 11 October 2011, points 20–27; and e-Curia: conditions of use applicable to assistants, done at Luxembourg on 11 October 2011, points 20–27.

[67] The rules set forth in the CST Rules of Procedure concerning time limits (Arts 100–101) generally follow those set forth in the ECJ Rules of Procedure and the EGC Rules of Procedure. For further discussion of time limits in relation to staff cases, see para. 18.25. Any time limit prescribed by the Union courts pursuant to the Rules of Procedure (such as the time limit for lodging the defence, reply, or rejoinder) may be extended: ECJ Rules of Procedure, Art. 52; EGC Rules of Procedure, Art. 103; CST Rules of Procedure, Art. 101. By contrast, time limits imposed by the Treaties, such as the time limit for bringing an action for annulment (Art. 263, sixth para., TFEU) or for failure to act (Art. 265, second para., TFEU) cannot be extended.

[68] Art. 263, sixth para., TFEU.

[69] Statute, Art. 56.

[70] See, e.g. ECJ (judgment of 8 November 2012), Case C-469/11 P *Evropaïki Dynamiki v Commission*, not reported, para. 50 (and further citations therein).

Procedural time limits are different from limitation periods, for example in the context of an action for damages against the Union.[71] Expiry of a limitation period leads to the extinction of a legal action, which is a matter of substantive law, since it affects the enforceability of a subjective right which the person concerned can no longer effectively assert before the relevant court.[72] On the one hand, a limitation period protects the interests of the aggrieved party, while on the other hand, it protects the party responsible for the harm from a claim for damages unrestricted in time. A limitation period is thus not laid down to serve the public interest. Consequently, a claim that a limitation period has been breached cannot be examined by the Union courts of their own motion.[73]

B. Preliminary objection

The correct calculation of procedural time limits is of utmost importance for a litigant being able to avail himself of judicial protection before the Union courts, since if a party lodges its application after the expiry of the procedural time limit concerned, its application will be held inadmissible. Moreover, if a defendant considers that the applicant has lodged its action out of time, that defendant may lodge by separate document an objection of inadmissibility on such grounds without even having to go into the merits of the case (see further para. 25.41).[74] **23.27**

C. Main steps in the calculation of procedural time limits

The calculation of a procedural time limit prescribed by the Treaties, Statute, or Rules of Procedure of the Union courts can generally be summarized as involving four main steps, which are each elaborated further in this section. **23.28**

The first step concerns the determination of the *dies a quo*, or the day on which time starts running, and there is special consideration in the case of actions for annulment where the contested measure has been published in the *Official Journal of the European Union*.

The second step concerns the counting of the duration of the particular procedural time limit, e.g. two months in the case of an application for an action for annulment,[75] six weeks from publication of the notice of the application in the *Official Journal* in the case of

---

[71] ECJ, Case C-469/11 P *Evropaïki Dynamiki v Commission*, para. 49. Another example bearing out this distinction is the revision of a judgment: whereas the time limit for bringing an application for revision is within three months of the date on which the facts on which the application is founded came to the applicant's knowledge (ECJ Rules of Procedure, Art. 159(2); EGC Rules of Procedure, Art. 125; CST Rules of Procedure, Art. 119(1), second para.), the Statute prescribes a limitation period of ten years from the date of judgment, after which time no application for revision may be made (Statute, Art. 44, third para.). For further discussion of revision, see para. 25.116.
[72] Statute, Art. 44, para. 52.
[73] Statute, Art. 44, para. 51.
[74] See ECJ Rules of Procedure, Art. 151; EGC Rules of Procedure, Art. 114.
[75] See Art. 263, sixth para., TFEU. In addition to the present section, for further discussion of the calculation of time limits in the context of an action for annulment, see para. 7.207.

intervention,[76] or two months after service in the case of the filing of the defence to an application.[77]

The third step involves adding on ten days for distance.

The fourth step concerns the determination of the *dies ad quem*, or the final day on which time stops running, including whether such day falls on a Saturday, Sunday, or official holiday, in which case it must be carried over to the next business day.

These steps must all be followed and in the right order, i.e. there should be no checking whether the applicable day falls on a Saturday, Sunday, or official holiday until the last step, which is sometimes an error made by parties.

D. *Dies a quo*

23.29 As far as the day from which time starts running (*dies a quo*) is concerned, the following is important. Time limits calculated from the moment at which an event occurs or an action takes place start to run on the day *after* the event occurs or the action takes place.[78]

E. Starting point in case of publication

23.30 This principle is further specified in the case of publication of the contested measure in the *Official Journal*:

> Where the time-limit allowed for initiating proceedings against a measure adopted by an institution runs from the publication of that measure, that time-limit shall be calculated . . . from the end of the 14th day after publication of the measure in the *Official Journal of the European Union*.[79]

Since 1 July 2013, only the *Official Journal* published in electronic form is authentic and produces legal effects.[80]

In particular, this rule applies in the case of lodging an action for annulment which, in the absence of notification, must in principle be instituted within two months of the

---

[76] ECJ Rules of Procedure, Art. 130(1); EGC Rules of Procedure, Art. 115(1). See further para. 25.70. For an example of the calculation of the time limit for intervening, see CFI (order of the President of 11 July 2001), Case T-339/00 *Bactria v Commission*, not reported, para. 10.

[77] ECJ Rules of Procedure, Art. 124(1); EGC Rules of Procedure, Art. 46(1). See further para. 25.28.

[78] ECJ Rules of Procedure, Art. 49(1)(a); EGC Rules of Procedure, Art. 101(1)(a).

[79] ECJ Rules of Procedure, Art. 50; EGC Rules of Procedure, Art. 102(1). This rule applies to all acts published in the electronic version of the *Official Journal of the European Union* and not only to acts whose publication is necessary in order for them to enter into effect (see CFI (order of 25 May 2004), Case T-264/03 *Schmoldt and Others v Commission* [2004] E.C.R. II-1515, paras 51–62). This rule also applies if an act is only published on the website of an Union institution, body, office, or agency and not in the *Official Journal of the European Union* (see ECJ (judgment of 26 September 2013), Case C-625/11 P *PPG and SNF v ECHA*, not reported, paras 30–37). An action against an act can, however, be brought prior to its publication if the applicant has knowledge of the existence of such act at such an earlier date: ECJ (judgment of 26 September 2013), Case C-626/11 P *PPG and SNF v ECHA*, not reported, para. 41.

[80] Council Regulation (EU) No. 216/2013 of 7 March 2013 on the electronic publication of the *Official Journal of the European Union*, [2013] O.J. L69/1, Arts 1(2) and 5.

publication of the contested measure in accordance with the sixth paragraph of Art. 263 TFEU (see further para. 7.211).[81]

Further to this, where the contested act constitutes a restrictive measure vis-à-vis a natural or a legal person, the Union institutions are under an obligation to communicate as soon as possible after the publication of the act in the *Official Journal* the grounds on which that measure is based. Time limits do not start to run in respect of the affected natural or legal person as long as the measure has not been notified or otherwise communicated to him.[82]

F. Duration of the period

As far as the running and duration of the period are concerned, it should first be noted that **23.31** Saturdays, Sundays, official holidays, and judicial vacations count towards the period.[83] In other words, they are included as part of the calculation; it is only if the last day on which time stops running (the *dies ad quem*) falls on a Saturday, Sunday, or official holiday that time must be extended as discussed below.

G. Extension of ten days on account of distance

In addition, all procedural time limits are currently subject to a standard extension of ten **23.32** days on account of distance.[84] This extension applies to all parties, including Union institutions, bodies, offices, and agencies.[85]

Formerly, there were different extensions on account of distance for different countries. The idea behind this was that, even though procedural documents were validly served at the parties' address for service in Luxembourg, an extension of time was necessary for parties who resided or were established a long way away so as to give all the parties the same time in which to prepare for their participation in the proceedings before the Union judicature. These extensions were subsequently replaced with a blanket extension of 10 days, irrespective of what country a party comes from.

---

[81] This rule also applies in the case of the lodging of an application initiating third-party proceedings which must be submitted within two months of publication of the contested decision in the *Official Journal*: see ECJ Rules of Procedure, Art. 157(3); EGC Rules of Procedure, Art.123(1), third para. See further para. 25.111.

[82] See, e.g. EGC (order of 11 January 2012), Case T-301/11 *Ben Ali v Council*, not reported, paras 18–20. See in this respect also ECJ (judgment of 23 April 2013), Joined Cases C-478/11 to C-482/11 *Gbagbo and Others v Council*, not reported, paras 53–64. See further para. 7-211.

[83] ECJ Rules of Procedure, Art. 49(1)(d) and (e); EGC Rules of Procedure, Art. 101(1)(d) and (e). For the current list of official holidays (which according to ECJ Rules of Procedure, Art. 24(6) are now published annually in the *Official Journal of the European Union*), see the Decision of the ECJ of 19 November 2013 on official holidays and judicial vacations ([2013] O.J. C359/2), which is applicable to the General Court (EGC Rules of Procedure, Art. 101(2), second para.) and the Civil Service Tribunal (CST Rules of Procedure, Art. 100(2), second para.). Under Art. 1 of this Decision, ten official holidays are listed: New Year's Day, Easter Monday, 1 May, Ascension Day, Whit Monday, 23 June, 15 August, 1 November, 25 December, and 26 December.

[84] Statute, Art. 45, first para.; ECJ Rules of Procedure, Art. 51; EGC Rules of Procedure, Art. 102(2).

[85] See, e.g. ECJ Case C-137/92 P *Commission v BASF and Others* [1994] E.C.R. I-2555, paras 40–42; ECJ, Case C-245/95 P *Commission v NTN Corporation and Koyo Seiko* [1998] E.C.R. I-401, paras 19–23.

The extension on account of distance is not to be regarded as separate from the procedural time limit, but merely as a prolongation of it.[86]

As the five-year limitation period for bringing an action for damages[87] is not a procedural time limit,[88] no extension on account of duration is applicable when such action is lodged.[89]

H. *Dies ad quem*

23.33 As far as the day on which time stops running (*dies ad quem*) is concerned, two aspects must be borne in mind.

First, there is the rule that if the period would otherwise end on a Saturday, Sunday, or an official holiday, it is extended until the end of the first following working day.[90]

Second, the last day of the period is determined as follows: 'A time-limit expressed in weeks, months or in years shall end with the expiry of whichever day in the last week, month or year is the same day of the week, or falls on the same date, as the day during which the event or action from which the time-limit is to be calculated occurred or took place. If, in a time-limit expressed in months or years, the day on which it should expire does not occur in the last month, the time-limit shall end with the expiry of the last day of that month; where a time-limit is expressed in months and days, it shall first be calculated in whole months, then in days.'[91]

It should be noted that the key day for determining the last day of a period is the actual day corresponding to the one on which the event or action occurred which caused time to start running, and not the day after, even though that is the day on which time actually started to run. Although this may appear contradictory, it is in fact quite logical, as the following example shows: if the period for bringing an action for annulment starts running as a result

---

[86] CFI (order of 20 November 1997), Case T-85/97 *Horeca-Wallonie v Commission* [1997] E.C.R. II-2113, para. 26; EGC (order of 15 July 2011), Case T-213/11 P(I) *Collège des représentants du personnel de la EIB and Others v Bömcke*, not reported, para. 10. Consequently, the last day of the time limit is the day on which the procedural time limit, together with the time on account of distance, runs out. This is important in order to determine whether the time limit may be extended because the last day is a Saturday, a Sunday, or an official holiday (see para. 23.33). In the *Horeca-Wallonie* case, the applicant argued that the procedural time limit, the 'last' day of which fell on Easter Monday—an official holiday—had to be extended, after which, on account of distance, time started to run. The then Court of First Instance rejected this argument. See also CFI (order of 19 January 2001), Case T-126/00 *Confindustria and Others v Commission* [2001] E.C.R. II-85, para. 18.

[87] Statute, Art. 46.

[88] See para. 23.26.

[89] ECJ (judgment of 8 November 2012), Case C-469/11 P *Evropaïki Dynamiki v Commission*, not reported, para. 59. For further discussion of the limitation period for actions for damages against the Union, see para. 11.86. The time limits for bringing the defence, reply, and rejoinder are, however, extended on account of distance, even in the context of an action for damages, since they constitute procedural time limits.

[90] ECJ Rules of Procedure, Art. 49(2); EGC Rules of Procedure, Art. 101(2), first para. For the list of official holidays, see n. 83.

[91] ECJ Rules of Procedure, Art. 49(1)(b) and (c); EGC Rules of Procedure, Art. 101(1)(b) and (c). These provisions on the *dies ad quem* codify the rule in *Misset* which used to be applied alongside the ECJ Rules of Procedure. See ECJ, Case 152/85 *Misset v Council* [1987] E.C.R. 223, para. 8; ECJ, Joined Cases 281/85, 283/85 to 285/85, and 287/85 *Germany and Others v Commission* [1987] E.C.R. 3203, paras 5–6.

of notification of the contested act on 3 April, then the two months within which the action must be brought run from 4 April at 0 hours (i.e. the *dies a quo*, being the day after notification) to 3 June at 24 hours (i.e. the *dies ad quem*, that it to say, the day which falls on the same date as 'the day during which the event or action from which the period is to be calculated occurred or took place', namely the date of notification). Thus, the period amounts to precisely two months.

I. Applications

A further example involving notification of the contested measure may be used to illustrate **23.34** the rules set out above: a Commission decision is notified to an undertaking established in the Netherlands on 15 October 2012. The usual two-month time limit ends at midnight on 15 December 2012, but is extended by ten days on account of distance, i.e. to midnight on 25 December 2012, an official holiday, which produces a further extension to midnight of the first working day, i.e. Thursday, 27 December 2012.[92]

Two other notable examples involving publication of the contested measure come from the case-law. In the first case, an application for annulment was lodged on 21 June 2001 against a Commission regulation published in the *Official Journal of the European Union* on 27 March 2001. The General Court held first, however, that time for bringing proceedings began to run from the end of the fourteenth day after publication, i.e. 10 April 2001. As a result, the two-month period laid down by former fifth paragraph of Art. 230, EC (now sixth paragraph of Art. 263 TFEU) ran out on Sunday, 10 June 2001, but was extended by time on account of distance to Wednesday, 20 June 2001. Accordingly, the application served on 21 June was out of time. In this connection, it was irrelevant that the 'original' deadline expired on a Sunday. This is because time on account of distance forms part of the complete limitation period, which ran out on a normal working day.[93]

In the second case, an application for annulment was lodged on 11 July 2011 against a Commission implementing regulation published in the *Official Journal of the European Union* on 14 April 2011. Pursuant to Art. 102(1) of the EGC Rules of Procedure, 14 days had to be added, pushing the date of publication forward to 28 April 2011. The time limit of two months for bringing an action for annulment (sixth paragraph of Art. 263 TFEU) expired on 28 June 2011 at 24h. Adding 10 days on account of distance resulted in Friday, 8 July 2011 as the *dies ad quem*. The General Court declared the action brought on Monday 11 July 2011 inadmissible, since it was brought out of time.[94]

J. The Court is never closed

On a practical note, documents may be handed in at the entrance of the Court of Justice **23.35** and the General Court at any time of the day or night; the security guard will note the exact time of receipt and this will be decisive evidence.

---

[92] This is because 26 December is an official holiday.
[93] CFI, Joined Cases T-142/01 and T-283/01 *OPTUC v Commission* [2004] E.C.R. II-329, paras 36–42.
[94] See EGC (order of 22 September 2011), Case T-374/11 *Libyan Investment Authority and Others v Council and Commission*, not reported, paras 10–19.

K. Lodgment at the Registry

23.36 Under Art. 57(6) of the ECJ Rules of Procedure and Art. 43(3) of the EGC Rules of Procedure, the day to be taken into account for calculating procedural time limits is the date of lodgment of the original at the Registry. The date on which a pleading or other document is registered at the Registry is therefore not determinative.[95]

L. Lodgment by telefax, e-Curia, or any other means of communication

23.37 Where a pleading is lodged with the appropriate Registry by telefax or any other technical means of communication available to the Court of Justice or the General Court (i.e. e-mail), the date of receipt is deemed to be the date of lodgment,[96] provided that the signed original of the pleading is lodged at the Registry no later than ten days thereafter.[97]

Such requirement does not exist for lodgments made by means of e-Curia. For the calculation of time limits, a procedural document is deemed to have been lodged by means of e-Curia at the time of the party representative's validation of lodgment of that document.[98]

A party's representative lodging documents by telefax has to take into account the average transmission time between two telefaxes. Only the time of receipt at the Registry will constitute the time of lodgment, not the time of sending as confirmed by the telefax of the representative. This is of particular importance if applications are lodged by telefax only minutes before the expiry of the time limit.[99]

M. Excusable error, unforeseeable circumstances, or *force majeure*

23.38 Finally, it should be mentioned that the expiry of a procedural time limit cannot be pleaded if the other party proves the existence of an excusable error, unforeseen circumstances, or

---

[95] CFI, Case T-145/98 *ADT Projekt v Commission* [2000] E.C.R. II-387, para. 80.

[96] The time zone of the seat of the Union courts applies, which is Luxembourg time. This should be taken into account when lodging applications from a different time zone. See, e.g. EGC (order of 1 April 2011), Case T-468/10 *Doherty v Commission* [2011] E.C.R. II-1497, para. 16; EGC (order of 1 April 2011), Case T-469/10 *Conneely v Commission*, not reported, para. 16; EGC (order of 1 April 2011), Case T-470/10 *Oglesby v Commission*, not reported, para. 16.

[97] ECJ Rules of Procedure, Art. 57(7); EGC Rules of Procedure, Art. 43(6). The period of ten days is not a procedural time limit and cannot be extended by the period on account of distance (see para. 23.32). In the event of any discrepancy between the signed original and the copy previously lodged, only the date of lodgment of the signed original will be taken into consideration (ECJ Practice Directions, point 43; EGC Practice Directions, point I.A.1.7). For an example, see CFI (order of 8 May 2003), Case T-63/03 *El Corte Inglés v OHIM*, not reported: the application was inadmissible because the original was not lodged with the Registry within ten days.

[98] ECJ Decision of 13 September 2011 on the lodging and service of procedural documents by means of e-Curia ([2011] O.J. C289/7), Art. 5; EGC Decision of 14 September 2011 on the lodging and service of procedural documents by means of e-Curia ([2011] O.J. C289/9), Art. 5.

[99] EGC (order of 1 April 2011), Case T-468/10 *Doherty v Commission* [2011] E.C.R. II-1497, para. 22.

force majeure.[100] This exceptional rule is applicable to any procedural time limit, but the Union courts take an extremely strict view.

The typical case of a clerical error made by the representative of one of the parties is not enough to bring the rule into play.[101] *Force majeure* will also not be accepted when a representative is faced with a temporary disfunctioning of the Registry's telefax while sending a large number of applications just before the expiry of the time limit.[102] A terrorist attack which would preclude a party from utilizing either the post or electronic means of communication for a period of time may suffice to prove *force majeure*, depending on the particular circumstances. Nonetheless, to rely on this exceptional rule remains a great—and hence unwarranted—risk.[103]

V. Procedures for Dealing with Cases

A. General

(1) Written and oral part

In general, without prejudice to the special provisions laid down in the Statute or the Rules of Procedure of the Union courts,[104] the procedure before the respective Union court consists of a written part and an oral part.[105] In essence, the purpose of the written part of the procedure is to define the subject-matter of the action and to put before the Court of Justice or the General Court all of the facts, pleas, arguments of the parties, interested   **23.39**

---

[100] Statute, Art. 45, second para. On the distinction between an excusable error, on the one hand, and an unforeseeable circumstance or *force majeure*, on the other, see ECJ (judgment of 22 September 2011), Case C-426/10 P *Bell & Ross v OHIM* [2011] E.C.R. I-8849, paras 47–48; EGC (order of 11 January 2012), Case T-301/11 *Ben Ali v Council*, not reported, paras 29–32; EGC (judgment of 18 June 2013), Case T-404/08 *Fluorsid and Minmet v Commission*, not reported, paras 60–61.

[101] See para. 7.208.

[102] See, e.g. EGC (order of 1 April 2011), Case T-468/10 *Doherty v Commission* [2011] E.C.R. II-1497, paras 20–22; EGC (order of 1 April 2011), Case T-469/10 *Conneely v Commission*, not reported, paras 20–22; EGC (order of 1 April 2011), Case T-470/10 *Oglesby v Commission*, not reported, paras 20–22. In these cases, the representative tried to lodge seven applications just before midnight. Only one application reached the General Court before the expiry of the time limit. The representative claimed that this was caused by a temporary dysfunctioning of the Registry's telefax between 23.53 and 23.57 while sending the first application, which reached the Court in time. The General Court rejected this argument, stating that as a result of the average transmission time the other applications would have never reached the Registry before midnight, even if the Registry's telefax had functioned correctly.

[103] See, e.g. ECJ (order of 7 May 1998), Case C-239/97 *Ireland v Commission* [1998] E.C.R. I-2655, paras 7-10, in which the fact that a courier service had not been able to deliver the application to the Registry on time because of technical difficulties was not considered to constitute *force majeure*, particularly since the applicant had waited until the day before time was due to run out (including time on account of distance) before sending the application from Ireland. See also CFI (order of 21 March 2002), Case T-218/01 *Laboratoire Monique Rémy v Commission* [2002] E.C.R. II-2139, para. 30, in which the application was sent by registered post a few days before time ran out but was not delivered to the Registry of the General Court until after time had run out; ECJ (order of 18 January 2005), Case C-325/03 P *Zuazaga Meabe v OHIM* [2005] E.C.R. I-403, paras 21–28; EGC (order of 8 May 2012), Case T-675/11 *Maxcom v OHIM*, not reported, para. 14.

[104] See, e.g. ECJ Rules of Procedure, Art. 76; EGC Rules of Procedure, Arts 135a and 146. Furthermore, no hearing is held when the Rules of Procedure allow the Court to determine a case by means of reasoned order. See further para. 23.40.

[105] Statute, Art. 20 (applicable to the General Court under Art. 53, first para., and to the Civil Service Tribunal under Annex I, Art. 7); ECJ Rules of Procedure, Art. 53(1); CST Rules of Procedure, Arts 33 and 48.

persons within the meaning of Art. 23 of the Statute, or others involved in the proceedings, and the forms of order sought by way of procedural documents or pleadings,[106] whereas the purpose of the oral part of the procedure (except where a case is dealt with under an expedited or urgent procedure) is to afford the parties (and others involved in the proceedings) the opportunity to present oral arguments, to develop their claims, and to clarify any issues or questions before the respective Court.[107]

(2) Reasoned order

23.40 Where it is clear that the Court of Justice or the General Court, as the case may be, has no jurisdiction to hear and determine a case or where a request or application is manifestly inadmissible, the Court concerned may decide at any time, after hearing the Advocate-General, to give a decision by reasoned order without taking any further steps in the proceedings.[108] The General Court can do the same where the action manifestly lacks any foundation in law.[109]

(3) Priority

23.41 Generally, the Court of Justice and the General Court take cognizance of cases brought before them in order, depending on when the preparatory inquiry is completed (see para. 23.56).[110] In special circumstances, however, the President of the respective Court may decide that a particular case be given priority over others.[111] He or she may do so of his or her own motion, although parties may request him or her to do so.

(4) Expedited procedures

23.42 A case before the Court of Justice or the General Court may be dealt with under an expedited procedure in accordance with the applicable rules of the Statute and Rules of Procedure.[112] An expedited procedure may be used in respect of direct actions (see para. 25.79)[113] and preliminary rulings proceedings (see para. 24.17).[114] A reference for a preliminary ruling may also be dealt with under an urgent procedure applicable in the Area of Freedom, Security and Justice (see para. 22.06).[115] Such procedures essentially

---

[106] See ECJ Practice Directions, point 9.

[107] See ECJ Practice Directions, point 45.

[108] ECJ Rules of Procedure, Art. 53(2); EGC Rules of Procedure, Art. 111. See also CST Rules of Procedure, Art. 76.

[109] The words 'or manifestly lacking any foundation in law' were added to Art. 111 of the EGC Rules of Procedure in order to make it clear that the General Court cannot deal with a case under that provision where the outcome of the proceedings depends on an assessment of the facts. For an example, see EGC (order of 24 October 2012), Case T-442/11 *Evropaïki Dynamiki v Commission*, not reported, para. 42.

[110] EGC Rules of Procedure, Art. 55(1); CST Rules of Procedure, Art. 47(1).

[111] ECJ Rules of Procedure, Art. 53(3); EGC Rules of Procedure, Art. 55(2), first para.; CST Rules of Procedure, Art. 47(2).

[112] See ECJ Rules of Procedure, Art. 53(4); EGC Rules of Procedure, Art. 76a(1). There is no expedited procedure in proceedings before the Civil Service Tribunal.

[113] ECJ Rules of Procedure, Art. 133; EGC Rules of Procedure, Art. 76a.

[114] ECJ Rules of Procedure, Arts 105–106.

[115] ECJ Rules of Procedure, Arts 53(5) and 107–114. For the distinction between the expedited and urgent procedure for preliminary rulings, see para. 22.19. See also V. Skouris, 'De nouveaux défis pour la Cour de justice dans une Europe élargie' ERA Forum (2008) 106.

allow the Court of Justice and the General Court, as the case may be, to deal with the particular case on a more speedy basis than the normal procedure.[116]

B. Joinder of cases

(1) Connection between cases

The President of the Court of Justice[117] or the President of the Chamber concerned at the General Court may, at any time after hearing the Judge-Rapporteur and the Advocate-General[118] and the parties (save in the case of preliminary ruling proceedings), order that two or more cases concerning the same subject-matter be joined, on account of the connection between them, for the purposes of the written or oral procedure or of the final judgment.[119] The President may refer the decision to the Court of Justice or the General Court, as the case may be.

23.43

Cases will be regarded as sufficiently connected, *inter alia*, where they contest the same act[120] using the same submissions,[121] or where the same parties are involved in different proceedings based on similar facts.[122]

In contrast to the former Rules of Procedure, the ECJ Rules of Procedure explicitly state that only cases 'of the same type' may be joined.[123] A joinder of direct and indirect actions is therefore precluded. Furthermore, Art. 77 of the ECJ Rules of Procedure now expressly precludes the organization of a joint hearing for cases of a different type but with the same subject-matter.[124] This constitutes a departure of an established practice under the former

---

[116] K. Lenaerts, 'An Overview of the Accelerated and Urgency Procedure in the Area of Freedom, Security and Justice' (2011) Evropeiski praven pregled 32–61.

[117] This power was conferred on the President in order to speed up proceedings: see V. Christianos and F. Picod, 'Les modifications récentes du règlement de la Cour de justice des Communautés européennes' (1991) Rec. Dalloz, Chronique 278–82.

[118] This only applies when the cases have already been assigned.

[119] ECJ Rules of Procedure, Art. 54(1) and (2); EGC Rules of Procedure, Art. 50. EGC Rules of Procedure, Art. 50(2) further provides that 'the agents, advisers or lawyers of all the parties to the joined cases, including interveners, may examine at the Registry the pleadings served on the parties in the other cases concerned' and adds that the 'President may, however, on application by a party, exclude [...] secret or confidential documents from that consultation'.

[120] ECJ, Joined Cases 19/74 and 20/74 *Kali & Salz and Kali-Chemie v Commission* [1975] E.C.R. 499, para. 2; CFI, Case T-1/89 *Rhône-Poulenc v Commission* [1991] E.C.R. II-867, para. 232; CFI, Joined Cases T-67/00, T-68/00, T-71/00, and T-78/00 *JFE Engineering and Others v Commission* [2004] E.C.R. II-2501; EGC, Joined Cases T-259/02 to T-264/02 and T-271/02 *Raiffeisen Zentralbank Österreich and Others v Commission* [2006] E.C.R. II-5169.

[121] ECJ, Joined Cases 112/73, 144/73, and 145/73 *Campogrande and Others v Commission* [1974] E.C.R. 957, para. 5; EGC, Joined Cases T-494/08 to T-500/08 and T-509/08 *Ryanair v Commission* [2010] E.C.R. II-5723.

[122] ECJ, Joined Cases 7/54 and 9/54 *Groupement des Industries Sidérurgiques Luxembourgeoises v High Authority* [1954 to 1956] E.C.R. 175; ECJ, Joined Cases C-305/86 and C-160/87 *Neotype Techmashexport v Commission and Council* [1990] E.C.R. I-2945.

[123] ECJ Rules of Procedure, Art. 54(1). Compare former ECJ Rules of Procedure, Art. 43 which merely specified 'two or more cases concerning the same subject-matter'. The EGC Rules of Procedure do not contain a similar rule since cases of a different type (i.e. a direct action, on the one hand, and an appeal or proceedings relating to intellectual property rights, on the other hand) brought before the General Court will in any event not concern the same subject-matter.

[124] ECJ Rules of Procedure, Art. 77 provides: 'If the similarities between two or more cases of the same type so permit, the Court may decide to organise a joint hearing of those cases.'

Rules in which the Court of Justice organized a joint hearing involving both direct and indirect actions, for instance, a joint hearing for a reference for a preliminary ruling and infringement proceedings.[125] Cases of a different type having the same subject-matter will henceforth be heard in sequence, either on the same day or during a number of consecutive days.[126]

(2) Objective

23.44 Cases are joined in order to facilitate the processing of cases by avoiding unnecessary repetition of procedural acts. Joinder has sometimes been justified on the grounds that it avoids conflicting interpretations of judgments.[127]

(3) Effect

23.45 In principle, joinder has no effects on the parties' legal position.[128] It does not preclude separate examination of the cases in the judgment.[129] Furthermore, it is possible for one of the cases to be declared inadmissible after joinder. The arguments put forward in the case declared inadmissible may be taken into account in determining the second or other cases joined.[130]

The President may at any time disjoin cases.[131]

C. Stay of proceedings

(1) Circumstances

23.46 The proceedings before the Court of Justice and the General Court, as the case may be, may be stayed in a variety of circumstances, which predicate the procedure to be followed before the respective Court.[132]

---

[125] See, e.g. ECJ, Case C-318/05 *Commission v Germany* [2007] E.C.R. I-6957 and ECJ, Case C-76/05 *Schwarz and Gootjes-Schwarz* [2007] E.C.R. I-6849, both dealing with a rule of German income tax legislation limiting a tax deduction for school fees to school fees paid to German private establishments. While both cases were not joined for the purposes of the final judgment, a common hearing was organized, and the Advocate-General issued a common opinion (Opinion of Advocate-General C. Stix-Hackl of 21 September 2006 in Case C-76/05 *Schwarz and Gootjes-Schwarz* and in Case C-318/05 *Commission v Germany*).

[126] See M. A. Gaudissart, 'La refonte du règlement de procédure de la Cour de justice', (2012) C.D.E 631–2.

[127] ECJ, Joined Cases 36/59 to 38/59 and 40/59 *Präsident Ruhrkohlen-Verkaufsgesellschaft and Others v High Authority* [1960] E.C.R. 423, at 438.

[128] Consequently, after joinder, the Court may not rely, as against one party, on documents from the case-file of another party to which the first party did not have access. See ECJ, Case C-480/99 P *Plant and Others v Commission and South Wales Small Mines Association* [2002] E.C.R. I-265, paras 24–34.

[129] ECJ, Joined Cases 7/54 and 9/54 *Groupement des Industries Sidérurgiques Luxembourgeoises v High Authority* [1954 to 1956] E.C.R. 175, at 188.

[130] ECJ, Joined Cases 26/79 and 86/79 *Forges de Thy-Marcinelle and Monceau v Commission* [1980] E.C.R. 1083, para. 4. See also CST (judgment of 13 January 2010), Joined Cases F-124/05 and F-96/06 *A and G v Commission*, not reported, para. 143.

[131] ECJ Rules of Procedure, Art. 54(3); EGC Rules of Procedure, Art. 50(1). For examples, see ECJ, Case 261/78 *Interquell Stärke-Chemie v EEC* [1982] E.C.R. 3271, para. 4; ECJ (order of the President of 17 November 2004), Joined Cases C-131/03 P and C-146/03 P *Reynolds Tobacco and Others v Commission*, not reported, para. 8; ECJ, Case C-422/10 *Georgetown University and Others* [2011] E.C.R. I-12157, para. 22; CFI, Case T-318/00 *Freistaat Thüringen v Commission* [2005] E.C.R. II-4179, para. 62.

[132] EGC Rules of Procedure, Art. 77 lists four circumstances. The applicable rules on the stay of proceedings with respect to the Civil Service Tribunal are comparable to those governing the General Court: see CST Rules of Procedure, Arts 71–72.

In all cases except for those specified in the third paragraph of Art. 54 of the Statute (where the Court of Justice and the General Court are validly seized of cases in which the object is identical or similar: see para. 2.55), the proceedings may be stayed before the Court of Justice or the General Court by decision of the President of the Court of Justice or the President of the Chamber concerned of the General Court, adopted after hearing the Judge-Rapporteur, the Advocate-General, and the parties (except in the case of references for preliminary rulings).[133] However, in the circumstances specified in the third paragraph of Art. 54 of the Statute, the proceedings before the Court of Justice may be stayed by order of the Court, made after hearing the Advocate-General[134] and thus not merely by a decision of the President.

For both Courts, the proceedings may be resumed following the same procedure.[135]

The order or decision of the Court of Justice or the General Court, depending on the circumstances, is served on the parties, or in the case of preliminary ruling proceedings, on the 'interested persons' within the meaning of Art. 23 of the Statute.[136]

(2) Effect and time limits

The stay of proceedings takes effect on the date indicated in the order or decision of stay, or in the absence of such indication, on the date of that order or decision.[137] While proceedings are stayed, time ceases to run for the parties or interested persons within the meaning of Art. 23 of the Statute for the purposes of procedural time limits.[138]   **23.47**

Where the order or decision does not fix the length of the stay, it ends on the date indicated in the order or decision of resumption or, in the absence of such indication, on the date of the order or decision of resumption.[139] From the date of the resumption of proceedings following a stay, the suspended procedural time limits are replaced by new time limits, and time begins to run from the date of that resumption.[140]

D. Deferment of the determination of a case

The President of the Court of Justice or the President of the Chamber concerned of the General Court, as the case may be, may in special circumstances, either of his own motion or at the request of at least one of the parties, defer a case to be dealt with at a later date, after hearing the Judge-Rapporteur, the Advocate-General, and the parties.[141]   **23.48**

---

[133] ECJ Rules of Procedure, Art. 55(1)(b); EGC Rules of Procedure, Art. 78. This only applies when the case has already been assigned.
[134] ECJ Rules of Procedure, Art. 55(1)(a).
[135] ECJ Rules of Procedure, Art. 55(2); EGC Rules of Procedure, Art. 78.
[136] ECJ Rules of Procedure, Art. 55(3); EGC Rules of Procedure, Art. 78.
[137] ECJ Rules of Procedure, Art. 55(4); EGC Rules of Procedure, Art. 79(1), first para.
[138] ECJ Rules of Procedure, Art. 55(5); EGC Rules of Procedure, Art. 79(1), second para. However, according to the EGC Rules of Procedure, time continues to run, notwithstanding the stay of proceedings with respect to applications to intervene.
[139] ECJ Rules of Procedure, Art. 55(6); EGC Rules of Procedure, Art. 79(2), first para.
[140] ECJ Rules of Procedure, Art. 55(7); EGC Rules of Procedure, Art. 79(2), second para.
[141] ECJ Rules of Procedure, Art. 56; EGC Rules of Procedure, Art. 55(2), second para.

VI. Written Part of the Procedure

A. Lodging of procedural documents

23.49 As part of the written part of the procedure, there are common procedural rules dealing with the lodging of procedural documents, irrespective of the type of action (for example, direct actions, preliminary ruling proceedings, and appeals), before the respective Union court.

The lodging of a procedural document means that it is handed in to the Registry of the respective Court or is sent by post, telefax, or any other technical means available to that Court.[142]

B. e-Curia

23.50 The use of e-Curia allows a party's representative to submit a procedural document via electronic means only, without the need for such lodging to be confirmed by post.[143] The procedural documents lodged will be considered to be the original documents when lodgment is effected by using the representative's user identification and password; such identification is deemed to constitute the signature of the document concerned.[144]

The choice to submit certain procedural documents (for example, the application or the defence in the case of a direct action) via e-Curia does not preclude the lodging of subsequent documents via other means provided for in the Rules of Procedure of the respective Court, if so required by the nature of the document. In that case, the procedural rules applying to applications sent by post, telefax, or any other technical means of communication apply.

C. Original procedural documents must be signed

23.51 The original of every procedural document must be signed by the party's agent or lawyer, or in the case of observations submitted in the context of preliminary ruling proceedings, that of the party to the main proceedings or his representative, if the national rules of procedure applicable to those main proceedings permit that party to bring court proceedings without being represented by a lawyer.[145]

---

[142] ECJ Rules of Procedure, Art. 57(7); EGC Rules of Procedure, Art. 43(6). Fax number of the ECJ: (352) 4337 66; e-mail address of the ECJ: ECJ.Registry@curia.europa.eu. Fax number of the EGC: (352) 4303 2100; e-mail address of the EGC: GeneralCourt.Registry@curia.europa.eu.

[143] ECJ Decision of 13 September 2011 on the lodging and service of procedural documents by means of e-Curia ([2011] O.J. C289/7), Art. 4, second para.; EGC Decision of 14 September 2011 on the lodging and service of procedural documents by means of e-Curia ([2011] O.J. C289/9), Art. 4, second para. By contrast, with respect to the date and time on which a particular procedural document is lodged, a procedural document sent by telefax or any other technical means of communication has to be confirmed by lodging the original document at the respective Court within ten days of its transfer by telefax or any other technical means of communication: see ECJ Rules of Procedure Art. 57(7); EGC Rules of Procedure, Art. 43(6).

[144] ECJ Decision of 13 September 2011 on the lodging and service of procedural documents by means of e-Curia ([2011] O.J. C289/7), Art. 3; EGC Decision of 14 September 2011 on the lodging and service of procedural documents by means of e-Curia ([2011] O.J. C289/9), Art. 3.

[145] ECJ Rules of Procedure, Art. 57(1); EGC Rules of Procedure, Art. 43(1). For some examples of the application of this requirement in the context of direct actions, see CFI, Case T-158/99 *Thermenhotel Stoiser Franz and Others v Commission* [2004] E.C.R. II-1, paras 41–46; EGC (judgment of 29 November 2012),

If the procedural document has not been signed accordingly, it will not be registered by the Registrar[146] and will be returned to the party concerned.[147] Notably, in the case of applications, defects concerning the signature that come to light after the expiry of the time limit for bringing the action cannot be rectified and will lead to the inadmissibility of the action.[148]

The obligation for individuals to have each pleading signed by a lawyer is designed to ensure that what is submitted to the Court of Justice or the General Court consists of only legal opinions and explanations of fact which are considered by a lawyer to be fit to be put forward.[149] Save for circumstances in the context of preliminary ruling proceedings where a party to the main proceedings is allowed to represent himself (see para. 23.14), a pleading which was drafted by the party himself and merely formally signed by his lawyer may be regarded, in the light of all the circumstances, as being an inadmissible pleading.[150]

Documents lodged via e-Curia will considered to be signed if that lodging has been done by the representative using his user identification number and password.[151]

D. Copies and translations

The original, accompanied by all annexes referred to therein and a schedule listing them (see para. 23.53), must be lodged together with five copies for the Court of Justice or the General Court, as the case may be, and in the case of proceedings other than preliminary **23.52**

Case T-590/10 *Thesing and Bloomberg Finance v ECB*, not reported, para. 16 (appeal pending: ECJ, Case C-28/13 P *Thesing and Bloomberg Finance v ECB*); EGC (judgment of 18 June 2013), Case T-406/08 *ICF v Commission*, not reported, para. 55. The fact that the applicant is a lawyer himself does not detract from the obligation to have the procedural document, *in casu* the application, signed by the party's representative: EGC (order of 5 May 2011), Case T-157/11 *Adămuţ and Others v Romania*, not reported, para. 9.

[146] Art. 21(1) of the ECJ Rules of Procedure and Art. 24(1) of the EGC Rules of Procedure require the respective Registrars to keep a register in which all pleadings and supporting documents have to be entered.

[147] ECJ, Joined Cases 220/78 and 221/78 *ALA and ALFER v Commission* [1979] E.C.R. 1693, paras 3–5; CFI (order of 29 November 1993), Case T-56/92 *Koelman v Commission* [1993] E.C.R. II-1267, para. 1.

[148] ECJ (judgment of 22 September 2011), Case C-426/10 P *Bell & Ross v OHIM* [2011] E.C.R. I-8849, para. 42; CFI (order of 24 February 2000), Case T-37/98 *FTA v Council* [2000] E.C.R. II-373, para. 28; CFI, Case T-223/06 P *European Parliament v Eistrup* [2007] E.C.R. II-1581, para. 59.

[149] This suggestion was put forward by Advocate-General K. Roemer in ECJ, Case 108/63 *Merlini v High Authority* [1965] E.C.R. 1, at 16. For those reasons, the lawyer signing the pleading must be a 'third party' collaborating in the administration of justice and being required to provide, in full independence and in the overriding interests of justice, such legal assistance as his or her client needs. For instance, an application which is signed by a lawyer who is also a director of the company submitting the application will be inadmissible on the grounds that since the lawyer is an organ of the company, he or she cannot be regarded as being an independent third party (CFI (order of 8 December 1999), Case T-79/99 *Euro-Lex v OHIM* [1999] E.C.R. II-3555, paras 27–30).

[150] ECJ, Case 108/63 *Merlini v High Authority*, at 9. In its judgment, the Court of Justice seems to have gone further than the Opinion of the Advocate-General, who considered the merely formal signature of a pleading by a lawyer only as 'negligence by the lawyer in his conduct of the proceedings' which might perhaps be considered incompatible with the requirements of the proper administration of justice (ECJ Rules of Procedure, Art. 46(1); EGC Rules of Procedure, Art. 41(1)). All the same, this judgment should be approached with some caution, given that the Court of Justice held that the pleading drafted by the applicant itself, which the lawyer had signed and lodged as the reply, should be rejected not only as being in breach of Art. 20 of the ECSC Statute and Art. 57 of the ECJ Rules of Procedure, but also because it 'rais[ed] fresh submissions and arguments' (Art. 20 of the ECSC Statute and Art. 57 of the ECJ Rules of Procedure).

[151] ECJ Decision of 13 September 2011 on the lodging and service of procedural documents by means of e-Curia ([2011] O.J. C289/7), Art. 3; EGC Decision of 14 September 2011 on the lodging and service of procedural documents by means of e-Curia ([2011] O.J. C289/9), Art. 3.

ruling proceedings, a copy for every other party to the proceedings. Copies must be certified by the party lodging them.[152]

In addition, the Union institutions are required to produce, within time limits set down by the respective Court, translations of any procedural documents into the other languages provided for by Art. 1 of Council Regulation No. 1, that is to say, the other official languages of the European Union, again with five copies for the respective Court and a copy for every other party to the proceedings, save for preliminary ruling proceedings.[153]

E. Annexes and schedule

23.53 There must be annexed to every procedural document a file containing the items and documents relied on in support of it, together with a schedule listing them.[154]

Where, in view of the length of a particular item or document, only extracts are annexed to the procedural document, the whole item or document or a full copy of it must be lodged at the Registry.[155]

F. All procedural documents must be dated

23.54 All procedural documents must be dated, but for the purposes of the calculation of procedural time limits, only the date and time of lodgment of the original at the Registry is taken into account (i.e. the date on and time at which that document arrives at the Registry).[156]

Where, however, a copy of a signed original of a procedural document is received by the Registry (together with the schedule of items and documents) by telefax or any other technical means of communication available to the Court of Justice or the General Court, the date of lodgment for the purposes of compliance with the procedural time limits is deemed to be the date of receipt of that copy, provided that the signed original[157] of the pleading, accompanied by the annexes and copies, is lodged at the Registry no later than 10 days thereafter.[158] The Registrar is not obliged to bring

---

[152] ECJ Rules of Procedure, Art. 57(1), (2), and (4); EGC Rules of Procedure, Art. 43(1). Failure to initial the stamp on the first page of a procedural document certifying that the copy is true to the original is a formal error that does not render the lodging of the document inadmissible: EGC, Case T-336/09 *Häfele v OHIM* [2011] E.C.R. II-4*, Summ. pub., para. 17.

[153] ECJ Rules of Procedure, Art. 57(3); EGC Rules of Procedure, Art. 43(2).

[154] ECJ Rules of Procedure, Art. 57(4); EGC Rules of Procedure, Art. 43(4).

[155] ECJ Rules of Procedure, Art. 57(5); EGC Rules of Procedure, Art. 43(5).

[156] ECJ Rules of Procedure, Art. 57(6); EGC Rules of Procedure, Art. 43(3). A party has the right to lodge a document instituting legal proceedings at any time up to the last working day of the period set by the Statute. This means that, prior to the expiry of that period, he or she must be allowed to withdraw a first document instituting legal proceedings in order to replace it, within the same period, by a new version of that document (ECJ, Case C-274/00 P *Simon v Commission* [2002] E.C.R. I-5999, para. 30).

[157] According to ECJ Rules of Procedure, Art. 57(8) and EGC Rules of Procedure, Art. 43(7), the Court 'may by decision determine the criteria for a procedural document sent to the Registry by electronic means to be deemed to be the original of that document. That decision shall be published in the *Official Journal of the European Union*'. See in this respect n. 160.

[158] ECJ, Rules of Procedure, Art. 57(7); EGC Rules of Procedure, Art. 43(6). In the event of any discrepancy between the signed original and the copy previously lodged, only the date of lodgment of the signed original will be taken into consideration: ECJ Practice Directions, point 43; EGC Practice Directions, point I.A.1.7. For an application, see, e.g. CFI (order of 8 May 2003), Case T-63/03 *El Corte Inglés v OHIM*,

promptly to the attention of a representative the existence of procedural defects in this regard.[159]

This condition does not apply when documents are lodged through e-Curia.[160] Instead, for lodgments via e-Curia, a procedural document is deemed to have been lodged at the time of the representative's validation of lodgment of that document (according to Luxembourg time).[161]

G. Length of procedural documents

The Union courts may, by decision, set the maximum length of written pleadings or observations lodged before it.[162] To date, this has not yet occurred (see further para. 25.56).   **23.55**

VII. The Preliminary Report and Assignment of Cases

When the written part of the procedure is closed (for example, in the case of direct actions,   **23.56** after the rejoinder has been lodged or the parties have refrained from lodging a reply or a rejoinder, or the General Court has decided that the application and the defence do not need supplementing), the President fixes the date on which the Judge-Rapporteur is to present a preliminary report to the Court of Justice or the General Court, as the case may be.[163]

The preliminary report is not published. It is intended for the general administrative meeting of the Court of Justice (the Judges, the Advocates-General, and the Registrar) or for the competent Chamber of the General Court (the Judges and the Registrar).[164]

The preliminary report contains proposals as to whether particular measures of organization of procedure or measures of inquiry should be undertaken (see para. 23.57), and in the case of the Court of Justice, whether requests for clarification to the referring court or tribunal should be made in the context of preliminary ruling proceedings.[165]

Furthermore, in proceedings before the Court of Justice, the Judge-Rapporteur proposes the formation which will deal with the case (three- or five-Judge Chamber, Grand

---

not reported (application inadmissible because the original was not lodged with the Registry in time). See also EGC (order of 29 November 2011), Case T-345/11 *ENISA v CEPD*, not reported, paras 15–17: both the electronic copy and the signed original were lodged with the Registry in time. However, the lawyer's signature on the electronic application was not identical to the lawyer's signature on the signed original. Consequently, the General Court took only the original application into account. Since the time limit for bringing the action had expired in the ten-day period between the lodging of the electronic copy and the signed original, the action was declared inadmissible because the application was not lodged in time.

[159] ECJ (order of 12 September 2012), Case C-69/12 P *Noscira v OHIM*, not reported, para. 14.
[160] ECJ Decision of 13 September 2011 on the lodging and service of procedural documents by means of e-Curia ([2011] O.J. C289/7), Art. 4; EGC Decision of 14 September 2011 on the lodging and service of procedural documents by means of e-Curia ([2011] O.J. C289/9), Art. 4.
[161] ECJ Decision of 13 September 2011 on the lodging and service of procedural documents by means of e-Curia ([2011] O.J. C289/7), Art. 5; EGC Decision of 14 September 2011 on the lodging and service of procedural documents by means of e-Curia ([2011] O.J. C289/9), Art. 5.
[162] ECJ Rules of Procedure, Art. 58; at present the EGC Rules of Procedure do not contain a similar provision. The EGC Practice Directions (as well as the ECJ Practice Directions), however, contain recommendations in this respect.
[163] ECJ Rules of Procedure, Art. 59(1); EGC Rules of Procedure, Art. 52(1).
[164] ECJ Rules of Procedure, Art. 59(1); EGC Rules of Procedure, Art. 52(1).
[165] ECJ Rules of Procedure, Art. 59(2); EGC Rules of Procedure, Art. 52(2).

Chamber, or the Full Court) in the preliminary report, which may also include proposals as to whether to dispense with the oral hearing and/or an Opinion of the Advocate-General pursuant to the fifth paragraph of Art. 20 of the Statute.[166] In contrast, before the General Court a case will normally be handled by the three-Judge Chamber of which the Judge-Rapporteur is a member. The Judge-Rapporteur will therefore deal with the question of the formation in the preliminary report only where he recommends the case should be referred to the Grand Chamber, a five-Judge Chamber, or a single Judge.[167]

The Court of Justice and the General Court decide on the Judge-Rapporteur's proposals set forth in the preliminary report, after hearing the Advocate-General.[168]

The respective Court may decide to open the oral proceedings without proceeding to measures of organization of procedure or measures of inquiry. If so, the President fixes the opening date.[169] The President will generally also fix the date for the hearing where only measures of organization of procedure are taken, such as preparatory measures requested by the Advocate-General or the Judge-Rapporteur.[170] Measures of inquiry decided upon have to have been completed before the President fixes the date for the opening of the oral part of the procedure.[171] After the inquiry, the Court of Justice or the General Court, as the case may be, may prescribe a time limit within which the parties are to submit written observations. The oral part of the procedure follows after that time limit has expired. In addition, during the oral part of the procedure, measures of organization of procedure or measures of inquiry may still be prescribed.[172]

VIII. Measures of Organization of Procedure and Measures of Inquiry

A. Burden of proof on the parties and role played by the Union courts in fact-finding

(1) General

23.57 The purpose of measures of organization of procedure is in particular to ensure efficient conduct of the written and oral procedure and to facilitate the taking of evidence, and also

---

[166] ECJ Rules of Procedure, Art. 59(2).
[167] EGC Rules of Procedure, Art. 52(2).
[168] ECJ Rules of Procedure, Art. 59(3); EGC Rules of Procedure, Art. 52(2), second para. This is invariably the case for the Court of Justice, but only exceptionally for the General Court where a Judge is designated to act as Advocate–General.
[169] ECJ Rules of Procedure, Art. 60(4); EGC Rules of Procedure, Art. 53. Where the expedited procedure applies before the Court of Justice, the President of the Court fixes the date of the hearing almost immediately after the defence has been lodged or at the time when the decision is taken to have recourse to the expedited procedure where that decision is taken after lodgment of the defence (ECJ Rules of Procedure, Art. 135(1)).
[170] ECJ Rules of Procedure, Art. 62(1).
[171] ECJ Rules of Procedure, Art. 75(1); EGC Rules of Procedure, Art. 54.
[172] For an example, see CFI, Joined Cases T-79/89, T-84/89 to T-86/89, T-89/89, T-91/89 to T-92/89, T-94/89, T-96/89, T-98/89, T-102/89, and T-104/89 *BASF and Others v Commission* [1992] E.C.R. II-315, para. 25. See also Opinion of Advocate-General P. Mengozzi in ECJ (judgment of 4 July 2013), Case C-287/11 P *Commission v Aalberts Industries and Others*, not reported, point 9: measures taken after hearing.

to determine the points on which the parties must present further argument or which call for measures of inquiry.[173] Measures of inquiry are intended to prove the veracity of the facts alleged by one of the parties in support of its pleas in law. They are taken by order and have a binding character.[174]

Generally, measures of organization of procedure and measures of inquiry may be employed in all types of proceedings before the Union courts, although in the context of preliminary ruling proceedings, measures of inquiry are in principle not availed of when such proceedings relate to the interpretation, as opposed to the validity, of Union law (see para. 24.23).

The development of each of these types of measures is situated against the backdrop of the interplay between the parties and the Union courts in fact-finding.

(2) Active role played by the Union courts

Fact-finding is the outcome of a complex interplay between the parties and between the parties and the Union courts.[175] The classic apportionment of the burden of proof, whereby each party proves the facts on which its claim or defence is based, also applies in Union law.[176] The Court may adjust this by means of presumptions designed to mitigate the substantive inequality between the parties in terms of their ability to prove the necessary facts.[177] For this reason too, a party not having to discharge the burden of proof may nevertheless be obliged to release information to which only it has access, in order to enable its opponent to provide the necessary evidence.[178]

23.58

The Court may further play an active role in fact-finding provided, however, that the parties have been able to define their position as regards the facts on which the Court

---

[173] EGC Rules of Procedure, Art. 64(1) and (2). See also CFI, Case T-141/01 *Entorn v Commission* [2005] E.C.R. II-95, paras 129–130 and EGC, Case T-560/08 P *Commission v Meierhofer* [2010] E.C.R. II-1739, para. 64 for the distinction between measures of organization of procedure and measures of inquiry.

[174] EGC Rules of Procedure, Art. 64(1) and (2). See also CFI, Case T-141/01 *Entorn v Commission* [2005] E.C.R. II-95, paras 129–130 and EGC, Case T-560/08 P *Commission v Meierhofer* [2010] E.C.R. II-1739, para. 64.

[175] For a more extensive discussion, see M. Berger, 'Beweisaufname vor dem Europäischen Gerichtshof', in P. Gottwald and H. Roth (eds), *Festschrift für Ekkehard Schumann zum 70. Geburtstag* (Mohr Siebeck, Tübingen, 2001), 27–41; K. Lenaerts, 'Rechter en partijen in de rechtspleging voor Hof en Gerecht' (2002) S. E.W. 231–7, in particular the part relating to the passive role played by the Court of Justice and the General Court. See also R. Barents, 'Rechter en partijen in het EU-procesrecht' (2010) S.E.W. 141–54.

[176] For example, the undertaking submitting that the excessive length of the administrative procedure has had an impact on the exercise of its rights of defence must demonstrate to the requisite legal standard that it experienced difficulties in defending itself against the Commission's allegations because of that excessive length. Merely stating that evidence had disappeared as a result of the lapse of time without indicating specific circumstances or events that have caused the evidence to disappear does not comply with the required legal standard: ECJ, Joined Cases C-201/09 P and C-216/09 P *Arcelor Mittal Luxembourg v Commission* [2011] E.C.R. I-2239, paras 118–124. See K. Lenaerts, 'Some Thoughts on Evidence and Procedure in European Community Competition Law' (2007) Fordham Int'l L.J. 1463–95.

[177] ECJ, Case 10/55 *Mirossevich v High Authority* [1954 to 1956] E.C.R. 333, at 343–4.

[178] ECJ, Case 45/64 *Commission v Italy* [1965] E.C.R. 857, at 867; pursuant to Art. 4(3) TEU, Member States are under a duty to provide the Commission with the information necessary in order for it to monitor whether Union law is being complied with. If a Member State fails to comply with that duty, this in itself is enough to justify proceedings under Art. 258 TFEU. In the course of such proceedings, the Court of Justice may put questions to Member States and order measures of inquiry, see ECJ, Case 96/81 *Commission v Netherlands* [1982] E.C.R. 1791 and ECJ, Case 97/81 *Commission v Netherlands* [1982] E.C.R. 1819. With respect to an action for annulment, see ECJ (order of 15 November 2006), Case C-273/04 *Poland v Council*, not reported, paras 1–7.

grounds its decision.[179] This involvement in fact-finding originates in the mission of the Court of Justice and the General Court of ensuring that the law is observed.[180] They may do so only if the facts on which the application of the law is based accord with reality. At the same time, the decisions of the Court of Justice and the General Court often affect the general interest, alongside the individual interest of the parties concerned. The potential ramifications of their decisions may prompt the Court of Justice and the General Court to prescribe *measures of inquiry*.

Finally, sometimes the facts and the law are so closely intertwined that it is difficult to make a hard-and-fast distinction between fact-finding and making determinations of law.[181] The allocation of duties as between the Court and the parties which is encapsulated in the maxim *da mihi factum, dabo tibi jus* cannot be unqualifiedly applied in the context of Union law. Moreover, as discussed in Chapter 2 (see para. 2.35), the jurisdiction transferred from the Court of Justice to the General Court was primarily to hear and determine cases requiring a thorough investigation of complex facts, the aim being to relieve the Court of Justice of the time-consuming task of making findings of fact. For its part, the General Court incorporated in its Rules of Procedure provisions specifically designed to facilitate greater interaction between that Court and the parties with a view to this task. This highlights the importance of *measures of organization of procedure*.[182] The General Court makes avid use of such measures, acting in a more inquisitorial manner than the Court of Justice formerly did.

(3) Parties must prove their assertions

23.59   The fact that the Court has the power to order measures of organization of procedure to be carried out does not release the parties from their obligation to prove their assertions. This is because the judicial contribution to fact-finding is only optional and complementary. Evidence offered in support by the parties[183] must make out a plausible case for their allegations and so constitute at least *prima facie* evidence. This means, for instance, where a party asks the Court to order the opposite party to produce documents in its possession, that the party requesting production must identify the documents requested and provide at least minimum information indicating the utility of those documents for the purposes of the proceedings.[184] It is only if the evidence satisfies those conditions that the Court will decide, in an appropriate case, to investigate the allegations further by means of measures of organization of procedure or measures of inquiry.[185] Whether the Court does so decide will be largely determined by the context of the proceedings. In this way, the Court's decision to take particular measures may be influenced by the fact that one party has difficulty, by

---

[179] ECJ (order of 27 September 2004), Case C-470/02 P *UER v Commission*, not reported, paras 63–74.

[180] Art. 19(1), first para., TEU.

[181] K. Lenaerts, 'Le Tribunal de première instance des Communautés européennes: genèse et premiers pas' (1990) J.T. 409, at 413.

[182] See ECJ Rules of Procedure, Arts 61–62; EGC Rules of Procedure, Art. 64.

[183] ECJ Rules of Procedure, Art. 120; EGC Rules of Procedure, Art. 44(1) as regards the application; ECJ Rules of Procedure, Art. 124(1); EGC Rules of Procedure, Art. 46(1) as regards the defence; ECJ Rules of Procedure, Art. 132(2); EGC Rules of Procedure, Art. 116(4) as regards statements in intervention.

[184] ECJ, Case C-185/95 P *Baustahlgewebe v Commission* [1998] E.C.R. I-8417, para. 93; CFI, Case T-141/01 *Entorn v Commission* [2005] E.C.R. II-95, para. 132.

[185] CFI (order of 21 November 1996), Case T-53/96 *Syndicat des Producteurs de Viande Bovine and Others v Commission* [1996] E.C.R. II-1579, para. 26; CFI (order of 4 February 2005), Case T-20/04 *Aguar Fernandez and Others v Commission*, not reported, para. 36.

comparison with its opponent, in obtaining evidence or by the fact that the parties agree on the existence of certain facts. Furthermore, the Union judicature is obliged to order measures of inquiry where this is necessary in order to be able to rule on whether a plea is well-founded.[186]

(4) Inadmissible means of proof

Union law does not lay down any specific rules on the use of evidence. All means of proof **23.60** are admissible, except for evidence obtained improperly[187] and internal documents, such as an opinion of the legal service of an institution.[188] Internal documents should not be disclosed in the framework of proceedings before the Union courts, unless such production has been authorized by the institution concerned or ordered by the Court concerned.[189] However, it may happen that an applicant adduces as evidence internal and/or confidential documents which were not lawfully obtained. If the Union judicature finds, having regard to the subject-matter and the particular nature of the action brought, that such documents are manifestly relevant for determining the dispute, it will order that the documents must remain in the case-file. In that event, an application from the defendant to remove the documents from the file and return them to it will be rejected.[190]

(5) The adversarial principle

As a rule, the Union courts will base their decision only on evidence to which the parties to **23.61** the proceedings have had access.[191] However, in some cases, it may be necessary for certain information to be withheld from the parties in order to preserve the fundamental rights of a third party or to safeguard an important public interest. Any restriction to the adversarial

---

[186] For an example in which the Court of Justice held that the then Court of First Instance had wrongly rejected a party's request for the production of documents, see ECJ, Case C-119/97 P *Ufex and Others v Commission* [1999] E.C.R. I-1341, para. 111.

[187] ECJ, Joined Cases 197/80 to 200/80, 243/80, 245/80, and 247/80 *Ludwigshafener Walzmühle and Others v Council and Commission* [1981] E.C.R. 3211, para. 16; CFI (order of 26 May 2004), Case T-266/03 *Groupement des Cartes Bancaires 'CB' v Commission*, not reported, para. 19; CFI, Case T-141/01 *Entorn v Commission* [2005] E.C.R. II-95, paras 37–39 (evidence will be admissible if applicant could have obtained the evidence properly).

[188] ECJ (order of 30 September 2004), Case C-36/04 *Spain v Council*, not reported, paras 1–5. See also ECJ (order of 9 September 2005), Case C-432/04 *Commission v Cresson*, not reported, paras 2–7.

[189] ECJ (order of 23 October 2002), Case C-445/00 *Austria v Council* [2002] E.C.R. I-9151, para. 12; CFI (order of 10 January 2005), Case T-357/03 *Gollnisch and Others v European Parliament* [2005] E.C.R. II-1, para. 34; EGC (order of the President of 30 April 2010), Case T-18/10 R *Inuit Tapiriit Kanatami and Others v Commission* [2010] E.C.R. II-75*, Summ. pub., paras 19–23; EGC, Case T-576/08 *Germany v Commission* [2011] E.C.R. II-1578, paras 42–43.

[190] ECJ, Case 232/84 *Commission v Tordeur* [1985] E.C.R. 3027; ECJ (order of 15 October 1986), Case 31/86 *LAISA v Council*, not reported; CFI, Case T-192/99 *Dunnett and Others v EIB* [2001] E.C.R. II-813, paras 32–34; EGC, Case T-149/09 *Dover v European Parliament* [2011] E.C.R. II-69*, Summ. pub., paras 60–64. Cf., however, ECJ (order of 30 September 2004), Case C-36/04 *Spain v Council*, not reported; CFI, Joined Cases T-228/99 and T-233/99 *Westdeutsche Landesbank Girozentrale v Commission* [2003] E.C.R. II-435, paras 90–91; EGC (order of 19 March 2013), Case T-331/11 *Besselink v Commission*, not reported.

[191] ECJ, Joined Cases 42/59 and 49/59 *SNUPAT v High Authority* [1961] E.C.R. 53, 84; ECJ, Case C-480/99 P *Plant and Others v Commission and South Wales Small Mines* [2002] E.C.R. I-265, para. 24; ECJ, Case C-199/99 P *Corus UK v Commission* [2003] E.C.R. I-11177, para. 19; ECJ, Case C-89/08 P *Commission v Ireland and Others* [2009] E.C.R. I-11245, paras 52–55 (the adversarial principle also, as a rule, implies a right for the parties to be apprised of pleas in law raised by the Union courts of their own motion, on which they intend to base their decisions, and to discuss them).

principle must be limited to what is strictly necessary to preserve such rights or safeguard such public interest.[192]

B. Measures of organization of procedure

(1) Court of Justice

23.62   Art. 61 of the ECJ Rules of Procedure delineates the measures of organization of procedure which may be prescribed by the Court of Justice. In addition to the measures which may prescribed under Art. 24 of the Statute,[193] the Court may invite the parties or the interested persons within the meaning of Art. 23 of the Statute in the context of preliminary ruling proceedings to answer certain questions in writing, within a certain time limit set by the Court, or at the hearing.[194] Where a hearing is organized, the Court invites the parties, insofar as possible, to concentrate their oral pleadings on one or more specified issues.[195]

Pursuant to Art. 62 of the ECJ Rules of Procedure, measures of organization may also be prescribed by the Judge-Rapporteur or the Advocate-General to which the case has been assigned. Each may request the parties or the interested persons within the meaning of Art. 23 of the Statute to submit within a specified period all such information relating to the facts, and all such documents or other particulars, as they may consider relevant.[196] Moreover, the Judge-Rappporteur or the Advocate-General may send to the parties or such interested persons questions to be answered at the hearing.[197] This power serves to facilitate the preparation of the Court's decision and the Advocate-General's Opinion. There is no equivalent provision in the EGC Rules of Procedure.[198] However, similar to those Rules, the measures of organization of procedure prescribed by the Court of Justice, the Judge-Rapporteur, or the Advocate-General are less formal than measures of inquiry and are not issued by means of orders.

---

[192] See ECJ, Case C-450/06 *Varec* [2008] E.C.R. I-581, para. 47; ECJ (judgment of 4 June 2013), Case C-300/11 *ZZ*, not reported, paras 65–66; ECJ (judgment of 18 July 2013), Joined Cases C-584/10 P, C-593/10 P, and C-595/10 P *Commission and Others v Kadi*, not reported, paras 119–130. At present Art. 67(3), third para., of the EGC Rules of Procedure provides that where a document to which access has been denied by a Union institution has been produced before the General Court in proceedings relating to the legality of that denial, that document will not be communicated to the other parties, but will be examined by the Court *in camera*: see ECJ (judgment of 21 June 2012), Case C-135/11 P *IFAW v Commission*, not reported, paras 73–75; EGC (judgment of 19 March 2013), Case T-301/10 *Sophie in 'Veld v Commission*, not reported, paras 33, 143, 149, and 153.

[193] Art. 24 of the Statute provides in relevant part that the Court of Justice 'may require the parties to produce all documents and to supply all information which the Court considers desirable', as well as 'require the Member States and institutions, bodies, offices and agencies not being parties to the case to supply all information which the Court considers necessary for the proceedings'.

[194] ECJ Rules of Procedure, Art. 61(1).

[195] ECJ Rules of Procedure, Art. 61(2).

[196] ECJ Rules of Procedure, Art. 62(1). As provided therein, the replies and documents provided in response to such requests are communicated to the other parties or interested persons within the meaning of Art. 23 of the Statute. Such measures can also be taken after the hearing: see Opinion of Advocate-General P. Mengozzi in ECJ, Case C-287/11 P *Commission v Aalberts Industries and Others*, not reported, point 9.

[197] ECJ Rules of Procedure, Art. 62(2).

[198] EGC Rules of Procedure, Art. 64(5) only provides that if the Court prescribes measures of organization of procedure and does not undertake such measures itself, it entrusts the task to the Judge-Rapporteur.

(2) General Court

Art. 64 of the EGC Rules of Procedure enables the General Court to prescribe measures in **23.63** order to ensure that 'cases are prepared for hearing, procedures carried out and disputes resolved under the best possible conditions'.[199]

In the light of the General Court's tasks as discussed, the rules on measures of organization of procedure are more elaborate in the EGC Rules of Procedure as compared to the ECJ Rules of Procedure. Such measures may, in particular, include: putting questions to the parties; inviting them to make submissions on certain aspects of the proceedings; requesting the parties to concentrate their oral pleadings on one or more specified issues; asking them or third parties for information or particulars; asking for documents or any papers relating to the case to be produced; and summoning the parties' agents or the parties in person to meetings.[200]

Measures of organization of procedure are relatively informal. They do not have the compelling nature of measures of inquiry and—unlike such measures—are not prescribed by order, but notified to the parties by letter from the Registrar. In fact, any party may, at any stage of the procedure, propose the adoption or modification of measures of organization of procedure, in which case the other parties must be heard before any measures are prescribed.[201] If a request for measures of organization of procedure is intended to obtain new factual evidence and is made at a stage in the procedure when the production of new evidence is in principle no longer allowed,[202] it is necessary in particular for the party requesting those measures to set out the reasons why the request could not have been made earlier.[203]

Where the procedural circumstances so require, the Registrar has to inform the parties of the measures envisaged by the General Court and give them an opportunity to submit comments orally or in writing.[204] The Judge-Rapporteur may be given the task of putting the measures into effect.[205] The General Court makes frequent use of this type of measure in order to streamline somewhat the processing of large or complex case-files. The General Court may, without infringing Art. 48(2) of its Rules of Procedure, base its judgment or order on matters which came to its knowledge from replies to questions put to the parties as measures of organization of procedure on which the parties had the opportunity to state their views in the course of the proceedings.[206]

---

[199] EGC Rules of Procedure, Art. 64(1).
[200] EGC Rules of Procedure, Art. 64(3).
[201] EGC Rules of Procedure, Art. 64(4). This is not provided for in the ECJ Rules of Procedure.
[202] See para. 25.18.
[203] ECJ (judgment of 14 April 2005), Case C-243/04 P *Gaki-Kakouri v Court of Justice*, not reported, para. 33; EGC (judgment of 14 March 2013), Case T-588/08 *Dole Food Company and Dole Food Germany v Commission*, not reported, paras 41–42; CFI, Case T-51/07 *Agrar-Invest-Tatschl v Commission* [2008] E.C.R. II-2825, para. 57; CFI, Case T-141/01 *Entorn v Commission* [2005] E.C.R. II-95, para. 132.
[204] EGC Rules of Procedure, Art. 64(4).
[205] EGC Rules of Procedure, Art. 64(5).
[206] ECJ, Case C-259/96 P *Council v De Nil and Impens* [1998] E.C.R. I-2915, para. 31. See also para. 23.62.

C. Measures of inquiry

(1) General

23.64 To recall, measures of inquiry are intended to prove the veracity of the facts alleged by one of the parties in support of its pleas in law.[207] Such measures of inquiry as the Court of Justice or the General Court should deem necessary are prescribed by order.[208] The order sets out the facts to be established. Before prescribing such measures, the respective Court hears the Advocate-General.[209] The Court of Justice or the General Court, as the case may be, may entrust the undertaking of the inquiry to the Judge-Rapporteur (or to the Chamber to which the case was originally assigned if the measures are ordered by the Grand Chamber of the General Court).[210] During the inquiry, evidence may be submitted in rebuttal and further evidence may be adduced.[211] The parties may be present at measures of inquiry.[212]

The Rules of Procedure of the ECJ and the EGC prescribe the following five types of measures of inquiry which may be adopted: personal appearance of the parties; a request for information and production of documents; oral testimony; the commissioning of an expert's report; and an inspection of a place or a thing.[213]

(2) Personal appearance of the parties

23.65 The Court of Justice and the General Court may summon parties to appear personally in order to provide explanations about the case or answer questions.[214] Unlike experts and witnesses, they are not heard under oath.[215] A party who does not comply with a summons from the Court of Justice or the General Court may not be fined, unlike a witness. As in the case of any hearing, minutes are kept, in which the appearance of parties is recorded. The President (of the Chamber) and the Registrar sign the minutes.[216]

---

[207] CFI, Case T-175/97 *Bareyt and Others v Commission* [2000] E.C.R.-SC I-A-229 and II-1053, para. 90; CFI, Case T-141/01 *Entorn v Commission* [2005] E.C.R. II-95, para. 130.

[208] Generally, the Court of Justice decides in its general meeting whether a measure of inquiry is necessary, but where the case has already been assigned to a formation of the Court, the decision on measures of inquiry is taken by that formation: ECJ Rules of Procedure, Art. 63. It is the Chamber of the General Court to which the case has been assigned which takes the decision regarding the measure of inquiry.

[209] ECJ Rules of Procedure, Art. 64(1); EGC Rules of Procedure, Art. 66(1) which further states that the parties are also heard where the General Court proposes to hear oral testimony, to commission an expert's report, or to inspect a place or a thing. Where a party makes an application for measures of inquiry after the oral procedure is closed, such a request may be admitted only if it relates to facts which may have a decisive influence on the outcome of the case and which the party concerned could not put forward before the close of the oral procedure (ECJ, Case C-200/92 *ICI v Commission* [1999] E.C.R. I-4399, para. 60).

[210] ECJ Rules of Procedure, Art. 65(1); EGC Rules of Procedure, Art. 67(1).

[211] ECJ Rules of Procedure, Art. 64(3); EGC Rules of Procedure, Art. 66(2). See also CFI, Case T-141/01 *Entorn v Commission* [2005] E.C.R. II-95, para. 130.

[212] ECJ Rules of Procedure, Art. 65(3); EGC Rules of Procedure, Art. 67(2).

[213] ECJ Rules of Procedure, Art. 64(2); EGC Rules of Procedure, Art. 65. As provided therein, this is without prejudice to Arts 24 and 25 of the Statute, which essentially reiterate requests for documents, information, and expert opinions.

[214] It is not because parties may 'plead' only through their representatives (Statute, Art. 29) that they themselves may not even address the Court in an inquiry based on the appearance of the parties. For an example, see CFI (order of 6 December 1989), Case T-59/89 *Yorck von Wartenburg v European Parliament*, not reported.

[215] Statute, Art. 28.

[216] ECJ Rules of Procedure, Art. 74(1); EGC Rules of Procedure, Art. 76(1).

(3) Requests for information and production of documents

The Court of Justice and the General Court have the power to require parties—and even **23.66** Member States and Union institutions not parties to the proceedings—to produce all documents and to supply all information which the Court considers desirable.[217] The Court of Justice and the General Court may request only the production of documents which are relevant, having regard to the subject-matter of the proceedings.[218] Formal note is taken of any refusal.[219] No formal sanctions attach to a refusal to provide information or to produce documents, but this may possibly affect the outcome of the case.[220]

A claim that a document produced is allegedly confidential[221] puts the Court under a duty to exercise care in disclosing it in *inter partes* proceedings.[222] It may do so, after carefully weighing the interests at stake, only where the document is genuinely necessary in order for it to decide the case or in order to respect the rights of defence.[223]

Where a document to which access has been denied by a Union institution has been produced before the General Court in proceedings relating to the legality of that denial, that document will not be communicated to the other parties.[224]

---

[217] Statute, Art. 21. For examples, see ECJ (order of 15 November 2006), Case C-273/04 *Poland v Council*, not reported, paras 1–7; CFI, Case T-2/90 *Ferreira de Freitas v Commission* [1991] E.C.R. II-103, paras 20–21; CFI (order of the President of 7 May 2000), Case T-306/01 R *Aden and Others v Council and Commission* [2002] E.C.R. II-2387, para. 34.

[218] CFI (order of 18 November 1997), Case T-367/94 *British Coal v Commission* [1997] E.C.R. II-2103, para. 24; CFI, Case T-192/99 *Dunnett and Others v EIB* [2001] E.C.R. II-813, paras 38–39. Internal documents of the institutions are not to be communicated to the applicants, unless the circumstances of the case are exceptional and the applicants make out a plausible case for the need to do so (CFI, Case T-9/99 *HFB and Others v Commission* [2002] E.C.R. II-1487, para. 40). Where, however, the Commission spontaneously joins internal documents to the case-file, the other parties cannot prevent it from doing so (CFI (order of 26 May 2004), Case T-266/03 *Groupement des Cartes Bancaires 'CB' v Commission*, not reported, para. 19). See also para. 23.60.

[219] Statute, Art. 24.

[220] See, e.g. ECJ, Case 155/78 *M v Commission* [1980] E.C.R. 1797, paras 20–21; ECJ (judgment of 18 July 2013), Joined Cases C-584/10 P, C-593/10 P and C-595/10 P *Commission and Others v Kadi*, not reported, paras 119–130 and 151–165.

[221] A document may be confidential on grounds, for instance, of State security (Art. 346(1) TFEU) or professional or business secrecy. See also para 23.61.

[222] Under Art. 67(3), first para., of the EGC Rules of Procedure, the General Court is to take into consideration only those documents which have been made available to the lawyers and agents of the parties and on which they have been given an opportunity of expressing their views. However, if the General Court has to review the confidentiality of a document that may be relevant for the determination of a dispute, that document will not be disclosed to the parties at the stage of the review. In addition, the General Court may consider the substantive accuracy of a non-confidential summary of a confidential document without disclosing the confidential document to the party with respect to which that document is confidential (see CFI, Case T-5/02 *Tetra Laval v Commission* [2002] E.C.R. II-4381, paras 78 and 116–117). See also S. Papasavvas, 'Confidentiality Issues in Competition Law. The Impact of Confidentiality Issues on Proceedings before the CFI', in H. Kanninen, N. Korjus, and A. Rosas (eds), *EU Competition Law in Context: Essays in Honour of Virpi Tiili* (Oxford and Portland Oregon, Hart Publishing, 2009), 221–232.

[223] ECJ (order of 9 September 2005), Case C-432/04 *Commission v Cresson*, not reported, paras 5–6; ECJ (judgment of 18 July 2013), Joined Cases C-584/10 P, C-593/10 P, and C-595/10 P *Commission and Others v Kadi*, not reported, paras 119–130. See also para. 23.61.

[224] EGC Rules of Procedure, Art. 67(3), third para. For an application, see, e.g. CFI (order of 19 February 2001), Case T-111/00 *British American Tobacco International (Investments) v Commission*, not reported; EGC (order of 23 September 2011), Case T-63/10 *Jurašinović v Council*, not reported; EGC (judgment of 19 March 2013), Case T-301/10 *Sophie in 'Veld v Commission*, not reported, paras 33, 143, 149, and 153.

(4) Oral testimony and experts' reports

(a) Witnesses

23.67 Occasionally, the Court of Justice or the General Court may, either of its own motion or on an application by a party, order that certain facts be proved by witnesses.[225] The Court's order sets out the facts about which the witness is to be examined.[226] Witnesses give their main evidence, after which the President (of the Chamber), the Judges, the Advocate-General and, subject to the control of the President (of the Chamber), the parties' representatives may put questions to them.[227] The hearing may be in open court or, on application, *in camera*.[228] After giving his or her main evidence, the witness takes the oath, although he or she may be released from this requirement.[229] The Registrar takes minutes, in which the evidence is reproduced. The minutes are checked by the witness and signed by him or her, the President (of the Chamber), or the Judge-Rapporteur responsible for conducting the examination of the witness and the Registrar.

On penalty of a fine, a witness who has been duly summoned must attend the hearing, give evidence, and take the oath.[230] Proceedings for perjury are taken at the instance of the Court in the competent court of the Member State concerned.[231] Member States are obliged to treat any violation of an oath by witnesses as if the offence had been committed before one of its courts with jurisdiction in civil proceedings.[232]

(b) Experts

23.68 The Court of Justice and the General Court may also order that an expert's report be obtained.[233] The order appointing the expert defines his or her task and sets a time limit within which the report is to be made.[234] After making his or her report, the expert is sworn in,[235] unless exempted from taking an oath.[236] The Court may order that the expert be examined.[237] The rules on perjury and non-compliance of witnesses are applicable to experts.[238]

---

[225] ECJ Rules of Procedure, Art. 66(1); EGC Rules of Procedure, Art. 68(1). A party applying for a witness to be heard must state precisely about what facts and for what reasons the witness should be examined, failing which the General Court may decline the request without considering whether it is appropriate to hear the person in question (CFI, Case T-9/99 *HFB and Others v Commission* [2002] E.C.R. II-1487, paras 34–38).

[226] For the full content of such an order, see Art. 66(3) of the ECJ Rules of Procedure; Art. 68(2) of the EGC Rules of Procedure.

[227] ECJ Rules of Procedure, Art. 67(2) to (4); EGC Rules of Procedure, Art. 68(4).

[228] Statute, Art. 31. See, e.g. CFI, Case T-172/01 *M v Court of Justice* [2004] E.C.R. II-1075, para. 29 (*in camera*).

[229] ECJ Rules of Procedure, Art. 68(2); EGC Rules of Procedure, Art. 68(5). Art. 71 of the EGC Rules of Procedure provides that witnesses may take the oath in a manner laid down by their national law.

[230] ECJ Rules of Procedure, Art. 69; EGC Rules of Procedure, Art. 69. Yet, as provided therein, this is only where the witness, 'without good reason' fails to appear, give evidence, or take the oath.

[231] Statute, Art. 30. See further ECJ Supplementary Rules, Arts 6–7 and Annex III.

[232] Statute, Art. 30. See further ECJ Supplementary Rules, Arts 6–7 and Annex III.

[233] For examples, see ECJ, Joined Cases C-89/85, C-104/85, C-114/85, C-116/85 to C-117/85, and C-125/85 to C-129/85 *Ahlström and Others v Commission* [1993] E.C.R. I-1307, paras 31–32; CFI, Case T-169/89 *Frederiksen v European Parliament* [1991] E.C.R. II-1403, paras 38–48; CFI, Case T-90/95 *Gill v Commission* [1997] E.C.R.-SC II-1231, para. 15; CFI (order of 21 November 2001), Case T-20/00 OP *Commission v Camacho-Fernandes*, not reported, para. 25; CFI (order of 10 July 2003), Case T-313/01 *R v Commission*, not reported.

[234] ECJ Rules of Procedure, Art. 70(1); EGC Rules of Procedure, Art. 70(1).

[235] ECJ Rules of Procedure, Art. 71(1); EGC Rules of Procedure, Art. 70(6).

[236] ECJ Rules of Procedure, Art. 71(2); EGC Rules of Procedure, Art. 70(6).

[237] ECJ Rules of Procedure, Art. 70(2)–(4); EGC Rules of Procedure, Art. 70(5). Notably, this includes questions put by, *inter alia*, the representatives of the parties, subject to the control of the President.

[238] See ECJ Supplementary Rules, Arts 6–7 and Annex III; EGC Rules of Procedure, Art. 72.

(c) Compensation

Witnesses and experts are entitled to reimbursement of their travel and subsistence **23.69**
expenses.[239] In addition, witnesses are entitled to compensation for loss of income and
experts to fees for their services.[240]

(d) Objection to a witness or an expert

Parties may object to a witness or an expert on the grounds that he or she is not a competent **23.70**
or a proper person to act as such or for any other reason.[241] An objection to a witness or an
expert must be raised within two weeks after service of the order summoning the witness or
appointing the expert; the statement of objection must set out the grounds of objection and
indicate the nature of any evidence offered.[242] The Court of Justice or the General Court, as
the case may be, decides on the objection.

(e) Letters rogatory

In order to obtain a statement from witnesses or experts who cannot appear before the Court of **23.71**
Justice or the General Court, letters rogatory may be issued for the purpose of having them
examined.[243] The competent national authority obtains the statements and sends the resulting
documents to the Registrar of the Court of Justice or the General Court, as appropriate.

(5) Inspections of the place or thing in question

To date, the Court of Justice has only undertaken two inspections of a place.[244] Possibly on **23.72**
account of their infrequency, even after the recent modifications, the Rules of Procedure of
the ECJ and the EGC contain no specific provisions on the conduct of an inspection.

IX. Oral Part of the Procedure

A. Opening of the oral part of the procedure

(1) Timing

When the Court of Justice or the Chamber concerned of the General Court decides, upon **23.73**
examination of the preliminary report of the Judge-Rapporteur, to open the oral procedure,
the President of the Court or of the Chamber, as the case may be, will fix the date of the
hearing.[245] They may decide to open the oral proceedings without proceeding to measures
of organisation of procedure or measures of inquiry.

---

[239] ECJ Rules of Procedure, Art. 73(2); EGC Rules of Procedure, Art. 74(1).
[240] ECJ Rules of Procedure, Art. 73(3); EGC Rules of Procedure, Art. 74(2).
[241] ECJ Rules of Procedure, Art. 72(1); EGC Rules of Procedure, Art. 73(1).
[242] ECJ Rules of Procedure, Art. 72(2); EGC Rules of Procedure, Art. 73(2).
[243] Statute, Art. 29. See further ECJ Supplementary Rules, Arts 1–3 and Annex I; EGC Rules of
Procedure, Art. 75.
[244] ECJ, Case 14/59 *Société des Fonderies de Pont-à-Mousson v High Authority* [1959] E.C.R. 215, at 224;
ECJ, Joined Cases 42/59 and 49/59 *SNUPAT v High Authority* [1961] E.C.R. 53. For a number of examples
in which a request for an inspection was rejected, see CFI, Case T-7/05 *Commission v Parthenon* [2006] E.C.R.
II-100*, Summ. pub., para. 76; EGC (judgment of 10 July 2012), Case T-587/10 *Interspeed v Commission*,
not reported, para. 84.
[245] ECJ Rules of Procedure, Art. 60(4); EGC Rules of Procedure, Art. 53. Where the expedited procedure
applies before the Court of Justice, the President of the Court fixes the date of the hearing almost immediately

When the Court of Justice adopts measures of inquiry and when the General Court adopts measures of organization of procedure or measures of inquiry, the President of the Court or of the Chamber, as the case may be, will fix the date for the opening of the oral part of the procedure only upon completion of the measures concerned.[246]

(2) Optional character of the hearing before the Court of Justice

23.74 Under an *a contrario* reading of Art. 76 of the ECJ Rules of Procedure, the Court of Justice may decide a case without the oral part of the procedure if none of the parties or interested persons within Art. 23 of the Statute have submitted a reasoned request for a hearing.

The reasoned request must be submitted within a period of three weeks after service on the parties or the interested persons within the meaning of Art. 23 of the Statute of the notification of the close of the written part of the procedure.[247] In practice, it is rare for a hearing to be organized in the absence of such a request. Even if a duly reasoned request has been submitted by one of the parties, the Court of Justice has the final say. It may indeed decide, on the proposal of the Judge-Rapporteur (see para. 23.56 concerning the preliminary report) and after hearing the Advocate-General, not to hold a hearing when it considers, on reading the written pleadings or observations lodged during the written part of the procedure, that it has sufficient information to give a ruling.[248] Yet, such a decision is foreclosed where a reasoned request has been submitted by an interested person within Art. 23 of the Statute who did not participate in the written part of the procedure.[249]

In any event, this does not mean that the oral part of the procedure will only be opened in exceptional circumstances. A hearing will be organized as soon as the Court is of the opinion that it will have an added value.

At present, the procedure before the General Court always consists—save in exceptional circumstances[250]— of a written and an oral part.

(3) Reasoned request

23.75 The reasoned request pursuant to Art. 76(1) of the ECJ Rules of Procedure must specify why the party or interested person within the meaning of Art. 23 of the Statute wishes to be heard. That reasoning must be based on a real assessment of the benefit of a hearing to the party in question and must indicate the documentary elements or arguments which that party considers it necessary to develop or disprove more fully at a hearing. It is not sufficient

---

after the defence has been lodged or at the time when the decision is taken to have recourse to the expedited procedure where that decision is taken after lodgment of the defence (ECJ Rules of Procedure, Art. 135(1)).

[246] ECJ Rules of Procedure, Art. 75; EGC Rules of Procedure, Art. 54. Measures of organization of procedure or measures of inquiry may still be prescribed during the oral part of the procedure: see EGC Rules of Procedure, Art. 54 ('Without prejudice to any measures of organisation of procedure or measures of inquiry which may be arranged at the stage of the oral procedure'). For an example, see CFI, Joined Cases T-79/89, T-84/89 to T-86/89, T-89/89, T-91/89 to T-92/89, T-94/89, T-96/89, T-98/89, T-102/89, and T-104/89 *BASF and Others v Commission* [1992] E.C.R. II-315, para. 25.

[247] ECJ Rules of Procedure, Art. 76(1). Yet, as provided therein, that time limit may be extended by the President. According to the ECJ Practice Directions, point 48, such request may not exceed three pages.

[248] ECJ Rules of Procedure, Art. 76(2).

[249] ECJ Rules of Procedure, Art. 76(3).

[250] See EGC Rules of Procedure, Arts 111, 113, 114, 135a, and 146.

to provide a general statement of reasons referring to the importance of the case or of the questions to be decided.[251]

B. Course of the oral procedure

(1) General

Before the hearing begins, the agents or lawyers are called to a short meeting with the **23.76** relevant formation of the Court of Justice or the General Court, as the case may be, in order to plan the hearing. At that point, the Judge-Rapporteur and the Advocate-General may indicate the matters they wish to hear developed in the arguments.[252]

The proceedings are opened and directed by the President (of the Chamber).[253] In principle, they are open to the public, unless the Court of Justice or the General Court decides otherwise, of its own motion or on application by the parties, for serious reasons.[254]

(2) Report for the hearing

The report for the hearing sets out the facts, an outline of the procedure up to the date of **23.77** the hearing, and a summary of the forms of order sought and of the parties' pleas and arguments. The requirement that a report for the hearing should be established has been abolished in the new ECJ Rules of Procedure, which entered into force on 1 November 2012. Henceforth, the report for the hearing will only be used by the General Court.

The judgment of the General Court will be largely based on the report for the hearing and so it is important for the parties that its contents are accurate. Therefore, it is sent to the parties a few weeks before the hearing. At the beginning of the sitting, the President (of the Chamber) mentions that the report has been sent out and invites comments.

(3) Oral argument

Oral argument is heard from the parties and any interveners (on intervention, see paras **23.78** 25.58–25.78).[255] Each party may address the Court of Justice or the General Court for 15 minutes.[256] This time may be extended by parties making a reasoned application to the Registry at least 14 days before the hearing.

Oral argument is intended to clarify the pleas and arguments raised during the written procedure, of which the Judges are already apprised, and to touch on certain aspects of them. In pleading before the respective Court, the parties may not raise any new pleas unless they

---

[251] ECJ Practice Directions, point 46.
[252] ECJ Practice Directions, point 48.
[253] ECJ Rules of Procedure, Art. 78; EGC Rules of Procedure, Art. 56.
[254] Statute, Art. 31; ECJ Rules of Procedure, Art. 78(1); EGC Rules of Procedure, Art. 57: some proceedings must be held *in camera* (see Art. 348 TFEU).
[255] Very often, the Judges and Advocate-General will listen to oral argument via simultaneous interpretation. In order to make that interpretation possible, agents and lawyers should speak at a natural and unforced pace and use short sentences of simple structure. To facilitate interpretation, parties' representatives are requested to send any text or written notes for their submissions to the Directorate for Interpretation in advance either by fax ((+352) 4303 3697) or by email (<http://interpret@curia.europa.eu>) (ECJ Practice Directions, point 57; EGC Pratice Directions, points 119–120).
[256] ECJ Practice Directions, point 52; EGC Practice Directions, point 125 (interveners may address the General Court for ten minutes).

are based on matters of law or of fact which have come to light in the course of the proceedings[257] or it is a question of pleas which the Union courts have to raise of their own motion.[258] Exceptionally, new evidence may be presented at the hearing, although an explanation must be given as to why it was not tendered during the written procedure.[259]

(4) Questions

23.79 After the parties have presented their oral arguments, the President (of the Chamber), the Judges, and the Advocate-General may put questions to the agents, advisers, or lawyers of the parties.[260] This affords an opportunity to elucidate any aspects of the case-file remaining unclear and may result in measures of inquiry being repeated or expanded, this being ordered by the Court of Justice or the General Court after hearing the Advocate-General.

(5) Closure of the oral part of the procedure

23.80 The oral stage of the procedure is closed by the President (of the Chamber) after the Advocate-General has presented his or her Opinion. The Advocate-General reads out his or her proposal for the operative part generally a few weeks after the hearing.[261] Where it considers that the case raises no new point of law, the Court of Justice may decide, after hearing the Advocate-General, that the case shall be determined without a submission from the Advocate-General.[262] In that case, the oral part of the procedure will be closed after the hearing.

In proceedings before the General Court, where an Advocate-General has not been designated in a case, the President (of the Chamber) declares the oral part of the procedure closed at the end of the hearing.[263] The President (of the Chamber) also declares the oral proceedings closed where an Advocate-General has been designated in a case and he or she delivers his or her Opinion in writing by lodging it at the Registry.[264]

(6) No right to respond to the Advocate-General's Opinion

23.81 The parties do not have the possibility under the Statute and the Rules of Procedure of the Court of Justice and the General Court of submitting written observations in response to the Advocate-General's Opinion.[265]

---

[257] ECJ Rules of Procedure, Art. 127(1); EGC Rules of Procedure, Art. 48(2).

[258] CFI, Case T-27/02 *Kronofrance v Commission* [2004] E.C.R. II-4177, para. 30.

[259] ECJ Rules of Procedure, Art. 128(2); at present the EGC Rules of Procedure do not contain a similar provision.

[260] ECJ Rules of Procedure, Art. 80; EGC Rules of Procedure, Art. 58.

[261] A document which is lodged after the Advocate-General has read out his or her proposal for the operative part will be inadmissible. However, the Court of Justice may decide to reopen the oral proceedings (ECJ, Case C-380/01 *Schneider* [2004] E.C.R. I-1389, paras 14 and 19).

[262] Statute, Art. 20, fifth para.; ECJ Rules of Procedure, Art. 59(2) and (3).

[263] EGC Rules of Procedure, Art. 60.

[264] EGC Rules of Procedure, Art. 61.

[265] See ECJ (order of 4 February 2000), Case C-17/98 *Emesa Sugar* [2000] E.C.R. I-665, paras 8–20: having regard to both the organic and the functional link between the Advocate-General and the Court, the Court considers that the fact that it is impossible for a party to submit written observations in response to the Advocate-General's Opinion does not violate the right to adversarial proceedings. See also ECJ, Case C-266/09 *Stichting Natuur en Milieu and Others* [2010] I-13119, para. 28 (and further citations therein); ECJ (judgment of 6 September 2012), Case C-262/10 *Döhler Neuenkirchen*, not reported, para. 29; ECJ (judgment of 18 July 2013), Joined Cases C-584/10 P, C-593/10 P, and C-595/10 P *Commission and Others v Kadi*, not reported, para. 57.

C. Reopening of the oral procedure

(1) Objective

The Court of Justice or the General Court may, after hearing the Advocate-General, order the **23.82** reopening of the oral procedure.[266] It will do so if an apparently determinative matter only becomes apparent after the oral procedure has been closed or, even more generally, if the Court needs further clarification on a certain point.[267] When the quorum of three Judges in the case of three- or five-Judge Chambers and of eleven Judges in the case of the Grand Chamber is no longer met, the Court will in principle also decide to reopen the procedure.[268]

If the procedure is reopened, the parties may make further written submissions,[269] additional measures of inquiry may be ordered and, following further oral argument, the Advocate-General may deliver a supplementary Opinion.[270]

Under the same conditions, the Court of Justice may order the opening of the oral procedure in a case where it had previously decided not to organize a hearing in the first place.[271]

---

[266] ECJ Rules of Procedure, Art. 83; EGC Rules of Procedure, Art. 62. The Court of Justice ordered the oral procedure to be reopened (in preliminary ruling proceedings) after the Advocate-General had delivered an Opinion in which he criticized very severely another judgment of the Court which had been given after the end of the oral procedure. In the order re-opening the oral procedure, the Court asked the parties, the institutions, and Member States concerned to concentrate their oral observations on a number of specific questions (ECJ (order of 18 June 2002) Case C-280/00 *Altmark Trans and Regierungspräsidium Magdeburg*, not reported; see also ECJ (order of 17 September 1999), Case C-35/98 *Verkooijen*, not reported). For other examples, see ECJ, Case C-304/02 *Commission v France* [2005] E.C.R. I-6263; ECJ, Case C-382/08 *Neukirchinger* [2011] E.C.R. I-139, para. 18. In contrast, in *Wouters*, the Court of Justice refused to reopen the oral procedure as applied for by the applicant in the main proceedings on the grounds that it was in possession of all the necessary facts, observing that those facts had been the subject of argument at the hearing (ECJ, Case C-309/99 *Wouters and Others* [2002] E.C.R. I-1577, paras 40–43). See also ECJ, Case C-184/01 P *Hirschfeldt v European Environment Agency* [2002] E.C.R. I-10173, paras 29–32; ECJ, Case C-273/00 *Sieckmann* [2002] E.C.R. I-11737, para. 22; ECJ (order of 2 September 2010), Case C-46/08 *Carmen Media Group*, not reported; ECJ (order of 4 July 2012), Case C-62/11 *Feyerbacher*, not reported.

[267] ECJ (order of 21 October 2005), Case C-475/03 *Banca popolare di Cremona*, not reported, para. 5; ECJ, Case C-58/09 *Leo-Libera* [2010] E.C.R. I-5189, paras 18–19; ECJ, Case C-221/09 *ADJ Tuna* [2011] E.C.R. I-1655, para. 36. In ECJ (order of 25 October 2011), Case C-262/10 *Döhler Neuenkirchen*, not reported, para. 5, the Court reopened the oral procedure because it appeared after the closing of the oral procedure that the interpretation of Art. 204(1)(a) of the Customs Code could possibily have a noticeable impact on EU customs law.

[268] In the General Court, the Grand Chamber quorum is at present still nine judges. A new hearing will not be held if the main parties (as well as the Advocate-General) renounce it. See, e.g. EGC, Case T-314/06 *Whirlpool Europe v Council* [2010] E.C.R. II-5005, paras 54–57.

[269] See e.g. ECJ (order of 21 October 2005), Case C-475/03 *Banca popolare di Cremona*, not reported, para. 5.

[270] For examples, see ECJ, Case 383/85 *Commission v Belgium* [1989] E.C.R. 3069, at 3077–8; ECJ, Case C-2/90 *Commission v Belgium* [1992] E.C.R. I-4431, at I-4472; see ECJ, Case C-304/02 *Commission v France* [2005] E.C.R. I-6263, at I-6319 and I-6321. That being said, the Court of Justice may reopen the oral procedure before the Advocate-General has delivered his or her Opinion, ECJ, Case 56/77 *Agence Européenne d'Intérims v Commission* [1978] E.C.R. 2215, at 2230, or when it had initially been decided that no Opinion would be rendered by the Advocate-General, see ECJ (judgment of 6 September 2012), Case C-262/10 *Döhler Neuenkirchen*, not reported, paras 24 and 32.

[271] ECJ Rules of Procedure, Art. 83. See, e.g. ECJ (order of 21 April 2010), Case C-382/08 *Neukirchinger*, not reported, para. 3.

(2) Request for reopening

23.83 In refusing to reopen the oral procedure after the judgment in the *PVC* cases,[272] the then Court of First Instance equated the circumstances in which a request to that effect might be granted with the conditions which have to be met in order to obtain revision of a judgment. On appeal, the Court of Justice confirmed that this is the case.[273] The oral procedure will be reopened only if the applicant or the defendant adduces a fact or reasonable evidence of a fact of which neither it nor the Court could have been aware at the time of the hearing and which possibly had a decisive bearing on the case. Naturally, the fact must be connected with the case in issue. Indications of a general nature or declarations made in other proceedings are not sufficient.[274] Consequently, the deliberations will be only upset for serious reasons in the same way as the authority of a judgment as *res judicata* may be revised only very exceptionally (see para. 25.117).

(3) Absence during initial hearing

23.84 In addition, a party may apply to have the oral procedure reopened if it was not present when it was originally held. Such an application will be granted if the party in question proves that its absence was due to *force majeure*, which, according to settled case-law, means abnormal difficulties, independent of the will of the party concerned and apparently inevitable, even if all due care is taken.[275] If the person providing the address for service for the absent party forgets to forward the summons to attend the hearing, this does not constitute a sufficient ground for ordering the oral procedure to be reopened.[276]

---

[272] CFI, Case T-9/89 *Hüls v Commission* [1992] E.C.R. II-499, paras 382–385; CFI, Case T-10/89 *Hoechst v Commission* [1992] E.C.R. II-629, paras 372–375; CFI, Case T-11/89 *Shell v Commission* [1992] E.C.R. II-757, paras 372–374; CFI, Case T-12/89 *Solvay v Commission* [1992] E.C.R. II-907, paras 345–347; CFI, Case T-13/89 *ICI v Commission* [1992] E.C.R. II-1021, paras 399–401; CFI, Case T-14/89 *Montedipe v Commission* [1992] E.C.R. II-1155, paras 389–391; CFI, Case T-15/89 *Chemie Linz v Commission* [1992] E.C.R. II-1275, paras 393–395; EGC, Joined Cases T-40/07 P and T-62/07 P *de Brito Sequeira Carvalho v Commission* [2009] E.C.R.-SC II-551, para. 131; EGC (judgment of 4 July 2012), Case T-12/12 *Laboratoires CTRS v Commission*, not reported, paras 22–24. See also ECJ, Case 77/70 *Prelle v Commission* [1971] E.C.R. 561, para. 7; ECJ, Case C-415/93 *Bosman* [1995] E.C.R. I-4921, para. 53; CFI, Joined Cases T-236/01, T-239/01, T-244/01 to T-246/01, T-251/01, and T-252/01 *Tokai Carbon and Others v Commission* [2004] E.C.R. II-1181 para. 484; ECJ (judgment of 18 July 2013), Joined Cases C-584/10 P, C-593/10 P and C-595/10 P *Commission and Others v Kadi*, not reported, paras 56–57 (and case-law cited).

[273] See, e.g. ECJ, Case C-199/92 P *Hüls v Commission* [1999] E.C.R. I-4287, para. 127; ECJ, Case C-200/92 P *ICI v Commission* [1999] E.C.R. I-4399, para. 61 (the General Court is probably obliged to order the procedure to be reopened when these conditions are met); ECJ, Case C-235/92 *Montecatini v Commission* [1999] E.C.R. I-4539, para. 102.

[274] See, e.g. ECJ, Case C-199/92 P *Hüls v Commission* [1999] E.C.R. I-4287, para. 130; ECJ, Case C-235/92 *Montecatini v Commission* [1999] E.C.R. I-4539, para. 105; ECJ (judgment of 18 July 2013), Joined Cases C-584/10 P, C-593/10 P and C-595/10 P *Commission and Others v Kadi*, not reported, paras 56–57 (and case-law cited).

[275] CFI, Case T-12/90 *Bayer v Commission* [1991] E.C.R. II-219, para. 44.

[276] CFI, Case T-235/94 *Galtieri v European Parliament* [1996] E.C.R.-SC II-129, para. 17 (English abstract at I-A-43).

X. Judgments and Orders

A. The judgment or order

(1) General

The decision of the Court of Justice or of the General Court which brings the proceedings **23.85** to an end takes the form of a judgment or order.[277] Occasionally, however, a judgment is given which determines only some of the issues. Examples are a judgment merely declaring the action admissible[278] or one finding the Union non-contractually liable but not making any determination of the amount of damages to be paid.[279]

(2) Orders

Orders are given by the Court of Justice or the General Court in a variety of circumstances **23.86** (for example, as mentioned earlier, in the context of a stay of proceedings involving circumstances of the third paragraph of Art. 54 of the Statute (see para. 23.46)).[280] Specifically in certain cases, the order must be reasoned (for example, as mentioned earlier, where it is clear that the Court of Justice or the General Court do not have jurisdiction or the case is manifestly inadmissible or manifestly lacking any foundation in law (see para. 23.40).[281]

(3) Timing

There is no principle of immediacy in Union law on the basis of which the Court of Justice **23.87** and the General Court are bound to give judgment shortly after the hearing. This is because there is at present no provision of the Statute or the Rules of Procedure which stipulates that the judgments or orders of the respective Court must be delivered within a specified period after the close of the oral procedure, if there is one. Nevertheless, the general principle of Union law, derived from Art. 6(1) of the European Convention for the Protection of Human Rights and Fundamental Freedoms (ECHR) and codified in Art. 47 of the Charter

---

[277] As regards the Civil Service Tribunal, the provisions on judgments and orders are comparable to those governing the Court of Justice and the General Court: see CST Rules of Procedure, Arts 79–83.

[278] ECJ, Case C-70/88 *European Parliament v Council* [1990] E.C.R. I-2041, operative part.

[279] ECJ, Case C-152/88 *Sofrimport v Commission* [1990] E.C.R. I-2477, operative part; ECJ, Case C-440/07 P *Commission v Schneider Electric* [2009] E.C.R. I-6413, operative part (as well as the order of 9 June 2010 in the same case [2010] E.C.R. I-73*, Summ. pub.); EGC, Joined Cases T-8/95 and T-9/95 *Pelle and Konrad v Council and Commission* [2007] E.C.R. II-4117, operative part.

[280] For other instances in which orders are involved, see, e.g. as regards common procedural rules, ECJ Rules of Procedure, Arts 64(1) concerning measures of inquiry; ECJ Rules of Procedure, Art. 83 on the reopening of the oral part of the procedure. With particular regard to preliminary ruling proceedings, see, e.g. ECJ Rules of Procedure, Art. 103 on rectification; ECJ Rules of Procedure, Art. 116(4) on legal aid. With further regard to direct actions and appeals, see ECJ Rules of Procedure, Art. 131(3) in the context of intervention; ECJ Rules of Procedure, Art. 145(1) concerning a dispute concerning costs; ECJ Rules of Procedure, Art. 154 on rectification; ECJ Rules of Procedure, Art. 159(5) concerning revision; ECJ Rules of Procedure, Art. 187(3) concerning legal aid in the context of appeals.

[281] For other instances in which reasoned orders are involved, see, e.g. ECJ Rules of Procedure, Art. 46(2) concerning exclusion of a party's representative from the proceedings; ECJ Rules of Procedure, Art. 66(3) concerning oral testimony. With regard to preliminary ruling proceedings, see, e.g. ECJ Rules of Procedure, Art. 99; with further regard to direct actions and appeals, see, e.g. ECJ Rules of Procedure, Art. 149 concerning cases that do not proceed to judgment; ECJ Rules of Procedure, Art. 150 on absolute bar to proceeding with a case; ECJ Rules of Procedure, Art. 162(1) concerning interim measures; ECJ Rules of Procedure, Arts 181 and 182 concerning appeals.

of Fundamental Rights of the European Union, that everyone is entitled to fair legal process applies, with the result that the respective Court has to render its decision within a reasonable period.[282]

B. Content and formal requirements

(1) Content

23.88 Judgments and orders of the Court of Justice and the General Court essentially consist of three parts: the introductory part (the facts, relevant Union and other law, and procedural background), the grounds for the decision (the Court's reasoning), and the operative part (the Court's holding typically in bold at the end). In the recently revised ECJ Rules of Procedure, there is now an explicit distinction drawn between judgments and orders, on the one hand, and between orders and reasoned orders, on the other, in relation to their content.

A judgment must contain the following fourteen items: (1) a statement that it is the judgment of the respective Court; (2) an indication as to the formation of the respective Court; (3) the date of delivery; (4) the names of the President (of the Chamber) and of the Judges who took part in the deliberations, with an indication as to the name of the Judge-Rapporteur; (5) the name of the Advocate-General, if designated; (6) the name of the Registrar; (7) a description of the parties or the 'interested persons' within Art. 23 of the Statute who participated in the proceedings; (8) the names of their representatives; (9) in the case of direct actions and appeals, a statement of the form of order sought by the parties; (10) where applicable, the date of the hearing; (11) a statement that the Advocate-General has been heard and, where applicable, the date of his or her Opinion; (12) a summary of the facts; (13) the grounds for the decision; and (14) the operative part of the judgment including, where appropriate, the decision as to costs.[283]

An order must contain basically eleven of the fourteen items listed above (all except for points (9), (10), (12), and (13)), with certain modification on account of the nature of the orders; for example, there is an additional specification that there must be an indication as to the legal basis of the order.[284]

---

[282] For examples involving infringement of that principle, see, e.g. ECJ, Case C-185/95 P *Baustahlgewebe v Commission* [1998] E.C.R. I-8417, paras 21 and 52; ECJ, Case C-385/07 P *Der Grüne Punkt—Duales System Deutschland v Commission* [2009] E.C.R. I-6155, para. 188. See also Opinion of Advocate-General E. Sharpston in ECJ (judgment of 26 November 2013), Case C-58/12 P *Groupe Gascogne v Commission*, not reported, points 70–150. For examples where duration of period justified and no infringement of that principle, see, e.g. ECJ (order of 5 June 2002), Case C-217/00 P *Buzzi Unicem v Commission*, not reported, para. 86 and in particular para. 91, in which the Court of Justice held that that principle was concerned not so much with the passage of time but with any unjustified delay in the proceedings which could be attributed to the Union judicature; ECJ, Joined Cases C-238/99 P, C-244/99 P, C-245/99 P, C-247/99 P, C-250/99 P, C-251/99 P, C-252/99 P, and C-254/99 P *Limburgse Vinyl Maatschappij and Others v Commission* [2002] E.C.R. I-8375, paras 179 and 208–222; ECJ, Joined Cases C-403/04 P and C-405/04 P *Sumitomo Metal Industries and Nippon Steel v Commission* [2007] E.C.R. I-729, paras 116–123; ECJ, Joined Cases C-120/06 P and C-121/06 P *FIAMM and Others v Council and Commission* [2008] E.C.R. I-6513, paras 212–214; EGC (judgment of 5 June 2012), Case T-214/06 *Imperial Chemical Industries v Commission*, not reported, paras 317–318.
[283] Statute, Art. 36; ECJ Rules of Procedure, Art. 87(a)–(n); EGC Rules of Procedure, Art. 81.
[284] See ECJ Rules of Procedure, Art. 89(1)(a)–(k). At present, the EGC Rules of Procedure do not contain a specific provision determining the content of an order.

Where an order must be reasoned, it must contain three additional items, which track points (9), (12), and (13), that is to say, it must also include a statement of the forms of order sought by the parties in the case of direct actions and appeals, a summary of the facts, and the grounds for the decision.[285]

(2) Language

The judgment or order is given in the language of the case (see further paras 23.02–23.05).[286]   **23.89**
The judgment or order in that language is the only authentic version,[287] and it is translated into the other official languages of the European Union as the case may be.[288]

(3) Delivery and service of judgments

The judgment is delivered in open court, and the parties or interested persons within the   **23.90**
meaning of Art. 23 of the State are informed of the date of delivery of a judgment.[289]

The original of the judgment, signed by the President (of the Chamber), by the Judges who took part in the deliberations and by the Registrar, is sealed and deposited at the Registry, and certified copies are served on the parties, and where applicable, the referring court or tribunal, the interested persons referred to in Art. 23 of the Statute, and the General Court.[290]

(4) Signature and service of orders

Much the same holds true for orders as for judgments, save that orders are not delivered in   **23.91**
open court; they are adopted, as opposed to delivered.[291] The original of the order, signed by the President (of the Chamber), and the Registar, is sealed and deposited at the Registry, and certified copies are served on the parties and, where applicable, the referring court or tribunal, the interested parties referred to in Art. 23 of the Statute, the Court of Justice, the General Court, or the Civil Service Tribunal.[292]

(5) Publication

A notice containing only the date and the operative part of the judgment or order of the   **23.92**
respective Court which closes the proceedings is published in the *Official Journal of the European Union*.[293]

---

[285] ECJ Rules of Procedure, Art. 89(2)(a)–(c). See also CST Rules of Procedure, Art. 81(2).

[286] ECJ Rules of Procedure, Art. 38(1); EGC Rules of Procedure, Art. 35(3), first para.

[287] CFI (order of 5 February 2001), Case T-334/00 *Goldstein v Court of Justice*, not reported, para. 6.

[288] As far as the Court of Justice is concerned, judgments given by Chambers of three Judges are no longer published. The same applies to judgments given by Chambers of five Judges without an Advocate-General's Opinion. In contrast, judgments in preliminary ruling proceedings are always published.

[289] Statute, Art. 37; ECJ Rules of Procedure, Arts 86 and 88(1); EGC Rules of Procedure, Art. 82(1).

[290] Statute, Art. 37; ECJ Rules of Procedure, Art. 88(2); EGC Rules of Procedure, Art. 82(2).

[291] See, in this regard, CFI (order of 31 July 2009), Case T-213/08 REV *Marinova v Université Libre de Bruxelles and Commission*, not reported, para. 26: contrary to the applicant's assertion, the fact that an order was not signed by all the Judges of a Chamber and that it does not bear the seal is explained by compliance with the requisite formalities of Art. 37 of the Statute, applicable by analogy to the signing of orders, and thus does not in any way signify that it was not adopted in the regular manner by that Chamber.

[292] ECJ Rules of Procedure, Art. 90. At present, no similar provision exists in the EGC Rules of Procedure.

[293] ECJ Rules of Procedure, Art. 92; EGC Instructions to the Registrar, Art. 18.

C. Legal force

(1) Binding nature of judgments and orders

23.93 A judgment of the Court of Justice and the General Court is binding from the date of its delivery,[294] whereas an order is binding from the date of its service.[295]

However, a judgment which annuls a regulation takes effect only as from the date of the expiry of the period for bringing an appeal or, if an appeal is lodged within that period, as from the date of dismissal of the appeal.[296] Apart from this, an appeal has no suspensory effect (see para. 16.26).

(2) Judgments are enforceable

23.94 The fact that the judgment is binding means that anyone to whom it applies is bound to take the necessary steps to comply with it. That obligation stems from the Treaty articles which specify the effects of judgments.[297] On a more general level, it also arises because of the function performed by judicial pronouncements. The principle of *res judicata* extends only to matters of fact and law actually or necessarily settled by the judicial decision in question.[298]

Judgments imposing a pecuniary obligation on natural or legal persons are enforceable per se.[299] They have an order for enforcement appended to them by the competent national authority without any review as to their substance[300] and are enforced in accordance with domestic law, if necessary with the cooperation of the competent judicial and other authorities.[301]

---

[294] ECJ Rules of Procedure, Art. 91(1); EGC Rules of Procedure, Art. 83.

[295] ECJ Rules of Procedure, Art. 91(2). At present, no similar provision exists in the EGC Rules of Procedure.

[296] Statute, Art. 60, second para.; EGC Rules of Procedure, Art. 83. Compare CST Rules of Procedure, Art. 83(1) and (2), making the binding nature of judgments and orders subject to provisions of Art. 12(1) of Annex I of the Statute, stipulating in relevant part that 'an appeal before the General Court shall not have suspensory effect'.

[297] See, *inter alia*, Arts 260, 266, 280, and 299 TFEU.

[298] See also para. 7.227.

[299] Art. 280 TFEU, under which Art. 299 TFEU applies to judgments of the Court of Justice of the European Union.

[300] In the United Kingdom, application to append to a judgment the order for enforcement is made to the Secretary of State. The person concerned then applies to the High Court in England or Wales or in Northern Ireland or the Court of Session in Scotland for the judgment to be registered, and that court must register the judgment forthwith (European Communities (Enforcement of Community Judgments) Order 1972, SI 1972/1590, Art. 3(1); see also European Communities Act, s. 3(3)). Once registered, the judgment has for all purposes of execution, the same force and effect as if it had been a judgment or order given by the High Court or Court of Session on the date of registration; proceedings may be taken on it and any sum payable under it carries interest as if it had been such a judgment or order (Order 1972, SI 1972/1590, Art. 4).

[301] Art. 299 TFEU provides that enforcement may be suspended only by a decision of the Court of Justice. In *Comune di Montorio al Vomano v Commission* (ECJ (order of the President of 30 May 2001), Case C-334/97 R-EX *Comune di Montorio al Vomano v Commission* [2001] E.C.R. I-4229, paras 20–21), the President of the Court of Justice rejected an application made by the municipality of Montorio on the basis of former Arts 244 and 256 EC (now Arts 280 and 299 TFEU, respectively) for suspension of the enforcement of the Court's judgment of 10 June 1999 (ECJ, Case C-334/97 *Commission v Comune di Montorio al Vomano* [1999] E.C.R. I-3387).

24

PROCEDURE IN THE CASE OF REFERENCES FOR A PRELIMINARY RULING

Apart from the common procedural rules governing the procedure before the Court of **24.01** Justice covered in Chapter 23, there are specific rules governing the procedure in the case of references for a preliminary ruling which have to do with the order for reference, the written and oral parts of the procedure, the expedited and urgent preliminary ruling procedures, and other special characteristics that distinguish this procedure from other types of proceedings.

I. The Order for Reference

A. Formal and substantive requirements

(1) Order for reference made by a national court

The order for reference is to be sent by the national court directly to the Court of Justice by **24.02** registered post.[1] Upon arrival, it will be registered at the Registry. This is when the case receives its serial number.

Notice is given of the request for a preliminary ruling in the *Official Journal of the European Union*.[2]

The Registry requests the national court to lodge the whole of the case-file so that the Court of Justice may be better placed to give a useful answer.

(2) Content of the order for reference

The decision by which a national court or tribunal refers a question to the Court of Justice **24.03** for a preliminary ruling may be in any form allowed by national law as regards procedural steps. The order for reference must be succinct but sufficiently complete and contain all the relevant information to give the Court and the parties entitled to submit observations a clear understanding of the factual and legal context of the main proceedings. In particular, the order for reference must contain:

---

[1] Recommendations to national courts and tribunals in relation to the initiation of preliminary ruling proceedings ([2012] O.J. C338/1), point 33 (Recommendations). It should be addressed to the Registry of the Court of Justice of the European Union, Rue du Fort Niedergrünewald, L-2925 Luxembourg, telephone number: +352-4303-1.
[2] ECJ Rules of Procedure, Art. 21(4).

- a summary of the subject-matter of the dispute and the relevant findings of fact as determined by the referring court or tribunal, or at least, an account of the facts on which the questions are based;[3]
- the tenor of any national provisions applicable in the case and, where appropriate, the relevant national case-law;[4]
- a statement of the reasons which prompted the referring court or tribunal to inquire about the interpretation or validity of certain provisions of Union law, and the relationship between those provisions and the national legislation applicable to the main proceedings.[5]

Furthermore, the national court or tribunal may include the following information:

- an accurate identification of the Union law provisions relevant to the case;[6]
- a brief summary of the relevant arguments of the parties to the main proceedings.[7]

Finally, if it feels itself able to do so, the national court or tribunal may briefly state its view on the answer to be given to the question referred for a preliminary ruling.[8]

(3) Length of the order for reference

24.04 The reference should in principle not exceed ten pages.[9] The question or questions themselves should appear in a separate and clearly identified section of the order for reference, generally at the beginning or the end. It must be possible to understand them without referring to the statement of the grounds for the reference.[10]

(4) Anonymity

24.05 The Court will respect in the proceedings before it the decision of the referring judge to grant anonymity.[11] The Court itself may also grant anonymity, either at the request of the referring judge, at a duly reasoned request of a party to the main proceedings, or of its own motion.[12]

B. Notification

(1) Notification of the order for reference

24.06 The order for reference is immediately translated into the other official languages of the European Union.[13] The Registrar of the Court of Justice notifies it to the parties to the main proceedings (i.e. to all 'parties' to the case, including any interveners), the Member States (a copy of the original order for reference and a translation in an official language of

---

[3] ECJ Rules of Procedure, Art. 94(a).
[4] ECJ Rules of Procedure, Art. 94(b).
[5] ECJ Rules of Procedure, Art. 94(c).
[6] Recommendations, point 23.
[7] Recommendations, point 23.
[8] Recommendations, point 24.
[9] Recommendations, point 22.
[10] Recommendations, point 26.
[11] ECJ Rules of Procedure, Art. 95(1).
[12] ECJ Rules of Procedure, Art. 95(2).
[13] But see para. 24.08.

the Member State in question), and the Commission.[14] Notice is given by registered letter with a form for acknowledgement of receipt, addressed to the lawyers of the parties to the main proceedings or, if the parties are not represented, to their personal address as set out in the order for reference; notice is given to the Member States by registered letter with a form for acknowledgment of receipt, addressed to the Ministry of Foreign Affairs (with a copy to the Permanent Representation in Brussels).

(2) Notification to other institutions, bodies, offices, or agencies of the Union

The Registrar of the Court of Justice further notifies the order for reference to the institution, **24.07** body, office, or agency which adopted the act the validity or interpretation of which is in dispute.[15] In exceptional cases, the order for reference is also notified to other institutions, bodies, offices, or agencies of the Union if the Court of Justice wishes to obtain information from them (for example, if the preliminary question has a bearing on their prerogatives).[16] The Registrar also notifies the order for reference to the States, other than Member States, which are parties to the EEA Agreement and to the EFTA Surveillance Authority.[17]

(3) Notification to the Member States

The Member States are notified by service of a copy of the original version of the decisions of **24.08** national courts and tribunals, accompanied by a translation in the official language of the recipient Member State.[18] Where appropriate on account of the length of the national court's decision, such translation is replaced by the translation into the official language of the State to which it is addressed of a summary of the decision, which will serve as a basis for the position to be adopted by that State.[19] States party to the EEA Agreement which are not Member States and the EFTA Supervisory authority receive a copy of the original version and a translation of the decision or, where appropriate, of a summary, in the official language of their choice.[20]

II. The Written Part of the Procedure

A. Written observations

The parties to the main proceedings, the Member States,[21] the Commission and, where **24.09** appropriate, the institution, body, office, or agency which adopted the act which is in

---

[14] Statute, Art. 23, first para.

[15] Statute, Art. 23, first para.

[16] Such a request for information is based on Art. 24 of the Statute. For an example, see ECJ, Case 20/85 *Roviello* [1988] E.C.R. 2805. See also ECJ, Case C-408/95 *Eurotunnel and Others* [1997] E.C.R. I-6315 (the European Parliament was heard in a case concerning the validity of a Council directive).

[17] Statute, Art. 23, third para.

[18] ECJ Rules of Procedure, Art. 98(1).

[19] ECJ Rules of Procedure, Art. 98(1). The summary includes the full text of the question or questions referred for a preliminary ruling. It also contains, insofar as that information appears in the national court's decision, the subject-matter of the main proceedings, the essential arguments of the parties in the main proceedings, a succinct presentation of the reasoning in the reference for a preliminary ruling, and the case-law and provisions of Union law and domestic law relied on.

[20] ECJ Rules of Procedure, Art. 98(2).

[21] For the involvement of Member States in preliminary ruling procedures, see M. P. Granger, 'When Governments Go to Luxembourg...: The Influence of Governments on the Court of Justice' (2004) E.L. Rev. 3–31.

dispute are entitled to submit statements of case or written observations within two months of notification of the order for reference.[22] States party to the EEA Agreement which are not Member States and the EFTA Supervisory Authority may likewise submit written observations within two months if the national court's decision concerns one of the fields of application of the EEA Agreement.[23]

Where an agreement relating to a specific subject-matter, concluded by the Council and one or more non-Member States, provides that those States are to be entitled to submit written observations where a court or tribunal of a Member State refers to the Court of Justice for a preliminary ruling a question falling within the scope of the agreement, the decision of the national court or tribunal containing that question shall also be notified to the non-Member States concerned.[24] Within two months of such notification, those States may lodge at the Court written observations.[25]

B. Calculation of the two-month period for submission of written observations

24.10 The two-month period is calculated according to the common procedural rules on time limits, including the extension of ten days for distance (see paras 23.26–23.33). Time starts to run as from notification, which is determined from the form for acknowledgment of receipt attached to the registered letter sent by the Court. The fact that a Member State received an advance notice of the reference for a preliminary ruling does not detract from that.[26] The two-month period may be extended only in the event of 'unforeseeable circumstances or *force majeure*' within the meaning of Art. 45 of the Statute.

Late submissions will be sent back to the interested person's representative and not taken into account by the Court.[27] This does not preclude participation in the oral part of the procedure.[28]

---

[22] Statute, Art. 23, second para.; see also ECJ Rules of Procedure, Art. 96(1)(a)–(d). Whatever distinction was meant between 'statements of case' and 'written observations' in various provisions of the Statute and ECJ Rules of Procedure on the preliminary ruling procedure (see Arts 20, second para., Art. 23, second–fourth paras, and 23a, second para., of the Statute and Arts 1(2)(c), 105(3)–(4), 109(2), and 110 of the ECJ Rules of Procedure) has in practice been lost: see D. Anderson and M. Demetriou, *References to the European Court* (2nd edn, London, Sweet & Maxwell, 2002), para. 10.12.

[23] Statute, Art. 23, third para.; see also ECJ Rules of Procedure, Art. 96(1)(e).

[24] Statute, Art. 23, fourth para.; see also ECJ Rules of Procedure, Art. 96(1)(f). According to ECJ Rules of Procedure, Art. 98(3), the original version of the decision of the national court or tribunal will be communicated to it together with a translation of the decision, or where appropriate of a summary, into one of the languages to be chosen by the non-Member State concerned which are mentioned in ECJ Rules of Procedure, Art. 36.

[25] Statute, Art. 23, fourth para.

[26] ECJ, Case C-137/08 *VB Pénzügyi Lízing* [2010] E.C.R. I-10847, paras 26–35. Such an advance notice does not create an imbalance between the interested persons involved in the proceedings. The two-month period has only the effective administration of justice as its object and not the procedural equality of arms. See Opinion of Advocate-General V. Trstenjak in ECJ, Case C-137/08 *VB Pénzügyi Lízing* [2010] E.C.R. I-10847, points 78–82.

[27] For an example, see Opinion of Advocate-General E. Sharpston in ECJ (judgment of 19 December 2012), Case C-364/11 *Mostafa Abed El Karem El Kott and Others*, not reported, point 21.

[28] ECJ Rules of Procedure, Art. 96(2).

C. No second exchange of written observations

The written procedure consists solely of this opportunity to submit observations to the **24.11**
Court. The observations received are sent to all those to whom the order for reference was
notified. There is no 'reply' as between those who have submitted observations should they
disagree with each other's views. This follows from the fact that the preliminary ruling
procedure is not, formally speaking, a dispute between 'parties'.

D. No intervention

A request by a natural or legal person to intervene in preliminary ruling proceedings— **24.12**
pursuant to Art. 40 of the Statute—in order to submit observations is inadmissible.[29] This
is because a preliminary ruling procedure is not a 'case before the Court' within the
meaning of Art. 40 of the Statute. A natural or legal person that wants to be joined to
preliminary ruling proceedings must become a party to the dispute before the national
court, since all parties to the main proceedings may participate in the procedure before the
Court of Justice.[30]

III. The Oral Part of the Procedure

A. Oral observations

The Court of Justice also allows parties who have not exercised their right to submit written **24.13**
observations to take part in the hearing.[31] This signifies that a failure to make use of the
time limit for submitting written observations does not mean that there is no right to state
one's case orally and answer any questions put by the Court.

This is important, since generally the so-called non-contentious nature of preliminary-
ruling proceedings appears to be no more than a fiction. Indeed, note should be taken, for
instance, of the case where a Member State submits written observations contending that a
part of its national law is compatible with Union law[32] or where a party to the main

---

[29] ECJ (order of the President of 26 February 1996), Case C-181/95 *Biogen* [1996] E.C.R. I-717, para. 4;
ECJ (order of the President of 30 March 2004), Case C-453/03 *ABNA and Others*, not reported, paras 13–16;
ECJ (order of the President of 25 May 2004), Case C-458/03 *Parking Brixen and Others*, not reported, paras
5–8; ECJ (order of the President of 12 September 2007), Case C-73/07 *Satakunnan Markkinapörssi and
Satamedia* [2007] E.C.R. I-7075, paras 8–13 (no right to intervene for the European Data Protection
Supervisor); ECJ (order of the President of 16 December 2009), Joined Cases C-403/08 and C-429/08
Football Association Premier League and Others, not reported, paras 5–11; ECJ (order of the President of 13
January 2010), Joined Cases C-92/09 and C-93/09 *Volker und Markus Schecke*, not reported, paras 4–9.
[30] ECJ Rules of Procedure, Art. 97(1) and (2). But see, however, ECJ (order of the President of
16 December 2009), Joined Cases C-403/08 and C-429/08 *Football Association Premier League and Others*,
not reported, paras 5–11, in which the ECJ dismissed the applications to participate in the preliminary
proceedings of persons which had become parties in the proceedings before the national court only with a view
to participation in the preliminary proceedings.
[31] ECJ Rules of Procedure, Art. 96(2).
[32] See, e.g. ECJ, Case 26/62 *Van Gend & Loos* [1963] E.C.R. 1, at 8; ECJ, Case 293/83 *Gravier* [1985]
E.C.R. 593, para. 12.

proceedings seeks implementation of an agreement while the other party claims that the agreement is contrary to Union law.[33]

Even if written observations are lodged by all involved, the oral part of the procedure affords a full opportunity for explanations and counter arguments to be presented. This fits within the underlying rationale of the preliminary ruling procedure, which is in effect a 'debate' before the Court of Justice requiring the largest possible participation in the written and oral parts of the procedure, especially since the preliminary ruling will have binding effects on the referring court as well as other national courts.

B. Reopening of the oral part of the procedure

24.14 As such, in line with the common procedural rules governing the reopening of the oral procedure (see para. 23.82), the Court may, after hearing the Advocate-General, order the reopening of the oral procedure of its own motion[34] if it considers that it is insufficiently informed or that the case should be decided on the basis of an argument on which no discussion has taken place between the parties and other interested persons within the meaning of Art. 23 of the Statute.[35]

C. Cases in which no hearing is held

24.15 First, as already mentioned, notwithstanding a reasoned request submitted by an interested person within the meaning of Art. 23 of the Statute, the Court may decide that no oral hearing is needed where it considers that it has sufficient information based on the pleadings or observations submitted during the written part of the procedure (see para. 23.74).[36] However, the Court is bound by a reasoned request for a hearing when it has been submitted by an interested person referred to in Art. 23 of the Statute who did not participate in the written part of the procedure.[37]

Second, the ECJ Rules of Procedure further provide that the Court may answer the question referred for a preliminary ruling without a hearing by reasoned order where the question is identical[38] to a question on which the Court has already ruled, where the answer

---

[33] See, e.g. ECJ, Case 261/81 *Rau* [1982] E.C.R. 3961, para. 4.

[34] ECJ Rules of Procedure, Art. 83. For examples, see ECJ (order of 17 September 1999), Case C-35/98 *Verkooijen*, not reported; ECJ (order of 18 June 2002), Case C-280/00 *Altmark Trans and Regierungspräsidium Magdeburg*, not reported; ECJ (order of 7 March 2007), Case C-110/05 *Commission v Italy*, not reported; ECJ, Case C-382/08 *Neukirchinger* [2011] E.C.R. I-139, para. 18. When the quorum of three Judges in the case of three- or five-Judge Chambers and of eleven Judges in the case of the Grand Chamber is no longer met, the Court will in principle also decide to reopen the procedure (see para. 23.82).

[35] ECJ (order of 4 February 2000), Case C-17/98 *Emesa Sugar* [2000] E.C.R. I-665, para. 18; ECJ, Case C-309/99 *Wouters and Others* [2002] E.C.R. I-1577, para. 42; ECJ (judgment of 13 November 2003), Case C-209/01 *Schilling and Fleck-Schilling* [2003] E.C.R. I-13389, para. 19; ECJ (order of 21 October 2005), Case C-475/03 *Banca popolare di Cremona*, not reported, para. 5; ECJ, Case C-205/06 *Commission v Austria* [2009] E.C.R. I-1301, para. 13; ECJ (judgment of 6 September 2012), Case C-262/10 *Döhler Neuenkirchen*, not reported, para. 30.

[36] ECJ Rules of Procedure, Art. 76(2).

[37] ECJ Rules of Procedure, Art. 76(3).

[38] The wording used need not be exactly identical. It is enough for the questions to be essentially identical: ECJ (order of 8 June 2004), Joined Cases C-250/02 to C-253/02 and C-256/02 *Telecom Italia Mobile*, not reported, paras 9–10.

to such a question may be clearly deduced from existing case-law, or where the answer to the question referred admits of no reasonable doubt.[39] The Court will then refer to an earlier judgment or to the relevant case-law.[40] The Court may at any time give its decision by reasoned order, on a proposal from the Judge-Rapporteur and after hearing the Advocate-General.[41]

Finally, the case will be decided by order—without an oral hearing—where the Court has no jurisdiction to take cognizance of the reference or where the action is manifestly inadmissible.[42]

IV. Expedited and Urgent Preliminary Ruling Procedures

A. General

There are at present two types of procedures that allow the Court of Justice to deliver its preliminary ruling on a speedier basis than the normal procedure for preliminary ruling proceedings: the expedited and the urgent preliminary ruling procedures (for a distinction between the two, see para. 22.19).   **24.16**

B. Expedited preliminary ruling procedure

(1) General

At the request of the national court or, exceptionally, of his own motion, the President may decide, after hearing the Judge-Rapporteur and the Advocate-General, to apply an   **24.17**

---

[39] ECJ Rules of Procedure, Art. 99. While similar, these circumstances allowing the Court to deliver a preliminary ruling by reasoned order are not the same thing as the so-called *CILFIT* conditions in respect of excusing the national courts of last instance from their obligation to make a reference for a preliminary ruling under Art. 267, third para., TFEU: see paras 3.51–3.55.

[40] For applications, see ECJ (order of 20 October 2000), Case C-242/99 *Vogler* [2000] E.C.R. I-9083; ECJ (order of 5 April 2001), Case C-518/99 *Gaillard* [2001] E.C.R. I-2771; ECJ (order of 2 May 2001), Case C-307/99 *OGT Fruchthandelsgesellschaft* [2001] E.C.R. I-3159 (question not identical but the answer was sufficiently clear from the case-law); ECJ (order of 22 November 2001), Case C-80/01 *Michel* [2001] E.C.R. I-9141 (answer sufficiently clear from the case-law); ECJ (order of 24 July 2003), Case C-166/02 *Messejana Viegas*, not reported (answer sufficiently clear from the case-law); ECJ (order of 27 January 2004), Case C-428/01 *Fratelli Costanzo and Others*, not reported (identical question); ECJ (order of 27 January 2004), Case C-259/02 *La Mer Technology and Others* [2004] E.C.R. I-1159 (answer to all the questions—with the exception of the last—sufficiently clear from the case-law; there was no reasonable doubt about the answer to the last question). See also ECJ (order of 18 April 2013), Case C-413/11 *Germanwings*, not reported; ECJ (order of 8 May 2013), Case C-542/12 *Fidenato*, not reported; ECJ (order of 20 June 2013), Case C-352/12 *Consiglio Nazionale degli Ingegneri*, not reported.

[41] ECJ Rules of Procedure, Art. 99. See, e.g. ECJ (order of 16 May 2013), Case C-564/11 *Consulta Regionale Ordine Ingegneri Della Lombardia and Others*, not reported; ECJ (order of 8 May 2013), Case C-542/12 *Fidenato*, not reported.

[42] ECJ Rules of Procedure, Art. 53(2). Where the Court manifestly lacks jurisdiction to deliver a preliminary ruling (e.g. where the reference was not made by a national court or tribunal within the meaning of Art. 267 TFEU or where the reference is manifestly inadmissible), the Court may, after hearing the Advocate-General, at any time decide to give a decision by reasoned order without taking further steps in the proceedings. For examples, see ECJ (order of 11 July 2003), Case C-161/03 *CAFOM and Samsung Electronics France*, not reported, paras 10–17; ECJ (order of 11 February 2004), Joined Cases C-438/03, C-439/03, C-509/03, and C-2/04 *Cannito and Others* [2004] E.C.R. I-1605, paras 9–13; ECJ (order of 8 May 2013), Case C-73/13 *T*, not reported, paras 9–15. See further para. 23.40.

expedited procedure where the nature of the case requires that a ruling on the question put to the Court is delivered in a short time.[43]

(2) Conditions

24.18 Generally, this requires the existence of exceptional urgency, meaning a situation in which a decision of the Court is necessary to prevent the risks that would be incurred in case the procedure would follow its normal course.[44] Also, the importance to the Union of the area of law in which the order for reference has been made will be taken into account.[45]

The President has ruled that the following circumstances by itself do not justify recourse to the expedited procedure: the large number of persons or legal situations concerned;[46] the interest a party has in obtaining a rapid decision on the rights conferred upon him by Union law;[47] economic interests;[48] damaging effects;[49] the risk of an economic loss;[50] the existence of conflicting case-law;[51] the fact that the reference was made in the context of summary proceedings;[52] the length of criminal proceedings before a national court;[53] the fact that a large number of similar cases is pending before the referring judge;[54] or the sensitive

---

[43] ECJ Rules of Procedure, Art. 105(1). In the former version of the ECJ Rules of Procedure, there had been an expedited procedure in the case of direct actions (Art. 62a), whereas for preliminary ruling proceedings, this was called an accelerated procedure (Art. 104a). With the recent revision of the ECJ Rules of Procedure, the terminology has been streamlined, and the expression 'expedited procedure' has been taken over for preliminary ruling proceedings as well.

[44] ECJ (order of the President of 21 November 2005), Case C-385/05 *Confédération générale du travail and Others*, not reported, para. 9; ECJ (order of the President of 15 July 2010), Case C-296/10 *Purrucker*, not reported, para. 7. Conversely, when the expedited procedure would not lead to a judgment within time to prevent the risk from materializing, the application will be rejected: ECJ (order of the President of 18 March 2005), Case C-300/04 *Eman and Sevinger*, not reported, para. 18.

[45] ECJ (order of the President of 1 March 2010), Case C-550/09 *E and F*, not reported, para. 10 (fight against terrorism); ECJ (order of the President of 12 May 2010), Joined Cases C-188/10 and C-189/10 *Melki and Abdeli*, not reported, para. 14 (Area of Freedom, Security and Justice; the functioning of Article 267 TFEU).

[46] ECJ (order of the President of 3 July 2008), Case C-201/08 *Plantanol*, not reported, para. 9; ECJ (order of the President of 19 October 2009), Case C-310/09 *Accor*, not reported, para. 9; ECJ (order of the President of 31 January 2011), Case C-573/10 *Micşa*, not reported, para. 9; ECJ (order of the President of 8 March 2012), Case C-6/12 *P*, not reported, para. 8.

[47] ECJ (order of the President of 7 May 2004), Joined Cases C-154/04 and C-155/04 *Alliance for Natural Health and Others*, not reported, para. 8; ECJ (order of 29 November 2010), Case C-416/10 *Križan*, not reported, paras 8–9; ECJ (order of the President of 16 March 2010), Case C-3/10 *Affatato*, not reported, para. 13; ECJ (order of 31 January 2011), Case C-573/10 *Micşa*, not reported, para. 10.

[48] ECJ (order of the President of 19 October 2009), Case C-310/09 *Accor*, not reported, para. 10.

[49] ECJ (order of the President of 23 March 2007), Case C-12/07 *Autostrada dei Fiori and AISCAT*, not reported, para. 8; ECJ (order of 29 September 2008), Case C-375/08 *Pontini and Others*, not reported, para. 11; ECJ (order of the President of 16 March 2010), Case C-3/10 *Affatato*, not reported, para. 13.

[50] ECJ (order of the President of 3 July 2008), Case C-201/08 *Plantanol*, not reported, para. 9; ECJ (order of the President of 4 December 2008), Case C-384/08 *Attanasio Group*, not reported, para. 11; ECJ (order of the President of 16 March 2010), Case C-20/10 *Cosimo Damiano Vino*, not reported, para. 10; ECJ (order of the President of 8 March 2012), Case C-6/12 *P*, not reported, para. 9.

[51] ECJ (order of the President of 28 June 2013), Case C-140/13 *Altmann and Others*, not reported, para. 13.

[52] ECJ (order of the President of 23 March 2007), Case C-12/07 *Autostrada dei Fiori and AISCAT*, not reported, para. 7.

[53] ECJ (order of the President of 29 September 2008), Case C-375/08 *Pontini and Others*, not reported, para. 10.

[54] ECJ (order of the President of 24 October 2005), Case C-330/05 *Granberg*, not reported, para. 8. But see ECJ (order of the President of 3 December 2008), Case C-439/08 *VEBIC*, not reported, para. 7.

economic or social nature of a case.[55] The application of the expedited procedure will also be rejected where the outcome of the main proceedings will only have an impact at a point in the far future.[56] Further to this, the expedited procedure cannot be used to allow the concomitant treatment of similar references for a preliminary ruling.[57] Conversely, the fact that a national judge is required to decide the case pending before it within a specific time limit may justify recourse to the expedited procedure.[58] This is motivated by the spirit of cooperation characterizing the relationship between the Court of Justice and the national courts.[59] The President has also accepted exceptional urgency where a decision on a point of Union law was necessary to rule on the legality of the continued detainment of persons;[60] where uncertainty about the validity of a Union law measure would adversely affect the financial stability of the euro area,[61] and where uncertainties about the application of Union law prevented the parties in the main proceedings from living a normal family life.[62]

In a number of cases, the President rejected the application for an expedited procedure because the national judge provided very few or no elements substantiating the request or because he merely referred to the arguments of the parties before him without making an assessment on the exceptional urgency of his own.[63] Therefore, since the President did not rule on the merits of the reasons adduced, it is uncertain, for instance, whether the existence of a threat to public health[64] will constitute an extreme urgency warranting the application of the expedited procedure.

(3) Procedure

The expedited procedure does not substantially differ from the ordinary procedure. The **24.19** treatment of the case is expedited, which means that shorter terms are respected not only by the parties and interested persons, but also by the Court internally. Therefore, as soon as it is decided to apply the expedited procedure, the President immediately fixes the date for the hearing and the period (not less than 15 days) within which parties and other interested

---

[55] ECJ (order of the President of 8 November 2007), Case C-456/07 *Mihal*, not reported, para. 8; ECJ (order of the President of 3 July 2008), Case C-201/08 *Plantanol*, not reported, para. 9; ECJ (order of the President of 16 March 2010), Case C-20/10 *Cosimo Damiano Vino*, not reported, para. 10.

[56] ECJ (order of the President of 15 July 2010), Case C-264/10 *Kita*, not reported, paras 7–9.

[57] ECJ (order of the President of 31 August 2010), Case C-228/10 *UEFA and British Sky Broadcasting*, not reported, para. 6.

[58] ECJ (order of the President of 1 October 2010), Case C-411/10 *N.S.*, not reported, para. 8.

[59] ECJ (order of the President of 1 March 2010), Case C-550/09 *E and F*, not reported, para. 11; ECJ (order of the President of 12 May 2010), Joined Cases C-188/10 and C-189/10 *Melki and Abdeli*, not reported, para. 15. But see ECJ (order of the President of 3 April 2007), Case C-33/07 *Jipa*, not reported, para. 7.

[60] Art. 267, fourth para., TFEU. For examples, see ECJ (order of the President of 1 March 2010), Case C-550/09 *E and F*, not reported, paras 13–14; ECJ (order of the President of 12 May 2010), Joined Cases C-188/10 and C-189/10 *Melki and Abdeli*, not reported, paras 13–14. On the relationship between the expedited procedure and the urgent procedure, see para. 22.19.

[61] ECJ (order of the President of 4 October 2012), Case C370/12 *Pringle*, not reported, para. 7.

[62] ECJ (order of the President of 17 April 2008), Case C-127/08 *Metock and Others*, not reported, para. 16, with a case note by N. Cambien (2009) Colum.J.Eur.L. 321–41.

[63] ECJ (order of the President of 15 November 2005), Case C-341/05 *Laval un Partneri*, not reported, paras 8–9; ECJ (order of the President of 29 November 2010), C-416/10 *Križan*, not reported, paras 10–11. When the national judge refers both to the urgent preliminary ruling procedure and the expedited procedure, the President of the Court of Justice will first examine whether the conditions of the urgent procedure are met: see ECJ (order of the President of 24 October 2013), Case C-369/13 *Gielen and Others*, not reported, paras 8–9.

[64] ECJ (order of the President 23 October 2009), Case C-240/09 *Lesoochranárske zoskupenie*, not reported, para. 12.

persons may lodge written observations.[65] The expedited preliminary ruling procedure is generally concluded within three to six months.[66]

C. Urgent preliminary ruling procedure

(1) General

24.20 An urgent preliminary ruling procedure exists for questions in the areas covered by Title V of Part Three of the TFEU (see para. 22.07).[67] On average, it takes around 66 days for an urgent preliminary ruling procedure to be completed, with no case exceeding a duration of three months.

(2) Procedure

24.21 The urgent preliminary ruling procedure is characterized by the importance of the oral part of the procedure, the Court having the possibility to omit the written part of the procedure in cases of extreme urgency.[68] The specific characteristics of the procedure are set out in paragraphs 22.13 *et seq.*[69]

V. Special Characteristics

A. General

24.22 After the written observations have been submitted or none have been received within the prescribed period, the Judge-Rapporteur draws up the preliminary report for submission to the general meeting of the Court (see para. 23.56) and the case is assigned to a particular formation of the Court—three- or five-Judge Chamber, Grand Chamber, or the Full Court (see para. 2.10). From that point onwards, the procedure for preliminary ruling proceedings—from the oral part of the procedure to delivery of the judgment or order by the Court of Justice—is the same as in the case of other types of actions before the Court of Justice. Nevertheless, some aspects warrant special attention.

B. Measures of organization of procedure and measures of inquiry

24.23 In principle, the Court of Justice will not prescribe measures of inquiry in preliminary ruling proceedings relating to the interpretation of Union law, since it is for the national

---

[65] ECJ Rules of Procedure, Art. 105(2) and (3). The President may request the interested persons within the meaning of Art. 23 of the Statute to restrict the matters addressed in their written observations to the essential points of law raised by the request for a preliminary ruling. For the first application of the expedited procedure in a preliminary procedure, see ECJ, Case C-189/01 *Jippes and Others* [2001] E.C.R. I-5689, with a case note by Spaventa (2002) C.M.L. Rev. 1159–70. See, e.g. also ECJ, Joined Cases C-188/10 and C-189/10 *Melki and Abdeli* [2010] E.C.R. I-5667; ECJ, Case C-550/09 *E and F* [2010] E.C.R. I-6213; ECJ (judgment of 27 November 2012), Case C-370/12 *Pringle*, not reported. See also Recommendations, points 37–46.

[66] Sometimes the procedure is concluded within a shorter period: see, e.g. ECJ, Case C-189/01 *Jippes and Others* [2001] E.C.R. I-5689 (2 months and 14 days); ECJ, Joined Cases C-188/10 and C-189/10 *Melki and Abdeli* [2010] E.C.R. I-5667 (2 months and 6 days).

[67] Statute, Art. 23a, first para.; ECJ Rules of Procedure, Art. 107(1).

[68] ECJ Rules of Procedure, Art. 111.

[69] See also Recommendations, points 37–46.

court to make the findings of fact in relation to the main proceedings and to draw the necessary conclusions for the purposes of reaching its decision.[70] Moreover, the Court may not verify the facts placed before it.[71] However, where the question relates to the validity of an act of Union law, the Court's role is similar to the one in the context of an annulment action. The examination of the validity of a Union act may compel the Court to order a measure of inquiry.[72]

Further to this, the Court may, after hearing the Advocate-General, request clarification from the national court.[73]

The Court (as well as the Judge-Rapporteur and the Advocate-General) may also prescribe measures of organization of procedure, such as addressing questions to the interested persons within the meaning of Art. 23 of the Statute and inviting the participants to the hearing to concentrate on one or more specified issues (see para. 23.62).[74]

C. Representation

As far as representation of the parties to the main proceedings and their attendance at the Court are concerned, the Court has regard to the rules of procedure applicable to the referring court or tribunal.[75] Consequently, parties do not have to be represented by a lawyer, unlike the position in the case of a direct action (see para. 23.14). **24.24**

D. Withdrawal of the reference for a preliminary ruling

A referring judge has the possibility of withdrawing a reference for a preliminary ruling.[76] This may happen, for instance, when the parties before the national court have come to an amicable settlement or proceedings were discontinued. The Court will in principle grant such a request since, in the context of Art. 267 TFEU, it only has jurisdiction if an actual dispute is pending before the referring judge. Delivering a preliminary ruling in the context of proceedings that are no longer pending before the referring judge amounts to the delivery of a general opinion or answering of hypothetical questions.[77] **24.25**

However, for reasons of procedural economy, the Court will not take the request for withdrawal into account when it has been made after the notice of the date of delivery of the judgment has been served on the interested persons referred to in Art. 23 of the

---

[70] ECJ, Case 17/81 *Pabst & Richarz* [1982] E.C.R. 1331, para. 12. See para. 6.21.
[71] ECJ, Case 104/77 *Oehlschläger* [1978] E.C.R. 791, para. 4. See para. 6.21.
[72] For an example, see ECJ (order of 15 June 2011), Case C-338/10 *GLS*, not reported, para. 8.
[73] ECJ Rules of Procedure, Art. 101(1). For an example, see ECJ (order of 12 March 2004), Case C-54/03 *Austroplant-Arzneimittel*, not reported, para. 14; ECJ, Joined Cases C-436/08 and C-437/08 *Haribo and Salinen* [2011] E.C.R. I-305, para. 19; ECJ (judgment of 26 April 2012), Case C-92/12 PPU *Health Service Executive*, not reported, paras 19, 49, and 55; ECJ (judgment of 27 June 2013), Case C-492/11 *Di Donna*, not reported, para. 19.
[74] ECJ, Rules of Procedure, Arts 61–62.
[75] ECJ Rules of Procedure, Art. 97(3).
[76] ECJ, Rules of Procedure, Art. 100(1).
[77] See Chs 3 and 6.

Statute.[78] That being said, the Court may at any time declare that the conditions of its jurisdiction are no longer fulfilled.[79]

E. Costs

24.26 The question of the costs incurred by the parties to the main proceedings on account of the reference for a preliminary ruling—in practice, lawyers' fees and expenses, since the actual procedure before the Court of Justice is free of charge—is a matter for the national court.[80] The Court of Justice merely adverts to this in its judgment. The costs incurred by Member States and Union institutions as a result of their intervention in preliminary ruling proceedings are not recoverable.[81]

Costs which under national procedural rules have to be borne by a successful party to the main proceedings may not be the subject of an action for damages against the Union under Art. 268 TFEU and the second paragraph of Art. 340 TFEU, even though the judgment in the main proceedings was based on a declaration made in a preliminary ruling that an act of a Union institution was invalid. This is because to hold the Union liable in damages on this head would place in question the existence and exercise of the exclusive jurisdiction which national courts enjoy in the matter of the costs of the reference for a preliminary ruling under Art. 102 of the ECJ Rules of Procedure.[82]

F. Legal aid

24.27 Parties to the main proceedings unable to meet the costs of the proceedings before the Court of Justice may apply at any time for legal aid.[83] The applicant should submit all documents necessary to allow the Court to assess its financial situation.[84] A certificate issued by the competent national authorities attesting to the financial situation of the applicant is required.[85] The Court will also take into account whether the applicant received legal aid before the referring court.[86]

---

[78] ECJ Rules of Procedure, Art. 100(1).

[79] ECJ Rules of Procedure, Art. 100(2).

[80] ECJ Rules of Procedure, Art. 102. Arts 137–146 and Art. 184 of the ECJ Rules of Procedure are concerned with costs in relation to direct actions brought before the Court of Justice. In view of the essential difference between direct actions and proceedings under Art. 267 TFEU, which are only a step in the proceedings before the national court, those provisions do not cover the recovery of costs and the recoverability of expenses incurred in the main proceedings in connection with a reference for a preliminary ruling. The applicable national provisions must be applied to determine how the costs are to be allocated in such a case: ECJ, Case 62/72 *Bollmann* [1973] E.C.R. 269, paras 5–6.

[81] For an example, see ECJ (judgment of 19 December 2012), Case C-364/11 *Abed El Karem El Kott and Others*, not reported, para. 82.

[82] See CFI, Case T-167/94 *Nölle v Council and Commission* [1995] E.C.R. II-2589, paras 37–39.

[83] ECJ Rules of Procedure, Art. 115(1).

[84] Note that since the entry into force of the current version of the ECJ Rules of Procedure on 1 November 2012, the Court of Justice no longer requires the applicant to prove that he is suffering from a lack of means. The Court of Justice will henceforth assess the financial situation of the applicant. Compare ECJ Rules of Procedure, Art. 115(2) to former ECJ Rules of Procedure, Art. 76(1), second para.

[85] ECJ Rules of Procedure, Art. 115(2).

[86] ECJ Rules of Procedure, Art. 115(3).

The decision on the application for legal aid is taken by the smallest formation to which the Judge-Rapporteur in the case has been assigned.[87] The application for legal aid can be granted in whole or in part. The order refusing the application for legal aid, either wholly or partially, shall be reasoned.[88]

The order granting the legal aid sets out the conditions under which the Court's cashier shall be responsible for the costs involved. Parties and their representatives may request an advance on those costs to be paid.[89]

Legal aid may be withdrawn where the circumstances which led to its being granted change in the course of proceedings to such an extent that legal aid is no longer required.[90]

G. Language of the case

In principle, the language of the case is the language of the national court or tribunal which **24.28** made the reference for a preliminary ruling.[91] This means that written observations must be drawn up and the parties have to plead in that language.[92] Yet this is subject to a number of derogations: Member States may use their official language or one of their official languages when taking part in preliminary ruling proceedings (including both written and oral observations);[93] and States other than Member States of the European Union which are party to the EEA Agreement, the EFTA Surveillance Authority, and non-Member States taking part in preliminary ruling proceedings pursuant to the fourth paragraph of Art. 23 of the Statute (involving an agreement relating to a specific subject-matter concluded by the Council and one or more non-Member States providing for their participation in such proceedings) may be authorized to use an official language of the European Union other than the language of the case when they take part in preliminary ruling proceedings (again, with respect to both written documents and oral statements).[94]

Moreover, at the duly substantiated request of one of the parties to the main proceedings, the use of another official language of the European Union may be authorized, after the other party to the main proceedings and the Advocate-General have been heard, but this is only in respect of the oral part of the procedure, and where granted, such authorization applies in respect of all interested persons referred to in Art. 23 of the Statute.[95]

---

[87] ECJ Rules of Procedure, Art. 116(1)–(3).
[88] ECJ Rules of Procedure, Art. 116(4). See, e.g. ECJ (order of 21 October 2004), Case C-73/04 AJ *Klein*, not reported; ECJ (order of 10 February 2009), Case C-127/08 AJ *Metock*, not reported; ECJ (order of 10 December 2010), Case C-509/09 AJ *eDate*, not reported; ECJ (order of 8 December 2011), Case C-329/11 AJ *Achughbabian*, not reported.
[89] ECJ Rules of Procedure, Art. 117.
[90] ECJ Rules of Procedure, Art. 118.
[91] ECJ Rules of Procedure, Art. 37(3).
[92] ECJ Rules of Procedure, Art. 38(1).
[93] ECJ Rules of Procedure, Art. 38(4).
[94] ECJ Rules of Procedure, Art. 38(5)–(6).
[95] ECJ Rules of Procedure, Art. 37(3).

H. No appeal

24.29   No appeal will lie before the Court of Justice[96] from parties to the main proceedings, Member States, or Union institutions, bodies, offices, and agencies against a preliminary ruling, since it is only for national courts and tribunals to decide whether to make a reference and, if so, what its subject-matter should be.[97] Consequently, they decide whether they have received sufficient guidance from the preliminary ruling and whether they consider it necessary to make a further reference to the Court of Justice.[98]

I. No interpretation

24.30   No request for the interpretation of a preliminary ruling can be made.[99] Doubts as to the meaning or the scope of the preliminary ruling can only give rise to a new reference.[100] The parties to the main proceedings may urge the national court to make an new reference,[101] but they have no right to apply to the Court of Justice directly.

J. Revision

24.31   It is not possible to seek revision of a preliminary ruling, since there are no parties to the proceedings and Arts 41–44 of the Statute relating to exceptional pleas are not applicable.[102]

K. Rectification

24.32   On a request of an interested person referred to in Art. 23 of the Statute or of its own motion, the Court may rectify clerical mistakes, errors in calculation, and obvious inaccuracies affecting judgments or orders.[103] The decision to rectify a judgment or an order is taken by the Court after hearing the Advocate-General.[104] The original of the rectified

---

[96] To be distinguished, certainly, an order referring a question to the Court of Justice may be the subject of an appeal in the national procedural framework (though subject to the requirements of Union law pursuant to the referring court's right to refer under Art. 267 TFEU): see para. 3.30.

[97] ECJ (order of 16 May 1968), Case 13/67 *Becher* [1968] E.C.R. 196, at 197.

[98] ECJ Rules of Procedure, Art. 104(2). See also ECJ (order of 18 October 1979), Case 40/70 *Sirena* [1979] E.C.R. 3169, at 3170-71; ECJ (order of 5 March 1986), Case 69/85 *Wünsche* [1986] E.C.R. 947, paras 15–16; ECJ (order of 28 April 1998), Case C-116/96 Rev. *Reisebüro Binder* [1998] E.C.R. I-1889, paras 6–9; ECJ (judgment of 13 November 2012), Case C-35/11 *Test Claimants in the FII Group Litigation*, not reported, para. 2.

[99] ECJ Rules of Procedure, Art. 104(1). See, e.g. ECJ (order of 17 December 2010), Case C-262/88 INT *Peinado*, [2010] E.C.R. I-174*, Summ. pub., ECJ (order of 9 February 2011), Case C-345/09 INT *Fokkens*, [2011] E.C.R. I-11*, Summ. pub.

[100] See ECJ Rules of Procedure, Art. 104(2): it is for the national courts or tribunals to assess whether they consider that sufficient guidance is given by a preliminary ruling or whether it appears to them that a further reference to the Court is required.

[101] ECJ Rules of Procedure, Art. 104. See, e.g. ECJ (judgment of 13 November 2012), Case C-35/11 *Test Claimants in the FII Group Litigation*, not reported, paras 22–24.

[102] ECJ (order of 28 April 1998), Case C-116/96 Rev *Reisebüro Binder* [1998] E.C.R. I-1889, paras 6–9.

[103] ECJ Rules of Procedure, Art. 103(1). See e.g. ECJ (order of 7 May 2013), C-617/10 REC *Åkerberg Fransson*, not reported.

[104] ECJ Rules of Procedure, Art. 103(2).

order is annexed to the original of the rectified decision, and a note of this order is made in the margin of the original of the rectified decision.[105]

No other requests and applications relating to judgments and orders similar to those applicable to direct actions (i.e. third-party proceedings and failure to adjudicate: see paras 25.107 and 25.136) are possible in relation to preliminary rulings.

L. EEA Agreement

Special features of the procedure followed in preliminary ruling proceedings brought before **24.33** the Court of Justice pursuant to Art. 111(3) of the EEA Agreement and Art. 1 of Protocol No. 34 to that Agreement are prescribed in Art. 204 of the ECJ Rules of Procedure.

---

[105] ECJ Rules of Procedure, Art. 103(3).

25

PROCEDURE IN THE CASE
OF DIRECT ACTIONS

25.01 As presented in Chapter 23, the procedure in the case of direct actions before the Court of Justice and the General Court consists in principle of two parts: the written procedure and the oral procedure.[1]

This chapter delves into the specific procedural rules applicable to direct actions before the Court of Justice and the General Court[2] with respect to the written part of the procedure, intervention, the expedited procedure, discontinuance, cases that do not proceed to judgment, preliminary issues, and various aspects related to the closure of the proceedings, including costs, legal aid, and several kinds of requests and applications relating to judgments and orders after they have been given (i.e. third-party proceedings, revision, interpretation, rectification, and failure to adjudicate).

I. The Written Procedure

A. The application

(1) Lodging of an application

25.02 A case is brought before the Court of Justice or the General Court by addressing an application to the Registrar.[3] The common procedural rules on the lodging of procedural documents apply to applications, i.e. the application must be signed, dated, and accompanied by the requisite annexes, schedule, and number of copies (see paras 23.49–23.55).

---

[1] See para. 23.39.
[2] The general procedural rules applicable to direct actions before the General Court also apply to proceedings before the Civil Service Tribunal. The specific rules applicable to proceedings before the Tribunal are mainly set out in Ch. 18 and in some instances in the present chapter.
[3] Statute, Art. 21, first para.

(2) Content of application

(a) Requirements

The identity of the parties, the subject-matter of the proceedings, and the pleas in law   **25.03**
adduced are determined by the application.[4] In the course of the procedure, the application
may not, or only exceptionally, be modified in these respects.

The following must appear at the beginning of each application:

- the applicant's name and address;
- the name and capacity of the applicant's agent or lawyer;[5]
- the identity of the party or parties against whom the action is brought;
- the address for service and/or agreement to service by telefax or any other technical
  means of communication.[6]

The application must also state:

- the subject-matter of the proceedings, the pleas in law and arguments relied on, and a
  summary of the pleas in law on which the application is based;
- the form of order sought by the applicant;
- where appropriate, the nature of any evidence offered in support.[7]

(b) Name and address of the applicant

This requirement raises few problems. Nevertheless, the General Court was once faced with   **25.04**
the question whether the applicant's details could be altered at the request of the defendant.
The latter contended that the partnership which had brought the action had no capacity to
bring proceedings and asked the Court to designate the two sole partners as applicants. The
Court joined the partners as applicants after finding that they had signed the authority of
the lawyer acting in the case.[8]

An application may be lodged on behalf of several parties,[9] provided that it has the same
subject-matter and raises the same pleas in law as regards each of them.[10] An applicant's
successors are entitled to continue proceedings started by the deceased.[11] If there are no
successors or if the successors decline the succession, the proceedings will become devoid of

---

[4] Art. 57 of the ECJ Rules of Procedure and Art. 43 of the EGC Rules of Procedure set out general
conditions with which every pleading must comply. For the desiderata of the Court of Justice and the General
Court as to the structure and layout of the application, see ECJ Practice Directions, points 12, 13, and 34–39;
EGC Practice Directions, points 18–28.

[5] ECJ Rules of Procedure, Art. 57(1); EGC Rules of Procedure, Art. 43(1).

[6] ECJ Rules of Procedure, Art. 121; EGC Rules of Procedure, Art. 44(1); EGC Practice Directions, point
19. Note that the ECJ Rules of Procedure, in contrast to the current Art. 44(2) of the EGC Rules of
Procedure, no longer require an address for service in Luxembourg.

[7] ECJ Rules of Procedure, Art. 120; EGC Rules of Procedure, Art. 44(1).

[8] CFI (order of 30 March 1994), Case T-482/93 *Weber v Commission*, not reported, para. 4. See also CFI,
Case T-174/95 *Svenska Journalistförbundet v Council* [1998] E.C.R. II-2289, paras 33–44; CFI, Case T-185/
02 *Ruiz-Picasso and Others v OHIM* [2004] E.C.R. II-1739, paras 19–22.

[9] The unintentional omission of the name of one of the applicants can be subsequently remedied if the
defendant does not object: see ECJ, Case 21/58 *Felten und Guilleaume Carlswerk Eisen- und Stahl and
Walzwerke v High Authority* [1959] E.C.R. 99, at 101.

[10] ECJ, Case 13/57 *Wirtschaftsvereinigung Eisen- und Stahlindustrie and Others v High Authority* [1957 and
1958] E.C.R. 265, at 277.

[11] ECJ, Case 92/82 *Gutmann v Commission* [1983] E.C.R. 3127, para. 2.

purpose.[12] A legal person resulting from the merger of legal persons which have brought proceedings before the General Court—or an appeal before the Court of Justice—may continue the proceedings where that person has acquired the rights and obligations of the original applicants/appellants.[13]

(c) Address for service

25.05 At present, the General Court requires the applicant to have an address for service in Luxembourg at which all pleadings may be served.[14] As regards the Court of Justice, the ECJ Rules of Procedure only require the application to 'state an address for service' without any reference to Luxembourg.[15] To this end, the application must state the name of the person who is authorized and has expressed willingness to accept all service.[16] However, in addition to, or instead of, specifying an address for service, an application brought before the General Court or the Court of Justice may state that the lawyer or agent agrees that service is to be effected on him by telefax or any other technical means of communication.[17]

If either of these two requirements are not satisfied, all service on the applicant for the purpose of the proceedings will be effected for so long as the defect has not been cured by registered letter addressed to the agent or lawyer of the party. Service is then deemed to be duly effected by the lodging of the registered letter at the post office in the place where the respective Court has its seat.[18] Any applicable procedural time limits start to run as from the said deemed service, which means that the entire risk of delay in the post is borne by the applicant in the event that he has neglected to provide a more reliable address for service.[19] In this context, it would even be hard to argue that a postal strike constitutes *force majeure*.

(d) Designation of the party against whom the application is made

(i) General

25.06 The requirement that the application states the name of the party against whom it is made is satisfied if it is sufficiently clear from the application as a whole against whom the action is being brought. The omission of the defendant's name by an oversight does not necessarily mean that the application is inadmissible, provided that the rights of the defence are not impaired.[20] It is sufficient for the judgment to designate the defendant correctly.[21] The defendant's identity may also emerge from the contested act.[22] However, it is not possible

---

[12] CFI (order of 14 July 2004), Case T-360/02 *Yorck von Wartenburg v Commission*, not reported, paras 5–10; EGC (order of 17 December 2012), Case T-228/11 *Barbin v European Parliament*, not reported, para. 9.

[13] ECJ, Case 294/83 *Les Verts v European Parliament* [1986] E.C.R. 1339, paras 15–18.

[14] EGC Rules of Procedure, Art. 44(2).

[15] ECJ Rules of Procedure, Art. 121(1).

[16] ECJ Rules of Procedure, Art. 121(1), first para.; EGC Rules of Procedure, Art. 44(2), first para.

[17] ECJ Rules of Procedure, Art. 121(2); EGC Rules of Procedure, Art. 44(2), second para.

[18] ECJ Rules of Procedure, Art. 121(3); EGC Rules of Procedure, Art. 44(2), third para.

[19] Formerly, the stricter sanction of holding the application to be inadmissible applied: ECJ (order of 29 January 1986), Case 297/84 *Sahinler v Commission* [1986] E.C.R. 443.

[20] ECJ (order of 3 July 1986), Case 85/86 *Commission v EIB* [1986] E.C.R. 2215 (the application, which stated that the defendant was the 'European Investment Bank' instead of the 'Board of Governors of the European Investment Bank' was declared admissible on the ground that it appeared from that pleading that the action brought under former Art. 180(b) EEC, subsequently former Art. 237(b) EC (now Art. 271(b) TFEU) was directed against the EIB's Board of Governors).

[21] Opinion of Advocate-General G. Reischl in ECJ, Case 44/76 *Milch-, Fett- und Eier-Kontor v Council and Commission* [1977] E.C.R. 393, at 413. See also CFI (order of 12 July 2005), Case T-163/04 *Schäfer v OHIM*, not reported, para. 23.

[22] ECJ, Joined Cases C-184/02 and C-223/02 *Spain and Finland v European Parliament and Council* [2004] E.C.R. I-7789, para. 17.

to extend the application to include a defendant who is not designated in the application and whose identity does not emerge therefrom.[23]

(ii) Measure imputable to another institution, agency, or body

In some areas of Union law, agencies have been given the power to adopt decisions of a **25.07** binding nature. For example, the European Agency for the Evaluation of Medicinal Products indirectly has the power to refuse market authorizations. Since the division of power between such an agency and the Commission is not always clear, applicants will designate both the Commission and the agency as the party against whom the application is made. The respective Union court will then determine whether the measure is imputable to the Commission or to that agency.[24]

(iii) Staff cases

Actions relating to disputes between the Union and its servants[25] must be brought against **25.08** the institution in which the applicant is or was employed, in which his or her predecessor was employed, or where he or she took part in a recruitment procedure.[26] As regards the non-contractual liability of the Union,[27] actions for damages must be brought against the institution(s) whose conduct gave rise to the alleged liability.[28]

(e) Subject-matter of the proceedings and the pleas in law and arguments on which the application is based

(i) General

The application must set out a brief summary of the facts and the subject-matter of the **25.09** proceedings. This means that both its purpose and, where appropriate, the act against which the proceedings are brought must be specified. In addition, the application must contain the pleas in law and arguments relied on and a summary of those pleas in law.[29]

(ii) Subject-matter and pleas must be clearly stated

The Court of Justice and the General Court require the subject-matter of the proceedings **25.10** and the pleas raised to be stated clearly and precisely in order that the defendant may prepare its defence and the Court may give judgment without having to have further

---

[23] ECJ (order of 10 November 1977), Case 90/77 *Stimming v Commission* [1977] E.C.R. 2113, paras 1-4.
[24] EGC, Case T-439/08 *Agapiou Josephides v Commission and EACEA* [2010] E.C.R. II-230*, Summ. pub., paras 33–39 (act imputable to the EACEA); CFI (order of 5 December 2007), Case T-133/03 *Schering-Plough v Commission and EMEA*, not reported, paras 16–23 (act imputable to the Commission). However, if the challenged act is imputable to the Commission and if that institution is not designated as a defendant, the action will be inadmissible: see EGC (order of 4 June 2013), Case T-213/12 *Elitaliana v Eulex Kosovo*, not reported, paras 19–35.
[25] Art. 270 TFEU.
[26] See, e.g. ECJ, Case 18/63 *Wollast (née Schmitz) v EEC* [1964] E.C.R. 85, at 96: ECJ, Case 27/63 *Raponi v Commission* [1964] E.C.R. 129, at 135–6; ECJ, Joined Cases 79/63 and 82/63 *Reynier and Erba v Commission* [1964] E.C.R. 259, at 265; CFI, Case T-497/93 *Hogan v Court of Justice* [1995] E.C.R. II-703, para. 31. When the recruitment procedure is organized by EPSO, the action should be brought against the Commission: see Art. 4 of Decision 2002/620/EC of the European Parliament, the Council, the Commission, the Court of Justice, the Court of Auditors, the Economic and Social Committee, the Committee of the Regions, and the European Ombudsman of 25 July 2002 establishing a European Communities Personnel Selection Office ([2002] O.J. L197/53).
[27] Art. 268 and Art. 340, second para., TFEU.
[28] See para. 11.19.
[29] ECJ Rules of Procedure, Art. 120(c); EGC Rules of Procedure, Art. 44(1)(c).

particulars.[30] In order to secure legal certainty and the sound administration of justice, the essential facts and law on which the application is based must be set out—at least summarily—in the text of the application itself in a coherent and comprehensible manner.[31] If the application fails to provide details of the underlying facts and circumstances, it will be inadmissible on the grounds that the Court is unable to rule on it.[32]

The text of the application may be elucidated by references to passages in documents appended to it, but a general reference to such documents cannot constitute a statement of the essential facts and law on which the action is based.[33] These must be included in the application itself.[34] Annexes will only be taken into account insofar as they support pleas or arguments expressly set out in the application and to the extent that it is possible to determine precisely what are the matters they contain that support or supplement those

---

[30] See, e.g. ECJ, Case 281/82 *Unifrex v Council and Commission* [1984] E.C.R. 1969, para. 15; CFI, Case T-21/90 *Generlich v Commission* [1991] E.C.R. II-1323, paras 31–32; CFI (order of 28 April 1993), Case T-85/92 *De Hoe v Commission* [1993] E.C.R. II-523, para. 20, upheld by ECJ (order of 7 March 1994), Case C-338/93 P *De Hoe v Commission* [1994] E.C.R. I-819, para. 29; CFI (order of 29 November 1993), Case T-56/92 *Koelman v Commission* [1993] E.C.R. II-1267, para. 21; CFI, Case T-575/93 *Koelman v Commission* [1996] E.C.R. II-1, para. 33; CFI, Case T-84/96 *Cipeke v Commission* [1997] E.C.R. II-2081, paras 30–31; CFI, Case T-5/97 *Industrie des Poudres Sphériques v Commission* [2000] E.C.R. II-3755, paras 192–195; EGC (judgment of 29 January 2013), Joined Cases T-339/10 and T-532/10 *Cosepuri v EFSA*, not reported, para. 28; CFI, Case T-70/05 *Evropaïki Dynamiki v EMSA* [2010] E.C.R. II-313, para. 78. For actions for damages, see CFI (order of 14 May 1998), Case T-262/97 *Goldstein v Commission* [1998] E.C.R. II-2175, paras 19–30; CFI, Case T-13/96 *TEAM v Commission* [1998] E.C.R. II-4073, para. 29 (an application initiating an action for damages must contain particulars which make it possible to determine what conduct the applicant attributes to the institution, the grounds for which the applicant considers that there is a causal link between that conduct and the alleged damage, and the nature and extent of the damage. As far as the damage is concerned, it is sufficient for the application to provide sufficient evidence on the basis of which its nature and extent can be assessed and so as to allow the defendant institution to prepare its defence. The applicant must supplement this information in its reply by figures, thereby enabling the defendant to discuss them in its rejoinder and at the hearing.) See also as regards actions for damages: CFI, Joined Cases T-215/01, T-220/01, and T-221/01 *Calberson v Commission* [2004] E.C.R. II-587, paras 176–180; CFI (order of 20 February 2004), Case T-319/03 *French and Others v Council and Commission* [2004] E.C.R. II-769, paras 11–25; EGC, Case T-107/08 *Kazchrome and ENRC Marketing v Council and Commission* [2011] E.C.R. II-8051, para. 85.

[31] See, e.g. CFI (order of 26 March 1992), Case T-35/92 TO 2 *Buggenhout and Others*, not reported, paras 16–17; CFI, Case T-338/99 *Schuerer v Council* [2000] E.C.R. II-2571, E.C.R.-SC I-A-131, II-599, para. 19; EGC (order of 20 January 2012), Case T-315/10 *Groupe Partouche v Commission*, not reported, paras 22–39; EGC (order of 19 March 2012), Case T-273/09 *Associazione 'Giùlemanidallajuve' v Commission*, not reported, para. 28; EGC (judgment of 17 October 2012), Case T-447/10 *Evropaïki Dynamiki v Court of Justice*, not reported, para. 28.

[32] See, e.g. ECJ, Case C-52/90 *Commission v Denmark* [1992] E.C.R. I-2187, paras 17–18; ECJ (judgment of 14 October 2004), Case C-55/03 *Commission v Spain*, not reported, paras 24–29; ECJ (order of 11 November 2004), Case C-114/03 P *Piscioneri v European Parliament*, not reported, paras 7–9; ECJ, Case C-400/08 *Commission v Spain* [2011] E.C.R. I-1915, paras 45–47; CFI (order of 25 November 2003), Case T-85/01 *IAMA Consulting v Commission* [2003] E.C.R. II-4973, paras 58–59; CFI (judgment of 13 July 2004), Case T-115/02 *AVEX v OHIM*, not reported, para. 11 (trade mark case); CFI (order of 2 July 2004), Case T-256/03 *Bundesverband der Nahrungsmittel- und Speiseresteverwertung and Kloh v Commission*, not reported, paras 29–30; EGC, Case T-34/08 *Berliner Institut für Vergleichende Sozialforschung v Commission* [2011] E.C.R. II-305*, Summ. pub., paras 28–29.

[33] See, e.g. ECJ, Case C-52/90 *Commission v Denmark* [1992] E.C.R. I-2187, para. 17; CFI (order of 29 November 1993), Case T-56/92 *Koelman v Commission* [1993] E.C.R. II-1267, para. 21; CFI, Case T-84/96 *Cipeke v Commission* [1997] E.C.R. II-2081, paras 33–34; CFI, Case T-127/02 *Concept-Anlagen v OHIM* [2004] E.C.R. II-1113, paras 17–21; EGC (judgment of 14 March 2013), Case T-587/08 *Fresh Del Monte Produce v Commission*, not reported, para. 269.

[34] See, e.g. EGC (judgment of 27 February 2013), Case T-387/11 *Nitrogénművek Vegyiparti v Commission*, not reported, paras 21–23; EGC (judgment of 29 March 2012), Case T-336/07 *Telefónica and Others v Commission*, not reported, para. 59 (appeal pending: ECJ, Case C-295/12 P *Telefónica and Others v Commission*).

pleas or arguments.[35] It is not for the Court to seek out and identify in those annexes the pleas and arguments relied on in the application, since the annexes have a purely evidential and instrumental function.[36] Furthermore, information may not be provided at the hearing in order to fill gaps in the application.[37]

The degree of precision required of an application depends on the circumstances of the particular case.[38] Yet, the Court of Justice and the General Court may not go so far in specifying the subject-matter of the application as to impair the rights of the defence or of interested third parties.[39]

(iii) Union courts are bound by the subject-matter of the case

The Union courts are bound by the subject-matter of the case as stated in the application.[40] **25.11** A dispute between the applicant and the defendant about the demarcation of the subject-matter of the litigation will not have any bearing on the admissibility of the application so long as the Court is able to define the subject-matter of the action precisely on the basis of the application.[41]

(iv) Presentation of pleas

The application must contain the pleas and arguments relied on. This means that it must be **25.12** possible to identify from the text of the application what the applicant's specific complaints

---

[35] EGC, Case T-201/04 *Microsoft v Commission* [2007] E.C.R. II-3601, para. 99; EGC (judgment of 14 March 2013), Case T-588/08 *Dole Food and Others v Commission*, not reported, para. 462. Annexes going beyond their purely evidential function by providing fresh arguments will only be taken into consideration insofar as they support pleas and arguments set out in the application: EGC, Case T-461/07 *Visa Europe and Visa International v Commission* [2011] E.C.R. II-1719, paras 52–53.
[36] CFI Case T-340/03 *France Télécom v Commission* [2007] E.C.R. II-107, para. 167 (appeal dismissed: ECJ, Case C-202/07 P *France Télécom v Commission* [2009] E.C.R. I-2369); CFI, Case T-201/04 *Microsoft v Commission* [2007] E.C.R. II-3601, para. 94; EGC, Case T-432/05 *EMC Development v Commission* [2010] II-1629, paras 48–50; EGC, Case T-30/09 *Engelhorn v OHIM* [2010] E.C.R. II-3803, para. 19; EGC, Case T-369/08 *EWRIA and Others v Commission* [2010] E.C.R. II-6283, para. 49; EGC (order of 20 September 2011), Case T-330/10 *M v Commission*, not reported, paras 6–7; EGC (judgment of 14 November 2012), Case T-135/09 *Nexans France and Nexans v Commission*, not reported, para. 112 (appeal pending: ECJ, Case C-37/13 P *Nexans and Nexans France v Commission*); EGC (judgment of 14 March 2013), Case T-588/08 *Dole Food and Others v Commission*, not reported, para. 463; EGC (judgment of 14 March 2013), Case T-587/08 *Fresh Del Monte Produce v Commission*, not reported, para. 270.
[37] CFI, Case T-195/91 *Guérin Automobiles v Commission* [1997] E.C.R. II-679, para. 26; CFI, Case T-247/01 *eCopy v OHIM* [2002] E.C.R. II-5301, para. 17; EGC, Case T-108/09 *Ravensburger v OHIM* [2010] E.C.R. II-99*, Summ. pub., para. 42 (appeal dismissed: ECJ, Case C-369/10 P *Ravensburger v OHIM* [2011] E.C.R. I-26*, Summ. pub.).
[38] See, e.g. CFI, Case T-20/94 *Hartmann v Council and Commission* [1997] E.C.R. II-595, para. 37. See also EGC (order of 13 April 2011), Case T-320/09 *Planet v Commission* [2011] E.C.R. II-1673, para. 23.
[39] ECJ, Case 30/68 *Lacroix v Commission* [1970] E.C.R. 301, paras 21–28; CFI, Case T-168/95 *Eridania Zuccherifici Nazionali and Others v Counci* [1999] E.C.R. II-2245, para. 37.
[40] ECJ, Case 232/78 *Commission v France* [1979] E.C.R. 2729, para. 3; ECJ, Case C-508/03 *Commission v United Kingdom* [2006] E.C.R. I-3969, para. 61; ECJ, Case C-543/08 *Commission v Portugal* [2010] E.C.R. I-11241, para. 20; CFI, Case T-89/07 *VIP Car Solutions v European Parliament* [2009] E.C.R. II- 1403, para. 110. See also Opinion of Advocate-General Y. Bot in ECJ (judgment of 10 December 2013), Case C-272/12 P *Commission v Ireland and Others*, not reported, point 48.
[41] ECJ, Case 168/78 *Commission v France* [1980] E.C.R. 347, paras 17–25; ECJ, Case 270/83 *Commission v France* [1986] E.C.R. 273, at 300–1; ECJ (judgment of 8 November 2012), Case C-342/10 *Commission v Finland*, not reported, paras 17–23; CFI (order of 19 June 1995), Case T-107/94 *Kik v Council and Commission* [1995] E.C.R. II-1717, para. 29; EGC (order of 13 April 2011), Case T-320/09 *Planet v Commission* [2011] E.C.R. II-1673, paras 21–27.

are and the legal and factual particulars on which they are based.[42] The resulting exposition must enable the defendant to protect its interests and the Court to carry out judicial review.[43]

An application should thus be clear, coherent, and well-structured.[44] Apart from these substantive requirements, the applicant is not bound to set out its pleas in any particular way.[45] It is also unnecessary for express reference to be made to the provision of Union law which has allegedly been breached[46] or for a legal categorization to be given to the pleas raised in the application,[47] provided that the pleas emerge sufficiently clearly from the application.[48] Even an error in citing the provision of Union law on which a plea is based will not cause that plea to be inadmissible.

---

[42] ECJ, Case 111/63 *Lemmerz-Werke v High Authority* [1965] E.C.R. 677, at 696; ECJ, Joined Cases 26/79 and 86/79 *Forges de Thy-Marcinelle and Monceau v Commission* [1980] E.C.R. 1083, para. 4; ECJ, Case C-347/88 *Commission v Greece* [1990] E.C.R. I-4747, para. 28; ECJ, Case C-52/90 *Commission v Denmark* [1992] E.C.R. I-2187, para. 17; ECJ, Case C-456/03 *Commission v Italy* [2005] E.C.R. I-5335, para. 23; ECJ (judgment of 6 September 2012), Case C-150/11 *Commission v Belgium*, not reported, para. 26; CFI (order of 28 April 1993), Case T-85/92 *De Hoe v Commission* [1993] E.C.R. II-523, para. 22; CFI (order of 28 March 1994), Case T-515/93 *B v Commission* [1994] E.C.R.-SC II-379, para. 12; CFI (order of 4 February 2005), Case T-20/04 *Aguar Fernandez and Others v Commission*, not reported, paras 44–47. It is possible that the summary of some pleas satisfy this condition and the summary of others does not. In this event, the Union judicature will declare inadmissible only those pleas which are not sufficiently defined and not the application as a whole (CFI, Joined Cases T-9/96 and T-211/96 *Européenne Automobile v Commission* [1999] E.C. R. II-3639, para. 57; CFI, Case T-251/97 *T. Port v Commission* [2000] E.C.R. II-1775, paras 90–92; CFI, Case T-308/05 *Italy v Commission* [2007] E.C.R. II-5089, para. 72; EGC, Case T-177/07 *Mediaset v Commission* [2010] E.C.R. II-2341, para. 24; EGC (judgment of 12 December 2012), Case T-457/07 *Evropaiki Dynamiki v EFSA*, not reported, para. 225).

[43] ECJ, Case C-267/09 *Commission v Portugal* [2011] E.C.R. I-3197, para. 28; EGC, Case T-432/05 *EMC Development v Commission* [2010] E.C.R. II-1629, para. 45; EGC (judgment of 12 December 2012), Case T-457/07 *Evropaiki Dynamiki v EFSA*, not reported, para. 225.

[44] EGC (order of 20 September 2011), Case T-267/10 *Land Wien v Commission* [2011] E.C.R. II-303*, Summ. pub., paras 14–26.

[45] CFI, Case T-145/98 *ADT Projekt v Commission* [2000] E.C.R. II-387, para. 67.

[46] *A fortiori* it is not necessary to submit pleas or complaints in respect of the particular provisions of a contested act if an action for annulment is brought against the act in its entirety: ECJ (judgment of 29 March 2012), Case C-505/09 P *Commission v Estonia*, not reported, para. 36.

[47] ECJ, Joined Cases 19/60 and 21/60, 2/61 and 3/61 *Société Fives Lille Cail and Others v High Authority* [1961] E.C.R. 281, at 295; CFI, Case T-35/93 *Cucchiara and Others v Commission* [1994] E.C.R.-SC II-413, paras 26–27 (English abstract at I-A-126); EGC (judgment of 8 November 2012), Case T-415/11 *Hartmann v OHIM*, not reported, para. 11.

[48] ECJ, Joined Cases 7/56 and 3/57 to 7/57 *Algera and Others v Common Assembly* [1957 and 1958] E.C. R. 39, at 64–5; ECJ, Joined Cases 2/63 to 10/63 *Società Industriale Acciaierie San Michele and Others v High Authority* [1963] E.C.R. 327, at 341; ECJ, Case 62/65 *Serio v Commission* [1966] E.C.R. 561, at 568 (it must be sufficiently clear from the application as a whole what legal principles the applicant considers have been breached); CFI, Case T-18/90 *Jongen v Commission* [1991] E.C.R. II-187, para. 13; EGC, Case T-224/10 *Association belge des consommateurs test-achats v Commission* [2011] E.C.R. II-7177, paras 71–72; EGC (judgment of 13 June 2012), Case T-542/10 *XXXLutz Marken v OHIM*, not reported, paras 19–21. But see CFI, Case T-224/95 *Tremblay and Others v Commission* [1997] E.C.R. II-2215, paras 79–82, in which it was held that the claim that the defendant had 'infringed the Treaty', which was only briefly enlarged upon in general terms in the application, did not enable it to determine the subject-matter of the proceedings sufficiently precisely and so did not enable the Commission effectively to defend itself. Similarly, the General Court held in EGC (judgment of 7 March 2013), Case T-370/11 *Poland v Commission*, not reported, para. 113, that claiming 'that the contested decision must comply with European Union law in its entirety' did not specify the provision allegedly infringed 'to the requisite legal standard'. See also EGC, Case T-262/09 *Safariland v OHIM* [2011] E.C.R. II-1629, para. 100.

A mere enumeration of pleas, however, does not suffice.[49] The application must set out the facts and reasoning on which each plea is based.[50] Unsupported arguments will be declared inadmissible.[51] It is not for the Court to speculate about the reasoning and precise observations that lie behind an action.[52] A reference to pleas raised in another case, even if the two cases are linked, does not constitute a sufficient statement of the pleas in law on which the application is based.[53] The same goes for references to proceedings before the OHIM Board of Appeal in intellectual property disputes.[54] Such a reference, however, will not render the application inadmissible if, leaving aside that reference, the application contains all the necessary particulars.[55]

(v) New pleas

New pleas—that is to say, pleas not raised in the application—may not be introduced in the course of the proceedings unless they are based on matters of law or of fact which come to light in the course of the proceedings.[56]

25.13

---

[49] EGC (judgment of 29 March 2012), Case T-398/07 *Spain v Commission*, not reported, para. 44; EGC (judgment of 29 March 2012), Case T-336/07 *Telefónica and Others v Commission*, not reported, para. 59 (appeal pending: ECJ, Case C-295/12 P *Telefónica and Others v Commission*).

[50] ECJ, Joined Cases 19/60 and 21/60, 2/61 and 3/61 *Société Fives Lille Cail and Others v High Authority* [1961] E.C.R. 281, at 295; ECJ, Case C-52/90 *Commission v Denmark* [1992] E.C.R. I-2187, para. 18. See also case-law in cited n. 42. An application by which an action for damages is brought must contain the following particulars: the evidence from which the conduct alleged against the institution can be identified, the reasons for which the applicant considers that there is a causal link between the conduct and the damage it claims to have suffered, and the nature and extent of that damage: CFI, Case T-64/89 *Automec v Commission* [1990] E.C.R. II-367, para. 73; CFI, Case T-167/94 *Nölle v Council and Commission* [1995] E.C.R. II-2589, para. 32; CFI, Case T-38/96 *Guérin Automobiles v Commission* [1997] E.C.R. II-1223, para. 42; CFI, Case T-277/97 *Ismeri Europa v Court of Auditors* [1999] E.C.R. II-1825, paras 28–30, 65, and 81; CFI, Case T-210/00 *Biret & Cie v Council* [2002] E.C.R. II-47, para. 34; EGC, Case T-436/09 *Julien Dufour v ECB* [2011] E.C.R. II-7727, para. 194; EGC, Case T-432/05 *EMC Development v Commission* [2010] II-1629, para. 47. See further para. 11.34.

[51] EGC, Case T-152/09 *Rintisch v OHIM* [2011] E.C.R. II-460*, Summ. pub., para. 48 (appeal dismissed: ECJ (judgment of 3 October 2013), Case C-122/12 P *Rintisch v OHIM*, not reported); EGC (judgment of 13 September 2012), Case T-369/11 *Diadikasia Symbouloi Epicheiriseon v Commission and Others*, not reported, para. 63.

[52] EGC (judgment of 15 March 2012), Case T-236/09 *Evropaïki Dynamiki v Commission*, not reported, para. 115.

[53] ECJ, Case 9/55 *Société des Charbonnages de Beeringen and Others v High Authority* [1954 to 1956] E.C.R. 311, at 325; ECJ, Joined Cases 19/63 and 65/63 *Prakash v Commission* [1965] E.C.R. 533, at 546; CFI, Case T-209/01 *Honeywell International v Commission* [2005] E.C.R. II-5527, paras 63–68. But see CFI, Case T-37/91 *ICI v Commission* [1995] E.C.R. II-1901, para. 47, in which the General Court accepted a reference made in one case to another on account of the specific circumstances; namely a close link existed between two cases which had not been joined (the parties, the agents, and the lawyers were the same, the actions had been brought before the Court on the same day, the cases had been assigned to the same Chamber, and the same Judge-Rapporteur and the contested decisions related to aspects of competition on the same market).

[54] EGC (judgment of 29 February 2012), Joined Cases T-77/10 and T-78/10 *Certmedica International and Lehning entreprise v OHIM*, not reported, para. 28; EGC, Case T-207/09 *El Jirari Bouzekri v OHIM* [2011] E.C.R. II-324*, Summ. pub., para. 20; EGC (order of 8 July 2010), Case T-211/10 *Strålfors v OHIM* [2010] E.C.R. II-143*, Summ. pub., para. 8. See also para. 20.19.

[55] ECJ, Case 4/69 *Lütticke v Commission* [1971] E.C.R. 325, paras 2–4.

[56] ECJ Rules of Procedure, Art.127(1); EGC Rules of Procedure, Art. 48(2), first para. The fact that the applicant became aware of a factual matter during the course of the procedure before the Court of Justice or the General Court does not mean that that element constitutes a matter of fact coming to light in the course of the procedure. A further requirement is that the applicant was not in a position to be aware of that matter previously (CFI, Case T-139/99 *AICS v European Parliament* [2000] E.C.R. II-2849, para. 62; CFI, Case T-76/02 *Messina v Commission* [2003] E.C.R. II-3203, paras 36–37; CFI, Case T-340/04 *France Télécom v Commission* [2007] E.C.R. II-573, para. 164; EGC, Case T-303/08 *Tresplain Investments v OHIM* [2010] E.C.R. II-5659, para. 167). For instances in which a new plea was not admitted, see ECJ, Case 11/81 *Dürbeck v Commission* [1982] E.C.R. 1251, paras 13–15; ECJ, Case 108/81 *Amylum v Council* [1982] E.C.R. 3107,

An amendment, in the course of proceedings, of the contested measure constitutes a new factor which allows the applicant to amend its pleas and the form of order sought.[57] Similarly, new pleas may be introduced where a relevant provision of Union law is annulled or declared invalid by the Union courts after the submission of the application.[58]

Given the absence of express, unequivocal rules on the matter, a new plea does not have to be submitted immediately, or within a particular period, after the matters of fact or law to which it refers come to light, in order to avoid being time-barred.[59]

If a new plea in law is presented in the course of proceedings, the President may prescribe a time limit in which the other party may respond to that plea. This is without prejudice to the decision to be taken on the admissibility of that new plea.[60]

(vi) Elaboration of pleas raised in the application

25.14 The rule that, in principle, new pleas may not be entered does not mean to say, however, that pleas adduced in the application may not subsequently be enlarged

---

paras 23–26; ECJ, Case 59/83 *Biovilac v EEC* [1984] E.C.R. 4057, paras 24–25; ECJ, Case 5/85 *AKZO Chemie v Commission* [1986] E.C.R. 2585, paras 13–17; ECJ, Joined Cases 279/84 to 280/84, 285/84, and 286/84 *Rau v Commission* [1987] E.C.R. 1069, para. 38; CFI, Case T-521/93 *Atlanta and Others v EC* [1996] E.C.R. II-1707, paras 39–40; CFI, Case T-252/97 *Dürbeck v Commission* [2000] E.C.R. II-3031, para. 44. A judgment which merely confirms a point of law which ought to have been known to the applicant when it brought an action cannot be regarded as a new matter allowing a fresh plea to be raised: ECJ, Case 11/81 *Dürbeck v Commission* [1982] E.C.R. 1251, para. 17; CFI, Case T-106/95 *FFSA and Others v Commission* [1997] E.C.R. II-229, para. 57; CFI (order of 25 July 2000), Case T-110/98 *RJB Mining v Commission* [2000] E.C.R. II-2971, para. 36; CFI, Case T-3/99 *Bananatrading v Council* [2001] E.C.R. II-2123, para. 49; EGC (judgment of 12 September 2012), Case T-154/10 *France v Commission*, not reported, para. 56. In the course of an action for damages, a submission which changes the very basis of liability constitutes a new plea in law which cannot be introduced in the course of proceedings. Accordingly, the applicant cannot submit for the first time in its reply that the Union is non-contractually liable for a lawful regulatory act, even if the plea, in common with the alleged liability for an unlawful act of the application, is based on the second para. of Art. 340 TFEU: ECJ, Joined Cases 279/84, 280/84, 285/84, and 286/84 *Rau and Others v Commission* [1987] E.C.R. 1069, para. 38; (ECJ, Case C-104/97 P *Atlanta v EC* [1999] E.C.R. I-6983, para. 27). Considerations relating to economy of procedure or respect for the rights of the defence cannot justify extending the exceptions to the rule which prevents new pleas in law beyond those expressly provided for in the Rules of Procedure (Case C-104/97 P *Atlanta*, para. 28). For cases in which a new plea was admitted, see ECJ, Case 14/81 *Alpha Steel v Commission* [1982] E.C.R. 749, para. 8; CFI, Case T-43/89 RV *Gill v Commission* [1993] E.C.R. II-303, paras 47–49; CFI, Case T-22/92 *Weissenfels v European Parliament* [1993] E.C.R. II-1095, paras 33–35; CFI, Case T-109/92 *Lacruz Bassols v Court of Justice* [1994] E.C.R.-SC II-105, para. 67 (English abstract at I-A-31); CFI, Case T-508/93 *Mancini v Commission* [1994] E.C.R.-SC II-761, paras 33–34 (English abstract at I-A-239); CFI, Case T-32/91 *Solvay v Commission* [1995] E.C.R. II-1825, paras 35–42. It is also possible for only part of a new plea to be declared admissible where, following a measure of organization of procedure by which all the applicants are granted access to the file (also those which did not enter a plea alleging infringement of their right of access to the file), a party introduces a new plea based on documents of which they had cognizance only in the course of the proceedings: ECJ, Joined Cases C-238/99 P, C-244/99 P, C-245/99 P, C-247/99 P, C-250/99 P, C-251/99 P, C-252/99 P, and C-254/99 P *Limburgse Vinyl Maatschappij and Others v Commission* [2002] E.C.R. I-8375, paras 366–375; CFI, Case T-19/95 *Adia Interim v Commission* [1996] E.C.R. II-321, paras 22–24. The fact that a party had initially misinterpreted a provision of Union law does not allow that party to introduce a new plea at a later stage of the procedure: EGC (order of 4 September 2012), Case T-381/08 *DAI v Commission*, not reported, paras 34–35.

[57] CFI, Case T-36/99 *Lenzing v Commission* [2004] E.C.R. II-3597, para. 54; EGC, Case T-299/08 *Elf Aquitaine v Commission* [2011] E.C.R. II-2149, para. 241. See also para. 25.17.

[58] EGC (judgment of 7 November 2012), Case T-574/08 *Syndicat des Thoniers Méditerranéens and Others v Commission*, not reported, para. 53 (appeal pending: ECJ, Joined Cases C-12/13 P *Buono and Others v Commission* and C-13/13 P *Syndicat des Thoniers Méditerranéens and Others v Commission*).

[59] CFI, Case T-32/91 *Solvay v Commission* [1995] E.C.R. II-1825, para. 40.

[60] ECJ Rules of Procedure, Art.127(2); EGC Rules of Procedure, Art. 48(2), second para.

upon.[61] Even pleas only raised impliedly may be extended in this way.[62] Accordingly, the applicant is entitled to raise additional arguments in the reply in support of pleas raised in the application.[63] This means that the Court will often have to make a subtle distinction between a new plea and a new argument.[64] In addition, the applicant may clarify in the reply the factual basis on which its pleas are based.[65] Obviously, however, the applicant may 'clarify' only pleas which have already been raised in the application.

The rule that—in principle—no new pleas may be raised applies only to the parties, not to the General Court or the Court of Justice.[66] Accordingly, the rule does not prevent the General Court and the Court of Justice from raising pleas of their own motion.[67]

(vii) Submissions supplementing the application

Despite the lack of express mention in the Statute and the Rules of Procedure of the Union **25.15** courts, submissions supplementing the application initiating proceedings which were submitted after the application was lodged but before the deadline for bringing procedings have been held admissible by the General Court.[68]

---

[61] ECJ, Joined Cases 9/60 and 12/60 *Vloeberghs v High Authority* [1961] E.C.R. 197, at 215; ECJ, Case 18/60 *Worms v High Authority* [1962] E.C.R. 195, at 203; ECJ, Case C-430/00 P *Dürbeck v Commission* [2001] E.C.R. I-8457, para. 17; ECJ, Case C-412/05 P *Alcon v OHIM* [2007] E.C.R. I-3569, paras 38–40; ECJ, Case C-71/07 P *Campoli v Commission* [2008] E.C.R. I-5887, para. 63; ECJ, Case C-485/08 P *Gualtieri v Commission* [2010] E.C.R. I-3009, para. 37; ECJ (judgment of 29 March 2012), Case C-504/09 P *Commission v Poland*, not reported, para. 34. Pleas can be amended when, in the course of proceedings, the contested decision is amended (CFI, Case T-36/99 *Lenzing v Commission* [2004] E.C.R. II-3597, para. 54; EGC, Case T-299/08 *Elf Aquitaine v Commission* [2011] E.C.R. II-2149, para. 241). See also para. 25.17 and para. 7.11.

[62] ECJ, Case 306/81 *Verros v European Parliament* [1983] E.C.R. 1755, paras 9–10; ECJ (judgment of 29 March 2012), Case C-504/09 P *Commission v Poland*, not reported, para. 34; CFI, Case T-37/89 *Hanning v European Parliament* [1990] E.C.R. II-463, para. 38; CFI, Case T-216/95 *Moles García Ortúzar v Commission* [1997] E.C.R.-SC II-1083, para. 87 (English abstract at I-A-403); CFI, Case T-217/95 *Passera v Commission* [1997] E.C.R.-SC II-1109, para. 87 (English abstract at I-A-413); CFI, Case T-204/99 *Mattila v Council and Commission* [2001] E.C.R. II-2265, para. 32; EGC, Case T-194/06 *SNIA v Commission* [2011] E.C.R. II-3119, paras 73–76 ; EGC, Case T-488/08 *Galileo International Technology v OHIM* [2011] E.C.R. II-350*, Summ. pub., para. 55.

[63] ECJ, Case 2/54 *Italy v High Authority* [1954 to 1956] E.C.R. 37, at 51; ECJ, Case C-66/02 *Italy v Commission* [2005] E.C.R. I-10901, paras 85–89; EGC, Case T-342/07 *Ryanair Holdings v Commission* [2010] E.C.R. II-3457, para. 325.

[64] See, e.g. ECJ, Case C-37/03 P *BioID v OHIM* [2005] E.C.R. I-7975, paras 56–58; ECJ, Case C-412/05 P *Alcon v OHIM* [2007] E.C.R. I-3569, paras 38–40; EGC (judgment of 13 April 2013), Case T-451/08 *Stim v Commission*, not reported, paras 65–72. See also Opinion of Advocate-General Y. Bot in ECJ (judgment of 10 December 2013), Case C-272/12 P *Commission v Ireland and Others*, not reported, point 66.

[65] ECJ, Case 74/74 *CNTA v Commission* [1975] E.C.R. 533, para. 4; ECJ Case C-456/03 *Commission v Italy* [2005] E.C.R. I-5335, paras 32–34; CFI, Case T-21/90 *Generlich v Commission* [1991] E.C.R. II-1323, para. 32; CFI, Case T-109/92 *Lacruz Bassols v Court of Justice* [1994] E.C.R.-SC II-105, para. 67 (English abstract at I-A-30); CFI, Case T-35/93 *Cucchiara and Others v Commission* [1994] E.C.R.-SC II-413, paras 26–29 (English abstract at I-A-127); CFI, Case T-369/06 *Holland Malt v Commission* [2009] E.C.R. II-3313, para. 32.

[66] ECJ, Case C-252/96 P *European Parliament v Gutiérrez de Quijano y Lloréns* [1998] E.C.R. I-7421, para. 30.

[67] See para. 7.146.

[68] EGC (judgment of 14 June 2012), Case T-338/08 *Stichting Natuur en Milieu and Pesticide Action Network Europe v Commission*, not reported, paras 16–25 (appeal pending in ECJ, Joined Cases C-404/12 P and C-405/12 P *Council and Commission v Stichting Natuur en Milieu and Pesticide Action Network Europe*).

(f) Form of order sought by the applicant

(i) Form of order sought must be unequivocal

25.16 The form of order sought (also referred to as 'conclusions' or 'claims') sets out the decision which the applicant is claiming that the Court should give.[69] It generally takes the form of the operative part of a judgment or order. However, the Court may also infer that a particular form of order is sought from the wording of the application.[70]

The form of order sought must be unequivocal and set out at the beginning or the end of the application[71] so that the Court is spared from either giving judgment *ultra petita* or from failing to give judgment on one of the heads of the form of order sought. This also protects the rights of the defence.[72] A head of claim set out in the form of order sought which is unclear will be regarded as inadmissible.[73] Since the form of order sought flows from the subject-matter of the proceedings and the pleas in law and arguments put forward in the application, it may only exceptionally be amended in the course of the proceedings.[74] The condition that no new plea in law may be introduced in the course of proceedings unless it is based on matters of law or fact which come to light in the course of the procedure is, *a fortiori*, applicable in the case of a modification of the form of order sought.[75] However, such modification may not alter the subject-matter or the nature of the proceedings,[76] for example by transforming an action for failure to act into an action for annulment.[77] Further to this, the applicant can 'clarify' the form of order sought in its reply

---

[69] ECJ, Case 55/64 *Lens v Court of Justice* [1965] E.C.R. 837, at 841.

[70] ECJ, Case 8/56 *ALMA v High Authority* [1957 and 1958] E.C.R. 95, at 99–100; ECJ, Case 80/63 *Degreef v Commission* [1964] E.C.R. 391, at 408; ECJ (order of 7 February 1994), Case C-388/93 *PIA HiFi v Commission* [1994] E.C.R. I-387, para. 10; EGC (order of 13 April 2011), Case T-320/09 *Planet v Commission* [2011] E.C.R. II-1673, para. 23; EGC, Case T-156/08 P *R v Commission* [2009] E.C.R.-SC II-B-1-51, paras 36–37.

[71] ECJ Practice Directions, point 12; EGC Practice Directions, point 22.

[72] ECJ, Joined Cases 46/59 and 47/59 *Meroni and Others v High Authority* [1962] E.C.R. 411, at 419; EGC (order of 13 April 2011), Case T-320/09 *Planet v Commission* [2011] E.C.R. II-1673, para. 22.

[73] ECJ, Case 188/73 *Grassi v Council* [1974] E.C.R. 1099, paras 5–9; CFI (order of 7 June 2001), Case T-202/00 *Costacurta v Commission*, not reported, para. 54. But see CFI, Case T-123/04 *Cargo Partner v OHIM* [2005] E.C.R. II-3979, para. 34: the applicant formally asked for the case to be sent back to the OHIM. The form of order was considered to be admissible, since it was clear from the application that the applicant sought, in substance, the annulment of the contested decision.

[74] ECJ, Case 232/78 *Commission v France* [1979] E.C.R. 2729, paras 2–4; ECJ, Case 124/81 *Commission v United Kingdom* [1983] E.C.R. 203, paras 5–7; CFI, Case T-398/94 *Kahn Scheepvaart v Commission* [1996] E.C.R. II-477, para. 20; CFI, Case T-24/00 *Sunrider v OHIM* [2001] E.C.R. II-449, para. 12; CFI, Case T-28/03 *Holcim v Commission* [2005] E.C.R. II-1357, paras 41–46. A form of order sought which is unsupported by any plea will be inadmissible (CFI, Case T-310/02 *Theodorakis v Council* [2004] E.C.R.-SC II-427, paras 21–22).

[75] ECJ, Case 83/63 *Krawczynski v Commission* [1965] E.C.R. 623, 785; CFI, Case T-494/04 *Wineke Neirinck v Commission* [2006] E.C.R.-SC I-A-2-259, para. 30; EGC, Case T-236/07 *Germany v Commission* [2010] E.C.R. II-5253, para. 28. See also EGC (order of 24 May 2011), Case T-176/09 *Government of Gibraltar v Commission* [2011] E.C.R. II-150, paras 46–47; EGC (order of 4 September 2012), Case T-381/08 *DAI v Commission*, not reported, paras 34–37.

[76] CFI, Case T-210/00 *Biret et Cie v Council* [2002] E.C.R. II-47, para. 49; CFI, Case T-28/03 *Holcim v Commission* [2005] E.C.R. II-1357, para. 45; CFI (order of 9 June 2005), Case T-265/03 *Helm Düngemittel v Commission* [2005] E.C.R. II-2009, para. 60; CFI (order of 14 February 2002), Case T-406/03 *Ravailhe v Committee of the Regions* [2005] E.C.R.-SC I-A-19, para. 53; CFI (order of 27 October 2005), Case T-89/05 *GAEC Salat v Commission* [2005] E.C.R. II-16*, Summ. pub., para. 28; CFI, Case T-494/04 *Wineke Neirinck v Commission* [2006] E.C.R.-SC-I-A-2-259, paras 29 and 66.

[77] ECJ, Case 125/78 *GEMA v Commission* [1979] E.C.R. 3173, para. 26; CFI, Case T-28/90 *Asia Motor France and Others v Commission* [1992] E.C.R. II-2285, paras 43–44.

or at the hearing,[78] for instance, by restricting the scope of its claims in an action for annulment.[79]

(ii) Contested act replaced by a new act

In the exceptional circumstance where the institution concerned replaces the contested act by an act which does not essentially diverge from it, the applicant may adjust its form of order sought accordingly. It would not be in the interests of the proper administration of justice or of the requirements of procedural economy to oblige the applicant to make a fresh application to the Court against the new act.[80] This is because the actual subject-matter of the proceedings is not changed.[81] It is also possible for the applicant to amend the form of order sought in this way where a contested implied decision is replaced by an express decision with the same content.[82] However, the act against which the original application was brought must be an act against which an action would lie. If that is not so and the original act is replaced by a challengeable act, the form of order sought may not be amended because that would change the subject-matter of the proceedings contrary to Art. 21 of the Statute.[83]

25.17

The form of order sought must in principle be adjusted within two months of the replacement of the contested act. The two-month time limit does not apply if the new act has the same object, grounds, and content as the repealed act.[84]

(g) Supporting evidence

The applicant must adduce, where appropriate, evidence in support of its pleas. It is apparent from the expression 'where appropriate' that the application does not necessarily have to contain offers of evidence.[85] The only sanction concerning offers of evidence is that they may

25.18

---

[78] Case C-456/03 *Commission v Italy* [2005] E.C.R. I-5335, paras 39–40; CFI, Joined Cases T-178/00 and T-341/00 *Pflugradt v ECB* [2002] E.C.R. II-4035, para. 34; ECJ.

[79] CFI (order of 11 May 2001), Case T-178/96 *Eridania and Others v Council*, not reported, para. 42; CFI, Case T-177/03 *Strohm v Commission* [2005] E.C.R.-SC II-651, para. 21. The subject-matter of the proceedings is not extended where the Commission, after alleging that a Member State has failed to transpose a directive at all, specifies in its reply that the transposition pleaded for the first time by the Member State concerned in its defence is in any event incorrect or incomplete so far as certain provisions of the directive are concerned. Such a complaint is necessarily included in the complaint alleging a complete failure to transpose and is subsidiary to that complaint (ECJ, Case C-456/03 *Commission v Italy* [2005] E.C.R. I-5335, para. 40).

[80] EGC, Case T-291/04 *Enviro Tech v Commission* [2011] E.C.R. II-8281, para. 94 (upheld on appeal in ECJ (order of 24 January 2013), Case C-118/12 P *Enviro Tech v Commission*, not reported); EGC (order of 24 May 2011), Case T-176/09 *Government of Gibraltar v Commission* [2011] E.C.R. II-150, para. 47; EGC, Joined Cases T-267/08 and T-279/08 *Région Nord-Pas-de-Calais and Communauté d'agglomération du Douaisis v Commission* [2011] E.C.R. II-1999, paras 22–24; EGC (judgment of 21 March 2012), Joined Cases T-439/10 and T-440/10 *Fulmen and Others v Council*, not reported, paras 37–38; EGC (judgment of 25 April 2012), Case T-509/10 *Manufacturing Support & Procurement Kala Naft v Council*, not reported, para. 41. See also para. 7.11.

[81] ECJ, Case 14/81 *Alpha Steel v Commission* [1982] E.C.R. 749, para. 8; ECJ, Joined Cases 351/85 and 360/85 *Fabrique de Fer de Charleroi v Commission* [1987] E.C.R. 3639, paras 8–11; CFI, Case T-36/99 *Lenzing v Commission* [2004] E.C.R. II-3597, para. 54; CFI (order of 15 February 2005), Case T-229/02 *PKK and Others v Council* [2005] E.C.R. II-539, para. 29; CFI, Case T-306/01 *Yusuf and Al Barakaat International Foundation v Council and Commission* [2005] E.C.R. II-3533, paras 72–76. However, once the claims have been adjusted, the new measure becomes the sole object of the action before the General Court. Pleas on appeal relating to the initial measure cannot lead to the setting aside of the judgment of the General Court and will therefore be regarded as immaterial: see ECJ, Joined Cases C-402/05 P and C-415/05 P *Kadi and Al Barakaat International Foundation v Council and Commission* [2008] E.C.R. I-6351, paras 159–160.

[82] ECJ, Case 103/85 *Stahlwerke Peine-Salzgitter v Commission* [1988] E.C.R. 4131, paras 11–12.

[83] CFI, Case T-64/89 *Automec v Commission* [1990] E.C.R. II-367, paras 68–69.

[84] EGC (judgment of 5 December 2012), Case T-421/11 *Qualitest v Council*, not reported, paras 21–28.

[85] CFI, Case T-19/01 *Chiquita Brands International and Others v Commission* [2005] E.C.R. II-315, para. 71.

be rejected on account of delay if they are submitted for the first time, and without justification, at the reply or rejoinder stage.[86] The ECJ Rules of Procedure provide that, in exceptional circumstances, evidence may even be offered or produced after the close of the written part of the procedure.[87] The General Court interprets its Rules of Procedure in a similar way.[88]

All evidence offered in support must be expressly and accurately indicated, in such a way as to show clearly the facts to be proved:[89]

– documentary evidence offered in support must refer to the relevant document number in a schedule of annexed documents.[90] Alternatively, if a document is not in the possession of the party concerned, the pleading must clearly indicate where and how the document may be obtained;
– where oral testimony is sought to be given, each proposed witness or person from whom information is to be obtained must be clearly identified.[91]

As already indicated, if evidence is offered in the course of the proceedings rather than in the application, reasons must be given for the delay in tendering it.[92]

(h) Accompanying documents

25.19 Certain documents must accompany the application in order for the action to be validly brought.

(i) Certificate of the lawyer

25.20 The lawyer assisting or representing the applicant must lodge at the Registry a certificate that he or she is entitled to practise before a court of a Member State or of a State party to the EEA Agreement.[93] He or she must provide evidence of the authority conferred on him

---

[86] CFI, Case T-19/01 *Chiquita Brands International and Others v Commission*, para. 71. ECJ Rules of Procedure, Art. 128(1); EGC Rules of Procedure, Art. 48(1). See, e.g. EGC (judgment of 27 September 2012), Case T-303/10 *Wam Industriale v Commission*, not reported, paras 68–72. See, however, the case-law cited in n. 90.

[87] ECJ Rules of Procedure, Art. 128(2).

[88] EGC, Case T-296/09 *EFIM v Commission* [2011] E.C.R. II-425*, Summ. pub., para. 22 (under appeal in ECJ, Case C-56/12 P *EFIM v Commission*, not reported); EGC (judgment of 14 March 2013), Case T-588/08 *Dole Food and Dole Germany v Commission*, not reported, para. 41. Note that no express provision has been made for this in the EGC Rules of Procedure. Art. 48(1) of the EGC Rules of Procedure only states that, 'In reply or rejoinder a party may offer further evidence.'

[89] EGC Practice Directions, point 26.

[90] ECJ Rules of Procedure, Art. 57(4) provides: '[t]o every procedural document there shall be annexed a file containing the items and documents relied on in support of it, together with a schedule listing them'. A similar provision can be found in EGC Rules of Procedure, Art. 43(4). See para. 23.53. The case-law shows that non-compliance with that obligation may entail the inadmissibility of the action if it is of such a kind as to hamper the other parties in the preparation of their arguments. See, in this respect, CFI, Case T-293/01 *Ineichen v Commission* [2003] E.C.R.-SC I-A-83, II-441, paras 29 *et seq.*; CFI, Case T-19/01 *Chiquita Brands International and Others v Commission* [2005] E.C.R. II-315, para 72.

[91] EGC Practice Directions, point 26.

[92] ECJ Rules of Procedure, Art. 128(1)(2); EGC Rules of Procedure, Art. 48(1). See, e.g. CFI, Case T-172/01 *M v Court of Justice* [2004] E.C.R. II-1075, paras 43–46; EGC (judgment of 27 September 2012), Case T-303/10 *Wam Industriale v Commission*, not reported, paras 68–72; EGC (judgment of 14 March 2013), Case T-588/08 *Dole Food and Dole Germany v Commission*, not reported, paras 41–42; EGC (order of 7 March 2013), Case T-198/09 *UOP v Commission*, not reported, para. 32.

[93] ECJ Rules of Procedure, Art. 119(3); EGC Rules of Procedure, Art. 44(3). A university teacher who, albeit not a practitioner, has rights of audience in his or her Member State is deemed to be a 'lawyer' for this purpose. See para. 23.17. Statute, Art. 19, seventh para.; ECJ Rules of Procedure, Art. 47(1); EGC Rules of Procedure, Art. 42.

or her by the client.[94] Failure to provide the requested documents might ultimately lead to the inadmissibility of the action.[95]

(ii) Contested act

25.21 If the annulment of an act is sought, the application must be accompanied by the contested act.[96] If the application is for failure to act, documentary evidence must be provided of the date on which the relevant institution was requested to act.[97] An application pursuant to an arbitration clause contained in a contract must be accompanied by a copy of the contract which contains that clause.[98]

(iii) Documents relating to legal persons

25.22 If the applicant is a legal person governed by private law, the application must be accompanied by proof of its 'existence in law'. Such proof consists of the instrument or instruments constituting or regulating that legal person or a recent extract from the register of companies, firms, or associations, or any other proof.[99] The fact that the legal person is governed by private law is determined by the law of its country of origin. At the same time, the applicant must adduce proof that the authority granted to its lawyer has been properly conferred on him or her by someone authorized for that purpose.[100]

(iv) Disputes relating to intellectual property rights

25.23 An application bringing a dispute relating to intellectual property before the General Court[101] in the form of an action against the Office for Harmonisation in the Internal Market (Trade Marks and Designs) or against the Community Plant Variety Office must also contain the names of all the parties to the proceedings before the Board of Appeal and the addresses they had given for the purposes of the notifications to be effected in the course of the proceedings before the Board of Appeal.[102] In addition, the contested decision has to be appended to the application and the date on which the applicant was notified of it must be indicated.[103]

(v) Summary for publication

25.24 The Court of Justice and the General Court require each application to be accompanied by a summary (not more than two pages long) of the pleas in law and main arguments relied on designed to facilitate publication of the notice in the *Official Journal of the European Union*.[104]

---

[94] ECJ Rules of Procedure, Art. 119(2); EGC Rules of Procedure Art. 44(5). There is no need for the power of attorney to make an express mention of the contested act the applicant seeks to challenge: EGC, Case T-320/07 *Jones and Others v Commission* [2011] E.C.R. II-417*, Summ. pub., para. 56. See also paras 23.17–23.19.

[95] ECJ Rules of Procedure, Art. 119(4); EGC Rules of Procedure Art. 44(6). See, e.g. EGC (order of 14 October 2010), Case T-296/10 *Varga and Haliu v Council*, not reported, paras 7–10; EGC (order of 15 October 2012), Case T-107/12 *LTTE v Council*, not reported, paras 25–28 (authority to represent a legal person); EGC (order of 13 November 2012), Case T-400/12 *Hârsulescu v Romania*, not reported, paras 7–11 (lawyer's certificate). Similarly, if a party has ended a representative's mandate and has not replaced him with a new representative within the period required by the Union courts, the action will become devoid of purpose: EGC (order of 2 September 2010), Case T-123/08 *Spitzer v OHIM*, not reported, paras 4–8.

[96] Statute, Art. 21, second para.; ECJ Rules of Procedure, Art. 122(1); EGC Rules of Procedure, Art. 44(4).

[97] Statute, Art. 21, second para.; ECJ Rules of Procedure, Art. 122(1); EGC Rules of Procedure, Art. 44(4).

[98] ECJ Rules of Procedure, Art. 122(2); EGC Rules of Procedure, Art. 44(5a).

[99] EGC Rules of Procedure, Art. 44(5)(a).

[100] EGC Rules of Procedure, Art. 44(5)(b).

[101] Art. 65 of Regulation No. 207/2009; Art. 73 of Regulation No. 2100/94; and Art. 61 of Regulation No. 6/2002. See further Ch. 20.

[102] EGC Rules of Procedure, Art. 132(1), first para.

[103] EGC Rules of Procedure, Art. 132(1), second para.

[104] ECJ Rules of Procedure, Art. 120(c); ECJ Practice Directions, point 13; EGC Practice Directions, point 25.

(3) Consequences

(a) Case becomes pending

25.25 The lodging of the application at the Registry causes the case to become pending before the Court of Justice or the General Court, as the case may be. The Registrar enters the case in the register and gives it a serial number reflecting the order in which it was lodged.

The case numbers of the Court of Justice are preceded by the letter 'C' (for the French 'Cour'), those of the General Court by the letter 'T' (for the French 'Tribunal'), and those of the European Union Civil Service Tribunal by the letter 'F' (for the French 'Tribunal de la *fonction* publique').

(b) Role of the Registry

25.26 The Registrar[105] serves the application on the defendant[106] by dispatch of a copy by registered post with a form for acknowledgement of receipt or by personal delivery against a receipt[107] and, in disputes relating to intellectual property, on the relevant Office and on all parties to the proceedings before the Board of Appeal, after determining the language of the case in accordance with Art. 131(1) of the EGC Rules of Procedure.[108] Alternatively, documents shall be served by means of e-Curia if a party's representative has expressly accepted this method of service.[109]

The Registrar ensures that notice is given in the *Official Journal of the European Union* of the date of registration of the application initiating proceedings, the names and addresses of the parties, the subject-matter of the proceedings, the form of order sought by the applicant, and a summary of the pleas in law and of the main supporting arguments.[110] The purpose of the notice in the C series of the *Official Journal* is to put Union institutions, Member States, and natural and legal persons on notice of the proceedings, giving them the opportunity of intervening.[111] Where the European Parliament, the Council, or the Commission is not a party to the case, the Registrar sends them copies of the application and of the defence, without the annexes thereto, to enable them to assess whether the inapplicability of one of its acts is being invoked under Art. 277 TFEU.[112]

(c) Regularization of the application

25.27 If the application does not comply with certain requirements or if the requisite accompanying documents are not appended to it, the Registrar prescribes a reasonable period within which the applicant is to comply with these requirements, either by putting the application in order or by producing any documents missing.[113] However, it cannot be

---

[105] ECJ Rules of Procedure, Art. 20(1); EGC Rules of Procedure, Art. 25(1).
[106] ECJ Rules of Procedure, Art. 123; EGC Rules of Procedure, Art. 45.
[107] ECJ Rules of Procedure, Art. 48; EGC Rules of Procedure, Art. 100.
[108] EGC Rules of Procedure, Art. 133(1).
[109] ECJ Decision of 13 September 2011 on the lodging and service of procedural documents by means of e-Curia ([2011] O.J. C289/7), Art. 6; EGC Decision of 14 September 2011 on the lodging and service of procedural documents by means of e-Curia ([2011] O.J. C289/9), Art. 6.
[110] ECJ Rules of Procedure, Art. 16(6); EGC Rules of Procedure, Art. 24(6).
[111] See para. 25.70.
[112] ECJ Rules of Procedure, Art. 125; EGC Rules of Procedure, Art. 24(7).
[113] ECJ Rules of Procedure, Art. 119(4) and Art. 122(3); EGC Rules of Procedure, Art. 44(6) and Art. 132(2). The requirements in question are those set out in Art. 119(2) to (3) and Art. 122(1) and (2) of the ECJ Rules of Procedure and in Art. 44(3) to (5a) and Art. 132(1) of the EGC Rules of Procedure.

reproached to the Registrar that he failed to detect a procedural irregularity.[114] If the applicant fails to comply with the Registrar's directions, the Court of Justice or the General Court, as the case may be, decides whether this renders the application formally inadmissible.[115]

Service of the application on the defendant will be effected as soon as the application has been put in order or the Court has declared it admissible, notwithstanding the failure to observe the formal requirements in question.[116]

B. The defence

(1) Lodging the defence

(a) Time limit

The defendant has two months following service upon it of the application in which to lodge a defence.[117] The President of the Court of Justice or the General Court, as the case may be, may exceptionally extend this time limit on a reasoned application by the defendant, which must be lodged before the original time limit runs out.[118] **25.28**

(b) Defence must be signed and dated

As a pleading, the defence is subject to the same formal requirements as the application initiating the proceedings and all other procedural documents (see paras 23.49–23.55 and 25.02–25.22). It must therefore be signed by an agent or a lawyer. Inobservance of this requirement leads to the inadmissibility of the defence.[119] **25.29**

(c) Disputes relating to intellectual property rights

In disputes relating to intellectual property rights, the Office, as defendant, and interveners within the meaning of Art. 134(1) of the EGC Rules of Procedure may submit responses to the application within a period of two months from the service of the application.[120] Since, in such disputes, interveners may apply for a form of order and put forward pleas in law not applied for or put forward by the main parties, the other parties to the proceedings may, **25.30**

---

[114] ECJ (order of 12 September 2012), Case C-69/12 P *Noscira v OHIM*, not reported, para. 16.

[115] ECJ (order of 10 July 1984), Case 289/83 *GAARM v Commission* [1984] E.C.R. 2789, at 2791; ECJ (order of 21 September 2012), Case C-69/12 P *Noscira v OHIM*, not reported, para. 16; CFI (order of 8 February 1993), Case T-101/92 *Stagakis v European Parliament* [1993] E.C.R. II-63, paras 9–11; CFI (order of 22 June 1995), Case T-101/95 *Zedelmaier v Council and Commission*, not reported. However, not all irregularities can be rectified: see para. 23.51.

[116] ECJ Rules of Procedure, Art. 123; EGC Rules of Procedure, Art. 45.

[117] ECJ Rules of Procedure, Art. 124(1); EGC Rules of Procedure, Art. 46(1). In ECJ, Case C-59/99 *Commission v Pereira Roldão & Filhos and Others* [2001] E.C.R. I-8499, para. 19, the Court of Justice found that the application could not be served on one of the defendants. The applicant then informed the Court that the proceedings were to be pursued in relation to the other two defendants, thereby implicitly abandoning the proceedings so far as the untraceable party was concerned.

[118] ECJ Rules of Procedure, Art. 124(3); EGC Rules of Procedure, Art. 46(3). The fact that the defendant applies for an extension of time for lodging its defence does not prevent it from raising an objection of inadmissibility pursuant to Art. 114 of the EGC Rules of Procedure on the basis of facts which were already known at the time the extension was applied for. This does not render the application for an extension an abuse (CFI (order of 10 July 2002), Case T-387/00 *Comitato organizzatore del convegno internazionale v Commission* [2002] E.C.R. II-3031, para. 359).

[119] The applicant may then apply for the form of order sought to be granted by default: see ECJ (judgment of 24 February 2005), Case C-279/03 *Commission v Implants*, not reported, paras 22–23.

[120] EGC Rules of Procedure, Art. 135(1).

within two months of service of the responses, submit replies or rejoinders, in response to the form of order sought and pleas in law put forward by an intervener for the first time. The President may exceptionally extend the time limit.[121]

(2) Judgments by default and applications to set them aside

(a) Default judgment

25.31 If, despite the fact that the application was duly served on the defendant, the latter fails to lodge a defence in the proper form within the time prescribed, the applicant may apply for the form of order sought to be granted.[122] The Court of Justice or the General Court may then give judgment by default.[123]

The application for judgment by default is served on the defendant.[124] No special formal requirements apply, although the application must comply with the general requirements laid down for pleadings.[125]

Before giving judgment by default, the Court of Justice or the General Court, as the case may be, after hearing the Advocate-General, considers whether the application initiating proceedings is admissible, whether the appropriate formalities have been complied with, and whether the application appears well-founded.[126]

The respective Court may decide to open the oral procedure relating to the application to grant the applicant's claims.[127] Naturally, only the applicant will be heard. The Court of Justice may adopt measures of organization of procedure or order measures of inquiry.[128] The General Court may also order a preparatory inquiry.[129]

---

[121] EGC Rules of Procedure, Art. 135(3).

[122] The applicant may waive the right to avail itself of the procedure for judgment by default (ECJ, Case C-32/02 *Commission v Italy* [2003] E.C.R. I-12063, paras 11–12).

[123] ECJ Rules of Procedure, Art. 152(1); EGC Rules of Procedure, Art. 122(1), first para.; for disputes relating to intellectual property rights, see EGC Rules of Procedure, Art. 134(4). For some examples, see, e.g. ECJ, Case C-274/93 *Commission v Luxembourg* [1996] E.C.R. I-2019, para. 9; ECJ, Case C-285/96 *Commission v Italy* [1998] E.C.R. I-5935, para. 13; ECJ, Case C-172/97 *Commission v SIVU and Hydro-Réalisations* [1999] E.C.R. I-3363, para. 16; ECJ, Case C-356/99 *Commission v Hitesys* [2000] E.C.R. I-9517, para. 18; ECJ, Case C-365/99 *Portugal v Commission* [2001] E.C.R. I-5645, para. 13; ECJ, Case C-77/99 *Commission v Oder-Plan Architektur and Others* [2001] E.C.R. I-7355, para. 25; ECJ, Case C-59/99 *Commission v Pereira Roldão & Filhos and Others* [2001] E.C.R. I-8499, para. 18; ECJ, Case C-29/03 *Commission v ITEC* [2003] E.C.R. I-12205, paras 18–20; ECJ (judgment of 8 July 2004), Case C-127/03 *Commission v Trendsoft*, not reported, paras 20–21; ECJ (judgment of 24 February 2005), Case C-279/03 *Commission v Implants*, not reported, paras 22–23 (defence had not been submitted by a lawyer authorized to practice before a court of a Member State); CFI, Case T-85/94 *Branco v Commission* [1995] E.C.R. II-45, para. 19; CFI, Case T-42/89 *Yorck von Wartenburg v European Parliament* [1990] E.C.R. II-31, paras 3–5; CFI (judgment of 14 October 2004), Case T-44/02 *Dresdner Bank v Commission*, not reported, paras 40–42; EGC, Case T-562/10 *HTTS v Council* [2011] E.C.R. II-8087, para. 23; EGC (judgment of 17 October 2012), Case T-220/10 *Commission v EU Research Projects*, not reported, paras 24–26.

[124] ECJ Rules of Procedure, Art. 152(2); EGC Rules of Procedure, Art.122(1), second para.

[125] ECJ Rules of Procedure, Art. 57; EGC Rules of Procedure, Art. 43.

[126] ECJ Rules of Procedure, Art.152(3); EGC Rules of Procedure, Art. 122(2). See, e.g. EGC, Case T-136/09 *Commission v Benjamin Gal-Or* [2010] E.C.R. II-221*, Summ. pub., para. 30; EGC, Case T-120/08 *Arch Chemicals and Others v Commission* [2011] E.C.R. II-298*, Summ. pub., para. 33; EGC, Case T-562/10 *HTTS v Council* [2011] E.C.R. II-8087, para. 29.

[127] ECJ Rules of Procedure, Art. 152(2); EGC Rules of Procedure, Art. 122(1), second para.

[128] ECJ Rules of Procedure, Art. 152(3).

[129] EGC Rules of Procedure, Art. 122(2).

A judgment by default is enforceable, although the Court of Justice or the General Court, as the case may be, may grant a stay of execution until the Court concerned has given its decision on any application to set it aside, or it may make execution subject to the provision of security. In the latter case, the security will be released if no application to set the default judgment aside is made or if such an application fails.[130]

(b) Application to set aside a default judgment

25.32 An application to set aside a judgment by default must be made within one month of service of the judgment[131] and submitted in the form prescribed for applications initiating proceedings (see paras 25.02–25.22).[132]

After the application has been served, the President prescribes a period within which the other party may submit written observations.[133] After a possible preparatory inquiry, the oral procedure takes place.[134] Finally, the Court concerned gives judgment.[135] No application may be made to have that judgment set aside.[136]

(c) Consequences

25.33 If an application to set aside a default judgment is rejected,[137] the default judgment remains in place. Conversely, if the application is successful,[138] the judgment setting aside the judgment by default takes its place.

(3) Content

(a) Requirements

25.34 In addition to the case-number and the applicant's name, the following must appear at the beginning of each defence:

— the defendant's name and address;
— the name and capacity of the defendant's agent or lawyer;
— an address for service and/or agreement to service by telefax or other technical means of communication.[139]

---

[130] ECJ Rules of Procedure, Art. 152(4); EGC Rules of Procedure, Art. 122(3).

[131] Statute, Art. 41. For calculation of time limits, see paras 23–026 *et seq.*

[132] ECJ Rules of Procedure, Art. 156(2); EGC Rules of Procedure, Art. 122(4).

[133] ECJ Rules of Procedure, Art. 156(3); EGC Rules of Procedure, Art. 122(5).

[134] However, a judgment can be delivered without holding a hearing: see, e.g. ECJ, Case C-172/97 OP *SIVU du plan d'eau de la Vallée du Lot v Commission* [2001] E.C.R. I-6699, para. 26.

[135] See, e.g. ECJ, Case C-172/97 OP *SIVU du plan d'eau de la Vallée du Lot v Commission* [2001] E.C.R. I-6699; ECJ, Case C-279/03 OP *Implants (International) v Commission* [2006] E.C.R. I-16*, Summ. pub.; CFI, Joined Cases T-44/02 OP, T-54/02 OP, T-56/02 OP, T-60/02 OP, and T-61/02 OP *Dresdner Bank and Others v Commission* [2006] E.C.R. II-3567.

[136] ECJ Rules of Procedure, Art. 156(5); EGC Rules of Procedure, Art. 122(6).

[137] CFI, Case T-42/89 OPPO *European Parliament v Yorck von Wartenburg* [1990] E.C.R. II-299; CFI, Case T-85/94 OPPO *Commission v Branco* [1995] E.C.R. II-2993.

[138] ECJ, Case C-172/97 OP *SIVU du plan d'eau de la Vallée du Lot v Commission* [2001] E.C.R. I-6699 (by which the default judgment was partially annulled).

[139] ECJ Rules of Procedure, Art. 124(2); EGC Rules of Procedure, Art. 46(1), first para.; EGC Practice Directions, point 30. The ECJ Rules of Procedure that entered into force on 1 November 2012 no longer require an address for service in Luxembourg.

The defence further contains:

– the pleas in law and arguments relied on;
– the form of order sought by the defendant;
– where appropriate, any evidence produced or offered.[140]

(b) Name and address of the defendant

25.35 The defence is subject to the same requirements as the application, for instance, as regards the address for service, assistance, or representation by a lawyer and proof of the existence in law of a legal person governed by private law.[141]

(c) Pleas in law and arguments relied on

(i) Pleas and arguments must be clearly set out

25.36 The arguments of fact and law relied on must be clearly set out in the defence.[142] If any fact alleged by the applicant is contested it must be clearly indicated, and the basis on which it is challenged must be stated explicitly.[143]

(ii) New pleas

25.37 The defendant is limited to pleas set out in the defence. In subsequent pleadings, the defendant may introduce new pleas in law only if they are based on matters of law or of fact which come to light in the course of the proceedings.[144] Consequently, 'new pleas' have the same standing for both the applicant and the defendant[145] in order to secure observance of the principle *audi alteram partem*. If the defendant could keep its defence pleas undisclosed until it lodged the rejoinder or, *a fortiori*, until the hearing, the applicant would lose any chance of making a 'reply' and of preparing its counter arguments for the hearing, which would jeopardize proper debate, with both parties putting forward pleas and counter pleas.

The defence has to take issue only with pleas raised by the applicant. A counter claim may be made, provided that it is related to the applicant's claim.[146]

(d) Form of order sought by the defendant

25.38 Generally, the form of order sought by the defendant, which must be precisely specified at the beginning or the end of the defence,[147] will claim that the application and the claims set out therein should be dismissed and the applicant ordered to pay the costs.

---

[140] ECJ Rules of Procedure, Art. 124(1); EGC Rules of Procedure, Art. 46(1), first para.

[141] ECJ Rules of Procedure, Art. 124(2); EGC Rules of Procedure, Art. 46(1), second para. The defendant may be a person governed by private law where a Union institution asserts a claim against such a person pursuant to an arbitration clause within the meaning of Art. 272 TFEU (see Ch. 19).

[142] See, e.g. EGC, Case T-133/07 *Mitsubishi Electric v Commission* [2011] E.C.R. II-4219, para. 25.

[143] ECJ Practice Directions, point 15; EGC Practice Directions, point 33.

[144] ECJ Rules of Procedure, Art. 127(1); EGC Rules of Procedure, Art. 48(2). See ECJ, Case C-136/92 P *Commission v Brazzelli and Others* [1994] E.C.R. I-1981, para. 58; ECJ, Case C-526/08 *Commission v Luxembourg* [2010] E.C.R. I-6151, paras 49–51; ECJ, Case C-351/09 *Commission v Malta* [2010] E.C.R. I-180*, Summ. pub., paras 21–24; CFI, Case T-81/97 *Regione Toscana v Commission* [1998] E.C.R. II-2889, para. 41.

[145] The German version of the provisions cited accordingly refers to '*Angriffs- und Verteidigungsmittel*'. For an example, see ECJ, Case C-471/98 *Commission v Belgium* [2002] E.C.R. I-9681, paras 41–43.

[146] ECJ, Case 250/78 *DEKA v EEC* [1983] E.C.R. 421, para. 5: in this case, the Commission sought to set off against compensation which what was then the Community had to pay the applicant a claim which had been assigned to the Commission for repayment of an amount which had been wrongly paid to the applicant by way of export refunds and monetary compensatory amounts for exports of maize gritz. As a 'defence plea', the claim for repayment of the amounts wrongly paid was apparently admissible. See also ECJ, Case C-87/01 P *Commission v Conseil des communes et régions d'Europe* [2003] E.C.R. I-7617, para. 56.

[147] EGC Practice Directions, point 31.

The claim for a costs order is very important, since both the Court of Justice and the General Court will order the unsuccessful party to pay the costs only 'if they have been applied for in the successful party's pleadings'.[148] This means that the defendant, too, should not omit to ask the Court to make a costs order against the applicant in case—as it naturally hopes—it is successful in its defence on the substance (see also para. 25.94).

(e) Any evidence produced or offered in support

At the first possible opportunity—i.e. in the defence—the defendant should tender any **25.39** supporting evidence. If, subsequently, the defendant offers further evidence in the rejoinder or at the hearing, it must give reasons for the delay in tendering it.[149] In this respect, too, the positions of the defendant and the applicant are parallel. Once again, it is the quality of debate before the Court which necessitates each party putting forward supporting evidence at a time when the other can still effectively put forward a counter argument.

(f) Accompanying documents

Just as in the case of the application, documents may have to be submitted with the defence **25.40** (see paras 25.18–25.22).

(4) The preliminary objection of inadmissibility

(a) Preliminary objection by separate act

Instead of lodging a defence, the defendant may submit an application, by separate act, to **25.41** the Court of Justice or the General Court (within the time prescribed for lodging a defence) for a decision on an objection of inadmissibility or lack of competence (or other preliminary objection: see further para. 25.86)[150] without a ruling on the substance of the case.[151] In that event, the President prescribes a period within which the opposite party may submit in writing his pleas in law and the form of order sought.[152]

(b) Separate decision or decision reserved for final judgment

When it receives the objection and the response to it, the Court of Justice or the General **25.42** Court, as the case may be, decides as soon as possible after hearing the Advocate-General, on the application for a decision on the preliminary objection or, where special circum stances so justify, reserves its decision until it rules on the substance of the case.[153]

If the respective Court decides to reserve its decision, the President prescribes new time limits for the further steps in the proceedings (in practice, this means that the defendant is

---

[148] ECJ Rules of Procedure, Art. 138(1); EGC Rules of Procedure, Art. 87(2), first para.
[149] ECJ Rules of Procedure, Art. 128(1); EGC Rules of Procedure, Art. 48(1). See, e.g. CFI, Case T-172/01 *M v Court of Justice* [2004] E.C.R. II-1075, paras 36–42; CFI (order of 26 May 2004), Case T-266/03 *Groupement des Cartes Bancaires 'CB' v Commission*, not reported, paras 15–19; EGC, Case T-51/07 *Agrar-Invest-Tatschl v Commission* [2008] E.C.R. II-2825, para. 57; EGC (judgment of 14 March 2013), Case T-588/08 *Dole Food Company and Dole Germany v Commission*, not reported, paras 40–41.
[150] For other preliminary objections, such as the objection that the action has become devoid of purpose and that there is no longer any need to adjudicate, the two-month time limit is not applicable.
[151] ECJ Rules of Procedure, Art. 151(1); EGC Rules of Procedure, Art. 114(1).
[152] ECJ Rules of Procedure, Art. 151(3); EGC Rules of Procedure, Art. 114(2).
[153] ECJ Rules of Procedure, Art. 151(5); EGC Rules of Procedure, Art. 114(4), first para.

given a new time limit for lodging the defence and hence for the resumption of the written procedure on the substance).[154]

If the respective Court decides to rule on the objection of inadmissibility, it is dealt with orally in principle and a date is fixed for a hearing, unless the Court of Justice or the General Court, as the case may be, decides differently.[155] If the action is clearly inadmissible, there is a tendency to uphold the objection without holding a hearing. In such a case, the Court concerned, after hearing the Advocate-General, declares the action inadmissible by reasoned order.[156]

If a judgment is given refusing the application on the preliminary objection and declaring the action admissible, the President prescribes new time limits for the further steps in the proceedings.[157]

(c) Examination of the substance without examining objection of inadmissibility

25.43   The Union courts might rule immediately on the substance of the case without examining the objection of inadmissibility if this is justified by the proper administration of justice. This will be the case when it appears clearly that the action will not succeed on the merits.[158]

(d) Moment in time taken into account to determine the admissibility of an action

25.44   The admissibility of an action is judged by reference to the situation prevailing when the application was lodged.[159] Therefore, new rules on standing for natural or legal persons cannot be adduced to assess the admissibility of an action if the application was lodged before the entry into force of those new rules.[160]

More interesting is the situation of *lis pendens* (often used interchangeably with *lis alibi pendens*), where two successive actions with identical parties, subject-matter, and submissions

---

[154] ECJ Rules of Procedure, Art. 151(6); EGC Rules of Procedure, Art. 114(4), second para.

[155] ECJ Rules of Procedure, Art. 151(4); EGC Rules of Procedure, Art. 114(3). See also ECJ (order of 29 October 2004), Case C-360/02 P *Ripa di Meana v European Parliament* [2004] E.C.R. I-10339, para. 35 and ECJ (order of 30 March 2006), Case C-113/05 P *European Federation for Cosmetic Ingredients v European Parliament and Council* [2006] E.C.R. I-46*, Summ. pub., para. 26 (no obligation for the General Court to organize an oral hearing).

[156] ECJ Rules of Procedure, Art. 53(2); EGC Rules of Procedure, Art. 111. For examples, see ECJ (orders of 26 September 1994), Case 216/83 *Les Verts v Commission and Council* [1984] E.C.R. 3325; Case 296/83 *Les Verts v European Parliament* [1984] E.C.R. 3335; Case 297/83 *Les Verts v Council* [1984] E.C.R. 3339; ECJ (order of 9 December 2003), Case C-224/03 *Italy v Commission* [2003] E.C.R. I-14751; CFI (order of 26 November 1993), Case T-460/93 *Tête and Others v EIB* [1993] E.C.R. II-1257; CFI (order of 14 December 1993), Case T-29/93 *Calvo Alonso-Cortés v Commission* [1993] E.C.R. II-1389; CFI (order of 20 July 1994), Case T-45/93 *Branco v Court of Auditors* [1994] E.C.R.-SC II-641, para. 21 (English abstract at I-A-197); EGC (order of 3 June 2010), Case T-173/09 *Z v Commission* [2010] E.C.R. II-105*, Summ. pub., para. 27; EGC (order of 27 September 2012), Case T-318/12 *Communicaid Group v Commission*, not reported, para. 3; EGC (order of 17 December 2012), Case T-532/12 *Morea v Commission*, not reported, para. 3.

[157] ECJ Rules of Procedure, Art. 151(6); EGC Rules of Procedure, Art. 114(4), second para.

[158] See, e.g. ECJ, Case C-23/00 P *Council v Boehringer* [2002] E.C.R. I-1873, para. 52; ECJ, Case C-233/02 *France v Commission* [2004] E.C.R. I-2759, para. 26; ECJ (judgment of 11 July 2013), Case C-439/11 P *Ziegler v Commission*, not reported, para. 45; ECJ, Case T-319/05 *Swiss Confederation v Commission* [2010] E.C.R. II-4265, para. 55; EGC, Joined Cases T-400/04, T-402/04 to T-404/04 *Arch Chemicals and Arch Timber Production and Others v Commission* [2011] E.C.R. II-296*, Summ. pub., para. 56; EGC, Case T-561/08 *Jürgen Gutknecht v Commission* [2011] E.C.R. II-364*, Summ. pub., paras 22–23.

[159] ECJ, Case 50/84 *Bensider and Others v Commission* [1984] E.C.R. 3991, para. 8; CFI (order of 15 February 2005), Case T-229/02 *PKK and Others v Council* [2005] E.C.R. II-539, para. 30; ECJ, Joined Cases C-71/09 P, C-73/09 P and C-76/09 P *Comitato 'Venezia vuole vivere' and Others v Commission* [2011] E.C.R. I-4727, para. 31.

[160] EGC, Case T-291/04 *Enviro Tech v Commission* [2011] E.C.R. II-8281, para. 98.

are pending before the Union courts.[161] If both actions are still pending at the moment where the Court of Justice or the General Court rules on the admissibility of the action, only the second action will be declared inadmissible on account of *lis pendens*.[162] This is logical, as the situation of *lis pendens* only existed in respect of the second action at the time of lodging. The situation becomes more complicated when the first action has been declared inadmissible. Applying the rule that the admissibility of an action should be assessed by reference to the situation prevailing when the application was lodged might also lead to the inadmissibility of the second action since, at the time of lodging the application, there was a situation of *lis pendens*. The Union courts, however, have rejected such a reasoning. It was held that the dispute arising from the first action ceased to exist when the action was declared inadmissible and thus caused the situation of *litis pendens* to disappear.[163] Consequently, the second action could not be declared inadmissible on account of *lis pendens*. The reasoning also applies when the first action has been withdrawn by the parties.[164]

(e) Reasoned order

As already mentioned, the Court of Justice or the General Court may decide by reasoned **25.45** order, without taking further steps in the proceedings and without hearing the parties (although it is obliged to hear the Advocate-General) that it has no jurisdiction to hear and determine the case or that the application is manifestly inadmissible.[165] The General Court can also decide by reasoned order that an action manifestly lacks any foundation in law (see para. 23.40).[166] It is not clear whether the defendant can raise an objection by which it calls on the General Court to declare, by order, that an action is manifestly ill-founded in law.[167]

C. The reply and the rejoinder

(1) General

After the defence has been lodged, the applicant may supplement its application by lodging **25.46** a reply within a time limit prescribed by the President of the Court of Justice or the General

---

[161] ECJ, Joined Cases 172/83 and 226/83 *Hoogovens Groep v Commission* [1985] E.C.R. 2831, para. 9; ECJ, Joined Cases 358/85 and 51/86 *France v European Parliament* [1988] E.C.R. 4821, para. 12; EGC (order of 21 June 2012), Case T-531/11 *Hamas v Council*, not reported, para. 15.

[162] EGC, Case T-378/06 *IMI and Others v Commission* [2011] E.C.R. II-62*, Summ. pub., paras 28–32.

[163] ECJ, Joined Cases 146/85 and 431/85 *Diezler and Others v ESC* [1987] E.C.R. 4283, para. 12; ECJ, Joined Cases C-71/09 P, C-73/09 P and C-76/09 P *Comitato 'Venezia vuole vivere' and Others v Commission* [2011] E.C.R. I-4727, para. 31.

[164] ECJ, Joined Cases C-71/09 P, C-73/09 P and C-76/09 P *Comitato 'Venezia vuole vivere' and Others v Commission* [2011] E.C.R. I-4727, para. 32.

[165] ECJ Rules of Procedure, Art. 53(2); EGC Rules of Procedure, Art. 111.

[166] EGC Rules of Procedure, Art. 111. The words 'or manifestly lacking any foundation in law' were added to Art. 111 of the EGC Rules of Procedure in order to make it clear that the General Court cannot deal with a case under that provision where the outcome of the proceedings depends on an assessment of the facts. For an example, see EGC (order of 24 October 2012), Case T-442/11 *Evropaïki Dynamiki*, not reported, para. 42.

[167] Art. 114(1) of the EGC Rules of Procedure does not seem to afford any basis for the defendant's doing so, since it expressly provides that the General Court is to rule on an application made in this way which does not 'go to the substance of the case'. Of course, the defendant may claim at any time in its defence that the application is manifestly ill-founded in law and ask the General Court to rule on that claim without taking further steps in the written procedure. For examples, see CFI (order of 10 December 1997), Case T-334/96 *Smets v Commission* [1997] E.C.R. II-2333, para. 16; CFI (order of 29 April 1998), Case T-367/94 *British Coal v Commission* [1998] E.C.R. II-705, paras 22–26; EGC (order of 8 October 2012), Case T-62/12 *ClientEarth v Council*, not reported, para. 10.

Court.[168] The defendant may then lodge a rejoinder on the same terms.[169] The parties are not obliged to lodge a reply and a rejoinder.[170]

Either party may apply to the President for an extension of time.[171] If a party allows the relevant period to expire without lodging such a pleading or if it waives its right to do so, the proceedings continue.

In proceedings before the Court of Justice, the President may specify the matters to which the reply or the rejoinder should relate.[172] In proceedings before the General Court, it is expressly provided that the Court may decide, after hearing the Advocate-General, that a second exchange of pleadings is unnecessary because the documents before it are sufficiently comprehensive to enable the parties to elaborate their pleas and arguments in the course of the oral procedure.[173] However, the General Court may authorize the parties to supplement the documents if the applicant presents a reasoned request to that effect within two weeks from the notification of that decision.[174] The President fixes the time limits within which these pleadings are to be lodged.[175]

(2) Formal requirements

25.47 No specific formal requirements are laid down for replies and rejoinders, although they do have to comply with the general requirements which all procedural documents have to satisfy (see paras 23.49–23.55).[176]

(3) Objective

25.48 The reply and the rejoinder afford each party an opportunity to supplement the application and the defence, respectively, in the light of its opponent's observations. They may contain supplementary arguments supporting or clarifying the pleas raised by the parties.

As already noted, if a party offers further evidence in the reply or the rejoinder (or possibly even at a later stage in the proceedings), reasons must be given for the delay in tendering it.[177] However, parties may tender evidence in rebuttal and the amplification of the offers of

---

[168] ECJ Rules of Procedure, Art. 126(1) and (2); EGC Rules of Procedure, Art. 47(1) and (2).

[169] ECJ Rules of Procedure, Art. 126(1); EGC Rules of Procedure, Art. 47(1).

[170] By virtue of the use of the term 'may' in ECJ Rules of Procedure, Art. 126(1); and EGC Rules of Procedure, Art. 47(1).

[171] If no extension of time is requested, a rejoinder lodged out of time will not be joined to the file (CFI, Case T-208/01 *Volkswagen v Commission* [2003] E.C.R. II-5141, para. 11).

[172] ECJ Rules of Procedure, Art. 126(2).

[173] EGC Rules of Procedure, Art. 47(1). See, e.g. CFI, Case T-277/03 *Vlachaki v Commission* [2005] E.C.R.-SC II-243, para. 23; CFI, Case T-216/05 *Mebrom v Commission* [2007] E.C.R. II-1507, para. 49; CFI, Case T-380/06 *Vischim v Commission* [2009] E.C.R. II-3911, para. 38; EGC (judgment of 10 April 2013), Case T-671/11 *IPK International v Commission*, not reported, para. 20.

[174] EGC Rules of Procedure, Art. 47(1).

[175] EGC Rules of Procedure, Art. 47(2).

[176] ECJ Rules of Procedure, Art. 57; EGC Rules of Procedure, Art. 43. See, e.g. EGC, Case T-320/07 *Jones and Others v Commission* [2011] E.C.R. II-417*, Summ. pub., paras 62–68; EGC (judgment of 24 May 2012), Case T-111/08 *MasterCard and MasterCard Europe v Commission*, not reported, paras 68–69.

[177] ECJ Rules of Procedure, Art. 128(1); EGC Rules of Procedure, Art. 48(1). See, e.g. CFI, Case T-172/01 *M v Court of Justice* [2004] E.C.R. II-1075, paras 39–40 (admissible evidence) and paras 43–46 (inadmissible evidence); EGC, Case T-335/08 *BNP Paribas and BNL v Commission* [2010] E.C.R. II-3323, para. 176 (inadmissible evidence); EGC, Case T-342/07 *Ryanair v Commission* [2010] E.C.R. II-3457, paras 327–328 (inadmissible evidence); EGC (judgment of 2 February 2012), Case T-83/08 *Denki Kagaku Kogyo Kabushiki Kaisha and Denka Chemicals v Commission*, not reported, paras 69–70 (inadmissible evidence); EGC (judgment of 27 September 2012), Case T-303/10 *Wam Industriale v*

evidence submitted in response to evidence in rebuttal contained in the defence or reply of the other party. Naturally, they do not have to give further reasons for this.[178]

(4) No new pleas

As has also already been observed, neither the reply nor the rejoinder may raise new pleas, **25.49** unless they are based on matters of law or of fact which have come to light in the course of the proceedings[179] or constitute pleas which the Union courts have to examine of their own motion.[180] This will not be the case where, although the party raising the new plea was not previously aware of a matter of fact on which the new substantive plea is based, it could have known of it at the time when the application or the defence, as the case may be, was lodged.[181] If, in contrast, a matter of fact is mentioned for the first time in the defence, the applicant is entitled to raise a plea based thereon in the reply.[182] Finally, new claims made in the reply or the rejoinder are inadmissible.[183]

(5) Improper use of procedural documents

Parties may not make improper use of procedural documents to which they have access in **25.50** the course of the proceedings. They may use such documents only for the purpose of pursuing their own case. If a party uses some of the procedural documents of other parties for other purposes, such as for provoking public criticism of the other parties' arguments as a result of the disclosure of the documents in question, it infringes a general principle of the due administration of justice according to which parties have the right to defend their interests free of external influences, and particularly from influences on the part of the public. Such an abuse of process may be penalized in the order for costs.[184] However, a

---

Commission, not reported, paras 68–72 (inadmissible evidence); EGC (judgment of 14 March 2013), Case T-588/08 *Dole Food Company and Dole Germany v Commission*, not reported, paras 40–48 (inadmissible evidence).

[178] ECJ, Case C-185/95 P *Baustahlgewebe v Commission* [1998] E.C.R. I-8417, para. 72; EGC, Case T-189/08 *Forum 187 v Commission* [2010] E.C.R. II-1039, paras 65–66; EGC (order of 7 March 2013), Case T-198/09 *UOP v Commission*, not reported, para. 32.

[179] ECJ Rules of Procedure, Art. 127(1); EGC Rules of Procedure, Art. 48(2). See, e.g. ECJ, Case C-471/98 *Commission v Belgium* [2002] E.C.R. I-9681, paras 41–43; ECJ, Case C-526/08 *Commission v Luxembourg* [2010] E.C.R. I-6151, paras 49–50; ECJ, Case C-351/09 *Commission v Malta* [2010] E.C.R. I-180*, Summ. pub., paras 21–24; EGC, Case T-186/06 *Solvay v Commission* [2011] E.C.R. II-2839, paras 418–419. See also para. 25.13.

[180] CFI, Case T-27/02 *Kronofrance v Commission* [2004] E.C.R. II-4177, para. 30; EGC, Case T-284/08 *People's Mojahedin Organization of Iran v Council* [2008] E.C.R. II-3487, para. 25.

[181] ECJ, Case 110/81 *Roquette Frères v Council* [1982] E.C.R. 3159, para. 31; ECJ, Case C-110/10 P *Solvay v Commission* [2011] E.C.R. I-10439, para. 58; CFI, Case T-139/99 *AICS v European Parliament* [2000] E.C.R. II-2849, para. 62; CFI, Case T-76/02 *Messina v Commission* [2003] E.C.R. II-3203, paras 36–37; CFI, Case T-340/04 *France Télécom v Commission* [2007] E.C.R. II-573, para. 164; EGC, Case T-303/08 *Tresplain Investments v OHIM* [2010] E.C.R. II-5659, para. 167.

[182] ECJ, Joined Cases 12/64 and 29/64 *Ley v Commission* [1965] E.C.R. 107, at 118–19; EGC, Case T-189/08 *Forum 187 v Commission* [2010] E.C.R. II-1039, paras 65–66; EGC (order of 7 March 2013), Case T-198/09 *UOP v Commission*, not reported, para. 32.

[183] CFI, Case T-22/92 *Weissenfels v European Parliament* [1993] E.C.R. II-1095, para. 27; CFI, Case T-146/95 *Bernardi v European Parliament* [1996] E.C.R. II-769, para. 31; CFI, Case T-494/04 *Wineke Neirinck v Commission* [2006] E.C.R.-SC-I-A-2-259, para. 30; EGC, Case T-236/07 *Germany v Commission* [2010] E.C.R. II-5253, para. 28. See also EGC (order of 4 September 2012), Case T-381/08 *DAI v Commission*, not reported, paras 34–37.

[184] See, e.g. CFI, Case T-174/95 *Svenska Journalistförbundet v Council* [1998] E.C.R. II-2289, paras 135–139, where the applicant published the Council's defence on the Internet, requesting the public to

party may join an application by which another party has brought other proceedings as a document to its own application if the third party agrees. This is because there is no rule or provision to prevent parties from disclosing their pleadings to third parties.[185]

(6) Disputes relating to intellectual property rights

25.51　In disputes relating to intellectual property rights, parties may submit replies and rejoinders only if the President, on a reasoned application made within two weeks of service of responses or replies, considers such further pleading necessary and allows it in order to enable the party concerned to put forward its point of view.[186]

D. Directions for preparing procedural documents

(1) General

25.52　Procedural documents lodged by the parties must be submitted in a form which can be processed electronically by the Court of Justice or the General Court and which, in particular, makes it possible to scan documents and to use character recognition.[187] For that purpose, the following requirements must be complied with:

- the paper must be white, unlined, and A4 size;
- the text must be easily legible and appear on one side of the page only;
- paper documents produced must be assembled in such a way as to be easily separable (they must not be bound together or permanently attached by means such as glue or staples);
- the text must be in a commonly used font (such as Times New Roman), in at least 12 pt in the body of the text and at least 10 pt in the footnotes, with at least single line spacing and upper, lower, left, and right margins of at least 2.5 cm;[188]
- the pages of the documents must be numbered consecutively in the top right-hand corner. That numbering must also cover all the pages of any annexes to the pleading, so as to make it possible to check that all the pages of the annexes have been duly scanned.

(2) First page

25.53　The following information must appear on the first page of the procedural document:[189]

- the title of the document (application, appeal, defence, response, reply, rejoinder, application for leave to intervene, statement in intervention, observations on the statement in intervention, objection of inadmissibility, etc.);
- the case number, if it has already been notified by the Registry;

---

inform the Council of their comments. See also EGC (judgment of 14 November 2012), Case T-135/09 *Nexans France and Nexans v Commission*, not reported, para. 108.

[185] ECJ (order of 3 April 2000), Case C-376/98 *Germany v European Parliament and Council* [2000] E.C.R. I-2247, para. 10. See also CFI, Case T-36/04 *API v Commission* [2007] E.C.R. II-3201, para. 88; CFI (order of 15 October 2009), Case T-459/07 *Hangzou Duralamp Electronics v Council* [2009] E.C.R. II-4015, para. 14.

[186] EGC Rules of Procedure, Art. 135(2).

[187] ECJ Practice Directions, point 35; EGC Practice Directions, point 12.

[188] Line spacing of 1.5 is, however, requested by the ECJ Practice Directions, point 35.

[189] ECJ Practice Directions, point 36; EGC Practice Directions, point 9.

– the names of the applicant and of the defendant;
– the name of the party on whose behalf the pleading is lodged.

(3) Procedural documents lodged by means of e-Curia

The Court of Justice has established a user manual clearly setting out how procedural **25.54**
documents lodged by means of e-Curia should be presented.

The file by which the procedural document is lodged should contain a name identifying the
document (for example, Pleadings, Annex Part 1, etc.). The document does not have to
bear a handwritten signature—the login details of the party's representative lodging the
document will constitute a signature for the purposes of the Rules of Procedure—and must
include the schedule of annexes. The text of the document can immediately be saved in
PDF format without scanning the document. Annexes to a procedural document must be
contained in a separate file.[190]

(4) Paragraphs need to be numbered

Each paragraph of the pleading must be numbered.[191] The signature of the agent or lawyer **25.55**
acting for the party concerned must appear at the end of the pleading.[192]

(5) Brief submissions

The pleadings should be as short as possible in order to expedite the disposal of the **25.56**
case. In its Practice Directions, the General Court lays down the maximum number of
pages for a series of pleadings. The maximum number of pages for an application and
a defence should not, in principle, exceed 50. The corresponding figures are 25 for the
reply and the rejoinder, 20 for an objection of inadmissibility and observations thereon,
and 20 pages for statements in intervention.[193] These limits may be exceeded in cases
involving particularly complex legal or factual issues.[194] The ECJ Practice Directions
state that, save in exceptional circumstances, an application and a defence should not
exceed 30 pages, and a reply and a rejoinder should not exceed 10 pages.[195] In the
future, the Court of Justice might, pursuant to Art. 58 of the ECJ Rules of Procedure,
adopt a decision setting the maximum length of written pleadings or observations lodged
before it.

(6) Annexes

Only those documents mentioned in the actual text of a pleading which are necessary in **25.57**
order to prove or illustrate its contents may be submitted as annexes.[196]

---

[190] ECJ Practice Directions, point 41; EGC Practice Directions, point 14.
[191] ECJ Practice Directions, point 35; EGC Practice Directions, point 10.
[192] EGC Practice Directions, point 11.
[193] EGC Practice Directions, point 15. Non-compliance with these Practice Directions can lead to an
unfavourable costs order for the party concerned: see CFI, Joined Cases T-191/98, T-212/98 to T-214/98
Atlantic Container Line and Others v Commission [2003] E.C.R. II-3275, paras 1645–1647.
[194] EGC Practice Directions, point 16.
[195] ECJ Practice Directions, points 12, 15, and 16.
[196] ECJ Practice Directions, point 39; EGC Practice Directions, point 57.

Annexes will be accepted only if they are accompanied by a schedule indicating, for each document annexed: the number of the annex, a short description of the document (for example, 'letter'), followed by its date, author, and addressee and its number of pages, the page reference and paragraph number in the pleading where the document is mentioned, and its relevance is described.[197] Where annexes are documents which themselves contain annexes, they must be arranged and numbered in such a way as to avoid all possibility of confusion.[198]

Each reference to a document lodged must state the relevant annex number as given in the schedule of annexes in which it appears and indicate the pleading to which it is annexed.[199]

II. Intervention

A. Aim and manner in intervention

(1) Objective

25.58 The outcome of proceedings before the Union courts may affect both Union institutions, bodies, offices, or agencies, and natural or legal persons, even though they are not parties. Intervention generally allows them to join voluntarily in the proceedings on the side of one of the parties. This enables the Court concerned to take their interests into account in deciding the case.

(2) Pleas which an intervener may raise

25.59 Intervention does not constitute a means for third parties to enter the proceedings by the back door as parties thereto. In the first place, interveners' submissions must be limited to supporting, in whole or in part, the form of order sought by one of the parties (see paras 25.16 and 25.38).[200] The intervener may therefore only raise pleas and arguments in support

---

[197] ECJ Practice Directions, point 39; EGC Practice Directions, point 58. For the General Court, an annex should also be numbered in such a way as to identify the procedural document in which it is produced (thus, for example, Annex A.1, A.2, etc. in an application; Annex B.1, B.2, etc. in a defence; Annex C.1, C.2, etc. in a reply; Annex D.1, D.2, etc. in a rejoinder). See further ECJ Rules of Procedure, Art. 57(4); EGC Rules of Procedure, Art. 43(4)–(5).

[198] EGC Practice Directions, point 60.

[199] ECJ Practice Directions, point 39; EGC Practice Directions, point 61.

[200] Statute, Art. 40, fourth para.; ECJ Rules of Procedure, Art. 129(1). The Court of Justice seems to interpret this provision flexibly, depending on the particular circumstances of the proceedings before it. If it appears from the statement in intervention as a whole and from the context that the intervener intends to cast further light on the dispute and so contribute to the success of the claim of the party which it is supporting, the 'form of order sought' set out in the statement in intervention is intended to support the party in favour of whom intervention is made, even if its literal wording seems to refer to another aim (ECJ, Case C-377/98 *Netherlands v European Parliament and Council* [2001] E.C.R. I-7079, paras 7–11). In other cases, the ECJ takes a stricter approach: see, e.g. ECJ (judgment of 13 January 2005), Case C-38/03 *Commission v Belgium*, not reported, paras 7–9; EGC (judgment of 28 March 2012), Case T-190/10 *Egan and Hackett v European Parliament*, not reported, paras 25–26.

of this form of order.[201] Although an intervener cannot submit claims which go beyond those in support of which it makes its intervention, it may support those claims only partly.[202]

(3) Pleas, arguments, and procedural rights

The intervener is at liberty to put forward its own (different) arguments. Indeed, if it were not **25.60** able to do so, intervention would serve no purpose, as the intervener would have to confine itself to repeating the arguments put forward by the party which it supported.[203] Thus, an intervener is not bound to discuss the whole of the argument underlying the application.[204]

However, an intervener is not entitled to raise an objection of inadmissibility not raised by the defendant.[205] The reason for this is that submissions in an application to intervene must be limited to supporting the submissions of one of the parties[206] and that the intervener must accept the case as it finds it at the time of its intervention.[207] This means that the intervener is bound by any acts which have already been carried out in the course of the proceedings and that new arguments adduced by it are admissible only insofar as they do

---

[201] ECJ, Case C-155/91 *Commission v Council* [1993] E.C.R. I-939, paras 22–25; ECJ, Case C-50/08 *Commission v France* [2011] E.C.R. I-4195, paras 26–31; CFI, Joined Cases T-125/96 and T-152/96 *Boehringer v Council and Commission* [1999] E.C.R. II-3427, para. 183; EGC, Case T-237/05 *Éditions Odile Jacob v Commission* [2010] E.C.R. II-2245, para. 37 (not affected by appeal in ECJ (judgment of 28 June 2012), Case C-404/10 P *Commission v Éditions Odile Jacob*, not reported). A party which intervenes on appeal and was not a party to the proceedings before the General Court cannot therefore claim that the annulment pronounced by that Court in the contested judgment should apply equally to it: ECJ, Case C-245/95 P *Commission v NTN Corporation and Koyo Seiko* [1998] E.C.R. I-401, para. 24.

[202] CFI, Case T-171/02 *Regione Autonoma della Sardegna v Commission* [2005] E.C.R. II-2123, para. 93.

[203] ECJ, Case 30/59 *De Gezamenlijke Steenkolenmijnen in Limburg v High Authority* [1961] E.C.R. 1, at 18; ECJ, Case C-248/99 P *France v Monsanto and Commission* (appeal brought by France) [2002] E.C.R. I-1, para. 56; ECJ (judgment of 21 December 2011), Case C-28/09 *Commission v Austria*, not reported, paras 50–53; CFI, Case T-459/93 *Siemens v Commission* [1995] E.C.R. II-1675, paras 21–23; CFI, Case T-37/97 *Forges de Clabecq v Commission* [1999] E.C.R. II-859, para. 93.

[204] ECJ, Case C-156/93 *European Parliament v Commission* [1995] E.C.R. I-2019, para. 15; CFI, Case T-459/93 *Siemens v Commission* [1995] E.C.R. II-1675, paras 21–23.

[205] ECJ, Case C-313/90 *CIRFS and Others v Commission* [1993] E.C.R. I-1125, paras 19–22; ECJ, Case C-225/91 *Matra v Commission* [1993] E.C.R. I-3203, paras 11–12; EGC, Case T-576/08 *Germany v Commission* [2011] E.C.R. II-1578, paras 38–39; cf. ECJ, Joined Cases 42/59 and 49/59 *SNUPAT v High Authority* [1961] E.C.R. 53, at 75 (where an objection of inadmissibility not raised by the defendant was allowed to be raised on the ground that it sought the rejection of the form of order sought by the applicant). The broad wording employed in that judgment was qualified in ECJ, Joined Cases C-305/86 and C-160/87 *Neotype Techmashexport v Commission and Council* [1990] E.C.R. I-2945, para. 18. The Court of Justice left it undecided whether an intervener is entitled to raise a plea of inadmissibility not raised by the party it is supporting because it held that the objection was one based on public policy which the Court could raise of its own motion under Art. 150 of the ECJ Rules of Procedure. In both the *CIRFS* and the *Matra* cases, the Court refused to entertain the possibility that the intervener could raise an objection of inadmissibility, but then considered the plea of its own motion on the grounds that it involved public policy considerations. See also ECJ, Case C-107/99 *Italy v Commission* [2002] E.C.R. I-1091, para. 29; cf. ECJ, Case C-13/00 *Commission v Ireland* [2002] E.C.R. I-2943, paras 3–6, in which in proceedings for failure to fulfil obligations, the United Kingdom submitted that the Court should declare that it had no jurisdiction to rule in the dispute. This was held to be inadmissible, since the defendant Member State, Ireland, accepted that it had failed to fulfil an obligation and had not contested the Court's jurisdiction. See also CFI, Case T-266/94 *Skibsværftsforeningen and Others v Commission* [1996] E.C.R. II-1399, paras 38–39; CFI, Case T-19/92 *Leclerc v Commission* [1996] E.C.R. II-1851, paras 50–51; CFI, Case T-174/95 *Svenska Journalistförbundet v Council* [1998] E.C.R. II-89, paras 77–78. See further CFI, Case T-184/97 *BP Chemicals v Commission* [2000] E.C.R. II-3145, para. 39, in which the then Court of First Instance rejected an objection of inadmissibility raised by France on the grounds that it went further than the form of order sought by the Commission and there was no reason for which the Court should consider of its own motion the admissibility of the application as regards the whole of the contested decision (in fact, the Court held the application to be partially inadmissible).

[206] Statute, Art. 40, fourth para.

[207] ECJ Rules of Procedure, Art. 129(3); EGC Rules of Procedure, Art. 116(3).

not alter the framework of the dispute as defined by the applicant.[208] Consequently, in principle an intervener cannot raise new pleas.[209]

In proceedings for interim relief, in which the urgency of an application for interim measures is assessed in the light of the extent to which they are necessary in order to avoid serious and irreparable damage, the intervener may assert its interests, but cannot widen the subject-matter of the dispute by laying claim to a personal right to interim legal protection.[210]

Finally, the ECJ Rules of Procedure provide that the intervention does not give rise to any right for the interveners to request that a hearing be held.[211]

B. Substantive requirements

(1) Who can intervene?

25.61 Union institutions, Member States, and States that are parties to the EEA Agreement as well as the EFTA Surveillance Authority, insofar as the case falls within the field of application of the EEA Agreement, are entitled to intervene in cases before the Court of Justice or the General Court.[212]

---

[208] ECJ, Case C-195/02 *Commission v Spain* [2004] E.C.R. I-7857, paras 26–32: the arguments of the intervener (in support of the defendant) which differed in part from those put forward by the Spanish Government purported to show that the Commission's application should be dismissed and were therefore admissible; CFI, Joined Cases T-447/93, T-448/93, and T-449/93 *AITEC and Others v Commission* [1995] E.C.R. II-1971, para. 122: the intervener stepped outside the framework of the dispute by contesting that a measure constituted State aid within the meaning of Art. 107 TFEU, whereas the applicant had not questioned its nature as State aid; CFI, Case T-243/94 *British Steel v Commission* [1997] E.C.R. II-1887, paras 70–73: an argument based on the EEA agreement raised by the intervener was held to be inadmissible because the applicant had not alleged that the Agreement had been breached. Consequently, the argument fell outside the framework of the dispute. See also CFI, Joined Cases T-125/96 and T-152/96 *Boehringer v Council and Commission* [1999] E.C.R. II-3427, paras 183–184. Arguments raised by an intervener supporting the form of order sought by the Commission (dismissal of an action for annulment), which would permit a finding that the contested decision is unlawful are inadmissible since consideration by the Court of such arguments would have the effect of altering the framework of the dispute as defined in the application and the defence: CFI, Case T-2/03 *Verein für Konsumenteninformation v Commission* [2005] E.C.R. II-1121, paras 49–53.

[209] CFI, Case T-114/02 *BaByliss v Commission* [2003] E.C.R. II-1279, paras 416–419 (and the case-law cited therein). An intervener may raise new arguments. The distinction between a new argument and a new plea is not always very clear (see ECJ, Case C-185/00 *Commission v Finland* [2003] E.C.R. I-14189, paras 91–92). In later case-law, the then Court of First Instance ruled that the intervener has the right to set out arguments as well as pleas independently. Yet, since the new pleas have to be connected with a plea already raised by the party supported by the intervener, this case-law confirms that only new arguments can be invoked by the intervener. Indeed, the framework of the dispute as defined in the application and the defence cannot be altered by the intervener (CFI, Case T-171/02 *Regione Autonoma della Sardegna v Commission* [2005] E.C.R. II-2123, paras 152–153; EGC, Joined Cases T-394/08, T-408/08, T-453/08, and T-454/08 *Regione autonoma della Sardegna v Commission* [2011] E.C.R. II-6255, para. 42; EGC (judgment of 14 March 2013), Case T-587/08 *Fresh Del Monte Produce v Commission*, not reported, paras 536–538).

[210] ECJ (order of the President of 18 November 1999), Case C-329/99 P (R) *Pfizer Animal Health v Council* [1999] E.C.R. I-8343, paras 93–94. With respect to interventions in interim proceedings, see further CFI (order of the President of 7 July 2004), Case T-37/04 R *Região autónoma dos Açores v Council* [2004] E.C.R. II-2153, para. 59; CFI (order of the President of 26 July 2004), Case T-201/04 R *Microsoft v Commission* [2004] E.C.R. II-2977, para. 32.

[211] ECJ Rules of Procedure, Art. 129(1). At present the EGC Rules of Procedure do not contain a similar provision.

[212] Statute, Art. 40, first and third paras.

The same right is 'open to bodies, offices and agencies of the Union and to any other person establishing an interest in the result of any case submitted to the Court'.[213] The term 'case' refers only to contentious procedures before the Court of Justice or the General Court, designed to settle a dispute. Consequently, an application by a natural or legal person to intervene—pursuant to Art. 40 of the Statute—in order to submit written observations in preliminary ruling proceedings before the Court of Justice will be inadmissible.[214]

The expression 'any other person' covers both natural and legal persons. Entities not formally having legal personality may be given leave to intervene if they have the ability, however circumscribed, to undertake autonomous action and to assume liability. This is because those characteristics constitute the basis for legal personality.[215] Consequently, an entity within the EU framework which takes decisions that have legal effects only within the Union institution of which it constitutes a part has no autonomy vis-à-vis third parties and hence does not possess characteristics such as to entitle it to intervene.[216]

(2) Privileged interveners

Union institutions[217] and Member States[218] are privileged interveners and do not have to establish an interest in the outcome of the case.[219]   **25.62**

(3) Non-Member States

States party to the EEA Agreement, not being Member States of the European Union, and   **25.63** the EFTA Surveillance Authority may intervene in cases before the Court of Justice or the General Court where one of the fields of application of that Agreement is concerned.[220]

---

[213] Statute, Art. 40, second para.

[214] See, e.g. ECJ (order of the President of 26 February 1996), Case C-181/95 *Biogen* [1996] E.C.R. I-717, para. 4; ECJ (order of the President of 30 March 2004), Case C-453/03 *ABNA and Others*, not reported, paras 13–16; ECJ (order of the President of 25 May 2004), Case C-458/03 *Parking Brixen and Others*, not reported, paras 5–8; ECJ (order of the President of 12 September 2007)), Case C-73/07 *Satakunnan Markkinapörssi and Satamedia* [2007] E.C.R. I-7075, paras 8–13 (no right to intervene for the European Data Protection Supervisor); ECJ (order of the President of 16 December 2009), Joined Cases C-403/08 and C-429/08 *Football Association Premier League and Others*, not reported, paras 5–11; ECJ (order of the President of 13 January 2010), Joined Cases C-92/09 and C-93/09 *Volker und Markus Schecke*, not reported, paras 4–9.

[215] ECJ (order of 11 December 1973), Joined Cases 41/73, 43/73 to 48/73, 50/73, 111/73, 113/73, and 114/73 *Générale Sucrière and Others v Commission* [1973] E.C.R. 1465, para. 3.

[216] See, in connection with the staff committee of the European Parliament, ECJ (order of 14 November 1963), Case 15/63 *Lassalle v European Parliament* [1964] E.C.R. 31, at 36, and the Opinion of Advocate-General M. Lagrange, at 52–57.

[217] The European Economic and Social Committee is not an institution and therefore not a privileged intervener (ECJ (order of the President of 17 March 2004), Case C-176/03 *Commission v Council*, not reported, paras 9–10).

[218] Similar to the action for annulment, regional entities cannot be considered to be a Member State for the purposes of Art. 40, first para. of the Statute and must prove an interest in the result of the case in accordance with Art. 40, second para. of the Statute: CFI (order of the President of 14 October 2008), Case T-68/08 *FIFA v Commission*, not reported, para. 10.

[219] ECJ, Case 138/79 *Roquette Frères v Council* [1980] E.C.R. 3333, paras 17–21; ECJ, Case 139/79 *Maizena v Council* [1980] E.C.R. 3393, paras 17–21: if the institutions' right to intervene were to be restricted, it would adversely affect their institutional position.

[220] Statute, Art. 40, third para. See ECJ (order of the President of 15 July 2010), Case C-493/09 *Commission v Portugal*, not reported, para. 9; ECJ (order of the President of 16 April 2012), Case C-239/11 P *Siemens v Commission*, not reported, paras 3–8; CFI, Case T-115/94 *Opel Austria v Council* [1997] E.C.R. II-39, para. 29, and para. 138; CFI, Joined Cases T-371/94 and T-394/94 *British Airways and Others v Commission* [1998]

Conversely, they must establish an interest in the outcome of the case if they want to intervene in a case where none of the fields of application of the EEA Agreement is concerned. Furthermore, they are not allowed to intervene in cases between Member States, between the institutions of the Union, or between Member States and institutions of the Union.[221]

(4) Bodies, offices, and agencies of the Union

25.64 Bodies, offices, and agencies of the Union that can establish an interest in the result of a case submitted to the Union courts[222] or can establish that the intervention falls within the scope of the tasks conferred upon them[223] may intervene. They cannot intervene in cases between Member States, between the institutions of the Union, or between Member States and institutions of the Union, unless a provision of Union law specifically entitles them to intervene in such proceedings.[224]

(5) Non-privileged interveners

25.65 Any other natural or legal person must make out a reasonable case that it has an interest in the result of a case brought before the Court of Justice or the General Court.[225] Furthermore, natural and legal persons are not allowed to intervene in cases between Member States, between Union institutions, or between Member States and Union institutions.[226]

Such an interest will exist if the intervener's legal position or economic situation[227] may actually be directly affected by the operative part of the decision to be taken by

---

E.C.R. II-2405, para. 27; EGC (order of 19 January 2012), Case T-289/11 *Deutsche Bahn and Others v Commission*, not reported, paras 9–12.

[221] Statute, Art. 40, second and third paras; ECJ (order of the President of 1 October 2010), Case C-542/09 *Commission v Netherlands*, not reported, paras 4–8 (and further citations therein).

[222] Statute, Art. 40, second para.

[223] EGC (order of the President of 4 September 2009), Case T-82/09 *Gert-Jan Dennekamp v European Parliament*, not reported, para. 7.

[224] See in this respect Art. 47(1)(i) of Regulation (EC) No. 45/2001 of the European Parliament and of the Council of 18 December 2000 on the protection of individuals with regard to the processing of personal data by the (Union) institutions and bodies and on the free movement of such data ([2001] O.J. L8/1) and ECJ (order of 17 March 2005), Case C-317/04 *European Parliament v Council* [2005] E.C.R. I-2457; ECJ (order of 17 March 2005), Case C-318/04 *European Parliament v Commission* [2005] E.C.R. I-2467 (with respect to the European Data Protection Supervisor who was given leave to intervene). Compare ECJ (order of the President of 17 March 2004), Case C-176/03 *Commission v Council*, not reported: the European Economic and Social Committee was not given leave to intervene.

[225] Statute, Art. 40, second para.

[226] Statute, Art. 40, second para. See, e.g. ECJ (order of the President of 30 January 2008), Case C-393/07 *Italy v European Parliament*, not reported; ECJ (order of the President of 30 June 2010), Case C-40/10 *Commission v Council*, not reported.

[227] CFI (order of 29 May 1997), Case T-89/96 *British Steel v Commission* [1997] E.C.R. II-835, paras 20–21; CFI (order of the President of 11 July 2001), Case T-339/00 *Bactria v Commission*, not reported, paras 12–14, in which the President recognized that a party had an interest in intervening insofar as the decision in the pending case would considerably affect the substantive situation, rules, and procedures on the basis of which it marketed its products. In CFI (order of the President of 26 June 2002), Case T-210/01 *General Electric v Commission*, not reported, paras 28–29, the President recognized that competitors of undertakings which had brought an action against a Commission decision declaring a merger incompatible with the internal market had an interest in intervening in support of the Commission; CFI (order of the President of 9 December 2008), Case T-111/08 *Mastercard v Commission*, not reported, paras 13–14, ruling that a number of banks had an interest in intervening in an action for annulment brought by Mastercard against a Commission decision determining that the so-called 'fallback interchange fees' merchants had to pay to their acquiring bank for accepting payment cards in the EEA was in breach of Art. 101 TFEU, since the loss of the fallback interchange

the Court of Justice or the General Court.[228] The interest can therefore not be assessed in the light of abstract legal arguments that go beyond the specific subject-matter of a case.[229]

In addition, the interest must be safeguarded by the form of order sought by the party in support of whom the intervener seeks to join in the proceedings.[230] It is not sufficient for the intervener to be in a similar situation to one of the parties to the proceedings and for it to maintain on that ground that it has an indirect interest in the grounds of the decision to be given by the Court of Justice or the General Court.[231] A person's interest in one of the pleas raised by a party to the proceedings succeeding or failing is insufficient if the operative part of the decision to be taken by the Court has no bearing on that party's legal position or

---

fee affected them financially. See also CFI (order of the President of 19 October 2009), Case T-422/08 *SACEM v Commission*, not reported, para. 11.

[228] ECJ (order of 4 October 1979), Case 40/79 *P v Commission* [1979] E.C.R. 3299, at 3300; EGC (order of the President of 14 December 2010), Case T-537/08 *Cixi Santai Chemical Fiber and Others v Council*, not reported, paras 16–17. See also CFI (order of 26 March 1992), Case T-35/89 TO 1 *Ascasibar Zubizarreta and Others* [1992] E.C.R. II-1599, paras 32–35, in which an application seeking to initiate third-party proceedings was dismissed as inadmissible because the applicants could have intervened. By the same token, an undertaking which is the subject of a complaint made to the Commission for infringing Art. 102 TFEU has an interest to intervene in proceedings for failure to act (Art. 265 TFEU) brought by the person who made the complaint against the Commission for failing to take any action. This is because the intervener has an interest in the complaint not causing the Commission to take binding measures against it and therefore in the Court of Justice or the General Court not declaring the Commission's failure to act contrary to Union law: CFI (order of 13 May 1993), Case T-74/92 *Ladbroke Racing v Commission* [1993] E.C.R. II-535, paras 8–9. Conversely, an undertaking which has lodged a complaint which has resulted in the Commission's initiating a procedure and adopting a decision finding an infringement of competition law has an interest in the outcome of proceedings brought against the Commission by undertakings to which the decision is addressed. It may therefore intervene in support of the Commission: CFI (order of 28 November 1991), Case T-35/91 *Eurosport v Commission* [1991] E.C.R. II-1359, paras 1–6. Similarly, an undertaking who applied before the national courts for the nullity of a contract on the basis of Art. 101 TFEU has an interest in intervening in a case by which the other party to the contract is challenging a Commission decision finding an infringement of Art. 101 TFEU: ECJ (order of the President of 20 October 2000), Case C 36/09 P *Transportes Evaristo Molina v Commission*, not reported, paras 5–10. The fact that a company had an independent right of action against a decision finding an infringement of Art. 101 TFEU but did not bring the action within the prescribed time limit is irrelevant for the purposes of determining whether that company has established an interest in intervening in the case: EGC (order of 17 February 2010), Case T- 587/08 *Fresh Del Monte Produce v Commission*, not reported, paras 30–31. For examples of the interest required for an individual to intervene in appeal proceedings, see ECJ, Case C-200/92 P *ICI v Commission* [1999] E.C.R. I-4399, para. 25; ECJ, Joined Cases C-172/01 P, C-175/01 P, C-176/01 P, and C-180/01 P *International Power and Others v Commission* [2003] E.C.R. I-11421, paras 49–53; ECJ (order of the President of 5 February 2009), Case C-550/07 P *Akzo Nobel Chemicals and Akros Chemicals v Commission and Others*, not reported, paras 7–15.

[229] ECJ (order of the President of 5 February 2009), Case C-550/07 P *Akzo Nobel Chemicals and Akcros Chemicals v Commission*, not reported, paras 8–9.

[230] ECJ (order of 25 November 1964), Case 111/63 *Lemmerz-Werke v High Authority* [1965] E.C.R. 716, at 717–18; ECJ (order of 12 April 1978), Joined Cases 116/77, 124/77, and 143/77 *Amylum and Others v Council and Commission* [1978] E.C.R. 893, para. 7; ECJ (order of the President of 16 April 2012), Case C-422/11 *Prezes Urzędu Komunikacji Elektronicznej and Poland v Commission*, not reported, para. 7 (and case-law cited therein); EGC (order of the President of 17 February 2010), Case T-587/08 *Fresh Del Monte Produce v Commission*, not reported, para. 25.

[231] ECJ (order of the President of 6 March 2003), Case C-186/02 P *Ramondín and Others v Commission* [2003] E.C.R. I-2415, paras 14–17; ECJ (order of the President of 9 February 2007), Case C-301/05 P *Wilfer v OHIM*, not reported, paras 4–9; CFI (order of 8 December 1993), Case T-87/92 *Kruidvat v Commission* [1993] E.C.R. II-1375, paras 12–13; EGC (order of 16 December 2009), Case T-370/08 *Csepeli Áramtermelő v Commission*, not reported, para. 12.

economic situation.[232] The strict interpretation of the notion 'interest in the result of a case submitted' is motivated by guarding the effectiveness and the proper course of the procedure.[233]

(6) Intervention within the framework of an action for damages

25.66 In the context of an action for damages, while in principle intervention is not precluded, in practice it is difficult for a person in a similar situation to the applicant to show that he or she has a 'direct and continuing' interest. Since the form of order sought by the applicant in such an action is directed only towards obtaining compensation for the damage sustained by it, a would-be intervener does not have a direct interest in the outcome of the application, but at the most an indirect interest in a judgment whose grounds might influence the manner in which the defendant institution(s) would deal with the intervener's own situation. Such an interest is insufficient.[234]

(7) Intervention within the framework of an action for annulment

25.67 A natural or legal person to whom a particular Union measure is addressed—for example, a decision finding an infringement of the Union competition rules under Art. 101 TFEU—has an interest in intervening in annulment proceedings brought by another addressee of the decision.[235] A person having an independent right of action must be considered as having an interest in the result of a case brought by another addressee.[236] The fact that said person did not bring an action for annulment himself does not detract from that.[237]

A competitor of an undertaking which allegedly violated Art. 102 TFEU has an interest in intervening in support of the form of order sought by the Commission.[238] This is because

---

[232] ECJ (order of the President of 17 June 1997), Joined Cases C-151 and C-157/97 P(I) *National Power and PowerGen v British Coal and Commission* [1997] E.C.R. I-3491, para. 57; EGC (order of the President of 17 February 2010), Case T-587/08 *Fresh Del Monte Produce v Commission*, not reported, para. 25 (and case-law cited); ECJ (order of 16 April 2012), Case C-422/11 P *Prezes Urzędu Komunikacji Elektronicznej and Poland v Commission*, not reported, para. 8.

[233] CFI (order of the President of 20 November 2008), Case T-167/08 *Microsoft v Commission*, not reported, para. 66.

[234] See, e.g. CFI (order of the President of 17 July 1995), Case T-517/93 *Van Parijs v Council and Commission*, not reported, paras 8–13; CFI (order of 7 March 1997), Case T-184/95 *Dorsch Consult v Council and Commission* [1997] E.C.R. II-351, paras 15–21. Member States are privileged interveners and can intervene also in the framework of an action for damages: see, e.g. CFI, T-139/01 *Comafrica and Dole Fresh Fruit Europe v Commission* [2005] E.C.R. II-409, compare paras 53 and 54.

[235] ECJ (order of 14 February 1996), Case C-245/95 P *Commission v NTN Corporation* [1996] E.C.R. I-559, para. 9; CFI (order of 28 November 1991), Case T-35/91 *Eurosport v Commission* [1991] E.C.R. II-1359, para. 15; EGC (order of 17 February 2010), Case T-587/08 *Fresh Del Monte Produce v Commission*, not reported, para. 30: the individual may intervene in support of the applicant. His or her interest is not defeated by the fact that he or she did not bring an action to annul the decision. But he or she may only act as intervener, i.e. only support the form of order sought by the applicant.

[236] ECJ (order of 14 February 1996), Case C-245/95 P *Commission v NTN Corporation* [1996] E.C.R. I-559, para. 9; CFI (order of 28 November 1991), Case T-35/91 *Eurosport v Commission* [1991] E.C.R. II-1359, para. 15; EGC (order of 17 February 2010), Case T-587/08 *Fresh Del Monte Produce v Commission*, not reported, para. 30. However, an addressee of a decision regarding the application of Art. 101 TFEU cannot intervene to support the form of order sought by the Commission (CFI (order of 16 December 2004), Case T-410/03 *Hoechst v Commission* [2004] E.C.R. II-4451, paras 13–22).

[237] EGC (order of 17 February 2010), Case T-587/08 *Fresh Del Monte Produce v Commission*, not reported, para. 31.

[238] CFI (order of the President of 26 July 2004), Case T-201/04 R *Microsoft v Commission* [2004] E.C.R. II-2977, para. 91.

such an undertaking has indeed a direct interest that the decision finding an abuse of a dominant position and obliging the addressee of the decision to put an end to the abuse be upheld. Conversely, an undertaking has an interest to intervene in an action for annulment brought by a competitor against a Commission decision rejecting a complaint on the basis of Art. 102 TFEU.[239] In contrast, where the prospective intervener only establishes an interest in the result of the case by reason of similarities between his situation and that of one of the parties in the main proceedings, his application will be dismissed.[240] This will be the case, for instance, where a local authority refers only to the similarity of an aid regime applicable in its region to that applicable in another region in an action for annulment of a Commission decision finding the latter aid regime incompatible with the internal market.[241]

After granting a party leave to intervene, the Court of Justice or the General Court may consider the admissibility of the application afresh if the circumstances warrant this.[242]

(8) Intervention within the framework of interim proceedings

An application for leave to intervene in the framework for interim proceedings should be assessed in relation to the specific interest the applicant has in the outcome of the interim proceedings.[243] A direct interest in the outcome of the main action is thus not sufficient to establish an interest to intervene in interim proceedings.[244] **25.68**

(9) Associations

Associations have the right to intervene if the outcome of the proceedings is liable to affect the collective interest defended by the association in question.[245] The aims pursued by an **25.69**

---

[239] EGC (order of the President of 12 January 2010), Case T-119/09 *Protégé International v Commission*, not reported, para. 8.

[240] CFI (order of 15 June 1993), Joined Cases T-97/92 and T-111/92 *Rijnoudt and Hocken v Commission* [1993] E.C.R. II-587, paras 14–26; CFI (order of 8 December 1993), Case T-87/92 *Kruidvat v Commission* [1993] E.C.R. II-1375, paras 12–13; CFI (order of 18 September 1995), Case T-375/94 *European Passenger Services v Commission*, not reported, paras 20–26; CFI (order of 20 March 1998), Case T-191/96 *CAS Succhi di Frutta v Commission* [1998] E.C.R. II-573, paras 31–32. See also ECJ (order of the President of 23 July 1998), Case C-155/98 P *Alexopoulou v Commission* [1998] E.C.R. I-4935, paras 12–18; ECJ (order of the President of 6 March 2003), Case C-186/02 P *Ramondín and Others v Commission* [2003] E.C.R. I-2415, paras 14–17.

[241] ECJ (order of the President of 6 March 2003), Case C-186/02 P *Ramondín and Others v Commission* [2003] E.C.R. I-2415, paras 14–17. However, where an aid scheme in a region has a direct and present effect on the economic situation of a neighbouring region, either by causing the relocation of some undertakings or by adversely affecting the competitive position of other undertakings, the authorities of the neighbouring region have a direct, present interest in seeing the form of order sought by the Commission granted (ECJ, Case C-186/02 P *Ramondín and Others v Commission*, para. 9).

[242] CFI, Case T-158/96 *Acciaierie di Bolzano v Commission* [1999] E.C.R. II-3927, para. 33.

[243] See, e.g. CFI (order of the President of 26 July 2004), Case T-201/04 R *Microsoft v Commission* [2004] E.C.R. II-2977, para. 33; EGC (order of the President of 11 February 2011), Case T-520/10 R *Comunidad Autónoma de Galicia v Commission* [2011] E.C.R. II-27*, Summ. pub., paras 29–31; EGC (order of the President of 11 March 2013), Case T-462/12 R *Pilkington Group v Commission*, not reported, para. 21. See also para. 13.042.

[244] But see CFI (order of the President of 14 December 2000), Case T-5/00 R *Nederlandse Federatieve Vereniging voor de Groothandel op Elektrotechnisch Gebied v Commission* [2000] E.C.R. II-4121, para. 25, in which it was held that a party which has already been given leave to intervene in support of a party in the main action has in principle an interest in supporting the form of order sought by the latter in interim proceedings. See also EGC (order of the President of 24 January 2011), Case T-533/10 R *DTS Distribuidora de Televisión Digital v Commission*, not reported.

[245] ECJ (order of 24 October 1962), Joined Cases 16/62 and 17/62 *Confédération Nationale des Producteurs de Fruits et Légumes and Others v Council* [1962] E.C.R. 487, at 488–489; ECJ (order of 11 December

association should, however, be sufficiently closely connected to the questions raised in the proceedings in which it seeks to intervene.[246] Thus, an association of undertakings which did not participate in the prior administrative procedure before the Commission for the application of the Union competition rules may be given leave to intervene only if: (1) it represents an appreciable number of the undertakings active in the sector concerned; (2) its objects include that of protecting its members' interests; (3) the case may raise questions of principle affecting the functioning of the sector concerned; and (4) the interests of its members may therefore be affected to an appreciable extent by the forthcoming judgment.[247]

Furthermore, in the area of anti-dumping, an association which has brought the complaint on the basis of which an anti-dumping regulation was adopted and which has actively taken part in the administrative procedure leading to the adoption of the regulation at issue has, in principle, an interest to intervene in an action for annulment brought against that regulation.[248]

In contrast to the case of natural persons applying to intervene, associations therefore do not have to show that their own legal position or economic situation is likely to be affected by the outcome of the case. An association will be regarded as having an interest in intervening if it coincides with that of its members in a context in which the association's intervention will enable the Court of Justice or the General Court better to assess the background to the case.[249] This somewhat more flexible approach with regard to the interest required to be established by an association wishing to intervene makes up to some extent for the strict approach taken to applications by individuals for leave to intervene. However, like individuals, associations are not entitled to intervene in cases between Member States, between

---

1973), Joined Cases 41/73, 43/73 to 48/73, 50/73, 111/73, 113/73, and 114/73 *Générale Sucrière and Others v Commission* [1973] E.C.R. 1465, paras 7–9; ECJ (order of the President of 16 April 2012), Case C-422/11 P *Prezes Urzędu Komunikacji Elektronicznej and Poland v Commission*, not reported, para. 9; CFI (order of 8 December 1993), Case T-87/92 *Kruidvat v Commission* [1993] E.C.R. II-1363, para. 10; CFI (order of 8 December 1993), Case T-87/92 *Kruidvat v Commission* [1993] E.C.R. II-1369, paras 12–14; CFI (order of 18 March 1997), Case T-135/96 *UEAPME v Council* [1997] E.C.R. II-373, para. 9; EGC (order of the President of 18 October 2012), Case T-245/11 *ClientEarth v ECHA*, not reported, para. 12 (and case-law cited therein).

[246] CFI (order of the President of 5 February 2009), Case C-550/07 P *Akzo Nobel Chemicals and Akcros Chemicals v Commission*, not reported, para. 14.

[247] CFI (order of 8 December 1993), Case T-87/92 *Kruidvat v Commission* [1993] E.C.R. II-1375, para. 14; CFI (order of 28 May 1997), Case T-120/96 *Lilly Industries v Commission*, not reported, para. 24; ECJ (order of the President of 28 September 1998), Case C-151/98 P *Pharos v Commission* [1998] E.C.R. I-5441, para. 6; CFI (order of the President of 23 March 1998), Case T-18/97 *Atlantic Container Line and Others v Commission* [1998] E.C.R. II-589, paras 10–19 (no interest in intervening in an action for annulment of a Commission decision withdrawing immunity from fines under then Art. 15(6) of Regulation No. 17); CFI (order of the President of 26 July 2004), Case T-201/04 R *Microsoft v Commission* [2004] E.C.R. II-2977, para. 37; EGC (order of the President of 18 October 2012), Case T-245/11 *ClientEarth v ECHA*, not reported, para. 12.

[248] CFI (order of the President of 16 February 2009), Case T-192/08 *ENRC Marketing v Council*, not reported, para. 12.

[249] In the context of an application for the partial suspension of a Regulation governing, *inter alia*, fishing activities within Azorean waters, the President of the then Court of First Instance gave leave to Porto de Abrigo—a cooperative defending the interests of fishermen active in the Azores—to intervene in the proceedings, but rejected the request of the WWF on the grounds that its interests were too wide and general to be significantly affected by the outcome of the proceedings (CFI (order of the President of 7 July 2004), Case T-37/04 R *Autonomous Region of the Azores v Council* [2004] E.C.R. II-2153, paras 57–71); EGC (order of the President of 14 December 2010), Case T-537/08 *Cixi Santai Chemical Fiber and Others v Council*, not reported, paras 14 and 18. Associations who are themselves members of an umbrella organization have to show a specific interest if they want to be granted a leave to intervene at the same time and to the same effect as the umbrella organization: ECJ (order of the President of 5 February 2009), Case C-550/07 P *Akzo Nobel Chemicals and Akcros Chemicals v Commission*, not reported, para. 13 (order concerning the Law Society of England and Wales).

Union institutions, or between Member States and Union institutions[250] unless a provision of Union law specifically entitles them to intervene in such proceedings.

C. Formal requirements

(1) Time limits and requirements

An application to intervene must be made within six weeks of publication in the *Official* **25.70** *Journal of the European Union* of the notice 'of the date of registration of an application initiating proceedings, the names of the parties, the form of order sought by the applicant and a summary of the pleas in law and of the main supporting arguments'.[251]

Consideration may be given by the Court of Justice or the General Court to an application to intervene which is made after the expiry of this six-week period, but before the decision to open the oral procedure.[252] An application to intervene in support of the defendant may be lodged before the defence is lodged. In that case, the intervener runs the risk of supporting a form of order sought whose content is still unknown to it.[253]

(2) Disputes relating to intellectual property rights

In the case of disputes concerning intellectual property rights in which a decision of the Office **25.71** for Harmonisation in the Internal Market (Trade Marks and Designs) or of the Community Plant Variety Office is brought before the General Court, special rules on intervention apply as regards parties other than the applicant or the defendant Office who were involved in the proceedings before the relevant Board of Appeal. Such parties may take part as interveners in the proceedings before the General Court.[254] They have the same procedural rights as the main parties.[255] In addition, they may, unlike 'ordinary' interveners, apply for a form of order and put forward pleas in law independently of those applied for and put forward by the main parties.[256]

(3) General requirements applicable to pleadings

Applications to intervene have to comply with the general requirements applicable to **25.72** procedural documents.[257] Each application has to contain a description of the case, a description of the parties, the intervener's name and address, the intervener's address for

---

[250] Statute, Art. 40, second para. For an example, see ECJ (order of the President of 30 June 2010), Case C-40/10 *Commission v Council*, not reported, paras 4–5.

[251] ECJ Rules of Procedure, Art. 130(1); EGC Rules of Procedure, Art. 115(1). See also ECJ Rules of Procedure, Art. 21(4); EGC Rules of Procedure, Art. 24(6). For the calculation of time limits, see paras 23.26 *et seq*.

[252] ECJ Rules of Procedure, Art. 129(4) (if the President allows the intervention, the intervener may submit his observations during the hearing, if it takes place); EGC Rules of Procedure, Art. 116(6). Where the six-week period has expired and there is no oral procedure (where, for instance, the case is dispatched by order), the application to intervene will be inadmissible (ECJ (order of the President of 28 June 2004), Case C-445/02 P *Glaverbel v OHIM* [2004] E.C.R. I-6267). While applications made within the six-week period set in motion a mandatory procedure, consideration of applications made after the expiry of that period is a mere possibility: ECJ (order of the President of 17 November 2009), Case C-550/07 P *Akzo Nobel Chemicals and Akcros Chemicals v Commission*, not reported, para. 8.

[253] CFI (order of 11 December 2000), Case T-158/00 *ARD v Commission*, not reported, paras 5–8.

[254] EGC Rules of Procedure, Art.134(1).

[255] EGC Rules of Procedure, Art.134(2), first para.

[256] EGC Rules of Procedure, Art.134(2), second para.

[257] ECJ Rules of Procedure, Art. 130(4); EGC Rules of Procedure, Art. 115(2), second para. They must also be represented: ECJ Rules of Procedure, Art. 130(3); EGC Rules of Procedure, Art. 115(3)).

service—in Luxembourg when intervening in a case before the General Court—the form of order sought in support of which the intervener is applying for leave to intervene and, except in the case of applications made by Member States or Union institutions, a statement of reasons establishing the intervener's interest in the result of the case.[258]

(4) Language

25.73 Applications to intervene are to be lodged in the language of the case (see para. 23.03).[259] Member States, however, are always entitled to use their official language when intervening in a particular case (see para. 23.08).[260]

Under the case-law so far, a request by an intervener (other than a Member State) to use a language other than the language of the case during the oral procedure may be granted.[261]

(5) Application to intervene is served on the parties

25.74 The application to intervene is served on the parties, who are given the opportunity to submit written or oral observations.[262]

(6) Decision on the application to intervene

25.75 Where an application to intervene is submitted to the Court of Justice by a Member State, a Union institution, a State that is a party to the EEA Agreement, or the EFTA Surveillance Authority, the President of the Court of Justice will decide on the intervention by way of a simple decision.[263] The intervention will be allowed, provided that the parties in the case have not put forward observations on the application to intervene or identified secret or confidential items or documents within 10 days after the service of the application to intervene.[264]

In any other case, and before the General Court, the President decides on an application to intervene by order.[265] Alternatively, the President may refer the application to the Court of

---

[258] ECJ Rules of Procedure, Art. 130(2); EGC Rules of Procedure, Art. 115(2).

[259] Art. 7(5), third para., of the Instructions to the Registrar of the General Court provides, however, that where an application to intervene originating from a third party other than a Member State is not drawn up in the language of the case, the Registrar will require the application to be put in order before it is served on the parties. If, however, a version of such an application drawn up in the language of the case is lodged within the period prescribed for this purpose by the Registrar, the date on which the first version, not in the language of the case, was lodged shall be taken as the date on which the document was lodged for the purposes of registration.

[260] ECJ Rules of Procedure, Art. 38(4); EGC Rules of Procedure, Art. 35(3), fourth para.

[261] See, e.g. CFI (order of 12 June 1995), Case T-371/94 *British Airways and Others v Commission*, not reported, para. 13, and CFI (order of 12 June 1995), Case T-394/94 *British Midland Airways v Commission*, not reported, para. 13; CFI (order of 16 August 1995), Case T-290/94 *Kaysersberg v Commission* [1995] E.C.R. II-2247, paras 3–8 (granting the request of the intervener, above the objection of the applicant, for the oral part of the procedure, but rejecting the request for the written part of the procedure); CFI (order of 17 November 1995), Case T-330/94 *Salt Union v Commission* [1995] E.C.R. II-2881, paras 25–28 (emphasizing that the Court takes a flexible approach where the request submitted by the intervener relates only to the oral procedure and no justified objection has been made by the parties); EGC (order of 26 October 2009), Case T-353/08 *vwd Vereinigte Wirtschaftsdienste v Commission*, not reported; EGC (order of 19 January 2012), Case T-289/11 *Deutsche Bahn and Others v Commission*, not reported, paras 15–18 (request from EFTA Authority granted for both written and oral procedures). However, see also para. 23.05.

[262] ECJ Rules of Procedure, Art. 131(1); EGC Rules of Procedure, Art. 116(1).

[263] ECJ Rules of Procedure, Art. 131(2).

[264] ECJ Rules of Procedure, Art. 131(2).

[265] ECJ Rules of Procedure, Art. 131(3); EGC Rules of Procedure, Art. 116(1), third para.

Justice or the General Court, as the case may be, which then decides by order.[266] If the application is rejected, the order will be reasoned.[267] A decision granting leave to intervene does not prevent the Court of Justice or the General Court, as the case may be, from reconsidering the admissibility of the application to intervene in the final judgment and declaring it wholly or partially inadmissible.[268]

(7) Statement in intervention

If the application to intervene is granted, the intervening party may submit a statement in **25.76** intervention. The statement in intervention has to contain a statement of the form of order sought by the intervener, the pleas in law and arguments relied on by the intervener and, where appropriate, the nature of any evidence offered.[269] With a view to expediting the proceedings, the statement should be as short as possible.[270] The intervener receives a copy of every procedural document served on the parties.[271] However, in its observations on an application to intervene, a party may ask the Court of Justice and the General Court to treat certain documents in the case as confidential and not send them to the intervener.[272] An

---

[266] ECJ Rules of Procedure, Art. 131(3); EGC Rules of Procedure, Art. 116(1), third para.

[267] This is specifically prescribed by Art. 116(1), third para., of the EGC Rules of Procedure, since an appeal may lie against the order (see para. 16.12). In fact, all orders concerning applications to intervene are reasoned.

[268] ECJ, Case C-199/92 P *Hüls v Commission* [1999] E.C.R. I-4287, para. 52; ECJ, Case C-200/92 P *ICI v Commission* [1999] E.C.R. I-4399, para. 25; ECJ, Case C-235/92 *Montecatini v Commission* [1999] E.C.R. I-4539, para. 75.

[269] ECJ Rules of Procedure, Art. 132 (2); EGC Rules of Procedure, Art. 116(4).

[270] For the Court of Justice, 10 pages (ECJ Practice Directions, point 29), for the General Court, maximum 20 pages (EGC Practice Directions, point 15).

[271] ECJ Rules of Procedure, Art. 131(2) and (4); EGC Rules of Procedure, Art. 116(2).

[272] ECJ Rules of Procedure, Art. 131(3) and (4); EGC Rules of Procedure, Art. 116(2). To this end, it is necessary for the Court of Justice or the General Court to ascertain, in respect of each document on the Court's file for which confidential treatment is claimed, the extent to which a reconciliation will in fact be effected between the applicant's legitimate concern to prevent substantial damage to its business interests and the interveners' equally legitimate concern to have the necessary information for the purpose of being fully in a position to assert their rights and to state their case before the Court: CFI (order of 4 April 1990), Case T-30/89 *Hilti v Commission* [1990] E.C.R. II-163, para. 11; CFI (order of 29 May 1997), Case T-89/96 *British Steel v Commission* [1997] E.C.R. II-835, para. 23. If documents in the case-file contain confidential information about natural or legal persons who are not parties to the proceedings, such persons have the right, in principle, to have the confidential nature of that information protected unless they have business relations with the intervener or the information is known to third parties: CFI (order of 19 March 1996), Case T-24/93 *CMBT and Others v Commission*, not reported, para. 7. In proceedings for interim relief, it is sufficient for the information for which confidential treatment is sought to appear, at first sight, to comprise business secrets: see CFI (order of the President of 13 May 1993), Case T-24/93 R *CMBI v Commission* [1993] E.C.R. II-543, para. 17; CFI (order of the President of 7 July 1998), Case T-65/98 R *Van den Bergh Foods v Commission* [1998] E.C.R. II-2641, para. 32; CFI (order of the President of 15 July 1998), Case T-73/98 R *Prayon-Rupel v Commission* [1998] E.C.R. II-2769, para. 18. Because the assessment of whether items in the case-file are or are not confidential is relatively onerous, the General Court proceeds as follows. The party claiming confidentiality is asked to put together a non-confidential file. This is communicated to the intervener. If the intervener then contests the confidentiality of certain documents, the General Court will determine by order (of the President of the Chamber concerned) whether or not the contested documents are confidential; see CFI (order of the President of 15 October 2002), Case T-203/01 *Michelin v Commission*, not reported; CFI (order of the President of 4 March 2005), Case T-289/03 *BUPA and Others v Commission*, not reported; CFI (order of the President of 11 May 2009), Case T-354/08 *Diamanthandel A. Spira v Commission*, not reported, paras 12–13; EGC (order of the President of 7 December 2011), Case T-151/11 *Telefónica Móviles España v Commission*, not reported; EGC (order of the President of 10 May 2012), Case T-354/08 *Diamanthandel A. Spira v Commission*, not reported, paras 33–64; EGC (order of the President of 5 October 2012), Case T-258/10 *France Télécom v Commission*, not reported.

application for confidential treatment must accurately identify the particulars or passages to be excluded and briefly state the reasons for which each of those particulars or passages is regarded as confidential. Such an application must be strictly limited to material which is genuinely confidential and may not cover the entirety of a pleading. The application must be accompanied by a non-confidential version of each pleading or document concerned with the confidential material deleted.[273]

If the request for confidential treatment is not granted, the party concerned may ask for certain documents to be removed from the case-file, but that request will not necessarily be granted.[274]

Where an application to intervene is made after the expiry of the period of six weeks after publication of the notice in the *Official Journal*, the intervener may only submit oral observations (if an oral procedure takes place). In proceedings before the General Court, the intervener will prepare its observations on the basis of the report for the hearing. In proceedings before the Court of Justice, the intervener will receive a copy of every document served on the parties.[275]

(8) Reply to the statement in intervention

25.77 Parties may, where this is deemed necessary by the President, reply to the statement in intervention.[276]

(9) Time limits

25.78 A party intervening before the Court of Justice may submit its statement in intervention within one month after the communication to it of all procedural documents served on the parties. On a duly reasoned request, the President of the Court of Justice may extend the time limit.[277] No time limit is specified in the EGC Rules of Procedure. Parties have to submit their statement in intervention within the period prescribed by the President of the General Court.[278]

No time limits have been prescribed for a reply to a statement in intervention. The President of the Court of Justice or of the General Court, as the case may be, will prescribe an appropriate time limit.[279]

---

[273] EGC Practice Directions, point 90.

[274] ECJ (order of 28 March 1979), Case 30/78 *Distillers v Commission*, referred to in the report for the hearing in Case 30/78 *Distillers v Commission* [1980] E.C.R. 2229, at 2237.

[275] ECJ Rules of Procedure, Arts 129(4) and 131(4); EGC Rules of Procedure, Art. 116(6). See CFI, Joined Cases T-142/01 and T-283/01 *OPTUC v Commission* [2004] E.C.R. II-329, para. 24: a statement lodged by the intervener was not joined to the file. This was because the intervener was only allowed to make its observations orally at the hearing. Where there is no hearing (for instance, where a case is dispatched by order), the application to intervene will be inadmissible: ECJ (order of the President of 28 June 2004), Case C-445/02 P *Glaverbel v OHIM* [2004] E.C.R. I-6267. Even if unforeseeable circumstances or *force majeure* prevented the intervener from making its application to intervene within six weeks of the publication in the *Official Journal of the European Union* of the notice of initiation of the action, he will not be allowed to file written submissions (CFI (order of the President of 28 April 2005), Case T-201/04 *Microsoft v Commission* [2005] E.C.R. II-1491, paras 19–20 and 46–47).

[276] ECJ Rules of Procedure, Art. 132(3); EGC Rules of Procedure, Art. 116(5).

[277] ECJ Rules of Procedure, Art. 132(1).

[278] EGC Rules of Procedure, Art. 116(4), first para.

[279] ECJ Rules of Procedure, Art. 132(3); EGC Rules of Procedure, Art. 116(5). See, e.g. ECJ (order of the President of 13 June 2008), Case C-28/08 P *Commission v Bavarian Lager*, not reported, operative part.

III. The Expedited Procedure

A. General

On application by the applicant or the defendant, the President of the Court of Justice **25.79** (after hearing the other party, the Judge-Rapporteur, and the Advocate-General)[280] or the Chamber concerned of the General Court (after hearing the other party and the Advocate-General),[281] may decide that a case is to be determined pursuant to an expedited procedure where the nature of the case requires that it be dealt with within a short time.[282]

B. Separate document

An application for a case to be decided under an expedited procedure must be made by a **25.80** separate document lodged at the same time as the application initiating the proceedings or the defence, as the case may be.[283] The party concerned must briefly state the reasons for the particular urgency of the case.[284] In proceedings before the General Court, the application may state that certain pleas in law or arguments or certain passages of the application initiating the proceedings or the defence are raised only in the event that the case is not decided under an expedited procedure.[285]

C. Importance of the oral part of the procedure

The Court of Justice and the General Court are not bound to accept such an application.[286] **25.81** If the application is accepted, in principle the parties may not lodge a reply or a rejoinder unless the President of the Court of Justice, after hearing the Judge-Rapporteur or the

---

[280] Exceptionally, the President of the Court of Justice may also take such decision of his own motion: ECJ Rules of Procedure, Art. 133(3).

[281] In contrast to the expedited procedure before the Court of Justice, it is the General Court that rules upon the application for an expedited procedure and not the President of the General Court.

[282] ECJ Rules of Procedure, Art. 133(1); EGC Rules of Procedure, Art. 76a(1), first para., which refers to the 'particular urgency and the circumstances of the case'.

[283] ECJ Rules of Procedure, Art. 133(2); EGC Rules of Procedure, Art. 76a(1), first para. The General Court has directed that an application in respect of which the expedited procedure is requested must not in principle exceed a maximum of 25 pages (EGC Practice Directions, point 69).

[284] ECJ Practice Directions, point 17; EGC Practice Directions, point 70.

[285] EGC Rules of Procedure, Art. 76a(1). A similar provision is not set forth in the ECJ Rules of Procedure.

[286] For a case in which such an application was rejected, see ECJ (order of the President of 10 February 2004), Case C-540/03 *European Parliament v Council*, not reported. The Court of Justice considered that this case, in which the annulment was sought of a directive which had to be implemented by the Member States only 22 months following lodgment of the application, was not particularly urgent. The Court further held that the fact that a large number of persons would be affected by the provisions of the directive did not in itself warrant recourse to the expedited procedure. A similar reasoning was used in ECJ (order of the President of 26 February 2010), Case C-40/10 *Commission v Council*, not reported, para. 12. See also ECJ (order of the President of 21 September 2004), Case C-317/04 *European Parliament v Council*, not reported; ECJ (order of the President of 21 September 2004), Case C-318/04 *European Parliament v Commission*, not reported; ECJ (order of the President of 18 July 2007), Case C-193/07 *Commission v Poland*, not reported. Also, a significant economic loss cannot by itself justify recourse to an expedited procedure: ECJ (order of the President of 23 October 2009), Case C-69/09 P *Makhteshim-Agan Holding and Others v Commission*, not reported, para. 10. See also ECJ (order of the President of 14 December 2011), Joined Cases C-478/11 P to C-482/11 P *Gbagbo v Council*, not reported, para. 7.

Advocate-General, or the General Court, as the case may be, considers this to be necessary.[287] The same goes for the statement in intervention.[288]

The key point here is the important role of the oral part of the procedure, in the course of which parties may supplement their arguments and offer evidence (reasons must be given for any delay in tendering it).[289] Thus, this is in contrast to the normal procedure before the Court of Justice, in which there is in principle no oral hearing unless there is a reasoned request made by one of the parties (see para. 23.74).

In practice, where an application for the expedited procedure is accepted, the Court of Justice[290] and the General Court[291] generally reach a final decision within an average period of three to nine months.

IV. Discontinuance, Cases that Do Not Proceed to Judgment, and Preliminary Issues

A. Discontinuance

(1) Amicable settlement of the dispute

25.82   If, before the Court of Justice or the General Court has given its decision, the parties notify the Court in question that they have reached a settlement of their dispute and that they

---

[287] ECJ Rules of Procedure, Art. 134(1); EGC Rules of Procedure, Art. 76a(2). Under an expedited procedure brought before the General Court, the period for lodging the defence is one month. The ECJ Rules of Procedure do not specify a shorter than the usual two-month time limit.

[288] ECJ Rules of Procedure, Art. 134(2); EGC, Rules of Procedure, Art. 76a(2).

[289] ECJ Rules of Procedure, Art. 135(2); EGC, Rules of Procedure, Art. 76a(3).

[290] For some examples before the Court of Justice, see ECJ, Case C-27/04 *Commission v Council* [2004] E.C.R. I-6649, relating to the measures taken by the Council in connection with the excessive budget deficits of two Member States; a decision of the Court of Justice was necessary within the shortest possible period for the purposes of the sound operation of Economic and Monetary Union (see ECJ (order of the President of 13 February 2004), Case C-27/04 *Commission v Council*, not reported). The Court of Justice has further applied the expedited procedure in appeals (ECJ, Case C-39/03 P *Commission v Artegodan* [2003] E.C.R. I-7885) and in references for a preliminary ruling (see ECJ, Case C-189/01 *Jippes and Others* [2001] E.C.R. I-5689; ECJ, Joined Cases C-188/10 and C-189/10 *Melki and Abdeli* [2010] E.C.R. I-5667; ECJ (judgment of 27 November 2012), Case C-370/12 *Pringle*, not reported). The expedited procedure has also been applied in infringement proceedings (ECJ (judgment of 6 November 2012), Case C-286/12 *Commission v Hungary*, not reported). It is not possible to use the expedited procedure in the case of an application for an opinion on the compatibility with the Treaties of an international agreement to be concluded by the Union pursuant to Art. 218(11) TFEU (ECJ (order of the President of 29 April 2004), Opinion 1/04, not reported).

[291] As far as the General Court is concerned, see in particular CFI, Joined Cases T-195/01 and T-207/01 *Gibraltar v Commission* [2002] E.C.R. II-2309; CFI, Case T-211/02 *Tideland Signal v Commission* [2002] E.C.R. II-3781; CFI, Case T-310/01 *Schneider Electric v Commission* [2002] E.C.R. II-4071; CFI, Case T-5/02 *Tetra Laval v Commission* [2002] E.C.R. II-4381; CFI, Case T-114/02 *BaByliss v Commission* [2003] E.C.R. II-1279; CFI, Joined Cases T-346/02 and T-347/02 *Cableuropa and Others v Commission* [2003] E.C.R. II-4251; CFI (order of 10 January 2005), Case T-209/04 *Spain v Commission* [2005] E.C.R. II-29 (in relation to an action for failure to act); CFI, Case T-390/08 *Bank Melli Iran v Council* [2009] E.C.R. II-3967; EGC (judgment of 26 October 2012), Case T-63/12 *Oil Turbo Compressor v Council*, not reported; EGC (judgment of 26 October 2012), Case T-53/12 *CF Sharp Shipping Agencies v Council*, not reported. In the *Solvay Pharmaceuticals* case (CFI (order of the President of 11 April 2003), Case T-392/02 R *Solvay Pharmaceuticals v Council* [2003] E.C.R. II-1825, para. 104), the President of the then Court of First Instance held that the fact that the Court had rejected an application for the expedited procedure did not mean that an application for interim measures would also have to be rejected for want of urgency.

have abandoned their claims, the President orders the case to be removed from the register and gives a decision as to the costs.[292]

Where parties to proceedings for interim measures reach an amicable settlement whereby the applicant declares that it will withdraw its application for interim relief, the Judge hearing the application must of his or her own motion order the application to be removed from the register if the applicant does not honour the undertaking given in the amicable settlement. This is because the amicable settlement is legally binding and, as such, must be enforced by the Judge.[293]

(2) Unilateral discontinuance

The applicant may also discontinue proceedings without the agreement of the opposite **25.83** party.[294] It does so by informing the Court of Justice or the General Court, as the case may be, in writing. In this case, too, the President orders the case to be removed from the register and decides as to the costs.[295]

B. No need to proceed to judgment

(1) Action devoid of purpose

The Court of Justice or the General Court, as the case may be, may decide that there is no need **25.84** to proceed to judgment on the grounds that the action has become devoid of purpose.[296] The respective Court may do so at any time of its own motion on a proposal from the Judge-Rapporteur and after hearing the parties and the Advocate-General, by way of reasoned order.[297] If the respective Court makes a finding to this effect, this closes the proceedings.[298]

---

[292] ECJ Rules of Procedure, Art. 147; EGC Rules of Procedure, Art. 98, first para. Those provisions do not apply to proceedings under Arts 263 and 265 TFEU. The decision on costs is taken in accordance with Art. 141 of the ECJ Rules of Procedure or Art. 87(5) of the EGC Rules of Procedure, as the case may be.

[293] CFI (order of the President of 12 August 1998), Case T-42/98 R *Sabbatucci v European Parliament* [1998] E.C.R. II-3043, para. 30.

[294] ECJ Rules of Procedure, Art. 148; EGC Rules of Procedure, Art. 99. The defendant cannot object to the other party's discontinuing the proceedings: see ECJ (order of the President of 19 March 1996), Case C-120/94 *Commission v Greece* [1996] E.C.R. I-1513, paras 10–13. The applicant may also partly discontinue proceedings: ECJ, Case C-331/94 *Commission v Greece* [1996] E.C.R. I-2675, paras 5–6; ECJ, Case C-503/04 *Commission v Germany* [2007] E.C.R. I-6153, para. 12; ECJ, Case C-188/08 *Commission v Ireland* [2009] E.C.R. I-172*, Summ. pub., para. 86.

[295] Again, the decision on costs is taken in accordance with Art. 141 of the ECJ Rules of Procedure or Art. 87(5) of the EGC Rules of Procedure, as the case may be.

[296] ECJ Rules of Procedure, Art. 149; EGC Rules of Procedure, Art. 113. This can also be done by way of judgment, see ECJ (judgment of 19 November 2013), Case C-66/12 *Council v Commission*, not reported.

[297] ECJ Rules of Procedure, Art. 149; EGC Rules of Procedure, Art. 113.

[298] For examples, see ECJ, Case 377/87 *European Parliament v Council* [1988] E.C.R. 4017, paras 10–12; ECJ (order of the President of 18 May 2011), Case C-337/09 P-R *Council v Zhejiang Xinan Chemical Industrial Group*, not reported, paras 39–49 (with respect to interim measures); CFI, Case T-140/89 *Della Pietra v Commission* [1990] E.C.R. II-717; EGC, Case T-411/09 *Terezakis v Commission* [2011] E.C.R. II-1, para. 21 (act against which the action for annulment was brought repealed: no need to adjudicate); EGC (order of 21 September 2011), Case T-141/05 RENV *Internationaler Hilfsfonds v Commission* [2011] E.C.R. II-6495, para. 23 (the referral by the Court of Justice of a case back to the General Court cannot derogate from the principle that the General Court can rule on a request for an order that there is no need to adjudicate which concerns an absolute bar to proceedings, such as a lack of interest in bringing proceedings). Where the applicant dies and his or her successors do not take over the proceedings, the application becomes to no purpose: CFI (order of 6 December 1999),

Where the Court decides that there is no need to give judgment in an action which has ceased to have any purpose, it is not necessary for it to examine the admissibility of that action.[299]

(2) Absolute bar to proceeding with a case

25.85 The Court of Justice and the General Court may also decide at any time, of its own motion, after hearing the parties (and the Advocate-General in the case of the Court of Justice) to rule by reasoned order on whether there exists any absolute bar to proceeding with a case.[300]

C. Preliminary issues

(1) General

25.86 A party may make an application to the Court of Justice or the General Court, as the case may be, under Art. 151 of the ECJ Rules of Procedure or Art. 114 of the EGC Rules of Procedure, respectively, for a decision on a preliminary objection or other preliminary issue which relates to the course of the proceedings but does not go to the substance of the case.

This possibility is frequently used by the defence in order to raise an objection of inadmissibility or lack of jurisdiction (see para. 25.41), but any other application may also be made, such as a request by a party for measures of inquiry,[301] for documents to be

---

Case T-81/98 *Boyes v Commission* [1999] E.C.R. II-3501, paras 3–9. Exceptionally, proceedings can become to no purpose as a result of the passiveness of the applicant, in particular where he or she repeatedly fails to lodge certain procedural documents: see, e.g. CFI (order of 1 March 2004), Case T-210/99 *Gankema v Commission* [2004] E.C.R. II-781; CFI (order of 26 May 2004), Case T-165/02 *Lloris Maeso v Commission*, not reported; EGC (judgment of 24 April 2012), Case T-166/10 *Samskip Multimodal Container Logistics v Commission*, not reported; EGC (order of 27 September 2010), Case T-365/08 *Hidalgo v OHIM*, not reported; EGC (order of 9 September 2010), Case T-365/08 *Phoenix-Reisen v OHIM*, not reported; EGC (order of 16 December 2010), Case T-164/09 *Kitou v ECDP*, not reported.

[299] ECJ, Joined Cases C-15/91 and C-108/91 *Buckl and Others v Commission* [1992] E.C.R. I-6061, paras 14–17; ECJ (order of 10 June 1993), Case C-41/92 *Liberal Democrats v European Parliament* [1993] E.C.R. I-3153, para. 4; ECJ, Joined Cases C-302/99 P and C-308/99 P *Commission and France v TF1* [2001] E.C.R. I-5603, para. 28; EGC (order of 8 April 2011), Case T-291/10 *Martin v Commission*, not reported, para. 23. But see CFI (order of 22 May 2000), Case T-103/99 *Associazione delle Cantine Sociali Venete v European Ombudsman and European Parliament* [2000] E.C.R. II-4165, para. 41, in which the then Court of First Instance held that it can rule on whether the application is to no purpose only after it has determined that the application is admissible.

[300] ECJ Rules of Procedure, Art. 150; EGC Rules of Procedure, Art. 113. See, e.g. ECJ, Case C-298/00 P *Italy v Commission* [2004] E.C.R. I-4087, para. 35 (examination *ex officio* by the Court of Justice of the question whether the applicant was individually concerned by the contested measure); CFI, Joined Cases T-142/01 and T-283/01 *OPTUC v Commission* [2004] E.C.R. II-329, para. 30 (examination *ex officio* by General Court of the expiration of the time limit for bringing an action); CFI, Case T-27/02 *Kronofrance v Commission* [2004] E.C.R. II-4177, para. 30 (examination *ex officio* by the General Court of the question whether the applicant was individually concerned by the contested measure); CFI, Case T-29/02 *GEF v Commission* [2005] E.C.R. II-835, para. 72 (examination *ex officio* by the General Court of its jurisdiction to hear the case); CFI, Joined Cases T-228/00, T-229/00, T-242/00, T-243/00, T-245/00 to T-248/00, T-250/00, T-252/00, T-256/00 to T-259/00, T-265/00, T-267/00, T-268/00, T-271/00, T-274/00 to T-276/00, T-281/00, T-287/00 to T-296/00 *Gruppo ormeggiatori del porto di Venezia and Others v Commission* [2005] E.C.R. II-787, paras 38–40 (*exceptio lis pendens* examined *ex officio* by the General Court). See also para. 7-217.

[301] See, e.g. ECJ (order of 2 June 1960), Joined Cases 33/59, 46/59, and 47/59 *Compagnie des Hauts Fourneaux de Chasse and Others v High Authority*, not reported; ECJ (order of 20 June 1960), Joined Cases 24/58

excluded from the proceedings[302] or to be treated as confidential,[303] a request that the Court concerned declare that there is no need to proceed to judgment (see para. 25.84), or a request to remedy alleged procedural defects.[304]

(2) Separate document

The application for a decision on a preliminary objection or issue 'not going to the substance of the case' must be made by separate document[305] and state the pleas of law and arguments relied on, together with the form of order sought, and any supporting documents must be annexed to it.[306]   **25.87**

As soon as the application has been lodged, the President prescribes a period during which the opposite party may lodge a document containing its pleas and the form of order sought.[307] The remainder of the proceedings is oral, unless the Court of Justice or the General Court, as the case may be, decides to reach its determination on the basis of the documents submitted by the parties. The Court, after hearing the Advocate-General, will decide on the application by order or reserve its decision for the final judgment.[308] If the Court refuses the application or reserves its decision, the President will prescribe new time limits for the further steps in the proceedings.[309]

---

and 34/58 *Chambre Syndicale de la Sidérurgie de l'Est de la France v High Authority*, not reported; CFI (order of the President of 27 July 2004), Case T-148/04 R *TQ3 Travel Solutions Belgium v Commission* [2004] E.C. R. II-3027, paras 60–63; EGC, Case T-481/08 *Alisei v Commission* [2010] E.C.R. II-117, paras 32, 33, and 104; EGC, Case T-346/10 *Borax Europe v ECHA* [2011] E.C.R. II-6629, paras 49–51.

[302] ECJ (order of 10 March 1966), Case 28/65 *Fonzi v Commission* [1966] E.C.R. 506, at 507; CFI, Case T-62/99 *Sodima v Commission* [2001] E.C.R. II-655, paras 22–25, where the Commission successfully applied to the then Court of First Instance to have an internal document accidentally communicated to a third party in another case removed from the file. See also ECJ (order of 30 September 2004), Case C-36/04 *Spain v Council*, not reported; CFI, Joined Cases T-228/99 and T-233/99 *Westdeutsche Landesbank Girozentrale v Commission* [2003] E.C.R. II-435, paras 90–91; EGC (order of 19 March 2013), Case T-331/11 *Besselink v Commission*, not reported.

[303] See, e.g. ECJ (order of 20 March 1985), Case 260/84 *Minebea v Council*, not reported; ECJ (order of the President of 17 August 2010), Case C-458/09 P *Italy v Commission*, not reported; CFI (order of 4 April 1990), Case T-30/89 *Hilti v Commission* [1990] E.C.R. II-163; CFI (order of 15 November 1990), Joined Cases T-1/89 to T-4/89 and T-6/89 to T-15/89 *Rhône-Poulenc and Others v Commission* [1990] E.C.R. II-637; CFI (order of the President of 11 June 2007), Case T-266/02 *Deutsche Post v Commission*, not reported; EGC (order of the President of 8 May 2012), Case T-108/07 *Spira v Commission*, not reported.

[304] CFI (order of 14 December 1992), Case T-47/92 *Lenz v Commission* [1992] E.C.R. II-2523.

[305] As such, however, not every plea of inadmissibility must be raised by a separate document. The lodging of a separate document is required only if the party submitting it applies for a decision on admissibility 'not going to the substance of the case': ECJ, Case C-401/09 P *Evropaïki Dynamiki v ECB* [2011] E.C.R. I-4911, paras 43–46; EGC (judgment of 22 May 2012), Case T-17/09 *Evropaïki Dynamiki v Commission*, not reported, para. 33. Therefore, it is not required that a plea only seeking the partial inadmissibility of an action was raised formally: EGC (judgment of 10 October 2012), Case T-172/09 *Gem-Year Industrial and Zhejiang v Council*, not reported, para. 20.

[306] ECJ Rules of Procedure, Art. 151(1) and (2); EGC Rules of Procedure, Art. 114(1).

[307] ECJ Rules of Procedure, Art. 151(3); EGC Rules of Procedure, Art. 114(2).

[308] ECJ Rules of Procedure, Art. 151(5) (which specifies that the Court shall decide 'as soon as possible' and that it shall reserve its decision until it rules on the substance of the case 'where special circumstances so justify'); EGC Rules of Procedure, Art. 114(4), first para.

[309] ECJ Rules of Procedure, Art. 151(6); EGC Rules of Procedure, Art. 114(4), second para.

V. The Closure of Proceedings

A. The judgment or order

25.88 The decision of the Court of Justice or of the General Court which brings the proceedings to an end takes the form of a judgment or order (see generally, paras 23.85–23.92).

Occasionally, however, a judgment is given which determines only some of the issues. Examples are a judgment merely declaring the action admissible[310] or one finding the Union liable, but not making any determination of the amount of damages to be paid.[311]

B. Costs

(1) Decision in the judgment or order

25.89 The order for costs is contained in the final judgment or order which closes the proceedings.[312]

(2) What costs are recoverable?

(a) Proceedings are free of charge

25.90 Proceedings before the Court of Justice or the General Court are free of charge. Exceptionally, a party may be ordered to refund avoidable costs which it has caused the Court of Justice or the General Court to incur, or to pay for, in respect of excessive copying or translation work carried out at the party's request.[313]

(b) Recoverable costs

25.91 Recoverable costs are sums payable to witnesses and experts and expenses necessarily incurred by the parties for the purposes of the proceedings, in particular travel and subsistence expenses, the remuneration of agents, advisers, or lawyers,[314] and office costs.[315]

The costs must have been caused by bringing the proceedings before the Union courts. This means that costs incurred during the pre-litigation stage of a staff case or during the administrative investigation into a purported infringement of competition law are not

---

[310] ECJ, Case C-70/88 *European Parliament v Council* [1990] E.C.R. I-2041, operative part. Exceptionally, the action may be declared partly inadmissible: see EGC (judgment of 6 June 2013), Case T-279/11 *T & L Sugars and Sidul Açúcares v Commission*, not reported, operative part.

[311] ECJ, Case C-152/88 *Sofrimport v Commission* [1990] E.C.R. I-2477, operative part; ECJ, Case C-440/07 P *Commission v Schneider Electric* [2009] E.C.R. I-6413, operative part (as well as order of 9 June 2010 in the same case [2010] E.C.R. I-73*, Summ. pub.); EGC, Joined Cases T-8/95 and T-9/95 *Pelle and Konrad v Council and Commission* [2007] E.C.R. II-4117, operative part.

[312] ECJ Rules of Procedure, Art. 137; EGC Rules of Procedure, Art. 87(1).

[313] ECJ Rules of Procedure, Art. 143; EGC Rules of Procedure, Art. 90.

[314] ECJ Rules of Procedure, Art. 144; EGC Rules of Procedure, Art. 91.

[315] ECJ (order of 6 January 2004), Case C-104/89 DEP *Mulder and Others v Council and Commission* [2004] E.C.R. I-1, para. 70 (the office costs were set at a flat rate of 50 per cent of the fees).

recoverable, since they are not related to the judicial proceedings.[316] Similarly, costs incurred in submitting complaints to the European Ombudsman before instituting proceedings before the Union courts are not recoverable.[317] The expense of paying a litigation insurance premium is not considered to be an indispensable expense unless in exceptional circumstances the party concerned can prove that it would not have been able to bring its action without such an insurance policy.[318] In intellectual property cases, costs necessarily incurred by the parties for the purposes of the proceedings before the Board of Appeal and costs incurred for the purposes of the production of translations of pleadings or other documents into the language of the case[319] are regarded as recoverable costs.[320]

All costs incurred for the purposes of the judicial proceedings, including the costs of any interlocutory proceedings, may be recoverable on condition, of course, that they were necessary.[321] Fees relating to the period after the oral procedure (such as lawyers' fees for considering the Advocate-General's Opinion) cannot be regarded in principle as being necessary costs incurred in connection with the proceedings.[322] The same goes for fees relating to a long period of inactivity before the oral hearing.[323]

---

[316] ECJ (order of 21 October 1970), Case 75/69 *Hake v Commission* [1970] E.C.R. 901, para. 1; ECJ (order of 30 November 1994), Case C-294/90 DEP *British Aerospace v Commission* [1994] E.C.R. I-5423, para. 12; CFI (order of 11 July 2005), Case T-294/04 *Internationaler Hilfsfonds v Commission* [2005] E.C.R. II-2719, paras 50–55; confirmed on appeal in ECJ, Case C-331/05 P *Internationaler Hilfsfonds v Commission* [2007] E.C.R. I-5475, paras 25–27). A party cannot, by way of an action for damages, seek to recover costs which are in principle not recoverable: see CFI, Case T-48/05 *Franchet and Byk v Commission* [2008] E.C.R. II-1585, para. 414 (and citations therein); CFI (order of 27 August 2009), Case T-367/08 *Abouchar v Commission* [2009] E.C.R. II-128*, Summ. pub., para. 42; EGC (order of 6 July 2010), Case T-401/09 *Marcuccio v Court of Justice*, not reported, para. 31 (appeal dismissed in ECJ (order of 14 April 2011), Case C-460/10 P).

[317] ECJ, Case C-331/05 P *Internationaler Hilfsfonds v Commission* [2007] E.C.R. I-5475, paras 25–27.

[318] CFI (order of 27 November 2000), Case T-78/99 (92) *Elder v Commission* [2000] E.C.R. II-3717, paras 17–18.

[319] Pursuant to EGC Rules of Procedure, Art. 131(4), second para.

[320] EGC Rules of Procedure, Art. 136(2). For examples, see CFI, Case T-32/00 *Messe München v OHIM* [2000] E.C.R. II-3829, paras 10–12; CFI, Case T-135/99 *Taurus-Film v OHIM* [2001] E.C.R. II-379, para. 36; CFI, Case T-136/99 *Taurus-Film v OHIM* [2001] E.C.R. II-397, para. 35; CFI, Case T-34/00 *Eurocool Logistik v OHIM* [2002] E.C.R. II-683, paras 54–56; CFI (order of 15 December 2004), Case T-129/01 DEP *Alejandro v OHIM*, not reported, paras 7–20; EGC (judgment of 17 July 2012), Case T-240/11 *L'Oréal v OHIM*, not reported, paras 11–19. See also para. 20.08.

[321] CFI (order of 17 September 1998), Case T-271/94 (92) *Branco v Commission* [1998] E.C.R. II-3761, paras 15–25.

[322] ECJ (order of 10 September 2009), Case C-204/07 P-DEP *C.A.S. v Commission* [2009] E.C.R. I-140*, Summ. pub., para. 25; EGC (order of 2 December 2010), Case T-270/06 DEP *Lego Juris v OHIM*, not reported, para. 57. See further ECJ (order of 6 January 2004), Case C-104/89 DEP *Mulder and Others v Council and Commission* [2004] E.C.R. I-1, paras 48–50: fees relating to negotiations conducted by the parties in order to establish the amount of damages payable by agreement where the Court of Justice itself expressly called upon the parties in the operative part of an interlocutory judgment to inform it of the amount of such damages within a specific period dating from the date of delivery of the judgment may not be excluded from the category of necessary costs. Where, in the interests of procedural economy, the Court of Justice itself does not rule on the amounts due but calls on the parties to reach agreement on them, the successful party would be placed at a disadvantage if the recovery of the costs incurred because of those negotiations was not taken into account.

[323] ECJ (order of 10 September 2009), Case C-204/07 P-DEP *C.A.S. v Commission* [2009] E.C.R. I-140*, Summ. pub., para. 24; CFI (order of 2 June 2009), Case T-47/03 DEP *Sison v Council* [2009] E.C.R. II-1483, para. 52; EGC (order of 3 September 2010), Case T-455/05 DEP *Componenta v Commission*, not reported, para. 44.

The salaries of officials who represent a Union institution before the Court of Justice or the General Court do not constitute recoverable costs, since a salary is by law paid, not as a fee for representing the institution, but for the purposes of fulfilling an obligation imposed on the institution concerned by the Staff Regulations. However, the travel and subsistence expenses of such officials are recoverable, as is the fee payable to a practitioner assisting the institution.[324]

(c) Disputes about the amount of the recoverable costs

25.92 Under the ECJ Rules of Procedure, the party concerned may bring a dispute about the amount of recoverable costs before the smallest Chamber to which the Judge-Rapporteur who dealt with the case is assigned.[325] The EGC Rules of Procedure do not contain a similar rule, but disputes about the amount of the recoverable costs will generally be decided by the Chamber that initially dealt with the case. The Chamber decides by order against which no appeal will lie, after hearing the opposite party.[326]

Such an application for the taxation of costs is admissible only if it genuinely relates to a dispute about the amount of recoverable costs.[327] As far as the costs of the proceedings for the taxation of costs are concerned, the Court of Justice and the General Court do not take a separate decision thereon. The reason for this is that, in determining the recoverable costs, the Union courts take account of all the circumstances of the case up to the time of their decision on the taxation of costs.[328] As the right to recover costs has its basis in the order of the Court of Justice or the General Court fixing the amount recoverable, interest thereon is payable only from the date of that order.[329]

---

[324] EGC (order of 3 May 2012), Case T-264/07 DEP *CSL Behring v Commission and EMA*, not reported, paras 15–16.

[325] ECJ Rules of Procedure, Art. 145(1).

[326] ECJ Rules of Procedure, Art. 145(1) and (2); in the Court of Justice, the Advocate-General is also heard; EGC Rules of Procedure, Art. 92(1). If the parties cannot agree on the amount of the recoverable costs, the interested party must bring the dispute before the Court of Justice or the General Court, as the case may be. A party cannot enforce the payment of such costs by offsetting in the event that the other party refuses to pay them: CFI, Case T-214/00 *X v Commission* [2001] E.C.R.-SC I-A-143, II-663, paras 28–41.

[327] EGC (order of 24 October 2012), Case T-227/12 *Saobraćajni institute CIP v Commission*, not reported, para. 20. The application becomes devoid of purpose when it concerns only the costs of the (initial) procedure before the General Court in the event that the Court of Justice annuls the judgment of the General Court and refers the case back to the General Court. In such case, the General Court will have to take in its final judgment a new decision with respect to the costs taking into account the proceedings both before the General Court and the Court of Justice: see CFI (order of 7 December 2004), Case T-237/00 DEP *Reynolds v European Parliament*, not reported, paras 10–17.

[328] ECJ (order of 6 January 2004), Case C-104/89 DEP *Mulder and Others v Council and Commission* [2004] E.C.R. I-1, para. 87; CFI (order of 15 September 2004), Case T-178/98 DEP *Fresh Marine v Commission* [2004] E.C.R. II-3127, para. 43; CFI (order of 20 December 2004), Case T-123/00 DEP *Thomae v Commission*, not reported, para. 37; ECJ (order of 4 February 2004), Case C-77/99 DEP *Commission v Oder-Plan Architektur and Others* [2004] E.C.R. I-1267, paras 24 and 25 (the recoverable costs relating to the taxation were estimated at 400 euro); EGC (order of 9 February 2011), Case T-429/08 DEP *Millers v OHIM*, not reported, para. 53; EGC (order of 14 May 2013), Case T-298/10 DEP *Gross v OHIM*, not reported, para. 38.

[329] ECJ (order of 18 April 1975), Case 6/72 *Europemballage and Continental Can v Commission* [1975] E.C.R. 495, para. 5; ECJ (order of 6 January 2004), Case C-104/89 DEP *Mulder and Others v Council and Commission* [2004] E.C.R. I-1, para. 86; CFI (order of 9 June 1993), Case T-78/89 DEP *PPG Industries Glass v Commission* [1993] E.C.R. II-573, paras 25–29; EGC (order of 3 May 2011), Case T-239/08 DEP *Comtec Translations v Commission*, not reported, paras 39–40.

An application for an order for costs to be reviewed is not considered a dispute about the amount of recoverable costs and thus is inadmissible.[330]

(d) Disputes over legal fees

If the dispute relates to the amount of a lawyer's fees, the Court of Justice or the General **25.93** Court, as the case may be, does not rule on whether the fees were appropriate, but only on the extent to which they are recoverable.[331] In the absence of provisions of Union law relating to tariffs or to the necessary working time of lawyers, the Court makes an assessment of the costs on a case-by-case basis.[332] In so doing, it takes account of the subject-matter and the character of the proceedings,[333] the importance of the dispute from the point of view of Union law, the volume of work involved for the lawyer,[334] and the economic importance of the case for the parties concerned.[335]

---

[330] CFI (order of 15 July 1993), Joined Cases T-33/89 and T-74/89 DEP *Blackman v European Parliament* [1993] E.C.R. II-837, paras 5–6.

[331] ECJ (order of 16 May 2013), Case C-498/07 P-DEP *Deoleo v Aceites del Sur—Coosur*, not reported, para. 30; CFI (order of 28 November 1996), Case T-447/93 DEP *AITEC v Commission* [1996] E.C.R. II-1631, para. 19; CFI (order of 7 March 2000), Case T-2/95 (92) *Industries des Poudres Sphériques v Council* [2000] E.C.R. II-463, para. 34.

[332] ECJ, Joined Cases C-12/03 P-DEP and C-13/03 P-DEP *Tetra Laval v Commission* [2010] E.C.R. I-67*, Summ. pub., para. 44.

[333] Whether a case raises questions already raised in other cases may have a bearing on this: see CFI (order of 11 July 1995), Cases T-23/90 (92) and T-9/92 (92) *Peugeot v Commission* [1995] E.C.R. II-2057, para. 30; CFI (order of 13 December 1995), Case T-138/95 (92) *Engelking v Council and Commission*, not reported, para. 14; CFI (order of 15 September 2004), Case T-178/98 DEP *Fresh Marine v Commission* [2004] E.C.R. II-3127, paras 33–34; CFI (order of 19 March 2009), Joined Cases T-333/04 DEP and T-334/04 DEP *House of Donuts International v OHIM*, not reported, para. 21; EGC (order of 2 December 2010), Case T-270/06 DEP *Lego Juris v OHIM*, not reported, para. 40.

[334] The Court will look at the nature of the documents submitted, the length of those documents, whether a hearing has taken place, whether the facts were disputed, whether the legal issues were complex, etc. See EGC (order of 25 November 2010), Case T-139/07 DEP *Pioneer Hi-Bred International v Commission*, not reported, para. 37; EGC (order of 9 February 2011), Case T-429/08 DEP *Grain Millers v OHIM*, not reported, para. 43; EGC (order of 28 February 2011), Case T-35/07 DEP *Leche Celta v OHIM*, not reported, para. 26. Further to this, the Court will assess whether the hours declared in relation to certain tasks, such as the study or drafting of documents, does not appear to be excessive. For instance, in CFI (order of 6 October 2009), Case T-95/06 DEP *Federación de Cooperativas Agrarias de la Comunidad Valenciana v CPVO*, not reported, paras 53–61, the Court held that the declaration of 30 working hours for an oral hearing of three hours was excessive, just as was the nine working hours declared for the study of a reply containing 24 pages. As regards costs incurred by an intervener, see ECJ (order of 7 June 2012), Case C-451/10 P-DEP *France Télévisions v TF1*, not reported, para. 26; CFI (order of 24 January 2005), Joined Cases T-346/02 and T-347/02 DEP *Cableuropa and Others v Commission*, not reported, paras 28 and 32.

[335] ECJ (order of 21 October 1970), Case 75/69 *Hake v Commission* [1970] E.C.R. 901, para. 2; ECJ (order of 26 November 1985), Case 318/82 *Leeuwarder Papierwarenfabriek v Commission* [1985] E.C.R. 3727, para. 3; ECJ (order of 6 January 2004), Case C-104/89 DEP *Mulder and Others v Council and Commission* [2004] E.C.R. I-1, para. 51; CFI (order of 25 February 1992), Joined Cases T-18/89 and T-24/89 *Tagaras v Court of Justice* [1992] E.C.R. II-153, para. 13; CFI (order of 9 June 1993), Case T-78/89 DEP *PPG Industries Glass v Commission* [1993] E.C.R. II-573, para. 36; CFI (order of 5 July 1993), Case T-84/91 DEP *Meskens v European Parliament* [1993] E.C.R. II-757, para. 13. An applicant has a very significant financial interest in proceedings brought against a measure freezing the funds of the applicant: EGC (order of 20 November 2012), Case T-121/09 DEP *Al Shanfari v Council and Commission*, not reported, paras 20–21. Regarding fines in the field of competition law, it was held that the economic importance of an action contesting a decision of the Commission imposing a fine on an undertaking was rather limited, since the fine only corresponded to a small percentage of the turnover (*in casu* 1.8 per cent) of the undertaking concerned and was only a fraction (i.e. less than one-fifth) of the maximum fine that could have been imposed: EGC (order of 14 January 2013), Case T-25/10 DEP *BASF v Commission*, not reported, para. 31. Conversely, an action brought against a fine corresponding to 60 per cent of the profits of an undertaking was deemed to be of

In general, the fees for one lawyer will be accepted as being recoverable costs.[336] In complex cases, however, the fees of more than one lawyer will only be recoverable within reasonable limits,[337] taking into account the number of hours' work objectively necessary for the purposes of the proceedings concerned and not the number of lawyers working on the case.[338] Coordination costs for the joint preparation of the pleadings will not be recoverable if not asked for by the Court.[339]

The Union courts are not bound by national scales of lawyers' fees[340] or by any agreement concluded by the applicant with its lawyer.[341] Particularly in the context of proceedings under the EU competition rules, where the contested Commission decision is largely based on economic considerations, the involvement of one or more economic advisers or experts

---

considerable economic interest to the applicant: ECG (order of 13 June 2012), Case T-40/06 DEP *Trioplast Industrier v Commission*, not reported, para. 43.

[336] EGC (order of the President of 22 October 2010), Case T-306/10 AJ *Yusef v Commission*, not reported, para. 15 (and case-law cited therein). The Court requires a detailed statement of costs broken down according to the work carried out: EGC (order of 9 February 2011), Case T-429/08 DEP *Grain Millers v OHIM*, not reported, paras 45–46. Failure to provide a detailed statement will lead the Court to adopt a strict approach in assessing the costs applied for: EGC (order of 23 March 2012), Case T-266/08 P-DEP *Kerstens v Commission*, not reported, paras 24–25.

[337] ECJ (order of 6 January 2004), Case C-104/89 DEP *Mulder and Others v Council and Commission* [2004] E.C.R. I-1, para. 62; ECJ (order of 3 September 2009), Case C-326/05 P-DEP *Industrias Químicas del Vallés v Commission* [2009] E.C.R. I-133*, Summ. pub., para. 47; ECJ (order of 16 May 2013), Case C-498/07 P-DEP *Deoleo v Aceites del Sur—Coosur*, not reported, para. 27; CFI (order of 8 November 1996), Case T-120/89 (92) *Stahlwerke Peine-Salzgitter v Commission* [1996] E.C.R. II-1547, para. 31; CFI (order of 28 November 1996), Case T-447/93 DEP *AITEC v Commission* [1996] E.C.R. II-1631, para. 23; CFI (order of 30 October 1998), Case T-290/94 (92) *Kaysersberg v Commission* [1998] E.C.R. II-4105, para. 20 (this order also gives an insight into the recovery of costs by an intervener). As far as the involvement of a barrister and a solicitor in proceedings before the General Court are concerned, see CFI (order of 28 June 2004), Case T-342/99 DEP *Airtours v Commission* [2004] E.C.R. II-1785, paras 40–53. The VAT paid by a VAT taxable person on lawyers' and experts' fees cannot be regarded as a cost (in view of the possibility to deduct VAT) and is therefore not recoverable (CFI (order of 28 June 2004), Case T-342/99 DEP *Airtours v Commission* [2004] E.C.R. II-1785, para. 79). See, in contrast, CFI (order of 8 July 2004), Joined Cases T-7/98 and T-208/98 DEP and T-109/99 DEP *De Nicola v EIB* [2004] E.C.R.-SC II-973, para. 37, as regards non-VAT-taxable persons. An appeal procedure will normally not justify the recourse to more than one counsel. This is because an appeal is limited to points of law (ECJ (order of 8 July 2004), Case C-286/95 P-DEP *ICI v Commission* [2004] E.C.R. I-6469, para. 26).

[338] ECJ, Joined Cases C-12/03 P-DEP and C-13/03 P-DEP *Tetra Laval v Commission* [2010] E.C.R. I-67*, Summ. pub., para. 56.

[339] CFI (order of 29 October 2004), Case T-77/02 DEP *Schneider Electric v Commission*, not reported, para. 61; CFI (order of 12 December 2008), Case T-417/05 DEP *Endesa v Commission*, not reported, para. 47.

[340] ECJ (order of 16 May 2013), Case C-498/07 P-DEP *Deoleo v Aceites del Sur—Coosur*, not reported, para. 31; CFI (order of 20 January 1995), Case T-124/93 *Werner v Commission* [1995] E.C.R. II-91, para. 10; CFI (order of 5 June 1996), Case T-228/94 (92) *Rusp v Council and Commission*, not reported, para. 11; CFI (order of 8 November 2001), Case T-65/96 DEP *Kish Glass v Commission* [2001] E.C.R. II-3261, para. 19. A rate of 210 euro per hour was deemed to be acceptable and recoverable in CFI (order of 20 December 2004), Case T-123/00 DEP *Thomae v Commission*, not reported, para. 37.

[341] CFI (order of 7 December 2000), Case T-77/95 DEP *Ufex and Others v Commission*, not reported, para. 29. In a merger case, an hourly rate of 400 euro was held to be recoverable: CFI (order of 29 October 2004), Case T-77/02 DEP *Schneider Electric v Commission*, not reported, para. 62; EGC (order of 14 May 2013), Case T-298/10 DEP *Arrieta D. Gross v OHIM*, not reported, para. 25 (an hourly rate of 297 euros in a trademark case was recoverable). Remuneration at a high hourly rate is appropriate only for the services of professionals who are capable of working efficiently and rapidly, the *quid pro quo* being that, in such a case, an assessment must be made—which must be rigorous—of the total number of hours of work necessary for the purposes of the proceedings concerned: see EGC (order of 22 March 2010), Case T-93/06 DEP *Mülhens v OHIM*, not reported, para. 22 (and the case-law cited therein).

may sometimes prove necessary and entail recoverable costs in proceedings before the General Court.[342]

(3) Who has to pay the costs?

(a) Principle

In principle, the Court of Justice or the General Court orders the unsuccessful party to pay **25.94** the costs if they have been applied for in the successful party's pleadings.[343] Thus, this highlights the importance of including such a request in the pleadings of the parties. It is possible to apply for costs for the first time at the stage of the oral procedure.[344]

(b) Other possibilities

An order may be made that the costs be shared or that the parties bear their own costs where **25.95** each party succeeds on some and fails on other heads or where the Court so decides on specific grounds[345] or for reasons of equity.[346]

In addition, Art. 136(1) of the EGC Rules of Procedure provides that where an action against a decision of a Board of Appeal is successful, the General Court may order the Office to bear only its own costs. In such a case, the General Court may order the intervener to pay the applicant's costs.

---

[342] CFI (order of 28 June 2004), Case T-342/99 DEP *Airtours v Commission* [2004] E.C.R. II-1785, paras 55–61; CFI (order of 29 October 2004), Case T-77/02 DEP *Schneider Electric v Commission*, not reported, para. 69; EGC (order of 31 March 2011), Joined Cases T-5/02 DEP and T-80/02 DEP *Tetra Laval v Commission*, not reported, para. 83.

[343] ECJ Rules of Procedure, Art. 138(1); EGC Rules of Procedure, Art. 87(2). See ECJ, Joined Cases 23/63 to 24/63 and 52/63 *Usines Emile Henricot and Others v High Authority* [1963] E.C.R. 217, at 225; ECJ, Joined Cases 188/80 to 190/80 *France and Others v Commission* [1982] E.C.R. 2545, para. 39. But see ECJ, Joined Cases 40/73 to 48/73, 50/73, 54/73 to 56/73, 111/73, 113/73, and 114/73 *Suiker Unie and Others v Commission* [1975] E.C.R. 1663, para. 627. An application that the other party be ordered to pay the costs must be made without ambiguity: see, e.g. CFI, Case T-277/03 *Vlachaki v Commission* [2005] E.C.R.-SC II-243, para. 97.

[344] CFI, Case T-64/89 *Automec v Commission* [1990] E.C.R. II 367, para. 79; CFI, Case T-13/92 *Moat v Commission* [1993] E.C.R. II-287, para. 50; CFI, Case T-423/04 *Bunker & BKR v OHIM* [2005] E.C.R. II-4035, para. 84. See, however, ECJ, Case 298/83 *CICCE v Commission* [1985] E.C.R. 1105, para. 32, where costs were claimed in the rejoinder, and this was considered to be too late and therefore the claim was inadmissible. This shows a tolerance of the Union courts vis-à-vis private parties. In *CICCE*, the private party lost its case and would therefore have had to pay the costs. In *Moat*, the individual was successful, and his claim was not regarded as having been made too late.

[345] ECJ Rules of Procedure, Art. 138(3); EGC Rules of Procedure, Art. 87(3), first para. For examples, see CFI, Case T-38/96 *Guérin Automobiles v Commission* [1997] E.C.R. II-1223, paras 48–50; CFI, Joined Cases T-191/98, T-212/98 to T-214/98 *Atlantic Container Line and Others v Commission* [2003] E.C.R. II-3275, paras 1645–7 (the application was too voluminous; by their conduct the applicants substantially added to the burden of dealing with the case, thus needlessly adding in particular to the costs of the defendant); EGC (order of 21 October 2011), Case T-335/09 *Groupement Adriano, Jaime Ribeiro, Conduril v Commission* [2011] E.C.R. II-7345, paras 37–38 (the Commission did not use clear and unequivocal language in drafting the debit note, which gave rise to the impression in the applicant's mind that the debit note concerned was a reviewable act within the meaning of Art. 263 TFEU).

[346] At present, under Art. 97(4) of the EGC Rules of Procedure, a determination of the costs can only be made on grounds of equity where a recipient of legal aid has been unsuccessful. Art. 97(4) provides: 'Where the recipient of [legal] aid is unsuccessful, the General Court may, in its decision, as to costs, closing the proceedings, if equity so requires, order that one or more parties should bear their own costs or that those costs should be borne, in whole or in part, by the cashier of the General Court by way of legal aid.' See also CST Rules of Procedure, Art. 87(2).

(c) Unreasonable or vexatious procedure

25.96 The successful party may be ordered to pay costs which the Court considers it to have unreasonably or vexatiously caused the other party to bear.[347] Thus, where within the framework of infringement proceedings, the defendant Member State fails to provide all the relevant information to the Commission in the pre-litigation procedure, the Court of Justice will order the Member State to bear (part of) the costs. This is because in such circumstances, it cannot be held against the Commission that it brought an infringement action before the Court of Justice, even though the action is ill-founded.[348]

The fact that the successful party has raised a number of unsuccessful arguments cannot lead to the conclusion that it has caused vexatious costs. This does not mean, however, that any argument can be made. A successful party will be ordered to pay the costs if it has deliberately raised 'worthless' arguments.[349] Furthermore, an institution may be ordered to pay the costs of the opposite party where the dispute is attributable in part to the conduct of that institution.[350]

(d) Staff cases

25.97 The Civil Service Tribunal rules on the costs. Subject to the specific provisions of the Rules of Procedure, the unsuccessful party will be ordered to pay the costs.[351] However, if equity so requires, the Tribunal may decide that an unsuccessful party is to pay only part of the costs, or even that he is not to be ordered to pay any.[352] Where there are several unsuccessful parties, the Tribunal will decide how the costs are to be shared.[353] Even a successful party may be ordered to bear the costs if he or she has made the other party incur unreasonable or vexatious costs.[354] Thus, where the representative of the servant does not appear at the oral hearing without any notice, the servant will have to support the cost incurred of the defendant institution as a result of its attending the hearing.[355]

---

[347] ECJ Rules of Procedure, Art. 139; EGC Rules of Procedure, Art. 87(3), second para. For examples, see ECJ, Joined Cases 35/62 and 16/63 *Leroy v High Authority* [1963] E.C.R. 197, at 208; ECJ, Joined Cases 23/63, 24/63, and 52/63 and 52/63 *Usines Emile Henricot and Others v High Authority* [1963] E.C.R. 217, at 225; ECJ, Case 148/79 *Korter v Council* [1981] E.C.R. 615, paras 19–20; ECJ, Case 263/81 *List v Commission* [1983] E.C.R. 103, paras 30–31; CFI, Case T-311/00 *British American Tobacco v Commission* [2002] E.C.R. II-2781, paras 62–67; CFI, Case T-40/01 *Scan Office Design v Commission* [2002] E.C.R. II-5043, paras 123–125; CFI (order of 11 July 2005), Case T-294/04 *Internationaler Hilfsfonds v Commission* [2005] E.C.R. II-2719, para. 53; CFI (order of the President of 5 September 2008), Case T-466/07 *Osram v Council*, not reported, para. 8.

[348] ECJ, Case C-456/03 *Commission v Italy* [2005] E.C.R. I-5335, paras 110–115.

[349] CFI (order of 9 November 2009), Case T-45/01 DEP *Sanders v Commission* [2009] E.C.R. II-4093, para. 20.

[350] EGC (judgment of 19 April 2012), Case T-49/09 *Evropaïki Dynamiki v Commission*, not reported, paras 135–136; EGC (judgment of 10 October 2012), Case T-247/09 *Evropaïki Dynamiki v Commission*, not reported, paras 183–184. The same applies to other bodies of the European Union: EGC (judgment of 10 October 2012), Case T-247/09 *Evropaiki Dynamiki v Commission*, not reported, para. 184; EGC (order of 16 December 2010), Case T-164/09 *Kitou v European Data Protection Supervisor*, not reported, paras 25–26.

[351] Statute, Annex I, Art. 7(5); CST Rules of Procedure, Art. 87(1).

[352] CST Rules of Procedure, Art. 87(2).

[353] CST Rules of Procedure, Art. 89(1).

[354] CST Rules of Procedure, Art. 88. For an example prior to the creation of the CST, see CFI, Case T-203/03 *Rasmussen v Commission* [2005] E.C.R.-SC II-1287, paras 88–89.

[355] CFI, Joined Cases T-120/01 and T-300/01 *De Nicola v EIB* [2004] E.C.R.-SC II-1671, para. 331; CFI, Case T-398/03 *Castets v Commission* [2005] E.C.R.-SC II-507, paras 39–40.

(e) Interveners

As interveners, Member States, institutions, EEA States, and the EFTA Supervisory **25.98**
Authority bear their own costs.[356] Other interveners may also be ordered to bear their
own costs, even if they intervened in support of the successful party.[357] Generally, however,
an intervener which intervened in support of the successful party will recover its costs from
the unsuccessful party.[358] An intervener which supported the form of order sought by the
unsuccessful party may be ordered to pay the costs together with that party. In particular,
the Court of Justice and the General Court may allow the successful party to recover the
costs it incurred as a result of the intervention of the intervener.[359]

(f) Proceedings which are discontinued

If a party discontinues or withdraws from proceedings (see paras 25.82–25.83), that party will **25.99**
be ordered to pay the costs if they have been applied for in the other party's observations on the
discontinuance or withdrawal.[360] Depending on the circumstances of the withdrawal, such
costs may also constitute vexatious costs.[361] However, the party discontinuing or withdrawing
from proceedings may apply for an order for costs against the other party if this appears justified
by that party's conduct.[362] Where the parties have come to an agreement on costs, the decision
on costs will be in accordance with that agreement. If costs are not claimed, the parties bear their
own costs.[363]

(g) Action becomes devoid of purpose

Where a case does not proceed to judgment, the costs are at the discretion of the Court of **25.100**
Justice or the General Court, as the case may be.[364]

[356] ECJ Rules of Procedure, Art. 140(1) and (2); EGC Rules of Procedure, Art. 87(4), first and second paras.
[357] ECJ Rules of Procedure, Art. 140(3); EGC Rules of Procedure, Art. 87(4), third para.
[358] CFI, Case T-2/93 *Air France v Commission* [1994] E.C.R. II-323, para. 106; EGC (order of
2 December 2010), Case T-270/06 DEP *Lego Juris v OHIM*, not reported, para. 62.
[359] See, e.g. ECJ, Case 113/77 *NTN Toyo Bearing v Council* [1979] E.C.R. 1185, para. 31; ECJ, Case 118/
77 *ISO v Council* [1979] E.C.R. 1277, para. 62; ECJ, Case 119/77 *Nippon Seiko v Council and Commission*
[1979] E.C.R. 1303, para. 38; ECJ, Case 120/77 *Koyo Seiko v Council and Commission* [1979] E.C.R. 1337,
para. 63; ECJ, Case 121/77 *Nachi Fujikoshi v Council* [1979] E.C.R. 1363, para. 29; EGC, Case T-427/08
CEAHR v Commission [2010] E.C.R. II-5865, para. 180; EGC, Case T-250/08 *Batchelor v Commission*
[2011] E.C.R. II-2551, para. 98.
[360] ECJ Rules of Procedure, Art. 141(1); EGC Rules of Procedure, Art. 87(5), first para.
[361] CFI (order of the President of 5 September 2008), Case T-466/07 *Osram v Council*, not reported,
para. 8.
[362] ECJ Rules of Procedure, Art. 141(2); EGC Rules of Procedure, Art. 87(5), first para. Where the
Commission discontinues proceedings for failure to fulfil obligations because the Member State has brought
the infringement to an end, it will normally claim that the Member State concerned be ordered to pay the
costs. For examples, see ECJ (order of 11 July 2000), Case C-271/99 *Commission v Belgium*, not reported,
para. 4; ECJ (order of 21 October 2003), Case C-80/03 *Commission v Netherlands*, not reported, paras 3–4.
Where the Commission withdraws the decision of which the annulment is sought, the action pursuant to Art.
263 TFEU becomes devoid of purpose; in that case, the Commission will have to bear the costs (CFI (order of
2 September 2004), Case T-291/02 *González y Diéz v Commission*, not reported, paras 17–23).
[363] ECJ Rules of Procedure, Art. 141(3) and (4); EGC Rules of Procedure, Art. 87(5), second and third
paras. For examples, see CFI (order of 16 October 1995), Case T-561/93 *Tiercé Ladbroke v Commission*
[1995] E.C.R. II-2755, paras 12–21; CFI (order of 22 October 1996), Case T-19/96 *Carvel and Guardian
Newspapers v Council* [1996] E.C.R. II-1519, paras 22–33; EGC (order of the President of 20 September
2012), Case T-116/12 *Tioxide Europe and Others v Council*, not reported, para. 4; EGC (order of the President
of 14 June 2013), Case T-13/13 *MasterCard International v OHIM*, not reported, para. 3.
[364] ECJ Rules of Procedure, Art. 142; EGC Rules of Procedure, Art. 87(6). See, e.g. ECJ (order of 18 September
2012), Case C-588/11 P *Omnicare v OHIM*, not reported, paras 14–17; ECJ (judgment of 19 November 2013),

C. Legal aid

(1) General

25.101 A party who is wholly or in part unable to meet the costs of the proceedings may at any time apply for legal aid.[365] The application, which need not be made through a lawyer,[366] has to be accompanied by evidence of the applicant's need of assistance, in particular by a document from the competent authority under national law certifying his or her lack of means.[367] Before the General Court, only natural persons qualify at present for legal aid.[368]

(2) Application may be made prior to proceedings

25.102 An application for legal aid may be made prior to proceedings which the applicant wishes to commence. If such an application is made, it must briefly state the subject of the proceedings.[369] The introduction of an application for legal aid suspends the period prescribed for the bringing of the action until the date of notification of the decision of the Court with respect to the legal aid.[370]

(3) Decision of the Court

25.103 Orders of the General Court relating to legal aid are not amenable to appeal.[371] If the application for legal aid is refused, the order will state the reasons for such refusal.[372] If circumstances alter during the proceedings, the Court may at any time, either of its own

---

Case C-66/12 *Council v Commission*, not reported, paras 23–25; CFI, Case T-56/92 *Koelman v Commission* [1993] E.C.R. II-1267, paras 29–32; EGC (order of 9 June 2010), Case T-293/08 *BASF Plant Science and Others v Commission*, not reported, para. 14; EGC (order of 14 July 2010), Case T-165/10 *Grupo Osborne v OHIM*, not reported, para. 4; EGC (order of 30 June 2011), Case T-4/10 *Al Saadi v Commission*, not reported, paras 12–13; EGC (order of 19 February 2013), Case T-418/12 *Beninca v Commission*, not reported, paras 21–22.

[365] Taking into account the allocation of jurisdiction between the Union courts, it should be pointed out that legal aid in direct actions is only relevant in proceedings before the General Court and the Civil Service Tribunal. This explains why there are no provisions on legal aid included in the specific title on direct actions in the ECJ Rules of Procedure, as compared to that concerning preliminary ruling proceedings (see para. 24.27) and appeals (see para. 26.10). See further ECJ Supplementary Rules, Arts 4–5 and Annex II.

[366] An application for legal aid may be made without the assistance of a lawyer not only before proceedings have been brought, but also after the application has been lodged by a lawyer: see EGC Rules of Procedure, Art. 95(1). See also CFI (order of 19 February 1997), Case T-157/96 *Affatato v Commission* [1997] E.C.R. II-155, at II-157-II-159.

[367] EGC Rules of Procedure, Art. 95(2) (a legal aid application form is available on the website of the Court of Justice and should be used to this effect). See, e.g. ECJ (order of 16 November 2004), Case C-374/03 AJ *Gürol*, not reported: legal aid was granted to a party with a monthly income of 700 euros; EGC (order of the President of 18 August 2010), Case T-101/09 AJ *Maftah v Council and Commission*, not reported (with respect to restrictive measures); CST (order of the President of 1 December 2006), Case F-101/06 AJ *Atanasov v Commission*, not reported, paras 12–18 (application dismissed, since it did not comply with the conditions of the Rules of Procedure).

[368] EGC Rules of Procedure, Art. 94(2). See, e.g. CFI, Case T-316/07 *Commercy v OHIM* [2009] E.C.R. II-43, paras 17–30 (also rejecting an attempt to treat the receiver of the company concerned in insolvent proceedings as a natural person entitled to legal aid). See also CST Rules of Procedure, Art. 95(2), first para. (referring to '[a]ny natural person'). Compare ECJ Rules of Procedure, Art. 115(1) (preliminary ruling proceedings) and Art. 185(1) (appeals), both of which allows 'a party' to make such request. Recently, the practice of the Union courts with respect to legal aid was highlighted in the context of preliminary ruling proceedings involving national law treating applications for legal aid by legal persons more strictly than those submitted by natural persons: see ECJ, Case C-279/09 *DEB* [2010] E.C.R. I-13849; and particularly, the accompanying Opinion of Advocate-General P. Mengozzi, points 72–75.

[369] EGC Rules of Procedure, Art. 95(2), second para.

[370] EGC Rules of Procedure, Art. 96(4).

[371] EGC Rules of Procedure, Art. 96(6).

[372] EGC Rules of Procedure, Art. 96(2), second para.

motion or on application, withdraw legal aid.[373] In the General Court, the President decides whether legal aid should be granted.[374]

(4) Legal aid is granted

If legal aid is granted, the cashier of the General Court advances the necessary funds. An **25.104** order granting legal aid may specify an amount to be paid to the lawyer appointed to act for the person concerned or fix a limit which the lawyer's fees and disbursements may not, in principle, exceed.[375] Subsequently, the Court may recover these costs from the opposite party if a costs order is made against it.[376]

(5) Necessity

The principal reason why legal aid must be available is that individuals must invariably be **25.105** represented before the General Court by a lawyer. In the event that they were unable to pay lawyer's fees, they would have no access to the Union courts.[377] This is why the budget of the Court of Justice of the European Union contains an item covering legal aid.

D. Requests and applications relating to judgments and orders

(1) General

There are certain exceptional procedures set down in the Statute and the Rules of Procedure **25.106** of the Union courts relating to judgments and orders, namely third-party proceedings against a judgment or order and the revision, interpretation, and rectification[378] of a judgment or order.[379] As such, these procedures must be distinguished from the review procedure set forth Arts 256(2) and (3) TFEU by which decisions of the General Court

---

[373] EGC Rules of Procedure, Art. 96(5).
[374] EGC Rules of Procedure, Art. 96(2), first para. Under the current Rules of Procedure, the President may refer the matter to the General Court.
[375] EGC Rules of Procedure, Art. 96(3).
[376] EGC Rules of Procedure, Art. 97. CFI, Case T-11/00 *Hautem v EIB* [2000] E.C.R.-SC II-4019, I-A-283, II-1295, para. 60; EGC, Joined Cases T-135/06 to T-138/06 *Al-Faqih and Others v Council* [2010] E.C.R. II-208*, Summ. pub., para. 49. Under normal circumstances, legal aid does not cover the expenses of the other party. Since the risk for the impecunious party of having to bear the other party's costs in the event that he or she loses the case may in itself constitute an impediment to access to justice, Art. 97(4) of the EGC Rules of Procedure provides: 'Where the recipient of the aid is unsuccessful, the General Court may, in its decision as to costs, closing the proceedings, if equity so requires, order that one or more parties should bear their own costs or that those costs should be borne, in whole or in part, by the cashier of the General Court by way of legal aid.'
[377] However, an application for legal aid made by the defendant at the moment the General Court had already decided to give judgment under the default procedure without opening the oral procedure does not serve any purpose and will be dismissed: see EGC, Case T-464/09 *Commission v New Acoustic Music Association and Hildibrandsdottir* [2011] E.C.R. II-133*, Summ. pub., paras 72–75. Indeed, as a rule legal aid must be restricted to covering the costs of proceedings incurred either at the same time as, or after, the making of the application: see EGC (order of the President of 28 April 2009), Case T-320/07 AJ *Jones v Commission*, not reported, para. 10.
[378] The rectification of a judgment or order can concern clerical errors (ECJ Rules of Procedure, Art. 154; EGC Rules of Procedure, Art. 84), as well as a failure of the Court to adjudicate on a specific head of claim or on costs (ECJ Rules of Procedure, Art. 155; EGC Rules of Procedure, Art. 85 which only refers to an omission to give a decision on costs).
[379] They also include applications to set aside a default judgment: see paras 25.32 *et seq.*

may be subject to review by the Court of Justice where there is a serious risk of the unity or consistency of Union law being affected (see Ch. 17).[380]

(2) Third-party proceedings

(a) Subject-matter

25.107 Judgments or orders of the Court of Justice or the General Court, as the case may be, may be prejudicial to the rights of third parties. Notwithstanding the force of *res judicata*, third parties are therefore entitled in exceptional circumstances to contest such decisions.[381]

Art. 42 of the Statute refers only to 'judgments', but as elaborated further in Art. 157 of the ECJ Rules of Procedure[382] third-party proceedings may pertain to judgments or orders of the Court concerned (as for the distinction between the two, see paras 23.85–23.86).

(b) Substantive requirements and time limits

(i) Third parties

25.108 Third-party proceedings may be brought by Member States, Union institutions, bodies, offices, and agencies, and any other natural or legal persons 'to contest a judgment rendered without their being heard, where the judgment is prejudicial to their rights'.[383]

Consequently, an application to bring third-party proceedings on the part of an intervener will be inadmissible. Third-party proceedings instituted by interested third parties who did not have good reasons for failing to intervene in the original proceedings will also be inadmissible.[384]

The notice published in the *Official Journal of the European Union* setting out the subject-matter of the proceedings, the form of order sought, and the pleas in law and main supporting arguments[385] is specifically intended to enable third parties to intervene in proceedings whose outcome may be prejudicial to their rights. Only diligent third parties who were unable to become aware on the basis of that notice that their rights might be affected can claim that they were not put on notice and thus an application to bring third-party proceedings by such a party will be admissible.[386] The duty of care is assessed in the

---

[380] See CFI (order of 31 July 2009), Case T-213/08 REV *Marinova v Université Libre de Bruxelles and Commission*, not reported, para. 34 (and cited case-law therein) in which the Court underlined that this review procedure should be distinguished from applications for revision of a judgment, which constitutes 'an exceptional review procedure that allows an applicant to call in question the authority of *res judicata* attaching to a judgment bringing the proceedings to an end on the basis of the findings of fact relied upon by the Court' and 'presupposes the discovery of elements of a factual nature which existed prior to the judgment and which were unknown at that time to the court which delivered it as well as to the party applying for revision and which, had the court been able to take them into consideration, could have led it to a different determination of the proceedings'.

[381] See, e.g. CFI (order of 17 September 2009), Case T-284/08 TO *Avaessian Avaki and Others v People's Mojahedin Organization of Iran and Others*, not reported, para. 14.

[382] At present, Art. 123 of the EGC Rules of Procedure only refers to judgments. See also CST Rules of Procedure, Art. 117 which uses the term 'decision'.

[383] Statute, Art. 42.

[384] ECJ, Joined Cases 42/59 and 49/59 Third-party proceedings *Breedband v Société des Aciéries du Temple and Others* [1962] E.C.R. 145, paras 2–3; CFI (order of 17 September 2009), Case T-284/08 TO *Avaessian Avaki and Others v People's Mojahedin Organization of Iran and Others*, not reported, para 15.

[385] ECJ Rules of Procedure, Art. 21(4); EGC Rules of Procedure, Art. 24(6).

[386] ECJ, Joined Cases 9/60 and 12/60 Third-party proceedings *Belgium v Vloeberghs and High Authority* [1962] E.C.R. 171, at 182.

light of the circumstances of the case and with due concern not to detract unnecessarily from the authority as *res judicata* of the contested decision in the interests of legal certainty. The bar is therefore set very high. Accordingly, a decision on the part of an interested third party not to intervene in the original proceedings does not satisfy the duty of care where that decision was based on the party's own assessment of the probable outcome of the case in light of the information as to the facts and law known by such party at the time the action was started. This is because further facts may emerge in the course of the proceedings to influence the outcome of the dispute. Moreover, it is not unforeseeable that the Union courts may depart from settled case-law in the proceedings.[387]

(ii) Third parties which could have taken part in the main proceedings
Third-party proceedings may be brought only by parties who could have taken part—at least in theory— in the main proceedings. For example, since natural or legal persons are not entitled to intervene in proceedings brought under Arts 258–260 TFEU, they may not bring third-party proceedings against a judgment closing such proceedings.[388] **25.109**

(iii) Contested decision must be prejudicial to the rights of the third party
The contested decision must be prejudicial to the rights of the third party. It is not enough that the third party has a legitimate interest to protect.[389] The prejudice to the third party's rights must ensue from the operative part or the grounds of the judgment or order itself.[390] The alleged prejudice may be material or non-material.[391] **25.110**

(iv) Time limits
Third-party proceedings must be brought within two months of publication of the contested decision in the *Official Journal of the European Union*.[392] **25.111**

(v) Third-party proceedings and appeal
Where an appeal before the Court of Justice and an application initiating third-party proceedings before the General Court contest the same decision of the latter Court, the General Court may, after hearing the parties, stay proceedings until the Court of Justice has delivered its ruling.[393] However, the Court of Justice may defer hearing the appeal pursuant **25.112**

---

[387] CFI (order of 26 March 1992), Case T-35/89 TO 1 *Ascasibar Zubizarreta and Others v Albani* [1992] E.C.R. II-1599, paras 33–35; CFI (order of 17 September 2009), Case T-284/08 TO *Avaessian Avaki and Others v People's Mojahedin Organization of Iran and Others*, not reported, para. 17.

[388] ECJ (order of the President of 6 December 1989), Case C-147/86 TO 1 *POIFXG and Others v Greece and Commission* [1989] E.C.R. 4103, paras 11–12; ECJ (order of the President of 6 December 1989), Case C-147/86 TO 2 *PALSO and Others v Greece and Commission* [1989] E.C.R. 4111, paras 11–12; ECJ (order of the President of 6 December 1989), Case C-147/86 TO 3 *PSIITENSM v Greece and Commission* [1989] E.C.R. 4119, paras 11–12.

[389] ECJ Rules of Procedure, Art. 157(1)(b); EGC Rules of Procedure, Art. 123(1)(b). See, e.g. ECJ (order of 22 September 1987), Case 292/84 TO *Bolognese and Others v Scharf and Commission* [1987] E.C.R. 3563, para. 7; CFI (order of 17 September 2009), Case T-284/08 TO *Avaessian Avaki and Others v People's Mojahedin Organization of Iran and Others*, not reported, para. 23.

[390] ECJ, Joined Cases 9/60 and 12/60 Third-party proceedings *Belgium v Vloeberghs and High Authority* [1962] E.C.R. 171, at 183–4; ECJ, Case 267/80 TO *Dreher v Riseria Modenese, Council, and Commission* [1986] E.C.R. 3901, paras 9–10; CFI (order of 17 September 2009), Case T-284/08 TO *Avaessian Avaki and Others v People's Mojahedin Organization of Iran and Others*, not reported, para. 24.

[391] ECJ, Joined Cases 9/60 and 12/60 Third-party proceedings *Belgium v Vloeberghs and High Authority* [1962] E.C.R. 171, at 183–4, and the Opinion of Advocate-General K. Roemer, at 190; CFI (order of 17 September 2009), Case T-284/08 TO *Avaessian Avaki and Others v People's Mojahedin Organization of Iran and Others*, not reported, paras 19, 25–26.

[392] ECJ Rules of Procedure, Art. 157(3); EGC Rules of Procedure, Art. 123(1), third para. On the calculation of time limits, see paras 23.26 *et seq.*

[393] EGC Rules of Procedure, Art. 123(4).

to Art. 54 of the Statute until such time as the General Court has dealt with the application for third-party proceedings.

(c) Formal requirements

(i) General requirements

25.113 The application initiating third-party proceedings must comply with the general requirements applicable to procedural documents (see paras 23.49–23.55) and with the specific requirements relating to applications (see paras 25.02–25.22).[394] In addition, the application must specify the contested judgment or order, state how the contested decision is prejudicial to the rights of the third party, and indicate the reasons why the third party was unable to take part in the original case.[395]

(ii) Application addressed to the parties to the original case

25.114 The application is addressed to all the parties to the original case.[396] If the contested judgment or order is varied, the variation may be relied upon against all the parties to the original proceedings since they were summoned to the third-party proceedings.

(d) Consequences

25.115 If the third-party proceedings are successful, the contested judgment or order will be varied on the points on which the submissions of the third party are upheld.[397]

The original of the judgment in the third-party proceedings is annexed to the original of the contested decision and a note of the judgment in the third-party proceedings is made in the margin of the contested decision.[398]

(3) Revision

(a) General

25.116 Revision affords an opportunity of varying the decision of the Court of Justice or the General Court after a 'new fact' has come to light.[399] Similar to third-party proceedings, although reference is made only to judgments in Art. 44 of the Statute, the ECJ Rules of Procedure[400] indicate that revision applies to judgments and orders of the respective Court.

(b) Substantive requirements and time limits

(i) New fact

25.117 Under the first paragraph of Art. 44 of the Statute, an application for revision of a judgment of the Court of Justice or of the General Court may be made on discovery of a fact which is of such a nature as to be a decisive factor and which, when the judgment was delivered or the order served, was unknown to the Court and to the party claiming the revision.[401] Consequently, revision is not a form of appeal, but an exceptional review

---

[394] ECJ Rules of Procedure, Arts 157(1) and 120 to 122; EGC Rules of Procedure, Arts 123(1) and 43 and 44.
[395] ECJ Rules of Procedure, Art. 157(1); EGC Rules of Procedure, Art. 123(1), first para.
[396] ECJ Rules of Procedure, Art. 157(2); EGC Rules of Procedure, Art. 123(1), second para.
[397] ECJ Rules of Procedure, Art. 157(5); EGC Rules of Procedure, Art. 123(3), first para.
[398] ECJ Rules of Procedure, Art. 157(6); EGC Rules of Procedure, Art. 123(3), second para.
[399] Statute, Art. 44; ECJ Rules of Procedure, Art. 159; EGC Rules of Procedure, Arts 125–128.
[400] ECJ Rules of Procedure, Art. 159. At present, Art. 125 of the EGC Rules of Procedure only refers to judgments.
[401] The Court of Justice, prior to the recent modification of its Rules of Procedure (ECJ Rules of Procedure, Art. 159), had already extended this provision of the Statute to cover orders producing the same effects as a judgment (ECJ, Joined Cases C-199/94 P and C-200/94 P-Rev *Inpesca v Commission and Pevasa*

procedure that allows an applicant to call into question the authority of *res judicata* attaching to a final judgment or order on the basis of the findings of fact relied upon by the Court.[402]

In order for revision proceedings to be admissible, the following three conditions have to be satisfied: (1) matters of a factual nature which existed prior to the decision must have been discovered; (2) those matters must have been unknown at that time to the Court which delivered the judgment or issued the order, as well as to the party applying for revision; and (3) the matters must be such that, if the Court had been able to take them into consideration, they might have led it to a different determination of the proceedings.[403]

(ii) Late discovery not attributable to applicant

The late discovery of the new fact must not be attributable to the applicant for revision. **25.118** Accordingly, where the applicant was aware of the existence of a given report but not of its content at the time of the original proceedings, the report in question did not constitute a new fact.[404] This was because the party's failure to ask for the content of the report to be communicated to it or to apply to the Court for measures of inquiry was part of the reason why the applicant was not apprised of the content of the report before the decision was given. The Court of Justice or the General Court, as the case may be, must also not have been aware of the allegedly 'new' fact at the time when judgment was delivered or the order was served. Accordingly, the Court is aware of the content of a document produced before the end of the oral procedure, even though it was not drawn up in the language of the case but in another official language of the European Union. There is an irrebuttable presumption that the Court of Justice and the General Court master all the official languages, and hence they may have cognizance of such a document.[405]

[1998] E.C.R. I-831, para. 16). Accordingly, it is possible to obtain the revision of an order declaring an appeal partially inadmissible or partially unfounded because such an order has the same effects as a judgment declaring an appeal partially inadmissible or partially unfounded (ECJ (judgment of 7 November 2002), Case C-301/00 P-Rev. *Meyer v Commission*, not reported, paras 19 and 20; EGC (order of 16 April 2012), Joined Cases T-40/07 REV and T-62/07 REV *de Brito Sequiera Carvalho v Commission*, not reported, paras 11–18 (revision declared inadmissible as no new facts present)).

[402] ECJ (order of 29 November 2007), Case C-12/05 P-REV *Meister v OHIM* [2007] E.C.R. I-167*, Summ. pub., para. 16; EGC (order of 21 June 2010), Case T-442/09 REV *Chacón de la Torre v Spain*, not reported, para. 7.

[403] ECJ (order of 25 February 1992), Case C-185/90 P-Rev. *Gill v Commission* [1992] E.C.R. I-993, paras 11–12. In that case, the application for revision of a judgment given by the Court of Justice on appeal setting aside a judgment of the then Court of First Instance was held to be manifestly inadmissible. In its judgment on appeal, the Court of Justice had given a decision on points of law only and did not adopt a view on the facts as found by the Court of First Instance. Moreover, the Court of Justice had referred the case back to the Court of First Instance and hence the new fact could have been raised before that court. See also ECJ (order of 29 November 2007), Case C-12/05 P-REV *Meister v OHIM* [2007] E.C.R. I-167*, Summ. pub., paras 19–20; CFI (order of 26 March 1992), Case T-4/89 Rev. *BASF v Commission* [1992] E.C.R. II-1591, paras 8–9. Naturally, an application for revision which makes no mention of any new fact will be inadmissible: see ECJ, Case C-295/90 Rev. *Council v European Parliament and Others* [1992] E.C.R. I-5299, paras 4–5; see also ECJ, Case 13/69 *Van Eick v Commission* [1970] E.C.R. 3, para. 33; ECJ, Case C-130/91 Rev. *ISAE/VP and Interdata v Commission* [1995] E.C.R. I-407, paras 6–8; CFI, Case T-8/89 Rev. *DSM v Commission* [1992] E.C.R. II-2399, para. 14; CFI, Case T-14/89 Rev. *Montecatini v Commission* [1992] E.C.R. II-2409, para. 10; CFI, Case T-77/99 Rev. *Ojha v Commission* [2002] E.C.R.-SC I-A-29, II-131, para. 12 (and the case-law cited therein).

[404] ECJ, Case 56/70 Rev. *Mandelli v Commission* [1971] E.C.R. 1, paras 9–12.

[405] ECJ, Case 1/60 *FERAM v High Authority* [1960] E.C.R. 165, at 16970.

(iii) Fact had already occurred when decision was given

25.119 As has been mentioned, the fact on which the application for revision is based must have already occurred at the time when the decision was given.[406] The fact must have been in existence—yet unknown—at that time.[407] For that reason, subsequent case-law of the Court of Justice or the General Court cannot be regarded as a new fact for the purposes of Art. 44 of the Statute.[408]

(iv) Decisive factor for the outcome of the case

25.120 Finally, the fact must be of such a nature as to be a decisive factor for the outcome of the case.[409] The new fact must potentially form the basis for amending the operative part of the contested judgment or order. A new fact which is relevant only to an additional ground, but cannot unsettle the judgment or order itself, does not satisfy that requirement.[410]

The application for revision must contest the determination made in the contested decision, not the order for costs or any measures taken in order to give effect to the decision.[411]

(v) Time limits and limitation period

25.121 An application for revision of a judgment or order must be made within three months of the date on which the facts on which the application is based came to the applicant's knowledge.[412] No application for revision may be made after the lapse of 10 years from the date of the judgment or order.[413]

---

[406] ECJ, Case C-130/91 Rev. II *ISAE/VP and Interdata v Commission* [1996] E.C.R. I-65, para. 6; ECJ (order of 29 November 2007), Case C-12/05 P-REV *Meister v OHIM* [2007] E.C.R. I-167*, Summ. pub., paras 19–20; EGC (order of 11 September 2012), Case T-241/03 REV *Marcuccio v Commission*, not reported, para. 16.

[407] ECJ, Case 116/78 Rev. *Bellintani v Commission* [1980] E.C.R. 23, para. 2. Assertions or personal opinions which have no official authority relating to facts which might possibly be classified as new facts cannot in themselves constitute such facts (ECJ, Case C-2/98 P *De Compte v European Parliament* [1999] E.C.R. I-1787, para. 32). See also ECJ, Case C-255/06 P-REV *Yedaş Tarim ve Otomotiv Sanayi ve Ticaret v Council and Commission* [2009] E.C.R. I-53*, para. 16.

[408] ECJ, Case C-403/85 Rev. *Ferrandi v Commission* [1991] E.C.R. I-1215, para. 13; CFI (order of 26 March 1992), Case T-4/89 Rev. *BASF v Commission* [1992] E.C.R. II-1591, para. 12. Cf. ECJ, Case 56/75 *Elz v Commission* [1977] E.C.R. 1617, para. 7, where the Court of Justice held with regard to a judgment of a national court that '[t]he mere fact that the judgment of the Tribunal was subsequent to the judgment of the Court [of Justice] cannot of itself prevent the first-mentioned judgment from being considered as the discovery of a new fact'. However, the national court's judgment merely confirmed earlier judgments of a lower court which were known to the Court of Justice and to the parties, and 'drew the foreseeable legal consequences from that confirmation'. As a result, the national court's judgment was not a 'new fact' and the application for revision was declared inadmissible.

[409] ECJ, Case 28/64 Rev. *Müller v Council* [1967] E.C.R. 141, at 144; ECJ, Case 37/71 Rev. *Jamet v Commission* [1973] E.C.R. 295, para. 3; ECJ, Case 107/79 Rev. *Schuerer v Commission* [1983] E.C.R. 3805, para. 7; ECJ, Case 285/81 Rev. I and II *Geist v Commission* [1984] E.C.R. 1789, paras 9–10; ECJ, Case 267/80 Rev. *Riseria Modenese v Council and Others* [1985] E.C.R. 3499, para. 12; ECJ, Case C-119/94 P Rev. *Coussios v Commission*, not reported, para. 10; ECJ (order of 29 November 2007), Case C-12/05 P-REV *Meister v OHIM* [2007] E.C.R. I-167*, Summ. pub., para. 19; CFI (order of 2 February 2009), Case T-367/03 REV *Yedaş Tarim ve Otomotiv Sanayi ve Ticaret v Council and Commission*, not reported, para. 20.

[410] ECJ, Case 40/71 *Richez-Parise v Commission* [1972] E.C.R. 73, para. 21; CFI (order of 1 July 1994), Case T-106/89 Rev. *Norsk Hydro v Commission* [1994] E.C.R. II-419, para. 14.

[411] ECJ, Case 235/82 Rev. *Ferriere San Carlo v Commission* [1986] E.C.R. 1799, para. 9.

[412] ECJ Rules of Procedure, Art. 159(2); EGC Rules of Procedure, Art. 125. See, e.g. CFI (order of 2 February 2009), Case T-367/03 REV *Yedaş Tarim ve Otomotiv Sanayi ve Ticaret v Council and Commission*, not reported, para. 19.

[413] Statute, Art. 44, third para.

(c) Formal requirements

(i) General requirements

The application must be made against all parties to the case in which the contested decision was [414] given and must be lodged in the language of the procedure of the decision to be revised.[415]   **25.122**

An application for revision must comply with the general requirements for procedural documents (see paras 23.49–23.55) and with the specific requirements for applications (see paras 25.02–25.22).[416] In addition, it must specify the judgment or order contested, indicate the points on which the judgment or order is contested, set out the facts on which the application is based, and indicate the nature of the evidence to show that there are facts justifying revision of the judgment, and that the applicable time limit has been observed.

(ii) Procedure

Without prejudice to its decision on the substance, the Court of Justice or the General Court, as the case may be, decides on the admissibility of the application in the form of an order after hearing the Advocate-General and having regard to the written observations of the parties.[417]   **25.123**

If the application is admissible, the Court proceeds to consider the substance of the application and gives its decision in the form of a judgment.[418] As underlined in the case-law, this division of the procedure into two stages is due to the strict conditions applying to revision, which is understandable having regard to the fact that it affects the principle of *res judicata*.[419]

(iii) Successful action

The original of the revising judgment is annexed to the original of the judgment or order revised. A note of the revising judgment is made in the margin of the original of the judgment or order revised.[420]   **25.124**

(4) The interpretation of judgments or orders

(a) General

If the meaning or scope of a judgment or order is in doubt, application may be made to the Court of Justice or the General Court, as the case may be, to construe it.[421] Although reference is made only to judgments in Art. 43 of the Statute, the ECJ Rules of Procedure[422] indicate that this procedure also applies to orders.[423]   **25.125**

---

[414] ECJ Rules of Procedure, Art. 159(4); EGC Rules of Procedure, Art. 126(2).

[415] ECJ (order of 20 May 2010), Case C-64/98 P-REV *Petrides v Commission* [2010] E.C.R. I-65*, paras 12–16.

[416] ECJ Rules of Procedure, Arts 159(3) and 120–122; EGC Rules of Procedure, Arts 126(1), 43, and 44.

[417] ECJ Rules of Procedure, Art. 159(5); EGC Rules of Procedure, Art. 127(2).

[418] ECJ Rules of Procedure, Art. 159(6); EGC Rules of Procedure, Art. 127(3).

[419] ECJ, Case 116/78 *Bellintani and Others v Commission* [1980] E.C.R. 23, para. 3; ECJ, Case C-5/93 P *DSM v Commission* [1999] E.C.R. I-4695, paras 66–67.

[420] ECJ Rules of Procedure, Art. 159(7); EGC Rules of Procedure, Art. 127(4).

[421] Statute, Art. 43; ECJ Rules of Procedure, Art. 158; EGC Rules of Procedure, Art. 129.

[422] By contrast, Art. 129 of the EGC Rules of Procedure only refers to judgments.

[423] However, an application relating to an order was dismissed under the former ECJ Rules of Procedure, Art. 102, since that provision only referred to judgments: see ECJ (order of 24 September 2008), Case C-502/06 P-INT *Correia de Matos v European Parliament*, not reported.

An application for interpretation of a judgment or order must seek only to resolve an obscurity or ambiguity relating to the determination made in the judgment.⁴²⁴ Questions concerning the implications of the judgment or order for other disputes or the content of measures needed in order to give effect to it or points not decided by the judgment or order do not constitute questions of interpretation for this purpose and hence are inadmissible.⁴²⁵ Such questions, however, may form the subject-matter of new proceedings.

(b) Who can bring an application for interpretation?

(i) Applicant

25.126   An application for interpretation of a judgment or order may be made by any party to the proceedings.⁴²⁶ An intervener in the original proceedings may make an application, irrespective as to the stance taken by the party in whose support it intervened.⁴²⁷

In the case of parallel proceedings, based on the same complaints, in which a decision is given in one or more cases by reference to a judgment or order in an initial case, all parties involved are entitled to apply for an interpretation of that latter judgment or order, even if they were not parties to those particular proceedings.⁴²⁸ In contrast, an application for interpretation of a judgment or order which is concerned merely to define the consequences of an earlier judgment or order constitutes an application to interpret that initial judgment, and so only parties to those proceedings are entitled to bring an application for interpretation.⁴²⁹

(ii) Special position of Union institutions

25.127   A Union institution⁴³⁰ which establishes an interest in having a judgment interpreted may bring an application for interpretation even if it was not a party to the proceedings which culminated in the judgment whose interpretation is sought.⁴³¹

---

⁴²⁴ ECJ (order of 20 April 2010), Case C-114/08 P(R)-INT *Pellegrini v Commission* [2010] E.C.R. I-48*, Summ. pub., paras 6–15 (application inadmissible because an interpretation was sought of a question not determined in the judgment); ECJ (order of 11 July 2013), Case C-496/09 INT *Italy v Commission*, not reported, paras 7–12 (application inadmissible, since there was no ambiguity with respect to meaning or scope of judgment).

⁴²⁵ ECJ, Case 70/63 bis *High Authority v Cllotti and Court of Justice* [1965] E.C.R. 275, at 279; ECJ, Case 110/63 A *Willame v Commission* [1966] E.C.R. 287, at 292; ECJ (order of 29 September 1983), Case 9/81-Interpretation *Court of Auditors v Williams* [1983] E.C.R. 2859, paras 9 and 13; ECJ (order of 29 September 1983), Case 206/81 A *Alvarez v European Parliament* [1983] E.C.R. 2865, para. 8; ECJ (order of 11 December 1986), Case 25/86 *Suss v Commission* [1986] E.C.R. 3929, para. 9; ECJ (order of 20 April 1988), Joined Cases 146 and 431/85-Interpretation *Maindiaux and Others v ESC* [1988] E.C.R. 2003, para. 6; ECJ (order of the President of 20 April 2010), Case C-114/08 P(R)-INT *Pellegrini v Commission* [2010] E.C.R. I-48*, Summ. pub., para. 13; CFI (order of 14 July 1993), Case T-22/91 INT *Raiola-Denti and Others v Council* [1993] E.C.R. II-817, para. 6.

⁴²⁶ Statute, Art. 43. See also ECJ Rules of Procedure, Art. 158(1); EGC Rules of Procedure, Art. 129.

⁴²⁷ ECJ (order of 20 April 1988), Joined Cases 146/85 and 431/85-Interpretation *Maindiaux and Others v ESC* [1988] E.C.R. 2003, para. 4; ECJ, Case C-245/95 P-INT *NSK and Others v Commission* [1999] E.C.R. I-1, para. 15.

⁴²⁸ ECJ, Case 5/55 *ASSIDER v High Authority* [1954 to 1956] E.C.R. 135, at 141–2.

⁴²⁹ ECJ, Case 24/66 bis *Gesellschaft für Getreidehandel v Commission* [1973] E.C.R. 1599, para. 3.

⁴³⁰ Art. 43 of the Statute (as well as Art. 158(1) of the ECJ Rules of Procedure) refer to 'any institution of the Union' and thus does not expressly mention Union bodies, offices, and agencies as compared to other provisions, e.g. the provision directly above it (Art. 42 of the Statute) relating to third-party proceedings. However, for the purposes of the ECJ Rules of Procedure, the term 'institutions' is meant to include both the official Union institutions listed in Art. 13(1) TEU and bodies, offices, and agencies of the Union established by the Treaties or by act adopted in implementation thereof: see ECJ Rules of Procedure, Art. 1(2)(a). Conceivably, Art. 158(1) of the ECJ Rules of Procedure dealing with interpretation could cover both. Yet, these provisions are framed as being in accordance with Art. 43 of the Statute. As such, arguably, Union bodies, offices, and agencies could apply for interpretation under circumstances where they are a party to the proceedings, but would not be accorded the special position given to the (official) Union institutions.

⁴³¹ Statute, Art. 43. See also ECJ Rules of Procedure, Art. 158(1).

(c) Substantive and formal requirements

(i) Doubt as regards the meaning or the scope of a judgment or order

In order for there to be a doubt as to the meaning or scope of a judgment or order within the meaning of Art. 43 of the Statute, it is sufficient that parties give differing meanings to it.[432] **25.128**

The doubt must relate to an issue determined by the judgment or order in question. It must therefore attach to the operative part or to one of the grounds determining it. An application for interpretation may not be made to the Court of Justice or the General Court for interpretation of an ancillary matter which supplements or explains those basic grounds.[433]

Finally, there must be a real obscurity or ambiguity in the judgment or order.[434] The applicant must expressly identify that obscurity or ambiguity.

(ii) General requirements

The application for interpretation must comply with the general requirements for proce- **25.129**
dural documents (see paras 23.49–23.55) and with the specific requirements for applications (see paras 25.02–25.22).[435] It must also specify the decision in question and the
passages of which interpretation is sought.[436]

The application must be made against all the parties to the case in which the decision in
question was given.[437]

(iii) Time limit

The ECJ Rules of Procedure require that an application for interpretation should be made **25.130**
within two years after the date of the delivery of the judgment or the service of the order.[438]
At present, no time limit is prescribed in the EGC Rules of Procedure.

(d) Procedure and consequences

(i) Procedure

The Court of Justice or the General Court, as the case may be, gives its decision after having **25.131**
given the parties an opportunity to submit their observations and after hearing the
Advocate-General.[439]

---

[432] ECJ, Case 5/55 *ASSIDER v High Authority* [1954 to 1956] E.C.R. 135, at 142.

[433] ECJ, Case 5/55 *ASSIDER v High Authority*, at 142. EGC, Case T-284/08 INT *People's Mojahedin Organization of Iran v Council* [2008] E.C.R. II-334*, Summ. pub., paras 8–12 (and case-law cited therein).

[434] Observations of Advocate-General P. VerLoren van Themaat in ECJ (order of 29 September 1983), Case 206/81 bis *Alvarez v European Parliament* [1983] E.C.R. 2865, at 2876; CFI (order of 14 July 1993), Case T-22/91 INT *Raiola-Denti and Others v Council* [1993] E.C.R. II-817, paras 7–10.

[435] ECJ Rules of Procedure, Arts 158(3) and 120–122; EGC Rules of Procedure, Arts 129(1), 43, and 44.

[436] ECJ Rules of Procedure, Art. 158(3); EGC Rules of Procedure, Art. 129(1).

[437] ECJ Rules of Procedure, Art. 158(4); EGC Rules of Procedure, Art. 129(1), second para.

[438] ECJ Rules of Procedure, Art. 158(2).

[439] ECJ Rules of Procedure, Art. 158(5); EGC Rules of Procedure, Art. 129(3), first para. These provisions do not specify whether the Court may do so by judgment or order. Of course, if the application for interpretation is manifestly inadmissible, the Court may dismiss it by order (ECJ Rules of Procedure, Art. 53(2); EGC Rules of Procedure, Art. 111). For an example, see CFI (order of 14 July 1993), Case T-22/91 INT *Raiola-Denti and Others v Council* [1993] E.C.R. II-817. The Court decides by judgment when it proceeds to a formal interpreta-tion: see ECJ, Joined Cases 41/73, 43/73 and 44/73-Interpretation *Générale Sucrière and Others v Commission* [1977] E.C.R. 445 and in ECJ, Case C-245/95 P-INT *NSK and Others v Council* [1999] E.C.R. I-1; EGC, Case T-348/05 INTP *JSC Kirovo-Chepetsky Khimichesky Kombinat v Council* [2009] E.C.R. II-116* Summ. pub.

(ii) Effect

25.132   If the application for interpretation is successful, the original of the interpreting decision is annexed to the original of the decision interpreted, and a note of the interpreting decision is made in the margin of the original of the decision interpreted.[440]

The interpreting decision is binding not only on all parties to the proceedings in which the interpreted decision was given, but also on parties to proceedings in which a judgment was given containing a passage 'exactly similar' to the passage interpreted.[441]

(5) Rectification of clerical errors

(a) General

25.133   Clerical mistakes, errors in calculation, and obvious inaccuracies in a judgment or an order may be rectified by the Court of Justice or the General Court by order setting out the rectified text.[442]

(b) Procedure

25.134   The Court of Justice or the General Court, as the case may be, may take this step of its own motion or at the request of a party (including an intervener) made within two weeks after delivery of the judgment or service of the order.[443]

The parties are entitled to lodge prior written observations. Under the ECJ Rules of Procedure, this possibility is limited to rectifications of the operative part or of one of the grounds constituting the necessary support for the operative part.[444]

The Court of Justice takes its decision after hearing the Advocate-General.[445] The General Court takes a decision in closed session.[446]

(c) Effect

25.135   The original of the rectification order is annexed to the original of the rectified decision, and a note of the order is made in the margin of the rectified decision.[447]

---

[440] ECJ Rules of Procedure, Art. 158(6); EGC Rules of Procedure, Art. 129(3), second para. See, e.g. ECJ, Joined Cases 41/73, 43/73, and 44/73-Interpretation *Générale Sucrière and Others v Commission* [1977] E.C. R. 445; ECJ, Case C-245/95 P-INT *NSK and Others v Council* [1999] E.C.R. I-1; EGC, Case T-348/05 INTP *JSC Kirovo-Chepetsky Khimichesky Kombinat v Council* [2009] E.C.R. II-116*.

[441] ECJ, Joined Cases 41/73, 43/73 and 44/73-Interpretation *Générale Sucrière and Others v Commission* [1977] E.C.R. 445, para. 29 ('This means that an interpreting judgment is binding not only on the applicants but also on any other party, insofar as that party is affected by the passage in the judgment which the Court is asked to interpret or by a passage exactly similar thereto').

[442] ECJ Rules of Procedure, Art. 154; EGC Rules of Procedure, Art. 84. For examples, see ECJ (order of 28 October 2004), Case C-299/02 *Commission v Netherlands*, not reported; ECJ (order of 20 October 2005), Case C-464/02 *Commission v Denmark*, not reported; ECJ (order of 10 July 2009), Case C-474/07 *European Parliament v Commission*, not reported; ECJ (order of 7 April 2011), Case C-50/10 *Commission v Italy*, not reported; CFI (order of 15 September 1995), Joined Cases T-466/93, T-469/93, T-473/93, T-474/93, and T-477/93 *O'Dwyer and Others v Council*, not reported; CFI (order of 3 June 2009), Joined Cases T-211/04 REC and T-215/04 REC *Government of Gibraltar v Commission*, not reported; EGC (order of 14 June 2010), Case T-289/07 REC *Caisse Nationale des Caisses d'Épargne et de Prévoyance v Commission*, not reported.

[443] ECJ Rules of Procedure, Art. 154(1); EGC Rules of Procedure, Art. 84(1). See ECJ (order of 19 March 2013), C-301/11 REC *Commission v Netherlands*, not reported, para. 2 (rectification at the request of interveners).

[444] ECJ Rules of Procedure, Art. 154(2); EGC Rules of Procedure, Art. 84(2).

[445] ECJ Rules of Procedure, Art. 154(3).

[446] EGC Rules of Procedure, Art. 84(3).

[447] ECJ Rules of Procedure, Art. 154(4); EGC Rules of Procedure, Art. 84(4).

(6) Failure to adjudicate

(a) General

If the Court of Justice or the General Court has failed to adjudicate—that is to say, failed to give a decision on a specific head of claim or on costs—that omission can be rectified on application by any party for the Court to supplement its decision.[448]   **25.136**

(b) Procedure

The application must be lodged within one month after service of the decision in question.[449] It is served on the opposite party, and the President prescribes a period within which that party may lodge written observations.[450] After that, the Court decides both on the admissibility and on the substance of the application (after hearing the Advocate-General in the case of the Court of Justice).[451]   **25.137**

---

[448] ECJ Rules of Procedure, Art. 155(1); EGC Rules of Procedure, Art. 85. Note that under the current EGC Rules of Procedure, this procedure only applies in relation to a decision on costs. The omission of the General Court to examine a form of order sought by the applicant in any event constitutes an error of law which may lead to the annulment of the decision of the General Court in the context of appeals proceedings (ECJ (order of 3 June 2005), Case C-396/03 P *Killinger v Germany, Council and Commission* [2005] E.C.R. I-4967, paras 11–13; ECJ, Case C-167/06 P *Komninou and Others v Commission* [2007] E.C.R. I-141*, Summ. pub., paras 22–28; ECJ, Case C-200/10 P *Evropaïki Dynamiki v Commission* [2011] E.C.R. I-67*, Summ. pub., paras 30–43).

[449] ECJ Rules of Procedure, Art. 155(1); EGC Rules of Procedure, Art. 85, first para.

[450] ECJ Rules of Procedure, Art. 155(2); EGC Rules of Procedure, Art. 85, second para.

[451] ECJ Rules of Procedure, Art. 155(3); EGC Rules of Procedure, Art. 85, third para. For examples, see ECJ (order of 20 January 1994), Joined Cases C-89/85, C-104/85, C-114/85, C-116/85, C-117/85, and C-125/85 to C-129/85 *Ahlström Osakeyhtiö and Others v Commission* [1994] E.C.R. I-99; CFI (order of 11 October 1990), Case T-50/89 *Sparr v Commission* [1990] E.C.R. II-539.

26

PROCEDURE IN THE CASE OF APPEALS AGAINST DECISIONS OF THE GENERAL COURT

26.01 This chapter focuses on the procedural rules applicable on appeals[1] brought before the Court of Justice against decisions of the General Court.[2] Similar rules apply to appeals brought before the General Court against decisions of the Civil Service Tribunal.[3]

The procedure before the Court of Justice in the case of an appeal brought against a decision of the General Court consists of a written part and an oral part.[4] The language of the case is the language of the decision of the General Court against which the appeal is brought.[5]

I. The Written Part of the Procedure

A. Appeal

26.02 The written part of the procedure is limited in principle to two documents: the appeal and the response. The appeal must be lodged at the Registry of the Court of Justice or of the General Court.[6] The appeal must be brought within two months of the notification of the decision appealed against.[7] It must seek to have set aside, in whole

---

[1] An appeal should be distinguished from an application for revision of a judgment as provided in Art. 44 of the Statute: see ECJ, Case C-12/05 P-REV *Meister v OHIM* [2007] E.C.R. I-167*, Summ. pub., paras 15–16.
[2] Art. 256(1) TFEU; Statute, Arts 55–61; ECJ Rules of Procedure, Arts 167–190.
[3] Arts 256(2) and 257 TFEU; Statute, Annex I, Arts 9–13; EGC Rules of Procedure, Arts 136a–149.
[4] Statute, Art. 59, first sent.
[5] ECJ Rules of Procedure, Art. 37(2)(a). For a general discussion of the language of a case, see Ch. 23.
[6] ECJ Rules of Procedure, Art. 167(1).
[7] Statute, Art. 56, first para. As regards rules relating to service, see Arts. 48, 121, and Art. 168(2) of the ECJ Rules of Procedure, which incorporates the rules on service for direct actions; see generally para. 23.24. For some applications of the rules on service in the context of appeals, see, e.g. ECJ (order of 29 October 2004), Case C-360/02 P *Ripa di Meana v European Parliament* [2004] E.C.R. I-10339, paras 21–25; ECJ, Joined Cases C-442/03 P and C-471/03 P *P&O European Ferries (Vizcaya) and Others v Commission* [2006] E.C.R. I-4845, paras 21–29.

or in part, the decision of the General Court as set out in the operative part of that decision.[8]

The appeal has to comply with certain requirements generally applying to applications.[9]

The following must appear at the beginning of each appeal: the appellant's name and address; the name and capacity of the appellant's agent or lawyer; the identification of the decision of the General Court appealed against (type of decision, formation of the Court, date and number of the case), and the names of the parties before the General Court; the date on which the decision of the General Court was served on the appellant; and an address for service and/or agreement to service by telefax or other technical means of communication.[10] The appeal must also contain the pleas in law and legal arguments relied on, a summary of those pleas in law, and the form of order sought.[11] The decision appealed against must be attached to the appeal.[12] If the appeal complies with those requirements,[13] it will be served on all the parties to the proceedings before the General Court.[14]

An appeal must indicate precisely the contested elements of the judgment which the appellant seeks to have set aside, and also the legal arguments specifically advanced in support of the appeal.[15] An appeal which confines itself to repeating or reproducing word

---

[8] ECJ Rules of Procedure, Art. 169(1). See, e.g. ECJ (order of 17 March 2009), Case C-251/08 P *Ayyanarsamy v Commission and Germany* [2009] E.C.R. I-36*, Summ. pub., para. 26; ECJ (order of 2 September 2010), Case C-28/10 P *Bayramoglu v European Parliament and Council* [2010] E.C.R. I-108*, Summ. pub., paras 12–14; compare ECJ (order of 4 October 2011), Case C-272/11 P *Ngele v Commission and Others* [2011] E.C.R. I-145*, Summ. pub., paras 11–12.

[9] ECJ Rules of Procedure, Art. 168(2), which refers to ECJ Rules of Procedure, Arts 119 (obligation to be represented), 121 (information relating to service) and 122(1) (annexes to the application). A clerical error in an application, for instance, an incorrect reference to a provision of the Statute as constituting the basis for an appeal, which has no effect on the subsequent course of the proceedings is not grounds for finding the appeal inadmissible: ECJ (order of the President of 19 July 1995), Case C-149/95 P(R) *Commission v Atlantic Container Line and Others* [1995] E.C.R. I-2165, para. 14.

[10] ECJ Rules of Procedure, Art. 168(1)(a)–(c) and Art. 168(3); ECJ Practice Directions, point 20. If the Court of Justice finds that the appeal was lodged within the prescribed period starting from the date on which the General Court gave judgment, failure to mention the names of other parties to the relevant case before the General Court and the date on which the judgment was served on does not make the appeal inadmissible: ECJ, Case C-91/95 P *Tremblay and Others v Commission* [1996] E.C.R. I-5547, paras 10–11. Mention in the appeal of a wrong address is not 'so substantial' an irregularity as to make the appeal inadmissible where the correct address can be found from other documents in the case-file, such as the contested judgment annexed to the appeal: ECJ, Case C-161/97 P *Kernkraftwerke Lippe-Ems v Commission* [1999] E.C.R. I-2057, para. 55. See also with respect to documents referred to in the appeal but not annexed to it, ECJ, Case C-82/01 P *Aéroports de Paris v Commission* [2002] E.C.R. I-9297, paras 8–13 (the defect was not sufficient to render the appeal inadmissible, since those documents were known to the parties).

[11] ECJ, Rules of Procedure, Art. 168(1)(d)–(e); see also ECJ Practice Directions, points 25 and 36. If the appellant requests that the case be referred back to the General Court if the decision appealed against is set aside, he must set out in the appeal the reasons why the state of the proceedings does not permit a decision by the Court of Justice: ECJ Rules of Procedure, Art. 170(2). In any event, the Court is not obliged to carry out this request: see, e.g. ECJ, Case C-200/10 P *Evropaïki Dynamiki v Commission* [2011] E.C.R. I-67*, Summ. pub., paras 98–102.

[12] Art. 168(2) which refers to Art. 122(1) of the ECJ Rules of Procedure.

[13] See ECJ Rules of Procedure, Art. 168(4).

[14] ECJ Rules of Procedure, Art. 171(1).

[15] See ECJ Rules of Procedure, Art. 169(2); ECJ (order of 11 November 2003), Case C-488/01 P *Martinez v European Parliament* [2003] E.C.R. I-13355, paras 40–41; ECJ (order of 10 June 2010), Case C-498/09 P *Thomson Sales Europe v Commission* [2010] E.C.R. I-79*, Summ. pub., para. 81.

for word the pleas in law and arguments previously submitted to the General Court does not satisfy that requirement.[16]

B. Response

26.03 Within a period of two months after service of the appeal, which may not be extended, any of the parties to the proceedings before the General Court 'having an interest in the appeal being allowed or dismissed' may lodge a response.[17]

The following heads must appear at the beginning of the response: the name and address of the party lodging it; the name and capacity of the agent or lawyer acting for that party; the date on which the appeal was served on that party; and an address for service and/or agreement to service by telefax or any other technical means of communication.[18] The response must also contain the pleas in law and legal arguments relied on, and the form of order sought.[19]

C. Cross-appeal

26.04 Any party entitled to submit a response may submit a cross-appeal, which must be introduced by a document separate from the response.[20]

The cross-appeal must contain: the name and address of the party bringing the cross-appeal; the date on which the appeal was served on that party; the pleas in law and legal arguments relied on; and the form of order sought.[21]

---

[16] ECJ, Case C-48/96 P *Windpark Groothusen v Commission* [1998] E.C.R. I-2873, para. 56; ECJ (order of 16 July 1998), Case C-252/97 *N v Commission* [1998] E.C.R. I-4871, paras 17–19; ECJ, Case C-221/97 P *Schröder and Others v Commission* [1998] E.C.R. I-8255, para. 35; ECJ (order of 12 December 2003), Case C-258/02 P *Bactria Industriehygiene-Service v Commission* [2003] E.C.R. I-15105, para. 31; ECJ, Case C-499/03 P *Biegi Nahrungsmittel and Commonfood v Commission* [2005] E.C.R. I-1751, paras 37–38; ECJ (order of 10 June 2010), Case C-498/09 P *Thomson Sales Europe v Commission* [2010] E.C.R. I-79*, Summ. pub., para. 82.

[17] ECJ Rules of Procedure, Art. 172.

[18] ECJ Rules of Procedure, Art. 173(1)(a)–(b); ECJ Practice Directions, point 22. Under Art. 173(2) of the ECJ Rules of Procedure, Arts 119 (obligation to be represented) and 121 (information relating to service) of the ECJ Rules of Procedure apply to responses.

[19] ECJ Rules of Procedure, Art. 173(c)–(d). See also ECJ Practice Directions, point 22. A response that does not seek to have the appeal allowed or dismissed, in whole or in part, as provided under Art. 174 of the ECJ Rules of Procedure, is inadmissible: see, e.g. ECJ, Case C-263/09 P *Edwin v OHIM* [2011] E.C.R. I-5853, paras 83–85 (dismissing claim for amendment of judgment under appeal).

[20] ECJ Rules of Procedure, Art. 176. The Court of Justice has ruled that there is nothing to preclude a party from bringing both an appeal and a cross-appeal against a judgment of the General Court: ECJ, Joined Cases C-501/06 P, C-513/06 P, C-515/06 P, and C-519/06 P *GlaxoSmithKline Services and Others v Commission* [2009] E.C.R. I-9291, paras 31–39.

[21] ECJ Rules of Procedure, Art. 177(1). Under Art. 177(2) of the ECJ Rules of Procedure, Arts 119 (obligation to be represented), 121 (information relating to service), 122(1) and (3) (annexes to the application) of the ECJ Rules of Procedure apply to cross-appeals. Both Art. 122(1) and (3)—not just Art. 122(1)—apply in relation to cross-appeals, since for the appeal, there is already a provision similar to Art. 122(3) set forth in Art. 168(4). In particular, by virtue of the cross-reference to Art. 119 of the ECJ Rules of Procedure, agents and lawyers must lodge at the Registry an official document or an authority to act issued by the party whom they represent (Art. 119(2)). The fact that such authority is annexed only as a document to the application brought before the General Court does not make the appeal inadmissible: see ECJ, Case C-234/06 P *Il Ponte*

A cross-appeal must seek to have set aside, in whole or in part, the decision of the General Court; it may also seek to have set aside an express or implied decision relating to the admissibility of the action before the General Court.[22] The pleas in law and legal arguments relied on must identify precisely those points in the grounds of the decision of the General Court which are contested and must be separate from those relied on in the response.[23]

Where a cross-appeal is brought, the applicant at first instance or any other party to the relevant case before the General Court having an interest in the cross-appeal being allowed or dismissed may submit a response, which must be limited to the pleas in law relied on in that cross-appeal, within a period of two months after the cross-appeal being served on him, with no extensions being allowed.[24]

D. Reply and rejoinder

The appeal and the response may be supplemented by a reply and a rejoinder only where **26.05** the President, on a duly-reasoned application[25] made by the appellant within seven days of service of the response, considers such further pleading necessary, after hearing the Judge-Rapporteur and the Advocate-General, in particular to enable the appellant to present his views on a plea of inadmissibility or on new matters relied on in the response.[26] The President fixes the date by which the reply is to be submitted and, upon service of that pleading, the date by which the rejoinder is to be submitted; in so doing, the President may limit the number of pages and the subject-matter of those pleadings.[27] Similar rules apply in connection with the submission of a reply and rejoinder on a cross-appeal.[28]

II. The Oral Part of the Procedure

A. Submission of reasoned request

As with other types of proceedings before the Court of Justice (see para. 23.74), a party **26.06** must submit a reasoned request for an oral hearing within three weeks after service on the parties of notification of the close of the written part of the procedure.[29]

Finanziaria v OHIM [2007] E.C.R. I-7333, paras 21–22. Moreover, depending on the wording of the power of attorney, it may be deemed to cover proceedings before the Court of Justice, although not explicitly mentioning that Court as such: see ECJ, C-401/09 P *Evropaiki Dynamiki v ECB* [2011] E.C.R. I-4911, paras 34–39.

[22] ECJ Rules of Procedure, Art. 178(1)–(2). Importantly, as made clear by the language now inserted in the ECJ Rules of Procedure, it is not necessary that the cross-appeal be against the operative part of the General Court's decision, since this would generally deprive the cross-appeal of useful effect.

[23] ECJ Rules of Procedure, Art. 178(3).

[24] ECJ Rules of Procedure, Art. 179.

[25] In principle, such application must not exceed 3 pages and must be confined to summarizing the precise reasons for which, in the appellant's opinion, a reply is necessary. The request must be comprehensible in itself without any need to refer to the appeal or the response. See ECJ Practice Directions, point 25.

[26] ECJ Rules of Procedure, Art. 175(1).

[27] ECJ Rules of Procedure, Art. 175(2); ECJ Practice Directions, point 26.

[28] ECJ Rules of Procedure, Art. 180.

[29] ECJ Rules of Procedure, Art . 76(1). For an example, see ECJ (order of 9 March 2000), Case C-291/98 P *Sarrió v Commission* [2000] E.C.R. I-1213, para. 11, in which the appellant had spontaneously forgone

B. Cases in which no hearing is held

26.07 Consequently, as already mentioned, the parties do not have a right to an oral hearing. Indeed, on a proposal from the Judge-Rapporteur and after hearing the Advocate-General, the Court may decide not to hold a hearing if it considers on reading the written pleadings or observations lodged during the written part of the procedure that it has sufficient information to give a ruling.[30]

Furthermore, the powers of the Court of Justice to dispose of appeals (and cross-appeals) by reasoned order may also result in no oral hearing being held. Where an appeal or cross-appeal is, in whole or in part, manifestly inadmissible or manifestly unfounded, the Court of Justice may at any time, acting on a proposal from the Judge-Rapporteur and after hearing the Advocate-General, decide by reasoned order to dismiss that appeal or cross-appeal in whole or in part.[31] Moreover, where the Court has already ruled on one or more questions of law that are identical to those raised by the pleas in law of the appeal or cross-appeal and considers the appeal or cross-appeal to be manifestly well-founded, it may, acting on a proposal from the Judge-Rapporteur and, after hearing the parties and the Advocate-General, decide by reasoned order in which reference is made to the relevant case-law to declare the appeal or cross-appeal manifestly well-founded.[32]

III. Application of General Rules and Special Characteristics

A. Provisions applicable to appeals

26.08 In addition to the common procedural provisions set down in Title II of the ECJ Rules of Procedure which govern all types of proceedings before the Court of Justice including appeals (see Ch. 23), a series of provisions of the ECJ Rules of Procedure regarding direct actions is stated to be applicable to the procedure before the Court of Justice on appeals against decisions of the General Court.[33] In addition to those rules

---

applying for leave to submit a reply so that it was hard for it to argue that the written procedure had not enabled it to defend its point of view in full.

[30] ECJ Rules of Procedure, Art. 76(2). See also Statute, Art. 59.

[31] ECJ Rules of Procedure, Art. 181. For examples, see ECJ (order of 27 February 1991), Case C-126/90 P *Bocos Viciano v Commission* [1991] E.C.R. I-781; ECJ (order of 20 March 1991), Case C-115/90 P *Turner v Commission* [1991] E.C.R. I-1423; ECJ (order of 24 January 1994), Case C-275/93 P *Boessen v ESC* [1994] E.C.R. I-159; ECJ (order of 7 May 2013), Case C-584/11 P *Dow AgroSciences and Others v Commission*, not reported; ECJ (order of 7 May 2013), Case C-418/12 P *TME v Commission*, not reported. See ECJ (order of 5 June 2002), Case C-211/00 P *Ciments Français v Commission*, not reported, and other orders given on the same day in the 'Cement' case', by which the Court dismissed by order a number of pleas which were manifestly inadmissible or manifestly unfounded. The remainder of these cases proceeded to judgment: see ECJ, Joined Cases C-204/00 P, C-205/00 P, C-211/00 P, C-213/00 P, C-217/00 P, and C-219/00 P *Aalborg Portland and Others v Commission* [2004] E.C.R. I-123. The Court may also declare arguments inadmissible which are raised in connection with pleas that are admissible per se, for instance, where the arguments do not contest the legal assessment but rather the findings of fact made by the General Court on the basis of the documents submitted as evidence (ECJ, Case C-449/99 *EIB v Hautem* [2001] E.C.R. I-6733, paras 46–49).

[32] ECJ Rules of Procedure, Art. 182.

[33] ECJ Rules of Procedure, Art. 190.

specified in relation to the content of the appeal, response, and cross-appeal,[34] the provisions relate to:

- the general bar on introducing new pleas in the course of the proceedings (Art. 127);
- intervention (Arts 129–132);[35]
- the expedited procedure (Arts 133–136);[36]
- costs (Arts 137–146, subject to what is provided in Art. 184);[37]
- amicable settlement (Art. 147);
- discontinuance (Art. 148);
- cases that do not proceed to judgment (Art. 149);
- absolute bar to proceeding with a case (Art. 150);
- assignment of cases to formations of the Court (Art. 153);
- rectification (Art. 154);
- failure to adjudicate (Art. 155);
- third-party proceedings (Art. 157);
- interpretation (Art. 158);
- revision of judgments (Art. 159);
- interim measures (Arts 160–164);
- applications to suspend the enforcement of a decision of the Court of Justice or of any measure adopted by the Council, Commission, or the European Central Bank pursuant to Arts 280 and 299 TFEU and Art. 164 EAEC (Art. 165); and
- compulsory inspections under Art. 81 EAEC (Art. 166).

As a result, unless otherwise provided for, the rules applicable to these matters are the same as for direct actions.[38] Moreover, Art. 95 of the ECJ Rules of Procedure on anonymity in the context of references for a preliminary ruling applies, *mutatis mutandis*, to the procedure before the Court of Justice concerning appeals against decisions of the General Court.[39]

Nevertheless, there are certain special characteristics of the procedure involving appeals.

B. No measures of inquiry

Although the ECJ Rules of Procedure do not formally exclude the application of the common procedural rules with respect to measures of inquiry[40] in appeal proceedings, the Court of Justice will, in principle, not order such measures in such proceedings.

26.09

---

[34] See ECJ Rules of Procedure, Art. 168(2), Art. 173(2), and Art. 177(2), respectively.

[35] However, by way of derogation from Art. 130(1), an application to intervene must be made within one month, as opposed to six weeks, of the publication of the notice of appeal as referred to in Art. 21(4): ECJ Rules of Procedure, Art. 190(2). A natural or legal person can intervene in an appeal before the Court of Justice even if that person was not a party to the proceedings before the General Court (provided the conditions for intervention are met): see e.g. ECJ, Joined Cases C-241/91 P and C-242/91 P *RTE and ITP v Commission* [1995] E.C.R. I-743, para. 3; ECJ (order of the President of 24 March 2009), Case C-60/08 P(R) *Cheminova and Others v Commission* [2009] E.C.R. I-43*, para. 15; ECJ, Case C-385/07 P *Der Grüne Punkt-Duales System Deutschland v Commission* [2009] E.C.R. I-6155, para. 62.

[36] See, e.g. ECJ Case C-39/03 P *Commission v Artegodan* [2003] E.C.R. I-7885.

[37] ECJ Rules of Procedure, Art. 184(1).

[38] The common procedural provisions of the ECJ Rules of Procedure also apply to appeals: see Ch. 23. These include, *inter alia*, the provisions on the calculation of time limits (see Art. 49).

[39] ECJ Rules of Procedure, Art. 190(3). See para. 24.05.

[40] ECJ Rules of Procedure, Arts 63–75.

Measures of inquiry would indeed exceed the bounds of an appeal, since it is limited to questions of law and is based on the facts as found by the General Court.[41]

C. Legal aid

26.10 There are specific provisions concerning legal aid in appeals as set forth in Arts 185–189 of the ECJ Rules of Procedure. By and large, they parallel the procedural rules governing legal aid in direct actions before the General Court (see paras 25.101–25.105). However, there are some differences. In particular, legal aid is not limited to natural persons and may instead by claimed by '[a] party who is wholly or in part unable to meet the costs of the proceedings'.[42] Moreover, there are specific rules regarding the formation of the Court that gives the decision on the application for legal aid.[43]

D. Effect on cross-appeal of dismissal of the appeal

26.11 Dismissal of the main appeal does not necessarily have an effect on the treatment of the cross-appeal, though this very much depends upon the pleas submitted. The Court of Justice may examine the cross-appeal even if the main appeal is dismissed.[44] It may happen that the Court of Justice first examines the cross-appeal and then decides that there is no longer any need to adjudicate on the main appeal.[45] Conversely, the Court may find that in the light of its findings regarding the main appeal, the cross-appeal must be dismissed as unfounded.[46]

In any event, by virtue of Art. 183 of the ECJ Rules of Procedure, a cross-appeal becomes devoid of purpose in the following three situations: (a) if the appellant discontinues the appeal; (b) if the appeal is declared manifestly inadmissible for non-compliance with the time limit for lodging an appeal; and/or (c) if the appeal is declared manifestly inadmissible on the sole ground that it is not directed against those kinds of decisions of the General Court in which an appeal will lie, namely a final decision of the General Court or a decision disposing of the substantive issues in part only or disposing of a procedural issue concerning a plea of lack of competence or inadmissibility within the meaning of the first paragraph of Art. 56 of the Statute.[47]

---

[41] ECJ, Case C-199/92 P *Hüls v Commission* [1999] E.C.R. I-4287, paras 90–91; ECJ, Case C-235/92 P *Montecatini v Commission* [1999] E.C.R. I-4539, paras 109–110; ECJ, Case C-198/99 P *Ensidesa v Commission* [2003] E.C.R. I-1111, paras 30–32. See also para. 16.24.

[42] ECJ Rules of Procedure, Art. 185(1).

[43] See ECJ Rules of Procedure, Art. 187.

[44] See, e.g. ECJ, Case C-234/02 P *European Ombudsman v Lamberts* [2004] E.C.R. I-2803, paras 72–94. But see, however, ECJ Rules of Procedure, Art. 183.

[45] See, e.g. ECJ, Case C-486/01 P *Front National v European Parliament* [2004] E.C.R. I-6289, para. 48: the General Court had dismissed the application of the Front National on the merits and the Front National appealed against that judgment; the European Parliament, in its cross-appeal, successfully alleged that the action brought before the General Court should have been declared inadmissible. In these circumstances, there was no longer need to adjudicate on the main appeal. It may also be the case that the Court will address the cross-appeal first, since it is only necessary to address the main appeal if the cross-appeal is dismissed: see, e.g. ECJ, Case C-362/05 P *Wunenberger v Commission* [2007] E.C.R. I-4333, para. 25.

[46] See, e.g. ECJ (judgment of 28 June 2012), Case C-404/10 P *Commission v Editions Odile Jacob*, not reported, paras 137–138.

[47] ECJ Rules of Procedure, Art. 183.

E. Procedure when a case is referred back to the General Court

The procedure followed where the Court of Justice sets aside a decision of the General **26.12** Court and refers the case back to that Court is set forth in Arts 117–121 of the EGC Rules of Procedure. In particular, where the written procedure before the General Court has been completed when the judgment referring the case back to it is delivered, the course of the procedure is as follows:[48]

(a) Within two months from the service upon him or her of the judgment of the Court of Justice, the applicant may lodge a statement of written observations.
(b) In the month following the communication to him or her of that statement, the defendant may lodge a statement of written observations. The time allowed to the defendant for lodging it may in no case be less than two months from the service upon him or her of the judgment of the Court of Justice.
(c) In the month following the simultaneous communication to the intervener of the observations of the applicant and the defendant, the intervener may lodge a statement of written observations. The time allowed to the intervener for lodging it may in no case be less than two months from the service upon him or her of the judgment of the Court of Justice.

Where the written procedure before the General Court has not been completed when the judgment referring the case back to the General Court was delivered, it is to be resumed at the stage which it had reached.[49] The General Court decides on the costs relating to the proceedings instituted before it and to the proceedings on the appeal before the Court of Justice.[50]

---

[48] EGC Rules of Procedure, Art. 119(1).
[49] EGC Rules of Procedure, Art. 119(2). The General Court may, if the circumstances so justify, allow supplementary statements of written observations to be lodged: EGC Rules of Procedure, Art. 119(3).
[50] EGC Rules of Procedure, Art. 121. See, e.g. CFI (judgment of 14 September 2004), Case T-156/94 *Siderúrgica Aristrain Madrid v Commission*, not reported, paras 45–52; CFI, Case T-229/02 *PKK v Council* [2008] E.C.R. II-45*, Summ. pub., paras 71–73; EGC (judgment of 22 January 2013), Joined Cases T-225/06 RENV, T-255/06 RENV, T-257/06 RENV and T-309/06 RENV *Budějovický Budvar v OHIM*, not reported, paras 67–69.

INDEX

Aarhus Convention 6.15
abuse of dominant position 7.49
abuse of process 11.10, 25.50
access
  to a court 4.07
  to documents 7.67, 7.135, 7.138, 18.27
  to file, refusal 11.51
accession of new Member States 6.04, 7.75
Accession Treaties and Acts 7.178
ACP States 7.73
acquis communautaire 3.02
acte clair 3.54, 3.58
acte éclairé 3.53
acts
  affecting jurisdiction of Court of Justice of the EU 5.19
  of bodies established by international
    agreements 6.15, 10.07
  cluster of 5.53
  of committees established under Union law 6.12
  excluded from review 10.03
  of general application 10.10
  of individual application, exclusion of 9.07
  invalidity 3.06
  non-binding 5.18
  pursuing authorized and unauthorized aims 7.182
  type of and status of party invoking objection 9.06
  of Union, bodies, offices or agencies 6.08–6.10,
    7.69–7.75, 10.06
  see also admissibility based on type of act;
    reviewable act
address for service 23.24, 23.32, 23.84, 25.03, 25.05,
  25.34–25.35, 26.02–26.03
adjudication, failure of 25.136–25.137
administrative meeting 2.12, 2.24, 23.56
administrative practice 5.10
admissibility based on type of act 7.85–7.110
  actio popularis 7.88
  acts not entailing implementing measures 7.106
  addresses of merger decision 7.87
  aid programmes 7.96
  associations 7.104
  Commission, authorization by of act
    of Member State 7.95
  constitutionally autonomous regions and devolved
    authorities 7.103
  contested act addressed to applicant 7.86–7.87
  contested act criteria 7.91
  contested act is measure of general
    application 7.99
  contested act is measure of individual
    application 7.98
  contested act is regulatory act *see* **regulatory act**
  contested act not addressed to individual
    applicant 7.88–7.104

contested act should be a 'decision' 7.85
contested measure must directly affect applicant's
  legal situation 7.92
contested measure must leave no discretion to
  addressees entrusted with implementation 7.93
decisions finding violation of Art. 101 and/or Art. 102
  TFEU or rejecting complaint 7.86
definition 7.90, 7.97
direct concern 7.90–7.96, 7.109
directives 7.94
effective judicial protection 7.105
exceptional circumstances 7.100
individual concern *see* **individual concern, concept of**
institution, refusal of 7.101
Les Verts judgment 7.102
no implementing measures 7.109
'regulatory act', concept of *see* **regulatory act**
adversarial principle 23.61
adverse effect, acts having 5.62, 5.64, 6.07, 7.22,
  7.23, 7.100, 11.82, 18.03–18.06
Advocate-General 2.05–2.06, 2.12, 2.20, 22.17
  Court of Justice 2.04, 2.15, 2.16
  General Court 2.24
  no right to respond to Opinion 23.81
  review procedure 17.01, 17.04–17.07
AETR case 7.17, 10.05
agents 23.16
agreements concluded by the Union and Member
  States 6.13–6.14
aid
  agriculture 5.25
  existing 5.22, 7.52, 7.53, 7.55, 7.57, 7.61, 7.63
  financed by Commission 7.96
  new 5.24, 7.52, 7.54–7.55, 7.57, 7.118
  see also **State aid**
Åland Islands 3.13
Amsterdam Treaty 1.06, 6.10
annulment, action for 1.07, 7.01–7.227, 11.11
  acknowledgment of facts 7.185
  action for failure to act 8.09–8.10
  acts imputed to Union institution, body,
    office or agency 7.69–7.75
  admissibility 7.82–7.84, 7.137
  see also **admissibility based**
    on type of act
  anti-dumping proceedings 7.188
  applicants/application 7.219–7.221 7.76–7.144,
    7.219–7.221
  application for annulment 7.219–7.221
  arrangements in secondary Union law 7.71
  capacity to bring action on behalf of another 7.84
  conditions 7.81
  conduct during administrative procedure and
    admissibility of pleas 7.185–7.189

annulment, action for (*cont.*)
  constitutionally autonomous regions and devolved
    authorities *see* **constitutionally autonomous**
    regions
  defendants 7.69–7.75
  dismissal of application 7.227
  EAEC and former ECSC Treaties 7.06
  European Central Bank, Court of Auditors and
    Committee of the Regions 7.79–7.80
  European Parliament, Council, Commission and
    Member States 7.76–7.78
  ex officio examination 7.217
  ex tunc effect 7.221
  individual concern *see* **individual concern,**
    concept of
  interest *see* **interest in annulment of contested act**
    requirement
  intervention for direct actions 25.67
  judgment, authority of 7.222–7.227
  legal personality 7.83
  Lisbon Treaty, changes brought by 7.03, 7.05
  merger control 7.186
  natural and legal persons 7.81–7.82
  nemo auditur 7.189
  nullity, declaration of 7.222–7.226
  objection of illegality 9.18
  partial annulment 7.220
  power of Union courts limited to annulment 7.219
  preliminary rulings on validity 10.14
  privileged applicants 7.76
  regulatory act *see* **regulatory act**
  reviewable act *see* **reviewable act**
  role in judicial protection 7.02
  second and third pillars (former) 7.04
  semi-privileged applicants 7.79
  State aid proceedings 7.187
  subsidiarity principle, violation of 7.80
  time frame 7.218
  time limits *see* **time limits**
  Treaty amendments 7.75
  Union institutions, bodies, offices or agencies 7.73,
    7.78
  see also **annulment, grounds for**
annulment, grounds for 7.145–7.184
  anti-dumping 7.166
  application of Arts 101 and 102 TFEU 7.163
  arbitration clause or special agreement 19.12
  competence, lack of 7.146, 7.148–7.157
  competence, lack of
    different aspects 7.148
    powers, delegation of 7.152
    substantive competence 7.149–7.150
    territorial competence 7.151
  confidentiality, duty of 7.167
  delegation and implementation
    in decision-making 7.153
  delegation to agencies 7.155
  delegation to Commission 7.156
  delegation to international bodies 7.154
  delegation to staff members 7.157
  discretion, margin of 7.180

  duty to seek an opinion 7.159
  infringement 7.179
  infringement of essential procedural
    requirement 7.158–7.175
  infringement of rights of defence 7.162
  infringement of Treaties or any rule of law
    relating to application 7.176–7.180
  internal procedural rules 7.168–7.169
  legal basis of contested act, failure to provide 7.172
  material inaccuracy 7.171
  merger control 7.164
  pleas raised by applicant 7.145
  pleas raised by Union judicature of its own
    motion 7.174, 7.146
  powers, misuse of 7.181–7.184
  publication and notification of contested
    act 7.175
  requirement to consult 7.159–7.160
  requirement to hear addressee 7.161–7.166
  rule of law 7.178
  State aid cases 7.165
  statement of reasons 7.170–7.174
  time-frames 7.147, 7.160, 7.173
  Treaties 7.177
anonymity 24.05
anti-dumping 7.64–7.66, 7.130–7.134, 7.138,
    7.205–7.206
  conduct during administrative procedure and
    admissibility of pleas 7.187 7.188
  damages, action for 11.54
  direct actions 25.69
  infringements of essential procedural
    requirement 7.166
  preliminary rulings on validity 10.08
appeals 16.01–16.32
  appellant 16.14
  appraisal of evidence by General Court 16.04
  confined to points of law 16.02–16.11
  consequences 16.29
  costs, appeal as to 16.13
  Court of Justice 2.22, 16.03, 16.30
  damages, assessment of 16.10
  dismissal 16.27
  distortion of evidence or content
    of contested act 16.05
  errors of law 16.02, 16.08, 16.19
  Civil Service Tribunal 2.44
  evidence on which parties were not heard
    at first instance 16.06
  final decisions 16.12
  General Court 16.11–16.13, 16.31
  injury suffered as result of bringing
    of appeal 16.23
  inquiry, measures of 16.24
  interim measures before Union courts 13.14
  interveners 16.15
  legal categorization of facts 16.07
  pleas 16.18, 16.21–16.22
  statement of reasons 16.09
  subject-matter 16.20
  successful 16.28

suspensory effects, none 16.26
third-party proceedings 25.112
time limits 16.25
two-tier legal protection 16.01
Union institutions and Member States
    16.16, 16.32
see also **appeals, procedure in case of**
appeals, procedure in case of 26.01–26.12
  appeal 26.02
  case referred back to General Court 26.12
  cross-appeal 26.04, 26.11
  dismissal of appeal 26.11
  general rules and special
    characteristics 26.08–26.12
  legal aid 26.10
  no hearing is held 26.07
  no measures of inquiry 26.09
  oral part 26.06–26.07
  provisions 26.08
  reasoned request submission 26.06
  reply and rejoinder 26.05
  response 26.03
  written part 26.02–26.05
appointing authority 13.27, 18.02, 18.06,
    18.13–18.18, 18.21–18.23, 18.25–18.26
arbitration clause/special agreement 19.01–19.27
  any party to the contract 19.13
  applicable law 19.16–19.19
  arbitration clause 19.01
  'arbitration clause' is misleading 19.08
  Art. 334 TFEU 19.27
  choice of the parties 19.16
  contract concluded by or on behalf of Union 19.05
  contract law rules 19.17
  contracts concerned 19.05–19.12
  contractual liability versus annulment claims 19.12
  contractual provisions 19.19
  contractual versus non-contractual liability
    claims 19.11
  disputes between Member States 19.22, 19.26
  disputes relating to subject-matter of Treaties 19.25
  EAEC and former ECSC Treaties 19.04, 19.23
  General Court: jurisdiction 19.10
  judgment enforceability 19.21
  jurisdiction of national and Union
    courts 19.07–19.12
  legal capacity of the parties 19.14
  Lisbon Treaty, changes brought by 19.03
  objectives 19.02
  procedure before Union courts 19.20
  procedure relating to direct actions 19.20
  special agreement 19.24
  substantive law and procedure rules 19.18
  Union institutions, bodies, offices or agencies 19.06
  validity 19.15
Area of Freedom, Security and Justice (AFSJ) 1.06,
    1.07, 3.02, 3.33, 21.01–22.19, 22.03–22.05
  Advocate-General's view 22.17
  circumstances warranting application of 22.11
  designated Chamber and urgent preliminary
    procedure 22.10

electronic transmission of documents 22.15
expedited procedures 22.19, 23.42
extension of Union model 22.05
former Treaty framework 22.02–22.04
Lisbon Treaty, changes brought by 22.05
national court, request by 22.08
no other jurisdiction in former third pillar 22.04
oral stage 22.16
questions concerning 22.07
reference may become devoid
    of purpose 22.12
request by Court of its own motion 22.09
restrictions, removal of 22.02–22.05
scope 22.07–22.12
substance, decision on 22.18
written stage 22.14
assets, reduction in 11.64
assignment of cases 23.56
Association Council 6.15
associations 7.104, 7.126–7.129, 25.69
audi alteram partem 11.50, 23.37, 25.37

Benelux Court of Justice 3.14, 3.47
Bergaderm **judgment** 4.46, 11.37, 11.45,
    11.48–11.50, 11.57
Boards of Appeal
  direct actions 25.13, 25.23, 25.71, 25.91, 25.95
  intellectual property 20.02, 20.14, 20.19, 23.04
Brussels Convention 6.17, 21.02, 21.07
Bundesfinanzhof 3.49
Bundesgerichtshof 3.50, 3.54
burden of proof 5.63–5.64, 23.57–23.61
  adversarial principle 23.61
  assertions, proof of 23.59
  inadmissible means of proof 23.60
  judge, active role played by 23.58

certificate of lawyer 25.20
Chambers
  Civil Service Tribunal 2.42
  Court of Justice 2.10, 2.12
  General Court 2.29–2.30
Channel Islands 3.13
Chernobyl **case** 7.79
Chief Adjudication Officer 3.09
Chief Social Security Commissioner 3.09
CILFIT **case** 3.50, 3.54–3.55, 3.56
CIRFS **case** 7.128
civil courts 4.40
Civil Service Tribunal 2.37–2.44
  appeals 2.44
  Chambers 2.42
  composition 2.39
  creation 2.38
  direct actions 25.97
  interim measures, proceedings before Union
    courts 13.27
  jurisdiction 2.39, 2.53
  President 2.40
  procedure 2.43
  Registrar 2.41

Civil Service Tribunal (*cont.*)
role 1.04
staff cases 18.08–18.09, 18.13, 18.15, 18.18,
18.24–18.30
claims for damages *see under* **Member State liability** *and*
damages, action for
clerical errors, rectification of 25.133–25.137
closed class 7.98–7.99, 7.112, 7.136
closure of proceedings for direct actions 25.88–25.137
costs 25.89–25.100
action becomes devoid of purpose 25.100
decision in judgment or order 25.89
discontinued proceedings 25.99
disputes 25.92–25.93
free of charge proceedings 25.90
interveners 25.98
legal fees 25.93
recoverable 25.90–25.93
staff cases 25.97
unreasonable or vexatious procedure 25.96
who pays 25.94–25.100
judgments and orders 25.88, 25.106–25.137
adjudication, failure of 25.136–25.137
formal requirements 25.113–25.114
interpretation 25.125–25.132
late discovery 25.118
new fact 25.117
procedure and consequences 25.131–25.132
rectification of clerical errors 25.133–25.137
revision 25.116–25.124
substantive and formal
requirements 25.128–25.130
successful action 25.115, 25.124
third-party proceedings 25.107–25.115
legal aid 25.101–25.105
necessity 25.105
Codorníu case 7.100
College of Commissioners 5.31, 5.46
collegiate decisions 2.14
Committee of the Regions 7.79–7.80
annulment, action for 7.03
jurisdiction, allocation of 2.51
preliminary rulings on interpretation 6.12
Common Foreign and Security Policy
(CFSP) 1.06–1.07, 3.02, 10.04
annulment, action for 7.04, 7.70, 7.81
arbitration clause/special agreement 19.03
damages, action for 11.02, 11.20
illegality, objection of 9.05
infringement 5.04–5.05
international agreements and Union law
compatibility 12.06
preliminary rulings on interpretation 6.05
Community Patent Court 3.14
Community Plant Variety Office 2.45, 2.53, 20.01,
23.04, 25.23, 25.71
compensation 4.52, 7.224, 11.28, 11.69, 11.95,
11.72, 23.69
competence 7.181
lack of *see under* **annulment, grounds for**
competent authority 4.09, 25.101

competition cases, standard of review in 7.190–7.206
anti-dumping cases 7.205–7.206
applicant, role of 7.191
compatibility of aid measure 7.202
compliance with Commission Guidelines 7.203
comprehensive review as general rule 7.190
doubt benefits applicant 7.192
enforcement of Arts 101 and 102
TFEU 7.190–7.195
lawfulness assessed on basis of fact and
law 7.200
lawfulness assessed in light of information available
when decision adopted 7.204
legal characterization of measure as aid 7.201
merger control 7.196–7.200
procedural guarantees 7.198
prospective analysis 7.196
review of compliance with Commission Guidelines
and Notices 7.195, 7.199
review of legality regarding fines 7.195
review takes into account complex nature of economic
and technical appraisals 7.193
review takes into account margin of discretion
of Commission 7.197
State aid cases 7.201–7.204
competition law (bank guarantees) 13.39
complainants 7.43, 7.132
anti-dumping cases 7.132, 7.166
competition cases 7.38, 7.43
access to file 7.43
infringement proceedings 7.18
State aid cases 7.60–7.62, 7.118, 7.165
complaint
failure to act, action for 8.20 *see* **failure to act,**
action for
infringement proceedings 7.13, 7.18
pursuant to Regulation No. 1/2003 7.43
regarding infringement of Art. 101 or Art. 102
TFEU 8.20
rejection 5.33, 7.86
partial dismissal 7.16
relating to violation of Art. 106(3) TFEU 7.44
right to file 7.60
State aid 7.23, 7.57, 7.61
staff cases 18.15, 18.22–18.23, 18.26
conferral principle 1.04
confidentiality, duty of 7.167
conflict avoidance 4.37
conflicting national rules, inapplicability of 4.36
Conseil d'Etat
France 3.54
Luxembourg 3.09
constitutional charter 1.03, 6.04
constitutional court
Court of Justice's function as 2.21
constitutionally autonomous regions
7.77, 7.103, 7.125
constitutional traditions common to Member
States 4.07, 4.11, 7.106
consumer associations 7.115
consumer protection law 4.41

contested act 7.08–7.12
  see also under admissibility based on type of fact;
    interest in annulment
    of contested act
contract law rules 19.17
contractual liability 19.11–19.12
contractual obligations, applicable law 19.16, 21.03
convention on the protection of financial
    interests 21.11
conventions between Member States 5.08, 21.01
conventions concluded by Member States: jurisdiction
    of Court of Justice 21.01–21.15
  Brussels Convention 21.02, 21.07
  Convention on the protection of financial
    interests 21.11
  conversion into Union instruments 21.04
  direct actions 21.09–21.11, 21.13, 21.15
  disputes between Commission and Member
    States 21.10
  disputes between Member States 21.09
  EU Treaty, based on 21.05, 21.08
  preliminary references 21.12, 21.14
  preliminary rulings 21.06–21.08
  procedure before Court 21.12–21.13
  Rome Convention 21.03, 21.07
cooperation
  enhanced 2.50, 2.53, 7.181
  judicial 6.19
  sincere 2.02, 4.40, 4.47, 5.64, 11.27
Coreper 7.72
costs
  appeals 16.13
  damages 8.21
  direct actions 25.89
  equal treatment 4.08
  failure to act 8.21
  fine reimbursement 7.226
  interest may disappear 7.142
  interim measures 13.45
  preliminary ruling 24.26
  staff cases 18.27, 18.29
  see also under closure of proceedings for
    direct actions
Council 2.37
  annulment, action for 7.14, 7.76–7.78, 7.69
  damages, action for 11.20, 11.18
  failure to act, action for 8.02, 8.08, 8.11–8.12
  jurisdiction 2.49–2.50, 2.53
  preliminary rulings on interpretation 6.10, 6.12
  preliminary rulings on validity 10.06
counterclaims 19.10
Courage case 4.53–4.54
court, access to 4.07
Court of Auditors 6.10, 7.79–7.80
  annulment, action for 7.69
  damages, action for 11.20
  failure to act, action for 8.12
  preliminary rulings on validity 10.06
Court of First Instance 1.06, 2.03, 2.38, 2.45–2.46
  effective judicial protection 4.11
  jurisdiction, allocation of 2.45, 2.48–2.49

Nice Treaty 2.47
  see also General Court
Court of Justice 1.06, 2.04–2.22
  Advocate-General 2.04, 2.15–2.16
  appeals 16.03, 16.30
  arbitration clause or special agreement 19.07
  basic functions 2.21–2.22
  Chambers 2.10, 2.12
  collegiate decisions of the Court 2.14
  composition 2.04–2.09
  constitutional court and supreme court 2.21
  cooperation *see* preliminary ruling: national courts
    and Court of Justice, cooperation between
  court of last resort for constitutional issues 2.22
  damages, action for 11.07–11.08
  deliberations 2.13
  divergence from case-law in preliminary ruling 3.61
  internal organization 2.10–2.20
  Judge-Rapporteur 2.15
  judges 2.04–2.05
  jurisdiction 1.07, 2.46, 2.47, 2.49, 2.53, 6.20
  see also conventions concluded by Member States;
    jurisdiction of Court of Justice
  language arrangements 23.11–23.13
  no ruling on facts and points of national law 6.21
  oath and immunity 2.06
  oral part of procedure 23.74
  organization of procedure 23.62
  preliminary hearing request 3.23
  preliminary rulings on validity 10.13, 10.18
  President 2.07, 2.17
  quorum 2.11
  Registrar 2.09, 2.19
  role 1.04
  sole power to declare Union act invalid 3.06
  staff 2.20
  Vice-President 2.08, 2.18, 13.23
Court of Justice of the European Union 2.03, 5.19
  annulment, action for 7.69
  damages, action for 11.04, 11.20
  failure to act, action for 8.12
  judgments 6.11
  jurisdiction 5.19
  preliminary rulings on interpretation 6.10
  see also Civil Service Tribunal; Court of Justice;
    General Court
criminal proceedings 2.06, 4.11, 4.45, 22.11, 24.18

Da Costa en Schaake case 3.52
damage
  serious and irreparable 13.36, 13.41
damages
  see under Member State liability; damages,
    action for; loss or damage; substantive
    requirements for liability
damages, action for 11.01–11.97
  annulment action 11.11
  applicants/application 11.13–11.17, 11.34
  compensation, obligation to pay 11.95
  contractual liability 11.06
  defendants 11.18–11.32

damages, action for (*cont.*)
  defendants
    broad interpretation 11.20
    damage caused by institutions 11.20
    damage caused by servants of
      institutions 11.21–11.23
    institution to which harmful act or conduct is
      attributable 11.19
    see also **liability concurrent with that of**
      Member States
  direct actions, intervention for 25.66
  EAEC and former ECSC Treaties 11.03
  equitable damage 11.66
  exclusive jurisdiction 11.04
  future damage 11.64, 11.89
  improper use 11.10
  independent form of action 11.09
  interim measures 13.11
  inter partes effect 11.97
  judgment 11.95–11.97
  judicial protection 11.12
  limitation period 11.86–11.94
    commencement and duration 11.86–11.93
    continuous damage 11.88
    expiry of must be raised by defendant 11.93
    future damage 11.89
    interruption of 11.94
    legislative and individual acts 11.90
    materialization of damage causes time to start
      running 11.87
    objective inquiry 11.91
    period of five years 11.86
    unawareness of event giving rise to damage 11.92
  Lisbon Treaty, changes brought by 11.02
  loss or damage *see* **loss or damage**
  Member States 11.17
  natural or legal person 11.13–11.16
  non-contractual liability 11.06–11.07
  non–material damage 11.64
  objective and conditions 11.01
  premature claim 11.35
  requirements 11.33
  staff disputes 11.05
  substantive requirements *see* **substantive**
    requirements for liability
  symbolic damage 11.66
  unjust enrichment 11.08
  unlawfulness, test for 11.42–11.51
da mihi factum, dabo tibi ius 25.58
deceit 4.35
declaratory judgment 5.69
declaratory relief 4.10–4.11
default and compensatory interest 11.72
default judgments 25.31–25.33
defence 25.28
definition of a position 8.10, 8.19–8.20
Deggendorf line of case-law 10.11, 7.122, 10.11
delegation *see under* **annulment, grounds for**
deliberations 2.06, 2.13, 2.17, 2.31, 12.19, 23.11,
  23.83, 23.88, 23.90
derogating provisions, misuse of 5.28

designs *see* **Office for Harmonisation in the Internal**
  Market relating to Community trademarks
  and designs
devolved authorities 7.77, 7.103, 7.125
Dieckmann case 11.53
dies ad quem 23.28, 23.31, 23.33–23.34
dies a quo 23.28–23.29
Dirección General de Defensa de la Competencia 3.11
direct actions, procedure in 25.01–25.137
  absolute bar to proceeding with case 25.85
  action devoid of purpose 25.84
  amicable settlement of dispute 25.82
  closure of proceedings *see* **closure of proceedings**
    for direct actions
  discontinuance 25.82–25.83
  expedited procedure 25.79–25.81
  illegality, objection of 9.16
  interim measures 13.09
  intervention *see* **intervention for direct actions**
  no need to proceed to judgment 25.84–25.85
  oral part of procedure 25.81
  preliminary issues 25.86–25.87
  representation of the parties 23.14
  separate document 25.80, 25.87
  written procedure *see* **written procedure**
    for direct actions
Directeur des Contributions Directes et Accises 3.09
directives, transposition of 4.49, 5.15–5.16
disciplinary proceedings 4.45, 11.51
discontinuance 25.01, 25.82–25.83
discretion
  of courts 5.78
  European Commission 5.27, 5.30, 5.62
  margin of 4.48, 7.180, 7.197
  substantive requirements for liability
    11.52–11.59, 11.61
discrimination, prohibition of 4.08, 6.22, 11.48, 11.50
divorce 21.07
documents, access to 7.67, 7.135, 7.138
duty of care 25.108
Dzodzi case-law 6.16–6.17

e-Curia 23.25, 23.50, 23.54–23.55, 25.26
EAEC Treaty 1.06, 11.03
  annulment, action for 7.06, 7.178
  arbitration clause or special agreement 19.04, 19.23
  damages, action for 11.03
  infringement 5.03
  interim measures 13.03
  international agreements 12.06
  preliminary rulings on interpretation 6.03–6.04
  sanctions 15.03
ECSC Treaty (former) 1.06
  annulment, action for 7.06
  arbitration clause or special agreement 19.04, 19.23
  damages, action for 11.03
  infringement 5.03
  interim measures 13.03
  preliminary ruling 3.04, 3.23
  sanctions 15.03
  unlawful act or conduct 11.43

EC Treaty 1.06, 7.04
EEA Agreement 3.15, 5.07, 12.13
  annulment, action for 7.72
  direct actions 25.20, 25.61, 25.63, 25.75
  preliminary ruling 24.07–24.09, 24.28, 24.33
EEA Joint Committee 7.72
EEA States 23.08, 23.16–23.17, 25.98
effective judicial protection principle 4.06–4.12
  court, access to 4.07
  deficiencies in system pre-Lisbon Treaty 4.10
  equal treatment 4.08
  interim relief 4.61
  Lisbon Treaty 4.12
  solutions identified in case-law 4.11
  statement of reasons 4.09
effectiveness principle 4.01, 4.05, 4.15, 4.25
  claims for an advantage due 4.34
  claims for damages 4.51
  sanctions 4.44
EFTA States 3.15
EFTA Supervisory Authority 24.08–24.09, 25.98
EFTA Surveillance Authority 23.08
  agents 23.16
  direct actions 25.61, 25.63, 25.75
  preliminary ruling, references for 24.07, 24.28
enhanced cooperation 2.50, 2.53, 7.181
environmental law 4.18
Epitropi Antagonismou 3.11
equal treatment 4.08
equivalence principle 4.01, 4.05, 4.14, 4.24, 4.44, 4.51
erga omnes effect 6.30–6.32, 6.34
  annulment, action for 7.88, 7.222
  preliminary rulings on validity 10.18, 10.21
error of law 4.47, 4.50, 16.02, 16.04, 16.29, 17.01
essential procedural requirement, infringement of 7.146
Etoile Commerciale case 11.25
European Agency for the Evaluation of Medicinal
    Products 25.07
European Anti–Fraud Office (OLAF) 9.11, 11.51,
    18.04, 18.06
European Atomic Energy Community Treaty
    see EAEC Treaty
European Central Bank 2.46, 3.02, 7.79–7.80
  annulment, action for 7.69
  arbitration clause/special agreement 19.14
  damages, action for 11.02, 11.20
  failure to act, action for 8.02, 8.11–8.12
  jurisdiction 2.49, 2.53
  preliminary rulings on interpretation 6.10
  preliminary rulings on validity 10.06
  staff cases 18.01
European Coal and Steel Community *see* ECSC
European Commission 2.38
  aid programmes 7.96
  annulment, action for 7.14, 7.69, 7.76–7.78
  authorization by of act of Member State 7.95
  burden of proof 5.63–5.64
  collegiate responsibility 5.46
  damages, action for 11.20
  disclosure of documents to third parties 7.38
  discretion 5.27, 5.30, 5.62, 7.197

  failure to act, action for 8.02, 8.06, 8.08, 8.11–8.12
  guidelines, compliance with 7.194, 4.199, 7.203
  infringement 5.31, 5.34
  jurisdiction 2.49–2.51, 2.53
  margin of discretion 7.197
  and Member States, disputes between 21.10
  preliminary rulings on interpretation 6.10, 6.12
  preliminary rulings on validity 10.06
  refusal to give access to file to parties under
      investigation 7.36
  rejection of request for protection of document under
      legal professional privilege 7.37
European Common Aviation Area 12.13
European Convention of Human Rights (ECHR) 6.24
European Council
  annulment, action for 7.03
  damages, action for 11.02, 11.20
  failure to act, action for 8.11–8.12
  jurisdiction, allocation of 2.51
  preliminary rulings on interpretation 6.10
  preliminary rulings on validity 10.06
  see also Pringle judgment
European Court of Human Rights 3.14, 4.12, 7.72,
    8.11, 11.18
European Court Reports 2.19
European Economic and Social Committee 6.12
European Investment Bank 2.53, 11.20, 18.01
European Ombudsman 7.67, 8.11, 11.20, 11.55,
    11.85, 25.91
European Parliament 2.37
  annulment, action for 7.69, 7.76–7.79
  Committee on Petitions 7.17
  damages, action for 11.20
  failure to act, action for 8.02, 8.08–8.09, 8.11–8.12
  jurisdiction 2.49, 2.51, 2.53
  preliminary rulings on interpretation 6.10, 6.12
  preliminary rulings on validity 10.06
European Schools 3.16
evidence
  supporting 25.18, 25.39
exchange rate 11.73
exclusive jurisdiction 2.52, 3.14, 3.59
  annulment, action for 7.02, 7.61
  appeals 16.03
  arbitration clause/special agreement 19.11
  damages, action for 11.02, 11.04, 11.31
  garnishee order 14.02
  infringement, action for 5.13, 5.60, 5.80
  preliminary ruling 24.26
  preliminary rulings on interpretation 6.17, 6.19, 6.21
  staff cases 18.27
excusable error 7.208, 7.214, 18.19
existing aid 5.22, 7.52, 7.53, 7.55, 7.57, 7.61, 7.63
ex nunc 7.141
ex officio examination 7.217
ex parte order 13.24
expedited procedure 22.19, 23.42, 24.17–24.19,
    25.79–25.81
experts 9.16, 23.06, 23.13, 23.67–23.71, 25.91, 25.93
  see also oral testimony and experts' reports
ex tunc effect 6.33, 7.141, 7.221, 10.22

failure to act, action for 8.01–8.23
  act must be capable of having legal effects 8.08
  admissibility 8.21
  and annulment, relationship between 8.09–8.10
  applicants 8.12–8.14
  basic elements 8.03
  complaint 8.20
  Court, procedure before 8.21–8.22
  defendants 8.11
  duty to act 8.06
  identification of act to be taken 8.07
  interim measures 13.10
  judgment 8.23
  judicial review 8.01, 8.14
  letter of formal notice 8.16, 8.18
  liability for failure to act 11.46
  Lisbon Treaty, changes brought by 8.02
  natural and legal persons 8.13, 8.15
  omission to take decision 8.05
  pleas in law 8.22
  pre-litigation procedure 8.15–8.20
  preliminary rulings on validity 10.12
  subject matter 8.04
  Union institutions, bodies, offices and
    agencies 8.11–8.12, 8.17, 8.19
federated State 4.51, 7.77
FIAMM 11.07
fines 5.78, 7.195, 15.09
  imposition of 7.33, 7.41–7.42, 9.08
  reimbursement 7.226
fixed–term work 4.45
Foglia v Novello 3.42
force majeure 5.68, 7.208, 7.214, 23.84
formal mistake 2.54
form of order 25.38
Foto-Frost case 3.06, 3.59–3.60, 10.13
Francovich case 4.49, 5.02
French overseas departments 3.13
Fresh Marine case 11.54
fumus boni juris 13.34
fumus non mali juris 13.34
fundamental rights 1.03, 1.06, 2.21, 3.39, 5.06,
    6.06–6.07, 6.20, 6.24, 7.73, 11.50, 23.61
  defence 11.51
  fair trial 11.51
  freedom of the press 11.51
  presumption of innocence 11.51
  private and family life 11.51
  right freely to exercise a trade or
    profession 11.50–11.51
  right to property 11.50–11.51
  see also **right to be heard; right to effective legal
    protection**

**garnishee order, proceedings for leave
    to serve** 14.01–14.07
  applicants 14.03, 14.07
  competent court 14.02
  defendants 14.04
  immunity, automatic 14.05
  jurisdiction, limited 14.06

  principle and purpose 14.01
GATT 10.08
GE Betz case 20.10
General Court 2.23–2.36
  Advocates-General 2.24
  appeals 16.04, 16.11, 16.12–16.13, 16.31
    see also **appeals against decisions of General Court**
  arbitration clause or special agreement 19.07, 19.10
  basic function 2.35–2.36
  Chambers 2.29–2.30
  composition 2.23–2.28
  intellectual property *see* **intellectual property,
    jurisdiction of Union courts over disputes
    relating to**
  internal organization 2.29–2.34
  judges 2.23
  jurisdiction 2.49, 2.53
  Nice, Treaty of and subsequent institutional
    developments 2.36
  oath and immunity 2.25
  organization of procedure 23.63
  President 2.26, 2.33, 13.23
  procedure 2.32
  purpose 2.35
  quorum 2.31
  Registrar 2.28, 2.33, 17.04, 17.06
  role 1.04
  staff 2.34
  Vice-President 2.27
  see also **Court of Justice of the European Union;
    Court of First Instance**
general principles
  Member States 4.11, 4.46, 7.153, 11.01–11.02,
    11.44, 11.69, 11.78, 11.85, 19.17
  Union Law 4.44, 5.05–5.06, 5.15, 6.07, 6.22, 6.24,
    7.102, 7.178, 11.49, 11.51, 16.04
Giudice Conciliatore 3.45
good faith, acting in 6.34

illegality, objection of 9.01–9.19
  act of general application 9.05, 9.08
  acts, of individual application, exclusion of 9.07
  act, type of and status of party invoking
    objection 9.06
  admissibility, requirements for 9.14–9.15
  annulment, action for 9.18
  'any party' 9.09
  courts 9.13
  direct action 9.16
  essential function 9.03
  inter partes effects 9.19
  judicial protection 9.04
  Lisbon Treaty, changes brought about by 9.02
  natural or legal persons 9.10
  not an independent right of action 9.01
  objection cannot be raised in proceedings for
    preliminary ruling 9.17
  objection raised by parties and exceptionally by
    Union Courts 9.13
  pleas in law 9.18
  Union bodies, offices and agencies 9.11–9.12

immunity
  automatic 14.05
  see also oath and immunity
implementing measures 2.50, 3.20, 4.10–4.11, 4.31,
    7.90, 7.94, 7.109
  Community act requiring no 4.10–4.12, 7.03,
    7.81, 7.85, 7.106, 7.107, 7.109, 7.110,
    8.13, 9.10, 10.11
importers 7.133–7.134
import licences 7.98, 11.30
inadmissibility, preliminary objection
    of 25.41–25.45
in camera 5.28, 23.67
individual concern, concept of 4.11, 7.03,
    7.111–7.136
  admissibility based on type of act 7.85,
    7.88–7.89, 7.94, 7.97, 7.102,
    7.107–7.108, 7.110
  anti-dumping cases 7.130–7.134
  application of Arts 101 and 102 TFEU 7.112
  closed class *see* closed class
  Codorníu see **Codorníu**
  competitors 7.113, 7.136
  complainants 7.132 *see* complainants
  consumer associations 7.115
  decision addressed to another person 7.135
  documents, access to 7.135
  general application measures 7.130
  importers 7.133–7.134
  individual applicant is not addressee
    of contested act 7.111
  merger control 7.113–7.116
  national authorities, referral to 7.116
  natural and legal persons 7.81
  original equipment manufacturers 7.134
  Plaumann see **Plaumann**
  producers and exporters 7.131
  procedural safeguards 7.132
  public contracts 7.136
  regulatory acts *see* regulatory act
  representatives of employees 7.114
  State aid cases 7.117–7.129
  State aid cases 7.61–7.62
  State aid cases
    associations 7.126–7.129
    beneficiaries, position of and their
      competitors 7.117–7.119, 7.121–7.122
    competitors of recipient 7.124
    constitutionally autonomous regions
      and devolved authorities 7.125
    decisions addressed to Member States 7.117
    decisions relating to general aid 7.120–7.122
    decisions relating to individual aid 7.123–7.124
    decisions taken on basis of preliminary
      procedure 7.118
    decision taken upon completion of
      procedure 7.119
    general application measures 7.120
    recipients 7.123
    trade unions 7.129
information injunction 7.59

infringement by a Member State 5.01–5.81
  see also Member State, failure of to fulfil obligation
    under Treaties; Member State liability
infringement by private parties
  Courage *see* **Courage**
  Manfredi 4.54
infringement proceedings *see* Member State, failure of
    to fulfil obligation under Treaties
inquiry, measures of 23.58, 23.64–23.72
  inspections of place or thing 23.72
  personal appearance of the parties 23.64–23.65
  preliminary ruling 24.23
  purpose 23.65
  requests for information and production of
    documents 23.66
  see also oral testimony and experts' reports
intellectual property, jurisdiction of Union courts over
    disputes relating to 20.01–20.22
  Administration of Trade Marks and Legal
    Division 20.02
  adverse effect by contested decision 20.11
  appeal 20.22
  applicant 20.11
  Board of Appeal 20.02
  Community Trade Mark 20.06
  content of application 20.19
  contested decision, review of 20.13
  costs of proceedings 20.08
  defendant 20.09–20.10
  dismissal of action 20.21
  forms of order 20.10
  General Court 20.03–20.08
  illegality 20.17
  jurisdiction 20.03–20.08
  legality control 20.03
  legal protection 20.02
  no declaratory or confirmatory judgments 20.07
  no power to issue injunction to office 20.06
  Office is defendant 20.09
  Opposition Divisions 20.02, 20.14
  pleas in law 20.12–20.17
  subject-matter 20.15–20.16
  successful action 20.20
  time limits 20.18
intellectual property rights disputes, procedure in the
    case of 23.04, 25.23, 25.51, 25.71, 25.91
interest 4.30
interest in annulment of contested act 7.138–7.144
  balanced approach 7.143
  concept 7.138
  interest may disappear 7.142
  no interest in challenging act 7.139
  personal interest 7.140
  pleas in law 7.144
  vested and present interest 7.141
interim measures 7.39, 13.10
interim measures before Union courts,
    proceedings for 13.01–13.46
  admissibility 13.25
  ancillary nature of proceedings 13.07–13.14
  appeals 13.14

interim measures before Union courts,
    proceedings for (*cont.*)
    damages, action for 13.11
    direct action 13.09
    failure to act, action for 13.10
    infringement, action for 13.12
    judge may not assume role of defendant
        institution 13.08
    preliminary ruling proceedings 13.13
  appeal 13.14, 13.46
  applicant 13.17–13.19
  competent judge 13.23
  costs 13.45
  defendant 13.20–13.22
  EAEC and now-expired ECSC Treaties 13.03
  interest 13.19
  interim relief tailored to the case 13.06
  interveners 13.18
  Lisbon Treaty, changes brought by 13.02
  no prejudgment of decision to be given in main
    proceedings 13.16
  objective 13.01
  opponent in main proceedings 13.20
  procedure before Court 13.24
  provisional nature 13.15–13.16, 13.44
  separate application 13.28–13.30
  staff cases 13.27
  substantive requirements 13.31–13.43
    avoidance of damage 13.40
    balance of interests 13.42–13.43
    competition law (bank guarantees) 13.39
    fumus non mali juris 13.34
    prima facie case 13.33–13.34
    public contracts 13.38
    reasonable diligence 13.37
    serious and irreparable damage 13.36, 13.41
    urgency 13.35–13.41
  summary procedure 13.24
  suspension of operation of contested act 13.04
  third parties 13.21
  time limits 13.15, 13.26–13.27
  types of measure 13.04–13.06
  Union bodies, offices and agencies 13.22
interim proceedings, intervention in 3.46, 25.68
interim relief, before national courts 4.60–4.64
  allegedly illegal national measure 4.61–4.62
  appeal against a national decision 4.63
  counterpart 4.64
interinstitutional disputes 2.49
interlocutory proceedings 3.16–3.17, 3.46, 4.61,
  13.01, 13.32, 25.91
internal market 5.28
  see also Office for Harmonisation in the Internal
    Market relating to Community trademarks
    and designs
internal security 22.02–22.03, 22.05
  see also security
international agreements 5.13
  acts of bodies established by 6.15
  preliminary rulings on interpretation 6.09,
    6.13–6.14

  preliminary rulings on validity 10.05, 10.07–10.08
  see also opinions on the compatibility of international
    agreements with Union law
International Court of Justice 2.14, 3.14
International Labour Organisation 12.12
international law 5.37, 5.65, 7.151, 7.178, 10.08,
  12.07, 12.12, 19.16, 21.04
inter partes effects 6.30–6.31, 9.19, 10.21, 11.97
interpretation *see* preliminary rulings
  on interpretation
interpretation of judgment, application for 6.11,
  25.125–25.132
interveners 23.78
  appeals 16.15
  closure of proceedings for direct actions 25.98
  direct actions 25.30, 25.59–25.60, 25.71, 25.98
  intellectual property 20.11, 20.15
  interim measures 13.18
  non-privileged 25.65
  preliminary ruling 24.06
  privileged 25.62
  staff cases 18.30
intervention for direct actions 25.58–25.78
  annulment, action for 25.67
  application to intervene served on the
    parties 25.74
  arguments and procedural rights 25.60
  associations 25.69
  damages, action for 25.66
  decision on application to intervene 25.75
  formal requirements 25.70–25.78
  intellectual property rights disputes 25.71
  interim proceedings 25.68
  language 25.73
  non-Member States 25.63
  non-privileged interveners 25.65
  objective 25.58
  pleas 25.59–25.60, 25.72
  privileged interveners 25.62
  reply to statement in intervention 25.77
  statement in intervention 25.76
  substantive requirements 25.61–25.69
  time limits 25.70, 25.78
  Union bodies, offices and agencies 25.64
  who can intervene 25.61
Inuit Tapiriit Kanatami 7.108 *see also* regulatory act
invalidity, declaration of 10.19–10.21
Irish Creamery Milk Suppliers Association
  case 3.25
Irish Goods Council 5.39
Isle of Man 3.13

Jégo–Quére case 4.11–4.12, 7.106, 7.110
joinder of cases 23.43–23.45
Judge-Rapporteur 2.10, 2.12–2.13, 2.15
judges 2.05–2.07, 2.10–2.14, 2.20
  active role played by 23.58
  Court of Justice 2.04–2.05
  General Court 2.23–2.26, 2.29–2.31, 2.34
judgments and orders 23.85–23.94
  binding nature 23.93

closure of proceedings for direct actions 25.88
content 23.88
declaratory judgment 5.69
default judgments 25.31–25.33
delivery and service of 23.90
enforceability 23.94
failure to act 8.23
formal requirements 23.88–23.92
language 23.89
legal force 23.93–23.94
publication 23.92
signature and service of 23.91
time limits 23.87, 25.108–25.112, 25.117–25.121,
    25.130
see also under closure of proceedings for direct
    actions; interpretation of judgment
judicial panels 2.03, 2.37, 2.38, 2.47–2.48
judicial protection 1.03
    challenges underlying system of 1.05
    coherent system of 1.02
    complete system of 1.02
    illegality, objection of 9.04
    problem of 7.105
    see also effective judicial protection
judicial remedy 3.48–3.49
judicial review 8.01, 8.14
judicial supervision 4.03
jurisdiction, allocation of 2.45–2.55
    Civil Service Tribunal 2.53
    Committee of the Regions 2.51
    Court of First Instance 2.45, 2.48
    Court of Justice 2.46–2.47, 2.53
    European Council 2.51
    exceptions 2.50
    General Court 2.53
    identical or similar object of cases pending before
        different courts 2.55
    infringement actions and preliminary references 2.52
    Nice Treaty 2.47–2.48
    pre Nice Treaty 2.45–2.46
    present allocation 2.49–2.55
    present system 2.49
    procedural document submitted to wrong court 2.54
justice and home affairs 21.01

Köbler 3.58, 4.50
Kühne & Heitz case 4.56–4.57

languages 23.02–23.13
    authentic text 23.10
    case, language of 23.02, 23.05
    Court of Justice 23.11–23.13
    determination of language of a case 23.03
    direct actions 25.91
    intellectual property rights disputes 23.04
    intervening States 23.08
    intervention for direct actions 25.73
    judgments and orders 23.89
    language service 23.13
    Members of the Court 23.07
    preliminary ruling 24.28

publications 23.12
Registrar responsibilities 23.09
witnesses and experts 23.06
working language 23.11
law enforcement services 22.03, 22.05
lawyers 23.17
legal aid 24.27, 25.101–25.105, 26.10
legal basis 7.19, 7.172, 15.01
legal certainty principle 5.66, 6.34
legal fees 25.93
légalité externe 7.146
légalité interne 7.146
legality of national provisions, assessment
    of 4.36–4.38
legal order, Union 1.03, 1.06, 1.09, 2.02, 2.16, 2.22,
    2.35, 2.74
    annulment, action for 7.152, 7.178, 7.198, 7.206,
        7.221–7.222
    equivalence and effectiveness 4.05, 4.10–4.11, 4.34,
        4.40, 4.45, 4.58–4.59, 4.61
    failure to act, action for 8.22
    infringement 5.65, 5.71
    preliminary ruling, references for 3.04–3.06, 3.21,
        3.27–3.28
    preliminary rulings on interpretation 6.13,
        6.161, 6.34
    preliminary rulings on validity 10.20
legal personality 7.83
legal persons *see* natural and legal persons
Les Verts judgment 1.03, 1.05, 7.70, 7.102,
    9.04, 10.10
letter of formal notice 5.41–5.44, 5.48, 5.52–5.57
    failure to act, action for 8.15, 8.16, 8.18
    infringement by Member State 5.41–5.44
letters rogatory 23.71
liability concurrent with that of Member
    States 11.24–11.32
liability
    contractual 19.11–19.12
    non-contractual 11.06–11.07, 19.11–19.12
    Member State 4.46, 4.50–4.51, 5.73, 11.60
    subjective 11.42
    see also liability concurrent with that of Member
        States; Member State liability; substantive
        requirements for liability
liability concurrent with that of Member States
    actual injury 11.31
    claim secures full compensation 11.28
    genuine discretion 11.26
    grounds on which an act may be attributed to Union
        or Member State 11.25
    liability principle 11.27
    pecuniary loss 11.27–11.32
    principle 11.24
    undue payment to national authority 11.29
    unlawful joint action of Union and Member
        State 11.32
    unlawful refusal to effect payment or perform
        an act 11.30
liability for lawful act 11.07, 11.08 *see also FIAMM;*
    Masdar

limitation periods in actions for damages 23.26
  see also under **damages, actions for**
limitation periods under national law 4.19
  claims for an advantage due 4.32
  equivalence and effectiveness 4.25
  rules of evidence 4.23, 4.26
lis alibi pendens 19.09, 25.44
lis pendens 7.217, 25.44
locus standi 1.07, 4.17–4.18, 7.89, 7.121, 7.124
Lomé Convention 7.25
loss or damage 4.48, 5.73
  actual 4.54
  assessment 16.10
  breach of superior law 3.58, 4.47
  causal connection 4.47, 11.74, 11.78
  claim 3.58
  compensation 4.52
  Courage see **Courage**
  damage passed on to others 11.71
  diligence 4.52
  discretion 11.56
  extent 11.57
  future loss or damage 11.67
  infringement 4.51
  Member State liability *see* **Member State liability**
  reality 11.63
  see also under **substantive requirements for liability**
Lucchini case 4.58 *see also under* **res judicata**
lump sum and/or penalty payment 5.77–5.79

Magorrian and Cunningham case 4.34
mandatory rules of Union law 4.39–4.40
Masdar judgment 11.08
material inaccuracy 7.171
matrimonial matters 21.04, 21.07
Meilicke case 3.28, 6.34
Member State, failure of to fulfil obligation under
    Treaties
  act or failure to act 5.14
  acts affecting jurisdiction 5.19
  administrative practice 5.10
  agriculture aid 5.25
  any shortcoming 5.09
  applicant 5.31–5.35
  Commission 5.31, 5.34
  complaint rejection 5.33
  Conventions between Member States 5.08
  defendant 5.36–5.39
  derogating provisions, misuse of 5.28
  directive transposition, failure of 5.15–5.16
  duty to take necessary measures 5.70
  general principles of Union law 5.06
  individuals, position of 5.72
  infringements 5.11
  interim measures before Union courts, proceedings
    for 13.12
  international agreements 5.13
  judgment may constitute basis for State liability 5.73
  judicial practice 5.12 jurisdiction, allocation of 2.52
  legal force of judgment and failure to fulfil
    obligations 5.70–5.74

legal provision no longer applied 5.17
legislature, executive and judiciary 5.38
letter of formal notice 5.41–5.44
Lisbon Treaty, changes brought by 5.04
Member State 5.35–5.37
mixed agreements 5.07
national rules violating treaties but complying with
    secondary law 5.20
nature of the action 5.01
non-binding acts 5.18
no standing for individuals 5.32
objective 5.40
preliminary ruling, failure to request a 3.56
pre-litigation stage 5.40–5.50
private companies controlled by public
    authorities 5.39
procedure 5.03
public procurement contracts 5.29–5.30
public undertakings 5.26–5.27
purpose 5.02
reasoned opinion 5.45–5.50
result of action 5.69
rules of non-CFSP Union law 5.05
sanctions for failure to comply with judgment
    5.75–5.81
  Art 258 TFEU 5.76
  Art. 260(2) TFEU 5.75–5.76
  court's discretion 5.78
  lump sum and/or penalty payment 5.77
  new failure to comply with judgment 5.81
  pecuniary sanctions 5.80
  retroactive pecuniary sanctions 5.79
State aid 5.22–5.25
temporal effects, limiting 5.71
time frame and compliance with judgment 5.74
violation of obligation to notify aid 5.24
Member States
  accession 6.04, 7.75
  annulment 7.76–7.78
  damages, action for 11.17
  illegality, objection of 9.11
  infringement *see* **Member State, failure of to fulfil**
      obligation under Treaties
  jurisdiction 2.49, 2.50
  preliminary ruling, references for 24.08
  preliminary rulings on interpretation 6.13
  State aid 7.117
  see also **Member State, liability**
Member State liability 4.46–4.52
  compensation 4.52
  conditions 4.47
  directives, transposition of 4.49
  discretion, margin of 4.48
  equivalence and effectiveness principles
    4.51, 4.51
  last instance, decisions of national courts
    adjudicating at 4.50
  State liability principle 4.46
merger control
  annulment, action for 7.138
  competition cases 7.196–7.200

conduct during administrative procedure and
    admissibility of pleas 7.186
individual concern, concept of 7.113–7.116
infringements of essential procedural
    requirement 7.164
see also under reviewable act
Merger Treaty 6.04
Miles 3.14
mistake of law 4.29, 5.37
mixed agreements 5.07, 6.14
Mulder case 11.25

national administrative body
    possibility to refer: *see under* preliminary rulings:
        national courts and Court of Justice,
        cooperation between
    reopening/withdrawal of decision 4.55–4.56
national competition authorities 3.11
national courts 2.01–2.02
    AFSJ: urgent preliminary ruling procedure 22.08
    arbitration clause or special agreement 19.09
    order for reference made by 24.02
    preliminary rulings on interpretation 6.25,
        6.27–6.32
    role of 1.04, 2.02
    see also preliminary ruling: national courts and Court
        of Justice
national procedural autonomy, equivalence and
    effectiveness 4.01–4.64
    autonomy 4.02
    constraints 4.04, 4.13–4.59
    effectiveness principle *see* effectiveness principle
    equivalence principle 4.14, 4.44, 4.51
    infringements by private parties *see* infringements
        by private parties
    interim relief 4.60–4.64
    judicial supervision 4.03
    legality of national provisions 4.36–4.38
    limitation periods 4.19
    locus standi and interest in bringing proceedings
        4.17–4.18
    national procedural autonomy principle 4.41
    pleas, raising of 4.39–4.41
    res judicata effects of national judicial decisions
        4.58–4.59
    rules of evidence 4.20–4.35
        burden of proof 4.28
        claims for an advantage due 4.32–4.35
        claim based on directive not implemented
            in time 4.33
        deceit 4.35
        effectiveness principle 4.34
        limitation periods 4.32
        constraints 4.22
        effectiveness principle 4.25
        equivalence principle 4.24
        heterogeneity of national systems 4.21
        interest 4.30
        limitation periods 4.23, 4.26
        payment under protest 4.29
        State aid, unlawful, recovery of 4.31

third parties, charge passed on to 4.27
unlawful charges, recovery of 4.21–4.30
withdrawal of a decision that has become final
    4.55–4.57
national security measures 5.28
natural or legal persons 23.18
    annulment, action for 7.03, 7.43, 7.81–7.82, 7.85,
        7.100, 7.109, 7.138
    damages, action for 11.13–11.16, 11.18
    failure to act, action for 8.13, 8.15
    illegality, objection of 9.10
    nationality, irrelevance of 7.82
negotorium gestio 11.08
nemo auditur 7.189
new aid 5.24, 7.52, 7.54–7.55, 7.57, 7.118
new facts 7.23, 13.44, 16.03, 18.20, 20.15
new plea 18.26, 23.78, 26.08
    annulment, action for 7.11, 7.209,
    appeals 16.20, 16.22, 16.29, 18.26
    direct actions 25.13–25.14, 25.16, 25.37
Nice Treaty 1.06, 2.36, 2.38
    annulment, action for 7.79
    jurisdictional allocation 2.47–2.49
non-contractual liability 11.06–11.07, 11.46,
    19.11–19.12
non-material damage 11.66, 13.14
notification 5.55, 7.46, 7.175, 7.213–7.215, 24.06
nullity, declaration of 7.222–7.226, 10.21

oath and immunity 2.06, 2.25
object of case
    identical or similar 2.55
Office for Harmonisation in the Internal Market
    relating to Community trademarks and designs
    (OHIM) 2.45, 2.53, 20.01, 20.08, 20.13
    direct actions 25.23, 25.71
    failure to act, action for 8.11
    languages 23.04
official holidays 23.31
officials 7.33, 7.128, 7.157, 11.13, 18.01,
    18.05–18.07, 25.91
operative part 23.80, 23.88, 23.92, 26.02
    annulment, action for 7.22, 7.34, 7.56, 7.223
    appeals 16.01, 16.27, 16.29
    direct actions 25.16, 25.65, 25.110, 25.120,
        25.128, 25.134
    infringement, action for 5.80
    intellectual property 20.06, 20.20
    preliminary rulings on interpretation 6.27
    staff cases 18.28
Opinion 1/09 3.14
opinions on the compatibility of international agreements
    with Union law 12.01–12.21
    adverse opinion 12.20
    'agreement envisaged' 12.08
    applicants 12.09
    Court, procedure before 12.18–12.19
    EAEC Treaty, comparable provisions of 12.06
    ex ante judicial control 12.02, 12.14
    favourable opinion 12.21
    jurisdiction, extent of 12.11–12.13

opinions on the compatibility of international agreements
with Union law (*cont.*)
  Lisbon Treaty, changes introduced by 12.04
  non-contentious nature of procedure 12.18
  no obligation 12.10
  no suspensory effect of request 12.17
  objective 12.01
  opinion 12.19
  participation of the Union 12.08
  relationship with other remedies in the
    Treaties 12.03
  review 12.11–12.13
  second and third pillars (former) 12.05
  subject-matter of envisaged agreement must
    be known 12.15
  time limit 12.14–12–17
  Union must not yet be bound by agreement 12.16
oral part of procedure 23.73–23.84
  absence during initial hearing 23.84
  closure 23.80
  course of 23.76–23.81
  no right to respond to Advocate-General's
    Opinion 23.81
  opening 23.73–23.75
  optional character of hearing before Court
    of Justice 23.74
  oral argument 23.78
  questions 23.79
  reasoned request 23.75
  reopening 23.82–23.84
  report for hearing 23.77
  timing 23.73
oral testimony and experts' reports 23.67–23.71
  compensation 23.69
  experts 23.68
  letters rogatory 23.71
  objection to witness or expert 23.70
  witnesses 23.67
order for enforcement 23.94
order for reference
  appeal brought against 3.30
  inadmissibility 3.26
  requirements for 3.25
orders *see* judgments and orders
organization of procedure, measures of 23.58,
  23.62–23.63, 24.23
original equipment manufacturers 7.134
overseas countries and territories 3.13
own motion
  annulment, action for 7.138, 7.146, 7.158, 7.174,
    7.193, 7.207, 7.217, 7.221
  appeals 16.14, 16.22
  Areas of Freedom, Security and Justice 22.06,
    22.09, 22.19
  damages, action for 11.92
  direct actions 25.14, 25.49, 25.82,
    25.84–25.85, 25.134
  equivalence and effectiveness 4.05, 4.36, 4.39–4.41,
    4.57–4.58
  illegality, objection of 9.13
  infringement, action for 5.31, 5.52

inquiry, measures of 23.67
intellectual property 20.12, 20.15
interim measures 13.15
language 23.05
oral part of procedure 23.76, 23.78
preliminary ruling, references for 3.09, 3.12, 3.19,
  3.44, 24.05, 24.17, 24.32
preliminary rulings on interpretation 6.22
preliminary rulings on validity 10.11, 10.15
procedure for dealing with cases 23.41, 23.48
sanctions 15.04, 15.08
staff cases 18.13, 18.26
time limits 23.26

Pardini case 3.16
Parfums Christian Dior 3.14
Passenger Name Record (PNR) data 12.17
pecuniary loss 11.27–11.32
penalty payment 5.79
perjury 23.67–23.68
personal appearance of parties 23.64–23.65
Pigs Marketing Board case 3.31
pillars of the Treaties (second and third) 1.06, 6.05,
  7.04, 10.04, 12.05, 22.04
  see also **Common Foreign and Security Policy; Police
    and Judicial Cooperation in Criminal Matters**
Plaumann case 4.11, 7.106, 7.110, 7.122
pleadings
  appeals 16.29, 26.05, 26.07
  direct actions
    closure of proceedings 25.91, 25.93–25.94
    intervention 25.72
    written procedure 25.05, 25.31, 25.37–25.38,
      25.46, 25.50, 25.54, 25.56
  intellectual property 20.08, 20.15
  interim measures 13.29
  language 23.05
  oral part of procedure 23.74
  organization of procedure, measures of 23.62–23.63
  preliminary ruling, references for 24.15
  procedures for dealing with cases 23.39
  written part of procedure 23.55
Police and Judicial Cooperation in Criminal
  Matters 1.06–1.07, 3.02, 10.04, 22.04
  annulment, action for 7.04, 7.70
  arbitration clause/special agreement 19.03
  conventions concluded by Member States 21.01
  damages, action for 11.02, 11.20
  infringement 5.04–5.05
  international agreements and Union law
    compatibility 12.05
  preliminary rulings on interpretation 6.05
powers, misuse of 7.181–7.184
praeter legem preliminary ruling, obligation
  to request 3.59–3.61
pre-litigation procedure
  failure to act 8.15–8.20
  infringement by Member State 5.40–5.50
  see also under **staff cases**
preliminary issues 25.86–25.87
preliminary references 2.52

preliminary report 23.56
preliminary rulings: national courts and Court of Justice, cooperation between 3.01–3.61
  administrative bodies 3.10
  annulment of request 3.29–3.30
  appeal brought against order for reference 3.30
  arbitrators 3.12
  Benelux Court of Justice 3.47
  Court of Justice: sole power to declare Union act invalid 3.06
  Court of Justice, divergence from case-law of 3.61
  court or tribunal of a Member State 3.08–3.15
  damages, claim in 3.58
  determination of relevance of request 3.31–3.42
  difficulties 3.57
  dispute must be pending before national court 3.16
  duty to request 3.43–3.61
  EAEC Treaty 3.03
  ECSC Treaty (former) 3.04
  Foto-Frost 3.59–3.60
  highest courts 3.44
  infringement action 3.56
  initiative for requesting 3.08–3.30
  interim proceedings 3.46
  international courts 3.14
  judicial remedy 3.48–3.49
  jurisdictional issues 3.18
  limits 3.34–3.42, 3.50–3.55
    acte clair 3.54
    answer can be clearly deduced from case-law (*acte éclairé*) 3.53
    Charter of Fundamental Rights of the EU 3.39
    cross-border elements 3.38
    disputes 3.37, 3.40–3.42
    general or hypothetical questions 3.35
    identical or similar question 3.52
    irrelevant questions 3.36–3.39, 3.50
    post-*CILFIT* case-law 3.55
    reference bears no relation to dispute 3.36
    relevance, presumption of 3.34
  Lisbon Treaty, changes brought by 3.02
  lower court, no remedy available against decision of 3.45
  national competition authorities 3.11
  national court, task of 3.31–3.33
  objectives 3.05
  obligation enforcement 3.56–3.58
  praeter legem preliminary rulings 3.59–3.61
  proceedings, types of 3.17
  relevance of questions must appear from order for reference 3.33
  relevance, responsibility for assessment of 3.31
  rulings must contribute to resolution of dispute 3.32
  third countries' courts 3.15
  timing and content of request 3.19–3.28
    Court of Justice and questions reformulation 3.23
    factual and legal context 3.27
    higher courts, binding rulings of 3.21
    initiative with national court 3.19
    national court, content determined by 3.22
    national court's discretion 3.28
    national court's right to refer 3.20
    reference, inadmissibility of 3.26
    reference, requirements for 3.25
    topics to be discussed 3.07
  Vaassen criteria *see* **Vaassen criteria**
preliminary rulings on interpretation 6.01–6.34
  acts of bodies established by international agreements 6.15
  acts of committees established under Union law 6.12
  acts of Union institutions, bodies, offices or agencies 6.08–6.10
  agreements concluded by the Union and Member States 6.13–6.14
  binding effect 6.27, 6.30
  Court of Justice does not rule on facts and points of national law 6.21
  Court of Justice, limits placed on jurisdiction of 6.20
  declaratory nature 6.31
  Dzodzi case-law 6.16–6.17
  ex tunc effect 6.33
  issues raised must fall within scope of Union law 6.24
  judgments of Court of Justice of European Union 6.11
  judicial cooperation 6.19
  national courts 6.27–6.32
    binding effect 6.27, 6.30
    jurisdiction 6.26
    new reference possible 6.28
    reference back to 6.25
    sanctions for non-compliance 6.29
  no jurisdiction to rule on compatibility of national rules 6.23
  provisions of Union law to which national law refers 6.16–6.17
  questions, reformulation of 6.22
  temporal effects 6.33–6.34
  Treaties 6.04–6.07
  uniformity in application of Union law 6.32
  versus application 6.18
preliminary rulings, procedure in case of 24.01–24.33
  anonymity *see* **anonymity**
  calculation of two-month period for submission 24.10
  content 24.03
  costs 24.26
  EEA Agreement 24.33
  expedited procedure 24.17–24.19
  formal and substantive requirements 24.02–24.05
  inquiry, measures of 24.23
  language of the case 24.28
  legal aid 24.27
  length 24.04
  national court 24.02
  no appeal 24.29
  no hearing is held 24.15
  no interpretation 24.30
  no intervention 24.12
  no second exchange 24.11
  notification 24.06–24.08
  oral observations 24.13–24.15
  order of reference 24.02–24.08

preliminary rulings, procedure in case of (*cont.*)
organization of procedure, measures of 24.23
rectification 24.32
reopening 24.14
representation 24.24
revision 24.31
urgent procedure 24.20–24.21
withdrawal of reference 24.25
written observations 24.09–24.12
preliminary rulings on validity 10.01–10.23
acts of bodies established by international
agreements 10.07
acts excluded from review 10.03
acts of general application 10.10
acts of Union institutions, bodies, offices
or agencies 10.06
annulment, action for 10.14
assessment of validity 10.16
binding and non-binding Union acts 10.09
Court of Justice ruling 10.18
declaration of invalidity 10.20, 10.19, 10.21
declaration of nullity 10.21
fact-finding to assess legality 10.17
failure to act 10.12
grounds on which validity may
be contested 10.15
individual acts and *Deggendorf* 10.11
see also *Deggendorf* line of case-law
international agreements 10.05
review of legality of Union acts reserved to Court of
Justice under
Foto-Frost 10.13
review of Union acts in light of international
agreements 10.08
temporal effects 10.22–10.23
Union acts in former second and third pillars
of Union (PJCCM and CFSP) 10.04
preparatory measures 7.65, 18.06, 23.56
President
Chambers 2.10
Court of Justice 2.07, 2.17
Civil Service Tribunal 2.40
General Court 2.26, 2.33
presumption of innocence 7.192
primacy of Union law 2.02, 3.20, 4.04, 4.58, 19.09
prima facie case 13.31–13.34
Pringle judgment 2.52, 6.08, 7.69, 7.75, 10.03, 19.25
private international law 19.16, 21.04
private law 2.53, 21.07, 25.35, 25.53
private law
annulment, action for 7.152, 7.155
contract 19.05
infringement 5.39
international 19.16, 21.04
legal person governed by 23.18, 25.22
qualification waiver 23.22
privileged applicants 7.03, 7.21, 7.76–7.77, 7.138,
9.06, 9.11
Privileges and Immunities Protocol 11.51
procedural safeguards 7.132
procedures for dealing with cases 23.39–23.48

circumstances 23.46
connection between cases 23.43
deferment of determination of case 23.48
effect 23.45, 23.47
expedited procedures 23.42
joinder of cases 23.43–23.45
objective 23.44
priority 23.41
procedure 23.48
reasoned order 23.40
stay of proceedings 23.46–23.47
time limits 23.47
written and oral part 23.39
proceed to judgment 2.43
no need to 25.01, 25.82–25.87, 25.100, 26.08
Procureur Général 2.15
producers and exporters 7.131
publication 7.175 7.210–7.213, 23.12, 23.30, 23.92,
25.24, 25.54
public contracts 7.136, 13.38
public policy 4.41, 7.217, 18.26
time–limit as matter of 7.207, 23.26
public procurement contracts 5.29–5.30,
7.17, 7.68
public tender procedure 7.73, 7.136
public undertakings 5.26–5.27

questions
general or hypothetical 3.35
identical or similar 3.52
irrelevant 3.36–3.39, 3.50
reformulation 6.22
quorum 2.11, 2.31

reasonable diligence 13.37
reasoned opinion 5.45–5.50, 5.52–5.59, 5.61
see also under Member State, failure of to fulfil
obligation under Treaties
reasoned order 25.45
recitals 7.22–7.29
recovery injunctions 7.58
reformatio in pejus, prohibition of 4.40
Registrar 2.20, 23.09
Court of Justice 2.09, 2.19
Civil Service Tribunal 2.41
General Court 2.28, 2.33
written procedure for direct actions 25.26
regulatory act 7.105–7.110
concept of 'regulatory act' 7.108
direct concern 7.109
effective judicial protection 7.105
Inuit Tapiriit Kanatami 7.108
no implementing measures 7.109
see also implementing measures
representation of the parties 23.14–23.23
reply and rejoinder see under written procedure for
direct actions and appeals, procedure in case of
representation of the parties
agents 23.16
direct actions and preliminary ruling proceedings 23.14
exclusion from proceedings 23.23

immunity 23.20
intermediaries 23.15
lawyers 23.17
legal persons 23.18
privileges and facilities 23.21
qualification and waiver 23.22
regularization 23.19
rights and obligations 23.20–23.23
res judicata 3.12, 7.227
  damages, action for 11.11
  direct actions 25.107–25.108, 25.123
  effects of national judicial decisions *see under*
    national procedural autonomy, equivalence
    and effectiveness; *Lucchini*
  illegality, objection of 9.15
  infringement actions 5.70, 5.76
  judgments and orders 23.94
  oral part of procedure 23.83
  preliminary ruling 3.30
resolutions 7.24
retroactive pecuniary sanctions 5.79
review procedure 2.22, 17.01–17.09
  decision whether to review 17.06
  effects 17.09
  exceptional 6.28
  initiation 17.04
  judgment on substance of case 17.07
  justification for 17.02
  no review necessary 17.03
  procedure 17.04–17.08
  Reviewing Chamber 17.05
  suspensory effect 17.08
reviewable act 7.08–7.68
  access to documents 7.67
  act of a contractual nature 7.15
  act intended to produce legal effects 7.20–7.29
  action inadmissible if act mere declaration of
    intent 7.24
  act no longer in force 7.10
  act not listed in Art. 288 TFEU 7.17
  act relating to execution of decision imposing
    a fine 7.42
  act replacing withdrawn act 7.11
  anti-dumping cases 7.64–7.66
  binding act, requirement for 7.13–7.15
  bonding on institution concerned 7.26
  Commission's disclosure of documents
    to third parties 7.38
  Commission's refusal to give access to its file to parties
    under investigation 7.36
  Commission's rejection of request for protection of
    document under legal professional privilege 7.37
  commitments 7.40
  complainant, position of 7.43
  complaint 7.44
  confirmatory acts 7.23
  content 7.16–7.19
  contested act, requirement for 7.08–7.12
  definitive measures 7.66
  definitive statement of position 7.27
  existing act 7.08

fine, imposition of 7.33, 7.41
infringement 7.34, 7.41
inspections 7.32
institution's rejection of confirmatory application
  is a reviewable act 7.67
interim measures 7.39
internal instructions and guidelines 7.25–7.26
internal procedure, measure concluding 7.28
irregularities in preparatory acts 7.29
legal effects 7.20
legitimate legal basis 7.19
merger control 7.45–7.51
  ancillary restrictions 7.48
  commitments 7.51
  dominant position 7.49
  final decisions on notification 7.46
  initiation of procedure 7.47
  national authorities 7.50
  regulatory framework 7.45
no legal effects vis-à-vis third parties 7.25
non-existent act 7.12
notice pursuant to Art. 27(4) of Regulation
  No. 1/2003 7.35
only final decision is reviewable 7.68
operative part and recitals 7.22
preparatory acts and measures laying down
  definitive position 7.27–7.29
preparatory measures 7.65
public procurement 7.68
refusal 7.18
regulatory framework 7.30
resolutions 7.24
silence on part of an institution 7.14
standard applicable to privileged and non-privileged
  applicants 7.21
State aid cases 7.52–7.63
  complaint 7.60–7.61
  existing aid 7.53
  final decisions 7.55
  information injunction 7.59
  initiation of procedure 7.57
  mere correspondence with complainants 7.62
  new aid 7.54
  refusal to take appropriate measures 7.63
  regulatory framework 7.52
  suspension and recovery injunctions 7.58
  undertakings by Member State concerned 7.56
  statement of objections 7.34
revision 24.31, 25.116–25.124
right to be heard 7.100, 7.115, 7.158, 7.161,
  11.50–11.51, 11.54, 13.21, 16.04
right to effective legal protection 4.12, 4.44,
  7.110, 10.07
rights 23.20
  of the defence
    annulment, action for 7.34, 7.36, 7.158,
      7.162–7.164, 7.166
    direct actions 25.06, 25.10, 25.16
    equivalence and effectiveness 4.40
    infringement, action for 5.26–5.27, 5.62
    preliminary rulings on interpretation 6.07

rights (*cont.*)
   procedural 13.21, 20.11, 25.60, 25.71
   procedural
      annulment, action for 7.43, 7.93, 7.104,
        7.115, 7.118
Rome Convention 21.03, 21.07
rule of law 1.03, 3.57, 9.18, 19.11
   annulment, action for 7.145, 7.176–7.180, 7.211
   damages, action for 11.06, 11.37, 11.45,
      11.47–11.50, 11.54, 11.60, 11.74, 11.82
   intellectual property rights 20.03, 20.12

sanctions: unlimited jurisdiction 15.01–15.09
   criteria 15.08
   EAEC Treaty and former ECSC Treaty 15.03
   fine, reduction or increase of 15.09
   force of 15.09
   Lisbon Treaty, changes brought by 15.02
   objective 15.04
   pecuniary 5.79–5.80
   reasonableness 15.07
   review 15.06
sanctions
   for non-compliance 6.29
   see also under **infringement by a Member State;**
      sanctions: unlimited jurisdiction
Schöppenstedt **test** 11.45, 11.48–11.50
Schutznorm **doctrine** 11.48, 11.50
security for costs 4.08
semi–privileged applicants 7.03, 7.79
servants (of the Union) 2.34, 2.38–2.39, 2.41, 2.45,
   18.01, 18.09, 25.08
   damages, action for 11.01–11.02, 11.05, 11.13,
      11.18, 11.20–11.24
   see also **staff**
sincere cooperation principle 2.02, 4.40, 4.47,
   5.64, 11.27
social policy 4.45, 6.09
special agreement *see* **arbitration**
   clause/special agreement
staff
   Court of Justice 2.20
   disputes 11.05
   Civil Service Tribunal 2.41
   General Court 2.34
   see also **staff cases**
staff cases 18.01–18.31
   action brought 18.27
   adverse effect 18.03–18.06
   any member of staff 18.08
   appeal 18.30
   applicants 18.08–18.10
   binding act 18.04
   bodies or agencies 18.09, 18.12
   closure of proceedings for direct actions 25.97
   costs 18.27, 18.29
   defendants 18.11–18.12
   disputes 18.01
   exclusive jurisdiction 18.27
   general measures 18.05
   institutions 18.11
   interest, requirement for 18.07

interim measures 13.27
measures for an action 18.03–18.07
personal interest 18.07
pre-litigation procedure 18.13–18.26
   complaint and application, parallelism
      between 18.26
   complaints 18.15, 18.22
   content of decision rejecting complaint 18.23
   course 18.14–18.15
   Civil Service Tribunal 18.24–18.26, 18.28
   excusable errors 18.19
   formal requirements 18.21
   new facts 18.20
   no requirement as to form 18.21
   requests 18.14
   substantive requirements 18.22–18.23
   time limits 18.16–18.20, 18.25
preparatory measures 18.06
review 18.31
Staff Regulations 18.02
trade unions and staff associations 18.10
written procedure for direct actions 25.08
State aid
   annulment, action for 7.26, 7.57, 7.61, 7.93,
      7.126, 7.128, 7.138
   competition 7.201–7.204
   conduct during administrative procedure and
      admissibility of pleas 7.187
   failure to act, action for 8.06
   infringement by a Member State 5.22–5.25
   infringements of essential procedural requirement 7.165
   unlawful, recovery of 4.31
State liability 4.46, 4.50–4.51, 5.73, 11.60 *see also*
   Member State liability
statement in intervention 25.53, 25.76, 25.77,
   25.78, 25.81
statement of reasons 4.09, 7.170–7.174, 16.09
subjective liability 11.42
subsidiarity 7.80, 7.216, 13.32
substantive mistake 2.54
substantive requirements for liability 11.36–11.85
   burden of proof is on applicant 11.40
   causal link 11.78–11.85
      case-by-case assessment 11.80
      damage attributable to omission to act 11.83
      damage attributable to Union institution
        or body 11.81
      damage attributable to unlawful act 11.82
      must be direct 11.78
      reasonable diligence of applicant 11.85
      rejection of broad definition of 11.79–11.80
      too remote in chain of causation 11.84
   classic conditions 11.36
   cumulative conditions 11.38
   development in case-law 11.37
   loss or damage, reality of 11.63–11.77
      applicant bears burden of proof 11.75
      Bergaderm conditions 11.74
      compensation in kind 11.69
      damage in case of unlawful collection of charge or
        withholding of payment 11.70
      damage must be actual and certain 11.64–11.74

damage passed on to others 11.71
default and compensatory interest 11.72
exchange rate 11.73
existence and extent of damage 11.64–11.74
factual evidence 11.76
future loss or damage 11.67
loss of profit 11.65
non-material damage 11.66
proof of damage 11.75–11.77
quantum, determination of 11.68
uncertainty about extent of damage 11.77
no particular order of assessment 11.39
unlawful act or conduct 11.41–11.62
any rule of Union law 11.49
Bergaderm judgment 11.45
case-by-case assessment 11.54
case-law prior to *Bergaderm* judgment 11.50
discretion 11.52–11.59, 11.61
ECSC Treaty, former 11.43
European Ombudsman 11.55
extent of loss or damage 11.57
fault and unlawfulness 11.42
general/individual, legislative/non-legislative
    nature of act is irrelevant 11.52
infringement proceedings 11.47
institution does not have discretion 11.58
intended to confer rights on individuals 11.48
justifications 11.59–11.62
non-contractual liability on account of failure
    to act 11.46
rules of law intended to confer rights on individuals
    following *Bergaderm* 11.51
sufficiently serious breach 11.52–11.62
TEU and TFEU 11.44
unlawfulness, test for 11.42–11.51
Supreme Court 2.21
Court of Justice's function as 2.21
Denmark 3.30
Italy 3.57, 4.59
Netherlands 3.44
Sweden 4.61
UK 3.44
suspension 2.40, 16.26
annulment, action for 7.57
equivalence and effectiveness 4.10, 4.61–4.63
infringement, action for 5.29
interim measures 13.01, 13.04–13.07,
    13.10–13–12, 13.14, 13.17, 13.39,
    13.42–13.43
recovery injunctions 7.58
Syfait case 3.11

Telmarsicabruzzo case 3.26, 3.28
third countries 3.15, 6.14
third parties 4.27, 13.21, 25.107–25.115
tierce–opposition 3.49
time limits 23.26–23.38
admissibility 5.61–5.62
annulment 7.147, 7.160, 7.173, 7.207–7.216
appeals 16.25
applications 23.34
calculation 23.26–23.38

cases 23.47
Court always open 23.35
dies ad quem 23.28, 23.31, 23.33, 28.33–28.34
dies a quo 23.28–23.29
direct actions 25.28, 25.70, 25.78
duration of period 23.31
equivalence and effectiveness 4.38
excusable error, unforeseeable circumstances or *force*
    majeure 23.38
infringement by Member States 5.71, 7.74
intellectual property 20.18
interim measures 13.15, 13.26–13.27
international agreements 12.14–12.17
judgments and orders 25.108–25.112,
    25.117–25.121, 25.130
limitation periods 7.207
lodgment at registry 23.36
lodgment by telefax, e-curia or other means 23.37
preliminary objection 23.27
procedural time limits and limitation periods,
    distinction between 23.26
publication, starting point in case of 23.30
staff cases 18.16–18.20
ten day extension on account of distance 23.32
trade associations 7.60, 7.103–7.104, 7.118,
    7.132, 11.15
trademarks *see* Office for Harmonisation in the Internal
    Market relating to Community trademarks and
    designs
trade unions 7.129, 18.10, 23.14
Treaties 1.03, 1.04, 6.04–6.07
Treaty amendments 7.75
Tribunal de Defensa de la Competencia 3.11
TRIPS 6.14

ultra petita 15.09, 25.16
unforeseeable circumstances 7.208, 7.214
Unified Patent Court 3.14
Unified Patent Litigation System (Draft Agreement) 3.14
Unión de Pequeños Agricultores case 4.11–4.12,
    7.106, 7.110
Union Laitière Normande case 3.25
United States 12.17
unjust enrichment 11.08
unlawful act or conduct 11.46
    see also under substantive requirement for liability
unlawful charges, recovery of 4.21–4.30
unlimited jurisdiction 7.195
    see also sanctions
urgency 13.35–13.41

Vaassen criteria 3.08–3.09, 3.12
administrative bodies 3.10
arbitrators 3.12
Benelux Court of Justice 3.14, 3.47
Direcciòn General de Defensa de la Competencia 3.11
Directeur des Contributions Directes et Accises 3.11
Epitropi Antagonismou 3.11
International courts 3.14
Miles 3.14
Opinion 1/09 3.14
Parfums Christian Dior 3.14

Vaassen criteria (*cont.*)
   Syfait 3.11
   Third countries' courts 3.15
   Tribunal de Defensa de la Competencia see Tribunal
     de Defensa de la Competencia
vacations (judicial) 23.31
validity *see* preliminary rulings on validity
Van der Kooy case 7.128
Vedial case 20.10
Vice-President
   Court of Justice 2.08, 2.18, 13.23, 13.24
   General Court 2.27
visas, asylum and other policies related to free
     movement of persons 1.06, 3.02, 22.01

witnesses 23.06, 23.65, 23.67–23.69, 23.71, 25.91
Woodpulp case 7.34, 7.226
written part of procedure 23.49–23.55
   annexes and schedule 23.53
   copies and translations 23.52
   dating of documents 23.54
   e-Curia 23.50
   length of documents 23.55
   signing of original documents 23.51
   see also written procedure for direct actions
   see also under preliminary rulings, procedure in case of
written procedure for direct actions 25.02–25.57
   application 25.02–25.27
     accompanying documents 25.19–25.24
     address for service 25.05
     case becomes pending 25.25
     certificate of lawyer 25.20
     consequences 25.25–25.27
     content 25.03–25.04
     designation of party against whom application is
       made 25.06–25.08
     form of order 25.16–25.17
     intellectual property rights disputes 25.23
     legal persons 25.22
     lodgment 25.02

     measure imputable to another institution, agency
       or body 25.07
     name and address of applicant 25.04
     pleas 25.10, 25.12–25.14
     Registrar 25.26
     regularization 25.27
     requirements 25.03
     staff cases 25.08
     subject-matter 25.10–25.11
     submissions supplementing application 25.15
     summary for publication 25.24
     supporting evidence 25.18
   defence 25.28–25.45
     accompanying documents 25.40
     content 25.34–25.40
     default judgments 25.31–25.33
     evidence produced or offered in support 25.39
     form of order 25.38
     inadmissibility 25.41–25.45
     intellectual property rights disputes 25.30
     lodgment 25.28–25.31
     name and address of defendant 25.25
     pleas in law and arguments relied on
       25.36–25.37
     reasoned order 25.45
     signature and date 25.29
     time limit 25.28
   preparation 25.52–25.57
     annexes 25.57
     brief submissions 25.56
     e-Curia 25.54
     first page 25.53
     paragraph numbering 25.55
   reply and rejoinder 25.46–25.51
     formal requirements 25.47
     improper use of documents 25.50
     intellectual property rights disputes 25.51
     no new pleas 25.49
     objective 25.48
WTO Agreement 6.14, 10.08, 11.07, 11.51

9 780198 707349